HUMAN SKELETON

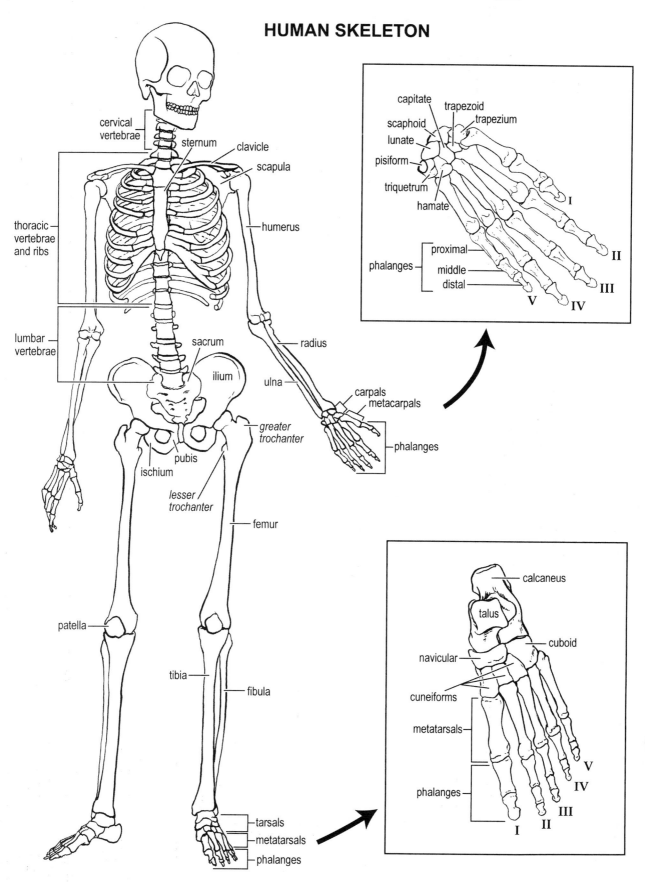

cervical vertebrae

sternum

clavicle

scapula

thoracic vertebrae and ribs

humerus

lumbar vertebrae

sacrum

ilium

radius

ulna

greater trochanter

pubis

ischium

carpals

metacarpals

phalanges

lesser trochanter

femur

patella

tibia

fibula

tarsals

metatarsals

phalanges

capitate

trapezoid

trapezium

scaphoid

lunate

pisiform

triquetrum

hamate

phalanges

proximal

middle

distal

I

II

III

V

IV

calcaneus

talus

cuboid

navicular

cuneiforms

metatarsals

phalanges

V

IV

III

II

I

The Human Evolution
Source Book

Advances in Human Evolution
A Prentice Hall College Division Series of Texts and Monographs

Advances in Human Evolution is committed to the timely publication of texts, monographs, and major edited works on all aspects of human evolution. The series' dedication to an interdisciplinary approach emphasizes new avenues of research in human evolution through biomolecular and DNA studies, developmental and evolutionary anatomy, paleoecological and paleobehavioral studies, ethnoarchaeological studies, as well as current debates on evolution from a biocultural perspective. Colleagues are invited to share these books with their undergraduate and graduate students as course texts or as supplemental readings. In addition to being of high scientific quality, books in this series advance our understanding of what it means to be human.

Series Editor:

Prof. Russell L. Ciochon, The University of Iowa

Editorial Board:

Prof. Robert Corruccini, Southern Illinois University – Carbondale
Prof. Dean Falk, Florida State University – Tallahassee
Prof. John Fleagle, Stony Brook University – Stony Brook
Prof. Henry McHenry, University of California – Davis
Prof. Erik Trinkaus, Washington University – St. Louis
Prof. Mark Weiss, Physical Anthropology Program – National Science Foundation

Series Titles:

The Human Evolution Source Book, Second Edition (2006)
Russell L. Ciochon and John G. Fleagle (Editors)

The Epic of Evolution: Science and Religion in Dialogue (2004)
James B. Miller (Editor)

The New Physical Anthropology: Science, Humanism, and Critical Reflection (1999)
Shirley C. Strum, Donald G. Lindburg, and David Hamburg (Editors)

The Biological Basis of Human Behavior: A Critical Review, Second Edition (1999)
Robert W. Sussman (Editor)

Integrative Paths to the Past: Paleoanthropological Advances in Honor of F. Clark Howell (1994)
Robert S. Corruccini and Russell L. Ciochon (Editors)

Forthcoming:

Debating Humankind's Place in Nature Since 1860
Richard Delisle

The Primate Evolution Source Book
Russell L. Ciochon and John G. Fleagle (Editors)

The Human Evolution Source Book

Second Edition

Russell L. Ciochon
The University of Iowa, Iowa City, IA

John G. Fleagle
Stony Brook University, Stony Brook, NY

Advances in Human Evolution Series

PEARSON
Prentice
Hall

Upper Saddle River, New Jersey 07458

Library of Congress Cataloging-in-Publication Data

The human evolution source book / [edited by] Russell L. Ciochon, John G. Fleagle.—2nd ed.
      p. cm.—(Advances in human evolution)
    Includes bibliographical references.
    ISBN 0-13-032981-9 (pbk.)
      1. Human evolution.   I. Fleagle, John G.   II. Advances in human evolution series.

GN281.H8475 2006
599.93′8—dc22

2004063104

Editorial Director: Leah Jewell
AVP/Publisher: Nancy Roberts
Editorial Assistant: Lee Peterson
Senior Marketing Manager: Marissa Feliberty
Marketing Assistant: Anthony DeCosta
Manufacturing Buyer: Ben Smith
Cover Art Director: Jayne Conte
Cover Design: Bruce Kenselaar
Composition: Interactive Composition Corporation
Printer/Binder: Bind-Rite
Typeface: 10/11 New Baskerville
Cover Photo: Javier Trueba/Madrid Scientific Films

Pearson Education LTD.
Pearson Education Singapore, Pte. Ltd
Pearson Education Canada, Ltd
Pearson Education-Japan
Pearson Education Australia PTY, Limited

Pearson Education North Asia Ltd
Pearson Educación de Mexico, S.A. de C.V.
Pearson Education Malaysia, Pte. Ltd
Pearson Education, Upper Saddle River, NJ

10 9 8 7 6 5 4 3 2 1
ISBN: 0-13-032981-9

Contents

PART I

Geological Background to Human Evolution   1

PART II

The Earliest Hominids: Biomolecular and Morphological Evidence   31

PART III

Australopithecus, Paranthropus and Relatives   73

PART IV

Origin of the Genus *Homo* and Early Evolution in Africa   219

PART V

Evolution and Dispersal of *Homo erectus*   293

PART VI

Middle Pleistocene Hominids in Africa, Europe, and Asia   393

PART VII

The Neandertals   447

PART VIII

Origin of Modern Humans   509

PART IX

Evolution of *Homo sapiens*   601

Glossary   686

Preface

It has been more than a decade since the first edition of *The Human Evolution Source Book* appeared. The first edition, published in 1993, assembled the key papers of paleoanthropological research of the previous four decades and has been widely used by undergraduate and graduate students at institutions around the world. Since the field of paleoanthropology and the publications that present and interpret new finds have grown dramatically in the past decade, it became clear that there was a need for a second edition. However, in designing this new edition we debated whether we should update the first edition by adding new articles or whether we should produce a second edition that augmented, rather than replaced, the first edition. Because of the tremendous volume of new discoveries and interpretations, we finally chose the latter. Consequently, this edition does not adhere to the historical approach we followed in the first edition. Instead, it consists almost entirely of articles published during the last decade, with over half of the articles appearing between 2000 and 2004. The number of chapters has grown to 75, yet the length of the volume is about the same as that of the first edition, as we have focused on including shorter contributions that are direct and to the point. This focus should be appreciated by students bogged down with onerous reading assignments in other classes and by their professors who want full topical coverage of the field of human evolution. This second edition provides a comprehensive treatment of the subject without overloading students with readings they cannot complete.

With the appearance of the second edition of *The Human Evolution Source Book*, the central theme of the volume has not changed. This collection is designed for use by students in anthropology, paleontology, and evolutionary biology. *The Human Evolution Source Book* brings together the major ideas and publications on human evolution of the past decade to provide the reader with an opportunity to examine the original articles that have shaped the recent development of this exciting and often controversial field. Although the emphasis in this edition of *The Human Evolution Source Book* is on the fossil record, the articles survey the entire scope of human evolutionary inquiry, including paleontology, archaeology, geology, genetics, paleoecology, functional anatomy, primate behavior, and human ecology. Each part is preceded by an editorial introduction to assist the reader in focusing on the major issues being debated. *The Human Evolution Source Book* closes with a glossary of key terms used throughout the text.

Part I, Geological Background to Human Evolution, presents the geological and chronometric background for interpreting the fossil record of human evolution in the early twenty-first century. Issues of context, dating, and taphonomy have moved center-stage in our quest to understand the human fossil record. These brief articles provide an introduction to many of the principles of geological studies and dating techniques that are essential for understanding many of the arguments presented in subsequent chapters. **Part II, The Earliest Hominids: Biomolecular and Morphological Evidence,** presents the latest evidence from the hominid fossil record, which now extends back to the late Miocene, some 7 million years ago (mya). This evidence comes from disparate areas such as molecular anthropology and from studies of the behavior and ecology of living primates. **Part III, *Australopithecus, Paranthropus,* and Relatives,** discusses the adaptive diversity and phylogenetic relationships of early fossil hominids from the middle Pliocene to the early Pleistocene of Africa. Included are well-known taxa, such as *Australopithecus* and *Paranthropus,* as well as newly proposed genera, such as *Kenyanthropus.* The evolution of hominid bipedalism is also considered here.

Part IV, Origin of the Genus *Homo* and Early Evolution in Africa, summarizes the earliest evidence of the genus *Homo* and the first appearance of stone artifacts in the fossil record. This has been an area of intense research over the last decade with many new discoveries shedding light on the origin of the human genus. **Part V, Evolution and Dispersal of *Homo erectus,*** explores the evolution and biogeography of the first hominids to leave Africa—*Homo erectus*—from the perspective of new discoveries in places such as the Republic of Georgia, as well as new finds and new contextual information from the well-known sites of Zhoukoudian (China) and Sangiran/Sambungmacan (Java). The early and widespread dispersal of *Homo erectus,* its late survival on the island of Java, and the discovery of its dwarfed descendant, *Homo floresiensis,* on the island of Flores are among the most dramatic new discoveries in the field of human evolution in recent years. **Part VI, Middle Pleistocene Hominids in Africa, Europe, and Asia,** chronicles current knowledge in one of the most poorly understood and rapidly unfolding areas of study in human evolution—the period between the dispersal of *Homo erectus* out of Africa into Asia (and probably Europe) and the appearance of Neandertals in Eurasia and modern humans in Africa. This section ends with the remarkable discovery of wooden spears from the 400,000-year-old site of Schöningen in Germany. **Part VII, The Neandertals,** presents a diverse collection of reports documenting many aspects of the biology of these distinctive and controversial middle and late Pleistocene hominids from Eurasia. The chapters in this part address the origin and evolution of Neandertals as well as many aspects of their biology, including adaptations for cold climate, comparisons of patterns of cranial ontogeny in Neandertals and modern humans, evidence for cannibalism, and the first discovery of Neandertal mtDNA.

Part VIII, Origin of Modern Humans, considers the evidence for the origin of modern humans (*Homo sapiens*) in sub-Saharan Africa from both an anatomical and a behavioral perspective. This has been a major area of research for nearly two decades. In particular, there are major debates regarding the timing of the first appearance of modern behavior and its relationship to modern anatomy. Defining what it means to be modern is not an easy task, and several chapters review criteria that have been put forth as evidence of modern behavior. **Part IX, Evolution of *Homo sapiens*,** reviews various models for the origin of diversity in modern *Homo sapiens,* comparing and contrasting the multiregional, out of Africa replacement, and various assimilation models. These include morphological, archaeological, and genetic studies aimed at understanding both current patterns in human diversity and our evolutionary origins. Chapters in this part also review the spread of humans to North and South America and the role of stone tools in our understanding of the evolution of human culture.

This volume represents many thousands of hours of editorial and computer preparation at the University of Iowa and at Stony Brook University. Numerous students at the University of Iowa and at Stony Brook University have had significant roles in the volume's preparation. K. Lindsay Eaves-Johnson, Chris Gilbert, Jason Kamilar, Justin Ledogar, Lisa Paciulli, Danielle Royer, Devra Sheffer, Krista Schroeder, Rick Young, and Jessica White assisted with editorial matters and proofreading; Erin Schembari, Autumn Noble, Alexis Pollitz, Nathan Totten, and Michael Zimmerman helped with computer graphics. K. Lindsay Eaves-Johnson and Erin Schembari deserve special thanks: Lindsay for acting as the "student copy editor," and Erin, for acting as the "illustrations editor," both in the final stages of the volume's preparation. Krista Schroeder also deserves special credit for her critical role in the final manuscript's preparation and proofing. Finally, Georgia Millward joined the editorial team to assist with copy editing and with the addition of the final chapters and artwork. She also helped with correction of the page proofs. We acknowledge Luci Betti-Nash for drawing the artwork and maps for the inside cover illustrations. At Prentice Hall we thank our editor Nancy Roberts for giving us the opportunity to produce a truly comprehensive reader/text on human evolution. As with the first edition, Nancy has given us the intellectual freedom to assemble the book we wanted even though it exceeded the page limitations originally allocated for the work. Also at Prentice Hall we thank our production editor, Joan Stone, for dealing with numerous problems during the production of this book. Many of these issues were outside her area of expertise but she was always able to find a solution.

Financial support during the preparation of this volume was provided by the Leakey Foundation, the Office of the Dean, College of Liberal Arts and Sciences, University of Iowa (UI), a Collaborative Interdisciplinary Programs (CIP) grant from the UI Office of the Vice President for Research, the Human Evolution Research Fund at the University of Iowa Foundation, and finally Prentice Hall through its generous support of the Advances in Human Evolution Editorial Fund in the UI College of Liberal Arts and Sciences. Special thanks go to Eric Delson who personally helped obtain permission from Mayfield Press to reprint 12 entries from the *Encyclopedia of Human Evolution* that he co-edited. Finally, we thank all of our paleoanthropological colleagues for allowing us to reprint their research in this volume. Clearly, without their support, *The Human Evolution Source Book* would not have become a reality. We also wish to note that the order of our names on the title page and preface of this work was determined alphabetically.

Russell L. Ciochon
John G. Fleagle

About the Authors

RUSSELL L. CIOCHON, Professor of Anthropology at the University of Iowa, received his Ph.D. from the University of California at Berkeley. He is the author of more than 100 research papers and 10 books, among them *The Primate Anthology* (with Richard Nisbett) and *Dragon Bone Hill: An Ice Age Saga of Homo erectus* (with Noel Boaz). Professor Ciochon specializes in paleoanthropological fieldwork in Asia, a region he has traveled in extensively over the past 25 years. He has organized paleoanthropological expeditions to Burma, India, China, Vietnam, Cambodia, and Indonesia. His most recent expeditions (1999–2005) have taken him to the *Homo erectus* localities of Sangiran on the island of Java. There he is working with an international team of geologists and archaeologists to date the first arrival of humans in Asia and to decipher the habitat and climate that drew early humans to this remote corner of the world nearly 1.6 million years ago.

Professor Ciochon is editor of *Advances in Human Evolution,* a series of college- and university-level texts. He is also co-editor (with Bernard Wood) of the *Human Evolution Series,* an advanced book series.

JOHN G. FLEAGLE, Distinguished Professor of Anatomical Sciences at Stony Brook University, received his Ph.D. from Harvard University in 1976. He has published more than 100 research papers on many aspects of primate evolution and comparative anatomy and is the author or editor of numerous books, including *Primate Adaptation and Evolution; Primate Communities* (with C. H. Janson and K. E. Reed); and *Primate Biogeography* (with Shawn Lehman). Professor Fleagle has conducted field research in Asia, Africa, and South America. His current research is an investigation of the early evolution of modern humans in the Kibish Formation of southwestern Ethiopia. He is a member of the Scientific Executive Committee of the L. S. B. Leakey Foundation, a Guggenheim Fellow, and a MacArthur Fellow.

Professor Fleagle is the founding editor of *Evolutionary Anthropology,* an interdisciplinary journal that provides mini-reviews of current research on human evolution from many different disciplines, and a co-organizer of the Stony Brook Human Evolution Workshops.

List of Contributors*

Leslie C. Aiello
The Wenner-Gren Foundation for
  Anthropological Research
470 Park Avenue South, 8th floor
New York, NY 10016

Peter Andrews
Department of Paleontology
Natural History Museum
Cromwell Road
London SW7 5BD, United Kingdom

Susan C. Antón
Department of Anthropology
New York University
New York, New York 10003

Antonio Ascenzi (deceased)
Istituto Italiano di Paleontologia
  Umana
Piazza Mincio 2
Rome 00198, Italy

Berhane Asfaw
Rift Valley Research Service
Box 5717
Addis Ababa, Ethiopia

Fachroel Aziz
Laboratory of Vertebrate
  Paleontology
Geological Research and Development
  Center
JL Diponegoro 57
Bandung 40122, Indonesia

Hisao Baba
Department of Anthropology
National Science Museum
Hyakunincho Shinjuku-ku
Tokyo 169-0073, Japan

Ofer Bar-Yosef
Department of Anthropology
Peabody Museum
Harvard University
Cambridge, Massachusetts 02138

José María Bermúdez de Castro
Museo Nacional de Ciencias Naturales
Departamento de Paleobiologia
J. Gutiérrez Abascal 2
Madrid 28006, Spain

Yonas Beyene
Department of Anthropology
  and Archaeology
ARCCH
Ministry of Youth Sports and Culture
Addis Ababa, Ethiopia

Robert J. Blumenschine
Center for Human Evolutionary
  Studies
Department of Anthropology
131 George Street
Rutgers University
New Brunswick, New Jersey
  08901-1414

Nicholas G. Blurton Jones
Departments of Anthropology
  and Psychiatry
University of California
Los Angeles, California 90095

Gunter Bräuer
Institute of Human Biology
University of Hamburg
Allende, Platz 2
Hamburg 20146, Germany

Alison Brooks
Department of Anthropology
George Washington University
Washington, District of
  Columbia 20052

Frank H. Brown
Dean, College of Mines &
  Earth Sciences
209 WBB
University of Utah
Salt Lake City, Utah 84112

Peter Brown
Department of Archaeology and
  Palaeoanthropology
University of New England
Armidale, New South Wales 2351,
  Australia

Michel Brunet
Faculté des Sciences et
Université de Poitiers
40, avenue du Recteur Pineau
Poitiers Cedex 86022, France

Eudald Carbonell
Laboratori d' Arqueologia
Universitat Rovira i Virgili
Plaza Imperial Tarraco 1
Tarragona 43005, Spain

Sean B. Carroll
R. M. Bock Laboratories
University of Wisconsin–Madison
1525 Linden Drive
Madison, Wisconsin 53706

Rachel Caspari
Paleoanthropology Laboratory
Department of Anthropology
University of Michigan
Ann Arbor, Michigan 48109-1382

Steven E. Churchill
Department of Biological
  Anthropology & Anatomy
Box 90383
Duke University
Durham, North Carolina 27708

Russell L. Ciochon
Department of Anthropology
University of Iowa
Iowa City, Iowa 52242-1322

J. Desmond Clark (deceased)
Department of Anthropology
University of California
Berkeley, California 94720

Els Cornelissen
Musée Royal de l' Afrique
  Centrale
Section de Prehistoire
Tervuren B-3080, Belgium

Michael H. Day
Department of Paleontology
Natural History Museum
Cromwell Road
London SW7 5BD,
  United Kingdom

* Due to space limitations, only the first three authors of each article are listed in this section. The complete list of authors for each article may be found on the article title page.

Alban Defleur
Laboratoire d'Anthropologie
UMR 6569 du CNRS
Boulevard Pierre Dramart
Marseille Cedex 20 13916, France

David DeGusta
Department of Anthropological
    Sciences
Building 360
Stanford University
Stanford, California 94305-2117

Jean de Heinzelin (deceased)
Institut Royal de Sciences
Naturelles de Belgique
rue Vautier 29
Bruxelles B-1000, Belgium

Francesco d'Errico
UMR 5808 du CNRS
Institut de Préhistoire et Géologie
    du Quaternaire
Bâtiment B18-Géologie
Talence 33405, France

Todd R. Disotell
Department of Anthropology
New York University
New York, New York 10003

E. James Dixon
Department of Anthropology
Denver Museum of Natural History
2002 Colorado Boulevard
Denver, Colorado 80205-5798

Dean Falk
Department of Anthropology
1847 West Tennessee Street
Florida State University
Tallahassee, Florida 32306-4531

Carlos Ferràndez-Canyadell
Departamento de Estratigrafia y
    Paleontologia
Universidade de Barcelona
Martí Franquès s/n
Barcelona 08028, Spain

Robert A. Foley
Department of Biological
    Anthropology
University of Cambridge
Downing Street
Cambridge CB2 3DZ, United Kingdom

David W. Frayer
Department of Anthropology
University of Kansas
Lawrence, Kansas 66045-7556

Leo Gabunia (deceased)
Institute of Paleobiology
Republic of Georgia National Academy
    of Sciences
Tbilisi 380007, Republic of Georgia

Josep Gibert
Institut de Paleontología M. Crusafont
Escola Industrial 23
Sabadell 08201, Spain

Lluís Gibert
Institut Paleontología M. Crusafont
Escola Industrial 23
Sabadell 08201, Spain

W. Henry Gilbert
Department of Integrative Biology
Laboratory for Human Evolutionary
    Studies
University of California
Berkeley, California 94720

Paul Goldberg
Department of Archaeology
Boston University
675 Commonwealth Avenue
Boston, Massachusetts 02215

Dominique Gommery
UPR 2147 CNRS
44, rue de l'Amiral Mouchez
Paris 75014, France

Frederick E. Grine
Departments of Anthropology
    and Anatomy
Stony Brook University, SUNY
Stony Brook, New York 11794-4364

Franck Guy
Faculté des Sciences et
CNRS UMR 6046
Université de Poitiers
40, avenue du Recteur Pineau
Poitiers Cedex 86022, France

John Guyer
Department of Anthropology
University at Albany, SUNY
Albany, New York 12222

Yohannes Haile-Selassie
Cleveland Museum of Natural History
1 Wade Oval Drive, University Circle
Cleveland, Ohio 44108-1767

Kristen Hawkes
Department of Anthropology
University of Utah
Salt Lake City, Utah 84112

John D. Hawks
Department of Anthropology
University of Wisconsin
5321 Observatory Drive
Madison, Wisconsin 53706

Christopher S. Henshilwood
Iziko Museums of Cape Town
South Africa Museum
Box 61
Cape Town 8000, South Africa

Andrew Hill
Department of Anthropology
Yale University
Room 3, 158 Whitney Avenue
New Haven,
    Connecticut 06520-8277

Trent W. Holliday
Department of Anthropology
1021 Audubon Street
Tulane University
New Orleans, Louisiana 70118

Yamei Hou
Institute of Vertebrate Paleontology
    and Paleoanthropology
Chinese Academy of Sciences
Box 643
Beijing 100044, China

Jean-Jacques Hublin
Department of Human Evolution
Max-Planck-Institut für evolutionäre
    Anthropologie
Deutscher Platz 6
D-04103 Leipzig, Germany

Donald C. Johanson
Institute of Human Origins
Arizona State University
Box 874101
Tempe, Arizona 85287-4101

Yousuka Kaifu
Department of Anthropology
National Science Museum
Hyakunincho Shinjuku-ku
Tokyo 169-0073, Japan

William H. Kimbel
Institute of Human Origins
Arizona State University
Box 874101
Tempe, Arizona 85287-4101

Richard G. Klein
Department of Anthropological
    Sciences
Building 360 MC: 2117
Stanford University
Stanford, California 94305-2117

Matthias Krings
Zoological Institute
University of Munich
Box 202136
Munich D-80021, Germany

Steven L. Kuhn
Department of Anthropology
University of Arizona
Tucson, Arizona 85721

Marta Mirazon Lahr
Duckworth Laboratory
University of Cambridge
Downing Street
Cambridge CB2 3DZ,
    United Kingdom

Roy Larick
Shore Cultural Center
23745 Lake Shore Drive
Euclid, OH 44123

Meave G. Leakey
Division of Palaeontology
National Museum of Kenya
Box 40658
Nairobi, Kenya

David Lordkipanidze
Department of Geology
    and Paleontology
Republic of Georgia
    State Museum
3 Purtseladze Street
Tbilisi 380007, Republic
    of Georgia

C. Owen Lovejoy
Department of Anthropology
Division of Biomedical Sciences
Kent State University
Kent State, Ohio 44242

Francesco Mallegni
Istituto Italiano di Paleontologia
    Umana
Piazza Mincio 2
Rome 00198, Italy

Giorgio Manzi
Istituto Italiano di Paleontologia
    Umana
Piazza Mincio 2
Rome 00198, Italy

Jonathan Marks
Department of Sociology
    and Anthropology
904 B Fretwell
UNC–Charlotte
Charlotte, North Carolina 28223

María Martinón-Torres
Museo Nacional de Ciencias
    Naturales-CSIC
Departamento de Paleobiología-Equipo
    de Atapuerca
C/José Gutiérrez Abascal 2
28006 Madrid, Spain

Fidelis T. Masao
Paleo-Cultural and Environmental
    Research
Box 70566
Dar es Salaam, Tanzania

Henry M. McHenry
Department of Anthropology
University of California
Davis, California 95616

Michael J. Morwood
Department of Archaeology
    & Palaeoanthropology
University of New England
Armidal, New South Wales 2351,
    Australia

James F. O'Connell
Department of Anthropology
University of Utah
Salt Lake City, Utah 84112

Charles R. Peters
Department of Anthropology and
    Institute of Ecology
Baldwin Hall
University of Georgia
Athens, Georgia
    30602-1619

Martin Pickford
Chaire de Paléoanthropologie
UMR 8569 du CNRS
8, rue Buffon
Paris 75005, France

David R. Pilbeam
Peabody Museum
Harvard University
11 Divinity Avenue
Cambridge, Massachusetts 02138

Frank E. Poirier
3707 Longford Circle
Ormond Beach,
    Florida 32174

Marcia S. Ponce de León
Anthropologisches Institut
Universitat Zurich-Irchel
Winterhurerstrasse 190
Zurich CH-8057, Switzerland

Richard Potts
Human Origins Program
National Museum of Natural History
Smithsonian Institution
Washington, District of
    Columbia 20560-0112

John C. Redmond, Jr.
Department of Anthropology
University at Albany, SUNY
Albany, New York 12222

Kaye E. Reed
Institute of Human Origins
Arizona State University
Box 874101
Tempe, Arizona 85287-4101

John H. Relethford
Department of Anthropology
College at Oneonta, SUNY
Oneonta, New York 13820

G. Phillip Rightmire
Department of Anthropology
Binghamton University
Binghamton, New York 13902-6000

William Jack Rink
Department of Geology
McMaster University
Hamilton, Ontario,
    Canada L8S 4M1

Christopher B. Ruff
Department of Cell Biology
    & Anatomy
Johns Hopkins University
    Medical School
725 North Wolfe Street
Baltimore, Maryland 21205

Oliver A. Ryder
Center for Reproduction of
    Endangered Species
Zoological Society of San Diego
San Diego, California
    92112-0551

Ralf W. Schmitz
Rheinisches amt für
    Bodendenkmalpflege
Endenicher Strasse 133
Bonn D-53115, Germany

Henry P. Schwarcz
Department of Geography
    and Geology
McMaster University
Hamilton, Ontario,
    Canada L8S 4M1

Sileshi Semaw
CRAFT Research Center and
    Stone Age Institute
Indiana University
419 North Indiana
Bloomington, Indiana 47405-7000

Brigitte Senut
Laboratoire de Paléontologie du
    Muséum National d'Histoire
    Naturelle
GDR 983 ct. UMR 8569 du CNRS
8, rue Buffon
Paris 75005, France

Fred Spoor
Department of Anatomy and
    Developmental Biology
University College
London WC1E 6JJ, United Kingdom

Rebecca L. Stauffer
Department of Biology and
    Institute of Molecular
    Evolutionary Genetics
Pennsylvania State University
University Park, Pennsylvania 16802

Jack T. Stern, Jr.
Department of Anatomical Science
Health Sciences Center
Stony Brook University (SUNY)
Stony Brook, New York 11794-8081

Anne Stone
Department of Anthropology
Arizona State University
Tempe, Arizona 85287

David S. Strait
Department of Anthropology
University at Albany (SUNY)
Albany, New York 12222

Christopher B. Stringer
Department of Paleontology
Natural History Museum
London SW7 5BD,
    United Kingdom

Thomas Sutikna
Indonesian Centre for
    Archaeology
Jl. Raya Condet Pejaten Number 4
Jakarta 12001, Indonesia

Gen Suwa
University Museum
University of Tokyo
7-3-1 Hongo, Bunkyo-ku
Tokyo 113-8654, Japan

Carl C. Swisher III
Department of Geological Sciences
Rutgers University
Wright Chemistry Building,
    Busch Campus
New Brunswick, New Jersey 08903

Mark F. Teaford
Department of Cell Biology
    and Anatomy
Johns Hopkins University School
    of Medicine
725 North Wolfe Street
Baltimore, Maryland 21205

Alan R. Templeton
Department of Biology
Washington University
St. Louis, Missouri 63130-4899

Hartmut Thieme
Niedersächsisches Landesamt für
    Denkmalpflege
Scharnhorststrasse 1
Hanover 30175, Germany

Erik Trinkaus
Department of Anthropology
Washington University
Campus Box 114,
    One Brookings Drive
St. Louis, Missouri 63130-4899

Peter S. Ungar
Department of Anthropology
University of Arkansas
Old Man 330
Fayetteville, Arkansas 72701

Patricia Valensi
Laboratoire de Préhistoire du Lazaret
33, bis Boulevard
Frank Pilatte
Nice 06300, France

John A. Van Couvering
Ph.D. Program in Anthropology
CUNY Graduate Center
365 Fifth Avenue
New York, New York 10016-4309

Abesalom Vekua
Republic of Georgia National
    Academy of Sciences
Tbilisi 380007, Republic of Georgia

Alan Walker
Department of Anthropology
Pennsylvania State University
409 Carpenter Building
University Park,
    Pennsylvania 16802-3404

Robert C. Walter
Department of Earth and Environment
Franklin and Marshall University
Box 3003
Lancaster, PA 17604-3003

Carol V. Ward
Department of Anthropology
University of Missouri–Columbia
107 Swallow Hall
Columbia, Missouri 65211

Steve Weiner
Department of Structural Biology
Weizmann Institute of Science
Rehovot 76100, Israel

Tim D. White
Department of Integrative Biology
University of California, Berkeley
Valley Life Sciences Building #3140
Berkeley, California 94720-3140

Milford H. Wolpoff
Department of Anthropology
University of Michigan
Ann Arbor,
    Michigan 48109-1382

Bernard A. Wood
Department of Anthropology
George Washington University
2110 G Street Northwest
Washington, District of
    Columbia 20052

Richard Wrangham
Department of Anthropology
Peabody Museum
Harvard University
Cambridge,
    Massachusetts 02138

Xinzhi Wu
Institute of Vertebrate Paleontology
    and Paleoanthropology
Chinese Academy of Sciences
Box 643
Beijing 100044, China

Fie Xie
Institute of Cultural Relics
Hebei Province
Shijiazhuang 050000, China

Qinqi Xu
Institute of Vertebrate Paleontology
    and Paleoanthropology
Academica Sinica
Chinese Academy of Sciences
Box 643
Beijing 100044, China

Royden Yates
Iziko Museums of Cape Town
South Africa Museum
Box 61
Cape Town 8000, South Africa

John E. Yellen
Archaeology Program
National Science Foundation
4201 Wilson Boulevard
Arlington, Virginia 22230

Baoyin Yuan
Institute of Geology and Geophysics
Chinese Academy of Sciences
Box 9825
Beijing 100029, China

Yahdi Zaim
Department of Geology
Institute of Technology Bandung
Jalan Ganesha 10
Bandung 40132, Indonesia

Rixiang Zhu
Institute of Geology and Geophysics
Chinese Academy of Sciences
Beijing 100029, China

Christoph P. E. Zollikofer
Anthropologisches Institut
Universitat Zurich-Irchel
Winterhurerstrasse 190
Zurich CH-8057, Switzerland

I

Geological Background to Human Evolution

As the name indicates, paleoanthropology (including paleontology and archaeology) is a historical science that is concerned with reconstructing and understanding events and processes that took place in the distant past. Fossils and archaeological remains are found in a geological context; it is this geological context that provides information about their age and the ecological conditions surrounding their life, death, subsequent preservation, and recovery by present-day scientists. An appreciation of geology and geological processes and techniques is a necessary prerequisite for understanding interpretations in paleoanthropology. This first section contains a series of short articles that provide an introduction to the geological concepts and terms that are critical for understanding the fossil record of human evolution. Many of the individual chapters focus on the methods used to obtain absolute and relative ages for fossils or the rocks in which these fossils have been found.

Chapter 1, "Stratigraphy Explained," by Francis H. Brown and John A. Van Couvering, discusses the basic principles used to describe, characterize, and interpret layered sequences of rocks. The most basic of these are the Principle of Superposition, which states that, in an undisturbed sequence, younger strata overlie older strata; the Principle of Original Horizontality, which states that strata are normally nearly horizontal when they are deposited; and the Principle of Original Lateral Continuity, which states that all parts of a stratum, however disrupted by later activity, once formed a single connected layer. The authors then consider the alternative ways in which layered strata may be characterized and described and the rules that have been adopted to unify these descriptions. The alternative ways include lithostratigraphy, biostratigraphy, chronostratigraphy, magnetostratigraphy, isotope stratigraphy, and cyclostratigraphy. Concise definitions of these terms appear in the glossary at the end of this volume.

The second chapter, "Cyclostratigraphy," by John A. Van Couvering, describes the repetitive features of the earth's stratigraphic record that appear to be driven by astronomical cycles. In particular, eccentricities in the earth's orbit around the sun, precession of the location of the earth's axis of rotation, and precession of the

equinoxes are discussed. Each of these astronomical processes operates on a different periodicity, but they all affect the climate of the earth. Just as lunar and solar cycles interact to produce extreme tides, these long-term astronomical cycles should interact to produce major climatic cycles on a geological time scale that are evident in the geological record. Most notably, the interaction of these variables is thought to have given rise to the major climatic cycles associated with the Pliocene and Pleistocene glaciations (Ruddiman, 2001).

Chapter 3, by Francis H. Brown, is on "Geochronometry: Measurement of Geologic Time." As an accurate assessment of the age of paleontological and archaeological material, geochronometry is critical for an understanding of many aspects of our past. These aspects include the sequence in which changes took place, the rate of evolutionary or cultural change, and likelihood that two species or events were contemporary. This chapter provides an overview of different methods of geological dating that are discussed more thoroughly in subsequent chapters.

The fourth chapter, by Henry P. Schwarcz, is on "Radiocarbon Dating." This technique, based on the decay of the radioactive isotope carbon-14 (^{14}C) to stable nitrogen (^{14}N), is applicable to many organically formed materials containing carbon, such as wood, charcoal, hair, coprolites, bones, and shells. Using this method, researchers can reliably calculate ages from the present to approximately 40,000 years ago (kya); beyond 40 kya, the amount of original carbon remaining in the sample is so small that reliable dates are difficult to obtain.

Chapter 5, by Francis H. Brown, is on "Potassium-Argon Dating." This dating technique is based on the spontaneous decay of the potassium-40 isotope (^{40}K) to argon-40 (^{40}Ar). Most recent applications of this technique rely on measurement of two argon isotopes, ^{40}Ar and ^{39}Ar, because of their greater analytical precision. Although this technique is limited to dating igneous rocks, and geological sections associated with them, it is applicable over a wide range of ages between roughly 1 kya (in special circumstances) and 1,000,000,000 (1 bya). The initial development of this technique, and its application in 1961 in dating Bed 1 of Olduvai Gorge at nearly 2 mya, revolutionized our appreciation of the time involved in human evolution (Leakey, Curtis, and Everndon, 1961; Curtis and Everndon, 1962).

Chapter 6, by Henry P. Schwarcz, "Electron Spin Resonance Dating, Fission-Track Dating, Thermoluminescence Dating and Uranium-Series Dating," is a composite of several short articles that describe a suite of dating techniques that have become increasingly applied to the later stages of human evolution. These later stages have been difficult to date using either ^{14}C or potassium-argon, requiring the use of alternate techniques. Although these techniques have not yet proved to be as reliable in yielding consistent results as ^{14}C or potassium-argon methods, they are being refined constantly. These methods are widely applied to materials that are too old for ^{14}C dating, or from depositional environments such as caves or clastic deposits that lack igneous rocks suitable for potassium-argon dating.

Electron spin resonance (ESR) is a technique that measures the accumulated radiation damage that occurs in a solid material over time. Alpha, beta, and gamma radiation cause electron "holes" that can last for significant periods of time in undisturbed solids. An ESR spectrometer uses microwave energy and a varying magnetic field to detect the number of these holes. By knowing the radiation dose rate for the sample and comparing the sample's ESR signal to signals obtained from experimentally irradiated samples, the age of the sample can be determined. This technique works best in caves where the samples have been shielded from external sources of radiation. Though the technique requires numerous assumptions about the stability of the sample over geological time, it is potentially applicable to a wide range of materials, including tooth enamel, speleothems (flowstone), mollusk shells, and corals.

Another technique that measures trapped electron charges is thermoluminescence dating (TL). This technique is possible because some materials give off visible light when heated. The temperature at which light energy is released from the electron traps is based on the time since the traps were formed, with the oldest traps yielding energy peaks at the highest temperatures. This technique has been used to date both sediments that were exposed to light before burial and to archaeological materials that may have been exposed to heat, such as ceramics or lithics made of quartz or flint. In the case of sediments, such as sands, it dates the time since the sediments were buried and no longer exposed to light. For archaeological remains, it dates the time elapsed since they were last at high temperatures, either through firing or through use in cooking.

Fission-track dating is based on the observation that radioactive uranium contained in the crystals of igneous minerals and glasses undergoes spontaneous fission, and that the fission particles leave tracks in the mineral. Because fission takes place at a constant rate for any sample, the time since the sample was formed can be estimated by determining the spontaneous fission rate for the sample and by counting the tracks. The reliability of the technique can be limited by the amount of uranium in the sample and by tracks being obliterated through recrystallization, often due to reheating.

Uranium-series dating (also known as thorium dating or thorium-uranium dating) is based on the decay of uranium into several radioactive daughter isotopes, and ultimately into thorium. By measuring the ratio of the isotopes, it is possible to determine the age of the material being dated. The technique is limited to material that initially contained uranium, but not thorium, and that has been closed to outside sources of uranium since it was formed. It has been widely applied to speleothems and travertines in caves, as well as to calcretes in soils. Efforts to date biological materials such as mollusk shells or bones have not yielded reliable dates because of the introduction of uranium after fossilization.

Chapter 7, "Paleomagnetism and Human Evolution," by Francis H. Brown, describes the use of changes in the earth's magnetic field to determine the age of rocks. The earth's magnetic field has varied unpredictably through geological time in both the polarity (the north-south directions) of the poles and their exact geographic positions. Most rocks contain iron oxide minerals that act as magnets and record the direction and polarity of the poles when the rocks are formed. By measuring the paleomagnetism in rocks, one can estimate when the rocks were formed by comparing these features with the sequence of polarity and position changes in the poles that have been determined from well-dated rocks. In this article, Brown reviews the ways in which different rocks acquire their magnetic record and the way in which the geomagnetic polarity time scale has been developed.

The final chapter in this section, Chapter 8, "Taphonomy in Human Evolution," by Andrew Hill, explains the use of this technique in understanding the human fossil record. Taphonomy is the study of all the things that happen to an organism between its death and its recovery many years later as a fossil. Taphonomy seeks to explain why, and more significantly how, the assemblages found as fossils differ from the living communities from which they were derived. By understanding the processes that cause some animals to be more or less likely to become fossilized, and some parts of animals more or less likely to be preserved, we can better reconstruct the actual animals and communities of animals as they lived in earlier epochs.

REFERENCES

Curtis, G. H., and J. P. Everndon. 1962. Age of basalt underlying Bed I, Olduvai. *Nature* 194:610–612.
Leakey, L. S. B., G. H. Curtis, and J. P. Everndon. 1961. Age of Bed I, Olduvai Gorge, Tanganiyika. *Nature* 191:478–479.
Ruddiman, W. F. 2001. *Earth's Climate Past and Future.* W. H. Freeman and Company, New York.

1

Stratigraphy Explained

F. H. Brown and J. A. Van Couvering

Stratigraphy is the study of the origin, physical characteristics, and spatial relationships of stratified rocks, primarily to understand the history of events documented in the strata. Layers of sediment are the principal object of study, but layered volcanic rocks, and even metamorphosed strata, can also be interpreted according to the three great principles of stratigraphy. The *principle of superposition* states that in an undisturbed sequence each stratum is younger than the one beneath; the *principle of original horizontality* states that strata are horizontal or nearly so when they are deposited; and the *principle of original lateral continuity* states that all parts of a stratum, however disrupted by later activity, were once joined in a single connected layer.

Rock strata may be classified by any of their properties or by inferred attributes, such as the time or environment of origin. In general, the units based on one set of properties do not coincide with units based on another, and a different set of units is thus needed for each classification. The three most common criteria by which strata are classified are lithology, fossil content, and age, and these give rise to the three main branches of stratigraphy: *lithostratigraphy, biostratigraphy,* and *chronostratigraphy,* respectively. Magnetostratigraphy, isotope stratigraphy, and cyclostratigraphy are also coming into wide use. Lithostratigraphic and biostratigraphic units are always limited because they depend on features that have finite vertical and lateral extent. Magnetostratigraphy, isotope stratigraphy, and cyclostratigraphy are based on global phenomena that, in theory, affect all sedimentary environments (and, in the case of magnetostratigraphy, igneous environments as well), but observing them is highly dependent on favorable circumstances. Only chronostratigraphic units are recognizable globally under all circumstances, because they are based on specified intervals of deposition rather than on specified processes of deposition.

Each of the stratigraphic categories has its own particular terminology, and the names of units in general do not overlap from one classification to another.

The thickness of lithostratigraphic units is not related explicitly to the passage of time, but in all other classifications there are exact geochronological equivalents. None of the stratigraphic-time units are inherently measurable in terms of years. On the one hand, magnetostratigraphy, isotope stratigraphy, and cyclo-

stratigraphy are related to age-calibrated models, while, on the other hand, chronostratigraphic and biochronological time units are scaled to the rock record. In the stratigraphies that relate to year-calibrated ideal models, the distinction between the stratigraphic unit and time tends to be blurred by the fact that the identification of these units conveys an immediate age value to the rocks. The distinction between magnetozone and chron, for instance, is very seldom considered, and most writers use *chron* as if it were being observed directly in the strata; thus, *lower Matuyama Chron* is commonly used where the modifier *early* would be more appropriate. As for isotope stages and orbitally induced cycles, no attempt has been made to erect geochronological equivalents, because the lithologic expressions of these stratigraphies and the chronometric models are always treated as one.

In chronostratigraphy, however, the difference between rocks and time is essential. This relationship is made clear by a two-aspect terminology, so that Tertiary, for instance, is both a System of rocks and a Period of time. In order to express this, stratigraphers conscientiously use the modifiers *lower* and *upper* to refer to strata, and *early* and *late* to refer to age. The word *middle* is used for both position and time, although some stratigraphers prefer *medial* for time units. With this in mind, it is logically impossible to speak of a Lower Pleistocene age or an Early Pleistocene formation. These positional modifiers are capitalized, as a matter of taste, when they mean an exact and complete subdivision of a rock or time unit; lowercase is employed where the meaning is intentionally vague or where the terms are simply comparative.

The rock record is far from complete. It is broken by myriad gaps of varying length, which are expressed as buried surfaces. There are two primary genetic types of gap: *diastems,* which are due to the inherent transitions or pauses in a continuing depositional process—e.g., the intervals between floods on a floodplain—and *discontinuities,* which are due to changes or interruptions in the depositional process itself. These range from *condensed sections,* where deposition was markedly slowed, to *disconformities,* where deposition was completely interrupted. Disconformities are usually marked by indications of exposure such as weathering, chemical alteration, or signs of organic habitation (burrowing, root casts), as well as a difference between the strata. Erosion during exposure leads to the extreme discontinuity called an *unconformity,* in which previously buried strata are eroded. In some circumstances, diastems involving contemporaneous facies can mimic erosional unconformities—e.g., in delta systems where migrating gravel-filled distributary channels carve their way laterally through fine-laminated overbank deposits.

Lateral relationships between strata are of great importance, particularly in the reconstruction of ancient landscapes. Sands may be deposited along the shoreline of a lake at the same time that finer sediments are being deposited farther offshore and gravels are being laid down in stream channels. As a result, rock types change as the strata within a defined unit are traced laterally; these features are called *facies*. In treating facies, it is imperative to maintain accurate time correlation because the objective of studying facies is to document the lateral variations in lithology and paleontology (as lithofacies and biofacies, respectively) in order to understand the environmental conditions under which the strata were formed. The term *facies* has also been used to mean the rocks of a particular sedimentary environment, without regard to coeval lateral relationships, but such a unit is properly termed a *lithotope*. The equivalent paleontological term for an environmentally governed set of fossils is a *biotope*.

Depositional environments are not fixed in geographic position but change position as time passes. Thus, the shoreline of a lake advances and retreats as its water budget changes or as subsidence in the lake basin waxes or wanes. As the position of the shoreline changes, so, too, do the kinds of sediments being deposited at a particular spot. The fact that the sediments of coeval adjacent facies will also be deposited adjacent to one another in vertical succession is known as *Walther's Law*.

Factors that control the distribution of stratigraphic facies are manifold. In regard to lithofacies, some of the more important are the amount of sediment supplied to an area of deposition, the climate in the immediate region and also in the source area of the sediments, tectonic movements, changes in base level (for whatever reason), changes in the kind or degree of biological activity, and chemical changes in water bodies associated with the site of deposition. In regard to biofacies, external factors include geology, topography, water supply, water depth, latitude, and seasonality, but the internal dynamics of the biosphere also play a major role. Climatic changes and geological movements are completely or largely insensitive to changes in the other factors but may induce large changes in them, so climate and tectonics may be viewed as more basic controlling factors than the others.

STANDARDS IN STRATIGRAPHIC PRACTICE

Stratigraphy is strictly governed by international guidelines, based on earlier national stratigraphic codes of the United States, the United Kingdom, and the former USSR. The guidelines spell out standards for defining and using units, with a modern emphasis on unambiguous physical definitions—i.e., type sections and boundary-stratotypes—rather than interpretations of paleoclimate, biological evolution, or geological events. Another distinction of the modern guidelines is the accommodation of new stratigraphies that are based on instrumental or mathematical analysis of layered sequences.

LITHOSTRATIGRAPHY

Every stratigraphic unit is based on the lithified crust of the Earth, but lithostratigraphic units are the only ones based on rocks alone. Because such units are the basis of geological mapping, their only requirement is that they are clearly and reliably recognizable across a reasonable distance. The least lithostratigraphic unit is a *bed*, which is simply the smallest unit that can be depicted on geological maps, and, in fact, the term is very often applied to units that are made up of smaller, unmappable beds (i.e., laminae or strata). The basic unit of lithostratigraphy is the *formation*, which is any well characterized set of beds with consistent mappable characteristics and clear stratigraphic boundaries. The division of formations into *members*—or the combination of formations into *groups*—is a matter of convenience, and the same strata may be included in different formations where regional points of view overlap. Formations may consist of several lithic phases, or *facies* (for instance, alternating conglomerates and shales), and it is common for formations to grade laterally or vertically with others through facies changes. Two terms for regionally mappable units, from the old USSR code, are *horizon*, a lithological level that can be recognized throughout a wide region by some distinctive fossil or mineral property, and *suite*, a composite unit like a group but organized laterally, rather than vertically, by the inclusion of coeval facies, in order to have a regional scope (e.g., the lake beds, river gravels, and peats of an interior montane valley).

A formation is defined in terms of a designated type section where the rocks can be best described, measured, and revisited. The type sections of subsurface formations and beds, or formations that are badly exposed at the surface, can be designated in boreholes or mines. The names of formations consist of a unique title, usually taken from a local cultural or geographic feature, and a descriptive appellation that may be generic (i.e., Formation, Member) or specific (i.e., Shale, Grit, Trachyte). The combinations are always capitalized: Jebel Qatrani Formation, Kabarnet Trachyte, Lubur Grits. Members and beds can have titles like formations, or they can have completely descriptive names (Lower Member, White Tuff, Upper Gravels). There are many exceptions to standard nomenclature, especially in the older literature—e.g., the Old Red Sandstone, the Millstone Grit, or the Kupferschiefer—and custom still allows much variation. The Olduvai Beds, for instance, are a formation, and its members are both numbered (Bed I, Bed II) and named (Lemuta Member).

BIOSTRATIGRAPHY

Biostratigraphy classifies rock strata according to their included fossils, without reference to the evolutionary relationships or absolute age of the remains. The use of fossils to distinguish bodies of rock predates Darwin by a century or more and is still widely applied. The most commonly used criterion for the boundary of a biozone is the presence or absence of designated fossils, but other criteria, such as the morphology or evolutionary stage of the fossils, or the frequency or relative abundance of the fossils, are also employed. Being defined on the basis of organisms, biozones tend to be recognized over much greater lateral extent than formations and through greater thicknesses of strata. Certain marine planktonic microfossils, in particular, result from dispersal so rapid and extensive that their biozone boundaries have virtually the same geologic age around the globe.

Modern biostratigraphers recognize that the observations of fossils in the rock do not provide an accurate record of true biological history, because of incomplete preservation, incomplete sampling, and the human nature of paleontologists. For this reason, the limit of occurrence of a fossil in rock is known as a *datum level,* emphasizing that the stratigraphic observations are necessarily different from the inferred historical events— evolution, immigration, extinction—that they only approximately record. Some paleontologists use the acronyms FAD (First Appearance Datum) and LAD (Last Appearance Datum) to distinguish the bottom and top of a fossil taxon's observed stratigraphic range. In biochronology, *datum event* is used to refer to the historical equivalent of a datum level.

Among the several kinds of biozones, an *assemblage-zone* (or faunal-zone in vertebrate paleontology) is a body of strata defined by the joint occurrence of a group of specified fossils. *Range-zones,* which are bodies of strata defined by the fossils of one or two specified taxa, fall into several variants. A *total-range-zone* is the strata between the FAD and the LAD of a designated taxon; a *partial-range-zone* is the strata between the FADs of two designated taxa (or, rarely, the interval between the LADs of two designated taxa); and a *concurrent-range-zone* is the strata in which two designated taxa overlap. An *acme-zone* is a body of strata defined by the relatively high abundance of a designated taxon. All biostratigraphic units are identified by the name or names of their characterizing fossil taxa and the type of zone (e.g., the *Globorotalia margaritae* partial-range zone of tropical planktonic foraminifera in the lowermost Pliocene).

CHRONOSTRATIGRAPHY

Rocks that form during a specified interval of time are classified in time-stratigraphic (= chronostratigraphic) units. The objective of chronostratigraphy is to put all strata of the same age into the same chronostratigraphic unit. The boundaries of time-stratigraphic units are isochronous planes, independent of rock types or thickness. They are also independent of absolute-age measurement, and their application depends strictly on the first principle of stratigraphy: that the age of any stratum relative to another is established by their superpositional relationship. Chronostratigraphy is, therefore, capable of classifying strata in terms of their age relative to another stratum with great precision, no matter how old the rocks are. The extension of chronostratigraphic boundaries accurately from region to region, known as *time-stratigraphic correlation,* is one of the great and never-

finished tasks of stratigraphers. For many years, regional correlations depended almost entirely on comparisons of biostratigraphic data, but radiometric dating, magneto-stratigraphy, isotope stratigraphy, and cyclostratigraphy have brought new levels of accuracy to this procedure.

Chronostratigraphic units are hierarchal, and, in principle, the greater are defined in terms of the lesser, such that the boundaries of a system are defined by the boundaries of its oldest and youngest included series, and so on. *Stages* are the smallest units that are, in theory, capable of being correlated globally, and, therefore, stage boundaries (at least potentially) define all others in the hierarchy. One difficulty is that there have been many stages defined around the world, and it has been necessary to rule that the sequence of marine stages of western Europe are to be considered as the global standard stages.

A stage is characterized in a *stage-stratotype,* which establishes its basic character and scope, but, because stratotype sections are designated in different places, there are usually stratigraphic overlaps and gaps between one stratotype and the next. To address this fact of life, the international guidelines recommend that "base defines boundary," so that the base of each unit is simultaneously the top of the one beneath, regardless of the upper limits of its stratotype. This makes the base all important, and the guidelines, therefore, recommend that every stage (and, thus, every unit in the hierarchy) eventually must be defined at its base by a *boundary-stratotype,* or unique physical reference point, to which the boundary is correlated around the world. This point, sometimes referred to as a *golden spike,* is a single stratigraphic plane in an accessible, appropriate, and easily correlatable section of beds—preferably, but not necessarily, located in the stage-stratotype section. Once defined, the boundary-stratotype may not be moved without formal action, even if new fossil finds or other evidence indicate that the reasons cited for its placement were in error. A number of boundary-stratotypes have been approved by the International Union of Geological Sciences for the status of GSSP, or Global-Boundary Stratotype Section and Point.

MAGNETOSTRATIGRAPHY

Paleomagnetic polarity is a feature that should be characteristic of all strata deposited during particular time intervals, because the magnetic field of the Earth is a global phenomenon. The isochronous boundaries between normal and reversed magnetozones are thus, in theory, ideal correlation tools. The practice, however, is more difficult, because many strata do not preserve paleomagnetic orientation. Furthermore, in those that do, paleomagnetic polarity reversals are indistinguishable from one another. This means that the identity of a particular reversal must be narrowed down in some way before a tenable correlation can be proposed. The usual method is to apply an external time scale, through correlation to a dated level or by direct dating of the magnetostratigraphic section. Another method is to match the studied section to the model of the calibrated paleomagnetic time scale, according to the thickness pattern of reversals or to the variations in geomagnetic intensity.

Another feature of magnetostratigraphic correlations that must be kept constantly in mind is that the isochroneity of the reversal boundaries is actually somewhat fuzzy because transitions—the interval in which the Earth has essentially no magnetic field—require at least 5 Kyr. Furthermore, the imprinting of a new polarity regime on strata can be delayed by thousands of years in certain environments. Bioturbation disorders the acquired polarity of seafloor sediments, and the fixation of detrital geomagnetic orientation in open-ocean marine deposits normally does not take place until the material is buried to ca. 40 cm. The time required for this depth of burial varies and is, of course, much longer in slowly deposited sediments. The age of a microfossil specimen is, therefore, synchronous not with the remanent magnetization in the horizon in which it occurs, but with that of a horizon ca. 40 cm below. Thus, the apparent microfossil "date" of a paleomagnetic horizon is always somewhat younger in deep-sea sediments than in the more rapidly deposited shallow marine equivalents.

ISOTOPE STRATIGRAPHY AND CYCLOSTRATIGRAPHY

These classifications, which reflect astronomically forced climate change, are not depicted as bounded units but as data curves in which the peaks are numbered starting from the present. The astronomical cycles are assumed *a priori* to have had globally synchronous effects, if not everywhere expressed in the same way or with the same intensity. All of the medium-high-frequency (10 to 100 Kyr) variations in oxygen and carbon isotope ratios in the later Cenozoic have now been related to astronomical cycles, and it is probable that this will prove to be the case in older strata as well. The correlation of isotope and insolation-cycle curves between one region and another is analogous to the correlation of tree rings or magnetostratigraphy, in that external evidence of age is combined with pattern recognition.

FURTHER READINGS

Ager, D. V. (1981). The Nature of the Stratigraphical Record. New York: Halsted/Wiley.

Dunbar, C. O., and Rodgers, J. (1957). Principles of Stratigraphy. New York: Wiley.

Eicher, D. L. (1976). Geologic Time. Englewood Cliffs, N.J.: Prentice-Hall.

Salvador, A., ed. (1994). International Stratigraphic Guide, 2nd ed. Boulder: Geological Society of America.

2

Cyclostratigraphy

J. A. Van Couvering

Cyclostratigraphy is the analysis of rhythmic features in the stratigraphic record according to astronomical cycles and, in particular, the Earth-orbital cycles with periodicities between 0.1 and 1.0 Myr that support an orbital-forcing time scale (OFT). Precision in OFT dating does not decrease with increasing age because the cyclic effects are stratigraphic features that are directly observable in the rocks. The accuracy of OFT dates, which depends on the extrapolation of orbital and rotational cycles into the past, is also well controlled because the cycles are independent and can be cross-checked against one another, and because changes in the astronomical periodicities over time can be calculated with great confidence. Other appellations for this relatively new discipline include *"cosmostratigraphy," "orbital stratigraphy,"* and *astrochronology.*

MILANKOVITCH CYCLES

The frequency spectrum of astronomical-motion periodicities ranges from pulsar spin, measured in milliseconds, through rotational and orbital periods of Earth, moon, and sun, to galactic cycles measured in tens of millions of years. Using the present sidereal year as the unit of measurement, this spectrum has been subdivided for convenience into frequency bands: calendar ($1/\text{yr} \times 10^{-3}$ to $1/\text{yr}$), solar ($1/\text{yr}$ to $1/\text{yr} \times 10^3$), Milankovitch ($1/\text{yr} \times 10^3$ to $1/\text{yr} \times 10^6$), and galactic ($1/\text{yr} \times 10^6$ to $1/\text{yr} \times 10^9$). The effects of calendar- and solar-frequency astronomical motion, such as tidal, seasonal, annual, and sunspot cycles, have long been recognized in growth stages of fossilized organisms and in fine-laminated sediments. At the turn of the twentieth century, G. K. Gilbert was proposing that such astronomical cycles might be useful in geochronology, but the known cycles were of too high frequency or, like cyclothems, were too episodic and noisy, to be of any practical use in this regard. M. Milankovitch, beginning in 1920, argued a direct relationship between the broad fluctuations of Pleistocene climate and the calculated variations of insolation (the flux of solar energy reaching the atmosphere at a given latitude) that could result from cyclic patterns in three different orbital motions—precession of the equinoxes, obliquity wobble, and eccentricity—and proposed that this could be used to determine the age of paleoclimatic features.

Milankovitch's calculations have been significantly extended and refined in massive computerized treatments that bring out the internal complexity of the orbital oscillations. It should be kept in mind that the numerical values used in general discussion are only convenient approximations or averages and that the effect of each cycle is different from the others in quality as well as timing. Over the duration of the Phanerozoic, the rotation of the Earth has slowed appreciably, and the moon's orbit has contracted, with effects on the computed orbital-forcing functions that must also be incorporated. The obliquity wobble, for instance, is now 40 percent faster than in the Silurian. The resultant of the three Milankovitch cycles is projected as a family of latitude-dependent insolation curves, with that of 65°N considered as the standard.

Precession

This refers to the shift of seasons with regard to the Earth's orbit, due to the combined effect of a 26-Kyr swing in the orientation of the Earth's rotational axis with regard to the orbit, and an independent, separate progression of the perihelion-aphelion nodes (nearest and farthest points in orbit) around the orbital path. This has the effect of causing the seasons to precess with respect to perihelion in periods of 19 and 23 Kyr, with an effective quasi period or average of insolation variation at 21.7 Kyr. The effects of precession are opposite in the Northern and Southern Hemispheres because aphelion (colder) winters and perihelion (warmer) summers in one hemisphere will be synchronous with perihelion winters and aphelion summers in the other hemisphere. At present, the Earth is approaching the peak of northern perihelion summers.

Obliquity

Also known as *tilt*, this refers to the angle between the Earth's rotational axis and the plane of the ecliptic. Tilt variations have greatest effect at the poles, and higher obliquity means warmer summers and colder winters at high latitudes in both hemispheres. Currently, the tilt of the axis varies between 22° and 24°30′, with a major quasi periodicity of 41 Kyr and minor components at 29 and 54 Kyr. The present angle of tilt is 23°27′, and it is in decrease toward the minimum. In addition, the amplitude of the variation in tilt changes by almost 100 percent on a cycle of 1.3 Ma. Intervals of high-amplitude obliquity coincide with clusters of the most severe glacial phases, but the obliquity amplitude at present is close to a minimum.

Eccentricity

This term refers to the degree of ellipticity (deviation from roundness) in the Earth's orbit. Eccentricity is caused by interactions with other planets, with major periods at 120, 100, and 95 Kyr, leading to a quasi period of insolation that varies around a mean of 100 Kyr. Eccentricity is declining from a recent maximum. The amplitude of eccentricity cycles also varies, with a major quasi period of 410 Kyr. Eccentricity significantly modulates the effects of both obliquity and precession.

Considering the entire year and integrating over the entire planet, the precession and tilt variations do not result in a change in total insolation, but only in its distribution. Only eccentricity cycles have an effect on total received insolation. Thus, eccentricity and precession dominate the signal at the equator, while obliquity is the primary influence on radiation received at the poles.

STRATIGRAPHY AND CYCLES: PROXY CURVES

The insolation of the past cannot be measured directly, of course, and cyclostratigraphy depends on sedimentary features whose variations are a proxy, or reflection, of the Milankovitch periods. None, however, of the various proxy curves in common use are completely faithful reproductions of the calculated net insolation curves. For one thing, the Milankovitch cycles probably affect insolation by only 5 to 10 percent and must be enhanced by feedback in climatic-oceanic systems in order to produce a sedimentary signal that is strong enough to be filtered from background variability. The amplification of the feedback, in turn, depends greatly on the degree of instability in the global climatic-oceanic system. The sedimentary imprint of Milankovitch cycles on Mesozoic and Lower Cenozoic strata is relatively muted because the warm oceans of that period buffered insolation-driven variations. In the later Cenozoic, however, the contrast between increasingly refrigerated ocean masses and the sun-warmed surfaces meant that global climates were much less stable, so that effects of the Milankovitch cycles were more influential. To make matters more complex, the climatic-oceanic system tends to respond independently to each of the three primary Milankovitch cycles.

Fortunately, the proxy curves, however distorted in amplitude, record insolation periodicities fairly well. The most detailed and reliable studies of Milankovitch cycles are based on proxy responses in three climate-sensitive systems: (1) stable isotopes of carbon and oxygen in the open ocean, (2) sapropels, and (3) marl-limestone rhythmites in sediments of protected basins.

Stable-Isotope Ratios

Milankovitch's theories were taken lightly until the mid-1960s, when the micropaleontologist Cesare Emiliani at the University of Miami began to present evidence for global climate changes that corresponded with the Milankovitch predictions. Emiliani and his students had found that the ratio of the two most common isotopes

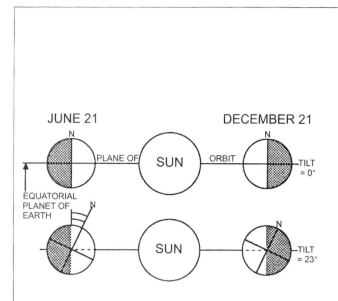

Axial tilt. When tilt is increased, polar regions receive more sunlight, since the summer sun is higher in the sky, while intensity of winter light is little changed. When tilt is low, regions close to the pole receive pratically no sunlight the year round.

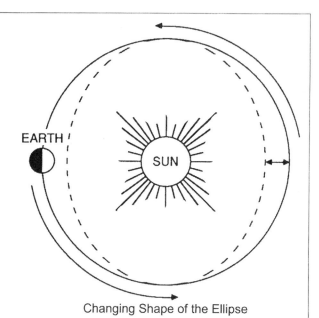

Changing Shape of the Ellipse

Orbital eccentricity. The shape of the earth's orbit changes from nearly circular to more elliptical, in cycles that repeat at irregular intervals concentrating around 100,000 and 400,000 years.

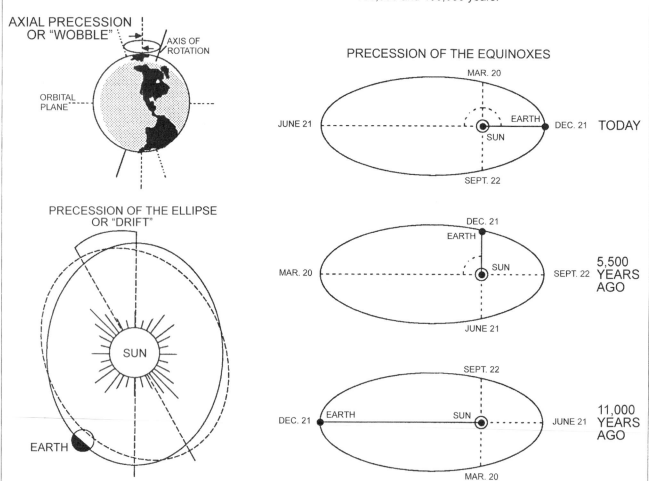

Precession of axial tilt and orbit. "Wobble" and "drift" together result in a cycle of 22,000 years in the timing of the seasons with regard to the orbit. Today the winter solstice in the nothern hemisphere occurs when the Earth is near the sun: 11,000 years ago it occurred when the Earth was far from the sun.

of carbon, ^{12}C and ^{13}C, (written as $\delta^{13}C$), in the shells of the surface-floating planktonic foraminiferan *Globigerina* varied according to the temperature of the water in which the shells had formed. Looking at this ratio in the fossilized tests of this foraminifer in sea-floor cores, it was found that the $\delta^{13}C$ varied with depth below the ocean floor, indicating historical changes in water temperatures that synchronized with Milankovitch's calculations. The primitive state of core sampling and geochronometry at that time prevented Emiliani from conclusively identifying Milankovitch cycles below Upper Pleistocene levels. In the following years, data from the Deep Sea Drilling Project and concurrent advances in dating abundantly substantiated and extended these pioneer findings.

In addition to the carbon-isotope ratios, it was found that the ratio of the common oxygen isotopes ^{16}O to ^{18}O (written as $\delta^{18}O$) in the carbonate of the fossil shells also varied with geologic age in curves that closely (but not exactly) matched the carbon-isotope curves. There is no difference, however, between oxygen-isotope ratios in modern marine seas from the poles to the tropics, so the observed geologic variations in $\delta^{18}O$ cannot be a reflection of changes in local water temperature. Instead, oxygen isotopes in seawater are fractionated by surface evaporation that takes up the lighter isotope preferentially, making airborne water much lighter isotopically than seawater. Considering the size of the oceans, a perceptible long-term variation in the oxygen-isotope ratio of surface waters requires a significant change in the amount of fresh water that is held separate from the ocean. Calculations indicate that only the growth and melting of major continental ice sheets could affect the $\delta^{18}O$ of seawater with the extent and rapidity observed in the Late Cenozoic. In other words, the oxygen-isotope record of the ocean reflects worldwide variation in continental ice sheets, while the carbon-isotope record reflects variation in sea surface temperature (SST) in the sample area.

Since the mid-1960s, the undisturbed, microfossil-rich sediments in the abyssal basins have been probed by hundreds of deep-drilled cores (and thousands of gravity cores) all around the globe, providing a strongly reinforced record of ocean history in unprecedented detail and accuracy. Several sets of these cores have been analyzed to give a continuous, standardized stable-isotope curve that extends to the base of the Pliocene, where the abnormal conditions of the Messinian event remain to be bridged, at least in terms of this proxy if not in others (see below). Because SST is subject to large, unpredictable local biases, the temperature curve from carbon-isotope ratios in planktonic foraminifera is considered to be a less reliable indicator of global climate change than the ice-volume curve described by the oxygen-isotope ratios. By convention, the major stable-isotope peaks are numbered from the present, so that warm (ice-minimum) peaks have odd numbers, and cold (ice-maximum) peaks have even numbers. For instance, the base of the Pleistocene, in the Eburonian glacial advance, is identified with isotope peak 64.

Sapropels

Variations in the carbon content of laminated strata in certain marine and lacustrine sequences have been found to accurately proxy both the relative intensity and the duration of Milankovitch-forced climatic cycles. To consider sapropels first, these are distinct, fine-laminated layers found in certain deep basins, such as the Eastern Mediterranean, that have anomalously high amounts of unreduced organic carbon (2 percent or more by weight) compared to negligible amounts in enclosing strata. Individual sapropel beds can be traced over wide areas, and in diluted form (as *sapropelic laminites*) into areas of higher sedimentation, clearly as the result of events of regional or wider significance.

Characteristically, sapropels and laminites are rich in diatoms and contain undisturbed fish skeletons, indicating high surface productivity and anoxic bottom conditions. In outcrop, they tend to stand out as distinct soft, dark bands, sometimes with a white gypsiferous efflorescence from the weathering of pyrite.

The modern consensus is that sapropels and sapropelic laminites tend to form at perihelion summer peaks, termed precession minima, in the 21-Kyr precession cycle. Analysis of sapropels supports the contention that the transient change in the carbon cycle is associated with weaker winter storms and higher summer rainfall in temperate regions at such times. As a result, circulation is markedly slowed, at these latitudes, in semiclosed basins (such as the Balearic Basin and the eastern Mediterranean) where seasonal convection overturn is the primary source of oxygenated water to the depths. Simultaneously, even as ventilation of deep water is reduced or cut off completely, the supply of limiting nutrients such as iron, phosphate, and nitrogen into the surface waters may be increased through higher levels of summer erosion and runoff. Whether or not surface waters become more productive, an excess of unreduced carbon will accumulate in response to the stagnation during perihelion peaks.

Carbonate Cycles

Experiments in connection with *global warming* amply demonstrate the role of atmospheric CO_2 as a heat trap. That its variation amplifies orbital effects, and those of precession-driven cycles in particular, is indicated by geological observations. For example, it has been found that, in Antarctic ice cores, layers with elevated carbon-dioxide content appear to be synchronous with intervals in the $\delta^{18}O$ curve that represent reduced ice volume. Atmospheric CO_2 is, however, largely controlled by the much greater CO_2 content of oceanic surface water. This is, in turn, influenced by conditions in the atmosphere, in what appears to be a complex interplay of deep water upwelling in response to wind velocity, terrestrial biotic activity, sea surface temperature, and the areal extent of limestone deposition in reefs and shallows. In this system, the increase and decrease of atmospheric CO_2 appears to involve self-reinforcing feedback that is set in motion by insolation changes.

The higher summer temperatures of precession minima mean lowered solubility of calcium carbonate and CO_2 in surface waters. At these times, the boundary of carbonate-saturated water deepens, and more carbonate is precipitated (or less is dissolved) in shallow- and medium-depth sediments. In outcrops of strata that were deposited under the migrating boundary, the precession rhythm is clearly seen in the alternation of soft marls and harder, more limy strata. In some basins, where both oxygen and carbon dioxide were at sensitive levels, precession cycles are recorded by superimposed sapropel and carbonate signals, and the two-layered marl-limestone rhythmite is replaced by a four-layered marl-limestone-sapropel-limestone unit.

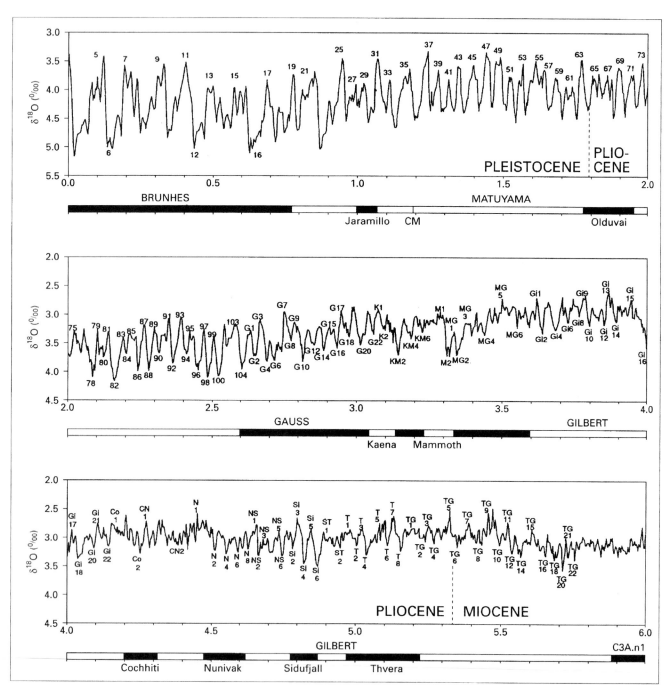

Standard oxygen isotope stages of the upper Cenozoic. The variation of the oxygen isotope ratio in the world ocean, due to changes in ice volume on land, show how orbital cycles have increased their influence as the ocean cooled and climate became increasingly sensitive to slight changes in annual insolation. Analysis of fine-layered marine deposits has shown that variation in carbonate and organic content, storm-related dust, and debris dropped from icebergs, all related to climate change, can be matched precisely to each isotopic peak and valley. The stratigraphic records of East African lakes, Chinese loess, and vegetational successions have also been closely matched to the cyclostratigraphic "time scale." Courtesy of N.J. Shackleton.

Cycle Groups

In sections with well-developed cyclic lithology, groupings of stronger and weaker (or missing) precession-driven peaks are evident and bespeak the influence of longer-term orbital cycles. The 100-Kyr eccentricity cycle, which strongly moderates the amplitude of the 21.7-Kyr precession cycle, is presently the dominant overprint in the stable-isotope record; prior to the Elsterian glaciation peak, broadly centered at 450 Ka, the 41-Kyr obliquity cycle had more effect, suggesting that the Arctic climate was less stable (i.e., warmer during obliquity maxima) than today. Over longer intervals, the interaction of the 410-Kyr periodicity in eccentricity-amplitude and higher-frequency cycles produced beats widely recognized as "major cold-climate peaks" at 2.5, 1.8, 0.9, 0.6–0.45, and 0.1 Ma. The 1.3-Myr. cycle in obliquity amplitude appears to have augmented the Elsterian peak (0.45), and also the Eburonian peak

(1.8) at the beginning of the Pleistocene. The overprint of the longer cycles is extremely useful in controlling the count of precession cycles.

Calibration

The first successful correlation of the geological time scale to cyclostratigraphy produced some striking results. Recognition of the 21-Kyr precession cycles through the Pleistocene and into the Middle Pliocene was first achieved by oxygen-isotope analysis of microfossils in Pacific deep-sea cores obtained during the Ocean Drilling Program in the late 1980s. Direct counting of the cycles demonstrated that the existing radiometric calibration of the geomagnetic polarity reversals, as seen in the same cores, was from 2 to 7 percent too old. A series of high-resolution laser-fusion $^{40}Ar/^{39}Ar$ dates on key sections, including several containing the Brunhes-Matuyama boundary as well as the type section

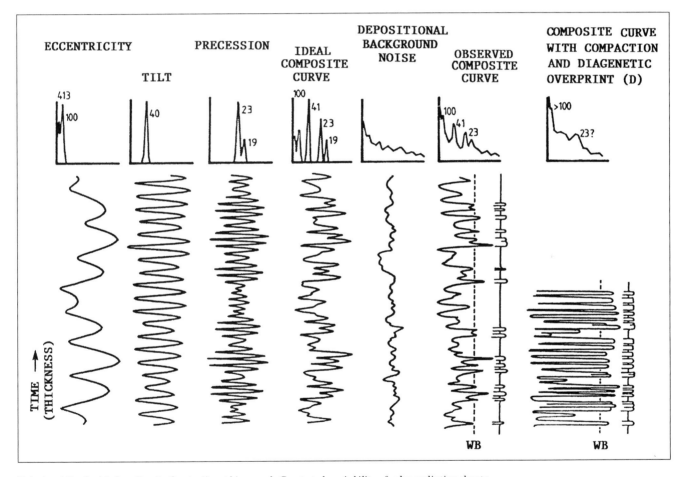

Relationship of orbital motion to the stratigraphic record. Computed variability of solar radiation due to orbital eccentricity, axial tilt (or obliquity), and equinoctial precession is indicated in the three left-hand columns, as are their cycle durations. The ideal composite insolation curve for a temperate latitude shows the 41 Kyr obliquity cycle as the dominant influence, as in the early Pleistocene. The insolation signal, although degraded by random variation in sedimentation ("background noise") and modified by CO_2 feedback (not considered here), is imprinted on receptive stratigraphic sequences as alternating bands of sediment reflecting cyclic climate change. The distorted signal is shown on the left and the resulting banding pattern on the right side of the observed composite column. Cutoff sensitivity of the depositional system to the orbitally forced climate shifts (line WB), and the effects of post-depositional change such as sediment compaction, cause further loss of orbital information in the resulting sedimentary sequence. After Einsele, G., Ricken, W., and Seilacher, A. (eds.), 1991. Cycles and Events in Stratigraphy. Berlin: Springer Verlag.

of the Olduvai Subchron, has since confirmed the orbitally corrected time scale. The extension of the OFT into the Miocene is proceeding, based on lithological cyclostratigraphy in the western Mediterranean region.

The larger and more persistent lake basins—those in rift basins, above all—may well contain sequences with useful cyclostratigraphic data, in terms of stable-isotope variations or sedimentary patterns. In the African Rift basins, however, the detection of precession cycles may be complicated by the fact that, in the tropics, the opposite signals of precession in Northern and Southern hemispheres could be confused.

FURTHER READINGS

Hays, J. D., Imbrie, J., and Shackleton, N. J. (1976). Variations in the Earth's Orbit: Pacemaker of the Ice Ages. Science 194: 1121–1132.

Hilgen, F. J., Krijgsman, W., Langereis, C. G., Lourens, L. J., Santarelli, A., and Zachariasse, W. J. (1995). Extending the astronomical (polarity) time scale into the Miocene, Earth, and Planetary Sciences Newsletters 136: 495–510.

Wadleigh, M. A. (1995). Applications of oxygen isotopes to Quaternary chronology. In N. W. Rutter and N. R. Catto (eds.): Dating Methods for Quaternary Deposits. St. Johns, Newfoundland: Geological Society Canada, pp. 51–60.

3

Geochronometry

Measurement of Geologic Time

F. H. Brown

The quantitative measurement of geologic time is called geochronometry. *Geochronology* is the broader subject, which includes both quantitative age determinations and relative methods of dating, such as biochronology, to determine the order of events in Earth history. Most geochronometric methods are based on the fact that the decay of long-lived radioactive isotopes leaves a meaningful record in the rocks, either as daughter isotopes, physical damage, electrons trapped in energy wells, or deviation of the isotopic composition of a sample from that of similar material being formed at present. A second method of obtaining the age of a stratum, that of counting backward from the present on the basis of cyclic events in the geologic record, has taken on new vitality with the validation beginning in the 1980s of Milankovitch's 1930–1940 calculations of an orbital imprint on past climates.

In addition, some progressive chemical changes in geological and fossil materials, such as racemization of organic molecules, fluorine uptake, and hydration, are used to estimate age in circumstances in which effects of external environmental influences (primarily temperature and groundwater chemistry) can be eliminated from analyses.

Placing an event in time must be distinguished from establishing the time interval over which a process has operated. In varved (annually or otherwise periodically

layered) sedimentary sequences, ice layers, tree rings, coral growth, and other seasonally inflected records, it may be possible to state quite accurately the duration of a counted interval or the amount of time that separates two events in the counted interval, without being able to state the age of the interval itself with anything like comparable accuracy. For some purposes this is sufficient, but more commonly the age of the strata is desired as well.

Some iterative (i.e., successive but not predictable) features of the geological record are useful in geochronology, although they do not yield quantitative geochronometric measures of geologic time by themselves. Once a relatively complete and accurate model of an iterated sequence has been developed, the age calibration of a few points gives chronological meaning to the rest. This can provide dating in situations that cannot be gained in any other way, but they are not geochronometric methods since they depend on other dating techniques for their calibration.

Isotopic dating methods that provide reasonably precise ages for Tertiary and Quaternary strata are of greatest interest in paleoanthropology. Methods such as uranium-lead dating do not provide sufficiently precise ages for geologically young materials to be of much use. Other methods (e.g., ^{210}Pb dating and some uranium-disequilibrium methods) are applicable over too short a time period to be used in paleoanthropology but are of value in archaeology. The methods of greatest importance to hominid studies are potassium-argon (K/Ar) and its variants; fission-track dating; and uranium-disequilibrium dating. Radiocarbon dating is applicable

Major Geochronometric Methods with Age Ranges, Typical Error Estimates and Types of Material Suitable for Dating

Method	Age-sensitive Ratio (esp. isotopic)	Age Range (yr)	Typical Error Percentages	Examples of Datable Material
Carbon-14	$^{14}C/^{12}C$	$10^2–5 \times 10^4$	± 1–5%	Organic materials, carbonates
K/Ar	$^{40}Ar/^{40}K$	$10^4–10^9$	± 1–5%	Feldspar, biotite, amphibole, fine-grained lava, Mn-oxides from paleosol, glauconite
Ar/Ar	$^{40}Ar/^{39}Ar$	$10^3–10^9$	± 0.1–1%	Feldspar, biotite, amphibole, fine-grained lava, Mn-oxides from paleosol, glauconite
Trapped-charge: TL, OSL, ESR	Quantity of trapped electrons vs. annual dose	$10^3–10^6$	± 5–15% (TL, OSL) ± 10–20%(ESR)	Quartz, calcite (bone, tooth enamel)
Fission-track (FT)	Track density vs. U concentration	$10^3–10^9$	± 1–5%	Zircon, sphene, apatite, glass, etc.
Rb/Sr	$^{87}Sr/^{87}Rb$	$10^6–10^9$	± 1–5%	Igneous rocks and minerals (normally requires analysis of more than one mineral in sample)
Th/U	$^{230}Th/^{234}U$	$10^2–10^5$	± 1–5%	Marine and non-marine carbonates including speleothems and travertines
Pa/U	$^{231}Pa/^{235}U$	$10^3–10^5$	± 1–5%	Marine and non-marine carbonates including speleothems and travertines
Pa/Th	$^{231}Pa/^{230}Th$	$10^3–10^5$	± 1–5%	Marine and non-marine carbonates including speleothems and travertines
Amino-Acid	D/L isomers	$10^3–10^6$	?	Ratite eggshell; other egg and mollusc shell

TL = Thermoluminescence; OSL = Optically stimulated luminescence; ESR = Electron spin resonance

to Late Pleistocene materials. In general, these methods cannot be applied to fossil materials themselves, so attribution of an age to a fossil requires thorough understanding of the stratigraphic relation between the dated materials and the fossils.

Some methods of interest in paleoanthropology and primate paleontology are tabulated in the above table.

Each method records the time elapsed after an event that "starts the clock." For crystalline solid systems, the starting event is the moment at which some blocking temperature is reached, below which daughter products cannot escape or be erased (e.g., K/Ar, Ar/Ar, Rb/Sr, fission track). In other systems, it is the moment of crystallization itself (e.g., uranium-disequilibrium series, K/Ar in part, carbon-14 in part). In still other systems, the event may be the moment at which input stops, either by the death of the organism (e.g., carbon-14) or by burial (electron trapping in part). One principal task of a geochronologist is to determine how the event that is being dated is related to the item of interest, and this requires all of the geological skill that can be brought to bear on the subject.

Even though determination of age-sensitive ratios in samples may be precise analytically, the ratios may yet be inaccurate because the relations between the materials measured and the event in question are not properly understood. For example, a measured K/Ar age on a mineral separate may yield an age of 10 ± 0.1 Ma and be a perfectly good determination in the analytical sense. If, however, this age is associated with fossils of Pleistocene age, it is patently inaccurate, probably from contamina-

tion of the sample by older grains. Unfortunately, inaccuracies are not always so obvious, and misplaced values, even for important events, may remain undetected for many years; the history of geochronometry is replete with painful case histories. The controversies over East African dating of the Rusinga *Proconsul*, the KBS Tuff, the Afar hominines, and the *Homo erectus* at Yuanmou (China) and Sangiran (Java) are vivid examples in the field of paleoanthropology.

Ages obtained on isolated samples and without independent backup should be regarded with great caution. Each method of dating has inherent weaknesses that can lead to inaccuracy. For all methods, however, the most difficult errors to detect are those hidden in small perturbations, and those for which independent information about the timing of the dated events is meager. It has become the hallmark of a good dating program to reduce random error and sample accidents by systematically overdoing everything. Internal redundancy is achieved by analyzing duplicate samples, by analyzing the same sample several times, and by collecting and analyzing samples from parallel traverses wherever possible. Nevertheless, the analysis or interpretation of a whole set of samples may be biased by some external influence, such as a regional thermal event or geological miscorrelation of the dated section, and such pervasive systematic errors are exposed only by comparison with the timing of similar or identical events from other geographic localities, by repeat analyses in different laboratories, or by the application of a different dating method.

FURTHER READINGS

Bishop, W. W., ed. (1978) Geological Background to Human Evolution. Edinburgh: Scottish Academic Press.
Rutter, N. W., and Catto, N. R., eds. (1995) Dating methods for Quaternary deposits. St. Johns, Newfoundland: Geological Society of Canada. Geotext 2.

4

Radiocarbon Dating

H. P. Schwarcz

Radiocarbon dating is a method of age determination based on measurements of the decay of the radioactive isotope carbon-14 (^{14}C, or radiocarbon) to stable nitrogen-14 (^{14}N) by emission of an electron charge (beta- particle) from the nucleus, leaving a proton in place of a neutron. The half-life of carbon-14 is 5,730 years; beyond about 10 half-lives (i.e., ca. 60 Kyr), the amount that remains is generally too small to measure with any accuracy. Carbon-14 is produced in the upper atmosphere by the reaction of cosmic rays with ^{14}N, and it oxidizes there to CO_2. The radioactive CO_2 enters the biosphere when the gas is taken up by plants and protists during organosynthesis and is recycled

until it enters the fossil state. The present-day concentration of this nuclide in living organisms corresponds to a radioactivity of 13.6 disintegrations per minute per gram of carbon. The age (t, in years) of any ancient carbon sample can be calculated from measurement of its remaining ^{14}C activity, A, according to the equation

$$t = [T\tfrac{1}{2}/0.6932] \ln (A/Ao)$$

where $T\tfrac{1}{2}$ is the half-life, 5,730 years, Ao is the ^{14}C activity in atmospheric carbon dioxide at the time that the sample was formed, and ln is the natural logarithm (base e).

The value for A in the equation can be determined either by counting the beta-decay events directly or by establishing the concentration of remaining ^{14}C atoms in the sample with an accelerator mass spectrometer (AMS). For measurement of β-activity, the carbon sample is converted into a liquid (usually benzene, C_6H_6),

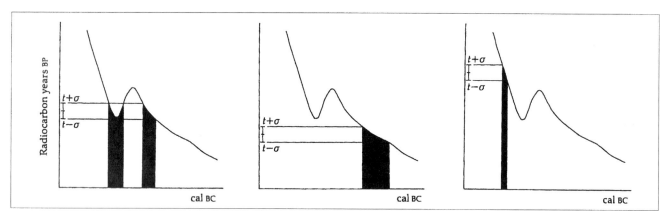

Calibration of ^{14}C ages. Radiocarbon ages do not necessarily increase steadily with time because the amount of ^{14}C in the environment is not constant, thanks to secular variation in the amount of CO_2 and CH_3 exposed to cosmic radiation in the upper atmosphere. In the figured example of a calibration curve, the difference between analyzed "radiocarbon years" (vertical axis) and counted calendar years (horizontal axis) in tree-ring sequences and ice cores is illustrated for the interval from 6–3 Ka. Some "wiggles" in the calibration curve are so severe, as in this segment, that the same radiocarbon age range can be one of two different calendar age ranges (left-hand figure). Note that the more precise a single radiocarbon age may be, the more likely it may fit to two different points in a wiggly calibration curve, but that locating the ambiguously dated sample in a stratigraphically ordered series of ages will resolve such conundrums. Note also that radiocarbon ages with the same error range can represent either a relatively precise (narrow) or imprecise (broad) range of calendar years depending on whether they fall on steeply or shallowly sloping parts of the correction curve (central and right hand figures, respectively). Copyright © 1990 The British Museum.

or to a gas (usually acetylene, C_2H_2), with a high carbon content. In liquid samples, the β-activity is measured by scintillometry, by adding a phosphor that emits a light flash when struck by a β-particle. In gas samples, the level of radioactivity is measured in a proportional counter similar to a Geiger counter. Both methods require very careful shielding to control natural background radioactivity.

Mass-spectrographic analysis of the ^{14}C isotope is done on purified carbon (graphite) extracted from the sample and activated as positive ions to differentiate the ^{14}C from the background ^{14}N, which has the same mass. The main advantage of AMS is its ability to analyze samples as small as a few micrograms, whereas conventional β-counting requires the use of several grams to several milligrams (in the most modern, ultra-low-background systems) to provide a reliable date. The upper age limit of AMS dating is ca. 40 Ka, whereas β-counting can reach ages as old as 60 Ka.

Radiocarbon dating is principally applicable to samples of organically formed materials, including wood, charcoal, hair, coprolites, bones, and shells. Samples to be dated must meet stringent criteria of purity in order to exclude radiocarbon atoms introduced after the sample enters stratigraphic context, which would give an erroneously young age. For example, buried samples typically contain root hairs, fungal growths, or deposits from burrowing animals, which contribute younger carbon. A lesser risk is the introduction of "dead" carbon from rocks or groundwater, leading to erroneously old ages. Ideally, purified biochemicals such as cellulose (from wood) or collagen (from bone) should be analyzed. The carbonate of bone mineral is less useful because of the common effect of ion exchange with soil carbonate.

Inorganically deposited carbonates, such as travertine and speleothems, can be dated by radiocarbon, but a large correction must be made for dead carbon, because carbonate in springs and cave seepages has equilibrated with the carbonate in limestone or dolomite, which has essentially zero ^{14}C activity. Modern spring deposits can show less than 50 percent of modern atmospheric ^{14}C activity.

however, over the time that carbon-14 dating is applicable, due primarily to the fact that the cosmic radiation flux in the upper atmosphere, and thus the production of radioactive carbon, varies inversely with the strength of the Earth's magnetic field. For the interval of 0 to 10 Ka, a correction curve has been built up through empirical calibration against counted tree rings, buttressed by dating of varved sequences in glaciers and lake beds. At many points in that interval, measured ^{14}C activity can be attributed to more than one age, because of "wiggles" in the curve of activity vs. time. In such instances, the age may be resolved by independent criteria, or it may be related to a stratigraphic set of ages that exhibits a characteristic variation curve. Calibration of the radiocarbon scale from 10 to 20 Ka is based on ^{14}C analyses of corals whose ages have been independently measured to ±1 percent by mass-spectrometric $^{230}Th/^{234}U$ dating. The carbon-14 dates on marine shells and corals require further correcting for the lowered ^{14}C activity of carbon in sea water. This is the *reservoir effect*, a term for the prolonged sequestration of huge volumes of dissolved carbonate ion in the virtually abiotic water masses below the eutrophic zone. Finally, in the interval from 20 Ka to the lower limit of measurable activity, correction is based on the long-term variation in the magnetic-field strength recorded in paleomagnetic studies.

The small-sample capability of AMS opens the possibility for dating single amino acids or other uniquely biogenic molecules from samples of bone or wood, but the need for extreme purification of the sample greatly increases the cost. The most interesting applications of ^{14}C dating to human evolution are near the limit of the AMS dating range (40 Ka), where extreme care is necessary to obtain samples of adequate purity. Many ^{14}C dates from near this limiting time are probably erroneously young due to contamination. A 40 Ka sample contains less than 1 percent of its original ^{14}C content, and contamination by only 1 percent of modern carbon will decrease its apparent age to ca. 35 Ka (about one half-life).

CORRECTION FACTORS

Unadjusted dates, in which Ao is simply set equal to present-day ^{14}C activity, are said to be in *radiocarbon years*. There have been large variations in atmospheric Ao,

FURTHER READINGS

Aitken, M. (1990). Science-Based Dating in Archaeology. London: Longman.

Arnold, L. D. (1995). Conventional radiocarbon dating. In N. W. Rutter and N. R. Catto (eds.): Dating Methods for Quaternary Deposits. St. Johns, Newfoundland: Geology Society of Canada, pp. 107–116.

Cabrera Valdes, V., and Bischoff, J. (1989). Accelerator ^{14}C dates for early Upper Paleolithic (basal Aurignacian) at El Castillo Cave (Spain). J. Archaeol. Sci. 16:577–584.

Litherland, A. E., and Beukens, R. P. (1995). Radiocarbon dating by atom counting. In N. W. Rutter and N. R. Catto (eds.): Dating Methods for Quaternary Deposits. St. Johns, Newfoundland: Geology Society of Canada, pp. 117–124.

Taylor, R. E. (1987). Radiocarbon Dating: An Archaeological Perspective. Orlando: Academic.

5

Potassium-Argon Dating

F. H. Brown

Potassium-Argon dating is a method of radiometric dating based on spontaneous decay of the unstable ^{40}K isotope. The decay of ^{40}K is relatively slow, with a half life of ca. 1.25 Myr, and the isotope occurs in only one out of 8,600 atoms of potassium. Most ^{40}K decay events proceed to ^{40}Ca by emission of a beta particle, and only 10.5 percent involve electron capture and gamma emission with decay into the ^{40}Ar isotope instead. Nevertheless, because of the abundance of potassium in granitic rock, it is calculated that the dual decay of this isotope is responsible for approximately one-third of the geothermal heat flow, nearly all of the background radioactive flux, and more than 99 percent of the argon in the atmosphere (ca. 1 percent of the total by weight). Radiogenic ^{40}Ca cannot be distinguished from the natural ^{40}Ca isotope of calcium, but *all* ^{40}Ar is radiogenic. This means that the amount of ^{40}Ar trapped within a mineral is a function of the age of the crystal and the amount of original ^{40}K (as a fixed percentage of total K, noted above). Applying the constant for the number of ^{40}K decay events per year ($\lambda = 5.543 \times 10^{-10}$ yr^{-1}) and a correction for any background, or atmospheric, ^{40}Ar that may have been incorporated at the beginning, year-ages can be calculated directly from the ratio of the parent and daughter isotopes.

Argon is a noble gas and does not combine or dissolve with other elements. Its atomic radius, however, is considerably larger than that of potassium, so that once the ^{40}Ar atom appears in place of its parent ^{40}K atom in the interlocked three-dimensional array of atoms that make up the *crystal lattice* of a mineral, it is mechanically (not chemically) trapped for as long as the lattice is not degraded, or dilated by heat. This property of the K/Ar system has been ingeniously exploited in the step-heating analysis procedure, described below.

SAMPLING

Dating a stratum, such as a paleomagnetic boundary or a fossil bed, requires a potassium-bearing mineral whose isotopic age can be related to the age of the stratum. A second requirement is that changes, if any, to the argon or potassium content of the mineral after it crystallizes must be measureable. There are few such datable minerals that actually form within sediments at the time of deposition, as opposed to many (i.e., zeolites) that form postdepositionally. The potassium salt sylvinite is well suited on all accounts, but its occurrence is confined to certain rare types of playas. Glauconite (*green earth*), a hydrous iron-potassium silicate that forms abundantly on the seafloor under reducing conditions, has been used extensively by some laboratories, but doubts remain as to its reliability except under ideal conditions. By far the greatest number of K/Ar ages applied to Cenozoic stratigraphy, therefore, have been obtained on tuffs and lava flows interbedded with strata of interest, because eruptive rocks can be considered to crystallize at the geological moment that they are deposited in the sequence.

The K-bearing phases in igneous rocks are among the last to solidify. Most of the potassium in lavas and tuffs, therefore, is in the frozen matrix surrounding the larger, earlier-formed crystals. In the early days of Cenozoic dating, the analytical systems were still relatively insensitive, and it was often necessary to run dates on pulverized samples of the whole rock in order to get enough argon to measure accurately. This is still done in instances in which low-potassium rocks (e.g., olivine basalts) are dated, but it is difficult to control for weathering and argon loss in the relatively unstable matrix, even in the freshest-looking samples. Improved techniques and equipment have allowed researchers to concentrate on the more homogenous and less alteration-prone large crystals, or phenocrysts. The K-bearing igneous minerals that commonly occur as phenocrysts in eruptive rock are biotite mica, amphibole (hornblende), potassium feldspars (sanidine, anorthoclase, and the more potassic plagioclases), leucite, and nepheline.

$^{40}K/^{40}Ar$ TOTAL-FUSION METHOD

The application of argon radioisotope dating to Cenozoic rocks requires accurate measurement of extremely small amounts of radiogenic argon. The basic breakthrough came in the mid-1950s at the University of California, Berkeley, when techniques were developed for extraction and concentration of argon in an ultrahigh-vacuum environment that included a mass spectrometer. This remains the basic procedure in all Cenozoic argon-isotope dating today, since it is only the near-exclusion of atmospheric gases that makes it practical to process the tiny amounts of gas occluded in such

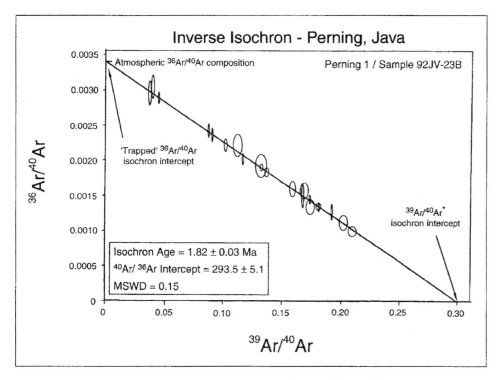

Isotope-correlation diagram ("isochron plot") of the ratios of ^{36}Ar and ^{39}Ar to ^{40}Ar obtained in incremental heating of neutron-irradiated hornblende crystals from Perning (Java). Dispersion about the isochron line is measured as MSWD (mean sum of weighted deviations). A low deviation, as in this example, represents the ideal in which all trials yield closely similar ages. MSWD over ca. 2.5 usually results from mineral or sample inhomogeneity. The isotope-correlation plot is more accurate than a simple weighted mean of the calculated ages because the atmospheric $^{36}Ar/^{40}Ar$ ratio in the sample is determined from the "y" intercept and not simply assumed. The ratio at the "x" intercept depends on the juvenile or radiogenic ^{40}Ar in the sample, and from these two points the isochron age, taking into account the neutron flux and other independent variables, can be calculated. From A. Deino, P. R. Renne and Carl C. Swisher, III, 1998, Evol. Anthropol. © 1998; reprinted with permission of Wiley-Liss, Inc., a subsidiary of John Wiley & Sons, Inc.

young samples. In models of the original design, an external microwave radiator is used to fuse the samples inside an evacuated chamber, and the expelled gas phase is passed through getters and condensers to further concentrate the argon. The amount of postcrystallization Ar is the residual after subtracting initial atmospheric, or background, radiogenic argon. This correction is based on measurement of the natural isotope ^{36}Ar in the sample, and the fact that the ratio of $^{40}Ar/^{36}Ar$ in air and (usually) in magma is 295:1. The ^{40}K values are derived from wet chemical analysis of total potassium in separate splits of the samples. Multiple analyses, and careful attention to reagents and standards, bring the precision of K/Ar dates obtained in this way close to 0.7 percent (double standard deviation) under the best circumstances.

The basic accuracy of the $^{40}K/^{40}Ar$ total-fusion method (as opposed to its analytical precision) is vulnerable to several sources of error. One is the necessity of making argon and potassium determinations on separate splits of a sample of pulverized rock or separated crystals, the homogeneity of which can never be completely assured. Another source of error, at least in the

early days, was the need to fuse relatively large samples (1 to 10 g) in order to obtain enough argon; under these circumstances, the potential for contamination by weathered (argon-deficient) or older (argon-amplified) material was very real, and often realized. A single fragment of Precambrian feldspar from a bit of wall rock caught up in a Pliocene eruption would contribute enough ^{40}Ar to seriously distort the age-signal from a thousand crystals of authigenic sanidine. A third potential source of error lies in compositional inhomogeneity of the phenocrysts themselves—in cases where the core portions of the mineral are isotopically older than the later phases—formed just before eruption. A fourth source of error is abnormalities in the isotopic ratios of ^{36}Ar and ^{40}K, which have been reported in some older rocks with complex thermal histories.

Step-Heating

Differences in lattice chemistry of minerals, including even small changes in the relative proportions within the same mineral, affect the temperature at which argon can escape. In minerals with zones of hydrothermally

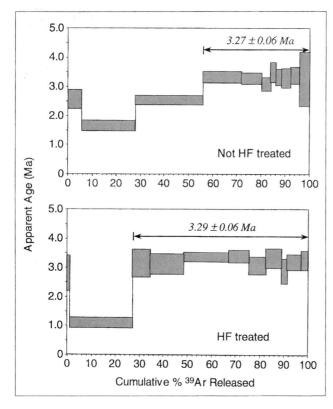

Step-heating ages in a whole-rock sample, the Kadada Moumou basalt, Hadar (Ethiopia). A spectrum of ages (shown on the vertical axis with 2 error envelopes) is obtained when different crystal phases release argon with increasing temperature, as monitored by incremental release of neutron-generated [39]Ar. Discordant younger ages are seen to come from low-temperature alteration products, while the age plateau at higher temperatures reflects older, more refractory unaltered phases, and represents the true or starting age of the sample. Dilute hydrofluoric acid treatment cleans the sample of weathering products and improves the signal from the original minerals. From A. Deino, P. R. Renne and Carl C. Swisher, III, 1998, Evol. Anthropol. © *1998; reprinted with permission of Wiley-Liss, Inc., a subsidiary of John Wiley & Sons, Inc.*

altered or weathered material in which argon leakage has reduced the apparent age, heating a sample in increments up to final fusion releases argon from the younger, lower-temperature phases before the older, less altered phases. Step-heating can, in theory, also separate the eruption age, recorded in the outermost zone of a phenocryst, from a significantly older core age and can isolate the geochronometric "noise" of older contaminant minerals. It cannot, however, distinguish mixed

ages (i.e., as the result of partial thermal overprinting) in a compositionally uniform sample, since all argon would be released at the same temperature.

[39]Ar/[40]Ar DATING

This technique, now almost universally applied, irradiates samples with carefully metered neutron emissions at energies designed to convert a controlled percentage of the common [39]K isotope to [39]Ar, a relatively short-lived isotope that no longer exists in nature. In this way, the age of the sample can be calculated on a single extract of argon gas, in which [36]Ar gives the atmospheric correction, [39]Ar is a function of the potassium content, and [40]Ar is a function of the time since the crystal reached isotopic closure. Standard samples of known age and potassium content (usually sanidines from the Miocene Fish Creek Tuff of Nevada) are irradiated at the same time to control for variations in the neutron flux. The [39]Ar/[40]Ar method can be combined with step-heating to obtain more precise dates of compositional phases. It offers greater accuracy than K/Ar step-heating, because the wet chemical assay of the latter technique gives only the potassium average of the whole sample.

Laser-probe fusion and customized mass spectrometers characterize the most advanced [39]Ar/[40]Ar systems, capable of age measurements in suitable minerals as young as 0.1 Ma, even less. The microfocus of laser beams, projected through a transparent vacuum barrier, allows analysis of extremely small samples, often a single crystal. The interior volume of a laser line is orders of magnitude less than a radio frequency (RF) line, making higher vacuums attainable, while hand-picked small samples and crystals are less likely to be affected by contamination. Ultrasensitive mass spectrometers, created solely to measure the nuclides between mass 36 and 40, are required to analyze the microvolumes of gas liberated in this way. Extraordinarily well controlled and precise dating, at the younger limit of argon-isotope dating, is attained by step-heating. The temperature of the sample is gradually raised by incrementally tightening the beam of a defocused laser.

[39]Ar/[40]Ar laser total-fusion dating can be highly efficient, since it is possible to automate the travel and firing of a laser across an array of dozens of tiny samples in a precisely machined carrier. Purification, mass spectroscopic analysis, computation, reporting, and purging can also be set to run automatically, even overnight, so that most of the time and effort in dating is loading the samples and checking equipment calibration.

FURTHER READINGS

Chen, Y., Smith, P. E., Evensen, N. M., York, D., and Lajoie, K. R. (1996). The edge of time: Dating young volcanic ash layers with the [40]Ar-[39]Ar laser probe. Science 274:1176–1178.

Dickin, A. P. (1995). Radiogenic Isotope Geology. Cambridge: Cambridge University Press.

McDougall, I. (1995). Potassium-argon dating in the Pleistocene. In N. W. Rutter and N. R. Catto (eds.): Dating Methods for Quaternary Deposits. St Johns, Newfoundland: Geological Society of Canada, pp. 1–14.

6

Electron Spin Resonance Dating, Fission-Track Dating, Thermoluminescence Dating, and Uranium-Series Dating

H. P. Schwarcz

ESR (ELECTRON SPIN RESONANCE) DATING

ESR dating is a technique for the dating of archaeological material and Quaternary strata according to the electron spin resonance (ESR) of solid materials. As one of the methods of trapped-charge dating, ESR spectrometry measures free electron charges at defects within mineral lattices that resonate at distinct frequency peaks (with distinct "g" values) representing different trap sites. The intensity (amplitude) of the peaks reflects the number of trapped electron charges that have accumulated in the sample through the effects of background radiation since the trap sites were formed, or since they were last zeroed. The original peak intensity is calculated from the equivalent radiation dose (DE) by the additive-dose method using controlled artificial radiation. The ratio of the additive-dose energy to the increased activity in the sample after dosing is a function of its age.

To be used for dating, the ESR signal sites must be sensitive to background radiation, so that the signal intensity is directly proportional to the natural dose rate, and must have lifetimes at least an order of magnitude greater than the age of the sample. The sites must also be robust (not subject to fading other than the thermal effect) and must not have been recrystallized or otherwise affected so that the number of traps is changed. Most, but not all, ESR-datable materials are carbonates or phosphates and are zeroed at the time of deposition because they were freshly crystallized. Materials that meet the above criteria are usually tooth enamel, speleothems (stalagmites and the like), mollusc shells, or corals. The lifetimes of ESR signals in these materials are close to or greater than 1.0 Myr, and all are radiation sensitive and relatively stable. Zeroing due to heating is also possible for flint or other siliceous artifacts.

Unsuitable materials include calcretes and spring-deposited travertines, which often display a significant initial signal, and bone tissue. The hydroxyapatite in bone is extremely susceptible to postmortem recrystallization, and bone usually takes up about 10 times as much ambient uranium as fossil teeth do.

Tooth enamel from archaeological sites is the most widely used subject for ESR dating, using the frequency peak at g = 2.0018, closely followed by analyses of speleothems using g = 2.0005. Dosimetry must be carefully determined and includes corrections for attenuation by the activity of β-particles, which may be emitted from radioisotopes in adjacent sediment or from within the fossil material itself. In tooth enamel, for instance, the signal is often modified significantly by ambient uranium ions that exchange with the phosphorus of dentine and enamel, and by evolution *in situ* of radioactive daughter isotopes of uranium. The ESR dating limit of enamel is more than 2 Ma, with a precision of ca. 10 percent of the age, and Miocene ESR ages have been reported. The minimum sample size is ca. 1 g of tooth enamel; therefore, only the teeth of larger animals (bovids, cervids, equids) are generally useful.

For analysis of tooth material, the enamel and dentine are reduced to a powder. Weighed portions of the enamel powder are exposed to gamma rays to determine the dose-response curve, while the uranium concentration is measured in both the enamel and the dentine. In cases in which the internal, U-generated radiation dose is large, the calculated age critically depends on the history of uranium uptake. The possible U-uptake models include early uptake (EU), in which the present U-content is assumed to have been established soon after deposition, and linear uptake (LU), which assumes a constant rate of uptake since deposition. The EU model leads to a calculation of the lowest possible age for a set of ESR data. Using U-series analyses of the enamel and dentine, it is possible to test which of these models best describes the U-uptake history of a tooth. Analyses of teeth from Israeli sites have suggested early U-uptake for most samples, while sites in other countries exhibit more continuous, quasi-linear uptake.

ESR dating has been used in assessing the age of numerous paleoanthropological sites, ranging in age from Acheulean levels in Morocco to the "archaic *Homo sapiens*" (or *Homo heidelbergensis*) site of Petralona (Greece), the "early modern human" sites at Qafzeh and Skhūl in Israel and Border Cave and Klasies River Mouth in South Africa, and Neanderthal sites such as Krapina. ESR studies of the australopith site at Sterkfontein (South Africa) indicate an age beyond the maximum limit of the technique, or more than 2 Ma.

FURTHER READINGS

Blackwell, B. (1995). Electron spin resonance dating. In N. W. Rutter and N. R. Catto (eds.): Dating Methods for Quaternary Deposits. St. Johns, Newfoundland: Geological Society of Canada, pp. 209–268.

Grun, R. (1993). Electron spin resonance dating in paleoanthropology. Evol. Anthropol. 2:172–181.

Grun, R., and Stringer, C. B. (1991). Electron spin resonance dating and the evolution of modern humans. Archaeometry 33:153–199.

Rhodes, E. J., Raynal, J.-P., Geraads, D., and Fatima-Zora, S. (1994). Premières dates RPE pour l'Acheuléen du Maroc atlantique (Grotte des Rhinocéros, Casablanca). C. R. Acad. Sci. (Paris), ser. 2, 319:1109–1115.

FISSION-TRACK DATING

Age measurements according to the accumulation of crystal defects, or *tracks,* caused by spontaneous fission of ^{238}U (uranium) nuclei in igneous minerals and glasses is called fission-track dating. This fission is relatively slow, but the technique is exquisitely sensitive because the measurements are made on single atoms. The damage caused by the massive particles resulting from each fission event appears as elongated, tear drop–shaped pits tapering toward the final resting place of the fission particle when a polished surface or flat crystal face is etched with an appropriate reagent, such as hydrofluoric or phosphoric acid. The tracks, which range in length from ca. 10 to 20 μm depending on the mineral and the etching procedure, are commonly counted in an acetate film peeled from the etched surface, in order to reduce the optical interference from flaws and reflections in the sample itself. The number of tracks per unit area, or *track density,* is determined under an optical microscope at 500 to 2500× magnification. The sample is then irradiated with a measured dose of neutrons in a

Grain mount showing spontaneous tracks in the individual grains

External detector mount showing induced tracks defining grain outlines

The use of an external detector allows a comparison between naturally accumulated fission tracks in a mineral grain, and the fission tracks induced by a measured dose of thermal neutrons. Since the natural decay rate of uranium is known, the age of the grain can be calculated by a comparison of the spontaneous fission tracks generated over time, and the concentration of parent uranium in the grain as represented by the induced tracks. The method has the advantage of providing fission-track age determinations for each individual mineral grain. Spontaneous tracks in a grain are exposed by chemical etching of a freshly cleaved or cut surface and counted. A uranium-free detector (plastic, or more often muscovite mica) is sealed against the surface and the sample is then irradiated. The detector is etched to reveal a mirror image of the grains showing induced tracks only. Reprinted with permission from K. Gallagher, R. Brown and C. Johnson, Fission track analysis and its applications to geological problems, Annual Reviews of Earth and Planetary Science, *Volume 26:519–572. © 1998 by Annual Reviews, www.annualreviews.org.*

research reactor, and the surface is reground, etched under the same conditions, and the track density is re-counted. The increment in fission tracks, from induced fission of the much rarer isotope ^{235}U, allows calculation of its abundance in the sample and thus the quantity of ^{238}U according to the natural ratio of the two isotopes. Thus, the age can be determined from the ratio of the induced to the spontaneous tracks, in a calculation that also takes into account the unrelated (and trackless) decay of ^{238}U by alpha-particle emission. A standard of known uranium content is normally irradiated along with the sample to monitor the neutron flux in the reactor.

The most suitable minerals for fission-track analysis are high-U minerals such as zircon, sphene, and apatite. Low-U materials such as feldspar and obsidian have much lower track densities and require several days of laborious counting to record a sufficient number of tracks for an accurate age. Normally, only minerals found in volcanic deposits are used to date surface sites, since these crystals were formed, or heat-annealed, close at the time of deposition. In principle, it is also possible to date nonvolcanic materials that have been heated sufficiently to anneal any preexisting tracks. Archaeological materials, however, would seldom be sufficiently heated to assure complete annealing, except for glass and ceramic glazes, or obsidian artifacts that have been heated almost to the point of melting. When volcanic ash layers are sampled, primary volcanic ejecta must be distinguished from reworked volcanic sediment. Furthermore, some U-rich igneous materials—of which apatite and volcanic glass are the prime examples—tend to anneal over time through recrystallization and chemical attack. Sphene, and especially zircon, is more stable. Controlled heat-annealing and recounting in irradiated samples are used to calculate a correction for the susceptibility of spontaneous tracks to be lost over time.

Fission-track dating is applicable over an age range from a few hundred thousand years to billions of years before present. For any particular material, the practical lower dating limit is determined by the time allocated for counting an adequate number of tracks. Assuming that no more than 20 hours is allocated per sample to find at least 100 tracks in a material with a total uranium content of 5 ppm, such as a typical obsidian, then the youngest age that can be measured is ca. 20 Ka. Archaeological and hominid-bearing deposits have been dated by fission-track analysis in East Africa (e.g., in studies of the KBS Tuff) and in Java, and the technique has been widely used by vertebrate paleontologists.

FURTHER READINGS

Gleadow, A. J. W. (1980). Fission track age of the KBS Tuff and associated hominid remains in northern Kenya. Nature 284:225–230.

Naeser, C. W., and Naeser, N. D. (1988). Fission track dating of Quaternary events. In D. J. Easterbrook (ed.): Dating of Quaternary Sediments. Special Paper 227. Geol. Soc. Am. pp. 1–12.

Westgate, J. A. (1988). Isothermal plateau fission-track age of the Late Pleistocene Old Crow tephra, Alaska. Geophys. Res. Lett. 15:376–379.

Westgate, J. A., and Naeser, N. D. (1995). Tephrochronology and fission-track dating. In N. W. Rutter and N. R. Catto (eds.): Dating Methods for Quaternary Deposits. St. Johns, Newfoundland: Geological Society of Canada, pp. 15–28.

TL (THERMOLUMINESCENCE) DATING

Thermoluminescence dating is a technique for dating archaeological and geological deposits based on the emission of light from heated samples; one of the methods of *trapped-charge dating*. Thermoluminescence depends on the fact that raising the temperature of some materials releases energy, stored as trapped electron charges, in measurable amounts of visible light. A few milligrams of finely granulated sample are placed beneath a high-sensitivity light detector on an electrically heated platform in a vacuum chamber. The sample is heated at a constant rate (usually $5°C/sec$), and a *glow curve* is constructed from measurements of the amount of light emitted at each increment. Energy from specific electron-charge traps is liberated at characteristic temperatures, with the longest-lived traps giving peaks at the highest temperatures. Thus, in mixtures of different minerals, such as in a pottery sample, the emitted light exhibits high-intensity peaks in particular wavelengths (seen as colors) in certain temperature ranges on the glow curve.

TL-datable materials from archaeological sites include quartz, feldspar, and flint (microcrystalline quartz) that have been zeroed by heating in cooking fires or in ceramic firing, and freshly formed calcite from stalagmites and tufa deposits. The age of ceramics can be determined with a precision of ca. 5–10 percent. Artifacts (e.g., points or knives) made of quartz or flint can be dated from the last time of heating; heated ("burned") flints can be recognized by the development of characteristic microfractures. The TL signal in quartz is stable up to at least 500 Ka and can be used to date Paleolithic sites where fire was used.

Burial age of Quaternary sediments can be approximately dated by TL, because the trapped-charge content in quartz and feldspar grains is gradually reduced during exposure to sunlight to values near (but not equal to) zero. The most datable sediments are those made up of grains that have been thoroughly exposed prior to burial, such as loess, dune sand, or beach sand. The apparent age is corrected by artificially bleaching a split of the sediment and subtracting for the residual TL activity.

Two sites at which burned flint was dated by TL are the cave of Qafzeh in Israel, where burials of anatomically modern humans were shown to date from 92 ± 5 Ka, and Le Moustier in the Dordogne region of France, where layers containing Mousterian artifacts gave mean ages ranging from 56 ± 5 (at the base) to 40 ± 3 Ka just below the Châtelperronian, which gave a date of 43 ± 4 Ka. The ages increase downward and indicate a resolution of a few thousand years.

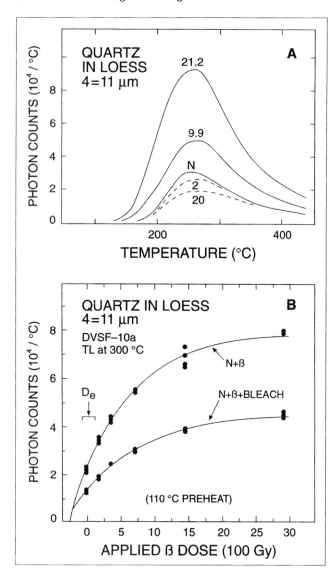

Top: *glow-curve for a sedimentary sample zeroed by solar bleaching. Each curve shows the light intensity emitted (as photon counts) as temperature is increased at 5°C/sec. N is glow-curve for the natural sample; solid curves are for samples with added doses of 990 and 2200 Gy (gray); dashed curves are for samples which were bleached and then irradiated. The height of the glow curves at 300°C was used to construct additive dose curve.*

Bottom: *additive-dose curve for determination of equivalent dose (DE). N + β shows the height of the glow curve at 300°C and for added dose (multiple points represent repeat measurements). N + β + BLEACH shows 300°C points for samples that were bleached before β-dosing.*

FURTHER READINGS

Aitken, M., and Valladas, H. (1992). Luminescence dating and the origin of modern man. In M. J. Aitken, C. B. Stringer, and P. A. Mellars (eds.): The Origin of Modern Humans and the Impact of Chronometric Dating. Princeton: Princeton University Press, pp. 27–39.

Berger, G. W. (1988). Dating Quaternary events by luminescence. In D. Easterbrook (ed.): Dating Quaternary Sediments (Special Paper No. 227). Boulder: Geological Society of America, pp. 13–25.

Berger, G. W. (1995). Progress in luminescence dating methods for Quaternary sediments. In N. W. Rutter and N. R. Catto (eds.): Dating Methods for Quaternary Deposits. St. Johns, Newfoundland: Geological Society of Canada, pp. 81–104.

Feathers, J. K. (1996). Luminescence dating and modern human origins. Evol. Anthropol. 5:25–36.

Hütt, G. I., and Raukas, A. (1995). Thermoluminescence dating of sediments. In N. W. Rutter and N. R. Catto (eds.): Dating Methods for Quaternary Deposits. St. Johns, Newfoundland: Geological Society of Canada, pp. 73–80.

URANIUM-SERIES DATING

Age determinations based on decay of the short-lived isotopes of uranium and their daughter isotopes are referred to as uranium-series dating. The principally used system, generally known as the *thorium-uranium system* or just *thorium dating,* employs the slow decay of uranium-238 (^{238}U) to the moderately radioactive uranium-234 (^{234}U; half-life = 248,000 years), which decays, in turn, to thorium-230 (^{230}Th; half-life = 75,200 years). In most near-surface environments, uranium is soluble in groundwater while thorium is not. Therefore, chemically and biologically deposited materials at archaeological sites may initially contain some uranium but will lack radiogenic daughter ^{230}Th. After the deposit is formed, a new crop of this isotope will begin to accumulate and grow toward equilibrium with the parent ^{234}U. Thus, the age can be measured from the $^{230}Th/^{234}U$ ratio. The

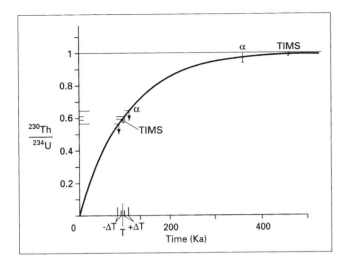

Variation of 230Th/234U activity ratio with time. The ratio in a sample is shown by a point on the x-axis. Here, for a sample with a true ratio of 0.6, are shown the error bars corresponding to alpha-spectrometric measurement (a, light line) and TIMS (heavy line). Note the corresponding errors (?T) in the ages (on the horizontal axis), and that the age errors are asymmetric. The upper age limit for the method is determined by the point at which the error bar for the Th/U ratio overlaps the infinite-age value of 1.0.

primordial isotope of thorium, ^{232}Th, serves as a control for any original thorium in the sample.

Uranium-235 (^{235}U) is the parent of another short-lived isotope, protactinium-231 (^{231}Pa; half-life = 34,300 years), which can also be used to date surficial deposits. Like thorium, protactinium is insoluble in groundwater, and chemical or biological processes will separate it from the parent isotope during deposition in archaeological sites. The maximum activity of ^{231}Pa, however, is only 1/22 that of ^{230}Th, due to the fact that its parent ^{235}U is much less abundant, and it is, therefore, harder to detect.

Materials selected for U-series dating must meet three criteria: (1) they must have been formed at the time of interest; (2) they must have initially contained uranium but no (or very little) thorium, as is usually the case with chemically or biologically deposited materials; and (3) they must have been closed systems since deposition, neither gaining nor losing atoms except by internal radioactive conversions. Materials at archaeological sites that satisfy these criteria are listed here in order of preference for U-series dating.

Speleothems, or coalesced stalagmitic floors (also called *plancher stalagmitique*, or *flowstone*), are deposits of calcite formed in caves and rockshelters, sometimes found interstratified with archaeological strata or bone-bearing silts; they may be contaminated with detritus containing nonradiogenic (i.e., common) thorium, but they can still be dated using the isochron method.

Travertine is spring-deposited limestone, which can be deposited at intermittent habitation sites. Many travertines are very porous and tend to alter after depo-

sition, but coarsely crystalline layers are suitable for dating.

Freshwater marls (clayey limestones) in some lake bed sequences may be associated with tools, bones, or living sites, and, although these may be highly contaminated with detritus, they are amenable to isochron dating.

Calcretes are calcitic layers, or hardpan, that form by evaporation of soil water in the subsurface *B-zone* of soils in arid and subarid regions. They are usually highly contaminated with detritus, but, if the host sediment is noncalcareous (e.g., volcanic, siliceous), isochron dating is possible.

Other types of carbonate precipitates, such as *kunkar* deposits in coastal flats, are also datable. With regard to biologically precipitated carbonate, such as the aragonite and calcite of marine shells, only corals are amenable to dating. This is because molluscs (i.e., bivalves, snails, limpets) and echinoderms (i.e., sea urchins) contain no initial uranium and absorb post-mortem uranium gradually over time. In general, poor agreement has been found between uranium-series dates and carbon-14 (^{14}C) dates on corals, and coral is seldom found in archaeological contexts. Vertebrate bones and teeth also contain no initial uranium, but they may take up significant amounts soon after death during the fossilization process. Agreement between uranium-series dates and ^{14}C dates on bone is also poor, although tooth enamel appears to be better behaved.

U-series analyses are carried out by measuring the ratios ^{230}Th/^{234}U and ^{234}U/^{238}U in one of three ways. Measurement of the relative radioactivities of the unstable isotopes such as ^{230}Th with an α-particle spectrometer requires 10–30 g of sample and has a precision error of 5–10 percent of the date. Counting the number of atoms of each isotope using a thermal ionization mass spectrometer (TIMS) takes 0.1–5 g of sample and is precise to within 1 percent. Counting gamma rays emitted by each isotope requires 50–500 g of sample and is precise only within 10–20 percent. Using the TIMS method, the lower and upper dating limits of uranium-series dating are 0.5 Ka and 500 Ka, respectively, while the upper dating limit for α-spectrometry is 350 Ka.

Examples of U-series dating are numerous. At La Chaise de Vouthon (France), stalagmitic layers were dated from 240 to 70 Ka, interposed between detrital cave-filling sediments containing Paleolithic artifacts and hominid (Neanderthal) skeletal remains. At Ehringsdorf (Germany), where quarrying of travertine deposits near Weimar revealed layers containing Paleolithic artifacts and hominid remains, a U-series isochron date of 230 Ka was obtained for the lower travertine, corresponding to the interglacial of isotope Stage 7. At El Castillo Cave (Spain), a travertine layer separating Acheulean and Mousterian deposits is part of the thick detrital fill. Although badly contaminated with common Th, it gave a Th/U date of 89 ± 11 Ka, which is a minimum age for the transition from Early to Middle Paleolithic culture at this site.

FURTHER READINGS

Schwarcz, H. P. (1992). Uranium series dating in paleoanthropology. Evol. Anthropol. 1:56–62.

Schwarcz, H. P. (1994). Uranium series dating. In R. E. Taylor and M. Aitken (eds.): Chronology of Archaeological Sites. New York: Plenum.

Schwarcz, H. P., and Blackwell, B. (1991). Archaeometry. In M. Ivanovitch and R. S. Harmon (eds.): Uranium Series

Disequilibrium: Application to Environment Problems in the Earth Sciences, 2nd ed. Oxford: Oxford University Press, pp. 513–552.

Taylor, R. E. and Aitken, M. J. (eds.) (1997). Chronometric Dating in Archaeology. New York: Plenum.

7

Paleomagnetism and Human Evolution

F. H. Brown

Paleomagnetism is the geological record of the Earth's magnetic field. Most rocks contain iron-oxide minerals, which tend, with more or less scattering, to be aligned within the Earth's contemporaneous magnetic field when the rock is formed. The fossilized magnetic orientation in rock samples produces a field that, while almost indetectable, can be measured quite accurately with sensitive modern magnetometers in magnetically isolated conditions.

Two principal uses have been made of paleomagnetic data in the study of hominid paleontology. The first is chronological, based on the fact that frequent reversals in the polarity of the Earth's magnetic field during the Cenozoic have been accurately dated, which means that the identification of such a reversal in a fossiliferous sequence can afford a very reliable age determination. The second is geographical and is based on the fact that the Earth's magnetic field has remained relatively fixed with respect to the poles of rotation while large parts of the outer part of the Earth (the lithosphere) have moved. Observations of paleomagnetic directions in rocks of a given age permit reconstruction of the latitudinal, if not longitudinal, position of landmasses at the time and also the rotation of the landmasses during platetectonic movement. The presence of accreted microplates and foreign terranes within a continent can also be detected by their anomalous paleomagnetism.

The Earth's magnetic field has both horizontal and vertical components. If a magnetized needle is left free to rotate, the needle aligns itself in the magnetic field with the ends seeking the magnetic poles, thus revealing the horizontal component, or *declination*. If the needle is balanced on a point, it does not (in general) remain horizontal but fixes itself at a definite angle of inclina-

tion to the Earth's surface, revealing the vertical component, or *inclination*. This angle grows steeper near the poles and shallower near the equator, with the dependency given, to a first approximation by

$$\tan \text{inclination} = 2 \tan \text{latitude}.$$

In the Northern Hemisphere, the north-seeking, or "positive," end of a magnet also inclines downward, and the same for the south, or "negative," end in the Southern Hemisphere. The magnetic pole is where the inclination is vertical, or 90°, and the magnetic equator is where the inclination is horizontal, or zero.

If the declination and inclination of the field are mapped at a large number of points, the actual field is found to have a complex form. The magnetic equator is only approximately circular, and the magnetic poles are only approximately opposite each other. The magnetic field constantly changes its shape and orientation, but it can be reasonably estimated by imagining a stationary dipole magnet situated in the center of the Earth and aligned with the rotational axis. The calculated magnetic field produced by such a theoretical dipole is called the *geomagnetic field*. While the magnetic poles do not necessarily coincide with the rotational poles at any given time, it has been found that, when the positions of the actual magnetic poles are averaged over a long time period, the geomagnetic poles do coincide with the rotational poles. The long-term average of the Earth's magnetic field is called the *axial geocentric dipole field*, and the position of paleomagnetic poles from the rock record is computed with respect to this model field. During periods when the magnetic field was reversed, the end of a magnetized needle that we call "positive," or "north," would point to the South Pole and would be inclined upward rather than downward with respect to the magnetic pole in the Northern Hemisphere. It was this contradictory effect, found in the 1950s in certain Miocene lavas in Germany being examined for fossilized declination, that gave the first clue that the polarity of the Earth's magnetic field had been reversed in the geological past.

When igneous rocks cool from high temperatures in the earth's magnetic field, they acquire magnetization because their iron minerals tend to crystallize parallel to the field existing at that time. This is referred to as *thermoremanent magnetization* (TRM). Detrital fragments of the same minerals give a preferred magnetic orientation to sedimentary rocks when they settle in alignment with the Earth's field onto the depositional surface. This is *detrital remanent magnetization* (DRM). The crystallization of hematite in altered, secondarily reddened sediments also records contemporaneous magnetic orientation known as *chemical remanent magnetization* (CRM). Previously crystallized magnetic minerals may be overprinted with subsequent geomagnetic orientations through the influence of short, high-intensity fields *(isothermal remanent magnetization,* or IRM), such as those associated with lightning strikes, or by the influence of low-intensity magnetic fields over longer periods of time *(viscous remanent magnetization,* or VRM). If

viscous effects for a sample are large, the sample is not suitable for paleomagnetic work. It is often possible, however, to "clean" the sample to remove the effects of both VRM or IRM by heating it in the absence of a magnetic field or by subjecting the sample to an alternating-frequency field. These procedures preferentially randomize the less stable, secondary magnetic phases and reveal the primary magnetization of a sample. The magnetization measured before any cleaning is the *natural remanent magnetization* (NRM).

The timing of reversals of geomagnetic polarity is reasonably well known from the Jurassic to the present. It is especially well known for the last 10 Ma and can be used to refine the chronology at hominid fossil sites. The magnetic field is usually in one of the two opposed states, normal or reversed, but the intensity of the magnetic field may vary markedly, sometimes declining to such low levels as to be indeterminate. There is no practicably measurable difference, however, between the

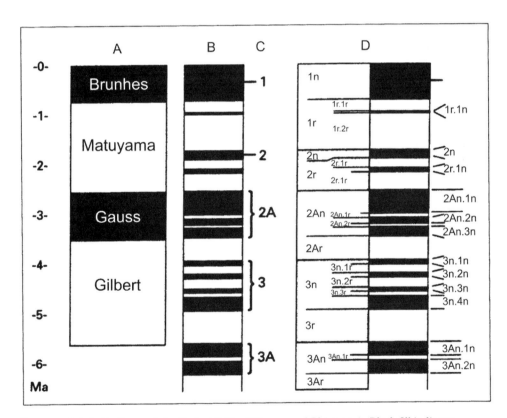

Geomagnetic polarity time scale for the last 5 Myr (Pliocene and Pleistocene). Black fill indicates intervals of normal polarity. Column A shows the named chrons (previously epochs) or major time intervals—chrons older than Gilbert are numbered rather than named. Column B increases the detail to show shorter intervals of opposite polarity within chrons, known as subchrons (previously events); those in the named chrons are also named (usually after the site where they were found), for example the Jaramillo normal subchron in the late Matuyama Chron, at about 1 Ma. An alternative system of numbering chrons and subchrons began with research on field reversals on the deep sea floor, where so-called magnetic anomalies were numbered outward from spreading ridges, as in column C. The modern system, in column D, incorporates the anomaly numbering system, so that chrons are numbered 1, 2, 2A, 3, 3A, 4, 5, etc., and the letters n or r appended to indicate normal or reversed polarity, respectively. In turn, subchrons are numbered following a decimal point in order from youngest to oldest. Thus, 2An.2r is the second reversed subchron and 2An.3n the third normal subchron, within the mainly normal chron 2A. From Kappelman (1993) Evol. Anthropol. © 1993; reprinted with permission of Wiley-Liss, Inc., a subsidiary of John Wiley & Sons, Inc.

present declination and inclination of the normal field and those in the past. Consequently, the age of a rock sequence must be already approximately known before the polarity zonation can yield its chronological information. This preliminary age estimate may be based on radiometric dates or paleontological age. If a stratigraphic section is extremely thick, and there is reason to believe that the rate of sedimentation was more or less constant, a very rudimentary age estimate may be sufficient to find that part of the model polarity-reversal time scale that fits the pattern in relative thicknesses of the magnetic zones in the sequence. Because of the discontinuous nature of deposition in most continental settings, however, care must be taken to control for hiatuses through detailed geological analysis and by running parallel sampling traverses in widely spaced sections. Even so, short magnetozones may escape notice. In addition, certain rock types are more susceptible than others to remagnetization by viscous process and can lead to spurious local magnetozones that have no chronological significance because they arise from effects other than geomagnetic-field reversals.

The position of landmasses at various times in the past has been determined by paleomagnetic studies on the continents and by study of plate motions revealed by the geometry of linear magnetic anomalies on the ocean floor. Times of contact and separation between continents can be estimated, with obvious import for possible routes of primate dispersal. The paleolatitude, which emerges from remanent-inclination analysis, must be considered when making paleoclimatic reconstructions. Also, marked changes in oceanic circulation are clearly related to changing continental configurations as documented by sea-floor anomaly patterns. These circulatory changes are linked to other regional, and even global, climatic change.

Estimation of the times of reversal of the polarity of the Earth's magnetic field have been obtained in several ways. Initially, a Geomagnetic Polarity Time Scale (GPTS) was constructed for the past 4 Myr or so, and extended with less certainty back to ca. 12 Ma, by measuring radiometric ages of volcanic rocks in paleomagnetically analyzed sequences. The GPTS was refined and extended to earlier times by analogizing symmetrical magnetic intensity patterns, known as *marine magnetic anomalies,* in the sea-floor lavas paralleling midoceanic spreading centers. These anomalies are zones of positive and negative polarity in the remanent magnetism of the lavas, acquired as the lavas were emplaced along the spreading centers. The width of the anomalies presumably reflects the duration of a given geomagnetic polarity state if it is assumed that the rate of sea-floor spreading was constant, and, thus, when the dated GPTS was fitted to the youngest part of the pattern near the spreading centers, it was a simple matter to extrapolate the same time/distance ratio to more distant anomalies. To minimize the possibility that a given transect might be biased by local changes in the spreading rate, a global model anomaly pattern was developed by statistically "stacking" transects from different ocean basins. Interestingly, the transect in the South Atlantic from which the first approximation of an anomaly-based GPTS was developed proved to have one of the steadiest spreading rates of all.

The final refinement to the GPTS has been achieved by paleomagnetic analysis of oriented deep-sea cores, which sample the fine-laminated bathyal strata in which deposition was essentially continuous and sediment accumulation rates were notably constant. In these cores, which span the entire Cenozoic in numerous overlapping segments, the circumglobal biostratigraphy of planktonic marine microfossils is so detailed that each geomagnetic reversal has its own unique place in the evolutionary zonation of the microfossil groups. This helps control for missing or duplicated sections that distort the observed paleomagnetic profile, and greatly enhances the accurate correlation of any given paleomagnetic reversal to the model.

The deep-sea cores also preserve evidence of cyclic variations in the Earth's climate that are due to regular periodicities in axial tilt, equinoctal precession, and orbital shape. The timing of the cycles, as originally calculated by M. Milankovich and recently refined by computers, is so precisely known, and the cycles are so closely spaced and regular, that the age of paleomagnetic reversals identified in this context can be established to a very high degree of accuracy, and with a level of precision approaching 10 Kyr. When this independent procedure for counting time was applied to magnetostratigraphy in Italian Pliocene and Pleistocene sections by researchers such as F. J. Hilgen the Paleomagnetic Laboratory of Utrecht University beginning in the 1980s, in a procedure that came to be known as *orbital tuning,* it confirmed earlier suspicions that the previously accepted radiometric dating of reversals in this period was on average ca. 6 percent too old. The corrected calibration has since been corroborated by new argon-argon (^{40}Ar/^{39}Ar) dating of the Olduvai Event at Olduvai Gorge (Tanzania) and by a similar redating of the Brunhes/Matuyama boundary.

FURTHER READINGS

Barendregt, R. W. (1995). Paleomagnetic dating methods. In N. W. Rutter and N. R. Catto (eds.): Dating Methods for Quaternary Deposits. St. Johns, Newfoundland: Geological Society Canada, pp. 29–50.

Hilgen, F. J. (1991). Astronomical calibration of Gauss to Matuyama sapropels in the Mediterranean and implications for the Geomagnetic Polarity Time Scale. Earth Planet. Sci. Lett. 104:226–244.

Kappelman, J. (1993). The attraction of paleomagnetism. Evol. Anthropol. 2:89–99.

McElhinny, M. W. (1973). Paleomagnetism and Plate Tectonics. Cambridge: Cambridge University Press.

Strangway, D. W. (1970). History of the Earth's Magnetic Field. New York: McGraw-Hill.

8

Taphonomy in Human Evolution

A. Hill

Taphonomy, the study of the processes affecting organic remains prior to fossilization, began as an ancillary field to paleoecology. The Russian geologist I. A. Efremov originated the term in 1940 to identify what he called the "transition of animal remains from the biosphere into the lithosphere." The word derives from the Greek *taphos*, ("burial") and *nomos* ("law").

Taphonomy considers two basic facts of paleontology. The first fact is that fossils (with rare exceptions such as insects in amber or animals smothered by volcanic ash or sandstorms) normally do not preserve the organism as it was precisely at the moment of death. Ancillary to this is the fact that fossil assemblages, likewise, are not (usually) the instantaneously preserved living communities. Animal fossils are just the remains of decomposed individuals, commonly the hardest parts, that become buried in sediments. In the case of vertebrates, we face the problem of discovering the meaning of piles of broken bones, in biological terms. To answer this question, and to reconstruct the paleoecology of these creatures with any confidence, we must assess the degree to which fossil assemblages constitute representative samples of the communities of animals from which they were derived.

Taphonomy encompasses a number of other concerns, some of which were already being debated when the word was invented. German scientists in the 1920s had coined a few relevant terms, such as *biostratonomy* (the study of the embedding of fossils in sediments) and *aktuo-* or *aktualpaläontologie* (the investigations of modern remains of animals in the contemporary environment). The goal of aktuopaläontologie, in particular, was to discover and understand the environments and events for which fossils are the only remaining evidence. This is really no more than a branch of actualism, or C. Lyell's uniformitarianism: the idea that the present is the key to the past.

Most of this early work concerned animals in the marine environment, but, in the early 1960s, E. C. Olson reintroduced the word *taphonomy* in his consideration of Late Permian terrestrial vertebrates of the United States and the (former) USSR. He stressed its importance and the need to keep it distinct from paleoecology, although the two subjects were closely related.

The science of taphonomy has developed along fairly independent lines around the world and has focused on slightly different subjects, depending mostly on the paleontological interests of the investigator. Much research in taphonomy has been carried out with a particular problem in mind, often of a paleoecological nature, beginning as a reaction to some other concern. The intention has often been to rectify preservational bias in an assemblage so as to reveal matters of paleoecological interest or to allow the assumptions and limitations of paleoecological conjecture to be more clearly stated.

Taphonomy is sometimes described as the study and evaluation of *information loss*. Others, however, see it as *information gain,* because the state of fossil material may provide unique data about the agents that cause preservational bias. Often, the agent of modification or collection can be of as much paleoecological interest as the fossil remains themselves.

This positive approach has led to investigations that are less disparate and more united in their aims. Such work has generated much basic information that has permitted the formulation of more general rules and principles that find wider application. Consequently, the relevance of taphonomy to matters other than paleoecology is also becoming realized. In a more recent and broader formulation, as the study of ways in which preservation affects the fossil record, it has important implications for biostratigraphy and evolutionary questions.

SUBJECT MATTER OF TAPHONOMY

Efremov's simple description of taphonomy as the transition of animals from the biosphere to the lithosphere, although accurate, is operationally difficult because there are so many ways in which animals can become fossils.

A more direct, and perhaps more objective, approach to the practice of taphonomy is to enumerate and then explain the differences between fossil collections and living communities of animals. Most questions about sites and assemblages can then be framed and possibly answered in terms of these differences. For vertebrates, the most relevant organisms for hominid sites, they include the following: the animals are dead; there are usually no soft parts preserved; the skeletons are often disarticulated; bones are often concentrated together; bones are mostly damaged; parts of the skeleton occur in proportions different from their occurrence in life; remains are buried in sediment or other rock; bones are sometimes preferentially oriented within the rock; bones are altered chemically.

The list only partly illustrates the scope of taphonomy. For one thing, these distinctions all apply to individual animals. The question of how whole communities are represented in the fossil record also involves the association of different species and their numbers or relative proportions, or the numbers of individuals of different age or sex groups within each species.

There are two complementary lines of approach for tackling these issues. One, which could be referred to as *paleotaphonomy*, examines the content and context of fossil or archaeological sites in greater detail than has been usual. Another, *neotaphonomy*, is close to the idea of aktuopaläontologie and concentrates on the modern environment to find analogies to fossil situations. This can be in the form of observations of modern situations where bones naturally accumulate, such as a hyena den, and preferably in an environment where the modern animals are reasonably well known, permitting the relation between the modern bone assemblage and the community from which it is derived to be more easily understood. Alternatively, the work may be more experimental in nature, perhaps in laboratory situations, to study the effect of a limited and controlled range of specific processes on bones or standard forms. For example, experiments have been performed with flume tanks, or artificial stream tables, to investigate the effects of moving water on different skeletal elements and different kinds of bones.

The resolution of taphonomical studies extends from highly detailed work on specific fossil sites, from microstratigraphy or the analysis of microscopic scratches on bone, to matters on a much larger scale. Some environments, for example, are much more likely to preserve bone than are others. Fossils may have been more likely to be preserved at particular times in the past than during others. Such factors as these directly pertain to large-scale issues of paleobiogeography and evolution.

TAPHONOMY AND THE HOMINID RECORD

Taphonomic factors clearly affect the nature of the hominid fossil record. On a global scale, taphonomical considerations largely constrain the availability of sites where hominids may be preserved. East Africa is famous for fossil sites in the Rift Valley, where a combination of richly productive habitats surrounding highly alkaline and rapidly subsiding sedimentary basins that were periodically flooded with lavas produced conditions highly favorable to the accumulation and preservation of bone. This rather unusual set of circumstances has had an undue impact on interpretations of the distribution of hominids on a world scale. In the rest of Africa and Eurasia, the right geological and paleoenvironmental conditions—basically, those in which the factors promoting the accumulation of fossiliferous strata were present and in which, at the same time, hominids were numerous—were much more limited. From this point of view, the abundance and diversity of fossil hominids in the East African fossil record obviously reflects local taphonomical rather than regional paleobiological factors.

Taphonomical factors have their effects on the distribution of hominids in time as well, and this, in turn, affects not only paleoecological inference but also how we see evolution as having taken place. If so many circumstances conspire to influence the preservation of a fossil, how can we know how accurately the first and last occurrences of the fossils of a particular species in the stratigraphic record actually represent the time of its local appearance and disappearance, let alone its true time of biological appearance and its final extinction worldwide? Taphonomy helps answer questions of time resolution in the fossil record that are essential for understanding the mode of evolution, such as discriminating between punctuated or gradualistic models. Taphonomy is also vital to questions of the influence of external forcing factors on evolution. It may provide insight into the question of whether events of speciation and climate that appear contemporaneous in the fossil record are truly synchronous.

On a finer scale, the contribution of taphonomy to paleoanthropology is to expose the factors that control and modify bone assemblages, to distinguish natural effects from the effects of human behavior. Paleoanthropologists and archaeologists have a vital interest in the accumulations of bone that may represent the food debris of hominids, as evidence of technology, domestication, social structure, and foraging strategies. Since the late 1960s, a good deal of taphonomical work, mainly in Africa, has specifically aimed at understanding hominid sites and behavior. Fundamental anthropological problems addressed by taphonomy include the identification of sites as having been produced by hominids; the recognition of bone tools; the determination of whether early hominids were hunters or scavengers; the analysis of butchery practices; the identification of human-inflicted vs. natural violence on human remains; the description of the meat component of the diet; and the distinctions between domesticated vs. hunted items. At the same time, taphonomy is valuable for critically examining the often wildly exaggerated claims of human activity in newly discovered bone assemblages.

These issues are often interrelated. The first of them, the identification of sites as having been produced by hominids, is fundamental. It applies particularly, but not exclusively, to early hominid localities: How is hominid involvement in a site to be recognized? This question has arisen a number of times since the beginning of the nineteenth century. A classic recent example relates to South African cave sites where australopiths have been found. Were the bones associated with the early hominids collected by them, or were they, along with the hominids, the food remains of carnivores? The recognition of the australopith remains as predator garbage involved some of the earliest serious taphonomical work on hominids, carried out by C. K. Brain, among others.

Normally, for an occurrence to be regarded as a site, bones must be present in some quantity. The problem of the objective differences between a fossil collection and a living community initially relates to the concentration of remains: What processes result in bones becoming accumulated together? Not only hominids but also other carnivores, such as hyenas and leopards, collect bones, and a good deal of taphonomical work has studied such animals, distinguishing their collections from others. Flowing water also concentrates bones, prompting research on the effect of moving water on different parts of the skeleton. In practice, the question of bone-collecting agency leads to a close study of some of the other objective differences, notably damage to bones and the differential representation of skeletal parts. These factors, such as carnivores and moving water, leave their imprint on bone collections, but how do their effects differ from those of hominids?

Two of the notable features of the South African cave collections were the markedly different proportions in which parts of the animal skeletons were represented and the fact that the remains were broken in consistently repeated ways. R. A. Dart suggested, plausibly at the time (the 1940s), that the bones were the deliberately selected and modified tools and weapons of the hominids. Taphonomical work has since shown that the different proportions can be explained by such factors as the relative robusticity of different bones, their specific gravity, and the time of epiphysis fusion. The anomaly does not require human intervention. These factors also explain the characteristic patterns of damage, and, nowadays, with increasing knowledge of bone breakage by nonhuman agencies, researchers are generally much more critical of claims concerning bone tools.

A more recent example of this issue concerns the peopling of the New World. The earliest putative evidence for the arrival of humans in North America takes the form of bones claimed to show the effects of human working, some of them alleged to be artifacts. Taphonomical work on bone damage assists in discriminating between human agencies and other factors potentially responsible for creating these bone objects. In neither of these cases, the South African cave sites and the North American occurrences, have damaged bones been found with stone tools. Association of bones with artifacts has traditionally been axiomatic in affirming hominid involvement at a site, but even this criterion has come into question, some regarding certain associations as fortuitous. This objection has resulted in increased subtlety in taphonomical analysis, which has, for example, established microscopic distinctions between scratch marks produced by humans using stone tools and marks made by teeth of other carnivores. In turn, this endeavor has led to attempts to discriminate between scavenging and hunting behavior on the part of early hominids.

Inferences concerning the butchery practices of early humans here come into play, and the matter is a more explicit object of inquiry in other contexts. Part of the process of butchery is the dismemberment of carcasses. It is interesting to discover the ways in which skeletons fall apart under natural conditions and to compare this information with sequences of disarticulation deduced from archaeological sites. It appears that, like damage to bones, it is the nature of the skeleton that fundamentally controls sequences of dismember-

ment rather than the idiosyncrasies of any external agent. Consequently, human butchery practices are sometimes less distinctive than has been supposed.

Evidence of breakage and damage to human bones has been called upon to answer questions regarding human violence to other humans. Apparently unusual fractures on human specimens have frequently been attributed to violent or cannibalistic behavior. Rarely were they considered in the context of other possible causes. Taphonomy has demonstrated the need for caution in such assertions, refining the analysis of human remains in this respect.

Other anthropological issues rely upon the ability to answer questions regarding the numbers, or at least the relative proportions, of different species in an assemblage or paleocommunity. These questions are particularly difficult to answer because they require far more information about relative taxonomic and skeletal preservation if our reconstructions are to be treated with any confidence. Among these problems is the perennial one of estimating the relative amount of different meat food items at an archaeological site and what this means in terms of diet. Many of the obvious questions, such as how much meat of each particular species is consumed and how often, are hard to answer. Taphonomical work is helpful primarily by being critical of rash suggestions but also by providing positive information about the time interval represented by the accumulation of bones at particular sites.

Inferences about animal domestication and hunting also sometimes depend upon an estimation of the relative proportions of different age groups in a bone assemblage, and here again taphonomical factors are important. It is essential to be able to assess the relative survivorship of skeletons from animals of different individual age.

TAPHONOMY TODAY

These examples show, in brief, the relevance of taphonomy to important paleoanthropological issues. Most of our information about past hominids comes from fossil sites, and the essence of taphonomy is to understand the true nature of our data. Taphonomy began by assimilating procedures and information that many scientists were already considering. Is it simply, as someone once insisted, just a matter of doing paleoecology properly? Partly, but not entirely: By drawing together relevant information from a variety of fields, taphonomy focuses attention on an area that is not otherwise adequately examined. In the past, interpretation of bone assemblages associated with hominids was anthropocentric, with little concern for the many other natural processes involved in the formation of such accumulations. Today, a large number of studies with an explicitly taphonomical orientation have produced a formidable body of information regarding the nature and dynamics of such processes. Workers are coming to see this information as being applicable to much broader problems that rely on the interpretation of the fossil and archaeological records, involving not just paleoecology but global paleobiogeography and the mode and tempo of evolution. Present-day taphonomical work is decreasingly a reaction to narrow problems at particular sites, although this remains valuable, and is increasingly designed to formulate rules, almost the laws Efremov hoped for, that are of much more general applicability.

FURTHER READINGS

Andrews, P. (1990). Owls, Caves and Fossils. Chicago: University of Chicago Press.

Behrensmeyer, A. K., and Hill, A. (1980). Fossils in the Making. Chicago: University of Chicago Press.

Behrensmeyer, A. K., and Kidwell, S. M. (1985). Taphonomy's contribution to paleobiology. Paleobiology 11:105–119.

Brain, C. K. (1981). The Hunters or the Hunted? An Introduction to African Cave Taphonomy. Chicago: University of Chicago Press.

Hill, A. (1978). Taphonomical background to fossil man. In W. W. Bishop (ed.): Geological Background to Fossil Man. London: Geol. Soc. London, pp. 87–101.

Lyman, R. L. (1994). Vertebrate Taphonomy. Cambridge: Cambridge University Press.

Shipman, P. (1981). The Life History of a Fossil. Cambridge, Mass.: Harvard University Press.

The Earliest Hominids
Biomolecular and Morphological Evidence

The chapters in this part are devoted to hominid[*] origins. They approach the topic from a variety of perspectives: the behavior and ecology of living apes, biomolecular studies of primate phylogeny, and the fossil record. Since the divergence of our lineage from that leading to living chimpanzees and bonobos is a real event that took place sometime in the geological past, all of these approaches should ultimately converge on when, where, and how this divergence took place. Nonetheless, we are still far from a consensus, both within these diverse approaches and between them. Many of the articles in this section openly address these uncertainties and conflicting interpretations.

In Chapter 9, "African Apes as Time Machines," Richard Wrangham and David Pilbeam examine what we can determine about the common ancestor of African apes and humans from our knowledge of the behavior, morphology, and development of living apes. Although there is near uniform agreement that the genus *Pan* contains our closest primate relatives, the two species of *Pan,* common chimpanzees (*P. troglodytes*) and bonobos (*P. paniscus*), differ in many aspects of their morphology and behavior. Modern humans share some behavioral features with one species and some with the other. By reviewing what is known about the developmental patterns that have led to the differentiation of living African apes, including gorillas, Wrangham and Pilbeam attempt to reconstruct the evolutionary history of these human behaviors and determine whether the last common ancestor resembled chimpanzees, bonobos, or neither.

Drawing extensively from the work of Brian Shea (e.g., 1989) they argue that the common ancestor of African apes and humans most closely resembled chimpanzees and that the morphological and behavioral

differences between chimpanzees and bonobos reflect a subsequent process of developmental neoteny, in which bonobos have retained many aspects of juvenile morphology and behavior as adults. They then argue that the juvenile features in bonobos are the result of selection for reduced male aggression because of reduced scramble competition during foraging in that species. In this scenario, the features that living humans share with chimpanzees, but not with bonobos, such as lethal intergroup raids, group hunting, and male dominance over females, are retained from our last common ancestor. Features that we share with bonobos, but not with chimpanzees, such as extensive nonreproductive sexuality, friendships among females, and egalitarian males, are more recent aspects of human behavior that have been acquired independently in bonobos and humans, perhaps for similar reasons.

In Chapter 10, "Molecular Anthropology and the Molecular Clock," Jon Marks provides a brief introduction to the genetic studies used to reconstruct primate phylogeny. In a roughly historical fashion he reviews studies of immunology, the molecular clock, cytogenetic data, DNA studies, and levels of evolution. Most of these approaches were initially applied to primate and human evolution in the 1960s and 1970s and their use has continued to increase ever since. The concept of a molecular clock that could be used to date the time of divergence of living species has been a major source of debate in paleoanthropology since the concept was first applied by Sarich and Wilson (1967) to date the origin of the human lineage in the late 1960s. When first proposed, the results of the molecular clock were soundly attacked by both paleontologists and many molecular systematists, because the molecular clock data were in dramatic conflict with current interpretations of the fossil record concerning the origin of the hominid lineage. Despite ongoing debates over calibration of the clock and evidence that different molecules have evolved at different rates, as well as ongoing disagreements between the chronologies reconstructed from fossils and those reconstructed from many studies in molecular systematics, the concept of a molecular clock is now fully accepted.

Chapter 11, "Human and Ape Molecular Clocks and Constraints on Paleontological Hypotheses," by Rebecca

---

[*]*Hominid* is used in its generally accepted sense of a member of the family Hominidae, composed of humans and their bipedal fossil relatives. Some specialists use the term *hominin* to refer to this grouping, which is a taxonomic term for a zoological tribe. In our usage, hominids are a separate family distinct from the families of apes: the ape and human families are included in the superfamily Hominoidea. We have chosen to use the term *hominid* throughout this text to reflect the usage of the majority of the contributing authors.

L. Stauffer and colleagues, is a recent attempt to use the latest data from studies of molecular phylogeny to estimate the divergence dates in ape and human phylogeny. Stauffer and colleagues compare the dates from biomolecular studies with paleontological hypotheses based on the fossil record to see which hypotheses are congruent with their genetic results. This is a very important paper because of its efforts to integrate information from both the fossil record and molecular systematics. As mentioned earlier, the fossil record and the genetic composition of living species are both the results of the same evolutionary past. However, attempts to reconstruct that past from either source are subject to many potential sources of error. The challenge is to eliminate, or correct for, as many sources of error as possible in the hope of finding the common and correct history.

The remaining four chapters discuss fossil taxa that have been identified in recent years as the earliest possible hominids. These exciting new discoveries come from Ethiopia, Kenya, and Chad and have been placed in three different genera. Moreover, each find is known from different parts of the skeleton, making direct comparisons difficult. Not surprisingly, the relative phylogenetic positions of these earliest hominids are far from settled and the authors offer conflicting interpretations. Any consensus must await additional discoveries and comparisons.

In "*Ardipithecus ramidus,* a Root Species for *Australopithecus*" (Chapter 12), Tim White, Berhane Asfaw, and Gen Suwa discuss the history of the description of this species in the context of the Middle Awash Project and their views of early hominid evolution. The type specimen of *Ardipithecus ramidus,* an associated partial upper and lower subadult dentition, comes from deposits at the locality of Aramis that are bracketed by two tuffs dated at 4.4 mya. Additional skeletal and dental elements have also been recovered from numerous sites, but have not yet been described. *Ardipithecus ramidus* is more primitive than *Australopithecus* in having thinner enamel on the molars and canines, relatively large canines, and a distinctive morphology of the deciduous and permanent premolars; and the authors suggest that it may be the sister taxon to all later hominids. The authors find no reason to believe that the base of the hominid tree was very speciose or bushy.

In Chapter 13, "First Hominid from the Miocene (Lukeino Formation, Kenya)," Brigitte Senut and colleagues describe *Orrorin tugenensis,* from 6 mya deposits in northern Kenya. Like *Ardipithecus, Orrorin* has large canines and a primitive premolar morphology, but it differs from *Ardipithecus* in having small molars with thick enamel. Several limb elements are known for *Orrorin,* including femora that show that this species was bipedal

(see also Pickford et al., 2002) and a humerus and manual phalanx that suggest arboreal adaptations. The reconstruction of early hominid phylogeny offered by Senut and colleagues is strikingly different from that proposed by White et al., in Chapter 12. Senut and colleagues argue that *Orrorin* is a direct ancestor of the lineage leading to the genus *Homo,* but that *Ardipithecus* is in the ancestry of chimps and gorillas. They also suggest that *Australopithecus* is a side branch in hominid evolution characterized by increasing megadonty, whereas the small teeth of *Homo* are retained from an *Orrorin* ancestry.

Chapter 14, "Late Miocene Hominids from the Middle Awash, Ethiopia," by Yohannes Haile-Selassie, describes numerous hominid fossils from the Middle Awash of Ethiopia dated at 6.5–5.2 mya. These include both dental and skeletal remains attributed to a subspecies of *Ardipithecus, A. ramidus kadabba.* Like the younger remains of *Ardipithecus,* these fossils show a mixture of primitive and derived features. The third molar retains a primitive morphology characteristic of Miocene apes, while the canines and premolars suggest that this taxon shares with later hominids the loss of a canine-premolar honing complex. An isolated pedal phalanx from the youngest deposits (5.2 mya) is similar to phalanges of *Australopithecus afarensis* and shares a "dorsally canted proximal joint surface," as found in later bipedal hominids. The author disagrees with the views of Senut et al. (Chapter 13) that *Ardipithecus* is on the lineage leading to African apes, and questions their proposed phylogenetic position of *Orrorin.*

In Chapter 15, "A New Hominid from the Upper Miocene of Chad, Central Africa," Michel Brunet and a host of coauthors describe yet another early hominid from the Miocene of Africa, *Sahelanthropus tchadensis.* In contrast with *Ardipithecus* and *Orrorin, Sahelanthropus* is known from a nearly complete, but crushed, cranium and several dental remains, including a lower jaw with four teeth. *Sahelanthropus* has a small neurocranium and a large, relatively flat face with a massive supraorbital torus, the largest seen in any hominoid, living or extinct. Like *Ardipithecus,* there is evidence that the canine-premolar honing complex, characteristic of apes, was in the process of being reduced so that the canines show apical wear. The molar enamel is thicker than in *Pan* but less than in *Australopithecus.* A reliable assessment of the phylogenetic position of *Sahelanthropus* is hindered by the crushed condition of the cranium (but see Zollikofer et al., 2005) and by the lack of comparable anatomical parts in other late Miocene taxa, such as *Ardipithecus* and *Orrorin.* Nevertheless, the authors suggest that *Sahelanthropus* lies near the divergence of hominids and chimpanzees and that it demonstrates that hominids were widespread in Africa during the latest Miocene.

REFERENCES

Pickford, M., B. Senut, D. Gommery, and J. Treil. 2002. Bipedalism in *Orrorin tugenensis* revealed by its femora. *Comptes Rendus Palevol* 1:191–203.

Sarich, V. M., and A. C. Wilson. 1967. Immunological time scale for hominoid evolution. *Science* 158:1200–1203.

Shea, B. T. 1989. Heterochrony in human evolution: the case for neoteny reconsidered. *Yearbook of Physical Anthropology* 32:69–104.

Zollikofer, C. P. E., M. S. Ponce de León, D. E. Lieberman, F. Guy, D. Pilbeam, A. Likius, H. T. Mackaye, P. Vignaud, and M. Brunet. Virtual cranial reconstruction of *Sahelanthropus tchadensis. Nature* 434:755–759.

9

African Apes as Time Machines

R. Wrangham and D. Pilbeam

INTRODUCTION

"About 5 million years ago forest-ranging, knuckle-walking apes—very much like living chimpanzees—evolved ... into the earliest humans ... " (Zihlman, 1978:4). This view has successfully challenged alternatives such as the prebrachiationist model (descent from a generalized terrestrial quadrupedal ape), the gibbon model (descent from a terrestrial gibbon), and the Miocene fossil model (descent from a thick-enameled megadont hominoid) (Latimer et al., 1981; Pilbeam, 1996). Increasingly strong support has come from our growing confidence in the molecular evidence that human and chimpanzee lineages diverged after the split with gorillas (Ruvolo, 1997); the recognition that *Pan* is little changed phenotypically from the African ape ancestor (Groves, 1986, 1988); and the discovery that the earliest known australopithecine fossils (probably within 1–2 million years of their likely split from the chimpanzee lineage) have more chimpanzee-like features than do later species (Richmond and Strait, 2000; White et al., 1994; Wood, 1994a; Zihlman, 1996a). For such reasons, "the common ancestor of humans and chimpanzees was probably chimpanzee-like, a knuckle-walker with small thin-enameled cheek teeth" (Pilbeam, 1996:155).

"Chimpanzee-like," in the above conclusion, refers equally to chimpanzees *(Pan troglodytes)* and bonobos *(P. paniscus)*. In this chapter we ask whether we can discriminate more finely. To what extent can the common ancestor be reconstructed as having similar features to those found currently in either *P. troglodytes* (hereafter called "chimpanzees") or *P. paniscus* (hereafter "bonobos")?

Before bonobos were well known, chimpanzees were assumed to provide a good model of the ancestral state. Then, following an early 'scala naturae' argument by Coolidge (1933), Zihlman and her colleagues proposed bonobos to be more similar to the common ancestor, on the basis that they were "the most generalized of the African apes and have many 'primitive' features, particularly the shorter humerus relative to femur" (Zihlman and Cramer, 1978:92; see also Zihlman, 1979; Zihlman et al., 1978). Although Zihlman's idea provoked considerable research into the comparative morphology of African hominoids, it has been neither fully supported nor fully refuted. The consensus is much as Wood (1994b:31) concluded, "it is at present unclear with

which of the two extant species of *Pan* the modern *H. sapiens* should be compared."

In this chapter, we suggest a different kind of conclusion. We do not ask which species provides a better model. Instead, given that we know the pattern of genetic relationships, we aim to characterize traits that differ between chimpanzees or bonobos as being either homologies or homoplasies with respect to gorillas (or humans). In many cases, there is no clear answer. However, following Shea (1983) and others, we note that the pattern of ontogenetic development of chimpanzees appears to be homologous with the pattern in gorillas, whereas it is derived in bonobos. If this conclusion is correct, the pattern of cranial ontogeny in the common ancestor was chimpanzee-like, and not bonobo-like. Inasmuch as morphologies can be interpreted correctly as reflections of behavior, therefore, this suggests that the common ancestor was likely to have been more chimpanzee-like than bonobo-like in aspects of its behavior that were correlated with cranial development. Accordingly, we briefly consider the implications for behavioral evolution.

DIFFICULTIES OF CHARACTERIZING THE COMMON ANCESTOR

Genetic data are sometimes invoked to aid in characterizing the common ancestor. For example, de Waal (1998:407) characterized bonobos and chimpanzees as "equally close, and equally relevant to an understanding of human evolution," and was accordingly puzzled about "why attempts are still being made to push it (the bonobo) to the sidelines" in discussions of human behavioral evolution (cf. Zihlman, 1996b). But this puzzle is easily solved. Genetic relationship is not the relevant dimension of comparison, because the rate of morphological evolution can vary from stasis across millions of years to rapid change in a few thousand years, and is therefore not necessarily correlated with the molecular clock. This means that in the absence of other kinds of information genetic relationships cannot be used to reconstruct the nature of ancestors. The relevant process is change in phenotypes, not genotypes.

The morphological similarities among chimpanzees, bonobos, and gorillas are profound, including dietary traits such as thin-enameled molars, and locomotor adaptations for arm-hanging and knuckle-walking. When size is taken into account, the similarities become even greater. With a few exceptions (such as the small incisors of gorillas), these apes are to a considerable extent "size variants in a single morphotypic series, going stepwise from the smaller *P. paniscus* to the large male gorilla" (Zihlman et al., 1978:744; see also Groves, 1970; Hartwig-Scherer, 1993; Jungers and Susman, 1984; McHenry, 1984; Shea, 1981, 1986; Taylor, 1997). Indeed, the crania of large chimpanzees are so difficult to distinguish from those of small gorillas that they were once thought to belong to their own intermediate-sized species (the kooloo-kamba, Shea, 1984a). These clearly homologous similarities explain why, until genetic data showed that humans had evolved subsequent to the split from gorillas, the three African apes were widely considered to be both each other's closest relatives, to the exclusion of humans, and even congeneric (in the genus *Pan*, Groves, 1970; Tuttle, 1968). Such fundamental similarity means that in many cases of traits differing between chimpanzee and bonobo, gorillas are sufficiently similar to these apes to allow a meaningful comparison. Extensive change in the lineage leading to humans (Hartwig-Scherer, 1993), by contrast, means that comparisons between bonobos or chimpanzees and humans offer few convincing cases of homology.

In theory, therefore, degrees of phenotypic difference from gorillas (or occasionally humans) allow us to evaluate whether traits that differ between bonobos and chimpanzees are likely to be primitive or derived. This is true whenever gorillas (or humans) are similar to only one of these other apes. Thus, if an identifiably homologous trait is shared between gorillas and only one of the *Pan* species, it is expected to have occurred in the common ancestor. The alternative version of the trait, found in the other *Pan*, would be considered derived, and absent in the ancestor.

Unfortunately, this formula is generally ineffective despite the presence of many phenotypic differences between bonobos and chimpanzees (Groves, 1986; Izor et al., 1981; Johnson, 1981; Jungers and Susman, 1984; Kinzey, 1984; Leigh and Shea, 1996; Socha, 1984; Stanyon et al., 1986). First, it is sometimes difficult to decide whether traits represent homology or homoplasy, even among the closely related set of bonobos, chimpanzees, and gorillas. For example, de Waal and Lanting (1996) note that bonobos and gorillas have wide nostrils, unlike chimpanzees. Because the genetics and functional significance of nostril width are unknown, however, the similarity of this trait in bonobos and gorillas may well be due to homoplasy. Given this uncertainty, the primitive condition cannot be confidently reconstructed. A closely related problem is the difficulty of identifying a biologically meaningful trait. Bonobos and gorillas have darker faces than chimpanzees, for instance (Groves, 1986). This suggests that dark faces are primitive, and would therefore have occurred in the ancestor. But bonobos, unlike chimpanzees or gorillas, have pink lips. This means that the character under selection might be the whole face color ("pink lips against a dark face"), rather than "dark face." If so, gorillas are similar to neither bonobos nor chimpanzees, and again, the ancestral state cannot be reconstructed. The absence of rules for selecting phenotypic, as opposed to genetic, traits means that, in theory, different researchers can reach different conclusions from the same data.

And they do. For example, the combination of short arms and long legs in bonobos was proposed by Zihlman (1979) to be homologous with australopithecines and therefore to be primitive, compared to the longer arms and shorter legs of chimpanzees. By contrast, Hartwig-Scherer (1993) noted that larger apes have longer arms in relation to leg length. She concluded that the arm:leg length ratio of bonobos was much as expected from their body length, and was accordingly homologous with the ratio in chimpanzees and gorillas. Shea (1983), on the other, hand, considered the relatively short arms of bonobos to be a pedomorphic character, derived from the chimpanzee-gorilla pattern. This unresolved problem illustrates the difficulty of identifying homologous and biologically relevant traits. As a result, most morphologists agree that it is impossible to characterize the common ancestor as being, overall, more like chimpanzees or bonobos. A typical comment is McHenry's evaluation of the ancestor's postcranial anatomy: "no living species can be considered as being the least derived in all of its anatomy" (McHenry, 1984:222). Similarly Shea (1989:94) concluded "it is far from clear that *P. paniscus* is more derived in its morphology and behavior than *P. troglodytes.*"

DEVELOPMENTAL PATTERN: A PRIMITIVE, HOMOLOGOUS TRAIT IN CHIMPANZEES AND GORILLAS

In spite of the problems reviewed above, extensive agreement has emerged concerning the polarity of change for one particular set of traits. "(The bonobo's) reduced masticatory apparatus and paedomorphic skull are probably not primitive, however, but instead are derived from a more robust ancestor" (McHenry, 1984:222). This conclusion has a long history (e.g., Coolidge, 1933; Tuttle, 1975), and has been extensively buttressed by comparisons of skull size (Cramer, 1977; Shea, 1983, 1984b, 1989), skull gracility (Latimer et al., 1981), face shape (McHenry, 1984), the pattern of basicranial flexion (Laitman and Heimbuch, 1984), mandible and tooth size (Cramer, 1977; Latimer et al., 1981; Zihlman and Cramer, 1978), and the degree of sexual dimorphism in teeth (Kinzey, 1984), brains, and crania (Cramer, 1977) (see also McHenry, 1984; McHenry and Corruccini, 1981). It is based on three strong allometric patterns (Shea, 1983, 1989). At any given body length, the post-cranial linear dimensions of all three African apes are strikingly close. In a similar way, skull length predicts the cranial dimensions of each of the African apes as well as if the three apes were members of a single species. Both post-cranially and cranially, therefore, the three species fall on the same ontogenetic regressions. However, when the sizes of the cranium and the post-cranial skeleton are compared to each other, only chimpanzees and gorillas fall on the same line. Bonobos are outliers because their skulls are distinctly smaller in relation to body size (Hartwig-Scherer, 1993; Shea, 1983, 1984b, 1989).

Shea (1983, 1989) has argued explicitly that the small skull of bonobos is neotenous, i.e., achieved by a change in developmental timing. This proposal is supported not only by the relatively small size of the bonobo skull, but also by its juvenilized shape compared to chimpanzees, as well as by the marked reduction in cranial and dental sexual dimorphism. A variety of other bonobo traits are also pedomorphic, such as their high-pitched calls (Groves, 1986), white anal tail tuft (Groves, 1986), and shape and pattern of sexual swelling (Dahl, 1986). Evidence of cranial neoteny suggests that selection on a few genes controlling development could be responsible for a series of changes characterized by the cranium ceasing its development relatively earlier in bonobos (i.e., in relation to body length) than in the other apes. Accordingly, it implies that the small, juvenilized skull and associated traits constitute a biologically meaningful character or set of characters, derived from an ancestral state that continues to be expressed in a homologous way in chimpanzees and gorillas.

Compared to chimpanzees and gorillas, neither orangutans *(Pongo pygmaeus)* nor australopithecines show evidence of small skulls in relation to body length. Orangutans fall on the same ontogenetic curve of brain volume to body mass as chimpanzees and gorillas (Schultz, 1941), while australopithecines are estimated to have had marginally larger brains in relation to body mass than chimpanzees (Kappelman, 1996). The conclusion that the small, juvenilized skull is a derived trait in bonobos can therefore be rejected only by arguing that the pattern of cranial ontogeny found in the other great apes has evolved independently several times. Because this is unlikely, the chimpanzee-gorilla pattern of ontogeny, including their relatively large crania in relation to body size, is appropriately regarded as a primitive character that would have been found in the common ancestor. Fossils will eventually test this prediction.

THE COMMON ANCESTOR OF THE LIVING AFRICAN APES

With the exception of gorillas and humans, female great apes show a remarkably consistent pattern of body mass. Among chimpanzees, bonobos, *Australopithecus, Paranthropus,* and orangutans, female body mass falls in the range of 29–46 kg (Table 1). Gorilla females average at least 25 kg higher, at 71–97 kg. The elevated body mass of gorillas (two to three times the other apes) suggests a shift to a new digestive strategy, because it is their large body that supposedly gives this species its unique ability to survive and grow on foliage foods of low nutritional quality. The argument from parsimony suggests that the common ancestor of African apes, before the line leading to gorillas split off around 8–9 mybp, was more generalized, that is, still a committed ripe-fruit-eater. Accordingly, the common ancestor should have had a female size range that conforms to the other great apes, i.e., 29–46 kg.

In this size range, our 6 mybp ancestor can be expected to have shown traits shared by bonobos, chimpanzees, and gorillas. It would have been thin-enameled and knuckle-walking, and females would have had black body coats. In addition, it would have had the cranial morphology of chimpanzees rather than bonobos and, like chimpanzees, would have been committed to fruit-eating even during periods when fruits were scarce. In view of the pedomorphic character of the white anal tail tuft, high-pitched calls, and female genitals of bonobos, it seems likely that the ancestor would have been more chimpanzee-like than bonobo-like in these traits also.

Table 1. Body Mass in Great Apes

Species		Female Mass (kg)	Male Mass (kg)	Reference
Orangutan	*Pongo pygmaeus abelli*	36	78	Smith and Jungers, 1997
Orangutan	*P. p. pygmaeus*	36	79	Smith and Jungers, 1997
Bonobo	*Pan paniscus*	33	45	Smith and Jungers, 1997
Chimpanzee	*Pan troglodytes verus*	42	46	Smith and Jungers, 1997
Chimpanzee	*P.t. troglodytes*	46	60	Smith and Jungers, 1997
Chimpanzee	*P.t. schweinfurthii*	34	43	Smith and Jungers, 1997
Australopithecus	*A. afarensis*	29	45	McHenry, 1992
Australopithecus	*A. africanus*	30	41	McHenry, 1992
Australopithecus	*A. robustus*	32	40	McHenry, 1992
Australopithecus	*A. boisei*	34	49	McHenry, 1992
Homo	*H. habilis*	32	52	McHenry, 1992
Gorilla	*Gorilla gorilla gorilla*	71	170	Smith and Jungers, 1997
Gorilla	*G. g. beringei*	97	162	Smith and Jungers, 1997
Gorilla	*G. g. graueri*	71	175	Smith and Jungers, 1997
Human	Central African Republic	42	48	Smith and Jungers, 1997
Human	Guatemala	46	54	Smith and Jungers, 1997
Human	Melanesia	50	58	Smith and Jungers, 1997
Human	Australia	54	60	Smith and Jungers, 1997
Human	Saudi Arabia	56	63	Smith and Jungers, 1997
Human	Japan	52	65	Smith and Jungers, 1997
Human	Denmark	62	72	Smith and Jungers, 1997
Human	Western Samoa	73	78	Smith and Jungers, 1997
Human	Median human (from above)	53	61.5	

However, our confidence in this resemblance between chimpanzees and the common ancestor stops there. Because of the problems with identifying homologous traits, we have less confidence in our ability to reconstruct traits such as the ratio of arm length to leg length, pelvis structure, foot morphology, face color, ear size, nostril width, or other aspects of external appearance.

WHY ARE BONOBOS JUVENILIZED?

The principal explanation for bonobos having smaller heads, reduced sexual dimorphism, lighter bodies, and more juvenilized features than chimpanzees and gorillas is Shea's proposal that these changes resulted from selection for reduced sexual dimorphism in morphology and behavior (Shea, 1983, 1984b, 1989). Here we elaborate Shea's idea with the specific suggestion that reduced sexual dimorphism functioned to reduce aggressive behavior by adult males.

Reduced aggression, in turn, has been attributed ultimately to bonobos having larger foraging parties than do chimpanzees (Blount, 1990; Wrangham, 1986, 1993, 2000). In the most specific formulation of this idea, Wrangham (1993) suggested that selection for the bonobo phenotype was initiated by the loss of gorillas within the distributional range of a chimpanzee-like, proto-bonobo population around 2.5 mybp. The absence of gorillas made high-quality foliage more available for proto-bonobos than for chimpanzees. As a result, proto-bonobos experienced a reduced intensity of scramble competition compared to chimpanzees (Wrangham, 2000). Reduced scramble competition allowed more stable parties, which then made several forms of aggression more dangerous and costly, and less beneficial, to the aggressors. This change in the economics of violence led through various social consequences to female-female alliances, concealed ovulation, and reduced individual vulnerability to gang attacks. All these favored a reduction in the propensity for male aggressiveness (Wrangham and Peterson, 1996).

The idea that selection for reduced male aggressiveness produces bonobo-like features is supported by data on domesticated mammals. In dogs (*Canis familiaris*), a reduction in aggressiveness compared to their wolf ancestors (*C. lupus*) is correlated with a juvenilized morphology as adults. Bonobo-like morphology in dogs includes relatively smaller heads, smaller teeth, and smaller brains than in wolves of the same body mass (Coppinger and Schneider, 1995). As in bonobos compared to chimpanzees, the reduction in cranial dimensions from wolves to dogs is around 15–20%. In a further 14 species of domesticated mammals reviewed by Hemmer (1990), domesticates also have small brains compared to their wild ancestors. We suggest that this brain reduction may have resulted from selection for reduced aggression, as we also propose for bonobos.

Although the genetic processes underlying neoteny are not well understood, it is known that selection for tameness can produce change in various correlated features (Coppinger and Schneider, 1995). For example, by selecting wild foxes (*Vulpes vulpes*) for tameness over 20 generations, Belyaev (1979) produced various dog-like (juvenilized) traits including drooping ears and curly tail. By analogy with dogs, therefore, the tameness hypothesis suggests that smaller heads, reduced sexual dimorphism, and more juvenilized features in bonobos could all result from selection for reduced male aggression.

IMPLICATIONS FOR BEHAVIOR

Humans share important aspects of behavior differentially with chimpanzees and bonobos (Table 2), differences that may tend to reflect different historical pathways. Thus, if bonobo cranial neoteny indeed results from a reduced level of scramble competition, as suggested, the chimpanzee pattern of relatively intense scramble competition is reconstructed as ancestral. Accordingly, behaviors found in chimpanzees that are consequences of intense scramble competition are good candidates for ancestral phenotypes, whereas behaviors found in bonobos that are consequences of relaxed scramble competition are likely to be derived.

This distinction has limited value, however, because phylogenetic continuity is impossible to confirm when it must traverse the great unknowns of 5 million years of hominid evolution. And more importantly, it has no explanatory value. The reasons why a behavior is shared

Table 2.   Human Behaviors Found in Chimpanzees or Bonobos, but Not Both. "Similar to H?" asks whether chimpanzees or bonobos are more similar to humans with respect to that trait. C = chimpanzee, B = bonobo.

Behavior	Reference	Similar to H?
Lethal raiding	Wrangham, 1999	C
Traditions of material culture	Whiten et al., 1999	C
Group hunting	Stanford, 1998	C
Intense male-bonding	de Waal, 1982	C
Male dominance over females	Smuts and Smuts, 1993	C
Extensive non-conceptive sexuality	Blount, 1990	B
Friendships among adult females	Kano, 1992	B
Relatively egalitarian males	de Waal and Lanting, 1996	B
Sexual conciliatory behavior	de Waal, 1990	B
Potentially relaxed intergroup interactions	Kano, 1992	B

Note: This list is illustrative only; it is not meant to be comprehensive.

must still be articulated for each species, whether in terms of functions or constraints.

In the case of lethal raiding, for example, an adaptive hypothesis suggests that in chimpanzees and humans it can be ultimately attributed partly to imbalances of power that arise from scramble competition varying in its intensity between neighboring communities (Wrangham, 1999). An accompanying argument suggests that the reduction of group hunting in bonobos is an incidental outcome of psychological changes resulting from selection against intra-specific violence, rather than against group hunting *per se* (Wrangham, 1999). Even these examples remain controversial, and in other cases (such as cultural traditions, shared between chimpanzees and humans) no detailed hypotheses have been advanced.

Homoplasies may be even harder to explain but are potentially fruitful in suggesting heuristic hypotheses. For example, in the case of increased female sexuality, the ultimate cause of the homoplasy may have been a reduced intensity of scramble competition (Blount, 1990). This can be expected to have occurred in bonobos around 2.5 mybp, when individuals were first able to form relatively permanent and stable defensive alliances within groups (Wrangham and Peterson, 1996). A parallel argument might therefore suggest that female sexuality became intensified in the human lineage at a time of reduced scramble competition. The obvious time for this was when foraging strategies changed from ape-like to human-like, presumably around 1.9 mybp

(Wrangham et al., 1999). Thus chimpanzees and bonobos both provide useful models in which to generate explanatory hypotheses, regardless of how we reconstruct their ancestral behaviors.

Unfortunately, there has been a tendency to polarize between favoring chimpanzee or bonobo models when reconstructing human evolution. But suppose, against all odds, that convincing evidence emerges to show that lethal raiding is 6 million years old in humans, whereas concealed ovulation is "only" 1.9 million years old. Should this matter to our sense of ourselves, that violence is 4.1 million years older than peace? Not at all. Our convergences with either species are as evolutionarily real and as behaviorally significant as our behaviors shared by common descent. They demand explanation in terms of evolutionary benefits and constraints, and both provide numerous opportunities for helping us to think about evolutionary processes in fossil hominids.

ACKNOWLEDGMENTS

Our thanks to Brian Hare for drawing our attention to the literature on dogs, to Christopher Boehm, Laurie Godfrey, Jamie Jones, Cheryl Knott, Andy Marshall, Martin Muller, Brian Shea, Andrea Taylor, and Frans de Waal for comments, and to the Institute for Human Origins, University of Arizona, for their February 2000 symposium "First Cousins: Chimpanzees and Human Origins" which provoked this paper.

REFERENCES

Belyaev, D. K., 1979, Destabilizing selection as a factor in domestication, *J. of Heredity* 70:301–308.

Blount, B. G., 1990, Issues in bonobo *(Pan paniscus)* sexual behavior, *Amer. Anthro.* 92:702–714.

Coolidge, H. J., 1933, *Pan paniscus:* Pygmy chimpanzee from south of the Congo River, *Amer. J. of Phys. Anthro.* 18:1–57.

Coppinger, R. and Schneider, R., 1995, Evolution of working dogs. Pp. 21–50 in: (Ed. J. Serpell), *The Domestic Dog: Its Evolution, Behaviour, and Interactions with People,* Cambridge: Cambridge University Press.

Cramer, D. L., 1977, Craniofacial morphology of *Pan paniscus:* A morphometric and evolutionary appraisal, *Contributions to Primatol.* 10:1–64.

Dahl, J., 1986, Cyclic perineal swelling during the intermenstrual intervals of captive female pygmy chimpanzees *(Pan paniscus), J. of Hum. Evol.* 15:369–385.

Groves, C. P., 1970, *Gorillas,* London: Arthur Baker.

Groves, C. P., 1986, Systematics of the great apes. Pp. 187–217 in: *Comparative Primate Biology, Vol. 1: Systematics, Evolution and Anatomy,* New York: Alan R. Liss.

Groves, C. P., 1988, The evolutionary ecology of the Hominoidea, *Annuario de Psicología* 39:87–98.

Hartwig-Scherer, S., 1993, *Allometry in Hominoids: A Comparative Study of Skeletal Growth Trends.* Ph.D. dissertation, Zurich University, Switzerland.

Hemmer, H., 1990, *Domestication: The Decline of Environmental Appreciation.* Cambridge: Cambridge University Press.

Izor, R. J., Walchuk, S. L., and Wilkins, L., 1981, Anatomy and systematic significance of the penis of the pygmy chimpanzee, *Pan paniscus, Folia Primatologica* 35:218–224.

Johnson, S. C., 1981, Bonobos: Generalized hominid prototypes or specialized insular dwarfs? *Current Anthro.* 22:363–375.

Jungers, W. L. and Susman, R. L., 1984, Body size and skeletal allometry in African apes. Pp. 131–178 in: (Ed. R. L. Susman), *The Pygmy Chimpanzee,* New York, Plenum Press.

Kano, T., 1992, *The Last Ape: Pygmy Chimpanzee Behavior and Ecology,* Stanford, CA: Stanford University Press.

Kappelman, J., 1996, The evolution of body mass and relative brain size in fossil hominids, *J. of Hum. Evol.* 30:243–276.

Kinzey, W. G., 1984, The dentition of the pygmy chimpanzee, *Pan paniscus.* Pp. 65–88 in: (Ed. R. L. Susman), *The Pygmy Chimpanzee,* New York: Plenum Press.

Laitman, J. T. and Heimbuch, R. C., 1984, A measure of basicranial flexion in *Pan paniscus,* the pygmy chimpanzee. Pp. 49–64 in: (Ed. R. L. Susman), *The Pygmy Chimpanzee,* New York: Plenum Press.

Latimer, B. M., White, T. D., Kimbel, W. H., and Johanson, D. C., 1981, The pygmy chimpanzee is not a living missing link in human evolution, *J. of Hum. Evol.* 10:475–488.

Leigh, S. R. and Shea, B. T., 1996, Ontogeny of body size variation in African apes, *Amer. J. of Phys. Anthro.* 99:43–65.

McHenry, H. M., 1984, The common ancestor: A study of the postcranium of *Pan paniscus, Australopithecus* and other hominoids. Pp. 201–232 in: (Ed. R. L. Susman), *The Pygmy Chimpanzee.* New York: Plenum Press.

McHenry, H. M., 1992, How big were early hominids?, *Evolutionary Anthro.* 1:15–20.

McHenry, H. M. and Corruccini, R. S., 1981, *Pan paniscus* and human evolution, *Amer. J. of Phys. Anthro.* 54:355–367.

Pilbeam, D. R., 1996, Genetic and morphological records of the hominoidea and hominid origins: A synthesis, *Molecular Phylogenetics and Evolution* 5:155–168.

Richmond, B. G. and Strait, D. G., 2000, Evidence that humans evolved from a knuckle-walking ancestor, *Nature* 404:382–385.

Ruvolo, M., 1997, Molecular phylogeny of the hominoids: Inferences from multiple independent DNA sequence data sets, *Molecular Biology and Evolution* 14:248–265.

Schultz, A. H., 1941, Relative size of the cranial capacity in primates, *Amer. J. of Phys. Anthro.* 28:273–287.

Shea, B. T., 1981, Relative growth of the limbs and trunk of the African apes, *Amer. J. of Phys. Anthro.* 56:179–202.

Shea, B. T., 1983, Paedomorphosis and neoteny in the pygmy chimpanzee, *Science* 222:521–522.

Shea, B. T., 1984a, Between the gorilla and the chimpanzee: A history of debate concerning the existence of the *kooloo-kamba* or gorilla-like chimpanzee, *J. of Ethnobiology* 4:1–13.

Shea, B. T., 1984b, An allometric perspective on the morphological and evolutionary relationships between pygmy (*Pan paniscus*) and common *(Pan troglodytes)* chimpanzees. Pp. 89–130 in: (Ed. R. L. Susman), *The Pygmy Chimpanzee*, New York: Plenum Press.

Shea, B. T., 1986, Scapula form and locomotion in chimpanzee evolution, *Amer. J. of Phys. Anthro.* 70:475–488.

Shea, B. T., 1989, Heterochrony in human evolution: The case for neoteny reconsidered, *Yearbook of Phys. Anthro.* 32:69–104.

Smith, R. J. and Jungers, W. L., 1997, Body mass in comparative primatology, *J. of Hum. Evol.* 32:523–559.

Smuts, B. B. and Smuts, R. W., 1993, Male aggression and sexual coercion of females in nonhuman primates and other mammals: Evidence and theoretical implications, *Advances in the Study of Behavior* 22:1–63.

Socha, W. W., 1984, Blood groups of pygmy and common chimpanzees: A comparative study. Pp. 13–42 in: (Ed. R. L. Susman), *The Pygmy Chimpanzee*, New York: Plenum Press.

Stanford, C. B., 1998, The social behavior of chimpanzees and bonobos: Empirical evidence and shifting assumptions, *Current Anthro.* 39:399–407.

Stanyon, R., Chiarelli, B., Gottlieb, K., and Patton, W. H., 1986, The phylogenetic and taxonomic status of *Pan paniscus*: A chromosomal perspective, *Amer. J. of Phys. Anthro.* 69:489–498.

Taylor, A. B., 1997, Scapula form and biomechanics in gorillas, *J. of Hum. Evol.* 33:529–553.

Tuttle, R. S., 1968, Quantitative and functional studies on the hands of the Anthropoidea. I: The Hominoidea, *J. of Morphology* 128:309–364.

Tuttle, R. S., 1975, Parallelism, brachiation, and hominoid phylogeny. Pp. 447–480 in: (Eds. W. P. Luckett and F. S. Szalay), *Phylogeny of the Primates*, New York: Plenum Press.

de Waal, F. B. M., 1982, *Chimpanzee Politics: Power and Sex Among Apes*, New York: Harper and Row.

de Waal, F. B. M., 1990, Sociosexual behavior used for tension regulation in all age and sex combinations among bonobos. Pp. 378–393 in: (Ed. T. Feierman), *Pedophilia: Biosocial Dimensions*, New York: Springer.

de Waal, F. B. M., 1998, "Comment" on Stanford (1998), *Current Anthro.* 39:407–408.

de Waal, F. B. M. and Lanting, F., 1996, *Bonobo: The Forgotten Ape*, Berkeley, CA: University of California Press.

White, T. D., Suwa, G., and Asfaw, B., 1994, *Australopithecus ramidus*, a new species of early hominid from Aramis, Ethiopia, *Nature* 371:306–312.

Whiten, A., Goodall, J., McGrew, W. C., Nishida, T., Reynolds, V., Sugiyama, Y., Tutin, C. E. G., Wrangham, R. W., and Boesch, C., 1999, Chimpanzee cultures, *Nature* 399:682–685.

Wood, B., 1994a, The oldest hominid yet, *Nature* 371:280–281.

Wood, B., 1994b, The age of australopithecines, *Nature* 372:31–32.

Wrangham, R. W., 1986, Ecology and social evolution in two species of chimpanzees. Pp. 352–378 in: (Eds. D. I. Rubenstein and R. W. Wrangham), *Ecology and Social Evolution: Birds and Mammals*, Princeton: Princeton University Press.

Wrangham, R. W., 1993, The evolution of sexuality in chimpanzees and bonobos, *Human Nature* 4:47–79.

Wrangham, R. W., 1999, The evolution of coalitionary killing, *Yearbook of Physical Anthro.* 42:1–30.

Wrangham, R. W., 2000, Why are male chimpanzees more gregarious than mothers? A scramble competition hypothesis. Pp. 248–258 in: (Ed. P. Kappeler), *Male Primates,* Cambridge: Cambridge University Press.

Wrangham, R. W. and Peterson, D., 1996, *Demonic Males: Apes and the Origins of Violence,* Boston: Houghton Mifflin.

Wrangham, R. W., Jones, J. H., Laden, G., Pilbeam, D., and Conklin-Brittain, N. L., 1999, The raw and the stolen: Cooling and the ecology of human origins, *Current Anthro.* 40:567–594.

Zihlman, A. L., 1978, Women and evolution, Part II: Subsistence and social organization among early hominids, *Signs: Journal of Women in Culture and Society* 4:4–20.

Zihlman, A. L., 1979, Pygmy chimpanzee morphology and the interpretation of early hominids, *S. African J. of Sci.* 75:165–168.

Zihlman, A. L., 1996a, Reconstructions reconsidered: Chimpanzee models and human evolution. Pp. 293–304 in: (Eds. W. C. McGrew, L. F. Marchant, and T. Nishida), *Great Ape Societies*, New York: Cambridge University Press.

Zihlman, A. L., 1996b, Looking back in anger, *Nature* 384:35–36.

Zihlman, A. L. and Cramer, D. L., 1978, Skeletal differences between pygmy (*Pan paniscus*) and common chimpanzees (*Pan troglodytes*), *Folia Primatologica* 29:86–94.

Zihlman, A. L., Cronin, J. E., Cramer, D. L., and Sarich, V. M., 1978, Pygmy chimpanzee as a possible prototype for the common ancestor of humans, chimpanzees, and gorillas, *Nature* 275:744–746.

10

Molecular Anthropology and the Molecular Clock

J. Marks

MOLECULAR ANTHROPOLOGY

Molecular anthropology is the systematic study of primate taxa using comparative genetic methods. Since evolutionary change involves change in the genes, a study of the genetic systems of primates should reveal the relationships of species. The subfield dates to G. Nuttall's pioneering work in 1902 on the immuno-

logical cross-reactions between the bloods of different species. Little progress was made in this area, however, until the studies of M. Goodman in the 1960s.

As immunological distances are a rough measure of protein (and, therefore, genetic) similarity, the first use of these data involved primate phylogeny and established that the African apes (chimpanzee and gorilla) are more closely related to humans than to orangutans. Another method that became available in the 1960s was the direct sequencing of the amino acids composing specific proteins, a more direct reflection of the genetic material. Protein-sequence data not only confirmed the immunological results, but also showed that humans,

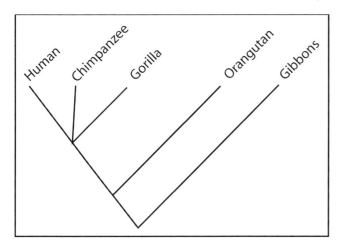

Molecular data show humans, chimpanzees, and gorillas to be approximately equally closely related to one another, but place the orangutan clearly apart from the African apes and humans. Courtesy of Jon Marks.

chimpanzees, and gorillas were genetically more similar to one another than had previously been imagined.

Concurrently, empirical data and theoretical advances pointed to the conclusion that most evolutionary changes in proteins are nonadaptive and not subject to the operation of natural selection. The spread of these *neutral* changes is governed by *genetic drift*, a statistical process. Consequently, any neutral mutation has a (low) probability of spreading through a population over time, and the spread of these mutations is simply a function of how often neutral mutations arise. Natural selection is here relegated to a primarily constraining role, limiting the rate at which a given protein can change but not affecting its evolution in a constructive, directional way.

Thus, although the vast majority of neutral mutations are lost shortly after arising, the laws of probability permit a few to spread through a population. They do so at a rate that fluctuates in the short run but approximates a constant rate in the long run. The amount of genetic difference between two species, therefore, could be taken as a measure of how long two species have been separated from each other.

Molecular Clock

The findings that molecular evolution proceeds at a roughly constant rate and that humans, chimpanzees, and gorillas are unexpectedly similar genetically can be reconciled in two ways, which represent the poles of a long-unresolved controversy.

Goodman and coworkers inferred that, since humans and the African apes are so similar genetically, the rate of molecular evolution in these species has been slowing down. Alternatively, A. Wilson, V. Sarich, and coworkers inferred that, since molecular evolution is constant, humans and the African apes must have diverged more recently than 4 Ma.

Sarich and Wilson argued that the prevailing opinion in 1967, that humans and African apes had diverged

from each other by 15 Ma because the fossil *Ramapithecus* was a uniquely human ancestor, was flawed. Time has borne out their conclusion, but it also appears that the divergence dates calculated by Sarich and Wilson are somewhat underestimated and that there was, indeed, a slowdown in the rate of molecular evolution among the great apes and humans. These facts are being used to study the microevolutionary history of the human species, and of other primate species, using mitochondrial DNA (deoxyribonucleic acid) as genetic markers.

Recent technological advances have permitted trace amounts of DNA to be amplified into analyzable quantities, via the polymerase chain reaction (PCR). This opens the door to the study of DNA samples from prehistoric (unfossilized) bones, as well as from hair follicles, which can be collected noninvasively.

Cytogenetic Data

Techniques were developed in the 1970s for distinguishing the 23 chromosome pairs in the human karyotype, and, while these techniques have been most useful in clinical applications, they have generated evolutionary data as well.

Chimpanzees and gorillas share several chromosomal inversions, inherited from a recent common ancestor, as well as a unique distribution of C-bands. In humans, these bands, which distinguish areas where the DNA is more tightly condensed than elsewhere, appear only at the centromere of each chromosome; below the centromere of chromosomes 1, 9, and 16; and on the long arm of the Y chromosome. In the African apes, however, they appear at the tips of most chromosomes.

In general, the chromosomes of humans and the African apes appear highly similar when prepared by

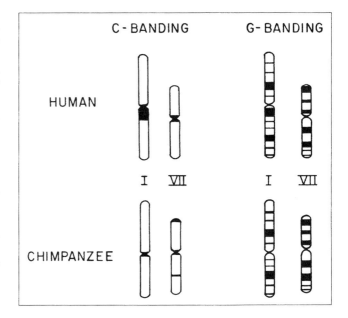

Despite some differences in C-banding (left) humans and chimpanzees share overwhelming similarities in their fine structure, as revealed by G-banding (right). Pictured are two chromosomes (1 and 7) from the human and their counterparts in the chimpanzee. Courtesy of Jon Marks.

the common procedure of G-banding. The most significant difference seems to be a recent fusion of two chromosomes in the human lineage, reducing the number of chromosome pairs from 24 (retained in the great apes) to 23 and creating what we now recognize as chromosome 2 in the human karyotype.

Rates of chromosomal change vary widely across primate taxa. We find rapid rates of chromosomal evolution in the gibbons and the most arboreal cercopithecine monkeys, slow chromosomal evolution in the baboons, and a moderate rate in the great apes and humans.

DNA Studies

The development of molecular genetics in the late 1970s brought studies of molecular evolution away from phenotypes (even a protein or antibody reaction is, properly speaking, a phenotype) and down directly to the genotype. These studies examine direct aspects of the DNA nucleotide sequence itself or indirect measures of DNA divergence. As phylogenetic data, the results obtained from DNA studies support those obtained from protein analyses. For example, the specific relations among human, chimpanzee, and gorilla are as unclear in their DNA as in their proteins, yet these species all still cluster apart from the orangutan.

Mitochondria are organelles that exist in the cytoplasm of each bodily cell. Although subcellular structures, they contain their own genetic machinery and information encoded in a circular piece of DNA (which is ca. 16,500 nucleotides long in humans). While the evolutionary rules that govern change in mitochondrial DNA are still unclear, in primates their rate of change seems to be about tenfold higher than that of nuclear DNA. Moreover, mitochondria are inherited exclusively through the mother, in contrast to nuclear DNA. These facts have already been used to study the genetic splitting of the human races, using mitochrondrial DNA as genetic markers. It has recently been proposed, based on the rate of change in this DNA, that the principal human groups diverged from one another ca. 200 Ka, a considerably more ancient date than usually thought.

Studies of DNA sequences across species have established that the neutral theory of molecular evolution is more applicable to DNA than to proteins. This is because the genome is now known to be very complex. Although a gene codes for a protein, only a portion of the gene actually consists of coding instructions. These regions *(exons)* are interrupted by DNA segments *(introns)* that do not become translated into part of the protein molecule. Untranslated regions are also found at the beginning and the end of each gene. Further, most of the DNA in the genome consists of *intergenic* DNA (i.e., DNA that lies between genes). It is now clear that, between any two species, intergenic DNA is most different, intron DNA is slightly more similar, and exon DNA is least different. Further, differences in exon DNA fall into two categories: those that direct a different amino acid to become part of the protein *(replacement mutations)* and those that do not change the protein *(silent mutations)*. Silent mutations far outnumber replacement mutations in any gene compared across two species.

What this means is that the neutral theory proposed to explain protein evolution is really only a first approximation, since the mutations that actually are detectable in protein evolution represent the slowest-evolving part of the genome. These replacement mutations are affected by the constraints of natural selection to a greater degree than silent mutations, intron and untranslated mutations, or intergenic mutations.

Levels of Evolution

While evolutionary change is genetic change, and ultimately molecular change, it is impossible at present to associate any adaptive anatomical specialization of humans with any particular DNA change. We may analogize to what is known about phenotypic evolution in other organisms, such as the fruitfly, but we have never located a gene for bipedalism or cranial expansion, and it is likely that there are no genes "for" these traits in the sense that there is a gene "for" cytochrome C or beta-hemoglobin.

Thus, while it is certain that the processes of bone growth and remodeling are under genetic control, as are the processes that govern the development of facultative responses to stresses on bone growth, such genes have not been located. Further, it is difficult to envision at this point how such genes work or what their primary product might be, much less how to isolate such a product.

Consequently, we are not able to explain at present how the primarily nonadaptive changes we find in the DNA account for the primarily adaptive morphological changes we find in the anatomy of the animal. This seems attributable less to any flaws in contemporary evolutionary theory than to our ignorance of how one gets phenotypic expressions out of genotypic information. It is, therefore, useful to conceive of evolution as a multilevel system: first, a level of the genome, where changes are clocklike over the long run and primarily unexpressed and nonadaptive; second, a level of the karyotype, where chromosomal rearrangements are primarily unexpressed and nonadaptive but may generate reproductive incompatibilities that facilitate the process of speciation; and third, a level of morphology, where changes usually track the environment, and individuals with certain anatomical characters outreproduce those with other similar anatomies, on the average.

FURTHER READINGS

Buettner-Janusch, J., and Hill, R. L. (1965). Molecules and monkeys. Science 147:836–842.

Devor, E. J., ed. (1992). Molecular Applications in Biological Anthropology. New York: Cambridge University Press.

Gillespie, J. (1986). Variability in evolutionary rates of DNA. Ann. Rev. Ecol. Syst. 17:637–665.

Goodman, M., Tashian, R., and Tashian, J., eds. (1976). Molecular Anthropology. New York: Plenum.

King, M.-C., and Wilson, A. C. (1975). Evolution at two levels in humans and chimpanzees. Science 188:107–116.

Marks, J. (1983) Hominoid cytogenetics and evolution. Yrbk. Phys. Anthropol. 25:125–153.

Marks, J. (1994). Blood will tell (won't it?): A century of molecular discourse in anthropological systematics. Am. J. Phys. Anthropol. 94:59–80.

Wilson, A. C., Cann, R. L., Carr, S. M., George, M., Gyllensten, U. B., Helm-Bychawski, K. M., Higuchi, R., Palumbi, S. R., Prager, F. M., Sage, R. D., and Stoneking, M. (1985). Mitochondrial DNA and two perspectives on evolutionary genetics. Bio. J. Linn. Soc. 26:375–400.

Weiss, M. (1987). Nucleic acid evidence bearing on hominoid relationships. Yrbk. Phys. Anthropol. 30:41–73.

MOLECULAR CLOCK

Comparative studies of protein structure suggested the *molecular-clock hypothesis* to E. Zuckerkandl and L. Pauling in 1962: that proteins evolve at statistically constant rates and that a simple algorithm might, therefore, relate the amount of protein difference between two species and the time since divergence of those species from their last common ancestor. It presents a sharp contrast to anatomical evolution, in which rates of evolution are usually related to environmental exigencies and may fluctuate widely. The concept of a molecular clock was used by V. Sarich and A. Wilson in 1967 to modify earlier assumptions about the remoteness of common ancestry between humans and the African apes.

M. Kimura, a theoretical population geneticist, showed mathematically in the late 1960s that, if most genetic changes had no adaptive effect on the organism, the evolution of these *neutral* mutations would be essentially constant over the long run. While predictions of the neutral theory accord well with the empirical data of protein evolution, it is also possible that models based on natural selection can account for these data.

It is now clear that each protein has its own characteristic rate of change. The most fundamental proteins (e.g., histones, which package cellular DNA) evolve slowly, while globins (which transport oxygen) evolve more rapidly. Further, this rate may fluctuate in the short run, but it averages to a constant rate over the long run. DNA (deoxyribonucleic acid) evolution can be modeled along the same lines as protein evolution. The discovery that most of the genomic DNA is not transcribed or expressed makes it likely that most DNA evolution is more nearly neutral than protein evolution. This makes noncoding DNA a good candidate for the mathematical models of the neutral theory.

FURTHER READINGS

Avise, J. C. (1994). Molecular Markers, Natural History, and Evolution. New York: Chapman and Hall.

Gillespie, J. H. (1992). The Causes of Molecular Evolution. New York: Oxford University Press.

Kimura, M. (1983). The Neutral Theory of Molecular Evolution. New York: Cambridge University Press.

Li, W.-H., and Graur, D. (1991). Fundamentals of Molecular Evolution. Sunderland, Mass.: Sinauer.

11

Human and Ape Molecular Clocks and Constraints on Paleontological Hypotheses

R. L. Stauffer, A. Walker, O. A. Ryder, M. Lyons-Weiler, and S. Blair Hedges

ABSTRACT

Although the relationships of the living hominoid primates (humans and apes) are well known, the relationships of the fossil species, times of divergence of both living and fossil species, and the biogeographic history of hominoids are not well established. Divergence times of living species, estimated from molecular clocks, have the potential to constrain hypotheses of the relationships of fossil species. In this study, new DNA sequences from nine protein-coding nuclear genes in great apes are added to existing datasets to increase the precision of molecular time estimates bearing on the evolutionary history of apes and humans. The divergence of Old World monkeys and hominoids at the Oligocene-Miocene boundary (approximately 23 million years ago) provides the best primate calibration point and yields a time and 95% confidence interval of 5.4 ± 1.1 million years ago (36 nuclear genes) for the human-chimpanzee divergence. Older splitting events are estimated as 6.4 ± 1.5 million years ago (gorilla, 31 genes), 11.3 ± 1.3 million years ago (orangutan, 33 genes), and 14.9 ± 2.0 million years ago (gibbon, 27 genes). Based on these molecular constraints, we find that several proposed phylogenies of fossil hominoid taxa are unlikely to be correct.

Reprinted with permission from *Journal of Heredity,* Vol. 92, pp. 469–474. Copyright © 2001 The American Genetic Association, by permission of Oxford University Press.

Fossils of the earliest hominoids (21 million years ago) and the cercopithecoids (Old World monkeys; 19 million years ago) are known from the early Miocene (Gebo et al., 1997; Lewin, 1999; Miller, 1999; Pilbeam, 1996). Between then and the end of the Miocene (approximately 5 million years ago), hominoids decreased and cercopithecoids increased in diversity in the fossil record (Fleagle, 1999). Relating the Miocene apes to living species has proven to be problematic (Pilbeam, 1996). There is no fossil species that is clearly a close relative of the gorilla, chimpanzee, or gibbon. It has been debated whether *Sivapithecus* (8–13 million years ago) or other Eurasian fossil apes are close relatives of the orangutan lineage (Pilbeam, 1996; Ward, 1997). Although the skull of one particular *Sivapithecus* species from 8 million years ago is orangutan-like, postcranial features and the morphology of the cheek teeth have suggested affinities with archaic hominoids (Pilbeam, 1996). With this uncertainty, the orangutan divergence is of limited value as a calibration point for molecular time estimates. The absence of Plio-Pleistocene fossil apes from Africa contrasts strongly with the rich hominid fossil record during that same period and is most likely explained by ecological and preservation biases (Fleagle, 1999). All of these factors make it difficult to impose time constraints on the origin of living species of hominoids.

With such uncertainty in the hominoid fossil record, considerable attention has been focused on molecular clocks during the last three decades. During the first half of the 20th century, anthropologists assumed that the great apes formed a single evolutionary group distinct from the human lineage, with a divergence time of approximately 30 million years ago (Lewin, 1999). However, the first applications of molecular techniques to this problem showed that humans are closer to African apes than to Asian apes (Goodman, 1962) and the human-African ape divergence occurred only 5 million years ago (Sarich and Wilson, 1967). Many molecular studies have been published since then (Easteal et al., 1995) and have clarified the branching order ((((human, chimpanzee) gorilla) orangutan) gibbon). However, divergence time estimates have varied considerably (Figure 1). If the ratios of the distances or time estimates are considered, the results are more consistent among studies. This suggests that variation in time estimates is largely attributable to the calibration used in each study.

To gain better and more precise estimates of hominoid splitting we have collected new sequence data from nine nuclear protein-coding genes in selected apes. Analyses of these data, along with all other available sequence data, have helped to constrain hypotheses concerning the phylogenetic placement of important fossil hominoids. One major element of uncertainty is the time of the human-chimpanzee divergence. Although the hominid fossil record is relatively good, there are no undisputed Pliocene fossils of African apes (chimpanzees and gorillas) and no Miocene ape fossils that clearly constrain a lower limit to that divergence. An advantage of molecular time

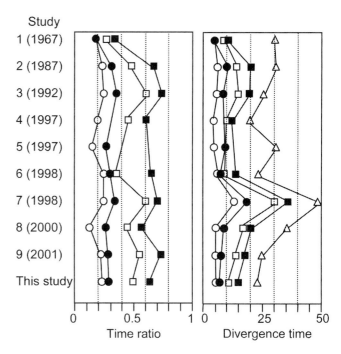

Figure 1. *Molecular divergence time estimates for apes and human. The results of selected studies published during the last four decades are shown, where an Old World monkey (cercopithecoid) also was included. Left panel shows the ratio of the human-ape divergence time divided by the hominoid-cercopithecoid divergence time. Right panel shows the actual divergence times. Symbols represent the following divergences: human-chimpanzee (open circles), human-gorilla (closed circles), human-orangutan (open squares), human-gibbon (closed squares), and human-cercopithecoid (open triangles). The data are from the following studies: 1 (Sarich and Wilson, 1967), 2 (Sibley and Ahlquist, 1987), 3 (Bailey et al., 1992), 4 (Easteal and Herbert, 1997), 5 (Takahata and Satta, 1997), 6 (Kumar and Hedges, 1998), 7 (Arnason et al., 1998), 8 (Yoder and Yang, 2000), and 9 (Page and Goodman, 2001).*

estimates is that they measure the mean time of separation rather than the minimum, and the amount of molecular data available has increased in recent years. However, even the most recent molecular studies (Arnason et al., 1998, 2001; Easteal and Herbert, 1997) have resulted in widely spaced estimates (3.6–14 million years ago) for the human-chimpanzee split. Because several major oscillations in global climate occurred over intervals of a few million years in the late Miocene and Pliocene (Crowley and North, 1991; Pagini et al., 1999), much greater precision in time estimation is necessary to establish postulated relationships between the origin of hominids themselves and bipedal locomotion (the first major hominid adaptation) and environmental change. It also is possible that extinction rather than speciation events are correlated with climate change (Foley, 1994).

MATERIALS AND METHODS

Portions of complementary DNAs (cDNAs) from the following nine nuclear genes were amplified and sequenced for *Gorilla gorilla* and *Pongo pygmaeus*: acyl-coA:

cholesterol acyltransferase I, alcohol dehydrogenase 1, beta-glucuronidase, Cd 46, CMP-N-acetylneuraminic acid hydroxylase, interleukin-α_1, prostaglandin D_2 synthase, chemokine receptor 2, and muscarinic acetylcholine receptor 5. A cDNA pool for each species was created by reverse transcription polymerase chain reaction (RT-PCR) (Perkin-Elmer RNA Core kit). RNA was extracted using the RNAqueous kit (Ambion, Inc., Austin, TX) from fibroblast cell cultures established and characterized at the Zoological Society of San Diego (www.sandiegozoo.org/cres/frozen.html). Primers were designed from conserved regions of the cercopithecoid and human sequences in the public databases. Gene fragments were amplified (PCR) and complimentary strands were sequenced. Gene fragments for each gene were combined and aligned using CLUSTAL W (Thompson et al., 1994). All primer sequences, alignments, and sequence accession numbers for this project are available at http://www.evogenomics.org/publications/data/primate/.

The other nuclear genes analyzed were 5-hydroxytriptamine receptor 1a, alpha 1,3 galactosyltrasferase, alanine: glyoxylate aminotransferase, atrophin, beta-nerve growth factor, blue opsin, carbonic anhydrase, c-myc oncogne, cytochrome oxidase subunit 4, DDX5 (p68 RNA helicase), decay accelerating factor, dopamine 4 receptor, dystrophin, eosinophil-derived neurotoxin, fusin, glycophorin A, hemoglobin $\alpha1$, hemoglobin β, hemoglobin ϵ, hemoglobin γ-α, histamine receptors H_1 and H_2, homeodomain proteins OTX1 and OPTX2, intracellular adhesion molecule 1, interleukin (IL)-3, IL-$\beta8$ receptor, IL-16, involucrin, L-selectin, leptin, lysozyme C, muscarinic acetylcholine receptors 2 and 3, myelin basic protein, myoglobin, olfactory receptor, preproinsulin, protamine p2, relaxin, rhesus-like factor, RNase k6, Sp100-HMG, testis-specific protein Y, and zinc finger Y. All genes included in the analyses satisfied two criteria: (1) a sequence was available for *Homo* and at least one other ape genus (*Pan, Gorilla, Pongo, Hylobates*), and (2) at least one calibration species (from Cercopithecidae, Artiodactyla, or Rodentia) and a mammalian or avian outgroup species sequence was available for relative rate testing. Furthermore, all *Pan* and *Gorilla* sequences that were identical to the corresponding *Homo* sequence were deemed uninformative and were therefore eliminated. All analyses were performed on both the group of rate-constant genes only and on the entire dataset.

The relatively low pairwise distances for most protein coding genes in these comparisons of closely related species, combined with limited sequence lengths, favors the more variable nucleotide data (all three codon positions) instead of amino acid data. For time estimation, the Kimura (1980) two-parameter with gamma model was used, which accounts for rate variation among sites. The gamma parameter was estimated by maximum likelihood estimation (Yang, 1997) for each gene. Between-group distance estimation was made using PHYLTEST (Kumar, 1996), and two methods of time estimation were used. The multigene method uses the mean (or mode) of single-gene time estimates (Hedges et al.,

1996; Kumar and Hedges, 1998). The average distance method is similar, but averages the concatenated distances, each weighted by sequence length (Lynch, 1999; Nei et al., 2001). Rate tests (Takezaki et al., 1995) were made for all comparisons using PHYLTEST.

We used the hominoid-cercopithecoid divergence, set at 23.3 million years ago, as the primate calibration point. It is a fossil calibration point, because the earliest fossils of each lineage are known from 19–21 million years ago (see above). The specific date used (23.3 million years ago) is the geologic boundary between the Oligocene and Miocene epochs (Harland et al., 1990). Most boundaries between geologic periods are times of major or catastrophic change in Earth history or climate, resulting in a greater than average number of extinctions followed by adaptive radiation. The resulting faunal change provides a sharp delineation or time marker in the fossil record. Thus, not considering other factors, it is more likely that the speciation event leading to these two major groups occurred at the boundary rather than slightly earlier or later. Also, the same time of 23.3 million years ago for the hominoid-cercopithecoid divergence was obtained by analysis of protein sequences from 56 nuclear genes calibrated with non-primate divergences (Kumar and Hedges, 1998).

We compared the results obtained using the primate calibration with application of a nonprimate calibration. Two nonprimate calibration points were selected: one was the divergence between ferungulates (carnivores and artiodactyls) and primates (92 million years ago) and the other was the divergence between rodents and primates (110 million years ago). These two calibration points are themselves molecular time estimates from an analysis of 333 and 108 nuclear proteins, respectively (Kumar and Hedges, 1998). In turn, they derive from a fossil calibration of 310 million years ago for the separation of reptiles and mammals. The advantage of these particular calibrations is the availability of sequences of cattle (*Bos taurus*) and mouse (*Mus musculus*) for most of the genes used. For the nonprimate calibration, we obtained an average rate by linear regression, with the regression line fixed through the origin.

For comparison of our results with previous studies, we also analyzed the complete mitochondrial genomes of *Homo sapiens, Pan troglodytes, Pan paniscus, Gorilla gorilla, Pongo pygmaeus, Hylobates lar,* and *Papio hamadryas,* using the same methods described above. As in previous studies by other authors, we excluded NADH6 from the analysis due to its unusual location on the opposite strand, and COXII because of its accelerated rate of evolution (in primates) compared with other mitochondrial genes. Because of the long branch length of *Pongo* in trees of mtDNA, possibly causing a bias, the divergence time of *Pongo* was also calculated using a lineage-specific method described elsewhere (Schubart et al., 1998). Essentially the time was estimated using only the *Homo* + *Pan* + *Gorilla* lineage. Furthermore, *Pongo* mtDNA was excluded from pairwise length calculations of *Pan, Gorilla, Hylobates,* and *Papio* to prevent possible skewing of results caused by extended branch length.

RESULTS

Of the genes newly sequenced, only beta-glucuronidase, Cd46, chemokine receptor 2, IL-α1, and prostaglandin d2 synthase demonstrated nucleotide substitution rate constancy. In addition, IL-α1 and alcohol dehydrogenase 1 could not be amplified for *Pongo*, and so the new sequences contributed 7082 base pairs of *Gorilla* sequence and 5556 base pairs of *Pongo* sequence to the analyses for these two species. The new sequences in this article have been deposited in the GenBank database (accession nos. AF354622–AF354638).

Total aligned nucleotide sites and the number of genes (in parentheses) examined for each species divergence (compared with human lineage) are *Pan* 40,668 sites (47 genes), *Gorilla* 29,999 sites (39 genes), *Pongo* 32,966 sites (41 genes), and *Hylobates* 19,307 sites (28 genes). The effects of eliminating the earliest and latest date from the arithmetic and weighted averages to account for possible paralogy problems (Kumar and Hedges, 1998) were examined and found to have little effect on divergence estimates (not shown).

Remarkably, divergence times were relatively consistent across genomes (mitochondrial versus nuclear), calibrations (primate and non-primate), rate consistency of gene, and time estimation methods (Table 1). Across all of these variables the divergence time estimates for human versus chimpanzee ranged from 4.2 to 6.3 million years ago, although most estimates were between 5 and 6 million years ago. The optimal method of analysis involves nuclear genes, primate calibration, and multigene method. Divergence times (and 95% confidence intervals) between the human lineage and apes using that method (Table 1) are 5.4 ± 1.1 million years ago (chimpanzee), 6.4 ± 1.5 million years ago (gorilla), 11.3 ± 1.3 million years ago (orangutan), and 14.9 ± 2.0 million years ago (gibbon) (Figure 2).

The difference between time estimates from rate-constant genes versus all genes is relatively small, and therefore the use of all genes is preferred because it

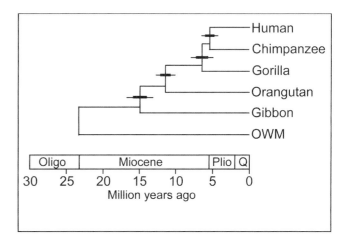

Figure 2. *Time tree of catarrhine primates based on divergence time estimates from this study (nuclear genes, Table 1). Time estimates are shown with ± 1 SE (heavy bar) and 95% confidence interval (narrow bar). Abbreviations are Oligo (Oligocene), OWM (Old World monkey), Plio (Pliocene), and Q (Quaternary).*

yields a lower variance. The multigene method yielded similar estimates to the average distance method except in the case of the human-chimpanzee divergence, where it was slightly low (4.3 million years ago). A variety of weighting schemes can be used with the average distance (or "concatenated distance") method, besides the one used here (sequence length), but the statistical properties of this method are not well known and deserve further study (Nei et al., 2001). We include those estimates here for comparison, but emphasize the better-known multigene method.

The time estimates from mtDNA (Table 1) are similar to those from nuclear DNA. However, we present these times only for comparison with the nuclear results and with previous studies. The relatively large amount of rate variation in this molecule makes it less desirable for use in time estimation and may explain (in part)

Table 1.   Divergence Time Estimates (million years ago) Between the Four Major Lineages of Hominoid Primates and the Human Lineage Based on Analyses of Nuclear and Mitochondrial DNA

	Chimpanzee			Gorilla			Orangutan			Gibbon		
	Time	SE	Genes	Time	SE	Genes	Time	SE	Genes	Time	SE	Genes
Nuclear												
Primate calibration, MG	**5.41**	0.55	36	**6.41**	0.74	31	**11.29**	0.68	33	**14.94**	1.01	27
	(4.87)	(0.52)	(25)	(5.49)	(0.65)	(22)	(10.64)	(0.70)	(23)	(14.56)	(1.07)	(21)
Nonprimate calibration, MG	4.65	0.68	22	6.35	1.43	18	10.54	1.29	16	10.73	2.12	6
	(4.54)	(1.07)	(12)	(4.48)	(0.76)	(10)	(8.07)	(1.01)	(10)	(9.28)	(2.99)	(4)
Primate calibration, AD	4.31			6.21			10.03			12.99		
Mitochondrial												
Unadjusted, MG	5.9	0.49	11	7.8	0.59	11	13.2	0.76	11	15.4	0.63	11
Adjusted, MG	4.8	0.59	11	6.4	0.71	11	12.3	0.83	11	14.6	0.70	11

The four comparisons are chimpanzees (*Pan*) versus humans, gorillas (*Gorilla*) versus humans + chimpanzees, orangutans (*Pongo*) versus humans + chimpanzees + gorillas, and gibbons (*Hylobates*) versus humans + other apes. In all cases, a gamma model was used. Results using only genes passing rate constancy tests are shown in parentheses. AD = average distance method; MG = multigene method. For the mitochondrial DNA estimates, results are based on a primate calibration; rate-adjusted times involve a correction for the long branch in orangutan. Time estimates based on the optimal combination of data and methods are indicated in bold.

why previous time estimates and time ratios from mtDNA have varied (Arnason et al., 1996, 1998; Yoder and Yang, 2000) (Figure 1).

DISCUSSION

Hominoid Divergence Times

The divergence time estimates and time ratios from these new sequence data are robust to different methods and calibrations (Table 1). In general, calibrations that are closer to the time estimate are preferred because they require less extrapolation and therefore we advocate use of the primate (hominoid-cercopithecoid) calibration. Using this calibration as a reference point, and the nucleotide-gamma method (Table 1), the resulting time ratios (divergence with human lineage) are 0.23 (chimpanzee), 0.28 (gorilla), 0.48 (orangutan), and 0.64 (gibbon). Here we have assumed that the hominoid-cercopithecoid divergence was 23 million years ago, for the reasons described above. In the future, additional molecular evidence will give increased precision to these distance and time ratios, but the actual time estimate will continue to depend on the calibration. For example, if hominoid or cercopithecoid fossils are found at 30 million years ago, the molecular time estimates would be pushed back by 30%, yielding (for example) a human-chimpanzee split of 6.9 million years ago. However, a similar increase in the synapsid-diapsid (mammal-bird) divergence, to approximately 400 million years ago, would place it earlier than the fish-tetrapod transition in the fossil record (Benton, 1997), which would be unlikely. The fact that the non-primate and primate calibrations now yield similar time estimates suggests some stability to the calibrations used here.

In theory, the divergence times estimated here may be overestimates of the actual population divergences because of coalescence (earlier divergence) of alleles within ancestral populations (Edwards and Beerli, 2000; Takahata and Satta, 1997). The overestimation is likely to be greatest in recently diverged populations and negligible in ancient splitting events of species (Edwards and Beerli, 2000). The amount of overestimation depends on knowledge of population parameters (e.g., population size and generation time) that are difficult to estimate for extinct species in the distant past. However, the closeness of our molecular time estimate of the human-chimpanzee divergence to the fossil record constraint (Haile-Selassie, 2001) suggests that the overestimation due to coalescence may be small.

Noncoding DNA sequences also have been used to time human and ape divergences, although higher rates of sequence change limit comparisons to closely related species. Therefore the cercopithecoid calibration usually is not available. In a recent study (Chen and Li, 2001) using approximately 24 kb of noncoding sequence, the time ratio (extrapolated from orangutan) for gorilla versus human (0.26) was similar to the coding DNA value reported here, but the human-

chimpanzee ratio (0.20) was lower than the corresponding value here (0.23). Assuming the orangutan divergence time estimated here (11.3 million years ago), the resulting human-chimpanzee divergence time with those noncoding data (4.7 million years ago) still is within the 95% confidence limit of our estimate (5.4 ± 1.1 million years ago).

Mitochondrial DNA has figured prominently in the timing of human and ape divergences in recent years. In large part, this is because of the availability of complete mitochondrial genomes for the species. However, much of the variability in divergence time estimates and time ratios concerns different analyses of these same data (Figure 1). For example, in some studies (Arnason et al., 1996, 1998, 2001) time estimates were two to three times greater than in other studies, whereas the time ratios were not unusually large or skewed, suggesting that the difference was in the calibration. In another case (Yoder and Yang, 2000), both the time estimates and time ratios were skewed (e.g., human-chimpanzee divergence was one-seventh of hominoid-cercopithecoid divergence) compared with other studies (Figure 1). Most or all of these problems with timing primate divergences using mtDNA probably stem from the well-known rate increase in the primate lineage in this molecule (Penny et al., 1998) and use of nonprimate calibrations. Although rate adjustments can and have been made, in cases like this where such major rate differences are known, it might be best to avoid using the molecule (especially with many nuclear genes available) or to use only a primate calibration. Taking the latter course in this study, we have obtained time estimates and time ratios for mtDNA more consistent with the fossil record and other molecular datasets.

In one recent study (Easteal and Herbert, 1997) the time estimate for the human-chimpanzee divergence (3.6 million years ago) postdates the first appearance of hominid fossils. This raised the possibility that chimpanzees evolved from an upright hominid such as *Australopithecus* (Easteal and Herbert, 1997) and that chimpanzees later lost the many morphological adaptations to bipedalism. Our dates using a larger dataset are more consistent with the hominid fossil record.

Temporal Constraints on Hominoid Evolution

Knowledge of an accurate timescale of primate evolution can help constrain interpretations of phylogeny and the relationships of fossil to living taxa. For example, the Early Miocene (21 million years ago) *Morotopithecus* from Uganda was suggested to be either a primitive great ape or the sister taxon of all living hominoids (Gebo et al., 1997). Under the timescale supported here, the first alternative can be rejected because the split between the great and lesser apes is estimated as 14.9 ± 2.0 million years ago and 21 million years ago is not included in the 95% confidence interval. The second hypothesis is not rejected by our data. Phylogenetic interpretations of some Eurasian fossil apes provide another example. The divergence of the

Table 2. Comparisons of Paleontological Hypotheses of Primate Phylogeny with Molecular Time Estimates

Fossil Genus of Group	Age (million years ago)	Postulated Fossil Relationship or Event	Reference	Consistent with Molecular Timescale
Orrorin	6	Stem hominid	Pickford and Senut (2001)	Yes
Orrorin	8.5	African ape-hominid split	Pickford and Senut (2001)	No
Ouranopithecus	9.5	Stem African ape	Andrews et al. (1997)	Yes
Ouranopithecus	9.5	Stem hominid	DeBonis and Koufos (1997)	No
Samburupithecus	9.5	Stem African ape	Ishida and Pickford (1997)	Yes
Dryopithecus	10	Stem African ape	Begun and Kordos (1997)	Yes
Dryopithecus	10	Orangutan clade	Moya-Sola and Kohler (1996)	Yes
Otavipithecus	13–12	Stem African ape	Pickford et al. (1997)	Yes
Sivapithecus	12.75	Orangutan clade	Ward (1997)	Yes
Proconsul	20	Stem great ape	Walker and Teaford (1989)	No
Proconsul	20	Stem hominoid	Walker (1997)	Yes
Gibbons	20	Pre-*Proconsul* divergence	Rae (1997)	No
Morotopithecus	21	Stem hominoid	Gebo et al. (1997)	Yes
Morotopithecus	21	Stem great ape	Gebo et al. (1997)	No
Small Miocene apes	23	Gibbon clade	Andrews et al. (1997)	No

Different hypotheses of relationships may be inferred from the morphological characters of a single fossil. Here a selection of fossil genera and groups is listed along with relationships (hypotheses) postulated by different authors. The age of the fossil places a temporal constraint on each hypothesis of relationship. Consistency between the paleontological hypothesis and the molecular time estimate (95% confidence interval) for the corresponding divergence among living hominoids is indicated.

orangutan lineage from the African ape and hominid lineage, 11.3 ± 1.3 million years ago, is only barely consistent with *Sivapithecus* (12.75–7.0 million years ago) (Ward, 1997) being on the orangutan lineage; a smaller confidence interval would reject that hypothesis for at least the earlier specimens of *Sivapithecus*. New hominoid fossils named *Orrorin tugenensis* from the approximately 6.0-million-year-old deposits of the Lukeino Formation of Kenya (Pickford and Senut, 2001; Senut et al., 2001) are said to be the earliest hominids, and this date is included in our 95% confidence interval for the chimpanzee-human split. However, the describers of these fossils postulate that African great apes and hominids split 8.5 million years ago, and this is not supported by our estimate. The recently described hominid fossils of *Ardipithecus* from Ethiopia (Haile-Selassie, 2001), dated at between 5.2 and 5.8 million years ago (WoldeGabriel et al., 2001), show signs of being close to the split between humans and chimpanzees, which again is consistent with our time estimate. The author discounts claims by Senut et al., (2001) that *Ardipithecus* is on the lineage leading to chimpanzees, and that *Orrorin* possesses characters placing it on the hominid lineage (Haile-Selassie, 2001). Other recent hypotheses concerning the relationships of extinct hominoids can be addressed by our divergence times (Table 2).

Molecular time estimates also can provide insight into the historical biogeography of hominoid primates. It is assumed that the living and fossil hominoids of Eurasia represent an early dispersal out of Africa. However, the origin of the African great apes and humans (AAH) has been debated. Either they arose from a preexisting lineage of African hominoids, or, as has been suggested (Sarich and Cronin, 1976; Stewart and Disotell, 1998), they represent dispersal back to Africa. In the recent revival of the "back to Africa" hypothesis (Stewart and Disotell, 1998), that scenario was deemed

more parsimonious when fossil taxa were considered because it required fewer dispersal events. However, the relationships of fossil hominoids are controversial (Pilbeam, 1996) and two African taxa are from a critical period. *Samburupithecus,* an approximately 9.5-million-year-old large hominoid from Kenya (Ishida and Pickford, 1997) is postulated on morphological and chronological grounds to be a close relative of the AAH clade. Our time estimates do not rule out this possibility. Similarly, the African *Otavipithecus* (13–12 million years ago) has been thought to be a close relative of the AAH clade (Pickford et al., 1997). Although our mean estimate of the splitting time between the orangutan clade and AAH is 11.3 million years ago, we are unable to reject this hypothesis based on overlap of the 95% confidence interval (12.6–10.0 million years ago) with the time of the fossils of *Otavipithecus.* Considering these fossils, the possibility that the ancestors of the gibbon lineage may have lived in Africa, and the general uncertainty of fossil hominoid relationships, an African origin for the AAH clade is perhaps more likely than a Eurasian origin. More evidence is needed before either hypothesis can be robustly supported.

The larger number of nuclear genes that will be available for analysis in the future will permit increased precision in time estimation and the opportunity to further test these and other hypotheses. This increased precision also will mean that calibration error will take on greater importance. Because fossil calibrations represent minimum (not average) time estimates for the divergence of two lineages, the use of many poorly constrained calibration points may yield a calibration that is a significant underestimate. A more accurate calibration (and resulting time estimate) may be obtained by using only the best-constrained calibration point or points.

REFERENCES

Andrews, P., Begun, D. R., and Zylstra, M., 1997. Paleoecology of Miocene hominoids. In: Function, phylogeny, and fossils (Begun, D. R., Ward, C. V., and Rose, M. D., eds). New York: Plenum; 29–58.

Arnason, U., Gullberg, A., Burgeuete, A. S., and Janke, A., 2001. Molecular estimates of primate divergences and new hypotheses for primate dispersal and the origin of modern humans. Hereditas 133:217–228.

Arnason, U., Gullberg, A., and Janke, A., 1998. Molecular timing of primate divergences as estimated by two nonprimate calibration points. J Mol Evol 47:718–727.

Arnason, U., Gullberg, A., Janke, A., and Xu, X., 1996. Pattern and timing of evolutionary divergences among hominoids based on analyses of complete mtDNAs. J Mol Evol 43:560–661.

Bailey, W., Hayasaka, K., Skinner, C., Kehow, S., Sieu, L., Sightom, J., and Goodman, M., 1992. Reexamination of the African hominoid trichotomy with additional sequences from the primate beta globin gene cluster. Mol Phylogenet Evol 1:97–135.

Begun, D. R. and Kordos, L., 1997. Phyletic affinities and functional convergence in *Dryopithecus* and other Miocene living hominids. In: Function, phylogeny, and fossils (Begun, D. R., Ward, C. V., and Rose, M. D., eds). New York: Plenum; 291–316.

Benton, M. J., 1997. Vertebrate paleontology. New York: Chapman and Hall.

Chen, F.-C. and Li, W.-H., 2001. Genomic divergences between humans and other hominoids and effective population size of the common ancestor of humans and chimpanzees. Am J Hum Genet 68:444–456.

Crowley, T. J. and North, G. R., 1991. Paleoclimatology. New York: Oxford University Press.

DeBonis, L. and Koufos, G., 1997. In: Function, phylogeny, and fossils (Begun, D. R., Ward, C. V., and Rose, M. D., eds). New York: Plenum; 317–326.

Easteal, S., Collet, C., and Betty, D., 1995. The mammalian molecular clock. Austin, TX: R. G. Landes.

Easteal, S. and Herbert, G., 1997. Molecular evidence from the nuclear genome for the time frame of human evolution. J Mol Evol 44:S121–S132.

Edwards, S. V. and Beerli, P., 2000. Gene divergence, population divergence, and the variance in coalescence time in phylogeographic studies. Evolution 54:1839–1854.

Fleagle, J. G., 1999. Primate adaptation and evolution. San Diego: Academic Press.

Foley, R. A., 1994. Speciation, extinction, and climatic change in hominid evolution. J Hum Evol 26:275–289.

Gebo, D. L., MacLatchy, L., Kityo, R., Deino, A., Kingston, J., and Pilbeam, D., 1997. A hominoid genus from the Early Miocene of Uganda. Science 276:401–404.

Goodman, M., 1962. Evolution of the immunologic species specificity of human serum proteins. Hum Biol 34:104–150.

Haile-Selassie, Y., 2001. Late Miocene hominids from the Middle Awash, Ethiopia. Nature 412:178–181.

Harland, W. B., Armstrong, R. L., Cox, A. V., Craig, L. E., Smitch, A. G., and Smith, D. G., 1990. A geologic time scale. Cambridge: Cambridge University Press.

Hedges, S. B., Parker, P. H., Sibley, C. G., and Kumar, S., 1996. Continental breakup and the ordinal diversification of birds and mammals. Nature 381:226–229.

Ishida, H. and Pickford, M., 1997. A new Late Miocene hominoid from Kenya: *Samburupithecus kiptalami* gen. et sp. nov. C. R. Acad Sci Paris II A 325:823–829.

Kimura, M., 1980. A simple method for estimating evolutionary rates of base substitutions through comparative studies of nucleotide sequences. J Mol Evol 16: 111–120.

Kumar, S., 1996. Phyltest: a program for testing phylogenetic hypotheses. University Park, PA: Institute of Molecular Evolutionary Genetics, Pennsylvania State University.

Kumar, S. and Hedges, S. B., 1998. A molecular timescale for vertebrate evolution. Nature 392:917–920.

Lewin, R., 1999. Human evolution. Malden, MA: Blackwell Science.

Lynch, M., 1999. The age and relationships of the major animal phyla. Evolution 53:319–325.

Miller, E. R., 1999. Faunal correlation of Wadi Moghara, Egypt: implications for the age of *Prohylobates tandyi*. J Hum Evol 36:519–533.

Moya-Sola, S. and Kohler, M., 1996. A *Dryopithecus* skeleton and the origins of great-ape locomotion. Nature 379:156–159.

Nei, M., Xu, P., and Glazko, G., 2001. Estimation of divergence times from multiprotein sequences for a few mammalian species and several distantly related organisms. Proc Natl Acad Sci USA 98:2497–2502.

Page, S. L. and Goodman, M., 2001. Catarrhine phylogeny: noncoding DNA evidence for a diphyletic origin of the mangabeys and for a human-chimpanzee clade. Mol Phylogenet Evol 18:14–25.

Pagini, M., Freeman, K. H., and Arthur, M., 1999. Late Miocene atmospheric CO_2 concentrations and expansion of C4 grasses. Science 285:876–879.

Penny, D., Murray-McIntosh, R. P., and Hendy, M. D., 1998. Estimating times of divergence with a change of rate: the orangutan/African ape divergence. Mol Biol Evol 15:608–610.

Pickford, M. and Senut, B., 2001. The geological and faunal context of Late Miocene hominid remains from Lukeino, Kenya. C R Acad Sci Paris II A 332:145–152.

Pickford, M., Sola, S. M., and Kohler, M., 1997. Phylogenetic implications of the first African Middle Miocene hominoid frontal bone from Otavi, Namibia. C R Acad Sci Paris II A 325:459–466.

Pilbeam, D., 1996. Genetic and morphological records of the Hominoidea and hominid origins: a synthesis. Mol Phylogenet Evol 5:155–168.

Rae, T. C., 1997. The early evolution of the hominoid face. In: Function, phylogeny, and fossils (Begun, D. R., Ward, C. V., and Rose, M. D., eds). New York: Plenum; 59–77.

Sarich, V. M. and Cronin, J. E., 1976. Molecular systematics of the primates. In: Molecular anthropology (Goodman, M., Tashian, R. E., and Tashian, J. H., eds). New York: Plenum; 141–170.

Sarich, V. M. and Wilson, A. C., 1967. Immunological time scale for hominid evolution. Science 158:1200–1203.

Schubart, C. D., Diesel, R., and Hedges, S. B., 1998. Rapid evolution to terrestrial life in Jamaican crabs. Nature 393:363–365.

Senut, B., Pickford, M., Gommery, D., Mein, P., Cheboi, K., and Coppens, Y., 2001. First hominid from the Miocene (Lukeino formation, Kenya). C R Acad Sci Paris II A 332:137–144.

Sibley, C. G. and Ahlquist, J. E., 1987. DNA hybridization evidence of hominoid phylogeny: results from an expanded data set. J Mol Evol 26:99–121.

Stewart, C. and Disotell, T., 1998. Primate evolution—in and out of Africa. Curr Biol 8:R582–R588.

Takahata, N. and Satta, Y., 1997. Evolution of the primate lineage leading to modern humans: phylogenetic and demographic inferences from DNA sequences. Proc Natl Acad Sci USA 94:4811–4815.

Takezaki, N., Rzhetsky, A., and Nei, M., 1995. Phylogenetic test of the molecular clock and linearized trees. Mol Biol Evol 12:823–833.

Thompson, J. D., Higgins, D. G., and Gibson, T. J., 1994. CLUSTAL W: improving the sensitivity of progressive multiple sequence alignment through sequence weighting, position-specific gap penalties and weight matrix choice. Nucleic Acids Res 22:4673–4680.

Walker, A., 1997. *Proconsul*: function and phylogeny. In: Function, phylogeny, and fossils (Begun, D. R., Ward, C. V., and Rose, M. D., eds). New York: Plenum; 209–224.

Walker, A. and Teaford, M., 1989. The hunt for *Proconsul*. Sci Am 260:76–82.

Ward, S., 1997. The taxonomy and phylogenetic relationships of *Sivapithecus* revisited. In: Function, phylogeny, and fossils (Begun, D. R., Ward, C. V., and Rose, M. D., eds). New York: Plenum; 269–290.

WoldeGabriel, G., Haile-Selassie, Y., Renne, P. R., Hart, W. K., Ambrose, S. H., Asfaw, B., Helken, G., and White, T., 2001. Geology and paleontology of the Late Miocene Middle Awash valley, Afar rift, Ethiopia. Nature 412:175–178.

Yang, Z., 1997. PAML: a program package for phylogenetic analysis by maximum likelihood. CABIOS 13:555–556.

Yoder, A. D. and Yang, Z., 2000. Estimation of primate speciation dates using local molecular clocks. Mol Biol Evol 17:1081–1090.

12

Ardipithecus ramidus, a Root Species for *Australopithecus*

T. White, B. Asfaw, and G. Suwa

HISTORY

Fossils belonging to the Middle Miocene primate *Ramapithecus* had been adopted by the paleontological community as the exclusive hominid ancestor by the early 1970s. Many paleontologists were then willing to identify species of *Proconsul* as the exclusive ancestors of modern chimpanzees and gorillas. *Ramapithecus* was linked to later hominids, then primarily South African *Australopithecus,* by its relatively large postcanine dentition, its thinner enamel, and a series of other conjectures such as delayed maturation and bipedal locomotion.

Given the then widespread belief in these direct phylogenetic linkages between Miocene fossils and their putative Plio-Pleistocene descendants, initial biochemical results suggesting a more recent common ancestry for African apes and modern humans (Sarich and Wilson, 1967) were generally dismissed. Although biomolecular approaches to hominoid phylogeny have since been greatly strengthened by advances in molecular biology, biochemically-based estimates of divergence among African apes and humans have consistently indicated a late Miocene time frame for what was, on a coarse scale, a trifurcation of the lineage leading to the two chimpanzees, the gorilla, and humans.

Molecular techniques have multiplied but it was paleontological discoveries that swayed the paleontological community. This community today accepts a more recent divergence as roundly as it condemned it two decades ago. What happened to shift the consensus? Predictions of an early divergence held that *Ramapithecus,* when it became better known, would conform to an early hominid pattern. Additional remains from this and closely related genera were, indeed, recovered from sites in Eurasia and Africa, testing this interpretation. These fossils showed that many of the Middle Miocene hominoids were adapted to heavily masticated diets relative to modern hominoids, and that this adaptation had anatomical consequences that reflected diet rather than direct descent. More importantly, however, was the recovery of even earlier hominid fossils from eastern Africa.

Reprinted with permission from *The First Humans and Their Cultural Manifestations,* F. Facchini, ed. Colloquium VII: Evolutive Modalities in Ancient Hominids and Phyletic Relationships between Australopithecines and the Genus *Homo.* XII International Congress of Prehistoric and Protohistoric Sciences. Copyright © 1996 by A.B.A.C.O., Forlì, Italy.

THE IMPACT OF *AUSTRALOPITHECUS AFARENSIS*

Predictions derived from an early divergence model were that the familiar Plio-Pleistocene hominid anatomy would extend well into the late Miocene. Indeed, when specimens such as the Lukeino molar and Lothagam mandible were recovered, they were attributed by many to *A. africanus,* a species demonstrated to be hominid in the 1950s (the Garusi specimens of *A. afarensis* were also placed in *A. africanus* at the time). However, the nearly simultaneous recovery of large fossil hominid samples from the Ethiopian site of Hadar and the Tanzanian site of Laetoli in the mid-1970s made it possible to evaluate early hominids based on many skeletal parts. The postcranial skeletons were similar to those already known from southern Africa, but craniodentally the Hadar and Laetoli fossils showed more primitive features. These features were used by Johanson and White to recognize the species *Australopithecus afarensis* and to reconsider phylogenetic relationships between then-known hominid taxa (Johanson and White, 1979). As the craniodentally primitive nature of *A. afarensis* became widely known, the notion of a more recent hominid/pongid divergence became more acceptable to paleontologists and focused additional attention on the extremely poor record of late Miocene and earliest Pliocene hominids.

Key sites spanning the period between 4 and 7 million years ago in Africa include, from south to north, Langebaanweg (c. 5 myr and without hominoids), Manonga (c. 3–6 myr and without hominoids), the Lower Laetolil Beds (c. 4.5 myr and without hominoids), Baringo Tabarin (c. 4.5 myr and with a mandible fragment and proximal humerus), Kanapoi and Allia Bay (3.5–4.1 myr, with a newly-recovered set of hominid fossils), Lothagam (c. 5–6 myr; with a mandible fragment and other small fragments; White, 1986), and Sahabi (c. 5.0 myr, without definitive hominoids). Substantial faunas have been recovered from these localities, but hominoid fossils have remained elusive. As a result, the ancestry of *A. afarensis* has remained largely in the realm of speculation.

New research at Hadar has clarified the temporal placement of this important sample of early hominids, and has yielded more complete remains from the time period between 3.0 and 3.4 myr (Kimbel et al., 1994; Walter, 1994; Aiello, 1994). These new discoveries include the first fairly complete skull of the taxon, a very large specimen. Because additional specimens representing very small individuals have also been recovered from Hadar, it is unlikely that the debate over the number of species represented here will soon be resolved.

Based on the new Hadar skull, Kimbel et al. (1994) also recently proposed to extend the known period of stasis within *A. afarensis* by c. 0.5 myr. This interpretation was based on comparisons between the frontal bone of the new specimen from Hadar (one of the youngest *A. afarensis* specimens known), and the c. 3.9 myr-old Belohdelie frontal from the Middle Awash (Asfaw, 1987). Assessment of evolutionary pace and pattern among hominids is difficult due to the fragmentary nature of their fossil record. This is why there is no consensus among paleoanthropologists on this topic. Basing conclusions about evolutionary mode and tempo on isolated segments of the anatomy is a hazardous undertaking, particularly when it is known that hominid evolution shows strong mosaicism (indeed, the taxon most important in demonstrating mosaic evolution is *A. afarensis*). For these reasons, the proposal of a million-year period of stasis in this taxon is premature, a point made by recent discoveries at Kanapoi (Leakey et al., 1995; see below).

THE MIDDLE AWASH STUDY AREA

The Middle Awash research area straddles the modern Awash River (Figure 1). This semiarid, relatively inaccessible region is inhabited by pastoralist Afar people. Geological work began in 1938 (Gortani and Bianchi, 1973). Taieb further explored the area, found fossils and artifacts, and did mapping and stratigraphic profiling as part of his Awash Basin survey (Taieb, 1974). Taieb and associates Coppens, Johanson, and Kalb began intensive work at Hadar in 1972—work that yielded the first Afar hominids (Johanson et al., 1982) and continues today with the Hadar and Gona projects investigating study areas to the north of the Middle Awash. In 1975 Jon Kalb left the Hadar group, created the Rift Valley Research Mission in Ethiopia (RVRME), and began further Middle Awash exploration. In 1976 Alemayehu Asfaw of the RVRME recovered the area's first hominid fossil from Middle Pleistocene deposits at Bodo (Kalb et al., 1980; Conroy et al., 1978). RVRME project fieldwork ended in 1978 and was summarized in a series of 1982 publications (for example, Kalb et al., 1982a,b,c). The RVRME proposed a stratigraphic nomenclature for the entire southern Afar based on air photo interpretation and preliminary reconnaissance (Kalb, 1993), but no radioisotopic dating or geochemistry of the abundant volcanic horizons was done.

Our group began work in the Middle Awash in 1981. Archaeological excavations were undertaken at Bodo and Hargufia, the first radioisotopic dates were made available, and Pliocene hominids were recovered (Clark et al., 1984). Following the Ethiopian research ban from 1982–90, we resumed fieldwork under an ongoing permit. Our 1990–91 focus was on Pliocene and Pleistocene deposits east of the Awash River (Clark et al.,

1993; White et al., 1993). We began intensive survey and collection west of the river in 1992.

Our team, led by Desmond Clark, Tim White, and Giday WoldeGabriel, includes colleagues from many disciplines, institutions, and nations who have collaborated since 1981. Our results show that the basin's tectonic, depositional, and evolutionary histories are recorded by windows of deposits now cropping out on both sides of the modern Awash River. We now know that several of these windows open on important time periods and access rich biological and geological data. We have shown that the eastern and western sides of the Awash are complementary. These, in turn, are complementary to Hadar, with little overlap in represented time. We have discovered a variety of new archaeological occurrences and fossil vertebrates, including 66 hominid specimens from six separate Middle Awash time horizons spanning 4.4 myr.

The entire depositional record of the Middle Awash spans over six million years. The study area is very large, but far less than 10% of it offers accessible and mappable sedimentary outcrop. Patches of exposed sediment within the study area are separated by expanses of basalt, water, riverine forest, grass, younger pediments, and residual lag. Correlation between fossiliferous patches is difficult and time-consuming, often depending on geochemical fingerprinting of volcanic units. Regional geology is extremely complex due to the active tectonic setting. Interpretation and correlation are hindered by syn- and postdepositional faulting, rapid facies change, and repetitive depositional regimes.

A primary research goal of the Middle Awash project has been sampling volcanic horizons for correlative and chronometric assessment, and relating these horizons to the paleontological and archaeological occurrences above and below them. We have sampled >300 different volcanic outcrops spanning the Middle Awash depositional column. This work has substantially revised and extended previous interpretations (Kalb et al., 1982c; Kalb, 1993), sometimes reordering entire members within formations. We are revising the RVRME stratigraphic nomenclature because of serious problems with its original definitions, descriptions, mapping, and formation boundaries. Single crystal Ar/Ar dating has established firm ages for many of the fossiliferous horizons. Tephrochemical analyses have allowed correlation among localities in modern Middle Awash catchments and ties to sediments deposited in the Turkana Basin and the Gulf of Aden (sampled from Deep Sea Drilling Project cores).

One of these correlations was very important in providing evidence of the early existence of *A. afarensis* in the Middle Awash. Here, at Wee-ee, we found the Sidiha Koma tuff (SHT) which was identified geochemically and radioisotopically dated to c. 3.4 myr. This volcanic ash is also known from the Turkana Basin and cores from the Gulf of Aden. The Maka hominids found in 1981 and 1990 were attributed to *A. afarensis*. They include the most complete male humerus and mandible from this species (White et al., 1993), and an extremely well-preserved proximal femur (Clark et al., 1984).

THE ARAMIS DISCOVERIES

With the presence of *A. afarensis* documented east of the modern Awash River, Middle Awash paleontologists and geologists began intensive work on the Central Awash Complex (CAC) to the west in December of 1992 (Figure 1). This is a stratigraphic succession now known to span the period from c.3.8 to c. 5.2 myr. Stratigraphic and geochronological work is still underway, but results from the middle portion of the local sequence, from the Aramis catchment, have been published (WoldeGabriel et al., 1994, 1995). The widespread Gàala Vitric Tuff Complex (GATC) is a key marker horizon between the Haradaso and Aramis members. A succession of overlying basaltic and vitric tuffs makes correlation between key vertebrate localities in the area possible and has afforded chronometric control over this part of the section. The GATC and overlying Daam Aatu Basaltic Tuff (DABT) are both dated to 4.4 million years. These horizons sandwich a unique vertebrate fauna that includes (as of October, 1995) 44 specimens of *Ardipithecus ramidus* among the thousands of fossil vertebrate, invertebrate, and macrobotanical specimens so far recovered from Aramis. Several overlying and underlying horizons with datable crystals have been sampled to complement the full paleomagnetic section at Sagantole and Aramis collected by the geological team. There is now no doubt that the mid-Pliocene succession exposed in the CAC and eastern margin of the Middle Awash will be a standard reference for the early Pliocene of Africa.

The first hominid discovered from Aramis was an upper molar. This was followed, over the next few days in December of 1992, by the recovery of a humeral shaft, an associated partial lower dentition, a partial child's mandible with deciduous molar, and more isolated teeth. The next field season saw the recovery of additional associated skeletal elements at Aramis. What would become the holotype specimen, an associated partial upper and lower subadult dentition, was recovered from Aramis Locality 6. More teeth and a basicranium were also found in 1993. At an adjacent locality, Locality 7, Alemayehu Asfaw found an associated radius, ulna and humerus from a single individual's left arm. After comparative analysis of this postcranial evidence, and with the firm dating of this part of the stratigraphic succession, the Aramis results were published eight months after the 1993/4 field discoveries (White, Suwa and Asfaw, 1994).

NAMING A NEW SPECIES AND GENUS, *ARDIPITHECUS RAMIDUS*

Species differentiation of the Aramis hominid fossils from *Australopithecus afarensis* was based on dramatic differences from homologous skeletal and dental parts preserved in the Hadar, Laetoli, and Maka specimens. Most significant among these are primitive traits of the dentition (absolutely and relatively thinner molar and canine enamel, relatively larger canines, lower first deciduous molar morphology, upper and lower premolar

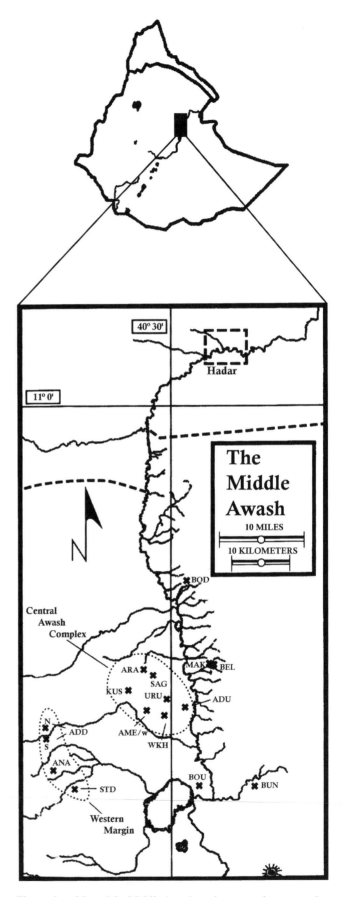

Figure 1. *Map of the Middle Awash study area to show some of the key areas discussed in the text.*

morphology, the lack of a definable articular eminence on the temporal bone). As we noted in our initial publication, generic attribution of the Aramis fossils to *Australopithecus* was a conservative taxonomic stance given that *A. ramidus* stood in obvious sister-group relationship to other hominids. At the urging of several colleagues subsequent to the publication of the new species—and based on the characters described previously—we provided a new genus name, *Ardipithecus,* to accommodate the species (White, Suwa and Asfaw, 1995).

Scrutiny of the naming and interpretation of any new hominid species is likely to involve three dimensions—taxonomy, chronology, and phylogenetic placement. Such scrutiny of *A. afarensis* generated decades of paleoanthropological debate that continues unabated to this day. It is likely that the description of *Ardipithecus ramidus* will precipitate parallel discussions.

Generic distinction is, ultimately, a completely subjective matter. For this reason, taxonomists cannot decide whether the living African apes, the chimpanzees and gorilla (species for which we have biochemistry, behavior, soft tissue anatomy, and blood), belong in a single genus *Pan,* or in two genera. In this light, what hope is there for resolving genus-level taxonomy for fossil species where the lack of data is compounded by the difficulty of applying static labels to dynamic evolutionary change through time? We are confident that the separation of *Ardipithecus* from *Australopithecus* is warranted from either grade- or clade-based concepts of the genus, but some investigators will prefer to retain *ramidus* in *Australopithecus.* The morphology and size of the first deciduous molar alone are so distinctive as to warrant the separation, and other features such as premolar morphology and enamel thickness indicate adaptive differences from later *Australopithecus.*

At the species level, also in the arena of taxonomy, some colleagues will maintain that the name *ramidus* is a junior synonym of Ferguson's (1989) *"Homo antiquus praegens."* However, the holotype for this subspecies is not diagnostic. This specimen, an eroded mandible fragment from Baringo Tabarin, was attributed, after exhaustive study by its discoverers, to *A.* cf. *afarensis.* We and others consider the name *"praegens"* (inextricably tied to that specimen) to be a nomen dubium—a name whose application will be forever in doubt. We explained this in our original work (White et al., 1994).

Fortunately, chronological control for the Aramis fossils is fairly straightforward. Nevertheless, some colleagues have questioned our first dates for the Aramis hominids (Kappelman and Fleagle, 1995). The fact that these fossils are sandwiched between volcanic strata with indistinguishable ages of 4.4 myr (WoldeGabriel et al., 1995) will convince most that the age is as originally stated, but additional radioisotopic and paleomagnetic studies are underway at Aramis to provide even more detailed calibration of the remains.

Phylogenetic placement of the *Ardipithecus* fossils from Aramis was also straightforward. Here was a taxon that antedated the earliest *Australopithecus afarensis* fossils (Laetoli at c. 3.6) by nearly 1 myr. It was a taxon characterized by more primitive teeth and basicrania. A

hypothesis of an ancestor-descendant linkage between these two species was favored in the absence of additional evidence.

ARDIPITHECUS RAMIDUS AND AUSTRALOPITHECUS ANAMENSIS

The description of fossils attributed to early *Australopithecus* from the Turkana Basin (Fleagle et al., 1991; Heinrich et al., 1993; Coffing et al., 1994; Leakey et al., 1995, Andrews, 1995) is an important event relative to the Aramis discoveries. Leakey and colleagues have recognized a new species of *Australopithecus, A. anamensis,* based on craniodental and postcranial remains from Kanapoi and Allia Bay dated to between 3.5 and 4.1 myr. Compared to *A. ramidus, A. anamensis* is derived in the direction of *A. afarensis* (Leakey et al., 1995). Although it is too early to address hominid evolutionary mode and tempo between 3.5 (Laetoli) and 4.4 myr (Aramis), the *A. anamensis* sample occupies an intermediate position in both time and anatomy, with its thicker enamel and larger postcanine teeth. It retains primitive mandibular and dental anatomy shared with *A. ramidus.*

The >4.0 myr discoveries have prompted some to speculate about an early diversification among the first hominids (Kappelman and Fleagle, 1995), but the known data are readily accommodated in the time-successive, ancestral-descendent series of *A. ramidus–A. anamensis–A. afarensis.* As the earliest and most primitive species in this series, *A. ramidus* serves as the outgroup for phylogenetic studies among all later hominids. For this reason, our recovery in 1995 of multiple skeletal and dental elements, from several Aramis individuals, is important.

In the 1960s and early 1970s there was excessive "pruning" of the hominid evolutionary tree. The 1970s brought a host of new fossils. The simultaneous co-development of cladistic methodology and rectangular evolutionary expectations added more branches to the hominid tree. The recovery of *A. ramidus* and *A. anamensis* adds still more data. Some have suggested that fossils attributed to *A. anamensis* might represent evidence for a diversification of early hominids shortly after the acquisition of bipedality (Leakey, 1995; Andrews, 1995). Others (Kappelman and Fleagle, 1995) have described the situation as follows: "It thus appears that the phylogeny of hominids, like that of many other mammalian groups is very bushy at its base." We question these assertions. We see nothing in the available chronological and anatomical data themselves as a warrant for such arguments. Furthermore, we see no theoretical reasons to suspect a "very bushy" tree at the base of a modest (even by mammalian standards) adaptive radiation. In the heyday of "pruning," misplaced appeal to ecological theory brought us the "single species hypothesis." Now, in the heyday of splitting, misplaced appeal to systematic theory may be generating equally invalid trees. Even bushes have trunks, and it is unlikely that hominid phylogeny, at its bushiest ca. 2.0 myr (after the appearance of robust *Australopithecus* species) was ever "very" bushy.

Finally, it is evident that relative to *Ardipithecus,* both *A. anamensis* and *A. afarensis* were the products of selection for craniodental morphology and size adaptations to more heavily masticated diets. It would be possible to atomize the characteristics of the masticatory apparatus among these taxa, group them, and thereby reach the ill-founded conclusion that *A. afarensis* was derived in the direction of later robust *Australopithecus,* (and therefore not ancestral to later *Homo* species). We believe that such a superficial analysis would probably lead to incorrect conclusions. Given the amount of demonstrated parallelism in hominid evolution, the susceptibility of these craniofacial characters to dietary selection, and the interdependence among the characters, we think that such phylogenetic conclusions would be premature because so few characters exclude *A. afarensis* from *Homo* ancestry. However, we predict (unfortunately for both living and phylogenetic trees) that such analyses and conclusions will be made and contended in the years which follow the description of *A. ramidus.*

CONCLUSIONS AND FUTURE RESEARCH

The unexpectedly primitive nature of the Aramis remains, even more than the *A. afarensis* remains found twenty years earlier, reinforces biochemically-based estimates for pongid-hominid divergence. The uniquely primitive morphology of the Aramis fossils, combined with the near "trifurcation" between *Gorilla, Pan* and *Homo* (Ruvolo et al., 1994), show that lineages in all three modern genera have evolved much since the last common ancestor. Fossils from sediments at 5 and 6 million years will be vital in identifying and understanding the last common ancestor of these three genera. With the biochemical estimates, and with the recovery of *Ardipithecus ramidus* at Aramis, it is now possible to strongly predict that remains of the last common ancestor will be found in sediments between 4.5 and 6.0 myr. Sediments dating to this time period are known in the Middle Awash study area, at localities stratigraphically below Aramis (Kuseralee Dora, Amba, Ambul Hareli, Gawto) and along the western margin of the study area (Saitune Dora, Asa Ali, Adu Dora). Our team is actively investigating these sediments and proceeding with the excavation of two partial skeletons of 4.4 myr *A. ramidus* at Aramis.

ACKNOWLEDGMENTS

Thanks go to the following institutions and individuals who have supported the Aramis research: The Physical Anthropology Program of the National Science Foundation (SBR-9318698; SBR-9512534), the UC Collaborative Research Program of the Institute of Geophysics and Planetary Physics at Los Alamos National Laboratory, the Government of Ethiopia, the Afar people, and all of our colleagues on the Middle Awash Project. Thanks to the organizers of the XIII Congress of the U.I.S.P.P. for inviting us to participate in the Colloquium.

REFERENCES

Aiello, L. C. (1994). Variable but singular. *Nature* 368:399–400.

Andrews, P. (1995). Paleontology—Ecological apes and ancestors. *Nature* 376:555–556.

Asfaw, B. (1987). The Belohdelie frontal: New evidence of early hominid cranial morphology from the Afar of Ethiopia. *Journal of Human Evolution* 16:611–624.

Asfaw, B. (1988). Pliocene Cranial Remains from Ethiopia: New Perspectives on the Evolution of the Early Hominid Frontal Bone. Ph.D. Dissertation, The University of California at Berkeley.

Clark, J. D., Asfaw, B., Harris, J. W. K., Walter, R. C., White, T. D. and Williams, M. A. J. (1984). Paleoanthropological discoveries in the Middle Awash Valley, Ethiopia. *Nature* 307:423–428.

Coffing, K., Feibel, C., Leakey, M. G., and Walker, A. (1994). Four-million-year-old hominids from East Lake Turkana, Kenya. *American Journal of Physical Anthropology* 93:55–65.

Ferguson, W. (1989). Taxonomic status of the hominid mandible KNM-ER TI 13150 from the Middle Pliocene of Tabarin, in Kenya. *Primates* 30:383–387.

Fleagle, J. G., Rasmussen, D. T., Yirga, S., Bown, T. M. and Grine, F. E. (1991). New hominid fossils from Fejej, Southern Ethiopia. *Journal of Human Evolution* 21:145–152.

Gortani, M. and Bianchi, A. (1973). *Missione Geologica Dell'azienda Generale Italiana Petroli (A. G. I. P.) Nella Dancalia Meridionale e Sugli Altipiani Hararini (1936–1938).* 4 volumes and 1 atlas. Rome: Accademia Nazionale dei Lincei.

Heinrich, R. E., Rose, M. D., Leakey, R. E., and Walker, A. C. (1993). Hominid radius from the Middle Pliocene of Lake Turkana, Kenya. *American Journal of Physical Anthropology* 92:139–148.

Johanson, D. C. and White, T. D. (1979). A systematic assessment of early African hominids. *Science* 202:321–330.

Kalb, J. E. (1993). Refined stratigraphy of the hominid-bearing Awash Group, Middle Awash Valley, Afar Depression, Ethiopia. *Newsletters on Stratigraphy* 29:21–62.

Kalb, J. E., Oswald, E. B., Tebedge, S., Mebrate, A., Tola, E. and Peak, D. (1982a). Geology and stratigraphy of Neogene deposits, Middle Awash Valley, Ethiopia. *Nature* 298:17–25.

Kalb, J. E., Jolly, C. J., Mebrate, A., Tebedge, S., Smart, C., Oswald, E. B., Cramer, D., Whitehead, P., Wood, C. B., Conroy, G. C., Adefris, T., Sperling, L., and Kana, B. (1982b). Fossil mammals and artefacts from the Middle Awash Valley, Ethiopia. *Nature* 298:25–29.

Kalb, J. E., Oswald, E. B., Mebrate, A., Tebedge, S. and Jolly, C. (1982c). Stratigraphy of the Awash Group, Middle Awash Valley, Afar, Ethiopia. *Newsletter on Stratigraphy* 11:95–127.

Kappelman, J. and Fleagle, J. G. (1995). Age of early hominids. *Nature* 376:558–559.

Kimbel, W. H., Johanson, D. C. and Rak, Y. (1994). The 1st skull and other new discoveries of *Australopithecus afarensis* at Hadar, Ethiopia. *Nature* 368:449–451.

Leakey, M. G., Feibel, C. S., McDougall, I., and Walker, A. (1995). New four-million-year-old hominid species from Kanapoi and Allia Bay, Kenya. *Nature* 376:565–571.

Ruvolo, M., Disotell, T. R., Allard, M. W., Brown, W. M. and Honeycutt, R. L. (1994). Resolution of the African hominoid trichotomy by use of a mitochondrial gene sequence. *Proceedings of the National Academy of Science, USA* 88:1570–1574.

Sarich, V. M. and Wilson, A. C. (1967). Immunological time scale for hominid evolution. *Science* 158:1200–1203.

Taieb, M. (1974). *Évolution Quaternaire du Bassin de l'Awash.* Unpublished Thesis, University of Paris VI, 327pp.

Walter, R. C. (1994). Age of Lucy and the first family: Single-crystal 40Ar/39Ar dating of the Denan Dora and lower Kada Hadar Members of the Hadar Formation, Ethiopia. *Geology* 22:6–10.

Ward, S. C. and Hill, A. (1987). Pliocene hominid partial mandible from Tabarin, Baringo, Kenya. *American Journal of Physical Anthropology* 72:21–37.

White, T. D. (1986). *Australopithecus afarensis* and the Lothagam mandible. *Anthropos* (Brno) 23:79–90.

White, T. D., Suwa, G., Hart, W. K., Walter, R. C., WoldeGabriel, G., de Heinzelin, J., Clark, J. D., Asfaw, B., and Vrba, E. (1993). New discoveries of *Australopithecus* at Maka, Ethiopia. *Nature* 366:261–265.

White, T. D., Suwa, G. and Asfaw, B. (1994). *Australopithecus ramidus*, a new species of early hominid from Aramis, Ethiopia. *Nature* 371:306–312.

White, T. D., Suwa, G. and Asfaw, B. (1995). Corrigendum: *Australopithecus ramidus*, a new species of early hominid from Aramis, Ethiopia. *Nature* 375:88.

WoldeGabriel, G., White, T. D., Suwa, G., Renne, P., de Heinzelin, J., Hart, W. K. and Heiken, G. (1994). Ecological and temporal placement of early Pliocene hominids at Aramis, Ethiopia. *Nature* 371:330–333.

WoldeGabriel, G., Renne, P., White, T. D., Suwa, G., deHeinzelin, J., Hart, W. K., and Heiken, G. (1995). Age of early hominids. *Nature* 376:559.

13

First Hominid from the Miocene (Lukeino Formation, Kenya)

B. Senut, M. Pickford, D. Gommery, P. Mein, K. Cheboi, and Y. Coppens

ABSTRACT

Remains of an early hominid have been recovered from four localities in the Lukeino Formation, Tugen Hills, Kenya, in sediments aged ca 6 Ma. 13 fossils are known, belonging to at least five individuals. The femora indicate that the Lukeino hominid was a biped when on the ground, whilst its humerus and manual phalanx show that it possessed some arboreal adaptations. The upper central incisor is large and robust, the upper canine is large for a hominid and retains a narrow and shallow anterior groove, the lower fourth premolar is ape-like, with offset roots and oblique crown, and the molars are relatively small, with thick enamel. A new genus and species is erected for the remains.

1. INTRODUCTION

The new genus of hominid described in the mid 90's (*Ardipithecus ramidus*) [28, 29] was interpreted as being ancestral to *Australopithecus anamensis* [13] and thus the oldest known hominid. However, several features of the Ethiopian fossil suggest that it may well not be a hominid *sensu stricto*, considering the numerous features close to *Pan paniscus*, which have been described. Bipedality in *Ardipithecus* still needs to be demonstrated as no detailed studies have been published since 1995. New discoveries made in Kenya last fall by the Kenya Palaeontology Expedition, a cooperative project between the Collège de France, Paris and the Community Museums of Kenya, Nairobi shed new light on the question of ape/human divergence and the phylogeny of hominids. The geological and faunal contexts were described by Pickford and Senut [17].

2. SYSTEMATIC DESCRIPTION

Order Primates Linnaeus, 1758
Suborder Anthropoidea Mivart, 1864
Superfamily Hominoidea Gray, 1825
Family Hominidae Gray, 1825
Genus *Orrorin* nov.

2.1. Type Species

Orrorin tugenensis nov. sp.

2.2. Generic Diagnosis

Hominid with jugal teeth smaller than those of Australopithecines; upper central incisor large and not shovel-shaped, with thick enamel; upper canine short with a shallow and narrow vertical mesial groove, apical height low; small triangular upper M^3s; *corpus mandibularis* relatively deep below M_3; lower P_4 with offset roots and oblique crown; small *Homo*-like rectangular lower M_2 and M_3s; thick enamel on lower cheek teeth; buccal notch well developed which imparts a bilobate profile to the buccal surface; no cingulum on molars. Femur with a spherical head rotated anteriorly, neck elongated and oval in section, lesser trochanter medially salient with strong muscle insertions, deep digital fossa; humerus with a vertical brachioradialis crest; proximal manual phalanx curved; dentition small relative to body size.

2.3. Differential Diagnosis

Orrorin is distinguished from *Australopithecus* by the morphology of the jugal teeth, which are smaller and less elongated mesio-distally; it differs from *Ardipithecus* by the greater thickness of enamel. It differs from both genera by the presence of a mesial groove on the upper canine. Postcranially, it differs from Australopithecines by the morphology of the proximal femur, which is more human-like than those of australopithecines or African apes.

2.4. Etymology

The generic name *Orrorin* (plural *Orroriek*) means 'original man' in Tugen. Note the pronunciation of the first two syllables, similar to the French word 'aurore' (dawn, daybreak). The specific name refers to the Tugen Hills, where the material was found.

Species *Orrorin tugenensis* nov.

2.5. Type Locality

Kapsomin (00°45′10.5″N: 35°52′29.9″E), Lukeino Formation, Baringo district, Kenya.

2.6. Age

Late Miocene (6 Ma)

2.7. Holotype

BAR 1000′00, a fragmentary mandible in two pieces; BAR 1000a′00: fragment of left mandible with M_{2-3} and BAR 1000b′00: fragment of right mandible with M_3 (figure 1).

2.8. Paratypes

The paratypes (Figure 1) are from four different sites in the Lukeino Formation: Cheboit [15], Kapsomin, Kapcheberek and Aragai. Table 1 lists the holotype and paratype series.

2.9. Species Diagnosis

As for the genus.

2.10. Description

2.10.1. Dental Descriptions (Table 2)

2.10.1.1. Upper Dentition. The lightly worn upper central incisor is robust, massive, relatively large mesiodistally, but smaller than those of Australopithecines and equivalent in size to that of *Ardipithecus ramidus.*

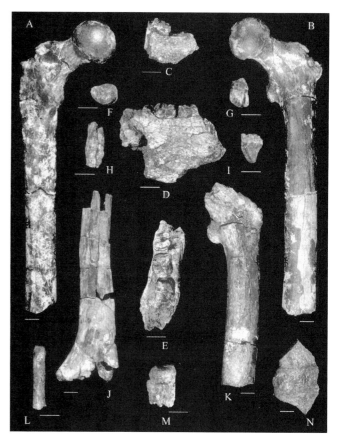

Figure 1. Orrorin tugenensis *nov. gen. nov. sp.* **A***: BAR 1002′00, left femur, posterior view;* **B***: BAR 1002′00, left femur, anterior view;* **C***: BAR 1000′00, right mandibular fragment with* M_3*, buccal view;* **D***: BAR 1000′00, left mandibular fragment with* M_{2-3}*, lingual view;* **E***: BAR 1000′00, left mandibular fragment with* M_{2-3}*, occlusal view;* **F***: BAR 1900′00, right* M^3*, occlusal view;* **G***: BAR 1390′00, right* P_4*, distal view;* **H***: BAR 1001′00, upper* I^1*, labial view;* **I***: BAR 1425′00, right* C̲*, lingual view;* **J***: BAR 1004′00, right distal humerus, posterior view;* **K***: BAR 1003′00, proximal left femur, anterior view;* **L***: BAR 349′00, manual proximal phalanx, superior view;* **M***: BAR 1426′00, left* M^3*, distal view;* **N***: BAR 1215′00, fragmentary right proximal femur, posterior view. Scale bars = 1 cm.*

The wear facet is inclined lingually. The labial face is almost vertical and slightly mesiodistally convex; the cervical outline is an open oval, almost circular. The lingual surface, which is planar, slopes strongly from apex to cervix as in chimpanzees and differs from

Table 1.   Hypodigm of *Orrorin tugenensis* nov. gen. nov. sp.

Catalogue No	Locality	Specimen	Collector	Date
KNM LU 335	Cheboit	lower molar	Martin Pickford	1974
BAR 349′00	Kapcheberek	manual phalanx	Evalyne Kiptalam	13 October 2000
BAR 1000′00	Kapsomin	2 mandible fragments	Kiptalam Cheboi	25 October 2000
BAR 1002′00	Kapsomin	left femur	Martin Pickford	4 November 2000
BAR 1004′00	Kapsomin	right humeral shaft	Brigitte Senut	5 November 2000
BAR 1003′00	Kapsomin	proximal left femur	Dominique Gommery	5 November 2000
BAR 1001′00	Kapsomin	upper central incisor	Samuel Chetalam	10 November 2000
BAR 1215′00	Aragai	proximal right femur	Martin Pickford	11 November 2000
BAR 1390′00	Kapsomin	lower fourth premolar	Samuel Chetalam	13 November 2000
BAR 1425′00	Kapsomin	upper right canine	Kiptalam Cheboi	16 November 2000
BAR 1426′00	Kapsomin	upper left third molar	Evalyne Kiptalam	17 November 2000
BAR 1900′00	Kapsomin	upper right third molar	Joseph Chebet	23 November 2000

Table 2. Dental Measurements of *Orrorin tugenensis* nov. gen. nov. sp. Compared to Those of Pliocene Hominids

		n	Mesio-Distal	*n*	Labio/Buccolingual
I¹	*Orrorin tugenensis*				
	BAR 1001'00 right	1	10e	1	8.7
	Ardipithecus ramidus	1	(10)	2	7.5–8.2
	Australopithecus anamensis				
	KNM-KP 29283 right	1	8.4	1	8.6
	KNM-KP 30202 right	1	10.5	1	9.0
	Australopithecus afarensis	3	10.8–11.8	5	7.1–8.6
C̲	*Orrorin tugenensis*				
	BAR 1425'00 right	1	11.0	1	9.3
	Ardipithecus ramidus	2	(11.2)–11.5	2	11.1–11.7
	Australopithecus anamensis				
	KNM-KP 29283 right	1	11.7	1	9.2
	Australopithecus afarensis	9	8.9–11.6	10	9.3–12.5
M³	*Orrorin tugenensis*				
	BAR 1426'00 left	1	10.2	1	13.1
	BAR 1900'00 right	1	10.3	1	12.9
	Ardipithecus ramidus	1	10.2	1	12.3
	Australopithecus anamensis				
	KNM-KP 29283 left	1	12.7	1	13.8
	KNM-KP 30200 right	1	(11.0)	1	(12.0)
	Australopithecus afarensis	8	10.5–14.3	8	13.0–15.5
P₄	*Orrorin tugenensis*				
	BAR 1390'00	1	8.0e	1	9.0e
	Ardipithecus ramidus	2	7.5–8.9	2	9.5–9.7
	Australopithecus anamensis				
	KNM-KP 29281 right	1	8.2	1	10.6
	KNM-KP 29281 left	1	8.4	1	10.0
	KNM-KP 29286 right	1	9.6	1	11.6
	KNM-KP 29286 left	1	9.7	1	11.7
	Australopithecus afarensis	15	7.7–11.1	14	9.8–12.8
M*	*Orrorin tugenensis*				
	KNM LU 335	1	11.4	1	10.6
M₂	*Orrorin tugenensis*				
	BAR 1000'00 left	1	11.5e	1	11.8e
	Ardipithecus ramidus	1	(13.0)	1	11.9
	Australopithecus anamensis				
	KNM-KP 29281 right	1	13.2	1	12.5
	KNM-KP 29281 left	1	13.0	1	12.7
	KNM-KP 29286 right	1	14.6	1	13.6
	KNM-KP 29286 left	1	14.6	1	13.7
	Australopithecus afarensis	23	12.4–16.2	22	12.1–15.2
M₃	*Orrorin tugenensis*				
	BAR 1000'00 right	1	12.4e	1	11.2
	BAR 1000'00 left	1	12.3e	1	10.4
	Ardipithecus ramidus	1	12.7	1	11.0
	Australopithecus anamensis				
	KNM-KP 29281 right	1	14.8	1	12.3
	KNM-KP 29281 left	1	14.5	1	12.4
	KNM-KP 29286 right	1	13.8	1	12.3
	KNM-KP 29286 left	1	14.4	1	12.8
	Australopithecus afarensis	14	13.7–16.3	14	12.1–14.9

*The measurements for *Ardipithecus ramidus* and *Australopithecus afarensis* are from [28] and for *Australopithecus anamensis* from [12] (e = estimated measurement).

Australopithecus afarensis [27] in which clear lingual grooves can be observed.

The upper canine is triangular in labial view, the cervical outline is not strongly mesio-distally compressed and a swelling but not a true cingulum occurs above the cervix. This swelling is clearly marked at the base of the distal and mesial crests. No lingual ridges can be observed. A shallow, narrow, vertical groove is present mesially. This groove does not occur in Australopithecines or *Homo*, nor in *Ardipithecus ramidus*, but is frequent in Miocene and modern apes. The apex of the canine is pointed (height above cervix = 13.4 mm), almost sectorial, recalling those of extant female chimpanzees. Perikymata are visible on the labial surface of the crown.

The upper M³'s are moderately to heavily worn and the details of the crowns cannot be properly seen (the left one is more worn than the right one). The teeth are trapezoidal, almost triangular in occlusal outline with small metacone and large protocone and are not strongly trapezoidal as in *Australopithecus afarensis*. The crown is low and the fovea are reduced; the distal fovea is located on the distobuccal corner of the tooth, unlike the pattern seen in Australopithecines. The occlusal surface is wrinkled but not as strongly as in Australopithecines. The roots of M_3 are long (35 mm on the distal root).

2.10.1.2. Lower Dentition.   The lower P_4 is ovoid in occlusal outline and compressed mesiodistally and has two offset roots. The enamel is missing from the anterior, lingual and posterior surfaces. The distal fovea is large as in extant and fossil nonhuman hominoids. The protoconid is higher than the metaconid and has a pointed apex from which two ridges run lingually and distally.

The lower left M_2 and right and left M^3 are preserved in BAR 1000'00. The teeth are broken and the enamel is missing from anterior and lingual surfaces of the left molars and from the mesial surface of the right molar which is also missing a chip of enamel distally. Enamel thickness at the apex on the paraconid is 3.1 mm. This is comparable to other hominids, *Ardipithecus* excluded. The occlusal outline of the M_2 is a round cornered rectangle, being slightly elongated mesiodistally. The distal fovea is not preserved except on the left M_2. The cusps are low and bunodont. The teeth are lightly worn. The lingual cusps on the lower left M_3 are damaged, but on the right M_3 the lingual cusps are pointed and slightly higher than the buccal ones. The lingual surface is vertical and there is no cingulum. The depth of the mandibular corpus below M_3 is 35.5 mm.

The lower molar (M_1 or M_2) KNM LU 335 has been the subject of a debate [4, 5, 7, 14, 16, 26, 31], which was summarised by Senut [20] and Hill [6]. Similarities to both chimpanzees and humans have been pointed out.

2.10.2. Postcranial Descriptions.   The two left femora (BAR 1002'00 and BAR 1003'00) are the best preserved but both lack the *trochanter major*. BAR 1002'00 is the most complete, including the femoral head, it preserves two thirds of the bone. The line of fusion of the head is visible and suggests that it belonged to a young adult. The well-defined head is spherical (33.0 mm in anteroposterior diameter and 33.0 mm perpendicular diameter) with a distinct and moderately wide *fovea capitis* and is slightly rotated anteriorly. It faces craniomedially, but less than in AL 288.1ap [11]. The proximal part of the shaft is antero-posteriorly flattened; the neck is elongated and compressed antero-posteriorly (estimated length: 20.5 mm; minimal height: 20.9 mm; width: 15.9 mm), giving a flattened ovoid section. The bulky *trochanter minor* is large (18.0 mm × 12.4 mm) and medially salient. There is an intertrochanteric groove, which runs from a small and moderately deep *fossa trochanterica* to an area situated just above the *trochanter minor*. This feature has been related to frequent bipedalism [22–25]. Below the *trochanter major* runs a crest for the insertion of the *m. vastus lateralis;* the well marked *tuberositas glutea* runs distally for approximately 46 mm.

A short *linea pectinea* is visible below the *trochanter minor* and runs distally as a low rugosity to meet the ridge which issues from the *tuberositas glutea* thereby forming a low and wide (9.0 mm) *linea aspera*. The general morphology of the proximal femur is clearly distinct from that of AL 288.1ap. The size of the head relative to the neck is also different. The preserved length of the femur is approximately 215 mm. The shaft is convex anteriorly and concave posteriorly, strongly flattened anteroposteriorly below the *trochanter minor* (anteroposterior diameter = 21.5 mm and medio-lateral diameter = 29.3 mm) but less than in AL 288.1ap at the same level [8] (a-p diameter = 18.3 mm; m-l diameter = 27.0 mm). Cortical thickness at midshaft is 5.2 mm (anterior), 5.2 mm (posterior), 7.4 mm (medial) and 5.5 mm (lateral). The neck-shaft angle is estimated to be between 120° and 130° (at present there is not a very good contact between two pieces of the femur).

Compared to modern humans, the head is smaller proportionally to the shaft, but it is proportionally larger than that of AL 288.1ap.

The humerus, represented by a distal shaft, shows a straight lateral crest, onto which inserts the *m. brachioradialis*. The same feature occurs in modern chimpanzees [19] and *A. afarensis* and it has been linked with climbing adaptations [18]. The same morphology is also present at Hadar [8, 18, 21] and in the Maka specimen [30], which we consider to be a male *Australopithecus afarensis*.

In lateral view, the proximal manual phalanx (preserved length: 33.8 mm; distal breadth: 7.1 mm) is curved recalling those of extant climbing primates as well as *A. afarensis*, a feature previously linked with grasping and climbing adaptations [22–25]. From the upper limb morphology, it appears that *Orrorin* was adapted to arboreal activities.

2.11. Phylogeny

Orrorin confirms that small, thick enamelled molars are an archaic feature for the hominid lineage, which is retained in *Homo*. Australopithecines retained thick enamel but developed megadonty, which increased through time. In contrast, *Ardipithecus* has thin enamelled cheek teeth, which may be a derived trait for the Gorillidae. If so, then the common ancestor of hominids and gorillids would have possessed small teeth with thick enamel. This scenario is comforted by the presence of the hominoid *Samburupithecus* in the Late Miocene of Kenya (9.5 Ma) [9, 10] (Figure 2).

2.12. *Orrorin* and the East Side Story

From the point of view of the timing of the dichotomy between African apes and hominids, the presence of the hominid *Orrorin* at 6 Ma accords with the East Side story proposed by Coppens [1–3].

3. CONCLUSIONS

On the basis of dental and postcranial morphology, it appears that *Orrorin* belongs to the hominid lineage, which was already present 6 Ma ago. This confirms the

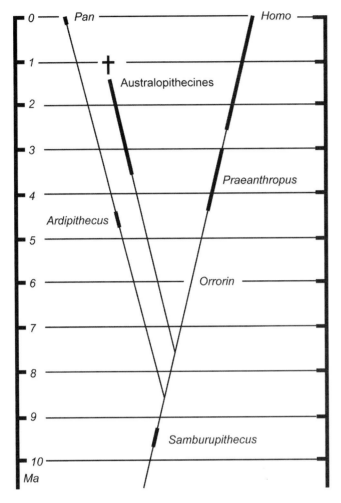

Figure 2. *Phylogenetic position of* Orrorin tugenensis *nov. gen. nov. sp.*

more ape-like, being closer in morphology to teeth of female chimpanzees. The molar enamel is thick. Another important feature is the relatively great depth of the *corpus mandibularis,* which is an archaic feature among hominids. Compared to later hominids, it seems that small jugal teeth relative to body size would be a primitive feature, inherited from the common ancestor of African apes and hominids, and retained in the *Homo* lineage. If this is so, then Australopithecines would have progressively developed megadonty—large jugal teeth and relatively small bodies. The postcranial evidence suggests that *Orrorin tugenensis* was already adapted to habitual or perhaps even obligate bipedalism when on the ground, but that it was also a good climber. Many scholars have considered that the earliest hominids were small animals; the femur and humerus of *Orrorin* are 1.5 times larger than those of AL 288.1, probably equivalent in size to a female common chimpanzee, indicating that the ancestor may have been larger than previously envisaged.

ACKNOWLEDGMENTS

The Kenya Palaeontology Expedition thanks the Community Museums of Kenya (Mr E. Gitonga) for local affiliation and the Kenyan Office of the President for research permission to M.P. (OP/13/001/28C 212) and B.S. (OP/13/001/29c 139). Funding was provided by the Collège de France (Prof. Y. Coppens), the Laboratoire de paléontologie of the Muséum national d'histoire naturelle, Paris (Prof. P. Taquet) and CNRS–UMR 8569, UPR 2147 and GDR 983. The KPE is anxious to thank all the personnel of the Community Museums of Kenya for their indispensable aid. We thank our field team (N. Kiptalam, E. Kiptalam, D. Chebor, S. Chetalam and J. Chebet) and all the other workers for logistics. We also thank the District Commissioner at Kabarnet (Mr L. N. Lenayapa), the Chief of the Kipkata location (Mr I. Tobole) and the Sub-Chief and villagers of Rondinin for their cheerful support and efficient help. Thanks to Mr M. Deville (Agence Gamma) for the photographs and to D. Serrette and P. Loubry for preparing Figure 1.

hypothesis that the divergence between apes and humans took place prior to 6 Ma, and probably between 9 and 7 Ma (Figure 2). The molars are smaller than those of Australopithecines and are closer in size to those of *Ardipithecus.* The anterior teeth, upper incisor and canine, as well as the lower P_4 are less hominid-like and

REFERENCES

1. Coppens, Y., Les plus anciens fossiles d'Hominidae, in: Recent Advances in the Evolution of Primates, Pontificiae Academiae Scientiarum Scripta Varia, Vol. 50, 1983, pp. 1–9.
2. Coppens, Y., Hominoïdés, Hominidés et Hommes, La vie des Sciences, Comptes rendus 1 (1984) 459–486.
3. Coppens, Y., L'évolution des hominidés, de leur locomotion et de leurs environnements, in: Coppens Y., Senut B. (Eds.), Origine(s) de la bipédie chez les Hominidae, Cah. Paléoanthrop., CNRS, Paris, 1991, pp. 295–301.
4. Corruccini, R., McHenry, H., Cladometric analysis of Pliocene hominoids, J. Human Evol. 9 (1980) 209–221.
5. Hill, A., Late Miocene and Early Pliocene Hominoids from Africa, in: Corruccini, R. S., Ciochon, R. L. (Eds.), Integrative Paths to the Past: Paleoanthropological Advances in Honour of F. Clark Howell, Prentice-Hall, Englewood Cliffs, NJ, 1994, pp. 123–145.
6. Hill, A., The Baringo Basin, Kenya: from Bill Bishop to BPRP, in: Andrews, P. J., Banham, P. (Eds.), Late Cenozoic Environments

and Hominid Evolution: A Tribute to Bill Bishop, Geological Society, London, 1999, pp. 85–97.
7. Hill, A., Ward, S., Origin of the Hominidae: the record of African large hominoid evolution between 14 My and 4 My, Yrbk Phys. Anthrop. 31 (1988) 49–83.
8. Johanson, D. C., Lovejoy, C. O., Kimbel, W. H., White, T. D., Ward, S. C., Bush, M. E., Latimer, B. M., Coppens, Y., Morphology of the Pliocene partial hominid skeleton (A.L. 288-1) from the Hadar Formation, Am. J. Phys. Anthrop. 57 (4) (1982) 403–451.
9. Ishida, H., Pickford, M., A new Late Miocene hominoid from Kenya: *Samburupithecus kiptalami* gen. et sp. nov., C. R. Acad. Sci. Paris, série IIa 325 (1998) 823–829.
10. Ishida, H., Pickford, M., Nakaya, H., Nakano, Y., Fossil anthropoids from Nachola and Samburu Hills, Afr. Stud. Monog. Suppl. 2 (1984) 73–85.
11. Johanson, D. C., White, T. D., Coppens, Y., Dental remains from the Hadar Formation, Ethiopia, Am. J. Phys. Anthrop. 57 (4) (1982) 545–603.

12. Leakey, M. G., Feibel, C. S., McDougall, I., Walker, A., New four-million-year-old hominid species from Kanapoi and Allia Bay, Kenya, Nature 376 (1995) 565–571.
13. Leakey, M. G., Ward, C. V., Walker, A., The new hominid species *Australopithecus anamensis*, in: Raath, M. A., Soodyall, H., Barkhan, D., Kuykendall, K. L., Tobias, P. V. (Eds.), Abstracts of Contributions, Dual Congress, Sun City, 1998, p. 21.
14. McHenry, H., Corruccini, R., Late Tertiary hominoids and human origins, Nature 285 (1980) 397–398.
15. Pickford, M., Stratigraphy and Palaeoecology of Five Late Cainozoic Formations in the Kenya Rift Valley, PhD thesis, University of London, 1974, pp. 1–219.
16. Pickford, M., Late Miocene sediments and fossils from the northern Kenya Rift Valley, Nature 256 (1975) 279–284.
17. Pickford, M., Senut, B., The geological and faunal context of Late Miocene hominid remains from Lukeino, Kenya, C. R. Acad. Sci. Paris, série IIa 332 (2001) 145–152.
18. Senut, B., L'humérus et ses articulations chez les hominidés plio-pléistocènes, Cah. Paléont., CNRS, Paris, 1981, pp. 1–141.
19. Senut, B., Le coude des primates hominoïdes: anatomie, fonction, taxonomie, évolution, Cah. Paléanthrop., CNRS, Paris, 1989, pp. 1–281.
20. Senut, B., Les grands singes fossiles et l'origine des hominidés: mythes et réalités, Primatologie 1 (1998) 93–134.
21. Senut, B., Tardieu, C., Functional aspects of Plio-Pleistocene hominid limb bones: implications for taxonomy and phylogeny, in: Delson E. (Ed.), Ancestors: The Hard Evidence, Alan R. Liss, New York, 1985, pp. 193–201.
22. Stern, J. T., Susman, R. L., The locomotor anatomy of *Australopithecus afarensis*, Am. J. Phys. Anthrop. 60 (1983) 279–317.
23. Stern, J. T., Susman, R. L., 'Total morphological pattern' versus the 'magic trait': conflicting approaches to the study of early hominid bipedalism, in: Coppens, Y., Senut, B. (Eds.), Origine(s) de la bipédie chez les hominidés, Cah. Paléoanthrop., CNRS, Paris, 1991, pp. 99–111.
24. Susman, R. L., Stern, J. T., Jungers, W. L., Arboreality and bipedality in the Hadar hominids, Folia primatol. 43 (1984) 113–156.
25. Tuttle, R. H., Evolution of hominid bipedalism and prehensile capabilities, Philos. Trans. Roy. Soc. London B 292 (1981) 89–94.
26. Ungar, P. S., Walker, A., Coffing, K., Reanalysis of the Lukeino molar (KNM LU 335), Am. J. Phys. Anthrop. 94 (1994) 165–173.
27. White, T. D., Johanson, D. C., Pliocene hominid mandibles from the Hadar Formation, Ethiopia: 1974–1977 collections, Am. J. Phys. Anthrop. 57 (4) (1982) 501–544.
28. White, T. D., Suwa, G., Asfaw, B., *Australopithecus ramidus*, a new species of early hominid from Aramis, Ethiopia, Nature 371 (1994) 306–312.
29. White, T. D., Suwa, G., Asfaw, B., Corrigendum: *Australopithecus ramidus*, a new species of early hominid from Aramis, Ethiopia, Nature 375 (1995) 88.
30. White, T. D., Suwa, G., Hart, W. K., Walter, R. C., WoldeGabriel G., de Heinzelin, J., Clark, J. D., Asfaw, B., Vrba, E., New discoveries of *Australopithecus* at Maka in Ethiopia, Nature 366 (1993) 261–265.
31. Wood, B., Plio-Pleistocene hominins from the Baringo Region, Kenya, in: Andrews, P. J., Banham, P. (Eds.), Late Cenozoic Environments and Hominid Evolution: A Tribute to Bill Bishop, Geological Society, London, 1999, pp. 113–122.

14

Late Miocene Hominids from the Middle Awash, Ethiopia

Y. Haile-Selassie

ABSTRACT

Molecular studies suggest that the lineages leading to humans and chimpanzees diverged approximately 6.5–5.5 million years (Myr) ago, in the Late Miocene[1–3]. Hominid fossils from this interval, however, are fragmentary and of uncertain phylogenetic status, age, or both[4–6]. Here I report new hominid specimens from the Middle Awash area of Ethiopia that date to 5.2–5.8 Myr and are associated with a wooded palaeoenvironment[7]. These Late Miocene fossils are assigned to the hominid genus Ardipithecus *and represent the earliest definitive evidence of the hominid clade. Derived dental characters are shared exclusively with all younger hominids. This indicates that the fossils probably represent a hominid taxon that postdated the divergence of lineages leading to modern chimpanzees and humans. However, the persistence of primitive dental and postcranial characters in these new fossils indicates that* Ardipithecus *was phylogenetically close to the common ancestor of chimpanzees and humans. These new findings raise additional questions about the claimed hominid status of* Orrorin tugenensis[8], *recently described from Kenya and dated to ~6 Myr[9].*

The western margin of the Middle Awash contains predominantly Late Miocene sediments mostly predating the Kuseralee Member at the base of the Sagantole Formation of the Central Awash Complex (CAC)[10]. Palaeontological work since 1992 has yielded abundant vertebrate fossils, including hominids that date to 5.2–5.8 Myr (Table 1). Environmental indicators suggest a wooded habitat[7]. To date, 11 hominid specimens (Figure 1) have been recovered at five localities since the first (a partial mandible) was recovered from Alayla in 1997. They represent at least five individuals and seem to represent a single taxon, a new subspecies of *Ardipithecus* (see Methods).

Table 1. Fossil Specimens of *Ardipithecus ramidus kadabba*

Specimen No.	Year Collected	Element	Discoverer	Dental Dimensions (mm)
AME-VP-1/71	1999	Proximal foot phalanx	L. Hlusko	
ALA-VP-2/10	1997–99	Right mandible with M_3 and associated teeth	Y. Haile-Selassie	RM_3 (13.3)MD; LI_2 6.3MD, 8.3LL; L_C 11.2MD, 7.8LL, (13.1+)CH; LP_4 (8.1)MD, 10.0BL; LM_2 (12.7)MD, 11.8BL
ALA-VP-2/11	1997	Intermediate hand phalanx fragment	S. Eshete	
ALA-VP-2/101	1999	Left humerus and ulna	T. White	
ASK-VP-3/78	1998	Left distal humerus	Y. Haile-Selassie	
ASK-VP-3/160	2001	LP^3	Group	7.6MD, 11.3BL
DID-VP-1/80	1998	Proximal hand phalanx fragment	Y. Haile-Selassie	
STD-VP-2/61	1998	R_C	M. Humed	10.8MD, 7.8LL, 14.3CH
STD-VP-2/62	1998	LM^3	Y. Haile-Selassie	10.9MD, 12.2BL
STD-VP-2/63	1999	LM^1	Group	(10.6)MD, 12.1BL
STD-VP-2/893	1998	Left clavicle fragment	Y. Haile-Selassie	

Numbers in parentheses are estimates. BL, buccolingual; LL, labiolingual; MD, mesiodistal, CH, crown height.

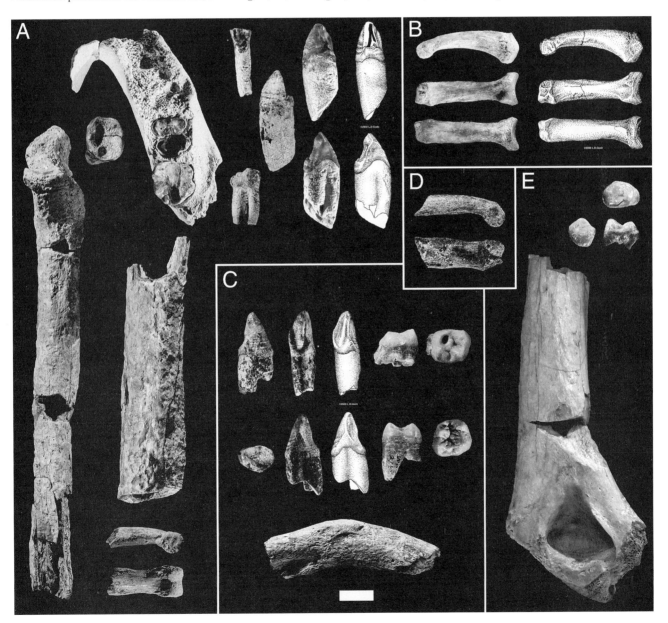

Figure 1. *Fossil hominid remains from the Late Miocene Middle Awash deposits. **A**, ALA-VP-2/10, mandible and all associated teeth; ALA-VP-2/120, ulna and humerus shaft; ALA-VP-2/11, hand phalanx. **B**, AME-VP-1/71, lateral, plantar and dorsal views of foot phalanx. **C**, STD-VP-2, teeth and partial clavicle. **D**, DID-VP-1/80, hand phalanx. **E**, ASK-VP-3/160, occlusal, mesial and buccal views; ASK-VP-3/78, posterior view. All images are at the same scale. Scale bar, 1 cm. Line drawings by L. Gudz.*

The first specimen recovered was the subspecific holotype, ALA-VP-2/10, a right mandible with M_3. (Note that subscripts indicate lower teeth, superscripts upper teeth.) Four isolated left lower teeth (I_2, L_C, P_4 and M_2) are associated by spatial proximity, colour, perimortem root fracture and wear. The left I_2 is metrically and morphologically comparable to known later hominid incisors and distinctively narrower than the lateral incisors of chimpanzees (*Pan troglodytes*). The P_4 has a well developed talonid and a Tome's root rather than the single roots reported for Aramis *A. ramidus*[11].

The associated lower canine is worn apically and distally. Its mesial crown shoulder is elevated relative to the condition usually seen in modern female apes. A distinct marginal ridge is formed on the mesial lingual face. Its distal face has an exposed dentine strip from apex to distal tubercle. The large distal tubercle is shared with Aramis homologues, but the posterior orientation of the wear facet is also shared by apes with a honing canine–premolar complex. However, the distal tubercle in apes is usually worn diagonally as the upper canine extends in full occlusion below the cervico–enamel junction of the lower canine. The distal tubercle in *Ardipithecus* is worn horizontally. The functional implication of this distinction is a possible absence of a fully functional honing canine–premolar complex in *Ardipithecus*.

The M_3 shows small occlusal wear facets on the buccal slopes of the spiky metaconid and entoconid. The buccal cusps are highly worn, with a deep, cupped, coalesced dentine exposure centred at the protoconid. The M_3 of ARA-VP-1/128 (*A. ramidus*) shows a different wear pattern in which both protoconid and metaconid exhibit small apical perforations in the enamel. All later hominids have cusps that are more rounded before wear. The ALA-VP-2/10 and ARA-VP-1/128 lower third molars are similar in mesiodistal dimension. However, ALA-VP-2/10 is absolutely smaller than the known ranges of *A. anamensis* ($n = 5$) and *A. afarensis* ($n = 14$), and absolutely larger than homologues in a sample of 20 common chimpanzees. The M_2 displays a buccal occlusal half deeply excavated by wear, with a large, oval, cupped dentine exposure spanning the protoconid and hypoconid and a separate deep, round exposure at the hypoconulid position. As with the M_3, this wear pattern is different from that of later hominids owing to the extreme wear differential between the lingual and buccal cusps.

A periodontal abscess affects the P_4/M_1 area, and consequent lateral corpus swelling resulted in only slight hollowing from P_4 to posterior M_1. The submandibular fossa is shallow anteriorly. The circular, anterosuperiorly opening mental foramen is positioned at or mesial to P_4 at approximately midcorpus. The preserved corpus is comparable in absolute size to AL 288-1 (*Australopithecus afarensis*) but is less robust at the M_2 and M_3 levels than AL 288-1 or KNM-LT 329 (the Lothagam mandible).

ASK-VP-3/160 is a left P^3 crown at an early wear stage. The root is entirely missing. The occlusal crown morphology is similar to Aramis homologues, but the mesial fovea is shallower. In mesial aspect, the mesial marginal ridge of ASK-VP-3/160 is below midcrown level. Its lingual extension bears an occlusal facet suggesting a prominent P_3 protoconid. It lacks the strong mesiobuccal crown extension commonly seen in *Pan* P^3 teeth.

STD-VP-2/61 is a narrow, pointed, unworn lower right canine with three strong horizontal buccal hypoplastic lines. The distal tubercle is less prominent than on ALA-VP-2/10. The mesial crown shoulder is lower (at midcrown) than the contemporary Alayla lower canine. One morphological feature that this canine shares with chimpanzees rather than later hominids is the flattening of the mesiolingual face with an absence of a distinct marginal ridge defined by a vertical mesiolingual groove. The weak development of later hominid lower canine traits on STD-VP-2/61, as well as the tall, narrow apex, makes this the most primitive hominid canine yet found.

STD-VP-2/62 is a fully erupted and minimally worn LM^3. The protocone apex bears a small wear facet. Occlusal outline is a buccolingually elongated rectangle with the distal half slightly buccolingually shorter than the mesial. With all four cusps well defined, this molar does not show the noticeable distal tapering usually seen in later hominids, and the occlusal surface is less crenulated than in chimpanzees. The mesial fovea is shallow and not as broad as in chimpanzees. The specimen is similar in size to the reported Aramis M^3 (ref. 11).

STD-VP-2/63 is LM^1 with both protocone and paracone exhibiting deeply pitted dentine exposures. It is absolutely smaller than known *A. afarensis* M^1 teeth. It is differentiated from chimpanzee M^1 teeth by the absence of strong occlusal crenulation.

The teeth of these Late Miocene *Ardipithecus* specimens show a mosaic of primitive and derived morphological features. Studies of enamel thickness are underway, but the available broken and little-worn teeth suggest that molar enamel thicknesses in the STD and ALA hominids were comparable to, or slightly greater than, those of the younger Aramis samples of *A. ramidus*. The presence of four distinct cusps and the absence of the distal tapering of the M^3 are primitive features shared with most Miocene hominoids. The lower canines are of particular interest. The development of the distal tubercle on these new *Ardipithecus* lower canines and the observed variation in the position of the mesial crown shoulder and expression of the mesial marginal ridge are best interpreted as representing early manifestations of the evolution of an incisiform canine, a definitive feature of later hominids.

ALA-VP-2/11 is the distal half of an intermediate hand phalanx. Dorsal shaft curvature is minimal. The concave palmar surface is marked by deep, bilateral fossae for the *m. flexor digitorum superficialis*. It is larger than but morphologically similar to most *A. afarensis* intermediate hand phalanges. Head diameter is larger than the largest *A. afarensis* intermediate hand phalanx (AL 333x-46) and comparison indicates that it was very probably longer than the longest *A. afarensis* homologue. DID-VP-1/80 is the distal half of a proximal hand phalanx. Ridges for the *m. flexor retinaculum* are not as developed as in most *A. afarensis* specimens. The overall degree of curvature of DID-VP-1/80 is similar to that of *A. afarensis*.

ASK-VP-3/78 is a left distal humerus fragment preserving some of the trochlea, the base of the medial epicondyle, the olecranon fossa and part of the distal shaft. The medial aspect of the proximal edge of the trochlear joint surface shows post-mortem subchondral erosion and minor arthritic lipping. The specimen is slightly smaller than ARA-VP-7/2 (*A. ramidus ramidus*)[11] and absolutely larger than small *A. afarensis* specimens such as AL 288-1m and AL 322-1. Radial and coronoid fossae are separated by a prominent ridge (but not by a 'Hershkovitz' tubercle). ASK-VP-3/78 is similar to ARA-VP-7/2 in having a relatively sharp lateral trochlear crest (as in most modern apes and some *A. afarensis*). The olecranon fossa of ASK-VP-3/78 differs from later hominids, which have more elliptical and shallower fossae.

ALA-VP-2/101 is an associated humeral mid-shaft and proximal ulna. The humeral mid-shaft is smaller than that of ARA-VP-7/2 and matches the smallest *A. afarensis*. The ulna is more complete. Most of its shaft is preserved but abraded. The coronoid and olecranon processes and the radial facet are damaged. The insertion area for the *brachialis* muscle is neither excavated nor medially or laterally well marked. Despite being incomplete, the ulnar shaft appears more curved than is typical of most later hominids.

The chronologically younger (5.2 Myr) AME-VP-1/71 is a complete left fourth proximal foot phalanx with a maximum length of 31.9 mm. It is close in maximum length to AL 333-71 (32.5 mm) (ref. 12). In lateral view, the shaft shows strong plantar curvature also comparable to AL 333-71. The distal half of the shaft is dorsoventrally compressed, whereas the proximal half is mediolaterally compressed with a prominent constriction above the base. AME-VP-1/71 shows a mosaic of features shared with both apes and *A. afarensis*. The proximal pedal phalanges of *A. afarensis* are unique in combining both strong phalangeal curvature (similar to apes) with a dorsally canted proximal joint surface (similar to later hominids)[13]. The dorsal orientation of this surface in AME-VP-1/71 may therefore constitute important evidence of a unique pedal morphology in this specimen similar to that in Hadar.

STD-VP-2/893 is the lateral half of a left clavicle lacking the acromial extremity. The deltoid muscle attachment is well marked on the superior surface. The shaft cortex is thick, with an oval cross-section immediately medial to the deltoid attachment. The conoid tubercle is a mediolaterally elongate, roughened surface comparable in overall robustness to AL 333x-9 and absolutely more robust than in chimpanzees.

The Middle Awash fossils described above share some dental characters exclusively with later hominids, and do so to the exclusion of all fossil and extant apes. These characters include lower canines with developed distal tubercles and expressed mesial marginal ridges. In addition, the proximal foot phalanx from Amba, dated at 5.2 Myr, is derived relative to all known apes and is consistent with an early form of terrestrial bipedality. Because of this combination of characters, the Middle Awash fossils described here are classified as cladistically hominid. They are currently distinguishable from the later *A. ramidus* at the subspecies level by more primitive dental characters consistent with their antiquity (see Methods). However, larger samples may reveal additional evidence that will require elevation of this subspecies to species rank.

Another candidate for hominid ancestry is the recently described *Orrorin tugenensis*[8]. The authors report thick molar enamel and suggest that *Ardipithecus* and African apes are commonly derived in having 'thin' enamel. However, enamel thickness is a complex character and intraspecifically variable, and its within-tooth three-dimensional patterning is characteristically expressed both serially and taxonomically. Therefore, the simplistic dichotomous characterization of enamel as either 'thick' or 'thin' on the basis of unspecified measurements of naturally broken sections (as was done in the *Orrorin* report[8]) is problematic.

The upper canine morphology of *O. tugenensis* is quite primitive, as it lacks the derived, elevated crown shoulders shared by *Ardipithecus* and all other hominids. Furthermore, the locomotor anatomy of *Orrorin* remains uncertain at this time because its description lacked comment on characters directly diagnostic of bipedality, such as the presence of an obturator externus groove[14] or an asymmetrical distribution of cortex in the femoral neck[15]. Given its antiquity and characters, as currently described, there is nothing to preclude *Orrorin* from representing the last common ancestor, and thereby antedating the cladogenesis of hominids. It is equally plausible that it represents a previously unknown African hominoid with no living descendants, or an exclusive precursor of chimpanzees, gorillas or humans.

The phylogeny proffered in the description of the *Orrorin* fossils interprets *Ardipithecus* as a chimpanzee ancestor[8]. The authors state that this view is consistent with early hominids evolving east of the African rift system and chimpanzees and gorillas evolving to the west. But how could a putative chimpanzee ancestor found east of the rift (*A. ramidus* according to ref. 8) be consistent with such a model? It is vastly more likely that *Ardipithecus* is not a member of the chimpanzee clade, because of the many derived characters it shares with later hominids[11]. It is also clear that more information will be needed to resolve the role of *Orrorin* in hominoid phylogeny.

Likewise, the phylogenetic and taxonomic status of the Middle Awash fossils described here will require review as hypodigms increase. They appear to represent a hominid situated temporally and anatomically close to the last common ancestor of chimpanzees and humans. These Late Miocene fossils are followed temporally in the Middle Awash by a 5-Myr succession of increasingly derived hominid taxa, including *Ardipithecus ramidus*, *Australopithecus afarensis*, *Australopithecus garhi* and species of *Homo*.

METHODS

Description

Primates Linnaeus, 1758
Anthropoidea Mivart, 1864
Hominoidea Gray, 1825
Hominidae Gray, 1825
Ardipithecus White, Suwa and Asfaw, 1995
Ardipithecus ramidus (White, Suwa and Asfaw, 1994)
Ardipithecus ramidus kadabba subsp. nov.

Etymology. The subspecific name, kadabba, is taken from the Afar language. It means basal family ancestor.

Holotype. ALA-VP-2/10 (Figure 1) is a right mandibular corpus with M_3, left I_2, C, P_4, M_2 and M_3 root fragment. Holotype and referred material are housed at the National Museum of Ethiopia, Addis Ababa. Holotype from Alayla Vertebrate Paleontology Locality Two (ALA-VP 2); differentially corrected GPS coordinates 10° 16.483′ N and 40° 15.313′ E; elevation 690 m.

Referred material. ALA-VP-2/11 (intermediate hand phalanx); ALA-VP-2/101 (left humerus and ulna); ASK-VP-3/78 (distal humerus); ASK-VP-3/160 (left P^3); DID-VP-1/80 (proximal hand phalanx fragment); STD-VP-2/61 (right lower canine); STD-VP-2/62 (LM^3); STD-VP-2/63 (LM^1); STD-VP-2/893 (left clavicle fragment); AME-VP-1/71 (proximal foot phalanx).

Localities. Saitune Dora (STD-VP-2), Alayla (ALA-VP-2), Asa Koma (ASK-VP-3) and Digiba Dora (DID-VP-1) are all located along the western margin of the Middle Awash study area in the Afar depression of Ethiopia. Amba East (AME-VP-1) is in the CAC[7,10].

Horizons. The four western-margin hominid localities discussed here are within the Asa Koma Member of the Adu Asa Formation and bracketed by an overlying basaltic flow dated to 5.54 ± 0.17 Myr and an underlying basaltic tuff dated to 5.77 ± 0.08 Myr[7]. The Amba hominid is from the Kuserale Member of the Sagantole Formation of the CAC and is bracketed to 5.2–5.6 Myr[10].

Diagnosis. On the limited available evidence, a subspecies of *Ardipithecus* distinguished from Aramis *A. ramidus* (*A. ramidus ramidus*) by sharp M_3 lingual cusps that retain their prominence even in extreme crown wear; squared distal outline to M^3 with four distinct cusps; shallow mesial fovea on P^3; tendency for less relief on the mesiolingual crown face of the lower canines (one of two specimens); mesiolingually-to-distobuccally compressed lower canines.

Ardipithecus ramidus kadabba is distinguished from fossil and extant apes in its tendency toward incisiform lower canines, comparable to the condition of Aramis *A. ramidus*, with a developed distal tubercle and variants with high mesial crown shoulder placement and some expression of the mesial marginal ridge.

ACKNOWLEDGMENTS

The National Science Foundation, the Wenner-Gren Foundation, and the University of California at Berkeley provided funding. The Authority for Research and Conservation of Cultural Heritage of the Ministry of Information and Culture granted field permits, and the National Museum of Ethiopia granted access to the Paleoanthropological Laboratory before 13 February 2001. The success of this research is largely owed to the members of the Middle Awash research project and the Afar people. This contribution is dedicated to our late friend Neina Tahiro, who suggested the name 'kadabba,' and to whom I give special thanks. G. WoldeGabriel played a major role in discovering fossiliferous hominid-bearing localities along the western margin of the Middle Awash study area and also studied the geology of the region. I thank T. White, B. Latimer, K. Geleta, H. Gilbert, D. DeGusta, L. Hlusko, E. Güleç, C. Pehlevan, B. Asfaw, M. Black, G. Suwa, S. Yosef, A. Amzaye, M. Asnake and H. Saegusa for their participation in survey and excavations. Sheikh Ebrahim and Sheikh Oumer helped coordinate the Afar labour force. I thank B. Latimer, O. Lovejoy and S. Simpson for their assistance during the comparative studies conducted at the Cleveland Museum of Natural History. O. Lovejoy, T. White and G. Suwa provided insights and comments. Advice, support and encouragement to conduct research along the western margin of the Middle Awash study area were extended by T. White and B. Asfaw.

REFERENCES

1. Ruvolo, M. Molecular phylogeny of the hominoids: inferences from multiple independent DNA sequence data sets. *Mol. Biol. Evol.* **14**, 248–265 (1997).
2. Horai, S., Hayasaka, K., Kondo, R., Tsugane, K. and Takahata, N. Recent African origin of modern humans revealed by complete sequences of hominoid mitochondrial DNAs. *Proc. Natl Acad. Sci. USA* **92**, 532–536 (1995).
3. Chen, F.-C. and Li, W.-H. Genomic divergences between humans and other hominoids and the effective population size of the common ancestor of humans and chimpanzees. *Am. J. Hum. Genet.* **68**, 444–456 (2001).
4. Hill, A. Late Miocene and early Pliocene hominoids from Africa, in *Integrative Paths to the Past: Paleoanthropological Advances in Honor of F. Clark Howell* (eds R. S. Corruccini and R. L. Ciochon) 123–145 (Prentice Hall, Englewood Cliffs, 1994).
5. McDougall, I. and Feibel, C. Numerical age control for the Miocene–Pliocene succession at Lothagam, a hominoid-bearing sequence in the northern Kenya Rift. *J. Geol. Soc. Lond.* **156**, 731–745 (1999).
6. Leakey, M. G. et al., A record of faunal change in the late Miocene of East Africa. *J. Vert. Paleontol.* **16**, 556–570 (1996).
7. WoldeGabriel, G. et al., Geology and palaeontology of the Late Miocene Middle Awash valley, Afar rift, Ethiopia. *Nature* **412**, 175–178 (2001).
8. Senut, B. et al., First hominid from the Miocene (Lukeino Formation, Kenya). *C.R. Acad. Sci. Ser. IIa* **332**, 137–144 (2001).

9. Pickford, M. and Senut, B. The geological and faunal context of Late Miocene hominid remains from Lukeino, Kenya. *C.R. Acad. Sci. Ser. IIa* **332**, 145–152 (2001).
10. Renne, P. R., WoldeGabriel, G., Hart, W. K., Heiken, G. and White, T. D. Chronostratigraphy of the Miocene–Pliocene Sagantole Formation, Middle Awash Valley, Afar rift, Ethiopia. *Geol. Soc. Am. Bull.* **111**, 869–885 (1999).
11. White, T. D., Suwa, G., and Asfaw, B. *Australopithecus ramidus*, a new species of hominid from Aramis, Ethiopia. *Nature* **371**, 306–312 (1994).
12. Latimer, B., Lovejoy, C. O., Johanson, D. C. and Coppens, Y. Hominid tarsal, metatarsal, and phalangeal bones recovered

from the Hadar Formation: 1974–1977 collections. *Am. J. Phys. Anthropol.* **57**, 701–719 (1982).
13. Latimer, B. and Lovejoy, C. O. Metatarsophalangeal joints of *Australopithecus afarensis. Am J. Phys. Anthropol.* **83**, 13–23 (1990).
14. Day, M. H. Femoral fragment of a robust australopithecine from Olduvai Gorge, Tanzania. *Nature* **47**, 230–233 (1969).
15. Ohman, J. C., Krochta, T. J., Lovejoy, C. O., Mensforth, R. P. and Latimer, B. Cortical bone distribution in the femoral neck of hominoids: implications for the locomotion of *Australopithecus afarensis. Am. J. Phys. Anthropol.* **104**, 117–131 (1997).

15

A New Hominid from the Upper Miocene of Chad, Central Africa

M. Brunet, F. Guy, D. Pilbeam, H. Taisso Mackaye, A. Likius, D. Ahounta, A. Beauvilain, C. Blondel, H. Bocherens, J.-R. Boisserie, L. De Bonis, Y. Coppens, J. Dejax, C. Denys, P. Duringer, V. Eisenmann, G. Fanone, P. Fronty, D. Geraads, T. Lehmann, F. Lihoreau, A. Louchart, A. Mahamat, G. Merceron, G. Mouchelin, O. Otero, P. Pelaez Campomanes, M. Ponce de Leon, J.-C. Rage, M. Sapanet, M. Schuster, J. Sudre, P. Tassy, X. Valentin, P. Vignaud, L. Viriot, A. Zazzo, and C. Zollikofer

ABSTRACT

The search for the earliest fossil evidence of the human lineage has been concentrated in East Africa. Here we report the discovery of six hominid specimens from Chad, central Africa, 2,500 km from the East African Rift Valley. The fossils include a nearly complete cranium and fragmentary lower jaws. The associated fauna suggest the fossils are between 6 and 7 million years old. The fossils display a unique mosaic of primitive and derived characters, and constitute a new genus and species of hominid. The distance from the Rift Valley, and the great antiquity of the fossils, suggest that the earliest members of the hominid clade were more widely distributed than has been thought, and that the divergence between the human and chimpanzee lineages was earlier than indicated by most molecular studies.

From their initial description in 1925[1] until 1995, hominids from the Pliocene (5.3–1.6 million years, Myr) and late Upper Miocene (~7.5–5.3 Myr) were known only from southern and eastern Africa. This distribution led some authors to postulate an East African origin for the hominid clade (where the term 'hominid' refers to any member of that group more closely related to extant humans than to the extant

chimpanzee, *Pan*)[2,3]. The focus on East Africa has been especially strong in the past decade, with the description of several new forms from Kenya and Ethiopia, including *Kenyanthropus platyops* (3.5 Myr; ref. 4); *Australopithecus anamensis* (3.9–4.1 Myr; ref. 5); *Ardipithecus ramidus ramidus* (4.4 Myr; ref. 6); *Ardipithecus ramidus kadabba* (5.2–5.8 Myr; ref. 7) and *Orrorin tugenensis* (~6 Myr; refs 8, 9). The discoveries of *A. ramidus ramidus*, *A. r. kadabba* and *O. tugenensis* have extended the human lineage well back into the Miocene. However, the discovery of *Australopithecus bahrelghazali* in Chad, central Africa[10,11], demonstrated a considerably wider geographic range for early hominids than conventionally expected.

Since 2001, the Mission Paléoanthropologique Franco–Tchadienne (MPFT), a scientific collaboration between Poitiers University, Ndjamena University and Centre National d'Appui à la Recherche (CNAR) (Ndjaména), has recovered hominid specimens, including a nearly complete cranium, from a single locality (TM 266) in the Toros-Menalla fossiliferous area of the Djurab Desert of northern Chad (Table 1). The constitution of the associated fauna suggests that the fossils are older than material dated at 6 Myr from Lukeino, Kenya[8,9]. Preliminary comparison with the fauna from the Nawata formation at Lothagam, Kenya[12,13], suggests that the fossils are from the Late Miocene, between 6 and 7 Myr old. All six recovered specimens are assigned to a new taxon that is, at present, the oldest known member of the hominid clade.

SYSTEMATIC PALAEONTOLOGY

Order Primates L., 1758
Suborder Anthropoidea Mivart, 1864
Superfamily Hominoidea Gray, 1825
Family Hominidae Gray, 1825
Sahelanthropus gen. nov.

Etymology.   The generic name refers to the Sahel, the region of Africa bordering the southern Sahara in which the fossils were found.

Generic Description.   Cranium (probably male) with an orthognathic face showing weak subnasal prognathism, a small ape-size braincase, a long and narrow basicranium, and characterized by the following morphology: the upper part of the face wide relative to a mediolaterally narrow and anteroposteriorly short lower face; a large canine fossa; a small and narrow U-shaped dental arch; orbits separated by a very wide interorbital pillar and crowned with a large, thick and continuous supraorbital torus; a flat frontal squama with no supratoral sulcus but with a marked postorbital constriction; a small, posteriorly located sagittal crest and a large nuchal crest (at least, in presumed males); a flat and relatively long nuchal plane with a large external occipital crest; a large mastoid process; small occipital condyles; a short, anteriorly narrow basioccipital; the long axis of the petrous temporal bone oriented roughly 30° relative to the sagittal plane; the biporion line touching the basion; a round external auditory porus; a broad glenoid cavity with a large post-glenoid process; a robust and superoinferiorly short mandibular corpus associated with a wide extramolar sulcus; a large, anteriorly opening mental foramen centred beneath lower teeth P_4–M_1, below midcorpus height; relatively small incisors; distinct marginal ridges and multiple tubercles on the lingual fossa of upper I^1; small (presumed male) upper canines longer mesiodistally than buccolingually; upper and lower canines with extensive apical wear; no lower c–P_3 diastema; upper and lower premolars with two roots; molars with low rounded cusps and bulbous lingual faces, M^3 triangular and M_3 rounded distally; enamel thickness of cheek teeth intermediate between *Pan* and *Australopithecus*.

Differential Diagnosis.   *Sahelanthropus* is distinct from all living great apes in the following respects: relatively smaller canines with apical wear, the lower showing a full occlusion above the well-developed distal tubercle, probably correlated with a non-honing C–P_3 complex (P_3 still unknown).

Sahelanthropus is distinguished as a hominid from large living and known fossil hominoid genera in the following respects: from *Pongo* by a non-concave lateral facial profile, a wider interorbital pillar, superoinferiorly short subnasal height, an anteroposteriorly short face, robust supraorbital morphology, and many dental characters (described below); from *Gorilla* by smaller size, a narrower and less prognathic lower face, no supratoral sulcus, and smaller canines and lower-cusped

cheek teeth; from *Pan* by an anteroposteriorly shorter face, a thicker and more continuous supraorbital torus with no supratoral sulcus, a relatively longer braincase and narrower basicranium with a flat nuchal plane and a large external occipital crest, and cheek teeth with thicker enamel; from *Samburupithecus*[14] by a more anteriorly and higher-placed zygomatic process of the maxilla, smaller cheek teeth with lower cusps and without lingual cingula, and smaller upper premolars and M^3; from *Ouranopithecus*[15] by smaller size, a superoinferiorly, anteroposteriorly and mediolaterally shorter face, relatively thicker continuous supraorbital torus, markedly smaller but mesiodistally longer canines, apical wear and large distal tubercle in lower canines, and thinner postcanine enamel; from *Sivapithecus*[16] by a superoinferiorly and anteroposteriorly shorter face with nonconcave lateral profile, a wider interorbital pillar, smaller canines with apical wear, and thinner cheek-teeth enamel; from *Dryopithecus*[17] by a less prognathic lower face with a wider interorbital pillar, larger supraorbital torus, and thicker postcanine enamel.

Sahelanthropus is also distinct from all known hominid genera in the following respects: from *Homo* by a small endocranial capacity (preliminary estimated range 320–380 cm^3) associated with a long flat nuchal plane, a longer truncated triangle-shaped basioccipital, a flat frontal squama behind a robust continuous and undivided supraorbital torus, a large central upper incisor, and non-incisiform canines; from *Paranthropus*[18] by a convex facial profile that is less mediolaterally wide with a much smaller malar region, no frontal trigone, the frontal squama with no hollow posterior to glabella, a smaller, longer and narrower braincase, the zygomatic process of the maxilla positioned more posterior relative to the tooth row, and markedly smaller cheek teeth; from *Australopithecus*[19–21] by a less prognathic lower face (nasospinale–prosthion length shorter at least in presumed males) with a smaller malar (infraorbital) region and a larger, more continuous supraorbital torus, a relatively more elongate braincase, a relatively long, flat nuchal plane with a large external occipital crest, non-incisiform and mesiodistally long canines, and thinner cheek-teeth enamel; from *Kenyanthropus*[4] by a narrower, more convex face, and a narrower braincase with more marked postorbital constriction and a larger nuchal crest; from *Ardipithecus*[6,7] by upper I^1 with distinctive lingual topography characterized by extensive development of the crests and cingulum; less incisiform upper canines not diamond shaped with a low distal shoulder and a mesiodistal long axis, bucco-lingually narrower lower canines with stronger distal tubercle, and P_4 with two roots; from *Orrorin*[8] by upper I^1 with multiple tubercles on the lingual fossa, and non-chimp-like upper canines with extensive apical wear.

Type Species.   *Sahelanthropus tchadensis* sp. nov.

Etymology.   In recognition that all specimens were recovered in Chad.

Holotype.   TM 266-01-060-1, a nearly complete cranium with the following: on the right—I^2 alveolus, C (distal part), P^3–P^4 roots, fragmentary M^1 and M^2, M^3; and on the left—I^2 alveolus, C–P^4 roots, fragmentary M^1–M^3 (Figure 1 and Tables 1–5). Found by D. A. on 19 July 2001.

After study, the holotype and paratype series will be housed in the Département de Conservation des Collections, Centre National d'Appui à la Recherche (CNAR) in Ndjaména, Chad. The holotype has been dubbed 'Toumaï'; in the Goran language spoken in the Djurab Desert, this name is given to babies born just before the dry season, and means 'hope of life'.

Paratypes. See Table 1 for a list of paratypes, and Figure 2 for illustrations.

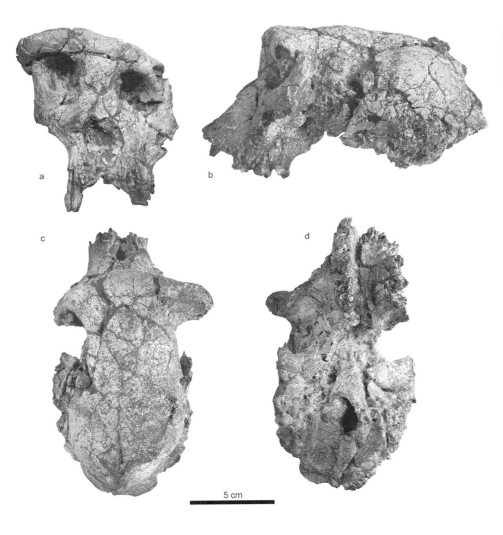

Figure 1. *Cranium of* Sahelanthropus tchadensis *gen. et sp. nov. holotype (TM 266-01-060-1).* ***a,*** *Facial view.* ***b,*** *Lateral view.* ***c,*** *Dorsal view.* ***d,*** *Basal view.*

5 cm

Table 1. Specimens of *Sahelanthropus tchadensis* gen. et sp. nov.

Specimen Number	Collected	Element	Discoverer	Dental Dimensions (mm)
TM 266-01-060-1 (holotype) (Figure 1)	2001	Cranium	D. A.	RC, BL = 10.2; RM^1, MD = 10.9; RM^2, MD = 13.0, BL = (12.8); RM^3, MD = 10.8, BL = 14.9; LM^1, MD = 11.5
TM 266-01-060-2	2001	Symphyseal fragment with I and C alveoli	Group	
TM 266-01-447	2001	Right M^3	Group	RM^3, MD = 10.7, BL = 12.7
TM 266-01-448 (Figure 2a)	2001	Right I^1	Group	RI^1, MD = (13.3), BL = 8.9
TM 266-02-154-1 (Figure 2b, c)	2002	Right mandible, (P_3) P_4–M_3	D. A.	RP_4, MD = 8.0; RM_1, MD = 11.0, BL = 11.9; RM_2, MD = 12.5; RM_3, MD = 13.3, BL = 12.2
TM 266-02-154-2 (Figure 2d, e)	2002	Right c	D. A.	Rc, MD = 11.0, BL = 8.5

Fossil hominids recovered from Toros-Menalla between July 2001 and February 2002. BL, buccolingual; L, left; MD, mesiodistal; R, right. Parentheses indicate estimated measurements–(P_3) indicates that only the roots are known.

Table 2. Comparative Dental Measurements

		Mesiodistal					Buccolingual				
		n	Min.	Max.	Mean	s.d.	*n*	Min.	Max.	Mean	s.d.
Upper dentition											
I[1]	*S. tchadensis*	1	—	—	(13.3)	—	1	—	—	8.9	—
	O. tugenensis[8]	1	—	—	(10.0)	—	1	—	—	8.7	—
	A. r. ramidus[6]	1	—	—	(10.0)	—	2	7.5	8.2	—	—
	A. anamensis[20]	3	10.5	12.4	11.3	1.0	3	8.2	9.3	8.8	0.6
	A. afarensis[6]	3	10.8	11.8	11.2	0.6	5	7.1	8.6	8.2	0.6
	P. t. troglodytes[26]	14	—	—	12.2	0.8	14	—	—	9.4	0.8
C	*S. tchadensis*	—	—	—	—	—	1	—	—	10.2	—
	O. tugenensis[8]	1	—	—	11.0	—	1	—	—	9.3	—
	A. r. ramidus[6]	2	(11.2)	11.5	—	—	2	11.1	11.7	—	—
	A. anamensis[20]	2	(10.6)	11.7	—	—	2	10.2	11.2	—	—
	A. afarensis[6]	9	8.9	11.6	10.0	0.8	10	9.3	12.5	10.9	1.1
	P. t. troglodytes[26]	15	—	—	15.6	2.1	15	—	—	11.3	1.37
M[1]	*S. tchadensis*	2	(10.9)	(11.5)	—	—	—	—	—	—	—
	A. r. kadabba[7]	1	—	—	(10.6)	—	1	—	—	12.1	—
	A. anamensis[20]	7	10.3	12.9	11.7	0.8	6	11.7	14.1	13.0	0.9
	A. afarensis[25]	14	10.5	13.8	12.2	1.0	12	12.0	15.0	13.4	0.9
	P. t. troglodytes[26]	14	—	—	10.5	0.5	14	—	—	11.3	0.6
M[2]	*S. tchadensis*	1	—	—	13.0	—	1	—	—	(12.8)	—
	A. r. ramidus[6]	2	(11.8)	11.8	—	—	2	(14.1)	(15.0)	—	—
	A. anamensis[20]	6	10.9	14.2	12.5	1.2	6	13.2	16.3	14.8	1.0
	A. afarensis[6]	5	12.1	13.5	12.8	0.5	6	13.4	15.1	14.7	0.6
	P. t. troglodytes[26]	16	—	—	10.7	0.6	16	—	—	11.7	0.8
M[3]	*S. tchadensis*	2	10.7	10.8	—	—	2	12.7	14.9	—	—
	O. tugenensis[8]	2	10.2	10.3	—	—	2	12.9	13.1	—	—
	A. r. kadabba[7]	1	—	—	10.9	—	1	—	—	12.2	—
	A. r. ramidus[6]	1	—	—	10.2	—	1	—	—	12.3	—
	A. anamensis[20]	7	11.1	15.7	12.4	1.6	5	13.0	14.7	13.8	0.6
	A. afarensis[6]	8	10.5	14.3	11.9	1.4	8	13.0	15.5	13.8	1.0
	P. t. troglodytes[26]	16	—	—	9.9	0.6	16	—	—	10.8	1.0
Lower dentition											
c	*S. tchadensis*	1	—	—	11.0	—	1	—	—	8.5	—
	A. r. kadabba[7]	2	10.8	11.2	—	—	2	7.8	7.8	—	—
	A. r. ramidus[6]	—	—	—	—	—	1	—	—	11.0	—
	A. anamensis[20]	7	6.6	10.4	9.0	1.3	6	9.2	11.4	10.2	1.0
	A. afarensis[27]	11	7.5	11.7	8.9	1.2	13	8.8	12.4	10.4	1.1
	P. t. troglodytes[26]	15	—	—	14.0	1.5	15	—	—	11.4	1.4
P$_4$	*S. tchadensis*	1	—	—	8.0	—	—	—	—	—	—
	O. tugenensis[8]	1	—	—	(8.0)	—	1	—	—	(9.0)	—
	A. r. kadabba[7]	1	—	—	(8.1)	—	1	—	—	10.0	—
	A. r. ramidus[6]	2	7.5	8.9	—	—	2	(9.9)	(11.5)	—	—
	A. anamensis[20]	8	7.4	9.8	8.8	1.0	9	9.6	11.9	10.7	0.8
	A. afarensis[6]	15	7.7	11.1	9.7	1.0	14	9.8	12.8	10.9	0.8
	P. t. troglodytes[26]	15	—	—	8.1	0.6	16	—	—	8.8	0.8
M$_1$	*S. tchadensis*	1	—	—	11.0	—	1	—	—	11.9	—
	A. r. ramidus[6]	2	11.0	11.1	—	—	2	(10.2)	10.3	—	—
	A. anamensis[20]	11	11.5	13.8	12.6	0.9	12	10.5	14.8	12.1	1.3
	A. afarensis[6]	17	11.2	14.0	13.0	0.6	16	11.0	13.9	12.6	0.8
	P. t. troglodytes[26]	15	—	—	10.7	0.4	15	—	—	9.2	0.6
M$_2$	*S. tchadensis*	1	—	—	12.5	—	—	—	—	—	—
	O. tugenensis[8]	1	—	—	(11.5)	—	1	—	—	(11.8)	—
	A. r. kadabba[7]	1	—	—	(12.7)	—	1	—	—	11.8	—
	A. r. ramidus[6]	1	—	—	(13.0)	—	1	—	—	11.9	—
	A. anamensis[20]	8	13.0	15.9	14.1	1.4	11	12.3	15.1	13.5	0.9
	A. afarensis[6]	23	12.4	16.2	14.3	1.0	22	12.1	15.2	13.5	0.9
	P. t. troglodytes[26]	15	—	—	11.3	0.5	15	—	—	10.6	0.9
M$_3$	*S. tchadensis*	1	—	—	13.3	—	1	—	—	12.2	—
	O. tugenensis[8]	2	(12.3)	(12.4)	—	—	2	10.4	11.2	—	—
	A. r. kadabba[7]	1	—	—	13.3	—	—	—	—	—	—
	A. r. ramidus[6]	1	—	—	12.7	—	1	—	—	11.0	—
	A. anamensis[20]	6	13.7	17.0	14.6	1.2	6	11.9	13.4	12.8	0.7
	A. afarensis[6]	14	13.7	16.3	14.8	0.8	14	12.1	14.9	13.3	0.8
	P. t. troglodytes[26]	16	—	—	11.0	0.6	16	—	—	9.6	0.8

Parentheses indicate estimated measurements.

Table 3.   Hominid Alveolar Height Measurements

Taxon	Alveolar Height (mm)
S. tchadensis (TM 266-01-060-1)	(22)
A. afarensis[21] (AL 417-1, AL 444-2)	30, 33
A. africanus[28] (mean and range, *n* = 11)	25.7 (21.1–30.0)
P. boisei[28]	42.2
H. habilis[28] (KNM-ER 1470, KNM-ER 1813)	31.0, 25.0

Alveolar height from nasospinale to prosthion. Parentheses indicate estimated measurements from a preliminary three-dimensional reconstruction.

Table 4.   Cranio-Facial Measurements of *S. tchadensis*

Cranio-Facial Features	Size (mm)
Orbital height × width	(36 × 35)
Maximum breadth	
Bicarotid chord	(45)
Bimastoid (at the nuchal crest level)	(108)
Biporion	(102)
Mastoid mesiodistal length	54.5
Nuchal plane length (opisthion–inion)	(47)

Measurements are from TM 266-01-060-1. Parentheses indicate estimated measurements from a preliminary three-dimensional reconstruction.

Table 5.   Measurements and Indices of Hominoid Frontal Bones

	Postorbital Breadth* (*a*) (mm)	Superior Facial Breadth† (*b*) (mm)	Fronto-Facial Breadth Index (*a/b* × 100)
P. troglodytes (10 males)[19]	71.0 (62.0–76.5)	110.1 (99.4–129.0)	64.4 (58.1–68.5)
P. troglodytes (10 females)[19]	70.1 (65.0–76.0)	102.2 (87.3–112.0)	68.8 (66.6–74.5)
G. gorilla (10 males)[19]	69.5 (60.5–77.0)	135.1 (127.7–144.0)	51.5 (47.4–59.4)
G. gorilla (10 females)[19]	68.5 (65.5–73.5)	115.5 (108.0–127.0)	59.5 (57.0–63.4)
P. pygmaeus (5 males)[19]	63.8 (59.0–69.5)	105.7 (88.3–116.2)	61.2 (51.7–72.5)
P. pygmaeus (4 females)[19]	64.0 (61.5–65.5)	90.1 (87.8–94.0)	71.1 (68.1–74.0)
S. tchadensis gen. et sp. nov. (TM 266-01-060-1)	(60)	(102)	(59)
A. afarensis (AL 444-2)[21]	77.0	118.6	64.9

Values are mean and range. Values for *S. tchadensis* were estimated from a preliminary three-dimensional reconstruction.
*The least-frontal breadth.
†Left frontomalare temporale to right frontomalare temporale (outer biorbital breadth).

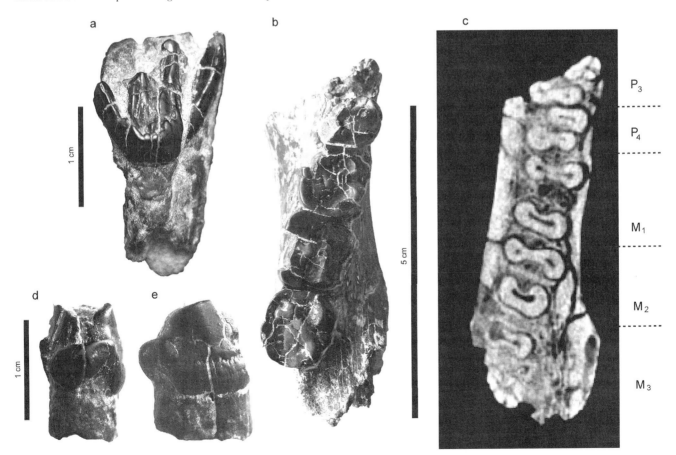

Figure 2.   Sahelanthropus tchadensis *gen. et sp. nov. paratypes.* **a,** *Right upper I¹, lingual view (TM 266-01-448).* **b, c,** *Right lower jaw (TM 266-02-154-1), occlusal view (***b***) and axial CT scan (***c***).* **d, e,** *Right lower canine (TM 266-02-154-2), distal view (***d***) and buccal view (***e***).*

Locality. Toros-Menalla locality TM 266, a single quarry of about 5,000 m², 16° 14′ 30″–16° 15′ 30″ N, 17° 28′ 30″–17° 30′ 00″ E (western Djurab Desert, northern Chad).

Horizon. All hominid specimens were found in the Toros-Menalla anthracotheriid unit (AU) and come from a perilacustrine sandstone[12]. The associated fauna is biochronologically[12] older than fossils from Lukeino, Kenya (~6 Myr; refs 8, 9), and more closely resembles material from the Nawata formation at Lothagam, Kenya, which is radio-isotopically dated to 5.2–7.4 Myr (ref. 13). Biochronological studies are still underway and TM 266 fauna can be tentatively dated between 6 and 7 Myr (ref. 12).

Diagnosis. Same as for genus.

PRESERVATION

All specimens are relatively well preserved, but almost the entire cranium has been flattened dorsoventrally and the entire right side is depressed. The cranium exhibits broken but undistorted bone units and matrix-filled cracks (Figure 1). Estimated measurements are given from a preliminary three-dimensional reconstruction. It will soon be possible to use computer tomography (CT) scans to generate a definitive three-dimensional reconstruction and stereolithographic casts.

COMPARATIVE OBSERVATIONS

Cranial comparisons of comparably aged hominids are limited to a fragmentary basicranium and temporal bone: ARA-VP1/500 and ARA-VP1/125 (ref. 6) from 4.4 Myr *Ardipithecus ramidus ramidus*. The next-oldest maxillary and cranial specimens are younger: KNM-KP-29283 (*A. anamensis*[5,20]), KNM-WT40000 (*Kenyanthropus platyops*[4]), and *A. afarensis* specimens, which include the well-preserved AL 444-2 (ref. 21). The most notable anatomical features of the *S. tchadensis* cranium for comparative purposes are to be found in the face, which shows a mosaic of primitive and derived features. The face (Figure 1a) is tall with a massive brow ridge, yet the mid-face is short (in the superoinferior dimension) and less prognathic than in *Pan* or *Australopithecus* (Table 3). This unusual combination of features is in turn associated with a relatively long braincase, comparable in size to those of extant apes (Figure 1b, c). Preliminary comparisons with *Pan* suggest an endocranial volume of 320–380 cm³.

Although the *Sahelanthropus* cranium is considerably smaller than that of a modern male *Gorilla*, its supraorbital torus is relatively and absolutely thicker. This is probably a sexually dimorphic character (see Figure 3), presumably reflecting strong sexual selection. If this is a male, then the combination of a massive brow ridge with small canines suggests that canine size was probably not strongly sexually dimorphic. The interorbital pillar is wide (Figure 1a). The zygomatic process of the maxilla emerges above the mesial margin of M¹ and is therefore more posterior relative to the cheek teeth than in *Australopithecus*[19–21] and *Paranthropus*[18]. The infraorbital plane (from the lower orbital margin to the inferior malar margin) is similar to that of *Pan* and differs from both *Gorilla* and larger *Australopithecus*, in which this region is absolutely and relatively taller. The canine fossa is similar to that in AL 444-2 (ref. 21) and there is no diastema between the alveoli of I² and C in the Chadian specimen. There is no supratoral sulcus. Between the temporal lines, the frontal squama is slightly depressed but not like the frontal trigone usually seen in *P. boisei*[18]. The temporal lines converge behind the coronal suture as in crested *Pan*, whereas their junction is more anterior than generally seen in some large *A. afarensis* (for example, AL 444-2; ref. 21). The sagittal crest is a little larger posteriorly than in either AL 444-2 (ref. 21) or KNM-WT 40000 (ref. 4). The compound temporal–nuchal crest is marked as in KNM-ER 1805 (ref. 22) and much larger than in the male *A. afarensis* AL 444-2 (ref. 21), suggesting a relatively large posterior temporalis muscle. The postorbital breadth (Figure 1c) is absolutely smaller than the *Pan–Gorilla* average, and similar to that in AL 444-2 and AL 417-1 (ref. 21) (Table 5).

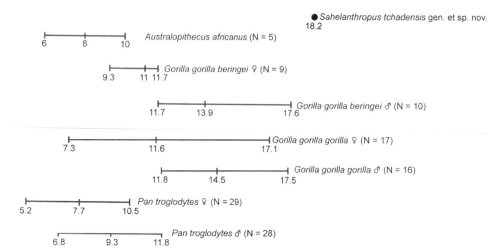

Figure 3. *Vertical (superoinferior) thickness of the supraorbital torus in extant hominoids, A. africanus and S. tchadensis gen. et sp. nov. Measurements are in millimetres at the highest point of the superior orbital margin. Data for apes and A. africanus are from ref. 28.*

The basicranium (Figure 1d) has small occipital condyles associated with an apparently large foramen magnum. Despite damage, the foramen magnum seems to be longer than wide, and not like the rounded shape typical of *Pan*. As in *A. ramidus*, the basion is intersected by the bicarotid chord; the basion is posterior in large apes and anterior in some of the later hominids. The *Sahelanthropus* basioccipital is correlatively short and shaped like a truncated triangle as in *Ardipithecus*[6]; it is not as triangular as in other early hominids.

Like *Pan*, *Australopithecus*[21] and *Ardipithecus*[6], the orientation of the petrous portion of the temporal is approximately 60° relative to the bicarotid chord, instead of 45° as is typical of *Paranthropus* and *Homo*. Unlike *Gorilla*, *Pan* and *Ardipithecus*[6], the posterior margin of the tympanic tube does not have a crest-like morphology. Compared with known *Ardipithecus* (ARA-VP-1/500)[6], the glenoid cavity is larger and the postglenoid process mediolaterally wider, so the pronounced squamotympanic fissure is situated more medially to the postglenoid process. The height of the relatively flat temporomandibular joint above the tooth row suggests a high ascending ramus of the mandible more similar in absolute size to *Gorilla* than to *Pan*. The large pneumatized mastoid process is anteroposteriorly long, more so than in *Ardipithecus*[6] and *Australopithecus* (AL 444-2, AL 333)[19,21]. The flat nuchal plane is relatively longer (Figure 1b, d and Table 4) than in *Pan*, *Gorilla*, AL 444-2 and AL 333, and with crests as marked as those of *Gorilla*, implying the presence of relatively large superficial neck muscles. The horizontally oriented nuchal plane is much flatter than the convex nuchal plane of *Pan*. There is not yet sufficient information to infer reliably whether *Sahelanthropus* was a habitual biped. However, such an inference would not be unreasonable given the skull's other basicranial and facial similarities to later fossil hominids that were clearly bipedal.

Little is preserved of the mandibular corpus in TM-266-02-154-1 or the symphysis in TM-266-01-060-2 to permit much discussion of mandibular anatomy. However, the former, presumably a male, has a thick corpus with a wide extramolar sulcus (Figure 2a).

In dentition, both lower incisor roots are small. The lingual surface of upper I^1 displays distinct marginal ridges converging basally onto a narrow gingival eminence and with several tubercles extending incisally into the lingual fossa (Figure 2a). The smaller upper I^2 alveolus is situated, in frontal view, lateral to the lateral edge of the nasal aperture (Figure 1a), a probable symplesiomorphy with *Pan*. The upper and lower canines are small (Tables 1, 2). Given the absolutely and relatively massive supraorbital torus of the cranium (Figures 1a and 3), possibly reflecting strong sexual selection, and the thick corpus of the mandible (Figure 2b, c), which probably indicate male status, we infer that *Sahelanthropus* canines were probably weakly sexually dimorphic. The upper canine (Figure 1d) has both distal and apical wear facets whereas M^3 is unworn. The lower canine (Figure 2d, e) has a strong distal tubercle that is separated from a distolingual crest by a fovea-like groove; the large apical wear zone at a level above this distal tubercle implies a non-honing C–P_3 complex (the

P_3 is still unknown). The upper canine, judging from the steep, narrow distal wear strip reaching basally, we believe had a somewhat lower distal shoulder than *Ardipithecus*[6,7], suggesting an earlier evolutionary stage. Moreover, a small, elliptical contact facet for P_3 on the distobuccal face of the distal tubercle indicates the absence of a lower c–P_3 diastema. *Sahelanthropus* thus probably represents an early stage in the evolution of the non-honing C–P_3 complex characteristic of the later hominids[7].

The cheek teeth are small (Tables 1, 2), within the size range of *A. ramidus* and the lower end of *A. afarensis*. Lower c and the lower and upper premolars each have three pulp canals and two roots (Figure 2c). The P_3 has a 2R:MB + D pattern (terminology following ref. 22: R, root; M, mesial; MB, mesiobuccal; D, distal) with a small mesiobuccal root and two partially fused, larger oblique distal roots. The P_4 has two transverse roots (2R:M + D), with the mesial one smaller than the distal; in both premolars the distal root has two pulp canals (Figure 2c). The P_4 teeth of *Ardipithecus* have more-derived root patterns, with either a Tome's root (*A. r. kadabba*)[7] or a single root (*A. r. ramidus*)[6]. *S. tchadensis* has a P_4 with a large talonid and well-marked grooves on the buccal face. The molar size gradient is M2 > M3 > M1. The upper molars have three roots, two buccal and one lingual, which is large and mesiodistally elongated. The M^3 crowns are triangular whereas the M_3 teeth are rectangular and rounded distally. The lower molar root pattern is 2R:M + D: a mesial root with two pulp canals and a distal root with only one canal (Figure 2c).

The radial enamel thickness is 1.71 mm at paracone LM^3 and 1.79 mm at hypocone LM^2. The molar enamel is therefore thicker than in *Pan*, possibly thicker than in *Ardipithecus ramidus ramidus*, but thinner than in *Australopithecus*[6]. Given individual and intraspecific variation, further study using high-resolution imaging (CT scanning) is needed for useful comparisons[7].

DISCUSSION

Sahelanthropus has several derived hominid features, including small, apically worn canines—which indicate a probable non-honing C–P_3 complex—and intermediate postcanine enamel thickness. Several aspects of the basicranium (length, horizontal orientation, anterior position of the foramen magnum) and face (markedly reduced subnasal prognathism with no canine diastema, large continuous supraorbital torus) are similar to later hominids including *Kenyanthropus* and *Homo*. All these anatomical features indicate that *Sahelanthropus* belongs to the hominid clade.

In many other respects, however, *Sahelanthropus* exhibits a suite of primitive features including small brain size, a truncated triangular basioccipital bone, and the petrous portion of the temporal bone oriented 60° to the bicarotid chord. The observed mosaic of primitive and derived characters evident in *Sahelanthropus* indicates its phylogenetic position as a hominid close to the last common ancestor of humans and chimpanzees. Given the biochronological age of *Sahelanthropus*, the divergence of the chimpanzee and human lineages must have occurred before 6 Myr, which is earlier than suggested by some authors[23,24]. It is not yet possible to discern phylogenetic relationships between *Sahelanthropus* and Upper Miocene hominoids outside the hominid clade. *Ouranopithecus*[15] (about 2 Myr older) is substantially larger, with quadrate orbits, a very prognathic and wide lower face, large male canines with a long buccolingual axis, and cheek teeth with very thick enamel. *Samburupithecus*[14] (about 2.5 Myr older) has a low, posteriorly positioned (above M^2) zygomatic process of the maxilla, cheek teeth with high cusps (similar to *Gorilla*), lingual cingula, large premolars and a large M^3.

Sahelanthropus is the oldest and most primitive known member of the hominid clade, close to the divergence of hominids and chimpanzees. Further analysis will be necessary to make reliable inferences about the phylogenetic position of *Sahelanthropus* relative to known hominids. One possibility is that *Sahelanthropus* is a sister group of more recent hominids, including *Ardipithecus*. For the moment, productive comparisons of *Sahelanthropus* with *Orrorin* are difficult because described craniodental material of the latter is fragmentary and no *Sahelanthropus* postcrania are available. However, we note that in *Orrorin*, the upper canine resembles that of a female chimpanzee. The discoveries of *Sahelanthropus* along with *Ardipithecus*[6,7] and *Orrorin*[8] indicate that early hominids in the late Miocene were geographically more widespread than previously thought.

Finally, we note that *S. tchadensis*, the most primitive hominid, is from Chad, 2,500 km west of the East African Rift Valley. This suggests that an exclusively East African origin of the hominid clade is unlikely to be correct (contrary to ref. 8). It will never be possible to know precisely where or when the first hominid species originated, but we do know that hominids had dispersed throughout the Sahel and East Africa[10] by 6 Myr. The recent acquisitions of Late Miocene hominid remains from three localities, as well as functional, phylogenetic and palaeoenvironmental studies now underway,

promise to illuminate the earliest chapter in human evolutionary history. *Sahelanthropus* will be central in this endeavour, but more surprises can be expected.

ACKNOWLEDGMENTS

We thank the Chadian Authorities (Ministère de l'Education Nationale de l'Enseignement Supérieur et de la Recherche, Université de N'djaména, CNAR). We extend gratitude for their support to the French Ministries, Ministère Français de l'Education Nationale (Faculté des Sciences, Université de Poitiers), Ministère de la Recherche (CNRS), Ministère des Affaires Etrangères (Direction de la Coopération Scientifique, Universitaire et de Recherche, Paris, and SCAC Ambassade de France à N'djaména), to the Région Poitou-Charentes, the Département de la Vienne, the Association pour le Prix scientifique Philip Morris, and also to the Armée Française (MAM and Epervier) for logistic support. For giving us the opportunity to work with their collections, we are grateful to the National Museum of Ethiopia, the National Museum of Kenya, the Peabody Museum and Harvard University, the Institute of Human Origins and the University of California. Special thanks to Scanner-IRM Poitou Charentes (P. Chartier and F. Perrin), for industrial scanner to EMPA (A. Flisch Ing. HTL) and to Multimedia Laboratorium-Computer Department, University of Zurich-Irchel (P. Stucki). Many thanks to all our colleagues and friends for their help and discussion, and particularly to F. Clark Howell, A. Garaudel, Y. Haile-Selassie, D. Johanson, W. Kimbel, M. G. Leakey, D. Lieberman, R. Macchiarelli, M. Pickford, B. Senut, G. Suwa, T. White and Lubaka. We especially thank all the other MPFT members who joined us for the field missions, and V. Bellefet, S. Riffaut and J.-C. Bertrand for technical support. We are most grateful to G. Florent for administrative guidance. We dedicate this article to J. D. Clark. All authors are members of the MPFT.

REFERENCES

1. Dart, R. A. *Australopithecus africanus,* the man-ape of South Africa. *Nature* **115,** 195–199 (1925).
2. Kortlandt, A. *New Perspectives on Ape and Human Evolution* 9–100 (Stichting voor Psychobiologie, Amsterdam, 1972).
3. Coppens, Y. *Le singe, l'Afrique et l'Homme* (Fayard, Paris, 1983).
4. Leakey, M. G. et al. New hominin genus from eastern Africa shows diverse middle Pliocene lineages. *Nature* **410,** 433–440 (2001).
5. Leakey, M. G., Feibel, C. S., McDougall, I. & Walker, A. C. New four-million-year-old hominid species from Kanapoi and Allia Bay, Kenya. *Nature* **376,** 565–571 (1995).
6. White, T. D., Suwa, G. and Asfaw, B. *Australopithecus ramidus,* a new species of hominid from Aramis, Ethiopia. *Nature* **371,** 306–312 (1994).
7. Haile-Selassie, Y. Late Miocene hominids from the Middle Awash, Ethiopia. *Nature* **412,** 178–181 (2001).
8. Senut, B. et al. First hominid from the Miocene (Lukeino Formation, Kenya). *C. R. Acad. Sci. Paris* **332,** 137–144 (2001).
9. Deino, A. L., Tauxe, L., Monaghan, M. & Hill, A. $^{40}Ar/^{39}Ar$ geochronology and paleomagnetic stratigraphy of the Lukeino and lower Chemeron Formations at Tabarin and Kapcheberek, Tugen Hills, Kenya. *J. Hum. Evol.* **42,** 117–140 (2002).
10. Brunet, M. et al. The first australopithecine 2500 kilometres west of the Rift Valley (Chad). *Nature* **378,** 273–275 (1995).
11. Brunet, M. et al. *Australopithecus bahrelghazali,* une nouvelle espèce d'Hominidé ancien de la région de Koro Toro (Tchad). *C. R. Acad. Sci. Paris* **322,** 907–913 (1996).
12. Vignaud, P. et al. Geology and palaeontology of the Upper Miocene Toros-Menalla hominid locality, Chad. *Nature* **418,** 152–155 (2002).
13. McDougall, I. and Feibel, C. S. Numerical age control for the Miocene–Pliocene succession at Lothagam, a hominoid-bearing sequence in the northern Kenya Rift. *J. Geol. Soc. Lond.* **156,** 731–745 (1999).
14. Ishida, H. and Pickford, M. A new Late Miocene hominoid from Kenya: *Samburupithecus kiptalami* gen. et sp. nov. *C. R. Acad. Sci. Paris* **325,** 823–829 (1998).
15. Bonis, L. de and Koufos, G. D. The face and the mandible of *Ouranopithecus macedoniensis:* description of new specimens and comparisons. *J. Hum. Evol.* **24,** 469–491 (1993).
16. Pilbeam, D. New hominoid skull material from the Miocene of Pakistan. *Nature* **295,** 232–234 (1982).
17. Kordos, L. and Begun, D. R. A new cranium of *Dryopithecus* from Rudabanya, Hungary. *J. Hum. Evol.* **41,** 689–700 (2001).
18. Tobias, P. V. *The Cranium and Maxillary Dentition of Australopithecus (Zinjanthropus) boisei, Olduvai Gorge* (Cambridge Univ. Press, London, 1967).

19. Kimbel, W. H., White, T. D., and Johanson, D. C. Cranial morphology of *Australopithecus afarensis*; A comparative study based on a composite reconstruction of the adult skull. *Am. J. Phys. Anthropol.* **64**, 337–388 (1984).

20. Ward, C. V., Leakey, M. G., and Walker, A. Morphology of *Australopithecus anamensis* from Kanapoi and Allia Bay, Kenya. *J. Hum. Evol.* **41**, 235–368 (2001).

21. Kimbel, W. H., Johanson, D. C., and Rak, Y. The first skull and other new discoveries of *Australopithecus afarensis* at Hadar, Ethiopia. *Nature* **368**, 449–451 (1994).

22. Wood, B. *Koobi Fora Research Project: Hominid Cranial Remains* Vol. 4 (Clarendon, Oxford, 1991).

23. Kumar, S. and Hedges, B. A molecular time scale for vertebrate evolution. *Nature* **392**, 917–920 (1998).

24. Pilbeam, D. in *The Primate Fossil Record* (ed. Hartwig, W.) 303–310 (Columbia Univ. Press, New York, 2002).

25. Kimbel, W. H. Systematic assessment of a maxilla of *Homo* from Hadar, Ethiopia. *Am. J. Phys. Anthop.* **103**, 235–262 (1997).

26. Uchida, A. *Intra-Species Variation among the Great-Apes: Implications for Taxonomy of Fossil Hominoids* Thesis, Harvard Univ. (1992).

27. Lockwood, C. A., Kimbel, W. H., and Johanson, D. C. Temporal trends and metric variation in the mandibles and dentition of *A. afarensis. J. Hum. Evol.* **39**, 23–55 (2000).

28. Lockwood, C. A. Sexual dimorphism in the face of *Australopithecus africanus. Am. J. Phys. Anthropol.* **108**, 97–127 (1999).

Australopithecus, Paranthropus, and Relatives

The chapters in this part describe the early hominids from the Pliocene and early Pleistocene of eastern and southern Africa. Compared with the earlier and more primitive taxa described in Part II, many of these fossil hominid taxa are known from numerous dental, cranial, and postcranial remains. As a result, there is extensive literature and ongoing debate about many details of their systematics, adaptations, and evolutionary relationships.

Chapter 16, "The Australopithecines in Review," by Leslie C. Aiello and Peter Andrews, provides a broad, historically based overview of the current status of research on early hominid phylogeny and evolution. Compared with many later chapters in this part, Aiello and Andrews adopt a conservative systematic arrangement and place most of the Pliocene species in a single genus, *Australopithecus*. Many subsequent chapters recognize additional taxa, including *Paranthropus*, *Praeanthropus*, and the recently described *Kenyanthropus*. There is a general consensus among most authorities that early hominid evolution in the Pliocene was characterized by several lineages and a diversity of species that occupied a range of habitats. As the authors note, ideas about the phylogeny of this group have become increasingly diverse and complex with the discovery of additional taxa, a trend that continues unabated, as described in several of the following chapters.

In Chapter 17, Carol Ward, Meave Leakey, and Alan Walker describe "The New Hominid Species *Australopithecus anamensis*." This species is from deposits dated between 3.8 and 4.2 mya near Lake Turkana in northern Kenya. *Australopithecus anamensis* is very similar to the younger and better known *Australopithecus afarensis* but differs in having lower-crowned molar teeth and more asymmetrical canines and premolars. *A. anamensis* differs from *A. afarensis* and from living apes in the shape of the maxillary tooth rows. In addition, *A. anamensis* also differs from *A. afarensis* and later hominids in lacking a distinct articular eminence on the temporal bone. In all of these features, *A. anamensis* is more primitive and also resembles *Ardipithecus*. The few skeletal elements known for *A. anamensis* resemble those of *A. afarensis*, including a tibia that shows adaptations for bipedalism. *A. anamensis* is one of the few fossil hominids whose phylogenetic position is not debated. Virtually all authorities consider it to be a lineal ancestor of *A. afarensis*.

Meave Leakey and colleagues describe another fossil hominid from Lake Turkana in Chapter 18, entitled "New Hominin Genus from Eastern Africa Shows Diverse Middle Pliocene Lineages." This new genus and species, *Kenyanthropus platyops*, is from the western side of Lake Turkana and dates to 3.5 mya. The type specimen is a largely complete but crushed and distorted cranium. *Kenyanthropus* is the same age as *Australopithecus afarensis* but differs primarily in having a flat face and moderate subnasal prognathism. In its facial morphology, *Kenyanthropus* is similar to KNM-ER 1470, the type specimen of *Homo rudolfensis*. *Kenyanthropus* likely indicates a greater diversity of hominid lineages in the middle Pliocene than had been recognized previously. However, some researchers have questioned whether it deserves separate generic status due to its crushed and distorted condition (White, 2003).

Chapter 19, by Henry M. McHenry, "Tempo and Mode in Human Evolution," discusses broad trends in early hominid evolution based on phylogenetic analyses. McHenry argues that the pattern of morphological evolution among early hominids was not uniform. Rather, early hominids retain a relatively primitive, ape-like cranium in conjunction with a more derived postcranial skeleton associated with bipedalism. Moreover, he argues that the evolution of bipedalism was a rapid event and was accomplished by the time of *Australopithecus afarensis*. In contrast, human-like craniodental features only appeared in the later stages of human evolution. The increase in relative brain size in human evolution is more difficult to assess because of the problems in obtaining reliable body weights for fossil hominids (see Kappelman, 1996). McHenry also observes that attempts to evaluate the patterns of evolutionary change in hominid evolution are intimately linked with the criteria used to define paleospecies. Nevertheless, it seems evident that there was morphological change both within and between species in the fossil record of hominid evolution.

In Chapter 20, D. S. Strait and F. E. Grine present a phylogenetic analysis of early hominid evolution in "Inferring Hominoid and Early Hominid Phylogeny Using Craniodental Characters: The Role of Fossil Taxa." Using 198 cranial and dental characters, they address the argument of Collard and Wood (2000) that phylogenetic analyses of such data do not yield clado-grams that are in accord with phylogenies of extant hominoids based on the results of molecular systemat-ics. In contrast, Strait and Grine find that when fossil hominid taxa are included in the analysis, the relative positions of extant hominoid taxa in the resulting cladograms are consistent with molecular phylogenies (see also Lockwood et al., 2004), therefore demonstrat-ing that cranial and dental data can be used to recon-struct phylogeny. Thus they move on to the analysis of fossil hominids. The results of their analyses indicate that the robust australopith taxa form a clade that is the sister taxon of *Homo.* They evaluate various hypotheses regarding the phylogenetic position of other fossil taxa that are advanced in other chapters of this book. They find some support for the hypotheses that *Sahelanthropus* (Chapter 15) and *Ardipithecus* (Chapter 14) are each near the base of hominid phylogeny. *Australopithecus anamensis* (Chapter 17) is also a sister taxon of many later hominids. However, they find no sup-port for the view that *Australopithecus garhi* (Chapter 29) is the sister taxon of *Homo* or that *Kenyanthropus platyops* (Chapter 18) bears any special relationship to *Homo rudolfensis.* All of their analyses indicate that the genus *Australopithecus,* as normally used, is paraphyletic.

As discussed in Chapter 19 by McHenry, the evolu-tion of bipedal walking was a major adaptive break-through in Pliocene hominids that separates hominids from apes. While there is no doubt that early hominids were bipedal, the nature of that bipedalism, the reasons it evolved, and whether it precluded other types of lo-comotion are topics that have been extensively debated in the past two decades. Chapter 21 and Chapter 22 summarize the opposing views in this debate.

In Chapter 21, "Evolution of Human Walking," C. Owen Lovejoy reviews the biomechanics of human bipedal walking and demonstrates that the pelvis of *Australopithecus afarensis* was that of a biped. Indeed, he argues that the early hominid pelvis was more efficient biomechanically for bipedal walking than is the modern human pelvis. He then argues that because *A. afarensis* had adaptations for bipedal walking, it was incapable of any other type of locomotor activity, such as arboreal climbing. In Lovejoy's view, human bipedalism evolved as part of a novel reproductive strategy that included provisioning by males (see Lovejoy, 1981).

In "Climbing to the Top: A Personal Memoir of *Australopithecus afarensis,*" Jack T. Stern, Jr., provides an autobiographic review of his own efforts to demon-strate that early bipedal hominids, and especially *A. afarensis,* had a locomotor behavior that was differ-ent from that of modern hominids. In contrast with Lovejoy, who sees bipedal walking as an all-or-none

activity, Stern emphasizes the many ways in which the skeleton of *A. afarensis* differs from that of modern humans and resembles that of living, climbing apes. He argues that many aspects of the skeletal anatomy of this extinct species indicate that its locomotion entailed a significant amount of arboreal climbing behavior in addition to bipedal walking (see Stern and Susman, 1983; Susman et al., 1984). Stern reviews not only the history of the debate but also his personal adventures, including his *courageous* travels to foreign museums, problems dealing with his inept coauthors, and the rise and fall of his scientific career.

In "Early Hominid Brain Evolution: A New Look at Old Endocasts" (Chapter 23), Dean Falk and colleagues report new studies on the surface morphology and vol-umes of cranial endocasts using new reconstructions of the entire brain. In particular, they find an unusual shape of the frontal lobe in *Paranthropus* species that af-fects reconstructions of brain size. Arguing that previ-ous reconstructions of brain size for *Paranthropus* species were too high, they find no support for the view that *Paranthropus* had a cranial capacity larger than *Australopithecus* or that the cranial capacity of the robust lineage increased through time in parallel with in-creases in the *Homo* lineage. This study supports earlier claims that the brain of *Australopithecus africanus* shows a surface morphology most suitable for the ancestry of the genus *Homo.*

Chapter 24, "Diet and the Evolution of the Earliest Human Ancestors," by Mark F. Teaford and Peter S. Ungar, summarizes reconstructions of the dietary habits of early hominids based on studies of many variables—tooth size, tooth shape, enamel structure, dental mi-crowear, and mandibular biomechanics. Dietary recon-structions have long played a role in efforts to explain early hominid diversity. Teaford and Ungar find that de-spite differences among taxa, early hominids as a group show teeth and jaws adapted for harder, more brittle foods than do those of Miocene apes. Moreover, early hominids lack any adaptations for eating tough foods, which suggests no dental preadaptation for meat eating.

Most attempts to explain evolutionary changes in human evolution appeal to some kind of ecological adaptations, either in responses to global and local climatic change (e.g., Vrba, 1988) or to a shift in habitat utilization (e.g., Stanley, 1992). In Chapter 25, "Early Hominid Evolution and Ecological Change through the African Plio-Pleistocene," Kaye E. Reed provides a reconstruction of habitats occupied by early hominids based on the ecomorphological characteristics of the mammalian fauna found in association with them at different fossil sites. She finds that *Australopithecus* is associated with mammals found in woodland environ-ments, while *Paranthropus* is associated with mammals from more open habitats and edaphic grasslands. Fossils of *Homo* are associated with mammalian fauna charac-teristic of arid, open landscapes. This contrasts with the traditional view that the initial emergence of bipedalism was associated with a savanna habitat. Only with early *Homo,* a larger, more adept biped, is there consistent evidence for a savanna adaptation (e.g., Stanley, 1992).

REFERENCES

Collard, M., and B. A. Wood. 2000. How reliable are human phylogenetic analyses? *Proc. Natl. Acad. Sci. USA* 97:5003–5006.

Kappelman, J. 1996. The evolution of body mass and relative brain size in fossil hominids. *Journal of Human Evolution* 30:243–276.

Lockwood, C. A., W. H. Kimbel, and J. M. Lynch. 2004. Morphometrics and hominoid phylogeny: Support for a chimpanzee-human clade and differentiation among great ape subspecies. *Proc. Natl. Acad. Sci. USA* 101:4356–4360.

Lovejoy, C. O. 1981. The origin of man. *Science* 211:341–350.

Stanley, S. M. 1992. An ecological theory for the origin of *Homo. Paleobiology* 18:237–257.

Stern, J. T., and R. L. Susman. 1983. The locomotor anatomy of *Australopithecus afarensis. American Journal of Physical Anthropology* 60:279–317.

Susman, R. L., J. T. Stern, and W. L. Jungers. 1984. Arboreality and bipedality in the Hadar hominids. *Folia Primatologica* 43:113–156.

Vrba, E. 1988. Late Pliocene climatic events and hominid evolution. In: *Evolutionary History of the "Robust" Australopithecines* (F. E. Grine, Ed.), pp. 405–426. Aldine, New York.

White, T. D. 2003. Early hominids: diversity or distortion. *Science* 299:1994–1997.

16

The Australopithecines in Review

L. C. Aiello and P. Andrews

ABSTRACT

*Over the past 75 years since the discovery of the first australop-
ithecine at Taung in southern Africa there has been a growing
realisation that there is no simple, linear ancestor-descendant
relationship connecting the australopithecines to later* Homo.
*There are currently at least ten recognised species of australop-
ithecine, including two species of early* Homo, *that have been
recently transferred to the genus Australopithecus. These
known species span the period between about 4.2–1.2 Ma and
throughout the majority of this period there are multiple contemporaneous hominin species in eastern and southern Africa.
This contribution reviews current knowledge about the australopithecine species and their inferred relationships to each
other and to the genus* Homo. *At present it is impossible to resolve the phylogenetic relationships of the australopithecines
with any degree of confidence. There is a growing realisation of
the 'bushy' nature of hominin evolution throughout the australopithecine period and also of the inevitability that additional early hominin species remain to be discovered.*

The term australopithecine comes from the genus
name *Australopithecus*. This genus was established in
1925 by Raymond Dart for an infant's skull (face,
mandible and natural endocranial cast) that had been
discovered the previous year at the Buxton lime quarry
at Taungs in the northern Cape Province of South
Africa. Although the name *Australopithecus* means
southern ape (australo = southern; pithecus = ape),
Dart emphasised the human-like reduced face and dentition of the Taung Child. He also noted that it most
probably had a more erect posture than do the living
apes. The foramen magnum was situated well forward,
suggesting that the head would have been balanced on
the vertebral column as it is in bipedal humans. Dart
also felt that the endocranial cast suggested that the
brain of the Taung Child had a more human-like organisation than that found in living apes, an assertion
that is still actively contested (Falk, 1985, Holloway,
1985). The australopithecines, as represented by this
child, were to Dart's mind intermediate between humans and apes. He called them man-apes and suggested
that they be placed in their own taxonomic family, the
Homo-simidae.

Today, seventy-five years after the discovery of the
Taung Child, we have many more australopithecine
fossils from both southern and eastern Africa and, as a
consequence, we have a much better idea of what these
hominins[1] were like. There are now at least eight
species of australopithecine that span the period
between approximately 4.2–1.2 Ma (Figure 1). The australopithecines have traditionally been divided into
two groups, the 'gracile' australopithecines and the
'robust' australopithecines and this distinction is still
heuristically useful. The 'gracile' australopithecines
lived between about 4.2 and 2.0 Ma and include
A. anamensis and *A. afarensis* as well as the original
species that Dart established for the Taung child,
A. africanus. An additional species, *A. bahrelghazali*,
from Chad is dated to between 3.0 and 3.5 million
years ago (Brunet et al., 1995). Too little is currently
known about this species to say how it relates to the
other 'gracile' australopithecines. Most recently, a new
species of *Australopithecus*, *A. garhi*, has been established for material from the Middle Awash Valley,
Ethiopia that dates to about 2.5 million years ago
(Asfaw et al., 1999). It has been suggested to have been
in the right place and at the right time to be the
evolutionary link between the earlier *A. afarensis* and
Homo. At the minimum, the growing number of
'gracile' australopithecine species suggests that the
picture of hominin evolution at this time may be more
complicated than the present fossil evidence indicates.
The 'robust' australopithecines generally occur later in
time than do the 'gracile' australopithecines, between
about 2.7–1.2 Ma. They include *A. aethiopicus*, *A. robustus*
and *A. boisei*.

Recently it has also been suggested that two species
of early *Homo*, *Homo habilis* and *Homo rudolfensis*, be
transferred to the genus *Australopithecus* (Wood and
Collard, 1999). This is based on the fact that the morphology of the fossils referred to these species, as well
as their inferred behavioural and lifehistory adaptations, are more similar to the australopithecines than
to later and more convincing members of the genus
Homo.

All of the australopithecines, including *Australopithecus habilis* and *Australopithecus rudolfensis*, share with
modern humans the ability to walk on two legs. Over
the years there have been a variety of explanations for
the origin of bipedal locomotion (Rose, 1991). These
include freeing the hands to carry and use tools
(Bartholomew and Birdsell, 1953; Washburn, 1967;
Marzke, 1986), enabling the hominins to see longer
distances in an open environment (Ravey, 1978),

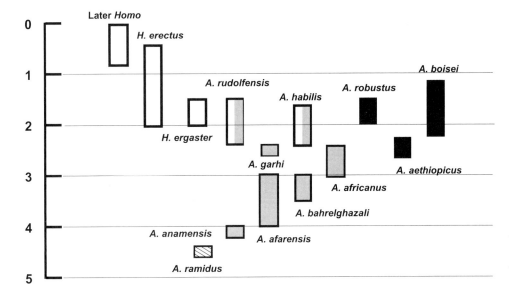

Figure 1. *Plot of approximate time ranges of the hominin species. Black boxes = 'robust' austalopithecines (paranthropines), grey boxes = 'gracile' australopithecines, hatched box =* Ardipithecus ramidus, *empty boxes =* Homo, *and half-empty and half-grey boxes =* Australopithecus habilis *and* Australopithecus rudolfensis *that have recently been transferred from the genus* Homo *(Wood and Collard, 1999).*

increasing locomotor efficiency (Rodman and McHenry, 1980; but see Streudel, 1994), aiding the transport of food or offspring (Dubrul, 1962; Sinclair et al., 1987), displaying or warning (Wescot, 1967; Jablonski and Chaplin, 1993), feeding (Jolly, 1970; Hunt, 1994) and thermoregulation (Wheeler, 1984, 1985, 1991a, 1991b, 1992a, 1992b, 1992c, 1993, 1994a, 1994b; but see Chaplin et al., 1994).

Because the reconstructed habitats of the 'gracile' australopithecines indicate that they lived in more wooded habitats than previously thought (Reed, 1997), many anthropologists now see australopithecine bipedalism as a forest adaptation. For example, Hunt (1994) has proposed that bipedalism is a specific adaptation to feeding on small fruits in open-forest trees, where food was gathered either by standing on the ground or in the trees. This may be the case, but chimpanzees that feed in this fashion have not developed bipedal features of the pelvis and hindlimbs. Furthermore the Laetoli footprints suggest that early australopithecine bipedalism was for loco-motion rather than merely postural. Because bipedal-ism is unique to hominins among primates and involves major skeletal modifications, it is logical to assume that its selective advantage relates to some unique aspect of the early australopithecine, or pre-australopithecine, niche. Wooded habitats are not nec-essarily homogenous and there is evidence that these early hominins occupied a variety of wooded habitats from closed forest to relatively open savannah-woodland. Few mammal species manage to live in both forest and open conditions, and the ability to exploit this range of habitats might have been the unique niche of the australopithecines. If this is the case hy-potheses for the origin of bipedalism that incorporate energy efficiency (e.g. Isbell and Young, 1996) and/or thermoregulation (e.g. Wheeler, 1984) may have also been important in the early evolution of this unique locomotor adaptation.

Australopithecine bipedalism and body form were not like those found in modern humans or in early members of the genus *Homo*. Currently available evi-dence suggests that all of the australopithecines, with the possible exception of the newly described *A. garhi*, had shorter legs in relation to their forelimb lengths than does *Homo* (Jungers, 1982; Garuz et al., 1988; Wood and Collard, 1999; but see McHenry and Berger, 1998a) and a pelvis that is considerably different in form from that of more modern hominins (Tauge and Lovejoy, 1986; Berge et al., 1984; Berge and Kazmierczak, 1986). They were also heavily muscled for their stature, like modern apes (Aiello, 1992). Furthermore, many aspects of their skeletons, and par-ticularly of their trunks, forelimbs, hands and shoul-ders, suggest that although bipedal when on the ground, they still were at home in the trees (Stern and Susman, 1983; Abitbol, 1995; Hunt, 1994). Recent esti-mates of australopithecine body mass show that there was little difference in size between the 'robust' and 'gracile' australopithecines (McHenry, 1992, 1994). Average species body masses for all of the austral-opithecines range between about 40–49 kgs, with the females about 65–75% the mass of the males. There is also accumulating evidence that all of the aus-tralopithecines, including *Australopithecus habilis* and *Australopithecus rudolfensis*, had growth and develop-ment patterns that were more similar to the rapid growth in modern apes than to the slower growth in modern humans (Dean et. al., 1993; Smith, 1994; Wood and Collard, 1999; but see Lampl et al., 1993).

Little is known about the postcranial skeleton of the 'robust' australopithecines and currently the main difference between the two groups of australop-ithecines seems to be in the size of their teeth, jaws and faces. The 'robust' australopithecines tend to have more megadont cheek teeth, and smaller ante-rior teeth in relation to these cheek teeth, than do the 'gracile' australopithecines. Their jaws and faces are much more robust (Wood and Aiello, 1998). This implies that there was considerable variation in dietary adaptation between these two groups. This difference, its morphological correlates and the assumption that all of the 'robust' australopithecines are monophyletic, has led some palaeoanthropologists to place the 'robust' australopithecines in their own genus, *Paranthropus.*

THE 'GRACILE' AUSTRALOPITHECINES

The two best-known species of 'gracile' australopithecine are *Australopithecus africanus* and *Australopithecus afarensis.* The remaining species: *A. bahrelghazali, A. anamensis* and *A. garhi* are less well represented by fossils and, because of their more recent establishment, are less well understood. An additional taxon, *Ardipithecus ramidus,* (White et al., 1995) was originally referred to the genus *Australopithecus* (White et al., 1994). This taxon was established on the basis of 17 fossils from the Middle Awash, Ethiopia, that date between about 4.5 and 4.3 Ma (White et al., 1994). Over 90 additional specimens making up about 45% of a single skeleton were found in 1994 (Gee, 1995b) but these specimens have yet to be fully reported. The currently described specimens do not include fossils of the pelvis or lower limbs which would confirm that *A. ramidus* was bipedal. *A. ramidus* has deciduous molars that are similar to ape deciduous molars and permanent teeth that may be smaller in relation to inferred body size than is the case in the larger 'gracile' australopithecines. These two features would suggest that *A. ramidus* had not yet evolved the dietary adaptations and associated dental morphology that characterise the australopithecine species. At present all that can be said is that *Ardipithecus ramidus* represents a more primitive level of adaptation than the known australopithecines and is possibly ancestral to them.

I. *Australopithecus africanus*

In the years since the discovery of the Taung child, *A. africanus* fossils have been found at three other southern African sites: Sterkfontein and Gladysvale in the central Transvaal and Makapansgat in the northern Transvaal. Sterkfontein is by far the most prolific of the *A. africanus* sites, having yielded over 500 *A. africanus* fossils since it was first excavated in 1936 (Clarke, 1994). Makapansgat has produced 29 *A. africanus* specimens since 1947 (Rayner et al., 1993) while Gladysvale, the most recently discovered site, yielded 2 tooth germs in 1992 (Berger et al., 1993). No additional hominin specimens have been recovered from Taung (McKee and Tobias, 1994).

The main *A. africanus* deposits at Sterkfontein (Member 4) are dated between approximately 2.8 and 2.2 Ma (Vrba, 1982). Based on faunal comparisons, Makapansgat may be earlier than this at about 3 Ma while Gladysvale may be the most recent, dating between about 2.5 and 1.7 Ma (Berger et al., 1993). There

is no evidence that any of these sites were living sites nor is there evidence of stone or bone tools in the deposits containing *Australopithecus africanus.* The australopithecine fossils seem to have been accumulated by carnivores, particularly leopards at Sterkfontein, hyenas at Makapansgat and eagles at Taung (Berger and Clark, 1995). Palaeoenvironmental reconstructions suggest that *A. africanus* may have lived in a sub-tropical forest environment at Makapansgat (Rayner et al., 1993) and in a more open environment at Sterkfontein. Stable carbon isotope analysis of *A. africanus* teeth from Makapansgat suggests that even these earlier hominins may have exploited relatively open environments such as woodlands or grasslands for food (Sponheimer and Lee-Thorpe, 1999). These analyses suggest that the australopithecines not only ate fruits and leaves like modern chimpanzees, but also large quantities of Carbon-13 enriched foods such as grasses and sedges or animals that ate these plants or both. The authors speculate that *A. africanus* may have consumed quantities of high-quality animal foods, a diet generally thought to be exclusive to the genus *Homo.*

There are two well-known *A. africanus* fossils from Sterkfontein, both found in 1947, which confirmed in adult specimens the bipedal hominin morphology that Dart had inferred for *A. africanus* on the basis of the Taung child. The first of these is a virtually complete skull (Sts 5), that is still affectionately known as 'Mrs. Ples' after one of the early taxonomic designations for the hominins from Sterkfontein, *Plesianthropus transvaalensis* (Broom, 1937). The second is a partially complete skeleton (Sts 14) comprising a distorted pelvis, a crushed femur, 15 vertebrae and some fragmentary ribs. Up until fairly recently, the general interpretation of *Australopithecus africanus* was that it represented a relatively homogenous taxon of bipedal hominin. Recent publication of a very large, presumed male *A. africanus* skull (Stw 505) (Conroy et al., 1998) and analysis of the plethora of other hominin fossils from Member 4 at Sterkfontein has begun to change this interpretation. McHenry and Berger's (1998a, 1998b) initial analysis of inferred body masses and relative limb lengths suggest that *A. africanus* was more ape-like in its body proportions than at least *A. afarensis,* while analyses of the tibia suggest that, although bipedal on the ground, *A. africanus* would also have had the capability to move efficiently in the trees (Berger and Tobias, 1996). Furthermore, there has been some suggestion that more than one species is represented among the *A. africanus* fossils. Quite extreme variation in size and morphology has been recognised among the mandibles from Makapansgat (Pilbeam, 1972), while Clarke (1988, 1994) believes that the variation in crania from Sterkfontein justifies the conclusion that some fossils (e.g. Sts 252 and Sts 36) might represent a species ancestral to the 'robust' australopithecines while others such as Sts 5 and Sts 52 would represent *A. africanus.* More recently, Lockwood (1999) has shown that the degree of variation in the *A. africanus* face, including the large Stw 505 cranium, is less than that found within *Australopithecus boisei* and compatible in pattern with the variation found within modern humans. The growing realization of the degree of size and morphological variation in the *A. africanus* collection, as well as in the other Plio-Pleistocene hominins, is one of the exciting current themes in australopithecine research.

Recently Sterkfontein also produced what is the earliest known hominin from southern Africa. This hominin skeleton (Stw 573) comes from Member 2 which is currently thought to be between 3.2 and 3.6 million years old. The foot bones suggest that it may have been more aboreally adapted than either *Australopithecus afarensis* or the later *Australopithecus habilis* (*Homo habilis*) (Clarke and Tobias, 1995). In this respect Stw 573 is consistent with the newer interpretations of the postcranial remains from the later Member 4 australopithecines. Whether Stw 573 proves to be *A. africanus* or another contemporary australopithecine, such as *A. afarensis*, must await further analysis of the remainder of this new discovery.

II. *Australopithecus afarensis*

Up until 1978 *Australopithecus africanus* was the only known 'gracile' australopithecine. But in that year Johanson and his co-workers established a new species, *A. afarensis*, for fossils from the site of Hadar in Ethiopia and Laetoli in Tanzania (Johanson et al., 1978). In 1979 Johanson and White suggested that it represented the common ancestor for all later australopithecines on the one hand and *Homo* on the other. Since 1979, fossils from Koobi Fora and Tabarin, Kenya and the Omo, Ethiopia have been referred to this taxon (Boas, 1988) as have further Ethiopian fossils from the Middle Awash (White et al., 1993) and Hadar itself (Kimbel et al., 1994).

A. afarensis is reasonably well dated by Potassium-Argon methods. The oldest currently known *A. afarensis* is a fragmentary frontal bone from the site of Belohdelie in the Middle Awash that is 3.9 Ma while the most recent is a relatively complete skull (AL 444-2) from Kada Hadar Member at Hadar that is 3.0 Ma (Johanson et al., 1994). Palaeoenvironmental reconstruction of a number of *A. afarensis* sites suggested that it occupied a spectrum of environments from closed forest of the SH Member at Hadar to more open conditions at Laetoli, Tanzania (White et al., 1993; but see Andrews, 1989).

By far the most well-known *A. afarensis* fossil is AL 228-1, a 40% complete skeleton that is affectionately known as Lucy. AL 288-1 was discovered in 1974 at Hadar, and because of its completeness it forms the basis for much that is known of *A. afarensis* skeletal anatomy. Careful reconstruction of the entire skeleton shows that Lucy would have stood 106 cm high (Schmid, 1983), about the height of a 4.5 year old European child. The pelvis is less distorted than, but similar to, the Sts 14 pelvis, and has sparked a heated controversy over the efficiency of *A. afarensis* bipedal locomotion (Lovejoy, 1988; Stern and Susman, 1983). There is little doubt, however, that *A. afarensis* was more capable of bipedal locomotion than are modern apes. Aspects of the knee, ankle joint and foot confirm this

interpretation and show that during the stride her body weight would have been transferred in a straight line over the foot, passing directly over the toes at the end of the stride (Latimer et al., 1987). As modern humans, *A. afarensis* would have also had moderate hip mobility and a more adducted femur (MacLatchy, 1996).

Many other aspects of *A. afarensis* anatomy are primitive. For example, the size of the birth canal in relation to the inferred size of an *A. afarensis* infant suggests that Lucy would have had no trouble in bearing an infant at the relatively advanced stage of development common for today's apes (Leutenegger, 1987; but see Hausler and Schmid, 1995). The less developed condition of modern human neonates is a derived adaptation permitting birth before the infant's head becomes too large to pass through the constricted human birth canal. *A. afarensis* also has an ape-like funnel-shaped rib cage (Schmid, 1983, 1991) that is consistent with an adaptation to climbing in the trees (Hunt, 1994). The wide rib-cage and broad pelvis would also have provided room for a capacious gut, suggesting that *A. afarensis* did not have the high quality diet, and correspondingly relatively small gut, that is a necessary energetic concomitant of the enlarged brain in *Homo* (Aiello and Wheeler, 1995). Many additional parts of the skeleton, such as curved hand and foot phalanges, the shape of the scapula, the relatively mobile knee joint, and details of the humerus and elbow joint suggest *A. afarensis* was able to climb in the trees with much more agility than modern humans (Stern and Susman, 1983; Aiello and Dean, 1990).

There are no living primates that show in their skeletons the same mosaic of bipedal and arboreal features as does *A. afarensis*, and one of the main questions today is precisely how terrestrial *A. afarensis* was in its day-to-day locomotion. The remarkably preserved footprints at Laetoli, Tanzania, which date to between 3.6–3.75 Ma, clearly demonstrate that a hominin existed at this time that walked with an apparently efficient striding bipedal locomotion. The environment of Laetoli at the time of the footprint trail was open savannah-woodland. Raindrops preserved along with the footprints indicate that they were made at the beginning of the rainy season (Hay and Leakey, 1982) and the accompanying prints of many migratory animal species suggest that the hominins may have been participating in the annual game migrations. Some anthropologists suggest that the footprints are too modern to have been made by *A. afarensis* (Tuttle, 1981) and that another, more modern hominin species must have been in existence at the same time as *A. afarensis*. However, White and Suwa (1987) have argued convincingly that the footprints are compatible with what is known of *A. afarensis* foot morphology. The evidence of the Laetoli footprints, together with the many aboreally-adapted features of the *A. afarensis* skeleton, suggest that these hominins had a mosaic locomotor pattern. This would have involved bipedalism while on the ground coupled with an arboreal adaptation that facilitated feeding and sleeping in the trees (Kimbel et at., 1994; Aiello, 1994a; but see White et al., 1993).

AL 288-1 is just one of a large number of fossils that have been referred to *A. afarensis* and a marked feature of the entire collection is an impressive difference in size. When the mandible, femur or humerus of AL 288-1, one of the smallest individuals, is compared to larger individuals, the degree of size difference is outside the range that would be expected in modern chimpanzees or humans, and just within the 95% confidence limits for gorillas and orang-utans (Richmond and Jungers, 1995). This is an impressive degree of dimorphism for a species that has a relatively small average body size. This fact, together with possible morphological differences between the large and small individuals, has lead some researchers to suggest that more than one species is present in the *A. afarensis* collection (Olson, 1981; Senut and Tardieu, 1985). Other anthropologists argue that some of the morphological differences have been misinterpreted (Kimbel et al., 1984), or that they are merely a result of size (Asfaw, 1985) and/or have no functional significance (Latimer et al., 1987).

At present the question of multiple species in the *A. afarensis* collection cannot be resolved. Discoveries in the Middle Awash and Hadar (Kimbel et al., 1994; White et al., 1993) suggest that the variation in size is continuous in time and space and cannot be sorted in two (or more) clear morphs that could be interpreted as different species. Furthermore, although the degree of dimorphism in *A. afarensis* is large, it is of the same order of magnitude as that found in other australopithecine species (McHenry, 1992, 1994; Aiello, 1994a). It may be unusual for modern humans and chimpanzees, but not for the australopithecines. Evidence for very large and robust arm bones from both Hadar and the Middle Awash goes a long way to dispel earlier ideas (Stern and Susman, 1983; Lovejoy, 1981) that the larger morph of *A. afarensis* was any less adapted to arboreal locomotion than was the smaller morph. At present the fossil evidence is most consistent with the interpretation that *A. afarensis* was a highly dimorphic taxon with a mosaic locomotor pattern.

III. *Australopithecus anamensis*

Australopithecus anamensis was established in 1995 on the basis of nine hominin dental, cranial and postcranial specimens from Kanapoi, Kenya and 12 specimens from Allia Bay, Kenya (Leakey, M. G. et al., 1995). Subsequently further fossil material has been recovered from both sites and the antiquity has been established at between 4.17 ± 0.03 and 4.07 ± 0.02 million years ago (Leakey, M. G. et al., 1998). Not only is *A. anamensis* older than *A. afarensis* but it is also more primitive in certain aspects of its dental anatomy, and particularly in its large canine teeth. In these aspects it resembles more closely the earlier *A. afarensis* material from Laetoli, Tanzania, than the later material from Hadar, Ethiopia (Leakey, M. G. et al., 1995). Its distal humerus is similar to that of *A. afarensis* (Lague and Jungers, 1996), the morphology of its 1st lower deciduous molar is intermediate between *Ardipithecus ramidus* and *A. afarensis*, and its capitate is more ape-like than any other known

hominin. Based on current assessment of its morphology and on what is presently known of *Ardipithecus ramidus*, *Australopithecus anamensis* could well be an intermediate species linking the earlier *Ardipithecus* with the later *A. afarensis*. Little is known from these early time periods, however, and the true evolutionary picture may prove to be considerably more 'bushy' than the present species suggest.

IV. *Australopithecus garhi*

The taxon *Australopithecus garhi* was established in 1999 for hominin fossils from the Hata Member of the Bouri Formation in the Middle Awash, Ethiopia. This material dates to 2.5 million years ago (Asfaw et al., 1999). The taxon is roughly contemporaneous with *A. africanus* and post-dates the remainder of the 'gracile' australopithecines. The species name, *garhi*, means surprise in the Afar language, and the morphology of this australopithecine was a surprise. It is distinguished from *A. afarensis* by its absolutely very large postcanine dentition, from the 'robust' australopithecines by the absence of their distinctive dental, facial and cranial features, and from *A. africanus*, *A. habilis* and *A. rudolfensis* by its primitive cranial and facial anatomy. Skeletal material from a nearby site, which most probably belongs to this taxon, also suggests that its femora were elongated in relation to its humeri as is the case in *Homo ergaster* and all more recent members of the genus *Homo*. It differs from *Homo* in retaining relatively long forearms for its upper arms, however. Animal bones found at the sites also show clear evidence of cutmarks indicating butchery (Heinzelin et al., 1999). Although no stone tools have been found at the Hata sites, nearly contemporary deposits at Gona (96 km to the north) have abundant stone tools dated to 2.6 Ma. The inferred environment at Hata was a featureless, grassy lake margin. The absence of stone tools may reflect the absence of ready sources of raw materials and indicate that the hominins were 'curating' their tools and not leaving them behind. Although it is not possible to say with confidence that *A. garhi* made stone tools and carried out the butchery, it is the only contemporary hominin in the deposits. If Asfaw and colleagues are correct in their attribution of these new fossils to *Australopithecus*, and if this taxon was responsible for the tool making and butchery, it would indicate that australopithecines in East Africa were both tool makers and meat eaters. As a result, the contemporary *A. africanus* in South Africa would not be the only australopithecine for which there is evidence of a high quality diet (Sponheimer and Lee-Thorpe, 1999).

THE 'ROBUST' AUSTRALOPITHECINES

Of the three species of 'robust' australopithecine, one (*Australopithecus robustus*) occurs in South Africa and two (*Australopithecus aethiopicus* and *Australopithecus boisei*) occur in East Africa with *A. boisei* known as far south as Malawi (Schrenk and Bromage, in press). The earliest 'robust' australopithecine, *A. aethiopicus,* is known from Kenya and Ethiopia and appears at about 2.7 Ma, while *A. boisei* appears about 2.3 Ma and *A. robustus* about 2.0 Ma.

The 'robust' australopithecines lived contemporaneously with either 'gracile' australopithecines or members of *Homo* throughout their time range. The extreme masticatory system of the 'robust' australopithecines may indicate a divergence in dietary adaptation that would avoid competition with early *Homo.* Foley (1987) has suggested that if the environment was becoming increasingly seasonal, the 'robust' australopithecines might have opted for processing larger quantities of foods of relatively low nutritional value, while the more gracile hominins adopted a strategy whereby they broadened their dietary base to include a range of high quality food items such as animal-based products (see also Potts, 1998).

Australopithecus robustus

The first 'robust' australopithecine was found in 1938 by a schoolboy at the site of Kromdraai, which is not far from Sterkfontein in the Transvaal, South Africa (Broom and Schepers, 1946). This original discovery was a partial skeleton including a fragmentary skull, a mandible and parts of the postcranium. On the basis of the large teeth and robust jaws, this material was originally placed in a new taxon, *Paranthropus robustus.* Although some anthropologists continue to use the genus name *Paranthropus* for all of the 'robust' australopithecines (e.g. Dean, 1985; Grine, 1985; Wood and Collard, 1999), many prefer to use *Australopithecus* and thereby to recognise the grade similarities in adaptation shared with the 'gracile' australopithecines. The nearby site of Swartkrans has produced fossils representing 124 individuals of *A. robustus* since it was first excavated in 1948 (Brain, 1993a, 1994) and most recently 'robust' australopithecine teeth have been found at Sterkfontein (Member 5) (Kuman, 1994; Clarke, 1994) and at Gondolin in the Northwest Province of South Africa (Kuykendall, 1999). 'Robust' australopithecine fossils have also been found at the site of Drimolin but these remain to be published.

Based on faunal comparisons, the australopithecine-bearing deposits at Swartkrans (Members 1–3) span the period between about 1.8–1.0 Ma (Brain, 1993a), while those at Sterkfontein (Member 5) are approximately 2.0–1.7 Ma (Kuman, 1994). The deposits at Kromdraai may be more similar in age to the material from Sterkfontein than to that from Swartkrans. Deciduous molar teeth from Kromdraai are similar to the newly discovered teeth from Sterkfontein and different from Swartkrans deciduous molars. Grine (1982) feels that this difference is great enough to separate the fossils into two different species, *Paranthropus robustus* for the material from Kromdraai and *Paranthropus crassidens* for the material from Swartkrans. He also feels that the Swartkrans material is more specialised, and therefore more recent, than

the Kromdraai fossils. Faunal comparisons also suggests an early date for Kromdraai (McKee et al., 1995).

Swartkrans has yielded some fascinating insights into the behaviour of the 'robust' australopithecines (Brain, 1993a, 1994). Stable carbon isotope analysis of *A. robustus* tooth enamel suggests that these hominins were generalised feeders and could have included a significant component of animal-based foods in their diet (Lee-Thorpe and van der Merwe, 1993; Lee-Thorpe et al., 1994). This is consistent with interpretations drawn from their brain sizes which suggest that *A. robustus* could not have survived on a low-quality, vegetarian diet that has often been inferred for them on the basis of their robust masticatory anatomy (Aiello and Wheeler, 1995).

Bone tools found throughout the deposits show wear patterns that suggest repeated use as digging implements (Brain and Shipman, 1994). It is possible that they may have been used to reach edible bulbs or tubers in the rocky terrain around the site. Other bone tools show wear that is consistent with working animal skins, and there are also stone tools throughout the deposits. It is currently impossible to determine whether *A. robustus* was the toolmaker. The reason is that early *Homo* is also found at Swartkrans in the same deposits as *A. robustus.* Susman (1988, 1994) argues that hand bones from the site indicate that *A. robustus* would have at least had the same manual ability to make and use tools as *Homo habilis,* but other anthropologists acknowledge the possibility that these hand bones may actually belong to *Homo* rather than to *A. robustus* (Trinkaus and Long, 1990; Aiello, 1994b).

The fossils at Swartkrans were largely accumulated as the result of carnivore predation. The smaller percentage of hominins in Member 3 (5.1%) in relation to the earlier Members 1 and 2 (9%, 16.7%) might even suggest that the Member 3 hominins were better at predator avoidance than the earlier hominins (Brain, 1993b, 1994). There is evidence for the controlled use of fire in Member 3 (Sillen and Hoering, 1993; Brain, 1993b, 1994) and the only hominins currently known from this member are the 'robust' australopithecines. Brain (1993b, 1994) suggests that Swartkrans in Member 3 times may have been a sleeping site for the 'robust' australopithecines, and that the decline in percentage representation of hominins in these deposits resulted from the protection provided by the presence of fires.

Australopithecus boisei

Australopithecus robustus is only known from South Africa and *Australopithecus boisei* is only found at sites in Tanzania, Kenya, Ethiopia and Malawi. The first *A. boisei* fossil, a relatively complete and undistorted cranium, was found in 1959 by Mary Leakey at Olduvai Gorge, Tanzania. It is generally similar in form to the *A. robustus* crania from Kromdraai and Swartkrans, but has bigger molar teeth and more extreme facial features: the cheek bones are both higher and more flaring. The facial structure of *A. boisei* completes the trend seen in

A. africanus and *A. robustus* towards the generation of increased chewing force (Rak, 1983). Discovery of the most complete *A. boisei* skull and mandible from Konso, Ethiopia, however, shows that there was considerable variation in the *A. boisei* skull (Suwa et al., 1997).

This first *A. boisei* skull (Olduvai Hominid 5) was initially put in a separate taxon, *Zinjanthropus boisei* (L. S. B. Leakey, 1959), but Robinson (1960) almost immediately suggested that it should be put in *Paranthropus boisei*. In 1967 Tobias reclassified it as *Australopithecus boisei*, pointing out the numerous similarities between it and the South African 'robust' australopithecines. Olduvai has only produced a few other *A. boisei* fossils (isolated teeth, parts of a fragmentary cranium, a fragmentary proximal femur and an almost complete ulna) that come from Beds I and II and date between about 1.85–1.20 Ma (Aiello et al., 1999). During this time there was a saline lake in the area and the sites were located close to fresh water streams. Recent palaeoenvironmental analyses suggest a riparian to grassy woodland environment, at least Bed I times (Sikes, 1994; Plummer and Bishop, 1994).

In the years since the first discovery at Olduvai, further *A. boisei* material has come from Peninj in Tanzania, from Chesowanja, West Turkana and Koobi Fora in Kenya, the Omo in Ethiopia and in Malawi. The most important of these sites have been the Omo and Koobi Fora. Over 200 hominin specimens were recovered from the Omo between 1967–1976 and the Omo is also important because it has provided a well dated stratigraphic sequence for the Turkana Basin. Although the great majority of the Omo fossils are very fragmentary, we know that robust and non-robust hominins co-occur between about 2.7–1.4 Ma (Shungura Formation members C-K) (Suwa et al., 1996). The robust fossils from the earlier members (C-F) represent a different taxon, *Australopithecus aethiopicus* (see below and Wood, 1991, for a review).

Koobi Fora has been by far the most prolific of the East African hominin sites, and *Australopithecus boisei* is the most common hominin found. *A. boisei* fossils at Koobi Fora are found in the Upper Burgi, KBS and Okote Members and span the period from approximately 2.0–1.4 Ma. During this period there was a marked change in the environment in the Turkana basin. Between about 1.8–1.9 Ma there was a saline lake and sites are located along the lake margin as well as near river channels (Rogers et al., 1994). After 1.7 Ma the lake disappeared to be replaced by a river. The climate also seems to have become drier (Rogers et al., 1994; Cerling, 1992). Whereas earlier australopithecines lived in fairly wooded, well watered environments, *A. boisei* (as well as the other 'robust' australopithecines) also lived in more open environments, but always near wetlands (Reed, 1997; see also Behrensmeyer, 1985; Shipman and Harris, 1988). *Homo* is the first hominin to be adapted to open and relatively arid environments.

Two of the most important of the many *A. boisei* fossils from Koobi Fora are a virtually complete large cranium (KNM-ER 406) and a smaller half-cranium (KNM-ER 732). Both of these are from the KBS member and date to about 1.65–1.70 Ma. KNM-ER 406 is similar in its morphology to Olduvai Hominid 5 and both are presumed to be males. KNM-ER 732 is much smaller in size, but it preserves many features in common with the larger specimens. These include a large, inflated mastoid process, elongated glenoid fossa (articulation for the jaw) and a dish-shaped face. The size difference between KNM-ER 406 and KNM-ER 732 is commonly taken to represent the high level of sexual dimorphism present in *A. boisei*. A further important *A. boisei* fossil from Koobi Fora is the KNM-ER 1500 partial skeleton. This is from the Upper Burgi Member and is therefore older than the two crania, dating to about 1.88-1.90 Ma. Although this skeleton is very fragmentary and its allocation to *A. boisei* has been questioned (Aiello et al., 1999), it has body proportions similar to those of *A. afarensis* (Grausz et al., 1988), with relatively small hindlimbs in relation to the forelimbs.

Considerable archaeological work has been carried out at Koobi Fora. Before about 1.6 Ma the stone tool assemblages were primarily restricted to relatively closed environments next to perennial water sources (Harris and Capaldo, 1993). After this time stone tools are found in a variety of habitat contexts and in varying densities. There is one site at Koobi Fora (FxJj 20 Main) which dates to 1.6 Ma and has evidence of controlled fire use in a context, like Swartkrans, that would suggest that the fire served as a source of light, heat and predator protection (Bellomo, 1994). Whether or not *A. boisei* was responsible for any of the archaeology at Koobi Fora is again impossible to determine with certainty. But Rogers et al. (1994) argue that the first appearance of early *Homo erectus* (*Homo ergaster*) and the apparent change in artifact distribution and occurrence around 1.6 Ma may be more than a coincidence. These authors strongly favour *Homo* as the tool user and fire maker at least in these later deposits.

V. *Australopithecus aethiopicus*

In 1985 two 'robust' australopithecine specimens, a skull and a mandible, were found at two different localities on the Western shore of Lake Turkana (Walker et al., 1986). The skull, found in the Lomekwi drainage, dates to about 2.50 Ma, while the mandible, from the nearby Kangatukuseo drainage, dates to about 2.45 Ma. This material is at least 500,000 years older than any of the previously known 'robust' australopithecines from sites other than the Omo, Ethiopia. The surprising thing about these fossils is not their age, but the fact that they represent a type of 'robust' australopithecine that was previously unknown. In particular, the skull (KNM-WT 17000) has a relatively small brain size and features of the occipital region that are characteristic of *A. afarensis*. But the teeth are among the largest 'robust' australopithecine teeth known and the face is massive and heavily buttressed. At an age that is roughly equivalent to *A. africanus* in South Africa, this specimen did not fit into the expected trend in facial evolution that had been previously established by Rak (1983).

KNM-WT 17000 was originally assigned to *Australopithecus boisei* on the grounds of overall resemblance

(Walker et al., 1986) and the fact that it probably represents an early part of the evolving *A. boisei* lineage (see also Walker and Leakey, 1988). Other authors have pointed out that of the many features used in comparison, only a small number (e.g. heart shaped foramen magnum, temporoparietal overlap at asterion) actually link this fossil exclusively with *A. boisei* (Delson, 1986; see also Kimble et al., 1988). The great majority of cranial features are either primitive, or link KNM-WT 17000 with all or some of the other 'robust' and 'gracile' australopithecines.

The taxon *Paraustralopithecus aethiopicus* was established by Arambourg and Coppens (1968) for an edentulous (without teeth) mandible (Omo 18-1967-18) from the Omo Shungura Member C (about 2.6 Ma). Because of the many features in which KNM-WT 17000 differs from *A. boisei,* and because of some similarities between the Omo 18-1967-18 mandible, other early Omo mandibular fossils and the Kangatukuseo mandible, Kimbel et al. (1988) have referred both of the West Turkana specimens to the species *aethiopicus* and placed this species in the genus *Australopithecus*. *A. aethiopicus* is now considered to be a taxon that is more primitive than *A. boisei* (or *A. robustus*), but most probably in the *A. boisei* clade.

AUSTRALOPITHECINE PHYLOGENY

Ideas about australopithecine phylogeny have changed radically over the years with the discovery of each new taxon. In the 1950s the South African australopithecine sites had yet to be as precisely dated as they are today, but faunal comparisons suggested that the *A. africanus* sites of Sterkfontein and Makapansgat were older than the *A. robustus* sites of Kromdraai and Swartkrans. Robinson (1963) felt that the then known 'robust' australopithecines represented late survivors of an ancestral stock from which *A. africanus* and *Homo* evolved (Figure 2a). He argued for a 'hominidizing' trend from *A. robustus* through *A. africanus* to *Homo*. This hypothesis lost support with the discovery of *A. boisei* at Olduvai in 1959 and the realisation that the large teeth and massive facial structure of the 'robust' australopithecines most probably represented specialised features that could easily have been derived from a more primitive *A. africanus*-like ancestor (Tobias, 1967). Because the Olduvai material was considered at that time to be roughly contemporaneous with the *A. africanus* deposits in South Africa, Tobias (1967) suggested that a postulated Upper Pliocene australopithecine with teeth similar to *A. africanus* was ancestral to the contemporaneous

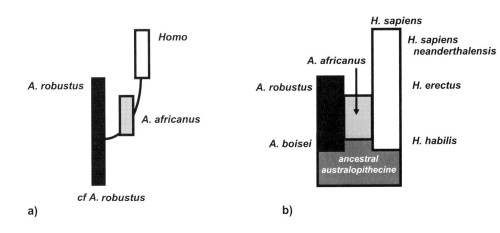

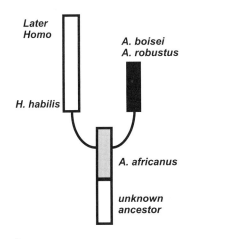

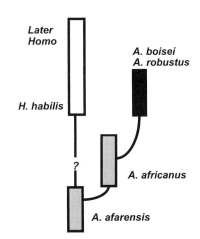

Figure 2. *Historical interpretations of australopithecine phylogeny. (a) after Robinson (1963), (b) after Tobias (1967), (c) a phylogeny popular in the early 1970's, (d) after Johanson and White (1979).*

Lower Pleistocene *A. africanus, A. boisei* and *Homo habilis* (Figure 2b). A rival hypothesis saw *A. boisei* and *Homo habilis* in East Africa as males and females of the same species, with a similar relationship between *A. africanus* and *A. robustus* in South Africa (Wolpoff, 1968). The 'single species hypothesis', as this idea came to be called, was not completely rejected until the mid-1970's. By this time the *A. africanus* levels of the South African cave sites were known not only to pre-date the *A. robustus* levels, but also to significantly pre-date the appearance of *Homo habilis* and *A. boisei* in East Africa. Furthermore, a skull of early *Homo erectus* (*Homo ergaster*) (KNM-ER 3733) had been found in the same stratigraphic horizon as the *A. boisei* skull, KNM-ER 406 at Koobi Fora, Kenya (Leakey and Walker, 1976). The morphological variation of contemporaneous Plio-Pleistocene hominins was now too great, and the temporal duration too long, to be compatible with the 'single species hypothesis'.

For a few years in the late 1970s, it seemed clear that *A. africanus* was the probable common ancestor of the 'robust' australopithecines on the one hand and *Homo habilis* on the other (Eldredge and Tattersall, 1975; Delson et al., 1977; Tattersall and Eldredge, 1977) (Figure 2c). However, the announcement of *A. afarensis* in 1978 resulted in yet another phylogenetic rethink. *A. afarensis* was not only older than *A. africanus*, but also more primitive. In 1979 Johanson and White put forward the hypothesis that *A. afarensis* was the common ancestor of all of the other australopithecines on the one hand and of *Homo* on the other (Johanson and White, 1979) (Figure 2d). In contrast, Tobias (1980) argued that *A. afarensis* was just an East African variant of the South African *A. africanus* and continued to support the idea that *A. africanus* was the common ancestor of *Homo* and the 'robust' australopithecines. Other anthropologists thought that the phylogeny was more complicated and recognised more than one species in the *A. afarensis* collection of fossils. In

particular, Olson (1981) argued that both *Homo* and *A. africanus* were present, the smaller *A. afarensis* fossils representing an early species of *Homo* which lead through *A. africanus* (reclassified as *Homo africanus* by Olson) to modern humans. The larger *A. afarensis* fossils represented an early species of *Paranthropus* that was ancestral to the later robust forms (see also Falk, 1986, 1987).

During the 1980s there were numerous attempts to determine australopithecine phylogeny through the application of cladistic methodology (e.g. Skelton, McHenry and Drawhorn, 1986; Wood and Chamberlain, 1986). These analyses tended to produce conflicting results that depended primarily on which aspects of cranial morphology were used in the analyses. The phylogenetic confusion has been compounded more recently by the discovery of additional australopithecine taxa, and particularly by the discovery of the 'Black Skull' (KNM-WT 17000) in 1985 and the resulting acceptance of the taxon *Australopithecus aethiopicus,* by *Australopithecus anamensis* in 1995 and by *Australopithecus garhi* in 1999. Figure 3 illustrates two recent cladograms depicting the relationships between the various taxa. The cladistic hypothesis put forward by Wood and Collard (1999) (Figure 3a) illustrates a monophylum *Homo ergaster* and all more recent members of the genus *Homo,* a monophylum for the 'robust' australopithecines (paranthropines), an equivocal position for *Australopithecus habilis* and *Australopithecus rudolfensis* and a more primitive basal position for *Australopithecus africanus* and *Australopithecus afarensis.* Note that these authors follow Strait et al. (1997) in preferring the nomen *Praeanthropus africanus* for *Australopithecus afarensis* and also employ *Paranthropus* as the genus for the 'robust' australopithecines. This nomenclature avoids the problem of paraphyly for the genus *Australopithecus* and accurately reflects the branching patterns in their cladistic hypothesis. They recognise, however, that by

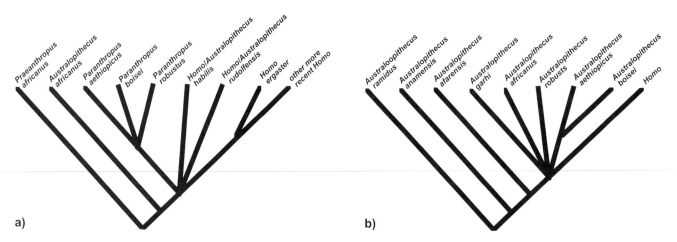

Figure 3.   *Two recently published cladograms depicting relationships between hominin taxa. (a) after Wood and Collard (1999), (b) after Suwa et al. (1999). See text for discussion.*

transferring *Homo habilis* and *Homo rudolfensis* to the genus *Australopithecus* they are resurrecting the paraphyletic nature of the genus *Australopithecus* (Wood and Collard, 1999).

The second cladogram (Figure 4b) includes both *Ardipithecus ramidus* and *Australopithecus garhi* (Asfaw et al., 1999). With the exception of the sister group relationship between *Australopithecus aethiopicus* and *Australopithecus boisei,* it postulates an unresolved polychotomy for *Australopithecus garhi* and all more recent australopithecines and *Homo*. Figure 4 provides some alternative phylogenies from Asfaw et al. (1999) some of which the authors note are not consistent with their cladogram. At present all that can be concluded is that it is not possible to resolve the phylogenetic relationships of the australopithecines with any degree of certainty. One implication of these phylogenetic uncertainties is the realisation of the 'bushiness' of hominin evolution. It is also inevitable that additional species remain to be discovered.

On the basis of present evidence it is probable that all of the australopithecines represent a single grade of evolution that was not only different from that of the genus *Homo* but also different from any extant primate. They mixed bipedal locomotion with an apparent arboreal capability, occupied a spectrum of habitats from closed forest to relatively open woodland, had a level of encephalization that was within the range of living primates (Aiello and Wheeler, 1995), and most probably had not developed the extended periods of infant dependency that are characteristic of modern humans. The major difference among the species is in the size of their masticatory apparatus which indicates an increasing reliance on foodstuffs requiring a greater degree of masticatory force in the later robust forms. This trend may have arisen in response both to environmental change and to competition not only with members of the genus *Homo*, but also with other terrestrial primates that were contemporaneous with them in both South and East Africa. The australopithecines represented a highly successful hominin adaptation that lasted for well over 3 million years. The only obvious explanation for their ultimate disappearance is that they finally lost the competitive struggle with the other primates, including members of the genus *Homo*, that were occupying similar niches in the African early Pleistocene.

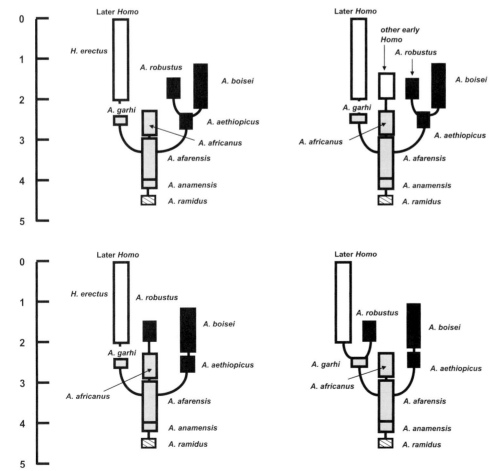

Figure 4. *Some possible alternative phylogenies for hominin evolution (after Suwa et al., 1999).*

ACKNOWLEDGMENTS

We would like to thank Professor Emiliano Aguirre for inviting LA to speak at the International Symposium of the Ramón Areces Foundation in Madrid (11–13 March, 1998) and for the opportunity to prepare this paper for publication. We would also like to thank the Ramón Areces Foundation for making the symposium possible and for outstanding hospitality while in Madrid. We are also grateful to Bernard Wood and Mark Collard for numerous stimulating discussions on the problems and pitfalls of hominin cladistics and phylogenetic reconstruction.

REFERENCES

Abitbol, M. M. 1995. Lateral view of *Australopithecus afarensis:* primitive aspects of bipedal positional behavior in the earliest hominids. *Journal of Human Evolution* **28:** 211–229.

Aiello, L. C. 1992. Size and shape in human evolution. *Journal of Human Evolution* **22:** 127–147.

Aiello, L. C. 1994a. Variable but singular. *Nature* **368:** 399–400.

Aiello, L. C. 1994b. Thumbs up for our early ancestors. *Science* **265:** 1540–1541.

Aiello, L. C. and Dean, M. C. 1990. *An Introduction to Human Evolutionary Anatomy.* London: Academic Press.

Aiello, L. C. and Wheeler P. 1995. The expensive-tissue hypothesis: the brain and the digestive system in human and primate evolution. *Current Anthropology* **36.**

Aiello, L. C., Wood, B. A., Key, C. and Lewis, M. 1999. Morphological and taxonomic affinities of the Olduvai ulna (OH 36). *American Journal of Physical Anthropology* **109:** 89–110.

Andrews, P. 1989. Palaeoecology of Laetoli (Lead Review). *Journal of Human Evolution* **18:** 173–181.

Arambourg, C. and Coppens, Y. 1968. Découverte d'un Australopithécien nouveau dans les gisements de l'Omo (Ethiopie). *South African Journal of Science* **64:** 58–59.

Asfaw, B. 1985. Proximal femur articulation in Pliocene hominids. *American Journal of Physical Anthropology* **68:** 535–538.

Asfaw, B., White, T., Lovejoy, O, Latimer, B., Simpson, S. and Suwa, G. 1999. *Australopithecus garhi:* A new species of early hominid from Ethiopia. *Science* **284:** 629–635.

Bartholomew, G. A. and Birdsell, J. B. 1953. Ecology and the proto-hominids. *American Anthropologist* **55:** 481–498.

Berge, C. and. Kazmierczak, J.-B. 1986. Effects of size and locomotor adaptations on the hominid pelvis: evaluation of australopithecine bipedality with a new multivariate method. *Folia Primatologia* **46:** 185–204.

Berger, C., Orban-Segebarth, R. and Schmid, P. 1984. Obstetrical interpretation of the australopithecine pelvic cavity. *Journal of Human Evolution* **13:** 573–587.

Berger, L. R. and Clarke, R. J. 1995. Birds of prey and the taphonomy of the Taung child. *Journal of Human Evolution* **29:** 275–299.

Berger, L. R. and Tobias, P. V. 1996. A chimpanzee-like tibia from Sterkfontein, South Africa and its implications for the interpretation of bipedalism in *Australopithecus africanus. Journal of Human Evolution.* **30.** 343–348.

Berger, L. R., Menter, C. G. and Thackeray, J. F. 1994. The renewal of excavation activities at Kromdraai, South Africa. *South African Journal of Science* **90:** 209–210.

Berger, L. R., Keyser A. W. and Tobias, P. V. 1993. Brief Communication: Gladysvale: First Early Hominid Site Discovered in South African Since 1948. *American Journal of Physical Anthropology* **92:** 107–111

Behrensmeyer, A. K., 1985. Taphonomy and the paleoecologic reconstruction of hominid habitats in the Koobi Fora Formation. In *L'Environment des Hominidés au Plio-Pléistocene* (Y. Coppens, ed.) Paris: Masson, pp. 309–324.

Bellomo, R. V. 1994. Methods of determining early hominid behavioral activities associated with the controlled use of fire at FxJj 20 Main, Koobi Fora, Kenya. *Journal of Human Evolution* **27:** 173–196.

Boas, N. 1988. The status of *Australopithecus afarensis. Yearbook of Physical Anthropology.* **31:** 85–113.

Brain, C. K. 1993a. *Swartkrans: A Cave's Chronicle of Early Man.* Transvaal Museum Monograph No. 8. Transvaal Museum, Pretoria.

Brain, C. K. 1993b. The occurrence of burnt bones at Swartkrans and their implications for the control of fire by early hominids. In *Swartkrans: A Cave's Chronicle of Early Man* (C. K. Brain, ed.) Transvaal Museum Monograph No. 8. pp. 229–242.

Brain, C. K. 1994. The Swartkrans Palaeontological research project in perspective: results and conclusions. *South African Journal of Science* **90:** 220–223.

Brain, C. K. and Shipman, P. 1993. The Swartkrans bone tools. In *Swartkrans: A Cave's Chronicle of Early Man* (C. K. Brain, ed.) Transvaal Museum Monograph No. 8. pp. 195–216.

Broom, R. 1937. The Sterkfontein ape. *Nature* **136:** 326.

Broom, R. and Schepers, G. W. H. 1946. *The South African Fossil Ape-Man. The Australopithecinae. Part I. The Occurrence and General Structure of the South African Ape-Men.* Transvaal Museum Memoir 2.

Brunet, M., Beauvilain, A., Coppens, Y., Heintz, E., Moutaye, A. H. E. and Pilbeam, D. 1995. The first australopithecine 2,500 kilometers west of the rift valley (Chad). *Nature* **378:** 273–275.

Cerling, T. 1992. Development of grasslands and savannas in East Africa during the Neogene. *Palaeogeography, Palaeoclimatology and Palaeoecology* **97:** 241–247.

Chaplin, G., Jablonski, N. G. and Cable, N. T. 1994. Physiology, thermoregulation and bipedalism. *Journal of Human Evolution* **27:** 497–510.

Clarke, R. J. 1988. A new *Australopithecus* cranium from Sterkfontein and its bearing on the ancestry of *Paranthropus.* In *Evolutionary History of the 'Robust' Australopithecines* (F. Grine, ed.). New York: Aldine de Gruyter, pp. 285–292.

Clarke, R. J. 1994. On some new interpretations of Sterkfontein stratigraphy. *South African Journal of Science* **90:** 211–214.

Clarke, R. J. and Tobias, P. V. 1995. Sterkfontein Member 2 foot bones of the oldest South African hominid. *Science* **269:** 521–524.

Conroy, G. C., Weber, G. W., Seidler, H., Tobias, P. V., Kane, A. and Brunsden, B. 1998. Endocranial capacity in an early hominid cranium from Sterkfontein, South Africa. *Science* **280:** 1730–1731.

Dart, R. A. 1925. *Australopithecus africanus:* the man-ape of South Africa. *Nature* **115:** 195–199.

Dean, M. C. 1985. The eruption pattern of the permanent incisors and first permanent molars in *Paranthropus robustus. American Journal of Physical Anthropology* **54:** 63–71.

Dean, M. C., Beynon, A. D., Thackeray, J. F. and Macho, G. A. 1993. Histological reconstruction of dental development and age at death of a juvenile *Paranthropus robustus* specimen, SK 63, from Swartkrans, South Africa. *American Journal of Physical Anthropology* **91:** 401–419.

Delson, E. 1986. Human phylogeny revised again. *Nature* **322:** 496–497.

Delson, E., Eldredge, N. and Tattersall, I. 1977. Reconstruction of hominid phylogeny: a testable framework based on cladistic analysis. *Journal of Human Evolution* **6:** 263–278.

DuBrul, E. L. 1962. The general phenomenon of bipedalism. *American Zoologist* **2:** 205–208.

Eldredge, N. and Tattersall, I. 1975. Evolutionary models, phylogenetic reconstruction and another look at hominid phylogeny. *Contributions to Primatology* **5:** 218–242.

Falk, D. 1985. Apples, oranges and the lunate sulcus. *American Journal of Physical Anthropology* **67:** 313–315.

Falk, D. 1986. Evolution of cranial blood drainage in hominids: enlarged occipital/marginal sinuses and emissary foramina. *American Journal of Physical Anthropology* **70:** 311–324.

Falk, D. 1987. Hominid palaeooneurology. *Annual Review of Anthropology* **16:** 13–30.

Foley, R. 1987. *Another Unique Species*. Harlow, Essex: Longman Group Limited.

Gee, H. 1995a. Uprooting the human family tree. *Nature* **373**: 15.

Gee, H. 1995b. New hominid remains found in Ethiopia. *Nature* **373**: 272.

Grausz, H. M., Leakey, R. E., Walker, A. C. and Ward, C. V. 1988. Associated cranial and postcranial bones of *Australopithecus boisei*. In: *Evolutionary History of the 'Robust' Australopithecines* (F. E. Grine, ed.) New York: Aldine de Gruyter, pp. 127–132.

Grine, F. 1982. A new juvenile hominid (Mammalia: Primates) from Member 3, Kromdraai Formation, Transvaal, South Africa. *Annals of the Transvaal Museum* **33**: 165–239.

Grine, F. E. 1985. Australopithecine evolution: the deciduous dental evidence. In *Ancestors: The Hard Evidence* (E. Delson, ed.) New York: Alan R. Liss, pp. 153–167.

Harris, J. W. K. and Capaldo, S. D. 1993. The earliest stone tools: their implications for an understanding of the activities and behaviour of late Pliocene hominids. In *The Use of Tools by Human and Non-Human Primates* (A. Berthelet and J. Chavaillon, eds.) Oxford: Clarendon Press, pp. 196–220.

Hausler, M. and Schmid, P. 1995. Comparison of the pelves of Sts 14 and AL 288-1: Implications for birth and sexual dimorphism in australopithecines. *Journal of Human Evolution*. **29**: 363–383.

Hay, R. L. and Leakey, M. D. 1988. The fossil footprints of Laetoli. *Scientific American* **246**: 38–45.

Heinzelin, J. de, Clark, J. D., White, T., Hart, W., Renne, P., WoldeGabriel, G., Beyene, Y. and Vrba, E. 1999. Environment and behavior of 2.5 million year old Bouri hominids, *Science* **284**: 625–629.

Holloway, R. 1973. Endocranial volumes of early African hominids and the role of the brain in human mosaic evolution. *Journal of Human Evolution* **2**: 449–458.

Holloway, R. L. 1985. The past, present and future significance of the lunate sulcus in early hominid evolution. In *Hominid Evolution: Past, Present and Future* (P. V. Tobias, ed.) New York: Alan R. Liss, pp. 47–62.

Hunt, K. 1994. The evolution of human bipedality: ecology and functional morphology. *Journal of Human Evolution* **26**: 183–202.

Isbell, L. A. and Young, T. P. 1996. The evolution of bipedalism in hominids and reduced group size in chimpanzees—alternative responses to decreasing resource availability. *Journal of Human Evolution* **30**: 389–397.

Jablonski, N. G. and Chaplin, G. 1993. Origin of habitual terrestrial bipedalism in the ancestor of the Hominidae. *Journal of Human Evolution* **24**: 259–280.

Johanson, D. C., White, T. and Coppens, Y. 1978. A new species of the genus *Australopithecus* (Primates: Hominidae) from the Pliocene of eastern Africa. *Kirklandia*, no. 28, pp. 1–14.

Johanson, D. C. and White, T. D. 1979. A systematic assessment of early African hominids. *Science* **203**: 321–330.

Jolly, C. J. 1970. The seed-eaters: a new model of hominid differentiation based on a baboon analogy. *Man* **5**: 1–26.

Jungers, W. L. 1982. Lucy's limbs: skeletal allometry and locomotion in *Australopithecus afarensis*. *Nature* **297**: 676–678.

Kimbel, W. H., White, T. C. and Johanson, D. C. 1984. Cranial morphology of *Australopithecus afarensis*: a comparative study based on a composite reconstruction of the adult skull. *American Journal of Physical Anthropology* **64**: 337–388.

Kimbel, W. H., White T. D. and Johanson, D. C. 1988. Implications of KNM-WT 17000 for the evolution of 'robust' australopithecines. In *The Evolutionary History of the 'Robust' Australopithecines* (F. Grine, ed.) New York: Aldine de Gruyter, pp. 259–268.

Kimbel, W. H., Johanson, D. C. and Rak, Y. 1994. The first skull and other new discoveries of *Australopithecus afarensis* at Hadar, Ethiopia. *Nature* **368**: 449–451.

Kuykendall, K. L. 1999. Description of the Gondolin teeth: Hyper-robust hominids in South Africa? *American Journal of Physical Anthropology* **108(28)**: 176–177 (abstract).

Kuman, K. 1994. The archaeology of Sterkfontein—past and present. *Journal of Human Evolution* **27**: 471–495.

Lague, M. R. and Jungers, W. L. 1996. Morphometric variation in Plio-Pleistocene hominid distal humeri. *American Journal of Physical Anthropology* **101**: 401–427.

Lampl, M., Monge, J. M. and Mann, A. E. 1993. Further observations on a method for estimating hominoid dental developmental patterns. *American Journal of Physical Anthropology* **90**: 113–128.

Latimer, B., Ohman, J. C. and Lovejoy, C. O. 1987. Talocrural joint in African hominoids: implications for *Australopithecus afarensis*. *American Journal of Physical Anthropology* **74**: 155–175.

Leakey, L. S. B. 1959. A new fossil skull from Olduvai. *Nature* **184**: 491–493.

Leakey, M. G., Feibel, C. S., McDougall, I., and Walker, A. 1995. New 4-million year old hominid species from Kanapoi and Allia Bay, Kenya. *Nature* **376**: 565–571.

Leakey, M. G., Feibel, C. S., McDougall, I., Ward, C. and Walker, A. 1998. New specimens and confirmation of an early age for *Australopithecus anamensis*. *Nature* **393**: 62–66.

Leakey, R. E. F. and Walker, A. C. 1976. *Australopithecus* and the single species hypothesis. *Nature* **261**: 572–574.

Lee-Thorpe, J. and van der Merwe, N. J. 1993. Stable carbon isotope studies of Swartkrans fossils. In *Swartkrans: A Cave's Chronicle of Early Man* (C. K. Brain, ed.) Transvaal Museum Monograph No. 8. pp. 251–256.

Lee-Thorpe, J., van der Merwe, N. J. and Brain, C. K. 1994. Diet of *Australopithecus robustus* at Swartkrans from stable carbon isotopic analysis. *Journal of Human Evolution* **27**: 361–372.

Lockwood, C. A. 1999. Sexual dimorphism in the face of *Australopithecus africanus*. *American Journal of Physical Anthropology* **108**: 97–127.

Lovejoy, C. O. 1974. The gait of australopithecines. *Yearbook of Physical Anthropology* **17**: 147–161.

Lovejoy, C. O. 1981. The origin of man. *Science* **211**: 341–350.

Lovejoy, C. O. 1988. Evolution of human walking. *Scientific American* **259**: 82–89.

Leutenegger, W. 1987. Neonatal brain size and neurocranial dimensions in Pliocene hominids: implications for obstetrics. *Journal of Human Evolution* **16**: 291–296.

MacLatchy, L. M. 1996. Another look at the australopithecine hip. *Journal of Human Evolution*. **31**: 455–476.

Marzke, M. W. 1986. Tool use and the evolution of hominid hands and bipedality. In *Primate Evolution* (J. Else and P. Lee, eds.) Cambridge: Cambridge University Press, pp. 203–209.

McHenry, H. 1982. The pattern of human evolution: studies on bipedalism, mastication, and encephalization. *Annual Review of Anthropology* **11**: 151–173.

McHenry, H. 1992. Body size and proportions in early hominids. *American Journal of Physical Anthropology* **87**: 407–431.

McHenry, H. 1994. Behavioral ecological implications of early hominid body size. *Journal of Human Evolution* **27**: 77–87.

McHenry, H. and Berger L. R. 1998a. Limb lengths in *Australopithecus* and the origin of the genus *Homo*. *South African Journal of Science* **94**: 447–450.

McHenry, H. M. and Berger L. R. 1998b. Body proportions in *Australopithecus afarensis* and *A. africanus* and the origin of the genus *Homo*. *Journal of Human Evolution* **35**: 1–22.

McKee, J. K. and Tobias, P. V. 1994. Taung stratigraphy and taphonomy: preliminary results based on the 1988–1993 excavations. *South African Journal of Science* **90**: 233–235.

McKee, J., Thackeray, F. and Berger, L. 1995. Faunal assemblage seriation of southern African Pliocene and Pleistocene fossil deposits. *American Journal of Physical Anthropology* **96**: 235–250.

Olson, T. R. 1981. Basicranial morphology of the extant hominoids and Pliocene hominids: the new material from the Hadar formation, Ethiopia, and its significance in early human evolution and taxonomy. In *Aspects of Human Evolution* (C. B. Stringer, ed.) London: Taylor and Francis, pp. 99–128.

Pilbeam, D. 1972. *The Ascent of Man*. New York: Macmillan.

Plummer, T. W. and Bishop, L. C. 1994. Hominid paleoecology at Olduvai Gorge, Tanzania as indicated by antelope remains. *Journal of Human Evolution* **27**: 47–75.

Potts, R. 1998. Environmental hypotheses of hominin evolution. *Yearbook of Physical Anthropology*. **41**: 93–136.

Rak, Y. 1983. *The Australopithecine Face*. Academic Press, London.

Ravey, M. 1978. Bipedalism: an early warning system for Miocene hominoids. *Science*, **199**: 372.

Rayner, R. J., Moon, B. P. and Masters, J. C. 1993. The Makapansgat australopithecine environment. *Journal of Human Evolution* **24**: 219–231.

Reed, K. E. 1997. Early hominid evolution and ecological change through the African Plio-Pleistocene. *Journal of Human Evolution* **32**: 289–322.

Robinson, J. T. 1960. The affinities of the new Olduvai australopithecine. *Nature* **186**: 456–458.

Robinson, J. T., 1963. Adaptive radiation in the australopithecines and the origin of man. In *African Ecology and Evolution* (G. Kurth, ed.) Stuttgart: Gustav Fischer, pp. 120–140.

Robinson, J. T. 1972. *Early Hominid Posture and Locomotion.* Chicago: University of Chicago Press.

Rodman, P. S. and McHenry, H. M. 1980. Bioenergetics and the origin of hominid bipedalism. *American Journal of Physical Anthropology* **52:** 103–106.

Rogers, M. J., Feibel, C. S. and Harris, J. W. K. 1994. Changing patterns of land use by Plio-Pleistocene hominids in the Lake Turkana Basin. *Journal of Human Evolution* **27:** 139–158.

Rose, M. D. 1991. The process of bipedalization in hominids. In *Origine(s) de la Bipedie chez les Hominides (Cahiers de Paleoanthropologie* (Y. Coppens and B. Senut, eds.) Paris: Editions du CNRS, pp. 37–48.

Schmid, P. 1983. Eine Rekonstrucktion des Skelettes von A. L. 288-1 (Hadar) und deren Konsequenzen. *Folia Primatologia* **40:** 283–306.

Schmid, P. 1991. The trunk of the australopithecines. In *Origine(s) de la bipedie chez les hominides* (Y. Coppens and B. Senut, eds.) Paris: Éditions du CNRS, pp. 225–234.

Schrenk, R., Bromage, T. G., Betzler, C. G., Ring, U. and Juwayeyi, Y. 1993. Oldest *Homo* and Pliocene biogeography of the Malawi Rift. *Nature* **365:** 833–836.

Senut, B. and Tardieu, C. 1985. Functional aspects of Plio-Pleistocene hominid limb bones: implications for taxonomy and phylogeny. In *Ancestors, The Hard Evidence* (E. Delson, ed.) New York: Alan R. Liss, pp. 193–201.

Shipman, P. and Harris, J. M. 1988. Habitat preference and paleoecology of *Australopithecus boisei* in Eastern Africa. In *Evolutionary History of the 'Robust' Australopithecines* (F. Grine, ed.) New York: Aldine de Gruyter, pp. 343–382.

Sikes, N. E. 1994. Early hominid habitat preferences in East Africa: Paleosol carbon isotopic evidence. *Journal of Human Evolution* **27:** 25–45.

Sillen, A. and Hoering, T. 1993. Chemical characterization of burnt bones from Swartkrans. In *Swartkrans: A Cave's Chronicle of Early Man* (C. K. Brain, ed.) Transvaal Museum Monograph No. 8. pp. 243–250.

Sinclair, A. R. E, Leakey, M. D. and Norton-Griffiths, M. 1986. Migration and hominid bipedalism. *Nature* **324:** 307–308.

Skelton, R. R. and McHenry, H. M. 1992. Evolutionary relationships among early hominids. *Journal of Human Evolution* **23:** 309–350.

Skelton, R. R., McHenry, H. M. and Drawhorn, G. M. 1986. Phylogenetic analysis of early hominids. *Current Anthropology* **27:** 21–43.

Smith, B. H. 1994. Patterns of dental development in *Homo, Australopithecus, Pan,* and *Gorilla. American Journal of Physical Anthropology* **94:** 307–326.

Sponheimer, M. and Lee-Thorpe, J. 1999. Isotopic evidence for the diet of an early hominid, *Australopithecus africanus. Science* **283:** 368–370.

Stern, J. T. and Susman, R. L. 1983. The locomotor anatomy of *Australopithecus afarensis. American Journal of Physical Anthropology* **60:** 279–317.

Strait, D. S., Grine, F. E. and Moniz, M. A. 1997. A reappraisal of early hominid phylogeny. *Journal of Human Evolution* **32:** 17–82.

Steudel, K. L. 1994. Locomotor energetics and hominid evolution. *Evolutionary Anthropology* **3:** 42–48.

Susman, R. L. 1988. Hand of *Paranthropus robustus* from Member 1, Swartkrans: fossil evidence for tool behavior. *Science* **240:** 781–784.

Susman, R. L. 1994. Fossil evidence for early hominid tool use. *Science* **265:** 1570–1573.

Suwa, G., White, T. D. and Howell, F. C. 1996. Mandibular postcanine dentition from the Shungura Formation, Ethiopia: Crown morphology, taxonomic allocations, and Plio-Pleistocene hominid evolution. *American Journal of Physical Anthropology* **101:** 247–282.

Suwa, G., Asfaw, B., Beyene, Y., White, T. D., Katoh, S., Nagaoka, S., Nakaya, H., Uzawa, K., Renne, P. and WoldeGabriel, G. 1997. The first skull of *Australopithecus boisei. Nature* **389:** 489–492.

Tague, R. G. and Lovejoy, C. O. 1986. The obstetric pelvis of A. L. 288-1 (Lucy). *Journal of Human Evolution* **15:** 237–255.

Tattersall, I. and Eldredge, N. 1977. Fact, theory and fantasy in human paleontology. *American Scientist* **65:** 204–211.

Tobias, P. V. 1967. *Olduvai Gorge. Vol 2: The Cranium and Maxillary Dentition of Australopithecus (Zinjanthropus) boisei.* Cambridge University Press: Cambridge.

Tobias, P. V. 1981. *"Australopithecus afarensis"* and *A. africanus:* critique and an alternative hypothesis. *Palaeontol. Afr.* **23:** 1–17.

Trinkaus, E. and Long, J. C. 1990. Species attribution of the Swartkrans Member 1 first metacarpals: SK 84 and SKX 5020. *American Journal of Physical Anthropology* **83:** 419–424.

Tuttle, R. H. 1981. Evolution of hominid bipedalism and prehensile capabilities. *Philosophical Transactions of the Royal Society B* **292:** 89–94.

Vrba, E., 1982. Biostratigraphy and chronology, based particularly on Bovidae, of southern hominid-associated assemblages: Makapansgat, Sterkfontein, Taung, Kromdraai, Swartkrans; also Elandsfontein (Saldanah), Broken Hill (now Kabwe) and Cave of Hearths. *Congres International de Paléontologie Humaine, 1er Congres.* Tome 1, pp. 707–752, Nice: CNRS.

Walker, A. and Leakey, R. E. 1988. The evolution of *Australopithecus boisei.* In *The Evolutionary History of the 'Robust' Australopithecines* (F. Grine, ed.) New York: Aldine de Gruyter, pp. 247–258.

Walker, A., Leakey, R. E., Harris, J. M. and Brown, F. H. 1986. 2.5 Myr *Australopithecus boisei* from west of Lake Turkana, Kenya. *Nature* **322:** 517–522.

Washburn, S. L. 1967. Behavior and the origin of man. *Proceedings of the Royal Anthropological Institute* **3:** 21–27.

Wescott, R. W. 1967. The exhibitionistic origin of human bipedalism. *Man* **2:** 630.

Wheeler, P. E. 1984. The evolution of bipedality and loss of functional body hair in hominids. *Journal of Human Evolution* **13:** 91–98.

Wheeler, P. E. 1991a. The thermoregulatory advantages of hominid bipedalism in open equatorial environments: the contribution of increased convective heat loss and cutaneous evaporative cooling. *Journal of Human Evolution* **21:** 107–115.

Wheeler, P. E. 1991b. The influence of bipedalism on the energy and water budgets of early hominids. *Journal of Human Evolution* **21:** 116–136.

Wheeler, P. E. 1992a. The influence of the loss of functional body hair on the energy and water budgets of early hominids. *Journal of Human Evolution* **23:** 379–388.

Wheeler, P. E. 1992b. The thermoregulatory advantages of large body size for hominids foraging in savannah environments. *Journal of Human Evolution* **23:** 351–362.

Wheeler, P. E. 1993. The influence of stature and body form on hominid energy and water budgets: a comparison of *Australopithecus* and early *Homo* physiques. *Journal of Human Evolution* **24:** 13–28.

Wheeler, P. E. 1994a. The thermoregulatory advantages of heat storage and shade-seeking behaviour to hominids foraging in equatorial savannah environments. *Journal of Human Evolution* **26:** 339–350.

Wheeler, P. E. 1994b. The foraging times of bipedal and quadrupedal hominids in open equatorial environments (a reply to Chaplin, Jablonski and Cable, 1994. *Journal of Human Evolution* **27:** 511–518.

White, T. D. and Suwa, G. 1987. Hominid footprints at Laetoli: facts and interpretations. *American Journal of Physical Anthropology* **72:** 485–514.

White, T. D., Suwa, G., Hart, W. K., Walter, R. C., WoldeGabriel, G., Heinzelin, J. de, Clark, J. D., Asfaw, B. and Vrba, E. 1993. New discoveries of *Australopithecus* at Maka in Ethiopia. *Nature* **366:** 261–265.

White, T. D., Suwa, G. and Asfaw, B. 1994. *Australopithecus ramidus,* a new species of early hominid from Aramis, Ethiopia. *Nature* **371:** 280–281.

White, T. D., Suwa, G. and Asfaw, B. 1995. *Australopithecus ramidus,* a new species of early hominid from Aramis, Ethiopia (correction). *Nature* **375:** 88.

Wolpoff, M. H. 1968. *Telanthropus* and the single species hypothesis. *American Anthropologist* **70:** 477–493.

Wood, B. A. 1991. *Koobi Fora Research Project, Vol. 4: Hominid Cranial Remains.* Oxford: Clarendon Press.

Wood, B. A. 1993. Four legs good, two legs better. *Nature* **363:** 587–588.

Wood, B. A. 1994. The oldest hominid yet. *Nature* **371:** 280–281.

Wood, B. A. and Chamberlain, A. T. 1986. *Australopithecus:* grade or clade? In *Major Topics in Primate and Human Evolution* (B. A. Wood, L. Martin and P. Andrews, eds.) Cambridge: Cambridge University Press, pp. 220–248.

Wood, B. A. and Aiello, L. C. 1998. Taxonomic and functional implications of mandibular scaling in early hominins. *American Journal of Physical Anthropology* **105:** 523–538.

Wood, B. A. and Collard, M. 1999. The human genus. *Science,* **284:** 65–71.

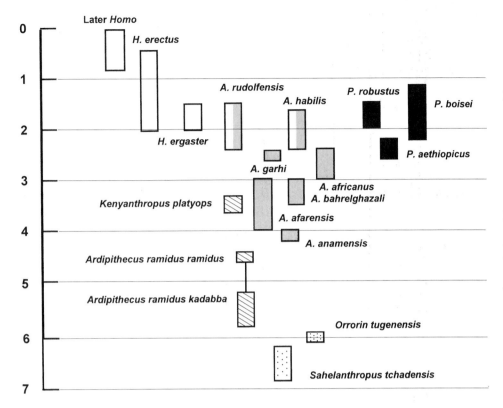

Figure 5. *Plot of approximate time ranges of the hominin species. Black boxes = 'robust' australopithecines (paranthropines), grey boxes = 'gracile' australopithecines, empty boxes = * Homo, *and stippled and hatched boxes = hominins belonging to genera other than* Homo *or* Australopithecus. *The half-grey boxes represent* Australopithecus habilis *and* Australopithecus rudolfensis *that have been transferred recently from the genus* Homo *(Wood and Collard, 1999). Similarities between* Kenyanthropus platyops *and* Australopithecus rudolfensis *suggest that* A. rudolfensis *might represent a later-occurring species of* Kenyanthropus *(Lieberman, 2001).*

APPENDIX: EARLY HOMININ UPDATE

Since the first publication of this paper in 2000, four new taxa of early hominin have been announced (Figure 5). The first of these is a new genus and species, *Kenyanthropus platyops,* from West Turkana in Kenya, that dates to between 3.5 and 3.4 Ma (Leakey et al., 2001; see also Lieberman, 2001). The second is another new genus and species, *Orrorin tugenensis,* from the Lukeino Formation of the Tugen Hills in Kenya, that dates to about 6 Ma (Senut et al., 2001; see also Aiello and Collard, 2001). The third is a new subspecies of *Ardipithecus ramidus, Ardipitheus ramidus kadabba,* from the Middle Awash area of Ethiopia, that dates between 5.2 and 5.7 Ma (Haile-Selassie, 2001; see also Gee, 2001). The last is another new genus and species, *Sahelanthropus tchadensis,* from Toros-Menalla in the Djurab Desert in Chad, that dates between 6 and 7 Ma (Brunet, 2002; see also, Wood 2002).

These new discoveries considerably extend the temporal and geographic range of known hominins and demonstrate a large degree of morphological diversity among them. If the hominin status of all of the new taxa stands up to detailed analysis, we will have at least 14 known hominin species that fall into 5 genera (*Sahelanthropus, Orrorin, Ardipithecus, Australopithecus,* including *Paranthropus,* and *Kenyanthropus*) from Africa that either predate or are contemporaneous with the first convincing member of the genus *Homo, Homo ergaster* (early African *Homo erectus;* Wood and Collard, 1999). These discoveries strongly suggest that the course of early human evolution was more complicated than previously thought. The number of new taxa that have been recently found also suggests that additional hominin species remain to be discovered.

REFERENCES

Aiello, L. C. and Collard, M. 2001. Palaeoanthropology—our newest oldest ancestor? *Nature* 410: 526–527.

Brunet, M., Guy, F., Pilbeam, D., Mackaye, H. T., Likius, A., Ahounta, D., Beauvilain, A., Blondel, C., Bocherens, H., Boisserie, J.-R., De Bonis, L., Coppens, Y., Dejax, J., Denys, C., Duringer, P., Eisenmann, V., Fanone, G., Fronty, P., Geraads, D., Lehmann, T., Lihoreau, F., Louchart, A., Mahamat, A., Merceron, G., Mouchelin, G., Otero, O., Pelaez Campomanes, P., Ponce De Leon, M., Rage, J.-C., Sapanet, M., Schuster, M., Sudre, J., Tassy, P., Valentin, X., Vignaud, P., Viriot, L., Zazzo, A. and Zollikofer, C. 2002. A new hominid from the Upper Miocene of Chad, Central Africa. *Nature* 418: 145–151.

Gee, H. 2001. Palaeontology—return to the planet of the apes. *Nature* 412: 131–132.

Haile-Selassie, Y. 2001. Late Miocene hominids from the Middle Awash, Ethiopia. *Nature* 412: 178–181.

Leakey, G. M., Spoor, F., Brown, F. H., Gathogo, P. N., Kiarie, C., Leakey, L. N. and McDougall, I. 2001. New hominin genus from eastern Africa shows diverse middle Pliocene lineages. *Nature* 410: 433–440.

Lieberman, D. E. 2001. Another face in our family tree. *Nature* 410: 419–420.

Senut, B., Pickford, M., Gommery, D., Mein, P., Cheboi, K. and Coppen, Y. 2001. First hominid from the Miocene (Lukeino Formation, Kenya). *C.R. Acad. Sci. II* A 332(2): 137–144.

Wood, B. 2002. Hominid revelations from Chad. *Nature* 418: 133–135.

Wood, B. and Collard, M. 1999. The human genus. *Science* 284: 65–71.

17

The New Hominid Species
Australopithecus anamensis

C. Ward, M. G. Leakey, and A. Walker

ABSTRACT

Australopithecus anamensis[1] *is the earliest species of this genus to have been found. Fossils attributed to* A. anamensis *have been recovered from sediments dating to between 3.8 and 4.2 mya at the sites of Kanapoi and Allia Bay in northern Kenya.* A. anamensis *is still poorly known in comparison with other early hominid species, but the material discovered so far displays primitive features along with more derived characteristics typical of later* Australopithecus *species. This mix of features suggests that* A. anamensis *belongs near the ancestry of this genus. Indeed, it may eventually be determined that this was the earliest* Australopithecus *species.*

HISTORICAL BACKGROUND

Bryan Patterson of Harvard University[2] found the first *A. anamensis* fossil, a distal humerus at Kanapoi in 1965. Patterson's expeditions were exploring the South Turkana localities of Lothagam, Kanapoi, and Ekora.[3,4] In 1967, Patterson thought the Kanapoi fauna dated to about 2.5 mya, based on whole-rock potassium-argon dates on the capping lava. This date was uncertain, however, because K/Ar determinations on relatively young rocks were difficult in those days, whole-rock determinations were even more so than those made on samples of sorted crystals. By 1970, the difficulty of dating the capping lava at Kanapoi, together with the early state of the development of a detailed paleomagnetic time scale, had created problems for Patterson's team. The later age determinations on the lava capping the sequence at Kanapoi had a wide spread, from greater than 2.9 ± 0.3 to 2.5 ± 0.2 mya, and thus could not be brought into concordance with the geomagnetic polarities then known. Luckily, however, the pioneering multidisciplinary program of deciphering the geological and faunal history of the Turkana Basin[5] had by then begun to bear fruit. Using faunal correlation with other dated sites, Patterson was able to estimate the age of the Kanapoi fauna to be between 4.0 and 4.5 mya.[4] The capping lava at Kanapoi is still recalcitrant to dating. McDougall[1] has carried out whole-rock $^{40}Ar/^{39}Ar$ dating and made

determinations of 3.11 ± 0.04 and 3.41 ± 0.04 mya, which he regards as minima for the actual age.

The Kanapoi fossil humerus was mentioned occasionally in reviews of the forearm anatomy of early hominids, with some researchers claiming *Homo* status for the fossil.[6] Still, the uncertainty about its geological age meant that the humerus received little attention. Apart from a brief exploratory expedition led by Richard Leakey in the early 1980s, which was cut short for security reasons, Kanapoi was not surveyed again until recently. One of us (M. G. L.) has led a series of expeditions to Kanapoi during each of the past four years. These expeditions have produced important new hominid fossils, including the holotype of *A. anamensis*, as well as new faunal specimens. They have also been important in allowing our colleagues Craig Feibel, of Rutgers University, and Ian McDougall, of the Australian National University, to undertake new geological and geochronological investigations.

Work at Allia Bay, East Lake Turkana, was part of the East Turkana Project, which was run by Richard Leakey and Glynn Isaac from 1968 onward. The site of 261-1 was discovered by J. Kithumbi, Kamoya Kimeu's brother-in-law. He found a single hominid upper molar on the surface where a pavement of bone fragments marked the place where a bone bed was exposed. This site lies near a Neolithic burial site and so, over the years, students and staff from the Koobi Fora Field School searched the surface and found a few more hominid teeth. Subsequent sieving of surface material at the site produced additional isolated hominid teeth. A small test trench yielded a small piece of mandible with two teeth in situ. Coffing and coworkers[7] described these early surface finds and attributed them to *Australopithecus* cf. *A. afarensis*. Still later, Musa Kyeva discovered a radius in beds that are laterally equivalent at the nearby Sibilot Hill. This radius was described and analyzed by Heinrich and colleagues,[8] who noted its similarities to other *Australopithecus* radii. Excavations at the Allia Bay 261-1 site were carried out for three seasons, from 1995 through 1997, and resulted in the recovery of a maxilla, more isolated teeth, and a more complete fauna. Craig Feibel and Ian McDougall were also involved in explicating the geology and dating at this site.

The list of hominid specimens attributed to *A. anamensis* is growing every season. It now includes several maxillae and mandibles, more than 50 isolated teeth, a piece of temporal bone, and parts of the humerus,

From C. Ward, M. G. Leakey, and A. Walker, *Evolutionary Anthropology,* Vol. 7, pp. 197–205. Copyright © 1999 by Wiley-Liss, Inc. This material is reprinted with permission of Wiley-Liss, Inc., a subsidiary of John Wiley & Sons, Inc.

radius, capitate, manual phalanx, and tibia from different individuals.[9]

GEOLOGICAL AND PALEOECOLOGICAL BACKGROUND

The two sites at which *A. anamensis* has been found are united by their geological setting. They can be placed in solid geological and temporal contexts, thanks to the pioneering work of Frank Brown, Craig Feibel, and their students and colleagues.

The present-day Lake Turkana lies in a basin that has had a varied history. There was a lake in this basin for only a small fraction of the last four million years.[10] Between 4.2 and 4.0 mya, a lake called Lonyumun filled the basin. The ancestral Kerio River drained into lake Lonyumun from the south, over time building a delta out into the lake. The fossiliferous sediments at Kanapoi are from channel deposits of this river, including those filling the dissected Miocene volcanics and those associated with the Kerio river delta. Three tuffaceous horizons have been dated by the single-crystal laser fusion ^{40}Ar/^{39}Ar method. The upper and lower of these dates bracket all but one of the Kanapoi hominid fossils to between 4.17 ± 0.03 and 4.07 ± 0.02 mya.[9] A presumed male mandible recovered from sediments immediately above the 4.07 mya tuff cannot be much younger than it is. Most of the fossil hominids are bracketed by the lower two of these dated tuffs, and so are dated to between 4.17 ± 0.03 and 4.12 ± 0.02 mya.[1]

The 261-1 site at Allia Bay was formed after the filling of Lonyumun lake. By about four million years ago, sediments from the ancient Omo, Turkwel, Kerio, and smaller rivers had filled the basin, and these rivers continued to flow over their extensive flood-plains. The ancestral Omo was then, as it is now, the dominant river.[10] The Allia Bay site is associated with a channel of this great river, and is probably a meander-splay concentration of bones. The bone bed itself consists primarily of bones of aquatic species, mainly fish and reptiles. Many of the fossils in this bed are rolled and weathered, indicating transport from a distance, reworking from older sediments, or both. At the top of the bed there are better-preserved fossils, including those of mammals, which probably are from animals that lived close to the channel.

The mainly fluvial sedimentary sequences at Allia Bay have tuffs in them. A thick outcrop of the Moiti Tuff is exposed in the hill just above the site and about 5 m stratigraphically above the bone bed. This has been dated elsewhere in the basin and near the source in the Ethiopian highlands to about 3.9 mya.[11] The age of the bone bed can be extrapolated, assuming uniform sedimentary rates, to $3.95 + 0.05$ mya. Thin tuffaceous horizons beneath the bone bed do not have crystals suitable for dating, but may provide correlative power through chemical fingerprinting (Craig Feibel, personal communication) and thus give a maximum age for the site.

The strata at Sibilot, where the radius was found,[8] are clearly bracketed by the Moiti and Lokochot Tuffs and are, therefore, between 3.92 ± 0.3 and $3.50 \pm .10$ mya. Further, Craig Feibel (personal communication) places the radius site below the Topernawi Tuff ($3.75 \pm .25$ mya) and estimates by stratigraphic extrapolation that it is about 3.8 mya. Thus, all *A. anamensis* fossils come from sites dated to between 3.8 and 4.2 mya.

Reconstructing the habitat preferences of *A. anamensis* is difficult because the relationship between a death assemblage and the habitat preferences of animals is a complex one. Even assuming that the hominids from Kanapoi and Allia Bay once lived near the areas where their bones are found, it is by no means certain that they preferred to live near the depositional environment itself. Also, habitat changes can be sudden in the East African Rift. A large river such as the Omo can dominate an otherwise arid environment to the point at which only narrow ecotone exists between desert and forest. Seasonal flooding can lead to habitats that support a large mammal biomass without much local rainfall. As far as we can tell, all Kanapoi hominid fossils have been damaged by carnivores, and the Allia Bay ones also may have been. These carnivores may have carried dead hominids or parts of them for a considerable distance before discarding them. Therefore, the fact that the hominids have been found in fluviatile and deltaic deposits in the ancient Turkana Basin does not mean that they lived in a riparian environment, although it is possible that they did. We know from the micromammals that dry woodland and bushland conditions existed close to the river that deposited the sediments, and we can be reasonably sure that the river would have supported a gallery forest. The Allia Bay hominids are among the fossils that are unrolled and so probably did come from environments more proximal to the ancient river.

As far as can be determined, the riverine woodlands and gallery forest habitats sampled at Kanapoi and Allia Bay are similar to those reconstructed for *A. afarensis* sites. Laetoli probably had open grassland with scattered trees and nearby woodland.[12] Hadar ranged from open and closed woodland to bush and grassland.[13] All of these sites contrast with the paleoenvironmental reconstruction of the *A. ramidus* site of Aramis, which is interpreted as having been closed woodland.[14]

COMPARATIVE ANATOMY

A. anamensis is intermediate in time between *Ardipithecus ramidus* and *Australopithecus afarensis,* and is morphologically distinct from both in several ways. The new genus and species *Ardipithecus ramidus* was named for fossils from horizons at Aramis in Ethiopia that have been securely dated by single-crystal ^{40}Ar/^{39}Ar laser fusion dating to just less than 4.4 mya.[14-16] So far, the brief publications regarding the fossils have not allowed a detailed comparison between the two species, but *A. ramidus* clearly is distinguished from all *Australopithecus* species in that it has 1) absolutely and relatively thinner tooth enamel; 2) canines larger relative to the postcanine teeth; 3) a distinctively small deciduous first molar resembling that of *Pan paniscus;* 4) a marked inclination of the distal radial articular surface; 5) a strong lateral condylar ridge on the distal humerus; and 6) an elongate, superoposteriorly extended lateral humeral epicondyle.[15] Because *A. anamensis* had not been named in 1994, there were a few features, such as lack of a clearly defined articular eminence on the temporal bone, that were originally thought to differentiate *A. ramidus* from all *Australopithecus* species, but that we now know probably do not.

Australopithecus afarensis is perhaps the best-known species of its genus. It has been found in Tanzania, Ethiopia, and Kenya in deposits ranging in age from about 3.7 mya to 3.0 mya (see Kimbel et al.[17] for recent discoveries, dates, and references). The large collections of *A. afarensis* fossils give a picture of this species as a habitually bipedal hominid with body size and sexual dimorphism at the levels seen in *Gorilla gorilla.*[18,19] All parts of the skeleton known for *A. anamensis* are also known for *A. afarensis,* so comparisons are easily made between these species.

The definitions of *A. anamensis* and *A. afarensis* are similar in many respects. Both species exhibit thick tooth enamel, as do all *Australopithecus* species, with that in robust species being especially thick. This appears, on the basis of comparisons with living African apes and *Ardipithecus,* to be a shared derived feature of the genus *Australopithecus,* although it must be noted that many, if not most, Miocene hominoids also had thick enamel.

A. anamensis and *A. afarensis* are similar in their degrees of postcanine megadontia, although the range of size variation in the sample of *A. anamensis* molars is just slightly larger than that in *A. afarensis.* There also is considerable overlap between size distributions of molars in these two species (Figure 1). Tooth size variability was at least as great in *A. anamensis,* if not greater. Given that molar size is generally related to body size, this may mean that body size variability in *A. anamensis* was also considerable.

The teeth of *A. anamensis* and *A. afarensis* differ in several aspects of morphology. Both the upper and lower molars of *A. anamensis* have lower crowns with

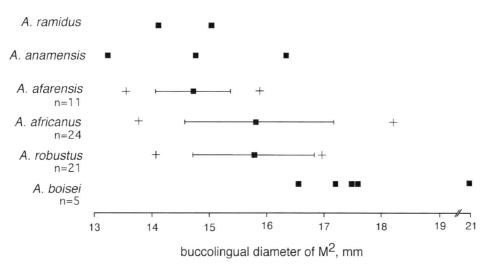

Figure 1. *Maximum buccolingual breadths of mandibular and maxillary second molar crowns for several* Australopithecus *taxa. Sample means, standard deviations, and ranges are indicated for most taxa. Individual data points are shown for* A. ramidus, A. anamensis, *and maxillary specimens of* A. boisei. *Comparative data for* A. africanus, A. robustus, *and* A. boisei *from*[51-52], A. ramidus *data from*[12]. A. afarensis *data kindly provided by William H. Kimbel.* A. anamensis *teeth are comparable in size to those of* A. afarensis, *but have a slightly greater observed size range.*

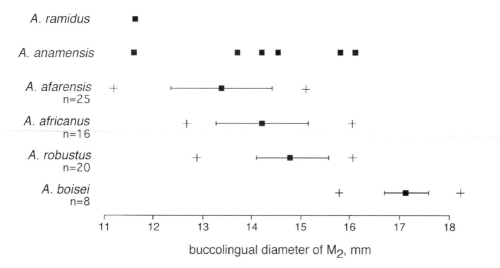

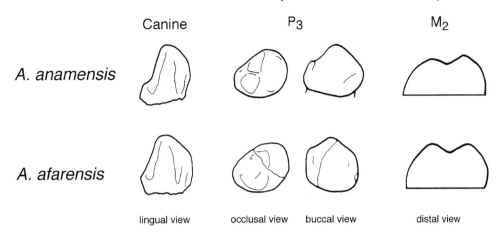

Canine   P₃   M₂

A. anamensis

A. afarensis

lingual view   occlusal view   buccal view   distal view

Figure 2.   *Mandibular canine, third premolar, and second molar crowns of* Australopithecus anamensis *compared with those of* A. afarensis. *Canines (*A. anamensis *KNM-KP 29286 and* A. afarensis *LH 3) are shown in lingual view. Third premolars (*A. anamensis *KNM-KP 29286 and* A. afarensis *LH 3, the latter reversed for comparison) are shown in occlusal and buccal views. Molars (composite outlines from Hlusko[53]) are shown in distal view.* A. anamensis *canines are more asymmetrical than those of* A. afarensis. A. anamensis *premolars have larger buccal cusps with very little lingual cusp development; and molar crowns are lower with more sloping sides.*

more sloping buccal and lingual sides (Figure 2). The lower third premolars of *A. anamensis* are more asymmetrical than are those of *A. afarensis* (Figure 2). They have a large, centrally placed buccal cusp that occupies most of the crown surface area in occlusal view. The lingual cusp is considerably smaller, and is barely distinguishable from the distal marginal ridge. *A. afarensis* lower third premolars, on the other hand, have much greater lingual cusp development, so that the two cusps are more equal in size. The lower fourth premolars are similarly more asymmetrical in *A. anamensis* than in *A. afarensis*.

A. anamensis canines are similar to those of *A. afarensis* in size and shape, but their crowns tend to be more asymmetrical (Figure 2). Relative to the size of the postcanine teeth, however, the lower canines of *A. anamensis* are slightly larger, on average, than those of *A. afarensis* (Figure 3). Despite the slightly larger canines of *A. anamensis*, the ranges of variation are similar for both species, demonstrating that they most likely had a similar pattern of canine size dimorphism. An index of largest to smallest canine crown area is 1.35 for *A. anamensis*, about the same as that for *A. afarensis* and less than that in African apes.

There is some evidence, however, that male canine size in *A. anamensis* was greater than we have estimated. A mandibular fragment from Allia Bay has a very large canine root. In addition, a new presumed male mandible from Kanapoi has a large left canine alveolus, although the fact that a piece of the lateral alveolar wall is missing makes it possible that the alveolus appears larger now than it was in life. The alveolus on the right has the lower part of the canine root still in place. CT scans taken by Fred Spoor through both bodies at the level of the mental foramina show that the large left alveolus is not distorted. It seems, then, that male *Australopithecus* canines were sometimes much larger in the earlier species.

Several maxillae and mandibles are known for *A. anamensis*, and they also differ morphologically from those of *A. afarensis*. They have a striking primitive feature not found in *A. afarensis:* Their postcanine tooth rows are set parallel to one another (Figure 4). Living apes have postcanine maxillary tooth rows that converge slightly posteriorly; in contrast, those of humans diverge strongly posteriorly. *A. anamensis* postcanine tooth rows are roughly parallel, while those of *A. afarensis* are more derived, ranging from nearly parallel to slightly divergent. In addition, the *A. anamensis* palate is narrower and shallower than that of *A. afarensis*, although it must be noted that the original Garusi maxillary fragment from Laetoli has also been reconstructed as having been narrow and shallow.[20]

The narrow, parallel tooth rows in all three mandibles of *A. anamensis* are correlated with the characteristic oblique long axes of the symphyseal cross-sections (Figure 5).[21] This leads to *A. anamensis* mandibles having a strongly receding symphyseal contour, a feature that distinguishes both of these mandibles from those of all other *Australopithecus* species.[21]

A left temporal fragment of *A. anamensis* is instructive in that it shows extensive pneumatization of the squama, a barely definable articular eminence, and a tiny external acoustic meatus.[22] These three primitive features are found also in *A. ramidus*.[15] The articular eminence is more pronounced and the acoustic meatus larger, however, in *A. afarensis* and other species of *Australopithecus*. It is almost certain that the small acoustic meatus has nothing to do with hearing or the size of the pinna.

Postcranially, *A. anamensis* is very like *A. afarensis*, despite some workers seeing derived human-like features in the humerus[2,6,23,24] and tibia.[25,26] The humerus, radius, and tibia can be almost exactly matched in size and morphology to the *A. afarensis* collections from Hadar.[27–29] These elements are as large as and sometimes

Mandibular canine size relative to postcanine tooth size

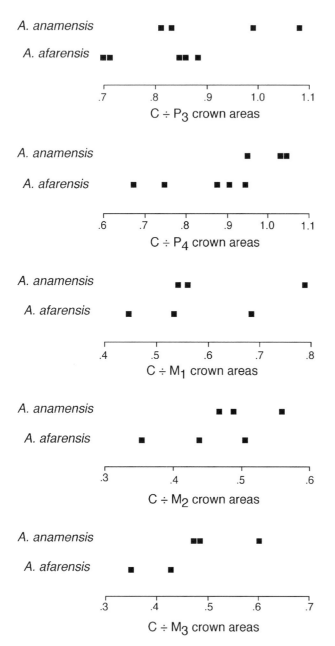

Figure 3. *Mandibular canine occlusal area, calculated as crown breadth times length, compared with crown areas, breadth times length, of each mandibular postcanine tooth. Data are presented as ratios of canine area to the area of each of the postcanine teeth. Only associated specimens are included. Individual values for* A. anamensis *and* A. afarensis *are shown. Sample ranges of both species overlap in all comparisons. In all cases,* A. anamensis *canines are slightly larger relative to the postcanine teeth than is the case in* A. afarensis, *although the magnitude of size variation is similar in both species.*

a little larger than any known for *A. afarensis.* This suggests that some *A. anamensis* individuals may have had body sizes exceeding those of the largest *A. afarensis* individuals, which are estimated to have weighed about 45 kg[30,31] or even up to 80 kg.[32]

The radius of *A. anamensis*[8] is too long to fit the longest ulna from Hadar, A. L. 438-1a.[17] However, this radius is morphologically very similar to others of *A. afarensis,* down to the unusual division of the lunate and scaphoid surfaces, where the lunate area rather than the scaphoid predominates, as in African apes and humans.[8] If the long radius is a guide, at least the largest of this species had forearms as long as those of human males over six feet tall. We think this suggests that *A. anamensis* had relatively long forearms compared with humans, a conclusion also reached by Kimbel, Johanson, and Rak[17] about the arm proportions of *A. afarensis.*

The humerus does not show the extant African ape-like conditions in the distal articular surface and epicondyle to the degree seen in *A. ramidus.*[15] The phenetic affinities of the *A. anamensis* humerus are with other *Australopithecus* distal humeri. However, some authors[23,24] also have found similarities between *A. anamensis* and *Homo* distal humeri, raising potentially interesting questions about relations among these taxa. But because many of these features are quite variable, with poorly understood functional and developmental bases, their value as taxonomic indicators is uncertain.

The partial phalanx is as large as the largest of the Hadar specimens and is similar in shape, curvature, and degree of development of the flexor sheath ridges. The capitate is damaged, but enough detail is preserved to say that it lacked a facet for the third metacarpal styloid process, and in this is similar to apes and all other *Australopithecus* capitates. It still, however, retains the primitive condition of having the facet for the second metacarpal facing directly laterally, and in this it is unlike *A. afarensis,*[33,34] *Australopithecus africanus,*[35,36] and *Homo sapiens,* including Neandertals.[37,38]

The tibia is matched closely in morphology by the largest Hadar tibia, A. L. 333-42, although it is a little larger than that one. It also shows unequivocal adaptations to habitually bipedal gait. The tibial shaft is oriented orthogonally relative to the talar joint surface, placing the knee directly over the foot in bipedal stance.[39] This vertical reorientation of the long axis of the tibia, which is found in all bipedal hominids, contrasts markedly with the varus angle of the shank in apes (Figure 6). The *A. anamensis* tibial metaphyses are markedly flared proximally and distally, another feature found only in hominid bipeds. The Kanapoi tibia also displays a reduced fibular articulation,[1] but is still lunate in shape, as in other *Australopithecus* tibias. The clear adaptations to bipedal posture and locomotion seen in the Kanapoi tibia indicate that terrestrial bipedality had been selectively advantageous for *A. anamensis* and its immediate ancestors, beginning some time prior to 4.2 mya.

EVOLUTIONARY PERSPECTIVE

Several other hominid fossils that date to this period were previously referred to *Australopithecus afarensis.* With the discovery of *A. anamensis* and the earlier discovery of *A. ramidus,* however, it is now not easy to decide to which species they belong. These fossils

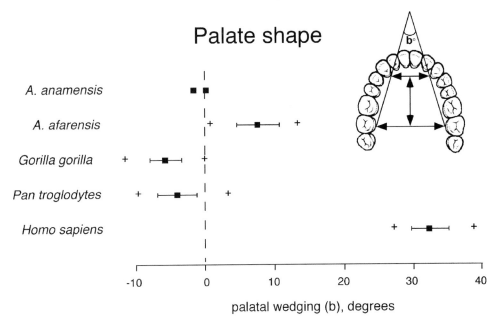

Palate shape

Figure 4. *Shape of the maxillary dental arcade computed as the angle of tooth row divergence between minimum distances between canine and second molar crowns, calculated using formula published by Digiovanni, Scoles, and Latimer[54] and considering anteroposterior distance between canines and second molars. Equivalent results can be obtained by using distances between P³'s instead of canines, or by computing a simple ratio between anterior and posterior breadths. Sample means, standard deviations, and observed ranges are depicted for comparative taxa and individual data points for* A. anamensis. *Extant taxa are represented by 20 individuals each and* A. afarensis *by 8 specimens from Hadar (data provided by W. H. Kimbel).* A. anamensis *maxillary dental arcades have roughly parallel sides, retaining an ape-like condition, while those of* A. afarensis *have postcanine tooth rows that diverge posteriorly. (The only exception is the Garusi specimen, which is not included here but appears to have parallel postcanine tooth rows). The same pattern is seen in mandibular shape. Canine size does not affect these results; there are no differences between male and females of any species.*

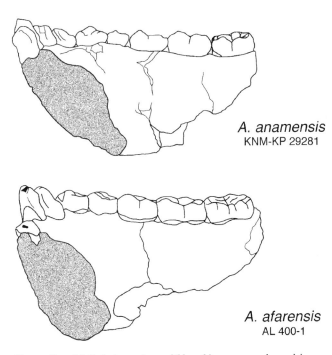

Figure 5. *Medial views of mandibles of* A. anamensis *and* A. afarensis, *with symphyseal cross-sections stippled. Both sufficiently well-preserved* A. anamensis *mandibles have more sloping symphyses than any known for* A. afarensis, *and correspondingly long postincisive plana.*[21]

include the femur from Maka,[40] the frontal bone from Belohdelie,[41] and the teeth from Fejej,[42] all in Ethiopia. There are, as yet, no femora known from *A. anamensis*, but in view of the fact that the *A. anamensis* tibia resembles those of *A. afarensis* in some detail, it would not be surprising to find that the femora of these two species were also similar. The frontal bone of *A. anamensis* is also unknown. Until one is found, there is really no way of determining if the Belohdelie frontal really belongs to *A. afarensis* or *A. anamensis,* or whether these species had equivalent frontal bone morphology.

The case of the 4.00 to 4.18 mya teeth from Fejej[42,43] is not much easier, as only one tooth in the sample has much of its crown left. Fejej is also less than 100 miles from Allia Bay. Tooth size ranges of *A. anamensis* and *A. afarensis* overlap considerably. The crown of the Fejej P_4 can be matched easily in size and morphology with some of those from Allia Bay and Kanapoi. The Fejej teeth also have thick enamel, which, as noted earlier, is a derived trait shared by all *Australopithecus* species, but not the earlier *Ardipithecus ramidus.*[15,16] Thus, we cannot be certain whether these specimens should be attributed to *A. afarensis* or *A. anamensis.*

There is no temporal overlap between *A. anamensis* and *A. afarensis.* Consequently, we feel that it is premature to decide that more than one hominid species necessarily existed around 4 mya,[43] even though there is no

Inclination of tibial shaft

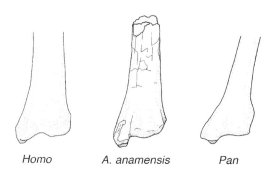

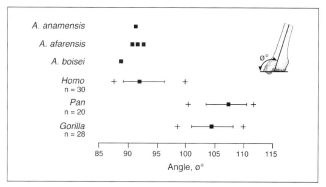

Figure 6. *Top, posterior views of a distal tibia of* Homo sapiens, Australopithecus anamensis *(KNM-KP 29285), and* Pan troglodytes *oriented so that the talocrural joint surfaces are horizontal. Bottom, graph of angles of inclination relative to the talar surface in extant and fossil taxa (adapted from Latimer, Ohman, and Lovejoy[39]). Hominids have vertically oriented tibial shafts relative to the talar joint surface, whereas chimpanzees and gorillas have sharply inclined tibial shafts that place the knee well lateral to the ankle in plantigrade posture. The Kanapoi tibia resembles that of all other hominids and differs from those of all African apes in having its knee placed directly over its ankle joint.*

theoretical reason for only one hominid species to have existed at any one time. If these few earlier *A. afarensis* examples are later shown to belong to *A. anamensis,* then an ancestor-descendent relationship between *A. anamensis* and *A. afarensis* might explain their distribution in time.

The simplest hypothesis that can be made to accommodate the new early hominid fossils is that there was one evolving lineage of hominids. Future fossil discoveries may reveal a bushier phylogenetic tree, but currently there are no data that support such a hypothesis. At present, we believe that no compelling evidence rules out the phylogenetic position of *A. anamensis* as intermediate between *A. ramidus* and *A. afarensis.* If we could be certain that these three taxa represent a single evolving lineage that was the result of a single splitting event, it would not be necessary to designate *A. anamensis* as a new species. But this has not yet been demonstrated, so placing the *A. anamensis* fossils in either of the other taxa on the basis that they might be from an intermediate part of a single lineage would obscure and restrict any other possible phylogenetic interpretations.

SUMMARY

The following scenario can be constructed from the available evidence, and might have taken place. *Ardipithecus ramidus* is known from relatively high altitude, closed-canopy woodlands of Ethiopia. This species may have been ancestral to *A. anamensis,* known from riverine woodlands and gallery forests of the Turkana Basin. *A. anamensis,* in turn, preceded the ecologically widespread species *A. afarensis,* known from forest, woodlands, and more open country across East Africa, and possibly Central Africa. This scenario would accord with the changes in the teeth in these successive species. The dentition, tooth row, palate and temporal bone of *A. anamensis* suggest a change in diet and chewing mechanism from the primitive African ape-like ones in *A. ramidus.* With its primitive dentition and thin enamel, *A. ramidus* was probably much like a chimpanzee in diet, an omnivore that relied heavily on fruit. A shift appears to have been made first to thicker tooth enamel in *A. anamensis,* perhaps indicating a dietary shift to harder foods.[44,45] Later, changes occurred in the geometry of the mandible and maxilla in *A. afarensis,* along with heightened molar tooth crowns. These traits were carried to extremes in the later species *A. aethiopicus* and *A. boisei.*

We do not yet know how long before 4.2 mya the shift to habitual bipedality was made. Little has been published about the postcranial skeleton or locomotor adaptations of *Ardipithecus ramidus.* The postcranial fossils of *Australopithecus anamensis* show that it was a habitually bipedal species that still retained some primitive features of the upper limb skeleton, perhaps even more so than did *A. afarensis.* Controversy exists, and will not easily be resolved, about whether these primitive retentions were adaptive and thus indicate that arboreality was a significant part of *Australopithecus* locomotion, or whether they were merely the result of differential rates of adaptive change between the fore and hindlimbs (see reviews in Latimer[46] and Susman, Stern, and Jungers[47]).

Molecular estimates for the divergence time of chimpanzees and humans range from 15 to 2.5 mya, but converge on 5 mya.[48–50] Because of the early date of *A. anamensis,* its craniodental and postcranial skeletal morphology is providing new and much-needed clues to the origin of our lineage.

ACKNOWLEDGMENTS

The authors thank the field crew that discovered the *Australopithecus anamensis* fossils and the trustees, directors, and staff of the National Museums of Kenya. We thank William H. Kimbel for providing data on *A. afarensis.* Field research at Kanapoi was funded by the National Geographic Society, Washington, DC (USA) and fieldwork at Allia Bay was funded by the National Science Foundation (USA). Caltex (Kenya) donated fuel.

REFERENCES

1. Leakey, M. G., Feibel, C. S., McDougall, I., Walker, A. 1995. New four-million-year-old hominid species from Kanapoi and Allia Bay, Kenya. Nature 376:565–571.

2. Patterson, B., Howells, W. W. 1967. Hominid humeral fragment from early Pleistocene of Northwestern Kenya. Science 156:64–66.

3. Patterson, B. 1966. A new locality for early Pleistocene fossils in northwestern Kenya. Nature 212:577–581.

4. Patterson, B., Behrensmeyer, A. K., Sill, W. D. 1970. Geology and fauna of a new Pliocene locality in northwestern Kenya. Nature 226:918–921.

5. Coppens, Y., Howell, F. C., Isaac, G. L., Leakey, R. E. F., editors. 1976. Earliest man and environments in the Lake Rudolf Basin. Chicago: University of Chicago Press.

6. Senut, B. 1981. L'humerus et ses articulations chez les Hominidés Plio-Pleistocene. Paris: CNRS.

7. Coffing, K., Feibel, C., Leakey, M., Walker, A. 1994. Four-million year old hominids from East Lake Turkana, Kenya. Am J Phys Anthropol 93:55–65.

8. Heinrich, R. E., Rose, M. D., Leakey, R. E., Walker, A. C. 1993. Hominid radius from the middle Pliocene of Lake Turkana, Kenya. Am J Phys Anthropol 92:139–148.

9. Leakey, M. G., Feibel, C. S., McDougall, I., Ward, C. V., Walker, A. 1998. New specimens and confirmation of an early age for *Australopithecus anamensis*. Nature 363:62–66.

10. Brown, F. H., Feibel, C. S. 1991. Stratigraphy, depositional environments, and palaeogeography of the Koobi Fora Formation. In: Harris, J. M. editor. The fossil ungulates: Geology, fossil artiodactyls, and palaeoenvironments. Oxford: Clarendon Press. p 1–30.

11. White, T. D., Suwa, G., Hart, W. K., Walter, R. C., WoldeGabriel, G., Heinzelin, J. D., Clark, J. D., Asfaw, B., Vrba, E. 1993. New discoveries of *Australopithecus* at Maka in Ethiopia. Nature 366:261–265.

12. Harris, J. M. 1987. Summary. In: Leakey, M. D., Harris, J. M., editors. Laetoli: A Pliocene site in northern Tanzania. Oxford: Clarendon Press. p 524–531.

13. Johanson, D. C., Taieb, M., Coppens, Y. 1982. Pliocene hominids from the Hadar Formation, Ethiopia (1973–1977): Stratigraphic, chronologic and paleoenvironmental contexts, with notes on hominid morphology and systematics. Am J Phys Anthropol 75:373–402.

14. WoldeGabriel, G., White, T. D., Suwa, G., Renne, P., de Heinzelin J, Hart, W. K., Helken, G. 1994. Ecological and temporal placement of early Pliocene hominids at Aramis, Ethiopia. Nature 371:330–333.

15. White, T. D., Suwa, G., Asfaw, B. 1994. *Australopithecus ramidus*, a new species of early hominid from Aramis, Ethiopia. Nature 371:306–312.

16. White, T. D., Suwa, G., Asfaw, B. 1995. Corregendum. Nature 375:88.

17. Kimbel, W. H., Johanson, D. C., Rak, Y. 1994. The first skull and other new discoveries of *Australopithecus afarensis* at Hadar, Ethiopia. Nature 368:449–451.

18. Lockwood, C. A., Richmond, B. G., Jungers, W. L., Kimbel, W. H. 1996. Randomization procedures and sexual dimorphism in *Australopithecus afarensis*. J Hum Evol 31:537–548.

19. Richmond, B., Jungers, W. L. 1995. Size variation and sexual dimorphism in *Australopithecus afarensis* and living hominoids. J Hum Evol 29:229–245.

20. Puech, P. F., Cianfarani, F., Roth, H. 1986. Reconstruction of the maxillary dental arcade of Garusi Hominid 1. J Hum Evol 15:325–332.

21. Sherwood, R. J., Emch, V. C., Hlusko, L. J., Walker, A. 1997. The mandibular symphysis of *Australopithecus*. J Hum Evol 32A:19–20.

22. Kimbel, W. H., Johanson, D. C. 1984. Cranial morphology of *Australopithecus afarensis*: A comparative study based on a composite reconstruction of the adult skull. Am J Phys Anthropol 64:337–388.

23. Baker, E. W., Malyango, A. A., Harrison, T. 1998. Phylogenetic relationships and functional morphology of the distal humerus from Kanapoi, Kenya. Am J Phys Anthropol 26(suppl):66.

24. Senut, B., Tardieu, C. 1985. Functional aspects of Plio-Pleistocene hominid limb bones: Implications for taxonomy and phylogeny.

In: Delson, E., editor. Ancestors: The hard evidence. New York: Alan R. Liss. p 193–201.

25. Andrews, P. 1995. Ecological apes and ancestors. Nature 376:555–556.

26. Johanson, D. C., Edgar, B. 1996. From Lucy to language. New York: Simon and Schuster.

27. Johanson, D. C., Lovejoy, C. O., Kimbel, W. H., White, T. D., Ward, S. C., Bush, M. E., Latimer, B. M., Coppens, Y. 1982. Morphology of the Pliocene partial hominid skeleton (A.L. 288-1) from the Hadar formation, Ethiopia. Am J Phys Anthropol 57:403–452.

28. Lovejoy, C. O., Johanson, D. C., Coppens, Y. 1982. Hominid upper limb bones recovered from the Hadar formation: 1974–1977 collections. Am J Phys Anthropol 57:637–650.

29. Lovejoy, C. O., Johanson, D. C., Coppens, Y. 1982. Hominid lower limb bones recovered from the Hadar formation: 1974–1977 collections. Am J Phys Anthropol 57:679–700.

30. McHenry, H. M. 1992. How big were early hominids? Evol Anthropol 1:15–20.

31. McHenry, H. M. 1992. Body size and proportions in early hominids. Am J Phys Anthropol 87:407–431.

32. Jungers, W. L. 1988. New estimates of body size in australopithecines. In: Grine F. E., editor. Evolutionary history of the "robust" australopithecines. New York: Aldine de Gruyter. p 115–125.

33. Marzke, M. W. 1983. Joint functions and grips of the *Australopithecus afarensis* hand, with special reference to the region of the capitate. J Hum Evol 12:197–211.

34. McHenry, H. M. 1983. The capitate of *Australopithecus afarensis* and *A. africanus*. Am J Phys Anthropol 62:187–198.

35. Broom, R., Schepers, G. W. H. 1946. The South African ape-men: The Australopithecinae. Trans Mus Mem 2:1–272.

36. Robinson, J. T. 1972. Early hominid posture and locomotion. Chicago: University of Chicago Press.

37. Niewoehner, W. A., Weaver, A. H., Trinkaus, E. 1997. Neandertal capitate-metacarpal articular morphology. Am J Phys Anthropol 103:219–233.

38. Trinkaus, E. 1983. The Shanidar neandertals. New York: Academic Press.

39. Latimer, B., Ohman, J. C., Lovejoy, C. O. 1987. Talocrural joint in African hominoids: Implications for *Australopithecus afarensis*. Am J Phys Anthropol 74:155–176.

40. Clark, J. D., Asfaw, B., Assefa, G., Harris, J. W. K., Kurashina, H., Walter, R. C., White, T. D., Williams, M. A. J. 1984. Palaeoanthropological discoveries in the Middle Awash Valley, Ethiopia. Nature 307:423–428.

41. Asfaw, B. 1987. The Belohdelie frontal: New evidence of early hominid cranial morphology from the Afar of Ethiopia. J Hum Evol 16:611–624.

42. Fleagle, J. G., Rasmussen, D. T., Yirga, S., Bown, T. M., Grine, F. E. 1991. New hominid fossils from Fejej, Southern Ethiopia. J Hum Evol 21:145–152.

43. Kappelman, J., Swisher, C. C., Fleagle, J. G., Yirga, S., Bown, T. M., Feseha, M. 1996. Age of *Australopithecus afarensis* from Fejej, Ethiopia. J Hum Evol 30:139–146.

44. Dumont, E. R. 1995. Enamel thickness and dietary adaptation among extant primates and chiropterans. J Mamm 76:1127–1136.

45. Kay, R. F. 1981. The nut-crackers—a new theory of the adaptations of the Ramapithecinae. Am J Phys Anthropol 55:141–151.

46. Latimer, B. 1991. Locomotor adaptations in *Australopithecus afarensis*: The issue of arboreality. In: Coppens Y, Senut B, editors. Origine(s) de la bipédie chez les hominidés. Paris: Centre National de la Recherche Scientifique. p 169–176.

47. Susman, R. L., Stern, J. T., Jungers, W. L. 1984. Arboreality and bipedality in the Hadar hominids. Folia Primatol 43:113–156.

48. Easteal, S., Herbert, G. 1997. Molecular evidence from the nuclear genome for the time frame of human evolution. J Mol Evol 44:S121–132.

49. Horai, S., Satta, Y., Hayasaka, K., Kondo, R., Inuoe, T., Ishida, T., Hayashi, S., Takahata, N. 1992. Man's place in Hominoidea revealed by mitochondrial DNA genealogy. J Mol Evol 35:32–43.

50. Morin, P. A., Moore, J. A., Chakraborty, R., Jin, L., Goodall, J., Woodruff, D. S. 1994. Kin selection, social structure, gene flow and the evolution of chimpanzees. Science 265:1193–1201.

51. White, T. D., Johanson, D. C., Kimbel, W. H. 1981. *Australopithecus africanus:* Its phylogenetic position reconsidered. S Afr J Sci 77:445–470.
52. Wood, B. 1991. Koobi Fora research project, Vol. 4: hominid cranial remains. Oxford: Clarendon Press.

53. Hlusko, L. 1998. Euclidean distance matrix analysis of early *Australopithecus* molars. M.A. Thesis, Pennsylvania State University.
54. Digiovanni, B. F., Scoles, P. V., Latimer, B. M. 1989. Anterior extension of thoracic vertebral bodies in Scheuermann's kyphosis. Spine 14:712–716.

18

New Hominin Genus from Eastern Africa Shows Diverse Middle Pliocene Lineages

M. G. Leakey, F. Spoor, F. H. Brown, P. N. Gathogo, C. Kiarie, L. N. Leakey, and I. McDougall

ABSTRACT

Most interpretations of early hominin phylogeny recognize a single early to middle Pliocene ancestral lineage, best represented by Australopithecus afarensis, *which gave rise to a radiation of taxa in the late Pliocene. Here we report on new fossils discovered west of Lake Turkana, Kenya, which differ markedly from those of contemporary* A. afarensis, *indicating that hominin taxonomic diversity extended back, well into the middle Pliocene. A 3.5 Myr-old cranium, showing a unique combination of derived facial and primitive neurocranial features, is assigned to a new genus of hominin. These findings point to an early diet-driven adaptive radiation, provide new insight on the association of hominin craniodental features, and have implications for our understanding of Plio–Pleistocene hominin phylogeny.*

The eastern African hominin record between 4 and 3 Myr is represented exclusively by a single species, *A. afarensis,* and its possible ancestor, *Australopithecus anamensis,* which are commonly thought to belong to the lineage ancestral to all later hominins[1,2]. This apparent lack of diversity in the middle Pliocene contrasts markedly with the increasingly bushy phylogeny evident in the later hominin fossil record. To study further the time interval between 4 and 3 Myr, fieldwork in 1998 and 1999 focused on sites of this age at Lomekwi in the Nachukui Formation, west of Lake Turkana. New hominin discoveries from Lomekwi, as well as two mandibles and isolated molars recovered previously[3] (Table 1), indicate that multiple species existed between 3.5 and 3.0 Myr. The new finds include a well-preserved temporal bone, two partial maxillae, isolated teeth, and most importantly a largely complete, although distorted, cranium. We assign the latter specimen to a new hominin genus on the basis

Reprinted by permission from *Nature,* Vol. 410, pp. 433–440.

of its unique combination of primitive and derived features.

DESCRIPTION OF *KENYANTHROPUS PLATYOPS*

Order Primates LINNAEUS 1758
Suborder Anthropoidea MIVART 1864
Superfamily Hominoidea GRAY 1825
Kenyanthropus gen. nov.

Etymology. In recognition of Kenya's contribution to the understanding of human evolution through the many specimens recovered from its fossil sites.

Generic Diagnosis. A hominin genus characterized by the following morphology: transverse facial contour flat at a level just below the nasal bones; tall malar region; zygomaticoalveolar crest low and curved; anterior surface of the maxillary zygomatic process positioned over premolars and more vertically orientated than the nasal aperture and nasoalveolar clivus; nasoalveolar clivus long and both transversely and sagittally flat, without marked juga; moderate subnasal prognathism; incisor alveoli parallel with, and only just anterior to, the bicanine line; nasal cavity entrance stepped; palate roof thin and flexed inferiorly anterior to the incisive foramen; upper incisor (I^1 and I^2) roots near equal in size; upper premolars (P^3, P^4) mostly three-rooted; upper first and second molars (M^1 and M^2) small with thick enamel; tympanic element mediolaterally long and lacking a petrous crest; external acoustic porus small. *Kenyanthropus* can be distinguished from *Ardipithecus ramidus* by its buccolingually narrow M^2, thick molar enamel, and a temporal bone with a more cylindrical articular eminence and deeper mandibular fossa. It differs from *A. anamensis, A. afarensis, A. africanus* and *A. garhi* in the derived morphology of the lower face, particularly the moderate subnasal prognathism, sagittally and transversely flat nasoalveolar clivus, anteriorly

Table 1.   Hominin Specimens from the Lower Lomekwi and Kataboi Members

KNM-WT	Description	Year	Discoverer	Locality	Measurements (mm)
8556	Mandible fragment: symphysis, right body with RP_3–RM_1, isolated partial RM_2, RM_3, LP_3	1982	N. Mutiwa	LO-5	RP_3, 9.8, 12.4; RP_4, 11.3, 12.6; RM_1, 13.7, 12.9; RM_2, NA, NA; RM_3, (17.5), (14.1); LP_3, 9.8, 12.5
8557	$LM_{1/2}$	1982	N. Mutiwa	LO-4	NA, (11.5)
16003	RM^3	1985	M. Kyeva	LO-5	13.3, 14.6
16006	Left mandible fragment with M_2 fragment and M_3	1985	N. Mutiwa	LO-4E	M_2, NA, NA; M_3, 15.3, 13.1
38332	Partial RM^3 crown	1999	M. Eregae	LO-4E	NA, 14.8
38333	$LM_{1/2}$ crown	1999	M. Eregae	LO-4E	13.1, 12.1
38334	$LM_{1/2}$	1999	M. Eregae	LO-4W	12.1, 11.5
38335	$RM_{1/2}$ crown fragment	1999	M. Eregae	LO-4E	NA
38337	$RM^{1/2}$	1999	R. Moru	LO-4E	11.5, 12.3
38338	Partial $RM^{1/2}$ crown	1999	N. Mutiwa	LO-4E	NA
38339	$LM_{1/2}$ crown	1999	J. Erus	LO-4W	12.8, 12.7
38341	Partial $LM_{2/3}$	1999	G. Ekalale	LO-4E	NA
38342	$LM_{1/2}$ crown	1999	J. Erus	LO-4E	12.8, (11.3)
38343	Right maxilla fragment with I^2 and P^3 roots and partial C; mandible fragment with partial P_4 and M_1 roots	1999	J. Erus	LO-4W	NA
38344	$RM_{1/2}$ crown	1998	M. Eregae	LO-9	12.8, 12.2
38346	Partial $RM^{1/2}$	1998	M. Mutiwa	LO-5	NA
38347	LdM_2 crown	1998	R. Moru	LO-5	11.7, 9.6
38349	$RM_{1/2}$ crown	1998	W. Mangao	LO-5	13.5, 12.6
38350	Left maxilla fragment with P^3 and P^4 roots and partial M^1	1998	B. Onyango	LO-5	LM^1: (10.5), (12.0)
38352	Partial $RM_{1/2}$	1998	W. Mangao	LO-5	NA, 11.5
38355	Partial $RM^{1/2}$ crown	1998	M. Eregae	LO-9	NA
38356	Partial $RM^{1/2}$ crown	1998	M. Eregae & J. Kaatho	LO-9	12.8, NA
38357	$RM_{1/2}$	1998	G. Ekalale	LO-5	12.8, 11.8
38358	Associated RI^2, LM_2 fragment, LM_3, RM^3 fragment, four crown fragments	1998	G. Ekalale	LO-5	RI^2, 7.5, 7.5, 9.1; LM_3, 15.3, 13.2
38359	Associated RM_1, RM_2	1998	M. Eregae	LO-5	RM_1, 12.7, 11.6; RM_2, 13.9, 12.2
38361	Associated (partial) germs of I^1, LI^2, R$\underline{C}$, LRP^3, LRP^4	1998	R. Moru	LO-5	I^1, NA, (8.0), (11.5); LI^2, 7.6, >5.9, 8.3; LP^3, (9.3), (12.0)
38362	Associated partial $LM^{1/2}$, $RM^{1/2}$	1998	R. Moru	LO-5	$RM^{1/2}$, 12.9, 14.3
39949	Partial LP_4	1998	R. Moru	LO-5	NA
39950	RM_3	1998	R. Moru	LO-5	16.0, 14.5
39951	$RM_{1/2}$ fragment	1998	R. Moru	LO-5	NA
39952	$LM_{1/2}$	1998	R. Moru	LO-5	NA
39953	$LM_{1/2}$ fragment	1998	R. Moru	LO-5	NA
39954	Two tooth fragments	1998	R. Moru	LO-5	NA
39955	$L\underline{C}$ fragment	1998	R. Moru	LO-5	NA
40000	Cranium	1999	J. Erus	LO-6N	RM^2, 11.4, 12.4
40001	Right temporal bone	1998	P. Gathogo	LO-5	NA

Dental measurements taken as in ref. 34. Mesiodistal crown diameter followed by buccolingual or labiolingual diameter, and for incisors and canines, labial crown height. Values in parentheses are estimates. NA, Not available. L or R in the 'Description' column indicates the left or right side. $\underline{C}$, upper canine; d, deciduous.

positioned maxillary zygomatic process, similarly sized I^1 and I^2 roots, and small M^1 and M^2 crowns. From *A. afarensis* it also differs by a transversely flat midface, a small, external acoustic porus, and the absence of an occipital/marginal venous sinus system, and from *A. africanus* by a tall malar region, a low and curved zygomaticoalveolar crest, a narrow nasal aperture, the absence of anterior facial pillars, a tubular, long and crestless tympanic element, and a small, external acoustic porus. *Kenyanthropus* lacks the suite of derived dental and cranial features found in *Paranthropus aethiopicus*, *P. boisei* and *P. robustus* (Table 2), and the derived cranial features of species indisputably assigned to *Homo* (For example, *H. erectus s.l.* and *H. sapiens,* but not *H. rudolfensis* and *H. habilis*)[4].

Type Species.   *Kenyanthropus platyops* sp. nov.

Etymology.   From the Greek *platus,* meaning flat, and *opsis,* meaning face; thus referring to the characteristically flat face of this species.

Specific Diagnosis.   Same as for genus.

Types.   The holotype is KNM-WT 40000 (Figure 1a–d), a largely complete cranium found by J. Erus in August 1999. The paratype is KNM-WT 38350 (Figure 1e), a partial left maxilla found by B. Onyango in August 1998. The repository is the National Museums of Kenya, Nairobi.

Table 2. Derived Cranial Features of *Paranthropus,* and Their Character State in *K. platyops* and *H. rudolfensis*

	Paranthropus aethiopicus	Paranthropus boisei	Paranthropus robustus	Kenyanthropus platyops	Homo rudolfensis
Upper molar size	Large	Large	Moderate	Small	Moderate
Enamel thickness	Hyperthick	Hyperthick	Hyperthick	Thick	Thick
Palatal thickness	Thick	Thick	Thick	Thin	Thin
Incisor alveoli close to bicanine line[*]	Present	Present	Present	Present	Present
Nasoalveolar clivus	Gutter	Gutter	Gutter	Flat	Flat
Midline subnasal prognathism	Strong	Moderate	Moderate	Weak	Weak
Upper I² root to lateral nasal aperture	Medial	Medial	Medial	Lateral	Lateral
Nasal cavity entrance	Smooth	Smooth	Smooth	Stepped	Stepped
Zygomaticoalveolar crest	Straight, high	Straight, high	Straight, high	Curved, low	Curved, low
Anteriorly positioned zygomatic process of maxilla[*]	Present	Present	Present	Present	Present
Midface transverse contour	Concave, dished	Concave, dished	Concave, dished	Flat	Flat
Malar region	Wide	Wide	Wide	Tall	Tall
Malar orientation to lateral nasal margin	Aligned	Aligned	Aligned	More vertical	More vertical
Facial hafting, frontal trigone	High, present	High, present	High, present	Low, absent	Low, absent
Postorbital constriction	Marked	Marked	Marked	Moderate	Moderate
Initial supraorbital course of temporal lines	Medial	Medial	Medial	Posteromedial	Posteromedial
Tympanic vertically deep and plate-like	Present	Present	Present	Absent	Absent
Position external acoustic porus	Lateral	Lateral	Lateral	Medial	Medial
Mandibular fossa depth	Shallow	Deep	Deep	Moderate	Moderate
Foramen magnum heart shaped	Present	Present	Absent	Absent	Absent
Occipitomarginal sinus	Unknown	Present	Present	Absent	Absent

Hypodigm of *H. rudolfensis* as in ref. 35. See refs 1, 8, 11, 36–40 for detailed discussions of the features.

[*] Character states shared by *Paranthropus* and *K. platyops.*

Localities. Lomekwi localities are situated in the Lomekwi and Topernawi river drainages in Turkana district, northern Kenya (Figure 2). The type locality LO-6N is at 03° 54.03′ north latitude, 035° 44.40′ east longitude.

Horizon. The type specimen is from the Kataboi Member, 8 m below the Tulu Bor Tuff and 12 m above the Lokochot Tuff, giving an estimated age of 3.5 Myr. The paratype is from the lower Lomekwi Member, 17 m above the Tulu Bor Tuff, with an estimated age of 3.3 Myr.

CRANIAL DESCRIPTION AND COMPARISONS

The overall size of the KNM-WT 40000 cranium falls within the range of *A. afarensis* and *A. africanus.* It is preserved in two main parts, the neurocranium with the superior and lateral orbital margins, but lacking most of the cranial base; and the face, lacking the premolar and anterior tooth crowns and the right incisor roots. Most of the vault is heavily distorted, both through postmortem diploic expansion and compression from an inferoposterior direction (Figure 1a, b). The better preserved facial part shows some lateral skewing of the nasal area, anterior displacement of the right canine, and some expansion of the alveolar and zygomatic processes (Figure 1c–d), but allows for reliable assessment of its morphology.

Only the right M² crown is sufficiently preserved to allow reliable metric dental comparisons. It is particularly small, falling below the known ranges of other early hominin species (Figure 3a). Likewise, the esti-

mated M¹ crown size of KNM-WT 38350 (Table 1) corresponds to minima for *A. anamensis, A. afarensis* and *H. habilis,* and is below the ranges for other African early hominins[5-7]. Molar enamel thickness in both specimens is comparable to that in *A. anamensis* and *A. afarensis.* CT scans show that both P³ and P⁴ of KNM-WT 40000 have a lingual root and two well-separated buccal roots. This morphology, thought to be the ancestral hominoid condition[8], is commonly found in *Paranthropus,* but is variable among species of *Australopithecus.* The P³ of KNM-WT 38350 has three well-separated roots (Figure 1e). Its P⁴ seems to be two-rooted, but the deeply grooved buccal root may split more apically. Relative to M² crown size, the canine roots of KNM-WT 40000 are smaller in cross-section at the alveolar margin than in *Ardipithecus ramidus* and *A. anamensis,* similar in size to *A. afarensis, A. africanus* and *H. habilis,* and larger than in *P. boisei.* Exposed surfaces and CT scans demonstrate that the I¹ and I² roots in KNM-WT 40000 are straight and similar in size. At the level of the alveolar margin the cross-sectional area of the I² root is about 90% of that of the I¹ root, whereas this is typically 50–70% in other known hominid taxa.

The incisor alveoli of KNM-WT 40000 are aligned coronally, just anterior to the bicanine line, and the overlying nasoalveolar clivus is flat both sagittally and transversely. There is no canine jugum visible on the preserved left side, reflecting the modest size of the canine root. At 32 mm (chord distance nasospinale to prosthion) the clivus is among the longest of all early hominins. Subnasal prognathism is moderate, expressed by a more vertically orientated clivus than in nearly all specimens of *Australopithecus* and *Paranthropus*

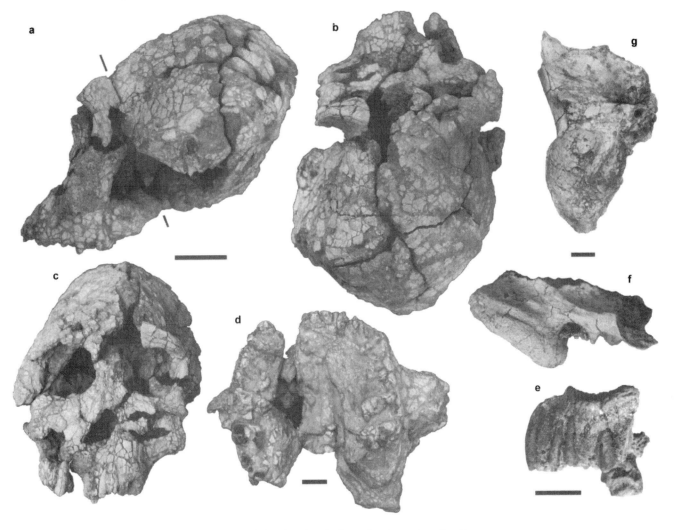

Figure 1. *Holotype KNM-WT 40000 **a**, left lateral view (markers indicate the plane separating the distorted neurocranium and the well-preserved face). **b**, Superior view. **c**, Anterior view. **d**, Occlusal view of palate. Paratype KNM-WT 38350. **e**, Lateral view. KNM-WT 40001. **f**, Lateral view. **g**, Inferior view. Scale bars: **a–c**, 3 cm; **d–g**, 1 cm.*

(Figure 3b). The nasal aperture lies in the same coronal plane as the nasoalveolar clivus and there are no anterior facial pillars (Figure 1a–c). The nasal aperture is small and narrow, in contrast to the large, wide aperture in *A. africanus* and *P. robustus*. The midface of KNM-WT 40000 is dominated by the tall malar region (Figure 3c) with a low and curved zygomaticoalveolar crest. At a level just below the nasal bones the transverse facial contour is flat (Figure 1b). In both KNM-WT 40000 and KNM-WT 38350 the anterior surface of the zygomatic process of the maxilla is positioned between P^3 and P^4 (Figure 1a, d, e), as is commonly seen in *Paranthropus*, but more anteriorly than in most *Australopithecus* specimens[9] or in *H. habilis*. The supraorbital region is *Australopithecus*-like, lacking both a frontal trigon as seen in *Paranthropus*, and a supratoral sulcus as seen in *H. habilis* (but not *H. rudolfensis*). Relative postorbital constriction (frontofacial index) of KNM-WT 40000 is similar to that in *Australopithecus*, *H. rudolfensis* and *H. habilis*, and less than in *P. boisei* (estimated frontofacial index[9] = 70). Its temporal lines converging on the frontal squama have a posteromedial course throughout (Figure 1b). Around bregma the midline morphology is not well preserved, but the posterior half of the parietals show double, slightly raised temporal lines about 6 mm apart. These contribute posteriorly to indistinct compound temporal/nuchal lines. The original shape of the severely distorted mastoids cannot be reconstructed, but other parts of the left temporal are well preserved. The tubular tympanic lacks a petrous crest and forms a narrow external acoustic meatus with a small aperture. This combination constitutes the primitive hominin morphology, also seen in *Ar. ramidus* and *A. anamensis* (Figure 3d). The mandibular fossa resembles that of specimens of *A. afarensis* and *A. africanus*. It is moderately deep, and the articular eminence, missing its lateral margin, is cylindrical with a moderately convex sagittal profile. The preserved posterior half of the foramen magnum suggests that it was probably oval in shape, rather than the heart shape seen in *P. boisei* and probably *P. aethiopicus*. Regarding the endocranial aspect, the reasonably well preserved

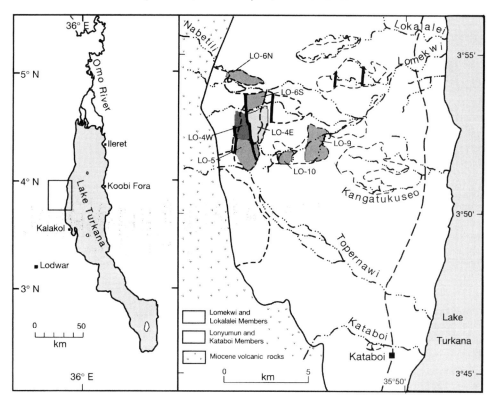

Figure 2. *Map showing localities of fossil collection in upper Lomekwi and simplified geology. The boundary between the Kataboi and Lomekwi Members is the base of the Tulu Bor Tuff, indicated as a dashed line through LO-4E and LO-4W. Faults are shown as thick lines; minor faults are omitted. LO-4E and LO-4W are of different shades to distinguish them from each other.*

occipital surface lacks any indication of the occipital/marginal venous sinus system characteristic of *A. afarensis, P. boisei* and *P. robustus.* Bilateral sulci suggest that the transverse/sigmoid sinus system was well developed. Endocranial capacity is difficult to estimate because of the distorted vault. However, comparing hominin glabella–opisthion arc lengths[8] with that of KNM-WT 40000 (259 mm; an estimate inflated by diploic expansion) suggests a value in the range of *Australopithecus* or *Paranthropus.*

The sex of KNM-WT 40000 is difficult to infer. Interpretation of the canine root size proves inconclusive without a suitable comparative context. The small M^2 crown size could suggest that the specimen is female. However, the close proximity and slightly raised aspect of the temporal lines on the posterior half of the parietals is not seen in known female hominin crania, including the *Paranthropus* specimens KNM-ER 732, KNM-ER 407 and DNH7, and suggests that KNM-WT 40000 could be male.

With incisor alveoli close to the bicanine line and anteriorly positioned zygomatic processes, the face of KNM-WT 40000 resembles the flat, orthognathic-looking faces of both *Paranthropus* and *H. rudolfensis* cranium KNM-ER 1470. However, KNM-WT 40000 lacks most of the derived features that characterize *Paranthropus* (Table 2), and its facial architecture differs from the latter in much the same way as has been described for KNM-ER 1470 (refs 8, 10). Facial flatness in *Paranthropus* results from the forward position of the anteroinferiorly sloping malar region, whose main facial surface approximates the plane of the nasal aperture, but whose orientation contrasts with the more horizontally inclined nasoalveolar gutter[11]. In KNM-WT 40000 and KNM-ER 1470, it is the flat and orthognathic

nasoalveolar clivus that aligns with the plane of the nasal aperture, whereas the anteriorly set, tall malar region is more vertically orientated. KNM-WT 40000 lacks the derived short nasal bones and everted lateral nasal margin of KNM-ER 1470, and is less orthognathic in the midfacial region than this specimen; however, on balance this is the hominin face that KNM-WT 40000 most closely resembles.

ADDITIONAL MATERIAL

The right maxilla fragment KNM-WT 38343A preserves three well-separated P^3 roots, and its damaged canine seems low-crowned when compared with *A. afarensis* canines of similar size and degree of wear. The right temporal bone KNM-WT 40001 lacks the squama and petrous apex, but is otherwise well preserved (Figure 1f, g). It shows a combination of characters not seen in any other hominin specimen. The projecting mastoid process is rounded, with an anteriorly positioned tip. It has a well-developed digastric fossa in the form of a deep, narrow groove that runs posterolaterally from the stylomastoid foramen, fully demarcating the mastoid process from the adjacent nuchal plane. The tympanic element is long, inferosuperiorly shallow and lacks a petrous crest. The external acoustic porus is the smallest of any known hominin temporal bone (Figure 3d). The articular eminence is as broad mediolaterally (38 mm) as in *P. aethiopicus* and *P. boisei,* and similar to the largest found in *A. afarensis.* Compared with KNM-WT 40000 the eminence is relatively flat sagittally, and the mandibular fossa is shallow.

The partial mandibles KNM-WT 8556 and KNM-WT 16006 have been assigned to *A. afarensis*[3]. However, KNM-WT 8556 shows a more derived morphology than

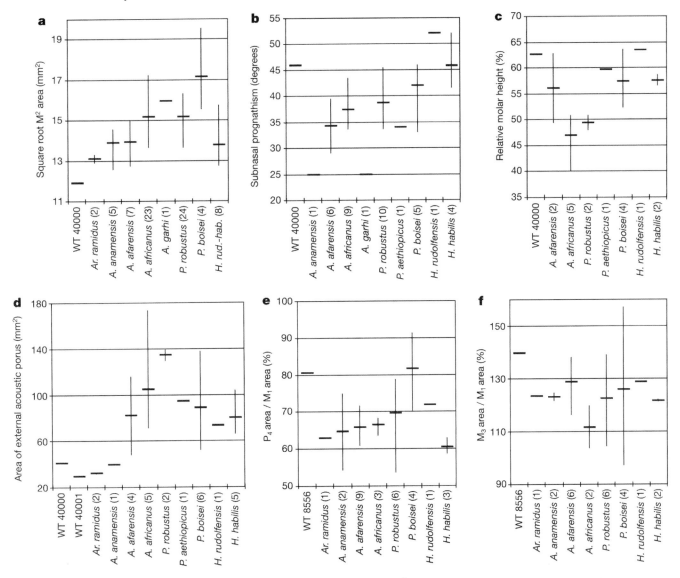

Figure 3. *Mean and range of characters of specified hominins.* **a,** *Square root of M^2 crown area (buccolingual $\times$ mesiolingual diameters).* **b,** *Angle of subnasal prognathism (nasospinale–prosthion to postcanine alveolar plane).* **c,** *Malar height[8] relative to orbitoalveolar height (orbitale to alveolar margin aligned with malar surface).* **d,** *Area of the external acoustic porus ($\pi \times$ long axis $\times$ short axis).* **e,** *Crown area of P_4 relative to that of $M^1 \times 100$.* **f,** *Crown area of M_3 relative to that of $M_1 \times 100$. All measurements are taken from originals, directly or as given in refs 8, 9, 14, 18, 37, 41–44, except for some South African crania taken from casts. Numbers in parentheses indicate sample size.*

this species by having a flat, more horizontal post-incisive plane, a more superiorly positioned genioglossal pit, a molarized lower fourth premolar (P_4) and a large M_3 (ref. 3). Indeed, relative to its *Australopithecus*-sized M_1 (refs 5, 6, 12, 13), the P_4 and M_3 crowns of KNM-WT 8556 are enlarged to an extent only seen in *P. boisei* (Figure 3e, f). All unworn molars in the Lomekwi sample are characterized by low occlusal relief and numerous secondary fissures. Most of the lower molars, including the KNM-WT 16006 M_3, have a well-developed protostylid, a feature that is usually absent in *A. afarensis*, but common in *A. africanus*[14]. The two I^2s are lower crowned than in *A. afarensis, A. africanus*[14] and

P. robustus[14]. Inability to distinguish between first and second molars makes meaningful intertaxon comparisons of these elements difficult.

TAXONOMIC DISCUSSION

The hominin specimens recovered from the Kataboi and lower Lomekwi Members show a suite of features that distinguishes them from established hominin taxa, including the only contemporaneous eastern African species, *A. afarensis*. Compared with the latter, the morphology of *K. platyops* is more derived facially, and more primitive in its small external acoustic porus and the absence of an occipital/marginal sinus system. These finds not only provide evidence for a taxonomically more diverse middle Pliocene hominin record, but also show that a more orthognathic facial morphology emerged significantly earlier in hominin evolutionary history than previously documented. This early facio-dental diversity concerns morphologies that functionally are most closely associated with mastication. It suggests a diet-driven adaptive radiation among hominins in this time interval, which perhaps had its origins considerably earlier. Furthermore, the presence in *K. platyops* of an anteriorly positioned zygomatic process in combination with a small M^1 and M^2 indicates that such characters are more independent than is suggested by developmental and functional models that link such facial morphology in *Paranthropus* with post-canine megadontia[11,15].

At present it is unclear whether the Lomekwi hominin fossils sample multiple species. Apart from the paratype maxilla KNM-WT 38350 with its small molar size and anteriorly positioned zygomatic process, the other specimens cannot be positively associated morphologically with the *K. platyops* holotype. These are therefore not included in the paratype series, and are left unassigned until further evidence emerges. Differences between the tympanic and mandibular fossa morphologies of the KNM-WT 40000 and KNM-WT 40001 temporal bones can perhaps be accommodated within a single species, but their shared primitive characters do not necessarily imply conspecificity. Affiliation of the KNM-WT 8556 mandible with the *K. platyops* types is not contradicted by its molarized P_4, which is consistent with an anteriorly positioned zygomatic process. However, its M_1 is larger than would be inferred from the smaller upper molars of the types, and with a 177 mm^2 crown area it is also larger than any in the combined sample of ten isolated M_1s and M_2s (139–172 mm^2). One isolated $M^{1/2}$ (KNM-WT 38362) is significantly larger than the molars of the *K. platyops* types, whereas another (KNM-WT 38337) is similar in size to the holotype's M^2.

The marked differences of the KNM-WT 40000 cranium from established hominin taxa, both with respect to individual features and their unique combination, fully justify its status as a separate species. It is worth noting that comparisons with *Australopithecus bahrelghazali* cannot be made directly, because this species was named on the basis of the limited evidence provided by an anterior mandible fragment[16]. Specific distinction of *A. bahrelghazali* from *A. afarensis* has yet to be confirmed[17], and Lomekwi specimens differ from *A. bahrelghazali* in symphyseal morphology and incisor crown height.

The generic attribution of KNM-WT 40000 is a more complex issue, in the absence of consensus over the definition of the genus category[4]. The specimen lacks almost all of the derived features of *Paranthropus* (Table 2), and there are no grounds for assigning it to this genus unless it can be shown to represent a stem species. However, the fact that the facial morphology of KNM-WT 40000 is derived in a markedly different way

renders this implausible. As KNM-WT 40000 does not show the derived features associated with *Homo*[4] (excluding *H. rudolfensis* and *H. habilis*) or the strongly primitive morphology of *Ardipithecus*[18], the only other available genus is *Australopithecus*. We agree with the taxonomically conservative, grade-sensitive approach to hominin classification that for the moment accepts *Australopithecus* as a paraphyletic genus in which are clustered stem species sharing a suite of key primitive features, such as a small brain, strong subnasal prognathism, and relatively large postcanine teeth. However, with its derived face and small molar size, KNM-WT 40000 stands apart from species assigned to *Australopithecus* on this basis. All it has in common with such species is its small brain size and a few other primitive characters in the nasal, supraorbital and temporal regions. Therefore, there is no firm basis for linking KNM-WT 40000 specifically with *Australopithecus*, and the inclusion of such a derived but early form could well render this genus polyphyletic. In a classification in which *Australopithecus* also includes the 'robust' taxa and perhaps even species traditionally known as 'early *Homo*'[4], this genus subsumes several widely divergent craniofacial morphologies. It could thus be argued that the inclusion of KNM-WT 40000 in *Australopithecus* would merely add yet another hominin species with a derived face. This amounts to defining *Australopithecus* by a single criterion, those hominin species not attributable to *Ardipithecus* or *Homo*, which in our view constitutes an undesirable approach to classification. Thus, given that KNM-WT 40000 cannot be grouped sensibly with any of the established hominin genera, and that it shows a unique pattern of facial and dental morphology that probably reflects a distinct dietary adaptive zone, we assign this specimen to the new genus *Kenyanthropus*.

Despite being separated by about 1.5 Myr, KNM-WT 40000 is very similar in its facial architecture to KNM-ER 1470, the lectotype of *H. rudolfensis*. The main differences amount to the more primitive nasal and neurocranial morphology of KNM-WT 40000. This raises the possibility that there is a close phylogenetic relationship between the two taxa, and affects our interpretation of *H. rudolfensis*. The transfer of this species to *Australopithecus* has been recommended[4,19], but *Kenyanthropus* may be a more appropriate genus. The identification of *K. platyops* has a number of additional implications. As a species contemporary with *A. afarensis* that is more primitive in some of its morphology, *K. platyops* weakens the case for *A. afarensis* being the sister taxon of all later hominins, and thus its proposed transfer to *Praeanthropus*[1,20]. Furthermore, the morphology of *K. platyops* raises questions about the polarity of characters used in analyses of hominin phylogeny. An example is the species' small molar size, which, although probably a derived feature, might also imply that the larger postcanine dentition of *A. afarensis* or *A. anamensis* does not represent the primitive hominin condition. Finally, the occurrence of at least one additional hominin species in the middle Pliocene of eastern Africa means that the affiliation of fragmentary specimens can now be reassessed. For example, the attribution of the 3.3 Myr old KNM-ER 2602 cranial fragment to *A. afarensis*[21] has been questioned[8], and evaluating its affinities with *K. platyops* is now timely.

GEOLOGICAL CONTEXT AND DATING

KNM-WT 40000 was collected near the contact of the Nachukui Formation with Miocene volcanic rocks in the northern tributary of Lomekwi (Nabetili). It is situated 12 m above the Lokochot Tuff, and 8 m below the β-Tulu Bor Tuff (Figure 4). Along Nabetili, the Lokochot Tuff is pinkish-grey and contains much clay and volcanic detritus. It is overlain by a volcanic pebble conglomerate, followed by a pale brown quartz-rich fine sandstone that includes a burrowed fine-sandstone marker bed 10–15 cm thick. The Lokochot Tuff is replaced by a thick volcanic clast conglomerate in the central part of Lomekwi. The contact between the fine

sandstone and the overlying dark mudstone can be traced from Nabetili to the hominin locality. Locally the mudstone contains volcanic pebbles at the base, and it has thin pebble conglomerate lenses in the upper part at the hominin locality, and also contains $CaCO_3$ concretions. The hominin specimen and other vertebrate fossils derive from this mudstone. Overlying the dark mudstone at the hominin site is a brown mudstone (8 m) that directly underlies the β-Tulu Bor Tuff.

New $^{40}Ar/^{39}Ar$ determinations on alkali feldspars from pumice clasts in the Moiti Tuff and the Topernawi Tuff, stratigraphically beneath the Lokochot Tuff, were instrumental in re-investigating the lower portion of this section. The new results yield a mean age for the Topernawi Tuff of 3.96 ± 0.03 Myr; this is marginally older than the pooled age for the Moiti Tuff of 3.94 ± 0.03 Myr. Previous investigations[22,23] placed the

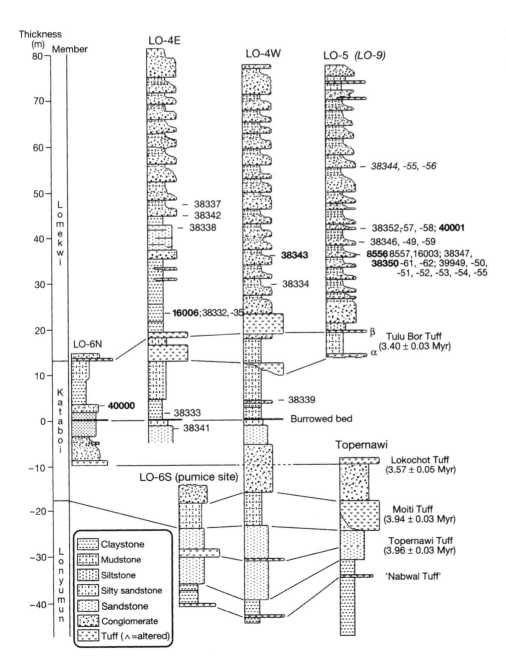

Figure 4. *Stratigraphic sections and placement of hominin specimens at sites in upper part of the Lomekwi drainage, west of Lake Turkana, northern Kenya. Specimen numbers are given without the prefix KNM-WT, and those in bold are discussed in the text. Placement of specimens is relative to the nearest marker bed in the section. Italicized numbers show the relative placement of specimens at LO-9 on section LO-5. The burrowed bed, a useful local marker, is used as stratigraphic datum (0 m). The date for the Tulu Bor Tuff is taken as the age of the Sidi Hakoma Tuff at Hadar[25], which is consistent with the age of the Toroto Tuff (3.32 ± 0.03 Myr)[45] that overlies the Tulu Bor at Koobi Fora. The age of the Lokochot Tuff is assigned from its placement at the Gilbert/Gauss Chron boundary[24,46]. The tuff formerly thought to be the Moiti Tuff at Lomekwi[22] has been informally called the 'Nabwal Tuff'[47]. Ages on the Tulu Bor and the Lokochot Tuffs are consistent with orbitally tuned ages of correlative ash layers in Ocean Drilling Program Core 722A in the Arabian Sea[48].*

Topernawi Tuff above the Moiti Tuff, mainly on the basis of the K/Ar ages on alkali feldspar from pumice clasts in the Topernawi Tuff (3.78, 3.71, 3.76 and 3.97 Myr, all ± 0.04 Myr)[23]. The older determination (3.97 Myr) was thought to result from contamination by detrital feldspar. South of Topernawi, however, the Topernawi Tuff has now been shown to underlie the Moiti Tuff, and to be in turn underlain by a tephra informally termed the 'Nabwal tuff', previously thought to be a Moiti Tuff correlative. The correct sequence is shown in Figure 4, and the new ^{40}Ar/^{39}Ar age data on the Moiti Tuff and Topernawi Tuff are provided elsewhere.

Linear interpolation between the Lokochot Tuff (3.57 Myr old)[24] and Tulu Bor Tuff (3.40 Myr)[25] yields an age of 3.5 Myr for KNM-WT 40000, and 3.53 Myr for the burrowed bed. KNM-WT 38341 from immediately below the burrowed bed has an age near 3.53 Myr. KNM-WT 38333 and 38339, from between the burrowed bed and the α-Tulu Bor Tuff lie between 3.4 and 3.5 Myr. Other specimens from LO-4, LO-5, and LO-6 lie 16–24 m above the β-Tulu Bor Tuff, with ages near 3.3 Myr. Assuming linear sedimentation between the Tulu Bor Tuff and the Lokalalei Tuff (2.5 Myr)[23], specimens from LO-9 are around 3.2 Myr. The probable error on these age estimates is less than 0.10 Myr.

Palaeogeographically, the mudstone that contained KNM-WT 40000 at LO-6N was deposited along the northern margin of a shallow lake that extended to Kataboi and beyond[26,27]. Laterally discontinuous volcanic pebble conglomerates within the mudstone record small streams draining from hills to the west. Carbonate concretions at the hominin level are probably pedogenic, and indicate regional conditions with net evaporative loss. Other specimens between the burrowed bed and the Tulu Bor Tuff were also preserved in lake-margin environments, as is the case for KNM-WT 38341 that was collected below the burrowed bed. At LO-5, and in the upper part of LO-4E, strata were laid down by ephemeral streams draining the basin margin, principally the ancestral Topernawi, which deposited gravels in broad, shallow channels, and finer grained materials in interfluves. Specimens preserved in floodplain deposits of the ancestral Omo River that occupied the axial portion of the basin include those at LO-9, those less than 6 m above the Tulu Bor Tuff at LO-4E, and KNM-WT 38338. Thus, there is evidence for hominins occupying floodplains of major rivers, alluvial fans, and lake-margin environments 3.0–3.5 Myr ago. There is reasonable evidence that water sources were available to these hominins in channels of the ephemeral streams, and also possibly as seeps or springs farther out into the basin.

PALAEOECOLOGY AND FAUNA

Faunal assemblages from Lomekwi sites LO-4, LO-5, LO-6 and LO-9 indicate palaeoenvironments that were relatively well watered and well vegetated. The relative proportions of the bovids in the early collections from these sites indicate a mosaic of habitats, but with predominantly woodland and forest-edge species dominat-

ing[22]. Comparisons of the Lomekwi faunal assemblages with those from the few known hominin sites of similar age, Laetoli in Tanzania, Hadar in Ethiopia and Bahr el Ghazal in Chad, are of interest in view of the different hominin taxa represented. Hadar and Bahr el Ghazal, like Lomekwi, represent lakeshore or river floodplain palaeoenvironments[28,29], whereas Laetoli was not located near a water source; no aquatic taxa nor terrestrial mammals indicative of swamp or grassy wetlands were recovered[30]. The faunal assemblages of all four sites indicate a mosaic of habitats that seems to have included open grasslands and more wooded or forested environments[22,28,29,31,32]; the assemblages differ primarily in the indication of the nature of the dominant vegetation cover.

Although the mammalian faunal assemblage from Lomekwi is more similar to that from Hadar than to that from Laetoli, some mammalian species represented are different. At Lomekwi, *Theropithecus brumpti* is common and is the dominant cercopithecid, as it is elsewhere in the Turkana Basin at this time. This species is generally considered to indicate more forested or closed woodland habitats. In the Hadar Formation, *Theropithecus darti* is the common *Theropithecus* species and is associated with lower occurrences of the water-dependent reduncines and higher occurrences of alcelaphines and/or *Aepyceros*, which indicates drier woodlands and grasslands[33]. Differences in the representation of other common species at the two sites that are less obviously linked to habitat include *Kolpochoerus limnetes, Tragelaphus nakuae* and *Aepyceros shungurensis* at Lomekwi, as opposed to *K. afarensis, T. kyaloae* and an undescribed species of *Aepyceros* at Hadar (K. Reed, personal communication). The general indication is that the palaeoenvironment at Lomekwi may have been somewhat more vegetated and perhaps wetter than that persisting through much of the Hadar Formation. At both sites more detailed analyses will be essential to further develop an understanding of how subtle temporal changes in the faunal assemblages relate to hominin occurrences.

Note added in proof: If the hominin status of the recently published Lukeino craniodental specimens[49] is confirmed, this would support the suggestion that small molar size is the primitive rather than the derived hominin condition.

ACKNOWLEDGMENTS

We thank the Government of Kenya for permission to carry out this research and the National Museums of Kenya for logistical support. The National Geographic Society funded the field work and some laboratory studies. Neutron irradiations were facilitated by the Australian Institute of Nuclear Science and Engineering and the Australian Nuclear Science and Technology Organisation. We also thank the Ethiopian Ministry of Information and Culture, the National Museum of Ethiopia, B. Asfaw, Y. Bayene, C. Howell, D. Johanson, W. Kimbel, G. Suwa and T. White for permission to make comparisons with the early Ethiopian hominins and numerous people including N. Adamali,

B. Asfaw, C. Dean, C. Feibel, A. Griffiths, W. Kimbel, R. Kruszynski, K. Kupczik, R. Leakey, D. Lieberman, J. Moore, K. Patel, D. Plummer, K. Reed, B. Sokhi, M. Tighe, T. White and B. Wood for their help. Caltex (Kenya) provided fuel for the field expeditions, and R. Leakey allowed us the use of his aeroplane. The field expedition members included U. Bwana, S. Crispin, G. Ekalale, M. Eragae, J. Erus, J. Ferraro, J. Kaatho, N. Kaling, P. Kapoko, R. Lorinyok, J. Lorot, S. Hagemann, B. Malika, W. Mangao, S. Muge, P. Mulinge, D. Mutinda, K. Muthyoka, N. Mutiwa, W. Mutiwa, B. Onyango, E. Weston and J. Wynn. A. Ibui, F. Kyalo, F. Kirera, N. Malit, E. Mbua, M. Muungu, J. Ndunda, S. Ngui and A. Mwai provided curatorial assistance. The Leakey Foundation awarded a grant to F.B.

REFERENCES

1. Strait, D. S., Grine, F. E. and Moniz, M. A. A reappraisal of early hominid phylogeny. *J. Hum. Evol.* **32,** 17–82 (1997).
2. Ward, C., Leakey, M. and Walker, A. The new hominid species *Australopithecus anamensis. Evol. Anthrop.* **7,** 197–205 (1999).
3. Brown, B., Brown, F. and Walker, A. New hominids from the Lake Turkana Basin, Kenya. *J. Hum. Evol.* **41,** 29–44 (2001).
4. Wood, B. A. and Collard, M. C. The human genus. *Science* **284,** 65–71 (1999).
5. Leakey, M. G., Feibel, C. S., McDougall, I. and Walker, A. C. New four-million-year-old hominid species from Kanapoi and Allia Bay, Kenya. *Nature* **376,** 565–571 (1995).
6. Leakey, M. G., Feibel, C. S., McDougall, I., Ward, C. and Walker, A. New specimens and confirmation of an early age for *Australopithecus anamensis. Nature* **393,** 62–66 (1998).
7. Kimbel, W. H., Johanson, D. C. and Rak, Y. Systematic assessment of a maxilla of *Homo* from Hadar, Ethiopia. *Am. J. Phys. Anthrop.* **103,** 235–262 (1997).
8. Wood, B. A. *Koobi Fora Research Project* Vol. 4 (Clarendon Press, Oxford, 1991).
9. Lockwood, C. A. and Tobias, P. V. A large male hominin cranium from Sterkfontein, South Africa, and the status of *Australopithecus africanus. J. Hum. Evol.* **36,** 637–685 (1999).
10. Bilsborough, A. and Wood, B. A. Cranial morphometry of early hominids: facial region. *Am. J. Phys. Anthrop.* **76,** 61–86 (1988).
11. Rak, Y. *The Australopithecine Face* (Academic, New York, 1983).
12. Lockwood, C. A., Kimbel, W. H. and Johanson, D. C. Temporal trends and metric variation in the mandibles and dentition of *Australopithecus afarensis. J. Hum. Evol.* **39,** 23–55 (2000).
13. Moggi-Cecchi, J., Tobias, P. V. and Beynon, A. D. The mixed dentition and associated skull fragments of a juvenile fossil hominid from Sterkfontein, South Africa. *Am. J. Phys. Anthrop.* **106,** 425–465 (1998).
14. Robinson, J. T. The dentition of the Australopithecinae. *Transv. Mus. Mem.* **9,** 1–179 (1956).
15. McCollum, M. A. The robust australopithecine face: a morphogenetic perspective. *Science* **284,** 301–305 (1999).
16. Brunet, M. et al. *Australopithecus bahrelghazali,* une nouvelle espèce d'Hominidé ancien de la région de Koro Toro (Tchad). *C.R. Acad. Sci. Ser. IIa* **322,** 907–913 (1996).
17. White, T. D., Suwa, G., Simpson, S. and Asfaw, B. Jaws and teeth of *A. afarensis* from Maka, Middle Awash, Ethiopia. *Am. J. Phys. Anthrop.* **111,** 45–68 (2000).
18. White, T. D., Suwa, G. and Asfaw, B. *Australopithecus ramidus,* a new species of early hominid from Aramis, Ethiopia. *Nature* **371,** 306–312 (1994).
19. Wood, B. and Collard, M. The changing face of genus *Homo. Evol. Anthrop.* **8,** 195–207 (2000).
20. Harrison, T. in *Species, Species Concepts, and Primate Evolution* (eds Kimbel, W. H. and Martin, L. B.) 345–371 (Plenum, New York, 1993).
21. Kimbel, W. H. Identification of a partial cranium of *Australopithecus afarensis* from the Koobi Fora Formation. *J. Hum. Evol.* **17,** 647–656 (1988).
22. Harris, J. M., Brown, F. and Leakey, M. G. Stratigraphy and paleontology of Pliocene and Pleistocene localities west of Lake Turkana, Kenya. *Cont. Sci. Nat. Hist. Mus. Los Angeles* **399,** 1–128 (1988).
23. Feibel, C. S., Brown, F. H. and McDougall, I. Stratigraphic context of fossil hominids from the Omo Group deposits, northern Turkana Basin, Kenya and Ethiopia. *Am. J. Phys. Anthrop.* **78,** 595–622 (1989).
24. McDougall, I., Brown, F. H., Cerling, T. E. and Hillhouse, J. W. A reappraisal of the geomagnetic polarity time scale to 4 Ma using data from the Turkana Basin, East Africa. *Geophys. Res. Lett.* **19,** 2349–2352 (1992).
25. Walter, R. C. and Aronson, J. L. Age and source of the Sidi Hakoma Tuff, Hadar Formation, Ethiopia. *J. Hum. Evol.* **25,** 229–240 (1993).
26. Brown, F. H. and Feibel, C. S. in *Koobi Fora Research Project,* Vol. 3, *Stratigraphy, artiodactyls and paleoenvironments* (ed. Harris, J. M.) 1–30 (Clarendon, Oxford, 1991).
27. Feibel, C. S., Harris, J. M. and Brown, F. H. in *Koobi Fora Research Project,* Vol. 3, *Stratigraphy, artiodactyls and paleoenvironments* (ed. Harris, J. M.) 321–346 (Clarendon, Oxford, 1991).
28. Johanson, D. C., Taieb, M. and Coppens, Y. Pliocene hominids from the Hadar Formation, Ethiopia (1973–1977): stratigraphic, chronologic and paleoenvironmental contexts, with notes on hominid morphology and systematics. *Am. J. Phys. Anthrop.* **57,** 373–402 (1982).
29. Brunet, M. et al. The first australopithecine 2,500 kilometres west of the Rift Valley (Chad). *Nature* **378,** 273–240 (1995).
30. Leakey, M. D. and Harris, J. M. *Laetoli, a Pliocene Site in Northern Tanzania* (Clarendon, Oxford, 1987).
31. Harris, J. M. in *Laetoli, a Pliocene Site in Northern Tanzania* (eds Leakey, M. D. and Harris, J. M.) 524–531 (Clarendon, Oxford, 1987).
32. Kimbel, W. H. et al. Late Pliocene *Homo* and Oldowan tools from the Hadar Formation (Kadar Hadar Member), Ethiopia. *J. Hum. Evol.* **31,** 549–561 (1996).
33. Eck, G. G. in *Theropithecus, the Rise and Fall of a Primate Genus* (ed. Jablonski, N. G.) 15–83 (Cambridge Univ. Press, 1993).
34. White, T. D. New fossil hominids from Laetolil, Tanzania. *Am. J. Phys. Anthrop.* **46,** 197–230 (1977).
35. Wood, B. Origin and evolution of the genus *Homo. Nature* **355,** 783–790 (1992).
36. Suwa, G. et al. The first skull of *Australopithecus boisei. Nature* **389,** 489–492 (1997).
37. Keyser, A. W. The Drimolen skull: the most complete australopithecine cranium and mandible to date. *S. Afr. J. Sci.* **96,** 189–193 (2000).
38. Kimbel, W. H., White, T. D. and Johanson, D. C. Cranial morphology of *Australopithecus afarensis:* a comparative study based on a composite reconstruction of the adult skull. *Am. J. Phys. Anthrop.* **64,** 337–388 (1984).
39. Walker, A., Leakey, R. E., Harris, J. H. and Brown, F. H. 2.5-Myr *Australopithecus boisei* from west of Lake Turkana, Kenya. *Nature* **322,** 517–522 (1986).
40. Kimbel, W. H., White, T. D. and Johanson, D. C. in *Evolutionary History of the "Robust" Australopithecines* (ed. Grine, F. E.) 259–268 (Aldine de Gruyter, New York, 1988).
41. Asfaw, B. et al. *Australopithecus garhi:* A new species of early hominid from Ethiopia. *Science* **284,** 629–635 (1999).
42. Grine, F. E. and Strait, D. S. New hominid fossils from Member 1 "Hanging Remnant" Swartkrans Formation, South Africa. *J. Hum. Evol.* **26,** 57–75 (1994).
43. Johanson, D. C., White, T. D. and Coppens, Y. Dental remains from the Hadar Formation, Ethiopia: 1974–1977 collections. *Am. J. Phys. Anthrop.* **57,** 545–603 (1982).
44. Tobias, P. V. in *Olduvai Gorge* Vol. 4 (Cambridge Univ. Press, 1991).
45. McDougall, I. K-Ar and $^{40}Ar/^{39}Ar$ dating of the hominid-bearing Pliocene–Pleistocene sequence at Koobi Fora, Lake Turkana, northern Kenya. *Geol. Soc. Am. Bull.* **96,** 159–175 (1985).

46. Brown, F. H., Shuey, R. T. and Croes, M. K. Magnetostratigraphy of the Shungura and Usno Formations, southwestern Ethiopia: new data and comprehensive reanalysis. *Geophys. J. R. Astron. Soc.* **54,** 519–538 (1978).
47. Haileab, B. *Geochemistry, Geochronology and Tephrostratigraphy of Tephra from the Turkana Basin, Southern Ethiopia and Northern Kenya.* Thesis, Univ. Utah (1995).
48. deMenocal, P. B. and Brown, F. H. in *Hominin Evolution and Climatic Change in Europe* Vol. 1 (eds Agustí, J., Rook, L. and Andrews, P.) 23–54 (Cambridge Univ. Press, 1999).
49. Senut, B. et al. First hominid from the Miocene (Lukeino Formation, Kenya). *C.R. Acad. Sci. Paris* **332,** 137–144 (2001).

19

Tempo and Mode in Human Evolution

H. M. McHenry

ABSTRACT

The quickening pace of paleontological discovery is matched by rapid developments in geochronology. These new data show that the pattern of morphological change in the hominid lineage was mosaic. Adaptations essential to bipedalism appeared early, but some locomotor features changed much later. Relative to the highly derived postcrania of the earliest hominids, the craniodental complex was quite primitive (i.e., like the reconstructed last common ancestor with the African great apes). The pattern of craniodental change among successively younger species of Hominidae implies extensive parallel evolution between at least two lineages in features related to mastication. Relative brain size increased slightly among successively younger species of Australopithecus, *expanded significantly with the appearance of* Homo, *but within early* Homo *remained at about half the size of* Homo sapiens *for almost a million years. Many apparent trends in human evolution may actually be due to the accumulation of relatively rapid shifts in successive species.*

I n the 50 yr since the publication of Simpson's *Tempo and Mode in Evolution* (1) the paleontological record of Hominidae has improved more than a 100-fold. The improvements include precise geological dating and rich collections of well-preserved fossil hominids. Particularly valuable are newly discovered postcranial remains of early species that permit body-size estimation (2–4). These new data show that the pattern of morphological change in the hominid lineage was mosaic. Different parts of the body evolved at different times and at various rates. This report focuses on hominid phylogeny and the tempo and mode of evolution of bipedalism, the hominid dental configuration, and encephalization.

Abbreviations: Myr, million year(s); EQ, ratio of brain volume and expected volume.

Reprinted with permission from H. M. McHenry, *Proceedings of the National Academy of Sciences, USA,* Vol. 91, pp. 6780–6786. Copyright © 1994 National Academy of Sciences, U.S.A.

SPECIES, CLADES, AND PHYLOGENY

Views differ on the definitions of fossil hominid species and their phylogenetic relationships for many reasons but especially because of (*i*) the difficulty in identifying paleospecies (5–8) and (*ii*) the pervasiveness of homoplasy (9). One view (9) consists of five species of *Australopithecus* (*A. afarensis, A. aethiopicus, A. africanus, A. boisei,* and *A. robustus*) and three of *Homo* (*H. habilis, H. erectus,* and *H. sapiens*). Table 1 presents the geological dates and the estimated body, brain, and tooth sizes of these species.

Analysis of the states of 77 craniodental characters in these species of *Australopithecus* and *H. habilis* (9) reveals that the cladogram in Figure 1A is the most parsimonious (tree length = 12,796, consistency index = 0.72). The two late "robust" australopithecines, *A. robustus* and *A. boisei* are the most highly derived and form a sister group with early *Homo.* This branch links with *A. africanus* to form a clade containing *A. africanus, A. robustus, A. boisei,* and early *Homo. A. aethiopicus* branches from this clade next with *A. afarensis* as a sister species to all later hominids.

Figure 1B displays the phylogenetic tree implied by the most parsimonious cladogram. This phylogeny implies that *A. afarensis* is the most primitive hominid and that all later hominids shared a common ancestor that was more derived than *A. afarensis.* This post-*afarensis* hypothetical ancestor may someday be discovered. Its morphology can be reconstructed by observing the many ways *A. aethiopicus* resembles later hominids (especially *A. africanus*) and not *A. afarensis.* For example, the canine eminences of the face are prominent in the outgroup and in *A. afarensis* but are reduced or absent in all other species of hominid, which implies that the common ancestor of all post-*afarensis* species had canine eminences that were also reduced. This hypothetical ancestor would have a strongly developed metaconid on the lower first premolar. It would not, however, resemble *A. aethiopicus* in traits related to masticatory hypertrophy (heavy chewing), nor would it resemble any other post-*afarensis* species because they are all too derived in flexion of the base of the skull,

Table 1. Species of *Australopithecus, Homo,* and Modern African Apes with Geological Ages, Estimated Body Weights, Brain Volumes, Relative Brain Sizes (EQ), Cheek-tooth Area, and Relative Cheek-tooth Area (MQ)

Species	Dates, Myr	Body Weight, kg[*] Male	Female	Brain Volume,[†] cm³	EQ[‡]	Tooth Area,[§] mm²	MQ[¶]
A. afarensis	4–2.8	45	29	384	2.2	460	1.7
A. africanus	3–2.3	41	30	420	2.5	516	2.0
A. aethiopicus	2.7–2.3			399		688	
A. boisei	2.1–1.3	49	34	488	2.6	756	2.5
A. robustus	1.8–1.0	40	32	502	2.9	588	2.2
H. habilis	2.4–1.6	52	32	597	3.1	502	1.7
Early *H. erectus*	1.8–1.5	58	52	804	3.3	377	1.0
Late *H. erectus*	0.5–0.3	60	55	980	4.0	390	1.0
H. sapiens	0.4–0	58	49	1350	5.8	334	0.9
Pan paniscus	0	38	32	343	2.0	227	0.9
Pan troglodytes	0	49	41	395	2.0	294	0.9
Gorilla gorilla	0	140	70	505	1.7	654	1.0

[*]See refs. 2 and 10.

[†]Endocranial volume is transformed into brain volume by formula 4 in ref. 11.

[‡]Expected brain volume is 0.0589 (species body weight in g)$^{0.76}$; see ref. 12.

[§]Tooth area is the sum of the md × bl diameters of P_4, M_1, and M_2; see ref. 13.

[¶]MQ, ratio of observed tooth area and expected area; expected area is 12.15 (species body weight in kg)$^{0.86}$; see ref. 13.

[‖]Two species may be represented in this sample. Using Wood's 1988 classification, I calculate the values for *H. habilis sensu stricto* and *Homo rudolfensis* as follows: male body weight, 37 and 60 kg; female body weight, 32 and 51 kg; brain volume, 579 and 709 cm³; EQ, 3.5 and 3.0; tooth area, 478 and 570 mm²; MQ, 1.9 and 1.5 kg; see ref. 10.

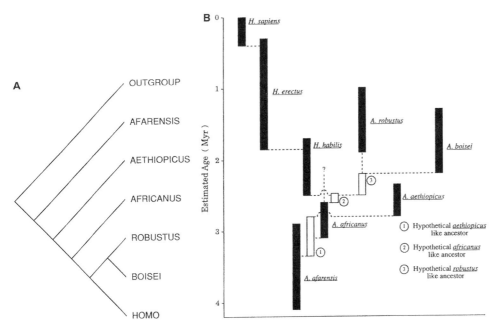

Figure 1. *(A) The most parsimonious cladogram using all 77 traits or using summary scores from the analyses of five functional complexes or seven anatomical regions. Tree length is 12,796 and consistency index is 0.722. (B) The phylogeny implied by the most parsimonious cladogram. Three hypothetical ancestors are predicted.*

orthognathism (flat faced), and encephalization to have been the ancestor of *A. aethiopicus*. After the divergence of *A. aethiopicus*, this phylogeny depicts a common ancestor of *A. afarensis, A. robustus, A. boisei,* and *Homo* that resembled *A. africanus* in its development of anterior dentition, basicranial flexion, orthognathism, and encephalization. A second hypothetical common ancestor appears in Figure 1*B* to account for the numerous derived traits shared by *A. robustus, A. boisei,* and early *Homo* that are not seen in *A. africanus*. This ancestor would have the degree of basicranial flexion and orthognathism seen in early *Homo* and the amount of encephalization seen in *A. robustus* and *boisei*. This

phylogeny proposes a third hypothetical ancestor that would be at the root of the lineage leading to *A. robustus* and *A. boisei*. This ancestor probably resembled *A. robustus* in traits related to heavy chewing.

Although the most parsimonious cladogram implies this phylogeny, other cladograms are possible but less probable. A cladogram linking *A. aethiopicus* to *A. boisei* and *robustus* as one branch and *A. africanus*/early *Homo* as another requires more evolutionary steps (tree length = 13332; consistency index = 0.69) because the later "robusts" resemble early *Homo* in so many features. These features include many aspects of basicranial flexation, loss of prognathism (muzzle), changes in the anterior dentition, and encephalization. The postcrania, although not included in this analysis, support the view that at least *A. robustus* and early *Homo* are monophyletic relative to other species of early hominid.

Whatever the true phylogeny is, and there can be only one, the fact remains that homoplasy is commonplace. Some resemblances appeared independently and not because of evolution from a common ancestor that possessed the same feature. Either adaptations for heavy chewing evolved twice or basicranial flexion, orthognathism, reduced anterior dentition, and encephalization each evolved more than once.

BIPEDALISM AND THE POSTCRANIUM

However the specific phylogeny of Hominidae is reconstructed, the important point is that these species are closely related to *H. sapiens,* and, in general, the more recent in time the species is, the more derived features it shares with our species. The earliest species, *A. afarensis,* is the most primitive in the sense that it shares the fewest of these derived traits and retains a remarkable resemblance to the common ancestor of African apes and people in many craniodental features. Its postcranium, however, is highly derived (14). It is fundamentally reorganized from that typical of apes to that specific to Hominidae (14–24).

Figure 2 presents features in which the postcranium of *A. afarensis* differs from African apes and approaches the condition characteristic of humans. The most significant features for bipedalism include shortened iliac blades, lumbar curve, knees approaching midline, distal articular surface of tibia nearly perpendicular to the shaft, robust metatarsal I with expanded head, convergent hallux (big toe), and proximal foot phalanges with dorsally oriented proximal articular surfaces. A

Lumbar lordosis and sacral retroflexion

Sacral ala expanded laterally

Sacroiliac and hip joints closely approximated

Pelvis with:
- Mediolaterally expanded, superinferiorly shortened, and anteriorly rotated iliac blades
- Robust anterior iliac spines
- Distinct sciatic notch
- Distinct iliopsoas groove
- Rugose and large area for sacrotuberous ligament
- Retroflexed auricular surface with extensive retroauricular area
- Robust posterior superior iliac spine
- Sigmoid curvature of iliac crest
- Dorsoventrally thickened pubic symphysis
- Retroflexion of hamstring tuberosity
- Shortened ischial shank

Femoral neck long with human-like distribution of cortical and spongy bone

Distal femur with:
- High bicondylar angle
- Elliptical lateral condyle
- Deep patellar groove with high lateral lip

Calcaneus with:
- Massive body
- Deep dorsoplantar dimension
- Ovoid transverse section
- Horizontally oriented sustentacular shelf

Midtarsal region is:
- Stout
- Anteroposteriorly expanded
- Strong transverse and longitudinal arch

Relative small forelimbs

Proximal humerus with open and shallow bicipital groove

Distal humerus with:
- Rounded lateral wall of olecranon fossa
- Gracile lateral epicondyle
- Moderate-sized and cranially facing medial epicondyle
- Moderate development of supracondylar ridge

Radiocarpal joint perpendicular to shaft axis

Capitate with:
- Proximodistally shortened axis
- Single and elongated facet for MCII
- Shallow excavations for MCIII articulations

Metacarpals II-V relatively short with no dorsal transverse ridge on heads

Phalanges relatively short

Tibia with straight shaft

Distal tibia with articular surface nearly perpendicular to shaft axis

Metatarsal I with:
- Robust and triangular diaphysis
- Expanded head

Metatarsals II-V with:
- Heads expanded superiorly
- MTV powerfully built with large tuberosity

Hallux is convergent

Toes relatively short

Proximal phalanges with dorsally oriented proximal articular surfaces

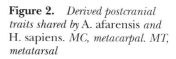

Figure 2. *Derived postcranial traits shared by* A. afarensis *and* H. sapiens. *MC, metacarpal. MT, metatarsal*

commitment to bipedalism in *A. afarensis* is also shown by the 3.5 million year (Myr) Laetoli footprints, which show very human-like proportions, arches, heel strike, and convergent big toes (24–27).

The nature of *A. afarensis* implies that bipedalism evolved well before the appearance of most other hominid characteristics. The appearance of bipedalism is sudden in the sense that it involved a complex alteration of structure in a relatively short period of time. Unfortunately, the fossil record does not yet include hominid postcrania predating 4.0 Myr that would document the transition from ape-like to hominid locomotion. The fundamental changes had already taken place in *A. afarensis.*

These bipedal alterations seen in *A. afarensis* are incomplete relative to modern *H. sapiens*, however (23, 28–40). Figure 3 presents traits in which this species differs in its postcranium from later species of Hominidae. These plesiomorphies probably imply that the bipedalism of *A. afarensis* was kinematically and energetically different from modern humans and may imply that they were more efficient tree climbers than modern humans. This arborealism would have been different from ape-like tree climbing, however, because the hindlimb was specialized for bipedality and had lost essential climbing adaptations such as hallucial divergence.

The pattern of change in these traits in later species of Hominidae is complex. Most of the postcranial

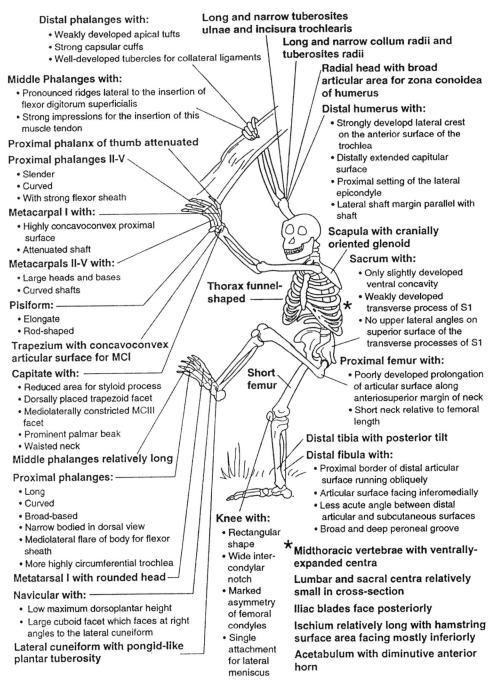

Distal phalanges with:
• Weakly developed apical tufts
• Strong capsular cuffs
• Well-developed tubercles for collateral ligaments

Middle Phalanges with:
• Pronounced ridges lateral to the insertion of flexor digitorum superficialis
• Strong impressions for the insertion of this muscle tendon

Proximal phalanx of thumb attenuated

Proximal phalanges II-V
• Slender
• Curved
• With strong flexor sheath

Metacarpal I with:
• Highly concavoconvex proximal surface
• Attenuated shaft

Metacarpals II-V with:
• Large heads and bases
• Curved shafts

Pisiform:
• Elongate
• Rod-shaped

Trapezium with concavoconvex articular surface for MCI

Capitate with:
• Reduced area for styloid process
• Dorsally placed trapezoid facet
• Mediolaterally constricted MCIII facet
• Prominent palmar beak
• Waisted neck

Middle phalanges relatively long

Proximal phalanges:
• Long
• Curved
• Broad-based
• Narrow bodied in dorsal view
• Mediolateral flare of body for flexor sheath
• More highly circumferential trochlea

Metatarsal I with rounded head

Navicular with:
• Low maximum dorsoplantar height
• Large cuboid facet which faces at right angles to the lateral cuneiform

Lateral cuneiform with pongid-like plantar tuberosity

Long and narrow tuberosites ulnae and incisura trochlearis

Long and narrow collum radii and tuberosites radii

Radial head with broad articular area for zona conoidea of humerus

Distal humerus with:
• Strongly developd lateral crest on the anterior surface of the trochlea
• Distally extended capitular surface
• Proximal setting of the lateral epicondyle
• Lateral shaft margin parallel with shaft

Scapula with cranially oriented glenoid

Sacrum with:
• Only slightly developed ventral concavity
• Weakly developed transverse process of S1
• No upper lateral angles on superior surface of the transverse processes of S1

Proximal femur with:
• Poorly developed prolongation of articular surface along anteriosuperior margin of neck
• Short neck relative to femoral length

Distal tibia with posterior tilt

Distal fibula with:
• Proximal border of distal articular surface running obliquely
• Articular surface facing inferomedially
• Less acute angle between distal articular and subcutaneous surfaces
• Broad and deep peroneal groove

Thorax funnel-shaped

Short femur

Knee with:
• Rectangular shape
• Wide inter-condylar notch
• Marked asymmetry of femoral condyles
• Single attachment for lateral meniscus

✱Midthoracic vertebrae with ventrally-expanded centra

Lumbar and sacral centra relatively small in cross-section

Iliac blades face posteriorly

Ischium relatively long with hamstring surface area facing mostly inferiorly

Acetabulum with diminutive anterior horn

Figure 3. *Primitive postcranial traits of* A. afarensis *shared with the reconstructed common ancestor of African apes and humans. MC, metacarpal.*

elements that can be directly compared reveal a period of stasis with no change between *A. afarensis* and *A. africanus* (23, 32). This is particularly striking in the capitate bone in the wrist and pelvis. Both have the identical combination of modern pongid, modern human, and unique characteristics. In the metacarpals and hand phalanges, however, *A. africanus* has some *Homo*-like features absent in *A. afarensis* (41, 42). The distal thumb phalanx of *A. africanus,* for example, is very human-like with its broad apical tuft that contrasts sharply with the relatively narrow, chimp-like tufts of the distal phalanges of *A. afarensis.* Limb proportions remain similar to *A. afarensis* in all species until the appearance of *H. erectus* at 1.7 Myr (2). Even *H. erectus* retains some primitive characteristics relative to *H. sapiens* (7). The most conspicuous of these is the relatively small cross-sectional area of the lumbar and sacral bodies (43). Narrow pelvic inlets and long femoral necks are characteristic of *A. afarensis, A. africanus,* and *H. erectus* and are probably related to parturition of smaller-head neonates (21, 44–49).

Body size remains relatively small in all species of *Australopithecus,* including the surprisingly petite bodies of the "robust" australopithecines (refs. 2–4, 49; Table 1, column 3). Sexual dimorphism in body size decreases from *A. afarensis* to *A. africanus* to *A. robustus.* Specimens attributed to *H. habilis* vary enormously in size and may imply (with other evidence) the existence of two species (3, 10, 14, 50). A sudden change occurs at 1.8 Myr with the appearance of *H. erectus* with body weights as high as 68 kg and a substantial reduction in sexual dimorphism. There is no evidence of a gradual trend of increased body weight through time, as might be expected from Cope's law.

MASTICATION

The distinction between the hominid and pongid dental pattern was sharply delineated before the discovery of *A. afarensis* (51), but that species bridged the gap (52, 53). Overall, the dentition of the earliest species of hominid is more similar to the inferred last common ancestor than it is to *H. sapiens.* Most notable primitive traits include large central and small lateral upper incisors, projecting upper canine with marginal attrition facets, small metaconid of the lower first premolar and parallel or convergent tooth rows. The positions of the masticatory muscles are also primitive, particularly the posterior placement of the main fibers of the temporalis. But there are numerous derived features shared with later hominids as well. The most conspicuous of these is the reduced canines with apical wear.

Hominid species postdating *A. afarensis* lose this species' primitive dental characteristics. *A. africanus* is variable in size and shape of its anterior teeth, but some specimens are more *Homo*-like (5, 50). Its lower first premolar is decidedly bicuspid. The mass of the temporalis muscle has moved forward into a more *Homo*-like position. Prognathism is reduced. The primitive dental features of *A. afarensis* are lost in hominid species postdating the appearance of *A. africanus.*

One unexpected characteristic of all early hominid species is postcanine megadontia and associated features related to heavy chewing (9, 13, 54–63). Relative to body size, the cheek-teeth of *A. afarensis* are 1.7 times larger than expected from that seen in modern species of Hominoidea (Table 1, column 8). Relative cheek-tooth size is higher in *A. africanus* (2.0) and higher still in *A. robustus* (2.2) and *A. boisei* (2.5). The appearance of *Homo* is marked by a reduction to 1.7. From the earliest *Homo* species to *H. erectus* to *H. sapiens* there has been dental reduction. Presumably the masticatory hypertrophy within species of *Australopithecus* is related to diet and to the amount of grit entering the mouth. Reduction of tooth size in *Homo* may reflect dietary change, but also it is probably related to the use of tools in preparing food.

The phylogeny presented in Figure 1*B* implies traits related to heavy chewing evolved by parallel evolution in two lineages. One of these is the lineage from *A. afarensis* to *A. aethiopicus.* The second is the lineage from *A. afarensis* to *A. africanus* to the late "robust" australopithecines, *A. robustus* and *A. boisei.* This is a surprising result because *A. aethiopicus* and *A. boisei* share a suite of unique character states such as extreme anterior projection of the zygomatic bone, huge cheek teeth, enormous mandibular robusticity, a heart-shaped foramen magnum, and temporoparietal overlap of the occipital at asterion (at least in males).

All of these traits, except for the heart-shaped foramen magnum, are related to the functional complex of heavy chewing. The huge cheek-teeth and robust mandibles of both species are obviously part of masticatory hypertrophy. The anterior projection of the zygomatic bones brings the masseter muscles into a position of maximum power. The encroachment by the root of the zygomaticoalveolar crest obscures the expression of the anterior pillars and upper canine jugae. Even the morphology of the temporoparietal overlap with occipital is related to the function of the forces generated by the chewing muscles (9).

Theoretically, it is understandable how such detailed similarity could be due to parallel evolution. These species are closely related and share "... so much in common in their constitution" (64) that similar selective forces produce similar morphologies. The selective forces in this case are related to a feeding adaptation that is associated with a specialized ecological niche. As Mayr (ref. 65, p. 125) points out "... most adaptations for special niches are far less revealing taxonomically than they are conspicuous. Occupation of a special food niche and the correlated adaptations have a particularly low taxonomic value." In fact, many of the same traits characteristic of *A. aethiopicus* and the other "robust" australopithecines reappear in distantly related species adapted to heavy chewing. Expansion of the cheek-teeth, shortening of the muzzle, and anterior migration of the attachment areas of the chewing muscles are seen in other primates whose diet requires heavy chewing (e.g., *Hadropithecus, Theropithecus,* probably *Gigantopithecus,* and *Ekmowehashala*).

ENCEPHALIZATION

Table 1, column 5 presents brain sizes in species of Hominidae. Absolute brain volume has more than tripled from *A. afarensis* to *H. sapiens,* and relative size has more than doubled (6, 8, 11, 12, 22, 66–84). Given the very human-like postcranium of *A. afarensis,* it is interesting that this species has a relative brain size very close to that of modern chimpanzees. Lamarck, Huxley, Haeckel, and Darwin speculated that bipedalism preceded encephalization, but they had no fossil proof (78). The early species of *Australopithecus* confirm their prediction.

Both absolute and relative brain size increase through time in the series from *A. afarensis* [384 cc, 2.2 ratio of brain volume and expected volume (EQ)] to *A. africanus* (420 cc, 2.5 EQ) to *A. boisei* (488 cc, 2.6 EQ) to *A. robustus* (502 cc, 2.9 EQ). Superficially, this increase through time appears to be by gradual increments, but samples are small and body weight determinations are inexact (2). The sample of endocasts of *A. afarensis* consists of three specimens and of these, all are fragmentary, and one is the estimated adult size from a 2.5-yr-old child (68). Although there are six endocasts of *A. africanus,* three of these needed substantial reconstruction (74). There is only one endocast of *A. robustus,* four of *A. boisei,* seven of *H. habilis,* five for early *H. erectus,* and five for late *H. erectus.* Body weight estimates may be off the mark, but the sample of postcranial specimens is sufficient to show that body weight remained at about the same relatively small size in all species of *Australopithecus.* This result implies that the apparent increase in brain size through time in species of *Australopithecus* is not due merely to an increase in body size. Body size and brain size are variable in specimens attributed to *H. habilis* with individuals as small as 32 kg and 484 cc and others as large as 57 kg and 709 cc. Although there are reasons to keep *H. habilis* as a single species (6), dividing the sample into two species is justifiable (8, 50). With either taxonomy, the absolute brain sizes of these early *Homo* specimens lie between *Australopithecus* and *H. erectus,* although relative brain

sizes of early members of *H. erectus* overlap the range of the smaller-bodied specimens of *H. habilis.* The relative brain size of early *H. erectus* is surprisingly small because body size is so large. By 1.7 Myr, individuals attributed to *H. erectus* grew to >180 cm, and by 1.5 Myr one individual (KNM-WT 15000) may have stood 185 cm and weighed 68 kg as an adult (4). Despite the fact that the average early *H. erectus* brain was >200 cc larger than the average brain of *H. habilis,* the relative brain sizes are only slightly different (EQ = 3.1 and 3.3).

The pattern of encephalization since early *H. erectus* is difficult to interpret because geological dates are less accurate, variability is high, and body weights are difficult to establish. Figure 4 plots brain size against time. For its first million years, *H. erectus* has absolute brain volumes that do not increase through time and therefore represent a period of stasis (85). It is difficult to establish whether relative brain sizes increased because there are very few postcranial fossils of *H. erectus* after 1.5 Myr from which to estimate body size. The few femora that are known are similar in size to those from early *H. erectus.* When taken over its entire range, the current sample of *H. erectus* does show a weak, but significant, positive increase in brain size through time (76). The sample of archaic *H. sapiens* (0.4–0.125 Myr) shows a strong positive trend (76). Variability is high. Many specimens as old as 0.4 Myr are within the modern human range of variation, and after 0.25 Myr all specimens are within this range. The average for the Neanderthals is 1369 cc compared with 1462 cc for early modern *H. sapiens.*

STASIS, PUNCTUATION, AND TRENDS

It is useful to regard evolutionary change in the hominid lineage from the point of view of Mayr's peripatric theory of speciation (86). Presumably, most of our samples derive from central populations of species and not from the small, isolated, and peripheral groups that are the most likely source of new species. When one of these peripheral isolates becomes reproductively isolated from the central species and its geographical range

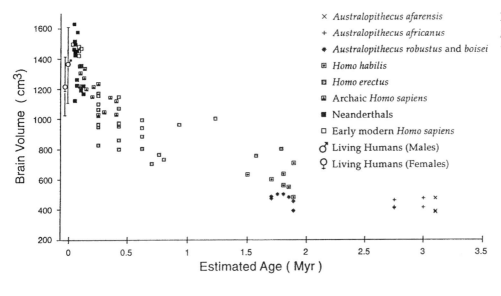

Figure 4.   *Brain size (in cm³) plotted against time (Myr) for specimens attributed to Hominidae.*

× *Australopithecus afarensis*

+ *Australopithecus africanus*

✳ *Australopithecus robustus* and *boisei*

⊞ *Homo habilis*

▣ *Homo erectus*

▦ Archaic *Homo sapiens*

■ Neanderthals

□ Early modern *Homo sapiens*

♂ Living Humans (Males)

♀ Living Humans (Females)

expands, it may overlap with the parent species, resulting in the coexistence of ancestral and descendant species. As depicted in Figure 1*B,* ancestral species overlap in time with descendants in most cases in hominid evolution, which is not what would be expected from gradual transformations by anagenesis (87). Trends through time observed in the fossil record are not necessarily the result of gradual change but rather "... an accumulation of discrete speciation events" (ref. 86; p. 223).

These events can be obscured by defining paleospecies too broadly, however. For example, it is conventional to define *H. erectus* as including specimens from deposits as old as 1.8 Myr and as young as 0.2 Myr (85). There is a slight trend in brain-size increase in this series (76), but the earliest and smallest brained specimens are regarded by some as a separate species, *Homo ergaster* (50, 88, 89). Another example is the inclusion of specimens into *H. sapiens* that date back to perhaps 0.5 Myr, despite their decidedly archaic features. By this attribution, there is a strong positive trend in brain size through time (76). An argument can be made, however, that this sample consists of several species (90).

This view does not exclude the presence of change through time within species, however. As the original proponents of the theory of punctuated equilibrium point out (86), this view concerns the relative frequency of stasis, punctuation, and phyletic gradualism. Even within the multiple-species hypothesis of Middle to Late Pleistocene *Homo* (90), all change through time does not occur at speciation events. For example, brain size and cranial morphology change from early to late specimens referred to *Homo neanderthalensis.* It is interesting, however, how little change occurs within most hominid species through time.

ACKNOWLEDGMENTS

I thank the organizers of this symposium and particularly Francisco Ayala and Walter Fitch for the invitation to contribute this paper. I am indebted to my colleague, R. R. Skelton, with whom I did the phylogenetic analysis reported here. I thank all those whose work led to the discovery of the fossils and especially M. D. Leakey, R. E. Leakey, F. C. Howell, D. C. Johanson, Tadessa Terfa, Mammo Tessema, C. K. Brain, P. V. Tobias, the late A. R. Hughes, and T. White for many kindnesses and permission to study the original fossil material. I thank the curators of the comparative samples used in this study. Partial funding was provided by the Committee on Research of the University of California, Davis.

REFERENCES

1. Simpson, G. G. (1944) *Tempo and Mode in Evolution* (Columbia Univ. Press, New York).
2. McHenry, H. M. (1992) *Am. J. Phys. Anthropol.* **87,** 407–431.
3. McHenry, H. M. (1994) *J. Hum. Evol.* **27,** 77–87.
4. Ruff, C. B. and Walker, A. (1993) in *The Nariokotome Homo erectus Skeleton,* eds. Walker, A. and Leakey, R. (Harvard Univ. Press, Cambridge, MA), pp. 234–265.
5. Kimbel, W. H. and Martin, L. B. (1993) in *Species, Species Concepts, and Primate Evolution,* eds. Kimbel, W. H. and Martin, L. B. (Plenum, New York), pp. 539–553.
6. Tobias, P. V. (1991) *Olduvai Gorge Volume 4: The Skulls, Endocasts and Teeth of Homo habilis* (Cambridge Univ. Press, Cambridge, U.K.).
7. Walker, A. and Leakey, R. (1993) in *The Nariokotome Homo erectus Skeleton,* eds. Walker, A. and Leakey, R. (Harvard Univ. Press, Cambridge, MA).
8. Wood, B. A. (1991) *Koobi Fora Research Project IV: Hominid Cranial Remains from Koobi Fora* (Clarendon, Oxford).
9. Skelton, R. R. and McHenry, H. M. (1992) *J. Hum. Evol.* **23,** 309–349.
10. McHenry, H. M. (1996) in *Power, Sex, and Tradition: The Archaeology of Human Ancestry,* eds. Shennan, S. and Steele, J. (Routledge and Kegan Paul, London), 91–109.
11. Aiello, L. C. and Dunbar, R. I. M. (1993) *Curr. Anthropol.* **34,** 184–193.
12. Martin, R. D. (1981) *Nature (London)* **293,** 57–60.
13. McHenry, H. M. (1984) *Am. J. Phys. Anthropol.* **64,** 297–306.
14. McHenry, H. M. (1994) in *Integrative Pathways to the Past: Paleoanthropological Papers in Honor of F. Clark Howell,* eds. Corruccini, R. S. and Ciochon, R. L. (Prentice–Hall, Engelwood Cliffs, NJ), pp. 251–268.
15. Berge, C. (1993) *L'Évolution de la Hanche et du Pelvis des Hominidés: Bipedie, Parturition, Croissance, Allometrie* (Presses du CNRS, Paris).
16. Johanson, D. C., Taieb, M. Coppens, Y. (1982) *Am. J. Phys. Anthropol.* **57,** 373–402.
17. Latimer, B. (1991) in *Origine(s) de la Bipédie chez les Hominidés,* eds. Coppens, Y. and Senut, B. (Presses du CNRS, Paris), pp. 169–176.
18. Latimer, B. M. and Lovejoy, C. O. (1989) *Am. J. Phys. Anthropol.* **78,** 369–386.
19. Latimer, B. and Lovejoy, C. O. (1990) *Am. J. Phys. Anthropol.* **82,** 125–134.
20. Latimer, B. and Lovejoy, C. O. (1990) *Am. J. Phys. Anthropol.* **83,** 13–23.
21. Lovejoy, C. O. (1988) *Sci. Am.* **259,** 118–126.
22. McHenry, H. M. (1982) *Annu. Rev. Anthropol.* **11,** 151–173.
23. McHenry, H. M. (1986) *J. Hum. Evol.* **15,** 177–191.
24. McHenry, H. (1991) in *Origine(s) de la Bipédie chez les Hominidés,* eds. Coppens, Y. and Senut, B. (Presses du CNRS, Paris), pp. 133–142.
25. Leakey, M. D. and Hay, R. L. (1979) *Science* **278,** 317–323.
26. Tuttle, R. H. (1987) in *Laetoli: A Pliocene Site in Northern Tanzania,* eds. Leakey, M. D. and Harris, J. M. (Clarendon, Oxford), pp. 503–523.
27. White, T. D. (1980) *Science* **208,** 175–176.
28. Deloison, Y. (1991) in *Origine(s) de la Bipédie chez les Hominidés,* eds. Coppens, Y. and Senut, B. (Presses du CNRS, Paris), pp. 177–186.
29. Jungers, W. L. (1982) *Nature (London)* **297,** 676–678.
30. Jungers, W. L. (1988) *J. Hum. Evol.* **17,** 247–266.
31. Senut, B. (1981) *L'Humérus et Ses Articulations chez les Hominidés Plio-Pléistocene* (Presses du CNRS, Paris).
32. McHenry, H. M. (1983) *Am. J. Phys. Anthropol.* **62,** 187–198.
33. Schmid, P. (1983) *Folia Primatol.* **40,** 283–306.
34. Schmid, P. (1991) in *Origine(s) de la Bipédie chez les Hominidés,* eds. Coppens, Y. and Senut, B. (Presses du CNRS, Paris), pp. 225–234.
35. Senut, B. and Tardieu, C. (1985) in *Ancestors: The Hard Evidence,* ed. Delson, E. (Liss, New York), pp. 193–201.
36. Senut, B. (1991) in *Origine(s) de la Bipédie chez les Hominidés,* eds. Coppens, Y. and Senut, B. (Presses du CNRS, Paris), pp. 245–258.
37. Stern, J. T. and Susman, R. L. (1983) *Am. J. Phys. Anthropol.* **60,** 279–318.
38. Susman, R. L., Stern, J. T. and Jungers, W. L. (1984) *Folia Primatol.* **43,** 113–156.
39. Tardieu, C. (1983) *L'articulation du Genou* (Presses du CNRS, Paris).
40. Tuttle, R. H. (1981) *Philos. Trans. R. Soc. London B* **292,** 89–94.
41. Ricklan, D. E. (1987) *J. Hum. Evol.* **16,** 643–664.
42. Ricklan, D. E. (1990) in *From Apes to Angels: Essays in Honor of Phillip V. Tobias,* ed. Sperber, G. H. (Wiley-Liss, New York), pp. 171–183.
43. Latimer, B. and Ward, C. V. (1993) in *The Nariokotome Homo erectus Skeleton,* eds. Walker, A. and Leakey, R. (Harvard Univ. Press, Cambridge, MA), pp. 266–293.

44. Berge, C., Orban-Segebarth, R., and Schmid, P. (1984) *J. Hum. Evol.* **13**, 573–587.
45. Lovejoy, C. O. (1978) in *Early Hominids of Africa*, ed. Jolly, C. J. (St. Martins, New York), pp. 403–429.
46. McHenry, H. M. (1975) *J. Hum. Evol.* **4**, 343–356.
47. Tague, R. G. and Lovejoy, C. O. (1986) *J. Hum. Evol.* **15**, 237–255.
48. Walker, A. (1993) in *The Nariokotome Homo erectus Skeleton*, eds. Walker, A. and Leakey, R. (Harvard Univ. Press, Cambridge, MA), pp. 411–430.
49. Walker, A. and Ruff, C. B. (1993) in *The Nariokotome Homo erectus Skeleton*, eds. Walker, A. and Leakey, R. (Harvard Univ. Press, Cambridge, MA), pp. 221–233.
50. Wood, B. A. (1992) *Nature (London)* **355**, 783–790.
51. Clark, W. E. L. (1967) *Man-Apes or Ape-Men* (Holt, Rinehart and Winston, New York).
52. Johanson, D. C. and White, T. D. (1979) *Science* **203**, 321–330.
53. White, T. D., Johanson, D. C. and Kimbel, W. H. (1981) *S. Afr. J. Sci.* **77**, 445–470.
54. Aiello, L. and Dean, C. (1990) *An Introduction to Human Evolutionary Anatomy* (Academic, London).
55. Grine, F. E., ed. (1988) in *Evolutionary History of the Robust Australopithecines* (de Gruyter, New York), 509–510.
56. Rak, Y. (1983) *The Australopithecine Face* (Academic, New York).
57. Tobias, P. V. (1967) *Olduvai Gorge: The Cranium and Maxillary Dentition of Australopithecus (Zinjanthropus) boisei* (Cambridge Univ. Press, Cambridge, U.K.).
58. Tobias, P. V. (1991) in *Evolution of Life: Fossils, Molecules, and Culture*, eds. Osawa, S. and Honjo, T. (Springer, Tokyo), pp. 363–377.
59. Turner, A. and Wood, B. (1993) *J. Hum. Evol.* **24**, 301–318.
60. Turner, A. and Wood, B. (1993) *J. Hum. Evol.* **24**, 147–168.
61. Walker, A., Leakey, R. E. F., Harris, J. M. and Brown, F. H. (1986) *Nature (London)* **322**, 517–522.
62. Wood, B. A. (1988) in *Evolutionary History of the "Robust" Australopithecines*, ed. Grine, E. F. (de Gruyter, New York), pp. 269–284.
63. Wood, B. A. and Chamberlain, A. T. (1987) *J. Hum. Evol.* **16**, 625–642.
64. Darwin, C. (1872) *The Origin of Species* (Random House, New York), 6th Ed.
65. Mayr, E. (1969) *Principles of Systematic Zoology* (McGraw-Hill, New York).
66. Begun, D. and Walker, A. (1993) in *The Nariokotome Homo erectus Skeleton*, eds. Walker, A. and Leakey, R. (Harvard Univ. Press, Cambridge, MA), pp. 326–358.
67. Blumenberg, B. (1983) *Curr. Anthropol.* **24**, 589–623.
68. Falk, D. (1987) *Annu. Rev. Anthropol.* **16**, 13–30.
69. Foley, R. A. (1992) in *Evolutionary Ecology and Human Behaviour*, eds. Smith, E. A. and Winterhalder, B. (de Gruyter, New York), pp. 131–164.
70. Godfrey, L. and Jacobs, K. H. (1981) *J. Hum. Evol.* **10**, 255–272.
71. Gould, S. J. (1975) *Contrib. Primatol.* **5**, 244–292.
72. Hofman, M. A. (1983) *Brain Behav. Evol.* **22**, 102–177.
73. Holloway, R. L. and Post, D. G. (1982) in *Primate Brain Evolution: Methods and Concepts*, eds. Armstrong, E. and Falk, E. (Plenum, New York), pp. 57–76.
74. Holloway, R. L. (1983) *Hum. Neurobiol.* **2**, 105–114.
75. Jerison, H. (1973) *Evolution of the Brain and Intelligence* (Academic, New York).
76. Leigh, S. R. (1992) *Am. J. Phys. Anthropol.* **87**, 1–13.
77. Martin, R. D. (1983) *Human Brain Evolution in an Ecological Context* (Am. Mus. Nat. Hist., New York).
78. McHenry, H. M. (1975) *Science* **190**, 425–431.
79. McHenry, H. M. (1974) *Am. J. Phys. Anthropol.* **40**, 329–340.
80. Parker, S. T. (1990) in *"Language" and Intelligence in Monkeys and Apes*, eds. Parker, S. T. and Gibson, K. R. (Cambridge Univ. Press, Cambridge, U.K.), pp. 129–154.
81. Passingham, R. E. (1985) *Brain Behav. Evol.* **26**, 167–175.
82. Pilbeam, D. R. and Gould, S. J. (1974) *Science* **186**, 892–901.
83. Shea, B. T. (1987) *Int. J. Primatol.* **8**, 139–156.
84. Tobias, P. V. (1971) *The Brain in Hominid Evolution* (Columbia Univ. Press, New York).
85. Rightmire, G. P. (1990) *The Evolution of Homo erectus* (Cambridge Univ. Press, Cambridge, U.K.).
86. Gould, S. J. and Eldredge, N. (1993) *Nature (London)* **366**, 223–227.
87. MacFadden, B. J. (1992) *Fossil Horses: Systematics, Paleobiology, and Evolution of the Family Equidae* (Cambridge Univ. Press, Cambridge, U.K.).
88. Groves, C. P. (1989) *A Theory of Human and Primate Evolution* (Clarendon, Oxford).
89. Wood, B. (1993) in *Species, Species Concepts, and Primate Evolution*, eds. Kimbel, W. H. and Martin, L. B. (Plenum, New York), pp. 485–522.
90. Stringer, C. B. (1994) in *Issues in Hominid Evolution*, ed. Howell, F. C. (California Acad. Sci., San Francisco), in press.

20

Inferring Hominoid and Early Hominid Phylogeny Using Craniodental Characters

The Role of Fossil Taxa

D. S. Strait and F. E. Grine

ABSTRACT

Recent discoveries of new fossil hominid species have been accompanied by several phylogenetic hypotheses. All of these hypotheses are based on a consideration of hominid craniodental

morphology. However, Collard and Wood (2000) suggested that cladograms derived from craniodental data are inconsistent with the prevailing hypothesis of ape phylogeny based on molecular data. The implication of their study is that craniodental characters are unreliable indicators of phylogeny in hominoids and fossil hominids but, notably, their analysis did not include extinct species. We report here on a cladistic analysis designed to test whether the inclusion of fossil taxa affects the ability of morphological characters to recover the molecular ape phylogeny. In the process of doing so, the study tests both

Collard and Wood's (2000) hypothesis of character reliability, and the several recently proposed hypotheses of early hominid phylogeny. One hundred and ninety-eight craniodental characters were examined, including 109 traits that traditionally have been of interest in prior studies of hominoid and early hominid phylogeny, and 89 craniometric traits that represent size-corrected linear dimensions measured between standard cranial landmarks. The characters were partitioned into two data sets. One set contained all of the characters, and the other omitted the craniometric characters. Six parsimony analyses were performed; each data set was analyzed three times, once using an ingroup that consisted only of extant hominoids, a second time using an ingroup of extant hominoids and extinct early hominids, and a third time excluding Kenyanthropus platyops.

Results suggest that the inclusion of fossil taxa can play a significant role in phylogenetic analysis. Analyses that examined only extant taxa produced most parsimonious cladograms that were inconsistent with the ape molecular tree. In contrast, analyses that included fossil hominids were consistent with that tree. This consistency refutes the basis for the hypothesis that craniodental characters are unreliable for reconstructing phylogenetic relationships. Regarding early hominids, the relationships of Sahelanthropus tchadensis *and* Ardipithecus ramidus *were relatively unstable. However, there is tentative support for the hypotheses that* S. tchadensis *is the sister taxon of all other hominids. There is support for the hypothesis that* A. anamensis *is the sister taxon of all hominids except* S. tchadensis *and* Ar. ramidus. *There is no compelling support for the hypothesis that* Kenyanthropus platyops *shares especially close affinities with* Homo rudolfensis. *Rather,* K. platyops *is nested within the* Homo + Paranthropus + Australopithecus africanus *clade. If* K. platyops *is a valid species, these relationships suggest that* Homo *and* Paranthropus *are likely to have diverged from other hominids much earlier than previously supposed. There is no support for the hypothesis that* A. garhi *is either the sister taxon or direct ancestor of the genus* Homo. *Phylogenetic relationships indicate that* Australopithecus *is paraphyletic. Thus,* A. anamensis *and* A. garhi *should be allocated to new genera.*

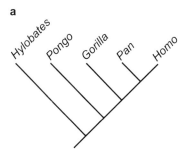

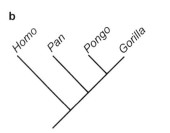

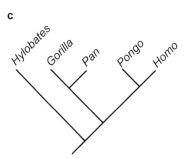

Figure 1. *Phylogenetic relationships among hominoids. (a) Cladogram supported by most molecular studies (e.g., Goodman et al., 1994; Ruvolo, 1997). Cladograms found by Collard and Wood's (2000) analysis of quantitative (b) and qualitative (c) craniodental characters.*

INTRODUCTION

The phylogenetic relationships of the earliest hominids remain a point of contention (Wood, 1991, 1992; Skelton and McHenry, 1992, 1998; Lieberman et al., 1996; Strait et al., 1997; Strait and Grine, 1998, 1999, 2001). The discovery of new species (White et al., 1994; Leakey et al., 1995; Brunet et al., 1996; Asfaw et al., 1999a; Senut et al., 2001; Ward et al., 2001; Leakey et al., 2001; Brunet et al., 2002) has fueled, rather than resolved, this debate, although a common assumption shared by these studies is that the pattern of early hominid phylogeny can be ascertained through analysis of craniodental morphology. Recently, however, this premise has been questioned (Collard and Wood, 2000), and consequently, doubts have been raised about the reliability of all phylogenetic hypotheses pertaining to early hominids. Collard and Wood (2000) have argued that the generally accepted molecular phylogeny of hominoids (Figure 1a) (e.g., Goodman et al.,

1994; Ruvolo, 1997; Shi et al., 2003; Wildman et al., 2003; Salem et al., 2003; but see Marks, 1993; Bailey, 1993; Deinard et al., 1998; Deinard and Kidd, 1999) can be used to test the phylogenetic reliability of morphological characters, and that craniodental characters produce cladograms that are grossly inconsistent with the molecular tree (Figure 1b,c). The implication of Collard and Wood's (2000) study is that because craniodental characters are inadequate indicators of phylogeny in living hominoids, they will also be inadequate to the task of resolving the relationships among our extinct ancestors and relatives.

The observation of incongruence between molecular and morphological data is not unique to the hominoids. A variety of studies have revealed that molecular and morphological data do not show complete congruence with regard to a number of disparate taxonomic groups, including primates (e.g., Shoshani et al., 1996; Baker et al., 1998; Horowitz et al., 1998; Liu and Miyamoto, 1999; Wiens and Hollingsworth, 2000; Gatesy and Arctander, 2000; Gatesy and O'Leary, 2001; Yoder et al., 2001; Masters and Brothers, 2002; Freudenstein et al., 2003). This raises the question of how incongruence is to be interpreted. Collard and

Wood (2000) took the position that, with respect to the hominoids, molecular data should be preferred and can be used to evaluate morphological data.

A factor not considered by Collard and Wood (2000), however, is the role that fossil taxa may play in resolving apparent incongruencies between morphological and molecular data sets. Fossil species preserve unique suites of primitive and derived characters, and therefore have a strong influence on patterns of character transformation (Eernisse and Kluge, 1993; Springer et al., 2001). In particular, fossils can play a key role in establishing phylogenetic linkages between morphologically derived extant species (Gauthier et al., 1988). As aptly noted by Gatesy et al. (2003:409):

> Certain fossils are expected to preserve ancestral morphologies that have been radically altered in extant taxa and might allow more precise hypotheses of homology in divergent anatomical systems. By including fossils, more characters and taxa (especially primitive taxa with unique combinations of morphological character states) can be utilized in phylogenetic analysis.

Thus, fossils serve to extend taxon sampling (Gauthier et al., 1988), which has been shown to increase overall phylogenetic accuracy (Wheeler, 1992; Zwickl and Hillis, 2002). Studies of quite disparate taxonomic groups have demonstrated that fossil taxa generally stabilize relationships and elucidate otherwise ambiguous patterns of character evolution (Eernisse and Kluge, 1993; O'Leary, 1999; Gatesy and O'Leary, 2001; Springer et al., 2001; Gatesy et al., 2003; Mallat and Chen, 2003).

Over a decade ago, Begun (1992) argued that morphological characters can recover the molecular phylogeny of apes so long as extinct species are included. To date, however, no study has reconstructed the phylogeny of both early hominids and living hominoids. In this paper, we test Collard and Wood's (2000) hypothesis by determining whether parsimony analysis of craniodental characters can yield a phylogeny of extant hominoids and extinct early hominids that is consistent with the ape molecular tree. As a result of testing Collard and Wood's (2000) hypothesis, it is also possible to test several recently proposed hypotheses of hominid phylogeny.

Regarding the fossil hominid taxa included herein, it is worth noting that, with the exception of *Australopithecus anamensis* (Ward et al., 2001), none of the recently discovered early hominid species has been comprehensively described, and the relevant specimens are not yet available for study. Thus, the present analysis of these species relies heavily on their initial published descriptions. In this regard, the proposed reconstruction of early hominid phylogeny relies on the accuracy of these initial descriptions and interpretations, some of which have been called into question. In particular, the validity of the species diagnosis of *Kenyanthropus platyops* has been questioned by White (2003), who implied that many of the defining features of the type specimen are artifacts of post-depositional distortion. We have no independent means of evaluating this claim, and thus we performed analyses that both included and excluded this taxon.

HYPOTHESES

Two levels of hypotheses are tested here. The first is Collard and Wood's (2000) hypothesis of *character reliability*. The others are hypotheses of *hominid phylogeny*.

Hypothesis of Character Reliability

Collard and Wood (2000) hypothesized that craniodental characters are unreliable for phylogenetic analysis of hominoids because such characters do not recover the pattern of hominoid phylogeny indicated by a majority of studies employing molecular data (e.g., Goodman et al., 1994; Ruvolo, 1997; Shi et al., 2003; Salem et al., 2003; Wildman et al., 2003). It is worth noting that some molecular data conflict with this tree (Marks, 1993; Bailey, 1993; Deinard et al., 1998; Deinard and Kidd, 1999), so it would be inaccurate to characterize hominoid phylogeny as being known with certainty. Nevertheless, the basis for Collard and Wood's (2000) hypothesis would be rejected if craniodental characters yielded the molecular phylogeny shown in Figure 1a.

A key concept underlying the hypothesis of Collard and Wood (2000) is that of congruence. Most systematists agree that when independent data sets are phylogenetically congruent, there is reason to conclude that a given cladogram may be accurate. However, Collard and Wood (2000) adopt a stronger interpretation of the meaning of congruence, namely that when given two data sets, one can be used to test the reliability of the other. In such a congruence test, one data set is considered to be "true" a priori, and the validity of the other data set is evaluated against it. If the two data sets produce equivalent results, then the set being tested is considered valid, and likely to provide reliable phylogenetic information (e.g., Gibbs et al., 2000). If not, then the characters in question fail the test and are considered unreliable. As noted by Collard and Wood (2000:5003), "This approach ... assumes that congruence between the morphological and molecular phylogenies indicates that equivalent hominin fossil evidence yields reliable phylogenies, whereas incongruence indicates the converse."

We do not subscribe to the logic of the congruence test as outlined above. However, insofar as the congruence test provides the framework for Collard and Wood's (2000) hypothesis, and given that the present study examines that hypothesis, the congruence test may be legitimately applied in this instance as a means to evaluate their conclusions.

Hypotheses of Hominid Phylogeny

The other hypotheses concern the phylogenetic relationships of early hominids, and are derived from the descriptions of recently discovered hominid species (White et al., 1994; Leakey et al., 1995; Asfaw et al., 1999a; Leakey et al., 2001; Brunet et al., 2002). These hypotheses are potentially difficult to test using cladistic analysis because they specify ancestor-descendant relationships without specifying sister-group relationships. However, cladistic analysis can indirectly test such hypotheses, because phyletic relationships imply sister-group

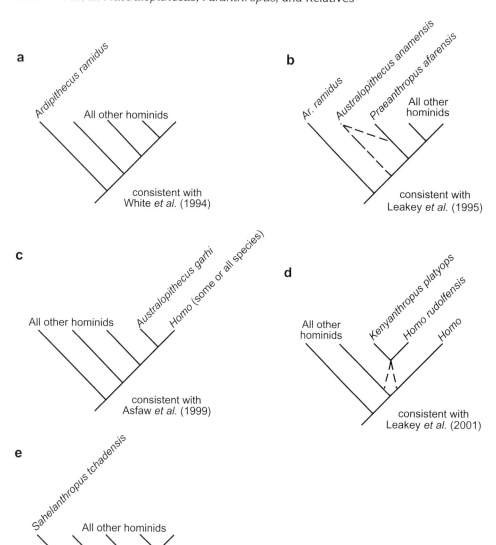

Figure 2. *Cladograms representing recently proposed hypotheses of early hominid relationships. Cladogram consistent with (a) White et al. (1994), (b) Leakey et al. (1995), (c) Asfaw et al. (1999a), (d) Leakey et al. (2001), and (e) Brunet et al. (2002). Dashed lines represent alternative branching patterns.*

relationships. In particular, it is an accepted principle that a species can only be considered a potential ancestor of another taxon if it is the sister species of that taxon, and if its character states resemble those reconstructed as being present in the relevant internal node of a cladogram (Szalay, 1977; Smith, 1994; Wagner and Erwin, 1995; O'Keefe and Sander, 1999). Accordingly, five phyletic hypotheses are evaluated here through reconstruction of sister-group relationships.

Ardipithecus ramidus *Hypothesis.* White et al. (1994) suggested that *Ar. ramidus* lies near the ancestry of all other hominids, and that it may be the actual ancestor of those species. A cladogram consistent with this hypothesis would place *Ar. ramidus* as the sister taxon of a clade that includes all other hominid species (Figure 2a).

Australopithecus anamensis *Hypothesis.* Leakey et al. (1995; Ward et al., 2001) have suggested that

A. anamensis is more closely related to later hominids than is *Ar. ramidus*, and may be directly ancestral to *Praeanthropus afarensis* (more commonly referred to as *Australopithecus afarensis*[1]). A cladogram consistent

[1]Note that *Praeanthropus afarensis* refers to the hypodigm usually attributed to *Australopithecus afarensis*. In a cladistic classification, this species should not be referred to *Australopithecus* because its inclusion within the genus has the effect of making it paraphyletic. Strait et al. (1997; see also Day et al., 1980; Harrison, 1993) referred to this species as *Pr. africanus* because the first specimen described in the hypodigm (the Garusi maxilla) had been assigned the name *Meganthropus africanus* Weinert 1950, and had subsequently been transferred to the genus *Praeanthropus* by Senyürek (1955). Recently, the International Commission on Zoological Nomenclature (1999) voted to override the principle of priority and to suppress the species name *Meganthropus africanus* (see also Groves, 1999). However, they recognized *Praeanthropus* as a valid genus name to which *A. afarensis* could be attributed. Thus, *Pr. afarensis* is employed here.

with this hypothesis would depict *A. anamensis* diverging from a higher node on the hominid tree than *Ar. ramidus*, and being the sister taxon of all later hominids (Figure 2b). An alternative topology that might also be consistent with the phyletic hypothesis would make *A. anamensis* the sister taxon of *Pr. afarensis*.

Australopithecus garhi *Hypothesis.* Asfaw et al. (1999a) implied that *A. garhi* could be a suitable ancestor for *Homo*, although they were careful to note that the exact phylogenetic relationships of this species remained unresolved. They presented a cladogram in which *A. garhi*, *A. africanus*, *Paranthropus robustus*, *P. boisei*, *P. aethiopicus* and *Homo* form a clade, but in which relationships within that clade were left unresolved[2]. However, they presented four phyletic trees, and in three of those, *A. garhi* was posited to be an ancestor of at least some members of the genus *Homo*. Moreover, they (Asfaw et al., 1999a:632) stated that "If *A. garhi* proves to be the exclusive ancestor of the *Homo* clade, a cladistic classification would assign it to genus *Homo*." Such a classification would only be valid if *A. garhi* and at least some of the *Homo* species form a monophyletic group, as in Figure 2c. Furthermore, in reference to the morphology of *A. garhi*, they (Asfaw et al., 1999a:634) stated that "its lack of derived robust characters leaves it as a sister taxon to *Homo* but absent many derived *Homo* characters." The hypothesis being tested here therefore represents a subset of the phylogenetic possibilities proposed by Asfaw et al. (1999a).

Kenyanthropus platyops *Hypothesis.* Leakey et al. (2001) noted that *Kenyanthropus platyops* appeared to share several derived character states exclusively with *H. rudolfensis*. They posited that this might imply that these two species had a particularly close relationship, and that their relationships to other early hominids were unclear (see also Lieberman, 2001). A cladogram consistent with this hypothesis (Figure 2d) would have *K. platyops* and *H. rudolfensis* as sister taxa.

Sahelanthropus tchadensis *Hypothesis.* Brunet et al. (2002:151) noted that *S. tchadensis* appears to be "the oldest and most primitive member of the hominid clade, close to the divergence of hominids and chimpanzees." The authors were cautious about the precise phylogenetic relationships of the species, but noted the possibility that *Sahelanthropus* is the sister taxon of all other hominids, including *Ardipithecus*. A cladogram consistent with this hypothesis would have *Sahelanthropus* as the basal branch of the hominid clade (Figure 2e). Wolpoff et al. (2002) suggested instead that *Sahelanthropus* may be more closely allied with *Pan* or *Gorilla* than with hominids.

---

[2] Asfaw et al. (1999) provided no information about the methods used to derive the cladogram, and stated elsewhere that they (Asfaw et al., 1999a:631) "caution against numerical cladistic application" of the trait list used to help diagnose *A. garhi*.

MATERIALS AND METHODS

Alpha Taxonomy of Ingroup Taxa

Hominid taxa examined here include the five species referred to above (*Ar. ramidus*, *A. anamensis*, *K. platyops*, *A. garhi*, *S. tchadensis*) and the nine species examined by Strait et al. (1997: Table 1) (*Pr. afarensis*, *A. africanus*, *P. aethiopicus*, *P. boisei*, *P. robustus*, *H. habilis*, *H. rudolfensis*, *H. ergaster* and *H. sapiens*). Specimens assigned to these species hypodigms are presented in Table 1. Three other early hominid taxa, *Ardipithecus kadabba* (Haile-Selassie et al., 2004), *Orrorin tugenensis* (Senut et al., 2001), and *A. bahrelghazali* (Brunet et al., 1996), were not examined here because their known fossils preserve very few relevant morphological characters.

The species hypodigms examined here do not include postcranial remains because, with the exception of partial skeletons, such specimens can only rarely be attributed to particular species with a high degree of confidence. Moreover, the postcranial skeletons of most species are poorly known, and thus the cladistic utility of postcranial features would be compromised. Accordingly, in this study, only specimens preserving cranial, dental and/or mandibular morphology were examined.

In addition to the fossil hominid species, extant hominoids were represented by samples of *Homo sapiens*, *Pan troglodytes*, *Gorilla gorilla*, *Pongo pygmaeus*, and a mixed-species sample of *Hylobates* (*H. lar* and *H. hoolock*).

Outgroup Taxa

As a generalization, multiple species should be employed in the outgroup in order to obviate the problem of species-specific specializations biasing character polarity (Maddison et al., 1993). Collard and Wood (2000) relied on a single outgroup species, *Colobus guereza*. Two outgroup taxa were employed in the present study, *C. guereza* and a mixed-species sample of *Papio* (*P. anubis* and *P. ursinus*). Because *Colobus* and *Papio* are so distinct morphologically, it is unlikely that their autapomorphies will be reconstructed as being primitive for the hominoid clade.

Character Analysis

Types of Characters. Collard and Wood (2000) examined two types of characters, which are categorized here as *craniometric* and *traditional*. Craniometric characters represent size-adjusted linear dimensions measured between standard cranial landmarks. Traditional characters represent those most commonly employed in systematic studies of apes and early hominids over the past quarter century. Traditional characters may be quantitative or qualitative, but when they are quantitative, they typically measure an aspect of morphology that has also been qualitatively described (e.g., a quantitative measurement of postorbital constriction).

Table 1.   Specimens Included in the Hypodigms of Early Hominid Species

Sahelanthropus tchadensis:		*Paranthropus robustus:*	
TM	266-01-060-1	DNH	7
Ardipithecus ramidus:		SK	6, 12, 13/14, 23, 34, 46, 47, 48, 49,
ARA-VP	6/1, 1/128, 1/500		52, 55, 65, 79, 83, 848, 1586
KNM-TH	13150	SKW	5, 8, 11, 29, 2581,
KNM-LT	329	SKX	265, 4446, 5013
Australopithecus anamensis:		TM	1517
KNM-KP	29181, 29283, 29286	*Paranthropus boisei:*	
Praeanthropus afarensis:		OH	5
A.L.	33-125, 58-22, 128-23, 145-35,	KGA	10-506, 10-525
	162-28, 188-1, 198-1, 199-1,	KNM-CH	1
	200-1, 207-13, 266-1, 277-1,	KNM-ER	403, 404, 405, 406, 407, 725,
	288-1, 311-1, 333-1, 333-2,		727, 728, 729, 732, 733, 801,
	333-45, 333-105, 333w-1,		805, 810, 818, 1468, 1469,
	333w-12, 333w-60,		1483, 1803, 1806, 3229, 3230,
	400-1a, 417-1, 444-2		3729, 3954, 5429, 5877, 13750,
Garusi	1		15930, 23000
KNM-ER	2602	KNM-WT	16841, 17400
LH	4	L	7a-125, 74a-21
MAK-VP	1/12	Natron	
Australopithecus garhi:		Omo	323-76-896
BOU-VP	12/130	*Homo habilis:*	
Australopithecus africanus:		A.L.	666-1
MLD	1, 2, 6, 9, 12, 22, 29, 34,	L	894-1
	37/38, 40, 45	OH	7, 13, 24, 62
Sts	5, 7, 17, 20, 26, 36, 52a and b,	KNM-ER	1478, 1501, 1502, 1805, 1813, 3735
	67, 71	SK	15, 27, 45, 847
Stw	13, 73, 252, 384, 404, 498,	Sts	19
	505, 513	Stw	53
Taung	1	*Homo rudolfensis:*	
TM	1511, 1512	KNM-ER	819, 1470, 1482, 1483, 1590, 1801,
Kenyanthropus platyops			1802, 3732, 3891
KNM-WT	38350, 40000	UR	501
Paranthropus aethiopicus:		*Homo ergaster:*	
KNM-WT	16005, 17000	KNM-ER	730, 820, 992, 1507, 3733, 3883
L	55s-33, 338y-6, 860-2	KNM-WT	15000
Omo	18-1967-18, 44-1970-2466,		
	57-4-1968-41		

Many fragmentary specimens and isolated teeth were also included in the study but are not listed.

All of the characters examined here are described in Tables 2 and 3. Characters were selected primarily from two sources, Collard and Wood (2000) and Strait and Grine (2001; Strait et al., 1997). Strait and Grine (2001) examined 69 traditional characters. An additional character (extensive mesial groove on upper canine) has been added here to those employed by Strait and Grine (2001), for a total of 70 characters. Collard and Wood (2000) examined 129 craniometric and 96 traditional characters. Their craniometric characters were drawn from Wood (1975) and Chamberlain (1987), and their traditional characters were compiled from several other sources (Delson and Andrews, 1975; Schwartz, 1984; Groves, 1988; Andrews, 1987; Braga, 1995; Shoshani et al., 1996).

For the purposes of this paper, the characters derived from Strait and Grine (2001) were labeled SG and then were numbered. The traditional characters derived from Collard and Wood (2000) were labeled CW and then are numbered. The Strait and Grine (2001) and Collard and Wood (2000) data sets share fourteen traditional characters. These characters are given both SG and CW labels (e.g., SG51 = CW7). Regarding craniometric characters, Collard and Wood (2000) organized their traits according to anatomical region, and gave them labels accordingly: palatal characters (P), mandibular characters (M), facial characters (F), and cranial vault/base characters (C). Within each group, the characters are numbered. This convention is adopted here.

Character Selection.   The craniometric characters examined by Collard and Wood (2000) comprise shape indices in which a linear measurement was divided by a geometric mean of other linear dimensions. Of the 129 craniometric traits examined by them, 40 mandibular features were omitted by us because shape indices could not be calculated for fossil hominid species in which there are no associated mandibles and crania (i.e., the geometric mean representing overall cranial size could not be calculated for isolated mandibles; see below). All other craniometric characters employed by Collard and Wood (2000) were employed in the present study.

Examination of the traditional characters used by Collard and Wood (2000) revealed that a large number of CW characters were either redundant with other traits or phylogenetically uninformative

Table 2. Craniometric Characters Derived from Collard and Wood (2000)

Variable	Definition	Source of data	Variable	Definition	Source of data	Variable	Definition	Source of data
P1	I^1 labiolingual diameter	1	F1	Right orbital breadth	1	C1	Glabella-Opisthocranion	1
P2	I^1 mesiodistal diameter	1	F2	Right orbital height	1	C2	Minimum post-orbital breadth	1
P3	I^2 labiolingual diameter	1	F3	Interorbital breadth	1	C3	Basion-Bregma	1
P4	I^2 mesiodistal diameter	1	F4	Biorbital breadth	1	C4	Maximum bi-parietal breadth	1
P5	C^1 mesiodistal diameter	1	F5	Nasion-Rhinion	1	C5	Biporionic width	1
P6	C^1 labiolingual diameter	1	F6	Nasion-nasospinale	1	C6	Mastoid length	1
P7	C^1 labial height	1	F7	Maximum nasal width	1	C7	Coronale-Coronale	1
P8	P^3 labiolingual diameter	1	F8	Nasospinale-Prosthion	1	C8	Opisthion-Inion	1
P9	P^3 mesiodistal diameter	1	F9	Bijugal breadth	1	C9	Bimastoid width	1
P10	P^4 labiolingual diameter	1	F10	Bizygomatic breadth	1	C10	Posterior skull length	1
P11	P^4 mesiodistal diameter	1	F11	Upper facial breadth	1	C11	Breadth across tympanic plates	2
P12	M^1 labiolingual diameter	1	F12	Lower facial breadth	1	C12	Breadth between carotid canals	2
P13	M^1 mesiodistal diameter	1	F13	Breadth between infraorbital foramina	1	C13	Breadth between petrous apices	2
P14	M^2 labiolingual diameter	1	F14	Lower nasal bone breadth	1	C14	Breadth between foramen ovale	2
P15	M^2 mesiodistal diameter	1	F15	Facial height	1	C15	Breadth between infratemporal crests	2
P16	M^3 labiolingual diameter	1	F16	Height of infraorbital foramen	1	C16	Breadth of mandibular fossa	2
P17	M^3 mesiodistal diameter	1	F17	Height of orbital margin	1	C17	Length of tympanic plate	2
P18	Outer alveolar breadth at M^3	1	F18	Upper malar height	1	C18	Length of petrous temporal	2
P19	Inter upper canine breadth	1	F19	Lower malar height	1	C19	Position of foramen ovale	2
P20	Palate length	1	F20	Upper facial prognathism	1	C20	Position of infratemporal crest	2
P21	Inner alveolar breadth at M^3	1	F21	Lower facial prognathism	1	C21	Length of foramen magnum	2
P22	Palate depth at M^1	1	F22	Malar prognathism	1	C22	Breadth of foramen magnum	2
P23	Prosthion to plane of M^3	1	F23	Naso-frontal subtense	2	C23	Length of infratemporal fossa	2
P24	Maxillo-Alveolar breadth (M^2B-M^2B)	2	F24	Maxillary subtense	2	C24	Breadth of infratemporal fossa	2
P25	Breadth between upper second molars (M^2L-M^2L)	2				C25	Opisthion-infratemporal subtense	2
P26	Palate depth at incisive fossa	2				C26	Basiooccipital length	2
P27	Palate depth at upper second molars	2				C27	Parietal thickness at Lambda	2
P28	Maxillary alveolar subtense	2				C28	Frontal sagittal chord	2
P29	Upper incisor alveolar length	2				C29	Parietal sagittal chord	2
P30	Upper premolar alveolar length	2				C30	Parietal coronal chord	2
P31	Upper molar alveolar length	2				C31	Occipital sagittal chord	2
						C32	Frontal sagittal arc	2
						C33	Occipital sagittal arc	2
						C34	Auricular height	2

All characters represent linear dimensions divided by a geometric mean of other cranial dimensions.

1 = Wood (1975)

2 = Chamberlain (1987)

Table 3.   Traditional Characters Derived from Strait and Grine (2001) and Collard and Wood (2000)

Label	Character	Colobus/Papio	Hylobates	Pongo	Gorilla	Pan	S. tchadensis	Ar. ramidus	A. anamensis
SG1.	Projection of nasal bones above frontomaxillary suture	Colobus: 2 Not projected Papio: 0 Projected, tapered	2 Not projected	3 Variable	0 Projected, tapered	0 Projected, tapered	?	?	?
SG2.	Inferior orbital margin rounded laterally	0 No	0 No	0 No	1 Variable	0 No	0 No	?	?
SG3.	Infraorbital foramen location	0 High	0 High	0 High	0 High	0 High	2 Low	?	?
SG4.	Anterior pillars	0 Absent	0 Absent	0 Absent	0 Absent	0 Absent	0 Absent	?	?
SG5.	Nasoalveolar clivus contour in coronal plane	0 Convex	0 Convex	0 Convex	0 Convex	0 Convex	?	?	?
SG6.	Protrusion of incisor alveoli beyond bicanine line (basal view)	0 Yes	0 Yes	0 Yes	0 Yes	0 Yes	?	?	?
SG7. (= CW4,23, 33,65,71,72)	Nasal cavity entrance	3 Stepped, no overlap	3 Stepped, no overlap	1 Smooth, overlap	0 Stepped, overlap	0 Stepped, overlap	?	?	?
SG8.	Palate thickness	0 Thin	0 Thin	0 Thin	0 Thin	0 Thin	?	?	0 Thin
SG9.	Height of the masseter origin	0 Low	0 Low	0 Low	0 Low	0 Low	?	?	?
SG10.	M-L thickness of zygomatic arch at root of frontal process	0 Thin	0 Thin	0 Thin	0 Thin	0 Thin	?	?	?
SG11.	Anterior projection of zygomatic bone relative to piriform aperture (dishing)	0 Posterior	0 Posterior	0 Posterior	0 Posterior	0 Posterior	0 Posterior	?	?
SG12. (= CW23)	Anterior palatal depth	0 Shallow	0 Shallow	2 Deep (shelved)	0 Shallow	0 Shallow	?	?	0 Shallow
SG13.	Index of palate protrusion anterior to sellion (facial prognathism)	Colobus: 1 Prognathic Papio: 0 Hyper-prognathic	1 Prognathic	0 Hyper-prognathic	1 Prognathic	1 Prognathic	3 Mesognathic	?	?
SG14.	Masseteric position relative to sellion	0 At or posterior	0 At or posterior	1 At or anterior	0 At or posterior	0 At or posterior	0 At or posterior	?	?
SG15.	Maxillary trigon (zygomatico-maxillary step)	0 Absent	0 Absent	0 Absent	0 Absent	0 Absent	0 Absent	?	?
SG16. (= CW62)	Cranial capacity	0 Small	0 Small	0 Small	0 Small	0 Small	0 Small	?	?
SG17.	Cerebellar morphology	0 Lateral flare, posterior protrusion	0 Lateral flare, posterior protrusion	0 Lateral flare, posterior protrusion	0 Lateral flare, posterior protrusion	0 Lateral flare, posterior protrusion	?	?	?
SG18.	O-M sinus present in high frequency	?	?	0 No	0 No	0 No	?	?	?
SG19. (= CW28,37)	Anteromedial incursion of the superior temporal lines	2 Moderate	3 Strong	3 Strong	2 Moderate	2 Moderate	2 Moderate	?	?
SG20. (= CW37)	Sagittal crest present, at least in presumptive males	Colobus: 1 No Papio: 0 Yes	1 No	0 Yes	0 Yes	1 No	0 Yes	?	?

A. garhi	K. platyops	Pr. afarensis	P. aethiopicus	A. africanus	P. robustus	P. boisei	H. habilis	H. rudolfensis	H. ergaster	H. sapiens
?	?	1 Projected, expanded	1 Projected, expanded	3 Variable	1 Projected, expanded	1 Projected, expanded	2 Not projected	2 Not projected	2 Not projected	2 Not projected
?	0 No	0 No	2 Yes	0 No	2 Yes	0 No	0 No	0 No	0 No	0 No
?	?	0 High	2 Low	1 Variable	2 Low	1 Variable	0 High	?	0 High	0 High
0 Absent	0 Absent	0 Absent	0 Absent	1 Variable	2 Present	0 Absent	1 Variable	0 Absent	0 Absent	0 Absent
0 Convex	1 Straight	0 Convex	2 Concave (gutter)	1 Straight	2 Concave (gutter)	2 Concave (gutter)	1 Straight	1 Straight	1 Straight	0 Convex
0 Yes	1 No	0 Yes	1 No	0 Yes	1 No	1 No	0 Yes	1 No	0 Yes	0 Yes
0 Stepped, overlap	0 Stepped, overlap	0 Stepped, overlap	1 Smooth, overlap	0 Stepped, overlap	1 Smooth, overlap	1 Smooth, overlap	1 Smooth, overlap	?	1 Smooth, overlap	2 Smooth, no overlap
0 Thin	0 Thin	0 Thin	1 Thick	0 Thin	1 Thick	1 Thick	0 Thin	0 Thin	0 Thin	0 Thin
0 Low	0 Low	0 Low	1 High	1 High	1 High	1 High	0 Low	0 Low	0 Low	0 Low
?	?	0 Thin	1 Thick	0 Thin	1 Thick	1 Thick	0 Thin	?	0 Thin	0 Thin
0 Posterior	2 Intermediate	0 Posterior	3 Anterior (dished)	1 Variable post.-inter.	3 Anterior (dished)	3 Anterior (dished)	0 Posterior	2 Intermediate	0 Posterior	0 Posterior
0 Shallow	2 Deep (shelved)	0 Shallow	0 Shallow	2 Deep (shelved)	0 Shallow	1 Variable	1 Variable	2 Deep (shelved)	2 Deep (shelved)	2 Deep (shelved)
1 Prognathic	3 Mesognathic	1 Prognathic	1 Prognathic	2 Variable prog.-mesog.	3 Mesognathic	3 Mesognathic	3 Mesognathic	3 Mesognathic	4 Orthognathic	4 Orthognathic
?	1 At or anterior	1 At or anterior	1 At or anterior	0 At or posterior	1 At or anterior	1 At or anterior	0 At or posterior	?	0 At or posterior	0 At or posterior
0 Absent	?	0 Absent	2 Present	0 Absent	2 Present	1 Variable	0 Absent	0 Absent	0 Absent	0 Absent
0 Small	0 Small	0 Small	0 Small	0 Small	0 Small	0 Small	1 Intermediate	2 Large	2 Large	3 Very Large
?	?	0 Lateral flare, posterior protrusion	0 Lateral flare, posterior protrusion	0 Lateral flare, posterior protrusion	1 Tucked	1 Tucked	1 Tucked	1 Tucked	1 Tucked	1 Tucked
?	0 No	2 Yes	0 No	1 Intermediate	2 Yes	2 Yes	0 No	0 No	?	1 Intermediate
2 Moderate	2 Moderate	2 Moderate	3 Strong	2 Moderate	3 Strong	3 Strong	1 Variable mod.-weak	0 Weak	0 Weak	0 Weak
0 Yes	0 Yes	0 Yes	0 Yes	0 Yes	0 Yes	0 Yes	0 Yes	1 No	1 No	1 No

(continued on next page)

Table 3. (continued)

Label	Character	Colobus/Papio	Hylobates	Pongo	Gorilla	Pan	S. tchadensis	Ar. ramidus	A. anamensis
SG21.	Compound T/N crest, at least in presumptive males	Colobus: 2 Partial Papio: 0 Extensive	2 Partial	0 Extensive	0 Extensive	0 Extensive	0 Extensive	?	?
SG22.	Asterionic notch	2 Absent	2 Absent	0 Present	0 Present	0 Present	?	?	?
SG23.	Parietal overlap of occpital at asterion, at least in males	0 No	0 No	0 No	0 No	0 No	?	?	?
SG24.	Squamosal suture overlap extensive, at least in males	0 Not extensive	0 Not extensive	0 Not extensive	0 Not extensive	0 Not extensive	?	?	?
SG25.	Lateral inflation of mastoid process relative to supramastoid crest	0 Not inflated	0 Not inflated	0 Not inflated	0 Not inflated	0 Not inflated	?	?	?
SG26.	Postorbital constriction	1 Moderate	1 Moderate	0 Marked	0 Marked	1 Moderate	0 Marked	?	?
SG27.	Pneumatization of temporal squama	Colobus: 2 Reduced Papio: 0 Extensive	2 Reduced	0 Extensive	0 Extensive	0 Extensive	0 Extensive	0 Extensive	0 Extensive
SG28. (= CW28)	Facial hafting	Colobus: 0 Low Papio: 1 High	0 Low	0 Low	0 Low	0 Low	?	?	?
SG29.	Supraglenoid gutter width	Colobus: 0 Narrow Papio: 1 Wide	0 Narrow	1 Wide	1 Wide	0 Narrow	?	?	?
SG30. (= CW12)	External cranial base flexion	Colobus: 1 Flat Papio: 3 Flexed	1 Flat	0 Retroflexed	1 Flat	1 Flat	?	?	?
SG31.	Horizontal distance between TMJ and M^2/M^3	0 Long	0 Long	0 Long	0 Long	0 Long	0 Long	?	?
SG32.	Relative depth of mandibular fossa	0 Shallow	0 Shallow	0 Shallow	2 Intermediate	0 Shallow	0 Shallow	0 Shallow	0 Shallow
SG33.	Postglenoid process size and position	0 Large and anterior	1 Mid-sized, fused or unfused	0 Large and anterior	0 Large and anterior	0 Large and anterior	0 Large and anterior	?	?
SG34.	Configuration of tympanic	0 Tubular (or weak crest)	0 Tubular (or weak crest)	0 Tubular (or weak crest)	0 Tubular (or weak crest)	0 Tubular (or weak crest)	0 Tubular (or weak crest)	0 Tubular (or weak crest)	0 Tubular (or weak crest)
SG35.	Medio-lateral position of external auditory meatus	Colobus: 0 Medial Papio: 2 Lateral	0 Medial	0 Medial	2 Lateral	0 Medial	?	2 Lateral	0 Medial
SG36.	Vaginal process	Colobus: 2 Moderate to large Papio: 0 Small or absent	0 Small or absent	0 Small or absent	0 Small or absent	0 Small or absent	?	?	?
SG37.	Eustachian process of tympanic	Colobus: 1 Variable Papio: 0 Present and prominent	0 Present and prominent	0 Present and prominent	0 Present and prominent	0 Present and prominent	0 Present and prominent	?	?
SG38.	Petrous orientation	0 Sagittal	0 Sagittal	0 Sagittal	0 Sagittal	0 Sagittal	0 Sagittal	?	?
SG39.	Heart shaped foramen magnum	0 Absent	0 Absent	0 Absent	0 Absent	0 Absent	0 Absent	?	?

A. garhi	K. platyops	Pr. afarensis	P. aethiopicus	A. africanus	P. robustus	P. boisei	H. habilis	H. rudolfensis	H. ergaster	H. sapiens
?	2 Partial	0 Extensive	0 Extensive	3 Absent	?	1 Variable	2 Partial	3 Absent	3 Absent	3 Absent
?	?	0 Present	0 Present	2 Absent	2 Absent	2 Absent	1 Variable	2 Absent	2 Absent	2 Absent
?	?	0 No	1 Yes	0 No	0 No	1 Yes	0 No	0 No	0 No	0 No
?	?	0 Not extensive	1 Extensive	0 Not extensive	?	1 Extensive	0 Not extensive	0 Not extensive	0 Not extensive	0 Not extensive
?	?	0 Not inflated	2 Inflated	0 Not inflated	2 Inflated	2 Inflated	1 Variable	0 Not inflated	0 Not inflated	0 Not inflated
1 Moderate	1 Moderate	1 Moderate	0 Marked	1 Moderate	0 Marked	0 Marked	1 Moderate	1 Moderate	1 Moderate	2 Slight
?	?	0 Extensive	0 Extensive	0 Extensive	2 Reduced	1 Variable	2 Reduced	2 Reduced	2 Reduced	2 Reduced
0 Low	0 Low	0 Low	1 High	0 Low	1 High	1 High	0 Low	0 Low	0 Low	0 Low
?	?	0 Narrow	1 Wide	0 Narrow	1 Wide	1 Wide	0 Narrow	0 Narrow	0 Narrow	0 Narrow
?	?	?	1 Flat	2 Moderate	3 Flexed	3 Flexed	3 Flexed	?	3 Flexed	3 Flexed
?	?	0 Long	0 Long	0 Long	0 Long	0 Long	1 Short	0 Long	1 Short	1 Short
?	2 Intermediate	0 Shallow	0 Shallow	2 Intermediate	2 Intermediate	3 Deep	2 Intermediate	2 Intermediate	1 Variable shallow-inter.	3 Deep
?	?	0 Large and anterior	1 Mid-sized, fused or unfused	1 Mid-sized, fused or unfused	3 Small and fused to tympanic	2 Variable mid.-small	2 Variable mid.-small	1 Mid-sized, fused or unfused	3 Small and fused to tympanic	3 Small and fused to tympanic
?	0 Tubular (or weak crest)	0 Tubular (or weak crest)	1 Crest with vertical plate	1 Crest with vertical plate	1 Crest with vertical plate	2 Crest with inclined plate	1 Crest with vertical plate	?	1 Crest with vertical plate	1 Crest with vertical plate
?	0 Medial	0 Medial	0 Medial	0 Medial	2 Lateral	2 Lateral	1 Variable	0 Medial	0 Medial	0 Medial
?	?	0 Small or absent	0 Small or absent	0 Small or absent	2 Moderate to large	2 Moderate to large	1 Variable	?	2 Moderate to large	2 Moderate to large
?	?	2 Absent or slight	2 Absent or slight	0 Present and prominent	0 Present and prominent	2 Absent or slight	2 Absent or slight	?	2 Absent or slight	2 Absent or slight
?	?	1 Intermediate	2 Coronal	1 Intermediate	2 Coronal	2 Coronal	2 Coronal	2 Coronal	2 Coronal	2 Coronal
?	0 Absent	0 Absent	2 Present	0 Absent	0 Absent	2 Present	0 Absent	?	1 Variable	0 Absent

(*continued on next page*)

Table 3. (continued)

Label	Character	Colobus/Papio	Hylobates	Pongo	Gorilla	Pan	S. tchadensis	Ar. ramidus	A. anamensis
SG40.	Inclination nuchal plane	1 Steeply inclined	1 Steeply inclined	0 Extremely steep	1 Steeply inclined	1 Steeply inclined	2 Intermediate	?	?
SG41.	Position of foramen magnum relative to bi-tympanic line	*Colobus:* 0 Well posterior *Papio:* 3 Well anterior	0 Well posterior	0 Well posterior	0 Well posterior	0 Well posterior	1 At bi-tympanic line	1 At bi-tympanic line	?
SG42.	Inclination of foramen magnum	0 Strongly inclined (posterior)	0 Strongly inclined (posterior)	0 Strongly inclined (posterior)	0 Strongly inclined (posterior)	0 Strongly inclined (posterior)	?	?	?
SG43.	Origin of digastric muscle	0 Broad, shallow fossa	0 Broad, shallow fossa	0 Broad, shallow fossa	0 Broad, shallow fossa	0 Broad, shallow fossa	?	1 Deep, narrow notch	?
SG44. (= CW77)	Mandibular cross-sectional area at M_1	0 Small	0 Small	0 Small	1 Variable	0 Small	0 Small	?	0 Small
SG45.	Orientation of mandibular symphysis	0 Receding	0 Receding	0 Receding	0 Receding	0 Receding	?	?	0 Receding
SG46.	Direction of mental foramen opening	*Colobus:* 1 Variable *Papio:* 2 Lateral	1 Variable	1 Variable	1 Variable	0 Anterior	0 Anterior	0 Anterior	2 Lateral
SG47.	Hollowing above and behind mental foramen	0 Present	0 Present	0 Present	0 Present	0 Present	?	0 Present	0 Present
SG48.	Width of mandibular extramolar sulcus	*Colobus:* 2 Wide *Papio:* 0 Narrow	2 Wide	2 Wide	2 Wide	0 Narrow	2 Wide	0 Narrow	0 Narrow
SG49.	Mandibular deciduous canine shape	1 Apex mesial, mesial convexity high	1 Apex mesial, mesial convexity high	0 Apex central, mesial convexity low	0 Apex central, mesial convexity low	0 Apex central, mesial convexity low	?	?	?
SG50.	Incisal reduction	*Colobus:* 1 Moderate *Papio:* 0 No	2 Very	0 No	0 No	0 No	0 No	1 Moderate	1 Moderate
SG51. (= CW7)	Canines reduced	0 No	0 No	0 No	0 No	0 No	1 Somewhat	1 Somewhat	1 Somewhat
SG52.	Prominence of median lingual ridge of mandibular canine	0 Prominent	0 Prominent	0 Prominent	0 Prominent	0 Prominent	?	?	?
SG53.	Premolar crown area	0 Smallest	0 Smallest	2	3	0 Smallest	1	1	1
SG54.	Molar crown area	0 Smallest	0 Smallest	1	2	0 Smallest	0	0	1
SG55.	d M_1 mesial crown profile	0 MMR absent, protoconid anterior, fovea open	0 MMR absent, protoconid anterior, fovea open	0 MMR absent, protoconid anterior, fovea open	0 MMR absent, protoconid anterior, fovea open	0 MMR absent, protoconid anterior, fovea open	?	0 MMR absent, protoconid anterior, fovea open	1 MMR slight, protoconid anterior, fovea open
SG56.	Distal marginal ridge of d M_2	0 Low	0 Low	0 Low	0 Low	0 Low	?	?	?
SG57.	Positions of buccal and lingual cusps relative to crown margin (states as for mandibular teeth; reverse for maxillary teeth)	1 Lingual cusps approximate margin; buccal cusps slightly lingual to margin	0 Buccal and lingual cusps approximate crown margin	0 Buccal and lingual cusps approximate crown margin	0 Buccal and lingual cusps approximate crown margin	0 Buccal and lingual cusps approximate crown margin	1 Lingual cusps approximate margin; buccal cusps slightly lingual to margin	2 Lingual cusps approximate margin; buccal cusps moderately lingual to margin	2 Lingual cusps approximate margin; buccal cusps moderately lingual to margin

A. garhi	K. platyops	Pr. afarensis	P. aethiopicus	A. africanus	P. robustus	P. boisei	H. habilis	H. rudolfensis	H. ergaster	H. sapiens
?	?	2 Intermediate	3 Weakly inclined	3 Weakly inclined	3 Weakly inclined	3 Weakly inclined	3 Weakly inclined	3 Weakly inclined	3 Weakly inclined	3 Weakly inclined
?	?	1 At bi-tympanic line	1 At bi-tympanic line	1 At bi-tympanic line	3 Well anterior	3 Well anterior	2 Variable at or anterior	?	1 At bi-tympanic line	1 At bi-tympanic line
?	?	?	?	0 Strongly inclined (posterior)	1 Roughly horizontal	1 Roughly horizontal	1 Roughly horizontal	?	2 Strongly inclined (anterior)	1 Roughly horizontal
?	?	0 Broad, shallow fossa	?	0 Broad, shallow fossa	1 Deep, narrow notch	0 Broad, shallow fossa	1 Deep, narrow notch	?	1 Deep, narrow notch	1 Deep, narrow notch
?	?	0 Small	2 Large	0 Small	2 Large	2 Large	0 Small	1 Variable	0 Small	0 Small
?	?	1 Intermediate	2 Vertical	1 Intermediate	2 Vertical	2 Vertical	2 Vertical	2 Vertical	2 Vertical	2 Vertical
?	?	1 Variable	2 Lateral	1 Variable	2 Lateral	2 Lateral	2 Lateral	2 Lateral	2 Lateral	3 Posterior
?	?	0 Present	2 Absent	1 Variable	2 Absent	2 Absent	2 Absent	1 Variable	2 Absent	2 Absent
?	?	0 Narrow	2 Wide	1 Variable	2 Wide	2 Wide	1 Variable	0 Narrow	0 Narrow	0 Narrow
?	?	0 Apex central, mesial convexity low	?	0 Apex central, mesial convexity low	1 Apex mesial, mesial convexity high	1 Apex mesial, mesial convexity high	?	?	0 Apex central, mesial convexity low	0 Apex central, mesial convexity low
1 Moderate	?	1 Moderate	1 Moderate	1 Moderate	2 Yes	2 Yes	1 Moderate	1 Moderate	1 Moderate	2 Yes
1 Somewhat	1 Somewhat	1 Somewhat	1 Somewhat	1 Somewhat	2 Very	2 Very	1 Somewhat	1 Somewhat	2 Very	2 Very
?	?	0 Prominent	?	1 Variable	2 Weak	2 Weak	2 Weak	2 Weak	2 Weak	2 Weak
4	?	1	4	2	3	5 Largest	1	2	1	0 Smallest
2	0	1	3 Largest	2	2	3 Largest	1	2	0 Smallest	0 Smallest
?	?	1 MMR slight, protoconid anterior, fovea open	2 MMR thick, protoconid even with metaconid, fovea closed	1 MMR slight, protoconid anterior, fovea open	2 MMR thick, protoconid even with metaconid, fovea closed	2 MMR thick, protoconid even with metaconid, fovea closed	?	?	1 MMR slight, protoconid anterior, fovea open	1 MMR slight, protoconid anterior, fovea open
?	?	0 Low	?	0 Low	1 High	1 High	0 Low	0 Low	?	0 Low
1 Lingual cusps approximate margin; buccal cusps slightly lingual to margin	?	1 Lingual cusps approximate margin; buccal cusps slightly lingual to margin	4 Lingual cusps moderately buccal to margin; buccal cusps strongly lingual to margin	3 Lingual cusps slightly buccal to margin; buccal cusps moderately lingual to margin	4 Lingual cusps moderately buccal to margin; buccal cusps strongly lingual to margin	4 Lingual cusps moderately buccal to margin; buccal cusps strongly lingual to margin	1 Lingual cusps approximate margin; buccal cusps slightly lingual to margin	1 Lingual cusps approximate margin; buccal cusps slightly lingual to margin	1 Lingual cusps approximate margin; buccal cusps slightly lingual to margin	1 Lingual cusps approximate margin; buccal cusps slightly lingual to margin

(continued on next page)

Table 3.   (continued)

Label	Character	Colobus/Papio	Hylobates	Pongo	Gorilla	Pan	S. tchadensis	Ar. ramidus	A. anamensis
SG58. (= CW94)	Frequency of well developed P_3 metaconid	0 Absent	0 Absent	0 Absent	0 Absent	0 Absent	?	0 Absent	0 Absent
SG59. (= CW57,73)	Relative enamel thickness	0 Thin	0 Thin	1 Thick	0 Thin	0 Thin	0 Thin	0 Thin	1 Thick
SG60. (= CW87,88)	Dental development rate	?	0 Delayed	0 Delayed	0 Delayed	0 Delayed	?	?	?
SG61.	Mesiobuccal protrusion of P_3 crown base	0 Strong	0 Strong	0 Strong	0 Strong	0 Strong	?	1 Moderate	1 Moderate
SG62. (= CW86)	Orientation of mandibular premolar row (dental arcade shape)	0 Premolar row parasagittal (U-shaped arcade)	0 Premolar row parasagittal (U-shaped arcade)	0 Premolar row parasagittal (U-shaped arcade)	0 Premolar row parasagittal (U-shaped arcade)	0 Premolar row parasagittal (U-shaped arcade)	0 Premolar row parasagittal (U-shaped arcade)	0 Premolar row parasagittal (U-shaped arcade)	0 Premolar row parasagittal (U-shaped arcade)
SG63.	Parietal tuber	0 Absent	0 Absent	0 Absent	0 Absent	0 Absent	?	?	?
SG64.	Parietomastoid angle	*Colobus:* 1 Weak *Papio:* 0 Strong	1 Weak	0 Strong	0 Strong	0 Strong	?	?	?
SG65.	External auditory meatus size	0 small	0 small	0 small	0 small	0 small	?	0 small	0 small
SG66.	Separation of mandibular tooth rows	*Colobus:* 0 Widely separated *Papio:* 1 Narrow separation	0 Widely separated	0 Widely separated	1 Narrow separation	0 Widely separated	1 Narrow separation	?	1 Narrow separation
SG67.	Configuration of the superior orbital fissure	0 Foramen	0 Foramen	0 Foramen	0 Foramen	0 Foramen	?	?	?
SG68.	Size of *Longus capitis* insertion	*Colobus:* 1 Small *Papio:* 0 Large	0 Large	0 Large	0 Large	0 Large	?	?	?
SG69.	Height of articular eminence above occlusal plane	1 Near plane	1 Near plane	0 High above plane	0 High above plane	1 Near plane	0 High above plane	?	?
SG70. (= CW38)	Extensive mesial groove on upper canine	0 Yes	0 Yes	0 Yes	0 Yes	0 Yes	?	1 No	1 No
CW 1	Depth of subarcuate fossa	0 Deep	1 Moderately deep to shallow	2 Very shallow to absent	2 Very shallow to absent	2 Very shallow to absent	?	?	?
CW 2	Orientation and length of the post-incisive planum	0 Long, weakly inclined	1 Intermediate	1 Intermediate	0 Long, weakly inclined	1 Intermediate	?	?	0 Long, weakly inclined
CW 3	Distinctiveness of angular process of mandible	1 Not distinct	0 Distinct, with posterior projection	1 Not distinct	1 Not distinct	1 Not distinct	?	?	?
CW 9	Depth of middle ear	0 Shallow	0 Shallow	0 Shallow	1 Deep	1 Deep	?	?	?
CW 10	Axis of ear bones	0 Right angle or more	1 Acute angle	1 Acute angle	0 Right angle or more	0 Right angle or more	?	?	?
CW 11	Area of inner ear	0 Low	0 Low	0 Low	1 Higher	1 Higher	?	?	?
CW 17	Presence/ absence of frontal sinus	0 Absent	0 Absent	0 Absent	1 Present	1 Present	?	?	?

A. garhi	K. platyops	Pr. afarensis	P. aethiopicus	A. africanus	P. robustus	P. boisei	H. habilis	H. rudolfensis	H. ergaster	H. sapiens
?	?	1 Infrequent	2 Frequent	2 Frequent	2 Frequent	2 Frequent	2 Frequent	2 Frequent	2 Frequent	2 Frequent
1 Thick	1 Thick	1 Thick	2 Hyperthick	1 Thick	2 Hyperthick	2 Hyperthick	1 Thick	1 Thick	1 Thick	1 Thick
?	?	0 Delayed	?	0 Delayed	2 Accelerated	2 Accelerated	?	0 Delayed	1 Intermediate	1 Intermediate
3 Weak or absent	?	2 Variable	3 Weak or absent	3 Weak or absent	3 Weak or absent	3 Weak or absent	3 Weak or absent	3 Weak or absent	3 Weak or absent	3 Weak or absent
?	?	0 Premolar row parasagittal (U-shaped arcade)	1 Premolar row obliquely oriented (parabolic arcade)	1 Premolar row obliquely oriented (parabolic arcade)	1 Premolar row obliquely oriented (parabolic arcade)	1 Premolar row obliquely oriented (parabolic arcade)	1 Premolar row obliquely oriented (parabolic arcade)	1 Premolar row obliquely oriented (parabolic arcade)	1 Premolar row obliquely oriented (parabolic arcade)	1 Premolar row obliquely oriented (parabolic arcade)
0 Absent	?	0 Absent	0 Absent	0 Absent	0 Absent	0 Absent	1 Present	1 Present	1 Present	1 Present
1 Weak	?	0 Strong	0 Strong	1 Weak	1 Weak	1 Weak	1 Weak	1 Weak	1 Weak	1 Weak
?	0 Small	1 Large	1 Large	1 Large	1 Large	1 Large	1 Large	?	1 Large	1 Large
?	?	0 Widely separated	0 Widely separated	0 Widely separated	0 Widely separated	0 Widely separated	0 Widely separated	0 Widely separated	0 Widely separated	0 Widely separated
?	?	0 Foramen	1 Comma-shaped	0 Foramen	?	1 Comma-shaped	0 Foramen	?	?	1 Comma-shaped
?	?	?	1 Small	0 Large	1 Small	1 Small	1 Small	?	1 Small	1 Small
?	?	1 Near plane	0 High above plane	0 High above plane	0 High above plane	0 High above plane	1 Near plane	?	1 Near plane	1 Near plane
1 No	?	1 No	?	1 No	1 No	1 No	1 No	1 No	1 No	1 No
?	?	2 Very shallow to absent	?	2 Very shallow to absent	2 Very shallow to absent	2 Very shallow to absent	2 Very shallow to absent	?	?	2 Very shallow to absent
?	?	1 Intermediate	1 Intermediate	1 Intermediate	1 Intermediate	1 Intermediate	1 Intermediate	1 Intermediate	1 Intermediate	2 Short, steeply inclined
?	?	1 Not distinct	?	1 Not distinct	1 Not distinct	1 Not distinct	1 Not distinct	?	1 Not distinct	1 Not distinct
?	?	?	?	?	?	?	?	?	?	1 Deep
?	?	?	?	?	?	?	?	?	?	0 Acute angle
?	?	?	?	?	?	?	?	?	?	1 Higher
?	?	1 Present	?	1 Present	1 Present	1 Present	1 Present	?	?	1 Present

(continued on next page)

Table 3. (continued)

Label	Character	Colobus/Papio	Hylobates	Pongo	Gorilla	Pan	S. tchadensis	Ar. ramidus	A. anamensis
CW 19	Position of infraorbital foramen relative to orbit	Colobus: 1 Foramen beneath medial third of orbital breadth Papio: 0 Foramen beneath middle third of orbital breadth	1 Foramen beneath medial third of orbital breadth	0 Foramen beneath middle third of orbital breadth	0 Foramen beneath middle third of orbital breadth	0 Foramen beneath middle third of orbital breadth	0 Foramen beneath middle third of orbital breadth	?	?
CW 20	Orientation of zygomatic bone	Colobus: 2 Fronto-lateral Papio: 0 Frontal	3 Lateral	0 Frontal	2 Fronto-lateral	2 Fronto-lateral	2 Fronto-lateral	?	?
CW 22	Glabellar prominence relative to sella	Colobus: 2 Weak, recessed behind sella Papio: 1 Intermediate, at the level of sella	1 Intermediate, at the level of sella	2 Weak, recessed behind sella	0 Strong, projects anterior to sella	0 Strong, projects anterior to sella	0 Strong, projects anterior to sella	?	?
CW 25	Supraorbital expression	Colobus: 1 Intermediate Papio: 2 Torus-like	1 Intermediate	0 Weak	2 Torus-like	2 Torus-like	2 Torus-like	?	?
CW 26	Supraorbital contour	2 Less arched	0 Arched	0 Arched	2 Less arched	0 Arched	2 Less arched	?	?
CW 32	Position of zygomatic foramina	Colobus: 1 Above plane of orbital rim Papio: 0 At or below plane of orbital rim	0 At or below plane of orbital rim	1 Above plane of orbital rim	0 At or below plane of orbital rim	0 At or below plane of orbital rim	?	?	?
CW 35	Patency of premaxillary suture in adults from frontal view	0 Patent	1 Variable	1 Variable	1 Variable	2 Obliterated	?	?	?
CW 36	Petrous apex ossified beyond spheno-occipital synchondrosis	1 Ossified, with projection	1 Ossified, with projection	1 Ossified, with projection	1 Ossified, with projection	1 Ossified, with projection	?	?	?
CW 40	I^2 similar in shape to I^1	0 Dissimilar	0 Dissimilar	0 Dissimilar	0 Dissimilar	2 Similar	?	?	?
CW 41	Robusticity of canines	0 Slender	0 Slender	1 More robust	1 More robust	1 More robust	0 Slender	1 More robust	1 More robust
CW 42	Basal keel of lower canine	0 Present	0 Present	0 Present	0 Present	1 Reduced	1 Reduced	?	1 Reduced
CW 43	Basal area of paracone of P^3	0 Paracone much larger than protocone	0 Paracone much larger than protocone	1 Paracone larger than protocone	2 Paracone equals protocone	1 Paracone larger than protocone	?	1 Paracone larger than protocone	2 Paracone equals protocone
CW 44	Molar cingulum	1 Reduced, incomplete	1 Reduced, incomplete	3 Frag-mented or absent	1 Reduced, incomplete	3 Frag-mented or absent	3 Frag-mented or absent	3 Frag-mented or absent	3 Frag-mented or absent
CW 46	Metaconid of dp_3	0 Absent or poorly defined	0 Absent or poorly defined	0 Absent or poorly defined	0 Absent or poorly defined	0 Absent or poorly defined	?	0 Absent or poorly defined	1 Well defined
CW 48	Talonid basin of dp_3	1 Closed distally	0 Open distally	0 Open distally	0 Open distally	0 Open distally	?	0 Open distally	?
CW 50	Distal trigonid crest on dp_4	1 Reaches protoconid apex	1 Reaches protoconid apex	1 Reaches protoconid apex	0 Does not reach protoconid apex	0 Does not reach protoconid apex	?	?	?

A. garhi	K. platyops	Pr. afarensis	P. aethiopicus	A. africanus	P. robustus	P. boisei	H. habilis	H. rudolfensis	H. ergaster	H. sapiens
?	?	0 Foramen beneath middle third of orbital breadth	?	0 Foramen beneath middle third of orbital breadth	0 Foramen beneath middle third of orbital breadth	0 Foramen beneath middle third of orbital breadth	0 Foramen beneath middle third of orbital breadth	?	0 Foramen beneath middle third of orbital breadth	0 Foramen beneath middle third of orbital breadth
?	?	?	?	1 Variable	2 Fronto-lateral	1 Variable	2 Fronto-lateral	2 Fronto-lateral	2 Fronto-lateral	2 Fronto-lateral
0 Strong, projects anterior to sella	?	?	0 Strong, projects anterior to sella	0 Strong, projects anterior to sella	0 Strong, projects anterior to sella	0 Strong, projects anterior to sella	0 Strong, projects anterior to sella	0 Strong, projects anterior to sella	0 Strong, projects anterior to sella	0 Strong, projects anterior to sella
2 Torus-like	1 Inter-mediate	2 Torus-like	2 Torus-like	1 Inter-mediate	2 Torus-like	2 Torus-like	2 Torus-like	1 Inter-mediate	2 Torus-like	0 Weak
2 Less arched	?	2 Less arched	2 Less arched	1 Variable	0 Arched	1 Variable	0 Arched	0 Arched	0 Arched	0 Arched
?	?	0 At or below plane of orbital rim	?	0 At or below plane of orbital rim	0 At or below plane of orbital rim	0 At or below plane of orbital rim	0 At or below plane of orbital rim	?	0 At or below plane of orbital rim	0 At or below plane of orbital rim
?	?	2 Obliterated	?	1 Variable	2 Obliterated	2 Obliterated	2 Obliterated	?	2 Obliterated	2 Obliterated
?	?	?	1 Ossified, with projection	1 Ossified, with projection	?	1 Ossified, with projection	1 Ossified, with projection	?	?	0 Not ossified
?	?	2 Similar	?	2 Similar	0 Dissimilar	0 Dissimilar	1 Variable	?	2 Similar	2 Similar
1 More robust	?	1 More robust	?	1 More robust	1 More robust	1 More robust	1 More robust	1 More robust	1 More robust	1 More robust
?	?	2 Absent	?	2 Absent	2 Absent	2 Absent	2 Absent	?	2 Absent	2 Absent
2 Paracone equals protocone	?	2 Paracone equals protocone	2 Paracone equals protocone	2 Paracone equals protocone	2 Paracone equals protocone	2 Paracone equals protocone	2 Paracone equals protocone	2 Paracone equals protocone	2 Paracone equals protocone	2 Paracone equals protocone
?	?	3 Frag-mented or absent	3 Frag-mented or absent	2 Variable	3 Frag-mented or absent	3 Frag-mented or absent	3 Frag-mented or absent	3 Frag-mented or absent	3 Frag-mented or absent	3 Frag-mented or absent
?	?	1 Well defined	?	1 Well defined	1 Well defined	1 Well defined	1 Well defined	?	1 Well defined	1 Well defined
?	?	1 Closed distally	?	1 Closed distally	1 Closed distally	1 Closed distally	1 Closed distally	?	?	1 Closed distally
?	?	0 Does not reach protoconid apex	?	0 Does not reach protoconid apex	1 Reaches protoconid apex	0 Does not reach protoconid apex	0 Does not reach protoconid apex	?	0 Does not reach protoconid apex	0 Does not reach protoconid apex

(continued on next page)

Table 3.   (continued)

Label	Character	Colobus/Papio	Hylobates	Pongo	Gorilla	Pan	S. tchadensis	Ar. ramidus	A. anamensis
CW 52	Protocone of dp^3, in occlusal view	1 Smaller than paracone	1 Smaller than paracone	1 Smaller than paracone	0 Larger than paracone	0 Larger than paracone	?	?	?
CW 54	Crista obliqua of dp^4	0 Weak	1 Moderate	1 Moderate	2 Strong	2 Strong	?	?	2 Strong
CW 55	Protocristid groove of lower molars	0 Prominent	1 Barely visible	1 Barely visible	0 Prominent	1 Barely visible	?	?	?
CW 56	Lingual marginal ridges of molars	0 Hardly appreciable	1 More prominent	1 More prominent	2 Very prominent	1 More prominent	?	?	?
CW 59	Insertion of genioglossus	0 Above inferior transverse torus	0 Above inferior transverse torus	1 On inferior transverse torus	1 On inferior transverse torus	1 On inferior transverse torus	?	?	?
CW 60	Insertion of geniohyoideus	0 Basally on inferior transverse torus	1 Higher on inferior transverse torus	0 Basally on inferior transverse torus	1 Higher on inferior transverse torus	2 Above inferior transverse torus	?	?	?
CW 61	Insertion of digastric	0 Posterior to inferior transverse torus	0 Posterior to inferior transverse torus	2 Not on symphysis	0 Posterior to inferior transverse torus	1 Inferior transverse torus	?	?	?
CW 64	Condylar canal	0 Absent or infrequent	0 Absent or infrequent	0 Absent or infrequent	1 Frequently present	1 Frequently present	?	?	?
CW 66	Molar dentine horns	0 High	0 High	1 Low	0 High	0 High	?	?	?
CW 69	Ethmo-lacrimal contact	0 c. 100%	0 c. 100%	0 c. 100%	1 Variable (49%)	1 Variable (79%)	?	?	?
CW 76	Fovea posterior	1 Well developed	0 Absent or weak	0 Absent or weak	1 Well developed	0 Absent or weak	?	0 Absent or weak	0 Absent or weak
CW 78	Mandibular corpus depth along tooth row	*Colobus:* 0 Shallow mesially *Papio:* 3 Deepens mesially	3 Deepens mesially	1 Constant	1 Constant	1 Constant	?	?	?
CW 79	Ethmo-sphenoid contact	0 Usually absent (0–25%)	0 Usually absent (0–25%)	3 Present (c. 100%)	1 Variable (c. 50%)	2 Usually present (c. 75%)	?	?	?
CW 89	I^1 lingual crenulations	0 Absent	0 Absent	2 Whole surface	1 Marginal	1 Marginal	2 Whole surface	?	?
CW 92	Canine sexual dimorphism	0 Hyper dimorphic	4 Mono-morphic, large canines	1 Strongly dimorphic	1 Strongly dimorphic	2 Moderately dimorphic	3 Mono-morphic, small canines	2 Moderately dimorphic	2 Moderately dimorphic
CW 96	Sulcus obliqus	0 Weak to moderate	0 Weak to moderate	1 Strong	1 Strong	0 Weak to moderate	?	?	?

(Table 4). These traits were either omitted or combined with other characters, which resulted in only 53 of their original 96 characters being employed here. However, when possible, these characters were coded independently in the present study. Thus, several of the character state assignments employed here differ from those of Collard and Wood (2000) and the sources from which they obtained their character data (Delson and Andrews, 1975; Schwartz, 1984; Groves, 1986; Andrews, 1987; Braga, 1995; Shoshani et al., 1996).

Sixty of the traditional characters derived from Strait and Grine (2001) were described in detail in the appendix of Strait et al. (1997). The remaining traits (SG 61-SG 70) are described in Appendix A [in the full published version of Strait and Grine (2004), also online at Science Direct], along with thirteen of the original Strait et al. (1997) traits that required revision or other explanation.

A. garhi	K. platyops	Pr. afarensis	P. aethiopicus	A. africanus	P. robustus	P. boisei	H. habilis	H. rudolfensis	H. ergaster	H. sapiens
?	?	0 Larger than paracone	?	0 Larger than paracone	0 Larger than paracone	?	0 Larger than paracone	0 Larger than paracone	0 Larger than paracone	0 Larger than paracone
?	?	2 Strong	?	2 Strong	2 Strong	2 Strong	2 Strong	?		2 Strong
?	?	?	?	?	?	?	?	?	?	0 Prominent
?	?	?	?	?	?	?	?	?	?	1 More prominent
?	?	?	?	?	?	?	?	?	?	0 Above inferior transverse torus
?	?	?	?	?	?	?	?	?	?	2 Above inferior transverse torus
?	?	?	?	?	?	?	?	?	?	1 Inferior transverse torus
?	?	0 Absent or infrequent	?	0 Absent or infrequent	1 Frequently present	1 Frequently present	0 Absent or infrequent	?	0 Absent or infrequent	1 Frequently present
?	?	?	1 Low	0 High	1 Low	1 Low	0 High	?	?	0 High
?	?	?	?	?	?	?	?	?	?	0 c. 100%
?	?	0 Absent or weak	?	0 Absent or weak	0 Absent or weak	1 Well developed	0 Absent or weak	0 Absent or weak	0 Absent or weak	0 Absent or weak
?	?	1 Constant	1 Constant	1 Constant	2 Variable	1 Constant	1 Constant	1 Constant	1 Constant	1 Constant
?	?	?	?	?	?	?	?	?	?	3 Present (c. 100%)
?	?	1 Marginal	?	1 Marginal	1 Marginal	?	?	1 Marginal	1 Marginal	1 Marginal
?	?	3 Mono-morphic, small canines	?	3 Mono-morphic, small canines	3 Mono-morphic, small canines	3 Mono-morphic, small canines	3 Mono-morphic, small canines	2 Moderately dimorphic	3 Mono-morphic, small canines	3 Mono-morphic, small canines
?	?	?	?	?	?	?	?	?	?	0 Weak to moderate

In summary, 198 characters were employed in the present study, including 89 craniometric and 39 traditional characters derived from Collard and Wood (2000), 56 traditional characters derived from Strait and Grine (2001), and 14 traditional characters derived from both Collard and Wood (2000) and Strait and Grine (2001).

Published data on extant primates (Delson and Andrews, 1975; Wood, 1975; Schwartz, 1984; Groves, 1986; Andrews, 1987; Chamberlain, 1987; Braga, 1995; Shoshani et al., 1996; Collard and Wood, 2000) were supplemented by observations by the authors on specimens housed at the American Museum of Natural History. Collard and Wood's craniometric data set was expanded to include data on *Papio* and *Hylobates* (Table 5). For most characters, these data derived from measurements on 20 *P. anubis* and 20 *H. lar* specimens compiled by Chamberlain (1987). Remaining craniometric characters were supplemented with

Table 4. Omitted or Conflated Characters

Character	Explanation
CW 4 (Direction of incisive foramen)	Redundant with SG 7 (Nasal cavity entrance) because the relationship between the clivus and palate will determine the direction of the opening of the incisive foramen.
CW 5 (Carotid canal morphology)	Autapomorphic for gibbons as coded by Collard and Wood (2000), and thus uninformative in the present analysis.
CW 6 (Size of I^1 relative to I^2)	Redundant with P2, P4, which are MD diameters of I^1 and I^2.
CW 7 (Canine honing in males)	Redundant with P7, SG 51, which reflect canine size. Honing only occurs in taxa with large canines.
CW 8 (Interorbital pillar width)	Redundant with F3 (Interorbital breadth).
CW 12 (Klinorynchy)	Redundant with SG 30 (Cranial base flexion), as both reflect the relationship between the face and base.
CW 13 (Frontozygomatic suture)	Autapomorphic for orangs as coded by Collard and Wood (2000), and thus uninformative in the present analysis.
CW 14 (Relative height of upper face)	Redundant with F15 (Facial height), and not clearly defined in Shoshani et al. (1996).
CW 15 (Facial index: height to breadth)	Redundant with F11 (Upper facial breadth) and F15 because these are the components of the facial index.
CW 16 (Height of mandibular symphysis relative to toothrow)	Groves (1988) described extensive overlap of values between species, and thus we do not recognize distinct states.
CW 18 (Pyriform aperture)	Redundant with F7 (Nasal width).
CW 21 (Frontal bone)	We cannot recreate the character states listed in Shoshani et al. (1996) based on the character description.
CW 23 (Number of incisive formina)	Redundant with SG 7 (Nasal cavity entrance) and SG 12 (Anterior palatal depth). Double foramina are caused by the vomer, which inserts onto the posterior pole of the clivus. If the foramen is a long canal, then a single opening is observed. If a short canal or simply a foramen is present, then double foramina are observed. Having a smooth, overlapping nasal cavity entrance produces a long canal. Humans have a long canal because of their deep anterior palate.
CW 24 (Maxillary sinus)	Autapomorphic for orangs as coded by Collard and Wood (2000), and thus uninformative in the present analysis.
CW 27 (Orbits)	Autapomorphic for orangs as coded by Collard and Wood (2000), and thus uninformative in the present analysis.
CW 28 (Supraorbital trigon)	Strait et al. (1997) omitted this character, deeming it to be redundant with SG 19 (Anteromedial incursion of temporal lines) and SG 28 (Facial hafting).
CW 29 (Nasal width)	Autapomorphic for orangs as coded by Collard and Wood (2000), and thus uninformative in the present analysis.
CW 30 (Length of nasals)	Redundant with F 5 (Nasion-Rhinion chord length).
CW 31 (Size of zygomatic foramina)	Autapomorphic for orangs as coded by Collard and Wood (2000), and thus uninformative in the present analysis.
CW 33 (Size of incisive foramina)	Redundant with SG 7 (Nasal cavity entrance). The foramen is small if the clivus and palate overlap.
CW 34 (Size and shape of palatine foramina)	Autapomorphic for orangs as coded by Collard and Wood (2000), and thus uninformative in the present analysis.
CW 37 (Posterior convergence of temporal lines)	Redundant with SG 19 (Anteromedial incursion of superior temporal lines) and SG 20 (Sagittal crest present in males).
CW 38 (Mesial groove on male canine)	Redundant with SG 70 (Extensive mesial groove on upper canine). Also, we disagree with the characterization of *Pongo* in Shoshani et al. (1996).
CW 39 (Relative height of upper canine)	Redundant with P7 (Upper canine labial height) and P5 (Upper canine M-D diameter).
CW 45 (Protoconid apex on dp$_3$)	Dependent on CW 46 (Presence of metaconid on dp$_3$) because protoconid will only be buccal if the metaconid is present.
CW 47 (Protocristid of dp$_3$)	Orientation of this crest is dependent on position of protoconid (CW 45), which, in turn, is dependent on the presence of a metaconid (CW 46).
CW 49 (Metaconid dp$_4$)	We do not recognize the distinctions between taxa reported in Shoshani et al. (1996).
CW 51 (Talonid basin of dp$_4$)	We do not recognize the distinctions between taxa reported in Shoshani et al. (1996).
CW 53 (Preprotocista of dp^4)	Autapomorphic for gibbons as coded by Collard and Wood (2000), and thus uninformative in the present analysis.
CW 57 (Thickness of molar enamel)	Redundant with SG 59 (Relative enamel thickness).
CW 58 (Proportion of pattern 3 enamel)	This character has yet to be adequately quantified in any of the ingroup taxa.
CW 62 (Encephalization)	Redundant with SG 16 (Cranial capacity).
CW 63 (Retro-articular canal)	Autapomorphic for orangs as coded by Collard and Wood (2000), and thus uninformative in the present analysis.
CW 65 (Incisive fossa)	Redundant with SG 7 (Nasal cavity entrance) because the fossa will be deep if stepped, absent if smooth, and will extend through the palate as a foramen if no overlap.
CW 67 (Molar enamel wrinkling)	Autapomorphic for orangs as coded by Collard and Wood (2000), and thus uninformative in the present analysis. Although some early hominids have wrinkled enamel, it is restricted in these species to the third molar.

Table 4.   (continued)

Character	Explanation
CW 68 (Postorbital sulcus)	Redundant with CW 25 (Supraorbital torus development). Moreover, we disagree with their (Collard and Wood, 2000) characterization of *Homo*.
CW 70 (Fronto-maxillary contact in orbits)	Redundant with CW 69 (Ethmo-lacrimal contact) because fronto-maxillary contact is possible only if the ethmoid and lacrimal are separated.
CW 71 (Nasal floor morphology)	Redundant with SG 7 (Nasal cavity entrance).
CW 72 (Palatine fenestra size)	Redundant with SG 7 (Nasal cavity entrance) because a palatine fenestra is equivalent to a large incisive foramen, which is related the degree of overlap of the palate and clivus.
CW 73 (Cheek tooth height)	Redundant with SG 59 (Enamel thickness) and CW 66 (Molar dentine horn height).
CW 74 (M_3 smaller than M_2)	Size of lower teeth should be related to the size of the upper teeth against which they occlude, and the absolute dimensions (M-D and B-L diameters) of those teeth have already been considered (P14–P17).
CW 75 (Number of zygomatic foramina)	Our observations indicate a higher degree of variability than reported by Schwartz (1984).
CW 77 (Relative depth of mandible)	The dimension being compared to mandibular depth was not specified. Strait et al. (1997) omitted one relative measurement, robusticity, because of excessive intraspecific variability. Moreover, relative depth is at least partially redundant with SG 44 (Mandibular cross-sectional area at M_1).
CW 80 (Zygomatic bone)	Redundant with CW 20 (Orientation of zygomatic bone).
CW 81 (Relative face height)	Redundant with F15 (Facial height).
CW 82 (Male canine length as a percentage of M^1)	Redundant with P5 (Upper canine M-D diameter) and P13 (M^1 M-D diameter).
CW 83 (Female canine length as a percentage of M^1)	Redundant with P5 (Upper canine M-D diameter) and P13 (M^1 M-D diameter).
CW 84 (Male canine length as a percentage of P^4)	Redundant with P5 (Upper canine M-D diameter) and P11 (P^4 M-D diameter).
CW 85 (Female canine length as a percentage of P^4)	Redundant with P5 (Upper canine M-D diameter) and P11 (P^4 M-D diameter).
CW 86 (Angle between toothrows)	Redundant with SG 62 (Orientation of mandibular premolar row = dental arcade shape).
CW 87 (Eruption after I^2)	Redundant with SG 60 (Dental development rate).
CW 88 (Eruption after I_2)	Redundant with SG 60 (Dental development rate).
CW 90 (I^1 cingulum tubercle)	This character is too variable to be of use.
CW 91 (Number of I^1 ridges)	Redundant with CW 89 (I^1 crenulations).
CW 93 (Canine elongation)	Redundant with P5 (Upper canine M-D diameter) and P6 (Upper canine B-L diameter) and CW 41 (Robusticity of canines).
CW 94 (P_3 metaconid)	Redundant with SG 58 (Frequency of well-developed P_3 metaconid).
CW 95 (Trigonid basin)	Distinctions between species as recognized by Groves (1988) are not observed due to high levels of intraspecific variability.

measurements by the authors on 20 *H. hoolock,* 13 *P. ursinus,* and 4 *P. anubis* specimens. Data on fossil hominids were obtained principally from Wood (1991) and Chamberlain (1987) and descriptions of recently discovered early hominid species (White et al., 1994; Leakey et al., 1995; Asfaw et al., 1999a; Ward et al., 2001; Leakey et al., 2001; Brunet et al., 2002). These were supplemented by the character data already compiled in Strait and Grine (2001) and Strait et al. (1997) and observations and measurements recorded by the authors.

Character Independence and Redundance. A critical component of any cladistic analysis should be an assessment of the independence of the features selected for analysis. If characters are not independent, they will bias an analysis by numerically overweighting what should essentially be considered a single character state change (e.g., Farris, 1983; Kluge, 1989). There are at least three reasons why characters might not be independent. First, characters might be descriptively redundant such that a single morphological feature might be

described in multiple ways. For example, characters CW 69 (Ethmo-lacrimal contact) and CW 70 (Fronto-maxillary contact) both describe the pattern by which

Table 5.   Sample Sizes of Extant Taxa Used for Craniometric Characters

Species	Data from Wood (1975)	Data from Chamberlain (1987)	Data from Present Study
Colobus guereza	24[1]	20[1]	—
Papio ursinus	—	—	13[2]
Papio anubis	—	20[2]	4[2]
Hylobates lar	—	20[2]	—
Hylobates hoolock	—	—	20[2]
Pongo pygmaeus	41[1]	20[1]	—
Gorilla gorilla	37[1]	20[1]	—
Pan troglodytes	35[1]	20[1]	—
Homo sapiens	70[1]	20[1]	—

[1] Data employed by Collard and Wood (2000).

[2] Data used to supplement that employed by Collard and Wood (2000).

bones articulate on the medial wall of the orbit, but the state of one character is a structural necessity of the other: if the ethmoid and lacrimal bones articulate, then the frontal and maxillary bones cannot.

Characters might also lack independence if they describe different parts of the same feature. Such characters might not be descriptively redundant in the strictest sense, but they nonetheless might partially or substantially depend on each other. For example, characters P 22 (Palate depth at M^1) and P 27 (Palate depth at M^2) are not identical measurements, but they are both basically expressions of posterior palate depth.

Finally, characters might describe different features, but those features might be morphologically integrated such that they evolve as a unit (Olson and Miller, 1958; Cheverud, 1982, 1995, 1996; Zelditch, 1987, 1988; Chernoff and Magwene 1999; Ackermann and Cheverud, 2000; Strait, 2001). For example, McCollum (1999a) has hypothesized that characters SG3 (Infraorbital foramen location), SG7 (Nasal cavity entrance), SG8 (Palate thickness), SG26 (Postorbital constriction), and SG28 (Facial hafting) are integrated as a result of developmental processes related to vomeral insertion.

Our study accounted for two of the three sources of character correlation described above. We omitted characters that are obviously descriptively redundant (Table 4), and downweighted characters that describe different parts of the same character complex (Table 6). Decisions about the conflation and omission of characters were made prior to the performance of any parsimony analysis. The third source of character correlation mentioned above is integration. We have argued elsewhere (Strait et al., 1997; Strait and Grine, 1998; Strait,

2001) that hypotheses of integration should be tested before being incorporated into phylogenetic analysis, because, unlike characters that describe the *same* feature, characters thought to be integrated describe *different* features. In our opinion, such characters should have the presumption of independence until shown otherwise. Indeed, when Strait (2001) examined the hominid cranial base, he found that untested hypotheses of integration tended to greatly overstate the number of characters that actually might be integrated. Hypotheses of integration in other cranial regions have yet to be tested with respect to early hominids, and it would be inappropriate to address the problem of integration in one region but not others. Thus, this study did not formally attempt to correct for the effects of morphological integration.

Scale-Adjustment. A difference between the present study and that of Collard and Wood (2000) concerns the definition of the geometric mean used to scale-adjust the craniometric characters. Because Collard and Wood's (2000) data were compiled from two sources (Wood, 1975; Chamberlain, 1987), each measurement was scale-adjusted by being divided by the geometric mean of all of the measurements contained in the data set from which it was derived. Thus, they employed two geometric means. This approach could not be applied to an analysis of fossil hominids because fossil specimens are rarely complete. As a result, no single specimen would preserve all of the characters necessary to create the geometric mean. In order to maximize the number of fossil specimens that can be included, it is necessary to employ a geometric mean based on relatively few characters. Thus, in the present study, a single geometric

Table 6. Complexes of Characters That Describe Different or Overlapping Parts of the Same Feature

Complex	Composition of Complexes	Weight of Each Character in the ALL CHARACTERS Data Set[1]	Weight of Each Character in the TRADITIONAL Data Set[1]
Incisor size	P1-4,29; SG50	0.167	1.000
Canine size	P5-7; SG51	0.250	1.000
Premolar size	P8-11,30: SG53	0.167	1.000
Molar size	P12-17,31; SG54	0.125	1.000
Palate/oral cavity breadth	P18,19,21	0.333	None included
Palate length	P20,23	0.500	None included
Posterior palate depth	P22,27	0.500	None included
Orbit/upper facial breadth	F1,4,11	0.333	None included
Nasal breadth	F7,13	0.500	None included
Nasal length	F5,6; SG1	0.333	None included
Bizygomatic breadth	F9,10; SG29	0.333	1.000
Malar height	F18,19	0.500	None included
Postorbital breadth	C2,7; SG26	0.333	1.000
Cranial length	C1,10,25,28-30,32	0.143	None included
Occipital length	C31,33	0.500	None included
Anterior basicranial breadth	C13-15	0.333	None included
Posterior basicranial breadth	C11,12	0.500	None included
Foramen magnum size	C21,22	0.500	None included
Infratemporal fossa size	C23,24	0.500	None included

[1] In cladistic analyses, independent characters are each assigned a weight of 1.000. Collectively, all of the characters in a complex equal the weight of an independent character. Note that the two data sets employed in this study contained different combinations of characters, and may exclude one or more of the characters in a complex. Thus, the weights of the included characters differ depending on the data set being examined. For example, in the ALL CHARACTERS data set, all of the six characters in the "incisor size" complex are included, and thus each character is given a weight of 0.167. However, in the TRADITIONAL data set, only one of the characters in this complex is included (SG 50), and so that character receives a weight of 1.000.

mean was constructed for each specimen based on four linear measurements (F7 [maximum nasal width], F10 [bizygomatic breadth], C1 [glabella-opisthocranion], and C5 [biporionic width]). These measurements were chosen because they are all preserved on a number of fossil hominid specimens, and because they are present in the two data sets (Wood, 1975; Chamberlain, 1987) employed by Collard and Wood (2000).

Assigning Character States.   The traditional characters were all assigned states according to the procedures outlined in Strait et al. (1997). With respect to qualitative traditional characters, a fossil species was characterized as exhibiting a particular morphology only if it was present in every relevant specimen in the hypodigm. If two or more morphological variants were observed within a species, then it was considered variable for that character, and assigned an intermediate numerical code (i.e., absent = 0, variable = 1, present = 2).[3] Exceptions to this rule occur when a given character state has been described as being present in varying frequencies. A modified criterion was used to code qualitative characters in extant species, because larger samples are generally available for those taxa, and therefore morphological outliers are more likely to be observed. Thus, in extant species, a variable character state was assigned to a taxon only if two or more morphologies were present in sizeable proportions, namely, if a second variant was present in more than 15% of the sample. The 15% value is a compromise. With respect to most qualitative characters, sample sizes for most fossil hominid species are so small that each specimen represents more than 15% of the sample. Thus, the 15% value accomodates the variation expected in extant taxa (in which there are large samples), but is consistent with the coding criterion applied to the extinct taxa (in which there are small samples).

States for quantitative traditional characters were determined using a range-based method such that taxa were assigned different states when their observed ranges were discontinuous or exhibited minimal overlap (Almeida and Bisby, 1984). The range-based method applied to quantitative characters is broadly analogous to the criterion described above for qualitative characters in that both methods assign states by recognizing clearly delineated morphological boundaries. Thus, states for all of the traditional characters examined here (both qualitative and quantitative) were determined in a similar fashion.

States for craniometric characters were obtained using homogeneous subset coding (HSC) (Simon, 1983; see also Rae, 1997). In HSC, taxa are subjected to an analysis of variance with respect to each character, and all possible pairwise comparisons between taxa are performed. HSC assigns to taxa the same state if they are statistically homogenous, but share the same pattern of statistical differences. That is, they share a state

when they are not significantly different from each other, but they are significantly different from the same set of taxa.

HSC was chosen because it is very similar to divergence coding (DC) (Thorpe, 1984), the method employed by Collard and Wood (2000). The two methods assign character states in the same rank order. As typically applied, HSC and DC produce weighted character states such that not all states are separated by the same number of steps, but we follow Farris (1990) in using unweighted (i.e., equally weighted) states. Like all quantitative coding methods, HSC works best when sample sizes are large, and this is clearly not the case with fossil species. As a result, a special procedure was developed that allowed HSC to be applied to fossil hominids [see Appendix B in Strait and Grine (2004)]. In particular, this procedure minimizes the complications stemming from the fact that it is difficult to establish statistically significant differences between species when sample sizes are small. The character states assigned to the craniometric characters are presented in Appendix C in Strait and Grine (2004).

As applied to craniometric characters, HSC differs from the range-based method applied to quantitative traditional characters insofar as HSC assigns different character states to taxa even when taxon ranges overlap extensively. Thus, HSC tends to recognize more states, and therefore subdivide taxa more finely, than the range-based method. Indeed, the taxon ranges observed in many of the craniometric characters overlap so extensively that the range-based method would have assigned all taxa the same state, implying that the characters were phylogenetically uninformative. It is difficult to argue that one coding procedure is better than the other, but at a minimum, it seems possible that character type and associated coding methods may have an impact on results.

Data Sets.   The coding differences described above suggest that traditional and craniometric characters, as employed here, are not strictly comparable. Moreover, whereas traditional characters are capable of describing many aspects of morphology, the craniometric characters employed here are only capable of describing the relative size of a linear dimension. Many of the craniometric characters were first compiled for use in a study of primate sexual dimorphism (Wood, 1975), and in that context, it may be desirable to have a data set dominated by breadths and lengths. However, it could be argued that in a cladistic data set it might be better to have a more nuanced set of characters. In order to test whether character type has an effect on results, the characters were examined in different combinations.

Characters were partitioned into two data sets. The ALL CHARACTERS data set included both craniometric and traditional characters (198 characters labelled F, P, C, CW, and SG [Tables 2, 3]). The TRADITIONAL data set included only the traditional characters (109 characters labelled CW and SG [Table 3]). By comparing analyses of these two data sets, it was possible to assess the effect of character type on the resulting phylogenetic reconstructions. A potential third data set, consisting only of craniometric characters, was not

---

[3] Note that this definition does not imply that the states assigned to fossil taxa cannot accommodate a certain degree of morphological variation. For example, a species in which anterior pillars are present may include specimens in which pillars are weak or strong. The degree of variation that can be accommodated by a given character state depends on how the state is defined.

constructed because these characters are not available for several of the early hominid taxa. As a result, such a data set would have limited comparative value.

Cladistic Analyses

Three analyses were performed on each data set, for a total of six analyses. Each data set was examined first using an ingroup composed only of extant taxa. The data sets were then re-examined following the addition of all fossil hominids. Finally, the data sets were examined after the exclusion of *K. platyops*. In this fashion, comparisons between analyses of the same data set allow one to assess the impact that extinct species have on resulting cladograms, as well as the impact of recognizing *K. platyops* as a distinct species. Comparisons between analyses that use different data sets allow an assessment of the impact of character type.

   Analysis 1 (AC-EXTANT): Parsimony analysis of the ALL CHARACTERS data set using only extant taxa.
   Analysis 2 (AC-ALL TAXA): Parsimony analysis of the ALL CHARACTERS data set using all extant and extinct taxa.
   Analysis 3 (AC-OMIT K): Parsimony analysis of the ALL CHARACTERS data set using all taxa except *K. platyops.*
   Analysis 4 (T-EXTANT): Parsimony analysis of the TRADITIONAL data set using only extant taxa.
   Analysis 5 (T-ALL TAXA): Parsimony analysis of the TRADITIONAL data set using both extant and extinct taxa.
   Analysis 6 (T-OMIT K): Parsimony analysis of the TRADITIONAL data set using all taxa except *K. platyops.*

Configuration of Analyses. In all analyses, preferred cladograms were found using maximum parsimony and the branch and bound search option of PAUP 4.0b10 (Swofford, 1998). Parsimony settings were fixed such that multistate taxa were considered polymorphic. All characters were considered ordered except SG1, SG7, SG34, SG46, SG60, CW61, and CW92, which were unordered. The outgroup taxa, *Colobus* and *Papio,* were constrained to be monophyletic. In all analyses, the most parsimonious cladogram is reported along with standard tree statistics.

Assessing Clade Stability

Although the logic of parsimony dictates that the most parsimonious tree should be preferred over others, the topology of this tree is rarely accepted at face value. In particular, it is reasonable to assess clade stability in terms of how strongly those clades are supported by parsimony. Three ways of assessing clade stability are employed here, and it is not obvious that any one of the three should be preferred over the others.

   First, a decay index (i.e., branch support) (Faith, 1991; Donoghue et al., 1992; Källersjö et al., 1992; Davis, 1993; Bremer, 1994) was calculated for every node in the most parsimonious cladogram. A decay index is simply the number of steps needed to collapse the clade. As a practical matter, the decay index is

calculated by sequentially examining topologies less parsimonious than the preferred one. Thus, if a given clade is present in all trees two steps longer than the preferred cladogram, but is missing in some of the trees that are three steps longer, then that clade has a decay index of three. As the decay index increases, so does the stability of the clade.

   A second method of assessing clade stability is to examine as a group trees that are marginally less parsimonious than the preferred cladogram (Strait et al., 1997). Thus, a 50% majority-rule consensus tree of all of the topologies within 1% of the length of the most parsimonious tree is presented. These topologies are the most reasonable alternatives to the most parsimonious tree, and thus, if a given clade is present in most of them, then the clade is well supported by the character matrix under the parsimony criterion.

   Finally, a third method of assessing clade stability is through the use of bootstrapping techniques. According to this method (Felsenstein, 1985), a cladistic data set is resampled with replacement and each resulting new data set is subjected to parsimony analysis. A majority-rule consensus tree is then employed to indicate the proportion of resampled data sets in which particular clades are supported. This procedure, employed by Collard and Wood (2000), is said to produce a confidence limit for each clade. However, there are significant problems with the application of bootstrapping to cladistic data (see Kitching et al., 1998, for review). Foremost among these is the assumption that the characters in the data matrix represent a random sampling of all possible characters. This is almost certainly not the case, because in nearly every cladistic study, characters are non-randomly selected for analysis specifically because there is reason to suspect that they might be phylogenetically informative. Regardless of these limitations, bootstrapping has become conventional in cladistic analyses, and thus the method is employed here.

   It should be noted that none of the methods discussed above assesses whether or not a particular clade is an accurate hypothesis of phylogeny. Rather, they merely indicate the internal consistency of a given data set.

RESULTS

Analysis 1 (AC-EXTANT)

The first parsimony analysis examined all characters using an ingroup of extant hominoids. A single most parsimonious cladogram was obtained that is inconsistent with the ape molecular tree in that *Hylobates* is the sister taxon of *H. sapiens, Pan* is the sister taxon of this clade, and *Gorilla* is the sister taxon of the *Hylobates* + *Homo* + *Pan* clade (Figure 3a). Decay indices indicate strong support for each of the internal nodes of the cladogram, although bootstrap support for them is only modest (Figure 3c). Consideration of marginally less parsimonious trees (i.e., trees within 1% of the length of the most parsimonious tree) is uninformative because only one other tree falls into this category. It differs substantially from the most parsimonious one, and thus a consensus of these two trees is an unresolved polytomy (Figure 3b).

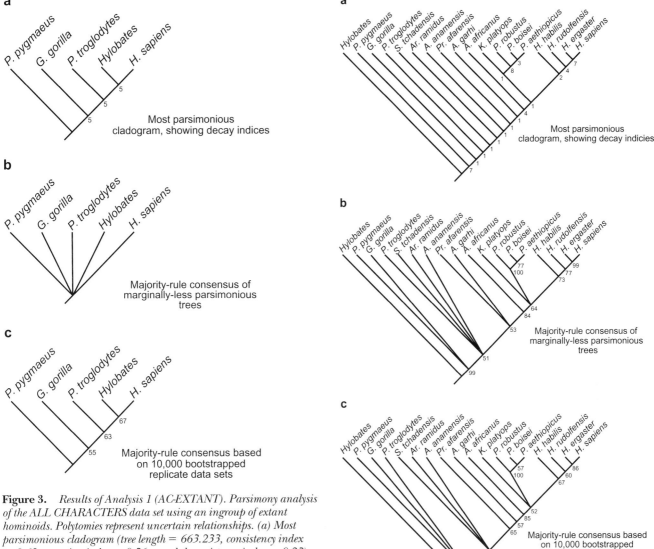

Figure 3. *Results of Analysis 1 (AC-EXTANT). Parsimony analysis of the ALL CHARACTERS data set using an ingroup of extant hominoids. Polytomies represent uncertain relationships. (a) Most parsimonious cladogram (tree length = 663.233, consistency index = 0.62, retention index = 0.36, rescaled consistency index = 0.23). Numbers at nodes represent decay indices (i.e., the number of additional steps needed to collapse the clade). (b) Majority-rule consensus of all topologies within 1% of the length of the shortest tree (2 trees, tree length ≤ 669.865). (c) Majority-rule consensus of 10,000 bootstrapped replicates. Numbers at nodes in (b) and (c) represent the proportion of included trees that support the given node.*

Analysis 2 (AC-ALL TAXA)

The second parsimony analysis examined all of the characters using an ingroup that included both extant hominoids and extinct hominids. It supported a single most parsimonious cladogram that is fully consistent with the ape molecular tree (Figure 4a). This tree finds that *Homo* and *Paranthropus* are each monophyletic, and that *Kenyanthropus* is the sister taxon of *Paranthropus*. All other hominid taxa branch off individually from the stem of the hominid clade. *Sahelanthropus tchadensis* represents the basal branch, followed, in sequence, by *Ar. ramidus*, *A. anamensis*, *Pr. afarensis*, *A. garhi* and *A. africanus*.

Decay indices suggest that the great ape and human clade is extremely stable, but that the clades corresponding to the divergences of *Gorilla* and *Pan* are

Figure 4. *Results of Analysis 2 (AC-ALL TAXA). Parsimony analysis of the ALL CHARACTERS data set using an ingroup of extant hominoids and fossil hominids. Polytomies represent uncertain relationships. (a) Most parsimonious cladogram (tree length = 1,077.431, consistency index = 0.43, retention index = 0.52, rescaled consistency index = 0.23) showing decay indices. (b) Majority-rule consensus of all topologies within 1% of the length of the shortest tree (60,646 trees, tree length ≤ 1,088.205). (c) Majority-rule consensus of 10,000 bootstrapped replicates.*

minimally stable. With respect to hominids, there is strong support for a *Paranthropus* clade, and a clade that includes *A. africanus, Kenyanthropus, Paranthropus* and *Homo*. A *Homo* clade has modest support, and nodes within the *Homo* clade are well supported. Most other hominid clades exhibit minimum stability.

Certain of the branches in the most parsimonious cladogram are lost in marginally less parsimonious trees, as indicated by a 50% majority rule consensus tree based on the 60,646 topologies within 1% of the shortest tree length (Figure 4b). Note that the large number of marginally less parsimonious trees is almost certainly influenced by the fact that craniometric characters were missing for several hominid species (*S. tchadensis, Ar. ramidus, A. anamensis, Pr. afarensis, A. garhi, K. platyops*), either because the relevant specimens are not yet available for general study, or because available specimens are not sufficiently complete as to allow the calculation of the geometric mean used for scale-correction. The consensus tree shows strong support for the nodes representing the great ape and human clade, the *Paranthropus* clade, and the clade including *Homo, Paranthropus, Kenyanthropus,* and *A. africanus.* There is moderate support for a monophyletic *Homo* clade. Within the great ape and human clade, the precise relationships of *Pan, Gorilla, Pongo* and the species at the base of the hominid clade are unstable.

Bootstrapping yields a consensus tree (Figure 4c) that is broadly comparable to that obtained by marginally less parsimonious trees (see above). Stability is greatest in the great ape and human clade, the *Paranthropus* clade, and the clade containing *Homo, Paranthropus, Kenyanthropus,* and *A. africanus.*

Analysis 3 (AC-OMIT K)

The third parsimony analysis examined all of the characters but omitted *K. platyops* from the ingroup. A single most parsimonious cladogram was found (Figure 5a) that is otherwise identical to that obtained when this species was included (Figure 4a). Decay indices indicate that nodes within the *A. africanus* + *Homo* + *Paranthropus* clade are well supported, as is the great ape and human clade. Other nodes are minimally stable. An equivalent pattern of stability is indicated by the consensus of 12,810 marginally less parsimonious trees (Figure 5b). Bootstrapping also indicates a similar pattern, but stability at certain nodes is somewhat lower.

Analysis 4 (T-EXTANT)

The fourth parsimony analysis examined traditional characters using an ingroup of extant hominoids. A single most parsimonious cladogram was found that was inconsistent with the ape molecular phylogeny (Figure 6a). Although it resembles the molecular tree in that great apes and humans form a clade, it departs from the molecular phylogeny by indicating that *Pan* is the sister taxon of a *Gorilla* + *Pongo* clade. Decay indices and bootstrap values (Figure 6c) both indicate that the great ape and human clade is very stable, while the *Pongo* + *Gorilla* clade is moderately stable. As was the case with Analysis 1 (AC-EXTANT), a consideration of marginally less parsimonious trees is uninformative because only two trees were available to construct the consensus (Figure 6b).

Analysis 5 (T-ALL TAXA)

The fifth parsimony analysis examined traditional characters using an ingroup that included both extant hominoids and extinct hominids. This analysis yields three most parsimonious trees (Figure 7a), each of which is consistent with the ape molecular phylogeny.

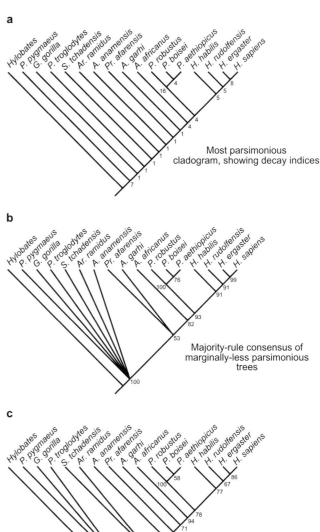

Figure 5. *Results of Analysis 3 (AC-OMIT K). Parsimony analysis of the ALL CHARACTERS data set using an ingroup of extant hominoids and fossil hominids that excluded K. platyops. Polytomies represent uncertain relationships. (a) Most parsimonious cladogram (tree length = 1,071.181, consistency index = 0.44, retention index = 0.52, rescaled consistency index = 0.23) showing decay indices. (b) Majority-rule consensus of all topologies within 1% of the length of the shortest tree (12,810 trees, tree length ≤ 1,081.893). (c) Majority-rule consensus of 10,000 bootstrapped replicates.*

In one tree, *Kenyanthropus* is the sister taxon of a *Homo* + *Paranthropus* clade, while in the other two, *Kenyanthropus* is the sister taxon of *Paranthropus* alone. Moreover, in two trees, *H. rudolfensis* is the sister taxon of other species within the genus *Homo*, while in the remaining tree, this position is filled by *H. habilis*. In all other respects, the three trees are identical to that in Figure 4a except that *P. robustus* rather than *P. aethiopicus* is the sister taxon of *P. boisei.*

Decay indices indicate that most of the clades in the cladogram are moderately to very stable, including all

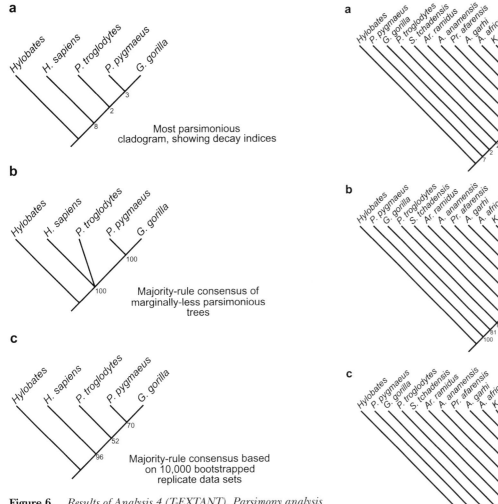

Figure 6. *Results of Analysis 4 (T-EXTANT). Parsimony analysis of the TRADITIONAL data set using an ingroup of extant hominoids. Polytomies represent uncertain relationships. (a) Most parsimonious cladogram (tree length = 235, consistency index = 0.62, retention index = 0.45, rescaled consistency index = 0.31) showing decay indices. (b) Majority-rule consensus of all topologies within 1% of the length of the shortest tree (2 trees, tree length ≤ 237). (c) Majority-rule consensus of 10,000 bootstrapped replicates.*

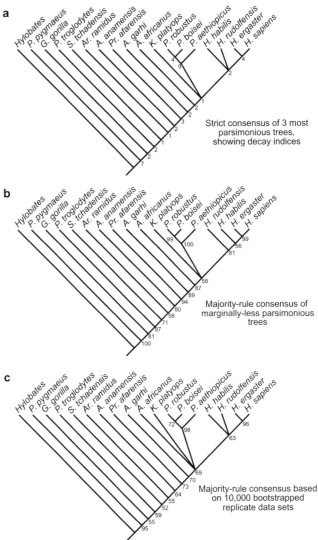

Figure 7. *Results of Analysis 5 (T-ALL TAXA). Parsimony analysis of the TRADITIONAL data set using an ingroup of extant hominoids and fossil hominids. Polytomies represent uncertain relationships. (a) Strict consensus of three equally most parsimonious cladograms (tree length = 424, consistency index = 0.47, retention index = 0.66, rescaled consistency index = 0.31) showing decay indices. (b) Majority-rule consensus of all topologies within 1% of the length of the shortest tree (333 trees, tree length ≤ 428). (c) Majority-rule consensus of 10,000 bootstrapped replicates.*

of those pertaining to the divergence of the extant ape species. The only relatively unstable nodes correspond to the *Kenyanthropus + Paranthropus + Homo* clade, and the divergences of *S. tchadensis* and *Ar. ramidus*. Consideration of 333 marginally less parsimonious trees yields a similar pattern, but the level of stability at most nodes is higher (Figure 7b). Bootstrapping produces the same basic pattern, but the level of stability is lower (Figure 7c).

Analysis 6 (T-OMIT K)

The sixth parsimony analysis examined traditional characters but excluded *K. platyops* from the ingroup. A single most parsimonious tree was obtained that reconstructs *H. habilis* as the basal branch of the *Homo* clade (Figure 8a). In all other respects, this cladogram is equivalent to that obtained when *K. platyops* was included (Figure 7a). Decay indices, a consensus of 118

marginally less parsimonious trees, and bootstrapping all (Figure 8) indicate that most nodes in the cladogram are at least moderately stable, but that the nodes corresponding to the divergence of *S. tchadensis* and *Ar. ramidus* are minimally stable.

DISCUSSION

The Role of Fossil Taxa in Phylogeny Reconstruction

The inclusion of fossil taxa in the cladistic analyses had a substantial impact on the relationships of extant hominoids. The two analyses that examined only extant taxa found cladograms that were inconsistent both with each

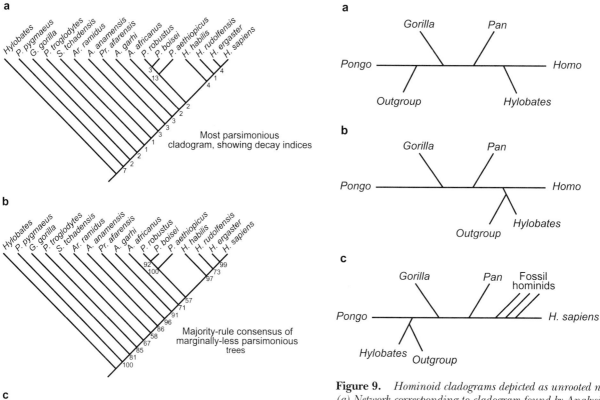

Figure 8. *Results of Analysis 6 (T-OMIT K). Parsimony analysis of the TRADITIONAL data set using an ingroup of extant hominoids and fossil hominids that excluded K. platyops. Polytomies represent uncertain relationships. (a) Strict consensus of three equally most parsimonious cladograms (tree length = 417, consistency index = 0.48, retention index = 0.67, rescaled consistency index = 0.32) showing decay indices. (b) Majority-rule consensus of all topologies within 1% of the length of the shortest tree (118 trees, tree length ≤ 421). (c) Majority-rule consensus of 10,000 bootstrapped replicates.*

Figure 9. *Hominoid cladograms depicted as unrooted networks. (a) Network corresponding to cladogram found by Analysis 1. (b) Network corresponding to cladogram found by Analysis 4. The networks in (a) and (b) are identical except with respect to the position of the outgroup taxon. (c) Network corresponding to a schematic representation of the cladograms found by Analyses 2, 3, 5 and 6. The network in (c) differs from those in (a) and (b) in that the addition of fossil hominids necessitates a shift in the position of* Hylobates.

other and with the ape molecular phylogeny (Figures 3a, 6a). When these analyses were modified to include fossil taxa, they produced cladograms that agreed with each other and the molecular tree (Figures 4a, 5a, 7a, 8a). These observations are consistent with those of other studies indicating that the inclusion of fossil taxa can often help resolve apparent conflicts between morphological and molecular data sets (Eernisse and Kluge, 1993; O'Leary, 1999; Gatesy and O'Leary, 2001; Springer et al., 2001; Gatesy et al., 2003; Mallat and Chen, 2003).

The importance of fossil taxa can be elucidated further by considering in greater detail the cladograms obtained when only extant taxa are considered (Figures 3a, 6a). Although the differences between these cladograms appear to be substantial, when the trees are depicted as unrooted networks (Figure 9a,b) it is clear that the topologies of the ingroup taxa are identical. Thus, the differences between the cladograms depicted in Figures 3a and 6a are a function of the position of the outgroup. The key component of these networks is that *Hylobates* and *Homo* diverge from a common node. This is likely due to the fact that these taxa superficially resemble one another in possessing small, flat faces and globular braincases in comparison to the great apes (Creel, 1986). When fossil taxa are added (Figure 9c), they act as morphological intermediates between *Pan* and *H. sapiens*. *Homo sapiens* resembles the fossil hominids with respect to some derived features, and the fossil hominids, in turn, resemble *Pan* with respect to some primitive features. These resemblances numerically outweigh the similarities between *Hylobates* and *H. sapiens*, and thus the link between these taxa is broken. As a result, the position of *Hylobates* in the network is shifted. Fossil hominids therefore act in precisely the fashion described by Gauthier et al. (1988), who predicted that fossil taxa can significantly improve the power of phylogenetic analyses when such taxa are generally plesiomorphic, but share some apomorphies with one of the extant species. Thus, the cladistic relationships of living taxa are affected by the inclusion of extinct taxa in the analysis. It follows, then, that the absence of fossil taxa in Collard and Wood's (2000) study may have been a factor that contributed to the inability of their analyses to recover the ape molecular phylogeny.

Character Type

Character type had a subtle impact on the results of the various cladistic analyses. The ALL CHARACTERS and TRADITIONAL data sets produced conflicting cladorams when only extant taxa were considered (Figures 3a, 6a), but, as noted above, the key distinction between them concerns how the ingroup network is rooted (Figure 9a,b). In both cases, the resulting cladograms were inconsistent with the ape molecular tree.

When fossil taxa were included, the principal difference between the data sets concerned clade stability. Analyses of the ALL CHARACTERS data set (Figures 4, 5), which included craniometric characters, were notably less stable than those of the TRADITIONAL data set (Figures 7, 8), in which craniometric characters were excluded. There are a number of possible explanations for this pattern. One explanation might be that the craniometric and traditional characters each support slightly different tree topologies, so that when the characters are examined together the resulting tree is less well supported. Another explanation might be that the craniometric characters do not produce a coherent phylogenetic signal, and thus acted as noise in the ALL CHARACTERS data set that partially obscured the phylogenetic signal imparted by the traditional characters. Finally, the instability associated with the craniometric characters might be due to missing data, as these characters were unavailable for several early hominid species. Missing data can have a deleterious effect on clade stability because there may be several equally parsimonious ways of reconstructing the missing character states for these taxa. Unfortunately, the missing data also make it difficult to evaluate which of the three explanations is most plausible.

The Effect of *Kenyanthropus platyops* on Hominid Cladistic Relationships

Hominid cladistic relationships were almost unaffected by the inclusion or exclusion of *K. platyops*. Analyses based on the ALL CHARACTERS data set (Figures 4, 5) revealed that the omission of *K. platyops* from the ingroup increased stability at many nodes within the *A. africanus* + *Homo* + *Paranthropus* clade, but did not affect tree topology. Analyses based on the TRADITIONAL data sets (Figures 7, 8) also obtained this result. In addition, in these latter analyses, the removal of *K. platyops* resolved relationships at the base of the *Homo* clade such that *H. habilis* became the sister taxon of the other *Homo* species.

Hypothesis of Character Reliability

As a result of their analysis of living hominoids, Collard and Wood (2000) hypothesized that craniodental characters are unreliable for reconstructing ape and human phylogeny. A large proportion of the characters employed by Collard and Wood (2000) were included here, albeit in a somewhat modified form. All analyses that included extinct taxa (Analyses 2, 3, 5, 6) yielded most parsimonious cladograms that recovered the molecular phylogeny of the extant apes (Figures 4a, 5a, 7a, 8a). Although certain nodes pertaining to extant apes were unstable when all of the characters were considered (Analyses 2, 3; Figures 4, 5), they were more stable when only traditional characters were examined (Analyses 5, 6, Figures 7, 8). Clearly, parsimony analysis of craniodental characters is able to retrieve the molecular phylogeny of hominoids, albeit with levels of stability that vary according to the data set employed.

According to the congruence test outlined by Collard and Wood (2000), these results refute the contention that craniodental characters either lack phylogenetic utility, or are less reliable than other types of morphological data (Collard and Wood, 2000; Gibbs et al., 2000) with respect to hominoid phylogenetic relationships. Even if one is not a proponent of the congruence test, one must nonetheless conclude, at a minimum, that the basis of Collard and Wood's (2000) hypothesis has been removed. Their claim that craniodental characters are unreliable was based on the inability of their analysis to recover the ape molecular tree, yet in the present study, analyses of data sets derived substantially from them yield the molecular tree.

Other studies of ape phylogeny that employed a variety of both hard and soft tissue characters have also found results consistent with molecular data (Begun, 1992; Shoshani et al., 1996; Gibbs et al., 2000; see also Lockwood et al., 2004). Collectively, those studies and the present one suggest that the perceived inconsistency between morphological and molecular data does not necessarily exist with respect to hominoids.

Does the observed congruence between craniodental and molecular data imply that the early hominid cladograms obtained here are reliable? Such a conclusion would be the logical outcome of the congruence test. However, the congruence test is inherently flawed because it is impossible to know the phylogeny of any group with certainty. It is encouraging when data sets are congruent, but when they are not, the most that one can conclude is that at least one of the data sets is wrong; which of the two is wrong is not a question that can be answered easily (e.g., O'Leary, 1999). In such cases, a total evidence analysis, in which the data sets are examined simultaneously (Kluge, 1989), may be preferable to dismissing an entire data partition. Indeed, a total evidence analysis might even reveal that neither of the cladograms supported separately by the data sets should be preferred, but that a novel cladogram is most parsimonious (Barrett et al., 1991; Chippendale and Wiens, 1994; Olmstead and Sweere, 1994).

Even if the consensus ape molecular phylogeny is accurate, the fact that some morphological data are incongruent with it does not necessarily mean that such data lack utility for reconstructing hominid phylogeny. This is because characters (of any type) can act in different ways at different levels of the phylogenetic hierarchy. Such characters violate the implicit assumption of the congruence test, which is that traits that are useful for investigating one group of primates should be equally useful for investigating other groups. For example, both Shoshani et al. (1996) and Collard and Wood (2000) used the facial index (upper facial height divided by facial breadth) as a character in their analyses. This character is consistent with the *cercopithecine* molecular phylogeny insofar as it helps define the papionins as a clade distinct from cercopithecins, but it is inconsistent with the *hominoid* molecular phylogeny because it identifies non-human great apes as a clade (Shoshani et al., 1996). In the present study, character CW 35 (patency of premaxillary suture) supports a chimpanzee-hominid clade, but would exclude *A. africanus* from the hominids. These examples demonstrate that character optimizations are complex. Characters are not simply homoplastic or homologous, but can exhibit both homology and homoplasy at different hierarchical levels.

Thus, congruence with the ape molecular phylogeny does not suggest that the proposed hominid phylogeny is correct. Rather, this study refutes the notion of an a priori reason for suspecting that craniodental data are either unsuitable for phylogenetic reconstruction, or are less suitable than other types of data.

Cladistic Relationships of Early Hominids

The analyses that included early hominids supported very similar tree topologies (Figures 4a, 5a, 7a, 8a). The strict consensus of these topologies is shown in Figure 10. In this consensus, the pattern of hominid phylogeny is unbalanced such that many species branch off by themselves from the base of the tree, while the top of the tree is dominated by two multi-species clades, *Homo* and *Paranthropus*. *Sahelanthropus* and *Ardipithecus* are, respectively, the first two branches of the tree, with subsequent branches successively represented by *A. anamensis, Pr. afarensis, A. garhi,* and *A. africanus*. If *K. platyops* is a valid species, then its position within the *Homo* + *Paranthropus* clade is unresolved; it is either the sister taxon of the clade, or of *Paranthropus*. Relationships within *Paranthropus* are also unresolved, with *P. boisei* being the sister taxon of either *P. aethiopicus* or *P. robustus*. The position of *H. habilis* relative to *H. rudolfensis* is unresolved, but it is clear that one or the other is the basal branch of the *Homo* clade. *Homo ergaster* and *H. sapiens* are sister taxa. On the basis of this consensus tree, it is possible to evaluate recently proposed phylogenetic hypotheses (White et al., 1994; Leakey et al., 1995; Ward et al., 2001; Asfaw et al., 1999a; Leakey et al., 2001; Lieberman, 2001; Brunet et al., 2002). The robusticity of each evaluation depends on clade stability.

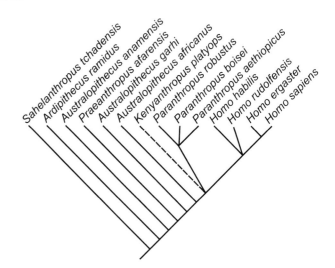

Figure 10.   *Early hominid cladistic relationships. Strict consensus of the most parsimonious cladograms found by Analyses 2, 3, 5 and 6. Polytomies represent uncertain relationships. Dashed line reflects uncertainty regarding whether or not* K. platyops *should be considered a distinct species.*

Ardipithecus ramidus Hypothesis

White et al. (1994) posited that *Ar. ramidus* is either the ancestor or near the ancestry of all other hominids. The present study suggests that *Ar. ramidus* is the sister taxon of all hominids except *Sahelanthropus* (Figure 10), although the relationships of both *Ar. ramidus* and *S. tchadensis* are unstable in every relevant analysis (Figures 4, 5, 7, 8). This instability precludes a definitive test of this hypothesis, but it is supported in a general sense insofar as *Ar. ramidus* branches off near the base of the hominid tree, if not necessarily at the basal node.

Australopithecus anamensis Hypothesis

Leakey et al. (1995; Ward et al., 2001) suggest that *A. anamensis* is likely to be the sister taxon of all hominids except *Ardipithecus* (and, presumably, *Sahelanthropus*). Results from the present study are consistent with this hypothesis (Figure 10), but the relationships of *A. anamensis* are stable only with respect to the analyses of TRADITIONAL characters (Figures 7, 8). The unstable position of *A. anamensis* in the analyses of the ALL CHARACTERS data set (Figures 4, 5) may be influenced by the fact that craniometric characters were not available for this species.

Australopithecus garhi Hypothesis

Asfaw et al. (1999a) suggested that *A. garhi* belongs to a clade that also includes *A. africanus, Paranthropus* and *Homo*. The current study is consistent with this hypothesis insofar as *A. garhi* is reconstructed as the sister taxon of a clade comprising those taxa (Figure 10). In addition, the relationships of *Ar. ramidus, A. anamensis* and *Pr. afarensis* obtained here (Figure 10) are equivalent to those proposed by Asfaw et al. (1999a). However, Asfaw et al. (1999a) also suggested that *A. garhi* may be ancestral to all or part of the genus *Homo*. Cladistic analysis fails to find a sister group relationship between *Homo* and *A. garhi* (Figure 10). Moreover, *A. garhi* is excluded from a stable clade that includes only *Homo, Paranthropus, A. africanus,* and, when included in the analysis, *K. platyops* (Figures 4, 5, 7, 8). Thus, there is no support for the hypothesis that *A. garhi* and *Homo* are sister taxa, so *A. garhi* is unlikely to be the direct ancestor of *Homo*. In order to force *A. garhi* and *Homo* to be sister taxa, it is necessary to reconstruct the characters missing in *A. garhi* to be extremely *Homo*-like, particularly with respect to the mandible and cranial base (see also Strait and Grine, 2001). However, in the present study, parsimony analyses reconstructed these missing character states as being more like those seen in apes or *Pr. afarensis*. These differences highlight the importance that future fossil discoveries will have in evaluating the phylogenetic relationships of this species.

Kenyanthropus platyops Hypothesis

On the basis of facial similarities, Leakey et al. (2001; see also Lieberman, 2001) suggest that *K. platyops* might share especially close affinities with *H. rudolfensis*, even to the point of removing the latter from the *Homo* clade. If *K. platyops* is a valid species, then its cladistic relationships appear to be inconsistent with this hypothesis (Figure 10). None of the analyses that included this species found most parsimonious trees supporting a sister group relationship between *H. rudolfensis* and *K. platyops* (Figures 4, 7). Rather, those analyses find that *Kenyanthropus* is the sister taxon of either *Paranthropus* or the *Homo* + *Paranthropus* clade. However, the position of *K. platyops* relative to *Homo* and *Paranthropus* is unstable, so inferences about the relationships of *K. platyops* must be tentative. Nevertheless, there is no strong evidence supporting the hypothesis that *H. rudolfensis* and *K. platyops* are sister taxa, and thus the transfer of *H. rudolfensis* to the genus *Kenyanthropus* is, at present, unwarranted. One implication of these results is that some of the facial features shared between *H. rudolfensis* and *K. platyops* may be primitive for the *Homo* + *Paranthropus* clade, while others may be convergent. Another implication concerns the timing of early hominid cladogenic events. If *K. platyops* is a valid species, then its age (3.3–3.5 Ma) and cladistic relationships suggest that *Homo* and *Paranthropus* may have diverged from other hominid taxa up to 700 kyr prior to the earliest known specimens currently attributed to those genera (Suwa et al., 1996). It follows, therefore, that this divergence would not be explained by the Turnover Pulse Hypothesis (e.g., Vrba, 1988) because the divergence would have predated the dessication event that was widespread in Africa between 2.7 and 2.3 Ma. These two clades may have each diversified during this period, but their origins are likely to have occurred earlier in the fossil record.

Sahelanthropus tchadensis Hypothesis

Brunet et al. (2002) discuss the possibility that *Sahelanthropus* is the sister taxon of all known hominid species, including *Ardipithecus*. The present study is consistent with this hypothesis insofar as *Sahelanthropus* was found to be the basal branch of the hominid clade (Figure 10), although the position of this species is unstable in all analyses (Figures 4, 5, 7, 8).

Genus-Level Taxonomy

The genus *Australopithecus*, as commonly defined (Skelton and McHenry, 1992; White et al., 1994; Leakey et al., 1995; Brunet et al., 1996; Asfaw et al., 1999a; Ward et al., 2001; Leakey et al., 2001), is manifestly paraphyletic. In recent years, it has become conventional in primatology to transfer species out of paraphyletic groups in order to maintain the monophyly of genera (e.g., *Lophocebus* out of *Cercocebus, Eulemur* out of *Lemur* [see Groves, 2001]). Monophyly is desirable because the allocation of multiple species to a single genus carries with it the implication that they are all more closely related to each other than they are to other species. This is clearly not the case with respect to the species commonly attributed to *Australopithecus*. Continued usage of *Australopithecus* sensu lato perpetuates the erroneous notion that these species form a monophyletic group. In order to make *Australopithecus* monophyletic, it is necessary to place *A. anamensis* and *A. garhi* in different genera. Indeed, new genera may need to be designated in order to accommodate these species. This is preferable to retaining them in a genus, *Australopithecus,* that is little more than a wastebasket taxon. Certainly, there are circumstances in which reference to grade-level, paraphyletic groups is appropriate, but informal names should be applied to them (i.e., "australopiths," "gracile australopiths," "early *Homo,*" "early hominids"). It is misleading to classify these unnatural groups in a formal taxonomy.

Another subject pertaining to genus-level taxonomy is the definition of the genus *Homo*. Wood and Collard (1999) have argued that genus names should correspond to both grades and clades. Noting that *H. habilis* and *H. rudolfensis* appear to belong to the australopith grade, Wood and Collard (1999) advocated removing them from *Homo* and attributing them to *Australopithecus*. However, because the addition of these species to *Australopithecus* contributes to the paraphyly of the genus (Figure 10), if the species are to be removed from *Homo*, they should be assigned new genus names. This possibility is not advocated here, because in a cladistic classification clade membership is more critical than grade membership with respect to supraspecific taxonomy (Hennig, 1966). For example, *Tarsius* is classified in the Haplorhini rather than the Prosimii, even though tarsiers are clearly of prosimian grade (e.g., Groves, 2001). It is convenient and desirable for grades and clades to correspond, but when they do not, taxonomic names should be assigned to clades. Thus, *H. rudolfensis* and *H. habilis* should be removed from

Homo only if there is evidence that their inclusion in *Homo* makes the genus paraphyletic. Wood and Collard (1999) cite three cladistic studies supporting *Homo* paraphyly, but of those, two (Chamberlain and Wood, 1987; Chamberlain, 1987) use an alpha taxonomy of early *Homo* that is no longer in common useage (i.e., they combined ER 1470 and ER 1813 into a single species distinct from another species at Olduvai Gorge). The third study, (Lieberman et al., 1996:105) employed a trait list in which half of the characters "emphasize the major cranial differences among early *Homo*," and half pertain to other hominids. With such a data set, it might not be surprising that paraphyly was observed. The few other cladistic studies that have examined the relationships of early *Homo* (Wood, 1991, 1992; Strait et al., 1997; Strait and Grine, 1999, 2001) have found that *Homo* is monophyletic. In the present study, the *Homo* clade is moderately stable (Figures 4, 5, 7, 8). Thus, from a purely cladistic perspective, there is no compelling reason to remove *H. habilis* and *H. rudolfensis* from the genus.

CONCLUSION

Craniodental characters represent the core data of much of vertebrate paleontology. There is disagreement as to how to interpret such characters when morphological and molecular data are contradictory (Eernisse and Kluge, 1993; Bull et al., 1993; Collard and Wood, 2000; Masters and Brothers, 2002). However, when they are congruent, as was found here, one need not suspect a priori that morphology is unreliable. Such a finding does not imply that morphology-based phylogenies are necessarily correct, but, at a minimum, paleontologists need not be pessimistic about the possibility of reconstructing the pattern of early hominid evolution.

In the present study, fossil hominids had a critical impact on the cladistic relationships of the extant apes. These results demonstrate the fundamental importance of fossil species in phylogeny reconstruction. In particular, fossil taxa increase taxon sampling, which minimizes the difficulty inherent in reconstructing phylogenetic relationships among highly derived extant species.

Regarding recently discovered hominid species, cladistic analysis reveals that *S. tchadensis, Ar. ramidus* and *A. anamensis* are the basal members of the hominid clade. A sister group relationship between *A. garhi* and *Homo* was not observed. If *K. platyops* is a valid species, then it is nested relatively high in the hominid tree given its chronological age. These hypothesized relationships may be tested by future fossil discoveries, and by more detailed investigations of the character data on which the hypothesis is based. In particular, hypotheses of morphological integration and character independence need to be rigorously tested.

ACKNOWLEDGMENTS

We are grateful to M. Collard and B. Wood for graciously making their data available to us, and to A. Walker and M. Leakey for allowing us to examine casts of *A. anamensis* and *K. platyops*. We thank N. Simmons and R. Randall for permission to examine primate specimens in the Department of Mammalogy at the American Museum of Natural History. This manuscript benefitted greatly from comments by M. O'Leary, M. Collard, M. Drapeau, J. Fleagle, T. Harrison, W. Jungers, W. Kimbel, R. O'Keefe, D. Pilbeam, B. Richmond, B. Wood, and three anonymous reviewers.

REFERENCES

Ackermann, R. R., Cheverud, J. M., 2000. Phenotypic covariance structure in tamarins (genus *Saguinus*): a comparison of variation patterns using matrix correlation and common principal component analysis. Am. J. Phys. Anthropol. 111, 489–501.

Aiello, L., Dean, C., 1990. An Introduction to Human Evolutionary Anatomy. Academic Press, San Diego.

Almeida, M. T., Bisby, F. A., 1984. A simple method for establishing taxonomic characters from measurement data. Taxon 33, 405–409.

Andrews, P., 1987. Aspects of hominoid phylogeny. In: Patterson, C. (Ed.), Molecules and Morphology in Evolution: Conflict or Compromise? Cambridge University Press, Cambridge, pp. 23–53.

Asfaw, B., White, T., Lovejoy, O., Latimer, B., Simpson, S., Suwa, G., 1999a. *Australopithecus garhi*: a new species of early hominid from Ethiopia. Science 284, 629–635.

Asfaw, B., White, T., Lovejoy, O., Latimer, B., Simpson, S., Suwa, G., 1999b. Cladistics and early hominid phylogeny. Response. Science 285, 1210–1211.

Bailey, W. J., 1993. Hominoid trichotomy: a molecular overview. Evol. Anthropol. 2, 100–108.

Baker, R. H., Yu, X., DeSalle, R., 1998. Assessing the relative contribution of molecular and morphological characters in simultaneous analysis trees. Mol. Phylogenet. Evol. 9, 427–436.

Barrett, M., Donoghue, M. J., Sober, E., 1991. Against consensus. Syst. Zool. 40, 486–493.

Begun, D. R., 1992. Miocene fossil hominoids and the chimp-human clade. Science 257, 1929–1933.

Begun, D., Walker, A., 1993. The endocast. In: Walker, A., Leakey, R. (Eds.), The Nariokotome *Homo erectus* Skeleton. Harvard University Press, Cambridge, pp. 326–358.

Braga, J., 1995. Emissary canals in the Hominoidea and their phylogenetic significance. Folia Primatol. 65, 144–153.

Bremer, K., 1994. Branch support and tree stability. Cladistics 10, 295–304.

Brunet, M., 2002. *Sahelanthropus* or '*Sahelpithecus*'? Reply. Nature 419, 582.

Brunet, M., Beauvillain, A., Coppens, Y., Heintz, E., Moutaye, A. H. E., Pilbeam, D. R., 1996. Australopithecus bahrelghazali, une nouvelle espece d'Hominide ancien de la region Koro Toro. C. R. Acad. Sci. Paris 322, 907–913.

Brunet, M., Guy, F., Pilbeam, D., Mackaye, H. T., Likius, A., Ahounta, D., Beauvilain, A., Blondel, C., Bocherens, H., Boisserie, J.-R., DeBonis, L., Coppens, Y., Dejax, J., Denys, C., Duringer, P., Eisenmann, V., Fanone, G., Fronty, P., Geraads, D., Lehmann, T., Lihoreau, F., Louchart, A., Mahamat, A., Merceron, G., Mouchelin, G., Otero, O., Campomanes, P. P., DeLeon, M. P., Rage, J.-C., Sapanet, M., Schuster, M., Sudre, J., Tassy, P., Valentin, X., Vignaud, P., Viriot, L., Zazzo, A., Zollikofer, C., 2002. A new hominid from the upper Miocene of Chad, central Africa. Nature 418, 145–151.

Bull, J. J., Huelsenbeck, J., Cunningham, C., Swofford, D., Waddell, P., 1993. Partitioning and combining data in phylogenetic analysis. Syst. Biol. 42, 384–397.

Chamberlain, A. T., 1987. A taxonomic review and phylogenetic analysis of *Homo habilis*. Ph.D. Dissertation, The University of Liverpool, Liverpool.

Chamberlain, A. T., Wood, B. A., 1987. Early hominid phylogeny. J. Hum. Evol. 16, 119–133.

Chernoff, B., Magwene, P. M., 1999. Morphological integration: forty years later. In: Olson, E. C., Miller, R. L. (Eds.), Morphological Integration. University of Chicago Press, Chicago, pp. 319–348.

Cheverud, J. M., 1982. Phenotypic, genetic, and environmental morphological integration in the cranium. Evolution 36, 499–516.

Cheverud, J. M., 1995. Morphological integration in the saddleback tamarin (*Saguinas fuscicolis*) cranium. Am. Nat. 145, 63–89.

Cheverud, J. M., 1996. Developmental integration and the evolution of pleitropy. Am. Zool. 36, 44–50.

Chippendale, P. T., Wiens, J. J., 1994. Weighting, partitioning, and combining characters in phylogenetic analysis. Syst. Biol. 43, 278–287.

Collard, M., Wood, B. A., 2000. How reliable are human phylogenetic hypotheses? Proc. Natl. Acad. Sci. 97, 5003–5006.

Creel, N., 1986. Size and phylogeny in hominoid primates. Syst. Zool. 35, 81–99.

Davis, J. I., 1993. Character removal as a means for assessing the stability of clades. Cladistics 9, 201–210.

Day, M. H., Leakey, M. D., Olson, T. R., 1980. On the status of *Australopithecus afarensis*. Science 207, 1102–1103.

Dean, M. C., 1985. The comparative myology of the hominoid cranial base. II: The muscles of the prevertebral and upper pharyngeal region. Folia Primatol 44, 40–51.

Deinard, A., Kidd, K., 1999. Evolution of a HOXB6 intergenic region within the great apes and humans. J. Hum. Evol. 36, 687–703.

Deinard, A., Sirugo, G., Kidd, K., 1998. Hominoid phylogeny: inferences from a sub-terminal minisatellite analyzed by repeat expansion detection (RED). J. Hum. Evol. 35, 313–317.

Delson, E., Andrews, P., 1975. Evolution and interrelationships of the catarrhine primates. In: Luckett, W. P., Szalay, F. S. (Eds.), Phylogeny of the Primates: A Multidisciplinary Approach. Plenum, New York, pp. 405–446.

Donoghue, M. J., Olmstead, R. G., Smith, J. F., Palmer, J. D., 1992. Phylogenetic relationships of Dipsacales based on *rbc*L sequences. Ann. Missouri Bot. Gardens 79, 672–685.

Eernisse, D. J., Kluge, A. G., 1993. Taxonomic congruence versus total evidence, an amniote phylogeny inferred from fossils, molecules, and morphology. Mol. Biol. Evol. 10, 1170–1195.

Faith, D. P., 1991. Cladistic permutation tests for monophyly and nonmonophyly. Syst. Zool. 40, 366–375.

Farris, J. S., 1983. The logical basis of phylogenetic analysis. In: Platnik, N., Funk, V. (Eds.), Advances in Cladistics, vol. 2. Columbia University Press, New York, pp. 7–36.

Farris, J. S., 1990. Phenetics in camouflage. Cladistics 6, 91–100.

Felsenstein, J., 1985. Confidence limits on phylogenies: an approach using the bootstrap. Evolution 39, 783–791.

Freudenstein, J. V., Pickett, K. M., Simmons, M. P., Wenzel, J. W., 2003. From basepairs to birdsongs: phylogenetic data in the age of genomics. Cladistics 19, 333–347.

Gatesy, J., Amato, G., Norell, M., DeSalle, R., Hayashi, C., 2003. Combined support for wholesale taxic atavism in gavialine crocodylians. Syst. Biol. 52, 403–422.

Gatesy, J., Arctander, P., 2000. Hidden morphological support for the phylogenetic placement of *Pseudooryx nghetinhensis* with bovine bovids: a combined analysis of gross anatomical evidence and DNA sequences from five genes. Syst. Biol. 49, 515–538.

Gatesy, J., O'Leary, M. A., 2001. Deciphering whale origins with molecules and fossils. Trends Ecol. Evol. 16, 562–570.

Gauthier, J., Kluge, A., Row, T., 1988. Amniote phylogeny and the importance of fossils. Cladistics 4, 105–209.

Gibbs, S., Collard, M., Wood, B. A., 2000. Soft-tissue characters in higher primate phylogenetics. Proc. Natl. Acad. Sci. 97, 11130–11132.

Goodman, M., Bailey, W. J., Hayasaka, K., Stanhope, M. J., Slightom, J., Czelusniak, J., 1994. Molecular evidence on primate phylogeny from DNA sequences. Am. J. Phys. Anthropol. 94, 3–24.

Groves, C., 1988. Systematics of the great apes. In: Swindler, D. R., Erwin, J. (Eds.), Comparative Primate Biology, vol. 1, Systematics, Evolution and Anatomy. Alan R. Liss, New York, pp. 187–217.

Groves, C. P., 1999. Nomenclature of African Plio-Pleistocene hominins. J. Hum. Evol. 37, 869–872.

Groves, C., 2001. Primate Taxonomy. Smithsonian Institution Press, Washington.

Haile-Selassie, Y., Suwa, G., White, T. D., 2004. Late Miocene teeth from Middle Awash, Ethiopia, and early hominid dental evolution. Science 303, 1503–1505.

Harrison, T., 1993. Cladistic concepts and the species problem in hominoid evolution. In: Kimbel, W. H., Martin, L. B. (Eds.), Species, Species Concepts, and Primate Evolution. Plenum Press, New York, pp. 345–371.

Hennig, W., 1966. Phylogenetic Systematics. University of Illinois Press, Urbana.

Holloway, R. L., 1988. "Robust" australopithecine brain endocasts: some preliminary observations. In: Grine, F. E. (Ed.), Evolutionary History of the "Robust" Australopithecines. Aldine de Gruyter, New York, pp. 97–106.

Holloway, R. L., Yuan, M. S., 2004. Endocranial morphology of A. L. 444-2. In: Kimbel, W. H., Rak, Y., Johanson, D. C. (Eds.), The skull of *Australopithecus afarensis*. Oxford University Press, New York, pp. 123–135.

Horowitz, I., Zardoya, R., Meyer, A., 1998. Platyrrhine systematics: a simultaneous analysis of molecular and morphological data. Am. J. Phys. Anthropol. 106, 261–268.

International Commission on Zoological Nomenclature., 1999. Opinion 1941. *Australopithecus afarensis* Johanson, 1978 (Mammalia, Primates): specific name conserved. Bull. Zool. Nomencl. 56, 223–224.

Källersjö, M., Farris, J. S., Kluge, A. G., Bult, C., 1992. Skewness and permutation. Cladistics 8, 275–287.

Keyser, A. W., 2000. The Drimolen skull: the most complete australopithecine cranium and mandible to date. S. Afr. J. Sci. 96, 189–193.

Kitching, I. J., Forey, P. L., Humphries, C. J., Williams, D. M., 1998. Cladistics, 2nd Edition: The Theory and Practice of Parsimony Analysis. Oxford University Press, Oxford.

Kluge, A. G., 1989. A concern for evidence and a phylogenetic hypothesis of relationships among *Epicrates* (Boidae, Serpentes). Syst. Zool. 38, 7–25.

Leakey, M. G., Feibel, C. S., McDougall, I., Ward, C., Walker, A. C., 1995. New four-million-year-old hominid species from Kanapoi and Allia Bay, Kenya. Nature 376, 565–571.

Leakey, M. G., Spoor, F., Brown, F. H., Gathogo, P. N., Kiarie, C., Leakey, L. N., McDougall, I., 2001. New hominin genus from eastern Africa shows diverse middle Pliocene lineages. Nature 410, 433–440.

Leonard, W. R., Hegmon, M., 1987. Evolution of P_3 morphology in *Australopithecus afarensis*. Am. J. Phys. Anthropol. 73, 41–63.

Lieberman, D. E., 2001. Another face in our family tree. Nature 410, 419–420.

Lieberman, D. E., Wood, B. A., Pilbeam, D. R., 1996. Homoplasy and early *Homo*: an analysis of the evolutionary relationships of *H. habilis sensu stricto* and *H. rudolfensis*. J. Hum. Evol. 30, 97–120.

Liu, F.-G. R., Miyamoto, M. M., 1999. Phylogenetic assessment of molecular and morphological data for eutherian mammals. Syst. Biol. 48, 54–64.

Lockwood, C. A., Kimbel, W. H., Lynch, J. M., 2004. Morphometrics and hominoid phylogeny: support for a chimpanzee-human clade and differentiation among great ape subspecies. Proc. Natl. Acad. Sci. 101, 4356–4360.

Maddison, W. P., Donohue, M. J., Maddison, D. R., 1993. Outgroup analysis and parsimony. Syst. Zool. 33, 83–103.

Mallat, J., Chen, J.-Y., 2003. Fossil sister group of craniates: predicted and found. J. Morph. 258, 1–31.

Marks, J., 1993. Hominoid heterochromatin: terminal C-bands as a complex genetic trait linking chimpanzee and gorilla. Am. J. Phys. Anthropol. 90, 237–246.

Masters, J. C., Brothers, D. J., 2002. Lack of congruence between morphological and molecular data in reconstructing the phylogeny of the Galagonidae. Am. J. Phys. Anthropol. 117, 79–93.

McCollum, M. A., Grine, F. E., Ward, S. C., Kimbel, W. H., 1993. Subnasal morphological variation in extant hominoids and fossil hominids. J. Hum. Evol. 24, 87–111.

McCollum, M. A., 1999a. The robust australopithecine face: a morphogenetic perspective. Science 284, 301–305.

McCollum, M. A., 1999b. Cladistics and early hominid phylogeny: response. Science 285, 1211.

McCollum, M. A., 2000. Subnasal morphological variation in fossil hominids: a reassessment based on new observations and recent developmental findings. Am. J. Phys. Anthropol. 112, 275–283.

O'Keefe, F. R., Sander, P. M., 1999. Paleontological paradigms and inferences of phylogenetic pattern: a case study. Paleobiology 25, 518–533.

O'Leary, M. A., 1999. Parsimony analysis of total evidence from extinct and extant taxa and the cetacean-artiodactyl question (Mammalia, Ungulata). Cladistics 15, 315–330.

Olmstead, R. G., Sweere, J. A., 1994. Combining data in phylogenetic systematics: an empirical approach using three molecular data sets in the Solanaceae. Syst. Biol. 43, 467–481.

Olson, E., Miller, R., 1958. Morphological Integration. Univ. of Chicago Press, Chicago.

Rae, T. C., 1997. The early evolution of the hominoid face. In: Begun, D. R., Ward, C. V., Rose, M. D. (Eds.), Function, Phylogeny and Fossils: Miocene Hominoid Evolution and Adaptations. Plenum Press, New York, pp. 59–77.

Rak, Y., Kimbel, W. H., Johanson, D. C., 1996. The crescent of foramina in *Australopithecus afarensis* and other early hominids. Am. J. Phys. Anthropol. 101, 93–100.

Ruvolo, M., 1997. Molecular phylogeny of the hominoids: inferences from multiple independent DNA sequence data sets. Mol. Biol. Evol. 14, 248–265.

Salem, A.-H., Ray, D. A., Xing, J., Callinan, P. A., Myers, J. S., Hedges, D. J., Garber, R. K., Witherspoon, D. J., Jorde, L. B., Batzer, M. A., 2003. Alu elements and hominid phylogenetics. Proc. Nat. Acad. Sci 100, 12787–12791.

Schwartz, J. H., 1984. Hominoid evolution: a review and a reassessment. Curr. Anthropol. 25, 655–672.

Senyürek, M., 1955. A note on the teeth of *Meganthropus africanus* Weinert from Tanganyika Territory. Belleten 19, 1–57.

Senut, B., Pickford, M., Gommery, D., Mein, P., Cheboi, K., Coppens, Y., 2001. First hominid from the Miocene (Lukeino formation, Kenya). C. R. Acad. Sci. Paris, Sci. Terre Plan 332, 137–144.

Shi, J., Xi, H., Wang, Y., Zhang, C., Jiang, Z., Zhang, K., Shen, Y., Jin, L., Zhang, K., Yuan, W., Wang, Y., Lin, J., Hua, Q., Wang, F., Xu, S., Ren, S., Xu, S., Zhao, G., Chen, Z., Jin, L., Huang, W., 2003. Divergence of the genes on human chromosome 21 between human and other hominoids and variation of substitution rates among transcription units. Proc. Natl. Acad. Sci, 100, 8331–8336.

Shoshani, J., Groves, C. P., Simons, E. L., Gunnell, G. F., 1996. Primate phylogeny: morphological vs. molecular results. Mol. Phylogenet. Evol. 5, 102–154.

Simon, C., 1983. A new coding procedure for morphometric data with an example from periodical cicada wing veins. In: Felsenstein, J. (Ed.), Numerical Taxonomy. Springer-Verlag, Berlin, pp. 378–382.

Skelton, R. R., McHenry, H. M., 1992. Evolutionary relationships among early hominids. J. Hum Evol. 23, 309–349.

Skelton, R. R., McHenry, H. M., 1998. Trait list bias and a reappraisal of early hominid phylogeny. J. Hum. Evol. 34, 109–113.

Smith, A. B., 1994. Systematics and the Fossil Record. Blackwell Scientific, London.

Springer, M. S., Teeling, E. C., Madsen, O., Stanhope, M. J., de Jong, W. W., 2001. Integrated fossil and molecular data reconstruct bat echolocation. Proc. Natl. Acad. Sci. 98, 6241–6246.

Strait, D. S., 1998. Evolutionary integration in the hominid cranial base. Ph.D. Dissertation. State University of New York, Stony Brook.

Strait, D. S., 2001. Integration, phylogeny, and the hominid cranial base. Am J. Phys. Anthropol 114, 273–297.

Strait, D. S., Grine, F. E., 1998. Trait list bias? A reply to Skelton and McHenry. J. Hum. Evol. 34, 115–118.

Strait, D. S., Grine, F. E., 1999. Cladistics and early hominid phylogeny. Science 285, 1210.

Strait, D. S., Grine, F. E., 2001. The systematics of *Australopithecus garhi*. Ludus Vitalis 9, 17–82.

Strait, D. S., Grine, F. E., 2004. Inferring hominoid and early hominid phylogeny using craniodental characters: The role of fossil taxa. J. Hum. Evol. 47, 399–452.

Strait, D. S., Grine, F. E., Moniz, M. A., 1997. A reappraisal of early hominid phylogeny. J. Hum. Evol. 32, 17–82.

Suwa, G., Asfaw, B., Beyene, Y., White, T. D., Katoh, S., Nagaoka, S., Nakaya, H., Uzawa, K., Renne, P., Wolde-Gabriel, G., 1997. The first skull of *Australopithecus boisei*. Nature 389, 489–492.

Suwa, G., White, T. D., Howell, F. C., 1996. Mandibular postcanine dentition from the Shungura Formation, Ethiopia: crown morphology, taxonomic allocations and Plio-Pleistocene hominid evolution. Am. J. Phys. Anthropol. 101, 247–282.

Swofford, D. L., 1998. PAUP: Phylogenetic Analysis Using Parsimony (version 4). Sinauer Associates, Sunderland, MA.

Szalay, F. S., 1977. Ancestors, descendants, sister groups, and testing of phylogenetic hypotheses. Syst. Zool. 26, 12–18.

Thorpe, R. S., 1984. Coding morphometric characters for constructing distance Wagner networks. Evolution 38, 244–255.

Vrba, E. S., 1988. Late Pliocene climatic events and hominid evolution. In: Grine, F. E. (Ed.), Evolutionary History of the "Robust" Australopithecines. Aldine de Gruyter, New York, pp. 405–426.

Wagner, P. J., Erwin, D. H., 1995. Phylogenetic tests of speciation models. In: Erwin, D. H., Antsy, R. L. (Eds.), New Approaches to Speciation in the Fossil Record. Columbia University Press, New York, pp. 87–122.

Ward, C. V., Leakey, M. G., Walker, A., 2001. Morphology of *Australopithecus anamensis* from Kanapoi and Allia Bay, Kenya. J. Hum. Evol. 41, 255–368.

Weinert, H., 1950. Uber die Neuen Vor- und Frühmenschenfunde aus Afrika, Java, China und Frankreich. Z. Morph. Anthropol. 42, 113–148.

Wheeler, W. C., 1992. Extinction, sampling and molecular phylogenetics. In: Novacek, M. J., Wheeler, Q. D. (Eds.), Extinction and Phylogeny. Columbia University Press, New York, pp. 205–215.

White, T. D., 2003. Early hominids—diversity or distortion? Science 299, 1194–1997.

White, T. D., Johanson, D. C., Kimbel, W. H., 1981. *Australopithecus africanus*: its phyletic position reconsidered. S. Afr. J. Sci. 77, 445–470.

White, T. D., Suwa, G., Asfaw, B., 1994. *Australopithecus ramidus*, a new species of early hominid from Aramis, Ethiopia. Nature 371, 306–312.

Wiens, J., Hollingsworth, B., 2000. War of the iguanas: conflicting molecular and morphological phylogenies and long-branch attraction in iguanid lizards. Syst. Biol. 49, 143–159.

Wildman, D. E., Uddin, M., Liu, G., Grossman, L. I., Goodman, M., 2003. Implications of natural selection in shaping 99.4% nonsynonymous DNA identity between humans and chimpanzees: enlarging genus *Homo*. Proc. Natl. Acad. Sci. 100, 7181–7188.

Wolpoff, M. H., Senut, B., Pickford, M., Hawks, J., 2002. *Sahelanthropus* or '*Sahelpithecus*'? Nature 419, 581–582.

Wood, B. A., 1975. An analysis of sexual dimorphism in primates. Ph.D. Dissertation. University of London, London.

Wood, B. A., 1991. Koobi Fora Research Project, volume 4: Hominid Cranial Remains. Clarendon Press, Oxford.

Wood, B. A., 1992. Early hominid species and speciation. J. Hum. Evol. 22, 351–365.

Wood, B. A., Collard, M. C., 1999. The human genus. Science 284, 65–71.

Yoder, A. D., Irwin, J. A., Payseur, B. A., 2001. Failure of the ILD to determine data combinability for slow loris phylogeny. Syst. Biol. 50, 408–424.

Zelditch, M. L., 1987. Evaluating models of developmental integration in the laboratory rat using confirmatory factor analysis. Syst. Zool. 36, 368–380.

Zelditch, M. L., 1988. Ontogenetic variation in patterns of phenotypic integration in the laboratory rat. Evolution 42, 28–41.

Zwickl, D. J., Hillis, D. M., 2002. Increased taxon sampling greatly reduces phylogenetic error. Syst. Biol. 51, 588–598.

21

Evolution of Human Walking

C. O. Lovejoy

Asked to choose the most distinctive feature of the human species, many people would cite our massive brain. Others might mention our ability to make and use sophisticated tools. A third feature also sets us apart: our upright mode of locomotion, which is found only in human beings and our immediate ancestors. All other primates are basically quadrupedal, and with good reason: walking on two limbs instead of four has many drawbacks. It deprives us of speed and agility and all but eliminates our capacity to climb trees, which yield many important primate foods, such as fruits and nuts.

For most of the twentieth century, evolutionary theorists have held that human ancestors evolved this strange mode of locomotion because it freed their hands to carry the tools their larger brains enabled them to make. Over the past two decades, however, knowledge of the human fossil record has expanded. Neither a unique brain nor stone tools are in evidence among our earliest known ancestors, the australopithecines of three million years ago and more. Yet these same ancestors do clearly show many of the hallmarks of bipedal walking.

How long had human ancestors been walking upright? Was bipedality fully developed in the hominids of three million years ago, or did they sometimes revert to using all four limbs for running or climbing? The answers can help to solve the puzzle of bipedality's role in early human evolution. If upright walking was well established by the time of *Australopithecus*, its advent could date back as far as the earliest hominids, whose lineage probably diverged from other primates some eight or 10 million years ago. The development of erect walking may have been a crucial initiating event in human evolution.

I have proposed that bipedality accompanied a set of behavioral adaptations that became the key evolutionary innovation of humanity's earliest ancestors. These adaptations included, in effect, the nuclear family: lasting monogamy together with care of the offspring by both parents. The male's contribution took the form of providing high-energy food, which expanded the mother's ability to nurture and protect each infant and also enabled her to give birth more often. Bipedality figured in this new reproductive scheme because by freeing the hands it made it possible for the male to carry food gathered far from his mate. These developments must have come long before the current hominid fossil record begins.

Upright walking should therefore have been perfected by the time of an australopithecine female whose fossil has become a test case for early walking. In 1974 the continuing search for human ancestors in the Afar

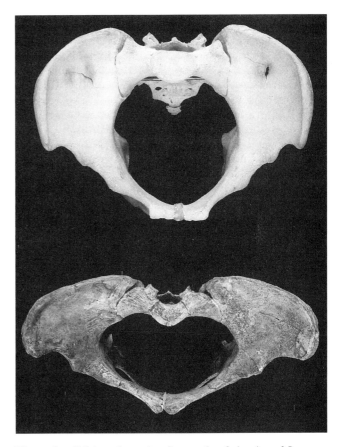

Figure 1. *Pelvises of a modern human female* (top) *and Lucy* (bottom) *are separated by three million years of evolution but bear the same hallmarks of upright walking. The major change visible in this view—the more ovoid form of the human pelvis—accompanied an expansion of the birth canal, needed because of the increase in brain size since Lucy. The author and Barbara Brown restored the Lucy pelvis from the fragmented fossil; Larry Rubens of Kent State University made the photograph.*

Triangle of Ethiopia, led by Donald C. Johanson of the Institute of Human Origins in Berkeley, Calif., was splendidly rewarded by the recovery of the "Lucy" skeleton, known formally as A.L. 288–1. Although the skeleton is not quite complete, it preserves far more detail than any comparable fossil. In particular, it includes many of the lower-limb bones, one of the innominate bones that, in a mirror-image pair, make up the primate pelvis, and an intact sacrum (the fused vertebrae at the back of the pelvis). Upright walking is so dependent on this structure that an analysis of Lucy's pelvis can reveal how well she and her contemporaries walked.

The distinctive pelvic features of a biped reflect the very different mechanics of two- and four-legged locomotion. In order to propel itself any terrestrial mammal must apply a force against the ground in a direction opposite to the direction of travel. It does so by extending the joints of its legs, which lie between the ground and the animal's center of mass. Lengthening a leg produces a "ground reaction" that propels the torso in a direction determined by the angle between the leg and the ground.

In the quadrupedal posture of most primates the center of mass lies well forward of the hind limbs. Hence extending the hind limbs generates a ground reaction that has a large horizontal component. Because the hip and knee joints of the hind limbs are tightly flexed at the start of each cycle, their extension can be prolonged and powerful.

Our upright posture, in contrast, places our center of mass almost directly over the foot. If we stand erect and lengthen our legs by straightening the knee and rotating the ankle, the ground reaction is directed vertically and we end up on tiptoe. In order to propel our upright trunk we must reposition our center of mass ahead of one leg. The trailing limb is lengthened to produce a ground reaction while the other leg is swung forward to keep the trunk from falling. The strength of the ground reaction is limited, because much of it is still directed vertically and also because the trailing limb is already near its limit of extension owing to our upright posture: the hip joint is fully extended and the knee joint nearly so.

With the new bipedal strategy there came new roles for most of the muscle groups in the lower limb—roles that in turn required changes in the muscles' structure or position and hence in the design of the pelvis. A comparison of the human pelvis with that of our closest living relative, the chimpanzee, highlights these changes in mechanical design.

The need to stabilize an upright torso dictated the most dramatic change in musculature that has come with the adoption of bipedality: the transformation of the gluteus maximus, a relatively minor muscle in the chimpanzee, into the largest muscle in the human body. The gluteus maximus originates over much of the back of the pelvis and is attached to the back and side of the upper femur, or thighbone. As such it is defined as a hip extensor, and many classical anatomists believed it serves as the major propulsive muscle in upright walking. By straightening the hip, it was thought, the

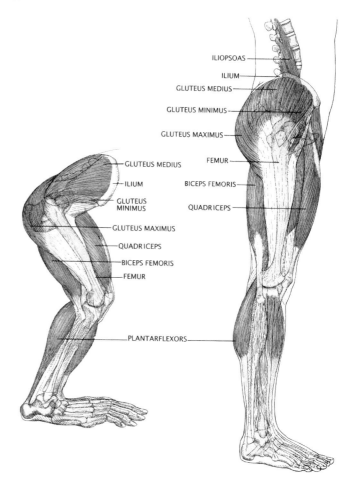

Figure 2. *Pelvis and leg of a chimpanzee* (left) *and a human being* (right) *reflect the differing demands of quadrupedal and bipedal locomotion. The musculature of the chimpanzee pelvis is dominated by the gluteus medius and gluteus minimus, which help to propel the animal by extending its hip joint. They are joined in that task by the hamstrings, which include the biceps femoris. In humans the gluteus maximus dominates the pelvis; it serves the new function of stabilizing the upright trunk. (The shortening of the ilium lowers the trunk's center of mass and makes it easier to control.) Other major muscles, such as the gluteus medius and minimus, the hamstrings and the iliopsoas, also play new auxiliary roles in upright walking. Only two muscle groups—the quadriceps and plantarflexors—are left to provide propulsion.*

gluteus maximus contributes to the ground reaction imparted by the trailing leg.

Actually, because the hip is almost completely extended in the first place during erect walking and running, the muscle's contribution to ground reaction is limited. Its hypertrophy in human beings reflects a quite different function. When we run, our upright trunk tends to flex forward at each foot strike owing to momentum. The gluteus maximus has taken on the role of preventing the trunk from pitching forward.

A major modification of the pelvis has made the muscle's stabilizing task considerably easier. Each innominate bone in the pelvis is topped by a blade of bone called an ilium; most of the lower viscera are cradled in the space between the two ilia. In the chimpanzee and other primates the ilia are much longer than they are in

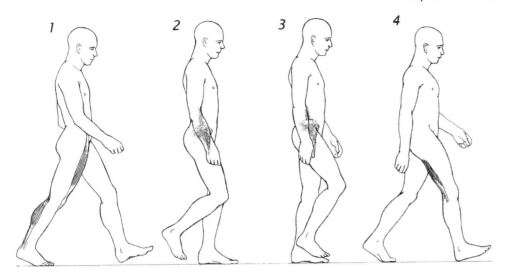

Figure 3. *Muscle activity during human striding is diagrammed. As the weight-bearing leg (here the right leg) becomes angled behind the torso (1), two muscle groups contract to extend it, generating a "ground reaction" that propels the body; they are the plantarflexors, which rotate the foot around the ankle, and the quadriceps, which straighten the knee. The foot then leaves the ground as weight is tranferred to the left leg. Contraction of the iliopsoas begins to tug the right leg forward (2) while the knee flexes passively (3). Near the end of the leg's swing the hamstrings contract to stop it, and the foot is planted (4). The left leg in turn generates ground reaction.*

humans. The long ilia have the effect of lengthening the torso; when these primates rear up, their center of mass lies well above their hip joints. In the language of engineering, their trunk has a long lever arm. A gluteus maximus working to hold such a trunk upright would tire rapidly. The dramatically shortened human ilium shortens the torso and brings the trunk's center of mass much closer to the hip joints, thereby reducing the muscle's mechanical disadvantage.

The ilium is long in the apes to accommodate a second muscle group that was transformed as our ancestors began walking upright: the anterior gluteals, composed of the gluteus medius and the gluteus minimus. In the chimpanzee these muscles contract between attachment points near the top of the ilium and on the outside of the upper femur. Their position enables them to serve as powerful hip extensors during quadrupedal locomotion, and because the ilium is long, the muscles have a large range of contraction. Human beings can forgo this almost universal skeletal feature of other primates because hip extension contributes very little to bipedal locomotion. Our anterior gluteals have been freed to assume a new role.

This new role is best understood by imagining a head-on view of a person walking. Soon after the heel of the leading foot strikes the ground, the trailing leg leaves the surface and begins to swing forward. While it does so the trunk is supported by only one hip, which lies well to the side of the trunk's center of mass. On their own the pelvis and trunk would tip toward the unsupported side at each step, causing rapid fatigue; they are prevented from doing so by the action of the anterior gluteals, which are also referred to as abductors in human beings.

The transformation of the anterior gluteals from propulsive muscles to stabilizing ones required major changes in their position. A top view of the human and chimpanzee pelvises reveals a radical reorientation of the iliac blades in the human pelvis. In the chimpanzee the blades are flat and lie more or less in a single plane across the back of the torso. In humans each ilium has been rotated forward, carrying with it the upper attachment point of the gluteals. Their lower attachment point falls on the outside of the upper femur, where the bone forms a neck that angles in to meet the pelvis at the hip joint. The abductors are thus disposed laterally in humans, away from the hip joints, which puts them in position to balance the pelvis against the weight of the trunk.

The reorientation of the ilia required two other changes in pelvic design not dictated directly by the mechanics of bipedality. If the ilia had simply been rotated forward, the space between them would have been sharply narrowed, leaving no room for the lower viscera. In compensation the sacrum, which separates the ilia at the back of the pelvis, has grown wider and the ilia have changed in shape: they are dished, so that the bending that has reoriented the abductors takes place well to the side, leaving ample room within the pelvis.

By increasing the distance between the hip joints, however, this widening of the central pelvis placed the abductors in a position of considerable mechanical disadvantage. The force the abductors must exert to offset the weight of the trunk depends in part on how far to the side of the trunk's center of mass each hip joint lies. The greater the separation of the hip joints is, the longer the trunk's lever arm will be and the harder these muscles will have to contract to offset its weight. They will be more likely to tire during walking, and the safety of the hip joint itself may be threatened, since the joint is subjected to both the weight of the torso and the abductors' force of contraction.

A front view of the human pelvis reveals the evolutionary solution. The abductors' own lever arm can be increased, and their work made easier, if their upper and lower attachment points are moved farther out from the hip joint. Two features of the human pelvis serve that purpose. The complex curvature of the human ilium includes an outward flare, which displaces the upper attachment point of the abductors to the side of the hip. In addition the human femoral neck is longer than that of the chimpanzee. The longer femoral neck serves to move the abductors' lower attachment point outward as well, adding to their leverage.

One set of muscles—the anterior gluteals—that help to propel chimpanzees has thus become co-opted to stabilize the human pelvis. A new role is also evident for another set of propulsive muscles in the chimpanzee: the hamstrings. They connect the lower pelvis to the back of the femur; in quadrupedal locomotion they serve as powerful hip extensors, which contribute even more to ground reaction than the anterior gluteals do. In bipedal walking, in contrast, they serve not to extend the limb but to control it.

A biped must swing each leg forward rapidly when it is not bearing weight. Because the limb is carried almost fully extended in a biped rather than tightly flexed, as it is in a quadruped, its center of mass lies well away from the pelvis. Like a long pendulum, an extended leg has a large moment of inertia, and it takes powerful muscle impulses to start and stop its swing. The iliopsoas, a muscle that originates within the pelvis and extends forward to an attachment point on the femur just below the hip joint, contracts to tug the limb forward. Once the leg has completed its arc, its swing must be checked. The position of the hamstrings, which is largely unchanged from the position in other primates, enables them to contract and decelerate the limb.

In human beings, then, the demands of stabilizing the pelvis and controlling the limb occupy several muscle groups that serve for propulsion in the chimpanzee. Only two muscle groups, the quadriceps and the plantarflexors, are left in positions that enable them to

produce a ground reaction. The quadriceps are a mass of four muscles that make up most of the front of the human thigh. They end in a stout tendon, which crosses the patella, or kneecap, and is anchored to the top of the tibia, the main bone of the lower leg.

As the weight-bearing leg becomes angled behind the torso during walking or running, this powerful muscle mass contracts and straightens the knee. The plantarflexors, which originate at the back of the lower leg and are attached to the heel by the Achilles tendon, contract in synchrony with the quadriceps and cause the foot to rotate about the ankle. The extension of the knee and the rotation of the foot together lengthen the trailing leg, producing a strong ground reaction.

How well developed was this set of muscular adaptations by the time of Lucy and her kin, according to the fossil evidence? The discovery included a largely intact sacrum, but the innominate bone that accompanied it had been broken and partially crushed; it consisted of about 40 separate pieces fused into a single mass by the matrix of stone in which it was preserved. Often a fossil in this condition can be reduced to its separate pieces and then reassembled like a jigsaw puzzle. The pieces of Lucy's innominate, however, could not safely be separated. Instead I took a cast of each piece and assembled the casts in proper anatomical juxtaposition; the restored innominate was then mirror-imaged to create its opposite number. The result was a complete pelvis of an almost three-million-year-old human ancestor.

The pelvis bears all the hallmarks of bipedality seen in our own. Its ilia are much shorter than those in the pelvis of an ape. The shortening would have lowered the trunk's center of mass and made it easier to keep upright. The ilia have also become bent around to provide lateral attachment for the abductor muscles that stabilize the bipedal pelvis when it is supported on one leg. The attachment points for the gluteus maximus, abductors and quadriceps can be seen, and they indicate that in Lucy these muscles had attained a size and

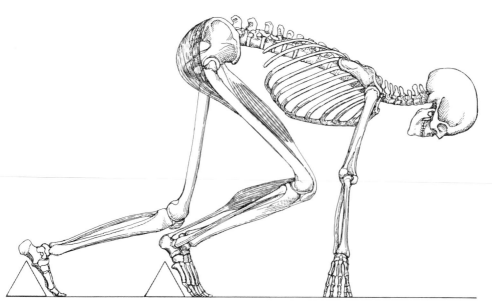

Figure 4. *Sprinter on the starting block briefly recovers the advantages of being quadrupedal: the hip and knee joints are tightly flexed, preparing the limbs for prolonged and powerful extension, and the center of mass is positioned well forward of the legs, which gives the ground reaction a strong horizontal component. Ordinary walking or running sacrifices these advantages. An upright posture requires the hip and knee joints to be almost fully extended and places the body's center of mass almost directly over the legs. Both factors tend to limit the strength of the ground reaction.*

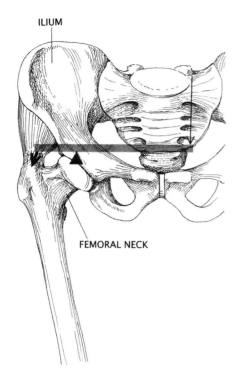

ILIUM

FEMORAL NECK

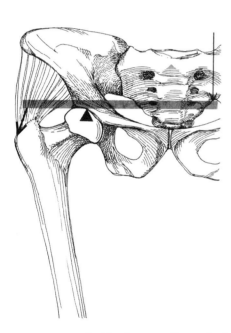

Figure 5. *Abductor muscles (the gluteus medius and minimus) contract to counterbalance the torso when the human pelvis is supported on only one leg. The hip joint acts as a fulcrum, with the weight of the torso and unsupported leg bearing down on one side and the abductors acting on the other (top). The abductors are at a mechanical disadvantage: the hip joint lies well to the side of the torso's center of mass, giving the body weight a long lever arm. In the Lucy pelvis (bottom) the body-weight lever arm was even longer, but greater lateral flare of the ilium and a longer femoral neck placed the abductors farther from the hip joint, increasing their mechanical advantage.*

disposition remarkably similar to our own arrangement. The same is true for the iliopsoas, the hip flexor that initiates the swing of the leg: a groove on the brim of the pelvis, ahead of the hip joint, matches the groove that indicates the muscle's course in the human pelvis.

In one respect Lucy seems to have been even better designed for bipedality than we are. Her ilia flare outward more sharply than those of a modern pelvis and her femoral necks are longer. Her abductor muscles thus enjoyed a greater mechanical advantage than these muscles do in modern females. Some of the abductors' advantage merely compensated for the slightly wider separation of her hip joints (which gave her trunk a longer lever arm). Yet accurate measurements of both the abductor and the trunk lever arms—possible because the Lucy pelvis is so complete—show that her abductor advantage is still greater than our own. Her abductors had to exert less force to stabilize the pelvis, which also reduced the pressure on the hip-joint surfaces.

Why should a three-million-year-old hominid have had this mechanical advantage over her descendants? The answer lies in the accelerated growth of the human brain during the past three million years. Lucy's pelvis was almost singularly designed for bipedality. The flaring ilia and long femoral necks increased her abductors' lever arm, but they yielded a pelvis that in top view was markedly elliptical, resulting in a birth canal that was wide but short from front to back. The constriction was tolerable because Lucy predated the dramatic expansion of the brain; her infant's cranium would have been no larger than a baby chimpanzee's. The process of birth in Lucy and her contemporaries would have been slightly more complex than in an ape, but much easier than the modern human birth process [*see illustration on page 156*].

As human ancestors evolved a larger brain, the pelvic opening had to become rounder. The pelvis had to expand from front to back, but at the same time it contracted slightly from side to side. In the process the flare of the ilia was reduced, leaving us with a somewhat shorter abductor lever arm than Lucy's. (These changes are less pronounced in the modern male pelvis, where the abductors retain some of their former mechanical advantage.) Meanwhile the head of the modern femur has become enlarged to withstand increased pressure from the harder-working abductors. The difficulty of accommodating in the same pelvis an effective bipedal hip joint and an adequate passage for a large infant brain remains acute, however, and the human birth process is one of the most difficult in the animal kingdom.

The close resemblance of Lucy's pelvis to that of a modern human and its dramatic contrast to the pelvis of a chimpanzee make it clear that she walked fully upright. But was her bipedal progression truly habitual? Had she forsaken all other kinds of locomotion? The muscular rearrangements that enabled her to walk upright would not have allowed efficient quadrupedal movement on the ground. Perhaps, however, she often took to the trees and climbed, as most primates do, using all four limbs.

Basic evolutionary principles provide one kind of verdict on the possibility. A species cannot develop detailed

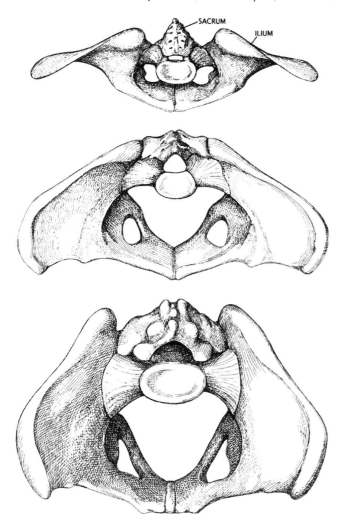

Figure 6. *Rotation of the ilia took place as human ancestors began walking upright. In a quadrupedal ape such as a chimpanzee (top) the ilia (seen here from above) lie almost flat against the back of the torso. In Lucy (middle) they have become bent around, providing lateral attachment points for the abductor muscles, which stabilize the pelvis during walking. The bending takes place well away from the center of the pelvis, leaving room for the viscera; in addition the sacrum, which separates the ilia, has widened. These changes are retained in the modern human pelvis (bottom), which has also become longer from front to back to create a more ovoid birth canal.*

anatomical modifications for a particular behavior, such as bipedality, unless it consistently employs that behavior. For natural selection to have so thoroughly modified for bipedality the skeleton Lucy inherited, her ancestors must already have spent most of their time on the ground, walking upright. Analysis of the Lucy fossil, however, can yield more direct evidence.

The analysis focuses on the neck of the femur, where much of the stress of locomotion is concentrated. When the leg is bearing weight, the hip joint transmits the weight of the torso to the femoral neck. The neck acts as a cantilevered beam: a beam that is anchored at one end to a supporting structure (the shaft of the femur) and carries a load at the other end. Cantilevering results in high bending stresses at the beam's anchorage—compression along the bottom of

the beam and tension along the top—and the stresses increase with the length of the beam. A long femoral neck such as Lucy's reduces pressure on the hip joint by improving the leverage of the abductors, but the neck itself is subject to higher bending stresses.

The femoral neck of the chimpanzee is much shorter than the modern human one; nonetheless, it is robustly engineered to withstand the loads imposed by the animal's terrestrial and arboreal acrobatics. A cross section of the bone reveals a central marrow-filled channel surrounded by a thick layer of dense bone. Dense bone is weaker under tension than it is under compression, and so the upper surface of the structure, which will be subjected to tension when the neck is bent, carries a markedly thicker layer of bone. With this ridge of thick bone (a bone "spike" in cross section), the chimpanzee femoral neck imitates the principle of an I beam: material is placed where it can best resist bending stresses.

Because the human femoral neck is longer than the chimpanzee's and must resist the combined force of body weight and abductor contraction, one would expect it to be even more robustly constructed. A cross section of the human bone reveals a surprise: the outer ring of solid bone is thick only at the bottom, and the rest of the neck is bounded by a thin shell of bone and filled in by a lattice of fine bone plates called trabeculae. Such porous bone, as one might expect, is weaker than solid material. The upper part of the femoral neck, where tensile stresses are presumably the highest, actually contains less bone than any other part of the structure. How can our femoral neck survive the greater stresses imposed by its length and function when it seems so much less sturdy than the femoral neck of the chimpanzee?

The answer lies in the action of muscles that operate only in bipedal locomotion: the abductors. These muscles have lines of action that are not vertical but are sharply inclined, which makes them roughly parallel to the femoral neck. When they contract, they push the femoral neck into the hip socket, compressing the neck along its length. This compressive stress combines with the stresses that result from bending (tension on the top of the femoral neck and compression on the bottom). The effect is to eliminate tension at the top of the femoral neck and create a gradient of increasing stress running from the top of the femoral neck, where stress is now minimal, to the bottom, where stress is very high but purely compressive. The bottom of the human femoral neck has a robust layer of solid bone, and even the porous bone that fills in the rest of the section is reasonably strong as long as it remains under compression.

Other muscles work with the abductors to keep the femoral neck under compression when it is loaded. The most important of them is the piriformis, which originates on the front of the sacrum and extends to the outer end of the femoral neck. That orientation enables the muscle to increase the femoral neck's level of compression. The synchronized action of all these muscles when body weight is supported on one leg makes it possible for this seemingly fragile bone to cope with its load.

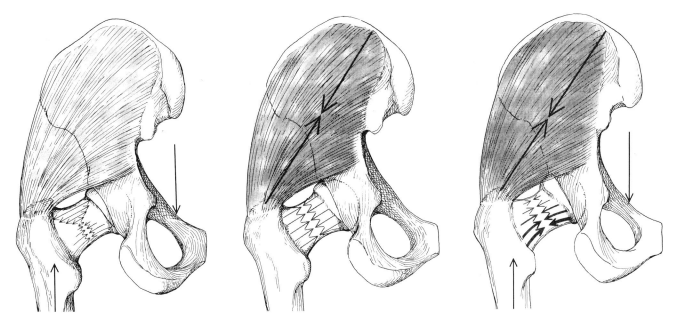

Figure 7. *Neck of the femur (shown from the back) is subjected to stress from two sources during human walking. Body weight imposes bending stress: tension on the top of the neck and compression on the bottom (left). At the same time the abductors, acting almost parallel to the femoral neck, subject its entire diameter to compression (middle). The sum of the two stress patterns is a gradient of stress running from low stress at the top to high compressive stress at the bottom (right).*

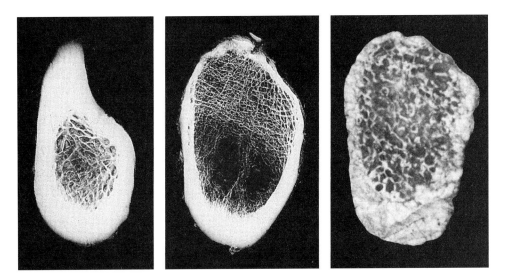

Figure 8. *Internal structure of the femoral neck distinguishes habitual bipeds. Seen in cross section, the femoral neck of the chimpanzee (left) has a robust thickness of bone together with a reinforcing ridge (visible in this section as a spike) at the top. These features enable the chimpanzee femoral neck to withstand the high bending stresses imposed by climbing and leaping. The human femoral neck (middle) has only a thin layer of bone at the top. It is suited only to the stresses of upright walking and running, when the abductor muscles counteract tension on the top of the neck. A fossil femoral neck from a contemporary of Lucy (right) has the same structure as the human one; it was designed exclusively for bipedal walking.*

Because of its distribution of bone, however, the femoral neck is indeed vulnerable if the abductors and other muscles do not act in the proper synchrony. The femoral neck is a primary site of fracture in old age, and not just because bone quality is reduced in old people. These "broken hips" are also a product of reduced muscular coordination. Thus the design of the human femoral neck requires the muscular action of bipedal

walking. The bone is poorly engineered for climbing and arboreal acrobatics, where it would be frequently subjected to bending stresses without being compressed at the same time by the abductors.

The femoral neck in *Australopithecus*, because it was even longer than that of modern humans, was subject to even greater bending stresses. If these human ancestors had often taken to the trees, stressing their femoral

CHIMPANZEE   LUCY   HUMAN

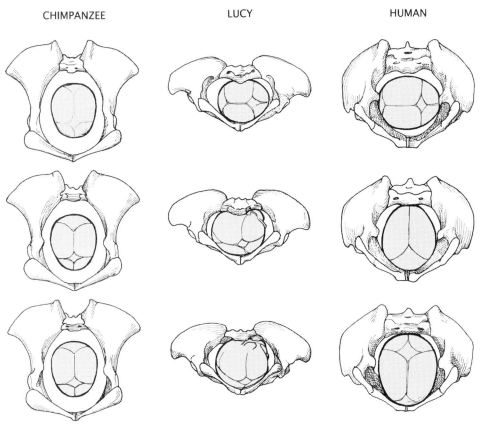

Figure 9. *The birth process has competed with bipedality in shaping the modern human pelvis. In the chimpanzee pelvis (shown from the back) the head of the fetus descends without difficulty through the inlet (top), midplane (middle) and outlet (bottom) of the birth canal. In Lucy the birth process was somewhat more difficult: her short, flaring ilia were well suited to bipedality but resulted in a birth canal that was broad but constricted from front to back. Her infant's cranium could pass through only if it was first turned sideways and then tilted. The much larger brain in the human infant demands a rounder birth canal. The necessary lengthening of the pelvis reduced the flare of the ilia and hence the mechanical advantage of the abductor muscles; even so, the human birth process is complex and traumatic, requiring a second rotation of the fetal cranium within the birth canal. The illustration is based on one by Robert G. Tague of Louisiana State University and Linda Budinoff of Kent State.*

neck without coordinated compression by the abductors, the bone would have had to have been even more robust than it is in the apes. Was it? The same site where Lucy was found also yielded several femurs that had broken during their long burial, affording a view of the neck's internal structure. Each specimen clearly shows the human feature of thin bone on the upper part of the femoral neck. Lucy's femoral neck, then, was suited exclusively for bipedality. She was not just capable of walking upright; it had become her only choice.

I have concentrated on the pelvic anatomy of Lucy because the hallmarks of bipedality are so vivid there. A review of the rest of her skeleton and of other *Australopithecus* skeletons would reveal equally dramatic modifications that favor bipedality and rule out other modes of locomotion. The knee, for example, is adapted for withstanding greater stress during complete extension than the knee of other primates, and its design brings the femur and the tibia together at a slight angle, so that the foot can easily be planted directly under the body's center of mass when body weight is supported on

one leg. The ankle is also modified for supporting the entire body weight, and a shock-absorbing arch helps the foot to cope with the added load. The great toe is no longer opposable, as it is in quadrupedal apes, but runs parallel to the other digits. The foot is now a propulsive lever for upright walking rather than a grasping device for arboreal travel. The arms have also become less suited to climbing: both the limb as a whole and the fingers have grown shorter than they are in the apes.

Lucy's ancestors must have left the trees and risen from four limbs onto two well before her time, probably at the very beginning of human evolution. I have suggested an explanation of why bipedality, with its many disadvantages, appeared long before our ancestors could have put their freed hands to use in carrying tools or weapons: it was part of a novel reproductive strategy that included provisioning by the male, a strategy that enabled the first hominids to flourish and diversify. The explanation will continue to be debated, but the evidence is conclusive that this curious form of locomotion was among the first anatomical characteristics to mark the ascent to cognitive life.

FURTHER READING

Human Walking. Verne T. Inman, Henry J. Ralston and Frank Todd. Williams & Wilkins, 1981.

Lucy: The Beginnings of Humankind. Donald C. Johanson and Edey Maitland. Simon and Schuster, 1981.

The Origin of Man. C. Owen Lovejoy in *Science,* Vol. 211, No. 4480, pages 341–350; January 23, 1981.

The Obstetric Pelvis of A. L. 288–1 (Lucy). Robert G. Tague and C. Owen Lovejoy in *Journal of Human Evolution,* Vol. 15, No. 4, pages 237–255; May, 1986.

22

Climbing to the Top

A Personal Memoir of *Australopithecus afarensis*

J. T. Stern, Jr.

Last autumn marked the 25th anniversary of the discovery of "Lucy." While that certainly was a momentous event in paleoanthropology, it had no less profound an effect on my academic life, for it presaged my eventual seduction into the arena of hominid fossil interpretation. My friend John Fleagle, editor of *Evolutionary Anthropology*, says I may introduce this paper with a history of that experience. He assures me this is appropriate because I have now reached the age when young people in the field have no idea who I am.

DOWN THE GARDEN PATH

Just a few months before the A.L. 288-1 partial skeleton was found, I had seen the first published picture of the A.L. 129 knee.[1] It was obviously valgus, a trait expressed most markedly in bipedal hominids, and the discoverers described the morphology of the distal femur as "tres humaine." The following year yielded a published photograph of Lucy.[2] While it was difficult to discern from the picture what she would tell us about the origins of bipedalism, the authors commented that the pelvis had some similarities to that of Sts 14 (*Australopithecus africanus*), and that the knee bones were virtually identical to the A.L. 129 specimens. Like many other physical anthropologists, I looked forward to what future analyses of the Hadar finds would reveal. In January 1976 there appeared an abstract stating that the high bicondylar angle, deep patellar groove, and elliptical lateral femoral condyle of the A.L. 129 knee indicated mechanical features that characterize the modern human knee, including "the capacity of hyperextension."[3] The following year came the first abstract of potential interest for reconstructing Lucy's locomotor behavior.[4] It reported that "the degree of medial rotation of the tibia on the talus during dorsiflexion was 3 to 4 times greater than that of modern humans."

The 1979 meeting of the American Association of Physical Anthropologists contained a special session devoted to the Hadar finds. Owen Lovejoy[5] presented his reconstruction of the A.L. 288-1 pelvis, concluding that it "exhibits adaptation to full bipedality," and making special note of the broad iliac blade and the mechanically advantageous position of the anterior gluteals. That same year, Leakey and Hay[6] formally presented the discovery of the Laetoli hominid footprints, which they said evinced a "fully upright, bipedal and free striding gait." In 1980 Lovejoy's[7] abstract on the role of reproductive-behavioral adaptations in hominid evolution referred to the "fully developed adaptation to bipedality" of *A. afarensis,* and two analyses of the Laetoli footprints found them to be indicative of a modern human-like form of bipedalism.[8,9]

Meanwhile, other workers were making some rather different observations. While not disputing that the Hadar hominids were bipedal, Senut[10,11] noted traits of the upper limb (the narrow, deep intertubercular sulcus of the humerus, the well-developed lateral margin of the humeral trochlea, the relatively proximal origin of the lateral epicondyle of the humerus, the relatively distal position of the ulnar tuberosity, and the long and narrow neck of the radius) that were so similar to those of apes as to "signify a certain ability and possible propensity on the part of these hominids to climb trees."[11] Tardieu's[12,13] thorough analysis of the knee identified traits of the A.L. 129 and/or A.L. 288-1 specimens that suggested to her a shorter stride, less frequent total extension of the knee, absence of terminal locking rotation of the knee, and freer voluntary rotation of the tibia. These included modest development of the lateral lip of the patellar groove on the femur, an incipiently elliptical lateral femoral condyle, anteroposteriorly short femoral condyles, the relatively narrow anterior region of the medial femoral condyle, the incipient development of a human-shaped femoral intercondylar notch, narrowness of the tibial intercondylar eminence relative to the width of the femoral intercondylar notch, and the convex articular surface of the lateral tibial condyle. Tardieu concluded that the smaller of the Hadar hominids represented an early stage in the development of hominid bipedality and that it probably maintained a certain aptitude for arboreal locomotion.

This was the state of affairs in December 1980, six years after Lucy's discovery, when my colleague Randy Susman walked into my office to proclaim his opinion that we were as well qualified as anyone to perform a comprehensive functional analysis of the Hadar postcranial material. I immediately realized that Randy was half right. He further suggested that we should visit Ethiopia to look at the fossils. Not being able to find

Reprinted from J. T. Stern, *Evolutionary Anthropology,* Vol. 9, pp. 113–133. Copyright © 2000 by Wiley-Liss, Inc. This material is reprinted with permission of Wiley-Liss, Inc., a subsidiary of John Wiley & Sons, Inc.

Ethiopia on a map of Long Island, I was reluctant, but eventually agreed. A trip was planned for the summer of 1981. Randy thought it would be wise to prepare for our study of the original fossils by taking a look at casts of the *A. afarensis* material in the Cleveland Museum of Natural History. Bill Jungers asked to come along so he could take some measurements of Lucy's body proportions. In May of 1981, the Stony Brook contingent of three arrived at the Cleveland Museum of Natural History, where Don Johanson graciously gave us complete access to all the casts of the Hadar material and the original specimen of the A.L. 333-115 foot. We collected many measurements, made extensive notes, and took numerous photographs, most of which were overexposed because Randy was not the excellent photographer he had claimed to be. (Randy redeemed himself on a 1992 visit to Addis during which he studied the original fossils and took fairly good pictures.) We left Cleveland with the tentative conclusion that the portrayals of *A. afarensis* locomotion by Senut and Tardieu were not far off the mark.

Although we did not learn so until several months later, it turned out that some of our observations we thought to be novel had also been made by Russell Tuttle.[14] While we were in Cleveland, he published a paper noting the markedly curved pedal proximal phalanges of Hadar foot specimens, the broad peroneal groove on the fibula, and somewhat laterally oriented iliac blades. Such features caused him to conclude that the Hadar hominids were rather recently derived from arboreal bipeds and may have engaged in a notable degree of tree climbing. Because Tuttle found the shapes of the Laetoli footprints to be indistinguishable from those made by striding humans who habitually go barefoot, he found it difficult to assign their maker to the same species as that represented by the A.L. 333-115 foot.

We arrived in Ethiopia in August of 1981. British Airways lost my luggage. I was not only anxious about being in a country that had street signs preaching the evils of Uncle Sam, but also was not adjusting well to having only one of each clothing item. (I absolutely refused Randy's offer to share his underwear.) To make a long story short, Randy and I were denied permission to look at the Hadar fossils and, while Randy was sleeping, I received a phone call from an Ethiopian government official advising us to leave the country immediately.

Upon our return, we decided to complete our work on reconstructing *A. afarensis* locomotor behavior using casts instead of original material. Don Johanson saw to it that the material we needed was sent to Stony Brook. As we were completing our analysis of the Hadar postcrania, Johanson's and Edey's[15] book *Lucy* was published. Here it was stated that the Hadar hominid was not a climber, despite having slightly long arms for its size, a tendency for the fingers to curl a bit more, some ape-like wrist bones, arched and relatively long pedal phalanges, and metatarsal heads having a shape intermediate between those of apes and humans. Rather, as shown by the pelvis, knee, hallux, and joints of the toes, *A. afarensis* was said to be a fully erect bipedal creature that could walk at least as well as a modern human, a conclusion said to be confirmed by the Laetoli

footprints. Lucy's ability to run as fast as a modern human was considered debatable.

The April 1982 issue of the American Journal of Physical Anthropology was devoted to detailed descriptions of the Hadar hominids, but it contained no functional interpretations of the postcranial material. That summer, Bill Jungers' paper on the proportions of Lucy's limbs was published.[16] He showed that Lucy's humerus, compared to that of a modern human, was not relatively long, but that her femur was relatively short. Bill concluded that Lucy's ability to climb was less than an ape's, and that her relatively short stride length suggested a greater cost and lower maximum speed of bipedal locomotion. In September 1982, Marc Feldesman published a multivariate study of distal humeral dimensions showing that the Hadar specimens are "quite primitive, and may be close to the point where hominids and pongids diverged."[17]

Mine and Randy's paper on the locomotor anatomy of *A. afarensis* was published in March of 1983.[18] One month later, three of us from Stony Brook went west to participate in Don Johanson's symposium on *A. afarensis* locomotion. There began a change in my career that I had not anticipated. Virtually overnight, I was transformed from an obscure electromyographer into someone being quoted in the New York Times and featured in Discover magazine. Over the course of the next few years, four separate television crews visited Stony Brook to tape us (mainly Randy) talking about the origin of bipedalism. I became alienated from Owen Lovejoy, a person whom I have always considered one of the most creative and insightful workers in our field. I became such a staunch advocate for one position that I am no longer certain of my objectivity. Sometimes I hope we will be proven wrong, just so I won't feel aggravated when I see a paper by Owen, Bruce Latimer, or Jim Ohman. But this desire quickly passes, as will soon become evident.

JACK OF TWO TRADES, MASTER OF NEITHER

There is no real dispute that *A. afarensis* progressed bipedally when on the ground (but see Sarmiento[19,20] for the sole contrasting view) nor that this was such an important part of its overall locomotor repertoire as to have engendered anatomic changes promoting its performance. The chief evidence for these conclusions comprises the shortened ilium, the posterior displacement of its auricular surface relative to the acetabulum, the presence of an iliac pillar, and a high bicondylar angle of the femur. However, while acknowledging this, our papers[18,21–25] claimed that:

1. *A. afarensis* also possessed anatomic adaptations for movement in trees (Table 1 and Figure 1).

2. Certain anatomic traits long thought to be diagnostic of a completely human-like form of bipedalism are not truly diagnostic of such behavior or are not actually present on Hadar specimens. These include an iliopsoas groove on the os coxae, an anterior inferior iliac spine, a femoral intertrochanteric line, an obturator externus groove on the femoral neck, and thin superior cortical bone coupled with thick inferior cortical bone in the femoral neck.

Table 1. Postcranial Traits Identified by Stern and Susman,[18] Jungers and Stern,[21] and Susman and Coworkers[22] as Distinguishing *A. afarensis* from Modern Humans

Relatively short hindlimb (A[*], N[**])	Lateral lip of patellar groove weakly developed for degree of valgus at knee (N)
Relatively long foot (N)	Medial femoral condyle wider than lateral condyle (N)
Elongated, rod-shaped pisiform (A)	Distal articular surface of Lucy's tibia angled to face posteriorly (N)
Finger metacarpals with large heads and bases relative to parallel-sided and somewhat curved shafts (A)	Proximal margin of talar facet on fibula is oblique (A)
Finger proximal phalanges slender and markedly curved, with a bilateral expansion of shaft correlated with strong expression of flexor sheath ridges (A)	Peroneal groove on fibula is wide, deep, and has prominent medial lip (A)
Trochleae of finger proximal phalanges subtend large angles and are deeply grooved (A)	Anterior limit of lateral margin of talar trochlea is extended distally (A)
Strong impressions for insertion of flexor digitorum superficialis on finger middle phalanges (A)	Calcaneus has large peroneal trochlea and small lateral plantar process (N)
Glenoid cavity of scapula faces more superiorly (A)	Hallucal tarsometatarsal joint is curved (A)
Relatively larger moment arm of hamstrings (A, N)	Head of hallucal metatarsal is mediolaterally very curved (A, N)
Relatively wide tuberoacetabular sulcus (N)	Lack of mediolateral widening of dorsal region of metatarsal heads (N)
Hamstring surface of ischial tuberosity makes a sharp angle to adductor magnus surface (N)	Pedal proximal phalanges II-V are slender, relatively long (N), and markedly curved (A)
Absence of falciform crest on medial aspect of ischial tuberosity (N)	Pedal proximal phalanges II-V have bilateral expansion in region of well developed flexor sheath attachments (A)
Ventral concavity of sacrum slightly developed (N)	Trochleae of pedal proximal phalanges II-IV subtend large angles (A)
Sacrum lacks well developed upper lateral angles (N)	Lack of dorsoplantar expansion at base of pedal proximal phalanges II-V (N)
Acetabular lunate articular surface has a diminutive anterior horn (N)	Proximal phalanx of toe II is shorter than that of toe III (A)
Absence of iliopubic eminence (N)	Pedal middle phalanges are relatively long compared to proximal phalanges (A, N)
Iliac blades more coronally oriented (N)	Laetoli footprints have small impression or none for ball of big toe (N)
Superior articular margin of femoral head runs from posterolateral to anteromedial (A)	Laetoli footprints show variable length of impressions for lateral toes (N)

[*]A = interpreted as being related to an arboreal component of behavior.

[**]N = interpreted as being related to a novel form of bipedalism

3. *A. afarensis* possessed anatomic traits suggesting that its bipedalism lacked human-like extension at the hip and knee during stance phase (Table 1 and Figure 1), and that early in the stance phase of bipedal walking the lesser gluteal muscles controlled side-to-side balance at the hip by acting as medial rotators of the partly flexed thigh.[26] Even if these particular claims are incorrect, the relatively short lower limb and relatively long foot of *A. afarensis* point to an energetically more costly form of bipedalism[16,21] and a kinematically distinctive swing phase.[27]

At the same time or shortly after the publication of our earliest papers on *A. afarensis* locomotion, there appeared a spate of other contributions reporting a mosaic of human-like and ape-like features in its postcranial anatomy. Clearly, these were based on work that had been done simultaneously with or even before our own. Marzke,[28] analyzing bones and joints of the wrist, and McHenry,[29] focusing on the capitate, seemed willing to recognize the possibility of some degree of arboreality in *A. afarensis* locomotor behavior but were reluctant to actually draw this conclusion. Rose,[30] who made many of the same observations on the Hadar feet and hands that we did, showed no such reluctance, nor did Schmid,[31] who focused on the ribs and pelvis. Deloison's[32] study of

the Hadar calcanei led her to state explicitly that *A. afarensis* bipedalism must have been distinct from that of modern humans. In contrast, Wolpoff,[33,34] challenging Jungers's[16] claim that Lucy's lower limb was shorter than expected for a diminutive human-like biped, drew a picture of *A. afarensis* as an efficient terrestrial biped that also made extensive use of arboreal resources. Berge[35–37] seemed to have a difficult time deciding on the functional significance of her multivariate osteometric study of the A.L. 288-1 and Sts 14 innominates. She interpreted the lateral orientation of the iliac blade, the proximity of the iliac pillar to the anterior edge of the bone, and the beaked form of the anterior superior iliac spine as pointing to a type of bipedal adaptation differing from that of modern humans. Furthermore, she stated that the smallness of the acetabulum, auricular surface, and the portion of the ilium just above the hip joint indicate a limited adaptation for weight bearing. Yet Berge also stated that gracile australopithecines were "as bipedal as *Homo*," with an equally effective lateral balance mechanism and pelvic proportions that in no way provide evidence for an arboreal adaptation. Finally, the formal publication of Tardieu's[38] thesis contained a new section reporting that the knee of *A. afarensis* was distinctly nonhuman by virtue of having only a single

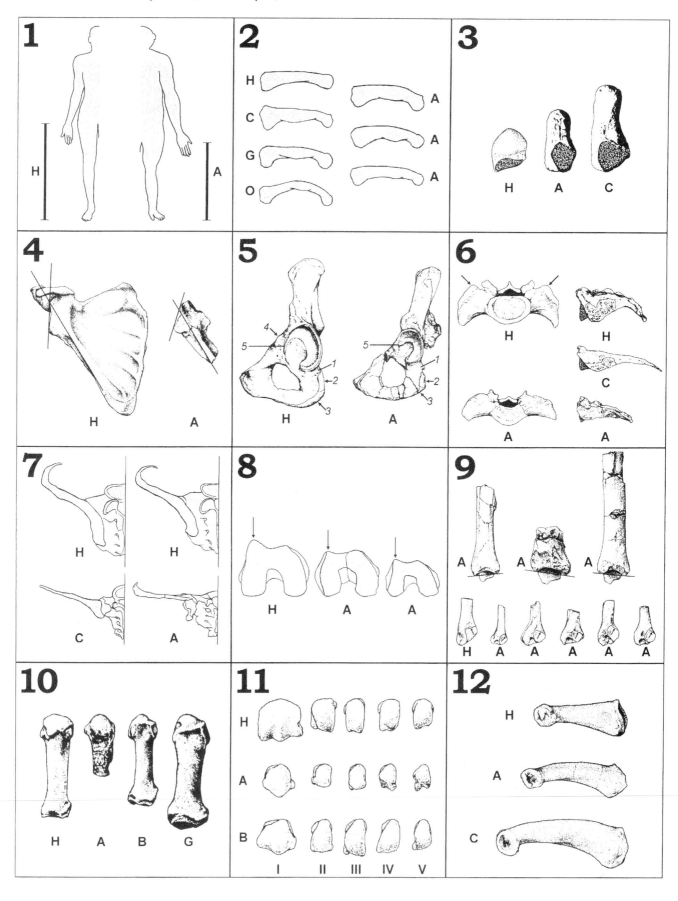

attachment of the lateral meniscus anterior to the external tibial spine. Tardieu[39,40] linked this trait to an enhanced range of lateral tibial rotation and said it would be useful if the foot were used as a prehensile organ.

From 1982 to 1985 there seemed to be a growing consensus that not only favored an adaptively important role for arboreality in the life of the Hadar hominids, but even recognized the possibility that their manner of bipedalism was recognizably different from that practiced by modern humans. Tardieu joined Senut in expressing the belief that both *Homo* and *Australopithecus* were represented at Hadar, and that the anatomy of the Hadar postcranial material indicated two different locomotor profiles, one human-like and one not. (More recently, Tardieu has attributed all the Hadar specimens to *A. afarensis* and makes no mention of a type with human-like locomotion.) In 1984, we expressed our opinion that there was one hominid species at Hadar and that all its members were distinctly nonhuman-like in locomotion, but that sexual dimorphism in the degree of arboreality was possible.[22]

During this period only one abstract was published portraying the Hadar hominid as a fully developed biped.[41] It dealt with the foot, reporting that metatarsophalangeal joint conformations provide evidence of the extreme dorsiflexion that occurs during toe-off in a habitual biped. Curved proximal phalanges were dismissed as "an adaptive response to large dorsoplantar bending moments," prehension as exhibited in the modern ape foot not being part of the *A. afarensis* locomotor repertoire. Longitudinal and transverse bony arches were said to exist and to indicate a bipedal foot. The arches were short-lived, however, for analysis of the navicular and cuboid from Hadar published a year later indicated that "*A. afarensis* possessed a more mobile transverse tarsal joint, and probably a wider and flatter tarsus than is characteristic of the normal modern human foot."[42]

THE EMPIRE STRIKES BACK

Of course there really was no consensus that the positional behavior of *A. afarensis* was distinct from that of

modern humans. The long-awaited response to such views was presented in a series of papers, largely emanating from Kent State University, between 1986 and 1990.[43–49] Table 2 lists and Figure 2 illustrates traits identified in these papers as proving the adaptive insignificance of arboreality in the life of *A. afarensis* and the human-like nature of its bipedality. Five of the seven papers were restricted to a consideration of the ankle and foot.

Many of the papers summarized in Table 2 contained suggestions to the effect that no significant adaptation to bipedalism can occur unless the commitment to this behavior is total. It was stated directly that hominoid arboreality is not to be viewed as a natural continuum and that arboreal capacity in early hominids should not be discussed in terms of "degrees" of adaptation.[44] A later contribution suggested that no selective advantage could accrue to an arboreal animal from any change that diminished its ability to climb.[50] Consequently, the presence of anatomic alterations for bipedalism that compromise climbing ability make it unlikely that arboreality remained adaptively significant. It was argued that if arboreality was adaptively significant for *A. afarensis*, its upper limb should have maintained, or even shown to a higher degree, all the features we have come to associate with pongid arboreality. In one way or another, the authors of all these papers agreed that "To suggest that *A. afarensis* still employed a significant degree of pongid-like arboreal behavior or that the stride pattern in this species included a 'primitive bent-hipped, bent-knee' gait (as has been recently suggested; see Stern and Susman, 1983; Susman et al., 1984) not only contradicts available anatomical evidence from the hip, knee, ankle, and foot but also completely contradicts the basic rudiments of neo-Darwinian theory."[47]

THE VIEW OF A CAST-OUT ANGEL

Can there be a home in neo-Darwinian heaven for those who do not believe the significance of derived traits overwhelms that of primitive traits for reconstructing the locomotor behavior of fossils? I have always had a simplistic way of looking at this

◄ **Figure 1.**   *Some of the traits identified in Table 1 as indicating that* A. afarensis *either possessed anatomic adaptations for movement in the trees or was not entirely human-like in its manner of terrestrial bipedality. A =* A. afarensis, *B = bonobo, C = chimpanzee, G = gorilla, H = human, O = orangutan. 1. Outline drawings of body shapes illustrating the relatively short lower limb of* A. afarensis. *2. Side views of manual proximal phalanges from ray IV showing the marked curvature of this bone in* A. afarensis. *3. Radial views of pisiform bones illustrating the rod-like nature of this bone in* A. afarensis. *4. Ventral views of scapulae illustrating that the glenoid cavity faces more cranially in* A. afarensis. *5. Lateral views of hip bones illustrating in the fossil the relatively wide tuberoacetabular sulcus (1), the relatively large distance from the center of the hip joint to the hamstring origin (2), the sharp angle between the area for origin of the hamstrings (2) and the area for origin of the adductor magnus (3), the absence of an iliopubic eminence (4), and the small size of the anterior horn of the acetabular lunate surface (5). 6. On the left, cranial views of sacra illustrating the poorly developed upper lateral angles in* A. afarensis; *on the right, side views of sacra illustrating the slight development of the ventral concavity in* A. afarensis. *7. Cranial views of iliac crests illustrating the coronal orientation of the iliac blades in* A. afarensis. *8. Distal views of femoral condyles illustrating that the patellar groove's lateral lip (arrow) is weakly developed in* A. afarensis. *9. On top, lateral views of distal tibiae (anterior to the left, posterior to the right) illustrating that in Lucy (leftmost specimen, reversed for ease of comparison) the distal articular surface is inclined posteriorly; on bottom, medial views of distal fibulae (anterior to the right, posterior to the left, some specimens reversed for ease of comparison) illustrating the obliquity of the talar facet's proximal margin (arrow) in* A. afarensis. *10. Dorsal views of hallucal metatarsals illustrating the marked mediolateral curvature of the head in* A. afarensis. *11. Distal views of metatarsal heads from rays I-V (dorsal toward the top, ventral toward the bottom) illustrating the lack of mediolateral widening of the dorsal regions in* A. afarensis. *12. Side views of pedal proximal phalanges from ray III illustrating the marked curvature of such bones in* A. afarensis.

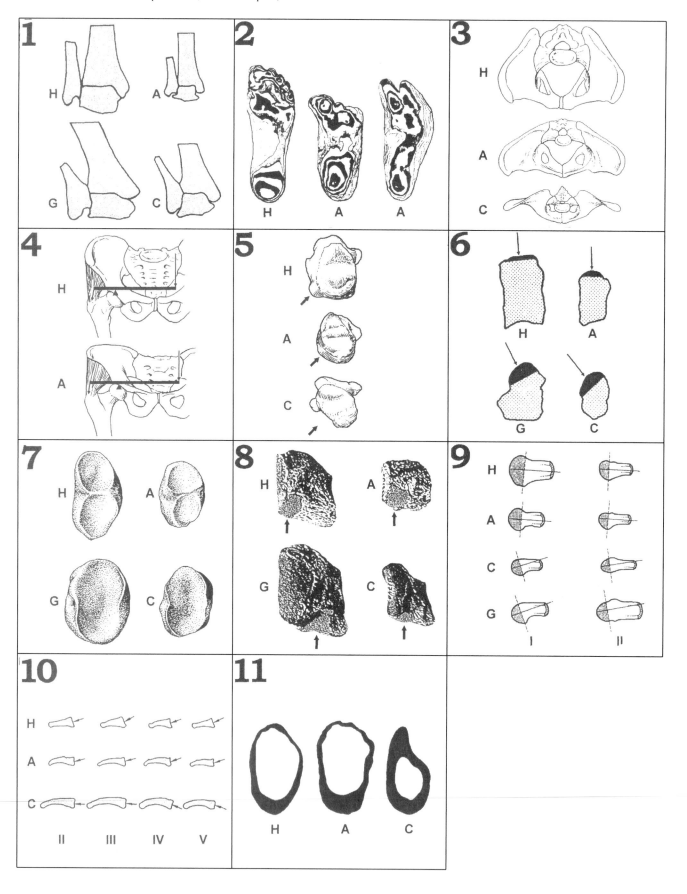

Table 2.   Traits Said to Indicate Human-Like Bipedality and Adaptive Insignificance of Arboreality in *A. afarensis*

The head of the first rib articulates with the body of only the T1 vertebra.[43] (I)
The deltoid muscle marking on the clavicle faces anteriorly.[43] (I)
The supratalar joint space is nearly perpendicular to the long axis of the tibia.[44] (I, H)
The flexion-extension axis of the talocrural joint is oriented so that there is little conjunct axial rotation of the tibia during flexion-extension movements at the ankle.[44] (I)
The Laetoli footprints have a fundamentally human-like total morphological pattern.[45] (H)
The ilia of Lucy are bent around to provide lateral attachment for the lesser gluteal muscles.[46] (H)
The attachment points and dispositions of the gluteus maximus and quadriceps are human-like.[46] (H)
An iliopsoas groove is present on the pelvis.[46,68] (H)
The hip abductors have a mechanical advantage surpassing that of the hip abductors in modern humans.[46] (H)
The foot has a shock-absorbing arch.[46] (H)
The upper limbs and fingers are relatively shorter than those of apes.[46] (I)
The inferolateral corner of the calcaneal corpus is expanded and a clearly defined lateral plantar process is present.[47] (H)
The posterior talar facet of the calcaneus is less convex and more vertically oriented than is that in apes.[47] (I, H)
The distal articular surface of the Hadar medial cuneiform faces more directly distally than does that in apes.[48] (I)
The proximal articular surface of the hallucal metatarsal is virtually divided into two separate facets by a slight transverse ridge.[48] (I)
The distal location of the "sub-bursal groove" for the tendon of tibialis anterior on the medial surface of the medial cuneiform is human-like.[48] (I)
The heads of metatarsals are inflated and angled dorsally.[49] (H)
The proximal articular surfaces of the pedal proximal phalanges are more superiorly oriented than are those of apes.[49] (H)
The superior cortical bone of the femoral neck is thin.[46] (I, H)

*I = interpreted as showing insignificance of arboreal behavior.

**H = interpreted as showing human-like bipedalism.

issue. The whale ancestor *Ambulocetus* shows anatomic adaptations for aquatic locomotion that have clearly diminished its terrestrial expertise.[51] Still, no one has suggested that terrestrial behavior was adaptively insignificant for *Ambulocetus*. Why then conclude that arboreal behavior was adaptively insignificant for *A. afarensis* because its anatomic adaptations for bipedal locomotion diminished its arboreal expertise? Other authors have thought and written more insightfully on this problem as it relates to human evolution. Rose[30,52] envisions the adoption of terrestrial bipedalism by a human ancestor as a process in which the animal moves through a series of compromise morphologies. "For an animal with a compromise morphology each of the component activities of the [locomotor] repertoire is performed less energetically efficiently than it would be given optimal design ... Although it is not maximally efficient, each activity within the repertoire is performed effectively, according to the purposes for which it was used."[52] Duncan and coworkers[53] stated that "Every species is composed of characteristics that reflect both its ancestry

as well as its unique evolutionary pathway; understanding the overall functional pattern of the organism requires an equal consideration of all its anatomical features, regardless of whether they are apomorphies, plesiomorphies, or homoplasies. This viewpoint serves to frame the fossil as a once fully functional living organism." I am persuaded by these arguments. If you are not, then without further ado you should accept *A. afarensis* as a fully committed and human-like terrestrial biped. You may proceed directly to the Acknowledgments; do not pass GO, do not collect $200.

JUST THE FACTS, MA'AM

Coffing[54] attributes much of the disagreement about reconstructing *A. afarensis* locomotor behavior to the previously mentioned differences in concepts of natural selection. However, it is also true that the opposing camps have doubted the accuracy, as well as the interpretation, of one another's data.

◄ **Figure 2.**   *Some of the traits identified in Table 2 as indicating human-like bipedality and the adaptive insignificance of arboreality in* A. afarensis. *A = A. afarensis, C = chimpanzee, G = gorilla, H = human. All drawings are modified from originals that appeared in the indicated references. 1. Outline tracings from midcoronally sectioned casts of ankle joints illustrating that the supratalar joint space is nearly perpendicular to the long axis of the tibia in humans and* A. afarensis.[44] *2. Contour maps of footprints said to illustrate the fundamentally humanlike pattern of the Laetoli footprints.[46] 3. Cranial views of pelves said to illustrate that the ilia of Lucy are bent around to provide lateral attachment for the lesser gluteal muscles.[46] 4. Anterior views of hip joints and pelves said to illustrate that the hip abductors of* A. afarensis *have a mechanical advantage surpassing that of the hip abductors in modern humans.[46] 5. Posterior views of left calcanei illustrating that the calcaneal corpus' inferolateral corner (arrow) is expanded and said to possess a clearly defined lateral plantar process.[47] 6. Transverse sections of right medial cuneiforms illustrating that in* A. afarensis *the distal articular surface faces more directly distally than it does in apes.[48] 7. Proximal articular surfaces of left hallucal metatarsals said to illustrate that this surface is virtually divided into two separate facets by a slight transverse ridge in both humans and* A. afarensis.[48] *8. Medial views of right medial cuneiforms illustrating the human-like distal location of the "sub-bursal groove" (arrow) for the tendon of tibialis anterior.[48] 9. Outline tracings of midsagittally sectioned casts of the first and second metatarsal heads said to illustrate that they are inflated and angled dorsally in both humans and* A. afarensis.[49] *10. Outline tracings of midsagittally sectioned casts of pedal proximal phalanges said to illustrate that in* A. afarensis *the proximal articular surfaces are more superiorly oriented than in apes.[49] 11. Drawings of the femoral neck's cortical bone seen on transverse sections (superior to the top) illustrating that the superior cortical bone of the femoral neck is thin in humans and* A. afarensis.[46]

Possible Errors by Randy and Bill

1. Using an adult intraspecific regression line of scapular bar-glenoid angle (Figure 1, part 4) versus glenoid length derived from 50 modern human scapulae, we predicted that a modern human of Lucy's size should have a bar-glenoid angle of 140 degrees, much greater than the 130 degrees observed in Lucy's scapula. Mensforth and coworkers[55] found our prediction to be in error. They reported that a similar analysis of 100 modern human scapulae yielded an expected value of ~130 degrees for the bar-glenoid angle of a Lucy-sized modern human scapula. More recently, Inouye and Shea[56] arrived at a value of 136 degrees, but pointed out that low correlations, together with the practice of extrapolating to a size below that found in one's modern sample, make any such estimate worthless. When Inouye and Shea included subadult human scapulae in their sample, the range of bar-glenoid angles encompassed Lucy's value, and the human regression line virtually ran through 130 degrees. (It appears from their graphs that Inouye and Shea used 2.25 cm, the value we reported, for Lucy's glenoid length. However, we did not include the supraglenoid tubercle in our measurement, whereas they reported doing so for all their specimens of extant species. The measurement of Lucy's glenoid length including the supraglenoid tubercle is 2.57 cm. If Inouye and Shea had used this value, they would have predicted a bar-glenoid angle for a Lucy-sized human of 137.5 degrees using the adult human regression line and one of 132 degrees using the ontogenetic human regression line.)

If the approach used by Inouye and Shea is appropriate for assessing the significance of Lucy's cranially directed glenoid cavity, then this trait no longer belongs on the list of characters suggesting arboreality. In accepting this possibility, I am being far more generous than Bill Jungers, who has conveyed to me his conviction that it is incorrect to apply an ontogenetic allometric trend to answer a question concerning the shape of a small adult. He is now scouring museums for a few adult human scapulae as small as Lucy's.

2. We asserted that the superior border of the articular margin of Lucy's femoral head exhibited a disposition found in apes but not in humans. We said this disposition was compatible with a greater range of abduction than occurs in modern humans. Asfaw,[57] using a much larger sample than ours, found the "ape-like" condition in 9% of human individuals. MacLatchy[58] showed that if the neutral posture of the femur is assumed to occur when the fovea capitis is centered in the acetabular fossa, the neutral position of Lucy's thigh was more adducted than that of modern humans. Furthermore, despite the fact that the lunate surface of Lucy's acetabulum was restricted dorsally and cranially relative to the acetabulum of modern humans, this difference was insufficient to allow greater abduction of the thigh.

These two studies cause me to doubt greatly the significance of our observations on the articular surface of Lucy's femoral head. Nonetheless, I wish to point out that limitation of hip abduction in modern humans is probably due to passive tension in the stretched adductor muscles. Although I am almost totally sedentary, I am able to abduct my extended thigh 40 to 50 degrees and my flexed thigh 50 to 60 degrees. Observations of gymnasts lead me to conclude that people who stretch their adductor muscles can abduct the thigh at least 90 degrees. So the question about the abductibility of the *A. afarensis* hindlimb is really a question of the rest-length of its hip adductors, which we will never know.

3. Tuttle described our statements on the Laetoli footprints as an example of "haste making paleontological waste."[59] He claimed that the chimpanzee footprints described by Manter and Elftman[60] and those produced by our own "incarcerated" chimpanzees[18] were atypical by having a somewhat adducted hallux and partially curled lateral toes. He also found that traits we identified as characteristic of modern human footprints are in fact commonly absent. White and Suwa[45] agreed, adding that we had incorrectly interpreted the footprint surface at Laetoli. We did not respond, but Deloison's[61] comparison of Laetoli footprints to those of chimpanzees and modern humans found the fossil pattern to be characterized by, among other things, a narrow impression for the heel, a depression likely to be caused by a large abductor hallucis, a partly abducted big toe, and folded lateral toes. Deloison concluded that the overall form was more similar to that of a chimpanzee than that of a human. The definitive word on the subject has yet to be uttered.

4. We asserted that the relatively long toes of *A. afarensis* were compatible with use of the foot for some kind of prehension in trees, and would also have increased the length of the foot in a way that would have affected the kinematics of bipedal swing phase. White and Suwa[45] reconstructed the length of Lucy's foot, finding the length of her toes relative to the rest of the foot to be halfway between that of a human and a gorilla, and 45% to 50% longer than that of the average human. Nonetheless, the authors claimed that the ratio of total foot length to femur length for Lucy was at the upper end of the modern human range of variation and, therefore, of minimal consequence for her manner of bipedalism. Latimer and Lovejoy[48] compared the length of Lucy's proximal pedal phalanx to four other postcranial measures and, despite its position intermediate between gorilla and human, concluded that the fossil toe was not particularly long. We had previously published two of the same comparisons[18,22] and, with very similar numbers, came to a quite different conclusion. Lucy's toes were probably as long as the fingers of a two-year old human. The lengths of the phalanges in the A.L. 333-115 foot are comparable to those in the hands of children between the ages of nine and ten years.[62] The real question seems to be how long is "particularly" long?

5. Our use of the superior edge of the talar facet on the fibula (Figure 1, part 9) to judge the range and set of plantarflexion at the ankle was said to be inaccurate because "talofibular joint congruence cannot be reliably assessed."[44] Latimer and colleagues[44] found no indication of a greater plantarflexion range in Lucy when

they manipulated her tibia upon her talus. On the other hand, when applied to chimpanzee bones, their method did not reveal the greater range of plantarflexion that we demonstrated by radiographic images of living animals.[22] My conclusion is that there is something very different about the talar facet of Hadar fibulae, but that we have not proven its functional significance.

6. Our comments on the size of the large peroneal trochlea and its relation to the lateral plantar process were described as inexplicable, inaccurate, and implausible.[47] While I admire the alliteration, I must point out that our assessment of the sizes of these bony bumps is fully concordant with that of Deloison.[32,63]

7. Whereas Wolpoff[33,34] criticized Jungers[16] for concluding that Lucy's lower limb was relatively short, and we responded with further evidence to support this contention,[21] Kramer[64] has recently published a mathematical simulation of Lucy's bipedalism purporting to show that Lucy was not energetically compromised by her short legs: "On a mass specific basis, the configuration developed from the fossil remains of AL 288-1 uses less energy to move than, and has the same cost of transport as, the modern human configuration." The assumptions underlying Kramer's conclusion are that Lucy had the same movement profile as a modern human, that the masses of Lucy's lower limb segments were proportionally the same as in a modern human, and that it is most appropriate to compare energy use of the two species when Lucy is walking at about 80% of the speed of a modern human.

If Lucy really had the same movement profile as a modern human, this alone would cause me, but not my colleagues, to classify her as a human-like biped regardless of energetic cost. Therefore, it is of little moment to me if the calculation of energy-use based on Kramer's assumptions is correct or not. For me, the issue is the implausibility of the assumptions. Furthermore, knowing that mathematical simulations are often highly dependent on the values of input parameters, it is troublesome that Kramer uses values for Lucy's segment masses and moments of inertia that are substantially different from the estimates provided by Crompton and coworkers.[65]

Do Unto Others As They Have Done Unto You

Those of you familiar with the history of the dispute about the locomotor behavior of *A. afarensis* know that we did not respond to criticism of our work by turning the other cheek. We, and sometimes other authors, claimed to have found the following flaws in the works of Latimer, Lovejoy, and Ohman.

1. Bill Jungers and I[66] said that Ohman's[43] claim about the uniqueness of the univertebral articulation of the human first rib was untrue. Schmid[67] pointed out that Ohman's description of Lucy's first rib as having only one facet on its head was contradicted by Johanson and coworkers,[68] who said it had a distinct double facet separated by a central ridge. Schmid also noted that Johanson and coworkers reported Lucy's clavicle as having a rounded superior surface presenting a roughened area for the attachment of the deltoid, whereas Ohman said it had the hominid condition of a deltoid attachment at the anterior edge of the bone. In the disagreements between Ohman and Johanson and coworkers, I do not know who is correct.

2. The calculation by Latimer and coworkers[44] that conjunct rotation of the tibia during flexion or extension movements of the ankle would have been minimal in Lucy directly contradicts the results reported by Christie,[4] which were based on manipulating the specimens.

3. Lovejoy's[46] assertion that the ilia of Lucy are bent around to provide lateral attachment for the lesser gluteal muscles to act as abductors (Figure 2, part 3) is the opposite of what we[18] and Schmid[67] claim (Figure 1, part 7).

4. The statement that the attachment points of the gluteus maximus and quadriceps femoris in Lucy indicate that they were as big as our own and similarly disposed[46] is unsupported by evidence.

5. Statements that an iliopsoas groove is present on Lucy's pelvis[46,68] are contrary to our observations.[18]

6. Lovejoy[46] stated that the greater outward flare of Lucy's ilia, coupled with a relatively long femoral neck, gave her abductors such a big moment arm that, despite the slightly greater interacetabular distance, they had a mechanical advantage surpassing our own (Figure 2, part 4), resulting in reduced hip joint pressure. This was disproved by Jungers[25] and Ruff.[69] Indeed, Ruff's analysis showed that if Lucy had walked as modern humans do, she would be expected to have a relatively larger acetabulocristal buttress, larger femoral head, and greater resistance of the femoral shaft to mediolateral bending than do humans. She does not.

7. We have already published[70] some of our complaints regarding the analysis of the Hadar calcanei conducted by Latimer and Lovejoy.[47] We pointed out temporal inconsistencies in their descriptions of the lateral plantar process (it grew to more human proportions from early to later papers) and their failure to include the ape-like A.L. 333-37 specimen when calculating cross-sectional areas of the calcaneal tuber.

There may also be a problem regarding their assessments of posterior talar facet curvatures in the fossil calcanei. The authors calculated the included angle of this facet to be 82 degrees for the A.L. 333-8 specimen (the lower the value of included angle, the flatter is the surface). Such a value is close to the mean of 78.5 degrees they report for humans and far from means they found in African apes (gorilla = 100 degrees, chimpanzee = 110 degrees). On the other hand, Deloison,[32] who calculated an undefined "index of curvature" of the same facet, found that the value in the fossil fell within the normal range of chimpanzees and outside that of modern humans.

Latimer and Lovejoy[47] stated that damage to the A.L. 333-55 calcaneus precluded reliable measurement of the included angle of its posterior talar facet, but they did offer an estimate of its radius of curvature equal to the value of 24.5 mm for A.L. 333-8 (the higher the value of radius of curvature, the flatter is the surface). Indeed, in A.L. 333-55, the facet is crossed by a longitudinal crack, but Latimer and associates[71] previously assured us that "owing to good apposition it is of no metric consequence." Using a cast of the specimen, I calculated the A.L. 333-55 posterior talar facet radius of curvature to be 16 mm and its included angle to be 96 degrees. Such values are concordant with Deloison's assessment of the better preserved A.L. 333-8 specimen.

8. The identification of the tibialis anterior "facet" on the Hadar medial cuneiform as being human-like in position and orientation[48] (Figure 2, part 8) has been challenged by Deloison,[72] who found this structure to be so variable in both humans and chimpanzees as to preclude any conclusion about affinities of the fossil.

9. Latimer and Lovejoy[48] described the proximal articular facet of the A.L. 333-54 hallucal metatarsal as having indentations in both its medial and lateral edges (Figure 2, part 7). They say this conformation was not found in their sample of African apes but is common in humans. Deloison[63] described the facet in chimpanzees as being bilaterally constricted, but that in humans as reniform. She concluded that the similarity is between the fossil and apes. Furthermore, she found both regions of the fossil's proximal articular surface to be concave, with radii of curvatures that match those in chimpanzees.[61]

10. The statement that in *A. afarensis* the proximal articular surfaces of the pedal proximal phalanges have the degree of superior orientation found in modern humans[48] (Figure 2, part 10) has been shown to be incorrect by Duncan and coworkers,[53] whose quantitative analysis proved that the orientation in the fossils is intermediate between that in humans and African apes.

11. Duncan and colleagues[53] pointed out inaccuracies in the statement that the metatarsal heads of *A. afarensis* are angled dorsally as in humans, but not pongids[48] (Figure 2, part 9). The same authors could not duplicate Latimer's and Lovejoy's results on metatarso-phalangeal joint excursion and suggested that the method used was unreliable.

12. Susman and I[23] disputed the statement that the thin superior cortical bone of the femoral neck in Hadar femora is a trait aligning them with humans and distinguishing them from arboreal primates[46] (Figure 2, part 11). I have to admit that of all the traits said to align the fossil with humans and push it away from apes, this was the one that gave me the most concern that we might be wrong. I have always been impressed by Pauwels'[73] explanation of why humans have this trait. Nonetheless, not knowing the condition in apes, Randy and I determined to see what comparable sections through human and nonhuman primate femoral necks would show. We did an extremely cursory job, looking only at one specimen each of *Homo, P. troglodytes, P. paniscus, Gorilla, Symphalangus,* and *Ateles.* All we could say was that most of the nonhuman primates in our sample also had thinner cortical bone on the superior aspect of the femoral neck than on its inferior aspect. We didn't quantify our results, and I expected that had we done so humans would have been at the extreme of the primate range, joined there by the A.L. 128-1 proximal femur and probably some other fossil specimens of the same period. Indeed, my fears were justified, for a few years later Ohman and coworkers[74] seemed to have demonstrated precisely this point in their thorough

quantitative comparison of humans and African apes. My only solace was the authors' concession that the trait no longer precluded arboreal behavior, but simply demonstrated that such behavior could only have been an insignificant component of the *A. afarensis* locomotor repertoire. Then along came a paper by Rafferty,[75] who extended the analysis of femoral neck structure to cercopithecoids and strepsirhines. She found the distribution of cortical bone in the femoral necks of these two groups, most species of which are predominantly arboreal, to be similar to that in humans. It seems that apes and atelines are unusual in having a more even distribution of cortical bone around the femoral neck. Rafferty surmised that this more even distribution was linked to the less stereotyped locomotor behavior of a climber-clamberer. So one conclusion would have to be that *A. afarensis* was not a pongid-like or ateline-like climber-clamberer. I feel comfortable with that view. I also believe that much is yet to be learned about what determines the distribution of cortical bone in the femoral neck. After all, radiographs of cerebral palsy patients, who walk with limited extension of the hip, appear to illustrate the same general pattern of femoral neck bone distribution as that found in people who walk normally[76] (Figure 3).

IS THERE HOPE FOR RESOLUTION?

I imagine that the scenario of argument and counterargument has become tiresome to many noncombatants. What hope is there for resolving the debate on *A. afarensis* locomotion? Maybe the answer lies in some truly novel ideas and data that have emerged in the last several years.

New Ideas About Old *Afarensis* Material

Rak,[77] accepting the notion that the sagittal plane excursions of Lucy's limbs were the same as those in modern humans, proposed a difference between Lucy's and modern humans' manners of walking with regard to rotation of the pelvis around a vertical axis. He suggested that Lucy's wide pelvis and long femoral neck enabled her to have a human-like stride length without suffering an increase in vertical excursion of the center of mass that would otherwise occur because of her short lower limbs. According to Rak, an increase in vertical excursion of the center of mass would have brought about both an increased cost of locomotion and increased joint reaction forces.

I am concerned that the relationships among energy cost, vertical excursion of the center of mass, and pelvic rotation are not as simple as Rak suggests. While it is true that for modern humans faster walking speeds are associated with longer strides and greater vertical oscillations of the center of mass,[78] for any speed there is an optimal stride length that minimizes energy cost.[79,80] At shorter stride lengths there will be less vertical oscillation but greater energy expenditure. When walking normally at any speed, we could always force ourselves to rotate the pelvis more in order to decrease the extent of center-of-mass fall, but we do not do so.[78] I presume there is an energy cost associated with pelvic rotation and that

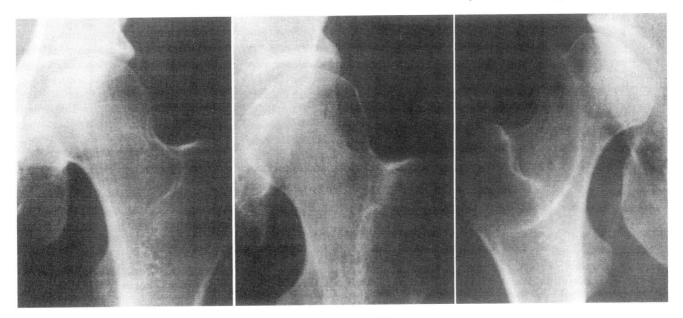

Figure 3. *Radiographs of the hips of three ambulatory cerebral palsy patients.[76] Despite the fact that such patients walk with abnormal flexion at the hips and knees, two of the radiographs (leftmost and rightmost) show a pattern of thin bone in the superior cortex of the femoral neck and thick bone in the inferior cortex. The resemblance of this pattern to that in people with normal gait suggests that the determinants of cortical bone distribution in the femoral neck have yet to be determined with sufficient precision to enable its use in the reconstruction of bipedal kinematics. (Reproduced with permission from* Clinical Radiology, *Vol. 35, pp. 317–319. Elsevier Ltd.,* © *The Royal College of Radiologists.)*

adopting more than is customary would offset any savings afforded by a reduced vertical oscillation of the center of mass. Nevertheless, if Rak's idea is correct, it would certainly mean that Lucy's gait would look different from that of a modern human even to a casual observer, though in a way far different than we suggested.

Berge[81–83] attempted to reconstruct the lines of action of muscles about the hip joint in A.L. 288-1, in one case assuming a human-like morphology and in another an ape-like disposition. She concluded that the ape-like disposition would actually have enabled Lucy to be a better biped. However, she stated that because extensors of the thigh in A.L. 288-1 had relatively longer moment arms than do those of humans, these muscles would have been more powerful in their ability to move the hip than to stabilize it. Berge further concluded that stability at the hip and knee in the coronal plane required a sort of waddling gait with large axial rotatory movements of the pelvis and counter-rotations of the shoulders, entailing a greater energy cost. Finally, her estimates of muscle torques led Berge to conclude that *A. afarensis* had a greater ability than humans do to move their lower limbs in different spatial positions, thereby promoting arboreal capability.

I have already mentioned Ruff's[69] demonstration that Lucy lacked certain osteologic traits expected to be present had she walked as do modern humans. Ruff concluded that Lucy may have walked bipedally in a way that allowed her trunk center of gravity to lie closer to a vertical line through the support-side hip joint. He suggested this could be accomplished if she laterally flexed her trunk toward the support side and elevated her pelvis on the nonsupport side. He likened this to the gait of a human with bilaterally painful hip joints because such individuals and Lucy would both have the goal of reducing hip joint reaction force.

Actually, the citation Ruff offered in support of this analogy provides a somewhat erroneous analysis of the gait of patients with a painful hip. It is true that during stance phase on the painful side, lateral lurch of the trunk toward that side is apparent,[84,85] but the majority of such patients exhibit a descent, not an elevation, of the pelvis on the nonsupport side.[84] Contralateral pelvic elevation could only be effective in reducing support-side hip joint force if it were brought about using muscles of the trunk. Use of support-side lesser gluteal muscles to accomplish this elevation would actually cause an increase in the hip joint reaction force. In this regard it is interesting to note that Schmid's[67] interpretation of Lucy's iliac blade orientation emphasizes increase in leverage of lateral flexors of the trunk.

Ruff also says that lateral trunk flexion and contralateral pelvic elevation probably characterize chimpanzee bipedalism, an assertion confirmed by the work of Tardieu.[86] Ruff's conclusion that Lucy's bipedal walking was less energetically efficient than that of modern humans is consistent with the view that although Lucy was a facultative biped, she probably was not a long-distance traveler.

Recently Ruff and colleagues[87] have drawn attention to the fact that Lucy and several other australopithecines have very robust femoral shafts relative to femoral head size. They concluded that overall mechanical loading of the skeleton was increased in these ancient hominids to about the same level as in modern African apes. As I read such statements, I wonder how this analysis of cortical stress would have been affected had Ruff not assumed full extension of the thigh during the support phase. Maybe walking with a less than fully extended hip and knee would necessitate relatively robust femoral shafts, but I am not smart enough to solve this problem.

Speaking of walking with a less than completely extended hip and knee, Crompton and coworkers[65] claim that their mathematical simulations of Lucy's bipedalism, bolstered by preliminary experimental data on humans, show that bent-hip, bent-knee gait is mechanically ineffective and likely to produce a rapid, large rise in core body temperature. My own response[88] to these arguments is that although bent-hip, bent-knee gait is more energetically costly than normal human bipedal walking, the cost is not as large as might be imagined and would not be prohibitive in an animal that used its bipedalism primarily as a feeding adaptation.[30,52,89,90] My reading of the relevant physiological literature has convinced me that such a mode of locomotion would be no more likely to result in an increased body temperature than would any other activity of comparable energetic cost. It is also worth mentioning that Schmitt and colleagues[91,92] have gathered force-plate and accelerometer data showing that the energetic disadvantage of bent-hip, bent-knee walking might be compensated for by an advantage in terms of joint-force reduction.

Some interesting functional analyses relating to vertebral morphology have been published in the last few years. Abitbol[93] argued that if Lucy had walked in the completely upright manner of a modern human, the superior surface of her sacrum would have been inclined only 20° from vertical as compared to an average of 60° in modern humans. Such a near-vertical superior sacral surface would require a truly extraordinary amount of lumbar lordosis to bring the trunk upright, and would place Lucy at great risk of spondylolisthesis. Abitbol suggested that Lucy would have walked either with her pelvis tilted backward or her trunk tilted forward, or a combination of both. Sanders[94] has recently published a functional analysis of two *A. afarensis* lumbar vertebrae (both probably L3) and the superior articular facets of Lucy's sacrum. One of the *A. afarensis* lumbar vertebrae is dorsally wedged, indicating lumbar lordosis; the other is not. The superior articular facets of the sacrum are relatively widely spaced, as in humans, and are relatively large, even larger than those of humans. Maybe such traits reflect a need to resist a relatively greater tendency toward spondylolisthesis.

Some fascinating new data on bony development in primates are quite relevant to an interpretation of *A. afarensis* locomotion. Responding to the notion that the curved fingers of *A. afarensis* might be primitive retentions that tell us little about actual use of the hand,[95] Paciulli[96] and Richmond[97,98] demonstrated a correlation between ontogenetic changes in phalangeal curvature and those in locomotor behavior for macaques, gibbons, chimpanzees, and gorillas. Richmond[98] concluded that "The sensitivity of phalangeal curvature to functional use in extant primates suggests that it faithfully reflects arboreal use in early hominids."

A second developmental study, this one on the distal femoral epiphysis of humans and apes, was undertaken by Christine Tardieu, no stranger to the debate on *A. afarensis* locomotion. Some of what she discovered runs counter to her own stated views. Tardieu observed that in juvenile humans the opposing surfaces of the distal femoral metaphysis and epiphysis are nearly flat, whereas in young apes these surfaces are characterized by interdigitating grooves and ridges. With respect to both characteristics, the immature Hadar femora match the human condition. Tardieu and Preuschoft[99] have interpreted the pongid state as being necessary for stabilization of the epiphysis during arboreal activities. If this is true, it is potent evidence against the practice of such activities by juvenile *A. afarensis*.

Tardieu[100] has also shown that the bony distal femoral epiphyses of human children between the ages of 10 and 12 years bear remarkable resemblances to the adult distal femora from Hadar in that they are mediolaterally wide, lack a pronounced lateral lip of the patellar groove, and have an almost circular lateral condyle. While Tardieu found no contradiction between these results and her longstanding view that *A. afarensis* was only a facultative biped, I consider the similarity in shape between the distal femur of a juvenile human and that of *A. afarensis* to be profoundly significant. If the shape of a juvenile distal femur is accurately reflected by its bony epiphysis, Tardieu has demonstrated that traits both she and I thought were essential for human-like bipedality are not so; they are absent in young humans, who are quite expert bipeds. This may indeed turn out to be the case, but in a more recent study Tardieu[101] has found that the cartilaginous distal femur of human fetuses is, in some cases, more similar in shape to that of an adult than are the juvenile bony epiphyses on which she previously reported. She recognizes the necessity of acquiring a growth series of cartilaginous epiphyses in order to resolve this issue.

New Fossils

Since our initial publications on *A. afarensis* locomotion, not only has additional postcranial material of this species been described, but there have been discoveries of other species, older, contemporaneous, and younger, that bear on the probability that *A. afarensis* was a partly arboreal, funny-walking biped.

Ardipithecus ramidus. The oldest of the australopithecines is *Ardipithecus ramidus*, dated to ~4.4 Myr. The first description of this species referred to portions of the humerus, radius, and ulna of a single individual.[102] The very preliminary description of these bones mainly served to convince me that the ulna lacked any features associated with knuckle-walking. Many people who are interested in the origins of bipedalism are keenly awaiting a more detailed presentation of the *A. ramidus* material. Meanwhile, we must content ourselves with a statement attributed to Tim White: "Let's just say *ramidus* had a type of locomotion unlike anything living today. If you want to find something that walked like it did, you might try the bar in Star Wars."[103]

Australopithecus anamensis. In 1994, Leakey and coworkers[104] combined ~4.1-Myr-old specimens from

Kanapoi and Allia Bay, Kenya, to create the new australopithecine species, *A. anamensis*. The evidence that *A. anamensis* was bipedal is provided by certain features of proximal and distal ends of a tibia that is larger than any found at Hadar: the articular surface of the lateral condyle is concave, the lateral condyle is nearly as large as the medial condyle, and the lateral facet of the distal articular surface faces inferiorly. Leakey and colleagues pointed out that the Kanapoi humerus, known for many years, has often been seen as human-like. They did not mention that Feldesman's multivariate analysis[17] found it to be further removed from that of *Homo* than are the humeri of living apes, or that Hill and Ward[105] had found its morphology to be consonant with the general pattern in *Australopithecus*. A recent multivariate study by Lague and Jungers[106] also concluded that the Kanapoi humerus "is not much more 'human-like' than any of the other australopithecine fossils, despite prior conclusions to the contrary." Indeed, it clustered with the Hadar specimens in a group that was unique among hominoids but was somewhat more chimp-like than human-like.

Another postcranial specimen from Allia Bay is a large radius that was described prior to the naming of *A. anamensis* but now is attributed to it. Heinrich and colleagues[107] portrayed this specimen as a larger version of Lucy's radius. Its ape-like traits, including an eccentrically placed proximal articular fovea associated with a beveled margin of the radial head, a long radial neck, and a well-developed crest for insertion of the brachioradialis, were interpreted as being well-suited to arboreal activity. The specimen also shared some human-like traits with A.L. 288-1: a robust radial neck, a relatively straight shaft, and a dorsally convex and ventrally concave distal shaft. The large lunate facet on the distal articular surface, and curvatures of this surface, are similar to features of the radii of Asian apes and, according to Heinrich and coworkers,[107] are also similar to the A.L. 288-1 radius. These characteristics were said to enhance flexibility in climbing.

More recent postcranial finds attributed to *A. anamensis* are a capitate and proximal manual phalanx from Allia Bay.[108] They also come from individuals comparable in size to, or larger than, the biggest Hadar individuals. The capitate is even more apelike than that of *A. afarensis* in that it has a facet for the second metacarpal that faces directly laterally, as opposed to distolaterally. The proximal phalanx from the hand is said to have the same degree of curvature and strong markings for the fibrous digital flexor sheath as do the manual proximal phalanges from Hadar.

More of *A. afarensis*. In 1993, White and coworkers[109] described a ~3.4-Myr-old humerus from the Maka site in Ethiopia. They ascribed it to an adult *A. afarensis* male. It is very robust, has a large deltoid tuberosity, an extremely well-developed supracondylar ridge, and human-like retroflexion. White and colleagues inferred that *A. afarensis* "retained a powerful upper limb, but an upper limb that lacked the key arboreal adaptation of great length." Jungers[110] replied with evidence that humans cannot be distinguished from African apes with

regard to humerus length relative to body mass. White[111] then said that Jungers should have included orangutans and gibbons in his comparison, and that every other aspect of *A. afarensis* anatomy shows that it was not at home in the trees, so who cares about its humeral length.

Kimbel and coworkers[112] reported on further discoveries at Hadar: a partial upper limb skeleton including a complete left ulna, dated at ~3.0 Myr, and a humeral shaft dated at ~3.4 Myr. Both specimens were considered to be from males. The ulna lacks any trait that could be construed as adaptive for knuckle-walking, and in this regard resembles human ulnae. The humerus is similar in all regards to that from Maka. The authors used these specimens to estimate the ulna-length/humerus-length index for an *A. afarensis* male (~91%) and compared to this index that of Lucy (~92.5%). They noted that the resulting values are distinctly closer to those of chimpanzees ($\bar{x} = 95\%$) than to those of modern humans ($\bar{x} = 80\%$). This seems to provide convincing evidence that the upper limbs of *A. afarensis* were relatively much longer than those of humans.

Ward and coworkers[113] recently described a capitate, hamate, lunate, the distal end of a metacarpal, and the proximal end of a proximal pedal phalanx from a single individual (KNM-WT 22944) found at the ~3.5 Myr old South Turkwel site in Kenya. On the whole, the morphologies of these specimens were said to be very similar, but not identical, to those of *A. afarensis* from Hadar. The authors found no reason to assign them to a different species. Some aspects of the carpal bones are ape-like, others are human-like. The distal metacarpal is said to be most similar to a human third metacarpal. The hamate has a massive hamulus, even larger than that of the Hadar hamate. This feature was said to indicate a large transverse carpal ligament, a deep carpal tunnel, and/or a strong flexor carpi ulnaris. However, because Neandertals also have large hamate hamuli, readers are warned against concluding that powerful forearm musculature is indicative of a climbing adaptation. The distal projection of the hamulus was said to suggest that its flexor carpi ulnaris was functionally more like that of extant apes than that of humans. Ward and associates conclude that there are no obvious indicators in the South Turkwel hand of specialized adaptations for climbing or suspension. They described the proximal part of the South Turkwel pedal phalanx as having an articular surface for the metatarsal that faces somewhat dorsally, making it resemble that of humans more closely than that of great apes. According to Leakey and coworkers,[108] "The dorsally-oriented metacarpal facet on the pedal phalanx of KNM-WT 22944 suggests that this individual was adapted for habitual bipedal locomotion."

South African *Australopithecus sp.* From Sterkfontein Member 2 (~3.5 Myr) come the four bones that comprise "Little Foot."[114] Clarke and Tobias described the talus and the tuberosity of the navicular as quite human-like. On the other hand, the navicular facets for the cuneiforms were said to be oriented as in apes, suggesting an abducted forefoot, and the medial cuneiform was said, in most respects, to be like that of an ape, forming a joint with the first metatarsal. That suggests a wide range of movement and a naturally abducted position of the hallux. The authors conclude that "It is becoming clear that *Australopithecus* was likely not an obligate terrestrial biped, but rather a facultative biped and climber." My joy at this discovery and its interpretation has been considerably lessened by, of all people, Randy Susman. He recently saw the original specimen and found the hallucal tarsometatarsal joint to be less ape-like than he had anticipated.

Australopithecus africanus. Berger and Tobias[115] have reported on proximal and distal tibial fragments from Sterkfontein Member 4 (~2.7 Myr). They describe the articular surface of the lateral tibial condyle as being extremely convex, and thus ape-like. A further resemblance to apes, and also to the Hadar proximal tibia, is the indication that the lateral meniscus had a single site of attachment anterior to the external tibial spine. Berger and Tobias also described ape-like attachment areas of the semimembranosus and tibialis posterior. While little of functional significance could be gleaned from the distal tibial fragment, its articular

surface appears to have a posterior tilt and thereby is allied to those of living apes and Lucy. In summary, the authors found these specimens to be the most ape-like of any Plio-Pleistocene hominid tibia and, indeed, even more ape-like than the tibia of *A. afarensis.*

McHenry and Berger[116] analyzed new finds from Sterkfontein Member 4 using an approach similar to that used by Oxnard[117] to study previously known material from South Africa. After assigning all the postcranial specimens to size categories, the authors found that 95% of those representing the upper limb were classified as medium or large, while 90% of those from the lower limb were classified as small. This strong indication that *A. africanus* was characterized by distinctly ape-like interlimb proportions was supported by an analysis of the Stw 431 associated material, which showed that the size of its elbow joint surfaces relative to the S1 body or acetabulum were comparable to those of apes and much larger than those of humans. Similar analyses on *A. afarensis* showed its intermediate position between apes and humans. McHenry and Berger also noted that the two associated skeletons attributed to *H. habilis* seem to have the same more ape-like interlimb proportions that characterize *A. africanus.* These authors conclude that because *A. afarensis* is craniodentally primitive as

Figure 4.   *A depiction of* Australopithecus *making a life for itself on the African savanna. This was the commonly accepted view in the early 1970s. Illustration adapted from* Emergence of Man: The Missing Link © *1972 Time-Life Books, Inc. All Rights Reserved.*

compared to both *A. africanus* and *H. habilis,* whereas its limb proportions are more human-like, the place of all these skecies in the human lineage is confused by extensive homoplasy. To me, their results also show that previous portrayals of *A. africanus* as having a fully human-like locomotor repertoire[118–120] should be viewed with the skepticism shown by Oxnard.[113,121–123]

Spoor and colleagues[124–126] offered a very different approach to understanding *A. africanus* locomotor behavior. They demonstrated that the posterior and anterior semicircular canals of humans are relatively larger than those of apes, whereas the lateral semicircular canal of humans is relatively smaller. Arguing that large vertical canals are probably an adaptation to human-like obligatory bipedalism, and finding that the three canals of *A. africanus* are of the same relative dimensions as those of apes, they concluded that this early hominid was probably a facultative biped, combining arboreal activities with a form of terrestrial bipedalism that lacked such complex movements as running and jumping.

Bouri Hata Hominids. Craniodental specimens assigned to the new taxon *A. garhi*[127] have been recovered from several different areas of the ~2.5 Myr old Hata beds, Bouri Formation, in the Ethiopian Middle Awash. In the same beds were found shafts of various long bones and a proximal pedal phalanx. Although the postcranial elements could not be conclusively assigned to *A. garhi,* they still are valuable indicators of hominid locomotor anatomy during this period. A number of the limb bone shafts are thought to come from a single individual and to enable calculation of reasonably accurate limb length proportions. Such calculations indicate that Bouri Hata hominids were distinguished from *A. afarensis* by relative femoral elongation resulting in a human-like humerofemoral index. On the other hand, they are said to share with *A. afarensis* a high brachial index. The Bouri Hata proximal pedal phalanx is said to be similar to that of *A. afarensis* in curvature.

Homo (Australopithecus?) habilis. As the debate about the locomotor anatomy of *A. afarensis* was unfolding, Johanson and coworkers[128] published their discovery of the ~1.8-Myr-old O.H. 62 partial skeleton from Olduvai Gorge, attributing it to *Homo habilis* based on craniodental evidence. The associated bits and pieces of its humerus, radius, ulna, femur, and tibia were said to be very similar to Lucy's, with one notable exception: the humerofemoral index of O.H. 62 was estimated at ≥ 95 as compared to values of 85 for Lucy, 74 for human pygmies, and 98 for bonobos.[21] Korey[129] pointed out that the error associated with calculating a humerofemoral index from the reconstructed lengths of the O.H. 62 limb bones is so great that one cannot justifiably assert either that it was significantly greater than in Lucy or significantly less than in a common chimpanzee ($\bar{x} = 102$). Asfaw and colleagues[127] claim that any statement that the humerofemoral index is more primitive in O.H. 62 than in

Lucy is erroneous because the length of the O.H. 62 femur cannot be accurately estimated. However, Hartwig-Scherer and Martin,[130] using a variety of other measurements on limb bones, confirmed that inter-limb proportions of O.H. 62 are far more pongid-like than are those of *A. afarensis.*

Emanating from East Lake Turkana and dated at ~1.9 Myr is the KNM-ER 3735 specimen comprising parts of the skull and of both the upper and lower limbs.[131] The postcranial material is in poor condition, but those measurements that could be taken indicate an upper limb that was much bigger than the lower limb, nearly to the degree found in a chimpanzee. Features of the distal humerus and proximal radius indicate climbing abilities as marked as in *Pan.* Phalangeal fragments were said to belong to a hand capable of extremely powerful flexion. Leakey and colleagues did not definitively assign the specimen to a known species, but considered the possibility that it might be a male *H. habilis.* Clearly, they were uncomfortable with the idea that a creature of this anatomy could evolve into *H. erectus* during the 200 Kyr time span available.

If the O.H. 62 and KNM-ER 3735 partial skeletons are indeed attributable to *Homo,* they present a picture of locomotor anatomy that differs markedly from that of all others members of our genus. This was a major consideration in Wood and Collard's[132] decision to transfer *Homo habilis* to *Australopithecus habilis.* One is then tempted to view *A. habilis* as a more craniodentally advanced descendent of something like *A. africanus.*

Were the Hominids Predating *A. afarensis* Less Well Adapted to Terrestrial Bipedalism Than Were Lucy and Her Hadar Relatives?

The postcranial material of *A. ramidus* has not been described in sufficient detail for any conclusion to be reached about its locomotion. The tibia of *A. anamensis* seems very much like that of *A. afarensis,* suggesting a no more primitive kind of bipedalism. The upper limb material, while pointing to an arboreal adaptation, also seems to be little different from that of *A. afarensis.*

Do New Finds of *A. afarensis* or The Contemporaneous Sterkfontein Member 2 *Australopithecus Sp.* Reveal Anything New About the Locomotion of 3.0–3.5 Myr Old Hominids?

New finds of *A. afarensis,* largely because they show great humeral robusticity and long forearms, add support to any suggestion that it possessed an adaptively significant component of arboreality. The analysis of "Little Foot" by its discoverers led them to claim it came from a creature with a grasping hallux. My colleague Randy Susman doubts it is more apelike than the hallux of *A. afarensis,* which we and others have stated possessed a modicum of mobility.

What Do Younger Australopithecines Tell Us About *A. afarensis* Locomotion?

Perhaps the most interesting new insights into early hominid locomotion come from discoveries of material that postdate *A. afarensis*. By virtue of having an elongated lower limb, the ~2.5-Myr-old Bouri Hata hominid appears further advanced toward the evolution of human-like bipedalism than was *A. afarensis*. It remains to be determined whether its relatively long forearm is a functionally irrelevant retention of a primitive trait or signifies that adaptively significant arboreal behavior coexisted with relatively advanced bipedalism, as we proposed for *H. habilis*.[133] On the other hand, despite possessing rather obvious osteologic signs of terrestrial bipedalism, *A. africanus* and *A. habilis* seem more arboreally adapted than *A. afarensis*. Implied in the reclassification of *H. habilis* to *Australopithecus*,[127] and in the suggestion that *A. garhi* might be the ancestor of true early *Homo*,[110] is the possibility that among the descendants of *A. afarensis* is one species (*garhi*) that was evolving toward a more human-like locomotor adaptation and another (*africanus* → *habilis*) that was evolving away from one. But what is the likelihood of this scenario if *A. afarensis* itself was a fully terrestrial human-like biped?

CONCLUSION

In 1986, after the first wave of papers on *A. afarensis* locomotion had appeared, Henry McHenry[134] acknowledged that he could no longer hold to his decade-long belief that all the primitive characters of australopithecine postcranial anatomy were simply evolutionary baggage that had little to do with locomotion: "The Hadar postcranial material sample of *A. afarensis* make this hypothesis much less likely." In 1991, after the second wave of analyses appeared, McHenry[135] had not changed his mind: "The host of 'ape-like' traits seen in these early hominids probably implies that their bipedalism was kinematically and energetically different than modern humans and may imply that they were more efficient tree-climbers than are modern humans. This arborealism was different from ape-like tree climbing, however, because the hindlimb was specialized for bipedality. . . ." Now, 25 years after Lucy's discovery, it remains my opinion that nothing has been discovered, no criticism offered, nor any analysis published that should cause rejection of McHenry's conclusions. Indeed, the majority of new information that has come to light points even more firmly to them.

In 1972, Time-Life Books portrayed *Australopithecus* as a human-like biped making a life for itself on the savanna of Africa (Figure 4). Three years ago, National Geographic portrayed the very same creature feeding high in the trees of the dense forest (Figure 5). While pictures in the popular press do not constitute evidence, they do reflect the fact that ever-increasing numbers of anthropologists are accepting arboreal behavior as an adaptively significant component of early australopithecine behavior.

Figure 5. *A depiction of* Australopithecus *making a life for itself in trees of the dense forest. This drawing, by Richard Schlecht, was published in the February 1997 issue of National Geographic Magazine as part of an article entitled The Dawn of Humans, The First Steps (Gore, R). Clearly, at least in popular depictions, the pendulum has swung regarding the importance of arboreality in the behavior of* Australopithecus.

I was never as certain about the nature of *A. afarensis* bipedalism as I was about its retained adaptations for movement in the trees. I am no more or less certain now. Whereas we suggested a form of bipedalism with less extension at the hip and knee than is characteristic of modern humans, others have proposed differences concerning axial rotation of the pelvis or lateral flexion of the trunk. Moreover, a significant number of people still hold to the view that early australopithecine bipedalism was fully human-like. I have often felt there is a bias in favor of viewing early hominid bipedalism as characterized by completely extended lower limbs because it is difficult for modern humans to walk with bent knees and hips. It seems inconceivable that such a manner of progression could last for more than the briefest of geologic times before evolving into our superior way of doing things. Returning to my simplistic analogy to cetacean evolution, I think if we were whales we would have great difficulty understanding how an ancestor could survive a million years while being such a poor swimmer. I have tried to overcome this bias. Along with others, I believe the bipedal adaptation first arose to improve access to food sources close to the ground, movement between such sources, or both.[30,52,89,90] Bipedalism probably persisted in this nascent but effective state for a million years, with no indication that it would be anything other than an evolutionary sidelight. Only later did some unknown event impel one of the creatures with this adaptation to abandon the trees more completely than any of its predecessors had done and become a tool-making hunter or tuber-gatherer.

This memoir is at its end. The siren calls of electrodes, strain gauges, and force plates beckon. For out of obscurity was I taken, and unto obscurity shall I return, at least until the *ramidus* material is made generally available and Randy walks into my office to proclaim that we are as well qualified as anyone to perform its comprehensive functional analysis.

ACKNOWLEDGMENTS

I am very grateful to Brigitte Demes, William Jungers, Susan Larson, and Randall Susman for their helpful comments on early versions of this paper. I am equally grateful to Henry McHenry, Bernard Wood, Richard Klein, Clark Howell, and one anonymous reviewer for comments made on the first submitted version of the manuscript. I thank Luci Betti-Nash for preparation of the illustrations. The research I and my Stony Brook colleagues conducted on the origins of hominid bipedalism has been supported by the National Science Foundation, most recently, by NSF Research Grant SBR9806291.

REFERENCES

1. Taieb, M., Johanson, D. C., Coppens, Y., Bonnefille, R., Kalb, J. 1974. Découverte d'hominidés dans les séries Plio-Pléistocènes d'Hadar (Bassin de l'Awash; Afar, Éthiopie). CR Acad Sci Paris, Sér D, 279:735–738.

2. Taieb, M., Johanson, D. C., Coppens, Y. 1975. Expédition internationale de l'Afar, Éthiopie (3ᵉ campagne 1974); Découverte d'hominidés dans les séries Plio-Pléistocènes a Hadar. CR Acad Sci Paris, Sér D, 281:1297–1300.

3. Johanson, D. C., Lovejoy, C. O., Burstein, A. H., Heiple, K. G. 1976. Functional implications of the Afar knee joint. Am J Phys Anthropol 44:188.

4. Christie, P. W. 1977. Form and function of the Afar ankle. Am J Phys Anthropol 47:123.

5. Lovejoy, C. O. 1979. A reconstruction of the pelvis of AL 288 (Hadar Formation, Ethiopia). Am J Phys Anthropol 50:460.

6. Leakey, M. D., Hay, R. L. 1979. Pliocene footprints in the Laetoli Beds at Laetoli, northern Tanzania. Nature 278:317–323.

7. Lovejoy, C. O. 1980. Hominid origins: the role of bipedalism. Am J Phys Anthropol 52:250.

8. White, T. D. 1980. Evolutionary implications of Pliocene hominid footprints. Science 208:175–176.

9. Day, M. H., Wickens, E. H. 1980. Laetoli Pliocene hominid footprints and bipedalism. Nature 286:385–387.

10. Senut, B. 1978. Etude comparative des piliers de la palette humerale. Cahiers d'Anthropol (Paris) n° 3:1–8.

11. Senut, B. 1980. New data on the humerus and its joints in Plio-Pleistocene hominids. Coll Anthropol 4:87–94.

12. Tardieu, C. 1979. Analyse morpho-fonctionelle de l'articulation de genou chez les primates. Application aux hominides fossiles. Theses, Universite Pierre et Marie Curie, Paris IV.

13. Tardieu, C. 1979. Aspects bioméchaniques de l'articulation du genou chez les Primates. Bull Soc Anat Paris n° 4:66–86.

14. Tuttle, R. H. 1981. Evolution of hominid bipedalism and prehensile capabilities. Proc Trans R Soc Lond B 292:89–94.

15. Johanson, D. C., Edey, M. A. 1981. Lucy, the beginnings of humankind. New York: Simon & Schuster.

16. Jungers, W. L. 1982. Lucy's limbs: skeletal allometry and locomotion in *Australopithecus afarensis*. Nature 297:676–678.

17. Feldesman, M. R. 1982. Morphometric analysis of the distal humerus of some Cenozoic catarrhines: the Late Divergence hypothesis revisited. Am J Phys Anthropol 59:73–95.

18. Stern, J. T. Jr., Susman, R. L. 1983. The locomotor anatomy of *Australopithecus afarensis*. Am J Phys Anthropol 60:279–317.

19. Sarmiento, E. E. 1987. Long bone torsions of the lower limb and its bearing upon the locomotor behavior of australopithecines. Am J Phys Anthropol 72:250.

20. Sarmiento, E. E. 1996. Quadrupedalism in the hominid lineage: 11 years after. Am J Phys Anthropol Suppl 22:208.

21. Jungers, W. L., Stern, J. T. Jr. 1983. Body proportions, skeletal allometry and locomotion in the Hadar hominids: a reply to Wolpoff. J Hum Evol 12:673–684.

22. Susman, R. L., Stern, J. T. Jr., Jungers, W. L. 1984. Arboreality and bipedality in the Hadar hominids. Folia Primatol 43:113–156.

23. Stern, J. T. Jr., Susman, R. L. 1991. In: Coppens, Y., Senut, B., editors. Origine(s) de la bipédie chez les hominidés. Paris: CNRS, p 99–111.

24. Stern, J. T. Jr., Larson, S. G. 1993. Electromyographic study of the obturator muscles in nonhuman primates: implications for interpreting the obturator externus groove of the femur. J Hum Evol 24:403–427.

25. Jungers, W. L. 1991. A pygmy perspective on body size and shape in *Australopithecus afarensis* (AL 288-1, "Lucy"). In: Coppens, Y., Senut, B., editors. Origine(s) de la bipédie chez les hominidés. Paris: CNRS, p 215–224.

26. Stern, J. T. Jr., Susman, R. L. 1981. Electromyography of the gluteal muscles in *Hylobates, Pongo,* and *Pan:* implications for the evolution of hominid bipedality. Am J Phys Anthropol 55:153–166.

27. Susman, R. L., Demes, A. B. 1994. Relative foot length in *Australopithecus afarensis* and its implications for bipedality. Am J Phys Anthropol Suppl 18:192.

28. Marzke, M. W. 1983. Joint functions and grips of the *Australopithecus afarensis* hand, with special reference to the region of the capitate. J Hum Evol 12:197–211.

29. McHenry, H. M. 1983. The capitate of *Australopithecus afarensis* and *A. africanus*. Am J Phys Anthropol 62:187–198.

30. Rose, M. D. 1984. Food acquisition and the evolution of positional behaviour: the case of bipedalism. In: Chivers, D. J., Wood, B. A., Bilsborough, A., editors. Food acquisition and processing in primates. New York: Plenum Press. p 509–524.

31. Schmid, P. 1983. Eine Rekonstruktion des Skelettes von A.L. 288-1 (Hadar) und deren Konsequenzen. Folia Primatol 40:283–306.

32. Deloison, Y. 1985. Comparative study of calcanei of primates and *Pan-Australopithecus-Homo* relationship. In: Tobias, P. V., editor. Hominid evolution: past, present and future. New York: Alan, R. Liss. p 143–147.

33. Wolpoff, M. H. 1983. Lucy's lower limbs: long enough for Lucy to be fully bipedal? Nature 304:59–61.

34. Wolpoff, M. H. 1983. Lucy's little legs. J Hum Evol 12:443–453.

35. Berge, C., Ponge, J-F. 1983. Les characteristiques du bassin des australopitheques (*A. robustus, A. africanus* et *A. afarensis*), sont-elles liees a une bipedie de type humain? Bull Mem Soc Anthropol Paris, ser XIII, 10:335–354.

36. Berge, C. 1984. Multivariate analysis of the pelvis for hominids and other extant primates: implications for the locomotion and systematics of the different species of australopithecines. J Hum Evol 13:555–562.

37. Berge, C., Kazmierczak, J-B. 1986. Effects of size and locomotor adaptations on the hominid pelvis: evaluation of australopithecine bipedality with a new multivariate method. Folia Primatol 46:185–204.

38. Tardieu, C. 1983. L'articulation du genou, analyse morpho-fonctionelle chez les primates et les hominidés fossiles. Paris: CNRS.

39. Tardieu, C. 1986. The knee joint in three primates: application to Plio-Pleistocene hominids and evolutionary implications. In: Taub, D. M., King, F. A., editors. Current perspectives in primate biology. New York: Van Nostrand. p 182–192.

40. Tardieu, C. 1986. Evolution of the knee intraarticular menisci in primates and some fossil hominids. In: Else, J. G., Lee, P. C., editors. Primate evolution, vol. 1. Cambridge: Cambridge University Press. p 183–190.

41. Latimer, B. 1983. The anterior foot skeleton of *Australopithecus afarensis*. Am J Phys Anthropol 60:217.

42. Gomberg, D. N., Latimer, B. 1984. Observations on the transverse tarsal joint of *A. afarensis,* and some comments on the interpretation of behaviour from morphology. Am J Phys Anthropol 63:164.

43. Ohman, J. C. 1986. The first rib of hominoids. Am J Phys Anthropol 70:209–229.

44. Latimer, B., Ohman, J. C., Lovejoy, C. O. 1987. Talocrural joint in African hominoids: implications for *Australopithecus afarensis*. Am J Phys Anthropol 74:155–175.

45. White, T. D., Suwa, G. 1987. Hominid footprints at Laetoli: facts and interpretations. Am J Phys Anthropol 72:485–514.

46. Lovejoy, C. O. 1988. Evolution of human walking. Sci Am 259:118–125.

47. Latimer, B., Lovejoy, C. O. 1989. The calcaneus of *Australopithecus afarensis* and its implications for the evolution of bipedality. Am J Phys Anthropol 78:369–386.

48. Latimer, B., Lovejoy, C. O. 1990. Hallucal tarsometatarsal joint in *Australopithecus afarensis*. Am J Phys Anthropol 82:125–133.

49. Latimer, B., Lovejoy, C. O. 1990. Metatarsophalangeal joints of *Australopithecus afarensis*. Am J Phys Anthropol 83:13–23.

50. Latimer, B. 1991. Locomotor adaptations in *Australopithecus afarensis:* the issue of arboreality. In: Coppens, Y., Senut, B., editors. Origine(s) de la bipédie chez les hominidés. Paris: CNRS, p 169–176.

51. Thewissen, J. G. M., Hussain, S. T., Arif, M. 1994. Fossil evidence for the origin of aquatic locomotion in archaeocete whales. Science 263:210–212.

52. Rose, M. D. 1991. The process of bipedalization in hominids. In: Coppens, Y., Senut, B., editors. Origine(s) de la bipédie chez les hominidés. Paris: CNRS, p 37–48.

53. Duncan, A. S., Kappelman, J., Shapiro, L. J. 1994. Metatarsophalangeal joint function and positional behavior in *Australopithecus afarensis*. Am J Phys Anthropol 93:67–81.

54. Coffing, K. E. 1999. Paradigms and definitions in early hominid locomotion research. Am J Phys Anthropol Suppl 28:109–110.

55. Mensforth, R. P., Latimer, B., Senturia, S. 1990. A review of the functional significance of the AL-288 axilloglenoid angle. Am J Phys Anthropol 81:267–268.

56. Inouye, S. E., Shea, B. T. 1997. What's your angle? size correction and bar-glenoid orientation in "Lucy" (A.L. 288-1). Int J Primatol 18:629–650.

57. Asfaw, B. 1985. Proximal femur articulation in Pliocene hominids. Am J Phys Anthropol 68:535–538.

58. MacLatchy, L. M. 1996. Another look at the australopithecine hip. J Hum Evol 31:455–476.

59. Tuttle, R. H. 1985. Ape footprints and Laetoli impressions: a response to the SUNY claims. In: Tobias, P. V., editor. Hominid evolution: past, present and future. New York: Alan R. Liss. p 129–133.

60. Elftman, H., Manter, J. 1935. Chimpanzee and human feet in bipedal walking. Am J Phys Anthropol 20:269 –279.

61. Deloison, Y. 1992. Empreintes de pas à Laetoli (Tanzanie). Leur apport à une meilleure connaissance de la locomotion des Hominidés fossiles.CR Acad Sci Paris, Sér II, 315:103–109.

62. Garn, S. M., Hertzog, K. P., Poznanski, A. K., Nagy, J. M. 1972. Metacarpophalangeal length in the evaluation of skeletal malformation. Radiology 105:375–381.

63. Deloison, Y. 1991. Les australopitheques marchaient-ils comme nous? In: Coppens, Y., Senut, B., editors. Origine(s) de la bipédie chez les hominidés. Paris: CNRS, p 177–186.

64. Kramer, P. A. 1999. Modelling the locomotor energetics of extinct hominids. J Exp Biol 202:2807–2818.

65. Crompton, R. H., Li, Y., Wang, W., Günther, M., Savage, R. 1998. The mechanical effectiveness of erect and "bent-hip, bent knee" bipedal walking in *Australopithecus afarensis*. J Hum Evol 35:55–74.

66. Stern, J. T. Jr., Jungers, W. L. 1990. The capitular joint of the first rib in primates: a re-evaluation of the proposed link to locomotion. Am J Phys Anthropol 82:431–439.

67. Schmid, P. 1991. The trunk of the australopithecines. In: Coppens, Y., Senut, B., editors. Origine(s) de la bipédie chez les hominidés. Paris: CNRS, p 225–234.

68. Johanson, D. C., Lovejoy, C. O., Kimbel, W. H., White, T. D., Ward, S. C., Bush, M. E., Latimer, B. M., Coppens, Y. 1982. Morphology of the Pliocene partial hominid skeleton (A.L. 288-1) from the Hadar Formation, Ethiopia. Am J Phys Anthropol 57:403–451.

69. Ruff, C. 1998. Evolution of the hominid hip. In: Strasser, E., Fleagle, J., Rosenberger, A., McHenry, H., editors. Primate locomotion, recent advances. New York: Plenum Press, p 449–469.

70. Susman, R. L., Stern, J. T. Jr. 1991. Locomotor behavior of early hominids: epistemology and fossil evidence. In: Coppens, Y., Senut, B., editors. Origine(s) de la bipédie chez les hominidés. Paris: CNRS, p 121–131.

71. Latimer, B. M., Lovejoy, C. O., Johanson, D. C., Coppens, Y. 1982. Hominid tarsal, metatarsal, and phalangeal bones recovered from the Hadar Formation: 1974–1977 collections. Am J Phys Anthropol 57:701–719.

72. Deloison, Y. 1992. Articulation cunéométatarsienne de l'hallux considérée comme un des éléments déterminants de la forme de locomotion à partir de son anatomie osseuse. Comparison entre l'australopitheque, l'homme et le chimpanzé. CR Acad Sci Paris, Sér II, 314:1379–1385.

73. Pauwels, F. 1958. Funktionnelle Anpassung durch Langenwachstum des Knochens. Verh Dtsch Orthop Ges, 45. Vers, p 34–56.

74. Ohman, J. C., Krochta, T. J., Lovejoy, C. O., Mensforth, R. P., Latimer, B. 1997. Cortical bone distribution in the femoral neck of hominoids: implications for the locomotion of *Australopithecus afarensis*. Am J Phys Anthropol 104:117–131.

75. Rafferty, K. L. 1998. Structural design of the femoral neck in primates. J Hum Evol 34:361–383.

76. Howard, C. B., Williams, L. A. 1984. A new radiological sign in the hips of cerebral palsy patients. Clin Radiol 35:317–319.

77. Rak, Y. 1991. Lucy's pelvic anatomy: its role in bipedal gait. J Hum Evol 20:283–290.

78. Inman, V. T., Ralston, H. J., Todd, F. 1981. Human walking. Baltimore: Williams Wilkins.

79. Zarrugh, M. Y., Radcliffe, C. W. 1978. Predicting metabolic cost of level walking. Eur J Appl Physiol 38:215–223.

80. Holt, K. G., Hamill, J., Andres, R. O. 1991. Predicting the minimal energy costs of human walking. Med Sci Sports Exerc 23:491–498.

81. Berge, C. 1991. Quelle est la signification fonctionelle du pelvis très large de *Australopithecus afarensis* (AL 288-1)? In: Coppens, Y., Senut, B., editors. Origine(s) de la bipédie chez les hominidés. Paris: CNRS, p 113–119.

82. Berge, C. 1993. L'évolution de la hanche et du pelvis des hominidés. Paris: CNRS.

83. Berge, C. 1994. How did the australopithecines walk? A biomechanical study of the hip and thigh of *Australopithecus afarensis*. J Hum Evol 26:259–273.

84. Murray, M. P., Gore, D. R., Clarkson, B. H. 1971. Walking patterns of patients with unilateral hip pain due to osteo-arthritis and avascular necrosis. J Bone Jt Surg 53A:259–273.

85. Murray, M. P., Gore, D. R. 1981. Gait of patients with hip pain or loss of hip joint motion. In: Black, J., Dumbleton, J. H., editors. Clinical biomechanics. A case history approach. New York: Churchill Livingstone, p 173–200.

86. Tardieu, C. 1992. Le centre de gravité du corps et sa trajetoire pendant la marche. Évolution de la locomotion des hommes fossiles. Paris: CNRS.

87. Ruff, C. B., McHenry, H. M., Thackery, J. F. 1999. Cross-sectional morphology of the SK 82 and 97 proximal femora. Am J Phys Anthropol 109:509–529.

88. Stern, J. T. Jr. 1999. The cost of bent-knee bent-hip bipedal gait. A reply to Crompton et al. J Hum Evol 36:567–570.

89. Hunt, K. D. 1994. The evolution of human bipedality: ecology and functional morphology. J Hum Evol 26:183–202.

90. Hunt, K. D. 1998. Ecological morphology of *Australopithecus afarensis:* traveling terrestrially, eating arboreally. In: Strasser, E., Fleagle, J., Rosenberger, A., McHenry, H., editors. Primate locomotion: recent advances. New York: Plenum Press, p 397–418.

91. Schmitt, D., Stern, J. T. Jr., Larson, S. G. 1996. Compliant gait in humans: implications for substrate reaction forces during australopithecine bipedalism. Am J Phys Anthropol Suppl 22:209.

92. Schmitt, D., Lemelin, P., Trueblood, A. C. 1999. Shock wave transmission through the human body during normal and compliant walking. Am J Phys Anthropol Suppl 28:243–244.

93. Abitbol, M. M. 1995. Lateral view of *Australopithecus afarensis:* primitive aspects of bipedal positional behavior in the earliest hominids. J Hum Evol 28:211–229.

94. Sanders, W. J. 1998. Comparative morphometric study of the australopithecine vertebral series Stw-H8/H41. J Hum Evol 34:249–302.

95. Gebo, D. L. 1996. Climbing, brachiation, and terrestrial quadrupedalism: historical precursors of hominid bipedalism. Am J Phys Anthropol 101:55–92.

96. Paciulli, L. M. 1995. Ontogeny of phalangeal curvature and positional behavior in chimpanzees. Am J Phys Anthropol Suppl 20:165.

97. Richmond, B. G. 1997. Ontogeny of phalangeal curvature and locomotor behavior in lar gibbons. Am J Phys Anthropol Suppl 24:197.

98. Richmond, B. G. 1999. Reconstructing locomotor behavior in early hominids: evidence from primate development. J Hum Evol 36:A20.

99. Tardieu, C., Preuschoft, H. 1996. Ontogeny of the knee joint in humans, great apes and fossil hominids: pelvi-femoral relationships during postnatal growth in humans. Folia Primatol 66:68–81.

100. Tardieu, C. 1998. Short adolescence in early hominids: infantile and adolescent growth of the human femur. Am J Phys Anthropol 107:163–178.

101. Tardieu, C. 1999. Ontogeny and phylogeny of femoro-tibial characters in humans and hominid fossils: functional influence and genetic determinism. Am J Phys Anthropol 110:365–377.

102. White, T. D., Suwa, G., Asfaw, B. 1994. *Australopithecus ramidus,* a new species of early hominid from Aramis, Ethiopia. Nature 371:306–312.

103. Gore, R. 1997. The first steps. Natl Geogr 191:72–99.

104. Leakey, M. G., Feibel, C. S., McDougall, I., Walker, A. 1995. New four-million-year-old hominid species from Kanapoi and Allia Bay, Kenya. Nature 376:565–571.

105. Hill, A., Ward, S. 1988. Origin of the Hominidae; the record of African large hominoid evolution between 14 My and 4 My. Yearbk Phys Anthropol 31:49–83.

106. Lague, M. R., Jungers, W. L. 1996. Morphometric variation in Plio-Pleistocene hominid distal humeri. Am J Phys Anthropol 101:401–427.

107. Heinrich, R. E., Rose, M. D., Leakey, R. E., Walker, A. C. 1993. Hominid radius from the middle Pliocene of Lake Turkana, Kenya. Am J Phys Anthropol 92:139–148.

108. Leakey, M. G., Feibel, C. S., McDougall, I., Ward, C., Walker, A. 1998. New specimens and confirmation of an early age for *Australopithecus anamensis.* Nature 393:62–66.

109. White, T. D., Suwa, G., Hart, W. K., Walter, R. C., WoldeGabriel, G., de Heinzelin, J., Clark, J. D., Asfaw, B., Vrba, E. 1993. New discoveries of *Australopithecus* at Maka in Ethiopia. Nature 366:261–265.

110. Jungers, W. L. 1994. Ape and hominid limb length. Nature 369:194.

111. White, T. D. 1994. Ape and hominid limb length—White replies. Nature 369:194.

112. Kimbel, W. H., Johanson, D. C., Rak, Y. 1994. The first skull and other new discoveries of *Australopithecus afarensis* at Hadar, Ethiopia. Nature 368:449–451.

113. Ward, C. V., Leakey, M. G., Brown, B., Brown, F., Harris, J., Walker, A. 1999. South Turkwel: a new Pliocene site in Kenya. J Hum Evol 36:69–95.

114. Clarke, R. J., Tobias, P. V. 1995. Sterkfontein Member 2 foot bones of the oldest South African hominid. Science 269:521–524.

115. Berger, L. R., Tobias, P. V. 1996. A chimpanzee-like tibia from Sterkfontein, South Africa and its implications for the interpretation of bipedalism in *Australopithecus africanus.* J Hum Evol 30:343–348.

116. McHenry, H. M., Berger, L. R. 1998. Body proportions in *Australopithecus afarensis* and *A. africanus* and the origin of the genus *Homo.* J Hum Evol 35:1–22.

117. Oxnard, C. E. 1975. Uniqueness and diversity in human evolution: morphometric studies of australopithecines. Chicago: University of Chicago.

118. Lovejoy, C. O., Heiple, K. G., Burstein, A. H. 1973. The gait of *Australopithecus.* Am J Phys Anthropol 38:757–780.

119. Lovejoy, C. O. 1975. Biomechanical perspectives on the lower limb of early hominids. In: Tuttle, R. H., editor. Primate functional morphology and evolution. The Hague: Mouton, p 291–326.

120. Lovejoy, C. O. 1978. A biomechanical review of the locomotor diversity of early hominids. In: Jolly, C. J., editor. Early hominids of Africa. New York: St. Martin's Press, p 403–429.

121. Lisowski, F. P., Albrecht, G. H., Oxnard, C. E. 1974. The form of the talus in some higher primates. Am J Phys Anthropol 41:191–216.

122. Oxnard, C. E., Lisowski, F. P. 1980. Functional articulation of some hominoid foot bones: implications for the Olduvai (Hominid 8) foot. Am J Phys Anthropol 52:107–117.

123. Oxnard, C. E. 1983. The order of man. A biomathematical anatomy of the primates. Hong Kong: Hong Kong University.

124. Spoor, F. 1993. The comparative morphology and phylogeny of the human bony labyrinth. Utrecht: F. Spoor.

125. Spoor, F., Wood, B., Zonneveld, F. 1994. Implications of early hominid labyrinthine morphology for evolution of human bipedal locomotion. Nature 369:645–648.

126. Spoor, F., Wood, B., Zonneveld, F. 1996. Evidence for a link between human semicircular canal size and bipedal behaviour. J Hum Evol 30:183–187.

127. Asfaw, B., White, T. D., Lovejoy, O., Latimer, B., Simpson, S., Suwa, G. 1999. *Australopithecus garhi:* a new species of early hominid from Ethiopia. Science 284:629–634.

128. Johanson, D. C., Masao, F. T., Eck, G. G., White, T. D., Walter, R. C., Kimbel, W. H., Asfaw, B., Manega, P., Ndessokia, P., Suwa, G. 1987. New partial skeleton of *Homo habilis* from Olduvai Gorge, Tanzania. Nature 327:205–209.

129. Korey, K. A. 1990. Deconstructing reconstruction: The OH 62 humerofemoral index. Am J Phys Anthropol 83:25–33.

130. Hartwig-Scherer, S., Martin, R. D. 1991. Was "Lucy" more human than her "child"? Observations on early hominid postcranial skeletons. J Hum Evol 21:439–449.

131. Leakey, R. E., Walker, A. C., Ward, C. V., Grausz, H. M. 1989. A partial skeleton of a gracile hominid from the Upper Burgi Member, of the Koobi Fora Formation, East Lake Turkana, Kenya. In: Giacobini, G., editor. Hominidae: Proceedings of the 2nd International Congress on Human Paleontology, Turin. Milan: Jaca, p 167–173.

132. Wood, B., Collard, M. 1999. The human genus. Science 284:65–71.

133. Susman, R. L., Stern, J. T. Jr. 1982. Functional morphology of *Homo habilis.* Science 217:931–934.

134. McHenry, H. M. 1986. The first bipeds: a comparison of the *A. afarensis* and *A. africanus* postcranium and implications for the evolution of bipedalism. J Hum Evol 15:177–191.

135. McHenry, H. M. 1991. First steps? Analyses of the postcranium of early hominids. In: Coppens, Y., Senut, B., editors. Origine(s) de la bipédie chez les hominidés. Paris: CNRS, p 133–141.

23

Early Hominid Brain Evolution

A New Look at Old Endocasts

D. Falk, J. C. Redmond, Jr., J. Guyer, G. C. Conroy, W. Recheis, G. W. Weber, and H. Seidler

ABSTRACT

Early hominid brain morphology is reassessed from endocasts of Australopithecus africanus *and three species of* Paranthropus, *and new endocast reconstructions and cranial capacities are reported for four key specimens from the* Paranthropus *clade. The brain morphology of* Australopithecus africanus *appears more human-like than that of* Paranthropus *in terms of overall frontal and temporal lobe shape. These new data do not support the proposal that increased encephalization is a shared feature between* Paranthropus *and early* Homo. *Our findings are consistent with the hypothesis that* Australopithecus africanus *could have been ancestral to* Homo, *and have implications for assessing the tempo and mode of early hominid neurological and cognitive evolution.*

INTRODUCTION

Much of what is known about hominid brain evolution has been learned from endocranial casts (endocasts) that reproduce details of the external morphology of the brain from the internal surface of the braincase. Because these endocasts are usually from fragmentary pieces of fossilized skulls, their missing parts must be reconstructed. Discoveries such as KNM-WT 17000 (*P. aethiopicus*) and KNM-WT 17400 (*P. boisei*) (Leakey & Walker, 1988; Walker et al., 1986; Brown et al., 1993) provide evidence of previously unknown parts of the *Paranthropus* brain. Prior to these discoveries, *Paranthropus* endocasts were sometimes reconstructed using endocasts of *A. africanus* (e.g., Sts 5) as a model (see below). In this study we compare endocasts of *Paranthropus* (including *P. robustus, P. aethiopicus, P. boisei*) with those of *Australopithecus africanus* and identify, quantify, and interpret previously unknown differences in the frontal and temporal lobe morphology between these genera. In addition, we provide revised estimates for the mean cranial capacity of *Paranthropus*.

MATERIALS AND METHODS

Previously unknown parts of the cerebral cortex in *Paranthropus* were observed and measured on both the endocast of KNM-WT 17000 (*P. aethiopicus*) and on a silicone endocast prepared from a cast of KNM-WT 17400 (*P. boisei*). Corresponding observations and measurements for *Australopithecus africanus* were obtained from silicone endocasts prepared from museum casts of Sts 5 (Mrs. Ples) and Stw 505 (Mr. Ples), as well as from a copy of the natural endocast of Sts 60. Other endocasts used for comparative purposes included KNM-ER 23000 (*P. boisei*), Sts 19 (*A. africanus*) and the Sterkfontein Number 2 natural endocast (*A. africanus*). Comparative endocast measurements were taken (by JG) from ten gorillas (*G. gorilla*), nine chimpanzees (*P. troglodytes*), nine bonobos (*P. paniscus*), and ten modern humans. Associated cranial capacities were obtained with mustard seed for the gorilla and chimpanzee sample and from the literature for the human, bonobo, and early hominid sample.

As a preliminary step, GWW and DF validated the size of the silicone endocasts for two of the specimens (Sts 5 and Stw 505) by comparing several measurements obtained using calipers with measurements taken on their corresponding virtual endocasts that had been acquired with 3D-CT technology from the original skulls (Conroy et al., 1998). The maximum length, height, and width obtained by measuring the virtual endocast of Sts 5 on the computer screen were 0.98, 1.00, and 1.00 of the respective measurements obtained with calipers from the silicone endocast. The length of the fragmentary Stw 505 virtual endocast and the distance between its left frontal and temporal poles were each 0.98 of the respective measurements obtained from the silicone endocast. A third measurement on the virtual endocast of Stw 505 (between its highest point on the dorsal surface and its lowest point at the anterior end of the temporal lobe) measured 0.99 of the comparable measurement of the silicone endocast. Thus, as detailed elsewhere (Weber et al., 1998), endocasts prepared from museum quality casts of skulls reproduce measurements obtained with 3D-CT technology from the braincases of the original specimens with a high degree of accuracy.

Eight measurements (described below) were obtained with calipers from basal views of endocasts and projected onto the basal plane. The procedure for orienting an endocast in basal view is to first determine the maximum antero-posterior diameter of the endocast in left lateral view (using the right hemisphere, if left is not present) that connects the frontal and occipital poles as described and illustrated by Connolly (1950:124–125). The endocast is then turned upside down and secured so that the maximum anterior-posterior diameter is in the horizontal or basal plane and the midsagittal plane is vertical. In cases of partial endocasts (e.g., Sts 60, Stw 505; KNM-WT 17400), basal orientations were estimated by aligning them next to correctly oriented full endocasts from the same genus (e.g., Sts 5; KNM-WT 17000). The fossil hominid measurements were from undistorted and unreconstructed portions of endocasts. In order to reduce potential observer error or bias, measurements were taken together by three observers (DF, JG, and JCR) on two different occasions and the results averaged. JG took the measurements with sliding calipers, while JR and DF confirmed his selection of landmarks and readings from the calipers, and made sure the calipers remained oriented so that measurements were projected onto the basal plane.

In order to quantify remeasurement error, the three workers together repeated all of the measurements on the fossil hominids one year after the first measurements were obtained and then compared their results with the earlier ones. For each of the eight measurements, remeasurement error was calculated as the mean of the absolute differences (determined for each specimen) between the first and second sets of measurements. Remeasurement error was then expressed as a percentage of the average length for each measurement. The results were 1% for measurements 1, 2, 6, and 8; and ranged from 2–8% for the other four measurements. The highest remeasurement errors expressed as percentages of mean lengths were for the shortest lengths. Similarly, JG remeasured 12 endocasts (three each from humans, bonobos, chimpanzees, and gorillas) one year after taking the initial measurements from these specimens. The results ranged from 1–8%, with the greatest relative remeasurement error associated with the shortest lengths.

The measurements included (Figure 1): (1) **bat–bat,** the distance between the most anterior points of the temporal lobes in basal view; (2) **mat–mat,** maximum width of the frontal lobes at the level of **bat;** (3) **mbat–rof(tan),** the shortest distance between the middle of the line connecting the two **bats** and the tangent to the most rostral point on the orbital surfaces of the frontal lobes (note that **rof** should not be confused with the frontal pole); (4) **mcp–mbat,** the shortest distance between the middle clinoid process (or anterior border of the sella turcica) and **mbat;** (5) **mcp–rof(tan),** the shortest distance between the middle clinoid process and **rof(tan);** (6) **cob–rof(tan),** the shortest distance between the caudal boundary of the olfactory bulbs (cribriform plate) and **rof(tan);** (7) **rob–rof(tan),** the shortest distance between the rostral boundary of the olfactory bulbs and

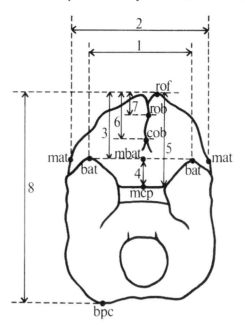

Figure 1. *Measurements obtained from basal views and projected onto the horizontal (basal) plane from endocasts of australopithecines, apes, and humans (see text for details and Table 1 for data). Landmarks: **bat,** most anterior point on temporal lobe from basal view; **mat,** most lateral point on endocast at the level of **bat** in basal plane; **mbat,** middle of the line connecting the two **bats;** **rof,** the most rostral point on the orbital surfaces of the frontal lobes; **mcp,** middle clinoid process; **cob,** caudal boundary of olfactory bulbs (cribriform plate) in midline; **rob,** rostral boundary of olfactory bulbs in midline; **bpc,** most posterior point on cerebella in basal view.*

rof(tan); (8) **rof(tan)–bpc(tan),** the shortest distance between **rof(tan)** and the tangent to the most posterior point on the cerebella in basal view (**bpc**).

Measurements 3, 6, 7, and 8 were used to calculate three additional lengths for each specimen: [3–6] the length between **mbat** and **cob;** [6–7], the length of the olfactory bulb (cribriform plate); and [8–3], the length of the basal aspect of the endocast caudal to **mbat.** Indices that express each measure as a percentage of endocast length in basal view were calculated by dividing these three lengths as well as measurements 1–7 by measurement 8 for the great ape and human samples, and for the two hominid endocasts for which measurement 8 was available (KNM-WT 17000 and Sts 5).

Descriptive statistics were provided for the lengths (Table 1) and indices (Table 2) obtained from endocasts of *Homo, Gorilla, Pan, Paranthropus* and *Australopithecus.* These data were first compared in living hominoids in order to establish a comparative basis for assessing endocasts representing *Australopithecus* and *Paranthropus.* For all of the comparisons in this study, there were significant differences between groups which were determined by post-hoc analyses of selected contrast within the general linear model (GLM) of *SPSS* (version 8.0). The alpha level was preset to $P \leq 0.05$ after correction with Bonferroni's method for multiple comparisons where the indicated *P*-values had been

Table 1. Endocast Measurements

	bat–bat 1	mat–mat 2	mbat–rof(tan) 3	mcp–mbat 4	mcp–rof(tan) 5	cob–rof(tan) 6	rob–rof(tan) 7	rof(tan)bpc(tan) 8	Cranial capacity (cm³) 9	Length mbat–cob [3–6]	Length olf. bulb [6–7]	Base–caudal to bat [8–3]
Homo (n=10)												
Mean	69.70	108.90	38.90	16.00	53.89	30.30	9.00	150.10	1350	8.60	21.30	111.20
S.D.	6.27	7.42	3.76	2.31	5.88	4.74	2.11	6.71	175.50	3.92	4.52	6.61
Range	(58.0–80.0)	(98.0–121.0)	(34.0–43.0)	(12.0–20.0)	(46.0–64.0)	(22.0–37.0)	(6.0–12.0)	(140.0–164.0)	—	(1.0–13.0)	(14.0–27.0)	(101.0–122.0)
Gorilla (n=10)												
Mean	49.00	77.60	34.00	5.70	40.90	16.60	4.60	120.90	483.50	17.40	12.00	86.90
S.D.	2.49	4.62	2.91	1.77	3.25	1.90	1.51	5.90	79.33	2.27	0.67	5.26
Range	(45.0–52.0)	(71.0–86.0)	(31.0–39.0)	(3.0–8.0)	(37.0–46.0)	(13.0–19.0)	(2.0–7.0)	(114.0–129.0)	(375.0–585.0)	(13.0–20.0)	(11.0–13.0)	(80.0–96.0)
Pan (n=18)												
Mean	47.30	74.94	31.41	8.56	40.29	16.44	4.79	107.56	392.67	14.76	11.26	76.33
S.D.	3.66	5.22	3.17	2.23	3.99	2.93	1.35	3.88	25.00	2.70	3.54	4.68
Range	(40.0–53.0)	(64.0–83.0)	(26.0–36.0)	(5.0–12.0)	(32.0–45.0)	(10.0–21.0)	(2.0–8.0)	(97.0–114.0)	(360.0–445.0)	(10.0–22.0)	(1.0–17.0)	(66.0–84.0)
Paranthropus												
WT 17000	50.00	74.00	34.00	5.00	39.00	20.00	7.00	114.00	410.00	14.00	13.00	80.00
WT 17400	45.00	68.00	29.00	4.00	33.00	14.00	7.00	—	390.00	15.00	7.00	—
Mean	47.50	71.00	31.50	4.50	36.00	17.00	7.00	—	400.00	14.50	10.00	80.00
S.D.	3.54	4.24	3.54	0.71	4.24	4.24	0.00	—	14.14	0.71	4.24	—
Range	(45.0–50.0)	(68.0–74.0)	(29.0–34.0)	(4.0–5.0)	(33.0–39.0)	(14.0–20.0)	(7.0–7.0)	—	(390.0–410.0)	(14.0–15.0)	(7.0–13.0)	—
Australopithecus												
Sts 5	56.00	85.00	39.00	14.00	53.00	30.00	14.00	118.00	485.00	9.00	16.00	79.00
Stw 505	—	—	33.00	11.00	44.00	29.00	11.00	—	515.00	4.00	18.00	—
Sts 60	62.00	—	31.00	11.00	42.00	—	—	—	428.00	—	—	—
Mean	59.00	—	34.33	12.00	46.33	29.50	12.50	—	476.00	6.50	17.00	—
S.D.	4.24	—	4.16	1.73	5.86	0.71	2.12	—	44.19	2.50	1.00	—
Range	(56.0–62.0)	—	(31.0–39.0)	(11.0–14.0)	(42.0–53.0)	(29.0–30.0)	(11.0–14.0)	—	(428.0–515.0)	(4.0–9.0)	(16.0–18.0)	—

Note: Descriptive statistics for measurements (see Figure 1) taken from endocasts of australopithecines, apes, and humans. Cranial capacities for gorillas and *Pan* were obtained from skulls, while those for humans are from Pakkenberg & Gundersen, 1997. Although the mean cranial capacity listed for *Pan* is for *P. troglodytes* only, a mean cranial capacity of 350 cm³ has been published elsewhere for *P. paniscus* (Cramer, 1977). For Stw 505, **mbat** was determined by the intersection of the tangent to the left **bat** with the intact midsagittal plane.

Table 2. Descriptive Statistics and P-Values for Endocast Indices

	1/8	2/8	3/8	4/8	5/8	6/8	7/8	[3–6]/8	[6–7]/8	[8–3]/8
Homo (n=10)										
Mean	0.46*	0.73*	0.26†	0.11*†	0.36	0.20*†	0.06*†	0.06*†	0.14*†	0.74†
S.D.	0.04	0.03	0.02	0.02	0.04	0.03	0.01	0.03	0.03	0.02
Range	(0.38–0.50)	(0.66–0.76)	(0.22–0.30)	(0.08–0.13)	(0.31–0.42)	(0.16–0.25)	(0.04–0.08)	(0.01–0.09)	(0.10–0.18)	(0.70–0.78)
Gorilla (n=10)										
Mean	0.41*‡	0.64*‡	0.28	0.05*‡	0.34‡	0.14*	0.04*	0.14*	0.10*	0.72
S.D.	0.02	0.03	0.02	0.01	0.02	0.02	0.01	0.02	0.008	0.02
Range	(0.37–0.44)	(0.57–0.69)	(0.25–0.31)	(0.03–0.06)	(0.30–0.60)	(0.10–0.16)	(0.02–0.06)	(0.11–0.17)	(0.09–0.11)	(0.69–0.75)
Pan (n=18)										
Mean	0.44†‡	0.69‡	0.29†	0.08†‡	0.37‡	0.15†	0.04†	0.14†	0.10†	0.71†
S.D.	0.03	0.04	0.03	0.02	0.04	0.03	0.01	0.02	0.03	0.03
Range	(0.38–0.49)	(0.62–0.77)	(0.25–0.34)	(0.05–0.11)	(0.30–0.42)	(0.09–0.20)	(0.02–0.08)	(0.01–0.20)	(0.01–0.16)	(0.66–0.75)
	*P<0.001	*P<0.001	†P=0.022	*P<0.001	‡P=0.04	*P<0.001	*P=0.001	*P<0.001	*P=0.004	†P=0.18
	‡P=0.026	‡P=0.003		†P=0.001		†P<0.001	†P=0.008	†P<0.001	†P=0.005	
				‡P<0.001						
Paranthropus										
KNM-WT 17000	0.44	0.65	0.30	0.04	0.34	0.18	0.06	0.12	0.11	0.70
Australopithecus										
Sts 5	0.47	0.72	0.33	0.12	0.45	0.25	0.12	0.08	0.14	0.67

Notes: Symbols represent a significant difference between groups: *Homo–Gorilla*; †*Homo–Pan*; ‡*Gorilla–Pan*.

Indices for endocasts in basal view were obtained by dividing the lengths of the variables provided in Table 1 by measurement 8. Significance tests were calculated with post-hoc multiple comparisons corrected with Bonferroni's method within the general linear model (type III) of SPSS. Indices were available for only one *Paranthropus* (KNM-WT 17000) and one *Australopithecus* (Sts 5) endocast. These are provided for comparative purposes, although they were not compared statistically with those of apes and humans.

adjusted (Tables 2 & 3). Differences in the mean lengths and indices were also tested for statistical significance between the two species of *Pan.* The only two measurements that were found to differ significantly between *P. troglodytes* and *P. paniscus* were variables 4 and 4/8. Consequently, for these two variables, results are reported separately for these two species. Endocasts of *Paranthropus* and *Australopithecus* were compared to each other and to endocasts from *Pan, Gorilla,* and *Homo* (Table 3) by computing mean differences, standard errors, and *P*-values from the data provided in Table 1. Finally, the above observations and statistically significant results were synthesized and the key features summarized for endocasts from apes, early hominids, and humans (Table 4).

Additionally, because previously unknown parts of *Paranthropus* endocasts are now available, new endocast reconstructions were made for *Paranthropus* specimens SK 1585 (*P. robustus*), OH 5 (*P. boisei*), KNM-ER 732 (*P. boisei*), and KNM-ER 407 (*P. boisei*), using appropriate *unreconstructed* parts of *Paranthropus* endocasts as models.

RESULTS

Gorilla, Pan, and *Homo*

Mean measurements from basal views of endocasts are presented in Table 1, and means of indices generated by dividing variables 1–7 and [3–6], [6–7] and [8–3] by endocast lengths are provided in Table 2. Not surprisingly, the means for larger-brained *Homo* are significantly greater than the means for smaller-brained *Gorilla* and *Pan* for variables 1–8, [6–7], and [8–3]. All *P*-values are <0.001 except for the *Homo-Gorilla* comparison for variable 3 (*P* = 0.021). Variable [3–6], on the other hand, is significantly shorter in *Homo* than in *Gorilla* or *Pan* (*P*< 0.001), which corresponds with an increased mean length of variable 4 in *Homo* (indicating a greater extent of temporal pole projection, see below). *Gorilla* is significantly longer than *Pan* for variables 8 (endocast length) and [8–3] (*P*< 0.001 for both comparisons). For variable 4, on the other hand, *P. troglodytes* is significantly longer than *Gorilla* (*P*< 0.001) and *P. paniscus* (*P*< 0.01), which do not differ significantly from each other (*P* = 0.82).

The mean indices (Table 2) that express variables as percentages of endocast lengths in basal view indicate that *Gorilla* differs significantly from *Homo* and *Pan* in having generally narrower endocasts at the level of the temporal poles (variable 2/8, *P*< 0.001 and *P* = 0.003 respectively), temporal poles that are relatively closer together (variable 1/8, *P*< 0.001 and *P* = 0.026), and temporal poles that do not project as far forward relative to sella (variable 4/8, *P*< 0.001 for both comparisons). The mean relative lengths of the orbital surfaces of the frontal lobes of *Gorilla* (variable 5/8) are significantly shorter than those of *Pan* (*P* = 0.04), while the mean relative lengths of the two most anterior regions of the frontal lobes (variables 6/8 and 7/8, *P* ≤ 0.001 for both comparisons) and olfactory bulbs (variable [6–7]/8, *P* = 0.004) are significantly shorter than those of *Homo.*

Endocasts of *Pan,* on the other hand, are similar to those of *Homo* and differ significantly from those of *Gorilla* in mean relative width at the level of the temporal poles (variable 2/8), mean relative distance between the temporal poles (variable 1/8), and mean relative length of the frontal lobes (variable 5/8) (*P* = 0.003, 0.026, 0.04 respectively). The mean relative length of the portion of the frontal lobes that is anterior to the temporal poles (variable 3/8), however, is significantly longer in *Pan* than *Homo* (*P* = 0.022), but not *Gorilla.* Corresponding to this, the mean relative length of the posterior portion of the endocast (variable [8–3]/8) is significantly shorter in *Pan* than in *Homo* (*P* = 0.018). The mean relative projection of the temporal poles (variable 4/8) does not differ from that for *Homo* or *P. troglodytes* (*P* = 0.63), but is significantly shorter in *P. paniscus* than for both *Homo* (*P* < 0.001) and *P. troglodytes* (*P*< 0.03). This variable is significantly greater in *P. paniscus* (*P* = 0.03) and *P. troglodytes* (*P*< 0.001) than it is for *Gorilla.* As is the case for *Gorilla,* the mean relative lengths of the two most anterior regions of the frontal lobes (variables 6/8 and 7/8) and olfactory bulbs (variable [6–7]/8) of *Pan* are significantly shorter than those of *Homo* (*P*< 0.001, 0.008 and 0.005 respectively).

Although the mean relative length of the entire frontal lobe in basal view (variable 5/8) does not differ significantly between *Homo* and either of the two apes, the mean relative lengths of certain subregions within the frontal lobe (variables 6/8, 7/8, and [6–7]/8) are significantly longer in *Homo* than they are in *Gorilla* and *Pan* (see Table 2 for *P*-values). The mean relative length of variable 4/8 is also significantly longer in *Homo* than in *Gorilla* (*P*< 0.001) and *P. paniscus* (*P*< 0.001), but not *P. troglodytes.* On the other hand, the relative length between the anterior end of the temporal poles and the posterior end of the olfactory bulbs (variable [3–6]/8) is significantly shorter in *Homo* than in either ape (*P*< 0.001 for both comparisons). As detailed in the discussion section, these findings support other comparative studies on actual brains of apes and humans, which show that the frontal lobes of *Homo* are reorganized compared to those of *Gorilla* and *Pan.*

To summarize the main findings regarding the relative proportion of endocasts from living hominoids: endocasts of gorillas are generally longer and narrower than those of *Pan* (variables 8, [8–3], 1/8, and 2/8) and narrower than those of *Homo* (variables 1/8 and 2/8), while endocasts from *P. troglodytes* (but not *P. paniscus* or *Gorilla*) further resemble those of humans in having relatively projecting temporal poles (variable 4/8). Although the overall length of the human frontal lobe (variable 5/8) does not differ significantly from those of *Pan* or *Gorilla,* the proportions of areas *within* human frontal lobes are dramatically different from those of apes (variables 6/8, 7/8, [6–7]/8, [3–6]/8 and, except for *Pan troglodytes,* 4/8). In particular, the most anterior regions (variables 6 and 7) of the frontal lobe are relatively longer in humans.

Paranthropus and *Australopithecus*

Table 3 presents mean differences, standard errors and *P*-values for comparisons of *Paranthropus* and *Australopithecus* with *Pan, Gorilla, Homo,* and each other

Table 3. Mean Difference, Standard Errors and *P*-Values for Comparisons with *Paranthropus* and *Australopithecus*

Comparison Groups (*Paranthropus*)

Group 1	Group 2	Mean Difference	Standard Error	*P*-Values
Variable 1: bat–bat				
Paranthropus	*Pan*	0.20	3.13	1.000
	Gorilla	−1.50	3.25	1.000
	Australopithecus	−11.17	3.83	0.059
	Homo	−22.20	3.25	<0.001*
Variable 2: mat–mat				
Paranthropus	*Pan*	−3.94	4.25	1.000
	Gorilla	−6.60	4.41	0.861
	Australopithecus			
	Homo	−37.90	4.41	<0.001*
Variable 3: mbat–rof(tan)				
Paranthropus	*Pan*	0.09	2.48	1.000
	Gorilla	−2.50	2.58	1.000
	Australopithecus	−2.83	3.04	1.000
	Homo	−7.40	2.58	0.066
Variable 4: mcp–mbat				
Paranthropus	*Pan*	−4.06	1.56	0.134
	Gorilla	−1.20	1.62	1.000
	Australopithecus	−7.50	1.91	0.004*
	Homo	−11.50	1.62	<0.001*
Variable 5: mcp–rof(tan)				
Paranthropus	*Pan*	−4.29	3.34	1.000
	Gorilla	−4.90	3.47	1.000
	Australopithecus	−10.33	4.09	0.158
	Homo	−17.89	3.47	<0.001*
Variable 6: cob–rof(tan)				
Paranthropus	*Pan*	0.56	2.42	1.000
	Gorilla	0.40	2.51	1.000
	Australopithecus	−12.50	2.96	0.001*
	Homo	−13.30	2.51	<0.001*
Variable 7: rob–rof(tan)				
Paranthropus	*Pan*	2.21	1.18	0.696
	Gorilla	2.40	1.23	0.583
	Australopithecus	−5.50	1.45	0.005*
	Homo	−2.00	1.23	1.000
Variable [3–6]: [mbat–cob]				
Paranthropus	*Pan*	−0.26	2.17	1.000
	Gorilla	−2.90	2.25	1.000
	Australopithecus	8.00	2.66	0.046*
	Homo	5.90	2.25	0.126
Variable [6–7]:				
[cob–rof(tan)–rob–rof(tan)]				
Paranthropus	*Pan*	−1.26	2.45	1.000
	Gorilla	−2.00	2.55	1.000
	Australopithecus	−7.00	3.00	0.251
	Homo	−11.30	2.55	0.001*

Comparison Groups (*Australopithecus*)

Group 1	Group 2	Mean Difference	Standard Error	*P*-Values
Variable 1: bat–bat				
Australopithecus	*Pan*	11.37	2.62	0.001*
	Gorilla	9.67	2.76	0.012*
	Homo	−11.03	2.76	0.003*
Variable 2: mat–mat				
Australopithecus	*Pan*	—	—	—
	Gorilla	—	—	—
	Homo	—	—	—
Variable 3: mbat–rof(tan)				
Australopithecus	*Pan*	2.92	2.08	1.000
	Gorilla	0.33	2.19	1.000
	Homo	−4.57	2.19	0.438
Variable 4: mcp–mbat				
Australopithecus	*Pan*	3.44	1.31	0.121
	Gorilla	6.30	1.38	0.001*
	Homo	−4.00	1.38	0.062
Variable 5: mcp–rof(tan)				
Australopithecus	*Pan*	6.05	2.80	0.368
	Gorilla	5.43	2.95	0.733
	Homo	−7.56	2.95	0.145
Variable 6: cob–rof(tan)				
Australopithecus	*Pan*	13.06	2.02	<0.001*
	Gorilla	12.90	2.13	<0.001*
	Homo	−0.80	2.13	1.000
Variable 7: rob–rof(tan)				
Australopithecus	*Pan*	7.71	0.99	<0.001*
	Gorilla	7.90	1.05	<0.001*
	Homo	3.50	1.05	0.018*
Variable [3–6]: [mbat–cob]				
Australopithecus	*Pan*	−8.26	1.81	0.001*
	Gorilla	−10.90	1.91	<0.001*
	Homo	−2.10	1.91	1.000
Variable [6–7]:				
[cob–rof(tan)–rob–rof(tan)]				
Australopithecus	*Pan*	5.74	2.05	0.080
	Gorilla	5.00	2.16	0.264
	Homo	−4.30	2.16	0.541

Endocasts for variables listed in Table 1. (*Pan* includes both *P. troglodytes* and *P. paniscus*.) Comparisons were done only for groups that contained two or more specimens for each variable, and significance tests were calculated with post-hoc multiple comparisons corrected with Bonferroni's method within the general linear model (type III) of SPSS (* indicates significant differences).

for the variables in Table 1. As shown by the *P*-values, *Paranthropus* does not differ significantly from either *Pan* or *Gorilla* for any variable listed in Table 3. On the other hand, *Paranthropus* endocasts are significantly smaller than those of *Homo* for the means of variables 1, 2, 4, 5, 6, and [6–7] ($P \le 0.001$ for all six comparisons), which is not surprising given the much larger cranial capacity of the latter (Table 1). *Paranthropus* endocasts are also smaller than those of *Homo* for variables 3 and 7, although these comparisons do not reach statistical significance ($P = 0.066$ and 1.0 respectively). Finally, *Paranthropus*, like both apes, is greater than *Homo* for variable [3–6], but not significantly so ($P = 0.126$). These statistics reveal that endocasts of *Paranthropus* are entirely ape-like in the absolute variables that reflect the gross morphology of the frontal and temporal lobes of the brain. [It should be noted, however (see below), that KNM-WT 17000 differs from apes for indices 6/8 and 7/8.]

In lateral view, the ape like variables of the frontal lobes of *Paranthropus* are manifested in orbital surfaces that have a beaked-shaped profile similar to that of chimpanzees and gorillas (Figure 2), and unlike the more flattened orbital rostrum of humans. Viewed dorsally (Figure 3), the rostral portions of the frontal lobes in *Paranthropus* specimens KNM-WT 17000 and KNM-WT 17400 are relatively pointed (Holloway, 1988*b*), being comparable to the unreconstructed portions of OH 5 (*P. boisei*) and KNM-ER 23000 (*P. boisei*). These specimens show that the ape like variables for the frontal lobes that are reproduced from endocasts in our *Paranthropus* sample are manifested in an overall teardrop shape when viewed dorsally [Figure 3(b)]. Compared to endocasts from *Homo* and *Australopithecus* (see below), the ape like variables for the temporal lobes of *Paranthropus* are manifested in rounded temporal poles [KNM-WT 17000 (*P. aethiopicus*), KNM-WT 17400 (*P. boisei*), SK 1585 (*P. robustus*)], shorter forward projections of the poles beyond the anterior borders of sella turcica (variable 4, Table 3; Figure 2), and shorter distances between the temporal poles when seen in basal view (measurement 1, Table 3; Figure 2).

The picture for endocasts of *Australopithecus* is quite different. Despite the fact that mean cranial capacity of the *Australopithecus* specimens listed in Table 1 (476 cm³) is between that of *Pan* (393 cm³) and *Gorilla* (484 cm³), a number of mean variables for *Australopithecus* are significantly larger than they are for either *Pan* or *Gorilla* (Table 3). These significant differences include variables 1 ($P = 0.001$ and 0.012 respectively), 6 ($P < 0.001$ for both comparisons), and 7 ($P < 0.001$ for both comparisons). For variable 4, *Australopithecus* is significantly larger than *Gorilla* and *P. paniscus* ($P = 0.001$ and 0.003 respectively), but not *P. troglodytes* ($P = 1.0$). On the other hand, *Australopithecus*, like *Homo*, is significantly smaller than both apes for variable [3–6] ($P \le 0.001$ for all four comparisons). In contrast to *Paranthropus*, and despite its small cranial capacity compared to *Homo*, endocasts of *Australopithecus* do not differ significantly from those

(KNM-WT 17000) (KNM-WT 17400) (KNM-WT 17000) (KNM-WT 17400)

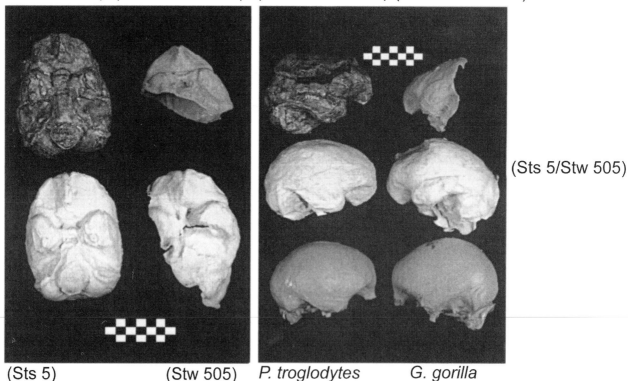

(Sts 5/Stw 505)

(Sts 5)   (Stw 505)   *P. troglodytes*   *G. gorilla*

Figure 2. *Basal (left) and lateral (right) views of endocasts from* A. africanus *specimens Sts 5 and Stw 505, and* Paranthropus *specimens KNM-WT 17000 and KNM-WT 17400. The lateral views are positioned frontal-lobe-to-frontal-lobe, and include a gorilla and chimpanzee for comparative purposes. Note the relatively expanded orbital surfaces of the frontal lobes of Sts 5 and Stw 505.*

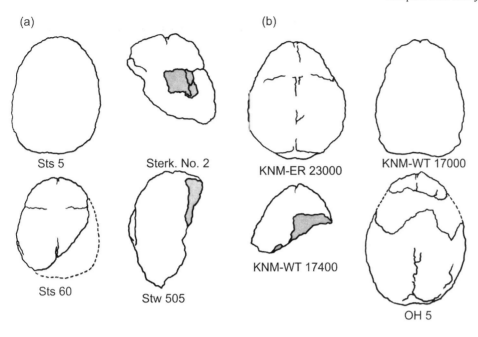

Figure 3. *Outlines of dorsal views of endocasts from (a)* A. africanus *(Sts 5, Stw 505, Sts 60, No. 2 specimen from Sterkfontein), and (b)* Paranthropus *(OH 5, KNM-WT 17000, KNM-ER 23000, KNM-WT 17400). Endocasts of* Paranthropus *appear more pointed, while those of* A. africanus *are wider at the rostral ends of the frontal lobes.*

of *Homo* for variables 4, 5, 6, and [6–7] (Table 3). Furthermore, variables 4, 6, and 7 are significantly larger in *Australopithecus* than in *Paranthropus* endocasts ($P = 0.004$, 0.001, and 0.005 respectively), while variable [3–6] is significantly smaller ($P < 0.05$).

The similarities between endocasts of *Australopithecus* and *Homo* are manifested in expanded and blunted, rather than beak-shaped, orbital rostra compared to apes and *Paranthropus* (variable 6, Tables 1 and 3; Figure 2), as well as cribriform plates (olfactory bulbs) that are longer on average (variable [6–7]). In *Australopithecus*, expansion of the frontal lobes in the region directly lateral to **rof** also produces a wider rostral end of the frontal lobe when viewed dorsally compared to that seen in *Paranthropus* (Figure 3). Compared to *Paranthropus*, endocasts of *Australopithecus*, like those from *Homo*, also have temporal poles that project more in an anterior and lateral direction relative to sella turcica (variables 4 and 1, Tables 1 and 3; Figure 2).

Because endocast indices can be obtained for only one *Paranthropus* (KNM-WT 17000) and one *Australopithecus* endocast (Sts 5) (Table 2), comparisons of these indices for the two genera cannot be statistically analyzed as was done for the variables presented in Table 1. One may note, however, that the *Paranthropus* endocast falls on or nearer the ape means while the *Australopithecus* endocast falls on or nearer the *Homo* means for relative variables 1/8, 2/8, 4/8, [3–6]/8, and [6–7]/8 (Table 2). Interestingly, the *Australopithecus* endocast is noticeably larger than those for *Paranthropus, Homo,* and both apes for relative variables 3/8, 5/8, 6/8, and 7/8; and noticeably smaller for relative variable [8–3]/8 (Table 2).

Summary of Key Features on Endocasts from *Gorilla, Pan, Paranthropus, Australopithecus* and *Homo*

The key findings regarding absolute and relative variables described above for endocasts of *Gorilla, Pan,*

Paranthropus, Australopithecus, and *Homo* are summarized in Table 4. Except for the indices for *Paranthropus* and *Australopithecus* (and unless otherwise stated in the legend), table entries for *Homo* indicate that its mean differs significantly from the means for apes, while entries for apes indicate that their means differ significantly from those for the apes that are not marked. This table is conservative. For example, although the mean [6–7] for *Australopithecus* is intermediate between that of apes and *Homo* (Table 1), this variable is not marked because the differences between the mean for *Australopithecus* and those for apes did not achieve statistical significance (Table 3). Conversely, the indices for *Paranthropus* and *Australopithecus,* could not be compared statistically with means from other groups because they are available for only one specimen each (i.e., KNM-WT 17000 and Sts 5). In these cases, entries indicate whether the index measured from one representative is closer to that for apes (G and/or P) or humans (H) (Table 2).

The observations in Table 4 are organized into four complexes, each of which contains interrelated (dependent) features. With regards to general size and shape of endocasts, the long (variable 8) and narrow (1/8 and 2/8) endocasts of *Gorilla* differ markedly compared to those of *Pan*. Endocasts of *Homo,* however, are associated with larger cranial capacities than those of apes, as well as longer relative lengths of the posterior portion of the brain [8–3]/8 compared to *Pan*. Two indices for *Australopithecus* (5/8, [8–3]/8) differ noticeably from those of apes because variables 3 and 5 of Sts 5 are increased greatly compared to apes while its overall length (variable 8) is not. These indices are smaller in *Homo* than *Australopithecus,* on the other hand, because *Homo* equals Sts 5 in the mean dimensions of variables 3 and 5, but has a much longer mean overall length.

The second set of variables in Table 4 pertain to subdivisions on the orbital surfaces of the frontal lobes and reveal that *Australopithecus* and *Homo* differ similarly in a number of key features compared to those of apes and

Table 4. Summary of Key Endocast Features for *Gorilla, Pan, Paranthropus, Australopithecus* and *Homo*

Description	Variable	*Gorilla*	*Pan*	*Paranthropus*	*Australopithecus*	*Homo*
General size and shape						
Cranial capacity	cm^3				+	
Absolute length endocast	8	+				+
Relative width bat–bat	1/8	–		P	H	+^{G}
Relative width mat–mat	2/8	–		G	H	+^{G}
Relative length mcp–rof	5/8		+	G	>G, P, H	
Absolute length mcp–rof	5					+
Relative length bpc–mbat	[8–3]/8			P	<G, P, H	+^{Pan}
Absolute length bpc–mbat	[8–3]	+				+
Frontal lobes						
Relative length mbat–rof	3/8			P	>G, P, H	–^{Pan}
Absolute length mbat–rof	3					+
Relative length mbat–cob	[3–6]/8			G, P	H	–
Absolute length mbat–cob	[3–6]				–	–
Relative length cob–rof	6/8			H	>G, P, H	+
Absolute length cob–rof	6				+	+
Relative length rob–rof	7/8			H	>G, P, H	+
Absolute length rob–rof	7				+	+
Olfactory bulbs						
Relative length cob–rob	[6–7]/8			G, P	H	+
Absolute length cob–rob	[6–7]					+
Temporal poles						
Relative length mcp–mbat	4/8		+$_{(P.\ troglodytes)}$	G	H	+$^{G, Pp}$
Absolute length mcp–mbat	4		+$_{(P.\ troglodytes)}$	–^{Pt}	+$^{G, Pp}$	+
Absolute width bat–bat	1				+	+

Based on statistical analyses of measurements obtained from basal views and illustrated in Figure 1. Symbols: + under *Homo* or *Australopithecus*, the mean for that variable is significantly *larger* than the means for apes; + under *Gorilla* or *Pan*, the mean is significantly larger than those for the unmarked apes; + with superscripts (e.g., +$^{G, Pp}$), the mean is significantly larger than the means for only the apes indicated by the superscript (superscripts: *G, Gorilla; Pan,* chimpanzees and bonobos; *Pp, Pan paniscus; Pt, Pan troglodytes*); + (*P. troglodytes*), the mean variable is significantly longer in *P. troglodytes* than either *P. paniscus* or *Gorilla;* – with and without superscripts, the same conventions as above, except that the means are significantly *smaller* than those for apes. Because indices could not be compared statistically with means from other groups for *Paranthropus* (KNM-WT 17000) and *Australopithecus* (Sts 5), *G* and/or *P,* or *H* indicate that a particular index is closer to the mean for *Gorilla* and/or *Pan* or *Homo* (Table 2); >G, P, H indicates that the index for Sts 5 is noticeably greater than the indices for *Gorilla, Pan,* and *Homo,* while <G, P, H means that the index for Sts 5 is noticeably smaller. Note that *Paranthropus* is similar to *Homo* for only two indices, and that none of its mean absolute variables differ significantly from those of apes in the same direction (+ or –) as *Homo. Australopithecus,* on the other hand, is similar to *Homo* for five indices, and the means of four of its absolute variables differ significantly from those of all apes in the same direction as *Homo.* These data have implications for understanding the sequence in which cortical reorganization occurred during hominid brain evolution.

Paranthropus. Again, the noticeably larger indices for the frontal lobes of *Australopithecus* compared to *Homo* (Table 2: 3/8, 6/8, and 7/8) are largely the result of a shorter variable 8 for Sts 5 than for *Homo.* These observations are consistent with the interpretation that, compared to endocasts from apes and *Paranthropus,* endocasts of *Australopithecus* are characterized by differentially lengthened frontal lobes and subdivisions thereof, concomitantly with relatively shortened posterior portions ([8–3]/8). This accounts for the comparatively expanded and squared-off appearance of the orbital rostra in *Australopithecus* endocasts (Figures 2 and 3).

Because olfactory regions represent a phylogenetically older part of the brain than neocortical areas (Finlay & Darlington, 1995), the two measurements pertaining to the olfactory bulbs are placed in a third complex (Table 4). As detailed in the discussion section, *Australopithecus* appears more like humans than apes in the size and shape of its olfactory bulbs. This is also true for the temporal poles described by the fourth complex of variables (Table 4), as confirmed by visual observation of endocasts from *Australopithecus* and *Homo* that share a forward (4/8, 4) and lateral (1) projection of the temporal poles (Figure 2).

In sum, Table 4 reveals that endocasts of *Paranthropus* are similar to those of *Homo* for only two indices, while none of its mean absolute variables differ significantly from those of apes in the same direction (+ or –) as the means from endocasts of *Homo.* In contrast, endocasts of *Australopithecus* are similar to *Homo* endocasts for five indices, and the means of four of its absolute variables differ significantly from those of all apes in the same direction as the means from *Homo.* The implications of these data for understanding the sequence in which cortical reorganization occurred during hominid brain evolution are explored in the discussion section.

NEW ENDOCRANIAL CAPACITIES

Because much of the above information was not available when endocasts of *Paranthropus* specimens SK 1585, OH 5, KNM-ER 407, and KNM-ER 732 were reconstructed (apparently with the endocast of Sts 5 as a

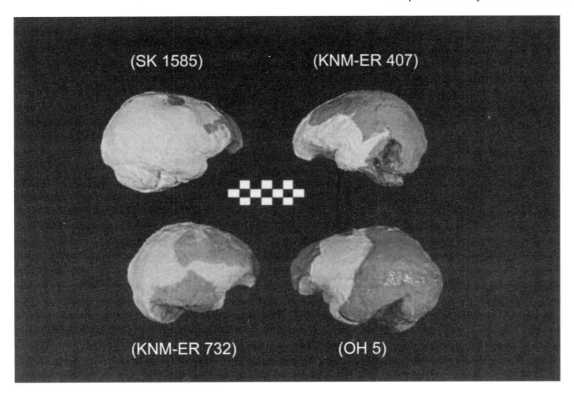

(SK 1585)   (KNM-ER 407)

(KNM-ER 732)   (OH 5)

Figure 4. *Newly reconstructed endocasts from four* Paranthropus *specimens. The reconstructed regions of SK 1585 are dark; those of KNM-ER 407, KNM-ER 732, and OH 5 are light. This endocast of SK 1585 contains matrix between the inferior border of the temporal lobe and the cerebellum that was removed in a subsequent procedure. These reconstructions reproduce the beak-shaped rostral orbital area that is found in* Paranthropus, *but not* Australopithecus.

frequent model), we reconstructed the endocasts of these specimens (Figure 4), using the *unreconstructed* parts of other *Paranthropus* endocasts as models and recalculated their endocranial capacities (Table 5).

Five water displacements of the newly reconstructed endocast of SK 1585 (*P. robustus*) resulted in a mean of 476 cm^3 (470–484 cm^3), 54 cm^3 *less than* the currently accepted estimate of 530 cm^3 (Holloway, 1972) (Figure 4).

Five cranial capacity estimates of the newly reconstructed endocast of OH 5 (*P. boisei*) resulted in a mean of 500 cm^3 (498–502 cm^3), 30 cm^3 *less than* the currently accepted estimate of 530 cm^3 (Tobias, 1967) (Figure 4). This loss is due mostly to reduction in the orbital olfactory region compared to the earlier reconstruction, which did not benefit from reference to *Paranthropus* specimens that were discovered subsequent to its reconstruction. Our reconstruction differs from the earlier one in having a smaller, beaked-shaped rostral orbital region, and somewhat less anteriorly extended temporal poles (Holloway, 1972, 1975).

Five cranial capacity estimates for the newly reconstructed endocast of KNM-ER 732 (*P. boisei*) result in a mean of 466 cm^3 (460–472 cm^3), 34 cm^3 *less than* the currently accepted estimate of 500 cm^3 (Holloway, 1988*a*) (Figure 4). Our reconstruction differs from the earlier one in having a smaller, beaked-shaped rostral orbital region.

Five cranial capacity estimates for the newly reconstructed endocast of KNM-ER 407 (*P. boisei*) result in a mean of 438 cm^3 (430–446 cm^3), 72 cm^3 *less than* the

currently accepted estimate of 510 cm^3 (Holloway, 1988*a*) and 68 cm^3 *less than* an earlier estimate of 506 cm^3 (Falk & Kasinga, 1983) (Figure 4). Our reconstruction differs from earlier ones in that most of the frontal lobe and temporal pole required reconstruction using the appropriate *Paranthropus* models.

Table 5 compares currently accepted endocranial capacities of *Paranthropus* with our revised values (estimates of other specimens in parentheses are considered acceptable). Our new estimates for these four *Paranthropus* specimens are all lower than earlier estimates, and the new mean of 450 cm^3 for eight specimens is significantly ($P < 0.05$, two-tailed) lower than one of the currently accepted means of 492 cm^3 (Table 5). However, the new mean does not differ significantly from that of 451 cm^3 for *Australopithecus* ($P \leq 0.95$), which contradicts the commonly held view that *Paranthropus* and early *Homo* had, on average, significantly larger brains than *Australopithecus* (Holloway, 1973).

DISCUSSION

The more human-like cortical morphology reproduced on *Australopithecus* endocasts is not due to allometric scaling because (1) the mean endocranial volume of the three *Australopithecus* specimens measured in this study is less than that for both gorillas and humans (Table 1), and (2) the mean endocranial volume of a wider sample of seven *Australopithecus* specimens does not differ

Table 5. Cranial Capacities for *Paranthropus* and *Australopithecus* Specimens. Those for *A. africanus* are from the Literature

Species	Dating (Ma)	Specimen	Cranial Capacity (cm³)	Reference	This Study	Method	Eval.
P. robustus	~1.8–1.7	SK 1585	530	1	**476**	B	1
P. aethiopicus	~2.5	KNM-WT 17000	410	2	(410)		
P. boisei	~2.4	Omo L338y-6	427	3	(427)		
	~1.88	KNM-ER 13750	450–480	4	—		
			or 500	5			
	~1.9	KNM-ER 23000	491	5	(491)		
	~1.8	KNM-WT 17400	390–400	4	(390)		
			or 500	5			
	~1.8	OH 5	530	6	**500**	A	1
	~1.7	KNM-ER 406	525	7	—		
	~1.85	KNM-ER 407	510	7	**438**	B	1–2
	~1.7	KNM-ER 732	500	7	**466**	B	1
	~2.2	Omo 323	490	5	—		
		Mean	479.4		**449.8**		
			or 492.1				
A. africanus	~3.0	MLD 37/38	425	8			
	~3.0–2.5	Sts 60	428	7			
		Sts 71	428	9			
		Sts 5	485	7			
		Sts 19	436	7			
	~2.8–2.6	Stw 505	515	10			
	~2.5–1.0?	Taung	440	7			
		Mean	**451**				

Revised cranial capacities for *Paranthropus* are in bold; those that are accepted from the literature are in parentheses. The first mean for *Paranthropus* includes estimates for KNM-ER 13750 and KNM-WT 17400 from Holloway (1988b); the second mean uses estimates for these two specimens from Brown et al. (1993). Our acceptance of the estimate for Omo L338y-6 is tentative pending an opportunity to do our own reconstruction. KNM-ER 13750 is excluded from the present study because of the disparity in estimates between Holloway (1988b) and Brown et al. (1993) and the fact that we do not have a copy of this specimen from which to make our own judgment. We accept the lower estimate for KNM-WT 17400 from Holloway (1988b) after comparing this specimen with a large number of ape and australopithecine endocasts in our collection. KNM-ER 406 is excluded because its capacity is based on external skull measurements and calculated from a formula that incorporates a factor (f) that is based on erroneous cranial capacity estimates for OH 5 and SK 1585 (Holloway, 1973). Omo 323 is excluded because it is too fragmentary to yield an accurate estimate. References: **1,** Holloway (1972); **2,** Walker et al. (1986); **3,** Holloway (1981); **4,** Holloway (1988b); **5,** Brown et al. (1993); **6,** Tobias (1967); **7,** Holloway (1988a); **8,** Conroy et al. (1990); **9,** Conroy et al. (2000); **10,** Conroy et al. (1998). Methods: **A,** water displacement of a full or hemi-endocast (times two) reconstructed in silicone with minimal distortion; **B,** volume of water contained by mold of hemi-endocast (times two). Evaluations of confidence in cranial capacity estimates due to completeness of original specimens: **1,** highest confidence; **2,** high confidence.

significantly from that of eight *Paranthropus* specimens ($P \leq 0.95$, Table 5). Furthermore, it is unlikely that the beak-shaped orbital rostra of endocasts from apes and *Paranthropus* are due to a high degree of postorbital constriction in their skulls, since skulls of *Australopithecus* that are also characterized by a high degree of postorbital constriction produce endocasts with orbital surfaces that are expanded and wide, rather than pointed (beak-shaped) and narrow at the very front (Figure 2). Thus, as others have suggested (Dean, 1988), endocranial aspects of the *cranial base*, while greatly influenced by the morphology of the brain, appear to be relatively independent from aspects of the masticatory system. It is also important to note that, although the cranial base of the skull has been shown to be affected by intentional deformation of the cranial vault (for cultural reasons) in Native Americans, the effect is indirect via the altered cranial vault's effects on brain growth (Cheverud et al., 1992; Kohn et al., 1993). These studies show that the cranial base responds directly to changes in brain growth.

An extensive literature based largely on comparative studies of actual brains indicates that the enlarged brain of *Homo sapiens* is derived compared to the brains of extant apes (Connolly, 1950; Holloway, 1988b; Falk,

1992; Semendeferi, 1994; Deacon, 1997; Tobias, 1997; Passingham, 1998; Semendeferi & Damasio, 2000). Within this context, frontal lobes have traditionally been of special interest to paleoneurologists because of their known functions with respect to language, abstract thought, planning, and execution of motor activities. For example, comparative studies on actual brains led both Deacon (1997) and Semendeferi (1994) to conclude that prefrontal regions of the frontal lobes are enlarged and derived in humans as a result of cortical reorganization that occurred during the evolution of their early hominid ancestors. Passingham (1998) arrived at the same conclusion regarding the inferior frontal cortex and temporal lobe. It is also important to note that brains need not be enlarged to be derived, i.e., that neurological evolution may entail cortical reorganization or redistribution of cortical tissues without an increase in brain size (Holloway, 1988b). The developmental mechanisms that are likely to have operated during the course of brain expansion and reorganization in mammals, including humans, have recently been elucidated within a framework that accommodates both allometric scaling and the evolution of neurological specializations (Finlay & Darlington, 1995).

Holloway's (1975, 1988*b*) long-held belief that cortical reorganization may already have been underway in australopithecines prior to the increase in brain size that occurred subsequently in *Homo* is supported by our observations for *Australopithecus*, but not *Paranthropus*. As detailed below, our morphological findings for the orbital surfaces of *Australopithecus* endocasts correspond with the reorganized cortical morphology that Semendeferi (1994) earlier hypothesized would have existed in the hominid ancestors of *Homo* and that would have been derived relative to the more primitive ape like morphology. Specifically, our analysis of endocasts has shown that the orbital surfaces of the frontal lobes of *Australopithecus* were expanded and the relative lengths of subareas rearranged (reorganized) compared to *Paranthropus*, which appears more ape like and less human like than *Australopithecus*.

Some Phylogenetic Speculations

Using *Australopithecus* as a hypothetical model for the ancestral *Homo* condition, it is possible to hypothesize about the sequence in which certain neurological features reorganized during the course of hominid evolution. It thus appears that the frontal lobes and temporal poles may have increased in size early on (i.e., in the australopithecine ancestors of *Homo*), followed by subsequent (additional) enlargement of posterior regions during the course of brain evolution in *Homo*. In addition to an increase in overall size of the frontal lobes (as indicated by length), the subregions within the orbital surfaces of the frontal lobes appear to have become reorganized with respect to one another in a sequential manner. For example, although human olfactory bulbs are estimated to be roughly 1/2 to 1/3 the volume of those of *P. troglodytes* and *Gorilla gorilla* (Stephan et al., 1981), inspection of endocasts shows that the shape of the human olfactory bulb is long and flattened compared to the shorter, more protuberant bulbs of apes. In keeping with this, the olfactory bulb measurement [6–7] of 21 mm is longer in humans than in apes and *Paranthropus* (Table 1). Measurement 6 (the length of the olfactory bulb plus measurement 7) averages 30 mm in both *Australopithecus* and humans. However, the mean length of the olfactory bulb in *Australopithecus* (17 mm) is 4 mm shorter than the mean for humans, while that of measurement 7 is 3.5 mm longer. These differences would disappear if the olfactory bulbs increased their length rostrally by 4 mm—i.e., to the human length while maintaining the overall length of measurement 6. These data are consistent with the hypothesis that the orbital surface of the frontal lobes was expanded in the region of **rof** in conjunction with some lengthening and flattening of the olfactory bulbs in *Australopithecus* compared to *Paranthropus*, and that the olfactory bulbs continued to lengthen in a rostral direction subsequent to this (i.e., in descendants of *Australopithecus* that may have given rise to *Homo*).

Our findings have wider implications for the evolution of cognition in early hominids. Both the blunt-shaped, relatively enlarged portions of the orbital surfaces of the frontal lobes and the anteriorly expanded, laterally pointed temporal poles of *Australopithecus* appear more human-like compared to *Paranthropus* and African apes. The area that is expanded near **rof** in the frontal lobes of *Australopithecus* corresponds to Brodmann's area 10 in both apes and humans, which has been shown experimentally to be involved in abstract thinking, planning of future actions, and undertaking initiatives (Semendeferi, 1994). Because the relative size of human area 10 is twice that of both bonobos and chimpanzees, Semendeferi (1994) suggested that this area of the cerebral cortex increased in relative size at some point along the line from the first hominids to the early representatives of the genus *Homo*. Our results support her suggestion, and further suggest that area 10 had begun to increase in size in *Australopithecus*.

Significantly, the temporal poles of chimpanzees (area TG) receive fibers from the orbital surface of the frontal lobe (area FF) (Bailey et al., 1950). In humans, the temporal poles (Brodmann's area 38) connect with the frontal lobes, limbic structures, and

> through their interconnections with visual and auditory association cortex, an elaborate association complex is built up in this anterior end of the temporal lobe. (Crosby et al., 1962:472).

Interestingly, the anterior lateral regions of the temporal poles of humans are activated during the recognition and naming of familiar human faces (Damasio et al., 1996).

Until now, received wisdom has been that brain size began to increase rapidly in the genus *Homo* around 2.0 Ma (Falk, 1992). Our findings that *Paranthropus* had smaller average cranial capacities than previously believed (Conroy et al., 1998; Falk, 1998), and that reorganization of the frontal and temporal lobes appears to have been underway in *Australopithecus* well before 2.0 Ma, suggest that the trends for increased brain size and cortical reorganization may have begun one million years earlier than previously believed, i.e., in the *Australopithecus* ancestors of *Homo* (Figure 5). Evidence pertaining to cranial blood flow, on the other hand, suggests that earlier hominid species, like *A. afarensis* from Hadar, Ethiopia (now placed in the genus *Praeanthropus* by Strait et al., 1997) could have been ancestral to *Paranthropus*, but not to the *Australopithecus–Homo* lineage (Falk & Conroy, 1983; Falk et al., 1995; Falk & Gage, 1998). These hypotheses are consistent with the recent findings of other workers based on analyses of postcrania (Berger, 1998; McHenry & Berger, 1998). As additional fossil hominids come to light, we look forward to learning more about wider areas of the cerebral cortex in early hominids, and to future tests of the ideas and hypotheses presented in this paper.

ACKNOWLEDGMENTS

This research is supported by NSF grant SBR-9729796 (DF), and was made possible by the cooperation of curators at the Transvaal Museum in Pretoria (C. K. Brain and E. Vrba), the Department of Anatomy at the University of Witwatersrand in Johannesburg (P. V. Tobias), and the National Museums of Kenya (R. Leakey) who generously

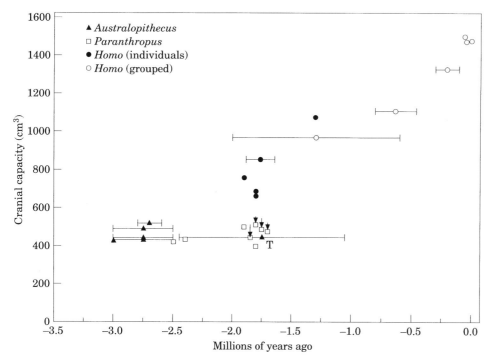

Figure 5. *Cranial capacities from* Australopithecus *and* Paranthropus *plotted against time (Table 5). For comparative purposes, cranial capacities are also provided for a number of key representatives of* Homo *(both individuals and groups; see Falk, 1987 for data). The relative dates for the South African specimens are indicated by error bars; the East African specimens (all* Paranthropus*) are associated with more precise radiometric dates. The age estimates for Taung are from Partridge (1986) and McKee (1993). The error bars for the dates for* Homo *provide the general range of dates that have been suggested by various workers for individuals or groups (Falk, 1987; Swisher et al., 1994). The four arrows illustrate the magnitude of the decrease in new cranial capacities reported on here compared to earlier estimates.* **T** *indicates the adult projection for Taung, which is the only hominid from its site and, although it is the type specimen for* A. africanus, *manifests a number of* Paranthropus-*like characteristics in its skull, teeth, and endocast (Falk et al., 1995). This graph and the morphological data pertaining to endocasts (see text) suggest that brain size may have begun to increase in australopithecine ancestors of* Homo *between 2.5 and 3.0 Ma.*

provided DF with casts and endocasts from original specimens. We thank Tim Gage and Bruce Dudek for statistical advice, Dieter zur Nedden for making his CT unit available to us, Alan Walker for helping us to obtain copies of hominid endocasts and for providing a copy of the occipital endocast of Omo L338y-6, R. MacPhee and F. Brady for permitting us to make endocasts from ape skulls at the American Museum of Natural History, and Terry Harrison for helpful suggestions regarding the manuscript.

REFERENCES

Bailey, P., Bonin, G. von & McCulloch, W. S. (1950). *The Isocortex of the Chimpanzee.* Urbana: University of Illinois Press.

Berger, L. R. (1998). The dawn of humans, redrawing our family tree? *Nat. Geog.* **194**, 90–99.

Brown, B., Walker, A., Ward, C. V. & Leakey, R. E. (1993). New *Australopithecus boisei* calvaria from east Lake Turkana. *Am. J. phys. Anthrop.* **91**, 137–159.

Cheverud, J., Kohn, L. A. P., Konigsberg, L. W. & Leigh, S. R. (1992). Effects of fronto-occipital artificial cranial vault modification on the cranial base and face. *Am. J. phys. Anthrop.* **88**, 323–345.

Connolly, J. C. (1950). *External Morphology of the Primate Brain.* Springfield, Illinois: Charles C. Thomas.

Conroy, G. C., Falk, D., Guyer, J., Weber, G., Seidler, H. & Recheis, W. (2000). Endocranial capacity in Sts 71 (*Australopithecus africanus*) by 3-dimensional computed tomography. *Anat. Rec.* **258**, 391–396.

Conroy, G. C., Vannier, M. W. & Tobias, P. V. (1990). Endocranial features of *Australopithecus africanus* revealed by 2- and 3-D computed tomography. *Science* **247**, 838–841.

Conroy, G. C., Weber, G. W., Seidler, H., Tobias, P. V., Kane, A. & Brunsden, B. (1998). Endocranial capacity in an early hominid cranium from Sterkfontein, South Africa. *Science* **280**, 1730–1731.

Cramer, D. L. (1977). Craniofacial morphology of *P. paniscus*: a morphometric and evolutionary appraisal. *Contrib. Primatol.* **10**, 1–64.

Crosby, E. C., Humphrey, T. & Lauer, E. W. (1962). *Correlative Anatomy of the Nervous System.* New York: Macmillan.

Damasio, H., Grabowski, T. J., Tranel, D., Hichwa, R. D. & Damasio, A. R. (1996). A neural basis for lexical retrieval. *Nature* **380**, 499–505.

Deacon, T. W. (1997). *The Symbolic Species.* New York: W. W. Norton.

Dean, M. C. (1988). Growth processes in the cranial base of hominoids and their bearing on morphological similarities that exist in the cranial base of *Homo* and *Paranthropus*. In (F. Grine, Ed.) *Evolutionary History of the "Robust" Australopithecines*, pp. 107–112. New York: Aldine de Gruyter.

Falk, D. (1983). Cerebral cortices of East African early hominids. *Science* **221**, 1072–1074.

Falk, D. (1987). Hominid paleoneurology. *Ann. Rev. Anthrop.* **16**, 13–30.

Falk, D. (1992). *Evolution of the Brain and Cognition in Hominids* (James Arthur Lecture). New York: American Museum of Natural History.

Falk, D. (1998). Hominid brain evolution: looks can be deceiving. *Science* **280**, 1714.

Falk, D. & Conroy, G. C. (1983). The cranial venous sinus system in *Australopithecus afarensis*. *Nature* **306**, 779–781.

Falk, D. & Gage, T. (1998). Radiators are cool: a response to Braga & Boesch's published paper and reply. *J. hum. Evol.* **35**, 307–312.

Falk, D. & Kasinga, S. (1983). Cranial capacity of a female robust australopithecine (KNM-ER 407) from Kenya. *J. hum. Evol.* **12**, 515–518.

Falk, D., Gage, T. B., Dudek, B. & Olson, T. R. (1995). Did more than one species of hominid coexist before 3.0 ma?: evidence from blood and teeth. *J. hum. Evol.* **29**, 591–600.

Finlay, B. L. & Darlington, R. B. (1995). Linked regularities in the development and evolution of mammalian brains. *Science* **268**, 1578–1584.

Holloway, R. L. (1972). New australopithecine endocast, SK 1585, from Swartkrans, South Africa. *Am. J. phys. Anthrop.* **37**, 173–186.

Holloway, R. L. (1973). New endocranial values for the East African early hominids. *Nature* **243**, 97–99.

Holloway, R. L. (1975). Early hominid endocasts: volumes, morphology and significance for hominid evolution. In (R. H. Tuttle, Ed.) *Primate Functional Morphology and Evolution*, pp. 391–415. The Hague: Mouton.

Holloway, R. L. (1981). The endocast of the Omo juvenile L338y-6 hominid specimen. *Am. J. phys. Anthrop.* **54**, 109–118.

Holloway, R. L. (1983). Human paleontological evidence relevant to language behavior. *Hum. Neurobiol.* **2**, 105–114.

Holloway, R. L. (1988*a*). Brain. In (I. Tattersall, E. Delson & J. van Couvering, Eds) *Encyclopedia of Human Evolution and Prehistory*, pp. 98–105. New York: Garland.

Holloway, R. L. (1988*b*). "Robust" australopithecine brain endocasts: some preliminary observations. In (F. Grine, Ed.) *Evolutionary History of the "Robust" Australopithecines*, pp. 97–105. New York: Aldine de Gruyter.

Kohn, L. A. P., Leigh, S., Jacobs, S. & Cheverud, J. (1993). Effects of annular cranial vault modification on the cranial base and face. *Am. J. phys. Anthrop.* **90**, 147–168.

Leakey, R. E. F. & Walker, A. (1988). New *Australopithecus boisei* specimens from east and west Lake Turkana. *Am. J. phys. Anthrop.* **76**, 1–24.

McHenry, H. M. & Berger, L. R. (1998). Body proportions in *Australopithecus afarensis* and *A. africanus* and the origin of the genus *Homo*. *J. hum. Evol.* **35**, 1–22.

McKee, J. K. (1993). Faunal dating of the Taung hominid fossil deposit. *J. hum. Evol.* **25**, 363–376.

Pakkenberg, B. & Gundersen, J. G. (1997). Neocortical neuron number in humans: effect of sex and age. *J. Comp. Neurol.* **384**, 312–320.

Partridge, T. (1986). Paleoecology of the Pliocene and lower Pleistocene hominids of southern Africa: how good is the chronological and paleoenvironmental evidence? *S. Afr. J. Sci.* **82**, 80–83.

Passingham, R. E. (1998). The specializations of the human neocortex. In (A. D. Milner, Ed.) *Comparative Neuropsychology*, pp. 271–298. Oxford: Oxford University Press.

Semendeferi, K. (1994). Evolution of the hominoid prefrontal cortex: a quantitative and image analysis of area 13 and 10. Ph.D. Dissertation, University of Iowa.

Semendeferi, K. & Damasio, H. (2000). The brain and its main anatomical subdivisions in living hominoids using magnetic resonance imaging. *J. hum. Evol.* **38**, 317–332.

Stephan, H., Frahm, H. & Baron, G. (1981). New and revised data on volumes of brain structures in insectivores and primates. *Folia primatol.* **35**, 1–29.

Strait, D. S., Grine, F. E. & Moniz, M. A. (1997). A reappraisal of early hominid phylogeny. *J. hum. Evol.* **32**, 17–82.

Swisher III, C. C., Curtis, G. H., Jacob, T., Getty, A. G., Suprijo, A. & Widiasmoro (1994). Age of the earliest hominids in Java, Indonesia. *Science* **263**, 1118–1121.

Tobias, P. V. (1967). *Olduvai Gorge, Volume 2 The Cranium and Maxillary Dentition of Australopithecus (Zinjanthropus) boisei*. Cambridge: Cambridge University Press.

Tobias, P. V. (1997). Evolution of brain size, morphological restructuring and longevity in early hominids. In (S. U. Dani, A. Hori & G. F. Walter, Eds) *Principles of Neural Aging*, pp. 153–174. Amsterdam: Elsevier.

Walker, A. C., Leakey, R. E., Harris, J. M. & Brown, F. H. (1986). 2.5-Myr *Australopithecus boisei* from west of Lake Turkana, Kenya. *Nature* **322**, 517–522.

Weber, G. W., Recheis, W., Scholze, T. & Seidler, H. (1998). Virtual anthropology (VA): methodological aspects of linear and volume measurements—first results. *Coll. Antropol.* **22**, 575–583.

24

Diet and the Evolution of the Earliest Human Ancestors

M. F. Teaford and P. S. Ungar

ABSTRACT

Over the past decade, discussions of the evolution of the earliest human ancestors have focused on the locomotion of the australopithecines. Recent discoveries in a broad range of disciplines have raised important questions about the influence of ecological factors in early human evolution. Here we trace the cranial and dental traits of the early australopithecines through time, to show that between 4.4 million and 2.3 million years ago, the dietary capabilities of the earliest hominids changed dramatically, leaving them well suited for life in a variety of habitats and able to cope with significant changes in resource availability associated with long-term and short-term climatic fluctuations.

Reprinted with permission from *Proceedings of the National Academy of Sciences, USA*, Vol. 97, pp. 13506–13511. Copyright © 2000 National Academy of Sciences, U.S.A.

Since the discovery of *Australopithecus afarensis*, many researchers have emphasized the importance of bipedality in scenarios of human origins (1, 2).

Surprisingly, less attention has been focused on the role played by diet in the ecology and evolution of the early hominids (as usually received). Recent work in a broad range of disciplines, such as paleoenvironmental studies (3, 4), behavioral ecology (5), primatology (6), and isotope analyses (7), has rekindled interests in early hominid diets. Moreover, important new fossils from the early Pliocene raise major questions about the role of dietary changes in the origins and early evolution of the Hominidae (8–10). In short, we need to focus not just on how the earliest hominids moved between food patches, but also on what they ate when they got there.

This paper presents a review of the fossil evidence for the diets of the Pliocene hominids *Ardipithecus ramidus, Australopithecus anamensis, Australopithecus afarensis,* and *Australopithecus africanus.* These hominids offer evidence for the first half of human evolution, from our split with prehistoric apes to the earliest members of our own genus, *Homo.* The taxa considered are viewed as a roughly linear sequence from *Ardipithecus* to *A. africanus,* spanning the time from 4.4 million to 2.5 million years ago. As such, they give us a unique opportunity to examine changes in dietary adaptations of our ancestors over nearly 2 million years. We also trace what has been inferred concerning the diets of the Miocene hominoids to put changes in Pliocene hominid diets into a broader temporal perspective. From such a perspective, it becomes clear that the dietary capabilities of the early hominids changed dramatically in the time period between 4.4 million and 2.3 million years ago. Most of the evidence has come from five sources: analyses of tooth size, tooth shape, enamel structure, dental microwear, and jaw biomechanics. Taken together, they suggest a dietary shift in the early australopithecines, to increased dietary flexibility in the face of climatic variability. Moreover, changes in diet-related adaptations from *A. anamensis* to *A. afarensis* to *A. africanus* suggest that hard, abrasive foods became increasingly important through the Pliocene, perhaps as critical items in the diet.

TOOTH SIZE

In 1970, Jolly (11) noted that australopithecines had relatively small incisors compared with molars and speculated that this might be associated with terrestrial seed eating, as seen in *Theropithecus* today. Although this idea has been the subject of some controversy (12), Jolly's efforts have stimulated considerable research on the origins of hominid adaptations and on relative incisor size in a wide variety of living and fossil primates. Hylander (13), for example, examined the relationship of incisor row length (relative to body size) in a range of living anthropoids and found that those species with larger incisors tend to consume larger, tougher fruits, whereas those with smaller front teeth tend to feed on smaller foods, or those that require less extensive incisal preparation, such as leaves or berries. Since the work of Jolly and Hylander, numerous workers have looked to incisor size in early hominids and other fossil primates for clues concerning diet.

What can incisor size tell us of the diets of Miocene apes? Unfortunately, not as much as one would like. Ideally, to consider relative incisor sizes among taxa, we need estimates of species body weights based on attributes independent of the dentition. Such estimates are unavailable for most taxa. Furthermore, Miocene apes as a whole evidently had small incisors compared with extant hominoids, in much the same way that platyrrhines as a whole have relatively smaller incisors than do catarrhines, regardless of diet (14). Such phylogenetic effects make it difficult to find an extant comparative baseline series with which to compare these basal taxa of uncertain phyletic affinities.

On the other hand, incisor size might give us some clues to diet and tooth use for the early australopithecines, and we have good, consistent weight estimates from independent studies (15, 16) for many of these taxa. If we look at a regression of maxillary central incisor breadth on body size for species representing a variety of catarrhine genera, we see a separation of cercopithecines (with relatively larger incisors) above the line and colobines below (Figure 1). Furthermore, more frugivorous chimpanzees and orangutans fall above the line, whereas gibbons and gorillas fall close to the line, with relatively smaller incisors. Indeed, values for the living frugivorous great apes fall above the 95% confidence limits of expected incisor size for modern catarrhines. The human values fall below the 95% confidence limits, indicating that we have very small incisors relative to body size.

Relative incisor sizes for the three "gracile" australopithecines are remarkably similar, and they fall very close to the regression line, much like the gorilla. These results are similar to those reported by Kay (21) and Ungar and Grine (17) and suggest that these

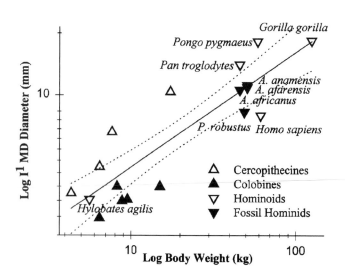

Figure 1. *Relative maxillary first incisor sizes in catarrhines. MD, mesiodistal. Dashed lines indicate 95% confidence limits of the least-squares regression plot (data from refs. 15 and 17–20).*

hominids used their incisors in ingestion to a similar degree, although they all probably used these teeth less than either the chimpanzee or orangutan. These data can also give us some idea of whether a taxon often eats foods that require incisal preparation. For instance, lar gibbons have much smaller incisors than orangutans, and they depend on smaller fruits requiring little incisal preparation (17, 22, 23). From this perspective, the australopithecines probably put less emphasis on foods that require substantial incisor use, such as those with thick husks and those with flesh adherent to large, hard seeds. Body weight estimates and incisor size data for *Ardipithecus ramidus* and *Australopithecus garhi* should provide even more insights.

One of the hallmarks of the australopithecines has always been their large, relatively flat molars (24–29). There are certainly differences in the amount of occlusal relief between gracile and robust australopithecines (30) (see below). However, by comparison with other primates, the australopithecines' molars are still flat and huge. Even in the earliest hominids, this can be seen in a simple plot of mandibular postcanine tooth area (MD × BL, the product of maximal mesiodistal and buccolingual diameters), where most taxa have teeth larger than those of the modern orangutan (Figure 2).

The only exception is *Ardipithecus*, which is more chimp-sized in the P_4–M_1 region, but intermediate between chimpanzees and orangutans in the M_2–M_3 region. Again, interpretations of such differences are hampered by the lack of body size estimates for *Ardipithecus*, but if a body size estimate of 51 kg is used for *A. anamensis* (the average of the two different estimates based on the tibia) (18), McHenry's "megadontia quotient" for this taxon is essentially identical to that for *A. afarensis* (Figure 3). In other words, its molars are large for a hominoid, but smaller than those of *A. africanus* or the "robust" australopithecines.

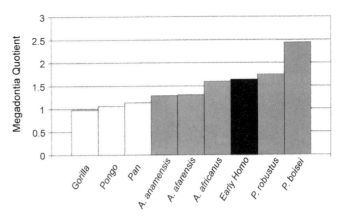

Figure 3. *Megadontia quotients for early hominids and extant primates (data from refs. 18, 20, 27, 31, and 38).*

As one might expect, the Miocene hominoids show a tremendous range of mandibular molar sizes (Figure 2). Many have postcanine tooth areas larger than that of *Ardipithecus,* and some (such as *Ouranopithecus*) even have larger postcanine tooth areas than that of *A. anamensis,* but as all body size estimates for them have been computed from dental remains, a megadontia quotient cannot be computed. The main message from a simple look at postcanine tooth size is that the earliest hominids make a nice progression leading into subsequent hominids, but they do not have larger postcanine teeth than all of the middle to late Miocene hominoids.

This might just mean that there are a variety of body sizes sampled in these taxa. However, as shown by the work of Lucas and colleagues (39), variations in tooth size are a means of adapting to changes in the external characteristics of foods, such as their size, shape, and abrasiveness. Clearly, some of these food characteristics were changing during the evolution of the earliest hominids, as postcanine teeth became relatively larger and larger. However, evidence from the middle to late Miocene shows that tooth size, by itself, cannot pinpoint the initial change to a hominid diet, at least not with the samples at hand.

One other way of looking at postcanine tooth size is to look at the ratio of the areas of M1 and M3 (Figure 4). Lucas et al. (39) showed that this ratio was inversely related to the percentage of leaves, flowers, and shoots in the diet; that is, anthropoids with a high ratio of M1 to M3 area consumed more fruit than did those with a low M1 to M3 ratio. When this is computed for the earliest hominids, plus a sample of Miocene apes, a clear separation is evident, with the early hominids, including *Ardipithecus,* showing higher ratios than the Miocene apes. So, does this indicate more fruit in the diet of the earliest hominids? To begin to answer this question, we must look at analyses of tooth shape.

TOOTH SHAPE

Variations in tooth shape are a means of adapting to changes in the internal characteristics of foods, such as their strength, toughness, and deformability (39–43).

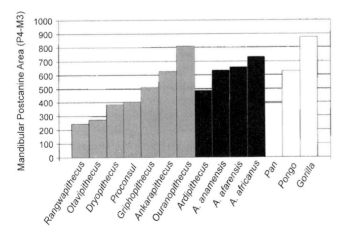

Figure 2. *Summed mandibular postcanine tooth areas (P4–M3) in Miocene apes, early hominids, and extant apes (data from refs. 8, 18–20, and 31–37).*

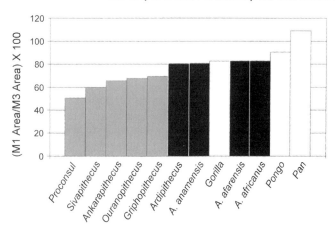

Figure 4.   *Ratios of M1 to M3 areas, defined as the products of maximal mesiodistal and buccolingual diameters (data from refs. 8, 18–20, and 31–37).*

Clearly, foods are complicated structures; thus it is impossible to describe all of the internal characteristics that might have confronted the earliest hominids' teeth. However, another approach is to describe the capabilities of those teeth.

For example, tough foods, those that are difficult to fracture, are generally sheared between the leading edges of sharp crests. In contrast, hard brittle foods, those that are easy to fracture but difficult to penetrate, are crushed between planar surfaces. As such, reciprocally concave, highly crested teeth have the capability of efficiently processing tough items such as insect exoskeletons and leaves, whereas rounder and flatter cusped teeth are best suited for a more frugivorous diet. Kay (21) has devised a "shearing quotient" as a measure of the relative shear potential of molar teeth. Basically, more folivorous species have the highest shearing quotients, followed by those that prefer brittle, soft fruits; finally, hard-object feeders have the lowest shearing quotients (21, 44).

Shearing crest studies have been conducted on early Miocene African apes and middle to late Miocene European apes. These studies suggest a considerable range of diets in these forms. For example, *Rangwapithecus* and *Oreopithecus* have relatively long shearing crests, suggesting folivory; *Ouranopithecus* has extremely short "crests," suggesting a hard-object specialization; whereas most other Miocene taxa studied, such as *Proconsul* and *Dryopithecus*, have the intermediate length crests of a frugivore (14, 45).

As for the early hominids, *A. africanus* had more occlusal relief than did *Paranthropus robustus*, suggesting a dietary difference between these species (30). Additional preliminary shearing quotient studies support this idea while reaffirming that the australopithecines, as a group, had relatively flat, blunt molar teeth and lacked the long shearing crests seen in some extant hominoids (28). By itself, this indicates that the earliest hominids would have had difficulty breaking down tough, pliant foods, such as soft seed coats and the veins and stems of leaves—although

they probably were capable of processing buds, flowers, and shoots.

Interestingly, as suggested by Lucas and Peters (46), another tough pliant food they would have had difficulty processing is meat. In other words, the early hominids were not dentally preadapted to eat meat—they simply did not have the sharp, reciprocally concave shearing blades necessary to retain and cut such foods. In contrast, given their flat, blunt teeth, they were admirably equipped to process hard brittle objects. What about soft fruits? It really depends on the toughness of those fruits. If they were tough, then they would also need to be precisely retained and sliced between the teeth. Again, early hominids would be very inefficient at it. If they were not tough, then the hominids could certainly process soft fruits.

In sum, Miocene apes show a range of adaptations, including folivory, soft-fruit eating, and hard-object feeding. This range exceeds that of living hominoids and especially the early hominids. Although studies of shearing crest length have been conducted on only some of the early hominids, all evidence indicates that the australopithecines had relatively flat molar teeth compared with many living and fossil apes. These teeth were well suited for breaking down hard, brittle foods, including some fruits and nuts, and soft, weak foods, such as flowers and buds; but again, they were not well suited for breaking down tough pliant foods such as stems, soft seed pods, and meat.

ENAMEL STRUCTURE

Another area of interest regarding dental functional anatomy is the study of enamel thickness. There are certainly methodological differences between studies (47–52), but the consensus still seems to be that the australopithecines had relatively thick enamel compared with living primates, and that many of the Miocene apes also had thick enamel (24, 28, 48–49, 51, 53–54). Interestingly, this perspective may be changing as we get glimpses of more and more new taxa. For instance, Conroy et al. (55) have noted that *Otavipithecus* may have had thin enamel, and White et al. (8) have made the same observation for *Ardipithecus*. Granted, in neither case do we have a detailed series of measurements over the tooth crown, but still, the figures that have been quoted (less than 1 mm for *Otavipithecus* and 1.1–1.2 mm for *Ardipithecus*) are far less than those quoted for the australopithecines.

So what might be the functional significance of enamel thickness? The most frequently cited correlations are between the consumption of hard food items, or abrasive food items, and thick molar enamel (58–59). There are many potential complicating factors (51, 56, 59–60); thus it is perhaps not surprising that the correlation between enamel thickness and diet is not a perfect one (57). Moreover, thick enamel by itself does not necessarily provide protection against hard objects, which commonly cause fracture of enamel (61). The best protection against this is prism or crystallite decussation or interweaving. Maas (62, 63), Rensberger

(64, 65), and others (42, 59) have shown that prism and crystallite orientations can give clues to intricate details of dental function, and that decussation can be an effective crack-stopping mechanism in many animals. Only anecdotal references to this phenomenon in Miocene apes and early hominids have been made thus far, largely because more detailed work generally requires the sectioning and etching of teeth. Still, after some discussion and debate (48–49, 53), a consensus now seems to be that they did have a significant degree of prism decussation. Thus, the thick enamel of the early hominids may have been a means of resisting breakage during the consumption of hard objects and an adaptation that prolonged the life of the tooth, given an abrasive diet.

DENTAL MICROWEAR

Numerous workers have recognized that microscopic wear on the incisors and molars of primates reflects tooth use and diet. For example, those primates that often use their front teeth in ingestion have high densities of microwear striations on their incisors. Furthermore, folivores have a high incidence of long narrow scratches on their molars, whereas frugivores have more pits on those surfaces. Among frugivores, hard-object feeders have even higher pit incidences than soft-fruit eaters. These and other relationships between microwear and feeding behaviors in living primates have been used to infer diet in fossil forms. Miocene apes have a remarkable range of microwear patterning, greatly exceeding that of living hominoids. For example, relatively high scratch densities suggest that *Micropithecus, Rangwapithecus*, and especially *Oreopithecus* (66) included more leaves in their diets. In contrast, high pit percentages suggest that *Griphopithecus* and *Ouranopithecus* (66) were hard-object specialists. Finally, intermediate microwear patterns suggest that most other species studied, such as *Gigantopithecus, Dendropithecus, Proconsul, Dryopithecus*, and, perhaps, *Sivapithecus* (66–68), had diets dominated by soft fruits. These data give us a glimpse of the extraordinary variation from which the last common ancestor of apes and hominids evidently arose.

Unfortunately, little is known about the microwear of early australopithecines. No microwear research has yet been published for either *Ardipithecus ramidus* or *A. anamensis*, although there has been some done on *A. afarensis* and *A. africanus*. The work done on *A. afarensis* has been largely qualitative and focused on the anterior teeth, and it suggests that these hominids were beginning to exploit savanna resources (69). Furthermore, Ryan and Johanson (70) argued that *A. afarensis* had a mosaic of gorilla-like fine wear striae and baboon-like pits and microflakes, indicating the use of incisors to strip gritty plant parts such as seeds, roots, and rhizomes. These authors also suggested that there was a functional shift in the P^3 complex from ape-like slicing and cutting to hominid puncture-crushing.

Work done on *A. africanus* has been more quantitative but has focused on comparing this taxon to *Paranthropus robustus* rather than to extant hominoids. Grine (71) found that *A. africanus* molars have lower incidences of pitting than seen for *Paranthropus*. *A. africanus* scratches are also longer and narrower and show more homogeneity in orientation. Grine argued that compared with the "robust" forms, *A. africanus* ate more soft fruits and leaves. Comparisons with work from Teaford (72) places *A. africanus* between *Cebus olivaceus* on one hand and *Pan troglodytes* on the other. Work on *A. africanus* incisors has shown that this taxon has higher microwear feature densities on all surfaces examined than does *Paranthropus* (17). This suggests that *A. africanus* processed a greater variety of foods with its front teeth, including larger, more abrasive ones, than were encountered by *Paranthropus*. Comparisons with an extant baseline series examined by Ungar (73) puts *Australopithecus* between *Pongo pygmaeus* and the seed predator/folivore *Presbytis thomasi* in degree of anterior tooth use in ingestion.

In sum, then, the microwear suggests that, by the end of the Miocene, hominoids had a wide range of diets. In contrast, *A. afarensis* probably focused on soft fruit but also began to incorporate into its diet abrasive, terrestrial resources that required incisal stripping. *A. africanus* may still have focused on soft fruit, particularly that which required a moderate amount of incisal preparation. Clearly, considerably more work is needed on these and other early hominids to put together a reasonable picture of diet based on microwear evidence.

MANDIBULAR BIOMECHANICS

Finally, there are other lines of evidence that we can examine to look for evidence of diet. Mandibular fragments are among the most common bony remains found at hominid fossil sites, and the architecture of this bone has been adapted to withstand stresses and strains associated with oral food processing. Thus its morphology probably reflects some aspects of diet. Analyses of australopithecine mandibular biomechanics have focused on corpus size and shape.

Comparisons with extant hominoids have shown that *A. afarensis* and *A. africanus* have relatively thick mandibular corpora (74, 75). The same pattern was also found for *Paranthropus boisei* and *P. robustus*. Figure 5 shows mandibular robusticity index values for extant great apes, some Miocene apes, and early australopithecines. The early hominids show relatively thicker mandibular corpora than extant great apes and Miocene catarrhines, suggesting a morphological shift in the former.

Both functional and nonfunctional interpretations have been offered to explain this phenomenon. For example, it may simply be that a thick mandibular corpus is an effect of large cheek teeth or a reduced canine. This is not a likely explanation, however, as australopithecines still have relatively broad mandibles when considered relative to molar size, and there appears to be no relationship between mandibular robusticity and relative canine size among the australopithecines (75).

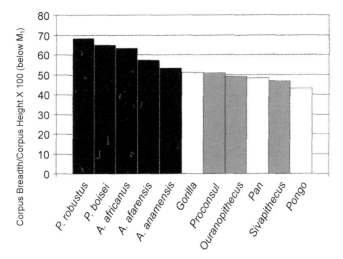

Figure 5. *Mandibular corpus shape (data from refs. 75, 76, and 85 and M. Leakey, personal communication).*

DISCUSSION

The australopithecines exhibited a complex of morphological features related to diet that are unique compared with living hominoids or Miocene apes. These early hominids all had small- to moderate-sized incisors; large, flat molars with little shear potential; a ratio of first to third molar area that was low compared with those of extant apes, but generally higher than those of Miocene apes; thick tooth enamel; and thick mandibular corpora. This suite of traits is distinctive of australopithecines and suggests a dietary shift at or near the stem of hominid evolution. Their thick-enameled, flattened molars would have had great difficulty propagating cracks through tough foods, suggesting that the australopithecines were not well suited for eating tough fruits, leaves, or meat. The dental microwear data agree with this conclusion, as the australopithecine patterns documented to date are most similar to those of modern-day seed predators and soft fruit eaters. Furthermore, given their comparatively small incisors, these hominids probably did not specialize in large, husked fruits or those requiring extensive incisal preparation. Instead, the australopithecines would have easily been able to break down hard, brittle foods. Their large flat molars would have served well for crushing, and their thick enamel would have withstood abrasion and fracture. Their mandibular corpora would probably have conferred an advantage for resisting failure, given high occlusal loads. In essence, for much of their history, the australopithecines had an adaptive package that allowed them ready access to hard objects, plus soft foods that were not particularly tough. The early hominids could also have eaten both abrasive and nonabrasive foods. This ability to eat both hard and soft foods, plus abrasive and nonabrasive foods, would have left the early hominids particularly well suited for life in a variety of habitats, ranging from gallery forest to open savanna.

Does this mean we can talk of a characteristic "australopithecine" dietary pattern? Perhaps to some extent, but although the australopithecines shared many features in common, they also differed from one another, suggesting a change in diet through time. Such morphological changes occurred as a mosaic, much as that seen for locomotor anatomy.

Much of the evidence for *Ardipithecus ramidus* is not yet available, but despite its thin molar enamel and absolutely smaller teeth than those of later hominids, it shows molar size proportions that may hint at dietary changes to come. *A. anamensis* shows the first indications of thicker molar enamel in a hominid, and its molar teeth were equivalent in size to those of *A. afarensis*. Still, its mandibular corpus is intermediate in robusticity between those of living great apes and later australopithecines. This combination of features suggests that *A. anamensis* might have been the first hominid to be able to effectively withstand the functional demands of hard and perhaps abrasive objects in its diet, whether or not such items were frequently eaten or were only an important occasional food source. *A. afarensis* was similar to *A. anamensis* in relative tooth sizes and probably enamel thickness, yet it did show a large increase in

Despite some inherent difficulties, it seems more likely that the unique shape of the australopithecine mandibular corpus relates to the functional demands of mastication. Thickened mandibles can act to resist extreme stresses associated with transverse bending (that is, "wishboning") and torsion. Because wishboning stresses decline toward the back of the corpus, torsion is likely a more important explanation. Corpus torsion can result from bite force and muscle activity during mastication. Therefore, it may be that australopithecine mandibular morphology reflects elevated stresses associated with unusual mechanical demands. Daegling and Grine (75) suggest that australopithecines may have eaten fibrous, coarse foods that required repetitive loading. While this fails to explain why colobines do not have thick corpora, it does suggest a fundamental difference between australopithecines and living great apes that may reflect a shift in diet in the early hominids.

Studies of corpus shape in *A. anamensis* and *Ardipithecus ramidus* will likely provide further clues regarding differences in mandibular architecture between great apes and later australopithecines. Corpus robusticity indices for *A. anamensis* below M_1 average 53.5 (M. Leakey, personal communication). These values fall at the upper range for extant hominoids (*Pan* = 39.2–57.8; *Gorilla* = 43.5–59.7; *Pongo* = 35.7–52.0) and at the lower end of the range for later fossil hominids (*A. afarensis* = 48.4–68.9, *A. africanus* = 54.8–79.0) (Figure 5) (data from Daegling and Grine and Lockwood et al.) (75, 85).

In sum, the architecture of the mandibular corpus suggests that the "gracile" australopithecines differed from living apes in their abilities to dissipate masticatory stresses. Taken with other lines of evidence, this certainly suggests a difference in diet between living apes and *A. anamensis*, and between *A. anamensis* and later hominids, with *A. anamensis* intermediate between the African ape and later australopithecine conditions.

mandibular robusticity. This increase may be due to changes in peak force magnitude or degree of repetitive loading in mastication. Either way, hard and perhaps abrasive foods may have become even more important components of the diet of *A. afarensis*. *A. africanus* shows yet another increase in postcanine tooth size, which by itself would suggest an increase in the sizes and abrasiveness of foods. However, its molar microwear does not show the degree of pitting one might expect from a classic hard-object feeder. Thus, even *A. africanus* has evidently not begun to specialize in hard objects, but rather has emphasized dietary breadth. In contrast, subsequent "robust" australopithecines do show hard-object microwear and craniodental specializations, suggesting a substantial departure in feeding adaptive strategies early in the Pleistocene.

In sum, diet was probably an important factor in the origin and early evolution of our family. The earliest australopithecines show a unique suite of diet-related features unlike those of Miocene apes or living hominoids. Such features suggest that the earliest hominids may have begun to experiment with harder, more brittle foods at the expense of softer, tougher ones early on. This does not mean that all of the australopithecines were specialized hard-object feeders. It merely means that, through time, they acquired the ability to feed on hard objects. Many modern primates need to consume critical "fall-back foods" at certain times of the year (6), and it may well be that the earliest australopithecines resorted to the consumption of hard objects only in such situations, whereas the robust australopithecines relied on them far more regularly.

Another important aspect of early hominid trophic adaptations is evident from data presented here—the dietary shift from apes to early hominids did not involve an increase in the consumption of tough foods, and so the australopithecines were not preadapted for eating meat. This conclusion runs counter to (*i*) recent isotope work suggesting that the australopithecines did in fact consume significant amounts of meat (7) and (*ii*) nutritional work suggesting that meat may have provided critical nutrients for both young and old hominids (77–79). There would seem to be three different ways to reconcile these perspectives. First, the present study has reviewed only craniodental features related to diet. If the australopithecines used other means for ingesting and processing meat (e.g., tools), they might have been able to process meat more efficiently than the craniodental evidence suggests (80, 81). Second, the heavy C3 signature found in *A. africanus* (7) may reflect the consumption of underground storage organs of C3 plants rather

than meat (82). Third, the functional analyses of the teeth assume that all meat has the same degree of toughness. This may not be the case. Studies of the physical properties of food have thus far focused on plant remains, with only brief mention of the toughness of materials like skin (40, 46). Variations in toughness between animal tissues might well be due to variations in the arrangement and density of collagen matrix. Furthermore, the physical effects of decomposition might render meat less tough and more readily processed by hominids. If this is so, it could be further evidence in support of scavenging as part of the early hominid way of life.

Investigators have tried to relate patterns of hominid evolution to patterns of climatic change for some time (3, 4). The focus of much of the recent work has been on the origin of the genus *Homo*. Can the dietary shifts in the earliest hominids also be tied to such changes? Whereas there is some evidence of large-scale climatic changes around the Mediterranean (83) and unusual faunal turnover in parts of western Asia (84), there are no large-scale changes evident in sub-Saharan Africa until after the earliest hominids have arrived on the scene (i.e., not until 1.5–2.5 million years ago). There is the slow and inexorable cooling and drying of the Miocene, but perhaps the crucial result of this was an increase in microhabitat variability. Certainly, there are limits to our paleoecological evidence from this period, but as Potts (4) has noted, "in general, the oldest hominids were associated with a diverse range of habitats." These included lake and river margins, woodland, bushland, and savanna. Potts (4) has emphasized that locomotor versatility was a crucial adaptation of the earliest hominids in the face of such varied environmental conditions. We feel that this perspective needs to be extended to the dietary adaptations of the earliest hominids as well. In such a land of variable opportunities, the generalized craniodental toolkit of the earliest hominids may have had a distinct advantage, as it allowed our forebears the flexibility to cope with short-term and long-term climatic variations and the resultant changes in resource availability.

ACKNOWLEDGMENTS

We are grateful to the Governments of Ethiopia, Kenya, and Tanzania and especially to the National Museums of Ethiopia, Kenya, and Tanzania for permission to study early hominid specimens in their care. This work was supported by National Science Foundation Grants SBR 9804882 and 9601766.

REFERENCES

1. Lovejoy, C. O. (1975) in *Primate Functional Morphology and Evolution*, ed. Tuttle, R. L. (Mouton, The Hague), pp. 291–326.
2. Susman, R. L., Stern, J. T. & Jungers, W. L. (1984) *Folia Primatol.* **43**, 113–156.
3. Vrba, E. S. (1995) in *Paleoclimate and Evolution, with Emphasis on Human Origins*, eds. Vrba, E. S., Denton, G. H., Partridge, T. C. & Burckle, L. H. (Yale Univ. Press, New Haven, CT), pp. 24–45.
4. Potts, R. (1998) *Yearbook Phys. Anthropol.* **41**, 93–136.
5. O'Connell, J. F., Hawkes, K. & Blurton Jones, N. G. (1999) *J. Hum. Evol.* **36**, 461–485.

6. Conklin-Brittain, N. L., Wrangham, R. W. & Hunt, K. D. (1998) *Int. J. Primatol.* **19**, 949–970.

7. Sponheimer, M. & Lee-Thorp, J. A. (1999) *Science* **283**, 368–370.

8. White, T. D., Suwa, G. & Asfaw, B. (1994) *Nature (London)* **371**, 306–312.

9. Asfaw, B., White, T., Lovejoy, O., Latimer, B., Simpson, S. & Suwa, G. (1999) *Science* **284**, 629–634.

10. Ward, C., Leakey, M. & Walker, A. (1999) *Evol. Anthropol.* **7**, 197–205.

11. Jolly, C. J. (1970) *Man* **5**, 1–26.

12. Dunbar, R. I. M. (1976) *J. Hum. Evol.* **5**, 161–167.

13. Hylander, W. L. (1975) *Science* **189**, 1095–1098.

14. Kay, R. F. & Ungar, P. S. (1997) in *Function, Phylogeny and Fossils: Miocene Hominoids and Great Ape and Human Origins,* eds. Begun, D. R., Ward, C. & Rose, M. (Plenum, New York), pp. 131–151.

15. Jungers, W. L. (1988) in *Evolutionary History of the "Robust" Australopithecines,* ed. Grine, F. E. (de Gruyter, New York), pp. 115–125.

16. McHenry, H. M. (1992) *Evol. Anthropol.* **1**, 15–20.

17. Ungar, P. S. & Grine, F. E. (1991) *J. Hum. Evol.* **20**, 313–340.

18. Leakey, M. G., Feibel, C. S., McDougall, I. & Walker, A. (1995) *Nature (London)* **376**, 565–571.

19. Wood, B. A. (1991) *Hominid Cranial Remains,* Koobi Fora Research Project (Clarendon, Oxford), Vol. 4.

20. Coffing, K., Feibel, C., Leakey, M. & Walker, A. (1994) *Am. J. Phys. Anthropol.* **93**, 55–65.

21. Kay, R. F. (1984) in *Adaptations for Foraging in Nonhuman Primates: Contributions to an Organismal Biology of Prosimians, Monkeys and Apes,* eds. Rodman, P. S. & Cant, J. G. H. (Columbia Univ. Press, New York), pp. 21–53.

22. Ungar, P. S. (1994) *Am. J. Phys. Anthropol.* **95**, 197–219.

23. Ungar, P. S. (1996) *Am. J. Primatol.* **38**, 145–156.

24. Robinson, J. T. (1956) *Mem. Transvaal Mus.* **9**, 1–179.

25. Wolpoff, M. H. (1973) *Am. J. Phys. Anthropol.* **39**, 375–394.

26. Wood, B. A. & Abbott, S. A. (1983) *J. Anat.* **136**, 197–219.

27. McHenry, H. M. (1984) *Am. J. Phys. Anthropol.* **64**, 297–306.

28. Kay, R. F. (1985) *Annu. Rev. Anthropol.* **14**, 315–341.

29. Suwa, G., Wood, B. A. & White, T. D. (1994) *Am. J. Phys. Anthropol.* **93**, 407–426.

30. Grine, F. E. (1981) *S. Afr. J. Sci.* **77**, 203–230.

31. Mahler, P. E. (1973) Ph.D. thesis (Univ. of Michigan, Ann Arbor).

32. Alpagut, B., Andrews, P. & Martin, L. (1990) *J. Hum. Evol.* **19**, 397–422.

33. Alpagut, B., Andrews, P., Fortelius, M., Kappelman, J., Temizsoy, I., Çelebi, H. & Lindsay, W. (1996) *Nature (London)* **382**, 349–351.

34. Andrews, P. (1978) *Bull. Br. Mus. (Nat. Hist.)* **30**, 85–224.

35. Begun, D. R. & Güleç, E. (1998) *Am. J. Phys. Anthropol.* **105**, 279–314.

36. de Bonis, L. & Melentis, J. (1984) *Cour. Forschungsinst. Senckenberg* **69**, 13–23.

37. Leakey, M. G., Feibel, C. S., McDougall, I., Ward, C. & Walker, A. (1998) *Nature (London)* **393**, 62–66.

38. McHenry, H. M. (1988) in *Evolutionary History of the "Robust" Australopithecines,* ed. Grine, F. E. (de Gruyter, New York), pp. 133–147.

39. Lucas, P. W., Corlett, R. T. & Luke, D. A. (1986) *Z. Morphol. Anthropol.* **76**, 253–276.

40. Lucas, P. W. & Teaford, M. F. (1994) in *Colobine Monkeys: Their Ecology, Behaviour and Evolution,* eds. Davies, A. G. & Oates, J. F. (Cambridge Univ. Press, Cambridge, U.K.), pp. 173–203.

41. Spears, I. R. & Crompton, R. H. (1996) *J. Hum. Evol.* **31**, 517–535.

42. Strait, S. G. (1997) *Evol. Anthropol.* **5**, 199–211.

43. Yamashita, N. (1998) *Am. J. Phys. Anthropol.* **106**, 169–188.

44. Meldrum, D. J. & Kay, R. F. (1997) *Am. J. Phys. Anthropol.* **102**, 407–428.

45. Ungar, P. S. & Kay, R. F. (1995) *Proc. Natl. Acad. Sci. USA* **92**, 5479–5481.

46. Lucas, P. W. & Peters, C. R. (2000) in *Development, Function and Evolution of Teeth,* eds. Teaford, M. F., Smith, M. M. & Ferguson, M. W. J. (Cambridge Univ. Press, Cambridge, U.K.), pp. 282–289.

47. Martin, L. B. (1985) *Nature (London)* **314**, 260–263.

48. Beynon, A. D. & Wood, B. A. (1986) *Am. J. Phys. Anthropol.* **70**, 177–193.

49. Grine, F. E. & Martin, L. B. (1988) in *Evolutionary History of the "Robust" Australopithecines,* ed. Grine, F. E. (de Gruyter, New York), pp. 3–42.

50. Beynon, A. D., Dean, M. C. & Reid, D. J. (1991) *Am. J. Phys. Anthropol.* **86**, 295–309.

51. Macho, G. A. & Thackeray, J. F. (1992) *Am. J. Phys. Anthropol.* **89**, 133–143.

52. Spoor, C. F., Zonneveld, F. W. & Macho, G. A. (1993) *Am. J. Phys. Anthropol.* **91**, 469–484.

53. Gantt, D. G. (1986) in *Comparative Primate Biology. Volume 1. Systematics, Evolution, and Anatomy.* Swindler, D. R. & Erwin, J. (Liss, New York), Vol. 1, pp. 453–475.

54. Andrews, P. & Martin, L. (1991) *Philos. Trans. R. Soc. London B* **334**, 199–209.

55. Conroy, G. C., Pickford, M., Senut, B., Van Couvering, J. & Mein, P. (1992) *Nature (London)* **356**, 144–148.

56. Martin, L. B. (1983) Ph.D. thesis (Univ. of London, London).

57. Maas, M. C. & Dumont, E. R. (1999) *Evol. Anthropol.* **8**, 133–152.

58. Kay, R. F. (1981) *Am. J. Phys. Anthropol.* **55**, 141–151.

59. Dumont, E. R. (1995) *J. Mammal.* **76**, 1127–1136.

60. Macho, G. A. & Berner, M. E. (1993) *Am. J. Phys. Anthropol.* **92**, 189–200.

61. Teaford, M. F., Maas, M. C. & Simons, E. L. (1996) *Am. J. Phys. Anthropol.* **101**, 527–544.

62. Maas, M. C. (1993) *Am. J. Phys. Anthropol.* **92**, 217–233.

63. Maas, M. C. (1994) *Am. J. Phys. Anthropol.* **95**, 221–242.

64. Rensberger, J. M. (1997) in *Tooth Enamel Microstructure,* eds. Koenigswald, W. v. & Sander, M. (Balkema, Rotterdam), pp. 237–257.

65. Rensberger, J. M.(2000) in *Development, Function and Evolution of Teeth,* eds. Teaford, M. F., Smith, M. M. & Ferguson, M. W. J. (Cambridge Univ. Press, Cambridge, U.K.), pp. 252–268.

66. Ungar, P. S. (1996) *J. Hum. Evol.* **31**, 335–366.

67. Teaford, M. F. & Walker, A. C. (1984) *Am. J. Phys. Anthropol.* **64**, 191–200.

68. Daegling, D. J. & Grine, F. E. (1994) *S. Afr. J. Sci.* **90**, 527–532.

69. Puech, P.-F. & Albertini, H. (1984) *Am. J. Phys. Anthropol.* **65**, 87–91.

70. Ryan, A. S. & Johanson, D. C. (1989) *J. Hum. Evol.* **18**, 235–268.

71. Grine, F. E. (1986) *J. Hum. Evol.* **15**, 783–822.

72. Teaford, M. F. (1988) *Scanning Microsc.* **2**, 1149–1166.

73. Ungar, P. S. (1998) *Evol. Anthropol.* **6**, 205–217.

74. Hylander, W. L. (1988) in *Evolutionary History of the "Robust" Australopithecines,* ed. Grine, F. E. (de Gruyter, New York), pp. 55–58.

75. Daegling, D. J. & Grine, F. E. (1991) *Am. J. Phys. Anthropol.* **86**, 321–339.

76. Smith, R. J. (1980) Ph.D. dissertation (Yale Univ., New Haven, CT).

77. Milton, K. & Demment, M. (1988) *Am. J. Primatol.* **46**, 45–52.

78. Milton, K. (1999) *Evol. Anthropol.* **8**, 11–21.

79. Speth, J. D. (1989) *J. Hum. Evol.* **18**, 329–343.

80. Blumenschine, R. J. & Cavallo, J. A. (1992) *Sci. Am.* **267**, 90–96.

81. de Heinzelin, J., Clark, J. D., White, T., Hart, W., Renne, P., WoldeGabriel, G., Beyene, Y. & Vrba, E. (1999) *Science* **284**, 625–629.

82. Lee-Thorp, J. (2001) in *The Evolution of Human Diet,* eds. Ungar, P. S. & Teaford, M. F. (Greenwood, New Haven, CT), in press.

83. Bernor, R. L. (1983) in *New Interpretations of Ape and Human Ancestry,* eds. Ciochon, R. L. & Corruccini, R. S. (Plenum, New York), pp. 21–64.

84. Barry, J. C. (1995) in *Paleoclimate and Evolution, with Emphasis on Human Origins,* eds. Vrba, E. S., Denton, G. H., Partridge, T. C. & Burckle, L. H. (Yale Univ. Press, New Haven, CT), pp. 115–134.

85. Lockwood, C. A., Kimbel, W. H. & Johanson, D. C. (2000) *J. Hum. Evol.* **39**, 23–55.

25

Early Hominid Evolution and Ecological Change through the African Plio-Pleistocene

K. E. Reed

ABSTRACT

The habitats in which extinct hominids existed has been a key issue in addressing the origin and extinction of early hominids, as well as in understanding various morphological and behavioral adaptations. Many researchers postulated that early hominids lived in an open savanna (Dart, 1925; Robinson, 1963; Howell, 1978). However, Vrba (1985, 1988) has noted that a major global climatic and environmental shift from mesic, closed to xeric, open habitats occurred in the late African Pliocene (approximately 2.5 m.y.a.), thus implying that the earliest hominids existed in these mesic, wooded environs. This climatic shift is also suggested to have contributed to a pulse in speciation events with turnovers of many bovid and possibly hominid species. Previous environmental reconstructions of hominid localities have concentrated on taxonomic identities and taxonomic uniformitarianism to provide habitat reconstructions (e.g., Vrba, 1975; Shipman & Harris, 1988). In addition, relative abundances of species are often used to reconstruct a particular environment, when in fact taphonomic factors could be affecting the proportions of taxa. This study uses the morphological adaptations of mammalian assemblages found with early hominids to reconstruct the habitat based on each species' ecological adaptations, thus minimizing problems introduced by taxonomy and taphonomy. Research presented here compares east and south African Plio-Pleistocene mammalian fossil assemblages with 31 extant mammalian communities from eight different habitat types. All communities are analyzed through ecological diversity methods, that is, each species trophic and locomotor adaptations are used to reconstruct an ecological community and derive its vegetative habitat. Reconstructed habitats show that Australopithecus *species existed in fairly wooded, well-watered regions.* Paranthropus *species lived in similar environs and also in more open regions, but always in habitats that include wetlands.* Homo *is the first hominid to exist in areas of fairly open, arid grassland. This change from closed to open habitats occurs gradually from about 4 m.y.a. until about 2 m.y.a. when there is a major increase in arid and grazing adapted mammals. Therefore, the appearance of open savannas do not appear to have influenced the origination or adaptations of the earliest hominids, but could have contributed to their demise. As Stanley (1992) hypothesized,* Homo *species appear the first to be adapted to open, arid environments.*

Reprinted from *Journal of Human Evolution*, Vol. 32, K. E. Reed, Early hominid evolution and ecological change through the African Plio-Pleistocene, pp. 289–322. Copyright © 1997 by Academic Press Ltd. Reprinted with permission from Elsevier.

INTRODUCTION

Many theories of early hominid evolution invoke environmental change to more open and xeric habitats as the causal agent for both origination and extinction events (Dart, 1925; Robinson, 1963; Howell, 1978; Vrba, 1985, 1988; Stanley, 1992). However, researchers have differences of opinion as to which species of hominids might have been the result of these aridification pressures: *Australopithecus, Paranthropus,* or *Homo?* Therefore, it is not only necessary to arrive at accurate habitat reconstructions for early hominid species, but to examine any alterations in those environments over time and compare those changes to appearances and disappearances of early hominids.

Much paleoecological research has centered on the study of single taxa or taxonomic groups and how the functional morphology of that taxonomic group is related to an animal's ecology, and thus its environment (Robinson, 1963; Vrba, 1974, 1975, 1980, 1988; Kay, 1975, 1978; Grine, 1981; Stern & Susman, 1983; Kappelman, 1988; Benefit & McCrossin, 1990; Ciochon, 1990; Spencer, 1995; Lewis, 1997). Community paleoecological analysis has traditionally concentrated on reconstructing the environment through the study of species organization and composition of the fossil fauna recovered from a locality (Dodd & Stanton, 1990). I use a combination of these two methodologies to reconstruct habitats for a variety of Pliocene hominid localities dating from 3.6 Ma until about 1 m.y.a. This is accomplished by first identifying the major trophic and locomotor adaptation of each fossil species through morphological analysis. These adaptations are then examined through ecological diversity analysis in a community perspective. Each fossil assemblage is thus a representative sample of a community of mammalian adaptations.

However, as with morphological studies that compare fossil animals to living ones, these fossil community assemblages had to be compared with modern analogs. Thus, a variety of modern habitats for which lists of large mammalian species were available were selected for this comparative study. These localities were taken from eight major vegetative habitat types, including forests, closed woodland, woodland–bushland transition, medium density woodland and bushland, open woodlands, shrubland, grasslands or plains, and desert.

Success of these paleoecological analyses is related to methods that minimize the effect of taphonomic processes. Accumulation of a fossil assemblage involves a number of processes that can alter the composition of the assemblage away from the original community. Therefore, I tested these methods on modern "death" assemblages. These assemblages consist of remains of mammals that have either died or been killed and left as surface assemblages or have been amassed by various carnivores and other animals. These death assemblages are all located within the modern vegetative habitats for which the entire community is known. Therefore, the results of the habitat reconstructions produced by the death assemblages are compared directly with the living community to determine if death assemblages reflect the habitat in which they were accumulated.

To address questions regarding hominid evolution and extinction, I use the habitat reconstructions of the Pliocene localities. First, I show how mammalian community composition alters with regard to proposed environmental changes that may have affected early hominids, such as suggested by Vrba (1988) at about 2.5 m.y.a. and at about 1.7 m.y.a. (Cerling, 1992; deMenocal, 1995). I also explore the possibility that particular species of hominids were adapted to specific vegetative habitat. Finally, I trace the ecological evidence provided by these fossil localities over time to see if the pattern of stasis purportedly exhibited in *Australopithecus* (Stanley, 1992) and *Paranthropus* (Wood et al., 1994) corresponds to any climatic stasis.

METHODS

Previous fauna-based environmental reconstructions of fossil localities include methods of taxonomic uniformitarianism (e.g., Vrba, 1974), functional or ecological morphology (e.g., Kappelman, 1988; Benefit & McCrossin, 1990), species diversity indices (e.g., Rose, 1981; Avery, 1982), faunal resemblance indices (e.g., Van Couvering & Van Couvering, 1976), and ecological structure analysis (e.g., Andrews et al., 1979; Andrews, 1989). To generate habitat reconstructions in this study, I use a combination of functional morphology and ecological structure analysis to minimize taphonomic overprint, as well as to make these hominid fossil localities more comparable with their modern analogs. Behrensmeyer (1991) has noted that broad-scaled paleoenvironmental reconstructions based on the presence of taxa are likely to be accurate despite the taphonomic history of the assemblage. Andrews et al. (1979) designed ecological structure analysis to enable comparisons of fossil localities with extant communities across time and geographic regions. In addition, using the complete macromammal community eliminates

problems encountered when deriving an environmental reconstruction from just one animal or group of animals, e.g., bovids, and provides an ecological reconstruction of a more complete community.

Ecological Structure Analysis

Fleming (1973) used this method to examine structural changes in faunal communities across latitudes. Andrews et al. (1979) recognized the significance of the method to compare communities across time and geographic regions without regard for taxonomic differences, and thus its usefulness for reconstructing habitats. At the basis of this analysis is the assignment of trophic, locomotor and body size ecological variables (ecovariables) to each mammal from each community. While Andrews et al. (1979) compared total spectra between communities (Figure 1), I examine abundance of each ecovariable (e.g., arboreality) from all habitats together (Figure 2). This type of examination shows a different perspective of ecological differences among habitats.

I use two categories of ecovariables for these reconstructions: locomotor and trophic. Preliminary analysis showed that body size was less effective for separating habitats than the trophic and locomotor adaptations (Reed, 1996). While these ecovariables are based on those of Andrews et al. (1979), I used additional trophic variables and different combinations of locomotor ecovariables for this study. These ecovariables are fairly broad, and therefore, can be readily identified from morphological analysis of fossil material.

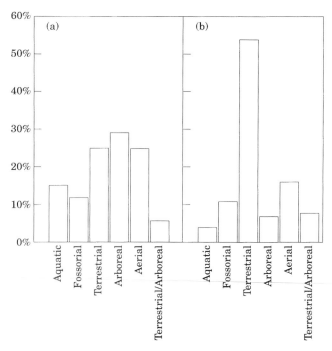

Figure 1. *The percentages of locomotor ecovariables compared in two African communities (after Andrews et al., 1979). (a) Nigerian rain forest; (b) Serengeti.*

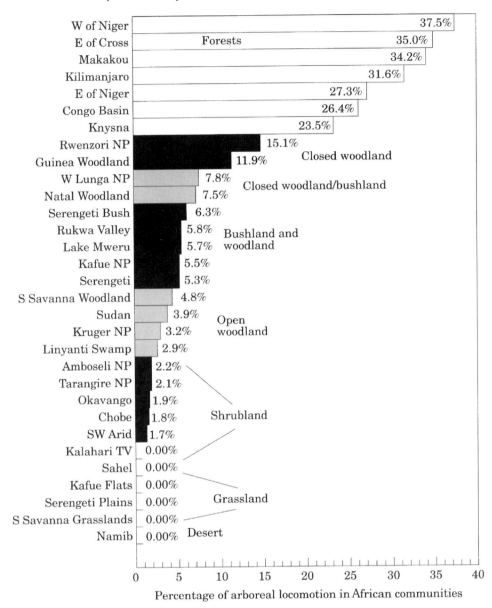

Figure 2. *The percentages of arboreal locomotion in vegetative habitats ranging from forests to desert. The percentages of arboreality decline as tree cover declines and tree cover declines as mean annual rainfall decreases (see Table 1).*

Locomotor categories include terrestrial, arboreal, aquatic, fossorial, and terrestrial/arboreal locomotion. Terrestrial locomotion refers to an animal that moves from place to place or feeds on the ground, for example, a bovid or a zebra. Arboreal locomotion describes a mammal that moves and feeds in trees at least 90% of the time, for example *Dendrohyrax arboreus,* the tree hyrax. Aquatic locomotion refers to animals that spend a major portion of their time in the water, and thus, water is a necessity. *Hippopotamus amphibius* is in this category. Fossorial locomotion describes an animal that utilizes or makes underground burrows, or uses its forelimbs to dig for food. An example is *Orycteropus afer,* the aardvark. Terrestrial/arboreal locomotion is a characteristic of animals that use the ground to move from place to place, but often feed or sleep in trees.

Examples of mammals that exhibit this type of adaptation are *Panthera pardus,* the leopard, and *Cercopithecus aethiops,* the vervet monkey. Because the assignment of the terrestrial/arboreal locomotion ecovariable from morphological analysis to fossils might have been equivocal, all of the locomotor ecovariables except arboreal locomotion were combined into total terrestrial locomotion for some analyses, that is, this percentage equals the relative abundances of aquatic, fossorial, terrestrial, and terrestrial/arboreal locomotion together.

There are 12 trophic ecovariables. Browsers are mammals that eat leaves. There are two ecovariables that encompass grazing animals: (1) grazers are mammals that eat relatively dry grass in bulk; and (2) fresh-grass grazers are mammals that eat specific types of grass from edaphic grasslands. (Edaphic grasslands are

Table 1. Modern African Habitat Localities

Locality	Rainfall	Category	Species	Arboreal	Aquatic	Frugivory	Terrestrial	Meat/Bone	Fresh Grass	Grass
W of River Niger, Nigeria	1600	Forest	33	37.50%	12.50%	40.63%	62.50%	0.00%	6.25%	0.09%
E of Cross River, Nigeria	1550	Forest	40	35.00%	17.50%	47.50%	65.00%	0.00%	5.00%	0.00%
Makakous, Gabon	1800	Forest	41	34.15%	7.32%	56.10%	65.85%	0.00%	7.32%	0.00%
Kilimanjaro, Tanzania	1050	Forest (montane)	19	31.58%	0.00%	42.11%	68.42%	0.00%	0.00%	0.00%
E of River Niger, Nigeria	1596	Forest	32	27.27%	15.15%	36.36%	72.73%	0.00%	9.09%	0.00%
Congo Basin, Zaire	1800	Forest	53	26.42%	13.21%	43.40%	73.58%	0.00%	1.89%	0.00%
Knysna Forests, South Africa	1016	Forest (some montane)	17	23.53%	5.88%	41.18%	76.47%	0.00%	0.00%	0.00%
Rwenzori NP, Uganda	900	Closed woodland	51	15.09%	9.43%	26.42%	81.13%	3.77%	11.32%	3.77%
Guinea Woodland, Nigeria	1000	Closed woodland	59	11.86%	8.47%	20.34%	88.14%	3.39%	11.86%	5.08%
W Lunga NP, Zambia	825	Closed woodland/bushland transition	44	6.67%	11.11%	17.78%	93.33%	2.22%	6.67%	11.11%
Natal Woodland, South Africa	875	Closed woodland/bushland transition	40	7.50%	7.50%	22.50%	92.50%	3.77%	9.43%	9.43%
Serengeti Bushland, Tanzania	803	Bushland	64	6.25%	4.69%	17.19%	93.75%	4.69%	4.69%	12.50%
Rukwa Valley, Tanzania	700	Bushland/woodland	52	5.77%	7.69%	19.23%	94.23%	3.85%	9.62%	9.62%
Lake Mweru, Zambia	850	Bushland/woodland/edaphic grasslands	35	5.71%	8.57%	22.86%	94.29%	5.71%	14.29%	11.43%
Kafue NP, Zambia	821	Medium density woodland	55	5.45%	10.91%	12.73%	94.55%	3.64%	12.73%	10.91%
Serengeti NP, Tanzania	750	Bushland/woodland	75	5.33%	8.00%	17.33%	94.67%	4.00%	6.67%	10.67%
S Savanna Woodland, South Africa	650	Open woodland	83	4.82%	6.02%	13.25%	95.18%	3.61%	6.02%	16.87%
Sudan Savanna, Nigeria	689	Open woodland	51	3.92%	5.88%	11.76%	96.08%	5.88%	7.84%	7.84%
Kruger NP, South Africa	675	Open woodland	63	3.17%	7.94%	12.70%	96.83%	4.76%	6.35%	12.70%
Linyanti Swamp, Botswana	650	Open woodland/swamp	35	2.86%	14.29%	11.43%	97.14%	2.86%	17.14%	17.14%
Amboseli NP, Kenya	600	Open/scrub woodland	46	2.17%	4.35%	8.70%	97.83%	4.35%	6.52%	15.22%
Tarangire NP, Tanzania	600	Open/scrub woodland	48	2.08%	2.08%	8.33%	97.92%	6.25%	4.17%	12.50%
Okavango Delta, Botswana	600	Shrubland with flood plain	54	1.85%	11.11%	7.41%	98.15%	3.70%	9.26%	16.67%
Chobe NP, Botswana	650	Scrub woodland with river	56	1.79%	8.93%	7.14%	98.21%	3.57%	10.71%	16.07%
SW Arid Region, South Africa	400	Shrubland	60	1.67%	6.67%	8.33%	98.33%	5.00%	3.33%	23.33%
Kalahari Thornveld, South Africa	450	Shrubland	15	0.00%	0.00%	6.67%	100.00%	6.67%	0.00%	13.33%
Sahel Savanna, Nigeria	450	Shrubland/grassland/edaphic grassland	31	0.00%	9.68%	6.45%	100.00%	3.23%	9.68%	6.45%
Serengeti Plains, Tanzania	500	Grasslands	19	0.00%	0.00%	0.00%	100.00%	15.79%	0.00%	26.32%
S Savanna Grasslands, South Africa	500	Grasslands	41	0.00%	9.76%	4.88%	100.00%	4.88%	2.44%	24.39%
Kafue Flats, Zambia	821	Edaphic grasslands	36	0.00%	14.29%	5.71%	100.00%	5.71%	14.29%	17.14%
Namib Desert, Namibia	125	Desert	18	0.00%	0.00%	11.11%	100.00%	11.11%	0.00%	11.11%

those in which the grasses grow in water-logged soils, such as might be found in wetlands or swamps.) Mixed feeders are mammals that eat both dicot and monocot leaves (browse and grass) in varying proportions. There are two ecovariables for frugivorous mammals: fruit–leaf eaters and fruit–insect eaters. Because these ecovariables had to be reconstructed through morphological analysis of fossil material, however, these two adaptations were collapsed into one ecovariable (total frugivory). Insectivores are mammals that eat only insects (irrespective of their taxonomic classification, e.g., the canid, *Otocyon megalotis*, is a carnivore that eats only insects). There are three meat-eating ecovariables: (1) meat-eaters are mammals that eat only meat; (2) meat/bone eaters include animals that ingest the bone as well as meat; and (3) meat/nonvertebrate eaters are mammals that eat both meat and insects, crustaceans, etc. Root and bulb eaters consume roots and tubers, e.g., the porcupine. Finally, an omnivore is an animal whose diet contains food from at least three of the other trophic categories without preference. *Mellivora capensis*, the honey badger, is an example of a mammal in this category.

Description and Collection of Data Sets

Modern African Habitats. The first part of this study entailed collecting data on biotic and abiotic factors from published accounts of African national parks, game reserves, etc. to create a comparative sample of diverse modern habitat types (Table 1). These modern habitat types are broadly characterized, for example, the "forest" category includes lowland rain, tropical temperate, and montane forests. Fossil assemblages are more likely to yield reconstructions of broadly defined biozones rather than by microhabitats contained within each habitat type. Categories of vegetative habitats include forests, closed woodlands, woodland–bushland transition, medium density woodland and bushland areas, open woodlands, shrublands (including scrub woodlands), grasslands and plains, and deserts (Figure 3). In general, these modern habitats provide an ecological gradient from areas that are well-watered throughout the year (forests) to those that are extremely dry or quite seasonal (shrubland and deserts). Between these two extremes, the structure of the vegetation shows a decreasing density of trees with decreasing rainfall. However, the

Figure 3. *Examples of eight habitat types used in this study. Scale in feet.*

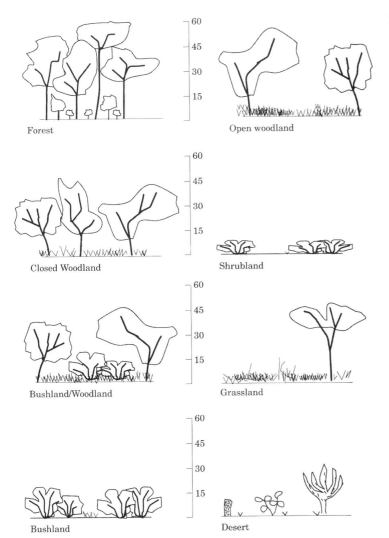

topological features of the landscape and the impact of fires, herbivores, and humans influence the plant life so that this gradient is not completely linear (Bourliere & Hadley, 1983).

I compiled lists of species from these habitats ranging in geographic breadth from western to eastern and southern African national parks, game reserves and specific vegetative regimes (Swynnerton, 1958; Lamprey, 1962; Child, 1964; Vesey-Fitzgerald, 1964; Sheppe & Osborne, 1971; Lind & Morrison, 1974; Kingdon, 1974a,b, 1977, 1979, 1982a,b; Ansell, 1978; Rautenbach, 1978; Smithers, 1978; Behrensmeyer et al., 1979; Perera, 1982; Bremen & de Wit, 1983; Emmons et al., 1983; White, 1983; Lanjouw, 1987; Happold, 1989; Skinner & Smithers, 1990). Areas in which species had been introduced, or habitats that were extremely altered by humans were not used. However, it should be noted that most African habitats have been altered by human intervention to some degree. Data on rainfall, vegetative cover, temperature and seasonality were also collected.

After preliminary investigations using both micro- and macromammals, I restricted the analysis to macromammals (Reed, 1996). At fossil sites, micromammals are often accumulated separately from macromammals and are sometimes poorly represented. Therefore, I avoided potential taphonomic problems by using only large mammalian taxa, i.e., those weighing greater than 500 g. Mammals from modern communities were assigned ecovariables based on behavioral observations and analysis of stomach contents (Kingdon, 1974a,b, 1977, 1979, 1982a,b; Delaney & Happold, 1979; Happold, 1989; Estes, 1991; Skinner & Smithers, 1990).

Death Assemblages. I included modern death assemblages in my analyses to see if biased samples taken from vegetative habitats in which the living community was known would accurately represent the environment in which they were collected. Thus, these death assemblage habitat reconstructions are compared directly with the living community to examine how accumulation factors influence habitat reconstructions.

Death assemblage data (Table 2) were taken from published accounts of mammals that produce bone assemblages (Kruuk, 1972; Schaller, 1976; Brain, 1981; Skinner et al., 1986; Kitchener, 1991) and of a surface bone collection experiment (Behrensmeyer et al., 1979).

Fossil Localities. Specimen lists of fossil assemblages (Table 3) were taken from the literature (Coppens et al., 1976; Harris, 1987; Brain, 1981; Leakey & Leakey, 1978; Leakey & Harris, 1987; Harris et al., 1988; Harris & Leakey, 1993; Brain, 1993) and from personal identification and examination of faunas from Makapansgat, Swartkrans, Sterkfontein, Kromdraai A and B, Hadar, and some of the Omo and Usno collections from the Shungura Formation. Some of the localities do not contain hominids (e.g., Kromdraai A), or contain very few hominids (e.g., Tulu Bor, Koobi Fora). These were included for comparison with the hominid-bearing localities. Fossil species were assigned trophic and locomotor ecovariables in three different ways. First, for the fossil

material I examined, morphological analyses were used to estimate trophic and locomotor preferences. These analyses (Reed, 1996) were based on methods from Van Valkenburgh (carnivores, 1987, 1989), Janis (ungulates, 1988), and Spencer (bovids, 1995). Second, other researchers have made morphological studies and assigned various trophic and locomotor behaviors to extinct taxa and these were used in many instances especially for material I did not examine (Geze, 1985; Benefit & McCrossin, 1990; Harris, 1987, 1991). Third, on occasion taxonomic uniformitarianism was used: a fossil taxon was assigned a trophic or locomotor category based on its relationship to an extant species, genus, tribe, or family. Assignments to trophic and locomotor ecovariables for all fossil taxa are listed in Reed (1996).

Analyses

Univariate Analyses. After trophic and locomotor ecovariables were assigned to each species, the percentage of each ecovariable from each category was recorded for each modern habitat (for variable percentages used here, see Table 1). Thus all locomotor ecovariables for each community totaled 100%, as did all trophic ecovariables for each community. The percentages of each ecovariable across habitats were placed in bar graphs arranged by habitat type, i.e., forests were grouped together, closed woodlands, etc. This identified ecovariables that appeared to separate vegetative habitats and also showed how communities from different habitats changed in ecological composition (Figure 2). Ecovariables that appeared to visually separate vegetative habitats (predictor ecovariables) were analyzed statistically (Table 4) and examined graphically with box and whisker plots (Figure 4).

Bivariate Analyses. The predictor ecovariables were used in bivariate plots to further analyze the communities (Figure 5). After modern habitats were analyzed, death assemblage data were plotted with and compared with their modern counterparts to see if they accurately reflected the vegetative habitat from which they were derived. Fossil locality data were then plotted with the modern community analogs to reconstruct the vegetative habitat for each fossil assemblage. Finally, the fossil localities were arranged in chronological order using grazing, total frugivorous, and arboreal adaptations to trace these ecovariables across time. These ecovariables were chosen to represent changing habitats across time.

RESULTS

Modern African Communities

By examining the ecovariables separately, i.e., in univariate analyses across habitats, several predictor ecovariables emerged. These predictor ecovariables are proportions of adaptations that are similar in the same vegetative habitat types and change consistently across habitats. Locomotor adaptations whose relative abundances predict habitats are: (1) percentage of arboreal

Table 2. Death Assemblages

Sites	Accumulator	Habitat	Species	Arboreality	Aquatic	Frugivory	Terrestrial	Meat/Bone	Fresh Grass	Grass
Amboseli	Bone transect	Shrubland	34	2.9%	5.9%	8.8%	97.1%	5.9%	5.9%	17.7%
Andrieskraal	Porcupine	Open woodland	15	0.0%	6.7%	13.3%	100.0%	0.0%	6.7%	13.3%
Kafue Flats	Lion	Edaphic grasslands	18	0.0%	0.0%	5.6%	100.0%	0.0%	27.8%	27.8%
Kalahari-Gemsbok	Brown hyena	Shrubland	17	0.0%	0.0%	5.9%	100.0%	5.9%	0.0%	17.7%
Kalahari-Gemsbok	Leopard	Shrubland	12	0.0%	0.0%	8.3%	100.0%	0.0%	0.0%	16.7%
Kalahari-Gemsbok	Porcupine	Shrubland	11	0.0%	0.0%	9.1%	100.0%	9.1%	0.0%	36.4%
Kruger NP	Spotted hyena	Open woodland	27	0.0%	3.7%	3.7%	100.0%	3.7%	11.1%	25.9%
Kruger NP	Leopard	Woodland/riparian	28	0.0%	4.2%	17.9%	100.0%	3.6%	7.1%	25.0%
Tai Forest	Leopard	Rain forest	22	31.8%	4.6%	50.0%	68.2%	0.0%	4.6%	0.0%
Serengeti NP	Leopard	Bushland/woodland	18	0.0%	0.0%	5.6%	100.0%	0.0%	11.1%	33.0%
Serengeti Plains	Spotted hyena	Bush/woodland/plains	16	0.0%	0.0%	0.0%	100.0%	0.0%	6.3%	43.8%
Ngorongoro Crater	Spotted hyena	Edaphic grasslands/woodland	12	0.0%	0.0%	0.0%	100.0%	8.3%	8.3%	41.7%

Table 3. Plio-Pleistocene Fossil Localities

Sites	Date (m.y.a.)	Species	Arboreality	Aquatic	Frugivory	Terrestriality	Meat/Bone	Fresh Grass	Grass
Laetoli 1	3.6	25	12.00%	0.00%	24.00%	88.00%	8.00%	0.00%	24.00%
Laetoli 7	3.6	28	10.71%	0.00%	21.43%	89.29%	3.57%	0.00%	17.86%
Sidi Hakoma	3.34–3.2	44	5.00%	6.81%	13.00%	95.00%	6.08%	12.50%	15.00%
Tulu Bor	3.36–2.68	38	2.60%	7.89%	7.89%	97.40%	2.60%	15.78%	21.05%
Usno	3.36–3.0	32	6.25%	6.25%	15.63%	93.75%	6.25%	6.25%	15.63%
Makapansgat 3	3.2–3.0	55	5.45%	1.82%	14.55%	94.55%	3.64%	3.64%	16.36%
Makapansgat 4	3.0	31	6.45%	0.00%	19.35%	93.55%	6.45%	3.23%	12.90%
Denen Dora	3.2–3.18	43	4.65%	6.98%	6.98%	95.35%	6.98%	9.30%	16.28%
Shungura B	2.95	44	13.33%	4.44%	20.00%	86.67%	2.22%	11.11%	22.22%
Shungura C	2.85	54	5.56%	5.56%	14.81%	94.44%	3.70%	11.11%	16.67%
Burgi Member	2.68–1.88	53	3.77%	9.43%	11.32%	96.23%	5.66%	13.21%	22.64%
Sterkfontein	2.6–2.4	30	3.33%	0.00%	16.67%	96.67%	3.33%	3.33%	23.33%
Shungura D	2.52	31	6.45%	6.45%	16.13%	93.55%	0.00%	12.90%	16.13%
WT 17000	2.5	39	2.56%	5.12%	20.51%	97.44%	2.56%	23.08%	17.95%
Shungura E	2.4	33	6.06%	6.06%	21.21%	93.94%	0.00%	9.09%	12.12%
Shungura F	2.36	44	4.55%	6.82%	13.64%	95.45%	2.27%	6.82%	20.45%
Shungura G	2.3	52	5.77%	5.78%	9.62%	94.23%	1.92%	13.46%	25.00%
Kromdraai B	2.0–1.5	15	0.00%	0.00%	26.67%	100.00%	6.67%	0.00%	13.33%
KBS Member	1.88–1.6	67	1.49%	7.46%	7.46%	98.51%	1.49%	14.93%	37.31%
Swartkrans 1	1.8	36	0.00%	5.56%	13.89%	100.00%	5.56%	2.78%	25.00%
Swartkrans 2	1.6	34	0.00%	5.88%	8.82%	100.00%	8.82%	0.00%	32.35%
Swartkrans 3	1.4	48	0.00%	6.25%	6.25%	100.00%	3.13%	4.17%	25.00%
Natoo Member	1.51	30	0.00%	10.00%	3.33%	100.00%	0.00%	16.67%	46.67%
Kromdraai A	1.5–1.0	41	2.44%	0.00%	9.76%	97.56%	7.32%	2.44%	21.95%
Okote Member	1.6–1.39	38	0.00%	10.53%	7.89%	100.00%	2.63%	18.42%	39.47%
Sterkfontein 5	1.0	16	0.00%	0.00%	0.00%	100.00%	0.00%	0.00%	43.75%
Makapan 5	1.0	13	0.00%	15.38%	0.00%	100.00%	0.00%	15.38%	15.38%

Table 4.   Ranges of Selected Predictor Ecovariables for Each Habitat Type

Habitat	Arboreality	Frugivory	Terrestriality	Grazing
Forests ($n = 7$)				
X	30.77%	43.9%	69.22%	0%
S.D. ($\pm$)	3.8%	4.68%	3.81%	—
Range	23.52–37.5%	36.36–56.09%	62.5–76.5%	—
*Closed wood ($n = 2$)				
X	13.47%	23.38%‡	84.63%	4.43%‡
S.D. ($\pm$)	1.61%	3.04%	3.5%	0.66%
Range	11.86–15.09%	20.3–26.46%	81.13–88.14%	3.77–5.08%
*Closed woodland bushland ($n = 2$)				
X	7.1%	20.14%‡	92.75%	10.27%‡
S.D. ($\pm$)	0.41%	2.36%	0.59%	0.83%
Range	6.67–7.5%	17.78–22.5%	92.16–93.33%	9.43–11.11%
Bushland ($n = 4$)				
X	5.7%†	19.15%‡	94.23%†	9.86%‡§
S.D. ($\pm$)	0.31%	2.28%	0.32%	1.51%
Range	5.33–6.25%	17.19–22.86%	93.75–94.67%	7.5–11.43%
Medium/open woodland ($n = 5$)				
X	4.05%†	12.37%	96.96%†	13.04%§
S.D. ($\pm$)	0.97%	0.06%	0.98%	3.58%
Range	2.85–5.45%	11.43–13.2%	95.54–97.14%	7.84–17.14%
Shrubland ($n = 7$)				
X	1.37%	7.58%	98.63%	14.79%
S.D. ($\pm$)	0.7%	0.66%	0.7%	3.77%
Range	0–2.17%	6.45–8.17%	97.82–100%	6.45–23.33%
Grasslands ($n = 3$)				
X	0%	3.53%	100%	22.61%
S.D. ($\pm$)	—	0.34%	—	5.47%
Range	—	0–5.71%	—	17.14–26.31%
Kruskal–Wallis test statistic	30.76	31.35	30.76	22.90

Krustal–Wallis showed significant differences between groups for all pairs of habitat types at $\chi^2_{0.001[6]} = 22.458$. *Combined for further analysis using Mann–Whitney U tests between each pair of communities. These tests showed significant differences at $P < 0.05$, except for: †no significant difference between bushland/open woodland; ‡no significant difference between closed woodland/bushlands; §$P < 0.10$ between bushland/open woodland.

locomotion (Figure 2); or (2) its antithesis, the percentage of total terrestrial locomotion (including terrestrial, aquatic, fossorial, and terrestrial/arboreal adaptations); and (3) the percentage of aquatic locomotion (Table 1). The relative abundance of these mammalian ecovariables is dependent upon the vegetative regime such that as tree presence changes, the percentages of arboreal and terrestrial animals change. If more water is present in the habitat, then there is a greater relative abundance of aquatic mammals.

Relative abundances of trophic ecovariables also characterize habitats. The best trophic predictor ecovariable is percentage of total frugivory. The proportion of total frugivory changes from high in forest regions to low or nonexistent in shrubland and plains regions. When this variable is used in combination with arboreality or terrestriality, each habitat category is separated from one another. In addition, the bushland communities are successfully separated from the medium density woodland habitat (Figure 5). Other trophic ecovariables that can be used to analyze habitats are proportions of grazing, fresh grass grazing, and meat-bone eating.

Through an analysis of each community of mammalian adaptations, patterns between the vegetation types and the mammals that live within them became apparent. Arboreal mammals are evident in forest and closed woodland communities in high numbers. As trees grow shorter and further apart due to lessening rainfall,

intense seasonality, and/or different soil content, the presence of arboreal animals decreases. As the total number of arboreal animals declines, animals with other locomotor adaptations become more common. For example, under arid conditions in poor soils (shrublands), more fossorial animals exist. It is interesting that it is the adaptations that are measurable and consistent, rather than the taxonomic identity. There are ecological equivalents existing in similar types of habitats whether the mammals are closely or distantly related.

This analysis shows that ecological proportions of mammals in communities are correlated with vegetative structure. This relationship is predictable in two ways. First, if one knows the vegetative regime of a particular area, the proportions and types of ecovariables that will be exhibited by the mammals in the habitat can be estimated. Second, and this is important for reconstructing paleocommunities, if the adaptations, i.e., the proportions of each ecovariable in communities can be reconstructed, then habitats can be predicted.

Death Assemblages

After the modern vegetative habitats were categorized by ecovariable proportions, I analyzed extant death assemblages in the same way. Table 2 shows the number of species and resultant ecovariable percentages for each of the death assemblages. The bar charts that I used to

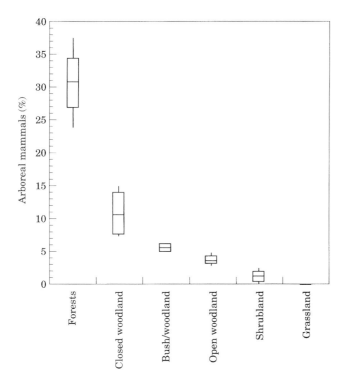

Figure 4. *Box and whisker diagram of the percentages of arboreal mammals. Whiskers indicate range, boxes represent two standard deviations, and the horizontal lines are the means for each vegetative habitat grouping. Closed woodland includes closed woodland–bushland transition regions.*

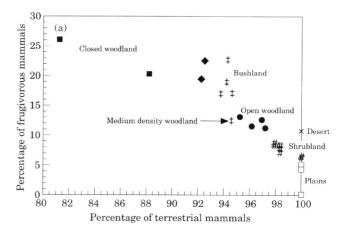

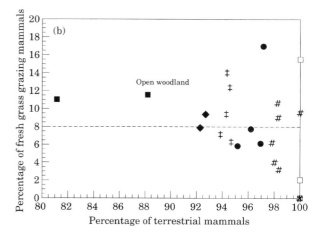

Figure 5. *(a) Bivariate plot of the percentages of total terrestrial mammals vs. frugivorous mammals in vegetative habitats ranging from closed woodlands to desert (forests are not presented in this and subsequent diagrams so that other habitats are more easily compared). Both ecovariables separate habitats according to tree cover and rainfall. In addition, the medium density woodland of Kafue National Park has been separated from the more bushland communities (‡) because the percentages of frugivory are higher in bushland regimes. (b) Bivariate plot of the percentages of total terrestrial mammals vs. fresh grass grazers in vegetative habitats ranging from closed woodlands to desert. Habitats that contain large amounts of water and thus edaphic grasslands are positioned above the 8% dashed line. Key: (■) closed woodland, (♦) closed woodland–bushland transition, (‡) bushland, (●) open woodland, (#) shrubland/scrub woodland, (□) grassland/plains, (×) desert.*

examine individual ecovariables are omitted here because of space limitations (but see Reed, 1996). The same results are obtained using bivariate plots, for example terrestriality *vs.* frugivory (Figure 6). The death assemblage based on leopard scats (Kitchener, 1991) from the Tai Forest predicted the vegetative habitat exactly. The Tai Forest assemblage exhibits high percentages of arboreal locomotion (31.82%) and total frugivory (50%), and no grazing nor meat–bone eating animals, all of which place the locality in a rain forest habitat.

The Amboseli Bone Transect (Behrensmeyer et al., 1979) was positioned near the Amboseli National Park in the scrub woodlands area of the graph [Figure 6(b)]. The smaller sample size of the bone transect increases the percentage of arboreality, and thus, it appears closer to the open woodlands than the shrublands. However, percentages of frugivory (8.82%) and grazing (17.65%) are within shrubland habitat ranges (Table 4).

The other death assemblages were created by carnivores and rodents that exist in more open habitats, and thus, the assemblages are classified as open using the total terrestrial locomotion ecovariable (100%). First, this reflects that some of these accumulators hunt in microhabitats that possess greater percentages of terrestrial animals than appear in the entire national park community, for example. Second, the sample sizes are smaller than those found in living and fossil communities with a bias against smaller animals. In open woodlands and shrublands usually the only arboreal animal is

a galago. Even if one of these creatures died and fell to the ground, a hyena would completely consume the remains, and a porcupine would not find the tiny skeletal elements of the galago appropriate for gnawing. Thus the death assemblages from the Kruger National Park and Andreiskraal are terrestrially aligned with more open and drier habitats than the living community. The modern Kalahari–Gemsbok communities contain small to no percentage of arboreal animals (1.29 and 0%), thus the three death assemblages from that region are positioned appropriately.

In the total fruit-eating ecovariable, however, all of the death assemblages are positioned with the habitats

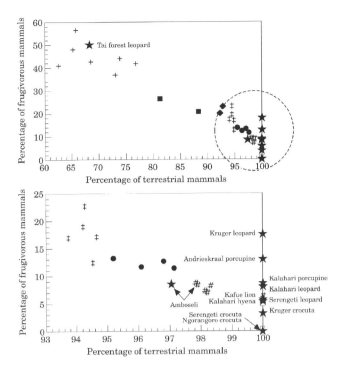

Figure 6. *Bivariate plots of the percentages of terrestrial vs. frugivorous mammals in vegetative habitats from forests to desert including death assemblages. The top figure shows all habitats and the Tai Forest leopard death assemblage aligning with other forest habitats. Bottom figure is expansion for the circle in the top figure. Key: (+) forests, (■) closed woodland, (♦) closed woodland–bushland transition, (‡) bushland, (●) open woodland, (#) shrubland/scrub woodland, (□) grasslands/plains, (×) desert, (★) death assemblages.*

from which they were derived. The Kafue National Park lion kills contained 5.56% frugivorous species and the living community contains 5.71% frugivorous species; the spotted hyena dens and the leopard kills from Kruger National Park have 3.7 and 17.86% frugivorous species, respectively. The difference reflects the fact that hyenas are prone to hunt and scavenge in more open woodland, while the leopards in Kruger are apt to hunt in the riparian and more bushland areas. The entire park contains 12.7% frugivorous species, about midway between the two death assemblage abundances of fruit-eaters. Finally, the three assemblages from the Kalahari–Gemsbok National Park contained 5.88% (brown hyenas), 8.33% (leopard), and 9.09% (porcupine) frugivorous species, while the modern habitats contain 6.67% (Kalahari Thornveld) and 8.33% (South West Arid Region). Thus, total frugivory is useful for predicting habitats as the death assemblages reflect finer habitat separations than expected.

These death assemblage samples show that although predators and collectors can bias samples, relatively accurate habitat reconstructions can be made based on them. Fossil assemblages are usually formed over longer periods of time and contain more species from the living communities than these death assemblages. Fossil localities that were carnivore accumulated may be depauperate in arboreal and/or aquatic species, and

this must be considered when reconstructing the paleo-habitat. Nevertheless, high percentages of frugivores and fresh grass grazers may also indicate bushlands, woodlands and wetlands. In addition, the presence of particular animals that are known to occupy fairly narrow habitats, such as forest-dwelling duikers, can also be used to help make final habitat reconstructions. Thus, death assemblages are biased in some ecovariables, but not others. However, the composite reconstructions of all of these death assemblages are fairly accurate predictions of the actual habitat.

Plio-Pleistocene Fossil Localities

Having shown that it is reasonable to expect that species found in death assemblages can predict the habitat in which they were found, I will now reconstruct the habitats for the Pliocene hominid sites based on fossil assemblages. Each individual assemblage, whether derived from a cave site, lacustrine environment, or surface landscape accumulation, is a sample of the living mammalian community, and as such, should provide fairly accurate habitat reconstructions. I will discuss southern African Plio-Pleistocene localities first, and then eastern African sites in chronological order. I will also compare these habitat reconstructions with previous environmental reconstructions that were based on geology, pollen, and faunal groups. Table 3 shows the number of species and resultant ecovariable percentages for each of the fossil localities.

Southern African Hominid Localities

Limeworks Cave, Makapan Valley. The Limeworks Cave is located in the northeastern part of the Transvaal in South Africa. The older deposits (Members 3 and 4) are suggested to be in the range of 3.2–2.7 Ma and are capped by a Pleistocene aged deposit (Partridge, 1979; MacFadden, 1980; Delson, 1984; Vrba, 1995).

MEMBER 3. This deposit contains an extremely large number of mammalian specimens (greater than 30,000), of which 24 are *Australopithecus africanus*. The deposit was accumulated in the cave by fossil hyaenid and porcupine species (Maguire, 1985; Reed, 1996). There are relatively high percentages of frugivorous species (14.95%) and some arboreal animals (5.45%). Thus the habitat is positioned with bushland and medium density woodlands. Fresh grass grazers (3.44%) and aquatic mammals (1.84%) indicate the presence of a river and some edaphic grasslands (Figures 7 and 8). Previous reconstructions have ranged from woodland (Vrba, 1980) to forest (Cadman & Rayner, 1989) to open savanna with nearby bushland (Dart, 1952; Wells & Cooke, 1956). However, the mammalian community suggests that this region was a habitat mosaic that contained riparian woodland, bushland, and edaphic grassland.

MEMBER 4. *A. africanus* is represented by only three specimens out of a total of 257 mammalian specimens. Cercopithecine monkeys make up 80% of the collection; and the likely accumulators were birds of prey and leopards (Reed, 1996).

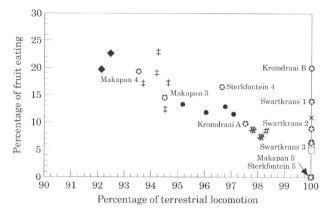

Figure 7.   *Bivariate plot of the percentages of terrestrial vs. frugivorous mammals in vegetative habitats ranging from closed woodlands to desert including southern African Plio-Pleistocene hominid localities. Key: (■) closed woodland, (♦) closed woodland–bushland transition, (‡) bushland, (●) open woodland, (#) shrubland/scrub woodland, (□) grasslands/plains, (×) desert, (☆) Plio-Pleistocene fossil localities.*

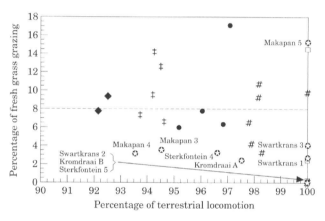

Figure 8.   *Bivariate plot of the percentages of terrestrial vs. fresh grass grazing mammals in vegetative habitats ranging from closed woodlands to desert including southern African Plio-Pleistocene hominid localities. Habitats that include rivers, wetlands, and edaphic grasslands are above the dashed line (8%). Key: (■) closed woodland, (♦) closed woodland–bushland transition; (‡) bushland, (●) open woodland, (#) shrubland/scrub woodland, (□) grasslands/plains, (×) desert, (☆) Plio-Pleistocene fossil localities.*

Member 4 deposits contain even greater percentages of arboreal (7%) and frugivorous (20%) species than Member 3, which suggests a more wooded habitat. However, this is probably a function of sample size and predation bias rather than a change of habitat. Because this member may have been accumulated by birds of prey, there may be an exclusion of many bovid species. This would skew the results to the more wooded habitat than the ecovariables suggest. Thus, because Member 3 and Member 4 are roughly contemporaneous in time, both assemblages probably represent a woodland–bushland habitat.

MEMBER 5. There have been no hominids or other primates recovered from this member. Member 5 is a Pleistocene deposit with very few species (13), and is included here for comparative purposes. The accumulating agent is not known, although as it is a cave deposit it is likely that either carnivores or hominids made the collection. There are aquatic animals (15.4%) and fresh grass grazers (15.4%) which indicate edaphic grasslands and a water source, but there are no frugivorous or arboreal mammals, indicating that the region might have been more open and xeric in the Pleistocene.

Sterkfontein, Sterkfontein Valley.   The Sterkfontein cave has been continuously excavated for the last 27 years. Over 850 hominid remains have been recovered (L. Berger, pers. comm.). Extensive analyses of faunal remains of this locality were done by Brain (1981) and Vrba (1976) and the analysis here is based on these original studies.

MEMBER 4.   *A. africanus* has been recovered from this member, which has been faunally dated to between 2.4 and 2.6 m.y.a. (Delson, 1984), and the deposit may be the result of carnivore activity (Brain, 1981). The mammalian community consists of few arboreal animals (3.33%), but a high percentage of frugivorous mammals (16.67%). There is also a fairly high percentage of terrestrial/arboreal animals (23.33%). There are no aquatic animals from this locality, and only 3.33% fresh grass grazers (Figures 7 and 8).

The fauna suggests a habitat reconstruction for Member 4 of an open woodland, with bushland and thicket areas. Other habitat reconstructions of this member at Sterkfontein have indicated a medium density woodland (Vrba, 1975), a moderately open savanna (Vrba, 1985), an open woodland to a forest (McKee, 1991), and an open savanna (Benefit & McCrossin, 1990). Thus, the mammalian community reconstruction is close to Vrba's 1975 interpretation. However, while there are few arboreal animals, the high percentage of frugivorous mammals falls within the range of bushland and medium density woodland, and this locality is likely similar to the more closed Makapansgat Member 3 deposit.

MEMBER 5.   Porcupines have gnawed a few of the specimens, as did carnivores, and likely they or the *Homo* sp. recovered from this member created the deposit (Brain, 1981). Other mammals recovered include 43.75% grazing animals with no arboreal or frugivorous species. These figures suggest an open or wooded grassland or plains region. Other habitat reconstructions (Vrba, 1975; McKee, 1991) suggest that the habitat at the time of this deposit was an open savanna, which agrees with the reconstruction presented here.

Kromdraai, Sterkfontein Valley.   The Kromdraai cave sites consist of narrow solution cavities that are no more than 17 m apart (Brain, 1981). The two non-contemporaneous deposits are designated A and B.

KROMDRAAI A.   Kromdraai A has produced no hominids, but is included here for comparative purposes (Figures 7 and 8). This deposit is the younger of the two and has been faunally dated to between 1.5 and 1.0 Ma old (Vrba, 1975; Delson, 1984). There are 2.44% arboreal and 9.76% frugivorous species. Kromdraai A has a relatively high percentage of grazers (21.95%) and no aquatic animals. These ecovariables reconstruct a vegetative habitat of scrub woodland with grasslands or perhaps wooded grasslands. Vrba (1975) suggested an open savanna for this site; my reconstruction agrees with that suggested by bovid tribe proportions.

KROMDRAAI B. *Paranthropus robustus* and three other primates were recovered from this site; there are very few other animals (11). This locality has been faunally dated to between 2.0 and 1.5 Ma (Vrba, 1983; Delson, 1984). Based only on the high percentages of terrestrially adapted animals (100%) it is likely that this was an open grassland. However, there is also a relatively high proportion (20%) of frugivorous species, indicating patches of riparian woodland. Vrba (1975), however, has also classified the habitat from Kromdraai B as an open savanna.

Swartkrans, Sterkfontein Valley.

The Swartkrans Cave was thoroughly excavated between 1979 and 1986 and the complete faunal assemblage was studied by Brain (1981, 1993) and Watson (1993). Although there are three distinct members, Brain (1993) has suggested that there is no difference in the fauna, and thus, all members are roughly the same age. This places them in a range of time from 1.8–1.2 m.y.a. The deposits were likely accumulated by carnivores, probably leopards (Brain, 1981).

MEMBER 1. *P. robustus* and *Homo* sp. are represented by this member. Although there are no arboreal species found in this Swartkrans deposit, there are 13.89% fruit and leaf eaters, as well as 5.56% aquatic animals (Figures 7 and 8). There is a small proportion of fresh grass grazers (2.78%). This gives the picture of an open habitat, with a river present as evidenced by aquatic animals. This river or stream probably supported a woodland or forest as suggested by the percentage of frugivorous mammals that fall in the range of medium density woodland and bushland. In addition, there would have been patches of edaphic grasslands to support the fresh grass grazers. Previous reconstructions of this member include a moderately open savanna (Vrba, 1975); a mesic, closed woodland (Benefit & McCrossin, 1990); and a savanna woodland with riparian woodland and reed beds (Watson, 1993). The reconstructed habitat here agrees with that of Watson (1993).

MEMBER 2. *P. robustus* and *Homo* sp. are recovered from this member. Despite the assertion that these deposits are roughly the same age (Brain, 1993), there appears to be a decline in fruit and leaf eaters from Member 1 (13.89%) to Member 2 (8.82%). There are no fresh grass grazers from this member, although there are still aquatic carnivores (5.88%). There is a very large percentage of meat–bone eaters (8.82%). There is also an increase to 32.35% grazing animals and 100% total terrestriality. Thus, this indicates a drier habitat than the previous member, perhaps a wooded grassland with wetlands. Vrba (1975) reconstructed the habitat of Member 2 as a moderately open savanna which agrees with the interpretation here.

MEMBER 3. Only *P. robustus* has been found in these deposits (Watson, 1993). There is a further drop in fruit

and leaf eaters in this member to 6.25%. However, there is also a decrease in grazing animals to 25%, which is accompanied by an increase in fresh grass grazing animals (4.17%). There are similar proportions of aquatic animals (6.25%) and fossorial animals (8.33%) to those in Member 2. Thus, the habitat of this member is reconstructed as an open grassland with a river or stream nearby supporting edaphic grasslands.

East African Deposits Greater than 2.5 Ma

Laetoli, Tanzania (3.6 Ma).

Australopithecus afarensis is found in the Laetolil Upper Beds. These are a conglomeration of localities that are separated by a variety of volcanic tuffs dating from 3.8–3.5 Ma. The vertebrate fauna does not appear until above Tuff 6 which is dated to about 3.6 Ma (Hay, 1987). Localities 1 and 7 are used here, rather than the complete fauna, in order to minimize time-averaging as both localities range from Tuff 6 to either the Yellow Marker Tuff or Tuff 8 (approximately 3.6–3.56 Ma). Specimens or foot prints of *A. afarensis* have been recovered from both localities.

There is a fairly high abundance of arboreal animals (12 and 10.71%) which are all primates. Even if some of these primates were terrestrial, Laetoli would still fall within the woodland–bushland range because of the high abundance of fruit eaters within the assemblage (24 and 25%). These localities are therefore reconstructed as closed woodlands (Figures 9 and 10).

The habitat of Laetoli has been previously reconstructed as a dry, open woodland because the deposits contain an abundance of dik-diks and other arid adapted grazing species (Harris, 1987). Andrews (1989), however, using the entire faunal list from the formation, also arrived at a more wooded habitat reconstruction. Walker (1987) suggests that there were trees in the vicinity because of the presence of galagos, and Gentry (1987) suggests that at least two of the bovid

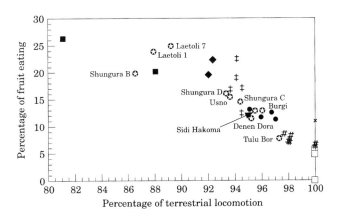

Figure 9. *Bivariate plot of the percentages of terrestrial vs. frugivorous mammals in vegetative habitats ranging from closed woodlands to desert including East African Pliocene localities from before 2.5 m.y.a. Key: (■) closed woodland, (◆) closed woodland–bushland transition, (‡) bushland, (●) open woodland, (#) shrubland/scrub woodland, (□) grasslands/plains, (×) desert, (☆) Plio-Pleistocene fossil localities.*

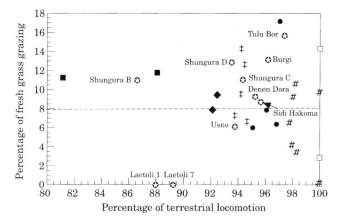

Figure 10. *Bivariate plot of the percentages of terrestrial vs. fresh grass grazing mammals in vegetative habitats ranging from closed woodlands to desert including East African Pliocene localities from before 2.5 m.y.a. Habitats that include rivers, wetlands, and edaphic grasslands are above the dashed line (8%). Key: (■) closed woodland, (◆) closed woodland–bushland transition, (‡) bushland, (●) open woodland, (#) shrubland/scrub woodland, (□) grasslands/plains, (×) desert, (☆) Plio-Pleistocene fossil localities.*

species were forest dwellers. Pollen analysis has indicated either wooded grassland with montane conifers in the vicinity or an evergreen bushland and *Acacia* savanna (Bonnefille & Riollet, 1987). Thus, my reconstructed habitat of a closed to medium density woodland is similar to those of Andrews (1989) and Walker (1987).

Hadar, Ethiopia (3.4–3.18 Ma). *A. afarensis* has been recovered from throughout the Hadar Formation in the Afar of Ethiopia. The data used here represent species lists from two geological members, as locality data are not yet analyzed. An overall habitat reconstruction emerges for these members, but fluctuations in climate that occur over 200,000 years will not be reflected in this analysis. Aronson & Taieb (1981) note that the paleoenvironment at Hadar consisted of fluviatile flood plains and lacustrine sediments.

SIDI HAKOMA. This member contains numerous fossils of extinct hippos, elephants, and crocodiles. Fresh grass grazing reduncines and hippos (8.7%) show that edaphic grasslands were present (Figures 9 and 10). The Sidi Hakoma falls within the ranges of extant medium to open density woodland communities rather than bushland, because of the lower percentage of fruit and leaf eaters (13.04%). There are 4.65% arboreal animals which is in the open woodland range, or could indicate the presence of a riparian woodland or forest. Because this member covers about 200,000 years, there must have been habitat fluctuations within that time span. However, it is likely that at no time during this period was there an open, arid habitat.

DENEN DORA. The Denen Dora spans from 3.2–3.18 m.y.a., and thus covers a relatively short amount of time. There is evidence of a lake with marshes in the early part of this member, but this changes to flood plains and deltas later in the section (Aronson & Taieb, 1981).

This member contains many of the same species present in the Sidi Hakoma and the habitat of the Denen Dora was also a woodland with forest regions near water sources and edaphic grasslands.

Other reconstructions of habitats for Hadar suggest wooded to treeless savanna (Boaz, 1977) and an open grassland with humid conditions (Harris, 1991). Pollen analysis suggests an evergreen bushland close to forest (Bonnefille, 1983). Thus the reconstruction predicted from the mammalian community is closest to that suggested by the pollen recovered from the deposits.

Koobi Fora Formation (3.4–1.6 Ma). This formation is in the Turkana basin of Kenya. Similar deposits to the north in Ethiopia include those of the Omo River, the Shungura and Usno Formations. Many of the volcanic tuffs between these two regions have been correlated (Brown & Feibel, 1991). The Koobi Fora Formation includes members that range from the Tulu Bor at 3.36 Ma (which is the earliest containing hominid fossils) to the Chari at about 1 Ma old. The faunal lists for Koobi Fora were derived from localities within each member reported in Leakey & Leakey (1978). The members for which habitats are reconstructed here include the Tulu Bor (3.36–3.0 Ma), the Burgi (3.0–2.0 Ma), the KBS (1.88–1.5 Ma), and the Okote (1.6 Ma). The Tulu Bor and Burgi Members are discussed here with the other early East African Pliocene localities. The KBS and Okote Members are discussed later.

TULU BOR. *A. afarensis* has been recovered from this member (Kimbel, 1988). Paleogeographic reconstructions of the Turkana Basin at 3.4 and 3.3 Ma indicate a river system with deposits laid down during axial flooding periods. These flood waters came from the Ethiopian Highlands, not from local rains (Brown & Feibel, 1991).

Fauna recovered from the Tulu Bor Member indicates fairly high percentages of aquatic animals (7.89%) and fresh grass grazing animals (15.78%) (Figures 9 and 10). However, the Tulu Bor deposits have very few arboreal animals (2.6%) and low percentages of fruit and leaf eaters (7.89%). Thus, this member appears to have been a scrub woodland region with a flooding river. Wetlands were probably extensive. Harris (1991) has noted that based on the fauna and pollen this member was probably a flood plain and gallery forest with edaphic grasslands to the south. The presence of a gallery forest is not reflected in the mammalian adaptations used to reconstruct this environment.

BURGI. There are two hominid species recovered from this member, *Homo* sp. and *Paranthropus boisei* (Harris, 1991). Brown & Feibel (1991) suggest this member was also an axially flooding river system. The faunal community has high abundances of aquatic animals (9.43%), fresh grass grazers (13.21%), and fruit and leaf eaters (11.32%). There is also a fairly high percentage (15.09%) of terrestrial/arboreal animals (Figures 9 and 10). It appears as if there was slightly more flooding or rainfall contributing to the presence of more herbaceous vegetation during this time period as compared to the Tulu Bor Member. I reconstruct this member as an open woodland with edaphic grasslands and a riparian woodland. Harris (1991) reconstructed this member as being a more closed woodland in the north and more open to the south.

Usno Formation. The Usno Formation is part of the Omo River Deposits in Ethiopia. The U-10 deposits have been correlated with the Tulu Bor Member in the Koobi Fora Formation (Feibel & Brown, 1993). Hominids from the Usno Formation have been attributed to *Australopithecus* sp. The Usno contains a higher percentage of arboreal (6.25%) and terrestrial/arboreal (28.13%) animals than the Tulu Bor Member, and thus the Usno is positioned with the bushland–woodland regions (Figures 9 and 10). There is a high abundance of aquatic animals (9.38%), but not very many fresh grass grazers (6.25%). This suggests a wooded riverine habitat without extensive edaphic grasslands. The abundance of fruit and leaf eaters (15.63%) indicates that there were probably bushland and thicket areas, as well as riverine forest and woodland.

Shungura Formation. This sequence of deposits occurs in the lower Omo Valley, Ethiopia. The Members (A–L) are divided by a series of tuffs that are dated from 3.6 to about 1.0 Ma. Some of these tephras have been correlated with those in the Usno and Koobi Fora Formations (Feibel & Brown, 1993). While the Shungura Formation has produced an abundance of mammalian material with exceptional specimens of bovids and monkeys, hominids are represented by fairly scrappy remains (pers. obs.).

MEMBER B. Hominids recovered have been assigned to *Australopithecus* sp. (Coppens et al., 1976). Deposits from Member B range from 3.36–2.8 Ma, and thus, fauna from Member B includes almost 600,000 years of material from various depositional systems. However, most of this fauna derives from B-10 and is thus more constricted in time to around 2.95 m.y.a. (G. G. Eck, pers. comm.). Therefore, a habitat reconstruction is possible. Geologically, deposits were formed by a perennial river system with occasional riverine flooding which created flood plains (de Heinzelin et al., 1976).

There is a high percentage of arboreal animals (13.33%) placing the locality within the closed woodland range (Figures 9 and 10). The percentage of frugivorous species is also quite high (20%), again within the range of closed woodland areas. Member B deposits also include some aquatic (4.54%) and some fresh grass grazing (11.11%) mammals. Member B fauna indicates a habitat of mostly closed woodland with riverine forest and edaphic grasslands. Other habitat reconstructions include a riverine forest based on pollen analysis (Bonnefille, 1984), and a wooded savanna and forest based on micromammals (Jaeger & Wesselman, 1976). The habitat reconstruction presented here agrees with both of these reconstructions.

MEMBER C. There are *Australopithecus* sp. remains from this member and Suwa (1990) indicates that *Paranthropus aethiopicus* is represented in unit C7. This member was also deposited along a meandering river under flooding conditions (de Heinzelin et al., 1976).

The fossil assemblage includes 5.56% arboreal, 14% frugivorous, and 5.56% aquatic animals (Figures 9 and 10). These percentages are in the ranges of modern woodlands and bushlands that also encompass riverine forest. There are high proportions of fresh grass grazers (11.11%) that indicate a fairly extensive edaphic grassland, and terrestrial/arboreal animals (22.22%). Therefore, the entire deposit appears to contain animals that are derived from an overall bushland–woodland regime with a riverine forest and edaphic grasslands. Bonnefille (1984) has noted that the pollen recovered from this member indicates a grassland habitat, but the faunal community does not agree with that unless the pollen is reflecting the edaphic grasslands.

MEMBER D. There are hominid remains from 10 localities in Member D which are attributed to *Australopithecus* sp. (Coppens et al., 1976) and to *P. aethiopicus* (Suwa, 1990). Tuff D was deposited on flood plains in which plants quickly grew (de Heinzelin et al., 1976). This was followed by extensive channeling of the river.

There are slightly higher percentages of arboreal animals (6.45%) and frugivorous species (16.13%) than those found in Member C (Figures 9 and 10). There are also 6.45% aquatic mammals and 12.9% fresh grass grazers. Therefore, this habitat consisted of riverine forests within a woodland–bushland regime and included edaphic grasslands. Bonnefille (1984) notes that the pollen from this member indicates woodland, and this agrees with the habitat indicated by the mammalian fauna.

East African Hominid Fossil Localities with Dates < 2.5 Ma

Koobi Fora Formation (1.88–1.6 Ma)

KBS MEMBER. Hominids from this member include *Homo erectus* and *P. boisei*. Lacustrine sediments are evident from the KBS, however, the lake was probably shallow and throughout much of the deposit there are no vertebrate fossils except fish (Brown & Feibel, 1991).

The KBS mammalian fauna includes many aquatic and fresh grass grazing animals (7.46 and 14.93%, respectively), but very low percentages of arboreal (1.49%) and terrestrial/arboreal (5.97%) adaptations (Figures 11 and 12). There are some adaptations to fruit and leaves (7.46%). The major change is in the percentage of grazing mammals (37%) which is greater than in any of the previous members at Koobi Fora. In addition, although KBS falls within the ranges of modern scrub woodland and arid shrubland for many of the ecovariables, it has many more grazing species. This implies that unlike the scrub woodland and shrubland habitats, there was an abundance of nonedaphic grasses present during the KBS depositional period.

Harris (1991) suggests dry open conditions for this member, based on percentages of various bovid tribes present. Two sets of pollen data indicate either a savanna or grassland/subdesertic steppe for the KBS Member (Bonnefille, 1984). Thus, all habitat reconstructions support a grassland or shrubland environment.

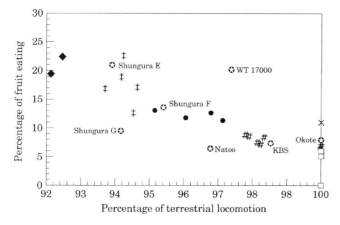

Figure 11. *Bivariate plot of the percentages of terrestrial vs. frugivorous mammals in vegetative habitats ranging from closed woodlands to desert including East African Pliocene localities after 2.5 m.y.a. Key: (■) closed woodland, (◆) closed woodland–bushland transition, (‡) bushland, (●) open woodland, (#) shrubland/scrub woodland, (□) grasslands/plains, (×) desert, (☼) Plio-Pleistocene fossil localities.*

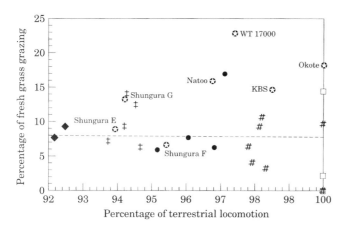

Figure 12. *Bivariate plot of the percentages of terrestrial vs. fresh grass grazing mammals in vegetative habitats ranging from closed woodlands to desert including East African Pliocene localities after 2.5 m.y.a. Habitats that include rivers, wetlands, and edaphic grasslands are above the dashed line (8%). Key: (■) closed woodland, (◆) closed woodland–bushland transition, (‡) bushland, (●) open woodland, (#) shrubland/scrub woodland, (□) grasslands/plains, (×) desert, (☼) Plio-Pleistocene fossil localities.*

OKOTE MEMBER. *P. boisei* has been recovered from this member. The Okote Member is again part of a river system, but the flooding was lateral rather than axial (Brown & Feibel, 1991). Fauna from this member includes no arboreal animals, and very few (5.26%) terrestrial/arboreal ones (Figures 11 and 12). There are very high proportions of aquatic adapted (10.53%) and fresh grass grazing animals (18.42%), plus a high abundance (39.47%) of grazing animals. Thus it appears that at 1.39 m.y.a., this region was similar to the wetlands and edaphic grasslands of Kafue Flats (as described by Perera, 1982).

Nachukui Formation, West Turkana. The Nachukui Formation is on the west side of Lake Turkana. The formation is part of the extensive Turkana Basin and Omo Group defined by de Heinzelin (1983).

LOMEKWI MEMBER/WT-17000 LOCALITY. The skull of *P. aethiopicus* was recovered 3.8 m below the Lokalalei Tuff in the Lomekwi Member. There is a great abundance of fresh grass grazing species (23.08%) from this locality. However, there are only 5.12% aquatic species (Figures 11 and 12). This suggests that the edaphic grasslands utilized by the fresh grass grazers were shallow wetlands or marshy swamps because there are few deep water aquatic species. There are 2.56% arboreal and 20.51% frugivorous species from this locality indicating the presence of trees and many fruiting plants, both trees and bushes. Walker et al. (1986) note that while alcelaphine and aepycerotine bovids dominate the horizons below this locality, this site is represented mostly by reduncine bovids, reflecting edaphic grasslands or marshes. I reconstruct the WT-17000 locality as an open woodland with bushland thickets, edaphic grasslands and wetlands, and a riparian woodland or forest.

NATOO MEMBER. The *H. erectus* skeleton, WT 15000 was probably recovered within this member as it is above the equivalent J-4 Tuff (1.64 Ma), but below the Lower Nariokotome Tuff (1.33 Ma) (Feibel & Brown, 1993). The Natoo Member is correlated with the Okote Member of the Koobi Fora Formation. The paleogeographic reconstruction of this depositional member includes three alternative water sources flowing into the region. There is speculation as to whether a lake or river existed in the region (Brown & MacDougall, 1993).

The presence of a lake or river system is evident in the percentages of aquatic (6.45%) and fresh grass grazing animals (16.13%). Like those found in the Lomekwi Member, these mammals could represent marshy wetlands. There are few arboreal animals (3.22%) and the percentage of frugivorous species is only 6.45% (Figures 11 and 12). The percentage of grazing animals is 46.67%. Thus the mammals of the Natoo deposits indicate wooded and edaphic grasslands, as well as swampy vegetation.

Shungura Formation, Omo, Ethiopia

MEMBER E. *P. boisei* (Feibel et al., 1989) and/or *P. aethiopicus* (Howell et al., 1987; Leakey & Walker, 1988; Suwa, 1990) have been recovered from this member. According to de Heinzelin et al. (1976), there is an absence of "illuvation" in the soils above Tuff E, and they therefore suggest a drier climate. However, the fauna does not indicate a particularly dry habitat. There is about the same percentage of arboreal species (6.06%) and a slightly higher percentage of frugivorous animals (21.21%) than found in the Member D deposits (Figures 11 and 12). There are also fewer grazing animals in Member E (12.12%) than D (16.13%). However, the abundance of fresh grass grazers (9.09%) and aquatic animals (6.06%) has dropped slightly from the percentages of these ecovariables in Member D. Therefore, fauna from this deposit seems to indicate a fairly well-watered woodland–bushland with a riparian woodland or forest. Bonnefille (1984) suggests grass-land pollen for this member, and while there probably was grass within the woodland and bushland, the total faunal assemblage does not indicate open grasslands for this member.

MEMBER F. *P. aethiopicus* has been recovered from this member (Suwa, 1990), which was deposited when there were flood plains present, although the tephras were deposited on sandy soils, rather than on water indicating that the flood plains were not particularly widespread (de Heinzelin et al., 1976). The terrestrial fauna from this member increases from previous members and thus, there appears to be less tree cover. There is also a decrease in fresh grass grazing animals to 6.82% and an increase in grazing animals to 20.45% (Figures 11 and 12). Therefore, there were few areas of edaphic grass-lands, and more open woodland at the time of these deposits, and high abundance of frugivorous species indicates the presence of bushland. Bonnefille (1984) notes that the pollen indicates grasslands, and Jaeger & Wesselman (1976) note that the micromammals indicate open, arid conditions. While my data do not indicate particularly arid conditions, the region was probably more open and slightly drier than preceding habitats. In fact, the mammalian fauna agrees with the paleogeography in that the flood plains are reduced (de Heinzelin et al., 1976).

MEMBER G. A *P. boisei* mandible has been recovered from unit G3 and a fragmentary skull attributed to *Homo habilis* has been found in unit G28 (Kimbel, 1995). This member has a very similar community structure to that of Member F. There are arboreal animals (5.77%) and frugivorous species (9.62%), as well as aquatic (5.78%) and fresh grass grazing species (13.46%). And there is a slight increase in grazing animals from 20 to 25% in this member (Figures 11 and 12). This locality also reflects the presence of a river surrounded by open woodland, and the flood plain seems to have again expanded from Member F to include edaphic grasslands as indicated by the fresh grass grazing species.

TRACING ECOVARIABLES ACROSS TIME

It has been postulated that there were major turnovers in bovid and hominid lineages at around 2.7–2.5 m.y.a. (Vrba, 1988, 1995; Vrba et al., 1989). These extinction and speciation events for bovids were proposed to be the result of a global cooling and drying event which produced more open grassland-type habitats in Africa. Cerling (1992), however, suggests that the first evidence of significant C4 grasslands, and thus evidence of major environmental change, is at about 1.7 m.y.a. Vrba (1995) shows significant bovid species turnover, as represented by an FAD (first appearance date) pulse at 2.7–2.5 m.y.a. Were there major climatic changes at either 2.7–2.5 m.y.a. or 1.7 m.y.a.? I examine this issue ecologically, rather than taxonomically, by charting specific ecological characteristics across time to see if there are trophic and/or locomotor changes in communities that would support the hypothesized climate changes at these times.

By plotting grazing, arboreal, and total frugivory predictor ecovariables from each eastern and southern African fossil locality against time, changes in community structure can be observed (Figure 13). While percentages of these ecovariables cannot be inferred in temporal gaps, it is probable that the fossil localities included represent the trends discussed. The relative abundances of grazing mammalian species, of which bovids, at least, are indicatory of more open woodlands and grasslands (Vrba, 1974, 1975), fluctuate in East African localities from 15–25% until approximately 1.8 m.y.a. [Figure 13(a)]. At that time grazing animals increase to higher percentages (45%) than previously recorded. Although South African hominid localities give evidence of having been more dry and bushy than

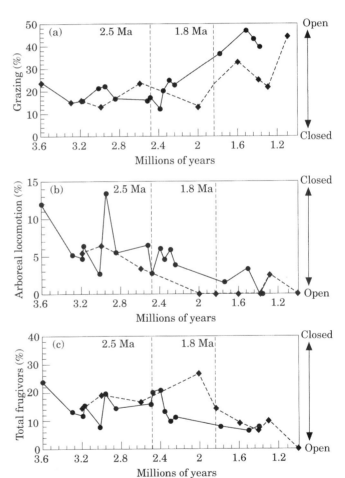

Figure 13. *Bivariate plot of the percentages of (a) grazing mammals, (b) arboreal animals, and (c) frugivorous mammals found in each hominid fossil locality against time. Vertical dotted lines represent 2.5 and 1.8 Ma. An increase in grazing occurs between 2.3 and 1.8 Ma in eastern and southern Africa. Arboreal locomotion declines sharply at the same time in both southern and eastern Africa. Frugivory declines between 2.5 and 1.8 Ma in eastern Africa. Interestingly, although southern Africa is relatively drier, frugivory is somewhat higher in those hominid localities indicating a bushier habitat than those of eastern Africa. Note: if the hominid locality encompassed a dating range (e.g., 3.36–2.68), then the mean date was used on the plot. (●) East Africa; (◆) South Africa.*

contemporaneous eastern African sites, percentages of grazing follow the same pattern.

The percentage of arboreality in East Africa at 3.6 m.y.a. is in closed woodland ranges (see Table 4). Percentages fluctuate between closed woodland and open woodland ranges until after 1.8 m.y.a. when they drop to shrubland and grassland ranges [Figure 13(b)]. The drops to open woodland ranges before 1.8 m.y.a. include the Tulu Bor Member of the Koobi Fora Formation and the WT-17000 locality from West Turkana which have already been recognized as slightly more open habitats. In southern Africa, arboreal percentages in mammalian communities begin in bushland–woodland ranges and fall into shrubland and grassland ranges. Because there is one site between 3.0 and 2.0 Ma, it is impossible to detect fluctuations in these variables. However, there is a definite change to open habitats from 3 to 2 m.y.a.

Percentages of frugivory in East African communities also fluctuate within woodland ranges until sometime between 2.45 and 1.88 m.y.a. when they drop to shrubland and grassland ranges. In South Africa, percentages of frugivory in communities remain relatively high from about 3.0 m.y.a. until about 1.8 m.y.a. when they drop into open woodland ranges and then to grassland levels at Sterkfontein 5 (Figure 13(c)).

Vrba (1988, 1995) reports a turnover in bovid species in Africa around 2.7–2.5 m.y.a. This taxonomic shift does not correspond to a dramatic increase in higher levels of grazing adaptations in bovids and other mammals. Although the percentages of grazing fluctuate until 1.8 m.y.a., a gradual decline in abundance of arboreal mammals within communities is apparent from around 3.4 Ma through 1 Ma, especially in South Africa. This could have been caused by either continuous, gradual climate aridification or an increase in seasonality. This gradual, but fluctuating, shift in ecological adaptations is supported by evidence for glacial cycles that began to fluctuate between 3.1 and 2.6 m.y.a. (deMenocal, 1995). Additionally, it has been reported (Kerr, 1996) that the Evolution of Terrestrial Ecosystems group at the Smithsonian Institution have not seen a taxonomic turnover pulse in any mammalian group from the Turkana Basin at 2.5 Ma, but did report a gradual taxonomic shift over about a million years. This study supports their detailed study of the Turkana Basin over a broader scaled examination of eastern and southern Africa. This pattern does not preclude various regions being more affected by local tectonism than by global climatic shifts. However, the overall pattern shows gradual aridification or change to more pronounced dry seasons that possibly precipitated the movement or extinction of arboreal and frugivorous mammals so that they are no longer found in great abundance in hominid assemblages after 1.8 m.y.a. Grazing mammals do not show great expansion until about 1.8 m.y.a. when they exceed 30% in many eastern African hominid localities. This spike coincides with Cerling's (1992) suggestion of an expansion of modern type C4 (secondary) grasslands in Africa, and deMenocal's

(1995) evidence of drier environments and seasonality at this time. Thus, it is likely that grazing adaptations did not increase substantially within communities until the development and expansion of secondary grasslands.

HABITATS ASSOCIATED WITH HOMINIDS

The goal of reconstructing paleohabitats and tracing changing environments across time is to illuminate the conditions in which hominid species lived. In this section, I describe the overall and perhaps preferred habitats in which each hominid species existed with regard to their evolution.

Australopithecus Species

The localities in this study that include *A. afarensis* or fossils that are only identified to the genus *Australopithecus* include Laetoli; Hadar Formation, Sidi Hakoma and Denen Dora Members; Shungura Formation, Members B, C (?), D (?), Usno (?); and Koobi Fora Formation, Tulu Bor Member. These localities have been reconstructed as closed to open woodland/bushland with edaphic grasslands. However, the fauna from the Tulu Bor Member is indicative of a shrubland with a deltaic flood plain, probably similar to the Okavango Delta. This reconstruction is interesting because this member contains just a few hominid specimens (Wood, 1994). It is possible that more hominids have not been recovered from the Tulu Bor because the paleohabitat was too open, i.e., the environment was not "preferred" by *A. afarensis.*

The Pliocene locality of Fejej from which *A. afarensis* has also been recovered has too few mammals to allow a thorough reconstruction of the community. However, the fauna from these Pliocene deposits includes crocodiles, cat fish, *Diceros bicornis, Nyanzachoerus* sp., *Tragelaphus* sp., and *Neotragini* sp. This preliminary faunal community reveals the presence of water and woodland–bushland animals, and as such it is similar to the constructions for the other early Pliocene localities.

A. afarensis is generally found in habitats containing water and trees. It is difficult to prove with habitat evidence alone that these early hominids had specific dietary, locomotor, or anti-predator adaptations that required trees or warm, mesic conditions. However, anatomical studies (e.g., Stern & Susman, 1983; Susman et al., 1984) have indicated that the anatomy of hominids indicated morphological adaptations for some arboreal locomotion.

The sites of Makapansgat and Sterkfontein are the only localities in this study that include *A. africanus.* The habitat derived from the Member 3 and Member 4 fauna from Makapansgat is woodland and bushland with riverine forest. This river system also supported patches of edaphic grasslands. The habitat of Sterkfontein Member 4, later in time, is also reconstructed as woodland, but it is more open than that of Makapansgat. Thus, *A. africanus* also existed in woodland areas, similar to those in which *A. afarensis* existed, albeit slightly drier. However, as these are cave sites and probably animal accumulated, there could be a bias against arboreal and aquatic animals. Thus, it is possible that *A. africanus* existed in more mesic, closed woodlands or bushlands than are represented by these reconstructions.

These woodland/bushland habitats with plentiful water suggest that the environment in which these *Australopithecus* spp. existed was fairly static, that is, the habitats in which these hominids could exist are constrained by minimum and maximum amounts of rainfall and tree cover. This agrees with the hypothesis of Stanley (1992) that *A. africanus,* at least, existed in a fairly static environment. Over time, as the mammalian communities indicate that Pliocene habitats became more open, these hominids disappear from the fossil record. Perhaps a gradual change to drier, more open habitats and/or a more pronounced dry season forced these australopithecines across an environmental tolerance limit around 2.8–2.5 m.y.a., and resulted in their extinction.

Paranthropus Species

P. aethiopicus has been recovered from the Shungura Formation, Members C–G (Suwa, 1990) and the West Turkana WT-17000 locality. Mammalian communities from these localities indicate that most were bushland to open woodland regions and all contain edaphic grasslands to greater or lesser extents. These habitats overlap with the more open end of those of *A. afarensis* and *A. africanus*. Because so few of these fossils have been recovered, it is not possible to make generalizations about the habitat preference of this species. However, these habitats appear to be more closed than those of later *Paranthropus* species.

P. boisei has been recovered from the KBS and Okote Members of the Koobi Fora Formation. These localities are fairly open (from woodland to scrub woodland), but all have edaphic grasslands and therefore plentiful water. Behrensmeyer (1978) has previously noted that *P. boisei* fossils were recovered from deltaic environments at Koobi Fora (KBS). In addition, Shipman & Harris (1988) indicate that Beds I and II at Olduvai sample lake margin regions, i.e., some edaphic grasslands. However, *contra* Shipman & Harris (1988) I found that this hominid does not necessarily prefer "closed" habitats (at least at non-Olduvai localities), but rather, habitats with abundant water and edaphic grasslands. This habitat differs from that of *P. aethiopicus* in being more open, but it cannot be considered dry.

P. robustus has been recovered from Swartkrans and Kromdraai. The habitats of Swartkrans have been reconstructed as an open or wooded/bushed grassland with edaphic grassland. Kromdraai B has been tentatively reconstructed as an open grassland, though it must be noted that this reconstruction is based on a small sample. Future excavations may recover fossils of aquatic or wetland mammals which could significantly affect this reconstruction. Nevertheless, the southern African *P. robustus* appear to be slightly more arid adapted than east African *P. boisei.*

Except for *Paranthropus* found at the Kromdraai B locality, the genus seems to have been recovered mostly from deltaic habitats that include edaphic grasslands. Wood et al. (1994) suggest that *P. boisei* exhibits evolutionary stasis throughout its existence in eastern Africa. It appears from this analysis that the habitats that are associated with *P. boisei* are extremely similar over its temporal range which supports the observations of Wood et al.

Grine (1981) has suggested that *Paranthropus* species had a diet that contained extreme amounts of grit, and perhaps the substances that they preferred in their diets were associated with river or lake margins and thus, edaphic grasslands. This study supports this suggestion as these species are always found in the vicinity of water courses with high percentages of mammals that eat the vegetation produced by this environment. *Paranthropus* is not found in early middle Pleistocene localities that were deposited in arid grassland environments. This suggests that as the environment became increasingly arid and open throughout the early Pleistocene, *Paranthropus* probably faced changing and diminishing resources. Further research into the time period between 1.2 million and 500,000 years ago may show that these flood plain habitats were also affected by seasonal changes. There was a drying event recorded in eolian dust after 1 m.y.a. (deMenocal, 1995). While other orders of mammals were able to withstand more arid or seasonal environments, perhaps these changes could have influenced the extinction of *Paranthropus* spp.

Homo Species

Several localities from which *Homo* species are known were included in this research: Koobi Fora KBS and Okote Members, Nachukui Formation Natoo Member, Swartkrans Members 1 and 2, and Sterkfontein Member 5. Two localities in this study in which only *Homo* species have been recovered are Sterkfontein 5 (an arid, plains habitat) and the WT 15000 locality of the Nachukui Formation (shrubland with possible riparian woodland). The differing reconstructions suggest that early *Homo* probably occupied a wider range of habitats than earlier hominids. However, it is worth emphasizing that there are several different species of *Homo* included in this analysis. Further study into hominid Pleistocene localities to examine habitats associated with various *Homo* species is necessary. Some of the earliest *Homo* species are found near edaphic grasslands, but are also found in habitats that have been reconstructed as open grasslands and dry shrublands. Many localities yield specimens of both *Homo* and *Paranthropus*. Perhaps *Homo* and *Paranthropus* were sympatric, but inhabiting different niches: *Paranthropus* foraging in edaphic grasslands and *Homo* utilizing other microhabitats. The appearance of later *Homo* in secondary grassland localities coincides with Stanley's

(1992) suggestion that *H. erectus* was the first hominid adapted to life on the "open savanna".

CONCLUSIONS

In conclusion, these ecological diversity studies have shown that modern habitat types can be predicted by the ecovariables of the mammals found in them. Tests of modern death assemblages showed that taxonomic and taphonomic overprint were minimized using this methodology. Using the same methodology, Plio-Pleistocene habitats were reconstructed through analyses of mammalian fossil assemblages.

Australopithecus species have been recovered from fossil assemblages that indicate fairly wooded regions. It is possible that these woodland areas provided some protection against predation, an important consideration for these small bipedal apes. Their anatomy shows that they were adept at climbing (Stern & Susman, 1983; Susman et al., 1984), and trees could have been used for not only predator avoidance, but also for sleeping and feeding. When *Australopithecus* disappeared from the fossil record, *Paranthropus* specimens become common and fossil assemblages associated with them indicate that they existed in slightly more open habitats that include wetlands. However, *P. aethiopicus* is not only associated with edaphic grasslands, but with woodland and bushland areas, i.e., in habitats that are similar to those utilized by *Australopithecus*. *Homo* species appear in the fossil record around 2 m.y.a. and are associated with habitats that also supported *Paranthropus* species. Later *Homo* species are also found in assemblages that indicate extremely arid and open landscapes. If these co-existing hominids partitioned the environment, it is possible that *Paranthropus* preferred edaphic grasslands and wetland regions, while *Homo* utilized the more open woodland and grassland habitats.

ACKNOWLEDGMENTS

I would like to thank Bruce Rubidge (Bernard Price Institute), Phillip V. Tobias and Lee R. Berger (University of the Witwatersrand Anatomy Department), Francis Thackeray (Transvaal Museum), Kessaye Begashaw and Solomon Werde Kel (Ethiopia National Museum), and Claude Guimotte (French Omo Collections) for allowing me to have access to the mammalian fossils in their care. I would also like to express my appreciation to all Plio-Pleistocene paleontologists who have published the results of their work and therefore made this research possible. I thank John Fleagle, Fred Grine, Charles Janson, Richard Klein and Curtis Marean for their suggestions and help; Peter Andrews for a long discussion and encouragement; Gerry Eck for discussions of Ethiopian fossil fauna; and John Fleagle for comments on an earlier draft of this manuscript. Thanks also to Peter Andrews, Tom Plummer, Mario Gagnon, and Lillian Spencer for their reviews of this manuscript. This research was supported by grants from the National Science Foundation (SBR-9312842), the L. S. B. Leakey Foundation, the Joel Reiss Scholarship for Field Work in Hadar, Ethiopia, and the American Association of University Women.

REFERENCES

Andrews, P. (1989). Paleoecology of Laetoli. *J. hum. Evol.* **18**, 173–181.

Andrews, P., Lord, J. M. & Nesbitt-Evans, E. M. (1979). Patterns of ecological diversity in fossil and modern mammalian faunas. *Bio. J. Linn. Soc.* **11**, 177–205.

Ansell, W. F. H. (1978). *The Mammals of Zambia.* Chilanga, Zambia: National Parks and Wildlife Service.

Aronson, J. L. & Taieb, M. (1981). Geology and paleogeography of the Hadar hominid site, Ethiopia. In (G. Rapp, Jr & C. F. Vondra, Eds) *Hominid Sites: Their Geologic Settings,* pp. 165–195. Boulder: Westview Press.

Avery, D. M. (1982). Micromammals as paleoenvironmental indicators and an interpretation of the late Quaternary in the Southern Cape Province. *Ann. S. Afr. Mus.* **85**, 183–374.

Behrensmeyer, A. K. (1978). The habitat of Plio-Pleistocene hominids in East Africa: taphonomic and microstratigraphic evidence. In (C. J. Jolly, Ed.) *Early Hominids of Africa,* pp. 165–190. London: Duckworth.

Behrensmeyer, A. K. (1991). Terrestrial vertebrate accumulations. In (P. A. Allison & D. E. G. Briggs, Eds) *Taphonomy: Releasing the Data Locked in the Fossil Record.* New York: Plenum.

Behrensmeyer, A. K., Western, D. & Dechant Boaz, D. E. (1979). New perspectives in vertebrate paleoecology from a recent bone assemblage. *Paleobiology* **5**, 12–21.

Benefit, B. R. & McCrossin, M. L. (1990). Diet, species diversity, and distribution of African fossil baboons. *Kroeber Anthrop. Soc. Papers* **71–72**, 79–93.

Boaz, N. (1977). Paleoecology of Plio-Pleistocene Hominidae of the Lower Omo Basin. PhD. Dissertation, University of California.

Bonnefille, R. (1983). Evidence for cooler and drier climate in the Ethiopian uplands towards 2.5 myr ago. *Nature* **309**, 487–491.

Bonnefille, R. (1984). Cenozoic vegetation and environments of early hominids in east Africa. In (R. O. Whyte, Ed.) *The Evolution of East Asian Environments.* Vol. II. Paleobotany, Paleozoology, and Paleoanthropology, Center of Asian Studies, University of Hong Kong.

Bonnefille, R. & Riollet, G. (1987). Palynological spectra from the Upper Laetolil Beds. In (M. D. Leakey & J. H. Harris, Eds) *Laetoli: A Pliocene Site in Northern Tanzania,* pp. 52–61. Oxford: Clarendon Press.

Bourliere, F. & Hadley, M. (1983). Present day savannas: An overview, pp. 1–17. In (F. Bourliere, Ed.) *Ecosystems of the World: Tropical Savannas.* Paris: UNESCO.

Brain, C. K. (1981). *The Hunters or the Hunted? An Introduction to African Cave Taphonomy.* Chicago: University of Chicago Press.

Brain, C. K., Ed. (1993). *Swartkrans: A cave's chronicle of early man.* Transvaal Museum Monograph. Pretoria: Transvaal Museum.

Bremen, H. & de Wit, C. T. (1983). Rangeland productivity and exploitation in the Sahel. *Science* **221**, 1341–1347.

Brown, F. H. & Feibel, C. S. (1991). Stratigraphy, depositional environments and palaeogeography of the Koobi Fora Formation. In (J. M. Harris, Ed.) *Koobi Fora Research Project, Volume 3 The Fossil Ungulates: Geology, Fossil Artiodactyls, and Palaeoenvironments,* pp. 1–29. Oxford: Clarendon Press.

Brown, F. H. & MacDougall, I. (1993). Geological Setting and Age. In (A. Walker & R. Leakey, Eds) *The Nariokotome Homo erectus Skeleton,* pp. 9–20. Cambridge: Harvard University Press.

Cadman, A. & Rayner, R. J. (1989). Climatic change and the appearance of *Australopithecus africanus* in the Makapansgat sediments. *J. hum. Evol.* **18**, 107–113.

Cerling, T. E. (1992). Development of grasslands and savannas in East Africa during the Neogene. *Paleogeog Paleoclimatol Paleoecol* (Global Planetary change Section) **97**, 241–247.

Ciochon, R. L. (1990). *Evolution of the Cercopithecoid forelimb: Phylogenetic and Functional Implications from Morphometric Analysis.* California: University of California Publications in Geological Science, 135.

Child, G. S. (1964). Some notes on the mammals of Kilimanjaro. *Tanganyika Notes Rec.* **64**, 77–89.

Coppens, Y., Howell, F. C., Isaac, G. Ll. & Leakey, R. E. F. (1976). *Earliest Man and Environments in the Lake Rudolph Basin: Stratigraphy, Paleoecology, and Evolution.* Chicago: University of Chicago Press.

Dart, R. A. (1925). *Australopithecus africanus:* The man ape of South Africa. *Nature* **115**, 195–199.

Dart, R. A. (1952). Faunal and climatic fluctuations in Makapansgat Valley: their relation to the geologic age and Promethean status of *Australopithecus.* In (L. S. B. Leakey & S. Cole, Eds) *Proceedings of the 1st Pan African Congress on Prehistory, Nairobi, 1947,* pp. 96–106.

de Heinzelin, J. (1983). The Omo Group. Musee Royale de l'Afrique Centrale, Tevuren, Belgique, Annales, Serie in 8°, Sciences Geologiques, No. 85.

de Heinzelin, J., Haesaerts, P. & Howell, F. C. (1976). Plio-Pleistocene formations of the Lower Omo Basin, with particular reference to the Shungura Formation, pp. 24–49. In (Y. Coppens, F. C. Howell, G. Ll. Isaac & R. E. F. Leakey, Eds) *Earliest Man and Environments in the Lake Rudolph Basin: Stratigraphy, Paleoecology, and Evolution.* Chicago: University of Chicago Press.

Delany, M. & Happold, D. C. D. (1979). *Ecology of African Mammals.* London: Longman.

Delson, E. (1984). Cercopithecid biochronology of the African Plio-Pleistocene: Correlation among eastern and southern hominid-bearing localities. *Cour. Forsch. Inst. Senckenberg* **69**, 199–218.

deMenocal, P. B. (1995). Plio-Pleistocene African Climate. *Science* **270**, 53–59.

Dodd, J. R. & Stanton, R. J. (1990). *Paleoecology: Concepts and Applications.* 2nd edn. New York: John Wiley and Sons.

Emmons, L., Gautier-Hion, A. & Dubost, G. (1983). Community structure of the frugivorous-folivorous mammals of Gabon. *J. Zool. Lond.* **199**, 209–222.

Estes, R. D. (1991). *The Behavior Guide to African Mammals.* Berkeley: University of California Press.

Feibel, C. S. & Brown, F. H. (1993). Microstratigraphy and paleoenvironments. In (A. Walker & R. Leakey, Eds) *The Nariokotome* Homo erectus *Skeleton,* pp. 21–39. Cambridge: Harvard University Press.

Feibel, C. S., Brown, F. & MacDougall, I. (1989). Stratigraphic context of fossil hominids from the Omo Group deposits: Northern Turkana Basin, Kenya and Ethiopia. *Am. J. phys. Anthrop.* **78**, 595–622.

Feibel, C. S., Harris, J. M. & Brown, F. H. (1991). Paleoenvironmental context for the Late Neogene of the Turkana Basin. In (J. M. Harris, Ed.) *Koobi Fora Research Project, Volume 3,* pp. 321–370. Oxford: Clarendon Press.

Fleming, T. H. (1973). Numbers of mammal species in North and Central American forest communities. *Ecol.* **54**, 555–563.

Gentry, A. W. (1987) Pliocene Bovidae from Laetoli. In (M. D. Leakey & J. M. Harris, Eds) *Laetoli: A Pliocene Site in Northern Tanzania,* pp. 378–408. Oxford: Oxford University Press.

Geze, R. (1985). Repartition paleoecologique et relations phylogenetiques des Hippopotamidae (Mammalia, Artiodactyla) du Neogene defrock orientals. In *L'Environnement des Hominides au Plio-Pleistocene,* pp. 81–100. Paris: Masson.

Grine, F. E. (1981). Trophic differences between "gracile" and "robust" australopithecines, a scanning electron microscope analysis of occlusal events. *S. Afr. J. Sci.* **77**, 203–230.

Happold, D. C. D. (1989). *The Mammals of Nigeria.* Oxford: Clarendon Press.

Harris, J. M. (1987). Summary. In (M. D. Leakey & J. M. Harris, Eds) *Laetoli: A Pliocene Site in Northern Tanzania,* pp. 524–532. Oxford: Clarendon Press.

Harris, J. M. (1991). *Koobi Fora Research Project, Vol. 3: The Fossil Ungulates: Geology, Fossil Artiodactyls, and Paleoenvironments.* Oxford: Clarendon Press.

Harris, J. M. & Leakey, M. (1993). The faunal context. In (A. Walker & R. Leakey, Eds) *The Nariokotome* Homo erectus *Skeleton,* pp. 54–62. Cambridge: Harvard University Press.

Harris, J. M., Brown, F. H. & Leakey, M. G. (1988). Stratigraphy and paleontology of Pliocene and Pleistocene localities west of Lake Turkana, Kenya. In *Contributions in Science, No. 399.* Los Angeles: Natural History Museum of Los Angeles County.

Hay, R. (1987). Geology of the Laetoli area. In (M. D. Leakey & J. M. Harris, Eds) *Laetoli: A Pliocene Site in Northern Tanzania,* pp. 23–47. Oxford: Clarendon Press.

Howell, F. C. (1978). Hominidae. In (V. J. Maglio & H. S. B. Cooke, Eds) *Evolution of African Mammals,* pp. 152–248. Cambridge: Harvard University Press.

Howell, F. C., Haesaerts, P. & deHeinzelin, J. (1987). Depositional environments, archaeological occurrences and hominids from Members E and F of the Shungura Formation (Omo Basin, Ethiopia). *J. hum. Evol.* **16**, 665–700.

Jaeger, J. J. & Wesselman, H. B. (1976). Fossil remains of micromammals from the Omo Group deposits, pp. 351–360. In (Y. Coppens, F. C. Howells, G. Ll. Isaac & R. E. F. Leakey, Eds) *Earliest Man and Environments in the Lake Rudolph Basin: Stratigraphy, Paleoecology, and Evolution.* Chicago: University of Chicago Press.

Janis, C. M. (1988). An estimation of tooth volume and hypsodonty indices in ungulate mammals, and the correlation of these factors with dietary preference. In (D. E. Russell, J-p. Santoro & D. Sigogneau-Russell, Eds) *Teeth Revisited, Proceedings of the VIIth International Symposium on Dental Morphology,* Paris, 1986. *Mem. Mus. natn. Hist. Nat., Paris (serie C)* **53**, 367–387.

Kappelman, J. (1988). Morphology and locomotor adaptations of the bovid femur in relation to habitat. *J. Morphol.* **198**, 119–130.

Kay, R. F. (1975). The functional adaptations of primate molar teeth. *Am. J. phys. Anthrop.* **43**, 195–216.

Kay, R. F. (1978). Molar structure and diet in extant Cercopithecidae. In (K. Joysey & P. Butler, Eds) *Development, Function, and Evolution of Teeth,* pp. 309–339. London: Academic Press.

Kerr, R. A. (1996). New mammal data challenge evolutionary pulse theory. *Science* **273**, 431–432.

Kimbel, W. H. (1988) Identification of a partial cranium of *Australopithecus afarensis* from the Koobi Fora Formation, Kenya, *J. hum. Evol.* **17**, 647–656.

Kimbel, W. H. (1995). Hominid speciation and Pliocene climatic change. In (E. S. Vrba, G. Denton, L. Burckle & T. Partridge, Eds) *Paleoclimate and Evolution with Emphasis on Human Origins,* pp. 425–437. New Haven: Yale University Press.

Kingdon, J. (1974a). *East African Mammals.* Vol. 1. Chicago: University of Chicago Press.

Kingdon, J. (1974b). *East African Mammals: Hares and Rodents.* Vol. IIB. Chicago: University of Chicago Press.

Kingdon, J. (1977). *East African Mammals: Carnivores.* Vol. IIIA. Chicago: University of Chicago Press.

Kingdon, J. (1979). *East African Mammals: Large Mammals.* Vol. IIIB. Chicago: University of Chicago Press.

Kingdon, J. (1982a). *East African Mammals: Bovids.* Vol. IIIC. Chicago: University of Chicago Press.

Kingdon, J. (1982b). *East African Mammals: Bovids.* Vol. IIID. Chicago: University of Chicago Press.

Kitchener, A. (1991). *The Natural History of the Wild Cats.* Ithaca: Comstock Publishing Associates.

Kruuk, H. (1972). *The Spotted Hyena: A Study of Predation and Social Behavior.* Chicago: University of Chicago Press.

Lamprey, H. F. (1962). The Tarangire Game Reserve. *Tanganyika Notes and Records* **60**, 10–22.

Lanjouw, A. (1987). *Data Review on the Central Congo Swamp and Floodplain Forest Ecosystem.* Royal Tropical Institute Rural Development Program.

Leakey, M. D. & Harris, J. M., Eds (1987). *Laetoli: A Pliocene Site in Northern Tanzania.* Oxford: Clarendon Press.

Leakey, M. G. & Leakey, R. E., Eds (1978). *Koobi Fora Research Project, Volume 1: The fossil hominids and an introduction to their context, 1968–1974.* Oxford: Clarendon Press.

Leakey, R. E. & Walker, A. (1988). New *Australopithecus boisei* specimens from East and West Lake Turkana, Kenya. *Am. J. phys. Anthrop.* **76**, 1–24.

Lewis, M. E. (1997) Carnivoran paleoguilds of Africa: implications for hominid food procurement strategies. *J. hum. Evol.* **32**, 257–288.

Lind, E. M. & Morrison, M. E. S. (1974). *East African Vegetation.* Bristol: Longman.

MacFadden, P. L. (1980). An overview of paleomagnetic chronology with special reference to the South African hominid sites. *Palaeont. afr.* **23,** 35.

Maguire, J. M. (1985). Recent geological, stratigraphic and palaeontological studies at Makapansgat Limeworks. In (P. V. Tobias, Ed.) *Hominid Evolution: Past, Present and Future,* pp. 151–164. New York: Alan R. Liss, Inc.

McKee, J. K. (1991). Paleo-ecology of the Sterkfontein hominids: a review and synthesis. *Palaeont. Afr.* **28,** 41–51.

Partridge, T. (1979). Reappraisal of the lithostratigraphy of Makapansgat Limeworks hominid site. *Nature* **279,** 484–488.

Perera, N. P. (1982). Ecological considerations in the management of the wetlands of Zambia. In (B. Gopal, R. E. Turner, R. G. Wetzel & F. F. Whighan, Eds) *Wetlands Ecology and Management,* pp. 21–30. Paris: UNESCO.

Rautenbach, I. L. (1978). Ecological distribution of the mammals of the Transvaal (Vertebrata: Mammalia). *Annals of the Transvaal Museum* **31,** 131–153.

Reed, K. E. (1996). The Paleoecology of Makapansgat and other African Pliocene Hominid Localities. Ph.D. Dissertation. State University of New York at Stony Brook.

Robinson, J. T. (1963). Adaptive radiation in the australopithecines and the origin of man. In (Howell, F. C. & Bourliere, F., Eds) *African Ecology and Human Evolution,* pp. 385–416. Chicago: Aldine.

Rose, K. D. (1981). Composition and species diversity in Paleocene and Eocene mammal assemblages: an empirical study. *J. Vert. Paleont.* **1,** 367–388.

Schaller, G. B. (1976). *The Serengeti Lion.* Chicago: University of Chicago Press.

Sheppe, W. & Osborne, T. (1971). Patterns of use of a flood plain by Zambian mammals. *Ecol. Mono.* **41,** 179–205.

Shipman, P. & Harris, J. M. (1988). Habitat preference and paleoecology of *Australopithecus boisei* in Eastern Africa. In (F. E. Grine, Ed.) *Evolutionary History of the "Robust" Australopithecines,* pp. 343–382. New York: Aldine de Gruyter.

Skinner, J. D. & Smithers, R. H. N. (1990). *The Mammals of the Southern African Subregion.* Pretoria: University of Pretoria Press.

Skinner, J. D., Henschel, J. R. & van Jaarsveld, A. S. (1986). Bone collecting habits of spotted hyaenas (*Crocuta crocuta*) in the Kruger National Park. *S. Afr. J. Zool.* **21,** 33–38.

Smithers, R. H. N. (1978). *A Checklist of the Mammals of Botswana.* Salisbury: Trustees of the National Museum of Rhodesia.

Spencer, L. M. (1995). Antelope and Grasslands: Reconstructing African Hominid Environments. Ph.D. Dissertation, State University of New York at Stony Brook.

Stanley, S. M. (1992). An ecological theory for the origin of *Homo. Paleobio.* **18,** 237–257.

Stern, J. T. J. & Susman, R. L. (1983). The locomotor anatomy of *Australopithecus afarensis. Am. J. phys. Anthrop.* **60,** 279–317.

Susman, R. L., Stern, J. T., Jr. & Jungers, W. L. (1984). Arboreality and bipedality in the Hadar hominids. *Folia Primatol.* **43,** 113–156.

Suwa, G. (1990). A comparative analysis of hominid dental remains from the Shungura and Usno Formations, Omo Valley, Ethiopia. Ph.D. Dissertation. University of California, Berkeley.

Swynnerton, G. H. (1958). Fauna of the Serengeti National Park. *Mammalia* **22,** 435–450.

Van Couvering, J. A. H. & Van Couvering, J. A. (1976). Early Miocene mammal fossils from East Africa: aspects of geology, faunistics, and paleoecology. In (G. L. Isaac & E. R. McCown, Eds) *Human Origins: Louis Leakey and the East African Evidence,* pp. 155–207. Menlo Park: Staples Press.

Van Valkenburgh, B. (1987) Skeletal indicators of locomotor behavior in living and extinct carnivores. *J. Vert. Paleontol.* **7,** 162–182.

Van Valkenburgh, B. (1989). Carnivore dental adaptations and diet: a study of trophic diversity within guilds. In (J. L. Gittleman, Ed.) *Carnivore Behavior, Ecology and Evolution,* pp. 410–435. Ithaca: Cornell University Press.

Vesey-Fitzgerald, D. F. (1964). Mammals of the Rukwa Valley. *Tanganyika Notes and Records* **62,** 61–72.

Vrba, E. S. (1974). Chronological and ecological implications of the fossil Bovidae at the Sterkfontein australopithecine site. *Nature* **250,** 19–23.

Vrba, E. S. (1975). Some evidence of chronology and palaeocology of Sterkfontein, Swartkrans, and Kromdraai from the fossil Bovidae. *Nature* **254,** 301–304.

Vrba, E. S. (1976) *The Fossil Bovidae of Sterkfontein, Swartkrans and Kromdraai.* Transvaal Mus. Mem. 21. Pretoria: Transvaal Museum.

Vrba, E. S. (1980). The significance of bovid remains as indicators of environment and prediction patterns. In (A. K. Behrensmeyer & A. Hill, Eds) *Fossils in the Making, Vertebrate Taphonomy and Paleoecology,* pp. 247–271. Chicago: University of Chicago Press.

Vrba, E. S. (1982) Biostratigraphy and chronology, based partly on Bovidae, of southern African hominid-associated assemblages: Makapansgat, Sterkfontein, Taung, Kromdraai, Swartkrans; also Elandsfontein (Saldanha), Broken Hill (now Kabwe) and Cave of Hearths. In (H. De Lumley & M. A. deLumley, Eds) *Proceedings of Congress International de Paleontologie Humaine,* Vol. 2., pp. 707–752. Nice: Union Internationale des Sciences Prehistoriques et Prohistoriques.

Vrba, E. S. (1985). Environment and evolution: alternative causes of the temporal distribution of evolutionary events. *S. Afr. J. of Sci.* **81,** 229–236.

Vrba, E. S. (1988). Late Pliocene climatic events and hominid evolution. In (F. E. Grine, Ed.) *Evolutionary History of the "Robust" Australopithecines,* pp. 405–426. New York: Aldine de Gruyter.

Vrba, E. S. (1995). The fossil record of African antelopes (Mammalia, Bovidae) in relation to human evolution and paleoclimate. In (E. S. Vrba, G. Denton, L. Burckle & T. Partridge, Eds) *Paleoclimate and Evolution with Emphasis on Human Origin,* pp. 385–424. New Haven: Yale University Press.

Vrba, E. S., Denton, G. H. & Prentice, M. L. (1989). Climatic influences on early hominid behavior. *Ossa* **14,** 127–156.

Walker, A. (1987). Fossil Galaginae from Laetoli. In (M. D. Leakey & J. M. Harris, Eds) *Laetoli: A Pliocene Site in Northern Tanzania,* pp. 88–90. Oxford: Clarendon Press.

Walker, A., Leakey, R. E., Harris, J. M. & Brown, F. H. (1986). 2.5 myr *Australopithecus boisei* from west of Lake Turkana. *Nature* **322,** 517–522.

Watson, V. (1993). Composition of the Swartkrans bone accumulations, in terms of skeletal parts and animals represented. In (C. K. Brain, Ed.) *Swartkrans: A Cave's Chronicle of Early Man,* pp. 35–74. Transvaal Museum Monograph No. 8. Pretoria: Transvaal Museum.

Wells, L. H. & Cooke, H. S. B. (1956). Fossil Bovidae from the Limeworks quarry, Makapansgat, Potgietersrust. *Palaeont. Afr.* **4,** 1–55.

White, F. (1983). *The Vegetation of Africa: A descriptive memoir to accompany UNESCO/AETFAT/UNSO vegetation maps of Africa.* Paris: UNESCO.

Wood, B. A., Wood, C. & Konigsberg, L. (1994). *Paranthropus boisei:* An example of evolutionary stasis? *Am. J. phys. Anthrop.* **95,** 117–136.

Wood, B. A. (1994). *Koobi Fora Research Project, Volume IV: Hominid Cranial Remains.* Oxford: Clarendon Press.

IV

Origin of the Genus *Homo* and Early Evolution in Africa

One of the most active and widely debated areas of research in human evolution today is the origin and early evolution of our own genus, *Homo*. As discussed in many chapters in Part III, several fossil taxa attributed to our own genus are present in fossil sites in eastern and southern Africa near the end of the Pliocene, at approximately the same time as stone tools first appear. As always, many of the fossils are fragmentary, and solid associations among cranial remains, limb elements, and stone tools are not firmly established. As a result, there are many areas of uncertainty and discussion: How many species are actually present in the fossil record? Which specimens belong to which species? Which should be placed in the genus *Homo* and which in *Australopithecus*? Who made the stone tools? What is the relationship of these tools to the origin of *Homo*? The chapters in Part IV address many of these questions and discuss the evolution of early members of the genus *Homo* in Africa. The initial spread of the genus *Homo* from Africa is discussed in Part V.

In the opening Chapter 26, Bernard A. Wood reviews "The History of the Genus *Homo*." He discusses the original descriptions and criteria used for assigning each of the species designated as belonging to this genus, especially the numerous species from the late Pliocene and early Pleistocene of Africa: *Homo habilis, Homo rudolfensis,* and *Homo ergaster.* Wood identifies two major controversies within the genus *Homo*. The first concerns the number of species in the genus and whether all hominids within *Homo* should be assigned to a single species, *H. sapiens,* because of the difficulty of identifying species boundaries (e.g., Wolpoff et al., 1994). The second controversy concerns the boundary of the genus *Homo* and specifically the inclusion of the African taxa *Homo habilis* and *Homo rudolfensis*. Wood argues that all evidence subsequent to their original descriptions has weakened the evidence that these taxa share derived functional attributes, such as habitual bipedalism and tool use, with *Homo ergaster.* Rather, both seem to share primitive locomotor and cultural abilities with *Australopithecus* and should be placed in that genus (see also Wood and Collard, 1999).

In Chapter 27, William H. Kimbel and colleagues describe "Late Pliocene *Homo* and Oldowan Tools from the Hadar Formation (Kada Hadar Member), Ethiopia." Although the divergence of the genus *Homo* from other hominids is generally agreed to have taken place between 3.0 and 2.0 mya, this date is based on collateral lines of evidence, including the presence of stone tools at 2.6 mya, the appearance of potential sister lineages such as *Paranthropus* at about 2.6 mya, and the diversity of species attributed to the genus *Homo* after 2.0 mya. This discovery is the earliest morphological evidence of the genus *Homo* in the fossil record, as well as the earliest association between *Homo* and stone tools in the context of a large mammal fauna. However, the authors were unable to find any features linking the maxilla with any particular species of *Homo*. Rather, the features it shares with members of the human genus are those found in all of the early species.

Chapter 28, by Robert J. Blumenschine and colleagues, "Late Pliocene *Homo* and Hominid Land Use from Western Olduvai Gorge, Tanzania," describes a new fossil hominid from Olduvai Gorge and the archaeological evidence for the behavior of these hominids. Olduvai Gorge is the type locality of the species *Homo habilis* (Leakey, Tobias, and Napier, 1964). However, the new maxilla show similarities to KNM-ER 1470, the type specimen of *Homo rudolfensis* from Lake Turkana, suggesting that the 1470 cranium may actually be referable to *Homo habilis,* a proposal previously put forth by Rightmire (1993). Since the early 1990s, most authorities have placed the specimens of early *Homo* from Lake Turkana with smaller teeth in the species *Homo habilis* and those that seemed to have larger teeth in the species *Homo rudolfensis* (e.g., Wood, 1992). However, if the more robust specimens of early *Homo* from Lake Turkana are assigned to *Homo habilis,* the proper taxonomic assignment for the more gracile specimens becomes unclear. More broadly, this calls into question the number of species of early *Homo* that are actually present in East Africa at the Plio-Pleistocene boundary.

Chapter 29, "*Australopithecus garhi*: A New Species of Early Hominid from Ethiopia," by Berhane Asfaw and colleagues, describes a new fossil hominid and additional skeletal and archaeological remains from the Middle Awash region of Ethiopia (see Chapter 14) dated at 2.5 mya. The authors argue that *A. garhi* is derived from *A. afarensis* (see also Chapter 20) and shows increased megadonty of the dentition. They mention similarities to some fossils of early *Homo* but refrain from assigning any phylogenetic position to this new species with respect to early *Homo*. From the same geological horizon, they report hominid limbs with human-like humerus to femur proportions and ape-like forearm to humerus ratio. These elements suggest that elongation of the femur, as in modern humans, took place before forearm reduction. However, the connection of the isolated limb elements to *A. garhi* remains unconfirmed.

The "Environment and Behavior of 2.5-Million-Year-Old Bouri Hominids" is the topic of Chapter 30, by Jean de Heinzelin and colleagues. The same geological horizon that yielded the fossil attributed to *Australopithecus garhi* also yielded faunal remains with cut marks, the earliest evidence of butchering behavior (see Chapter 30). No stone artifacts were found in the deposits, but early stone tools are known from several sites in the same region (see Chapters 26 and 31). Since bones with cut marks were not definitely associated with *A. garhi*, it is unclear whether *A. garhi* or some other taxon was the butcher.

In Chapter 31, Sileshi Semaw describes "The World's Oldest Stone Artefacts from Gona, Ethiopia: Their Implications for Understanding Stone Technology and Patterns of Human Evolution between 2.6–1.5 Million Years Ago." Primitive stone tools were first described and named from 1.8 mya deposits at Olduvai Gorge and were subsequently discovered in deposits as old as 2.3 mya in the Omo Valley of Ethiopia and near Lake Turkana in northern Kenya. In this and several other articles (Semaw et al., 1997, 2003; Roche et al., 1999; Merrick and Merrick, 1976; Plummer et al., 1999; Harris et al., 1987), stone tools have now been reported in deposits greater than 2.0 mya in several places. In general, the earliest tool assemblages show less diversity than assemblages from the early Pleistocene and seem to lack retouched flakes. Although these are the earliest record of stone tools, the excavated assemblages from this time period at Gona and elsewhere are extensive, yielding thousands of artifacts. These raise many additional questions, such as why do stone tools seem to appear abruptly in the geological record (see Panger et al., 2002) and which hominid(s) made these tools.

In Chapter 32, Alan Walker provides "Perspectives on the Nariokotome Discovery" of a nearly complete skeleton of *Homo erectus*. This fossil, dated to approximately 1.5 mya from the west side of Lake Turkana, is the most complete individual of *Homo erectus* known. This chapter summarizes the results of a large monograph devoted to this specimen (Walker and Leakey, 1993). Although WT 15000 was originally thought to be a teenager, it has been suggested that eight years is a more likely age estimate, given the faster rates of tooth growth and eruption in *Homo erectus* (Dean et al., 2001). Even at this young age, it is taller than any earlier fossil hominid and shows that *Homo erectus* (many authorities would refer this specimen to *Homo ergaster;* see Chapter 26) was similar to modern humans in height. Moreover, although this specimen had more robust bones than modern humans, like modern people living near the equator today, it seems to have had a slender body build as an adaptation for thermoregulation.

Part IV closes with Chapter 33, "Remains of *Homo erectus* from Bouri, Middle Awash, Ethiopia," where Berhane Asfaw and colleagues describe a cranium of *Homo* dated at approximately 1 mya from the site of Bouri in the Middle Awash, Ethiopia. The Bouri cranium, also called "Daka," is very similar to a cranium described earlier from Buia in Eritrea (Abbate et al., 1998). Asfaw and colleagues compare this new, relatively young specimen with other fossils attributed to *Homo erectus*, both in Africa and in other parts of the world. In a phylogenetic analysis of regional paleodemes (Howell, 1999) of early Pleistocene specimens placed in *Homo erectus* or *Homo ergaster,* they find that they are unable to distinguish the African fossils (many of which are often placed in a separate species, *Homo ergaster*) from Asian specimens attributed to *Homo erectus*. Thus, they argue that there is no justification for recognizing a separate species, *H. ergaster* (see also Manzi et al., 2003 and Gilbert et al., 2003). The specimens from Bouri and the Buia fossil from Eritrea are among the youngest fossils of *Homo erectus* known from Africa. Asfaw and colleagues suggest that there was a major climatic shift in the early Pleistocene between the last appearance of *Homo erectus* like the Bouri specimen and the first appearance of more advanced hominids from the early middle Pleistocene of Africa, often placed in the species *Homo heidelbergensis* (see Chapter 45).

REFERENCES

Abbate, E., A. Albianelli, A. Azzaroli, M. Benvenuti, B. Tesfamariam, P. Bruni, N. Cipriani, R. J. Clarke, G. Ficcarelli, R. Macchiarelli, G. Napoleone, M. Papini, L. Rook, M. Sagri, T. M. Tecle, D. Torre, and I. Villa. 1998. A one-million-year-old *Homo* cranium from the Danakil (Afar) Depression of Eritrea. *Nature* 393:458–461.

Dean, M. C., M. G. Leakey, D. Reid, F. Schrenk, G. T. Schwartz, C. Stringer, and A. C. Walker. 2001. Growth processes in teeth distinguish modern humans from *Homo erectus* and earlier hominins. *Nature* 414:628–631.

Gilbert, W. H., T. D. White, and B. Asfaw. 2003. *Homo erectus, Homo ergaster, Homo "cepranensis,"* and the Daka cranium. *Journal of Human Evolution* 45:255–259.

Harris, J. W. K., P. G. Williamson, J. Verniers, M. J. Tappan, K. Stewart, D. Helgren, J. de Heinzelin, N. T. Boaz, and R. V. Bellomo. 1987.

Late Pliocene hominid occupation of the Senga 5A site, Zaire. *Journal of Human Evolution* 16:701–728.

Howell, F. C. 1999. Paleo-demes, species, clades and extinctions in the Pleistocene homini record. *Journal of Anthropological Research* 55:191–243.

Leakey, L. S. B., P. V. Tobias, and J. R. Napier. 1964. A new species of the genus *Homo* from Olduvai Gorge. *Nature* 202:7–9.

Manzi, G., E. Bruner, and P. Passarello. 2003. The one-million-year-old *Homo* cranium from Bouri (Ethiopia): a reconsideration of its *H. erectus* affinities. *Journal of Human Evolution* 44:731–736.

Merrick, H. V., and J. P. S. Merrick. 1976. Archaeological occurrences of earlier Pleistocene age, from Shungura Formation. In: *Earliest man and environments in the Lake Rudolf Basin: Stratigraphy, paleoecology, and evolution* (Y. Coppens, F. C. Howell, G. L. Isaac, and

R. E. F. Leakey, Eds.), pp. 574–584, University of Chicago Press, Chicago.

Panger, M. A., A. S. Brooks, B. G. Richmond, and B. Wood. 2002. Older than the Oldowan? Rethinking the emergence of hominin tool use. *Evolutionary Anthropology* 11:235–245.

Plummer, T., L. C. Bishop, P. Ditchfield, and J. Hicks. 1999. Research on late Pliocene Oldowan sites at Kanjera South, Kenya. *Journal of Human Evolution* 36:289–322.

Rightmire, G. P. 1993. Variation among early *Homo* crania from Olduvai Gorge and the Koobi Fora Region. *American Journal of Physical Anthropology* 90:1–33.

Roche, H., A. Delanges, J. P. Brugel, D. Feibel, M. Kibunjia, V. Mourrel, and P. J. Texier. 1999. Early hominid stone tool production and technical skill 2.34 myr ago in West Turkana, Kenya. *Nature* 399:57–60.

Semaw, S., P. Renne, J. W. K. Harris, C. S. Feibel, R. L. Bernor, N. Fesseha, and K. Mowbray. 1997. 2.5-million-year-old stone tools from Gona, Ethiopia. *Nature* 385:333–336.

Semaw, S., M. J. Rogers, J. Quade, P. R. Renne, R. F. Butler, M. Dominguez-Rodrigo, D. Stout, W. S. Hart, T. Pickering, and S. W. Simpson. 2003. 2.6-million-year-old stone tools and associated bones from OGS-6 and OGS-7, Gona, Afar, Ethiopia. *Journal of Human Evolution* 45:169–177.

Walker, A. C., and R. E. Leakey, Eds. 1993. *The Nariokotome* Homo erectus *Skeleton*. Harvard University Press, Cambridge, MA.

Wolpoff, M. H., A. Thorne, J. Lelenick, and Z. Vinyun. 1994. The case for sinking *Homo erectus:* 100 years of *Pithecanthropus* is enough! *Courier Forschungs-Institut Senckenberg* 171:341–361.

Wood, B. A. 1992. Origin and early evolution of genus *Homo*. *Nature* 355:783–790.

Wood, B. A., and M. Collard. 1999. The human genus. *Science* 284:65–71.

26

The History of the Genus *Homo*

B. A. Wood

ABSTRACT

The genus Homo *was established by Carolus Linnaeus in 1758. During the course of the past 150 years, the addition of fossil species to the genus* Homo *has resulted in a genus that, according to the taxonomic interpretation, could span as much time as 2.5 Myr, and include as many as ten species. This paper reviews the fossil evidence for each of the species involved, and sets out the case for their inclusion in* Homo. *It suggests that while the case for the inclusion of some species in the genus (e.g.* Homo erectus) *is well-supported, in the case of two of the species,* Homo habilis *and* Homo rudolfensis, *the case for their inclusion is much weaker. Neither the cladistic evidence, nor evidence about adaptation suggest a particularly close relationship with later* Homo.

INTRODUCTION

When the genus *Homo* was introduced by Carolus Linnaeus it contained only two species, both of which were living forms (Linnaeus, 1758). One was referred to as a "nocturnal cave dweller" and given the name *Homo sylvestris*. The other, *Homo sapiens*, is the species to which modern humans belong. Since its introduction our understanding of *Homo* has been altered by the addition of fossil species. The incorporation of these species has nearly always involved relaxing the criteria for including taxa into the genus *Homo*. This review traces the history of this process of increasing inclusivity, beginning with the recognition of the Neanderthals and concluding with the latest proposals for the incorporation of the species *Homo antecessor*. As each species is introduced the fossil evidence that has accrued since its recognition is summarized and current taxonomic interpretations are reviewed. The year(s) given in parentheses are those in which the main fossil evidence for a species was discovered.

The review concludes by surveying contemporary interpretations of the genus *Homo*. These range from the view that it should be a monotypic genus, with *Homo sapiens* as the only species, to the judgment that *Homo* should be interpreted as containing more, rather than fewer, species. Finally, it will consider whether the relationships and adaptations of the more 'primitive' species are such that it would be more appropriate to attribute them to a genus other than *Homo*.

Reprinted with permission from *Human Evolution*, Vol. 15, pp. 39–49. Copyright © 2000 by International Institute for the Study of Man.

TAXONOMIC HISTORY

Homo sapiens Linnaeus, 1758

The first indication that modern humans were ancient enough to have fossilized representatives came with the discovery, in 1868, of skeletal remains at the Cro-Magnon rock shelter at Les Eyzies de Tayac, France. A male skeleton, Cro-Magnon 1, was made the type specimen of a new species, *Homo spelaeus* Lapouge, 1899, but it was not long before it was realized that it made no sense to place this material and living people in different species (Topinard, 1890; Keith, 1912).

The first fossil evidence from beyond Europe of populations that cannot be distinguished from the skeletons of contemporary local human populations came in 1924, from Singa, in the Sudan (Woodward, 1938). Thereafter more evidence from Africa came from the sites of Dire-Dawa, Ethiopia (1933); Dar es-Soltan, Morocco (1937–8); Border Cave, Natal, (1941–2 and 1974); Omo (Omo 1—Kibish Formation), Ethiopia, (1967) and from Klasies River Mouth, Cape Province (1968). It is probable that none of these remains exceeds 150 Kyr, and most date from less than 100 Kyr (Brauer et al., 1997). In the Near East comparable fossil evidence has been recovered from sites such as Mugharet Es-Skhul (1931–2) and Djebel Qafzeh (1933, 1965–75). In Asia and Australasia anatomically-modern human fossils have been recovered from sites that include Wadjak, Indonesia (1889–90), the Upper Cave at Zhoukoudian, China (1930), Niah Cave, Borneo (1958), Tabon, Philippines (1962) and the Willandra Lakes, Australia (1968 and thereafter). Few of these sites can be dated accurately, but new evidence suggests that anatomically-modern *H. sapiens* had penetrated Australia by as early as c.70 Kyr (Thorne et al., 1999).

Homo neanderthalensis King, 1864

The type specimen of *Homo neanderthalensis* consists of the fossil remains belonging to a single, adult, skeleton recovered from the Feldhofer Cave in the Neander Valley in Germany in 1856. With hindsight this was not the first fossil evidence of Neanderthals to come to light, for skulls of an adult and a child were found in 1829, at a site in Belgium called Engis (Schmerling, 1833), and a cranium recovered in 1848 from Forbes' Quarry in Gibraltar (Busk, 1865) also display the distinctive Neanderthal morphology. The next Neanderthal discovery in Europe was made in Moravia, at Sipka (1880). Thereafter came discoveries from Belgium at Spy (1886); Croatia, at Krapina (1899–1906); Germany, at

Ehringsdorf (1908–1925), and in France, at Le Moustier (1908 and 1914); La Chapelle-aux-Saints (1908); La Ferrassie (1909, 1910 and 1912), and at La Quina (1911), as well as in the Channel Islands, at St. Brelade (1911).

It was not until the 1920s that evidence of Neanderthals was found outside of Europe at Kiik Koba in the Crimea (1924–26). Thereafter came discoveries at Tabun cave on Mount Carmel, in the Levant (1929), and then in central Asia, at Teshik Tash, (1938). In the meantime two sites in Italy, Saccopastore (1929–35) and Guattari/Circeo (1939), had yielded the remains of Neanderthals. Further evidence was added after the 1939–45 war, first from Iraq (Shanidar, 1953 and 1957–60) and then from sites in Israel (Amud, 1961, 1964 and thereafter; Kebara, 1964 and thereafter) and more recently from sites in France and Spain (e.g. St. Cesaire, 1979, and Zafaraya, 1983 and 1992). The latter are the geologically most recent evidence of Neanderthals, with dates suggesting that they are just less than 30 Kyr-old (Hublin et al., 1995). Thus, Neanderthal remains have been found throughout Europe, with the exception of Scandinavia and the North German Plain, as well as in the Near East, the Levant and Western Asia. At one time it was suggested that Neanderthal-like remains were also to be found in Africa and Asia. However, there proved to be no sound evidence for a geographically more dispersed 'Neanderthal Phase' (Hrdlicka, 1927). It seems, therefore, that Neanderthals were a phenomenon confined to Europe and adjacent areas.

The characteristic Neanderthal morphology is seen throughout the cranial and postcranial skeletons. In the cranium it includes discrete and rounded supraorbital ridges, a face that projects anteriorly in the midline, laterally-projecting and rounded parietal bones, a rounded, posteriorly-projecting, occipital bone, an additional bony crest within the mastoid process, large incisor teeth, and postcanine teeth with large root canals. The postcranial peculiarities include short limb bones with stout shafts and relatively large joint surfaces, especially well-marked areas for the attachment of a muscle that helps to control the shoulder, and features of the pubic ramus of the pelvis that are likely to be related to the way the pelvis transmits the loading which takes place during locomotion.

Despite these peculiarities of the pelvis there is no indication that the Neanderthals were anything other than upright, obligate, long-range, bipeds. Their brains were as large, if not larger, than the brains of living *Homo sapiens*. For many years interpretations of Neanderthal physiognomy were influenced by Marcellin Boule's reconstruction of a skeleton recovered from La Chapelle-aux-Saints, in France. This is the skeleton of an aged male afflicted by osteoarthritis, and the curvature of the spine that is such a feature of the reconstruction is due to the effects of disease and is not a reliable indication of the habitus of non-pathological Neanderthal individuals.

Many elements of the characteristic morphology of the Neanderthals can be seen in remains recovered from sites such as Steinheim (Germany) and Swanscombe

(England) that date from c.200–300 Kyr. It is also apparently evident in precursor form in the remains that have been found in the Sima de los Huesos, Atapuerca, Spain. If so, this would extend the time of origin of the Neanderthals back to c.300 Kyr.

Homo heidelbergensis Schoetensack, 1908

This species was introduced for a hominin mandible found in 1907 during excavations to extract sand from a quarry at Mauer, near Heidelberg, Germany. The mandible has no chin and the body is a good deal larger than that of the mandibles of modern humans living in Europe today. The next evidence within Europe of fossil remains that showed equivalently archaic features came from Petralona (Greece), where in 1959 a cranium was recovered from a cave. Because of the lack of any sedimentary context its age of c.350–400 Kyr can only be approximate. A similar date is likely for comparable evidence from Arago (France, 1964–9), whereas the more fragmentary, but similarly morphologically archaic, material from Montmaurin (France, 1949), Vértesszöllös (Hungary, 1965) and Bilzingsleben (Germany, 1972–7, 1983 and thereafter) are apparently more recent (c.250 Kyr).

The first African evidence for 'archaic' *Homo sapiens* came in 1921, with the recovery of a c.250–300 Kyr cranium from a cave at the Broken Hill Mine at Kabwe, in what is now Zambia. Other morphologically-comparable remains have been found from the same time period in East Africa at Eyasi, Tanzania (1935). The earliest geological evidence of this African 'archaic' group comes from Ethiopia, at Bodo (1976, 1981 and 1990), which is dated at c.600 Kyr (Clark et al., 1994). Specimens intermediate in age (c.400 Kyr) include crania from southern Africa at Hopefield/Elandsfontein (1953), East Africa at Ndutu, Tanzania (1973), and North Africa, in Morocco at Sale (1971) and Thomas Quarry (1969/72). The Asian evidence for an 'archaic' form of *Homo* that does not qualify for inclusion in *Homo erectus*, comes from China at Dali (1978), Mapa, (1958), and India at Hathnora (1982). These fossils apparently range in age from c.100–200 Kyr.

What sets this material apart from *H. sapiens* is the morphology of the cranium and the robusticity of the postcranial skeleton. The brain cases are often, but not always, smaller than those of modern humans, but they are always more robustly built, with large ridges above the orbits and a thickened occipital region. Postcranially the shapes of the limb bones are much like those of *Homo sapiens* except that the shafts of the long bones are generally thicker, with higher robusticity indices.

For many years it was conventional to label this material as 'archaic' *Homo sapiens,* but there is now compelling evidence that this group of specimens, in terms of its overall cranial, dental and postcranial morphology, is distinct from that of *Homo sapiens*. Thus, it would be reasonable to place it in a separate species. If there is to be a single species name to cover all the archaic material, then the species name with priority is *Homo heidelbergensis* Schoetensack, 1908. However, if there was evidence that the main geographic regions, Europe,

Africa and Asia, each sampled 'good' species, then the name for the African species would be *Homo rhodesiensis* Woodward, 1921. Similarly, if the Ngandong material is not to be included in *Homo erectus* (see below) the appropriate species name for an Asian 'archaic' *Homo* species would be *Homo soloensis* Oppenoorth, 1932. Some workers have even suggested that within the African evidence there is room for a species, *Homo helmei*, between the more archaic remains within *H. heidelbergensis*, or *H. rhodesiensis*, and anatomically-modern *Homo sapiens* (Foley and Lahr, 1992; Lahr and Foley, 1994). Specimens that would be candidates for inclusion in *H. helmei* include Florisbad, Orange Free State (1932); Rabat, Morocco (1933); Cave of Hearths, Transvaal (1947); Jebel Irhoud, Morocco, (1961 and 1963); Omo 2 (Kibish Formation), Ethiopia, (1967); Laetoli 18, Tanzania, (1976); Eliye Springs (KNM-ES 11693), Kenya (1985) and Ileret (KNM-ER 999 and 3884), Kenya (1971 and 1976 respectively), (Brauer et al., 1997).

There is undoubtedly a gradation in morphology that makes it difficult to set a boundary between 'archaic' *Homo sapiens* and *Homo heidelbergensis*, but it is equally clear that unless a boundary is set then morphological variation within *Homo sapiens sensu lato* is then so great that it strains credulity (Brauer, 1992).

Homo erectus (Dubois, 1892) Mayr, 1944

In 1890 Eugene Dubois transferred his search for human fossils from Sumatra to Java, and in the same year found a mandible fragment at a site called Kedung Brubus. Less than a year later, in 1891, his workers unearthed the skull cap that was to become the type specimen of a new, and significantly more primitive, species of fossil hominin. In the initial publication about the Trinil finds, in 1892, Dubois placed the skull cap in the genus *Anthropopithecus*, but two years later he changed the generic designation to *Pithecanthropus*. What made the discovery of the Trinil braincase so significant was its small cranial capacity, c.850 cm^3, its low brain case and quite sharply-angulated occipital region. It was these features that led Dubois to think initially that the Trinil evidence may have belonged to an ape. The search for hominin remains in Java moved to Ngandong (1931–33), upstream of Trinil, where the Solo River cuts through the Plio-Pleistocene sediments of the Sangiran Dome. It was also in this region, in 1936, that Ralph von Koenigswald, a German palaeontologist, discovered a cranium that resembled the Trinil skull cap, but which had a substantially smaller, c.750 cm^3, brain size than the Trinil calotte. Research in this area continued until 1941, restarted in 1951, and has been taking place at varying levels of intensity ever since.

Excavations at a cave at Choukoutien, now called Zhoukoudian, near Beijing, in China, in 1921 and 1923, apparently recovered only quartz artefacts and non-hominin fossils. However, in 1926, Otto Zdansky realised that two teeth, an upper molar and a lower premolar, previously identified as ape-like were actually hominin. A year later the two teeth, together with a well-preserved left permanent first lower molar tooth (Ckn. A.1.1) found in 1927, were assigned to *Sinanthropus pekinensis* (Black, 1927). Excavations at Choukoutien were resumed by Black, Weng Wanhao and Anders Bohlin in 1927. The first human skull was found in 1929, and work continued there until its interruption by WW2. Similar-looking material has been found at other sites in China (e.g. Lantian, 1963–4; Hexian, 1980), and in southern Africa at Swartkrans, Gauteng (1949 and thereafter), East Africa (Olduvai [1960 and thereafter]; East Turkana [1970 and thereafter]; West Turkana [1975 and thereafter], and at Melka Kunture [1973 and thereafter]), and in North Africa at Tighenif (1954–5).

Despite the relatively large numbers of crania that had been recovered from Java, China and elsewhere, relatively little was known about the postcranial morphology of what was to become known as *Homo erectus*, and it was discoveries from East African sites that provided the crucial evidence. This came in the form of a pelvis and femur from Olduvai Gorge (OH 28), two fragmentary partial skeletons from East Turkana (e.g. KNM-ER 803 and 1800), and an especially rich source of evidence was the unusually well-preserved skeleton from West Turkana (KNM-WT 15000). There are morphological differences between this material and *Homo sapiens*, but all the postcranial elements are consistent with a posture that is habitually upright, and with a long-range bipedal mode of locomotion.

The crania of *Homo erectus* all have low vaults, with the greatest width being towards the base of the cranium. There is a substantial, essentially continuous, torus above the orbits, posterior to which there is usually a well-marked sulcus. There is both a sagittal torus, and an angular torus that runs towards the mastoid process. The occipital region is sharply-angulated, with a well-marked supratoral sulcus. The inner and outer tables of the cranial vault are thickened. The greatest width of the face is in the upper part. The palate has similar proportions to those of modern humans, but the buttressing is more substantial. The body of the mandible is more robust than that of modern humans and it lacks a well-marked chin. The tooth crowns are generally larger than those of modern humans, the third molar is usually smaller, or the same size, as the second. The roots of the premolar teeth tend to be more complicated than is usually the case in modern humans. The outer cortical bone of the postcranial skeleton is generally thick, and the limb bones have more robust shafts than is the case for modern humans. The shafts of the femur and the tibia are relatively flattened from front to back and from side to side, respectively, relative to those of modern humans; this is referred to as platymeria and platycnemia, respectively.

The two main regional subsets of this material were originally attributed to at least three genera. Two, *Pithecanthropus* and *Meganthropus*, were used for the Javanese evidence, one, *Sinanthropus*, for the Chinese component, and a fourth genus, *Atlanthropus*, for the evidence from North Africa. In 1943 Franz Weidenreich formally sank *Sinanthropus* into *Pithecanthropus*, and in 1944 Mayr proposed that the latter be sunk into *Homo*. Mayr went on to complete the process of taxonomic rationalization in 1950 by proposing that *Atlanthropus* be sunk into *Homo*. This, of course, had the effect of modifying the definition of *Homo* so that it could accommodate the relatively primitive remains that make up the new, combined, hypodigm of *Homo erectus*. In particular this meant that *Homo* now included a much wider range of cranial shape, brain size, and tooth and mandible shape and size than had been the case when the only fossil taxon included within the genus was *Homo neanderthalensis*.

Homo habilis Leakey, Tobias and Napier, 1964

A year after the discovery of a sub-adult fossil hominin cranium, OH5, the holotype of *Zinjanthropus boisei*, from Bed I at Olduvai Gorge, the Leakeys found evidence of an apparently more advanced hominin in the form of substantial parts of both parietal bones, much of a mandible and at least 13 hand bones of a juvenile skeleton (OH 7). The parietal bones of OH 7 did not show evidence of the bony crests that are such a distinctive feature of *Zinjanthropus boisei*, and the molar and premolar teeth were much smaller. In the next year, or so, further evidence of a 'non-robust' hominin was unearthed in Bed I (OH 4 and 6—skull fragments and teeth; OH 8—an adult foot; OH 14—juvenile cranial fragments, and OH 16—the fragmented cranial vault and maxillary dentition of a young adult) and Bed II (OH 13—the incomplete skull of an adolescent) of Olduvai Gorge.

In 1964 Louis Leakey, and his colleagues Phillip Tobias and John Napier, set out the case for recognizing a new species for these 'gracile' hominin remains from Olduvai, and they proposed that the new species be attributed to the genus *Homo*, as *Homo habilis* Leakey, Tobias and Napier, 1964. This decision meant that Le Gros Clark's 1955 diagnosis of the genus *Homo* needed to be amended. This involved relaxing some criteria, such as a brain size of 750 cm³ so that the relatively small-brained (c.600–700 cm³) crania from Olduvai would qualify. Leakey and his colleagues claimed that other criteria, such as dexterity, an upright posture and a bipedal gait did not need to be changed because Leakey et al.'s interpretation of the functional capabilities of *Homo habilis* suggested that the Olduvai fossils complied with these expectations.

The proposal to incorporate the new species within *Homo* did not go unchallenged. Some critics suggested that the new material was not sufficiently different from *Australopithecus africanus* to justify specific distinction. Other workers accepted the case for a new species, but challenged the view that it should be included within *Homo*. A third group took the view that specimens such as OH 13 were 'advanced' enough to be referred to *Homo erectus*, and claimed that *Homo habilis* was a mixture of *A. africanus*-like material from Bed I, and *Homo erectus*-like remains from Bed II. In due course more specimens from Olduvai were added to the hypodigm, the most significant being the cranium OH 24 and the fragmentary associated skeleton, OH 62. In their different ways, these specimens have helped to clarify the nature of *Homo habilis*. The discovery of OH 24 was

important because it resembled OH 13, but was found not in Bed II, but near the base of Bed I, making it the oldest of the specimens from Olduvai Gorge allocated to *H. habilis*. This meant that it was no longer possible to argue that there was a temporal cline in the morphology of the *H. habilis* remains, from the more 'primitive' specimens at the base of Bed I, to the morphologically 'more advanced' fossils in Bed II. The implications of the OH 62 associated skeleton were rather different. It is very fragmentary, but its estimated limb proportions are said to be more primitive than those of any other *Homo* species (Hartwig-Scherer and Martin, 1991). If OH 62 belongs to *H. habilis*, then it is clear that researchers can no longer be confident that *H. habilis* was both habitually upright and an obligate biped.

The most informative component of the *H. habilis* hypodigm comes from the site of Koobi Fora, initially known as East Rudolf and now also referred to as East Turkana. These remains include a skull, KNM-ER 1805, two well-preserved crania, KNM-ER 1470 and 1813, mandibles e.g. KNM-ER 1802 and isolated teeth, all found in 1972, or soon thereafter. Initially, many of these specimens were referred to as 'early *Homo*'. Some of the hominin fossils recovered from Members G and H of the Shungura Formation have been assigned to *H. habilis*, including a fragmented cranium, two mandibles and isolated teeth. A fragmentary cranium and some isolated teeth from Member 5 at Sterkfontein are also said to resemble *H. habilis*, and the same proposal has been made with respect to the so-called 'composite' cranium, SK 847, from Member 1 at Swartkrans. Suggestions that *H. habilis* remains have been recovered from sites beyond Africa have not received wide acceptance. Among remains that have been suggested as belonging to *H. habilis* are the hominin fragments from Ubeidiyah, Israel, and the material allocated to *Meganthropus palaeojavanicus* from Indonesia. In neither case have the researchers involved been able to make a convincing case that the remains should be allocated to *H. habilis*.

The material allocated to what some refer to as 'early *Homo*', and others as *Homo habilis sensu lato*, has a relatively variable cranial morphology (see below). The endocranial volume ranges from just less than 500 cm³ to c.800 cm³, and all the crania in this group are wider at the base than across the vault. The facial morphology varies (see below), with KNM-ER 1470 having its greatest width across the mid-face and little nasal projection, compared with KNM-ER 1813 which is broadest across the upper face. The mandibles vary in size and robusticity, with those from the larger individuals having robust bodies and premolar teeth with complex crowns and roots. Our knowledge of the postcranial skeleton of *H. habilis sensu lato* has traditionally come from the remains from Bed I at Olduvai Gorge, but although these were allocated to *Homo habilis* they may equally well belong to *Paranthropus boisei*. The only postcranial evidence from Olduvai Gorge that can, with confidence, be allocated to *Homo habilis* is the associated skeleton OH 62. Very little of the morphology of this specimen is preserved, but it is possible to determine that the skeleton had longer arms, relative to leg length, than any other *Homo* species. Thus, if OH 62 does belong to *Homo habilis*, then it would mean that the postcranial skeleton of at least one species of *Homo* could not be distinguished from that of *Australopithecus* and *Paranthropus*.

From the outset researchers have questioned the integrity of *H. habilis*. Initially, the main criticism was that within the linear, anagenetic model of evolution prevailing at the time of its discovery there was insufficient 'morphological space' for another taxon between *Australopithecus africanus* and *Homo erectus*. The criticism that *Homo habilis* was an amalgam of geologically older 'advanced' *Australopithecus africanus* fossils, and geologically younger 'primitive' *Homo erectus* remains has been countered by the demonstration that at Olduvai Gorge one of the most morphologically 'advanced' specimens, OH 24, was also geologically the oldest. Researchers have also shown that the characteristics of *Homo habilis* are not simply an admixture of the characteristics of *Australopithecus africanus* and *Homo erectus*, but are a distinctive combination of morphological features (Wood, 1992).

The third objection to *Homo habilis* was that it was too variable to make a plausible species. Views on this are polarized, with some researchers supporting the retention of a single taxon, *Homo habilis sensu lato*, for this material, and others supporting a 'two-taxon' solution. This debate will be explored in more detail in the section on *Homo rudolfensis*.

Homo ergaster Groves and Mazák, 1975

This taxon was introduced as part of a taxonomic review of the material from Koobi Fora allocated to 'early *Homo*'. The type specimen, KNM-ER 992, is an adult mandible that some workers had referred to *Homo erectus*, and the paratypes include the skull KNM-ER 1805. The only detailed analysis of the latter has concluded that KNM-ER 1805 should be referred to *Homo habilis sensu stricto*. Thus, decisions about whether *Homo ergaster* is a 'good' taxon hinge on whether researchers can demonstrate that the material referred to it can be distinguished from *Homo erectus*.

The features that have been claimed to distinguish *Homo ergaster* from *Homo erectus sensu stricto* fall into two groups. The first group consists of the ways in which *Homo ergaster* is more primitive than *Homo erectus sensu stricto*. The best evidence comes from the mandibular dentition, and in particular the mandibular premolars. It is claimed that the crowns and the roots of these teeth in *Homo ergaster* are more like those of the hypothetical common ancestor of the hominins than are those of *Homo erectus sensu stricto*. The second group consists of the ways that *Homo ergaster* is less specialised, or derived, in its cranial vault and cranial base morphology, than is *Homo erectus sensu stricto*. For example, *Homo ergaster* lacks some of the more derived features of *Homo erectus sensu stricto* cranial morphology, such as prominent sagittal and angular tori. Although some researchers support a taxonomic distinction between 'early African *H. erectus*', or *H. ergaster*, and *H. erectus sensu stricto*, (e.g. Wood, 1992, 1994; Bermudez de Castro et al., 1997),

others regard the morphological differences as warranting at best subspecific recognition (e.g. Turner and Chamberlain, 1989; Brauer and Mbua, 1992; Kramer, 1993; Brauer, 1994).

Homo rudolfensis (Alexeev, 1986; Groves, 1989)

As part of a comprehensive, although idiosyncratic, presentation of the evidence for human evolution, published in English in 1986, Valery Alexeev suggested that there were sufficient differences between the cranium KNM-ER 1470 and the material allocated to *Homo habilis* to justify referring the former to a new species, *Pithecanthropus rudolfensis* Alexeev, 1986. The proposal to include the new species in a genus that others had long ago sunk into *Homo* was an unusual one, but eccentricity is not sufficient reason to disregard Alexeev's proposal to establish a new species. Some workers have claimed that Alexeev either violated, or ignored, the rules laid down within The International Code of Zoological Nomenclature (Kennedy, 1999). However, there are no grounds for concluding that Alexeev's proposal did not comply with the *rules* of the Code, even if he did not follow all of its *recommendations* (Wood, 1999). Thus, Alexeev's species is available and if it is transferred to *Homo* it should be referred to as *Homo rudolfensis* (Alexeev, 1986), although there is evidence that Alexeev erected the taxon in a publication (Leney and Wood, in preparation).

Thus, if *Homo habilis sensu lato* is judged to subsume more variability than is consistent with a single species, and if KNM-ER 1470 belongs to a different species group than the type specimen of *Homo habilis sensu stricto*, then *Homo rudolfensis* (Alexeev, 1986) would be available as the name of a second early *Homo* taxon. This scenario appears to have some support, for several studies have shown that the degree of variation within *Homo habilis sensu lato* is greater than that which is expected in a single species. Researchers have recommended that the material be split into two species, *Homo habilis sensu stricto*, whose hypodigm consists of all the material attributed to the original taxon from Olduvai Gorge, together with a subset of the material attributed to *Homo habilis sensu lato* from Koobi Fora. That subset does not include KNM-ER 1470, thus making that specimen available as the type specimen of the second species, *Homo rudolfensis* (Alexeev, 1986) (Groves, 1989).

Homo rudolfensis and *Homo habilis sensu stricto* have different mixtures of primitive and derived, or specialised, features (Wood, 1992). For example, whereas the absolute size of the brain case is greater in *Homo rudolfensis*, the latter has a face that is widest in its mid-part, compared to *Homo habilis sensu stricto*, that has its greatest facial width superiorly. The primitive face of *Homo rudolfensis* is linked with a mandible that is robust, and with postcanine teeth that have larger crowns and more complex root systems than those of *Homo habilis sensu stricto*. Although we have a little information about the postcranial skeleton of *Homo habilis sensu stricto* from the associated skeleton, OH 62, there are no postcranial remains that can be reliably linked with *Homo rudolfensis*.

Homo antecessor Bermudez de Castro et al., 1997

The cave complex that provided the fossils from the Simo de los Huesos (see above) has also yielded remains from level 6 of the Gran Dolina (TD) site; this material is most likely at least 500 Kyr-old. The authors of the report claim that the material shows a combination of morphology not seen in any other hominin species. They contrast the remarkably modern human-like morphology of the face, with the relatively primitive crowns and roots of the teeth.

The authors consider that because *Homo heidelbergensis* shares some derived traits with *Homo neanderthalensis*, and because these derived features are not seen in the Gran Dolina material, then there are good grounds for not allocating the TD collection to *Homo heidelbergensis*. It is the apparent lack of these derived features, combined with differences from *Homo ergaster*, that compelled the authors to propose that the Gran Dolina fossils should be assigned to a new species, *Homo antecessor* Bermudez de Castro et al., 1997.

CONTROVERSIES

There are two major current debates about the genus *Homo*. The first is not concerned with the boundaries of the taxon, but with the number of species within it. One side of the debate takes the view that there was a major adaptive and morphological shift between *Ardipithecus, Australopithecus, Paranthropus*, on the one hand, and *Homo* on the other. They claim that once *Homo* had evolved then it is difficult, if not impossible, to identify species boundaries within *Homo*. The suggested solution is that there should be only one species within *Homo*, namely the type species, *Homo sapiens* Linnaeus, 1758 (e.g., Mayr, 1950; Jelínek, 1978; Wolpoff et al., 1994). According to the rules of zoological nomenclature all the other *Homo* species referred to above would be junior synonyms of *Homo sapiens*. The problem with this solution is that the species they propose, which we can call *Homo sapiens sensu lato*, would be so variable that it would not be equivalent to any other higher primate species, either fossil or living.

The second controversy is about the boundaries of *Homo*, and concerns the trend to relax the criteria for including species within the genus, combined with the discovery that some of the species included within *Homo* may not have the functional capabilities that have been attributed to them. The 'problem' species are *Homo habilis sensu stricto* and *Homo rudolfensis*. In the case of the former, the original fossils attributed to *Homo habilis sensu stricto* were believed to provide evidence that it was an animal which was habitually upright and bipedal, and that it was capable of the type of dexterity necessary to make the Oldowan stone tools. Unfortunately, since these assumptions were made nearly all of the functional studies of the relevant fossil evidence from Olduvai Bed I have tended to emphasize that these fossils are best interpreted as belonging to an animal that was not a committed biped, but one in which bipedalism was combined with the ability to climb. Likewise, there is nothing about the hand morphology of *Homo habilis sensu stricto* that distinguishes it functionally from hand fossils attributed to *Australopithecus* and *Paranthropus*. There are no anatomical reasons to identify it as the only possible maker of the Olduvai Bed I stone tools, and in any case stone artefacts now antedate fossil evidence of *Homo habilis sensu stricto* (Semaw et al., 1997). Thus, *Homo habilis sensu stricto* no longer matches the functional criteria for inclusion into *Homo* that were suggested by Leakey, Tobias and Napier (1964). As for *Homo rudolfensis*, although no postcranial remains can be linked with the taxon, there is no good evidence that it shows any significant advance over *Australopithecus* and *Paranthropus* in terms of its dietary adaptations. Thus, with hindsight, it seems that *Homo habilis sensu stricto* and *Homo rudolfensis* are insufficiently advanced in terms of their adaptations to justify their inclusion in *Homo*. If this is the case, then the boundaries of *Homo* should be adjusted so that *Homo ergaster* is included, but *Homo habilis sensu stricto* and *Homo rudolfensis* are excluded, and either transferred to *Australopithecus* (Wood and Collard, 1999), or placed in a new genus (Wood and Collard, 2000).

ACKNOWLEDGMENTS

Research incorporated in this review was supported by The Leverhulme Trust, The Wellcome Trust and The Henry Luce Foundation. BW is presently supported by The Henry Luce Foundation.

REFERENCES

Alexeev, V. P. 1986. *The origin of the human race.* Moscow: Progress Publishers.

Bermudez de Castro, J. M., Arsuaga, J. L., Carbonell, E., Rosas, A., Martinez I. and Mosqueria, M. 1997. *A hominid from the Lower Pleistocene of Atapuerca, Spain: Possible Ancestor to Neandertals and Modern Humans.* Science, 276:1392–1395.

Black, D. 1927. *On a lower molar hominid tooth from the Chou Kou Tien deposit.* Palaeontologia Sinica, New Series D, 7:1–28.

Brauer, G. 1992. *Africa's place in the evolution of Homo sapiens.* In: Continuity and Replacement: controversies in *Homo sapiens* evolution (eds. Brauer, G. and Smith, F. H.), pp. 83–98. Balkema: Rotterdam.

Brauer, G. 1994. *How different are Asian and African Homo erectus?* In: 100 years of *Pithecanthropus*. The *Homo erectus* problem (ed. J. L. Franzen), Courier. Forschungs-Institut Senckenberg, 171:301–318.

Brauer, G. and Mbua, E. 1992. Homo erectus *features used in cladistics and their variability in Asian and African Hominids.* Journal of Human Evolution, 22:79–108.

Brauer, G., Yokoyama, Y., Falgueres, C. and Mbua, E. 1997. *Modern human origins backdated.* Nature, 386:337–338.

Busk, G. 1865. *On a very ancient cranium from Gibraltar.* Report of the British Association Advancement of Science, (Bath, 1864):91–92.

Clark, J. D., de Heinzelin, J., Schick, K. D., Hart, W. K., White, T. D., Wolde Gabriel, G., Walter, R. C., Suwa, G., Asfaw, B., Vrba, E. and H. Selassie, Y. 1994. *African Homo erectus: old radiometric ages and young Oldowan assemblages in the Middle Awash Valley, Ethiopia.* Science, 264:1907–1910.

Dubois, E. 1892. *Palaeontogische anderzoekingen op Java*, in *Verslag van het Mijnwezen.* Batavia. 3:10–14.

Foley, R. A. and Lahr, M. M. 1992. *Beyond "out of Africa": reassessing the origins of* Homo sapiens. Journal of Human Evolution, 22:523–529.

Groves, C. P. and Mazák, V. 1975. *An approach to the taxanomy of the Hominidae: Gracile Villafranchian hominids of Africa.* Casopis Pro Mineralogii A Geologii, 20:225–247.

Hartwig-Schrerer, S. and Martin, R. D. 1991. *Was 'Lucy' more human than her child? Observations on early hominid postcranial specimens.* Journal of Human Evolution, 21:439–449.

Hrdlicka, A. 1927. *The Neanderthal phase of man.* Journal of the Royal Anthropological Institute, 57:249–274.

Hublin, J. J. Ruiz, C. B., Lara, P. M., Fontugne, M. and Reyss, J.-L. 1995. *The Mousterian site of Zafarraya (Andalucia, Spain): dating and implications of the peopling processes of Western Europe.* Comptes Rendus Academie des Sciences Paris (Series II a), 321:931–937.

Jelínek, J. 1978. Homo erectus *or* Homo sapiens? *Recent advances in Primatology,* 3:419–429.

Keith, A. 1912. *Ancient Types of Man.* Harper: London and New York.

Kennedy, G. E. 1999. *Is "Homo rudolfensis" a valid species?* Journal of Human Evolution, 36:119–121.

King, W. 1864. *The reputed fossil man of the Neanderthal.* Quarterly Journal of Science, 1:88–97.

Kramer, A. 1993. *Human taxonomic diversity in the Pleistocene: does* Homo erectus *represent multiple hominid species?* American Journal of Physical Anthropology, 91:161–171.

Lahr, M. M. and Foley, R. A. 1994. *Multiple dispersals and modern human origins.* Evolutionary Anthropology, 3(2):48–60.

Leakey, L. S. B., Tobias, P. V., and Napier, J. R. 1964. *A new species of the genus* Homo *from Olduvai Gorge.* Nature, 202:7–9.

Le Gros Clark, W. E. 1955. *The fossil Evidence for Human Evolution.* University of Chicago Press: Chicago.

Linnaeus, C. 1758. *Systema Naturae.* Laurentii Salvii: Stockholm.

Mayr, E. 1944. *On the concepts and terminology of vertical subspecies and species.* National Research Council Bulletin, 262:11–16.

Mayr, E. 1950. *Taxonomic categories in fossil hominids.* Cold Spring Harbor Symposia on Quantitative Biology, 15:109–118.

Schmerling, P. C. 1833. *Recherches sur des ossements fossiles decouverts dans les cavernes de la province de Liege,* Liege, pp. 59–62.

Schoetensack, O. 1908. *Der Unterkiefer des* Homo heidelbergensis *aus den Sanden von Mauer bei Heidelberg.* Leipzig, 1908:1–6.

Semaw, S., Renne, P., Harris, J. W. K., Feibel, C. S., Bernor, R. L., Fesseha, N. and Mowbray, K. 1997. *2.5-million-year-old stone tools from Gona. Ethiopia.* Nature, 385:333–336.

Thorne, A., Grün, R., Martinez. G, N. A. Simpson, J. J., McCulloch, M., Taylor, L. and Curnoe, D. *Australia's oldest human remains: age of the Lake Mungo 3 skeleton.* Journal of Human Evolution. 36:591–612.

Topinard, P. 1890. *Anthropology.* Chapman and Hall: London.

Turner, A. and Chamberlain, A. T. 1989. *Speciation. morphological change and the status of African* Homo erectus. Journal of Human Evolution. 18:115–130.

Wolpoff, M. H., Thorne, A. G., Jelinek, J. and Zhang, Y. 1994. *The case for sinking* Homo erectus. *100 years of* Pithecanthropus *is enough.* Courier Forschungs-Institut Senckenberg, 171:341–361.

Wood, B. A. 1992. *Origin and evolution of the genus* Homo. Nature, 355:783–790.

Wood, B. A. 1994. *Taxonomy and evolutionary relationships of* Homo erectus. Courier Forschungs-Institut Senckenberg, 171:159–165.

Wood, B. A. 1999. *'Homo rudolfensis' Alexeev, 1986—fact or phantom?* Journal of Human Evolution, 36:115–118.

Wood, B. and Collard. M. 1999. *The Human Genus.* Science, 284:65–71.

Wood, B. and Collard, M. 2000. *The changing face of* Homo. Evolutionary Anthropology, 18:195–228.

Woodward, A. S. 1938. *A fossil skull of an ancestral Bushman from the Anglo-Egyptian Sudan.* Antiquity. 12:193–195.

27

Late Pliocene *Homo* and Oldowan Tools from the Hadar Formation (Kada Hadar Member), Ethiopia

W. H. Kimbel, R. C. Walter, D. C. Johanson, K. E. Reed, J. L. Aronson, Z. Assefa, C. W. Marean, G. G. Eck, R. Bobe, E. Hovers, Y. Rak, C. Vondra, T. Yemane, D. York, Y. Chen, N. M. Evensen, and P. E. Smith

A broad consensus among paleoanthropologists holds that the *Homo* clade originated in Africa sometime between 2.0 and 3.0 Ma ago. However, a gap in the east African hominid fossil record spans the better part of this million year temporal interval. Although as many as three species of *Homo* greet the Pleistocene epoch in Africa [*Homo habilis*, *Homo rudolfensis*, and *Homo erectus* (= *ergaster*)], not one first appearance datum (FAD) for these taxa unequivocally predates 1.9 Ma (Kimbel, 1995; White, 1995), and their earlier Pliocene phylogenetic roots remain obscure (Wood, 1992). Therefore, any fossil specimen of *Homo* older than 2.0 Ma is potentially of great value.

In this preliminary report we describe the discovery of a maxilla of *Homo* closely associated with Oldowan stone tools and late Pliocene fauna in the upper part of the Kada Hadar Member, Hadar Formation, Ethiopia. Single-crystal ^{40}Ar/^{39}Ar laser probe analyses provide an age of 2.33 ± 0.07 Ma for this discovery which, therefore, represents the oldest association of hominid remains with stone tools, and possibly the earliest well-dated occurrence of the genus *Homo*.

RECOVERY

On 2 November 1994, during paleontological survey in a previously unexplored area containing deposits of the "upper" Kada Hadar Member, members of the Hadar project's hominid survey team (Ali Yesuf and Maumin Allahendu) recovered fragments of a hominid maxilla at a new locality, A.L. 666, a low, steep hill of undifferentiated silts capped by a small patch of a heavily weathered sandstone. The A.L. 666 outcrop occurs in a

Reprinted from *Journal of Human Evolution*, Kimbel et al., Late Pliocene *Homo* and Oldowan tools from the Hadar Formation (Kada Hadar member), Ethiopia, Vol. 31, pp. 549–561. Copyright © 1996 by Academic Press Limited. Reprinted with permission from Elsevier.

ca. 300 m × 600 m drainage basin of the Makaamitalu, a branch of the north (left) bank of the Awash River's Kada Hadar tributary.

The maxilla, A.L. 666-1, was found in two major portions comprising the left and right halves, broken cleanly along the intermaxillary suture. The left half, retaining P^3 and P^4 crown fragments and the roots of M^1, was spotted first, lying uncovered in a narrow gully draining the southeast facing slope of the hill. The right half, with P^3–M^1 crowns plus M^2–M^3 roots, was found topographically higher, on the surface of the southeast facing slope. Approximately 25 cm to the east of the right maxilla, alveolar bone, tooth crown and tooth root fragments from the left M^1–M^3 position were also found clustered on the surface. The latter occurrence marks the probable position on the slope from which the left maxilla tumbled into the gully. Intensive surface collecting followed by dry-sieving of the gully contents and adjacent slopes resulted in the recovery of nonhominid mammal elements and approximately 30 tooth crown, tooth root and bone fragments of the hominid maxilla.

All of these pieces, except a partial right C crown, fit cleanly on to the main portions of the maxilla. The specimen is well preserved, undistorted, and most breaks are fresh.

Fresh-appearing Oldowan flakes and "choppers" were present on the surface at the base of the A.L. 666 hill and surrounding outcrops. To identify the *in situ* horizon, a trial excavation was undertaken during the 1994 field season. Although no additional parts of the hominid maxilla were recovered in the initial 2 m^2 excavation, additional lithic elements and several non-hominid bone fragments were encountered.

STRATIGRAPHY

At least one disconformity, represented by an erosional surface with up to 8 m of relief, occurs high in the Kada Hadar Member above the 2.92 Ma BKT-2 marker tephra (Figure 1). Below the disconformity, from Sidi Hakoma up to middle Kada Hadar Member times, a meandering river system dominated the landscape, as recorded by

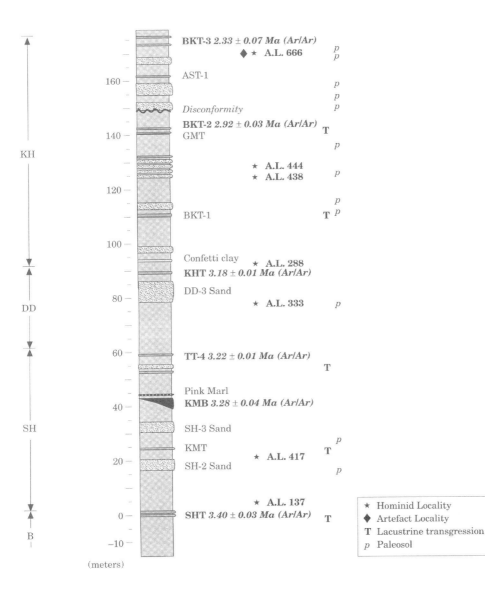

Figure 1. *Composite stratigraphic section of the Hadar Formation based on exposures in the Kada Hadar and Ounda Hadar drainages, with selected hominid localities and radioisotopic ages indicated. Member boundaries shown at left (B = Basal; SH = Sidi Hakoma; DD = Denen Dora; KH = Kada Hadar).*

several fining upward fluvial cycles, each comprising a sheet sandstone that gives way vertically to an overbank argillaceous siltstone or silty claystone often capped by a paleosol. Up to six lacustrine laminites interrupt the fluvial cycles. In contrast, above the disconformity sheet sandstones are replaced by coarse-grained conglomerates that are interbedded with sandy siltstones and paleosols, and lacustrine deposits are absent. The dramatic change in lithology above the disconformity reflects environmental change and/or faulting and downdropping of the Hadar basin.

The artefact-bearing horizon at A.L. 666, located 10–15 m above the disconformity and about 80 cm below the BKT-3 tephra (Figure 1), is a 3.5 m thick, massive to blocky pale brown siltstone containing minor amounts of pebble-size calcareous nodules and abundant white, calcified rhizoliths (root casts). Because the hill is eroded to an elevation lower than the tephra, BKT-3 does not occur at A.L. 666 itself. However, this same siltstone, with nodules, rhizoliths and artefacts, is observed 30 m to the northwest and 100 m to the southeast along the basin rim, where the sediment is directly overlain by BKT-3. Unique field characteristics among Hadar tephras (light brown color, occasionally cross-bedded, with root casts and brown clay-filled worm burrows) render BKT-3 a good stratigraphic marker in the upper Kada Hadar Member.

The position of freshly broken portions of the maxilla on a steep slope that was otherwise fairly devoid of accumulated overburden indicates that it had been exposed on the surface only a short time before discovery. We infer that it eroded from the silt horizon of the A.L. 666 hill based on the following circumstances: (1) silt matrix filled the maxillary sinus cavities and anterior

tooth alveoli on both sides of A.L. 666-1; (2) a root cast was present in one maxillary sinus; and (3) the *in situ* bone fragments show patina and preservation details identical to those of the hominid maxilla.

GEOCHRONOLOGY AND BIOCHRONOLOGY

The radiometric age of the BKT-3 tephra is the primary constraint on the age of the hominid maxilla and artefacts from A.L. 666. However, BKT-3 is not a primary airfall deposit and it contains no pumice fragments from which primary datable minerals can be extracted. Instead, ash-grade components of the BKT-3 eruption were transported by streams into Hadar's sedimentary record, presumably as a continuation of the deposition of the underlying flood plain silts. Conventional K/Ar and ^{40}Ar/^{39}Ar analyses, which employ bulk measurements that encompass thousands of grains, are not applicable to BKT-3 because such reworked tephras are prone to detrital contamination. Indeed, Miocene-age contaminants were detected in BKT-3 during fission-track analyses of zircons using the grain discrete external detector method, which produced an age of 2.3 ± 0.5 Ma (Walter, 1989). However, the large uncertainty did not instill confidence in the age.

Using the single-crystal ^{40}Ar/^{39}Ar laser microprobe method (York et al., 1981; Lobello et al., 1987), we have now dated three samples of BKT-3 from three separate localities: (1) H94-15, from an exposure 30 m northwest of A.L. 666; (2) H94-17, from an exposure ca. 500 m southwest of A.L. 666; (3) 76-B3 (Walter, 1981), from the tephra's type-locality, ca. 100 m west of A.L. 666.

Table 1 summarizes the results of 76 new single-grain analyses of the primary feldspar population, which

Table 1.   Summary of Single-Crystal ^{40}Ar/^{39}Ar Laser Microprobe Ages for BKT-3 Feldspars

Sample	Number of Grains	$(^{40}$Ar/^{36}Ar$)_i$[*]	MSWD[*]	Isochron Age[*] (Ma)	Integrated Age[†] (Ma)
H94-15	15	(299 ± 13	2.0	2.38 ± 0.47)	2.35 ± 0.16
H94-17	15	(288 ± 12	0.5	2.49 ± 0.22)	2.39 ± 0.21
76B3	46	(293 ± 3	0.8	2.32 ± 0.07)	2.32 ± 0.08
Total	**76**	**(295 ± 2**	**1.0**	**2.34 ± 0.06)**	**2.33 ± 0.07**

All grains are subhedral, clear, tabular crystals of plagioclase. Feldspars analyzed from H94-15 and H94-17 were about 0.5 mm wide and <1.0 mm long; those from 76B3 were, on average, 30% larger. Grains from each sample were placed in aluminium foil packets and inserted into a cadmium-shielded aluminium canister along with the neutron fluence monitor Fish Canyon sanidine (reference age of 27.84 Ma), and irradiated with fast neutrons for 2 h (4 MWh) in Position 5C at the McMaster Nuclear Reactor, Hamilton, Ontario. The samples and monitors were analyzed at the University of Toronto geochronology laboratory. Single grains of irradiated material were loaded into ca. 2 mm wide by 2 mm deep pits drilled into a disc of pure aluminium. The disc was loaded into the ultra-high vacuum extraction line, baked overnight at 190°C, and fused using a Spectra Physics 171 20W argon-ion laser. Extracted gases were purified using heated Zr alloy getters, and measured on a VG MS1200 mass spectrometer operated in the static mode, with an electron multiplier operating at 1.85 kV, and a gain of 1.51 × 10^5. Each analysis was preceded by a blank run. Argon isotopes were corrected for mass discrimination by measuring replicate aliquots of atmospheric Ar. Production of neutron-induced interferences was measured on irradiated K-glass and CaF$_2$ salt. Constants used are: λ=5.543 × 10^{-10}/a; ^{40}K/K=1.67 × 10^{-4} mol/mol. J values for each of the samples are: H94-14=4.618 ± 0.010 × 10^{-4}; H94-17=4.628 ± 0.007 × 10^{-4}; and 76B3=4.596 ± 0.016 × 10^{-4}. Uncertainties are 1σ, and propagate errors in peak measurements, interference corrections, and the measurement of standards and blanks.

[*]In the isochron method, $(^{40}$Ar/^{36}Ar$)_i$ ratios and ages are derived by fitting a line through the individual grain data on a diagram of ^{36}Ar/^{40}Ar versus ^{39}Ar/^{40}Ar. Straight lines of negative slope define grains of the same age (given by the ^{39}Ar/^{40}Ar intercept) that are variably mixed with contaminant argon of fixed composition (given by the ^{36}Ar/^{40}Ar intercept). Isochron calculations are based on the least-squares fitting algorithm of York (1969): no *a priori* assumptions are made about the initial ^{40}Ar/^{36}Ar ratio being atmospheric in value. However, all $(^{40}$Ar/^{36}Ar$)_i$ ratios derived by the fitting routine for BKT-3 are within errors of the atmospheric values of 295.5. MSWD is a reduced χ^2 statistic (ΣS/n-2), which measures how well the data are fitted to the line. This value should be about 1 if the observed and expected results are similar.

[†]Integrated ages are calculated by summing the Ar gas released from each single grain; such integrated ages are "model" ages because they assume that each grain formed with the same initial $(^{40}$Ar/^{36}Ar$)_i$ ratio of atmosphere (295.5).

consists of relatively fine-grained, low-K plagioclases (Ca/K = 4.0 ± 1.5, based on $^{37}Ar/^{39}Ar$ measurements). Eight additional grains, distinguishable on the basis of Ca/K, yielded Miocene ages between 7.7 ± 0.8 and 27.0 ± 0.1 Ma. The primary feldspar population yields single grain ages ranging from ca. 1–4 Ma, with an average relative error of 30%. Radiogenic argon in these grains is measured by subtracting contaminant atmospheric ^{40}Ar from total measured ^{40}Ar; in the unradiogenic BKT-3 samples these two values are nearly equal. Because the contaminant ^{40}Ar is determined by multiplying the ^{36}Ar peak by 295.5 (the atmospheric ^{40}Ar:^{36}Ar ratio), absolute errors in measuring the tiny ^{36}Ar peak are magnified and dominate the age. Despite care in measuring the ^{36}Ar peak accurately, large errors and scatter in the ages of individual grains are inevitable, and it is necessary to analyze many grains to reduce the error to acceptable values. The grains' low K content and small size make their age measurement comparable in difficulty to the age measurement of 13,000 year K-rich sanidines, analytically at the current threshold of feasiblity of the $^{40}Ar/^{39}Ar$ method (Hu et al., 1994). Because of the difficulty in determining the single-grain age for BKT-3, we prefer the *integrated age* as the best estimate of the formation age of the tephra. The integrated age sums the total gas from all grains in the subset (Table 1), excluding obvious contaminants. The combined ($n = 76$) integrated age of BKT-3 is 2.33 ± 0.07 Ma, statistically indistinguishable from the isochron age of 2.34 ± 0.06 Ma (Table 1). We conclude that the accurate and precise age of BKT-3 is 2.33 Ma, which is the minimum age for the A.L. 666 hominid and artefacts.

Biochronologic implications of the sparse fauna from the Makaamitalu basin (Table 2) are in broad agreement with the radioisotopic age of BKT-3. *Theropithecus oswaldi*, whose FAD in the Shungura Formation is in unit E-3, implies a *maximum* age of

ca. 2.4 Ma, while a notably small third molar most likely attributable to the poorly known *Metridiochoerus modestus* suggests an age of ca. 2.0 Ma, although the present state of knowledge of this suid species does not preclude an older age. A well-preserved lower molar of *Elephas recki atavus* corresponds to Morphotype I of Beden (1983), the characteristic form in lower Member G (below unit G-13) of the Shungura Formation, but not in Member F, suggesting an age range of 2.0–2.33 Ma (Beden, 1985; Feibel et al., 1989).

HOMINID MAXILLA

The morphology of the new Hadar maxilla distinguishes it not only from that of the well known Hadar hominid species *Australopithecus afarensis* (known only from sediments below the BKT-2 tephra) but also from that of other *Australopithecus* species (White et al., 1981; Rak, 1983; Ward & Kimbel, 1983; Kimbel et al., 1984, 1994; Leakey et al., 1995). Both maxillary and dental morphology tie the new Hadar specimen to the genus *Homo*.

The A.L. 666-1 maxilla features a relatively wide and deep palate with an evenly parabolic dental arcade. Subnasal prognathism is modest and the nasoalveolar clivus is sharply angled to the roof of the palate and to the floor of the nasal cavity. In anterior aspect, the maxilla appears deep and steep walled, and the frontal processes alongside the nasal aperture are mildly everted. The most inferior point on the zygomatic process root lies above M^1/M^2. The I^2 crown is strongly shovel-shaped; the canine is large but symmetric; M^1 shape is mesiodistally elongate; the M^2 occlusal outline is rhomboidal. Features that we attribute to male sex include inflated contours of the maxillary corpus and zygomatic process root due to expansive maxillary sinus cavities, absolutely long palate (est. orale–staphylion = 62.5 mm), and a fairly large canine (crown base area = 106 mm^2) that, though apically flattened by occlusal wear, projects below the level of the occlusal plane of the neighboring teeth (see Figure 2).

Relatively Broad Palate. At 63% the palatal breadth:length index for A.L. 666-1 falls above the values for the pooled *Australopithecus* sample (pooled n = 10, $\bar{x}$ = 54%, range = 48–59%) but among those for *H. habilis* and "early" African *H. erectus* (pooled n = 6, $\bar{x}$ = 67%, range = 60–71%).

Mild Subnasal Prognathism. Expressed as the ratio of the horizontal projected length to the direct chord length between nasospinale and prosthion, subnasal prognathism in A.L. 666-1 is less (at 63%) than in any *Australopithecus* specimen (pooled species n = 13, $\bar{x}$ = 75%, range = 65–84%), but is well within the range for the pooled early *Homo* sample (n = 6, $\bar{x}$ = 57%, range = 47–69%).

Flat Nasoalveolar Clivus Sharply Angled to Floor of Nasal Cavity at the Distinct Spinal Crest; Extensive Intranasal Platform Horizontally Separating Anterior Nasal Spine from Vomeral Insertion/Incisive Fossa. The former character is a synapomorphy of

Table 2. Makaamitalu Basin Faunal List

MAMMALIA	Artiodactyla
Primates	Suidae
Hominidae	*Metridiochoerus* cf. *modestus*
Homo sp.[*]	*Kolpochoerus* cf. *limnetes*
Cercopithecidae	Hippopotamidae
Theropithecus oswaldi[*]	Giraffidae
Rodentia	*Giraffa* sp.
Thryonomidae	Bovidae
Thryonomys cf. *swinderianus*	cf. *Syncerus*
Hystricidae	*Tragelaphus* sp.[*]
Hystrix cf. *cristatus*	Cephalophini sp.
Muridae	Hippotragini sp.
cf. *Golunda gurai*[*]	Reduncini sp.
cf. *Millardia coppensi*[*]	?*Parmularius* sp.
Carnivora	*Beatragus* sp.
Felidae	*Raphicerus* sp.[*]
Proboscicea	*Gazella* sp.[*]
Elephantidae	*Gazella praethomsoni*
Elephas recki atavus	
Perissodactyla	**REPTILIA**
Equidae	Crocodylia
	Crocodylidae
	Crocodylus sp.

[*]Taxa recovered from A.L. 666.

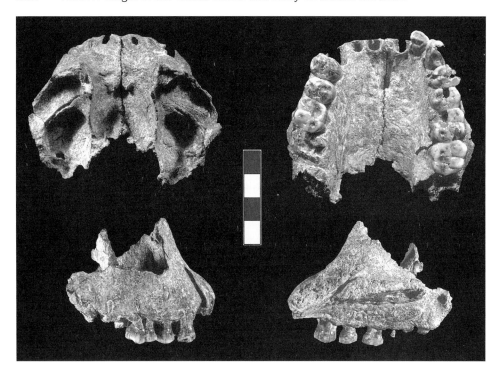

Figure 2. *The maxilla A.L. 666-1. Clockwise from top left: superior, palatal, left medial, right lateral. Scale = 4 cm. Tooth measurements (BL × MD corrected, in mm): LI^2, 7.0 × 7.4; RC, 10.2 × 10.4; RP^3, 12.5 × 9.2; RP^4, 12.6 × 9.0; RM^1, 12.4 × 12.9; LM^2, 14.4 × 13.5.*

Homo; the latter is the normative (arguably primitive) condition in *A. afarensis*, rare to absent in other species of *Australopithecus*, but retained in many early *Homo* maxillae. In combination they tie A.L. 666-1 to the early *Homo* sample (among which the resemblance to specimens such as O.H. 62, SK 847 and Sangiran 4 is particularly noteworthy).

***Square Anterior Maxillary Profile* (absence of the superomedial tapering of the midface in anterior aspect).** This configuration in A.L. 666-1 strongly diverges from the generalized triangular maxillary profile of *A. afarensis* and *Australopithecus africanus*, and in combination with flat, anterolaterally directed frontal processes, is similar to the morphology of specimens such as KNM-ER 1805, ER 1470, ER 3733 and Sangiran 4.

Narrow M^1 Crown. A buccolingually broad M^1 crown is the standard condition in *Australopithecus* (White et al., 1981; Leakey et al., 1995). The crown shape index (MD:BL) of 1.04 for the A.L. 666-1 M^1 indicates a significantly narrower tooth than in any *Australopithecus* species for which decent samples are available (*A. afarensis:* 0.92, SD = 0.06, n = 11; *A. africanus:* 0.92, SD = 0.05, n = 17; *A. robustus:* 0.91, SD = 0.05, n = 20). On the other hand, the A.L. 666-1 tooth is a little narrower than the mean (1.00, SD = 0.02, n = 12) for *H. habilis* [as constituted in Wood (1993)].

"Rhomboidal" Shape of M^2. The mesial cusps of the A.L. 666-1 M^2 dominate the distal cusps and the paracone bulges buccally relative to the metacone, creating an asymmetric rhomboidal occlusal outline. Brown & Walker (1993) suggest that this outline is typical of early African *H. erectus* M^2s (e.g., KNM-ER 3733, WT 15000, ER 807), but we would extend this description to the early African *Homo* sample writ large because it appears

to characterize most if not all known *H. habilis* M^2s (see also Tobias, 1991: pp. 636–637), as well as the only known M^2 of *H. rudolfensis* (KNM-ER 1590). Although a rhomboidal M^2 crown is not unknown in *A. afarensis* and *A. africanus*, a square occlusal outline tends to be the rule in these taxa and in "robust" *Australopithecus* species.

To which early species of *Homo* A.L. 666-1 should be attributed is problematic. None of the characters mentioned in support of the generic assignment of A.L. 666-1 affords a clear-cut taxonomic division within the early *Homo* sample. Three factors are responsible for this: variation within the boundaries of conventionally delineated taxa; very small sample sizes for some taxa (*H. rudolfensis*, early *H. erectus*); and, most important, the fact that many of the maxillary characters that bear on the taxonomy of the Hadar specimen appear to be apomorphic for the *Homo* clade as a whole, and thus not useful for sorting taxa within it. Preliminary comparisons indicate close dental morphological similarities between A.L. 666-1 and *H. habilis* specimens from Olduvai Gorge (e.g., O.H. 16, O.H. 39), but we do not at this time rule out other taxonomic assignments for the Hadar maxilla.

ARCHEOLOGY

Thirty-four stone tools were recovered from the A.L. 666 locality during 1994 field work, among which 14 were excavated *in situ* (Figure 3). The degree of association between the excavated and surface tools is not yet firmly established. However, lack of abrasion on the edges of the surface artefacts and their fresh condition suggest that they were neither exposed on the surface for a long time nor transported over nontrivial distances.

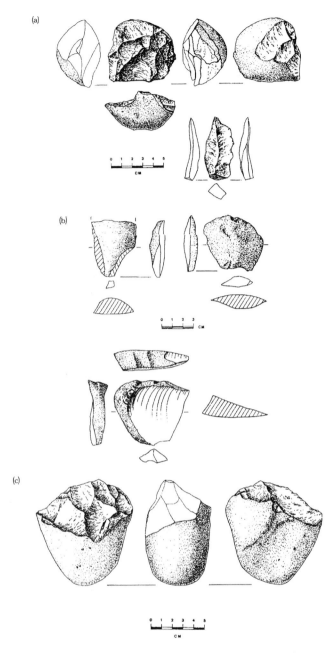

Figure 3. *A sample of lithics from A.L. 666. (a) Upper row:* in situ *core and flake conjoined (refit indicated by dark outline). Lower right: flake from the* in situ *assemblage. (b) Flakes from the* in situ *assemblage. (c) Bifacially flaked "end chopper" from the surface collection. Drawings by Julia Moskowitz.*

The surface and *in situ* stone tools from A.L. 666 are made out of volcanic and sedimentary raw materials, with basalt and chert the most abundant. The most frequent lithic types are "typical" Oldowan flakes (Toth, 1985) that preserve cortical and semi-cortical features and plain striking platforms. They exhibit a range of lengths and have irregular lenticular cross-sections and simple parallel scar patterns. Three specimens are an exception to this, with a complex scar pattern possibly indicating rotation of the core during knapping. The convex longitudinal profile of the dorsal surfaces of the flakes suggests they were struck from round river

cobbles. Although the surface collection has not yielded any typical core tools, we collected from the surface three bifacial "end-choppers" (Leakey, 1971) also made out of round river cobbles.

The trial excavation conducted on the southeastern face of A.L. 666 was limited to a 1.25 × 2.0 m grid and reached 80 cm below the surface. The density of lithics is low (11/m^3 of excavated sediment), a common feature among Plio-Pleistocene archeological sites (Leakey, 1971; Merrick, 1976; Isaac & Harris, 1978; Harris, 1983; Harris et al., 1987; Kaufulu & Stern, 1987; Kibunjia, 1994). *In situ* flakes were horizontally concentrated within a 90 × 80 cm area of the excavation and vertically clustered within 9 cm, although one flake was found 25 cm lower than this cluster. However, neither the vertical nor the horizontal limits of the artefact concentration have yet been identified, and further excavations at A.L. 666 may reveal clusterings in lithic and faunal density that may have behavioral significance.

The excavated lithic sample, which lacks utilized and retouched flakes, is morphologically similar to the surface collection. On both faces of the single *in situ* core knapping scars show removal of flakes from different striking platforms. We refit an *in situ* angular fragment to this core, which was located in the excavation about 1.6 m from it. This suggests some degree of horizontal dispersion of the artefacts, although we cannot presently determine whether this was the result of discard or postdepositional dispersion.

The technological traits of the small A.L. 666 assemblage (such as a dominance of end-struck flakes, generalized flake scar patterns, and low flake scar counts on the dorsal faces of flakes) resemble those described for the type assemblage of the "KBS Industry" (Isaac, 1976) and are typical of other Oldowan assemblages (Harris, 1983; Leakey, 1971).

Fossil vertebrate remains, including isolated teeth of *Theropithecus oswaldi*, a bovid horn core (*Raphicerus* sp.), and mandible fragments of Muridae, were collected at A.L. 666. Sieving the surface of the slope produced 51 additional bone fragments (not including those definitely attributable to the hominid maxilla), approximately 90% of which are highly fragmented long bone shaft segments that cannot be attributed to taxa. Some specimens preserve traces of carnivore and possibly hominid-induced modification. The excavated faunal remains are limited to three specimens, including a fragment of a small bovid scapula that exhibits what may be a stone tool cut mark.

PALEOENVIRONMENT

The Makaamitalu basin has produced a small (*n* = 83 specimens) but informative collection of fossil mammals identified at least to family level (Table 2). Bovids, mostly teeth, constitute 62% of the total mammalian sample. Of these, 33% represent Alcelaphini and Antelopini, which are grazers and usually arid-adapted mixed feeders, respectively. This is a substantial proportional increase over the representation of these tribes in the Sidi Hakoma (20%) and Denen Dora (18%) Members, although the lower Kada Hadar Member contains only slightly less (29%). High frequencies of these animals in fossil assemblages indicate open, dry habitats (Vrba, 1974). There are no Aepycerotini known in the Makaamitalu collection, whereas there are significant percentages in the Sidi Hakoma (32%), Denen Dora (18%), and lower Kada Hadar (10%) Members. Impalas are never found far from bush or woodlands (Estes, 1991), and their reduction or absence from a region in which they previously existed in great numbers suggests that the Hadar region became more "open" in later Pliocene times.

Tragelaphini and Reduncini are also represented in the Makaamitalu assemblage, indicating bush or tree cover and edaphic grasslands. Other mammals that indicate the presence of water include *Thryonomys* cf. *Thryonomys swinderianus*, the extant cane rat, which is known to inhabit reed beds in standing water, and specimens of Hippopotamidae. Finally, the only non-hominid primate present in these deposits is *Theropithecus oswaldi*, which is thought to have lived in lake margin and flood plain areas of more open habitats (Eck, 1987).

Based on the limited fossil evidence presently available, the paleohabitat of the Makaamitalu faunal community appears to have been predominantly open, with wetlands and bushed or wooded grasslands, and with stands of trees close to the water source. This contrasts with the generally more closed habitats of the *A. afarensis*-bearing deposits of the Hadar Formation (older than 2.92 Ma), which featured dry bush/woodland and riparian woodlands in the Sidi Hakoma Member, riverine forests and wetlands in the Denen Dora Member, and dry bush/woodland in the "lower" Kada Hadar Member.

CONCLUSIONS

Our preliminary research at A.L. 666 documents a late Pliocene locality with hominid remains in close spatiotemporal association with excavated lithics and a large-mammal fauna, a rare phenomenon at any East African Plio-Pleistocene site. The earliest evidence for such association comes from two sites, FLK-NN and FLK-*Zinjanthropus* in Bed I, Olduvai Gorge, dated to 1.8 and 1.75 Ma, respectively (Leakey, 1971; Walter et al., 1991), and FxJj38 NW in the lower KBS Member of the Koobi Fora Formation, about 1.85 Ma, though without fauna (Isaac and Harris, 1978; Feibel et al., 1989). A.L. 666 represents a still earlier spatiotemporal co-occurrence

of hominids, tools and fauna at a time when *Homo* as well as "robust" *Australopithecus* clades were flourishing—although there is no compelling evidence of direct association between the manufacture of Oldowan lithic technology and any particular hominid taxon.

There are few well-sampled fossiliferous African localities between 2.5 and 2.0 Ma. Recent claims for early *Homo* in this temporal interval (Hill et al., 1992; Schrenk et al., 1993; Kimbel and Rak, 1993) face one or more uncertainties of provenience, dating or phylogenetic affinity. The 2.33 Ma occurrence of *Homo* at A.L. 666 promises to add new insights on hominid paleobiology and behavior in this poorly understood time period. Further exploration and excavation during succeeding field seasons in the Makaamitalu basin and in other areas of Hadar that contain relatively young sediments should permit us to clarify archeological, paleontological and geological issues and to amplify the significance of these preliminary results.

ACKNOWLEDGMENTS

We thank the Center for Research and Conservation of Cultural Heritage (CRCCH) and the National Museum of Ethiopia, Ethiopian Ministry of Information and Culture, for their cooperation, assistance and permission to conduct field work at Hadar and laboratory research in Addis Ababa. The 1994 Hadar field season was funded by grants from the National Science Foundations (DBS 9222604) and the National Geographic Society. ^{40}Ar/^{39}Ar dating at the University of Toronto was supported by the Natural Science and Engineering Council of Canada and the Connaught Foundation of the University of Toronto. Thanks to Julia Moskowitz for the art work in Figure 3, and to Charlie Lucke for printing the photos in Figure 2. We extend our appreciation to Alan Walker and Carol Ward for helpful discussion and the loan of comparative materials. For invaluable logistical help in the field we are grateful to the Ethiopian Institute of Geological Surveys (Ministry of Mines) and SOGEA. Without the wise counsel and hard work of CRCCH representatives Tamrat Wodajo, Tesfaye Hailu and Ambachew Kebede, the 1994 Hadar field season would not have been successful. As always, we owe a huge debt of gratitude to the Afar people of Eloaha village for their friendship and assistance over many seasons of working and living together at Hadar.

REFERENCES

Beden, M. (1983). Family Elephantidae. In (J. M. Harris, Ed.) *Koobi Fora Research Project, Volume 2. The Fossil Ungulates: Proboscidea, Perissodactyla and Suidae*, pp. 40–129. Oxford: Clarendon Press.

Beden, M. (1985). Les proboscidiens des grand gisements à hominidés Plio-Pléistocènes d'Afrique orientale. In *L'environnement des Hominidés au Plio-Pléistocène*, pp. 21–44. Paris: Masson.

Brown, B. & Walker, A. (1993). The dentition. In (A. Walker & R. Leakey, Eds) *The Nariokotome* Homo erectus *Skeleton*, pp. 161–192. Cambridge, MA: Harvard University Press.

Eck, G. G. (1987). *Theropithecus oswaldi* from the Shungura Formation, lower Omo Basin, southwestern Ethiopia. In (G. G. Eck, N. G. Jablonski & M. G. Leakey, Eds) *Les Faunes Plio-Pléistocènes de la vallée de l'Omo (Éthiopie), Tome 3. Cercopithecidae de la Formation de Shungura*, pp. 124–139. Paris: CNRS.

Estes, R. D. (1991). *The Behavior Guide to African Mammals*. Berkeley: University of California Press.

Feibel, C. S., Brown, F. H. & McDougall, I. (1989). Stratigraphic context of fossil hominids from Omo Group deposits: northern Turkana basin, Kenya and Ethiopia. *Am. J. phys. Anthrop.* **78,** 595–622.

Harris, J. W. K. (1983). Cultural beginnings: Plio-Pleistocene archaeological occurrences from the Afar, Ethiopia. In (N. David, Ed.) *African Archaeological Review*, Vol. 1, pp. 3–31. Cambridge: Cambridge University Press.

Harris, J. W. K., Williamson, P. G., Verniers, J., Tappen, M. J., Stewart, K., Helgren, D., de Heinzelin, J., Boaz, N. T. & Bellomo, R. V. (1987). The setting, context and character of the Senga 5A site, Zaire. *J. hum. Evol.* **16,** 701–728.

Hill, A., Ward, S., Deino, A., Curtis, G. & Drake, R. (1992). Earliest *Homo. Nature* **355**, 719–722.

Hu, Q., Smith, P., Evensen, N. & York, D. (1994). Lasing the Holocene: extending the ^{40}Ar/^{39}Ar laser probe method into the carbon-14 range. *Earth Planet. Sci. Lett.* **123**, 331–336.

Isaac, G. Ll. (1976). Plio-Pleistocene artifact assemblages from East Rudolf, Kenya. In (Y. Coppens, F. C. Howell, G. Isaac & R. Leakey, Eds) *Earliest Man and Environment in the Lake Rudolf Basin*, pp. 552–564. Chicago: University of Chicago Press.

Isaac, G. Ll. & Harris, J. W. K. (1978). Archaeology. In (M. G. Leakey & R. E. Leakey, Eds) *Koobi Fora Research Project, Volume 1. The Fossil Hominids and an Introduction to Their Context*, pp. 64–85. Oxford: Clarendon Press.

Kaufulu, Z. M. & Stern, N. (1987). The first stone artefacts to be found *in situ* within the Plio-Pleistocene Chiwondo Beds in northern Malawi. *J. hum. Evol.* **16**, 729–740.

Kibunjia, M. (1994). Pliocene archaeological occurrences in the Lake Turkana basin. *J. hum. Evol.* **27**, 159–171.

Kimbel, W. H. (1995). Hominid speciation and Pliocene climatic change. In (E. S. Vrba, G. H. Denton, T. C. Partridge & L. H. Burckle, Eds) *Paleoclimate and Evolution, with Emphasis on Human Origins*, pp. 425–437. New Haven: Yale University Press.

Kimbel, W. H. & Rak, Y. (1993). The importance of species taxa in paleoanthropology and an argument for the phylogenetic concept of the species category. In (W. H. Kimbel & L. B. Martin, Eds) *Species, Species Concepts and Primate Evolution*, pp. 461–484. New York: Plenum.

Kimbel, W. H., Johanson, D. C. & Rak, Y. (1994). The first skull and other new discoveries of *Australopithecus afarensis* at Hadar, Ethiopia. *Nature* **368**, 449–451.

Kimbel, W. H., White, T. D. & Johanson, D. C. (1984). Cranial morphology of *Australopithecus afarensis*: a comparative study based on a composite reconstruction of the adult skull. *Am. J. phys. Anthrop.* **64**, 337–388.

Leakey, M. D. (1971). *Olduvai Gorge, Volume 3. Excavations in Beds I and II, 1960–1963*. Cambridge: Cambridge University Press.

Leakey, M. G., Feibel, C. S., McDougall, I. & Walker, A. (1995). New four-million-year-old hominid species from Kanapoi and Allia Bay, Kenya. *Nature* **376**, 565–571.

Lobello, P., Féraud, G., Hall, C., York, D., Lavina, P. & Berat, M. (1987). ^{40}Ar/^{39}Ar step heating and laser fusion dating of a Quaternary pumice from Neschers, Massif Central, France: the defeat of xenocrystic contamination. *Chem Geol* (Isotope Geoscience Section) **66**, 61–71.

Merrick, H. (1976). Recent archaeological research in the Plio-Pleistocene deposits of the lower Omo Valley, southwestern Ethiopia. In (G. Isaac & E. R. McCown, Eds) *Human Origins: Louis Leakey and the East African Evidence*, pp. 461–482. Menlo Park: Staples Press.

Rak, Y. (1983). *The Australopithecine Face*. New York: Academic Press.

Schrenk, F., Broamge, T., Betzler, C., Ring, U. & Juwayeyi, Y. (1993). Oldest *Homo* and Pliocene biogeography of the Malawi Rift. *Nature* **365**, 833–836.

Tobias, P. V. (1991). *Olduvai Gorge, Volume 4. The Skulls, Endocasts and Teeth of* Homo habilis. Cambridge: Cambridge University Press.

Toth, N. (1985). The Oldowan reassessed: a close look at early stone artifacts. *J. Archaeol. Sci.* **12**, 101–120.

Vrba, E. (1974). Chronological and ecological implications of the fossil Bovidae at the Sterkfontein australopithecine site. *Nature* **250**, 19–23.

Walter, R. C. (1981). The volcanic history of the Hadar early man site and surrounding Afar region of Ethiopa. Ph.D. Dissertation. Case Western Reserve University, Cleveland, Ohio.

Walter, R. C. (1989). Applications and limitations of fission-track geochronology to Quaternary tephras. *Quat. Int.* **1**, 35–46.

Walter, R. C., Manega, P. C., Hay, R. L., Drake, R. E. & Curtis, G. H. (1991). Laser-fusion ^{40}Ar/^{39}Ar dating of Bed I, Olduvai Gorge, Tanzania. *Nature* **354**, 145–149.

Ward, S. C. & Kimbel, W. H. (1983). Subnasal alveolar morphology and the systematic position of *Sivapithecus*. *Am. J. phys. Anthrop.* **61**, 157–171.

White, T. D. (1995). African omnivores: global climatic change and Plio-Pleistocene hominids and suids. In (E. S. Vrba, G. H. Denton, T. C. Partridge & L. H. Burckle, Eds) *Paleoclimate and Evolution, with Emphasis on Human Origins*, pp. 369–384. New Haven: Yale University Press.

White, T. D., Johanson, D. C. & Kimbel, W. H. (1981). *Australopithecus africanus*: its phyletic position reconsidered. *S. Afr. J. Sci.* **77**, 445–470.

Wood, B. A. (1992). Origin and evolution of the genus *Homo*. *Nature* **355**, 783–790.

Wood, B. A. (1993). Early *Homo*: how many species? In (W. H. Kimbel & L. B. Martin, Eds) *Species, Species Concepts and Primate Evolution*, pp. 485–522. New York: Plenum.

York, D. (1969). Least-squares fitting of a straight line with correlated errors. *Earth Planet. Sci. Lett.* **39**, 89–93.

York, D., Hall, C., Yanese, Y. & Hanes, J. (1981). ^{40}Ar/^{39}Ar dating of terrestrial minerals with a continuous laser. *Geophys. Res. Lett.* **8**, 1136–1138.

28

Late Pliocene *Homo* and Hominid Land Use from Western Olduvai Gorge, Tanzania

R. J. Blumenschine, C. R. Peters, F. T. Masao, R. J. Clarke, A. L. Deino, R. L. Hay, C. C. Swisher, I. G. Stanistreet, G. M. Ashley, L. J. McHenry, N. E. Sikes, N. J. van der Merwe, J. C. Tactikos, A. E. Cushing, D. M. Deocampo, J. K. Njau, and J. I. Ebert

ABSTRACT

Excavation in the previously little-explored western portion of Olduvai Gorge indicates that hominid land use of the eastern paleobasin extended at least episodically to the west. Finds included a dentally complete Homo *maxilla (OH 65) with lower face, Oldowan stone artifacts, and butchery-marked bones dated to be between 1.84 and 1.79 million years old. The hominid shows strong affinities to the KNM ER 1470 cranium from Kenya (*Homo rudolfensis*), a morphotype previously unrecognized at Olduvai. ER 1470 and OH 65 can be accommodated in the* H. habilis *holotype, casting doubt on* H. rudolfensis *as a biologically valid taxon.*

Reprinted with permission from *Science*, Vol. 299, pp. 1217–1221. Copyright © 2003 AAAS.

Bed I deposits at Olduvai Gorge that accumulated on the southeastern margin of paleo-Lake Olduvai yielded the first discoveries of *H. habilis* Leakey, Tobias, and Napier and *Paranthropus* (*Zinjanthropus*) *boisei* (Leakey) Robinson, along with a stone tool industry that became known as the Oldowan (*1–5*). Two additional late Pliocene hominid species known from East Turkana, Kenya [for example, (*6*)], the enigmatic *H. rudolfensis* (Alexeev) Groves and the *H. erectus*–like *H. ergaster* Groves and Mazak, have not been reported from Olduvai Gorge. In 1995, we recovered a hominid, designated OH 65, consisting of a maxilla with complete dentition and lower face. It was found in fluvial deposits from the western portion of the Bed I Olduvai lake basin (Figure 1) along with Oldowan stone artifacts and vertebrate fossils, some of which show evidence of butchery. The deposits were initially thought to be lower-most Bed II in age (*1*), but subsequent dating and stratigraphic analyses have shown them to be upper Bed I.

We excavated 11 trenches in the Bed I western basin (Figure 1). Fossils and artifacts described here are from one trench (Trench 57) in a zone 20 to 50 cm above the base of a 2.5-m-thick tuffaceous silty sandstone infilling a fluvially channelized incision (Figure 2). Geochemical correlatives of Tuffs IB and IC occur stratigraphically below the fossil-bearing unit. Tuffaceous material infilling the fossil-bearing channel is geochemically correlated with Tuff ID. The younger of two pumiceous air-fall tuffs at the top of the Bed I sequence has provisionally been correlated geochemically with Tuff IF.

Single-crystal, laser-fusion ^{40}Ar/^{39}Ar analysis of anorthoclase and sodic sanidine phenocrysts from four samples of Tuff IB (Table S1, Figure S1) yielded a mean age of 1.845 ± 0.002 (1 SE) million years old (Ma) (compare *7–9*; see Appendix at end of text). In the western basin, this tuff had been misidentified earlier (*1*) as Tuff IF. The overlying Tuff IC (Figure 2) yielded an age of 1.839 ± 0.005 Ma, the maximum age for the paleoanthropological assemblage.

We used paleomagnetic analysis to provide a minimum age for the assemblage of 1.785 Ma. Thermal and alternating-field demagnetization of 33 oriented block samples from 11 horizons through the Trench 57 sequence (Figure 2) showed normal geomagnetic polarity (see Appendix), which we equate to the Olduvai Geomagnetic Polarity Subchron, dated to be from 1.942 to 1.785 Ma (*10*).

OH 65 is a nearly complete maxilla. In facial view (Figure 3A), the rather flat naso-alveolar clivus of the maxilla extends laterally past the prominent canine root eminences, then curves sharply backward around the P^3 roots. In lateral view, the incisor region projects only slightly anteriorly to the canines, and the infero-anterior border of the zygomatic root is situated above the P^4–M^1 interface. In palatal view (Figure 3B), the incisor-canine row forms an arc, whereas on each side the cheek teeth form curving rows that diverge posteriorly. The palate shelves steeply back from the incisors to a maximum depth of 16.8 mm between the first molars, with an internal breadth of 36.7 mm between the P^3 lingual alveolar margins, widening to 39.2 mm between the M^3 lingual alveolar margins. In superior view, the short and broad naso-alveolar clivus is bordered posteriorly on each side by capacious maxillary sinuses that extend laterally to fill the roots of the zygomatic processes, which are consequently thin-walled. A small subdivision of the sinus occurs on its superior anteromedial corner.

The dental arcade is, in general, worn evenly, with dentine exposure on all teeth except the third molars (Figure 3). Wear on the incisors and canines is heavy, but lack of interstitial wear indicates premortem interdental spaces, possibly enlarged in part during or after fossilization. In contrast, interproximal wear between the canines and premolars is marked, whereas that

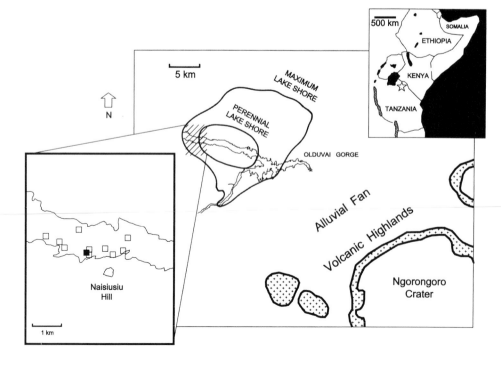

Figure 1. *Map of the Bed I Olduvai Lake Basin superimposed on present-day Olduvai Gorge. The area between the perennial and maximum paleo-lake shores [modified from (1)] defines the lake-margin zone. We excavated 11 trenches (squares in inset) into the Bed I western lake margin, including Trench 57 (solid square).*

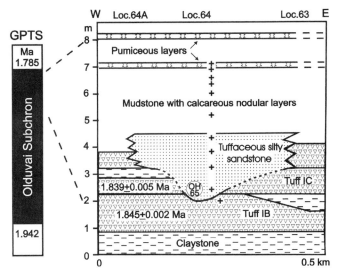

Figure 2. *Schematic stratigraphic profile of the upper part of Bed I in the vicinity of Trench 57, which lies in Geological Locality (Loc.) 64 (1). [See (1) for the location of Loc. 63. Loc. 64A lies between Locs. 64 and 65 in (1).] The profile shows major tuff units, the locations (+) of paleomagnetic samples, the correlation with the geomagnetic polarity time scale (GPTS), our new age determinations (Ma) for Tuffs IB and IC, and the location of OH 65. Correlations of tuffs with those previously described for the eastern basin (1) are determined from our mapping, ⁴⁰Ar/³⁹Ar dating, paleomagnetic analysis, and tuff geochemistry based on electron microprobe analysis of anorthoclase (Ca, Na, and K), augite (Mn, Al, Ti, Fe, Mg, and Ca), and titanomagnetite (Mn and Ti). In the lower part of the profile, a channelized incision cuts through Tuff IC down into Tuff IB. The incision contains an infill of channel deposits composed of tuffaceous silty sandstone with scattered pumices. At Trench 57, the basal 20 cm of the infill is a carbonate-cemented, locally pebbly, coarse quartzo-feldspathic sandstone. Samples of the tuffaceous material from the infill are geochemically comparable with Tuff ID as identified in the area of FLK in the eastern lake margin. The upper pumiceous layer near the top of the sequence correlates geochemically with Tuff IF.*

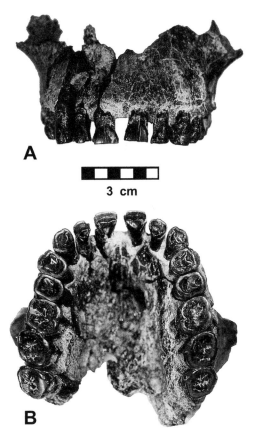

Figure 3. *(A) Anterior and (B) palatal views of OH 65. The specimen preserves the full upper dentition, roots of left and right zygoma, the lower right anterior margin of the nasal aperture, nasal floor, incisive canal, palate, maxillary sinuses, and lower face comprising the naso-alveolar clivus, extending from the alveolar margin to the base of the broken-away anterior nasal spine.*

Table 1. Maximum Observed Buccolingual (B-L) and Mesiodistal (M-D) Dimensions (in mm) of the Tooth Crowns of OH 65.

	Left		Right	
	B-L	**M-D**	**B-L**	**M-D**
I¹	8.0	9.2	8.0	10.2
I²	7.0	7.6	7.6	7.2
C	9.4	9.7	9.9	9.6
P³	12.8	9.2	12.6	9.4
P⁴	13.1	9.0	13.0	9.1
M¹	13.6	13.0	13.5	12.5
M²	14.4	12.8	14.3	13.4
M³	14.0	11.0	14.0	11.5

Despite large tooth roots, OH 65 was a relatively small-toothed individual [compare with KNM ER 1590 (6)], perhaps female.

between the premolars plus first molar is pronounced. Interproximal wear between the molars is moderate. Mesiodistal tooth measurements reflect this wear (Table 1). Occlusal striations, pitting, and polished chipping from dietary wear are present on the cheek teeth. Marked enamel hypoplasia is present. Several

teeth show apparent dietary acid etching and dental calculus. The latter is particularly apparent as a cluster of five small pearl-like concretions on the distal cervical margin of the right M^3. Before restoration, naturally broken alveolar bone revealed tooth roots that are massive relative to the crowns, including long canine roots (Figure 3A) that reach the level of the inferior nasal margin. M^3 is smaller than M^2 (Table 1, Figure 3B).

Although the lower face of OH 65 is broad and orthognathic and thus reminiscent of *Paranthropus*, it clearly does not belong to that genus. The naso-alveolar clivus of OH 65 does not possess the typical *Paranthropus* smooth gutter running from the floor of the nose onto the clivus. Instead, there is a sharp angulation between the floor of the nose and a flat clivus. The cheek teeth of OH 65 also lack the very large size relative to the anterior dentition that is seen in *Paranthropus*.

The morphology of the lower nasal region and roots of the zygoma of OH 65, together with its broad, flattened naso-alveolar clivus, which curves backward around the P^3 roots, is most similar to the late Pliocene KNM ER 1470 cranium (Table S2) from East Lake Turkana, Kenya, classified variously (Table S3) as *H. habilis* (*11, 12*) or *H. rudolfensis* (*13–16*). Horizontal contours across the anterior surface of the maxilla

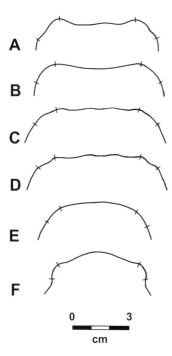

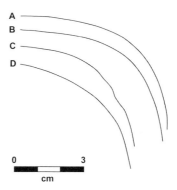

Figure 5. *Coronal contours of the external cranial surface midway along the left parietal: (**A**) OH 7 (the type specimen of H. habilis), (**B**) KNM ER 1470, (**C**) KNM ER 1813, and (**D**) Sts 5 (A. africanus).*

Figure 4. *Horizontal contours across the anterior surface of the maxilla, taken about halfway up the naso-alveolar clivus: (**A**) SK 12 (P. robustus), (**B**) OH 5 (P. boisei), (**C**) KNM ER 1470, (**D**) OH 65, (**E**) KNM ER 1813, and (**F**) Sts 52 (Australopithecus africanus). The crossmarks indicate positions of canine and P³. Note the hollowing caused by the naso-alveolar gutter in SK 12 and OH 5. The smaller brained specimens attributed to* H. habilis *are best represented by KNM ER 1813 because of its remarkably complete and undistorted condition. Although OH 13 is dentally virtually identical to ER 1813, it lacks a face, and the brain case is fragmentary. The cranium of the dentally similar OH 24 is distorted. Hence, only KNM ER 1813 has been used in Figures 4 and 5.*

(Figure 4) illustrate the strong resemblance of OH 65 to ER 1470. Also, the P³ is situated posterolaterally to the canine in both specimens. Although ER 1470 has no tooth crowns preserved, the size and placement of the roots (seen in broken horizontal and vertical sections, as well as in exposed incisor and canine sockets) are very similar to those of OH 65, in which, for example, the large flaring tooth roots of the molars have relatively small crowns.

The presence of OH 65 at Olduvai adds support to the hypothesis based upon cranial morphology that ER 1470 may belong to the same species as OH 7, the type specimen of *H. habilis*. OH 7 is composed of parts of a pair of juvenile parietals and a somewhat distorted partial juvenile mandible, presumably from the same individual (*3*). Considering the immaturity of OH 7, the parietals of ER 1470 and OH 7 match closely in size and shape (Figure 5). The OH 7 mandible is broad in its anterior dimension, with a well-developed postincisive shelf (lingual alveolar plane). Both of these features, which are apparent in the distorted condition of OH 7 (*17*) but strikingly revealed in photographic reconstruction (*5, 18*), appear to be compatible with the architecture of the maxilla and lower face in ER 1470 and OH 65, including the broad anterior alveolar arcade observed in both individuals (Table S2). This overall concordance of the ER 1470 and OH 65

morphologies with that of the type specimen of *H. habilis* casts doubt on *H. rudolfensis* as a biologically valid taxon. Consequently, *H. rudolfensis* (Alexeev) Groves would be a junior synonym for *H. habilis* Leakey, Tobias, and Napier (see Appendix).

The architectural similarities between OH 65 and ER 1470 support the judgement that late Pliocene hominids from Olduvai Gorge and East Lake Turkana usually assigned to *H. habilis* instead represent more than one species (*6, 11–15, 19*) (Table S3). On the basis of facial morphology (Table S2), parietal size and shape, and anterior mandibular morphology, the smaller brained, small-toothed hominids that have been placed in *H. habilis* [including OH 13, OH 24, OH 62, and ER 1813 (*5, 6, 20*)] do not appear to belong to that species. Phenetically they may be thought of as a gracile form of australopithecine, although cladistically they may be assigned to a primitive form of *Homo* (*13*). They lack, however, the larger neurocranium combined with raised nasal bones and everted lateral nasal margins characteristic of *Homo* and seen in ER 1470.

The environmental setting of the hominid locality was a stream in a small valley incised into the western lake margin during a period of low lake level. The fluvial sandstone containing the paleoanthropological assemblage displays an overall upward-fining in maximum grain and clast sizes (Figure 6). The lower meter best preserves evidence of fluvial processes, with very coarse sand or clast-filled channels underlain by trough cross-bedded and bar front planar cross-bedded units. The concentration of minor channels and channel lags near the base of the sandstone suggests that the paleoanthropological assemblage was disturbed somewhat. Still, the stone artifacts and fossils are orders of magnitude larger than the coarsest sand-fill, associated limb parts from each of three mammal individuals are present, and fluvially transportable and lag skeletal elements are evenly represented.

The admixed silt and clay in the channel sandstone suggests ephemeral fluvial flooding conditions. The presence of cemented aggregates of the small, benthic, freshwater clam *Corbicula* indicates well-oxygenated (flowing, shallow) water (*21*). The stream supported *Crocodylus*, *Hippopotamus*, and fish.

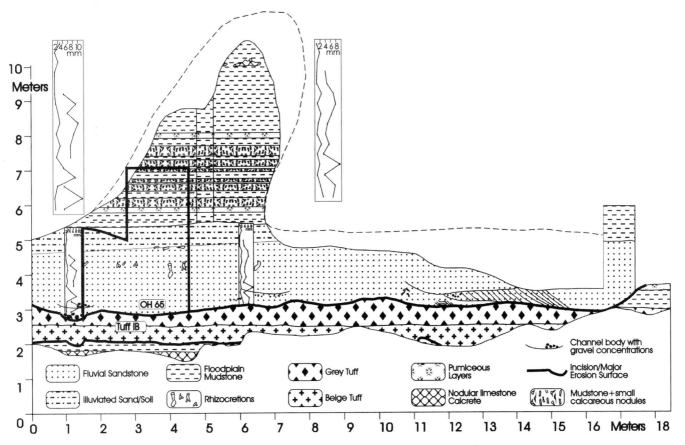

Figure 6. *Vertical exposure map of the rock face into which Trench 57 (bold polygon) was excavated, showing incision surfaces and lithofacies. Vertical variations in maximum matrix grain size and maximum size of contained clasts within the fossil-bearing sandstone are shown for two sections flanking Trench 57, and enlarged versions are shown above each for clarity. For the section on the left, the range of grain size is 0.8 to 8.0 mm, and the range of clast size is 2.0 to 10.0 mm. For the section on the right, the ranges are 0.8 to 2.0 mm and 2.0 to 10.0 mm, respectively. The major incision surface cuts down through Tuff IC locally into Tuff IB. Tuff IB, represented by two facies at this locality, also sits on a slightly incised surface cut into fluvial flood-plain facies. Channel and planar cross-bedded facies within the sandy incision-fill represent deposits within small fluvial channels that would have passed further downstream into paleo-Lake Olduvai. The top of the fluvial tuffaceous sandstone underwent bioturbation and pedogenic illuviation, followed by a return to fluvial floodplain facies. The uppermost pumiceous layer corresponds to the lower pumiceous layer of Figure 2.*

High $\delta^{13}C$ values (−3.6 to +1.2 per mil Peedee Belemnite standard) of tooth enamel from *Antidorcas, Beatragus* or *Connochaetes, Gazella* or *Aepyceros, Kobus, Megalotragus,* and *Parmularius* indicate that most of the mammalian herbivores drawn to the stream predominantly grazed plants that had the C_4 photosynthetic pathway [compare to (*22*)]. The presence of *Papio* and modern landscape analogs suggest that the stream may have supported a gallery woodland (*23*) (see Appendix). Such a wooded setting could explain the incidence of tooth marking (43% of the 72 larger mammal long-bone specimens with well-preserved surfaces) at about half of that expected if carnivores consumed the marrow and grease from all available bones (*24*).

Some of the animals were also exploited by hominids. Stone knife cut marks and hammerstone percussion marks are evident on 4.2% and 8.3%, respectively, of the larger mammal long-bone specimens, proportions that are three to five times lower than that expected if hominids extracted all available flesh and marrow (*24, 25*). This contrasts with the near-maximal occurrences of butchery marking in the FLK 22 (*Zinjanthropus* level) assemblage from the eastern Bed I lake margin (*24, 26*).

The stone artifacts (*n* = 234) found in the channel bed include a range of typically Oldowan core forms (*4*), 92% of which are made on quartzite like that found on outcrops near the western gorge. Three cores are made of lavas similar to those more commonly used by hominids in the Bed I eastern lake margin (*4*). These lavas were available at least 15 to 20 km from Trench 57, in streams draining the volcanic highlands in the southeastern basin (Figure 1).

The western basin, at the drier eastern edge of the Serengeti Plain, may have supported a resident hominid deme, at least during wetter time periods. However, the low occurrence of butchery marking and the lava artifacts are consistent with a hominid land-use model that emphasizes irregular, seasonal forays to the western basin streams from the ecologically more productive southeastern basin, which included drought refuges along its mountainsides (*27, 28*).

REFERENCES AND NOTES

1. R. L. Hay, *Geology of the Olduvai Gorge* (Univ. of California Press, Berkeley, CA, 1976).
2. L. S. B. Leakey, *Olduvai Gorge: 1951–1961, Vol. I* (Cambridge Univ. Press, Cambridge, 1965).
3. ———, P. V. Tobias, J. R. Napier, *Nature* **202**, 7 (1964).
4. M. D. Leakey, *Olduvai Gorge: Excavations in Beds I and II, 1960–1963* (Cambridge Univ. Press, Cambridge, 1971).
5. P. V. Tobias, *Olduvai Gorge, Vol. 4a and 4b: The Skulls, Endocasts and Teeth of* Homo habilis (Cambridge Univ. Press, Cambridge, 1991).
6. B. Wood, *Koobi Fora Research Project Vol. 4, Hominid Cranial Remains* (Clarendon, Oxford, UK, 1991).
7. G. H. Curtis, R. L. Hay, in *Calibration of Hominid Evolution*, W. W. Bishop, J. A. Miller, Eds.(Scottish Academic, Edinburgh, 1972), pp. 289–302.
8. R. C. Walter, P. C. Manega, R. L. Hay, R. E. Drake, G. H. Curtis, *Nature* **354**, 145 (1991).
9. R. C. Walter, P. C. Manega, R. L. Hay, *Quat. Int.* **13/14**, 37 (1992).
10. W. A. Berggren, D. V. Kent, C. C. Swisher III, M.-P. Aubry, *S.E.P.M. (Soc. Sediment. Geol.) Spec. Publ. No. 54* (1995), p. 129.
11. C. B. Stringer, in *Major Topics in Primate and Human Evolution*, B. Wood, L. Martin, P. Andrews, Eds.(Cambridge Univ. Press, Cambridge, 1986), pp. 266–294.
12. G. P. Rightmire, *Am. J. Phys. Anthropol.* **90**, 1 (1993).
13. C. P. Groves, *A Theory of Human and Primate Evolution* (Clarendon, Oxford, UK, 1989).
14. B. Wood, *Nature* **355**, 783 (1992).
15. ———, in *Species, Species Concepts, and Primate Evolution*, W. H. Kimbel, L. B. Martin, Eds. (Plenum, New York, 1993), pp. 485–522.
16. ———, *J. Hum. Evol.* **36**, 115 (1999).
17. L. S. B. Leakey, M. D. Leakey, *Nature* **202**, 5 (1964).
18. P. V. Tobias, *Nature* **209**, 953 (1966).
19. A. Walker, in Homo erectus: *Papers in Honor of Davidson Black*, B. A. Sigmon, J. S. Cybulski, Eds. (Univ. Toronto Press, Toronto, Canada, 1981), pp.193–215.
20. D. C. Johanson et al., *Nature* **327**, 205 (1987).
21. R. F. McMahon, in *The Mollusca: Vol. 6: Ecology*, W. D. Russell-Hunter, Ed. (Academic, New York, 1983), pp. 505–561.
22. J. A. Lee-Thorpe, N. J. van der Merwe, *S. Afr. J. Sci.* **83**, 712 (1987).
23. R. J. Blumenschine, C. R. Peters, *J. Hum. Evol.* **34**, 565 (1998).
24. R. J. Blumenschine, *J. Hum. Evol.* **29**, 21 (1995).
25. S. D. Capaldo, *J. Hum. Evol.* **33**, 555 (1997).
26. H. T. Bunn, E. M. Kroll, *Curr. Anthropol.* **27**, 431 (1986).
27. C. R. Peters, R. J. Blumenschine, *J. Hum. Evol.* **29**, 321 (1995).
28. ———, in *Four Million Years of Hominid Evolution in Africa: Papers in Honour of Dr. Mary Douglas Leakey's Outstanding Contribution in Paleoanthropology*, C. Magori, C. B. Saanane, F. Schrenk, Eds. (Kaupia, Darmstadter Beitrage zur Naturgeschichte, Darmstadt, Germany, 1996), pp. 175–221.
29. We thank the Tanzanian government for permission to conduct fieldwork at Olduvai; C. Kilembe, O. Kileo, C. Msuya, F. Ndunguru, G. K. Olle Moita, and J. Pareso for facilitating this work; T. D. White for comments on the hominid taxonomic interpretations; C. S. Feibel for identifying *Corbicula* and providing the reference on its environmental tolerances; S. C. Anton for comments on Table S2; and P. V. Tobias for comments on the submitted manuscript. S. R. Copeland, G. F. Mollel, J. Temba, G. Peter, and A. Venance provided excavation and mapping assistance. A. Venance and A. E. Cushing found OH 65 during excavation. The research was funded by NSF (grants SBR-9000099, SBR-9601065, and BCS-0109027), Rutgers University, Wenner-Gren Foundation for Anthropological Research, National Geographic Society, L. S. B. Leakey Foundation, Smithsonian Institution, Harvard University, University of Georgia, and Boise Fund.

APPENDIX

SUPPORTING TEXT

Supporting Text on the ^{40}Ar/^{39}Ar Dating Analyses: Walter et al. (*1, 2*) previously published single-crystal, laser-fusion ^{40}Ar/^{39}Ar ages for Tuffs IB and IC, as well as other Bed I tuffs at Olduvai Gorge from the central and eastern basin. For Tuff IB, they obtained a mean age for a lower, pre-ignimbritic air-fall tephra of 1.859 ± 0.007 Ma, distinctly older than the mean of 1.798 ± 0.004 Ma that they obtained for the ignimbrite and an upper pumice unit of Tuff IB. These ages, adjusted for subsequent revision in the age of the Fish Canyon sanidine standard used in their experiments (*3*), are 1.871 Ma and 1.810 Ma, respectively. At Loc. 64/Trench 57, the ignimbrite is not present, and it is not certain how the dated tephra correlates to the detailed stratigraphy of Tuff IB farther to the west. However, the new result of 1.845 ± 0.002 Ma for Tuff IB in the vicinity of Trench 57 is very close to the middle of the 0.06 Ma range of ages provided for Tuff IB by Walter et al. (*1, 2*). Their age for Tuff IC of 1.761 ± 0.028 Ma (revised age, 1.772 Ma) is 0.07 Ma younger than the age we report here for the geochemical correlative of Tuff IC in the vicinity of Trench 57. We have conducted a broad re-dating of Bed I units at Olduvai; in a later manuscript, we will analyze and compare these results to the ^{40}Ar/^{39}Ar ages provided by Walter and colleagues. Nonetheless, the conclusions of the current study regarding the age of the paleoanthropological assemblage would not be affected substantially if we use Walter's previous ages or our new ones.

Supporting Text on the Paleomagnetic Analysis: The average normal polarity direction of the 33 paleomagnetic samples is Dec. 357.6°, Inc. −18.4°, and is similar to that reported previously (*4*) and observed by us for the Olduvai Subchron elsewhere in the gorge. All specimens indicate small amounts of magnetization in goethite that appears to be removed by thermal demagnetization to 200°C. Most specimens showed stable normal directions between 200°C and 520°C (representing primary magnetization that likely resides in magnetite), and a drop in intensity and stability in direction above 550°C. In a few samples, indications of reverse polarity were observed above 600° C; although unstable, the results suggest the presence of small amounts of secondary magnetization in hematite of possible Matuyama age.

Supporting Text on *Homo habilis*:
Homo habilis Leakey, Tobias and Napier, 1964
    Revised hypodigm: including specimens from the terminal Pliocene of Olduvai Gorge, Tanzania, and Koobi Fora, Kenya. *Homo rudolfensis* (Alexeev, 1986)

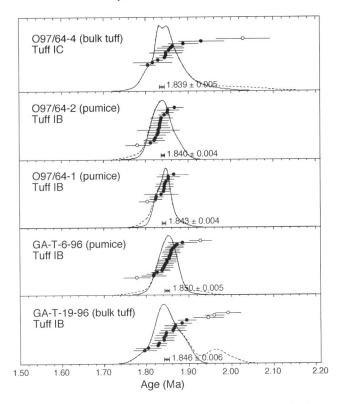

Figure S1. *Age-probability spectra for five samples of anorthoclase subjected to single-crystal $^{40}Ar/^{39}Ar$ dating from tuffaceous sediments in Tuff IB and Tuff IC (Figure 2). The age-probability spectra are generated by assuming that each analytical error is described by a normal probability distribution, and then summing the probabilities across all analyses of a particular sample. Individual analyses with 1σ analytical errors are superimposed on each spectrum. Open circles represent outliers excluded from the calculation of a weighted mean; age-probability spectra that include these analyses are shown by the dashed curves. Individual analyses are considered outliers if they occur more than 2σ from the weighted mean age of a primary age population, or if they appear to form a distinct subpopulation (the small peak at ~1.95 Ma in sample GA-T-19-96). Mean ages, weighted by the inverse analytical variance, and their 1σ standard error are shown for each sample.*

Groves, 1989, herein recognized as a junior synonym. Also, OH 65 included in the revised hypodigm. Revised diagnosis (in part): taxon differentiated by a unique combination of raised nasals, everted nasal margins, neurocranium larger than *Australopithecus africanus*, mid-face broader than upper face, position of anterior projection of origin of zygomatic root over P^4 or between P^4 and M^1, large tooth roots relative to crowns, *Australopithecus africanus*–like cranial profile in posterior view.

Supporting Text on Paleoenvironment: Stable carbon and oxygen isotope analysis conducted on seven paleosol carbonates from a claystone between Tuff IB and Tuff IC (Figure 2) yielded lower $\delta^{18}O$ values (–5.5 to –4.3‰ (PDB), $n = 7$) than the area's recent pedogenic carbonates (–1.1 to +1.0‰ (PDB), $n = 4$) (cf. *5*), suggesting a moister climate than prevails in the semi-arid Olduvai region today. The presence at the OH 65 locality of a mosaic of grassy woodland and wooded grassland is suggested by $\delta^{13}C$ values of –5.6 to –4.2‰ (PDB) for the seven paleosol carbonate samples. In modern East African lowland and mid-elevation environments, such values occur in settings with 45–55% C_3 woody plant biomass (*6, 7*). Because the paleosol carbonates likely formed prior to channel incision, their relevance to the climatic and vegetation contexts of the paleoanthropological assemblage is uncertain beyond providing a general environmental background to the Bed I western lake margin.

Table S1. $^{40}Ar/^{39}Ar$ Analytical Data for the Two Dated Stratigraphic Units in Figure 2

Sample Name	Lab ID#	N/n₀	MSWD	Ca/K ± 1σ	$^{40}Ar^*/^{39}Ar$ ± 1σ	Age (Ma) ± 1σ
Tuff IC						
O97/64-4	21081	11/12	1.3	0.18 ± 0.17	1.078 ± 0.003	1.839 ± 0.005
Tuff IB						
O97/64-2	21083/21084	17/18	1.2	0.11 ± 0.11	1.085 ± 0.002	1.840 ± 0.004
O97/64-1	21078	11/12	1.0	0.17 ± 0.09	1.092 ± 0.002	1.843 ± 0.004
GA-T-6-96	20881/20884	20/22	1.1	0.12 ± 0.06	1.156 ± 0.002	1.850 ± 0.005
GA-T-19-96	20888	13/16	1.5	0.07 ± 0.02	1.148 ± 0.003	1.846 ± 0.006
					Weighted mean age, Tuff IB:	1.845 ± 0.002

Data were obtained by complete fusion of individual feldspar phenocrysts under ultra-high vacuum using a focused Ar-ion laser, followed by measurement of five argon isotopes on a MAP-215 noble gas mass spectrometer (*8*). 'n/n_0' is the number of individual grain analyses accepted for calculation of the weighted-mean $^{40}Ar^*/^{39}Ar$ sample age, over the total number of analyses performed. 'MSWD' is the mean sum of weighted deviates of the individual ages. Ca/K is calculated from $^{37}Ar/^{39}Ar$ using a multiplier of 1.96. $^{40}Ar^*$ refers to radiogenic argon. Error in age is 1σ standard error of the mean, and incorporates error in the neutron fluence parameter, J (0.12–0.23%). The neutron fluence monitor is Fish Canyon Tuff sanidine, with a reference age of 28.02 Ma (*3*). Samples were irradiated for 3.5 hours in the Cd-shielded CLICIT facility of the Oregon State University TRIGA reactor, in three separate batches (GA-T-6-96 and GA-T-19-96; O97/64-1, 2, and 3; and O98/64-5). Isotopic interference corrections: $(^{36}Ar/^{37}Ar)Ca = 2.72 \times 10^{-4} \pm 1 \times 10^{-6}$, $(^{39}Ar/^{37}Ar)Ca = 7.11 \times 10^{-4} \pm 2.4 \times 10^{-6}$, $(^{40}Ar/^{39}Ar)K = 7 \times 10^{-4} \pm 3 \times 10^{-4}$. $\lambda = 5.543 \times 10^{-10}$ y⁻¹. Age-probability spectra of the five dated samples can be found in Figure S1.

Table S2. Characters of the Lower Mid-Face and Maxilla/Palate of OH 65 Compared to Other, Well-Preserved, Near-Contemporaneous Plio-Pleistocene Hominid Specimens

Character/Specimen	OH 5 *Paranthropus boisei*[*]	OH 65 *Homo habilis* (this paper)	ER 1470 *Homo habilis* (this paper)[†]	ER 1813 *Homo* or *Australopithecus*[‡]	ER 3733 *Homo ergaster*[§]
palate shape (note on depth)	long and narrow (deep)	**very broad (deep)**	very broad (deep)	"foreshortened" and moderately broad □□ (moderately deep)	short and narrow (very deep)
curvature of tooth rows (shape of alveolar arcade)	straight/divergent posteriorly	**arched**	arched	arched	arched/parallel sided[¶]
breadth of lower mid-face (anterior view of alveolar face)	broad lower mid-face (includes the alveoli of the buccal root of P³'s)	**very broad lower mid-face (includes the alveoli of the buccal root of P³'s)**	very broad lower mid-face (includes the alveoli of the buccal root of P³'s)	narrow lower mid-face (includes only the alveoli of the incisors and canines)	narrow lower mid-face (includes only the alveoli of the incisors and canines)
transition from the floor of the nasal aperture to the naso-alveolar clivus	smooth long gutter (long lower face), recessed nasal spine	**steep angulation, anterior nasal spine**	steep angulation** (area of anterior nasal spine not preserved)	steep angulation[††], anterior nasal spine	steep angulation[‡‡], anterior nasal spine
projection of the naso-alveolar contour beyond the bicanine line (in lateral view)	virtually absent	**weak**	virtually absent to weak	weak	weak (probably)
naso-alveolar clivus contours across the midline	concave	**flat to convex**	flat	convex	flat (probably)
position of the inferior anterior face of the maxillary root of the zygomatic process	anterior and flush with the slope of the lower and mid-face	**slightly posterior to the inferior lateral nasal margin (probably more vertical than the slope of the lower mid-face)**	slightly posterior to the inferior lateral nasal margin (probably more vertical than the slope of the lower mid-face)	posteriorly retracted and notably vertical	posteriorly retracted and notably vertical
position of the anterior projection of the origin of the zygomatic root	between P³ and P⁴	**between P⁴ and M¹**	mid-P⁴	M¹[§§]	M¹ (probably)

*Type specimen.

†*Homo rudolfensis* (Alexeev, 1986) Groves, 1989: lectotype (9); most complete cranium in the hypodigm (10, 11).

‡See Table S3. *Homo habilis sensu* Wood: most complete cranium (10).

§Most complete adult cranium (10, 12).

□□ Similar to OH 24 (10).

¶The canine and incisor alveoli lie in a smooth curve; the preserved portions of the arcade for the premolars and first and second molars appear parallel-sided (10): KNM ER 15000 is similar.

** According to Wood (10), there is no sharp nasal sill; the preserved nasal floor and the naso-alveolar clivus meet at an angle of about 70° (10).

††Low but discrete nasal sill; anterior nasal spine present (10). Also present in *Australopithecus africanus.*

‡‡Shallow prenasal fossa, but no sharp nasal sill; the plane of the nasal floor and the surface of the nasoalveolar clivus meet at a angle of 60°; low, rounded anterior nasal spine (10).

§§Similar to OH 24.

Table S3.   Taxonomic Groupings for Specimens Variously Included in *Homo habilis sensu lato*

Specimen/Author	1981 Walker (*13*)	1986 Stringer (*14*)	1989 Groves (*11*)	1991 Wood (*10*)	1993 Rightmire (*15*)
ER 1470	*Homo habilis**	*H. habilis*	*Homo rudolfensis*	*Homo* sp. nov.	*H. habilis*
ER 1590	*H. habilis*	*H. habilis*	*H. rudolfensis*	*Homo* sp. nov.	*H. habilis*
ER 1802	—	*H. habilis*	*H. rudolfensis*	*Homo* sp. nov.	*H. habilis*†
ER 1805	—	*Homo* sp. nov.	*Homo ergaster*	*H. habilis*	*Homo* sp. nov.
ER 1813	*Australopithecus* cf. *africanus*	*Homo* sp. nov.	*H. ergaster*	*H. habilis*	*Homo* sp. nov.
ER 3732	*H. habilis*	*H. habilis*	*H. rudolfensis*	*Homo* sp. nov.	*H. habilis*
OH 7 (type specimen)	*H. habilis*	*H. habilis*	*H. habilis*	*H. habilis*	*H. habilis*
OH 13	*Australopithecus* cf. *africanus*	*Homo* sp. nov.	*H. habilis*	*H. habilis*	*Homo* sp. nov.
OH 16	*H. habilis*	*Homo* sp. nov.	*H. habilis*	*H. habilis*	*Homo* sp. nov. ‡
OH 24	*Australopithecus* cf. *africanus*	*H. habilis*	*H. habilis*	*H. habilis*	*Homo* sp. nov.

*Australopithecine-like *Homo habilis*.

†"Possibly."

‡"Probably."

SUPPORTING REFERENCES

1. R. C. Walter, P. C. Manega, R. L. Hay, R. E. Drake, G. H. Curtis, *Nature* **354**, 145 (1991).
2. R. C. Walter, P. C. Manega, R. L. Hay, *Quat. Int.* **13/14**, 37 (1992).
3. P. R. Renne, et al., *Chem. Geol.* **145**, 117 (1998).
4. E. Tamarat, N. Thouveny, M. Taïeb, N. D. Opdyke, *Palaeogeogr. Palaeoclimatol. Palaeoecol.* **114**, 273 (1995).
5. T. E. Cerling, R. L. Hay, *Quat. Res.* **25**, 63 (1986).
6. T. E. Cerling, *Palaeogeogr. Palaeoclimatol. Palaeoecol.* **97**, 241 (1992).
7. N. E. Sikes, *J. Hum. Evol.* **27**, 25 (1994).
8. M. G. Best, E. H. Christiansen, A. L. Deino, C. S. Grommé, D. G. Tingey, *J. Geophys. Res.* **100**, 24593 (1995).
9. B. Wood, *J. Hum. Evol.* **36**, 115 (1999).
10. B. Wood, *Koobi Fora Research Project Vol. 4, Hominid Cranial Remains* (Clarendon, Oxford, 1991).
11. C. P. Groves, *A Theory of Human and Primate Evolution* (Clarendon, Oxford, 1989).
12. A. Walker, in *The Nariokotome* Homo erectus *Skeleton*, A. Walker, R. Leakey, Eds. (Harvard University Press: Cambridge, 1993), pp. 411–430.
13. A. Walker, in Homo erectus: *Papers in Honor of Davidson Black*, B. A. Sigmon, J. S. Cybulski, Eds. (Univ. Toronto Press, Toronto, 1981), pp. 193–215.
14. C. B. Stringer, in *Major Topics in Primate and Human Evolution*, B. Wood, L. Martin, P. Andrews, Eds. (Cambridge University Press, Cambridge, 1986), pp. 266–294.
15. G. P. Rightmire, *Am. J. Phys. Anthrop.* **90**, 1 (1993).

29

Australopithecus garhi

A New Species of Early Hominid from Ethiopia

B. Asfaw, T. White, O. Lovejoy, B. Latimer, S. Simpson, and G. Suwa

ABSTRACT

The lack of an adequate hominid fossil record in eastern Africa between 2 and 3 million years ago (Ma) has hampered investigations of early hominid phylogeny. Discovery of 2.5 Ma hominid cranial and dental remains from the Hata beds of Ethiopia's Middle Awash allows recognition of a new species of Australopithecus. This species is descended from Australopithecus afarensis and is a candidate ancestor for early Homo. Contemporary postcranial remains feature a derived humanlike humeral/femoral ratio and an apelike upper arm-to-lower arm ratio.

The succession of early hominid genera and species indicates diversification into at least two distinct adaptive patterns by ~2.7 Ma. A meager east African hominid record between 2 and 3 Ma has caused the pattern and process of this diversification to remain obscure. The *Australopithecus afarensis* (3.6 to 3.0 Ma) to *A. aethiopicus* (2.6 Ma) to *A. boisei* (2.3 to 1.2 Ma) species lineage is well corroborated by craniodental remains. In contrast, a suggested relationship between *A. afarensis* and early *Homo* has previously been evidenced only by relatively uninformative isolated teeth (*1*), a palate (*2*), and a temporal fragment (*3*).

The recovery of hominid remains from the Hata (abbreviation of Hatayae) Member of the Bouri Formation adds substantially to the inventory of fossils bearing on these phylogenetic issues. These remains comprise craniodental and postcranial elements from several areas in the Middle Awash. The first of these was discovered in 1990 at Matabaietu and Gamedah. Biochronology and Ar/Ar dating place these remains at ~2.5 Ma. They include a small left parietal fragment (GAM-VP-1/2) and an edentulous left mandible corpus from Gamedah (GAM-VP-1/1), as well as a distal left humerus from Matabaietu (MAT-VP-1/1). It is impossible to attribute the humerus and parietal fragments to a genus. However, the small, fluvially abraded Gamedah mandible retains tooth roots and corpus contours. These demonstrate that it is not a robust *Australopithecus*.

It was not until 1996–1998 that we recovered additional hominid remains of comparable antiquity west of the modern Awash, at Bouri. The proximal half of an adult hominid ulna (BOU-VP-11/1) was found on the surface of the Hata beds by T. Assebework on 17 November 1996. On 30 November, White found a proximal femur and associated forearm elements of a smaller individual, ~100 m to the WNW (BOU-VP-12/1A-G). Sieving and excavation revealed additional portions of this individual's femur in situ, 1 m above a 2.496 Ma volcanic ash, in a horizon with abundant catfish remains and medium-sized bovid fossils, the latter bearing cut marks (*4*).

This partial hominid skeleton includes fairly complete shafts of a left femur and the right humerus, radius, and ulna. A partial fibular shaft, a proximal foot phalanx, and the base of the anterior portion of the mandible were also found. There is no evidence that these remains represent more than one individual. Except for the in situ distal femoral shaft segment, all were surface finds lying within 2 m of one another. All are similarly preserved. Lengths can be accurately estimated for the phalanx, the femur, and the three arm elements. The foot phalanx is similar to remains of *A. afarensis* in size, length, and curvature. The mandible does not retain diagnostic morphology. No associated hominid teeth were found on the surface or in a large excavation.

Further search of the same ~2.5 Ma horizon led to the discovery, 278 m farther NNW, of a partial hominid cranium (BOU-VP-12/130) on 20 November 1997 by Y. Haile-Selassie (Figure 1). Another individual's crested cranial vault fragment (BOU-VP-12/87) was found 50 m south of the BOU-VP-12/1 skeleton excavation. At a more northerly locality in the Esa Dibo area ~9 km away, A. Defleur found a fairly complete mandible, with dentition, of another hominid individual (BOU-VP-17/1) on 17 November 1997. An additional hominid humeral shaft (BOU-VP-35/1) was found ~1 km farther north of

the location of the mandible, on 4 December 1998, by D. DeGusta. On biochronological grounds, these Esa Dibo specimens are about the same age as the more southerly cluster of hominid remains at Bouri localities 11 and 12 (*4*).

Great uncertainty has continued to confound the origin of *Homo* because of a lack of evidence from the interval between 2 and 3 Ma (*5*). The 2.5 Ma Bouri Hata hominids bear directly on these issues. In addition, they are closely associated with behavioral evidence of lithic technology (*4*). *Australopithecus africanus* from South Africa is roughly contemporary with the Hata remains. In eastern Africa, *A. aethiopicus* and at least one other putative lineage ancestral to early *Homo* are contemporaries in the Turkana Basin. The BOU-VP-12/130 cranial remains represent no previously named species. Only the recovery of additional specimens with associated crania and dentitions may allow the Bouri postcrania to be positively attributed to this new taxon. Therefore, the new species described below is established strictly on the basis of craniodental remains.

The following is a description of *Australopithecus garhi*, based on the BOU-VP-12/130 specimen: order, Primates Linnaeus 1758; suborder, Anthropoidea

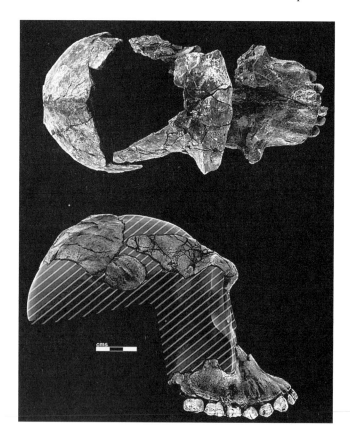

Figure 1. *Cranial parts of BOU-VP-12/130. (**Top**) Superior view of the original fossil. Nonstandard orientation (rotated posteriorly ~10° from Frankfurt horizontal) to show maximum anatomy. (**Bottom**) Lateral view of casts to show cranial and maxillary profiles. Note that neither Frankfurt horizontal nor placement of the maxilla relative to the vault can be accurately determined and that reconstructed portions (indicated by oblique lines) are speculative. Photos from National Museum of Ethiopia, Addis Ababa; © 1999 David L. Brill.*

Mivart 1864; genus, *Australopithecus* DART 1925; and species, *Australopithecus garhi*.

Etymology. The word garhi means "surprise" in the Afar language.

Holotype. ARA-VP-12/130 is an associated set of cranial fragments comprising the frontal, parietals, and maxilla with dentition. It was found by Y. Haile-Selassie on 20 November 1997. The holotype is housed at the National Museum of Ethiopia, Addis Ababa.

Locality. Bouri Vertebrate Paleontology locality 12 (BOU-VP-12) is on the eastern side of the Bouri peninsula, west of the modern Awash River, in the Middle Awash paleoanthropological study area, Afar depression, Ethiopia. The BOU-VP-12/130 holotype was found at 10°15.6199′N, 40°33.8445′E, at ~550 m elevation.

Horizon and Associations. The holotype was recovered from silty clays within 2 m of the top of the Maoleem vitric tuff, which has been dated to 2.496 Ma by Ar/Ar. Vertebrate fossils, including additional hominids, were found at the same stratigraphic horizon on nearby outcrops (*4*).

Diagnosis. *Australopithecus garhi* is a species of *Australopithecus* distinguished from other hominid species by a combination of characters presented in Table 1. It is distinguished from *A. afarensis* by its absolutely larger postcanine dentition and an upper third premolar morphology with reduced mesiobuccal enamel line projection and less occlusal asymmetry. *Australopithecus garhi* lacks the suite of derived dental, facial, and cranial features shared by *A. aethiopicus*, *A. robustus*, and *A. boisei*. *Australopithecus garhi* is distinguished from *A. africanus* and other early *Homo* species by its primitive frontal, facial, palatal, and subnasal morphology.

Dental Description. The postcanine dental size is remarkable, at or beyond the known nonrobust and *A. robustus* extremes (Figure 2). The anterior dentition is also large, with I1 and canine breadths equivalent to or exceeding those of their largest known *Australopithecus* and early *Homo* homologs. Thus, despite exceptional postcanine size, dental proportions of the holotype deviate markedly from the robust *Australopithecus* condition. The canine-to-premolar/molar size ratios are comparable to those of *A. afarensis*, *A. africanus*, and early *Homo*. Relative canine to incisor alveolar length is most similar to that of *A. africanus*. Postcanine wear, with developed angular facets and retention of buccal cusp saliency, differs distinctively from the robust *Australopithecus* pattern. The upper P3 is more derived than that of *A. afarensis* and most *A. africanus* specimens in exhibiting a reduced mesiobuccal crown quadrant and a weak transverse crest. The buccolingual narrowing of premolars and first molars often seen in early *Homo* is absent.

Cranial Description. The lower face is prognathic, with procumbent incisors. Canine roots are placed well lateral to the nasal aperture margin. The premaxillary surface is separated from the nasal floor by a blunt ridge and is transversely and sagittally convex. The palate is vertically thin (~3 mm at M1/M2 midline). The zygomatic roots originate above P4/M1. The dental arcade is U-shaped, with slightly divergent dental rows (Figure 3). The temporal lines encroach deeply on the frontal, past the midsupraorbital position, and probably met anterior to bregma. The postglabellar frontal squama is depressed in a frontal trigon. The localized frontal sinus is limited to the medial one-third of the supraorbital surface. Postorbital constriction is marked. The parietal bones have a well-formed, bipartite, anteriorly positioned sagittal crest that divides above lambda. An endocast was made from the aligned parietals and frontal and was completed by sculpting by R. Holloway. Cranial capacity was about 450 cm^3, as measured by water displacement.

Taxonomic Discussion. There is no current agreement about how many pre-*erectus* *Homo* species should be recognized or even on how the genus *Homo* should be defined. The traditional conservative definition emphasizes adaptive plateau. Ironically, by this definition, the early *Homo* species *H. rudolfensis* and *H. habilis* might be better placed in *Australopithecus*, as this would affiliate the major adaptive breakthroughs in anatomy and behavior that characterize *H. erectus* (*ergaster*) with the earliest defined occurrence of *Homo*. If *A. garhi* proves to be the exclusive ancestor of the *Homo* clade (see discussion below), a cladistic classification might assign it to genus *Homo*. Here we provisionally adopt the conservative, grade-sensitive alternative, emphasizing its small brain and large postcanine dentition by assigning the new Bouri species to *Australopithecus*. This attribution as well as our diagnosis and description may require emendation when additional individuals representing the species are recovered and firm postcranial associations are established (*6*).

Although the Bouri Hata postcrania cannot presently be assigned to the new species *A. garhi*, they illuminate aspects of hominid evolution. The past few years have witnessed a rash of attempts to estimate early hominid limb length proportions from fragmentary and unassociated specimens. These specimens have been used to generate a variety of functional and phylogenetic scenarios. Accurate estimates of the limb proportions of early hominids, however, must be confined to the very few specimens that actually preserve relevant elements, such as the A. L. 288-1 ("Lucy") specimen and KNM-WT 15000. The new Bouri VP-12/1 specimen is only the third Plio-Pleistocene hominid to provide reasonably accurate limb length proportions. The Olduvai Hominid 62 specimen of *Homo habilis* has been erroneously argued to show humerus-to-femur proportions more primitive than those of "Lucy" (*7, 8*), but its femur length cannot be accurately estimated. Other studies of limb proportions in early *Australopithecus* species are based on unassociated joints and not on actual (or even estimated) limb lengths (*7*).

The postcranial remains recovered from BOU-VP-11, -12, and -35 cannot be conclusively allocated to taxon.

Table 1. List of Characters Widely Used in Consideration of Hominid Phylogenetics (*11, 13*) that are Preserved on the BOU-VP-12/130 Holotype Cranium

	A. afarensis	*A. garhi* (*n = 1*)	Early *Homo*	*A. africanus*	*A. aethiopicus* (*n = 1*)	*A. robustus*	*A. boisei*
Dentition							
Canine to postcanine ratio	large	large	large	large	unknown	small	small
Incisor to postcanine ratio	large	smaller	large	smaller	smaller?	small	small
Postcanine absolute size	mod.	large	mod.	mod. to large	large	large	large
UP3 occlusal outline	asym.	more oval	more oval	more oval	oval	oval	oval
UP3 mesiobuccal line extension	frequent	absent	rare	rare	absent	absent	absent
Postcanine PM/M cusp wear	disp.	disp.	disp.	disp.	flat	flat	flat
Canine lingual shape	asym.	asym.	asym.	asym.	unknown	more sym.	more sym.
Premolar molarization	none	minor	minor	minor	pronounced	pronounced	pronounced
Enamel thickness	moderately thick	thick	thick	thick	hyperthick	hyperthick	hyperthick
Palate							
Ant. vertical thickness	thin	thin	thin	thin	thick	thick	thick
Dental arcade shape	rect.	rect.	para.	var.	rect.	para.	para.
Posterior dental arcade	conv.	div.	div.	div.	conv.	div.	div.
Ant. depth	shallow	shallow	deep	var.	shallow	usually deep	deep
UI2/UC diastema	common	present	rare	absent	absent	absent	absent
Incisor alveoli relative to bicanine line	ant.	ant.	var.	ant.	in line	in line	in line
Lower face							
C jugum	prom.	prom.	var.	prom.	weak	weak	weak
Ant. pillars	absent	absent	absent	present	absent	present	absent
Inferolateral nasal aperture margin	sharp	sharp	sharp	var.	blunt	var.	var.
UI2 root lateral to nasal aperture	lateral	in line	medial	medial	medial	medial	medial
Canine fossa	present	present	var.	present	absent	absent	absent
Maxillary fossula	absent	absent	absent	absent	absent	present	absent
Anterior zygomatic root position	M1	M1-P4	M1-P4	M1-P4	P4	P4-P3	P4/M1-P3
Zygomaticoalveolar crest	arched	arched	arched	var.	weak	var.	var.
Clivus contour	convex	convex	flat/convex	flat	concave	flat to concave	flat to concave
Subnasal prognathism	strong	strong	var.	var.	strong	weak	weak
Incisor procumbency	proc.	proc.	var.	var.	proc.	more vertical	more vertical
Subnasal to intranasal contours	discrete	discrete	discrete	var.	cont.	cont.	var.
Separation of vomeral/ant. septal insertion	strong	strong	usually strong	weak	weak	weak	weak
Lateral ant. facial contour	bipartite	bipartite	var.	var.	straight	straight	straight
Facial dishing	absent	absent	absent	absent	dished	dished	dished
Vault							
Frontal trigon	present	present	absent	absent	present	present	present
Costa supraorbitalis	present	present	torus	interm.	present	present	present
Temporal line's frontal convergence	mod.	mod.	weak	weak	strong	strong	strong
Postorbital constriction	mod.	mod.	mod.	mod.	marked	marked	marked
Sagittal crest in male	present	present	rare	rare	present	present	present
Relative size of posterior temporalis	large	interm.	interm.	interm.	large	small	small
Parietal transverse expansion/tuber	absent	absent	present	absent	absent	absent	absent
Parietomastoid angle	flared	weak	weak	weak	flared	weak	weak
Cranial capacity	small	small	enlarged	small	small	slightly enlarged	slightly enlarged

Because of arbitrary boundaries of presence or absence criteria, variability within species, limited sample sizes, and possible correlation between features, we caution against a numerical cladistic application of these tabulated data. Rather, this character list is meant to demonstrate the phenetic status of the single known *A. garhi* specimen with respect to features used to evaluate early hominid fossils. Note that despite the large postcanine dentition, no shared derived characters link *A. garhi* with *A. robustus* or *A. boisei*. The "early *Homo*" column comprises specimens assigned by various authors to both *H. habilis* and *H. rudolfensis*.

Abbreviations are as follows: mod., moderate; asym., asymmetric; disp., disparate; sym., symmetric; rect., rectangular; para., parabolic; var., variable; conv., convergent; div., divergent; ant., anterior; prom., prominent; proc., procumbent; cont., continuous; interm., intermediate.

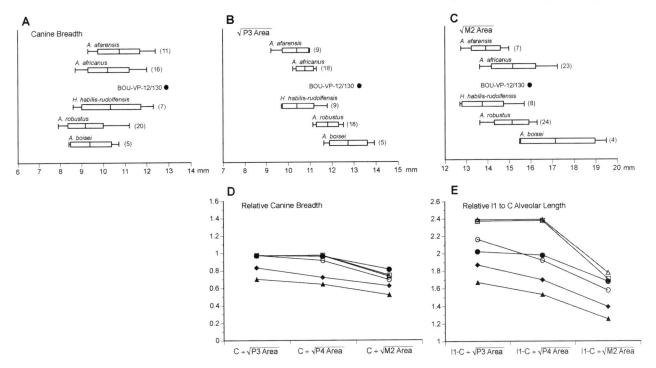

Figure 2. *Dental size of* A. garhi *compared with other early hominid taxa and specimens.* (**A**) *Canine breadth for various taxa.* (**B**) *The square root of calculated (MD × BL) premolar area.* (**C**) *The square root of calculated (MD × BL) second molar area.* (**D**) *Canine breadth relative to postcanine tooth size for various taxa.* (**E**) *Anterior alveolar length (mesial I1 to distal C) relative to postcanine tooth size. In (A) through (C), taxon means, standard deviations, ranges, and sample sizes (in parentheses) are given. All measures were taken by T. W. and G. S. on originals except for A. L. 444-2 and A. L. 417-1 (A. afarensis) and A. L. 666-1 (Homo), which are from (2, 14). Dental metrics for the BOU-VP-12/130 specimen are as follows (XX broken; parentheses = estimate; mesiodistal measure reported first, followed by buccolingual): RI1 XX, (9.2); RI2 6.9, 6.8; RC 11.6, 12.9; RP3 (11.0), 16.0; RP4 XX, XX; RM1 XX, XX; RM2 (14.4), (17.7); RM3 (15.2), 16.9; LI2 6.7, 7.0; LC 11.7, 12.9; LP3 (11.4), 16.0; LP4 (11.4), 16.0; LM1 (14.4), (16.5).* □, A. afarensis; ○, A. africanus; △, Homo; ◆, A. robustus; ▲, A. boisei; ●, BOU-VP-12/130.

The BOU-VP-12/1 specimen features a humanlike humeral/femoral ratio (Figure 4). This ratio may be an important derivation relative to *A. afarensis*, because it marks the earliest known appearance of the relative femoral elongation that characterizes later hominids. However, as in *A. afarensis*, the specimen's brachial index is apelike. This suggests that upper arm-to-lower arm ratios persisted into the basal Pleistocene and that the first hominid with modern forearm proportions was probably *Homo erectus* (*ergaster*). Because the *A. afarensis* forearm was also long relative to both the humerus and femur, the femur must have elongated before forearm shortening in early hominids.

The BOU-VP-11 ulna is from a larger individual, as is the BOU-VP-35/1 humeral shaft (estimated total humeral length = 310 to 325 mm). The latter is absolutely longer than the humerus of BOU-VP-12/1 but is less rugose and probably bore a smaller deltopectoral crest. These differences (in both size and rugosity) are well within the species ranges of extant hominoids. If both humeri represent the same taxon, they could reflect sexual dimorphism, which would be comparable to that currently seen in *A. afarensis*. However, it is

perilous to speculate on differences between only two specimens as they may reflect only fluctuating intraspecific variation in morphology and body mass.

The few and fragmentary nonrobust Turkana Basin hominids that span the 2.7 to 2.3 Ma time range are similar to the Bouri specimens in both size and aspects of morphology. Postcanine dental arcade length of BOU-VP-12/130 is equivalent to that of Omo 75-14, whereas individual teeth of the smaller Middle Awash mandibles (GAM-VP-1/1 and BOU-VP-17/1) are comparable in size to the smaller specimens of the Omo nonrobust collection. It is also important that BOU-VP-17/1 exhibits a derived lower P3 morphology (1) most similar to the Omo nonrobust and early *Homo* conditions and a dental arcade shape concordant with that of the holotype of *A. garhi*.

On the basis of size, BOU-VP-12/130 is a male. The craniodental size dimorphism documented for the closely related *A. afarensis* and *A. boisei* therefore predicts smaller individuals in *A. garhi*. The biochronologically contemporary and morphologically compatible BOU-VP-17/1 and GAM-VP-1/1 specimens are considerably smaller and may be females. This would suggest a

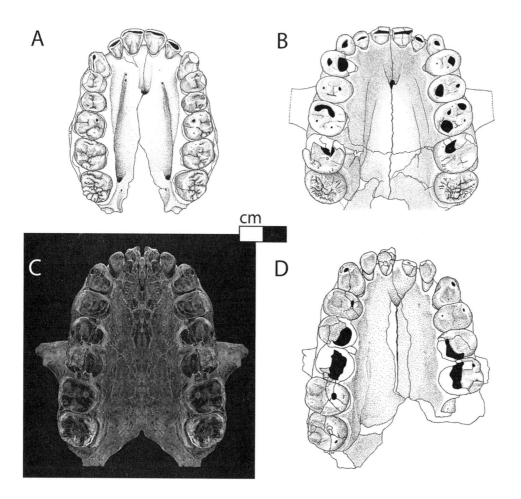

Figure 3.   *The most complete palates of* A. afarensis *(A. L. 200-1a; canine reset)* (*A*) *and* A. boisei *(OH-5)* (*B*) *compared with that of* A. garhi *(C and D). The photograph (National Museum of Ethiopia, Addis Ababa; © 1999 David L. Brill) was mirror-imaged on midline.* Australopithecus garhi *has relatively large canines like* A. afarensis *and absolutely large but morphologically nonrobust premolars and molars. Drawings © 1999 Luba Dmytryk Gudz/Brill Atlanta.*

shift in either or both body and dentognathic sizes to averages greater than in *A. afarensis*. More specimens are needed to test this hypothesis.

The discovery of *A. garhi* provides a strong test of many phylogenetic hypotheses that have addressed the relationships among Plio-Pleistocene hominid taxa. The South African species *A. africanus* was once widely considered to be the most primitive hominid. Discoveries of *A. afarensis* at Hadar and Laetoli displaced *A. africanus*. This more primitive sister species (*A. afarensis*) was in turn supplanted when the increasingly older and more primitive sister taxa *A. anamensis* (*9*) and *Ardipithecus ramidus* (*10*) were identified. However, the geometry of post-*afarensis* hominid phylogeny continues to be the focus of debate.

The position of *A. africanus* relative to the emergence of the genus *Homo* has been particularly difficult to resolve, even in the face of unduly elaborate phylo-

genetic analyses (*11*). One reason for this difficulty is the fundamental disagreement on whether early *Homo* comprises one sexually dimorphic (*H. habilis*) or two (*H. habilis* and *H. rudolfensis*) species. Most phylogenetic efforts have placed *A. africanus* as the link between *A. afarensis* and early *Homo*. This hypothesis has been widely, but not universally, accepted. Most predicted that a population of *A. africanus* would be found in eastern Africa when the 2.5 Ma gap there was filled by fossil discoveries.

The 2.5 Ma *A. garhi* is derived toward megadontia from *A. afarensis*, but in cranial anatomy it is definitively not *A. africanus*. Neither is it a representative of the contemporary *A. aethiopicus*. It is in the right place, at the right time, to be the ancestor of early *Homo*, however defined. Nothing about its morphology would preclude it from occupying this position. The close spatial and temporal association between *A. garhi* and behaviors

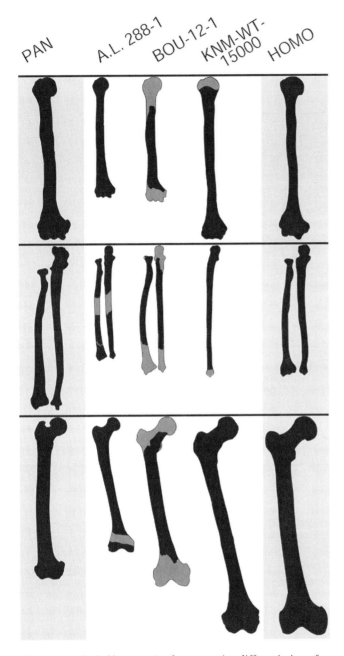

Figure 4. *Probable stages in the progressive differentiation of hominid long bone proportions (all bones shown to the same scale). The humerus (top), antebrachium (middle), and femur (bottom) are of about equal length in chimpanzees (Pan). Modern humans differ in two primary ways. Although our humerus is virtually the same length, the femur is elongated and the antebrachium is shortened. These changes appear to have emerged fully by ~1.5 Ma in H. erectus [all three limb segments are virtually complete in KNM-WT 15000 (15)]. On the basis of the other two partial skeletons in which long bone length can now be reliably estimated, the modern human pattern appears to have emerged in two stages: (i) elongation of the femur, which is intermediate in length relative to the humerus in A.L. 288-1 but exhibits modern proportions in BOU-VP-12/1; and (ii) shortening of the antebrachium, which retains primitive proportions in both specimens (16). Drawings © 1999 Luba Dmytryk Gudz/Brill Atlanta.*

thought to characterize later *Homo* provide additional circumstantial support. The temporal and possible phylogenetic placements of various hominid taxa relative to the new species from Bouri are reviewed in Figure 5.

Plio-Pleistocene hominid phylogenetics is bedeviled by atomization of functionally correlated character complexes that probably emanate from restricted genomic shifts as well as inadequate fossil samples (particularly for early *Homo*). Table 1 compiles characters available for *A. garhi* and related taxa bearing on phylogenetic placement. The discovery of the KNM-WT 17000 specimen of *A. aethiopicus* demonstrated the pervasiveness of homoplasy in hominid evolution (*12*). Specimens such as KNM-ER 1590, KNM-ER 1470, KNM-ER 1802, Malawi UR 501, and Omo 75-14 make it obvious that some early *Homo* specimens exhibit megadontia evolved in parallel with robust *Australopithecus*. *Australopithecus garhi* is certainly megadont, at least relative to craniofacial size. However, its lack of derived robust characters leaves it as a sister taxon to *Homo* but absent many derived *Homo* characters. A strictly cladistic analysis of available data has continually failed to resolve the issue of the position of *A. africanus* (*11*). The resulting currently unresolved polychotomy (Figure 5) stems from the fact that those characters most widely used in early hominid phylogenetic systematics are predominantly related to masticatory adaptation and are known to be both interdependent and susceptible to parallel evolution. Other characters such as cranial base flexion and craniofacial hafting are even more poorly understood. The atomization of such morphological complexes has led to lengthy trait lists, but the valence of the individual "characters" is clearly compromised. Such exercises have been useful in establishing the extensive homoplasy present among early hominids, but such confirmation only accentuates the precarious nature of phylogenetic reconstructions based on an incomplete and highly fragmentary fossil record.

Even a combination of all available temporal, spatial, and (circumstantial) behavioral evidence fails to resolve whether the origin of *Homo* was from South African *A. africanus* or east African *A. afarensis* (or both). We now know that a nonrobust species derived from *A. afarensis* persisted in eastern Africa until at least 2.5 Ma. Only additional fossils will confirm whether this form participated in a rapid evolutionary transition or transitions resulting in an early form or forms of *Homo*. Such rapid transition may be signaled by the recently described A. L. 266-1 palate from Hadar deposits that are claimed to be 2.33 Ma (*2*). This palate is more derived than that of *A. garhi*. If *A. garhi* is the direct ancestor of early *Homo*, as represented by such younger specimens as KNM-ER 1590 and KNM-ER 1470, additional major craniofacial changes must have occurred after 2.5 Ma, many of them as direct consequences of brain enlargement. Novel behavioral shifts associated with meat and marrow procurement by means of lithic technology may have played instrumental selective roles during this critical and perhaps short period of evolution.

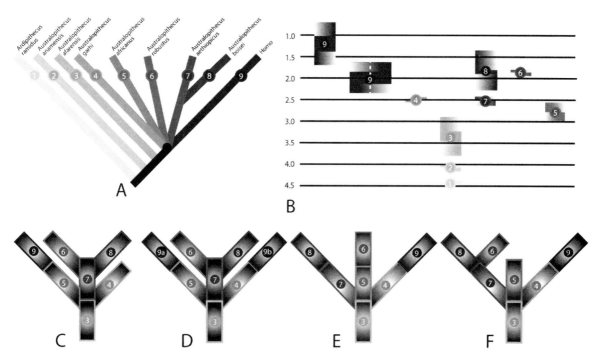

Figure 5. *(A) A cladogram depicting relationships among widely recognized early hominid taxa, including the new species A.* garhi. *Note that an additional clade is required when two contemporary forms of early* Homo *are recognized. A variety of possible cladograms have been generated from the data available in the hominid fossil record, but none of these satisfactorily resolve the polychotomy illustrated here (11). This cladogram adds* A. garhi *to the unresolved node. (B) The chronological relationships of early hominid taxa. Age is given in Ma. (C to F) Alternative phylogenies depicting possible relationships among early hominid taxa. Note that these alternatives do not exhaust the possibilities and that not all are entirely consistent with the cladogram. It is not presently possible to choose among these alternatives.*

REFERENCES AND NOTES

1. G. Suwa, T. D. White, F. C. Howell, *Am. J. Phys. Anthropol.* **101**, 247 (1996).
2. W. H. Kimbel et al., *J. Hum. Evol.* **31**, 549 (1996); D. C. Johanson and Y. Rak, *Am. J. Phys. Anthropol.* **103**, 235 (1997).
3. A. Hill, S. Ward, A. Deino, G. Curtis, R. Drake, *Nature* **355**, 719 (1992).
4. J. de Heinzelin et al., *Science* **284**, 625 (1999).
5. B. A. Wood, *Nature* **355**, 783 (1992).
6. The Chemeron temporal (3) has been called the earliest *Homo*, but the only two characters cited in support of this attribution (a medially positioned mandibular fossa and a sharp petrous crest) are missing from the Bouri holotype, and neither provides unambiguous evidence of brain expansion. Only additional discoveries will test whether Chemeron is a Kenyan representative of *A. garhi*.
7. H. M. McHenry and L. R. Berger, *J. Hum. Evol.* **35**, 1 (1998).
8. S. Hartwig-Scherer and R. D. Martin, *ibid.* **21**, 439 (1991).
9. M. G. Leakey, C. S. Feibel, I. McDougall, A. C. Walker, *Nature* **376**, 565 (1995).
10. T. D. White, G. Suwa, B. Asfaw, *ibid.* **371**, 306 (1994); *ibid.* **375**, 88 (1995).
11. A. T. Chamberlain and B. A. Wood, *J. Hum. Evol.* **16**, 119 (1987); R. R. Skelton and H. M. McHenry, *ibid.* **23**, 309 (1992); D. S. Strait, F. E. Grine, M. A. Moniz, *ibid.* **32**, 17 (1997); R. R. Skelton and H. M. McHenry, *ibid.* **34**, 109 (1997).
12. F. E. Grine, Ed., *Evolutionary History of "Robust" Australopithecines* (de Gruyter, New York, 1988); A. C. Walker, R. E. Leakey, J. M. Harris, F. H. Brown, *Nature* **322**, 517 (1986); H. M. McHenry, in *Contemporary Issues in Human Evolution*, W. E. Meikle, F. C. Howell, N. G. Jablonski, Eds. (California Academy of Sciences, San Francisco, 1996), pp. 77–92.
13. W. H. Kimbel, T. D. White, D. C. Johanson, *Am. J. Phys. Anthropol.* **64**, 337 (1984); G. Suwa et al., *Nature* **389**, 489 (1997); P. V. Tobias, *Olduvai Gorge, Volume 4: The Skulls, Endocasts and Teeth of* Homo habilis (Cambridge Univ. Press, Cambridge, 1991).
14. W. H. Kimbel, D. C. Johanson, Y. Rak, *Nature* **368**, 449 (1994).
15. A. C. Walker and R. E. Leakey, Eds., *The Nariokotome Homo erectus Skeleton* (Harvard Univ. Press, Cambridge, MA, 1993).
16. Femur and humerus length were virtually complete in A.L. 288-1 [D. C. Johanson et al., *Am. J. Phys. Anthropol.* **57**, 403 (1982)]. In BOU-VP-12/1, the femur is preserved from the intersection of the medial terminus of the neck with the (missing) femoral head (proximally) to a point on the medial supracondylar line just superior to the gastrocnemius impression (distally). This distance was measured in a sex- and species-balanced sample of *Pan, Gorilla,* and *Homo* ($N = 60$) and used to regress (least squares) femoral length [correlation coefficient (r^2) = 0.952; 95% confidence interval of estimate = ±0.28]. This regression computes the BOU-VP-12/1 femur at 348 mm. On anatomical grounds, we believe it to have actually been slightly shorter (about 335 mm). Much of the shaft of the BOU-12/1 humerus is preserved, including the point of confluence between the diaphysis and the medial epicondylar apophysis and the distalmost extent of the deltopectoral crest. This distance was used to regress humeral length with the same sample (length estimate = 226 mm; r^2 = 0.876; 95% confidence interval of estimate = ±0.40). On anatomical grounds, we estimate the humerus to have been slightly longer (about 236 mm). Radial length was estimated for A.L. 288-1 with multiple linear regressions from the same sample (breadth distal articular surface; maximum diameter radial head; length radial neck; r^2 = 0.929; 95% confidence interval of estimate = ±0.29) and for BOU-VP-12/1 (radial head to nutrient foramen; maximum diameter radial head; length radial neck; r^2 = 0.937; 95% confidence interval of estimate = ±0.27). These regressions estimate a length of 203 mm for A.L. 288-1 and 231 mm for BOU-VP-12/1. On anatomical grounds, the BOU-VP-12/1 estimate appears correct. However, we believe that the A.L. 288-1 radius is underestimated on the basis of a lack of sufficient "anatomical space" with which to accommodate all of the preserved pieces of the bone. A regression limited to a sample of common chimpanzees and bonobos ($N = 36$) estimates a length of 215 mm (r^2 = 0.529; 95% confidence interval of estimate = ±0.36). This result appears more probable. Only exceptionally pronounced errors in any of the above predictions would alter the conclusions

made in the legend of Figure 3, nor are these conclusions altered by regressions based only on single hominoid species.

17. The Middle Awash paleoanthropological project is multinational (13 countries), interdisciplinary research codirected by B. A., Y. Beyene, J. D. Clark, T. W., and G. WoldeGabriel. The research reported here was supported by the NSF. We thank N. Tahiro and A. Abdo for their assistance in naming the new species. We thank Y. Haile-Selassie for discovery of the BOU-VP-12/130 holotype and H. Gilbert and D. DeGusta for field and illustrations work. R. Holloway kindly allowed us to cite his BOU-VP-12/130 cranial capacity estimate. L. Gudz made the palate and postcranial drawings. D. Brill made the photographs. P. Reno provided comparative primate data. The Japan Ministry of Education, Science, Sports and Culture provided support to G. S. We thank the Ethiopian Ministry of Information and Culture, the Centre for Research and Conservation of the Cultural Heritage, and the National Museum of Ethiopia. We thank the Afar Regional Government and the Afar people of the Middle Awash for permission and support. We thank the many individuals who contributed to the camp, transport, survey, excavation, and laboratory work that stands behind the results presented.

30

Environment and Behavior of 2.5-Million-Year-Old Bouri Hominids

J. de Heinzelin, J. D. Clark, T. White, W. Hart, P. Renne, G. WoldeGabriel, Y. Beyene, and E. Vrba

ABSTRACT

The Hata Member of the Bouri Formation is defined for Pliocene sedimentary outcrops in the Middle Awash Valley, Ethiopia. The Hata Member is dated to 2.5 million years ago and has produced a new species of Australopithecus *and hominid postcranial remains not currently assigned to species. Spatially associated zooarchaeological remains show that hominids acquired meat and marrow by 2.5 million years ago and that they are the near contemporary of Oldowan artifacts at nearby Gona. The combined evidence suggests that behavioral changes associated with lithic technology and enhanced carnivory may have been coincident with the emergence of the* Homo *clade from* Australopithecus afarensis *in eastern Africa.*

Paleoanthropological research in the Middle Awash study area has revealed a hominid-bearing succession spanning the past 6 million years. The African hominid record is particularly ample from 3.0 to 4.0 million years ago (Ma). Numerous fossils of *Australopithecus afarensis,* which is widely thought to be ancestral to *Homo,* have been recovered from both the Middle Awash and other sites in Ethiopia, Kenya, Tanzania, and possibly Chad. Abundant *A. africanus* fossils are now available from 2.0-to 3.0-million-year-old cave deposits in South Africa. However, the east African record is relatively sparse for this same time period—one that witnessed the emergence of lithic technology and *Homo.* Asfaw et al. describe the discovery of 2.5-million-year-old hominids from Bouri in a companion paper (*1*). Here, we describe behavioral and environmental evidence demonstrating that early hominids used stone tools to butcher large mammal carcasses in an open lake margin habitat, and we also provide a stratigraphic context.

Active tectonics in the southern Afar triangle have shifted depocenters and drainages throughout the Plio-Pleistocene, creating a variety of habitats for hominid occupation and subsequently uplifting ancient sediments to modern erosional surfaces. The Bouri peninsula (Figure 1) is a tilted fault block transverse (NNW-SSE) to the Quaternary rift zone (NNE-SSW) of the southern Afar. This horst diverts the modern Awash River southward, toward the Ayelu Mountain, forming a partial dam for modern Yardi Lake. The Bouri horst resulted from multiple, closely spaced normal faults that formed a series of segmented half grabens tilted at 5° to 10° to the southwest. The parallel transverse faults are long (>20 km), dip steeply, and produce 50-m-high scarps that step eastward. These faults represent an accommodation zone [for example, (*2*)] that is apparent laterally but has been terminated centrally by recent major axial faults and buried under pyroclastic and lava flows from the Ayelu silicic and the adjacent basaltic shield volcanoes.

Kalb (*3*) followed Taieb's pioneering 1960s work in the Middle Awash. He mapped and described Bouri sediments as late middle Pleistocene, part of what he named the Wehaietu Formation. In this formation, Kalb et al. (*3*) described the Dakanihylo Member as succeeding the Bodo Member. The latter yielded the ~0.6-Ma Bodo hominid cranium in 1976, east of the modern Awash (*4, 5*). Our subsequent work has demonstrated that the geological situation at Bouri is considerably more complex. The Daka Member (abbreviation of Dakanihylo), which contains early Acheulean artifacts, is older, not younger, than the middle Pleistocene Bodo

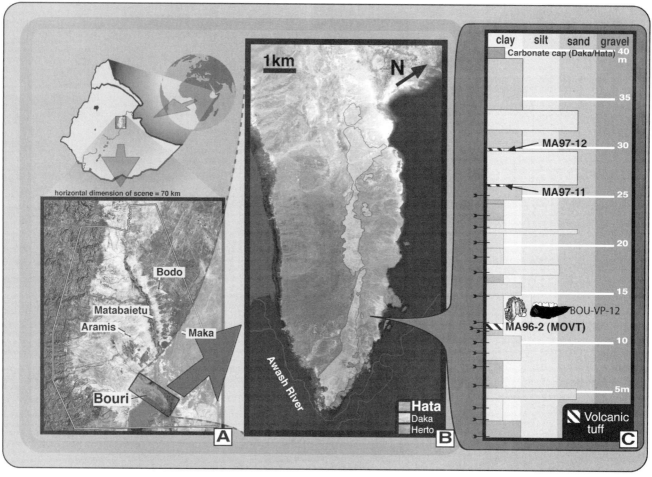

Figure 1.   *Geography and geology of the Bouri peninsula. (**A**) Landsat Thematic Mapper image showing the study area's most important fossil hominid localities. (**B**) Air photograph mosaic of the Bouri peninsula overlain by a geological map of the three members of the Bouri Formation. Faults are not shown at this scale, for clarity. (**C**) Stratigraphic column at the type locality of the Hata Member, showing the placement of the radiometrically dated MOVT and other volcanic markers (MA year, sample number), paleomagnetic sample locations (left arrows), hominid fossils, and hominid-modified bones.*

deposits (*4, 5*). Furthermore, at Bouri, this member is uncomfortably atop the previously unrecognized faunal, archaeological, and hominid-bearing Hata Member (abbreviation of Hatayae) that dates to 2.5 Ma. Stratigraphic fieldwork, biochronological analysis of collected faunas, assessment of archaeological remains, and radioisotopic dating of interbedded volcanic strata demonstrate that at least three discrete sedimentary packages spanning >2.5 million years crop out in the Bouri region. We name this succession the Bouri Formation, comprising three members with a combined thickness of ~80 m.

The youngest member of the Bouri Formation is the Herto Member, confined to the southwestern part of the Bouri horst. This member comprises ~15 m of silty clay, lacustrine limestone, beach sand with bentonite clasts, paleosols, and cross-bedded pumiceous sandstone. This member contains late Acheulean/Middle Stone Age artifacts, fauna, and hominid fossils. It has not yet been radioisotopically dated.

The underlying Daka Member contacts the Herto Member across a fault through the middle part of the

Bouri horst (Figure 1). The Daka Member is ~30 m thick and generally confined to the southern half of the Bouri horst. Its basal fluvial deposit is cross-bedded pumiceous sandstone named the Hereya Pumice unit (HPU) (Hereya is Afar for "warthog"), a horizon dated to ~1.0 Ma. The Daka Member contains early Acheulean artifacts, fauna, and hominids.

Most lithostratigraphic units of the Bouri horst are Pliocene and belong to the underlying Hata Member. At its type locality (10°15.5792′N, 40°34.0735′E), this member comprises ~40 m of variegated silty clay and paleosols, zeolitic and bentonitic tuffs, pedogenic carbonates, sandstone with bivalve and gastropod shells, and mudstone. These units were mostly deposited by fluvial processes associated with floodplains along distributary deltaic channels close to a shallow fluctuating lake. Only the upper contact of the Hata Member is exposed; the base of the formation is buried by the modern Awash River's alluvial plain.

Three volcanic units of variable thickness were identified in the Hata type section. The most prominent is the Maoleem Vitric Tuff (MOVT) (Maoleem is Afar for "dragonfly") (Figure 1). The relative scarcity of channel sand and the absence of shell beds in immediately superposed sediments indicate that it was deposited on flats surrounding the shallow lake. The MOVT is a yellow-green zeolitic tuff ~1 m thick. It contains patches of partially altered vitric material. It is exposed along strike for ~10 km and is mostly vitric in the northern part of the horst. A 6-cm diatomaceous tuff and a pinkish bentonitic tuff (4 cm thick) with abundant accretionary lapilli crop out at ~14 and 18 m above the MOVT, respectively. Both tuff layers are localized and discontinuous, are devoid of volcanic glass, and contain abundant Miocene feldspar xenocrysts. The upper Hata Member comprises poorly cemented yellow sandstone and dark-gray mudstone with bivalve fossils. This is capped by a 25-cm-thick, massive yellowish-orange pedogenic carbonate marking a major angular unconformity. Biochronological evidence indicates that the hominid-bearing sedimentary units ~9 km north of the type Hata section at Esa Dibo [Bouri Vertebrate Paleontological locality 17 (BOU-VP-17)] are roughly contemporary.

The antiquity of Hata Member sediments has been established with radioisotopic dating, paleomagnetic determinations, and biochronology. Sixty-six sanidine grains from the MOVT were analyzed individually with laser-total-fusion ^{40}Ar/^{39}Ar methods (6). Three grains were xenocrysts and yielded ages of 7 to 8 Ma. The remainder yielded mutually indistinguishable ages, whose weighted mean is 2.496 ± 0.008 Ma, based on 27.84 Ma for the Fish Canyon sanidine standard (7).

Magnetostratigraphic data were obtained from 21 samples from a 24-m interval bracketing the MOVT [methods in (6)] (Figure 1). Thermal demagnetization was performed in 12 to 15 steps per sample. Samples from this interval (Figure 1) show normal polarity overprints residing in geothite at low temperatures, but reverse polarity directions are shown above 350°C.

The age of ~2.5 Ma for the MOVT clearly identifies its reverse polarity as belonging to the Matuyama Chron [for example, (8)]. The absence of normal polarities below the MOVT indicates that the exposed 10.9-m Hata section below the MOVT is younger than the Gauss/Matuyama polarity transition, which is dated to 2.6 Ma. These observations indicate that the sub-MOVT stratigraphic interval represents ~100,000 years and, therefore, a sediment accumulation rate greater than 10.9 cm per 1000 years. The similarity of lithologies, lack of unconformities, and reversed polarities above the MOVT indicate that sedimentation rates above the MOVT were comparable to those below and therefore that the archeological, hominid, and faunal remains within 5 m above this tuff are likely to be no younger than 2.45 Ma (9).

Biochronological placement of the Hata Member fauna is in full accordance with the chronometric dating, paleomagnetic determinations, and sedimentological data. The presence of the bovids *Tragelaphus pricei*, *Beatragus whitei*, and *Damaliscus ademassui* and the suids *Metridiochoerus andrewsi* and *Kolpochoerus limnetes*, all sensitive time indicators, provides further temporal correlation with Shungura Formation (southern Ethiopia) members C to E.

We collected >400 vertebrate fossil specimens from the Hata Member (Table 1). Almost all of these come from within 3 m of the MOVT; most were found immediately above this unit. This assemblage largely reflects a mixture of grazers and water-dependent forms, which is broadly typical of later hominid-bearing Plio-Pleistocene occurrences and consistent with the sedimentological interpretation of the deposits as primarily lake marginal. Alcelaphine bovids are abundant and diverse. All indicators point to a broad featureless margin of a shallow freshwater lake. Minor changes in lake level, which were brought about by fluctuating water input, would probably have maintained broad grassy plains leading to the water's edge. As discussed below, hominids were active on this landscape.

Nearly contemporary deposits at Gona, only 96 km to the north, produced abundant surface and in situ 2.6-Ma Oldowan artifacts (10). In contrast, surveys and excavations of the Hata beds have so far failed to reveal concentrations of stone artifacts. Rare, isolated, widely scattered cores and flakes of Mode I technology appearing to have eroded from the Hata beds have been encountered during our surveys. Most of these surface occurrences are single pieces. Where excavations have been undertaken, no further artifacts have been found. However, our surveys and excavations have demonstrated that early hominids were actively using stone tools on the Pliocene Hata landscape. It is not currently possible to positively identify the creators of the earliest stone tools here or at Gona, even though *A. garhi* is currently the only recognized hominid taxon recovered from Hata sediments (1).

The first indication of hominid tool use in Hata times came during surface collection and excavation at the BOU-VP-12/1 partial skeleton locality (1), within 1 m above the MOVT. Here, several pieces of mammalian bone showed cut marks and percussion marks made by stone tools. Excavation revealed the left mandible of a medium-sized alcelaphine bovid with three successive, curvilinear striae on its posteromedial surface; these striae are unambiguous cut marks made by a sharp stone flake, presumably during tongue removal (Figure 2). At the same stratigraphic horizon 195.7 m to the south, fragments of a large bovid's tibia were found eroding from the surface. Reassembly across post-fossilization breaks showed a robust tibial midshaft segment without articular ends and with ancient fractures at both ends. The shaft bears cut marks, chop marks, and several diagnostic hammerstone impact scars on the external surface, as well as inner conchoidal scars proximally (Figure 2). Further excavation at that locality resulted in the recovery of a fairly intact, in situ *Hipparion* (three-toed horse) femur 1 m from the tibia. The femur bears stone-tool cut marks indicative of dismemberment and filleting. Our identification of these bone modifications follows procedures outlined elsewhere (11).

The bone modifications at these two excavated localities and at other localities from the same stratigraphic horizon across >2 km of outcrop demonstrate that stone tool–wielding hominids were active on the lake margin at 2.5 Ma. The bone modifications indicate that large mammals were disarticulated and defleshed and

Table 1.   Faunal List for the Hata Member, Bouri Formation

Class	Order	Family	Tribe	Genus	Species
Aves					
Reptilia					
	Lacertilia				
	Crocodilia				
	Chelonia				
Osteichthyes					
	Siluriformes	Clariidae			
Mammalia					
	Artiodactyla	Bovidae			
			Aepycerotini		
				Aepyceros	
			Alcelaphini		
				Beatragus	*whitei*
				cf. *Numidocapra*	*crassicornis*
				cf. *Rabaticeras*	*arambourgi*
				Connochaetes	*gentryi*
				Damaliscus	*ademassui*
				Megalotragus	*kattwinkeli*
				Parmularius	*rugosus*
			Antilopini	*Antidorcus*	sp.
				Gazella	*janenschi*
			Bovini	*Pelorovis*	sp.
				Syncerus	sp.
			Hippotragini	*Hippotragus*	*gigas*
				cf. *Oryx*	sp.
			Neotragini		
			Reduncini	*Kobus*	*kob*
				Kobus	*sigmoidalis*
			Tragelaphini	*Tragelaphus*	*nakuae*
				Tragelaphus	*strepsiceros*
				Tragelaphus	*pricei*
		Giraffidae		*Sivatherium*	sp.
				Giraffa	sp.
		Hippopotamidae		*Hexaprotodon*	sp.
		Suidae		*Kolpochoerus*	*limnetes*
				Metridiochoerus	*andrewsi*
				Notochoerus	sp.
	Carnivora	Felidae		*Homotherium*	sp. aff. *problematicum*
		Viverridae		*Genetta*	sp.
		Mustelidae		*Aonyx*	aff. *capensis*
	Perissodactyla	Equidae		*Hipparion*	sp.
	Primates	Hominidae		*Australopithecus*	*garhi*
		Cercopithecidae		*Theropithecus*	sp.
				Papio	sp.
	Proboscidea	Deinotheriidae		*Deinotherium*	cf. *bozasi*
		Elephantidae		*Elephas*	*recki shungurensis*

that their long bones were broken open, presumably to extract marrow, a new food in hominid evolution with important physiological, evolutionary, and behavioral effects. Similar patterns of marrow acquisition have been reported for younger sites such as Koobi Fora and Olduvai Gorge (*12*). However, the absence of abundant lithic assemblages at these Hata archaeology sites requires explanation.

At the nearby Gona site, abundant Oldowan tools were made and discarded immediately adjacent to cobble conglomerates that offered excellent, easily accessible raw materials for stone-tool manufacture. It has been suggested that the surprisingly advanced character of this earliest Oldowan technology was conditioned by the ease of access to appropriate fine-grained raw materials at Gona (*10*). Along the Karari escarpment at Koobi Fora (*13*), the basin margin at Fejej (*14*), and the lake margin at Olduvai Gorge (*12*), hominids also had easy access to nearby outcrops of raw material. In contrast, the diminutive nature of the Oldowan assemblages in the lower Omo [made on tiny quartz pebbles (*15*)] was apparently conditioned by a lack of available large clasts.

The situation on the Hata lake margin was even more difficult for early toolmakers. Here, raw materials were not readily available because of the absence of streams capable of carrying even pebbles. There were no nearby basalt outcrops. The absence of locally available raw material on the flat featureless Hata lake margin may explain the absence of lithic artifact concentrations. The bone modification evidence demonstrates that early hominids were transporting stone to the site of carcass manipulation. The paucity of evidence for lithic artifact abandonment at these sites suggests that these early hominids may have been curating their tools (cores and flakes) with foresight for subsequent use. Indications of tool curation by later hominids have been found at the more recent Pleistocene sites of Koobi Fora [Karari

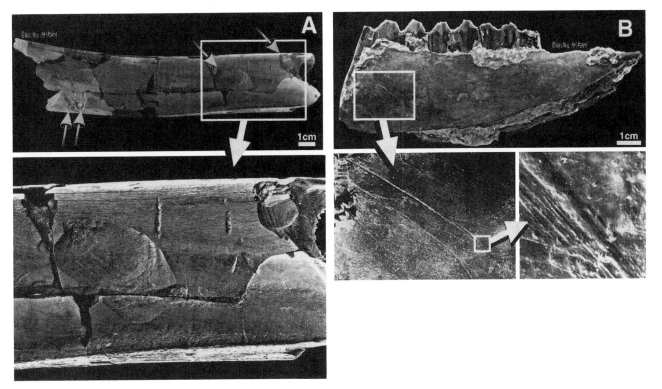

Figure 2. *Hominid modification to bovid bones from the Hata Member. Photographs © 1999 David L. Brill. White boxes show enlargement size. (A) Successive enlargements illustrating bone modifications on a large bovid's right tibial midshaft (BOU-VP-11/14). Gray arrows indicate direction of hammerstone impact deduced from striae in percussion pits. Note the large external conchoidal flakes driven off by the distal percussor impacts and the adjacent cut marks. These are the earliest documented percussion marks made by hominids who were presumably processing these bones for contained fatty marrow. (B) Successive enlargements illustrating cut marks on the medial surface of a medium-sized alcelaphine bovid's left mandible (BOU-VP-12/11), presumably made during tongue removal. Note the multiple striae and shoulder marks in the SEM (used with permission by G. Richards and B. Plowman). These are the earliest documented cut marks made by hominids.*

escarpment versus Ileret (*13*)] and Swartkrans [polished bone tools in a single repository (*16*)].

Additional research into the Hata beds may allow a determination of whether the butchery is related to hunting or scavenging. The Bouri discoveries show that the earliest Pliocene archaeological assemblages and their landscape patterning are strongly conditioned by the availability of raw material. They demonstrate that a major function of the earliest known tools was meat and marrow processing of large carcasses. Finally, they extend this pattern of butchery by hominids well into the Pliocene.

REFERENCES AND NOTES

1. B. Asfaw et al., *Science* **284**, 629 (1999).
2. N. J. Hayward and C. J. Ebinger, *Tectonics* **15**, 244 (1996).
3. J. E. Kalb et al., *Nature* **298**, 17 (1982). Eleven years later, J. E. Kalb et al. [*Newsl. Stratigr.* **29**, 21 (1993)] followed Clark et al. (*4*) in reversing Daka/Bodo Member order.
4. J. D. Clark et al., *Nature* **307**, 423 (1984).
5. J. D. Clark et al., *Science* **264**, 1907 (1994).
6. P. R. Renne, G. WoldeGabriel, W. K. Hart, G. Heiken, T. D. White, *Geol. Soc. Am. Bull.*, **111**, 869 (1999).
7. The age of this standard is now known to be slightly older [28.02 Ma (*17*)], but comparison with previous data (for example, from the Gona) is facilitated by retaining the standard age of 27.84 Ma. A table of the Ar isotopic data is available at www.sciencemag.org/feature/data/991110.shl.
8. F. J. Hilgen, *Earth Planet. Sci. Lett.* **107**, 249 (1991).
9. The sedimentation rate inferred is conservative because comparison of the ^{40}Ar/^{39}Ar age with the age of 2.6 Ma (*8*) for the Gauss/Matuyama boundary more properly requires the use of the older age of the standard (28.02 Ma) and indicates an ~10% greater sedimentation rate.
10. S. Semaw et al., *Nature* **385**, 333 (1997).
11. T. D. White, *Prehistoric Cannibalism at Mancos 5MTUMR-2346* (Princeton Univ. Press, Princeton, NJ, 1992); L. R. Binford, *Bones: Ancient Men and Modern Myths* (Academic Press, New York, 1981); R. J. Blumenschine, *J. Hum. Evol.* **29**, 21 (1995); S. D. Capaldo and R. J. Blumenschine, *Am. Antiq.* **59**, 724 (1994).
12. R. J. Blumenschine and F. T. Masao, *J. Hum. Evol.* **21**, 451 (1991).
13. G. L. Isaac, Ed., *Koobi Fora Research Project Volume 5: Plio-Pleistocene Archaeology* (Clarendon, Oxford, 1997).
14. B. Asfaw et al., *J. Hum. Evol.* **21**, 137 (1991).
15. F. C. Howell, P. Haeserts, J. de Heinzelin, *ibid.* **16**, 665 (1987).
16. C. K. Brain, Ed., *Swartkrans: A Cave's Chronicle of Early Man*, vol. 8 of *Transvaal Museum Monograph Series* (Transvaal Museum, Pretoria, 1993).
17. P. R. Renne et al., *Chem. Geol.* **145**, 117 (1998).
18. The Middle Awash paleoanthropological project is multinational (13 countries), with interdisciplinary research codirected by B. Asfaw, Y. Beyene, J. D. Clark, T. D. White, and G. WoldeGabriel. The research reported here was supported by NSF, the Ann and Gordon Getty Foundation (Berkeley Geochronology Center),

and the Institute of Geophysics and Planetary Physics of the University of California and the Earth Environmental Sciences Division at Los Alamos National Laboratory. Additional contributions were made by the Graduate School, the Office for Advancement of Scholarship and Teaching, and the Department of Geology at Miami University. We thank the Ethiopian Mapping Agency and the NASA Goddard Space Flight Center for imagery. We thank H. Gilbert for fieldwork and for work on the illustrations. D. Brill made the photographs and G. Richards and B. Plowman at the University of Pacific made the scanning electron microscope (SEM) image. T. Larson provided invaluable field and laboratory geology support. A. Defleur assisted in field survey and excavations at BOU-VP-11. We thank H. Saegusa for proboscidean identifications, D. DeGusta for primate identifications and excavations at BOU-VP-12/1, and F. C. Howell for carnivore identifications. We thank O. Lovejoy, G. Suwa, and B. Asfaw for helpful comments. We thank the Ethiopian Ministry of Information and Culture, the Centre for Research and Conservation of the Cultural Heritage, and the National Museum of Ethiopia. We thank the Afar Regional Government and the Afar people of the Middle Awash for permission and support. We thank the many individuals who contributed to the camp, transport, survey, excavation, and laboratory work that stands behind the results presented.

31

The World's Oldest Stone Artefacts from Gona, Ethiopia

Their Implications for Understanding Stone Technology and Patterns of Human Evolution between 2.6–1.5 Million Years Ago

S. Semaw

ABSTRACT

The systematic archaeological and geological survey and excavations at Gona between 1992–1994 led to the discovery of well-flaked stone artefacts which are currently the oldest known from anywhere in the world. More than 3000 surface and excavated artefacts were recovered at 15 localities documented east and west of the Kada Gona river. Based on radioisotopic dating ($^{40}Ar/^{39}Ar$) and magnetostratigraphy, the artefacts are dated between 2.6–2.5 million years ago (Ma). EG10 and EG12 from East Gona are the most informative with the highest density, providing the best opportunity for characterizing the oldest assemblages and for understanding the stone working capability of the earliest tool makers. Slightly younger artefact occurrences dated to 2.4–2.3 Ma are known from Hadar and Omo in Ethiopia, and from Lokalalei in Kenya. Cut-marked bones dated to 2.5 Ma from Bouri in Ethiopia are now providing important clues on the function of these artefacts. In addition, Australopithecus garhi *known from contemporary deposits at Bouri may be the best candidate responsible for the oldest artefacts. Surprisingly, the makers of the Gona artefacts had a sophisticated understanding of stone fracture mechanics and control similar to what is observed for Oldowan assemblages dated between 2.0–1.5 Ma. This observation was corroborated by the recent archaeological discoveries made at Lokalalei. Because of the similarities seen in the techniques of artefact manufacture during the Late Pliocene–Early Pleistocene, it is argued here that the stone assemblages dated between 2.6–1.5 Ma group into the Oldowan Industry. The similarity and simplicity of the artefacts from this time interval suggests a technological stasis in the Oldowan.*

Reprinted from *Journal of Archaeological Science*, Vol. 27, S. Semaw, The world's oldest stone artefacts from Gona, Ethiopia, pp. 1197–1214. Copyright © 2000 by Academic Press. Reprinted with permission from Elsevier.

INTRODUCTION

The results of the intensive archaeological survey, and systematic excavations between 1992–1994 have firmly established the significance of Gona for understanding the timing and context of the beginning of early stone technology (Semaw et al., 1997). The surface and excavated artefacts within the deposits exposed east of the Kada Gona below the level of a tuff named AST-2.75 are now firmly dated close to 2.6 million years ago (Ma) by a combination of Single Crystal Laser Fusion (SCLF) $^{40}Ar/^{39}Ar$ dating and magnetostratigraphy. These are currently the oldest known Late Pliocene stone artefacts, and by definition they are representatives of the earliest archaeology.

The two East Gona localities of EG10 and EG12 yielded close to 3000 surface and excavated artefacts providing the first large data set for analysing the composition and characteristics of the earliest stone assemblages, and for understanding the knapping skills of Late Pliocene hominids. Recent field research from the nearby contemporary deposits at Bouri in the Middle Awash has brought insights to the function of these artefacts by yielding evidence of bones with stone-tool cut-marks and hammerstone fractures dated to 2.5 Ma (de Heinzelin et al., 1999). It was argued for a long time that the appearance of flaked stones in the archaeological record signalled the beginning of a novel adaptation by Late Pliocene hominids with the incorporation of substantial meat in their diet (Harris, 1983; Pickford, 1990; Vrba, 1990). Thus, the two contemporary sites of Gona and Bouri are now shedding light on this issue by yielding complementary evidence, the former with abundant stone artefacts and the latter with evidence of use of such artefacts in butchery activities. An important addition from Bouri is also the discovery of *Australopithecus garhi*, the new hominid argued to be the species responsible for making the earliest stone tools (Asfaw et al., 1999). A handful of slightly younger Late Pliocene archaeological sites dated between 2.4–2.3 Ma are known from the nearby Hadar, in the Afar region of Ethiopia (Kimbel et al., 1996), Member F of the Shungura Formation in the Omo, from southern Ethiopia (Chavaillon, 1976; Merrick, 1976; Howell et al., 1987), and the Lokalalei sites of West Turkana, from northern Kenya (Roche, 1989, 1996; Kibunjia et al., 1992; Kibunjia, 1994; Roche et al., 1999).

The most informative Plio-Pleistocene archaeological sites in East Africa, providing major evidence for stone technology and the behavioural repertoire of Oldowan hominids between 2.0–1.5 Ma, are Olduvai Gorge from Tanzania (Leakey, 1971) and Koobi Fora from northern Kenya (Isaac & Harris, 1997). There are a large number of additional archaeological sites in this time period in the eastern, northern and southern parts of Africa. The archaeological sites from east Africa include Melka Kontoure, Middle Awash, Gadeb and Fejej from Ethiopia (Chavaillon et al., 1979; Clark & Kurashina, 1979; Clark et al., 1984, 1994; Asfaw et al., 1992) and Chesowanja from Kenya (Gowlett et al., 1981). Well-known sites of this interval with "pebble tools" (*galet aménagé*) from north Africa are Sidi Abderrahman from the Casablanca sequence in Morocco (Biberson, 1961; Clark, 1992) and Ain Hanech from Algeria (Balout, 1955; Sahnouni & de Heinzelin, 1998). Oldowan sites from the southern parts of the continent include Swartkrans Members 1 and 2 (Brain et al., 1988), Sterkfontein Member 5 (Kuman, 1994*a*, 1994*b*) and Kromdraai (Kuman et al., 1997). The ages of the sites from the northern and southern parts of Africa were estimated mainly based on magnetostratigraphy and faunal correlations with the East African sites, particularly with the faunal sequence documented from the well-dated Shungura sequence in the Omo.

The main artefact types found in all of the archaeological sites dated between 2.6–1.5 Ma are cores, whole and broken flakes, angular and core fragments, a small number of retouched pieces and in some instances unmodified stones transported to sites. The two basic Oldowan flaking techniques used were the hand-held percussion (for example on the volcanic rocks found at Gona and Lokalalei), and the bipolar flaking technique (the primary mode of stone working utilized on quartz, for example, at Omo). The 1.89 Ma "KBS Industry" from East Turkana has stone assemblages typical of the Oldowan. The absence of retouched pieces and spheroids/subspheroids was the criteria used for distinguishing the KBS (Isaac, 1976). Assemblages with a greater variety of artefact types including spheroids and retouched pieces become dominant later *c.* 1.5 Ma with

the so-called "Developed Oldowan". A few instances of probable retouched pieces were encountered at Gona, and there were some specimens identified into this category at Lokalalei 2C. The most distinctive of all the assemblages are the Karari scrapers from Koobi Fora dated to *c.* 1.6–1.5 Ma. These may be standardized cores probably made from split cobbles or large thick flakes (Harris, 1978).

The stone assemblages dated between 2.6–1.5 Ma conveniently group into the Oldowan Industry (*sensu* Leakey, 1971) because of similarities in the composition and simplicity of the artefacts, and in the knapping techniques practiced by the hominids. The Oldowan lasted for over 1 million years with little or no technological change and it was later replaced by an advanced stone working tradition—the Acheulian *c.* 1.5 Ma in Africa (Isaac & Curtis, 1974; Gowlett, 1988; Asfaw et al., 1992; Clark, 1994). A technological stasis for the Oldowan tradition is suggested because of its long persistency in the archaeological record (Semaw et al., 1997).

THE GONA STUDY AREA

The Gona Palaeoanthropological Research Project (GPRP) study area is located in the west-central Afar region of Ethiopia and it encompasses more than 500 km² area with artefact- and fossil-rich Plio-Pleistocene sediments (Figure 1). The study area is bounded to the east by the Hadar study area, to the north by the Mile-Bati Road, to the south by the Asbole River and to the west by the Western Ethiopian Escarpment. The major rivers within the study area, including the Kada Gona, the Ounda Gona, the Busidima and the Asbole, and associated small feeding streams, drain the surrounding areas flowing seasonally into the Awash River. A wealth of stone artefacts and fossil fauna are currently being exposed by these drainages.

More than 40 m of sediments are exposed along the Kada Gona drainage, with at least two artefact-bearing

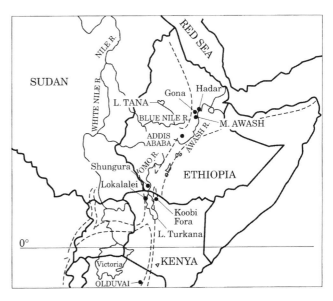

Figure 1. *A map showing Gona and Late Pliocene sites dated between 2.4–2.3 Ma.*

horizons documented in the time interval between 2.6–2.0 Ma. The deposits contain clays and silts, tuffaceous marker horizons and cobble conglomerates, which are prominent in the sections exposed within the Kada Gona and surrounding drainages. Erosion is rapid at Gona because of the high relief badlands topography, and artefacts and fauna are exposed by torrential rains and rapidly washed into modern drainages.

PREVIOUS FIELD RESEARCH AT GONA

The palaeoanthropological significance of much of the central Afar rift, including what are now recognized as the Gona, the Hadar and the Middle Awash study areas was first noticed in the late 1960s by Maurice Taieb while conducting a geological survey in the Awash river basin (Taieb, 1974 in Clark et al., 1984). More preliminary geological survey of the general area was later undertaken by Kalb (1993 and references therein). The presence of stone artefacts of great antiquity at Gona was known since the early 1970s, but the archaeology and geology of the area received only cursory attention while a wealth of remarkable fossil hominids of *Australopithecus afarensis* were being discovered from the contiguous Hadar deposits (Johanson et al., 1978, 1982).

The initial archaeological survey of the early 1970s led to the discovery of a low density scatter of surface artefacts east of the Kada Gona (Corvinus, 1976; Corvinus & Roche 1976, 1980; Roche & Tiercelin, 1977, 1980). The first archaeological locality was named Afaredo 1, and three further localities named Kada Gona 2, 3, and 4 were documented between two conglomerates identified east of the Kada Gona river. The artefacts were estimated to 2.5 Ma based on the age of the BKT-2 tuff from the Kada Hadar Member of the Hadar Formation then thought to correlate with the tuff found underlying the artefact horizon (Roche & Tiercelin, 1977, 1980). Subsequent field research by Harris (1983) in the area west of the Kada Gona resulted in the discovery of a low density of *in situ* artefacts from a small excavation opened at West Gona locality 1 (WG1 for short). There were no archaeological field studies undertaken in Ethiopia during much of the 1980s, and the first Gona field permit was issued in 1987. Two additional Oldowan localities (WG2 and WG3) were documented at West Gona during the brief survey undertaken that year (Harris & Semaw, 1989).

The first round of systematic archaeological and geological fieldwork at Gona was initiated between 1992–1994. The main objectives were to assess the palaeoanthropological potential of the general study area and to firmly resolve the age of the Kada Gona artefacts. Variable densities of surface and *in situ* artefacts were found from 12 new localities distributed east and west of the Kada Gona river (Figure 2(a)). The highest density and the most informative assemblages were those recovered from EG10 and EG12. Details of the results of this research, including the age of the artefacts and their archaeological significance, and their implications for understanding the behavioural evolution of Late Pliocene hominids, are presented here. Further intensive field and laboratory research is necessary to fully understand the geology, archaeology and palaeontology of the entire GPRP study area, and long-term systematic field studies are now under way by a large multidisciplinary team organized in 1999. The results of the new round of field and laboratory research at Gona will be reported in future publications.

STRATIGRAPHY

The GPRP study area lies within the sedimentary exposures of the Awash River basin. The Plio-Pleistocene Gona deposits are being dissected by the main rivers and their small tributaries which are currently exposing ancient sediments with extremely rich artefacts and fossil fauna. Following a preliminary geological survey of the Afar region, Kalb (1993) assigned the Gona sequence as "unconformable post-Hadar deposits" comparable in age to the Upper Pliocene Matabeitu Formation of the Middle Awash. Subsequent geological studies placed the Gona stratigraphy within the upper part of the Kada Hadar Member of the Hadar Formation (Taieb et al., 1976; Aronson et al., 1977, 1981; Semaw et al., 1997). However, the upper boundary of the Kada Hadar Member is still poorly studied, and its relationship to the Gona stratigraphy is uncertain.

Initially, three major Cobble Conglomerates and four tuffaceous marker horizons were recognized in the stratigraphic sequence exposed at Kada Gona (Roche & Tiercelin, 1977, 1980). Afaredo 1 was stratigraphically placed higher up in the section and Kada Gona 2, 3 and 4 were placed between the two conglomerates labelled as the Intermediate Cobble Conglomerate (*Conglomérat Intermédiaire*) and the Upper Cobble Conglomerate (*Conglomérat Supérieur*). The four marker tuffs from the oldest to the youngest were marked as ashes I–IV (*Cinérites* I–IV) and later three of these tuffs were relabelled by Walter (1980) as Artefact Site Tuffs 1–3 (AST-1, -2 and -3). The Kada Gona artefacts were stratified above the AST-2 tephra (Figure 2(b)). Unfortunately, the three tuffs were contaminated for K/Ar (or SCLF $^{40}Ar/^{39}Ar$) dating and have not yet yielded absolute ages for the artefacts. Geologist Craig Feibel (now at Rutgers University) was invited to work at Gona, and the first systematic and concentrated geological studies carried out between 1993–1994 provided a better resolution in terms of stratigraphic details and tephra chronology for the artefact localities found east of the Kada Gona (Semaw et al., 1997; Feibel & Wynn, no date).

The Kada Gona stratigraphic sequence can be separated into three intervals. At the base of the sequence are the lacustrine sediments with mollusc layers, a Green Marker Tuff, (a possible equivalent of the BKT-2L$_1$ of Hadar well-exposed near EG10), and an overlying tuff which may be a possible chemical correlate of the BKT-2L of Hadar. Above these are the six fluvial cycles with the three major conglomerates (and three additional less prominent ones), and the artefact-bearing layers containing the oldest artefacts and the interbedded marker tuffs (labelled from bottom to top as AST-1, -2, -2.5, -2.75 and AST-3). Uppermost in the sequence at East Gona are the capping strata characterized by fine-grained sediments and consolidated sand layers. The two

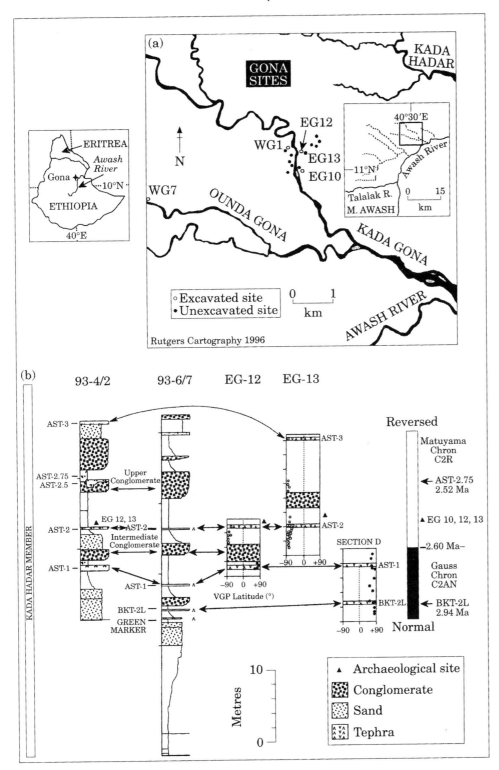

Figure 2. *(a) A map showing the excavated and surface-sampled Kada Gona localities. The excavated localities are shown with open circles. (b) Stratigraphy of the Kada Gona sites. Lithostratigraphy and markers from East Gona. The composite sections (93–4/2 and 93–6/7) are correlated with the magnetostratigraphy of EG12 and EG13. Stratigraphic markers are indicated next to the columns and correlations shown with solid lines. Normal polarity is indicated by filled circles, and reversed polarity by open circles. Absolute dates are provided with units of the magnetic polarity timescale (MPTS) on the right (figure after Semaw et al., 1997).*

new tuffs named AST-2.5 and AST-2.75 were identified in 1993 in the stratigraphic sequence exposed near EG10 and EG12. The AST-2.75 (discussed below) proved to be significant for absolute age determinations of the two excavated localities. The oldest Gona artefacts are exposed stratigraphically below the AST-2.75 and above the AST-2 tuffs. Slightly younger artefact occurrences, estimated to be *c.* 2.0 Ma are widely distributed within the capping strata. AST-2 is the only marker thus far identified west of

the Kada Gona, and it is found variably exposed below the artefact occurrences documented there.

DATING

Attempts were made earlier to tie the Gona AST tuffs to the three Bouroukie Tuffs (BKT-1, -2 and -3) identified within the Kada Hadar Member (Aronson et al., 1977). Initial age estimates for the Gona artefacts were made based on the age of the Hadar BKT-2 tuff. The age of the BKT-2 tuff was problematic because of several revised dates that ranged between 2.65–3.14 Ma, implying the approximate age of the artefacts to be anywhere between 2.5–3.0 Ma (Aronson et al., 1977, 1980, 1981; Walter, 1980; Walter & Aronson, 1982; Hall et al., 1985). Correlation and dating efforts were further complicated because the BKT-2 tuffs are exposed as duplets and triplets named BKT-2u, BKT-2L and BKT-2L$_1$ (Walter, 1980). The Gona AST-1 and -2 tuffs were suggested to be equivalent to the Hadar BKT-2L and BKT-2u tuffs, respectively (Walter, 1980; Tiercelin, 1986). Because of the wide margin of the dates for the BKT-2, the Gona artefacts were loosely and conservatively estimated to *c.* 2.5 Ma with no firm dates (Harris, 1983). Because of the lack of absolute dates for the Gona deposits, the 2.5 Ma age suggested for the artefacts was received with caution (for example, Isaac, 1984; Toth & Schick, 1986; Kibunjia, 1994). Therefore, resolving the age of the Gona deposits was among the major priorities of the field research undertaken during the early 1990s.

The plagioclase-phyric bentonite AST-2.75 tuff identified above the AST-2 marker at East Gona played a critical role in determining the age for the two excavated localities of EG10 and EG12 (Figure 2(b)). Volcanic crystals from AST-2.75 were dated by ^{40}Ar/^{39}Ar to 2.517+0.075. This tuff is stratigraphically placed *c.* 5 m above EG10 and EG12 (and directly above locality EG13), providing a minimum age of 2.52 Ma for the oldest Gona artefacts. A detailed palaeomagnetic analysis of the sediments sampled in 1993 from the stratigraphic sections exposed at the surface and excavated East Gona localities revealed that the 2.6 Ma Gauss-Matuyama polarity transition (McDougall et al., 1992) occurred within the Intermediate Cobble Conglomerate, which is stratigraphically located just below the artefact horizon and the AST-2 marker tuff. Therefore, the palaeomagnetic analysis gave a maximum age for the EG10 and EG12 artefacts, also corroborating the minimum 2.52 Ma ^{40}Ar/^{39}Ar date obtained for the AST-2.75 (Semaw et al., 1997). Stratigraphically, the artefacts are actually closer to the reversed magnetozone identified as the lowermost Matuyama chron (2.6 Ma). An ^{40}Ar/^{39}Ar analysis of the unnamed tuff (a possible chemical correlate of the Hadar BKT-2L), sampled from the base of the Kada Gona sequence stratigraphically below EG10, yielded an age of 2.940 + 0.006 Ma (Semaw et al., 1997). This date is consistent with the 2.95 Ma ^{40}Ar/^{39}Ar age reported for the main BKT-2L from the Kada Hadar Member (Kimbel et al., 1994; Walter, 1994). In addition, the BKT-2u from Hadar was dated to 2.92 Ma. The older date for the tuff sampled below EG10 is consistent with the stratigraphy of the Kada Gona sequence. The stratigraphic relationships between the Gona and Hadar deposits have yet to be resolved. The 1992–1994 research has shown that except for the possibility of the BKT-2L$_1$ and BKT-2L, there appears to be no apparent lithochronological or geochemical correlations between the AST Kada Gona tuffs and the BKT Hadar tuffs (Semaw et al., 1997).

THE GONA ARTEFACT LOCALITIES

A total of 12 new archaeological localities were identified at East and West Gona between 1992–1994. These are in addition to the previous Afaredo 1, Kada Gona 2, 3 and 4 localities of Roche and Tiercelin (1977, 1980), the WG1 locality discovered by Harris (1983), and the West Gona localities of Harris & Semaw (1989). During the 1992 survey, hundreds of stone artefacts were found eroding down steep slopes at EG10 and EG12, and the high density of the artefacts and their very fresh nature indicated that the materials had been exposed from the overlying sediments very recently. The surface artefacts exposed at EG10 and EG12 consisted of cores, flakes and a large number of smaller size angular fragments indicating a high probability of recovering undisturbed primary context assemblages through further excavations. Nearly 3000 artefacts were recovered from surface and systematic excavations carried out at the two localities (Table 1). Additional artefact concentrations were documented at several localities distributed within laterally extensive deposits traced above the AST-2 tephra. Surface occurrences with cores, flakes and angular fragments were sampled at several localities from the east and west sides of the Kada Gona. Most of the archaeological localities exposed on the east side of the Kada Gona were clearly associated with the AST-2 marker tuff and the Intermediate Cobble Conglomerate. Therefore, they are the same age as EG10 and EG12. Further detailed geological work is necessary to determine the age of the archaeological localities exposed within the capping strata. Localities WG1 and WG7 are the only excavated assemblages from west of the Kada Gona. WG7 was the furthest Oldowan locality documented at the time from the Ounda Gona, and its stratigraphic relationship to EG10 and EG12 needs further investigation.

THE TWO EXCAVATED LOCALITIES OF EG10 AND EG12

East Gona 10 (EG10)

A high density of fresh stone artefacts were found eroding down in the section exposed east of the Kada Gona approximately 5–7 km upstream from its confluence with the Awash river. Locality EG10 and the Kada Gona river are shown in Figure 3. The artefacts consisted of cores, whole and broken flakes and a high density of angular fragments. The volcanic tuffs including the Green Marker, the unnamed tuff (the possible equivalent of the BKT-2L from Hadar), the AST-1, and -2, and the Lower and the Intermediate Cobble Conglomerates are well exposed in the section (Figure 2(b)). An area of 38 m^2 was gridded at EG10 following the edge of the outcrops and 1549 artefacts were collected from the surface and surface scrapes. A total of 667 artefacts were excavated from an area of 13 m^2 (9 + 3 m^2 extensions added to the north and 1 m^2 to the southeast). The horizontal and vertical distribution of the excavated

Table 1. Composition and Percent of Artefact Types, the 2.5 Ma Gona and Late Pliocene Archaeological Sites Dated to 2.3–2.4 Ma

Artefact category	East Gona				West Turkana				Omo									
	EG10		EG12		Lokalalei 1		Lokalalei 2C		FtJi1		FtJi2		FtJi5		Omo 57		Omo123	
	Exc.	Surf.	Exc.	Surf.	Exc.	Surf.	Exc.	Surf.	Exc.	Surf.	Exc.	Surf.	Exc.	Surf.	Exc.	Surf.	Exc.	Surf.
Cores	0.97	2.40	0.97	2.03	11.99	6.12	2.61	2.91	0.26	7.00	1.35	4.60		3.90		3.68	1.56	2.37
Whole flakes	17.82	24.44	30.42	33.11	17.51	12.24	16.88	27.71	4.50	11.10	1.79	10.80	4.20	7.80	23.34	25.15	38.86	34.12
Flake fragments	6.13	7.65	12.62	11.71	55.63	81.64	57.14	55.62	2.10									
Angular fragments	73.53	63.27	54.05	50.90	11.99		16.06	12.02	93.30	81.85	96.90	84.60	95.80	87.00	70.00	65.03	56.45	56.31
Retouched pieces							0.44	0.78										
Piece*															6.66	9.81	0.26	0.30
Core fragments	1.55	2.25	1.62	2.25			0.44	0.19							6.66	6.14	2.35	6.90
Hammerstones							0.82											
Modified pebbles					2.88		3.34	0.78										
Unmodified pieces			0.32				2.27											
Total number of artefacts	1549	667	309	444	417	49	2067	516	375	270	223	130	24	77	30	193	767	1014

Exc.=Excavated, Surf.=Surface artefacts.

*The meaning of this category is not clear, and exists only in the inventory of Chavaillon (1976) (in Howell et al., 1987: p. 679).

Source for the Omo artefacts, Howell et al. (1987: p. 59). Broken flakes and small flakes are included together; all the core categories are included together, and broken cores are listed as core fragments.

Source for Lokalalei 2C, Roche et al. (1999: p. 59). Worked pebbles and broken pebbles are included together. Unmodified pebbles are listed under Unmodified pieces.

Source for Lokalalei 1, Kibunjia (1994: p. 164). Artefacts from both the 1987 and 1991 excavations are included together.

Data not yet available for Hadar.

Figure 3. *A photo showing the EG10 excavation and the Kada Gona river.*

artefacts are shown in Figure 4. There were no fossilized bones retrieved from the excavations. The sediments were fine-grained with well consolidated brown clay and glass shards from the altered AST-2 tephra chemically identified within and below the artefact levels. There were two artefact levels at EG10 separated by 40 cm thick deposits. The artefacts from both levels were restricted within 10 cm thick layers each suggesting minimal or no vertical displacement after discard. In addition, the fresh nature of the artefacts and the absence of discernible size sorting indicated a primary geological context. The presence of two horizontally discrete artefact levels may hint at repeated occupation at this locality which may be a result of its close proximity to raw material sources and water. The excavation was extended into a geological trench towards the north down to the level of the Intermediate Cobble Conglomerate, but there were no artefacts recovered from the underlying sediments. The fact that the artefact density is high in the south and southeast portion of the excavated area, and the presence of artefacts still eroding down the slope some 100 m to the south suggests that there may still be a high density of artefacts buried under the overburden.

East Gona 12 (EG12)

This locality is found in the Aybayto Dora stream, a small drainage feeding into Kada Gona from the east. EG12 is located *c.* 300 m north of the EG10 excavation and *c.* 100 m west of locality EG13. The two localities of EG12 and EG13 hold similar stratigraphic positions. All the volcanic marker tuffs and Cobble Conglomerates found in the section exposed at EG10 are also present here. The AST-2 tephra at EG12 is stratigraphically less than 0.5 m below the artefact horizon. The Upper Cobble Conglomerate is well-exposed *c.* 15 m above

EG12. A high density of surface artefacts were found exposed on a very steep-sided slope at EG12. The composition of the artefacts was similar to EG10. Following the edge of the outcrops, an area of 26 m² was gridded down to the level of the Intermediate Cobble Conglomerate. The horizontal and vertical distribution of the excavated artefacts are shown in Figure 5. A total of 309 artefacts were retrieved from surface and surface scrapes. About 1 m of overburden was removed before reaching the artefact horizon and an area of 8 m² (with additional 1 m² to the southwest) was excavated within fine-grained floodplain sediments yielding a total of 444 artefacts *in situ*. The artefacts were tightly clustered within 40 cm thick well-consolidated brown clay. Preservation and sediment characters were similar to EG10 and there were no fossilized bones recovered at EG12.

ASSEMBLAGE CHARACTERISTICS

The composition and characteristics of the artefacts from EG10 and EG12 are broadly similar to other Plio-Pleistocene Oldowan assemblages known in Africa from deposits dated between 2.6–1.5 Ma (Table 1). The Gona assemblages consist of cores, whole and broken flakes and a high density of angular fragments. Using criteria developed by Leakey (1971) for Olduvai Gorge Bed I and Lower Bed II, the Gona cores can be classified as choppers, discoids, polyhedrons and heavy duty core scrapers (Table 2, Figure 6). Almost 99% of the artefacts fall into the category of *débitage* which include whole and broken flakes, and angular and core fragments. A majority of the whole flakes from Gona show prominent bulbs of percussion and smooth release surfaces. Retouched pieces are very rare. There are no specimens identified as manuports except for one split cobble collected from the surface at EG12. Pitting and

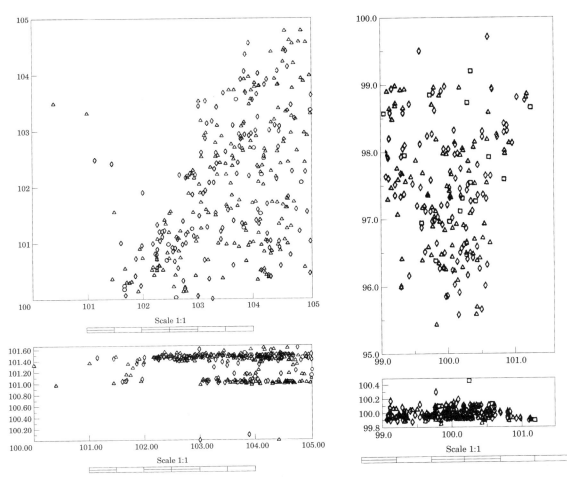

Figure 4. *Horizontal and vertical distribution of the EG10 excavated artefacts.*

Figure 5. *Horizontal and vertical distribution of the EG12 excavated artefacts.*

Table 2. Gona, Unifacially and Bi/Multifacially Flaked Pieces

	EG10				EG12			
	Surface		Excavated		Surface		Excavated	
	Uni	Bi/Multi	Uni	Bi/Multi	Uni	Bi/Multi	Uni	Bi/Multi
Side choppers	3	2	8	0	1	0	4	1
End choppers	3	0	0	0	1	0	0	0
Side and end choppers	2	2	2	1	0	0	0	3
Discoids	1	0	1	2	1	0	0	0
Core scraper	0	2	0	1	0	0	0	1
Polyhedron	0	0	0	1	0	0	0	0
Total	9	6	11	5	3	0	4	5
%	60.00	40.00	68.75	31.25	100.00	0.00	44.44	55.55

Uni=Unifacially worked, Bi/Multi=Bifacially or Multifacially worked.

bruising marks identified on some of the cores may hint to repeated bashing of the cobbles during the process of flaking or may be a result of utilization for pounding activities, for example as hammerstones for breaking bones for marrow. However, one has to exercise caution because field observations have shown that weathering may also mimic these features as a result of exfoliation of the cortex on some of the surface exposed cores.

Although a majority of the Gona cores were unifacially worked, they were very well-flaked, suggesting experienced knapping skills and mastery of the mechanics of conchoidal fracture by their makers (Figure 6). Following Leakey (1971), some of the bifacial cores made of elongated cobbles could have been classified as proto-bifaces. Current understanding of the Oldowan technology strongly suggests that Plio-Pleistocene

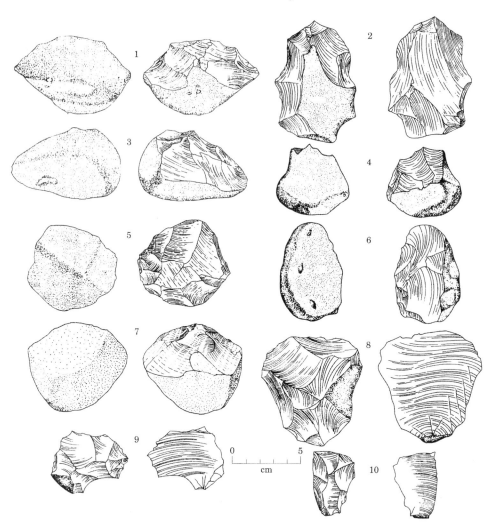

Figure 6. *Drawings of artefacts (cores and whole flakes), excavated from EG10 and EG12. (1) unifacial chopper, EG10, (2) discoid, EG10, (3) unifacial side chopper, EG12, (4) unifacial end chopper, EG12, (5) partial (irregular discoid), EG12, (6) unifacial side chopper, EG10, (7) unifacial side chopper, EG12, (8–10) whole flakes, EG10.*

hominids were mainly after the production of sharp-edged flakes for use as cutting implements, with no pre-determined design intended for the shape of the end product (Toth, 1982, 1985, 1987). For example, experimental replication of the artefacts from Koobi Fora has shown that the final shape of the Oldowan cores and flakes were dictated mainly by the size and morphology of the clasts available, the flaking quality of the raw materials and the extent of flaking afforded during the course of reduction of the cores (Toth, 1982, 1985, 1987). In order to avoid the functional implications inferred from Leakey's (1971) elaborate typology, Isaac et al. (1981) outlined a scheme for classifying early stone assemblages from a simple technological perspective. These were the *Flaked Pieces* (cores/choppers), *Detached Pieces* (flakes and fragments), *Pounded Pieces* (cobbles utilized as hammerstones, etc.) and *Unmodified Pieces* (manuports, stones transported to sites). This is a useful technological approach for describing early stone assemblages, but it may mask certain details important for examining behavioural changes in artefact manufacture and use during the Late Pliocene–Early Pleistocene. The use of Leakey's (1971) typology is still important for comparing early stone assemblages because most artefacts of this period have been described

following her conventions (for example, Chavaillon, 1976; Merrick, 1976; Isaac & Harris, 1997). Further technological studies may be essential for devising typological schemes standard for classifying early stone assemblages, and for understanding significant behavioural changes, if any, in Oldowan artefact manufacture through time.

The Cores

There were a total of 31 cores (16 *in situ*) from EG10 and a total of 12 cores (9 *in situ*) from EG12 (Table 2). A majority of the Gona cores were worked unifacially from rounded trachyte cobbles (very few on split cobbles). Although most were unifacial, the Gona cores were surprisingly very well-flaked for such an early age. The makers were involved in bold flaking, with excellent eye-hand coordination when seeking acute angles and removing large flakes from cobbles. Despite the unifacial pattern of flaking seen at Gona, some of the cores were exhaustively flaked with negative impression of several generations of scars present. In addition, they were selecting for fine-grained raw materials and a majority of the flakes removed had smooth release surfaces. Using the criteria of Leakey (1971), the majority of the cores (*Flaked Pieces* of Isaac et al., 1981) were identified as unifacial side choppers. Nearly 20% of the excavated cores from EG10, and 55% from EG12 were bifacially worked (Table 2). There were pieces identified as discoids, polyhedrons and core scrapers from EG10, but most of the cores from EG12 were side choppers and side and end choppers (except for 1 discoid recovered from the surface).

The *in situ* cores from EG10 range in maximum dimensions between 67–106 mm with a mean of 83 mm (s.d. = 10), and the EG12 cores vary in size between 58–92 mm with a mean of 77 mm (s.d. = 9). Scar counts on *in situ* cores vary between 8–14 scars at EG10 (mean = 11, s.d. = 1) and between 3–23 at EG12 (mean = 11, s.d. = 5). There are no pieces from EG10 and EG12 identified as hammerstones or unmodified pieces.

Débitage

The *Detached Pieces* (of Isaac et al., 1981) produced during the process of the reduction of the cores were classified as *débitage* following the criteria outlined by Leakey (1971). These include whole and broken flakes (split, snapped, and split and snapped), and angular and core fragments. Close to 99% of the artefacts from both EG10 and EG12 were identified into this category. The most informative in terms of hominid knapping skills and early stone technology are the whole flake category (details are discussed below). The other *débitage* categories are dealt with in greater detail in Semaw (1997) and will not be discussed here.

The Whole Flakes

The complete *Detached Pieces* with diagnostic striking platform, bulbs of percussion and a clear release surface were identified as whole flakes. There were a total of 438 (275 surface and 163 excavated) from EG10 and a total of 241 (94 surface and 147 excavated) whole flakes recovered from EG12. The whole flakes from EG10 account for 18% of the artefacts identified as *débitage*, where as 30% of the whole flakes from EG12 fall into this category. The most striking feature of the whole flakes from Gona is the presence of clear and prominent bulbs of percussion on a large number of the specimens (Figure 6). As is the case with the cores, trachyte was the dominant raw material.

The flake type system developed by Toth (1982) was used in order to examine the stages of flaking represented at these localities. Toth (1982, 1987) recognized six flake-types based on presence/absence of cortex on the striking platform and dorsal surface of whole flakes. These include Type I (cortex platform/cortex dorsal), Type II (cortex platform/part cortex dorsal), Type III (cortex platform/no cortex dorsal), Type IV (no cortex platform/cortex dorsal), Type V (no cortex platform/part cortex dorsal), and Type VI (no cortex platform/no cortex dorsal). Cortical flakes (Toth types I, II and IV) are rare, and the whole flakes are dominated by Toth types III, V and VI. Observations from experimental replicative work suggest that the preponderance of

Toth Type III in the whole flakes seem to be consistent with the abundance of extensively flaked unifacial cores at Gona (Toth, pers. comm.). Dorsal scar counts on the whole flakes attest that the hominids were actively working on reducing the cores. The number of dorsal scars on the *in situ* whole flakes from EG10 vary between 1–12 (mean = 3, s.d. = 2), and those from EG12 range between 0-7 counts (mean = 2, s.d. = 1). In terms of sizes, the maximum dimensions of the *in situ* whole flakes from EG10 range between 10–85 mm (mean = 38, s.d. = 16), and those from EG12 between 10–128 mm (mean = 34, s.d. = 16).

Raw Materials

Trachyte was the main raw material utilized for making the EG10 and EG12 excavated artefacts, accounting for more than 70% of the assemblages. The trachyte from Gona tends to be fine-grained, light-brown or grey in colour often with phenocrysts and dark brown cortex. The main raw material sources for the Gona tool-making hominids were stones from nearby ancient streams accessible in the form of water-worn, rounded, fist-sized cobbles. For example, the presence of a channel cut-and-fill geologically documented between EG12 and EG13 indicated that the clasts from the underlying Intermediate Cobble Conglomerate were readily available from nearby ancient streams for tool-making hominids *c.* 2.5–2.6 Ma. This same conglomerate is exposed laterally for more than 1 km, and a total of 103 cobbles suitable for making artefacts were randomly picked from the conglomerate exposed below EG10 for a preliminary assessment of the dominant raw material types accessible for making the Gona artefacts. The size of the clasts picked vary between 170–60 mm (mean = 105, s.d. = 28). About 48% of the raw material types were identified as trachyte (or trachytic ignimbrite). Raw materials identified as rhyolite accounted for 27%, lava for 23% and chalcedony and breccia for the remaining 2%. Artefacts made of rare and exotic raw materials such as chert are known from WG2 and EG13. The preponderance of trachyte (>70% of the EG10 and EG12 assemblage) at Gona implies that the hominids had a preference for this particular raw material, and they selected it over others because of its good flaking quality.

LATE PLIOCENE ARTEFACT ASSEMBLAGES FROM OTHER EAST AFRICAN SITES

There are only a handful of archaeological sites in Africa which are older than 2.0 Ma. These include the Omo, Hadar and Bouri localities from Ethiopia (Chavaillon, 1976; Merrick, 1976; Howell et al., 1987; Kimbel et al., 1996; de Heinzelin et al., 1999), and the Lokalalei sites from Kenya (Roche, 1989, 1996; Kibunjia et al., 1992; Kibunjia, 1994; Roche et al., 1999). With the exception of Gona and Bouri, the age of these sites cluster between 2.3–2.4 Ma. There are two sites, Senga 5a from Eastern Zaire and Mwimbi from the Chiwondo Beds in Malawi, with claims for the presence of archaeological sites with estimated ages of *c.* 2.2–2.3 Ma.

However, there are no absolute dates to corroborate these claims (Harris et al., 1987, 1990; Kaufulu & Stern, 1987).

It will be important to provide a brief review on the context and assemblage characteristics of the artefacts from the well-dated Late Pliocene Lokalalei sites for a better understanding of the issues raised by various researchers on the beginning of stone working technology and on the knapping skills of the earliest tool makers, and thereby for assessing the industrial affinity of the earliest artefact assemblages.

There are two Late Pliocene archaeological localities at West Turkana including Lokalalei 1 (GaJh5) excavated in 1987 and 1991 (Kibunjia et al., 1992; Kibunjia, 1994), and Lokalalei 2C (LA2C) excavated in 1997 (Roche et al., 1999). The artefacts at both localities were found within the same horizon traced stratigraphically above the Kalochoro tuff. This tuff was chemically correlated to tuff F of the Shungura Formation and the Lokalalei artefacts were dated to 2.3–2.4 Ma (Feibel et al., 1989). *Australopithecus boisei/aethiopicus* is the only hominid known thus far at West Turkana from deposits that are near contemporary with these artefacts (Walker et al., 1986). The Lokalalei assemblages are important for understanding Late Pliocene hominid stone working technology, and their behavioural implications require a closer examination.

Lokalalei 1 (GaJh5)

A total of 466 stone artefacts (417 excavated) including cores whole and broken flakes, angular fragments and pounded pieces were recovered at Lokalalei 1 (Kibunjia, 1994). The artefacts were in silty claystones, and they were fresh. Two bones with possible cut marks were identified from the excavations. More than 50 cores were identified which average close to 100 mm in size. The main raw material used was lava. According to Kibunjia (1994: p. 165), despite the presence of "opportune striking platforms on the cobbles", the cores were not intensively flaked, with only 1–12 flake scar counts. "About 80% of the flaking scars on these cores are characterized by step fractures and only a few instances of complete flake removals were observed.... Cores appear to have been abandoned after several attempts of flaking if most of the products obtained were the step/hinge flakes" (Kibunjia, 1994: p. 165). There were also some well-flaked cores at Lokalalei 1. The presence of two types of cores (several with lots of steps/hinges, and some well-flaked) was recognized, but the reasons for these differences were not adequately explained. Nonetheless, Kibunjia (1994: p. 165) concluded that "factors other than raw material account for the poor technology" and he named a new "Nachukui Industry" (also referred to as the "Nachukui facies") to differentiate Lokalalei 1 from assemblages that postdate 2.0 Ma. The "Shungura facies" earlier named by Chavaillon (1976) for the Omo was accepted as a distinct industry (facies), and both were assigned into a new Omo Industrial Complex. With no details yet available, the Gona artefacts were also included in this Industrial Complex (Kibunjia, 1994).

Lokalalei 2C (LA2C)

The artefact occurrences at LA2C are *c.* 1 km distance from Lokalalei 1 (Roche et al., 1999). LA2C yielded over 2500 stone artefacts which consisted of cores and *débitage* and some retouched pieces. Unique to the assemblages is the presence of a large number of refitting pieces, accounting for 20% of the excavated artefacts. There were no cut-marked bones at LA2C. Ten different raw materials were identified as potential sources, but basalt and phonolite were selected and used. The cobbles ranged from coarse to fine-grained basalt, with minimal flaking observed on the coarse-grained cobbles (Roche et al., 1999).

Remarkable differences in technology and motor skills are reported for the Lokalalei 1 and LA2C assemblages (Roche, 1989; Kibunjia, 1994; Roche et al., 1999). Despite the fact that both localities were traced within the same stratigraphic horizon separated by only *c.* 1 km, the Lokalalei 1 hominids were suggested to be less competent in striking flakes from cobbles (Roche, 1989, 1996; Kibunjia, 1994), and the LA2C artefacts were described as "sophisticated", and the hominids more advanced in cognitive and motor skills capable of striking flakes from prepared platforms (Roche et al., 1999). Furthermore, the two types of cores, i.e. the "less elaborate", apparently flaked from the coarse-grained basalt and the more elaborate struck from the fine-grained cobbles, were found in both the Lokalalei 1 and LA2C assemblages.

THE STONE WORKING TECHNOLOGY/ ARTEFACT TRADITION BETWEEN 2.6–1.5 MA

The industrial affinity of the stone assemblages known from archaeological sites that are dated between 2.6–2.0 Ma remained controversial until the discovery of a high density of well-flaked artefacts from EG10 and EG12 (Semaw, 1997; Semaw et al., 1997). Late Pliocene hominid understanding of the mechanics of conchoidal fracture, and their ability to strike workable flakes from cores prior to 2.0 Ma has been questioned by a number of archaeologists (Chavaillon, 1976; Piperno, 1989; Roche, 1989; Kibunjia, 1994). These researchers argued that the hominids who lived prior to 2.0 Ma had poor coordination and less knapping skills compared to the more competent stone knappers who made the Oldowan known later in the Early Pleistocene (for example at Olduvai and Koobi Fora). A "pre-Oldowan" phase was suggested by the main proponents of the idea (Roche, 1989, 1996; Piperno, 1989) to differentiate the pre-2.0 Ma assemblages from the "elaborate" Oldowan artefacts known later between 2.0–1.5 Ma. However, the validity of this assessment was put in to question following the discovery of the oldest well-flaked artefacts at Gona which were assigned to the Oldowan Industry (Semaw et al., 1997). The recent discovery from LA2C corroborates Semaw et al.'s (1997) earlier observation on the sophisticated understanding of stone flaking techniques by ancestral hominids prior to 2.0 Ma.

The two opposing views of Roche, (1) that all the artefact assemblages that are older than 2.0 Ma are technologically less elaborate and group into the "pre-Oldowan" (1989, 1996), and (2) that the 2.3–2.4 Ma artefacts from LA2C are "sophisticated" (Roche et al., 1999), were arguments forwarded based on ideas mainly derived from the study of the artefacts from the two spatio-temporally associated Lokalalei sites. Semaw et al. (1997) have shown that the hominids responsible for making the 2.5–2.6 Ma Gona artefacts understood the flaking properties of the raw materials available, that they selected for appropriate cobbles for making artefacts and that they were as competent as Early Pleistocene hominids in their knapping skills (Figure 6). Roche et al.'s (1999) discovery indicated that the hominids at LA2C had access to basalt (coarse-grained and fine-grained), and the majority of the refitted artefacts were made of the fine-grained type. This evidence clearly shows that the earliest tool makers selected for finer and better-flaking raw materials. In addition, albeit small quantity, the artefacts from Hadar are typical of the Oldowan tradition (Kimbel et al., 1996). Contemporary hominids at Omo had access to small sized quartz pebbles, and the small size of the artefacts at Omo was dictated by the size and flaking quality of the quartz raw materials (Merrick, 1976).

The main thrust of Semaw et al.'s (1997) argument was to show that the "pre-Oldowan" designation suggested earlier by Roche (1989, 1996; and Piperno, 1989), and the Omo Industrial Complex subsequently proposed by Kibunjia (1994) for assemblages older than 2.0 Ma are not warranted because of the presence of well-flaked artefacts from the Gona deposits and LA2C. Because of the similarities among the cores and the high level of flaking skills observed, the stone artefacts dated between 2.6–1.5 Ma group into the Oldowan Industry (*sensu* Leakey, 1971), and there is no compelling evidence for a "pre-Oldowan" phase. Differences in raw material types, quality of flaking and distances to sources may account for the relatively greater degree of core reductions shown for the Olduvai and Koobi Fora artefacts compared to Gona and other Late Pliocene assemblages (Semaw et al., 1997). Because of a lack of remarkable differences in the techniques and styles of artefact manufacture for over 1 million years (2.6–1.5 Ma), a technological stasis was suggested for the Oldowan Industry (Semaw et al., 1997). A recent study of the artefact assemblages from this time period by Ludwig & Harris (1998) is in agreement with the technological stasis proposed here.

Contrary to earlier views for Lokalalei 1, the LA2C excavated artefacts were argued to be "sophisticated" (Roche et al., 1999). How sophisticated were the LA2C artefacts compared to older, contemporary or younger Oldowan assemblages? This point is not clear from the refitting analysis. In addition, according to Roche et al. (1999: p. 59), "the stasis hypothesis cannot hold out against the detailed technological analysis of the LA2C". How the discovery of these abundant refitting pieces imply more "sophistication" and how their analysis refutes the "technological stasis" hypothesis need further explanations. The presence of a high

percentage of refitting pieces at LA2C at 2.3–2.4 Ma strongly suggests that the fine-grained basalt cobbles accessible for the Lokalalei hominids were of good flaking quality, the site was well-preserved and it was not disturbed by fluvial processes (for example, see Schick, 1986, 1987). There were two grades of basalt cobbles (coarse and fine-grained) used at Lokalalei 1 and LA2C. It is possible that the fine-grained cobbles flaked well yielding a large number of the refitting pieces, and the coarse-grained cobbles did not flake well and they were discarded after several attempts failed to produce flakes sustainable for use (see Kibunjia, 1994). It seems that experimental replicative work is required to determine the influence of the raw materials (for example, Toth, 1982; Jones, 1994), and to explain why there are "technologically sophisticated" and "less elaborate" cores within the assemblages of the spatio-temporally well-constrained Lokalalei sites which are within walking distance from each other. The flaking quality of the cobbles and the distances hominids had to travel to acquire raw materials had bearing on the nature and degree of core reductions seen in the assemblages documented during the Late Pliocene. The Omo artefacts were technologically simple and smaller in size because they were made of small size quartz brought from further distances (Merrick, 1976). The well-flaked nature of the Gona artefacts, and the presence of a high concentration at EG10 and EG12 can be explained by the fact that the hominids at Gona had easy access to well-flaking raw materials available from nearby ancient streams.

Simple unifacially and bifacially flaked cores, and a very high percentage of *débitage* are the main artefacts known in almost all of the Late Pliocene–Early Pleistocene Oldowan assemblages. Further investigations will be carried out to determine whether or not the preponderance of unifacial flaking was typical of the oldest Gona artefacts or a result of sampling bias. More bifacially/multifacially flaked cores including spheroids/subspheroids and retouched pieces appear later *c.* 1.6–1.5 Ma with the "Developed Oldowan". It is strongly argued here that there is no compelling evidence to warrant different facies or industries for the stone assemblages known between 2.6–1.5 Ma other than the Oldowan as originally defined by Leakey (1971).

THE MAKERS AND THE FUNCTION OF THE EARLIEST STONE TOOLS

There are no modified stones or bones with evidence of definite stone tool-cut marks known from deposits that are older than 2.6 Ma. Therefore, it is likely that *Australopithecus afarensis* was not involved in activities that required the use of modified stones. There are two hominids known *c.* 2.5 Ma in East Africa including *Australopithecus aethiopicus* originally identified in the Omo (Howell et al., 1987), and later at West Turkana (Walker et al., 1986); and *Australopithecus garhi* recently discovered from the Hata beds of the Bouri Formation in the Middle Awash (Asfaw et al., 1999). According to Suwa et al. (1996), both the non-robust and the robust lineages are represented *c.* 2.7 Ma in the Shungura

Formation. The robust lineage was identified as *Australopithecus aethiopicus* and it was sampled from Members C through F (2.7–2.3 Ma). The non-robust hominids from Members E-G are assigned to aff. *Homo* sp. indet. Those known *c.* 2.0–2.4. Ma are early representatives of the genus *Homo* and have similarities to species labelled as *Homo rudolfensis* (Suwa et al., 1996). Fossil remains of early *Homo* estimated to this time interval are also known from other parts of Africa (Hill et al., 1992; Schrenk et al., 1993). Thus far, the known range of *Australopithecus aethiopicus* is restricted to the Omo/Turkana basin, and *Australopithecus garhi* is identified only from the Afar region of Ethiopia. *Australopithecus garhi* is argued to be a strong candidate responsible for making and using the oldest known artefacts in the Afar, but some argue that there are no grounds for excluding *Australopithecus boisei* as maker and user of stone tools (Wood, 1997). Both hominid species are contemporary with the earliest stone tools dated between 2.5–2.6 Ma. Actually, the stone artefacts from Gona are close to 2.6 Ma, and a bit older than *Australopithecus garhi*. Therefore, there is a possibility for further discovery of the same species from older deposits, or the likelihood of finding a different species in the Afar region that may have lived between *Australopithecus afarensis* and *Australopithecus garhi* in the time interval between 2.9–2.5 Ma. The fossil remains of early *Homo* identified from the Omo (2.4–2.0 Ma) and Hadar (2.4–2.3 Ma) are contemporary with the Hadar, Omo and Lokalalei artefacts. Therefore, early *Homo* may be uncontested as the maker and user of stone artefacts, but the case for *Australopithecus garhi* as the first tool maker is also compelling.

Without associated fossilized animal bones bearing evidence of cut marks, the function of the oldest stone artefacts from Gona remained speculative for a long time. The recent cut-mark data from Bouri indicates that early hominids *c.* 2.5 Ma began incorporating some amount of high nutrient meat in their diet. Further detailed research is needed to determine why meat became an important food item by this time and how it was acquired. It is not clear whether or not the first stone artefacts were used for processing plant foods. There are certain indications from microwear studies on artefacts from Koobi Fora (Keeley & Toth, 1981) and from Gona (Beyries, 1993), but strong cases have yet to be made based on the archaeological record to demonstrate the use of flaked stones for processing plant food items.

SUMMARY

Late Pliocene hominids began manufacturing and utilizing flaked stones *c.* 2.6 Ma, and the Gona localities provide the earliest evidence of a high density of stone artefacts from laterally-extensive deposits exposed east and west of the Kada Gona river. The beginning of the use of modified stones was a major technological breakthrough which opened windows of opportunities for effective exploitation of available food resources including high nutrient meat and bone marrow from animals. The cut-mark and bone fracture evidence from Bouri provides strong evidence for the incorporation of meat in the diet of Late Pliocene hominids as early as 2.5 Ma. The sudden appearance of thousands of well-flaked artefacts documented from several localities in this time interval is intriguing. It may mean that the beginning of the manufacture and use of flaked-stones was a novel adaptive strategy which appeared abruptly *c.* 2.6 Ma and spread through populations quickly. On the other hand, there is a possibility of finding modified stones/and or bones from older deposits if the manufacture and use of flaked stones evolved gradually. Thus far, the evidence is strongly in favour of an abrupt appearance of modified stones in the archaeological record between 2.5–2.6 Ma or probably a bit earlier.

Research is still under way to address the question of what triggered early hominid beginning of the use of modified stones *c.* 2.6 Ma. Some link the appearance of stone tools and early *Homo* with the onset of the buildup of ice sheets in the northern hemisphere which resulted in major global cooling documented beginning *c.* 2.7–2.8 Ma (Vrba 1985, 1988, 1990, 1995; de Menocal, 1995; de Menocal & Bloemendal, 1995; Shackleton, 1995). Exactly how global cooling affected Africa and the causal links which led to the physical and behavioural changes seen in early hominids *c.* 2.6–2.5 Ma are not yet well understood. Others argue for regional uplifts and tectonic activities having a major impact on Late Pliocene hominids and the faunal community in Africa at this time (Denys et al., 1986; Pickford, 1990; Partridge et al., 1995). Future investigations at Gona of the palaeoenvironment from this critical time period based on faunal evidence, geological and isotope studies, can provide further crucial evidence for understanding the settings for the appearance of stone artefacts and to identify the makers (Cerling & Quade, 1993; Brown, 1995; Wesselman, 1995; White, 1995; Cerling et al., 1997).

The archaeological evidence from Gona at 2.6–2.5 Ma and the other Late Pliocene sites dated to 2.4–2.3 Ma and their implications for understanding early hominid behaviour can be summarized as follows.

1. The makers of the earliest Gona artefacts had a clear mastery of the mechanics of conchoidal fracture by *c.* 2.6 Ma and well-flaked artefacts are known from several archaeological sites dated to 2.3–2.4 Ma in East Africa.
2. Ancestral tool makers (beginning *c.* 2.6–2.5 Ma) chose appropriate size cobbles when making artefacts, selected for raw materials with good flaking quality, sought for acute angles when striking cobbles and produced sharp-edged implements used for cutting.
3. It seems that the main intent of Oldowan tool makers was the production of cores and flakes with sharp-edges which were probably used for cutting up carcasses to access high nutrient meat from animals (not yet clear whether hunted or scavenged). The absence of well-preserved high density of bones with stone tool-cut marks from the sites dated between 2.5–2.0 Ma may be a taphonomic bias, but some of the artefact occurrences of this period are found in association with numerous broken bones.
4. The makers of the earliest stone artefacts travelled long distances to acquire raw materials (for example at Omo and Bouri), implying greater mobility, long-term planning and foresight not recognized earlier. They

probably habitually carried artefacts (as suggested by the evidence from Bouri) and unmodified stones over the landscape.

5. The oldest archaeological traces known in Africa are thus far restricted to the Afar region and the Omo/Turkana basin. Although these occurrences are geographically restricted, the artefacts are of a high density character probably implying habitual tool use as early as 2.6 Ma.

6. Plio-Pleistocene hominids lived close to water and raw material sources, mainly along courses of ancient streams, where there were trees used as shelters and as refugee from predators.

7. The same stone working techniques and styles of tool manufacture persisted for over 1 million years (2.6–1.5 Ma) implying a technological stasis in the Oldowan.

Further palaeoanthropological multidisciplinary field and laboratory studies can help elucidate the environmental settings for the appearance of stone artefacts, for understanding of their adaptive significance, and for assessing the reasons for the behavioural and physical changes seen in Late Pliocene–Early Pleistocene hominids. The two contemporary Afar sites of Gona and Middle Awash have great potential for providing archaeological data for further detailed understanding of these questions. Furthermore, the identity of the makers may be clarified through further discoveries at Gona. A new round of multidisciplinary systematic research at Gona organized in 1999 has made a promising start in addressing these questions, and the results will be published in the near future.

ACKNOWLEDGMENTS

A field permit for the Gona research was issued by the Center for Research and Conservation of Cultural Heritage (CRCCH) of the Ministry of Information and Culture of Ethiopia. I would like to thank the L. S. B. Leakey Foundation, the National Science Foundation, the Boise Fund and Ann and Gordon Getty for their generous support for the 1992–1994 field seasons. EG10 and EG12 were excavated with Professor J. W. K. Harris (Rutgers University). He deserves special mention for his advice and time in the field. Dr Craig Feibel (Rutgers University) assisted in the field and laboratory with the details on the geology of Gona. Dr Paul Renne of the Berkeley Geochronology Center (BGC) is responsible for the paleomagnetic and ^{40}Ar/^{39}Ar dating, and I am grateful for his assistance in resolving the age of the Gona artefacts. I am grateful to Dr Nicholas Toth and Dr Kathy Schick (CRAFT, Indiana University) for offering me a postdoctoral fellowship, and for their invaluable comments on an earlier draft of this manuscript. I would like to thank Yonas Beyene, Berhane Asfaw, Tim White, Clark Howell, Desmond Clark, Manuel Dominguez-Rodrigo, Robert Blumenschine and John Cavallo for their support. I also thank Michael Rogers for his comments and kind assistance. My gratitude goes to the Afar people for their hospitality and support in the field. Part of the fellowship for my Graduate Studies was provided by the Institute of Human Origins and Rutgers University.

REFERENCES

Aronson, J. L., Schmitt, T. J., Walter, R. C., Taieb, M., Tiercelin, J. J., Johanson, D. C., Naesser, C. W. & Nairn, A. E. M. (1977). New geochronologic and paleomagnetic data for the hominid-bearing Hadar Formation, Ethiopia. *Nature* **267**, 323–327.

Aronson, J. L., Walter, R. C., Taieb, M. & Naeser, C. W. (1980). New geochronological information for the Hadar Formation and the adjacent Central Afar, Ethiopia. In (R. E. F. Leakey & B. A. Ogot, Eds) *Proceedings of the 8th Pan-African Congress of Prehistory and Quaternary Studies.* Nairobi: The International Louis Leakey Memorial Institute for African Prehistory, pp. 47–52.

Aronson, J. L. & Taieb, M. (1981). Geology and paleogeography of the Hadar hominid site, Ethiopia. In (G. J. Rapp & C. F. Vondra, Eds) *Hominid sites: their geologic settings.* American Association for the Advancement of Science Selected Symposium **63**. Boulder: Westview Press, pp. 165–195.

Asfaw, B., Beyene, Y., Suwa, G., Walter, R. C., White, T. D., WoldeGabriel, G. & Yemane, T. (1992). The earliest Acheulean from Konso-Gardula. *Nature* **360**, 732–735.

Asfaw, B., White, T., Lovejoy, O., Latimer, B., Simpson, S. & Suwa, G. (1999). *Australopithecus garhi*: a new species of early hominid from Ethiopia. *Science* **284**, 629–635.

Balout, L. (1955). *Préhistoire de l'Afrique du Nord. Essai de Chronologie.* Paris: Arts et Métiers Graphiques.

Beyries, S. (1993). Are we able to determine the function of the earliest palaeolithic tools? In (A. Berthelet & J. Chavaillon, Eds) *The use of tools by non-human primates.* Clarendon Press: Oxford, pp. 225–236.

Biberson, P. (1961). *Le Paléolithique Inférieur du Maroc Atlantique.* Rabat: Publications du Service Archeologique du Maroc.

Brain, C. K., Churcher, C. S., Clark, J. D., Grine, F. E., Shipman, P., Susman, R. L., Turner, A. & Watson, V. (1988). New evidence of early Hominids, their culture and environments from the Swartkrans cave, South Africa. *South African Journal of Science* **84**, 828–835.

Brown, F. H. (1995). The potential of the Turkana Basin for paleoclimatic reconstruction in East Africa. In (E. S. Vrba, G. H. Denton, T. C. Partridge & L. H. Burckle, Eds) *Paleoclimate and evolution, with emphasis on human origins.* New Haven and London: Yale University Press, pp. 319–330.

Cerling, T. E. & Quade, J. (1993). Stable carbon and oxygen isotopes in soil carbonates. In (P. Swart, J. A. McKenzie, K. C. Lohman, Eds) *Continental indicators of climate.* Proceedings of Chapman Conference, Jackson Hole, Wyoming, American Geophysical Union Monograph **78**, pp. 217–231.

Cerling, T. E., Harris, J. M., MacFadden, B. J., Ehleringer, J. R., Leakey, M. G., Quade, J. & Eiesnman, V. (1997). Global vegetation change through the Miocene/Pliocene boundary. *Nature* **389**, 153–157.

Chavaillon, J. (1976). Evidence for the technical practices of early Pleistocene Hominids, Shungura Formation, Lower Omo Valley, Ethiopia. In (Y. Coppens, F. C. Howell, G. Isaac & R. E. F. Leakey, Eds) *Earliest man and environments in the Lake Rudolf Basin.* Chicago: University of Chicago Press, pp. 565–573.

Chavaillon, J., Chavaillon, N., Hours, F. & Piperno, M. (1979). From the Oldowan to the Middle Stone Age at Melka-Kunture (Ethiopia). Understanding cultural changes. *Quaternaria* **21**, 87–114.

Clark, J. D. (1992). The Earlier Stone Age/Lower Palaeolithic in North Africa and the Sahara. In (F. Klees & R. Kuper, Eds) *New light on the Northeast African past.* Koln: Heinrich-Barth-Institut, pp. 17–37.

Clark, J. D. (1994). The Acheulian Industrial Complex in Africa and elsewhere. In (R. S. Corruccini & R. L. Ciochon, Eds) *Integrative paths to the past: palaeoanthropological advances in honor of F. Clark Howell.* New Jersey: Prentice Hall Publishers.

Clark, J. D. & Kurashina, H. (1979). Hominid occupation of the east central highlands of Ethiopia in the Plio-Pleistocene. *Nature* **282**, 33–39.

Clark, J. D., Asfaw, B., Assefa, G., Harris, J. W. K., Kurashina, H., Walter, R. C., White, T. D. & Williams, M. A. J. (1984). Palaeoanthropologic discoveries in the Middle Awash Valley, Ethiopia. *Nature* **307**, 423–428.

Clark, J. D., de Heinzelin, J., Schick, K. D., Hart, W. K., White, T. D., WoldeGabriel, G., Walter, R. C., Suwa, G., Asfaw, B., Vrba, E. & Selassie, Y. (1994). African *Homo erectus*: old radiometric ages and young Oldowan assemblages in the Middle Awash Valley, Ethiopia. *Science* **264**, 1907–1909.

Corvinus, G. (1976). Prehistoric exploration at Hadar, Ethiopia. *Nature* **261**, 571–572.

Corvinus, G. & Roche, H. (1976). La préhistoire dans la région de Hadar (Bassin de l'Awash, Afar, Ethiopie): premiers résultats. *L'Anthropologie* 80(2), 315–324.

Corvinus, G. & Roche, H. (1980). Prehistoric exploration at Hadar in the Afar (Ethiopia) in 1973, 1974, and 1976. In (R. E. F. Leakey & B. A. Ogot, Eds) *Proceedings, VIIIth Pan-African Congress of Prehistory and Quaternary Studies.* Nairobi: The International Louis Leakey Memorial Institute for African Prehistory, pp. 186–188.

de Heinzelin, J., Clark, J. D., White, T. W., Hart, W., Renne, P., WoldeGabriel, G., Beyene, Y. & Vrba, E. (1999). Environment and behavior of 2.5-million-year-old Bouri hominids. *Science* **284**, 625–629.

de Menocal, P. B. (1995). Plio-Pleistocene African climate. *Science* **270**, 53–59.

de Menocal, P. B. & Bloemendal (1995). Plio-Pleistocene climatic variability in subtropical Africa and the paleoenvironment of hominid evolution. In (E. S. Vrba, G. H. Denton, T. C. Partridge & L. H. Burckle, Eds) *Paleoclimate and evolution, with emphasis on human origins.* New Haven and London: Yale University Press, pp. 262–288.

Denys, C., Chorowicz, J. & Tiercelin, J. J. (1986). Tectonic and environmental control on rodent diversity in the Plio-Pleistocene sediments of the African Rift System. In (L. E. Frostick, R. W. Renaut, I. Reid & J. J. Tiercelin, Eds) *Sedimentation in the African rifts.* Oxford: Alden Press Ltd, pp. 362–372.

Feibel, C. S., Brown, F. H. & Mc Dougall, I. (1989). Stratigraphic context of hominids from the Omo Group deposits: northern Turkana basin, Kenya and Ethiopia. *American Journal of Physical Anthropology* **78**, 595–622.

Feibel, C. S. & Wynn, T. (no date). Preliminary report on the geologic context of the Gona archaeological sites. Unpublished manuscript.

Gowlett, J. A. J. (1988). A case of Developed Oldowan in the Acheulean? *World Archaeology* **20**(1), 13–26.

Gowlett, J. A. J., Harris, J. W. K., Walton, D. & Wood, B. A. (1981). Early archaeological sites, hominid remains and traces of fire from Chesowanja, Kenya. *Nature* **294**, 125–129.

Hall, C. M., Walter, R. C. & York, D. (1985). Tuff above "Lucy" is over 3 ma old. *Eos* **66**, 257.

Harris, J. W. K. (1983). Cultural beginnings: Plio-Pleistocene archaeological occurrences from the Afar, Ethiopia. *African Archaeological Review* **1**, 3–31.

Harris, J. W. K. (1978). *The Karari Industry: its place in East Africa prehistory.* Ph.D. Thesis. University of California, Berkeley.

Harris, J. W. K. & Semaw, S. (1989). Pliocene archaeology at the Gona River, Hadar. *Nyame Akuma* **31**, 19–21.

Harris, J. W. K., Williamson, P. G., Verniers, J., Tappen, M. J., Stewart, K., Helgren, D., de Heinzelin, J., Boaz, N. T. & Bellomo, R. (1987). Late Pliocene hominid occupation in Central Africa: the setting, context, and character of the Senga 5A site, Zaire. *Journal of Human Evolution* **16**, 701–728.

Harris, J. W. K., Williamson, P. G., Morris, P. J., de Heinzelin, J., Verniers, J., Helgren, D., Bellomo, R. V., Laden, G., Spang, T. W., Stewart, K. & Tappen, M. J. (1990). *Archaeology of the Lusso Beds.* Memoir 1. Martinsville: Virginia Museum of Natural History.

Hill, A., Ward, S., Deino, A., Curtis, G. & Drake, R. (1992). Earliest Homo. *Nature* **355**, 719–722.

Howell, F. C., Haesaerts, P. & de Heinzelin, J. (1987). Depositional environments, archaeological occurrences and hominids from Members E and F of the Shungura Formation (Omo Basin, Ethiopia). *Journal of Human Evolution* **16**, 665–700.

Isaac, G. Ll. (1976). Plio-Pleistocene artefact assemblages from East Rudolf, Kenya. In (Y. Coppens, F. C. Howell & G. Ll. Isaac, Eds) *Earliest man and environments in the Lake Rudolf Basin.* University of Chicago Press, pp. 552–564.

Isaac, G. Ll. (1984). The archaeology of human origins: studies of the Lower Pleistocene in East Africa 1971–1981. *Advances in World Archaeology* **3**, 1–87.

Isaac, G. Ll. & Curtis, G. H. (1974). Age of the Acheulian industries from the Peninj Group, Tanzania. *Nature* **249**, 624–627.

Isaac, G. Ll., Harris, J. W. K. & Marshall, F. (1981). Small is informative: the application of the study of mini-sites and least effort criteria in the interpretation of the Early Pleistocene archaeological record at Koobi Fora, Kenya. *Proc. Union Internacional de Ciencias Prehistoricas Y Protohistoricas; X Congress, Mexico City.* Mexico, pp. 101–119.

Isaac, G. Ll. & Harris, J. W. K. (1997). The stone artefact assemblages: a comparative study. In (G. Ll. Isaac, Ed.) *Koobi Fora Research Project, Vol. 3: The archaeology.* Oxford: Clarendon Press.

Johanson, D. C., White, T. D. & Coppens, Y. (1978). A new species of the genus *Australopithecus* (Primates: Hominidae) from the Pliocene of eastern Africa. *Kirtlandia* **28**, 1–14.

Johanson, D. C., Taieb, M. & Coppens, Y. (1982). Pliocene hominids from the Hadar Formation, Ethiopia (1973–1977): Stratigraphic, chronological, and paleoenvironmental contexts, with notes on hominid morphology and systematics. *American Journal of Physical Anthropology* **57**, 373–402.

Jones, P. R. (1994). Results of experimental work in relation to the stone industries of Olduvai Gorge. In (M. D. Leakey, Ed.) *Olduvai Gorge—excavations in Beds III, IV and the Masek Beds (1968–71)* (Vol. 5). Cambridge University Press.

Kalb, J. E. (1993). Refined stratigraphy of the hominid-bearing Awash Group, Middle Awash Valley, Afar Depression, Ethiopia. *Newsletters on Stratigraphy* **29**(1), 21–62.

Kaufulu, Z. M. & Stern, N. (1987). The first stone artefacts to be found *in situ* within the Plio-Pleistocene Chiwondo Beds in northern Malawi. *Journal of Human Evolution* **16**, 729–740.

Keeley, L. H. & Toth, N. P. (1981). Microwear polishes on early stone tools from Koobi Fora, Kenya. *Nature* **293**, 464–465.

Kibunjia, M. (1994). Pliocene archeological occurrences in the Lake Turkana basin. *Journal of Human Evolution* **27**, 159–171.

Kibunjia, M., Roche, H., Brown, F. H. & Leakey, R. E. F. (1992). Pliocene and Pleistocene archeological sites of Lake Turkana, Kenya. *Journal of Human Evolution* **23**, 432–438.

Kimbel, W. H., Johanson, D. C. & Rak, Y. (1994). The first skull and other new discoveries of *Australopithecus afarensis* at Hadar, Ethiopia. *Nature* **368**, 449–451.

Kimbel, W. H., Walter, R. C., Johanson, D. C., Reed, K. E., Aronson, J. L., Assefa, Z., Marean, C. W., Eck, G. G., Bobe, R., Hovers, E., Rak, Y., Vondra, C., Yemane, T., York, D., Chen, Y., Evensen, N. M. & Smith, P. E. (1996). Late Pliocene *Homo* and Oldowan tools from the Hadar Formation (Kada Hadar Member), Ethiopia. *Journal of Human Evolution* **31**, 549–561.

Kuman, K. (1994a). The archaeology of Sterkfontein—past and present. *Journal of Human Evolution* **27**, 471–495.

Kuman, K. (1994b). The archaeology of Sterkfontein: preliminary findings on site formation and cultural change. *South African Journal of Science* **90**, 215–219.

Kuman, K., Field, A. S. & Thackeray, J. G. (1997). Discovery of new artefacts at Kromdraai. *South African Journal of Science* **93**, 187–193.

Leakey, M. D. (1971). *Olduvai Gorge, Vol. III.* London: Cambridge University Press.

Ludwig, B. V. & Harris, J. W. K. (1998). Towards a technological reassessment of East African Plio-Pleistocene lithic assemblages. In (M. D. Petraglia & R. Korisettar, Eds) *Early human behavior in global context. The rise and diversity of the Lower Paleolithic Record.* London and New York: Routledge, pp. 84–107.

McDougall, I., Brown, F. H., Cerling, T. E. & Hillhouse, J. W. (1992). A reappraisal of the Geomagnetic Polarity Time Scale to 4 Ma using data from the Turkana Basin, East Africa. *Geophysical Research Letters* **19**(23), 2349–2352.

Merrick, H. V. (1976). Recent archaeological research in the Plio-Pleistocene deposits of the Lower Omo, southwestern Ethiopia. In (G. Ll. Isaac & I. McCown, Eds) *Human origins: Louis Leakey and the East African evidence.* Menlo Park: W. A. Benjamin.

Partridge, T. C., Wood, B. A. & deMenocal, B. (1995). The influence of global climatic change and regional uplift on large-mammalian evolution in East and South Africa. In (E. S. Vrba, G. H. Denton, T. C. Partridge & L. H. Burckle, Eds) *Paleoclimate and evolution, with emphasis on human origins.* New Haven and London: Yale University Press, pp. 331–355.

Pickford, M. (1990). Uplift of the roof of Africa and its bearing on the evolution of mankind. *Human Evolution* **5**(1), 1–20.

Piperno, M. (1989). Chronostratigraphic and cultural framework of the *Homo habilis* sites. In (G. Giacobini, Eds) *Hominidae. Proceedings of the 2nd International Congress of Human Paleontology.* Milan: Jaca Book, pp. 189–195.

Roche, H. (1989). Technological evolution in early hominids. *OSSA* **4**, 97–98.

Roche, H. (1996). Remarque sur les plus anciennes industries en Afrique et en Europe. Colloquium VIII Lithic Industries, language and social behaviour in the first human forms. *IUPSS Congress*, Forli, Italy, pp. 55–68.

Roche, H. & Tiercelin, J. J. (1977). Découverte d'une industrie lithique ancienne in situ dans la formation d'Hadar, Afar central, Ethiopie. *C. R. Acad. Sci. Paris D* **284**, 187–174.

Roche, H. & Tiercelin, J. J. (1980). Industries lithiques de la formation Plio-Pléistocène d'Hadar: campagne 1976. In (R. E. F. Leakey & B. A. Ogot, Eds) *Proceedings, VIIIth Pan-African Congress of Prehistory and Quaternary Studies.* Nairobi: The International Louis Leakey Memorial Institute for African Prehistory, pp. 194–199.

Roche, H., Delagnes, A., Brugal, J.-P., Feibel, C., Kibunjia, M., Mourre, V. & Texier, P.-J. (1999). Early hominid stone tool production and technical skill 2.34 Myr ago in West Turkana, Kenya. *Nature* **399**, 57–60.

Sahnouni, M. & de Heinzelin, J. (1998). The site of Ain Hanech revisited: new investigations at this Lower Pleistocene site in northern Algeria. *Journal of Archaeological Science* **25**, 1083–1101.

Schrenk, F., Bromage, T. G., Betzler, C. G., Ring, U. & Juwayeyi, Y. (1993). Oldest *Homo* and Pliocene biogeography of the Malawi Rift. *Nature* **365**, 833–836.

Schick, K. (1986). *Stone age sites in the making: experiments in the formation and transformation of archaeological occurrences.* Oxford: British Archaeological Reports, International Series **319**.

Schick, K. (1987). Modeling the formation of Early Stone Age artefact concentrations. *Journal of Human Evolution* **16**, 789–808.

Semaw, S. (1997). *Late Pliocene Archeology of the Gona River deposits, Afar, Ethiopia.* Ph.D. Thesis. Rutgers University, New Brunswick, NJ.

Semaw, S., Renne, P., Harris, J. W. K., Feibel, C. S., Bernor, R. L., Fesseha, N. & Mowbray, K. (1997). 2.5-million-year-old stone tools from Gona, Ethiopia. *Nature* **385**, 333–336.

Shackleton, N. J. (1995). New data on the evolution of Pliocene climatic variability. In (E. S. Vrba, G. H. Denton, T. C. Partridge & L. H. Burckle, Eds) *Paleoclimate and evolution, with emphasis on human origins.* New Haven and London: Yale University Press, pp. 242–248.

Suwa, G., White, T. & Howell, F. C. (1996). Mandibular postcanine dentition from the Shungura Formation, Ethiopia: crown morphology, taxonomic allocation, and Plio-Pleistocene hominid evolution. *American Journal of Physical Anthropology* **101**, 247–282.

Taieb, M., Johanson, D. C., Coppens, Y. & Aronson, J. L. (1976). Geological and paleontological background of Hadar hominid site, Afar, Ethiopia. *Nature* **260**, 288–293.

Tiercelin, J. J. (1986). The Pliocene Hadar Formation, Afar depression of Ethiopia. In (L. E. Frostick, R. W. Renaut, I. Reid & J. J. Tiercelin, Eds) *Sedimentation in the African rifts.* Oxford: Alden Press Ltd, pp. 225–240.

Toth, N. (1982). *The stone technologies of early hominids at Koobi Fora, Kenya: An experimental approach.* Ph.D. Thesis. University of California, Berkeley.

Toth, N. (1985). The Oldowan reassessed: a close look at early stone artefacts. *Journal of Archeological Science* **12**, 101–120.

Toth, N. (1987). Behavioral inferences from early stone artefact assemblages: an experimental model. *Journal of Human Evolution* **16**, 763–787.

Toth, N. & Schick, K. (1986). The first million years: the archaeology of protohuman culture. *Advances in Archaeological Method and Theory* **9**, 1–96.

Vrba, E. S. (1985). Environment and evolution: alternative causes of the temporal distribution of evolutionary events. *South African Journal of Science* **81**, 229–236.

Vrba, E. S. (1988). Late Pliocene climatic events and hominid evolution. In (F. Grine, Ed.) *The evolutionary history of the robust Australopithecine.* New York: Aldine de Gruyter, pp. 405–426.

Vrba, E. S. (1990). The environmental context of the evolution of early hominids and their culture. In (R. Bonnichsen & M. Sorg, Eds) *Bone modification.* Orono, Maine: Center for the study of the first Americans, pp. 27–42.

Vrba, E. S. (1995). On the connections between paleoclimate and evolution. In (E. S. Vrba, G. H. Denton, T. C. Partridge & L. H. Burckle, Eds) *Paleoclimate and evolution, with emphasis on human origins.* New Haven and London: Yale University Press, pp. 24–45.

Walker, A., Leakey, R. E., Harris, J. M. & Brown, F. H. (1986). 2.5-Myr *Australopithecus boisei* from west of Lake Turkana, Kenya. *Nature* **322**, 517–522.

Walter, R. C. (1980). *The volcanic history of the Hadar early man site and the surrounding Afar region of Ethiopia.* Ph.D. thesis. Case Western Reserve University.

Walter, R. C. (1994). Age of Lucy and the first family: single-crystal ^{40}Ar/^{39}Ar dating of the Denen Dora and lower Kada Hadar Members of the Hadar Formation, Ethiopia. *Geology* **22**, 6–10.

Walter, R. C. & Aronson, J. L. (1982). Revisions of K/Ar ages for the Hadar hominid site, Ethiopia. *Nature* **296**, 122–127.

Wesselman, H. B. (1995). Of mice and almost-men: regional paleoecology and human evolution in the Turkana Basin. In (E. S. Vrba, G. H. Denton, T. C. Partridge & L. H. Burckle, Eds) *Paleoclimate and evolution, with emphasis on human origins.* New Haven and London: Yale University Press, pp. 24–45, 356–368.

White, T. D. (1995). African omnivores: global climatic change and Plio-Pleistocene hominids and suids. In (E. S. Vrba, G. H. Denton, T. C. Partridge & L. H. Burckle, Eds) *Paleoclimate and evolution, with emphasis on human origins.* New Haven and London: Yale University Press, pp. 356–368.

Wood, B. A. (1997). The oldest whodunnit in the world. *Nature* **385**, 292–293.

32

Perspectives on the Nariokotome Discovery

A. Walker

ABSTRACT

Analysis of the Nariokotome skeleton and the new insights that it has given us in interpreting other, more fragmentary, specimens have led to several revisions of our view of human evolution. We have found few instances in our investigations where these early hominids differed substantially from modern humans, but those we have found testify to differences that are probably all ultimately and indirectly related to differences in higher mental function. The discovery of this 1.5-million-year-old skeleton has changed the narrative of our own evolution and illuminated yet other areas of our ignorance.

The nearly complete skeleton KNM-WT 15000 found at Nariokotome III by Kamoya Kimeu is one of the truly great discoveries in paleoanthropology. Eugene Dubois found the first *Homo erectus* in 1891, but up until 1971 only isolated parts of skeletons had been found in Asia and Africa. Meave Leakey found a fragmentary partial skeleton (KNM-ER 803) near Ileret, Lake Turkana, in 1971 and, although we did not know it at the time, this specimen was the first to include associated dental and postcranial material of *H. erectus*. The next year Kamoya Kimeu discovered the first associated bones of a single diseased individual (KNM-ER 1808); this specimen was more complete, but the long bones were covered with a surface layer of bone owing to a bout of periostitis. Although it was an interesting case for paleopathology (Walker et al., 1982), the fact that the individual had suffered the disease made comparative studies very difficult.

The discovery in 1984, then, of KNM-WT 15000 was the climax of nearly a century of diligent search. What we have found out already about this individual and his population's characteristics, about the life history strategies of this species and what they have to tell us about our own evolution, shows us that the search was worth it. I hope my colleagues and I have laid the groundwork for many future studies of this skeleton.

Although the chapters in *The Nariokotome* Homo erectus *Skeleton* cover a wide field of topics, there remain a few issues that have not been addressed. One wonders about the life history strategy of early African *H. erectus* populations, and in what sorts of environments they lived. What morphological features characterized the species? And what can this skeleton tell us about the evolution of our own lineage? The comments that follow are often only speculative, but they might lead other researchers to invent ways of answering some unresolved important questions.

THE SIZE AND WEIGHT OF EARLY AFRICAN *HOMO ERECTUS*

When we discovered the first limb bones of KNM-WT 15000 in 1984 we were surprised by their size. They were long for an individual whose second molars had just erupted and whose upper milk canines were still in place. When still in camp at Nariokotome, we thought that we must have found a rare, tall individual. But we found out on our return to Nairobi that we had underestimated the size of the incomplete bones that had been collected previously and that all known early African *H. erectus* individuals were tall. The results of the detailed study of body size and body shape (Ruff and Walker, 1993) have confirmed our initial assessment (Brown et al., 1985).

Six *H. erectus* individuals from East Africa have parts complete enough to predict their stature and body weight. These six probably include both males and females. The Nariokotome skeleton is almost certainly male on the basis of skull and pelvic characteristics. Walker et al. (1982) and Leakey and Walker (1985) thought that KNM-ER 1808 was a female, but McHenry

(1991) thought otherwise. Walker and Ruff (1993) have carried out computerized shape analyses on hip bones, but they were unable to apply that analysis to KNM-ER 1808 because the sciatic notch is not preserved in its entirety. McHenry contends that the sciatic notch is asymmetric and thus more similar to males, although he agrees that it appears to have been broad. We could match the remaining curvature of the notch in the fossil to either male or female, depending on how we oriented the specimen. We still maintain that the brow ridges, the depth of the mandible, and the size of the temporal make it more likely that the individual was female. The partial skeleton KNM-ER 803 is smaller in stature and in tooth dimensions and may be female, and the Olduvai femur and hip bone, OH 28, is definitely female, according to visual examination by Day (1971) and to Walker and Ruff (1993) by computerized shape analysis.

The average stature is 170 cm (158–185 cm) and the average weight is 58 kg (51–68 kg) for this population of early *H. erectus*. Any comparisons with modern humans can only be illustrative, for modern *H. sapiens* is an extremely diverse, polytypic species. But for the sake of illustration, we can look at the distributions of size and shape in various human populations around the world. Martin (1928) compiled data about body height and weight from many sources. For height he broke these populations down into 3 groups—small, medium, and large. The small group had 66, the medium group had 148, and the tall group had 44 populations.

As can be seen from Table 1, the early African *H. erectus* population, with a mean stature of 170, would be in the tallest 17% of modern human populations, even if we make the comparison only with modern males. The average female heights in these modern populations are about 10 cm shorter, so if the *H. erectus* sample included some females the population would be among an even smaller percentage of the tallest modern human populations. A smaller amount of body weight data is available for modern populations, but according to the data in Martin (1928) the body weights estimated for the early African *H. erectus* sample would match those of the middle-sized modern human populations. This is because the morphometric model used in the weight estimation allows for the elongated body shape that we know KNM-WT 15000 had.

Confirmation of this relatively large body size comes from a set of footprints found on the east side of Lake Turkana (Behrensmeyer and Laporte, 1981). These

Table 1. World Distribution, by Average Male Height in cm, of Modern Human Populations (data from Martin, 1928)

	Small (140.8–159.9)	Medium (160–169.9)	Large (170–200)
Africa	8	25	12
Europe	4	51	13
Asia	35	43	4
Oceania	9	10	4
New World	10	19	11
Total number of populations	66	148	44

footprints were apparently made by a *Homo erectus* individual walking across a sandy mudflat covered by shallow water. The prints are in sediments that are about the same age as those of the site of Nariokotome III (NK3). Feibel and Brown (1993) show that the sediments containing the prints are at virtually the same stratigraphic level as the footprint tuff at site NK3. Behrensmeyer and Laporte estimated, from the length of the footprints, a stature of between 1.6 and 1.7 meters for the individual. This estimate can be refined by using Tuttle's (1987) data on stature and foot length data in over 50 modern human populations. The regression equation is:

$$\text{Stature} = 5.366 \times \text{Foot length} + 28.97$$
$$(r^2 = .879, N = 52, p < .001)$$

This gives a calculated height of 1.685 meters for the individual and is very close to the average for stature of 1.7 meters calculated by Ruff and Walker (1993) from the bones of 6 individuals.

With good stature and body weight estimates on what is admittedly a small sample of early African *H. erectus,* together with knowledge of their body proportions, we can begin to answer some important questions about human evolution. The first is the problem of climatic adaptation and the second is the interpretation of the reduction of stature that seems to have taken place in many parts of the world with the advent of agriculture. We can also look into several aspects of life history strategy because body weight is correlated very strongly with many of them (Harvey, 1990).

BODY PROPORTIONS AND THERMOREGULATION

In an earlier publication (Leakey and Walker, 1989), we used Trinkaus's regression method (Trinkaus, 1981) to determine what mean annual temperature the KNM-WT 15000 individual was adapted to. We calculated values of 18.5 and 25.3 °C using the preliminary brachial and crural indices that we had estimated then. We now have better estimates of the radial length (see Ruff and Walker, 1993) and have also found that there is an error in the published regression equations. The correct equation for the hindlimb is:

$$\text{Mean annual temperature}$$
$$= 3.328 \times \text{Crural index} - 263.602$$

This gives a mean annual temperature of 29.2 °C using our crural index of 88. Using our new brachial index of 79.9 in Trinkaus's (1981) other equation, we calculate a mean annual temperature of 30.8 °C. These values are extremely close to one another and confirm the findings presented in Ruff and Walker (1993) that KNM-WT 15000 was adapted to a climate with extremely high mean annual temperatures. It is true, as Ruff and Walker (1993) pointed out, that ratios can be misleading if used over a wide range, but these two new temperature values are consistent with each other and with the results of other ways of looking at body proportions.

Feibel et al. (1991) report that the Lake Turkana region has had the same climate as today since about 1.5 Ma. They base this on many lines of evidence, from soil profiles to animal diversity, and point to the fresh and unweathered state of 1.5 Ma volcanic outflows as a clear sign of continuous aridity since then. If, as seems likely, the general climate of the Lake Turkana region then was much the same as it is today, and our deductions about the climatic adaptations of early *H. erectus* populations are correct (Ruff, 1991), then these early humans were shaped the way they were for efficient cooling. People cool off by sweating, not by panting or a combination of panting and sweating as do nearly all other mammals. A human needs a prodigious amount of water to keep cool in a hot climate—as all of us who have worked at Lake Turkana know! All this points to the conclusion that early *H. erectus* was under high radiant heat stress and was very dependent on water (see also Wheeler, 1991).

It is possible that early African *H. erectus* were salt-dependent too, for by relying only on sweating for cooling, people also lose a large amount of salt. Panting animals re-ingest most of their salt (Schmidt-Nielsen, 1975) and this enables them to cool themselves without depleting their salt resources. Many animal and human populations ingest salt directly by geophagy, and it is possible that early African *H. erectus* did so too. Another source of salt might have been animal blood and animal tissue, for it is virtually certain that these early humans were eating meat (Bunn, 1981; Potts and Shipman, 1981). And finally, Carrier (1984) put forward an argument based on energetic principles that early hominids had a physiology that allowed endurance running at speeds which forced prey to avoid them in an inefficient way. This, he hypothesized, made them effective predators who could run down prey without succumbing to overheating. What we have learned from the Nariokotome skeleton can be taken to support Carrier.

BODY SIZE AND THE ORIGINS OF AGRICULTURE

It used to be thought that agriculture brought health and happiness wherever it had developed, but lately there has been an increasing realization that agriculture can bring with it increased risk of disease, greater susceptibility to starvation, and poor nutritional status for its practitioners. The most useful recent compilation of data and ideas is Cohen and Armelagos (1984). As Cohen and Armelagos say in their summation, "The data point fairly clearly to a decline in health associated with the origin of agriculture." Some of these data are evident in several populations at different times and in different parts of the world of a reduction in stature. None of the contributors to the Cohen and Armelagos volume were dealing with the early paleolithic record and, of course, most concentrated their attention on the transition to agriculture. It is not surprising, then, that the beginnings of hunter-gathering practices were not considered. Cohen and Armelagos point out that the health trends before the adoption of agriculture are of great importance in interpreting trends subsequent to the start of it. But, they said, "Unfortunately, these trends are particularly hard to unravel in the absence of good early ('Paleo') hunter-gatherers."

The new evidence for stature in early *H. erectus* is of great help in looking at the problem of what agriculture does to people. It is most revealing to learn that populations of what might be the earliest hunter-gatherer humans were taller than most modern human ones. These hominids were living in equatorial Africa in extremely hot climates without the benefit of domesticated stock upon which the present-day people depend for survival. They also lived, we assume, in low population densities. Yet their tall statures support the conclusion that people living a hunter-gatherer existence might be healthier, better fed, and less subject to famine.

Antecedent populations in the same area of Africa were not as tall as the early *H. erectus* ones (McHenry, 1991; Ruff and Walker, 1993) if the small amount of data can be trusted. McHenry (1991) calculated almost exactly the same estimated statures that we do for the 3 individuals from the antecedent populations. His three averaged 146.6 cm while Ruff and Walker give the average as 147.0. Thus the earlier individuals seem to have been about 23 cm (about 14%) shorter on average than *H. erectus*. McHenry (1988) found the weight of these three early individuals to average 49.6 kg, while Ruff and Walker, using a different model, calculate the average as 46 kg. Thus the early sample could have averaged as much as 12 kg (about 20%) less than the early *H. erectus*. If this small sample gives a true indication of what was going on about 2 million years ago, then it would appear that both stature and body weight increased at the same time that a hunter-gatherer life-style was being established for the first time.

Five femurs about half a million years old have been recovered from Zhoukoudian (Weidenreich, 1941). C. B. Ruff has kindly calculated for me the body weights using his climate model of human proportions (Ruff, 1991). He reports an average of a little over 56 kg. This is very close to the mean of 58 kg calculated for the early African *H. erectus* population (Ruff and Walker, 1993). On this slim basis, then, it would appear that there were not any major changes in body weight in the evolving *H. erectus* lineage for over 1 Ma.

AN EXAMPLE OF STASIS OR OF GRADUAL EVOLUTION?

Rightmire and Wolpoff carried on a short exchange of papers on whether *Homo erectus* was an example of stasis in evolution or whether gradual evolution had taken place. Rightmire (1981) began with a regression analysis of four traits in a sample of *H. erectus* which included a few specimens, such as Olduvai Hominid 13 and Petralona, that are not usually thought of as belonging to this species. He found that the slopes of the regressions of traits versus geological time were not significantly different from zero when he dropped contentious specimens such as these from his analysis. He concluded that no significant trends can be observed and that stasis had occurred for over a million years before rapid evolutionary change began toward the end

of the Middle Pleistocene. Wolpoff's (1984) reply was based on an enlarged sample of *H. erectus* which he termed "conservative." He divided the sample into three "low-resolution" time spans and tested the differences between the means by Student's *t* tests. He found that there were significant changes in a number of skull and tooth features. Rightmire later (1986) said that Wolpoff had not composed his samples in a biologically reasonable way and, further, that some specimens included in Wolpoff's sample couldn't be measured properly. Wolpoff then (1986) dropped the offending samples and was still able to point to significant differences among his time samples.

It is worth pointing out that the two methods are very different and that, perhaps, the gradualist and punctuationist viewpoints have been forced into caricatures of extremes. Even ardent gradualists admit that there is little to no change in most systems of the body for most species for most of the time (Rose and Bown, 1992). And even those who promote the idea of punctuated equilibrium would have to admit to small, fluctuating changes through time as opposed to absolutely no change at all. The most telling point in the debate over change in the *H. erectus* lineage, as far as the issues go concerning KNM-WT 15000, is the composition of Wolpoff's early category. His sample for the Lower Pleistocene includes specimens from the earliest African ones, about 1.8 million years old, to later ones from Sangiran in Java. It seems more than likely that no hominids in Asia are much older than a million years. Three authorities (J. DeVos, J. Franzen, and Wu Rukang) agree that the earliest *H. erectus* populations in East and Southeast Asia might be no older than 700,000 years (in Wolpoff and Nkini, 1985). Thus Wolpoff's early category might cover over a million years of evolution. Any changes over that time period must, then, be relatively small. For example, the *Homo erectus* crania from Sangiran and Trinil in Java have an average cranial capacity of 931 cc with a range from 815 to 1059 cc. The average cranial capacity of early African *Homo erectus* from about 1.7–1.2 Ma is 907 cc with a range from 804 to 1067 cc (Begun and Walker, 1993). The shapes of the early and late skulls are also not very different.

Figure 1 shows computer shape envelopes generated in the same manner as for the sciatic notches by Walker and Ruff (1993) for early and late *Homo erectus*. Sagittal and coronal shape envelopes for later specimens from Indonesia and Java are shown in cross-hatching on the sagittal and coronal profiles. In solid black is the envelope generated for the two early specimens from Kenya, KNM-ER 3733 and 3883. As can be seen, this envelope falls within that of the later specimens.

Brown and Walker (1993) show that the teeth from KNM-WT 15000 are very like those described from 500,000-year-old Chinese *H. erectus* and that, as with stature and brain size, there is relatively little change over the million-year span. In any case, though there are some demonstrated small changes through the lineage, these appear dwarfed by the sudden changes in morphology that took place at about 1.8 million years ago and then again with the appearance of anatomically modern people.

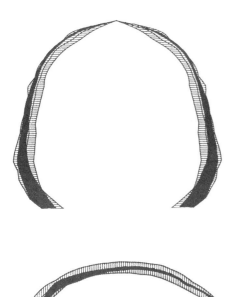

Figure 1. *Computer-generated shape envelopes for coronal and sagittal sections taken through Homo erectus crania. In cross-hatching are shown later crania from Indonesia and China, in solid black the two early crania KNM-ER 3733 and 3883.*

BRAIN WEIGHT AND BODY WEIGHT IN KNM-WT 15000

The Nariokotome skeleton is complete enough for us to estimate both the brain weight and body weight in the same individual. This cannot be accomplished for any other early hominid. Whole skeletons were hardly ever left for sedimentary burial, it seems, until the time humans began to bury the dead. Although partial skeletons of early hominids have been found before, none has a cranium preserved well enough to measure a cranial capacity.

In an influential paper on size and scaling in human evolution, Pilbeam and Gould (1974) looked at the scaling of the brain and the teeth in human evolution. They demonstrated that the African great apes were, in respect to the way the cranial capacity scaled to body weight, scaled versions of each other. They also showed that the three species of *Australopithecus* known then were also, in the same way, scaled versions of each other: the larger species were no more encephalized than the smaller but showed the usual mammalian relationship of brain size to body size. The difference between the ape and australopithecine samples did not lie in the slopes of the power functions calculated for them but in the intercepts. The hominids were more encephalized—the intercept of the line calculated to fit the hominid points was higher, but it had the same slope as the line calculated to fit the ape data. Thus both the African apes and the australopithecines were seen (in their relationship of these two features) to be series of animals differing only in size and not in design.

Pilbeam and Gould came to a different result when they applied this method to the human lineage. They used the sequence *Australopithecus africanus, Homo habilis, Homo erectus, Homo sapiens* to represent the human lineage. They found that the slope of the regression line calculated to fit the data for brain weight and body weight of this lineage was very different from the slopes of the lines for australopithecines and apes. The slope was 1.73, far greater than the other two slopes of .339 and .329 and far and away steeper than any slope representing functional equivalence. Pilbeam and Gould took this to show quite clearly that the brain had increased in size with marked positive allometry during our own evolution. Thus they concluded that "all australopithecines had brains equally expanded beyond the ape grade" but that in our lineage brain volume had increased dramatically. One reason *Homo habilis* should be in our genus, they added, was that it was the first species whose brain had increased beyond the australopithecine level.

We now have a chance to reevaluate this work. Another species of *Australopithecus* has been found since 1974 and we have better estimates for body weight and brain weight, especially for early *H. erectus*. The slope of the power function calculated for the australopithecines is not changed significantly by the addition of brain and body weight estimates for *A. afarensis*. The estimates for *H. habilis* and *H. erectus* do not now fit on the regression line for the human lineage calculated by Pilbeam and Gould. This is because the 68 kg adult body weight estimate for KNM-WT 15000 is much greater than the 53 kg that Pilbeam and Gould used for *H. erectus*, and the cranial capacity of the specimen is less than the value of 1050 cc that they used. The point representing *H. erectus* would still be very far from the line which Pilbeam and Gould calculated for the human lineage even if we were to use mean values for the early African *H. erectus* populations rather than the values for KNM-WT 15000 itself. This is because the body weight estimates are higher (58 kg) and the cranial capacity estimates lower (mean for four capacities = 907 cc). A line through the *H. habilis* and *H. erectus* points has a slope very close to regression lines calculated for the apes and australopithecines. This is especially remarkable because there are only two points. The straight line which Pilbeam and Gould could place through the points representing the human lineage can no longer be drawn. This is because the average body weight of early *H. erectus* is as big as those found in some modern populations with very big people, but the average cranial capacity of early *H. erectus* is much smaller than modern human cranial capacities. These authors would also have seen a more complicated picture had they used several human populations in their analysis. Their values for *H. sapiens* was a combined average of the data for male and female Australian aboriginal people. Figure 2 shows the data for several human populations, and these data, too, are scattered along a line with a slope very similar to the three others.

Figure 2 suggests an alternative view of brain and body scaling in human evolution. It seems there might be one scaling pattern for all hominoid groups rather than a separate pattern for members of the human lineage fundamentally different from those of the ape and

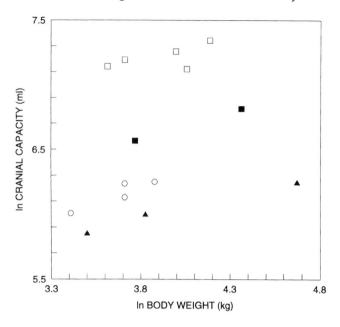

- ▲ African apes
- ○ Australopithecus species
- ■ H. habilis and H. erectus
- □ H. sapiens

Figure 2.   *Plot of estimates of body weights and brain weights (in logarithms) of four hominoid groups. Triangles: African apes (data from Pilbeam and Gould, 1974); circles: australopithecus species; filled squares: Homo habilis and Homo erectus (the point at upper right based on KNM-WT 15000 adult estimate); open squares: Homo sapiens (population means taken from Martin, 1928). Regression lines have not been drawn because the data points are so few, but the trends are apparent.*

australopithecine ones. We can postulate four allometric or scaling *grades* for the hominoid pattern: one each for African apes, australopithecines, *H. habilis—H. erectus*, and *H. sapiens*. Each of these groups scales in a similar way, which means that the animals in the group are similar in form but different in size. The difference between the groups is the level of encephalization. This view seems to be more likely, to my way of thinking, than the idea that there was a different set of relationships for our lineage alone.

Evolution from one grade to the next could have come about in several ways. Martin (1983) gives a theoretical discussion of them. Grade shifts require changes that result in vertical readjustments on the graph. It is theoretically possible that in this one respect, for instance, the chimpanzees could have given rise to australopithecines had their bodies but not their brains decreased in size. It is also possible that brain size could have increased while body size remained constant. And lastly it is possible that both body size and brain size increased. In the case of the three postulated scaling grades of hominids, it seems not to have been possible for the first to have happened, because the lowest brain values in the two later grades are bigger than the highest in the preceding ones. Correlated increases in both

body and brain size could have happened and dwarfing could have happened with brain size increase in the evolution of *H. sapiens* from *H. erectus*. If, as some believe (e.g., Andrews, 1984), Asian *H. erectus* were not on the lineage to modern humans, the same result applies. It is likely that most modern human populations have reduced body size relative to our early ancestors.

THE TAXONOMY OF EARLY AFRICAN *HOMO ERECTUS*

Leakey and Walker (1993) present a brief account of the problem of taxonomy of early African *H. erectus*. When KNM-ER 3773 was first found it was considered an early African representative of this species. It was earlier even than Olduvai Hominid 9, which has been almost unanimously considered to belong in *Homo erectus* (its finder, Louis Leakey, was an exception to the consensus—see Leakey, 1964). Walker and Leakey (1993) have given an account of all early African *H. erectus* specimens. I hope that this review will encourage people making taxonomic and phylogenetic assessments to take into consideration the high degree of variability to be found in the fossil sample.

The 1980s saw the rise of Hennegian cladistics as a common tool in taxonomy and phylogenetics in all branches of biology. There have been several cladistic studies of human taxonomy and phylogeny, but the one that I find most illuminating is that of Bilsborough and Wood (1986). They used two alternative methods to examine the questions of what *Homo erectus* really is and what were its origins and fate. The first was shape analysis, an analysis of a series of linear measurements using multivariate statistical procedures. The second was a cladistic analysis based upon the states of a selected series of characters.

The results of this study are illuminating because they give such different answers. The phenetic (or shape) analysis showed that early *H. erectus* from Africa are very close to late *H. erectus* from Asia but that there was a "distinct break" between the antecedent African fossils and early *H. erectus*.

The results of the cladistic study show major differences between some early *H. erectus* specimens from Africa and those from Asia. These differences are great enough to exclude two important early crania from Koobi Fora from the species *H. erectus*, because they lack the unique derived features of the Asian forms. The cladistic analysis links these early crania with those early *Homo* which immediately antedate them. The finding of no shared derived features with which one can link the early and late *H. erectus* contrasts strongly with the clear shape similarities. And yet the analysis links early *H. erectus* with specimens that do not look like them. This paradoxical result is illuminating in that it shows clearly that the two methods are unlikely to yield congruent answers when one is dealing with such closely related organisms.

Some practitioners of cladistics stick to a strict taxonomy that relies on splitting points. Changes of whatever magnitude within a species lineage cannot be used to define as species any isolated part of the lineage. Wiley

(1978) and Hull (1979), for instance, insist that, because an evolutionary species is in itself a lineage, it can give rise to other species only by branching. If this position is accepted, then all species of *Homo* back to the branching point from an ancestral species would be, by definition, in the same species. That species would be *Homo sapiens* for reasons of priority.

Rose and Bown (1993) give a clear exposition on the demerits of this sort of taxonomic scheme. As field paleontologists dealing with a very dense fossil record, they find such a scheme of little practical use, for, in the first and last members of their species, lineages might be composed of very different sorts of animals. I feel that taxonomy should be an aid to describing the real world and not a barrier. The real reason that cladistic treatments of very closely related organisms are difficult is the variability both within and between populations. When comparing closely related organisms it is difficult to find features that are discrete enough that all members of the populations have them. The use of continuous variables (or indices made from them) in cladistic analyses has grave problems—see Kennedy (1991) for a list of a few of them—and, further, makes it even more difficult to imagine that these "traits" are anything that would be genetically controlled in a straightforward way without being correlated very strongly with each other.

If evolution is the subject of interest, rather than taxonomy, the use of cladistics to sort out fossils in the genus *Homo* is frustrating. Evolution acts, as we have known since Darwin, upon the variability present in populations. By ignoring variability, in the attempt to make cleanly defined traits, much of the information in the fossil record can be lost. As Hopson (1989) says, "Although I am an advocate of cladistics, I find that the application of its methods to the dense fossil record of Cenozoic mammals, in which differences among closely related taxa often have a complex distribution, carries with it the danger of oversimplifying such distributions in the interest of clearcut results."

Several recent attempts to apply these methods have included *H. erectus* as an object of cladistic scrutiny (e.g., Andrews, 1984; Bilsborough and Wood, 1989; Chamberlain and Wood, 1987; Stringer, 1984, 1987; Wood, 1984, 1991). Kennedy's (1991) appraisal of supposed autapomorphic traits of *Homo erectus* is instructive in evaluating them. She looked at twelve possible traits that were said in several studies to be autapomorphic for the species and found that neither the qualitative discrete traits nor the quantitative traits were autapomorphic. She concluded that "*H. erectus*, as presently defined and using the methodology of phylogenetic systematics, cannot be considered a valid species." Brauer (1990) also attacked the idea that the Asian sample had a unique set of derived features. He looked at seven characters that Andrews (1984) believed were present in the Asian sample but not in the early African one. Brauer found that all seven could be found in the early African *erectus* grade sample. Most tellingly, Stringer, whose analyses in 1984 led him to conclude that the African fossils could be included in *H. erectus* only if a grade concept were being used, had by 1987 decided that they could be properly included in the *erectus* clade.

Finally, Turner and Chamberlain (1989) argue that cladistic analyses that attempt to define species using apomorphic character states may prove to be unworkable unless the characters themselves can be related to the fertilization system of the species. Here they follow Paterson (1985) by using his "recognition concept," which states that only those characters of sexual organisms that are related to mating and fertilization (or the bases for them) will necessarily be correlated with speciation itself. These authors do not attempt to give any details of *H. erectus* morphology that could be related to the specific mate recognition system of Paterson. Rather, they point out that most, if not all, of the autapomorphic characters used in prior cladistic analyses are hardly likely to have influenced early hominid sexual behavior. They believe that there is no consistent correlation between a speciation event and a change in morphology and that, when due recognition is given to the level of variation in early African *H. erectus* grade hominids, there is no good reason not to include them in the species.

This last point about variation seems very important, and without intending to belabor the issue, I shall give yet another example. It is often said that the crania of the early African sample have thinner vaults than later crania. Table 2 gives frontal bone thickness measured at bregma or as near as possible to bregma in the early African sample for comparison with the later Asian ones. Even counting KNM-WT 15000, which is a juvenile, and not counting Olduvai Hominid 9, which is from somewhat younger deposits, the mean for the early sample is 8.6 mm with a range of 7.3 to 10.0 mm. If Olduvai Hominid 9 is included, the mean is 8.75 mm. The mean and ranges for vault thickness near bregma for Zhoukoudian, according to Weidenreich (1943), is 8.78 mm with a range of 7.0 to 9.9 mm. Thus the vault thicknesses in these two samples are very nearly equal.

With all this in mind, we decided for the purposes of this volume to assign KNM-WT 15000 to *H. erectus*. The following alternatives to this assignment may or may not be testable in the future.

(1) For those who see speciation as occurring only by splitting, KNM-WT 15000 could be called one of three things. If there has been no split of the lineage leading to *Homo sapiens* since the early Pleistocene, it will be part of our species *by definition*. If there has been a split of the lineage, then KNM-WT 15000 might either be placed in the species *Homo erectus* or be declared a new species, depending on the distribution of derived traits.

(2) For those who believe that species can arise anagenetically, then time-successive species within the

Table 2. Thickness (mm) of Frontals At or Near Bregma

KNM-ER 730	8.5
KNM-ER 1466	10.0
KNM-ER 3883	8.0
KNM-ER 3892	9.2
KNM-WT 15000	7.3
KNM-ER 3733	(damaged here)
OH 9*	9.5

*Estimated from diagram of CT scan in Maier and Nkini, 1984.

genus *Homo* might be definable. If it becomes apparent that the early African sample is the same species as the later Asian ones, then it might be placed in *Homo erectus,* but if there are sufficient unique differences then it might be accommodated in a new species.

In either case, if a new name is needed for the species in which the early African sample belongs, then that name is, as suggested by Wood (1991, 1992), *H. ergaster.* This point is taken up in the next section.

THE STATUS OF OTHER FOSSILS

With a fairly complete skeleton of an early African *H. erectus,* it is now possible to know which other fossils belong in this species and which do not. The discovery of KNM-WT 15000, together with the recently discovered association of a mandibular fragment with a small *Australopithecus boisei* skeleton, means that we can sort most postcranial bones from the later part of the Turkana Basin succession into one or the other species. The task of sorting is still difficult for the period up to 1.7 Ma because it appears that some of these earlier postcranial bones could either be small *H. habilis* or *A. boisei.* Walker and Leakey (1993) have pointed out which other fossils from East and West Turkana can be certainly assigned to *H. erectus.* Table 3 gives a list of these.

The most important, as far as taxonomy goes, is KNM-ER 992, the type of *Homo ergaster.* A nearly complete mandible, KNM-ER 992 was discovered in 1971. Leakey et al. (1978) stated that this specimen belonged to the same taxon as cranium KNM-ER 1813 and that there were affinities with *Australopithecus africanus* from

Table 3.   Early *Homo erectus* Specimens from Lake Turkana

Specimen Number	Body Part	Stratigraphic Member
KNM-ER 164	Cranial fragment, vertebrae, phalanges	KBS
KNM-ER 730	Partial skull	KBS
KNM-ER 731	Mandible fragment	Okote
KNM-ER 736	Femur	Okote
KNM-ER 737	Femur	Okote
KNM-ER 741	Tibia	Okote
KNM-ER 803	Partial skeleton	Okote
KNM-ER 806	Isolated teeth	Okote
KNM-ER 807	Maxilla fragment	KBS
KNM-ER 808	Isolated teeth	Okote
KNM-ER 820	Juvenile mandible	Okote
KNM-ER 992	Mandible	Okote
KNM-ER 1466	Frontal fragment	Okote
KNM-ER 1808	Partial skeleton	KBS
KNM-ER 1821	Parietal fragment	KBS
KNM-ER 2592	Parietal fragment	Okote
KNM-ER 3733	Cranium	KBS
KNM-ER 3883	Cranium	Okote
KNM-ER 3892	Frontal fragment	Okote
KNM-ER 5428	Talus	KBS
KNM-WT 15000	Skeleton	Natoo
KNM-WT 16001	Cranial fragments	Natoo
KNM-WT 19700	Tibial fragment	Nachukui

South Africa. Groves and Mazak (1975) made the mandible the type specimen of *Homo ergaster* but, curiously, did not attempt to make a differential diagnosis between this specimen and those attributed to *H. erectus.* Wood (1976) concluded from a metrical study of the mandible that it could be allocated to *H. erectus.* Howell (1978) also placed it in that species.

Until KNM-WT 15000 was found, however, it was still difficult to establish the identity of this jaw. This was because only one of the mandibles from Lake Turkana was associated with an *erectus* grade cranium. This specimen (KNM-ER 730) also was an old adult with anterior alveolar resorption and with the three remaining teeth worn to the gum. Comparisons could be made with cranium KNM-ER 1813, which is not of *erectus* grade. Groves (1989) regards this comparison favorably and includes both KNM-ER 992 and 1813 in his *H. ergaster.* He made statements about the shape of the whole mandible that are not accurate. As noted in the original description (Leakey and Wood, 1973), the break between the two halves is not a simple one, and some crushing has occurred. Leakey and Wood wrote: "Breakage and displacement of bone at the anterior end of the body, especially on the left side, precludes accurate articulation of the hemi-mandibles, and requires that comments on the shape of the tooth row and dimensions of the whole mandible must await expert reassembly of the damaged area." This has not yet been done. The photograph in Groves (1989, figure 7.4) of the casts pushed together at the anterior break is misleading.

We can now compare the mandible of the Nariokotome specimen with the type of *H. ergaster.* When allowance is made for the juvenile state of the former and for the interstitial and occlusal wear of the latter (Brown and Walker, 1993), the similarities are striking, even down to details of the subocclusal morphology as revealed by X-ray. If, as Wood (1991) suggests, the early African *erectus*-grade hominids need their own taxon, then *H. ergaster* is the appropriate name for it. Two other mandibular specimens now known to be from this sample have been included here in Figures 3 and 4. These are KNM-ER 820 and KNM-ER 730. The first is a juvenile younger even than KNM-WT 15000 (see Smith, 1993) and the second is an old adult, older in terms of tooth-wear than KNM-ER 992. These four mandibles have been arranged in the figures in order of individual age, and they make a very impressive age series showing development of the body, mesial drift of the teeth, and, in the case of KNM-WT 15000 and KNM-ER 992, the development of the ramus.

THE FUNCTIONAL MORPHOLOGY OF EARLY AFRICAN *HOMO ERECTUS*

Many aspects of early African *H. erectus* morphology have been covered in the accounts presented in this volume. Here I review a few that deserve special mention.

The overall similarity between early *H. erectus* skeletons and those of modern humans is striking. As we

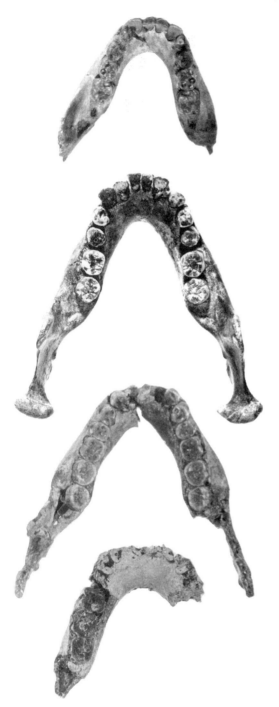

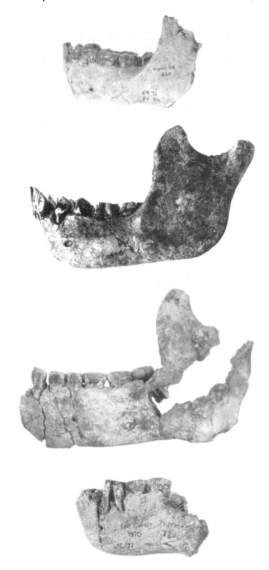

Figure 4. *Left lateral views of an age series of early Homo erectus mandibles.* Top to bottom: *KNM-ER 820, KNM-WT 15000 B, KNM-ER 992, and KNM-ER 730.*

Figure 3. *Occlusal views of an age series of early Homo erectus mandibles.* Top to bottom: *KNM-ER 820, KNM-WT 15000 B, KNM-ER 992, and KNM-ER 730.*

have shown, the limb proportions are those found in modern human populations who inhabit extremely hot, dry places. The facial skeleton seems remarkably modern in many aspects, although the paranasal sinus development is advanced for an individual of that dental age and the face as a whole is more prognathic. The upper limb skeleton is unremarkable from a modern human perspective. The thorax had already developed the unique human features of being barrel-shaped and having a ventrally invaginated thoracic column and ribs

that hang downwards and forwards. The vertebrae show that the lordotic and kyphotic curvatures typical of modern humans were already in place. Even the six lumbar vertebrae which seem to be typical of early hominids can be found in a small percentage of modern people. The major exceptions to a modern morphology are in the size and shape of the braincase, the size of the thoracic neural canal, the narrowness of the pelvis, the long femoral necks, the marked medullary cavity stenosis of the limb bones, and the markedly concave anterior borders of the fibulae.

These exceptions have been dealt with in the various chapters concerning them, but a few further remarks are necessary. Cranial capacities of early African *H. erectus* individuals were small by modern human standards. As an illustration, the capacity for an average individual that stood 1.7 meters tall and weighed nearly 60 kg was about 900 cc. As a crude illustration, this is about the cranial capacity of a human child between the ages of three and four whose stature might be around 1 meter and whose weight around 15 kg. There is, of course, no obvious correlation between mental abilities and brain size in people, but the gross difference in relative adult brain size between *H. erectus* and *H. sapiens* must point to differences in behavior. This difference should be enough to caution workers against using much of the behavior of modern people as a model for the behavior of these hominids 1.5 million years ago.

Despite this relative small brain size, however, the uniquely human trait of having secondarily altricial infants was already established among early hominids, as the extremely narrow pelvis of these specimens shows (Walker and Ruff, 1993). Selection for larger brains was already operating, then, despite stabilizing selection, which kept pelvises narrow and femoral necks long either for climatic or locomotor reasons. The abductor mechanism of the pelvis can be made more efficient by either decreasing the distance between the hip joints (and thereby narrowing the birth canal) or lengthening the femoral neck or both. *H. erectus* individuals had both narrow birth canals and long femoral necks and thus a more mechanically efficient abductor mechanism than modern *H. sapiens*. It is a matter of some importance to trace the subsequent development of the human condition and find reasons for the compromise of the abductor mechanism. This will require the finding of more complete fossil material, but a speculation can be offered here.

Stabilizing selection acting on the pelvis together with positive selection for larger brain size had led to secondarily altricial infants in *H. erectus* by 1.5 Ma. Modern humans could have evolved wide birth canals and kept primitively long femoral necks only if climatic conditions allowed a wide body build. This type of build is seen, in fact, among neandertals who had adapted to extreme cold and who had very wide pelvises and still retained relatively long femoral necks. A reasonable suggestion would be that modern humans had their origin in equatorial latitudes and that climatic stabilizing selection maintained the primitively narrow body condition, but that positive selection pressure for larger brains led to a compromise in the efficiency of the abductor mechanism. This led to wide birth canals and short femoral necks. An African origin of modern humans has been postulated for some time now (Stringer, 1990), and although present tree-making algorithms do not allow the mitochondrial DNA data to be interpreted as supporting or not an African origin for modern humans (Templeton, 1992), other genetic data hint at this conclusion. The very early modern human fossils from Qafzeh (Vandermeersch, 1969) also are considered to be African in affinities and are earlier in age than some neandertals in their region (Stringer, 1990).

The limb bones of early hominids are more robustly built than those of modern *H. sapiens*. Ruff et al. (1992) have demonstrated that "robusticity" (structural strength of bone relative to body mass) declines exponentially in the genus *Homo* from the early Pleistocene to the present day. There was little change in robusticity with the species *H. erectus*, however, because the decline is exponential. These changes probably reflect decreased mechanical loading of the skeleton and may not have any strong genetic basis. Early African *H. erectus* were, therefore, probably very active and placed high stresses on their postcranial skeletons.

THE ORIGINS OF SPEECH AND LANGUAGE

There are two schools of thought on the origin of human language. One believes that language of some sort appeared early in the human lineage, by the beginning of the Pleistocene at least. The other believes that human language and its use of speech appeared very late in our evolution, perhaps as late as 40,000 years ago. Several different sorts of evidence are used by both schools, but both use evidence from the morphology of the fossils and the nature of the archeological record. The morphological evidence involves the central nervous system and the pharyngeal airway. The primary evidence for speech noted by the first school is the size of the brain together with the presence of asymmetries and certain details on the endocranial surface. The second school holds as evidence of speech the bony parts from which it might be possible to make a reconstruction of the pharyngeal resonators. Other evidence includes the complexity of the archeological record, language capabilities of other primates, and the sequence of language development in human children. Noble and Davidson (1991) give a recent review of some of the arguments in this complex field. I shall deal here only with the evidence that can be gathered from the morphology of the fossils.

It has been thought for some time now that evidence of defined speech areas can be found on the endocasts of early hominids from at least 2.0 Ma. The two areas that might be expected to leave impressions are Broca's and Wernicke's (Begun and Walker, 1993). Tobias (1983) has claimed the presence of the former in hominids as early as *Australopithecus africanus* and the latter in the earliest members of the genus *Homo*. Tobias (1983, 1991), following Holloway (1969, 1983), links the development of language with stone tool complexity. As he puts it (1991, p. 836), "the complexity which archeologists have shown in, or inferred from, the lifestyle of *H. habilis* seems to the author to mark the point at which adequate and efficient transmission of cultural practices and advances to the offspring required at least rudimentary language."

Holloway (1983) gives the clearest account of what can and what cannot be learned about language from looking at endocasts of fossils. He suggests that four traits can be of use, but concludes that paleoneurological evidence can only corroborate or correlate with other evidence. He considers that the archeological record is the only "true" evidence for early human cognitive behavior. The four traits are brain size and evidence of well-defined areas for the motor control of speech, for Wernicke's area, and for cerebral asymmetries. Many advances in human and primate brain research have been made since Holloway's seminal paper (1969), and a summary of those that pertain to the origins of language can be made here.

Brain Size

As Holloway himself pointed out, brain size by itself cannot help one decide whether an early hominid could speak or not, even though some mimumum size must be required. Tobias (1983, 1991) calls attention to the coincidence of clear speech areas appearing at the same time as brain enlargment and encephalization became "obtrusive" and stone tools appear in the geological record. As Begun and Walker (1993) have pointed out, the evidence now suggests that *H. erectus* individuals were larger than had previously been suspected and that they are about as encephalized as *H. habilis*. If there was language in these two species, as Tobias thinks, then there seems to have been no corresponding increase in encephalization with changes in stone tool technology or during the dramatic spread of *H. erectus* over the Old World.

Broca's Area

As Begun and Walker have pointed out (1993), there now is good evidence from physiological studies on living people that the cortical area of the brain thought by Broca to be a motor area for speech is more likely to be associated with motor programming rather than with speech function. Tobias (1983) thought that the traditionally defined Broca's area was present in *A. africanus* but that Wernicke's area was not. This does not make much intuitive sense, since it is difficult to imagine how downstream parts of a command system could be selected for without the corresponding upstream parts. Holloway, in fact, pointed out (1983, p. 111) that Broca's caps could be found on chimpanzee endocasts. It could be argued, I suppose, that a language area deep to Broca's cap could be responsible for its development, but that is not very convincing.

Wernicke's Area

This is the most difficult area to assess. Most of the endocasts I know are distorted somewhat. That of KNM-WT 15000, for instance, is pushed over to the left and so features on the left side appear fuller. Tobias (1991, p. 729) says that the mark of the inferior parietal lobule shows strong development on all four of the Olduvai *H. habilis* endocasts. The following remarks can be made about the four endocasts. Olduvai Hominid 24 was squashed flat when found. Despite almost heroic efforts by R. J. Clarke to undo this distortion, he could not unflatten vault bones. Olduvai Hominid 16 has mainly fragments of vault bone, and the orientation of these pieces probably will never be completely settled. Olduvai Hominid 7 has most of the left and a piece of the right parietal. And Olduvai Hominid 13 has only the top part of the left parietal. In all of these cases it is very difficult to decide whether or not there were asymmetries in the configurations of the inferior parietal lobule impressions or even, I suspect, whether the impression itself is there. It is even more difficult to imagine how any such differences could be measured. Asymmetries of the sylvian sulcus impression are not necessarily indications of a well-developed speech area, as LeMay (1975) has proposed. This is because a longer left sylvian fissure is found in chimpanzees and *Macaca* (Falk et al., 1986).

Cerebral Asymmetries

It has been known for some time that human brains are often asymmetrical and also, since the work of R. W. Sperry, that in humans the left hemisphere is usually dominant in speech (see Williams et al., 1989, pp. 1064–1068, for a very clear review). It has been shown recently that it is the linguistic and not the symbolic or motor properties of language that are lateralized in the left hemisphere (Corina et al., 1992). It is also now known, however, that some Old World monkeys and chimpanzees are left hemisphere dominant for perception of meaningful (species-specific) vocalizations and that their brains are asymmetrical in ways similar to those of humans (Falk et al., 1990), including in sylvian fissure asymmetry (Falk et al., 1986). As Falk et al. (1990) conclude, the neurological substrate for brain lateralization may have been present during early anthropoid evolution. Thus care must be taken not to equate brain asymmetries necessarily with speech, even though in most humans the left hemisphere is the verbally skillful one.

There are definite associations between certain cerebral asymmetries and handedness in humans (LeMay, 1976). In KNM-WT 15000 the endocast shows a wider right frontal, right frontopetalia, and equal occipital petalia (Begun and Walker, 1993). In this the fossil is most like modern male right-handers. There are also asymmetries in the postcranial skeleton of this specimen. The right ulna is longer than the left and the clavicles have asymmetrical ligament pits and muscle scars. Schultz (1937) reviewed the asymmetries in lengths of long bones and found that right upper limb bones were usually longer in humans. He did not measure ulnas, but he found that the right radius was the longer in nearly 70% of cases and the left longer in 18%. The distributions are much more even in anthropoids. The fact that the clavicles of KNM-WT 15000 are asymmetrical and that the right ulna is longer suggests, together with the endocranial evidence, that this youth was right-handed. Since both brain asymmetries (LeMay, 1976) and limb asymmetries (Ruff and Jones, 1981) are known to be associated with handedness, it is likely that they are part of the same lateralization process. It is also likely that these combined asymmetries in the fossil skeleton show that this youth was right-handed for tool use. Toth (1985) has found evidence that early hominids at Lake Turkana had a preference for right-handedness in stone tool making. It does not necessarily follow, as I hope I have shown above, that he could speak because he was right-handed.

The Acheulean stone technologies which are associated with these early *H. erectus* populations require cores to be processed by reduction from large flakes. Sometimes such large flakes can be found already detached from their source rock, but in many instances these have to be removed from boulders or outcrops.

Practically the only means of removing large flakes that was available to these early hominids was the throwing of one boulder against another. Even if the spheroids and bifaces often found on these sites were not throwing objects, throwing must have been involved in flake removal. Darlington (1957, 1975) hypothesized that throwing was an important part of hunting behavior in early hominids and that selection for throwing efficiency would have brought about changes in those parts of the central and peripheral nervous system that were required in the complex act of "correlation of three moving objects (the animal, the object thrown, and another animal)." He suggests that such changes would then be preadaptive for later, more complex human faculties. This idea has been developed more fully by Calvin (1983) and others who see hammering and throwing as important skills which would have been selected for in early hominids and which would also lead to selection for handedness and increased circuitry in those parts of the central nervous system responsible for accurate throwing and the feedback required for it. Calvin himself thinks that the Acheulean bifaces were specialized objects purposefully made for throwing, but it is worth pointing out that at Olorgesalie, where bifaces abound in some places, only flakes struck from bifaces and not the bifaces themselves are found at butchery sites and, further, that edge wear is restricted to flakes (Rick Potts, personal communication). Perhaps the lateralization and the development of Broca's caps in early *H. erectus* is a reflection of throwing and hammering ability rather than of speech. Noble and Davidson (1991) hypothesize that selection for one-handed throwing could provide the neural mechanism for pointing, since pointing can be thought of as aiming without throwing.

The Spinal Cord

KNM-WT 15000 has many of its vertebrae preserved, enough for Latimer and Ward (1993) to show that he had all the spinal features associated with the fully human form of upright bipedalism. The vertebrae also allowed MacLarnon (1993) to examine whether or not the spinal canal was built in the same way as it is in humans. She found that the overall shape and proportions of the canal were most similar to humans among primates, and many of the features she examined were only found in humans. There was one important feature, however, in which *H. erectus* differed from modern humans—the relative size of the thoracic vertebral canal. In this feature MacLarnon found that KNM-WT 15000 was like other primates and not like humans, who have larger relative thoracic canals than all other primates. She concluded that *H. erectus* did not have the typically human increased bulk of grey matter in the thoracic cord nor enlarged thoracic spinal nerves. She also gave two possible explanations for this. The first is that improvements in the control of bipedalism might be responsible for the later enlargements in humans. This alternative I find unlikely since hominids had been bipedal for more than 2 million years by the time the Nariokotome boy was born. And, further, all parts of the locomotor system and body proportions in KNM-WT 15000 and the other fossils from that population seem to be completely human, even down to conforming to Allen's rule (Ruff and Walker, 1993). The second alternative is that the enlargement might be related to speech and that more control of the intercostal muscles and abdominal wall muscles is needed in modern people than was needed in *H. erectus*. If speech had not developed in *H. erectus,* then increased control over a normal primate thoracic cage and abdomen would not have been needed and the thoracic cord enlargement would not have been present. William Calvin (personal communication) also points out that the enlargement could have stabilized the thorax and abdomen for throwing.

The Upper Respiratory Tract

A great deal of interest and controversy has been generated since Leiberman and Crelin (1971) first concluded that neandertals could not speak. They based their analysis on studies of the upper pharynx and other resonators in the respiratory tract of humans and apes and on a reconstruction of the same in neandertals. Laitman and his colleagues, following this lead, have looked at the basicranial anatomy of early hominids (Laitman, 1985) and concluded that early African *H. erectus* (as exemplified by KNM-ER 3773) are the earliest hominids to have a cranial base that is derived relative to the basic mammalian condition. Laitman suggested further that the larynx may have been somewhat lowered in these populations and that the human type of upper respiratory tract might have begun to develop then. Laitman (personal communication) does not himself think that selection for laryngeal descent is related to the onset of human speech. Rather, he thinks a purely respiratory function would be selected for first.

Fransiscus and Trinkaus (1988) reviewed another part of the early hominid respiratory tract, the nose and nasal cavity, and concluded that early African *H. erectus* nasal morphology reflected the increased physiological demands of life in an arid environment. They point out that the change from an ape-like, flat, non-projecting nose to an anteriorly positioned external nose as in modern humans came first with these African populations. They argue that this new nasal structure allowed a greater volume of inhaled air to be moisturized with conserved exhaled moisture. They also pointed out that the appearance of the human type of nose in early African *H. erectus* followed the development of limbs that show a full adaptation to terrestrial bipedalism; it also coincided with the development of the Acheulean lithic complex and preceded the spread of the species out of Africa. The observations and ideas of Laitman and colleagues and Fransiscus and Trinkaus can be seen to converge, then, on the point that greater respiratory volume served as an adaptation for prolonged active bouts in arid environments. They might provide reasons for the initial respiratory adaptations from which efficient pharyngeal resonators could have developed, but they do not lend direct support to the presence of speech 1.5 million years ago.

CONCLUSION

The reader is referred to Noble and Davidson (1991) for a recent critical review of the origins of language. They reason that since the constituent signs of language are used symbolically, the earliest signs of language will be the archeological traces of symbols. They find no evidence of symbolic signs prior to 32,000 years ago and conclude that human language is a very late evolutionary event. Their review did not cover the morphology of early hominids, but from the brief review given above I feel that those who have done so and then claimed a very early origin for human language and speech are standing on ground that is steadily crumbling away. The reading of complex behaviors into the archeological record is all too easy and practically untestable. The notion that language is needed for cultural transmission if the inferred life-style and tools appear complex (Tobias, 1983) is testable, however. An experiment could be devised, for instance, whereby people are asked to make tools by following spoken instructions or by following an example. I suspect that it would be easier to make an Acheulean biface after watching someone else make one than to attempt the same by listening to instructions, let alone by reading an instruction manual! What such an experiment would tell us about hominid behavior 1.5 million years ago, though, is another matter. Potts (1991) has recently observed and measured a large sample of the Oldowan stone tool "culture" that impressed Tobias with its complexity and has concluded that standardized categories of broken stones cannot be found. Potts finds complete overlap in counts of scars, lengths of edges, and suchlike on cores and a complete spectrum of flake size and shape.

THE ORIGINS OF *HOMO ERECTUS*

Most authorities agree that the early African members of the genus *Homo* such as KNM-WT 15000 are from the early part of the human lineage, even if they do not agree on the name for them. But the origins of these populations are still a matter of dispute. With the exception of Groves (1989), who sees four species of the genus *Homo* about 2 million years ago, most workers fall into two groups. The first group thinks that there was only one non-*boisei* species at this time and that this species contained the populations antecedent to early African *H. erectus*. The second thinks that there were two non-*boisei* species at this time. The problem is not an easy one to solve, because there are about as many hypodigms of *H. habilis* as there are workers in the field. Whole crania can be placed in different species or even genera by different people. *H. habilis* (Leakey, Tobias, and Napier, 1964) was based on a broken, subadult mandible and some skull fragments that are probably associated with it and some postcranial pieces that are possibly associated with it. Tobias (1991) has now completed his analyses of the *H. habilis* fossils from Olduvai, but there are now many more fossils attributed to this species than there are from just that one site. These have been found in South Africa, Kenya, and Ethiopia. The variation to be seen in this species has increased

with the sample. For some people (e.g., Howell, 1978; Johanson, 1989; McHenry, 1991; Tobias, 1991; Wolpoff, 1980) there is only one, variable species. For others (e.g., Leakey and Walker, 1978; Rightmire, 1990; Stringer, 1986; Walker, 1991; Wood, 1991), the level of variability suggests that there is more than one species present. At present there is no way of resolving this issue. We need more and better fossil hominids from about 2 Ma. We can, however, give two alternative accounts from these two perspectives on the number of early *Homo* species about 2 million years ago.

If there was only one non-*boisei* hominid species antecedent to *H. erectus*, then the following can be said about the transition. *H. habilis* in this account would be a very variable, sexually dimorphic species with body size dimorphism approaching that of species of *Australopithecus*. Females were short, perhaps only a meter tall, and had humerofemoral proportions more like those of chimpanzees than humans (Johanson et al., 1987; Johanson, 1989). They were relatively megadont and had skulls which retained many features reminiscent of *Australopithecus* (Walker, 1976), including the flat pyriform aperture and nasal region. This species made a punctuational transition to *H. erectus* about 1.8 million years ago (OH 62 is about 1.8 Ma). The individuals of the new species were larger and displayed less sexual dimorphism. (That is, the females were as large as the males in the previous species). Brain size increased along with body size and limb proportions became essentially human. These physical changes coincided with major changes in lithic technology. This is the hypothesis put forward by the discoverers and describers of Olduvai Hominid 62 (Johanson et al., 1987) in the telegraphic form usually found in *Nature* articles and expanded a little in Johanson (1989).

The second account involves two non-*boisei* hominids co-existing about 2 million years ago. One of these species that are presently lumped together as one in *H. habilis* was ancestral to *H. erectus* and is represented by specimens such as KNM-ER 1470, 1471, 1590, and 3228. It is not, however, a very well-known taxon. The other species is better represented in both South and East Africa and includes specimens like Olduvai Hominids 24 and 62 and KNM-ER 1813. This hypothesis was put forward by Leakey and Walker (1978) and does not necessarily involve a punctuational event.

The testing of these two competing hypotheses is critical to our understanding of the origin of the genus *Homo*. The resolution of this problem should determine whether or not our lineage evolved in a punctuated evolutionary manner and whether or not major external stimulants such as global climatic shifts affected the course of our own evolution. Whether we can recognize any correspondence between morphological changes and major faunal changes or the appearance of new lithic technologies depends on our ability to sort out the phylogeny of the earliest members of the genus *Homo*. We have been able in the past to find new evidence to test hypotheses (e.g., Leakey and Walker, 1976), so it should be a matter of urgency that we plan field expeditions to look for the more complete fossils that will solve this problem.

REFERENCES

Adelola, A., K. R. Kattan, and F. N. Silverman. 1975. Thickness of the normal skull in the American blacks and whites. *American Journal of Physical Anthropology* 43: 23–30.

Andrews, P. J. 1984. An alternative interpretation of the characters used to define *Homo erectus*. *Courier Forschungsinstitut Senckenberg* 69: 167–175.

Begun, D., and A. Walker. 1993. The endocast. In *The Nariokotome Homo erectus Skeleton*, ed. A. Walker and R. Leakey, pp. 266–293. Cambridge: Harvard University Press.

Behrensmeyer, A. K., and L. F. Laporte. 1981. Footprints of a Pleistocene hominid in northern Kenya. *Nature* 289: 167–169.

Bilsborough, A., and B. A. Wood. 1986. The origin and fate of *Homo erectus*. In *Major Topics in Primate and Human Evolution*, ed. B. A. Wood, L. Martin, and P. Andrews, pp. 295–316. Cambridge: Cambridge University Press.

Brauer, G. 1990. The occurrence of some controversial *Homo erectus* cranial features in the Zoukoudian and East African hominids. *Acta Anthropologica Sinica* 9: 352–358.

Brown, B., and A. Walker. 1993. The dentition. In *The Nariokotome Homo erectus Skeleton*, ed. A. Walker and R. Leakey, pp. 161–192. Cambridge: Harvard University Press.

Brown, F., J. Harris, R. Leakey, and A. Walker. 1985. Early *Homo erectus* from west Lake Turkana, Kenya. *Nature* 316: 788–792.

Bunn, H. T. 1981. Archaeological evidence for meat-eating by Plio-Pleistocene hominids from Koobi Fora and Olduvai Gorge. *Nature* 291: 574–577.

Calvin, W. H. 1983. A stone's throw and its launch window: Timing precision and its implications for language and hominid brains. *Journal of Theoretical Biology* 104: 121–135.

Carrier, D. R. 1984. The energetic paradox of human running and hominid evolution. *Current Anthropology* 25: 483–495.

Chamberlain, A. T., and B. A. Wood. 1987. Early hominid phylogeny. *Journal of Human Evolution* 16: 119–133.

Cohen, M. N., and G. J. Armelagos. 1984. *Paleopathology at the Origins of Agriculture*. Orlando: Academic Press.

Corina, D. P., J. Vaid, and U. Bellugi. 1992. The linguistic basis of left hemisphere lateralization. *Science* 255: 1258–1260.

Darlington, P. R. 1957 *Zoogeography*. New York: Wiley.

——— 1975. Group selection, altruism, reinforcement, and throwing in human evolution. *Proceedings of the National Academy of Sciences* 72: 3748–3752.

Day, M. H. 1971. Postcranial remains of *Homo erectus* from Bed IV, Olduvai Gorge, Tanzania. *Nature* 221: 383–387.

Falk, D., J. Cheverud, M. W. Vannier, and G. C. Conroy. 1986. Advanced computer graphics technology reveals cortical asymmetry in endocasts of rhesus monkeys. *Folia Primatologica* 46: 98–103.

Feibel, C. S., and F. H. Brown. 1993. Microstratigraphy and paleoenvironments. In *The Nariokotome Homo erectus Skeleton*, ed. A. Walker and R. Leakey, pp. 21–39. Cambridge: Harvard University Press.

Feibel, C., J. M. Harris, and F. H. Brown. 1991. Palaeoenvironmental context for the late Neogene of the Turkana Basin. In *Koobi Fora Research Project*, vol. 3, ed. J. M. Harris. Oxford: Clarendon Press.

Fransiscus, R. G., and E. T. Trinkaus. 1988. Nasal morphology and the emergence of *Homo erectus*. *American Journal of Physical Anthropology* 75: 517–527.

Groves, C. P. 1989. *A Theory of Human and Primate Evolution*. Oxford: Clarendon Press.

Groves, C. P., and V. Mazek. 1975. An approach to the taxonomy of the Hominidae: Gracile Villafrancian hominids of Africa. *Casopis pro Mineralogii a Geologii* 20: 225–247.

Harvey, P. H. 1990. Life-history variation: Size and mortality patterns. In *Primate Life History and Evolution*, ed. C. J. DeRousseau, pp. 81–88. New York: Wiley-Liss.

Holloway, R. L. 1969. Culture: A *human* domain. *Current Anthropology* 10: 395–407.

——— 1983. Human paleontological evidence relevant to language behavior. *Human Neurobiology* 2: 105–114.

Hopson, J. A. 1989. Leonard Burton Radinsky (1937–1985). In *The Evolution of the Perissodactyls*, ed. D. R. Prothero and R. M. Schoch, pp. 3–12. Oxford: Oxford University Press.

Howell, F. C. 1978. Hominidae. In *Evolution of African Mammals*, ed. H. B. S. Cooke and V. J. Maglio, pp. 154–248. Cambridge: Harvard University Press.

Hull, D. L. 1979. The limits of cladism. *Systematic Zoology* 28: 416–440.

Johanson, D. C. 1989. A partial *Homo habilis* skeleton from Olduvai Gorge, Tanzania: A summary of preliminary results. In *Hominidae: Proceedings of the Second International Congress of Human Paleontology*, ed. G. Giacobini, pp. 155–166. Milan: Jaca Book.

Johanson, D. C., F. T. Masao, G. E. Eck, T. D. White, R. C. Walter, W. H. Kimbel, B. Asfaw, P. Manega, P. Ndessokia, and G. Suwa. 1987. New partial skeleton of *Homo habilis* from Olduvai Gorge, Tanzania. *Nature* 327: 205–209.

Kennedy, G. E. 1991. On the autapomorphic traits of *Homo erectus*. *Journal of Human Evolution* 20: 375–412.

Laitman, J. T. 1985. Evolution of the hominid upper respiratory tract: The fossil evidence. In *Hominid Evolution: Past, Present and Future*, ed. P. V. Tobias, pp. 281–286. New York: Alan R. Liss.

Latimer, B., and C. V. Ward. 1993. The endocast. In *The Nariokotome Homo erectus Skeleton*, ed. A. Walker and R. Leakey, pp. 326–358. Cambridge: Harvard University Press.

Leakey, L. S. B. 1964. Very early African Hominidae and their ecological setting. In *African Ecology and Human Evolution*, ed. F. C. Howell and F. Bourliere, pp. 448–457. London: Methuen.

Leakey, L. S. B., P. V. T. Tobias, and J. R. Napier. 1964. A new species of the genus *Homo* from Olduvai Gorge. *Nature* 202: 7–9.

Leakey, R. E., M. G. Leakey, and A. K. Behrensmeyer. 1978. The hominid catalogue. In *Koobi Fora Research Project*, vol. 1, ed. M. G. Leakey and R. E. Leakey, pp. 86–182. Oxford: Clarendon Press.

Leakey, R. E., and A. C. Walker. 1976. *Australopithecus*, *Homo erectus* and the single species hypothesis. *Nature* 261: 572–574.

——— 1978. The hominids of East Turkana. *Scientific American* 239: 54–66.

——— 1985. Further hominids from the Plio-Pleistocene of Koobi-Fora, Kenya. *American Journal of Physical Anthropology* 67: 135–163.

——— 1989. Early *Homo erectus* skeleton from west Lake Turkana, Kenya. In *Hominidae: Proceedings of the Second International Congress of Human Paleontology*, ed. G. Giacobini, pp. 209–215. Milan: Jaca Book.

Leakey R. E., and Walker A. C. 1993. Introduction. In *The Nariokotome Homo erectus Skeleton*, ed. A. Walker and R. Leakey, pp. 1–4. Cambridge: Harvard University Press.

Leakey, R. E. F., and B. A. Wood. 1973. New evidence for the genus *Homo* from East Rudolf, Kenya (II). *American Journal of Physical Anthropology* 39: 355–368.

Leiberman, P. E., and E. S. Crelin. 1971. On the speech of Neanderthal man. *Linguistic Inquiry* 2: 203–222.

LeMay, M. 1976. Morphological cerebral asymmetries of modern man, fossil man, and nonhuman primate. *Annals of the New York Academy of Sciences* 280: 349–366.

MacLarnon, A. 1993. The vertebral canal. In *The Nariokotome Homo erectus Skeleton*, ed. A. Walker and R. Leakey, pp. 359–390. Cambridge: Harvard University Press.

Maier, W., and A. Nkini. 1984. Olduvai Hominid 9: New results of investigation. *Courier Forschungsinstitut Senckenberg* 69: 123–130.

Martin, R. 1928. *Lehrbuch der Anthropologie*. Jena: Fischer.

Martin, R. D. 1983. *Human Brain Evolution in an Ecological Context: Fifty-second James Arthur Lecture on the Human Brain*. New York: American Museum of Natural History.

McHenry, H. M. 1988. New estimates of body weight in early hominids and their significance to encephalization and megadontia in "robust" australopithecines. In *Evolutionary History of the "Robust" Australopithecines*, ed. F. E. Grine, pp. 133–148. New York: Aldine de Gruyter.

——— 1991. Femoral lengths and stature in Plio-Pleistocene hominids. *American Journal of Physical Anthropology* 85: 149–158.

Noble, W., and I. Davidson. 1991. The evolutionary emergence of modern human behaviour: Language and its archeology. *Man* 26: 223–254.

Paterson, H. E. H. 1986. Environment and species. *South African Journal of Science* 82: 62–65.

Pilbeam, D. R., and S. J. Gould. 1974. Size and scaling in human evolution. *Science* 186: 892–901.

Potts, R. 1991. Why the Oldowan? *Journal of Anthropological Research* 47: 153–176.

Potts, R., and P. Shipman. 1981. Cutmarks made by stone tools on bones from Olduvai Gorge, Tanzania. *Nature* 291: 577–580.

Rightmire, P. G. 1981. Patterns in the evolution of *Homo erectus*. *Paleobiology* 7: 241–246.

———— 1990. *The Evolution of Homo erectus.* Cambridge: Cambridge University Press.

———— 1986. Stasis in *Homo erectus* defended. *Paleobiology* 12: 324–325.

Rose, K. D., and T. M. Bown. 1993. Species concepts and species recognition in Eocene primates. In *Species, Species Concepts and Primate Evolution,* ed. L. Martin and W. Kimbel. New York: Plenum.

Ruff, C. B. 1991. Climate and body shape in hominid evolution. *Journal of Human Evolution* 21: 81–105.

Ruff, C. B., and H. H. Jones. 1981. Bilateral asymmetry in cortical bone of the humerus and tibia—Sex and age factors. *Human Biology* 53: 69–86.

Ruff, C. B., E. Trinkaus, A. Walker, and C. S. Larson. 1993. Postcranial robusticity in *Homo,* I: Temporal trends and mechanical interpretation. *American Journal of Physical Anthropology* 91: 21–53.

Ruff, C. B., and A. Walker. 1993. Body size and body shape. In *The Nariokotome* Homo erectus *Skeleton,* ed. A. Walker and R. Leakey, pp. 234–265. Cambridge: Harvard University Press.

Schmidt-Nielsen, K. 1975. *Animal Physiology.* Cambridge: Cambridge University Press.

Schultz, A. H. 1937. Proportions, variability and asymmetries of the long bones of the limbs and the clavicles in man and apes. *Human Biology* 9: 281–328.

Smith, B. H. 1993. The physiological age of KNM-WT 15000. In *The Nariokotome* Homo erectus *Skeleton,* ed. A. Walker and R. Leakey, pp. 195–220. Cambridge: Harvard University Press.

Stringer, C. B. 1984. The definition of *Homo erectus* and the existence of the species in Africa and Europe. *Courier Forschungsinstitut Senckenberg* 69: 131–143.

———— 1987. A numerical cladistic analysis of the genus *Homo. Journal of Human Evolution* 16: 135–146.

———— 1990. The emergence of modern humans. *Scientific American* 264: 98–97.

Templeton, A. 1992. Human origins and analysis of mitochondrial DNA. *Science* 255: 737.

Tobias, P. V. 1988. Recent advances in the evolution of the hominids with especial reference to brain and speech. *Pontifical Academy of Sciences: Scripta Varia* 50: 85–140.

———— 1991. *Olduvai Gorge,* vol. 4. Cambridge: Cambridge University Press.

Toth, N. 1985. Archaeological evidence for preferential right-handedness in the lower and middle Pleistocene, and its possible implications. *Journal of Human Evolution* 14: 607–614.

Trinkaus, E. 1981. Neanderthal limb proportions and cold adaptation. In *Aspects of Human Evolution,* ed. C. B. Stringer, pp. 187–224. London: Taylor and Francis.

Turner, A., and A. Chamberlain. 1989. Speciation, morphological change and the status of African *Homo erectus. Journal of Human Evolution* 18: 115–130.

Tuttle, R. H. 1987. Kinesiological inferences and evolutionary implications from Laetoli bipedal trails G-1, G-2/3, and A. In *Laetoli: A Pliocene Site in Northern Tanzania,* ed. M. D. Leakey and J. M. Harris, pp. 503–523. Oxford: Clarendon Press.

Vandermeersch, B. 1969. Les nouveaux découvertes de restes humains dans les couches Levalloiso-Mousteriennes du gisement de Qafzeh (Israel). *Comptes Rendus, Académie des Sciences, Paris* 268: 2562–2565.

Walker, A. 1976. Remains attributable to *Australopithecus* in the East Rudolf succession. In *Earliest Man and Environments in the Lake Rudolf Basin,* ed. Y. Coppens, F. C. Howell, G. L1. Isaac, and R. E. F. Leakey, pp. 484–489. Chicago: University of Chicago Press.

———— 1991. The origin of the genus *Homo.* In *Evolution of Life,* ed. S. Osawa and T. Honjo, pp. 379–389. Tokyo: Spinger-Verlag.

Walker, A., M. R. Zimmerman, and R. E. F. Leakey. 1982. A possible case of hypervitaminosis A in *Homo erectus. Nature* 296: 248–250.

Walker, A., and R. E. Leakey. 1993. The skull. In *The Nariokotome* Homo erectus *Skeleton,* ed. A. Walker and R. Leakey, pp. 63–96. Cambridge: Harvard University Press.

Walker, A., and C. B. Ruff. 1993. The reconstruction of the pelvis. In *The Nariokotome* Homo erectus *Skeleton,* ed. A. Walker and R. Leakey, pp. 221–265. Cambridge: Harvard University Press.

Weidenreich, F. 1943. The skull of *Sinanthropus pekinensis. Palaeontologia Sinica,* new series D, 10: 1–291.

Wheeler, P. E. 1991. The thermoregulatory advantages of hominid bipedalism in open equatorial environments: The contribution of increased convective heat loss and cutaneous evaporative cooling. *Journal Human Evolution* 21: 107–115.

Wiley, E. O. 1978. The evolutionary species concept reconsidered. *Systematic Zoology* 27: 17–26.

Williams, P. L., R. Warwick, M. Dyson, and L. H. Bannister, eds. 1989. *Gray's Anatomy,* 37th ed. Edinburgh: Churchill Livingstone.

Wolpoff, M. H. 1980. *Paleoanthropology.* New York: Knopf.

———— 1984. Evolution in *Homo erectus:* The question of stasis. *Paleobiology* 10: 389–406.

———— 1986. Stasis in the interpretation of evolution of *Homo erectus:* A reply to Rightmire. *Paleobiology* 12: 325–328.

Wolpoff, M. H., and A. Nkini. 1985. Early and early middle Pleistocene hominids in Asia and Africa. In *Ancestors,* ed. E. Delson, pp. 202–205. New York: Alan R. Liss.

Wood, B. A. 1976. Remains attributable to *Homo* in the East Rudolf succession. In *Earliest Man and Environments in the Lake Rudolf Basin,* ed. Y. Coppens, F. C. Howell, G. L1. Isaac, and R. E. F. Leakey, pp. 484–489. Chicago: University of Chicago Press.

———— 1984. The origins of *Homo erectus. Courier Forschungsinstitut Senckenberg* 69: 99–111.

———— 1991. *Koobi Fora Research Project,* vol. 4. Oxford: Clarendon Press.

———— 1992. Origin and evolution of the genus *Homo. Nature* 355: 783–790.

33

Remains of *Homo erectus* from Bouri, Middle Awash, Ethiopia

B. Asfaw, W. H. Gilbert, Y. Beyene, W. K. Hart, P. R. Renne, G. WoldeGabriel, E. S. Vrba, and T. D. White

ABSTRACT

The genesis, evolution and fate of Homo erectus *have been explored palaeontologically since the taxon's recognition in the* late nineteenth century. Current debate[1] is focused on whether early representatives from Kenya and Georgia should be classified as a separate ancestral species (H. ergaster')[2–4], and whether H. erectus was an exclusively Asian species lineage that went extinct[5,6]. Lack of resolution of these issues has obscured the place of H. erectus in human evolution. A hominid calvaria and postcranial remains recently recovered

Reprinted by permission of *Nature,* Vol. 416, pp. 317–320. Copyright © 2002 by Macmillan Publishers Ltd.

from the Dakanihylo Member of the Bouri Formation, Middle Awash, Ethiopia, bear directly on these issues. These ~1.0-million-year (Myr)-old Pleistocene sediments contain abundant early Acheulean stone tools and a diverse vertebrate fauna that indicates a predominantly savannah environment. Here we report that the 'Daka' calvaria's metric and morphological attributes centre it firmly within H. erectus. *Daka's resemblance to Asian counterparts indicates that the early African and Eurasian fossil hominids represent demes of a widespread palaeospecies. Daka's anatomical intermediacy between earlier and later African fossils provides evidence of evolutionary change. Its temporal and geographic position indicates that African* H. erectus *was the ancestor of* Homo sapiens.

The Early Pleistocene Dakanihylo ('Daka') Member comprises 22 to ≤ 45 m of sediments unconformably atop the Pliocene Hatayae Member of the Bouri Formation[7] (Figure 1). These deposits contain abundant archaeological and palaeontological remains embedded in primarily alluvial deposits relating to lakeside beaches or shallow water deposits in distributary channels[8]. Initial interpretations identified Daka sediments as postdating hominid remains and Acheulean artefacts from Bodo[9]. However, the Daka artefacts clearly antedate those at Bodo, and single-crystal ^{40}Ar/^{39}Ar dating of a pumiceous unit at the base of the Member gave an age of 1.042 ± 0.009 Myr (ref. 8). The entire Dakanihylo Member is of reverse magnetic polarity, so the minimum age of its palaeoanthropological contents is ~0.8 Myr.

An extensive vertebrate fauna was recovered from the Daka Member. Faunas of this age are rare in Africa. Of 713 identified specimens (see Table 1 for faunal list), 377 are bovids, including three new species and two new genera[10]. The bovid assemblage is dominated by alcelaphine diversity and abundance not recorded at older African sites. Widespread open grassland habitats are thereby indicated. Adjacent water-margin habitats are evidenced by three *Kobus* species and abundant hippo fossils.

Table 1. Daka Member Faunal List

Bovidae
cf. *Aepyceros* sp.
Bouria anngettyae
Connochaetes taurinus
Gazella sp.
Kobus ellipsiprymnus
Kobus kob
Kobus sigmoidalis
Megalotragus kattwinkeli
Nitidarcus asfawi
Numidocapra crassicornis
Parmularius angusticornis
Pelorovis cf. *antiquus*
Rabaticeras sp.
Tragelaphus cf. *strepsiceros*

Carnivora
cf. *Pachycrocuta* aff. *brevirostris*
cf. *Panthera leo*

Giraffidae
Giraffa cf. *camelopardalis*
Sivatherium cf. *maurusium*

Hippopotamidae
Hippopotamus gorgops

Elephantidae
Elephas recki recki

Equidae
Equus sp.
Hipparion sp.

Rhinocerotidae
Ceratotherium sp.

Primates
Theropithecus cf. *oswaldi*
cf. *Colobus* sp.
Cercopithecinae gen. indet
Homo erectus

Suidae
Kolpochoerus majus
Kolpochoerus olduvaiensis
Metridiochoerus compactus
Metridiochoerus cf. *hopwoodi*
Metridiochoerus modestus

Rodentia
cf. *Thryonomys*

Non-Mammal
Aves
Osteichthyes
Chelonia
Crocodylia

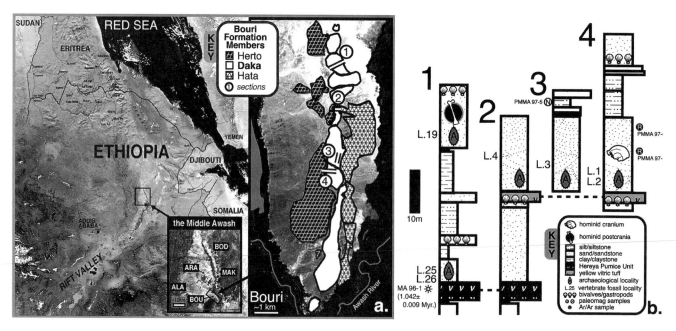

Figure 1. *Maps and generalized sections. **a**, Landsat and aerial photographic imagery showing the location of the Middle Awash study area, its major hominid-bearing localities, and the exposure of Bouri Formation sediments. The 1.0-Myr Daka Member of this formation is shown in white. **b**, Measured stratigraphic sections of this Member show the placement of Acheulean artefacts, hominid fossils, radiometric dates and geomagnetic polarity determinations (normal polarity in section 3 and cap of section 4 overlie the Daka Member).*

Daka Member archaeological sites are abundant. Bone modifications characteristic of the butchery of large mammals by hominids scar several equid, bovid and hippo postcrania. Lithic assemblages closely conform to African early Acheulean analogues. Handaxes and cleavers are ubiquitous elements, with invasive flake scars and fewer flake removals than later Acheulean counterparts[8].

A hominid calvaria (BOU-VP-2/66) was discovered *in situ* in Daka Member silty sand by W.H.G. on 27 December 1997. The specimen was orientated base-down, without associated artefacts, encrusted by fossilized root casts. Surface detail is well preserved, with no sign of fluvial transport or surface weathering. Its vault and supraorbitals exhibit perimortem scraping damage; the frontal and parietals bear multiple sets of subparallel striae, each with internal striations. The patterning and morphology of these marks is unusual and inconsistent with cutmarks made by hominids engaged in defleshing activities. We tentatively attribute this damage to animal gnawing.

The calvaria preserves a largely intact base and is only slightly distorted (plastic deformation skews the vault slightly to the individual's left (Figure 2)). Endocranial capacity is 995 cm^3 (measured repeatedly with teff seed). The thick supraorbital tori are strongly arched, with markedly depressed glabellar and supraglabellar regions. Radiographs reveal an asymmetrical frontal sinus extending to the left midorbital level. The frontal squama is bossed at midline and there is weak sagittal keeling there and on the parietals. The mandibular fossa is deep and anteroposteriorly short. Suprameatal and supramastoid crests and angular tori are weak. The damaged mastoids are small. There is no true occipital torus demarcated superiorly by a supratoral sulcus. Rather, the occipital squama rises vertically and curves anteriorly. Viewed posteriorly, the undistorted parietal walls would have been vertical. The cranial vault is smaller and shorter than Olduvai hominid OH-9 and is phenetically similar to the partly described Buia cranium from Eritrea[11]. Three isolated hominid femora and a proximal tibia were recovered from Daka deposits far removed from the calvaria (Figure 1). No femur is complete, but all display the marked platymeria and extremely thick midshaft cortex characteristic of *H. erectus*.

The new 'Daka' hominid fossils afford unique insights into unresolved spatial and temporal relationships of *H. erectus*. Most fossils attributed to this taxon came to light in Java, China, Europe and Africa during the twentieth century. Additional genus and species names were proposed before the application of modern systematics united them under *H. erectus* in the 1960s. The discovery of older Kenyan fossils in the 1970s and the application of cladistic methods in the 1980s produced a variety of phylogenetic and taxonomic assessments of Early and Middle Pleistocene *Homo*. In his 1985 distillation, Delson[1] identified two basic research problems involving *H. erectus*: whether the African fossils were conspecific with the Trinil holotype and other Asian representatives; and whether the species showed stasis or phyletic change through its 1.5-Myr span. Both

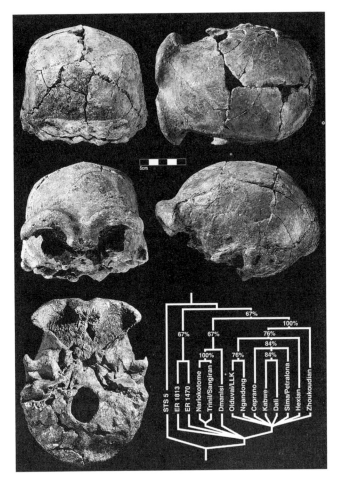

Figure 2. *Views of the Daka calvaria and cladograms representing majority rule (**a**) and strict consensus (**b**) of the 75 most parsimonious phylogenies generated by PAUP 4.0b8 (Sinauer). The Daka cranium is in the 'Olduvai/LLK' deme. Cladogram **b** is more conservative, showing the nodes that are stable across all equally parsimonious phylogenies. These branching diagrams are presented only to illustrate the limitations of a cladistic approach to phylogeny among this set of fossils, and the lack of calvarial evidence for a deep phylogenetic division between the African and Asian fossils.*

problems have persisted, and at ~1.0 Myr in the Horn of Africa the new Daka fossils now bear directly on them.

It has been proposed that the name *H. erectus* be restricted to a purported Asian clade (species) exemplified by fossils of disparate antiquity from Trinil, Sangiran, Zhoukoudian and Ngandong[5,6]. We examined the hypothesis that *H. erectus* was a specifically Asian clade by metrically and cladistically analysing the Daka calvaria. Its cranial metrics (see Tables 2 and 3) overlap with both Asian and African sample ranges and fail to distinguish the fossil consistently from either sample.

Previous applications of cladistics to *H. erectus* have been criticized on the basis of issues of character independence and variation [12-14], as well as the potentially confounding effect of gene flow[15,16]. We agree with these and other valid cautions[17,18]. However, to examine the hypothesis that *H. erectus* was a distinct African

Table 2. Cranial Metrics for the Daka Calvaria

Metrics (in mm) for BOU-VP-2/66:	Both	R.	L.
Maximum cranial length (Gl-Ops chord; GOL)	180±1		
Nasio-occipital length (Na-Ops chord; NOL)	175±1		
Basion-nasion length (Na-Ba chord; BNL)	95.5±1		
Cranial height (Ba-Br chord; BBH)	121±1		
Maximum cranial breadth (XCB)	141±2		
Maximum frontal breadth on coronal (XFB)	105±2		
Bistephanic breadth (STB)	101±2		
Biauricular breadth (Au-Au chord; AUB)	130±1		
Min. cranial breadth (WCB)	70±1		
Biasterionic breadth (ASB)	116±2		
Bifrontal breadth (Fma-Fma chord; FMB)	117±2		
Nasio-frontal subtense (NAS)	10		
Supraorbital projection (SOS)	16		
Glabella projection (GLS)	9		
Foramen magnum length (Ba-O chord; FOL)	36±1		
Frontal chord (Na-Br chord; FRC)	101±2		
Frontal subtense (Na-Br subtense; FRS)	18		
Nasion-subtense fraction (FRF)	55		
Parietal chord (Br-La chord; PAC)	94±1		
Parietal subtense (PAS)	16±1		
Bregma subtense fraction (PAF)	49±1		
Lambda-opisthion chord (OCC)	95±2		
Lambda-opisthion subtense (OCS)	34±1		
Lambda subtense fraction (OCF)	50±1		
Vertex radius (VRR)	95.5±2		
Nasion radius (NAR)	90.5±2		
Frontotemporale breadth	89±1		
Biparietal breadth (Bi-parietal chord)	133±2		
Biporionic breadth	128±1		
Frontal length (Gl-Br chord)	97±1		
Frontal arc (Gl-Br arc)	101±1		
Parietal arc (Br-La arc)	99±1		
Occipital scale length (La-In chord)	65±1		
Occipital scale arc (La-In arc)	75±1		
Nuchal length (In-Op chord)	47±2*		
Nuchal arc (In-Op arc)	48±2		
Occipital arc (La-Op arc)	122±2		
Maximum-minimum breadth across temporal fossae of frontal	95		
Maximum breadth on SOT wings	124		
Cranial capacity	995		
Interorbital breadth across nasion	33		
Basal breadth across depths of TMJ	96.5		
Supraorbital thickness		19	18
Vault thickness at:			
Bregma	7		
Opisthicranion	12		
Asterion		10.5	
Euryon		7.5–8.0	
Lambda	8.5		

*Inion very low on nuchal plane; metric not homologous with many published metrics on other specimens.

clade, we experimented with Hennigian parsimony analyses to investigate potential clustering of relevant crania. From recent published literature we compiled the 22 characters most widely and appropriately used in the cladistic analysis of calvarial anatomy in *H. erectus* and close relatives. We divided Early and Middle Pleistocene *Homo* fossils into operational taxonomic units on the basis of the palaeo-demes defined by Howell[19] (these are sets of fossils representing spatially and temporally bounded 'communities' below the species level).

Regardless of the software parameters used, or the removal of the later Asian demes, the hypothesis of a deep cladogenesis between African and Asian *H. erectus* is unsupported by our analyses (Figure 2). Previous cladistic efforts have noted difficulty with the African OH 9 specimen because it consistently aligned with the Asian fossils, thereby being interpreted as a sort of Tanzanian outpost of 'Asian' morphology[3] or as an evolutionary intermediate[20]. The recovery of the Buia and Daka fossils, almost certainly from the same eastern African deme, compounds such problems. Like OH 9, these new African specimens share many derived characters with Asian and European specimens. As a consequence, the cladistic method, regardless of serious questions concerning its applicability here, fails to support the division of *H. erectus* into Asian and African clades. Whether viewed metrically or morphologically,

Table 3. Morphological Observations on the Daka Calvaria

	Morphological Observations for BOU-VP-2/66:			Homo erectus (sensu lato) Ranges	
Feature	Technique	Daka Condition	Close Asian Match	Small	Large
Brain size	Direct measurement	995 cc	1004 cc = Sangiran 17	775 cc Dmanisi 2280	1251 cc Ngandong 6
Cranial vault shape (Length ÷ Height)	Index	1.49	1.55 = Ngangdong 7	1.49 Daka	1.87 Sangiran 17
Interorbital breadth (at Nasion)	Direct measurement	31.5	32.8 = Zhoukoudian III (cast)	27 mm KNM-ER 3733 (cast)	39 mm Ceprano (cast)
Cranial vault thickness (at Bregma)	Direct measurement	7	7 = Zhoukoudian XI	6.3 mm Buia	11 mm Sambungmachan 3
Postorbital constriction	Index	0.67	0.68 = Zhoukoudian Mean	0.58 Hexian	0.78 Ngandong 6
Supraorbital torus thickness above midorbit	Direct measurement	18.5	18 = Sangiran 17	8 mm KNM-ER 3733	22.1 mm Ceprano (cast)
Occipital angulation	Angle	115°	118° = Sangiran 2	92.1° Sangiran 17	110° Sambungmachan 3
Occipital/Nuchal scale index	Index	1.38	1.30 = Sangiran 17	0.8 Zhoukoudian XI	1.7 Dali
Glenoid fossa depth/Articular eminence height	Angle	120°	117° = Zhoukoudian III (cast)	105° Ngandong 12 (cast)	129.9° Dmanisi 2280 (cast)
Postglenoid projection	Direct measurement	4.6	4.2 = Sangiran 2 (cast)	3.9 mm Sambungmachan 1 (cast)	6.7 mm Zhoukoudian 11 (cast)
Temporal squama shape	Inspection, lateral view	High and arched	Dali		
Sutural keeling	Inspection	Present	Sambungmachen 1		
Forehead elevation	Inspection, lateral view	Prominent	Zhoukoudian III		
Glabellar inflexion	Inspection, superior view	Marked	None		
Supraorbital torus arching	Inspection, anterior view	Marked	Hexian		
Occipital torus	Inspection, posterior view	Absent	None		
Angular torus	Inspection, lateral view	Weak	Ngandong 7		
Parietal wall verticality	Inspection, posterior view	Vertical	Dali		
Juxtamastoid eminence	Inspection, basal view	Present	Zhoukoudian III		
Tympanic plate inclination	Inspection, basal view	Coronal	Sangiran 2		
Ossified styloid process	Inspection, basal view	Absent	Zhoukoudian		
Supramastoid/suprameatal shelf	Inspection, lateral view	Weak	Sangiran 2		
Not used in cladistic analysis:					
Orbital roof topography	Inspection, basal view	Arched	Sangiran 17		
Mastoid fissure	Inspection, basal view	Broken	—		
Mastoid process	Inspection, lateral view	Small, broken	Zhoukoudian III		

the Daka cranium confirms previous suggestions[15,16] that geographic subdivision of early *H. erectus* into separate species lineages is biologically misleading, artificially inflating early Pleistocene species diversity. Rather, the Daka calvaria is consistent with the hypothesis of a widespread, moderately polymorphic and polytypic species at ~1.0 Myr (refs 21, 22).

Because it is from a poorly sampled period[23], the newly discovered Daka calvaria is also important for assessing evolutionary mode and tempo in *H. erectus*. A key barrier to such assessment is the lack of chronological control for many Pleistocene Eurasian hominids—a persistent problem that confounds attempts to document patterns of morphological change across time. Chronometric placement is superior in eastern Africa, where the earliest fossils attributed to *H. erectus* (Nariokotome deme) date to ~1.78 Myr (ref. 2). These fossils have smaller braincases than later African species representatives, including Daka. This pattern could also characterize Eurasia, where the earliest hominid fossils from Sangiran, Java[24], and Dmanisi, Georgia[4], might be more primitive than younger regional counterparts (although the chronological placement of most Eurasian fossils is inadequate relative to what is now available for eastern Africa[25]).

Chronological and anatomical seriation of the African fossils from KNM-ER3733/3883 (Koobi Fora) to OH 9, to Daka/Buia to Bodo[26], is now available. In many features, including cranial capacity and its extensive developmental correlates, hominid crania in this eastern African succession comprise a morphocline consistent with the hypothesis that they sample a single evolving lineage. To recognize the basal fossils representing this apparently evolving lineage with the separate species name '*H. ergaster*' is therefore doubtfully necessary or useful[2]. At most, the basal members of the *H. erectus* lineage should be recognized taxonomically as a chronosubspecies (*H. erectus ergaster*). Suggestions that *H. ergaster* itself contains multiple species, even in a single locality[27], seem completely unsupported by the data[4].

The origins of the widespread, polymorphic, Early Pleistocene *H. erectus* lineage remain elusive. The marked contrasts between any potential ancestor (*Homo habilis* or other) and the earliest known *H. erectus* might signal an abrupt evolutionary emergence some time before its first known appearance in Africa at ~1.78 Myr. Uncertainties surrounding the taxon's appearance in Eurasia and southeast Asia make it impossible to establish accurately the time or place of origin for *H. erectus*. Available evidence is insufficient to detect the direction of its geographic dispersal. Given new perspectives afforded by the discoveries at Dmanisi in Eurasia, the assumption that the earliest *H. erectus* populations

emigrated from Africa to Eurasia[14,23,28,29], rather than invading Africa from Eurasia[30], is premature. Whatever its time and place of origin, and direction of spread, this species dispersed widely, and possibly abruptly, before 1.5 Myr. The Daka calvaria indicates that by 1 Myr the taxon had colonized much of the Old World without speciating—a finding of considerable biogeographic and behavioural significance. Through time and across its eastern hemispheric range, the technologies employed by this taxon ranged from Oldowan to Acheulean.

The resemblance of the Daka calvaria to Asian representatives of *H. erectus*, and its morphological intermediacy between earlier and later African specimens, provide strong evidence that it samples a widely distributed lineage that evolved during the million years after its Pliocene origin. The phylogenetic unity of *H. erectus* did not persist indefinitely. By ~0.5 Myr, very different hominid crania in Africa and Asia (Bodo versus Zhoukoudian) indicate that a hominid speciation event might have occurred in circum-Daka times[26]. Further sampling of the Daka to Bodo transition in Africa is needed to examine the rate of morphological change, as well as the hypothesis that the fractionation of *H. erectus* might have been related to the ~0.95-Myr onset of large magnitude global climatic oscillations.

ACKNOWLEDGMENTS

This paper is dedicated to the late J. Desmond Clark who initiated this research at Bouri in 1981. We thank A. Almquist, A. Asfaw, M. Asnake, T. Assebework, D. Brill, D. DeGusta, J. DeHeinzelin, A. Getty, Y. Haile-Selassie, B. Latimer, C. Pehlevan, K. Schick, S. Simpson, P. Snow, G. Suwa and Y. Zeleke for fieldwork and analytical studies. Electron microprobe and other support from the Earth Environmental Sciences Division, Los Alamos National Laboratory. Thanks to G. Suwa, D. DeGusta, C. Feibel, F. C. Howell, C. O. Lovejoy, F. Bibi, T. Stidham, J. Parham, J.-R. Boisserie and H. Saegusa for thoughtful review and/or assistance. We thank the Ministry of Youth, Sports and Culture, the Authority for Research and Conservation of the Cultural Heritage, and the National Museum of Ethiopia for permissions, and the Afar Regional Government and the Afar people of the Middle Awash, particularly H. Elema. Many additional individuals contributed. This research was supported by the NSF (USA) and the Institute of Geophysics and Planetary Physics (University of California at Los Alamos National Laboratory), with additional contributions by the Graduate School and Hampton Fund for International Initiatives, Miami University.

REFERENCES

1. Delson, E. Palaeobiology and age of African *Homo erectus*. *Nature* **316**, 762–763 (1985).
2. Walker, A. C. & Leakey, R. E. F. *The Nariokotome* Homo erectus *Skeleton* (Harvard Univ. Press, Cambridge, Massachusetts, 1993).
3. Wood, B. A. *Koobi Fora Research Project* Vol. 4 (Clarendon Press, Oxford, 1991).
4. Gabunia, L., Vekua, A. & Lordkipanidze, D. New human fossils from Dmanisi, eastern Georgia. *Archaeol. Ethnol. Anthropol. Eurasia* **2**(6), 128–139 (2001).
5. Andrews, P. J. An alternative interpretation of the characters used to define *Homo erectus*. *Courier Forschunginstitut Senckenberg* **69**, 167–175 (1984).

6. Groves, C. P. *A Theory of Human and Primate Evolution* (Clarendon Press, Oxford, 1989).

7. DeHeinzelin, J. et al. Environment and behavior of 2.5-million-year-old Bouri hominids. *Science* **284**, 625–629 (1999).

8. DeHeinzelin, J., Clark, J. D., Schick, K. D. & Gilbert, W. H. (eds) *The Acheulean and the Plio-Pleistocene Deposits of the Middle Awash Valley, Ethiopia* (Royal Museum of Central Africa, Tervuren, Belgium; *Ann. Sci. Geol.*, **104** (2000)).

9. Kalb, J. et al. Geology and stratigraphy of Neogene deposits, Middle Awash Valley, Ethiopia. *Nature* **298**, 17–25 (1982).

10. Vrba, E. S. New fossils of Alcelaphini and Caprinae (Bovidae: Mammalia) from Awash, Ethiopia, and phylogenetic analysis of Alcelaphini. *Palaeont. Afr.* **34**, 127–198 (1997).

11. Abbate, E. et al. A one-million-year-old *Homo cranium* from the Danakil (Afar) depression of Eritrea. *Nature* **393**, 458–460 (1998).

12. Brauer, G. & Mbua, E. *Homo erectus* features used in cladistics and their variability in Asian and African hominids. *J. Hum. Evol.* **22**, 79–108 (1992).

13. Kennedy, G. E. On the autapomorphic traits of *Homo erectus*. *J. Hum. Evol.* **20**, 375–412 (1991).

14. Kramer, A. Human taxonomic diversity in the Pleistocene: Does *Homo erectus* represent multiple hominid species? *Am. J. Phys. Anthropol.* **91**, 161–171 (1993).

15. Harrison, T. in *Species, Species Concepts, and Primate Evolution* (eds Kimbel, W. H. & Martin, L. B.) 345–371 (Plenum, New York, 1993).

16. Turner, A. & Chamberlain, A. Speciation, morphological change and the status of African *Homo erectus*. *J. Hum. Evol.* **18**, 115–130 (1989).

17. Lovejoy, C. O., Cohn, M. J. & White, T. D. Morphological analysis of the mammalian postcranium: A developmental perspective. *Proc. Natl Acad. Sci. USA* **96**, 13247–13252 (1999).

18. Trinkaus, E. Cladistics and the hominid fossil record. *Am. J. Phys. Anthropol.* **83**, 1–11 (1990).

19. Howell, F. C. Paleo-demes, species clades, and extinctions in the Pleistocene hominin record. *J. Anthropol. Res.* **55**, 191–243 (1999).

20. Martinez, I. & Arsuaga, J. L. The temporal bones from Sima de los Huesos Middle Pleistocene site (Sierra de Atapuerca, Spain). A phylogenetic approach. *J. Hum. Evol.* **33**, 283–318 (1997).

21. Rightmire, G. P. *The Evolution of* Homo erectus: *Comparative Anatomical Studies of an Extinct Human Species* (Cambridge Univ. Press, Cambridge, 1990).

22. Rightmire, G. P. Evidence from facial morphology for similarity of Asian and African representatives of *Homo erectus*. *Am. J. Phys. Anthropol.* **106**, 61–85 (1998).

23. Aguirre, E. Poor fossil record and major changes around 1 MaBP. *Hum. Evol.* **15**, 51–62 (2000).

24. Larick, R. et al. Early Pleistocene ^{40}Ar/^{39}Ar ages for Bapang Formation hominins, Central Java, Indonesia. *Proc. Natl Acad. Sci. USA* **98**, 4866–4871 (2001).

25. Olsen, J. W. New light on the earliest occupation of east Asia. *Anthropologie* **37**, 89–96 (1999).

26. Rightmire, G. P. The human cranium from Bodo, Ethiopia: Evidence for speciation in the Middle Pleistocene. *J. Hum. Evol.* **31**, 21–39 (1996).

27. Schwartz, J. H. Taxonomy of the Dmanisi crania. *Science* **289**, 55 (2000).

28. Ambrose, S. H. Paleolithic technology and human evolution. *Science* **291**, 1748–1753 (2001).

29. Bar-Yosef, O. Lower Paleolithic sites in South-western Asia: Evidence for 'Out of Africa' movements. *Anthropologie* **37**, 51–69 (1999).

30. Clarke, R. Out of Africa and back again. *Int. J. Anthropol.* **15**, 185–189 (2001).

V

Evolution and Dispersal of *Homo erectus*

It has long been recognized that the genus *Homo* was the first hominid to leave Africa and disperse into other major continental areas. However, recent, ongoing studies indicate that this earliest out of Africa dispersal was far earlier and more extensive than previously recognized. Moreover, the earliest members of our genus to leave Africa also appear to have survived much longer in Southeast Asia than suspected and to have given rise to a dwarf island species. The chapters in this part describe much of this new evidence for early dispersal from Africa. These articles chronicle not only the *Homo* pattern of dispersal and morphology but also the behavioral abilities that enabled early members of our genus to successfully colonize most of the Old World.

In Chapter 34, "The African Emergence and Early Asian Dispersals of the Genus *Homo*," Roy Larick and Russell L. Ciochon provide an overview of these early dispersals and speculate on the ecological factors contributing to the spread. They argue that "catchment scavenging" was the critical behavior that led to hominid expansion out of Africa. This behavior involves the use of a wide variety of resources in a sequential pattern and encourages wide movement (see also Antón et al., 2002, for additional discussion on the ranging behavior of *Homo erectus*). It was not until later that early hominids developed "territory scavenging," which involves the use of many small resources simultaneously and requires greater knowledge of local resources.

The late Leo Gabunia and colleagues, in Chapter 35, "Dmanisi and Dispersal," describe preliminary discoveries from the site of Dmanisi in the Republic of Georgia. These finds, initially discovered during excavation of a Medieval city, document the presence of early *Homo* at the "gateway" to Europe at the beginning of the Pleistocene, nearly 2 mya. These initial cranial specimens were described as most similar to *Homo ergaster* from Africa and *Homo erectus* from eastern Asia. The stone tools associated with the Dmanisi hominids are crude cores and flakes, most comparable to the Oldowan Industry of East Africa.

Chapter 36, "A New Skull of Early *Homo* from Dmanisi, Georgia," by Abesalom Vekua and colleagues, describes additional cranial material from Dmanisi. In contrast with the earlier discoveries, this new cranium has a much smaller cranial capacity. Although the authors attribute all of the Dmanisi material to *Homo erectus* (= *Homo ergaster*), they suggest that the Dmanisi remains are the best sample assigned to that species from anywhere in the world, and that they are very similar to *Homo habilis*. They suggest that the first hominids to disperse were a very primitive form of the genus *Homo*, similar to *Homo habilis*, a taxon that is also much in dispute (see Part IV). More recent excavations have supplied additional skulls as well as postcranial remains from this site. Most recently, in the last article authored by Leo Gabunia (Gabunia et al., 2002), another Dmanisi hominid has been described and given the name of *Homo georgicus* sp. nov. The type specimen, a mandible, contains a confusing mixture of primitive and derived traits not seen in other hominids of similar age or in the other hominid mandibles at Dmanisi. Future study should resolve the phylogenetic standing of this intriguing specimen.

The continuing discoveries at Dmanisi are revolutionizing our understanding of human evolution in many ways. In addition to expanding our knowledge of the biogeography of early hominids, the Dmanisi discoveries are providing a very large sample of early hominid crania from a single restricted site. This sample is likely to have profound effects on interpretations of the relationship between morphological and taxonomic diversity in other parts of the world.

In Chapter 37, by Josep Gibert and colleagues, "Venta Micena, Barranco León-5 and Fuentenueva-3: Three Archaeological Sites in the Early Pleistocene Deposits of Orce, South-East Spain," the authors provide evidence for early hominid tool users in Europe at the beginning of the Pleistocene. These sites most certainly document the earliest record of hominid expansion into Europe. The Orce region of Spain lies just across the Strait of Gibraltar from Africa, and in times of lower sea levels the two continents would have been separated by a distance of only 2 to 5 kilometers, dotted with small islands. Surveys over the past 25 years have led to the discovery of more than 20 paleontological and/or archaeological sites in the region. All three sites have yielded stone artifacts associated with large

293

mammal bones. At the Venta Micena site, the mammal bones show characteristic evidence of human butchering activities. The Venta Micena and the Barranco Léon-5 sites have also yielded fragmentary hominid fossils.

Rixiang Zhu and colleagues, in Chapter 38, "New Evidence on the Earliest Human Presence at High Northern Latitudes in Northeast Asia," report new ages for artifact-bearing sediments in the Nihewan Basin of China. The extensive assemblage of flakes and core forms is constrained by paleomagnetic reversals to an age of roughly 1.66 mya, an age that is also supported by faunal correlations. As noted in other articles in this part (Chapters 34, 41, 42, 43), there is increasing evidence of fossil hominids in tropical regions of Asia for nearly 2 million years, and it has been argued that early hominid cultures in Asia were dependent on tropical products such as bamboo. However, this article shows that these hominids were not so constrained to a single climatic regime. It provides the earliest evidence of humans in Asia at high latitudes (40° N) and indicates that early humans in Asia could occupy a wide range of habitats and produce a diversity of stone tool types similar to late Pliocene tools from Africa (see Chapter 28). Moreover, the archaeological remains also provide the earliest evidence of hominids using animal tissues, such as marrow processing, in Asia.

Chapter 39, "Mid-Pleistocene Acheulian-Like Stone Technology of the Bose Basin, South China," by Yamei Hou and colleagues, describes another new find in the artifact record of eastern Asia. The ovate large cutting tools (LCTs) from Bose are associated with tektites dated to 803 kya and are similar to Acheulean bifacial tools that are abundant and widespread in Africa and Europe between 1.6 and 0.2 mya, but rare in Asia east of the "Movius Line." These authors argue that the manufacture and use of these tools in the Bose Basin are associated with widespread forest destruction caused by the tektite fall.

For many decades, the site of Zhoukoudian in China has been recognized as demonstrating the earliest undoubted evidence for the use of controlled fire in human evolution. In Chapter 40, "Evidence for the Use of Fire at Zhoukoudian, China," Steve Weiner and colleagues show that the widely cited ash layers in Level 10 and Level 4 at Zhoukoudian are not ash or charcoal remnants at all. Rather, they represent loess (glacial dust) blown into the site from glacial activity in the north. Weiner and colleagues also found no evidence of hearths or campfires. However, the presence of burned bones associated with stone tools in these layers provides evocative evidence that humans at Zhoukoudian may have occasionally used fire.

In "*Homo erectus* and the Emergence of Sunda in the Tethys Realm: Contributions of Potassium-Based Chronology in the Sangiran Dome, Central Java" (Chapter 41), Roy Larick, Russell L. Ciochon, and Yahdi Zaim review the geological history of the Sunda Shelf, the broad area off the coast of Southeast Asia that contains the large islands of Borneo, Sumatra, and Java, as well as the discovery of fossil hominids in that region. They note that early fossils of *Homo erectus* are associated with active tectonic regions in both East Africa and Southeast Asia, and suggest that dispersal of *Homo erectus*

from Africa to Southeast Asia was facilitated by "open linear landscapes" along the Tethys Corridor extending across southern Asia. They further suggest that *Homo erectus* sought out unstable landscapes, presumably due to the relative abundance of resources. Although the initial dispersal of *Homo erectus* was accomplished by a relatively small-brained hominid without sophisticated stone tools, they argue that the African and Asian branches evolved increased brain size in parallel.

In Chapter 42, "*Homo erectus* Calvarium from the Pleistocene of Java," Hisao Baba and colleagues describe new *Homo erectus* cranial remains that are intermediate between the early Pleistocene fossils from Trinil and Sangiran and the more recent remains from Ngandong (Solo). The earlier *Homo erectus* fossils and the later material from Ngandong are distinct in many morphological features, such that the recognition of the *Homo erectus* affinities of the Ngandong material has long been a source of debate. This new material confirms that these two groups of Asian hominid fossils, separated by nearly 2 myr (see Chapter 43), are indeed part of a single lineage. Moreover, the authors suggest that in many cranial features, *Homo erectus* on Java became increasingly derived through time and increasingly distinct from the morphology found in modern humans. Thus, the *Homo erectus* lineage in Southeast Asia shows no evidence that it gave rise to modern humans.

In Chapter 43, "Latest *Homo erectus* of Java: Potential Contemporaneity with *Homo sapiens* in Southeast Asia," Carl C. Swisher III and colleagues report ages of 27,000 to 53,300 years for fossil bovid teeth associated with *Homo erectus* fossils in central Java. The fossils from Ngandong and Sambungmacan (often called the Solo skulls) have traditionally been identified as derived examples of *Homo erectus* (see Santa Luca, 1980) and were thought to be roughly 500,000 years old. The new ages are based on electron spin resonance and uranium-series dates of bovid teeth found in the same localities as the fossil hominids. They are much younger than the ages previously attributed to the latest *Homo erectus* fossils in Asia and indicate that *Homo erectus* was contemporary with *Homo sapiens* in Southeast Asia.

In Chapter 44, "A New Small-Bodied Hominin from the Late Pleistocene of Flores, Indonesia," Peter Brown and colleagues report one of the most spectacular discoveries in the history of human evolution. They describe numerous remains of a dwarfed hominid species, apparently related to *Homo erectus*, that survived on the Indonesian island of Flores as recently as 18,000 years ago (see also Morwood et al., 2005). The new species, which they named *Homo floresiensis*, stood just more than three feet tall and probably weighed between 40 and 70 pounds as an adult. The skull has a long, low cranial vault with distinct brow ridges and an ape-sized cranial capacity of 417 cm^3 (Falk et al., 2005). Archaeological deposits associated with the small hominid contained stone tools and remains of numerous other animals, including the Komodo dragon and a dwarf fossil elephant, *Stegodon* (Morwood et al., 2004). This small, archaic hominid on Flores overlapped extensively in time with modern humans, *Homo sapiens*, in the Sunda Shelf region but it is unknown if or how the two species might have interacted.

Additional discoveries of new individuals of *Homo floresiensis* have recently been announced (Morwood et al., 2005)—these confirm the small size of the species and add to the list of its unique anatomical features. Although the discovery of a new, dwarf species of our own genus living to the very end of the Pleistocene on an island in Southeast Asia is a remarkable and exciting find, in another sense it conforms almost exactly to expectations. Island faunas, because of their isolation, commonly contain relict species that have gone extinct on mainland areas where there is greater faunal turnover and exposure to new competitors and predators. For example, the tarsier was once widespread in Asia but is now confined to the islands of the Sunda Shelf (Beard, 1998). Similarly, island forms of animals larger than a rabbit are often smaller than their mainland relatives, presumably as a result of more limited food supplies and perhaps less predator pressure. Islands around the world are well known for their dwarf goats, dwarf elephants, dwarf deer, and many others. Thus the dwarf hominid of Flores is just what one would expect from an island species. In these respects, although exciting, the Flores hominid shows that human evolution follows many of the same ecological rules as that of other mammals. At the same time we can only wonder what other new discoveries await paleontologists and archaeologists on other islands around the world.

In the final article of Part IV, "Grandmothering and the Evolution of *Homo erectus*," James O'Connell and colleagues propose a new and radically different behavioral scenario for the evolution and geographic expansion of *Homo erectus*. They argue that current scenarios involving hunting and scavenging are based primarily on conventional wisdom and have been seriously questioned by recent research in primatology, archaeology, and modern human behavior. In their scenario, the evolutionary success of *Homo erectus* was based on a dramatic change in the pattern of foraging humans, in which older females became more actively involved in the provisioning of young children. This change would account for the distinctive life history features of modern humans that distinguish us from apes, including delayed maturity, higher fertility, and mid-life menopause (see also Hawkes et al., 2002). It would also explain the distinctive morphological features of *Homo erectus*, including larger female body size and greater cranial capacity than earlier hominids. In the view of these authors, hunting and scavenging in *Homo erectus*, presumably by males, was unlikely to have produced any substantial contribution to dietary needs. Instead, they argue that hunting and scavenging in *Homo erectus*, as in chimpanzees and many modern hunter-gatherers, was probably done more in conjunction with male display behavior (see O'Connell et al., 2002).

REFERENCES

Antón, S. C., W. R. Leonard, and M. L. Robertson. 2002. An ecomorphological model of the initial hominid dispersal from Africa. *Journal of Human Evolution* 43:773–785.

Beard, K. C. 1998. A new genus of Tarsiidae (Mammalian: Primates) from the middle Eocene of Shanxi Province, China, with notes on the historical biogeography of tarsiers. *Bulletin of the Carnegie Museum of Natural History* 34:260–277.

Falk, D., C. Hildebolt, K. Smith, M. J. Morwood, T. Sutikna, P. Brown, Jatmiko, E. Wahyu Saptomo, B. Brunsden, and F. Prior. 2005. The brain of LB1, *Homo floresiensis. Science* 308:242–245.

Gabunia, L. K., A. K. Vekua, M.-A. de Lumley, and D. O. Lordkipanidze. 2002. A new species of *Homo* represented by a fossil from the bottom part of the Pleistocene layer at Dmanisi, Georgia. *Archaeology, Ethnology, & Anthropology of Eurasia* 4:145–153.

Hawkes, K., J. F. O'Connell, and N. G. Blurton Jones. 2002. The evolution of human life histories: primate tradeoffs, grandmothering socioecology, and the fossil record. In *The Role of Life Histories in Primate Socioecology* (P. Kappeler and M. Pereira, Eds.), pp. 204–227, University of Chicago Press, Chicago.

Morwood, M. J., R. P. Soejono, R. G. Roberts, T. Sutikna, C. S. M. Turney, K. E. Westaway, W. J. Rink, J.–x Zhao, G. D. van den Bergh, Rokus Awe Due, D. R. Hobbs, M. W. Moore, M. I. Bird, and L. K. Fifield. 2004. Archaeology and age of a new hominin from Flores in eastern Indonesia. *Nature* 431:1087–1091.

Morwood, M. J., P. Brown, Jatmiko, T. Sutikna, E. Wahyu Saptomo, K. E. Westaway, Rokus Awe Due, R. G. Roberts, T. Maeda, S. Wasisto, and T. Djubiantono. 2005. Further evidence for small-bodied hominins from the Late Pleistocene of Flores, Indonesia. *Nature*, in press.

O'Connell, J. F., K. Hawkes, K. D. Lupo, and N. G. Blurton Jones. 2002. Male strategies and Plio-Pleistocene archaeology. *Journal of Human Evolution* 43:831–872.

Santa Luca, A. P. 1980. *The Ngandong Fossil Hominids.* Department of Anthropology, Yale University, New Haven.

34

The African Emergence and Early Asian Dispersals of the Genus *Homo*

R. Larick and R. L. Ciochon

More than a century ago, Dutch paleontologist Eugene Dubois suggested that human origins lay in Southeast Asia, and he soon found the undeniably earliest hominid skeletal remains on the island of Java. In the 1930s, many more fossils of similar primitive character came to light near Beijing, and the entire Asian collection became known as *Homo erectus*. Presumably arising from an Asian ape, "upright man" had evidently occupied a great swath of eastern Asia, and provided the logical precursor to the more advanced and younger Neanderthal and Cro-Magnon (*Homo sapiens*) fossils of Europe. In evolutionary terms, *Homo erectus* was thought to have emerged in Asia and later dispersed to Europe.

During the 1960s, the eastern Rift Valley region of eastern Africa began to yield contrary evidence in its many much older *Australopithecus* fossils as well as an ample number of fossils from *Homo*. By the 1970s, human origins were believed to lie in Africa, with a much later dispersal toward East Asia. Movement from Africa to Europe came yet later. The new African research, a collaborative effort among paleontologists, geologists, paleoclimatologists and others, also began to ask about the timing and cause of human emergence. In the light of new ecological theory and increasingly sensitive environmental evidence, paleoanthropologists could now advance relatively complex behavioral models.

Current evidence suggests that about 3.0 to 2.4 million years ago (mya), the relatively cool, dry climate of tropical Africa presented challenging new conditions for woodland-dwelling *Australopithecus*. In theory, the cooler climate cleared out some of the woodland to form new open habitats. It is at about this time that the earliest species of the genus *Homo* emerged, between 2.5 and 2.0 mya, to exploit the new habitats as a rather aggressive omnivorous scavenger.

Climate has been less useful for understanding the intercontinental dispersion of *Homo*. Until recently, the earliest *Homo* fossils in Asia appeared to be no more than 1.1 million years old, representing a time well after emergence and not directly related to significant climatic events. Paleoanthropologists have therefore explained dispersion as a separate stage of development, and as the result of "internal" factors, such as population saturation and technological advances in tool making and resource scavenging.

Recently, however, we and our Chinese colleagues have contributed to what has become a wave of new Asian fossil discoveries and technical reanalyses that change this picture. In tropical and subtropical East Asia, the age of newly discovered fossils of *Homo* and simple stone tools, as well as some revised dates for known remains now approach 2 million years, nearly 1 million years older than previous estimations. In temperate west Asia, a new hominid and associated tools reach 1.4 million years in age. This new evidence extends the pattern of well-known contemporary eastern Mediterranean archaeological sites northward to suggest a later—but still quite early—movement to the more temperate areas of the Middle East and mid-latitude west Asia.

The new finds and age determinations give distinctness and complexity as well as antiquity to the formerly late and amorphous pattern for Asian dispersal. Our interest lies in the initial dispersal of early *Homo* from tropical Africa eastward across tropical and subtropical habitats of South and East Asia. In fact, early *Homo* now seems to have arrived in East Asia so early that its African emergence and initial subtropical Asian dispersal must be linked. Thus the factors that triggered the evolution of *Homo* from *Australopithecus* also encouraged early *Homo* to leave Africa, at least initially. We reconsider the new evidence for early dispersals in the light of climatic, morphological, technological and behavioral factors hypothesized for the emergence of *Homo*. We find that the striding gait, the elementary stone tools and the simple, but expansive, pattern of scavenging that characterizes the emergence of *Homo* also served its initial dispersal. In contrast, later populations of *Homo* colonized more temperate habitats under more complex and less obvious conditions.

TIME, CLIMATE AND SPECIES

The most basic questions for human dispersal have remained hypothetical during the past two decades. When did hominids first leave Africa? Which species was the first to leave? Why did they leave? The issue of age has always overshadowed all others. In the eastern Rift Valley sites, fossils are usually recovered from relatively fine-grained deposits laid down by water and wind. These formations often include layers of volcanic ash that are easily dated using the potassium-argon (K-Ar) radiometric method. Alternatively, in Europe and subtropical Asia many fossils are found within the diverse and complex deposits that accumulate in caves, where depositional histories are difficult to interpret and volcanic materials are not present. The net effect is that the

Reprinted with permission from *American Scientist*, Vol. 84, pp. 538–551. Copyright © 1996 by Sigma XI, the Scientific Research Society.

Figure 1.   *An early hominid,* Homo ergaster, *depicted in this diorama from the American Museum of Natural History's Hall of Human Biology and Evolution, lived nearly 2 million years ago in the eastern Rift Valley of Africa. Until recently, anthropologists thought that such early hominids did not disperse from Africa to Asia until 1 million years ago. New fossil finds and dates from Asia, including the authors', now suggest that early* Homo *arrived in East and South Asia by 2 million years ago. Tying the new evidence to paleoclimate and ecological theory, the authors suggest that the physical adaptations of African emergence— among them, a ranging bipedal gait, stone technology, increased intelligence and extensive scavenging—may also have enabled early* Homo *to colonize subtropical Asia very quickly. (Courtesy of the Library, American Museum of Natural History)*

age of *Homo* fossils has been measured more precisely (and consistently older) in Africa than in Eurasia. Thus, the earliest *Homo erectus* (better termed *Homo ergaster*) fossils in the eastern Rift Valley appear fully developed by 1.9 mya, whereas the Javanese fossils (classic Asian *Homo erectus*), which are thought to be the earliest in Asia, have traditionally received broad age estimates of only 700,000 years to 1.1 million years. The nearly one-million-year disparity between the African emergence and the initial Asian arrival has for years been the basis of the conventional theory for a late dispersal.

Recent developments in techniques that provide the absolute ages of artifacts—such as paleomagnetism, electron-spin resonance (ESR), and single-crystal argon (Ar/Ar) methods—have shed new light on the arrival of *Homo* in Asia. Moreover, the discovery of new artifact-bearing sites makes the dispersal of *Homo* a much more

accessible question. At Riwat and Pabbi Hills in Pakistan, simple stone tools have a paleomagnetic age of about 1.9 million years. At Sangiran and Mojokerto in Java (Indonesia) the sedimentary contexts for three well-known cranial specimens of *Homo erectus* now have Ar/Ar age determinations of 1.6 to 1.8 million years. The most intriguing of the new finds for early Asian dispersal come from Longgupo, a cave in southeastern Sichuan Province, China. The Longgupo hominid teeth have affinities to early African *Homo* and the stone artifacts resemble early African tools. Last year, we and our Chinese colleagues, Huang Wanpo and Gu Yumin at the Institute for Vertebrate Paleontology and Paleoanthropology, published ESR and paleomagnetic analyses that indicated an age of 1.9 mya for the Longgupo remains. The growing number of Asian hominid fossils and stone-tool assemblages that

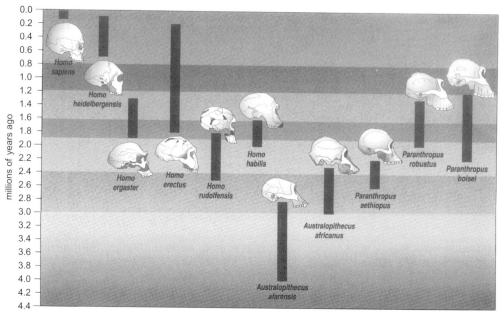

Figure 2.   *Evolution of the genus* Homo *from* Australopithecus *seems to be linked with global climate changes between 2 and 3 million years ago. Cooler temperatures diminished the tropical-woodland habitat of* Australopithecus *in favor of more open savanna. Several species of* Homo *evolved rapidly to occupy these new habitats, as did* Paranthropus, *another descendant of* Australopithecus. Paranthropus *became extinct by 1.2 million years ago. Early* Homo *maintained a generalized anatomy as it spread throughout tropical and subtropical Asia, but apparently became specialized with the evolution of* Homo erectus *by 1.8 million years ago. The much later European dispersal of African* Homo heidelbergensis *also seems to have resulted in the specialized Neanderthals. All of these early dispersals of* Homo *were apparently eclipsed by the late Eurasian dispersal of* Homo sapiens, *from Africa, some 100,000 years ago. The three darker bands indicate periods of greater relative aridity.*

approach 2.0 million years in age now suggests that an early population of *Homo* arrived in eastern Asia within a few hundred thousand years of arising in Africa. In the light of this new evidence for early dispersals, it appears *Homo* emerged not so much in adaptation to challenging conditions, but fully poised to dominate new resources in new territories.

Crucial aspects of hominid evolution and dispersal evidently relate to global climatic trends, particularly to the cooling and drying associated with glaciation in the northern hemisphere. Within the Rift Valley, such oscillations repeatedly added open components to woodlands, to effect more mixed or mosaic-like habitats. By implication, climatic trends prompted the large hominoids to develop new physical and behavioral adaptations, but the process and results are not always clearly related. For example, a cooling event during the Late Miocene epoch (about 6.0–5.3 mya) correlates well with the time at which apes and hominids diverged as estimated by molecular clocks. Although climate must have played a role in this speciation event, fossils from this period have yet to be found. Consequently, the crucial anatomical effects of climatic cooling and their relation to the divergence of the apes and the hominids are not known.

Fortunately, it is easier to link the emergence and dispersal of *Homo* with cooling during the Middle Pliocene (3.0–2.4 mya). During this period in Africa, many mammalian species were pushed toward extinction,

speciation or dispersion. Yale University paleontologist Elisabeth Vrba has documented extinctions for larger species of forest-adapted African bovids, particularly the antelopes, and the emergence of more cursorial, open-dwelling species that occupy grassland habitats to this day. Vrba also has shown that some six species of African bovids, a relatively large number for any period, dispersed to Eurasia during the Middle Pliocene. The dispersal of large bovids is especially interesting because their shift from the forest to the open resembles that hypothesized for the hominids. Moreover, since open-country bovids could have been hunted or scavenged by *Homo*, the two groups may have emerged and dispersed together.

Regarding the hominids, Middle Pliocene cooling underlies the divergence of *Australopithecus* into two evolutionary lines. One yielded *Paranthropus*, whose robust jaws and massive teeth reflect a rather specialized coarse vegetarian diet. In this robust line, *Paranthropus boisei* survived until 1.2 mya and may have developed stone tools. Nevertheless, in other ways *Paranthropus* was not substantially different from its australopith ancestors. With sexually dimorphic bodies and ape-sized brains, *Paranthropus* was confined to tropical habitats and never encountered its continental limits.

The second, more omnivorous line issued *Homo* in the African fossil record. From the discovery of Javanese finds in 1891 to the early 1960s, when Louis and Mary Leakey's work began to pay off in spectacular finds at Olduvai Gorge, our own genus comprised just two

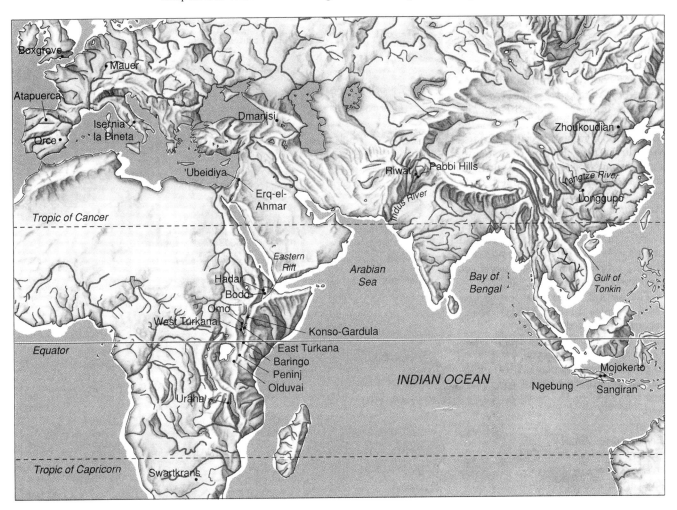

Figure 3.   *Hominids now known as* Homo erectus *were found on Java, Indonesia, in 1891, and at Zhoudoudian, near Beijing, in the 1930s. As* Homo erectus *was clearly more primitive than hominid fossils known in Europe, human beings were initially thought to have emerged in East Asia and dispersed westward. Since the early 1960s, numerous fossils from African localities in the eastern Rift Valley, Lake Malawi and South Africa have demonstrated an African emergence for* Homo. *In the 1990s, advances in dating methods and new finds at Dmanisi (Georgia), Riwat (Pakistan), two Javanese sites and Longgupo (China) show that early* Homo *had arrived in East Asia by 2 million years ago. Areas in white indicate land masses submerged since those early dispersals.*

species: *Homo erectus* (identified only later in Africa and, by some accounts, in Europe) and our own *Homo sapiens*. With the Leakeys' discoveries of *Homo habilis* at Olduvai, *Homo erectus*'s direct antecedent seemed to have appeared at 1.8 to 1.6 mya. When first found, *Homo habilis* presented a larger cranium and narrower teeth than the older autralopiths and yet still showed some primitive features such as small size. As fossil finds of *Homo habilis* have accumulated more recently, apelike long arms, short legs and australopith-like thigh anatomy have cast doubt on this relationship. *Homo habilis* is morphologically too primitive to be an ancestor of *Homo erectus*.

Concurrently, a number of fairly complete and well-preserved fossils from the Turkana Basin of northern Kenya (as well as a skull from Swartkrans, South Africa), indicate that Asian *Homo erectus* has an equally ancient sister species in Africa. By 1.9 mya *Homo ergaster* exhibited limb proportion and body size comparable to *Homo*

sapiens and to *Homo erectus*, and with a cranium larger than that of *Homo habilis*. Comparing the African and Asian forms yields subtle but significant differences. The skull of *Homo ergaster* is more generalized, having a higher or domed cranium, fairly thin cranial bones, weak brow ridges and a lightly built face, features that align the species more with *Homo sapiens*. Alternatively, Asian *Homo erectus* has always been defined on rather specialized features including a long cranium, a low forehead, thick cranial bones, large projecting brow ridges and a heavier face (compared to *Homo sapiens*). With the new earliest dates for *Homo erectus* in Asia at 1.8 mya, the two species seem to be evolutionary contemporaries (many do not even term them separate species). Although it is tempting to consider *Homo ergaster* as the more generalized African form of *Homo erectus*, and therefore the first colonizer of Asia, it is more likely that an older species ancestral to both forms left Africa more than 2.0 mya.

Table 1.   The Fossil Hominid and Stone Tool Assemblages That Trace the Emergence of *Homo* in Africa and Its Intercontinental Dispersals

Provenance, Age (millions of years)	Hominid Fossils	Stone-Tool Technology
Emergence Sites		
Hadar (Ethiopia)		
Kada Hadar (New), 2.3–2.2	mandible (*Homo* species indeterminate)	core-flake (Omo/Oldowan)
Kada Gona, 2.7–2.5		core-flake (Omo)
Omo Shungura (Ethiopia)		
Member E, 2.4–2.3	teeth (*Homo* sp. indet.)	core-flake (Omo)
Member D, 2.5–2.4	teeth (*Homo* sp. indet.)	
Koobi Fora (East Turkana)		
Okote, 1.65–1.50	skull ER 3883 (*H. ergaster*)	
	mandible ER 992 (*H. ergaster*)	
KBS, 1.78	skull ER 3733 (*H. ergaster*)	
Upper Burgi, 1.90–1.88	mandible ER 1812 (*H. ergaster*)	core-flake (Omo/Oldowan)
	occiput ER 2598 (*H. ergaster*)	
	pelvis ER 3228 (*H. ergaster*)	
	skull ER 1470 (*H. rudolfensis*)	
Nachukui (West Turkana)		
Lower Natoo, 1.5	skeleton WT 15000 (*H. ergaster*)	
Kalochoro, 2.35–1.9		core-flake (Omo)
Baringo (Kenya)		
Chemeron, 2.4	temporal BC 1 (*Homo* sp. indet.)	
Uraha (Malawi)		
Chiwondo Beds, 2.5–2.1	mandible UR 501 (*H. rudolfensis*)	
Swartkrans (South Africa)		
Member 1, 1.7–1.8	skull SK 847 (*H. ergaster*)	
Olduvai Gorge (Tanzania)		
Lower Bed II, 1.6		
Bed I, 1.8	skull OH 13 (*H. habilis*)	core-flake (Developed Oldowan)
	mandible OH 7 (*H. habilis*)	core-flake (Oldowan)
Early Acheulian Sites		
'Ubeidiya (Israel)		
'Ubeidiya Formation		
upper layers, 1.4		biface (Acheulian)
lower layers, 1.4		core-flake (Developed Oldowan)
Konso-Gardula (Ethiopia)		
KGA 4–KGA 12, 1.4	mandible KGA 10-1 (*H. ergaster*)	biface (Acheulian)
Peninj (Tanzania)		
Humbu, 1.4		biface (Acheulian)
Olduvai Gorge (Tanzania)		
upper Bed II, 1.25	skull OH 9 (*H. erectus*)	biface (Acheulian)
Early Dispersal Sites		
Longgupo (China)		
Middle Zone		
1.96–1.78	mandible CV.939.1 (*Homo* species indeterminate)	2 core tools
	incisor CV.939.2 (*Homo* sp. indet.)	
Sangiran (Java, Indonesia)		
Pucangan Formation, 1.66	2 skulls S 27, S 31 (*H. erectus*)	
Mojokerto (Java, Indonesia)		
Pucangan Formation, 1.81	skull Perning 1 (*H. erectus*)	
Ngebung (Java, Indonesia)		
Kabuh Formation, 0.75–0.25		core-flake (Sangiran Flake Industry)
Riwat (Pakistan)		
artifact horizon, 1.96–1.78		3 core tools
Pabbi Hills (Pakistan)		
fossil horizons, 2.0–0.9		core-flake (Omo)
Erq-el-Ahmar (Israel)		
Upper Erq-el-Ahmar, 1.96–1.78		2 core tools
Dmanisi (Georgia)		
hominid locality, 1.4	mandible (*H. erectus*)	core-flake
1.8 on underlying basalt		

Table 1. (continued)

Provenance, Age (millions of years)	Hominid Fossils	Stone-Tool Technology
	Later Dispersal Sites	
Atapuerca (Spain)		
Gran Dolina (TD) 6, 0.99–0.78	frontal, maxilla, mandible (*Homo* sp. indet.)	core-flake
Gran Dolina (TD) 4, 1.6–0.75		core-flake
Orce (Spain)		
Fuentenueva 3, 1.07–0.99	temporal (*Homo* sp. indet.)	core-flake
Isernia la Pineta (Italy)		
Sectors I and II		core-flake
0.99–0.78		
0.8–0.5		
	Acheulian Dispersal Sites	
Bodo (Ethiopia)		
Upper Bodo Sand Unit, 0.6	skull (*H. heidelbergensis*)	biface (Acheulian)
Elandsfontein (South Africa)		
Saldana Bay, 0.7–0.4	skull (*H. heidelbergensis*)	biface (Acheulian)
Boxgrove (England)		
Quarry 1, 0.5	tibia (*H. heidelbergensis*)	biface (Acheulian)
Mauer (Germany), 0.5	mandible (*H. heidelbergensis*)	

The earliest Asian finds date to almost 2 million years ago, contemporaneous with the fossils and artifacts of *Homo*'s emergence in Africa. A small first wave of elementary technology and poorly known early hominids is found in southern Europe just less than 1 million years ago. Relatively sophisticated stone tools of the Acheulian type first appear in Africa about 1.5 million years ago in association with *Homo ergaster*, but arrive in Europe only about 500,000 years ago, associated with the more advanced *Homo heidelbergensis*.

Scant evidence for this pre-*erectus* hominid—an emergent "early" *Homo*—comes from four other areas of the eastern Rift in addition to the Turkana Basin: the Hadar Basin of northeastern Ethiopia, the Omo Valley of southwestern Ethiopia, the Baringo locality of central Kenya and the Uraha locality of eastern Malawi. These areas have geological formations dating to middle–late Pliocene (2.5 to 1.8 mya), the end of the critical Pliocene cooling and the beginning of a period of climatic stability. Some early fossils have been termed *Homo rudolfensis*, a taxon having affinities with *Homo habilis* and possibly with *Homo ergaster/erectus*. Other finds (for example, the isolated teeth from Omo and the partial temporal bone from Baringo) are too fragmentary to classify with any specificity. In Hadar and in Omo, early *Homo* is associated stratigraphically with emergent stone-tool assemblages. Although a detailed understanding of early *Homo* awaits more fossil discoveries, the significant date of origin and the climatic link are incontrovertible.

EMERGENT BIOLOGICAL TECHNOLOGY

As typified by *Homo ergaster*, early *Homo* was the first hominid to develop a ranging bipedal gait, one that allowed it to cover a lot of ground in a short period. Long, well-muscled limbs on a lanky torso also conferred physical strength and defensive presence. Leverage and strength in the arms and hands gave early *Homo* the ability to make simple chopping and cutting implements. Whereas *Australopithecus* and *Paranthropus* had significant sexual dimorphism in body size and strength, early *Homo* did not. Among other primates, reduced sexual dimorphism usually means that both sexes perform similar economic activities, that males compete less physically among themselves for females and that males and females pair-bond for long periods. An enlarged cranium also typified early *Homo*. A larger brain may have bestowed a more flexible intelligence, useful for finding resources within new habitats, as well as the complex behavior *Homo* came to use against prey and predators.

The early specimens of *Homo* also exhibit the relatively diminished premolars and molars—the cheek teeth—of an omnivorous eater, one for which animal protein played a significant dietary role. As a part-time meat eater, early *Homo* probably relied on large carnivores to supply many usable packages of animal protein—very pragmatically scavenging the remains of what real carnivores could more effectively hunt. At the other dietary extreme, these hominids certainly consumed some hard, tough plant foods. In contrast to *Paranthropus*, whose digestion of such foods probably began inside its mouth, early *Homo* more often and more completely processed difficult animal and vegetal resources with stone-tool technology, which was employed to break, crush, split and cut up hard foods before ingesting them. Rather than being implements of predation, early tools underlay a technology that essentially added a new first stage to digestion. Indeed, we hypothesize a close relationship between Pliocene hominid biology and a very elementary technology, in effect a "biological technology" in which both the mass and the jagged edges of a few chipped rocks gave early *Homo* access to a wide range of nutritional resources. Simple stone tools represent immediate extensions of the forelimb and hand for breaking down or processing tough foodstuffs.

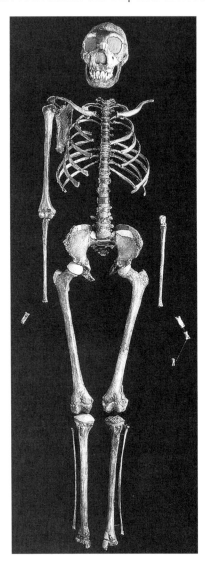

Figure 4.   *Earliest complete skeleton of* Homo *is that of a boy from the West Turkana region of Kenya.* Homo ergaster *already had many anatomical features of* Homo sapiens, *including a high, domed cranium with relatively light cranial and facial bones and a lanky torso with long, well-muscled limbs. The overall size and proportions of its skeleton gave* Homo ergaster *a ranging, bipedal gait as well as physical strength and a defensive presence. Leverage and strength in the arms and hands helped this hominid use simple stone tools effectively to chop and crush food. (Photograph provided by National Museums of Kenya, Nairobi; © 1985 David L. Brill.)*

Hominid biological remains may be difficult to classify, but stone tools present even greater problems of interpretation. One way to understand the development of early stone technology is to envision emergent and advanced stages separated by a transition. Currently, evidence for the emergent stage appears with the late–middle Pliocene (about 2.5 mya) in Hadar, Omo and Turkana. Mzalendo Kibunjia of the National Museums of Kenya has proposed the name Omo Industrial Complex for such assemblages, in which rocks were broken or casually chipped into very basic implements. Only a few general tool types can be defined for the Omo-type assemblages: simple core

choppers and rough flake scrapers. The basic technological characteristics of Omo-type core-flake assemblages vary by the raw materials available in each region. In Hadar and Turkana, where large volcanic cobbles are present, the tools tend to be large and the chipping technique a little more complex. In Omo, where small, tough quartz cobbles were used, the tools are much smaller and more haphazardly made. At present, the Omo-type localities and tools represent the initial threshold of stone technology at a date that correlates well with the emergence of *Homo* itself.

The advanced or Acheulian stage begins with the early Pleistocene, about 1.6 to 1.4 mya—well after *Homo ergaster* attains full development in the Turkana Basin. The Acheulian technological complex is achieved as the selection of raw materials, the preparation of the stone core and the chipping procedures become much more complex, and the tools themselves become somewhat specialized. Bifacial chipping is the hallmark of the Acheulian Industry. With this technique, a tool blank is chipped from two directions across a bisecting plane. The blank is worked around a circumferential edge to resemble a plump discus, or a double-sided tortoise shell, and the entire edge becomes the working part. Although earlier hominids had developed crude bifacial techniques by 2.0 mya, the method did not become the basis for a distinctive set of Acheulian biface tools until about 1.5 mya. The Acheulian appears to emerge in the eastern Rift in areas such as Konso-Gardula in Ethiopia, as well as Peninj and Olduvai Gorge in Tanzania. Nevertheless, Acheulian bifaces are found as far north as the Jordan Valley of Israel (at 'Ubeidiya) by 1.4 mya. When hominid remains and early Acheulian tools are associated within any site stratum in Africa, the species is always *Homo ergaster* or *Homo erectus,* not *Homo habilis* or *Paranthropus boisei.*

The period from about 2.0 to 1.5 mya is best seen as a long and important transition between the advent of chipping techniques and the achievement of standardized Acheulian biface tools. Much of this period is represented in the lower beds of Olduvai Gorge, Tanzania, where Mary Leakey of the National Museums of Kenya defined the well-known Oldowan Industry more than 30 years ago. At the time, the Oldowan was thought to be the earliest manifestation of stone technology and, indeed, the earliest assemblages in Bed I (the oldest levels of Olduvai) resemble those from Ethiopia and northern Kenya now deemed oldest. Nevertheless, most Oldowan tool kits reflect more care and skill in choosing raw materials and in preparing and striking cores to create usable flakes and core tools than do the Omo-type assemblages. Over the several hundred thousand years evident in Olduvai's stratigraphy, Oldowan assemblages undergo distinct refinement in chipping techniques and some standardization in tool form. By 1.7 to 1.6 mya, bifacial tools help to define the Developed Oldowan Industry. At Olduvai, the initial stone tool finds came in stratigraphic association with a new hominid, one with a larger brain and more gracile features than had the previous robust australopith skull found at Olduvai Gorge (*Paranthropus boisei*). The clear association of an advanced hominid with stone tools

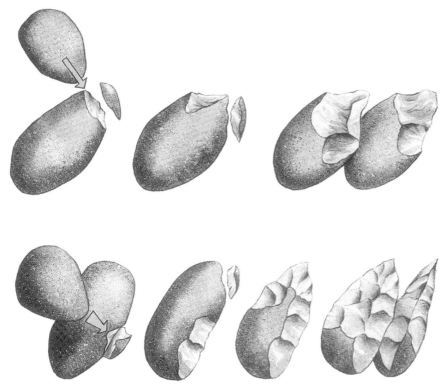

Figure 5. *Stone technology appears to have emerged in the eastern Rift Valley about 2.6 million years ago. At this time, tools of Omo Industrial Complex appeared, in which early* Homo *toolmakers chose a durable crystalline stone, often picked off the ground as a fist-sized cobble-stone, to break or chip into a core and several flakes (top). By 1.6 to 1.4 million years ago, raw-material selection, core preparation and chipping techniques had improved markedly. In reorienting the core and hammerstone,* Homo ergaster *toolmakers could chip flakes from a lenticular cobble around its periphery on both faces (bottom). Competent bifacial chipping, the hallmark of Acheulian artifacts, was a skill carried to Europe by* Homo heidelbergensis *about 600,000 years ago. Having attributes of both Omo and Acheulian tools, Oldowan artifacts, first recovered from Olduvai Gorge in the 1960s, reflect an intermediate technological stage lasting from about 2.0 to 1.5 million years ago.*

prompted the Leakeys to designate the new species *Homo habilis*, literally "handy man." It becomes clear that more than one species of *Homo*—and probably *Paranthropus boisei*—made Oldowan-type tools at Olduvai Gorge and elsewhere.

Given its relatively early appearance and greater complexity over the earlier stages as well as its association with *Homo ergaster*, the African Acheulian technology has often played into hypotheses for Eurasian dispersal. However, new dates and technological analyses make any such role unlikely in Asia. Although Acheulian tools always seemed to antedate the earliest tool assemblages in East Asia, the recently discovered stone tools at Longgupo and Riwat are as ancient and as simple in design as their Omo and early Oldowan counterparts in Africa. None of the older Asian assemblages contain handaxes, and few exhibit even the standardized chipping patterns of the Developed Oldowan or the Acheulian technologies.

The current and revolutionary evidence for a very early dispersal of hominids from Africa to Asia may be reiterated as follows. Fragmentary fossils representing the emergent genus *Homo* are consistently dated to nearly 2.5 mya at various points in the eastern Rift Valley. Likewise, as the earliest stone tools, also found in the eastern Rift, have equal antiquity, the emergence of one must be linked to the other. By 1.9 mya, *Homo ergaster* presents undeniable morphological features for moving great distances: long torso and limbs, narrow hips, a large brain and reduced dentition. With the new evidence from Longgupo, Java and Riwat, it becomes clear that early *Homo* (the immediate ancestor to *Homo ergaster* and *Homo erectus*) and simple

stone tools arrived in tropical and subtropical Asia by about 2.0 mya. The emergence of Acheulian technology in east Africa confirms the hypothesis for early Asian dispersal. Distinctive bifaces date to 1.5 mya in the eastern Rift Valley and the Middle East, and to 600,000 years ago in Europe. The absence of Acheulian bifaces at the early sites in South or East Asia suggests that *Homo* must have initially left Africa before the Acheulian stage appeared in Africa. Consequently, early *Homo* dispersed to subtropical Asia with a very elementary technology.

CATCHMENT SCAVENGING

Having established the Middle Pliocene climatic window, the coincident technological threshold and the early dates for arrival in Asia, it is now possible to hypothesize the process of early dispersal within a strong theoretical framework. We believe that the ecological context of emergence holds the key for understanding early Asian dispersal. Clearly, interactions between populations and their environments influence evolutionary change, including dispersion. Change in environmental conditions, such as climate, inevitably brings neighboring populations into competition for shelter, food and other resources. Populations may respond either by specializing to create a new niche within the old territory, or by dispersing to relieve pressure in the home territory and to establish or maintain the old niche in new territory. Alan Turner of the University of Liverpool has pioneered research that ties hominid dispersals to the better-known movements of more common mammalian species. His consistent point is that hominid evolution should not be viewed as unique or separate from the general processes that govern change in a host of related species.

Our ecological model addresses the scavenging behavior that we believe constitutes the primary behavioral factor for early dispersal. The model relies on the results of detailed regional survey and site excavation within the eastern Rift Valley by a number of archaeologists. Over years of research, the stone and bone detritus recovered at hominid occupation sites has been shown to reflect, quite sensitively, specific natural resources used and the ways in which resources were collected. Working together, archaeologists and paleoanthropologists have found that diverse research areas such as Olduvai Gorge, the Omo Valley and the Turkana Basin yield somewhat different patterns of early hominid occupation for any given period, based on the availability of stone raw materials for tools and water resources. Nevertheless, when compared through time, the localities exhibit basic similarities in hominid

scavenging practices and technological tradition that form the African background for early Asian dispersal. Jack Harris of Rutgers has been instrumental in bringing forth the earliest evidence for stone tools and their behavioral implications. Much of our model follows the lead of Harris and his colleagues and students.

In scavenging increasingly open terrain, early *Homo* was subject to two critical environmental factors. One was access to basic natural resources, including water, animal carcasses and stone for tools. The other was the ability to gain refuge from the heat of the sun, the cold of the night and the threat of carnivores. Two sequential patterns of subsistence behavior arose in relation to these factors. The first characterizes the earliest stone-tool sites that appear about 2.5 mya. The early sites are found on or near important natural features such as lake margins, stream confluences or rock outcrops. We term these locales and their immediate surroundings "catchments" to denote the presence of numerous complementary resources. Catchment sites often have rather large, diverse accumulations of bone and stone

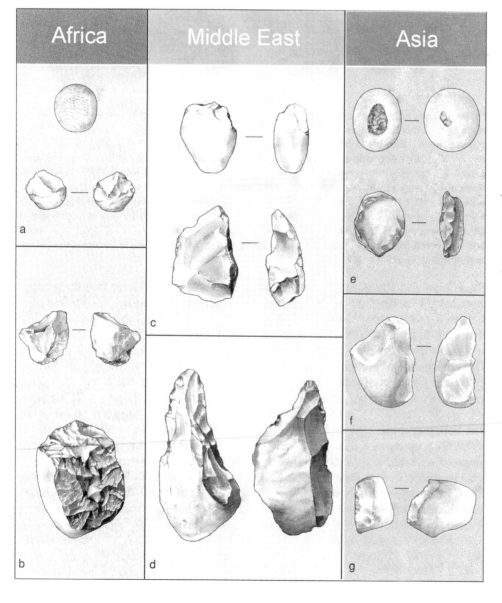

Figure 6. *Early stone artifacts show technological development in Africa and the Middle East, but none in subtropical Asia, where stone technology seems to have arrived and remained at Omo and Oldowan levels. Hammerstone and core tool from Olduvai Gorge, Tanzania (a), helped define the style of tool called Oldowan. Flake and core tools from Lokalalei, Kenya (b), are of the Omo type. Core tools of the Oldowan type were found in 'Ubeidiya, Israel (c), as were Acheulian bifaces (d). Core tools were found in Longgupo, China (e), Riwat, Pakistan (f), and Dmanisi, Georgia (g). Bars connect two views of the same tool. Scale bars are 1 inch = 15 centimeters*

refuse that indicate significant hominid occupation. It appears that early hominids congregated within catchments to use a number of resources for a fair amount of time. After exhausting one catchment's resources, the group would move on to another in a sequence of similar discrete movements. We term this form of subsistence behavior "catchment scavenging." It represents a way to use the resources of a large territory with a minimum of knowledge.

The second subsistence pattern appears after 2.0 mya and becomes common after 1.6 mya, and is generally associated with the Acheulian Industry. These later sites are found more often at locales offering just one or two resources, and they exhibit smaller and less-generalized stone and bone assemblages. Sites of this type may encompass many such small locales across a large area. A more complex behavior best fits this evidence, one in which small groups of hominids can manage the range of resources across a larger territory. A primary component of "territory scavenging" is the ability to work among small resource locales simultaneously or interdependently instead of sequentially. Even with this advance, the intensive localized knowledge required for territory scavenging could still be amassed at a prelinguistic, presymbolic and largely unconscious level— which would characterize the hominid groups that employed this type of scavenging style.

The distinction between catchment scavenging and territory scavenging provides a behavioral key for understanding early Asian dispersal. In leaving Africa before 2.0 mya, early *Homo* most likely employed the catchment strategy. In moving across numerous dispersed catchments, early *Homo* essentially could not invest in or manage a home territory in the way that modern *Homo sapiens* do. Moreover, as a spatially extensive strategy, catchment scavenging inherently dispersed hominid groups over a limited number of ideal points per given area. With the Middle Pliocene retreat of wooded refuge areas, the number of viable catchments probably diminished through time. Ranging ever more widely among fewer catchments, some hominid groups may have been forced north and east, and out of Africa before 2.0 mya. After this date, territory scavenging may have effectively kept remaining populations within the continent and raised intergroup competition for increasingly scarce resources. Territory scavenging may lie behind other particularly African technological advances, such as the development of the Acheulian Industry about 1.6 mya and the emergence and Eurasian dispersal of more advanced hominids, including *Homo heidelbergensis* about 600,000 years ago and anatomically modern *Homo sapiens* about 200,000 to 100,000 years ago.

EASTERN SUBTROPICAL HABITATS

Given the crucial technological advantages and catchment-scavenging strategies, early *Homo* should have out-competed other hominid and nonprimate scavengers within expanding open landscapes. This pattern of behavior created essentially a hegemonic ecological niche dependent on rapid, extensive and possibly aggressive movements. In this regard, South and East Asia offered new opportunities to scavenge and perhaps to hunt animals unaccustomed to the presence of hominids. Asia would also have presented fewer constraints in the form of large primate competitors and large carnivorous predators as well as endemic parasites and diseases. Moreover, an elementary stone-tool technology would suit catchment scavenging in Asia, as it does not require supplies of good-quality stone for specialized chipping and handaxe production. Fist-sized river cobbles of workable stone obviously served Asian hominids well enough. By gradually making its way among sparsely distributed open catchments, early *Homo* (now a global scavenger) could have reached East Asia within a few hundred thousand years of emerging in eastern Africa.

As mentioned, the earliest and most convincing new evidence for early Asian dispersal comes from Longgupo, Sichuan Province, China. Our Chinese colleagues, Huang and Gu, asked us to collaborate in analyzing the

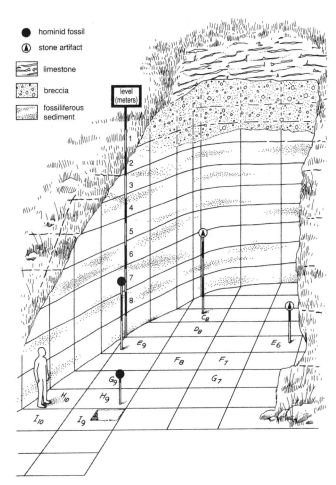

Figure 7. *Collapsed cave of Longgupo in eastern Sichuan Province, China, has recently yielded important hominid fossils and stone artifacts for which the authors have established a date of nearly 2 million years. The hominid remains and artifacts lie in geological association with many other mammalian fossils that provide sensitive evidence for species movement. In addition to the arrival of early* Homo, *the Longgupo fauna indicates that subtropical species of horses and pigs also moved to new northerly limits during the late Pliocene.*

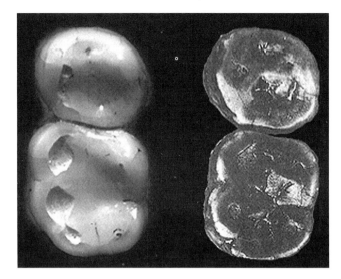

Figure 8. *Jaw fragment from Longgupo cave* (left), *which dates to about 1.9 million years ago, resembles an analogous specimen* (right) *from East Turkana (ER 992), dated to about 1.6 million years. Both fossils show more generalized hominid dental features in molar cusp patterns and premolar crown shape when compared with Asian* Homo erectus. *The Longgupo jaw is thus more primitive than* Homo erectus *and could represent the ancestral condition for that species. The Longgupo hominid best represents a population of early* Homo *arriving to East Asia about the time* Homo ergaster *appears in Africa. (Courtesy of Russell Ciochon)*

hominid teeth and artifacts, and in verifying the ancient age of the cave deposit. The finds at Longgupo include a jaw fragment with premolar and molar teeth, an isolated incisor and two stone artifacts. The incisor has a primitive form of "shoveling," where the sides and base extend rearward to form a depression on the center of the rear surface. This feature is well known for *Homo ergaster.* Fourth-premolar (second bicuspid) and first-molar cusp patterns also show affinities with *Homo ergaster.* The two artifacts are cobblestones of volcanic rock that have been slightly modified into tools for chopping and battering, much like the African Omo tools.

In introducing our argument, we noted that Eugene Dubois began collecting fossil hominids on the island of Java before the turn of our own century. Since Dubois's time, more than 80 cranial specimens of *Homo erectus* have been found at six principal localities. Although the localities generally have complex stratigraphies, the fossils have been collected without reliable stratigraphic information. However, two Javanese localities, Mojokerto and Sangiran, stand out for having *Homo erectus* fossils associated with the Pucangan Formation, which has been dated independently at nearly 2.0 mya. Recently, Carl Swisher at the Berkeley Geochronology Center and his colleagues have reconfirmed the geological associations and have applied Ar/Ar techniques to Pucangan deposits at these sites. Sediments from the Mojokerto site, in which a well-preserved juvenile skull has been found, yield an average age of 1.81 mya. Sediment from Sangiran, in which two other crania were found, gives 1.66 mya. The new ages for these three specimens show that the low cranial vault, thick cranial bones and massive face that characterize *Homo erectus* evolved rapidly after

early *Homo* arrived in Asia. Very recently, Truman Simanjuntak of the National Research Centre of Archaeology in Jakarta and François Sémah at the Musée National d'Histoire Naturelle at Paris have found simple but indisputable flake tools in the Kabuh Formation, which overlies the Pucangan. Although these artifacts were deposited more recently than the remains of the earliest hominids, the discovery puts tools in the hands of Javanese *Homo erectus* in general, for which any such association had been lacking.

The technological component of early dispersal also appears southeast of Rawalpindi, Pakistan, among some large tributaries of the Indus River. Two areas, Riwat and the Pabbi Hills, have been studied by British and Pakistani specialists. A small number of simple flaked quartzite tools were found at Riwat during the 1980s, and a larger core-flake assemblage was recovered from the Pabbi Hills locality. Geological associations and a paleomagnetic analysis suggest an age of nearly 2.0 million years for the Riwat deposit, and more circumstantial evidence points to a similar age at Pabbi Hills. The consistent technological feature of all the earliest Asian stone-tool assemblages is simplicity. Indeed, all assemblages, including the later tools from Sangiran, recall stone artifact assemblages from either the Omo or Oldowan technological complexes but not from the Acheulian.

How could groups of scavenging hominids employing the simplest of technologies spread across South and East Asia so quickly? Middle Pliocene cooling and drying also encouraged South Asian dispersal as a band of open tropical and subtropical environments appeared from the area that is now Saudi Arabia eastward south of the Himalayas and into Southeast Asia. Like the African grasslands, these habitats (of more mixed vegetation types) drew catchment-scavenging hominids. Moreover, by the late Pliocene a significant portion of the earth's moisture was locked in glacial ice mass, lowering the global sea levels to expose what is now the continental shelf as expansive areas of coastal plain or to reveal isthmuses where there are now straits. Two exposed areas would have facilitated eastward dispersal. The Bab-el-Mandab (linking Africa and Asia between modern-day Djibouti and Yemen) adjoins Hadar, with its very early stone-tool assemblages. This short isthmus would have produced the best departure point for eastward travel within the tropical zone. The presence of similar modern flora and fauna (including Hamadryas baboons) on both sides of the strait signal its importance for numerous dispersals. Departing Africa on this route, early *Homo* could trend east-northeast across the Arabian Peninsula to reach a much smaller Persian Gulf, possibly crossable at Hormuz. A short journey east along the Arabian Sea brings the Indus Valley and direct access to Riwat and Pabbi Hills. Thus, although these South Asian sites seem to be along way from Africa, the departure point of Hadar lies surprisingly close given late Pliocene geography. A route south of the Himalayas would have brought early *Homo* to Southeast Asia.

Within the lowland Southeast, hominid groups would have encountered the large land mass of the Sunda Shelf, which then linked the tropical Southeast Asian archipelagos (including the island of Java) to the mainland. In our own century, dredging and fishing on areas of the Sunda Shelf that are now offshore have yielded Pleistocene fossils of large mammals. Although modern-day Longgupo appears inaccessible from these lowlands because of the eastward drainage of the upper Yangtze River, during the Pliocene the river drained southeast toward the Gulf of Tonkin. Like northern Pakistan, inland south-central China could have been reached directly from the south by ascending a broad alluvial valley. Indeed, paleontologist John van der Made of the Rijksuniversiteit Utrecht notes that in association with the hominids at Longgupo, subtropical species of horse and pig appear rather early at their northerly limits.

WESTERN TEMPERATE HABITATS

If early *Homo* was able to disperse early and quickly across subtropical East Asia, why does it seem to arrive later in West Asia and yet later in Europe? For West Asia, the sites of 'Ubeidiya in the western Jordan Rift of Israel, and Dmanisi, southeast of Tblisi, Georgia, provide the most information on early occupation. 'Ubeidiya's 150 vertical meters of geological infill appear to have been deposited over a short period. The assemblage of animal fossils in the stratigraphic column suggests that much of the deposit dates to nearly 1.4 mya. The lower archaeological levels contain a range of stone flakes and tools, some having the standardized forms associated with contemporary assemblages in East Africa, but there are no biface tools. The upper levels, not greatly different in age, clearly have these Acheulian tools. As only a few isolated human teeth have been recovered from the site—only one in geological context—the hominids responsible for the stone tools remains unknown. Ofer Bar-Yosef of Harvard University interprets the sequence as the result of two separate hominid occupations within a relatively short time. Both groups shared an advanced core-tool technology; one group used biface tools, the other did not.

The deposits at Dmanisi were first excavated in the 1980s for their faunal remains. Later, an assemblage of simple flake and core tools was found and, finally, in 1991, a complete jaw of *Homo erectus*. The age of the hominid and the artifacts is debatable. The enveloping sediments have a paleomagnetic interpretation of about 1.8 mya and a potassium-argon determination on the underlying lava flow corroborates with 1.8 mya. Nevertheless, the hominid fossils and tools appear to lie in pockets having a younger paleomagnetic reading. A conservative biostratigraphic estimate for the remains is 1.4 mya, nearly identical with the dating of 'Ubeidiya. Combining the information from these two sites suggests

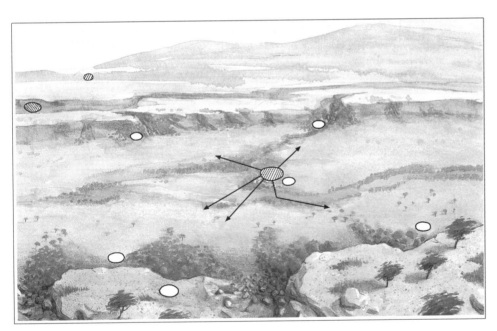

Figure 9. *Early* Homo *managed natural resources to minimize dependence on specific territories. The simple strategy for "catchment scavenging" is evident in eastern Rift Valley archaeological sites older than 2 million years. A group of hominids using this strategy established a camp conveniently close to multiple primary resources, such as water, stone and animal carcasses* (hatched marker in the foreground). *The catchment becomes the area around the camp within which resources are distributed sparsely but still readily available* (white markers). *Archaeological remains at catchment camps are rich and diverse, whereas little material is found at outlying points. After 2 million years ago,* Homo ergaster's *scavenging strategy became decentralized. This hominid ranged among more points within a larger "territory," a behavior that required more intimate knowledge of scattered resource points. Territory-site assemblages are thus smaller and more specialized, each reflecting localized resources. Rather than getting to know a landscape intimately, early* Homo *traveled widely among catchments* (hatched markers in the background), *thus increasing its ability and chance to disperse widely.*

that the Levant provided a corridor northward from Egypt and Saudi Arabia into Europe and northwestern Asia. Possibly, the eastern Mediterranean region has remained too rugged to support a Pliocene population of *Homo,* no matter how open the habitat. One other very enigmatic site plays into the timing of hominid dispersals to the Middle East. In the western Jordan Rift, the site of Erq-el-Ahmar has yielded a few probable core tools in a geological formation that antedates that of 'Ubeidiya. A paleomagnetic analysis indicates an age of about 1.8 mya, but some doubt remains about the date and the artifacts themselves.

As for Europe, it is fairly clear that mountain ranges, large watercourses and generally rigorous climates inhibited any significant early dispersal. It is certain, however, that a precursor to *Homo sapiens* colonized much of central and western Europe with the aid of a mature Acheulian technology. The earliest of those fossils and assemblages date to 600,000 years ago. Paleoanthropologists have argued for years about the name of this hominid species. Recently, Philip Rightmire of Binghamton University has proposed that a number of similar cranial and dental fossils from across Africa and Europe can be assigned to the species *Homo heidelbergensis,* which was first applied to a jaw found at Mauer, near Heidelberg, Germany, in 1908. *Homo heidelbergensis* is best described as a large-brained form of *Homo,* but still with a massive face. This hominid seems to have emerged in southern Africa around an advanced Acheulian technology at sites such as Bodo and Elandsfontein. The combination of a large brain and an advanced technology may account for the hominid's quick dispersion into Europe, as both *Homo heidelbergensis* and the Acheulian appear at sites such as Mauer and Boxgrove (in far northern Europe) by 500,000 years ago. In Europe, *Homo heidelbergensis* is the hominid that begins to show traits similar to the Neanderthals about 250,000 years ago, starting a trend of anatomical specialization that probably leads to extinction less than 30,000 years ago. Neither *Homo heidelbergensis* nor the Acheulian follows the path of early dispersal across southern Asia.

In Europe, as in Asia, recent finds and more penetrating age analyses bring up the possibility of African arrivals earlier than commonly hypothesized. Thus at Isernia la Pineta, in southern Italy, an elementary core-flake assemblage has a date of about 800,000 years ago, based on paleomagnetic and biostratigraphic methods. Even more intriguing are two Spanish sites where recent excavations have produced hominids and technological assemblages at an equally early age. At Atapuerca, in north-central Spain, core and flake tools accompany an early representative of *Homo* at greater than 780,000 years ago. Artifacts in a yet lower level of this locality may be significantly older. At Orce, in south-central Spain, excavators have recovered simple core and flake tools as well as purported hominid skull fragments and limb elements. Paleomagnetic analysis suggests an age of about 1.0 mya. Although hominid taxonomy and age determinations are tenuous at both localities, the Spanish sites represent possible evidence for an early species of *Homo* arriving from Africa before

Homo heidelbergensis and its Acheulian technology. It is also possible that *Homo* reached Europe via Gibraltar at least once.

EARLY DISPERSAL AND *HOMO SAPIENS*

If early *Homo* was able to leave Africa before 2.0 mya (and later), did these intercontinental quests contribute to the prehistoric distributions of *Homo sapiens,* our own species? The new evidence must be framed in terms of the ongoing debate over "multiregional" or "out-of-Africa" origins for *Homo sapiens.* The multiregional argument would use the new evidence to suggest that the early dispersals of early *Homo* set a complex stage for *Homo sapiens* to emerge at connected points across much of the Old World. For us, however, the new evidence suggests that both the early and later species of *Homo* had the ability to disperse across the continents. Given that *Homo sapiens* fossils appear to be much older in Africa than on any other continent, the answer seems obvious. Having emerged in Africa, *Homo sapiens* dispersed to Eurasia, replacing older populations of *Homo.*

Although there is little question that *Homo sapiens* emerged in Africa, the date of emergence, the technological associations and the dates for its Eurasian dispersals are debatable. It appears that our species originated between 200,000 and 100,000 years ago, somewhere in sub-Saharan Africa. Some recent discoveries in Zaire of ancient and finely crafted tool types (such as barbed-bone harpoons) indicate that the technology associated with this emergence may have been very advanced indeed, resembling the much later Upper Paleolithic of Europe. In the Levant, where *Homo sapiens* is evident about 90,000 years ago, a more archaic Middle Paleolithic technology still held sway. Consequently, we may not yet say whether the European dispersal of *Homo sapiens* was associated with either its emergence or a new technology.

CONCLUSION

In linking the early dispersal of early *Homo* with its emergence, we are describing a hominid very different from the australopiths, whose bipedal but still ape-like anatomy must have limited them to wooded locales. Thus the significance of an early dispersal to Asia is manifold. First, the climatic conditions of cool aridity that played a great role in the emergence of *Homo* itself also drew hominid populations out of Africa and into Asia. Emergence and dispersal are, to a great extent, a product of environmental change. Nevertheless, early *Homo* emerged with a radical, yet still generalized, set of characteristics that granted it ecological hegemony across the subtropical Old World. An early intercontinental distribution signifies a hominid not adapted to specific territorial conditions, but adapted to manage many local conditions through physical presence, technology and flexible social organization. Ironically, as the first species to use technology, early *Homo* colonized much of the subtropical Old World without the benefit of language, symbolic culture or individual consciousness as we know it.

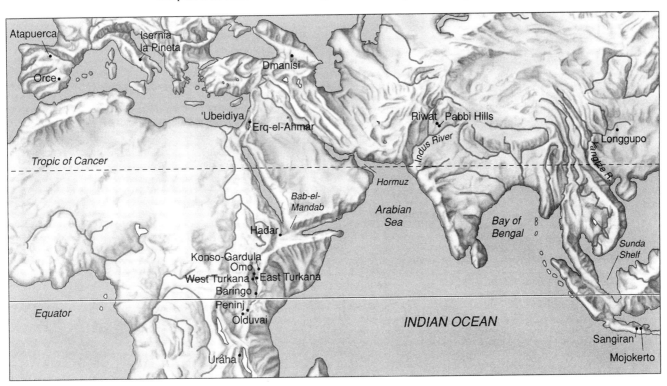

Figure 10. *Dispersal corridors opened out of Africa and across the Middle East into South and East Asia during the late Pliocene. Corridors formed primarily along coastal land masses, the product of expanding polar ice caps and resultant sea-level drawdown. Incipient development of the Red Sea rift also established departure routes through the Middle East. The drop in sea level in island Southeast Asia would have connected Sumatra, Java and Borneo with the mainland. Evolutionary analysis of fossil species, including antelopes, pigs and cats, indicates that large mammals dispersed along these routes sporadically during the late Pliocene and early Pleistocene. New fossil finds suggest that early* Homo *arrived in Asia some 1.8 to 1.9 million years ago, after departing Africa at least 100,000 years earlier.*

ACKNOWLEDGMENTS

This research is supported by the L. S. B. Leakey Foundation, the Wenner-Gren Foundation for Anthropological Research and the Human Evolution Research Fund at the University of Iowa Foundation. The authors acknowledge advice on early drafts of this work and on development of the illustrations from Noel Boaz, Frank Brown, Eric Delson, John Fleagle, F. Clark Howell, Philip Rightmire, Carl Swisher, Alan Turner and John Van Couvering.

REFERENCES

Asfaw, B., Y. Beyene, G. Suwa et al. 1992. The earliest Acheulean from Konso-Gardula. *Nature* 360:732–735.

Bar-Yosef, O. 1994. The lower Paleolithic of the Near East. *Journal of World Prehistory* 8:211–265.

Bräuer, G., and M. Schultz. 1996. The morphological affinities of the Plio-Pleistocene mandible from Dmanisi, Georgia. *Journal of Human Evolution* 30:445–481.

Bromage, T., and F. Schrenk. 1995. Biogeographic and climatic basis for a narrative of early hominid evolution. *Journal of Human Evolution* 28:109–114.

Cachel, S., and J. K. W. Harris. 1995. Ranging patterns, land-use and subsistence in *Homo erectus* from the perspective of evolutionary ecology. In *Proceedings of the Pithecanthropus Centennial, 1893–1993, Volume I, Palaeo-Anthropology: Evolution and Ecology of Homo erectus*, ed. J. R. F. Bower and S. Sartono. Leiden: Leiden University Press. pp. 51–66.

Carbonell, E., J. M. Bermudez de Castro, J. L. Arsuaga et al. 1995. Lower Pleistocene hominids and artifacts from Atapuerca-TD6 (Spain). *Science* 269:826–832.

Ciochon, R., V. T. Long, R. Larick et al. 1996. Dated co-occurrence of *Homo erectus* and *Gigantopithecus* from Tham Khuyen Cave, Vietnam. *Proceedings of the National Academy of Sciences* 93:3016–3020.

Clark, J. D., J. de Heinzelin, K. D. Schick et al. 1994. African *Homo erectus*: Old radiometric ages and young Oldowan assemblages in the Middle Awash valley, Ethiopia. *Science* 264:1907–1910.

Clarke, R. J. 1994. The significance of Swartkrans *Homo* to the *Homo erectus* problem. *Courier Forschungs-Institut Senckenberg* 171:185–193.

deMenocal, P. 1995. Plio-Pleistocene African climate. *Science* 270:53–59.

Dennell, R. W., H. M. Rendell, L. Hurcombe and E. A. Hailwood. 1994. Archaelogical evidence for hominids in Pakistan before one million years ago. *Courier Forschungs-Institut Senckenberg* 171:151–155.

Gabunia, L., and A. Vekua. 1995. A Plio-Pleistocene hominid from Dmanisi, East Georgia, Caucasus. *Nature* 373:509–512.

Haq, B. U., J. Hardenbol and P. R. Vail. 1987. Chronology of fluctuating sea levels since the Triassic. *Science* 235:1156–1167.

Hill, A., S. Ward, A. Deino et al. 1992. Earliest *Homo. Nature* 355:719–722.

Howell, F. C. 1994. A chronostratigraphic and taxonomic framework of the origins of modern humans. In *Origin of Anatomically Modern Humans*, ed. M. H. Nitecki and D. Nitecki. New York: Plenum Press.

Huang, W., R. Ciochon, G. Yumin et al. 1995. Early *Homo* and associated artefacts from Asia. *Nature* 378:275–278.

Johanson, D. C., F. T. Masao, G. G. Eck et al. 1987. New partial skeleton of *Homo habilis* from Olduvai Gorge, Tanzania. *Nature* 327:205–209.

Kibunjia, M. 1994. Pliocene archaeological occurrences in the Lake Turkana basin. *Journal of Human Evolution* 27:159–171.

Kimbel, W. H., R. C. Walter, D. C. Johanson et al. 1996. Late Pliocene *Homo* and Oldowan tools from the Hadar Formation (Kada Hadar Member), Ethiopia. *Journal of Human Evolution* 31:549–561.

Klein, R. G. 1995. Anatomy, behavior, and modern human origins. *Journal of World Prehistory* 9:167–198.

Pope, G. G. 1983. Evidence on the age of the Asian Hominidae. *Proceedings of the National Academy of Sciences* 90:4988–4992.

Potts, R. 1996. *Humanity's Descent: The Consequences of Ecological Instability.* New York: Morrow.

Ranov, V. A., E. Carbonell and X. P. Rodriguez. 1995. Kuldara: earliest human occupation in Central Asia in its Afro-Asian context. *Current Anthropology* 36:337–346.

Rendell, H. M., E. Hailwood and R. W. Dennell. 1987. Paleomagnetic dating of a two-million-year-old artefact-bearing horizon at Riwat, northern Pakistan. *Earth and Planetary Sciences Letters* 85:488–496.

Rightmire, G. P. 1996. The human cranium from Bodo, Ethiopia: Evidence for speciation in the Middle Pleistocene. *Journal of Human Evolution* 31:21–39.

Roe, D. 1995. The Orce Basin (Andalucía, Spain) and the initial Palaeolithic of Europe. *Oxford Journal of Archaeology* 14:1–12.

Schrenk, F., T. Bromage, C. G. Betzler et al. 1995. Oldest *Homo* and Pliocene biogeography of the Malawi rift. *Nature* 365:833–836.

Simanjuntak, T., and F. Sémah. 1996. A new insight into the Sangiran flake industry. *Indo-Pacific Prehistory Association Bulletin* 14:22–26 (Chiang Mai Papers, Vol. 1).

Stanley, S. 1992. An ecological theory for the origin of *Homo*. *Paleobiology* 18:237–257.

Swisher III, C., G. H. Curtis, T. Jacob et al. 1994. Age of the earliest known hominids in Java, Indonesia. *Science* 263:1118–1121.

Suwa, G., T. D. White and F. C. Howell. 1996. Mandibular postcanine dentition from the Shungura Formation, Ethiopia: crown morphology, taxonomic allocations, and Plio-Pleistocene hominid evolution. *American Journal of Physical Anthropology* 101:247–282.

Turner, A. 1984. Hominids and fellow travellers: Human migration into high latitudes as part of a large mammal community. In *Hominid Evolution and Community,* ed. R. Foley. London: Academic Press.

Vrba, E., G. Denton, T. Partridge and L. Burckle, eds. 1995. *Paleoclimate and Evolution with Emphasis on Human Origins.* New Haven: Yale University Press.

Vrba, E. 1994. An hypothesis of early hominid heterochrony in response to climate cooling. In *Integrative Paths to the Past,* ed. R. Corruccini and R. Ciochon. Englewood Cliffs, N.J.: Prentice Hall.

Walker, A., and R. Leakey, eds. 1993. *The Nariokotome* Homo erectus *Skeleton.* Cambridge, Mass.: Harvard University Press.

Walker, A., and P. Shipman. 1996. *The Wisdom of the Bones.* New York: Knopf.

Wood, B. 1992. Origin and evolution of the genus *Homo*. *Nature* 355:783–790.

Wood, B. 1994. Taxonomy and evolutionary relationships of *Homo erectus*. *Courier Forschungs-Institut Senckenberg* 171:159–165.

Wood, B., and A. Turner. 1995. Out of Africa and into Asia. *Nature* 378:239–240.

35

Dmanisi and Dispersal

L. Gabunia, S. C. Antón, D. Lordkipanidze, A. Vekua, A. Justus, and C. C. Swisher III

ABSTRACT

Evidence of early Pleistocene hominid dispersal outside of Africa is scant and controversial.[1-4] Most of the early evidence appeared to support a relatively late initial migration (after 1.0 Ma), suggesting that, for hominids, Acheulean technological innovation was one of the prerequisites of dispersal.[5,6] The past decade, however, has seen increasing evidence that suggests a substantially earlier dispersal, starting around 1.8 Ma. If that evidence is correct, such an early dispersal may be better envisioned as driven more strongly by biological and ecological factors than by technological breakthroughs.[7-10] The context and morphology of the first hominids to disperse from Africa is critical information for testing these two scenarios. Here we discuss recent discoveries from the early Pleistocene site of Dmanisi, Republic of Georgia, and their implications for models of early hominid dispersal.

Claims for early Pleistocene hominids in Asia generally have been met with various degrees of skepticism. The earliest of the potential early Pleistocene hominids are from China (Longuppo) and Java (Mojokerto and Sangiran). An early occupation at Longuppo, China,[3] is in doubt because the principal fossil evidence may not be hominid.[11,12] The early Indonesian remains are undeniably hominid, but their age is controversial. It is claimed that those from Mojokerto (Perning I) and the Sangiran formation of the Sangiran Dome (S 4, 27, 31, and IX) are of uncertain provenience.[13] However, careful archival and field work suggest that these claims have been broadly overstated.[14,15] However, even accepting that their stratigraphic position is known, their early age is sometimes questioned on the basis of its inconsistency with fission track ages, faunal indicators, or paleomagnetic evidence.[5,16]

Although not without controversy, the Dmanisi site in the Republic of Georgia goes a long way toward addressing the criticisms directed at other, potentially early dispersal sites and adds new dimensions, both geographically and morphologically, to our understanding of the first hominid dispersal from Africa. Although accidentally found during excavations of medieval ruins

Figure 1. *Ruins of the medieval castle sit atop the early Pleistocene site of Dmanisi. Both are perched on the Masavera basalt, dated to 1.85 Ma.*

(Figure 1), the Pleistocene portion of the Dmanisi site has been intensively and meticulously excavated by a German and Georgian team of scientists for more than a decade.[2,17–19] Thus, although the depositional history of the site is not simple, neither the provenience of the hominids nor the location of the site is at issue. Moreover, the early involvement of geologists and paleontologists from Georgia and abroad has ensured that the context of the hominids and stone tools is well-known relative to biological and geological dating indicators.

LOCATION AND YIELD

The Dmanisi site is located about 85 km southwest of Tbilisi, the capital city of the Republic of Georgia (Figure 2). The site sits on an erosional spur of the

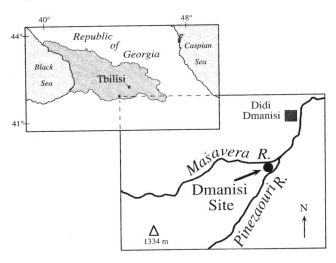

Figure 2. *Location of the Dmanisi site within the Republic of Georgia. Insert indicates the position of the site relative to the confluence of the Masavera and Pinezaouri rivers.*

Masavera Basalt, 80 m above the present-day water levels at the confluence of the Masavera and Pinezaouri rivers.

Excavations at Dmanisi have yielded four hominid fossils, thousands of vertebrate remains, and more than one thousand stone tools. The majority of this accumulation was recovered in stratigraphically similar contexts within the site, with the hominids being stratigraphically slightly lower than most of the stone tools. Three of the hominid fossils, the mandible (D211), found in 1991, and two partial crania (D2280 and D2282), found in 1999, were recovered from the same stratigraphic unit and 16 m² excavation pit (excavation I).[1,2,17,20] The hominid metatarsal (D2021) was recovered in 1997 from a similar but slightly higher stratigraphic level from excavation pit II, about 10 m east of excavation I.[21,22]

STRATIGRAPHY

So far the Dmanisi team has excavated about 150 m² within the volcanoclastic alluvium, approximately 2.5 to 4 m thick, that overlays the Masavera Basalt.[17] The exposed surface of the underlying basalt is relatively unweathered, suggesting that little or no erosion occurred before deposition of the first unit of sediments. The alluvium is divided into two major stratigraphic units (designated A and B) and their subdivisions (designated numerically) (Figure 3). Our description follows that of Gabunia and coworkers,[2] with cross-references to earlier stratigraphic schemes in parentheses.

The lowest alluvial unit, A1 (Layer VI of Dzaparidze and colleagues[17]), is variably thick, measuring up to 50 cm in some places. This unit is basaltic, tuffaceous loamy sand that fills low areas and crevasses of the Masavera Basalt. Unit A1 is conformably overlain by Unit A2 (Layers V and IV of Dzaparidze and coworkers[17]), a massive to thinly bedded dark grayish-brown to yellowish-brown tuffaceous loamy sand with

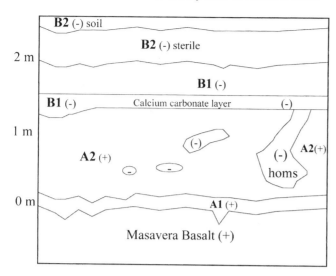

Figure 3. *Schematic stratigraphic section of the early Pleistocene Dmanisi site. Geomagnetic polarity of units is indicated by + (normal) and – (reversed). All the hominids and most of the vertebrate fauna have been recovered from the reverse polarity infills within Unit A.*

many carbonate veins and cavity linings. The upper boundary of Unit A2 is an erosional surface. Within Unit A, and especially in the lower part of Unit A2, are numerous lens-to-tunnel-shaped sedimentary structures that cross-cut horizontally bedded strata and are bounded by sharp marginal contacts. Where they are exposed, these structures can be several meters long and between 0.2 and 1.2 m wide. Most of the vertebrate fossils, including the hominids, and a few of the artifacts, come from these irregularly shaped structures (Figure 4). The cavities are lined by calcite that is continuous with the base of lower B1. The cavities themselves extend only to the A-B unit boundary and do not cross-cut unit B. The sediment enclosed within the structures consists of a mixture of Unit A sediments and a few elements similar to those in lower Unit B. Based on the morphology, cross-cutting relationships, and characteristics of the sediment within the structures, as well as their geomagnetic polarity, these cavities are likely to be intrusive fills within Unit A. Their structure suggests that they formed during erosion of Unit A before precipitation of the Unit B1 calcrete and deposition of Unit B sediments.

The A-B contact is an abrupt erosional surface along Unit A2 sediments. Units B1a and B1b are brown tuffaceous loamy sand colluvium that infills these erosional features and has locally concentrated pebble to small cobble colluvia. A zone 30 cm thick within the Unit B1a-b sands is cemented by calcium carbonate ("Kerki" or Layer III[17]) that occurred before and probably during soil formation in the upper B2 deposits. The base of the upper B2 deposits is continuous with the calcite linings of the large cavities of Unit A. The calcite cement, which envelops many artifacts and bones in Units B1a-b, is laterally continuous across the excavation areas. Because of its resistance, the calcite cement may have contributed to the preservation of the fossils in the underlying Unit A sediments. Lithic artifacts, fossil vertebrates, and cobble "manuports" have been recovered from Unit B1. Upper B1 (B1c) corresponds to Layer II of Dzaparidze and colleagues[17] and has yielded most of the artifacts. Unit B2 is devoid of any fossils or artifacts (Layer I of Dzaparidze and colleagues[17]). This 1.2 m thick dark yellowish brown tuffaceous, loamy sand exhibits a calcrete soil in its upper 50 cm that probably represents a long period of surface stability following deposition of Unit B sediments.

Figure 4. *Photograph of the northern wall of excavation I in 1999 showing articulated faunal remains within infills in Unit A.*

SITE FORMATION AND BONE ACCUMULATION

The accumulation and mixing of hominid remains, other vertebrates, and stone tools are likely to have resulted primarily from geological processes. The cavities in which most of the vertebrate remains have been found were probably created by ground water piping to the nearby river system and then subsequently infilled, possibly with the aid of carnivore activity.[2,23] The Unit A sediments were apparently washed in by low-energy water flow. The occurrence of articulated skeletal elements and the general preservation of the vertebrates indicate that little transport and little, if any, surface weathering of the remains occurred prior to their accumulation within the cavities. Unit B2 sediments were probably deposited by low-energy overbank flooding. Weathering of these sediments formed the soil in upper B2. Soil formation in Unit B may have limited bone preservation, but there is no evidence of significant erosion of this unit. There is also no evidence from either Unit A or B that the nearby rivers ever migrated across the area of the site. Rather, the rivers seem to have quickly incised their present canyons, sparing the site either additional erosion or sediment load.

The abundance of carnivore fossils, especially in Unit A, suggests their possible role in the accumulation of the other fauna. However, detailed taphonomic analyses are still to be completed, and there is little unequivocal evidence of carnivore modification of the remains. The lack of cut marks or any other indication of hominid modification of the bones also suggests that the hominids did not play a role in assemblage accumulation. The Unit B lithic assemblage also does not support the idea that the site was formed by hominid agency.

To date, Unit A has produced more faunal remains and greater faunal diversity than has Unit B, whereas Unit B has produced many more stone tools (Table 1). It should be noted, however, that field excavations between 1992 and 1996 were confined to Unit B sediments.[23] Because of its greater excavated area Unit B should have yielded more fauna than Unit A, yet it has yielded substantially fewer. While this difference may reflect ecological or use differences between Units A and B during the times they were formed, it is likely that the depauperate fauna of Unit B is in part attributable to the less hospitable environment for bone created during extensive soil development in that unit. The Unit B1 calcrete also seems to have served to cap and preserve bone in Unit A. Unlike differences in faunal yields that are not easily explainable by differences in excavated volume, the greater excavated volume of Unit B in part explains the larger artifactual assemblage found in it. However, the large disparity between the number of artifacts in these units (70 in Unit A versus 793 in Unit B) suggests that other factors may also be required to explain the difference in artifact abundance between the units. Further work on site formation and use should elucidate differences between Unit A and B assemblages.

Table 1. Minimum Numbers of Individuals for Vertebrate Taxa (Excluding Reptiles) Recovered from Dmanisi

Taxon	Unit A and Infills[a]	Unit B
Mimomys tornensis	1	
Mimomys ostramosensis	1	
Cricetus sp.	1	
Gerbillus sp.	1	
Parameriones cf. *obeidiensis*	3	
Kowalskia sp.	1	
Marmota sp.	1	
Ochonta cf. *lagreli*	1	
Hypolagus brachyagnatus	4	1
Apodemus dominans	3	
Struthio dmanisensis	1	
Panthera gombaszoegensis	1	
Pachycrocuta perrieri	3	1
Canis etruscus	9	3
Ursus etruscus	5	2
Martes sp.	1	
Megantereon megantereon	4	
Homotherium crenatidens	3	
Archidiskodon meriodionalis	9	2
Equus stenonsis	23	6
Dicerorhinus etruscus etruscus	9	2
Gazella borbonica	7	
Soergelia sp.	9	2
Dmanisibos georgicus	23	4
Eucladocerus aff. *Senezensis*	8	1
Cervidae cf. *Arvernoceros*	5	
Cervus perrieri	11	6
Dama nesti	18	1
Paleotragus sp.	2	1
Total MNI	156	33

[a] Data from Gabunia, Vekua, and Lordkipanidze.[18]

[b] Most of the Unit A fauna is from the Unit A infills. Exceptions to this include one mandible of *Dicerorhinus etruscus etruscus*.

AGE

The age of the Dmanisi hominids and fauna has been assessed using many different lines of evidence, including the geomagnetic polarity of the sediments, the radiometric age of the Masavera Basalt and Unit A1, estimates of the rate of deposition of sediments and soil formation, and biogeographic indicators of age, particularly micromammal fauna.[2,18] Geomagnetic polarity and $^{40}Ar/^{39}Ar$ analyses indicate an Olduvai Subchron age (1.78 Ma to 1.95 Ma) for the Masavera Basalt and Unit A (Figure 5). $^{40}Ar/^{39}Ar$ analyses of samples from the base, middle, and upper surface of the Masavera Basalt yielded a mean plateau age of 1.85 ± 0.01 Ma.[2] Samples from throughout the basalt and undisturbed Unit A sediments yielded normal geomagnetic polarity using thermal and alternating-field demagnetization techniques. However, neither the infillings within Unit A nor the hominids can be constrained within the normal Olduvai Subchron because they, like Unit B, yield reversed geomagnetic polarity. Given the age of Unit A, the infillings may be as old as the end of the Olduvai Subchron (1.78 Ma) or as young as the Matuyama/Jaramillo Subchron boundary (1.07 Ma). However, other evidence strongly supports a basal

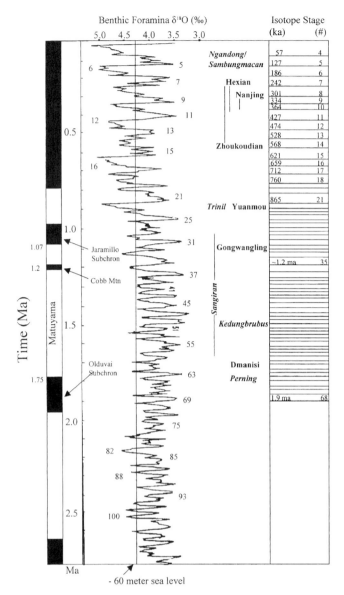

Figure 5. *Geological time scale correlated with geomagnetic polarity scale (white is reversed, black is normal), and oxygen isotope curves, with Dmanisi and major Asian* H. erectus *sites plotted. Indonesian* H. erectus *sites are in italics.* δ^{18}O *curve after Partridge (56; Data from SPECMAP stack for 0–0.62 Ma, from ODP Site 677 for 0.62–2.0 Ma, and from ODP Site 846 for 2.0–2.8 Ma). Even-numbered isotope stages indicate glacial periods. Colder periods have higher* δ^{18}O *values.*

Matuyama age (around 1.7 Ma) for the infillings and most of the hominid fossils.

The vertebrate fauna typifies the Late Villanyian (MN 17) and Early Biharian Mammal (MQ1) ages of Europe, indicating a late Pliocene to early Pleistocene age assignment (Table 1).[2,18] The large vertebrate fauna of Dmanisi includes a substantial archaic component, within which are ostriches (*Struthio dmanisensis*), hyenas (*Pachycrocuta perrieri*), deer (*Cervus perrieri* and cf *Avernoceros*), giraffes (cf Paleotraginae), gazelles (*Gazella* cf *borbonica*), and elephants (*Archidiskodon meridionalis taribanensis*). Much of this fauna, including the ostrich, hyena, and deer, is not known in strata younger than the

latest Pliocene or earliest Pleistocene at about 1.78 Ma (see Gabunia, Vekua, and Lordkipanidze[18] for detailed discussion). Some of the large vertebrates, such as *Panthera gomagazszoegensis, Ursus etruscus,* and *Equus stenonis,* although they occur in the Plio/Pleistocene, also occur in periods later than the earliest Pleistocene and thus do not provide an upper age limit for the site. Most significantly, the rodents *Mimomys ostramosensis* and *Mimomys tornensis* indicate a latest Pliocene (Olduvai Subchron) age. These rodents predate the occurrence of *Allophaiomys pliocaenicus,* which replaces them in Europe in the earliest Pleistocene (basal post-Olduvai Matuyama).[24] Thus, their presence, together with the absence of the later-occurring *Allophaiomys pliocaenicus,* constrains the age of the site to the very latest Pliocene or earliest Pleistocene.

Soil geomorphology also suggests a quick depositional history for the site and, by inference, a basal Matuyama age.[2] Given rates of weathering of basalt in similar settings, the soils suggest that the site, including both Units A and B and the Unit A infill, was isolated from fluvial activity about 10,000 to 15,000 years after deposition of the Masavera Basalt. This short time interval suggests a basal Matuyama date. Less conclusively, the Oldowan-like core and flake lithic artifacts and the morphology of the hominids recovered from Dmanisi are also consistent with an early Pleistocene age.[1,2,20,23,25]

PALEOECOLOGY

Paleontological and palynological remains suggest that during the early Pleistocene Dmanisi was in a mixed woodland environment with a slightly warmer and drier climate than that of the present day.[2] The fauna is of mixed European, Asian, and African origin but is heavily weighted toward Eurasian forms (Table 1). Species diversity and density decrease from Unit A to Unit B although, as mentioned previously, this may be the result of taphonomic processes related to soil formation in Unit B. The Unit A fauna contains a mix of closed- and open-habitat taxa, suggesting the availability of both forested (Cervids) and steppe (Ostrich) environments in the immediate vicinity. The flora also includes both arboreal forest taxa, such as *Betula* and *Pinus,* and shrubby elements such as *Artemesia* and *Ephedra,* as well as grasses and a high percentage of seeds, including hackberry (*Celtis*). Some of these may have been edible for hominids.[18]

STONE TOOLS AND BEHAVIOR

The stone tool assemblage from Dmanisi is a core and flake industry similar to the Oldowan chopping-tool industry of East Africa (Figure 6).[19,23,25] Stone tools are found throughout the Unit A cavities and in Unit B1, but are concentrated in B1. Thus the majority of the artifacts are stratigraphically higher than the hominid remains. All tools are made of local raw materials with clear selection of finer grained materials for tool manufacture, including an emphasis on quartzites and basalt.

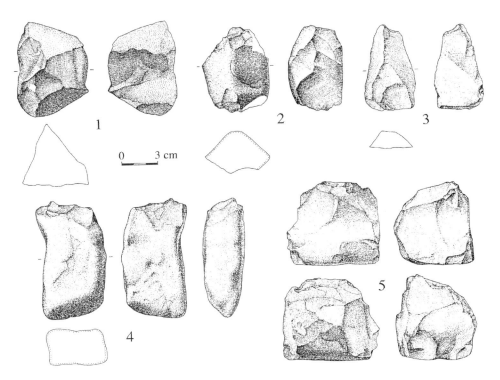

0   3 cm

Figure 6. *Representative core tools from Dmanisi.*

Although only the Unit B1 lithic assemblage is large enough for thorough analysis, no technological differences were seen between the assemblages in units A and B.[23] As of 1995, the Unit B1 assemblage totaled 5,748 pieces. Of these, 793 (14%) are certain artifacts, 1,215 are uncertain artifacts, 995 are intact cobbles larger than 4 cm, and 2,745 are naturally fractured stones or intact pebbles smaller than 4 cm. The vast majority of the certain artifacts (613, or 77%) are flakes. Of these, 19% exhibit limited (>5 mm), usually discontinuous retouch. Most flakes represent late stages in the reduction process, as indicated by the fact that fewer than 8% of all flakes, including small flakes (<2 cm), have a dorsal surface that is covered by cortex. The dorsal scar patterns on the flakes are simple; most have negatives only in the striking direction. The few flakes with complex dorsal patterns are thick and have no features on their striking platform that suggest they were resharpening flakes. Thus, no flakes from handaxes could be identified.

Most of the 149 core tools are unifacially worked, although some bifacial working occurs. There are no handaxes or cleavers. Spheroids and subspheroids are also absent, with only two possible hammerstones reported. Of the 31 special pieces, at least one multiple burin on a flake has been described.[19] No conjoins of any pieces have been found. The relative concentration of lithics throughout Unit B1 is related to the slope of the landscape: Higher areas yield few artifacts, while lower areas yield greater densities of both tools and unworked stone.[23]

Based on size classes, tool types, the absence of conjoins, and the rarity of small flakes, cortical flakes, and hammerstones, Justus and Nioradze[23] argue that Dmanisi Unit B1 cannot be interpreted as a knapping site. Rather, they suggest that the hominids were carefully selecting raw materials for knapping elsewhere and bringing the finished products to the vicinity of the site. In this sense, the B1 lithic assemblage is considered most similar to sites from Bed I and II of Olduvai Gorge such as HWK.E. However, in comparison to the Olduvai assemblages, Dmanisi is remarkable not only for its lack of spheroids and subspheroids, but, to date, the absence of evidence of butchery of vertebrate remains. Given the relatively small number of artifacts among stone objects, the predominance of flakes, and the absence of conjoins, the B1 lithic assemblage is similar to those recently retrieved from lake-edge contexts at Ubeidiya, although direct comparisons of the flaking techniques at these sites have not been made. The Ubeidiya assemblages have been interpreted as systematic tool abandonment at the point of food procurement.[26]

HOMINIDS

Four hominids have been recovered from Dmanisi. As luck would have it, the least taxonomically diagnostic of these, the mandible and metatarsal, were the first to be discovered.[1,21] These finds were followed in 1999 by the discovery of two partial crania, one with a nearly complete face (Figure 7).[2] Before the discovery of the crania there was considerable difference of opinion regarding the taxonomic affinities of the Dmanisi hominids. Some authors considered the mandible, in particular, to be quite similar to that of early African *H. erectus*,[1,17,27] while others thought it to be quite derived, possibly in the direction of later European hominids.[28,29]

The differences of opinion regarding the mandible are related in part to the fact that although the D211 mandibular corpus exhibits some of the primitive traits of early *Homo*,[30] including the location and form of the

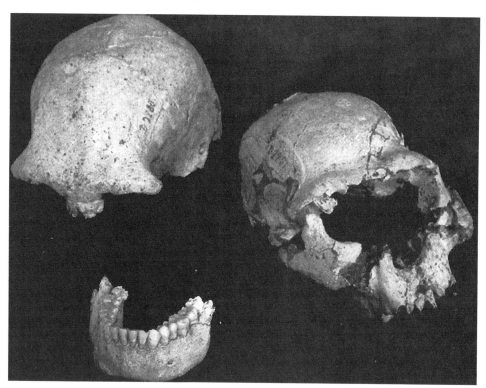

Figure 7. *Dmanisi cranial remains. Mandible D211, calvaria D2280, and calvaria with face D2282 were found in the same stratigraphic level and 16 m² excavation pit in 1991 and 1999 respectively.*

lateral prominence, the position of the anterior tubercle, and the long, narrow dental arcade, the mental trigone on the mandibular symphysis and some dental traits could be interpreted as derived conditions similar to those of later *Homo*.[29] However, Rosas and Bermudez de Castro[27] have convincingly argued that the mental trigone on the mandibular symphysis (without lateral tubercles) develops early in the African *Homo* lineage and should thus be considered a primitive condition in D211. Also difficult to interpret are the apparently derived dental traits, including molar size reduction from M_1 to M_3 and reduction of the P_4 talonid, resulting in the derived $P_3 > P_4$ size state. Particularly in the molar row, the size disparity between M_1 and M_3 is due partly to the presence of a protostylid complex. Once this accessory complex is removed, the remainder of the molar morphology is similar to that of early African *H. erectus*.[31]

The recently discovered crania (D2280 and D2282) clearly align the Dmanisi hominids with early African *H. erectus*. Despite their relatively small brain (both are less than 800 cc), the Dmanisi crania are easily differentiated from earliest African *Homo* (*H. rudolfensis* and *H. habilis*) and are quite similar to, although not identical with, early African *H. erectus* or *H. ergaster* (see Box 1). Relative to *H. rudolfensis* and *H. habilis*, the Dmanisi hominids are derived in the direction of *H. erectus* in that they have single-rooted upper premolars; well-developed supraorbital tori, the vertical thickness of which is well within the range of *H. erectus*; angulated cranial vaults; and large orbital areas. The Dmanisi crania are especially like early African *H. erectus*, and different from Asian *H. erectus*, in the moderate size of their supraorbital tori; their relatively tall, thin-walled,

narrow cranial vaults; small cranial capacities; and aspects of their lower dentition, including their buccolingually narrow anterior teeth and P/3, and the detailed occlusal morphology of their molars. The face of D2282 also exhibits a number of similarities to the faces of early African *H. erectus* (Figure 8), although its absolute pyriform (nasal) aperture width (28 mm) is small in comparison to that of other faces. Relative to the size of the D2282 cranium, as estimated by brain size, its pyriform aperture is not particularly narrow.

Although the similarities between early African *H. erectus* and the Dmanisi hominids are striking, and much greater than those between Asian and African *H. erectus* or between the Dmanisi hominids and Asian *H. erectus*, there are also ways in which the Dmanisi hominids differ from early African *H. erectus*. For the most part, these are relatively minor differences that might be expected given the geographic distance between the sites. However, some have argued that perhaps these features foreshadow later Asian hominids.[27] These features include the small buccolingual dimensions of the lower incisors and the overall shape of the occlusal surfaces of the mandibular dentition, which, in multivariate shape analyses, is similar to that in the Zhoukoudian specimens[27]; the shape and orientation of the subalveolar plane of the mandible, which is most similar to the mandibles of the larger Javanese *H. erectus* specimens[27]; the presence of accessory cusps, including Carabelli and protostylid complexes, which are similar to Asian dentitions as a whole; some minor characteristics of the vault, base, and facial skeleton.[31] The mandibular similarities to later Asian hominids are most likely primitive traits, whereas the dental similarities require further

Figure 8. *Facial skeletons of KNM-WT 15000 (cast) and D2282. Note the extensive postmortem deformation of D2282, which is currently undergoing three-dimensional CT reconstruction. Also note the similarities in the brow and pyriform areas, particularly in the formation of the nasal pillars.*

Table 2. Estimates of Body and Home-Range Size in Dmanisi and Other Hominids

	Brain Size	Stature (♂)	Stature (♀)	Body Wt (♂)	Body Wt (♀)	Home-Range Size
Dmanisi[a]	780 cc	—	148 cm	—	~50 kg	—
Extant *H. sapiens*	1350	175	161	58	49	598
Early African *H. erectus*	849	180	160	66	56	575
Asian *H. erectus*	974	—	—	—	—	—
H. rudolfensis	736	160	150	60	51	550
H. habilis	601	131	100	37	32	370
A. africanus	448	138	115	41	30	299

[a] Dmanisi brain size from D2280 only. D2282 experienced substantial postmortem deformation. Stature based on estimate from D2021 (see text for details). Body weight based on stature estimate.

Taxonomic groups and data as per McHenry and Coffing[32] except Asian *H. erectus* as per Antón and Swisher.[57] Home-range size, as estimated by Leonard, Antón, and Robertson[8] except that *H. rudolfensis* and *H. habilis* are adjusted for differences in mean body-weight estimates from the combined *H. habilis sensu lato* group used by Leonard and Robertson.[39]

evaluation, particularly in light of the effect of accessory cusp complexes on relative occlusal size and shape. These minor features aside, the Dmanisi hominids are assigned to the same taxon as the early Koobi Fora and West Turkana hominids, with an understanding that hominids like those from Dmanisi may have played an important role in the peopling of Eastern Asia.

The Dmanisi hominids are relatively small as compared to early African *H. erectus* (Table 2). It has been suggested that the two crania, the smaller of which is about 90% the size of the larger in many cranial dimensions, may represent a male and a female or may be smaller and larger individuals of the same sex. Although the mandible clearly belonged to a different individual than did either cranium, it is comparable in size, and especially molar morphology, to the smaller of the two crania (D2282). Among the shared aspects of molar morphology are the form of the mesial marginal ridge and anterior fovea, the presence of accessory cusp complexes, and the molar proportions. The third metatarsal is somewhat small and, based on its relative

robusticity, may be that of a female.[22] Although it is missing its distal articular end, the metatarsal yields a stature estimate of 1.48 m (SE = 65.4 mm) based on a maximal length estimate of about 60 mm and regression equations derived from modern human analogs. Such a stature is at the small end of the female range for early African *H. erectus* and is well encompassed by the stature estimates for specimens many have assigned to *H. rudolfensis*.[32]

IMPLICATIONS FOR DISPERSAL

For some time, Tchernov[33,34] has argued that by at least 1.4 Ma hominids were regular members of the faunal migrations that occurred when African ecological conditions expanded into the Levant. Others have argued that these movements were not true hominid dispersal events because they represent hominids moving with, rather than expanding out of their ecological niche.[5] However, much of the fauna at sites such as Ubeidiya in the Levant is Eurasian; only some is African. Thus, there

═══════ **BOX 1** ═══════

African and Asian *H. erectus.* One Species or Two?

Recently a lively debate has emerged regarding species concepts in paleoanthropology. That debate has focused on our ability to recognize species in the fossil record and our methods for doing so.[58,59] This spring the annual meeting of the American Association of Physical Anthropologists devoted an entire symposium ("Read Our Lips, No New Taxa") to arguments favoring the recognition of fewer species. These wider debates are reflected in recent studies of the composition of *H. erectus*, in which much work has focused on recognizing or refuting the significance of the differences between African and Asian *H. erectus.*[60–67]

Initially, *H. erectus* was known only in Asia.[68] The holotype for *H. erectus* is the Trinil calvaria from Java.[69] For much of the past century, the hypodigm for the species consisted only of Asian specimens, including, most importantly, the multiple calvaria from Zhoukoudian, China, and the various calvaria from Sangiran and Ngandong, Java.[70–80] Later discoveries from East Africa, the most important being some remains from Olduvai Gorge, Tanzania, and Koobi Fora and West Turkana, Kenya, have been referred to the species and have provided especially valuable information on the *H. erectus* face, a region of the cranium that is poorly represented in the Asian finds.[46,61,81–83] Some investigators have also referred specimens from northern Africa[82] and western Europe[84] to *H. erectus*, although there is less consensus as to whether *H. erectus* is represented in Europe than there is about whether it is present in Africa.

With the geographical and numerical enlargement of the *H. erectus* hypodigm, it became possible to consider the significance of the geographical variation. In these analyses, two main positions have emerged, one considering that the morphological variation indicates a single polytypic species[65–68,82,86] and the other suggesting that this variation encompasses two or more species.[47,62–64] The multiple-species position usually distinguishes early African *H. erectus* (fossils mostly from Koobi Fora and West Turkana) as *H. ergaster*, but leaves later African

H. erectus (for example, Olduvai Hominid 9) and the Asian fossils within *H. erectus*. A third, more extreme "lumping" position does not recognize *H. erectus* at all, viewing the entire genus as a single evolving lineage and, therefore, a single evolutionary species, *H. sapiens*.[12,85] Although this view does not recognize any speciation events within the lineage, it does recognize a number of morphological grades that in many, but not all ways, correspond to distinctions that others make between *H. erectus* and *H. sapiens.*

The argument between those who recognize both *H. ergaster* and *H. erectus* and those who recognize only *H. erectus* is essentially about the significance of certain morphological characters and, to a lesser extent, the recognition and distribution of these characters. While trait lists differ slightly among researchers, most of those who recognize *H. ergaster* argue that cranial superstructures such as metopic and sagittal keels and angular tori are unique derived characters (autapomorphies) that differentiate Asian *H. erectus* from early African forms (Table 3).[47,62,63,87] In addition, characters such as a tympanomastoid fissure, more robust supraorbital tori, thicker cranial vaults, and low, highly angulated crania, as well as, sometimes, unspecified facial and dental characters, are considered to differentiate the two groups at a specific level. In this view, Asian *H. erectus* is seen as more specialized than *H. ergaster.* The more generalized *H. ergaster* is often thought to be ultimately ancestral to later *H. sapiens*, whereas *H. erectus* is considered an extinct side branch.

Those who consider *H. erectus sensu lato* (in a loose sense) to be a widely distributed polytypic species recognize the same features in some African fossils or consider them to be primitive (that is, not taxonomically valent), or both.[61,64–66,83,86,88] They argue that given both the wide geographic and temporal spread of *H. erectus* fossils, both geographic and temporal variation are to be expected, and do not justify specific status. Furthermore "trait-list" comparisons between groups often

─────────────────────────────────

was some filtering of the African fauna, with hominids being a component of the fauna that did migrate. The geological age and faunal assemblage at Dmanisi suggest that hominids dispersed earlier and ranged further outside their ecological niche than had been the case in the Levant. Except for five nonhominid taxa, the Dmanisi fauna is exclusively Eurasian,[18] suggesting that Dmanisi represents a true hominid dispersal event by anyone's definition of the term.

It seems that early *H. erectus*, soon after appearing in Africa,[35] expanded its range well beyond the African continent and its normal ecological zone. This and subsequent hominid dispersals stand in contrast to the pattern seen in the rest of the Primate order, in which relatively r-selected monkeys radiated widely in Pliocene and recent times, while more k-selected apes underwent range retraction.[36] This suggests that k-selected hominids found some means of countering the normal restrictions placed on primates with their life-history variables and foraging strategies.[10,37,38] The Dmanisi hominids suggest that these solutions were in place soon after 1.8 Ma, if not before.[39]

What these solutions were is a source of great speculation. The early date and associated core-and-flake

industry at Dmanisi challenge the conventional wisdom that Acheulean technology was the catalyst for hominid dispersal but, at the same time, suggest that the foraging strategy associated with the Oldowan Industry may have facilitated dispersal.[7] The close morphological affinity between the Dmanisi hominids and early African *H. erectus* suggests the possibility that changes in body plan may also have facilitated dispersal.[10,40] Dispersal to Dmanisi suggests that home range expansion had occurred for early *H. erectus*, as does the increasing size of fossil postcrania, combined with positive scaling between home-range size and higher latitude in widely dispersed mammalian taxa.[32,39,40–43] Because home range is positively correlated with diet quality and group size,[40,44,45] an increase in home range was likely to be coupled with a shift in hominid foraging strategy toward a higher-quality diet.[40] Thus, shifts in body size, home range, and diet quality may be implicated in a web of ecomorphological factors that facilitated early hominid dispersal.[8,10]

A growing body of data suggests that the origin of *H. erectus* was associated with a significant biological shift associated and, perhaps, correlated with an increase in diet quality that facilitated activities involving increased energy expenditure.[10,32,46–49] These changes include

Table 3. Anatomical Features of *H. ergaster, H. erectus,* and the Dmanisi Hominids[a]

| Character | Africa *H. ergaster* | Asia *H. erectus* | Dmanisi | | |
			D2280	D2282	D211 (Mandible)
Cranial Vault					
Cranial capacity (in cc)	x = 800	range 750–1225	780	?650	—
Supraorbital torus	Moderate	Large	Mod/large	Moderate	—
Vault thickness	Thick	Really thick	Thick	Thick	—
Metopic and bregmatic eminences	Absent[b]	Present	Absent	Absent	—
Sagittal keel	Absent[b]	Present	Absent	Present	—
Angular torus	Absent	Present	Trace	Trace	—
Tympanomastoid fissure	Absent[b]	Present			—
Face					
Nasal pillars	Present	Absent	—	Present	—
Arcade shape	Long/narrow	Parabola (China)	—	Long/narrow	Long/narrow
Dental					
M_3/M_2 crown area ratio	1	~1–<1	—	—	<1
M^1 crown area	1440–1310	x = 1555 (Java)	—	1574	—
		x = 1365 (China)			
M_1 crown area	x = 1479	x = 1670 (Java)	—	—	1651
		x = 1480 (China)			

[a] *H. ergaster* includes "early African *H. erectus*" from Koobi Fora and West Turkana but excludes later African *Homo* erectus. Asian *H. erectus* excludes Ngandong for this table, however, its inclusion would affect only cranial capacity to 1251.

[b] Cranial superstructures are arguably present on some early African *H. erectus* although their structural similarity to corresponding features in Asian *H. erectus* has yet to be established. A tympanomastoid fissure is present in the juvenile KNM-WT 15000, but it can be argued that this is a result of its immature age.

overlook individual variation within groups. Comparisons of African and Asian fossils often ignore intra-Asian variation.[68] The "Asian morphotype" that frequently emerges is often explicitly or implicitly based on only one set of the Asian fossils, those from Zhoukoudian, China.[51] Yet Chinese and Indonesian *H. erectus* are easily separable not only on geographic, but also on morphological grounds.[51,72,73]

On whichever side of the *H. ergaster-H. erectus* debate you find yourself, the Dmanisi hominids clearly resemble early African fossils more closely than they do Asian *H. erectus* fossils (Table 3). They are the first fossil hominid evidence to be found outside Africa to bear such strong affinity to African hominid taxa. In the original publication,[2] these fossils were assigned to *H. ex gr. ergaster,* meaning "from the group of" *ergaster.* However, as we and others have noted,[27] they share some similarities with Asian forms. Discoveries of new fossils throughout this geographic range will elucidate the extent to which *H. ergaster* and *H. erectus* are separable.

increases in brain size and particularly body mass, changes in developmental pattern,[50] and perhaps the insertion of an adolescent growth spurt similar to that seen in modern humans.[51–54] In addition, the African archeological record becomes increasingly complex beginning just after the appearance of *H. erectus.*[38] Many have suggested that these changes reflect a greater dietary reliance on animal protein and fat resources.[7,8,55] The dispersal of these animal resources themselves might even have provided an impetus for hominid dispersal.[8] Whatever the proximate cause of dispersal, the Dmanisi hominids suggest that human dispersals beyond Africa occurred at least as early as the origin of *H. erectus.*

ACKNOWLEDGMENTS

This paper is dedicated to the memory of our friend and colleague Dr. Leo Gabunia. We thank the many Georgian, German, American, and other scientists who have contributed to the work at Dmanisi. Dr. Etty Indriati and Dr. Bill Leonard provided valuable discussion. The paper benefitted from the advice of five anonymous reviewers and Bernard Wood. We thank John Fleagle for the invitation to contribute to Evolutionary Anthropology, and for his patience.

REFERENCES

1. Gabunia L, Vekua A. 1995. A Plio-Pleistocene hominid from Dmanisi, East Georgia, Caucasus. Nature 373:509–512.
2. Gabunia L, Vekua A, Lordkipanidze D, Swisher CC, Ferring R, Justus A, Nioradze M, Tvalchrelidze M, Antón SC, Bosinski G, Joris O, de Lumley-M-A, Majsuradze G, Mouskhelishvili A. 2000. Earliest Pleistocene cranial remains from Dmanisi, Republic of Georgia: taxonomy, geological setting, and age. Science 288:1019–1025.
3. Huang W, Ciochon R, Yumin G, Larick R, Qiren F, Schwarcz H, Yonge C, de Vos, J, Rink W. 1995. Early *Homo* and associated artefacts from Asia. Nature 378:275–278.
4. Swisher CC III, Curtis GH, Jacob T, Getty AG, Suprijo A, Widiasmoro. 1994. Age of the earliest known hominids in Java, Indonesia. Science 263:118–1121.
5. Klein R. 1999. The human career. Chicago: University of Chicago Press.

6. Klein R. 2000. Archeology and the evolution of human behavior. Evol Anthropol 9:17–36.

7. Shipman P, Walker A. 1989. The costs of becoming a predator. J Hum Evol 18:373–392.

8. Leonard WR, Antón SC, Robertson MR. 1999. An ecomorphological model for the dispersal of *H. erectus*. Am J Phys Anthropol 28(suppl):182.

9. Bar-Yosef O, Belfer-Cohen A. 2000. Early human dispersals: the unexplored constraint of African diseases. In: Lordkipanidze D, Bar-Yosef O, Otte M, editors. Early humans at the gates of Europe. Etudes et Recherches Archéologiques de l'Université de Liège 92. Liège, Belgium. p. 79–86.

10. Antón SC, Aziz F, Zaim Y. 2001. Dispersal and migration in Plio-Pleistocene *Homo*. In: Tobias PV, Raath MA, Moggi-Cecchi J, Doyle GA, editors. Humanity from African naissance to coming millennia: colloquia in human biology and palaeoanthropology. Florence: Florence University Press. p. 97–108.

11. Schwartz JH, Tattersall I. 1996. Whose teeth? Nature 381:201–202.

12. Wolpoff MH. 1999. Paleoanthropology, 2nd ed. New York: McGraw Hill.

13. Langbroek M, Roebroeks W. 2000. Extraterrestrial evidence on the age of the hominids from Java. J Hum Evol 38:595–600.

14. Antón SC. 1997. Developmental age and taxonomic affinity of the Mojokerto child, Java, Indonesia. Am J Phys Anthropol 102:497–504.

15. Antón SC, Franzen JL. 1997. The occipital torus and developmental age of Sangiran-3. J Hum Evol 33:599–610.

16. DeVos J, Sondaar PY. 1994. Dating hominid sites in Indonesia. Science 266:1726.

17. Džaparidze V, Bosinski G, Bugianišvili TV, Gabunia L, Justus A, Klopotovskaja N, Kvavadze E, Lordkipanidze D, Majsuradze G, Mgeladze N, Nioradze M, Pavlenišvili E, Schmincke H-U, Sologašvili D, Tušabramišvili D, Tvalčrelidze M, Vekua A. 1992. Der altpaläolithische Fundplatz Dmanisi in Georgia (Kaukasus) Jahrb Römisch-Germanischen Zentralmuseums 36:67–116.

18. Gabunia L, Vekua A, Lordkipanidze D. 2000. The environmental contexts of early human occupation of Georgia (Transcaucasia). J Hum Evol 38:785–802.

19. Gabunia L, Vekua A, Lordkipanidze D, Ferring R, Justus A, Majsuradze G, Mouskhelishvili A, Nioradze M, Sologashvili D, Swisher CC, Tvalchrelidze M. 2000. Current research on the hominid site of Dmanisi. In: Lordkipanidze D, Bar-Yosef O, Otte M, editors. Early humans at the gates of Europe. Etudes et Recherches Archéologiques de l'Université de Liège 92. Liège, Belgium. p. 13–27.

20. Gabunia L, Joris O, Justus A, Lordkipanidze D, Muskhelishvili A, Swisher CC III, Nioradze M, Vekua A, Bosinski G, Ferring CR, Majsuradze G, Tvalcherelidze M. 1999. Neue Hominidenfunde das Altpaelalolitischen Fundplatzes Dmanisi im kontext aktualler Grabungsergebnisses. Archaeol Korrespondenzblatt 29:451–488.

21. Gabunia L, Vekua A, Lordkipanidze D. 1999. A hominid metatarsal from Dmanisi (Eastern Georgie). Anthropologie XXXVII:163–166.

22. Gabunia L, de Lumley M-A, Berillon G. 2000. Morphologie et fonction du troisième métatarsien de Dmanissi, Géorgie orientale. In: Lordkipanidze-D, Bar-Yosef O, Otte M, editors. Early humans at the gates of Europe. Etudes et Recherches Archéologiques de l'Université de Liège 92. Liège, Belgium. p. 29–41.

23. Justus A, Nioradze M. n.d. The lithic artefacts from the Lower Palaeolithic site of Dmanisi (Georgian Caucasus). In preparation.

24. Aguirre E. 1997. Plio-Pleistocene mammal faunas: an overview In: Van Couvering JA, editor. The Pleistocene boundary and the beginning of the Quaternary. Cambridge: Cambridge University Press. p. 114–128.

25. Nioradze M, Justus A. 1998. Stone tools of the ancient Palaeolithic site Dmanisi. In: Kopaliani D, editor. Dmanisi I. p 140–159.

26. Shea JJ, Bar-Yosef O. 1999. Lithic assemblages from the new (1988–1994) excavations at Ubeidiya: a preliminary report. J Isr Prehistoric Soc 28:5–20.

27. Rosas A, Bermudez de Castro JM. 1998. On the taxonomic affinities of the Dmanisi mandible. Am J Phys Anthropol 107:145–162.

28. Dean D, Delson E. 1995. *Homo* at the gates of Europe. Nature 373:472–473.

29. Brauer G, Schultz M. 1996. The morphological affinities of the Plio-Pleistocene mandible from Dmanisi, Georgia. J Hum Evol 30:445–481.

30. Henke W, Roth H, Simon C. 1995. Qualitative and quantitative analysis of the Dmanisi mandible. In: Radlanski RJ, Marketing HR, editors. Proceedings of the 10th international symposium on dental morphology, Berlin. p. 459–466.

31. Antón SC, Indriati E. n.d. The earliest ex-African hominids: Dmanisi and Sangiran 27 compared. In preparation.

32. McHenry HM, Coffing K. 2000. *Australopithecus* to *Homo*: transformations in body and mind. Ann Rev Anthropol 29:125–146.

33. Tchernov E. 1987. The age of the 'Ubeidiya Formation, an early Pleistocene hominid site in the Jordan Valley, Israel. Isr J Earth Sci 36:3–30.

34. Tchernov E. 1992. Biochronology, paleoecology, and dispersal events of hominids in the southern Levant. In: Akazawa T, Aoki K, Kimura T, editors. The evolution and dispersal of modern humans in Asia. Tokyo: Hokusen-Sha. p 149–188.

35. Feibel CS, Brown FH, McDougall I. 1989. Stratigraphic context of fossil hominids from the Omo group deposits: Northern Turkana Basin, Kenya and Ethiopia. Am J Phys Anthropol 78: 595–622.

36. Fleagle JG. 1988. Primate adaptation and evolution. Berkeley: Academic Press.

37. Jablonski N, Whitfort MJ, Roberts-Smith N, Quinqi X. 2000. The influence of life history and diet on the distribution of catarrhine primates during the Pleistocene in eastern Asia. J Hum Evol 39:131–158.

38. Cachel S, Harris JWK. 1998. The lifeways of *Homo erectus* inferred from archaeology and evolutionary ecology: a perspective from East Africa. In: Petraglia MD, Korisettar R, editors. Early human behaviour in global context: the rise and diversity of the lower Paleolithic record. Routledge, NY. p. 108–132.

39. Strait D, Wood B. 1999. Early hominid biogeography. Proc Natl Acad Sci 96:9196–9200.

40. Leonard WR, Robertson ML. 2000. Ecological correlates of home range variation in primates: implications for hominid evolution. In: Boinski S, Garber P, editors. On the move: how and why animals travel in groups. Chicago: University of Chicago Press.

41. Bergman C. 1847. Uber die verhaltnesse der warmeokonomie der tiere zu iherer grosse. Gottingen Studien 1:595–708.

42. Allen JA. 1877. The influence of physical conditions on the genesis of species. Radiol Rev 1:108–140.

43. Ehrlich PR. 1989. Attributes of invaders and the invading process: vertebrates. In: Drake JA, Mooney HA, di Castri F, Groves RH, Kruger FJ, Rejmanek M, Williamson M, editors. Biological invasions: a global perspective. New York: John Wiley & Sons. p 315–328.

44. McNab BK. 1963. Bioenergetics and the determination of home range size. Am Nat 97:133–140.

45. Milton K, May ML. 1976. Body weight, diet and home range in primates. Nature 259:459–462.

46. Walker A, Leakey R, editors. 1993. The Nariokotome *Homo erectus* skeleton. Cambridge: Harvard University Press.

47. Wood B, Collard M. 1999. The human genus. Science 284:65–71.

48. Aiello LC, Wheeler P. 1995. The expensive-tissue hypothesis: the brain and digestive system in human and primate evolution. Curr Anthropol 36:199–221.

49. Leonard WR, Robertson ML. 1997. Comparative primate energetics and hominid evolution. Am J Phys Anthropol 102:265–281.

50. Smith BH. 1993. The physiological age of KNM-WT 15000. In: Walker A, Leakey R, editors. The Nariokotome *Homo erectus* skeleton. Cambridge: Harvard University Press. p. 195–220.

51. Antón SC. n.d. Evolutionary significance of cranial variation in Asian *H. erectus*. Am J Phys Anthropol. Submitted.

52. Antón SC. 2001. Cranial growth in *Homo erectus*. In: Minugh-Purvis N, McNamara K, editors. Human evolution through developmental change. Baltimore: Johns Hopkins University Press.

53. Tardieu C. 1998. Short adolescence in early hominids: infantile and adolescent growth of the human femur. Am J Phys Anthropol 107:163–178.

54. Clegg M, Aiello L. 1999. A comparison of the Nariokotome *Homo erectus* with juveniles from a modern human population. Am J Phys Anthropol 110:81–94.

55. Walker A, Zimmerman M, Leakey R. 1982. A possible case of hypervitaminosis A in *Homo erectus*. Nature 296:248–250.

56. Partridge TC. 1997. Reassessment of the position of the Plio-Pleistocene boundary: is there a case for lowering it to the Gauss-Matuyama Paleomagnetic reversal? Quater Intl 40:5–10.

57. Antón SC, Swisher CC III. 2001. Evolution and variation of cranial capacity in Asian *Homo erectus*. In: Indriati E, editor. Festschrift in honor of the career of Dr. Teuku Jacob. Yogyakarta, Indonesia: In press.

58. Tattersall I. 2000. Paleoanthropology: the last half-century. Evol Anthropol 9:2–16.

59. Foley R. 2001. In the shadow of the modern synthesis? Alternative perspectives on the last fifty years of paleoanthropology. Evol Anthropol 10:5–14.

60. Wood B. 1994. Taxonomy and evolutionary relationships of *H. erectus*. In: Franzen JL, editor. 100 Years of Pithecanthropus, the *Homo erectus* problem. Courier Forschung Inst Senckenberg, 171:159–165.

61. Rightmire GP. 1998. Evidence from facial morphology of similarity of Asian and African representatives of *Homo erectus*. Am J Phys Anthropol 106:61–85.

62. Andrews P. 1984. On the characters that define *Homo erectus*. Courier Forschung Inst Senckenberg 69:167–175.

63. Stringer CB. 1984. The definition of *Homo erectus* and the existence of the species in Africa and Europe. Courier Forschung Inst Senckenberg 69:131–143.

64. Turner A, Chamberlain A. 1989. Speciation, morphological change and the status of African *Homo erectus*. J Hum Evol 18:115–130.

65. Bräuer G. 1990. The occurrence of some controversial *Homo erectus* cranial features in the Zhoukoudian and East African hominids. Acta Anthropol Sinica 9:350–358.

66. Bräuer G. 1994. How different are Asian and African *Homo erectus*? Courier Forschung Inst Senckenberg 171:301–318.

67. Bräuer G, Mbua E. 1992. *Homo erectus* features used in cladistics and their variability in Asian and African hominids. J Hum Evol 22:79–108.

68. Howells WW. 1980. *Homo erectus*—who, when and where: a survey. Yearbook Phys Anthropol 23:1–23.

69. Dubois E. 1884. *Pithecanthropus erectus*, eine menschenähnliche Uebergangsform aus Java. Batavia.

70. Black D. 1930. On an adolescent skull of *Sinanthropous pekinensis* in comparison with an adult skull of the same species and with other hominid skulls, recent and fossil. Palaeontol Sin Ser D 7:1–114.

71. Weidenreich F. 1936. The mandibles of *Sinanthropus pekinensis*: a comparative study. Palaeontol Sin Ser D 7:1–164.

72. Weidenreich F. 1943. The skull of *Sinanthropus pekinensis:* a comparative study on a primitive hominid skull. Palaeontol Sin Ser D 10:1–298.

73. Weidenreich F. 1951. Morphology of Solo man. Am Museum Nat Hist, Anthropol Pap 43: 207–290.

74. von Koengiswald GHR. 1936. Ein fossiler hominide aus dem Altpleistocän Ostjavas. De Ingenieur in Ned.-Indie. 8:149–158.

75. von Koengiswald GHR. 1940. Neue *Pithecanthropus*-Funde 1936–1938, Ein Beitrag zur Kenntnis der Praehominiden. Wetenschappelijke Mededeelingen no. 28. p 7–14.

76. von Koengiswald GHR. 1975. Early man in Java, catalogue and problems. In: Tuttle RH, editor. Paleoanthropology, morphology and Paleoecology. The Hague: Mouton. p. 303–309.

77. Dubois E. 1936. Racial identity of *Homo soloensis* Oppenoorth (including *Homo modjokertensis* von Koenigswald and *Sinanthropus pekinensis* Davidson Black. Koninklijke Akad Wetenschappen, Amsterdam. 34:1180–1185.

78. Jacob T. 1967. Some problems pertaining to the racial history of the Indonesian region. Utrecht: Drukkerij Neerlandia.

79. Jacob T. 1966. The sixth skull cap of *Pithecanthropus erectus*. Am J Phys Anthropol 25:243–260.

80. Sartono S. 1975. Implications arising from *Pithecanthropus* VIII. In: Tuttle RH, editor. Paleoanthropology, morphology and paleoecology. The Hague: Mouton. p. 327–360.

81. Wood B. 1991. Koobi Fora research project, vol. 4. Hominid Cranial Remains. Oxford: Clarendon Press.

82. Rightmire GP. 1993. The evolution of *Homo erectus*, comparative anatomical studies of an extinct human species. New York: Cambridge University Press.

83. Rightmire GP. 1979. Cranial remains of *Homo erectus* from Beds II and IV, Olduvai Gorge, Tanzania. Am J Phys Anthropol 20:23–35.

84. Ascenzi A, Biddittu I, Cassoli PF, Segre-Naldani E. 1996. A calvarium of late *Homo erectus* from Ceprano, Italy. J Hum Evol 31:409–423.

85. Wolpoff MH, Thorne AG, Jelinek J, Yinyun Z. 1994. The case for sinking *Homo erectus*. 100 years of Pithecanthropus is enough! Courier Forschung Inst Senckenberg 171:341–361.

86. Kennedy GE. 1991. On the autapomorphic traits of *Homo erectus*. J Hum Evol 20:375–412.

87. Delson E, Eldridge N, Tattersall I. 1977. Reconstruction of hominid phylogeny, a testable framework based on cladistic analysis. J Hum Evol 6:263–278.

88. Hublin J-J. 1986. Some comments on the diagnostic features of *Homo erectus*, fossil man, new facts-new ideas. Anthropos (Borno) 23:175–187.

36

A New Skull of Early *Homo* from Dmanisi, Georgia

A. Vekua, D. Lordkipanidze, G. P. Rightmire, J. Agusti, R. Ferring, G. Maisuradze, A. Mouskhelishvili, M. Nioradze, M. Ponce de Leon, M. Tappen, M. Tvalchrelidze, and C. Zollikofer

ABSTRACT

Another hominid skull has been recovered at Dmanisi (Republic of Georgia) from the same strata in which hominid remains have been reported previously. The Dmanisi site dated to ~1.75 million years ago has now produced craniofacial portions of several hominid individuals, along with many well-preserved animal fossils and quantities of stone artifacts. Although there are certain anatomical differences among the Dmanisi specimens, the hominids do not clearly represent more than one taxon. We assign the new skull provisionally to Homo erectus (=ergaster). *The Dmanisi specimens are the most primitive and small-brained fossils to be grouped with this species or any taxon linked unequivocally with genus* Homo *and also the ones most similar to the presumed* habilis-*like stem. We suggest that the ancestors of the Dmanisi population dispersed from Africa before the emergence of humans identified broadly with the* H. erectus *grade.*

The new Dmanisi cranium (D2700) and associated mandible (D2735) were found in squares 60/65 and 60/66 (Figure 1), embedded in the black to dark-brown tuffaceous sand immediately overlying the 1.85-million-year-old Masavera Basalt. Sedimentary horizons above the basalt also yielded two partial crania in 1999, along with mandibles discovered in 1991 and 2000 (*1–7*). The new hominid remains were associated with animal fossils that include an entire skull of *Stephanorhinus etruscus etruscus,* a skull of *Cervus perrieri* with a full rack of antlers, a *Dama nesti* antler, two crania of *Canis etruscus,* a complete mandible of *Equus stenonis,* and the anterior portion of a *Megantereon* cranium. Human occupation at Dmanisi is correlated to the terminal part of the (magnetically normal) Olduvai Subchron and immediately overlying (magnetically reversed) horizons of the Matuyama Chron, and is ~1.75 million years in age (*5, 6, 8*). Faunal remains also support the dating of Dmanisi to the end of the Pliocene or earliest Pleistocene (*8, 9*).

The evidence suggests that much of the Dmanisi fauna was buried rapidly after death, in many cases with ligaments still attached, and that the bones were buried very gently, with minimal transport. The protection afforded the bones in lower layers by the overlying calcareous horizon halted further diagenetic damage and compaction that normally occur. Sedimentological information and the appearance of all the fossils found nearby reinforce the conclusion that the hominid and faunal remains were deposited in a brief interval. Seventy percent of the assemblage is in weathering stage 0 or 1, and none in stages 4 or 5 (*10*). Rapid, low-energy deposition was followed by formation of petrocalcic horizons higher in the section, which arrested further destruction of bone. We estimate that in the sample of over 3000 vertebrate faunal remains recovered thus far, about 30% of the specimens are unbroken, and almost 90% are identifiable to genus if not species.

The diversity and high proportion of carnivores in the assemblage are paralleled by some tooth pits and characteristic carnivore breakage patterns, and also some hyena coprolites, but the general character of the assemblage in many ways does not fit conceptions of carnivore lairs (*11*).

The mammalian fauna includes new rodent species, which confirm that Dmanisi predates the holarctic dispersal of rootless voles (*Allophaiomys-Microtus* group). We also found a large, archaic *Mimomys,* which fits well in the *Mimomys pliocaenicus* group from the late Pliocene (Villanyian biozone) in European sites (Tegelen in the Netherlands, Val d'Arno in Italy, East and West Runton in England), a smaller vole of the *Tcharinomys (Pusillomimus)* lineage, abundant gerbils (*Parameriones* sp.), and hamsters (*Cricetus* sp., *Allocricetus bursae*) (*12*).

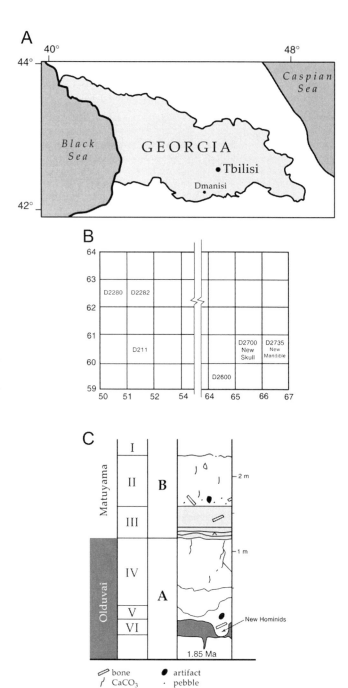

Figure 1. *(A) Location map of Dmanisi site. (B) The locations of hominid fossils (excavation units are 1-m squares). (C) General stratigraphic profile, modified after Gabunia et al. (5, 6). The basalt and the immediately overlying volcaniclastics (stratum A) exhibit normal polarity and are correlated with the terminus of the Olduvai Subchron. Slightly higher in the section, above a minor disconformity and below a strongly developed soil, Unit B deposits, which also contain artifacts, faunas and human fossils, all exhibit reversed polarity and are correlated with the Matuyama. Even the least stable minerals, such as olivine, in the basalt and the fossil-bearing sediments show only minor weathering, which is compatible with the incipient pedogenic properties of the sediments.*

Stone artifacts were found throughout the sediment section, but, as in the previously excavated areas, artifact concentrations are much larger in the upper deposits (Stratum B) than in the deeper sediments. All tools are produced out of local raw materials, and there is clear selection of finer grained stone such as quartzite and basalt for tool manufacture. The Dmanisi lithic assemblage belongs to a Mode 1 industry similar to the Oldowan of East Africa. The Dmanisi finds imply that early humans with primitive stone tool technology were able to expand out of Africa (*5, 8, 13*).

The D2700 cranium (Figures 2 and 3) carries four maxillary teeth: right M1 and M2 and left P4 and M2. The D2735 mandible (Figure 4) contains eight teeth: P3, P4, M1, and M2 are present on both sides, but the third molars are lacking. Ten isolated hominid teeth were also recovered. Of these, D2732 (upper right canine), D2678 (upper left canine), D2719 (upper right P4), D2710 (upper left M1), D2711 (upper right M3), and D2720 (upper left M3) fit well into the maxilla, but the dentition is still incomplete. When the upper and lower tooth rows are placed in occlusion, there is a good fit of the cranium to the lower jaw. Although the two fossils have separate field numbers, they represent one individual.

The skull is in remarkably fine condition (Figure 2). The maxillae are slightly damaged anteriorly, the zygomatic arches are broken, and both mastoid processes are heavily abraded. There is damage also to the orbital walls and to the elements of the interorbital region and the nasal cavity. The condyles are missing from the mandible. In other respects, the face, the braincase including the base, and the mandible are largely intact and undistorted. Computed tomography (CT) scans (Figure 3) show that internal anatomical structures are well preserved. As the maxillary M3s are only partly erupted (the occlusal surface is level with the base of the crown of M2), D2700/D2735 is a young individual whose age lies between that of the Nariokotome juvenile

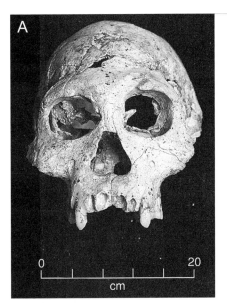
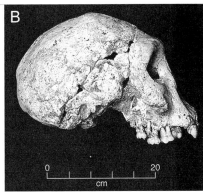
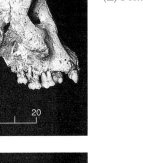
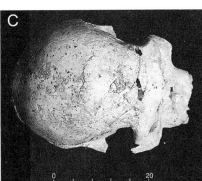
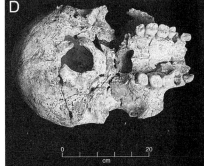
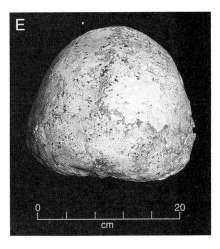

Figure 2. *The D 2700 cranium.*
*(**A**) Frontal view. (**B**) Lateral view.*
*(**C**) Superior view. (**D**) Inferior view.*
*(**E**) Posterior view.*

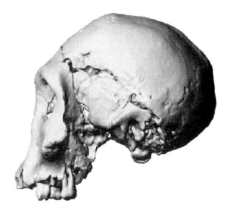

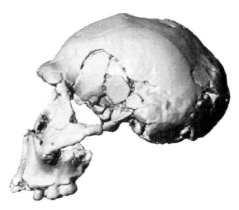

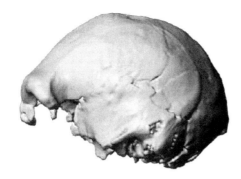

Figure 3. *The Dmanisi crania D2700 (top), D2282 (middle), and D2280 (bottom). The CT-based three-dimensional reconstructions of the specimens are oriented in the Frankfurt plane and shown in left lateral orthonormal view.*

(KNM-WT 15000) (*14, 15*) and D2282. The new specimen exhibits generally gracile morphology and may be a female. However, the upper canines carry large crowns and massive roots, and their size counsels caution in assessing sex.

In its principal vault dimensions, D2700 is smaller than D2280 and the specimens attributed to African *H. erectus* (Table 1; Figure 3). The new individual is closer in size to D2282 and equal to the latter in frontal and posterior vault widths. In cranial length and in most breadths, D2700 is larger than KNM-ER 1813 (attributed to *H. habilis*). The face is diminutive in comparison to that of either KNM-ER 3733 or KNM-ER 1470, and it is slightly larger in its transverse width and orbital and

nasal measurements than KNM-ER 1813. The new mandible (Figure 4) resembles D211 in its dimensions (Table 2), and there is no indication of a bony chin. In overall size and anatomical appearance, D2735 closely matches the mandible of the Nariokotome boy (KNM-WT 15000).

The face is surmounted by thin but well-defined supraorbital tori, curving gently upward from an inflated glabellar prominence. The nasion itself is set well forward from the orbital margins, as it is in D2280. The narrow nasal bones are waisted as in KNM-ER 1813 but broken inferiorly. The piriform aperture is similar in shape to, but smaller than that of, KNM-ER 3733, and there is a prominent incisive crest. The nasal sill is smooth, but by the criteria of McCollum et al. (*16*), the lateral border of the aperture is sharp. In its midfacial profile, D2700 resembles KNM-ER 1813, although the subnasal clivus is relatively flat, lacking vertical corrugations. The canine juga are expanded and reach upward to thicken the margin of the nose. The infraorbital walls are recessed, and a faint furrowlike sulcus is associated with the infraorbital foramen. A deeper sulcus is common in *H. erectus*. Laterally, the surfaces of the cheeks are hollowed, but these concavities are not comparable to the "canine fossa" of later humans. There is no malar tubercle. The zygomatic process is rooted above M1 and is substantially thickened—more so than in KNM-ER 1813 but resembling the condition in D2282. There is clear expression of a zygomaxillary incisure. A feature not seen in the other skulls occurs just anterior to the zygomatic pillar, in the wall of the alveolar process. Here on both sides, there is a distinct pit behind the canine jugum. The palate is shallow and like that of KNM-ER 1813 in its proportions.

There is no supratoral hollowing behind the brows. Postorbital constriction of the frontal bone is comparable to that in *H. habilis, H. erectus,* and the other Dmanisi individuals. There is faint midline keeling on the frontal, and this is more pronounced near bregma. Along the coronal suture, the frontal bone is raised relative to the parietal vault. Where they cross this suture, the temporal lines are 64 mm apart. The parietals themselves are long sagittally, and here there is definite midline keeling extending all the way to lambda. Indeed, the parietal surfaces are slightly depressed in relation to both the frontal and the occiput. This morphology, together with the inward sloping cranial walls above the supramastoid crests, gives the rear of the D2700 braincase a low and transversely flattened appearance, characteristic of both African and Asian *H. erectus*. No angular torus is present, but the supramastoid crests are moderately strong. The temporal squama is shaped like that of *H. erectus*, with a long, straight superior border passing downward toward asterion. In profile the upper scale of the occipital slopes slightly forward. The lambda-inion distance is longer than the inionopisthion chord as in *H. habilis* and KNM-ER 3733. The occiput is not strongly flexed, and its surface is smooth, with only light sculpting of the superior nuchal lines and a low linear tubercle. There is no transverse torus. This feature is also absent in D2282 and only slightly developed in D2280.

Table 1.   Cranial Measurements of the Dmanisi Hominids and Other Fossils from East Africa

Measurements (mm)	D2700	D2280	D2282	ER 1813	ER 1470	ER 3733	ER 3883	WT 15000
Cranial length	153	177	(167)	145	168	182	182	(175)
Max. cranial breadth	125	(136)	(125)	113	138	142	140	—
Max. biparietal breadth	115	118.5	116	100	120	131	134	—
Biauricular Breadth	119	(132)	—	112	135	132	129	—
Supraorbital torus thickness	9	11	10	9	8	8.5	11	—
Min. frontal breadth	66	74.5	65	65	71	83	80	73#
Biorbital chord	90	105	96	91	109	109	110	96#
Postorbital constriction index[*]	73.3	71.4	68.7	71.4	65.1	76.1	72.7	76#
Frontal arc	95	108	(81)	90	104	119	118	—
Frontal angle	147	149	—	139	140	139	140	—
Parietal arc	91	96	85	77	89	85	95	107#
Lambda-asterion arc	70	75	72	69	88	88	79	76#
Biasterionic breadth	104	104	103	93	108	119	115	106
Occipital arc	82	97	—	96	105	118	101	93#
Occipital angle	115	108	—	114	—	103	101	—
Occipital scale index[†]	81.8	102.1	—	72.7	75	92.9	106.2	131.5#
Nasion-prosthion length	63	—	—	64	90	81	—	77
Malar height	27	—	(30)	27	40	34	—	30
Nasion angle[‡]	136	139	—	153	151	155	151	138
Bimaxillary chord	96	—	—	86	98	101	—	100
Subspinale angle[§]	143	—	154	144	161	143	—	133
Orbit breadth	35	—	—	34	41	44	45	39
Orbit height	31	—	—	30	36	35	36	42
Nasal breadth	27	—	28	24	27	36	—	36
Nasal height	50	—	—	44	58	53	—	57

Numbers in parentheses indicate approximate values; dashes indicate unavailable data. Measurements were made on the original fossils by A. Vekua, D. Lordkipanidze, and G. P. Rightmire, except for those marked "#" which were taken from a cast by A. Walker.

[*]Calculated as the ratio of minimum frontal breadth to the biorbital chord. [†]Calculated as the ratio of the inion-opisthion chord to the lambda-inion chord. [‡]Calculated from the nasion subtense and one-half of the biorbital chord. [§]Calculated from the subspinale subtense and one-half of the bimaxillary chord.

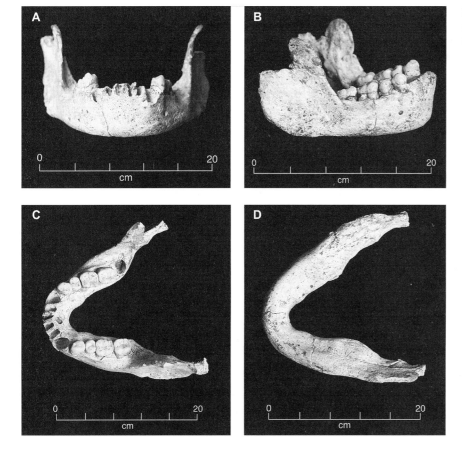

Figure 4.   *Views of D 2735 mandible.*
(A) Anterior view. (B) Lateral view.
(C) Superior view. (D) Inferior view.

Table 2. Measurements of the Dmanisi Mandibles (in mm)

Dmanisi Mandibles	D2600	D211	D2735
Height of symphysis	49.2	30.8	33.2
Maximum symphyseal thickness	22.4	17	16
Height at the level of the mental foramen	45	26.2	26
Breadth at the same point	23.3	17.8	19
Height at the level of M1	42.2	25.4	22
Breadth at the same point	23	20.4	20
Height at the level of M2	38	25.3	21
Breadth at the same point	22.8	20.4	21.5
Height at the level of M3	34	25.3	22
Breadth at the same point	24	24.9	23

The glenoid cavity is largely intact on both sides. Although relatively shallow and smaller in width, the temporomandibular joint surface resembles that of D2280 and KNM-ER 3733 in a number of details, including the forward curvature of the anterior wall, the lack of any barlike articular tubercle, the presence of a flattened preglenoid planum, and the extension of the cavity onto the underside of the zygomatic root. As in *H. erectus*, only the inner portion of the fossa lies below the braincase, while the outer part is lateral to the cranial wall above. However, the postglenoid process is large, as in some *H. habilis*. The inferior margin of the tympanic plate is not appreciably thickened but does exhibit a prominent petrosal spine. On the left, the petrous temporal is preserved. The long axis of the pyramid is angled so as to lie more nearly in the sagittal plane, relative to the transverse orientation of the tympanic plate. Such bending of the temporal axis was noted by Weidenreich (*17*) for the Zhoukoudian crania, and it is present also in the African representatives of *H. erectus*.

A comparison of the new skull to other specimens from Dmanisi, Koobi Fora, and West Turkana suggests that it has a number of similarities to early *H. erectus* (or *H. ergaster*) (Table 1). The cranium is exceptionally small, with a rounded occiput, and its face is like that of KNM-ER 1813, especially in profile. The canine juga of D2700, however, are well defined, and the zygomatic root (zygomaticoalveolar pillar) is very thick. Keeling along the sagittal midline, the generally depressed appearance of the parietal surfaces, the shape of the

temporal squama, and the transverse expansion of the base relative to the low vault all make the skull look more like a small *H. erectus* than *H. habilis*. There are other *erectus*-like traits of the glenoid cavity, tympanic plate, and petrous bone. In overall shape, D2700 is similar to D2280 and D2282, and D2735 resembles D211. Despite certain differences among these Dmanisi individuals, we do not see sufficient grounds for assigning them to more than one hominid taxon (*18*). We view the new specimen as a member of the same population as the other fossils, and we here assign the new skull provisionally to *Homo erectus* (=*ergaster*) (*19–21*).

Although the 1999 crania have been referred to *Homo ex gr. ergaster*, they exhibit some features indicating a degree of isolation from groups in Africa and the Far East (*5*, *22*). The mandible (D2600) (Table 2) discovered in 2000 underscores the fact that some Dmanisi fossils depart from the morphology characteristic of *H. erectus* (*7*, *23*). Nevertheless, the new skull may be regarded as an extremely small-brained representative of this species. Its endocranial volume of ~600 cm³ is substantially smaller than expected for *H. erectus* but near the mean for *H. habilis* (*sensu stricto*) (*24*). Although this individual is lightly built, it cannot be identified unequivocally as female. The extent of differences in size and other aspects of morphology within the Dmanisi population implies that reassessment of both the sex and the existing taxonomic assignments of the earliest *Homo* fossils from other localities (particularly in Africa) may be appropriate.

The Dmanisi hominids are among the most primitive individuals so far attributed to *H. erectus* or to any species that is indisputably *Homo* (*25*), and it can be argued that this population is closely related to *Homo habilis* (*sensu stricto*) as known from Olduvai Gorge in Tanzania, Koobi Fora in northern Kenya, and possibly Hadar in Ethiopia (*26–28*). The presence at Dmanisi of individuals like D2700 calls into question the view that only hominids with brains equivalent in size to those of mid-Pleistocene *H. erectus* were able to migrate from Africa northward through the Levantine corridor into Asia. It now seems more likely that the first humans to disperse from the African homeland were similar in grade to *H. habilis* (*sensu stricto*).

REFERENCES AND NOTES

1. L. Gabunia, *Jahrb. RGZM* **39**, 185 (1992).
2. ———, A. Vekua, *Dmanissian Fossil Man and Accompanying Vertebrate Fauna* (Metsniereba, Tbilisi, Georgia, 1993), pp. 1–71.
3. ———, *L'Anthropologie* **99**, 29 (1995).
4. L. Gabunia et al., *Archäol. Korrespond.* **29**, 451 (1999).
5. L. Gabunia et al., *Science* **288**, 1019 (2000).
6. L. Gabunia et al., in *Early Humans at the Gates of Europe*, D. Lordkipanidze, O. Bar-Yosef, M. Otte, Eds. (ERAUL 92, Liege, Belgium, 2000), pp. 13–27.
7. D. Lordkipanidze, A. Vekua, *J. Hum. Evol.* **42**, A20 (2002).
8. L. Gabunia et al., *Evol. Anthropol.* **10**, 158 (2001).
9. L. Gabunia, A. Vekua, D. Lordkipanidze, *J. Hum. Evol.* **38**, 785 (2000).
10. A. K. Behrensmeyer, *Paleobiology* **2**, 150 (1978).
11. M. Tappen et al., in *Current Topics on Taphonomy and Fossilization*, de Renzi et al., Eds. (Ajuntament de Valencia, Valencia, Spain, 2002), pp. 161–170.

12. *Mimomys* aff. *pliocaenicus* and *Tchardinomys* sp. from Dmanisi appear very close to *M. pliocaenicus* and *Tchardinomys tegelensis* from Tegelen discovered in sediments correlated with the upper part of the Olduvai Subchron (*29*, *30*).
13. A. Justus, M. Nioradze, *Mitt. Berl. Gesel. zur Anthrop. Ethn. Urg. Stuttgart* **21**, 61 (2001).
14. A. Walker, R. Leakey, *The Nariokotome Homo erectus Skeleton* (Harvard Univ. Press, Cambridge, MA, 1993), pp. 1–457.
15. C. Dean et al., *Nature* **414**, 628 (2001).
16. M. McCollum et al., *J. Hum. Evol* **24**, 87 (1993).
17. F. Weidenreich, *Paleontol. Sinica New Ser. D* **10**, 1 (1943).
18. L. Gabunia, A. Vekua, D. Lordkipanidze, *Science* **289**, 55 (2000).
19. We elect to group early African fossils (also called *H. ergaster*) with *H. erectus* [sometimes *H. erectus* (*sensu stricto*)] as known from the Far East. B. Asfaw et al. (*31*) report recent finds from Bouri in Ethiopia demonstrating that there is continuity in morphology between the paleodemes of *H. ergaster* in East Africa and *H. erectus*

in Asia. This evidence suggests that all the hominids may be treated as one polytypic species.

20. G. P. Rightmire, *The Evolution of Homo erectus. Comparative Anatomical Studies of an Extinct Human Species* (Cambridge Univ. Press, Cambridge, UK, 1990), pp. 1–260.
21. ———, *Am. J. Phys. Anthropol.* **106,** 61 (1998).
22. L. Gabunia, A. Vekua, D. Lordkipanidze, *Archeol. Ethnol. Anthropol. Eurasia* **2,** 128 (2001).
23. The large jaw (D2600) found in 2000 is high at the symphysis and has a long and relatively narrow alveolar arcade. The incisors (especially the I1s) are rather small-crowned. The canines are large but worn flat, with strong roots enclosed in massive juga. This specimen differs from D211 both in its dimensions and in the detailed morphology of the corpus, ascending ramus, and teeth. The index of robusticity is reduced as a result of great corpus height, shelving of the posterior face of the symphysis extends to the level of P4, canine juga are more pronounced, premolars are double-rooted, and the molars are larger, increasing slightly in size from M1 to M3 (see Table 2) (*32*).
24. B. Wood, *Nature* **355,** 783 (1992).
25. Several authors have argued that *H. habilis* (*sensu stricto*) and/or *H. rudolfensis* should be removed from *Homo* and placed instead with *Australopithecus.* J. T. Robinson (*33*) suggested this, and A. Walker (*34*) pointed out that the KNM-ER 1470 cranium exhibits a number of resemblances to *Australopithecus.* Recently, this view has been advanced by M. H. Wolpoff (*35*) and B. Wood and M. Collard (*36*).
26. P. V. Tobias, *Olduvai Gorge,* vol. 4, *The Skulls, Endocasts and Teeth of Homo habilis* (Cambridge Univ. Press, Cambridge, UK, 1991), pp. 1–921.
27. B. Wood, *Koobi Fora Research Project,* vol. 4, *Hominid Cranial Remains* (Clarendon, Oxford, UK, 1991).
28. W. H. Kimbel et al., *J. Hum. Evol.* **31,** 549 (1996).

29. W. H. Zagwijn, *Mededeling. Nederl. Ins. Toegepast. Geowetensch. TNO* **60,** 19 (1998).
30. A. S. Tesakov, *Mededeling. Nederl. Ins. Toegepast. Geowetensch. TNO* **60,** 71 (1998).
31. B. Asfaw et al., *Nature* **416,** 317 (2002).
32. L. L. Gabunia, M. A. De Lumley, A. Vekua, D. Lordkipanidze, *C. R. Acad. Sci.,* in preparation.
33. J. T. Robinson, *Nature* **205,** 121 (1965).
34. A. Walker, in *Earliest Man and Environments in the Lake Rudolf Basin,* Y. Coppens, F. C. Howell, G. Ll. Isaac, R. F. Leakey, Eds. (Univ. of Chicago Press, Chicago, IL, 1976), pp. 484–489.
35. M. H. Wolpoff, *Paleoanthropology* (McGraw-Hill, New York, ed. 2, 1999).
36. B. Wood, M. Collard, *Science* **284,** 65 (1999).
37. Research at Dmanisi is funded by the Georgian Academy of Sciences (grant N1318), National Geographic Society, and The Leakey Foundation (grants awarded to D.L.). Aspects of our interdisciplinary studies have been supported by Fulbright Foundation, Projects DGICYT-PB97-0157 (Spanish Ministry of Science) and ACE-38 (Generalitat de Catalunya), University of Zurich, the Eckler Fund of Binghamton University and the American School of Prehistoric Research, and the Peabody Museum of Harvard University. We thank all members of the 2001 Dmanisi research expedition, particularly J. Kopaliani, G. Kiladze, M. Mayer, G. Nioradze, S. Ediberidze, T. Shelia, D. Taktakishvili, and D. Zhvania. We are grateful to O. Bar-Yosef, F. C. Howell, H. de Lumley, M. A. de Lumley, and A. Walker for their help and assistance. Our work benefited from discussions with E. Delson, D. Lieberman, A. Justus, D. Pilbeam, O. Soffer, I. Tattersall, M. Wolpoff, and B. Wood. CT scans were produced at the Medical-Diagnostic Center of Tbilisi University. Photographs and illustrations were made by G. Davtiani, S. Holland, and G. Tsibakhashvili.

37

Venta Micena, Barranco León-5 and Fuentenueva-3

Three Archaeological Sites in the Early Pleistocene Deposits of Orce, South-East Spain

J. Gibert, L. Gibert, C. Ferràndez-Canyadell, A. Iglesias, and F. González

ABSTRACT

This contribution shows the results of twenty-five years of research in the region of Orce by a team led by one of the authors. During these years, more than twenty palaeontological localities have been discovered. Some of these are also archaeological sites but they have not all been excavated yet. After all these years of research, the Orce region has become a key area for understanding human biological and cultural evolution during the Lower Pleistocene. In this paper, we describe the three most important archaeological sites and their finds in the global context of the first dispersal of Homo *out of Africa. In our opinion, this took place rapidly and followed different routes, one of them across the Strait of Gibraltar.*

INTRODUCTION

Until 1976, the north-east sector of the Baza Basin (Orce region) was unknown from a palaeontological point of view. The site of Venta Micena was then discovered by a team from the Palaeontological Institute of Sabadell including N. Sànchez (now deceased), J. Agustí and J. Gibert who led the survey. Although no fossil remains had previously been reported from this area, its geological characteristics on the margin of a lake basin where shallow lacustrine, palustrine and alluvial sediments alternate, alerted the survey to the potential of new palaeontological sites. Thus, the first and most important site of Venta Micena was found. In subsequent surveys carried out in 1979 and 1981, further palaeontological localities were discovered. Then in 1982, the first excavation was carried out at Venta Micena. During this excavation a large collection of fossil material was recovered, and a human skull fragment was recognised amongst these fossils. Despite interruptions and difficulties, excavations led by J. Gibert have continued at various sites in the Orce region.

GENERAL SETTING

The archaeological sites of Venta Micena, Barranco León-5 and Fuentenueva-3 are situated in the north-east sector of the Guadix-Baza basin in south-east Spain (Figure 1). This part of the basin exposes a continental sedimentary sequence more than one hundred metres thick. Sedimentation in this basin was almost continuous from the Late Miocene up to the Upper Pleistocene. The Plio-Pleistocene deposits which outcrop in this sector represent seven major depositional cycles. These began with fluviatile sedimentation and ended with lacustrine. The archaeological sites of Orce are located in the lacustrine deposits of the Lower Pleistocene or 'Venta Micena' cycle (L. Gibert et al., 1999).

Venta Micena

The Venta Micena deposits correspond to a calcareous mud plain located close to a palaeolake shoreline and affected by edaphic processes. The bed containing abundant fossil mammal remains is about 75 cm thick, and it

Table 1.   Fauna Identified at Venta Micena

Class	Order	Species
Mammalia	Primates	*Homo* sp.
	Carnivora	*Homotherium latidens*
		Megantereon sp.
		Lynx sp.
		Canis etruscus
		Canis falconeri
		Vulpes praeglacialis
		Pachycrocuta brevirostris
		Meles sp.
		Ursus etruscus
	Perissodactyla	*Dicerorhinus etruscus brachycephalus*
		Equus granatensis
	Proboscidea	*Mammuthus meridionalis*
	Artiodactyla	*Hippopotamus amphibius antiquus*
		Praemegaceros sp.
		Cervidae indet.
		Hemitragus alba
		Soergelia minor
		Bubalus sp.
	Lagomorpha	*Apodemus* aff. *mystacinus*
		Prolagus calpensis
		Oryctolagus cf. *lacosti*
	Rodentia	*Allophaiomys pliocaenicus*
		Eliomys intermedius
		Castillomys crusafonti
		Hystrix major
	Insectivora	*Desmana* sp.
Amphibia	Anura	*Rana* sp.
Reptilia	Testudines	*Testudo* sp.
	Squamata	*Lacerta* sp.
Aves	Charadriiformes	indet.

can be traced for about two kilometres. The accumulation of mammal remains in these deposits can be attributed to the activities of carnivores close to the lake shore. During the last twenty years, the authorities have given permission for only six excavations at Venta Micena. Four of these were carried out in the 1980s and two in the 1990s. The last permit to excavate this site was granted in 1995. In the course of these excavations, 250 square metres were partially excavated of three different surfaces of the same fossiliferous bed. The excavations have produced 10,335 bones representing at least 214 individual animals. This profusion of material is one reason for considering Venta Micena to be one of the most important Lower Pleistocene palaeontological sites in Europe. The fossils include three human fragments which show signs of carnivore scavenging. The species represented at the site are listed in Table 1.

Barranco León

Site BL-5 at Barranco León is located in a fine sand bed that corresponds to the distal part of a small and ephemeral alluvial system. The thickness of this bed varies between 10 and 25 cm (Gibert et al., 1992a). Systematic work on this site was carried out in the summer of 1995, and the area excavated was 20 square metres.

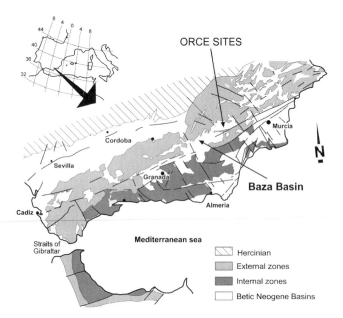

Figure 1.   *Geological location of the Baza Basin in south-east Spain.*

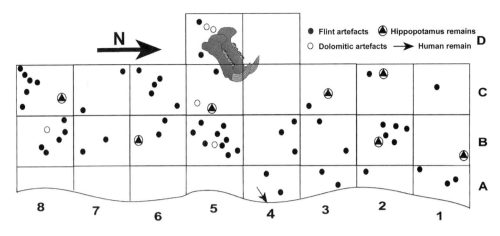

Figure 2. *Excavated surface at Barranco León.*

The excavation revealed the mandible of *Hippopotamus amphibius antiquus* surrounded by more than a hundred stone artefacts and associated with *Castillomys* cf. *crusafonti*, *Mimomys* sp., *Allophaiomys* sp., *Equus granatensis* and a human molar fragment (Figure 2) (Gibert et al., 1998b).

Fuentenueva-3

The Fn-3a site is located in a marginal zone of the basin. The sediments which outcrop there belong to a marginal lacustrine environment with different proportions of detrital material and organic matter in each level. The first stone artefacts were found on the surface together with fossil remains by J. Gibert and J. Serrallonga during a survey in 1990. In 1992, more artefacts turned up while an electricity company was at work nearby (Gibert et al., 1992a). This was followed by systematic excavations in 1995 when numerous stone artefacts were found in association with *Mimomys* sp., *Allophaiomys* sp., *Equus granatensis*, *Hippopotamus amphibius antiquus*, *Mammuthus meridionalis*, and indeterminate bovids. Most of the artefacts were closely associated with remains of large mammals (Gibert et al., 1998b).

CHRONOLOGY

Agustí et al. (1997) have reported a transition from reverse polarity to nine metres of normal polarity in the Barranco de Orce section. According to these authors, this normal polarity interval corresponds to the Olduvai event because of the presence of *Allophaiomys pliocaenicus* in the Orce-7 level. Stratigraphic correlations between the Orce-7 site and the archaeological site of Barranco León-5, show that both sites have a similar age (Gibert et al., 1998b).

New magnetostratigraphic data (Scott and Gibert 1999) revealed that the normal polarity reported by Agustí et al. (1997) from Barranco de Orce was in fact reversed. These new data, together with the stratigraphic framework (Gibert et al., 1998b) indicate that the site of Barranco León-5 is located in an epoch of reverse polarity. This was confirmed by new palaeo-

magnetic data from Barranco León (Oms et al., 2000). The new magnetic data show that up to now only reverse polarities have been found in the Orce area. The archaeological sites of Venta Micena, Barranco León-5 and Fuentenueva-3 are located in an epoch of reverse polarity between the Olduvai and Jaramillo events. The thickness of the lacustrine sediments of reversed polarity overlying these sites (12 metres at Fuentenueva-3; 15 metres at Barranco León-5) suggests that they are far from the Jaramillo epoch. This is confirmed by the presence of *A. pliocaenicus* at Venta Micena layers 1 and 2, and Barranco León layers 3 and 4, which indicates an early Lower Pleistocene age (Figure 3) (Berggren et al., 1995).

The site of Dmanisi, Georgia, is also located in a reverse polarity interval close to the Olduvai event (Gabunia et al., 2000). Faunal comparisons between this site and Venta Micena indicate a similar age although the Spanish site is slightly younger. The chronological frameworks for the deposits containing human fossil remains and stone artefacts in the Orce region are therefore based on palaeomagnetic, palaeontological and stratigraphic data. These data do not allow the age of the sites to be exactly determined. However, both the faunal assemblages and the presence of thick sections with reverse polarity overlying the sites argue for a first human presence in this region at about 1.5 myr.

EVIDENCE OF HUMAN ACTIVITY

Venta Micena

Human activity is represented at Venta Micena by stone artefacts, as well as cut marks and percussion fractured bones. The cut marks are similar to those observed on bones from East African sites (Olduvai and East Lake Turkana). Cut marks are distinguishable from other surface marks on the bone cortex by their characteristic location and grouping, as well as features such as micro striations which can be observed using a scanning electron microscope (Figure 4) (Gibert and Jiménez, 1991). Study of the fracture patterns on the bones from Venta Micena revealed percussion breaks attributable to

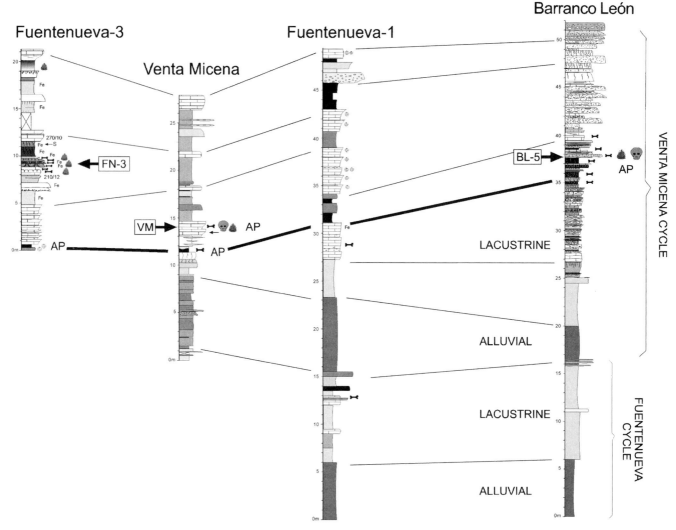

Figure 3. *Stratigraphic correlation between the sections at Venta Micena, Fuentenueva-3, Fuentenueva-1 and Barranco León. The correlation shows the relative position of the sites and the location of the beds with* Allophaiomys pliocaenicus *(AP).*

human action (Gibert and Ferràndez, 1989; Gibert et al., 1992b). The bones also show marks and fractures characteristic of carnivore activity, mainly that of hyaenids, thus suggesting competition between hominids and carnivores in obtaining proteins (Figure 5).

Stone Artefacts from Barranco León-5 and Fuentenueva-3

In 1995 excavations at Barranco León-5 (BL-5) yielded 116 stone artefacts and those at Fuentenueva-3a (Fn-3a) 100 artefacts. These are summarised by their raw materials in Table 2.

The flint from BL-5 is of good quality and mainly grey in colour. The cores are small (Figure 6) with a mean length of 43 mm. Their surfaces show centripetal flake removals. Flakes are abundant and range between 20 and 61 mm long, with a mean length of 40.7 mm (Figures 7 and 8). The butts are varied in

their morphology and the dorsal surfaces usually lack cortex. Two chopper-cores, one of flint and the other of dolomite, have worked edges (Figure 9). At Fn-3a, the flint is also of good quality but is uniformly white in colour. Some pieces have secondary iron oxide staining, and the cores exhibit centripetal flaking (Figure 6). Their mean length is 65 mm. The flakes have plain butts, and their mean length is 59 mm with a range of 21–64 mm (Figure 10). A chopper-core of

Table 2. Artefacts from Barranco León-5 and Fuentenueva-3 by Raw Material

Raw Material	BL-5	Fn-3a
Flint	114	98
Quartzite	1	1
Jurassic dolomite	1	1
Dolomite manuports	4	20

Figure 4. *SEM photomicrograph of cut marks on a fossil bone from Venta Micena (VM-1270). The enlargement shows the microstriations typical of such marks.*

Figure 6. *Cores from Barranco León-5 (left) and Fuentenueva-3 (right).*

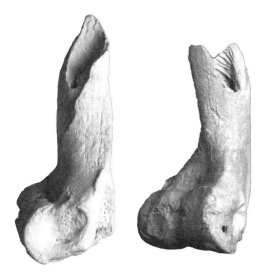

Figure 5. *Percussion (left) and carnivore (right) fractures of bone from Venta Micena.*

Figure 7. *Flakes from Barranco León-5.*

quartzite (Figure 9) is abraded on its cortical face and may have been used as a hammerstone. The local Jurassic limestone is slightly recrystallized and useful working edges can be obtained by percussion (Gibert et al., 1998b). Flakes from both BL-5 and Fn-3a show probable use traces but no microwear study has yet been attempted.

THE HUMAN REMAINS

Four human fossils have been described from the deposits in the Orce region, three of which are from Venta Micena and the fourth from Barranco León-5. The human remains from Venta Micena consist of a juvenile skull fragment (Figure 11) referred to as VM-0

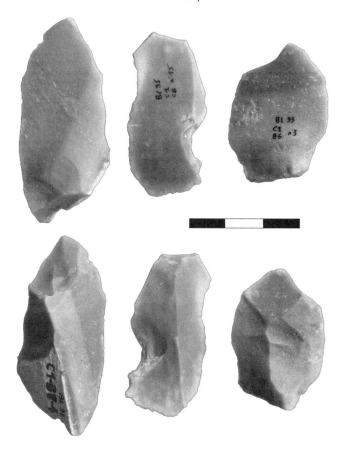

Figure 9. *Flint chopper-core from Barranco León-5 and another in quartzite from Fuentenueva-3.*

Figure 8. *Flakes from Barranco León-5.*

(Borja, 1999; Borja et al., 1992, 1997, Campillo, 1989, 1992; Campillo and Barcélo, 1989; Campillo et al., in press; Gibert and Palmqvist, 1995; Gibert et al., 1983, 1989a, 1989b, 1989c), a juvenile humeral shaft

(Figure 11), VM-1960 (Borja et al., 1997; Gibert et al., 1994a, 1999a; Sánchez et al., 1999), and an adult humeral shaft, VM-3691 (Gibert et al., 1994a; Sánchez et al., 1999). The only human fossil as yet identified at Barranco León is a molar fragment (Figure 12), BL-0 (Gibert et al., 1999b).

VM-0

The fragment of skull VM-0 consists of a small portion of the calvaria which includes the lambdoid region. The piece has some fracture lines, showing no signs of osseus regeneration but the deformation is of little importance. The maximum width is 76 mm and the maximum length is 80 mm. The borders of the occipital apex, which have been preserved, have a length of 17.5 mm at their right side and 10.5 mm at their left side, forming an angle of approximately 119°. The whole osseus surface is eroded forming a reticle with some considerably deep sulci which on occasion exceed one mm.

Figure 10. *Flakes from Fuentenueva-3.*

Figure 11. *Dorsal and ventral views of the human skull fragment VM-0 and humeral fragment VM-1960.*

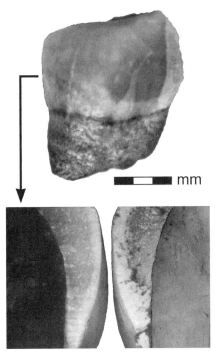

Figure 12. *Molar fragment from Barranco León-5 compared to a modern specimen to show the similarity in enamel thickness.*

It is worth noting the presence of important fracture lines. The first is located in the most external part of the right parietal bone, rectilinear and parallel to the sagittal suture. A second, transverse fissure, somewhat oblique (16°), crosses the sagittal suture at 31 mm from the lambda point. Finally, a right posterior transverse fracture originates in the lambda point. There is no significant deformation.

The sutures are quite simple. The sagittal suture becomes simpler still 18 mm from the lambda, as it usually occurs in the obelic region. All the sutures are free, preserving no signs of synostosis. There is no posthumous erosion of the endocranial surface. The thickness of the bone is between 2 mm, or even less, at the depth of the digital impressions, and 4 mm

approximately at the tips of the mammiliary protuberances. However, we must take into account the posthumous erosion of the exocranial surface. The whole of the surface appears quite dented due to the abundance of digital impressions which are more marked in the proximity of the lambdoid suture, and gradually fade as they move away from 35 mm of the lambda.

In the anterior part of the piece, the sagittal groove is practically imperceptible, becoming clearly visible from 32 mm of the lambda, where its width is approximately 7 mm and deepening along its trajectory. At 20 mm from the lambda, it has a width of 7.5 mm and depth of 1 mm, becoming separated from the middle line here and turning to the right. Just at the apex of the superior occipital angle, the groove is already at the right side in parasagittal position and its internal border (left side) has an osseus crest which originates in the middle line, rising rapidly and sticking out 5.5 mm with regards to the opening of the sagittal groove (7 mm including the thickness of the squama) at a distance of 15 mm from the apex. This crest is narrow, 1.8 mm in its higher point and 4 mm in its base, bending towards the right. The external border of the opening (the right one) is nearly imperceptible and it can only be perceived at 8 mm from the crest. In the same way as in the endocranium, sutures appear with no complications. The sagittal suture becomes irregularly dented from the lambda onwards, with no excessive complication, and at 18 mm its sinuosity diminishes, just as in the obelic region (Campillo, 1989).

Some authors (Agustí and Moyà, 1987; Moyà and Agustí, 1989; Moyà and Kölher, 1997) have questioned the identification of VM-0 as human and interpreted it as an equid. Their doubts are based mainly on the presence of a supposed coronal suture and have been rebutted. This supposed suture is actually a fracture, as has been demonstrated by radiological studies, as well as by comparative anatomical evidence (Campillo, 1989, 1992; Campillo and Barcélo, 1989; Campillo et al., 2003; Gibert et al., 1989c, 1998a).

Humeral Fragments

Two humeral fragments, VM-1960 and VM-3691, were excavated from the same faunal assemblage and stratigraphic level as the cranial fragment VM-0. The morphology, morphometry and paleoimmunology of the two fragments were studied using several complementary methods. The results of these studies place the humeral fragments inside the range of variability for *Homo* and separates them from humeri of similarly sized carnivores and cercopithecoid species, both recent and fossil, occurring in the Lower Pliocene of south-eastern Spain (Gibert et al., 1994a, 1999a).

Molar Fragment

The molar fragment from Barranco León, BL-0 (Figure 12), was studied in detail using various methods (Gibert et al., 1999b). Several characters indicate that it should be assigned to *Homo:* the first stria of the imbricate portion of the enamel, the enamel prism pattern, the arrangement of the Hunter-Schreger bands, the enamel thickness, and the presence of perikimatas. All these data exclude this fossil from being a non-human mammal.

Immunological Data

The fossils at Venta Micena are in a good state of preservation. They are found in almost pure, fine (micritic) carbonate sediments. This carbonate mud penetrated the trabecular bone and most probably helped to preserve the organic molecules found independently by two teams led by E. García-Olivares (University of Granada, Spain) and J. M. Lowenstein (University of California, USA). These immunological studies (Lowenstein, 1995) detected human albumin and IGg in the skull fragment VM-0, as well as equid and bovid proteins in equid and bovid bones respectively, from the same site (Borja, 1999; Borja et al., 1997).

THE STRAITS OF GIBRALTAR: A PLEISTOCENE BRIDGE TO EUROPE

The presence of human remains and Palaeolithic artefacts in the Lower Pleistocene of south-eastern Spain and Dmanisi, Georgia, suggests that the colonisation of Eurasia by *Homo* followed two routes, one via the Levant corridor, the other via the Straits of Gibraltar. At present, a distance of fourteen kilometers separates Europe from Africa across the Straits of Gibraltar. The possibility that *Homo* crossed such a wide marine barrier during the Lower Pleistocene is not one that is generally considered. However, when the evidence is analysed, the Straits become a probable alternative route for human dispersal out of Africa. Different kinds of data, palaeontological, geological, palaeogeographical, palaeoclimatic and oceanographic, all strengthen the hypothesis that *Homo* did cross the Straits of Gibraltar for the first time during the early Lower Pleistocene.

With regard to the palaeontological data, the presence of African mammal species in the Lower Pleistocene of the Iberian peninsula indicates the possibility of crossing the Straits during those times. The clearest evidence of faunal exchange between the two continents comes from the presence of *Theropithecus* cf. *oswaldi* in the Lower Pleistocene deposits of Cueva Victoria, Murcia, in south-east Spain. *Theropithecus* definitely has an African origin (Gibert et al., 1994b). Other species which might have an African origin and which are reported from Lower Pleistocene deposits in south-east Spain are *Hippopotamus amphibius antiquus* and *Equus granatensis*. At least one migration of a European species took place in the opposite direction to Africa. Geraads (1997) has reported *Ursus etruscus* from Upper Pliocene (2.4 myr) deposits in Morocco. This is a typical Plio-Pleistocene European species occurring in deposits dating between 3 myr (Etouaires, Villaroya) and 1.8–1.7 myr (Venta Micena, Olivola and Tasso). The available data do not allow the exact migra-

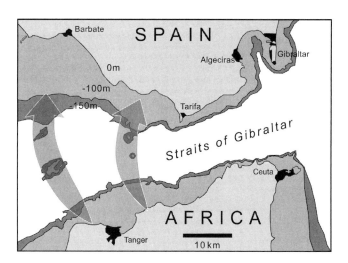

Figure 13. *Palaeogeographical reconstruction of the Straits of Gibraltar after a fall in sea level of 150 metres. The distance between Africa and Europe is reduced to 2–5 kilometres and islands appear. Topographic sea floor data obtained from Sanz et al. (1991).*

tion route of *U. etruscus* to Africa to be traced, although the Straits of Gibraltar cannot be excluded as a possibility. However, during the last three million years sea levels were lowered during various cold periods. Lowered sea levels considerably reduced the distance across water between Europe and Africa. This fact, together with the presence in the Iberian peninsula of African mammal species during the Lower Pleistocene, as well as the presence of at least one European species in north Africa during the Upper Pliocene, indicates that a faunal exchange took place between the continents.

A major Plio-Pleistocene fall of sea level of up to 130 m (Roberts, 1992) reduced the distance between Europe and Africa through the Straits of Gibraltar to less than 5 km (Figure 13), uncovering islands which might have acted as stepping stones for a selective crossing by land mammals. Such a distance probably did not represent a major barrier for organised groups of *Homo*. The penetration of *Homo* further north was probably constrained by colder climate.

CONCLUSION

Human remains, Palaeolithic artefacts and evidence of anthropic activity on bones occur in the Lower Pleistocene deposits of the Orce region. This evidence suggests a rapid dispersal of *Homo*, which probably reached the south-western part of Europe through the Straits of Gibraltar at the same time as migrating towards the east, to Georgia, China and Java.

ACKNOWLEDGMENTS

We are indebted to Professor Derek Roe. He was the first independent researcher to consider the lithic material from Orce as genuine artefacts during his first visit to the region in the summer of 1993. His support has helped us in our difficult research.

REFERENCES

Agustí, J. and Moyà, S. 1987. Sobre la identidad del fragmento craneal atribuido a *Homo* sp. de Venta Micena (Orce, Granada). *Estudios Geológicos* 42, 535–538.

Agustí, J., Oms, O. and Parès, J. M. 1997. Calibration of the Late Pliocene-Early Pleistocene transition in continental beds of the Guadix-Baza Basin (SE Spain). *Quaternary International* 40, 93–100.

Berggren, W. A., Kent, D. V., Swisher, C. C. and Aubry, M.-P. 1995. A revised Cenozoic geochronology and chronostratigraphy. In W. A. Berggren, D. V. Kent, M.-P. Aubry and J. Hardenbol (eds.) *Geochronology, Time Scales, and Global Stratigraphic Correlation*, 129–212. Society for Economic Palaeontology and Mineralogy Special Publication 54. Tulsa, Oklahoma.

Borja, C. 1999. Estudio de proteínas en fósiles. In J. Gibert, F. Sánchez, L. Gibert and F. Ribot (eds.) *The Hominids and Their Environment during the Lower and Middle Pleistocene of Eurasia*, 49–64. Ayuntamiento de Orce, Museo de Prehistoria y Paleontología J. Gibert, Orce.

Borja, C., García-Pacheco, M., Ramírez-López, J. P. and García-Olivares, E. 1992. Cuantificación y caraterización de la albumina fósil del craneo de Orce. In J. Gibert (ed.) *Presencia Humana en el Pleistoceno Inferior de Granada y Murcia*, 415–424. Museo de Prehistoria y Paleontología J. Gibert, Orce.

Borja, C., García-Pacheco, M., García-Olivares, E., Scheuenstuhl, G. and Lowenstein, J. 1997. Immunospecifity of albumin detected in 1.6 million year old fossils from Venta Micena in Orce, Granada, Spain. *American Journal of Physical Anthropology* 103, 433–441.

Campillo, D. 1989. Study of the Orce man. In J. Gibert, D. Campillo and E. García-Olivares (eds.) *Los Restos Humanos de Orce y Cueva Victoria*, 187–220. Institut Paleontològic Dr M. Crusafont, Sabadell. Diputacío de Barcelona.

Campillo, D. 1992. Estudio del hombre de Orce. In J. Gibert (ed.) *Presencia Humana en el Pleistoceno Inferior de Granada y Murcia*, 341–371. Museo de Prehistoria y Paleontología J. Gibert, Orce.

Campillo, D. and Barceló, J. A. 1989. Morphometric study of the internal surface of the squama occipitalis. In J. Gibert, D. Campillo and E. García-Olivares (eds.) *Los Restos Humanos de Orce y Cueva Victoria*, 109–186. Institut Paleontològic Dr M. Crusafont, Sabadell. Diputacío de Barcelona.

Campillo, D., Rovira, M., Sánchez-Sánchez, J. A., Vila, S., Gibert, J. and Gibert, L. 2003. Radiographical study of skull fragment of Venta Micena (VM-0) (Orce, Granada, Spain). *Human Evolution* 18:131–146.

Gabunia, L., Vekua, A., Lordkipanidze, D., Swisher, C. C., Ferring, R., Justus, A., Nioradze, M., Tvalchrelidze, M., Antón, S., Bosinski, G., Jöris, O., de Lumley, M.-A., Majsuradze, G. and Mouskhelishvili, A. 2000. Earliest Pleistocene hominid cranial remains from Dmanisi, Republic of Georgia: taxonomy, geological setting and age. *Science* 288, 1019–1025.

Geraads, D. 1997. Carnivores du Pliocène terminal de Ahl Al Oughlam (Casablanca, Maroc). *Geobios* 30, 127–164.

Gibert, J. and Ferràndez, C. 1989. Action anthropique sur les os à Venta Micena (Orce, Grenada, Espagne). In J. Gibert, D. Campillo and E. García-Olivares (eds.) *Los Restos Humanos de Orce y Cueva Victoria*, 295–327. Institut Paleontològic Dr M. Crusafont, Sabadell. Diputacío de Barcelona.

Gibert, J. and Jiménez, C. 1991. Investigations into cut-marks on fossil bones of Lower Pleistocene age from Venta Micena (Orce, Granada, Spain). *Human Evolution* 6, 117–128.

Gibert, J. and Palmqvist, P. 1995. Fractal analysis of the Orce skull sutures. *Journal of Human Evolution* 28, 561–575.

Gibert, J., Agustí, J. and Moyà, S. 1983. Presencia de *Homo* sp. en el yacimiento del Pleistoceno inferior de Venta Micena (Orce, Grenada). *Paleontologia i Evolució*, 1–9. Institut Paleontològic Dr M. Crusafont, Sabadell. Diputacío de Barcelona.

Gibert, J., Ribot, F., Ferràndez, C., Martínez, B. and Ruz, C. 1989a. Diagnosis diferencial del fragmento de cráneo de *Homo* sp. del yacimiento de Venta Micena (Orce, Granada). In J. Gibert, D. Campillo and E. García-Olivares (eds.) *Los Restos Humanos de Orce y Cueva Victoria*, 31–108. Institut Paleontològic Dr M. Crusafont, Sabadell. Diputacío de Barcelona.

Gibert, J., Ribot, F., Ferràndez, C., Martínez, B. and Caporicci, R. 1989b. Caracteristicas diferenciales entre el fragmento de cráneo de *Homo* sp. de Venta Micena (Orce, Granada) y los équidos. *Estudios Geologicos* 45, 121–138.

Gibert, J., Campillo, D., Caporicci, R., Ribot, F., Ferràndez, C. and Martínez, B. 1989c. Anatomical study: comparison of a hominid cranial fragment from Venta Micena (Orce, Spain) with fossil and extant mammals. *Human Evolution* 4, 283–305.

Gibert, J., Iglesias, A., Maillo, A. and Gibert, Ll. 1992a. Industrias líticas en el Pleistoceno inferior en la región de Orce. In J. Gibert (ed.) *Presencia Humana en el Pleistoceno Inferior de Granada y Murcia*, 219–283. Museo de Prehistoria y Paleontología J. Gibert, Orce.

Gibert, J., Ferràndez, C., Martínez, B., Caporicci, R. and Jiménez, C. 1992b. Roturas antrópicas en los huesos de Venta Micena y Olduvai. Estudio comparativo. In J. Gibert (ed.) *Presencia Humana en el Pleistoceno Inferior de Granada y Murcia*, 283–305. Museo de Prehistoria y Paleontología J. Gibert, Orce.

Gibert, J., Sánchez, F., Malgosa, A. and Martínez, B. 1994a. Découvertes des restes humains dans les gisements d'Orce (Granada, Espagne). *Comptes Rendus de l'Académie des Sciences de Paris* Series 2, 319, 963–968.

Gibert, J., Leakey, M., Ribot, F., Gibert, Ll., Arribas, A. and Martínez, B. 1994b. Presence of the cercopithecid genus *Theropithecus* in Cueva Victoria (Murcia, Spain). *Journal of Human Evolution* 28, 487–493.

Gibert, J., Campillo. D., Arqués, J. M., García-Olivares, E., Borja, C. and Lowenstein, J. 1998a. Hominid status of the Orce cranial fragment reasserted. *Journal of Human Evolution* 34, 203–217.

Gibert, J., Gibert, Ll. and Iglesias, A. 1998b. Two 'Oldowan' assemblages in the Plio-Pleistocene deposits of the Orce region, southeast Spain. *Antiquity* 72, 17–25.

Gibert, J., Malgosa, A., Sánchez, F., Ribot, F. and Walker, M. 1999a. Humeral fragments attributable to *Homo* sp. from Lower Pleistocene sites at Venta Micena (Orce, Granada, Spain). In J. Gibert, F. Sánchez, L. Gibert and F. Ribot (eds.) *The Hominids and Their Environment during the Lower and Middle Pleistocene of Eurasia*, 87–112. Ayuntamiento de Orce, Museo de Prehistoria y Paleontología J. Gibert, Orce.

Gibert, J., Albadalejo, S., Gibert, L., Sánchez, F., Ribot, F. and Gibert, J. 1999b. The oldest human remains of the Orce region. *Human Evolution* 14, 3–19.

Gibert, L., Maestro, E., Gibert, J. and Albadalejo, S. 1999. Plio-Pleistocene deposits of the Orce region (SE Spain): geology and age. In J. Gibert, F. Sánchez, L. Gibert and F. Ribot (eds.) *The Hominids and Their Environment during the Lower and Middle Pleistocene of Eurasia*, 127–144. Ayuntamiento de Orce, Museo de Prehistoria y Paleontología J. Gibert, Orce.

Lowenstein, J. M. 1995. Immunological reactions on fossil bones from Orce. Abstracts of the *International Conference on Human Palaeontology (Orce, Granada)*, 27.

Moyà, S. and Agustí, J. 1989. Una reinterpretación del fragmento craneal de Orce: *Equus stenonis*. In J. Gibert, D. Campillo and E. García-Olivares (eds.) *Los Restos Humanos de Orce y Cueva Victoria*, 447–451. Institut Paleontològic Dr M. Crusafont, Sabadell. Diputacío de Barcelona.

Moyà, S. and Köhler, M. 1997. The Orce skull: anatomy of a mistake. *Journal of Human Evolution* 33, 91–97.

Oms, O., Parès, J. M., Martínez-Navarro, B., Agustí, J., Toro, I., Martínez-Fernández, G. and Turq, A. 2000. Early human occupation of western Europe: paleomagnetic dates for two Palaeolithic sites in Spain. *Proceedings of the National Academy of Sciences* 97, 10666–10670.

Roberts, N. 1992. Climatic change in the past. In S. Jones, R. Martin and D. Pilbeam (eds.) *The Cambridge Encyclopaedia of Human Evolution*, 174–178. Cambridge University Press, Cambridge.

Sánchez, F., Gibert, J., Malgosa, A., Ribot, F., Gibert, Ll. and Walker, M. 1999. Insights into the evolution of child growth from Lower Pleistocene humeri at Venta Micena (Spain). *Human Evolution* 14, 63–82.

Sanz, J., Acosta, J., Esteras, M., Herranz, P., Palomo, C. and Sandoval, N. 1991. *Prospección Geofísica del Estrecho de Gibraltar*. Publicaciones Especiales 7, Institut Español de Oceanografia. Ministerio de Agricultura, Pesca y Alimentacíon, Madrid.

Scott, G. and Gibert, Ll. 1999. Evaluation of the Olduvai sub-chron in the Orce region. Abstracts of the EUROMAM workshop, *The Guadix-Baza Basin and the Chronostratigraphy of the Terrestrial Plio-Pleistocene in Europe (Orce, Spain)*, 11–12.

38

New Evidence on the Earliest Human Presence at High Northern Latitudes in Northeast Asia

R. X. Zhu, R. Potts, F. Xle, K. A. Hoffman, C. L. Deng, C. D. Shi, Y. X. Pan, H. Q. Wang, R. P. Shi, Y. C. Wang, G. H. Shi, and N. Q. Wu

ABSTRACT

The timing of early human dispersal to Asia is a central issue in the study of human evolution. Excavations in predominantly lacustrine sediments at Majuangou, Nihewan basin, north China, uncovered four layers of indisputable hominin stone tools. Here we report magnetostratigraphic results that constrain the age of the four artefact layers to an interval of nearly 340,000 yr between the Olduvai subchron and the Cobb Mountain event. The lowest layer, about 1.66 million years old (Myr), provides the oldest record of stone-tool processing of animal tissues in east Asia. The highest layer, at about 1.32 Myr, correlates with the stone tool layer at Xiaochangliang[1], previously considered the oldest archaeological site in this region. The findings at Majuangou indicate that the oldest known human presence in northeast Asia at 40° N is only slightly younger than that in western Asia[2,3]. This result implies that a long yet rapid migration from Africa, possibly initiated during a phase of warm climate, enabled early human populations to inhabit northern latitudes of east Asia over a prolonged period.

The Majuangou (MJG; 40° 13.517′ N, 114° 39.844′ E) section lies in the eastern margin of the Nihewan basin (Figure 1). It is a lacustrine sequence with brief intervals of wetland and lake-margin sediments, and consists mainly of greyish-yellow and greyish-green clay, silty clay and silt. It is underlain by red Jurassic volcanic breccia. Loess sediments at the top of the section have been subjected to erosion. The four artefact layers found in the MJG section are, from top to bottom, Banshan[4] (44.3–45.0 m), MJG-I (ref. 5; 65.0–65.5 m), MJG-II (73.2–73.56 m) and MJG-III (75.0–75.5 m) (Figure 2).

The Banshan artefact layer, discovered and excavated in 1990 (2 m² area, 70 cm thick), contained 95 stone artefacts in gravelly sandy silt[4]. Excavation of MJG-I in 1993 (20 m², 50 cm) yielded 111 stone tools in clayey silt[5]. Renewed excavation at Majuangou in 2001 and 2002 uncovered 226 artefacts in brown clayey silt of MJG-II (40 m², 36 cm) and 443 artefacts in greyish-black silty clay of MJG-III (85 m², 50 cm). The sediments, numerous molluscan shells (*Gyraulus chihliensis* and *Planorbis youngi*), and leaves and fruits of aquatic plants

(for example *Trapa* sp.) in MJG-III indicate a low-energy lakeshore or marsh environment rich in organic materials. The *in situ* artefact density in this layer was low overall (10.4 artefacts per m³), but artefacts and fauna in some 5-cm-thick units were as high as 170 specimens per m³ over the entire excavation and 620 specimens per m³ in a single square metre. These concentrations are comparable to those in African Plio-Pleistocene

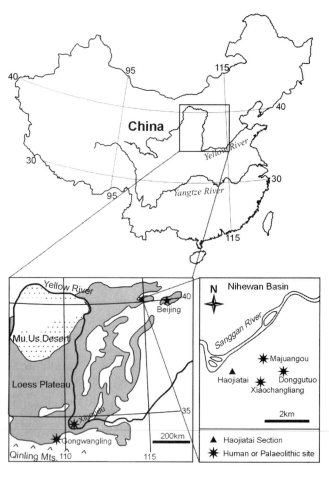

Figure 1. *Location of the Majuangou and Haojiatai sections in the Nihewan basin. Some sites mentioned in the text, Xiaochangliang, Donggutuo, Gongwangling and Xihoudu, are indicated. The Qinling Mountains (bottom left) are the traditional dividing line between north and south China. The Yellow River and Yangtze River are the major river systems in north and south China, respectively.*

Reprinted by permission from *Nature*, Vol. 431, pp. 559–562.

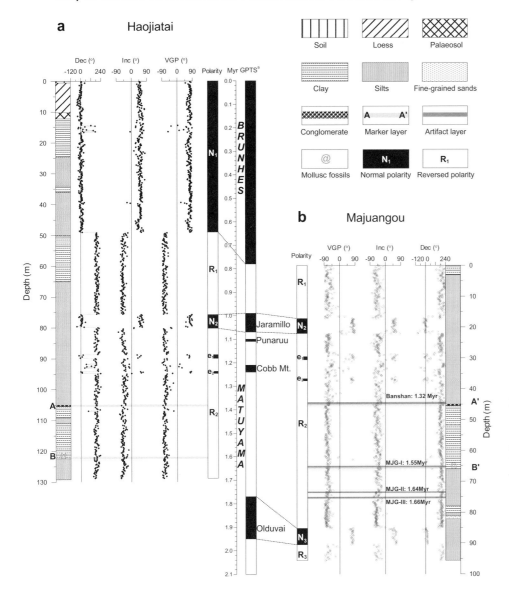

Figure 2. *Lithostratigraphy and magnetostratigraphy and correlation with the geomagnetic polarity timescale (GPTS)[6]. **a**, Haojiatai; **b**, Majuangou. The four artefact levels are shown. To confirm the palaeomagnetic results, two sets of parallel samples (black and grey circles in **b**) with independent orientation were measured on the Majuangou outcrop and well samples. Inc., inclination; Dec., declination; VGP, virtual geomagnetic pole.*

archaeological sites[6,7]. MJG-III exhibits remarkable preservation demonstrated by animal-trampled sedimentary surfaces, very fresh condition of the artefacts, and fossil bone surface details that include tool percussion marks and numerous fine scratches attributed to trampling.

The four Majuangou layers preserve indisputable stone tools indicative of repetitive stone-on-stone percussion flaking (Figure 3a–e). The assemblages are dominated by core fragments that exhibit truncated negative scars and by flakes with percussion platforms and bulbs. Each artefact layer also contained flaked cores that show striking platforms and multiple overlapping negative scars. The cores can be placed in artefact categories of chopper, scraper and polyhedron also known in African Plio-Pleistocene stone tool assemblages. The MJG cores were chipped from angular fragments of chert, sandstone, quartz and andesite, and thus differ from typical East African Oldowan artefacts made on rounded lava cobbles. The artefacts of MJG-I to MJG-III are significantly outsized clasts in very

fine-grain depositional contexts, which indicates the hominin transport of rocks from outcrop sources over an unknown distance.

Vertebrate fossil remains were best represented at MJG-III ($N = 1,014$), most of which are attributable to *Elephas* sp. Other taxa include horse *Equus sanmeniensis*, hyena *Pachycrocuta* sp., rhinoceros *Coelodonta antiquitatis*, deer *Cervus* sp., bovid *Gazella* sp., ostrich *Struthio* sp., and Carnivora gen. et sp. indet. The mammals from MJG-III and the Banshan layer are typical of the taxa recorded in the Xiaochangliang site[8]. Evidence of sedimentary abrasion due to trampling hinders an unambiguous identification of purposeful tool butchery marks at MJG; however, several diaphysis fragments of deer- and horse-sized mammalian long bones show tool percussion damage indicative of marrow extraction (Figure 3f). Although there was accumulation of tools and fossil bones during depositional hiatuses, there is no evidence of deflation surfaces that might have associated objects from separate strata. Accumulation of both artefacts and fossil animals was therefore

Figure 3. *Stone artefacts and modified bones from Majuangou.* **a,** *Notch made on a flake (MJG-III).* **b,** *Chopper made on an angular fragment (MJG-II).* **c,** *Multi-platform polyhedron made on an angular fragment (MJG-III).* **d,** *Scraper made on a flake (MJG-III).* **e,** *Hammerstone; arrow indicates the main battered end.* **f,** *Two mammalian long-bone shaft fragments with impact notches and flake scars (arrows) typical of tool percussion damage (MJG-III). Scale bars, 1 cm.*

contemporaneous, and the presence of tool-modified bones implies that hominins acquired food from the animal remains preserved in the MJG layers.

We examined the 95.6-m-thick MJG section palaeomagnetically and compared it with a 128.8-m-thick parallel section 1.5 km away named Haojiatai (HJT; 40° 13.240′ N, 114° 38.938′ E) (Figure 1). The HJT section, which consists of flat-lying beds exposed in deep gullies, preserves the entire upper part of the Nihewan sequence, including the Holocene soil and the last glacial loess (Figure 2). All HJT samples were collected from natural outcrops. Samples from the top of the MJG section to a depth of 75.2 m came from natural outcrops; two wells were dug to extend the MJG palaeomagnetic record. The first well, about 20 m southeast of the MJG-III site, recorded a depth interval from 75.2 to 86.2 m; the second well, about 50 m northwest of the site, recorded a depth interval from 75.2 to 95.6 m. The sedimentary sequences at MJG and HJT are well correlated by two distinctive marker layers: a

conglomerate layer (found at the 45-m depth at MJG and the 105-m depth at HJT) and a greyish-yellow clay layer with molluscan fossils (found at the 66-m depth at MJG and the 122.4-m depth at HJT) (Figure 2).

Rock magnetic methods, which included anisotropy of magnetic susceptibility, thermomagnetic analysis and hysteresis measurements, showed that magnetite of pseudo-single-domain grain size is the principal carrier of the magnetic remanence and that the sedimentary magnetic fabric had been unperturbed since deposition. After this check on the reliability of the two palaeomagnetic records, we established the polarity stratigraphy through stepwise demagnetization of the natural remanent magnetization. Complete information on rock magnetic methods and demagnetization of the natural remanent magnetization used here is given elsewhere.

After the removal of secondary remanent magnetization components from each sample through thermal and/or alternating field demagnetization procedures, virtual geomagnetic pole latitudes were determined from the characteristic remanent magnetization vector directions. These virtual geomagnetic poles were subsequently used to define the succession of magnetostratigraphic polarity in the two sections (Figure 2).

Four magnetozones are recognized in the HJT section: two with normal polarity, N1 (0–49.0 m) and N2 (75.8–80.2 m); and two with reverse polarity, R1 (49.0–75.8 m) and R2 (80.2–128.8 m). In the MJG section there are five magnetozones: two normal and three reverse. These magnetozones correlate to the polarity sequence at HJT as follows: N2 (17.2–22.0 m) and N3 (85.0–90.5 m); R1 (0–17.2 m), R2 (22.0–85.0 m) and R3 (90.5–95.6 m). The sediment layers containing stone artefacts all occur within magnetozone R2 at MJG.

Because the Holocene soil, the last glacial loess, and soil associated with the last interglacial overlay the HJT lacustrine sequence, the magnetozones determined for HJT can readily be correlated to the geomagnetic polarity timescale[9]. HJT magnetozones N1 and N2 correspond to the Brunhes chron and the Jaramillo subchron, respectively; thus, magnetozones N2 and N3 in the MJG section correspond to the Jaramillo subchron and the Olduvai subchron, respectively. Hence, these Nihewan basin sediments were deposited from just before the onset of the Olduvai subchron into the Brunhes normal chron.

The magnetostratigraphic correlation is strengthened in that the mammalian fauna from the Banshan and MJG-III layers is late Pliocene to early Pleistocene in age[8,10–12]. In addition, two short intervals of possible transitional field behaviour, labelled e1 and e2 in Figure 2, are recorded within magnetozone R2 at both MJG and HJT (e1, 29.5–30.5 m at MJG and 88.7–89.9 m at HJT; e2, 36.5–37.3 m at MJG and 94.1–94.7 m at HJT). Given that the duration of magnetozone R2 is about 0.70 Myr—between the termination of the Olduvai subchron (1.77 Myr) and the onset of the Jaramillo subchron (1.07 Myr)[9]—the interpolated ages for e1 and e2 are 1.16 Myr and 1.24 Myr, respectively, based on an averaged rate of sediment deposition. These values are remarkably similar to the ^{40}Ar–^{39}Ar age determinations of 1.10–1.11 Myr (ref. 13) and 1.21–1.24 Myr (ref. 9) for the Punaruu and Cobb Mountain geomagnetic events. It is therefore possible that the sediments in both sections record not only the coarse magnetostratigraphy of the Matuyama chron (that is, the Jaramillo and Olduvai normal polarity subchrons) but also some of its fine structure.

The Banshan, MJG-I, MJG-II and MJG-III artefact layers within magnetozone R2, reflecting brief episodes of wetlands or lakemargin deposition within a largely lacustrine sequence, have midway depths of 44.65, 65.25, 73.38 and 75.25 m, respectively (Figure 2). Again with the use of an averaged sediment accumulation rate for magnetozone R2 at MJG, the ages of these four artefact layers can be estimated at 1.32, 1.55, 1.64 and 1.66 Myr, respectively.

The ages for MJG-I, MJG-II and MJG-III are considerably older than previous age estimates of Palaeolithic sites in northern China[1] and indicate that humans might have reached northeast Asia earlier than previously thought. Along with estimated ages for the sites of Gongwangling (1.15 Myr)[14] and Xihoudu (1.27 Myr)[15] in the southern Loess Plateau and for Xiaochangliang (1.36 Myr)[1] and Donggutuo (1.1 Myr)[16] sites in the Nihewan basin, our new results imply an expansion and lengthy flourishing of human groups from northern to north-central China during the early Pleistocene.

The estimated age of 1.66 Myr for the MJG-III artefact layer predates the previous oldest age of unambiguous human presence at 40° N in East Asia by about 0.3 Myr. Our findings, particularly for the MJG-III layer, document the oldest coexistence of stone tools and man-made bone modifications in East Asia, indicating possible continuity with the oldest stone tools and artificial bone modifications reported in eastern Africa[17,18]. Archaeological evidence at MJG indicates the oldest known use of animal tissues, especially marrow processing, by early humans in Asia. The earliest archaeological level in the Nihewan basin is slightly younger than the 1.75 Myr estimated age for early humans at the Dmanisi site at 40° N latitude in western Eurasia[2,3]. Our estimated ages also fall within the 1.66–1.51-Myr range for the earliest known human fossils in southeast Asia[19,20]. The combined evidence suggests that, near the start of the Pleistocene, early human populations spread relatively rapidly across Asia, presumably from an African origin, and reached at least 40° N latitude. Our findings further establish that the earliest populations to reach northeast Asia were able to survive for at least 500 kyr before the mid-Pleistocene onset of high-amplitude climate oscillation[21-23].

ACKNOWLEDGMENTS

We thank R. J. Enkin for providing palaeomagnetic software. This work was supported by the National Natural Science Foundation of China and Chinese Academy of Sciences. R. P. was supported by the US National Science Foundation and the Smithsonian Human Origins Program. K. A. H. also received support from the US National Science Foundation.

REFERENCES

1. Zhu, R. X. et al. Earliest presence of humans in northeast Asia. *Nature* **413**, 413–417 (2001).
2. Gabunia, L. et al. Earliest Pleistocene hominid cranial remains from Dmanisi, Republic of Georgia: Taxonomy, geological setting, and age. *Science* **288**, 1019–1025 (2000).
3. Vekua, A. et al. A new skull of early *Homo* from Dmanisi, Georgia. *Science* **297**, 85–89 (2002).
4. Wei, Q. Banshan Paleolithic site from the lower Pleistocene in the Nihewan Basin in northern China. *Acta Anthropol. Sinica* **13**, 223–238 (1994).
5. HPICR, *Papers on Archaeology in Hebei Province* 30–45 (East, Beijing, 1998).
6. Potts, R. *Early Hominid Activities at Olduvai* (Aldine de Gruyter, New York, 1988).
7. Potts, R., Behrensmeyer, A. K. & Ditchfield, P. Paleolandscape variation and Early Pleistocene hominid activities: Members 1 and 7, Olorgesailie Formation, Kenya. *J. Hum. Evol.* **37**, 747–788 (1999).
8. Tang, Y. J., Li, Y. & Chen, W. Y. Mammalian fossils and the age of Xiaochangliang paleolithic site of Yangyuan, Hebei. *Vertebrata Palasiatica* **33**, 74–83 (1995).
9. Berggren, W. A., et al. in *Geochronology, Timescales, and Stratigraphic Correlation* (eds Berggren, W. A., Kent, D. V., Aubry, M. & Hardenbol, J.) 129–212 (SEPM Spec. Publ. 54, Tulsa, Oklahoma, 1995).
10. Wei, Q., et al. in *Evidence for Evolution—Essays in Honor of Prof. Chungchien Yong on the Hundredth Anniversary of His Birth* (ed. Tong, Y.) 193–207 (Ocean, Beijing, 1997).
11. Huang, W. P. & Fang, Q. R. *Wushan Hominid Site* 105–109 (Ocean, Beijing, 1991).
12. Qiu, Z. X. Nihewan fauna and Q/N boundary in China. *Quat. Sci.* **20**, 142–154 (2000).
13. Singer, B. S. et al. Dating transitionally magnetized lavas of the late Matuyama chron: Toward a new ^{40}Ar/^{39}Ar timescale of reversals and events. *J. Geophys. Res.* **104**, 679–693 (1999).
14. An, Z. S. & Ho, C. K. New magnetostratigraphic dates of Lantian *Homo erectus*. *Quat. Res.* **32**, 213–221 (1989).
15. Zhu, R., An, Z., Potts, R. & Hoffman, K. A. Magnetostratigraphic dating of early humans in China. *Earth Sci. Rev.* **61**, 341–359 (2003).
16. Quaternary Research Association of China, Li, H. M. & Wang, J. D. *Quaternary Geology and Environment of China* 33–38 (Ocean, Beijing, 1982).
17. Semaw, S. et al. 2.5-million-year-old stone tools from Gona, Ethiopia. *Nature* **385**, 333–336 (1995).
18. de Heinzelin, J. et al. Environment and behavior of 2.5-million-year-old Bouri hominids. *Science* **284**, 625–629 (1999).
19. Swisher, C. C. III et al. Age of the earliest known hominids in Java, Indonesia. *Science* **263**, 1118–1121 (1994).
20. Larick, R. et al. Early Pleistocene ^{40}Ar/^{39}Ar ages for Bapang Formation hominins, Central Java, Indonesia. *Proc. Natl Acad. Sci. USA* **98**, 4866–4871 (2001).
21. Potts, R. in *Human Roots: Africa and Asia in the Middle Pleistocene* (eds Barham, L. & Robson-Brown, K.) 5–21 (Western Academic & Specialist Press, Bristol, 2001).
22. Clark, P. U., Alley, R. B. & Pollard, D. Northern Hemisphere ice-sheet influences on global climate change. *Science* **286**, 1104–1111 (1999).
23. Tian, J., Wang, P., Cheng, X. & Li, Q. Astronomically tuned Plio-Pleistocene benthic δ^{18}O record from South China Sea and Atlantic–Pacific comparison. *Earth Planet. Sci. Lett.* **203**, 1015–1029 (2002).

39

Mid-Pleistocene Acheulean-Like Stone Technology of the Bose Basin, South China

Y. Hou, R. Potts, B. Yuan, Z. Guo, A. Deino, W. Wang, J. Clark, G. Xie, and W. Huang

ABSTRACT

Stone artifacts from the Bose basin, South China, are associated with tektites dated to 803,000 ± 3000 years ago and represent the oldest known large cutting tools (LCTs) in East Asia. Bose toolmaking is compatible with Mode 2 (Acheulean) technologies in Africa in its targeted manufacture and biased spatial distribution of LCTs, large-scale flaking, and high flake scar counts. Acheulean-like tools in the mid-Pleistocene of South China imply that Mode 2 technical advances were manifested in East Asia contemporaneously with handaxe technology in Africa and western Eurasia. Bose lithic technology is associated with a tektite airfall and forest burning.

A boundary between East Asia and western Eurasia/Africa was defined by Movius (*1, 2*) to mark a geographic separation in early human technology and behavioral competence during most of the Pleistocene. Movius and others (*3*) observed that technologically simple methods of stone flaking persisted in China and Southeast Asia during the period when ovate

large cutting tools (LCTs), specifically Acheulean bifacial handaxes and cleavers, characterized western Eurasia and Africa (currently dated at 1.6 to 0.2 million years ago). The boundary, known as the Movius Line, implies that Pleistocene East Asian populations were culturally and possibly genetically isolated (*4*), a situation that was reinforced by stable forest habitat east of the boundary (*2, 5*). Although the Movius Line has attracted criticism (*6–8*), little evidence to contradict it has been presented (*9, 10*). Analyses of Acheulean technology (*11, 12*) have concluded that the targeted manufacture of LCTs signifies an important advance in hominin behavior (enhanced planning and technical competence) for which evidence has been lacking in the early stone technology of East Asia.

Here we describe stone tools from the mid-Pleistocene of the Bose basin (*13*) in the Guangxi Zhuang Autonomous Region (Figure 1) of China that provide the oldest evidence of LCT manufacture in East Asia, contemporaneous with Acheulean LCTs in western Eurasia and Africa. The basin covers ~800 km² and is dissected by the Youjiang River from northwest to southeast. Laterized fluvial deposits of late Pliocene and Pleistocene age crop out as seven river terraces (T1 through T7) of differing elevation associated with episodic uplift of the Qinghai-Tibetan Plateau (*14*).

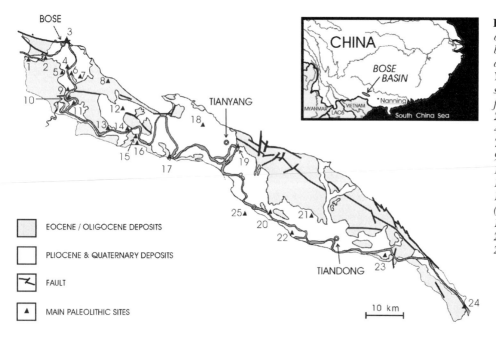

Figure 1. *Location of stone artifacts and tektites in the Bose basin. Artifact-bearing Quaternary deposits are distributed along the Youjiang River. Archeological surface and excavation sites are as follows: 1, Shangsong; 2, Dongzeng; 3, Hengshandao; 4, Dawan; 5, Shazhou; 6, Yangwu; 7, Cimu; 8, Nanposhan; 9, Jiangfeng and Datong; 10, Bogu; 11, Dafa; 12, Xiaguo; 13, Xiaomei and Nalian; 14, Damei; 15, Laikui; 16, Nayin (cave); 17, Napo; 18, Pinghepo; 19, Sanlei; 20, Xinzhou; 21, Ganlian; 22, Bodu; 23, Gaolingpo; and 24, Silin.*

Sediments of terrace 4 (T4) preserve concentrations of Paleolithic stone artifacts and dispersed tektites. The terrace, which has been fragmented by faulting, forms several platforms situated 25 to 100 m above the present river level. T4 consists of an upper sedimentary unit, 7 to 10 m thick, of poorly developed latosols underlain by reticular mottled red clay typical of laterites and of a lower unit, 5 to 20 m thick, of well-sorted cobble conglomerate. Tektites and artifacts are distributed in the upper unit within a zone 20 to 100 cm thick, which is typically 6 to 7 m above the top of the lower unit of T4. Paleolithic artifacts are abundant on the terrace surface and in three excavation localities tested between 1988 and 1996 (15) and have not been found in any of the other terraces.

The artifacts consist of extensively chipped cobbles of quartz, quartzite, sandstone, and chert and associated flakes (Figure 2). Raw materials were obtainable from the basal conglomerates of T5 through T7, which were exposed during the period of artifact manufacture

Figure 2. *Bifacial LCTs from the Bose basin. (A) Bogu 91001, no. 1, made on a large cobble. (B) Hengshandao 94, no. 3, made on a large flake with minimal retouching on the ventral surface. (C) Yangwu 91003, no. 1, made on a large flake. The right and left sides of the figure show opposite faces of each LCT. Scale bars at lower right of each image indicate 1 cm.*

and deposition on the fluvial floodplain of T4 before its uplift.

The age of the stone artifacts is established by $^{40}Ar/^{39}Ar$ analyses on three suspected Australasian tektites collected in situ from two localities (two tektites from Bogu and one from Yangwu) precisely associated with the artifacts of T4 (16, 17). Three to four replicate, 15- to 16-step, incremental heating experiments were performed on each sample. All experiments yielded plateaus (sequences of three or more steps in which the ages could not be mutually distinguished at the 95% confidence level), usually incorporating more than 80% of the total ^{39}Ar released (Table 1). Inverse isochron analysis ($^{36}Ar/^{40}Ar$ versus $^{39}Ar/^{40}Ar$) of plateau steps yielded ages concordant with plateau mean ages. The compositions of trapped argon inferred from the isochrons were within error of the atmospheric $^{40}Ar/^{39}Ar$ ratio, although there was an overall tendency toward greater-than-atmospheric ratios. Isochron ages are preferred over the straight weighted-mean calculation of ages from plateau steps because of the ability of the isochron analysis to accommodate deviations from atmospheric $^{40}Ar/^{36}Ar$ composition in the samples. Isochron ages range from 761 ± 17 to 816 ± 7 thousand years ago (ka). The best representative age is considered to be the overall weighted mean of the isochron ages from the three samples: 803 ± 3 ka (1σ). Previous $^{40}Ar/^{39}Ar$ ages of significant precision for the Australasian tektites are 783 ± 21 ka (18) and 784 ± 12 ka (19). These ages are concordant with our result, within error, and confirm the attribution of the tektites to the Australasian strewn field (20).

This result precisely calibrates the Bose artifacts and dates the sole period of Paleolithic toolmaking in the basin to the time of the strewn field. The age is well within the range of Acheulean assemblages of Africa and western Asia and is older than Acheulean occurrences in Europe and the elaboration of symmetry and craftsmanship in the late Acheulean (<500 ka) (12, 21).

The contrast between East Asian and western Eurasian/African toolmaking has been described in terms of Mode 1 (Oldowan-like, simple core/flake) versus Mode 2 (Acheulean-like, bifacial LCT) technology (22). Mode 1 is the oldest known type of stone flaking, well documented in excavated stone artifact samples from Beds I and II at Olduvai Gorge, Tanzania (23–25). Mode 2 provides the oldest evidence of targeted manufacture of large core/tool forms, such as handaxes, cleavers, knives, and picks. These LCT morphologies are typically ovate with distinctive tip ends (thin and convergent) and butt ends (thicker, sometimes unmodified). Mode 2 LCTs are made from large flakes, flat cobbles, or nodules whose properties enable thinning by percussion. Characteristics that differ from those of Mode 1 include manipulation and shaping of large rocks; production of flakes >10 cm, which were often the initial pieces on which LCTs were made; production of standardized tool forms (LCTs) that suggest the use of prescriptive procedures of percussion flaking (9, 26); large flake scar facets; and high flake scar counts. On a basinwide scale, moreover, Mode 2 artifacts tend to occur in a biased spatial distribution, with LCTs being abundant in delimited

Table 1. ^{40}Ar/^{39}Ar Analytical Results of Three Tektites (1 from Yangwu, 2 from Bogu) from the Bose Basin, South China

Sample	Lab ID#	Ca/K (± 1σ)	Incremental-Heating Plateaus				^{36}Ar/^{40}Ar *vs.* ^{39}Ar/^{40}Ar Isochrons	
			n in plateau	^{39}Ar$_{plateau}$/ ^{39}Ar$_{total}$ (%)	Plateau Age (ka ± 1σ)	MSWD	(^{40}Ar/^{38}Ar)$_{'trapped'}$ (± 1σ)	Isochron Age (ka ± 1σ)
AD-YW-3	21621-01	0.91 ± 0.07	8	80.7	797 ± 16	0.6	332 ± 75	788 ± 38
"	21621-02	0.91 ± 0.03	13	100.0	804 ± 8	0.8	294.9 ± 1.7	816 ± 7
"	21622/23-01	0.91 ± 0.06	5	52.1	813 ± 7	1.5	293 ± 8	811 ± 11
BOGU93/23/11	21628-01	0.80 ± 0.02	11	94.7	794 ± 8	0.6	307 ± 14	793 ± 10
"	21628-02	0.75 ± 0.06	13	100.0	818 ± 17	0.6	307 ± 6	812 ± 12
"	21628/29-01	0.80 ± 0.04	7	67.9	796 ± 5	0.4	295 ± 20	798 ± 11
AD-BG-3/A	21635-01	1.04 ± 0.03	13	92.5	789 ± 10	1.1	299 ± 3	795 ± 8
"	21635-02	1.03 ± 0.11	13	100.0	762 ± 18	0.3	300 ± 5	761 ± 17
AD-BG-3/A	21635/36-01	0.98 ± 0.09	11	95.1	806 ± 7	0.6	305 ± 5	799 ± 7
"	21636-01	1.02 ± 0.07	8	84.7	816 ± 9	1.1	303 ± 9	806 ± 11
					Overall weighted-mean plateau age: 802 ± 3		Overall weighted-mean isochron age: 803 ± 3	

Notes: Ca/K is calculated from ^{37}Ar/^{39}Ar using a multiplier of 1.96. MSWD refers to mean sum of weighted deviates. Isochrons are calculated from plateau steps only. Errors in age incorporate error in *J*, the neutron fluence parameter. Samples were irradiated for one-half hour in the Cd-shielded CLICIT facility of the Oregon State University TRIGA reactor. Sanidine from the Adler Creek rhyolite at Cobb Mountain was used as the irradiation monitor with a reference age of 1.194 (*32*). Flux monitoring was in sufficient detail to permit modeling both horizontal and vertical flux gradients. Isotopic interference corrections are: (^{36}Ar/^{37}Ar) Ca = 2.72 10^{-4} ± 1 × 10^{-6}, (^{39}Ar/^{37}Ar) Ca = 7.11 × 10^{-4} ± 2.4 × 10^{-6}, (^{40}Ar/^{39}Ar) K = 7 × 10^{-4} ± 3 × 10^{-4}. λ = 5.543 × 10^{-10} y^{-1}.

Table 2. Lithic Artifact Data from the Bose Basin Compared to Mode II (Acheulean) LCT Assemblages and Mode I (Oldowan and Developed Oldowan) Assemblages from Africa. Mean and SD (in parentheses) are given for all variables except percent made on flakes. Acheulean assemblages are from Olorgesailie Members 1 through 7 and Bed IV of Olduvai. Oldowan assemblages include DK 1-3, FLKNN-3, FLK Zinj, and FLKN-6; Developed Oldowan assemblages include HWKE-4, FLK Deinotherium, MNK Main, FCW Floor, and TK Upper (*60*). Bed IV Olduvai assemblages include PDK-IV, HEB-3, HEB-2a, HEB-2b, and WK (*32, 61, 62*). Olorgesailie data are from (*31*) and (*63*). The bifaciality index (ratio of the number of flake scars on each face) is calculated for LCTs only. n/av, no published data available; n/ap, measurement not applicable to the sample.

Site and Technology	Flaked Pieces	*n*	Maximum Dimension (mm)	Weight (g)	Percent Made on Flakes	Flake Scar Count	Maximum Flake Scar Length (mm)	Bifaciality Index
Bose	Unifacial LCTs	64	191 (41)	1906 (1362)	6	13.1 (6.0)	93.0 (24.1)	0.03 (0.11)
	Bifacial LCTs	35	180 (32)	1534 (766)	23	24.7 (10.5)	101.7 (24.4)	0.68 (0.22)
	Non-LCTs	74	158 (78)	894 (634)	5	7.8 (4.6)	80.4 (42.3)	n/ap
	All flaked pieces	173	178 (54)	1372 (1077)	9	13.3 (9.1)	89.9 (33.5)	n/ap
Mode II	Acheulean							
Olorgesailie	LCTs	913	165 (45)	714 (407)	31	20.0 (8.2)	n/av	0.62 (0.29)
Bed IV Olduvai	LCTs	333	136 (26)	n/av	74	16.2 (6.3)	n/av	n/av
Mode I	Oldowan							
Bed I Olduvai	All flaked pieces	156	75 (16)	287 (179)	0	6.2 (2.7)	42.4 (14.6)	n/ap
	Developed Oldowan							
Bed II Olduvai	All flaked pieces	437	83 (31)	385 (395)	2	6.5 (3.5)	41.6 (16.7)	n/ap
	Bifacial LCTs	39	123 (63)	731 (747)	13	9.8 (3.4)	61.1 (33.8)	n/av

areas (such as paleochannels) but rare elsewhere in laterally equivalent strata (such as floodplains) (*27, 28*). This spatial bias is unknown in Mode 1.

Bose stone technology exhibits all of these Mode 2 characteristics (Table 2). The analytical sample from Bose (*n* = 991 specimens) is composed of excavated (84%) and surface-collected (16%) artifacts in generally very fresh condition (sharp striking platforms and flake scar intersections). The sample is characterized by the manipulation of significantly larger pieces of raw material than in Mode 1 (*29*) and the detachment of flakes >10 cm in maximum dimension (*30*). After large flake removal, numerous smaller flakes (0.5 to 3.0 cm) were struck from either the modified cobbles or the large flakes, a combination that characterized

Acheulean LCT edge shaping. Unifacial and bifacial LCTs, which possess clearly defined tip and butt ends, make up 58% of all flaked pieces (*n* = 172), which is well above the minimum frequency (40%) defined by Leakey (*23*) for the African Acheulean. Because of the prevalence of thick asymmetrical cobbles as an initial form (91% of all flaked pieces; 80% of LCTs) and unifacial flaking (72% of all flaked pieces; 65% of LCTs), the overall artifact sample can be distinguished from Acheulean bifacial reduction of large flakes or soft-hammer thinning (*31–33*). Nonetheless, specific artifact forms closely match those of Acheulean LCTs (Figure 2). Although unifacial flaking dominates, a strong degree of bifacial flaking is present on 35% of LCTs in the Bose sample (Table 2, bifaciality index), nearly a quarter of which are made on large flakes and fall well within the morphological range of Acheulean handaxes, picks, or knives.

Bose LCTs represent a target morphology rather than a graded continuum with other tool forms (*34*). The number of flake scars, which increases over time in the Acheulean and is indicative of LCT refinement, is as high in the Bose LCT sample as in East African Acheulean bifaces of similar age (990 to 700 ka) from Olorgesailie, Kenya, and Beds III/IV of Olduvai, Tanzania (*35*). On the basis of extensive surface survey, there is a biased spatial distribution of unifacial and bifacial LCTs. Acheulean-like forms are delimited to the western third of the basin, whereas almost entirely unifacial forms occur in the eastern two-thirds (*36*). The area of bifacial LCTs coincides with the largest available clasts in the Bose basin, indicating that large flakes were made into bifacial LCTs where cobbles >20 cm in their maximum dimension were accessible.

Bose archeological assemblages therefore show evidence of flaking capabilities, strategies of lithic reduction, and spatial distributional patterns that are similar to those of the Acheulean (Figure 3). Although the tendency toward ovoid form and biconvex cross-sectional morphology that is typical of many Acheulean bifaces is rare in Bose lithic technology, prescriptive procedures were apparently applied in the selection and reduction of stone, as suggested by the concentrated thinning of LCT tips to a consistent shape, large-scale flaking of rock followed by intensive retouching, and the tendency to produce Acheulean-like bifacial forms on large flakes where raw materials of a particular size were available.

Bose stone technology is thus compatible with Mode 2 of western Eurasia/Africa just before the early-middle Pleistocene boundary. This finding implies similar technical, cultural, and cognitive capabilities on both sides of the Movius Line. The flow of population and cultural information across the line, however, may not have been extensive. The Bose basin is positioned between the Loess Plateau and South China Sea, where evidence of large environmental oscillation during the Quaternary has been documented (*37–41*). This location and the presence of poorly laterized loess at the top of the T4 section imply that Bose and South China generally were affected by significant Quaternary fluctuation. This observation implies that environmental stability did not reinforce the Movius Line throughout the Pleistocene.

Figure 3. *Opposing sides of a bifacially flaked large cutting tool (~803,000 years old) from the Bose basin, South China. The specimen (Bogu 91001, number 1; 20.7 cm in length) is representative of in situ tools recovered in a single stratum and associated with Australasian tektites and burned wood. The Bose artifacts provide the oldest known evidence of stone technology in eastern Asia equivalent to Acheulean handaxe technology in Africa and western Eurasia. [Photo: R. Potts and W. Huang.]*

One question is why stone tools are represented within a stratigraphically restricted interval in only one of the basin's fluvial terraces at about 803 ka, whereas Acheulean and other lithic traditions in western Eurasia and Africa span 10^5 to 10^6 years over numerous stratigraphic levels. One explanation is suggested by the presence of abundant charcoal and silicified wood fragments, detected during excavation and laboratory study, in precisely the same sediments containing the tektites and stone artifacts. On the basis of the co-occurrence of these remains, we suggest that the Paleolithic artifacts of Bose signal a behavioral adaptation to an episode of woody plant burning and widespread forest destruction initiated by the tektite event, which exposed cobble outcrops throughout the basin. Our findings indicate that when local or incoming populations made use of the stone available in the deforested setting, their technology and related behavioral capabilities were compatible with those of the western Old World.

REFERENCES AND NOTES

1. H. L. Movius Jr., *Trans. Am. Philos. Soc.* **38**, 330 (1949).
2. ———, in *Early Man in the Far East, Studies in Physical Anthropology*, no. 1, W. W. Howells, Ed. (Humanities Press, New York, 1969), pp. 17–77.
3. P. Teilhard de Chardin, *Early Man in China* (Institut de Géo-Biologie, Beijing, 1941).
4. Ideas advanced to explain the Movius Line include hominin migration to East Asia before the Acheulean's origin in Africa (*42*) and the loss of cultural knowledge about how to make Acheulean LCTs (*43*). Both ideas imply the isolation of toolmakers who were depauperate in the ability to produce Mode 2 LCTs after entering East Asia.
5. A stable tropical-to-subtropical setting, indicated by lateritized soils (*44*), is thought to have prompted the development in East Asia of simple lithic and nonlithic technology originally adapted to forested habitats, whereas the Acheulean developed in open savanna and Ice-Age environments of the western Old World (*45–48*).
6. S. Yi and G. A. Clark, *Curr. Anthropol.* **24**, 181 (1983).
7. V. Ranov, *Quat. Sci. Rev.* **14**, 731 (1995).
8. J. Leng, thesis, Washington University, St. Louis, MO (1992).
9. K. D. Schick, in *Integrative Paths to the Past*, R. S. Corruccini and R. L. Ciochon, Eds. (Prentice-Hall, Englewood Cliffs, NJ, 1994), pp. 569–596.
10. Previously reported East Asian sites with bifacial LCTs are dated >100 ka, but none are demonstrably older than 500 ka, including Chongokni (*49*), Dingcun (*50*), and Kamitakamori (*51*).

11. J. D. Clark, in *Integrative Paths to the Past*, R. S. Corruccini and R. L. Ciochon, Eds. (Prentice-Hall, Englewood Cliffs, NJ, 1994), pp. 451–469.

12. T. Wynn, *The Evolution of Spatial Competence* (Univ. of Illinois Press, Urbana, IL, 1989).

13. Bose is the local Zhuang spelling of Baise (Mandarin), a name by which the basin and lithic industry are also known (*52, 53*).

14. B. Yuan et al., *Acta Anthropol. Sin.* **18**, 215 (1999).

15. Excavation sites are Gaolingpo ($n = 770$ in situ artifacts), Bogu ($n = 26$), and Xiaomei ($n = 36$).

16. Assignment of the Bose T4 tektites to the Australasian group was suggested by a previous fission track analysis of a single tektite from Bogu (sample BG-93-18), which provided an initial age estimate of 732 ± 39 ka (*54*).

17. Analyses were done by incremental heating using a broad-beam CO_2 laser as the heating source (*55*). The tektites were splash-form in appearance, weighed 4.1 to 39.9 g, and consisted of exceedingly fresh, uniform black glass.

18. This number was recalculated from (*56*) on the basis of new standards (*57*). The error is a 95% confidence limit.

19. J. Kunz, K. Bollinger, E. K. Jessberger, D. Storzer, in *Ages of Australasian Tektites* (Lunar and Planetary Science Conference XXVI, Lunar and Planetary Institute, Houston, TX, 1995), p. 809.

20. Investigation of Ocean Drilling Program cores 767 and 769 from marginal seas of the Indonesian archipelago (*58*) indicates that the Australasian impact event preceded the Brunhes-Matuyama geomagnetic polarity reversal by ~12,000 years. Our result of 803 ± 3 ka for the Bose tektites can be used to predict an age of 791 ka for the reversal. This value agrees with an age for the boundary of 791 ± 2 ka obtained by $^{40}Ar/^{39}Ar$ analysis of lavas (*59*), adjusted to the Fish Canyon tuff sanidine standard used here (*57*). The Bose T4 section did not yield a coherent magnetostratigraphy.

21. W. Roebroecks and T. van Kolfschoten, Eds., *The Earliest Occupation of Europe* (Univ. of Leiden Press, Leiden, Netherlands, 1995).

22. G. Clark, *World Prehistory* (Cambridge Univ. Press, London, 1969).

23. M. D. Leakey, *Olduvai Gorge*, vol. 3 (Cambridge Univ. Press, Cambridge, 1971).

24. N. Toth, *J. Archaeol. Sci.* **12**, 101 (1985).

25. R. Potts, *J. Anthropol. Res.* **47**, 153 (1991).

26. In the early Acheulean (before 500 ka), LCT shape was also influenced by initial form; minimal secondary flaking of large flakes, for example, yielded the standard thin, ovate form typical of Acheulean bifaces.

27. R. L. Hay, *Geology of the Olduvai Gorge* (Univ. of California Press, Berkeley, CA, 1976).

28. R. Potts, A. K. Behrensmeyer, P. Ditchfield, *J. Hum. Evol.* **37**, 747 (1999).

29. Bose LCTs (unifacial and bifacial) are significantly larger in mean maximum dimension than Oldowan ($t = 22.56$, df = 270, $P < 0.001$) and Developed Oldowan ($t = 24.59$, df = 551, $P < 0.001$) flaked pieces, Developed Oldowan LCTs ($t = 6.94$, df = 120, $P < 0.001$), and even Acheulean LCTs from Olorgesailie, Kenya ($t = 4.32$, df = 994, $P < 0.001$). Bose bifacial LCTs, however, do not differ significantly from Acheulean LCTs from Olorgesailie ($t = 1.95$, df = 946, $P > 0.05$). The mean weight of Bose LCTs is greater than that of Oldowan and Developed Oldowan flaked pieces and of African Acheulean LCTs. Bose LCTs made on large flakes fall at the upper end of the range of mean weight variation at Olorgesailie.

30. Bose LCTs made on flakes (16.4 cm, $n = 12$) differ little in mean maximum dimension from Acheulean LCTs from Olorgesailie (16.3 cm, $n = 859$). The mean length of the largest flake scar for all Bose LCTs (9.6 cm, $n = 96$) indicates regular manufacture of flakes ≥ 10 cm. The mean scar length is significantly greater than that for Oldowan flaked pieces (4.2 cm; $t = 10.51$, df = 216, $P < 0.001$); for Developed Oldowan flaked pieces (4.2 cm; $t = 17.09$, df = 337, $P < 0.001$); and for Developed Oldowan bifacial LCTs (6.1 cm; $t = 4.62$, df = 107, $P < 0.001$).

31. G. Ll. Isaac, *Olorgesailie* (Univ. of Chicago Press, Chicago, IL, 1977).

32. M. D. Leakey, *Olduvai Gorge*, vol. 5 (Cambridge Univ. Press, Cambridge, 1994).

33. M. Roberts and S. Parfitt, *Boxgrove: A Middle Pleistocene Hominid Site at Eartham Quarry, Boxgrove, West Sussex* (English Heritage, London, 1999).

34. The overall thickness of Bose LCTs was determined by the size and shape of the original cobble (71% of LCTs were made on cobbles) or by flake size (29% were made on large flakes). Tip morphology, however, was determined by repetitive flaking procedures that thinned one end, produced a straight edge (viewed edge-on), and aligned the axis connecting the tip to the butt with the maximum dimension of the piece (99% of LCTs). On 75% of the LCTs, tip thinning produced a central ridge 25 to 60 mm from the tip, due to the intersection of flake scars from the converging edges. On the remainder, a single flake was usually detached at the tip, removing the central ridge. LCT shape ratios (for example, thickness/width at 20% of length from the tip and thickness 20%/thickness 50% of length from the tip) all had extremely low variances (range: 0.011 to 0.033), a level that Isaac (*31*) considered indicative of modal shaping of Acheulean LCTs.

35. The mean flake scar count for Bose LCTs (17.2, $n = 94$ LCTs) was significantly higher than for Oldowan flaked pieces (6.2, $t = 7.78$, df = 265, $P < 0.001$), Developed Oldowan flaked pieces (6.5, $t = 11.59$, df = 470, $P < 0.001$), and Developed Oldowan bifacial LCTs (9.8, $t = 4.19$, df = 123, $P < 0.001$). The mean scar count for bifacial LCTs from Bose (24.7, $n = 33$ LCTs) was higher than for Acheulean bifacial LCTs from Olorgesailie (20.0, $t = 3.17$, df = 890, $P < 0.01$).

36. Ninety-one percent of the bifacial LCT sample ($n = 35$ specimens) was from the western third of the Bose basin (Figure 1, sites 1 through 14).

37. T. Liu, Z. Ding, N. Rutter, *Quat. Sci. Rev.* **18**, 1205 (1999).

38. Z. Guo, T. Liu, N. Federoff, Z. An, *Chin. Sci. Bull.* **38**, 586 (1993).

39. P. Wang, *Quat. Sci.* **2**, 111 (1990).

40. K.-F. Wang, Y.-L. Zhang, H. Jian, *Chin. Sci. Bull.* **36**, 1721 (1991).

41. Z. Zhu et al., *Quat. Sci.* **8**, 276 (1995).

42. C. C. Swisher Jr. et al., *Science* **263**, 1118 (1994).

43. N. Toth and K. Schick, in *Tools, Language and Cognition in Human Evolution*, K. R. Gibson and T. Ingold, Eds. (Cambridge Univ. Press, Cambridge, 1992), pp. 346–362.

44. P. Teilhard de Chardin, C. C. Young, W. C. Pei, H. C. Chang, *Bull. Geol. Soc. China* **14**, 179 (1935).

45. K. Hutterer, in *Sunda and Sahul: Prehistoric Studies in Southeast Asia, Melanesia and Australia*, J. Allen, J. Golson, R. Jones, Eds. (Academic Press, New York, 1977), pp. 31–72.

46. G. G. Pope, in *The Palaeoenvironment of East Asia from the Mid-Tertiary*, J. S. Aigner, N. G. Jablonski, G. Taylor, D. Walker, P. Wang, Eds. (Centre of Asian Studies, Univ. of Hong Kong, Hong Kong, 1988), pp. 1097–1123.

47. H. Watanabe, *J. Anthropol. Archaeol.* **4**, 1 (1985).

48. J. D. Clark, *Trans. R. Soc. London Ser. B* **337**, 201 (1992).

49. K. Bai, thesis, University of California, Berkeley (1988).

50. T. Chen and S. Yuan, *Archaeometry* **30**, 59 (1988).

51. H. Kajiwara, S. Fujimura, T. Kamada, Y. Yokoyama, http://tfu-www.tfu.ac.jp/kenkyushitsu/kajiwara/KAJIWARA.html (1999).

52. W. Huang, *Quat. Res.* **28**, 237 (1989).

53. ———, J. Leng, X. Yuan, G. Xie, *Acta Anthropol. Sin.* **9**, 105 (1990).

54. S.-L. Guo, W. Huang, X.-H. Hao, B.-L. Chen, *Radiat. Meas.* **28**, 565 (1997).

55. W. Sharp and A. L. Deino, *Eos* **77**, F773 (1996).

56. G. A. Izett and J. D. Obradovich, *J. Geophys. Res.* **99**, 2925 (1992).

57. P. R. Renne et al., *Chem. Geol.* **145**, 117 (1998).

58. D. A. Schneider, D. V. Kent, G. A. Mello, *Earth Planet. Sci. Lett.* **111**, 395 (1992).

59. B. S. Singer and M. S. Pringle, *Earth Planet. Sci. Lett.* **139**, 41 (1996).

60. R. Potts, unpublished data on Oldowan and Developed Oldowan sites.

61. P. Callow, in *Olduvai Gorge*, vol. 5, M. D. Leakey, Ed. (Cambridge Univ. Press, Cambridge, 1994), pp. 235–253.

62. P. R. Jones, in *Olduvai Gorge*, vol. 5, M. D. Leakey, Ed. (Cambridge Univ. Press, Cambridge, 1994), pp. 254–298.

63. M. N. Noll, thesis, University of Illinois, Urbana-Champaign (2000).

64. We thank the government of the Guangxi Zhuang Autonomous Region and the Chinese Academy of Sciences for permission to conduct the Bose basin research. Supported by funds from the Smithsonian Institution's Human Origins Program and Scholarly Studies Program, by Chinese Academy of Sciences grant SEPP 9812, by National Natural Science Foundation of China grant 49894176, and by NSF. We thank W. G. Melson and F. M. Hueber for analytical assistance, M. N. Noll for data on Olorgesailie LCTs, and A. K. Behrensmeyer and A. S. Brooks for helpful discussions.

40

Evidence for the Use of Fire at Zhoukoudian, China

S. Weiner, Q. Xu, P. Goldberg, J. Liu, and O. Bar-Yosef

ABSTRACT

Zhoukoudian is widely regarded as having the oldest reliable evidence for the controlled use of fire by humans. A reexamination of the evidence in Layer 10, the earliest archaeological horizon in the site, shows that burned and unburned bones are present in the same layer with stone tools. However, no ash or charcoal remnants could be detected. Hence, although indirect evidence for burning is present, there is no direct evidence for in situ burning.

The use of fire was an important asset for our early ancestors, offering them protection against large carnivores, warmth, added nutrition, and light at night. The ability to make and maintain fire was probably a prerequisite for occupation of the higher latitudes of Eurasia. It is therefore important to know when humans acquired this skill. Some studies suggest that the use of fire goes back more than 1 million years (*1–3*), although the evidence presented for almost all sites older than 300,000 to 400,000 years is controversial (*4*).

The oldest reliable evidence has been thought to be from Locality 1 at Zhoukoudian (Peking Man Site) (*4–6*), which accumulated from about 500,000 to 200,000 years ago (*7, 8*). Over 60 years ago, the original investigators noted in Layers 10 and 4 the presence of "the evidently burnt condition of many of the bones, antlers, horn cores and pieces of wood found in the cultural layers, [and] a direct and careful chemical test of several specimens has established the presence of free carbon in the blackened fossils and earth. The vivid yellow and red hues of the banded clays constantly associated with the black layers is also due to heating or baking of the cave's sediments" [(*9*), p. 113]. Subsequent observations of Layer 10 as well as a few reported analyses of the bones and sediments have concurred with these early observations, although some doubts have been raised (*4, 9–14*).

The cave formed as an enlargement of a vertical fault in which silty and angular rockfall accumulated. Layer 10, the lowermost archaeological horizon, is about 50 to 65 cm thick and is composed of two lithological units. The upper part is quite compact and comprises pink to reddish-yellow silty clay, locally cemented with small rock fragments. The lower part consists of yellowish-red, dark reddish-brown, and reddish-brown silts that become increasingly well bedded with depth (*15, 16*) (Figure 1).

We examined the sediments in Layer 10 after cleaning the exposed section in 1996 and 1997. During the cleaning, we collected 42 bones of macrofauna and a considerably larger number of microfauna. Five of the macrofaunal bone fragments were uniformly black to grey in a freshly produced fracture surface; one had a turquoise hue. We extracted insoluble residues from the black bones after dissolution of the carbonated apatite by 1N hydrochloric acid (HCl) and the adhering silicate minerals by 40% hydrofluoric acid (HF) (*17*). Infrared (IR) spectra showed that the insoluble residues are all characteristic of burned bone organic matrix (Figure 2A). Most of the remaining bones were yellow with speckled black surface coloration. Those

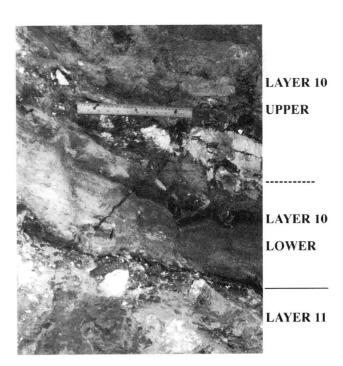

LAYER 10

UPPER

LAYER 10

LOWER

LAYER 11

Figure 1. *Photograph of Layer 10 showing the upper part, comprising light to dark brown fine-grained sediments and limestone boulders and the lower part comprising red- to yellow-colored finely laminated sediments.*

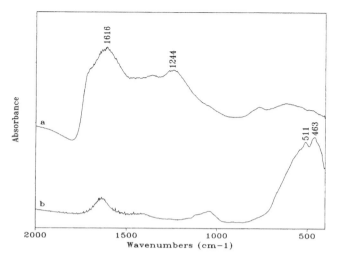

Figure 2. *Infrared spectra of the insoluble fractions of two black bones from the upper part of Layer 10 after treatment with HCl and HF (17). (**A**) Spectrum characteristic of burned organic matrix [see spectra in (17) and (26)]. (**B**) Spectrum characteristic of manganese and possible other oxides [see spectra in (17)].*

tested produced residues with IR spectra characteristic of oxides (Figure 2B). There was no appreciable acid-insoluble organic residue. Only seven of the bones from the microfauna were uniformly black and hence appear burned, out of a total of 278 collected. One of these was tested and confirmed as burned. Most of the bones, burned and unburned, were derived from the upper part of Layer 10. The small fragment with a distinct turquoise color was obtained from the lower part of Layer 10. None of the bones in the upper part were turquoise in color. We have reproduced this color experimentally by heating white- to yellow-colored fossil bones from Locality 1, including some from the upper part of Layer 10, to temperatures between 400° and 800°C for 2 hours. The optimal temperature is 600°C. Fresh bones turn black to grey under these conditions, and a black fossil bone from Layer 10 also turned turquoise.

The sediments of Layer 10 have often been described as ash (*6, 9, 10, 14–16*). Fresh wood ash is composed mainly of fine-grained calcite (*18*) and a minor amount (about 2% by weight) of a relatively insoluble phase. The latter is mainly an aggregate of soil-derived minerals embedded in a biologically produced amorphous matrix rich in Si, Al, Fe, and K. These have been called siliceous aggregates (*19, 20*). In prehistoric deposits containing bones, as in the upper part of Layer 10, ash if present should occur either as fine-grained calcite or as carbonated apatite (if the calcite reacted with phosphate in the ground water), with a small amount of siliceous aggregates (*20*). The three major components of the sediments from the upper part of Layer 10 are quartz (about 45%), carbonated apatite (about 40%), and clay (about 15%). We found no evidence of siliceous aggregates, even from the lowest density fraction after centrifugation in a heavy liquid (*21*). This fraction, composing about 0.6 weight % of the sample, did contain some mineral clusters that resemble siliceous aggregates

when observed in the back-scattering mode in the scanning electron microscope. They did not contain relatively large amounts of potassium, which is characteristic of other siliceous aggregates examined to date (*19*), or other properties, such as the association of characteristic phytoliths, that would reflect a biological origin. These clusters were also present in the lower part of Layer 10, in the breccia of Layer 8–9, and in Layer 4. According to micromorphological observations, they are of diagenetic origin. Infrared spectra as well as elemental analyses showed that the clays are secondarily silicified, and the aggregates are possibly a product of the silicification process. We thus infer from the above that the carbonated apatite present in the upper part of Layer 10 is not derived from ash, and that there is no evidence for the presence of wood ash in Layer 10.

The upper part of Layer 10 is rich in large bone fragments, many with sharp edges. In thin section, however, many of the microscopic pieces of bone are well rounded, possibly due to transport or to carnivore digestion, by hyenas for example. The lack of bedding and the massive loose nature of the sediments suggests bioturbation, an interpretation supported by the presence in thin section of numerous rounded silty clay aggregates (*22*).

The putative hearths in the lower part of Layer 10 are represented by (i) finely laminated silt and clay interbedded with reddish-brown and yellow-brown fragments of organic matter, locally mixed with limestone fragments, and (ii) dark brown finely laminated silt, clay, and organic matter. No charcoal was observed. The fine lamination of both sediment types, best visible in thin section (Figure 3), is indicative of accumulation in

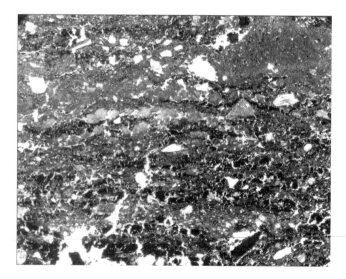

Figure 3. *Photomicrograph of Layer 10, illustrating the presence of massive sediments in the upper part and finely laminated, blackish organic matter (silts) in the lower part. The brighter colored material is a secondarily precipitated phosphate, probably carbonated apatite. Regardless of whether the dark-colored organic matter in the lower part is a result of actual burning or aging, it is certainly not in its primary context but is water laid. The image was made with plane-polarized light; the width of the photograph is about 3 mm.*

quiet water (*23*). The cave at this time was probably the locus of ponded water and was probably more open to the atmosphere.

The strongest evidence for fire associated with Layer 10 is the presence of burned macrofaunal bones. Layer 10 also contains an assemblage of stone artifacts composed mainly of quartzite (*9, 10*). During our examination of Layer 10, we observed several quartzite pieces, all of which came from the upper part of the section. There is thus a close association of the artifacts and the burned bones. Only 2.5% of the microfaunal bones were burned, as compared to 12% of the macrofaunal bones. These values are roughly similar to those obtained in much younger caves where fire was undoubtedly used by humans (*24*). As some of the sediments of Layer 10 were deposited under water, we cannot be sure that the bones, including the large burned and unburned bones, as well as the artifacts are in their original discard location. If fire was used at this location in the site, it is difficult to account for the absence of the insoluble fraction of wood ash.

At the base of Layer 4, there is also a close association of artifacts and macrofaunal bones, including many burned black bones. These sediments were similarly laminated and deposited under water in a low-energy environment. Here too we were not able to identify ash mineral remains. These bones, as well as many of the macrofaunal bones in the entire section, are present in a loess-like deposit (such as Layer 4) or in silt mixed with coarse angular limestone breccia (Layers 6 and 8–9). They were probably brought into the cave as runoff or in mud flows found between the breccia clasts.

The few burned bones we did observe above the base of Layer 4 and in the lower part of Layer 10 were turquoise colored, and we assume that they are fossil bones that were somehow burned by natural processes.

We conclude on the basis of the absence of ash or ash remnants (siliceous aggregates) and of in situ hearth features that there is no direct evidence for in situ burning in Layers 4 and 10. Most of the fine-grained sediments in the site were water laid, and even if ash remains could be recognized, it would be difficult to demonstrate where they were produced. The co-occurrence of burned black bones and quartzite artifacts in the same layers is only suggestive of a cultural association, and hence of the use of fire by humans, but does not prove it. As most of the site has, however, already been excavated, it is not now possible to determine the locations of any campfires in Locality 1 at Zhoukoudian.

REFERENCES AND NOTES

1. J. A. J. Gowlett, J. W. K. Harris, D. Walton, B. A. Wood, *Nature* **294**, 125 (1981).
2. M. Barbetti, *J. Hum. Evol.* **15**, 771 (1986).
3. C. K. Brain and A. Sillen, *Nature* **336**, 464 (1988).
4. S. R. James, *Curr. Anthropol.* **30**, 1 (1989).
5. K. Oakley, *Prehist. Soc.* **4**, 36 (1955).
6. S. Zhang, in *Palaeoanthropology and Palaeolithic Archaeology in the People's Republic of China*, W. U. Rukang and J. W. Olsen Eds. (Academic Press, London, 1985), pp. 147–186.
7. S. L. Guo et al., *Nucl. Tracks Radiat. Meas.* **19**, 719 (1991).
8. R. Grün et al., *Hum. Evol.* **32**, 83 (1997).
9. W. Pei and S. Zhang, *A Study of the Lithic Artifacts of Sinanthropus*, *Palaeontologica Sinica*, vol. 12 (Science Press, Beijing, 1985).
10. D. Black, T. De Chardin, C. C. Young, W. C. Pei, *Mem. Geol. Surv. China Ser. A* **11**, 1 (1933).
11. Z. Yang et al., in *Multi-Disciplinary Study of the Peking Man Site at Zhoukoudian*, W. Rukang et al., Eds. (Science Press, Beijing, 1985), pp. 1–85.
12. L. R. Binford and C. K. Ho, *Curr. Anthropol.* **26**, 413 (1985).
13. L. R. Binford and N. M. Stone, *ibid.* **27**, 453 (1986).
14. C. B. Stringer, *ibid.* **26**, 655 (1985).
15. Z. Liu, *Quat. Res.* **23**, 139 (1985).
16. _____, *Geoarchaeology* **3**, 103 (1988).
17. R. Shahack-Gross, O. Bar-Yosef, S. Weiner, *J. Archaeol. Sci.* **24**, 439 (1997).
18. G. S. Humphreys, P. A. Hunt, R. Buchanan, *Aust. J. Soil Res.* **25**, 115 (1987).
19. S. Schiegl, S. Lev-Yadun, O. Bar-Yosef, A. El-Goresy, S. Weiner, *Israel J. Earth Sci.* **43**, 267 (1994).
20. S. Schiegl, P. Goldberg, O. Bar-Yosef, S. Weiner, *J. Archaeol. Sci.* **23**, 763 (1996).
21. A 0.5-g aliquot of the sediment was treated with a mixture of 3N HCl and 3N HNO$_3$ for 30 min at 100°C. The acid was removed by centrifugation (at 6000 rpm for 2 min), and the pellet was washed twice with water. The pellet was resuspended in 5 ml of sodium polytungstate solution (density 2.4), thoroughly dispersed by sonication, and then centrifuged as above. The supernatant was removed and diluted with 1 ml of water, vortexed, and recentrifuged. This was repeated until no mineral remained in the supernatant.
22. P. Bullock, N. Federoff, A. Jongerius, G. J. Stoops, T. Tursina, *Handbook For Soil Thin Section Description* (Waine Research Publishers, Wolverhampton, UK, 1985).
23. M. A. Courty, P. Goldberg, R. Macphail, *Soils and Micromorphology in Archaeology* (Cambridge Univ. Press, Cambridge, 1989).
24. In Mousterian sediments in Kebara and Hayonim caves, Israel, the overall proportions of relatively large burned bones (based on their black color) are 5.2% (*25*) and 13% (M. C. Stiner, unpublished data), respectively. In Grotta dei Moscerini and Grotta di Sant'Agostini, Italy, the proportions vary between 1 and 7%, except for two levels in which they are 32 and 52% (*26*). At the Henderson site, New Mexico, the proportion of bison and ungulate burned bones is 8.6%, whereas for rodent bones it is 1.5% (*25*).
25. J. D. Speth, unpublished data.
26. M. C. Stiner, S. L. Kuhn, S. Weiner, O. Bar-Yosef, *J. Archaeol. Sci.* **22**, 223 (1995).
27. We thank L. Estroff for her help. This project was supported by grants from the Israel Science Foundation to S.W., from the L. S. B. Leakey Foundation to P.G., from the American School of Prehistoric Research (Peabody Museum, Harvard) to O.B.-Y., and from the Natural Science Foundation of China to Q.X.

41

Homo erectus and the Emergence of Sunda in the Tethys Realm

Contributions of Potassium-Based Chronology in the Sangiran Dome, Central Java

R. Larick, R. L. Ciochon, and Y. Zaim

Fossils of Java Man were first found on that Southeast Asian island 112 years ago. Although their origin was not recognized at the time, the finds represented *Homo erectus*, an early human species that presumably evolved

Reprinted with permission from *Athena Review*, Vol. 4, no. 1, pp. 32–39. Copyright © 2004 Athena Publications, Inc.

in equatorial Africa more than 2 million years ago. But the how, why, and when of *Homo erectus'* trek from Africa to island Southeast Asia have always been difficult questions.

The trek was indeed complex, and it appears that *Homo erectus'* arrival to current Java is an important factor for understanding why the species left highland

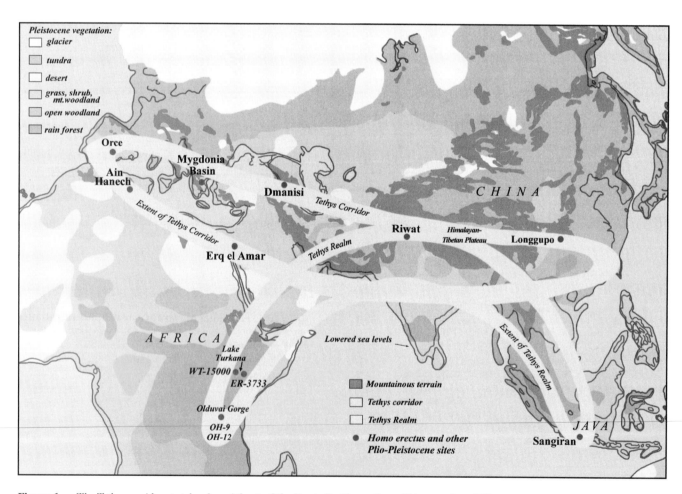

Figure 1. *The Tethys corridor stretches from Atlantic Gibraltar to Pacific southern China at about 32° north latitude. Between these points, the corridor follows geotectonically active coastlines and fore slopes along the southern margins of the Eurasian continental plate. Similar landscapes extend southward from the corridor along the Afro-Arabian rift system and along the Sunda subduction zone. During the Olduvai subchron, these areas together comprised the Tethys Realm, the maximum extent of early* Homo erectus *and associated large mammals (after National Geographic 1988).*

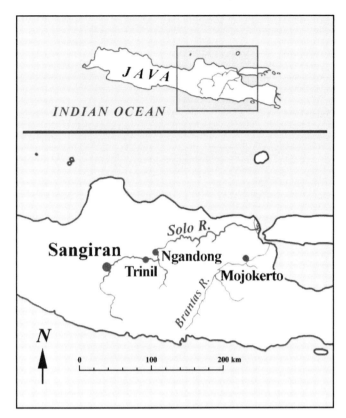

Figure 2. *Map showing concentration of sites with* Homo erectus *fossil finds in Central and East Java.*

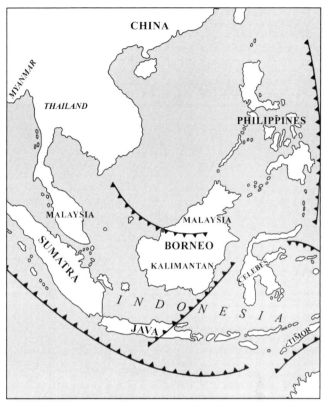

Figure 3. *Southeast Asia today with subduction zones* (Figures 2 and 3 after Djubiantono and Sémah 1993).

tropical Africa. We hope to shed light on the larger issues by delving into *Homo erectus'* significant relationship with volcanic and otherwise highly unstable landscapes in far Southeast Asia. *Homo erectus* seems to have sought out unstable landscapes, and this preference may explain this hominid's departure from Africa before 1.8 million years ago (mya) and its arrival to extreme Southeast Asia not long thereafter.

Our theory is based on two premises. First is the fact that early *Homo erectus* fossils are always found in the context of volatile geology and ragged geography. Second, the East African Rift and extreme Southeast Asia are endpoints on a grand east-west geotectonic pathway called the Tethys corridor (Figure 1). During a rather brief period called the Olduvai subchron (1.98–1.79 mya), the Tethys corridor was extremely unstable. *Homo erectus* and companion mammals took advantage of open linear landscapes to migrate north from the Rift to the Caucasus, and then both ways across the Tethys corridor—west toward Gibraltar, east to the Himalayan fore slope, and then far east to current Java. By the end of the Olduvai subchron, *Homo erectus* had dispersed throughout the greater Tethys Realm.

The immediate how of the Southeast Asian trek is perhaps the easiest to answer. We now know that *Homo erectus* did not navigate to present Java, but rather walked the length of the emergent Sunda continental shelf off East Asia's present south coast. Currently, the Indonesian archipelago's 14,000 tropical islands constitute the emergent landmass (Figure 3), but in the last 2 million years, the Sunda subcontinent (Figure 4) has

sometimes included much of the intervening sea bottom. Arriving to the area of present-day Thailand, *Homo erectus* groups spread south along a broad valley between the current Malay Peninsula and Sumatra. And they continued on to current Central Java, the extreme south coast of Sunda (Figure 2).

Much of Central Java lies directly above Sunda's highly volcanic subduction zone. Active volcanoes form the spine of the entire island but are especially large in the central zone (Figure 5), and their ash is slightly alkaline. Central Java is consequently blessed with rich volcanic soils; they are young and sweet. Using this resource of the central district, the entire island has supported a much larger historical human population than Sumatra, the Malay Peninsula, or Borneo—Java is earth's most densely inhabited agricultural island. Central Java's soil wealth probably explains why *Homo erectus* may have explored much of Sunda, but gravitated to this coast. As a hunter, this hominid also took advantage of eruptions that randomly cleared patches of rainforest. Such events provided rich graze for the large mammals upon which the early humans preyed.

THE SANGIRAN DOME

Central Java's Sangiran Dome lies squarely astride the subduction zone; large volcanoes rise to the east (Lawu) and to the west (Merapi) (Figures 5, 6). The dome is a window into one of earth's more important early human fossil beds and is now a UNESCO World

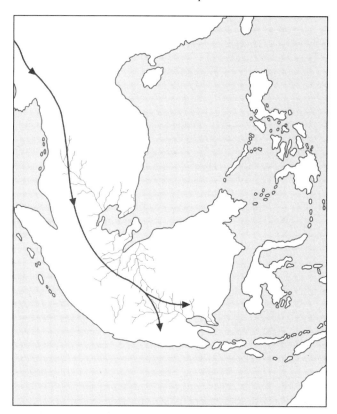

Figure 4.   *Schematic map of "Sundaland" at 2–1.5 mya, with probable migration path of* Homo erectus.

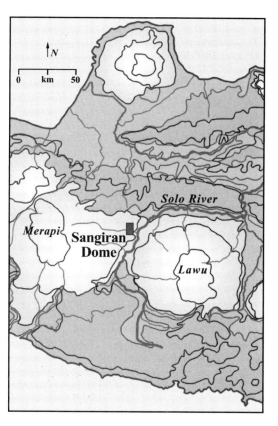

Figure 6.   *The Solo Basin, a segment of Java's east-west trending Central Depression, the current magmatic zone of the Indonesian volcanic island arc* (after Larick et al., 2001).

Figure 5.   *LANDSAT photograph of Central Java showing major* Homo erectus *find sites, associated rivers, and numerous volcanoes* (NASA/ JPL-LANDSAT).

Heritage Site (Box 1). During the last century, the dome's heavily eroded cliff faces have yielded more than 80 fragments of *Homo erectus* skeletons (Larick, Ciochon, and Zaim, 1999). The fossils represent an early human occupation of about 500,000 years' duration as Sunda emerged from the Java Sea.

Two million years ago, the area of the current dome lay on the southern edge of the submerged Sunda shelf. The edge emerged from the Java Sea as three base geological factors began to interplay. One was the slow but constant folding of Asian crust as the Indian Oceanic plate slid or subducted under it at the Java trench just

Fossil Finds in the Sangiran Dome

About 120,000 years ago, localized volcanic pressure began up-lifting the area around current Sangiran village. The pressure was enough to raise the local landscape several tens of meters above the surrounding plateau, but not strong enough to bring magma to the surface. During this geologically recent period, stream flow has outpaced the uplift; the domed area is consequently heavily eroded along the creek and river channels that still maintain crossings through it. One may draw analogy with the Colorado River outpacing the uplifting Colorado Plateau to form the Grand Canyon. While the scale is much reduced in the Sangiran Dome, a number of gorges have cut down into the rising Bapang and Sangiran formations and

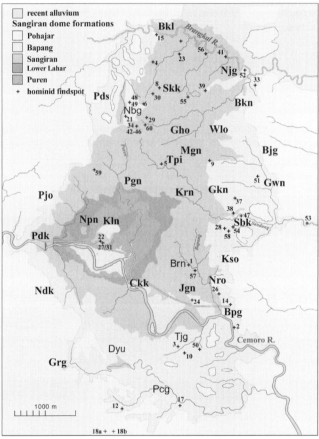

Figure 7. *Sangiran Dome, showing sedimentary levels and documented hominid fossil findspots. Abbreviations mark village localities* (after Larick et al., 2001).

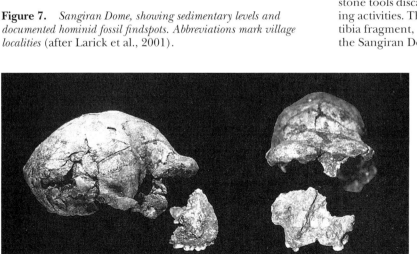

Figure 8. *Cranium of Sangiran 17, the most complete* Homo erectus *skull found in Asia, dated ca. 1.25 mya* (cast from American Museum of Natural History; photo: Athena Review).

even into the Puren limestone. Most Sangiran Dome hominid fossils (Figure 7) are found in these eroding gorge cliff faces.

In 1891, Eugene Dubois found early hominid fossils about 40 miles to the east at Trinil (Figures 4, 5), but his search in the Sangiran Dome was unsuccessful. In the mid 1930s, German paleoanthropologist Ralph von Koenigswald (affectionately known as "von K") came to the dome and paid local cultivators for fossils and information on their findspots. Von K had his first success in 1936 when his workers retrieved a sizable lower jaw fragment still holding most of its teeth. He eventually would recover eight significant hominid jaw and skull fragments and about ninety isolated teeth. In 1942, however, the invading Japanese terminated von K's fieldwork and imprisoned him for the duration of the war.

In the 1960s, two Indonesian paleoanthropologists, Teuku Jacob and Sastrohamijoyo Sartono, continued von K's reward system. To this day, most important finds in Sangiran are found by local farmers and workers, and very few have been recovered in scientific excavations. Probably due both to collection bias and differential preservation, most fossil evidence from Sangiran consists of teeth, jaws, and crania, such as Sangiran 17 (Figure 8), discovered in 1969 by a local farmer constructing agricultural terraces and Tjg 1993.05 (Figure 9), found in a similar fashion in 1993.

With refined survey and excavation techniques, archaeologists are now finding *Homo erectus* camp sites along the stream banks preserved in the Bapang formation. A Franco-Indonesian team has been excavating for years at a site in the Ngebung Hills. The finds there include a range of elementary stone tools discarded among faunal remains showing butchering activities. This excavation has also recovered a *Homo erectus* tibia fragment, the only postcranial bone recovered to date in the Sangiran Dome (Sémah et al., 1992).

Figure 9. Homo erectus *cranium (Tjg 1993.05) recently found in 1993 at the village locality of Tanjung in the Sangiran Dome* (photo: R. L. Ciochon).

south of the island. Another was the buildup of debris from volcanoes venting above the subduction zone. The critical factor was the coming of Pleistocene Ice Age around 2 mya. At this point, glacial ice accumulated rapidly on the northern hemisphere's continental masses. So much water was pulled out of the earth's atmosphere and locked up as ice that sea levels receded across the globe. While sea levels have fluctuated with glacial cycles over this period, the net effect has been lower water and a more emergent Sunda shelf.

The lowest formation exposed in the dome, the Puren limestone, represents this earliest stage of emergence. In its upper reaches, the Puren shows evidence for wave-cut benches, mangrove beaches, brackish lagoons, and hints of an island fauna. About 1.9 mya, a series of mass mudflows abruptly slid down a nearby volcanic cone to fill in local coastal areas. These lahars (slurries of wet ash mixed with larger rocks, tree trunks, and the occasional animal carcass) raised the local environment high enough to support freshwater lakes and swamps with higher, dryer ground inland. On top of the lahars, the Sangiran formation is mostly lacustrine clay with heavy organic content. Fossils of the first-arriving land mammals appear in these swamp deposits: water-loving species such as elephants, hippos, and certain deer.

As the Sangiran formation continued to build up, the lakes became shallower and more productive, and the nearby terrestrial landscapes must have been lush. *Homo erectus* arrived to such lakeside environments

along with the first large carnivore, *Panthera*. As the early humans settled in, the Sunda coast kept emerging, and the local landscape kept drying.

In yet another abrupt transition about 1.5 mya, local uplift and volcanic eruption took over the creation of area landforms. Local sedimentation changed from lacustrine to fully fluvial or riverine. The current dome area quickly took on much of its present aspect, a low terrestrial plateau framed with large volcanoes. This fluvial sediment mantle is known locally as the Bapang formation.

Active volcanism alternated with more peaceful times during the period represented by the Bapang formation. During the more energetic episodes, uplift increased stream gradients, and eruptions charged stream courses with volcanic detritus. As this sediment was transported seaward, the Sangiran locale found itself ever more distant from the coast. Thick layers of sand and gravel in fast-shifting stream beds typify the active phases. In quieter times, meandering rivers accumulated beds of fine tuffaceous sediment.

We count five two-phased cycles of sedimentation in the Bapang formation. Most large mammal fossils are found in the coarse sedimentary phases (Figure 10). We also find that the sedimentary cycles lose intensity through time. Rich bone beds lie just above the Bapang/Sangiran formations transition zone. The lower Bapang human fossils here are highly fragmented teeth and jaws. As one moves up through the Bapang sediment column, rock particles get finer and the fossils become more complete and well preserved (Table 1).

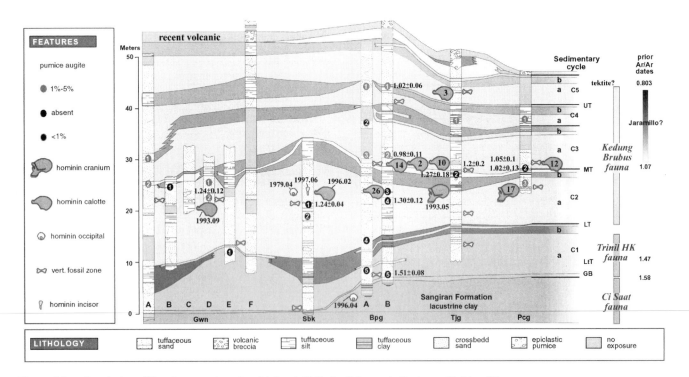

Figure 10. *Correlation of Sangiran stratigraphy with hominid finds. Columns indicate sampled localities, and numbered ovals indicate pumice samples tested for augite content, hornblende color, and* $^{40}Ar/^{39}Ar$ *age analysis. Skulls found into the mid-1970s are labeled with their "Sangiran" number (e.g., Sangiran 17). Later finds are referred to by the locality, year, and month of their discovery (e.g., Tjg 1993.05). Locality abbreviations, left to right (north to south, with no scale): Gwn—Grogolwetan; Sbk—Sendangbusik; Bpg—Bapang; Tjg—Tanjung; Pcg—Pucung (after Larick et al., 2001).*

Table 1. The Five Two-Phased Sedimentary Cycles of the Bapang Formation Have Produced a Differential Preservation of Fossil Hominids. The lowest cycle (1a) with more energy and courser rock particles has yielded fragmentary teeth and jaws. The upper cycles (2a to 5a) with lower energy levels and finer sediments have yielded better preserved calottes and crania. This figure links *Homo erectus* specimens with the sedimentary cycles that produced them. The bottom-most level depicts the oldest hominids found in the Sangiran Dome from the lacustrine Sangiran formation.

Sedimentary Cycles		Provenance	Institution		Specimen	S #	Pith #	Anatomy	Sex
tuff (unnamed)									
b									
a	Cycle 5a: ~1.0 mya	Tjg 1938.07	FS	F	calotte	3	III	posterior	f
Upper tuff									
b									
a	Cycle 4								
b									
tuff (unnamed)									
a	Cycle 3a: ~1.0 mya	Bpg 1937.08	FS	F	calotte	2	II		f
		Tjg 1963.05	GMU	Y	calotte	10	V	(+) left zygoma	m
		Pcg 1965.01	GRDC	B	calotte	12	VII	posterior	f
		Bpg 1966.01	GMU	Y	cranial frags	14		basilar-lateral	
		Sbk 1981	GMU	Y	calotte	38		mesio-posterior	m
		Brn 1986.06	GRDC	B	mandible	39		left fragment	
Middle tuff									
b									
a	Cycle 2a: ~1.25 mya	Pcg 1969.09	GRDC	B	cranium	17	VIII		m
		Bpg 1978	GMU	Y	cranial frags	26		parieto-temporal	
		Sbk 1979.04	GRDC	B	calotte	28		posterior	
		Sbk 1981.03	GRDC	B	mandible	37	G	left fragment	
		Nbg 1991.10	BA	J	molar	48		lower M2	
		Tjg 1993.05	IT	B	calotte	50	IX	(+) maxilla	f
		Gwn 1993.09	GMU	Y	calotte	51			f
		Sbk 1996.02	GMU	Y	calotte	54			m
		Sbk 1997.06	GRDC	B	incisor	58		lower left central	
Lower tuff									
b									
a	Cycle 1a: ~1.5 mya	Sbk 1952.09	GRDC	B	mandible	8	B	left fragment	
		Bkl 1969	GMU	Y	maxilla	15		right fragment	
		Bkl 1975.04	GMU	Y	endocast	23		basicranial	
		Brn 1979.05	GRDC	B	mandible	33	H	right fragment	
		Nbg 1980.12	GMU	Y	endocast	34		temporal	
		Njg 1986.06	GRDC	B	mandible	39		left fragment	
		Nbg 1988	BA	Y	mandible	42	A9	right fragment	
		Nbg 1988	BA	Y	cranial frags	43	A13	sagittal-parietal	
		Nbg 1988	BA	Y	molar	45	B13	right lower M1	
		Nbg 1988	BA	Y	teeth	46	A18	4 teeth in matrix	
		Nbg 1992	BA	J	femur	49	K11	left diaphysis	
		Nbg 1994	GRDC	B	frontal	52			
Grenzbank									
	Upper Sangiran Formation: >1.5 mya	Bkl 1939.12	FS	F	calotte	4	IV	(+) maxilla	m
		Kln 1978.07	GMU	Y	maxilla	27		(+) calotte in matrix	f
		Kln 1979.07	IT	B	calotte	31	M II	posterior	m
		Sbk 1989.04	BA	B	cranial frags	47	H1	16 calotte frags	
		Brn 1996.04	GRDC	B	occipital	57			f

a: Upper sedimentary facies
b: Lower sedimentary facies (shaded)

Provenance: village locality abbreviation and date of discovery
(see Figure 7 for map of localities)

BA: Balai Arkeologi   FS: Forschungsinstitut Senckenberg
GRDC: Geological Research and Development Center

GMU: Gadjah Mada University   IT: Institute of Technology

B: Bandung   F: Frankfurt

J: Jakarta   Y: Yogyakarta

S #: Sangiran hominid specimen number
(see Figure 7 for S # findspots)

Pith #: Pithecanthropus hominid number
(older numbering system)

While the formation names change, Bapang-like sedimentary cycles have continued right up to the present in Central Java. The human fossils, however, and most of the accompanying large mammal remains, are not present in the upper part of the Bapang formation itself. The time of disappearance must be about 800,000 years ago. For reasons not yet entirely clear, the well-entrenched early human population disappeared from the Sunda south coast after having lived there for more than a half million years.

In sum, the earliest *Homo erectus* groups arrived to the coastal swamps of south-central Sunda between 1.8 and 1.6 mya. At this point the hominids probably lived slightly inland of the Sangiran locale; their bones washing downstream after death. About 1.5 mya, fast-flowing streams began building and cutting beds of coarser sediment. The lower and middle Bapang formation stream banks represent the landscapes on which *Homo erectus* actually lived. About 800,000 years ago, the hominids and most other contemporary large mammals seem to have left the area. In the meantime, volcanic debris has continued to accumulate up to the present era.

AGE OF SUNDA *HOMO ERECTUS*

During the last century, age estimates for the earliest human fossils on Java have ranged from as little as a half million years to as much as 2 million years. As in other areas of human evolutionary research, the initial age estimates were young; newer geological findings and dating methods tend to push back the ages. Our collaboration with Indonesian geologists and American geochronologists applies the most advanced radiometric dating methods (Larick et al., 2001). There is now little question that early Sunda humans arrived toward the end of the Olduvai subchron.

The volcanic debris that preserves the Sangiran fossils also provides a means to understand their age (Box 2). Small quantities of deep earth minerals, such as hornblende and plagioclase, are expelled molten during eruptions. At the moment the droplets cool and crystallize outside the volcano, their potassium isotopes are maximally unstable. As the phenocrysts become part of the sediment column, the unstable isotopes decay at a constant rate. Radioactivity decreases as the stable decay byproducts increase. Given routine assumptions, the relative proportions of unstable and stable isotopes mark the time since the volcano has erupted. Geochronologists speak of this ratio as the mineral's eruption age. If a datable phenocryst and a human fossil have contemporaneous sedimentary origins, the mineral eruption age approximates the age of the fossil itself.

But there are some problems. Individual eruptions often produce tuffs, layers of air-fall volcanic ash that provide distinct horizons within a sedimentary sequence. In East Africa, such tuffs have been a heavenly gift for geochronologists. Phenocrysts dated from a tuff overlying fossil beds give a minimum age for any given fossil. Tuff minerals underlying a fossil bed produce maximum ages. In the humid environments of Southeast Asia, however, tuff layers are almost always reworked by surface runoff and stream action. Ash from a number of tuffs may be mixed together and then deposited against a stream bank from which older fossils are eroding.

These same conditions also increase the chemical weathering of the volcanic minerals. In the Sangiran dome, individual crystals are often too weathered to give true eruption ages. Moreover, Central Javan mineral crystals are often too small to analyze individually.

===== BOX 2 =====

Potassium-Based Age Analyses

The element potassium (K) makes up fully 2.4% of the mass of earth's crust. Volcanic rocks hold much of their K as components of minerals such as feldspar, hornblende, amphibole, and mica. A naturally radioactive isotope, ^{40}K, comprises about 0.01% of naturally occurring potassium. The abundance of ^{40}K makes it a good candidate for radiometric age analysis. The long half-life of ^{40}K, about 1.31 billion years, lends its decay analysis to volcanic minerals associated with early human fossils and archaeological sites. By way of comparison, the half-life of radiocarbon (^{14}C) is 7,530 years. Decay analysis of radiocarbon (from ^{14}C to ^{13}C) gives accurate ages for carbon samples up to about 40,000 years old. Analyzing ^{40}K decay produces accurate ages for volcanic minerals that range from about 100,000 to 4 billion years old.

Molecules of ^{40}K begin decaying as a molten volcanic phenocryst solidifies upon entering earth's atmosphere or cooling on its surface. The decay product is the inert gaseous element argon (^{40}Ar). Interest in ^{40}K-^{40}Ar decay analysis (commonly written K-Ar and verbalized as "potassium-argon dating") began in the 1950s. At that time, geochemists needed 10 grams of pure, unweathered mineral to determine an accurate and precise eruption age. One of the problems was that measurements of ^{40}K, a solid, and ^{40}Ar, a gas, required separate subsamples and instruments.

In the mid-1960s, Craig Merrihue and Grenville Turner worked to eliminate the major shortcomings of K-Ar dating.

The idea was to take advantage of another naturally occurring, but stable, potassium isotope (^{39}K), which can be converted into another argon isotope (^{39}Ar). The ^{39}Ar then substitutes for measuring ^{40}K in relation to ^{40}Ar. This strategy is known as $^{39}Ar/^{40}Ar$ analysis, or "argon-argon dating."

To proceed with $^{39}Ar/^{40}Ar$ analysis of Sangiran Dome hornblende in the laboratory, the bulk phenocryst sample is first bombarded with neutrons. This converts the ^{39}K to ^{39}Ar. The sample is then melted at a temperature around 1600°C to free the lab-created ^{39}Ar and the natural decay product, ^{40}Ar. These are then collected and their relative abundances are measured using high-resolution mass spectrometry.

Argon-argon dating still has limitations. First, chemical weathering of phenocryst minerals can reduce the amount of measurable isotopes and muddy their relative abundances. Second, the bracketing error range is several tens of thousands of years, although this is relatively small for eruption ages a million or more years old. Finally, no K-based technique can be used on a fossil itself—they offer only "indirect" means of knowing a fossil's age. In consequence, the K-based methods are only as good as the association of the datable volcanic mineral with the fossil of interest. Our work, therefore, is to understand the association of pumice clast hornblende with *Homo erectus* fossils as they are found together in streambed deposits within the Sangiran Dome.

In surmounting these problems, we have turned toward clastic (lumps of) pumice, the sponge-like glass debris common to island arc volcanoes in Southeast Asia. Pumice clasts usually contain numerous hornblende phenocrysts, and the encapsulation serves to hold back the weathering process. Moreover, pumice clasts are often found in the same coarse sediment as the human fossils themselves. Consequently, our geochronology uses bulk samples of pumice-encapsulated hornblende phenocrysts (Box 2).

In order to understand the associations of pumice clasts and human fossils, our Indonesian-American team has undertaken detailed study of the sedimentary framework for the Sangiran Dome (Figure 10). We are studying the sedimentary dynamics of fossil bones and pumice clasts in stream environments and are analyzing the petrographic variety in volcanic minerals throughout the dome. The final step is to calibrate these findings with hornblende eruption ages at a number of stratigraphic levels.

The rich bone beds of the Bapang formation provide abundant information. In the lowest Bapang sediments, coarse gravel holds highly fragmented human fossils. The pumice clasts contain green hornblende that yields eruption ages between 1.51 to 1.47 mya. Above the base, a second cycle of Bapang deposits holds less fragmented human cranial elements (Table 1). Middle range

pumice clasts have green and brown hornblende crystals with ages from 1.33 to 1.24 mya. Higher Bapang beds hold the youngest cranium in association with brown hornblende. The eruption ages cluster around 1 mya.

As already mentioned, the lahars at the base of the Sangiran formation contain pumice clasts and their hornblende gives eruption ages of 2 to 1.8 mya. Unfortunately, the Sangiran formation above the lahars has no pumice. For the present we are not able to include the most important early human fossil beds directly in our scheme. Nevertheless, the bracketing dated material indicates that *Homo erectus* arrived after 1.8 mya and before 1.6 mya.

Our results give the first radiometrically calibrated scheme for the emergence of this part of Sunda, as well as for the arrival, entrenchment, and disappearance of *Homo erectus*. This human ancestor occupied south Sunda for at least a half million years beginning more than 1.6 mya. With an occupation of this duration, we may speak of an evolutionary sequence for Sunda *Homo erectus*. With our sedimentary framework and argon-argon chronology, nearly 35 Sangiran Dome *Homo erectus* fossils can be seen in evolutionary sequence. Sunda *Homo erectus* followed a parallel evolutionary trajectory to that known for fossils in East Africa and the Caucuses. Cranial capacity increased and sex dimorphism became more nuanced (Box 3).

BOX 3

Evolutionary Trends in Sangiran *Homo erectus*

With our sedimentary framework and the pumice hornblende ages in place, a number of old and new Sangiran Dome cranial fossils may be seen in chronological sequence. Further, the Sangiran Dome evolutionary sequence can also be compared with a parallel sequence known from the East African Rift Valley and the Eurasian Caucasus (Dmanisi) in the western Tethys corridor.

It is now clear that the five Sangiran formation cranial fossils (Table 1, bottom) predate 1.51 mya and are penecontemporary with ER 3733, ER 3883, and WT 15000 from the East African Rift, and with D2280, D2282, and D2700 from the Caucasus (Gabunia et al., 2001; Vekua et al., 2002). These 11 Plio-Pleistocene specimens evince an early *Homo* cranial bauplan with significant regional variation. Relative to the Sangiran formation fossils, the western crania have less frontal angulation; moderated supraorbital tori; and varied supratoral sulci. Biorbital and bizygomatic breadths are narrow. Sangiran formation frontals, in contrast, are obliquely inclined and keeled, and prolong into a single, heavy supraorbital torus with a shallow supratoral sulcus. Biorbital breadth is greater and the zygomatics flare laterally.

Across the whole sample, sex dimorphism manifests primarily as a 15–20% difference in cranial capacity (mean for females = 730 cc; for males = 870 cc). The western crania are also dimorphic in cranial and facial superstructures. For instance, ER 3733 and D2282 (both female) exhibit gracile muscle attachments; this contrasts with the more marked muscle attachments seen in WT 15000 (sub-adult male), even though it is only a juvenile.

Sangiran formation cranial vaults show marked sex dimorphism in a slightly different way. Calottes S4 and S31 (males) have large mastoid processes and supramastoid crests; the vault bone is thickened posteriorly and along the sagittal midline. Occipital S57 (female), in contrast, has very thin vault bones and undeveloped superstructures. In sum, the early *Homo* cranial bauplan shows high and varied sex dimorphism from west to east.

The calottes found higher in the Bapang formation (C2a-C5a; Table 1, top) are penecontemporaneous with Olduvai upper Bed II specimens OH 9 and OH 12, with which they share encephalization features. The Bapang calottes are enlarged some 10–15% (mean for females = 835 cc; for males = 1030 cc) over their predecessors. Typically, calotte S54's temporal lines lie higher on the parietals, the occipital is expanded, and the nuchal and occipital plane lengths are nearly equal. The anterior features of all Bapang calottes (oblique frontals and a very heavy, continuous and projecting supraorbital torus with a shallow supratoral sulcus) continue to reflect a wide, prognathic face. Likewise, Bapang C2a–C5a sex dimorphism still favors the vault. Cranium S17 (male) has a thick vault that is keeled at the sagittal and temporal lines, and a heavy nuchal torus extending bilaterally to the supramastoid crests at asterion (Table 1). In contrast, cranium Tjg 1993.05 (female) has a thinly vaulted long, narrow, high calotte with a less angulated occipital and with a nuchal torus that is gracile and situated high (Figure 8). Many of these same features are apparent in Calotte S50 (female). Calotte S51 (female) has minimal cranial superstructures, thin vault bones (only 7 mm), and a slightly convex occipital squamous portion.

SUNDA *HOMO ERECTUS* IN GLOBAL CONTEXT

Fossils representing very early *Homo erectus* populations are now known from the highland Rift Valley of East Africa, the Caucasus Mountains that mediate southeast Europe and southwest Asia, and from the intensely volcanic slopes of the Sunda subduction zone. Circum-Mediterranean archaeological sites representing these groups may be present in northern Algeria (Ain Hanech), Andalusian Spain (Orce), and the Negev (Erq el Amar). Late Olduvai subchron archaeological sites are also known on the Himalayan fore slope (Riwat, Pakistan), and in southern China (Longgupo). The Plio-Pleistocene carnivores associated with humans are also known from Greece (Mygdonia Basin).

The commonalties among these sites call for a new interpretation of early *Homo erectus*. All these sites fall into the transcontinental Tethys geotectonic corridor, the grand suture at the southern margin of the Eurasian continental plate with southward extensions into the East African Rift and the Sunda subduction zone. A global time marker immediately precedes and overlaps with all sites, the Olduvai subchron (1.96 to 1.79 mya). With the corridor and the subchron, we can begin to talk about *Homo erectus* biogeography as neither African nor East Asian, but as Plio-Pleistocene Tethys.

The corridor's linear geotectonic structure includes convergent plate margins from Iberia to Sunda; rift valleys and plate imbrication zones from equatorial East Africa to the Caucasus. During the Olduvai subchron, major Tethys geotectonic events (including the Aullan sea regression in the west and the emergence of Sunda in the east) served to open virgin territory from west to east. With large body size, striding gait, carnivorous diet, and elemental technology—and a relatively small brain—early *Homo* apparently found advantage in the realm's linear structure and the subchron's geotectonic instability. Arising in the equatorial western realm near the beginning of the Olduvai subchron, early *Homo erectus* dispersed throughout the realm by or just after subchron end.

Biogeographically, early *Homo* is a Plio-Pleistocene Tethys lineage, with long-lived branches in East Africa and East Asia, and possibly in extreme southern Europe. Morphological variation across the realm is still incompletely known and potentially very complex. The new Sangiran data indicate that the two known equatorial populations (Sunda and East African Rift Valley) encephalized in parallel already by the early Pleistocene. Whatever their importance for later developments in *Homo*, neither a large brain nor a complex stone technology served this hominid's initial intercontinental dispersals. Alternatively, the Tethys geotectonic landscapes may have provided this early human species its greatest advantage and provided the distinction between it and the numerous preceding australopiths.

ACKNOWLEDGMENTS

For financial support, we thank the L.S.B. Leakey Foundation, the Collaborative Interdisciplinary Project (CIP) award program in the University of Iowa Office of the Vice President for Research, and the Human Evolution Research Fund at the University of Iowa Foundation. We also gratefully acknowledge a gift from Dr. Todd Roehr. Finally, we thank the Indonesian Institute of Sciences (Lembaga Ilmu Pengetahuan Indonesia) for making our research project in Indonesia possible.

REFERENCES

Djubiantono, T. and F. Sémah. 1993. "L'île de Java et son peuplement." In F. Sémah, A. -M. Sémah, and T. Djubiantono (eds.), *Le Pithecanthrope de Java*, pp. 12–19, Les Dossiers d' Archeologie, no. 184.

Gabunia L., S. C. Antón, D. Lordkipandze, A. Vekua, A. Justus, and C. C. Swisher III. 2001. "Dmanisi and Dispersal." *Evolutionary Anthropology* 10: 158–170.

Gibert, J., L. Gibert, C. Ferrández-Canyadell, A. Iglesias, and F. González. 2001. "Venta Micena, Barranco León-5 and Fuentenueva-3: Three Archaeological Sites in the Early Pleistocene deposits of Orce, South-East Spain." In S. Milliken and J. Cook (eds.), *A Very Remote Period Indeed: Papers on the Paleolithic Presented to Derek Roe*, pp. 144–152, Oxford, Oxbow Books.

Huffman, O. F. 2001. "Geologic Context and Age of the Perning/Mojokerto *Homo erectus*, East Java." *Journal of Human Evolution* 40: 353–362.

Koufus, G. D. 1992. "The Pleistocene Carnivores of the Mygdonia Basin (Macedonia, Greece)." *Annales de Paléontologie* 78: 205–257.

Larick, R., and R. L. Ciochon. 1996. "The African Emergence and Early Asian Dispersals of the Genus *Homo*." *American Scientist* 84: 538–552.

Larick, R., R. L. Ciochon, and Y. Zaim. 1999. "Fossil Farming in Java." *Natural History* 108(6): 54–57.

Larick, R., R. L. Ciochon, Y. Zaim, Sudijono, Suminto, Y. Rizal, and F. Aziz. 2000. "Lithostratigraphic Context for Kln-1993.05-SNJ, a Fossil Colobine Maxilla from Jokotingkir, Sangiran Dome." *International Journal of Primatology* 21: 731–759.

Larick, R., R. L. Ciochon, Y. Zaim, Sudijono, Suminto, Y. Rizal, F. Aziz, M. Reagan, and M. Heizler. 2001. "Early Pleistocene ^{40}Ar/^{39}Ar Ages for Bapang Formation Hominins, Central Jawa, Indonesia." *Proceedings of the National Academy of Sciences, USA* 98(9): 4866–4871.

Rendell, H. M., E. Hailwood, and R. W. Dennell. 1987. "Paleomagnetic Dating of a Two-Million-Year-Old Artefact-Bearing Horizon at Riwat, Northern Pakistan." *Earth and Planetary Sciences Letters* 85: 488–496.

Sémah, F., A. -M. Sémah, T. Djubiantono, and H. T. Simanjuntak. 1992. "Did They Also Make Stone Tools?" *Journal of Human Evolution* 23: 439–446.

Swisher III, C. C., G. H. Curtis, T. Jacob, A. G. Getty, A. Suprijo, and Widiasmoro. 1994. "Age of the Earliest Known Hominids in Java, Indonesia." *Science* 263: 1118–1121.

Vekua, A., D. Lordkipanze, G. P. Rightmire, J. Agusti, R. Ferring, G. Maisuradze, A. Mouskhelishvili, M. Noiradze, M. Ponce de Leon, M. Tappen, M. Tvalchrelidze, and C. Zollikofer. 2002. "A New Skull of Early *Homo* from Dmanisi, Georgia." *Science* 297: 85–89.

Wanpo, H., R. Ciochon, G. Yumin, R. Larick, F. Qiren, H. Schwarcz, C. Yonge, J. de Vos, and W. Rink. 1995. "Early *Homo* and Associated Artefacts from Asia." *Nature* 378: 275–278.

Zhu, R. X., K. A. Hoffman, R. Potts, C. L. Deng, Y. X. Pan, B. Guo, C. D. Shi, Z. T. Guo, B. Y. Yuan, Y. M. Hou, and W. W. Huang. 2001. "Earliest Presence of Humans in Northeast Asia." *Nature* 413: 413–417.

42

Homo erectus Calvarium from the Pleistocene of Java

H. Baba, F. Aziz, Y. Kaifu, G. Suwa, R. T. Kono, and T. Jacob

ABSTRACT

A Homo erectus calvarium [Sambungmacan 4 (Sm 4)] was recovered from Pleistocene sediments at Sambungmacan in central Java. Micro-computed tomography analysis shows a modern human-like cranial base flexion associated with a low platycephalic vault, implying that the evolution of human cranial globularity was independent of cranial base flexion. The overall morphology of Sm 4 is intermediate between that of earlier and later Javanese Homo erectus; apparent morphological specializations are more strongly expressed in the latter. This supports the hypothesis that later Pleistocene Javanese populations were substantially isolated and made minimal contributions to the ancestry of modern humans.

Javanese *Homo erectus* is best represented by the Early and Middle/Late Pleistocene remains found at Trinil, Sangiran, and Ngandong (*1–4*). Shared features of these hominids have led to the notion of continuous regional evolution in Java (*5–7*) as part of a broader *H. erectus* species distribution (*8, 9*). However, the actual evolution of Asian *H. erectus* is uncertain (*7, 8*), and phyletic relationships concerning *H. erectus*, other archaic *Homo*, and modern humans remain unresolved (*6–11*). Aside from the widely acknowledged increase of cerebral mass (*12*), the underlying morphogenetic basis of the transition from *H. erectus* to *H. sapiens* has only begun to be explored. Here we describe a new calvarium, Sambungmacan 4 (Sm 4). We analyzed Sm 4 by micro-computed tomography (micro-CT)–based visualization and compared it with other Javanese crania.

In the Sambungmacan area, two partial calvaria (Sm 1 and Sm 3) and a tibia fragment (Sm 2) of *H. erectus* were previously recovered (*13–15*). Affinities with the Ngandong series were suggested for the two calvaria (*13, 15*), although some regarded Sm 1 as intermediate between the Trinil/Sangiran and Ngandong hominids (*6*). The new adult calvarium, Sm 4, was discovered on 1 October 2001, between Mlale village of the Jenar district and Cemeng village of the Sambungmacan district in central Java (Figure 1). It was found 4 km west of where Sm 1 was found in 1973, and 100 m upstream from where Sm 3 was discovered in 1997 (*15*). The specimen was found along the Solo River during the collection of sand for construction material, but it shows no obvious signs of fluvial transport or surface weathering. Fossiliferous sediments of Middle Pleistocene age crop out upstream (*16*). Sm 4 preserves all calvarial elements, including those of the cranial base except the ethmoid. There is no obvious postmortem distortion, and osseous surface detail is excellent.

Sm 4 is larger than most other *H. erectus* specimens and probably belonged to a male. Most cranial sutures show minimal to moderate closure, suggesting that the individual was middle-aged or younger. There are several shallow depressions on the intact frontal squama and anterior parietals, the surfaces of which show characteristics of healed scars, as has been reported for several calvaria from Ngandong (*17*), 40 km east of Sambungmacan.

The overall morphology of Sm 4 is that of *H. erectus*, and it shares many features with Javanese representatives of the species (Figure 2, A to E). The vault is long and low, with the maximum breadth across the supramastoid crests. The thick supraorbital torus is relatively

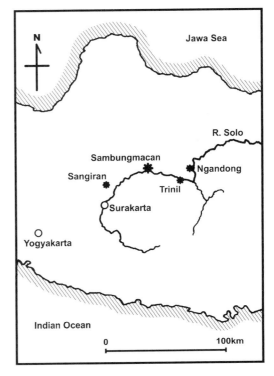

Figure 1. *Location map.*

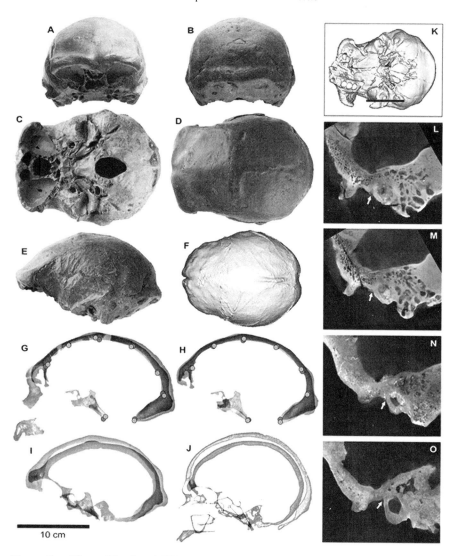

Figure 2.   *Views of Sm 4 and CT imagery of Sm 4 and comparative materials. Anterior (A), posterior (B), basal (C), superior (D), and lateral (E) views of Sm 4 are shown. (F) Superior view of virtual endocast. Superimposed midsagittal sections of Sm 4 (black) and Sangiran 17 (gray) (G) and of Sm 4 (black) and Ngandong 12 (gray) (H) are shown. (I) Mid- (gray) and parasagittal (black) sections of Sm 4 and (J) of a modern human cranium. Sagittal micro-CT sections of the mandibular fossa were taken just medial to the lateral edge of the tympanic, which position is shown for Sangiran 17 (K). The sections are Sangiran 17 right (L) and left (M), Sm 4 left (N), and Ngandong 12 left (O). Arrows indicate the position of the squamotympanic fissure. Landmarks plotted in (G) and (H) were determined from the serial micro-CT images as follows: anterior pole of the endocranium, midpoint on the internal endocranial contour between the anterior pole point and internal bregma, internal bregma, midpoint on the internal endocranial contour between the internal bregma and lambda, internal lambda, posterior pole of the endocranium, opisthion, and basion. The anterior and posterior pole points were defined as the most anterior and posterior points in an axis parallel to the glabella-inion line, in the serial parasagittal sections, projected onto the midsagittal section. Registration of Sm 4 and Sangiran 17 or Ngandong 12 was done by the Procrustes technique of superimposition (centroid size standardization and least-squares fit of the eight landmarks). Parasagittal sections of (I) and (J) were taken through the maximum anterior projections of the temporal pole of the middle cranial fossa. Images (L) to (O) were obtained by reformatting the serial micro-CT images. In Ngandong 12 (O), the entire squamous portion of the fossa inclines posterosuperiorly, so that the deepest part of the fossa occurs posteriorly at the squamotympanic fissure. Contrary to previous assessments (7, 15), Sangiran 17 does not show this peculiar morphology. The squamous portion of the fossa exhibits a broad and deep concavity placed anterior to the squamotympanic fissure. This is typical of both modern humans and other fossil hominids. The micro-CT image (M) reveals a postmortem crack passing through the deepest portion of the left mandibular fossa of Sangiran 17. Sm 4 is intermediate between Ngandong 12 and Sangiran 17.*

Table 1.   Cranial Base Metrics of Sm 4 and the Comparative Materials

		Cranial Base Angle						Temporal Pole Position			Orbital Roof Angle		
		CBA1			CBA4			TP1			ORA1		
		Mean	SD	Range	Mean	SD	Range	Mean	SD	Range	Mean	SD	Range
Modern human	This study, *n* = 9	136	4.7	128.5–141	110	8.5	98–122	0.40	0.046	0.35–0.50	11.9	3.58	6–18
	Spoor, 1997 (*35*), *n* = 48	138	4.9		—			—			—		
	McCarthy, 2001 (*34*), *n* = 60	136	5.2		111	6.8		—			—		
	Ross and Henneberg, 1995 (*22*), *n* = 93	—			112	7.4	92–135	—			—		
Sm 4	This study	141			97			0.30			20		
Ngandong 12	This study	—			—			(0.29)			—		
OH 9	Ross and Henneberg, 1995 (*22*)	—			93–104			—			—		

Cranial base angle 1 (CBA1) is the angle between the basion-sella and sella-foramen caecum and CBA4 is the angle between the clival plane and planum sphenoideum (*34*). TP1 is the ratio between the sella-temporal pole distance and the sella-foramen caecum length. The temporal pole point is defined as the most anterior point of the middle cranial fossa projected onto the midsagittal plane perpendicular to the sella-foramen caecum line. ORA1 is the angle between the sella-foramen caecum line and the line connecting the posterosuperior point of the tuberculum sellae and the anteroinferior pole of the anterior cranial fossa projected onto the midsagittal section. The anteroinferior pole point was defined on the parasagittal section passing through the middle of the foramen ovale. Values derived from the right and left sides were averaged in both TP1 and ORA1. The TP1 estimate of Ngandong 12 is based on its temporal pole position and preserved sella turcica floor. The approximate locations of the sella and foramen caecum were derived from Procrustes superimposition of Ngandong 12 with Sm 4.

straight in front view, as is typical in *H. erectus* of Java. The strong coronal and parietal keels are continuous with the weaker frontal keel via the bregmatic eminence. The occipital bone is sharply angled at the well-developed occipital torus. Suprameatal and supramastoid crests are marked, and angular tori are extensive on the mastoid angles of the parietals. The thick tympanic plates are coronally oriented. The styloid process is lacking. Sm 4 lacks characteristic features of Chinese *H. erectus* represented by the Zhoukoudian specimens, such as the continuous supratoral sulcus, steeply rising frontal squama with salient tuberosities, narrow occiput, relatively large biauricular breadths with markedly inclined temporal walls, and medially restricted petrosal crest (*5, 7, 17, 18*).

The endocranial capacity of Sm 4 is 1006 cm³, on the basis of volume rendering of 592 serial CT scans taken at a slice thickness and pitch of 340 μm (*19*). The virtual endocast (Figure 2F) exhibits left occipital petalia, as is common in other *H. erectus* remains and modern humans (*12*). The internal occipital crest is broad, and inion is widely separated from endinion. The frontal sinus is restricted relative to Euro-African specimens such as Kabwe and Petralona (*20*), with limited lateral and no posterior extensions.

Presumed male representatives of the Sangiran and Ngandong series, Sangiran 17 and Ngandong 12, that best preserve the cranial base were compared with Sm 4. In sagittal profile, the endocranial contour is comparably platycephalic in all three crania, but Ngandong 12 exhibits a slightly more depressed cranial base and higher frontal profile than does Sm 4 or Sangiran 17 (Figure 2, G and H). The thickness of the frontal bone at the glabella or nasion is weaker in Sm 4 and Ngandong 12 than in Sangiran 17. Overall, differences in cranial morphology tend to be more clearly manifested externally, whereas all three crania revealed a remarkably similar endocranial shape.

The cranial base flexion of *H. erectus* has hitherto been estimated in a single damaged specimen, OH 9, from the early Pleistocene of Africa. Our results show that the cranial base flexion of Sm 4 was as strong as in modern humans (Table 1 and Figure 2, I and J) (*21*), as was suggested by OH 9 (*22*), but reports of two Kenyan specimens from the earliest Pleistocene have left open the possibility that early *H. erectus* might have been characterized by a less flexed condition (*23*). The strong cranial base flexion of Javanese *H. erectus* suggests that midsagittal flexion did not play a decisive role in either the reduction of facial projection or the emergence of neurocranial globularity [compare with (*24, 25*)].

Despite the derived condition of the midsagittal endocranial base, the structure of the more lateral endocranial base of Javanese *H. erectus* is distinct from that of modern humans (Figure 2, I and J). The orbital axis of *Australopithecus* and, to a lesser degree, archaic *Homo* has been described as more anterodorsally oriented than in modern humans (*20, 22*). Although the same axis could not be measured in Sm 4, the inclination of the superior orbital roof is more anterodorsal than in modern humans (Table 1). In Sm 4 and Ngandong 12, the middle cranial fossa does not extend anteriorly as far as in modern humans (*26*) (Table 1). Changes in orbital orientation and temporal pole position are likely correlates of a general restructuring of anterior and middle cranial fossae associated with cerebral expansion. The length between the sella and the anterior temporal pole in our CT data sets corresponds to the "anterior sphenoid length" of previous radiographic studies (*24*). Our results indicate that the primitive condition of *Homo* was probably a shorter sphenoid, in concert with Spoor et al.'s (*27*) analysis of archaic *Homo*. The importance of the lateral cranial base in the development of facial form has been emphasized in modern humans (*28*), although such structural and developmental relations remain unclarified in evolutionary perspective.

Table 2. Cranial Characters That Differentiate the Javanese *H. erectus* Subgroups, and the Phenetic Condition of the Sambungmacan Calvaria (*19*)

Cranial Characters	Trinil/Sangiran	Sm 1	Sm 3	Sm 4	Ngandong
1. Cranial capacity (cm³)	813–1059	1035	918	1006	1013–1251
2. Relatively high vault	(–)	+	+	–	(+)
3. Moderately swollen frontal squama and posterior parietals	–	+	+	int	+
4. Postorbital constriction comparatively weaker	–	+	+	+	+
5. Strong temporal gutter	–	int	–	+	+
6. Reduced relative area of temporal muscle attachment	–	+	+	+	+
7. Extremely linear supraorbital torus in front view	–	+?	+	int	(+)
8. Laterally thickened supraorbital torus	–	int	+	+	+
9. No supraglabellar depression with right and left supratoral planes discontinuous	–	int	+	int	(+)
10. Extensive, plateau-like angular torus	(–)	+	+?	+	(+)
11. Anteroposteriorly elongated parietal incisura	–	int	+	int	+
12. Wide supramastoid sulcus	–	int	+	int	(+)
13. Large mastoid with triangular base	–	int	+	int	+
14. Specialized mandibular fossa morphology	–	int	+	int	+
15. Well-developed tympano-mastoid fissure	(–)	int	+	+	+
16. Less extensive digastric fossa associated with well-developed paramastoid crest	–	int	?	int	+
17. Vertically set occipital squama	–	+	+	+	+
18. Marked projection of occipital torus	(–)	–	–	+	(+)
19. Lower arm of occipital torus stronger than the upper	–	int	+	int	(+)
20. Extreme expression of an excavated nuchal planum	–	–	–	–	(+)
21. Opisthionic recess of foramen magnum present	–	?	+	+	+
22. Strong postcondyloid tuberosity	–	?	+	+	+

These characters were taken or modified from the literature (*5, 7, 8, 13, 15, 17*), except for item 11. For items 2 through 22, the morphological condition of interest is listed in the first column. Each subgroup/specimen exhibits either the listed condition "+," a different condition "–," or a partial expression of that condition "int." Parentheses indicate notably variable conditions. Item 14 refers to a mandibular fossa characterized not only by an anteroposteriorly short, deep fossa with the squamotympanic fissure situated in the deepest portion, but also by a laterally extended tympanic plate forming the "posterior wall" of the fossa and minimal or no development of the postglenoid process (Figure 2). The African *H. erectus* OH 9 differs in the latter aspects. Characters 7 to 10, 14, 16, 18, and 20 to 22 are possibly uniquely derived features characteristic of the Ngandong series.

The midsagittal cranial base flexion of archaic *H. sapiens* such as Kabwe has been suggested to be weaker than in modern humans by about 15° (*22, 24, 25*). The apparent contradiction of stronger cranial base flexion in Javanese *H. erectus* may reflect any of the following possibilities. First, it may simply reflect normal levels of intraspecific variation, with both *H. erectus* and archaic *H. sapiens* possessing comparable modal conditions. An inferred strong flexion in Bodo (*29*), another African example of archaic *H. sapiens*, supports this hypothesis. Second, a strong cranial base flexion might have been characteristic only of later *H. erectus* but not of *H. erectus* in general, a hypothesis contradicted by the OH 9 estimate. Finally, archaic *H. sapiens* may have secondarily acquired a more extended cranial base from the ancestral *H. erectus* condition. A possible mechanism for this might be a situation in which a slightly greater degree of postnatal extension of the cranial base occurred through interrelation with somatic growth.

Our analyses also offer new insights into the evolutionary history of Javanese *H. erectus* and into the ongoing controversy surrounding the origin of modern humans. Sm 4 is similar to Sangiran 17 and other Trinil/Sangiran specimens in its platycephalic cranial shape and lack of a strongly excavated nuchal plane. Sm 4 and Sm 1 are intermediate between Trinil/Sangiran and Ngandong, or close to Ngandong, in many other features (Table 2). Sm 4 also exhibits the rare presence of a foramen ovale subdivided by a bony bridge, as do some of the Ngandong specimens (*17*). In most of these features, Sm 3 exhibits the Ngandong series condition (*15*) (Table 2).

We conducted principal component analyses (PCAs) of several sets of metric data (*19*) to examine phenetic similarities among specimens without making a priori assumptions about grouping. A recent overview of Asian *H. erectus* contrasted the Javanese and Chinese samples from PCAs of cranial capacity and four cranial vault measurements (*7, 30*). Our results of five length, breadth, and height variables of the cranial vault (Figure 3) and evaluations of individual bones demonstrate the intermediate state of the Sambungmacan specimens within the Javanese series in relative cranial height and in temporal bone size and shape. In parietal and occipital bone size and shape, the Javanese crania cluster tightly, with subsample ranges of variation overlapping extensively.

The combined evidence suggests that Sm 4 (and Sm 1) represent a transition linking the Trinil/Sangiran and Ngandong hominids morphologically and possibly temporally. Our analysis also demonstrates that later Javanese *H. erectus* exhibits a suite of unique features (Table 2). These include aspects of mandibular fossa and foramen magnum morphologies (*15, 17*), which

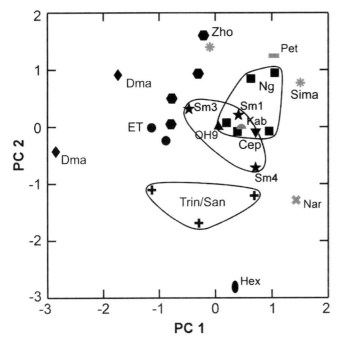

Figure 3. *First and second principal component (PC) scores of linear measurements of the whole vault. Variables are as follows: maximum cranial length, minimum frontal breadth, maximum cranial breadth, biasterionic breadth, and porion-bregma height. PC 1 (which accounts for 76% of the variance) gives greater scores if the vault is larger overall; PC 2 (which accounts for 11% of the variance) gives greater scores if the biasterionic breadth is narrower and the vault is higher.* H. erectus *specimens are black symbols and later archaic* Homo *specimens are gray symbols. Sm1, Sm3, Sm4, the Sambungmacan specimens, are indicated by stars. Hex, Hexian is indicated by an ellipse; Nar, Narmada is indicated by an X; Kab, Kabwe is indicated by a half circle; Cep, Ceprano is indicated by an inverted triangle; Pet, Petralona is indicated by a rectangle; Dma, Dmanisi is indicated by a diamond; Zho, Zhoukoudian is indicated by a hexagon; Ng, Ngandong is indicated by a square; OH9 is indicated by a triangle; Trin/San, Trinil/Sangiran is indicated by a +; ET, East Turkana is indicated by a circle; Sima, Sima de los Huesos is indicated by an asterisk.*

changed from an ancestral condition (the Trinil/Sangiran condition, which is closer to that seen in modern humans), to one more derived in later Javanese forms (Ngandong) (Figure 2, L to O). The morphological distinctiveness of the Javanese *H. erectus* lineage apparently intensified over time. This might have occurred through episodic range contraction and fragmentation, as glacial cycles recurred throughout the Pleistocene (*7, 31*). If *H. erectus* avoided tropical forest habitats, gene pool fragmentation was probably accentuated in peak interglacial periods, although details of the regional paleoenvironmental history and habitat preference of *H. erectus* are little known (*32, 33*).

REFERENCES AND NOTES

1. R. Larick et al., *Proc. Natl. Acad. Sci. U.S.A.* **98**, 4866 (2001).
2. M. Hyodo et al., *J. Hum. Evol.* **43**, 27 (2002).
3. G. D. Van den Bergh, J. De Vos, P. Y. Sondaar, F. Aziz, *Indo-Pac. Prehist. Assoc. Bull.* **14**, 7 (1996).
4. C. C. Swisher III et al., *Science* **274**, 1870 (1996).
5. A. P. Santa Luca, *The Ngandong Fossil Hominids: A Comparative Study of a Far Eastern Homo erectus Group* (Department of Anthropology, Yale Univ., New Haven, CT, 1980).
6. M. H. Wolpoff, *Paleoanthropology* (McGraw-Hill, New York, ed. 2, 1999).
7. S. C. Antón, *Am. J. Phys. Anthropol.* **118**, 301 (2002).
8. G. P. Rightmire, *The Evolution of Homo erectus: Comparative Anatomical Studies of an Extinct Human Species* (Cambridge Univ. Press, Cambridge, 1990).
9. B. Asfaw et al., *Nature* **416**, 317 (2002).
10. J. Hawks et al., *J. Hum. Evol.* **39**, 1 (2000).
11. C. Stringer, *Philos. Trans. R. Soc. London Ser. B* **357**, 563 (2002).
12. R. L. Holloway, in *Handbook of Human Symbolic Evolution*, A. Lock, C. R. Peters, Eds. (Blackwell, Oxford, 1999), pp. 74–125.
13. T. Jacob, in *Homo erectus: Papers in Honor of Davidson Black*, B. A. Sigmon, J. S. Cybulski, Eds. (Univ. of Toronto Press, Toronto, Canada, 1981), pp. 87–104.
14. S. Matsu'ura et al., *Curr. Anthropol.* **41**, 297 (2000).
15. E. Delson et al., *Anat. Rec.* **262**, 380 (2001).
16. Vertebrate fossils recovered from the Sm 4 findspot vary in preservation, suggesting a mixed assemblage composed of fossils from multiple sources upstream. Outcrops that we identified, within 6 km upstream of the find, include those that belong to the traditional Kabuh Formation of this area. On the basis of its adhering matrix, Sm 4 is likely to have derived from this series.
17. F. Weidenreich, *Anthropol. Pap. Am. Mus. Nat. Hist.* **43**, 205 (1951).
18. F. Weidenreich, *Palaeontol. Sin. New Ser. D* **10**, 1 (1943).
19. Materials and methods are available as supporting material in the Appendix.
20. H. Seidler et al., *J. Hum. Evol.* **33**, 691 (1997).
21. Our micro-CT analysis of Ngandong 12 revealed a damaged clivus and missing dorsum sellae, tuberculum sellae, and planum sphenoideum regions. This precludes a numerical evaluation of its cranial base flexion. The entire region from the sella turcica to the planum sphenoideum is missing in Sangiran 17. However, the floor of the sella turcica is preserved in Ngandong 12, and the clivus in Sangiran 17, allowing a comparison of approximate alignments with Sm 4 (Figure 2, G and H). This suggests a cranial base, in both Ngandong 12 and Sangiran 17, that is broadly compatible with the Sm 4 condition of flexion. As far as we are aware, no account of cranial base flexion of Ngandong 7 has been published.
22. C. Ross, M. Henneberg, *Am. J. Phys. Anthropol.* **98**, 575 (1995).
23. F. Spoor, *Am. J. Phys. Anthropol. Suppl.* **30**, 288 (2000).
24. D. E. Lieberman, C. F. Ross, M. J. Ravosa, *Yrbk. Phys. Anthropol.* **43**, 117 (2000).
25. D. E. Lieberman, B. M. McBratney, G. Krovitz, *Proc. Natl. Acad. Sci. U.S.A.* **99**, 1134 (2002).
26. In Sm 4, the anterior temporal pole outline intersects the midline cranial base profile close to the tuberculum sellae, whereas the same intersection in modern humans occurs at a position approximately at the middle of the planum sphenoideum (Figure 2, I and J).

27. F. Spoor, P. O'Higgins, C. Dean, D. E. Lieberman, *Nature* **397**, 572 (1999).
28. M. Bhat, D. E. Enlow, *Angle Orthodont.* **55**, 269 (1985).
29. F. Bookstein et al., *Anat. Rec.* **257**, 217 (1999).
30. S. Antón, S. Marquez, K. Mowbray, *J. Hum. Evol.* **43**, 555 (2002).
31. G. Hewitt, *Nature* **405**, 907 (2000).
32. G. D. van den Bergh, J. de Vos, P. Y. Sondaar, *Palaeogeogr. Palaeoclimatol. Palaeoecol.* **171**, 385 (2001).
33. F. J. Gathorne-Hardy, Syaukani, R. G. Davies, P. Eggleton, D. T. Jones, *Biol. J. Linn. Soc.* **75**, 453 (2002).
34. R. C. McCarthy, *J. Hum. Evol.* **40**, 41 (2001).
35. F. Spoor, *S. Afr. J. Sci.* **93**, 182 (1997).

36. We thank Darsono for the recovery of Sm 4; Sudijono, T. Sihombing, I. Kumiawan, A. Hikmat, E. Indriati, A. Suprijo, P. H. Sulistyarto, R. A. Suriyanto, J. M. Susanto, and people of Mlale and Cemeng for fieldwork; J. Arif for access to Tjg-1993.05; H. Otsuka for stratigraphic interpretations; T. Suzuki for observations of possible traumatic bone alteration on Sm 4; F. Spoor for comments on *H. erectus* cranial base lengths and flexion; S. Matsukawa and M. Chubachi for assistance; and T. White and E. Delson for suggestions. We thank the Geological Research and Development Centre, Bandung, for permission and support. This work was supported by the National Science Museum, Tokyo, and the Japan Society for the Promotion of Science.

APPENDIX

MATERIALS AND METHODS

The comparative Javanese sample of the present study consists of crania from the Trinil/Sangiran, Sambungmacan, and Ngandong groups, with sample sizes of 10, 2, and 9, respectively. Observed original specimens from Java are Sangiran 10, 12, 17, 37, 38; Tjg-1993.05, Sbk-1996.02; Sm1, 3; and Ngandong 1, 11, 12. Dento-gnathic evidence suggests significant morphological differences between the Sangiran assemblage from the Bapan [Kabuh] formation above the Grenzbank zone and that from the Grenzbank zone and upper Sangiran [Pucangan] F. (*S1*). Because of this, only cranial materials from the former were included in the Trinil/Sangiran sample of this study. Two specimens with indeterminate chronostratigraphic position, Trinil 2 and Sangiran 2, were tentatively included in the Trinil/Sangiran sample but exclusion of these does not affect the results. See Table S1 for a complete list of the comparative specimens. External morphological data of Sm 4 and other original specimens were taken by H.B. and Y.K., and the CT data were taken by G.S. and R.T.K.

CT analyses were performed on Sm 4, Ngandong 12, and Sangiran 17, using the microfocal X-ray CT system (TX225-Actis, Tesco/BIR) of the University Museum, University of Tokyo. Serial slices of 340-μm thicknesses were taken at 340-μm intervals (or 500-μm thickness and intervals in the case of Sangiran 17). Each section was reconstructed in 512 by 512 matrix size, with about 600 slices for a cranium. Multiplanar reformatting, three-dimensional volume rendering, and other image processing procedures were undertaken predominantly with Analyze 4.0 (Mayo Clinic). Our comparative modern human sample of the CT analysis is a multiethnic sample of nine modern humans, including four Australians, two Europeans, one Buriat, one Hawaiian, and one African crania. Cranial capacity of Sm 4 was estimated by determining the modal endocranial threshold value and digitally blocking the foramina at their endocranial openings.

Table S1. List of the Comparative Specimens

Specimen	Source of Data
Java	
Sambungmacan: Sm 1, 3	*S2*
Trinil/Sangiran: Trinil 2; Sangiran 2, 3, 10, 12, 17, 37, 38; Tjg-1993.05, Sbk-1996.02	*S2, S3, S4, S5*
Ngandong: Ngandong 1, 3, 5, 6, 7, 9, 10, 11, 12	*S2, S3, S4, S6*
East Eurasia	
Zhoukoudian (China): Skull 2, 3, 5, 10, 11, 12	*S3, S5*
Hexian (China), Dali (China), Narmada (India)	*S3, S7, S8, S9*
West Eurasia	
Dmanisi (Georgia); D2280, 2282	*S9, S10*
Ceprano (Italy), Petralona (Greece)	*S4, S11, S12*
Sima de los Huesos (Spain): Cranium 4, 5, 8; Occipital IV	*S13*
Africa	
East Turkana (Kenya): KNM-ER 3733, 3883	*S3, S4*
Olduvai (Tanzania): OH9	*S3, S4*
Daka (Ethiopia); Bodo (Ethiopia), Kabwe (Zambia), Ndutu (Tanzania)	*S3, S4, S12, S14*

Table S2. Measurements of Sm 4 (in mm)

Cranial capacity (cm^3)	1006
Maximum cranial length	198
Maximum cranial breadth	156
Minimum frontal breadth	110
Maximum frontal breadth	121
Biasterionic breadth	134
Porion-bregma height	102
Frontal sagittal chord	113
Frontal sagittal arc	123
Parietal sagittal chord	98
Parietal sagittal arc	102
Occipital sagittal chord	80
Occipital sagittal arc	113
Lambda-asterion chord (side average)	86
Lambda-asterion arc (side average)	93
Lambda-opisthokranion chord	54
Opisthokranion-opisthion chord	55
Supraorbital torus thickness (medial, side average)	14.5
Supraorbital torus thickness (lateral, side average)	16.5
Cranial thickness at bregma	10

REFERENCES AND NOTES

S1. Y. Kaifu et al., unpublished data.
S2. This study on the original specimens.
S3. This study on casts.
S4. G. P. Rightmire, *The Evolution of* Homo erectus. *Comparative Anatomical Studies of an Extinct Species* (Cambridge Univ. Press, Cambridge, 1990).
S5. F. Weidenreich, *Paleontol. Sinica New Ser. D* **10**, 1 (1943).
S6. A. P. Santa Luca, *The Ngandong Fossil Hominids. A Comparative Study of a Far Eastern* Homo erectus *Group* (Dept. of Anthropology, Yale Univ., New Haven, 1980).
S7. R. Wu, X. Dong, *Acta Anthropologica Sinica* **1**, 2 (1983).
S8. K. A. R. Kennedy, A. Sonakia, J. Chiment, K. K. Verma, *Am. J. Phys. Anthropol.* **86**, 475 (1991).

S9. A. Vekua et al., *Science* **297**, 85 (2002).
S10. L. Gabunia et al., *Science* **288**, 1019 (2000).
S11. A. Ascenzi, F. Mallegni, G. Manzi, A. G. Serge, E. Segre Naldini, *J. Hum. Evol.* **39**, 443 (2000).
S12. R. I. Murrill, *Petralona Man. A Descriptive and Comparative Study, with New Important Information on Rhodesian Man* (Charles C. Thomas, Springfield, 1981).
S13. J. L. Arsuaga, I. Martínez, A. Gracia, C. Lorenzo, *J. Hum. Evol.* **33**, 219 (1997).
S14. B. Asfaw et al., *Nature* **416**, 317 (2002).

43

Latest *Homo erectus* of Java

Potential Contemporaneity with *Homo sapiens* in Southeast Asia

C. C. Swisher III, W. J. Rink, S. C. Antón, H. P. Schwarcz, G. H. Curtis, A. Suprijo, and Widiasmoro

ABSTRACT

Hominid fossils from Ngandong and Sambungmacan, Central Java, are considered the most morphologically advanced representatives of Homo erectus. *Electron spin resonance (ESR) and mass spectrometric U-series dating of fossil bovid teeth collected from the hominid-bearing levels at these sites gave mean ages of 27 ± 2 to 53.3 ± 4 thousand years ago; the range in ages reflects uncertainties in uranium migration histories. These ages are 20,000 to 400,000 years younger than previous age estimates for these hominids and indicate that* H. erectus *may have survived on Java at least 250,000 years longer than on the Asian mainland, and perhaps 1 million years longer than in Africa. The new ages raise the possibility that* H. erectus *overlapped in time with anatomically modern humans* (H. sapiens) *in Southeast Asia.*

The geologic age and taxonomic affinity of hominid fossils from Ngandong and Sambungmacan, Central Java, bear directly on the controversy surrounding the origin of anatomically modern humans (*H. sapiens*). Proponents of a regional continuity model for the origin of *H. sapiens* consider that these fossils are both morphologically and temporally transitional between Javanese *H. erectus*, such as Sangiran 17, that are older

than 780,000 years ago (ka), and early robust Australian *H. sapiens*, such as Willandra Lakes Hominid (WLH) 50, that first appear about 30 ka (*1*, *2*). The opposing view is that *H. sapiens* arose in Africa less than 200 ka and only recently spread out over Europe and Asia, replacing existing populations of hominids with little or no interbreeding (*3*–*5*). Both views recognize strong morphological continuity between mid-Pleistocene Javanese *H. erectus* and the Ngandong and Sambungmacan hominids, but differ in how these hominids relate to *H. sapiens* (*1*, *3*, *6*, *7*). Here, we present geochronological data that suggest that *H. erectus* persisted in Southeast Asia much longer than in either Africa or mainland Asia, and may have coexisted in time with *H. sapiens*.

Hominid fossils were discovered at Ngandong in 1931, 40 years after the discovery of the type *H. erectus* specimen at Trinil (Figure 1). Between 1931 and 1933, the Dutch Geological Survey in Java conducted excavations in a 50 by 100 m area that yielded over 25,000 vertebrate fossils, including a total of 12 hominid calvaria and partial calvaria and two hominid tibiae (*8*). In excavations by Gadjah Mada University (GMU) between 1976 and 1980 in an adjacent 25 by 14 m area, an additional 1200 vertebrate fossils were recovered, including two partial hominid calvaria and hominid pelvic fragments (*9*). In both excavations, most of the 26,000 fossil vertebrates and all of the hominids were concentrated in an interval 50 cm or less thick near the base of a 0- to 3-m thick terrace deposit of the Solo River (Figure 1) (*8*). The Ngandong terrace, also referred to as the High

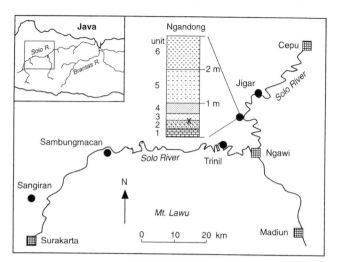

Figure 1.   *Map showing location of the Ngandong, Sambungmacan, and Jigar sites, Central Java, Indonesia. At Ngandong, a general stratigraphic section, modified slightly from (8), is shown adjacent to the site. Hominid and nonhominid fossils (X) were recovered from Unit 2 in volcaniclastic sandstone with cobbles of underlying Pliocene marl. In our test pit, we were not able to distinguish Units 4 and 5, whereas Unit 6 is probably recent alluvium. Similar findings were reported by Bartstra et al. (10).*

Terrace (*10*), is situated 20 m above the level of the present-day Solo River in the Kendeng Hills region and is traceable for some 15 km (*10*). The fossiliferous interval consists of volcaniclastic sandstone intermixed with marl cobbles from the unconformably underlying Pliocene Kalibeng Formation. Fossil accumulations at Ngandong, and in outcrops of the 20-m terrace deposit elsewhere, occur primarily at bends of the present-day Solo River (*11*), suggesting that the river had a similar course in the past and that the 20-m terrace is geomorphologically young.

The fragmentary nature of the fossils at Ngandong and their association with fluvial sediments suggest that they have been transported by water, although the presence in the nonhominid fossils of a few articulated vertebrae and a few crania with associated mandibles indicates that the amount of transport was minimal. Likewise, both hominid and nonhominid crania show little evidence of abrasion because fragile processes such as the pterygoid plates are preserved (*12*). Most of the fossils consist of isolated teeth, single and partial elements, and fragments (*8, 12*). Despite recent claims to the contrary (*6*), no complete skeletons were found (*13*). The lack of systematic study of the nonhominid fossils, rather than taphonomic processes, may explain why so few hominid postcranial elements (two tibiae and partial pelvic fragments) were reported from the Ngandong excavations because fragmentary hominid remains may have gone unidentified among the fauna (*6, 14*). Except for the few fossils described by von Koenigswald housed at the Geological Research and Development Center (GRDC), most of the 25,000 fossils from the original Dutch excavations appear to be lost (*15*).

Age estimates for the Ngandong fossil site have varied widely. Faunal correlations, as well as the geomor-phology of the site, indicate that the fossil site is late Pleistocene in age (*8, 16*). However, a mid-Pleistocene age has been suggested for the hominids on the basis of morphological comparisons with *H. erectus* fossils elsewhere and because the hominids might have been reworked from older deposits into the late Pleistocene faunal assemblage (*6, 17*). All of the available evidence, however, indicates that the hominid and nonhominid faunas from Ngandong are of the same age. Photographs of Ngandong hominid calvaria V and VI show that the hominids were found in situ among the nonhomind fauna in the same Solo River terrace (*7, 8, 18*). Similar bone preservation and chemistry of the hominid and nonhominid fauna (*12, 19–21*) and the improbability of selectively reworking 15 hominids from the underlying marine marls or from upstream mammalian fossil-bearing exposures (the nearest located 30 km away) argue against any differential age sorting of the nonhominid and hominid fauna (*11*).

Radioisotopic ages reported for the Ngandong and Sambungmacan hominids are based on dates on volcanic rocks within the Notopuro (Pojajar) Formation at Sangiran (*22, 23*). However, the fossil-poor Notopuro Formation has been shown to be older than the Solo River terraces (*10, 24, 25*). More recently, U-series dating of fossil bone chips from Ngandong have given ages between 31 and 101 ka (*10, 25*). Subsequent U-series dating of only the outer surface of the bone fragments yielded ages between 109 and 188 ka, whereas whole bone samples gave dates of 55 to 59 ka (*10, 25, 26*). These results showed that the outer surfaces of the bone had lost uranium long after uranium had been adsorbed by the bone and that ^{230}Th had grown partially into equilibrium with ^{234}U (*27*). Therefore, the true age may be younger than the whole bone analyses because these dates also incorporate a portion of the uranium-depleted bone (*26, 28*).

Our attempts to find primary volcanic material at Ngandong proved futile. ^{40}Ar/^{39}Ar analyses of detrital volcanic minerals collected from the overlying colluvium at the site gave dates ranging from over 400 to 100 ka (*29*), giving us a maximum age for the site. We decided to apply combined electron spin resonance (ESR) and U-series dating techniques to Ngandong fossil bovid tooth enamel (*30, 31*). We collected tooth samples from a 1-m-deep test pit in the terrace deposit at Ngandong, adjacent to the area quarried by Oppenoorth in the 1930s. At 220 cm below the present surface we encountered a zone consisting of volcaniclastic sandstone with cobbles of underlying Pliocene marl similar to that described by Oppenoorth as Layer 2 (Figure 1). Much of the upper 2 m appeared to represent colluvium, possibly including some of the debris from the original 1930's quarry. Layer 2 was only about 30 cm thick in our test pit, but was found to contain numerous vertebrate fossils. We excavated three small pits 10 to 20 cm in diameter down through the 30-cm-thick interval. In two of the pits, we recovered well-preserved fossil bovid teeth (95296 and 95297). The teeth and the adjacent sediment were collected for ESR and U-series dating. Five dosimeters were placed into the wall of the excavation at and above the fossil-bearing layer for external dose rates and left in the site for 1 year (*32*). We also collected a bovid tooth (95301) and associated sediment from a test pit in a terrace deposit located approximately 7 km downstream from Ngandong near the village of Jigar where GMU had recovered abundant fossil vertebrates. The terrace deposit at Jigar (Figure 1) is 19 m above the Solo River and its nonhominid fauna is considered to be similar to that of Ngandong (*33*).

To assure ourselves that we had excavated the same layer from which the Ngandong hominids were collected, we obtained bovid teeth from museum collections at GRDC and GMU. Bovid tooth GRDC 6679 was collected from Oppenoorth's layer 2, 15 February 1932, between the finds of Ngandong hominid calvaria IV (25 January 1932) and V (17 March 1932). A second bovid tooth was also obtained from the collections of the 1976–1980 GMU excavations from which Ngandong hominid calvarial fragments XIV and XV were discovered. The hominid calvaria and tibia from Sambungmacan (Figure 1) are considered morphologically similar to the Ngandong hominids (*34*). Fluorine analyses of the Sambungmacan hominid tibia gave similar values as the nonhominid fauna, indicating that they are of similar age (*34, 35*). We obtained a bovid tooth from the 1973 GMU excavation for direct age comparison with Ngandong.

ESR and U-series dating of bovid tooth enamel from Ngandong, Sambungmacan, and Jigar (Tables 1 and 2) were done at McMaster University following previously described preparatory and analytical methods (*30, 36, 37*). Two models of uranium uptake are generally considered in order to calculate an ESR age. In the early uptake (EU) model, it is assumed that all uranium in the tooth was adsorbed early in the burial history, whereas in the linear uptake (LU) model it is assumed that the uptake was continuous and constant throughout the burial history. The EU model yields the minimum age for a given data set provided that there has

been no loss of uranium. LU-ESR ages have often agreed well with ages from other dating methods (*31*), although EU-ESR ages have been shown to agree well with radiocarbon and U-series ages in many geological settings (*38, 39*).

The teeth from all of the sites contained high concentrations of uranium (Tables 1 and 2). The dentine values are particularly high, and exceed values for any previously measured site of similar age (*40*). The EU-ESR ages are consequently significantly lower than

Table 1. ESR Dates on Fossil Bovid Teeth from Central Java

Specimen Number	Lab No.[*]	U-en (ppm)	U-den (ppm)	LU Age (ka ± 1σ)	EU Age (ka ± 1σ)
Ngandong					
94NG-T1	95296A	6.2	186.4	48.1 ± 2.3	28.4 ± 1.3
	95296B	15.9	201.3	42.0 ± 2.5	24.1 ± 1.5
94NG-T2	95297A	11.9	192.2	48.6 ± 3.0	27.6 ± 1.7
	95297B	15.1	184.1	47.8 ± 3.1	27.0 ± 1.8
GRDC-1932	95393A	14.01	130.7	41.1 ± 4.8	23.7 ± 2.8
GDJM-1978	94762A	9.2	67.4	50.0 ± 5.8	30.4 ± 3.5
	Mean =			46.3 ± 3.7	26.9 ± 2.2
Jigar					
	95301A	0.5	78.1	39.9 ± 3.0	27.2 ± 1.9
	95301B	0.6	87.7	39.7 ± 2.3	26.6 ± 1.4
	Mean =			39.8 ± 0.1	26.9 ± 0.4
Sambungmacan					
(UGM-1973)	94761A	6.02	104.4	53.3 ± 4.0	32.4 ± 2.4

[*]A,B = samples prepared from different parts of the same tooth.

U-en, uranium concentration enamel; U-den, uranium concentration dentine. Uncertainty in uranium measurements are 1 ppm. EU and LU, uranium uptake modes; see text for full explanation. Neutron activation analysis yielded the following ranges of radioelements in the sediments from Ngandong: U—1.13 to 1.56 (±0.1) ppm; Th—4.41 to 6.27 (±0.17 to 0.36) ppm; and K—0.52 to 0.73 (±0.3 to 0.4) % by weight.

Table 2. U-Series Dates on Fossil Bovid Teeth from Ngandong, Central Java. All isotope ratios shown are activity ratios. Decay constant for ^{230}Th = 9.193 × 10^{-6} year^{-1}; ^{234}U = 2.833 × 10^{-6} year^{-1}. En, enamel; Den, dentine; ESD, micrometer's of enamel removed from outer (sediment) and inner (dentine) sides of tooth prior to dating. Uncertainties for uranium concentration, and ^{234}U/^{238}U, ^{230}Th/^{234}U, ^{230}Th/^{232}Th ratios are 2σ uncertainties in the last digits.

Material	ESD	U (ppm)	^{234}U/^{238}U	^{230}Th/^{234}U	^{230}Th/^{232}Th	Age ka ± 2σ
94NG-T1 (95296)						
Den	n.a.	188(1)	1.042(6)	0.548(5)	9315(100)	85.8 ± 1.2
En1	0/0	11.92(5)	1.082(5)	0.350(2)	713(2)	46.6 ± 0.3
En2	51/54	11.16(3)	1.078(3)	0.316(5)	486(8)	41.1 ± 0.8
94NG-T2 (95297)						
Den	n.a.	131(2)	1.07(13)	0.579(3)	3077(4)	92.8 ± 0.8
En1	0/0	17.12(7)	1.072(5)	0.30(1)	44(2)	37.6 ± 1.7[*]
En2	0/36	16.52(8)	1.084(5)	0.345(4)	111(1)	46.0 ± 0.7[*]
En5	69/0	17.56(8)	1.084(7)	0.317(8)	993(27)	41.3 ± 1.4
En4	29/0	15.78(8)	1.072(6)	0.271(5)	132(3)	33.8 ± 0.8[*]
GRDC-1932 (95393)						
En1	0/0	15.62(9)	1.030(6)	0.298(3)	2689(25)	38.5 ± 0.4
En2	32/25	19.39(8)	1.042(4)	0.249(1)	3355(7)	31.0 ± 0.2
En3	73/65	8.34(3)	1.027(4)	0.26(1)	423(20)	32.0 ± 1.8[*]
En4	109/102	9.18(3)	1.034(4)	0.252(3)	1040(5)	31.5 ± 0.2

[*]Age corrected for detrital thorium.

the LU-ESR ages, although both models yield late Pleistocene ages. All of the teeth from the three separate excavations at Ngandong using either model give similar ages, indicating that the fossils from the site are of a single age and are not differentially reworked from older deposits. Similar ESR ages were obtained on Sambungmacan and Jigar teeth supporting the temporal correlation of these three sites (Table 1).

In order to evaluate the appropriate uranium uptake model for the dated teeth, we made mass-spectrometric U-series analyses of Ngandong enamels and dentine. Grün et al. (*41*) showed that, if early uptake of uranium had occurred, then the U-series and EU-ESR ages should agree, because all U-series ages are computed on the assumption that uranium uptake was early. If uranium uptake had occurred continuously after deposition, the U-series age should be younger than the EU-ESR age (*39, 42*). However, at Ngandong the U-series ages (Table 2) are all older than the EU-ESR age (Table 1). This pattern could be a result of leaching of uranium from the teeth late in their burial history, leaving the less soluble ^{230}Th behind, thus increasing the ^{230}Th/^{234}U and the U-series age. To test for this, we analyzed teeth from which we had removed outer layers of enamel of varying thickness. In all cases where outer (sediment-side) enamel layers were removed, the ages were less than or equal to the age of the whole enamel (Table 2). This result confirms that uranium has been leached from the outer part of the enamel late in its burial history, causing an increase in the ^{230}Th/^{234}U ratio (and thus the apparent U-series age) of the whole enamel. Removal of the outer layers of the tooth generally resulted in a slight decrease in the uranium concentration of the remaining material, even though we argue that the stripped (outer) portion had lost uranium. This effect is attributed to the original distribution of uranium in the teeth prior to uranium loss from the outer (surface) enamel. As observed by fission track mapping of uranium in teeth from other young sites, the concentration of uranium is typically highest near the enamel's outer surface and decreases inward (*38*).

The decrease in age after stripping of the outer surfaces of enamel agrees with U-series analyses of surface bone from Ngandong that indicate uranium loss (*26*). Stripping enamel from the inner (dentine) side of one sample (95297Den) yielded a higher age compared with the whole enamel age, possibly because of uptake from the uranium-rich dentine (Table 2). Analysis of the dentine from the Ngandong teeth gave apparent ages near 90 ka (Table 2). These old ages are similar to those obtained on bone (*26*), further confirming the greater tendency of dentine and bone to lose uranium compared to denser enamel.

Even though the U-series ages of the tooth enamel, after removal of the outermost enamel layer, approach the EU-ESR ages (*37*), this is not proof that the EU model correctly describes the uranium uptake history of the teeth. The stripping experiments show that there has been some increase in age as a result of uranium loss; however, we cannot be sure exactly how much increase has occurred. If the ages before uranium loss occurred were significantly lower than the EU-ESR age, then an

LU model would be more appropriately applied to the ESR ages. A conservative conclusion from these experiments is that the true ages lie somewhere between the EU- and LU-ESR ages, but the complexities introduced by later uranium loss prevent a definitive assignment of an uranium uptake model. The EU and LU models give mean ESR ages of 27 ± 3 to 46 ± 4 ka for Ngandong, 27 ± 0.4 to 39.8 ± 0.1 ka for Jigar, and 27 ± 3 to 53 ± 4 ka for Sambungmacan (Table 1) (*37*), whereas our youngest U-series ages obtained from our Ngandong enamel stripping experiments was 31.0 ± 0.2 ka (Table 2).

The new dates from Ngandong and Sambungmacan are surprisingly young and, if proven correct, imply that *H. erectus* persisted much longer in Southeast Asia than elsewhere in the world. The youngest securely dated crania of African *H. erectus* come from Bed IV at Olduvai Gorge dated at older than 1 Ma (*43*), whereas the youngest mainland Asia *H. erectus* are older than 290 ka or 420 ka based on two U-series dating studies of the Layer 1-2 travertine at Zhoukoudian, China (*44–47*). Although the young ages for the Ngandong and Sambungmacan hominids might suggest that they should be grouped with early Australasian *H. sapiens* rather than with *H. erectus* (*1*), such an approach disregards morphological attributes unique to each of these groups of hominids. Although the Ngandong and Sambungmacan hominids possess a relatively large braincase for *H. erectus,* they retain Southeast Asian *H. erectus* autapomorphies, including cranial superstructures and vault shapes that distinguish them from the early Australasian *H. sapiens* (*3, 6, 48, 49*). On the other hand, the features shared by Ngandong *H. erectus* and the early Australasian *H. sapiens* are equally prevalent in fossil hominids from North Africa, suggesting that these features may be plesiomorphic (*49*).

If the Ngandong and Sambungmacan hominids represent a late-surviving sample of *H. erectus* (*50*), then the unilineal transformation in Southeast Asia from early and mid-Pleistocene *H. erectus* to the early Australasian *H. sapiens*—with Ngandong and Sambungmacan as intermediate steps, as proposed by the multiregional theory for the origin of *H. sapiens*—is no longer chronologically plausible. Rather, our ages for Ngandong and Sambungmacan indicate that *H. erectus* persisted in Southeast Asia into the latest Pleistocene overlapping in time with *H. sapiens* and raise the possibility that features shared by the two species are either homoplastic or the result of gene flow (*51*). In Africa and the Near East, *H. sapiens* first appear in the fossil record around 100 ka (*52*), and in mainland Asia perhaps by 67 ka (*45*). On Java, the oldest known *H. sapiens* date to less than 10 ka (*53*); however, evidence elsewhere in Southeast Asia indicates that *H. sapiens* arrived much earlier. Early *H. sapiens* date to about 30 ka in Australia (*54*) and possibly to 40 ka in Malaysia (*55*), whereas archaeological remains attributed to *H. sapiens* occur as early as 40 ka in New Guinea (*56*) and 50 ka (or greater) in Australia (*17, 57*). The temporal and spatial overlap between *H. erectus* and *H. sapiens* in Southeast Asia, as implied by our study, is reminiscent of the overlap of Neandertals (*H. neanderthalensis*) (*58*) and anatomically modern humans (*H. sapiens*) in Europe (*59*).

REFERENCES AND NOTES

1. M. H. Wolpoff, A. G. Thorne, J. Jelinek, Z. Yingun, *Cour. Forschungsinst. Senckenb.* **171**, 341 (1994).
2. A. G. Thorne and M. H. Wolpoff, *Am. J. Phys. Anthropol.* **55**, 337 (1981). Note, however, that Webb considers WLH-50 pathological [S. Webb, *Paleopathology of Aboriginal Australians: Health and Disease of a Hunter-Gatherer Continent* (Cambridge Univ. Press, Cambridge, 1995)].
3. G. P. Rightmire, *Cour. Forschungsinst. Senckenb.* **171**, 319 (1994).
4. C. B. Stringer and C. Gamble, *In Search of the Neanderthals* (Thames and Hudson, London, 1992); C. B. Stringer, in *Continuity or Replacement: Controversies in* Homo sapiens *Evolution*, G. Bräuer and F. H. Smith, Eds. (Balkema, Rotterdam, 1992), pp. 9–24.
5. G. Bräuer, in *Continuity or Replacement: Controversies in* Homo sapiens *Evolution*, G. Bräuer and F. H. Smith, Eds. (Balkema, Rotterdam, 1992), pp. 83–98.
6. A. P. Santa Luca, *Yale Univ. Publ. Anthropol.* **78** (1980).
7. F. Weidenreich, *Anthropol. Pap. Am. Mus. Nat. Hist.* **43**, 205(1951).
8. W. F. F. Oppenoorth, *Natur Mus.* **62**, 269 (1932); *Wet. Meded.* **20**, 49 (1932); *Kon. Ned. Aardr. Genootsch. Tijdschr.* **53**, 399 (1936); C. ter Haar, *Ing. Ned. Indië Mijning.* **4**, 51 (1934).
9. I. Moelyadi, *Proy. Penel. Paleoanthropol. Nas. Yogyak.*, (1982).
10. G.-J. Bartstra, S. Soegondho, A. van der Wijk. *J. Hum. Evol.* **17**, 325 (1988).
11. C. Swisher, personal field observation.
12. Personal observation of GRDC, and GMU museum collections by S. C. Antón and C. C. Swisher.
13. G. H. R. von Koenigswald, *Meeting Prehistoric Man* (Thames and Hudson, New York, 1956).
14. Unpublished notes, F. Weidenreich, in American Museum of Natural History, Department of Library Services.
15. F. Aziz, GRDC, personal communication
16. G. H. R. von Koenigswald, *Ing. Ned. Indië Mijning.* **1**, 185 (1934).
17. R. Klein, *The Human Career* (Univ. of Chicago Press, Chicago, 1989).
18. Unpublished G. H. R. von Koenigswald photographs, Senckenberg Museum, Frankfurt Am Main, Germany.
19. A. Bartsiokas and M. H. Day, *Proc. R. Soc. London B* **252**, 115(1993).
20. T. Jacob, in *Catalogue of Fossil Hominids, Part III: Americas, Asia, Australia.* K. P. Oakley, B. G. Campbell, T. I. Molleson, Eds. [British Museum (Natural History), London, 1975], pp. 103–115.
21. *F/P* = 0.06 for Ngandong calvaria V and *F/P* = 0.046 for nonhominid bone; *Catalogue of Fossil Hominids, Part III: Americas, Asia, Australia*, K. P. Oakley, B. G. Campbell, T. I. Molleson, Eds. [British Museum (Natural History), London, 1975].
22. M. Suzuki, Wikarno, Budisantoso, I. Saefundin, M. Itihara, in *Quaternary Geology of the Hominid Fossil Bearing Formations in Java*, N. Watanabe and D. Kadar, Eds. (Spec. Publ. 4, Geological Research and Development Centre, Bandung, Indonesia, 1985), pp. 309–358.
23. F. C. Howell, *L'Anthropologie* **90**, 447 (1986).
24. M. Itihara, T. Shibasaki, Sudijono, T. Hayashi, K. Furuyama, in (*22*), pp. 63–68.
25. G.-J. Bartstra, *Palaeohist. Gröningen* **29**, 1 (1987).
26. J. van der Plicht, A. van der Wijk, G. J. Bartstra, *Appl. Geochem.* **4**, 339 (1989).
27. A. Milard and R. Hedges, *Archaeol. Sci.* **22**, 200 (1995).
28. H. P. Schwarcz and B. Blackwell, in *Uranium Series Disequilibrium: Application to Environment Problems in Earth Science*, M. Ivanovich and R. S. Harmon, Eds. (Oxford Univ. Press, London, ed. 2, 1991), p. 513.
29. C. C. Swisher III, unpublished data.
30. R. Grün, H. P. Schwarcz, S. Zymela, *Can. J. Earth Sci.* **24**, 1022 (1987).
31. R. Grün and C. B. Stringer, *Archaeometry* **33**, 153 (1991).
32. The internal rates measured on the teeth are so high that the external dose as determined from the dosimeters will have no measurable affect on the calculated age.
33. G. Nitihaminoto and I. Moelyadi, *Pusat Penel. Purbak. Pening. Nas,* 1–40 (1977).
34. T. Jacob, in *Homo erectus: Papers in Honor of Davidson Black*, B. A. Sigmon and J. S. Cybulski, Eds. (Toronto University Press, Toronto, 1981), pp. 87–104; S. Matsu‡ura, N. Watanabe, F. Aziz, T. Shibasaki, M. Kondo, *Bull. Nat. Sci. Mus. Tokyo Ser. D (Anthropol.)* **16**, 19 (1990).
35. G. P. Rightmire, *The Evolution of* Homo erectus (Cambridge Univ. Press, Cambridge, 1993).
36. W.-X. Li, J. Lundberg, A. P. Dickin, D. C. Ford. H. P. Schwarcz, *Nature* **339**, 534 (1989); W. J. Rink et al., *J. Archaeol. Sci.* **21**, 839 (1994).
37. Associated sediment collected less than 10 cm from the in situ teeth was collected for estimation of beta and gamma dose rates. We used the in-situ sediment collected near 95297 at Ngandong to estimate dose rates to museum teeth 94762 and 95393 from Ngandong, and 94761 from Sambungmacan. The internal dose rates for all teeth are high, and slight variations in the composition of enclosing sediment used for museum samples would have negligible effect on the calculated ages. The ESR ages (Table 1) were calculated using the standard program DATA of R. Grün. The ESR ages were also calculated using new ESR dating software called ROSY (B. J. Brennan, W. J. Rink, E. L. McGuirl, H. P. Schwarcz, W. V. Prestwich, *Radia. Meas.*, **27**, 307 (1997)) using "One-Group" theory for beta dose attenuation in enamel. Using this method, both the EU- and LU-ESR ages are approximately 4000 years older than those using the DATA program. The mean EU age for Ngandong would be 31.4 ± 3.5 ka and agrees more closely with the U-series ages of 30 to 40 ka for the stripped enamels U-series ages.
38. C. R. McKinney, thesis, Southern Methodist University (1991).
39. R. Grün and F. McDermott, *Quat. Sci. Rev. (Quat. Geochronol.)* **13**, 121 (1994).
40. R. Grün and L. Taylor, *Ancient Thermolumia* **14**, 21 (1996).
41. R. Grün, H. P. Schwarcz. J. Chadam, *Nucl. Tracks* **14**, 237 (1988).
42. F. McDermott, R. Grün, C. B. Stringer, C. J. Hawkesworth, *Nature* **363**, 252 (1993).
43. E. Tamarat, N. Thouveny, M. Taieb, N. D. Opdyke, *Palaeogeogr. Palaeoclimatol. Palaeoecol.* **114**, 273 (1994).
44. C. Tiemei and Y. Sixun, *Archaeometry* **30**, 59 (1988).
45. Y. Sixun, C. Tiemei, G. Shijun, *Acta Anthropol. Sin.* **5**, 179 (1986); more recently, P. Brown [*Philos. Trans. R. Soc.* (1993)] has argued that there is no clear association of this date with the hominid skull at Liujiang.
46. Y. Sixun, C. Tiemei, G. Shijun, H. Yanqui, *Acta Anthropol. Sin.* **10**, 189 (1991).
47. S. Guanjun and J. Linhong, *ibid.*, p. 273; R. Ku, personal communication.
48. S. C. Antón, in preparation; P. Brown, *Archaeol. Oceania* **16**, 156 (1981); *Terra Aust.* **13** (1989); N. W. G. Macintosh and S. L. Lamach, in *The Origin of the Australians*, R. L. Kirk and A. G. Thorne Eds. (Humanities, Atlantic Highlands, NJ, 1976), p. 113; S. Webb, *Paleopathology of Aboriginal Australians: Health and Disease of a Hunter-Gatherer Continent* (Cambridge Univ. Press, Cambridge, 1995); N. W. G. Macintosh and S. L. Larnach, *Arch. Phys. Anthropol. Oceania* **7**, 1 (1972), and refs. 1 and 7 therein.
49. M. M. Lahr, *J. Hum. Evol.* **26**, 23 (1994).
50. F. C. Howell, in *Origins of Anatomically Modern Humans*, M. H. Nitecki and D. V. Nitecki, Eds. (Plenum, New York, 1994), p. 253.
51. J. H. Relethford and C. B. Stringer, in preparation.
52. H. P. Schwarcz and R. Grün, *Philos. Trans. R. Soc. London B* **337**, 145 (1992); H. Valladas et al., *Nature* **331**, 614 (1988).
53. P. Storm, *Scri. Geol.* **110**, 1 (1996); R. Shutler, in *Felicitation for R. P. Soejdono*, in press.
54. J. M. Bowler, A. G. Thorne, H. A. Polach, *Nature* **240**, 48 (1972).
55. D. R. Brothwell, *J. Sarawak Mus.* **323**, 1 (1960). There appears to be some question as to whether the ^{14}C dates are physically related to the Niah Cave hominid remains.
56. L. Groube, J. Chappell, J. Muke, D. Price, *Nature* **324**, 453 (1986).
57. R. G. Roberts, R. Jones, M. A. Smith, *ibid.* **345**, 153 (1990); P. G. Bahn, *ibid.* **383**, 577 (1996); R. L. K. Fullager, D. M. Prince, L. M. Head, *Antiquity* **70**, 751 (1996).
58. I. Tattersall and J. Schwartz, *Proc. Nat. Acad. Sci. U.S.A.* **96**, 7117 (1999).
59. Predecessors to Neandertals first appear by the Mid-Pleistocene in Western Europe [E. Carbonell et at., *Science* **269**, 826 (1995); H. de Lumley and M.-A. de Lumley, *C. R. Acad. Sci. Paris* **272**, 1729

(1971)], whereas classical Neandertals persist until nearly 30 ka [J. K. Kozlowski, *Excavations in the Bacho Kiro Cave, Bulgaria (final report)* (Paristwowe Wydaruynictwo, Naukowe, Warsaw, 1982); J. L. Bischoff, N. Soler, J. Maroto, R. J. Julia, *J. Archaeol. Sci.* **16**, 553 (1989)], overlapping in time and space with anatomically modern humans that first appear in Europe and Western Asia around 40 to 50 ka [J. J. Hublin, C. Barroso Ruiz, P. Medina Lara, M. Fontugni, J.-L. Reyss, *C. R. Acad. Sci. Paris* **321**, 931 (1995); J. J. Hublin, F. Spoor, M. Braun, F. Zonneveld, S. Condemi, *Nature* **381**, 224 (1996); C. B. Stringer and R. Grün, *ibid.* **351**, 701 (1991); M. H. Wolpoff and D. Frayer, *ibid.* **356**, 200 (1992); D. Frayer, in

Continuity or Replacement: Controversies in Homo sapiens Evolution, G. Bräuer and F. H. Smith, Eds. (Balkema, Rotterdam, 1992), pp. 179–188].

60. This project was supported by NSF (SBR-9405320) and L. S. B. Leakey Foundation grants to C.C.S. and G.H.C. Partial support for ESR and U-series dating was by NSF grant SBR-9410906 to H. Schwarcz; laboratory assistance was by K. Googer and J. Johnson. We would like to thank T. Jacob and F. Aziz for their help with field arrangements and museum specimens and C. B. Stringer, who provided valuable comments on an earlier draft of this manuscript.

44

A New Small-Bodied Hominin from the Late Pleistocene of Flores, Indonesia

P. Brown, T. Sutikna, M. J. Morwood, R. P. Soejono, Jatmiko, E. Wayhu Saptomo, and Rokus Awe Due

ABSTRACT

Currently, it is widely accepted that only one hominin genus, Homo, *was present in Pleistocene Asia, represented by two species,* Homo erectus *and* Homo sapiens. *Both species are characterized by greater brain size, increased body height and smaller teeth relative to Pliocene* Australopithecus *in Africa. Here we report the discovery, from the Late Pleistocene of Flores, Indonesia, of an adult hominin with stature and endocranial volume approximating 1 m and 380 cm³, respectively—equal to the smallest-known australopithecines. The combination of primitive and derived features assigns this hominin to a new species,* Homo floresiensis. *The most likely explanation for its existence on Flores is long-term isolation, with subsequent endemic dwarfing, of an ancestral* H. erectus *population. Importantly,* H. floresiensis *shows that the genus* Homo *is morphologically more varied and flexible in its adaptive responses than previously thought.*

The LB1 skeleton was recovered in September 2003 during archaeological excavation at Liang Bua, Flores[1]. Most of the skeletal elements for LB1 were found in a small area, approximately 500 cm^2, with parts of the skeleton still articulated and the tibiae flexed under the femora. Orientation of the skeleton in relation to site stratigraphy suggests that the body had moved slightly down slope before being covered with sediment. The skeleton is extremely fragile and not fossilized or covered with calcium carbonate. Recovered elements include a fairly complete cranium and mandible, right leg and left innominate. Bones of the left leg, hands and feet are less complete, while the

vertebral column, sacrum, scapulae, clavicles and ribs are only represented by fragments. The position of the skeleton suggests that the arms are still in the wall of the excavation, and may be recovered in the future. Tooth eruption, epiphyseal union and tooth wear indicate an adult, and pelvic anatomy strongly supports the skeleton being that of a female. On the basis of its unique combination of primitive and derived features we assign this skeleton to a new species, *Homo floresiensis*.

DESCRIPTION OF *HOMO FLORESIENSIS*

Order Primates Linnaeus, 1758

Suborder Anthropoidea Mivart, 1864

Superfamily Hominoidea Gray, 1825

Family Hominidae Gray, 1825

Tribe Hominini Gray, 1825

Genus *Homo* Linnaeus, 1758

Homo floresiensis sp. nov.

Etymology. Recognizing that this species has only been identified on the island of Flores, and a prolonged period of isolation may have resulted in the evolution of an island endemic form.

Holotype. LB1 partial adult skeleton excavated in September 2003. Recovered skeletal elements include the cranium and mandible, femora, tibiae, fibulae and patellae, partial pelvis, incomplete hands and feet, and fragments of vertebrae, sacrum, ribs, scapulae and clavicles. The repository is the Centre for Archaeology, Jakarta, Indonesia.

Referred Material. LB2 isolated left mandibular P_3. The repository is the Centre for Archaeology, Jakarta, Indonesia.

Localities. Liang Bua is a limestone cave on Flores, in eastern Indonesia. The cave is located 14 km north of Ruteng, the provincial capital of Manggarai Province, at an altitude of 500 m above sea level and 25 km from the north coast. It occurs at the base of a limestone hill, on the southern edge of the Wae Racang river valley. The type locality is at 08° 31′ 50.4″ south latitude 120° 26′ 36.9″ east longitude.

Horizon. The type specimen LB1 was found at a depth of 5.9 m in Sector VII of the excavation at Liang Bua. It is associated with calibrated accelerator mass spectrometry (AMS) dates of approximately 18 kyr and bracketed by luminescence dates of 35 ± 4 kyr and 14 ± 2 kyr. The referred isolated left P_3 (LB2) was recovered just below a discomformity at 4.7 m in Sector IV, and bracketed by a U-series date of 37.7 ± 0.2 kyr on flowstone, and 20 cm above an electron-spin resonance (ESR)/U-series date of 74^{+14}_{-12} kyr on a *Stegodon* molar.

Diagnosis. Small-bodied bipedal hominin with endocranial volume and stature (body height) similar to, or smaller than, *Australopithecus afarensis*. Lacks masticatory adaptations present in *Australopithecus* and *Paranthropus*, with substantially reduced facial height and prognathism, smaller postcanine teeth, and posteriorly oriented infraorbital region. Cranial base flexed. Prominent maxillary canine juga form prominent pillars, laterally separated from nasal aperture. Petrous pyramid smooth, tubular and with low relief, styloid process absent, and without vaginal crest. Superior cranial vault bone thicker than *Australopithecus* and similar to *H. erectus* and *H. sapiens*. Supraorbital torus arches over each orbit and does not form a flat bar as in Javan *H. erectus*. Mandibular P_3 with relatively large occlusal surface area, with prominent protoconid and broad talonid, and either bifurcated roots or a mesiodistally compressed Tomes root. Mandibular P_4 also with Tomes root. First and second molar teeth of similar size. Mandibular coronoid process higher than condyle, and the ramus has a posterior orientation. Mandibular symphysis without chin and with a posterior inclination of the symphysial axis. Posteriorly inclined alveolar planum with superior and inferior transverse tori. Ilium with marked lateral flare. Femur neck long relative to head diameter, the shaft circular and without pilaster, and there is a high bicondylar angle. Long axis of tibia curved and the midshaft has an oval cross-section.

DESCRIPTION AND COMPARISON OF THE CRANIAL AND POSTCRANIAL ELEMENTS

Apart from the right zygomatic arch, the cranium is free of substantial distortion (Figures 1 and 2). Unfortunately, the bregmatic region, right frontal, supraorbital, nasal and subnasal regions were damaged when the skeleton was discovered. To repair postmortem pressure cracks, and stabilize the vault, the calvarium was dismantled and cleaned endocranially before reconstruction. With the exception of the squamous suture, most of the cranial vault sutures are difficult to locate and this problem persists in computed tomography (CT) scans. As a result it is not possible to locate most of the standard craniometric landmarks with great precision.

The LB1 cranial vault is long and low. In comparison with adult *H. erectus* (including specimens referred to as *Homo ergaster* and *Homo georgicus*) and *H. sapiens* the calvarium of LB1 is extremely small. Indices of cranial shape closely follow the pattern in *H. erectus*. For instance, maximum cranial breadth is in the inflated supramastoid region, and the vault is broad relative to its height. In posterior view the parietal contour is similar to *H. erectus* but with reduced cranial height[2,3]. Internal examination of the neurocranium, directly and with CT scan data, indicates that the brain of LB1 had a flattened platycephalic shape, with greatest breadth across the temporal lobes and reduced parietal lobe development compared with *H. sapiens*. The cranial base angle (basion–sella–foramen caecum) of 130° is relatively flexed in comparison with both *H. sapiens* (mean 137°–138° (refs 4, 5)) and Indonesian *H. erectus* (Sambungmacan 4 141° (ref. 6)). Other small-brained hominins, for instance STS 5 *Australopithecus africanus*, have the primitive less-flexed condition.

The endocranial volume, measured with mustard seed, is 380 cm³, well below the previously accepted range for the genus *Homo*[7] and equal to the minimum estimates for *Australopithecus*[8]. The endocranial volume, relative to an indicator of body height (maximum femur length 280 mm), is outside the recorded hominin normal range (Figure 3). Medially, laterally and basally, the cranial vault bone is thick and lies within the range of *H. erectus* and *H. sapiens*[9,10]. Reconstruction of the cranial vault, and CT scans, indicated that for most of the cranial vault the relative thickness of the tabular bone and diploë are similar to the normal range in *H. erectus* and *H. sapiens*. In common with *H. erectus* the vault in LB1 is relatively thickened posteriorly and in areas of pneumatization in the lateral cranial base. Thickened vault bone in LB1, relative to that in *Australopithecus* and early *Homo*[2], results in a substantially reduced endocranial volume in comparison to Plio-Pleistocene hominins with similar external vault dimensions.

The occipital of LB1 is strongly flexed, with an occipital curvature angle of 101°, and the length of the nuchal plane dominates over the occipital segment. The occipital torus forms a low extended mound, the occipital protuberance is not particularly prominent compared with Indonesian *H. erectus* and there is a shallow supratoral sulcus. The endinion is positioned 12 mm inferior to the inion, which is within the range of *H. erectus* and *Australopithecus*[10]. Compared with *Australopithecus* and early *Homo*[2] the foramen magnum is narrow (21 mm) relative to its length (28 mm), and mastoid processes are thickened mediolaterally and are relatively deep (20.5 mm). In common with Asian, and some African, *H. erectus* a deep fissure separates the mastoid process from the petrous crest of the tympanic[10,11]. Bilaterally there is a recess between the tympanic plate and the entoglenoid pyramid. These two traits are not seen in modern humans, and show varied

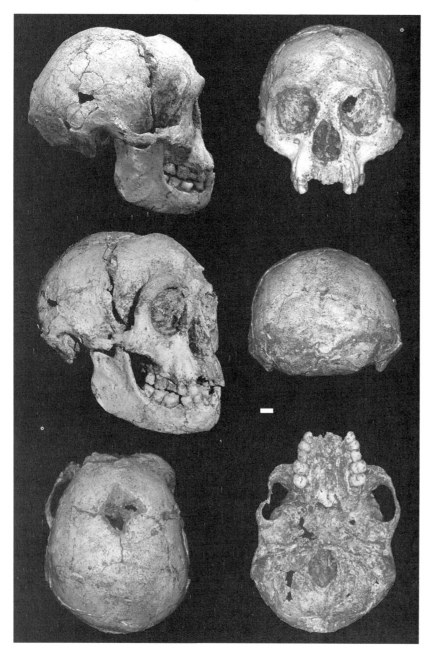

Figure 1. *The LB1 cranium and mandible in lateral and three-quarter views, and cranium in frontal, posterior, superior and inferior views. Scale bar, 1 cm.*

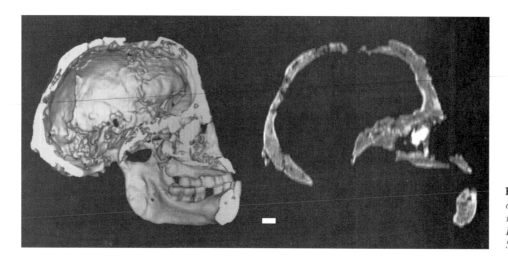

Figure 2. *Rendered three-dimensional and individual midsagittal CT section views of the LB1 cranium and mandible. Scale bar, 1 cm.*

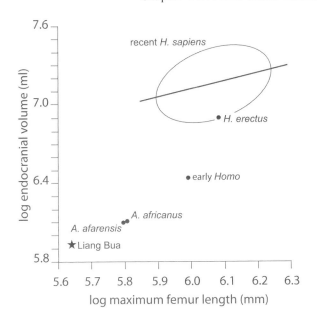

Figure 3. *Relationship between endocranial volume and femur length in LB1,* A. afarensis, A. africanus, *early* Homo sp., H. erectus *and modern* H. sapiens. *Modern human data, with least squares regression line and 95% confidence ellipse, from a global sample of 155 individuals collected by P.B.*

levels of development in Asian and African *H. erectus* and Pliocene hominins[10]. The depth and breadth of the glenoid fossae and angulation of the articular eminence are within the range of variation in *H. sapiens*. The inferior surface of the petrous pyramid has numerous similarities with Zhoukoudian *H. erectus*[12], with a smooth tubular external surface as in chimpanzees, and a constricted foramen lacerum. Styloid processes and vaginal crests are not present.

The temporal lines approach to within 33 mm of the coronal suture and have a marked posterior extension. There are no raised angular tori as is common in *H. erectus*[10] and some terminal Pleistocene Australians, and no evidence of parietal keeling. Posteriorly there is some asymmetrical obelionic flattening and CT scans indicate that the parietals reduce in thickness in this slightly depressed area (Figure 2). A principal component analysis (PCA) of five cranial vault measurements separates LB1, STS5 (*A. africanus*) and KNM-ER 1813 (early *Homo*) from other hominin calvaria in size and shape. Shape, particularly height and breadth relationships, placed LB1 closest to ER-3883, ER-3733 and Sangiran 2 *H. erectus*.

The face of LB1 lacks most of the masticatory adaptations evident in *Australopithecus* and its overall morphology is similar to members of the genus *Homo*[2,3]. In comparison with *Australopithecus*, tooth dimensions and the alveolar segment of the maxillae are greatly reduced, as are facial height and prognathism. The facial skeleton is dominated by pronounced canine juga, which form prominent pillars lateral to the nasal aperture. However, these are distinct from the anterior pillars adjacent to the nasal aperture in *A. africanus*[2,3]. The infraorbital fossae are deep with large infraorbital

foramina, the orbits have a particularly arched superior border and a volume of 15.5 cm³ (ref. 13). On the better preserved right-hand side, the supraorbital torus arches over the orbit and does not form a straight bar, with bulbous laterally projecting trigones, as in Indonesian *H. erectus*[11]. The preserved section of the right torus only extends medially slightly past mid-orbit, and the morphology of the glabella region and medial torus is unknown. In facial view the zygo-maxillary region is medially deep relative to facial height, and the inferior border of the malars are angled at 55° relative to the coronal plane. In lateral view the infraorbital region is orientated posteriorly as in other members of the genus *Homo*, rather than the more vertical orientation in *A. africanus*[2,3]. The root of the maxillary zygomatic process is centred above the first molar, and the incisive canal is relatively large and has an anterior location, contrasting with African and Javan *H. erectus*. In lateral view, curvature of the frontal squama is more similar to African early *Homo* and Dmanisi *H. ergaster*[3,14] than it is to the Javan hominins. The frontal squama is separated from the supraorbital torus by a supraorbital sulcus. In the middle third of the frontal there is a slight sagittal keel, extending into the remains of a low, broad prebregmatic eminence. On the midfrontal squama there is a circular healed lesion, probably the remains of a depressed fracture, which is about 15 mm across.

The mandible is complete, apart from some damage to the right condyle (Figure 4) and combines features present in a variety of Pliocene and Pleistocene hominins. Post-mortem breaks through the corpus at the right P_3 and M_2, and the left canine have resulted in some lateral distortion of the right ramus. There is a strong Curve of Spee. The ramus root inserts on the corpus above the lateral prominence, and in lateral aspect obscures the distal M_3. The ramus is broadest inferiorly, slopes slightly posteriorly and is thickened medio-laterally, and the coronoid process is higher than the condyle. The right condyle has a maximum breadth of 18 mm. There is a narrow and shallow extramolar sulcus and moderate lateral prominence. The anterior portion of the corpus is rounded and bulbous and without a chin. In the posterior symphyseal region the alveolar planum inclines postero-inferiorly, there is a moderate superior torus, deep and broad diagastric fossa, and the inferior transverse torus is low and rounded rather than shelf-like (Figure 4). There is a strong posterior angulation of the symphyseal axis, and the overall morphology of the symphysis is very similar to LH4 *A. afarensis* and unlike Zhoukoudian and Sangiran *H. erectus*. There are bilaterally double mental foramina, with the posterior foramina smaller and located more inferiorly. Double mental foramina are common in Indonesian *H. erectus*[15]. While the mandibular dental arch is narrow anteriorly, and long relative to its breadth, the axis of P_3–M_3 is laterally convex rather than straight (Figure 4).

The right P_4 is absent and the alveolus completely fused, the left P_4 was lost after death, and CT scans indicate that the maxillary right M^3 was congenitally absent. The relatively small and conical alveolus for the missing left M^3 suggests that it had a much smaller crown than

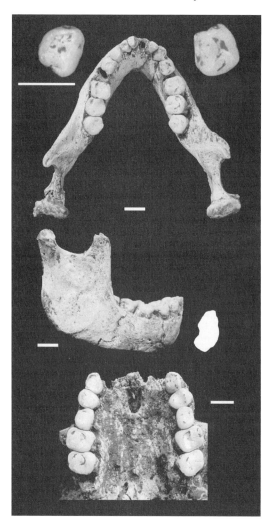

Figure 4. *Right lateral and occlusal views of the LB1 mandible, sagittal profile of the symphysis, occlusal view of the mandibular dentition and occlusal views of the mandibular premolars. Scale bars, 1 cm.*

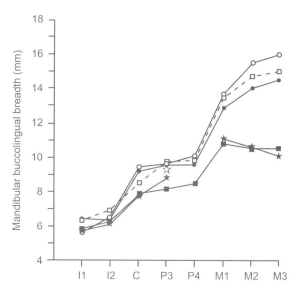

Figure 5. *Mean buccolingual tooth crown breadths for mandibular teeth in* A. afarensis *(filled circles),* A. africanus *(open circles), early* Homo *sp. (open squares), modern* H. sapiens *(filled squares), LB1 (filled stars) and LB2 (open stars). There are no mandibular P_4s preserved for LB1. Data for* Australopithecus *and early* Homo *are from ref. 49. Modern human data from a global sample of 1,199 individuals collected by P.B.*

M^1 and M^2. Size, spacing and angulation of the maxillary incisor alveoli, and absence of a mesial facet on the canines suggest that incisor I^2 was much smaller than I^1, and there may have been a diastema. Occlusal wear has removed details of cusp and fissure morphology from most of the maxillary and mandibular teeth. The canines have worn down to a relatively flat surface and there would have been an edge-to-edge bite anteriorly. Interproximal wear is pronounced and in combination with the loss of crown height means that mesio-distal crown dimensions convey little phylogenetic information. With the exception of P_3 the size and morphology of the mandibular teeth follow the pattern in *H. erectus* and *H. sapiens* (Figure 5). There is not a great deal of difference between the size of the molar teeth in each quadrant, and the size sequence for both mandibular and maxillary teeth is M1 ≥ M2 > M3. Using the megadontial quotient as a measure of relative tooth size[16], and substituting P_3 crown area for the missing P_4s, LB1 is megadont (1.8) relative to *H. sapiens* (0.9) and *H. ergaster* (0.9), but not

H. habilis (1.9) (ref. 8). The P_3s have a relatively great occlusal surface area (molariform) and when unworn had a prominent protoconid and broad talonid. Both P_3s have bifurcated roots and the alveolus for the left P_4 indicates a mesiodistally compressed, broad Tomes' root. A larger, less worn, isolated left P_3 from the deposit (LB2) has a more triangular occlusal outline, and a Tomes' root. Mandibular P_3s and P_4s with similar crown and root morphology have been recorded for *Australopithecus* and early *Homo*[17,18], and some Indonesian *H. erectus* mandibular premolars also have bifurcated or Tomes' roots[15]. Unusually, both maxillary P^4s are rotated parallel to the tooth row, a trait that seems to be unrecorded in any other hominin. Maxillary canines and P^3s have long roots and very prominent juga. The P^3 juga are emphasized by the rotation of the adjacent P^4 roots.

The pelvic girdle is represented by a right innominate, with damage to the iliac crest and pubic region, and fragments of the sacrum and left innominate. The right innominate, which is undistorted, has a broad greater sciatic notch suggesting that LB1 is a female (Figure 6). In common with all bipedal hominins, the iliac blade is relatively short and wide[19]; however, the ischial spine is not particularly pronounced. Compared with modern humans the LB1 ilium has marked lateral flare, and the blade would have projected more laterally from the body, relative to the plane of the acetabulum. The left acetabulum is of circular shape, and has a maximum width of 36 mm.

Apart from damage to the lateral condyle and distal shaft, the right femur is complete and undistorted (Figure 7). The overall anatomy of the femur is most consistent with the broad range of variation in *H. sapiens*,

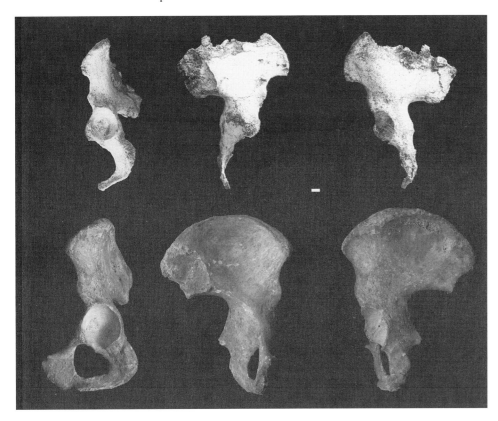

Figure 6. *Comparison of the left innominate from LB1 with a modern adult female* H. sapiens. *Lateral (external), and medial and lateral views of maximum iliac breadth. The pubic region of LB1 is not preserved and the iliac crest is incomplete. Scale bar, 1 cm.*

with some departures that may be the result of the allometric effects of very small body size. The femur shaft is relatively straight, and areas of muscle attachment, including the linea aspera, are not well developed. In contrast with some examples of Asian and African *H. erectus,* the femora do not have reduced medullary canals[20]. On the proximal end, the lesser trochanter is extremely prominent and the strong development of the intertrochanteric crest is similar to *H. sapiens* rather than the flattened intertrochanteric area in *Australopithecus* and *H. erectus* (KNM-ER 1481A, KNM-WT 15000). The biomechanical neck length is 55.5 mm and the neck is long relative to the femoral head diameter (31.5 mm), as is common to both *Australopithecus* and early *Homo*[19]. The neck–head junction is 31.5 mm long, with a shaft–neck angle of 130°, and the femur neck is compressed anteroposteriorly (Figure 7). Several indices of femoral size and shape, for example the relationship between femoral head size and midshaft circumference (66 mm), and femur length and sub-trochanteric shaft size[21], fall within the chimpanzee and australopithecine range of variation. The femur shaft does not have a pilaster, is circular in cross-section, and has cross-sectional areas of 370 mm² at the midshaft and 359 mm² at the midneck. It is therefore slightly more robust than the best-preserved small-bodied hominin femur of similar length (AL288-1; ref. 21). Distally there is a relatively high bicondylar angle of 14°, which overlaps with that found in *Australopithecus*[22].

The right tibia is complete apart from the tip of the medial malleolus (Figure 7). Its most distinctive feature, apart from its small size (estimated maximum length 235 mm, bicondylar breadth 51.5 mm) and the slight curvature in the long axis, is a shaft that is oval in cross-section (midshaft 347 mm²), without a sharp anterior border, and relatively thickened medio-laterally in the distal half. The relationship between the midshaft circumference and the length of the tibia is in the chimpanzee range of variation and distinct from *Homo*[21].

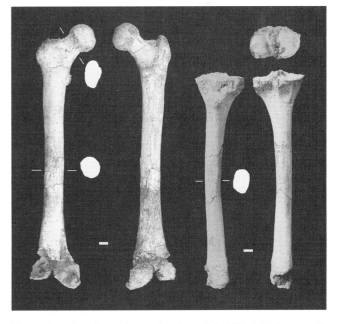

Figure 7. *Anterior and posterior views of the LB1 right femur and tibia, with cross-sections of the femur neck and midshaft, and tibia midshaft. The anterior surfaces of the medial and lateral condyles of the femur are not preserved. With the exception of the medial malleolus, the tibia is complete and undistorted. Scale bar, 1 cm.*

Additional evidence of a small-bodied adult hominin is provided by an unassociated left radius shaft, without the articular ends, from an older section of the deposit (74–95 kyr). The estimated maximum length of this radius when complete is approximately 210 mm. Although the arms of LB1 have not been recovered, the dimensions of this radius are compatible with a hominin of LB1 proportions.

Although there is considerable interspecific variation, stature has been shown to have phylogenetic and adaptive significance among hominins[23]. Broadly speaking, *Australopithecus* and the earliest members of the genus *Homo* are shorter than *H. erectus* and more recent hominins[8]. The maximum femur length of LB1 (280 mm) is just below the smallest recorded for *A. afarensis* (AL-288-1, 281 mm[24]) and equal to the smallest estimate for the OH 62 *H. habilis* femur (280–404 mm)[21]. Applying stature estimation formulae developed from human pygmies[25] gives a stature estimate of 106 cm for LB1. This is likely to be an overestimation owing to LB1's relatively small cranial height.

A stature estimate for LB1 of 106 cm gives a body mass of 16 to 28.7 kg, and a femur cross-sectional area of 525 mm^2 gives a mass of 36 kg. The brain mass for LB1, calculated from its volume[26], is 433.2 g; this gives an encephalization quotient (EQ)[27] range of 2.5–4.6, which compares with 5.8–8.1 for *H. sapiens*, 3.3–4.4 for *H. erectus/ergaster* and 3.6–4.3 for *H. habilis,* and overlaps with the australopithecine range of variation[28,29]. If LB1 shared the lean and relatively narrow body shape typical of Old World tropical modern humans then the smallest body weight estimate, based on Jamaican school children data[19], is probably most appropriate. This would support the higher EQ estimate and place LB1 within the *Homo* range of variation. Although neurological organization is at least as important as EQ in determining behavioural complexity, these data are consistent with *H. floresiensis* being the Pleistocene toolmaker at Liang Bua.

ORIGINS AND EVOLUTION

The LB1 skeleton was recovered from Flores, an island of 14,000 km^2 east of the Wallace Line, in Indonesia. It combines extremely small stature and an endocranial volume in the early australopithecine range, with a unique mosaic of primitive and derived traits in the cranium, mandible and postcranial skeleton. Both its geographic location and comparatively recent date suggest models that differ to those for more expected geological contexts, such as Pliocene eastern Africa. Among modern humans, populations of extremely small average stature were historically found in predominantly rainforest habitat in the equatorial zone of Africa, Asia and Melanesia[30,31]. Explanations for the small body size of these people generally focus on the thermoregulatory advantages for life in a hot and humid forest, either through evaporative cooling[32] or reduced rates of internal heat production[30]. For African pygmies, smaller body size is the result of reduced levels of insulin-like growth factor 1 (IGF-1) throughout the growth period[33], or reduced receptivity to IGF-1 (ref. 34). Although adult stature is reduced, cranio-facial proportions remain within the range of adjacent larger-bodied populations, as does brain size[35,36]. The combination of small stature and brain size in LB1 is not consistent with IGF-related postnatal growth retardation. Similarly, neither pituitary dwarfism, nor primordial microcephalic dwarfism (PMD) in modern humans replicates the skeletal features present in LB1 (refs. 37–40).

Other mechanisms must have been responsible for the small body size of these hominins, with insular dwarfing being the strongest candidate. Although small body size was an attribute of Pliocene australopithecines, the facial and dental characteristics of LB1 link it with larger-bodied Pleistocene *Homo*. In this instance, body size is not a direct expression of phylogeny. The location of these small hominins on Flores makes it far more likely that they are the end product of a long period of evolution on a comparatively small island, where environmental conditions placed small body size at a selective advantage. Insular dwarfing, in response to the specific ecological conditions that are found on some small islands, is well documented for animals larger than a rabbit[41,42]. Explanations of the island rule have primarily focused on resource availability, reduced levels of interspecific competition within relatively impoverished faunal communities and absence of predators. It has been argued that, in the absence of agriculture, tropical rainforests offer a very limited supply of calories for hominins[43]. Under these conditions selection should favour the reduced energy requirements of smaller individuals. Although the details of the Pleistocene palaeoenvironment on Flores are still being documented, it is clear that until the arrival of Mesolithic humans the faunal suit was relatively impoverished, and the only large predators were the Komodo dragon and another larger varanid. Dwarfing in LB1 may have been the end product of selection for small body size in a low calorific environment, either after isolation on Flores, or another insular environment in southeastern Asia.

Anatomical and physiological changes associated with insular dwarfing can be extensive, with dramatic modification of sensory systems and brain size[44], and certainly exceed what might be predicted by the allometric effects of body size reduction alone. Evidence of insular dwarfing in extinct lineages, or the evolution of island endemic forms, is most often provided by the fossil record. Whereas there is archaeological evidence of hominins being on Flores by approximately 840 kyr[45], there is no associated hominin skeletal material, and the currently limited evidence from Liang Bua is restricted to the Late Pleistocene. The first hominin immigrants may have had a similar body size to *H. erectus* and early *Homo*[21,46], with subsequent dwarfing; or, an unknown small-bodied and small-brained hominin may have arrived on Flores from the Sunda Shelf.

DISCUSSION

When considered as a whole, the cranial and postcranial skeleton of LB1 combines a mosaic of primitive, unique and derived features not recorded for any other hominin. Although LB1 has the small endocranial volume and stature evident in early australopithecines, it does not have the great postcanine tooth size, deep and prognathic facial skeleton, and masticatory adaptations common to members of this genus[2,47]. Instead, the facial and dental proportions, postcranial anatomy consistent with human-like obligate bipedalism[48], and a masticatory apparatus most similar in relative size and function to modern humans[48] all support assignment to the genus *Homo*—as does the inferred phylogenetic history, which includes endemic dwarfing of *H. erectus*. For these reasons, we argue that LB1 is best placed in this genus and have named it accordingly.

On a related point, the survival of *H. floresiensis* into the Late Pleistocene shows that the genus *Homo* is morphologically more varied and flexible in its adaptive responses than is generally recognized. It is possible that the evolutionary history of *H. floresiensis* is unique, but we consider it more likely that, following the dispersal of *Homo* out of Africa, there arose much greater variation in the morphological attributes of this genus than has hitherto been documented. We anticipate further discoveries of highly endemic, hominin species in locations similarly affected by long-term genetic isolation, including other Wallacean islands.

ACKNOWLEDGMENTS

We would like to thank F. Spoor and L. Aiello for data and discussion. Comments by F. Spoor and D. Lieberman greatly improved aspects of the original manuscript. Conversation with S. Collier, C. Groves, T. White and P. Grave helped clarify some issues. CT scans were produced by CT-Scan KSU, Medical Diagnostic Nusantara, Jakarta. S. Wasisto completed complex section drawings and assisted with the excavation of Sector VII. The 2003 excavations at Liang Bua, undertaken under Indonesian Centre for Archaeology Permit Number 1178/SB/PUS/BD/24.VI/2003, were funded by a Discovery Grant to M.J.M. from the Australian Research Council. UNE Faculty of Arts, and M. Macklin, helped fund the manufacture of stereolithographic models of LB1.

AUTHORS' CONTRIBUTIONS

P. B. reconstructed the LB1 cranium and was responsible for researching and writing this article, with M.J.M. T.S. directed many aspects of the Liang Bua excavations, including the recovery of the hominin skeleton. M.J.M. and R.P.S. are Principal Investigators and Institutional Counterparts in the ARC project, as well as Co-Directors of the Liang Bua excavations. E.W.S. and Jatmiko assisted T.S., and had prime responsibility for the work in Sector VII. R.A.D. did all of the initial faunal identifications at Liang Bua, including hominin material, and helped clean and conserve it.

REFERENCES

1. Morwood, M. J. et al. Archaeology and age of a new hominin from Flores in eastern Indonesia. *Nature* **431**, 1087–1091 (2004).
2. Wood, B. A. *Koobi Fora Research Project, Vol. 4: Hominid Cranial Remains* (Clarendon, Oxford, 1991).
3. Vekua, A. K. et al. A new skull of early *Homo* from Dmanisi, Georgia. *Science* **297**, 85–89 (2002).
4. Spoor, C. F. Basicranial architecture and relative brain size of STS 5 (*Australopithecus africanus*) and other Plio-Pleistocene hominids. *S. Afr. J. Sci.* **93**, 182–186 (1997).
5. Lieberman, D., Ross, C. F. & Ravosa, M. J. The primate cranial base: ontogeny, function, and integration. *Yearb. Phys. Anthropol.* **43**, 117–169 (2000).
6. Baba, H. et al. *Homo erectus* calvarium from the Pleistocene of Java. *Science* **299**, 1384–1388 (2003).
7. Tobias, P. V. *The Skulls, Endocasts and Teeth of* Homo habilis (Cambridge Univ. Press, Cambridge, 1991).
8. McHenry, H. M. & Coffing, K. E. *Australopithecus* to *Homo*: Transformations of body and mind. *Annu. Rev. Anthropol.* **29**, 125–166 (2000).
9. Brown, P. Vault thickness in Asian *Homo erectus* and modern *Homo sapiens*. *Courier Forschungs-Institut Senckenberg* **171**, 33–46 (1994).
10. Bräuer, G. & Mbua, E. *Homo erectus* features used in cladistics and their variability in Asian and African hominids. *J. Hum. Evol.* **22**, 79–108 (1992).
11. Santa Luca, A. P. *The Ngandong Fossil Hominids* (Department of Anthropology Yale Univ., New Haven, 1980).
12. Weidenreich, F. The skull of *Sinanthropus pekinensis*: a comparative study of a primitive hominid skull. *Palaeontol. Sin.* **D10**, 1–485 (1943).
13. Brown, P. & Maeda, T. Post-Pleistocene diachronic change in East Asian facial skeletons: the size, shape and volume of the orbits. *Anthropol. Sci.* **112**, 29–40 (2004).
14. Gabunia, L. K. et al. Earliest Pleistocene hominid cranial remains from Dmanisi, Republic of Georgia: taxonomy, geological setting, and age. *Science* **288**, 1019–1025 (2000).
15. Kaifu, Y. et al. Taxonomic affinities and evolutionary history of the Early Pleistocene hominids of Java: dento-gnathic evidence. *Am. J. Phys. Anthropol.* in press (2005).
16. McHenry, H. M. in *Evolutionary History of the 'Robust' Australopithecines* (ed. Grine, F. E.) 133–148 (Aldine de Gruyter, New York, 1988).
17. Wood, B. A. & Uytterschaut, H. Analysis of the dental morphology of the Plio-Pleistocene hominids. III. Mandibular premolar crowns. *J. Anat.* **154**, 121–156 (1987).
18. Wood, B. A., Abbott, S. A. & Uytterschaut, H. Analysis of the dental morphology of Plio-Pleistocene hominids. IV. Mandibular postcanine root morphology. *J. Anat.* **156**, 107–139 (1988).
19. Aiello, A. & Dean, C. *An Introduction to Human Evolutionary Anatomy* (Academic, London, 1990).
20. Kennedy, G. E. Some aspects of femoral morphology in *Homo erectus*. *J. Hum. Evol.* **12**, 587–616 (1983).
21. Haeusler, M. & McHenry, H. M. Body proportions of *Homo habilis* reviewed. *J. Hum. Evol.* **46**, 433–465 (2004).
22. Stern, J. T. J. & Susman, R. L. The locomotor anatomy of *Australopithecus afarensis*. *Am. J. Phys. Anthropol.* **60**, 279–317 (1983).
23. Ruff, C. B. Morphological adaptation to climate in modern and fossil hominids. *Yearb. Phys. Anthropol.* **37**, 65–107 (1994).
24. Jungers, W. L. Lucy's limbs: skeletal allometry and locomotion in *Australopithecus afarensis*. *Nature* **297**, 676–678 (1982).
25. Jungers, W. L. Lucy's length: stature reconstruction in *Australopithecus afarensis* (A. L. 288–1) with implications for other small-bodied hominids. *Am. J. Phys. Anthropol.* **76**, 227–231 (1988).
26. Count, E. W. Brain and body weight in man: their antecedants in growth and evolution. *Ann. NY Acad. Sci.* **46**, 993–1101 (1947).
27. Martin, R. D. Relative brain size and basal metabolic rate in terrestrial vertebrates. *Nature* **293**, 57–60 (1981).
28. Jerison, H. J. *Evolution of the Brain and Intelligence* (Academic, New York, 1973).
29. McHenry, H. M. in *The Primate Fossil Record* (ed. Hartwig, C. H.) 401–406 (Cambridge Univ. Press, Cambridge, 2002).

30. Cavalli-Sforza, L. L. (ed.) *African Pygmies* (Academic, Orlando, 1986).
31. Shea, B. T. & Bailey, R. C. Allometry and adaptation of body proportions and stature in African Pygmies. *Am. J. Phys. Anthropol.* **100**, 311–340 (1996).
32. Roberts, D. F. *Climate and Human Variability* (Cummings Publishing Co., Menlo Park, 1978).
33. Merimee, T. J., Zapf, J., Hewlett, B. & Cavalli-Sforza, L. L. Insulin-like growth factors in pygmies. *N. Engl. J. Med.* **15**, 906–911 (1987).
34. Geffner, M. E., Bersch, N., Bailey, R. C. & Golde, D. W. Insulin-like growth factor I resistance in immortalized T cell lines from African Efe Pygmies. *J. Clin. Endocrinol. Metab.* **80**, 3732–3738 (1995).
35. Hiernaux, J. *The People of Africa* (Charles Scribner's Sons, New York, 1974).
36. Beals, K. L., Smith, C. L. & Dodd, S. M. Brain size, cranial morphology, climate and time machines. *Current Anthropology* **25**, 301–330 (1984).
37. Rimoin, D. L., Merimee, T. J. & McKusick, V. A. Growth-hormone deficiency in man: an isolated, recessively inherited defect. *Science* **152**, 1635–1637 (1966).
38. Jaffe, H. L. *Metabolic, Degenerative and Inflammatory Disease of Bones and Joints* (Lea and Febiger, Philadelphia, 1972).
39. Seckel, H. P. G. *Bird-Headed Dwarfs* (Karger, Basel, 1960).
40. Jeffery, N. & Berkovitz, B. K. B. Morphometric appraisal of the skull of Caroline Crachami, the Sicilian "Dwarf" 1815?–1824: A contribution to the study of primordial microcephalic dwarfism. *Am. J. Med. Genet.* **11**, 260–270 (2002).
41. Sondaar, P. Y. in *Major Patterns in Vertebrate Evolution* (eds Hecht, M. K., Goody, P. C. & Hecht, B. M.) 671–707 (Plenum, New York, 1977).
42. Lomolino, M. V. Body size of mammals on islands: The island rule re-examined. *Am. Nat.* **125**, 310–316 (1985).
43. Bailey, R. C. & Headland, T. The tropical rainforest: Is it a productive habitat for human foragers? *Hum. Ecol.* **19**, 261–285 (1991).
44. Köhler, M. & Moyà-Solà, S. Reduction of brain and sense organs in the fossil insular bovid *Myotragus*. *Brain Behav. Evol.* **63**, 125–140 (2004).
45. Morwood, M. J.,O'Sullivan, P. B., Aziz, F. & Raza, A. Fission-track ages of stone tools and fossils on the east Indonesian island of Flores. *Nature* **392**, 173–176 (1998).
46. Walker, A. C. & Leakey, R. (eds) *The Nariokotome* Homo erectus *skeleton* (Harvard Univ. Press, Cambridge, 1993).
47. Rak, Y. *The Australopithecine Face* (Academic, New York, 1983).
48. Wood, B. A. & Collard, M. The human genus. *Science* **284**, 65–71 (1999).
49. Johanson, D. C. & White, T. D. A systematic assessment of early African Hominids. *Science* **202**, 321–330 (1979).

45

Grandmothering and the Evolution of *Homo erectus*

J. F. O'Connell, K. Hawkes, and N. G. Blurton Jones

ABSTRACT

Despite recent, compelling challenge, the evolution of Homo erectus *is still commonly attributed to big game hunting and/or scavenging and family provisioning by men. Here we use a version of the "grandmother" hypothesis to develop an alternative scenario, that climate-driven adjustments in* female *foraging and food sharing practices, possibly involving tubers, favored significant changes in ancestral life history, morphology, and ecology leading to the appearance, spread and persistence of* H. erectus. *Available paleoclimatic, environmental, fossil and archaeological data are consistent with this proposition; avenues for further critical research are readily identified. This argument has important implications for widely-held ideas about the recent evolution of long human lifespans, the prevalence of male philopatry among ancestral hominids, and the catalytic role of big game hunting and scavenging in early human evolution.*

*H*omo erectus presents an important and challenging problem to students of human evolution. A distinctive, well-defined fossil form, it was far more widely

Reprinted from *Journal of Human Evolution*, Vol. 36, O'Connell, J. F., K. Hawkes, and N. G. Blurton Jones. Grandmothering and the evolution of *Homo erectus*, pp. 461–485. Copyright © 1999 by Academic Press. Reprinted with permission from Elsevier.

distributed than any previous hominid, extant for more than a million years, and behaviorally different from both apes and modern humans, though in ways that are not yet entirely clear. Conventional wisdom has long associated its evolution and dispersal with big game hunting and paternal provisioning. These practices are thought to have stimulated the development of other modern human-like patterns of behavior, including extended periods of juvenile dependence, central place foraging, a sexual division of labor, and the nuclear family. Until recently, strong support for this argument came primarily from the archaeological record, particularly from the common association between stone artefacts made by *H. erectus* and the remains of large animals allegedly butchered and transported from kill sites to distant base camps for further processing, sharing, and consumption. The apparent match between this archaeological "signature" and those produced by modern hunter-gatherers led to the inference that other behaviors associated with the latter were also present in *H. erectus*. Key elements of the modern pattern, minus language and certain cognitive capabilities, were projected well back into the Pleistocene; arguments about the subsequent emergence of *Homo sapiens* were structured accordingly.

Appealing as this argument once was, the results of recent primatological, ethnographic, and archaeological research undercut it. Hunting is now known to be far more common among non-human hominoids than previously appreciated; yet it does not involve paternal investment. Big game hunting among modern tropical foragers, though sometimes productive, has been shown to be a poor strategy for feeding a family. Even the significance of archaeological assemblages formerly seen as providing clear evidence for ancient hunting is contested, some analysts arguing that they indicate little more than passive scavenging at kills made by other predators. If big game hunting, central place foraging, and paternal provisioning are eliminated from the *H. erectus* mix, then support for contingent inferences about modern human-like social organization and mating arrangements disappears. Reconstructions of its behavior are reduced to intriguing but somewhat disconnected inferences based on skeletal anatomy and archaeology; questions about its evolutionary origins and persistence are largely begged.

Here we offer a different model, one that has been foreshadowed in several ways over the past two decades, but only now developed in comprehensive form. We consider the proposition that *H. erectus* evolved as a result of climate-driven changes in *female* foraging and food sharing practices, possibly involving the exploitation of tubers. These changes may not only have had important effects on ancestral human ecology and physiology, but could also have provoked the first fundamental move away from hominoid life history patterns.

In the following pages, we briefly review the conventional wisdom on *H. erectus* ecology and the current critique thereof. We then turn to our alternative model, organizing empirical and theoretical elements developed elsewhere in terms of a series of predictions about relationships between past environmental change, adjustments in female foraging and food sharing, and their implications for hominid life history and ecology. We draw attention to recently proposed inferences about *H. erectus* life history; then review the evidence for anticipated climatic, environmental, and economic correlates. Though critical data are patchy, results are generally consistent with expectations. Potentially productive avenues for further research are clearly indicated. We comment on the implications of these results for widely held ideas about a much later date for the first appearance of long post-reproductive human lifespans, and for the notion that male philopatry and female dispersal are basic features of social organization among all members of the African ape clade, including ancestral hominids. We conclude with some remarks on the archaeological evidence that continues to shape conventional wisdom on *H. erectus*.

HOMO ERECTUS: A CRITIQUE OF CONVENTIONAL WISDOM

Homo erectus is a large-bodied hominid, similar in size and overall form to modern humans, but with a different cranium and a smaller brain (Rightmire, 1990, 1998; Walker & Leakey, 1993). The earliest examples (sometimes called *H. ergaster*, Wood, 1992) are from Africa, where they date to about 1.8 Ma (Feibel et al.,

1989; White, 1995). Near-contemporary specimens may be represented from the Caucasus, south China, and Indonesia (Brauer & Schultz, 1996; Gabunia & Vekua, 1995; Huang et al., 1995; Swisher et al., 1994), suggesting an early spread throughout the Old World tropics and into the temperate zone, a proposition consistent with emerging archaeological data (e.g., Dennell & Roebroeks, 1996; Dennell et al., 1988; Gibert et al., 1998; Tchernov, 1989). Once dispersed, *H. erectus* persisted, with little change in either physical form or geographical range, into the late Middle Pleistocene (<500 ka), when various populations evolved to or were displaced by *H. sapiens*.

Important inferences about *H. erectus* ecology and life history are drawn from its morphology, especially in contrast with that of contemporary and earlier hominids. Its modern human-like limb proportions are read to indicate fully terrestrial bipedality; its larger body size and more linear form a broader foraging range and higher tolerance for aridity; its thoracic cavity a simpler gut and correspondingly higher quality diet; its reduced sexual dimorphism the presence of multi-male, multi-female social groups; its dental eruption sequence and brain size and age at maturity and average adult lifespan intermediate between those of australopithecines and modern humans (Aiello & Wheeler, 1995; McHenry, 1994; Ruff, 1994; Smith, 1993; Walker & Leakey, 1993).

Until recently, equally important inferences about its behavior were drawn from the contemporary archaeological record. Generally speaking, early Pleistocene archaeological sites are larger in size, more diverse in terms of assemblage composition, and found in a broader range of habitats, both locally and globally, than those of the late Pliocene. Their associated faunal assemblages are often especially striking. Many include the remains of one or more (sometimes many more) large animals, mainly ungulates, often of several species. Many of the bones have been damaged, some by stone tools, apparently in connection with processing for consumption of associated meat and marrow.

These data were formerly interpreted by reference to presumed differences in the behavior of great apes and modern human foragers (e.g., Isaac, 1978; Leakey, 1971; Washburn & Lancaster, 1968; see also Binford, 1981; Fedigan, 1986; Hill, 1982; Isaac, 1984; Sept, 1992 for critical review). Special attention was drawn to nuclear families, central place foraging, and a sexual division of labor in which men hunt (mainly big game) to provision their wives and children; all thought to be typical of modern hunter-gatherers and pre-agricultural humans in general, but unrepresented among the great apes. Since some of the earliest faunal assemblages contained elements that had arguably been transported from distant kill sites, presumably by males who gave the meat to dependent mates and offspring, then other aspects of modern human behavior might be, and often were, inferred accordingly (see especially Isaac, 1978).

The evolution of this pattern was explained by appeal to a long-term trend toward cooler, drier climate that reduced the availability of previously important plant foods while favoring the spread of game-rich savannas. Ancestral hominid males were thought to have responded by adding large animals to their diets, thereby producing a potentially sharable resource. Hominid females paired with hunters to ensure access to the new food, which in turn enabled them to reduce their own foraging efforts. Nuclear families, a sexual division of labor, and paternal provisioning were established as a result. Female fertility and offspring survivorship were enhanced; an extended period of juvenile dependence, larger brain size, increased learning, and greater behavioral flexibility were all underwritten. Greater ability to cope with environmental variation, significant increases in geographical range, and long-term evolutionary success followed.

Over the past 20 years, this "hunting hypothesis" has been undercut in three important ways:

- Primates, particularly chimpanzees, are now known to hunt often (Boesch & Boesch, 1989; Stanford, 1996; Uehara et al., 1992; Wrangham & Bergman-Riss, 1990). Most hunting is done by males; the meat obtained is widely shared; yet there is no evidence for central place foraging or paternal provisioning.
- Evidence for pervasive paternal provisioning among modern human hunters has also been challenged (Hawkes, 1990, 1993; Hawkes et al., 1991, 1998). In the best known tropical foraging populations, men consistently pursue large game rather than other resources, despite the fact that returns are *highly* variable in the short run and impossible to defend from other claimants once in hand. If paternal provisioning were truly an important goal, they would do better by spending more time on small game and plant foods, both of which produce more reliable income and are often easily secured for family consumption. The fact that they target either less regularly than would meet this goal strongly suggests that big game hunting serves some other end, unrelated to provisioning wives and children.
- Archaeological evidence for big game hunting and paternal provisioning by *H. erectus* has also been re-evaluated. At some important sites, analysis of damage patterns on bones shows *no* evidence of hominid involvement (e.g., Binford, 1981; Klein, 1987). At others, the data can be read to indicate little more than "passive" hominid scavenging, mainly of long bone marrow and brain cavity contents (Binford, 1981; Blumenschine, 1991; Marean et al., 1992).[1] If accurate, this means that the amounts of edible tissue so acquired were probably too small and obtained too irregularly to provision juveniles (O'Connell et al., 1988b). Hunting and aggressive scavenging may also have been practised (Bunn & Ezzo, 1993; Capaldo, 1997; Dominguez-Rodrigo, 1997); but even if they were, it is unlikely that they were reliable enough to meet the *daily* nutritional needs of younger offspring, especially since active hunters with better weaponry (bows and poisoned

arrows) living in similar habitats today cannot do so consistently (Hawkes et al., 1991, 1998). Finally, there is no good evidence for the transport of meat by early hominids to distant "central places". The archaeological criteria formerly used to support this inference are now seen to be themselves unsupported (O'Connell et al., 1988*a*, 1990). Large animals represented in early archaeological assemblages may well have been processed and consumed by hominids at or near the point of initial acquisition (e.g., Marean et al., 1992; O'Connell, 1997).

These observations have very important implications: they eliminate all standard justifications for inferences about nuclear families and a modern human-like sexual division of labor in *H. erectus*. This raises key questions about *H. erectus* ecology and evolution. Current approaches to answering them fall into two categories: (1) those that entail continued insistence on the importance of big game hunting, central place foraging, and the prevalence of near-modern human patterns of social organization and reproduction in *H. erectus, despite* compelling challenge (e.g., Gowlett, 1993; Leakey & Lewin, 1992; Stanley, 1996); (2) those that respond to the challenge by treating the archaeological record much more inductively, using recent advances in taphonomy to reconstruct whatever possible about past hominid behavior, but with few exceptions about the shape it might take, apart from being "not modern" (e.g., Bunn & Ezzo, 1993; Potts, 1988; Rogers et al., 1994).

However commonly adopted, the first approach is indefensible. The second attends to archaeological evidence simply because it is easily recognized and relatively easily interpreted. The goal of accounting for it—of identifying and describing all the processes, human and non-human, involved in its creation—takes center stage. Though there are good historical reasons for the change in focus (compare Binford, 1981; Isaac, 1983), its net effect has been to beg the larger, ultimately more important ecological and evolutionary questions Pleistocene archaeology was once seen to address. The long-running dispute about whether early Pleistocene zooarchaeological assemblages represent hunting or some form of scavenging illustrates the problem. As currently phrased, and unlike the argument originally developed by Isaac (1978), *no other interesting questions about hominid behavior are resolved by the answer,* mainly because they are no longer asked. The only way of identifying such questions, and, by extension, the data pertinent to addressing them, is by developing and evaluating comprehensive models of early Pleistocene hominid ecology and evolution comparable to, but better-warranted than, the now-discredited hunting hypothesis.[2]

---

[1]Though it has long been assumed that FLK "Zinj" and other sites of similar age (~1.75 Ma) were produced in part by "early *Homo*" (cf. *habilis*, or more narrowly, *rudolfensis* [e.g., Bunn & Ezzo, 1993]), the earliest dates for African *H. erectus* (*ergaster*) (Feibel et al., 1989; White, 1995) and the coincident change in the archaeological record, marked by a sharp increase in assemblage diversity (compare Bunn, 1994; Kibunjia, 1994), now make it a better candidate for that role.

[2]Blumenschine and associates (e.g., Blumenschine & Peters, 1998; Blumenschine et al., 1994) and Rose & Marshall (1996) both take steps in this direction; but in each case the potential impact is limited by the narrow goal of accounting for certain features of the archaeological record (mainly faunal assemblage composition), rather than the larger evolutionary phenomenon of which it is a part.

THE GRANDMOTHER HYPOTHESIS[3]

One such model, the "grandmother hypothesis", has so far been developed as follows:

- Observations among modern hunter-gatherers show the importance of older women's foraging when mothers of child-bearing age rely on resources that weaned children cannot handle on their own. This suggests that mother–child food sharing could have favored the evolution of increased post-menopausal longevity that distinguishes humans from other hominoids.
- Several key life history attributes vary systematically with adult lifespans across the mammals generally and among primates in particular. If the underlying tradeoffs hold for humans, and longer adult lifespans are due to grandmothering, then the other departures from "typical ape" life histories that characterize our species may be (unexpectedly) explained as well.
- Since the ecological circumstances that would have favored increased mother–child food sharing and related changes in life history can be specified, the grandmother hypothesis provides the basis for an evolutionary scenario that can be evaluated in light of pertinent paleoclimatic, environmental, fossil and archaeological evidence.

Hadza Women's Foraging and Food Sharing

Our model is grounded on the results of fieldwork with the Hadza, a small population of traditional foragers living in the arid savanna woodlands of the Eastern Rift, northern Tanzania (Blurton Jones et al., 1996).

Apart from the very old and very young, Hadza of all ages are active, productive foragers. Time allocation and foraging returns are particularly striking for senior females and younger children. Women in their 60s and early 70s work long hours in all seasons, often with return rates equal to (sometimes greater than) those of their reproductive-age female kin (Hawkes et al., 1989, 1995, 1997). Hadza children are involved in the food quest virtually from the time they can walk, and by the age of five can and do supply, in some seasons, up to 50% of their daily nutritional requirements by their own efforts (Blurton Jones et al., 1989, 1994a, 1997; Hawkes et al., 1995, 1997).

Hadza mothers and grandmothers routinely capitalize on children's foraging capabilities by targeting resources that youngsters can take at high rates, notably fruit. Sometimes this involves bypassing items from which women earn better returns, but that children cannot handle. These choices mark an effort to maximize "team" returns, those earned by women and children together. In the wet season, when fruit is widely available, children's foraging opportunities largely determine adult female foraging strategies (Hawkes et al., 1995).

When resources easily taken by children are unavailable (especially in the dry season), Hadza women provision their offspring with foods they can procure reliably and efficiently. A good example is the woody rootstock, *Vigna frutescens* (Hadza: *//ekwa*), which favors deep stony soils and requires both substantial upper body strength and endurance to collect and the ability to make and control fire to process. Adult women, including seniors, take it often in all seasons, routinely earning up to 2000 kcal/h as a result (Hawkes et al., 1989, 1995, 1997; Vincent, 1985*a,b*). Pre-adolescents seldom pursue it, and rarely gain more than about 200 kcal/h when they do (Blurton Jones et al., 1989). Youngsters under 8 years old ignore it entirely.

This provisioning has an important ecological implication: it allows the Hadza to operate in habitats from which they would otherwise be excluded if, as among other primates, weanlings were responsible for their own subsistence.

It also creates the opportunity for another adult to influence a mother's birth-spacing: if someone else supplies food for her weaned but still dependent child, she can have the next baby sooner. Under these circumstances, grandmother, whose fertility has declined, can have a large impact on her own fitness by feeding the weaned children of her younger kin. Analyses of time allocation, foraging returns, and children's nutritional status (measured by seasonal changes in weight) provide a compelling measure of her effect (Hawkes et al., 1997). In families where mother is *not* nursing, children's nutritional status varies in accordance with mother's own foraging effort. At the arrival of a newborn, however, mother's foraging time drops and the correlation between her foraging effort and her weaned children's weight changes disappears. Instead, those weight changes vary closely with the effort of a related senior female, usually grandmother.

This suggests an hypothesis to account for the differences in average adult lifespans among the hominoids. Child-bearing careers in humans and apes are similar in length, but humans survive far longer after menopause. The dependence of weaned children on food from adults would have allowed ancestral human grandmothers to affect their fitness in ways that other apes could not, increasing the strength of selection against senescence, lowering adult mortality rates, and so lengthening average adult lifespans.

Female Food Sharing and the Evolution of Human Life Histories

Life histories differ widely among the mammals: some grow fast and die young; others mature slowly and live long adult lives (e.g., Harvey & Read, 1988). Although this variation correlates with body size, relationships among life history features persist even when the effect of body size is removed. Some are strong enough to be labeled "approximately invariant". Charnov (1993) has developed a model to account for them in which adult mortality rates set the tradeoffs that determine optimal age at maturity. Annual fecundity varies with both. Though very simple, the model also captures and

---

[3]Two very different versions of the grandmother hypothesis are discussed in the recent literature, one focusing on factors that might favor an "early" end to fertility, the other on the evolution of long post-reproductive lifespans. Here we are concerned only with the latter (see Hawkes et al., 1997; Hawkes et al., 1998*b*; Kaplan, 1997; Peccei, 1995 for discussion).

accounts for important differences between primates and other mammals (Charnov & Berrigan, 1993).

If the grandmother hypothesis explains extended human lifespans, and if human life histories maintain the broad patterning apparent across primates, then other human life history traits should be adjusted to predictable values relative to those observed in other living hominoids. Specifically, age at maturity should be delayed as a function of reduced adult mortality rates, but instead of the lower annual fecundity that normally goes with later age at maturity in other primates, grand-mother's help pays off in higher fertility. Comparison of averages for modern human foragers and wild populations of chimpanzees, gorillas, and orangutans yields results consistent with these expectations (Hawkes et al., 1998*a*). Not only do we have longer lifespans, but, as predicted by the combination of the grandmother hypothesis and Charnov's life history model, we also mature later and produce offspring at a higher rate.

An Evolutionary Scenario

Our analysis of Hadza women's foraging and food sharing leads us to propose a set of closely related hypotheses about the evolution of these distinctive features of human life history (Hawkes et al., 1997, 1998*a*,*b*). Imagine an ancestral hominid with life history characteristics and foraging patterns comparable to those of the modern chimpanzee. In particular (and unlike modern humans), age at maturity was about 10–12 years and fecundity was relatively low. Children were sometimes fed by mothers and older siblings, particularly with items they themselves could not handle, but the overall importance of these foods was marginal. The fertility of older females declined sharply in tandem with other aspects of physiology; maximum lifespan was about 50 years.

Imagine further a significant change in environment that reduced the availability of resources that younger juveniles could take on their own. Under these circumstances, local populations might have adjusted their foraging ranges, perhaps abandoning some areas entirely. Alternatively, they might have invested more in provisioning, especially with resources that may have been avoided before because although adults could handle them effectively, young children could not. For the strategy to be effective, returns must have been high enough to support the collector and at least one other individual. They must also have been available on a daily basis, with relatively low variance in returns between collecting bouts. Otherwise, their utility to small, growing youngsters would have been limited.

As provisioning became established, older females who were slightly more vigorous, despite declining fertility, could have assisted in the process, enhancing the survivorship of youngsters they helped while allowing the mothers of those offspring to begin a new pregnancy sooner. Less vigorous menopausal females would have provided less help. Higher reproductive success for the junior kin of more vigorous older females would have reduced the relative frequency of deleterious alleles expressed around menopause. Higher reproductive success for young adults with older helpers would also

alter the tradeoffs between allocation to current reproduction in early adulthood versus allocation to maintenance for later adaptive performance. The help of vigorous oldsters could more than compensate for reduced allocation to current reproduction by the junior kin themselves. Selection against senescence would be strengthened by both these pathways, decreasing adult mortality rates so that more would live to peri-menopausal, then post-menopausal ages. Longer adult lifespans would in turn have an effect on age at maturity. Lower adult mortalities increase the likelihood of reproducing before dying. Consistent with general mammalian (including primate) patterns (Charnov, 1993), delayed maturity, a longer period of growth, larger adult body size, and later age at maturity would have followed as a result. Extended fertility would *not* have been favored as it would have interfered with assistance to grandchildren and the enhanced fecundity at younger ages enjoyed by the daughters of older helpers. Instead, a fertile span similar to that of the other apes would have been conserved, the derived feature being extended post-menopausal longevity.

Increased offspring provisioning and related changes in fitness would also have had important ecological implications (Hawkes et al., 1997, 1998*b*). High juvenile mortality rates in modern primates are often attributable to feeding competition (van Schaik, 1989). If this were the case in the ancestral hominid population, then any increase in offspring provisioning should have reduced juvenile mortality. If the resources involved occurred in dense patches, with returns limited by handling requirements rather than by abundance, then their use should also have allowed the formation of larger foraging groups (Janson & Goldsmith, 1995; Wrangham et al., 1993). These would have been strongly favored by the requirements that grandmothers be near enough to daughters and grandchildren to support them. Where juvenile foraging capabilities previously limited habitat use, sharp increases in geographical range should also have been facilitated. To the degree that handling costs constrained adult returns from newly adopted resources, innovations in handling efficiency, including new technology, should also have been favored (Hawkes & O'Connell, 1992).

APPLYING THE ARGUMENT TO *HOMO ERECTUS*

Pursuing this hypothesis into the fossil and archaeological record has so far involved five steps: (1) marking the points in the hominid past at which life history changes are indicated, (2) examining the fit between changes inferred by paleoanthropologists and those predicted by the grandmother hypothesis in combination with Charnov's life history model; (3) assessing the evidence for coincident changes in climate and environment that might have reduced access to "children's" resources; (4) nominating resources previously unused but likely to have been adopted in response to these changes; (5) assessing the evidence that these resources were actually exploited more heavily coincident with changes in climate and hominid life history.

Homo erectus Life History

Significant changes in hominid life history are currently identified at two, possibly three points in the fossil record, one associated with the appearance of *H. erectus*, another with archaic *H. sapiens*, a third (least certainly, see below) with fully modern humans (Smith & Tompkins, 1995). Here we are concerned only with those changes associated with *H. erectus*. The appearance of this form is marked by shifts in brain size, dental eruption schedules and adult body weight, all read to indicate increased longevity and delayed maturity. Age at weaning should also have been adjusted, though the data needed to test this prediction have yet to be assessed:

- Estimates of longevity in fossil taxa are based on the correlation between brain size and longevity in living primates, including modern humans (Austad & Fisher, 1992; Sacher, 1959). Australopithecine brains were about the same size as those of modern chimpanzees (400–500 cc), suggesting similar adult mortality rates and, by this index, lifespans of about 50 years. Modern humans, with brain sizes of 1100–1700 cc, have much lower adult mortalities, with maximum lifespans estimated at 90–100 years. Brain sizes in *H. erectus* range from about 800–1100 cc, intermediate between values for australopithecines and modern humans, indicating similarly intermediate rates of adult mortality, and so intermediate maximum lifespans (Sacher, 1975).
- Dental eruption schedules provide an index of age at maturity (e.g., Beynon & Dean, 1988; Bromage & Dean, 1985; Smith, 1986, 1989, 1993). In australopithecines, M1, an important developmental marker closely correlated with other features of life history, including age at maturity, erupted at about age 3–3.5 years, the same age as in chimpanzees, but short of the 5.5–6 year figure for modern humans. In *H. erectus*, age at M1 eruption is estimated at about 4.5 years. These data suggest that australopithecines matured at about age 10, as do modern chimps, while *H. erectus* reached that threshold at about age 15.
- Adult body size is also an index of age at maturity. In Charnov's life history model, reduced adult mortality favors growing longer before switching production from growth into offspring. Maternal size is thus expected to increase with delayed maturity. Estimates of fossil hominid body weight are based on various postcranial indicators, notably the correlation between femoral head diameter and body weight in modern humans. This relationship suggests average adult weights of 35–40 kg for australopithecines, 55–60 kg for *H. erectus*, an increase of about 55% (McHenry, 1994; Ruff & Walker, 1993). The difference across females is especially striking: 30–35 kg for australopithecines, 50–55 kg for *H. erectus*, an increase of roughly 70%.
- Age at weaning in *H. erectus* should be no later than in apes and australopithecines. Although in mammals later age at maturity is usually correlated with lower annual fecundity, grandmothering raises the rate of baby production. Shorter interbirth intervals should be indicated by age at weaning, which in turn should be marked by changes in the chemical composition of permanent teeth that formed across the weaning period, specifically by lower post-weaning values for O^{18}, N^{15} and Sr/Ca, and higher values for C^{13}, all associated with the shift in trophic level and the adoption of solid foods (e.g.,

Wright & Schwarcz, 1998). It may also be indicated by an increase in the incidence of stress-related enamel hypoplasia (e.g., Goodman et al., 1984; cf. Hillson & Bond, 1997). These changes can be tracked relative to crown formation schedules (e.g., Wright & Schwarcz, 1998), or on the incremental growth features of individual teeth (Cerling & Sharp, 1996), both of which may in future allow estimates of age at weaning in *H. erectus*.

Based on general correlations, available brain and body weight and dental eruption data, though limited, can be read to indicate that longevity was increased and maturity delayed in *H. erectus* relative to the broader hominoid (including earlier hominid) pattern. In australopithecines, values for both were apparently similar to those in modern chimpanzees; in *H. erectus*, intermediate between those of australopithecines and modern humans.[4] Our model assumes that the length of the fertile period did not differ between *H. erectus* and australopithecines. This is difficult to assess in the fossil record, but given the apparent conservativeness of this attribute [fertile periods in chimpanzees and humans are essentially the same (Hill & Hurtado, 1996:463; Schultz, 1969)], it seems simplest to assume the same period for all ancestral hominids, including *H. erectus*.

Climate Change and "Children's" Resources

Our hypothesis leads us to expect that life history changes in *H. erectus* were prompted by a decline in the availability of resources easily taken by children (e.g., fruit). Generally speaking, such declines should have been associated with shifts toward cooler, drier, more seasonal climates. In tropical Africa, cooler, drier winters would have been especially critical. Plant foods accessible to humans are very limited in this season. Those that are available (e.g., seeds, nuts, underground storage organs) typically have relatively heavy handling costs (Peters & O'Brien, 1981; Peters et al., 1984).

Data from deep marine sediments indicate a general trend toward cooler climates world-wide over the past three million years, with marked steps in this direction at 2.8–2.5, 1.9–1.7, and 0.9–0.8 Ma (e.g., deMenocal, 1995). Terrestrial data (e.g., soil chemistry, pollen, fossil faunas) show progressive increases in aridity and seasonality and related expansion of open habitats in tropical Africa from 2.5–1.7 Ma (Behrensmeyer et al., 1997; Cerling, 1992; Cerling et al., 1988; Reed, 1997; Spencer, 1997; Vrba et al., 1995). These changes were evidently reinforced by continental uplift (Partridge et al., 1995), and a long term trend toward lower levels of atmospheric CO_2 (e.g., Street-Perrott et al., 1997).

---

[4]On brain and body weight criteria (e.g., McHenry, 1994), it might be argued that *H. habilis*, not *H. erectus*, is the earliest hominid to display distinctively non-pongid life history characteristics. Attempts to confirm this through analysis of dental eruption schedules have so far proven inconclusive (e.g., Dean, 1995; B. H. Smith, 1991; R. J. Smith et al., 1995). The issue is complicated by small sample size and continuing uncertainty about the taxonomy of key specimens (e.g., White, 1995). Even if *H. habilis* life history differed from the general hominoid pattern, available data indicate that *H. erectus* marked a more pronounced departure.

At least three lines of evidence mark the 1.9–1.7 Ma period bracketing the earliest dates for African *H. erectus* (Feibel et al., 1989; White, 1995) as especially critical from the perspective of our model:

- Soil carbonates indicate a sharp increase in the abundance of C4 biomass (an index of aridity and seasonality) in both the Turkana and Olduvai regions at about this time (Cerling, 1992). Prior to ca. 1.7 Ma, neither area had more than about 50% C4 biomass present; thereafter values jump to 60–80%.
- Feeding and habitat preferences of animals represented in early East African hominid sites show a complementary trend: arboreal and (more notably here) frugivorous animals formerly common in these localities are much less so after 1.8 Ma (Reed, 1997).
- Indicators of seasonal dietary stress are common in the teeth of fossil theropiths from Koobi Fora after 2.0 Ma (Macho et al., 1996).

"Tubers" as the Newly Exploited Resource

Resources adopted to provision juveniles in response to these changes must have been: (1) generally available, especially in the dry season, (2) capable of yielding returns high enough to support the collector and at least one other person, (3) reliable enough to provide those returns with little or no daily variance, and (4) open to exploitation by adults but not younger children. Many resources meet these criteria, notably certain varieties of small game, shellfish, nuts, seeds and the underground storage organs of plants. Here we restrict our attention to underground storage organs (hereafter "USOs" or, loosely, "tubers"), primarily because their availability and exploitation costs are relatively well understood, and because it has often been suggested that tubers were important in early hominid diets (e.g., Hatley & Kappelman, 1980; Isaac, 1980; McGrew, 1992; Peters & O'Brien, 1981; Stahl, 1984; Vincent, 1985a,b). Parallel treatment of other potential provisioning resources is clearly in order.[5]

USOs store water and carbohydrates (e.g., Anderson, 1987; Chapin et al., 1990). They take many forms, including bulbs, corms, rhizomes, taproots, tubers, and woody rootstocks, and are especially well-represented among the Liliaceae, Dioscoreaceae, Araceae, Taccaceae, and Icacinaceae (Raunkiaer, 1934; Thoms, 1989). Consistent with function, they are common in seasonally dry and/or cold habitats, often representing up to 20% of local species, sometimes occurring at densities of more than 1000 kg/hectare (e.g., Thoms, 1989; Vincent, 1985b). Edible carbohydrate content varies but generally represents 50–90% of dry weight in most species.

Wild forms are heavily exploited by modern humans in tropical through cool temperate latitudes on all continents (e.g., Bahuchet et al., 1991; Coursey, 1967;

Endicott & Bellwood, 1991; Gott, 1982; Hladik & Dounias, 1993; Hurtado & Hill, 1990; Johns, 1990; Lee, 1979; Malaisse & Parent, 1985; O'Connell et al., 1983; Thoms, 1989; Turner & Davis, 1993; Vainshtein, 1980; Vincent, 1985a,b; Watanabe, 1973). By contrast, they are rarely eaten by other primates except in arid, highly seasonal habitats, and even then only if they are found close to the ground surface (McGrew, 1992; McGrew et al., 1988; Moore, 1992; Peters & O'Brien, 1981; Whiten et al., 1992).

Although attractive as a potential energy source, tubers can present certain problems to human consumers: they may be heavily defended, either mechanically or chemically (Anderson, 1987; Coursey, 1973), and their carbohydrate content may be difficult to digest without pre-consumption processing (Thoms, 1989; Wandsnider, 1997). Mechanical defenses can often be countered by simple technology (e.g., digging sticks), chemical ones by a variety of techniques including maceration, leaching, boiling, baking, or roasting (Johns & Kubo, 1988; Lancaster et al., 1982; Spenneman, 1994; Stahl, 1984; Wandsnider, 1997).

Cooking also has an important effect on digestibility. The principal storage carbohydrates in tubers are starch, sucrose, and fructan (Banks & Greenwood, 1975; French, 1973; Lewis, 1984; Macdonald, 1980). Each occurs in a variety of molecular forms. Simpler types are water-soluble and easily handled raw by human digestive systems, though cooking usually improves nutrient yield. More complex forms definitely require cooking (French, 1973; Gaillard, 1987; Macdonald, 1980; Stahl, 1984; Wandsnider, 1997). Cooking also softens structural cellulose, which reduces intestinal "hurry", the speed with which high-fiber foods otherwise move through the gut. Slower passage generally increases nutrient yield (Macdonald, 1980; Stahl, 1984).

Two USOs favored by Native Americans, biscuit root (*Lomatium cous*) and camas (*Camassia quamash*), illustrate the effect of carbohydrate form on processing requirements. The primary storage medium in biscuit root is starch (dry weight fraction 40%; Yanovsky & Kingsbury, 1938). Under traditional conditions, this tuber was eaten raw, dried, or lightly boiled. It was also occasionally ground into flour and pressed into small cakes (Couture, 1978). No roasting or other extensive cooking was required. In contrast, the principal storage carbohydrate in camas is inulin (35–45% dry weight), a molecularly complex form of fructan only marginally digestible in raw form by humans. Traditional processing involved steaming the roots for 24–72 h in large rock-lined earth ovens, hydrolyzing the fructan to easily digested fructose (Konlande & Robson, 1972; Thoms, 1989). (See also Gott, 1983; Incoll et al., 1989; Turner & Kuhnlein, 1983; Turner et al., 1992; Wandsnider, 1997 for additional examples.)

The difficulties of coping with USO defenses and managing any required cooking are probably great enough to prevent pre-adolescent human children from exploiting many, perhaps most, USOs effectively. In the Hadza case, children as young as five often take shallow-growing *makalita* (*Eminia antenuliffera*), but cannot cook the starchy, fibrous roots for themselves if

---

[5]For data on age-related handling costs and nutrient returns for other potential provisioning resources, see (for example) Blurton Jones et al. (1994a, b), Boesch & Boesch (1984) and Peters (1987) on nuts, Bird & Bliege Bird (1997), Bliege Bird et al. (1995), and Meehan (1982) on shellfish.

Table 1. Some Post-Encounter Return Rates from Wild Tubers

Location	Resource	Type	Return (kcal/hr)
Central Australia	*Cyperus* sp.	Corm	≥4500[1]
	Ipomoea costata	Rhizome*	6200[1]
	Vigna lanceolata	Rootstock	1700[1]
East Africa	*Vigna frutescens*	Rootstock*	1000–3500[2,3]
	V. macrorhyncha	Rootstock*	3000[2]
	Vigna sp.	Rootstock*	900[2]
	Vatovaea pseudolablab	Rootstock*	2000[2]
South Africa	*Coccinea rehmannii*	Rootstock*	2900[4]
	Vigna diteri	Rootstock	3000[4]
Western North America	*Camassia quamash*	Bulb*	2000–4000[5]
	Lomatium spp.	Rootstock	1000–4000[6]
	Lewisia rediviva	Rootstock*	1200–1400[6,7]

*Item requires roasting, baking, or boiling.

[1] O'Connell & Hawkes, 1981; O'Connell et al., 1983.

[2] Vincent, 1985*a,b*.

[3] Hawkes et al., 1995.

[4] Blurton Jones et al., 1994*b*.

[5] Thoms, 1989.

[6] Couture, 1978; Couture et al., 1986.

[7] Simms, 1987.

fire kindled by an elder is unavailable. Thus, their returns may often be relatively low. The hard, sustained effort entailed in acquiring deeply buried //*ekwa* (the tuber favored by adults) prevents even older children from digging it efficiently, long after they can handle the necessary roasting.

These difficulties also constrain tuber use in chimpanzees. McGrew (1992:146) observes that the only USOs exploited by chimps are "either small bulbs simply pulled up by hand or surface roots directly gnawed". Though chimpanzees can make simple tools that might be suitable for collecting deeply buried tubers, and in some circumstances are even able to maintain fire [e.g., in connection with cigarette smoking (Brink, 1957)], they apparently never use either skill to take tubers in the wild, probably because other resources, easily taken by juveniles, are readily available in the habitats they occupy.

Quantitative data on return rates from wild tuber collecting are limited, but sufficient to show that they are often high enough to support the collector and one or more dependents, even where significant processing is required (Table 1). Values for a sample of tropical African and Australian and temperate North American forms range from 1000–6000 kcal/h (in patch). Assuming collectors spend about 4–6 h/day at the task (e.g., Hawkes et al., 1997; Thoms, 1989), daily returns from these resources would vary from roughly 4000–36,000 kcal/collector. Short-term variance in the best-controlled case (Hawkes et al., 1989, 1995) is low, ≤50%.[6] Observations among the Hadza, !Kung and Australian Alyawarra (Blurton Jones et al., 1994*a,b*; Hawkes et al., 1989, 1995; O'Connell et al., 1993) indi-

cate that returns of 8000–12,000 kcal/collector-day may be common in tropical savanna habitats. Thoms' (1989) summary of historical data on various Columbia Plateau groups suggests that in cool temperate steppe situations returns may be 2–3 times that high. Because tubers often occur at relatively high densities, such returns can be sustained for long periods of time (weeks or months) within daily foraging distance of a single residential base, even under intense collecting pressure (Hawkes et al., 1989, 1997; Thoms, 1989; Vincent, 1985*a,b*). Heavy culling may actually improve return rates in successive seasons (e.g., Anderson, 1987; Gott, 1983; Thoms, 1989).

The potential importance of tubers to ancestral hominids, specifically *H. erectus,* depended in part on their availability. Two lines of evidence point to greater abundance over the last 2.5 Ma, and especially after 1.8 Ma. One is overall pattern of tuber density in modern habitats. Surveys of African tropical forest communities show that tubers useful to humans are present at densities of about 1–10 kg/hectare (Hladik & Dounias, 1993). Similar assessments in African savanna and North American steppe situations indicate values in the range 1–100 T/hectare, *up to five orders of magnitude higher* (Thoms, 1989; Vincent, 1985*a,b*). Since these and other open habitats have become more common over the past 2–3 Ma, it seems reasonable to think that tuber abundance, diversity and distribution have increased accordingly, particularly after 1.8 Ma. The African paleontological record provides striking confirmation: suids, which rely heavily on USOs as a food resource, show a sharp increase in taxonomic diversity at ca. 1.8 Ma (White, 1995).

Archaeological and Fossil Evidence for Tuber Use

Archaeological evidence of tuber exploitation is often limited and indirect. Nevertheless, we can identify at

[6] Most of the return rate variance indicated for this case probably reflects differences in collector effort, not encounter rate. It is our impression that day-to-day variance in return rates for older women is *very* low, perhaps negligible.

least four patterns in the record consistent with the use of USOs beginning with the appearance of *H. erectus*:

- *Geographical Range.* Prior to ca. 1.8 Ma, hominids were confined to relatively well-watered parts of tropical and subtropical Africa (Reed, 1997). *H. erectus* was far more widespread, both within Africa and beyond, though never further north than about latitude 45–50 degrees (Dennell & Roebroecks, 1996; Gabunia & Vekua, 1995; Gibert et al., 1998; Roebroeks et al., 1992). Though the increase in range is often read to mean heavy reliance on hunting, this was unlikely to have been a productive strategy in many of the habitats newly occupied, particularly the more arid ones. Large animal biomass is typically low in such settings, implying high variance and low reliability in prey acquisition rates. USOs would have been much more dependable targets. Interestingly, latitude 50 marks not only the northern boundary of *H. erectus*, but also the approximate limit of reliance on tubers as a staple among ethnographically known hunter-gatherers in continental habitats (Thoms, 1989).[7]

- *Digging Tools.* Shallow-growing USOs can often be gathered by hand, but efficient acquisition of deeply buried forms requires, at minimum, a digging tool. Nearly a dozen pointed long-bone fragments, all showing damage to the tip said to be consistent with such use, are reported from Member 1 at Swartkrans Cave, dated at about 1.7 Ma (Brain, 1988). Stone tools suitable for the manufacture of wooden digging sticks (unifacial choppers and heavy scrapers) are common in the Oldowan Industry, which dates to ca. 2.5 Ma (Harris, 1983; Harris et al., 1987; Howell et al., 1987), but is especially well-known and widely encountered after 2.0 Ma (Isaac & Harris, 1978; Leakey, 1971). Keeley & Toth (1981) report damage consistent with woodworking on at least some early specimens. Later Acheulean and so-called "chopper-chopping tool" industries also include implements applicable to this task.

- *Evidence of Fire.* Some tubers may be eaten without preparation, but, as noted above, cooking typically improves the nutritional yield of even the simplest starches. Where storage carbohydrates are more complex and/or chemically defended, cooking is essential. Where cooking is practised, the likelihood of encountering archaeological evidence depends on the particular techniques employed. Some will be obvious [e.g., rock-filled earth ovens used in connection with camas processing (Thoms, 1989)]; others less so. Among the Hadza, for example, //ekwa roots are typically roasted for 5–15 min in large fires kindled on unprepared ground surfaces. Even where cooking sites are used repeatedly, archaeological evidence of this practice is likely to be ephemeral. The earliest unambiguous evidence for the use of fire by humans dates to the late Middle Pleistocene, 250–400 ka (Clark & Harris, 1985; James, 1989). Earlier indications include burned animal bones from Swartkrans, dated

1.0–1.5 Ma (Brain & Sillen, 1988), and small patches of reddened earth associated with stone tools and large animals bones at Chesowanja and East Turkana, dated 1.4–1.6 Ma (Bellomo, 1994; Gowlett et al., 1981; Isaac & Harris, 1978). Fire is indicated in all three cases; the question is whether hominids, specifically *H. erectus*, were involved in creating or maintaining it. In at least the eastern African cases, the associations with stone tools might be read to suggest that they were.

- H. erectus *Digestive Anatomy.* Milton & Demment (1988) report that modern human digestive tracts are smaller, relative to body size, than those of chimpanzees, probably as a function of differences in diet. The foods humans eat generally require less digestive processing than those favored by chimpanzees, partly because of pre-consumption processing, including cooking. Aiello & Wheeler (1995) argue on grounds of thoracic morphology that modern (or near-modern) human digestive systems first appeared with *H. erectus*. Earlier hominids display the funnel-shaped thorax typical of modern chimpanzees; *H. erectus* and later *H. sapiens* fossils all show the barrel shape found in modern humans. If Aiello and Wheeler are right, then beginning with *H. erectus*, humans either (1) narrowed the range of resources commonly exploited, focusing on those most readily digested, or (2) invested more effort in pre-consumption processing as means of reducing digestive costs. Tuber cooking is a good example of the latter strategy.

We can also point to at least two other potential tests for the importance of tubers in *H. erectus* diets. One involves analyses of dentition. Suwa et al. (1996) summarize evidence for reduced molar surface areas in early *H. erectus* relative to australopithecines, a pattern consistent with the idea of higher food quality and/or increased pre-consumption food processing just described. If tuber consumption produces distinctive damage patterns on teeth, then it might be implicated in these changes by inspection of the teeth in question.

The second test involves trace element analysis. Sillen & Lee-Thorp (1994) review research indicating differential concentration of strontium relative to calcium in plant storage organs, and discrimination against strontium across trophic levels. They further report that dietary fiber binds calcium more effectively than it does strontium; thus, all else equal, high-fiber eaters should display higher skeletal Sr/Ca than low-fiber eaters. These observations collectively suggest that if *H. erectus* relied heavily on tubers, their skeletons should display relatively high Sr/Ca ratios. If, on the other hand, and as generally believed, meat was the critical new element in *H. erectus* diets, their skeletal Sr/Ca ratios should be relatively low.

An Evolutionary Scenario Grounded in the Plio-Pleistocene

Data on *H. erectus* life history, climate, and resource use developed and integrated so far can be summarized along the following lines. By ca. 1.8 Ma, a long-term trend toward cooler, drier climate led to sharp reductions, at least seasonally, in the availability of plant foods previously exploited by hominids, especially juveniles. In some populations, adults and older juveniles

[7]An extensive literature review leads Thoms (1989:94) to observe: "Although there is considerable variation in the use of geophytes across [northern Eurasia], the overall pattern is one of minor use in the tundra and the northern part of the taiga zone, moderate use in the taiga zone, and comparatively heavy use along the southern margins of the taiga and the northern part of the steppe." The same review indicates a similar pattern in western North America. In both cases, the steppe/forest boundary falls at about latitude 50 degrees. Clearly, it would be useful to know more about the determinants of this pattern, as well as about whether and in what ways they may have limited the distribution of *H. erectus* in the past.

increased a previously infrequent practice of using resources that younger children could not acquire on their own, with mothers and older siblings providing shares to the younger ones. Without weanlings of their own, aging females were able to feed their daughter's youngsters. Those more vigorous could support a weanling fully, allowing their daughters to wean early and begin their next pregnancies sooner, with less impact on their weanlings' welfare. This increased selection against senescence, thereby lowering adult mortality rates and in turn favoring later maturity. Extended lifespans did not favor delaying menopause since females who continued to have babies of their own were unable to enhance their daughters' fertility. Lineages with higher fertility rates were those with post-menopausal helpers. Relaxation of the limits previously imposed on adult foraging by children's resource handling capabilities opened a broader range of habitats to exploitation. Longer-lived, and so later-maturing, larger-bodied, bigger-brained hominids, identifiable as *H. erectus*, quickly spread throughout the Old World tropics and into temperate latitudes.

Tubers may have been among the newly or increasingly used resources that enabled these changes. The same shift toward more open habitats that probably reduced access to "children's" foods almost certainly increased the availability of USOs. Whether they were exploited and, if so, how effectively depended on the handling problems they posed, and on the technology available to cope with them. Digging sticks could have been fashioned with then-extant stone tools and used to exploit deeply buried but chemically-undefended tubers, particularly those with simpler forms of carbohydrate storage. If fire could be made on demand, or at least maintained once "captured", then chemically more challenging forms might also have been accessible. If not, the returns potentially available from USOs, the advantages associated with provisioning, and related adjustments in life history would have been constrained accordingly. Apparent changes in hominid gut anatomy and evidence for fire at Lower Pleistocene sites might be read to indicate that tubers were cooked and consumed extensively. If so, they may well have played a critical role in the emergence and subsequent evolutionary success of *Homo erectus*.

DISCUSSION

Although this argument raises a wide range of issues, we comment here on just three: (1) a likely objection to the notion of long lifespans for *H. erectus*, (2) the implications of the grandmother hypothesis for current ideas about early human social organization, and (3) the importance of meat-eating in early human evolution.

Long Lifespans among Pre-Modern Humans

As applied to *H. erectus*, our model runs counter to the notion, widely held in some quarters, that long post-menopausal lifespans are a recent phenomenon, possibly the product of advances in medicine and basic sanitation made just in the last century or so, but definitely dating no earlier than the appearance of modern *H. sapiens* sometime in the early Upper Pleistocene (50–100 ka). There are good reasons to be skeptical of this proposition.

The idea that long lifespans are a very recent development stems at least in part from confusion over the implications of well-documented changes in *average life expectancy at birth*. This has increased substantially in some contemporary populations, largely due to sharp drops in infant and juvenile mortality rates. Low survivorship in the early years has a large effect on average lifespans. If, for example, half of those born die in the first year of life while everyone else lives to 100, life expectancy at birth must be near 50, even though all adults live well past that age. As it happens, old people, at least in their late 70s, are encountered everywhere, even in small populations, far from scientific medical care. Among the Ache, !Kung and Hadza, for example, average life expectancy at birth is about 35 years, yet average female life expectancy at age 45 is about 20 additional years (Blurton Jones et al., 1992; Hill & Hurtado, 1996; Howell, 1979). Again, this is an average: many live much longer. In all these cases, nearly 40% of adult women are post-menopausal.

The notion that long lifespans are restricted to modern *H. sapiens* is based on the fact that individuals identified as "old" (aged ≥50 yrs) are uncommon in the fossil record. Trinkaus (1995) and others appeal to a variety of skeletal indicators (e.g., epiphysial fusion, dental attrition, and long bone histomorphometry) in arguing that archaic *sapiens* routinely sustained high mortalities in young adulthood and seldom lived past age forty (see also Abbott et al., 1996; Bermudez de Castro & Nicolas, 1997). Though comparable analyses have yet to be undertaken on *H. erectus*, a similar argument might well be anticipated: long post-reproductive lifespans, predictable in theory, were seldom if ever actually achieved.

There are two important problems with this argument, either as applied to archaic *H. sapiens* or anticipated with respect to *H. erectus*:

- Older adults will *always* be under-represented in archaeological samples, simply because their remains are more susceptible to decay due to bone mineral depletion (e.g., Buikstra & Konigsberg, 1985; Galloway et al., 1997). The absence of elderly individuals in excavated cemetery populations of which they are *known*, on the basis of historical records, to have once been a part, illustrates the effect (e.g., Walker et al., 1988).
- Skeletally-based age estimates on adults over age 25 are notoriously inaccurate and commonly underestimate true age, sometimes by decades (e.g., Aiello & Molleson, 1992; Bocquet-Appel & Masset, 1982, 1996; Jackes, 1992; Konigsberg & Frankenberg, 1992; Paine, 1997).

Failure to appreciate the pervasive effects of these factors has sometimes led analysts to infer high young adult mortality rates and short lifespans even for modern human populations known archaeologically (e.g., Lovejoy et al., 1977). It is now generally recognized that such inferences are inappropriate (Aiello & Molleson, 1992; Bocquet-Appel & Masset, 1982, 1996; Howell,

1982; Jackes, 1992; Konigsberg & Frankenberg, 1992; Paine, 1997). Similar arguments about earlier hominid mortality and lifespan should be treated with equal skepticism.

Correlations between brain weight, maximum lifespan, and age at maturity documented across the primates (e.g., Austad & Fisher, 1992; Sacher, 1975) lead us to expect that long lifespans and late maturity have been typical of most humans since the late Middle Pleistocene (200–500 ka), when brain sizes in archaic *H. sapiens* reached the modern range (Leigh, 1992; Ruff et al., 1997). Though skeletal data enabling estimates of age at maturity in early *H. sapiens* are limited, the few available are consistent with the idea that this threshold was achieved late, at roughly the same age as in modern humans (e.g., Dean et al., 1986; Mann & Vandermeersch, 1997; Stringer & Dean, 1997; Stringer et al., 1990; Tompkins, 1996). The same reasoning leads us to expect earlier increases in average adult lifespan and age at maturity, beyond the hominoid range but short of those associated with *H. sapiens*, coincident with the first appearance of *H. erectus*. As indicated above, data on brain size, dental eruption schedules, and body weight are all consistent with this proposition.

Implications for *H. erectus* Social Organization

The grandmother hypothesis has important implications for current opinion about hominid social organization; in particular, for the suggestion, commonly made (e.g., Foley & Lee, 1989; Ghiglieri, 1987; Rodseth et al., 1991; Wrangham, 1987) and now widely echoed (e.g., Mellars, 1996), that evidence of male philopatry and female dispersal among chimpanzees and modern human hunter-gatherers implies that both were characteristic of *all* ancestral hominids, including *H. erectus*. Elsewhere (Hawkes et al., 1997), we have detailed reasons to be skeptical of this suggestion; among them, that patterns of residence, alliance, and dispersal vary widely among both chimps and modern hunters, and that all are evidently sensitive to local ecological conditions, especially as they affect female subsistence.

The grandmother hypothesis allows us to build on these observations more pointedly, specifically with reference to *H. erectus* social organization. Heavy reliance on high cost/high yield resources in connection with off-spring provisioning should have given daughters a strong incentive to remain with their natal group. As daughters grew, they acquired the strength and skill needed to feed younger siblings. When they matured, the assistance of aging mothers continued to enhance the benefits of proximity. From this perspective, long post-menopausal lifespans, late age at maturity, and high fertility suggest a pattern of co-residence among related females. The stronger the pattern, the greater the incentive for males to leave their natal group.

Grandmothers could certainly have improved their fitness by aiding sons, but the benefits associated with helping daughters are likely to have been much greater. Mothers and daughters face similar reproductive trade-offs: both do better by attending to offspring survivorship. Sons generally do better by investing in mating

(Anderson, 1994; Hawkes et al., 1995). A food-sharing mother might attract females to her son's group, but this would not assure her son paternity of those females' offspring. His fitness would depend on his success in competing with other males. Winners of that competition would enjoy higher reproductive success whether or not their mothers contributed to the fertility of their mates. Even if a grandmother could identify her son's offspring and single out grandchildren to feed, her potential fitness gains through increased fertility of "daughters-in-law" would be devalued by the uncertain paternity of subsequent children more quickly born to the mother of those grandchildren.

What about the Archaeological Evidence for Big Game Hunting and Scavenging?

This brings us a third issue, the common association between stone tools and the remains of large animals at sites of Lower and early Middle Pleistocene age that many continue to see as strong support for the hunting hypothesis. Though comprehensive consideration of these remains is well beyond us here, a brief comment grounded on our general argument seems pertinent.

As indicated above, heavy reliance on resources like tubers that occur at high densities, with returns limited primarily by handling requirements, should have favored larger group sizes. The associated predator-defense advantages should have reinforced the pattern, especially in more open habitats. Along with larger body size, larger group size should also have provided an important edge in "aggressive" or "confrontational" scavenging, where the kill is seized from the initial predator while still substantially intact (O'Connell et al., 1988b). Increased consumption of meat and marrow, and correspondingly increased evidence of such consumption in the archaeological record, should have been among the outcomes. There is little indication of meat consumption by hominids in the late Pliocene (Kibunjia, 1994). Instead, the earliest sites implicated in recent arguments about the hunting hypothesis date to the Plio-Pleistocene boundary (e.g., Bunn, 1994; Bunn & Kroll, 1986), coincident with the first evidence for African *H. erectus*. Recent analyses of cut- and tooth-mark distribution in the assemblage from the well-known "Zinjanthropus" site at Olduvai (Capaldo, 1997; Dominguez-Rodrigo, 1997) suggest that the sequence of carcass access there may have been carnivore–hominid–carnivore, consistent with the notion that hominids were successful in aggressive confrontations over large animal carcasses killed by other predators.

Success at acquiring carcasses need not have implied restricted mating access ("pair bonding") or paternal provisioning, any more than it does among chimpanzees. Neither would transport of parts to "central places" be indicated (cf. Bunn & Ezzo, 1993; Potts, 1988; Rose & Marshall, 1996): individuals or groups may simply have called attention to any carcass they encountered or acquired, just as do modern human hunters (O'Connell et al., 1988a,b, 1992). If the carcass had not yet been taken, the crowd so drawn could have done so, then consumed it on or near the spot, again just as modern hunters sometimes do (O'Connell et al., 1988*b*). The same advantages that helped secure the carcass initially—large body size and large group size—would often have deterred any counter-attack, either by the original predators or others arriving later. Repeated successes at the same spot, perhaps a dry season water source in a stream channel, would create archaeological sites very like those often identified as characteristic of the Lower Pleistocene record, particularly in East Africa. Subsequent density-dependent attrition of the bone assemblage would have sealed the match (Marean et al., 1992). Archaeological visibility notwithstanding, the sites so created need not indicate that large animal prey were either commonly acquired or an important part of *H. erectus* diets. On the contrary, their appearance might simply reflect changes in hominid group and body size stimulated largely if not entirely by prior changes in female foraging, food sharing, and life history.

SUMMARY

Clear-cut, probably widespread patterns in women's foraging and food sharing among modern tropical hunter-gatherers have an important effect on children's nutritional welfare. This observation is the basis for an hypothesis about the evolution of extended lifespans typical of all living humans. Because elements of mammalian life histories vary with each other systematically, other aspects of ancestral hominid life histories should have been entrained simultaneously. Longer adult lifespans favored by the payoffs for grandmothering when mothers provision their offspring should account for the delayed maturity, relatively high fertility and mid-

life menopause that collectively distinguish humans from other living hominoids. Here we have used this foundation to develop a scenario for the evolution of *Homo erectus;* then assessed it in light of the available data on *H. erectus* life history and anatomy, Plio-Pleistocene environment, the economics of tuber exploitation, and Lower Paleolithic archaeology. Results show that these lines of evidence are consistent with the proposition that grandmothering played a central role in the evolution and spread of this long successful taxon. Widely held ideas about the recent development of long human lifespans, the prevalence of male philopatry among ancestral hominids, and the catalytic role of hunting and scavenging in early human evolution are challenged accordingly.

ACKNOWLEDGMENTS

Research reported here was supported by the University of Utah, University of California (Los Angeles), and by the Division of Archaeology and Natural History, Research School of Pacific and Asian Studies, Australian National University. Useful assistance and advice (not always taken) was generously provided by Leslie Aiello, Jim Allen, Helen Alvarez, Margaret Avery, Thure Cerling, Ric Charnov, Joan Coltrain, Mike Cannon, Steve Donnelly, Jim Ehleringer, Jennifer Graves, Don Grayson, Geoff Hope, Richard Klein, Julia Lee-Thorp, Henry McHenry, Ric Paine, Doug Price, Alston Thoms, Eric Trinkaus, LuAnn Wandsnider, Tim White, Polly Wiessner and Richard Wrangham. We dedicate the paper to the late Bettina Bancroft, whose generous assistance made our initial fieldwork with the Hadza possible.

REFERENCES

Abbott, S., Trinkaus, E. & Been, D. B. (1996). Dynamic bone remodeling in later Pleistocene fossil hominids. *Am. J. phys. Anthrop.* **99**, 585–601.

Aiello, L. C. & Dean, C. (1990). *An Introduction to Human Evolutionary Anatomy.* London: Academic Press.

Aiello, L. C. & Molleson, T. (1992). Are microscopic aging techniques more accurate than macroscopic aging techniques? *J. Archaeol. Sci.* **20**, 689–704.

Aiello, L. C. & Wheeler, P. (1995). The expensive-tissue hypothesis: the brain and the digestive system in human and primate evolution. *Curr. Anthrop.* **36**, 199–221.

Anderson, D. C. (1987). Below-ground herbivory in natural communities: a review emphasizing fossorial animals. *Q. Rev. Biol.* **62**, 261–286.

Anderson, M. (1994). *Sexual Selection.* Princeton: Princeton University Press.

Austad, S. N. & Fisher, K. E. (1992). Primate longevity: its place in the mammalian scheme. *Am. J. phys. Anthrop.* **28**, 251–261.

Bahuchet, S., McKey, D. & de Garine, I. (1991). Wild yams revisited: is independence from agriculture possible for rain forest horticulturists? *Hum. Ecol.* **19**, 213–244.

Banks, W. & Greenwood, C. T. (1975). *Starch and Its Components.* Edinburgh: Edinburgh University Press.

Behrensmeyer, A. K., Todd, N. E., Potts, R. & McBinn, G. B. (1997). Late Pliocene faunal turnover in the Turkana Basin, Kenya and Ethiopia. *Science* **278**, 1589–1594.

Bellomo, R. V. (1994). Methods of determining early hominid behavioral activities associated with the controlled use of fire at FxJj 20 Main, Koobi Fora, Kenya. *J. hum. Evol.* **27**, 173–195.

Bermudez de Castro, J. M. & Nicolas, M. E. (1997). Paleodemography of the Atapuerca-Sima de los Huesos Middle Pleistocene hominid sample. *J. hum. Evol.* **33**, 333–355.

Beynon, A. D. & Dean, M. C. (1988). Distinct dental development patterns in early fossil hominids. *Nature* **335**, 509–514.

Binford, L. R. (1981). *Bones: Ancient Men and Modern Myths.* New York: Academic Press.

Bird, D. W. & Bliege Bird, R. L. (1997). Contemporary shellfish gathering strategies among the Meriam of the Torres Strait Islands, Australia: testing predictions of a central place foraging model. *J. Archaeol. Sci.* **24**, 39–63.

Bliege Bird, R. W., Bird, D. W. & Beaton, J. M. (1995). Children and traditional subsistence on Mer (Murray Island), Torres Strait. *Australian Aboriginal Studies* **1995**, 2–17.

Blumenschine, R. J. (1991). Hominid carnivory and foraging strategies and the socio-economic function of early archaeological sites. *Phil. Trans. R. Soc.,* series B **334**, 211–221.

Blumenschine, R. J. & Peters, C. (1998). Archaeological predictions for hominid land use in the paleo-Olduvai Basin, Tanzania, during lowermost Bed II times. *J. hum. Evol.* **34**, 565–608.

Blumenschine, R. J., Cavallo, J. A. & Capaldo, S. D. (1994). Competition for carcasses and early hominid behavioral ecology: a case study and conceptual framework. *J. hum. Evol.* **27**, 197–213.

Blurton Jones, N. G., Hawkes, K. & Draper, P. (1994*a*). Differences between Hadza and !Kung children's work: original affluence or practical reason? In (E. S. Burch, Ed.) *Key Issues in Hunter-Gatherer Research*, pp. 189–215. Oxford: Berg.

Blurton Jones, N. G., Hawkes, K. & Draper, P. (1994*b*). Foraging returns of !Kung adults and children: Why didn't !Kung children forage? *J. Anthrop. Res.* **50**, 217–248.

Blurton Jones, N. G., Hawkes, K. & O'Connell, J. F. (1989). Studying costs of children in two foraging societies: implications for schedules of reproduction. In (V. Standon & R. Foley, Eds) *Comparative Socioecology of Mammals and Man*, pp. 365–390. London: Blackwell.

Blurton Jones, N. G., Hawkes, K. & O'Connell, J. F. (1996). The global process and local ecology: how should we explain differences between the Hadza and !Kung? In (S. Kent, Ed.) *Cultural Diversity Among Twentieth Century Foragers: An African Perspective*, pp. 159–187. Cambridge: Cambridge University Press.

Blurton Jones, N. G., Hawkes, K. & O'Connell, J. F. (1997). Why do Hadza children forage? In (N. Segal, G. E. Weisfeld & C. C. Weisfeld, Eds) *Uniting Psychology and Biology: Integrative Perspectives on Human Development*, pp. 164–183. Washington DC: American Psychological Association.

Blurton Jones, N. G., Smith, L. C., O'Connell, J. F., Hawkes, K. & Kamuzora, C. (1992). Demography of the Hadza, an increasing and high density population of savanna foragers. *Am. J. phys. Anthrop.* **89**, 159–181.

Bocquet-Appel, J. P. & Masset, C. (1982). Farewell to paleodemography. *J. hum. Evol.* **11**, 321–333.

Bocquet-Appel, J. P. & Masset, C. (1996). Paleodemography: expectancy and false hope. *Am. J. phys. Anthrop.* **99**, 571–583.

Boesch, C. & Boesch, H. (1984). Possible cause of sex differences in the use of natural hammers by wild chimpanzees. *J. hum. Evol.* **13**, 415–440.

Boesch, C. & Boesch, H. (1989). Hunting behavior of wild chimpanzees in Tai National Park. *Am. J. phys. Anthrop.* **78**, 547–573.

Brain, C. K. (1988). New information from Swartkrans Cave of relevance to "robust" astralopithecines. In (F. Grine, Ed.) *Evolutionary History of the "Robust" Australopithecines*, pp. 311–316. Hawthorne, NY: Aldine.

Brain, C. K. & Sillen, A. (1988). Evidence from the Swartkrans cave for the earliest use of fire. *Nature* **336**, 464–466.

Brauer, G. & Schultz, M. (1996). The morphological affinities of the Plio-Pleistocene mandible from Dmanisi, Georgia. *J. hum. Evol.* **30**, 445–481.

Brink, A. S. (1957). The spontaneous fire-controlling reactions of two chimpanzee smoking addicts. *S. Afr. J. Sci.* **53**, 241–247.

Bromage, T. G. & Dean, M. C. (1985). Reevaluation of age at death of immature fossil hominids. *Nature* **317**, 525–527.

Buikstra, J. & Konigsberg, L. (1985). Paleodemography: critiques and controversies. *Am. Anthrop.* **87**, 316–333.

Bunn, H. T. (1994). Early Pleistocene hominid foraging strategies along the ancestral Omo River at Koobi Fora, Kenya. *J. hum. Evol.* **27**, 247–266.

Bunn, H. T. & Ezzo, J. A. (1993). Hunting and scavenging by Plio-Pleistocene hominids: nutritional constraints, archaeological patterns, and behavioural implications. *J. Archaeol. Sci.* **20**, 365–398.

Bunn, H. T. & Kroll, E. M. (1986). Systematic butchery by Plio/Pleistocene hominids at Olduvai Gorge, Tanzania. *Curr. Anthrop.* **27**, 413–452.

Capaldo, S. D. (1997). Experimental determinations of carcass processing by Plio-Pleistocene hominids and carnivores at FLK 22 (*Zinjanthropus*), Olduvai Gorge, Tanzania. *J. hum. Evol.* **33**, 555–597.

Cerling, T. E. (1992). Development of grasslands and savannas in East Africa during the Neogene. *Palaeog., Palaeoclimatol., Palaeoecol.* **97**, 241–247.

Cerling, T. E. & Sharp, Z. D. (1996). Stable carbon and oxygen isotope analysis of fossil tooth enamel using laser ablation. *Palaeogeog., Palaeoclimatol., Palaeoecol.* **126**, 173–186.

Cerling, T. E., Bowman, J. R. & O'Neil, J. R. (1988). An isotopic study of a fluvial-lacustrine sequence: the Plio-Pleistocene Koobi-Fora Sequence, East Africa. *Palaeogeog., Palaeoclimatol., Palaeoecol.* **63**, 335–356.

Chapin, F. S. III, Schulze, E-D. & Mooney, H. A. (1990). The ecology and economics of storage in plants. *Ann. Rev. Ecol. Syst.* **21**, 423–448.

Charnov, E. L. (1993). *Life History Invariants: Some Explorations of Symmetry in Evolutionary Ecology.* Oxford: Oxford University Press.

Charnov, E. L. & Berrigan, D. (1993). Why do female primates have such long lifespans and so few babies? Or life in the slow lane. *Evol. Anthrop.* **1**, 191–194.

Clark, J. D. & Harris, J. W. K. (1985). Fire and its roles in early hominid lifeways. *Afr. Archaeol. Rev.* **3**, 3–27.

Coursey, D. G. (1967). *Yams: An Account of the Nature, Origins, Cultivation and Utilization of the Useful Members of the Dioscoreaceae.* London: Longmans.

Coursey, D. G. (1973). Hominid evolution and hypogeous plant foods. *Man* **8**, 634–635.

Couture, M. D. (1978). Recent and contemporary foraging practices of the Harney Valley Paiute. Master's dissertation, Department of Anthropology, Portland State University.

Couture, M. D., Ricks, M. R. & Housley, L. (1986). Foraging behavior of a contemporary northern Great Basin population. *J. Calif. Great Basin Anthrop.* **8**, 150–160.

Dean, M. C. (1995). The nature and periodicity of incremental lines in primate dentine and their relationship to periradicular bands in OH16 (*Homo habilis*). In (J. Moggi Cecchi, Ed.) *Aspects of Dental Biology: Paleontology, Anthropology and Evolution*, pp. 239–265. Florence: International Institute for the Study of Man.

Dean, M. C., Stringer, C. B. & Bromage, T. G. (1986). Age at death of the neanderthal child from Devil's Tower, Gibraltar, and the implications for studies of general growth and development in neanderthals. *Am. J. phys. Anthrop.* **70**, 301–309.

deMenocal, P. B. (1995). Plio-Pleistocene African climate. *Science* **270**, 53–59.

Dennell, R. & Roebroeks, W. (1996). The earliest colonization of Europe: the short chronology revisited. *Antiquity* **70**, 535–542.

Dennell, R., Rendell, H. & Hailwood, E. (1988). Late Pliocene artifacts from northern Pakistan. *Curr. Anthrop.* **29**, 495–498.

Dominguez-Rodrigo, M. (1997). Meat-eating by early hominids at the FLK Zinjanthropus site, Olduvai Gorge (Tanzania): an experimental approach using cut-mark data. *J. hum. Evol.* **33**, 669–690.

Endicott, K. & Bellwood, P. (1991). The possibility of independent foraging in the rain forest of Peninsular Malaysia. *Hum. Ecol.* **19**, 151–185.

Fedigan, L. M. (1986). The changing role of women in models of human evolution. *Ann. Rev. Anthropol.* **15**, 25–66.

Feibel, C. S., Brown, F. & McDougall, I. (1989). Stratigraphic context of fossil hominids from the Omo Group deposits: Northern Turkana Basin, Kenya and Ethiopia. *Am. J. phys. Anthrop.* **78**, 595–622.

Foley, R. A. & Lee, P. C. (1989). Finite social space, evolutionary pathways, and reconstructing hominid behaviour. *Science* **243**, 901–906.

French, D. (1973). Chemical and physical properties of starch. *J. Anim. Sci.* **37**, 1048–1061.

Gabunia, L. & Vekua, A. (1995). A Plio-Pleistocene hominid mandible from Dmanisi, East Georgia, Caucasus. *Nature* **373**, 509–512.

Galliard, T. (Ed.) (1987). *Starch: Properties and Potential.* New York: John Wiley and Sons.

Galloway, A., Willey, P. & Snyder, L. (1997). Human bone mineral densities and survival of bone elements: A contemporary sample. In (W. D. Haglund & M. H. Sorg, Eds) *Forensic Taphonomy: The Postmortem Fate of Human Remains*, pp. 279–317. Boca Raton: CRC Press.

Ghiglieri, M. (1987). Sociobiology of the great apes and the hominid ancestor. *J. hum. Evol.* **16**, 319–358.

Gibert, J., Gibert, Ll., Iglesias, A. & Maestro, E. (1988). Two "Oldowan" assemblages in the Plio-Pleistocene deposits of the Orce region, southwest Spain. *Antiquity* **72**, 17–25.

Goodman, A. H., Armelagos, G. J. & Rose, J. C. (1984). The chronological distribution of enamel hypoplasias from prehistoric Dickson Mounds. *Am. J. phys. Anthrop.* **65**, 259–266.

Gott, B. (1982). The ecology of root use by Aborigines in southern Australia. *Archaeology in Oceania* **17**, 59–67.

Gott, B. (1983). Murnong—*Microseris scapigera*: A study of a staple food of Victorian Aborigines. *Australian Aboriginal Studies* **1983/2**, 2–18.

Gowlett, J. A. J. (1993). *Ascent to Civilization: The Archaeology of Early Humans* (2nd ed.). New York: McGraw-Hill.

Gowlett, J. A. J., Harris, J. W. K., Walton, D. & Wood, B. A. (1981). Early archaeological sites, hominid remains, and traces of fire from Chesowanja, Kenya. *Nature* **294**, 125–129.

Harris, J. W. K. (1983). Cultural beginnings: Plio-Pleistocene archaeological occurrences from the Afar, Ethiopia. *Afr. Archaeol. Rev.* **1**, 3–31.

Harris, J. W. K., Williamson, P. G., Veniers, J., Tappen, M. J., Stewart, K., Helgren, D., de Heinzelin, J., Boaz, N. T. & Bellomo, R. V.

(1987). Late Pliocene hominid occupation of the Senga 5A site, Zaire. *J. hum. Evol.* **16**, 701–728.

Harvey, P. H. & Reed, A. F. (1988). How and why do mammalian life histories vary? In (M. S. Boyce, Ed.) *Evolution of Life Histories: Patterns and Process from Mammals*, pp. 213–232. New Haven: Yale University Press.

Hatley, T. & Kappelman, J. (1980). Bears, pigs, and Plio-Pleistocene hominids: a case for the exploitation of below ground food resources. *Hum. Ecol.* **8**, 371–387.

Hawkes, K. (1990). Why do men hunt? Some benefits for risky strategies. In (E. Cashdan, Ed.) *Risk and Uncertainty in Tribal and Peasant Economies*, pp. 145–166. Boulder, CO: Westview Press.

Hawkes, K. (1993). Why hunter-gatherers work: an ancient version of the problem of public goods. *Curr. Anthropol.* **34**, 341–361.

Hawkes, K. & O'Connell, J. F. (1992). On optimal foraging models and subsistence transitions. *Curr. Anthropol.* **33**, 63–65.

Hawkes, K., O'Connell, J. F. & Blurton Jones, N. G. (1989). Hardworking Hadza grandmothers. In (V. Standen & R. Foley, Eds) *Comparative Socioecology of Mammals and Man*, pp. 341–366. London: Blackwell.

Hawkes, K., O'Connell, J. F. & Blurton Jones, N. G. (1991). Hunting income patterns among the Hadza: big game, common goods, foraging goals, and the evolution of the human diet. *Phil. Trans. R. Soc.*, series B **334**, 243–251.

Hawkes, K., O'Connell, J. F. & Blurton Jones, N. G. (1995). Hadza children's foraging: juvenile dependency, social arrangements and mobility among hunter-gatherers. *Curr. Anthropol.* **36**, 688–700.

Hawkes, K., O'Connell, J. F. & Blurton Jones, N. G. (1997). Hadza women's time allocation, offspring provisioning, and the evolution of post-menopausal lifespans. *Curr. Anthropol.* **38**, 551–578.

Hawkes, K., O'Connell, J. F. & Blurton Jones, N. G. (1998). Why do Hadza men hunt big animals?. Unpublished ms.

Hawkes, K., O'Connell, J. F., Blurton Jones, N. G., Charnov, E. L. & Alvarez, H. (1998a). Grandmothering, menopause, and the evolution of human life histories. *Proc. Nat. Acad. Sci. U.S.A.* **95**, 1336–1339.

Hawkes, K., O'Connell, J. F., Blurton Jones, N. G., Charnov, E. L. & Alvarez, H. (1998b). The grandmother hypothesis and human evolution. In (L. Cronk, N. Chagnon & W. Irons, Eds) *Evolutionary Biology and Human Behavior: 20 Years Later*. Hawthorne, NY: Aldine de Gruyter.

Hawkes, K., Rogers, A. R. & Charnov, E. L. (1995). The male's dilemma: increased offspring production is more paternity to steal. *Evol. Ecology* **9**, 1–16.

Hill, K. (1982). Hunting and human evolution. *J. hum. Evol.* **11**, 521–544.

Hill, K. & Hurtado, A. M. (1996). *Ache Life History: The Ecology and Demography of a Foraging People.* Hawthorne, NY: Aldine de Gruyter.

Hillson, S. & Bond, S. (1997). Relationship of enamel hypoplasia to the pattern of tooth crown growth: A discussion. *Am. J. phys. Anthrop.* **104**, 89–104.

Hladik, A. & Dounias, E. (1993). Wild yams of the African forest as potential food resources. In (C. N. Hladik, A. Hladik, O. F. Linares, H. Pagezy, A. Semple & M. Hadley, Eds) *Tropical Forests, Food and People: Biocultural Interactions and Applications to Development*, pp. 163–176. Paris: Parthenon Publishing Group.

Howell, F. C., Haesaerts, P. & de Heinzelin, J. (1987). Depositional environments, archaeological occurrences and hominids from Members E and F of the Shungura Formation (Omo Basin, Ethiopia). *J. hum. Evol.* **16**, 665–700.

Howell, N. (1979). *Demography of the Dobe !Kung.* New York: Academic Press.

Howell, N. (1982). Village composition implied by a paleodemographic life table: the Libben Site. *Am. J. phys. Anthrop.* **59**, 263–269.

Huang, W., Ciochon, R., Gu, Y., Larick, R., Fang, Q., Schwarcz, H., Yonge, C., De Vos, J. & Rink, W. (1995). Early *Homo* and associated artifacts from Asia. *Nature* **378**, 275–278.

Hurtado, A. M. & Hill, K. (1990). Seasonality in a foraging society: variation in diet, work effort, fertility and the sexual division of labor among the Hiwi of Venezuala. *J. Anthrop. Res.* **46**, 293–345.

Incoll, L. D., Bonnett, G. D. & Gott, B. (1989). Fructans in the underground storage organs of some Australian plants used for food by Aborigines. *J. Plant Physiol.* **134**, 196–202.

Isaac, G. Ll. (1978). The food sharing behavior of protohuman hominids. *Scientific American* **238**(4), 90–108.

Isaac, G. Ll. (1980). Casting the net wide: a review of archaeological evidence for early hominid land-use and ecological relations. In (L-K. Konigsson, Ed.) *Current Argument on Early Man: Proceedings of a Nobel Symposium Organized by the Royal Swedish Academy of Sciences and Held at Bjorkborns Herrgard, Karlskoga, Sweden, 21–27 May 1978, Commemorating the 200th Anniversary of the Death of Carolus Linnaeus*, pp. 226–251. Oxford: Pergamon.

Isaac, G. Ll. (1983). Bones in contention: competing explanations for the juxtaposition of early Pleistocene artifacts and faunal remains. In (J. Clutton-Brock & C. Grigson, Eds) *Animals and Archaeology*, Vol. 1, pp. 1–20. British Archaeological Reports 163.

Isaac, G. Ll. (1984). The archaeology of human origins: studies of the Lower Pleistocene in East Africa, 1971–1981. *Advances in World Archaeology* **3**, 1–87.

Isaac, G. Ll. & Harris, J. W. K. (1978). Archaeology. In (M. G. Leakey & R. E. F. Leakey, Eds) *Koobi Fora Research Project*, Vol. 1, pp. 64–85. Oxford: Clarendon.

Jackes, M. (1992). Paleodemography: problems and technique. In (S. R. Saunders & M. A. Katzenberg, Eds) *Skeletal Biology of Past Peoples: Theory and Methods*, pp. 189–224. New York: Wiley-Liss.

James, S. (1989). Hominid uses of fire in the Lower and Middle Pleistocene: a review of the evidence. *Curr. Anthrop.* **30**, 1–26.

Janson, C. H. & Goldsmith, M. L. (1995). Predicting group size in primates: foraging costs and predation risks. *Behavioral Ecology* **6**, 326–336.

Johns, T. (1990). *With Bitter Herbs They Shall Eat It: Chemical Ecology and the Origins of Human Diet and Medicine.* Tucson: University of Arizona Press.

Johns, T. & Kubo, S. (1988). A survey of traditional methods employed for the detoxification of plant foods. *Journal of Ethnobiology* **8**, 81–129.

Kaplan, H. (1997). The evolution of the human life course. In (K. W. Wachter & C. E. Finch, Eds) *Between Zeus and the Salmon: The Biodemography of Longevity*, pp. 175–211. Washington, D.C.: National Academy Press.

Keeley, L. H. & Toth, N. (1981). Microwear polishes on early stone tools from Koobi Fora, Kenya. *Nature* **293**, 464–465.

Kibunjia, M. (1994). Pliocene archaeological occurrences in the Lake Turkana Basin. *J. hum. Evol.* **27**, 159–171.

Klein, R. G. (1987). Problems and prospects in understanding how early people exploited animals. In (M. H. Nitecki & D. V. Nitecki, Eds) *The Evolution of Human Hunting*, pp. 11–45. New York: Plenum Press.

Klein, R. G. (1999). *The Human Career: Human Biological and Cultural Origins* (2nd ed.). Chicago: University of Chicago Press.

Konigsberg, L. W. & Frankenberg, S. R. (1992). Estimation of age structure in anthropological demography. *Am. J. phys. Anthrop.* **89**, 235–256.

Konande, J. E. & Robson, J. R. K. (1972). The nutritive value of cooked camas as consumed by Flathead Indians. *Ecology of Food and Nutrition* **1**, 193–195.

Lancaster, P. A., Ingram, J. S., Lim, M. Y. & Coursey, D. G. (1982). Traditional cassava-based foods: a survey of processing techniques. *Economic Botany* **36**, 12–45.

Leakey, M. D. (1971). *Olduvai Gorge, Volume 3: Excavations in Beds I and II 1960–1963.* Cambridge: Cambridge University Press.

Leakey, R. & Lewin, R. (1992). *Origins Reconsidered.* New York: Little, Brown.

Lee, R. B. (1979). *The !Kung San: Men, Women, and Work in a Foraging Society.* Cambridge: Cambridge University Press.

Leigh, S. R. (1992). Cranial capacity evolution in *Homo erectus* and early *Homo sapiens. Am. J. phys. Anthrop.* **87**, 1–13.

Lewis, D. H. (1984). Occurrence and distribution of storage carbohydrates in vascular plants. In (D. H. Lewis, Ed.) *Storage Carbohydrates in Vascular Plants*, pp. 1–52. Cambridge: Cambridge University Press.

Lovejoy, C. O., Meindl, R. S., Pryzbeck, T. R., Barton, T. S., Heiple, K. G. & Kotting, D. (1977). Paleodemography of the Libben Site, Ottowa County, Ohio. *Science* **198**, 291–293.

Macdonald, I. (1980). Suppliers of energy: carbohydrates. In (R. B. Alfin-Slater & D. Kritchevsky, Eds) *Nutrition and the Adult: Macronutrients*, pp. 97–116. New York: Plenum Press.

Macho, G. A., Reid, D. J., Leakey, M. O., Jablonski, N. & Beynon, A. D. (1996). Climatic effects on dental development of *Theropithecus oswaldi* from Koobi Fora and Olorgesailie. *J. hum. Evol.* **30**, 57–70.

Malaisse, F. & Parent, G. (1985). Edible wild vegetable products in the Zambezian woodland areas: a nutritional and ecological approach. *Ecology of Food and Nutrition* **18**, 43–82.

Mann, A. & Vandermeersch, B. (1997). An adolescent female neanderthal mandible from Montgaudier Cave, Charente, France. *Am. J. phys. Anthrop.* **103**, 507–527.

Marean, C. W., Spencer, L. M., Blumenschine, R. J. & Capaldo, S. D. (1992). Captive hyena bone choice and destruction, the Schlepp Effect, and Olduvai archaeofaunas. *J. Archaeol. Sci.* **16**, 101–121.

McGrew, W. C. (1992). *Chimpanzee Material Culture: Implications for Human Evolution.* Cambridge: Cambridge University Press.

McGrew, W. C., Baldwin, P. J. & Tutin, C. (1988). Diet of wild chimpanzees (*Pan troglodytes verus*) at Mt Assirik, Senegal: I. Composition. *Am. J. Primatol.* **16**, 213–226.

McHenry, H. M. (1994). Behavioral ecological implications of early hominid body size. *J. hum. Evol.* **27**, 77–87.

Meehan, B. (1982). *Shell Bed to Shell Midden.* Canberra: Australian Institute of Aboriginal Studies.

Mellars, P. (1996). *The Neanderthal Legacy: An Archaeological Perspective from Western Europe.* Princeton: Princeton University Press.

Milton, K. & Demment, M. W. (1988). Digestion and passage kinetics of chimpanzees fed high and low fiber diets and comparison with human data. *J. Nutri.* **118**, 1082–1088.

Moore, J. (1992). Savanna chimpanzees. In (T. Nishida, W. McGrew et al., Eds) *Topics in Primatology, Volume 1; Human Origins,* pp. 99–118. Tokyo: University of Tokyo Press.

O'Connell, J. F. (1997). On Plio/Pleistocene archaeological sites and central places. *Curr. Anthrop.* **38**, 86–88.

O'Connell, J. F. & Hawkes, K. (1981). Alyawara plant use and optimal foraging theory. In (B. Winterhalder & E. A. Smith, Eds) *Hunter-Gatherer Foraging Strategies: Ethnographic and Archaeological Analyses,* pp. 99–125. Chicago: University of Chicago Press.

O'Connell, J. F., Hawkes, K. & Blurton Jones, N. G. (1988a). Hadza hunting, butchering, and bone transport and their archaeological implications. *J. Anthrop. Res.* **44**, 113–162.

O'Connell, J. F., Hawkes, K. & Blurton Jones, N. G. (1988b). Hadza scavenging: Implications for Plio-Pleistocene hominid subsistence. *Curr. Anthrop.* **29**, 356–363.

O'Connell, J. F., Hawkes, K. & Blurton Jones, N. G. (1990). Reanalysis of large mammal body part transport among the Hadza. *J. Archaeol. Sci.* **17**, 301–316.

O'Connell, J. F., Hawkes, K. & Blurton Jones, N. G. (1992). Patterns in the distribution, site structure, and assemblage composition of Hadza kill-butchering sites. *J. Archaeol. Sci.* **19**, 319–345.

O'Connell, J. F., Latz, P. K. & Barnett, P. (1983). Traditional and modern uses of native plants among the Alyawara of central Australia. *Economic Botany* **37**, 83–112.

Paine, R. R. (1997). The need for a multidisciplinary approach to prehistoric demography. In (R. R. Paine, Ed.) *Integrating Archaeological Demography: Multidisciplinary Approaches to Prehistoric Population,* pp. 1–18. Occasional Paper 24, Center for Archaeological Investigations. Carbondale: Southern Illinois University.

Partridge, T. C., Wood, B. A. & deMenocal, P. S. (1995). The influence of global climatic change and regional uplift on large mammalian evolution in East and southern Africa. In (E. Vrba, G. Denton, T. Patridge & L. Buckle, Eds) *Paleoclimate and Evolution, with Emphasis on Human Origins,* pp. 331–355. New Haven: Yale University Press.

Peccei, J. S. (1995). The origin and evolution of menopause: the altriciality-lifespan hypothesis. *Ethology and Sociobiology* **16**, 425–449.

Peters, C. R. (1987). Nut-like oil seeds: food for monkeys, chimpanzees, humans and probably ape-man. *Am. J. phys. Anthrop.* **73**, 333–363.

Peters, C. R. & O'Brien, E. M. (1981). The early hominid plant food niche: insights from an analysis of plant exploitation by *Homo, Pan,* and *Papio* in eastern and southern Africa. *Curr. Anthrop.* **22**, 127–140.

Peters, C. R., O'Brien, E. M. & Box, E. O. (1984). Plant types and seasonality of wild plant foods, Tanzania to southwestern Africa: resources for models of the natural environment. *J. hum. Evol.* **13**, 397–414.

Potts, R. (1988). *Early Hominid Activities at Olduvai.* Hawthorne, NY: Aldine de Gruyter.

Raunkiaer, C. (1934). *The Life Forms of Plants and Statistical Plant Geography.* Oxford: Clarendon Press.

Reed, K. E. (1997). Early hominid evolution and ecological changes through the African Plio-Pleistocene. *J. hum. Evol.* **32**, 289–322.

Rightmire, G. P. (1990). *The Evolution of* Homo erectus: *Comparative Anatomical Studies of the Extinct Human Species.* Cambridge: Cambridge University Press.

Rightmire, G. P. (1998). Human evolution in the Middle Pleistocene: the role of *Homo heidelbergensis. Evol. Anthropology* **6**, 218–227.

Rodseth, L., Wrangham, R., Harrigan, A. & Smuts, B. (1991). The human community as primate society. *Curr. Anthrop.* **32**, 221–254.

Roebroeks, W., Conard, N. & van Kolfschoten, T. (1992). Dense forests, cold steppes and the paleolithic settlement of northern Europe. *Curr. Anthrop.* **33**, 551–586.

Rogers, M., Feibel, C. S. & Harris, J. W. K. (1994). Changing patterns of land use by Plio-Pleistocene hominids in the Lake Turkana Basin. *J. hum. Evol.* **27**, 139–158.

Rose, L. & Marshall, F. (1996). Meat eating, hominid sociality, and home bases revisited. *Curr. Anthrop.* **37**, 307–338.

Ruff, C. (1994). Morphological adaptations to climate in modern and fossil hominids. *Yearb. Phys. Anthrop.* **37**, 65–107.

Ruff, C. B., Trinkaus, E. & Holliday, T. W. (1997). Body mass and encephalization in Pleistocene *Homo. Nature* **387**, 173–176.

Ruff, C. B. & Walker, A. (1993). Body size and body shape. In (A. Walker & R. Leakey, Eds) *The Nariokotome Homo erectus Skeleton,* pp. 234–265. Cambridge: Harvard University Press.

Sacher, G. A. (1959). Relation of lifespan to brain weight and body weight in mammals. In (G. E. W. Wolstenholme & M. O'Connor, Eds) *Ciba Foundation Colloquia on Aging, Vol. 5, The Lifespan of Animals,* pp. 115–133. London: Churchill.

Sacher, G. A. (1975). Maturation and longevity in relation to cranial capacity in hominid evolution. In (R. Tuttle, Ed.) *Primate Functional Morphology and Evolution,* pp. 417–441. The Hague: Mouton.

Schultz, A. H. (1969). *The Life of Primates.* New York: Universe Books.

Sept, J. M. (1992). Archaeological evidence and ecological perspectives for reconstructuring early hominid subsistence behavior. In (M. B. Schiffer, Ed.) *Archaeological Method and Therapy,* pp. 1–56. Tucson: University of Arizona Press.

Sillen, A. & Lee-Thorp, J. (1994). Trace element and isotope aspects of predator–prey relationships in terrestrial food webs. *Palaeog., Palaeoclimatol., Palaeoecol.* **107**, 243–255.

Simms, S. R. (1987). *Behavioral Ecology and Hunter-Gatherer Foraging: An Example from the Great Basin.* British Archaeological Reports, International Series 381.

Smith, B. H. (1986). Dental development in *Australopithecus* and early *Homo. Nature* **323**, 327–330.

Smith, B. H. (1989). Dental development as a measure of life history in primates. *Evolution* **43**, 683–688.

Smith, B. H. (1991). Dental development and the evolution of life history in the Hominidae. *Am. J. phys. Anthrop.* **86**, 157–174.

Smith, B. H. (1993). The physiological age of KNM-WT 15000. In (A. Walker & R. Leakey, Eds) *The Nariokotome Homo erectus Skeleton,* pp. 195–220. Cambridge: Harvard University Press.

Smith, B. H. & Tompkins, R. L. (1995). Toward a life history of the Hominidae. *Ann. Rev. Anthrop.* **24**, 257–279.

Smith, R. J., Gannon, P. J. & Smith, B. H. (1995). Ontogeny of austalopithecines and early *Homo:* evidence from cranial capacity and dental eruption. *J. hum. Evol.* **29**, 155–168.

Spencer, L. M. (1997). Dietary adaptations of Plio-Pleistocene Bovidae: implications for hominid habitat use. *J. hum. Evol.* **32**, 201–228.

Spenneman, D. H. R. (1994). Traditional arrowroot production and utilization in the Marshall Islands. *Journal of Ethnobiology* **14**, 211–234.

Stahl, A. B. (1984). Hominid dietary selection before fire. *Curr. Anthrop.* **25**, 151–168.

Stanford, C. (1996). The hunting ecology of wild chimpanzees: implications for the evolutionary ecology of Pliocene hominids. *American Anthropologist* **98**, 96–113.

Stanley, S. M. (1996). *Children of the Ice Age.* New York: Random House.

Street-Perrott, F. A., Huang, Y., Perrott, R. A., Eglinton, G., Barker, P., Khelifa, L. B., Harkness, D. D. & Olago, D. O. (1997). Impact of atmospheric carbon dioxide on tropical mountain ecosystems. *Science* **278**, 1422–1426.

Stringer, C. B. & Dean, M. C. (1997). Age at death of Gibraltar 2: a reply. *J. hum. Evol.* **32**, 471–472.

Stringer, C. B., Dean, M. C. & Martin, R. D. (1990). A comparative study of cranial and dental development in a recent British population and neanderthals. In (C. J. DeRousseau, Ed.) *Primate Life History and Evolution* 14, pp. 115–152.

Suwa, G., White, T. D. & Howell, F. C. (1996). Mandibular postcanine dentition from the Shungura Formation, Ethiopia: crown morphology, taxonomic allocations, and Plio-Pleistocene hominid evolution. *Am. J. phys. Anthrop.* **101**, 247–282.

Swisher, C., Curtis, G., Jacob, T., Getty, A., Suprijo, A. & Widiasmoro (1994). Age of the earliest known hominids in Java. *Science* **263**, 1118–1121.

Tchernov, E. (1989). The age of the Ubiediya Formation. *Israel J. Earth Sci.* **36**, 3–30.

Thoms, A. (1989). The northern roots of hunter-gatherer intensification: Camas and the Pacific Northwest. Ph.D. dissertation, Department of Anthropology, Washington State Univ., Pullman.

Tompkins, R. L. (1996). Relative dental development of Upper Pleistocene hominids compared to human population variation. *Am. J. phys. Anthrop.* **99**, 103–116.

Trinkaus, E. (1995). Neanderthal mortality patterns. *J. Archaeol. Sci.* **22**, 121–142.

Turner, N. J. & Davis, A. (1993). "When everything was scarce": the role of plants as famine foods in northwestern North America. *J. Ethnobiol.* **13**, 171–202.

Turner, N. J., Johnson Gottesfeld, L. M., Kuhnlein, H. V. & Ceska, A. (1992). Edible wood fern root-stocks of Western North America: solving an ethnobotanical puzzle. *J. Ethnobiol.* **12**, 1–37.

Turner, N. J. & Kuhnlein, H. V. (1983). Camas (*Camassia* spp.) and riceroot (*Fritillaria* spp.): two liliaceous "root" foods of the Northwest Coast Indians. *Ecol. Food Nutri.* **13**, 199–219.

Uehara, S., Nishida, T., Hamai, M., Hasagawa, T., Hazaki, H., Huffman, M., Kawanaka, K., Kobayashi, S., Mitani, J., Takahata, Y., Takasaki, H. & Tsukahara, T. (1992). Characteristics of predation by chimpanzees in the Mahale Mountains National Park. In (T. Nishida, W. C. McGrew, P. Marler, M. Pickford & F. B. M. deWaal, Eds) *Topics in Primatology, Volume 1, Human Origins*, pp. 143–150.

Vainshtein, S. (1980). *Nomads of South Siberia* (Translated from the original [1972] Russian by M. Colenso). Cambridge: Cambridge University Press.

van Schaik, C. P. (1989). The ecology of social relationships amongst female primates. In (V. Standen & R. Foley, Eds) *Comparative Socioecology of Mammals and Man*, pp. 195–218. London: Blackwell.

Vincent, A. S. (1985a). Plant foods in savanna environments: a preliminary report of tubers eaten by the Hadza of northern Tanzania. *World Archaeology* **17**, 131–148.

Vincent, A. S. (1985b). Wild tubers as a harvestable resource in the East African savannas: ecological and ethnographic studies. Ph.D.

dissertation, Department of Anthropology, University of California, Berkeley.

Vrba, E., Denton, G., Partridge, T. & Buckle, L. (Eds) (1995). *Paleoclimate and Evolution, with Emphasis on Human Origins.* New Haven: Yale University Press.

Walker, A. & Leakey, R. E. F. (Eds). (1993). *The Nariokotome Homo erectus Skeleton.* Cambridge: Harvard University Press.

Walker, P. L., Johnson, J. R. & Lambert, P. M. (1988). Age and sex bias in the preservation of human skeletal remains. *Am. J. phys. Anthrop.* **76**, 183–188.

Wandsnider, L. A. (1997). The roasted and the boiled: food composition and heat treatment with special emphasis on pit-hearth cooking. *J. Anthrop. Archaeol.* **16**, 1–48.

Washburn, S. L. & Lancaster, C. S. (1968). The evolution of hunting. In (R. B. Lee & I. DeVore, Eds) *Man the Hunter*, pp. 293–303. Chicago: Aldine.

Watanabe, H. (1973). *The Ainu Ecosystem: Environment and Group Structure.* Seattle: University of Washington.

White, T. D. (1995). African omnivores: global climatic change and Plio-Pleistocene hominids and suids. In (E. Vrba, G. Denton, T. Partridge & L. Buckle, Eds) *Paleoclimate and Evolution, with Emphasis on Human Origins*, pp. 369–384. New Haven: Yale University Press.

Whiten, A., Byrne, R. W., Barton, R. A., Waterman, P. G. & Henzi, S. P. (1992). Dietary and foraging strategies of baboons. *Phil. Trans. R. Soc.*, series B **334**, 187–197.

Wood, B. (1992). Origin and evolution of the genus *Homo. Nature* **355**, 783–790.

Wrangham, R. (1987). The significance of African apes for reconstructing human social evolution. In (W. G. Kinzey, Ed.) *The Evolution of Human Behavior: Primate Models*, pp. 51–71. Albany: State University of New York Press.

Wrangham, R. & Bergmann-Riss, E. (1990). Rates of predation on mammals by Gombe chimpanzees, 1972–1975. *Primates* **31**, 157–170.

Wrangham, R. W., Gittleman, J. L. & Chapman, C. A. (1993). Constraints on group size in primates and carnivores: population density and day range as assays of exploitation competition. *Behav. Ecol. Sociobiol.* **32**, 199–209.

Wright, L. E. & Schwarcz, H. P. (1998). Stable carbon and oxygen isotopes in human tooth enamel: identifying breast feeding and weaning in prehistory. *Am. J. phys. Anthrop.* **106**, 1–18.

Yanovsky, E. & Kingsbury, R. M. (1938). *Analyses of some Indian food plants.* Contribution 138, Carbohydrate Research Division, Bureau of Chemistry and Soils. Washington, D.C.: United States Department of Agriculture.

VI

Middle Pleistocene Hominids in Africa, Europe, and Asia

Fossils from the middle Pleistocene of Africa, Europe, and, to some degree, Asia have been a source of confusion in human evolution. In their 1975 volume, *After the Australopithecines,* Karl Butzer and the late Glynn Isaac referred to this time period as the "muddle in the middle." As the chapters in Part VI demonstrate, this remains the case today. Many aspects of hominid evolution in the middle Pleistocene that are largely unresolved include the age of many fossils, the proper systematics, and their relationships to later hominid evolution. The chapters describe some of the morphological and behavioral diversity among these middle Pleistocene hominids while providing a few new solutions to this "muddle in the middle" Pleistocene time period.

In Chapter 46, "Human Evolution in the Middle Pleistocene: The Role of *Homo heidelbergensis,*" G. Philip Rightmire reviews the fossil record from the middle Pleistocene, and discusses alternative views on the systematics and phylogenetic relationships of the hominid fossils from this time period. As noted in the chapters in the preceding parts of this volume, *Homo erectus,* in the broadest sense, extended from Africa to Asia as early as 1.8 mya, and appears to have survived in Asia until the late Pleistocene. However, in the middle Pleistocene in Africa and Asia, *Homo erectus* is succeeded by a more advanced taxon, represented by African fossils such as those from Bodo in Ethiopia and Broken Hill (Kabwe) in Zambia and by Asian fossils such as Dali in Shaanxi Province, China. In Europe, similar fossils are found at Petralona in Greece, Arago in France, and more fragmentary remains at Mauer (Heidelberg) in Germany and Boxgrove in England. Until recently, many of these fossils were commonly referred to as archaic *Homo erectus* but lacked many derived features of modern *Homo sapiens*. Rightmire argues that these fossils indicate a speciation event from the primitive *Homo erectus* ancestor, and are best placed in a separate species, *Homo heidelbergensis.*

There are, however, additional questions regarding the relationships of these middle Pleistocene fossils to later hominids. Many of the European fossils seem to share features with later Neandertals that are not found in the African fossils (see Chapter 47). Furthermore, the middle Pleistocene fossils from Africa seem to grade slowly into modern humans (see Chapter 49). In this case, perhaps, the African fossils should be separated into yet another taxon, *Homo rhodesiensis* (see Bermúdez de Castro et al., 2003 for new support of this relationship). The relationship of middle Pleistocene fossils from China to either *Homo heidelbergensis* or modern humans is even more difficult to determine.

In Chapter 47, "The Atapuerca Sites and Their Contributions to the Knowledge of Human Evolution in Europe," José María Bermúdez de Castro and colleagues discuss the extraordinary new finds from the middle Pleistocene sites at Atapuerca, near Burgos, Spain. From a bone-filled pit deep in a cave, the Sima de los Huesos, have come more than 4000 hominid fossils representing at least 28 different individuals. These fossils have been dated by several different methods to between 200,000 and 500,000 years old (for a discussion of the dating at this site, see Bischoff and Shamp, 2003). The 4000 fossils seem to sample a population of middle Pleistocene hominids that is near the base of the Neandertal lineage. From the Gran Dolina site, a few hundred meters away, has come a new taxon, *Homo antecessor* (Bermúdez de Castro et al., 1997). This new species comes from the lower levels of a large cave filling, below the last major magnetic reversal at 780 kya (see original descriptions of the site by Carbonell and Bermúdez de Castro, 1995 and by Pares and Perez-Gonzolez, 1995). According to Bermúdez de Castro and colleagues, these remains are more advanced than *Homo erectus* but lack Neandertal features found in the fossils from the Sima de los Huesos and others attributed to *Homo heidelbergensis*. Instead, they show facial morphology more similar to modern *Homo sapiens* (see Bermúdez de Castro et al., 2003). There are also indications from cut marks and scraping marks made by stone artifacts on the hominid remains that this population engaged in cannibalism. Unfortunately, one of the most diagnostic specimens is a maxillary fragment of a juvenile individual, and it is possible that some of the distinctive features of the taxon may be the result of the immature morphology. That, and the considerable variability in the region among middle Pleistocene hominids from Africa and Europe, suggest caution to some authorities (see Chapter 59).

In Chapter 48, "A Cranium for the Earliest Europeans: Phylogenetic Position of the Hominid from Ceprano, Italy," Giorgio Manzi and colleagues describe another European fossil thought to be comparable in age to *Homo antecessor.* In a series of morphological analyses, the authors found that the Ceprano skull lacks many characteristic features of the cranium found in *Homo erectus,* but also lacks derived features found among European fossils assigned to *Homo heidelbergensis.* Therefore, it is the most primitive cranium known from Europe and seems related to the same stock that gave rise to the African fossils from Bodo and Broken Hill. The most parsimonious taxonomic assignment, they argue, is that the Ceprano skull represents the adult cranium of *Homo antecessor* (see also Manzi, 2004). However, there are no comparable remains known from the type locality that would confirm this allocation.

Chapter 49, "The KNM-ER 3884 Hominid and the Emergence of Modern Anatomy in Africa," by Gunter Bräuer, describes the broad pattern of hominid evolution in the middle and late Pleistocene of Africa. He reviews recent studies that have re-dated many near-modern fossils from Africa to the middle Pleistocene, including the KNM-ER 3884 cranium from Lake Turkana, the Florisbad hominid, and the Laetoli 18 hominid. The modern-looking African hominids are thus contemporary with Neandertals and some fossils assigned to *Homo heidelbergensis* in Europe. Bräuer argues for a gradual evolution of modern *Homo sapiens* in Africa during the middle Pleistocene, from more archaic fossils like Bodo in the early middle Pleistocene to nearly modern fossils in the late Pleistocene. In light of this gradual transition, he prefers to allocate all of the African fossils to *Homo sapiens* rather than recognizing an additional taxon such as *Homo heidelbergensis.*

In Chapter 50, Xinzhi Wu and Frank E. Poirier provide a description and brief interpretation of the Dali remains in "Dali, a Skull of Archaic *Homo sapiens* from China." The best dates for this skull indicate that it is from the middle Pleistocene, approximately 300–250 kya (Yin et al., 2001), and was found associated with a collection of small stone artifacts. In the reported measurements, this skull is intermediate between *Homo erectus* and modern *Homo sapiens,* and there are many different views on its most likely affinities. Some (Etler, 1996) have argued that it is a modern human derived from local populations of *Homo erectus;* others identify its affinities with *Homo heidelbergensis* from Europe (see Chapter 46).

Alternatively, it may represent a distinct Asian lineage that went extinct (see Chapter 59, Figure 3).

In Chapter 51, Chris Ruff and colleagues discuss "Body Mass and Encephalization in Pleistocene *Homo.*" Using new regressions based on femoral head diameter and skeletal dimensions, they find that from the early Pleistocene through the upper Paleolithic, extinct populations of *Homo* were much larger in size than modern people—some middle Pleistocene hominids were truly giants, with estimates of nearly 100 kg (220 lb) for fossils from Berg Alkas or Bodo. Moreover, this large body size shows no geographic pattern. These estimates agree with other estimates based on cranial dimensions (Kappelman, 1996; Aiello and Wood, 1994). Although brain size increased from the early Pleistocene to the late Pleistocene, with a major jump in the middle Pleistocene, when body size is taken into account there is no major trend in encephalization quotients. The authors suggest that sexual selection for male-male competition may have given rise to the larger male mass seen in the early Pleistocene (but see also Chapter 45). Perhaps most significantly, they note that the apparent increase in relative brain size among modern humans is largely the result of a decrease in body size. They find no correlation between technological innovation and the decrease in body size over the past 90,000 years, but note that the "less sturdily constructed skeleton" of modern humans suggests increasingly less active lifestyles.

Part VI closes with Chapter 52, "Lower Paleolithic Hunting Weapons from Schöningen, Germany—The Oldest Spears in the World." Here, Hartmut Thieme and colleagues describe the discovery of well-preserved wooden spears found in conjunction with butchered horses. At an age of approximately 400 kya, they are the oldest complete hunting weapons known. The spears were made from individual trees (usually spruce) that had been felled and stripped of their branches and sharpened at both ends. They resemble modern javelins in the position of the maximum thickness and weight along the length, suggesting they could have been thrown. Others have suggested they could have been used quite effectively as thrusting spears. These were truly massive weapons, approximately 2 m in length, with maximum diameters of 29 to 50 mm. This ties in well with the large size of middle Pleistocene hominids described in Chapter 51. Due to the density of weapons and skeletons, the authors believe that this site reflects an organized attack to kill an entire herd of horses.

REFERENCES

Aiello, L. C., and B. A. Wood. 1994. Cranial variables as predictors of hominine body mass. *American Journal of Physical Anthropology* 95:409–27.

Bermúdez de Castro, J. M., J. L. Arsuaga, E. Carbonell, A. Rosas, I. Martinez, and M. Mosquera. 1997. A hominid from the Lower Pleistocene of Atapuerca, Spain: possible ancestor to Neandertals and modern humans. *Science* 276:1392–1395.

Bermúdez de Castro, J. M., M. Martinon-Torres, S. Sarmiento, and M. Lozano. 2003. Gran Dolina-TD6 versus Sima de los Huesos dental samples from Atapuerca: evidence of discontinuity in the

European Pleistocene population? *Journal of Archaeological Science* 30:1421–1428.

Bischoff, J. L., and D. D. Shamp. 2003. The Sima de los Huesos hominids date to beyond U/Th equilibrium (> 350 kyr) and perhaps to 400–500 kyr: new radiometric dates. *Journal of Archaeological Science* 30:275–280.

Butzer, K. W., and G. L. L. Isaac (Eds.). 1975. *After the Australopithecines: Stratigraphy, Ecology, and Culture, Change in the Middle Pleistocene.* Aldine Publishers, Chicago.

Carbonell, E., and J. M. Bermúdez de Castro. 1995. Lower Pleistocene hominids and artifacts from Atapuerca-TD6 (Spain). *Science* 269:826–830.

Etler, D. A. 1996. The fossil evidence for human evolution in Asia. *Annual Review of Anthropology* 25:275–302.

Kappelman, J. 1996. The evolution of body mass and relative brain size in fossil hominids. *Journal of Human Evolution* 30:243–276.

Manzi, G. 2004. Human evolution at the Matuyama-Brunhes boundary. *Evolutionary Anthropology* 13:11–24.

Pares, J. M., and A. Perez-Gonzolez. 1995. Paleomagnetic age for hominid fossils at Atapuerca archaeological site, Spain. *Science* 269:830–832.

Yin, G., C. Falguères, G. Shen, and Y. Lu. 2001. The age of Dali man. XIVth Congress. Union Internationale des Sciences Préhistoriques et Protohistoriques (UISPP), Liège, 2–8 September 2001. Session 16.1, abstract C7.

46

Human Evolution in the Middle Pleistocene

The Role of *Homo heidelbergensis*

G. P. Rightmire

For paleoanthropologists working in the Middle Pleistocene, these are interesting times. New discoveries of artifacts and human fossils have been reported from western Europe, so that it now looks as though this continent was populated 800,000 years ago, if not earlier. One of the fossils, from Ceprano in Italy, is described as *Homo erectus*. Whether this ancient species ever reached Europe has been repeatedly questioned, but the Ceprano cranium is complete enough to provide some hard evidence.

Other finds from Spain are even more spectacular. The Sima de los Huesos ("Pit of Bones") in the Sierra de Atapuerca has yielded a wealth of skeletons that are best interpreted as early Neanderthals, perhaps close to 300,000 years in age. Older but unfortunately more fragmentary remains, also from Atapuerca, display no Neanderthal features and are claimed as representatives of a new species. *Homo antecessor* will require close study.

These European discoveries focus fresh attention on the evidence accumulating from Africa and Asia. Human bones are known from the earlier Middle Pleistocene of Africa at localities such as Bodo in Ethiopia and Broken Hill in Zambia. The crania show anatomical features that distinguish them from *Homo erectus*. In the Far East, the people at Dali and other sites are also more advanced than *Homo erectus*, but their affinities to groups in the West are uncertain.

This Middle Pleistocene record, still sparse but increasingly well dated, raises important questions. One concerns the fate of *Homo erectus* in different regions of the Old World. Another is how many distinct species should be recognized among the descendants of this ancient lineage. It is apparent that the traditional approach of lumping diverse humans together as "archaic" *Homo sapiens* will no longer work. The picture is highly complex, and several taxa probably are needed to accommodate the fossils. Evolutionary relationships among these populations must be clarified, but pose some major problems. I will address only a subset of these topics pertaining mainly to earlier Middle Pleistocene hominids.

HOMO ERECTUS IN PERSPECTIVE

This extinct species has been at the center of much controversy. At present, there is no firm consensus as to whether it should be defined as a long lasting, polytypic lineage or as a group of relatively specialized populations geographically confined to the Far East. In my view, *Homo erectus* originated in Africa and then spread to Eurasia. The hypodigm is made up of specimens from Java, Zhoukoudian, and other sites in China, Ternifine (now Tighenif) in Northwest Africa, Olduvai Gorge, the Turkana Basin, and Swartkrans in South Africa (Figure 1). Several fossils recently discovered in western Asia and in Europe probably should be counted as well. This species spans an interval of at least 1.5 million years. Indeed, some East Asian populations may have survived into later Pleistocene times.

As documented by Weidenreich, von Koenigswald, Le Gros Clark, and others, members of this taxon share a suite of characters by which they can be distinguished from recent humans. Some of the principal differences relate to cranial capacity, keeling on the midline of the vault, parietal length, occipital proportions, the anatomy of the cranial base, facial projection, the form of the mandibular symphysis, tooth size, the relative narrowness of the pelvis, and the length of the femoral neck. A large number of traits generally describe *Homo erectus* and diagnose this species relative to living people.

These assumptions have been challenged by several workers, on highly diverse grounds. One point of contention concerns the material from the Turkana Basin. It has been claimed that the early Kenyan crania lack special features developed by the Asian populations. A midline keel on the vault, an angular torus at the postero-inferior corner of the parietal bone, certain characters of the base, and overall thickening of the braincase are said to be absent from the specimens at Koobi Fora but well expressed in the remains from Trinil, Sangiran, and Zhoukoudian. These differences have prompted investigators, including Andrews,[1] Groves,[2] and Larick and Ciochon,[3] to recognize two species and to suggest that *Homo erectus* must be geographically restricted to the Far East. Wood[4,5] agrees, on the basis of facial measurements, perhaps some aspects of temporal bone morphology, and dental differences, that the early African hominids should be set apart from later *Homo erectus*. Wood now refers the Turkana Basin specimens to *Homo ergaster*, which, in his opinion, is more likely than *Homo erectus* to have played a role in the evolution of later people.

A quite different interpretation has been offered by Wolpoff and coworkers,[6] who now claim that the nomen *Homo erectus* is unnecessary and should be discarded altogether. Here the question is really whether there is continuity from earliest Pleistocene times right

Reprinted from G. P. Rightmire, *Evolutionary Anthropology*, Vol. 6, pp. 218–227. Copyright © 1998 by Wiley-Liss, Inc. This material is used by permission of Wiley-Liss, Inc., a subsidiary of John Wiley & Sons, Inc.

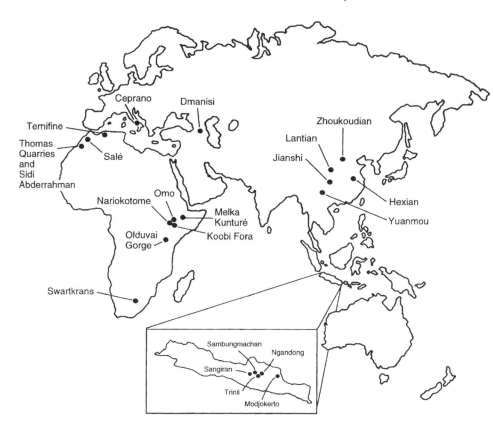

Figure 1. *A map showing the principal localities that have yielded fossil remains of* Homo erectus. *Ceprano in Italy is the first site to demonstrate that the species reached Europe, probably before the onset of the Middle Pleistocene.*

to the present; that is, whether just one long lineage, with no branches or extinctions, can be recognized. Such a lineage would include the ancient Turkana populations as well as those later resident in Africa and Eurasia. If it could be demonstrated that no splitting had occurred, one might argue that any division between taxa would have to be arbitrary. Wolpoff et al.[6] and Wolpoff[7] (see also Tobias[8]) go a step further and say that there simply is no basis for keeping more than one species, which must then be *Homo sapiens.*

It does not seem to me that either of these scenarios can be supported fully. Certainly there is geographic variation among the several assemblages of *Homo erectus,* but the fossils from the Turkana Basin, Olduvai Gorge, and other sites in Northwest Africa exhibit essentially the same set of traits as do those from the Far East.[9] Discrete characters said to be unique to the Asian populations are variable in their expression and, in fact, most can be identified in the earlier East African material.[10] Cranial dimensions show much overlap.[11,12] Vault thickness, as measured near the junction of the frontal and parietal bones, is about the same in the African and Asian samples.[13] The faces of KNM-ER 3733 from Koobi Fora and KNM-WT 15000 from Nariokotome conform in nearly all respects to the anatomy of *Homo erectus* as reconstructed from the Sangiran and Zhoukoudian specimens.[14] Also, the teeth from the Turkana Basin are close in size and shape to those from Zhoukoudian.[15] Apparently there are not many traits that can be used to diagnose *Homo ergaster,* and probably just one polytypic species should be recognized. Nevertheless, *Homo erectus,* as broadly defined, does possess many anatomical distinctions, extending not only to the skull and

teeth but to the postcranial skeleton as well. All of the better-preserved individuals, including even the late surviving ones from some of the Far Eastern sites, can be set apart from *Homo sapiens.* The boundary between these taxa is not arbitrarily defined.

NEW EVIDENCE FROM EURASIA

Although there is disagreement about taxonomy, most workers would concede that populations resembling *Homo erectus* dispersed from Africa into Eurasia well before 1.0 million years ago. These movements occurred probably over a long period. The hominids may have made repeated sorties, introducing crude chopping tools and stone flakes or Acheulean handaxes into different regions.[16]

Evidence documenting the spread of humans into western Asia comes from several sites, including Dmanisi in Georgia and 'Ubeidiya in Israel. At Dmanisi, a lithic industry and a well-preserved mandible with teeth have been recovered.[17] The jaw resembles those of *Homo erectus.*[18] The bone-bearing levels overlie a lava flow dated at 1.8 million years, but the age of the tools and fossils remains problematical.[16] At 'Ubeidiya, an extensive mammalian fauna excavated from lake sediments suggests a relatively cool climate at a date of perhaps 1.4 to 1.0 million years. In addition to the fauna, there are stone choppers, spheroids, picks, and bifaces, which Tchernov[19] compared to the lithic material from upper Bed II at Olduvai Gorge. How the differences between the non-Acheulean and Acheulean assemblages at this Jordan Valley site should be interpreted is unclear, but the tools most probably were used by groups of *Homo erectus.*

Ancient traces of hominid activity are found also in Europe, at French localities such as Le Vallonet, Isernia in Italy, and in the Neuwied Basin in Germany. This scattered archeological evidence, consisting mainly of core-choppers and flakes, sometimes found with broken animal bones taken to be food waste, may demonstrate a human presence in the Early Pleistocene[20] (but also see Roebroeks[21]). Unfortunately, the oldest European sites have not produced more than a few bits of human skeleton. A notable exception is Ceprano in central Italy. Here a fragmentary but fairly complete braincase was discovered in 1994.

The fossil was picked up in clay deposits, which contain no volcanic material that is directly datable. Potassium-argon dates have been obtained from volcanic sands higher in the stratigraphic sequence; these are said by Ascenzi and coworkers[22] to indicate an age greater than 700,000 years. Insofar as can be determined from the description provided by its discoverers, this hominid displays the heavy continuous brow, low vault, angled occiput, and thick cranial bones that are characteristic of *Homo erectus*. This is important information. Although the Ceprano specimen is damaged in some key respects, it seems to confirm the identity of one group of people who entered Europe in the Early Pleistocene.

Representatives of *Homo erectus* also reached the East Asian tropics before moving into more temperate regions. It has been assumed that movement into the Far East began 1.0 million years ago or slightly earlier, but radiometric dates from mineral samples collected at Modjokerto and Sangiran now suggest that the oldest Indonesian localities may be 1.8 to 1.6 million years old.[23] If this result can be verified, then it will look as though *Homo erectus* spread quite rapidly across the Old World. These hominids flourished for a long time. At sites including Zhoukoudian and Longtandong (Hexian) in China, the species is known from deposits of the later Middle Pleistocene, while at Ngandong in Java, at least one group of archaic people may have survived into the Late Pleistocene.[24] Populations such as that at Ngandong may document the last appearance of the lineage.

SPECIATION IN AFRICA?

The picture emerging is one of *Homo erectus* as a widespread, polytypic species, with groups persisting longer in some regions than in others. The pattern documented in China and especially in Java contrasts with that in the West, where *Homo erectus* seems to disappear from the record at a relatively early date.[25,26] Also, it is interesting that the Asian populations apparently are more specialized in the sense of exhibiting a higher incidence of some morphological characters associated with cranial robusticity. These traits are subject to geographic variation and do not mark a species boundary, but they may nevertheless delimit groups that had different evolutionary fates.

There is no reason to suppose that all demes of *Homo erectus* evolved further. The evidence is consistent with eventual extinction of some or all populations in the Far East. A less specialized branch of the species may well have given rise to later humans.[9,27] This budding of a daughter lineage from *Homo erectus* must have occurred very early in the Middle Pleistocene, if not before. African and western Asia are likely areas in which the first more advanced humans originated (Figure 2). An African locus is consistent with findings from archeology, environmental reconstruction, and patterns of animal dispersal.[28]

Fossils that shed light on this speciation event have turned up at several localities in Africa. One is Bodo in the Middle Awash region of Ethiopia. The Bodo cranium and, later, a broken parietal from a second individual, were found in conglomerates and sands containing mammalian bones and Acheulean artifacts.[29,30] Fauna from the site has been compared to that from Bed IV at Olduvai Gorge and Olorgesailie in Kenya, and an early Middle Pleistocene age is indicated. New argon-argon dates reported by Clark and colleagues[31] support this biochronology. The evidence from fauna, archeology, and laser-fusion determinations points to an age of about 600,000 years for the Bodo hominids.

The face and anterior portion of the braincase are reasonably complete; it can be established that Bodo is like *Homo erectus* in some features. The massive facial bones, projecting brow, low and constricted frontal with midline keeling, parietal angular torus, and thick vault give the specimen an archaic appearance. In other respects, the cranium is more advanced in its morphology. Brain size is close to 1,300 cc, which is substantially greater than is expected for *Homo erectus*. The frontal bone proportions, arched shape of the squamous temporal, and some traits of the cranial base are like those of more modern humans. Although the face is very broad and heavily constructed, the supraorbital tori are divided into medial and lateral segments, the margin of the nose is vertical rather than forward sloping, and the incisive canal opening into the front of the hard palate shows a derived condition present in recent *Homo*.[32]

This mix of characters suggests that the Middle Awash individuals are "intermediate" in their morphology. However, several of the resemblances to *Homo erectus* are plesiomorphies that cannot be considered diagnostic. Moreover, it is clear that the cranium shares other apomorphic features with more modern populations. It seems reasonable to group Bodo with the famous fossil from Broken Hill (Kabwe) in Zambia (Figure 3), along with specimens from Elandsfontein in South Africa, Lake Ndutu in Tanzania, and probably Eyasi, also in Tanzania. These localities are Middle Pleistocene in age. In addition to the human skullcap, deflation surfaces ("bays") at Elandsfontein have yielded a large fauna, together with Acheulean handaxes. Dating of this assemblage is complicated by the fact that several of the extinct mammal species are unknown elsewhere, but comparisons with other African sites imply that the bones were accumulated between 700,000 and 400,000 years ago.[33] Animal remains possibly associated with the Broken Hill cranium suggest an age within this same broad interval.[34]

As has been recognized for some time, the African hominids are similar to other, roughly contemporary

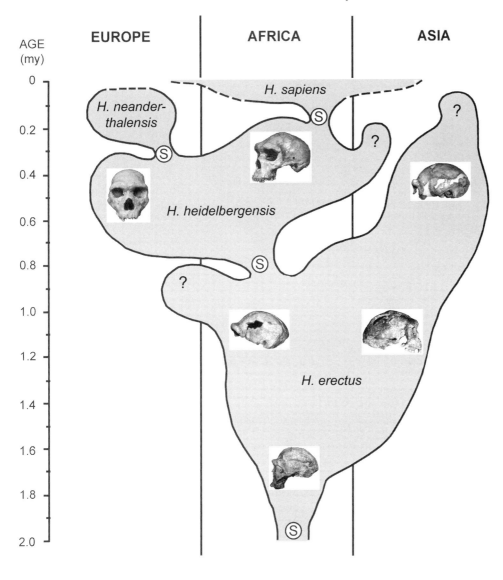

Figure 2. *A tree illustrating the evolution and geographic distribution of* Homo *in the Pleistocene.* Homo erectus *is assumed to have originated in Africa and then spread quickly to Asia and probably to Europe.* Homo heidelbergensis *is distributed from Africa into Eurasia during the Middle Pleistocene. Whether this species reached the Far East is still a question. European* Homo heidelbergensis *gave rise to the Neanderthals, while an African branch of* Homo heidelbergensis *is ancestral to modern humans. Four speciation events (S) are depicted.*

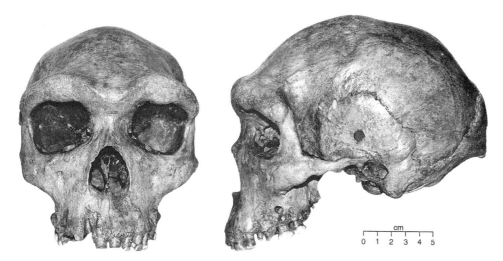

Figure 3. *Facial and lateral views of the Broken Hill cranium. Broken Hill is one of the most complete Middle Pleistocene specimens, here attributed to* Homo heidelbergensis. *Along with increased brain volume, the cranium exhibits features of the nasal region, palate, occiput and base that distinguish it from* Homo erectus.

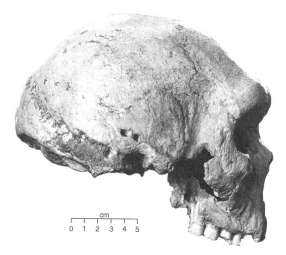
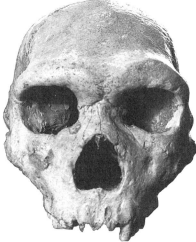

Figure 4. *Lateral and facial views of the Petralona cranium. This individual from Greece resembles that from Broken Hill in many metric features relating to facial proportions and vault shape. Whether the Petralona face also displays characters unique to the Neanderthal lineage is currently debated.*

people known from Europe. Like that from Broken Hill, the cranium from Petralona in Greece is particularly well preserved (Figure 4). Although there is doubt about both its original provenience within layers of stalagmite deposited on the cave floor and its association with animal bones, this individual is of Middle Pleistocene antiquity. Some of the flowstone may be about 200,000 years old,[35] but other fossils from the site imply a greater age for the cave contents (see Cook and coworkers[36] for a review). In any case, the Petralona and Broken Hill crania differ only slightly in orbit size, frontal proportions, and prominence of the torus crossing the occipital bone; in general, they are remarkably alike. Resemblances are apparent in the height, breadth, and massive construction of the upper face and cheek, several measures of projection in the facial midline, configuration of the thickened brows, and many aspects of vault shape.[9] Because the Bodo material is less complete, comparisons between it and the Greek cranium must be more limited in scope, but here also there are similarities.[32]

Multivariate studies of skull form have been carried out by several workers, who noted resemblances between the African and European specimens.[37–39] Van Vark[40] has used 17 dimensions of the face and braincase to construct a measure of generalized distance (D^2), which shows that the Broken Hill and Petralona specimens differ from one another less than is the case for Upper Paleolithic and recent humans. When a reconstruction of the partial cranium from Arago Cave in France is included in this analysis, it also falls close to that from Broken Hill. There seem to be good phenetic grounds for lumping these hominids together.

Other ancient European finds are more fragmentary. Human bones and teeth have been recovered from the quarry at Bilzingsleben in Germany and from several earlier Middle Pleistocene sites in Italy, while an occipital bone is on record from Vertesszöllös in Hungary. There is also the rear portion of a braincase from Swanscombe in England. The mandible from Mauer in Germany and a tibia associated with Acheulean bifaces at Boxgrove in England are arguably among the oldest hominids from Europe. Both are on the order of

500,000 years in age.[41] Of course there are questions about the affinities of this material, as few anatomical clues are preserved. But if the Mauer mandible is grouped with the other specimens from Europe and Africa, then the entire assemblage can be referred to *Homo heidelbergensis.*[9,42,43]

This species was named by Schoetensack in 1908 to accommodate the jaw found a year earlier in the basal sand and gravel complex of the Grafenrain pit near Heidelberg. Schoetensack was impressed with the primitive character of his fossil but recognized that it must be human, as the canines are reduced in size and the tooth crowns generally display the proportions expected for modern populations.

Later authors continued to emphasize the primitive appearance of the mandible. Howell[44] pointed to its massive construction, multiple mental foramina, and very thick symphysis, which lacks any indication of a chin, as characters shared by other early representatives of *Homo.* However, Howell was careful to note that other features of the specimen, including its ramus breadth, relatively great anterior depth of the corpus, and moderate size of the dentition, distinguish it from both Far Eastern *Homo erectus* and the Ternifine people. He argued that the Mauer hominid must be specifically distinct from archaic lineages in Asia or Northwest Africa. Howell left open the relationship of this isolated fossil to other European groups, including the Neanderthals. While there are still obvious difficulties with linking the mandible to individuals such as that from Petralona, for which no lower jaw has been recovered, the fossil can be lumped with earlier Middle Pleistocene humans in the way I have outlined. As defined on this basis, *Homo heidelbergensis* retains a number of archaic characters and may be the stem from which both Neanderthals and modern people are derived.

ALTERNATIVE VIEWS OF *HOMO HEIDELBERGENSIS*

Just as there is controversy about whether *Homo erectus* should be partitioned into two taxa, so there are questions about the make-up of *Homo heidelbergensis.* Some authorities hold that the European and African specimens should be set apart as representatives of distinct lineages. Proponents of this view agree that the French, German, and Greek fossils share a series of features with the hominids from Bodo and Broken Hill. But they claim that even the earliest Middle Pleistocene Europeans exhibit apomorphic traits that align them only with Neanderthals.[45-49]

In this reading of the evidence, the fossils from Mauer and probably Boxgrove, Arago Cave, Petralona, Bilzingsleben, Vertesszöllös, and Swanscombe document a single line evolving toward the populations at Steinheim in Germany and Atapuerca in Spain. These assemblages can be referred to *Homo heidelbergensis*. However, it is recognized that there is no clear separation of the latter from early Neanderthals such as those from Biache in France, Ehringsdorf in Germany, or Saccopastore in Italy. Eventually this same lineage produced the "classic" Neanderthals of the Late Pleistocene. So an alternative classification is possible in which not only the "classic" populations, but also all the older fossils, are placed in one species termed *Homo neanderthalensis*[50] (see also Carbonell and coworkers[51] and Arsuaga and coworkers[52]).

According to this "accretion" hypothesis, distinctive Neanderthal characters appear first in the facial skeleton. Advocates of the model argue that such traces can be identified in the Mauer and Arago remains. At later evolutionary stages, apomorphies accumulate in the occiput and finally in the temporal region. It is suggested that the ancestors of Neanderthals became increasingly isolated through time as a consequence of colder climate conditions. In the second half of the Middle Pleistocene, barriers formed by glaciers and associated tundra to the north, ice sheets in the mountains to the east, and the Mediterranean to the south reduced contact and gene exchange with people outside Europe.[49] Isolation in this relatively harsh environment led to the full expression of the morphology that distinguishes Neanderthal skulls and postcranial bones from those of other populations.

Much of this scenario seems sound. Certainly it is easy enough to track the Neanderthals back in time to Steinheim or even to Swanscombe. The occipital bones of both specimens display signs of a suprainiac fossa (a centrally placed elliptical depression with a pitted floor). Moreover, Swanscombe possesses a transverse torus that is weak near the midline but bilaterally projecting. These traits are diagnostic for the lineage. The Sima de los Huesos at Atapuerca confirms that Neanderthal features are present in an assemblage that may be close to 300,000 years in age.[53]

As described by Arsuaga and his colleagues,[47,52] the Sima skulls present a combination of plesiomorphic and derived characters. The well-preserved face of cranium 5 is quite large in relation to the braincase. This, by itself, is not a Neanderthal apomorphy, but the topography of the midface seems to anticipate that of later populations. The infraorbital surface and the side wall of the nose meet at a shallow angle, producing a slight concavity. The cheek region is thus not "inflated" in the extreme manner of Neanderthals, but can be interpreted

as intermediate in form. Also in the Sima sample, brows are very thick. Continuity of the supraorbital tori at glabella is said to be reminiscent of Neanderthals. At the rear of the cranium, the suprainiac area is large but not very depressed. This trait and the shape of the occipital torus seem to foreshadow the Neanderthal condition.

Earlier in the Middle Pleistocene, Neanderthal roots are more difficult to find. Some authors have pointed to Vertesszöllös or even Bilzingsleben as documenting evolutionary continuity, but most of this material is too fragmentary to provide convincing information. The jaw from Mauer is complete but, in fact, shows few if any traits that can be taken as specific links to later European populations. More crucial to the accretion hypothesis, or at least the version of it that encompasses the earliest fossils, are the crania from Arago and Petralona. Here the question is whether there are signs of "incipient" Neanderthal morphology, especially in the facial region.

The face of the partial cranium from Arago is largely complete but unfortunately damaged as a result of its long interment in compacted cave sediments. The frontal bone, interorbital pillar, nose, and cheeks show numerous cracks; localized areas of crushing are also present. The discoverers have been able to correct some of this damage in a reconstruction,[54,55] but significant distortion remains. In spite of these problems, some workers can discern definite resemblances to Neanderthals. Hublin[49] notes that the infraorbital surface of the maxilla is flattened and the cheek bones are obliquely oriented. Arsuaga and colleagues[52] suggest that the Arago midface is actually more Neanderthal-like than that of Sima cranium 5 in the extent to which the infraorbital plate and the side wall of the nose are continuous, and this surface is inflated or convex. Also, there is much forward protrusion of the face at subspinale (in the midline, just below the nasal opening). The nose itself is limited inferiorly by a sharp rim, as in Neanderthals.

These observations must be tempered by the fact that cracking and plastic deformation make it difficult to assess some key aspects of morphology. The wall of the Arago maxilla is generally flattened or even inflated in the manner characteristic of Neanderthals, but there is slight hollowing laterally, below the orbit. This cannot be discounted as due entirely to damage. Also, it is not clear that the zygomatic bone is swept back (obliquely oriented) as noticeably as it is in later populations. In facial forwardness at subspinale, as measured by the zygomaxillary angle of Howells,[56] the Arago cranium, at 113°, is in the Neanderthal range, and the Petralona specimen, at 118°, shows almost as much protrusion. But the value for Broken Hill is only 116°. Consequently, a low zygomaxillary angle does not necessarily align Arago and Petralona with Neandertals rather than with other Middle Pleistocene specimens. The sharp inferior margin of the Arago nose is indeed reminiscent of that in Neanderthals. However, there is variation in this feature. Petralona is rather less like the Neanderthals, while some later Europeans, including the Sima people, have a pattern of cresting on the nasal floor resembling that in the Broken Hill or Bodo fossils. Finally, it is worth noting that neither the Arago nor the Petralona cranium exhibits the apomorphic traits identified recently by Schwartz and Tattersall.[57] A medial projection from the inner margin of the nose and a swelling of the posterior nasal wall itself are present in Neanderthals but seem to be lacking in earlier Middle Pleistocene hominids.

Given this level of doubt concerning specific Neanderthal affinities of the Arago and Petralona crania or the Mauer jaw, perhaps it is premature to disassociate these specimens from contemporary Africans. In my view, all of the earlier Middle Pleistocene hominids share both *erectus*-like features and a suite of derived traits common to later humans. It is hard to find any morphological basis for restricting *Homo heidelbergensis* to Europe. This taxon may well have evolved elsewhere. However, these people did reach Europe at an early date. Sometime later, as climatic conditions changed and populations became isolated by ice barriers, speciation produced the first Neanderthals (Figure 2). Just when this event occurred is uncertain, but the ca. 300,000-year-old Sima fossils, as well as those from Steinheim and Swanscombe, foreshadow the Neanderthal condition. There are good reasons to postulate deep roots for the Neanderthal lineage, and here the accretion model must be broadly accurate.

MORE FOSSILS FROM SPAIN

New evidence challenging both the phylogenetic role of *Homo heidelbergensis* and the accretion model has been reported recently from Spain. The Sierra de Atapuerca contains many sites in addition to the Sima de los Huesos. One is a limestone cave deposit exposed by workers cutting a railway trench at the turn of the century. The collapsed cave of Gran Dolina is filled with a substantial thickness of sediments. The most ancient levels must be of Early Pleistocene age. Paleomagnetic sampling indicates that the TD6 layers may lie just below the Brunhes-Matuyama magnetic reversal, dated at 780,000 years.[58] Excavations in one of the TD6 strata have produced a collection of stone tools consisting of core-choppers and flakes, but no handaxes or cleavers. Along with the artifacts, there are human bones representing at least six different individuals. Given the uncertainties surrounding the age of the find at Ceprano in Italy, these Spanish discoveries may be the oldest anywhere in Europe.

Although many of the fossils are fragmentary, they provide information about the teeth, skull, and postcranial skeleton. Preliminary descriptions have been provided by Carbonell and colleagues[51] and Bermúdez de Castro and colleagues.[59] One important specimen is part of a lower jaw with the molars still in place. More teeth belonging to this hominid have been recovered and it is possible that a piece of frontal bone should also be assigned to the same individual, an adolescent about 14 years old. Differences from *Homo erectus* are apparent in the expansion of the lower incisor crowns, the size relationships of the premolar teeth, and the relative gracility of the mandibular body. Frontal breadth, which can be estimated as a minimum behind the brows, exceeds that for all but the largest of the *Homo erectus* crania from Asia.

Confirmation that the Gran Dolina people are more advanced than *Homo erectus* comes from a partial face discovered in 1995. The morphology of this specimen, representing another young individual, is said to be remarkably modern. Below the orbit, hollowing of the bone surface is accentuated by forward bending of the side wall of the nose. Such a degree of "flexion" of the maxilla is not seen in archaic hominids. That hollow, the canine fossa, is not well developed in specimens such as those from Bodo, Arago, or Petralona. As noted earlier, Neanderthal faces have quite a different appearance, with the cheek region inflated and swept to the rear. If the identification of the Ceprano braincase is corroborated, the Gran Dolina people may have coexisted with *Homo erectus* in the Mediterranean region. However, these people seem to be set apart, not only from *Homo erectus*, but also from *Homo heidelbergensis* and later Europeans.

The evidence from midfacial topography, along with other cranial, mandibular, and dental characters, has persuaded the Atapuerca researchers to name a new species, *Homo antecessor*.[59] As described so far, the fossils do not exhibit any of the derived features of Neanderthals and so do not fit neatly into the accretion model, which holds all early Europeans to be Neanderthal ancestors. Members of the new taxon can be interpreted as close relatives to Middle Pleistocene hominids such as Mauer and Arago. Moreover, some features of its mandibular body are very similar to those of the Sima population. This suggests evolutionary continuity with *Homo heidelbergensis*, taken to be a strictly European lineage. At the same time, *Homo antecessor* may be generalized enough in its morphology to be ancestral to more modern humans. The species from Spain thus seems to be a candidate for the stem from which both Neanderthals and *Homo sapiens* are descended. Here the role played by Middle Pleistocene populations in Africa is left unexplained, but Bodo and Broken Hill apparently are neither *antecessor* nor *heidelbergensis* and must represent still another (unnamed) taxon.

Undoubtedly, the exciting new material from Atapuerca will be subjected to further comparative study. In the meantime, there are questions. Attention has been focused particularly on the facial skeleton. The morphology of the ATD6-69 midface does seem to be distinctive with respect to other Middle Pleistocene hominids, and a well developed canine fossa is characteristic of more modern humans. A complication is that this Gran Dolina individual is juvenile, maybe only 10 or 11 years old. It is always tricky to compare children to adults, for little is known of the growth patterns in archaic people. Almost certainly, the shape of the maxilla changes as the sinuses expand and the teeth are fully erupted. In another (adult) specimen from the site, less hollowing of the cheek is present. So one must ask whether this feature is an appropriate component of the diagnosis of a new species. It seems to me that one can make a good case for attributing the Spanish fossils to *Homo heidelbergensis*, where the hypodigm for this taxon is defined broadly to include European and African remains. In this view, *Homo heidelbergensis*, like *Homo erectus*, was a wide-ranging species rather than just a short segment of a lineage sandwiched in between the Gran Dolina hominids and later Neanderthals.

CONTINUING QUESTIONS

Several questions about the evolutionary role of *Homo heidelbergensis* have still to be touched on. In my reading of the record, this species is ancestral *not* only to *Homo neanderthalensis* but also to modern humans. Figure 2 suggests speciation to *Homo sapiens* in Africa or western Asia sometime in the later Middle Pleistocene. However, there are more fossils from the Far East that complicate this picture. Particularly in China, many localities document the presence of humans more advanced than *Homo erectus,* certainly after 300,000 years ago and perhaps much earlier. Whether the skeletons should be lumped with *Homo heidelbergensis* is one issue; how they are related to recent Asian populations is another. Both are fraught with controversy.

Two important crania have been discovered in terrace deposits of the Han River at Yunxian in western Hubei.[60] The finds were made in a clay layer and both hominids were encased in hard calcareous matrix. The same level has produced mammalian fossils and some stone cores and flakes. The fauna suggests a Middle Pleistocene age. Paleomagnetic work coupled with other approaches now indicates that the Yunxian assemblage may be as much as 600,000 or even 800,000 years old.[61,62]

Unfortunately, the crania themselves are heavily damaged. One has been crushed nearly flat. In the other the face is reasonably well preserved, although the vault has been deformed and the base is filled with small cracks. There are some resemblances to *Homo erectus.* The brow is thickened and the vault is long and low, with an angled occiput. The cranial base is generally similar to that in the Zhoukoudian specimens and does not seem to exhibit the flexion apparent in later populations. At the same time, the Yunxian crania share many features with more advanced humans. The braincase is large and not very constricted behind the orbits, and the squamous temporal is arched. Some traits of the nose and palate may also be derived relative to *Homo erectus.* The midface of the second individual is described as especially "*sapiens*-like" in that a canine fossa is present and the infraorbital region is set at an angle to the flaring cheek. Given this mix of characters, Li and Etler[60] and Etler[61] choose to place the skulls with *Homo erectus,* but Zhang[63] identifies them with later humans.

Other fossils are known from later Middle Pleistocene localities in China. The Dali and Jinniushan specimens are often described as archaic or pre-modern *Homo sapiens.*[64] The Dali cranium is quite complete. Its massive brow, keeled frontal, and low vault are reminiscent of *Homo erectus.* In many other respects, the Dali braincase is more like that of later humans. Even when crushing of the maxilla is accounted for, the face must be relatively short. Also, the margin of the nose is vertically oriented and the incisive canal is placed anteriorly on the hard palate, as in Middle Pleistocene Africans and Europeans. As with one of the Yunxian faces, the wall of the cheek is hollowed to produce a canine fossa.

If it is accepted that these Chinese individuals (including Yunxian?) are not *Homo erectus,* then sorting them to *Homo heidelbergensis* is one alternative that must be explored. This is suggested in Figure 2. Depending on the age of the Yunxian material, the entrance of *Homo heidelbergensis* into eastern Asia might have occurred earlier than depicted. The taxon would then have persisted alongside *Homo erectus* for a substantial time. A question arises as to the fate of these Chinese populations. The scenario of Figure 2 shows eventual extinction, but a case for continuity with recent humans must be considered. In fact, this point is still difficult to resolve from the paleontological record. Comparative molecular studies keep open the possibility that there was some contribution from archaic Asians to the modern gene pool.[65]

Some workers elect instead to separate the Chinese hominids from Middle Pleistocene populations in the West. This preference is based largely on observations of the midface, which is said to show modern features at a relatively early date. These workers emphasize the development of a canine fossa, along with lateral prominence of the cheek. If these differences are taken to preclude an identification as *Homo heidelbergensis,* then the fossils may have to be allocated to a new taxon. However, as noted earlier, hollowing of the infraorbital surface can be documented for faces outside of China. Furthermore, the new finds from Gran Dolina suggest that this feature may appear in Europe at the beginning of the Middle Pleistocene. Such evidence will make it harder to argue for isolation of the major Old World geographic provinces. The spread of some populations of *Homo heidelbergensis* into the Far East cannot be ruled out.

CONCLUSIONS

In their well-known 1975 volume *After the Australopithecines,*[66] Karl Butzer and Glynn Isaac noted many uncertainties surrounding human evolution in the Middle Pleistocene. Almost a quarter of a century later, the "muddle in the middle" is still evident, especially in respect to systematics and classification of the hominids. Perhaps the most vexing questions concern fossils of earlier Middle Pleistocene antiquity. Specimens from Africa and Eurasia have most frequently been described as "archaic" representatives of our own species, but this situation is unsatisfactory for several reasons. Fossils such as those found at Bodo, Broken Hill, Arago, Petralona, and Dali retain many primitive *erectus*-like characters, and this anatomy sets them apart from recent humans. Simply lumping diverse ancient groups with living populations obscures these differences.

There is increasing acceptance of the suggestion that distinct lineages may have evolved during this period. One possibility is that fossils from Africa and Europe can be sorted together to a single taxon, appropriately called *Homo heidelbergensis.* This species may have originated in Africa. If the Gran Dolina fossils are also *Homo heidelbergensis,* then these people apparently reached Europe at an early date. In this region, populations isolated by glacial conditions perhaps were eventually ancestral to the Neanderthals. In other parts of the species range, including Africa, there are indications that later Middle

Pleistocene groups were evolving in the direction of *Homo sapiens*. *Homo heidelbergensis* is thus the stem from which both Neanderthals and modern humans are derived.

A problem is whether the same taxon can be identified in the East. Fossils such as those found at Dali and Jinniushan in China are more advanced than *Homo erectus* and exhibit some of the same derived characters as do the specimens from Africa and Europe. But it can be argued that the Chinese hominids are distinctive in aspects of their facial morphology. Some workers will prefer either to place them in a new species or lump them as early *Homo sapiens*. This question remains to be resolved.

ACKNOWLEDGMENTS

My studies of Pleistocene hominids have been conducted with the assistance of many individuals and institutions, and I am grateful for this help. The governments of China, Ethiopia, Indonesia, Kenya, and Tanzania granted me clearance to examine fossils in these countries. The L.S.B. Leakey Foundation and the Boise Fund supported much of the research on which this paper is based. R. G. Klein, R. Quam, and C. B. Stringer kindly commented on a version of the manuscript, as did several anonymous reviewers.

REFERENCES

1. Andrews, P. (1984). An alternative interpretation of characters used to define *Homo erectus*. Cour Forsch-inst Senckenberg *69*:167–175.
2. Groves, C. P. (1989). *A Theory of Human and Primate Evolution*. Oxford: Oxford University Press.
3. Larick, R., Ciochon, R. L. (1996). The African emergence and early Asian dispersals of the genus *Homo*. Am Sci *84*:538–551.
4. Wood, B. (1991). *Koobi Fora Research Project, Vol. 4. Hominid Cranial Remains*. Oxford: Clarendon.
5. Wood, B. (1994). Taxonomy and evolutionary relationships of *Homo erectus*. Cour Forsch-inst Senckenberg *171*:159–165.
6. Wolpoff, M. W., Thorne, A., Jelinek, J., Zhang, Y. (1994). The case for sinking *Homo erectus*: 100 years of *Pithecanthropus* is enough! Cour Forsch-inst Senckenberg *171*:341–361.
7. Wolpoff, M. W. (1996). *Human Evolution*. New York: McGraw-Hill.
8. Tobias, P. V. (1995). The place of *Homo erectus* in nature with a critique of the cladistic approach. In Bower, J. R. F., Sartono, S. (eds), *Human Evolution in Its Ecological Context, Vol. 1. Palaeoanthropology: Evolution and Ecology of Homo erectus*, pp 31–41. Leiden: Pithecanthropus Centennial Foundation.
9. Rightmire, G. P. (1990). *The Evolution of Homo Erectus. Comparative Anatomical Studies of an Extinct Human Species*. Cambridge: Cambridge University Press.
10. Bräuer, G., Mbua, E. (1992). *Homo erectus* features used in cladistics and their variability in Asian and African hominids. J Hum Evol *22*:79–108.
11. Kramer, A. (1993). Human taxonomic diversity in the Pleistocene: Does *Homo erectus* represent multiple hominid species? Am J Phys Anthropol *91*:161–171.
12. Bräuer, G. (1994). How different are Asian and African *Homo erectus*? Cour Forsch-inst Senckenberg *171*:301–318.
13. Walker, A. (1993). Perspectives on the Nariokotome discovery. In Walker, A., Leakey, R. (eds), *The Nariokotome Homo erectus Skeleton*, pp 411–430. Cambridge: Harvard University Press.
14. Rightmire, G. P. (1998). Evidence from facial morphology for similarity of Asian and African representatives of *Homo erectus*. Am J Phys Anthropol *106*:61–85.
15. Brown, B. (1994). Comparative dental anatomy of African *Homo erectus*. Cour Forsch-inst Senckenberg *171*:175–184.
16. Bar-Yosef, O. (1995). The role of climate in the interpretation of human movements and cultural transformations in western Asia. In Vrba, E. S., Denton, G. H., Partridge, T. C., Burckle, L. H. (eds), *Paleoclimate and Evolution with Emphasis on Human Origins*, pp 507–523. New Haven: Yale University Press.
17. Gabunia, L., Vekua, A. (1994). A Plio-Pleistocene hominid from Dmanisi, East Georgia, Caucasus. Nature *373*:509–512.
18. Bräuer, G., Schultz, M. (1996). The morphological affinities of the Plio-Pleistocene mandible from Dmanisi, Georgia. J Hum Evol 30:445–481.
19. Tchernov, E. (1987). The age of the 'Ubeidiya Formation, an Early Pleistocene hominid site in the Jordan Valley, Israel. Israel J Earth Sci *36*:3–30.
20. Villa, P. (1991). Middle Pleistocene prehistory in southwestern Europe: The state of our knowledge and ignorance. J Anthropol Res *47*:193–217.
21. Roebroeks, W. (1994). Updating the earliest occupation of Europe. Curr Anthropol *35*:301–305.
22. Ascenzi, A., Biddittu, I., Cassoli, P. F., Segre, A. G., Segre-Naldini, E. (1996) A calvarium of late *Homo erectus* from Ceprano, Italy. J Hum Evol *31*:409–423.
23. Swisher, C. C., Curtis, G. H., Jacob, T., Getty, A. G., Suprijo, A., Widiasmoro (1994). Age of the earliest known hominids in Java, Indonesia. Science *263*:1118–1121.
24. Swisher, C. C., Rink, W. J., Anton, S. C., Schwarcz, H. P., Curtis, G. H., Suprijo, A., Widiasmoro (1996). Latest *Homo erectus* of Java: Potential contemporaneity with *Homo sapiens* in southeast Asia. Science *274*:1870–1874.
25. Groves, C. P. (1994). The origin of modern humans. Interdisciplinary Sci Rev *19*:23–34.
26. Dean, D., Delson, E. (1995). *Homo* at the gates of Europe. Science *373*:472–473.
27. Harrison, T. (1993). Cladistic concepts and the species problem in hominoid evolution. In Kimbel, W. H., Martin, L. B. (eds), *Species, Species Concepts and Primate Evolution*, pp 345–371. New York: Plenum Press.
28. Foley, R., Lahr. M. M. (1997). Mode 3 technologies and the evolution of modern humans. Cambridge Archaeol J *7*:3–36.
29. Kalb, J. E., Wood, C. B., Smart, C., Oswald, E. B., Mabrate, A., Tebedge, S., Whitehead, P. (1980). Preliminary geology and palaeoecology of the Bodo d'Ar hominid site, Afar, Ethiopia. Palaeogeogr Palaeoclimatol Palaeoecol *30*:107–120.
30. Clark, J. D., Asfaw, B., Assefa, G., Harris, J. W. K., Kurashina, H., Walter, R. C., White, T. D., Williams, M. A. (1984). Paleoanthropological discoveries in the Middle Awash valley, Ethiopia. Nature *307*:423–428.
31. Clark, J. D., de Heinzelin, J., Schick, K. D., Hart, W. K., White, T. D., WoldeGabriel, G., Walter, R. C., Suwa, G., Asfaw, B., Vrba, E., H.-Selassie, Y. (1994). African *Homo erectus*: Old radiometric ages and young Oldowan assemblages in the Middle Awash valley, Ethiopia. Science *264*:1907–1910.
32. Rightmire, G. P. (1996). The human cranium from Bodo, Ethiopia: Evidence for speciation in the Middle Pleistocene? J Hum Evol *31*:21–39.
33. Klein, R. G., Cruz-Uribe, K. (1991). The bovids from Elandsfontein, South Africa, and their implications for the age, palaeoenvironment and origins of the site. Afr Archaeol Rev *9*:21–79.
34. Klein, R. G. (1994). Southern Africa before the Iron Age. In Corruccini, R. S., Ciochon, R. L. (eds), *Integrative Paths to the Past: Paleoanthropological Advances in Honor of F. Clark Howell*, pp 471–519. Englewood Cliffs: Prentice Hall.
35. Grün, R. (1996). A re-analysis of electron-spin resonance dating results associated with the Petralona hominid. J Hum Evol *30*:227–241.
36. Cook, J., Stringer, C. B., Currant, A. P., Schwarcz, H. P., Wintle, A. G. (1982). A review of the chronology of the European Middle Pleistocene hominid record. Yrbk Phys Anthropol *25*:19–65.
37. Stringer, C. B. (1974). A multivariate study of the Petralona skull. J Hum Evol *3*:397–404.
38. Stringer, C. B. (1983). Some further notes on the morphology and dating of the Petralona hominid. J Hum Evol *12*:731–742.
39. Bräuer, G. (1984). A craniological approach to the origin of anatomically modern *Homo sapiens* in Africa and implications for the appearance of modern Europeans. In Smith, F. H., Spencer,

F. (eds), *The Origins of Modern Humans: A World Survey of the Fossil Evidence*, pp 327–410. New York: Alan R. Liss.

40. Van Vark, G. N. (1995). The study of hominid skeletal remains by means of statistical methods. In Boaz, N. T., Wolfe, G. D. (eds), *Biological Anthropology: The State of the Science*, pp 71–90. Corvallis: Oregon State University Press.

41. Roberts, M. B., Stringer, C. B., Parfitt, S. A. (1994). A hominid tibia from Middle Pleistocene sediments at Boxgrove, UK. Nature 369:311–313.

42. Stringer, C. B. (1993). New views on modern human origins. In Rasmussen DT (ed), *The Origin and Evolution of Humans and Humanness*, pp 75–94. Boston: Jones and Bartlett.

43. Groves, C. P., Lahr, M. M. (1994). A bush not a ladder: Speciation and replacement in human evolution. Perspect Hum Biol 4:1–11.

44. Howell, F. C. (1960). European and northwest African Middle Pleistocene hominids. Curr Anthropol 1:195–232.

45. Vandermeersch, B. (1985). The origin of the Neandertals. In Delson, E. (ed), *Ancestors: The Hard Evidence*, pp 306–309. New York: Alan R. Liss.

46. Hublin, J.-J., Tillier, A.-M. (1991). L'*Homo sapiens* en Europe occidentale: Gradualisme et rupture. In Hublin, J.-J., Tillier, A.-M. (eds), *Aux Origines d'Homo Sapiens*, pp 291–327. Paris: Presses Universitaires de France.

47. Arsuaga, J. L., Martínez, I., Gracia, A., Carretero, J. M., Carbonell, E. (1993). Three new human skulls from the Sima de los Huesos Middle Pleistocene site in Sierra de Atapuerca, Spain. Nature 362:534–537.

48. Condemi, S. (1996). Does the human fossil specimen from Reilingen (Germany) belong to the *Homo erectus* or to the Neanderthal lineage? Anthropologie 34:69–78.

49. Hublin, J.-J. (1996). The first Europeans. Archaeology 49:36–44.

50. Stringer, C. B. (1995). The evolution and distribution of later Pleistocene human populations. In Vrba, E. S., Denton, G. H., Partridge, T. C., Burckle, L. H. (eds), *Paleoclimate and Evolution with Emphasis on Human Origins*, pp 524–531. New Haven: Yale University Press.

51. Carbonell, E., Bermúdez de Castro, J. M., Arsuaga, J. L., Diez, J. C., Rosas, A., Cuenca-Bescos, G., Sala, R., Mosquera, M., Rodriguez, X. P. (1995). Lower Pleistocene hominids and artifacts from Atapuerca-TD6 (Spain). Science 269:826–830.

52. Arsuaga, J.-L., Martínez, I., Gracia, A., Lorenzo, C. (1997). The Sima de los Huesos crania (Sierra de Atapuerca, Spain). A comparative study. J Hum Evol 33:219–281.

53. Bischoff, J. L., Fitzpatrick, J. A., Leon, L., Arsuaga, J. L., Falgueres, C., Bahain, J. J., Bullen, T. (1997). Geology and preliminary dating of the hominid-bearing sedimentary fill of the Sima de los Huesos chamber, Cueva Mayor of the Sierra de Atapuerca, Burgos, Spain. J Hum Evol 33:129–154.

54. Spitery, J. (1982). La face de l'homme de Tautavel. In de Lumley M-A (ed), *L'Homo Erectus et la Place de l'Homme de Tautavel Parmi les Hominidés Fossiles*, pp 110–136. Nice: CNRS.

55. De Lumley, M.-A., Spitery, J. (1982). Le maxillaire de l'homme de Tautavel. In de Lumley, M.-A. (ed), *L'Homo Erectus et la Place de l'Homme de Tautavel Parmi les Hominidés Fossiles*, pp 154–177. Nice: CNRS.

56. Howells, W. W. (1973). Cranial variation in man. A study by multivariate analysis of patterns of difference among recent human populations. Papers of the Peabody Museum 67:1–259.

57. Schwartz, J. H., Tattersall, I. (1996). Significance of some previously unrecognized apomorphies in the nasal region of *Homo neanderthalensis*. Proc Natl Acad Sci 93:10852–10854.

58. Pares, J. M., Peres-Gonzalez, A. (1995). Paleomagnetic age for hominid fossils at Atapuerca archaeological site, Spain. Science 269:830–832.

59. Bermúdez de Castro, J. M., Arsuaga, J. L., Carbonell, E., Rosas, A., Martínez, I., Mosquera, M. (1997). A hominid from the Lower Pleistocene of Atapuerca, Spain: Possible ancestor to Neandertals and modern humans. Science 276:1392–1395.

60. Li, T., Etler, D. (1992). New Middle Pleistocene hominid crania from Yunxian in China. Nature 357:404–407.

61. Etler, D. (1996). The fossil evidence for human evolution in Asia. Ann Rev Anthropol 25:275–301.

62. Chen, T., Yang, Q., Hu, Y., BaoW, Li, T. (1997). ESR dating of tooth enamel from Yunxian *Homo erectus* site, China. Q Sci Rev 16:455–458.

63. Zhang, Y. (1995). Fossil human crania from Yunxian: Morphological comparison with *Homo erectus* crania from Zhoukoudian. Acta Anthropol Sinica 14:1–7.

64. Wu, X. Z., Poirier, F. E. (1995). *Human Evolution in China. A Metric Description of the Fossils and a Review of the Sites*. New York: Oxford University Press.

65. Harding, R. M., Fullerton, S. M., Griffiths, R. C., Bond, J., Cox, M. J., Schneider, J. A., Moulin, D. S., Clegg, J. B. (1997). Archaic African and Asian lineages in the genetic ancestry of modern humans. Am J Hum Genet 60:772–789.

66. Butzer, K. W., Isaac, G. L. (1975). *After the Australopithecines*. The Hague: Mouton.

47

The Atapuerca Sites and Their Contributions to the Knowledge of Human Evolution in Europe

J. M. Bermúdez de Castro, M. Martinón-Torres, E. Carbonell, S. Sarmiento, A. Rosas, J. van der Made, and M. Lozano

ABSTRACT

Over the last two decades, the Pleistocene sites of the Sierra de Atapuerca (Spain) have provided two extraordinary assemblages of hominin fossils that have helped refine the evolutionary story of the genus Homo in Europe. The TD6 level of the

Gran Dolina site has yielded about one hundred remains belonging to a minimum of six individuals of the species Homo antecessor. These fossils, dated to the end of the Lower Pleistocene (800 kyr), provide the earliest evidence of hominin presence in Western Europe. The origin of these hominins is unknown, but they may represent a speciation event from Homo ergaster/Homo erectus. The TD6 fossils are characterized by a significant increase in cranial capacity as well as the appearance of a "sapiens" pattern of craniofacial architecture. At the Sima de los Huesos site, more than 4,000 human fossils belonging to a minimum of 28 individuals of a Middle

Reprinted from J. M. Bermúdez de Castro et al., *Evolutionary Anthropology*, Vol. 13, pp. 25–41. Copyright © 2004 by Wiley-Liss, Inc. This material is used by permission of Wiley-Liss, Inc., a subsidiary of John Wiley & Sons, Inc.

Pleistocene population (ca. 500–400 kyr) have been recovered. These hominins document some of the oldest evidence of the European roots of Neanderthals deep in the Middle Pleistocene. Their origin would be the dispersal out of Africa of a hominin group carrying Mode 2 technologies to Europe. Comparative study of the TD6 and Sima de la Huesos hominins suggests a replacement model for the European Lower Pleistocene population of Europe or interbreeding between this population and the new African emigrants.

Since the late 1980s, paleoanthropology has witnessed a paradigm shift in interpretation of the evolution of the genus *Homo*.[1] The anagenetic evolutionary model, which postulates an unbroken lineal temporal succession of the reproductive continuity of *Homo habilis, Homo erectus,* and *Homo sapiens,* representing three evolutionary grades, is gradually being replaced by the cladogenetic model of speciation, which recognizes several speciation events throughout the evolution of the genus *Homo.* These events (cladogenesis) might have been favored by successive dispersals of hominins out of Africa and migratory movements between Africa and Eurasia during the Pleistocene, as well as events of reproductive isolation due to climatic and ecological changes.

The anagenetic model divides the fossil record, or the morphological space of the genus *Homo,* into three evolutionary grades. As the morphospace is filled with new findings, it is becoming increasingly difficult to agree on the exact boundaries between species. The difficulties of this model are exemplified by the frequent use of terms such as "advanced," "primitive," "early archaic," "archaic," and "late archaic" to modify *Homo sapiens.* These terms and other similar ones[2,3] have no taxonomical validity, but suggest a need to describe morphological diversity.

The cladogenetic model also has difficulties. Cladistics requires the establishment of character polarities (the phylogeny of the characters), the selection of independent traits, and the identification of homoplasies. These difficulties have opened several debates concerning the recognition of one or more species in a given hypodigm. One of the most prominent examples concerns the possible partition of a large portion of the Early Pleistocene fossil record into two species, *Homo erectus,* Dubois, 1892, and *Homo ergaster,* Groves and Mazak, 1975. *Homo ergaster* would be restricted to Africa (if we consider the hominins found in the Dmanisi site, Republic of Georgia, to belong to a different species[4]), while *Homo erectus* may have representatives in Asia and Africa.[1] The distinctions are based on the absence of some specific traits in the African fossils that are present in the Asian ones, to which the species name *erectus* applies. These include a midline keel on the vault, strong reduction of the postglenoid process, an angular torus at the posterior-inferior corner of the parietal bone, overall thickening of the braincase, and reduced superstructures in the temporal-occipital region. Moreover, *Homo erectus ss* exhibits a styloid process, as well as differences in the size and shape of the supraorbital torus.[5–7] The debate about the partitioning of the fossil record is beyond the scope of this paper but, from this point on, we assign

the specimens of the African Early Pleistocene, including KNM-ER 992 (the holotype of the species), KNM-ER 3733, KNM-ER 3883, and KNW-WT 15000 (the Turkana boy) to the species *Homo ergaster.*

Most authors suggest the use of apomorphies (unique derived traits) for the recognition of a species in a strict application of the cladogenetic model.[8] However, trait exclusiveness is not as common in the fossil record as it might seem. Given this situation, criteria that are less strict, such as the presence of a unique combination of apomorphic (derived) and plesiomorphic (primitive) traits, frequently have been used.[9,10] Furthermore, due to the difficulties we have noted, some authors consider that the species diagnosis does not need a cladistic basis, but can be made through the phenetic determination of a distinctive morphotype.[11]

Despite the internal debate generated by the cladogenetic model, most authors have abandoned the gradualist model for the "phylogenetic species concept" and the recognition of a larger number of species in the fossil record of the genus *Homo.* This situation has triggered an ongoing debate about the number of cladogenetic events, the nomenclature of the identified species, and possible evolutionary scenarios. For the past thirty years, the research team of the Sierra de Atapuerca sites (Spain) has contributed to this debate through the discovery of two hominin fossil assemblages from the Sima de los Huesos and Gran Dolina sites. These assemblages, as well as other specimens discovered in the last decade in Africa and Europe, give insight into the relationship between Early Pleistocene *Homo* and the lineage that gave rise to *Homo sapiens.*

THE SIERRA DE ATAPUERCA SITES

The Sierra de Atapuerca is a small hill of about twelve square kilometers that rises 1,079 meters above sea level and approximately 100 meters above the alluvial flatness of the Arlanzón river. The Sierra de Atapuerca is located in northern central Spain (Duero Basin) fourteen kilometers east of the historical city of Burgos. It contains numerous karst cavities in Cretaceous limestones that are filled with Pleistocene sediments (Figure 1).

The Sima de los Huesos is a blind cavity of 8×4 m^2 located well inside the Cueva Mayor-Cueva del Silo cave system of the karst of Sierra de Atapuerca (Figure 1). The access to this chamber is a vertical conduit 14 m deep, which ends with a steep inclined ramp about 9 m long. The first human remains, associated with a large assemblage of cave-bear (*Ursus deningeri*) fossils, were found here in 1976.[12] This site has been systematically excavated since 1984. Over several decades, tons of sediment were turned over by cavers hunting for cave-bear teeth.[13] A meticulous and methodical excavation began in 1988.[14] Arsuaga and coworkers[14] described the stratigraphy and many other aspects of the Sima de los Huesos site and other nearby cavities. They also published cross-sectional diagrams of the Sima de los Huesos site and a map of the excavation grid. The stratigraphy, geological history, and preliminary dating of the site can be found in Bischoff and coworkers.[15] All the human fossils were recovered from the same unit,

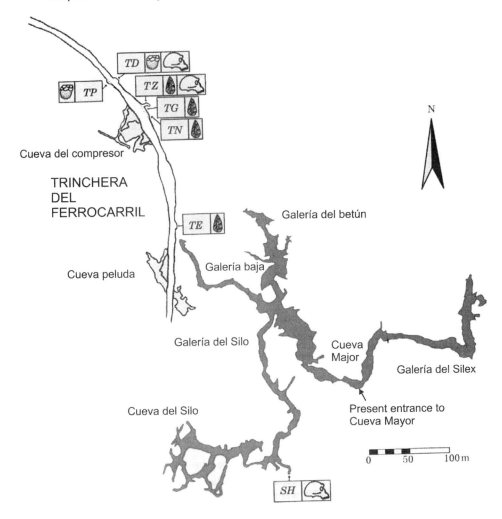

TRINCHERA
DEL
FERROCARRIL

Cueva del compresor

Cueva peluda

Galería del betún

Galería baja

Galería del Silo

Cueva Major

Galería del Silex

Cueva del Silo

Present entrance to
Cueva Mayor

N

Figure 1. *Map of the Trinchera del Ferrocarril and Cueva Mayor, showing the location of the main Atapuerca sites. TD: Gran Dolina; TG: Galería; TN: Trinchera Norte; TZ: Covacha de los Zarpazos; TE: Sima del Elefante; SH: Sima de los Huesos.*

which is shaped by breccias of clay-supporting bones, blocks, and clasts[15] of varying thickness along the site's profile. Apparently, all fossils were deposited in the site during the same sedimentation period.[15]

Previous radiometric and paleomagnetic analyses, as well as biochronological data, pointed to an age of 200 to 320 kyr (oxygen isotope stages 7 to 9) for the Sima de los Huesos hominins.[15–17] However, recent radiometric studies (U-series) of a 14-cm-thick in-situ speleothem overlying the mud-breccia containing the human bones has provided a minimum age of 350 kyr for these hominins.[18] An estimated age of 400 to 500 kyr (oxygen isotope stages 12 to 14) for these hominins is based on the rate of growth of the speleothem, correlation of the fauna (micro- and macro-mammals) at Sima de los Huesos with that at other Atapuerca sites (for example, TD6, TD8, TD10, and TD11 levels of Gran Dolina), and the normal magnetization of the Sima de los Huesos fossiliferous mud.[18]

The current hominin sample from Sima de los Huesos consists of more than 4,000 fossil remains. Considering all skeletal elements, it represents more than the 80% of the worldwide Middle Pleistocene record for the genus *Homo*.[18] The relative homogeneity of the sample and the fact that all fossils were recovered from the same level strongly support the notion that all of these hominins belonged to the same biological population.

The Sima de los Huesos hypodigm represents a minimum of 28 individuals. The most plausible explanation for this striking fossil accumulation is the use of this cavity by the human population of Atapuerca as a place to deposit corpses. The group may have died over a relatively short period or because of a catastrophic event.[14,19] In 1998, the finding of a handaxe with exceptional characteristics provided the first evidence of lithic industry at this site.[20] In our opinion, this discovery reinforces the hypothesis of the anthropic accumulation of the hominin remains with possible symbolical rituals.

Near the end of the nineteenth century, a British mining company opened a railway trench in the southwestern slope of the Atapuerca Hill less than 1 km from the entrance of the Cueva Mayor. Since 1978, some of the exposed cave infillings along the now-abandoned railway trench have been systematically explored, sampled, and excavated. The vertical section of one of these deposits, Gran Dolina, is 18 m high, formed by 11 successive levels deposited from the late Early Pleistocene to the end of the Middle Pleistocene.[21] The lowest stratigraphic levels (TD1 and TD2) contain sediments of interior facies typical of a closed cave. With the exception of TD9, the paleontological record (pollen and faunal remains) is continuous from TD3 to TD11 and some levels (TD4, 5, 6, 7, 10, and 11) contain abundant stone tools.

Table 1. Mesiodistal (MD) and Buccolingual (BL) Dimensions of the Canines and Postcanine Teeth of the Atapuerca Sima de los Huesos and TD6 Hominins

			Maxilla				Mandible			
			N	X	S.D.	Range	N	X	S.D.	Range
C	SH	MD	17	8.6	0.3	8.1–9.6	19	7.6	0.4	6.9–8.5
		BL	18	9.7	0.5	8.8–10.7	18	8.5	0.7	7.3–10.1
	TD6 H1	MD		8.9				8.1		
		BL		11.0				10.0		
P3	SH	MD	13	8.0	0.5	7.2–8.9	19	7.9	0.4	7.2–9.0
		BL	13	10.7	0.6	9.7–11.8	19	8.9	0.6	7.9–10.0
	TD6 H1	MD		8.4				8.8		
		BL		11.7				10.6		
	TD6 H3	MD		8.8						
		BL		12.1						
P4	SH	MD	12	7.6	0.5	7.1–8.4	23	7.2	0.5	6.0–8.0
		BL	13	10.4	0.6	9.5–11.3	23	8.6	0.6	7.2–10.1
	TD6 H1	MD		8.0				8.2		
		BL		11.7				10.2		
	TD6 H3	BL		11.6						
M1	SH	MD	16	11.1	0.6	9.9–12.3	23	11.2	0.5	10.3–12.1
		BL	16	11.5	0.7	10.3–13.0	23	10.4	0.5	9.6–11.6
	TD6 H1	MD		12.1				12.2		
		BL		13.1				11.8		
	TD6 H3	MD		11.9						
		BL		12.1						
M2	SH	MD	17	9.9	0.9	8.1–11.6	26	11.0	0.5	9.9–12.1
		BL	17	12.1	0.8	11.0–13.8	26	10.2	0.5	9.3–11.5
	TD6 H1	MD		12.1				13.5		
		BL		13.7				12.0		

In 1993, with the aim of performing a more detailed stratigraphic study of the Gran Dolina site, our team excavated an archeological survey pit of 6 m². In July 1994, the test pit reached level 6 (TD6). In one of its strata, known since then as the Aurora stratum, a rich assemblage of fossils and lithic industry was found.[22] The excavation of this stratum was completed in 1996. The human sample recovered includes a total of 86 hominin remains, 250 lithic pieces, and hundreds of macrovertebrate remains.

The first paleomagnetic investigation of the Gran Dolina site was performed by Parés and Pérez-González.[23] They found a paleomagnetic inversion of the TD7 level 1 m above the Aurora stratum, which they identify with the Matuyama-Brunhes boundary. Another study by these authors[21] confirmed that the lower levels (TD1–TD6) displayed reversed polarity, whereas the upper levels (TD7–TD11) were normal. At the bottom of the TD section, Parés and Pérez-González reported evidence of a short normal polarity event, which they interpreted as being the Jaramillo or Kamikatsura event. The electron spin resonance and U-series results obtained by Falguères and coworkers[24] also confirm an age range between 780 and 857 kyr for TD6.

Pollen studies of the Atapuerca sites by García Antón[25] suggest that the upper part of TD6, the Aurora stratum, corresponds to a Mediterranean forest composed of *Quercus* (oak, holm, galloak) and *Cupresaceae* (cypress), as well as *Olea, Celtis,* and *Pistacea.* The structure and composition of the mammals and avian paleocommunities are consistent with a Mediterranean climate similar to the present one.[26,27] Therefore, the Aurora stratum could be correlated with the oxygen isotope stage 21 (warm). The TD6 macromammals include

Vulpes sp., Canidae indet., Mustelidae indet., *Panthera* sp., *Felis silvestris, Ursus* sp., Proboscidea indet., *Equus* sp. *Stenoniano, Stephanorhinus etruscus, Sus scrofa, Dama dama vallonetensis, Cervus elaphus* cf. *acoronatus, Megaloceros* cf. *verticornis, Capreolus capreolus.*[28,29] The fauna is considered typical of the end of the Early Pleistocene and beginning of the Middle Pleistocene. Among microvertebrates, the presence of *Mimomys savini,* also represented in TD7 and TD8,[30] is noteworthy, as this taxon persisted at other European sites until 450 kyr ago.[31,32]

The TD6 human fossil record comprises more than 85 fragmented bones belonging to the cranial and postcranial skeleton. The sample includes more than 43 parts of clavicles, radii, femora, vertebrae, ribs, and patellae, metacarpal, and metatarsal bones, and pedal and manual phalanges. The cranial sample is represented by fragments of frontal, parietal, temporal, occipital, maxillary, zygomatic, sphenoid, and mandibular bones. A total of 30 deciduous and permanent teeth were identified as human. The human remains were assigned to a minimum of six individuals identified by the maxillae, mandibles, and teeth (Table 1). Two isolated lower incisors were attributed to two adult individuals whose age at death is difficult to assess, but were probably young adults.

THE ATAPUERCA HOMININS

Sima de Los Huesos

Study of the human fossils from Sima de los Huesos has revealed primitive features not found in Upper Pleistocene Neanderthals, transitional traits associated with the Neanderthal morphology, and some more derived Neanderthal traits, especially in the supraorbital torus, facial skeleton, and mandible.[33–36] The dental sample also displays a general morphology and proportions that are very similar to those observed in Neanderthals.[37,38] Therefore, this sample supports the European roots of Neanderthals deep in the Middle Pleistocene. This lineage can be tracked through the specimens recovered at other Middle Pleistocene European sites such as Arago, Montmaurin, Petralona, Pontnewydd, Steinheim, and Swanscombe. In all these specimens, we can observe one or more Neanderthal apomorphies in combination with primitive traits lost in Upper Pleistocene Neanderthals.[33,36,39]

According to Arsuaga and colleagues,[36] "Middle Pleistocene Europeans and Neanderthals represent the same 'evolutionary' species, an ancestral-descendant sequence of populations without rupture of the reproductive continuity." However, these authors also state that the European Middle Pleistocene population can be defined by a combination of various plesiomorphies not found in later Neanderthals, Neanderthal apomorphies, and incipient Neanderthal-like traits, suggesting the inclusion of these specimens in the species *Homo heidelbergensis* as a chronospecies of the European-Neanderthal lineage.

This taxon was proposed by Otto Schoetensack[40] to name the mandible found in 1907 in the fluvial deposits of the Neckar river near the small German locality of Mauer, nor far from the city of Heidelberg. The Mauer mandible is probably the oldest specimen from the European Middle Pleistocene population. This mandible shows clear affinities to other European specimens such as Arago 2, Arago 13, and the first mandible discovered at Sima de los Huesos (Atapuerca 1).[41,42] Rosas and Bermúdez de Castro[43] showed that the Mauer mandible displays a set of traits that form the structural basis through which Neanderthal apomorphies eventually were fully developed. Moreover, study of the Mauer mandible dental morphology and proportions reveals the proximity between it and the Sima de los Huesos and Neanderthal samples.[43,44] It is clear that during the Middle Pleistocene an independent hominin clade evolved into the Neanderthal human population, which, according to several authors, should be included in the species *Homo heidelbergensis*.[36,45,46]

Gran Dolina, TD6 Level

Studies of the TD6 human fossils reveal that most of the dental traits are plesiomorphic for the genus *Homo*, with a tendency toward enlarged anterior teeth. This appears to be a derived trait in *Homo ergaster* that is shared with European and African Middle Pleistocene populations. The TD6 mandible displays a generalized morphology in common with African, Early European, and Middle Pleistocene hominins. However, it does not demonstrate distinctive African traits such as corpus robustness and strong alveolar prominence.

The assessment of these traits, as well as the chronological and geographic situation of the TD6 level of Gran Dolina, initially led us to consider the Aurora

stratum hominins as a representation of a primitive form of *Homo heidelbergensis*.[22] However, the 1995 finding of several remains belonging to the facial skeleton drastically modified our original assessment. The most striking attribute of the find was the modern morphology in the facial skeleton, representing the earliest occurrence of a modern face in the fossil record. These TD6 human remains exhibit a unique combination of a modern face with a primitive dentition. They were subsequently attributed to a new species that the Atapuerca research team named *Homo antecessor.*[47] We further suggested that this species might represent the last common ancestor to both the Neanderthal and modern human lineages. This hypothesis implies that *Homo antecessor* had an ancestor-descendant relationship with both European and African Middle Pleistocene populations.

A SPECIATION EVENT IN THE LATE EARLY PLEISTOCENE?

In 1996, Rightmire[48] proposed that a speciation event occurred either in Africa or Western Eurasia early in the Middle Pleistocene or before. Rightmire reached this conclusion from his study of a cranium recovered in 1976 at the locality of Bodo, in the Middle Awash region of Ethiopia. The Upper Bodo Sand Unit, from which this specimen was collected, has been dated by the argon-argon method to about 640 kyr (Middle Pleistocene). This age was later ratified by archeological and paleontological evidence.[49] Rightmire[48] pointed to clear similarities between the Bodo cranium and the species *Homo erectus/Homo ergaster,* such as the great breadth and heavy buttressing of the face (massive zygomatic bones), very thick vault bones, the low and archaic appearance of the braincase, a flattened frontal profile, and a prominent angular torus. In combination with these primitive traits, Rightmire also described the Bodo cranium as having some synapomorphies with later Middle Pleistocene populations and modern humans. In particular, the cranial capacity of Bodo is around 1,300 cc, exceeding the upper limit of 1,100 cc in *Homo erectus.* The large capacity of the Bodo cranium, reflected in its broad midvault with signs of parietal bossing, the high contour of its temporal squama, and the minimum and maximum dimensions of its frontal breadth, exceeds the values for *Homo erectus/Homo ergaster.* Furthermore, the crista nasalis falls vertically from the rhinion, projecting the nose in a way similar to that in modern populations. Nevertheless, the Bodo cranium shows a very inflated maxilla without a canine fossa. Finally, the incisive canal follows a nearly vertical trajectory, having an anterior position 6 to 8 mm behind the septum separating the central incisor sockets. The Bodo cranium shares this trait with Middle Pleistocene European hominins, Neanderthals, and modern humans.

Consequently, the speciation suggested by Rightmire[48] would be characterized by the appearance of some derived traits in both the face and the braincase. According to his view, the most appropriate interpretation of the data would be to include the Bodo specimen in the species *Homo heidelbergensis*, together with other Middle Pleistocene specimens such as those from Arago, Mauer, or Petralona in Europe, Kabwe, Elandsfontein, and Ndutu in Africa, and maybe Dali, Jinniushan, and Yunxian in Asia. This fossil assemblage would represent the stem group for Neanderthals and modern humans. This model had been suggested previously by Stringer[50,51] and Stringer and McKie,[52] and defended by Tattersall,[53] reviving use of the designation *Homo heidelbergensis*.

The one-million-year-old specimen from Buia (Northern Danakil Depression, Eritrea), which was partially described by Abbate and coworkers,[54] displays primitive traits, including its 750 to 800-cc cranial capacity, that are characteristic of *Homo erectus/Homo ergaster*. However, this specimen also shows some "progressive traits," such as the high position of its greatest biparietal breadth. According to Abbate and colleagues,[54] the Buia cranium could provide the key to understanding the time, place, and model of the origins of *Homo sapiens*. Asfaw and coworkers[55] have recently described the calvarium recovered from the Dakanihylo Member of the Bouri Formation (Middle Awash, Ethiopia), which is from the same period as the Buia cranium. The Daka calvarium has a cranial capacity of 995 cc and has morphological similarities to the Buia specimen. Asfaw and associates[55] believe that this skull should be included in the species *Homo erectus*. They propose an evolutionary continuity in Africa, from fossils such as KNM-ER 3733 and KNM-ER 3883 to OH 9, Daka/Buia, and Bodo, but suggest that a speciation event in Africa may have taken place approximately one million years ago. Manzi, Bruner, and Passarello[56] agree

that the Daka calvarium should be considered as part of an African evolutionary lineage spanning the interval from approximately 1,800 kyr up to about 1,000 kyr. However, these authors do not believe that the Bodo and Kabwe Middle Pleistocene specimens indicate a continuation of the same African lineage.

The common idea underlying these studies is the presence of one or more evolved forms of *Homo erectus/Homo ergaster* having derived traits pointing to the origin of modern populations. This idea was proposed some years ago with the notion of "archaic" *Homo sapiens* (see, for instance, Wood[2], Stringer, Howell, and Melentis,[57] and Rightmire[58]). Following the concept of "evolutionary grade," this suggested a progression toward *Homo sapiens* and the Neanderthals. The TD6 hominin findings are crucial in solving this problem. The ATD6-69 maxilla (Hominid 3) has a fully modern pattern of midfacial morphology[59] (Figure 2). Clearly, this specimen belonged to an adolescent[47] with incomplete facial growth. However, ATD6-19 and ATD6-58, which represent two adults, also exhibit modern traits (see figures 3d and 3e in Arsuaga and coworkers[59]). ATD6-58 shows expansion of the maxillary sinus that reduces expression of the canine fossa.[59] From this evidence, we suggest that the face of *Homo sapiens* may have appeared by a paedomorphic process in which adults retained the facial developmental rate of juveniles.

Another derived trait of the TD6 hominins with respect to *Homo erectus/Homo ergaster* is the shape of the squamosal suture, which depicts a high arch (ATD6-20 specimen). Although there are no tools robust enough for precise estimation of the cranial capacity of the TD6 hominins, the estimated minimum frontal breadth of

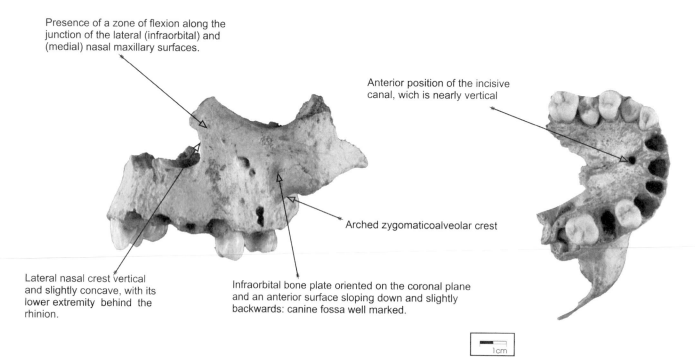

Presence of a zone of flexion along the junction of the lateral (infraorbital) and (medial) nasal maxillary surfaces.

Anterior position of the incisive canal, wich is nearly vertical

Arched zygomaticoalveolar crest

Lateral nasal crest vertical and slightly concave, with its lower extremity behind the rhinion.

Infraorbital bone plate oriented on the coronal plane and an anterior surface sloping down and slightly backwards: canine fossa well marked.

1cm

Figure 2. *The partial face ATD6-69 (Hominid 3 from TD6) exhibits a completely modern pattern of midfacial topography. ATD6-69 shares with Neanderthals and modern humans an anterior position of the incisive canal, which has a nearly vertical course.*

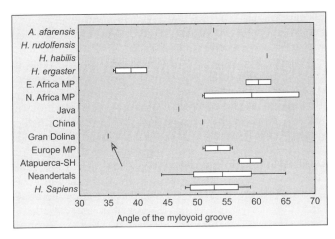

Figure 3.   *The angle of inclination of the mylohyoid groove in relation to the alveolar margin at the level of M1 and M2 is compared in different hominid samples. The mylohyoid groove in the ATD6-5 mandible forms a 34° angle and can be traced to the level of M2/M3. No other* Homo *mandible shows a mylohyoid groove located in such an extreme position. In OH13, attributed to* Homo habilis, *the mylohyoid groove is more vertical (about 60°), and ends at the distal end of the M3. Similar inclinations are found in African Middle Pleistocene mandibles such as Tighenif II and III, OH22, and BK67. However, in all of them the groove fails to reach M3. In the European hominids, the mylohyoid groove is more posterior and less inclined (x = c. 55°, n = 12). Thus, with regard to this feature, the Gran Dolina specimen is clearly different from the African and European Middle Pleistocene mandibles. Three mandibles in the fossil sample resemble ATD6-5: KNM-WT 15000, mandible C from Sangiran, and an Upper Palaeolithic specimen from Arene Candide (Italy).*

the ATD6-15 frontal bone (around 100 mm) suggests a cranial capacity greater than 1,000 cc for Hominid 3.[22] The TD6 hominins share three derived traits with modern humans, Neanderthals, and African and European Middle Pleistocene populations[59]; these are a convex superior border of the temporal squama, an anterior position of the incisive canal, and a marked nasal prominence. As a result, *Homo antecessor* appears to be the common ancestor of all of them.[59] With regard to the postcranial skeleton, Carretero, Lorenzo, and Arsuaga[60] and Lorenzo, Arsuaga, and Carretero[61] concluded that the more completely preserved specimens, which include clavicles, radii, a femur, vertebrae, and hand and foot bones, display morphological traits that resemble modern humans more than they do either Middle Pleistocene hominins or the Neanderthals.

The calvarium found in 1994 near the Italian locality of Ceprano has provided relevant information. The geostratigraphy and biostratigraphy of the Ceprano basin, as well as the available K/Ar dating, give an age to this fossil or more than 700 kyr, probably 800 to 900 kyr.[62] The first study of the Ceprano calvarium revealed similarities to *Homo erectus*, although some general traits related to the large cranial capacity of this specimen, estimated at 1,185 cc, suggested the need for prudence in its taxonomic assignment.[62] Later, Ascenzi and associates[63] assigned the specimen to late *Homo erectus*. A new reconstruction of the Ceprano calvarium by R. J. Clarke, M. A. de Lumley, and F. Mallegni confirmed the

previous taxonomic assessment.[63,64] More recently, Manzi, Mallegni, and Ascenzi[65] performed a comparative study of the Ceprano calvaria. They obtained a matrix of Manhattan phenetic distances. The unrooted trees generated from this matrix show that the Ceprano specimen occupies an intermediate position between *Homo erectus/Homo ergaster* specimens and the African and European Middle Pleistocene ones. Consequently, these investigators conclude that "Ceprano represents a unique morphological bridge between the clade *Homo ergaster/Homo erectus* and later Middle Pleistocene specimens commonly referred to *Homo heidelbergensis* (and/or to *Homo rhodesiensis*)." Manzi, Mallegni, and Ascenzi[65] subscribe to the notion of attributing the Ceprano calvarium to the species *Homo antecessor*, although this adult specimen cannot be directly compared to the immature TD6 hominins.

The TD6 hominins represent the earliest evidence of clear and unquestionable modern traits in the fossil record. These hominins, together with the Ceprano calvarium, are older than the Bodo cranium and more recent than the Buia and Daka specimens. Consequently, the appearance of *Homo antecessor* appears to be the best candidate for the speciation event that, around one million years ago, preceded the origin of later hominin lineages. Given this framework, several questions arise: Where did this speciation event take place? What is the origin of *Homo antecessor*? What are the possible evolutionary scenarios for the phylogenetic position of this species?

THE ORIGIN AND PHYLOGENETIC RELATIONSHIPS OF *HOMO ANTECESSOR*

Different evolutionary scenarios can be considered to explain the origins of the European Early Pleistocene population. One is the possibility that TD6 and the Dmanisi hominins are phylogenetically related. At the Dmanisi site, located in the Republic of Georgia, the entrance to Europe, the earliest evidence of hominins out of Africa has been recovered, dated to the Pliocene-Pleistocene boundary.[4,66–69] Perhaps this first dispersal out of Africa, which may have occurred at the end of the Pliocene, also reached southwestern Europe, but this has yet to be determined. The oldest archeological evidence of the presence of hominins in Europe comes from three Spanish localities: Sima del Elefante, also located in the railway trench of the Sierra de Atapuerca, and Barranco León and Fuente Nueva 3, in the Guadix-Baza basin (Andalucía). The lower levels of Sima del Elefante (E8–E12) give a reverse polarity. The micromammal association of these levels is consistent with the Matuyama chron, suggesting an age of about 1,000 kyr for a small sample of flint flakes recovered from the E11 level.[70] With regard to the paleomagnetic data and the faunal assemblages recovered from Barranco León and Fuente Nueva 3, the lithic artifacts (Mode 1) may be older than 1,070 kyr.[71]

The metrical and morphological differences between the hominins from Dmanisi and TD6 are remarkable,[66] a fact that could weaken this scenario. However, it is necessary to bear in mind that these hominins are one million years apart. This first scenario would explain the presence of Mode 1 in all of the European Early and early Middle Pleistocene sites.[72] Moreover, in this evolutionary scenario *Homo antecessor* would represent a speciation event in Eurasia after the first hominin dispersal out of Africa. This species could have disappeared or been absorbed by the subsequent arrival of an "Acheulean" population that originated in Africa. In this case, we should consider that the expression of "modern" traits in the skull happened more than once, in both Africa and Europe, and in populations that had been separated for almost one million years.

In relation to this first scenario, it is known that before 1,200 kyr a series of dispersals started in Eurasia, mainly involving mammals of Asiatic origin and probably related to climatic change.[73,74] More than 25 species of large mammals dispersed from Asia into western and central Europe in the next 500 kyr, many more than in any period of comparable length since the early Miocene.

A second scenario postulates a second major dispersal of hominins out of Africa across the Levant toward southwestern Europe at the end of the Early Pleistocene, around one million years ago or earlier. In this context, it is important to remember that the main dispersals of mammals from Africa to Europe during the Pleistocene occurred around 1,200, 900, and 500 to 600 kyr.[74,75] In this scenario, *Homo antecessor* could represent a speciation event that occurred either in Africa or Eurasia after the second major dispersal. If this event occurred in Africa, *Homo antecessor* would have persisted in Africa to originate the evolutionary lineage of *Homo sapiens*. If the species originated in Eurasia, or perhaps in the Near East, *Homo antecessor* must have gone back to the African continent to give rise to our species.

This second scenario is strengthened by the morphological similarities between the TD6 hominins and certain African hominins and hominins of Africa origin. Thus, the mandibular specimen ATD6-5 displays a remarkable position of the mylohyoid groove, comparable only to that found in immature specimens of *Homo ergaster* and, very rarely, in adult *Homo sapiens* (Figure 3). Furthermore, as stated earlier, the TD6 hominins share three derived traits with modern humans, Neanderthals, and African and European Middle Pleistocene hominins. Considering either of the two possibilities that might be expected in this second scenario, we would still need to know why this expansion occurred with Mode 1 technology when Mode 2 was already present in Africa and the Near East. According to suggestions made by Stringer and McKie,[52] Rightmire,[48] and Tattersall,[46] the origin of the European Middle Pleistocene population may be related to the dispersal toward Europe of an African Middle Pleistocene population that probably resembled the Bodo specimen. In this way, Mode 2 might have been carried to Europe by these new emigrants,[22,65] resulting in replacement of the autochthonous populations or, more likely, crossbreeding between them.[76]

If this is correct, then it is necessary to assume that another cladogenetic event took place in Africa at the beginning of the Middle Pleistocene, initiating the

geographic split between the European lineage, which then dispersed out of Africa, and the African lineage, which subsequently gave rise to *Homo sapiens*. This cladogenetic event could have been from the African population of the species *Homo antecessor*, if we accept that this species is the common ancestor of the Neanderthals and modern humans (Figure 4). For climatic and geographical reasons, the European lineage might have evolved during the Middle Pleistocene almost without genetic exchange with other people outside Europe, culminating in the "classic" Neanderthals of the early Upper Pleistocene. The appropriate name for this lineage is *Homo neanderthalensis* if we acknowledge that the Neanderthals do not represent a cladogenetic event in Europe but, instead, are the result of an

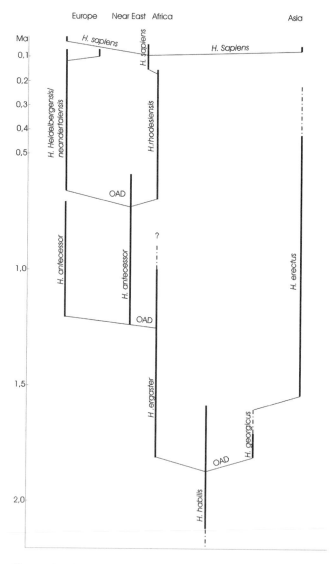

Figure 4. *In this scheme, we assume that the Dmanisi hominins represent a distinct species,* Homo georgicus,[102] *and that this species shares a common ancestor with* Homo ergaster. *A candidate for this common ancestor is* Homo habilis. *Although* Homo erectus *appears as a long-lasting lineage in China and Southeast Asia, the large variability of this species needs to be revised. Theoretically, the distribution of the species* Homo antecessor *would include Southern Europe, the Near East, and Africa. OAD = Out of Africa dispersal.*

evolutionary process of morphological "accretion" of the Neanderthal features.[36,45,77,78] For practical reasons, we can consider two chronospecies, *Homo heidelbergensis* and *Homo neanderthalensis* in this European lineage.[36] The Middle Pleistocene African fossils could be grouped in *Homo rhodesiensis* (see Stringer[45]). The African lineage followed a different trajectory that culminated in the last speciation event, which gave rise to the species *Homo sapiens* (Figure 4).

HOMO ANTECESSOR AND THE EUROPEAN MIDDLE PLEISTOCENE POPULATION

In both of the scenarios outlined, an essential question is whether or not there is an ancestor-descendant relationship between the European Early Pleistocene population, represented by TD6 and Ceprano, and the European Middle Pleistocene population. In other words, did *Homo antecessor* evolve in Europe into the Neanderthal lineage?

One of the most striking Neanderthal features is midfacial prognathism.[79,80] In these hominins, the infraorbital bone plate is not oriented in the coronal plane, as it is in modern populations, but rather exhibits a coronal-sagittal (or parasagittal) orientation, conforming to a uniplanar surface with the lateral nasal wall. This surface lacks a canine fossa and maxillary flexion. The zygomatico-alveolar crest is straight and oblique with its root low in the maxilla. Finally, the zygomatic bone is located at the M2 or M2–M3 level.[80] Midfacial prognathism, a derived trait of the Neanderthal facial skeleton, was already present in its Middle Pleistocene ancestors. According to Arsuaga and coworkers,[36] Arago 21, Petralona, and Cranium 5 of Sima de los Huesos also show midfacial prognathism (Figure 5), although differences from the classic Neanderthal pattern are still distinguishable.[79]

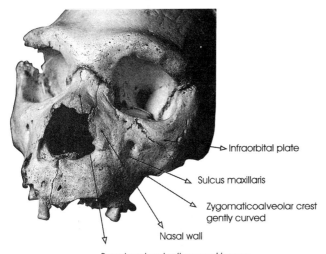
→ Infraorbital plate
→ Sulcus maxillaris
→ Zygomaticoalveolar crest gently curved
→ Nasal wall
Broad and projecting nasal bones

Figure 5. *Partial view of Cranium 5 from Sima de los Huesos (Individual XXI). This specimen exhibits midfacial prognathism. The infraorbital plate and the nasal wall do not form a uniplanar surface as they do in classic Neanderthals, but they meet at a wide angle. The zygomaticoalveolar crest is gently curved instead of straight and oblique as in classic Neanderthals.*

The TD6 Hominid 3 face is categorically modern, bearing no resemblance to the derived face of Neanderthals. ATD6-58 does not share any common trait with these hominins either.[59] However, Arsuaga and colleagues[59] believe that the Neanderthal face could be derived from a face like that of the TD6 hominin. According to these authors, specimens from Sima de los Huesos (AT-404) and Steinheim point to that possibility,[59] showing an intermediate morphology between the generalized midface[79] observed in certain hominins and modern populations and the derived midface of Neanderthals. They also point to the fact that the AT-404 and Steinheim specimens are clearly derived toward the Neanderthal direction.

The internal nasal cavity of ATD6-69 lacks the three Neanderthal apomorphies described by Schwartz and Tattersall[81]: development of an internal nasal margin bearing a well-developed and vertically oriented medial projection, swelling of the posterior-lateral wall of the nasal cavity as a result of a medially expanded maxillary sinus, and lack of an ossified roof over the lacrimal groove. Furthermore, nasal crests of ATD6-69 are similar to those of modern humans and lack the typical Neanderthal sharp lower margin formed by the lateral crest.[59]

Metric and shape features of the Early Pleistocene mandible specimen from TD6 show that ATD6-5 had a generalized morphology largely shared with both African and European Early and Middle Pleistocene samples.[82] However, distinctive African traits such as corpus robustness and strong alveolar prominence are absent in the Gran Dolina specimen. At the same time, none of the apomorphic features that characterize Middle and early Upper Pleistocene European hominins can be recognized in ATD6-5.

Study of the size, proportions, and morphology of the TD6 and Sima de los Huesos dental samples also provides important data. Due to their highly conserved genetic component, teeth are considered a valuable and reliable source of characters for phylogenetic analysis.[83,84] The sample for this analysis comprises the TD6 hypodigm, composed of 28 permanent and 2 deciduous teeth and the Sima de los Huesos sample, with 467 permanent and 8 deciduous teeth.

The relative size of the second premolar (P4) and the molars (M1–M3) is a remarkable feature characterizing the Sima de los Huesos sample. The mean mesiodistal and buccolingual diameters of the crowns are similar to those in modern populations.[85] Considering the reduced size of these teeth in other Middle Pleistocene fossils such as those from Steinheim, Pontnewydd, and Mauer, as well as some of the Arago specimens, the general trend toward posterior tooth reduction (except the first premolar, P3) in the European Middle Pleistocene is clear. This could represent a case of parallelism between the Middle Pleistocene populations and the lineage leading to modern populations.[85] In contrast, the mesiodistal and buccolingual dimensions of the TD6 posterior teeth are large and comparable to those of the African and Asian Early and Middle Pleistocene specimens.[47] As shown in Table 1, some of the dimensions of the Gran Dolina-TD6 posterior teeth are beyond the

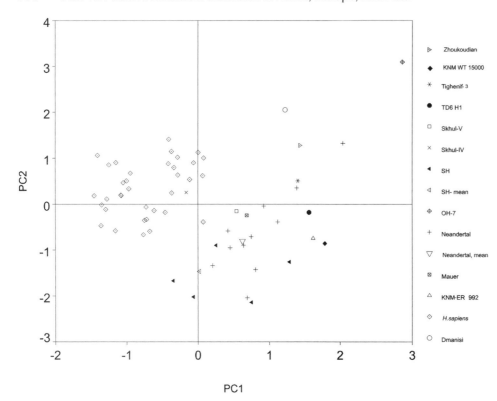

Figure 6. *Scatter diagram for the first and second principal components of dental variables: mesiodistal and buccolingual diameters of the mandibular I2-M2. Homo sapiens: Aboriginals from Gran Canaria, Canary Islands and individuals II, XII, and XXIII from the Atapuerca-Sima de los Huesos sample. (2): Individuals from the Neanderthal sample: Arcy II, Genay, Le Moustier, Ehringsdorf N, Spy II, Krapina D, Krapina E, Krapina H, Krapina L, and Valdegoba.*

Sima de los Huesos range of variation. This is true of the buccolingual dimension of the maxillary C mandibular and maxillary P3, and maxillary P4 and M1; the mesiodistal and buccolingual dimensions of mandibular P4, M1, and M2; and the mesiodistal dimension of maxillary M2. However, it is important to note that some specimens from Arago, such as Arago 13, have posterior teeth that are as large as or even larger than those of TD6.

The anterior teeth (incisors, canines, and the P3) from Sima de los Huesos are relatively large in comparison to the P4 and molars. The size imbalance of I1-P3 versus P4-M3 is an important trait that can be used to establish affinities and phylogenetic relationships among hominins.[38,44] As far as the mandibular dentition is concerned, some *Homo* specimens such as Dmanisi, OH7, or Zhoukoudian (mean values of this sample) show predominance of the posterior dentition over the anterior teeth. Hominid 1 from TD6 and other *Homo* specimens such as Mauer and Tighenif 3 show a balanced relationship between the size of the anterior and posterior dentitions. Finally, in the Sima de los Huesos hominins and most Neanderthals, anterior teeth are clearly larger than posterior teeth. Figure 6 and Table 2 show the results of an analysis of principal components (factors 1 and 2) illustrating this size relationship between anterior and posterior dentitions. It is important to highlight the fact that the size and shape of the dentition of the Mauer specimen (the holotype of *Homo heidelbergensis* Schoetensack, 1908) are very similar to those of the Neanderthal and Sima de los Huesos samples.[43,44]

With regard to the dental morphology and interdental indices (Table 3), we selected a total of 14 features that show the clear differences between the TD6 and Sima de los Huesos samples. The two samples share

some traits, but these traits do not necessarily imply a phylogenetic relationship between the TD6 and Sima de los Huesos populations. For example, shovel-shape, a plesiomorphic trait for the *Homo* clade, is present in all *Homo* species, including some *Homo sapiens* populations. The P3 dominating P4 (P3 > P4) sequence is also shared by the African Early and Middle Pleistocene hominins and the Neanderthals. Finally, the relatively broad M1, common in TD6 and the Sima de los Huesos hominins, is also present in African and Asian Middle Pleistocene hominins.

The Arago hominins display a set of dental traits that deserves special mention. Most Arago permanent teeth are large, especially those of the Arago 13 mandible. In this specimen, the crown of the P3 is symmetrical and lacks a cingulum and talonid. However, the apical fourth part of the root is divided into two components,

Table 2.   Principal Component Analysis of the Mandibular Dental Variables

		Factor 1	Factor 2
I2	MD	0.853	−0.257
	BL	0.805	−0.424
C	MD	0.912	−0.222
	BL	0.901	−0.246
P3	MD	0.936	−0.007
	BL	0.902	−0.239
P4	MD	0.842	0.340
	BL	0.906	−0.003
M1	MD	0.798	0.460
	BL	0.728	0.483
M2	MD	0.884	0.131
	BL	0.897	0.199
% of variance:		74.9	8.6
Cumulative variance:		74.9	83.5

Table 3. Comparison of the State of Dental Features in the Gran Dolina-TD6 and Sima de los Huesos Hominins from the Sierra de Atapuerca

Dental Traits	TD6	SH
Shovel-shaped upper incisors	Present	Present
Relative buccolingual dimension of the mandibular incisors with regard to the posterior teeth dimensions	Intermediate	Broad
Relative buccolingual dimension of the maxillary incisors with regard to the posterior teeth dimensions	Intermediate	Broad
Cingulum in mandibular canines and premolars	Present	Absent
Crown shape of the mandibular third premolar (P3)	Strongly asymmetrical	Symmetrical or moderately asymmetrical
Relative buccolingual dimension of the mandibular P3 with regard to the mesiodistal dimension	Broad	Broad/narrow
Talonid of the mandibular P3	Well developed	Small or absent
Mandibular premolar root morphology	2 roots; MB + DL[a]	1 Root
Mandibular P3/P4 size sequence for the crown area	P3 > P4	P3 > P4
Mandibular M1/M2 size sequence for the crown area[b]	M1 < M2	M1 > M2
Maxillary M1/M2 size sequence for the crown area	M1 < M2	M1 > M2
Hypoconulid in the mandibular M1 and M2[b]	Present and well developed	Frequently absent in M2, and less so in M1
Relative buccolingual dimension of the mandibular M1 with regard to the mesiodistal dimension	Broad	Broad
Taurodontism[c]	Hypotaurodontism	Hypo- to hypertaurodontism

[a] The TD6 premolars have two roots; the distolingual root is shorter than the plate-like mesiobuccal root. The dominant buccal component and the shorter and narrower mesial components of the mesiobuccal root have independent root canals.

[b] The Montmaurin mandible also exhibits the M1 > M2 size sequence. No hypoconulid is present in the M2 of this specimen or in the Arago 5 (M2) and Arago 6 (M2) specimens (personal observation of the originals by first author).

[c] Classification of Shaw (1928).

mesiobuccal and buccolingual, each with a single canal (observable on CT scans). The crown of the P4 exhibits a well-developed talonid, while the apical third of the root is also divided in two components, mesiobuccal and distolingual, as in the TD6 sample. Also, the mesiobuccal component has two-rooted canals. Hence, the root morphology of this tooth is similar to that of the corresponding tooth of Hominid 1 from TD6. On the other hand, Arago 13 and Arago 21 show a clear M1 < M2 size sequence; the M2 and M3 of Arago 13 are hypotaurodont and mesotaurodont, respectively. Arago 13 shows a combination of the Gran Dolina and Sima de los Huesos dental traits (see Table 1).

Since the 1997 publication regarding the species *Homo antecessor* and its possible phylogenetic position,[47] there have been new findings in Africa and Eurasia. Moreover, the question of the persistence of Mode 1 technology in Eurasia or, if preferred, the late arrival of Mode 2 to this continent, has been a source of debate in the scientific community. Given this context, we find it appropriate to review the Atapuerca evidence. The study of the skull, mandibles, and dental remains of TD6 has not revealed any Neanderthal apomorphic traits. Moreover, the size and shape differences between the TD6 and Sima de los Huesos specimens, as well as between TD6 and other specimens from the European Middle Pleistocene, are remarkable. Hence, the hypothesis of an ancestral-descendant sequence of populations without rupture of the reproductive continuity between the late Early Pleistocene and the Middle

Pleistocene in Europe does not seem clear. However, some of the Arago specimens might represent cross-breeding between the two populations.

CONCLUSIONS

The scattered nature of the fossil record has long undermined studies of human evolution in the period between 1,200 and 500 kyr. For Asia, there is a general consensus about the evolutionary continuity of the populations assigned to *Homo erectus*, probably from the beginning of the Early Pleistocene to the end of the Middle Pleistocene, seemingly with no cladogenetic events. However, it has been proposed that in Africa, or maybe in Western Asia, a speciation event modified the evolutionary landscape of the genus *Homo* around one million years ago.[7,48] This speciation event implied the origin of the hominin population that derived toward the "sapiens" pattern but retained plesiomorphic traits of its ancestral species *Homo ergaster* (or *Homo erectus,* if we accept the scheme of those who consider *Homo ergaster* to be the African form of a polytypic species distributed throughout Africa and Eurasia). The "sapiens" pattern is characterized by a substantial increase in the cranial capacity with subsequent modifications of the cranial vault and the appearance of certain modern traits in the facial skeleton. According to anagenetic and gradualist visions of human evolution, the presence of this hominin population was established in the Middle Pleistocene of Africa, Asia, and Europe. In the

BOX 1

The Origin of the Sima de los Huesos Hominin Assemblage

Including all the skeletal elements, the Sima de los Huesos hominin sample currently comprises more than 4,000 fossil remains. The minimum number of individuals was assessed through analysis of the maxilla, mandibles, and isolated teeth. The Sima de los Huesos hypodigm includes more than fifty remains of maxillae and mandibles. Some of these bones are nearly complete; others are less so. Moreover, the current sample includes a total of 479 teeth, 109 in situ and 370 isolated. The MNI evaluation has continued from the first excavation seasons.[86-88] At this moment, we have determined a MNI of 28.

Data obtained from the Sima de los Huesos hominins suggest that the time and pattern of dental development in the population represented by these hominins were similar to those in modern human populations.[89] Thus, we have used modern standards of human dental development to assess the relative mineralization stage of developing teeth in the immature individuals and to estimate their age at death. According to these standards, the third molars (M3) of the hominins appear systematically advanced in their formation as compared to second molars (M2), from 1.5 years in individual XVIII to 3.4 years in individual XXV. This observation implies that in these Middle Pleistocene populations M3s had their gingival eruption approximately at the age of 15 years, whereas the occlusal eruption occurred at about the age of 16 years.[90]

In order to estimate the age at death of the Sima de los Huesos adults we have applied the tooth-wear-based method developed by Miles[91] to the canines, premolars, and molars. This method takes as reference a group of individuals with estimated sex and incompletely developed dentitions. The degree of wear on a particular tooth is calculated in a qualitative way and applied to adult specimens. This method has the advantage of obtaining an internal variable for the population, in this case the wear rate, which is supposed to be similar for all individuals belonging to that population. (See Bermúdez de Castro and Nicolás[87] for a discussion of this method.) In our opinion, this method offers reasonable results for adults under the age of 30 years although, as tooth wear increases, its accuracy decreases. Nevertheless, only 3 individuals in the Sima de los Huesos sample are over 30 years old, so that the lack of precision at this stage does not really influence our mortality distribution assessment. Moreover, we have quantified the tooth-wear rate of lower incisors in immature individuals,[92] which allows us higher reliability and precision up to

the age of about 35 years. Concerning sex, the metrical and morphological variability of the Sima de los Huesos mandibles,[93] and the extremes of variability of dental size[88] suggest that 12 individuals are females and 8 are males, while sex determination for 8 individuals is inconclusive.

Figure 7 illustrates the age-at-death distribution for the Sima de los Huesos hominin sample. The most noteworthy results are the presence of a single individual under the age of 10, represented by a deciduous canine; the high percentage of those under the age of 20 years (64.3%); and the low percentage of individuals who died after the age of 35 years (10.7%).

When this mortality distribution is compared with theoretical models based on demographic parameters estimated for Middle Pleistocene populations,[94] we find that the peculiar Sima de los Huesos distribution fits neither an attritional profile nor a catastrophic one. The main reason is that this

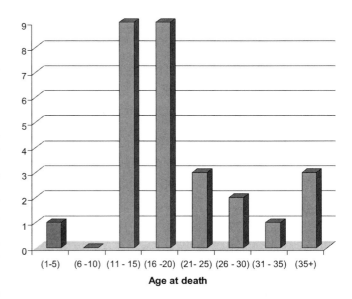

Figure 7. *Age-at-death distribution of the 28 individuals identified in the Atapuerca-Sima de los Huesos fossil hominin sample.*

last decade of the twentieth century, along with the move toward a cladogenetic understanding of human evolution, these hominins have been grouped as *Homo heidelbergensis*.

This model is not totally satisfactory, especially to those who see consistent and clear differences among the specimens assigned to *Homo heidelbergensis*, differences which seem sufficient for distinguishing two or more lineages within the group.[36] The excavations in the Pleistocene sites of Sierra de Atapuerca have yielded significant data to contribute to this debate. First, the study of the extraordinary human fossil assemblage recovered in the Sima de los Huesos site has undoubtedly shown that Europe was the home of the local evolution of a lineage that subsequently gave rise

to the so-called "classic" Neanderthals. This lineage started at least half a million years ago, probably originating in a hominin dispersal out of Africa that brought the Mode 2 to Europe. The most appropriate name for this lineage is *Homo neanderthalensis*, although it is also possible to admit, only for practical reasons, the succession of two chronospecies, *Homo heidelbergensis* and *Homo neanderthalensis*. In Africa, a different lineage gave rise to the species *Homo sapiens*. These two lineages probably shared a common ancestor, from which they increasingly differentiated during the Middle and early Upper Pleistocene.

At the point of origin of these two lineages, we should, according to protagonists of the previously mentioned speciation event, expect an ancestral species sample almost completely lacks infants and children, and has an abnormally high percentage of adolescents and prime-age adults. Also, the number of adults over the age of 20 years is lower than expected in these models.

The testimonial presence of only one individual under the age of 10 years in the Sima de los Huesos site could be explained by the action of taphonomic agents. The fragile and delicate remains of infants and children are more severely affected by the action of biostratinomic and fossildiagenetic agents than are bones from adolescents and adults.[95] Andrews and Fernández-Jalvo[96] have observed the presence of carnivore marks of a big felid, probably *Panthera leo fossilis,* and small scavengers, probably *Vulpes vulpes* on more than 50% of the human remains at Sima de los Huesos. These authors suggested that there was an initial anthropic accumulation of human corpses and that later the action of these animals eliminated all vestiges of the individuals younger than 10 years. However, very delicate bones have been recovered at the site, including small ear bones, as well as eight perfectly preserved deciduous teeth. This suggests extraordinary preservation conditions at the site. Consequently, it seems difficult to accept the idea that almost all evidence of infants, children, and juveniles disappeared in the manner suggested.

The presence of a high percentage of individuals under the age of 20 years is not expected in a mortality distribution of attritional type, where all individuals who died across a long period for diverse reasons are represented. In a distribution of this kind, we should expect a high number of individuals close to the age of the maximum longevity of that population.[97,98] In all populations, it is normal to find a certain number of adolescents who have died of different causes, generally accidental death or first births. However, adolescents and young adults represent the sector of the population that is most resistant to illness, which is a major cause of death for infants, children, and elderly members of the population.

Arsuaga and coworkers[14] also considered an anthropic origin for the accumulations, postulating that they were the result of a kind of mortuary practice because of the large minimum number of individuals. In a later work, Bocquet-Appel and Arsuaga[99] discarded the hypothesis that the site was a primitive cemetery, suggesting instead that the mortality distribution could be the result of a catastrophe, although they did not specify the origin of the accumulation.

The recent finding of a handaxe of exceptional characteristics provides the first evidence of lithic industry in this site.[20]

The tool is made of good-quality, reddish to light-brown veined quartzite, a raw material not commonly found among the thousand stone tools recovered so far from the Pleistocene sites of Atapuerca. It has an amygdaloid shape, and one of its sides is flat while the other is convex. It seems to have been made by means of soft hammer percussion after an initial reduction sequence of two main phases. The first phase was devoted to forming the volume, through flat, invasive extractions around both of its surfaces. The second phase was implemented by shaping the edges of the biface to achieve a convex distal conformation and a straight, sharp perimetral edge (Figure 8). Traceology studies reveal that the handaxe does not show use-wear traces. The finding of this unique stone tool together with the corpses of 28 individuals is difficult to explain as a natural accumulation that occurred without human intervention.

Figure 8. *Frontal surface view of the handaxe found at Sima de los Huesos (Atapuerca Hill).*

from the Early Pleistocene that fulfills the requirements of combining plesiomorphic *Homo ergaster/Homo erectus* traits with derived traits toward the "modern" pattern. Surprisingly, the first evidence of such morphology was discovered outside of Africa. The Gran Dolina site in the Sierra de Atapuerca and the Ceprano site[103] have provided fossils of a new species, *Homo antecessor,* which may represent the common ancestor of Neanderthals and modern populations. Different scenarios have been proposed to complete the puzzle of the available fossil record. However, there are still missing pieces waiting to be uncovered. These pieces undoubtedly would allow a more precise approach to the evolutionary history of the genus *Homo* and the origin of our species.

ACKNOWLEDGMENTS

We thank Professor Fleagle for his kind invitation to contribute a paper on the Sierra de Atapuerca sites and its contribution to the knowledge of human evolution. We are also grateful to the referees who, through their valuable comments, have helped us improve the paper. This research was supported by funding from the Dirección General de Investigación of the Spanish M.E.C., Project N° BXX2000-1258C03-01, the CSIC "Unidades Asociadas" Program, Fundación Atapuerca, Fundación Duques de Soria, and Fundación Caja Madrid. Field-work support came from Consejería de Cultura y Turismo of the Junta de Castilla y León and Fundación Atapuerca.

BOX 2

Human Cannibalism in the Aurora Stratum

One of the most interesting results of study of the Aurora stratum of the TD6 level has been the conclusion that the hominin assemblage originated through the practice of cannibalism.[100] It thus represents the oldest evidence of cannibalism recorded so far in hominin evolution.

The 30-cm deep Aurora stratum contained a large number of human and nonhuman remains, and stone tools. The distribution of the human remains, excavated in 1994 and 1995, seems to be random in the 7 m² area. There is not a clear pattern in the distribution of the different human skeletal parts, which are mixed with the faunal remains and stone tools. Furthermore, a random arrangement characterizes the distribution of the human and nonhuman fossil remains. Most of these remains show human-induced damage. Tool-induced surface modifications in the sample include frequent cutmarks; scraping marks resulting from the removal of periosteum and muscle by scraping the bone surface; and percussion marks, which indicate the use of a stone hammer to smash the bones (Figure 9). Adhered bone flakes are also frequent in the human and nonhuman remains. Such flakes are produced by striking bones with artifacts. Peeling is especially frequent in the remains of humans and small animals (roe deer, wild boars, and fallow deer). Peeling is defined as a roughened surface with parallel grooves or fibrous texture produced by bending the fresh bones between the hands.

All these butchering techniques were aimed at meat and marrow extraction. The presence of human remains in the assemblage suggests cannibalism for nutritional purposes. The species diversity recorded in the Aurora stratum is the richest found at any level in the Sierra de Atapuerca sites. The temperate climate inferred from the fossil record (pollen and mammal community) for TD6, as well as the abundance of hunting available to hominins, make it improbable that humans ate other humans as a survival strategy. Rather, it seems that the TD6 hominins consumed other members of their species as part of their regular diet (dietary or gastronomic cannibalism).

On the other hand, the skeletal-element representation in the Aurora stratum suggests that the small animals, including humans, were transported complete into the cave.[101] In contrast, the anatomical representation of large animals, which is biased in favor of elements rich in fat and marrow, suggests transport selection by hominins. Pending future excavations over the whole TD6 level, the Aurora stratum can be interpreted as a consumption site, whether it was a preferential central place or an occasional refuge.

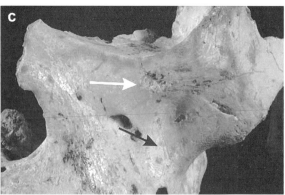

Figure 9.   *a: Scanning electron microscope image of the immature clavicle ATD6-55 exhibiting parallel cutmarks and a transversal fracture made when the bone was still fresh. b: Fragment of human temporal ATD6-16 showing numerous more-or-less parallel cut-marks (white arrow) affecting the area where the sternocleidomastoid muscle is attached. c: The face ATD6-69 shows an impact produced with a stone tool near the infraorbital border (white arrow), as well as some slicing and sawing marks near the zygomaticoalveolar crest (black arrow).*

REFERENCES

1. Wood, B. 1992. Origin and evolution of the genus *Homo*. Nature 355:783–790.
2. Braüer, G. 1984. The "Afro-European *sapiens* hypothesis" and hominid evolution in East Asia during the late Middle and Upper Pleistocene. Courier Forschungsinstitut Senckenberg 69:145–165.
3. Hublin, J. J., 1982. Les anténéandertaliens: presapiens ou prénéandertaliens. Geobios 6:345–357.
4. Gabunia, L., de Lumley, M. A., Vekua, A., Lordkipanidze, D., de Lumley, H. 2002. Découverte d'un nouvel hominidé à Dmanissi (Transcaucasie, Géorgie) C. R. Palevol 1:243–253.
5. Wood, B. 1994. Taxonomy and evolutionary relationships of *Homo erectus*. Courier Forschungsinstitut Senckenberg 171:341–361.
6. Martinez, I., Arsuaga, J. L. 1997. The temporal bones from Sima de los Huesos Middle Pleistocene site (Sierra de Atapuerca, Spain): a phylogenetic approach. J Hum Evol 33:283–318.
7. Rightmire, G. P. 1998. Human evolution in the Middle Pleistocene: the role of *Homo heidelbergensis*. Evol Anthropol 6:218–227.
8. Tattersall, I. 1986. Species recognition in human paleontology. J Hum Evol 15:165–175.
9. Tattersall, I. 1992. Species concepts and species identification in human evolution. J Hum Evol 22:341–349.
10. Kimbel, W. H., Rak, Y. 1993. The importance of species taxa in paleoanthropology and an argument for the phylogenetic concept of the species category. In: Kimbel, W. H., Martin, L. B. editors. Species, species concepts, and primate evolution. New York: Plenum Press. p. 461–485.
11. Harrison, T. 1993. Cladistic concepts and the species problem in hominoid evolution. In: Kimbel, W. H., Martin, L. B., editors. Species, species concepts, and primate evolution. New York: Plenum Press. p. 345–372.
12. Aguirre, E., Basabe, J. M., Torres, T. 1976. Los fósiles humanos de Atapuerca (Burgos): nota preliminar. Zephyrus 26–27:489–511.
13. Aguirre, E., Arsuaga, J. L., Bermúdez de Castro, J. M., Carbonell, E., Ceballos, M., Díez, C., Enamorado, J., Fernández, Y., Gil, E., Gracia, A., Martín-Nájera, A., Martínez, I., Morales, J., Ortega, A. I., Rosas, A., Sánchez, A., Sánchez, B., Sesé, C., Soto, E., Torres, T. 1988. The Atapuerca sites and the Ibeas hominids. Hum Evol 5:55–73.
14. Arsuaga, J. L., Martínez, I., Gracia, A., Carretero, J. M., Lorenzo, C., García, N., Ortega, A. I. 1997. Sima de los Huesos (Sierra de Atapuerca, Spain): the site. J Hum Evol 33:109–127.
15. Bischoff, J. L., Fitzpatrick, J. A., León, L., Arsuaga, J. L., Falguères, C., Bahain, J. J., Bullen, T. 1997. Geology and preliminary dating of the hominid-bearing sedimentary fill of the Sima de los Huesos Chamber, Cueva Mayor of the Sierra de Atapuerca, Burgos, Spain. J Hum Evol 33:129–154.
16. Cuenca-Bescós, G., Laplana-Conesa, C., Canudo, J. I., Arsuaga, J. L. 1997. Small mammals from Sima de los Huesos. J Hum Evol 33:175–190.
17. Parés, J. M., Pérez-González, A., Weil, A. B., Arsuaga, J. L. 2000. On the age of the hominid fossils at the Sima de los Huesos, Sierra de Atapuerca, Spain: paleomagnetic evidence. Am J Phys Anthropol 111:451–561.
18. Bischoff, J. L., Shampa, D. D., Aramburu, A., Arsuaga, J. L., Carbonell, E., Bermúdez de Castro, J. M. 2003. The Sima de los Huesos hominids date to beyond U/Th equilibrium (> 350 kyrs) and perhaps to 400–600 kyrs: new radiometric dates. J Archaeol Sci 30:275–280.
19. Bermúdez de Castro, J. M., Martinón-Torres, M., Bermúdez de Castro, A., Muela, A., Sarmiento, S., Lozano, M. n.d. Paleodemografía del yacimiento del Pleistoceno medio de la Sima de los Huesos (Sierra de Atapuerca, Burgos). Alcalá de Henares, Museo Arqueológico Regional de Madrid. In Press.
20. Carbonell, E., Mosquera, M., Ollé, A., Rodríguez, X. P., Sala, R., Vergés, J. M., Arsuaga, J. L., Bermúdez de Castro, J. M. 2003. Les premiers rites funeraires auraient-ils pris place a Atapuerca, il y a 340 000 ans? L'Anthropologie 107:1–14.
21. Parés, J. M., Pérez-González, A. 1999. Magnetochronology and stratigraphy at Gran Dolina section, Atapuerca (Burgos, Spain). J Hum Evol 37:325–342.
22. Carbonell, E., Bermúdez de Castro, J. M., Arsuaga-J.L., Díez, J. C., Rosas, A., Cuenca-Bescós, G., Sala, R., Mosquera, M., Rodríguez, X. P. 1995. Lower Pleistocene hominids and artifacts from Atapuerca-TD6 (Spain). Science 269:826–830.
23. Parés, J. M., Pérez-González, A. 1995. Paleomagnetic age for hominid fossils at Atapuerca site, Spain. Science 269:830–832.
24. Falguères, C., Bahain, J.-J., Yokoyama, Y., Arsuaga, J. L., Bermúdez de Castro, J. M., Carbonell, E., Bischoff, J. L., Dolo, J.-M. 1999. Earliest humans in Europe: the age of TD6 Gran Dolina, Atapuerca, Spain. J Hum Evol 37:343–352.
25. García Antón, M. 1989. Estudio palinológico de los yacimientos meso-pleistocenos de Atapuerca (Burgos): reconstrucción paisajística y paloclimática. Tesis Doctoral, Universidad Autónoma de Madrid.
26. Rodríguez, J. 1997. Paleoecología del Pleistoceno de Atapuerca. Tesis Doctoral, Universidad Autónoma de Madrid.
27. Sánchez-Marco, A. 1999. Implications of the avian fauna for paleoecology in the Early Pleistocene of the Iberian Peninsula. J Hum Evol 37:375–388.
28. van der Made, J. 1999. Ungulates from Atapuerca TD6. J Hum Evol 37:389–413.
29. García, N., Arsuaga, J. L. 1999. Carnivores from the early Pleistocene hominid-bearing Trinchera Dolina 6 (Sierra de Atapuerca, Spain). J Hum Evol 37:415–430.
30. Cuenca-Bescós, G., Laplana-Conesa, C., Canudo, J. I. 1999. Biochronological implications of the Arvicolidae (Rodentia, Mammalia) from the Lower Pleistocene hominid-bearing level of Trinchera Dolina 6 (TD6, Atapuerca, Spain). J Hum Evol 37:353–373.
31. Fejfar, O., Heinrich, W.-D., editors. 1990. Presented at International Symposium on Evolution, Phylogeny and Biostratigraphy of Arvicolids (*Rodentia, Mammalia*), Rohanov, Czechoslovakia.
32. Agustí, J., Moyà-Solà, S. 1992. Mammalian dispersal events in the Spanish Pleistocene. Courier Forschunginstitut Senckenberg 153:69–77.
33. Arsuaga, J. L., Martínez, I., Gracia, A., Carretero, J. M., Carbonell, E. 1993. Three new human skulls from the Sima de los Huesos Middle Pleistocene site in Sierra de Atapuerca, Spain. Nature 362:534–537.
34. Rosas, A., Bermúdez de Castro, J. M., Aguirre, E. 1991. Mandibules et dents d'Ibeas (Espagne) dans le contexte de l'evolution humaine en Europe. L'Anthropologie 4:89–102.
35. Rosas, A. 1995. 17 new mandibular specimens from the Atapuerca/Ibeas Middle Pleistocene hominids sample (1985–1992). J Hum Evol 28:533–559.
36. Arsuaga, J. L., Martínez, I., Gracia, A., Lorenzo, C. 1997. The Sima de los Huesos crania (Sierra de Atapuerca, Spain). A comparative study. J Hum Evol 33:219–281.
37. Bermúdez de Castro, J. M. 1988. Dental remains from Atapuerca/Ibeas (Spain) II. Morphology. J Hum Evol 17:279–304.
38. Bermúdez de Castro, J. M. 1993. The Atapuerca dental remains: new evidence (1987–1991 excavations) and interpretations. J Hum Evol 24:339–371.
39. Stringer, C. B. 1993. Secrets of the Pit of the Bones. Nature 362:501–502.
40. Schoetensack, O. 1908. Der Unterkiefer des *Homo heidelbergensis* aus den Sanden von Mauer bel Heidelberg: ein Beitrag zur Palaöntologie des Menschen. Leipzig: Engelmann.
41. Aguirre, E., de Lumley, M. A. 1977. Fossil men from Atapuerca, Spain: their bearing on human evolution in the Middle Pleistocene. J Hum Evol 6:681–688.
42. Rosas, A. 1987. Two new mandibular fragments from Atapuerca/Ibeas mandibles sample. J Hum Evol 16:417–427.
43. Rosas, A., Bermúdez de Castro, J. M. 1998. The Mauer mandible and the evolutionary significance of *Homo heidelbergensis*. Geobios 31:687–697.
44. Bermúdez de Castro, J. M., Rosas, A., Nicolás, M. A. 1999. Dental remains from Atapuerca-TD6 (Gran Dolina site Burgos, Spain). J Hum Evol 37:523–566.
45. Stringer, C. B. 1996. Current issues in modern human origins. In: Meikle, W. E., Howell, F. C., Jablonski, N. G., editors.

Contemporary issues in human evolution. San Francisco; California Academy of Sciences, Memoir 21. p. 115–133.

46. Tattersall, I. 2000. Paleoanthropology: the last half-century. Evol Anthropol 4:2–16.

47. Bermúdez de Castro, J. M., Arsuaga, J. L., Carbonell, E., Rosas, A., Martínez, I., Mosquera, M. 1997. A hominid from the Lower Pleistocene of Atapuerca, Spain: possible ancestor to Neandertals and modern humans. Science 276:1392–1395.

48. Rightmire, G. P. 1996. The human cranium from Bodo, Ethiopia: evidence for speciation in the Middle Pleistocene? J Hum Evol 31:21–39.

49. Clark, J. D., de Heinzelin, J., Schick, K. D., Hart, W. K., White, T. D., WoldeGabriel, G., Walter, R. C., Suwa, G., Asfaw, B., Vrba, E., H-Selassie, Y. 1994. African *Homo erectus:* old radiometric ages and young Oldowan assemblages in the Middle Awash valley, Ethiopia. Science 264:1907–1910.

50. Stringer, C. B. 1983. Some further notes on the morphology and dating of the Petralona hominid. J Hum Evol 12:731–742.

51. Stringer, C. B. 1985. Middle Pleistocene variability and the origin of Late Pleistocene humans. In: Delson, E. editor. Ancestors: the hard evidence. New York: Alan R. Liss, p. 289–295.

52. Stringer, C. B., McKie, R. 1991. African exodus: the origin of modern humanity. London: Jonathan Cape.

53. Tattersall, I. 1996. The last Neanderthal. New York: Macmillan.

54. Abbate, E., Albianelli, A., Azzaroli, A., Benvenuti, M., Tesfamariam, B., Bruni, P., Cipriani, N., Clarke, R. J., Ficcarelli, G., Macchiarelli, R., Napoleone, G., Papini, M., Rook, L., Sagri, M., Tecle, T. M., Torre, D., Villa, I. 1998. A one-million-year-old *Homo* cranium from the Danakil (Afar) Depression of Eritrea. Nature 393:458–460.

55. Asfaw, B., Gilbert, W. H., Beyene, Y., Hart, W. K., Renne, P. R., WoldeGabriel, G., Vrba, E. S., White, T. D. 2002. Remains of *Homo erectus* from Bouri, Middle Awash, Ethiopia. Nature 416:317–320.

56. Manzi, G., Bruner, E., Passarello, P. 2003. The one-million-year-old *Homo* cranium from Bouri (Ethiopia): a reconsideration of its *Homo erectus* affinities. J Hum Evol 44:731–736.

57. Stringer, C. B., Howell, F. C., Melentis, J. K. 1979. The significance of the fossil hominid skull from Petralona, Greece. J Archaeol Sci 6:235–253.

58. Rightmire, G. P. 1983. The Lake Ndutu cranium and early *Homo sapiens* in Africa. Am J Phys Anthropol 61:245–254.

59. Arsuaga, J. L., Martínez, I., Lorenzo, C., Gracia, A., Muñoz, A., Alonso, O., Gallego, J. 1999. The human cranial remains from Gran Dolina Lower Pleistocene site (Sierra de Atapuerca, Spain). J Hum Evol 37:431–457.

60. Carretero, J. M., Lorenzo, C., Arsuaga. J. L. 1999. Axial and appendicular skeleton of *Homo antecessor.* J Hum Evol 37:459–499.

61. Lorenzo, C., Arsuaga, J. L., Carretero, J. M. 1999. Hand and foot remains from the Gran Dolina Early Pleistocene site (Sierra de Atapuerca, Spain). J Hum Evol 37:501–522.

62. Ascenzi, A., Biddittu, I., Cassoli, P. F, Segre, A. G., Segre-Naldini, E. 1996. A calvarium of late *Homo erectus* from Ceprano, Italy. J Hum Evol 31:409–423.

63. Ascenzi, A., Mallegni, F., Manzi, G., Segre, A. G., Segre-Naldini, E. 2000. A reappraisal of Ceprano calvaria affinities with *Homo erectus,* after the new reconstruction. J Hum Evol 39:443–450.

64. Clarke, R. J. 2000. A corrected reconstruction and interpretation of the *Homo erectus* calvaria from Ceprano, Italy. J Hum Evol 39:433–442.

65. Manzi, G., Mallegni, F., Ascenzi, A. 2001. A cranium for the earliest Europeans: phylogenetic position of the hominid from Ceprano, Italy. Proc Natl Acad Sci USA 98:10011–10016.

66. Rosas, A., Bermúdez de Castro, J. M. 1998. On the taxonomic affinities of the Dmanisi mandible (Georgia). Am J Phys Anthropol 107:145–162.

67. Gabunia, L., Vekua, A. 1995. A Plio-Pleistocene hominid from Dmanisi East Georgia, Caucasus. Nature 373:509–512.

68. Gabunia, L., Vekua, A., Lordkipanidze, D., Swisher, C. C., Ferring, R., Justus, A., Nioradze, M., Tvalchrelidze, M., Antón, S. C., Bosinski, G., Jöris, O., de Lumley, M. A., Majsuradze, G., Mouskhelishvili, A. 2000. Earliest Pleistocene hominid cranial remains from Dmanisi, Republic of Georgia: taxonomy, geological setting, and age. Science 288:1019–1025.

69. Vekua, A., Lordkipanidze, D., Rightmire, G. P., Agusti, J., Ferring, R., Maisuradze, G., Mouskhelishvili, A., Nioradze, M., Ponce de León, M., Tappen, M., Tvalchrelidze, M., Zollikofer, C.

2002. A new skull of early *Homo* from Dmanisi, Georgia. Science 297:85–89.

70. Rosas, A., Pérez-González, A., Carbonell, E., van der Made, J., Sánchez, A., Laplana, C., Cuenca-Bescós, G., Parés, J. M., Huguet, R. 2001. Le gisement pléistocéne de la "sima del Elefante" (Sierra de Atapuerca, Espagne), L'Anthropologie 105:301–312.

71. Oms, O., Parés, J. M., Martínez-Navarro, B., Agustí, J., Toro, I., Martínez-Fernández, G., Turq, A. 2000. Early human occupation of Western Europe: paleomagnetic dates for two paleolithic sites in Spain. Proc Natl Acad Sci USA 97:10666–10670.

72. Carbonell, E., Mosquera, M., Rodríguez, X. P., Sala, R., Van der Made, J. 1999. Out of Africa: the dispersal of the earliest technical systems reconsidered. J Anthropol Archaeol 18:119–136.

73. van der Made, J. 2001. Les ongulés d'Atapuerca: stratigraphie et biogéographie. L'Anthropologie 105:95–113.

74. van der Made, J., Aguirre, E., Bastir, M. Fernández-Jalvo, Y., Huguet, R., Laplana, C., Márquez, B., Martínez, C., Martinón-Torres, M., Rosas, A., Rodríguez, J., Sánchez, A., Sarmiento, S., Bermúdez de Castro, J. M. El registro paleontológico y arqueológico de los yacimientos de la Trinchera del Ferrocarril en la Sierra de Atapuvverca. Col-Pa. In Press.

75. Maglio, V. J., Cooke, H. B. S., editors. 1978. Evolution of African mammals. Cambridge: Harvard University Press.

76. Bermúdez de Castro, J. M., Martinón-Torres, M., Sarmiento, S., Lozano, M. 2003. Gran Dolina-TD6 versus Sima de los Huesos dental samples from Atapuerca: evidence of discontinuity in the European Pleistocene population? J Archaeol Sci 30:1421–1428.

77. Hublin, J. J. 1990. Les peuplements paléolithiques de l'Europe: un point de vue paléobiogeographique. Mémoires du Musée de Prehist. D'Ile-de-France 3:29–37.

78. Rightmire, G. P. 1997. Deep roots for the Neanderthals. Nature 389:917–918.

79. Rak, Y. 1986. The Neanderthal: a new look at an old face. J Hum Evol 15:151–164.

80. Trinkaus, E. 1987. The Neandertal face: evolutionary and functional perpectives on a recent hominid face. J Hum Evol 16:429–443.

81. Schwartz, J. H., Tattersall, I. 1996. Significance of some previously unrecognized apomorphies in the nasal region of *Homo neanderthalensis.* Proc Natl Acad Sci USA 93:10852–10854.

82. Rosas, A., Bermúdez de Castro, J. M. 1999. The ATD6-5 mandibular specimen from Gran Dolina (Atapuerca, Spain): morphological study and phylogenetic implications. J Hum Evol 37:567–590.

83. Turner, C. G. II, Nichol, C. R., Scott, G. R., 1991. Scoring procedures for key morphological traits of the permanent dentition: the Arizona State University dental anthropology system. In: Kelley, M. A., Larsen, C. S., editors. Advances in dental anthropology. New York: Wiley-Liss, p. 13–22.

84. Irish, J. D. 1993. Biological affinities of Late Pleistocene through modern African aboriginal populations: the dental evidence. Ph.D. Dissertation, Arizona State University, Tempe, AZ.

85. Bermúdez de Castro, J. M., Nicolás, M. E. 1995. Posterior dental size reduction in hominids: the Atapuerca evidence. Am J Phys Anthropol 96:335–356.

86. Bermúdez de Castro, J. M. 1986. Dental remains from Atapuerca (Spain) I. Metrics. J Hum Evol 15:265–287.

87. Bermúdez de Castro, J. M., Nicolás, M. E., 1997. Palaeodemography of the Atapuerca-SH Middle Pleistocene hominid sample. J Hum Evol 33:333–355.

88. Bermúdez de Castro, J. M., Sarmiento, S., Cunha, E., Rosas, A., Bastir, M. 2001. Dental size variation in the Atapuerca-SH Middle Pleistocene hominids. J Hum Evol 41:195–209.

89. Bermúdez de Castro, J. M., Rosas, A. 2001. Pattern of dental development in Hominid XVIII from the Middle Pleistocene Atapuerca-Sima de los Huesos site (Spain). Am J Phys Anthropol 114:325–330.

90. Wolpoff, M. H. 1979. The Krapina dental remains. Am J Phys Anthropol 50:67–114.

91. Miles, A. E. W. 1963. The dentition in the assessment of individual age in skeletal material. In: Brothwell DR, editor. Dental anthropology. Oxford: Pergamon Press. p. 191–209.

92. Bermúdez de Castro, J. M., Martinón-Torres, M., Sarmiento, S., Lozano, M., Arsuaga, J. L., Carbonell, E. 2003. Rates of anterior teeth wear in Middle Pleistocene hominins from Sima de los Huesos (Sierra de Atapuerca, Spain). Proc Natl Acad Sci USA 100:11992–11996.

93. Rosas, A., Bastir, M., Martínez-Maza, C., Bermúdez de Castro, J. M. 2002. Sexual dimorphism in the Atapuerca-SH hominids: the evidence from the mandibles. J Hum Evol 42:451–474.

94. Bermúdez de Castro, J. M., Martinón-Torres, M., Bermúdez de Castro, A., Muela, A., Sarmiento, S., Lozano, M. n.d. Paleodemografía del yacimiento del Pleistoceno medio de la Sima de los Huesos (Sierra de Atapuerca, Burgos). In: Baquedano E, editor. Volumen Homenaje al Profesor Emiliano Aguirre. Alcalá de Henares: Publ. Museo Arqueológico Regional de la Comunidad de Madrid. In press.

95. Walker, P. L., Johnson, J. R., Lambert, P. M. 1988. Age and sex biases in the preservation of human skeletal remains. Am J Phys Anthropol 76:183–188.

96. Andrews, P., Fernández-Jalvo, Y. 1997. Surface modifications of the Sima de los Huesos fossil humans. J Hum Evol 33:191–217.

97. Lyman, R. L. 1994. Vertebrate taphonomy. Cambridge: Cambridge University Press.

98. Margerison, B. J., Knüsel, C. J. 2002. Paleodemographic comparison of a catastrophic and an attritional death assemblage. Am J Phys Anthropol 119:134–143.

99. Bocquet-Appel, J. P., Arsuaga, J. L. 1999. Age distributions of hominid samples at Atapuerca (SH) and Krapina could indicate accumulation by catastrophe. J Arachaeol Sci 26:327–338.

100. Fernández-Jalvo, Y., Díez, J.C., Cáceres, I., Rosell, J. 1999. Human cannibalism in the Early Pleistocene of Europe (Gran Dolina, Sierra de Atapuerca, Burgos, Spain). J Hum Evol 37:591–622.

101. Díez, J. C., Fernández-Jalvo, Y., Rosell, J., Cáceres, I. 1999. Zooarchaeology and taphonomy of Aurora Statum (Gran Dolina, Sierra de Atapuerca, Spain). J. Hum Evol 37:623–652.

102. Gabunia, L., de Lumley, M. A., Vekua, A., Lordkipanidze, D., de Lumley, H. 2001. Découverte d'un nouvel hominidé à Dmanissi (Transcaucasie, Géorgie). C R Palevol 1:243–253.

103. Manzi, G. 2004. Human evolution at the Matuyama-Brunhes boundary. Evol Anth 13:11–24.

48

A Cranium for the Earliest Europeans

Phylogenetic Position of the Hominid from Ceprano, Italy

G. Manzi, F. Mallegni, and A. Ascenzi

ABSTRACT

The human fossil evidence unequivocally pertaining to the first inhabitants of Europe at present includes the sample from Atapuerca-TD6 (Spain) and the incomplete adult calvaria discovered near Ceprano, in Southern Latium (Italy). On the basis of regional correlations and a series of absolute dates, the age of the Ceprano hominid is estimated to range between 800 and 900 kilo-annum (ka). In addition, the association with archaic (Mode 1) Paleolithic findings from the same area is suggested. After the completed reconstruction of the calvaria, we present here a new study dealing with the general and more detailed aspects of the morphology displayed by Ceprano, in comparison to fossil samples ranging between Early and Middle Pleistocene. According to our results, cranial features indicate that Ceprano represents a unique morphological bridge between the clade Homo ergaster/erectus *and later Middle Pleistocene specimens commonly referred to* Homo heidelbergensis *(and/or to* Homo rhodesiensis*), particularly those belonging to the African fossil record that ultimately relates to the origin of modern humans. In conclusion, given its geographical, chronological, and phylogenetic position, an attribution to the species* Homo antecessor *is considered, although the sample from Atapuerca-TD6 is not directly comparable to Ceprano. Alternatively, a new species—ancestral to later European and African hominines—should be named to accommodate such a unique fossil specimen.*

The presence of human populations in Europe before the 500-ka age range indicated by advocates of the so-called "short chronology" (1) has been claimed for a long time on the basis of archaeological discoveries in various corners of the continent. Examples of pre-500-ka localities are Le Vallonet, in France (2), Monte Poggiolo, in Italy (3), and those in the Guadix-Baza Basin, Spain (4). In 1994, unequivocal human fossil evidence pertaining to the time range at the boundary between Early and Middle Pleistocene was found in the sites of Atapuerca Gran Dolina (Spain; ref. 5), including a sample of fragmentary juvenile specimens and dental remains, and Ceprano (Italy; ref. 6), where an incomplete adult calvaria was discovered. Roughly one million years earlier, hominids are present at the "gates of Europe," in Georgia (7). It is, however, to be demonstrated that early *Homo* diffused in Europe at that time, whereas an occupation of East Asia can be inferred (8–10).

Acheulean assemblages are widely diffused in Europe from about 600 ka (11) and fossil human remains are also present in various sites, such as at Mauer, Arago, Bilzinsgleben, Vérteszöllös, Visogliano, and so on. According to the scenario indicated by some authors during the last decade (12, 13), these ancient Europeans can be referred to *Homo heidelbergensis*, a paleospecies that (according to the same point of view) also includes a large part of the Middle Pleistocene African fossil record, represented by specimens such as

Reprinted with permission from *Proceedings of the National Academy of Science*, Vol. 98, pp. 10011–10016. Copyright © 2001 National Academy of Sciences, U.S.A.

Abbreviations: ka, kilo-annum (thousand years ago); Ma, mega-annum (million years ago); NJ, neighbor-joining; UPGMA, unweighted pair group method using arithmetic averages.

Bodo, Kabwe, and others. At the same time, the more traditional notion of a single multiregional Middle Pleistocene phase—the so-called "archaic *Homo sapiens*"—has been abandoned by the majority of the authors. Alternatively, in the presence of a stem species named *Homo antecessor* (14), another scenario has to be considered in which the European and African clades are distinguished as separate morphotypes, respectively referable (if distinguished at the species level) to *H. heidelbergensis* and to *Homo rhodesiensis*. Concurrently, human populations from this general time span in the Far East are mostly regarded as representatives of another regional clade, the species *Homo erectus* (15, 16).

Given these alternative scenarios, the discovery and/or reevaluation of fossil specimens that may fill the chronological gap between the most ancient African evidence pertaining to the genus *Homo* and subsequent biogeographical human radiation in the Early and Middle Pleistocene is of critical importance. From this perspective, the recently discovered crania and mandible from Dmanisi, dated to about 1.7 mega-annum (Ma) (see ref. 7), can be regarded as the evidence of one of the earliest, if not the earliest, human diffusions out of Africa. Yet, the time span between 1.5 and 0.5 Ma still remains relatively poor in terms of human fossil evidence. In the late Early Pleistocene, in particular, there are very few well preserved fossils in Africa (17) or in Eurasia (see, e.g., ref. 13). Among them, the Ceprano calvaria occupies a crucial position, as far as its chronology and morphological features are concerned. In this framework, the present paper provides a comparative analysis of this fossil, based on a new reconstruction (18, 19). This study is aimed at evaluating the significance of the Italian specimen for the evolution of the genus *Homo*.

DATING AND GENERAL FEATURES OF CEPRANO

The circumstances of recovery of the fossil hominid by I. Biddittu at Campogrande near Ceprano, the geostratigraphy, the chronology, and the archaeology of the site have been described (see refs. 6 and 19–21). In brief, according to the interpretation given by Ascenzi and coworkers on the basis of regional correlations synthesized in Figure 1, the cranium should be referred to the time span between the Acheulean site of Fontana Ranuccio [about 458 ka (22)] and layers with volcaniclasts dated by ^{40}Ar/^{39}Ar to around 1 Ma (23, 24). In addition, given the absence in the sediments containing the cranium of any leucitic remnants of the more recent volcanic activity known in the region—that are referred to the range between 100 and 700 ka (25)—and the presence above the cranium itself of a clear stratigraphic unconformity that marks the lowest limit of the sandy leucitic pyroclasts, an age between 800 and 900 ka is at present our best chronological estimate.

As a consequence of the age estimate, a possible association of the hominid from Ceprano with pebble/flakes (i.e., Mode 1) assemblages in the same region

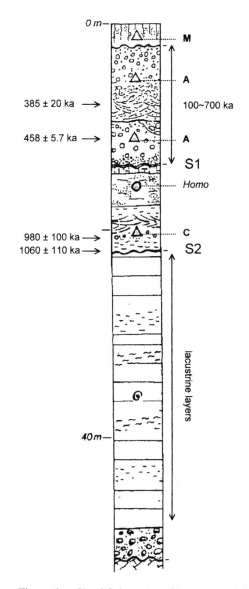

Figure 1. *Simplified stratigraphic sequence of the central Ceprano Basin composed by A. G. Segre from various test sections in the region (redrawn from ref. 17; see text for other references). The position of the human cranium is marked with a circle, whereas triangles indicate archaeological layers: M, Mousterian; A, Acheulean; C, "archaic" Paleolithic. In relationship with two major unconformities in the sequence, S1 and S2, indicate the lowest limits of sands with leucitic pyroclasts (younger volcanic activity; referred to the range between 100 and 700 ka) or without leucitic pyroclasts (volcanic activity older than 700 ka), respectively. Available K-Ar datings in the region are also reported on the left.*

(Southern Latium)—from sites such as Castro dei Volsci, Arce, and Fontana Liri (26)—has been suggested.

The current form of the Ceprano calvaria (Figure 2) is the result of a process started in 1994 and concluded in 1999. It is based on the original reconstruction by Ascenzi and coworkers (see ref. 6), subsequently corrected by R. J. Clarke (18) and further revised by M. A. de Lumley and F. M. (19). Looking at the cranium along its transversal contour, Ceprano is presently

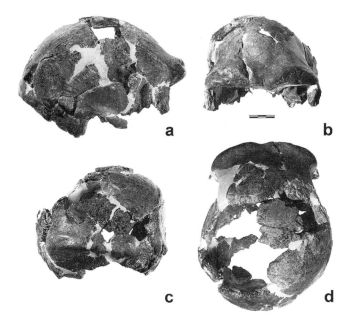

Figure 2. *The new reconstruction of the Ceprano calvaria in four views:* (a) *right lateral;* (b) *frontal;* (c) *occipital;* (d) *superior.*

constituted as follows. On the right side the virtually complete frontal bone articulates in two points with fragments of the parietal along the coronal suture and also with the greater wing of the sphenoid, which also articulates with the temporal squama (endocranial surface). The right parietal—well represented, particularly in its posterior component—articulates with both the temporal and the largely preserved occipital bone along the preserved segments of the lambdoid suture. Both the right and left mastoid portions of the temporal bones articulate with the occipital in the asterionic regions and for part of the occipitomastoid suture. On the left, the squama of the temporal bone is in connection with few residual fragments of the parietal and with the preserved part of the sphenoid; the latter, in turn, is connected with the frontal. Thus, cranial shape can be confidently examined, because all of the preserved cranial portions connect directly with each other.

The cranial vault of Ceprano is low and gently curved along the midsagittal profile; the maximum length is between glabella and inion, which is therefore coincident with the opistocranium. At the same time, however, the cranium is relatively short, with considerable transversal expansion. As a result, Ceprano is brachicranic, an unusual trait in archaic *Homo*. The maximum breadth is at the level of the supramastoid crests.

A massive and continuous torus with supratoral sulcus characterizes the receding squama of the frontal bone. In the supraorbital region we observe an interesting suite of traits. The glabella area is depressed in both superior and frontal views; on both sides, the torus shows a variable thickness, growing steeply from the midsagittal plane, reaching maximum height around midline of each orbit, and gradually decreasing laterally. We also observe torsion of the superficial aspect of the supraorbital ridges, with a flat and vermiculate

medial component clearly distinguishable from the more rounded and bulging lateral part. By contrast, the superior border of the orbits is almost rectilinear. The interorbital width is great, and frontal sinuses extend laterally and posteriorly. The cranium exhibits moderate postorbital constriction and marked temporal lines on both the frontal and (right) parietal bones. There are no indications of frontal, coronal, or parietal keelings, although a slight parabregmatic depression is visible. The parietal (right side) is square in shape, relatively flattened sagittally, and markedly angled in coronal sections at the level of the temporal lines. The superior border of the temporal squama is missing, but it can be hypothesized that it was relatively high and curved. The mandibular fossa (incompletely preserved) is relatively small and deep, and is bordered by a prominent entoglenoid process. The tympanic bones are bilaterally lost, and the mastoid processes are massive. The occipital squama is wide and flat; in lateral view, the occipital is angled, characterized by the presence of transverse occipital torus with supratoral sulcus. Inion and endinion are clearly separated. The torus does not reach the asterionic region on both sides, thus it is not continuous with the well defined angular torus or with the supramastoid crests. The nuchal plane is preserved only in part, and large areas of the cranial base are unfortunately missing or damaged. Thickness of the bones of the cranial vault is exceptional, reaching values above 20 mm (temporal asterion).

Metric data recorded on the new reconstruction of the Ceprano calvaria have recently been published in detail (19). The selection of bivariate metric comparisons shown in Figure 3 demonstrates that Ceprano fits within the variability of archaic *Homo* and is frequently associated with the more massive specimens in that sample, such as Sangiran 17, Petralona, and the Cranium 4 from Sima de los Huesos. One of the most peculiar traits of Ceprano is confirmed to be the relatively large breadth, especially compared with its maximum length, as clearly demonstrated by the diagram in Figure 3*a*. The considerable value of frontal expansion (Figure 3*b*) is closer to European specimens of the Middle Pleistocene generally referred to *H. heidelbergensis*. However, the distance between glabella and inion (Figure 3*a*), as well as the relationship between frontal and parietal midsagittal chords (Figure 3*c*), relate Ceprano with fossils from Zhoukoudian and give the Italian specimens a resemblance to *H. erectus* and/or to *Homo ergaster* in lateral profile. In addition, the proportions of the occipital bone reported in Figure 3*d* indicate that Ceprano has a wide upper scale, proportionally high (lambda-inion chord) and large (biasterionic breadth), leading to a position in the plot close to that of ER-3733.

DISCRETE TRAITS: A MULTIVARIATE COMPARATIVE ANALYSIS

From this overview of the general features displayed by Ceprano, the original preliminary attribution to *H. erectus* (ref. 6; see also ref. 18) does not appear completely

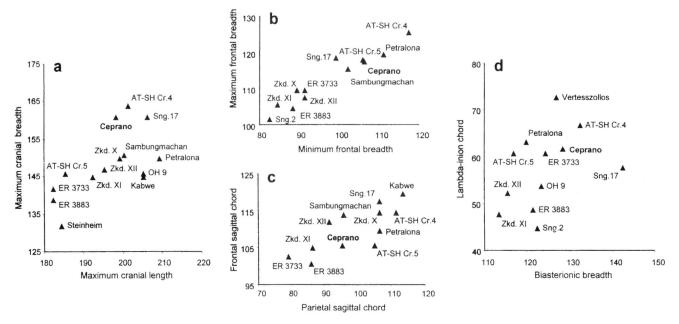

Figure 3. *Bivariate morphometric comparisons between Ceprano and archaic* Homo *samples.*
(a) *maximum cranial length vs. maximum cranial breadth;* (b) *minimum frontal breadth (Martin measurement n. 9) vs. maximum frontal breadth (n. 10);* (c) *parietal sagittal chord (from bregma to lambda) vs. frontal sagittal chord (from nasion to bregma);* (d) *biasterionic breadth vs. lambda-inion chord. A more extensive collection of measurements obtained on the new reconstruction of the Ceprano calvaria is reported in ref. 16. Site/specimen abbreviations are as in Table 1.*

satisfactory, and should be reconsidered. As a matter of fact, the variability of this taxon appears surprisingly extensive when the Italian specimen is included in the hypodigm. As we already stated elsewhere (19): "to assess its affinities to *H. erectus* additional comparisons will need to be made with other taxa, particularly *H. heidelbergensis* and *H. antecessor.*"

To shed some light on the phylogenetic and taxonomic position of Ceprano, thirty character states have been examined in a series of 20 specimens ranging between Early and Middle Pleistocene, sufficiently complete to be compared with the calvaria from Ceprano. Selection of traits derives from lists of distinctive features generally considered in describing *H. erectus* and related hominines [see table 2.11 in Wood (27)]. Given the peculiar character of the frontal region in Ceprano, special attention has been devoted to features describing the supraorbital structures. The traits that have been considered and specimens that have been examined are listed in Table 1, where the scores for presence or absence are also reported.

From these data, a matrix of Manhattan phenetic distances was calculated (Table 2). These distances have been used to generate unrooted trees respectively based on neighbor-joining (NJ) and unweighted pair group method using arithmetic averages (UPGMA; 28, 29); both these trees are reported in Figure 4. Consistent results were also obtained when applying multivariate analyses to raw discrete data, but with the limitation that several rows or, alternatively, columns had to be excluded because of missing scores.

In general, the distribution of the specimens in the trees appears consistent with the assumption that specimens with obvious affinities—like those coming from the same site (i.e., Dmanisi, Zhoukoudian, and Sima de los Huesos)—should cluster together as they actually do. Given this consistency with the expectations and merging the results reported in both the NJ-based and UPGMA-based trees with the *H. erectus* architectural resemblance of the Ceprano calvaria (see above), the position of the late Early Pleistocene Italian specimen appears of great interest for our knowledge on the relationships between populations/species of the genus *Homo*.

Two main clusters are evident in Figure 4 (*a* and *b*). Differences between the trees appear minimal and only concern the relative position of a few specimens. Particularly, Ceprano in the NJ-based tree stands in an isolate position (Figure 4*a*), whereas in the UPGMA-based tree is grouped with the African Middle Pleistocene sample (Figure 4*b*).

A first main cluster in both the trees includes the Asian specimens from Sangiran and Zhoukoudian, generally referred to *H. erectus* (*sensu stricto*), with the possible inclusion of the African OH-9. Another association of this same cluster includes fossils from both Turkana and Dmanisi. In this light, the two Georgian crania appear appropriately classified as *H. ergaster* (according to ref. 7). A second cluster describes a completely separate area of the two graphs, as it groups Middle Pleistocene specimens from Africa and Europe that find in Ceprano a plausible ancestral morph.

Table 1. Alternative Character States in Ceprano and Comparative Samples

	Africa						Asia								Europe					
	ER 3733	ER 3883	OH 9	Bodo	Kabwe	Saldanha	Dmn. 2280	Dmn. 2282	Sng. 2	Sng. 17	Zkd. III	Zkd. X	Zkd. XI	Zkd. XII	Ceprano	Arago	Steinheim	Petralona	At-SH Cr.4	At-SH Cr.5
Long cranial vault	1	1	1	1	1	1	1	1	1	1	1	1	1	1	0	1	1	1	0	1
Low cranial vault	1	1	1	1	1	1	1	1	1	1	1	1	1	1	1	1	1	1	1	1
Maximum breadth across the angular torus or supramastoid crest	1	1	1	—	1	—	1	1	1	1	1	1	1	1	1	—	0	1	1	1
Thick vault bones (parietal)	0	1	1	1	0	1	1	—	1	1	1	1	1	0	1	0	0	0	1	1
Pronounced postorbital constriction	1	1	1	0	1	0	1	1	1	1	1	1	1	1	0	0	0	0	0	0
Frontal keel or ridge	1	0	0	0	1	0	1	0	0	1	1	1	1	0	0	0	0	0	0	0
Straight junction of torus and frontal squama	0	0	0	1	1	1	1	0	1	0	0	0	0	0	0	0	0	1	0	1
Coronal ridge	1	1	—	0	0	0	1	1	1	1	1	1	1	1	0	0	0	0	0	0
Flattened parietal	1	0	1	0	0	0	1	1	1	1	1	1	1	1	1	1	0	0	0	0
Rectangular parietal	0	0	0	—	1	1	1	1	0	1	0	1	0	0	0	0	0	1	1	0
Low temporal squama	0	1	1	0	0	—	1	1	1	1	1	1	1	1	0	—	0	0	0	0
Flat superior border of the temporal squama	0	1	1	0	0	0	0	0	1	1	1	1	1	1	0	—	0	0	0	0
Small mastoid process	1	0	1	—	0	—	1	1	1	1	1	1	1	1	0	—	1	0	0	0
Opisthocranion coincident with inion	1	1	1	—	0	1	1	1	1	1	1	1	1	1	1	—	0	1	0	0
Sharply angulated occipital profile	1	0	1	—	0	1	1	1	0	1	1	1	1	1	1	—	0	0	0	0
Broad nasal bones	0	0	1	1	1	—	0	—	—	1	1	1	1	1	1	1	1	1	1	1
Horizontal inferior border of the supraorbital torus	0	0	1	1	0	0	0	0	1	1	0	1	1	1	0	0	0	0	0	0
Continuous thickness of the supraorbital torus	1	1	1	0	0	0	0	0	1	1	1	1	1	1	0	1	1	1	1	1
Glabellar inflexion in superior view	1	1	1	1	1	1	0	—	—	0	1	0	0	0	1	1	1	1	1	1
Ceprano-like "torsion" of the supraorbital torus	0	0	0	1	1	1	1	1	0	0	0	0	0	0	1	1	0	0	0	0
Bilateral discontinuity (ridges) of the supratoral sulcus	0	0	0	1	1	1	1	0	0	0	0	0	0	0	1	1	1	1	0	0
Prominent angular torus at mastoid angle	0	0	1	—	0	1	1	1	0	1	1	1	1	1	1	0	1	0	1	1
Marked supramastoid crests	1	1	0	—	1	—	1	1	1	1	1	1	1	1	1	—	0	1	1	1
Marked mastoid crests	1	0	1	—	1	—	1	1	0	0	0	1	1	0	0	—	0	—	1	1
Occipitomastoid ridge	0	0	0	—	1	—	—	—	1	1	1	1	1	1	1	—	1	—	1	1
Juxtamastoid ridge absent	0	1	0	—	1	—	—	—	1	1	1	1	1	1	1	—	0	—	1	1
Suprameatal tegmen	1	0	1	—	1	—	1	1	1	1	1	1	1	1	1	—	0	1	0	0
Occipital torus with supratoral sulcus	0	0	0	—	1	0	0	0	1	0	1	1	1	1	1	—	0	1	1	1
Occipital torus continuous with angular torus and supramastoid crest	0	0	0	—	1	1	0	0	1	1	1	0	0	0	0	—	0	0	1	0
Mid-sagittal depression of the occipital torus	0	0	0	—	—	0	0	0	0	0	0	0	0	0	0	—	1	0	1	1

0/1 = absent/present. Site/specimen abbreviations: At-SH = Atapuerca Sima de los Huesos; Dmn. = Dmanisi; ER = East Turkana; Ngd. = Ngandong; OH = Olduvai; Sng. = Sangiran; Zkd. = Zhoukoudian.

Table 2. Matrix of Phenetic Distances Based on Data in Table 1

	ER 3733	ER 3883	OH 9	Bodo	Kabwe	Saldanha	Dmn. 2280	Dmn. 2282	Sng. 2	Sng. 17	Zkd. III	Zkd. X	Zkd. XI	Zkd. XII	Ceprano	Arago	Steinheim	Petralona	At-SH Cr.4	At-SH Cr.5
ER 3733	0.000																			
ER 3883	0.333	0.000																		
OH 9	0.276	0.345	0.000																	
Bodo	0.688	0.625	0.533	0.000																
Kabwe	0.517	0.586	0.714	0.250	0.000															
Saldanha	0.524	0.476	0.550	0.071	0.300	0.000														
Dmn. 2280	0.286	0.464	0.370	0.563	0.481	0.381	0.000													
Dmn. 2282	0.280	0.360	0.292	0.538	0.458	0.421	0.120	0.000												
Sng. 2	0.393	0.321	0.296	0.571	0.556	0.500	0.385	0.440	0.000											
Sng. 17	0.367	0.367	0.310	0.688	0.552	0.524	0.321	0.360	0.143	0.000										
Zkd. III	0.333	0.333	0.276	0.688	0.517	0.571	0.357	0.360	0.143	0.167	0.000									
Zkd. X	0.367	0.433	0.241	0.688	0.552	0.667	0.250	0.280	0.214	0.133	0.167	0.000								
Zkd. XI	0.333	0.400	0.207	0.688	0.586	0.714	0.286	0.320	0.179	0.167	0.133	0.033	0.000							
Zkd. XII	0.333	0.400	0.276	0.750	0.586	0.762	0.357	0.360	0.179	0.167	0.133	0.100	0.067	0.000						
Ceprano	0.533	0.533	0.448	0.188	0.448	0.381	0.500	0.440	0.429	0.500	0.400	0.433	0.400	0.400	0.000					
Arago	0.438	0.500	0.333	0.357	0.438	0.400	0.625	0.385	0.571	0.625	0.375	0.563	0.500	0.438	0.250	0.000				
Steinheim	0.433	0.500	0.483	0.375	0.517	0.476	0.714	0.560	0.607	0.600	0.567	0.667	0.633	0.567	0.500	0.125	0.000			
Petralona	0.444	0.444	0.500	0.250	0.269	0.333	0.519	0.417	0.520	0.593	0.481	0.481	0.519	0.481	0.333	0.250	0.407	0.000		
At-SH Cr.4	0.600	0.467	0.586	0.375	0.345	0.476	0.643	0.520	0.571	0.567	0.467	0.500	0.533	0.600	0.400	0.375	0.433	0.296	0.000	
At-SH Cr.5	0.533	0.400	0.517	0.250	0.345	0.476	0.571	0.520	0.500	0.633	0.467	0.500	0.467	0.533	0.400	0.313	0.367	0.222	0.133	0.000

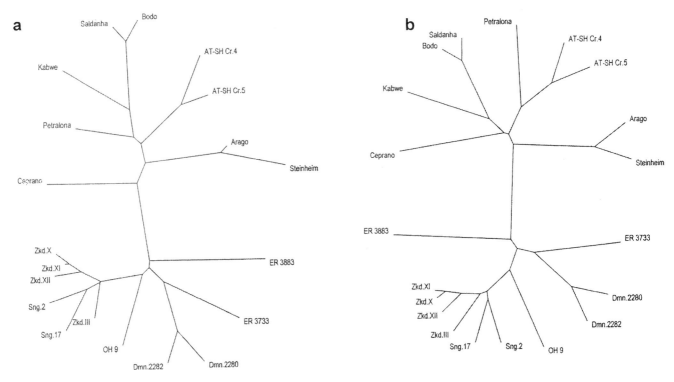

Figure 4. *NJ* (a) *and UPGMA* (b) *unrooted trees (28, 29) derived from weighted Manhattan distances reported in Table 2. Site/specimen abbreviations are as in Table 1.*

Consistent with its morphometric features (Figure 3), in fact, Ceprano appears in the trees—particularly looking at the NJ analysis (Figure 4a)—as a morphological "bridge" between the *H. ergaster/erectus* group and that composed by specimens commonly referred to *H. heidelbergensis*. In addition, the difference observed when using UPGMA to generate the tree (Figure 4b) is the more close clustering of the European Ceprano with the African Middle Pleistocene specimens: Bodo, Kabwe, and Saldanha. However, looking at both the trees, it should be borne in mind the general (architectural) resemblance in shape between Ceprano and fossils ascribed to *H. ergaster* and/or to *H. erectus* (see above)—a feature, actually a suite of features, that is not included in these analyses.

Affinities between Ceprano and Middle Pleistocene specimens from Africa and Europe include: absence of pronounced postorbital constriction, absence of clear keeling or ridges on the vault (with the exception of Kabwe), higher and more rounded temporal squama than in *H. erectus,* relatively large mastoids (with the exception of Steinheim), and features of the supraorbital torus (such as the presence of a glabellar inflexion). Some frontal features in particular—namely the discontinuous thickness of the torus, marked by a definite midorbit torsion (see above)—indicate a relationship between Ceprano and the Mid-Pleistocene fossil record from Africa closer than with the Anteneandertal European specimens (as evidenced by the UPGMA-based tree).

Interestingly, therefore, Ceprano appears as the most archaic—for the "*erectus*-like" parieto-occipital vault—

and the most ancient specimen to display this kind of morphology in the frontal region. Unfortunately, little can be said about the face (with a few exceptions, such as the relative dimension of the nasal bones). Taken as a whole, its morphological pattern is diverse from that shared by *H. ergaster* and *H. erectus*. Given the dating of the Italian specimen, it is also new with respect to later *Homo* referred to *H. heidelbergensis* (and to *H. rhodesiensis;* if a distinction at the species level of the African group is preferred). In this light, Ceprano can be considered as a good candidate to represent the last common ancestor for this latter group of hominines, ultimately between Neandertals and modern humans.

CONCLUSIONS: TOWARD AN INTERPRETATION

On the basis of these results and evaluations, we suggest that humans represented by Ceprano—bearing a new morphology and clear signs of greater encephalization (demonstrated, e.g., by the frontal proportions; see Figure 2b)—diffused into the northern hemisphere during the late Early Pleistocene, in association with Mode 1 Paleolithic technologies. According to the evidence furnished by Ceprano, part of this new morphology was subsequently lost during human evolution in Europe as a possible consequence of the arrival of Acheulean immigrants, whose presence seems to be widely attested in the continent only after 600 ka. At the same time, it should be concluded that this phenotype further developed in Africa during the Middle Pleistocene, as indicated by the affinities between Ceprano and specimens like Bodo or Kabwe.

Which species is then represented by Ceprano? Given its geographical, chronological, and possible phylogenetic position (as described above), the best comparison should be represented by the fossil sample unearthed from Gran Dolina (level TD6) at Atapuerca (Spain). Unfortunately, among the nearly 80 fossil pieces that have been found so far at that site, and referred to the species *H. antecessor* (5, 14, 30), none is directly or adequately comparable with Ceprano, at least in terms of completeness (as for some temporal bone fragments) or age at death (as in the case of the juvenile frontal TD6-15). It is not possible at present to predict the morphologies that could be discovered at Atapuerca, when level TD6 will be reached again by future excavations. However, we cannot exclude that affinities will emerge with what we observe now on Ceprano; in this case, this calvaria would describe for the first time the adult cranial morphology of *H. antecessor*. Alternatively, a less parsimonious scenario should be invoked, where two different human morphs were present during the same time span in Europe, and a new species should be named to accommodate the Italian specimen. Nevertheless, any scenario has to face the fact that the Ceprano morphological pattern does not appropriately fit in the known ranges of variability of *H. ergaster/erectus*, from one side, and *H. heidelbergensis/rhodesiensis* from the other.

ACKNOWLEDGMENTS

This paper is dedicated to the memory of A. Ascenzi. We gratefully acknowledge Prof. F. Clark Howell, who kindly followed and supported our work on Ceprano since its beginning, and the benevolent comments of three referees. Special thanks go to A. G. Segre, E. Segre-Naldini, and I. Biddittu for their suggestions and encouragement, to E. Bruner for his contribution in data analysis, to A. Gracia and I. Martinez for discussions about morphological features, and to D. Lordkipanidze, who kindly authorized the inclusion of observations made on the Dmanisi crania. This work was supported by grants attributed to the Italian Institute of Human Paleontology by the Italian Ministry of Cultural Heritage (MBAC) and the Italian Ministry of Scientific Research (MURST).

REFERENCES

1. Roebroeks, W. & van Kolfschoten, T. (1995) *Analecta Praehistorica Leidensia* **27**, 297–315.
2. de Lumley, H., Fournier, A., Krzepkowska, J. & Echassoux, A. (1988) *L'Anthropologie* **92**, 501–614.
3. Antoniazzi, A., Cattani, L., Cremaschi, M., Fontana, L., Peretto, C., Posenato, R., Proli, F. & Ungaro, S. (1988) *L'Anthropologie* **92**, 629–642.
4. Oms, O., Parés, J. M., Martínez-Navarro, B., Agustí, J., Toro, I., Martínez-Fernández, G. & Turq, A. (2000) *Proc. Natl. Acad. Sci. USA* **97**, 10666–10670. (First Published September 5, 2000; 10.1073/pnas. 180319797)
5. Carbonell, E., Bermudez de Castro, J. M., Arsuaga, J. L., Dìez, J. C., Rosas, A., Cuenca-Bescòs, G., Sala, R., Mosquera, M. & Rodrìguez, P. (1995) *Science* **269**, 826–830.
6. Ascenzi, A., Biddittu, I., Cassoli, P. F., Segre, A. G. & Segre Naldini, E. (1996) *J. Hum. Evol.* **31**, 409–423.
7. Gabunia, L., Vekua, A., Lordkipanidze, D., Swisher, C. C., III, Ferring, R., Justus, A., Nioradze, M., Tvalchrelidze, M., Antón, S. C., Bosinski, G., et al. (2000) *Science* **288**, 1019–1025.
8. Swisher, C. C., III, Curtis, G. H., Jacob, T., Getty, A. G., Supprijo, A. & Widiasmoro (1994) *Nature (London)* **263**, 1118–1121.
9. Larick, R. & Ciochon, R. L. (1996) *Am. Sci.* **84**, 538–551.
10. Manzi, G. (2001) in *Humanity from African Naissance to Coming Millenia*, eds. Tobias, P. V., Raath, M. A., Moggi-Cecchi, J. & Doyle, G. A. (Firenze Univ. Press, Firenze, Italy/Witwatersrand Univ. Press, Johannesburg), pp. 117–124.
11. Piperno, M., ed. (1999) *Notarchirico Un Sito del Pleistocene Medio Iniziale nel Bacino di Venosa* (Osanna, Venosa, Italy).
12. Stringer, C. B. (1993) in *The Origin and Evolution of Humans and Humanness*, ed. Rasmussen, D. T. (Jones and Bartlett, Boston), pp. 75–94.
13. Rightmire, G. P. (1998) *Evol. Anthropol.* **6**, 218–227.
14. Bermúdez de Castro, J. M., Arsuaga, J. L., Carbonell, E., Rosas, A., Martínez, I. & Mosquera, M. (1997) *Science* **276**, 1392–1395.
15. Rightmire, G. P. (1990) *The Evolution of Homo erectus. Comparative Anatomical Studies of an Extinct Human Species* (Cambridge Univ. Press, Cambridge, U.K.).
16. Franzen, J. L., ed. (1994) *Cour. Forch. Inst. Senckenberg* **171**.
17. Abbate, E., Albianelli, A., Azzaroli, A., Benvenuti, M., Tesfamariam, B., Bruni, P., Cipriani, N., Clarke, R. J., Ficcarelli, G., Macchiarelli, R., et al. (1998) *Nature (London)* **393**, 458–460.
18. Clarke, R. J. (2000) *J. Hum. Evol.* **39**, 433–442.
19. Ascenzi, A., Mallegni, F., Manzi, G., Segre, A. G. & Segre-Naldini, E. (2000) *J. Hum. Evol.* **39**, 443–450.
20. Ascenzi, A. & Segre, A. G. (1997) *Anthropologie (Brno)* **35**, 241–246.
21. Ascenzi, A. & Segre A. G. (2000) in *The Origin of Humankind*, eds. Aloisi, M., Battaglia, B., Carafoli, E. & Danieli, G. A. (IOS, Amsterdam), pp. 25–33.
22. Segre, A. G. & Ascenzi, A. (1984) *Curr. Anthropol.* **25**, 230–233.
23. Rammelzwaal, A. (1978) *Publ. Fysisch-Geogr. Bodenkundig Lab. Univ. Amsterdam* **28**, 1–310.
24. Sevink, J., Rammelzwaal, A. & Spaargaren, O. C. (1984) *Publ. Fysisch-Geogr. Bodenkundig Lab. Univ. Amsterdam* **38**, 1–144.
25. Fornaseri, M. (1985) *Rend. Soc. It. Mineral. Petrolog.* **40**, 74–106.
26. Biddittu, I. (1984) in *Il Paleolitico e il Mesolitico nel Lazio* (Ist. It. Preist. Protost., Firenze, Italy), pp. 31–37.
27. Wood, B. (1991) *Koobi Fora Research Project. Hominid Cranial Remains* (Clarendon Press, Oxford).
28. Felsenstein, J. (1993) PHYLIP: Phylogeny Inference Package, Version 3.5c (Univ. of Washington, Seattle).
29. Page, R. D. M. (1996) *Comput. Appl. Biosci.* **12**, 357–358.
30. Carbonell, E., Bermúdez de Castro, J. & Arsuaga, J. L., eds. (1999) *J. Hum. Evol.* **37**, 309–700.

49

The KNM-ER 3884 Hominid and the Emergence of Modern Anatomy in Africa

G. Bräuer

ABSTRACT

Although there can be little doubt that modern anatomy originated very early in Africa, new results indicate that the evolutionary process of modernization occurred even earlier than generally thought. Most recent indications for such a backdating are yielded by Uranium-series dates for two fragment of the KNM-ER 3884 cranium and a part of the KNM-ER 999 femur from Ileret, Kenya, suggesting ages of around 270,000 and 300,000 years, respectively. These results were surprising because of the near-modern morphology of the specimens. However, recent dating of Laetoli Hominid 18 (Tanzania) and Florisbad (South Africa) also support such an early age for late archaic Homo sapiens *in Africa. These results raise again the interesting question whether the evolution of modern anatomy followed a mosaic-like pattern in most of Africa or whether it took place predominantly in one part of the continent. Not only late archaic* H. sapiens, *but also early archaic* H. sapiens, *appear to have existed earlier than has long been assumed. Ar/Ar ages place the Bodo hominid from Ethiopia at around 600,000 years BP, indicating that at this time a form existed which was more derived than* H. erectus. *While some workers classify Bodo and similar specimens as (early) archaic* H. sapiens, *others, assign them to a species named* H. heidelbergensis. *The present paper discusses the current framework of Middle and early Late Pleistocene hominid evolution in Africa including questions of taxonomy.*

INTRODUCTION

The evolution of modern anatomy in Africa has been a much debated topic for many years. I have been personally involved in this question for more than 20 years, and looking over this time period I can say that there has been increasing evidence from both fossils and dating that support a very early origin of modern anatomy in Africa. The most recent evidence comes from the Ileret specimen, KNM-ER 3884, also known as the Guomde cranium (Figure 1). The date of the specimen has long been unknown because it was not possible to determine whether the cranium derived from undifferentiated later deposits of the Upper Chari Member of the Koobi Fora Formation or from the subsequent

Holocene Galana Boi Formation (Bräuer, Leakey & Mbua, 1992). It has therefore been unclear whether the cranium dates from more than 100,000, up to several hundred thousand years, or whether it could even be less than 10,000 years old (Feibel et al., 1989).

Figure 1. *Reconstruction of KNM-ER 3884 cranium from Ileret.*

In the 1980s, we carried out a preliminary analysis and comparison of the cranium (Bräuer, Leakey & Mbua, 1992), and we found that the posterior cranial vault was basically anatomically modern, whereas the supraorbital fragment seemed to tell a different story. It clearly exhibits a continuous supraorbital torus running over both orbits. We compared the torus morphology with that seen in the Galana Boi material and other East African Holocene and final Pleistocene specimens. We could find no similarities. We also included in our comparison robust modern remains like the cranial fragment from Lukenya Hill, which dates to roughly 17,000 years. This specimen clearly deviates from the morphology of KNM-ER 3884 in having a modern supraorbital pattern with a pronounced but well defined superciliary arch and a flattened supraorbital trigone. The supraorbital morphology of KNM-ER 3884, instead, showed closer affinities to archaic *Homo sapiens*.

RECENT DATING EVIDENCE

Over the years dating possibilities for the KNM-ER 3884 cranium have been sought, but only recently was a direct dating of the hominid possible using the nondestructive method of gamma-ray spectrometry. Yuji Yokoyama and Christophe Falguères of the Muséum National d'Histoire Naturelle in Paris were able to date two cranial fragments separately to 272,000 and 279,000 years respectively (Bräuer et al., 1997). To be on the safe side we also included in this dating project the so-called Guomde femur, KNM-ER 999, which derived from the same deposits as the KNM-ER 3884 cranium. The result of the gamma-ray spectrometry dating for the femur was about 300,000 years, which also supported the great age of the cranium. The morphology of the KNM-ER 999 femur was analysed by Trinkaus (1993), who found close similarities to early modern specimens from the Near East. Although the femur is thick-walled, it exhibits a number of derived features such as a pilaster development and a very low neck-shaft angle.

The great age of the Ileret specimen was indeed surprising, but other recent evidence has supported such an early presence of near-modern humans in Africa. A few months after the Ileret cranium was dated to around 270,000 years, Grün et al. (1996) published a new date for the Florisbad hominid of 259,000 (±35,000) years, based on ESR analysis of the single hominid tooth. The early presence of such near-modern humans in Africa has further been supported by new dating evidence for the Upper Ngaloba Beds in Tanzania, from which the Laetoli Hominid 18 cranium derived. Recent amino acid dates on ostrich eggshell material point to an age of more than 200,000 years for this specimen (Manega, 1995). Thus there are three different hominids, dated by different methods and different laboratories, all pointing to the presence of a near-modern or late archaic anatomy in Africa between 250,000 and 300,000 years ago. The partial cranium from Florisbad exhibits a quite derived, near-modern

anatomy which is especially evident from its canine fossa and the moderately developed supraorbital torus. The Laetoli Hominid 18 also shows a modern face and a slightly projecting supraorbital torus. A close look at the torus indicates that there is a division between the superciliary arch and the supraorbital trigone, as Magori (1980) pointed out in his dissertation.

Two further late archaic *Homo sapiens* crania from Jebel Irhoud, Morocco, might date to somewhat less than 200,000 years (Grün & Stringer, 1991). They also exhibit a derived supraorbital morphology and the face, only preserved in one specimen, appears quite modern. In view of these recent dates for late archaic *Homo sapiens*, a new comparative study of the Ileret cranium KNM-ER 3884 is currently under way (G. Bräuer and E. Mbua, in preparation).

THE MODERNIZATION PROCESS

The late archaic hominid specimens from Africa are followed by early anatomically modern humans (Figure 2). The Singa cranium from Sudan, dating to about 150,000 years (McDermott et al., 1996), can be

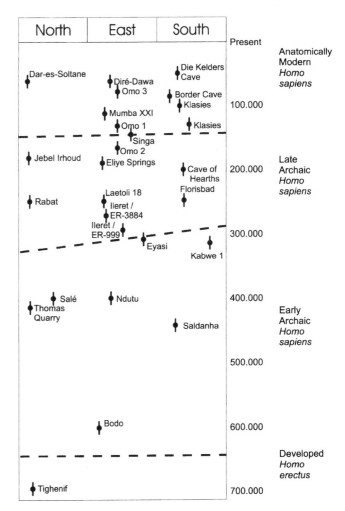

Figure 2. *Updated scheme of Middle and Late Pleistocene hominid evolution in Africa.*

regarded as being just on the threshold to modern humans. It has been classified both as late archaic and as anatomically fully modern.

Another important early anatomically modern specimen comes from the Omo Kibish Formation in Ethiopia. Uranium-series dates for the hominid level have yielded an age of around 130,000 years. This date has been questioned because it is based on mollusc material. However, mollusc shells tend to accumulate Uranium after deposition, which would normally lead to an *under*-estimation of age. The cranium and post-cranial remains of the Omo Kibish I hominid are fully anatomically modern, and I would not be surprised to find a similar skull among early modern Europeans.

Another important site which yielded early modern cranial and post-cranial remains lies on the south coast of Africa, at the Klasies River Mouth. The oldest human remains came from the LBS Member, which dates to the last interglacial period around 120,000 years ago. An analysis of the maxillary fragments found there has shown that the specimens fall into the range of a Holocene sample from Africa (Bräuer, Deacon & Zipfel, 1992). One of the best preserved specimens from Klasies River is a 100,000-year-old mandible (no. 41815) from the lower SAS Member, showing a well developed chin and a fully modern anatomy.

The famous frontal fragment from this site is about 80,000 years old and it also does not exhibit any archaic reminiscences. Its supraorbital margin is thin and it is quite unlikely that a supraorbital torus morphology could have developed, even if the specimen belonged to a sub-adult of around 15 or 16 years of age.

Nevertheless, the Klasies River human remains dated to between 60,000 and 80,000 years ago exhibit a rather great variability (Bräuer & Singer, 1996a,b). The mandibular specimens range from extremely gracile (no.16424) to robust ones with weak chin development (no.13400). Although much of this variation might be due to sexual dimorphism, the question arises whether some features should be regarded as archaic retentions.

As there is much subjectivity in the assessment of chin development, Lam et al. (1996) carried out a metrical analysis of the depth of the anterior incurvature and the protrusion of the chin, and found that some Klasies specimens are marginal to, but still within, the 95% range of recent samples. There are also less pronounced chins in the early modern remains from Qafzeh, Israel (Tillier, 1989). A similar situation is found in the postcranial specimens from Klasies River and Border Cave. Here, too, the morphology of some specimens seems to show archaic reminiscences, as for example the Klasies River ulna with regard to the relative height of its coronoid and olecranon processes. Nevertheless, Churchill et al. (1996) stated that the morphology of the Klasies River ulna could be matched in samples from recent San and other sub-recent Africans (see also Pearson & Grine, 1996). From Groves' (1998) Principal Components Analysis, the position of the Klasies River ulna is somewhere between archaic humans (Neanderthal, Baringo) and recent

moderns and could also be interpreted as being ancestral to more modern humans. Whether special conditions of certain features seen in an early modern sample like that from Klasies River should be regarded as archaic retentions or as common early anatomically modern conditions is difficult to decide, but also not of much relevance. I think the morphological range of variation seen in the Klasies River material is exactly what one would expect in such an early modern population: fully anatomically modern specimens, like some mandibles, the frontal fragment and others, as well as pieces showing more archaic-looking conditions marginal to the recent variation.

We cannot expect that the recent morphological variation will cover the total range of early anatomically modern variation (Trinkaus, 1993; Bräuer & Singer, 1996b). The range of variation will most likely be wider to the archaic and more robust side. Interestingly, Pfeiffer & Zehr (1996: 57) found in their analysis of the robust humerus from Border Cave not only similarities to Early Upper Palaeolithic and Later Stone Age specimens, but also "that the oldest males of the dated sample of LSA humeri show high values for bone mass and strength relative to their overall size, similar to Border Cave". Therefore, I do not see any problem in classifying the Klasies River and Border Cave materials as anatomically modern humans.

In summary, the fossil hominids and the most recent dating evidence clearly indicate that the evolution of modern anatomy occurred relatively early in Africa (Figure 2). Near-modern or late archaic humans already existed in eastern and southern Africa at least 250,000 years ago. This process of modernization and *sapiens* evolution can be traced back up to around 600,000 years to the earliest known specimen of early archaic *Homo sapiens*, the Bodo cranium from Ethiopia. This specimen deviates significantly from *Homo erectus* morphology in a number of features, as for example in its larger cranial capacity of around 1,300 cc, the broader frontal and also in some derived features of its supraorbital morphology (Rightmire, 1996). Thus, it is quite probable that a speciation process occurred around 700,000 years ago. Unfortunately, the hominid material from this time period is very sparse.

Another interesting question is whether the modernization process in Africa took place all over the continent in a mosaic-like pattern, or whether it occurred predominantly in one of the major areas of Africa and then spread to other regions. About 15 years ago it was widely believed that late archaic and modern humans appeared first in sub-Saharan Africa. At the end of the 1980s, new dates for the Jebel Irhoud hominids pointing to an age of up to 190,000 years have drawn attention to North Africa as a possible cradle of modern anatomy. However, as outlined above, the last three years have again yielded more important new evidence for an earlier presence of near-modern humans in sub-Saharan Africa. Further analysis of the African cranial material with regard to derived and primitive conditions might yield more clarity on the process.

PHYLOGENETIC PERSPECTIVES

Finally, how do we put the African sequence into a larger phylogenetic scheme? I think that the speciation process in Africa around 700,000 or 800,000 years ago took place between *Homo erectus* and archaic *Homo sapiens* followed by more or less gradual evolution from early to late archaic *Homo sapiens* and finally to anatomically modern humans, whereas in Europe the evolution led from Ante-Neanderthals to Neanderthals (for the Far East, see Bräuer, 2001). Rightmire (1996, 1998) has recently suggested a speciation from *Homo erectus* to *Homo heidelbergensis*, from which in Europe *Homo neanderthalensis*, and in Africa *Homo sapiens*, might be descended. However, the situation for Africa appears to be more difficult because the late archaic *Homo sapiens* group is already quite close to anatomically modern humans. In such a scenario, *Homo sapiens* could not be regarded as including only anatomically modern humans, as has been proposed by a number of authors, but it should also include the late archaic *Homo sapiens* group. On the other hand, it appears rather difficult clearly to distinguish early from late archaic *Homo sapiens* in Africa on a species or paleospecies level. Thus, to me it appears more plausible to consider the African sequence over the last 600,000 years as a rather gradual evolution of our own species, *Homo sapiens*.

ACKNOWLEDGMENTS

I would like to thank Giacomo Giacobini and Phillip Tobias for inviting me to take part in this Colloquium. I am also grateful to the organizers of the magnificent Dual Congress as well as to the German Research Foundation (DFG) for supporting my participation.

REFERENCES

Bräuer, G. (2001). The 'out-of-Africa' model and the question of regional continuity. In: Humanity from African Naissance to Coming Millennia, ed. P. Tobias, M. Raath, J. Moggi-Cecchi, & G. Doyle, pp. 183–197. Firenze: Firenze University Press.

Bräuer, G., Deacon, H. J. & Zipfel, F. (1992). Comment on the new maxillary finds from Klasies River, South Africa. Journal of Human Evolution, 23, 419–22.

Bräuer, G., Leakey, R. E. & Mbua, E. (1992). A first report on the ER 3884 cranial remains from Ileret/East Turkana, Kenya. In: Continuity or Replacement—Controversies in Homo sapiens Evolution, ed. G. Bräuer & F. H. Smith, pp. 111–19. Rotterdam: Balkema.

Bräuer, G. & Singer, R. (1996a). The Klasies zygomatic bone: archaic or modern? Journal of Human Evolution, 30, 161–65.

Bräuer, G. & Singer, R. (1996b). Not outside the modern range? Journal of Human Evolution, 30, 173–74.

Bräuer, G., Yokoyama, Y., Falguères, C. & Mbua, E. (1997). Modern human origins backdated. Nature, 386, 337–38.

Churchill, S. E., Pearson, O. M., Grine, F. E., Trinkaus, E. & Holliday, T. W. (1996). Morphological affinities of the proximal ulna from Klasies River Mouth Main Site: archaic or modern? Journal of Human Evolution, 31, 213–37.

Feibel, C. S., Brown, F. H. & McDougall, I. (1989). Stratigraphic context of fossil hominids from the Omo Group deposits, northern Turkana Basin, Kenya and Ethiopia. American Journal of Physical Anthropology, 78, 595–622.

Groves, C. P. (1998). The proximal ulna from Klasies River. Journal of Human Evolution, 34, 119–21.

Grün, R. & Stringer, C. B. (1991). Electron Spin Resonance dating and the evolution of modern humans. Archaeometry, 33, 153–99.

Grün, R., Brink, J. S., Spooner, N. A., Taylor, L., Stringer, C. B., Franciscus, R. G. & Murray, A. S. (1996). Direct dating of Florisbad hominid. Nature, 382, 500–01.

Lam, Y. M., Pearson, O. M. & Smith, C. M. (1996). Chin morphology and sexual dimorphism in the fossil hominid mandible sample from Klasies River Mouth. American Journal of Physical Anthropology, 100, 545–57.

Manega, P. (1995). New geochronological results from the Ndutu, Naisiusiu and Ngaloba Beds at Olduvai and Laetoli in Northern Tanzania: their significance for evolution of modern humans. Paper presented at the Conference "Preservation and use of Olduvai Gorge, Laetoli, rock art and other paleoanthropological resources in Tanzania." Bellagio, Italy.

Magori, C. C. (1980). Laetoli Hominid 18: Studies on a Pleistocene fossil human skull from Northern Tanzania. Unpublished Ph.D. Thesis, University College, London.

McDermott, F., Stringer, C., Grün, R., Williams, C. T., Din, V. K. & Hawkesworth, C. J. (1996). New Late-Pleistocene uranium-thorium and ESR dates for the Singa hominid (Sudan). Journal of Human Evolution, 31, 507–16.

Pearson, O. M. & Grine, F. E. (1996). Morphology of the Border Cave hominid ulna and humerus. South African Journal of Science, 92, 231–36.

Pfeiffer, S. & Zehr, M. K. (1996). A morphological and histological study of the human humerus from Border Cave. Journal of Human Evolution, 31, 49–59.

Rightmire, G. P. (1996). The human cranium from Bodo, Ethiopia: evidence for speciation in the Middle Pleistocene? Journal of Human Evolution, 31, 21–39.

Rightmire, G. P. (1998). Human evolution in the Middle Pleistocene: The role of Homo heidelbergensis. Evolutionary Anthropology, 6, 218–27.

Tillier, A.-M. (1989). The evolution of modern humans: evidence from young Mousterian individuals. In: The Human Revolution, ed. P. Mellars & C. B. Stringer, pp. 286–297. Edinburgh: Edinburgh University Press.

Trinkaus, E. (1993). A note on the KNM-ER 999 hominid femur. Journal of Human Evolution, 24, 493–504.

50

Dali, a Skull of Archaic *Homo sapiens* from China

X. Wu and F. E. Poirier

ABSTRACT

In 1978, Shuntang Liu, a geologist from the Geological Bureau of Shaanxi Province, fou an almost complete human skull at a loess terrace named Tianshuigou near Jiefang Village, Dali County, Shaanxi Province (109°40'E, 34°52'N) in northwestern China (Figure 1).

HUMAN FOSSILS

The following description is summarized from X. Wu (1981). The Dali skull is rather complete, except that the posterior superior part of the skullcap, the left zygomatic arch, and the pterygoid process are missing. The lower part of the face was deformed by the upward depression of the alveolar process. This depression was caused by pressure exerted by the earth deposits.

The skull is rather robust and probably from a male slightly less than 30 years of age (Figure 2). Its supraor-

bital torus is thick, and the temporal lines and the supramastoid ridges are well developed. The external cranial sutures are intact; however, the suture between the greater wing of the sphenoid and the temporal squama is obliterated.

In most measurements and indices the Dali skull falls within the range of variation of western early *H. sapiens* and is intermediate between *H. erectus* and late *H. sapiens*. Some measurements and indices are within the range of variation of the Zhoukoudian *H. erectus* skulls (Table 1).

In its nonmetric features, the Dali skull is more similar to early *H. sapiens* than to *H. erectus*. The broadest part of the skull vault is at the postero-superior margin of the temporal squama rather than near the cranial base. In a rear view, the upper part of the parietal is more horizontal than is true with *H. erectus,* while the lower part is more vertical than in *H. erectus*. Unlike the case with Neandertals, the posterior contour of the Dali skull is not spherical. The distance between the parietal tuberosities is close to the maximum breadth of the skull. The postorbital constriction is not as narrow as that in *H. erectus*.

A sagittal prominence on the frontal squama broadens at the middle and attenuates upward and downward. The upper end is slightly higher than the center

Figure 1. *The early* Homo sapiens *site of Dali.* (Courtesy of IVPP.)

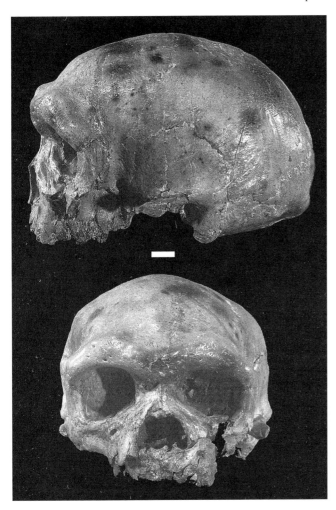

Figure 2. *Early* Homo sapiens *skull from Dali. (top) Lateral view. (bottom) Anterior view.* (Courtesy of IVPP.)

Table 1. Measurements of the Dali Skull (in mm or degrees)

Cranial length (g-op)	207
Cranial width (eu-eu)	149
Cranial height (ba-b)	118
Auricular bregmatic height	102.5
Cranial sagittal arc (n-o arc)	379
Cranial transverse arc (po-b-po arc)	299
Distance between parietal tuberosities	136
Orbital height (r)	34
Orbital width (mf-ek, r)	45
Height of zygomatic	52.6
Minimum distance between postorbital surfaces of both sides of frontal bone	106.4
Distance between most lateral points of both sides of the brow ridges	125
Height of temporal squama	46.5
Length of temporal squama	72
Distance between inion and endinion	11
Nasomalar angle (fmo-n-fmo)	143
Inclination angle of frontal bone I (b-n-i)	54°
Inclination angle of frontal bone II (b-n-o)	49°
Inclination angle of frontal squama I (b-g-i)	50°
Inclination angle of frontal squama II (b-g-o)	45°
Inclination angle of lower frontal bone I (m-g-i)	72°
Inclination angle of lower frontal bone II (m-g-o)	67°
Thickness of cranial bones:	
Center of frontal squama	9
Center of parietal tuberosity	11.2
Cerebellar fossa	3.9
Center of temporal squama	7
Cranial capacity	1120
Cranial index	72
Length-height index	57
Width-height index	79.2
Transverse curvature	47.5
Index of postorbital constriction	85.1
Length-height index of temporal squama	64.6
Ratio of dimensions of cerebral fossa to cerebellar fossa	3:2

Cited from X. Wu (1989 in Wu et al., 1989)

of the frontal squama. The lower end is about 2 cm above the glabella. A weak eminence, reminiscent of the cruciate eminence, exists at the bregmatic region. Between the left parietal and occipital bones is a small bone, perhaps the remaining part of an Inca bone, the lower border of which is horizontal. The adjoining part of the right parietal and occipital bones is missing.

The left parietal is rather complete, except for a small supero-posterior part. Only the anterior portion of the right parietal is preserved. Both parietals are slightly elevated near the sagittal border. There is a shallow groove along the sagittal suture between these elevations. The parietal tuberosity is distinct and located slightly below the center of the parietal bone. Both the superior and inferior temporal lines are distinct and rather broad. The inferior temporal line passes the parietal tuberosity where the distance between both temporal lines is 1 cm. Both temporal lines are separated on the parietal bone. The inferior temporal line terminates at the angular torus, close to the asterion, and is thinner than that in *H. erectus pekinensis*. This torus in the Dali skull is circular and about 2 cm in diameter.

The superior border of the temporal squama is formed by a short anterior and a longer posterior part.

The former is more horizontal. A small quadrilateral process of the supero-anterior part of the squama inserts between the parietal and the sphenoid bones, and connects with the frontal bone. The pteryon of both sides is of the I-type. The supramastoid ridge is robust and spindle-shaped and is almost in line with the zygomatic arch. Although it has a weak inclination in an upward direction, it is less inclined that that of the Neandertals. The small mastoid process points downward. The orifice of the auditory meatus is elliptically shaped with a vertically oriented longitudinal axis. A small, 4 cm in diameter, moundlike exostosis appears on the wall of the auditory meatus.

The upper border of the zygomatic process is lower than the Frankfurt Plane. The longitudinal axis of the zygomatic arch forms a 10° angle with the Frankfurt Plane. The elongation of this axis passes through the upper half of the auditory orifice. The right zygomatic arch is thin, with its thinnest part 7 mm high and 4.3 mm wide. The left arch is similar judging from its remaining part. The postglenoid process is well developed. The concavity and thickness of the tympanic plate is intermediate between *H. erectus pekinensis* and modern humans. The long axis of the petrous part forms a 40° angle with the sagittal plane.

No infratemporal ridge exists on the greater wing of the sphenoid, but the demarcation between the temporal and infratemporal surface is distinct. The occipital torus is thick in the middle but thins toward the lateral ends. There is a shallow supratoral sulcus. The glabellar region is receding. The infraglabellar notch is indented in lateral view.

The frontonasal and frontomaxillary sutures form an almost horizontal curve. The upper part of the nasal bone is much narrower than its lower part. The profile angle of the nasal bone is big, and the nasal saddle is flat. There is a median sagittal longitudinal narrow ridge on the nasal bone.

Both orbits are quadrangular. The medial part of the orbit is somewhat rounded, and the lateral part is slightly more angular. The right orbit is slightly higher than the left. The lacrimal depression of the orbit roof is shallower than that in modern humans and deeper than in "Peking Man." The superior orbital margin is evenly curved. There is no supraorbital notch, supraorbital foramen, or supraorbital tubercle. The inferolateral part of the orbital margin is rounded. The superior orbital fissure is similar to that of "Peking Man." However, the inferior zygomatico-orbital foramen is located on the lateral wall of the orbit, not on the elongating line of the inferior orbital fissure.

The pyriform orifice is pear shaped. The nasal process of the maxilla bulges supero-laterally to the orifice, as is also true for Neandertals. The distance between the infraorbital foramen and the inferior orbital margin is 8 mm. A maxillary sulcus runs downward from the infraorbital foramen. A well-developed canine jugum is located lateral to the lower segment of this sulcus.

The anterior surface of the zygomatic process of the maxilla faces forward and forms a shallow groove with the anterior surface of the maxilla. The lower margin of the zygomatic process and the lateral surface of the maxillary body form a deepened curve, which is slightly weaker than that in "Peking Man," which possesses a very deep malar notch. The juncture of the lower margin of the zygomatic process and the body of maxilla is distant from the alveolar margin. This point is located midway between the alveolar margin and the inferior orbital margin. A forward protruding process at the upper end of the zygomatic process makes a sharp turn at the junction of this process and the zygomatic bone. The sharp turn is especially distinct when viewed inferiorly.

The zygomatic bone is only 52.6 mm high. The anterolateral surface of the fronto-sphenoidal process of the zygomatic faces more forward than in Neandertals. A weak marginal process and an orbital tubercle appear on the posterior margin and the orbital margins of this process, respectively. There is a moderately developed tuberosity on the lateral surface of the bone.

There is a crista galli on the endocranial surface. A complete pattern of branching of the middle meningeal artery can be seen on the left side. The artery has three main branches. The fronto-parietal branch is slightly thicker than the superior temporal branch and terminates at the bregmatic and obelion regions. The superior temporal branch is the longest and is slightly thicker than the inferior temporal branch,

which runs almost parallel to the superior branch. This pattern of branching is somewhat similar to that of the latest Peking skull (no. 5 from Locus H). The impressions of the branches of the meningeal artery on the endocranial surface are clearer than in "Peking Man."

Table 1 shows the important measurements and indices of the Dali skull. Many figures are within the range of early *H. sapiens* and intermediate between *H. erectus pekinensis* and modern humans. These measurements are the maximum length, maximum width, height, median sagittal arc, transverse arc, transverse curvature, inclination angle of the frontal bone, post-orbital constriction, distance between the external and internal occipital protuberance, and the ratio of the dimension of the cerebral fossa to that of the cerebellar fossa.

The Dali skull also has many *H. erectus* traits. These include the low cranial vault, thick cranial wall, well-developed brow ridges, small superior orbital fissure, low position of the zygomatic arch, angular turn from the occipital to the nuchal plane of the occipital bone, the supratoral sulcus of the occipital bone, and the maxillary sulcus, among others.

Progressive features of the Dali skull include a low zygomatic bone, thin zygomatic arch, the absence of a supraorbital tubercle, the short distance between the infraorbital foramen and the inferior orbital margin, the zygomatico-orbital foramen located on the lateral orbital wall, and the presence of a crista galli, among others.

GEOLOGY

The Dali human skull was unearthed from the third terrace of Lohe River. The deposits consist of 15 layers (X. Wu and You, 1979). They are as follows from the surface downward:

Strata dating to the upper part of the Middle Pleistocene:

13. Grayish-yellow silty clay, 7.6 m thick
12. Light brownish-red paleosol, 3 m thick
11. Grayish-yellow silty clay with small gravels and concretions, 7 m thick
10. Light brownish red paleosol rich with concretions, 2.1 m thick
9. Grayish yellow fine sands and silt, 1.8 m thick
8. Brownish-yellow, orange yellow coarse sands with cross-bedding, rich with molluscs, 1.2 m thick
7. Yellow green clay, 0.5 m thick
6. Grayish-yellow sandy clay rich with molluscs, 2.5 m thick
5. Grayish-yellow silt, fine sands, 6.2 m thick
4. Light purple moderate-sized and coarse sands, with cross bedding, cemented, 0.5–18 m thick
3. Brown grayish, brown gravels, yielding the human skull, stone artifacts, vertebrate fossils, molluscs, and carbon particles, 0.5–1.2 m thick

———————unconformity———————

Strata dating to the upper part of the Lower Pleistocene:

2. Grayish-green sandy clay, 1.8 m thick
1. Light gray sands with gravel, exposed thickness, 2 m

According to X. Wu and You (1979) the vertebrate fossils associated with the hominid remains are as follows:

Primates
 Homo sapiens
Rodentia
 Myospalax sp.
 Castor sp.
Proboscidea
 Palaeoloxodon sp.
Perissodactyla
 Equus sp.
 Rhinocerus sp.
 Coelodonta sp.
Artiodactyla
 Megalocerose pachyosteus
 Megaloceros sp.
 Pseudais cf. *grayi*
 Bubulus sp.

Gazella przewalskyi
Gazella sp.
Bird
 Struthio anderssoni
Fishes
 Cypriniformes
 Siluroidea

Uranium series dates on ox teeth give an age of 209,000 ± 23,000 years ago (T. Chen et al., 1984).

ARCHAEOLOGY

Some small stone artifacts were found with the human fossils. Most of the stone tools are scrapers, others include points, a stone awl, and burins. Most tools were made by hammering, and the manufacture is simple and rough.

REFERENCES

Chen, T., Yuan, S., and Gao, S. (1984). The study of uranium series dating of fossil bones and an absolute age sequence for the main Paleolithic sites of north China. *Acta Anthropologica Sinica*, 3:259–268 (in Chinese with English abstract).

Wu, R., Wu, X., and Zhang, S., eds. (1989). *Early Humankind in China*. Science Press, Beijing (in Chinese).

Wu, X. and You, Y. (1979). A preliminary observation of the Dali Man site. *Vertebrata PalAsiatica*, 17:294–303 (in Chinese with English abstract).

Wu, X. (1981). The well preserved cranium of an early *Homo sapiens* from Dali, Shaanxi. *Scientia Sinica*, 24:200–206.

51

Body Mass and Encephalization in Pleistocene *Homo*

C. B. Ruff, E. Trinkaus, and T. W. Holliday

ABSTRACT

Many dramatic changes in morphology within the genus Homo *have occurred over the past 2 million years or more, including large increases in absolute brain size and decreases in postcanine dental size and skeletal robusticity. Body mass, as the 'size' variable against which other morphological features are usually judged, has been important for assessing these changes[1-5]. Yet past body mass estimates for Pleistocene* Homo *have varied greatly, sometimes by as much as 50% for the same individuals[2,3,6-12]. Here we show that two independent methods of body-mass estimation yield concordant results when applied to Pleistocene* Homo *specimens. On the basis of an analysis of 163 individuals, body mass in Pleistocene* Homo *averaged significantly (about 10%) larger than a representative sample of living humans. Relative to body mass, brain mass in late archaic* H. sapiens *(Neanderthals) was slightly smaller than in early 'anatomically modern' humans, but the major increase in encephalization within* Homo *occurred earlier during the Middle Pleistocene (600–150 thousand years before present (kyr* BP*)), preceded by a long period of stasis extending through the Early Pleistocene (1,800 kyr* BP*).*

It is generally acknowledged, even by those who have used other methods, that the best means of estimating body mass from skeletal or fossil remains, when feasible, is to use features that have some direct functional relationship to body mass[9,11,12]. For hominids, the skeletal dimensions used most often have been lower limb long bone diaphyseal and articular breadths[2,3,6,7,9]. Diaphyseal breadths of fossil hominids are problematic as body mass estimators because relative to body size they are systematically larger than modern humans, probably as a response to increased mechanical loading[5]. In contrast, articulations are much less environmentally sensitive[13,14], and thus are potentially better body-size indicators. The articular dimension used here as a body-mass estimator is femoral head breadth because it is available for many fossil *Homo* specimens, is easily measured and highly reproducible, and because several investigators have provided information on the relationship between femoral head breadth and body mass in modern humans[6,13,15] (see Methods).

The second method used here to estimate body mass does not rely on any assumptions about the mechanical relationship between a particular skeletal feature and body size (support of body weight). Rather, in this approach body mass is estimated directly from reconstructed stature and body breadth. A modern worldwide anthropometric sampling of 56 population/sex-specific means[16] was used to derive multiple regressions of body mass on stature and bi-iliac (maximum pelvic) breadth (Methods).

Figure 1 compares femoral head and stature/bi-iliac estimates of body mass for 75 Pleistocene *Homo* specimens. The mean absolute difference between estimates is about 5 kg (7.6%), and the mean directional difference is less than 1 kg (1.1%). Paired *t*-tests between results are not significant ($P \geq 0.30$). Thus, equations based on femoral head size and stature/bi-iliac breadth yield similar body mass estimates when applied to Pleistocene *Homo*, with very little systematic bias. Because the two techniques are based on different rationales and skeletal dimensions, yet nevertheless converge on the same result, this increases confidence in both.

Skeletal dimensions for 163 Pleistocene *Homo* specimens, dated 10–1,950 kyr BP, were derived from

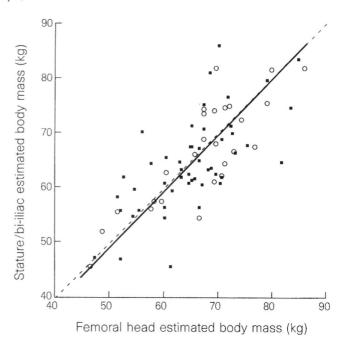

Figure 1. *Comparison between body mass estimated from stature and bi-iliac breadth and body mass estimated from femoral head breadth in 75 Pleistocene* Homo *specimens. Empty symbols, measured bi-iliac breadth; filled symbols, estimated bi-iliac breadth. Solid line, reduced major axis regression (y = 1.04 × x – 3.4; r = 0.738). Dotted line indicates equivalence of y and x.*

previously published sources and personal measurements[5,10,17]. Most regions of the Old World (except Australia) are represented, although the majority of the sample is from Europe (55%), with the remainder from Africa (27%), western Asia (15%) and eastern Asia (3%). The resulting body mass estimates are shown in Figure 2a, together with 51 sex/population-specific means for a worldwide sampling of living humans

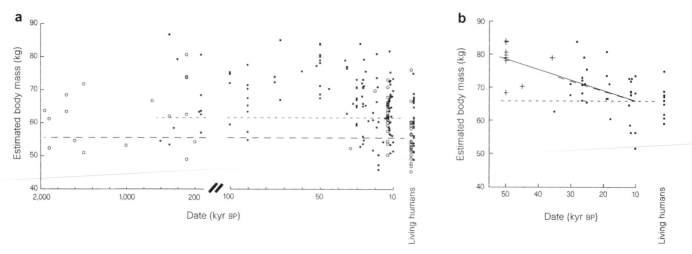

Figure 2. *Changes through time in body mass of* Homo. *a, Total sample. Empty symbols, lower latitude (<30° N) (dashed line through living mean); closed symbols, higher latitude (dotted line through living mean). Note change in temporal (x) axis scale at 100 kyr BP. b, Higher-latitude males. Crosses, archaic* H. sapiens; *squares, early anatomically modern (EAM) and living* H. sapiens *(dotted line through living mean). Solid line, least-squares regression through total Pleistocene sample (y = 0.318 × x + 62.6; r = 0.582); dashed line, least-squares regression through EAM sample (y = 0.299 × x + 62.9; r = 0.334).*

Table 1. Body-Mass and Brain-Mass Data

Sample	Temporal Range (kyr BP)	Body Mass (kg)* (mean ± s.e. (*n*))	Cranial Capacity (cc)[†] (mean ± s.e. (*n*))	Brain Mass (g)[‡] (mean ± s.e. (*n*))	Encephalization Quotient[‡]	
					Associated Specimens (mean ± s.e. (*n*))	Sample Means (mean)
living worldwide	—	58.2 ± 1.0 (51)	1,349	1,302	—	5.288
Pecos Pueblo	—	55.5 ± 1.2 (29)	1,308 ± 23 (29)	1,263 ± 22 (29)	5.349 ± .103 (29)	—
Late Upper Paleolithic	10–21	62.9 ± .9 (71)	1,466 ± 35 (23)	1,412 ± 33 (23)	5.479 ± .083 (18)	5.406
Early Upper Paleolithic	21–35	66.6 ± 1.3 (33)	1,517 ± 30 (15)	1,460 ± 28 (15)	5.467 ± .142 (10)	5.352
Late archaic *H. sapiens*	36–75	76.0 ± 1.4 (17)	1,498 ± 45 (14)	1,442 ± 42 (14)	4.984 ± .165 (8)	4.781
Skhul-Qafzeh	90	66.6 ± 2.2 (10)	1,501 ± 45 (6)	1,444 ± 42 (6)	5.369 ± .083 (4)	5.293
early Late Pleistocene	100–150	67.7 ± 2.4 (10)	1,354 ± 41 (8)	1,307 ± 39 (8)	4.682 (1)	4.732
late Middle Pleistocene	200–300	65.6 ± 5.1 (6)	1,186 ± 32 (17)	1,148 ± 30 (17)	—	4.257
middle Middle Pleistocene	400–550	67.9 ± 6.4 (5)	1,090 ± 38 (12)	1,057 ± 36 (12)	—	3.818
late Early to early Middle Pleistocene	600–1,150	58.0 ± 4.3 (3)	856 ± 52 (7)	835 ± 50 (7)	—	3.400
Early Pleistocene	1,200–1,800	61.8 ± 4.0 (5)	914 ± 45 (5)	890 ± 43 (5)	3.064 (1)	3.458

*Data from Figure 2, except that Early Pleistocene sample does not include earliest (pre-1,800 kyr BP) specimens (see text). Pecos Pueblo body weights from femoral head and bi-iliac/stature formulae.

[†]Average cranial capacity for living worldwide sample from Beals *et al.*[29]; Pecos Pueblo cranial capacities from Hooton's original grave cards[30]; Pleistocene *Homo* cranial capacities from the literature and personal measurement.

[‡]See Methods for derivation of brain mass from cranial capacity, and encephalization quotient.

(ref. 16, excluding five Pygmy data points). More than three-quarters (125/163) of the Pleistocene specimens fall above the living human mean. On average, Pleistocene specimens are 7.4 kg larger (mean ± s.e., 65.6 ± 0.7 kg) than living humans (58.2 ± 1.0 kg), a highly significant 12.7% difference in body mass ($P < 0.0001$, *t*-test).

There is some indication in Figure 2a that body mass is lower in the Early Pleistocene and rises to peak values in the Late Pleistocene. However, this is largely an artefact of two confounding variables: sex and geography. Modern and fossil *Homo* males are larger than females, and there is a bias towards males in our Late Pleistocene sample (72 of 114 sexable specimens). Ecogeographic patterning in body mass has been demonstrated in modern humans, with populations from higher latitudes being larger on average than those from lower latitudes[16]. The same is true for Pleistocene *Homo*: in our sample specimens from over 30° N latitude are significantly larger than those from under 30° N latitude (ANCOVA, controlling for sex and date, $P < 0.005$). All of the Pleistocene *Homo* specimens included here and dated before 600 kyr BP are from tropical regions (Figure 2a). The apparent sudden increase in average body mass during the later Middle Pleistocene is largely a result of the inclusion of higher-latitude specimens beginning during this time period. If the effects of latitude and sex are controlled through ANCOVA, the pooled Pleistocene *Homo* sample is still 9.2% larger on average than living humans ($P < 0.0001$).

Body mass appears to decline after about 50 kyr BP. Figure 2b shows that within higher-latitude (>30° N) males there is a significant decrease (16%, $P < 0.0001$) in average body mass between 50 and 10 kyr BP. The trend is very similar whether or not archaic *Homo sapiens* (Neanderthals) are included. By the Terminal Pleistocene (10–15 kyr BP) body mass is not significantly different from that of living higher-latitude males (0.3% difference). The same is also true of

higher-latitude females (3.7% difference). However, lower-latitude Terminal Pleistocene males and females are still significantly larger (11–12%, $P < 0.01$) than lower-latitude living samples.

The body-mass data are paired with cranial capacity and brain-mass data in Table 1, temporally subdivided within the Pleistocene. Because of uncertainty regarding the cranial–postcranial affinities of very early *Homo*[18], only specimens dated to 1,800 kyr BP or later are included in this analysis.

Early to early Middle Pleistocene (1,800–600 kyr BP) *Homo* was about one-third less encephalized than Recent humans, and there was no increase in encephalization quotient (EQ) throughout this time period (Table 1). By the early Late Pleistocene (150–100 kyr BP), EQ had increased to values within about 10% of those of Recent humans. However, early Late Pleistocene and late archaic *H. sapiens* are significantly lower in EQ than pooled 'early anatomically modern' (EAM) *H. sapiens* (Skhul-Qafzeh and Upper Palaeolithic samples) ($P < 0.01$, *t*-test of individually associated specimens). The same results holds true whether or not Recent humans are pooled with EAM *H. sapiens*, or the early Late Pleistocene individual with associated data (Tabun C1) is pooled with late archaic *H. sapiens*.

Because EQs in general, and any EQ in particular, are subject to a number of limitations, encephalization within *Homo* was also evaluated by plotting log(cranial capacity) against log(body mass) (Figure 3). Figure 3a is a plot of the sample mean data from Table 1. The data appear to be best characterized by three major 'trajectories': an Early to middle Middle Pleistocene trajectory, a late Middle to early Late Pleistocene to late archaic *H. sapiens* trajectory, and a trajectory that includes Recent and EAM *H. sapiens*. Variation in cranial capacity between these three groups with body mass as a covariate is highly significant ($P < 0.0001$, ANCOVA; Tukey tests, $P < 0.01$, all pairwise comparisons). Alternatively, the middle and late Middle Pleistocene

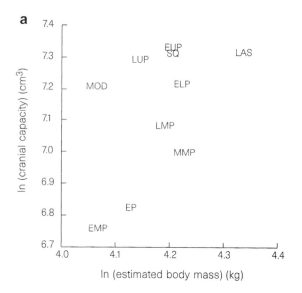
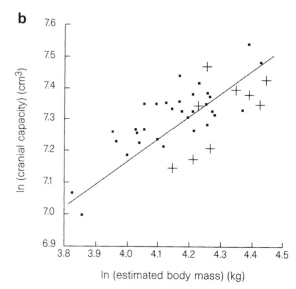

Figure 3. *Log-transformed brain mass versus body mass in Pleistocene* Homo. *a, Temporal group means. MOD, living humans; LUP, Late Upper Palaeolithic; EUP, Early Upper Palaeolithic; SQ, Skhul-Qafzeh; LAS, late archaic* H. sapiens; *ELP, early Late Pleistocene; LMP, late Middle Pleistocene; MMP, middle Middle Pleistocene; EMP, early Middle Pleistocene; EP, early Pleistocene (see Table 1).* **b,** *Late Pleistocene individuals. Squares, pooled EUP, LUP and SQ individuals; crosses, pooled LAS and ELP individuals; solid line, reduced major axis regression through total pooled sample.*

groups could be viewed as transitional between an earlier (EP–EMP) and later (ELP–LAS) trajectory, with Recent and EAM *H. sapiens* again forming a third trajectory; this interpretation would be more consistent with the EQ data in Table 1. Figure 3b is a plot of all of the individually associated brain and body masses for the Late Pleistocene samples. Although there is substantial overlap between archaic and EAM *H. sapiens,* they are significantly different ($P < 0.01$); this result holds true whether or not the one early Late Pleistocene specimen is included.

Pilbeam and Gould[1] suggested that the scaling of brain size to body size in *Homo* followed a single log-linear trajectory that eventually separated humans from australopithecines as well as other primates. Walker[19], in part on the basis of the discovery of the early *Homo* KNM-WT 15000, proposed that *Homo* was characterized by two brain-size/body-size scaling trajectories or 'grades': one for *H. habilis/H. erectus* and one for modern *H. sapiens.* With more specimens and more accurate means of estimating body mass, it now appears that there were at least three trajectories, or grades of brain size relative to body size within *Homo,* even excluding very early *H. habilis* or *H. rudolfensis* specimens, which may represent another grade[4]. Other previously proposed temporal trends may also now be evaluated with more confidence. For example, the presence of a directional trend in absolute brain size in Early to Middle Pleistocene *Homo* has been debated, with interpretations hampered by the lack of body-mass data for the same time period[20,21]. Our results support a stasis in relative brain size within *Homo* between 1,800 and at least 600 kyr BP. Opinions regarding the relative encephalization of Late Pleistocene archaic *H. sapiens* (Neanderthals) have varied widely[9,12]. Our findings

indicate that Neanderthals were slightly less encephalized than Recent and EAM *H. sapiens,* but closer in this respect to modern humans than to middle Middle Pleistocene and earlier *Homo.*

Our results also indicate that a decrease in average absolute brain size over the past 35,000 years within *H. sapiens* was paralleled by a corresponding decrease in average body size, supporting earlier suggestions of a general correlated size reduction in the human skeleton since the early Upper Palaeolithic[22]. This decrease continued through the Neolithic, at least in Europe[23]. Recent secular increases in body size have characterized European and many other higher-latitude populations, whereas many tropical populations have experienced flat or even negative secular trends in size over the same time period[24]. Our body mass results for tropical and higher latitude samples are consistent with these recent trends. Viewed in this light, although some living humans may be expressing a genetic potential for greater body size retained from earlier hunter-gatherer (Upper Palaeolithic) ancestors[25], this phenomenon has been largely limited to higher-latitude populations.

METHODS

Femoral Head Estimation of Body Mass

Equations from three studies of a diverse sampling of modern humans were used[6,13,15]. In one study, estimates had been derived for males and females separately[13]; in the other two only a combined sex sample had been analysed[6,15]. For the Pleistocene sample, the two combined sex equations were always used and the male or female equation used when sex could be determined (otherwise, a mean of the male and female equation results was used). All equations are for raw (non-logged) data (BM, body mass; FH, femoral head breadth (mm)):

$$BM = 2.239 \times FH - 39.9; r = 0.98 \quad (1)$$
(derived by us from raw published data) (ref. 6)

$$BM = 2.268 \times FH - 36.5; r = 0.92 \text{ (ref. 15)} \quad (2)$$

$$BM = 2.741 \times FH - 54.9; r = 0.50 \text{ (males)};$$
$$BM = 2.426 \times FH - 35.1; r = 0.411 \text{ (females)} \quad (3)$$
$$\text{(ref. 13)}$$

Estimates from equation (3) were adjusted downwards by 10% as recommended by the authors. When applied to 94 Pleistocene *Homo* specimens with intact femoral heads, correlations between pairs of body mass estimates using the above equations were all 0.97 or better, with a mean difference between results of 4%. The mean of the three estimates was used in the study.

Stature/Bi-Iliac Estimation of Body Mass

The stature/bi-iliac equations were derived from modern anthropometric data given in ref. 16 (BM, body mass (kg); ST, stature (cm); BI, bi-iliac breadth (cm)):

$$BM = 0.373 \times ST + 3.033 \times BI - 82.5;$$
$$r = 0.90 \text{ (males)};$$
$$BM = 0.522 \times ST + 1.809 \times BI - 75.5;$$
$$r = 0.82 \text{ (females)} \quad (4)$$

(Note that the equation for females is different from that published in ref. 16 because of correction of an error in one of the original data points (Aleut females: correct body mass = 53.4 kg)). The sex-specific formula was used when possible; otherwise the mean of the male and female formulae was used. Before applying these formulae, skeletal bi-iliac breadth was converted to living bi-iliac breadth using the equation (both dimensions in cm):

$$\text{living BI} = 1.17 \times \text{skeletal BI} - 3 \quad (5)$$

derived from comparisons within modern humans[16]. Bi-iliac breadth of the Pleistocene specimens was either measured directly or estimated from closely related fossils and/or from known clinal variation in bi-iliac breadth[16,17]. Stature was estimated from preserved long bone lengths using equations derived from appropriately proportioned modern reference samples.

Combined Body Mass Estimates

When both an intact femoral head and bi-iliac breadth were available, the mean of the femoral head and stature/bi-iliac estimates was used ($n = 26$). Otherwise, either the femoral head, when available ($n = 67$) or the estimated stature/bi-iliac ($n = 70$) estimate was used.

Brain Mass and EQ

Brain mass was derived from cranial capacity using a least-squares regression of 27 primate species that had data available for both parameters[26,27], corrected for logarithmic transformation bias:

$$\text{brain mass} = 1.147 \times \text{cranial capacity}^{0.976}$$
$$(r^2 = 0.995) \quad (6)$$

Encephalization quotient was derived from Martin's[28] relationship between brain mass (g) and body mass (kg) in mammals:

$$EQ = \text{brain mass}/(11.22 \times \text{body mass}^{0.76}) \quad (7)$$

Encephalization quotients (EQ) relating brain mass to body mass were derived in two ways, using individually associated crania and postcrania and using mean brain mass and body mass within temporally defined groups. The EQs derived using the group means are based on many more specimens, but because they do not use individually matched data they could potentially be biased in several ways. However, other methods of limiting these samples, for example by using only individuals from the same sites and/or sex, produce similar results. Also, where they can be compared, the individually associated and mean data values for the same temporal periods are similar (Table 1). For associated specimens, sex and latitudinal biases in EQ should be minimal: within the Pecos and Pleistocene EAM samples sex differences in EQ average less than 2%, and among modern humans higher- and lower-latitude populations appear to average less than a 4% difference in EQ (mean data from Beals et al.[29] and our worldwide sample[16]).

ACKNOWLEDGMENTS

We thank the many institutions and individuals who made available specimens for this study and T. Berger for help in finding the Pecos cranial capacity data. Supported in part by the National Science Foundation and the LSB Leakey Foundation.

REFERENCES

1. Pilbeam, D. & Gould, S. J. Size and scaling in human evolution. *Science* **186**, 892–901 (1974).
2. McHenry, H. M. Early hominid body weight and encephalization. *Am. J. Phys. Anthropol.* **45**, 77–84 (1976).
3. McHenry, H. M. in *Evolutionary History of the "Robust" Australopithecines* (ed. Grine, F. E.) 133–148 (Aldine de Gruyter, New York, 1988).
4. McHenry, H. Behavioral ecological implications of early hominid body size. *J. Hum. Evol.* **27**, 77–87 (1994).
5. Ruff, C. B., Trinkaus, E., Walker, A. & Larsen, C. S. Postcranial robusticity in *Homo*, I: temporal trends and mechanical interpretation. *Am. J. Phys. Anthropol.* **91**, 21–53 (1993).
6. McHenry, H. M. Body size and proportions in early hominids. *Am. J. Phys. Anthropol.* **87**, 407–431 (1992).
7. Rightmire, G. P. Body size and encephalization in *Homo erectus*. *Anthropos (Brno)* **23**, 139–149 (1986).
8. Gauld, S. C. Body size of Asian *Homo erectus*: estimation based on prediction models utilizing measures of cranial bone thickness (abstract). *Am. J. Phys. Anthropol.* **16** (suppl.) 93 (1993).

9. Hartwig-Scherer, S. Body weight prediction in fossil *Homo. Cour. Forsch.-Inst. Senckenberg* **171**, 267–279 (1994).
10. Ruff, C. B. & Walker, A. in *The Nariokotome* Homo Erectus *Skeleton* (eds Walker, A. & Leakey, R.) 234–265 (Harvard Univ. Press, Cambridge, 1993).
11. Aiello, L. C. & Wood, B. A. Cranial variables as predictors of hominine body mass. *Am. J. Phys. Anthropol.* **95**, 409–426 (1994).
12. Kappelman, J. The evolution of body mass and relative brain size in fossil hominids. *J. Hum. Evol.* **30**, 243–276 (1996).
13. Ruff, C. B., Scott W. W. & Liu, A. Y.-C. Articular and diaphyseal remodeling of the proximal femur with changes in body mass in adults. *Am. J. Phys. Anthropol.* **86**, 397–413 (1991).
14. Trinkaus, E., Churchill. S. E. & Ruff, C. B. Postcranial robusticity in *Homo*, II: humeral bilateral asymmetry and bone plasticity. *Am. J. Phys. Anthropol.* **93**, 1–34 (1994).
15. Grine, F. E., Jungers, W. L., Tobias, P. V. & Pearson, O. M. Fossil *Homo* femur from Berg Aukas, northern Namibia. *Am. J. Phys. Anthropol.* **97**, 151–185 (1995).
16. Ruff, C. B. Morphological adaptation to climate in modern and fossil hominids. *Yb. Phys. Anthropol.* **37**, 65–107 (1994).
17. Holliday, T. W. *Body Size and Proportions in the Late Pleistocene Western Old World and the Origins of Modern Humans.* (Thesis, Univ. New Mexico, Albuquerque, 1995).
18. Wood, B. Origin and evolution of the genus *Homo. Nature* **355**, 783–790 (1992).
19. Walker, A. in *The Nariokotome* Homo Erectus *Skeleton* (eds Walker, A. & Leakey, R.) 411–430 (Harvard Univ. Press, Cambridge, 1993).
20. Rightmire, G. P. Patterns in the evolution of *Homo erectus. Paleobiology* **7**, 241–246 (1981).
21. Leigh, S. R. Cranial capacity evolution in *Homo erectus* and early *Homo sapiens. Am. J. Phys. Anthropol.* **87**, 1–13 (1992).
22. Henneberg, M. Decrease of human skull size in the Holocene. *Hum. Biol.* **60**, 395–405 (1988).
23. Frayer, D. W. in *The Origins of Modern Humans: A World Survey of the Fossil Evidence* (eds Smith, F. H. & Spencer. F.) 211–250 (Liss, New York, 1984).
24. Tobias P. V. The negative secular trend. *J. Hum. Evol.* **14**, 347–356 (1985).
25. Brown, F., Harris, J., Leakey, R. & Walker, A. Early *Homo erectus* skeleton from West Lake Turkana, Kenya. *Nature* **316**, 788–792 (1985).
26. Martin, R. D. *Primate Origins and Evolution* (Princeton Univ. Press, Princeton, 1990).
27. Stephan, H., Bauchot, R. & Andy, O. J. in *The Primate Brain* (eds Noback, C. R. & Montague, W.) 289–297 (Appleton-Century-Crofts, New York, 1970).
28. Martin, R. D. Relative brain size and basal metabolic rate in terrestrial vertebrates. *Nature* **293**, 57–60 (1981).
29. Beals, K. L., Smith, C. L. & Dodd, S. M. Brain size, cranial morphology, climate, and time machines. *Curr. Anthropol.* **25**, 301–330 (1984).
30. Hooton, E. A. *The Indians of Pecos Puebla. A Study of Their Skeletal Remains. Papers of the Phillips Acad. SW Exped., No. 4* (Yale Univ. Press, New Haven, 1930).

52

Lower Palaeolithic Hunting Weapons from Schöningen, Germany—The Oldest Spears in the World

H. Thieme

ABSTRACT

Since 1983, the development of the lignite opencast mine at Schöningen in Eastern Lower Saxony has been accompanied by large-scale rescue excavations conducted by the Bodendenkmalpflege, Hannover, Office for the Preservation of Historical Monuments. In the course of these operations since 1992, in the Quaternary layers of the opencast mine, several Lower Palaeolithic sites from the time of Homo erectus have been discovered and partially investigated. One of these sites—a horse hunting camp—has now yielded, among other items, eight wooden javelins. With an age of 400,000 years, these implements are, up to now, the oldest-known completely preserved hunting weapons of mankind. They revise the common conception of the early hominid as a marginal scavenger and substantiate the existence of systematic, methodical big-game hunting and even hunting specialisation as well as high-level skills in wood-working at this early period.

Reprinted with permission from *Acta Anthropologica Sinica*, Vol. 19 supplement, pp. 140–147. Copyright © 2000 by Chinese Academy of Sciences.

INTRODUCTION

Finds of wooden tools from the Lower and Middle Palaeolithic are extremely rare. This is a result of unfavourable conditions prevailing in most sedimentary contexts after burial. In Europe, only two well preserved examples from this period are known: the lance tip from Clacton-on-Sea in Essex (England), discovered in 1911[1], and the lance from Lehringen in Lower Saxony (Germany), excavated in 1948[2], both made of yew (*Taxus*). These two examples have been dated to the Middle Pleistocene Holsteinian Interglacial and the Late Pleistocene Eemian Interglacial, respectively. This scarcity of material highlights the importance of the Lower Palaeolithic sites, excavated since 1992, in the brown coal mine at Schöningen, with numerous finds of diverse wooden implements, in a state of exceptional preservation.

LOCATION AND STRATIGRAPHY

The Schöningen opencast mine is situated in the northern part of Germany about 100 km east of Hannover, in the northern foreland of the Harz mountains, at the south-eastern edge of the Triassic limestone ridge called the Elm (323 m). This area belongs to the northern region of the 70 km long sub-herzynic basin between Helmstedt and Staßfurt. The mine covers an area of 6 km². In 1983 I initiated long-term archaeological excavations in order to secure any unknown prehistoric sites in danger of being destroyed. During the course of the ongoing mining operations, an area of more than 350,000 m² has been excavated,

mainly with Holocene sites dating from the Neolithic to Iron Age[3]. In addition to this the massive sediment layers of the Pleistocene exposures were constantly monitored and analysed by geological and environmental specialists[4-5].

The oldest Pleistocene deposits exposed in the mine are up to now the sediments of the Elster Glaciation (Figure 1). Above these sediments a series of six major erosional channels has been documented since 1992 in the southern part of the Schöningen opencast mine

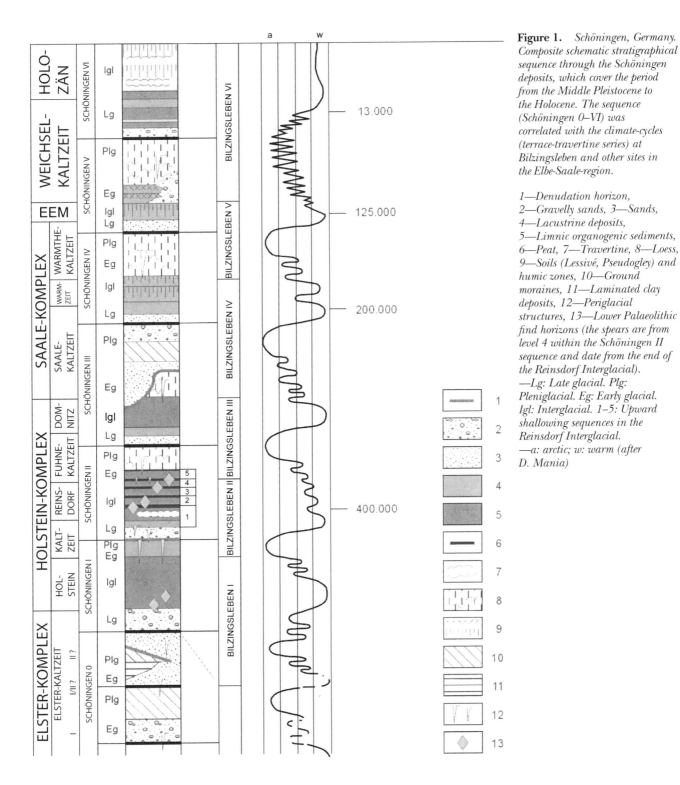

Figure 1. *Schöningen, Germany. Composite schematic stratigraphical sequence through the Schöningen deposits, which cover the period from the Middle Pleistocene to the Holocene. The sequence (Schöningen 0–VI) was correlated with the climate-cycles (terrace-travertine series) at Bilzingsleben and other sites in the Elbe-Saale-region.*

1—Denudation horizon, 2—Gravelly sands, 3—Sands, 4—Lacustrine deposits, 5—Limnic organogenic sediments, 6—Peat, 7—Travertine, 8—Loess, 9—Soils (Lessivé, Pseudogley) and humic zones, 10—Ground moraines, 11—Laminated clay deposits, 12—Periglacial structures, 13—Lower Palaeolithic find horizons (the spears are from level 4 within the Schöningen II sequence and date from the end of the Reinsdorf Interglacial). —Lg: Late glacial. Plg: Pleniglacial. Eg: Early glacial. Igl: Interglacial. 1–5: Upward shallowing sequences in the Reinsdorf Interglacial. —a: arctic; w: warm (after D. Mania)

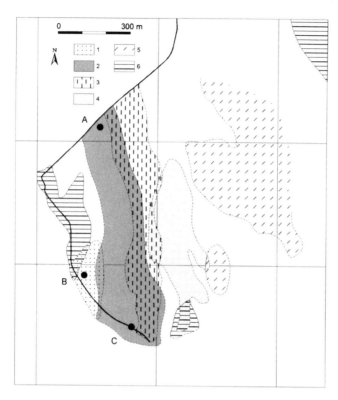

Figure 2.   *Schöningen, Germany. Course of the six Pleistocene/Holocene channels in an area of 1 km² in the southern part of the Schöningen open cast mine.*

1—Schöningen I, 2—Schöningen II, 3—Schöningen III, 4—Schöningen IV, 5—Schöningen V, 6—Schöningen VI. The Elsterian glacial deposits lie beneath all the channels; the channel of Schöningen III is covered by the glacial series of the Saalian glaciation sensu stricto (Drenthe). Channel Schöningen VI contains Holocene deposits.
Location of the Lower Palaeolithic sites mentioned in the text: A: Schöningen 12 (1992) with two archaeological find horizons. B: Schöningen 13 I (1994). C: Schöningen 13 II (since autumn 1994) with the "spear site" (Schöningen 13 II-4).

(Figure 2)[6]. The channels and their associated sediments represent a series of interglacial/glacial cycles that have been named Schöningen I–VI (Figures 1, 2) and suggest an age range from the Holsteinian to the Holocene[7]. Channels I–III, which contain limnic sediments, date to the period between the Elster and Saale glacial *sensu stricto*.

The oldest interglacial sediments (Schöningen I) probably date to the Holsteinian. The Schöningen II channel (Figure 1) is filled by sediments of the Reinsdorf Interglacial[8] and the ensuing Fuhne cold stage. The depositional sequence contains five levels of organic muds and peats (1–5). Level 1 represents both the early and interglacial maxima of the Reinsdorf Interglacial; the upper levels represent cool temperate phases and exhibit frost structures between Levels 4 and 5 (Figure 1). This interglacial is a new biostratigraphical unit between the Elster and Saale *sensu stricto:* palynological analysis by B. Urban[5] indicates that its vegetational history differs from both the preceding Holsteinian and the following Schöningen (III) interglacials, which is correlated to the Dömnitz

Interglacial[9]. The mollusc fauna of Level 1 of the Reinsdorf Interglacial is a thermophilous fauna rich in species with Mediterranean and SE-European elements (*Helicigona banatica* fauna), indicating temperatures 2 to 3 degrees warmer than the present day[6, 10]. The Schöningen IV channel is younger than the Saale glacial *sensu stricto* (Drenthe) and consists of an extensive double soil complex (Figure 1). The infill of channel V is correlated to the (last) Eemian Interglacial, whilst the sixth channel infill is of Holocene age. Work by D. Mania has established a correlation between the Schöningen sequence and the terrace-travertine series at Bilzingsleben (Thuringia, Germany)[11].

THE LOWER PALAEOLITHIC SITES AT SCHÖNINGEN

Since 1992, several Lower Palaeolithic sites have been discovered (from 8–15 m below the present ground surface) and excavated in Middle Pleistocene interglacial sediments, dating to the Holsteinian complex (Figure 1)[3]. Two of these sites (Schöningen 12 and Schöningen 13 II-4) (Figures 1, 2), dating to the upper part of the Holsteinian complex (the newly discovered Reinsdorf-Interglacial), yielded finds of diverse wooden implements.

Schöningen 13 I

The oldest evidence of human occupation, a lakeshore site, dates to the earliest part of the Holsteinian complex (channel Schöningen I) (Figure 1). This Lower Palaeolithic site was discovered and partially excavated (120 m²) in 1994 (Figure 2, B). It comprises flint tools, flakes and numerous burnt flints together with faunal remains of steppe elephant (*Mammuthus trogontherii*), bovids, horse and red deer[12]. A first result of a series of TL-measurements at burnt flints from this site (by D. Richter) indicates an age of more than 400 ka BP.

On the surface of an overlying organic mud the remains of a *Bison* skull and several tracks of large mammals were discovered (Figure 1).

Schöningen 12

The Lower Palaeolithic site Schöningen 12 (find layer 1) was discovered and excavated in the following interglacial in 1992 (Figure 2, A), with more than 150 m² in the course of three months' work[6, 8, 13]. Lakeshore deposits with gyttja sands from the Reinsdorf Interglacial (Schöningen II, Level 1) (Figure 1) contained numerous flint artefacts and more than one thousand large mammal bones (*Palaeoloxodon antiquus* fauna), from straight tusked elephant, rhinoceros (*Stephanorhinus kirchbergensis*) and so on[14]. Some of these bones exhibit cut marks from butchery, while a tibia shaft of *Ursus spelaeus* was probably used as a support[3], perhaps to cut organic materials. There are also numerous small mammals[15], including the water vole *Arvicola terrestris cantiana* and the beaver-like *Trogontherium cuvieri*, together with the remains of birds, fish and reptiles. Analysis of the *Arvicola* molars from Schöningen II,

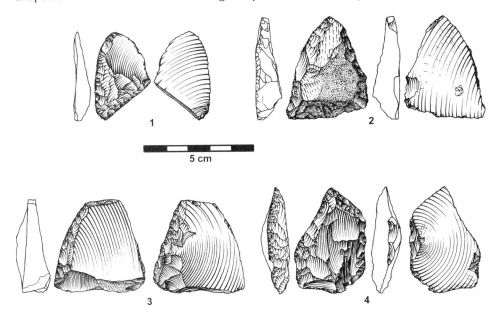

5 cm

Figure 3. *Schöningen, Germany. Site Schöningen 13 II-4: Flint tools: 1–2 Convex side scrapers; 3 Alternate retouched side scraper; 4 Déjeté scraper.*

Level 1 (the Reinsdorf Interglacial) suggests a correlation with the Bilzingsleben *Homo erectus* site[15–16].

Very important finds from this site are three worked branches of the common silver fir (*Abies alba*). These wooden tools (length 170, 191, 322 mm; width 36, 39, 42 mm), have a diagonal groove cut into one end probably for holding flint tools or sharp flakes to create a more efficient tool[3]. If this supposition is correct, these implements (cleft hafts) represent the oldest composite tools in the world. A forth cleft haft from this site (length about 120 mm) has grooves cut into both ends, and one can compare such tools with similar objects found in the Aboriginal culture in Australia. The raw material for these Lower Palaeolithic cleft hafts consists of the hard intact roots of the boughs of rotten trunks from the common silver fir (analysis by W. H. Schoch, who has made all the wood identifications in Schöningen)[17].

During excavations of find layer 1 a second archaeological horizon was discovered 2 m to 3 m higher up in peat sediments of the Reinsdorf Interglacial, Level 2 (Figure 1), with flint artifacts and butchered remains of large mammals in 30 m^2 (Schöningen 12, find layer 2)[8].

Schöningen 13 II-4

The Schöningen 13 II-4 site (the "spear site") was discovered in the autumn of 1994 in Level 4 (Figure 2, C) of the Schöningen II (Reinsdorf Interglacial) channel[18]. The archaeological material of this site lies in an organic mud which underlies a peat horizon (Figure 1). Analysis of the molluscan fauna by D. Mania and of the pollen spectra by B. Urban, suggests a boreal, cool-temperate climate; the vegetation is a mix of meadows and forest steppes. Until the end of 1999, the excavation yielded much more than 20,000 well preserved faunal remains, mainly of 19 horses (*Equus mosbachensis*), from an area of 2,500 m^2. Many of the bones display traces of butchery, in the form of cut marks and fracturing. The assemblage of flint artefacts includes points, carefully retouched scrapers (Figure 3) and about 1,200 spalls (retouch waste). Furthermore, some places were discovered where the chalky sediments had turned red and display fossil drying cracks, very probably under the influence of the heat of fires.

The first wooden tool from this site, discovered in October 1994, has a length of 0.78 m, a maximum diameter of 3 cm and is made of spruce (Figure 4). Both

Figure 4. *Schöningen, Germany. Site Schöningen 13 II-4: View of a Lower Palaeolithic throwing stick in the field in October 1994. Close to the stick is a larger bone fragment, on its left a flint scraper. Scale in cm.*

Figure 5.   *Schöningen, Germany. Site Schöningen 13 II-4: Situation of spear VI in May 1997 (length: about 2.50 m).*

ends are sharpened to a point[18]. The function of this implement was most probably a throwing stick, resembling in shape and size the throwing sticks used by the aborigines of Australia to hunt birds in flight.

The most spectacular wooden implements from the site first came to light in autumn 1995[19–20]. Since then a whole collection of more than half a dozen exceptionally well preserved spears with lengths varying between 1.82 m (spear III) to 2.5 m (spear VI, Figure 5) (max. diameter: 29–50 mm) have been excavated[21], in conjunction with abundant faunal remains. Most of the spears are made from spruce (*Picea* sp.); spear IV is made from pine (*Pinus* sp.). The wood selected exhibits a dense concentration of growth rings, implying slow growing conditions in a cool environment. The spears are made from individual trees, which were felled, debranched and debarked; the tip/distal ends (up to 60 cm long) are worked from the hardest part of the wood at the base of the tree. Although the points are symmetric, they are cut to avoid the pith ray. The tails are long and taper towards the proximal pointed end. With the maximum thickness and weight situated a third of the way from the tip, the spears resemble modern javelins and were used by the late *Homo erectus* to hunt horses on the shoreline of a long shallow lake (Figure 2).

The main find scatter of the Schöningen 13 II-4 site is more than 40 m long and about 10 m wide on the western upper banks of the lake[21], sometimes with more than 120 objects per square meter, with the wooden hunting spears and other wooden artifacts amongst the skeletal remains of a hunted and butchered herd of horses. According to their skulls, mainly completely preserved, the minimum number of individuals is 19 horses. Because of the density of finds, i.e. the close proximity of the artifacts and skeletal remains, one is led to believe that this was a planned and organised action in order to obtain a complete herd of horses with one blow. The aim was to secure enough meat and skins to ensure a constant supply of nourishment and warmth (for clothes and tents). This is the first indication of seasonal hunting in autumn, inferred from amongst others, the presence of specific plants on the bones[21].

CONCLUSIONS

Since 1992, several Lower Palaeolithic sites have been discovered and excavated in Middle Pleistocene interglacial sediments, dating to the Holsteinian complex (Figure 1). Two of these sites (Schöningen 12 and Schöningen 13 II-4), dating to the new discovered Reinsdorf Interglacial, yielded finds of diverse wooden implements. The wooden finds from the Lower Palaeolithic horse hunting site Schöningen 13 II-4 constitute, with an age of about 400,000 years, the world's oldest wooden throwing spears—so far the oldest complete hunting weapons of humankind. The spears from Schöningen suggest that systematic and co-ordinated hunting, involving fore-sight, planning and appropriate technology (with first indications of seasonal hunting etc.), was already a part of the behavioural repertoire of Middle Pleistocene hominids. Accordingly, meat from hunting may have provided a larger dietary contribution than many workers have been prepared to acknowledge[22–24].

ACKNOWLEDGMENTS

We are grateful to the Braunschweigische Kohlen-Bergwerke AG (BKB), Helmstedt, for the technical and organisational support of the long-term archaeological excavations in the Schöningen mine, especially for their efforts and their courtesy in enabling us to excavate and analyse the complete sedimentary sequence of the new Reinsdorf Interglacial up to an area of about 3,000 m² and about 6 m thickness—a unique chance for Pleistocene Archaeology! I thank the Deutsche Stiftung Denkmalschutz for a grant that supported the rescue excavations at the "spear site". Thanks are due to A. Pastoors (Cologne) for the drawings of Figures 1–2, B. Kaletsch (Marburg) for the drawing of Figure 3, P. Pfarr (Hannover) for the photographs of Figures 4–5 and W. Roebroeks (Leiden, The Netherlands) for reviewing this paper.

REFERENCES

1. Oakley, K. P., Andrews, L., Keeley, L. H. et al. A Reappraisal of the Clacton Spearpoint. Proc Prehis Soc, 1977, 43:13–30.
2. Thieme, H., Veil, S. Neue Untersuchungen zum eemzeitlichen Elefanten-Jagdplatz Lehringen, Ldkr. Verden. Kunde NF, 1985, 36:11–58.
3. Thieme, H., Maier, R. Archäologische Ausgrabungen im Braunkohlentagebau Schöningen, Landkreis Helmstedt. Hannover, 1995.
4. Urban, B., Lenhard, D., Mania, D. et al. Mittelpleistozän im Tagebau Schöningen, Ldkr. Helmstedt. Zeitschrift der deutschen geologischen Gesellschaft, 1991, 142:351–372.
5. Urban, B. Vegetations- und Klimaentwicklung des Quartärs im Tagebau Schöningen. In: Thieme, H., Maier, R. eds. Archäologische Ausgrabungen im Braunkohlentagebau Schöningen, Landkreis Helmstedt. Hannover, 1995, 44–56.
6. Thieme, H., Mania, D. "Schöningen 12"—ein mittelpleistozänes Interglazialvorkommen im Nordharzvorland mit paläolithischen Funden. Ethnographisch-Archäologische Zeitschrift, 1993, 34:610–619.
7. Mania, D. Die geologischen Verhältnisse im Gebiet von Schöningen. In: Thieme, H., Maier, R. eds. Archäologische Ausgrabungen im Braunkohlentagebau Schöningen, Landkreis Helmstedt. Hannover, 1995. 33–43.
8. Thieme, H., Mania, D., Urban, B. et al. Schöningen (Nordharzvorland). Eine altpaläolithische Fundstelle aus dem mittleren Eiszeitalter. Archäologisches Korrespondenzblatt, 1993, 23:147–163.
9. Urban, B. Palynological evidence of younger Middle Pleistocene Interglacials (Holsteinian, Reinsdorf and Schöningen) in the Schöningen open cast lignite mine (eastern Lower Saxony, Germany). Mededelingen Rijks Geologische Dienst, 1995, 52:175–186.
10. Mania, D. The earliest occupation of Europe: the Elbe-Saale region (Germany). In: Roebroeks, W., Kolfschoten, T. van eds. The Earliest Occupation of Europe. Leiden, 1995, 85–101.
11. Mania, D. Die Terrassen-Travertin-Sequenz von Bilzingsleben. Ein Beitrag zur Stratigraphie des Mittel- und Jungpleistozäns im Elbe-Saale-Gebiet. Ethnographisch-Archäologische Zeitschrift, 1993, 34:554–575.
12. Thieme, H. Der altpaläolithische Fundplatz Schöningen 13 I (Holstein-Interglazial). In: Thieme, H., Maier, R. eds. Archäologische Ausgrabungen im Braunkohlentagebau Schöningen, Landkreis Helmstedt. Hannover, 1995, 57–61.
13. Thieme, H. Die altpaläolithischen Fundschichten Schöningen 12 (Reinsdorf-Interglazial). In: Thieme, H., Maier, R. eds. Archäologische Ausgrabungen im Braunkohlentagebau Schöningen, Landkreis Helmstedt. Hannover, 1995, 62–72.
14. Kolfschoten, T. van. Faunenreste des altpaläolithischen Fundplatzes Schöningen 12 (Reinsdorf-Interglazial). In: Thieme, H., Maier, R. eds. Archäologische Ausgrabungen im Braunkohlentagebau Schöningen, Landkreis Helmstedt. Hannover, 1995, 85–94.
15. Kolfschoten, T. van. Die Vertebraten des Interglazials von Schöningen 12. Ethnographisch-Archäologische Zeitschrift, 1993, 34:623–628.
16. Heinrich, W.-D. Zur taphonomie, paläoökologie und biostratigraphie fossiler kleinsäugerfaunen aus dem mittelpleistozänen travertinkomplex Bilzingsleben in Thüringen. In: Mania, D., Mania, U. et al. eds. Bilzingsleben V. Homo erectus—seine Kultur und Umwelt. Bad Homburg/Leipzig: Verlag Ausbildung + Wissen, 1997, 121–134, 256–259.
17. Schoch, W. H. Hölzer aus der Fundschicht 1 des altpaläolithischen Fundplatzes Schöningen 12 (Reinsdorf-Interglazial). In: Thieme, H., Maier, R. eds. Archäologische Ausgrabungen im Braunkohlentagebau Schöningen, Landkreis Helmstedt. Hannover, 1995, 73–84.
18. Thieme, H. Ein altpaläolithischer Lagerplatz aus der Zeit des Urmenschen von Schöningen 13 II (Reinsdorf-Interglazial). In: Thieme, H., Maier, R. eds. Archäologische Ausgrabungen im Braunkohlentagebau Schöningen, Landkreis Helmstedt. Hannover, 1995, 95–106.
19. Thieme, H. Altpaläolithische Wurfspeere aus Schöningen, Niedersachsen.—Ein Vorbericht—.Archäologisches Korrespondenzblatt, 1996, 26:377–393.
20. Thieme, H. Lower Palaeolithic hunting spears from Germany. Nature, 1997, 385: 807–810.
21. Thieme, H. Altpaläolithische Holzgeräte aus Schöningen, Lkr. Helmstedt. Bedeutsame Funde zur Kulturentwicklung des frühen Menschen. Germania, 1999, 77(2):451–487.
22. Binford, L. R. Bones: Ancient Men and Modern Myths. New York/London, 1981.
23. Gamble, C. Man the Shoveler. In: Soffer, O. ed. The Pleistocene Old World. Regional Perspectives. New York, 1987, 81–98.
24. Nitecki, M. H. The idea of human hunting. In: Nitecki, M. H., Nitecki, D. V. eds. The Evolution of Human Hunting. New York/London, 1987, 1–9.

VII

The Neandertals

Neandertals were the first fossil hominids to be recovered and described, in the 1850s, and they remain at the center of debates over human evolution. Although this centrality is widely attributed to the fact that they are indigenous to Europe, where paleoanthropology has a long academic tradition, it is also true that Neandertals are among the best known of all fossil hominids. The chapters in this part review many of the current debates about Neandertals: Are Neandertals ancestral to modern Europeans or are they a dead end side branch in hominid evolution? Did Neandertals become more specialized over time, and, if so, how far back in time does their lineage extend? Are the distinctive features of Neandertals adaptations to a cold climate or are they the result of many separate morphological modifications or some simple developmental mechanism? These chapters demonstrate that even though Neandertal fossils have been known for more than 150 years, most of the questions about them remain unresolved. There is still much to learn through the use of modern techniques in genetics, morphometrics, and dating.

In Chapter 53, "Climatic Changes, Paleogeography, and the Evolution of Neandertals," Jean-Jacques Hublin provides a broad overview of the evolution of Neandertal morphology. He traces their morphological evolution from its nascence in some middle Pleistocene European fossils often classified as *Homo heidelbergensis* through its development into the "classic" Neandertals of the late Pleistocene. He argues that the evolution of Neandertal morphology took place by the accretion of successive modifications to a more primitive middle Pleistocene morphology. The frequency of the distinctive features varies not only with time but also in different contemporaneous populations. He relates the pattern of Neandertal evolution to the climatic and biogeographic consequences of the glacial geology of Europe during the Pleistocene.

Chapter 54, "The Accretion Model of Neandertal Evolution," by John D. Hawks and Milford H. Wolpoff, tests the model of Neandertal evolution proposed by Hublin (see also Stringer and Hublin, 1999; Maureille and Houet, 1998; Dean et al., 1998). Hawks and Wolpoff examined ten traits proposed to be unique or very common features of Neandertals, and tested to see if these features increased in frequency from pre-Neandertals to early Neandertals to late Neandertals. They also tested to see if these features were more common in Neandertals than in contemporary non-European populations. They found no evidence of the features accreting, and no general pattern of decreased variance in the Neandertal features through time. On the basis of their results, they argue that there is no morphological indication of decreased gene flow between Neandertals and other hominid populations during the late Pleistocene due to geographic isolation.

Matthias Krings and colleagues, in Chapter 55, "Neandertal DNA Sequences and the Origin of Modern Humans," report on their analysis of mitochondrial DNA (mtDNA) extracted from the humerus of the Neandertal type specimen from Germany. They find that Neandertals lie outside the range of variation among modern humans. They calculate that the age of the common ancestor of Neandertal and human mtDNA is four times greater than the age of the last common ancestor of all modern human DNA. They estimate the divergence of Neandertals and modern humans as being between 550 and 690 kya. Subsequent studies of genetic material from additional Neandertals have supported these results and indicate that genetic diversity among Neandertals, like that among modern humans, was much less than the genetic diversity among living apes. This suggests that Neandertals may also have evolved from a small initial population (see Krings et al., 2000; Schmitz et al., 2002). Similarly, recent studies of ancient DNA from a fossil modern human from Italy showed that the fossil DNA clustered with modern humans and was distinct from the Neandertal DNA (Caramelli et al., 2003).

In Chapter 56, "Cold Adaptation, Heterochrony, and Neandertals," Steven E. Churchill contrasts two different approaches for explaining the distinctive morphological features of Neandertals. Both approaches have been promoted by paleoanthropologists over the past century and a half. From a structuralist perspective, Neandertal features are seen as a coordinated set of changes that evolved in response to cold climates, perhaps genetically and developmentally linked, and probably the result of some simple mechanism. A more traditional, adaptationist (neo-Darwinian) approach sees each distinctive Neandertal feature as the result of independent selection. Empirical studies suggest that the truth lies somewhere in the middle. Some aspects of Neandertal limb proportions are correlated in the same way that these proportions are correlated among modern humans, but these integrated features account for less than half of the variance in either cranial or postcranial morphology. Churchill then reviews various developmental and physiological models that have been offered to suggest that a simple systemic change in endocrine levels or growth rates may account for the distinctive aspects of Neandertal morphological features, and finds that none of the proposed global explanations for Neandertal evolution is satisfactory. Moreover, while some aspects of Neandertal body form follow patterns associated with cold adaptation in other mammals, many do not. The evolution of Neandertals was probably the result of a unique mix of selective pressures involving climate, activity level, and foraging patterns.

Marcia S. Ponce de León and Christoph P. E. Zollikofer describe "Neanderthal Cranial Ontogeny and Its Implications for Late Hominid Diversity" in Chapter 57. They use computerized morphometrics to reconstruct fragmentary fossils (see Zollikofer et al., 1998) and to examine complex patterns of morpholog-

ical change during ontogeny. Their results show that many characteristic features of Neandertal cranial morphology appear early in development and are maintained throughout postnatal development. Ontogenetic shape changes in the crania of modern humans and Neandertals follow parallel, nonoverlapping trajectories (see also Rak et al., 1994), indicating that adult Neandertals are not just overgrown modern humans. The growth of their crania follows much the same pattern of ontogenetic change as seen in modern human growth, but is based on a different organization that was established from birth and undoubtedly has a unique genetic basis. Consequently, Neandertals are not a part of modern human variation.

In Chapter 58, Alban Defleur and colleagues provide new evidence of the behavior of Neandertals in "Neandertal Cannibalism at Moula-Guercy, Ardèche, France." Although cannibalism has been attributed to Neandertals for nearly a century, the evidence put forth has been repeatedly questioned (see Villa, 1992). In this chapter, Defleur and colleagues document identical patterns of bone modification in the remains of Neandertals and deer, indicating disarticulation, defleshing, and the breaking of shafts to expose the marrow cavity for food. As a result, it provides the best evidence to date for cannibalism among a population of Neandertals (for a broader review of cannibalism in the fossil record, see White, 2001).

REFERENCES

Caramelli, D., C. Lalueza-Fox, C. Vernesi, M. Lari, A. Casoli, F. Mallegni, B. Chiarelli, I. Dupanloup, J. Bertranpetit, G. Barbujani, and G. Bertorelle. 2003. Evidence for a genetic discontinuity between Neandertals and 24,000-year-old anatomically modern Europeans. *Proceedings of the National Academy of Sciences, USA* 100:6593–6597.

Dean, D., J.-J. Hublin, R. Holloway, and R. Ziegler. 1998. On the phylogenetic position of the pre-Neandertal specimen from Reilingen, Germany. *Journal of Human Evolution* 34:485–508.

Krings, M., C. Capelli, F. Tschentscher, H. Geisert, S. Meyer, and A. von Haeseler. 2000. A view of Neanderthal genetic diversity. *Nature Genetics* 26:144–146.

Maureille, B., and F. Houet. 1998. La variabilitie morpho-metrique du nez: derive genique dans la lignee Neandertalienne? *Biométrie Humaine et Anthropologie* 16:27–33.

Rak, Y., W. H. Kimbel, and E. Hovers. 1994. A Neanderthal infant from Amud Cave, Israel. *Journal of Human Evolution* 26:313–324.

Schmitz, R. W., D. Serre, G. Bonani, S. Feine, F. Hillgruber, H. Krainitzki, S. Paabo, and F. H. Smith. 2002. The Neander type site revisited: interdisciplinary investigations of skeletal remains from the Neander Valley, Germany. *Proceedings of the National Academy of Sciences, USA* 99:12927–12932.

Serre, D., A. Langaney, M. Chech, M. Teschler-Nicola, M. Paunovic, P. Mennecier, M. Hofreiter, G. Possnert, and S. Pääbo. 2003. No evidence of Neandertal mtDNA contribution to early modern humans. *PLoS Biology* 2:313–317.

Stringer, C., and J.-J. Hublin. 1999. New age estimates for the Swanscombe hominid and their significance for human evolution. *Journal of Human Evolution* 37:873–877.

Villa, P. 1992. Cannibalism in prehistoric Europe. *Evolutionary Anthropology* 1:93–104.

White, T. D. 2001. Once were cannibals. *Scientific American* 285:58–66.

Zollikofer, C. P. E., M. S. Ponce de León, and R. D. Martin. 1998. Computer assisted paleoanthropology. *Evolutionary Anthropology* 6:41–64.

53

Climatic Changes, Paleogeography, and the Evolution of the Neandertals

J.-J. Hublin

INTRODUCTION

Mainly because of historical reasons, Europe has provided the largest series of Middle and Upper Pleistocene hominids. Many of the sites which yielded these specimens can be placed in a reliable environmental and chronological framework, and they allow us to produce detailed evolutionary scenarios covering the entire last half a million years.

However, although this area was once used as a model for the entire Old World, it is actually marginal when considering the development of hominids using broader chronological and geographical scales. The evolutionary processes of the European population are indeed peculiar. At the center of this peculiarity are the Neandertals, a group of archaic humans that remains unknown outside of Western Eurasia (i.e., Europe and its oriental fringes). The rise, development, and extinction of Neanderthals can be traced in relation to the environmental and cultural changes in Europe.

It is easy to recognize the unique nature of the area that produced this original group. Europe is a long and rather narrow peninsula in the middle latitudes that became isolated by the development of seas and mountain chains. Located at the western extremity of Eurasia, it is far from the intertropical zone where most of the evolutionary processes of the early hominids took place. Another aspect of this European particularism is the dramatic climate changes that it experienced for most of the last million years. These changes caused tremendous contraction of the non-arctic bio-climatic zones and led to the periodic development of periarctic conditions in moderately high latitudes.

It is tempting to imagine a relationship between the peculiar paleobiogeographic history of Europe and the development of an odd lineage of hominids. In this perspective, the following questions arise: What series of phenomena could determine this link? When did the divergence of the European hominids from their Asian and African relatives begin? How fast was it? How far did it go biologically? What is the geographical extension of the process?

The goal of this paper is to review briefly the tempo of the development of European particularism in relation to the geographical and climatic changes, and then to question the boundaries of this process and the relationships between Europe and adjacent areas.

DEFINITION OF THE NEANDERTALS

The development in the late 1970s of cladistic methods in human paleontology led to a reassessment of the anatomical definition of the Neandertals. It allowed for a better understanding of the polarity of the anatomical features of the group, sorting out archaic retentions, derived features shared with modern humans, and proper Neandertal apomorphies. One of the main results of this new approach was the refutation of several previous models or hypotheses based on a misunderstanding of the "global morphological pattern." First, the so-called "European pre-*sapiens*," supposedly the ancestors of modern humans in the Middle Pleistocene of Europe, were demonstrated to be genuine pre-Neandertals. They were reminiscent in some respects of the modern morphology only because of symplesiomorphies. The African and Asian "Neandertaloids" appeared to be well-separated from the West Eurasian Neandertals with whom they essentially shared primitive retentions and robusticity.

However, the cladistic approach to the Neandertal problem suffered several criticisms. Phylogenetic analysis was mainly conducted on cranio-mandibular features, while post-cranial morphology did not yield very clear cut evidence. In particular, the limited knowledge of contemporary and immediately preceding out-groups made the phylogenetic interpretation of Neandertal post-cranial morphology difficult. Some, if not most, of the "Neandertal" post-cranial features that are missing in contemporary or later modern humans could be plesiomorphic retentions and thus would be observable in the direct ancestors of modern humans as well. In addition, the degree of homoplasy between closely related groups can be high. This is especially true when dealing with locomotor or climatic adaptations which shaped the morphology, robusticity, and proportion of the limbs and trunk of large bipedal hominids. Finally, the possible use of the cladist methodology within a species (*Homo sapiens*) was questioned on theoretical bases and heavily criticized as typological and non-biological (Trinkaus, 1990).

It may be said that dealing with the homoplasy was the fate of cladism from its dawn and that this does not invalidate the great progress that resulted from its use as a theoretical framework. Questioning evolutionary processes in paleobiological terms is certainly one of the major advances of paleoanthropology in the last two decades. Still, the baby should not be thrown out with the bath water. The adaptative perspective does not resolve all the questions raised by the fossil hominids, especially in terms of phylogeny and the pattern of peopling. Furthermore, the features which develop along the evolution of a fossil lineage do not all result from direct adaptive responses. Genetic drift and pleiotropic effects are also involved.

Regarding the possible (or impossible) use of the cladistic methodology within the species *Homo sapiens*, it must be said that the subspecific status of the Neandertals is still, at the least, debatable. However, in order to avoid the sin of "typologism," intrapopulational (or intraspecific) variation must always be taken into consideration. When dealing with metric features, clear overlaps are observed between the Neandertals and neighboring groups of hominids. Whenever possible, the occurrences of some morphological features should also be considered in terms of frequency (see for example Franciscus and Trinkaus, 1995). Yet there are almost no real problems in distinguishing the Neandertals and their close ancestors from contemporary groups. In a pragmatic way, cladism does work when dealing with the Neandertals. The question of whether cladism works because it is useful at a subspecific level or because Neandertals are a distinct species of the genus *Homo* is important theoretically, but it is also secondary.

The series of cranio-mandibular features presented in Table 1 were operational in distinguishing the

Table 1.   Neandertal Cranio-Mandibular Derived Features, Unique or Most Frequent in the Group

Upper face and mandible:
- Rounded supraorbital torus without distinct elements
- High orbits
- Mid-facial prognathism resulting in low subspinal angle, low nasiofrontal angle, large difference between M1 alveolus and zygomaxillare radii
- Infraorbital area horizontally flat or convex, obliquely receding in alignment with the antero-lateral surface of the zygomatic
- Posterior rooting of the facial crest
- Bucco-lingually expanded anterior dentition
- Extended taurodontism
- Laterally expanded mandibular condyle
- Mental foramina posteriorly set relatively to the dental arcade
- Retromolar space
- Oval horizontal shape of the mandibular foramen
- Large medial pterygoid tubercle

Cranial vault:
- Secondarily increased relative platycephaly
- "En bombe" cranial shape
- Low symmetrically arched temporal squama
- *Meatus acusticus externus* at the level of the posterior zygomatic arch with a strong inclination of the basal groove of this process
- Highly convex upper scale of the occipital

Basicranium:
- Flat articular eminence
- Mediolaterally developed postglenoid process
- Elongated foramen magnum
- Root of the stylomastoidian process medial to the anterior end of the digastric groove and stylomastoidian foramen
- Small and inferiorly situated posterior semicircular canal

Occipito-mastoid area:
- Laterally flattened mastoid process, medially oriented inferiorly
- Tuberculum mastoideum anterius
- Fully developed suprainiac fossa associated with a bilaterally protruding occipital torus

Neandertal specimens. Their possible occurrences in the Lower and Middle Pleistocene mark the milestones of Neandertal emergence.

STAGES OF THE NEANDERTALIZATION PROCESS

The Lower Pleistocene Group

Dating the earliest peopling of Europe has been the subject of a long-term debate. The sites of Soleihac and Le Vallonet (France) can be assigned to the Jaramillo event (from 0.99 to 1.07 My) on the basis of paleomagnetic evidence (Thouveny and Bonifay, 1984; de Lumley et al., 1988). Still, some doubts have been raised on the human origins of some of the artifacts and structures discovered in these two sites. However, indisputable late Lower Pleistocene artifacts and human remains are known in layer TD6 of the Gran Dolina of Atapuerca (Spain) (Carbonell et al., 1995). The area of Orce (Spain) has yielded even older archaeological evidence in two sites: Fuenta Nueva 3 and Barranco Leon 5. A recent reexamination of the biostratigraphic and paleomagnetic framework of the whole sedimentary basin indicates an immediately pre-Jaramillo age for the two sites, which would then be dated between 1.2 and 1 myrs (Turq et al., 1996). 'Ubeidiyeh (Israel) and Dmanisi (Georgia) might only be slightly older (Tchernov, 1986; Gabunia and Vekua, 1995; Bräuer and Schultz, 1996). It is likely that the early Lower Pleistocene witnessed the first attempts of colonization of the Mediterranean parts of Europe.

In any case, it is important to distinguish European Mediterranean areas from latitudes above 45 degrees. These were geographically well-separated and represented distinct ecological zones. If the supporters of the so-called "long chronology" recently had more success in the south of Europe, the supporters of the "short chronology" are still not defeated in the higher altitudes. Humans, as tropical animals primarily adapted to warm and open environments, seem to have colonized the temperate to cold environments only relatively recently. There is still no indisputable evidence of more or less permanent human occupation outside the Mediterranean area before 500 ky BP (Roebroeks et al., 1992). However, the paleontological and archaeological records become relatively abundant and continuous after this date.

The morphology of the Dmanisi mandible falls in the wide range of variation of *Homo erectus sensu lato*. Yet some features of this specimen can be interpreted as rather progressive, especially the morphology of the anterior part of the mandibular body and the size and proportion of the cheek teeth. According to Brauer and Schultz (1996), this morphology questions the previously proposed late Pliocene age of the specimen (Gabunia and Vekua, 1995), as the occurrence of "unexpectedly derived traits" in a nearly 1.6 or 1.8 my old hominid is deemed unlikely. However, the Dmanisi mandible gives us some indication of the possible nature of the first colonizers of Europe. Given its time range, it does not demonstrate a clear regional pattern.

In the preliminary description of the remains from the TD6 layer of the Gran Dolina of Atapuerca (Spain) (Carbonell et al., 1995), one dental and several mandibular features of this sample were claimed to demonstrate an evolutionary continuity between the TD6 hominids and much (?) later Middle Pleistocene hominids of Atapuerca-Simas de los Huesos (SH). One finds the buccolingual enlargement of the second lower incisors among them. On average, the Neandertals as a group clearly display this enlargement relative to older forms (Semal, 1988). Yet such a feature can display strong individual variation and is difficult to assess on isolated specimens. The Dmanisi mandible does not display this pattern and, in contrast, some African individuals assigned to *Homo erectus sensu lato* (e.g., WT 15000, Tighenif 1 and 3) do display buccolingual enlargement of the lower incisors comparable to that of the Neandertals.

The Early Middle Pleistocene Group

This group includes the specimens from Mauer (Germany), Boxgrove (England), Tautavel (France), Petralona (Greece), and Verteszöllos (Hungary). Regarding the last two specimens, some radiometric ages contradict the paleontological data and suggest a possible younger age (Schwarcz and Latham, 1984; Grün, 1996). More fragmentary remains from the late Cromerian come from Fontana Ranuccio and Visogliano in Italy. The specimen from Ceprano (Central Italy) is likely to be referred to this group or to be older (Ascenzi et al., 1996).

In this group, and for the first time, we see the development of an incipient but clearly Neandertal morphology. On Arago 21 and the Petralona skull, some facial features are reminiscent of the Neandertals. These include a flat or slightly convex horizontal profile of the maxilla between the nasal opening and the zygomaxillary suture, obliquely oriented posteriorly and followed by an obliquely oriented zygomatic. Some details of the nasal aperture including the shape of the nasal floor in Petralona are also reminiscent of the later Neandertals. The description of the material from the Sima de Los Huesos in Atapuerca, likely dating later (Bischoff et al., 1997) and displaying an even more obvious trend toward a Neandertal facial morphology and its so-called mid-facial prognathism (Arsuaga et al., 1997), has confirmed this observation.

The mandibles also display some Neandertal trends. Mauer, which could be the oldest specimen of the series, weakly displays this tendency. The size of the anterior teeth relative to the cheek teeth has been suggested to be a pre-Neandertal characteristic of the specimen (Wolpoff, 1982; Bermudez de Castro, 1986). On Arago 2 and 13, which are estimated to be nearly 450 kyrs old (de Lumley et al., 1984), one finds the lateral expansion of the mandibular condyle. In addition, Arago 2, which is much more gracile than Arago 13, displays an enlargement of the anterior part of the dental arcade and a mental foramen located under M1.

It should be emphasized that other anatomical areas in this early Middle Pleistocene group, such as the occipital, the temporal, and the cranial vault as a whole, still display a rather primitive aspect in contrast to the facial area. The skull exhibits a broad, simple, and midprojecting occipital torus quite different from the typical Neandertal aspect. The braincases have a pentagonal outline in posterior view distinctive from the "en bombe" shape characteristic of the Neandertals.

The "Holstein-Hoxnian" Group

A second step in the development of the Neandertal cranial morphology is marked by the development of a series of unique features on the occipital. The occurrence of a moderate occipital torus displaying a bilateral development instead of a medial maximal point of projection, associated with a horizontally extended well-marked suprainiac depression, is one of the most striking autapomorphic Neandertal features (Hublin, 1988a). This suprainiac fossa is first shallow and widely extended and later deep, long, and narrow. A genuine external occipital protuberance is always lacking. In Europe, this set of features appears clearly on specimens such as Steinheim and Swanscombe, which are respectively assigned to the Hoxnian and Holstein "interglacials." They would belong to the isotopic stages 11 or 9 and to a range of time between 430 and 300 ky. The specimens of Reilingen (Germany), Bilzingsleben (Germany), and possibly those from the Atapuerca SH (Spain) series are likely found in the same range of time. Reilingen clearly displays the same morphology as Swanscombe and Steinheim (Dean et al., 1998). Atapuerca SH skulls display a rough and/or porous suprainiac surface (Arsuaga et al., 1997). They fill the morphological gap between the middle projected and wide occipital torus of Verteszöllos and the Swanscombe-Steinheim-Reilingen group with their shallow and still ill-defined surpainiac fossa associated with a bilaterally projected occipital torus. In this group, Swanscombe seems to be the more derived, combining a rather Neandertal-like suprainiac area with a highly convex upper occipital scale. This observation calls into question its possible assignment to stage 11 (Bridgland, 1994). In contrast, one finds the primitive aspect of the occipital reminiscent of the previous group on one individual in Bilzingsleben, and a suprainiac fossa on another one (Condemi, 1998). If a late age for Verteszöllos is retained, this specimen would serve as another example of persistence of the occipital primitive condition at a relatively late period.

At this chronological stage, the trend toward the facial and mandibular Neandertal morphology is more expressed than in the previous group, as documented by SH skull 5. This specimen displays a strong pneumatization of the maxilla and frontal, a Neandertal-like supraorbital torus, midfacial projection, and flattened and receding infraorbital area simultaneously (Arsuaga et al., 1993, 1997). However, a rather primitive facial morphology still exists in Atapuerca 404. The "primitive" (but sometimes also said to be "modern-like") shape of Steinheim results at least partly from a severe distortion of the specimen.

On these specimens incipient and occasional Neandertal features are observed in the glenoid cavity and in the position of the stylomastoid foramen. A strong juxtamastoid eminence can be observed (Hublin, 1988b; Martinez and Arsuaga, 1997) but never reaches the Neandertal conditions. Yet many of the typical Neandertal aspects of the temporal are still missing, in particular in the mastoid area. On adult specimens, the mastoid process is usually strong and projects downward when it is preserved. There is no mastoidian anterior tubercle, with perhaps one exception: Atapuerca AT 86 (Elyatqine, 1995, but see Martinez and Arsuaga, 1997). In the series of Simas de los Huesos, on Steinheim and Reilingen, the outline of the temporal squama does not display the primitive low and angular pattern observed in *Homo erectus*. It is relatively short and high, contrasting also with the Neandertal conditions (relatively low and symmetrical) which appear to be derived. Castel de Guido (Italy) could be the first specimen where the Neandertal outline is observed (Elyatqine, 1995). The position of the posterior root of the zygomatic arch is still basically primitive with a weak inclination of the basal groove.

Regarding the vault shape, the pattern is still primitive relative to the Neandertals with a pentagonal shape on all the specimens. The lateral walls of the skull are either parallel or converge slightly upward. However, on some specimens (e.g., Swanscombe and Reilingen) the outline of the skull in posterior view is more rounded, forerunning the "en bombe" shape observed in the Neandertals. It should be noted that, as in the previous group, an exceptional angular torus can be observed. This superstructure, frequent in *Homo erectus* but unknown in the Neandertals, is present on Reilingen and some of the SH specimens (4 and 5) (Arsuaga et al., 1993).

The apparent simultaneous occurrence of ancestral or derived conditions for the same features, within this group, could sometimes derive from imperfections in our chronological calibration. However, it also clearly results from the actual coexistence of different morphologies in the same populations, the derived one becoming more frequent over time. This model applies to the occipital morphology as well as to the development of facial and mandibular derived features, which started earlier in the pre-Neandertal lineage. It explains the morphological contrasts observed within the series of Arago, Bilzingsleben, and Atapuerca SH.

The Saalian Group

There are no European specimens assigned clearly to isotopic stage 8. The group of specimens covering stages 7 and 6 includes the material from Biache-Saint-Vaast (France), Ehringsdorf (Germany), La Chaise-Suard (France), Fontechevade 2 (France), Le Lazaret (France), Pontnewydd (Wales), and possibly Montmaurin (France). In this series, it is already possible to recognize individually most if not all of the Neandertal derived features. They are still observed in combination with some primitive retentions on a rather complete individual, but some isolated bones could be practically indistinguishable from a stage 4 "classic" specimen. In particular, the evolution of the occipital morphology seems to be virtually completed. Already in stage 7, we find very derived conditions with the specimen of Biache-Saint-Vaast 1 (Auguste, 1995a). The "en bombe" shape of the vault in posterior view is observed for the first time, as well as a Neandertal-like temporal morphology. The mastoid process is small and flattened, obliquely oriented medio-inferiorly, and associated with a juxtamastoid eminence more inferiorly projecting than the mastoid process itself (Stringer et al., 1984). This specimen is not fully adult and the mastoid could have developed further. Yet La Chaise-Suard stage 6 temporal displays indisputable Neandertal conditions in the mastoid area (Condemi and Piveteau, 1988). The specimens from La Chaise and Ehringsdorf are the first in Europe to display a well-developed retromolar space on the mandible (Franciscus and Trinkaus, 1995).

The Eemian and Weschelian Groups

During stages 5, 4, and 3 we find Neandertal populations where the expression and frequency of the derived Neandertal features increased. Only with the "classical" (stage 4) specimens are all the details of the temporal morphology completed as well as the Neandertal vault shape (bombe-like in posterior view, strongly elongated antero-posteriorly, and ending with a highly convex upper occipital scale). But the positions of the mental foramina display a higher frequency of the Neandertal conditions in stage 5 than in stage 4 (Trinkaus, 1993).

ACCRETION OF THE NEANDERTAL FEATURES: A SHIFT IN FREQUENCY

This rapid review demonstrates that the development of the Neandertal morphology results from an *accretion* phenomenon beginning in the middle of the Middle Pleistocene, around 450,000 BP or a bit before. Not all the anatomical areas are effected simultaneously. In a simplistic view, the craniomandibular sequence seems to be: 1) upper facial and mandibular features; 2) occipital area features; 3) temporal area and vault shape features. However, as this accretion proceeds from an increase of the *frequency* of the derived conditions, complex combinations could result from the phenomenon. The mosaic of derived and primitive features may be different in two contemporaneous specimens. But this does not mean that we have different contemporary taxa inside Europe (Vlcek, 1993; Otte, 1996). As a matter of fact, the mosaic can also be different from one individual to another *within the same population* as documented by the Middle Pleistocene sites of Arago and Atapuerca SH. The change in frequency of the derived conditions is different from one anatomical area to another not only in terms of timing but also in terms of degree. One hundred percent of the known post-Holstein occipitals in Europe display more or less accentuated derived conditions. Yet for other anatomical areas, it is still possible to find the persistence of primitive conditions on some rather late individuals. Although the upper facial and mandibular area seems to be the first to exhibit Neandertal features, the Montmaurin mandible, which could be as late as early stage 5 (Tavoso, 1982), or the even younger Bagnoles specimen (Julia and Bischoff, 1991), are still very plesiomorphic. Amidst the late Neandertals, one isolated individual at Spy still displays a pentagonal shape of the vault in posterior view (Thoma, 1975).

This approach clearly discards the typological views on the Neandertals and their ancestors but its use results in various problems, such as the difficulty of sharply defining grades (Hublin, 1988b). Considering the mosaic nature of the accretion phenomenon, tracing clear divisions along the pre-Neandertals/Neandertals lineage is quite artificial. The chronological grades tentatively presented above are affected by consistent morphological overlaps.

Regarding the taxonomical problem, it seems difficult not to include in *Homo neanderthalensis* (or *Homo sapiens neanderthalensis*) all the specimens involved in this Neandertalization process, even if they display only a few derived Neandertal features. Separating the oldest sequence of the series as *Homo heidelbergensis* would lead to significant problems in the anatomical definition of the two taxa, especially if some African specimens are also included in *Homo heidelbergensis* (Rightmire, 1990; Stringer, 1991). If, in Europe, a taxon anatomically distinguishable from *Homo erectus sensu lato* was present before the development of the Neandertal lineage, its hypodigm should be restricted to the populations anterior to the development of the first Neandertal apomorphies. In this case, the term *Homo heidelbergensis* itself, with the Mauer mandible as a type specimen, would be inappropriate. Considering its fragmentary nature, this specimen is at least to be regarded as an *insertae sedis*, if it is not one of the first representatives of *Homo neanderthalensis*.

ENVIRONMENTAL CHANGES AND EVOLUTIONARY PROCESS

Adaptation to a new environment or ecological niche led the Neandertal ancestors to evolve under the pressures of selection. In particular, the body proportions of the European Neandertals are demonstrated to be hyper-arctic, contrasting with the conditions observed in the Pleistocene representatives of the genus *Homo* in lower latitudes and in the early modern humans in the Levant and in Europe (Trinkaus, 1981; Holliday, 1995). This adaptation clearly resulted from the colonization of higher latitudes but not necessarily from the constant exposure to peri-arctic conditions, if one considers the likely limited ability of Middle Pleistocene hominids to resist technically the climatic stress. In addition, moist conditions are demonstrated to result in effects similar to cold conditions (Holliday and Falsetti, 1995). As a matter of fact, climatic conditions during the last half million years were always notably colder than the present except during very brief episodes of stages 11, 9, and 5e. Besides the features which developed directly as adaptive responses to the environment, some Neandertal features may have developed secondarily from pleiotropic effects and therefore remain beyond the reach of simple interpretations. For example, similarities in the relative proportions of the phalanges in the foot and the hand (Trinkaus, 1983) could result from such a phenomenon.

In order for the Neandertals to develop as a subspecies of *Homo sapiens*, and even more as a separate species, some level of genetic isolation from adjacent populations of archaic humans was needed. Throughout the evolution of species, this isolation has usually resulted from peculiar geographical and/or ecological conditions. Howell (1960) emphasized the role of paleogeography in the rise of the Middle and Upper Pleistocene groups of hominids, underlining the possible effects of a glacial event on the isolation of Europe. As is best documented by the conditions of the last pleniglacial, the development of an ice sheet over northwestern Europe during a glacial maximum and the occurrence of a wide zone of permafrost all along this ice sheet dramatically reduced the possibilities of humans settling in the mid-latitudes. Very continental environments developed in Eastern Europe over broad areas. A strong glacial system covered the main mountain chains, in particular the Caucasus. In addition, the Caspian Sea, which was fed by a powerful glacial fluvial system, developed on the edge of the glacial sheet and was not regressive but rather transgressive and dramatically expanded toward the northwest. It extended beyond 50 degrees of north latitude and approached the southern end of the Ural Mountains, reaching a latitudinal limit that was never surpassed in the north by permanent Paleolithic settlements before stage 5. During the Pleistocene, it also periodically developed a channel along the Manytsch depression from its west bank to the Azov and Black Seas, thereby doubling the geographic barrier of the Caucasus. While the regression of the Atlantic Ocean increased the continental surface of Europe toward the west, the possibilities of exchange were very limited in the east.

When the isotopic climatic curves were first widely used, some attempts were made following Howell's model to match the development of the "Classic Neandertals" with the cold oscillation post-dating stage 5e (Boaz et al., 1982). However, this model can be criticized. Neandertals were known to occur already during this interglacial (Eemian), and the emergence of their lineage is now demonstrated to be much older, as demonstrated above. However, if this early development occurred between 500 and 400 ky BP, the isotopic curves do show a major change in the climatic history of Europe (Figure 1). Throughout the Pleistocene, there is a shift from a pattern of moderate climatic oscillations to alternation between contrasting cold and temperate periods. The isotopic curves established in the mid-Atlantic at latitude c. 41 degrees N demonstrate an increase in the amplitude and wave length around 0.7 my. In the Mediterranean Sea, the curve obtained by Vergnaud-Grazzini et al. (1990) in the Tyrrhenian basin demonstrates that the swing between cold to temperate conditions passed through two stages during which it significantly increased. In the first period, around 900,000 BP, a clear system of alternating cold and warm faunas is observed in Europe and glaciations are documented in Alpine deposits below the Matuyama/Bruhnes boundary (Audra and Rochette, 1993). A second stage in the increase of amplitude is observed near 450,000 BP. It is contemporary with the

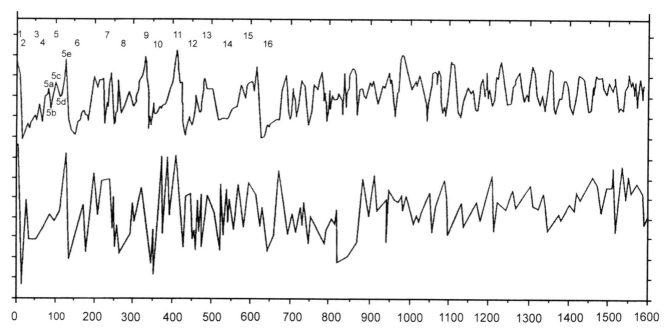

Figure 1.   *Top: The oxygen isotopic record in borehole (site 607) in the mid-Atlantic at latitude c. 418N (from Ruddiman et al., 1989). Bottom: The ^{18}O record of G. bulloides of ODP hole 653A in the Tyrrhenian Basin (Vergnaud-Grazzini et al., 1990).*

development of cold species of mammals and with the emergence of the European hominids' endemicity.

The warmest interglacial in the last million years (stage 11) followed an exceptionally severe glaciation (stage 12) (Shackleton, 1987). This increase in the amplitude of the climatic oscillations is associated with the occurrence of brief warm interglacials (the already mentioned stages as well as 11, 9, and 5e) which may have played a role in the peopling of the mid-latitudes of Europe (but see discussion in Gamble, 1986; Roebroeks et al., 1992). Stage 7, while "interglacial," witnessed the persistence of cool conditions while extensive ice caps remained present in the northern hemisphere (Shackleton, 1987). The period covering stages 8, 7, and 6 represents virtually a double glaciation of 150,000 years, which witnessed the final development of the Neandertal morphology.

During most of the last half million years, European climatic conditions were regionally cool to cold, limiting both the northern dispersal and the density of human peopling. The main exchanges between Europe and more easterly regions were then likely limited to the corridors between Anatolia and the Balkans. North of the Black Sea, few or no continuous human settlements above 50 degrees of latitude are demonstrated to predate stage 5e (Klein, 1973; Soffer, 1989). By this time, the differentiation of the European hominids as Neandertals was accomplished virtually entirely (although they are still sometimes called "Proto-Neandertal" or "early Neandertal").

As a whole, the European subcontinent was rather isolated when Neandertals emerged. However, the impact of these cold episodes was not only seen in increased isolation. The extreme conditions, although only found during rather relatively short periods, could also have

had a major impact on the distribution, demography, and subsequently the evolutionary processes of European peoples. In addition to a north-to-south change of the human population density, a west-to-east cline may also have developed. The pattern of raw material transport (Feblot-Augustins, 1993) suggests quite a different style in land occupation in Western versus Central/Eastern Europe during the Middle Paleolithic. This idea is supported by modern examples showing that the density of hunter-gatherer territorial exploitation in middle latitudes decreased significantly from the oceanic and more humid western areas to the inner and eastern zones that were exposed to continental conditions (Demars, 1996).

The conditions of stage 2, when modern humans had already peopled Europe, are better known. Almost a century and a half of archeological surveys and excavations demonstrated that, at the peak of stage 2, most of the European territories north of the Alps were abandoned by humans who were forced to find refuge in small pockets in the southern part of the continent. In the southwest, glaciers developed in the central Sierras of Spain. Most of the Solutrean sites are distributed along the coasts of the Iberic Peninsula within 50 km or less of the present coast. Farther north, other disconnected refuges are represented by the Dordogne and Charente area, the north facade or the Pyrenees Mountains, and the Gard-Ardèche-Provence area more to the east (Straus, 1991). Only eight percent of the French Solutrean sites are open air sites, which represents the lowest proportion observed in the local Upper Paleolithic (Demars, 1996). Only two sites are known in the Parisian basin (Arcy-sur-Cure and La Montagne de Segrez). The Solutrean is unknown further north. In the eastern areas, although Germany and most of Poland were abandoned, Italy, Greece, and the Balkans offered refuges comparable to those found in south-western Europe. The clustering effect of this climatic event on the animal populations resulted in faunal differentiation between Eastern and Western Europe (Delpech and Guadelli, 1992). It also affected the cultural evolution of Upper Paleolithic with the subsequent separation of Western European cultural lineages (Solutrean and then Magdalenian) from eastern branches (Epigravettian) (Djinjian, 1996).

If a pleniglacial episode had such a dramatic effect on Upper Paleolithic populations, who used needles to make clothing and had sophisticated dwellings, one can assume that it may have had a comparable if not stronger impact on Middle Pleistocene archaic humans. During the range of time when Neandertals emerged, the conditions of the last glacial maximum were significantly exceeded by stage 12 and perhaps marginally by stage 6 (Shackleton, 1987). Overall the latter witnessed less extreme temperatures than stage 2 but was much longer (Jouzel et al., 1993). Stage 10 was comparable to stage 2 in intensity. Aside from the intensity and length of these major glacial episodes, one can also question the effect of brutal climatic changes on the human settlements. Glaciological data demonstrate that in contrast to the extreme stability of the Holocene, the previous 250 ka have been characterized in the North Atlantic region by marked climatic instability (Dansgaard et al., 1993). Even during the culmination of the Eemian, brief but catastrophic events are recorded in the ice deposits of Greenland (Anklin et al., 1993). They witnessed average temperature fluctuations of 10 to 14°C within the time length of one or a few human generations.

During the second half of the Middle Pleistocene, glacial peaks provoked major contractions of the available European territory and certainly led to a disjunction of discrete populations in separate pockets. As in stage 2, local increases in population density may have occurred, supported by the development of new continental areas (Van Andel, 1989). Yet at the scale of the entire continent, it is likely that massive reductions in population size occurred. When they last for several thousand years, these phenomena inevitably lead to the reduction of genetic variability and to the promotion of genetic drift. It should be emphasized that similar effects are observed within the ungulate populations (Delpech, 1998). During both stage 2 and stage 6, after having extended their living area towards an extremely southwestern limit, populations of reindeer and saiga antelope were eventually reduced to isolates in southwestern France. These isolates were apparently totally separated from their more eastern representatives and suffered body size reduction as well as some local morphological change. This evolution certainly affected the available biomass and possibly the density of human peopling. It could also parallel some aspects of human biological evolution.

It has already been argued that the northern extension of the Neandertals and their direct ancestors was limited during the cold stages (Tuffreau, 1987; Hublin, 1990). Although a series of archeological sites is assigned to stage 6 in middle latitudes (Achenheim, Ariendorf 2, La Cotte St Brelade), none of these rare sites can be securely assigned to the peak of the pleniglacial conditions. In northern France, very few sites are reported to have been inhabited during the cold conditions of stage 4 (Auguste, 1995b). In the late Middle Pleistocene, the most numerous sites and the richest, e.g., Biache (Tuffreau and Sommé, 1988), are related to interglacial, interstadial, or early glacial periods. During most of the Lower and Middle Paleolithic, human occupation of European middle latitudes was discontinuous in space and pulsating, developing essentially during temperate to moderately cold climatic periods. In this situation, the difficulty in evaluating possible demographic crashes at the peak of the glacial episodes comes from the limited chronological resolution in the Middle Pleistocene. In fact, a relatively brief but intense cold episode comparable to that of stage 2, which could have resulted in major depopulation, would likely remain undetectable in the archaeological record.

EASTERN EXPANSION OF THE NEANDERTALS

As effective as it was, the isolation of the European populations was not complete. Although there is no evidence of significant biological exchange across the Strait of Gibraltar during the late Middle Pleistocene (Hublin, 1992), we do find Neandertals in the Near East. However, they are not documented in sites as old as those in Europe. The Zuttiyeh skull, with a possible age estimated between 200,000 and 280,000 years (stage 8 to 7) (Bar-Yosef, 1995; Vandermeersch, 1995), does not display clear Neandertal affinities (see Sohn and Wolpoff, 1993 for discussion and references) at a time when European Neandertal derived features are already observed. In addition, in contrast to the local early modern humans of stage 5, eastern Neandertals display some cold-adapted body proportions, although these are not as extreme as those of the western Neandertals (Trinkaus, 1981; Holliday, 1995). This is now usually interpreted as resulting from their origin in latitudes higher than those of the Levant area. Still, as documented by the European Upper Paleolithic record, a short period of time (less than 20 ka) is enough to allow significant changes in the climatic adaptation of body proportions (Holliday, 1995).

One can consider the occurrence of Neandertals in the Near East as late expansion out of their natural European territory. It has been proposed by Bar-Yosef (1988) that this movement could have been related to environmental pressure resulting from the glacial stage 4. For some authors, this hypothesis would be consistent with overall similarities between Near Eastern Neandertals and European Neandertals from stage 5 (Condemi, 1992). One may wonder why such a movement did not happen during an earlier cold stage, such as stage 6. A related question concerns determining the nature of the Mousterian peopling of Anatolia. Where was the southern boundary of the palearctic province peopled by Neandertals during the cold stages of the late Middle Pleistocene: along the paths between the Anatolian plateau and the Balkans, or the Taurus-Zagros line? Supporting the second hypothesis is the evidence for cultural affinities between the interglacial

Middle Paleolithic industries of the Balkans and northern Middle East (Zagros Group) (Kozlowski, 1992).

Another way to consider the expansion of Neandertal territory toward the southeast and the east is to emphasize the role of temperate rather than cold periods. In this view, the Neandertal peopling of the Near East would not result from environmental pressure during stage 4 but rather from their previous spread into the middle latitudes of Eastern Europe. As a matter of fact, stage 5e is certainly more exceptional as a warm stage than stage 4 is as a cold stage. The new conditions on the eve of stage 4 included the extension of the Neandertals' settlements not only into the Ukrainian and Russian plain but probably even more to the east. In this range of latitudes, Neandertal adaptations allowed their expansion beyond the northern shores of the Caspian Sea which, in contrast with the Mediterranean and Black Seas, underwent a regression during the interglacial. The occurrence of Neandertals further east at Teshik-Tash (Uzbekistan) could have resulted from the use of the northern and shortest route from Eastern Europe to Central Asia. Future discoveries will tell us how far east the Neandertal extension continued in the middle latitudes. This situation would also explain a later major movement into the Near East during the following cold stage (4).

An early occurrence of the Neandertals, at least in the northern part of the Near East, remains difficult to verify. It would, however, explain the morphological differences observed between them and the western Neandertals. It would also support the interglacial age of the Shanidar layer D hominid sample proposed by some authors (Trinkaus, 1995). However, the chronology of this site is still debated, as is the chronological position of the Tabun C1 hominid in the Levant. An assignment of this specimen to late stage 7 or early stage 6, predating the Skhul/Qafzeh sample (Mercier et al., 1995), would support an early age for the southernmost penetration of the Neandertals in the Near East. Yet Tabun C1 displays one of the most derived morphologies of the occipito-mastoid area amidst the Near East Neandertals. This feature could support a later age and an intrusive burial of the specimen in layer C of Tabun (see Bar-Yosef, 1995 for further comments). While the mastoid area is one of the last anatomical areas to develop a derived Neandertal morphology, this evolution is already observed in Europe on Saalian, stage 6, specimens. However, if the oldest estimation is retained for Tabun C1 dating (Vandermeersch, 1995), some of its derived temporal conditions would (perhaps surprisingly) predate the earliest indisputable occurrence of these features in Europe.

CONCLUSIONS

The first demonstrated attempts at the colonization of Europe are documented around 1 million years or slightly earlier. One or several distinct waves of populations entered the southern part of the subcontinent in the Mediterranean areas. However, it is not before 500 ky BP that a dense record of archeological sites is observed in higher latitudes. Even after this date, humans seem to have been primarily restricted to an area

south of 53 degrees north. This limit includes most of the sites dated to cold as well as relatively warm stages prior to the arrival of modern humans in Europe. This limit is effective not only in the west, where the last extension of the ice-sheet could have destroyed hypothetical sites further north, but is also observed in the Russian plain where the oldest significant extension of Middle Paleolithic settlements toward the north occurs during the exceptionally warm stage 5e.

Geographical and climatic constraints resulted in a relative isolation of the European populations, with possible genetic exchange through the Bosphorus corridor and an apparent biological isolation from northwestern Africa. This isolation was intensified periodically by the development of glacial conditions. The development of European endemicity is consistent with the occurrence of major cold stages after 450,000 BP.

Since this period, the European hominids display the development of derived morphological features relating all the known specimens to a unique lineage leading to the Neandertals. This evolution resulted from an *accretion process* characterized by the successive occurrence of new features and by an *increase in their frequency* within the pre-Neandertal populations. Because of this shift in frequency, and although some anatomical areas are affected earlier than others, clear cut stages can hardly be defined. From a taxonomic point of view, integrating all the specimens displaying this trend into a unique taxon (*Homo sapiens neanderthalensis* or *Homo neanderthalensis*) seems the best option.

The major cold stages of the last half million years increased the climatic stress resulting in the isolation of European hominids and the evolution of cold adaptations. These stages also had a major effect on the distribution and size of the Neandertal populations. The model developed by examining the effects of stage 2 on the Upper Paleolithic groups strongly suggests that the most extreme glacial conditions could have led to short but intense clustering of the European populations along with a dramatic reduction of their size. In particular, the peak of stage 12 (425–480 ky BP), which exceeded the cold conditions of stage 2, may have caused a significant demographic crash in the European populations and triggered their evolutionary divergence. Added to the founder effect following the initial colonization of Europe by small populations, such events would have produced genetic drift episodes resulting in the fixation of derived features. In this view, some of these features could have developed although they do not have a clear adaptive significance. This model would predict a decrease of the variability, as some studies suggest (Maureille, 1994; Elyatqine, 1995), in the pre-Neandertal/Neandertal populations that experienced major changes of their size.

Regarding the geographical distribution of the Neandertals, the exceptionally warm stage 5e played an important role in the eastern extension of Neandertals, allowing them to occupy territories between the Ural Mountains and the Caspian depression and eventually part of Central Asia. However, it would not be surprising to find earlier occurrences of the Neandertals between the Bosphorus and Levant corridors in cold episodes prior to stage 4.

REFERENCES

Anklin, M., J. M. Barnola, J. Beer, T. Blunier, J. Chappellaz, H. B. Clausen, D. Dahl-Jensen, W. Dansgaard, M. de Angelis, R. J. Delmas, P. Duval, M. Fratta, A. Fuchs, K. Fuhrer, N. Gundestrup, C. Hammer, P. Iversen, S. Johnsen, J. Jouzel, J. Kipfstuhl, M. Legrand, C. Lorius, V. Maggi, H. Miller, J. C. Moore, H. Oeschger, G. Orombelli, D. A. Peel, G. Raisbeck, D. Raynaud, C. Schott-Hvidberg, J. Schwander, H. Shoji, R. Souchez, B. Stauffer, J. P. Steffensen, M. Stievenard, A. Sveinbjrnsdottir, T. Thorsteinsson, and E. W. Wolff. 1993. Climatic instability during the last inter-glacial period recorded in GRIP ice core. *Nature* 364:203–7.

Arsuaga, J. L., I. Martinez, A. Gracia, J. M. Carretero, and E. Carbonell. 1993. Three new human skulls from the Sima de los Huesos Middle Pleistocene site in Sierra de Atapuerca, Spain. *Nature* 362:534–7.

Arsuaga, J. L., I. Martnez, A. Gracia, and C. Lorenzo. 1997. The Sima de los Huesos crania (Sierra de Atapuerca, Spain). A comparative study. *Journal of Human Evolution* 33:219–81.

Ascenzi A., I. Bidditu, P. F. Cassoli, A. G. Segre, and E. Segre-Naldini. 1996. A calvarium of late *Homo erectus* from Ceprano, Italy. *Journal of Human Evolution* 31(5):409–23.

Audra, P., and P. Rochette, 1993. Premières traces de glaciations du Pleistocène inférieur dans le massif des Alpes. Datation par paléo-magnétisme de remplissages à la grotte Vallier (Vercors, Isère, France). *Comptes Rendus de l'Académie des Sciences* 317(II): 1403–9.

Auguste, P. 1995a. Cadres biostratigraphiques et paléoécologiques du peuplement humain dans la France septentrionale durant le Pleistocène. Apports de l'étude paléontologique des grands mamm-ifères du gisement de Biache-Saint-Vaast (Pas-de-Calais). Ph.D. diss. Museum Nationale d'Histoire Naturelle. Paris.

Auguste, P. 1995b. Adaptation biologique et culturelle des prénéan-dertaliens et des néandertaliens aux modifications paléoé-cologiques et fauniques en France septentrionale, 99–117. In *Nature et Culture*, ed. M. Otte. Liège: ERAUL 68.

Bar-Yosef, O. 1988. The date of Southwest Asian Neandertals, 31–8. In *L'Homme de Neandertal*, No. 3, ed. E. Trinkaus. Liège: ERAUL 30.

Bar-Yosef, O. 1995. The Lower and Middle Palaeolithic in the Mediterranean Levant: Chronology and cultural entities, 247–63. In *Man and Environment in the Palaeolithic*. H. Ullrich ed. Liège: ERAUL 62.

Bermudez de Castro, J. M. 1986. Dental remains from Atapuerca (Spain) I. Metrics. *Journal of Human Evolution* 15:265–87

Bischoff, J. L., J. A. Fitzpatrick, L. Len, J. L. Arsuaga, C. Falguères, J. J. Bahain, and T. Bullen. 1997. Geology and preliminary dating of the hominid-bearing sedimentary fill of the Sima de los Huesos Chamber, Cueva Mayor of the Sierra de Atapuerca, Burgos, Spain. *Journal of Human Evolution* 33:129–54.

Boaz, N. T., D. Ninkovitch, and M. Rossignol-Strick. 1982. Paleoclimatic setting for *Homo sapiens neanderthalensis*. *Naturwissenschaften* 69:29–33.

Bräuer, G., and M. Schultz. 1996. The morphological affinities of the Plio-Pleistocene mandible from Dmanisi, Georgia. *Journal of Human Evolution* 30:445–81.

Brigland, D. R. 1994. *Quaternary of the Thames*. London: Chapman and Hall.

Carbonell, E., J. M. Bermudez de Castro, J. L. Arsuaga, J. C. Diez, A. Rosas, G. Cuenca-Bescos, R. Sala, M. Mosquera, and X. P. Rodriguez. 1995. Lower Pleistocene hominids and artifacts from Atapuerca-TD6 (Spain). *Science* 269:826–9.

Condemi, S. 1992. *Les Hommes fossiles de saccopastore et leurs relations phy-logénétiques*. Paris: CNRS Editions.

Condemi, S. 1996. Une origine européenne pour les néandertaliens du Proche-Orient? L'apport des nouvelles données chronologiques. Paper presented at the *121e Congrès National des Sociétés Historiques et Scientifiques*, Nice, October 26–31, 1996.

Condemi, S. 1998. *Le Peuplement de l'Europe au Pléistocène Moyen*. Habilitation à diriger des Recherches, Université de Bordeaux, synthèse d'habilitation, 150 pp.

Condemi, S., and J. Piveteau. 1988. L'os temporal Riss-Würm (BD 7) provenant de la grotte de La Chaise, abri Bourgeois-Delaunay, 105–10. In *L'Homme de Néandertal*, No. 3, ed. E. Trinkaus. Liège: ERAUL 30.

Dansgaard, W., S. J. Johnsen, H. B. Clausen, D. Dahl-Jensen, N. S. Gundestrup, C. U. Hammer, C. S. Hvidberg, J. P. Steffensen, A. E. Sveinbjörnsdottir, J. Jouzel, and G. Bond. Evidence for general

instability of past climate from a 250-kyr ice-core record. *Nature* 364:218–20.

Dean, D., J. J. Hublin, R. Holloway, and R. Ziegler. 1998. On the phy-logenetic position of the pre-Neandertal specimen from Reilingen, Germany. *Journal of Human Evolution* 34:485–508.

Delpech, F. 1998. Biomasse d'Ongulés et peuplement paléolithique au nord de l'arc alpin. In *Archéologie et inférences démographiques*, ed. J. P. Bocquet-Appel. *Bulletins et Mémoires de la Société d'Anthropologie de Paris*.

Delpech, F., and J. L. Guadelli. 1992. Les grands mammifères gravet-tiens et aurignaciens de la grotte de Temnata, 141–216. In *Temnata Cave. Investigations in Karlukovo Karst Area*, Vol. 1. Krakow: Jagellonia University Press.

Demars, P. Y. 1996. Démographie et occupation de l'espace au Paléolithique Supérieur et au Mésolithique en France. *Préhistoire Européenne* 8:3–26

Elyatqine, M. 1995. Variabilité et evolution de l'os temporal chez *Homo sapiens*. Comparaison avec *Homo erectus*. Ph.D. diss. University of Bordeaux I. Bordeaux.

Djindjian, F. 1996. Le cloisonnement du peuplement de Chasseurs-Cueilleurs au maximum glaciare en Méditerranée occidentale, 161–2. In abstracts volume of the *121e Congrès National des Sociétés Historiques et Scientifiques*, Nice, October 26–31, 1996.

Féblot-Augustins, J. 1993. Mobility strategies in the Late Middle Paleolithic of Central Europe and Western Europe: Elements of sta-bility and variability. *Journal of Anthropological Archaeology* 12:211–65.

Franciscus, R. G., and E. Trinkaus. 1995. Determinants of retromolar space presence in Pleistocene *Homo* mandibles. *Journal of Human Evolution* 28:577–95.

Gabunia, L., and A. Vekua. 1995. A Plio-Pleistocene hominid from Dmanisi, East Georgia, Caucasus. *Nature* 373:509–12.

Gamble, C. 1986. *The Palaeolithic Settlement of Europe*. Cambridge: Cambridge University Press.

Grün, R. 1996. A re-analysis of electron spin resonance dating results associated with the Petralona hominid. *Journal of Human Evolution* 30(3):227–41.

Holliday, T. W. 1995. Body size and proportions in the Late Pleistocene Western Old World and the origins of modern hu-mans. Ph.D. diss. University of New Mexico. Albuquerque.

Holliday, T. W., and A. B. Falsetti. 1995. Lower limb length of European early modern humans in relation to mobility and cli-mate. *Journal of Human Evolution* 29:141–53.

Howell, F. C. 1960. European and northwestern African Middle Pleistocene hominids. *Current Anthropology* 1:195–232.

Hublin, J. J. 1988a. Caractères derivés de la region occipito-mastoidi-enne chez les Neandertaliens, 67–73. In *L'Homme de Néandertal*, No. 3, ed. E. Trinkaus. Liège: ERAUL 30.

Hublin, J. J. 1988b. Les plus anciens représentants de la lignée prénéandertalienne, 81–94. In *L'Homme de Néandertal*, No. 3, ed. E. Trinkaus. Liège: ERAUL 30.

Hublin, J. J. 1990. Les peuplements paléolithiques de l'Europe, 29–37. In *Paléolithique Moyen Récent et Paléolithique Supérieur Ancien en Europe*, ed. C. Farizy. Nemours: APRAIF.

Hublin, J. J. 1992. Recent human evolution in northwestern Africa. *Philosophical Transactions of the Royal Society of London* 337B: 185–91.

Jouzel, J., N. I. Barkov, J. M. Barnola, M. Bender, J. Chappellaz, C. Genthon, V. M. Kotlyakov, V. Lipenkov, C. Lorius, J. R. Petit, D. Raynaud, G. Raibeck, C. Ritz, T. Sowers, M. Stievenard, F. Yiou, and P. Yiou. Extending the Vostock ice-core record of palaeocli-mate to the penultimate glacial period. *Nature* 364:407–12.

Julia, R., and J. Bischoff. 1991. Radiometric dating of Quaternary de-posits and the hominid mandible of Lake Banyolas, Spain. *Journal of Archaeological Science* 18:707–22.

Klein, R. G. 1973. *Ice-Age Hunters of Ukraine*. Chicago: University of Chicago Press.

Kozlowski, J. K. 1992. The Balkans in the Middle and Upper Paleolithic: The gate to Europe or a cul-de-sac? *Proceedings of the Prehistoric Society* 58:1–20.

Lumley, H. de, A. Fournier, J. Krzepkowska, and A. Echassoux. 1988. L'industrie du Pleistocène inférieur de la grotte du Vallonet Roquebrune-Cap-Martin, Alpes-Maritimes. *L'Anthropologie* 92:501–614.

Lumley, H. de, A. Fournier, Y. C. Park, Y. Yokoyama, and A. Demouy. 1984. Stratigraphie du remplissage pleistocène moyen de la

Caune de l'Arago à Tautavel. Etude de huit carottages effectués de 1981 à 1983. *L'Anthropologie* 88:5–18.

Martinez, I., and J. L. Arsuaga. 1977. The temporal bones from Sima de los Huesos Middle Pleistocene site (Sierra de Atapuerca, Spain). A phylogenetic approach. *Journal of Human Evolution* 33:283–318.

Maureille, B. 1994. La Face chez *Homo erectus* et *Homo sapiens*: Recherche sur la variabilité morphologique et métrique. Ph.D. diss. University of Bordeaux I. Bordeaux.

Mercier, N., H. Valladas, G. Valladas, and J. L. Reyss. 1995. TL dates of burnt flints from Jelinek's excavations at Tabun and their implications. *Journal of Archaeological Science* 22:495–509.

Otte, M. 1996. *Le Paléolithique Inférieur et moyen en Europe.* Paris: Armand Colin.

Rightmire, P. 1990. *The Evolution of* Homo erectus. Cambridge: Cambridge University Press.

Roebroeks W., N. J. Conard, and T. van Kolfschoten. 1992. Dense forests, cold steppes, and the Palaeolithic settlement of northern Europe. *Current Anthropology* 33(5):551–86.

Ruddiman, W. F., M. E. Raymo, D. G. Martinsin, B. M. Clement, and J. Backman. 1989. Pleistocene evolution: Northern hemisphere ice sheets and North Atlantic Ocean. *Paleoceanography* 4:353–412.

Semal, P. 1988. *Evolution et variabilité des dimensions dentaires chez* Homo sapiens *neanderthalensis*. Viroinval: Editions du Centre d'Etudes et de Documentation Archéologiques.

Schwarcz. H. P., and A. G. Latham. 1984. Uranium series age determinations of travertines from the site of Verteszöllös, Hungary. *Journal of Archaeological Science* 11:327–36.

Shackleton, N. J. 1987. Oxygen isotopes, ice volume and sea level. *Quaternary Science Reviews* 6:183–90.

Sohn, S., and M. H. Wolpoff. 1993. Zuttiyeh face: A view from the East. *American Journal of Physical Anthropology* 91:325–47.

Soffer, O. 1989. The Middle to Upper Paleolithic transition on the Russian Plain, 714–42. In *The Human Revolution*, ed. P. Mellars and C. B. Stringer. Edinburgh: Edinburgh University Press.

Straus, L. G. 1991. Southwestern Europe at the Last Glacial Maximum. *Current Anthropology* 32(2): 189–99.

Stringer, C. B. 1991. *Homo erectus* et *"Homo sapiens* archaïque." Peut-on définir *Homo erectus*? 51–74. In *Aux origines d'*Homo sapiens, ed. J. J. Hublin and A. M. Tillier. Paris: Presses Universitaires de France.

Tavoso, A. 1982. Le cadre chronologique de la mandibule de Montmaurin, examen des données disponibles. *First International Congess of Human Paleontology*. Nice: CNRS.

Tchernov, E., ed. 1986. *Les Mammifères du Pleistocène inférieur de la vallée du Jourdain à Oubeidiyeh*. Paris: Association Paléorient.

Thoma, A. 1975. Were the Spy fossils evolutionary intermediates between Classic Neandertal and modern Man? *Journal of Human Evolution* 4:387–410.

Thouveny, N., and E. Bonifay. 1984. New chronological data on European Plio-Pleistocene faunas and hominid occupation sites. *Nature* 308:355–8.

Trinkaus, E. 1981. Neandertal limb proportions and cold adaptation, 187–224. In *Aspects of Human Evolution*, ed. C. B. Stringer. London: Taylor and Francis.

Trinkaus, E. 1983. Functional aspects of Neandertal pedal remains. *Foot and Ankle* 3(6):377–90.

Trinkaus, E. 1990. Cladistics and the hominid fossil record. *American Journal of Physical Anthropology* 83:1–11.

Trinkaus, E. 1993. Variability in the position of the mental foramen and the identification of Neandertal apomorphies. *Rivista di Antropologia* 71(2):259–74.

Trinkaus, E. 1995. Near Eastern Late Archaic humans. *Paléorient* 21(2):9–24.

Tuffreau, A. 1987. Le Paléolithique inférieur et Moyen du Nord de la France (Nord, Pas-de-Calais, Picardie) dans son cadre stratigraphique. Ph.D. diss. University of Lille. Villeneuve d'Asq.

Turq, A., B. Martinez-Navarro, P. Palmqvist, A. Arribas, J. Agusti, and J. Rodriguez Vidal. 1996. Le Plio-Pleistocene de la région d'Orce, Province de Grenade, Espagne: Bilan et perspectives de recherche. *Paleo* 8:161–204.

Van Andel, T. H. 1989. Late Quaternary sea-level changes and archaeology. *Antiquity* 63:733–45.

Vandermeersch, B. 1995. Le rôle du Levant dans l'évolution de l'humanité au Pleistocène supérieur. *Paléorient* 21(2):25–34.

Vergnaud-Grazzini, C., J. F. Saliège, M. J. Urrutiaguer, and A. Iannace. 1990. Oxygen and carbon isotope stratigraphy of ODP Hole 653A and site 654: The Pliocene-pleistocene glacial history recorded in the Tyrrhenian basin (west Mediterranean), 361–86. In *Proceedings of the Ocean Drilling Program, Scientific Results*, Vol. 107, ed. K. A. Kastens, J. Mascle, J. et al.

Vlcek, E. 1993. Entwicklung der populationen im Pleistozän Europas, 167–79. In *Man and Environment in the Paleolithic*, ed. H. Ullrich. Liège: ERAUL 62.

Wolpoff, M. H. 1982. The Arago dental sample in the context of hominid dental evolution, 389–410. In *"L'*Homo erectus *et la place de l'Homme de Tautavel parmi les Hominidés,"* *1er Congrès International de Paléontologie Humaine, Prétirage* Nice: CNRS Editions.

54

The Accretion Model of Neandertal Evolution

J. D. Hawks and M. H. Wolpoff

ABSTRACT

The Accretion model of Neandertal evolution specifies that this group of Late Pleistocene hominids evolved in partial or complete genetic isolation from the rest of humanity through the gradual accumulation of distinctive morphological traits in European populations. As they became more common, these traits also became less variable, according to those workers who developed the model. Its supporters propose that genetic drift caused this evolution, resulting from an initial small European population size and either complete isolation or drastic reduction in gene flow between this deme and contemporary human populations elsewhere. Here, we test an evolutionary model of gene flow between regions against fossil data from the European population of the Middle and Late Pleistocene. The results of the analysis clearly show that the European population was not significantly divergent from its contemporaries, even in a subset of traits chosen to show the maximum differences between Europeans and other populations. The pattern of changes over time within Europe of the traits in this subset, does not support the Accretion model, either because the characters did not change in the manner specified by the model or because the characters did not change at all. From these data, we can conclude that special phenomena such as near-complete isolation of the European population during the Pleistocene are not required to explain the pattern of evolution in this region.

The Neandertals were the Late Pleistocene human populations living in Europe and parts of Western Asia until approximately 30,000 years ago, more or less. It has long been observed that this hominid group was morphologically different from its contemporaries and from later human populations. In several recent papers, a new theory, called "Accretion," has been proposed to describe and account for the evolution of the European Neandertals. In articulating the Accretion model, Hublin (1998, p. 307) noted:

> Since [450,000 B.P.], the European hominids display the development of derived morphological features relating all the known specimens to a unique lineage leading to the Neandertals. This evolution resulted from an *accretion process* characterized by the successive occurrence of new features and by an *increase in their frequency* within the pre-Neandertal populations.

All authors do not agree that the Neandertal features are new, but there is concurrence that they change in frequency during the Middle Pleistocene.

> [The] greater complexity in the patterns of Middle Pleistocene human evolution . . . supports the view that the accretion of Neanderthal features might result in a shift in the frequency of the derived conditions rather than from the clear cut emergence of new morphologies (Stringer and Hublin, 1999, p. 876).

How did this happen? Hublin (1998, p. 307) notes:

> The peak of stage 12 (425–480 ky BP) . . . may have caused a significant demographic crash in the European populations and triggered their evolutionary divergence. Added to the founder effect following the initial colonization of Europe by small populations, such events would have produced genetic drift episodes resulting in the fixation of derived features. In this view, some of these features could have developed although they do not have a clear adaptive significance. This model would predict a decrease of the variability . . . in the pre-Neandertal/Neandertal populations that experienced major changes of their size

Similarly, in a study of nasal variation, Maureille and Houet (1998) suggest that the level of metric variation in the isolated Neandertal population should be low compared to a nonisolated population because of the effect of genetic drift.

Two things are apparent from the quotations provided above. At one level, the Accretion model is no more than a hypothesis of pattern: morphological features in the European Middle and Late Pleistocene appear, at least to some researchers, to "accrete" over time. This usage is essentially a restatement of mosaic evolution. For this reason, the Accretion model entails a hypothesis of process: accretion in features in this particular geographically defined group over time is due, according to some researchers, to evolution by genetic drift, caused by the partial or complete isolation of this

lineage. As Dean et al. (1998, p. 505) commented, "The primary conclusion one draws from the Accretion model is that gene flow into Europe was restricted from the middle Middle Pleistocene well into the Late Pleistocene." Other researchers take an even stronger position, such as Hublin (2000, p. 163) who writes, "More probably, European and African populations remained isolated for most of the last half million years."

In this paper, we provide a test of the Accretion model, based on the expected phenotypic divergence of populations connected by gene flow. This perspective has been lacking in previous analyses, which depend on the observation of "distinctive" characteristics without making explicit explanations of what such "distinctiveness" actually means. Metric data from fossil Europeans and non-Europeans reflect the phenotypic divergence of these populations, and we test these data from traits that have been suggested to be "distinctive" among ancient Europeans to evaluate whether they refute a null hypothesis of interregional gene flow. Our results indicate that no model of isolation is required to explain the pattern of European metric data, and these data fail to indicate an accretion of features over time in the European population of the Middle and Late Pleistocene.

TESTING GENE FLOW

It was Howell (1952) who first systematically addressed the issue of interregional gene flow among ancient humans, assessing divergent evolutionary trends in the Western European Neandertals (then thought to be) dated to the last glaciation and attributing these divergent trends to the effects of isolation caused by the glaciation itself. But the Accretion model requires that this isolation extend over much of the Middle and Late Pleistocene, a much longer time period over which there are no geographic, climatic, or other factors that would appear to present barriers to gene flow to and from Europe for all or most of the relevent time span. Instead we may expect that Pleistocene glaciations, which periodically reduced the habitable land area of Europe by as much as two-thirds, resulted in a large amount of gene flow into and out of Europe as people tracked habitable zones and encountered populations in adjacent regions. This tracking has been one explanation for certain morphological similarities between Europeans and some West Asians of the Late Pleistocene. Indeed, the only possible source of isolation during this entire time period would seem to be simple geographic distance, which would imply some limit on the rate of gene flow, but not an absolute one. These factors argue that we cannot assume the complete isolation of European hominids, without first subjecting the hypothesis of gene flow to an appropriate test. A null hypothesis with respect to gene flow is then that the European population was connected to others in a pattern of isolation-by-distance. Within this framework, the specific level of gene flow may be unknown, but if a test fails to reject a particular level of gene flow, we will have no particular reason to believe that it did not occur.

As noted in the introduction, several researchers have indicated that the level of morphological distinctiveness of Pleistocene Europeans implies that the level of gene flow between this population and its contemporaries was very low or nonexistent. Historically, researchers have considered discrete traits among Pleistocene Europeans to be "distinctive" if they occur at low—though usually unspecified—frequencies in other human populations. Indeed, in light of the fact that no external isolating mechanism is apparent between Europe and other regions, some researchers have posited that these "distinctive" morphological features *themselves* caused isolation of the European population, by interfering with mate recognition among contemporary hominids. But as noted above, there is no nonmorphological reason to suspect very strong isolation of Pleistocene Europeans, and claims of isolation based on morphology have without exception been made without any formal test of either the frequencies of traits or their significance.

Although we agree that traits are sufficient to form a hypothesis of some limitation on the level of gene flow, they have not yet provided a test of a gene flow hypothesis (Løfsvold, 1988). What we need is some information about the probability distribution from which the distinctive traits of Pleistocene Europeans are drawn. Any random collection of traits, especially in a small sample, will contain some apparently "distinctive" characters whose frequencies are different among predefined groups. As we examine the small set of specimens more carefully, it is inevitable that we will find more such traits, or worse, that we will find many correlated traits and count them as independent ones. For Pleistocene Europeans, no one has yet tried to count the number or proportion of morphological features that are *not* distinctive. Because the number of such traits that we might have examined—but did not—is potentially very large, we cannot even arrive at an estimate of how "distinctive" the European population might have been, much less any estimate of the rate of gene flow. This is because even though we could choose to take observations on a large set of additional, nondistinctive features, there is nothing to tell us just how large a set we should choose, making any estimate of proportion meaningless. Further, for each additional character that we added, we would need estimates of its covariances with the other characters, but such estimates will have little accuracy on the limited set of fossil specimens available to us. Clearly for these reasons, no accurate picture of the distribution of distinctiveness in traits can be available to us.

Some have suggested that if Europeans were isolated during the Pleistocene, then we should expect to find that the population should have a low level of metric variability (Dean et al., 1998; Hublin, 1998; Maureille and Houet, 1998). But in general it is not true that a reduced level of genetic variation, whatever the cause, leads to a reduced level of phenotypic variation of metric characters (Falconer and Mackay, 1996). This is often because an inbred population with less genetic variation usually will exhibit increased nongenetic variance. For this reason and for the reason of small sample

sizes, we cannot feel confident about any assessment of the level of gene flow based only on the within-European level of phenotypic variation.

A distribution that is available to us is the distribution of how much phenotypic difference should exist among subpopulations connected by gene flow. In other words, although we do not know what proportion of traits among Pleistocene Europeans are divergent, we do know how divergent some "distinctive" traits are. We can use this distribution to test whether the level of phenotypic "distinctiveness" of those traits is surprising under the null hypothesis of gene flow. This distribution is model-specific, which means that we must specify an evolutionary model and from it derive the expected distribution of morphological change.

Such an analysis will allow the comparison of traits known to be "distinctive," to whatever degree, to a relevant probability distribution describing the level of difference that should exist between a subpopulation and the total population under the hypothesis of gene flow. It is important to note that this method does not allow an *estimate* of the level of gene flow. We intend to test a null hypothesis that an equilibrium level of gene flow connected the European human population with the rest of the world during the period from roughly 500,000 to 40,000 years ago. If the available data do not reject this hypothesis, then we must conclude that the distribution of skeletal traits in Pleistocene European populations is not unusual under a model of isolation-by-distance, and there is no need to posit extraordinary isolating factors, including speciation, to account for their evolution.

EVOLUTIONARY MODEL

Intuitively, it would seem that a greater level of isolation would cause a greater level of phenotypic divergence of subpopulations, which is the basic assumption of the Accretion model. However, in order to derive the distribution of phenotypic divergence, we will need to consider the genetic and nongenetic factors that cause phenotypic change to occur. These include two primary genetic causes—natural selection and genetic drift. They also include two primary nongenetic causes—changes in environmental variance and interaction variance. There is no consensus on the importance of any of these forces on any of the characters that we might observe in Pleistocene Europeans, and we cannot consider any of them to be a priori a more likely source of change. However, we are primarily interested in whether gene flow may be excluded by morphological data. The major weakness in examining this question is that under certain regimes of selection or changes in environment, no test of gene flow may be possible. For this reason, we first outline the conditions that may lead to significant change within the European population even if gene flow from other regions was always present.

The most obvious possible source of change over time in this population is selection. We cannot reject, and do not attempt to reject, the possibility that selection has exerted a primary influence on the pattern of morphological variation of Pleistocene Europeans. For many of the "distinctive" features found in this population, realistic selective regimes may be imagined that would have changed the distribution of phenotypic values in the observed way. Indeed, illuminating these selective explanations has been a primary goal of evolutionary research on this group (Trinkaus, 1992). Selection concerns us here primarily because if we find any unusual level of interpopulation difference in the phenotypic value of a trait, it may be the result of selection and not of restricted gene flow. This is a significant problem for the researcher attempting to confirm a hypothesis of isolation, because to refute gene flow with selection she or he would first have to refute every possible selective mechanism that may apply to the traits examined, which is the primary criticism that has been leveled at studies attempting to demonstrate European isolation from morphological characters. In the following, we attempt to test the hypothesis of gene flow *without* selection, leaving the consideration of selection to the discussion.

Other factors that may cause significant phenotypic change within the European population over time include changes in the environmental component of variance (V_E), presence of a significant interaction variance (V_I), and changes in the mutational variance (V_M). Of these factors, the least important is the last, because the mutation rate among coding loci is unlikely to have varied enough among human populations over the course of the past 400,000 years to cause a large difference in either the rate of phenotypic change or the level of phenotypic variance. Differences in V_E and V_I are more difficult to dismiss, both because of the unique character of the European environment compared to other regions during large stretches of the Middle and Late Pleistocene and because of the often rapid climatic changes that characterized this period of time. The actions of either of these factors are formally similar to selection, in that either of them may cause significant phenotypic divergence of populations even in the presence of gene flow. Like selection, V_E and V_I have been suggested as primary influences on morphological change in Pleistocene Europeans, although the persistence of particular phenotypic values for traits in vastly different climatic regimes partially belies such assertions. Nevertheless, we consider these factors in the same class as selection in their potential effects on phenotypic traits, and as in the case of selection, we attempt to refute a model in which they are assumed to have no effect. Therefore, the model that we describe here is a neutral model with gene flow between regions in which neither selection nor environmental effects have played any significant role in differentiating regions, keeping in mind the considerable probability that many traits may differentiate Europeans because of these other reasons.

Under this model, the expected genetic differentiation of subpopulations is a simple function of the past rate of migration between regions. The actual amount of migration in the past is unknown and probably varied over time. However, an interesting hypothesis to consider is that the genetic differentiation among humans today, with an F_{ST} between continental regions between 0.10 and 0.15, was caused by an equilibrium level of gene flow between the same regions in the past. Under this hypothesis, the expected variance in the phenotypic means of groups connected by gene flow is given by Rogers and Harpending (1983, eq. 15) as:

$$E\{\sigma_y^2\} = 2\sigma_a^2 \frac{R_0}{1-R_0} \quad (1)$$

where σ_y^2 is the variance in the phenotypic differences of the groups from the centroid, σ_a^2 is the within-group additive genetic variance, and R_0 is simply Wright's (1951) F_{ST}. The within-group additive genetic variance may be estimated as the within-group phenotypic variance, σ_P^2, divided by the heritability, h^2.

In a similar vein, Lande (1979, p. 410) provides a "scaled square of generalized genetic distance":

$$\frac{t}{N_e} \mathbf{y}^{\mathrm{T}} \bar{\mathbf{G}}^{-1} \mathbf{y} \quad (2)$$

which is distributed as χ^2 with one degree of freedom, where $\mathbf{y}$ is the vector of phenotypic difference of the subpopulation from the centroid, simply $z_1 - z_0$ in the case of a single trait. The scaling factor here, $(t/N_e)\bar{\mathbf{G}}^{-1}$, is the multiplicative inverse of the expected amount of phenotypic diversification of the subpopulation, assuming isolation (Lande, 1979, p. 409).

In the case of gene flow, we can substitute the inverse of the right half of equation 1, above, for the scaling factor in equation 2, obtaining:

$$\frac{(1 - F_{ST})(\bar{z}_1 - \bar{z}_0)^2}{2 F_{ST} h^2 \sigma_P^2} \quad (3)$$

as the square of phenotypic difference of the subpopulation from the centroid, scaled to the expectation of that difference under equilibrium migration, and distributed as χ^2 with one degree of freedom. For $F_{ST} = 0.15$, this reduces to:

$$2.83 \times \frac{(\bar{z}_1 - \bar{z}_0)^2}{h^2 \sigma_P^2} \quad (4)$$

We can use this expression to test the null hypothesis of equilibrium gene flow between the European population and the rest of the world during the Middle and Late Pleistocene. If our set of "distinctive traits" in fact are markers of evolutionary isolation of this lineage, then the level of morphological divergence of these traits should be very great, compared to the expectation under the hypothesis of gene flow. If none, or very few, of these traits are more divergent than expected under the hypothesis of gene flow, then certainly this hypothesis cannot be refuted by these traits. Therefore, we can compare the level of difference in this subset of traits with the 95% confidence limit of the χ^2 distribution with one degree of freedom. If these traits are not significantly different between the European population and other populations, then these data do not reject the hypothesis of gene flow.

MATERIALS AND METHODS

Following the categories used by Dean et al. (1998, Table 1), we examined three samples of European hominids to test the Accretion model of founder effect and/or isolation in Europe, especially during the last glaciation (Tables 1–6). Only adults or older juveniles when the morphology is not affected by increased age are used in the tables. Sex is not considered (as it is not in the other studies discussed here) because it cannot be reliably established for most of the fragmentary specimens.

Specimen Selection

Our selection of specimens and their group affiliations conform to Dean and colleagues (1998), with two exceptions. First, we added specimens such as the Ceprano vault (Ascenzi et al., 1996) and the Apidima crania (Coutselinis et al., 1991) that they did not include. Second, we did not consider any of the Asian specimens discussed in the Dean et al. (1998) and Maureille and Houet (1998) papers, in particular omitting Shanidar, Amud, and Teshik Tash. We regard our examination of the Accretion model as a question of isolation, drift, and independent evolution *in Europe;* the broader the area encompassed, the less likely that any model of isolation is valid. It was the *European* Neandertals who presumably were isolated during the last glaciation, and not those from Western Asia. By restricting the problem to a European one, we may more validly examine the possible isolation of Neandertals, and we are being conservative, in that it makes it more likely that the later Neandertals can be shown to have reduced variation, as the Accretion model predicts. The geographic areas represented in our three samples are more or less the same (an exact statement of area is impossible because each comparison we made incorporates somewhat different sample compositions since all cranial parts are not equally represented).

Sample Selection

Using the theory described above, it is possible to develop a very precise testing procedure based on the phenotypic values of individual specimens and conditioned on their chronological dates. However, sophisticated approaches using individual dates are of little use to us, because the dates for many of the specimens are very imperfectly known. For example, the earliest large site in our sample, Atapuerca, has estimates of geologic age varying by a factor of two, with a minimum date of 200,000 years ago and a maximum date of some 350,000 years (Parés et al., 2000). In view of the lack of temporal resolution for these specimens, we found it more easily defensible to follow precedent by collapsing the sample into three time segments: pre-Neandertals, early Neandertals, and Würm Neandertals. We chose samples as similar as possible to those that have been presented in support of Accretion, although we did not retain the four-sample division of Dean et al. (1998) because of uncertainties of data that make membership in those two pre-Neandertal groups problematic. The Accretion model stipulates that it is the comparison of pre-Neandertals with Neandertals that is of key importance, and we have retained these groups. Not all the specimens are radiometrically dated and in some cases

group membership was determined from geological or stratigraphic considerations. The ages represented for each sample group in Tables 1–6 differ, because the samples differ, but under the assumptions that they all sample the same groups, and that the specimens not directly dated fall within the ranges of the dated specimens for each sample, the three groups more or less extend across 20,000 years (Würm Neandertals), 40,000 years (Early Neandertals), and approximately 200,000 years (Pre-Neandertals). The consequences of the different age spans are reviewed in Table 9. All of the age-related questions are reviewed in Wolpoff (1999) and sources therein.

Tests of the three different time periods may not form independent tests of the hypothesis of gene flow, if the effective size of the population during these time periods was very large, because genetic drift will not equilibrate a very large population during the time spans involved. However, the worldwide effective size has been estimated on the basis of other evidence as less than 20,000 effective individuals (Harpending et al., 1998; Hawks et al., 2000). The effective size within Europe alone is unlikely to have exceeded one tenth of the worldwide amount, and therefore was apparently sufficiently small to allow independent tests of gene flow for the three temporal groups addressed here. A small effective size itself does not address the phylogenetic status of Pleistocene Europeans (Hawks et al., 2000).

Using the groupings presented in Dean et al. (1998), whether or not they are construed to be evolutionary stages, does not imply our acceptance of their validity. We do not necessarily agree with either the groupings or their purported evolutionary meaning. If this grouping does not support the Accretion model, however, it is reasonable to ask what more appropriate grouping we should have examined.

Trait Selection

We limited our examination to features that Dean et al. (1998), Rak et al. (1996), and/or Hublin (1998) propose to be unique or very frequent features of the Neandertals, because variation in these traits is explained by the Accretion model. We omitted traits with sample sizes too small for any determination of statistical significance in the comparisons. This selected sample is no less likely to exhibit evolutionary changes than other traits we might have chosen to examine, and the traits we examined are easily recognizable. We focused on features that could be quantified, rather than on discrete characters, in order to test the changes in means and in the magnitude of variation that the Accretion model requires, and to examine the conditions under which selection or drift could account for their change. Our features are not exhaustive, but were picked to maximize sample size and represent different parts of the cranium, face, and dentition. These include the height of the mastoid process below the digastric sulcus (the projection of the mastoid below the cranial base is minimal in Neandertals, Table 1), nasal breadth (large in Neandertals, Table 2), relatively and absolutely tall

Table 1.   Mastoid Height from the Digastric Sulcus (in mm)

Würm Neandertals	Mastoid Height	Early Neandertals	Mastoid Height	Pre-Neandertals	Mastoid Height
Spy 2	4.0	Krapina 38.12	3.1	Atapuerca AT 1122	6.6
Forbes Quarry	4.2	Biache	4.2	Ehringsdorf H	7.9
Spy 1	5.2	Krapina 39.1	4.6	Reilingen	8.1
La Quina 27	6.0	Krapina 38.7	5.2	Atapuerca Cr. 7	8.5
La Ferrassie 2	6.1	Krapina 39.16	6.0	Atapuerca AT 643	9.0
La Ferrassie 1	6.2	Krapina 38.13	6.1	Atapuerca Cr. 5	12.1
La Quina 5	7.4	Saccopastore 1	6.2	Atapuerca AT 84	13.6
La Chapelle	8.2	Saccopastore 2	6.4	Atapuerca Cr. 1	14.0
Guattari	9.1	Krapina 3	7.7	Atapuerca Cr. 4	15.7
		Krapina 39.13	7.9	Atapuerca Cr. 8	17.1
		Krapina 38.3	8.6		
		Krapina 39.13	8.9		
		Krapina 39.17	9.6		
		Krapina 38.15	9.8		
		Krapina 10	11.1		
		Krapina 5	11.8		
Mean[1]	6.3	Mean[1]	7.3	Mean	11.3
Standard Error	0.54	Standard Error	0.61	Standard Error	1.1
Standard Deviation[2]	1.7	Standard Deviation	2.5	Standard Deviation	3.7
Coefficient of Variation	27.5	Coefficient of Variation	34.4	Coefficient of Variation	32.7

[1]A one sided t-test shows this mean differs significantly from the Pre-Neandertal mean with a significance of $P = 0.01$.
[2]An F-test shows the variance differs significantly from the Pre-Neandertal variance with a significance of $P = 0.05$.

Table 2.   Nasal Breadths of European Hominids (in mm)

Würm Neandertals	Nasal Breadth	Early Neandertals	Nasal Breadth	Pre-Neandertals	Nasal Breadth
Vindija 259	26.2	Montmaurin 4	27.5	Arago 21	29.2
St. Césaire	27.7	Krapina 49	29.7	Apidima 2	31.0
Vindija 225	28.5	Krapina 3	30.0	Steinheim	31.6
Kůlna	30.0	Saccopastore 1	32.9	Atapuerca AT 1100	32.0
La Chapelle	33.2	Saccopastore 2	33.7	Castel del Guido	32.0
Arcy-sur-Cure	33.3			Petralona	36.4
La Ferrassie 1	34.0			Atapuerca AT 767/963	37.0
Forbes Quarry	34.1			Atapuerca Cr. 5	38.5
Guattari	35.1				
Mean	31.3	Mean	30.8	Mean	33.5
Standard Error	1.1	Standard Error	1.1	Standard Error	1.2
Standard Deviation	3.3	Standard Deviation	2.5	Standard Deviation	3.3
Coefficient of Variation	10.4	Coefficient of Variation	8.2	Coefficient of Variation	10.0

Table 3.   Orbit Shape (100 × height/breadth)

Würm Neandertals	Height (mm)	Index	Early Neandertals	Height (mm)	Index	Pre-Neandertals	Height (mm)	Index
La Chapelle	37.2	79.5	Krapina 6	33.4	82.5	Apidima 2	31.0	75.6
La Ferrassie	35.5	80.0	Saccopastore 2	36.9	82.6	Petralona	36.8	76.1
Guattari	38.6	86.5	Saccopastore 1	38	89.8	Atapuerca Cr. 5	33.0	80.1
Gibraltar	38.2	92.3	Krapina 3	37	90.0	Steinheim	32.1	82.7
Mean[1]	37.4[1]	84.6[2]	Mean	36.3	86.2[1]	Mean	33.2	78.6
Standard Error	0.7	3.1	Standard Error	1.0	2.1	Standard Error	1.3	1.7
Standard Deviation	1.4	6.1	Standard Deviation	2.0	4.2	Standard Deviation	2.5	3.4
Coefficient of Variation	3.7	7.2	Coefficient of Variation	5.5	4.9	Coefficient of Variation	7.6	4.3

[1]Differs from the Pre-Neandertal mean at $P = 0.01$.
[2]The mean difference from the Pre-Neandertals is almost significant at $P = 0.05$.

orbits (Table 3), flattening of the lambdoidal region (as expressed in the lambdoidal depression index, Table 4), foramen magnum elongation (Table 5), and relative maxillary incisor breadth (the lateral incisor is often as broad as or broader than the central one, Table 6). We also examined changes in cranial capacity (Table 7). Large cranial capacity is not distinctive in Neandertals to the exclusion of later humans, but important in subsequent discussion. Many authors contend its evolution, as revealed by the changes shown in Table 7, like the evolution of other features would have to be explained as a homoplasy if Neandertals were

Table 4.   Lambdoidal Depression Index (100 × lambda-inion chord/biasterionic diameter)

Würm Neandertals	Index	Early Neandertals	Index	Pre-Neandertal	Index
Spy 2	46	La Chaise (Suard) 2	43	Bilzingsleben	36
Le Moustier	48	Saccopastore 1	47	Vértesszöllös	39
Guattari	48	Krapina 5	49	Swanscombe	48
Forbes Quarry	48	La Chaise (Delaunay) 17	50	Ceprano	48
Lebenstedt	50	Biache	57	Atapuerca Cr. 4	51
La Chapelle	50			Atapuerca Cr. 5	52
La Ferrassie 1	50			Atapuerca Cr. 1	53
Spy 1	51			Petralona	53
La Quina 5	53			Reilingen	54
Mean	49	Mean	49	Mean	48
Standard Error	0.7	Standard Error	2.3	Standard Error	2.2
Standard Deviation[1]	2.1	Standard Deviation	5.1	Standard Deviation	6.5
Coefficient of Variation	4.2	Coefficient of Variation	10.4	Coefficient of Variation	13.4

[1]An F-test shows that variance of the Würm Neandertals differs significantly from the Early Neandertals and Pre-Neandertals at $P = 0.01$.

Table 5.   Foramen Magnum Elongation (percent of breadth/length)

Würm and Early Neandertals[1]	Relative Breadth	Pre-Neandertal	Relative Breadth
La Chapelle	68	Atapuerca Cr. 4	71
Gánovce	69	Swanscombe	73
Biache	74	Atapuerca Cr. 5	74
La Ferrassie 1	77	Petralona	85
Saccopastore 1	89		
Mean	75	Mean	76
Standard Error	3.8	Standard Error	3.2
Standard Deviation	8.4	Standard Deviation	6.3
Coefficient of Variation	11.2	Coefficient of Variation	8.3

[1]The Neandertal sample is too small to divide into Early and Würm groups, we consider them together because the foramen magnum should be relatively long in both according to the Accretion model.

genetically isolated from other human populations, and therefore hold its variation to be an argument against isolation. Metric data were collected by one of the authors (MHW) on the original specimens, except for measurements of Ceprano (Ascenzi et al., 1996), Apidima (Coutselinis et al., 1991), and the Atapuerca crania (Arsuaga et al., 1997; Martínez-Labarga and Arsuaga, 1997). The cranial capacities are from published sources.

Computational Methods

The mean and standard deviation for each character within each group of Europeans were estimated from the metric data. The worldwide mean during these time periods was also estimated, as the sample mean of all non-European specimens available, with the exception of those West Asian samples that have been considered to be Neandertals by some authors, notably the Shanidar hominids, Tabun 1, and Amud 1. The worldwide mean is therefore conservative, in that we excluded the European sample from it and all those specimens that have been suggested to have European affinities. Such conservatism is desirable considering that the European sample is relatively large compared to that from other regions, and its inclusion would likely shift the centroid closer to Europe. Interestingly, however, experimental inclusion of the West Asian specimens in the worldwide sample did not alter the results, because these specimens are apparently not specifically like Europeans for these metric characteristics.

Table 6.   Relative Maxillary Incisor Breadths of European Hominids

Würm Neandertals	100 × (I^2 Breadth/I^1 Breadth)	Early Neandertals	100 × (I^2 Breadth/I^1 Breadth)
Arcy-sur-Cure H1	94	Krapina D18	92
Hortus 8	95	Krapina D29	96
Teshik Tash	96	Krapina D17	97
La Quina 5	98	La Chaise (Delaunay) 18	98
Genay	100	Krapina 46	98
Marillac	100	La Chaise (Delaunay) 9	101
St. Césaire	101	Krapina 48	102
La Ferrassie 2	102	Ehringsdorf G	102
Hortus 12	103	Krapina 49	104
Le Moustier	105	Krapina 50	106
Hortus 7	105		
Mean	99.9[1]	Mean	99.6[1]
Standard Error	1.1	Standard Error	1.3
Standard Deviation	3.8	Standard Deviation	4.2
Coefficient of Variation	3.8	Coefficient of Variation	4.2

[1]Mean not significant to the nearest 10th, but presented to show slight difference between samples.

Table 7. Cranial Capacity for Adult Specimens of Younger Individuals Old Enough to Have Attained Adult Vault Size (in cc)

Würm Neandertals	Cranial Capacity	Early Neandertals	Cranial Capacity	Pre-Neandertal	Cranial Capacity
Forbes Quarry	1270	La Chaise (Suard) 1	1065	Steinheim	950
Spy 1	1305	Krapina 3	1200	Atapuerca Cr. 6	1100
Guattari	1367	Biache[1]	1200	Atapuerca Cr. 5	1125
La Quina 5	1367	Saccopastore 1	1258	Arago 21	1166
Feldhofer	1525	Saccopastore 2	1300	Ceprano	1185
Spy 2	1553	Gánovce	1320	Petralona	1220
Le Moustier	1564	Fontéchevade	1350	Vértesszöllös	1300
La Chapelle	1626			Swanscombe	1325
La Ferrassie 1	1641			Atapuerca Cr. 4	1390
				Reilingen	1430
				Ehringsdorf H	1450
Mean	1494	Mean[2]	1242	Mean[1]	1240
Standard Error	43	Standard Error	37	Standard Error	47
Standard Deviation	129	Standard Deviation	97	Standard Deviation	155
Coefficient of Variation	8.6	Coefficient of Variation	7.8	Coefficient of Variation	12.5

[1]This value is a likely minimum.
[2]A *t*-test shows this mean differs from the Würm Neandertal mean with a significance of $P = 0.01$. None of the variances differ significantly.

The lumping across timespans of the non-European sample is not ideal, but we followed it because of some significant sampling problems for non-Europeans during this time period. There have been significant difficulties in the dates of some of the non-European specimens. Both the relatively smaller sample size of this set of specimens and the fact that the dates of some individual specimens, such as the Ngandong hominids from Java, cannot be localized to within 200,000 years interfere both with our ability to divide the specimens into time periods and with our ability to recognize temporal trends in the data. Additionally, those specimens for which relatively accurate assessments of date do exist show a bias toward relatively more ancient specimens in some regions (East Asia) and relatively recent ones in others (West Asia), confounding the issues of temporal change with geographic variation. For these reasons, except as noted below, we assume that the non-European means did not change during the relevant time periods.

If changes in the non-European means did occur and rendered the European population more divergent during a time period than our estimate indicates, our assumption would be nonconservative because it would make the European population look more similar to the worldwide mean than it actually was. We checked for this possibility by looking for trends over time, as far as we could identify them, in the non-European sample. For many of the characters, including nasal breadth, foramen magnum shape, and orbit shape, the non-European specimens simply did not appear to change over time. However, in two cases, mastoid length and lambdoidal depression, the non-Europeans did appear to exhibit a trend opposite in direction to the direction of change within Europe. In these two cases, the later group of non-Europeans was more different from later Europeans than was the overall non-European mean, and in these cases we tested explicitly against contemporary samples rather than across time periods. In only one of these characters, the degree of lambdoidal depression, did the trend in non-European specimens make a difference in the result, causing the sample

mean of the Würm Neandertals to diverge from the sample non-European mean more than the expected amount, while it did not do so when compared to the full set of non-Europeans. For cranial capacity, the non-Europeans had a significant trend in the *same* direction as the Europeans, this resulted in later Europeans being more similar to later non-Europeans than to the overall non-European sample, as reported below.

With these data, the computation of our tests is quite straightforward. If the European phenotypic mean for a character is found to differ from the non-European mean by more than the 95% limit of the χ^2 distribution, then the character is surprisingly divergent in the European population during that time period, assuming our evolutionary model is correct. If few characters are found to be surprising using these criteria, then our evolutionary model, the hypothesis of neutral evolution with gene flow, will not be rejected by this procedure. The strength of this test depends on the accuracy of estimates of mean and standard deviation from the available data. Given the small sample sizes, the strength of the method is an appropriate concern, and we report the standard errors of all these estimates.

RESULTS

The results of the analysis are fairly unambiguous (Table 8). Of the 19 comparisons of groups, the sample mean of the European group was significantly different from the non-European sample mean only four times. Each of these four represented a sample difference between European and non-European groups that exceeded the 95% probability threshold of divergence, but these were the only four comparisons that did so, assuming that the heritability of the traits equals 0.5. The rest of the comparisons yielded no significant difference between the European and non-European sample means, and even taking the differences at face value, the levels of difference between the samples were well within the range expected for a subpopulation with gene flow.

Table 8. Results: Column 4 reports whether the sample means of European and non-European specimens are significantly different. Columns 6 and 8 report whether the level of difference between the sample means produces χ^2 greater than the 95% confidence threshold, which is 3.84 with one degree of freedom, with heritability of 0.5 and 0.25, respectively.

Character	Time Period	Absolute Difference	Significantly Different?	Equation 4, χ^2 with $h^2 = 0.5$	> 95% C.I.?	Equation 4, χ^2 with $h^2 = 0.25$	> 95% C.I.?
Mastoid height[1]	Pre	0.32	yes	5.48	yes	11.0	yes
	Early	0.12	no	0.58	no	1.17	no
	Würm	0.25	yes	4.61	yes	9.21	yes
Nasal breadth[1]	Pre	0.05	no	1.52	no	3.05	no
	Early	0.04	no	1.27	no	2.55	no
	Würm	0.02	no	0.19	no	0.39	no
Orbit shape	Pre	1.4	no	0.97	no	1.95	no
	Early	6.2	yes	12.2	yes	24.5	yes
	Würm	4.6	no	3.17	no	6.34	yes
Lambdoidal depression	Pre	1.4	no	0.26	no	0.52	no
	Early	0.4	no	0.305	no	0.071	no
	Würm	0.4	no	0.22	no	0.43	no
Foramen magnum	Pre	0	no	0	no	0	no
	Würm and Early	1	no	0.080	no	0.16	no
Relative maxillary incisor	Early	0.2	no	0.013	no	0.025	no
	Würm	0.1	no	0.0038	no	0.0076	no
Cranial capacity	Pre	10	no	0.023	no	0.047	no
	Early	12	no	0.086	no	0.17	no
	Würm	264	yes	23.7	yes	47.5	yes
Mastoid height[2]	Würm	0.32	yes	7.55	yes	15.1	yes
Lambdoidal depression[2]	Würm	5.4	yes	39.3	yes	78.7	yes
Cranial capacity[2]	Würm	77	no	2.02	no	4.04	yes

[1]Comparisons are made with ln-transformed data. This transform had no effect on the results.
[2]Comparisons made with later part of non-European sample only.

A finer temporal subsampling of the non-Europeans tends to make an additional comparison significant also, the lambdoidal depression in Würm Neandertals. However, such finer sampling renders the cranial capacity of the same group insignificant, so the overall result is unchanged. This same measurement is evaluated as divergent when compared to the entire set of non-Europeans if we disregard the lack of significant difference, under the assumption that heritability equals 0.25, this being the only measurement where this assumption of lower heritability changes the result.

If these characters are indeed representative of the "distinctiveness" of the Pleistocene European population, then we must conclude that the population is surprisingly not "distinctive" at all. Instead, they are no farther from the worldwide phenotypic mean for most of these "distinctive" characters than would be expected for a random set of characters in a population connected to others by gene flow. These data clearly do not justify an interpretation of isolation or other special explanations to explain the evolution of people in this region.

Do the Characters "Accrete"?

As we discuss the particular characters below, we caution that the observed changes in phenotype of these characters over time are obtained from a very small number of specimens. We describe changes in the characters here as an empirical exercise, because they make quite clear that the data, such as they are, do not sup-

port an interpretation of "accretion" of unique character states over time in the European sequence. Where these patterns of change over time are statistically significant, we make explicit the level of statistical significance in the tables and in our description.

One character is an exception to the apparent pattern of similarity between Europeans and non-Europeans and might illuminate the process of character accretion, if it occurred. Two of the significantly divergent group comparisons occurred for the mastoid height from digastric sulcus. Importantly, these two comparisons were significantly divergent in opposite directions: the Pre-Neandertals were unusually tall compared to non-Europeans, whereas the Würm Neandertals were unusually short. An examination of only the non-European specimens closest in time to these groups increases the significance of the comparisons. Empirically, it would seem that an early European population that had significantly diverged from other populations evolved first to be more similar to them and then to assume the opposite condition. The change between Pre-Neandertal and later samples, which is statistically significant ($P < 0.01$) does not support the Accretion model, which predicts that earlier European populations should diverge with less magnitude than later Europeans, but in the same direction.

The Accretion model is also not supported by change in other characters. For example, the orbit shape index is less in Pre-Neandertals than the non-European mean, then increases significantly ($P < 0.05$)

in Early Neandertals, and appears to decrease slightly, although not significantly, in Würm Neandertals in the direction of the non-European mean. This pattern of evolution clearly cannot be described as "accretion" in the sense of the Accretion model. Furthermore, unlike the first two characters, the remaining characters simply do not change significantly in Europe over time. Nasal breadth, lambdoidal depression, foramen magnum shape, and relative maxillary incisor breadth have no significant change in phenotype over time in the European sequence. This is strong evidence that the Accretion model does not provide an accurate account of evolutionary pattern in Europe.

Level of Variation

A second issue raised by the Accretion model is the level of phenotypic variation within European samples. Some researchers have examined the variance of metric features in Europe, expecting decreases in variance to be the result of genetic drift (e.g., Dean, 1998; Hublin, 1998; Maureille and Houet, 1998). As we have noted above, this issue is not especially relevant to evolutionary pattern because genetic drift does not typically reduce phenotypic variance in an inbred subpopulation (Falconer and Mackay, 1996). Nevertheless, the available data allow us to examine whether phenotypic variance decreased over time in Europe, and for most of these characters it did not. Orbit shape, nasal breadth, foramen magnum shape, and relative maxillary incisor breadth all show no significant change in variance between any time periods in Europe, and many of these appear to increase in variance over time rather than decrease. Only mastoid height and lambdoidal depression decrease significantly in variance over time between European samples. These two cases are interesting, because in both cases it is the reduced variation of Würm Neandertals that causes this group to differ significantly from the non-European mean, accounting for half the total cases of significant phenotypic divergence in Europe. The decreased variance of this group, which does not occur for other characters, would suggest that either selection or sample bias has given us a Würm sample with less than the expected amount of variance.

Cranial Capacity

Cranial capacity increases significantly within the European sample without a significant change in variability (Table 7). This increase results in the Würm Neandertals exhibiting a significant deviation from the overall non-European mean. Large cranial capacity, however, is not a Neandertal autapomorphy. It increases in the non-European sample over time also (Ruff et al., 1997), and its increase is usually and logically attributed to selection. This pattern of increase is fully consistent with a model of gene flow between these groups, as demonstrated by the non-significant difference between the Würm Neandertals and the Late Pleistocene subset of non-European specimens (Table 8).

Cranial capacity evolution differs from the other characters in that we can *show* that it is guided by selec-

Table 9. Change[1] for Neandertal Cranial Capacity (from Table 7)

Samples:	$\Delta(\bar{x})/\sigma$	t in 25 Year Generations	Minimum Selection	N_e
Early-Würm	1.63	3400	1.5×10^{-3}	1.2×10^3
Pre-Early	0.06	6800	2.1×10^{-5}	1.8×10^6

[1]Calculations as described in Lande (1976, equations 12 and 19), where the difference in means is given as the difference between the means of the ln-transformed data, divided by the average standard deviation of these data. Selection calculated is the minimum selective mortality (proportion culled per generation) in the absence of drift assuming $h^2 = 0.5$, and the effective population size (N_e) is the magnitude required for a 5% chance that a change at least as large as the observed change could be caused by drift in the complete absence of selection. Both drift and selection in a population connected to others by gene flow are possible explanations for the observed changes.

tion and not drift. Following Lande (1976) we examined the strength of selection and the minimum amount of genetic drift (measured by effective population size) necessary to explain the rate of change in cranial capacity among our European samples. These models are somewhat unrealistic because they assume no gene flow into Europe from elsewhere; we use it for illustration only. Examination of changes in cranial capacity under the drift hypothesis (based on data in Table 7) shows a pattern of N_e variation that *could* be compatible with neutral genetic drift in Europe alone (Table 9), but this hypothesis is unlikely considering that the worldwide human population, with N_e estimated at 10,000 to 20,000 individuals, appears to undergo approximately the same magnitude of change across the human range during the same time period (Ruff et al., 1997). Therefore drift is an unreasonable explanation. The strongest minimum pruning selection these changes require is on the order of 10^{-3}, which seems entirely credible for evolutionary changes in cranial capacity in ancient humans.

Though Würm Neandertals do not differ from non-Europeans more than we would expect if the populations exchanged genes, this group is larger than their non-European contemporaries in cranial capacity. This increased size could have several consequences reflected in the anatomical changes discussed here. One of these may be in orbit height, which shows a nonsignificant increase that may reflect increasing cranial capacity, because these two features are related in humans (Schultz, 1965). Another may be the projection of the mastoid process, suggested by the fact that whereas projection below the digastric sulcus decreases over time in Europe (Table 1), the projection of the mastoid below the Frankfurt Horizontal remains the same, and is the same in living Europeans (Dean et al., 1998; Martínez-Labarga and Arsuaga, 1997; Vallois, 1969). The difference between samples probably reflects the posterior-inferior expansion of the cranial base that follows from the increased cranial capacity among Neandertals (Table 7). Therefore, we cannot reject the hypothesis that the significant divergences observed between some European groups and contemporary non-Europeans are related to differences in cranial capacity observed in later Europeans.

All these characters are fully consistent with a model of gene flow between Pleistocene Europeans and non-Europeans. The data give us no reason to believe that any significant isolation occurred among these groups. Recalling the important possibility that selection or environmental variance may have influenced changes in any of these traits, we may question whether the data demonstrate Europeans to be particularly distinctive at all. It is certain that the hypothesis of gene flow is not refuted.

DISCUSSION

Obviously we would prefer to have a larger sample of fossil hominids to examine questions of gene flow, but we can only work with the sample at hand and accept its limitations. The Accretion model that we have addressed must depend on the same sample and, of course, has the same limitations. One could argue that the constraints imposed by the sample make *any* statement of evolutionary model imprecise to the point where it risks invalidity, and we sympathize with this view. Nonetheless, the Accretion model has been widely published and accepted as an explanatory hypothesis, and we cling to the simple principle that if there is sufficient reason to believe a hypothesis, there must be sufficient data to test it.

Given that the very data that have been used to generate the Accretion model apparently provide no support for it, we must wonder why the model exists. The reason is an artifact of the history of anthropology. The Accretion model is a variant of polygenism, much like the pseudo-evolutionary model proposed by Coon (1962) in which human subspecies were thought to have evolved in parallel, in virtual or complete isolation from each other. Today, no one contends that living human groups have independent origins early in the Pleistocene. But polygenism has been resurrected by scientists who assert that such separate origins do in fact exist: evolution in isolation for recent human groups in the Late Pleistocene (discussed by Templeton, 1998), and separate origins for ancient human groups in the Early Pleistocene, delineated for archaic Europeans by the Accretion model.

The key feature of pseudo-evolutionary polygenism is its reliance on massive parallelism to explain evolutionary trends shared by different groups. When researchers describe the phylogeny of our genus in terms of a "bush" of hominid species during the past two million years, usually unstated is the fact that whenever this "bushlike" pattern is subjected to phylogenetic analysis, hefty levels of homoplasy are the necessary result. Such homoplasy can be explained under this hypothesis only by the interpretation that any long-term evolutionary trends are parallel developments in separated genetic systems. Even explanations of behavioral evolution have come to require parallelism to account for what can be readily observed in the archaeological record (Mellars, 1989). As archaeologists grapple with the questions of how and where modern human behaviors arose in the Late Pleistocene, the fact that they appear in European Neandertals and sub-Saharan Africans at about the same time also requires that modern human behaviors evolved independently and in parallel (Zilhão and D'Errico, 1999), for those who assume that Neandertals are a different species.

The Accretion model, as a descriptive hypothesis, does not make explicit whether distinct lineages or separate demes within a single species are thought to underlie this pattern, but neither of these can resolve the problems raised by the underlying polygenic interpretation. Limiting our investigations to crania, the subject of this paper, the foremost evolutionary trend among all representatives of Pleistocene *Homo* is the expansion of brain size, but others include:

> (1) reduction in the cranial superstructures (central and lateral supraorbital and nuchal tori) and in cranial bone thickness; (2) expansion of the occipital plane of the occiput at the expense of the nuchal (muscle-bearing) plane; (3) expansion of the superciliary aspect of the supraorbital torus, while the lateral structures reduce and in some cases degenerate; (4) anterior dental reduction; and (5) nasal breadth reduction.

Any account of evolution within our genus must explain these facts. The only explanation provided by the Accretion model and other polygenic variants is parallelism.

At the extreme, Tattersall (1996, p. 52) defends an interpretation of multiple contemporary *Homo* species in the Pleistocene and explains the parallel evolutionary trends this interpretation requires as follows:

> Natural selection takes place at the level of the local population, and in similar circumstances closely related populations are likely to respond to ecological pressures or other agents of natural selection upon them in similar ways. These various considerations will hold true even when such local populations have become individual evolutionary entities. When, that is, speciation has intervened between them.

It is of interest to compare this with Wiley's (1981, p. 25) definition of the evolutionary species: "a single lineage of ancestral-descendant populations which maintains its identity from other lineages and which has its own evolutionary tendencies and historical fate." It is plain that if Tattersall is correct then the evolutionary species definition must be invalid, because different closely related species might be expected to have the same evolutionary tendencies. Alternatively, if the definition is valid and provides a means of comparing present and past species, then Tattersall is incorrect in presuming that a number of the same long-term evolutionary trends can take place in different species (especially in the human case; Wolpoff, 1994), when the purported species are wide-ranging and contiguous. We prefer the second alternative as by far a more likely, and more testable, proposition. Parallelism does occur in evolution and is more common among closely related species than among distantly related groups. However, the level of parallelism required to support a "bushlike" interpretation of our evolution is insupportable, when compared to the more parsimonious alternative of gene flow among groups. There is no scientific basis for any polygenic theory of human evolution (Wolpoff and Caspari, 1997).

By directly testing the hypothesis of gene flow among these ancient groups, we provide a novel way to address the ancestry of recent humans. Rogers (1995) points out the difficulty of testing the hypothesis of replacement of ancient humans isolated within regions with humans of geographically separate origins. However, the polygenic model based on replacement depends not only on the wholesale migration of recent humans from a single source, but also on the complete isolation of archaic humans before this dispersal event. The demonstration that we cannot substantiate any isolation between ancient regions directly weakens the hypothesis of replacement by showing that the geographic source population for recent humans, in the genetic sense, must extend across more than one ancient region of the world. Even if substantial migrations occurred during the Late Pleistocene, the genetic background of this expanding population reflects a prior equilibrium population with migration from several regions. This genetic continuity should be considered by researchers who compare recent and ancient groups. Our analysis suggests strongly that the observations of Relethford (1995), who examines the differences of recent human groups in terms of an equilibrium migration model with much larger population size in Africa than in other regions, provide an appropriate basis for understanding the genetic differentiation of recent and ancient humans.

In summary, our study demonstrates clearly that no special explanations or phenomena are required to account for the evolution of certain characters in Pleistocene Europeans that have been described as "distinctive" in this population. The hypothesis that this population was connected to other populations by gene flow during the Pleistocene has not been rejected by morphological evidence. This finding is consistent with molecular evidence from ancient DNA sequence variation, which shows a higher divergence between Neandertals and recent humans than among recent humans alone, but a threefold lower divergence than would be expected if these groups had diverged before the Late Pleistocene (Krings et al., 1997, 1999). It is also consistent with morphological evidence for genetic exchanges between Europeans and other populations after 40,000 years ago (Frayer, 1993). A simple and homogeneous model of gene flow at levels equal to recent humans between populations of unchanging sizes is without doubt too simple to fully describe the evolution of Pleistocene humans. We have every reason to believe that different human populations have experienced different selective, environmental, and demographic histories. Nevertheless, using the currently available data, as slim as they are in places, we are able to say with confidence that the morphological differences present between Neandertals and other populations are not the result of complete isolation of Europe from other regions. They do not have to be attributed to the genetic isolation of a unique Neandertal lineage. They are compatible with an antiparallelist explanation of selection and genic exchanges, and the results of isolation by distance across the broad range of territories occupied by the human species—in other words, Multiregional evolution.

ACKNOWLEDGMENTS

We thank the curators of the fossil Neandertal remains that we examined for permission to study the specimens in their care. We are grateful to K. Rosenberg, E. Trinkaus, and an anonymous reviewer for helpful comments and suggestions.

LITERATURE CITED

Arsuaga, J. L., I. Martinez, A. Gracia, and C. Lorenzo. 1997. The Sima de los Huesos crania (Sierra de Atapuerca, Spain). A comparative study. J. Hum. Evol. 33:219–281.

Ascenzi, A., I. Biddittu, P. F. Cassoli, A. G. Sergi, and E. Sergi-Naldini. 1996. A calvarium of late *Homo erectus* from Ceprano, Italy. J. Hum. Evol. 31:409–424.

Coon, C. S. 1962. The origin of races. Knopf, New York.

Coutselinis, A., C. Dritsas, and T. Pitsios. 1991. Expertise médicolégale du crâne Pléistocéne LA01/S2 (Apidima II), Apidima, Laconie, Grèce. L'Anthropol. 95:401–408.

Dean, D., J-J. Hublin, R. Holloway, and R. Ziegler. 1998. On the phylogenetic position of the pre-Neandertal specimen from Reilingen, Germany. J. Hum. Evol. 34:485–508.

Falconer, D. S., and T. F. C. Mackay. 1996. Introduction to quantitative genetics. 4th ed. Longman, Essex, U.K.

Frayer, D. W. 1993. Evolution at the European edge: Neanderthal and Upper Paleolithic relationships. Préhistoire Européenne 2:9–69.

Harpending, S., M. A. Batzer, M. Gurven, L. B. Jorde, A. R. Rogers, and S. T. Sherry. 1998. Genetic traces of ancient demography. Proc. Natl. Acad. Sci. USA 95:1961–1967.

Hawks, J., S-H. Lee, K. Hunley, and M. Wolpoff. 2000. Population bottlenecks and Pleistocene human evolution. Mol. Biol. Evol. 17:2–22.

Howell, F. C. 1952. Pleistocene glacial ecology and the evolution of "classic Neandertal" man. Southwest J. Anthropol. 8:377–410.

Hublin, J-J. 1998. Climatic changes, paleogeography, and the evolution of the Neandertals. Pp. 295–310 *in* T. Akazawa, K. Aoki, and O. Bar-Yosef, eds. Neandertals and modern humans in Western Asia. Plenum, New York.

———. 2000. Modern-nonmodern hominid interactions: a Mediterranean perspective. Pp. 157–182 *in* O. Bar-Yosef and D. Pilbeam, eds. The geography of Neandertals and modern humans in Europe and the greater Mediterranean. Peabody Museum of Archaeology and Ethnology, Harvard University, Cambridge, MA. Bulletin no. 8.

Krings, M., A. Stone, R. Schmitz, H. Krainitzid, M. Stoneking, and S. Pääbo. 1997. Neandertal DNA sequences and the origin of modern humans. Cell 90:1–20.

Krings, M., H. Heisert, R. W. Schmitz, H. Krainitzki, and S. Pääbo. 1999. DNA sequence of the mitochondrial hypervariable region II from the Neandertal type specimen. Proc. Natl. Acad. Sci. USA 96:5581–5585.

Lande, R. 1976. Natural selection and random genetic drift in phenotypic evolution. Evolution 30:314–334.

———. 1979. Quantitative genetic analysis of multivariate evolution, applied to brain:body size allometry. Evolution 33:402–416.

Løfsvold, D. 1988. Quantitative genetics of morphological differentiation in *Peromyscus*. II. Analysis of selection and drift. Evolution 42:54–67.

Martínez-Labarga, C., and J. L. Arsuaga. 1997. The temporal bones from Sima de los Huesos Middle Pleistocene site (Sierra de Atapuerca, Spain). A phylogenetic approach. J. Hum. Evol. 33:283–318.

Maureille, B., and F. Houet. 1998. La variabilité morpho-métrique du nez: dérive génique dans la lignée Neandertalienne? Biometr. Hum. Anthropol. 16:27–33.

Mellars, P. A. 1989. Major issues in the emergence of modern humans. Curr. Anthropol. 30:349–385.

Parés, J. M., A. Pérez-González, A. B. Weil, and J-L. Arsuaga. 2000. On the age of the hominid fossils at the Sima de los Huesos, Sierra de Atapuerca, Spain: paleomagnetic evidence. Am. J. Phys. Anthropol. 111:451–461.

Rak, Y., W. H. Kimbel, and E. Hovers 1996. On Neandertal autapomorphies discernible in Neandertal infants: a response to Creed-Miles et al. J. Hum. Evol. 30:155–158.

Relethford, J. H. 1995. Genetics and modern human origins. Evol. Anthropol. 4:53–63.

Rogers, A. R. 1995. How much can fossils tell us about regional continuity? Curr. Anthropol. 36:674–676.

Rogers, A. R., and H. C. Harpending. 1983. Population structure and quantitative characters. Genetics 105:985–1002.

Ruff, C. B., E. Trinkaus, and T. W. Holliday. 1997. Body mass and encephalization in Pleistocene *Homo*. Nature 387:173–176.

Schultz, A. H. 1965. The cranial capacity and orbital volume of hominoids according to age and sex. Homenaje a Juan Comas en su 65 Anniversario, 2. Libros de Mexico, Mexico City.

Stringer, C. B., and J-J. Hublin 1999. New age estimates for the Swanscombe hominid and their significance for human evolution. J. Hum. Evol 37:873–877.

Tattersall, I. 1996. Paleoanthropology and preconception. Pp. 47–54 *in* W. E. Meikle, F. C. Howell, and N. G. Jablonski, eds.

Contemporary issues in human evolution. Wattis Symposium Series in Anthropology, Calif. Acad. Sci. Mem. no. 21.

Templeton, A. 1998. Human races: a genetic and evolutionary perspective. Am. Anthropol. 100:632–650.

Trinkaus, E. 1992. Paleontological perspectives on Neanderthal behavior. Pp. 151–176 *in* M. Toussaint, ed. 5 Millions d'Années, l'Adventure Humaine. Étud. Recher. Archéol. l'Université Liège no. 56.

Vallois, H. V. 1969. Le Temporal Néandertalien H 27 de La Quina. Anthropologie. 73:365–400, 525–544.

Wiley, E. O. 1981. Phylogenetics: the theory and practice of phylogenetic systematics. John Wiley and Sons, New York.

Wolpoff, M. H. 1994. What does it mean to be human—and why does it matter? Evol. Anthropol. 3:116–117.

———. 1999. Paleoanthropology. 2d ed. McGraw-Hill, New York.

Wolpoff, M. H., and R. Caspari. 1997. Race and human evolution. Simon and Schuster, New York.

Wright, S. 1951. The genetical structure of populations. Ann. Eugen. 15:323–354.

Zilhão, J., and F. D'Errico 1999. The chronology and taphonomy of the earliest Aurignacian and its implications for the understanding of Neandertal extinction. J. World Prehist. 13:1–68.

55

Neandertal DNA Sequences and the Origin of Modern Humans

M. Krings, A. Stone, R. W. Schmitz, H. Krainitzki, M. Stoneking, and S. Pääbo

ABSTRACT

DNA was extracted from the Neandertal type specimen found in 1856 in western Germany. By sequencing clones from short overlapping PCR products, a hitherto unknown mitochondrial (mt) DNA sequence was determined. Multiple controls indicate that this sequence is endogenous to the fossil. Sequence comparisons with human mtDNA sequences, as well as phylogenetic analyses, show that the Neandertal sequence falls outside the variation of modern humans. Furthermore, the age of the common ancestor of the Neandertal and modern human mtDNAs is estimated to be four times greater than that of the common ancestor of human mtDNAs. This suggests that Neandertals went extinct without contributing mtDNA to modern humans.

INTRODUCTION

Neandertals are a group of extinct hominids that inhabited Europe and western Asia from about 300,000 to 30,000 years ago. During part of this time they coexisted

Reprinted from *Cell*, Vol. 90, M. Krings et al., Neandertal DNA sequences and the origin of modern humans, pp. 19–30. Copyright © 1997 by Cell Press. Reprinted with permission from Elsevier.

with modern humans. Based on morphological comparisons, it has been variously claimed that Neandertals: (1) were the direct ancestors of modern Europeans; (2) contributed some genes to modern humans; or (3) were completely replaced by modern humans without contributing any genes (reviewed in Stringer and Gamble, 1993; Trinkaus and Shipman, 1993; Bräuer and Stringer, 1997). Analyses of molecular genetic variation in the mitochondrial and nuclear genomes of contemporary human populations have generally supported the third view, i.e., that Neandertals were a separate species that went extinct without contributing genes to modern humans (Cann et al., 1987; Vigilant et al., 1991; Hammer, 1995; Armour et al., 1996; Tishkoff et al., 1996). However, these analyses rely on assumptions, such as the absence of selection and a clock-like rate of molecular evolution in the DNA sequences under study, whose validity has been questioned (Wolpoff, 1989; Templeton, 1992). An additional and more direct way to address the question of the relationship between modern humans and Neandertals would be to analyze DNA sequences from the remains of Neandertals.

The reproducible retrieval of ancient DNA sequences became possible with the invention of the polymerase chain reaction (Mullis and Faloona, 1987; Pääbo et al., 1989). However, theoretical considerations (Pääbo and Wilson, 1991; Lindahl, 1993a), as well as empirical studies (Pääbo, 1989; Höss et al., 1996a), show that DNA in fossil remains is highly affected by hydrolytic as well as oxidative damage. Therefore, the retrieval of DNA sequences older than about 100,000 years is expected to be difficult, if not impossible, to achieve (Pääbo and Wilson, 1991). Fortunately, Neandertal remains fall within the age range that in principle allows DNA sequences to survive. It is noteworthy, though, that even among remains that are younger than 100,000 years most fail to yield amplifiable DNA sequences (Höss et al., 1996b). In addition, contamination of ancient specimens extracts with modern DNA poses a serious problem (Handt et al., 1994a) that requires numerous precautions and controls. This is particularly the case when human remains are studied, since human DNA is the most common source of contamination. Therefore, a number of criteria need to be fulfilled before a DNA sequence determined from extracts of an ancient specimen can be taken to be genuine (Pääbo et al., 1989; Lindahl, 1993b; Handt et al., 1994a; Handt et al., 1996).

Since 1991, the Neandertal-type specimen, found in 1856 near Düsseldorf, Germany, has been the subject of an interdisciplinary project of the Rheinisches Landesmuseum Bonn, initiated and led by R. W. S. (Schmitz et al., 1995; Schmitz, 1996). As a part of this project, a sample was removed from the Neandertal specimen for DNA analysis. Here, we present the sequence of a hypervariable part of the mtDNA control region derived from this sample. We describe the evidence in support of its authenticity and analyze the relationship of this sequence to the contemporary human mtDNA gene pool.

RESULTS

Amino Acid Racemization

A 3.5 g section of the right humerus was removed from the Neandertal fossil (Figure 1). It has previously been shown that ancient specimens exhibiting high levels of amino acid racemization do not contain sufficient DNA

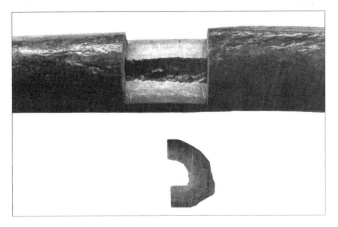

Figure 1. *Sample removed from the right humerus of the Neandertal type specimen.*

for analysis (Poinar et al., 1996). To investigate whether the state of preservation of the fossil is compatible with DNA retrieval, we therefore analyzed the extent of amino acid racemization. Samples of 10 mg were removed from the periostal surface of the bone, from the compact cortical bone, and from the endostal surface of the marrow cavity. Samples were also removed from remnants of a varnish, with which the specimen has been treated at least twice. The samples were hydrolyzed under acid conditions, and the released amino acids were analyzed using high performance liquid chromatography and fluorescent detection (Poinar et al., 1996). Table 1 shows that the total amounts of the amino acids detected in the Neandertal bone are 20%–73% of those in modern bone and more than two orders of magnitude higher than in the varnish, indicating that the results do not reflect the amino acid content of the varnish. Furthermore, the absolute and relative amounts of the amino acids analyzed (e.g., the ratio of glycine to aspartic acid) are similar in the three Neandertal samples and comparable to those of a contemporary bone. Most importantly, the ratio of the D to the L enantiomers of aspartic acid in the three

Table 1. Racemization Results for Three Neandertal Bone Samples, Varnish from the Neandertal Fossil, and Modern Bone

	Periostal Surface	Compact Bone	Endostal Surface	Varnish	Modern Bone
Total (ppm)	23,167	83,135	53,888	145	113,931
Aspartic acid (%)	7.8	8.3	7.4	10	8.3
Serine (%)	0.7	0.7	0.7	2	0.6
Glutamic acid (%)	20.2	20.1	20.2	22	19.9
Glycine (%)	49.5	49.0	50.2	22	51.8
Alanine (%)	14.4	14.0	14.0	11	11.1
Valine (%)	3.5	3.9	3.9	23	3.9
Isoleucine (%)	0.5	0.5	0.6	1	0.7
Leucine (%)	3.4	3.3	3.2	9	3.6
Glycine/aspartic acid	6.3	5.9	6.8	2.1	6.2
D/L aspartic acid	0.117	0.114	0.110	ND	0.05
D/L alanine	0.006	0.007	0.004	0.08	0.01
D/L leucine	0.005	ND	ND	ND	ND

Comparison of the amino acid analysis of the Neandertal bone, varnish removed from the bone surface, and a two-year-old bone sample. Given are the total amounts of the amino acids analyzed (ppm, parts per million), the amino acid compositions in percentages of the eight amino acids analyzed, and the D/L-ratios for three amino acids. ND, no detectable D form.

Neandertal samples varies between 0.11 and 0.12, which is in the range compatible with DNA survival (Poinar et al., 1996). Thus, the extent of amino acid racemization in the Neandertal fossil suggests that it may contain amplifiable DNA.

DNA Extraction and Amplification

DNA was extracted from 0.4 g of the cortical compact bone. Previous experience shows that ancient DNA tends to be degraded and damaged to an extent that makes amplification of segments of mtDNA longer than 100–200 bp difficult (Pääbo, 1989). Therefore, two primers (L16,209, H16,271) that amplify a 105-bp-segment of the human mtDNA control region (including primers) were used to perform amplifications from the bone extract as well as from an extraction control. An amplification product was obtained in the bone extract but not in the control (data not shown). In a subsequent experiment, this was repeated and the same results were obtained.

Sequence Variation of the Amplification Product

The two amplification products were cloned in a plasmid vector and 18 and 12 clones, respectively, were sequenced (Figure 2, extract A). Twenty-two of the 30 clones contained seven nucleotide substitutions and one insertion of an adenine residue, when compared to the standard human reference sequence (Anderson et al., 1981). Three of these eight differences to the reference sequence were individually lacking in a total of five of the clones. In addition, among the 27 clones were nine differences that each occurred in one clone, three differences that occurred in two clones and one that occurred in three clones, respectively. Such changes that are present in only a few clones are likely to be due to misincorporations by the DNA polymerase during PCR, possibly compounded by damage in the template DNA. In addition, some of these could be due to mitochondrial heteroplasmy, which may be more common in humans than often assumed (Comas et al., 1995; Ivanov et al., 1996) and is abundant in some mammalian species (Petri et al., 1996). Of the remaining three clones, two were identical to the reference sequence, and the third clone differed from the reference sequence at one position.

Thus, the amplification product was composed of two classes of sequences, a minor class represented by three clones that is similar to the human reference sequence, and another class represented by 27 clones that exhibits substantial differences from it. The former class of molecules probably reflects contamination of the specimen, which is likely to have occurred during handling and treatment of the specimen during the 140 years since its discovery. The other class of sequences is not obviously of modern origin. Further experiments were therefore performed to determine if this class is endogenous to the Neandertal fossil.

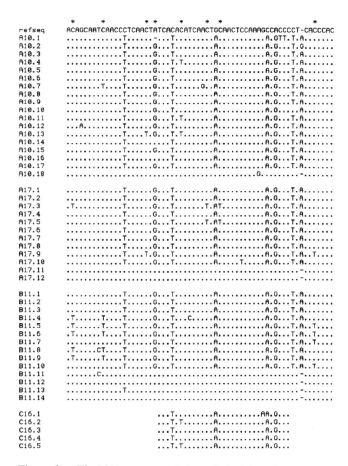

Figure 2. *The DNA sequences of clones derived from four amplifications of the mitochondrial control region from the Neandertal fossil.*

Dots indicate identity to a human reference sequence (Anderson et al., 1981) given above. The clone designations consist of a letter (A, B, C) indicating the DNA extract followed by a number indicating the amplification reaction, as well as a number after the period identifying the particular clone. Extracts A and B were performed at the University of Munich; extract C, at Penn State University. Clones derived from different amplifications are separated by a blank line. Asterisks identify sequence positions where more than one clone differs from the majority of sequences. For the three upper amplifications (performed at the University of Munich) primers L16,209 (5'-CCC CAT GCT TAC AAG CAA GT-3') and H16,271 (5'-GTG GGT AGG TTT GTT GGT ATC CTA-3') were used. For the bottom amplification (performed at Penn State University) the primers NL16,230 (5'-GCA CAG CAA TCA ACC TTC AAC TG-3') and NH16,262 (5'-GTA GAT TTG TTG ATA TCC TAG TGG GTG TAA-3') were used.

Quantitation of Putative Neandertal DNA

Amplifications that start from more than 1000 ancient template molecules tend to yield reproducible results, while amplifications starting from fewer molecules tend to yield results that vary between experiments, due to misincorporations during the early cycles of the PCR as well as due to sporadic contamination (Handt et al., 1996). Therefore, the number of template molecules representing the putative Neandertal sequence in the extract was determined by quantitative PCR. To this end, a molecule representing the putative Neandertal sequence but carrying a 12 bp deletion was

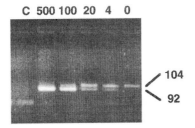

Figure 3. *Quantitation of the putative Neandertal mtDNA.*

A dilution series of a competitor construct carrying the putative Neandertal sequence with a 12 bp deletion was added to 2.5 μl of extract A from the fossil. Primers used were specific for the putative Neandertal sequence. Above the lanes, the approximate numbers of cd LWcompetitor molecules added are indicated. The control amplification (C) contained neither competitor nor Neandertal extract.

constructed. To each step in a dilution series of this construct, a constant amount of extract was added and amplifications were performed using primers that are specific for a 104 bp product of the putative Neandertal sequence and that do not amplify contemporary human sequences. The results (Figure 3) show that on the order of 10 putative Neandertal molecules exist per microliter of extract and thus that amplifications starting from 5 μl of extract are initiated from approximately 50 template molecules. However, due to variation in the efficiency of individual primer pairs, and stochastic variation in the number of template molecules added to an individual amplification, some amplifications may start from fewer (or even single) molecules. This makes nucleotide misincorporations in early cycles of the amplification reaction likely to affect a large proportion of the molecules in the final amplification product. Such misincorporations may be frequent since the template molecules are likely to carry miscoding base modifications (Höss et al., 1996a). To detect this type of sequence change, amplifications were performed such that each sequence position to be determined was covered by at least two independent PCR reactions. The products of each PCR reaction were independently cloned and the sequences determined from multiple clones.

Authenticity of Sequences

The inadvertent amplification of small amounts of contemporary DNA is a major source of erroneous results in the study of ancient DNA sequences (Pääbo et al., 1989; Lindahl, 1993b; Handt et al., 1994a). Such contamination may result in the amplification of not only contemporary organellar mtDNA but also of nuclear insertions of mtDNA (Collura and Stewart, 1995; van der Kuyl et al., 1995; Zischler et al., 1995). Several experiments were performed in order to exclude modern DNA, including a nuclear insertion of mtDNA, as the source of the putative Neandertal sequence.

Since nuclear insertions are less numerous than mitochondrial genomes in the organelles, any single insertion sequence is expected to represent a major proportion of an amplification product only in cases where a primer favors the amplification of an insertion sequence over the corresponding mtDNA sequence. This occurs when mismatches to the primer in the mtDNA make the priming of an insertion more efficient than that of the organellar mtDNA (Handt et al., 1996). Therefore, the preferential amplification of an insertion sequence is expected to be restricted to a particular primer. In order to elucidate whether the putative Neandertal sequence is seen only when a particular primer is used, primers were exchanged such that first the 5′ primer was replaced by a primer located outside the previous amplification product (L16,122), and 13 clones of this amplification product were sequenced (Figure 4, clones A7.1–13). All 13 clones showed the same eight differences from the reference sequence that were previously observed, as well as nine differences in the region that was not included in the earlier amplification. In addition, one difference was observed in one clone, as well as length variation in a homopolymer of cytosine residues, previously described to be of variable length in humans (Bendall and Sykes, 1995).

The 3′-primer from the first amplification was then replaced by a primer (H16,379) located outside the initial amplification product, and 13 clones of this amplification product were sequenced (Figure 5, clones A12.1–13). All 13 clones contained the same eight differences in the region overlapping the previous amplifications, as well as seven differences in the region not covered in the previous amplifications. In addition, two substitutions and one deletion occurred in one clone, and one other substitution occurred in a different clone. Furthermore, in a subsequent amplification from another extract where both primers (L16,254-H16,379) differed from the initial amplification, all four differences located in the segment included in the first amplifications were observed in all 8 clones sequenced (Figure 5, clones B13.1–8). Thus, the retrieval of the putative Neandertal sequence is not dependent on the primers used. Furthermore, most primer combinations yield a large excess of clones representing the putative Neandertal sequence over clones similar to contemporary human mtDNA.

To further exclude the possibility that the sequence may represent a nuclear insertion, primers for the putative Neandertal sequence were constructed that do not amplify human mtDNA. In control experiments where various amounts of a cloned copy of the putative Neandertal sequence were mixed with human DNA, these primers were able to detect about 20 copies of the cloned sequence in 50 ng of total human DNA, i.e., less than one copy per genome equivalent (data not shown). When these primers were used to amplify DNA isolated from 15 Africans, 6 Europeans, and 2 Asians, no amplification products were obtained (data not shown), indicating that this sequence is not present in the genome of modern humans.

To test whether the extraction and amplification of the putative Neandertal sequence is reproducible, an additional independent DNA extraction was performed from 0.4 g of the bone. When the primers L16,209 and H16,271 were used in an amplification from this extract

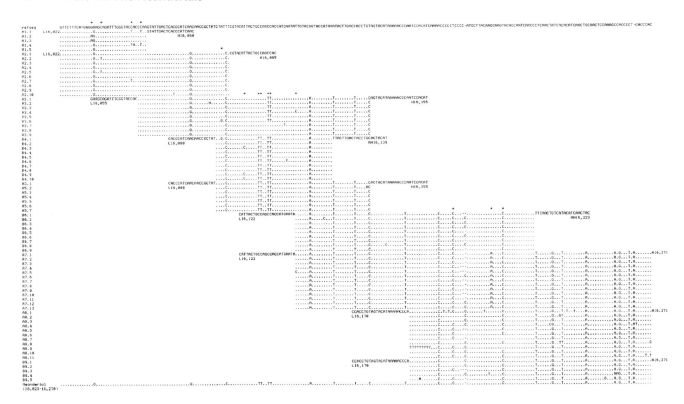

Figure 4. *The DNA sequences of clones used to infer the sequence of the hypervariable region 1 of the Neandertal individual.*

Above, the modern human reference sequence (Anderson et al., 1981) is given, below the sequence inferred for the Neandertal individual, numbered according to the reference sequence. The designations and sequences of primers used (reversed and complemented when the letter H occurs in the designations) are given for the first clone of each amplification, except for primers L16,022 (5'-CTA AGA TTC TAA TTT AAA CTA TTC CTC T-3') and H16,401 (5'-TGA TTT CAC GGA GGA TGG TG 3'). For primers L16,209 and H16,271 and further details, see legend to Figure 2. Ambiguities in the sequencing reactions are indicated by standard abbreviations.

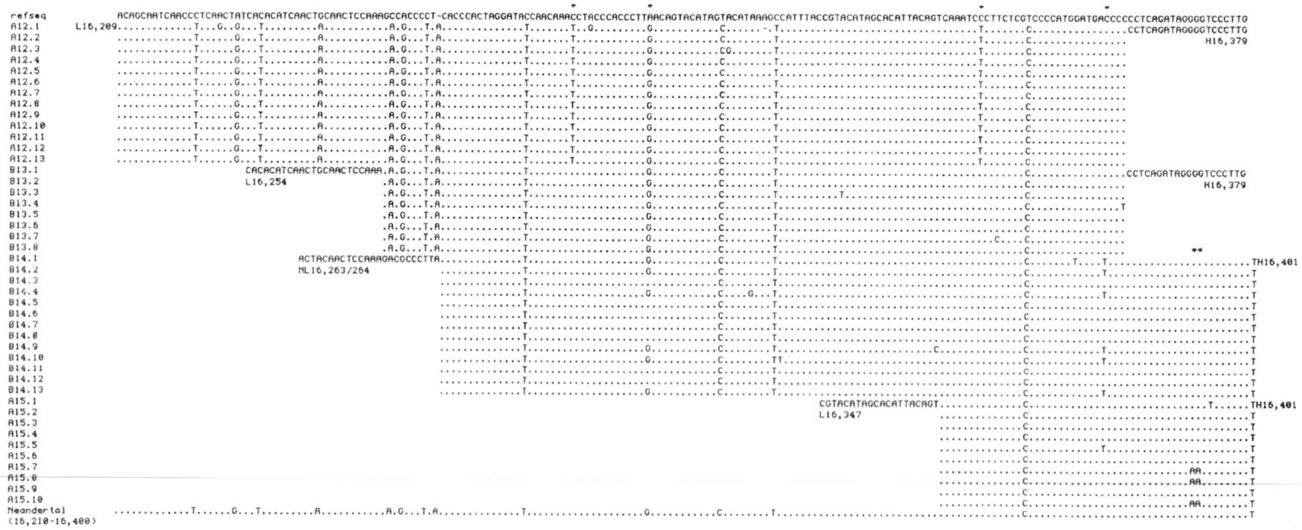

Figure 5. *The DNA sequences of clones used to infer the sequence of the hypervariable region 1 of the Neandertal individual.*

Above, the modern human reference sequence (Anderson et al., 1981) is given, below the sequence inferred for the Neandertal individual, numbered according to the reference sequence. The designations and sequences of primers used (reversed and complemented when the letter H occurs in the designations) are given for the first clone of each amplification, except for primers L16,022 (5'-CTA AGA TTC TAA TTT AAA CTA TTC CTC T-3') and H16,401 (5'-TGA TTT CAC GGA GGA TGG TG-3'). For primers L16,209 and H16,271 and further details, see legend to Figure 2. Ambiguities in the sequencing reactions are indicated by standard abbreviations.

and the product cloned (Figure 2, extract B), ten clones carried the eight differences from the reference sequence observed in the amplifications from the first extract, as well as two changes affecting single clones. In addition, three sequence positions carried changes occurring in five and four clones. These changes were not observed in combination in the previous four amplifications covering this sequence segment. Since they occurred in only one amplification product, they are probably due to polymerase errors in the early cycles of the PCR, possibly compounded by in vitro recombination induced by damage and degradation of template DNA molecules (Pääbo et al., 1990). Four clones were similar to the human reference sequence. Thus, although the amplification products clearly derive from few template molecules, the putative Neandertal sequence is present in a DNA extract independently prepared from the fossil.

To further investigate whether the results are due to laboratory-specific artifacts or contamination, an additional bone sample of 0.4g was sent to the Anthropological Genetics Laboratory at Pennsylvania State University where a DNA extraction was performed. When the primers (L16,209 and H16,271), which had previously resulted in a product that contained both the putative Neandertal sequence and contemporary human mtDNA sequences (Figure 2) were used in amplifications from this extract, 15 of the resulting clones yielded a DNA sequence that was identical to the experimenter (A. S.), while two yielded sequences that differed by one and two substitutions from the reference sequence, respectively. However, when primers specific for the putative Neandertal sequence (NL16,230 and NH16,262) were used, 5 out of 5 clones yielded the putative Neandertal sequence (Figure 2, extract C). Thus, while this third independent extract contains a larger amount of contemporary human DNA, probably stemming from laboratory contamination, it confirms that the putative Neandertal sequence is present in the fossil specimen.

In summary, these experiments indicate that the putative Neandertal sequence does not originate from a nuclear mtDNA insertion and that it is endogenous to the fossil. It furthermore falls outside the variation of the mtDNA gene pool of modern humans (see below). We therefore conclude that it is derived from the mitochondrial genome of the Neandertal individual.

Determination of the Neandertal mtDNA Sequence

The entire sequence of hypervariable region I of the mtDNA control region (positions 16,023 to 16,400; Anderson et al., 1981) was determined. Since the state of preservation of the DNA allowed only short fragments to be amplified, this was achieved by several overlapping amplifications. Furthermore, since the quantitation experiments indicated that some amplifications might start from single molecules, and thus that misincorporations in early cycles of the amplification might be misinterpreted as sequence differences (Handt et al., 1996), all sequence positions were determined from at least two independent amplifications. At five sequence positions, two amplifications yielded discordant results, i.e., all clones in one amplification differed at a position from all clones in another amplification. For these positions, clones from at least one more independent amplification were sequenced. In all cases, all clones from the subsequent amplification products carried one of the two bases at the five positions in question. At 23 positions, differences were found between two or more clones, either within one amplification or in different amplifications. In those cases, the sequence present in the majority of clones was scored. Figures 4 and 5 show how 123 clones from 13 amplifications were used to determine 379 bp from the Neandertal individual.

Sequence Comparisons

When the Neandertal DNA sequence is compared to the human reference sequence, 27 differences are seen outside the heteroplasmic cytosine homopolymer (Bendall and Sykes, 1995) (Figure 4). Of these 27 differences, 24 are transitions, two are transversions, and one represents an insertion of a single adenosine residue.

The Neandertal sequence was compared to a collection of 2051 human and 59 common chimpanzee sequences over 360 bp of the sequence determined from the Neandertal (positions 16,024 to 16,383). Among the 27 nucleotide differences to the reference sequence found in this segment, 25 fall among the 225 positions that vary in at least one of the human sequences, and one of the two remaining positions varies among the chimpanzees. Thus, the types of differences observed (e.g., an excess of transitions over transversions), and the positions in the Neandertal sequence where they occur, reflect the evolutionary pattern typical of mtDNA sequences of extant humans and chimpanzees.

The Neandertal sequence was compared to 994 contemporary human mitochondrial lineages, i.e., distinct sequences occurring in one or more individuals, found in 478 Africans, 510 Europeans, 494 Asians, 167 Native Americans and 20 individuals from Australia and Oceania (S. Meyer, personal communication). Whereas these modern human sequences differ among themselves by an average of 8.0 ± 3.1 (range 1–24) substitutions, the difference between the humans and the Neandertal sequence is 27.2 ± 2.2 (range 22–36) substitutions. Thus, the largest difference observed between any two human sequences was two substitutions larger than the smallest difference between a human and the Neandertal. In total, 0.002% of the pairwise comparisons between human mtDNA sequences were larger than the smallest difference between the Neandertal and a human.

The Neandertal sequence, when compared to the mitochondrial lineages from different continents, differs by 28.2 ± 1.9 substitutions from the European lineages, 27.1 ± 2.2 substitutions from the African lineages, 27.7 ± 2.1 substitutions from the Asian lineages, 27.4 ± 1.8 substitutions from the American lineages and 28.3 ± 3.7 substitutions from the Australian/Oceanic lineages. Thus, whereas the Neandertals inhabited the same geographic region as contemporary Europeans, the

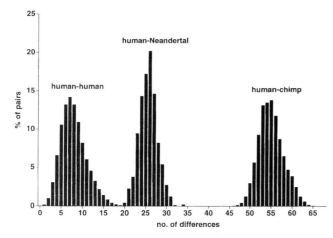

Figure 6. *Distributions of pairwise sequence differences among humans, the Neandertal, and chimpanzees.*

X axis, the number of sequence differences; Y axis, the percent of pairwise comparisons.

observed differences between the Neandertal sequence and modern Europeans do not indicate that it is more closely related to modern Europeans than to any other population of contemporary humans.

When the comparison was extended to 16 common chimpanzee lineages (Figure 6), the number of positions in common among the human and chimpanzee sequences was reduced to 333 (Morin et al., 1994). This reduced the number of human lineages to 986. The average number of differences among humans is 8.0 ± 3.0 (range 1–24), that between humans and the Neandertal, 25.6 ± 2.2 (range 20–34), and that between humans and chimpanzees, 55.0 ± 3.0 (range 46–67). Thus, the average number of mtDNA sequence differences between modern humans and the Neandertal is about three times that among humans, but about half of that between modern humans and modern chimpanzees.

An insertion of a portion of the mitochondrial control region on chromosome 11 has been inferred to represent an outgroup to the modern human mtDNA gene pool (Zischler et al., 1995). When its sequence was compared to the human and Neandertal sequences, 294 positions could be compared and the number of human lineages was reduced to 970. In this case, the differences between humans and the Neandertal sequence are 25.5 ± 2.1 (range 20–34) whereas between humans and the insertion sequence there are 21.3 ± 1.7 (range 16–27) differences. Thus, although the distributions of the distances overlap, they suggest that the insertion of a portion of the mtDNA control region to chromosome 11 may have occurred after the divergence of the Neandertal and modern human mtDNA gene pools. This is compatible with the notion that the Neandertal sequence diverged from the lineage leading to the current human mtDNA gene pool well before the time of the most recent common ancestor of human mtDNAs.

Phylogenetic Analyses

To further investigate the relationship of the Neandertal mtDNA sequence to contemporary human

mtDNA variation, phylogenetic tree reconstructions were performed. A neighbor-joining tree (Saitou and Nei, 1987) of the 16 chimpanzee lineages, the Neandertal sequence, and the 986 human lineages was constructed (Figure 7a). This tree shows the Neandertal sequence diverging prior to the divergence of the human mtDNA lineages. To estimate the support for this relationship, a likelihood mapping statistic (Strimmer and von Haeseler, 1997) was used. In this analysis, all possible quartets involving the Neandertal sequence, one of the chimpanzee lineages, and two representatives out of 100 human lineages (randomly selected from the 986 human lineages) were analyzed, and the likelihoods for the three possible groupings of the Neandertal, chimpanzee, and human sequences were plotted for each quartet. An example of this analysis is shown in Figure 7b. A different random subset of 100 human lineages was then chosen and the analysis repeated; in 40 such analyses, an average of 89% (range 84%–93%) of the quartets grouped the two human sequences together. Thus, the phylogenetic analyses agree with the pairwise comparisons of sequence differences in placing the Neandertal mtDNA sequence outside the variation of modern human mtDNA.

Age of the Neandertal/Modern Human mtDNA Ancestor

To estimate the time when the most recent ancestral sequence common to the Neandertal and modern human mtDNA sequences existed, we used an estimated divergence date between humans and chimpanzees of 4–5 million years ago (Takahata et al., 1995) and corrected the observed sequence differences for multiple substitutions at the same nucleotide site (Tamura and Nei, 1993). This yielded a date of 550,000 to 690,000 years before present for the divergence of the Neandertal mtDNA and contemporary human mtDNAs. When the age of the modern human mtDNA ancestor is estimated using the same procedure, a date of 120,000 to 150,000 years is obtained, in agreement with previous estimates (Cann et al., 1987; Vigilant et al., 1991). Although these dates rely on the calibration point of the chimpanzee–human divergence and have errors of unknown magnitude associated with them, they indicate that the age of the common ancestor of the Neandertal sequence and modern human sequences is about four times greater than that of the common ancestor of modern human mtDNAs.

Rooting of Modern Human mtDNA Gene Pool

The phylogenetic tree (Figure 7a) shows the first three human branches to be composed of seven African mtDNA sequences, with the first non-African sequences appearing only in the fourth branch. This branching pattern would indicate that the ancestor of the mtDNA gene pool of contemporary humans lived in Africa (cf. von Haeseler et al., 1996). When the statistical support for these branches was assessed with the likelihood mapping approach using the Neandertal sequence as an outgroup, these three branches were supported by

a

b

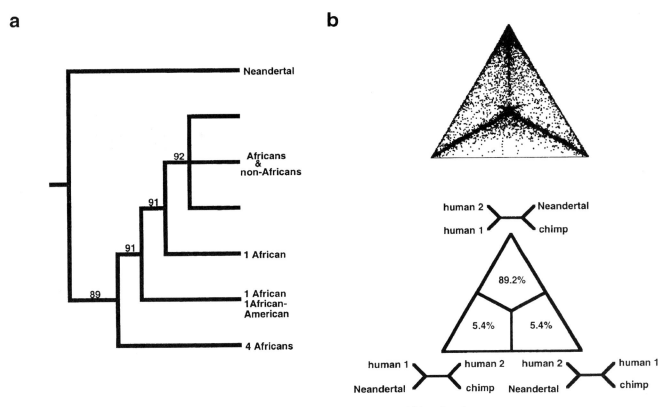

Figure 7. *A schematic phylogenetic tree relating the Neandertal mtDNA sequence to 986 modern human mtDNA sequences and likelihood mapping analysis showing the support for various groupings of Neandertal, human, and chimpanzee sequences.*

(a) The tree was rooted with 16 chimpanzee mtDNA lineages. For clarity, only the first five branches without their internal branching structures but with their geographical states are shown. Numbers on internal branches refer to quartet puzzling probabilities. To calculate these, all possible combinations of the Neandertal sequence, one of 16 chimpanzee lineages, and two of 100 lineages chosen at random from among 986 human lineages were analyzed.

(b) For each such quartet of sequences, the likelihoods for each of the three possible phylogenetic arrangements are plotted in a triangle (b, upper panel) where the tips indicate absolute support for one of the arrangements (b, lower panel). The percentage of the quartets favoring the grouping of the Neandertal sequence with the chimpanzee to the exclusion of the two human lineages is found in the upper of the three areas. A total of 40 such analyses with different random sets of human mtDNA lineages were carried out and the average of these is given in the tree. The other internal branches were similarly analyzed.

91%, 91%, and 92% of quartets, respectively. When the seven African sequences in the first three branches were tested together with the 684 non-African lineages in the database and the Neandertal sequence, they grouped with the latter in 97% of all quartets analyzed. Thus, overall, the results suggest an African origin of the human mtDNA gene pool, as has been claimed when chimpanzee sequences (Vigilant et al., 1991; Hedges et al., 1992) and a nuclear insertion of the mitochondrial control region (Zischler et al., 1995) were used in similar analyses.

DISCUSSION

DNA Preservation in the Neandertal Fossil

Based on its "classical" morphology, the undated Neandertal fossil is thought to be between 30,000 and 100,000 years old (Stringer and Gamble, 1993). It is thus among the oldest specimens for which the chemical stability of DNA would seem to allow for the retrieval of endogenous DNA (Pääbo and Wilson, 1991; Lindahl, 1993a). Furthermore, the extent of amino acid racemization indicates that preservation conditions of the Neandertal fossil have been compatible with DNA preservation (Poinar et al., 1996). In agreement with this, the quantitation shows that an extract of 0.4 g of bone contains about 1000–1500 Neandertal mtDNA molecules of length 100 bp. Thus, mitochondrial DNA sequences can be retrieved from the fossil. However, this result also indicates that single-copy nuclear DNA sequences, which are a hundred- to a thousand-fold less abundant than mtDNA in most cells, would be impossible to reproducibly amplify from the extracts. This is reminiscent of the situation in most other archaeological remains (e.g., Handt et al., 1994b, 1996).

Several factors complicate the determination of mtDNA sequences from the Neandertal fossil. The low number of preserved mtDNA molecules poses problems since misincorporations during the initial cycles of the amplification will become represented in a large fraction of the molecules in the final amplification product. Such misincorporations may be particularly likely in the case of ancient DNA, which often contains lesions that can enhance misincorporations (Höss et al., 1996a). In addition, the Neandertal extracts contain sequences that are probably derived from contemporary humans. This is not unexpected since the specimen has been extensively handled during 140 years. A further complication is that exogenous as well as endogenous molecules, both sometimes carrying substitutions from early cycles of the amplification, may recombine with each other during the amplification process. Such "jumping PCR" is induced by strand breaks and DNA damage and may itself introduce sequence changes (Pääbo et al., 1990).

Fortunately, neither misincorporations nor jumping phenomena are expected to show a great specificity for certain sequence positions. Therefore, even when an amplification starts from a single molecule and an error occurs in the first cycle of the PCR such that it becomes represented in all resulting molecules, one will be alerted to the problem if two independent amplifications are analyzed since they will yield different sequences. A third amplification can then be analyzed to determine which of the two sequences is reproducible and hence authentic. Taken together, the results (Figures 4 and 5) show that misincorporations are a fairly frequent phenomenon in the Neandertal extracts, contributing to variation seen at 64 of the 378 sequence positions determined. Furthermore, some amplifications start from very few or single molecules since amplifications yielded completely discordant results at five positions. In contrast, jumping PCR, which is a frequent phenomenon in extracts of some ancient specimens (Handt et al., 1994b), does not seem to play a major role in the case of the Neandertal fossil, although some clones (Figure 2, extract B) are likely to be the result of this process.

Implications for Modern Human Origins

Both pairwise sequence comparisons and phylogenetic analyses tend to place the Neandertal mtDNA sequence outside modern human mtDNA variation. Furthermore, the divergence between the Neandertal mtDNA sequence and the modern human mitochondrial gene pool is estimated to be about four-fold older than the diversity of the modern human mtDNA gene pool. This shows that the diversity among Neandertal mtDNA sequences would have to be at least four times larger than among modern humans in order for other Neandertal sequences to be ancestral to modern human sequences. Thus, although based on a single Neandertal sequence, the present results indicate that Neandertals did not contribute mtDNA to modern humans.

These results do not rule out the possibility that Neandertals contributed other genes to modern humans. However, the view that Neandertals would have contributed little or nothing to the modern human gene pool is gaining support from studies of molecular

genetic variation at nuclear loci in humans (Hammer, 1995; Armour et al., 1996; Tishkoff et al., 1996). It is also in agreement with assessments of the degree of morphological difference between Neandertal skeletal remains and modern humans (e.g., Rak, 1993; Zollikofer et al., 1995; Hublin et al., 1996; Schwartz and Tattersall, 1996) that would classify Neandertals and modern humans as separate species.

Given the placement of the Neandertal mtDNA sequence outside the range of modern human mtDNA variation, it can be used as an outgroup in phylogenetic analyses to assess the geographic origin of the human mtDNA ancestor. Initial claims that Africa was the most likely geographic source of contemporary human mtDNA variation (Cann et al., 1987; Vigilant et al., 1991) were challenged by subsequent reanalyses that found the original phylogenetic analyses to be inadequate (Maddison, 1991; Templeton, 1992; Hedges et al., 1992). However, new methods of phylogenetic analysis have continued to support an African origin of human mtDNA variation (Penny et al., 1995), as has the use of a nuclear mtDNA insertion as an outgroup (Zischler et al., 1995). When the Neandertal mtDNA sequence is used to root a neighbor joining tree of modern human mtDNA sequences (Figure 7a), the first three branches consist exclusively of African sequences. The Neandertal mtDNA sequence thus supports a scenario in which modern humans arose recently in Africa as a distinct species and replaced Neandertals with little or no interbreeding.

Implications for Neandertal Genetics

It is interesting to compare the mtDNA date for the divergence between Neandertals and modern humans of 550,000 to 690,000 years ago with dates derived from other sources of information. For example, the fossil record indicates a likely minimum date for the divergence between modern humans and Neandertals of 250,000–300,000 years (Stringer, 1998), while the archaeological record also puts the divergence between modern humans and Neandertals at about 300,000 years (Foley and Lahr, 1997). A date of over 500,000 years for the molecular divergence between Neandertal and human mtDNAs is in excellent agreement with the palaeontological and archaeological record since the divergence of genes is expected to predate the divergence of populations by an amount that reflects the level of polymorphism in the ancestral species (Nei, 1987). Thus, if the palaeontological and archaeological estimates for the divergence of the Neandertal and human populations are accurate, and the mtDNA estimate for the molecular divergence is also accurate, this would indicate that the diversity of the mtDNA gene pool in the ancestral species (presumably *Homo erectus*) from which Neandertals and humans evolved, was at least as great as that of modern humans.

It must be emphasized that the above conclusions are based on a single individual sequence; the retrieval and analysis of mtDNA sequences from additional Neandertal specimens is obviously desirable. If this proves possible, then the potential exists to address several questions concerning Neandertals that hitherto could be studied exclusively by morphological and archaeological approaches. For example, the genetic relationship between Neandertal populations in Europe and in western Asia could be explored, as could the demographic history of Neandertal populations, using methods that have been applied to investigate the demographic history of modern human populations (Harpending et al., 1993; von Haeseler et al., 1996).

A Cautionary Note

Remains of animals found in association with Neandertal remains in other parts of Europe have failed to yield amplifiable DNA and/or display levels of amino acid racemization that make the prospect of retrieving DNA bleak (A. Cooper and H. Poinar, personal communication). It is therefore possible that the type specimen may be fairly unique in containing amplifiable endogenous DNA. Thus, we strongly recommend that valuable Neandertal specimens should not be subjected to destructive sampling before the analysis of associated animal fossils, and/or the application of some other method that requires minimal destruction of specimens (such as amino acid racemization), has yielded evidence that DNA may survive in the fossil.

EXPERIMENTAL PROCEDURES

Sampling

Protective clothing was worn throughout the sampling procedure. Instruments used were treated with 1 M HCl followed by extensive rinsing in distilled water. After removal, the sample was immediately put into a sterile tube for transport to Munich. All subsequent manipulations of the sample, and experimental procedures prior to cycling of PCR reactions, were carried out in laboratories solely dedicated to the analysis of archaeological specimens, where protective clothing, separate equipment and reagents, UV irradiation, and other measures to minimize contamination are used routinely.

Amino Acid Analysis

Samples of 10 mg of bone powder and varnish were removed by drilling and were hydrolyzed in 1 ml 6 N HCl at 100°C for 24 hr. The hydrolysates were processed and analysed by reverse phase HPLC as described (Poinar et al., 1996). Amounts of the amino acid enantiomers were determined by comparison to standards after subtraction of the amino acid content determined in a negative control processed in parallel with the samples.

DNA Extraction

Bone pieces were removed using a drill saw. Subsequently, the surface of the pieces was removed with a grinding bit and furthermore treated by soaking in a 10% solution of NaClO for 10 s, and rinsing in double-distilled and UV-irradiated H_2O. The samples were then ground to powder in a Spex Mill (Edison, NJ) filled with liquid nitrogen. The powder was incubated in 1 ml of 0.5 M EDTA (pH 8.0), 5% sarkosyl on a rotary wheel at ambient temperature for ~40 hr. Ten microliters of proteinase K (10 mg/ml) were then added and the incubation continued at 37°C for another 40 hr. Tissue remains were removed by centrifugation and the supernatant extracted with phenol, phenol/chloroform, and chloroform/isoamyl alcohol as described (Ausubel et al., 1995). The aquaeous phase was concentrated by centrifugal dialysis using Microcon-30 microconcentrators (Amicon, Beverly, MA) and incubated with 40 μl silica suspension in 1 ml of 5 M guanidinium isothiocyanate, 0.1 M Tris-HCl (pH 7.4) for 15 min on a rotary wheel at ambient temperature as described (Höss and Pääbo, 1993). The silica was collected by centrifugation and washed twice with 1 ml 70% ethanol and once with 1 ml acetone, prior to air-drying. DNA was eluted into two aliquots of 65 μl TE (pH 8.0) at 56°C. The eluates were pooled, aliquoted, and stored at −20°C. An extraction control to which no bone powder was added was processed in parallel with each sample extraction.

PCR, Cloning, and Sequencing

A lower reaction mixture of 10 μl (67 mM Tris-HCl [pH 8.8], 2 mM $MgCl_2$, 2 mg/ml BSA, 2 μM of each primer and 0.25 mM of each dNTP) was separated prior to the first denaturation step by a wax layer from a 10 μl upper mixture (67 mM Tris-HCl [pH 8.8], 2 mM $MgCl_2$, 0.375 units Taq DNA polymerase [Perkin Elmer, Cetus], 5 μl bone extract). Forty cycles of PCR (15 s at 92°C, 1 min at 55°C or 60°C, 1 min at 72°C) were carried out in an MJ research PTC 200 cycler. Ten microliters of the reactions was electrophoresed in 3% agarose gels, stained with ethidium bromide, and visualized by UV transillumination. The bands, as well as the corresponding areas of the lanes where control amplifications were electrophoresed, were cut out of the gels, melted in 100 μl double-distilled H_2O and shock frozen in liquid nitrogen. After thawing during centrifugation, 5 μl of the supernatant was used in 50 μl amplification reactions (67 mM Tris-HCl [pH 8.8], 2 mM $MgCl_2$, 1 mg/ml BSA, 1 μM of each primer, 0.125 mM of each dNTP, 0.75 units Taq DNA polymerase). Thirty cycles identical to the initial amplification, except for an increase of 3°C in annealing temperature, were performed. If primer dimers or nonspecific bands were visible upon gel electrophoresis, reamplification products were gel purified prior to cloning. Alternatively, 10 μl of the reamplification volume were directly treated with T4 DNA polymerase (New England Biolabs) according to the supplier's protocol and ligated into a SmaI-cut pUC18 (Pharmacia Biotech, Uppsala, Sweden) vector in the presence of 10 units of SmaI at ambient temperature for 16 hr. E. coli SURE (Stratagene, La Jolla, CA) were transformed by electroporation using half of the ligation and grown in 1 ml SOC medium (Ausubel et al., 1995) for 20–25 min before plating on selective IPTG/X-gal agar plates.

White colonies were transferred into 12.5 μl PCR reactions (contents as in reamplifications) with "M13 universal" and "M13 reverse" primers. After 5 min at 92°C, 30 cycles of PCR (30 s at 90°C, 1 min at 50°C, 1 min at 72°C) were carried out and clones with inserts of the expected size were identified by agarose gel electrophoresis. Of these PCR products, 1.5 μl was sequenced with the Thermo Sequenase kit (Amersham, UK) according to the supplier's instructions, and half of the sequencing reactions were loaded onto a 6.5% denaturing polyacrylamide gel and analysed on an A.L.F. automated sequencer (Pharmacia Biotech, Uppsala, Sweden).

Quantitative PCR

A competitor standard was constructed (Förster, 1994; Handt et al., 1996) and cloned into pUC18. This molecule matches the Neandertal mtDNA sequence from base 16,190 to 16,290 but lacks 12 bases (16,210 to 16,221). The plasmid was purified from an overnight culture by alkaline lysis (Ausubel et al., 1995) and the DNA concentration determined by UV absorbance at 260/280 nm. The standard and Neandertal DNA extracts were used in amplifications with two primers (NL16,209: 5'-CCC CAT GCT TAC AAG CAA GC-3', NH16,262: 5'-GTA GAT TTG TTG ATA TCC TAG TGG GTG TAA-3') specific for the Neandertal sequence.

Sequence Analyses

In total, 27 amplifications of the mtDNA control region were performed from the Neandertal specimen. Of these, twelve amplifications yielded exclusively Neandertal sequences, whereas 6 amplifications contained sequences similar to the contemporary human reference sequence as well as Neandertal sequences. Figures 2, 4, and 5 give all Neandertal sequences determined except those from the quantitation reaction (Figure 3). In addition, 9 amplifications yielded exclusively sequences similar to the human reference sequence (not shown). In these cases, the primers used turned out to have one to four mismatches to the Neandertal sequence and thus to select against the latter. The Neandertal sequence was inferred using the sequences shown in Figures 2, 4, and 5.

The Neandertal sequence was compared to an mtDNA sequence database (S. Meyer, personal communication). Except for the scoring of variable positions, only human sequences where no insertions, deletions, or ambiguities occur were used. In the case of the 16 chimpanzee lineages, four are reported (Morin et al., 1994) with an ambiguity at position 16,049, and one each with ambiguities at positions 16,063 and 16,064. Pairwise sequence differences were determined using unpublished software by A. von Haeseler. Maximum likelihood distances and phylogenetic trees were computed using the PHYLIP package, version 3.5 (Felsenstein, 1994), assuming a transition/transversion ratio of 20. Support for internal branches was tested by likelihood mapping using the program Puzzle 3.0 (Strimmer and von Haeseler, 1997). Briefly, this algorithm analyzes all possible quartets of sequences, two from one side of an internal branch, two from the other. In each case, enough subsamples of sequences were analyzed to ensure with 95% probability that any particular sequence was sampled at least once.

For dating, the Tamura-Nei algorithm (Tamura and Nei, 1993) as implemented in Puzzle 3.0 was used to estimate 9 classes of substitution rates, rate heterogeneity parameters, transition/transversion ratios, pyrimidine/purine transition ratios and nucleotide frequencies for 5 datasets consisting of 100 random human sequences. The average values for these parameters were then used to calculate the distances within and between species.

ACKNOWLEDGMENTS

We are indebted to Drs. F. G. Zehnder and H.-E. Joachim (Rheinisches Landesmuseum Bonn) for permission to remove the sample; to H. Lüdtke and M. Schultz for support and advice in the sampling process; to S. Meyer and K. Strimmer for help with computer analyses; to W. Schartau for oligonucleotide synthesis; to M. Beutelspacher, H. Fröhlich, A. Greenwood, R. F. Grill, M. Höss, T. Merritt, H. Poinar, L. Vigilant, and H. Zischler for discussions and help; to the Deutsche Forschungsgemeinschaft (Pa 452/3–1), the Boehringer Ingelheim Fonds (M. K.), and the National Science Foundation (M. S.) for financial support. R. W. S. especially thanks his late Ph.D. supervisor W. Taute (University of Cologne).

REFERENCES

Anderson, S., Bankier, A. T., Barrell, B. G., de Bruijn, M. H. L., Coulson, A. R., Drouin, J., Eperon, I. C., Nierlich, D. P., Roe, B. A., Sanger, F., et al. (1981). Sequence and organization of the human mitochondrial genome. Nature 290, 457–474.

Armour, J. A. L., Anttinen, T., May, C. A., Vega, E. E., Sajantila, A., Kidd, J. R., Kidd, K. K., Bertranpetit, J., Pääbo, S., and Jeffreys, A. J. (1996). Minisatellite diversity supports a recent African origin for modern humans. Nature Genet. 13, 154–160.

Ausubel, F. A., Brent, R., Kingston, R. E., Moore, D. D., Seidman, J. G., Smith, J. A., and Struhl, K., eds. (1995). Current Protocols in Molecular Biology (New York: John Wiley & Sons).

Bendall, K. E., and Sykes, B. C. (1995). Length heteroplasmy in the first hypervariable segment of the human mtDNA control region. Am. J. Hum. Genet. 57, 248–256.

Bräuer, G., and Stringer, C. B. (1997). Models, polarization, and perspectives on modern human origins. In Conceptual Issues in Modern Human Origins Research, G.A. Clark and C.M. Willermet, eds. (New York: de Gruyer), pp. 191–201.

Cann, R. L., Stoneking, M., and Wilson, A. C. (1987). Mitochondrial DNA and human evolution. Nature 325, 31–36.

Collura, R. V., and Stewart, C.-B. (1995). Insertions and duplications of mtDNA in the nuclear genomes of Old World monkeys and hominoids. Nature 378, 485–489.

Comas, D., Pääbo, S., and Bertranpetit, J. (1995). Heteroplasmy in the control region of human mitochondrial DNA. Genome Res. *5*, 89–90.

Felsenstein, J. (1994). Phylip 3.5 (University of Washington, Seattle).

Foley, R., and Lahr, M. M. (1997). Mode 3 technologies and the evolution of modern humans. Cambridge Archaeol. J., *7*, 3–36.

Förster, E. (1994). An improved general method to generate internal standards for competitive PCR. Biotechniques *16*, 18–20.

Hammer, M. F. (1995). A recent common ancestry for human Y chromosomes. Nature *378*, 376–378.

Handt, O., Höss, M., Krings, M., and Pääbo, S. (1994a). Ancient DNA: methodological challenges. Experientia *50*, 524–529.

Handt, O., Richards, M., Trommsdorff, M., Kilger, C., Simanainen, J., Georgiev, O., Bauer, K., Stone, A., Hedges, R., Schaffner, W., Utermann, G., Sykes, B., and Pääbo, S. (1994b). Molecular genetic analyses of the Tyrolean ice man. Science *264*, 1775–1778.

Handt, O., Krings, M., Ward, R. H., and Pääbo, S. (1996). The retrieval of ancient human DNA sequences. Am. J. Hum. Genet. *59*, 368–376.

Harpending, H. C., Sherry, S. T., Rogers, A. R., and Stoneking, M. (1993). The genetic structure of ancient human populations. Curr. Anthropol. *34*, 483–496.

Hedges, B., Kumar, S., Tamura, K., and Stoneking, M. (1992). Human origins and analysis of mitochondrial DNA sequences. Science *255*, 737–739.

Höss, M., and Pääbo, S. (1993). DNA extraction from Pleistocene bones by a silica-based purification method. Nucleic Acids Res. *21*, 3913–3914.

Höss, M., Jaruga, P., Zastawny, T. H., Dizdaroglu, M., and Pääbo, S. (1996a). DNA damage and DNA sequence retrieval from ancient tissues. Nucleic Acids Res. *24*, 1304–1307.

Höss, M., Dilling, A., Currant, A., and Pääbo, S. (1996b). Molecular phylogeny of the extinct ground sloth Mylodon darwinii. Proc. Natl. Acad. Sci. USA *93*, 181–185.

Hublin, J.-J., Spoor, F., Braun, M., Zonneveld, F., and Condemi, S. (1996). A late Neanderthal associated with Upper Paleolithic artefacts. Nature *381*, 224–226.

Ivanov, P. L., Wadhams, M. J., Roby, R. K., Holland, M. M., Weedn, V. W., and Parsons, T. J. (1996). Mitochondrial DNA sequence heteroplasmy in the Grand Duke of Russia Georgij Romanov establishes the authenticity of the remains of Tsar Nicholas II. Nature Genet. *12*, 417–420.

Lindahl, T. (1993a). Instability and decay of the primary structure of DNA. Nature *362*, 709–715.

Lindahl, T. (1993b). Recovery of antediluvian DNA. Nature *365*, 700.

Maddison, D. R. (1991). African origin of human mitochondrial DNA recxamined. Syst. Zool. *40*, 355–363.

Morin, P. A., Moore, J. J., Chakraborty, R., Jin, L., Goodall, J., and Woodruff, D. S. (1994). Kin selection, social structure, gene flow, and the evolution of chimpanzees. Science *265*, 1193–1201.

Mullis, K. B., and Faloona, F. (1987). Specific synthesis of DNA in vitro via a polymerase-catalyzed chain reaction. Methods Enzymol. *155*, 335–350.

Nei, M. (1987). Molecular Evolutionary Genetics (New York: Columbia University Press).

Pääbo, S. (1989). Ancient DNA: extraction, characterization, molecular cloning and enzymatic amplification. Proc. Natl. Acad. Sci. USA *86*, 1939–1943.

Pääbo, S., and Wilson, A. C. (1991). Miocene DNA sequences—a dream come true? Current Biol. *1*, 45–46.

Pääbo, S., Higuchi, R. G., and Wilson, A. C. (1989). Ancient DNA and the polymerase chain reaction. The emerging field of molecular archaeology. J. Biol. Chem. *264*, 9709–9712.

Pääbo, S., Irwin, D. M., and Wilson, A. C. (1990). DNA damage promotes jumping between templates during enzymatic amplification. J. Biol. Chem. *265*, 4718–4721.

Penny, D., Steel, M., Waddell, P. J., and Hendy, M. D. (1995). Improved analyses of human mtDNA sequences support a recent African origin for Homo sapiens. Mol. Biol. Evol. *12*, 863–882.

Petri, B., von Haeseler, A., and Pääbo, S. (1996). Extreme sequence heteroplasmy in bat mitochondrial DNA. Biol. Chem. Hoppe-Seyler *377*, 661–667.

Poinar, H. N., Höss, M., Bada, J. L., and Pääbo, S. (1996). Amino acid racemization and the preservation of ancient DNA. Science *272*, 864–866.

Rak, Y. (1993). Morphological variation in Homo neanderthalensis and Homo sapiens in the Levant. A biogeographic modern. In Species, Species Concepts and Primate Evolution, W.H. Kimbel and L.B. Martin, eds. (New York: Plenum Press), 523–536.

Saitou, N., and Nei, M. (1987). The neighbor joining method: a new method for reconstructing phylogenetic trees. Mol. Biol. Evol. *4*, 406–425.

Schmitz, R. W. (1996). Das Alt- und Mittelpaläolithikum des Neandertals und benachbarter Gebiete. Doctoral dissertation, Prehistory, University of Cologne (Cologne, University Microfilms).

Schmitz, R. W., Pieper, P., Bonte, W., and Krainitzki, H. (1995). New investigations of the Homo sapiens neanderthalensis, found in 1856. In Advances in Forensic Sciences, Vol. 7: Forensic Odontology and Anthropology. Proceedings of the 13th Meeting of the International Association of Forensic Sciences, Düsseldorf, August 22nd to 28th, 1993, B. Jacob and W. Bonte, eds. (Berlin, Köster), pp. 42–44.

Schwartz, J., and Tattersall, I. (1996). Significance of some previously unrecognized apomorphies in the nasal region of Homo neanderthalensis. Proc. Natl. Acad. Sci. USA *93*, 10852–10854.

Strimmer, K. S., and von Haeseler, A. (1997). Likelihood mapping: a simple method to visualize phylogenetic content of a sequence alignment. Proc. Natl. Acad. Sci. USA, *94*, 6815–6819.

Stringer, C. (1998). Chronological and biogeographic perspectives on later human evolution. In Neandertals and Modern Humans in West Asia, O. Bar-Yosef and T. Akazawa, eds. (New York: Plenum Press), pp. 29–37.

Stringer, C., and Gamble, C. (1993). In Search of the Neanderthals (London: Thames and Hudson).

Takahata, N., Satta, Y., and Klein, J. (1995). A genetic perspective on the origin and history of humans. Annu. Rev. Ecol. Syst. *26*, 343–372.

Tamura, K., and Nei, M. (1993). Estimation of the number of nucleotide substitutions in the control region of mitochondrial DNA in humans and chimpanzees. J. Mol. Evol. *10*, 512–526.

Templeton, A. R. (1992). Human origins and analysis of mitochondrial DNA sequences. Science *255*, 737.

Tishkoff, S. A., Dietsch, E., Speed, W., Pakstis, A. J., Kidd, J. R., Cheung, K., Bonné-Tamir, B., Santachiara-Benerechetti, A. S., Moral, P., Krings, M., et al. (1996). Global patterns of linkage disequilibrium at the CD4 locus and modern human origins. Science *271*, 1380–1387.

Trinkaus, E., and Shipman, P. (1993). The Neandertals: Changing the Image of Mankind (New York: Knopf).

van der Kuyl, A., Kuiken, C. L., Dekker, J. T., Perizonius, W. R. K., and Goudsmit, J. (1995). Nuclear counterparts of the cytoplasmic mitochondrial 12s rRNA gene: a problem of ancient DNA and molecular phylogenies. J. Mol. Evol. *40*, 652–657.

Vigilant, L., Stoneking, M., Harpending, H., Hawkes, K., and Wilson, A. C. (1991). African populations and the evolution of mitochondrial DNA. Science *253*, 1503–1507.

von Haeseler, A., Sajantila, A., and Pääbo, S. (1996). The genetical archaeology of the human genome. Nature Genet. *14*, 135–140.

Wolpoff, M. H. (1989). Multiregional evolution: the fossil alternative to Eden. In The Human Revolution, C. Stringer and P. Mellars, eds. (Edinburgh: Edinburgh University Press).

Zischler, H., Geisert, H., von Haeseler, A., and Pääbo, S. (1995). A nuclear 'fossil' of the mitochondrial D-loop and the origin of modern humans. Nature *378*, 489–492.

Zollikofer, C., Ponce de Leon, M., Martin, R., and Stucki, P. (1995). Neanderthal computer skulls. Nature *375*, 283–285.

GENBANK ACCESSION NUMBER

The GenBank accession number for the Neandertal sequence reported here is AF011222.

56

Cold Adaptation, Heterochrony, and Neandertals

S. E. Churchill

ABSTRACT

Since the writings of Clark Howell and Carleton Coon, the distinctive craniofacial and postcranial morphology of Neandertals has been associated with the frigid glacial climates of Pleistocene Europe. Direct associations between Ice-Age climate and Neandertal form have been proposed: Large noses and large paranasal sinuses, big brains, and robust, muscular bodies with barrel chests and foreshortened limbs may have been thermal adaptations to harsh glacial conditions, especially in hominids that perhaps lacked the technological sophistication to shield themselves from the cold. Indirect associations between cold climate and Neandertal morphology have also been advanced: Midfacial prognathism, dolichocephaly, occipital bunning, and other characteristics may have been the consequences of genetic drift in small populations of foragers isolated from the rest of the world by Alpine and continental ice sheets. Either way, when we think of Neandertals we think of primitive humans that endured the climatic and ecological hardships of cold periglacial Europe. Accordingly, it makes sense to think their morphology should reflect this in some important way.

Cold-adapted body forms are produced by heterochronic alteration of ontogenetic programs relative to warm-adapted ancestors. Small changes in ontogenetic programs, especially if they occur early in development, can have myriad effects on adult morphology. Even moderate changes in organismal size can produce profound differences in body proportions and skeletal morphology. These changes may be manifest across the entire organism and may appear to be independent of one another when, in fact, they are all correlated responses to one or a few changes in ontogenetic timing. Given the links between climate, developmental programs, and myriad phenotypic traits, we are led to ask: Can the appearance of Neandertal morphology, with all of its distinctive features, be explained by reference to a few ontogenetic shifts related to adaptation to cold climate? Recent research indicates that there are undeniable intercorrelations between traits that paleontologists often treat as independent ones, and that some distinguishing features of Neandertals may be best interpreted as secondary consequences of

ontogenetic programs that were geared to produce cold-adapted body forms. However, it is also clear that the morphological appearance of Neandertals cannot be explained entirely, or even in majority, by reference to one or a few shifts in developmental timing. Selection or developmental plasticity related to specific behavior patterns must have shaped the form of some parts of their skeletons. What emerges from these considerations is the realization that morphological analyses must work on multiple levels, from the whole organism to the specific functional trait, to reach a more complete understanding of Neandertal adaptation.

INTELLECTUAL APPROACHES TO NEANDERTAL MORPHOLOGY

A full-grown Neandertal must have been a peculiar sight. Envision a relatively short, thickset body with a barrel-chest, wide trunk, and short, muscular limbs, topped with a large, elongated head. Add to this a forward-thrust, beetle-browed, and chinless face adorned with an enormous protruding nose. Seen through our modern eyes, the overwhelming visual impression would be one of a creature *squat, stocky,* and *strange*. Even shorn, shaved, bathed, and suitably attired, I think a Neandertal would still turn heads on a New York City subway.[1,2]

The list of anatomical features that distance Neandertals from living people is expanded when one considers skeletal morphology (Figure 1). Neandertal skeletons are characterized by a suite of craniofacial and postcranial features that, taken individually, may overlap the range of variation seen in living people, but which, in concert, appear only in these hominids. Naturally, the features that characterize Neandertals have been argued to reflect both phylogenetic and behavioral distance between these later Pleistocene humans and recent people. Of interest here are not the inferences that have been generated from these contrasts, but rather the intellectual approaches that have been applied to their analyses.

Paleoanthropologists have come at the study of Neandertal morphology from two perspectives. One approach has been to see these features as intercorrelated responses to larger-scale changes in body form, usually as the result of ontogenetic shifts that affected the morphogenesis of the whole organism. As I have noted before, there is a recurring idea in paleoanthropology that Neandertal morphology can be explained wholly or in part by a limited number of epigenetic

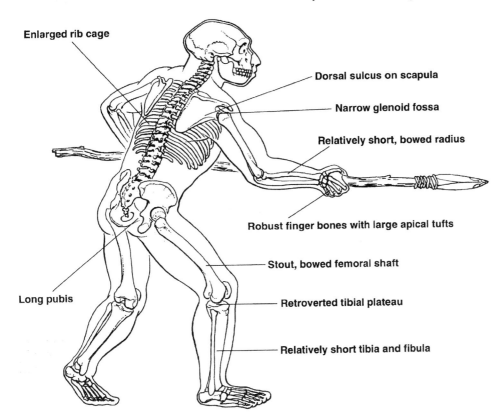

Enlarged rib cage

Dorsal sulcus on scapula

Narrow glenoid fossa

Relatively short, bowed radius

Robust finger bones with large apical tufts

Long pubis

Stout, bowed femoral shaft

Retroverted tibial plateau

Relatively short tibia and fibula

Figure 1. *Neandertal skeletons are characterized in part by dolichocephalic crania with occipital buns and suprainiac fossae, enlarged juxtamastoid eminences, and large, double-arched supraorbital ridges; midfacially prognathic faces with large nasal apertures and horizontally oriented distal nasal bones, expanded maxillary sinuses, and swept-back zygomatic arches; and chinless mandibles with retromolar spaces. Postcranially, their skeletons exhibit robust appendicular bones, long clavicles, broad scapulae with narrow glenoid fossae and with dorsal sulci on their axillary borders, narrow humeral deltoid tuberosities, anteriorly directed ulnar trochlear notches and medially directed radial bicipital tuberosities, anteroposteriorly and mediolaterally expanded rib cages, wide pelves with elongated superior pubic rami, and stout lower limb bones with large articular surfaces. Drawing by Stephen Nash.*

developmental shifts, the result of a periglacial cold climate having selected for a stocky, cold-adapted body build.[3–5] This approach follows from the intellectual tradition of structuralism, a paradigm that is generally concerned with biological organization at the organismal level.

The alternative approach has been to see the suite of features that characterize Neandertals as all having been more or less independently selected for as biomechanical or thermoregulatory adaptations in behaviorally primitive, technologically unsophisticated hominids living in cold periglacial Eurasia.[6] This perspective emerges from a Neo-Darwinian (or adaptationist) paradigm, an approach that emphasizes microevolutionary processes in explaining larger-scale patterns of morphological evolution. This paradigm can be recognized by a tendency to disarticulate organisms into discrete units of study—traits or trait complexes—and by an emphasis on natural selection as the dominant force in shaping the morphological evolution of lineages.

It must be kept in mind that these are broad conceptual approaches, not mutually exclusive paradigms. Structuralists are also generally concerned with the adaptive consequences of morphological change, and adaptationists fully appreciate the developmental and functional integration of trait complexes and their integration with other such complexes. The difference is one of emphasis on the whole organism versus a trait or trait complex in studying morphological change and its role in macroevolution. If anything, I have, as a heuristic measure, overstated the dichotomy between these approaches.

These conceptual paradigms have enormous implications for how we interpret the meaning of morphological contrasts between hominid groups. Morphologists engaged in classification or phylogenetic reconstruction often compare organisms on a trait-by-trait basis, tending to focus on problems of homology and homoplasy that affect the relevance of various traits in cross-taxa comparisons.[7] Less often are we consciously bothered by the interrelation of traits within an organism. Yet problems of pleiotropy, allometry, and functional or developmental covariance in characters can also confound phylogenetic analyses. It is possible that many Neandertal features were the correlated results of a change in a few regulatory genes. Moreover, this possibility has deep implications for both cladistic and phenetic approaches to late Pleistocene phyletic evolution. In cladistic analyses, the intercorrelation of characters may cause a single genetic shift to be counted multiple times. Because each affected character is treated as a separate autapomorphy in the analysis, this single genetic difference may be weighed too heavily in the resulting cladograms. In phenetic approaches, multiple morphological consequences of a change in a single gene may cause genetically close groups to appear more distant in morphospace, leading to overestimation of evolutionary distances between groups. Finally, an incomplete appreciation of size and shape allometry can lead to taxonomic oversplitting in taxa that vary considerably in size, as has been the case in both paleontological and neontological contexts.[8] An incomplete appreciation of integration, the traditional domain of structuralists, can lead to faulty phylogenetic reconstructions.

Glossary

Acceleration—faster rate of change of shape (i.e., growth of one structure relative to another) or of developmental events, resulting in peramorphosis of descendants relative to their ancestors.

Heterochrony—a change in the form of descendants relative to their ancestors that is brought about by an alteration in the timing of developmental events.

Hypermorphosis—extension of a growth allometry that is common to both ancestor and descendant to larger size in the descendant by prolongation of the growth period (delayed offset of growth).

Neoteny—heterochronic reduction in the developmental rate of change in shape, such that if the rate of growth in size and the ages at which growth begins and ends are the same in ancestor and descendant, the descendant will have an adult shape similar to that of a juvenile in the ancestor species (paedomorphic).

Paedomorphosis—the retention of ancestral juvenile shape in the adults of the descendant species.

Peramorphosis—"overdevelopment," or the development of traits in the descendant species beyond that seen in adult ancestors.

Postdisplacement—delayed onset of developmental change in shape. Assuming a common growth allometry between ancestor and descendant and similar ages of growth offset, postdisplacement will result in paedomorphic morphology in the descendant.

Predisplacement—early onset of developmental change in shape. Given common growth allometry between ancestor and descendant and similar ages of growth offset, predisplacement will result in peramorphic morphology in the descendant.

Progenesis—early cessation (offset) of a growth allometry (common to both ancestor and descendant), resulting in paedomorphic descendants.

Robusticity—one of the most variably defined yet frequently used words in describing premodern human morphology, robusticity has been loosely used in referring to everything from browridge size to degree of muscle scarring to overall bone size. In most modern usages, cranial robusticity refers to the degree of development of cranial vault superstructures and muscle attachment sites, while postcranial robusticity refers to the mechanical strength of skeletal elements relative to the overall size of the individual.

Sesquipedalianism—a tendency to use inappropriately long words when simpler words will do: highfalutin.

The issue of single ontogenetic shifts that have multiple morphological consequences is no less important in efforts to reconstruct hominid behavior and adaptation from skeletal morphology. Numerous features in the Neandertal skeleton have been argued to be functionally meaningful on the assumption that they were either shaped by selection for effective functional design or shaped by biomechanically stimulated bone modeling and remodeling processes.[9,10] This is clearly an adaptationist perspective and, if true, these traits provide information about the selection histories of fossil groups and possibly about the activity levels and patterns of the individual hominids themselves. Hence, potentially they can provide great resolution in behavioral inferences. For example, Trinkaus, Ruff, and I,[11–17] on the basis of recent work, have interpreted Neandertal and modern human contrasts in upper and lower limb long bone strength and shape as reflecting adaptively important differences in mobility, upper limb loading intensity, and behavior patterns. If, instead, these features are *only* correlated consequences of changes in the developmental timing necessary to produce relatively massive, thermally adaptive bodies, then we have erred in trying to attach behavioral meaning to between-group differences. If this is the case, morphological differences between Pleistocene and recent human groups may reflect broader-scale adaptive patterns such as eco-geographical patterning more than they do variation in hominid behavior.[18] Again, inattention to structuralist considerations of integration can potentially result in flawed behavioral inferences.

The normative approach in paleoanthropology has always been adaptationist: Structuralism has a long history in the field, but has never played a major role in guiding research. Structuralism is, however, increasingly coming to the fore, especially as paleoanthropologists devote more attention to the role of ontogenetic transitions in human evolution. My purpose here is to explore structuralism in Neandertal studies, specifically by examining two models that propose single genetic shifts to explain multiple Neandertal features.

STRUCTURALISM IN PALEOANTHROPOLOGY AND THE NEANDERTALS AS COLD-ADAPTED HETEROCHRONES

The 1977 publication of Gould's *Ontogeny and Phylogeny*[19] represented a landmark in the study of heterochrony and the role of morphogenesis in macroevolution. The work reflected growing attention on the part of English-speaking evolutionary biologists to the conceptual tradition of structuralism and opposed structuralism to the themes of adaptation, selection, and microevolution that have been prevalent since the modern synthesis.[8,20] Structuralism seeks to develop a theory, based on principles of generation of form, of biological organization at the organismal level. It further seeks to deduce from this theory both the role of developmental constraints on the action of natural selection and the role of developmental, epigenetic shifts in morphogenic transitions.[20] The role of epigenetic shifts in macroevolution emerges in Gould's work as a search for a global, heterochronic perturbation that would account for the evolutionary emergence of human morphology. Following on the arguments of Bolk and others, Gould saw retardation of development relative to a hominoid developmental baseline as that perturbation.[21] Paedomorphosis in general, and neoteny in particular, have been intensely investigated since Gould's work, and have not found support as explanations for human morphological divergence from other hominoids (see references in Godfrey and Sutherland).[21]

Structuralist arguments emerge in human paleontology as well. Thermoregulatory adaptations in hominid body size and shape may have been brought about by relatively simple heterochronic shifts.[8,22,23] It has been argued that evolutionary changes in developmental rate, specifically increased growth rate (acceleration) and increased time to maturity (hypermorphosis) in growth, are the mechanisms that provide the adaptive fit, as described by Bergmann's rule, between body size and mean annual temperature in cold-adapted endotherms.[22] It should be noted that cold-adapted humans are not larger in every way than humans from warm regions: They are generally more massive, yet not always as tall.[24] Body weight in cold-adapted humans, then, is likely to represent peramorphosis relative to warm-adapted ancestors. Conformity to Allen's rule, involving adaptive shortening of limb lengths in colder environments, most likely represents paedomorphosis relative to hominids adapted to warmer climes.[22] Foreshortened limbs are considered paedomorphic because human juveniles, both modern and, presumably, those of ancestral *Homo*, have limbs that are short relative to the trunk and head size of adults.[25] Shorter, paedomorphic limbs could be achieved through some combination of decelerated developmental rate (neoteny), later onset (postdisplacement), or earlier offset (progenesis) of growth in limb length relative to overall growth in body size. Thus it has been suggested that cold-adapted body forms in humans and other mammals may result from some combination of hypermorphosis and paedomorphosis ("hyperpaedomorphosis").[22] The combination of these two heterochronic trends has been advanced as an explanation for observed evolutionary trends in brain and body size in the genus *Homo* as an adaptive response to late Cenozoic global cooling.[22,26] Heterochronic models relating human morphological evolution to climatic change are very speculative and largely untested, yet there is compelling paleontological, comparative, and experimental evidence from other animals that climate effects developmental rates and patterns.[19,20,27–30] It is also clear that heterochronic differences between populations produce the ecogeographic patterns seen in extant human morphology. So while the interplay of heterochrony and climate is still questionable as a comprehensive explanation for the evolutionary trajectory of body form in *Homo*, heterochronic responses to climatic selection pressures do hold considerable potential for our understanding of human morphological variation in space and time.

Even slight heterochronic shifts can have profound effects on adult morphology.[23] If late Cenozoic global cooling trends *could* have produced developmental shifts in humans, resulting in altered body size and shape, as well as altered proportions between brain and body size, what might we expect to be the effect of extreme glacial climates on hominids with minimal cultural buffering against the cold? Neandertals have long been seen as having been cold-adapted. Recent accounts have increasingly referred to them as "arctic"[14] or even "hyperpolar"[31] with respect to some features of their morphology. As compared with earlier archaic humans and later modern *Homo sapiens*, it has been suggested that Neandertal craniofacial and postcranial form represents a specialized departure from the general *Homo* pattern.[32–34] A structuralist perspective leads to this question: To what extent can Neandertal features, from their unique craniofacial form and robust skeletons to their seemingly idiosyncratic characters such as long pubic rami and scapular dorsal sulci, be explained as the direct or pleiotropic results of climatic effects on heterochrony? At the risk of sesquipedalianism, we might ask: Were the Neandertals *hyper*hyperpaedomorphic variations on the basic *Homo* theme?

TESTING STRUCTURALIST MODELS

It is well known that growth allometry cannot be understood by reference to adult static allometry.[8] This limits our ability to explore heterochrony in evolutionary morphogenic transitions in fossil hominids for which ontogenetic series are limited (see, for example, Stringer and colleagues[35] Table 4 for Neandertals). However, analysis of covariance patterns between traits in adult samples can provide limited testing of heterochronic growth models. Predictions about the end products of heterochronic shifts, that is the adult morphological patterns, can be generated and tested by a variety of means. One such method is to specify patterns of trait covariation necessitated by the heterochronic model under consideration and to test the predicted relationships using any number of methods designed to analyze variance-covariance or correlation matrices (for example, quadratic assignment procedures or confirmatory factor analysis).[36,37] Another approach is to test for interdependence of metric and discrete data sets using correspondence analysis as a means of exploring integration of traits. Strong signals of integration may then point to developmental relationships among skeletal parts. Both approaches have been profitably applied to questions of the functional and developmental integration of archaic human cranial[38] and postcranial[13,39] morphology.

Hublin[40,41] suggested that cranial vault superstructures characteristic of *Homo erectus* might all be developmentally correlated, and thus should not be taken separately as independent characters in phylogenetic analyses. He also suggested that these superstructures might be pleiotropic correlates of cranial vault thickness. These possibilities have implications for understanding cranial morphology in *Homo* generally because superstructures and thick vault bones tend to co-occur in Neandertals and other premodern groups. The idea of developmental correlation of cranial superstructures received partial support in recent work by Lahr and Wright.[38] Using canonical correlation analysis, an extension of correspondence analysis, Lahr and Wright found that the expression of cranial vault superstructures was positively correlated with cranial size measures in a large pooled sample of recent and fossil humans. Specifically, they found that facial breadth, length, and protrusion, as well as cranial length, were most strongly associated with robust expression of such superstructures as supraorbital ridges and zygomatic trigones. They also reported a less important yet still significant relationship between cranial shape and superstructure expression, so that narrow skulls with large teeth tended to exhibit greater development of superstructures. Although Neandertals were not included in Lahr and Wright's study, it follows from their analysis that some aspects of Neandertal cranial morphology—specifically, the relatively strong development of supraorbital ridges—were perhaps developmentally or functionally related to their large and relatively dolichocephalic crania and tall, projecting faces.[42,43]

While Lahr and Wright[38] did find significant correlation between cranial metric and discrete traits, they also found that variation in cranial size and shape accounts, *at best,* for only 40% of the variation observed in the discrete traits. This and other studies show that even though there is a moderate signal of integration in cranial morphology, there is still substantial variation in metric and nonmetric traits that is unrelated to variation in other traits.[44–46] This work also serves as a clear example of how knowledge of morphological integration should guide selection of characters for taxonomic and phylogenetic studies. Lahr and Wright contend that early modern humans from Israel show that modern human cranial shape emerged before the reduction of cranial size and robusticity of superstructures. Since size and cranial robusticity are related, yet size and modern cranial shape are unrelated, cranial gracility (weak development of superstructures) cannot be used as a defining characteristic of modern humans.

Recently I reported on work that used confirmatory factor analysis to test the hypothesis that upper-limb traits characteristic of Neandertals (dorsal scapular axillary borders, narrow deltoid tuberosities, low humeral torsion angles) were functional or developmental correlates of a cold-adapted body form.[13,39] Using samples of Neandertals, early modern, and recent humans, I found that a model of body form and upper-limb trait integration[47] fit the data better than did a model of no integration. In particular, it appears that moderate to weak associations exist between chest shape and humeral shaft morphology and between measures of relative humeral strength and mechanical leverage in the upper limb. The association between chest shape and humeral shape likely reflects functional integration. With variation in chest shape and, accordingly, the orientation of the scapula, concerted changes must occur in humeral torsion, and hence in shaft shape, to maintain the axis of the elbow joint in a more-or-less coronal plane. The relationship detected between long bone robusticity and mechanical leverage probably reflects the parallel actions of dynamic bone modeling and natural selection in active populations. In groups in which high activity levels are critical to survival, dynamic bone modeling and remodeling in response to habitually high biomechanical loads is probably the major cause of robust limb bones. But it is also likely that genes contributing to enhanced skeletal robusticity

and genes for enhanced bone-muscle mechanical leverage were selectively advantageous in these groups. Thus, heightened skeletal strength and leverage may be expected to positively co-occur in populations with an evolutionary history of high activity. In sum, my investigation into upper-body integration revealed a clear signal of covariation and suggested that some variation in upper-limb traits is related to variation in body form.

Two other points became clear in the foregoing analysis. The first is that Neandertals do not differ from modern humans in patterns of trait covariance. This suggests that Neandertal form, at least for the upper postcranial skeleton, reflects extrapolations of ontogenetic scaling relationships that are seen in modern humans and that probably are characteristic of all members of the genus *Homo.* There is no evidence for a major dissociation of patterns of growth allometry. It thus seems unlikely that a *major* heterochronic shift separates Neandertals from other members of the genus, whether it be their ancestors or anatomically modern humans. The second thing, and this is in common with the finding of Lahr and Wright for the cranium, is that intercorrelation (integration) accounted for less than half of the observed variance in upper-limb morphology. From this I concluded that differences in overall body form are inadequate to account for the host of upper-limb features that differentiate Neandertals from modern human samples. More particulate modes of morphological evolution, such as natural selection operating on single traits or functional complexes, must also be invoked to explain Neandertal morphology.

From the perspective of structuralist models, the proverbial glass may be seen as being either half empty or half full. Studies of the intercorrelation of traits consistently detect a significant degree of covariance beyond that imposed by size, but this covariance never accounts for more than half of the observed variance in the data set. It is clear that we need structuralist models to understand shared variance in traits and adaptationist models to understand unique variance in traits. Only when these approaches are used in tandem will we fully understand morphology.[20] Adaptationist approaches to Neandertal morphology are common[9–17] and have been well summarized elsewhere.[9,10] Structuralist explanations are much less common. We can now turn our attention to two structuralist models that have been proposed to account for overall Neandertal form and evaluate their utility in accounting for the signal of integration detected in the previously mentioned studies. These are the endocrine-shift model first espoused, in incomplete terms, by Arthur Keith[48] and the accelerated basicranial growth model of Fred Smith and Michael Green.[71]

ENDOCRINE-SHIFT EXPLANATIONS FOR NEANDERTAL MORPHOLOGY

Keith[48] was a firm believer in the role of hormones in both interpopulational variation in body form in modern humans and variation in skeletal morphology between hominid taxa. Keith's emphasis on endocrine action may in part be a reflection of the novelty of endocrine physiology in the early part of this century and the potential the field held for the study of morphology. Nevertheless, Keith never went beyond unspecified statements of implication, and the possibilities of endocrinological explanations for hominid morphological evolution went largely ignored for 50 years. Endocrine models reemerged in the 1970s with the suggestion by Brothwell[3] that the distinctiveness of Neandertals might be explicable by reference to a single heterochronic perturbation, one involving an earlier onset or greater intensity of hormones regulating the adolescent growth spurt, perhaps under selection for the production of larger, more thermally adapted adults.

This structuralist model postulates an endogenous, epigenetic agent (in this case one that has an adaptive basis) for morphological distance between taxa. It also invokes the theme of integration, whereby change in many traits can be seen as functionally, developmentally, or pleiotropically correlated responses to other changes. Brothwell cogently sums up this point: "Might, for instance, such characters as the prominent nasal bridge and large upper face, long basi-cranial axis, short and broad ramus, small mastoids, large distinctive hands and the relatively large articular ends of the long bones of European neanderthalers be explainable in terms of a few programmed growth rate/sequence changes, rather than as a variety of small scale isolated morphogenetic trends?" (p. 162). This endocrine theme reemerges in various forms with some regularity in paleoanthropology,[40,41,49–52] and has even been taken to ridiculous extremes.[53,54]

In the years since Keith first proposed an endocrine mechanism behind skeletal variation, the role of hormones on skeletal development and maintenance has been greatly elucidated. While endocrine effects are enormously complex and still only partly understood, generalizations can be made about three endocrine axes that affect skeletal development (Figure 2). First, growth hormone, released by the anterior pituitary, operates in conjunction with growth factors produced by target tissues to stimulate growth and cell division[55] in a variety of growing tissues. In bones, growth hormone stimulates cortical bone deposition and growth at growth plates.[55] Growth hormone is critical to the adolescent growth spurt, as well as to normal somatic growth throughout childhood: A deficiency of the hormone results in pituitary dwarfism, while an overabundance leads to gigantism. Adolescent spurts in growth hormone production appear to be triggered by elevated levels of sex steroids, produced by the maturing gonads.[55] Second, these steroids, androgens and estrogens, also have direct effects on bone growth. Testosterone, for example, may directly activate bone and cartilage-forming cells, thus leading to longer, thicker, denser bones. Testosterone may, as well, have an indirect effect through stimulation of muscle development.[56] Steroids appear to play a critical role in the maturation of bony growth plates and fusion of epiphyses, simultaneously increasing growth rate yet hastening growth cessation. Finally, parathyroid hormone and calcitonin appear to have direct effects on the activity of bone-depositing and bone-resorbing cells, but seem to be more involved in bone and blood mineral transfer

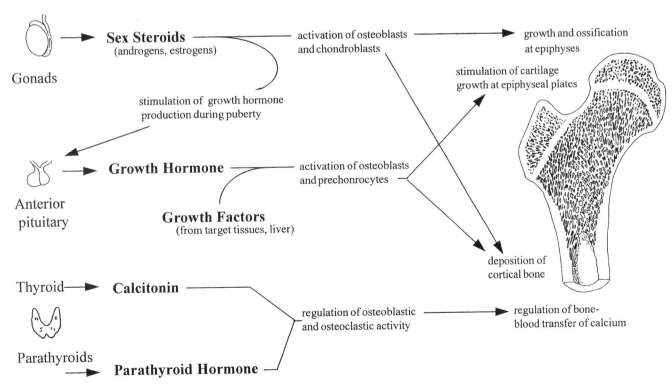

Figure 2. *Effects of three endocrine axes on osteogenic and chondrogenic cells, and their resultant effects on skeletal morphology. Note that only two of these axes, sex steroids and growth hormone, have a major effect on the gross morphology of skeletal elements.*

and regulation of serum calcium than they are in bone growth.

The timing and intensity of endocrine production thus affects bone growth at a systemic, organismal level, directly influencing bone sizes, cortical thicknesses, and relative joint sizes in the entire skeleton. There have also been claims that different bone-forming areas, namely the periosteal (outer) and endosteal (inner) surfaces of long bones, exhibit different sensitivities to osteogenic hormones. Accordingly, shifts in endocrine environment can alter the relative rates of deposition and resorption at these surfaces, and hence alter diaphyseal (shaft) cross-sectional shape. Most notably, it has been argued that heightened endosteal apposition and encroachment of the medullary space are characteristic of the hormonally intense adolescent growth spurt.[57,58]

The claim that the periosteal and endosteal surfaces of long-bone diaphyses experience different developmental histories has been substantiated in recent work by Ruff and colleagues,[59] in which they used radiographic data from professional tennis players. Combining data on asymmetry in playing versus non-playing limbs in humeral shaft cross-sectional areas (total, cortical, and medullary) with knowledge of the age at which each player began intensive tennis playing, these investigators were able to infer which osteogenic envelope, periosteal or endosteal, was most active in bone formation in response to heightened activity. Their results indicate that the periosteal or outer surface of long-bone shafts remain in a state of net bone formation throughout life, leading to ever-expanding diaphyses with age. Periosteal expansion largely keeps pace with somatic growth prior to maturity, and thus may be sensitive to circulating levels of growth hormone. The endosteal or inner surface, on the other hand, undergoes net resorption in childhood and early adolescence, net deposition from mid-adolescence to the fourth decade of life, and net resorption once again thereafter. The timing of changes in endosteal activity, corresponding as they do to changes in the intensity of sex steroid production, suggests that bone formation at this surface may be directly influenced by sex hormones.

Might elevated levels of these potent morphogenic agents be responsible for the skeletal features that characterize the Neandertals, as suggested by Brothwell and others? Neandertals and other premodern hominids appear to be peramorphic (that is, larger than *us*) in many aspects of musculoskeletal anatomy, including robust and heavily muscled limb bones with large joint surfaces, thick cranial vault bones, large brow ridges, projecting midfaces, and elongated crania. The clinical condition of precocious puberty mimics some of these features.[55,60] This disorder results from an early onset and elevated levels of sex steroid production, triggering increased growth hormone production and causing an early and drastic adolescent growth spurt. Individuals with this condition experience heightened cortical bone deposition on the endosteal surfaces of long bones, resulting in robust diaphyses with thick cortical bone and narrow medullary cavities. Narrowing of the

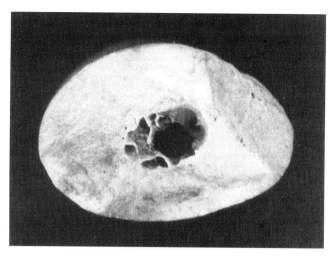

Figure 3. *Femoral shaft of a Neandertal from Krapina, Croatia, showing the thickened cortical tissue and medullary stenosis (narrowing) characteristic of premodern humans. Photo courtesy of Milford Wolpoff and the Croatian Natural History Museum.*

medullary space, or *medullary stenosis*, also happens to be a nearly ubiquitous feature of the robust limb bones of premodern and early modern humans (Figure 3). It has been argued that the pattern of stenosis in *Homo erectus* femora reflects greater bone deposition on the endosteal rather than periosteal surface.[49] This is consistent with the idea that the robusticity of long bones in premodern humans was caused by elevated "adolescent" bone growth through an earlier onset, greater intensity, or longer duration of sex-steroid-mediated endosteal apposition.[3]

Heightened levels of androgens, particularly testosterone, promote muscle development in the same way their synthetic cousins, the anabolic steroids, do. Large muscles can be inferred as a characteristic of Neandertal body form, based on the size and rugosity of muscle attachment sites. Long-bone development in a high-steroid environment results in early fusion of growth plates, causing relatively short bones and short adult stature, yet apparently normal development of joint surfaces. Thus the expected adult skeletal morphology would include robust, stenotic postcranial elements, with large rugose muscle insertion sites and relatively large joint surfaces, all of which are characteristic of the Neandertal postcranial skeleton[10] (Figure 4). Rapid somatic growth combined with heightened muscularity (acceleration resulting in peramorphosis), but with foreshortened limbs (paedomorphosis), would produce a short yet massive ("stocky") cold-adapted hominid that dutifully obeyed the ecogeographic rules of Bergmann and Allen. Furthermore, androgens and growth hormone stimulate cranial vault thickening and brow-ridge growth, as recognized initially by Keith[61] and documented more fully by recent research.[62] Brothwell's[3] suggestion that hormones could have large effects at the growth cartilages of the cranial base and face, and could also affect nasal, alveolar, and sinus development, as well as molar taurodontism, draws Neandertal craniofacial morphology under the endocrine umbrella as well (Figure 4).

Growth Hormone + Steroids

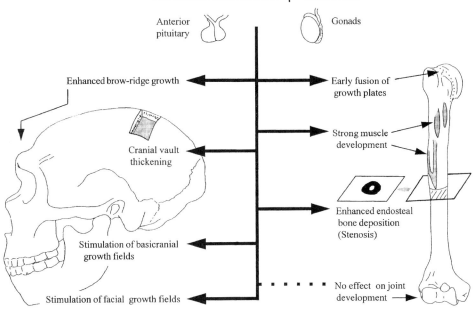

Figure 4. *Proposed effects of an epigenetic shift affecting the combined growth-hormone and sex-steroid axis on Neandertal skeletal morphology. In this model, increased production of osteogenically active hormones produces a myriad of seemingly independent Neandertal characteristics in the skeleton, ranging from unique craniofacial morphology to great postcranial robusticity.*

The obvious logical flaw in Brothwell's model is that Neandertals shared many of these features with other species of archaic *Homo*, including those from much warmer regions. In particular, heightened cranial and postcranial robusticity appears to be a universal feature of premodern *Homo*, thus negating the argument that heightened robusticity is caused by adaptation to cold. Subsequent arguments for endocrine models of robusticity[49,52] have not invoked cold adaptation as the ultimate cause, and have changed their focus from Neandertal morphology *per se* to heightened skeletal robusticity in premodern humans in general. The Neandertals, as well-known representatives of archaic *Homo*, can still be contrasted with modern humans to explore the possibility that the emergence of anatomically modern humans, wherever or from whomever that occurred, involved an epigenetic shift in hormonal control of growth and development.

The transition from archaic to modern human skeletal morphology was mosaic in the sense that some aspects of the skeleton maintained their robusticity across the transition, others became somewhat more gracile, and still others became markedly more gracile.[6,13] How can a mosaic pattern of gracilization be accommodated by systemic endocrine models? Reisenfeld[50] experimentally analyzed the effects of numerous hormones on skeletal robusticity in rats to explore the role of endocrine shifts in gracilization in human evolution. He showed that even a single hormone had different effects on different bones, resulting in mosaic patterns of change in robusticity with single changes to the endocrine system. While this work illustrates the inherent complexity in bone-hormone relationships, it nevertheless provides general support for endocrine shift models. It has also been argued that changes in single endocrine systems can result in ontogenetic scaling (i.e., allometric transformations[63]) between parts, which could enhance the perception of mosaic change. The

piecemeal nature of Pleistocene change in skeletal robusticity could thus be as easily explained by an endocrine shift as by a more particulate manner of evolution.[6,13]

ACCELERATED ENDOCHONDRAL GROWTH IN NEANDERTALS

The early appearance of distinctive traits in Neandertal ontogeny[35] and the relatively great robusticity of young Neandertals,[64–66] presumably before they experienced high adult activity levels, have been seen as general support for a claim of substantial genetic distance between these hominids and modern humans. Numerous adaptive arguments have been launched to explain the meaning of these features in adults.[10] However, the establishment of these features early in ontogeny has led some to wonder if our adaptive explanations have focused on the wrong stage of the life cycle. Might not selection have favored large, robust babies that would be better able to survive the harsh selective trials imposed by extreme cold than would small, metabolically disadvantaged, minimally culture-buffered infants?[4,5,67–69]

Questions such as these led Smith and Green[5,70–72] to raise the possibility of accelerated growth in endochondral anlagen, the cartilaginous precursors of bone, during late embryonic and early fetal development in Neandertals. Rates of development and growth of the sphenoid bone relative to surrounding bones can affect cranial vault shape, facial morphology, and the spatial relationships between the face and neurocranium.[73] A relatively minor change in growth rate of these basicranial cartilages at a very early developmental age, effectively producing predisplacement of craniofacial shape relative to size, could have produced differences between Neandertals and modern humans in midsagittal facial prognathism, relative flatness of the cranial base, overall cranial vault contours and elongation, and occipital morphology.

Noting that distinctive Neandertal postcranial traits also appear early in development, Smith[5] has suggested that this model may apply to early endochondral bone formation across the entire skeleton. Smith[74] has identified this heterochronic shift as perhaps the most significant morphogenic transition related to the emergence of modern humans: "The final factor that led to modern human anatomical form may have been a change in the regulatory part of the genome. Specifically, we suggest a change in the control mechanism of endochondral bone growth, which resulted in shorter, more flexed anterior cranial bases and changes in the forms of the long bones" (p. 60). While accelerated fetal growth models have been expressed before, they generally have been forwarded as explanations for differences in neonatal or adult body size.[67,68] Smith and Green presented a model that, by a subtle heterochronic shift in early ontogeny, explained craniofacial and postcranial *shape* differences.

Smith[5] has taken claims of accelerated developmental schedules in Neandertals as general support for the model. He points out that Neandertal subadults are larger than recent humans of the same developmental age, but that the rate of postnatal growth appears to be the same. Neandertal children started out bigger than their modern counterparts and stayed bigger than recent children. Comparisons of the Devil's Tower Neandertal child with recent European children, for example, indicate that Neandertals were on an advanced schedule for dental development and brain growth relative to modern children.[35,75] Overall, the developmental evidence suggests that Neandertal children were ahead of modern children in growth and development, but that developmental patterns did not differ from those of modern humans.[76–78] Thus the peramorphosis in craniofacial features, trunk size, and skeletal robusticity seen in Neandertals may be attributable to predisplacement, which is consistent with accelerated cartilage growth in the embryonic and fetal periods.

RECENT WORK ON ONTOGENY AND INTEGRATION IN NEANDERTALS

Three lines of research are providing new insights into the nature of the morphological contrasts between Neandertals and recent humans. These studies, many of which are still in progress or are only now being published, include investigations of craniofacial ontogeny, the ontogeny of postcranial robusticity, and the intercorrelation of postcranial robusticity measures. Studies of ontogenetic (growth) series of fossil hominids provide direct assessment of heterochronic differences between taxa, while morphometric analyses of covariance of traits in adult skeletons allow testing of models of trait integration specified by structural models.

The results of previous studies of developmental schedules in Neandertals have been mixed and difficult to interpret, in part because much of the work has been based on dental developmental rates, which are not an adequate reflection of somatic growth velocity.[79,80] Discordance in estimates of age from dental development versus those from long-bone epiphyseal fusion has been suggested in at least one Neandertal subadult.[81] Another problem concerns the availability of immature fossil hominids. Immature Neandertals, though not abundant, are available. However, immature remains of earlier *Homo* are rare. Thus, inferences about heterochrony in Neandertals must be made indirectly by comparison of Neandertal and modern human growth series. Despite the difficulties inherent in evaluating heterochronic differences between fossil and extant taxa, studies of premodern human ontogeny and morphological integration are becoming increasingly important to understanding the significance of adult morphology in extinct humans.

Recent studies of craniofacial ontogeny have produced intriguing yet somewhat contradictory results. Krovitz and colleagues[82] used Euclidean distance matrix analysis as a way of looking at changes in craniofacial shape in an ontogenetic series of Neandertals and recent humans. This method involves examination of changes in the linear distances between landmark points in the sequential age classes of the growth series, followed by comparison of these changes with those in other groups. Application of this method to a limited ontogenetic series of Neandertals and recent humans indicates that contrasts between groups in craniofacial growth are complex, entailing increased growth in some dimensions in Neandertals relative to modern humans, similar growth rates in other dimensions, and reduced growth rates in still others.[82] While this does not rule out an endocrine shift or some other change in the regulation of development, it does suggest that differences in the facial morphology of Neandertals and modern humans are the result of differences in growth rates at multiple growth fields throughout childhood, and not simply the result of predisplacement or acceleration of growth in all fields. However, it is also clear from this work that Neandertals did have an overall accelerated growth rate, with the craniofacial size normally seen in modern adults being achieved during adolescence in Neandertals.[82]

In contradistinction, Williams[83,84] has recently argued that Neandertals and modern humans are ontogenetically scaled in facial growth. Using measures of craniofacial shape plotted on age in growth series of Neandertals and modern humans, Williams argued that growth in both groups follows similar ontogenetic pathways, but terminates at different points along that pathway. Thus, modern humans and Neandertals share similar facial shapes, but at different developmental ages. Because Neandertals continued along this developmental pathway farther than do modern people, their peramorphic morphology relative to modern humans and, presumably, their ancestors, is attributable to hypermorphosis, not predisplacement as argued by Smith and Green's model (but see Krovitz and coworkers[82]).

There is also some evidence that contrasts between Neandertal and modern humans in facial projection are the result of different rates of growth in growth fields interposed between the cranial vault and face.[85]

Lieberman[85] found no significant difference in measures of relative facial anteroposterior length between archaic humans, including non-Neandertals, and modern humans. These groups did differ, however, in anterior cranial base length. Neandertals and other archaic humans have markedly longer anterior cranial base lengths, which, in turn, contribute to greater facial projection. Anterior cranial base length corresponds to the length of the sphenoidal sinus and the prechordal portion of the body. Hence, greater growth at the midsphenoidal synchondrosis during fetal development could account for much of the facial projection seen in Neandertals.

Of the studies reviewed, Lieberman's findings are the most consistent with Smith and Green's model of accelerated endochondral growth. However, it is important to note that Neandertals share the primitive pattern of elongated anterior cranial base length with non-Neandertal archaic humans, including those from subtropical regions (e.g., Kabwe). Neandertals therefore do not appear to exhibit heterochrony in this feature relative to their ancestors. Consequently, it is unlikely that this feature is related to cold-adapted morphology. Instead, it is modern humans who appear to exhibit postdisplacement in cranial vault growth and hence paedomorphism in facial projection. In sum, studies of craniofacial growth in Neandertals do not lend much support to either the endocrine-shift or accelerated endochondral growth models.

The ontogeny of postcranial robusticity has been explored by delineation of developmental trajectories in modern human growth series, with age-specific comparisons of relevant subadult fossil hominids to the recent human baseline. Ruff and coworkers[59] used this approach to assess percent cortical area, or cortical area as a percentage of total cross-sectional area, in the Nariokotome *Homo erectus* (*ergaster*), La Ferrassie 6, and Teshik-Tash 1 Neandertal juvenile skeletons relative to both an ontogenetic series of Native Americans from Pecos Pueblo and recent Europeans. Percent cortical area serves as a direct measure of medullary stenosis, which, in turn, appears to be conditioned by hormonally mediated bone deposition on the endosteal surface of the diaphysis. Comparison of immature fossil and recent humans with respect to diaphyseal percent cortical area may then help us to understand the age of onset of accelerated endosteal deposition and to make inferences about intergroup differences in circulating levels of sex steroids. The femora of the Nariokotome boy have percent cortical areas that are consistent with high activity levels in a child that had not yet shifted to the adolescent pattern of endosteal bone deposition (Figure 5). The data indicate that by the age of 11 or 12 years the Nariokotome youth had not yet reached puberty, suggesting that he was on a developmental trajectory similar to that of living humans.

What about the Neandertals? Both La Ferrassie 6 and Teshik Tash 1, the only two specimens of a handful of immature Neandertal skeletons for which femoral cross-sectional data are available, have extremely elevated percent cortical areas (Figure 5). The stenosis evident in these juvenile Neandertals does suggest a difference in developmental patterns in that endosteal deposition does not begin until adolescence in modern humans or, presumably, African *Homo erectus*. However, if Neandertal and modern human skeletal contrasts are attributable to differences in growth-active hormones, especially steroids, as suggested by the endocrine-shift model, these hormones must be present from a very early age. It is hard to imagine a three-year-old with adolescent concentrations of testosterone in his bloodstream, but it is possible that growth hormone and androgen levels were higher in Neandertals from an early age. This would support an endocrine explanation for robusticity in Neandertals but, barring the possibility that the Nariokotome skeleton is anomalous, leaves unexplained the heightened robusticity of earlier *Homo*. It is also possible that Neandertal longbone diaphyses started out more stenotic in early life and remained so into adulthood. Early development of stenosis could possibly be the result of reduced levels of bone resorption at the endosteal surface, perhaps due to either elevated activity levels in childhood or altered developmental programs controlling the early vascularization

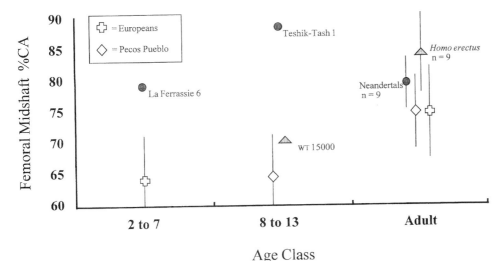

Figure 5. *Femoral midshaft cross-sectional percent cortical area (100*cortical area/total cross-sectional area) for recent and fossil humans in three age classes. Error bars represent ± one standard deviation about the group means. Note the elevated percent cortical area values of the immature Neandertals from La Ferrassie and Teshik-Tash relative to their age-specific comparative groups. Note also that the Nariokotome boy (WT 15000) has a percent cortical area value well below that of the juvenile Neandertal from Teshik-Tash. Data from Ruff et al.[59]*

and ossification of cartilaginous primordia. This latter possibility might be consistent with Smith and Green's model of predisplacement in early endochondral bone formation. At present, it remains unknown whether medullary stenosis in Neandertal children was caused by hormonally elevated endosteal bone deposition, predisplacement in long bone cortical tissue development, or high childhood activity levels.

Recently I have used analysis of covariance structure in measures of postcranial robusticity and muscularity to evaluate the endocrine-shift model as an explanation for between-group differences in robusticity.[13,86] The objective of this work was to explore how much of the variation in robusticity, both between hominid taxa (Neandertals and modern humans) and within modern human groups, could be explained with respect to a systemic agent. If variation in endocrine action is a major source of variation in skeletal robusticity, we would expect, based on the effects of sex steroids and growth hormone on skeletal development, to find a clear pattern of covariation in bone length, cortical tissue thickness, medullary stenosis, relative articular robusticity, and muscularity. I used data from Neandertals and modern humans with exploratory factor analysis to examine the pattern of covariation between measures of all these aspects of robusticity.

The factor analysis revealed a significant pattern of covariance in robusticity measures. The first factor in the analysis accounted for most of the shared variation in robusticity measures, yet explained less than half of the total variation in the data. The second factor, which explained only a very small amount of the total variance, was primarily driven by variation in medullary stenosis, which was unexplained on the first factor. Thus, there is considerable variation in robusticity measures that cannot be explained by reference to overall, or systemic, robusticity. Were it not for the work of Reisenfeld,[50] showing that a single hormone can have different effects on the strength of different bones, we would expect individuals who are robust in one aspect of their skeletons to be robust in others, since the regulating hormones are systemic in their action. Instead we find, consistent with Reisenfeld's results, that individuals are themselves robusticity mosaics, capable of being relatively robust in some features and relatively gracile in others. However, the model does not fit the observed pattern of covariance. The first factor accounted for most of the shared variance in robusticity measures, yet variation in medullary stenosis was virtually unexplained on this factor. The endocrine model predicts that medullary stenosis should have a strongly positive association with robusticity, yet in this analysis variation in medullary area was predominantly explained on a second factor that was unrelated to the first. When the condition that the factor axes must be orthogonal to one another is relaxed, correlations between factors reveal a mild tendency for more robust individuals to have *less stenotic* humeri than more gracile individuals, which is opposite to the prediction of the model. When humeral medullary and cortical areas are regressed on a measure of humeral robusticity (Figure 6), it becomes clear that individuals tend to increase humeral robus-

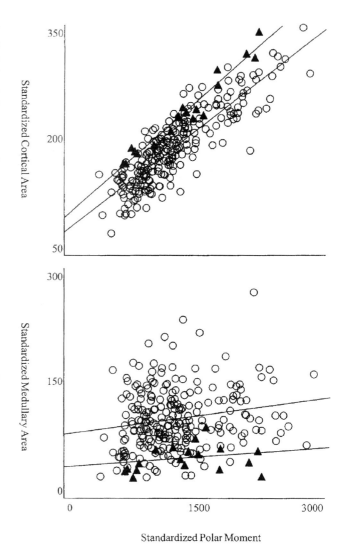

Figure 6. *Regressions of size-standardized humeral mid-distal cross-sectional cortical area and medullary area (both areas standardized as 10^5 *area/humeral length^2) on polar moment of inertia (standardized as 10^9 *polar moment/humeral length^4). Open circles represent recent modern humans; closed triangles represent Neandertals. Least squares regression lines are provided for each group. For cortical area on polar moment: modern humans, $y = 80.79 + 0.089x$, $r = 0.862$; Neandertals, $y = 100.78 + 0.100x$, $r = 0.974$. For medullary area on polar moment: modern humans, $y = 83.16 + 0.015x$, $r = 0.184$; Neandertals, $y = 39.68 + 0.008x$, $r = 0.250$ (not significant). Based on pooled fossil and recent samples, 73.9% of the variance in polar moment of inertia can be explained by variation in cortical area, while only 2.3% can be explained by variation in medullary area. Data from Churchill.[86]*

ticity by expanding cortical tissue *outwards,* not inwards into the medullary space. Contrary to the prediction of the endocrine model, there is a weak but significantly *positive* relationship between medullary area and bone strength, so that more robust individuals tend to have relatively larger medullary spaces.

Finally, mean factor scores (Figure 7) for the fossil and recent groups reveal no significant difference on the robusticity factor between Neandertals and European Upper Paleolithic modern humans. If the first factor could be construed as an endocrine-robusticity factor,

a)

b)

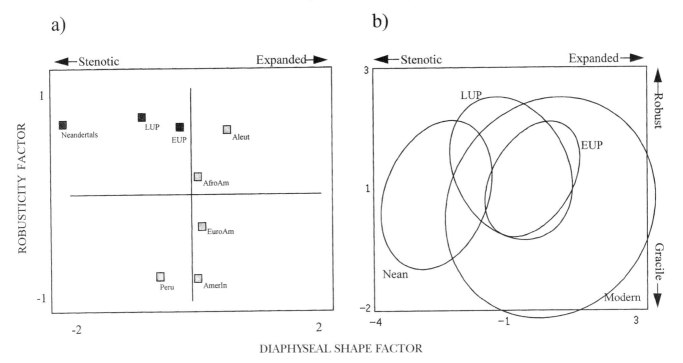

DIAPHYSEAL SHAPE FACTOR

Figure 7.   *Plots of mean factor scores from a factor analysis of upper-limb robusticity measures. The first factor (vertical) is a generalized or systemic robusticity factor. Factor two (horizontal) is a humeral diaphyseal shape factor that distinguishes individuals with stenotic cross-sections from those with expanded medullary areas. a) Sample means. Dark squares represent fossil groups (EUP = Early Upper Paleolithic modern humans; LUP = Late Upper Paleolithic modern humans) and light squares represent various recent human samples. b) Ellipses showing the total range of factor scores for Neandertals, Early (EUP), Late (LUP) Upper Paleolithic fossils, and a large sample of recent modern humans. Note that the Neandertals are not significantly different from early modern humans in generalized robusticity, which argues against an endocrine contrast between groups, and that medullary stenosis is unrelated to generalized robusticity, which again runs counter to the expectations of the endocrine-shift model. Data from Churchill.[86]*

then an endocrine shift does not separate Neandertals from early modern humans. Only one foraging group, western Aleutian Islanders, was included in this study and they were comparable to the fossil groups in their mean score on factor one. Factor one, then, separated foragers from nonforagers, not Neandertals from modern humans.

The shared variance in robusticity measures reflected in the first factor probably has three causes: genetic control over bone formative and regulatory processes played out over the entire skeleton, either through direct control of development or through endocrine agents; the parallel action of natural selection and activity-induced bone modeling and remodeling in structurally adapting whole functional systems like the upper limb for habitual loading regimes; and the effects of overall activity on systemic modeling and remodeling processes. This last cause is becoming increasingly appreciated now that the role of activity in stimulating growth hormone production, and hence, systemic increases in skeletal robusticity, has been more fully elucidated.[62] Experimental research (reviewed in Lieberman[62]) reveals a direct, positive relationship between exercise and growth hormone secretion and a stimulatory effect of growth hormone on cortical bone deposition. Thus, endocrine effects may well explain between-group variation in robusticity in the genus *Homo*, but not as agents of heterochronic transitions.

Given that growth hormone may be more active at the periosteal surface than it is at endosteal surfaces, this might explain, in part, the finding that more robust individuals tend to have expanded diaphyseal cortical areas without necessarily having contracted medullary spaces. The similarity of fossil and recent foragers on a generalized robusticity factor is most parsimoniously explained as a function of similar overall activity levels among foraging groups.

CONCLUSIONS

Taken together, the studies reviewed here indicate that heterochronic models do not serve well as *global* explanations for morphological contrasts between Neandertals and modern humans. Ontogenetic studies do suggest some intriguing heterochronic differences between these groups. Limited studies of covariance structure also reveal a consistent signal of integration in postcranial morphology, suggesting that some variability in trait expression may be attributable to changes in overall body form as the result of heterochrony. However, covariance patterns reveal that while some of the variation in postcranial robusticity and other features in the genus *Homo* can be explained by reference to variation in other traits, *most* of the variation cannot. In other words, developmentally derived covariance, the *sine qua non* of heterochronic explanations of

Neandertal morphology, is weak, at best. Furthermore, covariance observed in skeletal robusticity measures is better explained as the consequence of overall activity, through both mechanical and systemic (growth hormone) effects on bone modeling and remodeling across the entire skeleton. Thus, some of the morphological differences between Neandertals and modern humans are, wholly or in part, the result of differences in activity levels and patterning. All this suggests to me that broad heterochronic explanations, ones that try to account for virtually everything, are doomed to fail, whereas more narrowly construed heterochronic arguments may play a critical role in directing future research.

The endocrine-shift model, as an example of a global heterochronic model, does not fit the skeletal robusticity data. This model holds great intuitive appeal, especially since we can wander down to the local weight room and see, first hand, the morphogenic effects of synthetic sex steroids, or at least their effects on muscle tissue and brow ridge development. It is most probable that heterochronic shifts in the onset and intensity of hormone secretion are an evolutionary pathway to morphogenic change; it is also probable that many of the morphological features that distance Neandertals from us were influenced by subtle differences in circulating hormones. But as a comprehensive explanation, the endocrine model simply does not work.

The accelerated endochondral growth model of Smith and Green, as an example of a more narrowly constructed heterochronic argument, deserves further investigation. This model is valuable in that it provides a competing though not necessarily exclusive hypothesis, with a different selective agent, to the longstanding anterior dental loading hypothesis (reviewed in O'Connor, Franciscus, and Holton[87]) as an explanation for Neandertal craniofacial form. This model is also testable, both by comparing Neandertal juvenile crania with ontogenetic series of recent humans and by exploring the extent to which endochondral growth in the basicranium and postcranial skeleton are developmentally integrated in modern humans. Testing this model will tell us not only something of the Neandertals, but something of the nature of human skeletal morphogenesis in general.

There is no question that the Neandertals' stalwart bodies served them well in Pleistocene Europe. After all, they lasted more than 100,000 years there. There is also no question that they and most probably their European ancestors, as early as 500,000 years ago,[88] were adapted to the glacial climates that periodically gripped Europe during the Ice Ages. A full appreciation of the true extent to which their distinctive features were directly or indirectly related to the Neandertal's occupation of glacial Europe can come only from continued investigation of developmental and functional integration. The significance of certain features, such as mid-facial prognathism and long bone medullary stenosis, is still unclear. It remains to be determined if these are direct consequences of growth programs that were geared to produce stocky, cold-adapted bodies. Other features, such as reduced humeral torsion and elongated pubic bones,[89] may have been secondary consequences of cold adaptation, as adjustments to increased trunk dimensions and body mass in biomechanical systems that must be integrated to function. These possibilities must be fully explored before we can conclude that morphological differences equate with behavioral differences. But it is also clear that the evolution of a cold-adapted body form, as extreme as it may have been, cannot account for all of the features that distinguish the Neandertals from their ancestors, contemporaries, or predecessors. It is likely that the robusticity of their bones, the shapes and orientations of their joints, and the size, orientations and mechanical leverage of their muscles were only indirectly related to their habitation of cold climates. These features are largely unrelated to aspects of body shape, and most likely reflect an emphasis on the strength and endurance necessary to deal with temporal and spatial patchiness of resources in a cold-temperate environment, especially given a technologically and possibly organizationally simple foraging system. Many of these features suggest that Neandertals loaded their skeletons in different ways than do modern foragers, perhaps involving high mobility over uneven terrain, close-contact hunting with short-range weapons, and production of high reaction forces in the upper limb during flint knapping, woodworking, and subsistence activities. Many questions remain about the Neandertals, but it seems clear that continued discovery about these intriguing humans depends on our taking an integrated approach, giving due respect to structuralist and adaptationist perspectives, to the study of their morphology.

ACKNOWLEDGMENTS

My thanks to Matt Cartmill, John Fleagle, Gail Krovitz, Dan Lieberman, Rich Kay, Chris Ruff, Dan Schmitt, Kathleen Smith, Erik Trinkaus, Chris Wall, and two anonymous reviewers for fruitful discussions and helpful comments on earlier drafts of this paper. Thanks also to Laura Shackelford for comments and help with the figures. Stephen Nash drew Figure 1.

REFERENCES

1. Straus, W. L. Jr., Cave, A. J. E. (1957). Pathology and posture of Neanderthal man. Q Rev Biol 32:348–363.
2. Coon, C. S. (1939). The Races of Europe. New York: Macmillan.
3. Brothwell, D. R. (1975). Adaptive growth rate changes as a possible explanation for the distinctiveness of the Neanderthalers. J Archeol Sci 2:161–163.
4. Weaver, D. S. (1980). Catastrophe theory and human evolution. J Anthropol Res 36:403–410.
5. Smith, F. H. (1991). The Neandertals: Evolutionary dead ends or ancestors of modern people? J Anthropol Res 47:219–238.
6. Trinkaus, E., Smith, F. H. (1985). The fate of the Neandertals. In Delson, E. (ed), Ancestors: The Hard Evidence, pp. 325–333. New York: Alan R. Liss.
7. Fleagle, J. G. (1997). Beyond parsimony. Evol Anthropol 6:1.
8. Shea, B. T. (1993). Bone growth and primate evolution. In Hall, B. K. (ed), Bone, vol 7: Bone Growth–B, pp. 133–157. Boca Raton: CRC Press.

9. Trinkaus, E. (1983). Neandertal postcrania and the adaptive shift to modern humans. In Trinkaus, E. (ed), *The Mousterian Legacy*, pp. 165–200. British Archaeological Reports IS-164.
10. Trinkaus, E. (1986). The Neandertals and modern human origins. Ann Rev Anthropol *15*:193–218.
11. Trinkaus, E., Ruff, C. B. (1989). Cross-sectional geometry of Neandertal femoral and tibial diaphyses: Implications for locomotion. Am J Phys Anthropol *78*:315–316.
12. Trinkaus, E., Ruff, C. B. (1989). Diaphyseal cross-sectional morphology and biomechanics of the Fond de-Foret and the Spy 2 femur and tibia. Anthropol Prehist *100*:33–42.
13. Churchill, S. E. (1994). Human Upper Body Evolution in the Eurasian Later Pleistocene. Ph.D. Dissertation, University of New Mexico, Albuquerque.
14. Ruff, C. B., Trinkaus, E., Walker, A., Larsen, C. S. (1993). Postcranial robusticity in *Homo*, I: Temporal trends and mechanical interpretation. Am J Phys Anthropol *91*:21–53.
15. Trinkaus, E., Ruff, C. B., Churchill, S. E. (1998). Upper limb versus lower limb loading patterns among Near Eastern Middle Paleolithic hominids. In Akazawa, T., Aoki, K., Bar Yosef, O. (eds), *Neanderthals and Modern Humans in West Asia*. Princeton: Princeton University Press, pp 391–404.
16. Trinkaus, E., Churchill, S. E., Ruff, C. B., Vandermeersch, B. (n.d.) Long bone diaphyseal robusticity and body proportions of the Saint-Césaire 1 Neandertal. J Arch Sci, in press.
17. Churchill, S. E., Weaver, A. H., Niewoehner, W. A. (n.d.) Late Pleistocene human technological and subsistence behavior: Functional interpretations of upper limb morphology. In Bietti, A., Grimaldi, S. (eds), *Reduction Processes ("Chaînes Opératoires") in the European Mousterian*, Q Nova 6, in press.
18. Pearson, O. M. (1997). The distinctiveness of Neandertal diaphyseal robusticity. Am J Phys Anthropol Suppl *24*:184.
19. Gould, S. J. (1997). *Ontogeny and Phylogeny*. Cambridge: Harvard University Press.
20. Wake, D. B., Larson, A. (1987). Multidimensional analysis of an evolving lineage. Science *238*:42–48.
21. Godfrey, L. R., Sutherland, M. R. (1996). Paradox of peramorphic paedomorphosis: Heterochrony and human evolution. Am J Phys Anthropol *99*:17–42.
22. Vrba, E. S. (1996). An hypothesis of heterochrony in response to climatic cooling and its relevance to early hominid evolution. In Corruccini, R. S., Ciochon, R. L. (eds), *Integrative Paths to the Past: Paleoanthropological Advances in Honor of F. Clark Howell*, pp. 345–376. Englewood Cliffs: Prentice Hall.
23. Shea, B. T. (1992). Developmental perspective on size change and allometry in evolution. Evol Anthropol 1:125–134.
24. Eveleth, P. B., Tanner, J. M. (1976). *Worldwide Variation in Human Growth*. Cambridge: Cambridge University Press.
25. Bogin, B. (1988). *Patterns of Human Growth*. Cambridge: Cambridge University Press.
26. Chaline, J., Marchand, D., Berge, C. (1986). L'évolution de l'homme: Un modele gradualiste ou ponctualiste? Bull Soc R Belge Anthropol Prehist *97*:77–97.
27. Tihen, S. A. (1955). A new Pliocene species of *Ambystoma* with remarks on other fossil ambystomatids. Contrib Museum Paleontol Univ Michigan *12*:229–244.
28. Weaver, M. E., Ingram, D. L. (1969). Morphological changes in swine associated with environmental temperature. Ecology *50*:710–713.
29. Sterns, S. C. (1982). The role of development in the evolution of life histories. In Bonner, J. T. (ed), *Evolution and Development*, pp. 237–258. Berlin: Springer Verlag.
30. Raff, R. A., Kaufman, T. C. (1983). *Embryos, Genes and Evolution*. New York: Macmillan.
31. Holliday, T. W. (1997). Postcranial evidence of cold adaptation in European Neandertals. Am J Phys Anthropol *104*:245–258.
32. Howells, W. W. (1976). Neanderthal man: Facts and figures. Yearbook Phys Anthropol *18*:7–18.
33. Rak, Y. (1986). The Neanderthal: A new look at an old face. J Hum Evol *15*:151–164.
34. Rak, Y. (1993). Morphological variation in *Homo neanderthalensis* and *Homo sapiens* in the Levant: A biogeographic model. In Kimbel, W. H., Martin, L. B. (eds), *Species, Species Concepts and Primate Evolution*, pp 523–536. New York: Plenum Press.
35. Stringer, C. B., Dean, M. C., Martin, R. D. (1990). A comparative study of cranial and dental development within a recent British sample and among Neandertals. In De Rousseau, C. J. (ed),

36. Zelditch, M. L. (1987). Evaluating models of developmental integration in the laboratory rat using confirmatory factor analysis. Syst Zool *36*:368–380.
37. Cheverud, J. M., Wagner, G. P., Dow, M. M. (1989). Methods for the comparative analysis of variation patterns. Syst Zool *38*:201–213.
38. Lahr, M. M., Wright, R. V. S. (1996). The question of robusticity and the relationship between cranial size and shape in *Homo sapiens*. J Hum Evol *31*:157–191.
39. Churchill, S. E. (1996). Particulate versus integrated evolution of the upper body in late Pleistocene humans: A test of two models. Am J Phys Anthropol *100*:559–583.
40. Hublin, J. J. (1989). Les caractères dérivés d'*Homo erectus*: Relation avec l'augmentation de la massé of squelettique. In Giacobini, G. (ed), *Hominidae*, pp. 199–204. Milan: Jaca Book.
41. Hublin, J. J. (1992). *Homo erectus*: Are the "autapomorphies" reversible? Am J Phys Anthropol *14*(suppl):92.
42. Moss, M. L., Young, R. W. (1960). A functional approach to craniology. Am J Phys Anthropol *18*:281–292.
43. Hylander, W. L., Picq, P. G., Johnson, K. R. (1991). Masticatory-stress hypotheses and the supraorbital region of primates. Am J Phys Anthropol *86*:1–36.
44. Anton, S. C. (1989). Intentional cranial vault deformation and induced changes of the cranial base and face. Am J Phys Anthropol *79*:253–267.
45. Konigsberg, L. W., Kohn, L. A. P., Cheverud, J. M. (1993). Cranial deformation and nonmetric trait variation. Am J Phys Anthropol *90*:35–48.
46. Kohn, L. A. P., Leigh, S. R., Cheverud, J. M. (1995). Asymmetric vault modification in Hopi crania. Am J Phys Anthropol *98*:173–195.
47. Olson, E. C., Miller, R. J. (1958). *Morphological Integration*. Chicago: University of Chicago Press.
48. Keith, A. (1925). *The Antiquity of Man*. London: Williams & Norgate.
49. Kennedy, G. E. (1985). Bone thickness in *Homo erectus*. J Hum Evol *14*:669–708.
50. Reisenfeld, A. (1972). Endocrine control of skeletal robusticity. Acta Anat *91*:481–499.
51. Nelson, A. J. (1995). Cortical Bone Thickness in the Primate and Hominid Postcranium—Taxonomy and Allometry. Ph.D. Dissertation, University of California, Los Angeles.
52. Kennedy, G. E., Gauld, S. E., Nelson, A. J. (1991). Bone thickness in fossil hominids. In Dixon, A. D., Sarnat, B. G., Hoyte, D. A. N. (eds), *Fundamentals of Bone Growth: Methodology and Applications*, pp. 587–593. Boca Raton: CRC Press.
53. Ivanhoe, F. (1985). On the Neandertal pubis and acromegaly. Curr Anthropol *26*:526–527.
54. Trinkaus, E. (1985). Reply to Ivanhoe, F. On the Neandertal pubis and acromegaly. Curr Anthropol *26*:527–529.
55. Buchanan, C. R., Preece, M. A. (1992). Hormonal control of bone growth. In Hall, B. K. (ed), *Bone, vol. 6: Bone Growth–A*, pp. 53–89. Boca Raton: CRC Press.
56. Bouvier, M. (1989). The biology and composition of bone. In Cowin, S. C. (ed), *Bone Mechanics*, pp. 1–13. Boca Raton: CRC Press.
57. Garn, S. (1970). *The Earlier Gain and Later Loss of Cortical Bone in Nutritional Perspective*. Springfield: Charles C Thomas.
58. Frisancho, A. R., Garn, S. M., Ascoli, W. (1970). Subperiosteal and endosteal bone apposition during adolescence. Hum Biol *42*:639–664.
59. Ruff, C. B., Trinkaus, E., Walker, A. (1994). Postcranial robusticity in *Homo*, III: Ontogeny. Am J Phys Anthropol *93*:35–54.
60. Ucko, H. (1951). *Endocrine Diagnosis*. London: Staples Press.
61. Russell, M. D. (1985). The supraorbital torus: "A most remarkable peculiarity." Curr Anthropol *26*:337–360.
62. Lieberman, D. E. (1996). How and why recent humans grow thin skulls: Experimental evidence for systemic cortical robusticity. Am J Phys Anthropol *101*:217–236.
63. Shea, B. T. (1988). Heterochrony in primates. In McKinney, M. L. (ed), *Heterochrony in Evolution: A Multidisciplinary Approach*, pp. 237–266. New York: Plenum Press.
64. Vlcek, E. (1973). Postcranial skeleton of a Neandertal child from Kiik-Koba, U.S.S.R. J Hum Evol 2:537–544.
65. Heim, J. L. (1982). *Les Enfants Néandertaliens de La Ferrassie*. Paris: Masson.

Primate Life History and Evolution, pp. 115–152. New York: Wiley-Liss.

66. Tompkins, R. L., Trinkaus, E. (1987). La Ferrassie 6 and the development of Neandertal pubic morphology. Am J Phys Anthropol 73:233–239.

67. Wolpoff, M. H. (1980). *Paleoanthropology.* New York: Alfred A Knopf.

68. Brace, C. L. (1988). Comment on Rosenberg, K. R. The functional significance of Neandertal pubic length. Curr Anthropol 29:607–608.

69. Rosenberg, K. R. (1988). The functional significance of Neandertal pubic length. Curr Anthropol 29:595–617.

70. Green, M. (1990). Neandertal Craniofacial Growth: An Ontogenetic Model. M.A. Thesis, University of Tennessee, Knoxville.

71. Green, M., Smith, F. H. (1990). Neandertal craniofacial growth. Am J Phys Anthropol 81:232.

72. Smith, F. H., Green, M. (1991). Heterochrony, life history and Neandertal morphology. Am J Phys Anthropol 12(suppl):164.

73. Enlow, D. H. (1982). *Handbook of Facial Growth,* 2nd ed. Philadelphia: W.B. Saunders.

74. Smith, F. H., Falsetti, A. B., Donnelly, S. M. (1989). Modern human origins. Yearbook Phys Anthropol 32:35–68.

75. Dean, M. C., Stringer, C. B., Bromage, T. G. (1986). Age at death of the Neanderthal child from Devil's Tower, Gibraltar and the implications for studies of general growth and development in Neanderthals. Am J Phys Anthropol 70:301–309.

76. Trinkaus, E., Tompkins, R. L. (1990). The Neandertal life cycle: The possibility, probability, and perceptibility of contrasts with recent humans. In DeRousseau (ed), *Primate Life History and Evolution, Monographs in Primatology Vol 14,* pp. 153–180. New York: Wiley-Liss.

77. Tompkins, R. L. (1991). Relative Dental Development in Upper Pleistocene Fossil Hominids and Recent Humans. Ph.D. Dissertation, University of New Mexico, Albuquerque.

78. Abbott, S., Trinkaus, E., Burr, D. B. (1996). Dynamic bone remodeling in later Pleistocene hominids. Am J Phys Anthropol 99:585–601.

79. Simpson, S. W., Lovejoy, C. O., Meindl, R. S. (1991). Relative dental development in hominoids and its failure to predict somatic growth velocity. Am J Phys Anthropol 86:113–120.

80. Simpson, S. W., Lovejoy, C. O., Meindl, R. S. (1992). Further evidence on relative dental maturation and somatic developmental rate in hominoids. Am J Phys Anthropol 87:29–38.

81. Thompson, J. L., Nelson, A. J. (1997). Relative postcranial development of Neandertals. J Hum Evol 32: A23–A24.

82. Krovitz, G., Cole, T. M. III, Richtsmeier, J. T. (1997). Three-dimensional comparisons of craniofacial growth patterns in Neandertals and modern humans. Am J Phys Anthropol 24(suppl):147.

83. Williams, F. L. (1995). Similarity of craniofacial growth and development in Neandertals and modern humans. Am J Phys Anthropol 20(suppl): 222.

84. Williams, F. L. (1996). The use of non-linear models to map craniofacial heterochronies in fossil hominids. Am J Phys Anthropol 22(suppl):244.

85. Lieberman, D. E. (1997). A developmental approach to defining modern humans. Am J Phys Anthropol Suppl 24:155–156.

86. Churchill, S. E. (1997). Endocrine models of skeletal robusticity and the origins of gracility. Am J Phys Anthropol 24(suppl):92.

87. O'Connor, C. F., Franciscus, R. G., Holton, N. E. (2005). Bite force production capability and efficiency in Neandertals and modern humans. Am J Phys Anthropol 127:129–151.

88. Trinkaus, E., Stringer, C. B., Ruff, C. B., Hennessy, R. J., Roberts, M. B., Parfitt, S. A. (1996). The Boxgrove tibia. Am J Phys Anthropol Suppl 22:230–231.

89. Weaver, T. D., Franciscus, R. G., Karlin, C. D., Burson, E. A., Gust, K. A. (1998). 3-D coordinate analysis of the Kebara 2 Neandertal pelvis. Am J Phys Anthropol Suppl 26:228.

57

Neandertal Cranial Ontogeny and Its Implications for Late Hominid Diversity

M. S. Ponce de León and C. P. E. Zollikofer

ABSTRACT

Homo neanderthalensis *has a unique combination of craniofacial features that are distinct from fossil and extant 'anatomically modern'* Homo sapiens *(modern humans). Morphological evidence, direct isotopic dates[1] and fossil mitochondrial DNA from three Neanderthals[2,3] indicate that the Neanderthals were a separate evolutionary lineage for at least 500,000 yr. However, it is unknown when and how Neanderthal craniofacial autapomorphies (unique, derived characters) emerged during ontogeny. Here we use computerized fossil reconstruction[4] and geometric morphometrics[5,6] to show that characteristic differences in cranial and mandibular shape between Neanderthals and modern humans arose very early during development, possibly prenatally, and were maintained throughout postnatal ontogeny. Postnatal differences in cranial ontogeny between the two taxa are characterized primarily by heterochronic modifications of a common spatial pattern of development. Evidence for early ontogenetic divergence together with evolutionary stasis of taxon-specific patterns of ontogeny is consistent with separation of Neanderthals and modern humans at the species level.*

Comparative analyses of immature crania indicate that diagnostic Neanderthal characters appeared early during ontogeny[7,8] and that the Neanderthal ontogenetic process was fast relative to that of the modern humans[7,9–11]. Here, we use a new methodological approach to study the comparative ontogeny of Neanderthal and modern human skulls. After computerized reconstruction of fragmentary fossil specimens[4,12–14], we applied geometric morphometric methods (GMM)[5] to identify and visualize complex patterns of morphological change during ontogeny (see Methods). In GMM the form of a specimen is described by the spatial configuration of a set of three-dimensional anatomical landmarks. Size-corrected variation in shape can then be computed in terms of between-specimen rearrangements of landmark positions. To capture large trends in shape variation in ontogenetic samples of Neanderthals and modern humans, we used relative warp analysis[5,6], which separates shape variability into statistically independent factors. Each relative warp thus captures an independent aspect of shape variation in the sample (Figure 1) that can be plotted

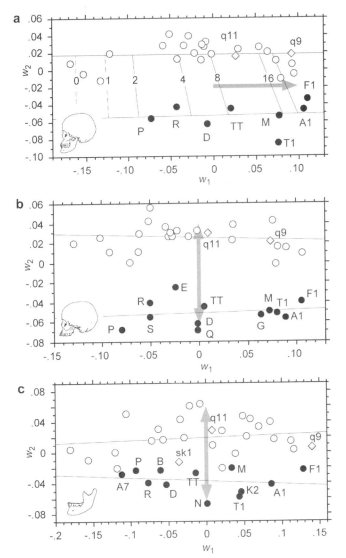

Figure 1. *Shape variability in an ontogenetic series of Neanderthals (filled circles; see Methods for specimen labels) and modern humans (open circles/diamonds indicate extant/fossil specimens, respectively) for craniomandibular (**a**), cranial (**b**) and mandibular (**c**) landmark configurations. The labels w_1 and w_2 represent factors of shape variation resulting from relative warp analysis[5,6]. Neanderthals and modern humans follow ontogenetic trajectories that are approximately parallel (lines are principal axes of within-taxon correlation). The arrow in **a** characterizes the shared Neanderthal/modern human mode of development as shown in Figure 3; taxon-specific trajectories are connected with lines at dental ages 0 (birth), 1, 2, 4, 8, 16 yr and adulthood. Arrows in **b** and **c** indicate differences in shape between Neanderthals and modern humans as shown in Figure 4.*

ontogenetically as temporal (Figure 2) and spatial (Figures 3 and 4) patterns of morphological change.

Our relative warp analyses are based on a large cross-sectional ontogenetic series of Neanderthal cranial and mandibular specimens that were reconstructed by computerized methods, and a comparative fossil/ recent modern human sample. The Neanderthal sample mostly comprises individuals from dental stage 3 (3–6 yr) to adulthood, but includes an early postnatal mandible (Amud 7, about 0.5 yr[8]) and a cranium and mandible from dental stage 2 (Pech de l'Azé, about 2.5 yr); the modern human sample includes individuals from all ontogenetic stages—from perinatal through to adulthood (see Methods and Appendix for sample details and landmark definitions). We computed the statistically independent relative warps for the combined craniomandibular landmark configurations (Figure 1a) and for cranial and mandibular configurations in isolation (Figure 1b, c), and plotted these against three additional factors: (1) individual age (dental age); (2) centroid size (S, the extent of the landmark configuration); and (3) taxon (Neanderthal compared to modern human).

In all three analyses, only the first two statistically independent relative warps (w_1 and w_2) covary significantly with age, S and taxon, which together account for about 60% of the total shape variability (see Methods and Appendix for details of relative warp analysis). There are clear patterns of covariation: w_1 describes shape variation related to size and age (Figures 1 and 2), whereas w_2 describes taxon-specific shape variation (Figure 1). Each w_1–w_2 coordinate in Figure 1 corresponds to a specific morphological configuration in physical space, and each vector (arrows along statistically independent relative warps in Figure 1) indicates a distinct spatial pattern of morphological change. The most important result of the analyses (evident from Figure 1) is that taxon-specific differences in craniomandibular shape are present by dental stage 2 and remain subsequently unchanged during ontogeny. This indicates that the characteristic morphologies that distinguish both Neanderthals and modern humans develop before dental stage 2, during early postnatal or possibly during prenatal ontogeny. From dental stage 2 onwards, Neanderthals and modern humans follow parallel ontogenetic trajectories along the direction of w_1 (Figure 1), demonstrating a shared spatial pattern of morphological change (Figure 3). The different lengths of the trajectories in Figure 1, however, indicate that there are heterochronic differences between the taxa in their postnatal ontogeny. Plots of the relationship between dental age, craniomandibular shape w_1 and size S (Figure 2) show that although the two taxa follow similar ontogenetic allometries (Figure 2a), Neanderthals compared to modern humans show rate hypermorphosis (faster rates of growth and development leading to greater adult values of size and shape) during ontogeny (Figure 2b, c). In all analyses, the fossil modern human subsample falls within the range of ontogenetic variability displayed by the extant modern human sample. In addition, the Neanderthals analysed here, which sample a long period of time[1], exhibit similar within-taxon ontogenetic variability, suggesting

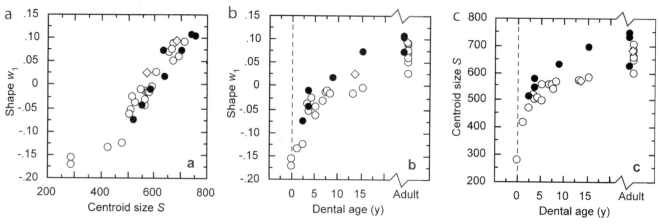

Figure 2. *Correlations between shape (w₁), centroid size S and dental age (in postnatal years) for craniomandibular morphologies of Neanderthals (filled circles) and extant/fossil modern humans (open circles/diamonds, respectively).* **a**, *Ontogenetic allometry (w₁ versus S).* **b**, *Development (w₁ versus dental age).* **c**, *Growth (S versus dental age). Compared to modern humans, Neanderthals show rate hypermorphosis during development and growth.*

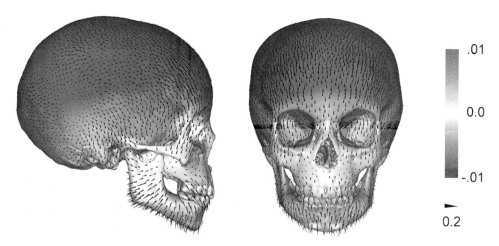

Figure 3. *Patterns of shape change during postnatal development in Neanderthals and modern humans. A Neanderthal/modern human consensus skull is shown. Changes in morphology (corresponding to transformation along the arrow in Figure 1a) are visualized with shading and vector fields (see Methods). Arrows indicate direction and magnitude of shape change tangential to the surface (all scales in units of centroid size, S). Note the projection and downward elongation of the face and mandible, as opposed to the relative 'contraction' of the cranial vault (size S is held constant).*

long-term stability of the modern human and Neanderthal patterns of ontogeny.

To further explore taxon-specific regional differences in cranial and mandibular growth, Figures 3 and 4 express statistically independent factors w_1 and w_2 as modifications of the Neanderthal/modern human consensus morphology (computed from a 5-year-old modern human specimen). Components of shape change were computed perpendicular and parallel to the craniomandibular surface and were visualized using vector fields (see Methods). Figure 3 shows the shared Neanderthal/modern human pattern of craniomandibular shape change from dental stage 2 to adulthood. The stability of this pattern over an extended phase of ontogeny (linear trajectories in Figure 1a) indicates that the spatial distribution of areas of bone deposition/resorption and the relative rates of growth in these areas were constant in both taxa[15].

Patterns of Neanderthal and modern human ontogeny from dental stage 2 onwards therefore apparently derive from generally similar growth processes.

Figure 4 shows quantitative differences between Neanderthal and modern human morphologies that are already established at dental stage 2 and that are consistent with previous characterizations of the differences between the taxa[1,8,16–19]. Relative to modern humans, Neanderthals have a low cranial vault that is expanded posterolaterally. The boundary between superior and inferior regions of the vault (as visualized by shading in Figure 4a–c) probably corresponds to the circumcranial reversal line that separates depository from resorptive growth fields on the internal surface of the braincase[20]. Increased drift and displacement in the inferior region of the Neanderthal cranial vault may therefore account for many of the Neanderthal apomorphies (derived characters) found, such as a broadened temporal

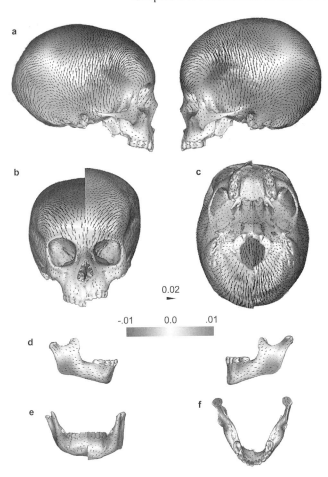

Figure 4. *Shape differences between Neanderthal and modern human skulls (**a–c**) and mandibles (**d–f**). Left panels show Neanderthal morphologies; right panels show modern human morphologies (corresponding to opposite tips of the arrows in Figure 1b, c). The shading patterns indicate the direction and magnitude of shape difference of each taxon relative to the other and can tentatively be interpreted as representing contrasts between modes of prenatal (and early postnatal) development. Arrows indicate differences tangential to surfaces (all scales in units of centroid size, S). An animated version (Neanderthal–modern human transition) is available at: http://www.nature.com/nature/journal/v412/n6846/extref/images/NeanderthalToSapiens.mov*

region, rounded lateral cranial walls[1], a more caudal position of the middle cranial fossa, an elongated foramen magnum[8], and a large occipital squama[21] (Figure 4a–c). The differences in growth fields that may account for these features probably reflect taxon-specific differences in interactions between cranial base shape and brain size/shape during early development[21].

Differential activity of growth fields may also explain many unique aspects of Neanderthal maxillofacial and mandibular morphology (Figure 4d–f). In the fetal/early postnatal mandible, the lingual surfaces of the corpus and the external and anterior surfaces of the rami are resorptive[20], such that differential growth patterns affect the inclination of the rami relative to the cranial midplane and their anteroposterior position relative to the dentition. Visualization of relative warp analyses suggests that, compared to modern humans, the Neanderthal mandible was characterized by rela-

tively less mediolateral growth and more anteroposterior growth: the rami are relatively inclined (having short condylar processes that are positioned laterally), and the corpus and rami are at a posterior position relative to the dentition (suggesting an early rather than late[19] ontogenetic origin of the retromolar space[16,17,22]). In humans, depository growth fields in the most anterior regions of the maxilla and mandible turn into resorptive fields shortly after birth, limiting facial projection during postnatal ontogeny[20,23]. According to our data, Neanderthals follow a similar postnatal pattern. Thus, increased rates of fetal growth and/or later reversal of growth fields may be responsible for many characteristic aspects of Neanderthal midfacial prognathism, such as expanded maxillae, a spacious nasal cavity, a receding cheek region (Figure 4a–c), and a longer persistence of the premaxillary suture[24]. Similar differences may generate the receding symphyseal region of the Neanderthal mandible.

The above analyses therefore indicate that most of the principal differences between Neanderthal and modern human skulls result from ontogenetically early differences in the relative timing and rates of activity at specific growth fields. These data thus support recent studies suggesting that early modifications of growth processes, notably in basicranial morphogenesis, have a principal role in generating evolutionary novelty in the hominid cranium[21,23,25,26]. Pronounced basicranial flexion at the spheno-occipital synchondrosis before 2 yr accounts for the unique position of the modern human face beneath the anterior cranial fossa[23,27]. It is therefore probable that the midfacial projection that is characteristic of Neanderthals[16–18] (Figure 4a, b) results, in part, from less basicranial flexion during early postnatal or possibly prenatal ontogeny[23]. The early appearance of taxon-specific features between Neanderthals and modern humans, the morphological distinctiveness of these taxa throughout later postnatal ontogeny, and the evidence for evolutionary stasis of taxon-specific patterns of ontogeny, all support the theory[8,12,18,25] that *Homo neanderthalensis* and *Homo sapiens* represent morphologically discrete, separate species, which belonged to distinct evolutionary lineages[28]. It remains to be tested whether the observed pattern of evolutionary developmental diversification—prenatal divergence in conjunction with postnatal parallelism of developmental patterns—is characteristic for hominid evolution in general.

METHODS

Sample Structure

The Neanderthal sample comprises 11 immature and 5 adult specimens, respectively: Amud 7 (A7; 0.5 yr); Pech de l'Azé (P; 2.2 yr); Barakai (B; 3 yr); Subalyuk 2 (S; 3.2 yr); Roc de Marsal (R; 3.5 yr); Devil's Tower (Gibraltar 2) (D; 3.5 yr); Engis 2 (E; 5.5 yr); La Quina 18 (Q; 6.5 yr); Teshik Tash (TT; 8.5 yr); La Naulette (N; 14 yr); Le Moustier 1 (M; 15 yr), all of which are immature; and Amud 1 (A1); La Ferrassie 1 (F1); Forbes' Quarry (Gibraltar 1) (G); Kebara 2 (K2); and Tabun 1 (T1), which are adult specimens. The fossil modern human sample comprises 3 specimens from the Near East: Skhul 1 (sk1; 3.5 yr); Qafzeh 11 (q11; 13.5 yr); and Qafzeh 9 (q9; adult), all of which are dated to about 100,000 yr ago[1]. The extant modern humans are represented by a pooled-sex sample of 22 specimens from Europe, Africa, Asia, America and Australia. This sample includes hyper-robust specimens from high north/south latitudes (for details see Appendix Table 1).

Ageing

We estimated ages at death of both Neanderthal and modern human specimens with modern standard scores of dental eruption[29]; we used ages based on perikymata where available[9]. Direct age estimates based on perikymata indicate that application of modern human dental scores may bias results towards higher ages in Neanderthals[9]. As Neanderthal cranial ontogeny tends to be slightly fast relative to modern humans[7,9,10], dental scoring yields conservative estimates for individual ages. To distinguish early versus late phases of postnatal ontogeny, we discern between dental stage 2 (after eruption of dc (lower deciduous canine) and before full crown development of I1) and dental stage 3 (crown of I1 fully developed and before eruption of M1).

Data Acquisition and Fossil Reconstruction

After acquisition of volume data with computer tomography, we generated three-dimensional, graphical object representations of all specimens. We reconstructed the fossil specimens by using special-purpose virtual reality tools[30]. Briefly, filling material was removed from earlier reconstructions, the isolated fossil fragments were re-composed on the computer screen, missing parts were completed with mirror-imaged counterparts, and taphonomic deformation was tentatively corrected, using the methods and anatomical criteria described elsewhere[4,12,14].

Landmark Data Registration

Three-dimensional coordinates of the anatomical landmarks were determined on the graphical representations of the specimens. Virtual registration allows landmark data acquisition on external and internal cranial surfaces[4]. The data set used in GMM analysis comprises 51 cranial (15 midsagittal and 18 bilateral pairs) and 22 mandibular (4 midsagittal and 9 bilateral pairs) landmarks (for details see Appendix Table 2). All landmarks were chosen to represent locations of between-specimen homology.

Analysis of Shape Variability

Relative warp analysis provides an effective means to detect and analyse patterns of correlated shape change in multi-landmark configurations. We performed relative warp analysis according to methods in ref. 6. To constrain modes of shape variation to bilateral symmetry, each specimen's landmark configuration was made sym-

metrical by generalized least-squares (GLS) superimposition with its mirror-imaged counterpart, and subsequent averaging. The form of each specimen is defined as the set of its three-dimensional landmark coordinates. As a linear measure of size, centroid size S is used, calculated as the square root of the sum of squared distances of all landmarks from the centre of gravity (the centroid) of the landmark configuration[5]. GLS fitting of the size-normalized ($S = 1$) landmark configurations of all specimens yields an average configuration (the consensus) and defines a linearized Procrustes space in which the shape of each specimen is given by its linear deviation (landmark by landmark) from the consensus. Using the thin plate spline (TPS) eigenfunctions of the consensus, each specimen is then expressed as a smooth deformation of the consensus, given by its partial warp scores[5]. An array of orthogonal basis vectors, the relative warps, were calculated to reduce the dimensionality of the resulting partial warp space. Relative warps are statistically independent factors of shape variation that account for the largest, second largest and successively smaller proportions of the total sample variance in shape (for details see Appendix Table 3).

Visualization of Shape Change

As relative warps are TPS functions, each point in the space of relative warps (see Figure 1) corresponds to one specific physical landmark configuration resulting from a deformation of the consensus. Similarly, the transformation between any two points in relative warp space (arrows in Figure 1) can be expressed as a TPS function. This TPS function defines a displacement vector at every point of the cranial surface. The resulting spatial pattern of shape change is visualized as follows: for each point on the cranial surface, the displacement vector is decomposed into its normal and tangential components, relative to the local orientation of the surface. The tangential component is visualized as a vector field, indicating its direction and magnitude (see Figures 3 and 4).

ACKNOWLEDGMENTS

We are grateful to R. D. Martin and P. Stucki for support of our research. C. B. Stringer's continuous help and advice is gratefully acknowledged. We thank C. Howell, J.-J. Jaeger, D. Lieberman, J. Schwartz and C. Pryce for valuable comments on an earlier version of this paper. We appreciate the help of the following curators in providing access to fossil specimens: J.-J. Cleyet-Merle, J.-M. Cordy, V. Kharitonov, M. Marinot, F. Menghin, R. Orban, I. Pap, Y. Rak, C. B. Stringer, B. Vandermeersch. We also thank the radiologists, physicists and technicians engaged in fossil computer tomography scanning: E. Berenyi, G. Bijl, P. Dondelinger, V. Dousset, W. Fuchs, S. Louryan, V. Makarenko, U. Shreter, N. Strickland and C. L. Zollikofer. This work was supported by the Swiss National Science Foundation and a habilitation grant of the Canton of Zurich.

REFERENCES

1. Stringer, C. B. & Gamble, C. *In Search of the Neanderthals: Solving the Puzzle of Human Origins* (Thames and Hudson, London, 1993).

2. Krings, M. et al. A view of Neandertal genetic diversity. *Nature Genet.* **26,** 144–146 (2000).

3. Ovchinnikov, I. V. et al. Molecular analysis of Neanderthal DNA from the northern Caucasus. *Nature* **404,** 490–493 (2000).

4. Zollikofer, C. P. E., Ponce de León, M. S. & Martin, R. D. Computer-assisted paleoanthropology. *Evol. Anthropol.* **6,** 41–54 (1998).

5. Bookstein, F. L. *Morphometric Tools for Landmark Data* (Cambridge Univ. Press, Cambridge, 1991).

6. Rohlf, F. J. in *Contributions to Morphometrics* (eds Marcus, L., Bello, E. & García-Valdecasas, A.) 131–159 (Consejo superior de investigaciones científicas, Madrid, 1993).

7. Tillier, A.-M. in *The Human Revolution. Behavioural and Biological Perspectives on the Origins of Modern Humans* (eds Mellars, P. & Stringer, C. B.) 286–297 (Edinburgh Univ. Press, Edinburgh, 1989).

8. Rak, Y., Kimbel, W. H. & Hovers, E. A Neanderthal infant from Amud Cave, Israel. *J. Hum. Evol.* **26,** 313–324 (1994).

9. Dean, M. C., Stringer, C. B. & Bromage, T. G. Age at death of the Neanderthal child from Devil's Tower, Gibraltar and the implications for studies of general growth and development in Neanderthals. *Am. J. Phys. Anthropol.* **70,** 301–309 (1986).

10. Stringer, C. B., Dean, M. C. & Martin, R. D. in *Primate Life History and Evolution* (ed. DeRousseau, C. J.) 115–152 (Wiley-Liss, New York, 1990).

11. Williams, F. l. E. in *Neanderthals on the Edge* (eds Stringer, C. B., Barton, R. N. E. & Finlayson, J. C.) 257–267 (Oxbow Books, Oxford, 2000).

12. Zollikofer, C. P. E., Ponce de León, M. S., Martin, R. D. & Stucki, P. Neanderthal computer skulls. *Nature* **375,** 283–285 (1995).

13. Ponce de León, M. S. & Zollikofer, C. P. E. New evidence from Le Moustier 1: computer-assisted reconstruction and morphometry of the skull. *Anat. Rec.* **254,** 474–489 (1999).

14. Ponce de León, M. S. *Neanderthal Ontogeny: a Geometric Morphometric Analysis of Cranial Growth.* PhD thesis, Univ. Zürich (2000).

15. O'Higgins, P. & Jones, N. Facial growth in *Cercocebus torquatus*: an application of three-dimensional geometric morphometric techniques to the study of morphological variation. *J. Anat.* **193,** 251–272 (1998).

16. Rak, Y. The Neanderthal: a new look at an old face. *J. Hum. Evol.* **15,** 151–164 (1986).

17. Trinkaus, E. The Neandertal face: evolutionary and functional perspectives on a recent hominid face. *J. Hum. Evol.* **16,** 429–443 (1987).

18. Schwartz, J. H. & Tattersall, I. Significance of some previously unrecognized apomorphies in the nasal region of *Homo neanderthalensis*. *Proc. Natl Acad. Sci. USA* **93,** 10852–10856 (1996).

19. Rosas, A. Occurrence of Neanderthal features in mandibles from the Atapuerca-SH site. *Am. J. Phys. Anthropol.* **114,** 74–91 (2001).

20. Enlow, D. H. *Facial Growth* 3rd edn (Saunders, Philadelphia, 1990).

21. Lieberman, D. E., Pearson, O. M. & Mowbray, K. M. Basicranial influence on overall cranial shape. *J. Hum. Evol.* **38,** 291–315 (2000).

22. Franciscus, R. G. & Trinkaus, E. Determinants of retromolar space presence in Pleistocene *Homo* mandibles. *J. Hum. Evol.* **28,** 577–595 (1995).

23. Lieberman, D. E. in *Development, Growth and Evolution* (eds O'Higgins, P. & Cohn, M. J.) 85–122 (Linn. Soc. Lond., London, 2000).

24. Maureille, B. & Bar, D. The premaxilla in Neandertal and early modern children: ontogeny and morphology. *J. Hum. Evol.* **37,** 137–152 (1999).

25. Lieberman, D. E. Sphenoid shortening and the evolution of modern human cranial shape. *Nature* **393,** 158–162 (1998).

26. Lieberman, D. E., Ross, C. F. & Ravosa, M. J. The primate cranial base: ontogeny, function, and integration. *Yb. Phys. Anthropol.* **43,** 117–169 (2000).

27. Lieberman, D. E. & McCarthy, R. C. The ontogeny of cranial base angulation in humans and chimpanzees and its implications for reconstructing pharyngeal dimensions. *J. Hum. Evol.* **36,** 487–517 (1999).

28. Tattersall, I. & Schwartz, J. H. Morphology, paleoanthropology and Neanderthals. *New Anat.* **253,** 113–117 (1998).

29. Ubelaker, D. H. *Human Skeletal Remains. Excavation, Analysis, Interpretation* (Chicago Univ. Press, Chicago, 1978).

30. Zollikofer, C. P. E. & Ponce de León, M. S. Tools for rapid prototyping in the biosciences. *IEEE Comp. Graph. Appl.* **15,** 48–55 (1995).

Supplementary information is available on *Nature's* World-Wide Web site (http://www.nature.com) or as paper copy from the London editorial office of *Nature*.

APPENDIX

Table 1. Description of the Neanderthal and the "Anatomically Modern" *Homo sapiens* (AMH) Sample

Specimen	Postnatal Dental Age (y)	Sex	Locality	Remarks
Recent AMH[*]				
AS 1601	–0.3		Africa	
AS 111	–0.2		Africa	
AS 52	1		India	
AS 177	2	m	Europe	
AS 807	3	m	Africa	
UHZ 4	3.5		India	
AS 174	4	f	Africa	
AIZ Wt	5		Switzerland	
AIZ 127	5		India	
AIZ 1006BV43	6.5		New Guinea	
NHM 86.4.27.5	7		Greenland	
AIZ 1000BV37	7.5		N-America	
AS 29	8	f	Africa	
AIZ 63BV3	13		Asia	
AIZ Po	15	f	Austria	
AIZ 4539	adult	m	Australia	robust
AIZ 5671	adult	m	Africa	
AIZ 8731	adult		India	
NHM BD1191	adult	f	Greenland	hyper-robust
NHM AM10_8540	adult	m	Greenland	hyper-robust
NHM 1025.4	adult		Tierra del Fuego	hyper-robust
NHM 1915.5.5.1	adult		Patagonia	hyper-robust

continued on next page

Table 1. (Continued)

Specimen	Postnatal Dental Age (y)	Sex	Locality	Remarks
Fossil AMH				
Skhul 1	3.5		Israel	
Qafzeh 11	13.5		Israel	
Qafzeh 9	adult		Israel	
Neanderthals				
Amud 7	0.5		Israel	
Pech de l'Azé (cast)	2.2		France	
Barakai	3		Russia	
Subalyuk 2	3.2		Hungary	
Roc de Marsal	3.5		France	
Devil's Tower - Gibraltar 2	3.5		Gibraltar	
Engis 2	5.5		Belgium	
La Quina 18 (cast)	6.5		France	
Teshik Tash	8.5		Uzbekistan	
La Naulette	14		Belgium	
Le Moustier 1	15		France	
Amud 1	adult		Israel	
LaFerrassie 1 (cast)	adult		France	
Forbes' Quarry - Gibraltar 1	adult		Gibraltar	
Tabun 1	adult		Israel	
Kebara 2	adult		Israel	

*AIZ: collection of the Anthropological Institute, Zurich. AS: A. Schultz collection, Zurich. NHM: Natural History Museum, London. UHZ: collection of the University Hospital, Zurich.

Table 2. Definitions of the Cranial and Mandibular Landmarks

Landmark	Definition*
Cranium	
Midsagittal	
prosthion	M
nasospinale	M
nasion	M
glabella	M
mid-nasion-bregma	midpoint of the arch nasion-bregma
bregma	M
mid-bregma-lambda	midpoint of the arch bregma-lambda
lambda	M
inion	M
opisthion	M
basion	M
sphenobasion	M
staphylion	M
foramen caecum	pit between crista frontalis and crista galli
internal occipital protuberance	midsagittal point at the height of the left/right sulci of the transverse sinuses
Bilateral	
2nd (pre)molar	buccal-most midpoint on crown of the second upper deciduous molar or of the second permanent premolar
foramen infraorbitale	midpoint of the foramen on the level of the maxillary bone surface
zygomaxillare	M
orbitale	M
maxillofrontale	M
foramen supraorbitale	midpoint of the foramen/notch along the supraorbital rim; if foramen not present: highest point of supraorbital rim
frontomalare orbitale	M
jugale	point on the posterior rim of the zygomatic bone, connecting the orbital and zygomatic processes
eminentia frontalis	point with highest Gaussian curvature on the squama of the frontal bone
stephanion	M
mid-coronale	midpoint of the arch bregma-pterion
eminentia parietalis	point with highest Gaussian curvature on the parietal bone
asterion	M
entomion	M
porion	M
mid-lambda	midpoint of the arch lambda-asterion
foramen stylomastoideum	midpoint of the foramen on the level of the bone surface
foramen caroticum	midpoint of the foramen on the level of the external bone surface
Mandible	
Midsagittal	
infradentale	M
gnathion	M

Table 2.   (Continued)

Landmark	Definition[*]
akanthion	M
mid-infradentale-gnathion	midpoint of the arch infradentale-gnathion
Bilateral	
canine	buccal-most midpoint on crown
2nd (pre)molar	buccal-most midpoint on crown of the second lower deciduous molar or of the second permanent premolar
foramen mentale	midpoint on the bone surface level
anterior border of ramus	intersection of alveolar plane with anterior-exterior margin of ramus
foramen mandibulae	midpoint on the bone surface level
gonion	M
processus coronoideus	tip of the coronoid process
incisura	lowest point of incisura mandibulae
mesokondylion	midpoint on the glenoid surface of the mandibular condyle

[*]M: according to Martin, R. (1914). *Lehrbuch der Anthropologie.* Jena: Gustav Fischer.

Table 3.   Statistics of Relative Warp Analyses of the Craniomandibular, Cranial, and Mandibular Landmark Configurations

Relative Warp	Craniomandibular Shape	Cranial Shape	Mandibular Shape
Variance proportions (%)			
w1	50.53	45.91	49.45
w2	10.06	10.41	8.97
w3	9.15	6.97	8.82
w4	3.92	4.95	6.77
w5	3.55	3.97	5.36
Influence of taxon (Nea/AMH[*]; ANOVA; *p*-values)			
w1	0.17	0.29	0.81
w2	<0.0001	<0.0001	<0.0001
w3	0.49	0.75	0.45
Correlation with centroid size *S* (*p*-values)			
w1	<0.0001	<0.0001	<0.0001
w2	0.46 (Nea); 0.71 (AMH)	0.72 (Nea); 0.57 (AMH)	0.71 (Nea); 0.51 (AMH)
w3	0.66	0.2	0.37
Correlation with dental age (*p*-values)			
w1	<0.0001	<0.0001	<0.0001
w2	0.89 (Nea); 0.34 (AMH)	0.21 (Nea); 0.37 (AMH)	0.53 (Nea); 0.19 (AMH)
w3	0.09	0.45	0.12

[*]Nea: *Homo neanderthalensis*. AMH: "anatomically modern" *Homo sapiens*.

58

Neandertal Cannibalism at Moula-Guercy, Ardèche, France

A. Defleur, T. White, P. Valensi, L. Slimak, and É. Crégut-Bonnoure

ABSTRACT

The cave site of Moula-Guercy, 80 meters above the modern Rhone River, was occupied by Neanderthals approximately 100,000 years ago. Excavations since 1991 have yielded rich paleontological, paleobotanical, and archaeological assemblages, including parts of six Neanderthals. The Neanderthals are contemporary with stone tools and faunal remains in the same tightly controlled stratigraphic and spatial contexts. The inference of Neanderthal cannibalism at Moula-Guercy is based on comparative analysis of hominid and ungulate bone spatial distributions, modifications by stone tools, and skeletal part representations.

Baume ("cave") Moula-Guercy is in southeastern France on the west bank of the Rhone River, in Ardèche. The stratigraphic sequence is exclusively Middle Paleolithic. A test excavation in 1991 revealed 12 hominid skeletal fragments, some with cut marks (*1*).

The lowest exposed units (levels XVI to XX) represent a cold period that is biochronologically dated to the terminal Middle Pleistocene (isotope stage 6). The upper units (levels IV to XI) represent a cool period corresponding to isotope stage 4. Level VI is volcanic tephra dated to 72,000 ± 12,000 years ago (2). A thick and homogenous deposit (levels XII through XV) between the upper and lower units contains an abundant fauna representative of a temperate forest. We interpret the data to indicate an Eemian age for the latter deposits (isotope stage 5, 80,000 to 120,000 years ago) (2). The Neanderthal fossils all derive from level XV, a tem-porary Mousterian (Middle Paleolithic) occupation thought to date to between 100,000 and 120,000 years ago on the basis of biochronologies of large and small mammals (2). Approximately 30% of the estimated volume of this unit has been excavated (Figure 1). Contemporary European sites are rare. Moula-Guercy's detailed paleoenvironmental and behavioral records complement its Neanderthal remains in illuminating the transition from the Middle to the Upper Pleistocene.

Level XV contains a lithic assemblage attributable to the Ferrassie Mousterian, a lithic tradition based on a

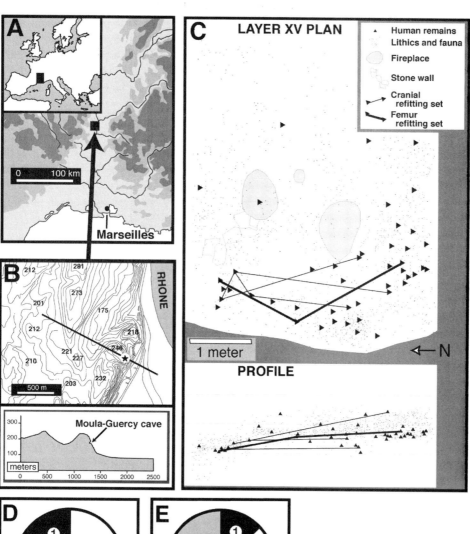

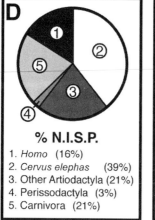

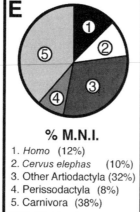

Figure 1. *The Moula-Guercy Mousterian occupation site and its contents. (**A**) Site placement within France. (**B**) Map and profile showing the position of Moula-Guercy in space and its elevation relative to the modern Rhone River. (**C**) Plan and projection of the excavation into level XV, the main Mousterian occupation. This shows lithics, nonhuman remains, hearths, hominid specimens, and refitting sets. (**D** and **E**) Taxonomic breakdowns of identifiable specimens (NISP) and minimum numbers of individuals (MNI) in level XV.*

high frequency of scrapers and Levallois [prepared core (3)] debitage. The lithics are not abundant in this unit, being mainly represented by tools rather than debitage and cores. This layer contains structural evidence in the form of three hearths and a stone wall (Figure 1). As of August 1998, there were 78 identified, unconjoined hominid fragments from level XV. Additionally, there were 392 taxonomically and anatomically identified nonhominid remains [number of identifiable specimens present (NISP)] among the 1527 cataloged macromammalian faunal specimens. The red deer *Cervus elaphus* is represented by at least five individuals [minimum number of individuals (MNI)]. The hominid and cervid remains evince parallel discard histories based on their spatial and stratigraphic commingling (Figure 1). The subsequent occupation (level XIV) was very different. There, the same kind of Mousterian assemblage is present but with abundant fauna and lithics and without hominid remains.

Preservation of the osteological remains from level XV is excellent. Even fetal ungulate remains were recovered. *Cervus elaphus* is the dominant taxon, followed by *Homo* and *Capra* (Figure 1). The 78 certain hominid fossils include cranial, dental, and postcranial remains that are attributable to a minimum number of six individuals. The only intact hominid bones are those of the hand and foot. Determining individual ages for such broken and isolated remains is difficult. At least one large and one smaller adult Neanderthal are represented by clavicles and calcaneal fragments. Two immature specimens are aged at 15 to 16 years, based on dental eruption. Two additional individuals aged 6 to 7 years are also present.

European fossil hominids recovered from deposits of similar antiquity are all Neanderthals. In regard to all anatomical areas in which character assessment can be accomplished, the Moula-Guercy level XV hominid remains represent Neanderthals. Neanderthal characters that are evident among the fragmentary remains currently include a double occipital suprainiac fossa; an occipital torus that fades laterally and is depressed near the midline; a posteriorly originating mandibular ascending ramus; incisor hypertrophy; taurodont molars and premolars; a long, thin, crested superior pubic ramus; hand and foot phalanx robusticity; wide terminal phalangeal apical tufts; a superoinferiorly flattened clavicular shaft; a relatively short third metacarpal styloid process; and thick long bone cortices in both adults and immatures. The larger adult individual is one of the largest Neanderthals known.

Qualitative and quantitative studies of modifications to the hominid and nonhominid faunal assemblages from the Moula-Guercy level XV demonstrate parallels in processing. The antiquity of modification of both faunal and hominid remains is demonstrated by matrix cover and manganese rosettes superimposed on cut marks, as well as by multiple cut marks crossing ancient fracture edges of refit pieces discovered in different parts of the cave. Only one identifiable *Cervus* specimen shows carnivore modification. None of the hominid remains do. In contrast, both hominid and deer bones show abundant and unequivocal evidence of hominid-induced modification. These modifications were studied and quantified according to criteria established elsewhere (4). Cut marks, percussion pits, anvil striae, adhering flakes, internal vault release, inner conchoidal scars, crushing of spongy bone, and peeling are all found on both the ungulate and hominid remains. In some instances, the cut and percussion marks show signature criteria to indicate successive strokes of the same implement in defleshing and percussing (Figure 2). There is similar post-discard polish on the hominid and nonhominid assemblages, possibly indicating that occupation of the cave continued after the butchery event or events had occurred. Refitting studies establish that fragments of fractured human bones were spread across 3 m of the cave and were distributed through ~30 to 40 cm of deposit (Figure 1).

The assessment of cannibalism in a prehistoric context depends on the demonstration that faunal and hominid remains were subjected to similar treatment (4, 5). In the case of Moula-Guercy, there is clear evidence to this effect. Table 1 provides quantitative data

Table 1. Comparison of Hominid-Induced Modifications on Different Skeletal Parts of *Homo* (Neanderthal) and *Cervus* (deer)

	Cut Marks		Fracture for Marrow or Brains	
	Hominid	Deer	Hominid	Deer
Cut Marks and Fracture				
Cranium	15/23	0/1	23/23	1/1
Mandible	2/2	1/5	2/2	5/5
Vertebrae	0/2	1/12	—	—
Ribs	2/2	1/8	—	—
Pelvis	0/3	0/0	—	—
Scapula	0/0	0/2	—	—
Humerus	0/0	4/9	—	—
Radius	1/2	—	—	—
Ulna	1/2	—	—	—
Radioulna	—	2/7	—	—
Carpal	0/1	0/3	—	—
Tarsal	1/7	1/5	—	—
Metapodial	1/3	9/36	0/3	43/43
Femur	3/5	7/15	—	—
Tibia/fibula	1/4	2/9	—	—
Phalanx	4/9	1/20	2/9	13/17
Clavicle	3/3	—	—	—
Limb bones	6/13	15/40	13/13	40/40
Inner Conchoidal Scars				
Total pieces	7.4%	10.7%		
Percussion Pits				
Total pieces	2.9%	2.0%		
Adhering Flakes				
Total pieces	1.5%	1.0%		
Anvil Striae				
Total pieces	1.5%	0.5%		

The anatomical differences between these taxa, particularly the larger crania and smaller metapodials of the Neanderthals, result in the observed differences in modification frequencies and element counts. Except where denoted as percentage values, the first number in each column is the number of specimens (NISP) with the modification. The second number is the total number of specimens observed.

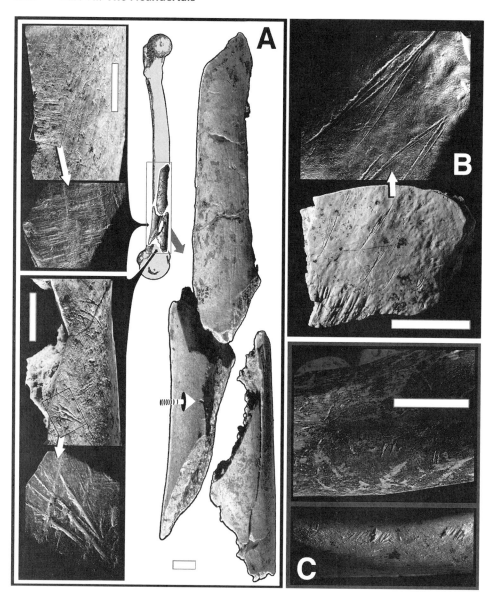

Figure 2. *Modifications to the Neanderthal skeletal remains illustrated by photographic and scanning electron microscope images. Scale bars equal 1.0 cm. (A) Refitting set CS-2, a distal left femur. The cut marks (lower left), percussion impact scar (white arrow), anvil striae on the opposite side (upper left), and internal conchoidal scars indicate defleshing before fracture by directed percussion by a hammerstone atop an anvil. (B) Ectocranial surface of the left parietal bone with cut marks. Note the successive signatures of the same stone tool edge, indicating filleting of the temporalis muscle. (C) The mandibular corpus of a juvenile Neanderthal (top) and a red deer (bottom) to show the similar position and form of cut marks made by a stone tool.*

on the representation and modifications of deer and Neanderthal bones. All crania and limb bones of both taxa are broken. There is an elevated frequency of hominid vault fragments relative to those of deer, presumably because fracture of the much larger hominid cranial vault produces more pieces. Furthermore, fracture of deer metapodials yields more marrow than does fracture of hominid metacarpals or metatarsals, generating differential fragmentation between the two taxa for these elements. Bone fracture is presumably related to processing for marrow and brains in both *Homo* and *Cervus*. The patterns of bone modification observed on the hominid and deer assemblages are also in parallel, except for functional differences between the taxa. For example, deer lack clavicles.

Anatomical assessment of the hominid bone modification leads to an understanding of the butchery practices used. For example, all three Neanderthals represented by the distal clavicle display cut marks on the lateral inferior surface of this bone, indicating disarticulation at the shoulder. In at least one individual each,

the Achilles' tendon, pedal phalangeal flexor tendons, and tendon of brachialis were cut transversely at the ankle, metatarsophalangeal, and elbow joints, respectively. The temporalis muscle was removed from two of the immature cranial vaults. Cut marks on the lingual surface of the juvenile mandible show that the tongue was cut out. Cut marks on the femoral shafts show that the thigh musculature was removed.

These bone modifications indicate that the human individuals were defleshed and disarticulated. After this, the marrow cavity was exposed by a hammer-on-anvil technique. Refitting of femoral pieces shows that the medial distal femoral shaft surface was struck with a percussor and fractured while supported on an anvil [conjoining set 2 (CS-2): three fragments of a very large adult's femur]. Cut marks, percussion pitting, inner conchoidal scars, and anvil striations on the contra-coup surface of this refitted specimen are evidence of marrow processing (Figure 2). Discarded conjoint shaft fragments were found, separated by 3 m (Figure 1).

The cervid and hominid remains at Moula-Guercy show parallel spatial distribution (discard history), element representation, and bone modifications. We interpret these data to indicate that the hominid and deer carcasses were butchered in a similar way, with the objective being the removal of soft tissues and marrow. An inference of cannibalism is therefore warranted for Moula-Guercy level XV. We find no evidence that modifications to the hominid or deer bones from Moula-Guercy represent any form of mortuary ritual for either species. Whether the cannibalism was motivated by resource stress or other social factors will require further investigation here and at other sites.

Cannibalism has been attributed to Neanderthals for nearly a century (6) and is a recurrent theme in considerations of their mortuary practices. Perimortem modifications are known from other Pleistocene localities, such as Krapina, Vindija (7), Marillac (8), Combe Grenal (9), Macassargues (10), Zafarraya (11), and even Europe's earliest occupation site, the Lower Pleistocene TD6 occurrence at Atapuerca's Dolina (12). Inferences of paleolithic cannibalism have been questioned on the basis of insecure spatial and stratigraphic data, as well as insecure identification of bone modifications. The largest skeletal series interpreted as evidence of cannibalism among Neanderthals is the Krapina assemblage from Croatia (13). The cannibalism interpretation was questioned by Trinkaus (14), who attributed the assemblage to other taphonomic factors. A subsequent analysis of perimortem cut marks on the Krapina Neanderthal bones by Russell (15) led her to conclude that there was: "postmortem processing of corpses with stone tools, probably in preparation for burial of cleaned bones" (p. 381). Both investigators deny any evidence of marrow processing of the Krapina Neanderthal limb bones (14, 16).

Moula-Guercy is a key site for understanding Mousterian occupation in Europe at the beginning of the Upper Pleistocene. It has now yielded spatial and associational data critical to the accurate assessment of prehistoric behavior. As a result, the Moula-Guercy fossils and their context are now the best evidence that some Neanderthals practiced cannibalism.

REFERENCES AND NOTES

1. A. Defleur et al., *Nature* **362**, 214 (1993).
2. A. Defleur, É. Crégut-Bonnoure, E. Desclaux, *C. R. Acad. Sci. Ser. II A Sci. Terre Planetes* **326**, 453 (1998); S. Sanzelle et al., *C. R. Acad. Sci. Ser. II A Sci. Terre Planetes* **330**, 541 (2000).
3. F. Bordes, *Typologie du Paléolithique Ancien et Moyen* (CNRS, Paris, 1961).
4. T. White, *Prehistoric Cannibalism at Mancos 5MTUMR-2346* (Princeton Univ. Press, Princeton, NJ, 1992).
5. P. Villa et al., *Science* **233**, 431 (1986); C. Turner and J. Turner, *Man Corn: Cannibalism and Violence in the Prehistoric American Southwest* (Univ. of Utah Press, Salt Lake City, UT, 1999).
6. D. Gorjanovíc-Kramberger, *Der Diluviale Mensch von Krapina in Kroatien* (C. W. Kreidel Verlag, Weisbaden, Germany, 1906).
7. M. Malez and H. Ullrich, *Palaeontol. Jugosl.* **29**, 1 (1982).
8. B. Vandermeersch, *Gallia Prehist.* **23**, 301 (1980).
9. C. Hughes, S. Garimond, S. Gagnière, P. Marcellin, *Ann. Paleontol.* **37** 155 (1951).
10. F. Le Mort, *Bull. Soc. Prehist. Fr.* **86**, 79 (1989).
11. J. Hublin et al., *C. R. Acad. Sci. Ser. II A Sci. Terre Planetes* **321**, 931 (1995).
12. Y. Fernández-Jalvo et al., *Science* **271**, 277 (1996).
13. F. Smith, *Univ. Tenn. Dept. Anthropol. Rep. Invest.* **15**, 1 (1976); H. Ullrich, *Anthropos (Brno)* **21**, 253 (1982); J. P. Bocquet-Appel and J. L. Arsuaga, *J. Archaeol. Sci.* **26**, 327 (1999).
14. E. Trinkaus, *J. Hum. Evol.* **14**, 203 (1985).
15. M. Russell, *Am. J. Phys. Anthropol.* **72**, 381 (1986).
16. ———, *ibid.,* p. 373.
17. We thank the Ministère de la Culture et de la Communication; le Service Régional de l'Archéologie (DRAC Rhône-Alpes); Monsieur le Président du Conseil-Général de l'Ardèche et le Vice-Président chargé de la Culture; Monsieur le Maire de Soyons et Monsieur le Conservateur du Musée Municipal; Fondation Singer-Polignac; Académie des Sciences de Paris; and D. DeGusta, H. Gilbert, L. Hlusko, J.-L. Arsuaga, J.-M. Carretero, F. C. Howell, N. Toth, and Y. Coppens.

VIII

Origin of Modern Humans

The chapters in Part VIII address one of most prominent topics in human evolution during the past two decades: the origin of modern humans. In many instances, these chapters overlap extensively with ones in the preceding and succeeding parts. Whereas many of the chapters in Part VII deal with the relationship between Neandertals and modern humans, and those of Part IX are concerned with the diversity of modern humans today, the chapters in this part focus more narrowly on the origins of *Homo sapiens* and on the evolution of the distinctive behavioral attributes of modern humans.

In the first chapter of this part, Chapter 59, Christopher B. Stringer sets the stage with a current summary of "Modern Human Origins: Progress and Prospects." In this wide-ranging paper, Stringer reviews much of the paleontological and genetic evidence of human evolution from the past 1 myr, addressing many of the issues discussed in previous parts of this book. He begins by reviewing the major models of modern human origins that have been debated for the last decade and continue to be debated today (see also Aiello, 1993) and how the models have developed over the years. These models are: (1) the recent African origin (and replacement) model; (2) the (African) hybridization and replacement model; (3) the assimilation model; and (4) the multiregional evolution model. In his view, the multiregional model has been debunked by available evidence. He then addresses the fossil evidence for the initial divergence of *Homo sapiens* and *Homo neanderthalensis*, arguing that *Homo heidelbergensis* was a species that ultimately gave rise to *H. neanderthalensis* in Europe and *H. sapiens* in Africa. This divergence, indicative of regional differentiation, was perhaps due to the glacial-interglacial cycles during the middle Pleistocene. He then focuses on the African record of modern human origins, where recent redating of remains have overturned the older view that human evolution in Africa was retarded compared with other continents. The new picture that emerges is of a mosaic, and perhaps gradual, evolution over the past 300 kyr from *H. heidelbergensis* to *H. sapiens,* which parallels the evolution of *H. neanderthalensis* in Europe. This, of course, raises the more difficult issue of how one defines "modern" in the evolution of modern humans.

The hominid fossil record in the Middle East is much more complicated than in Europe or Africa. In the Levant, Neandertals and modern humans seem to have occupied the region either sympatrically or alternatively for the past 150 kyr. Modern humans are first recorded in the region over 100 kya, with Neandertals present at 50–60 kya. Then Neandertals disappear and modern humans reappear in the Upper Paleolithic, approximately 40 kya (Shea, 2003). The Asian record is hindered by controversies over dating of the fossil hominids, but it appears that *Homo erectus* persisted in Southeast Asia until as recently as 27 kya (see Chapter 43).

In Stringer's view, all of the genetic data, from both extant populations and fossils, appear to support a recent African origin for modern humans (see Chapters 55, 63, 70, 71, 72, and 74 for a variety of views). In the closing sections of the paper, Stringer identifies what he sees as the current outstanding problems and the most promising areas of future research. These include the multiple dispersals model (see Chapter 62), the biology of hybridization, geometric morphometrics (see Chapter 57), and the more general issue of defining "modernity" in the evolution of human morphology and behavior (see Chapters 64, 65, and 67; see also McBrearty and Brooks, 2000; d'Errico, 2003; Henshilwood and Marean, 2003).

In Chapter 60, "A Reconsideration of the Omo-Kibish Remains and the *erectus-sapiens* Transition," Michael H. Day and Christopher B. Stringer discuss the fossil evidence that was most influential for Stringer (see Stringer and McKie, 1998) in developing the out of Africa hypothesis for modern human origins. The fossil hominids from the Kibish Formation in southwestern Ethiopia were discovered by Richard Leakey and colleagues in 1967, and were described by Michael Day (1969). One of the Kibish fossils, Omo I, was described as essentially modern in its cranial morphology, despite being dated at over 100 kyr. Since modern humans were not known elsewhere in the world before 40 kya, Day argued that modern humans must have originated in Africa and then spread to the rest of the world. The remarkably early date for modern humans indicated by the Omo I remains, and the limitations of dating techniques in 1969, have led many subsequent experts to question the actual age of this material. However, recent studies (McDougall, Brown, and Fleagle, 2005) summarized in the addendum to this article support the original conclusions of Butzer (1969) that the Omo I and Omo II crania are both from the upper part of Member I of the Kibish Formation and that these crania are the oldest known modern humans now dated to nearly 200,000 years old.

Chapter 61, "Pleistocene *Homo sapiens* from Middle Awash, Ethiopia," by Tim D. White and colleagues, reports on a series of modern human crania from the Middle Awash region of Ethiopia that date to between 154 and 160 kya (see also Clark et al., 2003). These exceptionally complete and well-dated fossil crania confirm the presence of modern humans in eastern Africa over 150 kya and expand our understanding of their anatomy and behavior. Like the Kibish remains, they document modern humans' anatomy in Africa well before modern humans are known from anywhere else in the world. These crania are associated with an assemblage of artifacts "traditionally classified as Final or Traditional Acheulean" and fauna suggesting both aquatic and grassland habitats. In a related article, Clark et al. (2003) report that the fossil crania show evidence of defleshing and possible manipulation.

Marta M. Lahr and Robert Foley discuss alternative models of modern human origins in Chapter 62, "Multiple Dispersals and Modern Human Origins." While they agree with Stringer that modern humans originated in Africa, they note that the first appearance of modern humans in other parts of the world is not concordant with a single dispersal. For example, dates for the colonization of Australia appear much earlier than the first appearance of modern humans in Europe. Accordingly, they suggest that the spread of modern humans may have taken place in several dispersals out of Africa and then from subsequent regional centers of radiation. In particular, they argue that the initial dispersal of modern humans to Australia followed a southern route through the Horn of Africa to the Arabian Peninsula. This multiple dispersal model agrees with the results of virtually all genetic studies that emphasize an extraordinary genetic diversity within Africa during the past 200 kyr (e.g., Chapters 70, 71, and 72; see also Templeton, 2002).

In Chapter 63, "Models, Predictions, and the Fossil Record of Modern Human Origins," John H. Relethford suggests that the morphological evidence for a recent African origin for all modern humans, with no contribution from hominids living in other regions, may reflect population differences rather than phylogeny. If the modern human population of Africa has been larger than that in other regions of the Old World for most of the past 100 kyr, then the "African genes" would effectively swamp out the genetic contributions by smaller regional populations and make the subsequent populations look more like Africans than their regional ancestors, despite interbreeding. Since any evidence of regional continuity would be surprising in the face of a larger African population, he argues that future research to test models of modern human origins should focus on regional continuity rather than similarity to early modern Africans.

Today, the evolution of modern human behavior is one of the most active areas of research and debate in paleoanthropology. It is often intimately connected to the out of Africa theory of human origins. In Chapter 64, "Fully Modern Humans," Richard G. Klein reviews the current status of debate on this topic. He summarizes his own view that although modern humans as a species first appeared in Africa over 100 kya (see previous chapters), modern human behavior involving symbolic art, ornamentation, and carved bone tools only appears much later with the late Stone Age of Africa and the Upper Paleolithic of Europe, between 50 and 40 kya. In Klein's most radical hypothesis, the appearance, or at least the coalescence, of modern behavior was the result of some type of brain mutation in an early modern human population in Africa. It was only after this abrupt shift in behavioral abilities that modern humans were able to successfully expand out of Africa into Eurasia. Recent genetic studies have indeed found evidence of a gene associated with language that appears to date roughly to 50 kya (Lai et al., 2001). However, Klein's view has many critics among archaeologists who offer considerable evidence that would appear to refute his hypothesis (see especially Chapter 67; see also McBrearty and Brooks, 2000). In his summary, Klein reviews all the contradictory evidence and in many cases offers alternative explanations for the seemingly disparate results; he suggests additional data that might resolve the controversy (see also Klein and Edgar, 2002).

In Chapter 65, "The Big Deal about Blades: Laminar Technologies and Human Evolution," Ofer Bar-Yosef and Steven L. Kuhn review the evolution of blade technologies in the archaeological record. Blade technologies have often been identified as a hallmark of modern human behavior and a characteristic behavioral attribute associated with the initial appearance of modern humans in the Upper Paleolithic of Europe. However, as Bar-Yosef and Kuhn point out, the production of blades as an artifact type is much more widespread in the archaeological record, and was achieved by different techniques in different industries. Blades are neither uniquely associated with modern humans nor found in all modern human lithic assemblages. Nevertheless, blade technologies came to dominate the archaeological record of western Eurasia in the upper Pleistocene, but were less important in other parts of the world. For that reason, they suggest that this proliferation of blades in the Upper Paleolithic industries may well indicate novel and significant patterns of human behavior associated with the development and use of composite tools.

In Chapter 66, "A Middle Stone Age Worked Bone Industry from Katanda, Upper Semliki Valley, Zaire," John E. Yellen and colleagues describe a collection of bone points and harpoons that date to nearly 100 kya and suggest that carefully crafted bone tools were present in Africa well before the Late Stone Age (see also Brooks et al., 1995). The Katanda artifacts include a variety of bone implements that are very unusual for this time period in Africa, but have also been reported from Blombos in South Africa (see Chapter 67). Other occurrences of bone harpoons in the African fossil record are mostly from the last 12 kyr (see Yellen, 1998). The early date for the Katanda tools, which contradicts Klein's hypothesis that modern behavior appeared only after 50 kya, has become a subject of debate (see Klein and Edgar, 2002).

Part VIII closes with Chapter 67, "Emergence of Modern Human Behavior: Middle Stone Age Engravings from South Africa," by Christopher S. Henshilwood and colleagues. This chapter reports additional evidence for "modern behavior" in the African Middle Stone Age of South Africa, over 70 kya. From the site of Blombos Cave, Henshilwood and colleagues describe several pieces of red ochre engraved with abstract designs, which they suggest is evidence of cognitive abilities characteristic of modern humans (see also Henshilwood and Marean, 2003). The engraved ochre

from Blombos Cave supports arguments from other archaeological evidence, such as standardized lithic tools, shaped bone points, and innovative subsistence strategies like fishing and shellfishing. The combined evidence suggests that the hominids had evolved modern human behavior in Africa well before "modern behavior" first appears in the fossil record of Europe approximately 35 kya (but see also d'Errico, 2003). More recently, Henshilwood et al. (2004) report the discovery of perforated shell beads from Blombos Cave dated by two complimentary techniques to about 75 kya. This discovery of personal ornaments (jewelry) at Blombos Cave is unambiguous evidence of symbolically mediated behavior characteristic of modern *Homo sapiens*. It provides further support that complex, symbolic thinking, "modern behavior" arose first in African early *Homo sapiens*.

REFERENCES

Aiello, L. C. 1993. The fossil evidence for modern human origins in Africa: A revised view. *American Anthropologist* 95:73–97.

Brooks, A. S., D. M. Helgren, J. S. Cramer, A. Franklin, W. Hornyak, J. M. Keating, R. G. Klein, W. J. Rink, H. P. Schwarcz, J. N. Leith Smith, K. Stewart, N. E. Todd, J. Verniers, and J. E. Yellen. 1995. Dating and context of three Middle Stone Age sites with bone points in the upper Semliki Valley, Zaire. *Science* 268:548–553.

Clark, J. D., Y. Beyene, G. WoldeGabriel, W. Hart, P. R. Renne, H. Gilbert, A. Defleur, G. Suwa, S. Katoh, K. R. Ludwig, J.-R. Boisserie, B. Asfaw, and T. D. White. 2003. Stratigraphic, chronological and behavioral contexts of Pleistocene *Homo sapiens* from Middle Awash, Ethiopia. *Nature* 423:747–752.

Day, M. 1969. The Omo skeletal remains. *Nature* 222:1135–1138.

d'Errico, F. 2003. The invisible frontier: a multiple species model for the origin of behavioral modernity. *Evolutionary Anthropology* 12:188–202.

Henshilwood, C. S., F. d'Errico, M. Vanhaeren, K. Van Niekerk, and A. Jacobs. 2004. Middle Stone Age shell beads from South Africa. *Science* 303:404.

Henshilwood, C. S., and C. W. Marean. 2003. The origin of modern human behavior. *Current Anthropology* 44:627–652.

Henshilwood, C. S., J. C. Sealy, R. J. Yates, K. Cruz-Uribe, P. Goldberg, F. E. Grine, R. G. Klein, C. Poggenpoel, K. L. Van Niekerk, and I. Watts. 2001. Blombos cave, southern Cape, South

Africa: preliminary report on the 1992–1999 excavations of the Middle Stone Age levels. *Journal of Archaeological Science* 28:421–448.

Klein, R. G., and B. Edgar. 2002. *The Dawn of Human Culture.* John Wiley, New York.

Lai, C. S. L., S. E. Fisher, J. A. Hurst, F. Vargha-Khadem, and A. P. Monaco. 2001. A fork-headed-domain gene is mutated in a severe speech and language disorder. *Nature* 413:519–523.

McBrearty, S., and A. Brooks. 2000. The revolution that wasn't: a new interpretation of the origin of modern human behavior. *Journal of Human Evolution* 39:453–563.

McDougall, I., F. H. Brown, and J. G. Fleagle. 2005. Stratigraphic placement and age of modern humans from Kibish, Ethiopia. *Nature,* 433:733–736.

Shea, J. J. 2003. Neandertals, competition, and the origin of modern human behavior in the Levant. *Evolutionary Anthropology* 12:173–187.

Stringer, C. B., and R. McKie. 1998. *African Exodus.* Henry Holt, New York.

Templeton, A. R. 2002. Out of Africa again and again. *Nature* 416:45–52.

Yellen, J. E. 1998. Barbed bone points: tradition and continuity in Saharan and sub-Saharan Africa. *African Archeological Review* 15:173–198.

59

Modern Human Origins

Progress and Prospects

C. B. Stringer

ABSTRACT

The question of the mode of origin of modern humans (Homo sapiens) has dominated palaeoanthropological debate over the last decade. This review discusses the main models proposed to explain modern human origins, and examines relevant fossil evidence from Eurasia, Africa and Australasia. Archaeological and genetic data are also discussed, as well as problems with the concept of 'modernity' itself. It is concluded that a recent African origin can be supported for H. sapiens, morphologically, behaviourally and genetically, but that more evidence will be needed, both from Africa and elsewhere, before an absolute African origin for our species and its behavioural characteristics can be established and explained.

INTRODUCTION

Over the past ten years, one topic has dominated palaeoanthropological debate—the origin of 'modern' humans. While it is generally agreed that Africa was the evolutionary homeland of Pliocene hominins (such as *Australopithecus*) and the earliest humans (members of the genus *Homo*), was it also the sole place of origin of our own species, *Homo sapiens*, during the Pleistocene (1.8–0.012 Myr ago) (see Figure 1)? Originally centred on the fossil record, the debate has more recently drawn on archaeological and genetic data. The latter have become increasingly significant, and now even include DNA from Neanderthal fossils. Yet, despite the growth of such data, and the availability of increasingly sophisticated methods of analysis, there is still a perception in some quarters that the debate about modern human origins is sterile and as far from resolution as ever. In this review, I wish to discuss the impact of recent discoveries and analyses, and give my own perspective on the current debate, as well as discussing possible future progress. I hope to show that there are rich and stimulating differences of opinion and approach, even within the polarized factions that have grown up during the current vigorous debate, and that further exciting developments are imminent.

As discussed later, there is no agreement about the number of human species that have existed during the Pleistocene. For some workers there may have been

Reprinted with permission from C. B. Stringer, *Philosophical Transactions of the Royal Society of London*, Series B, Vol. 357, pp. 563–579. Copyright © 2002 by The Royal Society.

only one—*H. sapiens* (e.g. Hawks et al., 2000*a*)—while for others, there may have been at least eight (e.g. Tattersall & Schwartz, 2000). My preference lies between these extremes, and for the rest of this paper I will recognize and use four species names: *H. erectus*, its probable descendant *H. heidelbergensis*, and two probable descendant species of *H. heidelbergensis*: *H. neanderthalensis* and *H. sapiens*.

First, I will concentrate on the fossil records of Africa and western Eurasia. In order to discuss these in a consistent fashion, I am going to use the following morphologically based terms: '*Recent H. sapiens*' are members of the clade containing all living *H. sapiens* and their closest past relatives, inclusive of the last morphological common ancestor of the whole group. '*Archaic H. sapiens*' are members of the stem group (Smith, 1994) of *H. sapiens*, more closely related to recent *H. sapiens* than are any members of the sister clade to *H. sapiens*, *H. neanderthalensis*, or the last common ancestor of *H. sapiens* and *H. neanderthalensis* which, in my view, is represented by the species *H. heidelbergensis*. *Homo sapiens* thus consists of the combination of the crown group of recent *H. sapiens* and the stem group of archaic *H. sapiens*. It should be noted that my usage of 'archaic *H. sapiens*' is distinct from, and more restricted

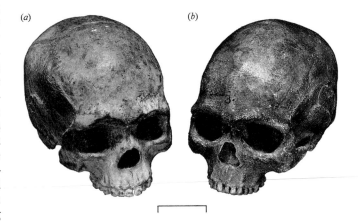

Figure 1. *This comparison of late Pleistocene crania from Liujiang, China (a), and Fish Hoek, South Africa (b), highlights a central issue in modern human origins research. The cranium from Liujiang is seen by some workers as a link between archaic and recent Chinese populations, yet this visual comparison conforms with metrical analyses in showing its close resemblance to an African fossil from over 10 000 km away. Does such a resemblance reflect the late Pleistocene dispersal of a shared 'modern' morphology, or gene flow between different regions? Scale bar, 50 mm.*

than, others that may include Neanderthal or early Middle Pleistocene fossils from Europe and Africa. *Homo neanderthalensis* forms the sister clade to *H. sapiens*, and may be divided in a comparable fashion into 'late *H. neanderthalensis*' and 'archaic *H. neanderthalensis*'. The more primitive *H. heidelbergensis* represents the putative Middle Pleistocene ancestral species for the *H. sapiens* and *H. neanderthalensis* clades, and is used here for both Eurasian and African fossils.

The growing body of archaeological, morphological and genetic evidence concerning modern human origins is still generally assessed against two contrasting models known as 'Recent African Origin' (also called 'Out of Africa', 'African Replacement', or simply 'Replacement' model) and 'Multiregional Evolution' (also sometimes called 'Regional Continuity'). However, as Aiello (1993) discussed, there are two other models of modern human evolution that also merit consideration (Figure 2). One ('Hybridization and Replacement') can be viewed as a variant of Recent African Origin, while the other ('Assimilation') combines elements of Recent African Origin and Multiregional Evolution. Aiello summarized them as follows (my editing [ ]):

1. [*Recent African Origin*] argues that modern humans first arose in Africa about 100 000 years ago and spread from there throughout the world. . . . Indigenous premodern populations in other areas of the world were replaced by the migrating populations with little, if any, hybridization between the groups [Figure 2*a*].
2. *The (African) Hybridization and Replacement Model* is similar to the above, but allows for a greater or lesser extent of hybridization between the migrating population and the indigenous premodern populations . . . [Figure 2*b*; Bräuer, 1992].
3. *The Assimilation Model* also accepts an African origin for modern humans. However, it differs from the previous models in denying replacement, or population migration, as a major factor in the appearance of modern human. . . . Rather, this model emphasizes the importance of gene flow, admixture, changing selection pressures, and resulting directional morphological change [Figure 2*c*].
4. [*Multiregional Evolution*] differs from the previous three in denying a recent African origin for modern humans. . . . It emphasizes the role of both genetic continuity over time and gene flow between contemporaneous populations in arguing that modern humans arose not only in Africa but also in Europe and Asia from their Middle Pleistocene forebears [Figure 2*d*].

I discussed the development of Recent African Origin models in Stringer (1994). From 1980 to 1986, early Recent African Origin proposals argued that modern humans evolved in Africa about 100 thousand years (kyr) ago, spread to Western Asia by about 45 kyr, and to Europe by about 35 kyr. However, uncertainties about the records from the Far East and Australasia led to greater caution about events there, and a reluctance to propose a global model. Some early Recent African Origin formulations were implicitly punctuational, with the assumption of a relatively late evolution of a package of 'modern' morphological and behavioural features, and their subsequent rapid spread from Africa. This package included, morphologically, a high and mid-sagittally rounded cranial vault, a mental eminence and a lightly built skeleton, and behaviourally, the presence of blade tools, symbolism and (inferred) complex language. At this stage total replacement models, in which it was argued that archaic populations living outside Africa had become completely extinct, were rarely articulated due to the lack of relevant fossil evidence from many regions and time periods. Thus, the distinction between models 1 and 2 was not made in early presentations of Recent African Origin models.

From 1986 two significant developments began to force modification of the original models. The first was the development and application of new dating techniques that could reach beyond the range of conventional radio-carbon dating (*ca.* 40 kyr), in particular, luminescence applied to burnt stone tools, and electron spin resonance applied to fossil mammal tooth enamel (Taylor & Aitken, 1997). These applications made their

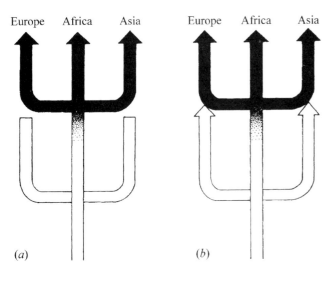

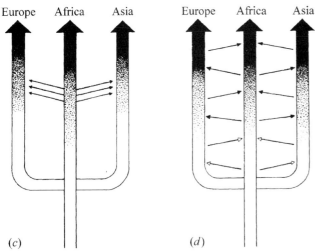

Figure 2. *Evolutionary models of modern human origins (modified from Aiello, 1993). (a) Recent African Origin; (b) (African) Hybridization and Replacement Model; (c) Assimilation Model; (d) Multiregional Evolution.*

greatest impact on the dating of Neanderthal and early modern human burial sites in Israel, although they have also affected reconstructions of events elsewhere (Grün & Stringer, 1991; Stringer, 2001a). The second development was the increasing impact of genetic data on the debate, leading to greater polarization and a hardening of some Recent African Origin proposals in the direction of complete replacement (model 1, above). Pioneering genetic work on the reconstruction of early human evolution had been conducted by researchers such as Cavalli-Sforza & Bodmer (1971) and Nei & Roychoudhury (1982), but it was not until the late 1980s that clearer resolution started to become possible using genetic systems such as beta-globins (e.g. Wainscoat et al., 1986) and, in particular, mitochondrial DNA (mtDNA; e.g. Cann et al., 1987).

The Assimilation Model (3, above) arose through integration of the emerging evidence for an important African role in modern human origins with multiregional views. It was developed by Smith (1992), who was originally a multiregionalist. Other multiregionalists also modified their position, although less explicitly. Aspects of the original Multiregional Model (4, above) can be found in Thorne & Wolpoff (1992, p. 83), where it is summarized as follows: 'Human evolution happened everywhere because every area was always part of the whole'. It was argued that each inhabited area showed a continuous anatomic sequence leading to modern humans, and those outside Africa showed no special African influence.

By 1997, Wolpoff and some colleagues had in many respects shifted to a position close to that of the Assimilation Model (Wolpoff & Caspari, 1997). Because this shift was not explicit, I have distinguished it from the original Multiregional Model by the designation 'Multiregional 2' (Stringer, 2001b). Multiregional 2 argues that an African influence predominated throughout Pleistocene human evolution because of larger population size, while populations outside Africa were more vulnerable to bottlenecking and extinctions. Thus, modern populations would mainly have African-derived genes and African-derived morphological characters, although these were predominantly acquired through gene flow, rather than via rapid replacement. It is argued that modern genes and characters accumulated over the entire Pleistocene within a genetic exchange network dominated by Africa (Hawks et al., 2000a).

There is now more than enough fossil evidence to demonstrate that most of the characters claimed to link archaic and recent populations in the same areas under multiregional evolution are either retained plesiomorphies or are not homologous (e.g. Stringer, 1992; Lahr, 1996). Neither the distinctive characteristics of the species H. sapiens, nor those of its modern regional variants, were present in the earlier Pleistocene, and this is supported by the absence of such characters even in Middle Pleistocene fossil samples that, on morphological grounds, may represent ancestors of Neanderthals and recent humans (see below). As is also discussed below, the estimated date for the mitochondrial last common ancestor of Neanderthals and recent humans is between 317 and 741 kyr, and this range of dates

would appear to set another maximum age for the appearance of recent characters that were not already present in the common ancestor with Neanderthals. The original version of Multiregional Evolution thus appears no longer tenable, even to its previous adherents, while the data just discussed appear sufficient to falsify the aspects of Multiregional 2 that really distinguish it from the Assimilation Model (i.e. stipulation of the entire Pleistocene time-scale for the establishment of novel H. sapiens characters rather than a later Pleistocene one). Moreover, despite the careful arguments of Relethford (1999), the level of gene flow required to spread the ubiquitous modern morphology under Multiregional 2 would appear incompatible with the claimed parallel long-term maintenance of regional features in small peripheral populations.

All of the remaining models focus on the central importance of Africa in modern human origins during the later Pleistocene, while differing over the mechanisms by which modern characters spread from the continent and the relative importance of any extra-African genetic input. Therefore, in the rest of this article I will concentrate on the following aspects of the Middle–Upper Pleistocene fossil evidence: the origin of H. neanderthalensis and H. sapiens; the early African record of H. sapiens; the western Eurasian record of H. neanderthalensis and H. sapiens; and the later Pleistocene records of eastern Asia and Australasia (see Figure 3). I will then discuss the relevance of recent genetic data and, finally, review recent and possible future developments in this research area, including a discussion of the concept of modernity.

THE ORIGIN OF *H. NEANDERTHALENSIS* AND *H. SAPIENS*

The European fossil human record of the Middle to Late Pleistocene has grown appreciably during the past decade, especially with the discovery of large skeletal samples from the Sierra de Atapuerca (Spain). This locality has produced important earlier (Gran Dolina—GD) and later (Sima de los Huesos—SH) fossil samples. The early component, dated at ca. 800 kyr, has been claimed to represent a new species ('H. antecessor'; Bermúdez de Castro et al., 1997) that was the last common ancestor of H. neanderthalensis and H. sapiens. It is argued that this species gave rise to H. heidelbergensis in Europe, which in turn evolved into H. neanderthalensis. A parallel African descendant lineage of 'H. antecessor' gave rise to H. sapiens. However, while I recognize the distinctiveness of the 'H. antecessor' material, I am cautious about its taxonomic status, and in particular about the phylogenetic significance placed on the 'modern' morphology of the infraorbital region of the immature individual ATD6-69. The adult form of this fossil may be represented by the approximately contemporaneous Ceprano cranium (Manzi et al., 2001), and if so, this shows much less similarity to H. sapiens. In addition, there is enough variation in the infraorbital region of African and European hominins from the Middle Pleistocene to warrant caution about the taxonomic value of this character. In my view (cf. Manzi et al., 2001),

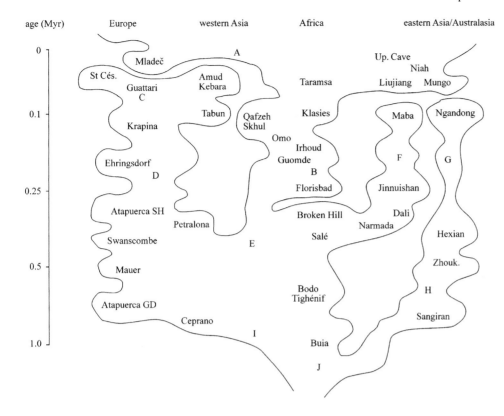

Figure 3. *Distribution of selected Pleistocene fossil hominins in time and space, showing possible taxonomic groupings and relationships. (A) Recent H. sapiens; (B) archaic H. sapiens; (C) late H. neanderthalensis; (D) archaic H. neanderthalensis; (E) H. heidelbergensis; (F) possible Asian H. heidelbergensis/H. neanderthalensis; (G) late H. erectus; (H) early H. erectus; (I,J) H. ergaster/early H. erectus. It is uncertain whether group (F) represents evidence of homoplasy, or affinities, with populations in western Eurasia. Abbreviations: St Cés., St Césaire; Up. Cave, Upper Cave; Zhouk., Zhoukoudian.*

the 'H. antecessor' material and Ceprano may represent a transitional form between *H. erectus* and *H. heidelbergensis*. Thus, for the moment, I still prefer to group early Middle Pleistocene European (e.g. Arago, Petralona and Mauer) and African (e.g. Bodo, Broken Hill and Salé) material in *H. heidelbergensis* as representing the common ancestral species for *H. neanderthalensis* and *H. sapiens*. This usage is very comparable to that of Rightmire (1998).

The Middle Pleistocene European sequence shows an accretional (mosaic and gradual) appearance of Neanderthal characters (Hublin, 1998; Stringer, 1998*b*), but I would argue that this process only becomes marked towards the end of the Middle Pleistocene, making a clade origination with 'H. antecessor' some 500 000 years earlier less probable. However, the apparent

gradual nature of Neanderthal evolution does make recognition of the species/clade origin difficult. This is an important question, because if *H. neanderthalensis* is our sister group, then its origin also marks the origin of our own clade (Stringer & Hublin, 1999). The inference of an early origin would imply that *H. sapiens* clade characters should be present in African fossils right through the Middle Pleistocene, but I would argue that these are not recognizable in fossils such as Bodo, Broken Hill and Salé, only appearing in the late Middle Pleistocene.

An alternative model of Neanderthal and recent human origins is that of Foley & Lahr (1997), who have hypothesized an even later divergence between Neanderthals and *H. sapiens*, ca. 250 kyr, linking this with the development of prepared core or levallois (Mode 3; Clark, 1968, and Table 1) technology in the

Table 1.   Time Relationships of Technological Categories in Western Eurasia and Sub-Saharan Africa

Age (kyr)	Stratigraphic	Western Eurasia	Category	Africa
12	—		—	
		Upper Palaeolithic		Later Stone Age
			(Mode 4)	
	Upper Pleistocene	—		—
		Middle Palaeolithic		Middle Stone Age
			(Mode 3)	
130	—		—	
	Middle Pleistocene			
790	—	Lower Palaeolithic		Early Stone Age
	Lower Pleistocene		(Modes 1–2)	
1800	—			

The earliest archaeological record extends beyond 1.8 Myr in Africa. The alternative 'Mode' nomenclature was introduced by Clark (1968).

'Mode 3 Hypothesis'. In turn, they relate this archaeo-logical innovation to the African species 'H. helmei', based on the Florisbad cranium (now directly dated to *ca.* 260 kyr; Grün et al., 1996). In their view, 'H. helmei' evolved from *H. heidelbergensis* in Africa and then dispersed to give rise to Neanderthals in Eurasia, and modern humans in Africa. 'H. helmei' carried the newly derived Mode 3 technology with it during its late Middle Pleistocene dispersal. For Lahr and Foley (Foley & Lahr, 1997; Lahr & Foley, 1998), 'H. helmei' is repre-sented by African fossils such as Florisbad and Jebel Irhoud, perhaps ultimately ancestral to *H. sapiens,* and European fossils such as Atapuerca SH and Ehringsdorf, ancestral to the Neanderthals. Their use of 'H. helmei' hence differs from mine (e.g. Stringer, 1996) when I argued that this species might lie within the modern clade, as an evolutionary intermediate between *H. heidelbergensis* and *H. sapiens.*

While I appreciate the rationale behind the Mode 3 hypothesis, I do not consider it provides a realistic model for the origins of *H. neanderthalensis* and *H. sapiens.* First, Neanderthal characteristics were already evolving in Europe prior to the hypothesized appearance and dispersal of 'H. helmei', e.g. in the Swanscombe speci-men, dated to *ca.* 400 kyr (Stringer & Hublin, 1999). Second, African specimens such as Florisbad and Jebel Irhoud make unparsimonious ancestors for the Neanderthals, since not only do they post-date the appearance of Neanderthal clade characters in Europe, but they appear to lack Neanderthal morphological characteristics that might be expected in a common ancestor. A large cranial capacity is cited by Lahr and Foley (Foley & Lahr, 1997; Lahr & Foley, 1998), but this is highly variable in Middle Pleistocene fossils and is more evident in the European fossils that might be assigned to 'H. helmei', such as Atapuerca SH4 and Ehringsdorf calvaria 9, than in African examples.

Usage of Mode 3 technology as an ancestral 'taxo-nomic' characteristic is also problematic, in my opin-ion. This is partly because technologies might transfer between distinct populations or even different species, as has been hypothesized for the spread of Upper Palaeolithic elements in Europe (see below), but also because the time and place of origin of prepared core techniques are currently unknown. These apparently existed in Europe and Africa (Roebroeks & Gamble, 1999; McBrearty & Brooks, 2000) by Oxygen Isotope Stage 9 (OIS 9 *ca.* 325 kyr ago), but it is unclear in which area, or areas, they originated. Their origin may have been African, as Lahr and Foley (Foley & Lahr, 1997; Lahr & Foley, 1998) propose, European or Asian, or the concept might even have been developed indepen-dently in different regions. But if Mode 3 technology does identify the ancestor of *H. neanderthalensis,* this was already present in Europe during OIS 9.

Thus, I question the evidence not only for an early Middle Pleistocene origin for the Neanderthal and modern human clades, based on 'H. antecessor' as the last common ancestor, but also for a late Middle Pleistocene divergence implied by the Mode 3 hypothe-sis. Instead, I believe that *H. heidelbergensis,* present in the Middle Pleistocene of both Europe and Africa,

represents the probable common ancestral species for *H. neanderthalensis* and *H. sapiens* in the later Middle Pleistocene. In principle, recognizing the origin of either descendant species (*H. neanderthalensis* or *H. sapiens*) would indicate the time of origin of our own species. Neanderthal mitochondrial DNA has been used to estimate a Neanderthal/*H. sapiens* clade separa-tion at *ca.* 600 kyr (see below), and this in turn has been used to support the view of a deep separation time for the Neanderthal–modern clades, as suggested by the 'H. antecessor' material. However, using the analogy of recent human diversification, a rather different conclu-sion can be reached. This is because genetic differenti-ation inevitably precedes population and specific differ-entiation. It is probable that *H. sapiens* has been diverging genetically for some 150 kyr, and yet we are unquestionably still a single species. Thus, for a period of time, mtDNA differences must have been accumulating *within* a Middle Pleistocene species (?*H. heidelbergensis*) prior to cladogenesis. Hence, an estimated mtDNA coa-lescent date of *ca.* 600 kyr in fact provides a *maximum* age for any specific separation of *H. neanderthalensis* and *H. sapiens.*

This also raises the question of the evolution of mor-phological characteristics, and again analogy with re-cent *H. sapiens* is useful. If human evolution was contin-uing to take its Pleistocene course, present human populations in, say, Africa, Europe or Australia might eventually form new species. Looked at from a perspec-tive half a million years in the future, it would be possi-ble to detect genetic or morphological apomorphies characterizing the nascent species *within* present-day populations, i.e. recent geographic variants of *H. sapi-ens* would contain clade features of the future distinct species. This illustrates a fundamental point that apo-morphies characterizing new species must necessarily originate within previously existing species. Therefore, the fact that some fossils attributed to *H. heidelbergensis* (such as Mauer and Petralona) display apomorphies characteristic of *H. neanderthalensis* does not necessarily require their attribution to the Neanderthal clade, con-trary to some arguments (e.g. those of Arsuaga et al., 1997; Bermúdez de Castro et al., 1997). As an example, metrical and morphological studies instead suggest that variation between the European Petralona cranium and the African Broken Hill cranium is comparable to the differences found today between geographically dis-tinct populations of *H. sapiens* (Seidler et al., 1997). I would argue that *H. heidelbergensis* was a geographically widespread and diverse species that gave rise to *H. neanderthalensis* in Eurasia, and *H. sapiens* in Africa (cf. Rightmire, 1998).

Finally, what might have driven the cladogenesis that culminated in *H. neanderthalensis* and *H. sapiens*? The ancestral, geographically dispersed populations would have been repeatedly bottlenecked as glacial–interglacial cycles intensified during the Middle Pleistocene. They would inevitably have diverged ge-netically and morphologically with the heightened effectiveness, during climatic changes, of biogeographic barriers such as an enlarged Caspian Sea and the cold, arid uplands of the Anatolian–Iranian plateau. Possible gene exchange between eastern Europe and the Levant would thus have been regularly disrupted or prevented. Surviving populations in the, at times, arid Levant would also have been increasingly genetically isolated from those south of the Sahara. Thus, in my view, regional characters began to develop and accumulate in *H. heidelbergensis,* including idiosyncratic 'Neanderthal' cranial features found in European material from Arago, Petralona and Swanscombe, as well as those that might be related to climatic adaptation (e.g. comparing the tibia from Boxgrove with that from Broken Hill; Stringer et al. (1998)). While I would argue that the Atapuerca SH material represents archaic *H. neanderthalensis,* I recognize that it can equally be regarded as a late and derived form of the ancestral species *H. heidelbergensis.*

THE AFRICAN RECORD

The pattern of human evolution in Africa remains less well understood than that of Europe, but the developing picture suggests that there are parallels between the two continents. Twenty-five years ago the prevailing view, based mainly on radiocarbon dating, was that although the earliest humans may have originated in Africa, subsequent human development lagged behind that of Europe. Thus, the earliest technological stage, the Lower Palaeolithic, was believed to have continued in Africa until *ca.* 50 kyr, whereas the subsequent Middle Stone Age may have only given way to the Later Stone Age at *ca.* 12 kyr, some 25 kyr later than the equivalent Middle–Upper Palaeolithic transition in Europe. The hominin sequence was thought to be comparably retarded, with the archaic Broken Hill cranium (Zambia) perhaps dated to 130 kyr, and the somewhat less archaic Florisbad (South Africa) specimen dated to *ca.* 40 kyr (Stringer, 2001*a*).

The situation now is dramatically different. Argon–argon dating has shown that stone tool making began in Africa by at least 2.3 Myr, and the whole timescale of the African Palaeolithic has been stretched back in time (Klein, 1999). The Middle Stone Age is now believed to have begun by at least 250 kyr and the transition to the Later Stone Age began prior to 45 kyr (Table 1). Thus, the African record can now be seen to be in concert with, or even in advance of, the record from Eurasia. The hominin record has been similarly reassessed. Biostratigraphic correlation suggests that the Broken Hill cranium (*H. heidelbergensis*) probably dates from at least 300 kyr (Klein, 1999), while a combination of electron spin resonance dating on human tooth enamel and luminescence dating of sediments suggests that the Florisbad cranium—an archaic *H. sapiens*—actually dates from *ca.* 260 kyr rather than the former estimate of *ca.* 40 kyr (Grün et al., 1996).

Fossil specimens showing mosaic archaic–modern *H. sapiens* characters from Guomde (Kenya) and Singa (Sudan) are now dated by gamma rays, and a combination of electron spin resonance and uranium series, to at least 150 kyr (Bräuer et al., 1997) and 133 kyr (McDermott et al., 1996). *Homo sapiens* fossils such as Omo Kibish 1 (Ethiopia), Border Cave 1 (South Africa) and those from the Middle Stone Age levels of the

Klasies River Mouth Caves (South Africa) are of comparable, or somewhat younger, age, although much of this material is fragmentary and difficult to date more precisely (Klein, 1999). Overall, the picture of human evolution in Africa over the last 300 kyr can now be seen to parallel that of Europe. Both regions appear to show a mosaic and perhaps gradual transition from *H. heidelbergensis* to a more derived species: in Europe *H. neanderthalensis,* and in Africa *H. sapiens* (Bräuer et al., 1997; Rightmire, 1998; Stringer, 1998*b*).

If this model of gradual regional evolution can be applied to the African fossil record, an accretional mode of *H. sapiens* evolution would consequently be expected (Stringer, 1998*b*). In which case, how can we recognize when identifiably 'modern' humans appear? So far, I have avoided further discussion of the term 'modern', but it will be necessary to discuss the use of this important but complex concept in detail later. However, the term is generally used to contrast the shared characteristics of recent humans (whether morphological, behavioural or cultural) with those of earlier (nonmodern or archaic) humans. Unfortunately, there are no generally agreed definitions or diagnoses of the term as applied to the fossil or archaeological record. Moreover, acceptance of a gradualistic scenario for the origin of modernity means that diagnosing 'modernity' will be dependent on the particular criteria selected. In addition, in the case of morphology, while individual anatomical characters may be used to recognize which fossils belong to the *H. sapiens* clade, membership of this clade will not necessarily be synonymous with modernity as an assemblage, since this may have evolved long after the cladistic origin of *H. sapiens* (which, in my view, was at the *H. neanderthalensis–H. sapiens* cladogenetic event). Thus, fossils such as Florisbad, Singa, and even those from Skhul and Qafzeh, probably belong to *H. sapiens* cladistically, but do not necessarily represent 'modern' humans.

THE WESTERN EURASIAN RECORD

The Levant occupies a unique geographical position linking Africa and Eurasia, but its Middle Pleistocene hominin record is much poorer than that of adjoining regions. Only fragmentary specimens from sites such as Zuttiyeh and the lower levels of Tabun provide physical evidence of the Levantine human populations before *ca.* 130 kyr, but they are insufficient to provide much information about the nature of those populations (Klein, 1999). Interpretations of the regional fossil record after this period have undergone some remarkable upheavals brought about by the application of new dating techniques. As late as 1985, it was believed by most workers that the pattern of population change in this area paralleled that of Europe, or rather preceded it by a small amount of time. Thus, Neanderthals at Israeli sites such as Tabun and Amud evolved into, or gave way to, early modern humans such as those known from Skhul and Qafzeh by *ca.* 40 kyr ago (e.g. Trinkaus, 1984). For some workers technological and biological changes were interlinked, leading to an evolution of modern humans in the region, and it was postulated that these early moderns could then have migrated into Europe, giving rise to the Cro-Magnons (the term used for Upper Palaeolithic–associated *H. sapiens* in Europe). One of the first applications of the newer chronometric techniques (thermoluminescence applied to burnt flint) seemed to reinforce this pattern, dating a recently discovered Neanderthal burial at Kebara in the anticipated time-range of *ca.* 60 kyr ago (Valladas et al., 1987).

Shortly afterwards, the first application was made to the site of the Qafzeh early modern material, giving a surprisingly old age estimate of *ca.* 90 kyr, more than twice the generally expected figure. Further applications of non-radiocarbon dating methods have amplified the pattern suggested by the age estimates for Qafzeh and Kebara (see reviews in Grün & Stringer, 1991; Klein, 1999). It seems probable that the early modern burials at Qafzeh and Skhul date from more than 90 kyr, and some may be as old as 130 kyr. The Neanderthal burials at Kebara and Amud date younger than this figure, in the range 50–60 kyr ago. As the intervening period approximates the transition from the supposedly predominantly interglacial stage 5 to predominantly glacial stage 4, this has led to a proposed scenario where Neanderthals only appeared in the Levant after the onset of glaciation further North (Akazawa et al., 1998).

In this context, it has been difficult to establish the age of the Tabun Neanderthal burial, for two different reasons. First, while age estimates for the stratigraphy at Tabun based on electron spin resonance and luminescence both considerably stretch the late Pleistocene time-scale previously proposed for the site into the Middle Pleistocene, the methods do not give compatible results. Luminescence estimates from burnt flint excavated from the rear of the cave are much older than electron spin resonance estimates from mammal teeth from correlated levels nearer the mouth of the cave (compare Grün et al., 1991 with Mercier et al., 1995). Second, the stratigraphic position of the Tabun burial cannot be established with certainty over 60 years after its excavation, giving further doubt about its actual age (Garrod & Bate, 1937; Bar-Yosef & Callander, 1999). Direct non-destructive gamma ray (uranium series) dating of the mandible and leg bones from this skeleton had suggested a surprisingly young age of less than 40 kyr (Schwarcz et al., 1998). However, the accuracy of this estimate was questioned (Millard & Pike, 1999; Alperson et al., 2000) and direct electron spin resonance dating of a tooth enamel fragment from a molar on the mandible has now given a much older age estimate of *ca.* 120 kyr (Grün & Stringer, 2000). Thus, the extent of Neanderthal–early modern contemporaneity in the Levant over the period 90–130 kyr ago is still an open question, but given that the region lies in the potential overlap zone of range expansions of either the evolving African *H. sapiens* lineage or that of Eurasian Neanderthals, this was certainly probable (Stringer, 1998*b*). Yet, after this time, the Neanderthals appear to have predominated in the region until *ca.* 45 kyr ago, when the development of new technology and behaviour by early modern humans may have fuelled major range expansions, heralding the eventual extinction of the Neanderthals.

Having discussed the beginning of the Neanderthal and modern human lineages and their presence in western Asia, I will now examine the fate of the Neanderthals. New luminescence and electron spin resonance dating, in concert with the accelerator radiocarbon technique (which requires much smaller samples of organic material than conventional methods), has generally confirmed previous views of the Middle/Upper Palaeolithic sequence, but with some additional complexity, especially in Europe. Upper Palaeolithic industries such as the Aurignacian, by inference associated with early modern humans, have been dated in parts of Eurasia (e.g. northern Spain and Hungary) by luminescence, electron spin resonance, uranium series or radiocarbon accelerator methods to *ca.* 40 kyr. Middle Palaeolithic (Mousterian) industries, actually or presumably associated with Neanderthals, start to disappear from some areas of Europe from about this time. However, both the old favoured models of rapid *in situ* evolution of Neanderthals into Cro-Magnons or a rapid replacement of Neanderthals by them can now be shown to be invalid. Late Neanderthal levels at French sites such as Le Moustier and Saint-Césaire have been dated in the range 35–40 kyr ago, while those at Arcy have been radiocarbon dated at *ca.* 32 kyr ago (Mellars, 1999). These dates may well be compatible, given that radiocarbon dates at this period could underestimate calendar ages by several millennia (Stringer & Davies, 2001). Moreover, Neanderthal fossils have now been dated at *ca.* 30 000 radiocarbon years in areas such as Southern Spain, Croatia and the Caucasus, and regions such as southern Iberia and the Crimea show a parallel persistence of Middle Palaeolithic industries (e.g. Hublin et al., 1995; Smith et al., 1999; Ovchinnikov et al., 2000). If these dates and associations are accurate, it appears that Neanderthals survived quite late in some regions, and had a potential coexistence with the Cro-Magnons of at least ten millennia.

The previous relatively clear picture of the Middle Palaeolithic/Neanderthal and Upper Palaeolithic/*H. sapiens* interface in Europe has also become cloudier since the identification of Neanderthal remains in Châtelperronian (early Upper Palaeolithic) levels at the French sites of Saint-Césaire and Arcy (Hublin et al., 1996). Moreover, there is an apparent association of Neanderthals with symbolic artefacts such as pendants at Arcy. Furthermore, it has been suggested that other industries with supposed Upper Palaeolithic affinities in central Europe (Szeletian) and Italy (Uluzzian) may also have been the handiwork of late Neanderthals (see reviews in d'Errico et al., 1998; Klein, 1999). Thus, the Neanderthals appear to show some of the same technological and behavioural innovations as the Cro-Magnons. For some researchers (e.g. Klein, 1999; Mellars, 1999), this late pattern of regionalization in the Neanderthals reflects the final fragmentation of their formerly continent-wide range, while in contrast the wide distribution of the Aurignacian reflects the dispersal of early modern humans across much of Europe. Present dating evidence no longer clearly demonstrates a wave of advance of the Aurignacian, since its oldest manifestations may be as ancient in northern Spain as in the east of the continent. The assumed external source for the Aurignacian and its manufacturers is also now unclear, and it remains possible that *H. sapiens* first arrived in the region with a pre-Aurignacian, even Middle Palaeolithic, technology. Such a precursor industry that might mark the appearance of early modern pioneers, although currently without diagnostic fossil material, is the Bohunician of eastern Europe, dated beyond 40 000 radiocarbon years (Stringer & Davies, 2001).

Workers such as Zilhão and Trinkaus have proposed still greater complexity in the European picture (e.g. d'Errico et al., 1998; Duarte et al., 1999). To them, Middle–Upper Palaeolithic transitions are indicative of complex and changing population dynamics as incoming Cro-Magnons mixed and merged with native Neanderthals over many millennia. In this scenario, the Neanderthals were arguably as culturally advanced as the Cro-Magnons, and were simply absorbed into a growing Cro-Magnon gene pool. It is even claimed that a hybrid child has been discovered at Lagar Velho in Portugal, dated to *ca.* 25 000 radiocarbon years (Duarte et al., 1999), but this claim remains unresolved until more detailed studies have been published. Whatever the outcome of that particular proposal (and I still consider that this may represent an unusually stocky modern human child), the impact of new dates and discoveries in Europe shows that the whole gamut of population interactions between the last Neanderthals and the first Cro-Magnons could, and perhaps did, occur, ranging from conflict to possible interbreeding. Nevertheless, the outcome of these processes was the extinction of the Neanderthals after a long period of survival in the challenging and unstable climates of Pleistocene Europe. MtDNA studies, discussed later, suggest that the genes of the earliest Cro-Magnons are not necessarily well represented in recent Europeans, because of intervening replacement or bottlenecking (Richards & Macaulay, 2000). Therefore, any small Neanderthal genetic component 30 kyr ago could easily have been subsequently lost.

THE LATER PLEISTOCENE RECORDS OF EAST ASIA AND AUSTRALASIA

Homo erectus was present in both China and Indonesia prior to 1 Myr ago (Culotta, 1995; Klein, 1999). The largest sample of Chinese material of this species, from the Zhoukoudian Lower Cave, is now dated at *ca.* 400–500 kyr by uranium series and electron spin resonance, and comparable southern Chinese material from Hexian is of similar, or somewhat younger, age (Grün et al., 1997, 1998). Other Middle Pleistocene fossils are indicative of morphological and perhaps, specific diversity, but limited knowledge of them has prevented their integration into the wider fossil record. Relatively complete, but heavily distorted, cranial material from the site of Yunxian (Etler, 1996) may exhibit variation away from the standard *H. erectus* pattern towards that of *H. heidelbergensis,* while a partial cranium from Nanjing, still not described in detail, even appears reminiscent of

Neanderthals in nasal, although not maxillary, morphology (C. Stringer, personal observation). These populations were apparently succeeded by more derived humans formerly attributed to 'archaic *H. sapiens*', represented by fossils from sites such as Jinniushan and Dali, and dated to *ca.* 250–300 kyr ago (Etler, 1996; Yin et al., 2001). Their affinities are still unclear, with some workers (e.g. Etler, 1996) seeing them as descended from local *H. erectus* antecedents, others (e.g. C. Stringer; Lahr, 1996; Rightmire, 1998) regarding them as possible eastern representatives of *H. heidelbergensis*. The isolated Narmada calvaria from India (Klein, 1999) may also represent such a population (Figure 3). Fragmentary early late Pleistocene fossils (*ca.* 100 kyr) from Chinese sites such as Xujiayo and Maba may record further local evolution, with Maba showing possible affinity to western Eurasian Neanderthals. However, the arrival of *H. sapiens* in the region is still poorly dated and poorly understood. That arrival must precede the modern human fossils known from the Upper Cave (Shandingdong) at Zhoukoudian, dated by radiocarbon on associated fauna to between 12 and 30 kyr ago, and might even extend back beyond 70 kyr if the Liujiang skeleton (Figure 1) is of that age (Shen & Wang, 2001). On the basis of cranial data, neither these specimens nor the late Pleistocene Minatogawa material from Japan seem very closely related to recent populations in the region (Brown, 1999; Stringer, 1999), and may provide evidence of early diversity that is either now lost or survives in the form of aboriginal isolates such as the Ainu of Hokkaido and the Andamanese Islanders.

In Indonesia, several *H. erectus* fossils have been indirectly dated to *ca.* 1.7 Myr ago using argon–argon dating on volcanic sediments (Klein, 1999), although some workers doubt that the fossils have been correctly associated with the dated rocks (Culotta, 1995). Other *H. erectus* fossils are dated by combinations of argon–argon, palaeomagnetics and biostratigraphy to between 500 kyr and 1.2 Myr ago (Klein, 1999). The Ngandong and Sambungmacan fossils have been even more controversially dated to less than 50 kyr by electron spin resonance and uranium series on associated fauna, implying a survival of *H. erectus* in Indonesia as late as Neanderthals survived in Eurasia (Swisher et al., 1996). Other workers have argued that these dates must be underestimates (Grün & Thorne, 1997), but further uranium series determinations, including direct measurements on the fossils, do support these dates (Falguères et al., 2001). The date of arrival of modern humans in the region is still uncertain, but given the evidence from Australia discussed below it must lie before 60 kyr. Known fossils such as Wajak (Java) and Niah (Sarawak) remain poorly dated, but may derive from the late Pleistocene.

Exactly when humans first arrived in Australia has been unclear until recently. Sites such as Malakunanja II, Nawalabila and Devil's Lair appear to contain artefacts or evidence of human–faunal interaction dating from at least 50 kyr, based on luminescence or minimum-age radiocarbon dates (Roberts et al., 1990, 1994; Turney et al., 2001). However, in none of these sites were associated human remains preserved, thus leaving the nature of the first Australians uncertain. Two different views have predominated in recent debate about the peopling of Australia. For some workers, there were two original colonizations of the continent (Thorne & Wolpoff, 1992; Frayer et al., 1993). An early colonization, originating from the archaic people of Java (here regarded as *H. erectus*, although regarded as early *H. sapiens* by some of the last group of authors) introduced a robust population at, perhaps, 50 kyr ago. This colonization event was supposedly represented by the Willandra Lakes human fossil known as WLH-50 (Willandra Lakes Human-50), and by subsequent populations sampled at sites such as Kow Swamp, Cohuna and Coobool Creek. A second colonization, purportedly derived from China, arrived via an eastern route and brought the more gracile people known from the Mungo fossils at *ca.* 30 kyr ago and sampled at later sites such as Keilor and King Island. Under this dual origin hypothesis, present day Australian Aboriginal variation is the result of Holocene hybridization between these robust and gracile peoples. A second, contrasting, view saw the robust and gracile peoples as parts of a single morphologically variable population. Their differences probably developed within Australia following a single colonization event, with recent Aborigines representing the end product of this process (Pardoe, 1991; Brown, 1992).

Recently, the Mungo 3 burial has been redated using a combination of the techniques of gamma ray uranium series dating on skull fragments, electron spin resonance on a piece of tooth enamel, uranium series on attached sediment, and optically stimulated luminescence applied to the sands containing the burial (Thorne et al., 1999). The dates obtained are 62 ± 6 kyr, approximately double the ages originally estimated from radiocarbon (Bowler & Thorne, 1976). By correlation, these new age estimates may also apply to the Mungo 1 cremated individual found nearby. There has been critical debate about the accuracy of these new determinations (Grün et al., 2000), although even critics appear to accept that Mungo 1 and 3 are older than previously thought.

If these new dates for Mungo 1 and 3 are indeed accurate, they imply that gracile people were the first inhabitants of Australia. This is because, in a related study, skull fragments of the supposedly more archaic fossil WLH-50 were dated by the gamma ray method, giving a preliminary age estimate of only *ca.* 14 kyr (Simpson & Grün, 1998). Thus this specimen, and the other robust fossils so far dated (Brown, 1992), all apparently postdated the last glacial maximum *ca.* 20 kyr ago. The sequence of morphologies supports a model of diversification within Australia, not derivation from separate ancestors. Otherwise, one would have to postulate the movement of 'gracile' people through Indonesia into Australia by 60 kyr ago, without replacement or interaction with existing 'robust' people, and then the arrival of surviving 'robust' people from Indonesia, who managed to disperse through Australia without significant intermixture with existing 'gracile' inhabitants.

Additionally, the description of the robust crania as archaic and *H. erectus*-like (e.g. Thorne & Wolpoff, 1992; Frayer et al., 1993) has been challenged by several workers who instead argue that their distinctive features can be related to large size, artificial deformation, or pathology (Brown, 1992; Lahr, 1996; Stringer, 1998*a;* Antón & Weinstein, 1999). Nevertheless, continued attempts have been made to demonstrate regional continuity between the WLH-50 calvaria and archaic Indonesian predecessors (Hawks et al., 2000*b*), but these have been idiosyncratic in the scoring of morphological characters (cf. Lahr, 1996) and failed to control for the confounding effect of size in metrical comparisons (cf. Stringer, 1998*a*).

Overall, it seems probable that a modern human dispersal had reached Australia, via boats, by *ca.* 65 kyr ago. This may have been the endpoint of a long-term coastal expansion from Africa (Stringer, 2000), but until more is known of the late Pleistocene populations of southern Asia, this will remain unclear. The relationship of the first Australians to later inhabitants of the continent is still uncertain. Late Pleistocene morphological diversity may well have been accentuated by the severity of the last glacial maximum, leading to isolation and the forcing of morphological change in some Australian populations. If archaic populations such as those known from Ngandong *did* survive into the late Pleistocene, an analogous situation to that in Europe might have obtained, raising the possibility of gene flow with dispersing *H. sapiens* (cf. Hawks et al., 2000*b*). Given previously discussed data from Europe and China, it is also possible that the genes of the first human colonizers are poorly represented in the aboriginal people of today because of extinctions, bottlenecking, or because later population expansions have largely overprinted their traces, physically, genetically and linguistically.

GENETIC DATA

Genetic data have assumed an increasing importance in reconstructions of recent human evolution over the past 15 years. Earlier studies had to work with population frequencies of genetic markers, the products of the genetic code (e.g. blood groups, proteins). By combining data from populations, attempts were made to reconstruct the genetic history of humans (Cavalli-Sforza & Bodmer, 1971; Nei & Roychoudhury, 1982). The advent of techniques that revealed individual molecular sequence data allowed phylogenetic trees or genealogies of specific genes or DNA segments to also be constructed. Two pioneering papers published in *Nature* in 1986 and 1987 illustrate, respectively, population-based and phylogenetic approaches using DNA markers called RFLPs (Restriction Fragmentation Length Polymorphisms). Using the former approach, Wainscoat et al. (1986) studied polymorphisms close to the beta-globin gene, and showed by genetic distance analyses that African populations were quite distinct from non-African ones. The following year, Cann et al. (1987) published their paper giving a genealogy of 134 mitochondrial DNA 'types' constructed from restriction maps of 148 people from different regions. The genealogy was used to reconstruct increasingly ancient hypothetical ancestors, culminating in one female, most parsimoniously located in Africa. Moreover, using a mtDNA divergence rate calculated from studies of other organisms, it was estimated that this hypothetical female ancestor lived *ca.* 200 kyr ago. These conclusions were extremely controversial, and were subjected to critical scrutiny concerning the samples, methods and calibration used (Templeton, 1993). Although it is now evident that Cann et al. (1987) were premature in the confidence with which they presented their results, much more extensive analyses (e.g. Ingman et al., 2000) have shown that they were fundamentally correct in their conclusions.

In the past ten years, with the development and application of PCR techniques, a wealth of sequenced data has been made available from autosomal (biparentally inherited) DNA, Y-chromosome DNA (inherited through males) and mitochondrial DNA (inherited through females). These data have been used to compare the DNA of human populations in ever greater detail (Tishkoff et al., 2000; Kayser et al., 2001), to estimate coalescent (last common ancestral) dates for various gene systems (Ingman et al., 2000), to reconstruct ancient demographic patterns (e.g. Rogers, 2001), and to develop phylogeographic studies to map ancient dispersal events (e.g. Richards & Macaulay, 2000; Underhill et al., 2001). While most of these data support a recent African origin for recent humans and their genetic diversity (e.g. Jorde et al., 2000; Ke et al., 2001), others may not (Zhao et al., 2000). Although the data are growing in power and resolution, analyses cannot yet resolve the precise time and place of our origins, nor establish whether there was only one or perhaps several significant dispersals of *H. sapiens* from Africa during the later Pleistocene.

Some genetic data, in the form of mtDNA, are now available from Neanderthal fossils (Krings et al., 2000) and these suggest a separation time of their lineage from that leading to recent humans of *ca.* 600 kyr (Krings et al., 2000; Ovchinnikov et al., 2000; Figure 4). As explained earlier, such estimates necessarily provide

maximum ages for evolutionary separation, since any population and species separations would inevitably post-date the first mitochondrial divergence by an unknown amount of time. But they are consistent with fossil evidence of an effective separation date of the *H. neanderthalensis* and *H. sapiens* lineages at *ca.* 300 kyr and also with subsequent genetic divergence among recent humans beginning less than 200 kyr ago (Stringer, 1998*b*). Both the morphological data and the limited amount of fossil DNA available suggest that Neanderthal–recent human differences were of the order of two or three times that found within recent humans. But even in this case, where genetic and morphological differences are clear, the data can be used to support a placing of Neanderthals and recent humans in either the same or different species, given the recency of common ancestry.

There have also been recent claims for the recovery of ancient DNA from Australian fossils. Adcock et al. (2001) reported that 10 out of 12 specimens tested from Willandra Lakes and Kow Swamp had yielded mitochondrial sequences. One of these, from Mungo 3, was claimed to form an outgroup with a previously reported mitochondrial nuclear insert, distinct from the other fossils and from recent human sequences. Adcock et al. (2001) claimed, moreover, that the distinctiveness of the Mungo 3 sequence undermined genetic support for a recent African origin. In an accompanying commentary, Relethford (2001) used the results to support alternative multiregional interpretations, and to question previous interpretations of Neanderthal DNA. However, Cooper et al. (2001) in turn criticized various aspects of the work. First, they observed that the claimed recovery rate for the Australian ancient DNA was exceptional compared with results from elsewhere, and that standard experimental protocols had not been employed, suggesting the possibility of contamination. Second, they reanalysed the data, using a larger number of recent Australian and African sequences, and demonstrated that the Mungo 3 sequence did not now form an outgroup to recent human mtDNA in the most parsimonious phylogeny. Third, they observed that even the original published phylogeny presented no serious challenge to Recent African Origin. Australian fossils classed by multiregionalists as 'robust' and 'gracile', purportedly derived from archaic Indonesian and Chinese ancestors respectively, grouped with the recent human sequences from regions such as Europe and Africa, while Mungo 3 was more closely related to all these than it was to the Neanderthal sequences used as an outgroup.

NEW APPROACHES TO MODERN HUMAN ORIGINS RESEARCH

In these concluding sections, I would like to draw together aspects of this review and also look at new approaches to some remaining problems. In my opinion, variants of one of the polar extremes in the debate about modern human origins discussed at the beginning of this paper—Multiregional Evolution—have

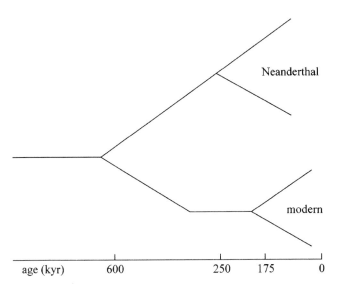

| age (kyr) | 600 | 250 | 175 | 0 |

Figure 4. *Schematic depiction of Neanderthal–modern human mtDNA relationships, with approximate coalescence dates (from data in Ovchinnikov et al. (2000) and Krings et al. (2000)). The small sample of Neanderthal sequences is sufficient to suggest comparable diversity to, but clear distinctiveness from, recent humans.*

been falsified, and the fundamental mode of modern human origins can be assumed to be that of a recent African origin. But until we have better records of late Pleistocene events in human history from regions such as China and Australia, we will continue to depend on genetic data to inform us whether a strict Recent African Origin model is likely to be adequate, rather than a variant incorporating a greater and more gradual (assimilation) or a lesser and more rapid (hybridization) degree of gene flow with contemporary populations outside Africa. However, even the strict Recent African Origin model has undergone considerable recent development in the Multiple Dispersals model of Lahr and Foley (1994, 1998), and this will be discussed next.

The Multiple Dispersals model proposes that significant recent human population subdivisions developed within Africa, and that there may then have been multiple dispersals of already differentiated populations from there, perhaps using different routes. This model has concentrated attention on the African fossil record of the late Middle Pleistocene. Other researchers recognized the high variation in these samples, but accepted that ancestors of recent humans were probably represented amongst them (Hublin, 1993; Bräuer et al., 1997; Rightmire, 1998; Stringer, 1998*b*). Lahr & Foley (1994, 1998) have taken this further in arguing that they might represent subdivided and distinct populations, with some or many not representing ancestors for recent *H. sapiens*. Following a bottleneck during OIS 6 (*ca.* 150 kyr), one African population recovered and spread into the Levant during OIS 5 (*ca.* 125 kyr), as represented by the Skhul–Qafzeh fossils. However, in the Multiple Dispersals model, these Levantine pioneers went extinct around the onset of OIS 4 (*ca.* 70 kyr). Surviving Africans, meanwhile, became divided into subgroups that were to form the ancestors of both African and non-African populations. A subsequent Middle Palaeolithic-associated dispersal occurred via Arabia and southern Asia, eventually reaching Australia, while later dispersals took the ancestors of recent European, Asian and Oriental people out of Africa following the development of Later Stone Age–Upper Palaeolithic technologies. Other workers have raised the possibility of separate early dispersals to Australia, but Lahr & Foley (1994, 1998) proposed a specific coastal route for this via the Straits of Hormuz (Bab el Mandeb). Subsequently, Stringer (2000), using new evidence of Middle Stone Age littoral adaptations, argued that coastal expansion around the Red Sea basin could have facilitated a range expansion of modern humans towards Australasia without necessarily using the Straits of Hormuz. By focusing attention on the development of diversity within Africa, the Multiple Dispersals model has provided fruitful hypotheses for testing from fossil, behavioural and genetic data.

A number of taxonomic issues in modern human origins remain unresolved. However, new ways of comparing past human taxic diversity with that of recent primates are being developed, and new techniques of investigation are adding further data from the expanding fossil record. One of the most serious remaining areas of uncertainty and confusion in studies of modern human origins is the question of species recognition. Some workers (e.g. Tattersall & Schwartz, 2000) argue that many distinct morphological groups in the fossil record warrant specific recognition, with the existence of at least eight such species of the genus *Homo* supported during the last two million years. Others (e.g. Thorne & Wolpoff, 1992) argue that only one species warrants recognition over that period—*H. sapiens*. An additional complication is that different species concepts may become confused—for example, some multi-regionalists have applied biological species concepts to the fossil record in an attempt to show that *H. neanderthalensis* and *H. sapiens* must have been conspecific. However, even if we accept controversial claims for the existence of supposed Neanderthal–modern hybrids (e.g. Duarte et al., 1999), it is well known that many closely related mammal species (including primates) can hybridize, and may even produce fertile offspring. However, if this is not a widespread or reproductively successful behaviour, it may have little or no impact on the populations that constitute the core of the different species or on future generations. The limited genetic data on Neanderthal–recent relationships show that Neanderthals and recent *H. sapiens* represent distinct but nevertheless closely related lineages, but are ambiguous about whether these samples represent different species. Thus, in fossils, morphological criteria necessarily remain the mode of species recognition, but recent research is providing better testing of the assumptions involved.

Harvati (2001) used differences in temporal bone morphology between common chimpanzees and specifically distinct bonobos to compare the level of difference between Neanderthals and recent *H. sapiens*. She concluded that Neanderthal–recent *Homo sapiens* differences in the temporal bone were at least as great as those between the two chimpanzee species. As she recognized, this result was based on only one cranial area, and further tests were required before reaching more definitive conclusions. In a similar study based on cranial measurements, Schillaci & Froehlich (2001) compared the level of differentiation of fossil (Upper Palaeolithic) *H. sapiens* and Neanderthals with that calculated between species of macaques that are known to hybridize, or not to hybridize. Again, the degree of difference between the fossil human cranial samples exceeded that found between the recent primate species. Thus, both these studies supported the distinctiveness of *H. neanderthalensis*. Apart from more cranial studies, it would be valuable to extend this approach to comparisons of mandibular morphology and metrics (e.g. extending the data of Humphrey et al. (1999)) and of dental morphology (see discussion of the work of Bailey (2000) below).

In recent years, traditional osteometric methods of recording the size and shape of fossil bones and teeth have been complemented and increasingly superseded by techniques that capture such information digitally through digitizing or scanning (Harvati, 2001). The medical technology of Computed Tomography (CT) has been particularly successful in extending such work

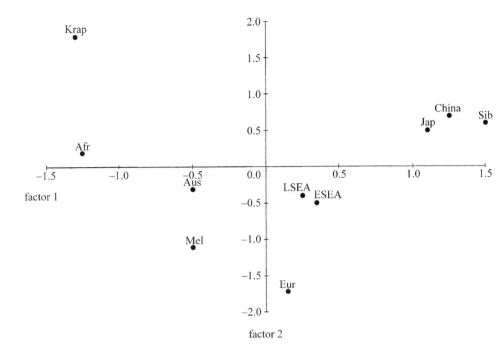

Figure 5. *Plot of first and second principal components using dental morphological data from Stringer et al. 1997 (redrawn from Stringer (1999), principal components analysis by L. Humphrey). The use of comparative data from the Krapina Neanderthals as a guide to polarity suggests that recent African and Australian populations may be closer to the ancestral modern human dental pattern than those of Southeast Asia (contra Turner, 1992). Abbreviations: Krap, Krapina; Afr, recent sub-Saharan African; Aus, recent Australian; Mel, recent Melanesian; Eur, Holocene European; LSEA, recent Southeast Asian; ESEA, Holocene Southeast Asian; Jap, recent Japanese; China, recent Chinese; Sib, recent Siberian.*

into anatomical structures that are either difficult to measure through traditional techniques (e.g. external and internal frontal bone shape: Bookstein et al. (1999)) or are otherwise inaccessible (e.g. inner ear bone shape: Hublin et al. (1996)). The techniques of geometric morphometrics are now being used to investigate both ontogeny and phylogeny (e.g. Ponce de León & Zollikofer, 2001). Much wider and more detailed comparisons of fossil and recent samples will undoubtedly have major impacts on future taxonomic and phylogenetic research on modern human origins.

Dental morphological variation provides an alternative and still rather neglected approach to reconstructing human population histories, despite the pioneering work of researchers such as Turner (1992) and K. and T. Hanihara (Hanihara, 1992). Turner's 'Out of Asia' scenario for recent human evolution was based on phenetic distance analyses and assumptions of relatively constant rates of dental evolution. It postulated that the 'Sundadont' aboriginal peoples of Southeast Asia were closest to the original modern human dental pattern and that this indicated the original source area for *H. sapiens*. However, this approach was unable to account for the relatively close phenetic distance between Australian and African dental patterns, and no attempt was made to test the hypothesis by the use of fossil data as an outgroup. These limitations were remedied in the work of Stringer et al. (1997), Irish (1998) and Tyrell & Chamberlain (1998), who found that the use of either a Neanderthal or archaic African outgroup supported a sub-Saharan, not Asian, root for recent human dental dendrograms or cladograms. Figure 5 shows the first two factors of a principal components analysis from the data of Stringer et al. (1997), with the inclusion of the Krapina Neanderthal sample as an outgroup. It is evident that if the Krapina dental sample is a representative outgroup, then European

and East Asian ('Sinodont') samples appear derived, 'Sundadont' samples are rather average for recent humans (as Turner and the Haniharas have reported), while Australian and sub-Saharan African samples are relatively plesiomorphic. The dental ancestor for recent humans thus probably combined characters most commonly found today in sub-Saharan Africans and Australians. Shields (1998), using a different dataset derived from digitized dental radiographs, also concluded that Australians displayed the most plesiomorphous morphology of non-African populations, while 'Mongoloid' and Native American samples were more derived. Thus, it appears that in both dental and morphological/metrical characters the 'Mongoloid' cranial form is very derived. Bailey (2000) has extended dental morphological studies to a wider range of fossils, including those of the western Eurasian Upper and Middle Palaeolithic. She concluded that Eurasian Neanderthals were similar to each other but quite distinct from other fossil, and recent, human samples. Both the Skhul–Qafzeh and Upper Palaeolithic groups showed recent affinities, with the former closer to sub-Saharan Africans, the latter to Europeans and North Africans.

PROBLEMS WITH THE CONCEPT OF "MODERNITY"

The fundamental problem of diagnosing ancient examples of 'modern' humans, morphologically and behaviourally, nevertheless persists because there is no agreement on how this should be carried out. In the past, I favoured the use of recent skeletal variation to diagnose whether a fossil could be termed 'modern' (Stringer, 1994). It is now apparent that recent skeletal variation is smaller than that recognized for *H. sapiens* in even the late Pleistocene, and members of the

H. sapiens clade in the African late Middle to early Late Pleistocene were much more distinct and diverse (Howells, 1989; Stringer, 1992; Lahr, 1996). While there seems little doubt that Aurignacian and Gravettian-associated humans from 25–35 kyr ago in Europe share enough morphological and behavioural features with recent populations to warrant the application of the term 'modern', problems arise as we move further back in time. The samples from Skhul and Qafzeh in Israel appear to represent a primitive form of *H. sapiens* (Trinkaus, 1984; Vandermeersch, 1989; Stringer, 1992; Lahr, 1996) but reassessments of their morphology, and that of samples from sites such as Klasies River Mouth, Omo Kibish, Singa, Ngaloba, Jebel Irhoud and Guomde (e.g. Lahr, 1996; Trinkaus, 1997; Pearson, 2000) show mosaic evolutionary patterns. This means that a morphological definition of modernity based on recent samples will be problematic when applied further back in time.

A further problem with the use of recent samples to assess fossils is that current 'regionality' appears to have evolved quite recently. In both China and Europe it may only really have developed during the last 20 kyr (e.g. Stringer, 1992; Lahr, 1996; Brown, 1999). Is this a reflection of a relatively late colonization of these regions by modern humans compared with Africa and Australia, or is it reflecting the impact of the last glacial maximum *ca.* 20 kyr ago, purging the earliest colonizers and followed by recolonization with the actual ancestors of today's inhabitants? While the combination of a morphological and metrical approach by Lahr (1996) undermined classic multiregional claims for the long-term persistence of regional characters, her studies did confirm the individuality of Australians in some respects. She argued that concepts of *H. sapiens* should not just be based on recent representatives, as in several aspects such as reduced size and robusticity we represent a restricted and atypical sample of the species as it was even in the late Pleistocene.

If, as suggested earlier, the characteristic morphology of modern humans evolved in a gradual, mosaic fashion, what of modern human behaviour? The concept of a 'Human Revolution', demarcating a punctuational origin of a package of recent human behaviours, such as complex language, symbolism and specialized technologies, has been central to much archaeological debate over the past ten years (Klein, 2000). Originally focused on apparent contrasts between the Middle and Upper Palaeolithic records in Europe, this concept has now been extended to the Middle to Later Stone Age transition in Africa (Table 1). It is argued that the major changes in human behavioural evolution occurred there by *ca.* 50 kyr (possibly related to mutations that enhanced brain function, leading to changes in cognition or language; Klein, 2000). In turn, this led to the successful expansion of modern humans and now-modern behaviour beyond Africa, and the replacement of the remaining archaic populations. Thus morphological and behavioural evolution were decoupled, since 'morphological modernity' may have evolved before 'behavioural modernity'. This pattern is counterintuitive for those who argue that behavioural change lay behind the transformation of the archaic skeletal pattern into that of modern humans. However, it is based on the fact that, despite their morphological 'modernity', fossil samples from sites such as Klasies River Mouth and Skhul or Qafzeh are associated with Middle Palaeolithic artefacts, comparable with those made by Neanderthals, and apparently lack other aspects of 'modern' behaviour. The contrast between their morphology and their inferred behaviour is sufficient for Klein (2000) to employ the term 'near-modern' for them, implying that they represent an evolutionary stage where modern anatomy was evolving *prior* to truly modern behaviour.

Workers such as Lahr & Foley (1998) and McBrearty & Brooks (2000) have instead argued that previous views of modern behavioural origins display a Eurocentric bias and a failure to appreciate the depth and breadth of an African Middle Stone Age record that precedes the supposed 'Human Revolution' by at least 100 kyr. In this view, 'modern' features, such as advanced technologies, increased geographic range, specialized hunting, aquatic resource exploitation, long distance trade and the symbolic use of pigments, occur across a broad spectrum of Middle Stone Age industries. This suggests a gradual assembly of the package of modern human behaviours in Africa during the late Middle–early Late Pleistocene, and its later export to the rest of the World. Thus the origin of our species, behaviourally and morphologically, was linked with the appearance of Middle Stone Age technology, dated in many parts of Africa to more than 250 kyr ago.

It is thus debatable whether African Middle Stone Age humans really lacked 'modern' behaviour. Moreover, the Middle Palaeolithic associated Skhul–Qafzeh samples display morphological signs of behavioural change (Churchill, 2001) as well as burials that apparently display evidence of 'modern' symbolic behaviour in the form of grave goods. There are also more remote indications that the dispersal of modern humans was not dependent on the appearance of the Later Stone Age/Upper Palaeolithic, and that symbolic behaviour existed before their development. As discussed earlier, there is growing evidence that Australia was colonized prior to 50 kyr ago and prior to the technological changes characterizing Mode 4 industries. Not only would this have required the development of maritime adaptations, but if the earliest Mungo fossils are representative of the first colonizers, these people were also engaging in complex behaviours such as burial with red ochre, and cremation.

In my opinion it is still too early to definitively determine when and where 'modern' morphology and behaviour developed, especially when these concepts are apparently so fluid. In my view, Africa was the ultimate source of the basic elements of both our anatomy and our behaviour. But it has also become evident that some claimed unique attributes of recent human behaviours were present even during the Middle Pleistocene outside Africa, for example, the evidence for systematic hunting of large mammals from sites such as Boxgrove and Schöningen, and the carefully crafted wooden javelins from the latter site (Dennell, 1997; Stringer et al., 1998). Additionally, the debate about Neanderthal, and specifically Châtelperronian, capabilities highlights the issue of potential versus performance. d'Errico et al. (1998) have argued that Neanderthals were developing 'modern' symbolic behaviour independently of a *H. sapiens* morphology, thus producing a contrasting decoupling of modern anatomy and behaviour from that envisaged by Klein (2000). Others (e.g. Mellars, 1999) argue that Neanderthals were developing complex behaviours only through contact with dispersing modern humans, not independently of them. The question of whether behavioural innovations arose regularly and independently in different populations in human prehistory (but were often lost during population crises or extinctions), or they spread widely by diffusion or dispersals, even between distinct populations and even species, remains unresolved.

While the temperate–cold climates of western Eurasia may well have influenced the evolution of the Neanderthals (e.g. Holliday, 1997), it is still unclear what drove the evolution of *H. sapiens* in Africa. The large habitable area of that continent, combined with dramatic changes in precipitation and vegetation, might have forced evolutionary change through isolation and adaptation. As discussed earlier, there is also growing evidence for the precocious appearance during the Middle Stone Age of aspects of modern human behaviour such as symbolism. It may well be that the predominance of Africa was fundamentally a question of its larger geographical and human population size (Relethford & Jorde, 1999), giving greater opportunities for innovations to both develop and be conserved (Shennan, 2001), rather than the result of a unique evolutionary pathway, perhaps based on mutations affecting cognition (Klein, 2000). The rapidity and repetition of late Pleistocene climatic oscillations outside Africa may well have continually disrupted long-term adaptation by its human populations, while Africa perhaps had shallower resource gradients (Foley, 1989), greater chances of isolation and endemism (Lahr & Foley, 1998), or encouragement of 'variability selection' responses to its environmental fluctuations (Potts, 1998). While the admittedly limited evidence does seem to point to a gradual assembly of recent human morphology and behaviour in Africa during the period from 300 to 100 kyr ago, rather than major punctuational events, genetic data are ambivalent on this question. Several genetic datasets suggest that there was at least one major population bottleneck during this time-period (Jorde et al., 2000; Ingman et al., 2000; Takahata et al., 2001), with effective population size reduced to only a few thousand individuals. Such population crashes might indeed have produced saltational changes in morphology and behaviour within what must have been a diverse early *H. sapiens* clade. However, other evidence of the conservation of older (?African) population subdivisions suggests that there cannot have been severe, localized bottlenecks, as these could not have conserved earlier geographical substructuring (e.g. Tishkoff et al., 2000; Watkins et al., 2001).

CONCLUDING REMARKS ON MODERN HUMAN ORIGINS

It seems to me that the ideas discussed, whether ultimately supported or falsified, are important for the way that they highlight difficulties inherent in any absolute concept of 'modernity', behavioural or morphological. Yet, such concepts are critical to the reconstruction of our origins. Was 'modernity' a package that had a unique African origin in one time, place and population or was it a composite whose elements appeared at different times and places, and were then gradually assembled to assume the form we recognize today? While I argue that variants of the Multiregional Model have lost their validity when applied globally, could there have been an African-based multiregional model where 'modern' behaviours, morphologies and genes coalesced from different parts of that continent during the Middle Pleistocene? If so, we will need, yet again, to account for the unique importance of Africa in human evolution. Foley & Lahr (1997) argued that the contrasting geographies of Eurasia and Africa would have favoured latitudinal expansions and contractions in Eurasia but longitudinal ones in Africa. Consequently, both a larger population size and geography would have facilitated dispersal from Africa, but not in the reverse direction. However, much more evidence from the African late Middle Pleistocene archaeological, palaeontological and palaeoenvironmental records will be required to test such ideas. The burgeoning genetic data from present and, to a lesser extent, past populations will continue to illuminate events in human prehistory. These will feed into new models of modern human origins and dispersal. It also seems likely that many questions concerning the origins of the peoples of eastern Asia, Australasia, the Americas and even Europe will only be fully answerable when Asia yields up a later Pleistocene record to compare with that already recovered from Europe and beginning to be recovered from parts of Africa. Only then will we be in a position to finally establish whether all the most significant events in the early history of *H. sapiens* occurred in Africa and whether, as evidence is now suggesting, the main morphological and behavioural components that characterize our species had already developed there by 100 kyr ago.

ACKNOWLEDGMENTS

The author thanks many colleagues for access to fossils and data, collaboration, and friendly discussions, all of which have directly, or indirectly, contributed to this review paper. More specifically, the Photographic Unit of The Natural History Museum produced Figure 1 and Philip Rye prepared Figure 2. The author also thanks five reviewers for their considerable help in improving this paper.

REFERENCES

Adcock, G., Dennis, E., Easteal, S., Huttley, G., Jermiin, L., Peacock, W. & Thorne, A. 2001 Mitochondrial DNA sequences in ancient Australians: implications for modern human origins. *Proc. Natl Acad. Sci. USA* **98**, 537–542.

Aiello, L. 1993 The fossil evidence for modern human origins in Africa; a revised view. *Am. Anthropol.* **95**, 73–96.

Akazawa, T. Aoki, K. & Bar-Yosef, O. (eds) 1998 *Neandertals and modern humans in western Asia.* New York: Plenum.

Alperson, N., Barzilai, O., Dag, D., Hartman, G. & Matskevich, Z. 2000 The age and context of the Tabun 1 skeleton: a reply to Schwarcz et al. *J. Hum. Evol.* **38**, 849–853.

Antón, S. & Weinstein, K. 1999 Artificial cranial deformation and fossil Australians revisited. *J. Hum. Evol.* **36**, 195–209.

Arsuaga, J. L., Bermúdez de Castro, J. M. & Carbonell, E. (eds) 1997 The Sima de los Huesos hominid site. *J. Hum. Evol.* **33**, 105–421.

Bailey, S. 2000 Dental morphological affinities among Late Pleistocene and Recent humans. *Dent. Anthropol.* **14**, 1–8.

Balter, M. 2002 What made humans modern? *Science* **295**, 1219–1225.

Barham, L. & Robson-Brown, K. (eds) 2001 *Human roots: Africa and Asia in the Middle Pleistocene.* Bristol: Western Academic and Specialist Press.

Bar-Yosef, O. & Callander, J. 1999 The woman from Tabun: Garrod's doubts in historical perspective. *J. Hum. Evol.* **37**, 879–885.

Bermúdez de Castro, J. M., Arsuaga, J., Carbonell, E., Rosas, A., Martinez, I. & Mosquera, M. 1997 A hominid from the lower Pleistocene of Atapuerca, Spain: possible ancestor to Neandertals and modern humans. *Science* **276**, 1392–1395.

Bookstein, F. (and 12 others) 1999 Comparing frontal cranial profiles in archaic and modern *Homo* by morphometric analysis. *Anat. Rec.* **257**, 1–9.

Bowler, J. & Thorne, A. 1976 Human remains from Lake Mungo: discovery and excavation of Lake Mungo III. In *The origin of the Australians* (ed. R. Kirk & A. Thorne), pp. 127–138. Canberra: Australian Institute of Aboriginal Studies.

Bräuer, G. 1992 Africa's place in the evolution of *Homo sapiens.* In *Continuity or replacement? Controversies in* Homo sapiens *evolution* (ed. G. Bräuer & F. Smith), pp. 83–98. Rotterdam, The Netherlands: Balkema.

Bräuer, G., Yokoyama, Y., Falguères, C. & Mbua, E. 1997 Modern human origins backdated. *Nature* **386**, 337–338.

Brown, P. 1992 Recent human evolution in East Asia and Australasia. *Phil. Trans. R. Soc. Lond.* B **337**, 235–242.

Brown, P. 1999 The first modern East Asians? Another look at Upper Cave 101, Liujiang and Minatogawa 1. In *Interdisciplinary perspectives on the origins of the Japanese* (ed. K. Omoto), pp. 105–131. Kyoto, Japan: International Research Center for Japanese Studies.

Cann, R., Stoneking, M. & Wilson, A. 1987 Mitochondrial DNA and human evolution. *Nature* **325**, 31–36.

Cavalli-Sforza, L. & Bodmer, W. 1971 *The genetics of human populations.* San Francisco, CA: Freeman.

Churchill, S. 2001 Hand morphology, manipulation, and tool use in Neandertals and early modern humans of the Near East. *Proc. Natl Acad. Sci. USA* **98**, 2953–2955.

Clark, J. G. 1968 *World prehistory: a new outline.* Cambridge University Press.

Cooper, A., Rambaut, A., Macaulay, V., Willerslev, E., Hansen, A. & Stringer, C. 2001 Human origins and ancient human DNA. *Science* **292**, 1655–1656.

Culotta, E. 1995 Asian hominids grow older. *Science* **270**, 1116–1117.

Dennell, R. 1997 The world's oldest spears. *Nature* **385**, 767–768.

d'Errico, F., Zilhão, J., Julien, M., Baffier, D. & Pelegrin, J. 1998 Neanderthal acculturation in Western Europe? A critical review of the evidence and its interpretation. *Curr. Anthropol.* **39**, S1–S44.

Duarte, C., Maurício, J., Pettitt, P. B., Souto, P., Trinkaus, E., van der Plicht, H. & Zilhão, J. 1999 The early Upper Paleolithic human skeleton from the Abrigo do Lagar Velho (Portugal) and modern human emergence in Iberia. *Proc. Natl Acad. Sci. USA* **96**, 7604–7609.

Etler, D. 1996 The fossil evidence for human evolution in Asia. *A. Rev. Anthropol.* **25**, 275–301.

Falguères, C., Sémah, F., Saleki, H., Yokoyama, Y., Jacob, T., Fontugne, M. & Féraud, G. 2001 Advancements in the dating of Solo Man. In

XIVth Congr. Union Int. des Sciences Préhistoriques et Protohistoriques (*UISPP*), Liège, 2–8 September 2001. Session 16.1 Abstract C15.

Foley, R. 1989 The ecological conditions of speciation: a comparative approach to the origins of anatomically-modern humans. In *The human revolution: behavioural and biological perspectives in the origins of modern humans* (ed. P. Mellars & C. Stringer), pp. 298–318. Edinburgh University Press.

Foley, R. & Lahr, M. 1997 Mode 3 technologies and the evolution of modern humans. *Camb. Archaeol. J.* **7**, 3–36.

Frayer, D., Wolpoff, M., Smith, F., Thorne, A. & Pope, G. 1993 The fossil evidence for modern human origins. *Am. Anthropol.* **95**, 14–50.

Garrod, D. & Bate, D. 1937 . *The Stone Age of Mount Carmel*, vol. 1. Oxford University Press.

Grün, R. & Stringer, C. 1991 Electron spin resonance dating and the evolution of modern humans. *Archaeometry* **33**, 153–199.

Grün, R. & Stringer, C. 2000 Tabun revisited: revised ESR chronology and new ESR and U-series analyses of dental material from Tabun C1. *J. Hum. Evol.* **39**, 601–612.

Grün, R. & Thorne, A. 1997 Dating the Ngandong humans. *Science* **276**, 1575–1576.

Grün, R., Stringer, C. & Schwarcz, H. 1991 ESR dating of teeth from Garrod's Tabun cave collection. *J. Hum. Evol.* **20**, 231–248.

Grün, R., Brink, J., Spooner, N., Taylor, L., Stringer, C., Franciscus, R. & Murray, A. 1996 Direct dating of Florisbad hominid. *Nature* **382**, 500–501.

Grün, R., Huang, P. H., Wu, X., Stringer, C., Thorne, A. & McCulloch, M. 1997 ESR analysis of teeth from the palaeoanthropological site of Zhoukoudian, China. *J. Hum. Evol.* **32**, 83–91.

Grün, R., Huang, P.-H., Huang, W., McDermott, F., Stringer, C., Thorne, A. & Yan, G. 1998 ESR and U-series analyses of teeth from the palaeoanthropological site of Hexian, Anhui Province, China. *J. Hum. Evol.* **34**, 555–564.

Grün, R., Spooner, N. A., Thorne, A., Mortimer, G., Simpson, J. J., McCulloch, M. T., Taylor, L. & Curnoe, D. 2000 Age of the Lake Mungo 3 skeleton, reply to Bowler & Magee and to Gillespie & Roberts. *J. Hum. Evol.* **38**, 733–741.

Hanihara, T. 1992 Dental and cranial affinities among populations of East Asia and the Pacific: the basic populations in East Asia IV. *Am. J. Phys. Anthropol.* **88**, 163–182.

Harvati, K. 2001 Analysis of Neanderthal temporal bone morphology using geometric morphometrics. *Am. J. Phys. Anthropol.* **S32**, 76–77.

Hawks, J., Hunley, K., Lee, S. & Wolpoff, M. 2000*a* Population bottlenecks and Pleistocene human evolution. *Mol. Biol. Evol.* **17**, 2–22.

Hawks, J., Oh, S., Hunley, K., Dobson, S., Cabana, G., Dayalu, P. & Wolpoff, M. 2000*b* An Australasian test of the recent African origin hypothesis using the WLH-50 calvarium. *J. Hum. Evol.* **39**, 1–22.

Holliday, T. 1997 Body proportions in Late Pleistocene Europe and modern human origins. *J. Hum. Evol.* **32**, 423–448.

Howells, W. W. 1989 Skull shapes and the map. In *Papers of the Peabody Museum, Harvard*, vol. 79.

Hublin, J.-J. 1993 Recent human evolution in northwestern Africa. In *The origin of modern humans and the impact of chronometric dating* (ed. M. Aitken, C. Stringer & P. Mellars), pp. 118–131. Princeton University Press.

Hublin, J.-J. 1998 Climatic changes, paleogeography, and the evolution of the Neandertals. In *Neandertals and modern humans in Western Asia* (ed. T. Akazawa, K. Aoki & O. Bar-Yosef), pp. 295–310. New York: Plenum.

Hublin, J.-J., Barroso Ruiz, C., Medina Lara, P., Fontugne, M. & Reyss, J.-L. 1995 The Mousterian site of Zafarraya (Andalucia, Spain): dating and implications on the Palaeolithic peopling processes of Western Europe. *Crit. Rev. Acad. Sci. Paris* IIa **321**, 931–937.

Hublin, J.-J., Spoor, F., Braun, M., Zonneveld, F. & Condemi, S. 1996 A late Neanderthal associated with Upper Palaeolithic artefacts. *Nature* **381**, 224–226.

Humphrey, L., Dean, M. C. & Stringer, C. B. 1999 Morphological variation in great ape and modern human mandibles. *J. Anat.* **195**, 491–513.

Ingman, M., Kaessmann, H., Pääbo, S. & Gyllensten, U. 2000 Mitochondrial genome variation and the origin of modern humans. *Nature* **408**, 708–713.

Irish, J. 1998 Ancestral dental traits in recent sub-Saharan Africans and the origins of modern humans. *J. Hum. Evol.* **34**, 81–98.

Jorde, L., Watkins, W., Bamshad, M., Dixon, M., Ricker, C., Seielstad, M. & Batzer, M. 2000 The distribution of human genetic diversity: a comparison of mitochondrial, autosomal, and Y-chromosome data. *Am. J. Hum. Genet.* **66**, 979–988.

Kayser, M. (and 11 others) 2001 An extensive analysis of Y-chromosomal microsatellite haplotypes in globally dispersed human populations. *Am. J. Hum. Genet.* **68**, 990–1018.

Ke, Y. (and 22 others) 2001 African origin of modern humans in East Asia: a tale of 12 000 Y chromosomes. *Science* **292**, 1151–1153.

Klein, R. 1999 *The human career.* University of Chicago Press.

Klein, R. 2000 Archeology and the evolution of human behavior. *Evol. Anthropol.* **9**, 17–36.

Krings, M., Capelli, C., Tschentscher, F., Geisert, H., Meyer, S., von Haeseler, A., Grossschmidt, K., Possnert, G., Paunovic, M. & Pääbo, S. 2000 A view of Neanderthal genetic diversity. *Nature Genet.* **26**, 144–146.

Lahr, M. 1996 *The evolution of modern human diversity: a study of cranial variation.* Cambridge University Press.

Lahr, M. & Foley, R. 1994 Multiple dispersals and modern human origins. *Evol. Anthropol.* **3**, 48–60.

Lahr, M. & Foley, R. 1998 Towards a theory of modern human origins: geography, demography, and diversity in recent human evolution. *Ybk Phys. Anthropol.* **41**, 137–176.

McBrearty, S. & Brooks, A. 2000 The revolution that wasn't: a new interpretation of the origin of modern human behavior. *J. Hum. Evol.* **39**, 453–563.

McDermott, F., Stringer, C., Grün, R., Williams, C. T., Din, V. & Hawkesworth, C. 1996 New Late-Pleistocene uranium–thorium and ESR dates for the Singa hominid (Sudan). *J. Hum. Evol.* **31**, 507–516.

Manzi, G., Mallegni, F. & Ascenzi, A. 2001 A cranium for the earliest Europeans: phylogenetic position of the hominid from Ceprano, Italy. *Proc. Natl Acad. Sci. USA* **98**, 10 011–10 016.

Mellars, P. 1999 The Neanderthal problem continued. *Curr. Anthropol.* **40**, 341–350.

Mercier, N., Valladas, H., Valladas, G., Reyss, J.-L., Jelinek, A., Meignen, L. & Joron, J.-L. 1995 TL dates of burnt flints from Jelinek's excavations at Tabun and their implications. *J. Archaeol. Sci.* **22**, 495–509.

Millard, A. & Pike, A. 1999 Uranium-series dating of the Tabun Neanderthal: a cautionary note. *J. Hum. Evol.* **36**, 581–585.

Nei, M. & Roychoudhury, A. 1982 Genetic relationship and evolution of human races. *Evol. Biol.* **14**, 1–59.

Ovchinnikov, I., Anders, G., Götherström, A., Romanova, G., Kharitonov, V., Lidén, K. & Goodwin, W. 2000 Molecular analysis of Neanderthal DNA from the northern Caucasus. *Nature* **404**, 490–493.

Pardoe, C. 1991 Competing paradigms and ancient human remains: the state of the discipline. *Archaeol. Oceania* **26**, 79–85.

Pearson, O. 2000 Postcranial remains and the origin of modern humans. *Evol. Anthropol.* **9**, 229–247.

Ponce de León, M. & Zollikofer, C. 2001 Neanderthal cranial ontogeny and its implications for late hominid diversity. *Nature* **412**, 534–538.

Potts, R. 1998 Environmental hypotheses of hominin evolution. *Ybk Phys. Anthropol.* **41**, 93–136.

Relethford, J. 1999 Models, predictions and the fossil record of modern human origins. *Evol. Anthropol.* **8**, 7–10.

Relethford, J. 2001 Ancient DNA and the origin of modern humans. *Proc. Natl Acad. Sci. USA* **98**, 390–391.

Relethford, J. & Jorde, L. 1999 Genetic evidence for larger African population size during recent human evolution. *Am. J. Phys. Anthropol.* **108**, 251–260.

Richards, M. & Macaulay, V. 2000 Genetic data and the colonization of Europe: genealogies and founders. In *Archaeogenetics* (ed. C. Renfrew & K. Boyle), pp. 139–151. Cambridge: McDonald Institute.

Rightmire, G. P. 1998 Human evolution in the Middle Pleistocene: the role of *Homo heidelbergensis. Evol. Anthropol.* **6**, 218–227.

Roberts, R., Jones, R. & Smith, M. 1990 Thermoluminescence dating of a 50 000 year old human occupation site in northern Australia. *Nature* **345**, 153–156.

Roberts, R., Jones, R., Spooner, N., Head, M., Murray, A. & Smith, M. 1994 The human colonization of Australia: optical dates of 53 000

and 60 000 years bracket human arrival at Deaf Adder Gorge, Northern Territory. *Quat. Sci. Rev. (Quat. Geochronol.)* **13**, 575–583.

Roebroeks, W. & Gamble, C. (eds) 1999 *The Middle Palaeolithic occupation of Europe.* University of Leiden.

Rogers, A. 2001 Order emerging from chaos in human evolutionary genetics. *Proc. Natl Acad. Sci. USA* **98**, 779–780.

Schillaci, M. & Froehlich, J. 2001 Nonhuman primate hybridisation and the taxonomic status of Neanderthals. *Am. J. Phys. Anthropol.* **115**, 157–166.

Schwarcz, H. P., Simpson, J. J. & Stringer, C. B. 1998 Neanderthal skeleton from Tabun: U-series data by gamma-ray spectrometry. *J. Hum. Evol.* **35**, 635–645.

Seidler, H., Falk, D., Stringer, C., Wilfing, H., Muller, G., zur Nedden, D., Weber, G., Recheis, W. & Arsuaga, J. L. 1997 A comparative study of stereolithographically modelled skulls of Petralona and Broken Hill: implications for future studies of middle Pleistocene hominid evolution. *J. Hum. Evol.* **33**, 691–703.

Shen, G. & Wang, W. 2001 Chronological evidence for early appearance of modern humans in southern China. *XIVth Congr. Union Int. des Sci. Préhistoriques et Protohistoriques (UISPP)*, Liège, 2–8 September 2001. Session 16.1 Abstract C8.

Shennan, S. 2001 Demography and cultural innovation: a model and its implications for the emergence of modern human culture. *Camb. Archaeol. J.* **11**, 5–16.

Shields, E. 1998 Australian aborigines represent the first branch from Eurasian antecedents: odontometric evidence. *J. Craniofac. Genet. Devl Biol.* **18**, 228–232.

Simpson, J. & Grün, R. 1998 Non-destructive gamma spectrometric U-series dating. *Quat. Sci. Rev. (Quat. Geochronol.)* **17**, 1009–1022.

Smith, A. 1994 *Systematics and the fossil record: documenting evolutionary patterns.* Oxford: Blackwell Scientific.

Smith, F. 1992 The role of continuity in modern human origins. In *Continuity or replacement? Controversies in* Homo sapiens *evolution* (ed. G. Bräuer & F. Smith), pp. 145–156. Rotterdam, The Netherlands: Balkema.

Smith, F., Trinkaus, E., Pettitt, P., Karavanić, I. & Paunović, M. 1999 Direct radiocarbon dates for Vindija G₁ and Velika Pećina late Pleistocene hominid remains. *Proc. Natl Acad. Sci. USA* **96**, 12 281–12 286.

Stringer, C. 1992 Reconstructing recent human evolution. *Phil. Trans. R. Soc. Lond.* B **337**, 217–224.

Stringer, C. 1994 Out of Africa—a personal history. In *Origins of anatomically modern humans* (ed. M. Nitecki & D. Nitecki), pp. 149–172. New York: Plenum.

Stringer, C. 1996 Current issues in modern human origins. In *Contemporary issues in human evolution* (ed. W. Meikle, F. C. Howell & N. Jablonski), *California Academy of Sciences Memoir* **21**, 115–134.

Stringer, C. 1998*a* A metrical study of the WLH-50 calvaria. *J. Hum. Evol.* **34**, 327–332.

Stringer, C. 1998*b* Chronological and biogeographic perspectives on later human evolution. In *Neandertals and modern humans in Western Asia* (ed. T. Akazawa, K. Aoki & O. Bar-Yosef), pp. 29–37. New York: Plenum.

Stringer, C. 1999 The origin of modern humans and their regional diversity. *Newslett. Interdisc. Stud. Origins Jpn. Peoples Cultures* **9**, 3–5.

Stringer, C. 2000 Coasting out of Africa. *Nature* **405**, 24–27.

Stringer, C. 2001*a* Dating the origin of modern humans. In *The age of the Earth: from 4004 BC to AD 2002* (ed. C. Lewis & S. Knell), pp. 265–274. London: Geological Society.

Stringer, C. 2001*b* Modern human origins—distinguishing the models. *Afr. Archaeol. Rev.* **18**, 67–75.

Stringer, C. & Davies, W. 2001 Those elusive Neanderthals. *Nature* **413**, 791–792.

Stringer, C. & Hublin, J.-J. 1999 New age estimates for the Swanscombe hominid, and their significance for human evolution. *J. Hum. Evol.* **37**, 873–877.

Stringer, C., Humphrey, L. & Compton, T. 1997 Cladistic analysis of dental traits in recent humans using a fossil outgroup. *J. Hum. Evol.* **32**, 389–402.

Stringer, C., Trinkaus, E., Roberts, M., Parfitt, S. & Macphail, R. 1998 The Middle Pleistocene human tibia from Boxgrove. *J. Hum. Evol.* **34**, 509–547.

Swisher, C., Rink, W., Anton, S., Schwarcz, H., Curtis, G., Suprijo, A., Widiasmoro 1996 Latest *Homo erectus* of Java: potential contemporaneity with *Homo sapiens* in southeast Asia. *Science* **274**, 1870–1874.

Takahata, N., Lee, S.-H. & Satta, Y. 2001 Testing multiregionality of modern human origins. *Mol. Biol. Evol.* **18**, 172–183.

Tattersall, I. & Schwartz, J. 2000 *Extinct humans.* Boulder, CO: Westview Press.

Taylor, R. & Aitken, M. (eds) 1997 *Chronometric dating in archaeology.* New York: Plenum.

Templeton, A. R. 1993 The 'Eve' hypothesis: a genetic critique and reanalysis. *Am. Anthropol.* **95**, 51–72.

Templeton, A. 2002 Out of Africa again and again. *Nature* **416**, 45–50.

Thorne, A. & Wolpoff, M. 1992 The multiregional evolution of modern humans. *Sci. Am.* **266**, 76–83.

Thorne, A., Grün, R., Mortimer, G., Spooner, N., Simpson, J., Mcculloch, M., Taylor, L. & Curnoe, D. 1999 Australia's oldest human remains: age of the Lake Mungo 3 skeleton. *J. Hum. Evol.* **36**, 591–612.

Tishkoff, S. (and 11 others) 2000 STRP-Alu haplotype variation at PLAT locus. *Am. J. Hum. Genet.* **67**, 901–925.

Trinkaus, E. 1984 Western Asia. In *The origins of modern humans* (ed. F. Smith & F. Spencer), pp. 251–293. New York: Alan R. Liss.

Trinkaus, E. 1997 Appendicular robusticity and the paleobiology of modern human emergence. *Proc. Natl Acad. Sci. USA* **94**, 13 367–13 373.

Turner III, C. 1992 Microevolution of east Asian and European populations: a dental perspective. In *The evolution and dispersal of modern humans in Asia* (ed. T. Akazawa, K. Aoki & T. Kimura), pp. 415–438. Tokyo: Hokusen-Sha.

Turney, C. (and 11 others) 2001 Early human occupation at Devil's Lair, southwestern Australia 50 000 years ago. *Quat. Res.* **55**, 3–13.

Tyrell, A. & Chamberlain, A. 1998 Non-metric trait evidence for modern human affinities and the distinctiveness of Neanderthals. *J. Hum. Evol.* **34**, 549–554.

Underhill, P., Passarino, G., Lin, A., Shen, P., Lahr, M., Foley, R., Oefner, P. & Cavalli-Sforza, L. 2001 The phylogeography of Y chromosome binary haplotypes and the origins of modern human populations. *Ann. Hum. Genet.* **65**, 43–62.

Valladas, H., Joron, J., Valladas, G., Arensburg, B., Bar-Yosef, O., Belfer-Cohen, A., Goldberg, P., Laville, H., Meignen, L. & Rak, Y. 1987 Thermoluminescence dates for the Neanderthal burial site at Kebara in Israel. *Nature* **330**, 159–160.

Vandermeersch, B. 1989 The evolution of modern humans: recent evidence from southwest Asia. In *The human revolution: behavioural and biological perspectives in the origins of modern humans* (ed. P. Mellars & C. Stringer), pp. 155–164. Edinburgh University Press.

Wainscoat, J. (and 10 others) 1986 Evolutionary relationships of human populations from an analysis of nuclear DNA polymorphisms. *Nature* **319**, 491–493.

Watkins, W., Ricker, C., Bamshad, M., Carroll, M., Nguyen, S., Batzer, M., Harpending, H., Rogers, A. & Jorde, L. 2001 Patterns of ancestral human diversity: an analysis of Alu-insertion and restriction-site polymorphisms. *Am. J. Hum. Genet.* **68**, 738–752.

Wolpoff, M. & Caspari, R. 1997 *Race and human evolution: a fatal attraction.* New York: Simon & Schuster.

Yin, G., Falguères, C., Shen, G. & Lu, Y. 2001 The age of Dali Man. *XIVth Congr. Union Int. des Sci. Préhistoriques et Protohistoriques (UISPP)*, Liège, 2–8 September 2001. Session 16.1 abstract C7.

Zhao, Z. (and 12 others) 2000 Worldwide DNA sequence variation in a 10-kilobase noncoding region on human chromosome 22. *Proc. Natl Acad. Sci. USA* **97**, 11 354–11 358.

60

A Reconsideration of the Omo-Kibish Remains and the *erectus-sapiens* Transition

M. H. Day and C. B. Stringer

ABSTRACT

The Omo-Kibish remains have been restudied in the light of new finds including those from Arago. The dating of the Kibish remains is reviewed and a new reconstruction of Omo 1 is presented.

The affinities of the Omo-Kibish crania have been reassessed making use of the newer principles of classification that have emerged in the last ten years. Working definitions of Homo erectus *and* Homo sapiens *are offered, based on distinctive within-group characters that can be identified objectively. These definitions are employed to assess the affinities of the Omo 1 and 2 crania in terms of a scoring system.*

The conclusion reached is that the Omo 1 cranium can be clearly aligned with anatomically modern Homo sapiens *while Omo 2 is closer to* Homo erectus *than to the Neanderthals or to anatomically modern* Homo sapiens *on the characters considered.*

The dating of the two specimens remains a problem in terms of absolute age and contemporaneity.

Comparison with Arago 21 shows that Omo 2 has more in common with this specimen than Omo 1, although Arago 21 and Omo 2 do not appear to be closely related. Their similarities are mainly symplesiomorphies retained from earlier Middle Pleistocene ancestors rather than synapomorphies.

From Day, M. H., & Stringer, C. B. (1982). A reconsideration of the Omo Kibish remains and the *erectus-sapiens* transition. In M. A. de Lumley, ed., *L'Homo erectus et la place de l'homme de Tautavel parmi les hominidés fossiles.* Congrès International de Paléontologie Humaine, 1er Congres Pretirage. Tome 2. Nice: Centre National de la Recherche Scientifique, pp. 814–846.

INTRODUCTION

In 1967 the Kenya Group of the International Omo Expedition, led by Mr. Richard Leakey, recovered parts of three skeletons including an incomplete calvaria with a number of associated postcranial bones (Omo 1), a nearly complete calvaria (Omo 2) and some cranial remains including a glabellar fragment (Omo 3). These remains have been the subject of several publications (Leakey, 1969; Day, 1969, 1972, 1973), as have the deposits from which the remains were taken (Butzer, 1969; Butzer & Thurber, 1969; Butzer, Brown & Thurber, 1969).

These initial publications concluded that the remains of Omo 1 and 2 were found in Member I of the Kibish Formation, a group of layers that overlie the Nkalabong Beds (Figure 1). The Omo 1 partial skeleton was found partly *in situ* in association with faunal remains that include a primitive modern elephant (*Loxodonta africana*), an advanced archaic elephant (*Elephas recki*), both white and black rhinoceros (*Ceratotherium simum* and *Diceros bicornis*) and a buffalo (*Syncerus caffer*). The dating of the site was found to be outside the range of the radiocarbon method but Member I has been dated at about 130,000 years B.P. by the Uranium/Thorium technique applied to molluscs (Butzer, 1969). Relative dating of the site was investigated by fluorine, nitrogen and uranium analysis and the fauna is consistent with an upper Middle Pleistocene or early Upper Pleistocene date. The only archaeological evidence is a few stone tools found with Omo 1 and they are undiagnostic of a recognised culture.

The Omo 2 calvarium which was discovered approximately 2.5 km from the site of Omo 1 (Figure 2) is less certainly dated since it was essentially a surface find with no clear stratigraphic, faunal or cultural context although the sedimentary sequence is reported to be the same on both sides of the Omo river in this area.

The Omo 3 fragments are thought to come from Member III of the Kibish formation and are thus slightly higher in the sequence, but still older than 37,000 years B.P. according to radiocarbon determinations on molluscs from Member III (Butzer, 1976).

Some of the initial conclusions concerning the dating of the Omo material remain essentially unchanged in that:

(a) Omo 1 is most clearly associated with Member I in that it was a partly *in situ* find that was properly excavated.

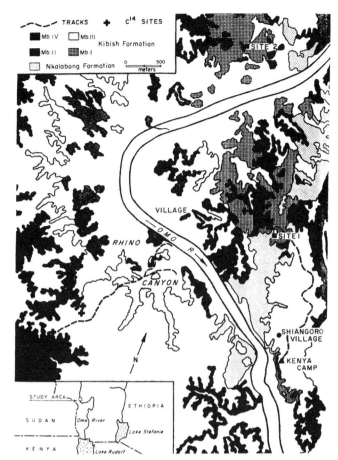

Figure 2. *Map of the Omo 1 and 2 hominid sites (courtesy Dr. K. W. Butzer).*

(b) The contemporaneity of Omo 1 and the associated faunal remains seems secure.
(c) The uncertainty concerning the precise stratigraphic level of the Omo 2 remains leaves some doubt as to its contemporaneity with Omo 1. Omo 3 certainly appears to be younger than Omo 1.
(d) The chronological date of 130,000 years B.P. for Member I by the Uranium/Thorium method remains unconfirmed by any other technique, but it is not contradicted by the limited available faunal and radiocarbon dating.

Since the initial excavation, the site has not been revisited and no further evidence as to its dating has been published.

In terms of dating, therefore, several questions can be posed. Is the relative dating evidence strong enough to demand that the material be treated as a single population sample? If the answer is yes, reconstruction and morphological analysis can operate within the bounds of variability of a local population of a single taxon. If the answer is no, then additional considerations arise in that the remains may represent samples of time—successive populations that are closely related to each other or they may represent evidence of population replacement rather than local *in situ* evolution.

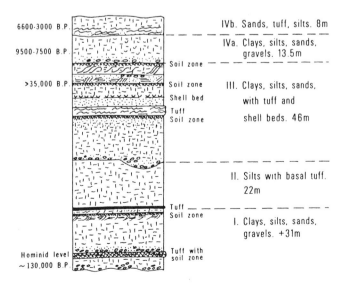

Figure 1. *Generalized stratigraphic column of the Kibish formation (courtesy Dr. K. W. Butzer).*

PREVIOUS WORK ON THE OMO-KIBISH REMAINS

The initial work on these remains included their cleaning, restoration and description. The initial assessment of the remains was based on anatomical evidence and concluded that while all three specimens should be attributed to *Homo sapiens,* specimens 1 and 2 show striking differences in skull form. The more complete calvaria having features in common with the Solo skulls, the Broken Hill skull and with *Homo erectus* (Day, 1969). Later work, including a discriminant function analysis of metrical skull data, emphasised the differences between Omo 1 and Omo 2 and that both could be distinguished from at least three populations of modern *Homo sapiens* (Day, 1973).

The Omo specimens were regarded as Neanderthals (in the grade sense) by Brose & Wolpoff (1971), who stated that no features of the specimens were outside the range of Neanderthal morphology. Omo 1 "would be identified as anatomically modern if found in another context," but at the same time they made the remarkable claim that the specimen was "extremely similar to Amud." Overall, the Omo crania were said to be Neanderthals (*Sensu lato*), transitional to "modern" *H. sapiens.* Howells (1974) strongly disagreed with Brose & Wolpoff's (1971) general approach and specifically criticised their conclusions about the Omo specimens. We fully endorse his criticisms.

Rightmire (Rightmire, 1976, 1980, 1981) favoured treating the specimens together as related forms, while admitting that Omo 2 was more like Broken Hill 1. As we also believe, Rightmire (1981) felt that the unpublished Guomde specimen (KNM-ER 3884) from East Turkana might be related to the Omo-Kibish fossils.

Stringer utilised multivariate analysis of cranial measurements (1974) and analyses of size, shape, angles and indices (1978) to compare the Omo-Kibish specimens. The results tended to accentuate the contrasts between the Omo crania, always aligning Omo 1 much more closely to anatomically modern (a.m.) *H. sapiens.* The multivariate analyses (Stringer, 1974) were based on measurements of Omo 2, and Omo 1 as reconstructed in 1972. However the new reconstruction presented here is only marginally different in frontal dimensions and cranial length from that of 1972, while parietal and occipital regions have been retained. Thus the 1974 multivariate results comparing Omo 1 and 2 are still relevant to the present discussion. The analysis which employed most measurements for the two specimens together utilised the following 13 measurements: biasterionic breadth (ASB); nasion-bregma chord, subtense and fraction (FRC, FRS, FRF); bregma-lambda chord, subtense and fraction (PAC, PAS, PAF); lambda-opisthion subtense and fraction (OCC, OCS, OCF); supraorbital projection (SOS—estimated for Omo 2); bistephanic breadth (STB); maximum cranial breadth (XCB).

Discrimination between the groups analysed was measured using the Mahalanobis D^2 statistic, and an extract from the results is provided here.

D^2 Distance between Omo Crania and Other Hominid Crania

	Omo 1	Omo 2
Choukoutien	49.1	42.8
Solo	32.2	18.3
Neanderthal	35.8	40.5
Skhūl 5	14.6	43.9
Upper Palaeolithic	18.6	48.1
Nearest modern (Norse)	16.1	46.1
Broken Hill	38.7	28.4
Irhoud 1	51.5	41.1
Singa	27.5	49.1
Petralona	59.5	60.5
Omo 1	—	24.3
Omo 2	24.3	—
Saccopastore	33.6	13.2

Omo 1 has nearest neighbours Skhūl 5, the Upper Palaeolithic group and a.m. Norse (all, in our opinion, representative of a.m. *H. sapiens*); Omo 2 has nearest neighbours Saccopastore 1, Solo, Omo 1 and Broken Hill. Of all the "non-modern" specimens, Omo 2 is closest to Omo 1. Shared differences from other archaic crania are the low SOS, large FRC, large PAC, large PAF, large OCC. Shared differences compared with a.m. *H. sapiens* crania include larger XCB, STB, ASB, FRC, FRF and PAF. Differences between Omo 1 and 2 mainly relate to contrasts in FRS (Omo 1 higher value—more domed frontal), PAS (Omo 1 higher value—more domed parietal), OCS (Omo 2 higher value—more projecting occiput), OCF (Omo 1 higher value—expanded occipital plane) and ASB (Omo 2 higher value—broader occipital base), and in every one of these differences Omo 1 is closer to the pattern of a.m. *H. sapiens* crania.

Thus the multivariate results confirmed that Omo 1 approximated to an anatomically modern pattern in these cranial measurements, while Omo 2 did not. The two crania do share, however, certain cranial characteristics suggesting that they are related, though temporally separated, members of an evolutionary lineage in northeast Africa leading from *erectus*-like hominids to a robust, but anatomically modern form. Alternatively, if we accept the published dating, the Omo 1 cranium could represent a late Middle Pleistocene/Upper Pleistocene spread of a.m. *H. sapiens* into the area accompanied by some degree of gene flow from a more archaic local population represented by Omo 2.

Clark Howell (1978) was skeptical of the Middle Pleistocene age estimates for the Omo-Kibish crania, and questioned Day's (1973) conclusions regarding their affinities. He emphasized their distinctiveness from *H. erectus* and *H. sapiens rhodesiensis* and concluded that they represented a late subspecies of *H. sapiens* closely related to modern man. He quoted Stringer's (1974) conclusions in support of this view, but these results do not justify Howell's interpretation, since Omo 2 is *not* closely related to recent *H. sapiens* but is similar to various archaic specimens.

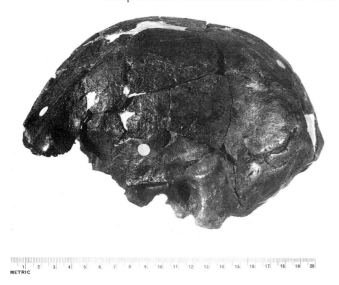

Figure 3. *Left lateral view of the Omo 2 calvaria (norma lateralis).*

THE RECONSTRUCTION OF THE OMO 1 CRANIUM

The problems of the Kibish remains can also be approached from the viewpoint of anatomical reconstruction, governed by the internal evidence of anatomical necessity rather than reconstruction by the amalgamation of several species (*vide* Arago).

The reconstruction of undistorted cranial fragments can proceed with confidence only if the fragments concerned are adjacent and capable of a demonstrable interlocking fit. Once those pieces that have such a fit are identified and joined other factors such as bilateral symmetry of skulls can aid reasonable reconstruction.

In the case of the Omo 2 calvaria (Figures 3 and 4) the four fragments fit perfectly and the specimen is undistorted. Any attempt to reconstruct the face would be purely speculative and of little or no scientific value.

Figure 4. *Superior view of Omo 2 (norma verticalis).*

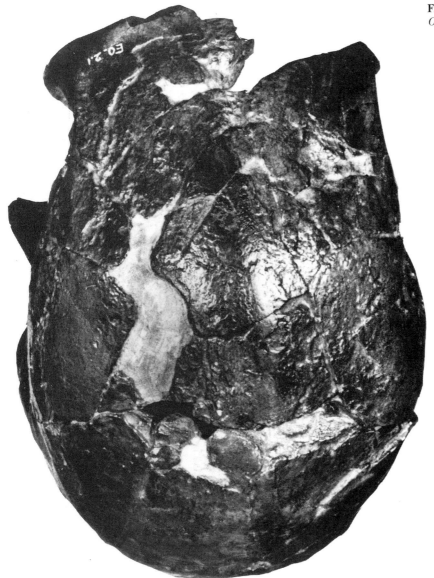

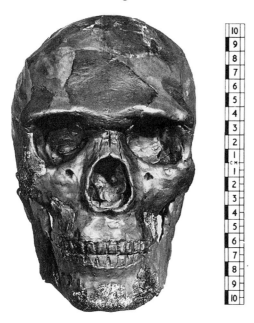

Figure 5.   *Omo 1 reconstruction: frontal view (norma frontalis).*

Figure 6.   *Omo 1 reconstruction: superior view (norma verticalis).*

Similarly with Omo 3, the paucity of fragments (one left fronto-parietal fragment and a glabellar fragment) does not allow any reasonable attempt at reconstruction to be made. It is the purpose of this paper to publish a reconstruction of Omo 1 and to discuss the problems encountered and to compare the Omo I reconstruction with the other Omo (Kibish) remains and with other specimens to comparable age from Africa and from Europe. This in turn, may throw some light on the problems of the *erectus-sapiens* transition and contribute to the current debate on punctuated equilibrium as opposed to gradualism in this period of human evolution.

Omo 1 has a posterior vault which can be reconstructed with some confidence, giving a decidedly "modern" appearance. To what extent should the reconstruction of the anterior region reflect this? We believe the robust but anatomically modern morphology of the posterior vault should be mirrored by an appropriate reconstruction of the frontal, face and mandible. Using early anatomically modern specimens from southwest Asia (Skhūl, Qafzeh) and more archaic specimens from Africa (Irhoud 1, Ngaloba L.H.18, Broken Hill 1), it is possible to reconstruct a face which is "modern" but which nevertheless reflects the robust morphology of other late Middle/early Upper Pleistocene hominids by displaying a wide upper face, large interorbital breadth and strong alveolar prognathism (Figure 5).

The frontal bone is very long, but some flexibility is possible in the degree of flatness chosen for the reconstruction (Figure 6). The mandible has a fairly narrow ascending ramus which would normally indicate a short body and overall length. However, given the constraints of the long frontal bone and our preference for a face with some degree of alveolar prognathism, rather than an orthognathic face, the mandible has been reconstructed with a long body, while avoiding the presence of retromolar spaces, not otherwise found in African Pleistocene hominids.

NEW ANALYSES AND THE CLASSIFICATION OF THE OMO-KIBISH REMAINS

Since the original studies of the Omo fossils, much new material has been discovered and described which is relevant to our interpretation of these specimens. The characteristics of African *H. erectus* are now better known, thanks to recent discoveries and descriptions (Rightmire, 1980), while material which throws light on the possible transition from *H. erectus* and *H. sapiens* has been described from sites such as Petralona, Arago and Bilzingsleben in Europe (see e.g. Stringer et al., 1979) and Ndutu and Bodo in Africa (Rightmire, 1980, 1981). Archaic hominid material from Broken Hill and possible early anatomically modern material from Florisbad may be more ancient than had been supposed, probably dating from the Middle Pleistocene and early Upper Pleistocene respectively (Rightmire, 1981), while other African material which may document the latter stages of hominid evolution has been described from sites such as Djebel Irhoud (Howell, 1978) and Ngaloba (Day et al., 1980). From Border Cave and Klasies Cave in Southern Africa, material which may represent anatomically modern hominids from the early Upper Pleistocene has been described (Rightmire, 1981).

From all this additional knowledge we should now be in a better position to assess the affinities of the Omo-Kibish crania than was possible ten years ago, but the intervening years have also seen reassessments of the principles to be used in classifying fossil hominids and a growing recognition of the problems we face in interpreting a fragmented fossil record with poor chronological control, against a background of debate about the fundamental mechanisms of evolutionary change. Following some common palaeoanthropological methods of classification we might use the "total morphological pattern" approach of Le Gros Clark (1964) or employ a multivariate approach (e.g. Stringer, 1974) to produce measures of overall similarity between fossil hominids and recent populations. But such approaches are primarily phenetic, often leading to the creation of grade systems, disguised by the use of subspecies names (Campbell, 1964; Howell, 1978) or overt in the application of numbered grades (Stringer et al., 1979). When one of us suggested a grade system for *H. sapiens*, it was because it was felt that the application of subspecies names to fossils was hindering rather than helping the progress of palaeoanthropology.

A numbered grade system should only be employed pending the creation of valid taxonomic units, and could not be a workable solution in the long term. As a first step towards a different approach to hominid classification we would like to propose simple working definitions of *H. erectus* and *H. sapiens* based on distinctive within-group characteristics which can be used to assess the affinities of the Omo-Kibish fossils. Most of the characters have previously been used in describing the two species but we have attempted to provide clear presence or absence data which can be assessed objectively and applied simply. Some of the metrical differences recognised can be shown to lie behind multivariate discrimination (see Stringer, 1974, 1978, and earlier discussion of the Omo multivariate results), although this is sometimes masked by amalgamation of size and shape differences. Once broad groupings (*H. erectus*, Neanderthals and a.m. *H. sapiens*) are established, it should be possible to recognise further subdivisions and identify other groupings for fossils which do not fit well into any of these categories. More detailed definitions based on more anatomical characters, including those most generally used (e.g. see Le Gros Clark, 1964; Howell,1978; Howells, 1980) would be desirable, but without clear character weighting it is difficult to classify fossil hominids which show only some of these features, or which have characters only partly developed.

It seems appropriate to begin with a definition of a.m. *H. sapiens* based on derived characters which can be assessed in the Omo specimens. There is a large body of data available (Howells, 1973). Indeed if we cannot provide a valid definition of the only living human species there is little hope of our recognising extinct taxa. Whether the species so recognised should also form the basis for recognising the species in the fossil record is a difficult problem, but it does seem somewhat inappropriate to include in the species fossil hominids which lack most of the derived characters defining *H. sapiens* today. But for the present we will equate our definition of *H. sapiens (Sensu stricto)* with the term a.m. *H. sapiens*, and leave the question of whether various archaic forms rightly belong within the species *H. sapiens* to future research. The criteria used here to define a.m. *H. sapiens* will not all be present in all modern specimens, but a majority should always be present. Because of population variability, some of these characters will also be found in fossil hominids which are

clearly not anatomically modern forms. But if either of the Omo-Kibish specimens can reasonably be classified as a.m. *H. sapiens*, we should expect over 50% of the "modern" characters to be present of those which can be tested.

Working Definition of Anatomically Modern *H. sapiens*

- Cranium short but high (ratio of basion-bregma height or vertex radius to glabello-occipital length should exceed 0.70 or 0.64 respectively);
- Parietal arch is long and high, inferiorly narrow, superiorly broad (parietal angle less than 138°, ratio of bregma-asterion chord to biasterionic breadth greater than 1.19);
- Frontal bone high (frontal angle less than 133°);
- Supraorbital torus not continuous, but divided into lateral and medial portions;
- Occipital bone well curved rather than angulated (occipital angle more than 114°);
- Mental eminence on mandible;
- Gracile limb bones—thin walled with relatively small articular surfaces.

For *Homo erectus*

Fossil material from Africa and Asia can similarly be used to produce a working definition of *H. erectus*. Material used here to formulate the morphological and metrical definition includes KNM-ER 3733 and 3883; Choukoutien; Sangiran 2,4,17; and Ngandong. The characters chosen exclude some of the useful traditional characters (e.g. thick occipital torus, presence of angular torus, presence of mid-sagittal keeling and parasagittal depressions) because these cannot be defined precisely or objectively. Such characters should also be assessed in any overall study of the Omo-Kibish material and have previously been investigated (e.g. Day, 1969, 1971). The characters chosen for Table 1 will all be present in some *H. erectus* crania, and the majority should be present in all *H. erectus* crania. Other fossils will display some *H. erectus* characters even though they are not members of the species *H. erectus*, since our working definition is primarily created to separate *H. erectus* most effectively from anatomically modern *H. sapiens* (see Table 2). Other characters would have to be utilised if we were trying to separate Neanderthals from *H. erectus*, since they share some of the characters which reflect the presence of a long, low skull, low frontal and short flat parietal arch, and this will have to be investigated in the future. But Neanderthal crania do not show a majority of the *H. erectus* characters, and a set of criteria differentiating Neanderthals from a.m. *H. sapiens* can also be created to test whether either of the Omo-Kibish crania could be regarded as "Neanderthal" (Table 3). If specimens are found that display combinations of characters typical of the various groups (or intermediate values for certain characters) this may indicate a) that they represent genuine morphological intermediates between the forms, b) that they are hybrids if it can be demonstrated that the morphologically distinct groups overlap in time, or c) that the characters used in the working definitions are inadequate and need modification.

Tables 1 and 2. Metrical and Morphological Characteristics of *H. erectus* and Anatomically Modern *H. sapiens*, and Their Occurrence in the Omo-Kibish Remains. Characters chosen are expected to be present in more than 75% of samples. The Arago 21 reconstruction is also tested using the same criteria.

Table 1

H. erectus (characters to differentiate from a.m. *H. sapiens*)	Omo 2	Omo 1	Arago 21 Recon.
1. BBH/GOL <0.62 or VRR/GOL <0.58	(c. 0.58) Marginal	No	—
2. Inion = opisthocranion	Yes	No	—
3. Thick cranium:			
(a) parietal bregma >8 mm	Yes ⎫ 2/3	Marginal ⎫	Marginal ⎫
(b) parietal asterion >14 mm	No ⎬ Yes	No? ⎬ = ½	Marginal ⎬ = ½
(c) occipital inion >14 mm	Yes ⎭	Yes ⎭	— ⎭
4. OCA <107°	Marginal	No	—
5. Inion-opisthion cd > lambda-inion cd	Yes	No	—
6. Inion >25 mm above internal occipital prot.	Yes	No	—
7. PAA >145.5°	Yes	No	Yes
8. BAC/ASB <1.14	No	No	No
9. FRA >136.5°	Yes	Marginal (c. 136°)	Yes
10. Cranial capacity <1150 ml	No	No	Marginal ½
	7/10 70%	1/10 10%	3/5 60%

Table 2

H. sapiens (characters of modern humans to differentiate from *H. erectus* [and Neanderthals])	Omo 2	Omo 1	Arago 21 Recon.
1. BBH/GOL >0.70 or VRR/GOL >0.64	No	Yes	—
2. PAA <138°	No	Yes	No
3. BAC/ASB >1.19	Marginal	Yes	Yes
4. FRA <133°	No	No	No
5. Clearly divided supraorbital torus, weakly developed lateral and medial portions	?	?	No
6. OCA >114°	No	Yes	—
7. Mental eminence	—	Yes	? No (other material)
8. Limb bones thin-walled with relatively small articular surfaces	—	Yes	? No (other material)
	½/5 10%	6/7 86%	1/6 17%

Table 3. Selected Metrical and Morphological Characters Which Distinguish between Neanderthal and a.m. *H. sapiens* (Stringer & Trinkaus, 1981). These are utilized to see whether either Omo-Kibish specimen can be described as "Neanderthal" rather than as related to *H. erectus* or a.m. *H. sapiens*.* The Arago 21 reconstruction is also tested.

Relevant Neanderthal Characters	Omo 2	Omo 1	Arago 21 Recon.
1. FRA >136° ⎫ primitive characters	Yes	Marginal	Yes
2. PAA >138° ⎬ partly shared with	Yes	No	Yes
3. BAC/ASB <1.15 ⎭ *H. erectus.*	No	No	No
4. Suprainiac fossa	No	No	—
5. Large occipitomastoid crest	No	No	—
6. Anterior mastoid tubercle	No	No	—
7. Cranial shape oval in occipital view max. diameter low on parietals	No	No	No
8. Nasio-frontal angle <141°	No? (Cannot be measured exactly)	—	No
9. Limb bones thick walled with relatively large articular surfaces	—	No	? Yes (other material)
	2/8 25%	½/8 6%	3?/6 50%

*Several of the more diagnostic Neanderthal characters of the face and post-cranium cannot be used because of the incomplete nature of the Omo-Kibish finds. The Arago 21 specimen does not show these most distinctive Neanderthal characters of the face and hence would not be classified as a Neanderthal using all available criteria.

Working Definition of *H. erectus*

- Cranium long and low (ratio of basion-bregma height or vertex radius height to glabello-occipital length is less than 0.62 or 0.58 respectively);
- Inion is coincident with opisthocranion;
- Thick cranial walls (for example parietal thickness at bregma exceeds 8 mm, at asterion exceeds 14 mm, on occipital at inion exceeds 14 mm);
- Angulated occipital bone (occipital angle less than 107°);
- Expanded nuchal portion of occipital bone (inion-opisthion chord exceeds lambda-inion chord);
- Inion more than 25 mm above internal occipital protuberance;
- Parietal arch flat, short and low, superiorly narrow, inferiorly broad (parietal angle exceeds 145.5°, ratio of bregma-asterion chord to biasterionic breadth is less than 1.14);
- Low frontal bone (frontal angle exceeds 136.5°);
- Cranial capacity generally below 1150 ml.

CONCLUSIONS: THE AFFINITIES OF THE OMO-KIBISH FOSSILS

In Tables 1, 2 and 3, it is evident from the characters considered that Omo 1 and 2 differ markedly in their affinities, far more than would be expected for one population. Omo 2 shows most resemblance to *H. erectus,* the main differences being related to larger cranial capacity and associated vertical expansion of the cranial vault reflected by a large vertex radius and bregma-asterion chord. The occipital bone shows various typical *erectus* characters but it is actually less angulated than the majority of other *erectus* crania. Omo 1 is clearly aligned with a.m. *H. sapiens* although the low and long frontal bone of the reconstructed cranium is exceptional and the robusticity of the specimen is indicated by relatively thick cranial walls. It would be premature to assign the Omo 2 fossil to the species *H. erectus* when some important anatomical areas are not represented (e.g. face, dentition, mandible, post-cranium) and there are clear departures in supraorbital torus morphology, cranial capacity and overall dimensions from the typical and fairly consistent sample of *H. erectus* crania from Africa and Asia. However the affinities of the specimen are certainly closer to *H. erectus* than to the Neanderthals or a.m. *H. sapiens* on the characters assessed here. For Omo 1 we feel we have sufficient evidence from the cranial parts, mandible and post-cranium to align the specimen positively with a.m. *H. sapiens*, despite its robusticity.

The main problems remaining are chronological. If both specimens are of late Middle/early Upper Pleistocene age, then two distinct but approximately contemporaneous populations are being sampled. One of them conformed to an anatomically modern pattern and would represent one of the most ancient if not the most ancient of such groups known. But a note of caution must be injected at this point. Further confirmatory absolute dating analyses have not been performed, neither has subsequent field work been conducted in the area to recover further material, including faunal remains which might be more diagnostic of a Middle or Upper Pleistocene age. Given the evidence from southern Africa (Rightmire, 1981) it is no longer implausible that anatomically modern hominids existed at the beginning of the Upper Pleistocene. What would be difficult to explain, however, is the occurrence of such widely separated early anatomically modern hominids when more archaic populations may still have existed in North Africa and in the intervening area of East Africa. Perhaps the dating of hominids in East Africa such as Eyasi, Broken Hill and Ngaloba may be significantly earlier than the more "modern" specimens, or there may have been a rapid population replacement in the early Upper Pleistocene. However this cannot be demonstrated within our present inadequate dating framework.

Alternatively the evolution of hominids resembling anatomically modern man may have occurred more or less independently in areas of Southern, Eastern and Northern Africa, in which case the Omo-Kibish remains may document a transition from an *erectus*-like (not Neanderthal) ancestor to a robust but "modern" skeletal form. Whichever model eventually proves most appropriate it is evident that relationships between the contrasting Omo-Kibish specimens will remain somewhat problematical until further evidence is available about their relative chronological positions.

THE OMO REMAINS AND THE ARAGO 21 CONSTRUCTION

One of the purposes of this symposium is to discuss the new reconstruction of the Arago 21 specimen,* and through comparative analyses, to place the specimen in relation to various other fossil hominids. Our reconstruction of the Omo 1 cranium was made using the available fragments, directly where possible, or indirectly as indicators of the probable morphology of missing parts. We did not use fragments of other fossil hominids in our reconstruction, but rather attempted to produce a reasonable reconstruction given the available fragments and the morphology of other late Middle/early Upper Pleistocene crania. For the Arago original reconstruction, modified parts of other fossils have been used to create a composite cranium containing fragments from specimens such as Sangiran 17, Swanscombe or Vertesszöllös to represent the missing parts of the skull.

Direct comparisons between the Arago cranium and the Omo fossils are difficult since the former specimen consists primarily of parts not well represented in the latter (upper dentition, palate, face, supraorbital region), and some of the most informative parts of the Omo crania (mastoid region occipital bone, mandible and post-cranium of Omo 1) are not present in the Arago 21 cranium itself. Comparisons can be made for the frontal bone and parietal region and except for the common feature of a long and flat frontal bone (accepting the Omo 1 reconstruction), there are immediate contrasts between the specimens. The Arago frontal certainly appears more archaic in its massive supraorbital torus and narrow dimensions, with a significant degree of postorbital constriction. The latter character is no doubt related to the lower cranial capacity of the Arago specimen.

In parietal morphology there are also contrasts since Omo 1 displays a much more modern form than Arago 47

---

* The new reconstruction consists of Arago 21 and Arago 47 combined.

(as reconstructed) while Omo 2 appears rather archaic in comparison, with a midsagittal keel, parasagittal flattenings and a broad base to the parietal arch. But some of the most important diagnostic characters which separate the Omo crania are in the occipital bone, which is unfortunately lacking in the Arago specimen. Given the morphology of the face and frontal bone, a more archaic occipital than that of the Swanscombe specimen was probably present and therefore the Vertesszöllös, Petralona or Bilzingsleben occipitals may be more appropriate models for the Arago reconstruction. It is true that the Arago 47 parietal may appear rather "advanced" in certain respects, but the arch has been reconstructed with a low biasterionic breadth in comparison with all other European Middle Pleistocene hominids except the Steinheim cranium. In addition, the parietal form of specimens such as Petralona, Biache, Steinheim and Ehringsdorf 9 is very "progressive" in certain respects, and this characteristic seems to be a significant derived character for European Middle Pleistocene hominids generally compared with *H. erectus* fossils. It is not always matched by the morphology of the occipital bone (*vide* Petralona). The strong angular torus of the Arago 47 parietal compared with the Petralona specimen may also be a clue to the robusticity to be expected in the occipital bone. Thus the Arago occipital bone would probably have been much more archaic than that of Omo 1, perhaps resembling that of Omo 2 more closely. The temporal bone of European Middle Pleistocene hominids (such as Petralona, Steinheim and perhaps Ehringsdorf 9) also shows distinctive, more modern characters compared with those of Asian *H. erectus* fossils, and therefore the Arago temporal bones may have resembled those of European hominids (or Broken Hill 1) rather than Sangiran 17.

As we have already discussed, we believe that Omo 1 must be classified as an a.m. *H. sapiens*. For Omo 2 and Arago 21, the choice is not so easy. Under the generally accepted system for hominid classification, the choice of taxon would lie between *H. erectus* and some form of "archaic" *H. sapiens*. In differentiating between *H. erectus* and *H. sapiens (sensu lato)* the ultimate classification depends entirely on which characters are considered most significant. If endocranial volume and supraorbital torus morphology are considered important, Arago 21 would probably be classified as *H. erectus* and Omo 2 as *H. sapiens*. If occipital morphology is emphasised, Omo 2 would probably be classified as *H. erectus* while Arago 21 could not even be assessed. In details of parietal form, the two specimens show different combinations of *erectus*-like and *sapiens*-like characters, but share a flat parietal bone, typical of *erectus*, with a parietal arch which is "advanced" in being higher, diagonally longer and (as reconstructed for Arago) relatively narrow inferiorly. If we define *H. erectus* only by the shared derived characters of the Asian and early African specimens then Arago 21 and Omo 2 both show significant, but distinct departures from this condition. If however we adopt a broader definition of *H. erectus* to include fossils often regarded as "archaic" *H. sapiens* (e.g. Broken Hill, Petralona) then both could be included in such a group. Yet another alternative is to recognise a third group for such specimens which display mosaic or intermediate characters. We have both suggested names for such a group in the past. Day (1973) proposed that they be regarded as a "Pithecanthropoid Intermediate" group, while Stringer et al. (1979) suggested the term "*H. sapiens* grade I." Either of these terms is still preferred by us to the allocation of sub-specific names which are of dubious applicability and usefulness.

Eventually it may be possible to recognise subsets within this grouping of "intermediate" fossils based on derived characters probably linking the Arago fossils with other European Middle Pleistocene specimens, and, perhaps ultimately, with the Neanderthals. But convincing synapomorphies with the Neanderthals are difficult to detect in the European hominids until the later Middle Pleistocene and the search for derived characters linking together the African fossils of this time is an even more difficult task. Ultimately the Arago and Omo 2 fossils will probably not be classified together except in a generalised grade framework. They do not appear to be closely related specimens and their grade similarities rest mainly on symplesiomorphies retained from earlier Middle Pleistocene ancestors rather than on synapomorphies. But we are unable to propose a definitive classification at the moment beyond suggesting that neither belong in *H. erectus sensu stricto* or *H. sapiens sensu stricto*.

REFERENCES

Brose, D. S. & Wolpoff, M. H. 1971. Early Upper Paleolithic man and late Middle Paleolithic tools. *American Anthropologist 73:* 1156–1194.

Butzer, K. W. 1969. Geological interpretation of two Pleistocene hominid sites in the Lower Omo Basin. *Nature 222:* 1133–1135.

Butzer, K. W. 1976. The Mursi, Nkalabong and Kibish Formations, Lower Omo Basin, Ethiopia. In *Earliest Man and Environments in the Lake Rudolf Basin* Ed. Y. Coppens, F. C. Howell, G. Ll. Isaac & R. E. F. Leakey. Chicago: University of Chicago Press. Pp. 12–23.

Butzer, K. W., Brown, F. H. & Thurber, D. L. 1969. Horizontal sediments of the Lower Omo Valley: the Kibish Formation. *Quaternaria 11:* 15–29.

Butzer, K. W. & Thurber, D. L. 1969. Some Late Cenozoic sedimentary formations of the Lower Omo Basin. *Nature 222:* 1138–1143.

Campbell, B. G. 1964. Quantitative taxonomy and human evolution. In *Classification and Human Evolution.* Ed. S. L. Washburn. Chicago: Aldine. Pp. 50–74.

Day, M. H. 1969. Omo human skeletal remains. *Nature 222:* 1135–1138.

Day, M. H. 1972. The Omo human skeletal remains. In *The Origin of Homo sapiens.* Ed. F. Bordes. Paris: UNESCO. Pp. 31–35.

Day, M. H. 1973. The development of *Homo sapiens.* In *L'origine Dell 'Uomo.* (Darwin Centenary Symposium on the origin of man). Roma: Accademia Nazionale Dei Lincei. Pp. 87–95.

Day, M. H., Leakey, M. D. & Magori, C. 1980. A new fossil hominid skull (L.H.18) from the Ngaloba Beds, Laetoli, northern Tanzania. *Nature 284:* 55–56.

Howell, F. C. 1978. Hominidae. In *Evolution of African Mammals.* Ed. V. J. Maglio & H. B. S. Cooke. Cambridge: Harvard University Press. Pp. 154–248.

Howells, W. W. 1973. Cranial variation in man: a study by multivariate analysis of patterns of difference among recent human populations. *Papers of the Peabody Museum.* 67: 1–259 (whole volume).

Howells, W. W. 1974. Neanderthals: names, hypotheses and scientific method. *American Anthropologist 76:* 24–38.

Howells, W. W. 1980. *Homo erectus*—who, when and where: a survey. *Yearbook of Physical Anthropology 23:* 1–23.

Leakey, R. E. F. 1969. Early *Homo sapiens* remains from the Omo River region of southwest Ethiopia: faunal remains from the Omo Valley. *Nature 222:* 1132–1133.

Le Gros Clark, W. E. 1964. *The Fossil Evidence for Human Evolution.* Chicago: University of Chicago Press.

Rightmire, G. P. 1976. Relationships of Middle and Upper Pleistocene hominids from sub-Saharan Africa. *Nature 260:* 238–240.

Rightmire, G. P. 1980. *Homo erectus* and human evolution in the African Middle Pleistocene. In *Current Argument on Early Man.* Ed. L.-K. Konigsson. Oxford: Pergamon. Pp. 70–85.

Rightmire, G. P. 1981. Later Pleistocene hominids of eastern and southern Africa. *Anthropologie Brno. 19:* 15–26.

Stringer, C. B. 1974. Population relationships of later Pleistocene hominids: a multivariate study of available crania. *Journal of Archaeological Science 1:* 317–342.

Stringer, C. B. 1978. Some problems in Middle and Upper Pleistocene hominid relationships. In *Recent Advances in Primatology, Vol. 3: Evolution.* Ed. D. J. Chivers & K. A. Joysey. London: Academic Press. Pp. 395–418.

Stringer, C. B., Howell, F. C. & Melentis, J. K. 1979. The significance of the fossil hominid skull from Petralona, Greece. *Journal of Archaeological Science 6:* 235–253.

Stringer, C. B. & Trinkaus, E. 1981. The Shanidar Neanderthal crania. In *Aspects of Human Evolution.* Ed. C. B. Stringer. London: Taylor & Francis. Pp. 129–165.

ADDENDUM

John G. Fleagle

Recent paleontological expeditions in the Kibish Formation have greatly expanded our understanding of the geological provenance and the age of the fossil hominids, as well as provided much greater documentation of the associated fauna and archaeological remains. As reported by McDougall, Brown, and Fleagle (2005), re-examination of the stratigraphy supports Butzer's earlier work (1969; also Butzer et al., 1969) indicating that both the Omo I partial skeleton and the Omo II cranium were associated with the upper part of Member I of the Kibish Formation. The published date for Member I and, hence, the fossil hominids, of 130,000 years based on a Uranium/Thorium analysis of molluscs has been questioned by many workers since its initial publication. However, recent $^{40}Ar/^{39}Ar$ ages of tuffs from Member III and Member I, and correlations between the members of the Kibish Formation and Mediterranean sapropels, indicate that the best estimate for the age of the Kibish hominids is 195,000 ± 5,000 years. This makes them the oldest well-dated fossils of *Homo sapiens* yet discovered and significantly older than the remains from Herto in the Middle Awash region of Ethiopia (Chapter 61).

REFERENCES

Butzer, K. W. 1969. Geological interpretation of two Pleistocene hominid sites in the Lower Omo Basin. *Nature 222:* 1133–1135.

Butzer, K. W., Brown, F. H., and Thurber, D. L. 1969. Horizontal sediments of the Lower Omo Valley: The Kibish Formation. *Quaternaria 11:* 15–29.

McDougall, I., Brown, F. H., and Fleagle, J. G. 2005. Stratigraphic placement and age of modern humans from Kibish, Ethiopia. *Nature 433:* 733–736.

61

Pleistocene *Homo sapiens* from Middle Awash, Ethiopia

T. D. White, B. Asfaw, D. DeGusta, H. Gilbert, G. D. Richards, G. Suwa, and F. C. Howell

ABSTRACT

The origin of anatomically modern Homo sapiens *and the fate of Neanderthals have been fundamental questions in human evolutionary studies for over a century*[1-4]. *A key barrier to the resolution of these questions has been the lack of substantial and accurately dated African hominid fossils from between 100,000 and 300,000 years ago*[5]. *Here we describe fossilized hominid crania from Herto, Middle Awash, Ethiopia, that fill this gap and provide crucial evidence on the location, timing and contextual circumstances of the emergence of* Homo sapiens. *Radioisotopically dated to between 160,000 and 154,000 years ago*[6], *these new fossils predate classic Neanderthals and lack their derived features. The Herto hominids are morphologically and chronologically intermediate between archaic African fossils and later anatomically modern Late Pleistocene humans. They therefore represent the probable immediate ancestors of anatomically modern humans. Their anatomy and antiquity constitute strong evidence of modern-human emergence in Africa.*

The fossilized crania of one immature and two adult hominids were recovered with more fragmentary remains in 1997 from Herto Bouri, a set of localities in the Herto Member of the Bouri Formation in the Middle Awash study area of Ethiopia's Afar depression[6]. These new remains are associated with archaeological assemblages containing elements of both Acheulean and Middle Stone Age technocomplexes[6]. The three crania display evidence of post-mortem mortuary practice[6].

Here we describe the Herto fossils and compare them with Eurasian Neanderthals, and with earlier and later African fossils, to investigate the emergence of anatomically modern humans. The following descriptions focus on characters relevant to the study of Late Pleistocene hominid affinities. Craniodental dimensions are provided in Tables 1–3. The specimens are illustrated in Figures 1 and 2.

The most complete specimen so far recovered from the Upper Herto Member of the Bouri Formation is an adult cranium from Bouri Vertebrate Paleontology Locality 16 (BOU-VP-16/1). Exposure before discovery led to loss of the left side of the calvarium, but vault distortion is limited to a slight movement of rigid plates; the right temporal process of the zygomatic is displaced about 3 mm posteromedially at the frontozygomatic suture, and the internasal midline is shifted

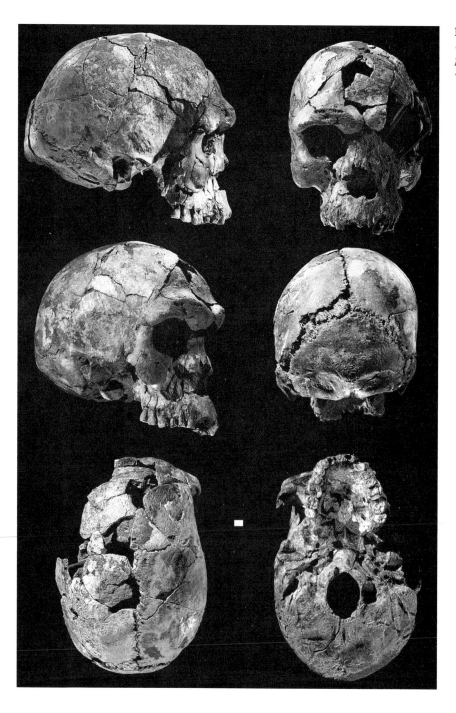

Figure 1. *The Herto BOU-VP-16/1 adult cranium in lateral, frontal, three-quarter, posterior, superior and inferior views. Scale bar, 1 cm.*

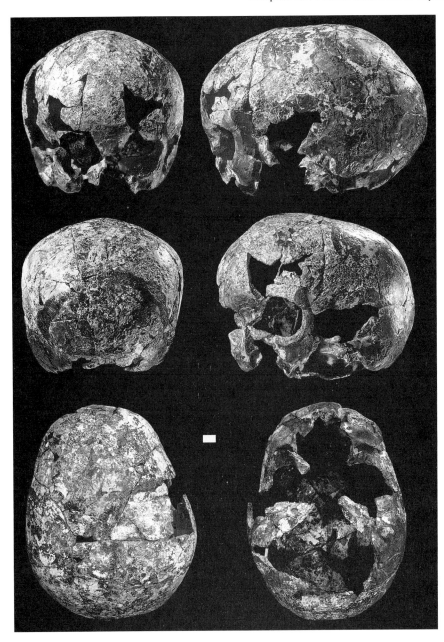

Figure 2. *The Herto BOU-VP-16/5 child's cranium in frontal, lateral, posterior, three-quarter, superior and inferior views. Scale bar, 1 cm.*

about 2 mm right-laterally. The palate is fairly intact, and the entire right facial skeleton is present. The specimen is fully adult, with patent vault sutures and a heavily worn dentition featuring progressively smaller M1, M2 and M3. Heavily worn premolars bear strong superolateral bevelling of the fully exposed dentine occlusal platforms (reminiscent of La Ferrassie 1). The cranium, interpreted here as a male, is generally large and robust, with a cranial capacity estimated by teff seed volume (right side doubled) at about 1,450 cm^3, at the high end of the modern human range.

The BOU-VP-16/1 cranium is long and high in lateral view (Figure 1). The distance between the cranial articular eminence and occlusal plane exceeds that observed in a sample of 2,000 modern human crania (American Indian and Predynastic Egyptian). The Baringo KNM-BK-62 mandible approximates the required ramal

height for articulation with the Herto specimen, but this mandible is too small in other dimensions for an appropriate fit. The Herto occipital is strongly flexed, with an occipital angle (103°) that is more acute than that in almost all modern humans[7] and marked by a prominent, massive, rugose external occipital protuberance. There is no occipital bun or suprainiac fossa. The mastoid processes are large and projecting, with a mastoid height (37 mm) much greater than the Neanderthal condition and exceeding all but a few modern humans. The zygomatic root is high relative to the level of the external auditory meatus. The superior margin of the temporal squama is high and arched. The root of the maxillary zygomatic process is centred above the first molar. The zygomatic bone is robust in the infraorbital region. The infraorbital plate is oriented paracoronally and marked by a distinct canine fossa.

In anterior view (Figure 1) the BOU-VP-16/1 cranium shows a broad upper and lower face, with moderate alveolar prognathism. The malar incisura is deep and bounded laterally by a robust malar tubercle. The broken nasal aperture is bounded inferiorly by a sharp nasal sill and prominent spine. The midface combines a broad interorbital area and tall, narrow nasal bones. The glabellar region is prominent, bilaterally arched, rugose, and projects anteriorly over the superomedial orbital corners. The frontal is moderately bossed and slightly receding, offset from the supraorbital torus by a supratoral sulcus. The supraorbital torus is differentiated into halves at the level of the (multiple) supraorbital foramina. The flat lateral portion is extremely broad anteroposteriorly (at zygofrontal suture, 18 mm from orbital rim to temporal line), and forms a superoanteriorly facing trigone. There is an extensive frontal sinus that extends laterally to mid-orbit. The great length of the cranium is evident in superior aspect. Its glabella-to-occipital length (219.5 ± 2 mm) exceeds that found in most other fossil hominids (including Skhul and Qafzeh) and a global sample of over 3,000 modern humans[7]. Prominent temporal lines reach to within 35 mm of the sagittal suture, and parallel the latter over most of the parietal's length. Bi-stephanic breadth is only 96 ± 3 mm, well below the modern human mean despite the specimen's size. The angular torus is not prominent, and is fully within the modern human range.

Despite slight distortion of the cranium evident in posterior view, its profile is clearly 'en-maison', with the greatest interparietal breadth high on the vault. The lambdoidal suture is highly complex, bearing numerous ossicles. In inferior view the palate is deep and broad (75.5 ± 1.5 mm external breadth; near modern human maximum). The foramen magnum is large and anteroposteriorly elongate (45 mm, well above the modern human mean). The digastric grooves are deep and bounded medially by prominent juxtamastoid crests. Relative to most modern humans, the masticatory apparatus is well developed, the dentition large and heavily worn, glenoid fossa broad and deep, and pterygoid plates large and flared.

The second major adult specimen (BOU-VP-16/2) was an even larger adult, as judged by matching parts of its preserved temporal bone. It is represented by portions of temporal, frontal, parietal, zygomatic and occipital. Its occipital is not so angled in sagittal profile as that of BOU-VP-16/1, but bears a more prominent occipital crest. Both vaults are thick (see Tables 1 and 2). A third adult individual represented by a left parietal fragment (BOU-VP-16/43) shows an extensive squamosal overlap of 24 mm, but might have been slightly smaller overall than the other two adults.

The immature cranium BOU-VP-16/5 was found on the surface after its erosion from an indurated sandstone. It had been shattered into more than 180 small fragments from which the cranial vault and facial portions were restored. A partial dentition comprises both left deciduous molars as well as unerupted fully formed canine and premolar crowns, and a first molar with wear facets. On the basis of modern human standards, we estimate the individual's age at death as 6–7 years. The cranium is morphologically compatible with the Herto adults. Its vault is pentagonal in posterior profile, and the face shows a clear canine fossa and strong malar incisura. The supraorbitals are poorly developed, with pronounced verticality and frontal bossing. As with the adults, the Herto child exhibits a character complex that is distinctly unlike that of Neanderthals[8].

The Herto crania are thus not Neanderthals. They exhibit none of the notably derived features that are common to those Eurasian specimens attributed to a Neanderthal lineage[9] represented by a multitude of fossils of successive ages, and culminating in the 'classic' Neanderthals. The Herto hominids are contemporaneous with obvious antecedents of the 'classic' Neanderthals, but do not resemble them. The Herto hominids also have derived characters not seen in *Homo erectus* and in other apparently older African specimens such as Bodo, Saldanha and Kabwe, and so cannot be assigned to those groups.

When BOU-VP-16/1 is compared metrically with a large global sample of modern human crania[7] (Figures 3 and 4), similarities and differences are apparent. The large overall size of BOU-VP-16/1 stands out, aspects of which are described above. Apart from its exceptionally great anterior–posterior length, the cranium exhibits large vault dimensions together with a deep, tall and broad face. However, the orbit and cheekbone dimensions are smaller, and facial projection anterior to the zygomatic is relatively weak. These metric aspects contribute to the comparatively modern gestalt of the face (contrary, for example, to Neanderthals or Kabwe). BOU-VP-16/1 is metrically indistinguishable from anatomically modern *Homo sapiens* (AMHS) in its high cranial vault and relatively large frontal and parietal sagittal dimensions as expressed in their size-standardized variables (by geometric means of 50 variables). Metric indices of neurocranial globularity and facial retraction have been proposed as diagnostic criteria for AMHS[10]. The former index is estimated at 0.54 in BOU-VP-16/1, within the range suggested to be characteristic of AMHS. Here again, though, the BOU-VP-16/1 parietal bone tends to be less curved, the occipital distinctly flexed, and supraorbitals projecting anteriorly, attesting to its retention of archaic morphology.

Among the global sample of modern humans, the Herto crania, both metrically and non-metrically, lack any derived affinity with modern African crania or with any other modern group, confirming earlier suggestions[11]. Instead, the closest approximations among modern individuals to the overall morphology, size and facial robusticity are found in some Australian and Oceanic individuals, although these are also clearly distinct from the Herto hominids. The Herto crania are likewise distinct from Pleistocene representatives of AMHS in some of the features outlined above. In supraorbital morphology and occipital construction and robusticity, BOU-VP-16/1 is distinguished from the later Klasies and Qafzeh specimens often identified as the earliest AMHS. Other African fossil crania that are possibly temporally intermediate between the early

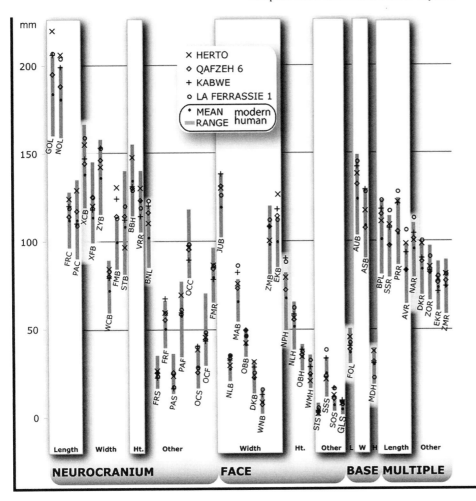

Figure 3. *Univariate comparisons, by anatomical region and dimension, of BOU-VP-16/1 with Qafzeh 6, Kabwe, La Ferrassie, and modern (recent) human males. All comparative data are from Howells[7,27] on original specimens. The listed means are the grand means of the male sample means for the skeletal populations studied by Howells[7,27]. The measurement abbreviations are as per Howells[7,27], and are also defined in Tables 1–3. Symbols: multiplication signs, Herto; diamonds, Qafzeh; plus signs, Kabwe; open circles, La Ferrassie 1; filled circles, means for modern humans; grey bars, range for modern humans. Ht, height.*

forms (such as Bodo and Kabwe—the 'early archaic *H. sapiens*' of Bräuer[12,13]) and AMHS exhibit considerable morphological diversity. The affinities of these specimens (such as Ngaloba, Omo 2, Eliye Springs and Jebel Irhoud— the 'late archaic *H. sapiens*' of Bräuer[12,13]) have proved difficult to assess. However, regardless of the particular relationships between these specimens, the general evolutionary position of the Herto sample is clear.

The morphology of the Herto crania falls between the more primitive morphology of the earlier African specimens (such as Bodo and Kabwe) and the more derived morphology of later AMHS (such as Klasies and Qafzeh). The Herto crania are intermediate, metrically and non-metrically, in an African series spanning about 600,000–100,000 years ago, although they are not the only such intermediates in the series. They sample a population that is on the verge of anatomical modernity but not yet fully modern (Figure 4). This conclusion is supported by comparative anatomical, metric and cladistic considerations, and has profound evolutionary and taxonomic implications.

Some genetic studies[14] have concluded that populations whose contributions quantitatively dominate the modern human gene pool were located in Middle Pleistocene Africa. However, fossil confirmation of these

predictions has been lacking. This has prompted some to assert that the sparse African record did not falsify the 'multiregional' evolution of AMHS in Europe and the Far East[15–17]. The Herto crania fail to confirm such 'multiregional' speculation and conform more closely to most molecular predictions[14,18–20]. They add direct fossil evidence about the anatomy of the populations ancestral to modern humans. The many morphological features shared by the Herto crania and AMHS, to the exclusion of penecontemporanous Neanderthals, provide additional fossil data excluding Neanderthals from a significant contribution to the ancestry of modern humans.

The Herto hominids, although clarifying evolutionary questions, raise taxonomic issues. Widely scattered, often poorly dated, and morphologically diverse Middle and Upper Pleistocene hominid crania from the eastern hemisphere have been assigned to various taxa. In addition to the difficulties inherent in partitioning lineages, several of the available species names are based on inadequate type specimens (such as *H. heidelbergensis*, Schoetensack, 1908; *H. helmei*, Dreyer, 1935; and *H. njarasensis*, Reck and Kohl-Larsen, 1936). Because the Herto hominids are morphologically just beyond the range of variation seen in AMHS, and because they differ from all other known fossil hominids, we recognize

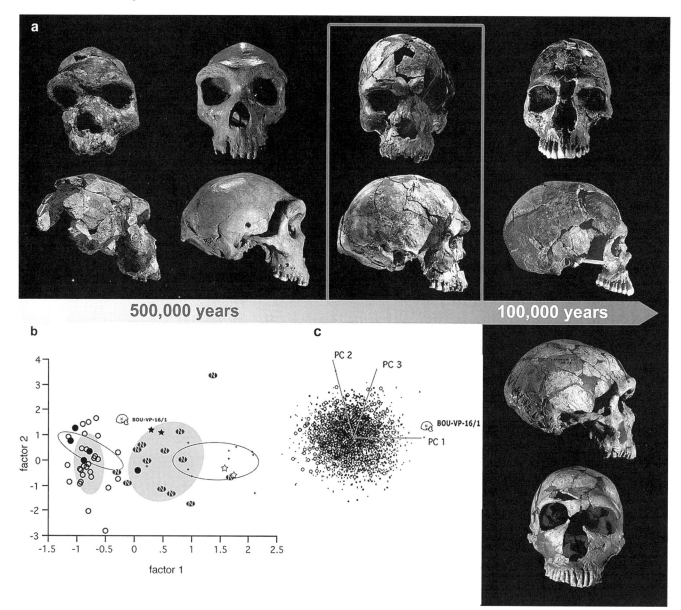

Figure 4.   *a, Comparative analysis of the Herto BOU-VP-16/1 adult cranium. **a**, From left to right, in anterior and lateral views, Bodo (The National Museum of Ethiopia, Addis Ababa), Kabwe (The Natural History Museum, London), Herto BOU-VP-16/1 (boxed), Qafzeh 9 (The Rockefeller Museum, Jerusalem), and, inset below, the La Ferrassie Neanderthal (Musée de L'Homme, Paris), all to the same scale, with approximate timeline. **b**, Plot of first two principal component scores, with the position of Herto BOU-VP-16/1 given by the fossil symbol marked 'x'*. Homo erectus, *includes KNM-ER 3733 and KNM-ER 3883 (open stars), and Sangiran, Ngandong and Zhoukoudian crania (plus signs). 'Neanderthals' (Amud, Atapuerca, Gibraltar, La Ferrassie, La Chapelle, La Quina, Monte Circeo, Petralona, Saccopastore, Shanidar, Steinheim and Tabun crania) are shown by circled letter N, Omo 2 and Kabwe by filled stars, and fossil AMHS (Qafzeh 6, 9, Skhul 5, Cro-Magnon and Predmostí 3 crania) by filled circles. Population means of 28 male modern human samples (shown by open circles) were taken from Howells[27] and included in the principal-components analysis (PCA). This was done to show the plot position of modern humans and the degree of inter-population variation. The ovals (line and shade) represent the 1 s.d. dispersion areas of the fossil AMHS sample, the Neanderthal sample, the Asian* H. erectus *sample, and the modern human population means. The measurements used for this analysis are those of the cranial vault (GOL, NOL, XCB, XFB, AUB, ASB, FRC and PAC; see Tables 1–3 for meanings of abbreviations). The raw measurements were standardized for size by the geometric mean of all eight variables. PCA was performed on the size-standardized variables so as to describe shape. The limited number of measurements is a necessary limitation when including fossil specimens. This graph thus illustrates the phenetic affinities as reflected in a limited part of the anatomy. The comparative data are from Arsuaga et al.[9] and Howells[27]. **c**, Plot of the first three principal components of the complete Howells[27] data set of 3,024 modern (recent) human individuals, plus Herto BOU-VP-16/1 (the fossil symbol marked 'x'). The principal components were generated from the natural-log-transformed data. This and other results of multivariate analyses demonstrate the phenetic distinctiveness of the Herto hominids relative to modern human crania. However, finer details of the relative position of Herto hominids in multidimensional morphometric space are difficult to interpret because of the necessary inclusion of estimated measurements. The measurements used are given in Tables 1–3.*

them here as *Homo sapiens idaltu,* a new palaeosubspecies of *Homo sapiens* (see Methods). The available evidence from comparative anatomy, multivariate analysis and cladistic considerations suggests that '*H. rhodesiensis*' (Bodo and Kabwe) was ultimately ancestral to *H. sapiens idaltu,* which in turn was ancestral to *Homo sapiens sapiens* (AMHS).

The Middle Awash valley of Ethiopia has now yielded a succession of hominids spanning the past 6 million years[21–26]. Within this study area, and within the genus *Homo,* there exists a chronologically ordered succession of increasingly derived hominids: from Daka (1.0 million years ago) to Bodo (500,000 years ago) to Herto (155,000 years ago). When considered with the evidence from other sites, this shows that modern human morphology emerged in Africa long before the Neanderthals vanished from Eurasia.

METHODS

Order Primates L., 1758

Suborder Anthropoidea Mivart, 1864

Superfamily Hominoidea Gray, 1825

Family Hominidae Gray, 1825

Homo sapiens idaltu subsp. nov.

Etymology. The subspecies name 'idàltu' is taken from the Afar language. It means 'elder'.

Holotype. BOU-VP-16/1 (Figure 1), an adult cranium with partial dentition. Holotype and referred material are housed at the National Museum of Ethiopia, Addis Ababa. Holotype from Bouri Vertebrate Paleontology Locality 16 (BOU-VP 16); differentially corrected GPS coordinates: 10° 15.5484′ N and 40° 33.3834′ E.

Referred Material. BOU-VP-16/2 cranial fragments; BOU-VP-16/3 parietal fragment; BOU-VP-16/4 parietal fragment; BOU-VP-16/5 child's cranium; BOU-VP-16/6 R. upper molar; BOU-VP-16/7 parietal fragment, BOU-VP-16/18 parietal fragments; BOU-VP-16/42 upper premolar, BOU-VP-16/43 parietal fragment.

Stratigraphy and Age. Bouri Formation, Upper Herto Member. Dated by $^{40}Ar/^{39}Ar$ to between 160,000 and 154,000 years ago (ref. 6).

Diagnosis. On the limited available evidence, a subspecies of *Homo sapiens* distinguished from Holocene anatomically modern humans (*Homo sapiens sapiens*) by greater craniofacial robusticity, greater anterior–posterior cranial length, and large glenoid-to-occlusal plane distance. *Homo sapiens idaltu* is distinguished from the holotype of *Homo rhodesiensis* (Woodward, 1921) by a larger cranial capacity, a more vertical frontal with smaller face, and more marked midfacial topography (for example, canine fossa). We consider the holotypes of *H. helmei* and *H. njarasensis* too fragmentary for appropriate comparisons.

ACKNOWLEDGMENTS

We thank A. Almquist, A. Asfaw, M. Asnake, T. Assebework, D. Brill, J. D. Clark, J. DeHeinzelin, A. Getty, Y. Haile-Selassie, B. Latimer, C. Pehlevan, K. Schick, S. Simpson, P. Snow and Y. Zeleka for fieldwork and analytical studies; J. L. Arsuaga, A. Gracia and N. Garcia for comparative metric data; C. O. Lovejoy for review; and F. Bibi, D. Brill, R. Cann, Y. Haile-Selassie, L. Hlusko, L. Jellema, R. Klein, J. Matternes and R. Paul for assistance. We thank the Ministry of Youth, Sports and Culture, the Authority for Research and Conservation of the Cultural Heritage, and the National Museum of Ethiopia for permissions; the Afar Regional Government and the Afar people of the Middle Awash, particularly the Bouri–Modaitu community and H. Elema; and many other individuals for contributing to our efforts. This research was supported by the NSF (US) and the Japan Society for the Promotion of Science.

REFERENCES

1. Mbua, E. N. *Patterns of Middle Pleistocene Hominid Evolution in Africa* Dissertation, Univ. Hamburg, (2001).

2. Stringer, C. B. Modern human origins: progress and prospects. *Phil. Trans. R. Soc. Lond. B* **357**, 563–579 (2002).

3. Howell, F. C. Paleo-demes, species clades, and extinctions in the Pleistocene hominin record. *J. Anthropol. Res.* **55**, 191–243 (1999).

4. Stringer, C. B. in *The Age of the Earth: From 4004 BC to AD 2002* (eds Lewis, C. L. E. & Knell, S. J.) 265–274, Geological Society of London, Spec. Publ. 190 (2001).

5. Rightmire, G. P. in *Humanity from African Naissance to Coming Millennia* (eds Tobias, P. V., Raath, M. A., Moggi-Cecci, J. & Doyle, G. A.) 231–236 (Firenze Univ. Press, 2001).

6. Clark, J. D. et al. Stratigraphic, chronological and behavioural contexts of Pleistocene *Homo sapiens* from Middle Awash, Ethiopia. *Nature* **423**, 747–752 (2003).

7. Howells, W. W. Cranial variation in man. *Pap. Peabody Mus. Archaeol. Ethnol.* **67**, 1–259 (1973).

8. Tillier, A.-M. in *The Evolution and Dispersal of Modern Humans in Asia* (eds Akasawa, T., Aoki, K. & Kimura, T.) 15–28 (Hokusensha, Tokyo, 1992).

9. Arsuaga, J. L., Martínez, I., Gracia, A. & Lorenzo, C. The Sima de los Huesos crania (Sierra de Atapuerca Spain): A comparative study. *J. Hum. Evol.* **33**, 219–281 (1997).

10. Lieberman, D. E., McBratney, B. M. & Krovits, G. The evolution and development of cranial form in *Homo sapiens*. *Proc. Natl Acad. Sci. USA* **99**, 1134–1139 (2002).

11. Sarich, V. M. in *Conceptual Issues in Modern Human Origins Research* (eds Clark, G. A. & Willermet, C. M.) 392–412 (Aldine, New York, 1997).

12. Bräuer, G. in *Humanity from African Naissance to Coming Millennia* (eds Tobias, P. V., Raath, M. A., Moggi-Cecci, J. & Doyle, G. A.) 191–197 (Firenze Univ. Press, 2001).

13. Bräuer, G., (eds Mellars, P. & Stringer, C. B.) 123–154 (Edinburgh Univ. Press, 1989).

14. Cann, R. Genetic clues to dispersal in human populations: Retracing the past from the present. *Science* **291**, 1742–1748 (2001).

15. Wolpoff, M. & Caspari, R. in *Conceptual Issues in Modern Human Origins Research* (eds Clark, G. A. & Willermet, C. M.) 28–44 (Aldine, New York, 1997).

16. Hawks, J. D. & Wolpoff, M. H. The four faces of Eve: Hypothesis compatibility and human origins. *Quat. Int.* **75**, 41–50 (2001).

17. Wolpoff, M. H., Hawks, J., Frayer, D. & Hunley, K. Modern human ancestry at the peripheries: A test of the replacement theory. *Science* **291**, 293–297 (2001).

18. Templeton, A. R. Out of Africa again and again. *Nature* **416**, 45–51 (2002).

19. Underhill, P. A. et al. The phylogeography of Y chromosome binary haplotypes and the origins of modern human populations. *Ann. Hum. Genet.* **65**, 43–62 (2001).

20. Ingman, M., Kaessmann, H., Pääbo, S. & Gyllensten, U. Mitochondrial genome variation and the origin of modern humans. *Nature* **408**, 703–713 (2000).

21. Haile-Selassie, Y. Late Miocene hominids from the Middle Awash, Ethiopia. *Nature* **412**, 178–181 (2001).

22. White, T. D., Suwa, G. & Asfaw, B. *Australopithecus ramidus,* a new species of hominid from Aramis, Ethiopia. *Nature* **371**, 306–312 (1994).

23. Lovejoy, C. O., Meindl, R. S., Ohman, J. C., Heiple, K. G. & White, T. D. The Maka femur and its bearing on the antiquity of human walking: Applying contemporary concepts of morphogenesis to the human fossil record. *Am. J. Phys. Anthropol.* **119**, 97–133 (2002).

24. White, T. D. et al. New discoveries of *Australopithecus* at Maka, Ethiopia. *Nature* **366**, 261–265 (1993).

25. Asfaw, B. et al. *Australopithecus garhi:* A new species of early hominid from Ethiopia. *Science* **284**, 629–635 (1999).

26. Asfaw, B. et al. Remains of *Homo erectus* from Bouri, Middle Awash, Ethiopia. *Nature* **416**, 317–320 (2002).

27. Howells, W. W. Skull shapes and the map. Craniometric analyses in the dispersion of modern *Homo. Pap. Peabody Mus. Archaeol. Ethnol.* **79**, 1–189 (1989).

APPENDIX

Table 1. Herto Crania: Howells' Metrics

Adult = BOU-VP-16/1
Child = BOU-VP-16/5

D = Measured on one side and doubled
L = Measured on left side
R = Measured on right side

Measurement	Abbr	Adult	Child
Glabella-occipital length	GOL	219.5 ± 2	176 ± 2
Nasio-occipital length	NOL	206 ± 2	172 ± 2
Basion-nasion length	BNL	110 ± 2	
Basion-bregma height	BBH	147.5 ± 2	
Maximum cranial breadth	XCB	155 ± 5	137 ± 2
Maximum frontal breadth	XFB	120 ± 5 D	114 ± 1
Bistephanic breadth	STB	96.3 ± 3 D	
Bizygomatic breadth	ZYB	142 ± 5 D	
Biauricular breadth	AUB	138 ± 2 D	
Minimum cranial breadth	WCB	84 ± 2 D	
Biasterionic breadth	ASB	117 ± 2	115 ± 3
Basion-prosthion length	BPL	111 ± 3	
Nasion-prosthion length	NPH	79 ± 3	
Nasal height	NLH	56 ± 3	
Orbit height, left	OBH	34 ± 1	29 ± 1
Orbit breadth, left	OBB	42 ± 2	33 ± 1
Bijugal breadth	JUB	130 ± 3 D	84 ± 2 D
Nasal breadth	NLB	29 ± 2 D	
Palate breadth external	MAB	75.5 ± 1.5	
Mastoid height	MDH	37 R	22 L
Bimaxillary breadth	ZMB	100 ± 2 D	65 ± 3
Zygomaxillary subtense	SSS	21 ± 2 D	
Bifrontal breadth	FMB	130 ± 2 D	82 ± 2 D
Biorbital breadth	EKB	126 ± 4 D	84 ± 3
Interorbital breadth	DKB	31 D	21 ± 1
Simotic chord (least nasal breadth)	WNB	8 ± 1 D	8.4
Simotic subtense	SIS	1.5	2
Cheek height	WMH	20 ± 1	27.4
Supraorbital projection	SOS	12 ± 0.5	
Glabella projection	GLS	7.5 ± 1	0
Foramen magnum length	FOL	45	
Nasion-bregma chord (frontal chord)	FRC	124 ± 3	104.8 ± 1
Nasion-bregma subtense (frontal subtense)	FRS	26 ± 1	29 ± 1
Nasion-subtense fraction	FRF	59	49
Bregma-lambda chord (parietal chord)	PAC	129 ± 1	113.4 ± 1
Bregma-lambda subtense (parietal subtense)	PAS	23	20
Bregma-subtense fraction	PAF	69 ± 1	56
Lambda-opisthion chord (occipital chord)	OCC	96	
Lambda-opisthion subtense (occipital subtense)	OCS	38	
Lambda-subtense fraction	OCF	45	

Table 1. (continued)

Measurement	Abbr	Adult	Child
Vertex radius	VRR	130 ± 4	109
Nasion radius	NAR	100 ± 4	90 ± 3
Subspinale radius	SSR	109 ± 3	
Prosthion radius	PRR	122	
Dacryon radius	DKR	98 ± 3	81 ± 3
Zygoorbitale radius	ZOR	85 ± 3	73 ± 3
Frontomalare radius	FMR	86 ± 2	70 ± 3
Ectochonchion radius	EKR	78 ± 4	61 ± 3
Zygomaxillary radius	ZMR	81 ± 3	57 ± 4
Molar alveolus radius	AVR	98 ± 3	

Notes on Measurements:
1. Measurement definitions are given in Howells (7).
2. The asterionic region in BOU-VP-16/1 is a complex intersection of sutures, and asterion was placed on the occipital edge as per Howells (7).
3. The lambdoidal area of BOU-VP-16/1 is suturally complex. Lambda was placed at the projected intersection of the main occipital sutures, as per Howells (7), which in this specimen is at the inferior-most point of the convergence of the sagittal and lambdoidal sutures.
4. In a number of cases, subtenses are not reported even though the individual measures and osteometric points they use are reported (e.g., the nasio-frontal subtense). This is generally because such measurements, being absolutely small, are effectively swamped by the error range. In addition, some subtenses are distorted in the dimension of the projection.
5. One "Howells metric," mastoid breadth (MDB), is not reported due to difficulties in applying the definition given in Howells (7), though the mastoids are well-preserved in both crania.
6. Distortion renders the EKB measurement of BOU-VP-16/1 (55 × 2 = 110) deceptively smaller than it was. The estimate corrects for this based in inferior projection from FMB. Of the two measures, FMB can be taken more precisely on the Herto specimen.

Table 2. Herto Crania: Other Cranial Metrics

Adult = BOU-VP-16/1	D = Measured on one side and doubled	E = Estimated
Child = BOU-VP-16/5	L = Measured on left side	N = Measured in vicinity of given osteometric point
	R = Measured on right side	I = Measured on fragment of indeterminate side

Measurement	Abbr	Adult	Child	BOU-VP-16/2	BOU-VP-16/4	BOU-VP-16/18	BOU-VP-16/43
Frontotemporale Breadth	FTB	112 ± 2 D	92 ± 2 D				
Biparietal Breadth	BPB	145 ± 5 D	137 ± 2				
Biporionic Breadth	BRB	130 ± 3 D	100 ± 2				
Glabella-Bregma Chord	GBC	125 ± 2	102 ± 1				
Glabella-Bregma Arc	GBA	137 ± 2	120 ± 1				
Parietal Arc	PAA	140 ± 3	123 ± 1				
Lambda-Inion Chord	LIC	66					
Inion-Opisthocranion Chord	IOC	48.2					
Inion-Opisthocranion Arc	IOA	48					
Lambda-Opisthocranion Arc	LOA	127					
Max-Min Frontal (ref. 27)	MMF	110 ± 3 D	92 ± 2 D				
Max Breadth of Supraorbital Tori Wings	MBS	138 ± 3 D	94 ± 2 D				
Bi-Mastoid Tip Breadth	BTB	109 ± 2	92 ± 2				
Cranial Capacity[*]	CRC	1450 D R	1250				
Max Bimastoid Breadth	MBB	142	117				
Interorbital Breadth at Nasion	ION	36 ± 3 D	25 ± 1				
Basal Breadth at Depth of TMJs	BBT	108 ± 2	84 ± 4 D				
Supraorbital Thickness at Midorbit	STM	16 ± 1					
Squamosal Sutural Overlap (Max)	SSO						24
Thickness at							
Frontal Boss	THF	8 ± 1		9.5			
Bregma	THB	10 ± 1		10			
Opisthocranion	THO	18					
Asterion	THA	11 L		12			
Euryon	THE	7 R			9.5 N L	9.5 N I	7 N L
Lambda	THL	7 ± 1 R		8			

[*]Preliminary determinations using teff seed. Adult estimate more reliable due to absence of much of the child's cranial base. Final determinations will require CT.

Table 3. Herto Crania: Dental Metrics

Adult = BOU-VP-16/1   ( ) = Estimate of current dimension
Child = BOU-VP-16/5   [ ] = Estimate of unworn dimension
                             { } = Measurement before correction for matrix expansion
                             W = Too worn to measure

	Adult		Child		BOU-VP-16/6		BOU-VP-16/42	
Tooth	Mesial-Distal	Buccal-Lingual	Mesial-Distal	Buccal-Lingual	Mesial-Distal	Buccal-Lingual	Mesial-Distal	Buccal-Lingual
RUC	7 ± 1	9 ± 1						
LUC	8 ± 1	9 ± 1		−7.3				
RUP3	7.2 [8.0]	W						
LUP3	7.7	W	7.5					
RUP4	8.4 [8.1]	W						
LUP4	8.5 ± 1	W	7.2	9.2			7.8	10.4
RUM1	11.5 [11.5 ± 1]	W			12.1	11.8		
LUM1			11.2					
RM2	11.1 [12.0]	12.8 {13.4}						
LM2	10.6 [11.8]	12.8 {13.4}						
RM3	8.6	11.9						
LM3	8.6	11.9						
LUDM1			6.4 [6.6]	9.2				
LUDM2			9.1 [9.2]					
LM4 root	AP = 4	BC = 6						

62

Multiple Dispersals and Modern Human Origins

M. M. Lahr and R. Foley

ABSTRACT

Despite a massive endeavour, the problem of modern human origins not only remains unresolved, but is usually reduced to "Out of Africa" versus multiregional evolution. Not all would agree, but evidence for a single recent origin is accumulating. Here, we want to go beyond this debate and explore within the "Out of Africa" framework an issue that has not been fully addressed: the mechanism by which modern human diversity has developed. We believe there is no clear rubicon of modern Homo sapiens, *and that multiple dispersals occurred from a morphologically variable population in Africa. Pre-existing African diversity is thus crucial to the way human diversity developed outside Africa. The pattern of diversity—behavioural, linguistic, morphological and genetic—can be interpreted as the result of dispersals, colonisation, differentiation and subsequent dispersals overlaid on former population ranges. The first dispersals would have originated in Africa from where two different geographical routes were possible, one through Ethiopia/Arabia towards South Asia, and one through North Africa/Middle East towards Eurasia.*

Reprinted from M. M. Lahr and R. Foley, *Evolutionary Anthropology,* Vol. 3, pp. 48–60. Copyright © 1994 by Wiley-Liss, Inc. This material is reprinted with permission of Wiley-Liss, Inc., a subsidiary of John Wiley & Sons, Inc.

A model of multiregional evolution was the first comprehensive theory of the evolution of modern humans from their hominid ancestors. Multiregional evolution in the Pleistocene explains both the origins of modern humans and subsequent regional diversity as resulting from the transformation of archaic hominid groups into modern populations in each part of the world. Modern human features have been superimposed on pre-existing regional ones. Weidenreich,[1] who first proposed the theory of multiregional evolution, explained regional differences in morphology between modern groups like Asians and Australians as resulting from relatively independent evolution from *Sinanthropus* and *Pithecanthropus.* The early multiregional models suffered from the lack of a mechanism for the maintenance of worldwide parallelisms.[1,2]

Recently however, Wolpoff and others [3–5] have proposed a modified version of this earlier theory in which gene flow takes a major role. Accordingly, the multiregional model proposes that each modern human regional population arose from archaic regional inhabitants, and that a balance between gene flow and isolation allowed regional differentiation without speciation and the maintenance of grade similarities worldwide.

The "Out of Africa" model is more recent. It is based on fossil evidence for an earlier appearance of modern humans in Africa than elsewhere. Howells[6] proposed the idea of a single and recent origin as the "Noah's Ark" model. This hypothesis has been elaborated in the last few years by several researchers.[7-10] This model highlights the discontinuity in the fossil record, suggesting a recent localized origin in Africa, followed by geographical expansion and replacement of archaic populations.

THE EVIDENCE FOR THE ORIGINS OF MODERN HUMANS

In recent years, the application of new dating techniques like electron spin resonance and thermoluminescence to Upper Pleistocene fossils has had a revolutionary effect on late hominid chronology.[11-13] These techniques, which date beyond the range of ^{14}C, have proven three significant points: that hominids with a modern morphology occurred in the Middle East around 100 ky ago;[14-16] that relatively gracile moderns lived in Africa around 70 ky ago;[17] and that Neanderthal remains in Europe and the Middle East date to 60 to 40 ky ago, postdating early modern forms.[11,18] Furthermore, the remains from Klasies River Mouth (KRM) in South Africa, presenting a variable but modern morphology,[19] are firmly associated with early last interglacial levels, and therefore are 120/100 ky old.[20,21]

This new chronology has also affected the archeological record. Now it is known that technologies based on the production of blades appear relatively late in the record, some 60,000 years after the appearance of morphologically modern people, although there is some evidence of more complex behavior in a Middle Stone Age tradition (the Howieson's Poort) between 85 and 60 ky in South Africa.[22-24] The first archeological assemblages that present blade tools are found around the Mediterranean.[25] In North Africa, there is evidence of a pre-Aurignacian tradition,[26] while early Upper Paleolithic assemblages have been identified in Boker Tachtit, Israel, and Ksar Akil, Lebanon, between 47 and 38 ky ago.[27,28] The Aurignacian seems to have spread rapidly through Europe as seen at 43 kya in Bulgaria (Bacho Kiro)[29] and at 40 kya in Spain (L'Abreda, El Castillo[30-32]). Associated with this geographical expansion process of Aurignacian peoples through Europe, the terminal Neanderthal industries, including the Chatelperronean, Szeletian, and Uluzzian, have been interpreted as the result of an acculturation process.[33,34]

To the fossil and archeological record, the molecular evidence should be added. In 1987, Cann and co-workers obtained a phylogenetic tree based on mtDNA in which one branch led solely to Africans and the other branch to Africans and other populations.[36] This tree reflected the fact that Africans present the greatest diversity of mtDNA lineages. This could be explained either by a faster rate of mutations in Africans than in the rest of the world or by a longer time during which mutational differences accumulated in this group. Given the lack of evidence from other sources of a faster mutation rate in Africans, the authors deduced that the evolution of modern humans started in Africa and then expanded to the rest of the world.

Since these results were first published, further research has both reinforced and undermined this conclusion. On the one hand, research on the mtDNA diversity of localized groups like the San and Papuans has thrown light on the levels of diversification of recent people.[36,37] In addition, mounting nuclear genetic evidence points strongly to an African origin of all modern groups.[38-40] On the other hand, Maddison[41] and Templeton[42] have shown that the statistical procedures for rooting the mtDNA phylogenetic tree and the statistical significance of the single African branch were incorrect. These technical problems are a major drawback in the technique. Indeed, it apparently is impossible at the moment to prove statistically the branching pattern of mtDNA lineages. However, contrary to what has been claimed,[43] these problems do not completely discredit the genetic evidence. The great diversity of African mtDNA lineages remains unchallenged.[44]

Recently, Rogers and Jorde challenged the notion that greatest diversity equates with greatest age and provided an explanation in terms of paleodemography.[45] They conclude that the mtDNA diversity patterns reflect the fact that Africa held a larger population than other regions throughout the period. Taking these demographic parameters into account, Harpending finds, through pairwise comparisons (mismatch distributions), that there is evidence of a leading wave signal in African samples, suggesting that Africa may have been the source of dispersal of modern humans.[46] Although it is clear that the mitochondrial data cannot be interpreted as tightly as the original "Eve hypothesis" proposed, the nuclear DNA evidence is increasingly robust and the genetic evidence, overall, strongly supports a recent African origin of modern people.[47]

The evolutionary interpretations of the genetic evidence have been in such extraordinary agreement with the "Out of Africa" model that the two concepts have been interlaced. It is often mistakenly assumed that the main evidence for a single origin of modern humans is genetic and not morphological or chronological. The conclusion that the available evidence strongly supports a recent, single African origin of modern people must follow if one takes into account the following points: the earliest modern people are found in Africa or the Middle East some 60,000 years before they appear in other regions;[8] different hominids overlap in time and space in the Middle East, Europe, and, probably, East Asia;[11] the archeological evidence in Europe points to a distinct replacement of local traditions;[34,48] the nuclear and mtDNA evidence indicates an African ancestry of all modern humans;[38] and there is an apparently strong correlation between recent linguistic differentiation and genetic differentiation.[49] In spite of all this, however, if morphological continuity from regional archaic hominids to modern regional populations can indeed be observed in the fossil record, there will still be evidence that multiregional evolution took place.

TESTING THE MODELS

The Multiregional Hypothesis

The basis for the Multiregional model is that we can observe unique regional patterns of morphological continuity across the transition from archaic to modern forms of hominids.[4,5] This interpretation of continuity makes two assumptions: that such features are indeed regional markers; and that they are not functionally determined.

Three recent studies have independently tackled the problem of regional morphological continuity.[50–52] Two of these dealt with the regional distribution of features identified as presenting continuity through time among worldwide archaic populations, and therefore, tested their uniquely Asian and Southeast Asian character in the past.[50,51] The authors of both studies found that these features were common in *Homo erectus* and "archaic" *Homo sapiens* fossils throughout the world, but reached somewhat different conclusions about their role in proving continuity. On the basis of their plesiomorphic character, Groves concluded that these features should not be used as evidence of phylogenetic relationships.[50] On the other hand, Habgood considered that the combined occurrence of features like supraorbital tori and zygomaxillary tuberosities in Javanese *H. erectus* and Australian aborigines can be used as evidence of morphological continuity.[51] In the third study, Lahr dealt with the regional distribution of features of continuity in recent populations and their relationship to metrical parameters of the skull, testing their uniquely Asian and Australian character in the present and the independence of that character from developmental processes.[52] Lahr found that of the thirty so-called Asiatic regional traits, twenty-one did indeed have a significant incidence in a particular region of the world. However, only ten of these traits actually occurred in the geographical area conventionally associated with them. In other words, the regional traits fail to characterize East Asians and, in Australians, do so only in terms of robusticity.[52,53] Furthermore, this work showed that the development of characteristics such as pronounced tori and ridges occurs regardless of geographical region among both modern and prehistoric populations with large cranial and dental dimensions. Another finding, that the development of a number of facial features depends on the presence of large supraorbital ridges,[52,53] is particularly relevant in the light of Habgood's conclusions regarding the combined occurrence of features of robusticity, which Lahr showed instead to be correlated with each other. The implication is that traits that have been claimed to show links between, for example, Javanese *Homo erectus* and Australian aborigines, are, in fact, evidence of the link between modern Australians and a robust modern ancestor anywhere in the world. The only conclusion to be drawn is that the morphological evidence does not support a multiregional model of modern human origins.

Two other lines of evidence related to the mechanisms of multiregional evolution also refute the basis of the multiregional model. One, a survey of the fossil evidence of subspeciation in animals with a wide geographical distribution, has shown that multiregional evolution as a mechanism is undocumented except, possibly, in the Javanese rhinoceros, and that the common pattern observed is one of interspecific or intraspecific replacement.[54] Second, recent assessments by Harpending and co-workers of the demographic density of *Homo erectus* populations suggest that these populations never achieved the critical size to maintain the levels of gene flow necessary for multiregional evolution to occur.[45,46]

Besides the chronology of the fossils and the genetic evidence for a single origin of modern people, these studies show that the multiregional hypothesis is based on incorrect premises of morphological continuity and demographic patterns. In addition, the recent dating of some of the *H. erectus* fossils of Java[56] takes the original expansion of *Homo erectus* (and, according to the multiregional model, the origin of regional differentiation) to around 1.8 MA. This early date is far outside of even the most generous confidence limits for the origin of modern mtDNA lineages.

The "Out of Africa" Model

If the basis of the Multiregional model can be discredited, can the "Out of Africa" model be taken as the best explanation for the origins of modern humans? The lines of evidence in support of that model, in terms of the continuity in form from archaic to modern fossils in Africa,[10] the discrepancy between the dates in African/Levantine modern humans and elsewhere, and the genetic data, are all compatible. However, there still are problems with this hypothesis. Those problems relate less to contradictory evidence than to the lack of specificity in both the model and the data. The model has three components, which, to some extent, can be treated independently: a single origin in Africa; a pattern of total replacement involving no admixture with other hominid populations; and a mechanism of dispersal across the world. Although current evidence supports a single African origin, the problem of replacement versus admixture remains a major issue. Moreover, a consistent mechanism for the world expansion of modern humans from their original African source has not been proposed. In this regard, the "Out of Africa" model lacks sufficient specificity to account for the regional patterns of modern human diversity and the specifics of both morphological and behavioral evolution over the last 100,000 years.

These problems highlight the need to develop more precise ideas about the origins of diversity. A theory of modern human origins has to be able to explain not only the appearance of modern people, but the origin of the diversity of modern populations.

THE EVIDENCE FOR THE ORIGINS OF HUMAN DIVERSITY

Human diversity refers to the biological and technological differences among modern populations today and in the recent past. Although many people consider the biological diversity of present-day humans to be vast, genetic studies show that it is very limited when compared to that of chimpanzees.[56–59] Modern humans are in fact an extraordinarily homogeneous species.[45] Nevertheless, differences in their morphology, genetics, and archeology are apparent for as long as there is evidence of modern people. It is the evolutionary origin of these differences from a recent common ancestor that we seek to explore. It is clear, and must be stressed, that there has been interbreeding between modern groups throughout the period, and that gene flow was one mechanism of change, although some subdivision of gene pools must have occurred in order for populations to have acquired and established their differences.

In order to investigate the origins of diversity, three points should be taken into account: first, that only scant evidence is available for the first part of the period; second, that at the point at which there is a record of modern people in various parts of the world, these populations are already different from each other; and third, that diversity increases with time, i.e., people become increasingly more different between wide geographical distances. Therefore, two sets of evidence are important, the patterns of diversity among the first occupants of each region for which there are records and the subsequent pattern of differentiation of each of these groups. Moreover, any theoretical model that attempts to explain the evolutionary process that created this diversity has to encompass a mechanism that would explain how modern people appeared in various regions, how these peoples acquired their early differentiation, and how they expanded and differentiated to produce modern levels of diversity. Clearly, the available data are not sufficient to answer all the relevant questions, especially those pertaining to differentiation. However, enough evidence has accumulated from diverse disciplines and groups of scholars to give us insight into how this process might have occurred.

The Modern Regional Populations

The point of origin of modern humans within Africa is unclear, but a case can be made for East Africa on the grounds that the earliest transitional forms (Omo) are found there.[10] Furthermore, East Africa, with its diverse habitat and potential for isolation, has been a major source of evolutionary novelty.[60] Geographical expansion probably led to the early differentiation of populations, as is suggested by the diversity of Middle Stone Age traditions.[61,62] The early modern fossils of Skhul and Qafzeh in the Middle East should be considered as an extension of North African populations, for they are accompanied by African faunas, at least in Qafzeh,[63] and do not seem to have expanded any further at this time.[64] Outside Africa, modern humans appeared at different regions at different times,[13] first in Australia and Asia, then later in Europe. Although this may be partly an artifact of a poor fossil record, some of these temporal patterns have remained relatively stable as new dates have been obtained in the last few years.

The evidence from different regions of the world after the appearance of modern humans is highly variable, both spatially and temporally, but vast (Figure 1). We do not presume to cover it here, but we will outline certain chronological, morphological, and archeological aspects that are relevant to the process of diversification of peoples.

Africa. About 100 ky ago, there were modern humans in East Africa (Omo),[9] North Africa/Middle East (Skhul, Qafzeh),[65] and South Africa.[66,67] In North Africa, the early moderns may have remained restricted to the area for a long period. There is no evidence supporting further expansion from the Middle East at this stage. In addition, biogeographic data show a movement of Palearctic faunas in the Levant between Stages 5 and 4 (70–60 ky).[64] It is possible that descendants of this early modern population developed the Aterian Middle Palaeolithic industry in North Africa, which shows certain derived characteristics.[68,69]

There is climatic,[70,71] faunal, and archeological[72] evidence of biogeographic movements across the Sahara around 50 ky ago. The lack of substantial fossil material from this time in this area precludes interpretations of the effect of gene flow from sub-Saharan Africa on North African populations, which eventually developed into the robust Mesolithic groups of Afalou, Taforalt, and Mechta.[73] In sub-Saharan Africa, the evidence after the first modern fossils, (Omo, KRM, Border Cave) is scant.

In South Africa, there is continuity of Middle Stone Age traditions until around 40 ky, after which date the area seems to have been essentially uninhabited until the Late Stone Age around 20 ky.[48] Genetic mtDNA and Y-chromosome studies have shown that the San and Pygmies are distinct, which suggests their early differentiation from other populations.[36,74,75] The main characteristic of these groups was a trend toward extreme gracilization. It is possible that this small body size adaptation allowed later colonization of the rainforests of western Africa. The close linguistic and genetic affinities of east and southern African hunter-gatherer populations[76] may be the result of subsequent movements. Within Africa, and superimposed on the early population patterns, are the recent expansions of farming communities, speakers of the Niger-Kordofanian languages, and from western Asia to North Africa, speakers of the Afro-Asiatic languages.

Australia and Island Melanesia. The first record of people in Australia is archeological. Roberts and colleagues recently obtained artifacts showing a relatively unsophisticated stone tool technology based on flakes dated to around 60 ky.[78,79] This technology, together with elaborate bone tools and art, characterized most of the subsequent Australian prehistory.[80] Around 40 ky ago, the number and geographical distribution of archeological sites in Australia increased sharply. At this moment, it is not known whether there was continuous occupation from 60 ky with a demographic expansion around 40 ky, or whether the large number of sites at 40 ky reflects a flow of people into Australia from outside. The archeological data suggest that Australian populations remained relatively isolated until very recent times, when microlithic tools and the dingo were introduced.[80] The first fossil evidence in Australia was found in the southeast, at the sites of Mungo and the Willandra Lakes system.[81,82] These fossils show remarkable variation in relation to the level of robusticity they present, the crania ranging from very gracile to more

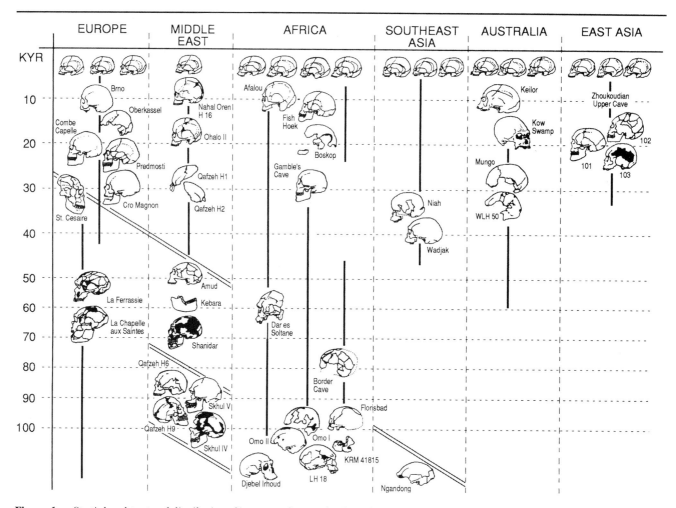

Figure 1.   *Spatial and temporal distribution of important human fossils in the Upper Pleistocene, together with a representation of present regional cranial variation. Continuous lines represent prehistoric occupation; diagonal double lines represent taxonomic distinctions within a region.*

robusticity than most modern ones, past or present.[83] They also show morphological features that clearly link them to recent Australian aborigines.[84,85] Most craniometric studies show the Australo-Melanesian population as that most closely related to African groups.[85–88] Therefore, a pattern of early colonization followed by relative isolation may be represented in Melanesia by the level of differences in mtDNA lineages among Papuan tribes[36] and of the comparatively high incidence of plesiomorphic archeological[89] and skeletal[52] traits.

Eastern Asia.   In eastern Asia, the archeological and paleontological record for the first half of the Upper Pleistocene is very poor. The first fossil evidence of modern people in Southeast Asia dates to around 40 ky ago (Niah, Wadjak, Tabon).[90] The Southeast Asian population of the late Pleistocene and its modern descendants can be identified cranially[91] and dentally (Sundadonts).[92] The range of this population reached beyond Southeast Asia into southern China, Japan (then connected to the mainland), and eventually Polynesia.[93,94] In eastern Asia, the best known early modern fossils are those of Zhoukoudian Upper Cave.

These fossils were first described as showing such variation as to resemble three different populations, Chinese, Eskimo, and Melanesian.[95] Recent northeastern Asians show a derived morphology, represented by the "Mongoloid" features of facial flatness and Sinodonty.[93,94,96–98] Turner has recognized Sinodont characteristics in the Upper Cave Zhoukoudian remains.[99] However, other authors have found that these fossils are not closely related to recent Asians,[100] which implies a relatively late appearance of the typical Mongoloid morphology. Holocene human remains with Mongoloid features are found in a wide area, from Eastern Siberia (where Turner identified a sharp east-west boundary in the incidence of Sinodonty in the region of Lake Baikal[99]), Mongolia, Korea, Japan, and the Americas. In Japan, the prehistoric Jomonese and recent Ainu, who show Sundadonty[99] and are cranially isolated from recent Japanese and Chinese,[91,96,97] must be survivors of the population before the Sinodont expansion.

It is not known how the Southeast Asian population represented by fossils like Niah and Tabon relates to the earliest Southeast Asian population from which Australians and New Guineans derive. It is not yet possible to determine whether the Southeast Asian population around 40 ky ago is the result of long-term differentiation of people present in the area for 20 to 30 ky, represents part of the widespread expansion of peoples from North Africa or the Middle East after 45,000 years ago, or a mixture of both. The evidence suggests that the first hypothesis is correct: current Southeast Asian populations are closer, both genetically[38] and archeologically,[89] to Australo-Melanesians than either is to Eurasians and Indians. Turner has proposed that East Asians derive from a southeast Asian source.[93] Cranial,[84,85,91,96–98,101–103] dental,[92] archeological,[89] and mtDNA[104] evidence further suggest that Southeast, East, and Northeast Asians are closely related, presenting a tight Mongoloid complex independent of Eurasia and India. However, nuclear genetic studies by Cavalli-Sforza[105] show that Northeast Asian (Japanese, Korean, Mongolian) and Amerindian populations are closer to Eurasians than to southern Chinese and Southeast Asians. A possible explanation for these differences is that the nuclear genetic patterns reflect invasions into northeastern Asia by Siberian peoples of Eurasian origin, either in the late Pleistocene, as indicated by archeological evidence,[106–110] or recently by peoples speaking the Altaic languages.[77]

There is also the question of Amerindian affinities. If the Americas were colonized early (40 to 20 kya[111–113]), the first inhabitants would have been derived from the less specialized Asian populations, whereas if they were colonized late (15 to 10 kya[114]), the first inhabitants would have been derived from relatively specialized East Asian groups. Evidence of a more robust and less specialized Asian morphology within the Americas has been suggested for Holocene remains[115,116] and for marginal native American groups (Fueguians, Patagonians).[117] On the other hand, Turner's finding that all Amerindian remains present a homogeneous Sinodont dental pattern[96] supports a recent migration into the New World (although his sample does not include southernmost South American groups). This hypothesis has been supported by genetic and linguistic data.[114] However, other genetic evidence shows that the timing and source of Amerindian differentiation is still unclear.[118]

Northern, Southern, and Western Asia. This area is not a unit in biogeographical terms. The area of the Middle East was at times an extension of African faunal distributions and at other times an extension of Eurasian ones.[64] The population history of the Middle East is complex. After the first appearance of modern humans in the last interglacial, the area was occupied by an archaic population with European Neanderthal affinities (Kebara, Amud).[119] Technologically, there is no clear distinction between the early modern and archaic populations; both are accompanied by Middle Paleolithic industries. Between 50–40 ky, the first technologies recognized as early Upper Paleolithic are found at Boker Tachtit and Ksar Akil, the latter associated with a modern human skeleton.[27,28] The subsequent pattern in the Middle East is one of continuity, from a robust modern Upper Paleolithic population (Qafzeh I and II,

Ohalo), to the Natufian pre-agriculturalists, to the first Neolithic farmers.

The paleoanthropology of the last 100 ky in the Indian subcontinent is virtually unknown. The first evidence of modern humans is found relatively late (28 ky) in Sri Lanka,[20] and most probably is not representative of the first population that occupied the area. This skeleton is accompanied by a stone tool industry similar to that of the European Upper Paleolithic.

In Northern Asian and Siberia, the archeological record indicates a date of first occupation between 35 and 20 ky by modern people manufacturing Upper Paleolithic-like stone tools.[48,121]

Europe. During most of the Upper Pleistocene, Europe was occupied by a Neanderthal population. The last known Neanderthals in Europe are those of St. Cesaire in France (36 ky)[122] and Zafarraya in Spain.[123] European Neanderthals were typically associated with Mousterian industries.[34] In St. Cesaire and other similarly late sites, the technology is Chatelperronian,[124] a Middle Paleolithic industry with elements similar to the Upper Paleolithic. Once considered as evidence of technological continuity between Neanderthals and modern humans in Europe, the Chatelperronian, being contemporaneous with the earliest Aurignacian sites, is currently interpreted as resulting from acculturation.[33,34] Similar interpretations apply to industries like the Szeletian of Eastern Europe or the Uluzzian of Italy. The first evidence of modern humans in Europe is mainly archeological, and is related to the spread of Aurignacian sites. The majority of cases of Upper Paleolithic fossils date to later periods and are accompanied by subsequent industries. These populations were robust and had larger crania[125] than more recent people, and, in many cases, were distinct from recent Europeans.[126,127]

Superimposed on these Paleolithic populations are the dispersals of agriculture-related peoples in the early Holocene.[128] Modern Europeans are cranially the most homogeneous of regional human populations.[52] If the model proposed by Renfrew is correct, and these agriculturalists brought with them a branch of the Indo-European family of languages,[77] then the Basques and Lapps must represent surviving Paleolithic groups.[128]

Multiple Dispersals as a Model for the Origins of Human Diversity

These patterns of differentiation suggest that modern populations changed at different rates during the Upper Pleistocene, depending on levels of gene flow and demographic pressures, and that geographical dispersal and expansion were main components of the process of differentiation. The "Out of Africa" model implies that it is dispersal beyond Africa that is critical. This ignores two things: the first is that because Africa itself is more than one third of the habitable Old World, dispersals within Africa are equally important; the second is that dispersal and divergence within Africa would lead to variable populations leaving Africa at different times and possibly by different routes. This means that the levels of differentiation in the populations colonizing the other continents were probably already high.

Beyond the original routes out of Africa, the data also point to a complex process of population differentiation involving the incomplete superimposition of dispersing populations on previously existing ones. In morphological terms, the temporal and spatial variation in the presence of common features suggests that modern humans differentiated, acquiring and losing traits in a stepwise manner, reducing at each step the communality of modern cranial traits.[52] The archeological remains also show uneven development of technologies during the Upper Pleistocene and the appearance of technological innovations at particular temporal and geographic points, suggesting a generally localized process of differentiation. Further, the genetic data available from contemporaneous populations show that degrees of differentiation and admixture vary markedly, some populations being the result of very recent expansions and differentiation and others being the result of previous expansions that may or may not have come into recent contact with other populations.[44] Therefore, the evolutionary origin of present populations may be extraordinarily varied. At this point, however, the evidence is only tentative. In eastern Asian and Australia, for example, we may be sampling three populations that resulted from three distinct dispersals. A population like the Australians may be the descendant of a group who left Africa between 100 and 60 ky, and hence present a high degree of morphological continuity with early and more robust moderns. A population like the Southeast Asians may be the result of long-term tropical differentiation in the area and geographical expansion. Differing amounts of gene flow, together with the effects of the break-up of the Sunda land mass, could account for the varying levels of distinctness of groups like the Andaman Islanders, Philippinos, and others. A population like the present east Asians may be

the result of a relatively recent adaptation, having undergone its own geographical expansion that included the Americas. Therefore, it is possible to see differentiation followed by population growth and dispersal as the mechanism of expansion of modern humans out of Africa and as the mechanism of development of subsequent regional populations.

THE MULTIPLE DISPERSALS MODEL

We have seen that the morphological basis of the multiregional model is incorrect. That fact, together with the chronological, archeological, and genetic evidence, indicates that the alternative single-origin explanation is more compatible with the available data. However, we have also seen that although the "Out of Africa" hypothesis explains the origins of modern humans from an archaic source, the model lacks a mechanism to explain the origins of human diversity. We propose a model to explain the diversity and disparity of the paleoanthropological data in the Upper Pleistocene based on the concept of geographical expansions and dispersals. This model is based on a single-origin hypothesis, followed by multiple dispersals out of Africa through two rather independent routes, then subsequent expansions and dispersals from secondary geographical sources.

A Mechanism: Dispersals and Evolutionary Change

Biogeographical comparisons suggest that the appearance of evolutionary novelty tends to occur in small areas and that successful populations can expand explosively, or at least relatively rapidly, from these centers of origins [129,130] (Figure 2). This seems to be the case with well-documented paleontological events, as well as historical ones involving humans and other species.[131-133] The process begins with dispersals into new regions and

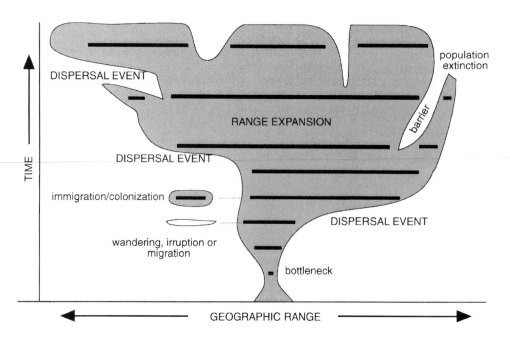

Figure 2. *Schematic representation of the geographical expansion of a species through time, showing localized origins, unsuccessful events, successful dispersal events, population isolation through the development of barriers, and superimposition of later dispersal events on the range of previous expansions. Adapted from Tchernov.[130]*

if colonization is successful, the available habitats of the colonized region would be occupied. Range expansion then takes place. Through time, this would be followed by differentiation as the population breaks up due to the appearance of barriers. Further dispersals would be superimposed on this pattern, resulting in a complex palimpsest of relic and recent populations. Range expansion, migrations, dispersals, colonizations, and differential survival of populations are the norms of evolutionary biogeography.[130–134] Furthermore, even if only a small proportion of invaders establish themselves,[134] they can be spectacularly successful. The mechanisms involved in the displacement of local populations by invading groups may be diverse, ranging from adaptive superiority, disease, habitat disturbance and destruction, and differential reproductive rates.[134] The processes of displacement ensuing from the expansion of modern human populations may have ranged from nonexistent (total interbreeding of local and incoming populations) to complete, either directly, through factors like disease, or indirectly, through the competition for resources and differential reproduction or demography. If such dispersal events occurred frequently during the later Pleistocene and were the primary mechanisms by which the human population diversified, then the mosaic of modern human diversity can be seen as the product of several events of differing geographical extent occurring over 100,000 years. This process would account for the pattern of modern human variability as a consequence of differential ancestral morphology occurring in successive dispersals followed by local adaptation. According to this view, Africa is unique only as the original source of populations, whereas the diversification process involved varied geographical foci, both African and non-African. Where modern populations were already present, dispersals would have acted as a primary mechanism of gene flow.

A Pattern: Routes of Dispersal and Levels of Differentiation

Traditionally, it has been assumed that expansions out of Africa occurred through the narrow corridor of northeastern Africa and the Middle East, a northern route. This assumption carries two implications. First, the direction of movement was across a major desert towards the Middle East, an area that certainly was populated at the time. Therefore, movement would have been strongly constrained by climatic conditions and competition with other hominids. Second, that there was morphological and genetic unity in the expanding population at any one time. However, another route of dispersal, through the Horn of Africa towards the Arabian Peninsula, a southern route, has been used by animals in the past. Use of this route by expanding early moderns has also been suggested[49,60] (Figure 3).

How would the existence of two different routes out of Africa affect the subsequent diversity of modern humans? Three main aspects of the expansion process would be affected. First, the climatic conditions necessary for northward expansion are very strict—faunal dispersals across the Sahara occurred during short episodes

of fast deglaciation, during which wet conditions prevailed in most of northern Africa. These strict climatic constraints would not have acted on populations expanding eastward toward Asia from East Africa. Second, the circum-Mediterranean area was certainly occupied by hominid populations during the last 200 ky. Hence, any movement into this region would imply competition with other groups. Although hominids were present throughout southern and eastern Asia in the late Pleistocene, the sizes and densities of populations may have been highly variable. The third and, perhaps, the most important aspect is that as hominids took different routes at different times, it is likely that the African source populations also differed from each other.

How does the available data fit the hypothesis of different routes of expansion? A northern faunal route of dispersal into the Nile Valley and across northern Africa has been intermittently used since the Miocene, and the Levantine corridor was alternatively occupied by Afro-Arabian or Palearctic elements.[64] As Tchernov[63,64] has argued, the paleoanthropological evidence suggests that an early modern population took an inland route to north Africa and the Middle East during the hypsithermal phase of the last interglacial.[70,135–137] However, this population, represented by the Skhul and Qafzeh fossils, seems to have faced a competitive or geographical barrier to further expansion at that stage. The main expansion of modern humans out of Africa through the Levantine corridor occurred around 45 ky,[48] but this event postdates the first occupation in Australia.[78,79] Furthermore, the morphological and archeological features of Middle Eastern and European population of 40 ky ago precludes them from the ancestry of many Australian fossils. If, however, another population, already genetically separated from other modern groups, expanded out of East Africa toward the Indian subcontinent at any time between 100 and 50 kya, this could explain some of the marked differences in morphology and technological traditions at the point of the first appearance of regional populations and the relatively early dates for the occupation of Australia.

Is the hypothesis of differentiation in Africa of populations ancestral to regional groups consistent with the available evidence? One way of interpreting the differences between regional modern populations when they appear in the archeological record is that these differences, in fact, reflect various levels of admixture between modern people and local archaic populations. Although it is commonly stated that there are two models of modern human origins, others have been proposed, such as the Afro-European Sapiens Hypothesis[138,139] and the Assimilation Hypothesis.[140,141] Both of these hypotheses are largely concerned with the level of genetic admixture between dispersing African populations and indigenous populations, especially European Neanderthals. They differ, however, in the amount of gene flow considered to have taken place. The Afro-European Sapiens model sees archaic genes persisting in a modern gene pool, whereas the Assimilation Hypothesis sees modern genes imposed on an archaic gene pool. The difference is therefore one of relative contribution. However, the absence of

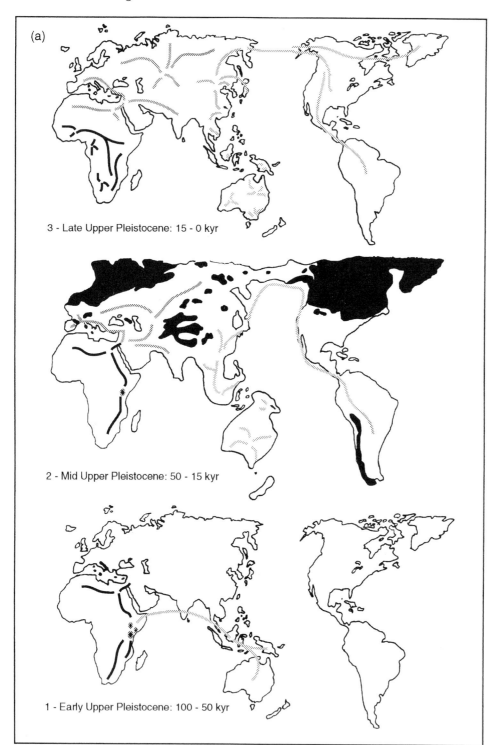

Figure 3. *Two views of the pattern of modern human divergence and dispersal according to the multiple dispersals model. (a) Possible Pleistocene dispersals: 1) In the early Upper Pleistocene (100–50 ky) there are dispersals within and out of Africa of early robust forms of modern humans; 2) The mid-Upper Pleistocene (50–15 ky) is the scene of world glaciations and the dispersals within southeast Asia and of Eurasian Upper Paleolithic populations; and 3) In the late Upper Pleistocene (15–0 ky), we see the recent dispersals, some associated with agricultural expansions, that have been superimposed on the Paleolithic human distribution.*

consistently transitional fossils throughout the world[10] argues against gene flow as the main process in the geographical expansion of modern morphology, making the Assimilation Hypothesis as unlikely as the multiregional model. Although some hybridization between modern humans and archaic populations might have occurred, it is not clear that the morphological features considered to reflect continuity between Neanderthals and early Upper Paleolithic Europeans (generally measures of robusticity, as is the case for the claimed similarities between Australians and *Homo erectus*), are

relevant phylogenetic markers. Furthermore, the mtDNA data show that no widely divergent lineage that could be attributed to Neanderthal descent has ever been sampled. The possibility of finding such a lineage remains, at least theoretically, until all people have been sampled, but its absence in the thousands of individuals studied so far indicates that even if such interbreeding took place, it did not have significant magnitude. This conclusion is further supported by recent research by Waddle using matrix correlation of Eurafrican fossils.[142]

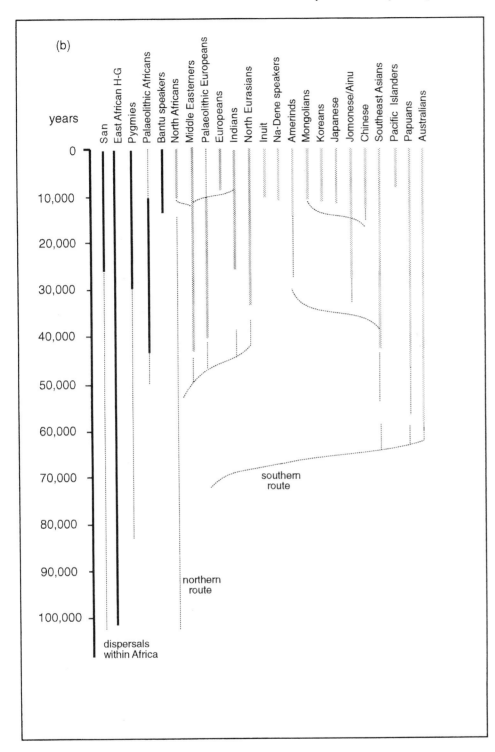

Figure 3. *(b) The implied time depth of the main populations of living* Homo sapiens.

Another way of explaining the original diversity of regional populations is that these populations were already different at the time they left Africa. In this case, a certain amount of prior differentiation and population subdivision would have taken place prior to expansion. There is little fossil data to support or refute this idea. Between 130 and 60 ky ago in Africa, there are fossils from South, East, and North Africa, but these are very few, localized, and early. The groups in these three regions do show marked population differences, and

indicate an even earlier date for the first appearance of a common morphology. They are also technologically diverse, although all present what are called Middle Stone Age or Middle Paleolithic stone tools. Therefore, both the fossil and archeological evidence tentatively suggests African diversification at this time. However, genetic evidence obtained by Harpending and co-workers strongly supports the idea of diversification of populations prior to geographical expansion, a model they have called the Weak Garden of Eden.[45,46,143] Their interpretation of mtDNA diversity through pairwise distributions indicates that modern humans underwent a bottleneck around 100 ky, that this bottleneck was followed by population subdivision and relative isolation of these diverse modern groups, and that demographic geographical expansion occurred between 70 and 40 ky, the youngest being that of Europeans. Therefore, molecular data show that a large amount of population differentiation occurred prior to expansion.

CONCLUSIONS

Although we believe that a recent single origin is the evolutionarily correct explanation for the appearance of *Homo sapiens,* we suggest that the "Out of Africa" model does not explain the temporal and geographical patterns of diversification observed in the Upper Pleistocene. The theoretical explanation of human diversity that best accounts for data on the dates of first occupation, morphological variation, and technological innovations involves multiple dispersal events. These dispersals would have taken different routes out of Africa, as well as different routes and directions from other subsequent non-African sources. The varying order and geographical extent of the early dispersals from Africa are proposed to explain the different times at which various regions of the world were first occupied. The incomplete geographical extent of subsequent dispersals is proposed to explain the persistence of relic populations as new populations were superimposed on the range of earlier groups. Finally, high levels of isolation, especially in tropical areas, are proposed to explain the differing rates of morphological, genetic, and technological change through time between long-standing adaptations and very recent colonizations.

Modern humans originated from a recent single evolutionary event, whereas modern human diversity is the result of multiple evolutionary events brought about by multiple geographical dispersals. Much remains to be done to document these various dispersals and their morphological, archeological, and genetic correlates. However, we also need to investigate further the possibility that one principal difference between modern humans and archaic hominids lay not in any major cognitive difference or any single edge of advantage, but simply in the social and ecological potential of modern humans to disperse at higher rates than could archaic hominids.

We are not naive or optimistic enough to suppose that this paper will end the debate between the multiregional and "Out of Africa" theories. We hope nonetheless, that by more fully developing the mechanisms for the evolution of modern human diversity and by emphasizing the importance of pre-existing variability at the origins of modern humans, albeit within Africa, rather than worldwide, we have at least brought something new to this discussion.

ACKNOWLEDGMENTS

We thank J. Fleagle for the invitation to write this paper, as well as C. Gamble, W. W. Howells, F. Lahr, and C. Stringer for commenting on an earlier version of it. Thanks also to R. Klein and six anonymous referees for their reviews. All errors that remain are our own. Special thanks to B. Arensburg, H. Harpending, R. Haydenblit, J. Nichols, and K. Robson Brown for stimulating discussions on the subject of modern human differentiation and to F. Lahr for his help with the figures. Financial support to MML was provided by CNPq, (Brazil), the Leakey Trust, and the CARE Foundation.

REFERENCES

1. Weidenreich, F. (1943). The skull of *Sinanthropus pekinensis:* A comparative study of a primitive hominid skull. Palarontol Sinica N. S., No. 10.
2. Coon, C. S. (1962). *The Origin of Races.* New York: Knopf.
3. Thorne, A., Wolpoff, M. H. (1981). Regional continuity in Australasian Pleistocene hominid evolution. Am J Phys Anthropol 55:337–349.
4. Wolpoff, M. H., Wu, X. Z., Thorne, A. (1984). Modern *Homo sapiens* origins: A general theory of hominid evolution involving the fossil evidence from East Asia. In Smith F. H., Spencer F. (eds), *The Origin of Modern Humans: A World Survey of the Fossil Evidence,* pp. 411–483. New York: Alan R. Liss.
5. Frayer, D. W., Wolpoff, M. H., Thorne, A. G., Smith, F. H., Pope, G. G. (1993). Theories of modern human origins: The palaeontological test. Am Anthropol 95:14–50.
6. Howells, W. W. (1976). Explaining modern man: Evolutionists versus migrationists. J Hum Evol 5:477–495.
7. Stringer, C. B. (1989). The origin of modern humans: A comparison of the European and non-European evidence. In Mellars, P., Stringer, C. B. (eds) *The Human Revolution,* pp. 232–244. Edinburgh: Edinburgh University Press.
8. Stringer, C. B. (1993). Reconstructing recent human evolution. In Aitken, M. J., Stringer, C. B., Mellars, P. A. (eds) *The Origin of Modern Humans and the Impact of Chronometric Dating,* pp. 179–195. Princeton: Princeton University Press.
9. Stringer, C. B., Hublin, J. J., Vandermeersch, B. (1984). The origin of anatomically modern humans in Western Europe. In Smith, F. H., Spencer, F. (eds) *The Origin of Modern Humans: A World Survey of the Fossil Evidence,* pp. 51–135. New York: Alan R. Liss.
10. Stringer, C. B., Andrews, P. (1988). Genetic and fossil evidence for the origin of modern humans. Science 239:1263–1268.
11. Grun, R., Stringer, C. B. (1991). Electron spin resonance dating and the evolution of modern humans. Archaeometry 33:153–199.
12. Aitken, M. J., Stringer, C. B., Mellars, P. A. (eds) (1993). *The Origin of Modern Humans and the Impact of Chronometric Dating.* Princeton: Princeton University Press.
13. Foley, R. A., Lahr, M. M. (1992). Beyond "Out of Africa": Reassessing the origins of *Homo sapiens.* J Hum Evol 22:523–529.
14. Valladas, H., Reyss, J. L., Valladas, G., Bar-Yosef, O., Vandermeersch, B. (1988). Thermoluminescence dating of Mousterian "Proto-Cro-Magnon" remains from Israel and the origin of modern man. Nature 331:614–616.
15. Schwarcz, H. P., Grun, R., Vandermeersch, B., Bar-Yosef, O., Valladas, H., Tchernov, E. (1988). ESR dates for the hominid burial site of Qafzeh in Israel. J Hum Evol 17:733–737.
16. Stringer, C. B., Grun, R., Schwarcz, H. P., Goldberg, P. (1989). ESR dates for the hominid burial site of Skhul in Israel. Nature 338:756–758.
17. Grun, R., Beaumont, P. B., Stringer, C. B. (1990). ESR dating evidence for early modern humans at Border Cave in South Africa. Nature 334:537–539.
18. Valladas, H., Joron, J. L., Valladas, G., Arensburg, B., Bar-Yosef, O., Belfer-Cohen, A., Goldberg, P., Laville, H., Meignen, L., Rak, Y., Tchernov, E., Tillier, A. M., Vandermeersch, B. (1987).

Thermoluminescence dates for the Neanderthal burial site at Kebara in Israel. Nature *330*:159–160.

19. Rightmire, P., Deacon, H. J. (1991). Comparative studies of late Pleistocene human remains from Klasies River Mouth, South Africa. J Hum Evol *20*:131–156.

20. Deacon, H. J. (1989). Late Pleistocene palaeoecology and archaeology in the southern Cape, South Africa. In Mellars, P., Stringer, C. B. (eds) *The Human Revolution*, pp. 547–564. Edinburgh: Edinburgh University Press.

21. Singer, R., Wymer, J. (1982). *The Middle Stone Age at Klasies River Mouth in South Africa*. Chicago: University of Chicago Press.

22. Brooks, A. S., Yellen, J. E. (1989). An archaeological perspective on the African origins of modern humans. Am J Phys Anthropol *78*:197.

23. Clark, J. D. (1982). The transition from Lower to Middle Palaeolithic in the African continent. In Ronen, A. (ed) *The Transition from Lower to Middle Palaeolithic and the Origin of Modern Man*, pp. 235–255. Oxford: BAR Int Series 151.

24. Deacon, H. J., Schuurman, R. (1992). The origins of modern people: The evidence from Klasies River. In Brauer, G., Smith, F. H. (eds) *Continuity or Replacement? Controversies in* Homo sapiens *Evolution*, pp. 121–129. Rotterdam: Balkema.

25. Gowlett, J. A. J. (1987). The coming of modern man. Antiquity *61*:210–219.

26. McBurney, C. B. M. (1967). *Haua Fteah and the Stone Age of the Southeast Mediterranean*. Cambridge: Cambridge University Press.

27. Marks, A. E. (1990). The Middle and Upper Palaeolithic of the Neareast and the Nile Valley: The problem of cultural transformations. In Mellars, P. (ed) *The Emergence of Modern Humans*, pp. 56–80. Ithaca: Cornell University Press.

28. Bergman, C. A., Stringer, C. B. (1989). Fifty years after: Egbert, an early Upper Palaeolithic juvenile from Ksar Akil, Lebanon. Paleorient *15*:99–111.

29. Smith, F. H. (1984). Fossil hominids from the Upper Pleistocene of central Europe and the origin of modern Europeans. In Smith. F. H., Spencer, F. (eds) *The Origin of Modern Humans: A World Survey of the Fossil Evidence*, pp. 137–209. New York: Alan R. Liss.

30. Bischoff, J. L., Soler, N., Maroto, J., Julia, R. (1989). Abrupt Mousterian/Aurignacian boundary at c 40 ka bp: Accelerator 14C dates from l'Abreda Cave (Catalunia, Spain). J Archeol Sci *16*:563–576.

31. Cabrera, V., Bischoff, J. L. (1989). Accelerator 14C dates for early Upper Palaeolithic (Basal Aurignacian) at El Castillo Cave (Spain). J Archeol Sci *16*:577–584.

32. Straus, L. G. (1989). Age of the modern Europeans. Nature *342*:476–477.

33. Mellars, P. (1991). Cognitive changes and the emergence of modern humans in Europe. J Cambridge Archeol *1*:63–76.

34. Mellars, P. (1993). Archaeology and the population-dispersal hypothesis of modern human origins in Europe. In Aitken, M. J., Stringer, C. B., Mellars, P. A. (eds) *The Origin of Modern Humans and the Impact of Chronometric Dating*, pp. 196–216. Princeton: Princeton University Press.

35. Cann, R. L., Stoneking, M., Wilson, A. C. (1987). Mitochondrial DNA and human evolution. Nature *325*:31–36.

36. Vigilant, L., Stoneking, M., Harpending, H. Hawkes, K., Wilson, A. (1989). African populations and the evolution of human mtDNA. Science *253*:1503–1507.

37. Stoneking, M., Jorde, L. B., Bhatia, K., Wilson, A. I. (1990). Geographic variation in human mitochondrial DNA from Papua New Guinea. Genetics *124*:717–733.

38. Wainscoat, J. S., Hill, A. V. S., Boyce, A. L., Flint, J., Hernandez, M., Thein, S. L., Old, J. M., Lynch, J. R., Falusi, A. G., Weatherall, D. J., Clegg, J. B. (1986). Evolutionary relationships of human populations from an analysis of nuclear DNA polymorphisms. Nature *319*:491–493.

39. Mountain, J., Lin, A. A., Bowcock, M., Cavalli-Sforza, L. L. (1993). Evolution of modern humans: Evidence from nuclear DNA polymorphisms. In Aitken M. J., Stringer, C. B., Mellars, P. A. (eds) *The Origin of Modern Humans and the Impact of Chronometric Dating*, pp. 69–83. Princeton: Princeton University Press.

40. Tishkoff, S. A., Kidd, K. K. (1994). Evidence for stability of a highly variable short tandem repeat polymorphism during recent human evolution. Am J Phys Anthropol Suppl *18*:195.

41. Templeton, A. R. (1992). Humans origins and analysis of mitochondrial DNA sequences. Science *255*:737.

42. Maddison, D. R. (1991). African origin of human mitochondrial DNA reexamined. Syst Zool *40*:355–363.

43. Wolpoff, M. H., Thorne, A. (1991). The case against Eve. New Scientist, 22 June:37–41.

44. Stoneking, M., Sherry, S. T., Redd, A. J., Vigilant, L. (1993). New approaches to dating suggest a recent age for the human mtDNA ancestor. In Aitken M. J., Stringer, C. B., Mellars, P. A. (eds) *The Origin of Modern Humans and the Impact of Chronometric Dating*, pp. 167–175. Princeton: Princeton University Press.

45. Rogers, A. R., Jorde, L. B. (1995). Genetic evidence on modern human origins. *Human Biology 61*:1–36.

46. Harpending, H., Sherry, S. T., Rogers, A. R., Stoneking, M. (1993). The genetic structure of ancient human populations. Curr Anthropol *34*:483–496.

47. Stoneking, M. (1993). DNA and recent human evolution. Evol Anthropol *2*:60–73.

48. Klein, R. G. (1992). The archaeology of modern human origins. Evol Anthropol *1*:5–14.

49. Cavalli-Sforza, L. L., Piazza, A., Menozzi, P., Mountain, J. (1988). Reconstruction of human evolution: Bringing together genetic, archaeological and linguistic data. Proc Nat Acad Sci *85*:6002–6006.

50. Groves, C. P. (1989). A regional approach to the problem of the origin of modern humans in Australasia. In Mellars, P., Stringer, C. B. (eds) *The Human Revolution*, pp. 274–285. Edinburgh: Edinburgh University Press.

51. Habgood, P. J. (1989). The origin of anatomically modern humans in Australasia. In Mellars, P., Stringer, C. B. (eds) *The Human Revolution*, pp. 245–273. Edinburgh: Edinburgh University Press.

52. Lahr, M. M. (1992). The origins of modern humans: A test of the Multiregional hypothesis. PhD dissertation, University of Cambridge.

53. Lahr, M. M. (1994). The Multiregional Model of modern human origins: A reassessment of its morphological basis. J Hum Evol *26*:23–56.

54. Groves, C. P. (1992). How old are subspecies? A tiger's eye-view of human evolution. Perspect Hum Biol 2/Archaeol Oceania *27*:153–160.

55. Swisher, C. C. III, Curtis, G. H., Jacob, T., Getty, A. G., Suprijo, A., Widiasmoro, (1994). Age of the earliest known hominids in Java, Indonesia. Science *263*:1118–1121.

56. Li, W. H., Sadler, L. A. (1991). Low nucleotide diversity in man. Genetics *129*:513–523.

57. Ferris, S., Brown, W., Davidson, W., Wilson, A. (1981). Extensive polymorphism in the mitochondrial DNA of apes. Proc Nat Acad Sci USA *78*:6319–6323.

58. Kocher, T., Wilson, A. (1991). Sequence evolution of mitochondrial DNA in humans and chimpanzees: Control region and a protein-coding region. In Osawa, S., Honjo, T. (eds) *Evolution of Life: Fossils, Molecules and Culture*, pp. 391–413. New York: Springer-Verlag.

59. Wilson, A., Cann, R., Carr, S., George, M., Gyllensten, U., Helm-Bychowski, K., Higuchi, R., Palumbi, S., Prager, E., Sage, R., Stoneking, M. (1985). Mitochondrial DNA and two perspectives on evolutionary genetics. Biol J Linnean Soc *26*:375–400.

60. Kingdon, J. (1993) *Self-Made Man and His Undoing*. London: Simon & Schuster.

61. Masao, F. T. (1992). The Middle Stone Age with reference to Tanzania. In Brauer, G., Smith, F. H. (eds) *Continuity or Replacement? Controversies in* Homo sapiens *Evolution*, pp. 99–109. Rotterdam: Balkema.

62. Clark, J. D. (1993). African and Asian perspective on the origins of modern humans. In Aitken, C. B., Stringer, C. B., Mellars, P. (eds) *The Origin of Modern Humans and the Impact of Chronometric Data*, pp. 201–215. Princeton: Princeton University Press.

63. Tchernov, E. (1992). Biochronology, paleoecology and dispersal events of hominids in the southern Levant. In Akazawa, T., Aoki, K., Kimura, T. (eds) *The Evolution and Dispersal of Modern Humans in Asia*, pp. 149–188. Tokyo: Hokusen-sha.

64. Tchernov, E. (1992). Eurasian-African biotic exchanges through the Levantine corridor during the Neogene and Quaternary. Cour Fors Senck *153*:103–123.

65. Vandermeersch, B. (1989). The evolution of modern humans: Recent evidence from Southwest Asia. In Mellars, P., Stringer, C. B. (eds) *The Human Revolution*, pp. 155–164. Edinburgh: Edinburgh University Press.

66. Deacon, H. J. (1993). Southern Africa and modern human origins. In Aitken, M. J., Stringer, C. B., Mellars, P. (eds) *The Origin of Modern Humans and the Impact of Chronometric Dating*, pp. 177–183. Princeton: Princeton University Press.

67. Rightmire, G. P., Deacon, H. J. (1991). Comparative studies of late Pleistocene human remains from Klasies River Mouth, South Africa. J Hum Evol *20*:131–156.

68. Close, A. E., Wendorf, F. (1990). North Africa at 18,000 BP. In Gamble, C., Soffer, O. (eds) *The World at 18,000 BP, Vol 2*, pp. 41–57. London: Unwin.

69. Debenath, A., Raynal, J. P., Roche, J., Texier, J. P., Ferembach, D. (1986). Stratigraphie, habitat, typologie et devenir de l'Aterian marocain: Donnes recentes. L'Anthropol *90*:233–246.

70. Petit-Marie, N. (1989). Interglacial environments in presently hyperarid Sahara: Paleoclimatic implications. In Leinen, M., Sarntheim, M. (eds) *Paleoclimatology and Paleometeorology: Modern and Past Patterns of Global Atmospheric Transport*, pp. 637–661. London: Kluwer Ac Press.

71. Fontes, J. C., Gasse, F. (1989). On the ages of humid and late Pleistocene phases in North Africa: Remarks on "Late Quaternary climatic reconstruction for the Maghreb (North Africa)" by P. Rognon. Pal Pal Pal *70*:393–398.

72. Wendorf, F., Schild, R., Siad, R., Haynes, C. V., Gautier, A., Kobusiewicz, M. (1976). The prehistory of the Egyptian Sahara. Science *193*:103–114.

73. Brauer, G., Rimbach, K. W. (1990). Late archaic and modern *Homo sapiens* from Europe, Africa and southwest Asia: Craniometric comparisons and phylogenetic implications. J Hum Evol *19*:789–807.

74. Lucotte, G. (1992). African pygmies have the more ancestral gene pool in studies for Y-chromosome DNA haplotypes. In Brauer, G., Smith, F. H. (eds) *Continuity or Replacement? Controversies in* Homo sapiens *Evolution*, pp. 75–81. Rotterdam: Balkema.

75. Stine, O. C., Dover, G. H., Zhu, D., Smith, K. D. (1992). The evolution of two west African populations. J Mol Evol *34*:336–344.

76. Ruhlen, M. (1990). An overview of genetic classification. In Hawkins, J. A., Gell-Mann, M. (eds) *The Evolution of Human Languages*, pp. 1–27. Addison-Wesley.

77. Renfrew, C. (1991). Before Babel: Speculation on the origins of linguistic diversity. Cambridge Archeol J *1*:3–23.

78. Roberts, R. G., Jones, R., Smith, M. A. (1990). Thermoluminescence dating of a 50,000 year old human occupation site in northern Australia. Nature *345*:153–156.

79. Roberts, R. G., Spooner, N. (1992). Luminescence dating of early occupation sites in northern Australia. Paper presented at the conference "Australia Day" University of Cambridge.

80. Kirk, R. L. (1981). *Aboriginal Man Adapting*. Oxford: Oxford University Press.

81. Thorne, A. G. (1977). Separation or reconciliation? Biological clues to the development of Australian society. In Allen, J. (ed) *Sunda and Sahul: Prehistoric Studies in Southeast Asia, Melanesia, and Australia*, pp. 187–204. London: Academic Press.

82. Thorne, A. G. (1984). Australia's human origins: How many sources? Am J Phys Anthropol *63*:227.

83. Habgood, P. J. (1985). The origin of the Australian Aborigines: An alternative approach and view. In Tobias, P. V. (ed) *Human Evolution: Past, Present and Future*, pp. 367–380. New York: Alan R. Liss.

84. Pietrusewsky, M. (1984). *Metric and Non-Metric Cranial Variation in Australian Populations Compared with Populations from the Pacific and Asia*. Canberra: Australian Inst. Aboriginal Studies.

85. Howells, W. W. (1989). *Skull shapes and the map*. Papers Peabody Museum, Arch Ethnol, vol 79, Cambridge: Harvard University Press.

86. Hedges, S. B., Kumar, S., Tamura, K., Stoneking, M. (1991). Comment on "Human origins and analysis of mitochondrial DNA sequences" by J. A. Templeton. Science *255*:737–739.

87. Vigilant, L., Stoneking, M., Harpending, H., Hawkes, K., Wilson, A. (1991). African populations and the evolution of human mitochondrial DNA. Science *253*:1503–1507.

88. Wright, R. V. S. (1992). Correlation between cranial form and geography in *Homo sapiens*: CRANID. A computer program for forensic and other applications. Perspect Hum Biol 2/Arch Oceania *27*:128–134.

89. Pope, G. G. (1988). Recent advances in Far Eastern palaeoanthropology. Ann Rev Anthropol *17*:43–77.

90. Jones, R. (1989). East of Wallace's Line: Issues and problems in the colonization of the Australian continent. In Mellars, P., Stringer, C. B. (eds) *The Human Revolution*, pp. 743–782. Edinburgh: Edinburgh University Press.

91. Brace, C. L., Brace, M. L., Dodo, Y., Leonard, W. R., Li, Y., Shao, X. Q., Sangvichien, S., Zhang, Z. (1990). Micronesians, Asians, Thais and relations: A craniofacial and odontometric perspective. Micronesia, Suppl *2*:323–348.

92. Turner, C. G. II (1987). Late Pleistocene and Holocene population history of East Asian based on dental variation. Am J Phys Anthropol *73*:305–321.

93. Turner, C. G. II (1990). The major features of Sundadonty and Sinodonty, including suggestions about East Asian microevolution, population history and late Pleistocene relationships with Australian Aborigines. Am J Phys Anthropol *82*:295–317.

94. Turner, C. G. II (1990). Origin and affinity of the people of Guam: A dental anthropological assessment. Micronesia, Suppl *2*:403–416.

95. Weidenreich, F. (1939). On the earliest representatives of modern mankind recovered on the soil of East Asia. Peking Nat Hist Bull *13*:205–224.

96. Brace, C. L., Brace, M. L., Leonard, W. R. (1989). Reflections on the face of Japan: A multivariate and odontometric perspective. Am J Phys Anthropol *78*:93–113.

97. Howells, W. W. (1984). Prehistoric human remains from China. In Schwidetzky I (ed) *Rassengeschichte der Menschheit*, pp. 29–38. Munich: R. O. Verlag.

98. Howells, W. W. (1986). Physical anthropology of the prehistoric Japanese. In Pearson R. J. (ed) *Windows on the Japanese Past: Studies in Archaeology and Prehistory*, pp. 85–99. Ann Arbor: Michigan Center for Japanese Studies.

99. Turner, C. G. II (1985). The dental search for Native American origins. In Kirk, R., Szathmary, E. (eds) *Out of Asia: Peopling of the Americas and the Pacific*, pp. 31–78. Canberra: Journal of Pacific History.

100. Kamminga, J., Wright, R. V. S. (1989). The Upper Cave at Zhoukoudian and the origins of the Mongoloids. J Hum Evol *17*:739–767.

101. Hanihara, K. (1985). Origins and affinities of the Japanese as viewed from cranial measurements. In Kirk, R., Szathmary, E. (eds) *Out of Asia. Peopling of the Americas and the Pacific*, pp. 105–112. Canberra: Journal of Pacific History.

102. Pietrusewsky, M. (1990). Craniofacial variation in Australasian and Pacific populations. Am J Phys Anthropol *82*:319–340.

103. Pietrusewsky, M., Li, Y., Shao, X., Nguyen, Q. Q. (1992). Modern and near modern populations of Asia and the Pacific: A multivariate craniometric interpretation. In Akazawa, T., Aoki, K., Kimura, T. (eds) *The Evolution and Dispersal of Modern Humans in Asia*, pp. 531–558. Tokyo: Hokusen-sha.

104. Ballinger, S. W., Schurr, T. G., Torroni, A., Gan, Y. Y., Hodge, J. A., Hassan, K., Chen, K. H., Wallace, D. C. (1992). Southeast Asian mitochondrial DNA analysis reveals genetic continuity of ancient Mongoloid migrations. Genetics *130*:139–152.

105. Cavalli-Sforza, L. L., Menozzi, P., Piazza, A. (1992). Genetic history and geography of Asia. In Akazawa, T., Aoki, K., Kimura, T. (eds) *The Evolution and Dispersal of Modern Humans in Asia*, pp. 613–623. Tokyo: Hokusen-sha Publ Co.

106. Bellwood, P. (1990). From late Pleistocene to early Holocene in Sundaland. In Gamble, G., Soffer, O. (eds) *The World at 18,000 BP, Vol 2*, pp. 155–163. London: Unwin Hyman.

107. Chen, C., Olsen, J. W. (1990). China at the last glacial maximum. In Soffer, O., Gamble, C. (eds) *The World at 18,000 BP, Vol 1*, pp. 276–295. London: Unwin Hyman.

108. Jia, L., Huang, W. (1985). The late Palaeolithic of China. In Wu, R., Olsen, J. W. (eds) *Palaeoanthropology and Palaeolithic Archaeology in the People's Republic of China*, pp. 211–223. Orlando: Academic Press.

109. Olsen, J. W. (1987). Recent developments in the Upper Pleistocene prehistory of China. In Soffer, O. (ed) *The Pleistocene Old World: Regional Perspectives*, pp. 135–146. New York: Plenum.

110. Reynolds, T. E. G., Kaner, S. C. (1990). Japan and Korea at 18,000 BP. In Soffer, O., Gamble, C. (eds) *The World at 18,000 BP, Vol 1*, pp. 296–311. London: Unwin Hyman.

111. Dillehay, T. D., Collins, M. B. (1988). Early cultural evidence from Monte Verde in Chile. Nature *332*:150–152.
112. Gruhn, R. (1987). On the settlement of the Americas: South American evidence for an expanded time frame. Curr Anthropol *28*:363–365.
113. Delibrias, G., Guidon, N. (1986). L'abri Toca do Boqueirao da sitio da Pedra Furada. L'Anthropol *90*:307–316.
114. Greenberg, J., Turner, C. G. II, Zegura, S. (1986). The settlement of the Americas: A comparison of the linguistics, dental and genetic evidence. Curr Anthropol *27*:477–497.
115. Steele, D. G., Powell, J. F. (1992). Peopling of the Americas: Paleobiological evidence. Hum Biol *64*:303–336.
116. Neves, W. A., Pucciarelli, H. M. (1991). Morphological affinities of the first Americans: An exploratory analysis based on early South American human remains. J Hum Evol *21*:261–273.
117. Lahr, M. M. (1993). Patterns of modern human diversification: Implications for Amerindian origins. Paper presented at the XIII ICAEJ, Mexico, Aug. 1993.
118. Szathmary, E. J. E. (1993). Genetics of aboriginal North Americans. Evol Anthropol *1*:202–220.
119. Bar-Yosef, O. (1993). The role of western Asian in modern human origins. In Aitken, M. J., Stringer, C. B., Mellars, P. A. (eds) *The Origin of Modern Humans and the Impact of Chronometric Dating*, pp. 132–147. Princeton: Princeton University Press.
120. Kennedy, K. A. R., Deraniyagala, S. U. (1989). Fossil remains of 28,000 year old hominids from Sri Lanka. Curr Anthropol *30*:394–399.
121. Morlan, R. E. (1987). The Pleistocene archaeology of Beringia. In Nitecki, M. H., Nitecki, D. V. (eds) *The Evolution of Human Hunting*, pp. 267–307. New York: Plenum.
122. Mercier, N., Valladas, H., Joron, J. L., Reyss, J. L., Leveque, F., Vandermeersch, B. (1991). Thermoluminescence dating of the late Neanderthal remains from Saint-Cesaire. Nature *351*:737–739.
123. Hublin, J. J. (pers. comm.)
124. Leveque, F., Vandermeersch, B. (1981). Le neanderthalien de Saint-Cesaire. Recherche *12*:242–244.
125. Kidder, J. H., Jantz, R. L., Smith, F. H. (1992). Defining modern humans: A multivariate approach. In Brauer, G., Smith, F. H. (eds) *Continuity or Replacement? Controversies in* Homo sapiens *Evolution*, pp. 157–177. Rotterdam: Balkema.
126. van Vark, G. N. (1990). A study of European Upper Palaeolithic crania, Fysisch-Antropol Mededelingen *2*:7–15.
127. van Vark, G. N., Bilsborough, A., Henke, W. (1992). Affinities of European Upper Palaeolithic *Homo sapiens* and later human evolution. J Hum Evol *23*:401–417.

128. Cavalli-Sforza, L. L. (1991). Genes, people and languages. Sci Am, November.
129. Foley, R. A. (1989). The ecological conditions of speciation: A comparative approach to the origins of anatomically modern humans. In Mellars, P., Stringer, C. B. (eds) *The Human Revolution*, pp. 298–320. Edinburgh: Edinburgh University Press.
130. Tchernov, E. (1992). Dispersal: A suggestion for a common usage of this term. Cour Fors Senck *153*:21–25.
131. Groves, R. H., Burdon, J. J. (1986). *Ecology of Biological Invasions*, Cambridge: Cambridge University Press.
132. Gray, A. J., Crawley, M. J,, Edwards, P. J. (eds) (1987). *Colonization, Succession and Stability*. Oxford: Blackwell Scientific.
133. Hengeveld, R. (1989). *Dynamics of Biological Invasions*. London: Chapman & Hall.
134. Lodge, D. M. (1993). Biological invasions: Lessons for ecology. TREE *8*:133–137.
135. Causse, C., Conrad, G., Fontes, J. C., Gasse, F., Gibert, E., Kassir, A. (1988). Le dernier "Humide" Pleistocene du Sahara nord-occidental daterait de 80–100,000 ans. C R Acad Sci Paris, t *306*, Serie II:1459–1464.
136. Causse, C., Coque, R., Fontes, J. C., Gasse, F., Gibert, E., Ben Ouezdou, H., Zouari, K. (1989). Two high levels of continental waters in the southern Tunisian chotts at about 90 and 150 ka. Geology *17*:922–925.
137. Gaven, C., Hillaire-Marcel, C., Petit-Marie, N. (1981). A Pleistocene lacustrine episode in southeastern Libya. Nature *290*:131–133.
138. Brauer, G. (1984). The "Afro-European sapiens hypothesis" and hominid evolution in East Asia during the late Middle and Upper Pleistocene. Cour Fors Senck *69*:145–165.
139. Brauer, G. (1992). L'hypothese Africaine de l'origine des hommes modernes. In Hublin, J. J., Tillier, A. M. (eds) *Aux Origines d'Homo sapiens*, pp. 181–215. Paris: Presses Université de France.
140. Smith, F. H. (1992). The role of continuity in modern human origins. In Brauer, G., Smith, F. H. (eds) *Continuity or Replacement? Controversies in* Homo sapiens *Evolution*, pp. 145–156. Rotterdam: Balkema.
141. Smith, F. H., Simek, J. F., Harrill, M. S. (1989). Geographical variation in supraorbital torus reduction during the later Pleistocene (c 80,000–15,000 B.P.). In Mellars, P., Stringer, C. B. (eds) *The Human Revolution*, pp. 172–193. Edinburgh: Edinburgh University Press.
142. Waddle, D. M. (1994). Matrix correlation tests support a single origin for modern humans. Nature *368*:452–454.
143. Sherry, S. T., Rogers, A. R., Harpending, H., Soodyall, H., Jenkins, T., Stoneking, M. (1994). Mismatch distributions of mtDNA reveal recent human population expansions. Hum Biol. *66*:761–775.

63

Models, Predictions, and the Fossil Record of Modern Human Origins

J. H. Relethford

It is clear from the recent contents of this journal and others that the debate about modern human origins continues unabated. My own foray into this subject has dealt with some of the genetic evidence. It has become increasingly clear to me that much of the genetic evidence is indeterminate and that both African replacement and multiregional models can explain observed patterns of genetic variation.[1,2] Consider, for example, the finding that many traits show higher genetic diversity within sub-Saharan African populations. While this finding can be interpreted as indicating a greater age for African populations, thus supporting a recent African origin, it can also be explained by a larger long-term African population size, which is compatible with both a recent African origin and multiregional evolution.

Population geneticists have long known of the problems of unraveling population history from genetic data. Relationships between populations can reflect either common ancestry or migration.[3–7] When considering the predictions of different models, it is critical to make sure that the predictions are unique to each model. I suggest that the problem of indeterminate results is also characteristic of some analyses of the fossil record. In particular, the results from several studies proclaimed as proof of a recent African origin are also compatible with a multiregional model.

One approach to analyzing the fossil record has been to compare fossil samples from different geographic regions across time by using some form of biological distance measure.[8–11] A useful comparison would be between fairly recent modern human fossil samples (<30 kya) and earlier samples (35 to 100+ kya) across the major geographic regions of the Old World.[10,11] The most relevant distances are those across time periods. Are the distances within regions less than the distances between regions? Several analyses have shown that more recent modern samples are morphologically more similar to earlier samples from Africa and the Middle East than to earlier samples within their geographic region. For example, it has been suggested that recent modern samples from Europe (e.g., Cro-Magnon) are more similar to older samples from Africa and the Skhul-Qafzeh samples in the Middle East than to earlier Europeans (Neandertals).[8–11] These findings are often taken as support for a recent African origin because this is the type of pattern we would expect to see if all recent modern humans came from Africa within the last 100,000 years.

I will not discuss here debates over sample composition, measurements used, or specifics of chronology. My purpose is to examine the underlying assumptions of such studies, and to that end I will take the reported distances as given. Further study can always help us refine our measurements and analyses, but this is of little utility if we do not examine underlying assumptions and make sure that our interpretations are based on valid predictions of the models.

Assuming that the distances between fossil samples across time and space are an accurate reflection of past history, it is clear that such results are compatible with a recent African origin. This finding would reject a multiregional model only if the results do not agree with the predictions of a multiregional model. What are these predictions? It is common to see statements to the effect that multiregional evolution predicts that the greatest similarity across time will be within geographic regions. According to this prediction, recent Europeans should be more similar to Neandertals than are fossil samples from other regions at roughly the same time period. This assumption is apparent in Waddle's design matrix for the multiregional model, in which she predicts that the smallest biological distances will occur within geographic regions.[10] The assumption was made most recently with reference to the extraction of Neandertal mitochondrial DNA:[12] Krings and colleagues stated that "whereas the Neandertals inhabited the same geographic region as contemporary

Europeans, the observed differences between the Neandertal sequence and modern Europeans do not indicate that it is more closely related to modern Europeans than to any other population of contemporary humans."

At first glance, this assumption seems to make sense. After all, given that multiregional evolution incorporates isolation by distance, we would expect, in any given generation, a pattern of population endogamy. At an aggregate level, this would translate into regional endogamy, so that the vast majority of a generation's genes would come from ancestors one generation earlier in the same geographic region. It is then assumed that the accumulated ancestry over many generations would reflect this pattern, so that most of the genes in Europe would derive from Europe, most genes in Asia would derive from Asia, and so on.

This last assumption is incorrect, and that leads to an incorrect prediction of the multiregional model. The problem arises from equating per-generation endogamy with accumulated ancestry over many generations. The easiest way to illustrate this problem is with a simple example of gene flow. Assume two populations, A and B, where population A consists of 4,000 reproductive adults and population B consists of 1,000 reproductive adults. Further assume that these sizes are constant over time. Now, let each population exchange 10 mates per generation. These numbers are easily visualized using a migration matrix, where the columns refer to offspring and the rows refer to their parents. In this simple example, the migration matrix is

$$
\begin{array}{c c c}
 & A & B \\
A & 3990 & 10 \\
B & 10 & 990.
\end{array}
$$

A matrix of probabilities is obtained by dividing each element of the matrix by its corresponding column total. This gives

$$
\begin{array}{c c c}
 & A & B \\
A & 0.9975 & 0.0100 \\
B & 0.0025 & 0.9900.
\end{array}
$$

This matrix has a standard meaning in population genetics. Each element represents the probability that a gene in column j came from row i. In this specific example, the probability of a gene in population A coming from population A (endogamy) is 0.9975, while the probability of a gene in A coming from population B (exogamy) is 0.0025.

These hypothetical values show that both populations are highly endogamous. Following the reasoning set forth earlier, we might at first expect that, given this endogamy, the greatest similarities over time would occur within each population. This is true for short periods, but over many generations the total accumulated ancestry in each population will change. Under a simple migration model, the matrix of accumulated ancestry after t generations can be derived by raising the above matrix to the power t.[13,14] For example, after 100 generations the matrix of accumulated ancestry is

	A	B
A	0.8569	0.5726
B	0.1431	0.4274.

After 100 generations of low gene flow, population A would have derived roughly 14% of its genes from population B, while population B would have derived roughly 57% of its genes from population A. In the latter case, we would now expect that population B would actually be closer to population A as it was 100 generations earlier! As the number of generations increases, these numbers change even more. After 200 generations, the matrix of accumulated ancestry would be

	A	B
A	0.8162	0.7354
B	0.1838	0.2646.

It is clear that by this time both populations A and B would have derived the majority of their ancestry from population A. The matrix will continue to change until an equilibrium is reached, as

	A	B
A	0.8000	0.8000
B	0.2000	0.2000.

At equilibrium, both populations would reflect 80% ancestry from population A and 20% ancestry from population B. Note that these numbers are equal to the relative sizes of the two populations. Population A (N = 4,000) accounts for 80% of the total population size (4,000 + 1,000 = 5,000), and population B (N = 1,000) accounts for 20% of the total population size. This is not coincidental; previous studies of migration matrices show that, given symmetric migrant numbers, the rows of the equilibrium matrix will be equal to the relative weights of the populations.[15,16] The situation is more complex with asymmetric migrant numbers, but the same tendency still applies. In any case, a symmetric model seems appropriate as a simplifying model for describing most human populations because the genetic effects of asymmetry are not very different from those expected under a symmetric model.[17]

What does this all mean? This simple example shows clearly that, given enough time, the accumulated ancestry of any population will be dominated by the largest population. This is intuitive: The larger the population, the greater the proportion of genes. This principle has a major implication for the analysis of hominid fossil samples across time. Many genetic studies have demonstrated that the long-term population size of Africa is larger than that of any other region.[4,18] A larger African population is also expected throughout most of prehistory, based on ecological arguments.[19,20] It is important to keep in mind that this model only makes the assumption that, over time, Africa was the largest. While archeological evidence suggests times during which parts of Africa were relatively depopulated,[21] the genetic evidence supports the hypothesis that the long-term average population was largest in Africa.

If the African population was the largest, then even under a model of low-level gene flow it would exert the greatest genetic impact. A comparison across many generations would show this effect. The more recent samples would all be more similar to earlier samples in Africa than to samples from anywhere else. While these results might seem paradoxical, there is no mystery. The common assumption of greater similarity within regions over long periods confuses per-generation endogamy with accumulated ancestry.

Of course, the above example relies on a simple and unrealistic model in which gene flow alone affects genetic history. However, the same results apply with more complex models. Konigsberg[22] has developed a general model for examining biological distances across space and time. This model incorporates gene flow, genetic drift, and linear systematic pressure, which includes mutation, long-range migration, and selection. He found that over time the biological distance within a region will increase and the biological distance between regions will decrease. The overall pattern is the same as illustrated in the simple example I used earlier.

The implications for the fossil record of modern human origins are clear. Given a larger long-term population size in Africa, both recent African origin and multiregional models predict that temporally recent fossil samples across the Old World will more closely resemble earlier populations in Africa. While this demonstration does not prove a multiregional model, it does show that previous biological distance analyses do not prove a recent African origin. Both models produce the same prediction. To further complicate matters, the same pattern could be produced by population expansion with admixture as well as gene flow among populations, depending on the rate of admixture.

Resolution of the debate is therefore not possible from analyses of overall biological distance. One possibility is to examine the relative occurrence of regional continuity in individual traits. My findings may seem contradictory to the prediction of regional continuity under a multiregional model, which is that the greatest similarity over time will be within regions. However, this prediction would be contradictory only if we expect all traits to show a pattern of regional continuity. However, proponents of the multiregional model do not suggest that all traits will show continuity. In reality, regional continuity is expected only for some traits as the result of genetic drift and selection acting to maintain high frequencies of a trait within a region in opposition to gene flow.[20,23,24] My model provides a prediction of the expected biological distance between samples averaged over many traits. We must also consider variation about these expected averages. Individual traits could show deviations from this expectation because of drift, selection, or both. Therefore, if the multiregional model is correct, we would expect to see regional continuity for a small number of traits, as well as greater similarity to earlier African samples when considering the average over many traits.

In this light, it is interesting to consider the findings of Lahr's[25] comprehensive analysis of continuity traits in East Asian and Australasian samples. Her analysis suggested continuity in 11 out of 30 (37%) traits. The remainder of the traits either did not show a regional pattern or showed higher frequencies in other regions. Although her analysis has been used to argue against a multiregional model, I contend that the presence of some continuity traits is consistent with the gene flow-drift model I have described. Given the nature of accumulated ancestry, we would not expect most traits to show regional continuity. The important finding is that some do, which is more difficult to explain from the perspective of an African replacement model. Further investigation is needed to determine whether similar patterns of continuity could be obtained under a replacement model as a consequence of recurrent mutation and drift. I am currently planning a set of simulation analyses to address these questions.

Population genetics models can provide us with valuable predictions for the fossil record of modern human origins. Two points are critical to future investigation. First, multiregional models do not predict that the lowest biological distance between time periods will be within geographic regions; instead, the lowest distance will be to the largest population. Second, this expectation applies to biological distances averaged over many traits, but not necessarily to each trait individually. By examining overall biological distance we can address the issue of accumulated ancestry and ancient population size. By looking at individual traits and comparing them to the average, we can assess claims of regional continuity. Based on these findings and the hypothesis of a larger long-term African population, I suggest that the multiregional model predicts that biological distances based on many traits will show that recent modern fossil samples are more similar to earlier samples from Africa than they are to samples from the same geographic region. I also suggest that regional continuity will be found in a small number of traits, but not all traits. Based on research to date, both predictions appear to be confirmed. Future resolution of the debate must focus on regional continuity because the first prediction also fits an African replacement model.

ACKNOWLEDGMENTS

My thanks to Henry Harpending, Lyle Konigsberg, and Milford Wolpoff for their comments.

REFERENCES

1. Relethford, J. H. 1995. Genetics and modern human origins. Evol Anthropol 4:53–63.
2. Relethford, J. H. 1998. Genetics of modern human origins and diversity. Ann Rev Anthropol 27:1–23.
3. Felsenstein, J. 1982. How can we infer geography and history from gene frequencies? J Theor Biol 96:9–20.
4. Relethford, J. H., Harpending, H. C. 1994. Craniometric variation, genetic theory, and modern human origins. Am J Phys Anthropol 95:249–270.
5. Relethford, J. H., Harpending, H. C. 1995. Ancient differences in population size can mimic a recent African origin of modern humans. Curr Anthropol 36:667–674.
6. Weiss, K. M., Maruyama, T. 1976. Archeology, population genetics, and studies of human racial ancestry. Am J Phys Anthropol 44:31–50.
7. Weiss, K. M. 1988. In search of times past: gene flow and invasion in the generation of human diversity. In: Mascie-Taylor, C. G. N., Lakser, G. W., editors. Biological aspects of human migration. Cambridge: Cambridge University Press, p 130–166.
8. Stringer, C. B. 1993. Reconstructing human evolution. In: Aitken, M. J., Stringer, C. B., Mellars, P. A., editors. The origin of modern humans and the impact of chronometric dating. Princeton: Princeton University Press. p 179–195.
9. Stringer, C. B. 1994. Out of Africa—a personal history. In: Nitecki, M. H., Nitecki, D. V., editors. Origins of anatomically modern humans. New York: Plenum Press. p 149–172.
10. Waddle, D. M. 1994. Matrix correlation tests support a single origin for modern humans. Nature 368:452–454.
11. Sokal, R. R., Oden, N. L., Walker, J., Waddle, D. M. 1997. Using distance matrices to choose between competing theories and an application to the origin of modern humans. J Hum Evol 32:501–522.
12. Krings, M., Stone, A., Schmitz, R. W., Krainitzki, H., Stoneking, M., Pääbo, S. 1997. Neandertal DNA sequences and the origin of modern humans. Cell 90:19–30.
13. Roberts, D. F., Hiorns, R. W. 1962. The dynamics of racial intermixture. Am J Hum Genet 14:261–277.
14. Roberts, D. F., Hiorns, R. W. 1965. Methods of analysis of the genetic composition of a hybrid population. Hum Biol 37:38–43.
15. Jaquard, A. 1974. The genetic structure of populations. New York: Springer-Verlag.
16. Harpending, H. C., Ward, R. H. 1982. Chemical systematics and human populations. In: Nitecki, M., editor. Biochemical aspects of evolutionary biology. Chicago: University of Chicago Press. p 213–256.
17. Rogers, A. R., Harpending, H. C. 1986. Migration and genetic drift in human populations. Evolution 40:1312–1327.
18. Relethford, J. H., Jorde, L. B. 1999. Genetic evidence for larger African population size during recent human evolution. Am J Phys Anthropol 108:251–260.
19. Thorne, A. G., Wolpoff, M. H., Eckhardt, R. B. 1993. Genetic variation in Africa. Science 261:1507–1508.
20. Wolpoff, M. H., Caspari, R. 1997. Race and human evolution. New York: Simon and Schuster.
21. Ambrose, S. H. 1998. Late Pleistocene human population bottlenecks, volcanic winter, and differentiation of modern humans. J Hum Evol 34:623–651.
22. Konigsberg, L. W. 1990. Analysis of prehistoric biological variation under a model of isolation by geographic and temporal distance. Hum Biol 62:49–70.
23. Wolpoff, M. H., Wu X, Thorne, A. G. 1984. Modern *Homo sapiens* origins: a general theory of hominid evolution involving the fossil evidence from East Asia. In: Smith F. H., Spencer F., editors. The origins of modern humans: a world survey of the fossil evidence. New York: Alan R. Liss. p 411–483.
24. Wolpoff, M. H. 1989. Multiregional evolution: The fossil alternative to Eden. In: Mellars, P. A., Stringer, C. B., editors. The human revolution: behavioral and biological perspectives on the origin of modern humans. Princeton: Princeton University Press. p 62–108.
25. Lahr, M. M. 1994. The multiregional model of modern human origins: a reassessment of its morphological basis. J Hum Evol 26:23–56.

64

Fully Modern Humans

R. G. Klein

INTRODUCTION

For decades paleoanthropologists have pondered whether modern humans evolved throughout the human geographic range or in only a small part. Debate continues, but the accumulating fossil, archaeological, and genetic evidence increasingly points to a restricted origin in Africa from which modern humans spread to replace or swamp their nonmodern contemporaries elsewhere. The case is particularly clear with regard to the replacement of the Neanderthals in Europe and western Asia beginning 50,000 to 40,000 years ago and more uncertain with respect to the fate of nonmodern people in eastern Asia. It is not that eastern Asia suggests a contrary result, but that it presents too few data for any persuasive conclusion.

Many important subsidiary details remain to be established, including above all how modern humans managed to spread. I argue here that the most essential factor was abrupt development of the fully modern capacity for culture. It is only after 50,000 to 40,000 years ago that the archaeological record unequivocally reflects the technological ingenuity, social formations, and ideological complexity of historic hunter-gatherers. The archaeology of people who lived before 50,000 to 40,000 years ago suggests that they were distinctly nonmodern in virtually every detectable aspect of their behavior, including their relatively unstandardized (informal) artifacts, the remarkable uniformity of their artifact assemblages through time and space, their failure to produce unequivocal art or ornaments, the simplicity of their burials, their failure to build structures that retain archaeological visibility, and their relatively limited ability to hunt and gather.

If my basic thesis is accepted, the advent of fully modern humans was a punctuational evolutionary event in the sense of Eldredge and Gould (1972). It was arguably the last and most significant of three such events that paleoanthropologists have so far detected. The previous ones were, first, the simultaneous emergence of the genus *Homo* and those uniquely human behaviors that produced the first archaeological sites roughly 2.5 million years ago (mya) and second, the development of *Homo ergaster* and the associated behavioral advances that allowed people to expand beyond tropical and subtropical African woodlands beginning roughly 1.7 mya.

FOSSILS, GENETICS, AND MODERN HUMAN ORIGINS

Genetic analyses indicate that chimpanzees and people last shared a common ancestor between 8 and 5 mya. The oldest known people, identified primarily by legs that were shaped for bipedal locomotion, date to roughly 4.5 mya. All subsequent people until roughly 2.5 mya were essentially bipedal apes who retained small ape-sized brains and long arms that were well suited for tree climbing. Brain expansion beyond the ape range first occurred in the emergence of *Homo* about 2.5 mya; enlarged brains help explain the concurrent appearance of the oldest known archaeological sites. These comprise clusters of stone artifacts that signal a uniquely human understanding of how to flake stone, together with fragmented animal bones that imply an equally humanlike investment in eating meat. The earliest people lived exclusively in Africa, but sometime between 1.7 and 1 mya, the relatively small-brained but otherwise typically human species, *Homo ergaster,* colonized Eurasia.

Paleoanthropologists agree that the far-flung descendants of this species then began to diverge morphologically, but they disagree strongly on how far the divergence proceeded and on its meaning for the origins of modern humans. At present the protagonists divide broadly between those who advocate "multiregional continuity" and those who favor the "Out of Africa" hypothesis.

Proponents of multiregional continuity argue that intercontinental gene flow constrained morphological differentiation and ensured that highly adaptive novelties (such as larger brains) spread rapidly to all populations (Frayer et al., 1993; Wolpoff, 1996). As a result, people everywhere remained on the same fundamental evolutionary track, and modern humans emerged more or less simultaneously wherever nonmodern humans had lived before—in Africa, Asia, and Europe. The multiregional theory depends on morphological traits that purportedly demonstrate regional continuity between nonmodern and modern populations in China, in Southeast Asia (including Australia and neighboring islands), and to a lesser extent in Europe. Critics have questioned both the regional restriction and the phylogenetic significance of key traits (Lahr, 1994; Lieberman, 1995), and they have pointed out that some apparent evidence for regional continuity is inevitable, as long as regional fossil samples remain small compared with the number of anatomical features among which multiregional advocates can search for similarities (Harpending, 1994). There is the further objection that multiregionalism requires an unrealistically large amount of gene flow among small hunter-gatherer populations scattered across three continents.

The Out of Africa theory might be better called "Out of Africa 2" (Stringer and Gamble, 1993) to distinguish it from the universally accepted initial African exodus before 1 mya. In essence, Out of Africa 2 posits that after the colonization of Eurasia morphological differentiation produced separate evolutionary lineages, culminating by 100,000 years ago in at least three continentally distinct human populations. In Africa there were early modern or near modern people, in Europe there were the Neanderthals, and in eastern Asia there were equally nonmodern people who could represent evolved end products of classic east Asian *Homo erectus.* It its most extreme form, Out of Africa 2 posits that modern people expanded from Africa beginning 60,000 to 50,000 years ago to replace the Neanderthals and equally archaic east Asians without gene exchange (or interbreeding) (Figure 1). An implicit corollary is that human populations on different continents actually belonged to different species (Figure 2). In its less extreme form, Out of Africa 2 allows for some gene flow between expanding moderns and resident archaic populations (Bräuer, 1992; Smith, 1994).

Out of Africa 2 depends primarily on human fossils that demonstrate the divergence of European and African lineages after 500,000 to 400,000 years ago. In both lineages, evolutionary change was apparently gradual, in contrast to the postulated punctuational events

that produced earliest *Homo, H. ergaster,* and fully modern *H. sapiens.* The key fossils that document a European lineage include those from Swanscombe in England (Hublin, 1996), Reilingen in Germany (Dean et al., 1994), and above all the Sima de los Huesos (Atapuerca) in Spain (Arsuaga et al., 1997) (Figure 3, right). The specimens in each case antedate 200,000 years ago, yet they clearly anticipate typical Neanderthals in one or more derived morphological features. These features do not seem to have evolved as an integrated morphological complex, and their development may have been due more to genetic drift than to natural selection. Early European populations certainly suffered repeated crashes during recurrent intervals of especially cold, dry climate, and the consequent bottlenecks enhanced the potential for significant drift (Hublin, 1998).

The relative roles of drift and natural selection aside, fossils from Biache-Saint-Vaast in northern France (Stringer et al., 1984) and Ehringsdorf in Germany (Grün and Stringer, 1991) suggest that typical Neanderthal morphology became fixed at or shortly after 200,000 years ago, and classic Neanderthal fossils are well known from numerous western and central European sites dated to between 130,000 and 50,000 to 40,000 years ago. The classic Neanderthals have often been regarded as late archaic humans, and the term is probably most apt with respect to their behavior. Their remarkable robusticity (Trinkaus, 1989), their extreme bodily adaptation to cold (Holliday, 1997), and the frequency and pattern of their injuries (Berger and

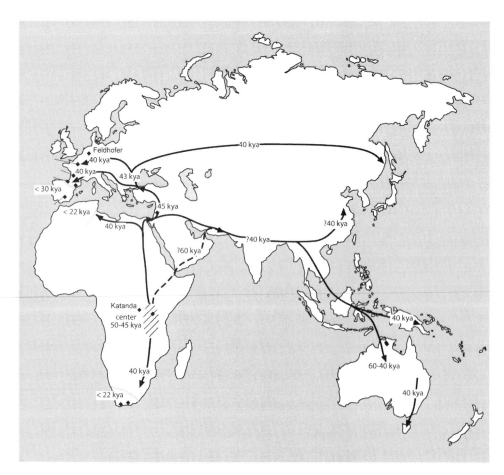

Figure 1. *The putative spread of fully modern humans from an east African center (modified after Bar-Yosef, 1998b, Figure 6). Key sites mentioned in the text are also shown. The arrows signify population expansions that arguably began in eastern Africa about 45,000 years ago and that may have taken 5000 years to reach western Europe and eastern Asia. A small number of dates suggests that modern humans spread to southwestern Asia and southeastern Europe 3000 to 5000 years before they reached western Europe (Mellars, 1993). However, the dispersion may have occurred so rapidly that it will ultimately appear instantaneous from the present perspective. The dotted line indicates a possible 60,000-year-old dispersion across the mouth of the Red Sea that could explain a postulated 60,000 to 50,000-year initial occupation of Australia.*

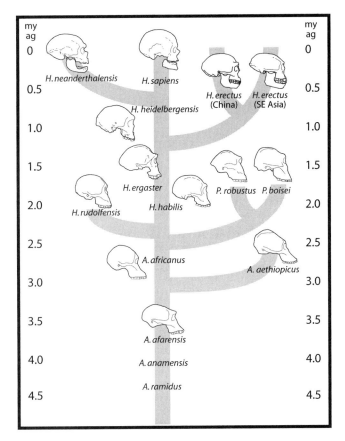

Figure 2. *A working phylogeny of the human family (A. =* Australopithecus, *P. =* Paranthropus, *H. =* Homo). *The Out of Africa theory of modern human origins all but requires the development of continentally distinct human species. The number of species may actually have been far greater (Tattersall, 1998), and fossils from Java and China suggest that at least two distinct human lines developed in eastern Asia.* H. heidelbergensis *is used here for the last shared ancestor of* H. neanderthalensis *and* H. sapiens *(Rightmire, 1998; Stringer and McKie, 1996), but some authorities use it to designate an early stage within the Neanderthal lineage (Arsuaga et al., 1997).*

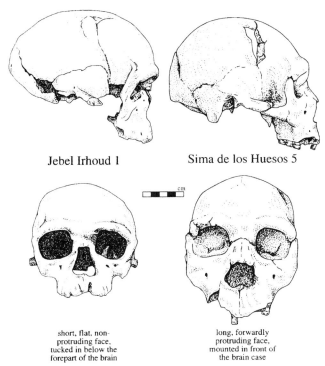

Figure 3. *Skulls from Jebel Irhoud Cave, Morocco, and the Sima de los Huesos (Pit of the Bones), Atapuerca, Spain (drawn by Kathryn Cruz-Uribe from photographs). The exact ages of both skulls remain to be established, but both are much older than 100,000 years. The Jebel Irhoud skull anticipates living humans in its short, flat face tucked in below the forepart of the brain. In contrast, the Sima de los Huesos skull anticipates the classic Neanderthals in the length and forward protrusion of the face, particularly along the midline. Differences in occipital morphology also imply that Irhoud people were near the line that produced modern humans, while the Sima de los Huesos people were close to the line that produced the Neanderthals.*

Trinkaus, 1995) confirm archaeological evidence that they were technologically inferior to their successors. However, in many details of their anatomy, including, for example, the unique structure of their bony inner ear (Spoor and Zonneveld, 1998), the Neanderthals were not so much primitive as different, and their uniquely derived features make them highly unlikely ancestors for any living people.

The key specimens that document a separate evolutionary trajectory in Africa constitute two groups—an earlier one dated between 300,000 and 100,000 years ago that includes especially the fossils from Florisbad in South Africa (Grün et al., 1996), Singa in Sudan (McDermott et al., 1996), and Jebel Irhoud in Morocco (Hublin, 1993) (Figure 3, left) and a later group dated between 130,000 and 80,000 years ago that embraces especially the fossils from the Klasies River Mouth Caves in South Africa (Rightmire and Deacon, 1991), Dar es Soltan 2 in Morocco (Hublin, 1993), and the Qafzeh and Skhul Caves in Israel (Bar-Yosef and Vandermeersch, 1993) (Figure 4). The Qafzeh and

Skhul fossils are included because associated Ethiopian animal fossils indicate that Africa had expanded ecologically to incorporate its southwest Asian periphery. The African fossils are variously contemporaneous either with the ante-Neanderthals or the classic Neanderthals referred to previously, yet none exhibit any Neanderthal specializations. Instead, the earlier African group anticipates the later group, and the morphology of the later group is modern or near modern.

The great antiquity of modern or near-modern morphology in Africa provides the principal evidence for Out of Africa 2. Moreover, in contrast to the multiregional theory, only Out of Africa 2 is fully compatible with two compelling genetic findings: first, that living humans are so similar genetically that they must share a common ancestor within the past 200,000 years (Harpending and Relethford, 1997; Manderscheid and Rogers, 1996; Relethford, 1995; Stoneking, 1993), and second, that Neanderthals were genetically so different from living humans that the last shared ancestor probably lived 600,000 to 500,000 years ago (Krings et al., 1997). The second finding is based on the spectacular recovery of mitochondrial DNA from the humerus of the original Neanderthal (Feldhofer Cave) fossil, and it

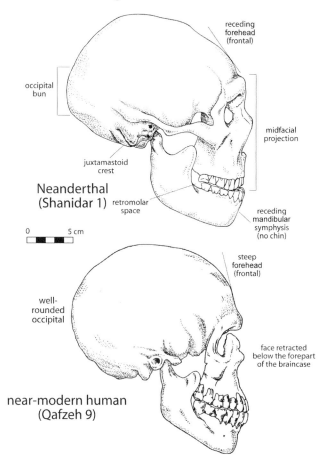

Figure 4. *Skulls of a Neanderthal from Shanidar Cave, Iraq, and of a near modern human from Qafzeh Cave, Israel, emphasizing cranial features that tend to distinguish Neanderthals and modern humans (drawn by Kathryn Cruz-Uribe from photographs). The Qafzeh skull dates from roughly 100,000 years ago. The age of the Shanidar skull is not established, but it is probably somewhat younger.*

archaics. The highly inadequate Far Eastern record cries out for fresh research.

ARCHAEOLOGY AND OUT OF AFRICA 2

A potentially fatal objection to Out of Africa 2 concerns the failure of near modern or modern people to expand immediately after they appeared in Africa, at least 100,000 years ago. Instead, they seem to have been confined to Africa until roughly 50,000 years ago, and it is even possible that they were replaced by Neanderthals on the southwest Asian margin of Africa (in what is now Israel) about 80,000 years ago (Tchernov, 1992). Archaeology offers a partial solution to the problem. The people who inhabited Africa between 100,000 and 50,000 years ago may have been modern or near modern in form, but in behavior they closely resembled the Neanderthals and other archaic humans (Bar-Yosef, 1994; Jelinek, 1994; Klein, 1994; Mellars, 1996). Admittedly, they were superb stone knappers; they often collected naturally occurring iron and manganese compounds that they could have used as pigments; they apparently built fires at will; they buried their dead, at least on occasion; and they routinely acquired large mammals as food. In all these respects and perhaps others they may have been advanced over yet earlier, archaic people. However, in common with earlier people and with their Neanderthal contemporaries, they manufactured a relatively small range of recognizable stone tool types (Figure 5); their artifact assemblages varied remarkably little through time and space (despite notable environmental variation); they obtained stone raw materials overwhelmingly from local (versus far distant) sources (suggesting relatively small home ranges or very simple social networks); they rarely, if ever, utilized bone, ivory, or shell to produce

must be regarded as more tentative than the first, pending the recovery of DNA from other fossil specimens.

The multiregional model cannot be dismissed, but the growing fossil and genetic records far more strongly favor Out of Africa 2. This is particularly true with respect to Europe and western Asia, where fossils and archaeology join to show that modern humans quickly replaced the Neanderthals beginning roughly 50,000 years ago. From a strictly fossil and archaeological perspective, the principal obstacle to Out of Africa 2 is the murkiness—multiregional advocates would say contrariness—of the east Asian evidence. Most relevant Chinese fossils—from Maba, Changyang, Dali, Dingcun, Xujiayao, and Yinkou (Jinniushan) (Wu and Poirier, 1995)—remain poorly described, weakly dated, or both, and the associated archaeological record is too sparse to show whether there was a cultural rupture roughly 50,000 to 40,000 years ago when modern invaders might have appeared. It thus remains possible that modern humans evolved independently in eastern Asia or that modern east Asians originated from gene exchange between invading Africans and resident

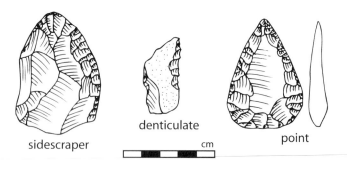

Figure 5. *The principal retouched stone tool types that early modern or near modern Africans and their European Neanderthal contemporaries produced before 50,000 years ago. The most common type is the sidescraper, and it has been subdivided into more than 20 subtypes, based mainly on the shape, number, and position of the retouched edges. However, the subtypes tend to intergrade, and the extent to which their makers distinguished them is highly questionable (Dibble and Rolland, 1992; Mellars, 1996). The number of basic tool types and of readily recognizable subtypes increased significantly after 50,000 to 40,000 years ago, and the increase was associated with dramatically accelerated artifactual variation through time and space.*

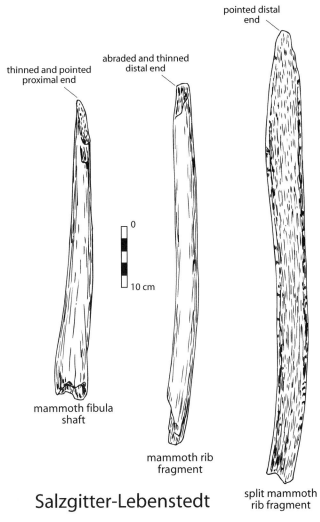

thinned and pointed
proximal end

abraded and thinned
distal end

pointed distal
end

0

10 cm

mammoth fibula
shaft

mammoth rib
fragment

split mammoth
rib fragment

Salzgitter-Lebenstedt

Figure 6. *Three of 28 supposed mammoth bone tools from the Mousterian site of Salzgitter-Lebenstedt, Germany (redrawn after Gaudzinski, 1999). The specimens are among the most persuasive bone artifacts from any Mousterian or Middle Stone Age site, but they were transported by river flow before burial, and this raises the possibility that they were thinned and abraded naturally. Only Upper Paleolithic/Later Stone Age people routinely turned bone and related substances into unequivocal artifacts.*

formal artifacts (Figure 6); they left little or no evidence for structures or for any other formal modification of their campsites (Figure 7); they were relatively ineffectual hunter-gatherers who lacked, for example, the ability to fish; their populations were apparently very sparse, even by historic hunter-gatherer standards (Figure 8); and they left no compelling evidence for art or decoration (Figure 9).

Based on what early near modern Africans did and did not do, it seems reasonable to conclude that they were cognitively human but not cognitively modern in the sense that all living people are. It was only when they became cognitively modern, with the fully modern capacity for culture, that they obtained an adaptive advantage over their archaic Eurasian contemporaries. If Out of Africa 2 is correct, we would expect Africa to provide the oldest secure evidence for art and other indicators of modern mental abilities. In fact, the oldest well-

documented ornaments come from Enkapune Ya Muto Cave in Kenya (Ambrose, 1998a), and the oldest securely dated bone artifacts come from Blombos Cave in South Africa (Henshilwood and Sealy, 1997, 1998). The Enkapune Ya Muto ornaments are ostrich eggshell beads similar to ones that Africans commonly produced after 40,000 years ago, but at Enkapune Ya Muto they antedate 40,000 or even 45,000 years ago. The Blombos bone artifacts include two carefully shaped points and about 20 "awls" that are unquestionably artifactual and that also antedate 40,000 years ago, perhaps by a substantial interval. No comparable artifacts are known in Europe until 40,000 years ago or later, and the Enkapune Ya Muto and Blombos findings thus support and supplement fossil evidence for an African origin of modern humans.

SOME PROBLEMS WITH OUT OF AFRICA 2

Out of Africa 2 is the most plausible and parsimonious explanation of the available fossil and archaeological data, but there are contradictory observations, and these cannot simply be ignored. Some specialists also believe that proponents of Out of Africa 2 have unwittingly imposed their intellectual preconceptions on highly contrary data, and this leads them to reject Out of Africa 2 a priori (Clark, 1997). Carried to its logical extreme, however, this perspective precludes any decision on Out of Africa 2, barring the unlikely development of data collection procedures that do not require advance assumptions or expectations. New intellectual frameworks or paradigms may yet prove helpful, but the aim of this section is to note some problems with Out of Africa 2 that are more evidentiary than epistemological. They are thus issues that could be resolved by fresh research.

What Explains the Relatively Abrupt Appearance of Modern Human Behavior (the Modern Capacity for Culture) 50,000 Years Ago?

The simplest answer is probably that it stemmed from a fortuitous mutation that promoted the fully modern brain. But this argument relies primarily on three circumstantial observations: that natural selection for more effective brains largely drove the earlier phases of human evolution, that increases in brain size and probably also changes in brain organization were associated with the first appearance of stone artifacts roughly 2.5 mya and with the first appearance of handaxes and other well-made bifacial tools about 1.7 to 1.6 mya, and finally, that the relationship between morphological and behavioral change shifted abruptly about 50,000 years ago. Before this time, morphology and behavior appear to have evolved more or less in tandem, very slowly, but after this time morphology remained relatively stable while behavioral (cultural) change accelerated rapidly. What could explain this better than a neural change that promoted the extraordinary modern human ability to innovate? This is not to say that the Neanderthals and their nonmodern contemporaries had apelike brains or that they were as biologically and behaviorally primitive

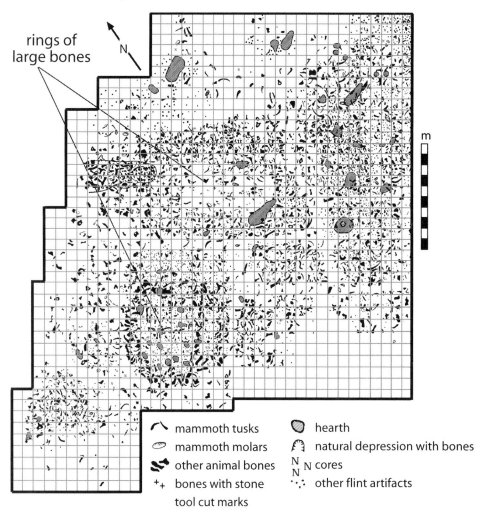

rings of
large bones

N

m

mammoth tusks   hearth

mammoth molars   natural depression with bones

other animal bones   N   N cores

bones with stone
tool cut marks   other flint artifacts

Molodova I, level 4

Figure 7. *Plan of the excavations in Molodova I, level 4, Ukraine (redrawn after Chernysh, 1982, Figure 8). The rings of large bones may mark the foundations of structures that local Middle Paleolithic (Mousterian) people built, but they might also have been created by slope wash. The evidence for "ruins" at other Middle Paleolithic sites is even less compelling. In stark contrast, indisputable structural remnants are common in Upper Paleolithic sites, postdating 50,000 to 40,000 years ago. More effective housing helps to explain how people after 50,000 to 40,000 years ago became the first to colonize the especially harsh environments of northeastern Europe and adjacent Asia (Siberia).*

as yet earlier humans. It is only to suggest that an acknowledged genetic link between morphology and behavior in yet earlier people persisted until the emergence of fully modern ones and that the postulated genetic change 50,000 years ago fostered the uniquely modern ability to adapt to a remarkable range of natural and social circumstances with little or no physiological change.

The central problem with the neural hypothesis is that it is currently untestable from fossils. The connection between behavioral and neural change earlier in human evolution is inferred from conspicuous increases in brain size, but humans virtually everywhere had achieved modern or near modern brain size by 200,000 years ago. Any neural change that occurred 50,000 years ago would thus have been strictly organizational, and fossil skulls so far provide only speculative evidence for brain structure. Neanderthal skulls, for example, differ dramatically in shape from modern ones (Figure 4), but they were as large or larger, and on present evidence it is not clear that the difference in form implies a significant difference in function.

In the circumstances, it might seem equally reasonable to argue that fully modern behavior originated among people who had long had the neural capacity for

it but who expressed their modern potential only after some biologically irrelevant technological or social change (Hayden, 1993; Soffer, 1990). If this is accepted, the origin and spread of modern humans from an African center might be likened to the much later origin and spread of agriculture from a southwest Asian heartland (Bar-Yosef, 1998b). A strictly historical social or technological explanation, however, is more circular than the neural (biological) alternative since it does not explain why social organization or technology changed so suddenly and fundamentally. It also assumes that an innovation analogous to plant or animal domestication triggered the spread of modern humans, when the stimulus appears to have been the far more fundamental development of the modern ability to innovate.

Moreover, unlike the origins of agriculture in southwestern Asia, which may have been a response to radical environmental change during the dramatic Younger Dryas cold snap 11,000 to 10,000 years ago (Bar-Yosef, 1998a; Moore and Hillman, 1992), the modern human diaspora cannot be clearly linked to any specific climatic event. It occurred during a long interval (global oxygen isotope stage 3) when climate often fluctuated between cool and very cool but did not, on present

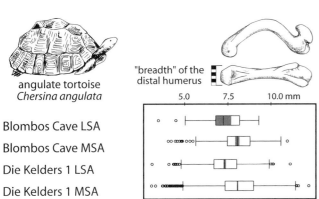

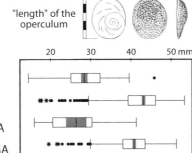

Figure 8. **Top:** *Boxplots summarizing the "breadth" of angulate tortoise distal humeri in the Middle Stone Age (MSA) and Later Stone Age (LSA) deposits of Blombos Cave (Henshilwood and Sealy, 1997) and of Die Kelders Cave 1 (Avery et al., 1997; Schweitzer, 1979).* **Bottom:** *Boxplots summarizing the "length" of Cape turban-shell opercula in the MSA and LSA layers of Blombos Cave and of the Klasies River Mouth Caves (Singer and Wymer, 1982). The Die Kelders MSA deposits do not preserve shells well enough for measurement, while the Klasies River Mouth deposits contain too few tortoise bones for numeric analysis. The key elements in each plot are the vertical line near the middle, which represents the median measurement or 50th percentile, and the open rectangles, which enclose the middle half of the measurements, between the 25th and 75th percentiles. Circles and asterisks indicate extreme values (outliers). The shaded rectangles mark the 95% confidence limits for the medians (Velleman, 1995). When shaded rectangles do not overlap, chance is unlikely to explain the difference between medians. More intense collection by denser human populations with more advanced technology probably explains the significantly smaller size of the LSA tortoises and turban shells. The MSA/LSA interface has been dated to 50,000 to 40,000 years ago, and only LSA people were fully modern in both anatomy and behavior.*

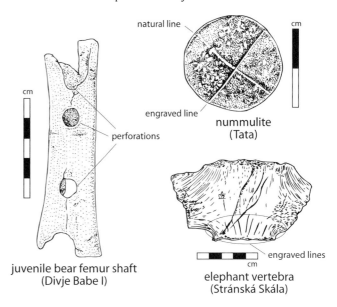

Figure 9. *Representative "art objects" from European Lower and Middle Paleolithic sites (the Tata nummulite and Stránská Skála elephant vertebra were redrawn after Bednarik, 1992; the Divje Babe bone "flute" was drawn from a photograph in Turk et al., 1997). Art objects are very rare before the Upper Paleolithic, and they are never as persuasively artistic as innumerable Upper Paleolithic examples. In many cases, they are not even convincingly artifactual. The perforations on the Divje Babe flute, for example, closely resemble holes that carnivore biting produces, and there is nothing in their size or morphology that requires human action (d'Errico et al., 1998a). Abrasion against sharp objects in the ground could account for the engraved lines on the Tata nummulite (a silicified marine invertebrate fossil) and on the Stránská Skála elephant vertebra. A natural origin is particularly likely at Stránská Skála, since the site has yet to provide unambiguous stone artifacts (Roebroeks, 1996).*

ago, they did not provoke a revolutionary cultural response. The lack of a response underscores artifactual evidence that people before 50,000 years ago were inherently less able to innovate than their fully modern successors.

In sum, then, it is certainly more economical to attribute the origin of modern human behavior to a selectively advantageous neural change such as those that must partly underlie earlier behavioral advances. Arguably the last key neural change promoted the modern capacity for rapidly spoken phonemic speech, that is, for "a fully vocal language, phonemicized, syntactical, and infinitely open and productive" (Milo and Quiatt, 1994:321). If this is agreed, then Neanderthals may always have been precluded from fully modern behavior because their vocal tracts could not produce a sufficient range of sounds (Lieberman et al., 1992). However, the shortcomings of the Neanderthal vocal apparatus are disputed (Arensburg et al., 1990; DeGusta et al., 1999; Houghton, 1993; Kay et al., 1998), and the suggestion that fully modern behavior stemmed from a linguistic advance depends primarily on the intimate bond between culture and language historically. Among living humans, language is vital not only for communication, but also for abstract modeling and for posing the kind of "what if" questions that enable the uniquely modern ability to innovate

evidence, include a specific event near 50,000 years ago that stands out in the manner of the Younger Dryas (van Andel and Tzedakis, 1996). Even if such an event is eventually detected, it will be difficult to explain why it prompted such a fundamental behavioral response, when yet earlier, equally or even more radical climatic spikes did not. The most notable earlier spike was the remarkable millennium-long bout of intense cold that followed the Mt. Toba volcanic supereruption in Sumatra 71,000 to 70,000 years ago (Ambrose, 1998b). The Mt. Toba eruption and its aftermath are obviously too old to explain the modern human diaspora, but they are noteworthy precisely because like other abrupt episodes of environmental change before 50,000 years

(Bickerton, 1990). It is above all a quantum advance in the ability to innovate that distinguishes the advent of fully modern humans.

Were Neanderthals Fundamentally Incapable of Fully Modern Behavior?

As outlined here, Out of Africa 2 postulates that the Neanderthals were replaced because they could not compete culturally with their modern human successors. The argument is bolstered over most of Europe by the relatively abrupt nature of the replacement. The earliest fully modern Europeans are often characterized popularly as Cro-Magnons, and Cro-Magnon bones are commonly associated with Upper Paleolithic artifacts. Neanderthal bones are generally found with Middle Paleolithic (or Mousterian) artifacts. At most sites, Cro-Magnon/Upper Paleolithic occupations overlie Neanderthal/Middle Paleolithic layers with no evidence for a major break in time or for any transition between the two, suggesting that the replacement took only decades, or at most centuries. However, there is the occasional discovery of artifact assemblages that constitute a blend of Neanderthal/Middle Paleolithic and Cro-Magnon/Upper Paleolithic artifact types. The most compelling examples come from western France and northern Spain, where they have been assigned to the Châtelperronian industry (Harrold, 1989). The exact age of the Châtelperronian remains to be established, but it probably existed for a few centuries or perhaps a millennium about 40,000 years ago; human remains from La Roche á Pierrot rockshelter, Saint-Césaire (Lévêque et al., 1993), and the Grotte du Renne, Arcy-sur-Cure (Hublin et al., 1996), indicate that the makers were Neanderthals.

At Arcy, the Neanderthals not only produced a mix of typical Middle and Upper Paleolithic stone artifacts, but they also manufactured typical Upper Paleolithic bone tools and personal ornaments (Farizy, 1990, 1994; Leroi-Gourhan, 1965). The Châtelperronian layers provided 142 bone artifacts, including some that appear decorated, and 36 animal teeth and pieces of ivory, bone, or shell that are pierced or grooved, presumably for hanging as beads or pendants (Bahn, 1998; D'Errico et al., 1998b). Nearly identical pierced teeth also have been found in the Châtelperronian layers of Quinçay Cave, France (Granger and Lévêque, 1997; White, 1998). In addition to manufacturing bone tools and ornaments, the Arcy people also modified their living space in a characteristically Upper Paleolithic fashion, and Arcy contains the least ambiguous structural "ruin" of any site that antedates the Upper Paleolithic in the narrow sense. One can argue that the Châtelperronian Neanderthals borrowed Upper Paleolithic cultural traits from fully Upper Paleolithic (Aurignacian) neighbors whose ultimate origin was in Africa. But even if this is accepted, it begs one fundamental question: If Upper Paleolithic culture was clearly superior and the Neanderthals could imitate it (that is, they were not biologically impeded from behaving in an Upper Paleolithic way), why didn't they acculturate more widely, with the result that they or their genes would

have persisted much more conspicuously into Upper Paleolithic times (after 40,000 to 35,000 years ago)? There is no compelling answer, and, of all the problems that beset "Out of Africa 2," the Châtelperronian is perhaps the most serious, since it may not be resolved simply by fresh discoveries and dates.

Did Neanderthals Manage to Survive in Parts of Europe for Thousands of Years after Modern People Arrived?

If so, this would suggest that they were behaviorally more competitive than I propose here, and it would enhance the likelihood of cultural and genetic exchange. At the moment, the most persuasive case comes from south of the Ebro and Tagus Rivers in southern Spain and Portugal (d'Errico et al., 1998b; Hublin et al., 1995; Straus, 1997), where it is based partly on dates near 30,000 years ago for layers with Mousterian artifacts and Neanderthal remains and partly on the absence of the basal Aurignacian early Upper Paleolithic industry. In the abrupt replacement model I favor, the basal Aurignacian is the cultural manifestation of modern human invaders in central and western Europe (Figure 10), and dates on early Aurignacian layers at Willendorf II in Austria (Damblon et al., 1996); Geissenklösterle Cave in southern Germany (Richter et al., 2000); Trou Magrite in Belgium (Otte and Straus, 1995); and El Castillo, L'Arbreda, Romaní, and Reclau Viver in northern Spain (Bischoff et al., 1989, 1994; Straus, 1997) place the early Aurignacian near 40,000 years ago in both central and western Europe. Early Aurignacian human remains are fragmentary and scarce, but where they are known, mainly in France, they are clearly modern (Gambier, 1989, 1997).

The possibility that Neanderthals persisted in southern Spain and Portugal to 30,000 years ago is intriguing, but it is founded mainly on a small number of radiocarbon determinations from only five or six sites. None are accelerator mass spectrometry (AMS) dates on charcoal such as those that place the Aurignacian in northern Spain at or shortly after 40,000 years ago, and there are also no corroborative luminescence or uranium-series dates on appropriate materials. In this circumstance, it remains possible that the available dates are minima only and that the Mousterian actually ended throughout Spain and Portugal by 40,000 years ago. The absence of the basal Aurignacian in the south and west may largely reflect adverse climatic conditions that restricted human occupation from 40,000 years or before until 30,000 years ago or later. Especially extreme aridity may account for a gap in nearby northwestern Africa between Aterian/Mousterian occupations that antedate 40,000 years ago and Upper Paleolithic (Iberomaurusian) occupations dated to 22,000 to 21,000 years ago (Camps, 1975; Close and Wendorf, 1990; Cremaschi et al., 1998; Wendorf, 1992). A similar hiatus also occurs at similar latitudes in southern Africa, where it separates Middle Stone Age occupations antedating 40,000 years ago from Later Stone Age layers postdating 22,000 years ago (Deacon and Thackeray, 1984; Klein, 1994), and widespread, recurrent aridity is

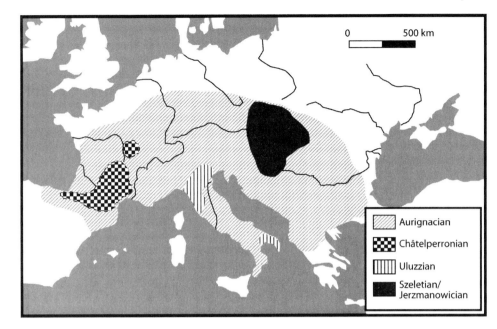

Figure 10. *The distribution of the Aurignacian, Châtelperronian, Uluzzian, and Szeletian/ Jerzmanowician Industries in Europe (redrawn after Mellars, 1993, Figure 1). The Châtelperronian, Uluzzian, and Szeletian/ Jerzmanowician are sometimes known as "transitional" industries because they combine elements of the Middle and Upper Paleolithic. Arguably, they resulted from contact between resident Middle Paleolithic people (Neanderthals) and invading Upper Paleolithic Aurignacians (Cro-Magnons).*

again a likely explanation. In southern Africa, a failure to appreciate the limitations of radiocarbon dating initially masked the hiatus and led investigators to miscorrelate the local Middle Stone Age with the European Upper Paleolithic (Vogel and Beaumont, 1972).

Dating aside, sedimentological studies could reveal the presence or absence of relevant occupational discontinuities in southern Spanish or Portuguese sites. Thus, of all the issues that may confound "Out of Africa 2," this particular one may be especially amenable to empirical resolution.

Why Weren't the Earliest Modern Humans as Heavily Built as the Neanderthals?

Neanderthal limb bones are remarkably robust, with very conspicuous muscle markings, implying that Neanderthals of both sexes were exceptionally powerful people. In spite of this, they often broke their bones, they commonly developed arthritis or other senile pathologies in their 20s or 30s, and they seldom survived beyond age 40 (Berger and Trinkaus, 1995; Brennan, 1991; Trinkaus, 1995; Trinkaus and Shipman, 1993a). The sum of the data suggests that they led extraordinarily stressful lives. In contrast, their fully modern, Cro-Magnon successors were much less heavily built, they broke their bones much less often, and their maximum life expectancy was significantly greater. Since Neanderthals were culturally (artifactually) much less sophisticated, a reasonable explanation for the difference is that Neanderthals often accomplished physically what later people accomplished culturally (technologically).

The downside of Neanderthal robusticity was that it required a great deal of energy to sustain, and it is presumably this that favored reduced robusticity in modern humans—the same number of calories could now support larger populations, and larger populations are a measure of evolutionary success. However, the most

completely known early modern contemporaries of the Neanderthals, from Qafzeh Cave in Israel, were much less heavily built than the Neanderthals, even though they made similar, relatively unsophisticated artifacts (Bar-Yosef and Vandermeersch, 1993; Trinkaus, 1992; Trinkaus and Shipman, 1993b). When the smaller body mass of the Qafzeh people is considered, they may have equaled the Neanderthals in the robusticity of their legs, but their arms were significantly less powerful (Trinkaus et al., 1998). To the extent that this casts doubt on the adaptive superiority of fully modern technology, it presents a problem for the version of Out of Africa 2 preferred here.

What Kind of People First Occupied the Americas and Australasia?

A probable corollary of Out of Africa 2 is that they were fully modern. With regard to the Americas, this follows from the likelihood that first entry was across a land bridge that linked northeastern Asia to Alaska during glacial periods (times of lowered sea level) and from archaeological evidence that northeastern Asia was itself first colonized only after 35,000 years ago (Goebel, 1995; Kuzmin and Orlova, 1998), when fully modern humans developed the housing, clothing, and other cultural wherewithal to survive in very harsh, continental climates. The colonization of the Americas by fully modern humans is fully consistent with the archaeology of North and South America, neither of which was indisputably occupied before the closing phases of the last glaciation, after 14,000 years ago (Haynes, 1992; Hoffecker et al., 1993; Meltzer, 1995). At least south of Alaska, human occupation before this time was probably precluded by an ice sheet that extended more or less continuously across Canada. In short, the American record presents no problem for Out of Africa 2.

The same may not be true for Australasia, (Australia, New Guinea, and Tasmania, which comprised a single landmass during glacial intervals), where the argument for an initial colonization by fully modern humans follows from the need to cross 80 to 100 km of open water, the minimum distance separating Australasia from southeastern Asia, even during periods of lowered sea level. It would be hard to deny an essentially modern capacity for culture to people who could produce sufficiently seaworthy watercraft. Until recently, it appeared that the first Australasians were, in fact, fully modern people who arrived between 40,000 and 30,000 years ago, bringing with them complex burial practices, fishing technology, art, and probably other modern behavioral markers (Jones, 1992). An entry at about 40,000 years ago could itself be regarded as an indicator of the modern human ability to innovate, this time with respect to water transport.

However, thermoluminescence (TL) and optically stimulated luminescence (OSL) readings on unburnt quartz sands enclosing and overlying artifacts at the Malakunanja II and Nauwalabila I sites in northern Australia now suggest that people colonized Australasia as much as 60,000 years ago (Roberts et al., 1994). The excavators have especially stressed the Nauwalabila I dates, since a layer dated by OSL to approximately 53,000 years ago contains ground hematite fragments that could have been used for painting. If so, the first Australians were behaviorally advanced over their European and African contemporaries for whom no such ancient art is known. On the other hand, the hematite might have been used for hide processing or some equally mundane purpose, and similar hematite fragments are common in Middle Paleolithic/Neanderthal sites, with no other evidence for art (Bordes, 1952; Combier, 1988). They also occur without apparent art at many (Middle Stone Age) sites antedating 50,000 years ago in southern Africa (Thackeray, 1992). Modified hematite fragments are actually more abundant in such sites than they are in much younger (Later Stone Age) ones, including some whose occupants surely painted on nearby rock faces.

For proponents of Out of Africa 2, then, the problem is not that 60,000 year old Australian dates need imply an especially early, non-African emergence of art, but that they raise two other fundamental questions. Is it possible that modern humans left Africa at least twice (Lahr and Foley, 1994), once in a migration roughly 60,000 years ago to southeastern Asia and Australasia and again after 50,000 years ago in a migration to western Asia and Europe? And assuming that two separate migrations occurred, what factors permitted modern humans to reach the far east (Australasia) 20,000 years before they reached the far west (France and Spain)? In this context it is important to note that the Middle Paleolithic/Upper Paleolithic interface in the far west cannot be much older than 40,000 years. This estimate is based not on ^{14}C dating, which provides only minimal ages in the 40,000 years range, but on TL dating at Le Moustier, France (Valladas et al., 1986) and on Uranium-series dates at Abric Romaní, Spain (Bischoff et al., 1988, 1994), which show that the Middle Paleolithic (Mousterian) survived in western Europe until roughly 40,000 years ago.

The answer to the conundrum may be that the Malakunanja and Nauwalabila artifacts were worked into older sands by bioturbation and trampling and that they are actually less than 40,000 years old (O'Connell and Allen, 1998). Human absence before 40,000 years ago may be implied by the failure of any Australasian archaeological site to provide a radiocarbon date of more than 40,000 years (O'Connell and Allen, 1998). Contamination by recent carbon could be responsible in many instances, but dates in excess of 40,000 years have been obtained at African and Eurasian sites, and they are also available at Australasian geologic localities. In this light, the Makalunanja and Nauwalabila results must be replicated elsewhere in Australasia before they present a serious obstacle to Out of Africa 2.

Was Out of Africa 2 Encouraged by a Significant Advance in Human Ability to Hunt and Gather 50,000 to 40,000 Years Ago?

The best evidence for such an advance comes from southern Africa, where bones from fish, airborne birds, and dangerous terrestrial mammals are significantly more abundant in Later Stone Age sites than in preceding Middle Stone Age ones (Klein, 1994). However, the pertinent Middle Stone Age sites are all older than 60,000 years ago, and the Later Stone Age sites are younger than 20,000 years ago. Sites dating from the intervening 40,000 years are rare, probably because increased aridity in southern Africa during the middle of the last glaciation drastically reduced plant and animal resources (Deacon and Thackeray, 1984). There is the further problem that sea level fell during the same interval and most sites that might reveal a sharp increase in fishing and fowling 50,000 to 40,000 years ago are probably located on the now-drowned continental shelf. Blombos Cave mentioned previously for its early bone artifacts may be an important exception, but its dating is problematic as discussed later. In the meanwhile, the case that economic advances promoted Out of Africa 2 is obviously incomplete.

Is It Really True That Modern Behavioral Markers Appeared Widely Only about 50,000 to 40,000 Years Ago?

With regard to art, for example, virtually all specialists agree that it becomes commonplace only after this time and that earlier examples are both rare and crude. But authorities disagree sharply on what this combination of rarity and simplicity implies. To some—for example, Bednarik (1992), Hayden (1993), and Marshack (1991)—it means that modern cognitive abilities were present but were weakly expressed before 50,000 years ago, whereas to others—for example, Chase and Dibble (1992, 1987), Davidson and Noble (1989), Mellars (1998), and me—it suggests that the fully modern capacity for culture may have appeared only about this time.

Some of the very rare art objects that antedate 50,000 years ago are probably younger intrusions that even the most careful excavation cannot detect, while others are probably the result of human or natural actions that will inevitably, on rare occasions, mimic crude human attempts at art. In this regard, credible claims for art or other modern human behavioral markers before 50,000 years ago must involve relatively large numbers of highly patterned objects from well-documented contexts. Using this criterion, perhaps the most serious obstacle to the Out of Africa scenario favored here is the discovery of unequivocal bone artifacts and accompanying evidence for fishing at the Katanda sites in the Democratic Republic of the Congo (Brooks et al., 1995; Yellen, 1998; Yellen et al., 1995) and at Blombos Cave in South Africa (Henshilwood, 1998; Henshilwood and Sealy, 1997). At Katanda, electron spin resonance (ESR) dates on associated hippopotamus teeth and TL dates on covering sands suggest an age between 155,000 and 90,000 years ago. At Blombos Cave, ESR, TL, and OSL suggest that the bone artifacts may be 100,000 years old. If the age estimates at both sites are valid, they imply that modern behavioral traits and modern morphology may have arisen together, at or before 100,000 years ago, and we will be forced to find a nonbehavioral explanation for why modern or near modern humans were confined to Africa until roughly 50,000 years ago. We also will have the difficult task of explaining why even larger, well-excavated artifact and bone assemblages from apparently contemporaneous African sites completely lack evidence either for formal bone working or for fishing.

The Katanda and Blombos dates illustrate a recurrent, nearly ubiquitous problem in the archaeology of modern human origins—the difficulty of obtaining reliable dates in the crucial interval between 200,000 years and 50,000 to 40,000 years ago. The most widely used dating methods at present are ESR and the luminescence methods (TL and OSL), as they have been applied at Katanda and Blombos. Both ESR and luminescence dating depend on the observation that irradiation by naturally occurring uranium, thorium, and radiopotassium causes electrons to accumulate in defects within crystalline substances. The aggregate number of trapped electrons can be measured, and the rate at which they accumulated can be estimated from the level of background radioactivity to which a substance was exposed. The number of trapped electrons divided by their annual accumulation rate (the annual radiation dose) then estimates the last time the crystal traps were empty. The luminescence methods are applied primarily to objects where heat or light emptied (or zeroed) the traps before burial, whereas ESR is applied mainly to dental enamel, where formation (precipitation during life) produced initially empty traps. The time range covered by the luminescence methods and ESR depends on the time it takes for traps to fill (or saturate) so that no more electrons can be added. This varies from substance to substance and from site to site, but in general the methods are applicable to materials that are between a few thousand and a few hundred thousand years old (Schwarcz and Grün, 1993).

ESR and the luminescence methods are more difficult to apply than ^{14}C, because they depend far more on site-specific variables, of which the annual radiation dose is the most important. In standard application, ESR and luminescence dating assume that the annual dose has been constant, but at any given spot the dose could have varied significantly through time, because ground water percolation subtracted (leached) or added uranium, because changes in soil moisture content variably buffered objects from irradiation, or because the texture of the surrounding deposit changed. Fine-grained deposits (e.g., unconsolidated sand) block irradiation less than lumpier ones (e.g., undecomposed sandstone blocks.) Dose rate estimation can be especially complicated for ESR, since teeth tend to adsorb uranium after burial, and the rate of adsorption can vary through time or across a site. Mistaken dose rate estimates will obviously produce erroneous dates, and luminescence dating also must confront the possibility that the target sands or burnt stones were incompletely zeroed before burial (that is, that bleaching or heating failed to release all trapped electrons.) Incomplete zeroing inevitably furnishes dates that are "too old".

Mistaken dose rate estimation may largely explain inconsistencies between paired ESR and luminescence dates in Israel (Bar-Yosef, 1998a). The methods agree on the roughly 100,000 year age of the Qafzeh-Skhul near modern people, and the luminescence dates at Qafzeh Cave seem particularly secure, because they have been replicated repeatedly (Mercier and Valladas, 1994). However, luminescence dates on older Israeli deposits tend to be significantly greater than their ESR counterparts, and the discrepancy grows with age. Incomplete zeroing probably affected the luminescence dating of sands at Katanda (Feathers, 1996), and their true age may be closer to 12,000 years than to 90,000 years ago or more. Most of the Katanda bone artifacts are finely crafted barbed points like those that usually postdate 12,000 years ago elsewhere in Africa. The associated stone artifacts at Katanda are insufficiently diagnostic for dating, and the associated animal bones tend to be much more abraded than the points. This may mean that most of the bones were particles in a gravel bar on which the points were subsequently dropped. Direct ^{14}C dating of the barbed points could perhaps settle the question.

Radiocarbon dating at Blombos confirms that the bone artifacts are older than 40,000 years; the issue, then, is whether they are truly 100,000 years old, which would seriously undermine the Out of Africa scenario offered here, or whether they are between 50,000 and 40,000 years old, which would strongly support it. The stone artifacts that accompany the bone artifacts at Blombos include numerous finely made Still Bay bifacial points, whose degree of standardization could be regarded as an additional indicator of fully modern behavior. The underlying levels, which lack bone artifacts and Still Bay points, have provided (Middle Stone Age) artifacts and faunal remains like those that have been dated to 75,000 to 65,000 years ago by ESR, TL, and OSL at nearby Die Kelders Cave 1 (Avery et al., 1997; Feathers and Bush, 2000). The Die Kelders dating suggests that the Blombos bone artifacts may be closer to 50,000 than to 100,000 years old, but the inconsistency can be resolved only with fresh age estimates from the widest possible range of methods and laboratories. The excavator of Blombos is vigorously seeking fresh dates now.

CONCLUSION

It was only in the late 1980s and 1990s that the evidence of fossils, dates, and genetics gelled to document the European roots of the Neanderthals and the recent African origin of modern humans. However, for a century or more, the European fossil and archaeological records have suggested that fully modern Cro-Magnon immigrants replaced the resident Neanderthals. Evidence that Cro-Magnon success was grounded in radically different behavior became available especially early. By the 1890s, French archaeologists had already outlined the succession of distinct Upper Paleolithic industries that we still accept today, but they spoke mainly of an undifferentiated and monotonous Mousterian (Oakley, 1964). For decades afterwards, to the extent that the Mousterian was subdivided, it was mostly between variants of prepared core (Levallois) and nonprepared cores. The great French archaeologist, François Bordes sought a finer subdivision, based on interassemblage differences in the frequencies of 62 carefully defined artifact types (Bordes, 1968). Many of his types probably represent stages in a manufacturing or use continuum, however (Dibble and Rolland, 1992), and the boundaries between his Mousterian variants blurred as his typology became more widely applied (Bordes, 1981; Freeman, 1980).

In contrast, discrete, uncontested Upper Paleolithic artifact types and assemblage variants continue to multiply, and the sum of more than a century of research thus implies that the Mousterian represents a fundamentally different behavioral system. In every detectable archaeological respect, this system is far harder to distinguish from the Lower Paleolithic that preceded it than from the Upper Paleolithic that followed, and only the Upper Paleolithic material record unequivocally anticipates

the record of many historically recorded hunter-gatherers. Since the European Mousterians were Neanderthals, their Upper Paleolithic successors were anatomically modern, and modern morphology appeared earlier in Africa than in Europe, it surely follows that the Neanderthals were replaced by modern African invaders. Only the precise nature and rapidity of the replacement remain debatable.

The case for a similar replacement of nonmodern east Asians is much less secure, mainly because the east Asian fossil and archaeological records remain sparse and poorly dated. Even in Europe, where the record is far denser, not all the evidence lines up squarely behind replacement, and it probably never will, if only because the fossil and archaeological records are inherently noisy. Some stratigraphic mixups are inevitable, and even the most reliable dating techniques sometimes provide erroneous results. The advantage in Europe is that the data are sufficient to separate noise from signal, and it is the strength of the signal that I have emphasized here.

This is not to say that there are no problems to resolve. We desperately need fresh research not only in eastern Asia, but also in Africa, where the number of early anatomically modern fossils remains frustratingly small and the archaeological evidence for an especially early shift to fully modern behavior is still meager. Site discovery, excavation, and analysis do not proceed quickly, and progress in paleoanthropology depends far more on serendipity than it does in the experimental sciences. Additional fossil and archaeological evidence may thus accumulate slowly, in fits and starts, but the need for more should not be allowed to obscure the very strong empirical base that now underpins the Out of Africa hypothesis.

ACKNOWLEDGMENTS

Kathryn Cruz-Uribe kindly helped with the illustrations and T. D. Price provided thoughtful criticisms of a draft.

REFERENCES

Ambrose, S. H., 1998a, Chronology of the Later Stone Age and Food Production in East Africa. *Journal of Archaeological Science* 25:377–392.

Ambrose, S. H., 1998b, Late Pleistocene Human Population Bottlenecks, Volcanic Winter, and Differentiation of Modern Humans. *Journal of Human Evolution* 34:623–651.

Arensburg, B., Schepartz, L. A., Tillier, A. M., Vandermeersch, B., and Rak, Y., 1990, Reappraisal of the Anatomical Basis for Speech in Middle Palaeolithic Hominids. *American Journal of Physical Anthropology* 83:137–146.

Arsuaga, J. L., Martínez, I., Gracia, A., and Lorenzo, C., 1997, The Sima de los Huesos Crania (Sierra de Atapuerca, Spain): A Comparative Study. *Journal of Human Evolution* 33:219–281.

Avery, G., Cruz-Uribe, K., Goldberg, P., Grine, F. E., Klein, R. G., Lenardi, M. J., Marean, C. W., Rink, W. J., Schwarz, H. P., Thackeray, A. I., and Wilson, M. L., 1997, The 1992–1993 Excavations at the Die Kelders Middle and Later Stone Age Cave Site, South Africa. *Journal of Field Archaeology* 24:263–291.

Bahn, P., 1998, Archaeology: Neanderthals Emancipated. *Nature* 394:719–721.

Bar-Yosef, O., 1994, The Contributions of Southwest Asia to the Study of the Origin of Modern Humans. In *Origins of Anatomically*

Modern Humans, edited by M. H. Nitecki, and D. V. Nitecki, pp. 23–66. Plenum, New York.

Bar-Yosef, O., 1998a, The Chronology of the Middle Paleolithic of the Levant. In *Neandertals and Modern Humans in Western Asia*, edited by T. Akazawa, K. Aoki, and O. Bar-Yosef, pp. 39–56. Plenum Press, New York.

Bar-Yosef, O., 1998b, On the Nature of Transitions: The Middle to Upper Palaeolithic and the Neolithic Revolution. *Cambridge Archaeological Journal* 8:141–163.

Bar-Yosef, O. and Vandermeersch, B., 1993, Modern Humans in the Levant. *Scientific American* April 1993:94–100.

Bednarik, R. G., 1992, Palaeoart and Archaeological Myths. *Cambridge Archaeological Journal* 2:27–42.

Berger, T. D. and Trinkaus, E., 1995, Patterns of Trauma Among the Neandertals. *Journal of Archaeological Science* 22:841–852.

Bickerton, D., 1990, *Language and Species*. University of Chicago Press, Chicago.

Bischoff, J. L., Julia, R., and Mora, R., 1988, Uranium-Series Dating of the Mousterian Occupation at Abric Romaní, Spain. *Nature* 332:668–670.

Bischoff, J. L., Ludwig, K., Garcia, J. F., Carbonell, E., Vaquero, M., Stafford, T. W. J., and Jull, A. J. T., 1994, Dating of the Basal

Aurignacian Sandwich at Abric Romaní (Catalunya, Spain) by Radiocarbon and Uranium-Series. *Journal of Archaeological Science* 21:541–551.

Bischoff, J. L., Soler, N., Marot, J., and Julia, R., 1989, Abrupt Mousterian/Aurignacian Boundary at c. 40 ka bp: Accelerator [14]C Dates from L'Arbreda Cave (Catalunya, Spain). *Journal of Archaeological Science* 16:563–576.

Bordes, F. H., 1952, Sur l'Usage Probable de la Peinture Corporelle dans Certaines Moustériennes. *Bulletin de la Société Préhistorique Française* 49:169–171.

Bordes, F. H., 1968, *The Old Stone Age*. McGraw-Hill, New York.

Bordes, F. H., 1981, Vingt-Cinq ans Après: Le Complexe Moustérien Révisité. *Bulletin de la Société Préhistorique Française* 78:77–87.

Bräuer, G., 1992, Africa's Place in the Evolution of *Homo sapiens*. In *Continuity or Replacement: Controversies in* Homo sapiens *Evolution*, edited by G. Bräuer, and F. H. Smith, pp. 83–98. A. A. Balkema, Rotterdam.

Brennan, M. U., 1991, *Health and Disease in the Middle and Upper Paleolithic of Southwestern France: A Bioarchaeological Study*, Ph.D. dissertation, New York University, New York.

Brooks, A. S., Helgren, D. M., Cramer, J. S., Franklin, A., Hornyak, W., Keating, J. M., Klein, R. G., Rink, W. J., Schwarcz, H. P., Leith Smith, J. N., Stewart, K., Todd, N. E., Verniers, J., and Yellen, J. E., 1995, Dating and Context of Three Middle Stone Age Sites with Bone Points in the Upper Semliki Valley, Zaire. *Science* 268:548–553.

Camps, G., 1975, The Prehistoric Cultures of North Africa: Radiocarbon Chronology. In *Problems in Prehistory: North Africa and the Levant*, edited by F. Wendorf and A. E. Marks, pp. 181–192. Southern Methodist University Press, Dallas.

Chase, P. G. and Dibble, H. L., 1987, Middle Paleolithic Symbolism: A Review of Current Evidence and Interpretations. *Journal of Anthropological Archaeology* 6:263–296.

Chase, P. and Dibble, H. L., 1992, Scientific Archaeology and the Origins of Symbolism: A Review of Current Evidence and Interpretations. *Cambridge Archaeological Journal* 2:43–51.

Chernysh, A. P., 1982, *Molodova I: A Unique Mousterian Settlement on the Middle Dnestr (in Russian)*. Nauka, Moscow.

Clark, G. A., 1997, The Middle-Upper Paleolithic Transition in Europe: An American Perspective. *Norwegian Archaeological Review* 30:25–53.

Close, A. E. and Wendorf, F., 1990, North Africa at 18,000 B.P. In *The World at 18,000 B.P.*, edited by C. Gamble, and O. Soffer, pp. 41–57. Unwin Hyman, London.

Combier, J., 1988, Témoins Moustériens d'Activités Volontaires. In *De Néandertal à Cro-Magnon*, edited by J.-B. Roy, and A.-S. LeClerc, pp. 69–72. Musée de Préhistoire de l'Ile de France, Nemours.

Cremaschi, M., Di Lernia, S., and Garcea, E. A. A., 1998, Some Insights on the Aterian in the Libyan Sahara: Chronology, Environment, and Archaeology. *African Archaeological Review* 15:261–286.

Damblon, F., Haesaerts, P., and van der Pflict, J., 1996, New Datings and Considerations on the Chronology of Upper Palaeolithic Sites in the Great Eurasiatic Plain. *Préhistoire Européene* 9:177–231.

Davidson, I. and Noble, W., 1989, The Archaeology of Perception: Traces of Depiction and Language. *Current Anthropology* 30:125–155.

Deacon, H. J. and Thackeray, J. F., 1984, Late Pleistocene Environmental Changes and Implications for the Archaeological Record in Southern Africa. In *Late Cainozoic Palaeoclimates of the Southern Hemisphere*, edited by J. C. Vogel, pp. 375–390. A. A. Balkema, Rotterdam.

Dean, D., Hublin, J.-J., Ziegler, R., and Holloway, R., 1994, The Middle Pleistocene Pre-Neanderthal Partial Skull from Reilingen (Germany). *American Journal of Physical Anthropology Supplement* 18:77.

DeGusta, D., Gilbert, W. H., and Turner, S. P., 1999, Hypoglossal Canal Size and Hominid Speech. *Proceedings of the National Academy of Sciences* of the USA 96:1800–1804.

d'Errico, F., Villa, P., Pinto Llona, A. C., and Ruiz Idarraga, R., 1998a, A Middle Palaeolithic Origin of Music? Using Cave-Bear Bone Accumulations to Assess the Divje Babe I Bone "Flute." *Antiquity* 72:65–79.

d'Errico, F., Zilhão, J., Julien, M., Baffier, D., and Pelegrin, J., 1998b, Neandertal Acculturation in Western Europe? A Critical Review of the Evidence and Its Interpretation. *Current Anthropology* 39:S1–S44.

Dibble, H. L. and Rolland, N., 1992, On Assemblage Variability in the Middle Paleolithic of Western Europe: History, Perspectives, and a New Synthesis. In *The Middle Paleolithic: Adaptation, Behavior, and Variability*, edited by H. L. Dibble and P. A. Mellars, pp. 1–28. Monograph 72. University of Pennsylvania Museum, Philadelphia.

Eldredge, N. and Gould, S. J., 1972, Punctuated Equilibrium: An Alternative to Phyletic Gradualism. In *Models in Paleobiology*, edited by T. Schopf, pp. 82–115. W. H. Freeman, San Francisco.

Farizy, C., 1990, The Transition from Middle to Upper Palaeolithic at Arcy-sur-Cure (Yonne, France): Technological, Economic and Social Aspects. In *The Emergence of Modern Humans: An Archaeological Perspective*, edited by P. Mellars, pp. 303–326. Cornell University Press, Ithaca, NY.

Farizy, C., 1994, Behavioral and Cultural Changes at the Middle to Upper Paleolithic Transition in Western Europe. In *Origins of Anatomically Modern Humans*, edited by M. H. Nitecki and D. V. Nitecki, pp. 93–100. Plenum, New York.

Feathers, J. K. 1996, Luminescence Dating and Modern Human Origins. *Evolutionary Anthropology* 5:25–36.

Feathers, J. K. and Bush, D. A., 2000, Luminescence Dating of Middle Stone Age Deposits at Die Kelders. *Journal of Human Evolution* 38:91–119.

Frayer, D. W., Wolpoff, M. H., Thorne, A. G., Smith, F. H., and Pope, G. G., 1993, Theories of Modern Human Origins: The Paleontological Test. *American Anthropologist* 95:14–50.

Freeman, L. G., 1980, Occupaciones Musterienses. In *El yacimiento de la Cueva de "El Pendo" (Excavaciones 1953–57)*, edited by J. González-Echegaray, pp. 29–74. Consejo Superior de Investigaciones Científicas, Madrid.

Gambier, D., 1989, Fossil Hominids from the Early Upper Paleolithic (Aurignacian) of France. In *The Human Revolution: Behavioural and Biological Perspectives on the Origins of Modern Humans*, edited by P. Mellars and C. Stringer, pp. 194–211. Edinburgh University Press, Edinburgh.

Gambier, D., 1997, Modern Humans at the Beginning of the Upper Paleolithic in France. In *Conceptual Issues in Modern Human Origins Research*, edited by G. A. Clark and C. M. Willermet, pp. 117–131. Aldine de Gruyter, New York.

Gaudzinski, S., 1999, Middle Palaeolithic Bone Tools from the Open-Air Site Salzgitter-Lebenstedt (Germany). *Journal of Archaeological Science* 26:125–141.

Goebel, T., 1995, The Record of Human Occupation of the Russian Subarctic and Arctic. *Byrd Polar Research Center Miscellaneous Series* M-335:41–46.

Granger, J.-M. and Lévêque, F., 1997, Parure Castelperronienne et Aurignacienne: Étude de Trois Séries Inédites de Dents Percées et Comparaisons. *Comptes Rendus de l'Académie des Sciences, Paris, Science de la Terre et des Planètes* 325:537–533.

Grün, R., Brink, J. S., Spooner, N. A., Taylor, L., Stringer, C. B., Franciscus, R. G., and Murray, A. S., 1996, Direct Dating of Florisbad Hominid. *Nature* 382:500–501.

Grün, R. and Stringer, C. B., 1991, Electron Spin Resonance Dating and the Evolution of Modern Humans. *Archaeometry* 33:153–199.

Harpending, H. C., 1994, Gene Frequencies, DNA Sequences, and Human Origins. *Perspectives in Biology and Medicine* 37:384–394.

Harpending, H. and Relethford, J., 1997, Population Perspectives on Human Origins Research. In *Conceptual Issues in Modern Human Origins Research*, edited by G. A. Clark, and C. M. Willermet, pp. 361–368. Aldine de Gruyter, New York.

Harrold, F. B., 1989, Mousterian, Chatelperronian and Early Aurignacian in Western Europe: Continuity or Discontinuity? In *The Human Revolution: Behavioural and Biological Perspectives on the Origins of Modern Humans*, edited by P. A. Mellars, and C. B. Stringer, pp. 677–713. Edinburgh University Press, Edinburgh.

Hayden, B., 1993, The Cultural Capacities of the Neanderthals: A Review and Re-evaluation. *Journal of Human Evolution* 24:113–146.

Haynes, C. V., 1992, Contributions of Radiocarbon Dating to the Geochronology of the Peopling of the New World. In *Radiocarbon After Four Decades*, edited by R. E. Taylor, A. Long, and R. S. Kra, pp. 355–374. Springer-Verlag, New York.

Henshilwood, C., 1998, Blombos Cave. In *Excursion Guide to Sites North and East of Cape Town: DUAL Congress 1998*, edited by H. J. Deacon, pp. 42–46. DUAL Congress 1998, Stellenbosch.

Henshilwood, C. and Sealy, J., 1997, Bone Artifacts from the Middle Stone Age at Blombos Cave, Southern Cape, South Africa. *Current Anthropology* 38:890–895.

Henshilwood, C. and Sealy, J., 1998, Blombos Cave: Exciting New Finds from the Middle Stone Age. *The Digging Stick* 15:1–4.

Hoffecker, J. F., Powers, W. R., and Goebel, T., 1993, The Colonization of Beringia and the Peopling of the New World. *Science* 259:46–53.

Holliday, T. W., 1997, Postcranial Evidence of Cold Adaptations in European Neanderthals. *American Journal of Physical Anthropology* 104:245–258.

Houghton, P., 1993, Neanderthal Supralaryngeal Vocal Tract. *American Journal of Physical Anthropology* 90:139–146.

Hublin, J.-J., 1993, Recent Human Evolution in Northwestern Africa. In *The Origins of Modern Humans and the Impact of Chronometric Dating*, edited by M. J. Aitken, C. B. Stringer, and P. A. Mellars, pp. 118–131. Princeton University Press, Princeton.

Hublin, J.-J., 1996, The First Europeans. *Archaeology* 49(1):36–44.

Hublin, J.-J., 1998, Climatic Changes, Paleogeography, and the Evolution of the Neandertals. In *Neanderthals and Modern Humans in Western Asia*, edited by T. Akazawa, K. Aoki, and O. Bar-Yosef, pp. 291–310. Plenum, New York.

Hublin, J.-J., Barroso Ruiz, C., Medina Lara, P., Fontugne, M., and Reyss, J.-L., 1995, The Mousterian Site of Zafarraya (Andalucia, Spain): Dating and Implications on the Palaeolithic Peopling Processes of Western Europe. *Comptes Rendus de l'Académie des Sciences, Paris* Série IIa, 321:931–937.

Hublin, J.-J., Spoor, F., Braun, M., and Zonneveld, F., 1996, A Late Neanderthal Associated with Upper Paleolithic Artifacts. *Nature* 381:224–226.

Jelinek, A. J., 1994, Hominids, Energy, Environment, and Behavior in the Late Pleistocene. In *Origins of Anatomically Modern Humans*, edited by M. H. Nitecki and D. V. Nitecki, pp. 67–92. Plenum, New York.

Jones, R., 1992, The Human Colonisation of the Australian Continent. In *Continuity or Replacement: Controversies in* Homo sapiens *Evolution*, edited by G. Bräuer and F. H. Smith, pp. 289–301. A. A. Balkema, Rotterdam.

Kay, R. F., Cartmill, M., and Balow, M., 1998, The Hypoglossal Canal and the Origin of Human Vocal Behavior. *Proceedings of the National Academy of Sciences of the USA* 95:5417–5419.

Klein, R. G., 1994, Southern Africa Before the Iron Age. In *Integrative Paths to the Past: Paleoanthropological Advances in Honor of F. Clark Howell*, edited by R. S. Corruccini, and R. L. Ciochon, pp. 471–519. Prentice-Hall, Englewood Cliffs, NJ.

Krings, M., Stone, A., Schmitz, R. W., Krainitzki, H., Stoneking, M., and Pääbo, S., 1997, Neanderthal DNA Sequences and the Origin of Modern Humans. *Cell* 90:19–30.

Kuzmin, Y. V. and Orlova, L. A., 1998, Radiocarbon Chronology of the Siberian Paleolithic. *Journal of World Prehistory* 12:1–53.

Lahr, M. M., 1994, The Multiregional Model of Modern Human Origins: A Reassessment of Its Morphological Basis. *Journal of Human Evolution* 26:23–56.

Lahr, M. M. and Foley, R., 1994, Multiple Dispersals and Modern Human Origins. *Evolutionary Anthropology* 3:48–60.

Leroi-Gourhan, A., 1965, Le Châtelperronien: Problème ethnologique. In *Miscelanea en Homenaje al Abate Henri Breuil*, Volume 2, edited by E. Ripoll Perello, pp. 75–81. Diputación Provincial de Barcelona, Instituto de Prehistoria y Arqueología, Barcelona.

Lévêque, F., Backer, A. M., and Guilbaud, M., 1993, *Context of a Late Neanderthal: Implications of Multidisciplinary Research for the Transition to Upper Paleolithic Adaptations at Saint-Césaire, Charente-Maritime, France*. Prehistory Press, Madison WI.

Lieberman, D. E., 1995, Testing Hypotheses About Recent Human Evolution from Skulls. *Current Anthropology* 36:159–197.

Lieberman, P., Laitman, J. T., Reidenberg, J. S., and Gannon, P. J., 1992, The Anatomy, Physiology, Acoustics, and Perception of Speech: Essential Elements in the Analysis of the Evolution of Human Speech. *Journal of Human Evolution* 23:447–467.

Manderscheid, E. J. and Rogers, A. R., 1996, Genetic Admixture in the Late Pleistocene. *American Journal of Physical Anthropology* 100:1–5.

Marshack, A., 1991, A Reply to Davidson on Mania and Mania. *Rock Art Research* 8:47–58.

McDermott, F., Stringer, C. B., Grün, R., Williams, C. T., Din, V. K., and Hawkesworth, C. J., 1996, New Late-Pleistocene Uranium-Thorium and ESR Dates for the Singa Hominid (Sudan). *Journal of Human Evolution* 31:507–516.

Mellars, P. A., 1993, Archaeology and the Population-Dispersal Hypothesis of Modern Human Origins in Europe. In *The Origin of Modern Humans and the Impact of Chronometric Dating*, edited by M. J. Aitken, C. B. Stringer, and P. A. Mellars, pp. 196–216. Princeton University Press, Princeton.

Mellars, P. A., 1996, *The Neanderthal Legacy: an Archaeological Perspective from Western Europe*. Princeton University Press, Princeton.

Mellars, P. A., 1998, Comment on "Neanderthal Acculturation in Western Europe? A Critical review." *Current Anthropology* 39:S25–S27.

Meltzer, D. J., 1995, Clocking the First Americans. *Annual Review of Anthropology* 24:21–45.

Mercier, N. and Valladas, H., 1994, Thermoluminescence Dates for the Paleolithic Levant. In *Late Quaternary Chronology and Paleoclimates of the Eastern Mediterranean*, edited by O. Bar-Yosef and R. S. Kra, pp. 13–20. American School of Prehistoric Research, Cambridge, MA.

Milo, R. G. and Quiatt, D., 1994, Language in the Middle and Late Stone Ages: Glottogenesis in Anatomically Modern *Homo sapiens*. In *Hominid Culture in Primate Perspective*, edited by D. Quiatt and J. Itani, pp. 321–329. University Press of Colorado, Niwot, CO.

Moore, A. T. M. and Hillman, C., 1992, The Pleistocene to Holocene Transition and Human Economy in Southwest Asia: The Impact of the Younger Dryas. *American Antiquity* 57:482–494.

O'Connell, J. F. and Allen, J., 1998, When Did Humans First Arrive in Greater Australia, and Why Is It Important to Know? *Evolutionary Anthropology* 6:132–146.

Oakley, K. P., 1964, The Problem of Man's Antiquity: An Historical Survey. *Bulletin of the British Museum (Natural History) Geology* 9:86–155.

Otte, M. and Straus, L. G., 1995, Conclusions et Résumé. In *Le Trou Magrite: Fouilles 1991–1992*, edited by M. Otte and L. G. Straus, pp. 229–238. Études et Recherches Archéologiques de l'Université de Liège 69. Centre de Recherches Archéologiques, Université de Liège, Liège.

Relethford, J. H., 1995, Genetics and Modern Human Origins. *Evolutionary Anthropology* 4:53–63.

Richter, D., Waiblinger, J., Rink, W. J., and Wagner, G. A., 2000, TL, ESR and ^{14}C-Dating of the Late Middle and Early Upper Palaeolithic Site of Geissenklösterle Cave, Southern Germany. *Journal of Archaeological Science* 27:71–81.

Rightmire, G. P., 1998, Human Evolution in the Middle Pleistocene: The Role of *Homo heidelbergensis*. *Evolutionary Anthropology* 6:218–227.

Rightmire, G. P. and Deacon, H. J., 1991, Comparative Studies of Late Pleistocene Human Remains from Klasies River Mouth, South Africa. *Journal of Human Evolution* 20:131–156.

Roberts, R. G., Jones, R., Spooner, N. A., Head, M. J., Murray, A. S., and Smith, M. A., 1994, The Human Colonisation of Australia: Optical Dates of 53,000 and 60,000 Years Bracket Human Arrival at Deaf Adder Gorge, Northern Territory. *Quaternary Science Reviews* 13:575–586.

Roebroeks, W., 1996, The English Palaeolithic Record: Absence of Evidence, Evidence of Absence and the First Occupation of Europe. In *The English Palaeolithic Reviewed*, edited by C. S. Gamble and A. J. Lawson, pp. 57–62. Trust for Wessex Archaeology, Wessex.

Schwarcz, H. P. and Grün, R., 1993, Electron Spin Resonance (ESR) Dating of the Origins of Modern Man. In *The Origin of Modern Humans and the Impact of Chronometric Dating*, edited by M. J. Aitken, C. B. Stringer, and P. A. Mellars, pp. 40–48. Princeton University Press, Princeton.

Schweitzer, F. R., 1979, Excavations at Die Kelders, Cape Province, South Africa: The Holocene Deposits. *Annals of the South African Museum* 78:101–233.

Singer, R. S. and Wymer, J. J., 1982, *The Middle Stone Age at Klasies River Mouth in South Africa*. University of Chicago Press, Chicago.

Smith, F. H., 1994, Samples, Species, and Populations in the Study of Modern Human Origins. In *Origins of Anatomically Modern Humans*, edited by M. H. Nitecki and D. V. Nitecki, pp. 227–249. Plenum, New York.

Soffer, O., 1990, Before Beringia: Late Pleistocene Bio-social Transformations and the Colonization of Northern Eurasia. In *Chronostratigraphy of the Paleolithic in North, Central, East Asia and America*, edited by Anonymous. Academy of Sciences of the USSR, Novosibirsk.

Spoor, F. and Zonneveld, F., 1998, Comparative Review of the Human Bony Labyrinth. *Yearbook of Physical Anthropology* 41:211–251.

Stoneking, M., 1993, DNA and Recent Human Evolution. *Evolutionary Anthropology* 2:60–73.

Straus, L. G., 1997, The Iberian Situation Between 40,000 and 30,000 B.P., in Light of European Models of Migration and Convergence. In *Conceptual Issues in Modern Human Origins Research*, edited by G. A. Clark and C. M. Willermet, pp. 235–252. Aldine de Gruyter, New York.

Stringer, C. and Gamble, C., 1993, *In Search of the Neanderthals*. Thames and Hudson, New York.

Stringer, C. B. and McKie, R., 1996, *African Exodus: The Origin of Modern Humanity*. Jonathan Cape, London.

Stringer, C. B., Hublin, J.-J., and Vandermeersch, B., 1984, The Origin of Anatomically Modern Humans in Western Europe. In *The Origins of Modern Humans: A World Survey of the Fossil Evidence*, edited by F. H. Smith and F. Spencer, pp. 51–135. Alan R. Liss, New York.

Tattersall, I., 1998, *Becoming Human: Evolution and Human Uniqueness*. Harcourt, Brace, New York.

Tchernov, E., 1992, Biochronology, Paleoecology, and Dispersal Events of Hominids in the Southern Levant. In *The Evolution and Dispersal of Modern Humans in Asia*, edited by T. Akazawa, K. Aoki, and T. Kimura, pp. 149–188. Hokusen-Sha, Tokyo.

Thackeray, A. I., 1992, The Middle Stone Age South of the Limpopo River. *Journal of World Prehistory* 6:385–440.

Trinkaus, E., 1989, The Upper Pleistocene Transition. In *The Emergence of Modern Humans: Biocultural Adaptations in the Later Pleistocene*, edited by E. Trinkaus, pp. 42–66. Cambridge University Press, Cambridge.

Trinkaus, E., 1992, Morphological Contrasts Between the Near Eastern Qafzeh-Skhul and Late Archaic Human Samples: Grounds for a Behavioral Difference. In *The Evolution and Dispersal of Modern Humans in Asia*, edited by T. Akazawa, K. Aoki, and T. Kimura, pp. 278–294. Hokusen-Sha, Tokyo.

Trinkaus, E., 1995, Neanderthal Mortality Patterns. *Journal of Archaeological Science* 22:121–142.

Trinkaus, E. and Shipman, P., 1993a, *The Neandertals: Changing the Image of Mankind*. Alfred A. Knopf, New York.

Trinkaus, E. and Shipman, P., 1993b, Neanderthals: Images of Ourselves. *Evolutionary Anthropology* 1:194–201.

Trinkaus, E., Ruff, C. B., and Churchill, S. E., 1998, Upper Limb versus Lower Loading Patterns Among Near Eastern Middle Paleolithic Hominids. In *Neanderthals and Modern Humans in Western Asia*, edited by T. Akazawa, K. Aoki, and O. Bar-Yosef, pp. 391–404. Plenum, New York.

Turk, I., Dirjec, J., Kavur, B., and Bastiani, G., 1997, Description and Explanation of the Origin of the Suspected Bone Flute. In *Mousterian "Bone Flute" and Other Finds from Divje Babe 1 Cave Site in Slovenia*, edited by I. Turk, pp. 157–175. Zanstvenoraziskovakni Center SAZU, Ljubljana.

Valladas, H., Geneste, J. M., Joron, J. L., and Chadelle, J. P., 1986, Thermoluminescence Dating of Le Moustier (Dordogne, France). *Nature* 322:452–454.

van Andel, T. H. and Tzedakis, P. C., 1996, Palaeolithic Landscapes of Europe and Environs: 150,000–25,000 Years Ago: An Overview. *Quaternary Science Reviews* 15:481–500.

Velleman, P. F., 1995, *Data Desk Version 5.0. Statistics Guide*. Data Description, Ithaca, NY.

Vogel, J. C. and Beaumont, P. B., 1972, Revised Radiocarbon Chronology for the Stone Age in South Africa. *Nature* 237:50–51.

Wendorf, F., 1992, The Impact of Radiocarbon Dating on North African Archaeology. In *Radiocarbon After Four Decades: An Interdisciplinary Perspective*, edited by R. E. Taylor, A. Long, and R. S. Kra, pp. 310–324. Springer-Verlag, New York.

White, R. K., 1998, Comment on "Neanderthal Acculturation in Western Europe? A Critical Review." *Current Anthropology* 39:S30–S32.

Wolpoff, M. H., 1996, *Human Evolution: 1996–1997 Edition*. McGraw-Hill, New York.

Wu, X. and Poirier, F. E., 1995, *Human Evolution in China: A Metric Description of the Fossils and a Review of the Sites*. Oxford University Press, New York.

Yellen, J. E., 1998, Barbed Bone Points: Tradition and Continuity in Saharan and Sub-Saharan Africa. *African Archaeological Review* 15:173–198.

Yellen, J. E., Brooks, A. S., Cornelissen, E., Mehlman, M. J., and Stewart, K., 1995, A Middle Stone Age Worked Bone Industry from Katanda, Upper Semliki Valley, Zaire. *Science* 268:553–556.

65

The Big Deal about Blades

Laminar Technologies and Human Evolution

O. Bar-Yosef and S. L. Kuhn

ABSTRACT

Despite the rapid expansion of archaeological knowledge of the Paleolithic over the past several decades, some generalized interpretive frameworks inherited from previous generations of researchers are remarkably tenacious. One of the most persistent of these is the assumed correlation between blade technologies, Upper Paleolithic industries, and anatomically (and behaviorally) modern humans. In this paper, we review some of the evidence for the production of early blade technologies in Eurasia and Africa dating to the late Lower and the Middle Paleolithic. The basic techniques for blade production appeared thousands of years before the Upper Paleolithic, and there is no justification for linking blades per se to any particular aspect of hominid anatomy or to any major change in the behavioral capacities of hominids. It is true that blades came to dominate the archaeological records of western Eurasia and Africa after 40,000 years ago, perhaps as a consequence of increasing reliance on complex composite tools during the Upper Paleolithic. At the same time, evidence from other regions of the world demonstrates that evolutionary trends in Pleistocene Eurasia were historically contingent and not universal.

During the nineteenth and early twentieth centuries, the pioneers of prehistoric research based the main subdivisions of the Stone Age largely on the forms of lithic artifacts found on river terraces and in stratified cave sites. The Lower Paleolithic was defined as consisting of assemblages with core choppers or large bifaces, the Middle Paleolithic was characterized by flake-based lithic industries and Levallois technique, and the Upper Paleolithic was identified with blade-dominated assemblages. Technologies based on geometric microliths and ground and polished implements characterized the postglacial Mesolithic and Neolithic, respectively. The transition from chopper to handaxe to flakes, blades, and finally ground-edged axes was often—and in some cases continues to be—equated with a generalized pattern of technological "progress" paralleling biological evolution within the genus *Homo*.

Although they were originally formulated on the basis of the relatively small number of archaeological sites then known within western Europe, these broad generalizations have held up remarkably well, and they remain the mainstay of textbooks and popular accounts of the evolution of early human technology. Inevitably, however, as both the number and geographic range of documented sites have increased, many exceptions have appeared. The development of new methods of radiometric dating has also enabled prehistorians to bypass the circular practice of "dating" assemblages based on apparent levels of technological development, further complicating—and enriching—the picture of technological change over the course of the Pleistocene. For example, it is now well documented that the "transitions" between different stages or phases were neither sudden nor smooth, so that "Lower Paleolithic" core-tool and "Middle Paleolithic" flake-tool assemblages with prepared cores were contemporaneous in some parts of the world (e.g., Rigaud, 1989:429–439). At this point, the major stages of the Paleolithic remain useful only as a crude first approximation of the evolutionary history of human technologies.

Despite the rapid expansion of the Paleolithic archaeological record over the past 50 years and the inevitable effects of this increased knowledge on the systems of classification inherited from previous generations of prehistorians, some generalizations have been remarkably tenacious. One of the most persistent of these is the equation of blade technologies, Upper Paleolithic industries, and anatomically (and behaviorally) modern humans. A heavy reliance on specialized methods for producing elongated, parallel-sided stone flakes (or blades) is often cited in textbooks as a defining characteristic of the lithic assemblages of anatomically modern human populations in Eurasia and Africa (the Upper Paleolithic and Late Stone Age) (e.g., Boyd and Silk, 1997:471; Foley and Lahr, 1997; Gamble, 1986:120; Relethford, 1997:329; Schick and Toth, 1993). The manufacture and use of blades is seen by some as a major threshold in the evolution of hominid technological capacities, a watershed event in the development of "modern" behavioral repertoires. Blade technologies are thought to possess a number of inherent advantages particularly suited for the "complex" and "efficient" technological adaptations of modern humans, and they are frequently included in archaeological trait lists used to define "fully modern behavior" in the Paleolithic (e.g., Clark and Lindly, 1989; Schick and Toth, 1993:293; Sherratt, 1997:283).

In fact, it has been clear for some time that the presumed associations between blade technology, modern anatomy, and modern behavior are far from clear cut. In this paper, we review some of the evidence of blade technologies in Eurasia and Africa. Many assemblages from Europe, the Near East, and Africa provide evidence for the production of blades and laminar flakes during the Middle Paleolithic/Middle Stone Age, and even the later Lower Paleolithic. While blade-based assemblages are somewhat scattered across both space and time prior to the Upper Paleolithic, there is no justification in maintaining that the development of laminar lithic technologies *per se* is linked to the appearance of either modern anatomy or "modern" behavior. At the same time, the recent prehistory of North America and Australia shows that blades are not part and parcel of complex, sophisticated or high-mobility adaptations of "modern" hunter-gatherers. These well-documented but little-discussed global patterns call into question assumptions of both the significance of blade technologies in human evolution and the putative superiority of these technological systems. The global data can also help in redefining questions about the nature of the technological transition from Middle to Upper Paleolithic in Eurasia. Although the Upper Paleolithic does not mark the first appearance of blades, they do come to dominate the archaeological record to an unprecedented degree. The real issue therefore, concerns the rapid *proliferation* of blade-based lithic technologies during the Upper Paleolithic of western Eurasia. In the concluding section, we propose a hypothesis to explain the redefined patterns, citing both historical factors and changes in the organization of technological systems.

WHAT ARE BLADES, AND WHAT HAVE PEOPLE SAID ABOUT THEM?

The standard morphological definition of a blade is any flake more than twice as long as it is wide, although some investigators prefer ratios of 2.5 or even 4 to 1. The technical definition is somewhat narrower, limiting use of the term to elongated blanks with parallel or slightly converging edges. Normally, technical blades possess one or more ridges running parallel to their long axes, giving them a triangular or trapezoidal cross-section. The sub-class of bladelets simply represents especially small, narrow blades. Although they may be made by very different methods, the distinction between blades and bladelets in the Old World is generally based on an arbitrary size threshold: the maximum width for bladelets is generally set between 1 and 1.5 cm, depending on local assemblage characteristics (Owen, 1988:2; Tixier, 1963). The "microblades" found in late Pleistocene and Holocene assemblages from northeast Asia and Alaska are often even smaller, and were produced by pressure flaking (Anderson, 1970; Andrefsky, 1987).

Blades and blade-like flakes can be manufactured in a surprising variety of ways. It is possible to draw a broad distinction between *prismatic* and *Levallois* methods. In classic prismatic blade production, one or more long ridges are prepared on the face of the core by bifacial flaking, creating the characteristic crested blade (*lame à crête*). A series of blades is then detached along part or all of the core's perimeter. The striking platforms of prismatic cores can be flat and unmodified or they may be prepared by flaking or abrasion. If multiple striking platforms are present, they are often located at opposing ends of the core, not infrequently somewhat offset. Levallois technology, better known as a technique for the production of flakes, was especially common during the Middle Paleolithic. In Levallois blade manufacture, blades are "peeled off" the gently-convex face of a generally flat core. Striking platforms are located on the core's perimeter. Typically, the angles and contours of striking platforms are adjusted by removal of small flakes, producing the characteristic faceted morphology: striking platforms may also be isolated by creating notches on either side, resulting in so-called "*chapeau de gendarme*" morphology. A crucial aspect of Levallois manufacture is the shaping of the face of detachment to an appropriate longitudinal and transverse convexity, a process that results in a number of distinctive byproducts (Boëda et al., 1990; Inizan et al., 1993). The so-called "Hummalian" technique (Boëda, 1995) may represent a third family of approaches to making elongated blanks, though it is much less widespread than Levallois or prismatic core technology.

There is considerable variation even within each of these broad categories of blade production. The variety of approaches to blade production that could be classified as prismatic or Levallois is vast, and it would be impractical to list every variant here. True Levallois blade technology may be less variable than prismatic blade technology. Levallois methods are confined largely to the Lower and Middle Paleolithic of Eurasia and Africa, although very closely allied techniques appear in contexts such as the Preclassic Maya "macroblade" production (Hester and Shafer, 1987:247–249). At least during the Middle Paleolithic, Levallois technique was executed using direct hard hammer percussion (Boëda et al., 1990), whereas prismatic blade cores may be exploited using hard hammer, soft hammer, or indirect percussion, as well as pressure. It is noteworthy that small bladelets or microblades are generally manufactured by prismatic reduction only.

Prismatic blade production has often been described as offering marked advantages over other means of manufacturing blanks for stone tools. One potential strong point concerns the economy of raw material, the number of blanks that can be produced from a given unit of stone. It is frequently stated that prismatic blade production can provide a vastly greater length of usable edge per unit of raw material than other blank manufacture techniques (e.g., Bordaz, 1970). In fact, the only empirical evaluation of this proposition (Sheets and Muto, 1972) involved replication of Mesoamerican pressure blade technology using obsidian, which represents a rather extreme case: there is no experimental literature on the relative productivity of hard hammer blade production. Boëda (1990, 1995) has argued that prismatic blade production differs from classical Levallois technology in how a piece of raw material is exploited. Essentially, Levallois production concentrates on the exploitation of a single surface of flake detachment, gradually flattening (and shortening) the core as reduction proceeds. In contrast, prismatic blade manufacture is thought to involve systematic exploitation of the entire volume of a nodule of raw material. The production of prismatic blades may thus consume a given volume of raw material more effectively and completely. One implication of these characteristics is that blade technologies might have provided distinct advantages to toolmakers where raw material was at a premium, due either to a scarcity of suitable stone or to limitations imposed by high residential mobility.

A number of additional potential advantages have been attributable to blade technologies. Prismatic core techniques, in particular, permit close control over the dimensions of blanks, sometimes resulting in a remarkable degree of standardization in the sizes and shapes of end products (e.g., Clark, 1987). Such uniformity of products could be a distinct advantage when manufacturing replaceable components of composite tools, a theme to which we will return, as well as in the context of mass production for sale or exchange. Laminar blanks may also provide greater potential for resharpening than flakes, particularly when the working edge is on the end of the blade.

Although they have some notable strong points, it is important to point out that blade technologies have a number of potential limitations as well. Blade production is risky, prone to "fatal" errors, mistakes that render a core useless without extensive reworking. The production of elongated, laminar blanks also tends to be quite demanding of raw materials. Long, thin blades are comparatively fragile, yet significant force is needed to detach them. The raw material must be brittle enough that a fracture will carry over the desired length of the blade, yet also sufficiently homogeneous and tough so that the blades will not shatter from the force of percussion or pressure. As a consequence, blades were most often manufactured on isotropic, fine-grained raw materials such as flint, jasper, chert, and obsidian, although coarser-grained materials were sometimes employed if they were sufficiently isotropic. The need for homogeneous material may in turn require stringent selection or importation of raw materials, at some cost in terms of time or effort in many geological contexts. Properly setting up a face of detachment for blades often requires extensive preparation, placing further limits on minimum sizes of nodules. Finally, production of large blades may be relatively rigid and not especially "portable," or at least not appropriate for transport and sporadic, occasional exploitation. Speaking of the manufacture of pressure blades, admittedly the most "sensitive" type of blade production technology, John Clark, an experienced flint knapper, observes:

> Each blade is produced by the same process as the one preceding it, a monotonous process. As with other skilled knapping, it also requires rhythm. . . . Blade removal takes only a fraction of a second; but setting up, and reawakening the needed "touch" for making blades, requires the most time. It takes about 10–15 minutes to make one blade and another four minutes to make 10–20 more, barring any major knapping errors. [1987:268]

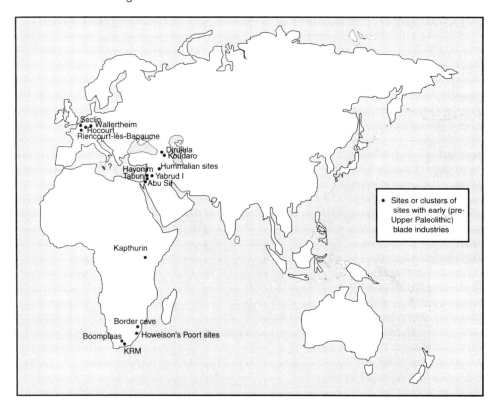

Figure 1. *Map showing locations of some sites yielding early (pre-Upper Paleolithic) blade industries.*

A question that naturally arises in the context of discussions of human evolution is whether blade manufacture is in some way more complicated than other forms of blank production, requiring a higher level of physical skill or cognitive sophistication. There is no evidence to indicate that the manufacture of blades is any more demanding than the making of handaxes or Levallois flakes. Although Boëda has long argued that Levallois and prismatic blade technologies entail *different* conceptions of how to exploit the volume of a piece of raw material, he does not assert that one conception is more sophisticated or complex than the other. It is our impression, based on an admittedly informal survey of modern-day knappers, that, if anything, the Levallois method is more difficult to master than is the production of blades from prismatic cores. If prismatic blades appear to be complex and sophisticated, it may only be because they seemed at one time so closely linked with the appearance of modern humans (Reynolds, 1990).

BLADE TECHNOLOGIES BEFORE THE UPPER PALEOLITHIC

Findings from throughout Europe, the Near East, and Africa show that, in some times and places, substantial numbers of blades and blade cores are present in layers long predating the appearance of other traits thought to define the Upper Paleolithic and/or the first appearance of anatomically modern humans. A brief summary of some of the global evidence is appropriate at this point. The following review is by no means comprehensive, and it is focused mainly on the areas with which the authors are most familiar: western Europe and the Levant. Figures 1 and 2 show the locations of some of the pre-Upper Paleolithic and early Upper Paleolithic sites discussed below.

In the Near East, the manufacture of blades first appears quite early, in the "pre-Aurignacian" of Yabrud rockshelter I and the Amudian at Tabun and Abri Zumoffen (Garrod and Kirkbride, 1961; Jelinek, 1981, 1982, 1990; Meignen, 1994) (Figure 3, nos. 1–6). Based on extrapolation from recent TL dates, the Amudian layers at Tabun cave (Mercier et al., 1995) appear to date to the later half of the Middle Pleistocene, between 270,000 and 330,000 years before present. Although blades are not the most common variety of tool blank in Amudian assemblages (Jelinek, 1990), they are nonetheless quite typical in form (Ronen, 1992). The so-called "pre-Aurignacian" assemblage from the Haua Fteah cave in Libya (McBurney, 1967) could represent a similar phenomenon, but this assemblage is extremely small and remains undated.

The earliest Mousterian assemblages of the Levant are typically even more laminar (blade-rich) than the Amudian. One of the defining characteristics of the so-called "Early Levantine" or "Tabun-D type" Mousterian, known from sites such as Tabun, Hayonim layer E (Meignen, 1994, 1998) (Figure 4), Abu Sif, Rosh Ein Mor (Crew, 1976; Marks and Monigal, 1995), 'Ain Difla (Lindly and Clark, 1987), and Douara layer IV (Nishiaki, 1989), is the predominance of blades and elongated points (pointed blades). The abundance of retouched points made on markedly elongated blanks in assemblages from Abu Sif and Tabun layer D attracted the attention of Bordes, who termed them "Abu Sif" points (1960). Both Levallois and non-Levallois methods were employed to produce blades, and sometimes they are found together in the same assemblage or geological layer. The presence of crested blades in some

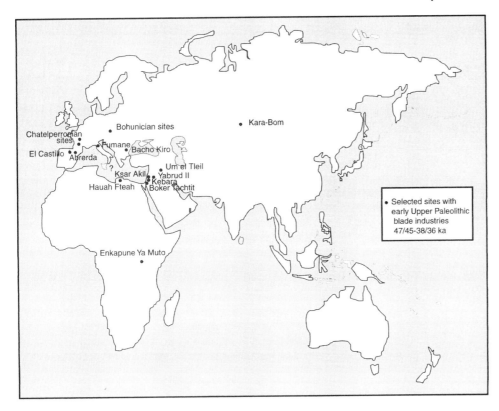

Figure 2. *Map showing locations of some sites yielding early Upper Paleolithic blade industries.*

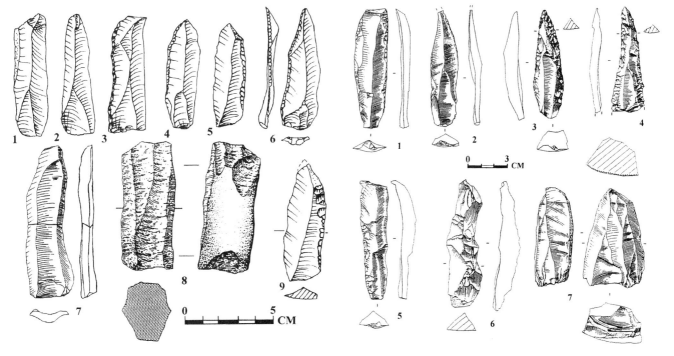

Figure 3. *Blade tools and core from the Amudian of Abri Zumoffen, Lebanon (nos. 1–6), and middle Pleistocene layers from the Kapthurin formation, Kenya (nos. 7–9) (after Garrod and Kirkbride, 1961; McBrearty et al., 1996).*

Figure 4. *Laminar artifacts and blade core from the early Mousterian (layer E) of Hayonim cave, Israel.*

assemblages indicates that the basic schemes of core exploitation were at least generally similar to later prismatic blade industries (e.g., Marks and Monigal, 1995). The majority of sites yielding these early Levantine Mousterian assemblages date to between 100 and 250 Ka B.P. (e.g., Grün et al., 1991; Mercier et al., 1995).

The Hummalian assemblages from El-Kowm, Syria (Boëda and Muhesen, 1993), also characterized by non-Levallois blades and elongated points, might date to approximately the same time as the early Levantine Mousterian, although there are inconsistencies between different dating techniques (Bar-Yosef, 1996).

Interestingly, the majority of the more recent Upper Pleistocene Mousterian strata in the Near East, including those yielding the early anatomically modern *Homo sapiens* burials at the site of Qafzeh, have produced decidedly non-laminar industries. The more recent Mousterian assemblages in the northern and central Levant are dominated by typical centripetal or convergent Levallois methods (Bar-Yosef, 1996; Meignen, 1995; Meignen and Bar-Yosef, 1991), which result in the manufacture of relatively short, wide blanks. It is not clear whether blade production reappears in the terminal Mousterian. Some investigators argue that "bladey" industries persist throughout the Mousterian in the southern Levant, so that so-called "early" and "late" versions of the Levantine Mousterian actually coexisted (e.g., Marks, 1990). In the refitted cores from the site of Boker Tachtit, the site's investigators see a smooth transition from essentially Mousterian to typical Upper Paleolithic prismatic blade production (e.g., Marks, 1983, 1990; Marks and Volkman, 1983). However, other non-laminar assemblages date to about the same time as the Boker Tachtit sequence (e.g., Boëda and Muhesen, 1993; Goren-Inbar, 1990).

Middle Paleolithic blade industries are also known from Transcaucasia, from the sites of Djrujula, Tsona, and Koudaro Caves (Liubin, 1977, 1989) (Figure 5). Mousterian assemblages from Koudaro I and Tsona, both high-elevation localities, are characterized by elevated frequencies of blades and retouched pieces, especially points, much like the Early Levantine Mousterian. Although neither site has been directly dated, blade-rich Middle Paleolithic levels in Koudaro I and Tsona are stratified directly above late Acheulean layers, suggesting that they are relatively ancient.

Despite the stereotypical view, pre-Upper Paleolithic assemblages dominated by blade blanks are now docu-

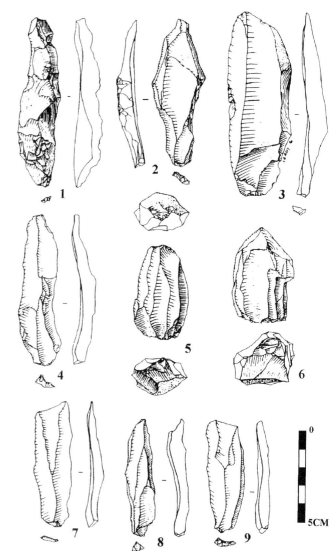

Figure 6.   *Mousterian blades and blade cores from Riencourt, Belgium (after Otte, 1994).*

mented in several parts of Europe. Twenty years ago, Bordes noted that even late Acheulean assemblages could contain substantial numbers of blades (Bordes, 1977). Northern Europe is especially rich in early blade industries, and literally dozens of Middle Paleolithic assemblages with a strong, even predominant, blade component are known from Germany (Conard, 1990), northern France (Meignen, 1994; Révillion, 1995; Révillion and Tuffreau, 1994), and Belgium (Otte, 1994). A variety of methods was employed in blade production, ranging from uni- and bidirectional recurrent Levallois at Biache-Saint-Vaast (Tuffreau and Somme, 1988) to more classic, Upper-Paleolithic-like methods involving prismatic cores (Otte, 1994; Révillion, 1995; Tuffreau et al., 1994) (Figure 6). It is noteworthy that many of the laminar Mousterian industries date to the late Middle or early Upper Pleistocene (between approximately 200,000 and 70,000 years ago), certainly well before the Middle-Upper Paleolithic transition. There is no evidence for a massive shift (or return) to the use of blade technologies at the end of the Middle

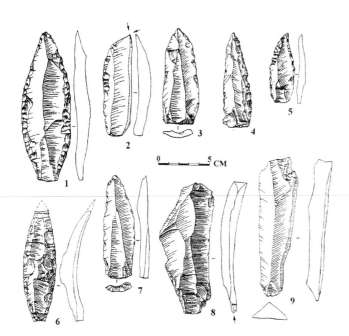

Figure 5.   *Mousterian blades from Koudara and Djrujula caves, Caucasus (after Liubin, 1989).*

Paleolithic in Europe, and in fact it may be the earliest assemblages that are richest in blades (Révillion, 1995:438–439). Mellars argues that, on the whole, blades are scarce in terminal Mousterian assemblages in Europe (1996:393; see also Harrold, 1989:691). In Italy, blade production increases towards the end of the Mousterian in some areas (e.g., Kuhn, 1995) and declines in others (Kuhn and Stiner, 1992; Palma di Cesnola, 1986). Some European "transitional" or initial Upper Paleolithic industries, such as the Bohunician (Svoboda and Skrdla, 1995), are decidedly laminar. Others, including the Castelperronian, appear to be technologically variable, encompassing both blade- and flake-dominated assemblages (Harrold, 1989; Kozlowski, 1990; Pelegrin, 1995). Still others, such as the Uluzzian of Italy, are essentially flake industries (Palma di Cesnola, 1993).

Assemblages containing substantial numbers of blades are also known from both east and south Africa as early as the later Acheulean (Clark, 1989:571). Middle Stone Age assemblages from southern Africa may contain many blades and elongated, pointed flakes (e.g., Clark, 1989; Sampson, 1974). In South Africa, the Howieson's Poort industry, dating to the early part of the Upper Pleistocene, contains many blades and backed pieces as well as flakes (Clark, 1989:573; Deacon, 1989). In the Kapthurin formation of Kenya, layers dated to around 240,000 years ago have yielded assemblages containing blades produced from large prismatic cores using the crested-blade technique (Cornelissen, 1995; McBrearty et al., 1996; Texier, 1996). Although the artifacts appear rather rough (Figure 3, nos. 7–9), this is probably attributable to the use of coarse-grained volcanic stone. Discussions of these early blade-rich assemblages from Pleistocene Africa sometimes link them hypothetically to the appearance of anatomically modern humans (e.g., Deacon, 1989; Stringer, 1989).

FLAKES, BLADES, AND BIFACES IN LATER ASSEMBLAGES

Not only were true blades sometimes systematically produced in very early time periods, they are by no means ubiquitous among stone-tool technologies attributed to modern humans. The notion that laminar technologies are somehow integral to the sophisticated foraging adaptations of anatomically modern humans simply does not hold up outside of western Eurasia and North Africa. Based on a review of the evidence from the Americas, Parry (1994) concludes that blade manufacture in the New World is more commonly associated with specialist (commoditized) production in urban settings rather than with mobile hunter-gatherers. With a few exceptions, including prismatic blades from Paleoindian (Clovis) caches and sites (Collins, 1990; Green, 1963), the early microblade industries of Alaska and the Pacific Northwest (Anderson, 1970; Andrefsky, 1987), and highly specialized microblade production in the Channel Islands of southern California (Arnold, 1985, 1987), most mobile New World hunter-gatherers based stone tool production on either flake or biface manufacture techniques (Kelly, 1988; Parry and Kelly,

1987). This includes many of the highly complex ethnographically documented technologies of the Arctic and Pacific coast. In Australia, the production of blades or elongated flakes from both Levallois and prismatic cores is known (Binford and O'Connell, 1984; Dortch and Bordes, 1977), but is also comparatively rare.

Even the Eurasian Upper Paleolithic, the source of ideas about the association between blade-based lithic technologies and modern humans, is not entirely uniform from this technological perspective (e.g., Clark and Lindly, 1989; Straus, 1990). Early Upper Paleolithic (Aurignacian and Castelperronian) assemblages from southwest Europe exhibit a wide range of variation in blank production. In northern Italy and Spain, the earliest Aurignacian assemblages from sites such as Arbreda cave, Riparo Mochi, and Grotta Fumane contain large numbers of blades and especially bladelets (e.g., Bartolomei et al., 1992; Kuhn and Stiner, 1998; Maroto and Fullola, 1996); the frequency of blades in the Aurignacian subsequently *declines* in these sites. The late Upper Paleolithic Badegoulian of France is an almost entirely flake-based industry (Sonneville-Bordes, 1960:387). In the Near East, the earliest Upper Paleolithic industries, termed Ahmarian, are heavily biased towards the production of elongated blanks. These assemblages, which first appear as early as 42,000 B.P., contain not only blades but also many small, marginally retouched bladelets: in the long run, the production of small bladelets may have more important behavioral implications. Interestingly, the later Levantine Aurignacian, which appears after the Ahmarian, is often described as a flake-based technology (Bar-Yosef and Belfer Cohen, 1988; Bar-Yosef et al., 1996; Gilead, 1991; Marks, 1983). In southern Africa, blades are common early in the Middle Stone Age and occur in some Late Stone Age industries, but they disappear again between 12,000 and 8000 B.P. (Deacon, 1984; Volman, 1984). In East Asia, the timing of the appearance of blade-based technologies is still unclear, but it is likely that they long postdate the early Upper Paleolithic of western Asia and Europe (e.g., Jia and Huang, 1985).

DISCUSSION

Several points are clear from the review presented above. First, blades and blade technologies are not exclusively associated with the Upper Paleolithic/Late Stone Age (LSA). Both Levallois and prismatic blade technologies are found throughout western Eurasia in Paleolithic assemblages dating back as far as the later Middle Pleistocene, or as early as 300,000 years ago. These early assemblages contain more than just a few elongated pieces: there is abundant evidence for stone-working techniques directed specifically at the production of blades. Second, pre–Upper Paleolithic blade technologies are found in many regions of the Old World. Although east Africa is home to one of the earliest cases of blade manufacture from prismatic cores (Kapthurin), blade-rich assemblages of similar antiquity are known from the Near East (some early Levantine Mousterian assemblages, for example). Laminar technologies appear somewhat later in Europe, but a number of cases do predate the last interglacial (120,000 years ago). Finally, in no region is there an unbroken sequence linking Middle or Lower Paleolithic blade technologies to the Upper Paleolithic/Late Stone Age. In most regions, including the Levant, southern Africa, and Europe, the use of blade technologies waxes and wanes markedly over time, and early blade-based assemblages are subsequently replaced by flake-based Middle Paleolithic or Middle Stone Age industries (see also Gamble, 1994). Finally, after the establishment of anatomically modern humans and the disappearance of archaic *Homo sapiens,* blade technologies became very widespread if not ubiquitous in *some* parts of the world, notably North Africa, western Asia, and Europe.

Many of the facts summarized above have been known for decades. Still, long-held assumptions about links between modern humans and blade technologies are remarkably tenacious. Some researchers continue to assert that the early appearance of blades in Africa and the Near East marks the first appearance of either anatomically modern humans or "modern behavior" (e.g., Ronen, 1992; le Tensorer and Muhesen, 1997:162). The emphasis placed on pre-LSA blades in Howieson's Poort assemblages from South Africa as support for the African origin of modern *Homo sapiens* (e.g., Deacon, 1989; Stringer, 1989) shows a similar, though less explicit assumption about the phylogenetic significance of blade production. Clearly, the data show that blades were made at many times and places prior to the Upper Paleolithic. However, the Upper Paleolithic is no longer synonymous with anatomically modern humans. Is it possible that blade technologies still are somehow linked with modern humans, whether before or after the appearance of the Upper Paleolithic?

The fossil record is of little immediate help in answering this question. Certainly, there is no direct evidence that the earliest blade industries are associated with anatomically modern fossils. There are few, if any, unambiguous hominid associations with the early industries containing blades in East Africa, the Near East, or Europe. In part, this reflects a general scarcity of fossil-bearing deposits and well-preserved human remains dating to the period between around 300,000 years ago and the appearance of the classic Neandertals. While there is currently no direct evidence that the "Tabun D-type" Mousterian or any similar assemblages were produced by anatomically modern populations, it is not clear to which hominid taxon or taxa these assemblages should be attributed. Of course, the earliest anatomically modern human burials known today (from Skhul and Qafzeh) are associated with Mousterian assemblages dominated by flakes obtained by centripetal Levallois method. On the other hand, several fossils of archaic members of the genus *Homo* have been found in layers yielding laminar lithic assemblages. The hominids from Biache-Saint-Vaast, which are closely affiliated with the Neandertals (Vandermeersch, 1978), were associated with artifact assemblages full of blades, albeit produced by Levallois method. Much later in time, Neandertal fossils from Saint-Césaire and Arcy-sur-Cure are associated with Castelperronian industries showing substantial evi-

dence for blade production by non-Levallois methods (Gouedo, 1990; Guilbaud, 1993).

Indirect evidence argues more strongly against any simple equation of blades with modern anatomy. The highly discontinuous spatio-temporal distribution of early blade technologies makes them an unlikely potential marker for the hypothetical early expansion of the first anatomically modern populations "out of Africa." If one wished to argue that the early presence of blades in East Africa, the Levant, and Europe also marked the presence of modern *Homo sapiens,* one would have to hypothesize either (1) a period of co-residence of early anatomically modern populations with Neandertals and their forebears throughout Europe and western Asia lasting between 100,000 and 250,000 years, with the latter dominating the fossil record, or (2) a series of brief expansions of blade-making modern humans as far as northern Europe, subsequent to which they either stopped making blades or were replaced by anatomically archaic human groups. Neither of these seems a very likely scenario. Of course, if one holds with a model of regional continuity and a late appearance of modern *Homo sapiens,* then blade industries older than 50,000 years or so should have nothing to do with modern humans. Similarly, the absence of local technological continuity between early blade industries and the Upper Paleolithic/Late Stone Age in many areas suggests that laminar technologies *per se* have little long-term phylogenetic significance.

In the absence of good fossil associations, the most parsimonious interpretation of current knowledge is that the pre–Upper Paleolithic blade technologies in Europe, the Near East, and Africa were produced by a variety of members of the genus *Homo*, perhaps including anatomically modern humans but certainly also including other taxa such as Neandertals or *H. heidelbergensis.* One lesson to be taken from the global evidence is simply that the knowledge of and ability to produce blades from either Levallois or prismatic cores has tremendous time depth in human prehistory. Since at least the late Middle Pleistocene, some humans have had both the capacity and *savoir faire* to make elongated blanks. Moreover, many notions about the general superiority and complexity of prismatic blade technologies stem from perceived associations between these types of technologies and anatomically modern populations. If these connections no longer seem so robust, then perhaps it is time to reevaluate ideas about the behavioral significance of making blades. The converse holds true as well. If it is not possible to equate blade making with modern humans or "modern behavior," whatever that may be, then the scarcity or absence of blades in early Upper Paleolithic assemblages can no longer be considered an "archaic" holdover. After all, in North America and Australia sophisticated, mobile hunter-gatherers got along quite well into the historic period with "only" flakes and bifaces.

We do not mean to deny that prismatic blade technologies can provide advantages over other methods of blank production, or that many Upper Paleolithic groups took advantage of the special properties of blades. However, the advantages are only situationally relevant. The simple fact that blade technologies come and go in many prehistoric sequences demonstrates that their advantages are hardly overwhelming. In order to argue that blade technologies would provide an advantage to populations using them it is first necessary to explain how their particular properties would have been locally beneficial. It may be true, for example, that the manufacture of prismatic blades yields more sharp edge per kilogram of stone than any other technique. However, it is relevant to ask whether the conservation of raw material is always of great advantage, or whether the need to save stone has always been a major driving force in human evolution.

Although it is not valid to attribute blade technologies exclusively to either modern humans or the Upper Paleolithic, or to assume that such systems or blank manufacture are inherently superior to all other modes of stone tool production, blade-dominated assemblages are still an important and interesting dimension of the Pleistocene archaeological record. Many of the broad patterns that stimulated researchers to investigate the connections between hominid anatomy and technology in the first place must still be explained. The questions must simply be reframed. First, it is clear that the Upper Paleolithic/modern human "blade phenomenon" is really confined largely to North Africa, northern and western Asia, and Europe. Second, the most important development in laminar technologies within this area is not in their simple presence but in their *ubiquity* (cf. Mellars, 1989:360). Many pre–Upper Paleolithic assemblages contain significant numbers of blades, but many do not. In contrast, the majority of Upper Paleolithic assemblages from western Eurasia and North Africa, especially the later ones, contain plentiful evidence for blade and bladelet production. Moreover, many other methods of blank production, including Levallois and classic discoid methods, seem to disappear almost completely from these areas at about the same time that blade technologies take over. Finally, if there is any major shift from Middle to Upper Paleolithic in the technology of blade production, it is seen in (1) the appearance of soft hammer and indirect (punch) percussion in blade manufacture, which result in finer, more symmetrical products (e.g., Meignen, 1994, 1996; Mellars, 1996; Pelegrin, 1990), and (2) the manufacture of small bladelets.

The two authors of this paper come from very different backgrounds and are inclined "paradigmatically" to pursue very different explanations for the widespread use of blades in the Upper Paleolithic and Epipaleolithic of west Asia and Europe. Nonetheless, we do agree on several aspects of a potential explanation for why laminar technologies become so dominant after 45,000 years ago. With the recognition that we are unable to offer a complete resolution to the question at present, we offer the following conjectures as a basis for further discussion.

First, the *chaînes opératoires* behind what we refer to generically as blade production techniques represent designs for producing tool blanks that were invented, abandoned, and reinvented due to a variety of factors, of which their success or failure in the techno-economic

sphere is only one. There are only a limited number of ways usable blanks can be produced from a block of stone, and these tend to appear repeatedly throughout prehistory. All blade (or biface, or Levallois) technologies need not have common origins. Second, it is important to recognize that the stereotypical progression from flakes to blades is not inevitable. Historical contingency plays a major role in shaping long-term evolutionary trends. Blades simply represent one alternative way of making tools to solve common problems that became well established in one part of the world (Europe and western Asia) where raw materials were conducive. The heavy reliance on biface production among mobile hunter-gatherers in North America represents an equally effective solution to some of the same kinds of problems.

While historical factors may well answer the question of "why blades?" (as opposed to flakes or bifaces), they alone cannot account for the spread and near-ubiquity of blade-based technologies in the Upper Paleolithic of western Eurasia. We still need to ask "why so many blades, in so many places," to seek out a more general explanation for the remarkable persistence and broad distribution of this family of blank production techniques. There should be some commonality in the widespread adoption of blade technologies in the Upper Paleolithic of the western Old World. There is no question that mobility patterns and functional considerations may favor the use of blade technologies in specific contexts (e.g., Henry, 1989; Kuhn, 1995; Marks, 1988; Parry, 1994). However, the range of environments in which laminar lithic technologies occurred during the late Pleistocene would argue against a single, overarching explanation of this type: social systems, land use strategies, and economies were simply too diverse. The same is true of general explanations relating to the conservation of raw material. In some areas, high quality raw material may have become increasingly scarce over the course of the Upper Pleistocene, which would favor the adoption of economical prismatic blade production techniques, but this needs to be demonstrated and should not be presupposed.

On the other hand, lithic technology was not the only thing to change with the origins of the Upper Paleolithic. It is likely that the widespread adoption of prismatic blade production was associated with other broadly metamorphosing aspects of technology and society. It has long been argued that the spread of prismatic blade technologies could well tie in to another aspect of technology that flourished during the Upper and Epi-Paleolithic, namely hafting and composite tools (e.g., Gamble, 1986:121, 1994; Sherratt, 1997). Although simple hafted knives, scrapers or points were part of Middle Paleolithic technological repertoires (Anderson-Gerfaud, 1990; Boëda et al., 1996; Freidman et al., 1994; Shea, 1989), there is much evidence that the number, diversity, and complexity of multi-component tools increased during the Upper Paleolithic (e.g., Clark, 1983; Mellars, 1989; Sherratt, 1997). Bone, antler, and ivory armatures are common in many European assemblages beginning with the early Upper Paleolithic. Even when such artifacts are not preserved, the presence of backed or marginally retouched bladelets too small and narrow to have been hand-held tools attests to the use of hafts or armatures of highly perishable materials such as wood. Although bladelets are often considered a hallmark of the later Upper Paleolithic, they are quite abundant in some early Upper Paleolithic assemblages from the Near East (e.g., Bar-Yosef and Belfer, 1977; Gilead, 1991; Jones et al., 1983; Phillips, 1988) and also from Europe (Bartolomei et al., 1992; Harrold, 1989; Kuhn and Stiner, 1998; Maroto and Fullola, 1996).

Greater reliance on composite tools in turn implies need for interchangeable parts. Blades, and especially bladelets, are ideal for this application. One often-stated advantage of blade technology is that it allows for greater standardization of the product. This does not necessarily mean that, taken together, *all* products and byproducts of blade production will be notably more standardized than the results of flake manufacture (cf. Chazan, 1995). However, prismatic blade techniques in particular do seem to permit an unusual degree of control over the dimensions and shapes of a limited range of products, namely the blades themselves. The fact that a blade tends to be fairly uniform in width and thickness over its entire length also means that smaller blanks of similar size and shape can be produced simply by sectioning them. In addition, several investigators have argued that one difference between Upper Paleolithic and earlier methods of blank production is the use of soft hammer and indirect (punch) percussion in the later time ranges (Meignen, 1994; Pelegrin, 1990). Soft hammer and indirect percussion permit one to achieve a more uniform final product than does hard hammer percussion. This high degree of control over blank morphology would in turn have obvious benefits when stone tools served as low-cost, replaceable components of composite implements.

We emphasize that this argument does not presuppose that everything in Upper Paleolithic assemblages was hafted, or even that all blade tools served as parts of composite implements. In fact, it is seldom the case that all tools in Upper Paleolithic assemblages were made using blade blanks. Other methods for working stone are likely to have been employed where they offered particular advantages, or where the potential benefits of prismatic blade production did not counterbalance the risk of failure or raw material requirements involved. At the same time, expertise in particular modes of production would be expected to bleed over into blank production for other purposes: skills acquired in making uniform blanks for use in composite tools would inevitably be turned to making larger blades to be used as blanks for hand-held implements.

The assertion that widespread adoption of prismatic blade production during the Upper Paleolithic is related to increasing use of composite tools has several implications. First, the defining characteristic of blades (elongation) may not be so important as the potential for producing uniform, standardized blanks. Second, not all blades are created equal. The appearance of small bladelets as well as the use of soft hammer, indirect percussion or pressure to make highly uniform

blade blanks are more significant technologically than is the simple preponderance of large blades in an assemblage. Most importantly, however, this account also begs the question of why humans might come to rely more and more on complex composite artifacts.

The burgeoning complexity of composite artifacts during the Upper Paleolithic reflects more than a simple increase in the cognitive capacity or technological competence of hominids: after all, hafting itself has a very long history. A more comprehensive explanation requires that one consider disadvantages and costs as well as benefits. The potential advantages of composite tools with interchangeable parts are numerous. Multipart artifacts with easily replaced components may offer increased effectiveness, reliability, *and* maintainability (*sensu* Bleed, 1986), although admittedly these properties have seldom been measured experimentally. The integration of tough, flexible components of bone, antler or hardwoods into weapons and other resource procurement tools reduces the likelihood of catastrophic failure. Moreover, the parts most likely to fail—brittle stone inserts—are inexpensively and easily replaced. Yet this improved functionality is not without costs. Elaborate tools may afford users increased effectiveness or time utility in the procurement and processing of resources, but they also require a greater investment of time and energy, effort which could in principle be put to other fitness-enhancing pursuits such as foraging, mate acquisition or child care. Implements involving parts of several materials bound, spliced or glued together are obviously "expensive" to produce, whether the currency measured is time or energy. Ethnologists (e.g., Osgood, 1940) and experimentalists (e.g., Julien, 1982; Knecht, 1997; Stordeur-Yedid, 1980) have documented the considerable effort and time required to produce complex composite tools and weapons with simple hand tools.

The increasing importance of elaborate composite tools in some parts of the world over the course of the Upper Paleolithic may reflect a significant shift in patterns of allocation of technological effort and a change in the social networks of the producers of these tools. The creation of elaborate technological aids to foraging or other work carries with it a significant amount of "frontloading," expenditure of time and energy well in advance of any possible return. On one hand, this requires a certain degree of foresight on the part of toolmakers. Perhaps more importantly, it requires a significant amount of cooperation and coordination of activities among members of a social group. The investment of significant amounts of time and labor in the production of elaborate items of technology, the potential benefits from which might not be realized for days, weeks or even years, means that individuals were free to divert this time and labor from more immediately pressing concerns such as getting food or shelter. If an individual is able to devote many hours or even days to the manufacture of an artifact, someone else must be carrying at least part of the load with respect to gathering and processing other resources. This "division of labor" might well have been transitory and minor compared with the kinds of occupational differentiation seen in later and larger-scale societies, and we are not arguing for rigid, permanent occupational specialization during the Upper Paleolithic. Nonetheless, the ability to shift the burden of daily subsistence labor onto another individual at least temporarily would be vital to the evolution of some of the complex technologies that began to appear in the Upper Paleolithic. Conversely, the absence of such options for cooperation would inhibit the amount of time and energy any single individual could afford to put into tool manufacture, regardless of the potential payoffs of having more elaborate implements.

Admittedly, the Upper Paleolithic is hardly a monolithic entity. The suite of traits generally thought to typify the Upper Paleolithic does not appear all at once (Clark and Lindly, 1989; Gamble, 1986; Straus, 1990; Straus and Heller, 1988). Moreover, one of the hallmarks of the period between 45,000 and 10,000 years ago is the variability of material remains. Some Upper Paleolithic assemblages contain few blades, and some have little evidence for composite tools. As for the first observation, we emphasize that the use of complex composite tools is neither a necessary nor sufficient condition for the proliferation of blade production. This hypothetical reorganization of technological labor would have rendered blade and bladelet technologies advantageous, but it would not have guaranteed their invention or adoption in all places. Multi-part tools can be made with flake inserts as well. However, if technologies requiring interchangeable components were widely established in the Upper Paleolithic, conditions would have been ideal for the adoption of techniques for blade and bladelet production. As for the second observation, there is no reason to expect that all Upper Paleolithic populations would have used elaborate composite tools, even given the potential to allocate labor to their production. Theories of artifact design predict that the complexity, variety, and labor "cost" of artifacts will vary among hunter-gatherer groups according to patterns of mobility and resource distributions, as well as social factors (e.g., Arnold, 1987; Bleed, 1986; Bousman, 1993; Hayden, 1981; Shott, 1986; Torrence, 1983, 1989). These theories lead us to expect that effective but "expensive" composite artifacts would have appeared most often in certain situations, such as when windows of opportunity for obtaining certain key resources were at their narrowest. The demographic changes which mark the later Upper Paleolithic (e.g. Clark and Straus, 1983; Gamble, 1986:372–373) could also have had important consequences in terms of both the opportunities to invest in elaborate items of material culture, and the benefits of such investment, whether in the context of procuring increasingly scarce game or in connection with exploiting newly important resources such as fish or birds.

What, then, of early (pre–Upper Paleolithic) blade technologies? In biological terms, the resemblance between early and late blade manufacture is likely to be an analogy rather than a homology. They are not in themselves sufficient evidence to argue the early appearance of complex composite tools of the type known for the Upper Paleolithic. Most importantly, the earliest blade technologies do not include those features (bladelet/

microblade production and soft hammer, pressure, or indirect percussion) that afford greatest control over blank form and would be most closely tied to the manufacture of interchangeable components for composite tools. Large, heavy hard hammer blades such as those found in the early Levantine Mousterian, the Hummalian or the Kapthurin formation would not be ideal for hafting in complicated armatures. The Howieson's Poort assemblages, which do contain geometric pieces, remain an exception and an anomaly. Cases such as the early Mousterian of northwestern Europe and the Howieson's Poort are also of a different spatial and chronological order from the proliferation of prismatic blade manufacture during the Upper Paleolithic, and we should not expect them to be amenable to the same kinds of explanations (*contra* Sherratt, 1997:283). Explanations of these more restricted technological phenomena are more appropriately structured in terms of locally relevant factors such as mobility, raw material availability, or artifact function (e.g., Ambrose and Lorenz, 1990; Henry, 1989; Kuhn, 1995; Marks, 1988).

SUMMARY AND CONCLUSION

Long-held and widespread views about the sophistication and utility of blade technologies and their exclusive association with anatomically modern humans and the Upper Paleolithic are based on observations of the limited and rather incomplete European archaeological record of decades past. Based on the archaeological record as it is known today, there is no clear association between the production of elongated blades—prismatic or Levallois—and any single feature of hominid anatomy or behavior. Prismatic blade production is the dominant mode of blank manufacture in most parts of Europe and western Asia during the Upper Paleolithic, but forms of blade technology had been around for tens of millennia before the appearance of modern humans or the Upper Paleolithic, and other modes of blank production continue to be used throughout the world even after the origins of modern humans.

Though hominids have been making blades since the late Middle Pleistocene, there is no denying the fact that blade technologies do come to dominate the archaeological record of western Eurasia and parts of Africa after around 45,000 years ago. Because the basic techniques had first appeared thousands of years earlier, however, this apparently sudden and widespread adoption of a fairly narrow range of methods for making stone tools cannot be attributed to either chance discovery or some specific change in the technological capacities of hominids. The ubiquity of blade technologies involving soft hammer or indirect percussion during the Upper Paleolithic in certain regions of western Eurasia may well have been tied to the use of complex composite tools with interchangeable cutting edges composed of blades or blade segments. Ultimately, the fact that blade technologies—as opposed to other methods of working stone—became predominant in western Eurasia during the late Upper Pleistocene may be simply a "frozen accident," in evolutionary terms equivalent to the fixation of a trait due to historical circumstances. After all, in late prehistoric Australia, microlithic components of composite tools were often manufactured using small flakes (Flood 1983:190). However, if the proliferation of blade and bladelet technologies during the Upper Paleolithic is in fact linked to composite tool manufacture, it may also reflect the emergence of novel and highly significant patterns of social and economic cooperation within human groups.

ACKNOWLEDGMENTS

Discussions with a number of colleagues have greatly influenced our thinking on the topics contained in this paper. We would like to acknowledge the contributions of Anna Belfer-Cohen, Arthur Jelinek, Janusz Kozlowski, Liliane Meignen, Nigel Goring-Morris, and Mary Stiner. Three anonymous reviewers provided cogent and much-needed criticism of an earlier version of this manuscript.

REFERENCES CITED

Ambrose, S., and K. Lorenz. 1990. Social and Ecological Models for the Middle Stone Age in Southern Africa. In The Emergence of Modern Humans: An Archaeological Perspective. P. Mellars, ed. Pp. 3–33. Ithaca, NY: Cornell University Press.

Anderson, D. 1970. Microblade Traditions in Northeastern Alaska. Arctic Anthropology 7(2):2–16.

Anderson-Gerfaud, P. 1990. Aspects of Behaviour in the Middle Paleolithic: Functional Analysis of Stone Tools from Southwest France. In The Emergence of Modern Humans: An Archaeological Perspective. P. Mellars, ed. Pp. 389–419. Ithaca, NY: Cornell University Press.

Andrefsky, W. 1987. Diffusion and Innovation from the Perspective of Wedge Shaped Cores in Alaska and Japan. In The Organization of Core Technology. J. Johnson and C. Morrow, eds. Pp. 13–44. Boulder, CO: Westview Press.

Arnold, J. 1985. The Santa Barbara Channel Islands Bladelet Industry. Lithic Technology 14:71–80.

Arnold, J. 1987. Technology and Economy: Microblade Core Production from the Channel Islands. In The Organization of Core Technology. J. Johnson and C. Morrow, eds. Pp. 207–237. Boulder, CO: Westview Press.

Bar-Yosef, O. 1996. The Middle/Upper Palaeolithic Transition: A View from the Eastern Mediterranean. In The Last Neanderthals, the First Anatomically Modern Humans. E. Carbonell and M. Vaquero, eds. Pp. 79–94. Tarragona, Spain: Universitat Rovira i Virgili.

Bar-Yosef, O., and A. Belfer. 1977. The Lagaman Industry. In Prehistoric Investigations in Gebel Mughara, Sinai. O. Bar-Yosef and J. Phillips, eds. Pp. 42–88. QEDEM 7. Jerusalem: Hebrew University.

Bar-Yosef, O., and A. Belfer-Cohen. 1988. The Early Upper Paleolithic in Levantine Caves. In The Early Upper Paleolithic: Evidence from Europe and the Near East. J. Hoffecker and C. Wolf, eds. Pp. 23–42. BAR International Series, 437. Oxford: British Archaeological Reports.

Bar-Yosef, O., M. Arnold, A. Belfer-Cohen, P. Goldberg, R. Housley, H. Laville, L. Meignen, N. Mercier, J. C. Vogel, and B. Vandermeersch. 1996. The Dating of the Upper Paleolithic Layers in Kebara Cave, Mt. Carmel. Journal of Archaeological Science 23:297–306.

Bartolomei, G., A. Broglio, P. F. Cassoli, L. Castelletti, L. Cattani, M. Cremaschi, G. Giacobini, G. Malerba, A. Maspero, M. Peresani, A. Sartorelli, and A. Tagliacozzo. 1992. La Grotte de Fumane. Un site Aurignacien au pied des Alpes. Preistoria Alpina 28(1):131–179.

Binford, L., and J. O'Connell. 1984. An Alyawara Day: The Stone Quarry. Journal of Anthropological Research 40:406–432.

Bleed, P. 1986. The Optimal Design of Hunting Weapons. American Antiquity 51:737–747.

Boëda, E. 1990. De la surface au volume. Analyse des conceptions des débitages Levallois et laminaire. In Paléolithique Moyen Récent et Paléolithique Supérieur Ancien en Europe. C. Farizy, ed. Pp. 63–68. Mémoires du Musée de Préhistoire d'Ile de France, No. 3.

Boëda, E. 1995. Levallois: Volumetric Construction, Methods, a Technique. In The Definition and Interpretation of Levallois Technology. H. Dibble and O. Bar-Yosef, eds. Pp. 41–68. Monographs in World Archaeology, No. 23. Madison, WI: Prehistory Press.

Boëda, E., J. Connan, D. Dessof, S. Muhesen, N. Mercier, H. Valladas, and N. Tisnerat. 1996. Bitumen as a Hafting Material on Middle Paleolithic Artifacts. Nature 380:336–338.

Boëda, E., J.-M. Geneste, and L. Meignen. 1990. Identification des chaînes opératoires lithiques du Paléolithique ancien et moyen. Paléo 2:43–80.

Boëda, E., and S. Muhesen. 1993. Umm El Tlel (El Kowm, Syrie): Étude préliminaire des industries lithiques du Paléolithique moyen et supérieur. Cahiers de l'Euphrate 7:47–91.

Bordaz, J. 1970. Tools of the Old and New Stone Age. New York: Natural History Press.

Bordes, F. 1960. Le Pré-Aurignacien de Yabroud (Syrie) et son incidence sur la chronologie du quaternaire en Moyen Orient. Bulletin of the Research Council of Israel 9G:91–103.

Bordes, F. 1977. Que sont le Pré-Aurignacien et le Yabroudien? In Eretz Israel 13 (Moshé Stekelis Memorial Volume). B. Arensburg and O. Bar-Yosef, eds. Pp. 49–55. Jerusalem: Israel Exploration Society.

Bousman, C. B. 1993. Hunter-Gatherer Adaptations, Economic Risk and Tool Design. Lithic Technology 18:59–86.

Boyd, R., and J. Silk. 1997. How Humans Evolved. New York and London: W. W. Norton and Co.

Chazan, M. 1995. The Language Hypothesis for the Middle-to-Upper Paleolithic Transition: An Examination Based on Multi-regional Lithic Analysis. Current Anthropology 36:749–768.

Clark, G., and J. Lindly. 1989. The Case for Continuity: Observations on the Biocultural Transition in Europe and Western Asia. In The Human Revolution: Behavioural and Biological Perspectives on the Origins of Modern Humans. P. Mellars and C. Stringer, eds. Pp. 626–676. Princeton, NJ: Princeton University Press.

Clark, G., and L. Straus. 1983. Late Pleistocene Hunter-Gatherer Adaptations in Cantabrian Spain. In Hunter-Gatherer Economy in Prehistory. G. Bailey, ed. Pp. 131–148. Cambridge: Cambridge University Press.

Clark, J. D. 1983. The Significance of Culture Change in the Earlier Later Pleistocene in Northern and Southern Africa. In The Mousterian Legacy: Human Biocultural Change in the Upper Pleistocene. E. Trinkaus, ed. Pp. 1–12. BAR International Series S164. Oxford: British Archaeological Reports.

Clark, J. D. 1989. The Origins and Spread of Modern Humans: A Broad Perspective on the African Evidence. In The Human Revolution: Behavioural and Biological Perspectives on the Origins of Modern Humans. P. Mellars and C. Stringer, eds. Pp. 565–587. Princeton, NJ: Princeton University Press.

Clark, J. E. 1987. Politics, Prismatic Blades, and Mesoamerican Civilization. In The Organization of Core Technology. J. Johnson and C. Morrow, eds. Pp. 259–284. Boulder, CO: Westview Press.

Collins, M. B. 1990. Observations on Clovis Lithic Technology. Current Research in the Pleistocene 7:73–74.

Conard, N. 1990. Laminar Lithic Assemblages from the Last Interglacial Complex in Northwestern Europe. Journal of Anthropological Research 46:243–262.

Cornelissen, E. 1995. Indications du post-Acheuléen (Sangoen) dans la formation Kapthurin, Baringo, Kenya. L'Anthropologie 99:55–73.

Crew, H. L. 1976. The Mousterian Site of Rosh Ein Mor. In Prehistory and Paleoenvironments in the Central Negev, vol. 1. A. Marks, ed. Pp. 75–112. Dallas, TX: Southern Methodist University.

Deacon, H. 1989. Late Pleistocene Paleoecology and Archaeology in the Southern Cape, South Africa. In The Human Revolution: Behavioural and Biological Perspectives on the Origins of Modern

Humans. P. Mellars and C. Stringer, eds. Pp. 547–564. Princeton, NJ: Princeton University Press.

Deacon, J. 1984. The Later Stone People and their Descendants in Southern Africa. *In* Southern African Prehistory and Paleoenvironments. R. Klein, ed. Pp. 221–328. Rotterdam: A. A. Balkema.

Dortch, C., and F. Bordes. 1977. Blades and Levallois Technology in Western Australia. Quartér 27/28:1–19.

Flood, J. 1983. Archaeology of the Dreamtime. Honolulu: University of Hawaii Press.

Foley, R., and M. M. Lahr. 1997. Mode 3 Technologies and the Evolution of Modern Humans. Cambridge Archaeological Journal 7(1):3–36.

Friedman, E., N. Goren-Inbar, A. Rosenfeld, O. Marder, and F. Burian. 1994. Hafting during Mousterian Times—Further Indications. Journal of the Israel Prehistoric Society 26:8–31.

Gamble, C. 1986. The Paleolithic Settlement of Europe. Cambridge: Cambridge University Press.

Gamble, C. 1994. Timewalkers: The Prehistory of Global Colonization. Cambridge, MA: Harvard University Press.

Garrod, D. A. E., and D. Kirkbride. 1961. Acheuléo-Jabrudian et pré-Aurignacien de la Grotte de Taboun, Mont Carmel: Étude stratigraphique et chronologique. Quaternaria 3:39–59.

Gilead, I. 1991. The Upper Paleolithic Period in the Levant. Journal of World Prehistory 5:105–153.

Goren-Inbar, N. 1990. Quneitra: A Mousterian Site on the Golan Heights. QEDEM, Monographs of the Institute of Archaeology. Jerusalem: Hebrew University.

Gouedo, J.-M. 1990. Les technologies lithiques du Châtelperronien de la couche X de la Grotte du Renne d'Arcy-sur Cure (Yonne). *In* Paléolithique Moyen Récent et Paléolithique Supérieur Ancien en Europe. C. Farizy, ed. Pp. 305–308. Mémoires du Musée de Préhistoire d'Ile de France, No. 3. Nemours: A.P.R.A.I.F.

Green, F. E. 1963. Clovis Blades: An Important Addition to the Llano Complex. American Antiquity 29:145–165.

Grün, R., C. B. Stringer, and H. P. Schwarcz. 1991. ESR Dating of Teeth from Garrod's Tabun Cave Collection. Journal of Human Evolution 20:231–248.

Guilbaud, M. 1993. Debitage from the Upper Castelperronian Level at Saint-Césaire: Methodological Approach and Implications for the Transition from Middle to Upper Paleolithic. *In* Context of a Late Neandertal. F. Lévêque, A. Backer, and M. Guilbaud, eds. Pp. 37–58. Madison, WI: Prehistory Press.

Harrold, F. 1989. Mousterian, Châtelperronian and Early Aurignacian in Western Europe: Continuity or Discontinuity? *In* The Human Revolution: Behavioral and Biological Perspectives on the Origins of Modern Humans. P. Mellars and C. Stringer, eds. Pp. 677–713. Princeton, NJ: Princeton University Press.

Hayden, B. 1981. Research and Development in the Stone Age: Technological Transitions among Hunter-Gatherers. Current Anthropology 22:519–528.

Henry, D. 1989. Correlations between Reduction Strategies and Settlement Patterns. *In* Alternative Approaches to Lithic Analysis. D. Henry and G. Odell, eds. Pp. 139–155. Washington, DC: Archaeological Papers of the American Anthropology Association, No. 1.

Hester, T., and H. Shafer. 1987. Observations on Ancient Maya Core Technology at Colha, Belize. *In* The Organization of Core Technology. J. Johnson and C. Morrow, eds. Pp. 239–258. Boulder, CO: Westview Press.

Inizan, M. L., H. Roche, and J. Tixier. 1993. Technology of Knapped Stone. Préhistoire de la Pierre Taillée, 3. Meudon: CREP.

Jelinek, A. J. 1981. The Middle Paleolithic in the Southern Levant from the Perspective of Tabun Cave. *In* Préhistoire du Levant. J. Cauvin and P. Sanlaville, eds. Pp. 265–280. Paris: Éditions du CNRS.

Jelinek, A. J. 1982. The Middle Paleolithic in the Southern Levant with Comments on the Appearance of Modern *Homo sapiens*. *In* The Transition from Lower to Middle Paleolithic and the Origin of Modern Man. A. Ronen, ed. Pp. 57–104. BAR International Series, 151. Oxford: British Archaeological Reports.

Jelinek, A. J. 1990. The Amudian in the Context of the Mugharan Tradition at Tabun Cave (Mount Carmel) Israel. *In* The Emergence of Modern Humans: An Archaeological Perspective. P. Mellars, ed. Pp. 81–90. Ithaca, NY: Cornell University Press.

Jia, L., and W. Huang. 1985. The Late Paleolithic of China. *In* Paleoanthropology and Paleolithic Archaeology in the People's Republic of China. R. Wu and J. Olsen, eds. Pp. 211–224. New York: Academic Press.

Jones, M., A. Marks, and D. Kaufman. 1983. Boker: The Artifacts. *In* Prehistory and Paleoenvironments in the Central Negev, Israel, vol. 3. A. Marks, ed. Pp. 283–329. Dallas, TX: Southern Methodist University.

Julien, M. 1982. Les Harpons Magdaléniens. XVII Supplément à Gallia Préhistoire. Paris: Éditions du CNRS.

Kelly, R. L. 1988. The Three Sides of a Biface. American Antiquity 53: 717–734.

Knecht, H. 1997. Projectile Points of Bone, Antler and Stone: Experimental Explorations of Manufacture and Use. *In* Projectile Technology. H. Knecht, ed. Pp.191–212. New York: Plenum Press.

Kozlowski, J. K. 1990. A Multiaspectual Approach to the Origins of the Upper Paleolithic. *In* The Emergence of Modern Humans: An Archaeological Perspective. P. Mellars, ed. Pp. 419–437. Edinburgh: Edinburgh University Press.

Kuhn, S. 1995. Mousterian Lithic Technology: An Ecological Approach. Princeton, NJ: Princeton University Press.

Kuhn, S., and M. Stiner. 1992. New Research on Riparo Mochi, Balzi Rossi (Liguria): Preliminary Results. Quaternaria Nova 2:77–90.

Kuhn, S., and M. Stiner. 1998. The Earliest Aurignacian of Riparo Mochi, Liguria. Current Anthropology 39 (supplement):S175–S189.

Lindly, J., and G. Clark. 1987. A Preliminary Lithic Analysis of the Mousterian Site of 'Ain Difla (WHS site 634) in the Wadi Ali, West-Central Jordan. Proceedings of the Prehistoric Society 3:48–76.

Liubin, V. P. 1977. Mousterian Culture in the Caucasus. Leningrad: Nauka (in Russian).

Liubin, V. P. 1989. Paleolithic of Caucasus. Leningrad: Nauka (in Russian).

Marks, A. 1983. The Middle to Upper Paleolithic transition in the Levant. *In* Advances in World Archaeology, vol. 2. F. Wendorf and A. E. Close, eds. Pp. 51–98. New York: Academic Press.

Marks, A. 1988. The Middle to Upper Paleolithic Transition in the Levant: Technological Change as an Adaptation to Increasing Mobility. *In* L'Homme de Néandertal, vol. 8, La Mutation. M. Otte, ed. Pp. 109–123. ERAUL 35. Liège: Université de Liège.

Marks, A. 1990. The Middle and Upper Paleolithic of the Near East and the Nile Valley: The Problem of Cultural Transitions. *In* The Emergence of Modern Humans: An Archaeological Perspective. P. Mellars, ed. Pp. 56–80. Ithaca, NY: Cornell University Press.

Marks, A., and K. Monigal. 1995. Modeling the Production of Elongated Blanks from the Early Levantine Mousterian at Rosh Ein Mor. *In* The Definition and Interpretation of Levallois Technology. H. Dibble and O. Bar-Yosef, eds. Pp. 267–278. Madison, WI: Prehistory Press.

Marks, A., and P. Volkman. 1983. Changing Core Reduction Strategies: A Technological Shift from the Middle to the Upper Paleolithic in the Southern Levant. *In* The Mousterian Legacy: Human Biocultural Change in the Upper Pleistocene. E. Trinkaus, ed. Pp. 13–33. BAR International Series S164. Oxford: British Archaeological Reports.

Maroto, J. S., and J. M. Fullola. 1996. Cultural Change between Middle and Upper Paleolithic in Catalonia. *In* The Last Neandertals, the First Anatomically Modern Humans. E. Carbonell and M. Vaquero, eds. Pp. 219–250. Tarragona, Spain: Universitat Rovira i Virgili.

McBrearty, S., L. Bishop, and J. Kingston. 1996. Variability in Traces of Middle Pleistocene Hominid Behavior in the Kapthurin Formation, Baringo, Kenya. Journal of Human Evolution 30:563–580.

McBurney, C. B. M. 1967. The Haua Fteah (Cyrenaica) and the Stone Age of the South-East Mediterranean. Cambridge: Cambridge University Press.

Meignen, L. 1994. Le Paléolithique moyen au Proche-Orient: le phénomène laminaire. *In* Les Industries Laminaires au Paléolithique Moyen. S. Révillion and A. Tuffreau, eds. Pp. 125–159. Paris: Editions du CNRS.

Meignen, L. 1995. Levallois Lithic Production Systems in the Middle Paleolithic of the Near East: The Case of the Unidirectional Method. *In* The Definition and Interpretation of Levallois

Technology. H. Dibble and O. Bar-Yosef, eds. Pp. 361–381. Madison, WI: Prehistory Press.

Meignen, L. 1996. Les prémices du Paléolithique superieur au proche orient. *In* The Last Neandertals, the First Anatomically Modern Humans. E. Carbonell and M. Vaquero, eds. Pp. 107–127. Tarragona, Spain: Universitat Rovira i Virgili.

Meignen, L. 1998. A Preliminary Report on the Hayonim Cave Lithic Assemblages in the Context of the Near Eastern Middle Paleolithic. *In* Neandertals and Modern Humans in Western Asia. T. Akazawa, K. Aoki, and O. Bar-Yosef, eds. Pp. 165–180. New York: Plenum Press.

Meignen, L., and O. Bar-Yosef. 1991. Les outillages lithiques Moustériens de Kébara. *In* Le Squelette mousterien de Kebara 2, Mt. Carmel, Israël. O. Bar-Yosef and B. Vandermeersch, eds. Pp. 49–76. Paris: Editions CNRS.

Mellars, P. 1989. Technological Changes at the Middle to Upper Paleolithic Transition: Economic, Social, and Cognitive Perspectives. *In* The Human Revolution: Behavioral and Biological Perspectives on the Origins of Modern Humans. P. Mellars and C. Stringer, eds. Pp. 338–365. Princeton, NJ: Princeton University Press.

Mellars, P. 1996. The Neanderthal Legacy. Princeton, NJ: Princeton University Press.

Mercier, N., H. Valladas, G. Valladas, J. L. Reyss, A. Jelinek, L. Meignen, and J. L. Joron. 1995. TL Dates of Burnt Flints from Jelinek's Excavations at Tabun and Their Implications. Journal of Archaeological Science 22(4):495–510.

Nishiaki, Y. 1989. Early Blade Industries in the Levant: The Placement of Douara IV Industry in the Context of the Levantine Early Middle Paleolithic. Paléorient 15(1):215–229.

Osgood, C. 1940. Ingalik Material Culture. Yale University Publications in Anthropology, 22. New Haven, CT: Yale University Press.

Otte, M. 1994. Rocourt (Liège, Belgique): Industrie laminaire ancienne. *In* Les Industries Laminaires au Paléolithique Moyen. S. Révillion and A. Tuffreau, eds. Pp. 179–186. Paris: Éditions du CNRS.

Owen, L. 1988. Blade and Microblade Technology: Selected Assemblages from the North American Arctic and the Upper Paleolithic of Southwest Germany. BAR International Series 441. Oxford: British Archaeological Reports.

Palma di Cesnola, A. 1986. Panorama del Musteriano Italiano. *In* I Neandertaliani. D. Cochi-Genick, ed. Pp. 139–174. Viareggio, Italy: Museo Preistorico e Archeologico "Alberto Carlo Blanc."

Palma di Cesnola, A. 1993. II Paleolitico Superiore in Italia: Introduzione allo studio. Firenze, Italy: Garlatti e Razzai Editori.

Parry, W. J. 1994. Prismatic Blade Technologies in North America. *In* The Organization of North American Prehistoric Chipped Stone Tool Technologies. P. J. Carr, ed. Pp. 87–98. Archaeological Series 7. Ann Arbor, MI: International Monographs in Prehistory.

Parry, W. J., and R. L. Kelly. 1987. Expedient Core Technology and Sedentism. *In* The Organization of Core Technology. J. Johnson and C. Morrow, eds. Pp. 285–304. Boulder, CO: Westview Press.

Pelegrin, J. 1990 Observations technologiques sur quelques séries du Châtelperronien et du MTA B du sud-ouest de la France: Un hypothèse d'évolution. *In* Paléolithique Moyen Récent et Paléolithique Supérieur Ancien en Europe. C. Farizy, ed. Pp. 39–42. Mémoirs du Musée de Préhistoire d'Ile de France, No. 3. Nemours: A.P.R.A.I.F.

Pelegrin, J. 1995. Technologie Lithique: Le Châtelperronian de Roc-du-Combe (Lot) et de La Côte (Dordogne). Cahiers du Quaternaire, N. 20. Paris: Éditions du CNRS.

Phillips, J. 1988. The Upper Paleolithic of the Wadi Feiran, Southern Sinai. Paléorient 14:183–200.

Relethford, J. 1997. The Human Species. 3rd edition. Mountain View, CA: Mayfield.

Révillion, S. 1995. Technologie du débitage laminaire au Paléolithique moyen en Europe Septentrionale: État de la question. Bulletin de la Société Préhistorique Française 92:425–441.

Révillion, S., and A. Tuffreau, eds. 1994. Les Industries Laminaires au Paléolithique Moyen. Paris: Éditions du CNRS.

Reynolds, T. 1990. The Middle-Upper Paleolithic Transition in Southwestern France: Interpreting the Lithic Evidence. *In* The

Emergence of Modern Humans: An Archaeological Perspective. P. Mellars, ed. Pp. 262–276. Ithaca, NY: Cornell University Press.

Rigaud, J.-P., ed. 1989. La Grotte Vaufrey: Paléoenvironnement, Chronologie, Activités Humains. Paris: Mémoires de la Société Préhistorique Française, Tome XIX.

Ronen, A. 1992. The Emergence of Blade Technology: Cultural Affinities. *In* The Evolution and Dispersal of Modern Humans in Asia. T. Akazawa, K. Aoki, and T. Kimura, eds. Pp. 217–228. Tokyo: Hokusen-Sha.

Sampson, C. G. 1974. The Stone Age Archaeology of Southern Africa. New York: Academic Press.

Schick, K., and N. Toth 1993. Making Silent Stones Speak: Human Evolution and the Dawn of Technology. New York: Simon and Schuster.

Shea, J. 1989. A Functional Study of the Lithic Industries Associated with the Hominid Fossils in the Kebara and Qafzeh Caves, Israel. *In* The Human Revolution: Behavioral and Biological Perspectives on the Origins of Modern Humans. P. Mellars and C. Stringer, eds. Pp. 598–610. Princeton, NJ: Princeton University Press.

Sheets, P., and G. Muto. 1972. Pressure Blades and Total Cutting Edge: An Experiment in Lithic Technology. Science 175:632–634.

Sherratt, A. 1997. Climatic Cycles and Behavioral Revolutions. Antiquity 71(272):271–287.

Shott, M. 1986. Settlement Mobility and Technological Organization: An Ethnographic Examination. Journal of Anthropological Research 42:15–51.

Sonneville-Bordes, D. 1960. Le Paléolithique Supérieur en Perigord. Bordeaux: Delmas.

Stordeur-Yedid, D. 1980. Harpons Paléo-Esquimaux de la Région d'Igloulik. Préhistoire: Enquêtes et Méthodes. Paris: Éditions ADPF.

Straus, L. G. 1990. The Early Upper Paleolithic of Southwest Europe. Cro-Magnon Adaptations in the Iberian Peripheries, 40,000–20,000 BP. *In* The Emergence of Modern Humans: An Archaeological Perspective. P. Mellars, ed. Pp. 276–302. Ithaca, NY: Cornell University Press.

Straus, L., and C. Heller. 1988. Explorations of the Twilight Zone: The Early Upper Paleolithic of Vasco-Cantabrian Spain. *In* The Early Upper Paleolithic: Evidence from Europe and the Near East. J. Hoffecker and C. Wolf, eds. Pp. 97–134. BAR International Series, 437. Oxford: British Archaeological Reports.

Stringer, C. 1989. The Origin of Early Modern Humans: A Comparison of the European and Non-European Evidence. *In* The Human Revolution: Biological and Behavioral Perspectives on the Origins of Modern Humans. P. Mellars and C. Stringer, eds. Pp. 232–244. Princeton, NJ: Princeton University Press.

Svoboda, J., and P. Skrdla. 1995. Bohunician Technology. *In* The Definition and Interpretation of Levallois Technology. H. Dibble and O. Bar-Yosef, eds. Pp. 432–439. Madison, WI: Prehistory Press.

le Tensorer, J.-M., and S. Muhesen. 1997. Les Premiers Hommes du Désert Syrien: Fouilles Syrio-Suisse à Nadaouiyeh Ain Askar. Paris: Éditions du Musée National d'Histoire Naturelle.

Texier, P.-J. 1996. Production en série. Pour la Science (232):22.

Tixier, J. 1963. Typologie de l'Epipaléolithique du Maghreb. Paris: C.R.A.P.E., 2.

Torrence, R. 1983. Time Budgeting and Hunter-Gatherer Technology. *In* Hunter-Gatherer Economy in Prehistory. G. Bailey, ed. Pp. 11–22. Cambridge: Cambridge University Press.

Torrence, R. 1989. Time, Energy, and Stone Tools. Cambridge: Cambridge University Press.

Tuffreau, A., and J. Somme, eds. 1988. Le Gisement Paléolithique Moyen de Biache-Saint-Vaast (Pas-de-Calais). Vol. 1, Stratigraphie, environment, études archéologiques. Mémoires de la Société Préhistorique Française, T. 21. Paris.

Tuffreau, A., S. Révillion, J. Somme, and B. Van Vliet-Lanoë. 1994. Le gisement Paléolithique moyen de Seclin (Nord). Bulletin de la Société Préhistorique Française 91:23–46.

Vandermeersch, B. 1978. Le crâne pré-Wurmien de Biache-Saint-Vaast (Pas-de-Calais). *In* Les Origines Humaines et les Époques de l'Intelligence. F. Bordes, ed. Pp. 153–157. Paris: Masson.

Volman, T. 1984. The Early Prehistory of Southern Africa. *In* Southern African Prehistory and Paleoenvironments. R. Klein, ed. Pp. 169–220. Rotterdam: A. A. Balkema.

66

A Middle Stone Age Worked Bone Industry from Katanda, Upper Semliki Valley, Zaire

J. E. Yellen, A. S. Brooks, E. Cornelissen, M. J. Mehlman, and K. Stewart

ABSTRACT

Three archaeological sites at Katanda on the Upper Semliki River in the Western Rift Valley of Zaire have provided evidence for a well-developed bone industry in a Middle Stone Age context. Artifacts include both barbed and unbarbed points as well as a daggerlike object. Dating by both direct and indirect means indicate an age of ~90,000 years or older. Together with abundant fish (primarily catfish) remains, the bone technology indicates that a complex subsistence specialization had developed in Africa by this time. The level of behavioral competence required is consistent with that of upper Paleolithic Homo sapiens sapiens. These data support an African origin of behaviorally as well as biologically modern humans.

Anatomically modern humans (*Homo sapiens sapiens*) appeared in Africa and the Levant before 90,000 years ago (ka) (*1*). By 50 ka, they had colonized Australia (*2*) and possibly east Asia (*3*). In the colder climates of Europe, central Asia, and Siberia, however, Neandertals (*Homo sapiens neandertalensis*) continued to predominate until as late as 35 ka. The middle to upper Paleolithic behavioral transition in Europe, central Asia, Siberia, and the Near East also occurred between 40 and 30 ka and is marked by the appearance of (i) new technologies, such as prismatic blade cores, specialized bone and antler tools, burins, and sophisticated hearths, (ii) more complex economic strategies, involving seasonally specific activities, storage, and long-distance procurement, (iii) larger scale social networks, reflected not only in the long-distance trade in raw materials but also in the use of personal ornaments, and (iv) an expanded use of symbols in art and daily life. Regionally specific styles of artifact manufacture in the early upper Paleolithic reflect this greater social complexity. In Europe, with a few exceptions from the transitional period (*4*), the evolutionary shifts in human morphology and behavior coincide; anatomically modern humans are associated with upper Paleolithic industries, whereas Neandertals are associated with middle Paleolithic or Mousterian industries.

In Africa, however, fossils of anatomically modern humans from between 130 and ~60 ka are associated with industries grouped as Middle Stone Age (MSA), which share broad technological parallels with the Mousterian–middle Paleolithic of western Eurasia (*5*). By ~40 ka, these flake and prepared-core industries begin to be replaced, at least in some areas, by Later Stone Age (LSA) industries based primarily on microlithic technology rather than on blades (*6*). This new technology is associated with other indicators of greater behavioral complexity such as bone tools, ostrich eggshell beads, and transport of raw materials over long distances. The extent to which the MSA differs from the Mousterian in foreshadowing this complexity is uncertain (*7*).

We have recently recovered evidence for early complex behavior in the MSA from three sites at Katanda (Kt2, Kt9, and Kt16), a multisite locality in the Upper Semliki Valley of eastern Zaire, ~6 km north of Ishango, where the Semliki River exits from Lake Rutanzige (formerly Lake Edward) (*8*). The Katanda materials include a formal (*9*) bone industry, consisting of barbed bone points, unbarbed points, and a flat dagger. Bone industries from other African sites are considerably younger. Upstream at Ishango, uniserial and biserial barbed points have been dated to ~25 ka (*10, 11*). Outside Africa, formal bone points with finished bases suggestive of hafting first appear in the European Aurignacian as early as 38 to 40 ka (*12*); barbed points, however, do not occur before ~14 to 12 ka (*13*) at sites throughout Eurasia. Here we describe the artifact horizon at Kt9 with occasional reference to materials from Kt2 and Kt16. Paleoenvironmental data (*8*) suggest that all three Katanda sites were located along the valley of a southward-flowing proto-Semliki River, fringed with relatively dense gallery forest in proximity to open savannas. Sediment analyses indicate that Kt9 was the closest of the three to the proto-Semliki channel (*14*).

Excavation at Kt2 began in 1986 and continued through 1990, exposing 21 m² in the MSA levels. Three horizons of MSA were distinguished. The lowest, resting on the ASB paleosol, is the most comparable stratigraphically to the MSA horizons at Kt9 and Kt16. Over 2700 lithics in quartz, quartzite, and chert and 1100 faunal remains of fish and mammals were recovered from this lower horizon. The upper two MSA horizons yielded a total of 3700 lithics, predominantly in quartz, and some 75 poorly preserved faunal remains of which only 10 fragments were identifiable. Discoidal cores were the most distinctive aspect of the lithic material; formal tools were rare. In 1990, a single large fusiform bone point was recovered from the lowest MSA horizon in contact with the paleosol.

At Kt9, the MSA horizon crops out on a steep cliff face below ~8 m of horizontally stratified sand and silt, carbonate paleosols, and volcanic deposits. This over-burden was intact over all but the extreme northwest and southwest corners of the excavated area at the cliff face. Removal of the overburden over an area of 35.2 m^2 revealed a dense concentration of artifacts and faunal remains (*15*).

The artifact concentration stopped abruptly on the north, east, and southeast. To the west and southwest, the original distribution had been truncated by erosion of the cliff face. The artifact horizon rested on a surface that sloped up 3° to the southeast. The thickness of the concentration averaged 5.5 cm but increased down-slope to a maximum of 16 cm. The abundance of artifacts (up to 289 pieces per 400 cm^2), the abrupt edges of the con-centration, and the dominance of chipped pieces over manuports or rolled quartz fragments, together with the nature of overlying cover and matrix sediments (medium to fine sands), suggest that the concentration itself is an anthropogenic feature or "pavement" (*16*).

The Kt9 concentration included over 8000 lithics, 7369 mammal and fish remains, and most remarkably, a series of 10 worked bone artifacts. This assemblage in-dicates the presence of a highly developed projectile technology and complex subsistence strategy. Fish re-mains and worked bone artifacts are rare in other MSA sites (*17–19*). The degree of abrasion and weathering on some of the lithic and faunal fragments suggests that the concentration may have been exposed for a signifi-cant period of time. Dating of the immediately overly-ing sands and teeth from the concentration suggests an age of 80 to 90 ka for the final burial of the site (*8*).

The lithic industry from Kt9 falls technologically and typologically within the broad range of the MSA. Local quartz and quartzites provided most of the raw material, although fragments of a nonlocal brown chert are also present. The percentage of recognizable cores, re-touched pieces, and other formal artifacts in the ana-lyzed sample of 7366 pieces is a low 8.2%. Core types were primarily discoidal but included examples with single and multiple platforms. Bipolar specimens are rare. Scrapers on retouched flakes are uncommon and do not conform to highly formalized patterns. Occasional spheroids and rubbing or grinding stones with intentionally ground flat faces are also present. The assemblage lacks formal bifacial or unifacial points or daggers, as well as hand axes, large core tools, blades, or microliths. Presence of the latter would have sug-gested inclusion within the LSA.

Highly formalized worked bone tools constitute the most remarkable aspect of the assemblage. These in-clude seven well-made uniserial barbed bone points, two unbarbed points, and a large dagger-shaped object of unknown function (Table 1). All are made from rib fragments or long bone splinters of large mammals. Replication experiments and low-power microscopic examination (*20*) indicate that the shape was obtained by grinding the bone on a stone anvil or with a stone grinder. The method for barb construction on all pieces was the same: The edge was first shaped and smoothed before parallel notches, all at the same oblique angle to the long axis of the point, were cut into it. Specialized lithic artifacts such as burins were unnecessary, as the barbs could have been cut with an unmodified quartz flake. The resultant barbs are shaped like a parallelo-gram with three distinct edges (Figure 1). This shape clearly distinguishes the Katanda points from later Ishangian counterparts (*21*), all of which have a trian-gular shape formed by the intersection of two edges.

Pieces where the butt end is preserved suggest that two hafting methods were used. Either several shallow

Table 1. Worked Bone from Katanda Sites

Site	Piece Number	State	Descriptive Notes	Maximum Width (mm)	Maximum Thickness (mm)
Barbed points					
Kt9	2	PF; tip AC; broken behind first barb	Rounded one face; medullary face flattened	19	9
Kt9	3	DF; last barb + portion of haft	Haft: two complete encircling incised grooves	17	11
Kt9	4	DF?; butt C; broken at haft incision	Markedly flattened both faces	17	8
Kt9	5	DF; butt C + five barbs	Rounded both faces; haft: three notches on barbed + three on unbarbed edge	14	7
Kt9	6	PF; tip AC + two barbs	Rounded one face; slightly flattened other	12	8
Kt9	7	AC; small fragment of tip missing; length, 142 mm.	Four barbs; slightly flattened one face; haft: three complete encircling incised grooves	19	13
Kt9	9	DF; butt C + one barb	Flattened both faces; haft: seven notches on barbed + seven on unbarbed edge	19	11
Kt16	1	AC: extreme tip and butt missing; length, 130 mm	Ten barbs; haft: nine notches barbed + nine unbarbed edge	19	9
Unbarbed pointed pieces					
Kt9	1	Pointed end C; broken across shaft	Flattened both faces; no haft indication	14	7
Kt9	8	Pointed end AC; broken across shaft	Rounded both faces; no haft indication	11	8
Kt2	1	Butt C + shaft fragment	Rounded; no haft indication		
"Knife"					
Kt9	10 (A, B, C, D)	Tip + portion of "blade" Tip = A + B + C D is a nonattached shaft fragment	Tip and edges rounded; flattened both faces	39	7

AC, almost complete; C, complete; DF, distal fragment; PF, proximal fragment.

Figure 1. *Worked bone from Kt9 and Kt16. Top row: Kt9:10, D through A (left to right); second row: Kt9:6, Kt16:1; third row: Kt9:7, A and B, Kt9:9; fourth row: Kt9:8, Kt9:5; fifth row: Kt9:1, Kt9:4, Kt9:3. See Table 1 for descriptions.*

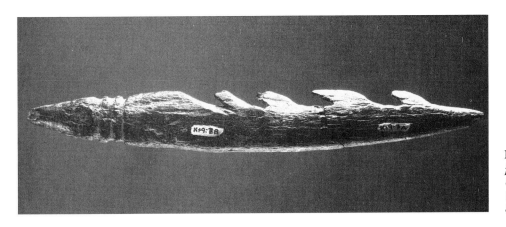

Figure 2. *Complete barbed bone point from Katanda 9, with circular grooves around the base. (Photo courtesy Chip Clark, Smithsonian Institution)*

grooves were incised around the circumference of the shaft (Figure 2) or a series of closely spaced notches were cut into the barbed and nonbarbed edges. It is possible that the points served as harpoons, which, by definition, detach from the shaft after contact with prey, but this is unlikely because it is difficult for this grooved butt shape to hold a line against pressure from the harpooned animal. It is more likely that they were permanently fixed to a shaft.

The blunt rounded point and edges of the dagger-like object suggest that it served neither to cut nor pierce; its function is unknown. Although the two non-barbed points probably served as weapons, their use is also uncertain. The number of clearly distinct artifact classes demonstrates that the Katanda people recognized that bone could serve as a workable plastic medium and be used for different purposes.

The barbed bone points are spatially associated with both fish and mammal remains, which are present in abundance at Kt9 as well as Kt2 and Kt16. Species captured by Katanda people (8) include *Clarias* and *Synodontis*, both catfish, which constitute the majority of the assemblage. Because of *Clarias*'s much larger size

(some specimens exceeded 2 m in length), this species could have provided the major meat input. *Clarias* is a bottom dweller that spawns in shallow water. The taxa represented in the samples from all three Katanda sites and the absence of individuals in juvenile size ranges are consistent with predation during spawning and suggest that the Katanda people visited the area repeatedly during limited seasons. *Clarias* and *Synodontis* spawn chiefly on floodplains in the rainy season, when they are easiest to catch (22).

The distribution of materials within the pavement suggests several inferences regarding behavior. Artifacts and fauna are particularly concentrated in two distinct clusters on the upslope portion of the pavement (23). These clusters cannot be attributed to materials settling into low points on the surface. Size sorting is evident (24) both overall and within each cluster, and larger pieces are located further downslope. Although the extent of abrasion on some of the bone and lithic pieces attests to extended exposure on the surface, the strong sorting by size over a short distance suggests that the deposits were redistributed slightly by low-energy transport. The effect of this was to blur the cluster edges.

Although one or more edges of each cluster have been truncated by erosion of the cliff face, analysis of the remainder suggests that each exhibits bilateral symmetry and that material is concentrated in the center. On this basis, it is possible to reconstruct the original shapes and sizes of the clusters. One cluster is somewhat larger than the other (4 and 3.4 m in maximum diameter). The two clusters contain similar proportions of artifacts and faunal remains. Neither the contemporaneity nor original causality of the clusters can be proven. In terms of cluster size, distance between clusters, and similarity in both faunal and lithic remains, the pattern conforms to that of ethnographically observed debris produced by hunter-gatherer nuclear families in which production tasks are replicated by each nuclear unit (25).

The Kt16 site, 400 m to the north of Kt9, was discovered and excavated in 1990. From 11 m² of a buried MSA horizon, we recovered ~1500 lithics, 650 mammalian faunal elements, and 9700 fish remains, together with a large barbed bone point. As at Kt9 and Kt2, the assemblage consisted largely of flakes and radial cores, with rare formal tools. In contrast to the other two sites, however, Kt16 also contained several large bifacial pieces, a few blades, and two large, carefully made grindstones on dioritic, gabbroic, or amphibolite rocks. Microliths and microcores such as those associated with the late Paleolithic Ishango horizons (8) are absent at all three sites.

The Katanda sites indicate that a complex bone industry and seasonal use of aquatic resources had developed by ~90 ka. The absence of known parallels within Africa may indicate the existence at this time of a geographically limited cultural tradition, with little contact between central and southern Africa, or it may reflect inadequate exposure or exploration of the ancient margins of large tropical rivers and lakes. The presence of other, geographically limited hafted projectile traditions within the MSA, such as the Lupemban or Bambata (26), reflects that African hominids not only possessed considerable technological capabilities at this time but also incorporated symbolic or stylistic content into their projectile forms. The fact that other early barbed bone points, although ~55,000 to 60,000 years younger, occur only 6 km away suggests the long-term continuity of regional adaptations (11). The Katanda people may have been living in nuclear family units and following a specialized subsistence pattern most often associated with a terminal Pleistocene to Holocene adaptation. Their archaeological traces suggest the early presence of modern behavioral capabilities in Africa along with the evidence for anatomically modern humans.

REFERENCES AND NOTES

1. H. Valladas et al., *Nature* **331**, 614 (1988); H. P. Schwarcz et al., *J. Hum. Evol.* **17**, 733 (1988); G. H. Miller, P. B. Beaumont, A. T. Jull, B. Johnson, *Proc. R. Soc. London Ser. B* **337**, 149 (1992); A. S. Brooks, P. E. Hare, J. E. Kokis, *Carnegie Inst. Washington Yearb.* **92**, 95 (1993); P. E. Hare, G. L. Goodfriend, A. S. Brooks, J. E. Kokis, D. W. Von Endt, *ibid.*, p. 80; R. Grun and C. B. Stringer, *Archaeometry* **33**, 153 (1991).

2. R. Jones, in *The Human Revolution: Behavioral and Biological Perspectives on the Origins of Modern Humans,* P. Mellars and C. Stringer, Eds. (Edinburgh Univ. Press, Edinburgh, 1989), pp. 743–782; R. G. Roberts, R. Jones, M. A. Smith, *Nature* **345**, 153 (1990).

3. A. S. Brooks and B. Wood, *Nature* **344**, 288 (1990).

4. F. Levêque, A. M. Backer, M. Guilbaud, *Context of a Late Neandertal: Implications of Multidisciplinary Research for the Transition to Upper Paleolithic Adaptations at Saint-Césaire (Charente-Maritime) France* (Monogr. in World Prehistory 16, Prehistory Press, Madison, WI, 1993); F. H. Smith and J. Ahern, *Am. J. Phys. Anthropol.* **93**, 275 (1994).

5. Relevant sites include Klasies River Mouth, Border Cave, Die Kelders, and Equus caves in South Africa, Mumba Cave in Tanzania, and the Omo River Kibish formation in Ethiopia. Dating by various direct and indirect techniques indicate ages of ~50,000 to greater than 105,000 years [R. Grun, N. J. Shackelton, H. J. Deacon, *Curr. Anthropol.* **31**, 427 (1990); H. J. Deacon, in *The Human Revolution: Behavioral and Biological Perspectives on the Origins of Modern Humans,* P. Mellars and C. B. Stringer, Eds. (Edinburgh Univ. Press, Edinburgh, 1989), pp. 547–564; A. S. Brooks et al., *Science* **248**, 60 (1990); M. J. Mehlman, *World Archaeol.* **11**, 80 (1979); *J. Archaeol. Sci.* **14**, 133 (1987); K. W. Butzer, F. H. Brown, D. L. Thurber, *Quaternaria* **11**, 15 (1969).

6. P. B. Beaumont, H. de Villiers, J. C. Vogel, *S. Afr. J. Sci.* **74**, 409 (1978); F. Van Noten, *Antiquity* **51**, 35 (1977); S. H. Ambrose, paper presented at the 11th Biennial Meeting of the Society of Africanist Archaeologists, Los Angeles, 26 to 29 March 1992; M. J. Mehlman and A. S. Brooks, paper presented at the 11th Biennial Meeting of the Society of Africanist Archaeologists, Los Angeles, 26 to 29 March 1992.

7. A. S. Brooks, in *Encyclopedia of Human Evolution and Prehistory,* I. Tattersal, E. Delson, J. Van Couvering, Eds. (Garland, New York, 1988), pp. 346–349; S. McBrearty, *Man* **25**, 129 (1990); R. G. Klein, *The Human Career* (Univ. of Chicago Press, Chicago, 1989).

8. A. S. Brooks et al., *Science* **268**, 548 (1995); See also discussion of large mammal remains in this paper.

9. Earlier bevel-shaped or pointed bone and ivory implements are known from several middle Pleistocene sites including Přezletice, Czech Republic [J. Fridrich, *Proceedings of the IXth International Union of Pre- and Proto-Historic Sciences Section VIII: Les Premieres Industries d'Europe* (Nice, France, 1976), pp. 8–23], Bilzingsleben, Germany [D. Mania and T. Weber, *Bilzingsleben III Veroffentlichungen des Landesmuseums fur Vorgeschichte in Halle* **39**, 9 (1986)], Kabwe, Zambia [J. D. Clark, in *From the Earliest Times to c. 500 BC*, vol. 1 of *The Cambridge History of Africa*. J. D. Clark, Ed. (Cambridge Univ. Press, Cambridge, 1982), pp. 248–341], and possibly the lower Pleistocene site of Swartkrans [C. K. Brain et al., *S. Afr. J. Sci.* **84**, 828 (1988)], but the shaping is simple and may be due in part to use. For a summary, see (12).

10. A summary of research history to 1988 is provided by J. Verniers and J. de Heinzelin, in *Evolution of Environments and Hominidae in the African Western Rift Valley*, N. T. Boaz, Ed. (Virginia Museum of Natural History Mem. 1, Martinsville, VA, 1990), pp. 17–39.

11. A. S. Brooks and C. C. Smith, *Afr. Archaeol. Rev.* **5**, 65 (1987); A. S. Brooks and P. Robertshaw, in *Low Latitudes*, vol. 2 of *The World at 18 000 BP*, C. S. Gamble and O. Soffer, Eds. (Unwin Hyman, London, 1990), pp. 121–169. On the basis of both radiocarbon and amino acid racemization dating of ostrich eggshell, barbed bone points and LSA lithics at White Paintings Shelter, Tsodilo Hills, Botswana, may be associated with a date as old as or older than the barbed points from Ishango (L. H. Robbins, personal communication).

12. H. Knecht, in "Hunting and Animal Exploitation in the Later Palaeolithic and Mesolithic of Eurasia," *Archaeol. Pap. Am. Anthropol. Assoc. 4*, G. L. Peterkin, H. M. Bricker, P. Mellars. Eds. (1993), p. 33; L. G. Straus, *ibid.*, p. 83; H. M. Bricker, A. S. Brooks, R. B. Clay and N. David. Les fouilles de H. L. Movius Jr. à l'Abri Pataud: généralités. In H. M. Bricker (ed.) *Le Paléolithique supérieur de l'abri Pataud (Dordogne): les fouilles de H. L. Movius, Jr.* pp. 11–30. Paris: Editions de la Maison des Sciences de l'Homme (1995); H. Knecht, *Sci. Am.* **271** (no. 1), 82 (1994).

13. J. Troenig, *Worldwide Chronology of Fifty-Three Prehistoric Innovations* (Acta Archaeol. Lund. Ser. 8° 21, Stockholm, 1993).

14. D. Helgren, personal communication.

15. We recorded these materials within 20 cm by 20 cm squares, together with the topography of the concentration in each square. All matrix was screened through 3-mm mesh.

16. We prefer to use "pavement" rather than the more usual archaeological designation "living floor." This avoids a priori assumptions about possible aggregating agents and hominid role.

17. Site 440 located near Wadi Halfa, Sudan, contained at least six species of fish in association with a Mousterian industry [P. H. Greenwood, in *The Prehistory of Nubia*, F. Wendorf, Ed. (Southern Methodist Univ. Press, Dallas, 1968), vol. 1, pp. 100–109; J. L. Shiner, *ibid.*, vol. 2, pp. 630–650].

18. L. Robbins, paper presented at the 11th Biennial Meeting of the Society for Africanist Archaeologists, Los Angeles, 26 to 29 March 1992. Ongoing excavation at White Paintings Shelter, Tsodilo Hills, Botswana, indicates the presence of fish associated with a MSA industry.

19. Two notched bone fragments and one unbarbed bone point occur in MSA and Howieson's Poort Industries at Klasies River mouth. Split and polished warthog or bush pig tusks have also been reported from Border Cave [R. Singer and J. Wymer, *The Middle Stone Age at Klasies River Mouth in South Africa* (Univ. of Chicago Press, Chicago, 1982); T. P. Volman, in *Southern African Prehistory and Paleoenvironments*, R. G. Klein, Ed. (Balkema, Boston, 1984), pp. 169–220]. Middle Paleolithic bone or ivory awls are known from the Khormusan industry of Egypt [A. E. Marks, in *The Prehistory of Nubia*, F. Wendorf, Ed. (Southern Methodist Univ. Press, Dallas, 1968), vol. 1, pp. 315–391] and from site Kostienki 17 on the Russian plain [M. Anikovich, *J. World Prehist.* **6**, 205 (1992)]. The complexity and formal nature of the Katanda industry, however, place it, we believe, in a cognitively distinct category.

20. C. Krupsha, thesis, George Washington University, Washington, DC (1993).

21. J. de Heinzelin, *Les Fouilles d'Ishango: Exploration du Parc National Albert, Mission J. de Heinzelin 1950*, Fasc. **2** (1957).

22. At Ishasha, south of Lake Rutanzige, in a swampy gallery forest environment similar to that implied for the Katanda MSA, large numbers of *Clarias* are taken annually by harpoon during the few days of the spawning season (T. E. Mugangu, personal communication).

23. Correlation of number of in situ lithics per square and depth of square below datum: $r^2 = 0.0370$; $n = 369$; $P = 0.01$.

24. A number of correlation analyses were conducted to examine the relation between lithic maximum length and depth below datum. These confirm that when controlled by both lithic type and raw material type, larger pieces have been displaced down-slope.

25. Distance between cluster "centers," as defined by maximum lithic and faunal density, is 4.2 m. Maximum cluster diameters are 4.0 and 3.4 m. For comparative data, see J. E. Yellen, *Archaeological Approaches to the Present: Models for Reconstructing the Past* (Academic Press, New York, 1977); R. A. Gould and J. E. Yellen, *J. Anthropol. Archaeol.* **6**, 77 (1987).

26. J. D. Clark. *J. World Prehist.* **2** (no. 3), 235 (1988).

27. We thank the people and the government of Zaire for facilitating this research, which was a collaborative effort involving almost 200 individuals from more than 15 countries. This study is based on work supported by the National Science Foundation under grants to N. T. Boaz, J. W. K. Harris, and A.S.B. (BNS85–07891, BNS86–08269, and BNS90–14092). Additional financial support was provided by the George Washington University Committee on Research, the L. S. B. Leakey Foundation, the Holt Family Foundation, the National Geographic Society, the National Science Foundation, the Smithsonian Institution, the Social Sciences and Humanities Research Council of Canada, and the Musée Royal de l'Afrique Centrale. Identification of the rocks used for grind stones was made by S. Sorensen. Artifact photographs by R. E. Clark Jr. (Smithsonian Institution).

67

Emergence of Modern Human Behavior

Middle Stone Age Engravings from South Africa

C. S. Henshilwood, F. d'Errico, R. Yates, Z. Jacobs, C. Tribolo, G. A. T. Duller, N. Mercier, J. C. Sealy, H. Valladas, I. Watts, and A. G. Wintle

ABSTRACT

In the Eurasian Upper Paleolithic after about 35,000 years ago, abstract or depictional images provide evidence for cognitive abilities considered integral to modern human behavior. Here we report on two abstract representations engraved on pieces of red ochre recovered from the Middle Stone Age layers at Blombos Cave in South Africa. A mean date of 77,000 years was obtained for the layers containing the engraved ochres by thermoluminescence dating of burnt lithics, and the stratigraphic integrity was confirmed by an optically stimulated luminescence age of 70,000 years on an overlying dune. These engravings support the emergence of modern human behavior in Africa at least 35,000 years before the start of the Upper Paleolithic.

Archaeological evidence associated with modern cognitive abilities provides important insights into when and where modern human behavior emerged (*1*). Two models for the origins of modern human behavior are current: (i) a late and rapid appearance at ~40 to 50 thousand years ago (ka) associated with the European Upper Paleolithic and the Later Stone Age (LSA) of sub-Saharan Africa (*2, 3*) or (ii) an earlier and more gradual evolution rooted in the African Middle Stone Age (MSA; ~250 to 40 ka) (*4, 5*). Evidence for modern behavior before 40 ka is relatively rare and often ambiguous (2, 6). However, in sub-Saharan Africa, archaeological evidence for changes in technology, economy, and social organization and the emergence of symbolism in the MSA may support the second model (4, 5, 7–9). Examples of these changes include standardized formal lithic tools (5, 8, 10), shaped bone implements (5, 7, 9, 11), innovative subsistence strategies such as fishing and shellfishing (10–12), and the systematic use of red ochre (10, 13).

Utilized ochre is found in almost all Stone Age occupations in southern Africa that are younger than 100 ka (13). The ochre may have served only utilitarian functions (e.g., skin protection or hide tanning) (3) or may have been used symbolically as pigment (4, 10, 13). Evidence for the latter is a persistent use of ochre with saturated red hues to produce finely honed crayon or pencil forms (10, 13). However, no ochre pieces or other artifacts older than ~40 ka provide evidence for abstract or depictional images, which would indicate modern human behavior (2, 14, 15).

We have recovered two pieces of engraved ochre from the MSA layers at Blombos Cave, South Africa. Situated on the southern Cape shore of the Indian Ocean, the cave is 35 m above sea level. A 5- to 60-cm layer of aeolian sand containing no archaeological artifacts (BBC Hiatus; Figure 1) separates the LSA from the

MSA occupation layers. The MSA is divided into three substages (9, 10) (Figure 1): (i) an upper series of occupational deposits, BBC M1, typified by abundant bifacially flaked, lanceolate-shaped stone points (Still Bay points) (10); (ii) a middle series, BBC M2, containing fewer Still Bay points but relatively abundant in deliberately shaped bone awls and points that were probably hafted (9, 11); and (iii) a lower BBC M3 series with few retouched pieces but with blades and flakes typical of the Mossel Bay/MSA 2b subphase (10). Associated, well-preserved faunal remains from all layers indicate that subsistence strategies were wide ranging and include terrestrial and marine mammals, shellfish, fish, and reptiles (10, 11).

More than 8000 pieces of ochre, many bearing signs of utilization, have been recovered from the MSA layers at Blombos Cave (10). Seven of nine pieces are potentially engraved and under study. We report here on the two unequivocally engraved pieces recovered in situ from layer CC, square E6a and layer CD, square H6a (Figure 1) (10) during excavations in 1999 and 2000, respectively. The engraved ochre piece from layer CC (SAM-AA 8937) was located adjacent to a small hearth, and that from layer CD (SAM-AA 8938) was surrounded by a number of small, basin-shaped hearths. Both specimens were located in a matrix of undisturbed and consolidated mixed ash and sand. There is no indication of perturbation in either the overlying 15 to 20 cm of MSA deposits or in the blanketing aeolian dune sand and no sign of intrusion of younger LSA materials (9, 10). All lithic artifacts in the ochre-bearing and overlying MSA layers are typologically MSA (9, 10).

On the 8937 piece (Figure 2, A and B), both the flat surfaces and one edge are modified by scraping and grinding. The edge has two ground facets, and the larger of these bears a cross-hatched engraved design. The cross hatching consists of two sets of six and eight lines partly intercepted by a longer line. The engraving on 8938 (Figure 2, C and D) consists of a row of cross hatching, bounded top and bottom by parallel lines and divided through the middle by a third parallel line that divides the lozenge shapes into triangles. Some of the lines are well-defined single incisions; others have parallel tracks along part or all of their lengths. Much of the parallel tracking may have resulted from a change in position of the engraving tool causing simultaneous scoring from more than one projection. The midline comprises three marking events. Examination of the intersections of the cross-hatched lines indicates that they were not executed as consecutive cross hatchings but that lines were made in first one direction and then another; the horizontal lines overlie the cross hatching. The preparation by grinding of the engraved surface, situation of the engraving on this prepared face, engraving technique, and final design are similar for both pieces, indicating a deliberate sequence of choices. Although the engraving on the 8937 ochre has fewer markings than the 8938 piece, it indicates that 8938 is not unique; the engraving on 8938 can be considered a complex geometric motif as the cross-hatched lines are bisected and framed by horizontals.

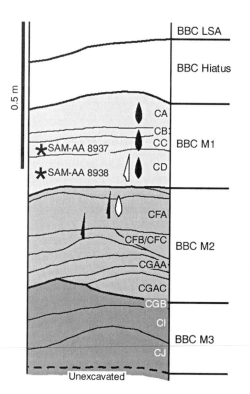

Figure 1. *Stratigraphy of Blombos Cave (34°25' S, 21°13' E). Sequence of MSA layers in square H6 showing relative location of engraved ochre pieces SAM-AA 8937 and SAM-AA 8938, bifacial Still Bay points (lanceolate shape), and bone tools. Closed and open symbols for bifacial points and bone tools indicate common and rare occurrences, respectively. The MSA layers consist principally of sands interlayered with consolidated beds, lenses, and stringers of marine shells, organic matter, and wood ash.*

Figure 2. *Engraved ochres from Blombos Cave. (A) SAM-AA 8937 is a flat piece of shale-like ochre that grades into silt on the reverse side: weight = 39.2 g; maximum length = 53.6 mm; breadth = 42.6 mm, depth = 11.7 mm; streak color notation 3060 Y65R (33). (B) Tracing of lines verified as engraved by study under magnification (scale bar, 5 mm). (C) SAM-AA 8938 is a rectangular slab of ochreous shale: weight = 116.6 g; maximum length = 75.8 mm; breadth = 34.8 mm; depth = 24.7 mm; streak color notation 4050 Y60R (30). Oblique lighting of specimen accentuates both engraved lines and irregularities of the surface, some created by grinding before the engraving and others by the process of engraving. (D) Tracing of lines verified as engraved by study under magnification, superimposed on flat-bed scan of engraved surface (scale bar, 10 mm).*

Assessing the significance of these engravings demands an accurate determination of their age (*16*). The engraved ochres were found within layers containing bifacially flaked stone points; in the South African MSA, these stone point types occur only within or below Howiesons Poort horizons (*10*) dated to ~65 to 70 ka (*17*). This association suggests that the engravings are older than 65 ka. To independently confirm and refine this time frame, we applied two luminescence-based dating methods to the Blombos Cave layers. Thermoluminescence (TL) dates were obtained for five burnt lithic samples from the MSA phase BBC M1 (Figure 1) (*18, 19*). The mean age for the lithic samples is 77 ± 6 ka (*20*). To confirm the stratigraphic integrity, we applied optically stimulated luminescence (OSL) dating to the aeolian dune (BBC Hiatus) separating the LSA and MSA layers (Fig. 1). Multiple grain measurements with a single aliquot regenerative (SAR) procedure (*21*) yielded a depositional age of 69 ± 5 ka (*22*). Single-grain SAR measurements (*23*) yielded consistent ages (*24*), indicating that the aggregate samples were not contaminated by grains of different ages (*25*). Because only 1.8% of the 1892 grains analyzed yielded reproducible growth curves, a more representative approach was also used (*26*), combining OSL signals from grains to generate synthetic aliquots. These provide a depositional age of 70 ± 5 ka (*20*) and confirm the antiquity of the engraved ochres.

Abstract images similar to the Blombos Cave engravings occur at Upper Paleolithic sites in Eurasia (*15*). The Blombos Cave motifs suggest arbitrary conventions unrelated to reality-based cognition, as is the case in the Upper Paleolithic (*15*), and they may have been constructed with symbolic intent, the meaning of which is now unknown. These finds demonstrate that ochre use in the MSA was not exclusively utilitarian and, arguably, the transmission and sharing of the meaning of the engravings relied on fully syntactical language (*5, 27*).

Genetic and fossil evidence suggests that humans were anatomically near modern in Africa before 100 ka (*5, 28, 29*). Key questions are whether anatomical and behavioral modernity developed in tandem (*5*) and what criteria archaeologists should use to identify modern behavior (*2, 4, 5*). For the latter, there is agreement on one criterion—archaeological evidence of abstract or depictional images indicates modern human behavior (*2, 14, 15*). The Blombos Cave engravings are intentional images. In the light of this evidence, it seems that, at least in southern Africa, *Homo sapiens* was behaviorally modern about 77,000 years ago.

REFERENCES AND NOTES

1. The term "modern human behavior" as used here has no chronological implication and means the thoughts and actions underwritten by minds equivalent to those of *Homo sapiens* today. Key among these is the use of symbols.
2. P. A. Mellars, K. Gibson, Eds., *Modelling the Early Human Mind* (McDonald Institute Monographs, Cambridge, 1996).
3. R. G. Klein, *The Human Career* (Chicago Univ. Press, Chicago, IL, 1999).
4. H. J. Deacon, J. Deacon, *Human Beginnings in South Africa: Uncovering the Secrets of the Stone Age* (David Philip, Cape Town, South Africa, 1999).
5. S. McBrearty, A. Brooks, *J. Hum. Evol.* **38**, 453 (2000).
6. F. d'Errico, P. Villa, *J. Hum. Evol.* **33**, 1 (1997).
7. J. Yellen, A. Brooks, E. Cornelissen, M. Mehlman, K. Stewart, *Science* **268**, 553 (1995).
8. S. Wurz, thesis, Stellenbosch University, Stellenbosch, South Africa (2000).
9. C. S. Henshilwood, F. d'Errico, C. W. Marean, R. Milo, R. Yates, *J. Hum. Evol.* **41**, 631 (2001).
10. C. S. Henshilwood et al., *J. Archaeol. Sci.* **28**, 421 (2001).
11. C. S. Henshilwood, J. C. Sealy, *Curr. Anthropol.* **38**, 890 (1997).
12. R. C. Walter et al., *Nature* **405**, 65 (2000).
13. I. Watts, in *The Evolution of Culture*, R. Dunbar, C. Knight, C. Power, Eds. (Edinburgh Univ. Press, Edinburgh, 1999), pp. 113–146.
14. G. A. Clark, C. M. Willermet, *Conceptual Issues in Modern Human Origins Research* (de Gruyter, New York, 1997).
15. P. Bahn, J. Vertut, *Journey Through the Ice Age* (Weidenfeld & Nicolson, London, 1997).
16. A sediment sample from Blombos was included in an earlier study of coastal sediments, in which it was found to date to oxygen isotope stage 5 (*30*). However, the dates obtained for un-etched quartz and feldspar grains with TL and infrared stimulated luminescence, respectively, were inconsistent.
17. J. C. Vogel, in *Humanity - from African Naissance to coming Millennia*, P. V. Tobias, M. A. Raath, J. Moggi-Cecchi, G. A. Doyle, Eds. (Univ. of Florence Press, Florence, Italy, 2000), pp. 261–268.
18. The five lithic specimens (a few cm in size and weighing between 6 and 35 g) came from the upper phase of occupational deposits BBC M1: Samples BBC24 and BBC23 are from CA/CB and BBC15, BBC20, and BBC22 are from CC. Examination of thin sections revealed the presence of quartz grains embedded in a siliceous matrix. The time since they were burnt was computed from TL analysis of 100- to 160-μm grains obtained by crushing after the samples' outer surfaces had been removed with a diamond saw (*31*). The equivalent dose (D_e) was determined with a combined additive and regenerative dose protocol (*19*). U, Th, and K concentrations of the lithic samples were measured by neutron activation analysis (*32*). The total dose rates (*20*) were calculated assuming that the quartz grains were free of radioactive impurities and that all radioisotopes were confined to and uniformly distributed within the surrounding siliceous matrix. In computing the alpha and beta dose rates received by the grains, attenuation factors appropriate for the mean grain size in each specimen were taken into account. To determine the gamma dose rates, we buried 24 dosimeters in the cave deposits for 1 year at points no farther than 1 m from each previously excavated lithic. The ages combine to provide a mean age of 77 ± 6 ka, which is consistent with the OSL age for the overlying dune layer.
19. N. Mercier, H. Valladas, G. Valladas, *Ancient TL* **10**, 28 (1992).
20. Supplementary data including a table containing dose rate, D_e, and age information for TL and OSL analyses and a supplementary figure showing a radial plot of OSL D_e values for the "synthetic" aliquot data are available on *Science* Online at www.sciencemag.org/cgi/content/full/1067575/DC1.
21. A. S. Murray, A. G. Wintle, *Radiat. Meas.* **32**, 57 (2000).
22. The depositional age of the dune layer was determined by OSL dating. OSL analyses on Aber/52-ZB-15 were undertaken on quartz grains to measure the radiation dose that they had received since their last exposure to daylight. Their equivalent dose (D_e) was determined with the SAR procedure. The total radiation dose rate to the grains (*20*) was measured with a combination of thick-source alpha counting, beta counting, and atomic absorption spectroscopy for potassium determination, and a water content of 10 ± 5% (weight water / weight dry sediment) was used, based on current moisture contents in the cave. The calculated gamma dose rate was consistent with that measured in the field, and the cosmic ray dose rate of 45 μGy/year was based on the thickness of the overlying rock. Quartz grains were extracted after treatment with 10% hydrochloric acid to remove carbonates and 30 vol of H_2O_2 to remove organics. The sample was sieved to obtain grains from 212 to 250 μm in diameter. Feldspars and heavy minerals were removed by density separation at 2.62 and 2.70 g/cm³. The alpha-irradiated outer layer of the grains was removed by etching in 48% hydrofluoric acid for 45 min. The initial set of luminescence measurements (stimulation at 470 nm with blue diodes) used 48 aliquots, each containing about 500 grains. A range of thermal pretreatments (preheats) from 160° to 300°C for 10 s was used. From 200° to 280°C, the D_e values from 30 replicate aliquots were reproducible and showed no systematic trend with temperature. A weighted mean was calculated, with the individual D_e values weighted according to their uncertainty. The uncertainty in the mean was divided by $\sqrt{N}$, where N is the number of independent estimates of D_e—in this case 30. D_e values were calculated with the package Analyst, which combines uncertainties due to the counting statistics of each OSL measurement and the error associated with the mathematical fitting of the growth curve to the luminescence data. The 30 aliquots gave a value of 47.9 ± 1.7 Gy, resulting in an age of 69 ± 5 ka.
23. L. Bøtter-Jensen, E. Bulur, G. A. T. Duller, A. S. Murray, *Radiat. Meas.* **32**, 523 (2000).
24. The single-grain SAR measurements were made in an automated reader based around a 10-mW, 532-nm Nd: YVO_4 laser, whose beam can be directed at individual grains (*23*). A single preheat at 220°C for 10 s was used, with the main OSL measurement (L) being followed by measurement of the OSL response (T) to a test dose as observed after a 160°C cut heat (*21*). Grains whose natural signal ratio (L_N/T_N) does not intersect the regeneration growth curve were not used in subsequent analyses. In addition, grains thought to contain some feldspar were also rejected. The presence of feldspar was identified by making additional measurements of a given regeneration dose on each grain. The first measurement is undertaken within the SAR procedure and yields the ratio L_1/T_1 used in the growth curve. For each grain, two additional measurements of L/T were made at the end of the SAR procedure. The first duplicates the previous measurement, as a test of the sensitivity correction. The second uses the same regeneration dose, but, before preheating, the grains are exposed to infrared (830 nm) radiation from a 500-mW laser diode for 100 s. If the grains contain feldspar, then the infrared exposure will have reduced the magnitude of L, and hence the ratio of these last two measurements of L/T will be substantially less than unity; for a quartz grain, the ratio will be consistent with unity. Of the 1892 grains that were measured, 22 were rejected on the basis of these criteria. The OSL signal from many of the remaining 1870 grains was close to instrumental background, and only 34 yielded reproducible growth curves.
25. R. G. Roberts et al., *Nature* **393**, 358 (1998).
26. Single-grain OSL measurements were made with 19 aluminum discs, with up to 100 grains on each disc. For each disc, the OSL signals from the unrejected grains were combined to generate "synthetic" aliquots consisting of between 93 and 100 grains. The D_e values for 18 "synthetic" aliquots were combined to give a weighted mean of 48.5 ± 1.2 Gy, giving a depositional age of 70 ± 5 ka (*20*).
27. L. Aiello, N. G. Jablonski, Eds., *The Origin and Diversification of Language* (Memoirs of the California Academy of Sciences, San Francisco, 1998).
28. C. B. Stringer, in *Contemporary Issues in Human Evolution*, W. Meikle, N. Jablonski, Eds. (California Academy of Sciences, San Francisco, 1996), pp. 115–134.
29. M. Ingman, K. Kaessmann, S. Pääbo, U. Gyllensten, *Nature* **408**, 708 (2000).
30. J. C. Vogel, A. G. Wintle, S. M. Woodborne, *J. Archaeol. Sci.* **26**, 729 (1999).
31. H. Valladas, *Quat. Sci. Rev.* **11**, 1 (1992).

32. J.-L. Joron, thesis, Université Paris-Sud (1974).
33. "Natural Color System Index" (Scandinavian Colour Institute, Stockholm, 1999).
34. This work was supported by grants to C.H. from the Anglo American Chairman's Fund, Centre National de la Recherche Scientifique OHLL, the Leakey Foundation, the National Geographic Society, NSF, the South African National Research Foundation, and the Wenner-Gren Foundation; to F.D. from CNRS Origine de l'Homme, du Langage et des Langues (OHLL) and the Service Culturel of the French Embassy in South Africa; to Z.J. from the Sir Henry Strakosch Memorial Trust and an Overseas Research Student award; to C.T. from CNRS OHLL; to G.D. from the Natural Environment Research Council; to J.S. from the South African National Research Foundation and the University of Cape Town; and to I.W. from the British Academy. We thank G. Avery at Iziko Museums of Cape Town, the South African Museum, and K. van Niekerk.

Evolution of *Homo sapiens*

As documented by the chapters in Part VIII, increasing evidence in the past decade from both fossils and studies of human genetics support the hypothesis that modern humans were present in Africa well before their appearance in other parts of the world. Moreover, it is also widely accepted that these "anatomically modern" humans expanded out of Africa approximately 50–70 kya to colonize other parts of the globe. However, there remains considerable debate over the exact timing of their first appearance on other continents and the fate of other, more archaic hominids already present in those regions. As discussed in Chapter 59, and other chapters in Part VIII, there are numerous, contrasting theories regarding the extent of genetic exchange between modern human populations from Africa and the regional populations they encountered as they dispersed throughout the world. Some authors argue for total replacement by modern humans, while others argue for varying degrees of interbreeding such that regional populations contributed to modern diversity. The chapters in this part deal more explicitly with regional diversity in modern humans and its evolution.

In Chapter 68, "Multiregional, Not Multiple Origins," Milford H. Wolpoff, John Hawks, and Rachael Caspari argue that the widely discussed multiregional model of modern human origins does not imply independent origins of modern human morphology in different parts of the Old World. More accurately, it is a model that is based on a hypothesis of global gene exchange between populations in different regions. In an effort to correct what they see as widespread misconceptions and misinterpretations of the theory of multiregional evolution, they review and critique many published "descriptions" of the multiregional model by its detractors. They then describe how their view of multiregionalism differs from these "descriptions" and how many of the attempts to falsify the multiregional model are inappropriate (see also Chapter 63). In their view, multiregional evolution is the antithesis of the independent origin of *Homo sapiens* from many regional populations of *Homo erectus* because it emphasizes genetic exchange as the basis of differentiation, geographic variation, and evolution. They suggest that much of the argument

against multiregional evolution is based on a misconception of the multiregional model.

Milford H. Wolpoff and colleagues, in Chapter 69, "Modern Human Ancestry at the Peripheries: A Test of the Replacement Theory," provide a test of the widely held theory that as modern humans spread from Africa throughout the rest of the world during the last 60 kyr, they completely replaced all regional populations with no contributions of the predecessor populations to the modern populations. In particular, they test the hypothesis that early modern human crania from Europe and Australia are more similar to the earliest anatomically modern humans from the Levant than they are to more archaic hominids from the same geographic regions. They find that early modern crania from the Czech Republic do not show more similarity to early modern humans from the Levant than they do to European Neandertals. Likewise, they find that early modern crania from Australia do not show greater similarity to early modern humans from the Levant than they do to fossils from Ngandong in Java, commonly assigned to *Homo erectus*. Accordingly, they argue that a dual ancestry (i.e., from both modern dispersers and from preexisting regional populations of modern humans in Europe and in Australia) cannot be eliminated, but a total replacement hypothesis is rejected.

Ever since the initial study by Cann, Stoneking, and Wilson in 1987, genetic studies of human population differences have played a major role in efforts to reconstruct the time and place of the origin of *Homo sapiens*. With the sequencing of the human genome, the pace of these studies has increased dramatically in recent years. Most studies have concurred with the original results of Cann et al. (1987) in supporting an African origin of modern humans sometime between 100 and 200 kya. However, there are also studies that have yielded different conclusions (see Chapter 72). In Chapter 70, "Origins of Modern Humans Still Look Recent," Todd R. Disotell reviews several genetic studies that argue for a relatively ancient origin of modern humans. These include analyses of the Neandertal mtDNA (Wolpoff, 1998) and studies of the human X chromosome (Hey, 1997). Disotell then reviews the methods and assumptions of each paper and argues that all are based on sampling problems or incorrect analysis. He suggests that all current genetic data support a recent origin of modern humans in Africa during the last 100 to 200 kya. Moreover, he emphasizes that human genetic diversity is extremely limited compared with that reported for other great apes, further supporting the view that our species has a very recent origin.

Alan R. Templeton, in Chapter 71, "Out of Africa Again and Again," reports on an extensive, comprehensive analysis of genetic data from many sources, including mtDNA, Y-Chromosomal DNA, X-linked regions, and six autosomal regions. His results agree with those of many others in finding genetic evidence for a major expansion out of Africa between 80 and 150 kya. However, he also finds evidence for older expansions out of Africa, one at approximately 1.7 mya and again between 420 and 840 kya. These three time periods accord roughly with the appearance of *Homo sapiens*, *Homo heidelbergensis*, and *Homo erectus* in the African fossil record. The presence of evidence from these earlier species in the genome of modern human populations is not compatible with a total replacement model, in which all modern humans are descended from a single recent common ancestor, as suggested by Disotell in Chapter 70. Rather, Templeton's results are more compatible with the assimilation model of Smith et al. (1989) or the multiregional model of Wolpoff et al. (2000, Chapter 68) and the "mostly out of Africa" model of Relethford (1999, Chapter 63).

In Chapter 72, "Genetics and the Making of *Homo sapiens*," Sean B. Carroll discusses the tremendous opportunities for understanding human origins that are becoming available through our new knowledge of the composition of the human genome. With the sequencing of the human genome, researchers are able to focus on the genetic basis of critical human features, such as brain size, brain organization, and speech, and broader features, such as the timing of growth and development. He discusses general features of human genetics—for example, most quantitative traits are likely to be polygenic; the rate of evolution is not a function of the number of genes involved; and many evolutionary changes are the result of regulatory genes. The chapter concludes with a general overview of how genome-scale investigations of human evolution will proceed in the coming years.

E. James Dixon, in Chapter 73, addresses another major event in the dispersal of modern humans in "Human Colonization of the Americas: Timing, Technology and Process." Most evidence indicates that North and South America were the last major continents to be successfully colonized by modern humans, but the timing and number of early colonizations have long been topics of debate. A preponderance of dated sites indicates that the initial colonization was approximately 11,500 years ago and involved large game hunters, characterized by the Clovis technological complex, traveling overland in a north to south front (e.g., Metzer, 1994; Hoffecker and Elias, 2003). However, excavations at Monte Verde, in southernmost South America (Dillehay, 2000), indicate an earlier

appearance. In addition, there are other, more controversial, sites suggesting an even older initial appearance of humans in the New World (e.g., Meadowcroft in Pennsylvania [see Adovasio et al., 1978], and Pedra Furada in Brazil [see Guidon and Delibras, 1986]). Dixon reviews the evidence for a pre-Clovis colonization of the New World and questions whether the concept of a single colonization is even realistic. He also evaluates the available evidence regarding the geographic spread of Paleo-Indians and their likely subsistence strategies and finds that these do not accord with an early wave of big game hunters sweeping through the Americas from north to south. In light of the many problems with the established Clovis theory, he proposes an alternative model involving human colonization of the Americas by repeated incidental coastal migration and subsequent spread inland. In this model, the western Plains of North America would have been one of the last areas to be colonized.

In Chapter 74, Alan R. Templeton reviews "Human Races: A Genetic and Evolutionary Perspective." He argues that although human evolution has long been characterized by many local populations, from a quantitative genetic perspective, the genetic differences between human populations are much smaller than differences between subspecies of other animals. Moreover, human populations show a distinct pattern of isolation by geographic distance; that is, populations that are separated farther geographically are more genetically distinct. The differences between human populations are not of long standing or indicative of distinct lineages. This type of genetic differentiation is not consistent with "tree" representations of human populations. Human evolution has long been characterized by locally differentiated populations which have been subject to genetic contact with other populations; there is little genetic justification for any major subdivisions within our species.

The volume closes with Robert Foley's and Marta M. Lahr's synthetic review "On Stony Ground: Lithic Technology, Human Evolution, and the Emergence of Culture." Given the wide scope of this chapter, which analyzes culture and lithic technology, it seemed an appropriate choice to conclude this anthology. In this chapter, Foley and Lahr discuss the role of the archaeological record of stone tools for understanding the nature of the evolution of culture. Efforts to understand the evolution of culture using only the modern behavior of humans, apes, and other primates is limited because of both the huge differences in the all-pervasive role of culture in human societies and the limited success in identifying bits and pieces of culture in the activities of other animals. Moreover, studies of culture in living taxa lack any great time depth for evolutionary patterns.

The authors note that interpretation of the factors driving changes in stone tool technology through time have alternated between different ideas. Earlier views saw this technological difference in stone artifacts as cultural characteristics of individual populations of extinct hominids; current views see the differences in stone tool technology as a reflection of the primary differences in adaptive needs and available raw materials, largely independent of the hominid taxa responsible for their manufacture. Foley and Lahr find that major patterns of stone tool technology over the past 2.5 million years indicate that there is a strong, but not totally simple, relationship between hominid phylogeny and the archaeological records of tool technology. This suggests that the cognitive abilities of individual taxa played an important role in the evolution of cultural abilities through time.

REFERENCES

Adovasio, J. M., J. D. Gunn, J. Donahue, and R. Stuckenrath. 1978. Meadowcroft Rockshelter 1977: an overview. *American Antiquity* 43:632–651.

Cann, R., M. Stoneking, and A. Wilson. 1987. Mitochondrial DNA and human evolution. *Nature* 325:31–36.

Dillehay, T. 2000. *The Settlement of the Americas: A New Prehistory.* Basic Books, New York.

Guidon, N., and G. Delibras. 1986. Carbon-14 dates point to man in the Americas 32,000 years ago. *Nature* 321:769–771.

Hey, J. 1997. Mitochondrial and nuclear genes present conflicting portraits of human origins. *Molecular Biology and Evolution* 14:166–172.

Hoffecker, J. F., and S. A. Elias. 2003. Environment and archeology in Beringia. *Evolutionary Anthropology* 12:34–49.

Metzer, D. J. 1994. Pleistocene peopling of the Americas. *Evolutionary Anthropology* 1:157–169.

Relethford, J. 1999. Models, predictions, and the fossil record of modern human origins. *Evolutionary Anthropology* 8:7–10.

Smith, F. H., A. B. Falscetti, and S. M. Donnelley. 1989. Modern human origins. *Yearbook of Physical Anthropology* 32:35–68.

Stringer, C. B. 2002. Modern human origins: progress and prospects. *Philosophical Transactions of the Royal Society of London* B 357:563–579.

Wolpoff, M. 1998. Concocting a divisive theory. *Evolutionary Anthropology* 7:1–3.

Wolpoff, M., J. Hawks, and R. Caspari. 2000. Multiregional, not multiple origins. *American Journal of Physical Anthropology* 112:129–136.

68

Multiregional, Not Multiple Origins

M. H. Wolpoff, J. Hawks, and R. Caspari

ABSTRACT

Multiregional evolution is a model to account for the pattern of human evolution in the Pleistocene. The underlying hypothesis is that a worldwide network of genic exchanges, between evolving human populations that continually divide and reticulate, provides a frame of population interconnections that allows both species-wide evolutionary change and local distinctions and differentiation. "Multiregional" does not mean independent multiple origins, ancient divergence of modern populations, simultaneous appearance of adaptive characters in different regions, or parallel evolution. A valid understanding of multiregional evolution would go a long way toward reducing the modern human origins controversy.

The past decade has seen very significant fossil (Duarte et al., 1999; Li and Etler, 1992; Lü, 1990; Pope, 1992) and genetic (Awadalla et al., 1999; Bower, 1999; Harding et al., 1997; Harris and Hey, 1999; Hey, 1997; Loewe and Scherer, 1997; Relethford, 1998; Wise et al., 1997, 1998) discoveries that directly address the modern human origins debate. Many believe they should have resolved it. But the debate has not been resolved. Several ideas about why the modern human origins debate continues unabated have been proposed, ranging from the influence of strong feelings and exacerbating personal comments in books and newspapers, to the contention that the debate cannot be resolved because the hypotheses are not sufficiently contradictory or even are untestable (see Clark and Willermet, 1997; Howell, 1996; Smith and Harrold, 1997). We believe there is a much simpler explanation. For whatever reason, or reasons (and we suspect there are more than one), there has been a continued pattern of misinterpreting or incorrectly describing multiregional evolution. These misinterpretations follow a theme, in which multiregional evolution is depicted as parallel or independent evolution (often involving simultaneous changes) in the different inhabited regions of the world,[1] and then is rejected because such a scheme is unlikely. There have been attempts to correct this (Frayer et al., 1993; Relethford, 1995, 1999; Smith, 1997; Wolpoff and Caspari, 1997).

There are historical reasons for this particular misinterpretation (Wolpoff and Caspari, 1997). Here we do not discuss these but rather focus on the literature of the past few years. The papers we discuss reflect the

consistent consequences of interpreting multiregional evolution to mean parallelism and the simultaneous evolution of modernity. More than any other source could, they demonstrate by example why it is that without a valid understanding of the multiregional model, it is not possible to examine its consequences, test it, or make progress toward resolving the modern human origins debate. We present several examples from genetics and paleoanthropology.

INTERPRETATIONS OF MULTIREGIONAL EVOLUTION

Independent Origin of *Homo sapiens* in China

As part of their analysis of microsatellite relationships between contemporary Chinese populations, Chu et al. (1998) discussed the multiregional evolution hypothesis and stated that it is incorrect because "genetic evidence does not support an independent origin of *Homo sapiens* in China" (Chu et al., 1998, p. 11763). Multiregional evolution does not predict the "independent" evolution of modern humans in China, or anywhere else in the Old World. It evokes diffusion across a network of genic exchanges, a mechanism that is the opposite of independent evolution, to account for the shared pattern of evolution across the human range combined with the presence of some regional continuities in various areas. The multiregional hypothesis is that a network of genic exchanges, promoted by but not necessarily dependent on exogamy rules,[2] provides a

---

[1] One of the reviews of this paper notes that "if you propose, and then espouse, a hypothesis about modern human origins and call it the 'Multiregional Hypothesis,' it is probably likely that people will think . . . that your hypothesis involved 'modern humanness' having more than one origin." But apart from the fact that multiregional evolution is a hypothesis about the *pattern* of human evolution, and not specifically about modern human origins (if there *is* such an event; see Wolpoff and Caspari, 1996), "multiregional" refers to nothing more or less than "many places" and there is no reason to assume it means "many places where the same things happen at the same time independently of each other."

[2] Native Australian marriage preference is defined by descent group, they must marry outside their clan, but they are not required to marry outside their "tribe" (defined by dialect and territory, these are the smallest breeding populations on the continent according to Birdsell, 1958). Yet even without "tribal" exogamy rules, the data of Tindale (1940) on Native Australian marriages show that for each generation, on average 13% of marriages were with a neighboring "tribe" and 1.6% were with "tribes" whose borders were not adjoining (Lasker and Crews, 1996). Ignoring population movements and reticulations (which would speed up the process), this is more than sufficient to insure a much greater magnitude of genic exchange than the less than one migrant per generation between regional populations that the multiregional model requires to work (Relethford, 1999; Relethford and Harpending, 1995).

frame of population interconnections that allows both species-wide evolutionary change and local distinctions and differentiation. As the evolving human populations continued to diverge and reticulate, this network has had several consequences. It encouraged geographic differentiation through isolation-by-distance for neutral traits. For traits that were not neutral, it allowed advantageous features, promoted by selection, to spread everywhere throughout humanity. Traits such as these are widely shared, but differentiation in other adaptive traits across this network reflects adaptive variation, tempered by historic differences.[3] Even when the distribution of the causes of adaptation are not clinal, there can be widespread gradations of variation maintained by gene flow balanced against selection differences or drift. Because of the key role played by genic exchanges in this model, multiregional evolution means that no human species, subspecies, or race can have multiple "independent origins" in different regions. If genetic loci have evolved in the absence of selection, as is often assumed for microsatellites such as those examined in Chu et al. (1998), then multiregional evolution predicts there will be a pattern of isolation-by-distance and expects reticulate evolution among populations.

However, Chu et al. (1998) provide no test of whether the Chinese microsatellite data fit an isolation-by-distance model, nor do they assess the effects of population reticulation on the observed population structure. Instead, they use a standard algorithm to fit their data to a branching model, or tree, of population relationships. Just as regression may be fit to any pair of metric variates, any matrix of population distances may be fit to a tree. However, as in the case of regression, we must evaluate a priori whether a tree is an appropriate model for the population relationships. In the case of these microsatellite data, there are two obvious hypotheses to explain the observed interpopulational distances. First, we may believe that a series of population divergences, perhaps accompanied by founder events, led to the differences. If this were true, a tree would be the appropriate model to fit to the data. Second, we may believe that differences in migration among the populations led to the differences, in which case a tree would be clearly inappropriate. Either of these two hypotheses will result in a matrix of population differences, and the observation of such a matrix is not sufficient to determine which hypothesis is the correct one (Relethford, 1995). They may be distinguished, however, by testing the goodness of fit of the data to a tree model, measuring the "treeness"[4] of the

data. In this case, Chu et al. (1998) do not report the treeness of the microsatellite data. This is an important omission, both because analysis of diverse human genetic data demonstrates that treeness can be rejected for global samples of living human groups (Templeton, 1998), and because a high treeness is the only way that distance data could refute an isolation-by-distance model for humans in China.

The further conclusion that "modern humans originating in Africa constitute the majority of the current gene pool in East Asia" (Chu et al., 1998, p. 11766) is also compatible with the multiregional hypothesis, given the stipulation, common to most modern human origins explanations, that until recently more people lived in Africa than in other parts of the world (Relethford, 1999). In this respect, multiregional evolution and uniregional replacement have similar expectations, since Africa makes up half or more of the inhabited land mass of the world prior to 100,000 years ago. In contrast, multiregional evolution can easily be disproved if it can be shown that all of the ancestors of living humans at some discrete time in the Middle or Late Pleistocene lived in only one area of the world. If this were the case, then we should be able to trace the ancestry of every human genetic locus to a single population existing at some time in the past million years. This testing is actively underway using genetic evidence, and no such time has yet been found at which every genetic locus resides in a single African population (Harris and Hey, 1999; Harding et al., 1997). However, such a test has not been performed on microsatellite data, and no such test is performed in this study.

Unique Descent

The commentary accompanying Chu et al. (1998) emphasized the inference that the majority of East Asian genes came from Africa, and concluded, "This should help refute the claim that there is a continuity of evolution from *Homo erectus* to modern humans in East Asia, as maintained by supporters of the multiregional hypothesis" (Cavalli-Sforza, 1998, p. 11502). This is a misrepresentation of the term "continuity" as explicitly employed in the multiregional model, by confusing the continuity of features with a claim of unique descent,[5] and as noted above, most modern human origins explanations agree about where the majority of Pleistocene humans lived.

---

[3] A new source of selection can only modify what is already present (Gould and Vrba, 1982), barring the unlikely occurrence of a useful mutation at just that moment. Therefore, while population differences in adaptive features reflect adaptive variation, the details of the differences may, in some cases, be found in variation created by random genetic drift at an earlier time. The same difference in selection does not necessarily cause the same difference in the morphological response to it, so population history can be a key element in this process even before the process has begun.

[4] "Treeness" is exhibited when all of the endpoints on one side of a split are equally related to all of the endpoints on the other side. If there were migration and genic exchanges between groups at the endpoints, then the relations would depend on the pattern of migration and not on the split. In this case, equal relationships would not be found.

[5] A claim of unique descent from ancient to modern Asian populations would not be *multiregional* evolution, but *polygenic* evolution. Regional continuity refers to the observation that very common features persist in different regions for long periods of time. It is not the claim that such features do not appear elsewhere; the genetic structure of the human species makes such a possibility unlikely to the extreme. There may be uniqueness in *combinations* of traits, but no single trait is likely to have been unique in a particular part of the world, although it might appear to be so because of the incomplete sampling provided by the spotty human fossil record. Neither is it the claim that such features persist for the entire period of habitation of a region, for such a claim would disregard population replacements and extinctions, as well as the action of natural selection for some features, all of which are usual evolutionary events.

The Neandertal Lynchpin

It is further stated (Cavalli-Sforza, 1998, p. 11502) that "another stronghold of the multiregional hypothesis was the transformation of Neanderthal into modern humans in Europe, and also this has been falsified by an analysis of DNA of the Neanderthal *par excellence.*" Europe (especially Western Europe) and the fate of the Neandertals have never been a "stronghold" of the multiregional evolution hypothesis, which was explicitly developed to account for the fossil evidence in *East* Asia (Wolpoff et al., 1984).

The interpretation by Cavalli-Sforza (1998) is based on the assumption that the Neandertal's distinct mtDNA lineage is a separate biological lineage, reflecting a population (or paleodeme) that diverged from humanity when the mtDNA lineage branched, and subsequently evolved in parallel with humans. But mtDNA lineages are not separate populations, and population genetics demonstrates that the reported Neandertal mtDNA cannot falsify *any* relevant evolutionary model for European origins (Nordborg, 1998; Wolpoff, 1998). To date, there is only one published partial sequence of Neandertal mtDNA, and it has not been compared with the mtDNA of its contemporaries, but instead only with that of living humans. The problem is, as Nordborg (1998) lays out, that only a very few ancestors of the world sample of human mtDNA were present in contemporaries of the Feldhofer Neandertal. This means that the total sample of mtDNA that *could* be compared is very small. At the moment, the analysis that has been done has demonstrated little more than what has been accepted paleontologically for over 100 years: Neandertals were biologically at the fringes of the range of variation of living humanity. No Neandertals can be found today, although most of their features remain, at differing frequencies (Frayer, 1992). Moreover, and perhaps most relevantly, multiregionalism could be a valid explanation for human evolution even if every Neandertal became extinct without issue. No human populations persist endlessly or continuously through time; all either become extinct, or merge with other populations.

An Extreme Theory of Multiple Origins

In another paper, multiregional evolution was portrayed as an "extreme version of the origin of modern humans (*Homo sapiens sapiens*) from *Homo erectus* . . . [with] multiple origins, one in almost every continent" (Li et al., 1999, p. 3796). There is a serious question about whether modernity can be defined in a way that would allow a statement like this to be valid (Wolpoff and Caspari, 1997), and no multiregionalist has proposed a subspecies taxonomy for modern humans, but even more serious, and disturbing, is the persistent contention that *multiregionalism means multiple origins.* The fundamental difference between multiregional evolution and all replacement theories is that multiregional evolution describes a process within a single evolving species and therefore is a reticulate model in which there is branching, extinction, and merging of populations. In contrast, replacement theories, such as the single recent African origin of modern humans, describe a process of evolution by branching alone, in which reticulations are impossible. The branching process is assumed a priori and is the basis of analyses to account for both the origin of modern humans and the differentiation of these humans into the different, widespread populations found today.

It is correct to say that multiregional evolution and evolution by replacement are extremes, because there is no process that can lie between them or be a compromise. But authors who continue to regard the multiregional hypothesis as a "candelabra theory" (Lewin, 1993; Seielstad et al., 1999) are simply incorrect. Ironically, it is the branching replacement model that must be described as a "candelabra" (Templeton, 1998), because branching is the only explanation this theory offers for variation. In the replacementist view, morphological variation in the Middle and Late Pleistocene is the result of branching of different species, and genetic variation among living humans is the result of the branching of ancestral human populations. By assuming population variation to be a reflection of the time since common ancestry of diverging populations, replacementists are forced to accept parallel evolution to explain Middle and Late Pleistocene changes across the human range, and complete population isolation to explain the observed worldwide pattern of genetic diversity in living humans.

Parallel Independent Evolution

The depiction of multiregional evolution as a polygenic theory of multiple origins and parallel evolution continues in paleontology as well as in human genetics. In the most recent paper by the two paleoanthropologists who disagree with multiregional evolution most strongly, we find the comment, "Frayer (1992) also proposes, on the basis of the persistence of traits across the Neandertal/modern boundary, a degree of continuity indicating 'some measure of genetic contribution of Neandertal to subsequent *Homo sapiens* populations' . . . this view no longer means regional evolution" (Bräuer and Stringer, 1997, p. 199). But given the reticulate nature of evolution within species, and the ethnogenic modeling that is part of the multiregional framework (Moore, 1994), what else *could* regional evolution mean *unless multiregional evolution is still being interpreted by these scholars as parallel independent evolution in different regions?* Elsewhere, Stringer and McKie (1996, p. 141) assert that "multiregionalism . . . holds that our brain development is an event of all-consuming global consequence towards which humanity strived in unison for nearly two million years. . . . to believe that humanity could be the product of a small, rapidly evolving African population who struck it lucky in the evolution stakes is therefore viewed as being worse than apostasy by these people." Gould (1994) writes, "Multiregionalism is awfully hard to fathom. Why should populations throughout the world, presumably living in different environments, under varying regimes of natural selection, all be moving on the same evolutionary pathway?" Howell (1996, p. 32) asserts, "MRE requires that natural selection drive African and African-derived hominin populations in Eurasia anagenetically and ineluctably toward the modern human condition. It has an almost omega-point inevitability about it."

Simultaneous Appearance of Modernity as Mutations Accumulate Because of Relaxed Selection

Natural selection is not the only force "posited" to drive simultaneous parallel evolution in these innovative depictions of multiregional evolution; there is also the *absence* of natural selection. Smith and Harrold (1997), writers who do not particularly support the Eve theory, provide an example which mistakes multiregional evolution for parallelism and uses the absence of selection to account for it. The model they describe as multiregional evolution is actually that of Brace (1991), i.e., "stages of human evolution."[6] Brace (1991, p. 52) asserts that multiregional evolution is, in actuality, no more than his PME (probable mutation effect), when he contends, "The idea of the emergence of modern human form gradually and simultaneously throughout the entire occupied world or 'in situ continuity' has recently been rechristened 'multiregional evolution.'"[7] According to Brace (1991), his worldwide evolutionary stages are based on a theory of parallel evolution that evokes human culture as the common source of parallel trends that cause simultaneous changes, and the accumulation of mutations in the absence of selection[8] as the mechanism that creates the parallelisms (culture removes selection, in Brace's view).

Simply put, Smith and Harrold (1997) turn to this cultural explanation for common parallel evolutionary trends in human populations because they do not believe there is enough gene flow for the multiregional model to work without it. They reject the interpretation of Templeton (1993) of mtDNA distribution as reflecting a long history of "restricted gene flow among Old World human populations with no single source population for all genetic variation." Instead, they cite Livingstone (1992), whose simple simulations "showed" that genes cannot move fast enough, Stringer and McKie (1996), who assert that the level of gene flow that multiregional evolution requires is "improbable," and Howell (1994, p. 304) who commented that the multiregional mechanism "stretches the bounds of credulity . . . there is serious need for normal procedures of evolutionary biology to prevail." This is all wrong. Several evolutionary biologists have calculated the magnitude of gene flow required for multiregional evolution to work, and it is very low. Estimates of the number of people who need move between continents each generation for isolation by distance to explain the existing

multiregional distribution of neutral genes average only a few each generation (Harpending et al., 1996; Relethford, 1998; Templeton, 1998). In fact, Relethford (1999) shows that on average, less than one migrant per generation is sufficient, hardly a large enough number to justify the comment that multiregional evolution must require an unacceptably large amount of migration in order to work. The estimate of Relethford (1999) is a *maximum* because it is for *neutral* genes. Genes under selection may have spread with much less migration, since their ultimate frequency and pattern of dispersion are controlled by the magnitude of selection, which in large populations is greater than the effect of migration on frequencies. Smith and Harrold (1997) accept the formulation of Brace (1991), in which culture relaxes selection and thereby creates parallel changes as structures reduce because of mutations, as being the multiregional model. It is not, and it is not necessary to accept so improbable an explanation as the probable mutation effect to account for the worldwide evolution of the human species.

DISCUSSION

"Multiregional" does not mean independent multiple origins, ancient divergence of modern populations, simultaneous appearance of adaptive characters in different regions, or parallel evolution. By depending on genic exchanges as the basis of its explanation of how differentiation, geographic variation, and evolutionary change within the human species take place, multiregional evolution is the antithesis of these. Therefore, the incorrect portrayals and invalid assumptions about the basis of multiregional evolution challenge our valid understanding of the issues, and undermine attempts to make progress in resolving them. One might gather from this essay that we contend that most authors who believe multiregional evolution is invalid, are in fact mistaking multiregional evolution for multiple origins. To a great extent this is correct. But it is not at all universally true. Prominent paleoanthropologists such as Tattersall (1997) and population geneticists such as Harpending et al. (1998) are truly exceptions to this generalization. They describe multiregional evolution correctly, but do not believe it is valid. There may be others who understand the model and yet disagree with it, but there are not many, and certainly not enough to suggest that misunderstanding multiregional evolution and the conviction it is wrong are unrelated.

Of course, the controversy does not persist solely because multiregional evolution is improperly understood, although misunderstandings have played an important role in how the controversy developed and their continuation has helped this controversy endure. Lying beneath this is a disagreement that mainly persists, and will continue to persist, because explanations of modern human origins through the mechanisms of complete replacement and worldwide evolution of a single species fully contradict each other. One of them must be wrong, and either is a valid refutation of the other. There is no compromise position to make it easier to find a synthesis of the views or form the basis of a consensus

---

[6] Although Brace's "stages of human evolution" is very different from multiregional evolution, he treats it as an only slightly modified version, and Smith and Harrold (1997) accept this.

[7] This, of course, is not true; it is neither a valid description of multiregional evolution, nor an accurate portrayal of its intellectual roots (see Wolpoff and Caspari, 1997).

[8] However, this "probable mutation effect" is not regarded as a valid evolutionary mechanism (Calcagno and Gibson, 1988).

that might make some more comfortable. Instead, we would predict that the posturing, spin-doctoring of new data, and repositioning will continue until one side admits it is mistaken, or more likely, turns its attentions

to other problems and, like the *Ramapithecus* debate, this one fades away. But we believe this can never happen until accuracy is achieved in portraying the evolutionary explanation that some authors are so sure is incorrect.

REFERENCES

Awadalla, P., Eyre-Walker, A., Smith, J. M. 1999. Linkage disequilibrium and recombination in hominid mitochondrial DNA. Science 286:2524–2525.

Birdsell, J. B. 1958. On population structure in generalized hunting and collecting populations. Evolution 12:189–205.

Bower, B. 1999. DNA's evolutionary dilemma: genetic studies collide with the mystery of human evolution. Sci News 155:88.

Brace, C. L. 1991. Cultural innovation and the mechanism for the emergence of modern morphology [abstract]. Am J Phys Anthropol [Suppl] 12:52.

Brace, C. L. 1995. Biocultural interaction and the mechanism of mosaic evolution. Am Anthropol 97:711–721.

Bräuer, G., Stringer, C. 1997. Models, polarization, and perspectives on modern human origins. In: Clark, G. A., Willermet, C. M., editors. Conceptual issues in modern human origins research. New York: Aldine de Gruyter. p. 191–201, 437–492.

Calcagno, J. M., Gibson, K. R. 1988. Human dental reduction: natural selection or the probable mutation effect. Am J Phys Anthropol 77:505–517.

Cavalli-Sforza, L. L. 1998. The Chinese human genome diversity project. Proc Natl Acad Sci USA 95:11501–11503.

Cavalli-Sforza, L. L., Menozzi, P., Piazza, A. 1993. Demic expansions and human evolution. Science 259:639–646.

Chu, J. Y., Huang, W., Kuang, S. Q., Wang, J. M., Xu, J. J., Chu, Z.T., Yang, Z. Q., Lin, K. Q., Li, P., Wu, M., Geng, Z. C., Tan, C. C., Du, R. F., Jin, L. 1998. Genetic relationship of populations in China. Proc Natl Acad Sci USA 95:11763–1178.

Clark, G. A. 1997. Through a glass darkly: conceptual issues in modern human origins research. In: Clark, G. A., Willermet, C. M., editors. Conceptual issues in modern human origins research. New York: Aldine de Gruyter. p. 60–76, 437–492.

Clark, G. A., Willermet, C. M. 1997. Introduction to conceptual issues in modern human origins research. In: Clark, G. A., Willermet, C. M., editors. Conceptual issues in modern human origins research. New York: Aldine de Gruyter. p. 1–8, 437–492.

Duarte, C., Maurício, J., Pettitt, P. B., Souto, P., Trinkaus, E., van der Plicht, H., Zilhão, J. 1999. The early Upper Paleolithic human skeleton from the Abrigo do Lagar Velho (Portugal) and modern human emergence in Iberia. Proc Natl Acad Sci USA 96:7604–7609.

Frayer, D. W. 1992. The persistence of Neandertal features in post-Neandertal Europeans. In: Bräuer, G., Smith, F. H., editors. Continuity or replacement? Controversies in *Homo sapiens* evolution. Rotterdam: Balkema. p. 179–188.

Frayer, D. W., Wolpoff, M. H., Smith, F. H., Thorne, A. G., Pope, G. G. 1993. The fossil evidence for modern human origins. Am Anthropol 95:14–50.

Gould, S. J. 1994. So near and yet so far. NY Rev Books 24–28.

Gould, S. L., Vrba, E. 1982. Exaptation—a missing term in the science of form. Paleobiology 8:4–15.

Harding, R. M., Fullerton, S. M., Griffiths, R. C., Bond, J., Cox, M. J., Schneider, J. A., Moulin, D. S., Clegg, J. B. 1997. Archaic African and Asian lineages in the genetic ancestry of modern humans. Am J Hum Genet 60:722–789.

Harpending, S., Batzer, M. A., Gurven, M., Jorde, L. B., Rogers, A. R., Sherry, S. T. 1998. Genetic traces of ancient demography. Proc Natl Acad Sci USA 95:1961–1967.

Harpending, H. C., Relethford, J. H., Sherry, S. T. 1996. Methods and models for understanding human diversity. In: Boyce, A. J., Mascie-Taylor, C. G. N., editors. Molecular biology and human diversity. Cambridge: Cambridge University Press. p. 283–299.

Harris, E. E., Hey, J. 1999. X chromosome evidence for ancient human histories. Proc Natl Acad Sci USA 96:3320–3324.

Hey, J. 1997. Mitochondrial and nuclear genes present conflicting portraits of human origins. Mol Biol Evol 14:166–172.

Howell, F. C. 1994. A chronostratigraphic and taxonomic framework of the origins of modern humans. In: Nitecki, M. H., Nitecki, D. V.,

editors. Origins of anatomically modern humans. New York: Plenum Press. p. 253–319.

Howell, F. C. 1996. Thoughts on the study and interpretation of the human fossil record. In: Meikle, W. E., Howell, F. C., Jablonski, N. G., editors. Contemporary issues in human evolution. Wattis symposium series in anthropology, California Academy of Sciences memoir. Volume 21. p. 1–45.

Lasker, G. W., Crews, C. E. 1996. Behavioral influences on the evolution of human genetic diversity. Mol Biol Evol 5:232–240.

Lewin, R. 1993. The origin of modern humans. New York: Scientific American Library.

Li, J., Underhill, P. A., Doctor, V., Davis, R. W., Peidong, S., Cavalli-Sforza, L. L., Oefner, P. J. 1999. Distribution of haplotypes from a chromosome 21 region distinguishes multiple prehistoric human migrations. Proc Natl Acad Sci USA 96:3796–3800.

Li, T., Etler, D. A. 1992. New Middle Pleistocene hominid crania from Yunxian in China. Nature 357:404–407.

Livingstone, F. B. 1992. Gene flow in the Pleistocene. Hum Biol 64:67–80.

Loewe, L., Scherer, S. 1997. Mitochondrial Eve: the plot thickens. Tree 12:422–423.

Lü, Z. 1990. La découverte de l'homme fossile de Jingniu-shan. Prem Etud Anthropol 94:899–902.

Moore, J. H. 1994. Putting anthropology back together again: the ethnogenetic critique of cladistic theory. Am Anthropol 96:925–948.

Nordborg, M. 1998. On the probability of Neanderthal ancestry. Am J Hum Genet 63:1237–1240.

Pope, G. G. 1992. Craniofacial evidence for the origin of modern humans in China. Yrbk Phys Anthropol 35: 243–298.

Relethford, J. H. 1995. Genetics and modern human origins. Evol Anthropol 4:53–63.

Relethford, J. H. 1998. Genetics of modern human origins and diversity. Annu Rev Anthropol 27:1–23.

Relethford, J. H. 1999. Models, predictions, and the fossil record of modern human origins. Evol Anthropol 8:7–10.

Relethford, J. H., Harpending, H. C. 1995. Ancient differences in population size can mimic a recent African origin of modern humans. Curr Anthropol 36:667–674.

Seielstad, M., Bekele, E., Ibrahim, M., Touré, A., Traoré, M. 1999. A view of modern human origins from Y chromosome microsatellite variation. Gene Res 9:558–567.

Smith, F. H. 1997. Modern human origins. In: Spencer, F., editor. History of physical anthropology. An encyclopedia. New York: Garland Publishing Inc. p. 661–672.

Smith, S. L., Harrold, F. B. 1997. A paradigm's worth of difference? Understanding the impasse over modern human origins. Yrbk Phys Anthropol 40:113–138.

Stringer, C. B., McKie, R. 1996. African exodus: the origins of modern humanity. London: Jonathan Cape.

Tattersall, I. 1997. Out of Africa again . . . and again? Sci. Am 276:60–67.

Templeton, A. R. 1993. The "Eve" hypotheses: a genetic critique and reanalysis. Am Anthropol 95:51–72.

Templeton, A. R. 1998. Human races: a genetic and evolutionary perspective. Am Anthropol 100:632–650.

Tindale, N. B. 1940. Distribution of Australian Aboriginal tribes: a field survey. Trans R Soc S. Austr 64:140–231.

Willermet, C. M., Hill, B. 1997. Fuzzy set theory and its implications for species models. In: Clark, G. A., Willermet, C. M., editors. Conceptual issues in modern human origins research. New York: Aldine de Gruyter. p 77–88, 437–492.

Wise, C. A., Sraml, M., Easteal, S. 1998. Departure from neutrality at the mitochondrial NADH dehydrogenase subunit 2 gene in humans, but not in chimpanzees. Genetics 148:409–421.

Wise, C. A., Sraml, M., Rubinsztein, D. C., Easteal, S. 1997. Comparative nuclear and mitochondrial genome diversity in humans and chimpanzees. Mol Biol Evol 14:707–716.

Wolpoff, M. H. 1998. Concocting a divisive theory. Evol Anthropol 7:1–3.

Wolpoff, M. H., Caspari, R. 1996. An unparalleled parallelism. Anthropologie (Brno) 34:215–223.

Wolpoff, M. H., Caspari, R. 1997. Race and human evolution. New York: Simon and Schuster.

Wolpoff, M. H., Wu, X., Thorne, A. G. 1984. Modern *Homo sapiens* origins: a general theory of hominid evolution involving the fossil evidence from east Asia. In: Smith, F. H., Spencer, F., editors. The origins of modern humans: a world survey of the fossil evidence. New York: Alan, R. Liss. p. 411–483.

Wolpoff, M. H., Thorne, A. G., Smith, F. H., Frayer, D. W., Pope, G. G. 1994. Multiregional evolution: a world-wide source for modern human populations. In: Nitecki, M. H., Nitecki, D. V., editors. Origins of anatomically modern humans. New York: Plenum Press. p. 175–199.

69

Modern Human Ancestry at the Peripheries

A Test of the Replacement Theory

M. H. Wolpoff, J. Hawks, D. W. Frayer, and K. Hunley

ABSTRACT

The replacement theory of modern human origins stipulates that populations outside of Africa were replaced by a new African species of modern humans. Here we test the replacement theory in two peripheral areas far from Africa by examining the ancestry of early modern Australians and Central Europeans. Analysis of pairwise differences was used to determine if dual ancestry in local archaic populations and earlier modern populations from the Levant and/or Africa could be rejected. The data imply that both have a dual ancestry. The diversity of recent humans cannot result exclusively from a single Late Pleistocene dispersal.

Two conflicting evolutionary models of modern (*1*) human origins have emerged in the past decade (*2*): complete replacement, in which modern humans are a new species that replaced all archaic populations, and multiregional evolution, in which modern humans are the present manifestation of an older worldwide species with populations connected by gene flow and the exchange of ideas, resembling each other because of similar adaptations to ideas and technologies that spread across the inhabited world and because of the dispersals of successful genes promoted by selection. One place where the models have quite different predictions is at the peripheries of the human range, where the replacement theory stipulates that the ancestry of early modern populations is not among their local archaic predecessors, who often are regarded as different human species (*3*). Multiregional evolution, a reticulate theory, is compatible with a dual ancestry for early moderns from the peripheries. Here we examine ancestry in Australia and Central Europe, two peripheral

areas with the best fossil record for the so-called transitional period, considering an early modern Australian cranium, Willandra Lakes Hominid (WLH) 50, and the two adult male crania from Mladeč, in Moravia, Czech Republic.

WLH-50 has been dated to about 15,000 to 13,000 years by gamma spectrometric U-series analysis (*4*) and to about double that time by electron spin resonance on bone (*5*). The calvarium exhibits many features that closely resemble earlier Indonesian hominids, including the Ngandong fossils of Java (*6*). WLH-50 is regarded as a modern human in all origins models (*6, 7*), whereas Ngandong fossils are often assessed as archaic humans or late surviving *Homo erectus* (*8*). The other possible ancestral population we tested for this male is the earlier modern human sample from Africa and the Levant of western Asia, which under the replacement theory must represent the only ancestors (Figure 1) of the first modern humans in Australia.

In Central Europe, over 100 fragmentary specimens unequivocally associated with an early Aurignacian industry (*9*) were recovered from the two Mladeč Caves in Moravia, Czech Republic (*10*). The most complete male calvaria are from the Quarry Cave. Mladeč 5 and 6 have been likened to the temporally earlier Neandertals (*11–13*) [although it is recognized that they are not themselves Neandertals (*10, 11*)]. Neandertals, then, are the local archaic predecessors of the Mladeč folk and are potentially their ancestors. The other potential ancestors are from Qafzeh and Skhul, the earlier modern human remains in western Asia (Figure 2), geographically and temporally the closest source of a replacing population.

The complete replacement model requires a unique relation between the early modern humans at these two peripheries and the earlier Levantines and/or Africans regarded as modern human. If evidence shows significant local ancestry for the peripheral samples, complete replacement must be wrong. To examine this issue, we tested for refutations of the hypotheses of dual

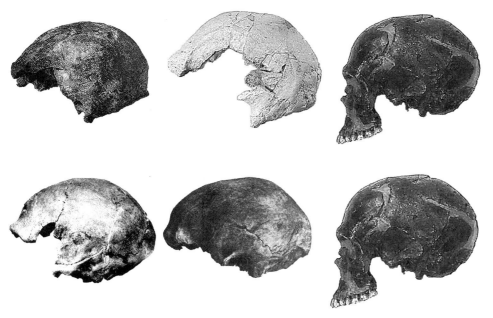

Figure 1. *Ngandong 1 (left) compared with WLH-50 (center, cast) and Qafzeh 9 (right, cast), shown in lateral view to the same scale. In its simplest form, the issue we address is which two are alike and which one is different. WLH-50 is the youngest of the three.*

Figure 2. *Mladeč 5 (center) compared with Qafzeh 9 (right, cast) and Spy 2 (left), in lateral view. As in Figure 1, we ask which two are alike and which one is different. The three specimens shown here are males, and Mladeč is the youngest of the three.*

ancestry (*14*) for WLH-50 and the Mladeč males. Obtaining a valid statistical test requires overcoming some formidable obstacles. There are only a few early modern crania complete enough to analyze, their dates are uncertain, the comparative samples are small and haphazardly preserved (*15*), and the traits may depend on each other in ways we cannot observe. In order not to compound these problems with extraneous assumptions, we used a simple method to address the relation among individuals that is independent of group assignments and the statistical structure of the groups. We collected details on certain nonmetric traits, scored as presence or absence to make unweighted sums of differences potentially informative (*16*). Using the scores on these nonmetric traits, we calculated the pairwise differences between specimens in the two early modern samples from the peripheries and each of the specimens in the earlier samples of potential ancestors. This kind of pairwise difference analysis is commonly applied to DNA sequence data to derive information about past population demography (*17*) and to estimate closeness of relation (*18*). Its use for nonmetric traits is tolerant of missing data—because we treat such cases as the absence of differences—as long as the missing data are either randomly distributed or are more strongly represented in the African or Levantine sample of potential ancestors predicted by the replacement theory. Additionally, we minimized missing data by appropriate choices of specimens and traits. The chance of a type I error is high with the pairwise test only if an early modern specimen is more similar in size to the local archaic sample and if the traits that are correlated with cranial size do not reflect geographic differences. We can reject both these conditions, as discussed below. If the early modern specimen is exclusively related to the earlier Africans and/or Levantines, then the probability of it looking more like the archaic sample should be effectively zero.

It may be claimed that because our analysis is a phenetic procedure, it is inappropriate to test the relations of these early modern humans with various putative ancestors because we do not take the polarity of the character states into account. We chose this procedure because we were unwilling to assume that the potential ancestors were different species; indeed, to do so would be to assume our conclusions. Character polarity is meaningless if the evolution of these groups included gene flow, which is one of the hypotheses under consideration. Moreover, although cladistic procedures might provide an implicit test of the replacementist assumption that archaic and modern peoples represent different species, the broad distribution of most of the nonmetric traits across groups, with very few traits unique to any group, leaves only a small number of potential synapomorphies required for phylogenetic analysis. The problem can be illustrated in the WLH-50 analysis. There are only eight traits unique to one potentially ancestral group or another in our nonmetric data. Of these eight character states that are uniquely in one sample, five are polymorphic within their samples, and only three are shared with WLH-50 (all three are shared between WLH-50 and Ngandong). The degree to which these nonmetric traits are shared among groups may itself suggest the conspecificity of the specimens involved, but we question the validity of this approach, which is why we did not take it.

For the WLH-50 analysis, we considered all of the specimens in the two earlier samples, regardless of sex, because we cannot reliably determine the sexes of the Ngandong calvaria. However, in the Mladeč analysis we restricted our comparisons to the males. We believe that our identification of males in Mladeč and in the earlier samples of potential ancestors is reliable, and note that females are poorly represented in the Skhul/Qafzeh cranial sample. The comparative samples are detailed in Tables 1 to 3.

Table 1. Pairwise Comparison of WLH-50 to Indonesian, African, and Levantine Specimens

Specimen	Number of Differences from WLH 50
Ngandong 5	2
Ngandong 9	3
Ngandong 10	3
Ngandong 11	3
Ngandong 4	4
Ngandong 1	5
Skhul 9	5
Ngandong 6	6
Jebel Irhoud 2	6
Omo 1	6
Qafzeh 6	7
Qafzeh 9	7
Skhul 5	7
Omo 2	8
Jebel Irhoud 1	10
Laetoli 18	10
Singa	12

The mean difference with the Ngandong specimens is 3.7; with the Levantine sample, 7.3; and with the Africans, 9.3. Unlike the Mladeč analyses (Tables 2 and 3), this analysis does not include Skhul 4 because it possesses only a few of the nonmetric traits listed below, mostly because of the parts preserved and the poor condition of the surface of the cranium. The features used in the Mladeč comparisons could be observed much more often. The 16 nonmetric features used in this pairwise comparison are as follows: angular torus; coronal keel; sagittal keel on frontal; lateral frontal trigone; *linea obliquus* strongly developed; mastoid crest; sagittal keel on parietal; postlambdoidal eminence; prebregmatic eminence; projecting inion; sulcus dividing the medial and lateral elements of the supraorbital torus or superciliary arches; superior margin of the orbit blunt (as opposed to sharp); suprainiac fossa; supramastoid crest; temporal line forms a ridge; and transversely extensive nuchal torus.

Most nonmetric observations were taken on the original fossil crania by at least one and often two of us; observations on casts of Laetoli Hominid 18 and the Omo crania were also used (see legends to Tables 1 and 2). In our scoring system, the presence of a trait was scored as 1, and its absence as 0. Some of these traits may reflect robustness, and for all such traits the more robust condition was scored as 1. In cases where a trait could not be observed on a specimen, we scored the trait as missing for that individual and treated it as not different in all comparisons involving that individual. We could unambiguously score 16 nonmetric traits on WLH-50. We avoided duplicating features that seemed to reflect the consequences of the same anatomical variation. These were scored in the Levant sample of four specimens and in six Late Pleistocene Africans, and were present in most cases. The pattern of missing data is random for the WLH-50 comparisons (Kruskal-Wallis test, $\chi^2 = 0.126$, $P = 0.939$). In the Mladeč analysis, we examined 30 nonmetric traits from all parts of the Mladeč 5 cranium (22 could be scored on the less complete Mladeč 6). These nonmetric traits were scored in four Neandertal and five Skhul/Qafzeh males and were present in virtually all instances. In this case, the pattern of missing data in the comparative samples is not random. The Skhul/Qafzeh crania have

Table 2. Pairwise Differences between Mladeč 5 and the Most Complete Neandertal Males (mean difference = 14.8) and Skhul/Qafzeh Males (mean difference = 14.0)

Specimen	Number of Differences from Mladeč 5
Skhul 4	8
Qafzeh 6	10
Skhul 9	11
Spy 2	12
La Chapelle	13
Qafzeh 9	15
La Ferrassie	15
Guattari	15
Skhul 5	23

Presence or absence of 30 nonmetric traits is scored in this analysis: anterior temporal fossa border angled; thick parietal at asterion (> 9 mm); broad frontal (> 125 mm); broad occiput (> 120 mm); central frontal boss; cranial rear rounded (as seen from back); external auditory meatus leans forward; frontal keel; long frontal (glabella-bregma length > 113); frontonasal suture arched; glabellar depression; glenoid articular surface flattened; thick occipital at lambda (> 8 mm); lateral supraorbital central thinning; mastoid process projects minimally; mastoid tubercle; mastoid-supramastoid crests well separated; medially tall supraorbital (> 19 mm); nuchal torus extends across occiput; occipital bun; long occipital plane (> 60 mm); occipitomastoid crest prominent; paramastoid crest prominent; retromastoid process prominent; sagittal groove along vault posterior; supraglenoid gutter long; elliptical suprainiac fossa; supraorbital center dips downward; "teardrop" shape (seen from top); and vertical occipital face short.

Table 3. Pairwise Differences between Mladeč 6 and the Most Complete Neandertal Males (mean difference = 7.8) and Skhul/Qafzeh Males (mean difference = 11.6)

Specimen	Number of Differences from Mladeč 6
Qafzeh 6	6
La Chapelle	7
Guattari	7
Spy 2	8
La Ferrassie	9
Skhul 4	11
Skhul 9	11
Qafzeh 9	14
Skhul 5	16

Presence or absence of 22 nonmetric traits is scored in this analysis, less than the number for Mladeč 5 because the vault is less complete. The eight traits from Table 2 not found on this specimen are as follows: thick occipital at lambda; prominent occipitomastoid crest; minimal projection of mastoid process; mastoid tubercle; long supraglenoid gutter; central thinning of lateral supraorbital; angled anterior temporal fossa border; and external auditory meatus leans forward.

more missing data than the Neandertals. This makes the analysis conservative because if all else is equal, the results will be biased to show more similarities with the Skhul/Qafzeh remains (i.e., will support replacement).

We examined whether there might be special similarities between the peripheral samples and their archaic predecessors because of robustness in the peripheral specimens created by their size, an explanation some have suggested (*19, 20*). To specify the relation, we examined each region for an influence of size on the robustness, as estimated by the sum of the nonmetric scores (*20*). We used endocranial capacity to estimate cranial size because it is not based on any particular observation in our analysis (*21*). The question of how robustness and size are related has different answers at different levels of analysis. For instance, within populations there is usually a clear relation between size and robustness because males are on average and in particular larger and more robust than females. There were no significant within-group associations of cranial size and presence of nonmetric traits in our samples (Africans: $P = 0.527$; Levantines: $P = 0.901$; Ngandong: $P = 0.580$; Mann-Whitney test). Between populations, on the other hand, the relation could be just the opposite. Comparing the African and Levantine samples, there is a positive association, indicating that any relation between cranial size and presence of nonmetric features must depend strongly on the geographic locations of the groups being compared. In the Australasian analysis, the extraordinary robustness of WLH-50 resembles one potential ancestor, and its size resembles the other. Of the 16 nonmetric variables used in the WLH-50 analysis, 6 were correlated with cranial capacity ($P = 0.05$, Kolmogorov-Smirnov test). In each instance where the presence of a nonmetric feature was correlated with cranial capacity, the specimens that possessed the feature had smaller cranial capacities than those lacking the feature. These relations exist because Ngandong is the most robust group in our sample (Figure 3) and has the smallest mean cranial capacity. The large size of WLH-50 ensures that if there is a significant nonmetric relation of WLH-50 with Ngandong, a rejection of the replacement hypothesis will be a conservative outcome.

A similar but weaker relation can be found in the Mladeč comparisons where the population with larger

crania is not the more robust one. The Neandertal males ($n = 8$) are more robust than the Skhul/Qafzeh males ($n = 5$), but their mean cranial capacity is smaller (1531 cm^3 compared with 1552 cm^3). It follows that the larger size of the early modern descendants cannot be posited as a cause of their robustness, so nonmetric similarities between earlier and later specimens within regions cannot have resulted from cranial size. The most parsimonious explanation for such similarities is ancestry.

We found significant differences among the groups for pairwise differences from WLH-50 (Table 1). Six of the seven Ngandong crania are closer to WLH-50 than are any other specimens, and the seventh is separated from the others by only one individual (Skhul 9). On average, WLH-50 possesses fewer differences from the Ngandong group (3.7 pairwise differences) than from either the African (9.3) or Levantine (7.3) groups. Mean pairwise differences between Ngandong and African, and Ngandong and Levantine groups are statistically significant at the 0.05 level (Mann-Whitney). The Ngandong mean pairwise difference from WLH-50 is significantly lower than both the African mean and the Levantine mean differences at the 0.05 level (Mann-Whitney). WLH-50 is most different from the Africans, although difference in the number of pairwise differences between the African and Levantine samples relative to WLH-50 is not significant. In sum, in its nonmetric traits WLH-50 is closer to the specimens from Ngandong than to any other group. If Ngandong was the expected ancestor under the replacement theory, this would disprove a dual-ancestry hypothesis. However, it is not, and a Ngandong ancestry disproves the replacement theory, so the conservative interpretation of these results is that the dual-ancestry hypothesis cannot be disproved.

We might expect a similar pattern for the Mladeč specimens. Examination of characteristics said to be unique for Neandertals (*22*) indicates that Mladeč 6 has a suprainiac fossa of elliptical form, extensive lambdoidal flattening, and a short posterior face on the occiput. Mladeč 5 has a Neandertal-like sagittal contour, a well-developed occipitomastoid crest, minimal mastoid projection, and evidence of midfacial prognathism, insofar as the marked anterior projection of the upper face predicts this.

The average pairwise difference between Mladeč 5 and the Neandertal sample is 14.8, and between Mladeč 5 and the Skhul/Qafzeh sample, 14.0—virtually the same (Table 2). On the other hand, for Mladeč 6 the corresponding comparisons are 7.8 and 11.6, so it is closer to the Neandertal sample (Table 3). A Sample Runs Test (*23*) was used to examine whether the ordering of Neandertal and Skhul/Qafzeh crania, based on the number of pairwise differences from the Mladeč crania, is random (the null hypothesis). Randomness can be rejected at the $P = 0.05$ level when there are two or less, or 9 or more, runs (*24*) from the same site, for a sample of this size. There are five runs for Mladeč 5 and three runs for Mladeč 6—randomness in the order of pairwise similarities cannot be rejected (*25*). Again, these data fail to reject the dual-ancestry hypothesis.

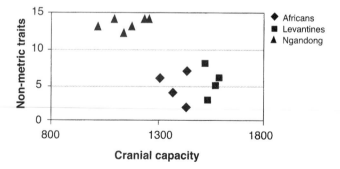

Figure 3. *Robustness and cranial size. The relation between presence of nonmetric traits used in the WLH-50 analysis, presented here as the sum of their scores for each individual, and cranial size, as measured by cranial capacity. The sum of the nonmetric scores is a measure of robustness because each was scored as 0 or 1, and whenever robustness characterized the difference, the more robust condition was scored as 1. The geographic affinities of the groups being compared provide the main source of variation.*

They imply that the Mladeč crania are not uniquely related to Skhul/Qafzeh.

Another way to examine this nonmetric variation is in terms of its distribution within and between the samples of putative Mladeč ancestors. Three of the nonmetric variables completely separated the Neandertal and Skhul/Qafzeh samples. Of these, the Mladeč crania were like the Neandertals in two, and like Skhul/Qafzeh in one. Seven additional traits almost completely separated the putative Mladeč ancestors (*26*). Of these, the Mladeč crania were like the Neandertals in four, and like Skhul/Qafzeh in two. For the seventh trait, one Mladeč cranium was like each comparative sample. In spite of the predominance of Neandertal resemblances for this subset of 10 traits, the normal approximation of the binomial distribution shows that an ancestry hypothesis in which dual ancestry is assumed to be equal ancestry cannot be rejected at the 0.05 level.

These tests show that a dual-ancestry model cannot be rejected for either of the geographically peripheral samples we have considered. There is no evidence suggesting that WLH-50 can be grouped with either Late Pleistocene Africans or Levantines to the exclusion of the Ngandong sample, or that the Mladeč males can be grouped with the Levantines to the exclusion of European Neandertals. This refutes the replacement theory and contradicts the interpretation that local archaic populations represent now-extinct human species (*27*). It means that Ngandong should not be classified as *H. erectus* (*6*). This result joins other evidence of sufficient Neandertal features in Upper Paleolithic Europeans to reject interpreting their variation as that of an extinct human species (*11, 13, 28–30*), because no matter how different Neandertals may seem, diagnostically Neandertal anatomy in later populations is an indication of sufficient Neandertal ancestry to reject such a species hypothesis.

Our analyses, like all discussions of modern human origins, are limited by the small sample sizes and ignorance of the underlying variance and covariance matrices for the data, and we interpret them with this in mind. However, their failure to disprove the hypothesis of dual ancestry for early moderns in two far-flung regions of the world adds to the improbability of a replacement explanation for modern human origins. We do not doubt that many prehistoric groups were replaced by others, but we conclude that the hypothesis that all living humans descended from a single geographically isolated group during the Late Pleistocene is false, and that the replacement explanation for the origin of these early modern Australians and Europeans can be ruled out.

REFERENCES AND NOTES

1. We use this word guardedly; we take "modern" to refer to all living humans and their immediate ancestors, but whether modernity originated at one time and place as a single entity, or whether it reflects the worldwide distribution of shared anatomies and behaviors, is the question examined in this paper.

2. M. H. Wolpoff, R. Caspari, *Race and Human Evolution* (Simon & Schuster, New York, 1997); C. B. Stringer, in *Origins of Anatomically Modern Humans*, M. H. Nitecki, D. V. Nitecki, Eds. (Plenum, New York, 1994), pp. 149–172; G. A. Clark, C. M. Willermet, Eds., *Conceptual Issues in Modern Human Origins Research* (Aldine de Gruyter, New York, 1997).

3. Although Ngandong has been considered *Homo erectus* (*8*) and Neandertals classified as *Homo neanderthalensis* (*27*), not all replacement theorists agree that there is a taxonomic difference at the species level. Some have suggested that Neandertals could have interbred with Upper Paleolithic Europeans but did not do so very often [G. Bräuer, in *Continuity or Replacement? Controversies in* Homo sapiens *Evolution*, G. Bräuer, F. H. Smith, Eds. (Balkema, Rotterdam, 1992), pp. 83–98; C. B. Stringer, *Nature* **356**, 201 (1992)]. However, others note that this is actually a variant of multiregional evolution [J. H. Relethford, *Evol. Anthropol.* **8**, 7 (1999); M. H. Wolpoff, J. Hawks, R. Caspari, *Am. J. Phys. Anthropol.*, **112**, 29 (2000)]. This is because models including population mixing are reticular, and enough mixing to be recognized in the fossil record is a disproof of replacement, not an example of it [A. R. Templeton, in *Conceptual Issues in Modern Human Origins Research*, G. A. Clark, C. M. Willermet, Eds. (Aldine de Gruyter, New York, 1997), pp. 329–360, 437–492].

4. J. J. Simpson, R. Grün, *Quat. Geochr.* **17**, 1009 (1998).

5. D. Caddie, D. Hunter, P. Pomery, H. Hall, in *Archaeometry: Further Australasian Studies*, W. Ambrose, J. Mummery, Eds. (Department of Prehistory, Australian National University, Canberra, 1987), pp. 156–166.

6. J. Hawks et al., *J. Hum. Evol.* **39**, 1 (2000).

7. C. Stringer, *J. Hum. Evol.* **34**, 327 (1998).

8. G. P. Rightmire, *The Evolution of* Homo erectus: *Comparative Anatomical Studies of an Extinct Human Species* (Cambridge Univ. Press, Cambridge, 1990); C. C. Swisher III et al., *Science* **274**, 1870 (1996).

9. J. Svoboda, *J. Hum. Evol.* **38**, 523 (2000).

10. J. Szombathy, *Eiszeit* **2**, 1, 73 (1925); F. H. Smith, in *History of Physical Anthropology. An Encyclopedia*, F. Spencer Ed. (Garland, New York, 1997), pp. 659–660.

11. J. Jelínek, *Anthropologie* (Brno) **21**, 57 (1983).

12. D. W. Frayer, *Anthropologie* (Brno) **23**, 243 (1986).

13. F. H. Smith, *Curr. Anthropol.* **23**, 667 (1982).

14. The dual-ancestry model, which is a multiregional one, depends on reticulation and is visible through evidence of regional continuity. In criticizing the multiregional explanation of modern human origins in Europe, G. Bräuer and H. Broeg [in *Origins and Past of Modern Humans: Towards Reconciliation*, K. Omoto, P. V. Tobias, Eds. (World Scientific, Singapore, 1998), pp. 106–125] state, "during the long period of coexistence, mixing and gene flow between Neandertals and the dispersing modern populations might have occurred to varying degrees in different regions . . . such gene flow could have mimicked some degree of continuity" (p. 106). To avoid confusion, we note that multiregional evolution is not mimicked by gene flow, but is based on it.

15. They have unequal numbers of males and females, and because of differences in preservation, the sample represented for one trait is often not the same as for another.

16. A trait, say, scored with four character states could contribute as much to a pairwise difference analysis as three traits scored as present or absent. We realize that our nonmetric characters are not formally equal to each other in complexity or heritability, but contend that our approach to scoring makes them as comparable as possible.

17. A. R. Rogers, *Evolution* **49**, 608 (1995).

18. M. Krings et al., *Cell* **90**, 1 (1997).

19. P. Brown, *Coobool Creek. Terra Australis* **13** (Department of Prehistory, Research School of Pacific Studies, Australian National University, Canberra, 1989).

20. M. M. Lahr, H. V. S. Wright, *J. Hum. Evol.* **31**, 157 (1996).

21. This helps to avoid spurious correlations that might result from using different measurements of the same thing as independent and dependent variables [B. Solow, *Acta Odontol. Scand.* **24** (suppl. 46), 1 (1966)].

22. J.-J. Hublin, in *Neandertals and Modern Humans in Western Asia*, T. Akazawa, K. Aoki, O. Bar-Yosef, Eds. (Plenum, New York, 1998), pp. 295–310.

23. F. S. Swed, C. Eisenhart, *Ann. Math. Stat.* **14**, 66 (1943).

24. A run is one or more crania from the same group in a row. For instance, the Mladeč 6 analysis (Table 3) has three runs.

25. With a larger sample and fewer runs in the WLH-50 analysis, randomness can be rejected at $P = 0.05$. Ngandong is significantly closer to WLH-50, which is compatible with dual ancestry but is a refutation of the replacement hypothesis, so the consequences are the same even though the significance test results were opposite.

26. Meaning that all of one sample were the same for the character state, and only one specimen in the other sample differed from the opposite character state.

27. I. Tattersall, *The Last Neanderthal: The Rise, Success, and Mysterious Extinction of our Closest Human Relatives*. (MacMillan, New York, 1995).

28. D. W. Frayer, *Préhist. Eur.* **2**, 9 (1993).

29. C. Duarte et al., *Proc. Natl. Acad. Sci. U.S.A.* **96**, 7604 (1999); A. E. Mann, J. Monge, M. Lampl, *Am. J. Phys. Anthropol.* **86**, 175 (1991); J. Szilvássy, H. Kritscher, E. Vlček, *Ann. Vienna Nat. Hist. Mus.* **89**, 313 (1987).

30. R. Caspari (University Microfilms, Ann Arbor, MI, 1991).

31. We thank A. Thorne (Australian National University) for allowing M.H.W. to study the original WLH-50 specimen. We are grateful to J. Jelínek (Moravian Museum, Brno), H. Kritscher, H. Poxleitner, L. Seitl, J. Szilvássy, and M. Teschler (Vienna Natural History Museum) for permission to work on the Mladeč specimens, and thank the many curators and museum directors with responsibility for the comparative samples we discuss here for access to the fossil collections in their care. Supported by NSF grants BNS 75-21756, BNS 76-82729, and BNS 85-09147; grants from the National Academy of Sciences, Eastern European Program; a grant from the Department of Prehistory, Research School of Pacific Studies, Australian National University; and grants from the Rackham Graduate School, University of Michigan.

70

Origins of Modern Humans Still Look Recent

T. R. Disotell

ABSTRACT

That modern humans have a relatively ancient origin has been suggested on the basis of fossil and genetic evidence. But DNA sequences from an extinct neanderthal, and phylogenetic analyses of hundreds of human and ape sequences, continue to support a recent origin for modern humans.

Perhaps the greatest controversy in studies of human evolution concerns the origins of modern humans and our relationship with the first fossils discovered that bear on this question—the neanderthals. Two main hypotheses have been put forth. The 'multiregional model' proposes that modern humans arose independently in different regions of the world, with sufficient gene flow between the regions to maintain the unity of the species, and share a most recent common ancestor who lived over one million years ago. The 'recent replacement model', in contrast, proposes that a single population, most likely of African origin, expanded and replaced archaic populations throughout the world, beginning around 200,000 years ago.

Starting with the original 'African Eve' hypothesis [1], mitochondrial DNA studies have generally supported a 200,000 year old African origin for modern humans mitochondrial variation [2,3]. Numerous studies of Y chromosome and autosomal variation have arrived at the same conclusion [2–4]. Given the relative paucity of the non-European fossil record of specimens dating to this crucial time period, it is not surprising that the most vehement arguments surround the fate of the well-known neanderthals who lived in Europe and western Asia between about 200,000 and 30,000 years ago. Did they evolve into modern Europeans, hybridize with incoming modern invaders, or were they replaced by an invading population?

A recently discovered, 24,500 year old skeleton of a four-year-old child found in Portugal has reignited the debate over the possibility that neanderthals and modern humans hybridized. Duarte et al. [5] claim that this child displays a mixture of neanderthal and modern traits. Given that neanderthals disappeared from western Europe approximately 29,000–30,000 years ago, this would mean neanderthal morphological traits persisted for over 200 generations of admixture. While this itself is extremely unlikely, reevaluation of the preserved traits has already led many researchers to voice skepticism about hybridization [6].

Although most of the skeletal features of this specimen look most similar to those of a modern human, the body proportions, and other features of the limbs and trunk, are interpreted by Duarte et al. [5] as being more similar to those of a neanderthal. Tattersall and Schwartz [6], however, rightly point out how difficult it is to reconstruct and interpret the postcranial skeleton of an immature individual, concluding that "the probability must thus remain that this is simply a chunky Gravettian child, a descendent of the modern invaders who had evicted the Neanderthals from Iberia several millennia earlier". Other claims of neanderthal–modern hybrids in central and eastern Europe have been similarly criticized. Given their many unique adaptations, most paleoanthropologists now view these people as a distinct sort of human and place them in their own species *Homo neanderthalensis*.

The more surprising evidence for separate evolutionary paths has come from analyses of neanderthal DNA. In 1997, Krings et al. [7] extracted mitochondrial DNA from the arm of the original neanderthal-type specimen from Feldhofer Cave in Germany's Neander Valley. Under extremely stringent conditions in their laboratory in Munich, which included testing multiple extracts (with one performed in an independent laboratory at Pennsylvania State University), Krings et al. [7] were able to amplify and sequence a 378 base-pair region of the mitochondrial control region. The sequence was found to differ significantly from all of their laboratory personnel and all humans sequenced to date, leading to the conclusion that it was indeed from the neanderthal's DNA. Compared to a human reference sequence, the neanderthal sequence differed by 26 nucleotide substitutions and a single base insertion event. Sequence comparisons revealed that the neanderthal sequence fell outside of the variation of modern humans [7]. Phylogenetic analysis suggested that the common ancestor of the neanderthal and modern humans existed around 600,000 years ago, four times the estimate for when the common ancestor of all modern humans existed based on this mitochondrial region.

Two years on, an additional 340 base sequence of the second highly variable region of the mitochondrial control region has been obtained from the same individual [8]. Further analyses of the combined sequences continue to demonstrate that the neanderthal sequence is not closely related to modern Europeans, as would be predicted by the multiregional model, but rather that it diverged around 465,000 years ago [8]. This date is slightly younger than the original estimate based upon a shorter sequence, but is still too old to support a neanderthal ancestry for modern Europeans, or any other modern humans for that matter.

Wolpoff, a leading paleoanthropologist who still supports the multiregional model, has reevaluated the neanderthal sequence data [9]. Using a pairwise approach, he compared the neanderthal sequence to a sample of 2051 modern human sequences, noting that 25 of the 27 differences between them varied within modern humans. From further comparison among 994 modern sequences of known geographic origin, Wolpoff [9] concluded "the most surprising finding was that several of the humans were found to differ from each other more than the Neanderthal differs from some humans". Unfortunately, these kinds of pairwise comparisons are not very useful, and indeed, can be misleading. Overall similarity is composed of three components, shared-ancestral traits, shared-derived traits, and homoplasies resulting from convergence or parallelism. Simple pairwise comparisons do not separate out these different kinds of similarity and therefore can yield a mistaken

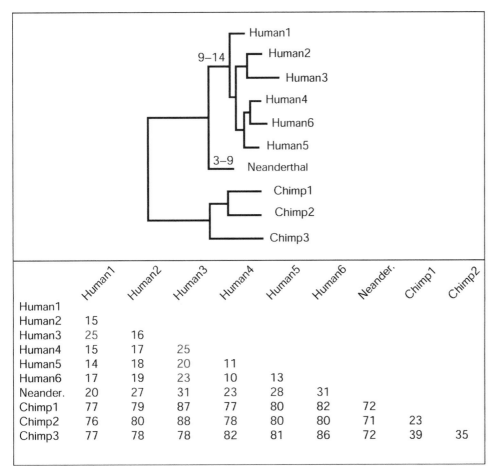

Figure 1. *Bottom: number of nucleotide substitutions in the region of the mitochondrial control region originally sequenced in the neanderthal [7] and reanalyzed by Wolpoff [9]. Note that, for four modern human pairs the differences are greater than or equal to those between some modern humans and the neanderthal. Top: maximum parsimony tree inferred from the same sequences. The numbers along the branches leading to the neanderthal and modern humans represent the range of nucleotide substitutions that are inferred to have occurred along each branch.*

	Human1	Human2	Human3	Human4	Human5	Human6	Neander.	Chimp1	Chimp2
Human1									
Human2	15								
Human3	25	16							
Human4	15	17	25						
Human5	14	18	20	11					
Human6	17	19	23	10	13				
Neander.	20	27	31	23	28	31			
Chimp1	77	79	87	77	80	82	72		
Chimp2	76	80	88	78	80	80	71	23	
Chimp3	77	78	78	82	81	86	72	39	35

impression of how close the two individuals are with respect to their true evolutionary relatedness [10].

To illustrate this, I have put together a small data set composed of the same mitochondrial region used above for six humans, three chimpanzees and the neanderthal. Pairwise differences, as well as the most parsimonious phylogenetic tree, are shown in Figure 1. For several pairwise comparisons among modern humans, the differences are greater than those between some of them and the neanderthal (Figure 1). Yet the most parsimonious tree unambiguously groups the humans together (Figure 1), with between 12 and 23 nucleotide substitutions occurring between the neanderthal and ancestral human branches (depending upon the model of nucleotide evolution used in the phylogenetic reconstruction).

Proponents of the multiregional model also like to cite several genetic studies which apparently contradict those that support the recent replacement hypothesis. Nearly all the studies using mitochondrial, Y chromosome and autosomal loci reveal greater genetic diversity among modern Africans, place the first branch of the modern human tree within Africa, and infer a date within the last 100,000 or 200,000 years for the derivation of non-African populations [2,3]. Several of these conclusions rest upon the assumption that the effective population size of the human species—or at least of the population that gave rise to modern people—was relatively small, on the order of 10,000 individuals, for tens of thousands of years. Numerous studies support this assumption and elaborate upon it by inferring that this so-called genetic 'bottleneck' existed for a long time, rather than as a relatively short singular event [11].

Two analyses of X chromosome loci, however, have yielded discordant results. An 8 kilobase segment of the X-linked *dystrophin* gene was characterized in 860 chromosomes from 13 populations [12]. Population genetic analyses are consistent with the view that this gene behaves as a neutrally evolving locus in a population with a long-term effective population size of approximately 10,000 [12]. Furthermore, the older alleles (determined by comparing them to those found in the great apes) have similar frequencies in African and non-African populations, while the younger alleles have more limited distributions, implying an African origin [12]. These inferences are in reasonable agreement with those based on the loci discussed above [3].

But the inferences drawn from analyses of another X-linked locus do not fit so easily with the majority view. The *PDHA1* locus was initially sequenced in eight males, including four of sub-Saharan African descent, for a total of 1,769 bases [13]. The sequences from the four non-African individuals do not vary at all, while the African sequences vary at only four sites. A comparison of the four polymorphisms in these sequences to those in the mitochondrial control region led Hey [13] to conclude that mitochondrial sequences have been under selection and therefore provided misleading estimates of ancestral effective population sizes and thus dates of common ancestry. This result was cited by paleoanthropologists [9] as conflicting with the recent replacement hypothesis. This *PDHA1* data set unfortunately is far too small to allow such inferences to be reached with any confidence.

To rectify this deficiency, a larger *PDHA1* data set was collected, comprising 4,200 nucleotides from 35 human (including eight Africans) and two common chimpanzee males [14]. Twenty-five polymorphic positions were discovered, from which population genetic parameters and a phylogenetic tree were inferred. Eight of the ten lineages in the resulting tree were solely of African origin, with the two European lineages being most closely related to the most divergent African lineage (Figure 2a). By observing the total divergence between the two chimpanzee and the human sequences, and assuming a divergence time of 5 million years, an estimate of the mutation rate was obtained. Applying this rate to the phylogenetic tree gave an estimate of 1.86 million years for the human common ancestral type of this *PDHA1* region [14]. Even though autosomal loci should yield coalescence times four times as old as those of mitochondrial or Y chromosome loci—three times in the case of the X chromosome—because of their larger effective population sizes, this date stands in opposition to most others, which vary between 200,000 years (for mitochondrial and Y chromosome sequences) and 800,000 years (for autosomal sequences).

Several flaws are also apparent in this study [14]. The sampling of only eight Africans and six Europeans

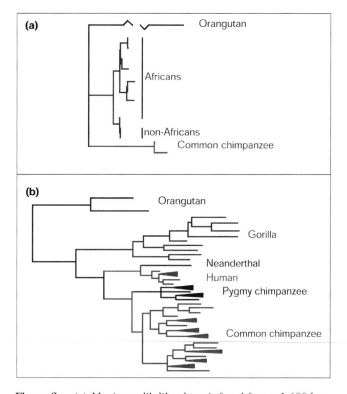

Figure 2. *(a) Maximum likelihood tree inferred from a 1,600 base subset of the* PDHA1 *region, with base frequency and probability of change parameters estimated from the data; the tree is drawn with proportional branch lengths (data kindly supplied by Jody Hey). The orangutan branch length is too long to display in full. (b) Neighbor-joining tree—pruned to remove closely related sequences—based on 1,158 mitochondrial control region 1 sequences, with proportional branch lengths (modified from [15]). (Note that (a) and (b) are not drawn to the same scale.)*

means that shared alleles were surely missed [3]. It is also surprising that the two chimpanzee sequences differ at only three positions. The massive data set of human (811) and ape (345) mitochondrial sequences collated and analyzed by Gagneux et al. [15] has revealed a tremendous amount of variation within chimpanzee populations, especially as compared to within-human variation (see Figure 2b). Further sampling of both humans and chimpanzees could significantly alter the shape and depth of the tree based on *PDHA1* sequences.

The time estimates are also dependent upon the assumption of equal rates of evolution along the chimpanzee and human lineages. The reanalysis shown in Figure 2a—using a smaller, 1,600 base portion of this *PDHA1* region that was also sequenced in the orangutan—yields a phylogenetic tree that clearly shows unequal rates of evolution. Such rate disparity often indicates the influence of selection, which would then call into question most of the population genetic

parameters and conclusions drawn. It would therefore seem to be premature to draw conclusions from the *PDHA1* data until additional human and chimpanzee sequences are collected and new analyses performed.

Thus, the results of Gagneux et al. [15] appear to have received considerable support from numerous other genetic systems [2,3]. As illustrated in the tree shown in Figure 2b, human populations are genetically depauperate compared to our great ape cousins. The single neanderthal sequence collected to date falls clearly outside of the modern human lineage, and is best estimated to share common ancestry with our lineage around a half million years ago. Therefore, the most strongly supported hypothesis to date suggests that our ancestry is derived from an African population that may have remained relatively isolated in Africa for tens of thousands of years before migrating out in the last 100,000 years or so, replacing archaic humans, including neanderthals, throughout the old world.

REFERENCES

1. Cann, R. L., Stoneking, M., Wilson, A. C.: Mitochondrial DNA and human evolution. *Nature* 1987, 325:31–36.
2. Disotell, T. R.: Sex-specific contributions to genome variation. *Curr Biol* 1999, 9:R29–R31.
3. Seielstad, M., Bekele, E., Ibrahim, M., Touré, A., Traoré, M.: A view of modern human origins from Y chromosome microsatellite variation. *Genome Res* 1999, 9:558–567.
4. Ruvolo, M.: A new approach to studying modern origins: hypothesis testing with coalescence time distributions. *Mol Phylogenet Evol* 1997, 5:202–219.
5. Duarte, C., Maurício, J., Pettitt, P. B., Souto, P., Trinkaus, E.: The early Upper Paleolithic human skeleton from the Abrigo do Lagar Velho (Portugal) and modern human emergence in Iberia. *Proc Natl Acad Sci USA* 1999, 96:7604–7609.
6. Tattersall, I., Schwartz, J. H.: Hominids and hybrids: the place of neanderthals in human evolution. *Proc Natl Acad Sci USA* 1999, 96:7117–7119.
7. Krings, M., Stone, A., Schmitz, R. W., Krainitzki, H., Stoneking, M., Pääbo, S.: Neanderthal DNA sequences and the origin of modern humans. *Cell* 1997, 90:19–30.
8. Krings, M., Geisert, H., Schmitz, R. W., Krainitzki, H., Pääbo, S.: DNA sequence of the mitochondrial hypervariable region II from the neanderthal type specimen. *Proc Natl Acad Sci USA* 1999, 96:5581–5585.
9. Wolfpoff, M.: Concocting a divisive theory. *Evol Anthrop* 1998, 7:1–3.
10. Stewart, C.-B.: The powers and pitfalls of parsimony. *Nature* 1993, 361:603–607.
11. Harpending, H. C., Batzer, M. A., Gurven, M., Jorde, L. B., Rogers, A. R., Sherry, S. S.: Genetic traces of ancient demography. *Proc Natl Acad Sci USA* 1998, 95:1961–1967.
12. Zietkiewicz, E., Yotova, V., Jarnik, M., Korab-Laskowska, M., Kidd, K. K., Modiano, D., Scozzari, R., Stoneking, M., Tishkoff, S., Batzer, M., et al.: Genetic structure of the ancestral population of modern humans. *J Mol Evol* 1998, 47:146–155.
13. Hey, J.: Mitochondrial and nuclear genes present conflicting portraits of human origins. *Mol Biol Evol* 1997, 14:166–172.
14. Harris, E. E., Hey, J.: X chromosome evidence for ancient human histories. *Proc Natl Acad Sci USA* 1999, 96:3320–3324.
15. Gagneux, P., Wills, C., Gerloff, U., Tautz, D., Morin, P. A., Boesch, C., Fruth, B., Hohmann, G., Ryder, O. A., Woodruff, D. S.: Mitochondrial sequences show diverse evolutionary histories of African hominoids. *Proc Natl Acad Sci USA* 1999, 96:5077–5082.

71

Out of Africa Again and Again

A. R. Templeton

ABSTRACT

The publication of a haplotype tree of human mitochondrial DNA variation in 1987 provoked a controversy about the details of recent human evolution that continues to this day. Now many haplotype trees are available, and new analytical techniques exist for testing hypotheses about recent evolutionary history using haplotype trees. Here I present formal statistical analysis of human haplotype trees for mitochondrial DNA, Y-chromosomal DNA, two X-linked regions and six autosomal regions. A coherent picture of recent human evolution emerges with two major themes. First is the dominant role that Africa has played in shaping the modern human gene pool through at least two—not one—major expansions after the original range extension of Homo erectus *out of Africa. Second is the ubiquity of genetic interchange between human populations, both in terms of recurrent gene flow constrained by geographical distance and of major population expansion events resulting in interbreeding, not replacement.*

Recent human evolution is an area of great controversy[1]. There is general agreement that the human lineage evolved in Africa, and then spread to southern Eurasia as *Homo erectus*. After *Homo erectus* spread out of Africa, the out-of-Africa replacement model[2] posits that populations in Africa, Europe and Asia had little genetic contact and evolved independently, with anatomically modern humans evolving only in Africa. After the evolution of modern humans in Africa, a second expansion occurred out of Africa about 100,000 years ago that resulted in the global replacement and genetic extinction of nonmodern human populations by anatomically modern humans. Under the multiregional trellis model[3,4] genetic contact between African and non-African *Homo erectus* populations was maintained although restricted by isolation by distance. Isolation by distance allowed local populations to become differentiated from one another, but gene flow prevented long-term independent evolution such that humanity evolved into modernity as a single evolutionary lineage.

Much of this controversy started with the publication of evolutionary trees of haplotype variation in human mitochondrial DNA (mtDNA)[5,6]. The estimation of these initial mtDNA haplotype trees was flawed[7,8], but many subsequent studies have generated more reliable haplotype trees for mtDNA[9–12], Y-chromosomal DNA regions (Y-DNA)[13], X-linked DNA regions[14,15] and several autosomal DNA regions[16–20]. Not all of these haplotype trees have been analysed with respect to models of recent human evolution. The purpose of this paper is to analyse several recently published haplotype trees and combine these new analyses with older analyses.

RECONSTRUCTING HUMAN EVOLUTION WITHOUT PREVIOUS MODELS

Instead of testing *a priori* hypotheses of recent human evolution, nested clade phylogeographic analyses[21] as implemented with the program GEODIS[22] are used to infer both historical events (such as range expansions) and recurrent events (such as gene flow) without regard to any prior model. Although it is relatively new[21], nested clade analysis has been validated by applying it to data sets with known *a priori* information and has been found to be accurate and not prone to false positives, although it fails to detect all known events[23]. This methodology has now become a standard tool in phylogeographic analyses (for example, see refs 24–27).

The nested clade analysis first tests the null hypotheses of no association between geography and the haplotype tree. Only when this null hypothesis is rejected at the 5% level of significance is there an attempt to interpret the pattern biologically. Inferences are thereby limited to patterns that are based upon sufficient sampling and genetic resolution to have a significant phylo-

geographic signal. The biological meaning of these significant signals is interpreted by using an inference key[21]. This key can lead to the conclusion that the sampling design was inadequate to make clear biological inferences. Therefore, only a subset of the statistically significant results lead to a biological interpretation. The use of an *a priori* inference key published well before the production of all the data sets to be analysed here prevents me from making *post hoc* explanations or trying to fit the results to a favoured hypotheses. The GEODIS program and the inference key are available at http://darwin.uvigo.es/software/geodis.html.

In choosing data for analyses from the recent literature, four criteria were used: (1) a minimum of four populations had to be sampled with at least one each in Europe, Asia and Africa; (2) the minimum sample size was 35 individuals; (3) haplotypes were determined, and the frequencies of these haplotypes within each sampled population were available; and (4) there was little or no recombination within the DNA region being investigated, allowing the estimation of a biologically meaningful haplotype tree. The data sets satisfying these criteria include a recent survey of complete mtDNA genome variation in humans[9], the X-linked gene coding for the pyruvate dehydrogenase *E1* α-subunit (*PDHA1*)[14], and five autosomal regions: these are the *MX1* locus on chromosome 21 (ref. 17), the gene coding for eosinophil-derived neurotoxin (*EDN*) on chromosome 14 (ref. 20), the gene coding for eosinophil cationic protein (*ECP*) on chromosome 14 (ref. 20), the gene coding for the melanocortin 1 receptor (*MC1R*) on chromosome 16 (ref. 18), and compound haplotypes generated in the MS205 hypervariable minisatellite region on chromosome 16 (ref. 19). The whole genome mtDNA survey estimated a haplotype tree that excluded the sites in the D-loop region to focus upon the older phylogenetic signal in the mtDNA[9], and the current analysis also excludes the D-loop. Haplotype trees were estimated by statistical parsimony[28] using the program TCS[29]. In all cases, the statistical parsimony tree is either identical to or is a topologically compatible but more resolved version of the haplotype tree estimated by the original authors, who usually used either maximum parsimony or neighbour-joining. In some cases, tree ambiguities were further resolved using coalescent criteria[30].

The results obtained from these DNA regions are combined with previously published nested clade analyses[13,23,31–33] of mtDNA data[10–12,34,35], the *SRY* and *YAP* regions on the Y chromosome[13], a non-coding, low-recombination region on the X chromosome called Xq13.3 (ref. 15), and the autosomal haemoglobin β-chain locus[16].

RESULTS

The biological inferences made from previously published nested clade analyses are summarized in Table 1. The geographical extent of sampling is indicated, with 'global' meaning that human populations in Africa, Europe, Asia and America were included. Only statistically significant (5% level) inferences are shown that

Table 1. Previously Published Inferences Using the GEODIS Program

DNA Region Reference Range	Mitochondrial DNA			SRY and YAP 13* Global	Xq13.3 15*, 35† Global	Haemoglobin β 16*, 34† Global
	36*, 37*, 33† Global	11*, 12*, 23† NE Asia and America	10*, 23† SE Asia and Pacific			
	IBD	IBD, LDC to America	IBD, LDD	RE out of Africa		RE out of Africa
			LDC to Pacific			
	IBD	IBD, RE to Siberia	IBD, RE and/or LDC to Pacific	IBD, RE out of Africa	IBD	IBD
		F (Asia versus America), IBD				
	IBD; RE to N Eurasia	IBD, LDD, RE within America	IBD, RE to Pacific	IBD, RE out of Asia	IBD	RE out of Asia

Inferences are shown from oldest (top) to most recent (bottom). IBD, recurrent gene flow restricted by isolation by distance; LDD, recurrent gene flow with some long-distance dispersal; RE, range expansion of populations to geographically contiguous areas; LDC, range expansion of populations through long-distance colonization; F, genetic fragmentation into two or more allopatric populations.

*Reference for the data.

†Reference for the analysis (if different).

Table 2. New Inferences Using the GEODIS Program

DNA Region Reference* Range	mtDNA 9 Global	PDHA1 14 Africa and Eurasia	MS205 19 Global	MC1R 18 Global	MX1 17 Global	EDN 20 Global	ECP 20 Global
	RE out of Africa	IBD	RE, origin ambiguous RE to Pacific and America	RE out of Africa	IBD RE to Pacific	IBD	IBD
	F (America)		IBD, RE to Pacific	RE to N Eurasia	IBD, RE to America	RE to America	

Inference abbreviations are the same as given in Table 1. Inferences are shown from oldest (top) to most recent (bottom).

*Reference for the data being analysed.

also resulted in an unambiguous biological interpretation. The inferences are ordered from the highest clade level in the nested analysis (the oldest contrasts in the haplotype tree) to the lowest clade level (the most recent contrasts). When no inference is indicated on the first inference line in Table 1, either no statistically significant associations were detected at the highest nesting level or their biological meaning was ambiguous. Similarly, if no entry occurs on the bottom line, no statistically significant, biologically unambiguous inference occurred at the most recent level of analysis. Inferences are ordered solely with respect to the nesting structure for a specific gene or DNA region. Table 1 does not give a temporal ordering of inferences across genes.

The output from even a single GEODIS analysis is lengthy, so the results of the new analyses are not given here. Table 2 presents the unambiguous biological inferences associated with statistically significant phylogeographic associations, with relative temporal ranks within each gene.

INTEGRATING INFERENCES ACROSS LOCI

There is no expectation that every haplotype tree should yield the same inferences. The inferences obtained from any one tree depend upon several sampling features, which are summarized in Table 3 for the data sets analysed. Table 3 reflects the numbers used in the actual GEODIS analyses, which may differ from the numbers given in the original references. For example, the genetic survey of a non-coding region on the X chromosome was performed on 69 individuals, each from a different location[15]. Having a sample size of one at every location precludes any assessment of within-population variation versus between-populations variation, so several nearby populations were pooled to reduce the total number of geographical sites to 29 for the purposes of the nested phylogeographic analysis[33].

One sampling constraint on inference is the spatial spread of the samples relative to the distribution of the species. Not all data sets covered the same geographic areas, and the inferences from any one data set are confined to the area sampled. Another constraint is the number of locations sampled, which varies from 4 to 35 (Table 3). For example, the analysis of the mtDNA of Torroni et al.[11,12] was unique in detecting range expansion, long-distance dispersal, and isolation by distance within the Americas. Most of the other data sets had only one native American population, thereby making inferences within the American continents impossible. As the number of locations within an area increases, the spatial scale of inference becomes finer.

A third aspect of sampling is sample size, which varies from 35 to 1,544 (Table 3). Biological inference is

Table 3.   Sampling Properties of the Data Sets Analysed in Tables 1 and 2

Locus or DNA Region and Reference	Pattern of Inheritance	Number of Individuals	Number of Locations	Number of Haplotypes	TMRCA* (Myr ago)
mtDNA[36,37]	Maternal haploid	1,389	12	77	0.24
mtDNA[11,12]	Maternal haploid	532	21	109	0.24
mtDNA[10]	Maternal haploid	1,178	14	127	0.24
mtDNA[9]	Maternal haploid	53	16	51	0.24
SRY and YAP[13]	Paternal haploid	1,544	35	10	0.23
X non-coding[15]	Haplo-diploid	69	29	33	0.67
PDHA1[14]	Haplo-diploid	35	8	11	1.91
Haemoglobin β[16]	Diploid	160	9	14	1.63
EDN[20]	Diploid	67	4	9	1.15
ECP[20]	Diploid	67	4	8	1.09
MC1R[18]	Diploid	121	6	7	0.85
MX1[17]	Diploid	354	21	10	8.5
MS205[19]	Diploid	389	15	15	1.25

*Time to the most recent common ancestral haplotype.

confined to statistically significant associations, so the number of individuals sampled is important. In general, the larger the sample size, the more power in making inferences. Also, there is generally more power to detect older events or processes that influence many populations and haplotypes than more recent events or forces. For example, the smallest sample in Table 3 (the X-linked *PDHA1* locus) could only detect a statistically significant signal at the highest level of nesting, a contrast that makes use of all 35 individuals sampled.

The DNA region sampled also determines inference properties. For example, only mtDNA detected the fragmentation event between native American populations and Old World (Asian) populations (Table 1). This event was too recent (perhaps only 14,000 years ago) to have much chance of being marked by mutations in the other genetic systems, owing to their slower rates of overall evolution. Moreover, major range expansions can occur that are not detected by a particular locus simply because mutations did not occur at the right time and place to mark the event[23]. Thus, although the nested analysis is not prone to false positives, any one haplotype tree may not detect certain events or processes owing to inadequate genetic resolution[23]. Genetic resolution also constrains what is meant by a 'recurrent' evolutionary process[21]. For example, when gene flow is inferred, it does not necessarily mean that gene flow occurred every generation, but rather that gene flow occurred recurrently relative to the mutation rate at that locus. Even for the rapidly evolving mtDNA, populations isolated from one another for a few thousand years would not be detected as fragmented in a nested clade analysis.

The temporal sampling period also varies across loci. A haplotype tree contains information up to but excluding the final coalescent event to a common ancestral molecule. Different genes have different expected coalescent times as a function of their pattern of inheritance (Table 4). Hence, the unisexual haploid elements (mtDNA and Y-DNA) are expected to detect only relatively recent events, whereas the bisexual X-linked and autosomal genes are expected to detect far older

events. There is also a large variance in coalescent times across loci sharing a common pattern of inheritance[36]. For example, the expected coalescent time for a large sample at an autosomal locus under neutrality is $4N_{ef}$ and the variance is about $4.64N_{ef}$ (ref. 2), where N_{ef} is the long-term inbreeding effective size of the population (see Table 4). Thus, different DNA regions sharing a common pattern of inheritance are expected to show considerable variation in their temporal depths, as is indeed found in the DNA regions analysed (Table 3).

The dates in Table 3 were obtained using the method of ref. 37 that estimates the time to the most recent common ancestral haplotype (TMRCA) by calculating the ratio of the average nucleotide differences within the human sample to one-half the average nucleotide difference between chimpanzees and humans and multiplying the ratio by an estimate of the divergence time between humans and chimpanzees. Takahata et al.[37] used 5 million years for this divergence time, but recent fossil finds[38,39] indicate that it is more likely to be at least 6 million years, a figure still compatible with the molecular data[40]. Hence, the estimates[37] for *PDHAI*, Xq13.3, the β-globin locus, mtDNA and Y-DNA are recalculated with a calibration point of 6 million years. This same estimator is applied to the remaining loci used in this study, with the results shown in Table 3. Two loci require special consideration. The first is *MX1*, which

Table 4.   Expected Coalescent Times for Different Inheritance Patterns

DNA Region	Pattern of Inheritance	Expected Coalescence Time in Generations
mtDNA	Maternal haploid	$2N_{eff} \approx N_{ef}$*
Y-Chromosomal DNA	Paternal haploid	$2N_{efm} \approx N_{ef}$
X-linked DNA	Bisexual haplo-diploid, equal sex ratio	$3N_{ef}$
Autosomal DNA	Bisexual diploid	$4N_{ef}$

*N_{ef} is the long-term inbreeding effective size of the population, N_{eff} the inbreeding effective size of females, and N_{efm} the inbreeding effective size of males. The approximations to the expected coalescence time are made under the assumption that $N_{eff} = N_{efm} = N_{ef}/2$.

has an estimated TMRCA of 8.5 million years ago, a date older than the chimpanzee–human divergence of 6 million years ago. A coalescent time older than the species is a true biological possibility known as trans-specific polymorphism. The TMRCA for *MS205* had already been estimated at 1 million years[41] with the calibration date of 5 million years, but is given as 1.2 million years in Table 3 using the 6 million year calibration date.

Rannala and Bertorelle[42] argue that phylogenetic dating approaches like that of ref. 37 are also appropriate for dating the ages of the older clades within a haplotype tree but are unreliable for the more recent clades. In particular, the procedure of ref. 37 ignores the sampling error in estimating the average nucleotide differences both within and between species and clades of haplotypes, and the error in the coalescent process itself due to genetic drift[40]. These errors can be quite large for recent haplotypes[42]. Therefore, the procedure[37] is used only to date the inferences at the higher (older) nesting levels in the GEODIS analyses. The age of an inferred process or event is estimated as the age of the youngest monophyletic clade that contributed in a statistically significant fashion to the inference. This represents the time in the population's history during which all haplotype lineages affected by the event were present but more derived haplotype lineages not affected by the event had not yet evolved. This method of ageing reflects the fact that the mutations that occur during the event or process provide the strongest signal for biological inference under a nested clade analysis. For example, a mutation that occurs in a population in the act of expanding into a new geographical area provides the signal used by the nested clade analysis to infer range-expansion events[21,23]. The age of the youngest clade marking an event or process is therefore expected to be largely coincident with the age of the event itself in most cases. However, there are exceptions. For example, a mutation occurring in a population shortly before a range expansion will have a large geographical range for its frequency once the expansion has occurred—another signal for range expansion in the nested clade analysis[21,23]. Alternatively, a mutation occurring in the new geographical area shortly after a range expansion could create a new haplotype with a limited geographical range that is located far from the geographical centre of its ancestral haplotype—yet another signal for range expansion in the nested clade analysis[21,23]. Thus, the estimated age of an event could sometimes be older or younger than the actual event.

Because the procedure of ref. 37 does not take into account the potentially large error associated with the coalescent process, I used my method[40] to fit a gamma distribution with a mean equal to the date estimated[37] and with a variance given by a neutral coalescent process given the amount of pairwise diversity observed within the monophyletic clade being dated. The ages of the inferred events and processes are therefore treated as random variables rather than constants. Because the dating of an event from any one gene could be either younger or older than the actual event and the error

associated with any one gene can be large, a conservative approach is taken in reserving hard inference only for those events for which there is significant overlap (5% or more) in the probability distributions of the inferred ages from more than one gene. By requiring cross-validation over genes, a parsimonious interpretation of the number of events is obtained, and the dating of these events can be averaged over the genes to minimize errors associated with any one gene. Any event that is not cross-validated is regarded as tentative and questionable. There is no biological reason why dates of inferences of recurrent processes such as gene flow should be concordant across loci. However, a conservative approach is taken here as well in which those time intervals indicating gene flow that are not cross-validated at the 95% level are regarded as tentative and questionable.

INFERENCES ON RECENT HUMAN EVOLUTION

All the inferences in Tables 1 and 2 can be placed into a single, internally consistent model of recent human evolution (Figure 1). This model accepts the fossil evidence that the human lineage started in Africa and initially spread out of Africa about 1.7 million years ago[43].

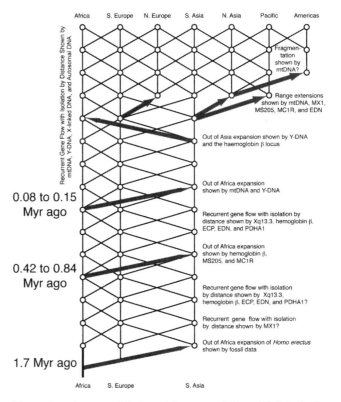

Figure 1. *A new model of recent human evolution. All statistically significant inferences in Tables 1 and 2 are incorporated into this single model. Major expansions of human populations are indicated by black arrows. Genetic descent is indicated by vertical lines, and gene flow by diagonal lines. The timing of inferences lacking resolution at the 5% level and/or not validated by more than one locus are indicated by question marks.*

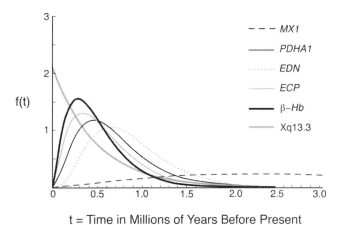

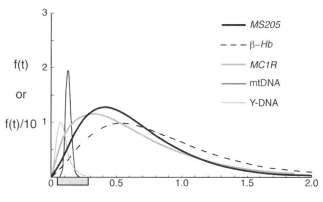

t = Time in Millions of Years Before Present

Figure 2. *The distributions for the ages of the youngest clade contributing to a significant inference of gene flow constrained by isolation by distance at the highest nesting level for the genes* MX1, PDHA1, EDN *and* ECP, *and at intermediate nesting levels for the β-globin (β-Hb) locus and the Xq13.3 region. The x axis gives the time in millions of years before present (BP), and the y axis gives the gamma probability distribution, f(t), that was fitted to the clade data.*

Figure 3. *The distributions for the ages of the youngest clade contributing to a significant inference of a population range expansion for mtDNA, Y-DNA, MC1R, MS205, and the β-globin (β-Hb) locus. The y axis gives the gamma probability distribution, f(t), that was fitted to the clade data. Because the probability mass of the gamma distributions for mtDNA and Y-DNA are heavily concentrated into a small, recent, time interval, their probability distributions divided by ten, f(t)/10, are plotted instead. The grey area on the time axis indicates the interval of most likely overlap among these five distributions.*

The oldest inferences for four genes (Table 2) are recurrent gene flow constrained by isolation by distance at the *MX1* locus (3.41 million years ago or Myr ago), *PDHA1* (0.86 Myr ago), *EDN* (0.69 Myr ago) and *ECP* (0.58 Myr ago). Two other genes yield the same inference in middle clades (Table 1) that date to a similar time period (β-globin, 0.49 Myr ago; and Xq 13.3, 0.48 Myr ago). Figure 2 shows the distributions for these ages. All of these six inferences of isolation by distance have broadly overlapping time intervals with the exception of *MX1*, the locus that samples the oldest time period (Table 3). The 95% confidence interval for the inference of isolation by distance from *MX1* ranges from 8.5 Myr ago to 0.61 Myr ago, indicating a low confidence in the timing of this gene flow. The spatial pattern of gene flow detected with *MX1* could not have existed until after there were human populations in Eurasia, so the fossil date of 1.7 Myr ago places a biological bound on the older limit of the age interval. This confidence interval is consistent with recurrent gene flow constrained by isolation by distance shortly after the original expansion out of Africa because 21% of the probability mass of this gamma distribution is associated with times less than 1.7 Myr ago. However, no other inference of isolation by distance has 5% or more of its probability mass extending that far back in time. Moreover, *MX1* is an outlier in TMRCA (Table 3), which raises the possibility that natural selection has shaped the coalescent process at this locus. Therefore, the evidence for recurrent gene flow among the *Homo erectus* populations shortly after they first came out of Africa is tentative and of questionable validity.

Figure 2 shows that as time progresses, the evidence for gene flow with isolation by distance among Old World human populations is increasingly cross-validated even when *MX1* is excluded. For example, all five remaining inferences of restricted gene flow have

more than 5% of their probability mass on times 1 Myr ago and older: *PDHA1* ($P = 0.32$), *EDN* ($P = 0.19$), *ECP* ($P = 0.13$), β-globin (0.08), and Xq13.3 (0.12) and the probability that one or more of these loci is detecting recurrent gene flow 1 Myr ago or older is 0.61. This probability increases to 0.95 by 0.61 Myr ago or older. These results indicate that recurrent gene flow occurred among Old World human populations from the present back to at least 600,000 years ago, and probably even further into the past.

The highest clade level inferences for five genes are range expansions out of Africa (mtDNA at 0.13 Myr ago; Y-DNA at 0.09 Myr ago; *MC1R* at 0.64 Myr ago; and β-globin at 0.82 Myr ago) and a range expansion of ambiguous origin (*MS205* at 0.63 Myr ago). Figure 3 shows the gamma distributions associated with the ages of these expansion events. The β-globin inference has 5.6% of its probability mass at 1.7 Myr ago or older, but all the other inferred range expansions have much less probability mass at 1.7 Myr ago or older. Hence, there is no cross-validated inference of marking the original expansion of *Homo erectus* out of Africa. Figure 3 shows that the five inferences fall into two broadly overlapping classes; the mtDNA and Y-DNA that are tightly clustered around an expansion event out of Africa at about 100,000 years ago, and the three autosomal loci with means between 0.64 to 0.82 Myr ago. To test the null hypothesis that all five loci are compatible with a single range expansion event, the lower age bound was found such that 0.1% of the β-globin probability distribution was above this age (this locus has the oldest inferred expansion event) and the upper age bound was found such that 0.1% of the Y-DNA probability distribution was below this age (this locus has the youngest inferred expansion event). Any age outside of this interval would be strongly rejected (at the 0.1% level) on the basis of Y-DNA or β-globin alone. This interval spans between 0.0474 to 0.2906 Myr ago and is shown in grey in Figure 3. The probability that all five loci are detecting an event in this age interval is 0.003. Because the expansion event detected with *MS205* is of ambiguous geographical origin, the calculation was repeated excluding that locus to focus specifically upon out-of-Africa expansion events. With this exclusion, the hypothesis of a single out-of-Africa expansion event is rejected with *P* = 0.018. The broad overlap of the mtDNA and Y-DNA distributions (Figure 3) indicates that the null hypothesis of these two genetic elements marking the same out-of-Africa range-expansion event cannot be rejected, and similarly the null hypothesis that the three nuclear markers in Figure 3 are marking the same expansion event cannot be rejected. The parsimonious explanation of Figure 3 is therefore a minimum of two out-of-Africa expansion events, both of which are cross-validated by more than one locus. Combining the three nuclear genes, the 95% confidence interval for the older out-of-Africa range-expansion event is 0.42 to 0.84 Myr ago. Combining the mtDNA and Y-DNA distributions, the 95% confidence interval for the more recent out-of-Africa expansion event is 0.08 to 0.15 Myr ago.

The GEODIS analyses indicate that the most recent out-of-Africa expansion event was not a replacement event. If it had been, the three significant genetic signatures of the older expansion event (Figure 3) and the six significant genetic signatures of older recurrent gene flow (Figure 2) would have been wiped away. Although there is considerable error in dating any single inference from only one gene, an out-of-Africa replacement event would require that all nine significant inferences found in all eight bisexually inherited nuclear loci examined would have to be in error simultaneously. Moreover, the dating errors would have to be large in all nine cases and in the same direction. The hypothesis of a recent out-of-Africa replacement event is therefore strongly rejected. Indeed, this is the most highly cross-validated conclusion of the entire analysis because every gene region that is expected to contain information about events or processes substantially older than 0.15 Myr ago leads to a rejection of recent replacement. Hence, this is a genome-wide conclusion and not a locus-specific conclusion. The out-of-Africa expansion that took place between 0.08 to 0.15 Myr ago therefore represented a major movement of peoples characterized by interbreeding and not replacement.

It is likely that the earlier out-of-Africa expansion event between 0.42 to 0.84 Myr ago was also characterized by interbreeding and not replacement. Even excluding the *MX1* result, the other distributions shown in Figure 2 jointly define a probability of 0.78 of recurrent gene flow before 0.84 Myr ago, a signal that would have been erased by replacement. Hence, the evidence suggests that the intermediate out-of-Africa expansion event shown in Figure 1 was also not a replacement event, but this suggestion must be regarded as tentative because the probability of such ancient gene flow is less than 0.95.

Proceeding downwards in the nested inferences shown in Tables 1 and 2, several recent interferences are encountered of recurrent but restricted gene flow and of population expansions. Rannala and Bertorelle[42] warned that recent events cannot be reliably dated phylogenetically. Their warning is confirmed by this analysis. The youngest clade marking many of these recent inferences is a tip haplotype that has no mutational derivatives, resulting in an average within-nucleotide difference of zero. It is impossible to use any method of phylogenetic dating in these cases. Even when the average within-nucleotide difference is greater than zero, the estimate is likely to be unreliable because the number of informative mutations for recent events is so small[42]. For example, the expansion of humans into the Americas as detected by *MS205* (Table 2) is dated phylogenetically at 449,000 years ago, with a 95% confidence interval of 1.18 Myr ago to 68,000 years ago. Even 68,000 years ago appears to be too old for this event[117]. The time estimate in this case depends upon just two mutational events, and as predicted[42], the resulting estimate seems to be unreliable. Rannala and Bertorelle[42] suggest that recent haplotypes should be dated instead through a population genetic approach that uses models of demography, mutation, and/or recombination to estimate allele age. However, the population genetic approach in turn is limited by the reliability of these underlying models. In light of these considerations, the recent inferences found in the lower hierarchical levels shown in Tables 1 and 2 will undoubtedly be more accurately dated by palaeontological and archaeological evidence than by genetic data. Therefore, no estimates of dates of these inferences will be given here.

Most of these recent inferences come from Y-DNA or mtDNA (Tables 1 and 2), and their nesting position means that they must be more recent than the most recent out-of-Africa expansion event found at the highest (oldest) nesting levels for Y-DNA and mtDNA. Many of these recent inferences are expansions of humans into areas not formerly occupied; such as northern Eurasia, the Pacific (including Australia), and the Americas. However, one of these recent expansion events did occur within the range of previous human occupation. Both the Y-DNA and β-globin locus detect a recent out-of-Asia expansion event that did not erase earlier genetic signals (Table 1) and therefore was an expansion/interbreeding event rather than an expansion/replacement event. Indeed, the failure to detect this recent out-of-Asia expansion event with mtDNA despite good sample sizes and genetic resolution may indicate that this recent out-of-Asia expansion event was primarily male-mediated, and therefore had to be characterized by interbreeding in order to leave a genetic signature.

Genetic contact among human populations after the latest out-of-Africa expansion is also indicated by several inferences at the lower clade levels of recurrent gene flow constrained by isolation by distance with occasional long-distance dispersal (Tables 1 and 2), a conclusion confirmed by other genetic analyses[32]. The only evidence for significant fragmentation (long-term genetic isolation) among the human populations who have left living descendants is the recent genetic isolation between Amerindians and the rest of humanity that followed the colonization of the Americas (Table 1). All of these inferences are summarized in Figure 1.

DISCUSSION

The model of recent human evolution shown in Figure 1 is dominated by genetic interchange and a special role for Africa. I consider first genetic interchange. African and Eurasian populations were linked by recurrent gene flow, certainly over the last half a million years, and probably longer. Overlaid upon this gene-flow trellis are occasional major movements out of Africa and out of Asia that enhanced gene interchange through interbreeding. More recently, population expansions acted to extend the geographical range of the human species and to establish additional areas linked by gene flow. This model emphasizes that genetic interchange among human populations, facilitated both by gene flow and range expansions coupled with interbreeding, has been a major force in shaping the human species and its spatial pattern of genetic diversity.

Second, Figure 1 reveals the special role that African populations have played in human evolution. There were at least two major movements of peoples out of Africa after the original spread of *Homo erectus*. This inference is consistent with the archaeological record of cultural expansions out of Africa (Acheulean) in the Middle Pleistocene[44–48]. These Acheulean cultural expansions broadly overlap the time frame of the middle out-of-Africa expansion event shown in Figure 1, indicating that this expansion involved both people and ideas coming out of Africa and interacting with local populations in Eurasia. This expansion is also compatible with the fossil data. After the initial expansion of *Homo erectus* out of Africa about 1.7 Myr ago, there was little change in average brain size up to 700,000 years ago[1]. By 400,000 to 500,000 years ago, average cranial capacities had shown a substantial increase[1]. The time period of this transition in cranial capacity overlaps extensively with the time period for the older out-of-Africa expansion event shown in Figure 3.

The most recent out-of-Africa expansion event shown in Figures 1 and 3 is also compatible with fossil evidence. Many 'modern' traits (such as high, rounded skulls; small brow ridges; a vertical forehead; and a noticeable chin) first appear in Africa about 130,000 years ago, followed by an expansion out-of-Africa more than 90,000 years ago[1]. This time frame overlaps extensively with the out-of-Africa expansion marked by the mtDNA and Y-DNA distributions in Figure 3, implying that many of these traits could have been carried into Eurasia by this African population range expansion. Other traits, however, do not display any significant changes before, during or after this most recent expansion out of Africa[1]. This later set of traits is difficult to reconcile with a population replacement, but is compatible with

this most recent out-of-Africa expansion event being characterized by interbreeding. With interbreeding, Mendelian inheritance allows some traits to spread while others do not. Moreover, living humans are still polymorphic for 'modern' traits, and the frequencies of different 'modern' traits show heterogeneity in their present geographical distributions[1]. The current spatial and frequency heterogeneity in 'modern' traits undercuts the idea of a global replacement of an 'archaic' type by a 'modern' type but is consistent with a trait-based evolution of humans that is allowed under expansion with interbreeding. The model in Figure 1 indicates the recent fossil evidence should be interpreted in terms of traits and not population types.

The genetic impacts of Africa upon the entire human species is large because of at least three major expansions out of Africa, although the genetic impact is not as complete as it would be under total replacement. This model is similar to earlier models that have emphasized the role of out-of-Africa population expansion coupled with gene flow and not replacement, such as the assimilation model of Smith et al.[49], the multiregional model with expansions followed by admixture of Wolpoff et al.[50], and the 'mostly out of Africa' model of Relethford[1].

The predicted large genetic impact of African populations explains the results of Takahata et al.[37] that about 90% of the haplotype trees in the nuclear genome appear to be rooted in Africa. These results[37] also falsify a total replacement hypothesis, which predicts that all haplotype trees with coalescent times greater than 100,000 years must be rooted in Africa. All of the haplotype trees considered[37] have expected coalescent times greater than 100,000 years, so 100% of such old trees should have African roots under complete replacement, and not the observed 90%.

The results given here show the importance of examining many DNA regions with a common analytical technique in making phylogeographic inferences. Indeed, the clearest result from Tables 1 and 2 is how incomplete our view of human evolution would be if it were based upon just one locus or DNA region. As more DNA regions are examined, additional insights into human evolution are sure to follow. However, this current analysis already demonstrates the inadequacies of both the out-of-Africa replacement model and of a simple trellis model. Humans expanded again and again out of Africa, but these expansions resulted in interbreeding, not replacement, and thereby strengthened the genetic ties between human populations throughout the world.

ACKNOWLEDGMENTS

I thank J. Brisson, J. Hess, R. Koch, M. Kramer, R. Robertson and J. Strasburg for suggestions on an earlier draft of this manuscript. I also thank E. Trinkaus and J. Relethford for their reviews. This work was supported in part by a Burroughs Wellcome Fund Innovation Award in Functional Genomics.

REFERENCES

1. Relethford, J. H. *Genetics and the Search for Modern Human Origins* (Wiley, New York, 2001).
2. Stoneking, M. & Soodyall, H. Human evolution and the mitochondrial genome. *Curr. Opin. Genet. Dev.* **6**, 731–736 (1996).
3. Wolpoff, M. H., Hawks, J. & Caspari, R. Multiregional, not multiple origins. *Am. J. Phys. Anthropol.* **112**, 129–136 (2000).
4. Weidenreich, F. *Apes, Giants, and Man* (Univ. Chicago Press, Chicago, 1946).
5. Cann, R. L., Stoneking, M. & Wilson, A. C. Mitochondrial DNA and human evolution. *Nature* **325**, 31–36 (1987).
6. Vigilant, L., Stoneking, M., Harpending, H., Hawkes, K. & Wilson, A. C. African populations and the evolution of human mitochondrial DNA. *Science* **253**, 1503–1507 (1991).
7. Maddison, D. R. African origin of human mitochondrial DNA reexamined. *Syst. Zool.* **40**, 355–363 (1991).
8. Templeton, A. R. Human origins and analysis of mitochondrial DNA sequences. *Science* **255**, 737 (1992).
9. Ingman, M., Kaessmann, H., Pääbo, S. & Gyllensten, U. Mitochondrial genome variation and the origin of modern humans. *Nature* **408**, 708–713 (2000).
10. Sykes, B., Leiboff, A., Low-Beer, J., Tetzner, S. & Richards, M. The origins of the Polynesians: an interpretation from mitochondrial lineage analysis. *Am. J. Hum. Genet.* **57**, 1463–1475 (1995).
11. Torroni, A. et al. Asian affinities and continental radiation of the four founding native American mtDNAs. *Am. J. Hum. Genet.* **53**, 563–590 (1993).
12. Torroni, A. et al. mtDNA variation of aboriginal Siberians reveals distinct genetic affinities with Native Americans. *Am. J. Hum. Genet.* **53**, 591–608 (1993).
13. Hammer, M. F. et al. Out of Africa and back again: Nested cladistic analysis of human Y chromosome variation. *Mol. Biol. Evol.* **15**, 427–441 (1998).
14. Harris, E. E. & Hey, J. X. Chromosome evidence for ancient human histories. *Proc. Natl Acad. Sci. USA* **96**, 3320–3324 (1999).
15. Kaessman, H., Heißig, F., Haeseler, A. V. & Pääbo, S. DNA sequence variation in a non-coding region of low recombination on the human X chromosome. *Nature Genet.* **22**, 78–81 (1999).
16. Harding, R. M. et al. Archaic African and Asian lineages in the genetic ancestry of modern humans. *Am. J. Hum. Genet.* **60**, 772–789 (1997).
17. Jin, L. et al. Distribution of haplotypes from a chromosome 21 region distinguishes multiple prehistoric human migrations. *Proc. Natl Acad. Sci. USA* **96**, 3796–3800 (1999).
18. Rana, B. K. et al. High polymorphism at the human melanocortin 1 receptor locus. *Genetics* **151**, 1547–1557 (1999).
19. Rogers, E. J., Shone, A. C., Alonso, S., May, C. A. & Armour, J. A. L. Integrated analysis of sequence evolution and population history using hypervariable compound haplotypes. *Hum. Mol. Genet.* **9**, 2675–2681 (2000).
20. Zhang, J. & Rosenberg, H. F. Sequence variation at two eosinophil-associated ribonuclease loci in humans. *Genetics* **156**, 1949–1958 (2000).
21. Templeton, A. R., Routman, E. & Phillips, C. Separating population structure from population history: a cladistic analysis of the geographical distribution of mitochondrial DNA haplotypes in the Tiger Salamander, *Ambystoma tigrinum*. *Genetics* **140**, 767–782 (1995).
22. Posada, D., Crandall, K. A. & Templeton, A. R. GeoDis: a program for the cladistic nested analysis of the geographical distribution of genetic haplotypes. *Mol. Ecol.* **9**, 487–488 (2000).
23. Templeton, A. R. Nested clade analyses of phylogeographic data: testing hypotheses about gene flow and population history. *Mol. Ecol.* **7**, 381–397 (1998).
24. Bernatchez, L. The evolutionary history of brown trout (*Salmo trutta* L.) inferred from phylogeographic, nested clade, and mismatch analyses of mitochondrial DNA variation. *Evolution* **55**, 351–379 (2001).
25. Gomez, A., Carvalho, G. R. & Hunt, D. H. Phylogeography and regional endemism of a passively dispersing zooplankter: mito-

chondrial DNA variation in rotifer resting egg banks. *Proc. R. Soc. Lond. B* **267**, 2189–2197 (2000).
26. Nielson, M., Lohman, K. & Sullivan, J. Phylogeography of the tailed frog (*Ascaphus truei*): Implications for the biogeography of the Pacific Northwest. *Evol.* **55**, 147–160 (2001).
27. Turner, T. F., Trexler, J. C., Harris J. L. & Haynes, J. L. Nested cladistic analysis indicates population fragmentation shapes genetic diversity in a freshwater mussel. *Genetics* **154**, 777–785 (2000).
28. Templeton, A. R., Crandall, K. A. & Sing, C. F. A cladistic analysis of phenotypic associations with haplotypes inferred from restriction endonuclease mapping and DNA sequence data. III. Cladogram estimation. *Genetics* **132**, 619–633 (1992).
29. Posada, D. TCS 1.06 (Provo, Utah, 2000); available at http://darwin.uvigo.es/software/geodis.html.
30. Crandall, K. A. & Templeton, A. R. Empirical tests of some predictions from coalescent theory with applications to intraspecific phylogeny reconstruction. *Genetics* **134**, 959–969 (1993).
31. Templeton, A. R. in *Conceptual Issues in Modern Human Origins Research* (eds Clark, G. A. & Willermet, C. M.) 329–360 (Aldine de Gruyter, New York, 1997).
32. Templeton, A. R. Human races: A genetic and evolutionary perspective. *Am. Anthropol.* **100**, 632–650 (1998).
33. Templeton, A. R. Using phylogeographic analyses of gene trees to test species status and processes. *Mol. Ecol.* **10**, 779–791 (2001).
34. Excoffier, L. & Langaney, A. Origin and differentiation of human mitochondrial DNA. *Am. J. Human. Genet.* **44**, 73–85 (1989).
35. Excoffier, L. Evolution of human mitochondrial DNA: evidence for departure from a pure neutral model of populations at equilibrium. *J. Mol. Evol.* **30**, 125–139 (1990).
36. Donnelly, P. & Tavare, S. Coalescents and genealogical structure under neutrality. *Annu. Rev. Genet.* **29**, 401–421 (1995).
37. Takahata, N., Lee, S.-H. & Satta, Y. Testing multiregionality of modern human origins. *Mol. Biol. Evol.* **18**, 172–183 (2001).
38. Haile-Selassie, Y. Late Miocene hominids from the Middle Awash, Ethiopia. *Nature* **412**, 178–181 (2001).
39. Pickford, M. & Senut, B. The geological and faunal context of the Late Miocene hominid remains from Lukeino, Kenya. *C. R. Acad. Sci. IIA* **332**, 145–152 (2001).
40. Templeton, A. R. The "Eve" hypothesis: a genetic critique and reanalysis. *Am. Anthropol.* **95**, 51–72 (1993).
41. Alonso, S. & Armour, J. A. L. A highly variable segment of human subterminal 16p reveals a history of population growth for modern humans outside Africa. *Proc. Natl. Acad. Sci. USA* **98**, 864–869 (2001).
42. Rannala, B. & Bertorelle, G. Using linked markers to infer the age of a mutation. *Hum. Mutat.* **18**, 87–100 (2001).
43. Gabunia, L. et al. Earliest Pleistocene hominid cranial remains from Dmanisi, Republic of Georgia: Taxonomy, geological setting, and age. *Science* **288**, 1019–1025 (2000).
44. Aguirre, E. & Carbonell, E. Early human expansions into Eurasia: The Atapuerca evidence. *Quat. Int.* **75**, 11–18 (2001).
45. Bar-Yosef, O. & Belfer-Cohen, A. From Africa to Eurasia—early dispersals. *Quat. Int.* **75**, 19–28 (2001).
46. Hou, Y. M. et al. Mid-Pleistocene Acheulean-like stone technology of the Bose basin, South China. *Science* **287**, 1622–1626 (2000).
47. Saragusti, I. & Goren-Inbar, N. The biface assemblage from Gesher Benot Ya'aqov, Israel: illuminating patterns in "Out of Africa" dispersal. *Quat. Int.* **75**, 85–89 (2001).
48. Otte, M. in *Archaeogenetics: DNA and the Population Prehistory of Europe* (eds Renfrew, C. & Boyle, K.) 41–44 (Univ. Cambridge, Cambridge, 1999).
49. Smith, F. H., Falsetti, A. B. & Donnelly, S. M. Modern human origins. *Yb. Physical Anthrop.* **32**, 35–68 (1989).
50. Wolpoff, M., Thorne, A. G., Smith, F. H., Frayer, D. W. & Pope, G. G. in *Origins of Anatomically Modern Humans* (eds Nitecki, M. H. & Nitecki, D. V.) 175–200 (Plenum, New York, 1994).

72

Genetics and the Making of *Homo sapiens*

S. B. Carroll

ABSTRACT

Understanding the genetic basis of the physical and behavioural traits that distinguish humans from other primates presents one of the great new challenges in biology. Of the millions of base-pair differences between humans and chimpanzees, which particular changes contributed to the evolution of human features after the separation of the Pan *and* Homo *lineages 5–7 million years ago? How can we identify the 'smoking guns' of human genetic evolution from neutral ticks of the molecular evolutionary clock? The magnitude and rate of morphological evolution in hominids suggest that many independent and incremental developmental changes have occurred that, on the basis of recent findings in model animals, are expected to be polygenic and regulatory in nature. Comparative genomics, population genetics, gene-expression analyses and medical genetics have begun to make complementary inroads into the complex genetic architecture of human evolution.*

What is a man,
If his chief good and market of his time
Be but to sleep and feed? a beast, no more.
Sure, he that made us with such large discourse,
Looking before and after, gave us not
That capability and god-like reason
To fust in us unused.
            W. Shakespeare, *Hamlet* IV:iv

What makes modern humans different from the great apes and earlier hominids? In what hominids and when in evolution did important physical traits and behaviours appear? Where in our larger brains do human-specific capabilities reside? These have been long-standing questions in palaeoanthropology and comparative anatomy, since the discovery of Neanderthal skulls and the first studies of great apes in the nineteenth century. Now, the mystery of human origins is expanding beyond the description and history of human traits, towards the genetic mechanisms underlying their formation and evolution. With the characterization of the human genome, and that of our chimpanzee cousin on the way, the quest to discover the genetic basis of the physical and behavioural traits that distinguish us from other apes is rapidly gaining momentum.

Genomes diverge as a function of time, and most of the sequence changes that accumulate between any two

Reprinted by permission from *Nature*, Vol. 422, pp. 849–857. Copyright © 2003 Macmillan Publishers Ltd.

related species are selectively neutral or nearly neutral in that they do not contribute to functional or phenotypic differences. The great challenge is to elucidate the number, identity and functions of genes, and the specific changes within them, that have shaped the evolution of traits. This has been accomplished for only a few traits in model systems, so it is a difficult task for human features about which we know little, and an enormous prospect to consider the whole arc of human evolution.

In this article, I will examine both the physical and genetic scope of human evolution and the approaches being used to try to understand it. I will first review the current state of our understanding of human evolution from the viewpoint of the fossil record, comparative anatomy and development. These disciplines point to many key traits to be considered, and define the magnitude and nature of evolutionary change in the human lineage. I will preview the picture of human evolution that we might expect to emerge in view of our current knowledge of the genetic architecture of trait evolution in model systems. I will then examine the variety of methods being used on a genome-wide scale and at the level of individual loci to identify genes that may have contributed to the evolution of key traits. I will discuss some of the crucial methodological challenges in distinguishing causative from potentially large numbers of candidate loci. Finally, I will address some of the disciplines in which future advances are likely to have a central role in furthering our knowledge of the genetic and developmental basis of human evolution.

HOMINID EVOLUTION

The Hominid Tree

To approach the origins of human traits at the genetic level, it is essential to have as a framework a history of our lineage and the characters that distinguish it. It is inadequate and misleading to consider just the comparative anatomy and development (or genomes) of extant humans, chimpanzees and other apes, and then to attempt to infer how existing differences might be encoded and realized. Each of these species has an independent lineage that reaches back as far or further than hominins ('hominins' refers to humans and our evolutionary ancestors back to the separation of the human and ape lineages; 'hominids' to humans and the African apes) (Figure 1). The evolution of 'modern' traits was not a linear, additive process, and ideas about the tempo, pattern and magnitude of change can only be tested through fossil evidence, which is always

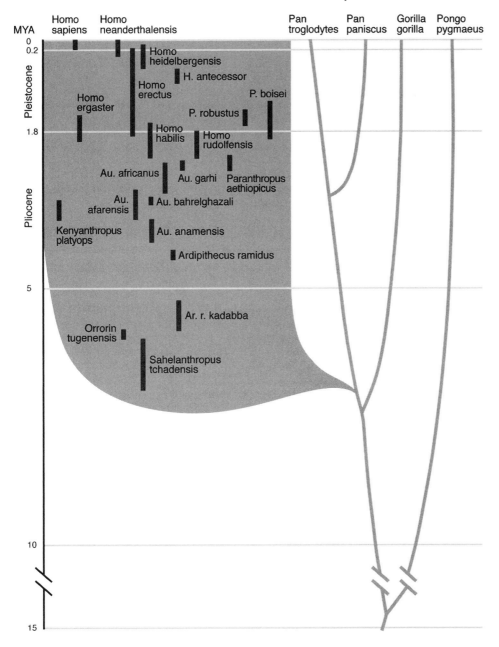

Figure 1. *The timescale and phylogeny of hominids. Ape relationships are shown in grey for the chimpanzee* (Pan troglodytes), *bonobo* (P. paniscus), *gorilla and orangutan* (Pongo pygmaeus). *The approximate times of divergence are derived from molecular data (summarized in ref. 89). The phylogenetic relationships among hominins (shaded) are uncertain. The solid bars denote the time span of the fossil species and/or the uncertainty of fossil ages. The identity of the last common ancestor of chimpanzees and humans (LCA) is not known. Note that the estimated age of* Sahelanthropus tchadensis *predates molecular estimates of the time of the chimpanzee–human divergence. This species could pre- or postdate the LCA. Also note that* Homo sapiens *represent only the last 3% of the time span of hominin evolution. Hominin distributions and nomenclature are based primarily on refs 1, 90.*

subject to revision by new finds. The fossil record continues to shape views of three crucial issues in hominid evolution. First, what distinguishes hominins from the apes? Second, what distinguishes modern humans (*Homo sapiens*) from earlier hominins? And third, what was the nature of the last common ancestor of hominins and the *Pan* lineage?

Inferences about the chronological order and magnitude of the evolution of hominin characters depend on a model of the hominin evolutionary tree. This has always been a contentious issue and remains unsettled, in part because of the pace of exciting new fossil finds over the past two decades. An emerging view portrays hominin evolution as a series of adaptive radiations in which many different branches of the hominin lineage were formed, but died out[1,2] (Figure 1). One prediction of this model is that various anatomical features would be found in

different combinations in hominins through their independent acquisition, modification and loss in different species. For example, the recent, stunning discovery of a 6–7-million-year (Myr)-old fossil cranium of *Sahelanthropus tchadensis* that had a chimpanzee-sized brain but hominin-like facial and dental features[3] is the sort of morphology that would be consistent with a radiation of ape-like animals from which the stem of the hominin lineage emerged (although the interpretation of this fossil's affinities is controversial[4]).

What Makes a Human?

Evolutionary Trends in Fossil Hominins. Ideally, if every possible fossil human and ape species were identified and many fairly complete specimens were available, one could reconstruct the emergence of human and

Selected Traits That Distinguish Humans from Other Apes[5-7]

Body shape and thorax

Cranial properties (brain case and face)

Relative brain size

Relative limb length

Long ontogeny and lifespan

Small canine teeth

Skull balanced upright on vertebral column

Reduced hair cover

Elongated thumb and shortened fingers

Dimensions of the pelvis

Presence of a chin

S-shaped spine

Language

Advanced tool making

Brain topology

Table 1. Evolution of Brain and Body Size in Hominids

Species	Estimated Age[1,3,7,86-88] (Myr ago)	Body Size[7] (kg)	Brain Size[3,7] (cm³)
Homo sapiens	0–0.2	53	1,355
H. neanderthalensis	0.03–0.25	76	1,512
H. heidelbergensis	0.3–1	62	1,198
H. erectus	0.2–1.9	57	1,016
H. ergaster	1.5–1.9	58	854
H. rudolfensis	1.8–2.4	—	752
H. habilis	1.6–2.3	34	552
Paranthropus boisei	1.2–2.2	44	510
Australopithecus africanus	2.6–3	36	457
Au. afarensis	3–3.6	—	—
Au. anamensis	3.5–4.1	—	—
Ardipithecus ramidus kadabba	5.2–5.8	—	—
Sahelanthropus tchadensis	6–7	—	~320–380

This list does not include all recognized species.

chimpanzee features through time. But that is not the case for most lineages; in fact, there are no identified archaic chimpanzee fossils. We must make do with a partial and often confusing picture of human trait evolution. From a rather extensive list of qualitative and quantitative features that distinguish humans from other apes[5,6] (Box 1), our large brain, bipedalism, small canine teeth, language and advanced tool-making capabilities[7,8] have been the focus of palaeoanthropology. The major physical traits are generally not singular elements, but entail concomitant changes in skeletal features involved in locomotion (for example, in the vertebral column, pelvis and feet, and in limb proportions), grasping (hand morphology and an opposable, elongated thumb) and chewing of food (the mandible and dentition), as well as life-history traits such as lifespan. It is fortunate that most of the skeletal features lend themselves to detailed quantitative studies of the fossil record.

Some trends in the evolution of body size, brain size and dentition are evident within the hominins. More recent species are characterized by larger body mass, relatively larger brains, longer legs relative to the trunk and small teeth, whereas earlier species had, in general, smaller brains and bodies (Table 1), shorter legs relative to the trunk and large teeth[7,9,10]. I highlight these traits to focus attention on the magnitude and timescale of character evolution, and on the (increasing) number of generally recognized hominin taxa. Whatever the branching pattern in the hominin tree, substantial relative changes occurred over an extended time span and a significant number of speciation events. There was a marked increase in absolute brain size by the Early Pleistocene and again in the Middle Pleistocene, with a long interval of perhaps 1 Myr during which brain size did not change significantly[9,11] (Table 1). With regard to modern *H. sapiens*, it is interesting to note that body and brain size were even greater in *H. neanderthalensis;*

there is no obvious physical explanation for the success of *H. sapiens* and the demise of *H. neanderthalensis*[11].

A Beautiful Mind: Insights from Comparative Neuroanatomy. The relative increase in brain size, although marked, is only a crude index of a potential increase in cognitive abilities. Because it has long been appreciated that there are discrete areas of the brain that process various cognitive, motor and sensory functions, comparative neuroanatomists have sought to identify areas that might be central to the evolution of human capacities. There is a longstanding notion that the frontal cortex (involved in planning, organization, personality, behaviour and other 'higher' cognitive functions) is disproportionately larger in humans[12], but this now seems not to be the case (it is larger, but not disproportionately so[13]). As gross anatomical differences do not account for cognitive capabilities, relative differences in the size, cellular composition, detailed cytoarchitecture and/or connectivity of human and great ape brain areas have been sought to explain the emergence of human capabilities.

Of paramount interest is the production and understanding of speech. Two areas in particular have commanded the greatest attention. One is Broca's area in the frontal lobe of the neocortex (Figure 2). This region is larger in the left hemisphere of the brain than in the right, an asymmetry that has been correlated with language ability. From magnetic resonance images of chimpanzees, bonobos and gorillas, a similar left–right asymmetry has been found in these great apes[14] (Figure 2). This indicates that the neuroanatomical substrate of left-hemisphere dominance in speech production preceded the origin of hominins. The left hemisphere also usually controls right-handedness, so it is interesting to note that in captive apes, manual gestures are right-hand biased, and this bias is increased when vocalization is combined with gesturing[15], indicating a left-hemisphere-controlled communication process.

A second area of interest is Wernicke's posterior receptive language area in the temporal lobe (Figure 2). A site within this area, the planum temporale, is implicated in human communication (both spoken and

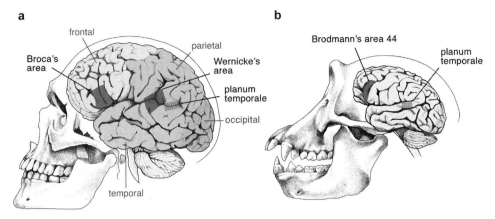

Figure 2. *Comparative neuroanatomy of humans and chimpanzees. Lateral views of the left hemispheres of a modern human and a chimpanzee brain. Although the overall skull sizes are roughly comparable, the human cranial capacity and brain are much larger. **a,** Two areas of the human brain that are associated with communication are shown: Broca's area in the frontal lobe and Wernicke's area, which overlaps the posterior temporal lobe and parts of the parietal lobe. In the left hemisphere, Broca's area is larger, as is the planum temporale, which lies below the surface in Wernicke's area. **b,** These asymmetries have been found in corresponding regions of chimpanzee brains[15,17], suggesting that the areas in humans might be elaborations of a pre-existing communication centre in a common ancestor of apes and humans.*

gestural) and musical talent, and also shows a left-hemisphere dominance. In most humans, the Sylvian fissure associated with the left planum temporale extends more posteriorly. Evidence for this asymmetry has been found in fossil endocasts in *H. habilis*, *H. erectus* and *H. neanderthalensis*[16]. More importantly, an asymmetrical planum temporale pattern has recently been demonstrated in chimpanzees[17,18] (Figure 2).

Several hypotheses have been forwarded to explain the presence of these two human-communication-associated neuroanatomical landmarks in great apes[14,17]. Although it is possible that they arose and acquired their functions independently in each lineage, the most parsimonious explanation is that the common ancestor of great apes and humans had asymmetrical centres that were involved in communication, and that these structures underwent independent evolutionary modifications in chimpanzees and hominins. If this is the case, then the challenge to comparative neuroanatomy is to identify more subtle differences in suborganization (that is, 'microanatomy') that affect the interconnections of cortical regions, in local circuitry and/or cytoarchitecture[19,20] that might be unique to human brains. Recently, it has been found that the dimensions of the vertical columns of neurons in the cortex, known as 'minicolumns', differ between humans and chimpanzees in the planum temporale[21]. In addition, area 10 of the prefrontal cortex, which is involved in higher cognitive functions, has been shown to be enlarged and specialized in humans relative to apes[22]. These observations suggest that human capacities are more a product of quantitative changes in specialized areas than of neuroanatomical novelties.

Development of Hominid Features

The morphological differences between modern humans, earlier hominins and the great apes are,

of course, the product of changes during development. Comparative studies of human and chimpanzee skull development[23], remarkably detailed examinations of Neanderthal craniofacial ontogeny[22,24–26], and early hominin dentition formation[27] have yielded crucial insights into a variety of developmental shifts that underlie modern human cranial size and morphology.

One of the long-appreciated, fundamental differences in chimpanzee and human development is the relative rate of skull growth and maturation. Human neonates have less mature skulls in terms of shape in comparison to young chimpanzees, but much larger skulls (and brains)[23,28]. These are classically described as heterochronic changes, which produce neotenic features in which maturation is retarded, size increases and shape resembles juvenile forms of ancestors[29]. Chimpanzee and human skulls eventually grow to the same size, reflecting further relative shifts in juvenile and adolescent growth periods, and marked differences in face size and cerebral volume. Importantly, all of the skeletal changes associated with bipedalism are structural innovations independent of neoteny. These observations suggest that the human brain is not a product of simple shifts in growth relationships, but of multiple, independent and superimposed modifications.

With respect to more recent hominin species, modern human craniofacial form appears to have been shaped by changes in elements that influence the spatial position of the face, neurocranium and cranial base. Modern humans are marked by greater roundedness of the cranial vault and facial retraction (the anteroposterior position of the face relative to the cranial base and neurocranium)[25]. Comparisons with Neanderthal skull development inferred from fossils of different aged individuals suggest that the characteristic cranial differences between Neanderthal and modern human features arise early in ontogeny[24,26].

Our prolonged childhood, delayed sexual maturation and long lifespan are life-history traits that shape important aspects of human society. Insights into the evolution of these development shifts in evolution are offered by detailed comparative analysis of dental development, which is correlated with stages of primate growth and development. Rates of enamel formation in fossil hominins suggest that tooth-formation times were shorter in australopiths and early members of the genus *Homo* than they are in modern humans[27]. This indicates that the modern pattern of dental formation and correlated developmental traits appeared late in human evolution. When considered in the context of other traits, such as brain size and body proportions, a mosaic pattern of evolution emerges with different traits appearing at different times and perhaps in different combinations in hominin history[30].

Was Human Evolution Special?

The magnitude, rate and pattern of change during hominin evolution, inferred from the fossil record, comparative neuroanatomy and embryology, provide the essential foundation for approaching the genetics of human evolution. From the studies discussed above, five key points emerge that have a bearing on attempts to reconstruct the genetic events that underlie the origin and modification of human traits.

First, trait evolution was nonlinear. The ~1,000-cm^3 increase in brain size over 5–7 Myr did not occur at the same relative rate in hominin phylogeny: it was static at times, faster in some intervals, and reversed slightly more recently. Second, most trait evolution can be characterized as simple quantitative changes (that is, traits are continuous). Third, evolutionary rates were not at all exceptional with respect to mammalian evolution. For example, fossil horse lineages in the late Pliocene–Pleistocene show similar rates of body-size and other character changes as do those of hominids[31]. Fourth, much evolutionary change preceded the origin of the *Homo* genus and of *H. sapiens*: the history of our species represents just the last 3% of the time span of hominin evolution (Figure 1). And fifth, many characters are present not only in humans, but also in apes. This suggests that modification of existing structures and developmental pathways, rather than the invention of new features, underlies much of human evolution.

These observations indicate that morphological evolution in hominins was not special, but the product of genetic and developmental changes typical of other mammals and animals.

GENETICS OF HUMAN EVOLUTION

Genetic Architecture of Trait Evolution

Given the dimensions of hominin evolution, inferred from the fossil record and comparative anatomy, what can we expect in terms of the genetic complexity underlying trait evolution? For example, there is a long-standing tendency for events that are perceived to be relatively 'rapid' in the fossil record to be ascribed to

perhaps one or a few radical mutations[32], including recent human evolution[33,34]. Could the relative increase in brain size over 5 Myr, or its expanded cognitive function, be due to just one or a few genetic changes? The best (and, at present, the only available) guides for this question are detailed genetic studies in model organisms, which have achieved success in dissecting the genetics of complex trait formation, variation and evolution. Six essential general concepts have been established in model systems that pertain to the potential genetic architecture of human trait evolution:

(1) Variation in continuous, quantitative traits is usually polygenic. Studies of variation in model species[35–38] reveal that many genes of small effect, and sometimes one or a few genes of large effect, control trait parameters. In humans, a study of variation in 20 anthropometric variables in two different ethnic human populations suggested that more than 50% of variation was polygenic[39].

(2) The rate of trait evolution tells us nothing about the number of genes involved. Studies of artificial selection[35,38,40] and of interspecific divergence[41] indicate that the intensity of selection and heritability are more important determinants of evolutionary rate than is the genetic complexity of the traits under selection. There is considerable standing variation in traits, including characters that might be thought of as highly constrained, such as limb morphology in tetrapods[42]. In general, the observed rates of evolution under natural selection are far slower than is potentially possible[43,44]. Genetic variation or genetic complexity is not the limiting factor[32]; indeed, considerable genetic variation underlies even phenotypically invariant traits[45–48]. Because the rate at which a trait emerges in the fossil record tells us nothing about genetic architecture, the temptation to invoke macromutational models for 'rapid change'[33,49] must be resisted in the absence of genetic evidence.

(3) Morphological variation and divergence are associated with genes that regulate development. Comparisons of the developmental basis of body-pattern evolution in animals suggest that morphological evolution is a product of changes in the spatiotemporal deployment of regulatory genes and the evolution of genetic regulatory networks[50–52]. Developmental changes in the human lineage are expected to be associated with genes that affect developmental parameters, such as those that encode transcription factors and members of signal-transduction pathways.

(4) Mutations responsible for trait variation are often in noncoding, regulatory regions. When it has been possible to localize variation in genes that underlie phenotypic variation or protein-level differences, insertions or substitutions in regulatory regions and non-coding regions are often responsible[53–57].

(5) Multiple nucleotide replacements often differentiate alleles. Fine-scale analysis of quantitative trait loci has often revealed that functional differences between alleles are due to multiple nucleotide differences[55,56]. It also indicates that non-additive interactions between sites within a locus may be key to the differentiation of alleles, and that the contribution of any individual site may be modest (and difficult to detect).

(6) There is some concordance between genes responsible for intraspecific variation and interspecies divergence. Genetic analyses of interspecies divergence is only possible under certain circumstances, when laboratory breeding can overcome species barriers and traits can be mapped. In some cases, it has been found that some of the same loci are involved in both within-species variation and between-species divergence[35,58]. This raises some hope that studies of intraspecific variation in humans could lead to genes that have been important in human history.

Since human trait evolution has followed a similar, incremental course as traits studied in model systems, these six concepts suggest that we should expect a highly polygenic basis for complex traits such as brain size, craniofacial morphology and development, cortical speech and language areas, hand and digit morphology, dentition and post-cranial skeletal morphology. We should also anticipate that multiple changes in non-coding regulatory regions and in regulatory genes are of great importance. But how can we find them?

The Arithmetic of Human Sequence Evolution

All genetic approaches to human origins are fundamentally comparative, and seek to identify genetic changes that occurred specifically in the human lineage and contributed to the differentiation of humans from our last common ancestor with either apes or other species of *Homo*. Our primary comparative reference is the genome of the chimpanzee (*Pan troglodytes*), our closest living relative, with whom we share a common ancestor that lived 5–7 Myr ago. The arithmetic that sets the problem for human evolutionary genetics is as follows: first, the most extensive comparison of chimpanzee and human genomic sequences indicates an average substitution level of ~1.2% in single-copy DNA[59]; second, the human genome comprises ~3×10^9 base pairs; third, it is reasonable to assume that one-half of the total divergence between chimpanzees and humans occurred in the human lineage (~0.6%); and fourth, this amounts to ~18×10^6 base-pair changes. In addition, there are an unknown number of gene duplications and pseudogene, transposon and repetitive element changes in each lineage. A recent small-scale survey indicated that insertions and deletions (indels) might account for another 3.4% of differences between chimpanzee and human genomes, with the bulk of that figure contributed by larger indels[60]. A good deal of genomic change might be the noise of neutral substitutions and the gain and loss of repetitive elements over long time spans (more than 46% of human DNA is composed of interspersed repeats), but some small fraction of the changes in genomic sequence is responsible for the hereditary differences between species. The crux of the challenge is how to identify specific changes that are biologically meaningful from the many that are not.

In the case of human evolution, there are three basic genetic issues that we would like to grasp. First, how many genes were directly involved in the origin of human anatomy, physiology and behaviour (a few, dozens, hundreds or thousands)? Second, which specific genes contributed to the emergence of particular human traits? And third, what types of change in these genes contributed to evolution (for example, gene duplications, amino-acid replacements or regulatory sequence evolution)? In the few pioneering studies that are directly addressing the genetic basis of human–chimpanzee divergence, different but somewhat complementary strategies are being pursued that are beginning to reveal the scope of human genetic evolution and, in some cases, specific genes that might have been under selection in the course of recent human evolution.

Comparative Genomics

The most readily detected differences between animal genomes are expansions or contractions of gene families. Although the full chimpanzee genome is not yet available, a partial comparative map indicates that there are regions of the human genome that might not be represented in chimpanzees or other apes[61]. Such regions could be due to duplications or insertions that occurred in the hominin lineage or to deletions in the chimpanzee lineage. One gene family, dubbed *morpheus*, underwent expansion as part of a segmental duplication on human chromosome 16 (ref. 62). This expansion is shared by other great apes, but it seems that there were human lineage-specific duplications as well.

On the basis of comparisons with other genomes, particularly the recently reported draft mouse sequence[63], such lineage-specific duplications are expected. In the 75 Myr or more since the divergence of the common ancestor of mice and humans, several dozen clusters of mouse-specific genes arose that are generally represented by a single gene in the human genome[63]. The shorter divergence time between humans and apes suggests that the human-specific gene set will be smaller. It is interesting to note that a significant fraction of the mouse gene clusters encode proteins with roles in reproduction, immunity and olfaction. This indicates that sexual selection, pathogens and ecology can shape the main differences in coding content between mammals. It should also be noted that 80% of mouse genes have a 1:1 orthologue in the human genome, and that more than 99% have some homologue[63]. These figures and synteny data suggest that there is a gene repertoire that is qualitatively nearly identical among mammals. The presence or absence of particular gene duplicates might reflect adaptively driven change, but further evidence will be necessary to determine whether positive selection has acted on genes.

Thousands of Adaptive Changes in the Human Proteome?

The first place that adaptive genetic changes have been looked for is in the coding sequences for proteins. If the 18×10^6 substitutions in the human lineage are evenly distributed throughout the genome, only a small fraction will be expected to fall within coding regions. Assuming that the average protein is ~400 amino acids in length, and that there are ~30,000 protein-coding genes, only ~3.5×10^7 base pairs (or a little more than 1.5% of the genome) consists of coding regions[64,65]. So, assuming neutrality and ignoring the selective removal of deleterious changes in protein sequences, ~1.5% of these 18×10^6 substitutions (or 270,000 sites) may contribute to protein evolution. A fraction of these (roughly one-quarter) are synonymous substitutions, so the total number of amino-acid replacements in the human lineage could be of the order of ~200,000. This figure is in good agreement with observed average rates of amino-acid replacement in mammals[66].

Various methods have been developed to detect whether amino-acid replacements could be the result of positive selection—that is, adaptive evolution[67,68]. To estimate the extent of positive selection in human protein evolution, Fay et al.[69] surveyed sequence-divergence data for 182 human and Old World monkey genes, and polymorphism data for a similar number of human genes. Taking into consideration the frequency of common polymorphisms (ignoring rare alleles), a greater-than-expected degree of amino-acid replacements was observed, which is evidence of selection. When extrapolated to the entire proteome, 35% of amino-acid substitutions between human and Old World monkeys were estimated to have been driven by positive selection. Applied to human–chimpanzee divergence, this would extrapolate to ~70,000 adaptive substitutions in the human lineage. This figure is substantially larger than would be expected if most mutations were neutral or nearly neutral[70]. If it is even the correct order of magnitude, it forecasts a nightmare for the identification of key genes under selection, because this figure suggests that, on average, two or more adaptive substitutions have occurred in every human protein in the last 5 Myr.

It is possible that the figure, based on the study of less than 0.5% of the human proteome, is an overestimate of the fraction or distribution of adaptive replacements. It is clear that some proteins are under strong pressure to remain constant, whereas others, especially those involved in so-called 'molecular arms races', are under pressure to change. For example, major histocompatibility complex proteins, which interact with diverse and changing foreign substances, show clear signatures of selection[71]. Proteins involved in reproduction that play a part in sperm competition or gamete recognition also appear to evolve faster and under some degree of positive selection[72]. A host of human male reproductive proteins have greater-than-average ratios of amino-acid replacements[73]. Although accelerated protein evolution can also be the consequence of relaxed constraints, the correlation of higher levels of amino-acid replacements in proteins that have a role in reproduction and immunity seems to be biologically and selectively driven.

The population genetics- and protein-sequence-based statistical estimates of adaptive evolution require three caveats regarding how much they tell us about human evolution. First, there are generally no direct functional data that either test or demonstrate whether a human protein is indeed functionally diverged from an ape orthologue. Second, the proteins for which signatures of selection have been detected generally do not affect development. And third, the proteome is just part of the whole picture of genome evolution. Non-coding sequences, including transcriptional *cis*-regulatory elements, the untranslated regions of messenger RNAs, and RNA-splicing signals, contribute considerably to evolution by affecting the time, place and level of gene expression (see above). Ever since the pioneering comparative analysis of ape and human protein-sequence divergence nearly three decades ago[74], it has generally been anticipated that changes in gene regulation are a more important force than coding-sequence evolution in the morphological and behavioural evolution of hominins.

Evolution of Human Gene Expression

How large is the functional compartment of non-coding sequences—the other 98% of the genome? A recent estimate suggests that perhaps twice as much non-coding DNA is under selection than coding DNA[63]. So, we would also expect a large number of substitutions in the human lineage, of the order of several hundred thousand, with potential functional consequences in noncoding DNA. Even if one applies a much smaller, more conservative estimate of the fraction of adaptive substitutions in non-coding DNA, such as 2% (ref. 75), one still reaches a figure of more than 10,000 adaptive substitutions in human genes and their regulatory regions. The problem is that regulatory sequences are more difficult to analyse: we have no algorithms that can infer biological function from tracts of intergenic or intronic sequence, let alone to decipher how base-pair changes affect function. It is therefore perhaps understandable why non-coding regions have received little attention at the level of population genetics. However, a growing body of work in quantitative genetics and on the evolution of development has shown that regulatory sequences are central to changes in gene expression and morphology. New methodologies have been required to detect the evolution of gene expression and regulatory sequences.

A first step towards the identification of human-specific gene-expression patterns was recently taken by Enard et al.[76], who used genome microarrays to analyse within- and between-species differences in primate gene expression. Analysis of RNA expression profiles from the left prefrontal lobe (Brodmann area 9, which is thought to be involved in cognitive functions) of adult male humans, chimpanzees and an orangutan, and from the neocortex of humans, chimpanzees and macaques, indicated an apparent acceleration of gene-expression differences in the human brain relative to other primates and to other tissues. Protein-expression analyses were also consistent with the idea that relative changes in protein-expression levels were accelerated in the evolution of the human brain, and could be detected for ~30% of the proteins surveyed. The concordance between RNA and protein-level data indicates that regulatory changes have occurred in a substantial fraction of genes. Indeed, a recent survey of humans heterozygous at 13 loci revealed allelic variation in gene-expression levels at 6 loci[77]. Both intraspecific variations and interspecific divergence in gene expression are probably due to substitutions in non-coding regions that influence transcript or protein abundance through transcriptional or post-transcriptional mechanisms. These data further suggest that quantitative changes in gene expression should be expected as a general feature that accompanies species divergence, and that the raw material for evolutionary changes in gene expression appears to be widely available in non-coding DNA.

The microarray experiments raise many challenges for future progress. Specifically, how can changes that contribute to human anatomy, physiology or behaviour be sorted out from those that don't? Gene-expression data are correlative, not definitive in terms of identifying cause and effect. Many developmental and genetic mechanisms could contribute to the overall pattern observed. For example, a change in the composition of a tissue (for example, the relative proportions of cell types) will be accompanied by altered expression profiles, but many of these changes will be an indirect consequence of a developmental change, not the cause. Similarly, changes in levels or activities of regulatory proteins may affect batteries of downstream genes, but again are indirect and do not necessarily involve substitutions at the loci whose expression changes. Therefore, different approaches have to be taken to identify primary changes in regulatory pathways.

Candidate Genes in Human Evolution

The ultimate goal of microarray analyses, quantitative trait genetics, population genetics or other comparative genetic methods is the identification of genes that are candidates for being causally associated with phenotypic divergence. Although genome-wide, large-scale surveys provide an overview, rigorous tests of causality demand a gene-by-gene approach. In choosing genes to be studied in greater detail, molecular geneticists will be opportunistic, focusing on those loci for which additional information from human or model-animal biology suggests an association with a trait of greater evolutionary interest, such as craniodental development[78]. Therefore, it is unlikely that all traits will be pursued with equal vigour or success.

To implicate a gene in human evolution, two types of data need to be assessed. First, functional evidence that a gene is involved in a developmental, behavioural or physiological trait is required to formulate hypotheses about the role of an individual gene. This may come from analysis of human mutations at a locus (see below). Second, the molecular evolution and population genetics of the locus need to be analysed for evidence of natural selection. Comparison of orthologues from chimpanzees and other primates and mammals, and analyses of intraspecific variation in humans, can reveal signs of positive selection at the sequence level or of a recent 'selective sweep' through a locus (Box 2). Evidence of positive selection has been found at several human loci[73,79–81]. Although these might be physiologically important (for example, in immunity or reproduction), most genes studied so far are not expected to contribute to the divergence of morphological or behavioural traits. More recently, attention has turned to candidate genes identified from human mutations that do affect such traits.

The Evolution of a Gene Affecting Speech. Human medical genetics has made substantial progress, and sophisticated mapping techniques for polymorphisms are accelerating the characterization of genes involved in complex traits, particularly those of medical interest. One of the most provocative reports of late was the identification of the gene *FOXP2* (forkhead box P2), mutations of which are associated with a speech and language disorder[82]. The gene encodes a transcription factor and is therefore expected to control the expression of other genes. The excitement surrounding *FOXP2* stems from the observation that affected individuals appear to have not an overt impairment, but a lesion in the neural circuitry that affects language processes[62,82,83].

Is this a novel human 'language' gene? No, the gene is found in other species. In fact, the human FOXP2 protein differs from the gorilla and chimpanzee sequence at just two residues, and from the orangutan and mouse sequences at three and four residues, respectively[76]. This history is typical of human and other species' genes, in that most genes have orthologues in other mammals and animals. However, there is the possibility that the two replacements in the FOXP2 protein that evolved in the human lineage are of functional significance to the origin of language.

To examine whether the *FOXP2* gene has been the target of selection during human evolution, a detailed analysis was undertaken of nucleotide variation over a 14-kilobase (kb) subregion of the large *FOXP2* locus, of amino-acid polymorphism in a segment of the protein, and of chimpanzee and orangutan sequences[84]. An unusual excess was found of rare alleles at the human *FOXP2* locus, and of high-frequency alleles. Reduced genetic variation in neutral linked regions is a predicted consequence of a selective sweep (Box 2), so these observations are consistent with natural selection acting on the *FOXP2* locus. Estimates of the time of fixation of the two amino-acid replacements place them within the last 200,000 yr of human evolution, an intriguing correlation with the estimated age of *H. sapiens*.

However, it should be noted that there are no biological data to support the hypothesis that these amino-acid replacements are functionally important. In the 14-kb region surveyed, more than 100 fixed differences exist; the entire *FOXP2* locus is large (267 kb), and more than 2,000 differences would be expected to exist between the *FOXP2* genes of humans and chimpanzees. No assessment has been made of potential non-coding regulatory sequences that might have contributed to a divergence in the role of FOXP2 in hominids. Trait differences are often due to changes in regulatory networks that govern development, and need not be in coding regions (although that would be much more convenient, given just two changes in the human FOXP2 protein). Because FOXP2 is a transcription factor, changes in *FOXP2* expression could be of functional and evolutionary significance.

========= BOX 2 =========

Selective Sweeps

If a change in a gene is favoured, then selection may drive the allele bearing that change to fixation (left and centre of the figure). In the process, neutral variation at linked sites 'hitch-hikes' along with the selected site; this is known as a 'selective sweep'. The physical limits of the sweep depend on the strength of the linkage between selected and adjacent sites. After a sweep, variation may again begin to build up, and initially there will be a relatively high frequency of rare polymorphisms (right of the figure). Tajima[91] proposed a statistic (D) that tests for selective neutrality. If the frequencies of polymorphisms are skewed, with an excess of rare types, this gives a negative value (neutral value = 0) and can be indicative of a recent selective sweep. Tajima's D is sensitive to other factors apart from selection that can also yield a negative value. A recent expansion in population size from a relatively small population will produce similar patterns of genetic variation and D values. In human populations, population history (for example, drift and expansion) and population structure (ethnicity, migration and immigration) will affect D values at all loci, whereas selection will affect D values at selected and linked loci. The mean D values for 437 loci range from –0.69 to –1.25, depending on sampling methods[92], indicating that population structure and history has had an effect. These negative values underscore a challenge in human evolutionary genetics to distinguish selective sweeps at loci from population-based effects. The D value obtained for the human *FOXP2* locus was –2.20, the second largest negative value among all human genes surveyed so far[84]. Other methods have been developed to detect positive selection: for example, by identifying areas of extended haplotype homozygosity[81]. It is important to emphasize that all of these methodologies detect signs of recent selection in the *Homo sapiens* lineage. The preceding 5–6 Myr of hominin genetic history, a period when we know from the fossil record that many human features arose, is not addressed by these methods.

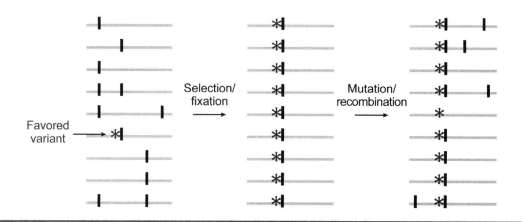

The typical genetic architecture that underlies complex traits makes it extremely unlikely that *FOXP2* was the only gene under selection in the evolution of our language capabilities. However, we have no means of assessing the relative contribution of *FOXP2* and other candidate genes. The encouraging lesson of *FOXP2* is that medical genetics has provided an interesting lead into a regulatory network that affects the development of speech ability. Further study of *FOXP2* should lead, at a minimum, to a better understanding of the neurodevelopmental biology of speech and language, and perhaps to more genes with interesting evolutionary histories.

The Functions of Selected Genes

The three genome-scale approaches highlighted here—population genetics, comparative genomics and gene-expression profiling—have all succeeded in finding what each sought: thousands of potential adaptive coding substitutions, regulatory differences in gene expression, and gene duplications and rearrangements. Each has yielded many candidates through which to sift and, interestingly, because of the different search regimens used, there is virtually no overlap in the sets of genetic changes that have been surveyed. It is almost certain that, as in other lineages, all of these types of genetic mechanism have contributed to hominid evolution. The crucial challenge now is to obtain functional data for individual genes and to scrutinize the molecular evolution of candidates for signatures of selection.

To place any candidate gene into a functional context of human trait evolution, advances in primate and human developmental neurobiology will be essential. Non-primates are limited as models of the development and function of primate and hominid neocortex, and thus as models of the function of proteins such as FOXP2 in the development and elaboration of neural networks. Direct empirical work on developing primates, which faces serious methodological constraints as well as bona fide ethical questions, will be necessary to advance beyond associations and correlations. Testing the functional role of what may be subtle changes in human orthologues of primate genes, a daunting task in the most technically developed model species, will be even more difficult.

There are two immediate avenues to increasing the power of human evolutionary genetics. First, we would increase the value of chimpanzee–human comparative genomics by sequencing the gorilla genome, which is the next earliest branching ape to humans and chimpanzees. This would help us to determine the polarity of genetic changes by distinguishing those changes in the human lineage from those in the chimpanzee lineage. Second, 6×10^9 interbreeding humans is a very large resource for identifying rare mutations (for example, in *FOXP2*) with subtle behavioural or developmental effects, and for mapping genetic variation that underlies morphological variation, both of which could lead to genes that govern the formation of human traits and that might have played a part in hominid evolution.

THE FINE PRINT BELOW THE HEADLINES

It is easy to foresee the media headlines that will announce the completion of the chimpanzee genome. One aim of this article has been to anticipate both the excitement that accomplishment warrants and the more sobering aspects of complex trait genetics and genome-scale evolution. Despite our enhanced understanding of functional genetic architecture, there remains a tendency to associate the development, function or evolution of a trait with single genes (genes 'for' speech, cancer and so on). The ghost of 'hopeful monsters' still haunts biology and is, unfortunately, a prevalent misconception in the scientific and general press. Perhaps wishful thinking is also an intrinsic part of human nature, but it seems unlikely that the traits that interest us most—bipedalism, skeletal morphology, craniofacial morphology, brain size and speech—were the products of selection of just a few major genes. Just as palaeoanthropology now recognizes a complex pattern of hominin phylogeny and the uncertainties in

identifying long-sought common ancestors, and comparative neurobiology now searches for more subtle explanations of human capabilities, the lessons of model-system genetics and comparative genomics should prepare us for the finding that the genetics of hominid trait evolution are, in fact, subtle and complicated.

I underscore this point not just for its scientific relevance, but also because of the larger issues at stake—the meaning of the pursuit of the material basis of human evolution. Evolutionary biology has always faced public resistance. It has been difficult enough to gain acceptance of fundamental ideas using humble finches or fruit flies as examples. We can anticipate even more hostile challenges to human evolutionary genetics. Opponents will be sure to exploit any instances where claims or hypotheses are founded on weak or contradictory data. Witness how the recent scrutiny of data supporting the classic paradigm of industrial melanism has been hijacked by the anti-evolution agenda[85]. The sequencing of the chimpanzee genome will reveal no more directly about the origin of human traits than the sequence of the human genome tells us about how to construct a healthy baby. Headlines may claim more, but we would be well advised to describe this as just the beginning of a large, complex and profoundly important story.

ACKNOWLEDGMENTS

Thanks to B. Hopkins and C. Cantalupo for guidance on Figure 2, and to L. Olds for illustrations; to B. Williams, A. Kopp, S. Paddock, A. Rokas, D. Bownds, J. Doebley, N. Shubin and J. Crow for comments on the manuscript; to P., N. and J. Carroll for inspiration, and to J. Carroll for preparation of the manuscript. S.B.C. is an Investigator of the Howard Hughes Medical Institute.

REFERENCES

1. Wood, B. Hominid revelations from Chad. *Nature* **418,** 133–135 (2002).
2. Leakey, M. et al. New hominin genus from eastern Africa shows diverse middle Pliocene lineages. *Nature* **410,** 433–440 (2001).
3. Brunet, M. et al. A new hominid from the Upper Miocene of Chad, Central Africa. *Nature* **418,** 145–151 (2002).
4. Wolpoff, M., Senut, B., Pickford, M. & Hawks, J. Palaeoanthropology: *Sahelanthropus* or '*Sahelpithecus*'? *Nature* **419,** 581–582 (2002).
5. Groves, C. P. in *Comparative Primate Biology* Vol. 1 (eds Swindler, D. R. & Erwin, J.) 187–218 (Alan R. Liss, New York, 1986).
6. Klein, J. & Takahata, N. *Where Do We Come From? The Molecular Evidence for Human Descent* (Springer, New York, 2002).
7. Wood, B. & Collard, M. The human genus. *Science* **284,** 65–71 (1999).
8. Relethford, J. H. *Genetics and the Search for Modern Human Origins* (Wiley–Liss, New York, 2001).
9. Ruff, C. B., Trinkaus, E. & Holliday, T. W. Body mass and encephalization in Pleistocene *Homo*. *Nature* **387,** 173–176 (1997).
10. Conroy, G. C. et al. Endocranial capacity in an early hominid cranium from Sterkfontein, South Africa. *Science* **280,** 1730–1731 (1998).
11. Conroy, G. C., Weber, G. W., Seidler, H., Recheis, W. & Zur Nedden, E. Endocranial capacity of the Bodo cranium determined from three-dimensional computed tomography. *Am. J. Phys. Anthropol.* **113,** 111–118 (2000).
12. Brodmann, K. Neue Ergebnisse über die vergleichende histologische Lokalisation der Grosshirnrinde mit besonderer Berücksichtigung des Stirnhirns. *Anat. Anz.* **41,** 157–216 (1912).
13. Semendeferi, K., Lu, A., Schenker, N. & Damasio, H. Humans and great apes share a large frontal cortex. *Nature Neurosci.* **5,** 272–276 (2002).
14. Cantalupo, C. & Hopkins, W. D. Asymmetric Broca's area in great apes. *Nature* **414,** 505 (2001).
15. Hopkins, W. D. & Leavens, D. A. The whole-hand point: The structure and function of pointing from a comparative perspective. *J. Comp. Psychol.* **112,** 95–99 (1998).
16. Holloway, R. L. Indonesian "Solo" (Ngandong) endocranial reconstructions: Some preliminary observations and comparisons with Neandertal and *Homo erectus* groups. *Am. J. Phys. Anthropol.* **53,** 285–295 (1980).
17. Gannon, P. J., Holloway, R. L., Broadfield, D. C. & Braun, A. R. Asymmetry of chimpanzee planum temporale: Humanlike pattern of Wernicke's brain language area homolog. *Science* **279,** 220–222 (1998).
18. Hopkins, W. D., Marino, L., Rilling, J. K. & MacGregor, L. Planum temporale asymmetries in great apes as revealed by magnetic resonance imaging (MRI). *NeuroReport* **9,** 2913–2918 (1998).
19. Hof, P. R., Nimchinsky, E. A., Perl, D. P. & Erwin, J. M. An unusual population of pyramidal neurons in the anterior cingulate cortex of hominids contains the calcium-binding protein calretinin. *Neurosci. Lett.* **307,** 139–142 (2001).

20. Nimchinsky, E. A. et al. A neuronal morphological type unique to humans and great apes. *Proc. Natl Acad. Sci. USA* **96,** 5268–5273 (1999).

21. Buxhoeveden, D., Switala, A., Litaker, M., Roy, E. & Casanova, M. Lateralization of minicolumns in human planum temporale is absent in nonhuman primate cortex. *Brain Behav. Evol.* **57,** 349–358(2001).

22. Semendeferi, K., Armstrong, E., Schleicher, A., Zilles, K. & Van Hoesen, G. W. Prefrontal cortex in humans and apes: A comparative study of area 10. *Am. J. Phys. Anthropol.* **114,** 224–241 (2001).

23. Penin, X., Berge, C. & Baylac, M. Ontogenetic study of the skull in modern humans and the common chimpanzees: Neotenic hypothesis reconsidered with a tridimensional procrustes analysis. *Am. J. Phys. Anthropol.* **118,** 50–62 (2002).

24. Ponce de León, M. S. & Zollikofer, C. P. E. Neanderthal cranial ontogeny and its implications for late hominid diversity. *Nature* **412,** 534–538 (2001).

25. Lieberman, D. E., McBratney, B. M. & Krovitz, G. The evolution and development of cranial form in *Homo sapiens. Proc. Natl Acad. Sci. USA* **99,** 1134–1139 (2002).

26. Williams, F. L., Godfrey, L. R. & Sutherland, M. R. in *Human Evolution through Developmental Change* (eds Minugh-Purvis, N. & McNamara, K. J.) 405–441 (Johns Hopkins Univ. Press, Baltimore, 2002).

27. Dean, C. et al. Growth processes in teeth distinguish modern humans from *Homo erectus* and earlier hominins. *Nature* **414,** 628–631 (2001).

28. Rice, S. H. in *Human Evolution through Developmental Change* (eds Minugh-Purvis, N. & McNamara, K. J.) 154–170 (Johns Hopkins Univ. Press, Baltimore, 2002).

29. Gould, S. J. *Ontogeny and Phylogeny* (Belknap, Cambridge, Massachusetts, 1977).

30. Moggi-Cecchi, J. Questions of growth. *Nature* **414,** 595–597 (2001).

31. MacFadden, B. J. Fossil horses from "Eohippus" (*Hyracotherium*) to *Equus:* Scaling, Cope's Law, and the evolution of body size. *Paleobiology* **12,** 355–369 (1986).

32. Charlesworth, B., Lande, R. & Slatkin, M. A neo-Darwinian commentary on macroevolution. *Evolution* **36,** 474–498 (1982).

33. Schwartz, J. H. Homeobox genes, fossils, and the origin of species. *Anat. Rec.* **257,** 15–31 (1999).

34. Klein, R. G. Archeology and the evolution of human behavior. *Evol. Anthropol.* **9,** 17–36 (2000).

35. Mackay, T. F. C. Quantitative trait loci in *Drosophila. Nature Rev. Genet.* **2,** 11–20 (2001).

36. Atchley, W. R., Plummer, A. A. & Riska, B. Genetic analysis of size-scaling patterns in the mouse mandible. *Genetics* **111,** 579–595 (1985).

37. Atchley, W. R. & Zhu, J. Developmental quantitative genetics, conditional epigenetic variability and growth in mice. *Genetics* **147,** 765–776 (1997).

38. Doebley, J. & Stec, A. Inheritance of the morphological differences between maize and teosinte: Comparison of results for two F2 populations. *Genetics* **134,** 559–570 (1993).

39. Livshits, G., Roset, A., Yakovenko, K., Trofimov, S. & Kobyliansky, E. Genetics of human body size and shape: Body proportions and indices. *Ann. Hum. Biol.* **29,** 271–289 (2002).

40. Brakefield, P. et al. Development, plasticity and evolution of butterfly eyespot patterns. *Nature* **384,** 236–242 (1996).

41. True, J. R., Liu, J., Stam, L. F., Zeng, Z. B. & Laurie, C. C. Quantitative genetic analysis of divergence in male secondary sexual traits between *Drosophila simulans* and *Drosophila mauritiana. Evolution* **51,** 816–832 (1997).

42. Shubin, N., Wake, D. B. & Crawford, A. J. Morphological variation in the limbs of *Taricha granulosa* (Caudata: Salamandridae): Evolutionary and phylogenetic implications. *Evolution* **49,** 874–884(1995).

43. Gingerich, P. D. Rates of evolution on the time scale of the evolutionary process. *Genetics* **112/113,** 127–144 (2001).

44. Gingerich, P. D. Rate of evolution: Effects of time and temporal scaling. *Science* **222,** 159–161 (1983).

45. Lauter, N. & Doebley, J. Genetic variation for phenotypically invariant traits detected in teosinte: Implications for the evolution of novel forms. *Genetics* **160,** 333–342 (2002).

46. Polaczyk, P. J., Gasperini, R. & Gibson, G. Naturally occurring genetic variation affects *Drosophila* photoreceptor determination. *Dev. Genes. Evol.* **207,** 462–470 (1998).

47. Rutherford, S. L. & Lindquist, S. Hsp90 as a capacitor for morphological evolution. *Nature* **396,** 336–342 (1998).

48. Gibson, G., Wemple, M. & van Helden, S. Potential variance affecting homeotic *Ultrabithorax* and *Antennapedia* phenotypes in *Drosophila melanogaster. Genetics* **151,** 1081–1091 (1999).

49. Goldschmidt, R. *The Material Basis of Evolution* (Yale Univ. Press, New Haven, Connecticut, 1940).

50. Carroll, S. B., Grenier, J. K. & Weatherbee, S. D. *From DNA to Diversity: Molecular Genetics and the Evolution of Animal Design* (Blackwell Scientific, Malden, Massachusetts, 2001).

51. Davidson, E. H. *Genomic Regulatory Systems: Development and Evolution* (Academic, San Diego, 2001).

52. Wilkins, A. S. *The Evolution of Developmental Pathways* (Sinauer Associates, Sunderland, Massachusetts, 2002).

53. Laurie, C. C. & Stam, L. F. Molecular dissection of a major gene effect on a quantitative trait: The level of alcohol dehydrogenase expression in *Drosophila melanogaster. Genetics* **144,** 1559–1564 (1996).

54. Long, A. D., Lyman, R. F., Morgan, A. H., Langley, C. H. & Mackay, T. F. C. Both naturally occurring insertions of transposable elements and intermediate frequency polymorphisms in the *achaete-scute* complex are associated with variation in bristle number in *Drosophila melanogaster. Genetics* **154,** 1255–1269 (2000).

55. Wang, R.-L., Stec, A., Hey, J., Lukens, L. & Doebley, J. The limits of selection during maize domestication. *Nature* **398,** 236–239 (1999).

56. Long, A. D., Lyman, R. F., Langley, C. H. & Mackay, T. F. C. Two sites in the *Delta* gene region contribute to naturally occurring variation in bristle number in *Drosophila melanogaster. Genetics* **149,** 999–1017 (1998).

57. Lai, C., Lyman, R. F., Long, A. D., Langley, C. H. & Mackay, T. F. C. Naturally occurring variation in bristle number and DNA polymorphisms at the *scabrous* locus of *Drosophila melanogaster. Science* **266,** 1697–1702 (1994).

58. Nuzhdin, S. V. & Reiwitch, S. G. Are the same genes responsible for intra- and interspecific variability for sex comb tooth number in *Drosophila. Heredity* **84,** 97–102 (2000).

59. Chen, F.-C. & Li, W.-H. Genomic divergences between humans and other hominoids and the effective population size of the common ancestor of humans and chimpanzees. *Am. J. Hum. Genet.* **68,** 444–456 (2001).

60. Britten, R. J. Divergence between samples of chimpanzee and human DNA sequences is 5%, counting indels. *Proc. Natl Acad. Sci. USA* **99,** 13633–13634 (2002).

61. Fujiyama, A. et al. Construction and analysis of a human–chimpanzee comparative clone map. *Science* **295,** 131–134 (2002).

62. Johnson, M. E. et al. Positive selection of a gene family during the emergence of humans and African apes. *Nature* **413,** 514–518 (2001).

63. Mouse Genome Sequencing Consortium. Initial sequencing and comparative analysis of the mouse genome. *Nature* **420,** 520–562 (2002).

64. Venter, J. C. et al. The sequence of the human genome. *Science* **291,** 1304–1323 (2001).

65. International Human Genome Sequencing Consortium. Initial sequencing and analysis of the human genome. *Nature* **409,** 860–921 (2001).

66. Li, W.-H. *Molecular Evolution* (Sinauer Associates, Sunderland, Massachusetts, 1997).

67. Kreitman, M. Methods to detect selection in populations with applications to the human. *Ann. Rev. Genomics Hum. Genet.* **1,** 539–559 (2000).

68. McDonald, J. H. & Kreitman, M. Adaptive protein evolution at the *Adh* locus in *Drosophila. Nature* **351,** 652–654 (1991).

69. Fay, J. C., Wyckoff, G. J. & Wu, C.-I. Positive and negative selection on the human genome. *Genetics* **158,** 1227–1234 (2001).

70. Ohta, T. Near-neutrality in evolution of genes and gene regulation. *Proc. Natl Acad. Sci. USA* **99,** 16134–16137 (2002).

71. Hughes, A. L. *Adaptive Evolution of Genes and Genomes* (Oxford Univ. Press, New York, 1999).

72. Swanson, W. J. & Vacquier, V. D. The rapid evolution of reproductive proteins. *Nature Rev. Genet.* **3,** 137–144 (2002).

73. Wyckoff, G. J., Wang, W. & Wu, C.-I. Rapid evolution of male reproductive genes in the descent of man. *Nature* **403,** 304–309 (2000).

74. King, M.-C. & Wilson, A. C. Evolution at two levels in humans and chimpanzees. *Science* **188,** 107–116 (1975).

75. Nachman, M. W. Single nucleotide polymorphisms and recombination rate in humans. *Trends Genet.* **17**, 481–485 (2001).

76. Enard, W. et al. Intra- and interspecific variation in primate gene expression patterns. *Science* **296**, 340–343 (2002).

77. Yan, H., Yuan, W., Velculescu, V. E., Vogelstein, B. & Kinzler, K. W. Allelic variation in human gene expression. *Science* **297**, 1143 (2002).

78. McCollum, M. A. & Sharpe, P. T. Developmental genetics and early hominid craniodental evolution. *BioEssays* **23**, 481–493 (2001).

79. Andolfatto, P. Adaptive hitchhiking effects on genome variability. *Curr. Opin. Genet. Dev.* **11**, 635–641 (2001).

80. Diller, K. C., Gilbert, W. A. & Kocher, T. D. Selective sweeps in the human genome: A starting point for identifying genetic differences between modern humans and chimpanzees. *Mol. Biol. Evol.* **19**, 2342–2345 (2002).

81. Sabetl, P. C. et al. Detecting recent positive selection in the human genome from haplotype structure. *Nature* **419**, 832–837 (2002).

82. Lai, C. S. L., Fisher, S. E., Hurst, J. A., Vargha-Khadem, F. & Monaco, A. P. A forkhead-domain gene is mutated in a severe speech and language disorder. *Nature* **413**, 519–523 (2001).

83. Pinker, S. Talk of genetics and vice versa. *Nature* **413**, 465–566 (2001).

84. Enard, W. et al. Molecular evolution of *FOXP2*, a gene involved in speech and language. *Nature* **418**, 869–872 (2002).

85. Coyne, J. A. Evolution under pressure. *Nature* **418**, 19–20 (2002).

86. Kimbel, W. H., Johanson, D. C. & Rak, Y. The first skull and other new discoveries of *Australopithecus afarensis* at Hadar, Ethiopia. *Nature* **368**, 449–451 (1994).

87. Haile-Selassie, Y. Late Miocene hominids from the Middle Awash, Ethiopia. *Nature* **412**, 178–181 (2001).

88. Asfaw, B. et al. Remains of *Homo erectus* from Bouri, Middle Awash, Ethiopia. *Nature* **416**, 317–320 (2002).

89. Hacia, J. G. Genome of the apes. *Trends Genet.* **17**, 637–645 (2001).

90. Richmond, B. G., Aiello, L. C. & Wood, B. A. Early hominid limb proportions. *J. Hum. Evol.* **43**, 529–548 (2002).

91. Tajima, F. Statistical method for testing the neutral mutation hypothesis by DNA polymorphism. *Genetics* **123**, 585–596 (1989).

92. Ptak, S. E. & Przeworski, M. Evidence for population growth in humans is confounded by fine-scale population structure. *Trends Genet.* **18**, 1–5 (2002).

73

Human Colonization of the Americas

Timing, Technology and Process

E. J. Dixon

ABSTRACT

Geological and archeological research indicates that humans first colonized the Americas with the use of watercraft along the southern coast of the Bering Land Bridge and the western coast of the Americas. Early dates from a number of archeological sites in the Americas indicate human colonization of the Americas began prior to ca. 13,000 BP. A review of archeological sites in eastern Beringia identifies several distinctive cultural traditions which had developed by 11,000–10,000 BP. Geological, biological, linguistic evidence, and dated human skeletal remains all suggest human occupation of the Americas prior to ca. 11,500 BP. Glacial geology indicates colonization could have begun ca. 14,000–13,000 BP along the western coasts of the Americas and ended about 5000 BP with deglaciation of the Canadian eastern Arctic and coastal Greenland. The use of watercraft and coastal navigation prior to 11,000 BP are inferentially demonstrated. A model for early coastal and subsequent inland colonization of the Americas along large ecological zones best fits current geologic and archeological data.

ORIGINS

Humans evolved in the Old World, beginning in Africa and subsequently colonizing Eurasia, Australia, and the Americas. Many archeologists believe that the first humans to enter the Americas came from northeast Asia via the Bering Land Bridge sometime ca. 12,000 years ago about the end of the Wisconsin glaciation, the last glacial stage of the Pleistocene Epoch in North America. However, this is not the only possible time for humans to have reached the New World. Some archeologists (Simpson et al., 1986; Irving et al., 1986; Carter, 1952, 1957; and others) believe humans may have come to the Americas 200,000–150,000 years ago during earlier glacial stages when the Bering Land Bridge formed as a result of lower sea levels (Hopkins, 1973). However, other researchers are of the opinion that humans first arrived in the Americas within the ca. 50,000 years ago during the Happy Interval (Hopkins, 1979, 1982), and more likely within the last 14,000 years (Hrdlička, 1928; Haynes, 1969; Griffin, 1979). Reliably dated human skeletal remains have not been found in the Americas which are older than 12,000 BP. This supports other evidence suggesting that humans first arrived in the Americas toward the end of the Wisconsin glaciation. Research dating late Pleistocene deglaciation indicates that terrestrial connections between eastern Beringia and areas south of the North American continental glaciers were not reestablished until about 11,000 BP (Jackson et al., 1997). This precludes a mid-continental route for human entry until ca. 11,000 BP.

BERINGIA AND THE ICE-FREE CORRIDOR

The Bering Land Bridge has been a cornerstone in American paleontology and archeology for hundreds of years. In addition to explaining the exchange of plants and large terrestrial mammals between Asia and North America, it is presumed that hunters of large terrestrial mammals probably first entered North America from Asia via the Land Bridge. The traditional explanation is that humans then moved south through central western Canada sometime about 11,500 BP, either through a hypothetical ice-free corridor or after the continental glaciers melted (Figure 1). According to this theory, the pattern of Old World mammoth hunting was transposed to North America near the end of the last ice age by peoples using Clovis or Clovis-like technology.

There is little evidence to support the traditional paradigm of mammoth hunters "expanding" from the Asian steppe into Beringia and southward through what is now interior Canada into more southern regions of the Americas. The only places from which there is firm evidence for mammoth hunting is on both sides of Beringia, not Beringia itself (Haynes, 1991, pp. 208–213). However, blood residues preserved on Northern Paleoindian projectile points suggests that

mammoth may have been hunted in eastern Beringia possibly as late as 10,500 BP (Dixon, 1993; Loy and Dixon, 1998).

North American glacial chronology establishes maximum and minimum limiting dates for human colonization of North America. Deglaciation along the northwest coast of North America was sufficiently advanced to enable human settlement by at least 13,000 BP. However, the interior Bering Land Bridge/midcontinental route was not deglaciated before ca. 11,000 BP. Extreme northeastern North America was not deglaciated until ca. 5000 BP, thus providing the last opportunity for large-scale colonization sometime shortly thereafter (Figure 8).

OLDEST ARCHEOLOGICAL SITES IN THE AMERICAS

There is no professional consensus on the time humans first colonized the Americas. There is widespread concurrence that the Clovis complex (11,500–11,000 BP) provides a minimum limiting date for human colonization. Some archeologists believe that the Clovis complex represents the tangible remains of America's first colonists. However, numerous archeological sites have been reported from North and South America that some archeologists believe predate Clovis and the deglaciation of central northern North America.

North American archeologists have established protocols to test the validity of Pleistocene archeological remains in the Americas (Haynes, 1967; Jennings, 1974; Griffin, 1979; Stanford, 1979). Some of the more important or better known North American sites include Meadowcroft Rock Shelter in Pennsylvania (Adovasio et al., 1977, 1978, 1980), the Dutton and Selby sites in Colorado (Stanford, 1979, 1983; Graham, 1981), the Manis Mastodon site (Gustafson et al., 1979), and Valsequillo in southeastern Mexico (Irwin-Williams, 1967, 1969, 1978). South American sites include Pedra Furada in northeast Brazil (Guidon and Delibrias, 1986; Delibrias et al., 1988; Parenti et al., 1990) Tiama-Tiama in northern Venezuela (Rouse and Cruxent, 1966; Cruxent and Ochsenius, 1979; Bryan, 1979; Bryan and Gruhn, 1979) and Monte Verde in southern Chile (Dillehay, 1989, 1997). While the age or the cultural origin of all these sites are controversial, Monte Verde is accepted as a pre-Clovis site.

Monte Verde, located in south-central Chile, is a campsite reflecting a wide range of human activity including residential structures and exceptionally well-preserved organic remains including bone, wood and other materials. The site has been scientifically excavated under the direction of Dillehay and his fellow researchers (Dillehay, 1997). A series of eight stratigraphic units (labeled youngest to oldest, MV-1 through MV-8) have been described and dated by seven concordant ^{14}C determinations. Artifacts and other evidence of human occupation have been recovered from MV-7, which is capped by a layer of peat that sealed and preserved the archeological materials.

Dillehay (1984, 1986, 1997; Collins and Dillehay, 1986) reports the remains of at least 12 dwellings,

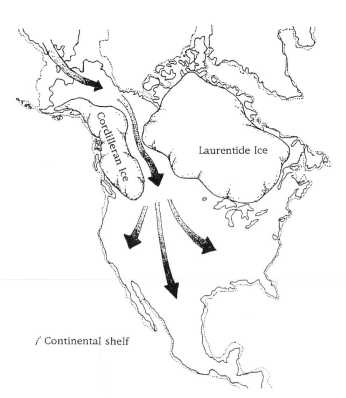

Figure 1. *Map depicting the traditional Beringian-midcontinental human route for human colonization of the Americas (modified from Dixon, 1999; courtesy of E. J. Dixon and the University of New Mexico Press).*

presumably covered with animal skins, containing shallow clay-lined braziers. Large "communal" hearths were found with the remains of edible seeds, nuts, fruits, and berries, and wood artifacts have been recovered including mortars, wooden hafts containing stone flakes, digging sticks, a pointed lance or spear, and vast amounts of worked wood. Although there are a few well-made bifacially flaked stone tools, most of the lithic industry consists of individual flakes, split pebbles and other stones exhibiting little modification from their natural states. There are many nearly spherical forms, a few of which are grooved and were possibly used as bola weights and/or stones for slings. Although no human remains were recovered, footprints of a child or small adolescent were preserved on the surface of MV-7. No geologic or other noncultural processes have been identified to suggest this suite of evidence could have been produced by any mechanism other than human occupation. Monte Verde meets, or exceeds, the criteria establishing pre-Clovis validity for archeological sites in the Americas (Meltzer et al., 1997).

Two hearth-like features suggest the possibility that there may be an even earlier occupation at the site. They were discovered stratigraphically below unit MV-7, about 70 m north of the main occupation (Dillehay and Collins, 1988; Dillehay, 1997). Two ^{14}C determinations from these features are 33,370 ± 530 (Beta-6754) and >33,020 (Beta-7825). Scattered about them were 26 naturally fractured stones, which appear to have been used by people. In the absence of other evidence, the investigators are not certain that these features present unequivocal evidence of human occupation.

HUMAN REMAINS

Unlike the Old World, the New World lacks human remains anatomically similar to very early human forms such as *Homo erectus, Homo sapiens neanderthalensis,* or even Archaic *Homo sapiens.* Human remains found in the New World appear to be completely modern humans, *Homo sapiens.* The only possible evidence to the contrary is the inconclusive identification of a human supraorbital ridge from the Chapala Basin, Mexico, which has been compared to the supraorbital ridge from Old World examples of *Homo erectus.* However, Solorzano (1990; Haley and Solorzano, 1991) cautions that this identification has been made on a small fragment of bone. Other researchers suggest that this bone may not be human, but rather derived from the fragmentary remains of another element from a different species. Another report of pre-*Homo sapiens* from the New World is a curious article and illustration of an archaic human calvarium (skull cap) by Bryan (1978, pp. 318–321) which, since his description, has disappeared.

The three oldest sets of reliably dated human remains from North America are from Fishbone Cave, in western Nevada; Arlington Springs on Santa Rosa Island, California; and the Anzick site, Montana. Radiocarbon dates of 11,555 ± 500 BP (no lab # cited) and 10,900 ± 300 BP (L-245) BP were reported from Fishbone Cave by Orr (1956, p. 3) for level 4. This level contains the partial remains of a human skeleton consisting of the burned remains of a left foot, a clavicle, and a fibula.

Two human femora, a humerus and an unidentified bone were found about 37.5 ft (11 m) below the surface on Santa Rosa Island (Orr, 1962, p. 418). Based on the size of the femora, Orr suggested they were the remains of an adult male. These remains have become known as Arlington Man. Chemical analysis demonstrated that the bone was fossilized, suggesting considerable antiquity (Oakley, 1963). Charcoal from the stratigraphic unit containing the human remains was ^{14}C dated to 10,400 ± 200 BP (L-568A) and 10,000 ± 200 (L-650) (Orr, 1962, p. 419). Although the human bone originally submitted was considered unsuitable for ^{14}C analysis (Morris, cited in Erlandson, 1994, p. 186), Berger and Protsh (1989, p. 59) were able to obtain a ^{14}C determination of 10,080 ± 810 BP from a long bone of Arlington Man. Controversy over the age of the human remains has focused on the large standard deviation associated with this date and the fact that there was only one ^{14}C determination. To address the controversy, additional AMS ^{14}C determinations were run by Johnson and Stafford (1997, pers. comm.) resulting in an AMS ^{14}C date of 10,970 ± 80 (CAMS-16810) on collagen from the human bone and another AMS ^{14}C determination of 11,490 ± 70 on *Peromyscus* sp. bone collagen directly associated with the human remains. Arlington Man also provides the earliest evidence for the use of watercraft in North America because Santa Rosa Island was not connected to mainland North America during the last ice age (Erlandson, 1994, p. 183).

The Anzick rock shelter located in Montana was accidentally discovered in 1968 (Jones and Bonnichsen, 1994). The site and context of the artifacts and human remains were largely destroyed by construction activities before they were examined by trained scientists. The burial(s) contained two individuals and an assemblage of more than 100 stone and bone artifacts. Both individuals are described as "subadults" (Wilke et al., 1991). Two very small pieces of human crania, one from each individual, were directly dated by the AMS method. One was bleached white and the other stained with hematite (ochre). The bleached crania dated 8600 ± 90 BP and the ochre-stained bone dated 10,680 ± 50 BP (Stafford, 1990, p. 121; 1994, pp. 49–51). More recently a second ^{14}C AMS date of 11,550 ± 60 (CAMS-35912) has been obtained on gelatin from the ochre-stained crania (Stafford, pers. comm., 1997). It is difficult to explain the difference in these two dates, and resolution of this problem will require additional dating.

Direct AMS dating of human bone provides unequivocal proof and limiting dates for humans in the Americas. The oldest human remains from Anzick, Fishbone Cave, and Arlington Springs appear to be between ca. 11,500–11,000 BP. This indicates that by this time human population density had achieved a level sufficient to assure the survival and discovery of fossil remains over a broad geographic area and from different depositional environments. Prior to ca. 11,000–11,500 BP the North American human population may have been extremely small or geographically restricted.

Toth (1991, p. 55) has suggested that if we assume a model for the colonization of the Americas as ever increasing population over time, the odds of documenting the very earliest evidence of human occupation are very slim.

BIOLOGICAL AND LINGUISTIC EVIDENCE

Linguistics and biological anthropology demonstrate that Native Americans most likely came to the Americas from northeast Asia. Turner (1983) has studied the dentition of Native Americans and northeast Asians. Based on about 20 dental traits, such as the shape of tooth crowns and the number of tooth roots, he has defined an overall dental pattern which he calls "Sinodonty". This distinctive dental pattern is shared among Native Americans and people from northeast Asia. However, Sinodonty is not found in people who originated in southern Asia, Africa, or Europe. Another less complex dental pattern, called Sundadonty, is shared among peoples of Southeast Asia and occurs in some early Native American skeletons, including Kennewick Man (Chatters, 1997). Turner (1992, p. 6) concludes that because there has been less dental evolution in the Americas, the New World has been occupied for less time than Asia, and that widespread Sinodonty demonstrates a northeast Asian origin for Native Americans. However, Merriwether et al. (1996) identify Mongolia as a more likely point of origin for New World founding populations based on their analysis of the mitochondrial DNA (mtDNA) of native Mongolians.

Turner (1983, 1985, 1992) recognizes three subdivisions of Sinodonty based on the dental characteristics, and proposes that colonization of the Americas occurred in three distinct migrations. The first were ancestors of the peoples of South America and southern North America. The second were ancestors of Native Americans residing in interior Alaska and along the Northwest Coast. The third were the Aleut-Eskimo who occupy the coastal fringes of Alaska. Some genetic research may support Turner's "three wave" model (Williams et al., 1985).

The dental evidence appears to correspond with linguistic data compiled by Greenberg (Greenberg et al., 1986; Greenberg, 1987, 1997). By applying a process called "*mass comparison*", he lumped Native American languages into three groups called Amerind, Na-Dene and Eskimo-Aleut. The linguistic data appear to correlate well with the dental evidence. It suggests that the first arrivals to settle the Americas were the ancestors of the Amerinds, the second "wave" were the ancestors of the Na-Dene and the last to emigrate to the New World were the Eskimo-Aleut (Greenberg et al., 1987).

The analysis of nuclear and mitochondrial DNA has led to alternative conclusions. In analyzing mtDNA from Native Americans, Schurr et al. (1990) recognized four basic mtDNA lineages, or haplogroups, which they labeled A–D. The fact that only four lineages could be identified suggests that the founding population(s) may have been very small. All four lineages occur in all Native American populations, but it is not clear how this

information can be interpreted properly. Based on mtDNA analysis, Torroni et al. (1992) conclude that Amerind and Na-Dene populations were founded by two separate migrations. However, research by Horai et al. (1996) draws the conclusion that the four haplogroups are evidence of four respective ancestral populations that migrated to the Americas gradually in different "waves". On the other hand, Merriwether et al. (1995) reason that because all four founding lineages are found in all Native American populations, the concept of a single migration with all four lineages being derived from the original founding population is probable. Other researchers (Bailliet et al., 1994; Lorenz and Smith, 1996) report evidence suggesting there may have been at least one more haplogroup in Native American populations prior to contact with Europeans. Although the conclusions drawn from this research are controversial, mtDNA research raises serious challenges to the "three wave" migration model based on the analysis of contemporary languages and prehistoric dental traits.

Archeologists have long recognized the difficulty in identifying genetic, ethnic, and linguistic "signatures" in the archeological record. Although much work remains to be done, it is clear that to establish migration of people, it is necessary to document a culture in one region and subsequently document it in another. To do this, it is necessary to identify material traits that can be reliably attributed to a specific culture. The early archeology of eastern Beringia and North America is so poorly understood, that this is impossible to do except at gross levels of comparison.

COLONIZATION PROCESSES

There is no need to think of human migration as a specific event. Humans may have populated the Americas in small numbers, or migratory "dribbles", over long periods of time (Meltzer, 1989). Some migrations may have been successful, and others may not have been. Some of these small groups of early migrants could have been genetically swamped by later groups, exterminated by warfare or by the introduction of disease, too small to be viable, or unable to adapt to new environments.

If the earliest immigrants were few in number, had technology derived from perishable organic material, and survived for only a short time, the evidence of their passing would be extremely difficult to detect in the archeological record. This would be even more difficult if these early peoples lacked what archeologists consider to be diagnostic artifact types, such as fluted stone projectile points. There would be no genetic or linguistic evidence in extant populations if the colonists did not survive, and there may not exist a continuous archeological record extending from the Pleistocene to later well-documented North American archeological sites. It is possible that there were sporadic colonization events that are not connected to subsequent development of New World archeology. Tracing the migration of specific groups of people is extremely difficult in the archeological record.

Some researchers believe that ecological disequilibrium may result in human dispersals and that initial contact between humans and select species may cause their extinction. Paul S. Martin (1967, 1973, 1974) has advanced the "overkill hypothesis" which postulates that the first human hunters to enter the Americas were responsible for the extinction of approximately 70 genera. According to this scenario, as humans moved into the Americas, they encountered large mammals that had developed no effective means of evading intelligent and sophisticated human predators, and humans quickly hunted these large mammals to extinction.

Kelley and Todd (1988; Kelly, 1996) have advanced a variation of Martin's model. They suggest that the first Paleoindians were technologically based foragers. Unlike modern foragers who are geographically based and generally confined by neighboring foraging groups, the earliest human groups in North America may have relied more on knowledge of animal behavior and technology rather than knowledge of geography. This may have enabled them to move from region to region exploiting various species, some of which may have been preferred. Such a subsistence strategy could result in comparatively rapid human "migration" and the extinction of select species.

Aquatic metaphors such as "waves", "trickles", "dribbles", and "drift" are frequently used to describe the peopling of the Americas. However, these "terms" tell us little, if anything, about the actual processes of human colonization. Currently there exist very few models for the peopling of the Americas. Mosimann and Martin (1975) demonstrated that humans could have colonized both North America and South America in approximately 1000 years and concurrently killed off the large Pleistocene mammals. Some scientists counter that dramatic change in climate caused the extinction of ice age mammals, while others suggest that a combination of both climatic change and human predators were the cause.

Wormington (1983, p. 192) believed that human colonization of the Americas took much longer than the model proposed by Mosimann and Martin. In her view, early hunters and gatherers needed more time to develop familiarity with their environment and its resources, and once they had gained this knowledge they were reluctant to move. She regarded environmental change and population pressure as the causal mechanisms for human groups to move. This type of model requires a much greater amount of time for humans to colonize the American continents than that advocated by Mosimann and Martin (1975).

In their attempt to model the human colonization of the Americas, Mosimann and Martin (1975) rely heavily on the work of Birdsell (1957), who derived his statistics from his research of human population expansion on Pitcarin—a remote Pacific island that was uninhabited until 1790, when it was colonized by nine mutineers from HMS *Bounty* and 19 Polynesians. While these data may be correct and useful in the contexts of the ecology of small islands, Beaton (1991a) suggests it is not applicable for Australia, a large landmass of continental proportion similar to the Americas. It may be inappro-

priate to extrapolate the human environmental impact from small Pacific islands to continental landmasses.

Furthermore, it is necessary to emphasize that the scale of investigative resolution fit the scale of the problem (Beaton, 1991a, p. 220). In other words, when attempting to address human colonization of continents, such as the initial peopling of the Americas or Australia, it is more useful to look at large, or macro, environmental zones. Such large environmental zones, or biomes, include regions such as coastlines, rather than smaller ecological areas such as estuaries or headlands. These macroenvironmental regions, or biomes, are what Beaton (1991a) calls "megapatches", which are large environmental zones or areas such as coasts, forests, deserts, and mountains.

The major physiographic and ecological regions of the Americas tend to be oriented linearly from north–south. For example, the western cordillera of North America forms a huge mountainous "spine" extending from Alaska to Arizona, the Plains extend from Alberta, Canada to northern Mexico, and the western coastal coniferous forest stretches from Alaska to California.

The bow wave model proposed by Mosimann and Martin (1973) is illustrated in Figure 2. It is characterized by bow-shaped lines, or "waves", symbolizing the sequential advance of the human population at approximately the same latitude. By comparison, the ecological

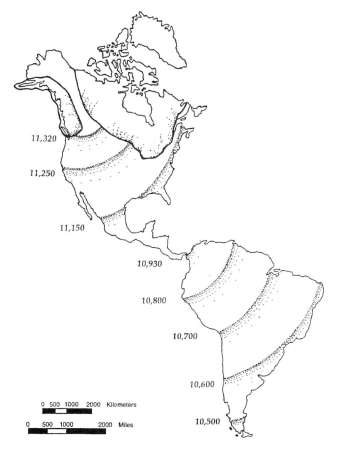

Figure 2. *The hypothetical bow wave model for the human colonization of the Americas from north to south (modified from Mosimann and Martin, 1975, and reproduced from Dixon, 1999, p. 36, courtesy of E. J. Dixon and the University of New Mexico Press).*

zone model illustrated in Figure 8 is characterized by more vertical lines that parallel the major environmental zones, such as the coast and the western cordillera.

Linear north-to-south colonization could have also occurred along ecotones, which are zones of transition between two or more biomes. These transitional environments may have been the "megapatch of choice", possibly being more productive than either of the adjacent biomes and possibly permitting people access to resources in adjacent biomes. On a very large (continental) level of analysis the coastal zone could be regarded as an ecotone, where the resources of both the marine and terrestrial biomes are available.

In relatively linear environmental zones such as river systems or coastal margins, colonization might be expected to be rapid, possibly resulting in high-velocity settlement in conjunction with the use of watercraft. In other types of ecological settings, colonization may have occurred at a much slower rate. With colonization occurring along major environmental zones, it may be reasonable to assume that different environmental regions of the Americas were colonized at different times. For example, coastal zones may have been inhabited long before the interior plains or deserts.

EARLY ARCHEOLOGY OF EASTERN BERINGIA

Three archeological traditions and two complexes have been identified in eastern Beringia and the Pacific Northwest. The earliest is the Nenana complex (older than 11,600–10,500 BP), discovered at several sites in interior Alaska. Archeologists have not ascertained the origins of the Nenana complex.

The second major cultural development is called the American Paleoarctic tradition (10,500–8,000 BP). It is derived from Asia and has its technological roots in the late Upper Paleolithic microblade industries of Eurasia. The hallmark of this tradition is microblade technology. The American Paleoarctic tradition is subdivided here into three regional variants: (1) the first retains the original name, the American Paleoarctic tradition, (2) the Denali complex, and (3) the Northwest Coast Microblade tradition.

The third major cultural development in eastern Beringia is the Northern Paleoindian tradition (ca. 10,500–8500 BP), believed to be a northern manifestation of the Paleoindian tradition of western North America. The American Paleoarctic tradition, the Northern Paleoindian tradition, and Denali complex are co-traditions. Co-traditions existed when people living in adjacent regions practiced different ways of life and made different types of tools during the same period of time. Each of these traditions is reviewed briefly to demonstrate how they support a coastal colonization model.

NENANA COMPLEX (ca. > 11,600–10,500 BP)

The Nenana complex (greater than 11,600 BP–10,500 BP) is defined on the basis of stone artifacts which date to the same time period found in Alaska's Nenana River valley (Powers and Hoffecker, 1990). Field research in the upper Tanana River valley in the early 1990s discovered similar artifact assemblages (Figure 3). Nenana complex peoples may have been confined to interior Alaska prior to melting of Brooks Range glaciers (Hamilton and Goebel, 1999). Artifact types that define the Nenana complex are: (1) triangular and "teardrop-shaped" projectile points and knives, (2) straight- or concave-based lanceolate projectile points, (3) perforators, (4) end and side scrapers, (5) burins, (6) hammer

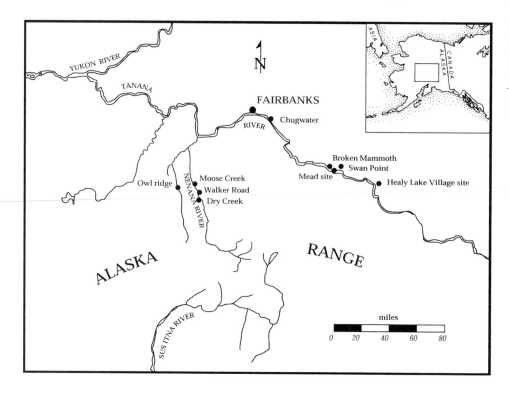

Figure 3. *Map depicting the location of important archeological sites and site components ascribed to the Nenana complex (modified from Dixon, 1993, and reproduced courtesy of E. J. Dixon and the University of New Mexico Press).*

and anvil stones, (7) unifacial knives and scrapers. Flakes, small stone wedges (*piece esquille'e*), and lithic debitage are also associated with these sites. These diagnostic types of stone artifacts have been found at Component I at the Dry Creek site, the Walker Road site and the Moose Creek site. Another Nenana complex site in the Teklanika River valley has been dated to 11,340 ± 150 BP and contains the same types of artifacts (Phippen, 1988).

Radiocarbon dates from Components I at the Walker Road and Dry Creek sites range between ca. 11,800 and 11,000 BP, averaging ca. 11,300 BP (Powers and Hoffecker, 1990, p. 278). Nenana complex sites are found near the bottom of thick sections of windblown sediments that began to accumulate during the early Birch interval (ca. 14,000 BP).

The earliest firmly dated archeological remains ascribed to the Nenana complex come from sites located in Alaska's Tanana River valley: the Broken Mammoth, Mead, and Swan Point sites. Extensive excavations have not been conducted at the Mead site. The oldest paleosol identified at the site is dated to ca. 11,600 BP, from which a cylindrical ivory object, a scraper, a few biface fragments and waste flakes, and possibly a small projectile point fragment were recovered.

The Broken Mammoth site has yielded more information. This site is important because it is well stratified, contains four major periods of cultural occupation, and exhibits concurrent ^{14}C determinations. It is possibly the oldest reliably dated site in Alaska. A series of nine ^{14}C determinations indicate Cultural Zone IV was occupied between ca. 11,700–11,000 BP. Cultural remains from Zone IV include waste flakes, a quartz "chopper/scraper/plane", retouched flakes, biface thinning flakes, scrap fossil ivory, and a cache of tools made of fossil ivory consisting of two cigar shaped "points" and a possible handle (Yesner, 1996).

At Swan Point the oldest cultural level (ca. 11,660 BP) contains worked mammoth tusk fragments (probably scavenged "fossil" ivory dated to 12,060 ± 70 (NSRL-2001, CAMS-17045)), microblades, microblade core preparation flakes, blades, split quartz pebble chopper/ planes, dihedral burins, and red ochre. The next oldest occupation, dated by one ^{14}C determination to 10,230 ± 80 BP, (BETA-56666, CAMS-4251) (Holmes et al., 1996), lacks microblades and contains small lanceolate points with convex/straight bases, thin triangular points, gravers made on broken points and quartz pebble choppers or hammers. Although the ca. 11,660 year old component appears anomalous based on the presence of a microblade technology, the later occupation dating to ca. 10,230 BP is consistent in its artifact assemblage with other Nenana complex sites.

Swan Point is an anomaly because it appears to have a microblade industry more than a thousand years earlier than anywhere else in interior Alaska, even earlier than similar assemblages from western Beringia. The Denali complex at Swan Point is dated by two ^{14}C samples. One was from mammoth ivory dating to 12,060 ± 70 (CAMS-17045) which was probably older scavenged ivory (Holmes et al., 1996, p. 323). The other dates, 11,660 ± 70 BP (BETA-56667, CAMS-4252) and 11,660 ± 60 BP

(BETA-71372, CAMS-12389), were run on willow and poplar charcoal derived from a cultural hearth associated with the microblades (Holmes et al., 1996, p. 321). Goebel and Hamilton (1999) suggest that the microblades may have been mixed with older charcoal immediately after the deposition of a pebbly colluvial layer and immediately before the overlying loess began to accumulate. The older dates could also result from other factors such as burning older "fossil" wood. Swan Point is still in the early stages of investigation and additional research is required to resolve the age of the early microblade component and its relationship to the Nenana complex.

The Healy Lake Village site contains distinctive "teardrop"-shaped bifaces, called "Chindadn" points, found in the lower levels (Cook, 1969, 1996). Chindadn points are generally small and occasionally ground on one lateral edge, suggesting they were dulled for hafting and used as knives. This distinctive artifact occurs in Nenana complex type sites, and other sites in the Tanana Valley. Component I of the Owl Ridge site also has been ascribed to the Nenana complex and radiocarbon dated to 11,340 ± 150 BP (Beta-11209) (Phippen, 1988).

The relationship between the Nenana complex and somewhat earlier Tanana Valley sites is not well understood. Preliminary data suggest that both groups of sites share a number of common traits, and may be regional and temporal variants of a larger tradition or complex. With the notable exception of Swan Point, all lack evidence of microblade technology. All contain small triangular bifacially flaked projectile points, some of which have concave bases and are basally thinned, and many sites contain distinctive pointed ovate "Chindadn" bifaces.

Except for the few gastroliths, the original evidence from Dry Creek suggested that Nenana complex peoples were big game hunters primarily hunting elk and sheep. However, additional data from the Broken Mammoth site demonstrates a more generalized opportunistic gathering economy which included harvesting waterfowl, gathering eggs, and hunting and/or trapping small mammals. Large mammal hunting, particularly for bison, elk and sheep, was important. Proboscidean remains (mammoth or mastodon ivory) resulted from collecting fossil ivory rather than mammoth or mastodon hunting.

Trace element analysis indicates that obsidian from the Wrangell Mountains occurs in the lowest levels at Broken Mammoth and Walker Road sites. Obsidian from the Batza Tena source on the south side of the Brooks Range also occurs in Tanana Valley Nenana complex sites. These discoveries demonstrate that a widespread trade network was already in place in interior Alaska probably as early as ca. 11,700 BP (Hamilton and Goebel, 1999).

All sites ascribed to the Nenana complex were small camps generally located on bluffs with panoramic views. They appear to have been occupied by small groups of people for brief periods of time. No human remains or evidence of structures have yet been found and fires appear to have been built directly on the surface of the ground with little or no preparation of the area. Charcoal is generally scattered and relatively scarce for dating purposes. Minute unidentifiable calcined bone fragments have been recovered frequently from these hearths, suggesting bone was burned as fuel, for ritual purposes, or to keep camps clean. Red ochre has been reported associated with several Nenana complex occupations (Goebel and Powers, 1989; Phippen, 1988, p. 118; Powers and Hoffecker, 1990, p. 281, Holmes et al., 1996).

Most sites were probably open-air camps probably using skin tents or temporary tent-like structures. Although no structural remains were discovered, the spatial distribution of more than 130 artifacts around a circular clay-lined hearth at the Walker Road site were interpreted to be the location of a circular tent about 5 m in diameter (Goebel and Powers, 1989; Powers et al., 1990). The full range of the Nenana complex settlement pattern and subsistence cycle is still poorly understood.

AMERICAN PALEOARCTIC TRADITION (ca. 10,500–7000 BP)

Anderson (1970, p. 69) first defined the American Paleoarctic tradition to include the Akmak and Band 8 assemblages from the Onion Portage site, the early microblades from the Trail Creek Caves, and various undated assemblages from the Brooks Range characterized by wedged-shaped microblade cores, microblades, and other artifact types. Since that time the American Paleoarctic tradition has been used to lump a wide variety of early microblade and microcore assemblages which are widely dispersed throughout eastern Beringia (Figure 4).

Because so many regional variants and different economic systems have been subsumed under the American Paleoarctic tradition, the term has lost much of its descriptive utility and is no longer very useful as a tradition in classic definition of the term. It has been divided into three basic units: (1) the American Paleoarctic tradition, (2) the Denali complex, and (3) the Northwest Coast Microblade tradition (Dixon, 2002).

The diagnostic lithic artifacts associated with the American Paleoarctic tradition include wedge-shaped microblade cores, microblades, blades and blade cores, core bifaces, antler arrow points slotted to receive microblades, grooved stone abraders, and waste flakes. The geographic distribution includes the coastal margins of Bering and Chukchi seas, the Arctic Ocean, and adjacent terrestrial environments. It extends south roughly to the limit of winter sea ice. Economically, it probably had two aspects, (1) marine mammal hunting, including winter sea ice hunting and (2) exploitation of adjacent non-coastal regions to fish and hunt for terrestrial mammals. When moving inland from the coast, it is difficult to identify where economies based solely on interior environments begin and coastal economic practices are abandoned. Perhaps these different economies are best viewed as gradational, with greater and greater reliance placed on non-marine resources as one moves away from the coast toward the interior.

1. Anangula
2. Ugashik Narrows
3. Kivichak Bay
4. Trail Creek Caves
5. Onion Portage
6. Gallagher Flint Station
7. Bluefish Caves
8. Campus Site
9. Dry Creek
10. Panguingue Creek
11. Susitna Sites
12. Healy Lake
13. Tangle Lakes
14. Beluga Point
15. Craig Point
16. Ground Hog Bay
17. Hidden Falls
18. PET-408
19. Chuck Lake
20. Thorne Bay
21. Skoglund's Landing
22. Arrow Creek 2
23. Namu
24. Glenrose Cannery

Figure 4. *Map depicting the location of important archeological sites and site components ascribed to the American Paleoarctic tradition (modified from Dixon, 1993, and reproduced courtesy of E. J. Dixon and the University of New Mexico Press).*

The archeological record is obscured along Bering and Chukchi Sea coasts because of Holocene sea level rise. However, the persistence of the American Paleoarctic tradition is suggested along the Bering Sea coast. For example, Anderson (1986, p. 313) suggests that the Lower Bench site at Cape Krusenstern may be a transitional microblade assemblage between the American Paleoarctic tradition and the later Arctic Small Tool tradition. Shortly after sea level stabilized, there is widespread recognition of the Arctic Small Tool tradition along the Bering and Chukchi Sea coast. In regions where tectonic uplift or isostatic rebound have outpaced sea level rise, such as Anangula Island, it is clear from the location of the sites adjacent to the sea that they were adapted to a marine economy.

A single ^{14}C determination from Locality 1 at the Gallagher Flint Station may suggest that American Paleoarctic populations may have been in place in interior areas adjacent to the coast possibly as early as ca. 10,500 (Dixon, 1975). On the Alaska Peninsula, Paleoarctic tradition occupations are documented from the lowest levels of the Ugashik Narrows site and at Kvichak Bay (Dumond, 1977; Dumond et al., 1976; Henn, 1978). Five radiocarbon determinations indicate that these assemblages range between ca. 9000 and 7000 BP. The Ugashik Narrows site, located along a river with a major salmon run, where large mammals such as caribou and moose may easily cross the river, suggests that fishing and large-mammal hunting were important economic activities.

THE DENALI COMPLEX (10,500–8000 BP)

Throughout interior Alaska and the Yukon Territory, a number of archeological sites have been documented to date between ca. 10,500 and 8000 BP and contain bifacial biconvex knives, end scrapers, large blades and blade-like flakes, prepared microblade cores, core tablets, microblades, burins, burin spalls, worked flakes, and retouched flakes. This suite of artifacts was defined by West (1967, 1974) as the Denali complex. Since that time the list of associated lithic traits has been increased to include large blade cores, straight and convex based projectile points with constricting sides, elongate bifaces, spokeshaves, and abraders. The term Denali complex is retained here because it has priority in the literature and is applied to a restricted region (interior regions of eastern Beringia lacking a coastal/marine economic component).

Component II at Dry Creek suggests that the Denali complex first appears in interior Alaska ca. 10,690 ± 250 based on the overall site stratigraphy and ^{14}C dating (Powers and Hoffecker, 1989). Component II at nearby Panguingue Creek has several ^{14}C determinations bracketing this occupation between 8500 and 7500 BP (Powers and Maxwell, 1986; Goebel and Bigelow, 1996). West (1996, pp. 375–380; West and others, 1996, pp. 381–408) reports numerous sites from glacial terrain in the Tangle Lakes region of the south-central Alaska Range which contain typical Denali complex assemblages. All are relatively shallow sites (less than 50 cm deep) primarily situated on the top of glacial features, some of which appear to have reliable radiocarbon determinations dating Denali complex occupations between ca. 10,500 and 8000 BP. Numerous other sites containing Denali complex occupations have been reported throughout the interior, including the Healy Lake Village site (Cook, 1969; Cook and Mckennan, 1970). In the upper Susitna River drainage, Dixon and Smith (1990) identified six sites which they ascribed to the Denali complex based on typological traits, stratigraphic position within a series of regional tephras, and radiocarbon dating. The Campus site is now considered to be late Holocene in age based on a reevaluation of the site and associated artifacts by Mobly (1991).

Numerous Denali complex sites have been reported from a variety of ecological settings throughout interior eastern Beringia. The ecological setting of interior sites indicate an economy which included large mammal hunting and freshwater aquatic resources. Faunal remains from Component II at Dry Creek include bison and sheep. Many of the sites in the Alaska Range and Susitna River drainage are ideally situated for caribou hunting. Although data are sketchy, most sites are relatively small, lacking evidence of structures or other features which might be indicative of permanent or semi-permanent settlements. Organic artifacts are rare and little is known about these residents of the interior.

THE NORTHWEST COAST MICROBLADE TRADITION (ca. 10,500– <7000 BP)

This tradition was first called the Early Boreal tradition (Borden, 1969, 1975), and later given a variety of names, including the Early Coast Microblade complex (Fladmark, 1975), the Microblade tradition (Carlson, 1979, 1981), Early Coast and North Coast Microblade complex (Fladmark, 1982), the Marine Paleoarctic tradition (Davis, 1989), and the Maritime Paleoarctic tradition (Jordan, 1992). Rather than add to this confusing nomenclature, this presentation simply uses the term Northwest Coast Microblade tradition, which is in keeping with Fladmark (1975) and descriptively includes both the geographic area and hallmark technological trait, the shared use of microblade technology. These sites extend from the Kodiak Archipelago southeastward along the Pacific Rim through southeast Alaska, British Columbia, Washington, Oregon and the northern Great Basin (Dumond, 1962).

A marine economy is indicated for most sites by faunal remains, ecological settings and isotope analysis of human remains from Prince of Wales Island (Dixon et al., 1997). The northern geographic limit of this tradition is difficult to ascertain, but could extend to the south side of the Alaska Peninsula where there is no winter pack ice. Marine subsistence in the Northwest Coast Microblade tradition is adapted to year-round open water, rugged forested coasts characterized by fjords, islands, and rocky headlands, calving glaciers, major salmon runs, salt water fishing and intertidal shellfish resources.

It has not been determined when this tradition first appeared along the Northwest Coast. Rising sea level inundated most coastal areas older than ca. 9500 BP. Preserved sites include Beluga Point ca. 7000–8000 BP (Reger, 1996, p. 434). Craig Point, 7790 ± 620 BP (Jordan, 1992), Component III, Ground Hog Bay 2, 10,180 ± 800 and 9130 ± 130 BP (Ackerman et al., 1979; Ackerman, 1996a, b). Hidden Falls, Component I, ca. 9000 BP (Davis, 1989, p. 194), Locality 1 at the Chuck Lake, Locality 1, ca. 8200 BP (Ackerman et al., 1985), Rice Creek, ca. 9000 BP (Ackerman, 1996a, b, pp. 127 and 130), and the Thorne River site ca. 7500 BP (Holmes, 1988; Holmes et al., 1989). Obsidian from Hidden Falls and Ground Hog Bay is from Sumez Island (adjacent to Prince of Wales in the Alexander Archipelago) and Mt. Edziza (upper Sitkine River, northern British Columbia) (Nelson, 1976, cited in Ackerman, 1996a, b). This early trade in obsidian required the use of watercraft (Ackerman, 1992; Davis, 1989; Erlandson et al., 1992), and implies that the area must have been occupied earlier in order to discover these obsidian sources and develop trade networks.

PET-408 is located on the northern end of Prince of Wales Island, southeast Alaska. Human skeletal remains from this site have been ^{14}C dated to ca. 9800 BP.

(Dixon et al., 1997). Isotopic values for the human bone indicate a diet based primarily on marine resources and $\delta^{13}C$ values for the human bone are similar to those obtained for ringed seal, sea otter, and marine fish. These data indicate a diet based primarily on sea foods and that the marine carbon reservoir has affected the accuracy of the ^{14}C determinations. In the Queen Charlotte Islands to the south, a ca. 600 year ^{14}C difference in the regional marine and atmospheric carbon cycles has been documented by comparison of ^{14}C determinations on wood and shell (Fedje, Mackie, McSporran and Wilson, 1996, p. 118). This suggests that the dates on the human remains from PET-408 should be corrected by subtracting ca. 600 ^{14}C years. Presuming this correction factor can be applied to Prince of Wales Island, the corrected age for the human is ca. 9200 BP.

The human remains from PET-408 are probably contemporaneous with a microblade bearing cultural horizon at the site which has been dated by ^{14}C wood charcoal to ca. 9200 BP (Dixon et al., 1997). This demonstrates a maritime adaptation by microblade-using peoples along the Northwest Coast by ca. 9200 BP. An individual bone tool, possibly an awl or punch, manufactured from terrestrial mammal bone from 49-PET-408 has been AMS dated to 10,300 ± 50 BP (CAMS-42381). This ^{14}C determination and other evidence suggest that PET-408 was occupied during the late Pleistocene.

Fedje and Josenhans (pers. comm., 1998) recovered a basalt blade-like flake from the continental shelf of British Columbia. Based on local sea level rise at the end of the Pleistocene, this locale would probably have been covered by rising sea level about or shortly before 10,000 BP, thus suggesting the site may have been occupied ca. 10,300 BP (Josenhans et al., 1997). Although these data and the ca. 10,300 BP date on a bone tool from PET-4089 are preliminary, they suggest humans occupied the Northwest Coast of North America at the end of the last ice age when sea level was lower and the continental margins of western North America were exposed as dry land.

In coastal British Columbia, Fladmark (1982) defined an early Holocene cultural complex contemporaneous with early southeast Alaska sites (Carlson, 1990, 1996; Fladmark, 1990; Stryd and Rousseau, 1996; Fedje et al., 1996; and others). Despite the more extensive research in British Columbia, there are few sites reported which can be demonstrated to be older than 10,000 BP (Hobler, 1978; Fladmark, 1979). Hobler (1978) reports flakes and flake cores from intertidal sites in the Queen Charlotte Islands which are presumed to have been deposited prior to sea level rise ca. 10,000 BP. The earliest cultural component at the Skoglund's Landing site is ca. 8500–9000 BP (Fladmark, 1979). Fedje et al. (1996) report early Holocene ^{14}C determinations of ca. 9200 BP for Arrow Creek 2.

Collectively, these sites demonstrate widespread occupation by maritime adapted humans in southeast Alaska and British Columbia beginning sometime prior to 10,000 BP. Lithic artifacts include blocky and wedge-shaped microblade cores, microblades, utilized, notched and waste flakes, flake cores, rare bifaces,

scrapers, gravers, and choppers. Obsidian was traded widely and the use of watercraft is inferentially demonstrated by the widespread trade in obsidian, fishing for off-shore bottom fish, marine mammal hunting, and the location of sites on islands and other settings accessible from the sea.

NORTHERN PALEOINDIAN TRADITION (ca. 10,500-8000 BP)

Fluted projectile points and related lanceolate forms have been found throughout eastern Beringia (Figure 5). The fluted projectile points from eastern Beringia have come from sites which either have not been dated or for which the dating is ambiguous. Most scholars have assumed a historical relationship between Paleoindian projectile points from eastern Beringia and those from the southern Plains of western North America based on their morphological similarity. Fluted projectile points have been found primarily in the northern areas of Beringia along the north and south sides of the Brooks Range. A few examples are also reported from regions in central interior Alaska.

Numerous sites containing fluted projectile points from eastern Beringia are part of the larger North American Paleoindian tradition usually associated with the western United States (Dixon, 1993, pp. 15–23). By including the northern examples within the larger Paleoindian tradition the underlying assumption is made that the peoples who made and used these tools in eastern Beringia were part of a larger population of peoples who shared a similar way of life and economic system. This assumption is supported by the fact that most of the northern sites appear to be situated in locales best suited for big game hunting, a strong economic focus of Paleoindians to the south.

There are three hypotheses which address the relationships between the northern and southern Paleoindian assemblages (Clark, 1984a, b): (1) northern Paleoindian artifacts were left by the first humans to reach Alaska and later moved southward, (2) fluted projectile points developed in the more southern regions of North America and spread northward into eastern Beringia, or (3) fluted points were independently invented in eastern Beringia thousands of years after those to the south. This technology could also have developed rapidly from the Nenana complex as it spread south (Goebel et al., 1991). While some Paleoindian sites are known to contain large blades and blade-like flakes, Paleoindian tradition peoples did not manufacture microblades or use side blade insets.

Comparative analysis using cumulative percentage curves and cluster analysis demonstrates a close relationship between the Nenana and Clovis complexes suggesting two explanations for the similarities: (1) (following Haynes, 1987; and others) that humans crossed the Bering Land Bridge sometime between 12,000 and 13,000 BP and rapidly moved south "through the Ice-Free Corridor" and that both Clovis and the Nenana complexes were derived from this migration, or (2) that both complexes are technologically derived from an

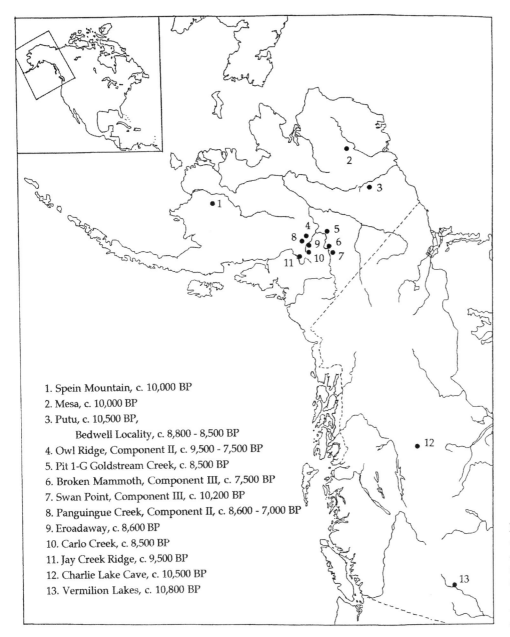

1. Spein Mountain, c. 10,000 BP
2. Mesa, c. 10,000 BP
3. Putu, c. 10,500 BP,
   Bedwell Locality, c. 8,800 - 8,500 BP
4. Owl Ridge, Component II, c. 9,500 - 7,500 BP
5. Pit 1-G Goldstream Creek, c. 8,500 BP
6. Broken Mammoth, Component III, c. 7,500 BP
7. Swan Point, Component III, c. 10,200 BP
8. Panguingue Creek, Component II, c. 8,600 - 7,000 BP
9. Eroadaway, c. 8,600 BP
10. Carlo Creek, c. 8,500 BP
11. Jay Creek Ridge, c. 9,500 BP
12. Charlie Lake Cave, c. 10,500 BP
13. Vermilion Lakes, c. 10,800 BP

Figure 5. *Map depicting the location of important archeological sites and site components ascribed to the Northern Paleoindian tradition (reproduced from Dixon, 1999, courtesy of E. J. Dixon and the University of New Mexico Press).*

earlier migration which hypothetically took place before the "closing of the Ice-Free Corridor" ca. 22,000–25,000 BP (Goebel et al., 1991).

It is also possible that the Nenana and Clovis complexes are inland adaptations derived from an earlier migration along the western coast of the Americas near the end of the Pleistocene ca. 13,500 BP (Dixon, 1993). This hypothesis is strengthened by evidence indicating that Clovis peoples may have used the coast. Several Clovis or Clovis-like sites have been reported near or adjacent to the west coast of North America. The Richie Roberts Clovis cache near Wenatchee, Washington is less than 150 km from the ocean. Clovis points have been reported from a coastal site in Mendocino County, California (Simons et al., 1985), and on the coast near Santa Barbara (Erlandson et al., 1987; Erlandson and Moss, 1996). Because sea level was lower at the time these sites were occupied their distance from the coast would have been somewhat greater than it is today.

The Mesa site has 14 radiocarbon determinations ranging between ca. 11,660 and 9730 BP, derived from 15 hearths at the site (Kunz and Reanier, 1996). Only two dates (derived from the same "split" charcoal sample) exceed 11,000 BP. They appear to be statistical outliers, possibly resulting from burning fossil wood (Hamilton and Goebel, 1999). All the remaining dates cluster around 10,000 BP, suggesting this is an accurate date for the Mesa occupation. The projectile points are typologically similar to Agate Basin projectile points from the high plains (Frison and Stanford, 1982). The two pre-11,000 BP dates and the geographic location of the site have led some researchers to suggest that Mesa "culture" may be ancestral to Agate Basin sites from more southern areas of North America (Kunz et al., 1994, 1995; Kunz and Shelley, 1994; Kunz and Reanier, 1996).

The Putu site has two localities which frequently have been treated as separate sites, the Putu and Bedwell sites (Alexander, 1974, 1987; Morlan, 1977; Dumond, 1980; Clark and Clark, 1983; Clark, 1984a, b, 1991; Kunz and Reanier, 1994). The lower component at the Putu locality contains fluted projectile points. A single radiocarbon date of 11,470 ± 500 was originally believed to date the fluted points, but reevaluation by Reanier (1995, 1996) demonstrates that two other dates, 8450 ± 130 and 8810 ± 60, probably more accurately date the lower component. Reanier (1995, 1996) obtained an AMS ^{14}C date on charcoal collected during the original excavation of the Bedwell locality which dated to 10,490 ± 70 (Beta 69895, CAMS-11032). Based on comparison of the projectile points with similar specimens from the Mesa site, Reanier suggests this ^{14}C determination may date the Bedwell occupation.

Spein Mountain extends the range of the Northern Paleoindian tradition to southwestern Alaska (Ackerman, 1996a, b), and is dated to 10,050 ± 90 (BETA-64471, CAMS-8281). The site lacks microblades or evidence of microblade technology and contains bifacially flaked lanceolate projectile points with constricting bases and other artifact types attributable to the Northern Paleoindian tradition that are similar to artifacts from the Mesa Site and Bedwell sites (Ackerman, 1996a, b, p. 460).

There are a number of isolated surface finds typologically characteristic of Northern Paleoindian tradition projectile points that have been found throughout Alaska and the Yukon Territory. In addition, Northern Paleoindian sites have been excavated in central interior Alaska which date between 10,500 and 8500 BP. These are Component I at the Carlo Creek site dating to ca. 8500 BP (Bowers, 1980), the Jay Creek Ridge site occupied ca. 9500 BP based on six ^{14}C AMS determinations (Dixon, 1993, pp. 85–87), the Eroadaway site (Holmes, 1988), the Eroadaway site dated to 8640 ± 170 BP (WSU-3683) (Holmes, 1988, p. 3), and Component II at the Owl Ridge site dated by four ^{14}C determinations between 7500 and 9500 BP (Phippen, 1988). Yesner et al. (1992) report occupations dating ca. 7500 BP from the Broken Mammoth and Mead sites which also lack evidence of microblade technology but which contain bifacial stone tools. Although Component II dating ca. 8600 and 7000 BP at Panguingue Creek (Powers and Hoffecker, 1989, p. 276, Powers and Maxwell, 1986) has been ascribed to the American Paleoarctic tradition, this component does not contain microblade technology but does contain bifacial tools.

A series of four ^{14}C determinations suggests that Cultural Zone III at the Broken Mammoth site was occupied ca. 10,300 BP. Zone III contains waste flakes, point fragments, two small "trianguloid" basally ground projectile points, large biface and point fragments, quartz hammer stones, and a small eyed bone needle (Holmes and Yesner, 1992b; Yesner et al., 1993; Yesner, 1996; Hamilton and Goebel, 1999). At the Swan Point site, Cultural Component III dated to 10,230 ± 80 BP (Beta-56666, CAMS-4252) contains strait and convex-based small lanceolate projectile points as well as thin triangular points.

Two exceptionally well-preserved bone projectile points recovered from Pit 1-G, on Goldstream Creek

were reported by Rainey (1939, p. 393). Two AMS ^{14}C radiocarbon determinations indicate they were probably manufactured ca. 8500 BP. These specimens were not slotted to receive microblade insets and they are probably atlatl dart points (Dixon, 1999).

Sites and site components ascribed to the Northern Paleoindian tradition all contain projectile points similar to Paleoindian sites elsewhere in North America. All lack evidence of a microblade industry. Several sites, including Carlo Creek and Eroadaway, suggest that the Northern Paleoindian tradition persisted for a considerable length of time in eastern Beringia. Although some of these sites might represent a continuum from the Nenana complex in Alaska's interior (Dixon, 1993), it is equally plausible that they are later regional manifestations of the Northern Paleoindian tradition, possibly incorporating both Nenana complex and Northern Paleoindian tradition technological traits.

Because the earliest reliable ^{14}C determinations for the Northern Paleoindian tradition are no older than ca. 10,500 BP, the Paleoindian tradition is younger in eastern Beringia than in more southern areas of North America. It appears that Paleoindian projectile point types derived from the northern Plains may have arrived in eastern Beringia beginning ca. 10,500 BP, following partition of the continental ice. This interpretation is supported by the discovery of a Clovis component at Charlie Lake Cave in northeastern British Columbia dated to ca. 10,550 BP (Fladmark et al., 1986; Driver, 1996; Driver et al., 1996), and at Vermilion Lake in Banff National Park in Alberta, Canada (Fedje et al., 1995). At Vermilion Lake, Fedje et al. (1995) have documented an assemblage ascribed to the "Late Fluted Point tradition" possibly dating as early as 10,800 BP based on ^{14}C determinations from other typologically similar sites.

Northern Paleoindian projectile points do not exhibit the full typological array of Paleoindian projectile points from the more southern regions of North America. While most of the early fluted types exhibit multiple flutes, concave bases and edge grinding, among the northern assemblages large Clovis points are rare and classic Folsom points have not been found. Later lanceolate forms resemble tapering stemmed forms similar to Agate Basin and Hell Gap points. These differences led some archeologists (Wormington, 1968; Dixon, 1976) to propose the south-to-north spread of Paleoindian technology based on the fact that the northern examples looked typologically later than the those found on the western Plains. Dixon (1976) suggested the south-to-north spread of this technology may have occurred ca. 10,000 BP, but more contemporary data suggest it may have been earlier, probably ca. 10,500 BP.

ARCHEOLOGICAL SUMMARY

The earliest archeology of eastern Beringia is ascribed to the Nenana complex, characterized by triangular bifacial projectile points and ovate knives. Widespread trade in obsidian was already established indicating occupation of Alaska prior to that time. The occurrence of "scavenged fossil ivory" at several sites implies that mammoth or mastodon remains were being scavenged by ca. 11,600 BP. No mammoth or mastodon kill sites have been found in eastern Beringia, although controversial blood residue analysis of fluted projectile points suggests that mammoth may have persisted until ca. 10,500 BP in some areas of eastern Beringia (Dixon, 1993; Loy and Dixon, 1998).

The Nenana complex begins sometime prior to 11,600 BP and persists until ca. 10,500 at which time it becomes difficult to distinguish from the Northern Paleoindian tradition in interior Alaska. This suggests a possible "blending" of technological traits of the Nenana complex and Northern Paleoindian tradition. Although not entirely conclusive, it appears that the Nenana complex did not manufacture microblades. The Northern Paleoindian tradition existed in regions of eastern Beringia as a co-tradition with the American Paleoarctic tradition between ca. 10,500–8000 BP. This tradition spread northward into eastern Beringia from the northern Plains.

Distinctive microblade technologies were introduced into eastern Beringia sometime around 10,500 BP and are contemporaneous with the Northern Paleoindian tradition. The Denali complex represents an inland adaptation by microblade using peoples. The American Paleoarctic and Northwest Coast Microblade traditions are found in near coastal areas suggesting subsistence activities related to coastal and adjacent inland resources. Trade in obsidian, site locations, and faunal remains inferentially demonstrate the use of watercraft prior to 10,000 BP along the Northwest Coast.

This analysis does not support the traditional Bering Land Bridge theory of human migration to the Americas, which postulates that hunters of large terrestrial mammal using Clovis-like projectile points crossed the Bering Land Bridge and descended from Beringia to the Plains of North America ca. 11,500 BP. Archeological research demonstrates that pre-Clovis sites exist at Monte Verde, in eastern Beringia, and probably at other sites throughout the Americas. The northern movement of the Paleoindian tradition ca. 10,500 BP demonstrates that humans were south of the continental glaciers prior to deglaciation ca. 11,000 BP and that the Clovis complex is an independent New World cultural development. Technological similarities between the contemporaneous Nenana and Clovis complexes may result from the fact that both are derived from a common cultural predecessor.

WEAPON SYSTEMS

The width of the projectile point at the place where it is hafted helps to define the size of the shaft to which it was attached. This along with the size and weight of Nenana, Clovis, and later Paleoindian projectile points suggests that they were attached to atlatl darts and not used to tip arrows. These projectile points are conceptually very different than composite projectile points

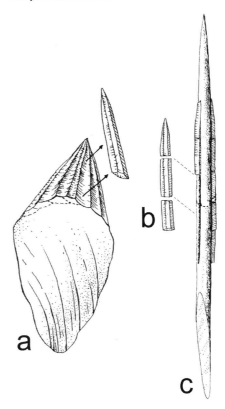

Figure 6. *The process of producing a composite projectile point with microblade insets. (a) microblade removal from a microblade core (view from core platform), (b) microblade, proximal, medial and distal segments, (c) medial fragment inset into an organic projectile point (modified from Dixon, 1999, reproduced courtesy of E. J. Dixon and the University of New Mexico Press).*

manufactured by setting microblades in organic points. The American Paleoarctic tradition used thin parallel sided stone microblades struck from specially prepared stone cores to create cutting edges. The microblades were inset along longitudinal grooves incised in bone, antler, or ivory projectile points to form razor-sharp cutting edges along the margins of projectile points manufactured from organic materials (Figure 6).

The bifacial stone and composite projectile point manufacturing techniques are fundamentally different approaches to producing the same type of artifact, the projectile point (Dixon, 1993). These two contrasting conceptual approaches to the manufacture of weapon systems suggest that other profound differences in technological and social concepts existed between these peoples.

The manufacture of microblades and composite projectile points is geographically restricted to Eurasia, Alaska and northwest Canada. The vast region of interior Alaska and adjacent Canada was a transitional area between more Eurasian-oriented microblade traditions and non-microblade bifacial traditions of North America. The boundaries between these technological traditions shifted repeatedly over time and consequently some archeological sites provide a sequence of non-microblade/microblade technologies when viewed at a single geographic locale.

COLONIZATION EVENTS

From a technological perspective, there appear to be two major colonizing events in the Americas. The first was an early migration by the ancestors of the Clovis/Nenana complexes sometime before ca. 11,500 BP and possibly as early as ca. 13,500 BP. These people used atlatl darts tipped with bifacially flaked stone end blades lashed to harpoon-like heads seated on bone foreshafts. They did not manufacture microblades and did not use the bow and arrow. The atlatl remained the primary weapon system in South America and temperate and southern regions of North America until Archaic times.

The second colonization event was by peoples bearing the American Paleoarctic tradition ca. 10,500 BP. Although they probably used the atlatl, they also introduced the bow and arrow. This included the complex technique of manufacturing composite projectile points which were characterized by insetting razor sharp stone microblades along the sides of bone and antler projectile points.

Although both populations required effective projectile points essential in hunter/gatherer societies, each developed unique approaches to manufacturing them. Nenana/Clovis peoples relied primarily on reducing a lithic core by flaking away excess rock to create a flaked stone projectile point, or biface. American Paleoarctic peoples engaged in a complex technological sequence of "building" projectile points by inserting microblades in slots carved along the sides of cylindrical bone or antler projectile points. These conceptually complex and different approaches successfully solved the same problem, suggesting that the differences result from learned behavior passed from generation to generation. Other profound differences may have existed between these two groups, possibly including biological and linguistic traits, as well as technological and social concepts.

The limited physical anthropological data also imply two distinct human groups emigrated to the Americas. Steele and Powell (1992) have concluded that the human cranial and facial characteristics from the Americas that are over 8500 BP are distinctively different than later Native Americans. Distinguishing features identified by physical anthropologists for these very early New World peoples are: longer, more narrow faces; and smaller more narrow nasal apertures (Steele and Powell, 1992; Chatters, 1997; Jantz and Owsley, 1997). These early remains from the Americas tend to display craniofacial features which are more similar to southern Asian and European populations.

They were followed by a second population bearing greater resemblance to contemporary northern Asians and Native Americans. Although rapid evolutionary change could explain the differences between the earlier (older than ca. 8000 BP) and later Native American populations, they more likely represent two distinct populations. The older group has been described as being more "Caucasoid" in appearance and they resemble the Ainu of northern Japan. If these comparisons are accurate, then both early technological evidence and physical anthropological data might suggest a possible point of origin for the earliest Americans in the maritime regions of northeast Asia.

COASTAL MIGRATION

Prior to the early 1970s, it had been assumed that the Cordilleran ice extended westward to the margins of the continental shelf thus creating a barrier to human migration (Coulter et al., 1965; Nasmith, 1970; Prest, 1969). More recent geologic and paleoecologic studies document deglaciation and the existence of ice-free areas throughout major coastal areas of British Columbia by ca. 13,000 BP (Blaise et al., 1990; Bobrowsky et al., 1990). It is now clear that areas of continental shelf and off-shore islands were not covered by ice during and toward the end of the last glacial. Vast areas along the coast may have been deglaciated beginning about 16,000 BP. Except for a 400-km coastal area between southwest British Columbia and Washington state, the Northwest Coast of North America was largely free of ice by ca. 16,000 years ago (Mann and Peteet, 1995). The exposed continental shelf and off-shore islands were available as a migration route between 13,500 and 9500 BP (Josenhans et al., 1995, 1997), possibly enabling people to colonize ice-free regions along the continental shelf exposed by lower sea level.

Because of the misleading early geologic interpretations, the region has not been subject to research equivalent to that which has occurred in non-coastal eastern Beringia, but significant advances are now being made. The remains of large omnivores, such as black and brown bears, and other land animals, including caribou, have been found in southeast Alaska dating between 12,500 and 10,000 BP (Heaton, 1995, 1996; Heaton and Grady, 1993; Heaton et al., 1996) demonstrating that sufficient subsistence resources were available to support humans (Dixon, 1995). The Northwest Coast Microblade tradition is documented as early as 10,000 BP in British Columbia and southeast Alaska. Archeological sites ascribed to this tradition share the use of microblades, and exhibit a marine economy documented by limited faunal remains and isotopic analysis of human remains (Dixon et al., 1997), and the ecological setting of the sites (Figure 7).

THE MODEL

The model for human colonization of the Americas suggested by the most current data are coastal migration with inland movement and settlement within broad environmental zones, or megapatches that extend from north to south throughout the Americas. Migration probably occurred in many directions at the same time. For example, some people may have been moving more rapidly southward along the Pacific Coast of the Americas while others were colonizing more slowly eastward from the coast to the interior of the continents.

This model is drastically different than the traditional Beringian crossing and subsequent unidirectional "migration" from north to south, cross-cutting

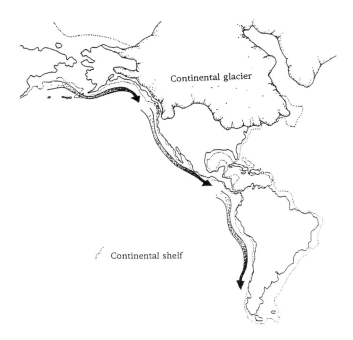

Figure 7. *Map depicting the hypothetical coastal migration hypothesis (reproduced from Dixon, 1999, courtesy of E. J. Dixon and the University of New Mexico Press).*

terrestrial mammal hunting are more dependent on a few strong adults to bring down large mammals. Large mammal hunting also requires greater territorial movement and presents greater difficulty for human groups, which realistically include the elderly, the very young, pregnant women, and the infirm. Current data from some of the earliest sites in the Americas, including the Aubery (Ferring, 1989, 1990, 1995), Horn Shelter in Texas (Forrester, 1985; Redder, 1985; Young, 1985; Young et al., 1987), a Clovis age rock shelter near the California–Oregon border (Beaton, 1991b), Lewisville (Stanford, pers. comm.), and numerous other sites, indicate subsistence traditions based on foraging rather than specialized large mammal hunting. Local abundance of marine and intertidal resources and predictable runs of anadromous fish concentrated human populations in specific locales such as sheltered bays, inlets, estuaries, and salmon spawning streams.

Temperate coastal technological adaptations rely heavily on readily available materials such as driftwood, marine mammal products, beach cobbles, and shell, which in many cases may have been already partially modified by noncultural processes. In such an environment, reliance on sophisticated lithic technologies was probably not as important as in other environments. For example, preshaped and prepolished sling and bola

environmental zones and a wide array of physical obstacles. Colonization along large environmental zones is more consistent with New World archeological data and enables seemingly conflicting evidence to be reconciled into a single rational model for colonization of the Americas. Figure 8 schematically portrays how colonization may have occurred along major environmental zones at arbitrary 500-year intervals beginning at ca. 13,000 BP. Extreme northeast North America and Greenland were not sufficiently deglaciated to permit colonization until about 5000 BP.

This alternative model proposes that initial human colonization of the Americas may have begun ca. 14,000–13,500 BP along the southern margin of the Bering Land Bridge and then southward along the Pacific Coast of the Americas. With the use of watercraft, the human population moved rapidly southward along the coastal–intertidal Pacific biome, or "megapatch". Even though evidence of this early migration may be obscured by rising sea level at the end of the last ice age, evidence might be expected to be found in adjacent areas of the interior, such as Monte Verde. Although it would have been somewhat further from the sea at the time it was occupied than it is today, Monte Verde is located along a river drainage only 15 km northeast of the Pacific Ocean. If this model is correct, the Pacific Coast of the Americas could have been occupied thousands of years before the continental ice in North America melted.

Coastal environments provide many ecological advantages for generalized foragers, an economic adaptation best suited for colonizing populations. For example, intertidal resources, such as shellfish, may be harvested by children and the elderly and simply eaten raw. On the other hand, hunters specializing in large

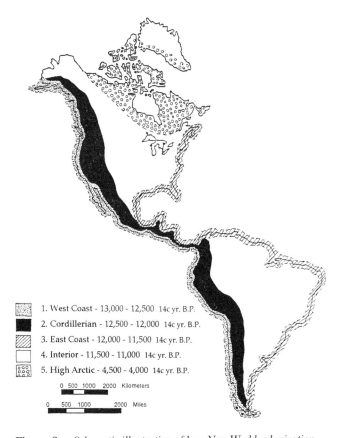

1. West Coast - 13,000 - 12,500 14c yr. B.P.
2. Cordillerian - 12,500 - 12,000 14c yr. B.P.
3. East Coast - 12,000 - 11,500 14c yr. B.P.
4. Interior - 11,500 - 11,000 14c yr. B.P.
5. High Arctic - 4,500 - 4,000 14c yr. B.P.

0 500 1000   2000 Kilometers

0 500 1000   2000 Miles

Figure 8. *Schematic illustration of how New World colonization may have occurred along major environmental zones at arbitrary 500 year intervals. Extreme northeast North America and Greenland were not sufficiently deglaciated to permit colonization until ca. 5000 BP (reproduced from Dixon, 1999, courtesy of E. J. Dixon and the University of New Mexico Press).*

Part IX: Evolution of *Homo sapiens*

stones, the only lithic material required for two effective, deadly weapons, can be easily and efficiently collected from noncultural beach deposits. Monte Verde provides a rare glimpse into this type of technological adaptation. At Monte Verde people produced and used few bifacially flaked stone tools and relied heavily on simple flakes and organic materials.

From an original and theoretical maritime subsistence strategy, several adaptive trajectories were possible as humans expanded across the landscape. Survival may have been best assured by the continuation of a pattern of general foraging, which could be adjusted or modified based on availability of resources and increasing knowledge of local geography and biological patterns. For example, along the west coast people may have continued their ancient adaptation to shellfish gathering, fishing, and marine mammal hunting. In interior regions of southern California, Arizona and Mexico the pattern of general foraging may have led to an increasing emphasis on harvesting and processing plant products and seed grinding. On the Plains general foraging persisted throughout the Paleoindian period, but people emphasized and refined large mammal hunting, particularly communal mass kills.

Although the initial colonization along the continental margins of the Americas may have occurred rather quickly, subsequent colonization of interior environments probably occurred more slowly. People probably first moved inland from the coast along rivers. As population increased and people adapted to interior environments, colonization probably continued to progress along environmental zones.

Given this scenario, the western Plains of North America may have been among the last to be settled as well as one of the least hospitable environmental regions of the continent. Separated from the Pacific Coast by the vast cordillera, adaptation to intervening mountainous regions may have occurred slowly. Classic Clovis sites, such as Blackwater Draw and Murray Springs, containing evidence of spectacular mammoth predation, may be representative of a rather unique cultural, technological and ecological adaptation during late Pleistocene. In other words, the spectacular and well-publicized Clovis kill sites may be the least typical and the least useful sites for interpreting the peopling of the Americas and early New World adaptations.

Although Clovis is often associated with mammoth hunting, other data demonstrate that Clovis people may have placed greater emphasis on generalized gathering. Only 12 sites have been documented in North America where Clovis points have been found in association with mammoth remains (Haynes, 1991, pp. 197–197, 206). A more realistic portrayal of Clovis economics suggests that mammoth kill sites occur in marginal habitats that may have been some of the last to be colonized. Although these sites may provide the earliest evidence of human occupation in the western interior of North America, this region may have been among the last to be colonized.

Analysis of Paleoindian dentition (Powell and Steel, 1994) supports the hypothesis that Clovis and other early New World cultures have their adaptive roots as generalized foragers rather than specialized big game

hunters. The characteristics of dental wear in the oldest human remains from the Americas are virtually identical to those of generalized foragers. This demonstrates that these early diets included a broad array of foods and large amounts of plant fiber.

TECHNOLOGY

The lithic technology found at Monte Verde is characterized by the selection and use of naturally occurring stone and minimal modification of stones and other useful items found in the natural environment. This type of technological system probably originates from a generalized coastal economy which might have only occasional and comparatively rare need for bifacial projectile points to serve as harpoon end blades or possibly knives.

An intriguing connection between coastal migrations and mammoth hunting may lay in understanding the Clovis weapon system. It is characterized by the atlatl, or spear thrower, used to propel a short light weight spear, or dart. The dart is tipped with bifacially flaked stone Clovis projectile point believed to be mounted in a split-shaft harpoon-like haft, that is attached to a bone foreshaft (Stanford, 1996). The end blade, harpoon, and foreshaft assembly used for marine mammal hunting is essentially the same as the Paleoindian foreshaft, dart head and Clovis projectile point assembly suggested by Stanford (1997) (Figure 9). This suggests that

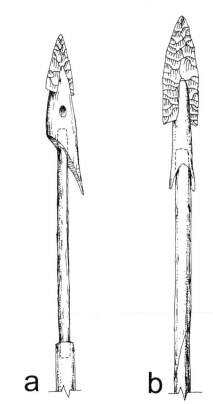

Figure 9. *Line drawing comparing the (a) detachable Clovis end blade, dart head, and foreshaft atlatl dart assembly (Stanford, 1996) and the (b) detachable marine mammal hunting end blade, harpoon head and foreshaft assembly used in marine mammal hunting (reproduced from Dixon, 1999, courtesy of E. J. Dixon and the University of New Mexico Press).*

the Clovis weapon system may have its origins in coastal marine mammal hunting technology that was subsequently adapted to hunting large terrestrial mammals. The diagnostic trait of basal thinning and fluting early Paleoindian projectile points may be derived from thinning the base of stone projectile points to make them fit easily into slotted harpoon heads designed for marine mammal hunting. This type of end blade assembly persisted until historic times among maritime hunters in northwestern North America and northeast Asia.

CONCLUSIONS

The initial colonization of the Americas used watercraft and occurred about 13,500 BP. This hypothesis is supported by the following:

1. The earliest deglaciated route was coastal. The deglaciated west coast of North America was first available for colonization by ca. 13,500. The interior route was blocked by the continental glaciers until about 11,000 when a deglaciation corridor developed between Beringia and the southern areas of North America ca. 11,000 BP.
2. Monte Verde, and other sites, predate the opening of the mid-continental route indicating peoples were south of the continental glaciers prior to deglaciation ca. 11,000 BP.
3. Reliably dated human remains first appear in North America between 11,000 and 11,500 BP, providing limiting minimum dates for human occupation and suggesting human colonization occurred earlier.
4. By about 11,000–12,000 BP regional cultural adaptation was well under way in North America, suggesting an earlier migration.
5. The Paleoindian tradition spread from south to north ca. 10,500 BP, indicating that people were south of the continental ice prior to deglaciation, ca. 11,000 BP.
6. Paleoindian subsistence data indicate an economic system rooted in general foraging, not specialized big game hunting.
7. The New World's first weapon system, the foreshaft/harpoon/end-blade atlatl dart assembly, may trace its origins to coastal marine mammal hunting, rather than large terrestrial mammal hunting.
8. Evidence from other regions of the world demonstrate that humans had watercraft and the ability to navigate near-shore ocean waters prior to 14,000 BP.
9. Technological and physical anthropological evidence suggests at least two major colonizing events, the first beginning possibly by ca. 13,500 BP using the atlatl and the second about 10,500 BP introducing the bow and arrow. However, the relationships, if any, between the two human physical types and the two major technological traditions are not clear.

Although it is imperative that New World archeologists keep their minds open to earlier human colonization of the Americas, the very limited data from the lower level at Monte Verde and controversial discoveries at other sites suggesting human occupation as early as 30,000–35,000 BP, are not adequate to demonstrate an earlier colonization event. A stronger suite of evidence will be required to convince most scientists, and most will be reluctant to accept a third and much earlier (ca. 30,000 BP) human migration to the Americas without additional evidence.

The coastal "corridor" provided the environmental avenue essential for the initial human entry to the Americas. The coast formed part of a continuous northern marine–intertidal ecosystem extending between northeast Asia and northwestern North America. It would have facilitated coastal navigation and provided similar subsistence resources in a continuous ecological zone linking the two hemispheres. Old World adaptations could have enabled rapid colonization without developing new technologies or subsistence strategies.

The intellectual dominance of the interior Beringian model for the colonization of the Americas by Eurasian large land mammal hunters has resulted in little archeological research directed toward New World colonization along the coastal regions of northeast Asia and the western coasts of the Americas. The concept of humans first entering the Americas via a Bering Land Bridge is almost 500 years old and was advanced and strengthened when science lacked the archeological and geologic evidence available today (de Acosta, 1604; Dawson, 1894; Johnston, 1933; Spinden, 1933; and others). Viewed in light of the coastal colonization hypothesis, the Bering Land Bridge played an important, but different, role in the peopling of the Americas. The Bering Land Bridge was essential for human colonization because it provided an uninterrupted marine–intertidal environment that facilitated intercoastal navigation connecting Eurasia and North America along its southern margin.

Archeological evidence necessary to evaluate the coastal migration hypothesis is difficult to find because rising sea level at the close of the Pleistocene inundated much of the continental shelf. If the coastal migration hypothesis is to be fully evaluated, the late Pleistocene coastal archeology of western North America requires research equivalent to that which has traditionally focused on the late Pleistocene/early Holocene archeology of mid-continental North America.

ACKNOWLEDGMENTS

The Denver Museum of Natural History supported the preparation of this manuscript and the University of New Mexico Press gave permission to use the figures. Special thanks to David M. Hopkins who was a catalyst for this paper and a mentor to so many of us who were able to participate in the 1997 Beringian Symposium.

REFERENCES

Ackerman, R. E., 1992. Earliest stone industries on the North Pacific coast of North America. Arctic Anthropology 29, 18–27.

Ackerman, R. E., 1996a. Early maritime culture complexes of the northern Northwest Coast. In: Carlson, R. L., Dallas Bona, L.

(Eds.), Early Human Occupation in British Columbia. University of British Columbia Press, Vancouver, pp. 123–132.

Ackerman, R. E., 1996b. Spein Mountain. In: West, F. H. (Ed.), American Beginnings. The University of Chicago Press, Chicago, pp. 456–460.

Ackerman, R. E., Hamilton, T. D., Stuckenrath, R., 1979. Early culture complexes on the northern Northwest Coast. Canadian Journal of Archaeology 3, 195–208.

Ackerman, R. E., Reir, K. C., Gallison, J. D., Roe, M. E., 1985. Archaeology of Heceta Island: a Survey of 18 Timber Harvest Units in the Tongass National Forest, Southeastern Alaska. Center for Northwest Anthropology, Washington State University, Pullman.

de Acosta, J., 1604. The Naturall and Morall Historie of the East and West Indies. Translated by Edward Grimston. Reprinted by Bart Franklin, New York, by permission of the Haakluyt Society.

Adovasio, J. M., Gunn, D., Donahue, J., Stuckenrath, R., 1977. Meadowcroft Rockshelter: retrospect 1976. Pennsylvania Archaeologist 47, 1–93.

Adovasio, J. M., Gunn, D., Donahue, J., Stuckenrath, R., 1978. Meadowcroft Rockshelter, 1977: an overview. American Antiquity 43, 632–651.

Adovasio, J. M., Gunn, D., Donahue, J., Stuckenrath, R., Guilday, E., Volman, K., 1980. Yes Virginia, it really is that old: a reply to Haynes and Mead. American Antiquity 45, 588–595.

Alexander, H. C., 1974. The association of aurignacoid elements with fluted point complexes in North America. In: Raymond, S., Schledermann, P. (Eds.), International Conference on Prehistory and Paleoecology of the Western North America Arctic and Sub Arctic. University of Calgary Archaeological Association, Calgary, pp. 21–31.

Alexander, H. L., 1987. Putu: a fluted point site in Alaska. Simon Fraser University Publication No. 17. Archaeology Press, Simon Fraser University, Burnaby, British Columbia.

Anderson, D. D., 1970. Akmak: an early archeological assemblage from Onion Portage, Northwest, Alaska. Acta Arctica, Fasc. XVI, 80 pp.

Bailliet, G., Rothhammer, F., Carnese, F. R., Bravi, C. M., Bianchi, N. O., 1994. Founder mitochondrial haplotypes in Amerindian populations. American Journal of Human Genetics 54, 27–33.

Beaton, J. M., 1991a. Colonizing continents: some problems for Australia and the Americas. In: Dillehay, T. D., Meltzer, D. J. (Eds.), The First Americans: Search and Research. CRP Press, Boca Raton, FL, pp. 209–230.

Beaton, J. M., 1991b. Paleoindian occupation greater than 11,000 yr B. P. at Tule Lake, northern California. Current Research in the Pleistocene 8, 5–7.

Berger, R., Protsh, R., 1989. UCLA radiocarbon dates XI. Radiocarbon 31, 55–67.

Birdsell, J. B., 1957. Some population problems involving Pleistocene man. Cold Spring Harbor Symposium Quantitative Biology 22, 47–69.

Blaise, B., Clague, J. J., Mathewes, R. W., 1990. Time of maximum Late Wisconsin glaciation, west coast of Canada. Quaternary Research 34, 282–295.

Bobrowsky, P. T., Catto, N. R., Brink, J. W., Spurling, B. E., Gibson, T. H., Rutter, N. W., 1990. Archaeological geology of sites in western and northwestern Canada. Geological Society of America, Centennial Special Vol. 4, pp. 87–122 (Chapter 5).

Borden, C. E., 1969. Early population movements from Asia into Western North America. Syesis 2, 113.

Bowers, P. M., 1980. The Carlo Creek site: geology and archaeology of an early Holocene site in the central Alaska Range. Anthropology and Historic Preservation, Cooperative Park Studies Unit, Occasional Paper, 27. Fairbanks, Alaska.

Bryan, A. (Ed.), 1978. Early man in America. Occasional Papers, Department of Anthropology, University of Alberta, Edmonton, No. 1., 327 pp.

Carlson, R. L., 1979. The early period on the central coast of British Columbia. Canadian Journal of Archaeology 3, 211–228.

Carlson, R. L., 1990. Cultural Antecedents. In: Sturtevant, W. C. (Ed.), Handbook of North American Indians, Vol. 7, Northwest Coast. Smithsonian Institution Press, Washington, DC, pp. 60–69.

Carter, G. F., 1952. Interglacial artifacts from the San Diego area. Southwestern Journal of Anthropology 8, 444–456.

Carter, G. F., 1957. Pleistocene Man at San Diego. The Johns Hopkins Press, Baltimore.

Chatters, J. C., 1997. Encounter with an ancestor. American Anthropological Association Newsletter, January, 9–10.

Clark, D. W., 1984a. Some practical applications of obsidian hydration dating in the subarctic. Arctic 37, 91–109.

Clark, D. W., 1984b. Northern fluted points: Paleo-Eskimo Paleo-Arctic, or Paleo-Indian. Canadian Journal of Anthropology 4, 65–81.

Clark, D. W., 1991. The northern (Alaska-Yukon) fluted points. In: Bonnichsen, R., Turnmire, K. L. (Eds.), Clovis: Origins and Adaptations. Center for the Study of the First Americans, Oregon State University, Corvallis, pp. 35–48.

Clark, D. W., Clark, A. M., 1983. Paleo-Indians and fluted points: sub-arctic alternatives. Plains Anthropologist 28, 283–291.

Collins, M. B., Dillehay, T. D., 1986. The implications of the lithic assemblage from Monte Verde for Early Man Studies. In: Bryan, A. L. (Ed.), New Evidence for the Pleistocene Peopling of the Americas. Center for the Study of Early Man, University of Maine at Orono, pp. 339–355.

Cook, J. P., 1969. The early prehistory of Healy Lake, Alaska. Ph.D. Dissertation, Department of Anthropology, University of Wisconsin, Madison.

Cook, J. P., 1996. Healy Lake. In: West, F. H. (Ed.), American Beginnings. The University of Chicago Press, Chicago, pp. 371–374.

Cook, J. P., Mckennan, R. A., 1970. The Village site at Healy Lake, Alaska, an interim report. Paper read at the 35th Annual Meeting of the Society for American Archeologists, Mexico City, Mexico.

Coulter, H. W., Hopkins, D. M., Karlstrom, T. N. V., Péwé, T. L., Wahrhaftig, C., Williams, J. R., 1965. Map showing extent of glaciations in Alaska. U.S. Geological Survey Miscellaneous Geologic Investigations Map, I-415, scale 1:2,500,00.

Davis, S. D., 1989. Cultural component I. In: Davis, S. D. (Ed.), The Hidden Falls Site. Alaska Anthropological Association Monograph Series, Vol. 5, pp. 159–198.

Dawson, G. M., 1894. Geological notes on some of the coasts and islands of Bering Sea and vicinity. Geological Society of America Bulletin 5, 117–146.

Dillehay, T. D., 1984. A late ice-age settlement in southern Chile. Scientific American 51, 100–109.

Dillehay, T. D., 1986. The cultural relationships of Monte Verde: a late Pleistocene settlement in the sub-Antarctic forest of south-central Chile. In: Bryan, A. L. (Ed.), New Evidence for the Pleistocene Peopling of the Americas. Center for the Study of Early Man, University of Maine at Orono, pp. 319–337.

Dillehay, T. D., 1997. Monte Verde A Late Pleistocene Settlement in Chile, Vol. 2: The Archaeological Context and Interpretation. Smithsonian Institution Press, Washington, DC.

Dillehay, T. D., Collins, M. B., 1988. Early cultural evidence from Monte Verde in Chile. Nature 332, 150–152.

Dixon, E. J., 1975. The Gallagher Flint Station, an early man site on the North Slope, Arctic Alaska and its role in relation to the Bering Land Bridge. Arctic Anthropology 12, 68–75.

Dixon, E. J., 1976. The pleistocene prehistory of Arctic North America. Proceedings of the Ninth International Congress of Anthropological Sciences, Nice, France, pp. 168–198.

Dixon, E. J., 1993. Quest for the Origins of the First Americans. University of New Mexico Press, Albuquerque.

Dixon, E. J., 1995. The significance of southeast Alaska karst. The Alaskan Caver 15, 1–3.

Dixon, E. J., 1999. Bones, Boats and Bison: Archeology and the First Colonization of Western North America. University of New Mexico Press, Albuquerque.

Dixon, E. J., 2002. How and when did humans first come to North America? Athena Review, Quarterly Journal of Archaeology, History, and Exploration. 3 (2), 23–27.

Dixon, E. J., Smith, G. S., 1990. A regional application of tephrochronology in Alaska. Geological Society of America Centennial Special Vol. 4, pp. 383–398 (Chapter 21).

Dixon, E. J., Heaton, T. H., Fifield, T. E., Hamilton, T. D., Putnam, D. E., Grady, F., 1997. Late Quaternary regional geoarchaeology of southeast Alaska karst: a progress report. Geoarchaeology 12, 689–712.

Driver, J. C., 1996. The significance of the fauna from the Charlie Lake Cave site. In: Carlson, R. L., Bona, L. D. (Eds.), Early Human Occupation in British Columbia. University of British Columbia Press, Vancouver, pp. 21–28.

Driver, J. C., Handly, M., Fladmark, K. R., Nelson, D. E., Sullivan, G. M., Preston, R., 1996. Stratigraphy, radiocarbon dating, and culture history of Charlie Lake Cave, British Columbia. Arctic 49, 265–277.

Dumond, D. E., 1980. The archeology of Alaska and the peopling of America. Science 209, 984–991.

Dumond, D. E., 1977. The Eskimos and Aleuts. Thames and Hudson, London.

Dumond, D. E., Henn, W., Stuckenrath, R., 1976. Archaeology and Prehistory on the Alaska Peninsula. Anthropological Papers of the University of Alaska 18, 17–29.

Erlandson, J. M., 1994. Early Hunter-Gatherers of the California Coast. Plenum Press, New York.

Fedje, D. W., White, J. M., Wilson, M. C., Nelson, D. E., Vogel, J. S., Southon, J. R., 1995. Vermilion Lakes site: adaptations and environments in the Canadian Rockies during the latest Pleistocene and early Holocene. American Antiquity 60, 81–108.

Fedje, D. W., Mackie, A. P., McSporran, J. B., Wilson, B., 1996. Early period archaeology in Gwaii Haanas: results of the 1993 field program. In: Carlson, R. L., Dalla Bona, L. (Eds.), Early Human Occupation in British Columbia. University of British Columbia Press, Vancouver, pp. 133–150.

Ferring, C. R., 1989. The Aubrey Clovis site: a Paleoindian locality in the Upper Trinity Drainage Basin, Texas. Current Research in the Pleistocene 6, 9–11.

Ferring, C. R., 1990. The 1989 investigations at the Aubrey Clovis site, Texas. Current Research in the Pleistocene 7, 10–12.

Ferring, C. R., 1995. The Late Quaternary geology and archaeology of the Aubrey site, Texas: a preliminary report. In: Johnson, E. (Ed.), Ancient Peoples and Landscapes. Texas Tech University Press, Lubbock, pp. 273–281.

Fladmark, K. R., 1975. A Paleoecological Model for Northwest Coast Prehistory. National Museum of Man, Mercury Series. Archaeological Survey of Canada Paper, 43, Ottawa.

Fladmark, K. R., 1979. Routes: alternative migration corridors for early man in North America. American Antiquity 44, 55–69.

Fladmark, K. R., 1982. An introduction to the prehistory of British Columbia. Canadian Journal of Archaeology 6, 95–156.

Fladmark, K. R., 1986. Getting one's Berings. Natural History 95, 8–19.

Forrester, R. E., 1985. Horn shelter number 2: the north end, a preliminary report. Central Texas Archeologist 10, 21–36.

Goebel, T. E., Powers, W. R., Bigelow, N., 1991. The Nenana complex of Alaska and Clovis origins. In: Bonnichsen, R., Turnmire, K. (Eds.), Clovis Origins and Adaptations. Center for the Study of the First Americans, Oregon State University, Corvalis, pp. 49–79.

Goebel, T., Powers, W. R., 1989. A possible paleoindian dwelling in the Nenana, Alaska: spatial analysis at the Walker Road site. Paper presented at the 16th annual meeting of the Alaska Anthropological Association March, 3.

Goebel, T., Bigelow, N. H., 1996. Panguingue Creek. In: West, F. H. (Ed.), American Beginnings. The University of Chicago Press, Chicago, pp. 366–370.

Graham, R. W., 1981. Preliminary report on late Pleistocene vertebrates from the Selby and Dutton archaeological/paleontological sites, Yuma County, Colorado. Contributions to Geology, University of Wyoming 20, 33–56.

Greenberg, J. H., Turner, C., Zegura, S. L., 1986. The settlement of the Americas: a comparison of the linguistic, dental, and genetic evidence. Current Anthropology 27, 477–497.

Griffin, J. B., 1979. The origin and dispersion of American Indians in North America. In: Laughlin, W. S., Harper, A. B. (Eds.), The First Americans: Origins, Affinities, and Adaptations. Gustav Fischer, New York, pp. 43–56.

Guidon, N., Delibrias, G., 1986. Carbon-14 dates point to man in the Americas 32,000 years ago. Nature 321, 769–771.

Gustafson, C., Daugherty, R., Gilbow, D., 1979. The Manis Mastodon site: early man on the Olympic Peninsula. Canadian Journal of Archaeology 3, 157–164.

Haley, S. D., Solorzano, F., 1991. The Lake Chapala first Mexicans project, Jalisco, Mexico. Current Research in the Pleistocene 8, 20–22.

Hamilton, T. D., Goebel, T., 1999. Late Pleistocene peopling of Alaska. In: Bonnichsen, R., Ice Age Peoples of North America. Center for the Study of the First Americans, Oregon State University, Corvallis.

Haynes Jr., C. V., 1967. Geology of the Tule Springs Area. Nevada State Museum Anthropological Papers 13, 15–104.

Haynes Jr., C. V., 1969. The earliest Americans. Science 166, 709–715.

Haynes Jr., C. V., 1987. Clovis origin update. The Kiva 52, 83–92.

Haynes Jr., C. V., 1991. Geoarchaeological and paleohydrological evidence for a Clovis-age drought in North America and its bearing on extinction. Quaternary Research 35, 438–450.

Heaton, T. H., Grady, F., 1993. Fossil grizzly bears from Prince of Wales Island, Alaska, offer new insights into animal dispersal, interspecific competition, and age of deglaciation. Current Research in the Pleistocene 10, 98–100.

Heaton, T. H., 1995. Middle Wisconsin bear and rodent remains discovered on Prince of Wales Island, Alaska. Current Research in the Pleistocene 12, 92–95.

Heaton, T. H., 1996. The late Wisconsin vertebrate fauna of On Your Knees Cave, northern Prince of Wales Island, Alaska. Journal of Vertebrate Paleontology 16, 40–41.

Henn, W., 1978. Archaeology on the Alaska Peninsula: the Ugashik Drainage, 1973–1975. University of Oregon Anthropological Papers No. 14, Eugene.

Hobler, P. M., 1978. The relationship of archaeological sites to sea levels on Moresby Island, Queen Charlotte. Canadian Journal of Archaeology 2, 1–14.

Holmes, C. E., 1988. An early post Paleo-Arctic site in the Alaska Range. Paper presented at the 15th Annual Meeting of the Alaska Anthropological Association, March 25–26. Fairbanks, Alaska.

Holmes, C. E., Dale, R. J., McMahn, J. D., 1989. Archaeological mitigation of the Thorne River Site (CRG- 177), Prince of Wales Island, Alaska. Office of History and Archaeology, Report Number 15. Division of Parks and Outdoor Recreation, Alaska Department of Natural Resources.

Holmes, C. E., VanderHoek, R., Dilley, T. E., 1996. Swan Point. In: West, F. H. (Ed.), American Beginnings. The University of Chicago Press, Chicago, pp. 525–536.

Hopkins, D. M., 1973. Sea level history in Beringia during the last 125,000 years. Quaternary Research 3, 520–540.

Hopkins, D. M., 1979. Landscape and climate of Beringia during Late Pleistocene and Holocene time. In: Laughlin, W. S., Harper, A. B. (Eds.), The First Americans: Origins, Affinities and Adaptations. Gustav Fischer, New York, pp. 15–41.

Hopkins, D. M., 1982. Aspects of the paleogeography of Beringia during the Late Pleistocene. In: Hopkins, D. M., Matthews Jr., J. V., Schweger, C. E., Young, S. B. (Eds.), Paleoecology of Beringia. Academic Press, New York, pp. 3–28.

Horai, S., Kondo, R., Sonoda, S., Tajima, K., 1996. The first Americans: different waves of migration to the New World inferred from mitochondrial DNA sequence polymorphisms. In: Akazawa, T., Szathmary, E. J. E. (Eds.), Prehistoric Mongoloid Dispersals. Oxford University Press, Oxford, pp. 270–283.

Hrdlička, A., 1928. The origin and antiquity of man in America. Bulletin of the New York Academy of Medicine 4, 802–816.

Irving, W. N., Jopling, A. V., Beebe, B. F., 1986. Indications of pre-Sangamon humans near Old Crow, Yukon, Canada. In: Bryan, A. L. (Ed.), New Evidence for the Pleistocene Peopling of the Americas. Center for the Study of Early Man, University of Maine, Orono, pp. 49–63.

Irwin-Williams, C., 1969. Comments on the associations of archeological materials and extinct fauna in the Valsequillo region, Puebla, Mexico. American Antiquity 34, 82–83.

Irwin-Williams, C., 1978. Summary of archaeological evidence from the Valsequillo region, Puebla, Mexico. In: Browman, D. L. (Ed.), Cultural Continuity in Mesoamerica, pp. 7–22.

Jackson Jr., L. E., Phillips, F. M., Shimamura, K., Little, E. C., 1997. Cosmogenic ^{36}Cl dating of the Foothills erratics train, Alberta, Canada. Geology 25, 195–198.

Jantz, R. L., Owsley, D. W., 1997. Pathology, taphonomy and cranial morphometrics of the Spirit Cave mummy (AHUR 2064). Nevada Historical Society Quarterly 40, 62–84.

Johnston, W. A., 1933. Quaternary geology of North America in relation to the migration of man. In: Jenness, D. (Ed.), The American Aborigines, Their Origins and Antiquity. University of Toronto Press, Toronto, pp. 9–46.

Jones, S., Bonnichsen, R., 1994. The Anzick Clovis burial. Current Research in the Pleistocene 11, 42–43.

Jordan, R. H., 1992. A maritime Paleoarctic assemblage from Kodiak Island, Alaska. Anthropological Papers of the University of Alaska.

Josenhans, H. W., Fedje, D. W., Conway, K. W., Barrie, J. E., 1995. Postglacial sea-levels on the western Canadian continental shelf: evidence for rapid change, extensive subaerial exposure, and early human habitation. Marine Geology 125, 73–94.

Josenhans, H. W., Fedje, D. W., Pienitz, R., Southon, J., 1997. Early humans and rapidly changing Holocene sea levels in the Queen

Charlotte Islands-Hecate Strait, British Columbia, Canada. Science 277, 71–74.

Kelley, R. L., 1996. Ethnographic analogy and migration to the western hemisphere. In: Akazawa, T., Szathmary, E. J. E. (Eds.), Prehistoric Mongoloid Dispersals. Oxford University Press, Oxford, pp. 228–240.

Kelley, R. L., Todd, L. C., 1988. Coming into the country: early Paleoindian hunting and mobility. American Antiquity 53, 231–244.

Kunz, M. L., Reanier, R. E., 1994. Paleoindians in Beringia: evidence from arctic Alaska. Science 263, 660–662.

Kunz, M. L., Reanier, R. E., 1996. Mesa site, Iteriak Creek. In: West, F. H. (Ed.), American Beginnings. The University of Chicago Press, Chicago, pp. 505–511.

Lorenz, J. G., Smith, D. G., 1996. Distribution of four founding mtDNA haplogroups among Native North Americans. American Journal of Physical Anthropology 101, 307–323.

Loy, L. H., Dixon, E. J., 1998. Blood residues on fluted points from eastern Beringia. American Antiquity 63, 21–46.

Martin, P. S., 1967. Prehistoric overkill. In: Martin, P. S., Wright, H. E. (Eds.), Pleistocene Extinctions: The search for a cause. Yale University Press, New Haven, pp. 75–120.

Martin, P. S., 1973. The discovery of America. Science 179, 969–974.

Meltzer, D. J., 1989. Why don't we know when the first people came to North America? American Antiquity 54, 471–490.

Meltzer, D. J., Grayson, D. K., Ardila, G., Barker, A. W., Dincauze, D. F. C., Haynes, V., Mena, F., Nuñez, L., Stanford, D. J., 1997. On the Pleistocene antiquity of Monte Verde, southern Chile. American Antiquity 62, 659–663.

Merriwether, D. A., Rothhammer, F., Ferrell, R. E., 1995. Distribution of the four founding lineage haplotypes in Native Americans suggests a single wave of migration for the New World. American Journal of Physical Anthropology 98, 411–430.

Merriwether, D. A., Hall, W. W., Vahlne, A., Ferrell, R. E., 1996. mtDNA variation indicates Mongolia may have been the source for the founding population of the New World. American Journal of Human Genetics 59, 204–212.

Mobly, C. M., 1991. The Campus Site: A Prehistoric Camp at Fairbanks, Alaska. University of Alaska Press, Fairbanks.

Morlan, R. E., 1977. Fluted point makers and the extinction of the arctic-steppe biome in eastern Beringia. Canadian Journal of Archaeology 1, 95–108.

Mosimann, J. E., Martin, P. S., 1975. Simulating overkill by Paleoindians. American Scientist 63, 304–313.

Nasmith, H. W., 1970. Pleistocene geology of the Queen Charlotte Islands and southern British Columbia. In: Smith, R. A., Smith, J. (Eds.), Early Man and Environments in Northwestern North America. University of Calgary Press, Calgary, pp. 5–9.

Oakley, K. P., 1963. Relative dating of Arlington Springs man. Science 141, 1172.

Orr, P. C., 1956. Pleistocene man in Fishbone Cave, Pershing County, Nevada. Bulletin of the Department of Archaeology, Nevada State Museum 2, 1–20.

Orr, P. C., 1962. The Arlington Springs site, Santa Rosa Island, California. American Antiquity 27, 417–419.

Phippen, P. G., 1988. Archaeology at Owl Ridge: a pleistocene-Holocene boundary age site in central Alaska. M. A. Thesis, University of Alaska, Fairbanks.

Powers, W. R., Hoffecker, J. F., 1989. Late Pleistocene settlement in the Nenana Valley, central Alaska. American Antiquity 54, 263–287.

Powers, W. R., Maxwell, H. E., 1986. Lithic remains from Panquinque Creek: an early Holocene site in the northern foothills of the Alaska Range. Alaska Historical Commission, Anchorage.

Prest, V. K., 1969. Retreat of Wisconsin and recent ice in North America. Geological Survey of Canada Map, 1257A.

Rainey, F., 1939. Archaeology in central Alaska. Anthropological Papers of the American Museum of Natural History 36, 351–405.

Redder, A. J., 1985. Horn Shelter number 2: the south end, a preliminary report. Central Texas Archeologist 10, 37–65.

Simpson, R. D., Patterson, L. W., Singer, C. A., 1986. Lithic technology of the Calico Mountains site, southern California. In: Bryan, A. L. (Ed.), New Evidence for the Pleistocene Peopling of the Americas. Center for the Study of Early Man, University of Maine, Orono, pp. 89–105.

Spinden, H. J., 1933. Origin of civilization in central America and Mexico. In: Jenness, D. (Ed.), The American Aborigines, Their Origin and Antiquity. University of Toronto Press, Toronto, pp. 217–246.

Stafford, T. D., 1990. Late Pleistocene megafaunal extinctions and the Clovis culture: absolute ages based on accelerator ^{14}C dating of skeletal remains. In: Agenbroad, L. D., Mead, J. I., Nelson, L. W. (Eds.), Megafauna and Man Discovery of America's Heartland. The Mammoth Site of Hot Springs, South Dakota, Scientific Papers Vol. 1, Hot Springs, South Dakota and Northern Arizona University, Flagstaff, Arizona, pp. 118–122.

Stanford, D., 1979. Afterward: resolving the question of New World origins. In: Humphrey, R. L., Stanford, D. (Eds.), Pre-Llano Cultures of the Americas: Paradoxes and Possibilities. The Anthropological Society of Washington, Washington, DC, pp. 147–152.

Stanford, D., 1983. Pre-Clovis occupation south of the ice sheets. In: Shutler Jr., R. (Ed.), Early Man in the New World. Sage Publications, Beverly Hills, CA, pp. 65–72.

Stanford, D., 1996. Foreshaft sockets as possible Clovis hafting devices. Current Research in the Pleistocene 13, 44–46.

Steele, G. D., Powell, J. F., 1992. Peopling of the Americas: paleobiological evidence. Human Biology 64, 303–336.

Stryd, A. R., Rousseau, M. K., 1996. The early prehistory of the mid Fraser-Thompson River area. In: Carlson, R. L., Dalla Bona, L. (Eds.), Early Human Occupation in British Columbia. University of British Columbia Press, Vancouver, pp. 177–204.

Toth, N., 1991. The material record. In: Dillehay, T. D., Meltzer, D. J. (Eds.), The First Americans—Search and Research. CRC Press, Boca Raton, pp. 53–76.

Turner II, C. G., 1983. Dental evidence for the peopling of the Americas. In: Shutler Jr., R. (Ed.), Early Man in the New World. Sage Publications, Beverly Hills, CA, pp. 147–158.

Turner II, C. G., 1985. The dental search for Native American origins. In: Kirk, R., Szathmary, E. (Eds.), Out of Asia: Peopling the Americas and the Pacific. Journal of Pacific History, Canberra, pp. 31–78.

Turner II, C. G., 1992. New World origins: new research from the Americas and the Soviet Union. In: Stanford, D., Day, J. (Eds.), Ice Age Hunters of the Rockies. Denver Museum of Natural History and University Press of Colorado, Boulder, 48 pp.

West, F. H. (Ed.), 1996. American Beginnings: The Prehistory and Paleoecology of Beringia. University of Chicago Press, Chicago.

Williams, R. C., Steinberg, A. G., Gershowitz, H., Bennet, P. H., Knowler, W. C., Pettitt, D. J., Butler, W., Baird, R., Dowd-Rea, L., Burch, T. A., Morse, H. G., Smith, C. G., 1985. Gm allotypes in Native Americans: evidence for three distinct migrations across the Bering Land Bridge. American Journal of Physical Anthropology 66, 1–19.

Wormington, H. M., 1983. Early man in the New World: 1970–1980. In: Shutler Jr., R. (Ed.), Early Man in the New World. Sage Publications, Beverly Hills, CA, pp. 191–195.

Yesner, D. R., 1996. Human adaptation at the Pleistocene-Holocene boundary (circa 13,000 to 8,000 BP) in eastern Beringia. In: Straus, L. G., Eriksen, B. V., Erlandson, J. M., Yesner, D. R. (Eds.), Humans at the End of the Ice Age: The Archaeology of the Pleistocene-Holocene Transition. Plenum Press, New York, pp. 255–272.

Yesner, D. R., Holmes, C. E., Crossen, K. J., 1992. Archaeology and paleoecology of the Broken Mammoth site, central Tanana Valley, interior Alaska, USA. Current Research in the Pleistocene 9, 1–12.

74

Human Races

A Genetic and Evolutionary Perspective

A. R. Templeton

ABSTRACT

Race *is generally used as a synonym for* subspecies, *which traditionally is a geographically circumscribed, genetically differentiated population. Sometimes traits show independent patterns of geographical variation such that some combination will distinguish most populations from all others. To avoid making "race" the equivalent of a local population, minimal thresholds of differentiation are imposed. Human "races" are below the thresholds used in other species, so valid traditional subspecies do not exist in humans. A "subspecies" can also be defined as a distinct evolutionary lineage within a species. Genetic surveys and the analyses of DNA haplotype trees show that human "races" are not distinct lineages, and that this is not due to recent admixture; human "races" are not and never were "pure." Instead, human evolution has been and is characterized by many locally differentiated populations coexisting at any given time, but with sufficient genetic contact to make all of humanity a single lineage sharing a common evolutionary fate.*

The word *race* is rarely used in the modern, non-human evolutionary literature because its meaning is so ambiguous. When it is used, it is generally used as a synonym for *subspecies* (Futuyma, 1986:107–109), but this concept also has no precise definition. The traditional meaning of a subspecies is that of a geographically circumscribed, genetically differentiated population (Smith et al., 1997). The problem with this definition from an evolutionary genetic perspective is that many traits and their underlying polymorphic genes show independent patterns of geographical variation (Futuyma, 1986:108–109). As a result, some combination of characters will distinguish virtually every population from all others. There is no clear limit to the number of races that can be recognized under this concept, and indeed this notion of subspecies quickly becomes indistinguishable from that of a local population. One way around this difficulty is to place minimal quantitative thresholds on the amount of genetic differentiation that is required to recognize subspecies (Smith et al., 1997). A second solution is to allow races or sub-

species to be defined only by the geographical patterns found for particular "racial" traits or characters. A similar problem is faced in defining species. For example, the biological species concept focuses attention on characters related to reproductive incompatibility as those important in defining a species. These reproductive traits have priority in defining a species when in conflict with other traits, such as morphology (Mayr, 1970). Unfortunately, there is no such guidance at the subspecies level, although in practice easily observed morphological traits (the very ones deemed not important under the biological species concept) are used. There is no evolutionary justification for this dominance of easily observed morphological traits; indeed, it merely arises from the sensory constraints of our own species. Therefore, most evolutionary biologists reject the notion that there are special "racial" traits.

Because of these difficulties, the modern evolutionary perspective of a "subspecies" is that of a distinct evolutionary lineage within a species (Shaffer and McKnight, 1996) (although one should note that many current evolutionary biologists completely deny the existence of any meaningful definition of subspecies, as argued originally by Wilson and Brown [1953]—see discussions in Futuyma [1986:108–109] and Smith et al. [1997:13]). The Endangered Species Act requires preservation of vertebrate subspecies (Pennock and Dimmick, 1997), and the distinct evolutionary lineage definition has become the de facto definition of a subspecies in much of conservation biology (Amato and Gatesy, 1994; Brownlow, 1996; Legge et al., 1996; Miththapala et al., 1996; Pennock and Dimmick, 1997; Vogler, 1994). This definition requires that a subspecies be genetically differentiated due to barriers to genetic exchange that have persisted for long periods of time; that is, the subspecies must have historical continuity in addition to current genetic differentiation. It cannot be emphasized enough that *genetic differentiation alone is insufficient to define a subspecies.* The additional requirement of historical continuity is particularly important because many traits should reflect the common evolutionary history of the subspecies, and therefore in theory there is no need to prioritize the informative traits in defining subspecies. Indeed, the best traits for identifying subspecies are now simply those with the best phylogenetic resolution. In this regard, advances in molecular genetics have greatly augmented our ability to resolve genetic variation and provide the best current resolution of recent evolutionary histories (Avise, 1994), thereby allowing the identification of evolutionary lineages in an objective, explicit fashion (Templeton, 1994b, 1998a, 1998b; Templeton et al., 1995).

The purpose of this paper is to examine the existence of races in humans using an evolutionary genetic perspective. The fundamental question is: Are human populations genetically differentiated from one another in such a fashion as to constitute either sharply genetically differentiated populations or distinct evolutionary sublineages of humanity? These questions will be answered with molecular genetic data and through the application of the same, explicit criteria used for the analyses of nonhuman organisms. This last point is critical if the use of the word *race* in humanity is to have any general biological validity. This paper will not address the cultural, social, political, and economic aspects of human "races."

ARE HUMAN "RACES" GEOGRAPHICALLY CIRCUMSCRIBED, SHARPLY DIFFERENTIATED POPULATIONS?

The validity of the traditional subspecies definition of human races can be addressed by examining the patterns and amount of genetic diversity found within and among human populations. One common method of quantifying the amount of within to among genetic diversity is through the F_{st} statistic of Wright (1969) and some of its more modern variants that have been designed specifically for molecular data such as K_{st} (Hudson et al., 1992) or N_{st} (Lynch and Crease, 1990). F_{st} and related statistics range from 0 (all the genetic diversity within a species is shared equally by all populations with no genetic differences among populations) to 1 (all the genetic diversity within a species is found as fixed differences among populations with no genetic diversity within populations). The F_{st} value of humans (based on 16 populations from Africa, Europe, Asia, the Americas, and the Australo-Pacific region) is 0.156 (Barbujani et al., 1997), thereby indicating that most human genetic diversity exists as differences among individuals within populations, and only 15.6% can be used to genetically differentiate the major human "races." To put the human F_{st} value into perspective, humans need to be compared to other species. F_{st}'s for many plants, invertebrates, and small-bodied vertebrates are typically far larger than the human value, but most of these organisms have poor dispersal abilities, so this is to be expected. A more valid comparison would be the F_{st} values of other large-bodied mammals with excellent dispersal abilities. Figure 1 shows the values of

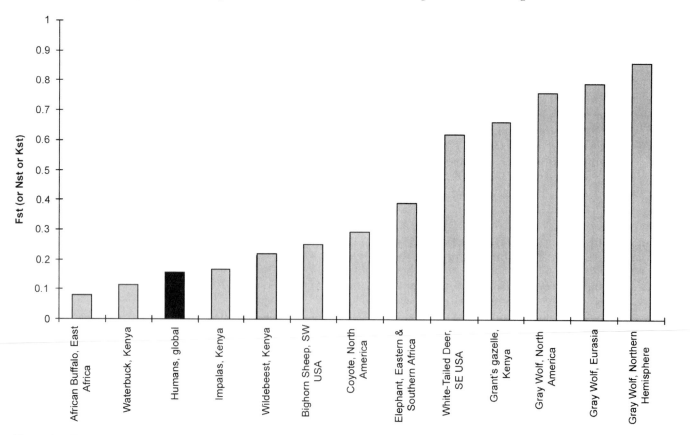

Figure 1. F_{st} (or K_{st} or N_{st}) values for various species of large-bodied mammals with excellent dispersal abilities. The figure shows F_{st} (or its multiallelic analogue, G_{st}) values for African buffalo (Templeton and Georgiadis, 1996), humans (Barbujani et al., 1997), bighorn sheep (Boyce et al., 1997), elephants (Georgiadis et al., 1994), and white-tailed deer (Ellsworth et al., 1994); K_{st} values for waterbuck, impalas, wildebeest, and Grant's gazelle (Arctander et al., 1996); and N_{st} values for coyotes (Lehman and Wayne, 1991) and wolves (Wayne et al., 1992). The geographical scale of the study is indicated by the species name. Values are given in order of size, with the human value indicated in black and nonhuman values in gray.

F_{st}'s and related statistics for several large-bodied mammals. As can be seen, the human F_{st} value is one of the lowest, even though the human geographical distribution is the greatest. A standard criterion for a subspecies or race in the nonhuman literature under the traditional definition of a subspecies as a geographically circumscribed, sharply differentiated population is to have F_{st} values of at least 0.25 to 0.30 (Smith et al., 1997). Hence, as judged by the criterion in the nonhuman literature, the human F_{st} value is too small to have taxonomic significance under the traditional subspecies definition.

This does not mean that the low human F_{st} value is without any evolutionary significance. Suppose for the moment that the F_{st} values in humans truly reflect a balance between gene flow versus local drift/selection and are not due to isolated human lineages. One convenient method for quantifying this balance is Nm, the product of local effective population size (N) with m, the migration rate between demes. Under the idealized population structure known as the island model, the relationship between F_{st} and Nm is (Wright, 1969):

$$F_{st} = \frac{1}{4Nm + 1} \qquad (1)$$

Most real populations do not fit an island model (which assumes that gene flow is independent of geographical distance). Nm is therefore not the actual number of individuals exchanged per generation, but rather is an effective number of migrating individuals per generation relative to this simple, idealized model of population structure. This allows comparisons across different species in effective amounts of gene flow with respect to a common standard. For the human F_{st} value of 0.156, $Nm = 1.35$. This result is consistent with the work of Santos et al. (1997) who examined several human data sets with a variety of statistical procedures and always obtained $Nm > 1$. With Nm on the order of 1, massive movements of large numbers of individuals are not needed to explain the level of genetic differentiation observed in humans. Moreover, $Nm = 1.35$ does not mean that precisely 1.35 effective individuals migrate among the "races" every generation; rather, this is the long-term average. Assuming a generation time of 20 years, the levels of racial differentiation in humanity could be explained by interchanging 1.35 effective individuals every 20 years, or 13.5 every 200 years, or 135 every 2,000 years. Since humans often move as populations, gene flow could be very sporadic on a time scale measured in thousands to tens of thousands of years and still yield an effective number of migrants of 1.35.

An Nm value of 1.35 would insure that the population evolves as a single evolutionary lineage over long periods of time (Crow and Kimura, 1970). Nevertheless, population genetic theory also indicates that fluctuations around an average Nm of order one is conducive both to the rapid spread of selectively favored genes throughout the species and to local population differentiation and adaptation (Barton and Rouhani, 1993). If anatomically modern traits did indeed first evolve in Africa, the human Nm value implies that such traits could rapidly spread throughout all of humanity through gene flow if selectively favored even though local populations could still display genetic differentiation for other loci. Studies on nonhuman organisms indicate that Nm values can be larger than those in humans and yet the species can still display much local differentiation and adaptation, as predicted by this theory. For example, populations of *Drosophila mercatorum* on the slopes versus the saddle of the Kohala mountains on the island of Hawaii (a distance of 3 km) have an estimated Nm of between 4 and 8 (DeSalle et al., 1987). Nevertheless, these populations show extreme differentiation and local adaptation for the abnormal abdomen syndrome, a complex polygenic suite of phenotypes that affects morphology, developmental time, female fecundity, male sexual maturation, and longevity in adaptively significant ways (Hollocher and Templeton, 1994; Hollocher et al., 1992; Templeton et al., 1993; Templeton et al., 1989). Similarly, garter snake populations in Lake Erie have an Nm value between 2.7 and 37.6 among sites with populations that differ greatly in the amount of melanism (King and Lawson, 1995, 1997; Lawson and King, 1996). These examples (and many more could have been given) clearly show that Nm values higher than the estimated Nm value for humans are still compatible with much local differentiation across space even though the gene flow is sufficiently high to ensure that the species as a whole evolves as a single lineage over time.

The above discussion was predicated upon the *assumption* that the human F_{st} value arose from the balance of gene flow versus local drift and selection. Unfortunately, the F_{st} statistic per se cannot discriminate among potential causes of genetic differentiation (Templeton, 1998a). Although human "races" do not satisfy the standard quantitative criterion for being traditional subspecies (Smith et al., 1997), this does not necessarily mean that races do not exist in the evolutionary lineage sense. Under the lineage concept of subspecies, all that is needed is sufficient genetic differentiation to define the separate lineages. If the lineages split only recently, the overall level of divergence could be quite small. Therefore, the quantitative levels of genetic diversity among human populations do not rule out the possibility that human "races" are valid under the evolutionary lineage definition of subspecies. The remainder of this paper will focus upon this more modern definition of subspecies.

ARE HUMAN "RACES" DISTINCT EVOLUTIONARY LINEAGES?

Models of Human Evolution and Human Races

When a biological race is defined as a distinct evolutionary lineage within a species, the question of race can only be answered in the context of the recent evolutionary history of the species. The two dominant models of recent human evolution during the last half

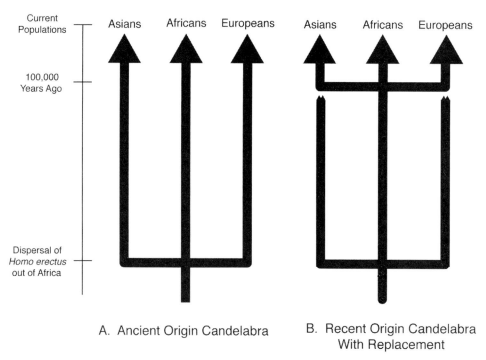

Figure 2.   *Candelabra models of recent human evolution. Part A illustrates the ancient origin version of the candelabra model. Under this hypothesis, the major human "races" split from one another at the time of dispersal of* Homo erectus *out of Africa. After that initial split, the various "races" behaved as separate evolutionary lineages and independently evolved into their modern forms. Part B illustrates the recent origin version of the candelabra model with replacement. Under this hypothesis, an initial candelabra existed as illustrated in part A. However, anatomically modern humans then arose in Africa and dispersed out of Africa around 100,000 years ago. This second dispersal event was marked by the complete genetic extinction of the earlier* Homo erectus *populations (indicated by the broken lineages in B) and by a split of these anatomically modern humans into separate evolutionary lineages that then independently acquired their modern "racial" variation.*

of this century are the candelabra (Figure 2) and trellis (Figure 3) models. Both models accept the evolutionary origin of the genus *Homo* in Africa and the spread of *Homo erectus* out of Africa a million years ago or more. Candelabra models posit that the major Old World geographical groups (Europeans, sub-Saharan Africans, and Asians) split from one another and since have had nearly independent evolutionary histories (but perhaps with some subsequent admixture). Therefore, the evolutionary relationships among Africans, Europeans, and Asians can be portrayed as an evolutionary tree—in this case with the topology of a candelabra (Figure 2). The major human geographical populations are portrayed as the branches on this candelabra and are therefore valid "races" under the evolutionary lineage definition. The ancient origin candelabra model regarded the split between the major "races" as occurring with the spread of *Homo erectus* (Figure 2A) followed by independent evolution of each "race" into its modern form. This version has been thoroughly discredited and has no serious advocates today. However, a recent origin candelabra model known as the out-of-Africa replacement hypothesis (Figure 2B) has become widely accepted. Under this model, anatomically modern humans evolved first in Africa. Next, a small group of these anatomically modern humans split off from the African population and colonized Eurasia about 100,000 years

ago, driving the *Homo erectus* populations to complete genetic extinction everywhere (the "replacement" part of the hypothesis). The ancient (Figure 2A) and recent (Figure 2B) candelabra models differ only in their temporal placement of the ancestral node but share the same tree topology that portrays Africans, Europeans, and Asians as distinct branches on an evolutionary tree. It is this branching *topology* that defines "races" under the evolutionary lineage definition, and not the *time* since the common ancestral population. Hence, human "races" are valid evolutionary lineages under either candelabra model.

The trellis model (Figure 3) posits that *Homo erectus* populations not only had the ability to move out of Africa but also back in, resulting in recurrent genetic interchange among Old World human populations (Lasker and Crews, 1996; Wolpoff and Caspari, 1997). It is also important to note that, under the trellis model, the taxonomic designations of *Homo erectus* and *H. sapiens* only have morphological significance and do not imply reproductive isolation as under the biological-species concept (Mayr, 1970). Therefore, anatomically modern traits could evolve anywhere in the range of *Homo erectus* (which includes Africa) and subsequently spread throughout all of humanity by selection and gene flow. Hence, an African origin for anatomically modern humans is compatible with both the trellis and

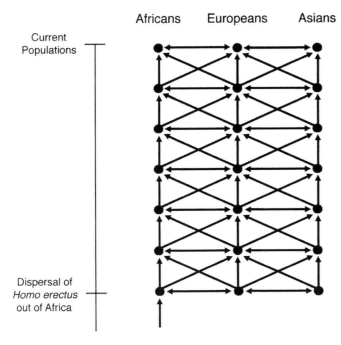

Figure 3. *The trellis model of recent human evolution. Under this hypothesis,* Homo erectus *dispersed out of Africa and established populations in Africa and southern Eurasia, as indicated by the large dots. These populations were interconnected by gene flow so that there were no evolutionary sublineages of humanity or independent evolution of the various "races." Arrows with heads on both ends indicate gene flow among contemporaneous populations, and arrows with single heads indicate lines of genetic descent.*

candelabra models. The two models do differ in their interpretation of interpopulational genetic differences. Populational genetic differences reflect the time of divergence from a common ancestral population under the candelabra models. With the trellis model, the genetic distances reflect the amount of genetic interchange and not time of divergence from an ancestor. However, the most important distinction between the candelabra and trellis models for the discussion at hand is that under the trellis model there was no separation of humanity into evolutionary lineages, and hence human "races" are not valid subspecies. In summary, human "races" as evolutionary lineages do exist under the candelabra models but do not exist under the trellis model.

Although these two models are frequently presented as mutually exclusive alternatives (Wolpoff and Caspari, 1997), there is no biological reason why some human populations may be genetically differentiated because they are historical lineages, whereas other populations are differentiated because of recurrent but restricted gene flow. Moreover, the genetic differences between any two human populations may represent a mixture of both gene flow and historical events. Much genetic evidence is equally compatible with both models and hence is noninformative. The emphasis in this paper will therefore be upon data sets that discriminate between gene flow and historical splits as non-mutually exclusive causes of differentiation among human populations.

Genetic Diversity Levels within and among Human Populations

Do the levels of genetic diversity found within and among human "races" discriminate between evolutionary lineage and genetic interchange models of recent human evolution? As pointed out earlier, *F* statistics and related measures of within to among diversity levels do not discriminate per se. However, one conclusion reached in that section has great relevance to the debate over the validity of human races as evolutionary lineages; namely, that the estimated gene flow levels in humans are compatible with local differentiation across geographical space even though the species as a whole could evolve as a single lineage over time. Much skepticism about the trellis model stems from the belief that a delicate balance is required between gene flow (to insure all humans are a common evolutionary lineage over time) and local genetic drift/selection (to maintain humans as a polytypic species at any given moment in time) (Aiello, 1997; Nei and Takezaki, 1996). Indeed, even proponents of the trellis model have argued that only rarely can a species be polytypic under a trellis model. For example, Wolpoff and Caspari (1997:282) state that "the human pattern . . . of a widespread polytypic species with many different ecological niches . . . is a very rare one." However, polytypic species are not rare (Futuyma, 1986; Mayr, 1970). Moreover, as illustrated by the examples given earlier, polytypic species occur over a broad range of values for *Nm* and are a robust evolutionary outcome. There is no difficulty either in population genetic theory or observation for the conclusion that humans can be both a polytypic species and a single evolutionary lineage.

Although *F* statistics are compatible with either model of human evolution, the claim is made in much of the recent literature that within "race" diversity levels support the recent candelabra model. Africans have higher amounts of genetic diversity than non-Africans for many nuclear loci (Armour et al., 1996; Jorde et al., 1997; Perez-Lezaun et al., 1997), mitochondrial DNA (mtDNA) (Comas et al., 1997; Francalacci et al., 1996), and some regions of Y-DNA (Hammer et al., 1997). These results are often interpreted as supporting the recent candelabra model by assuming that only a small number of individuals left Africa to colonize Eurasia with little or no subsequent gene flow. As a result, a bottleneck effect reduced the levels of genetic variation in non-Africans. This interpretation of genetic diversity also implies that at least Africans and non-Africans are distinct evolutionary lineages and hence are valid races. However, alternative explanations of diversity levels exist. Under the neutral theory, the expected heterozygosity for a DNA region (a standard measure of genetic diversity) is given by:

$$\text{Heterozygosity} = \frac{1}{1+4N_e\mu} \quad (2)$$

where N_e is an effective size of the population and μ is the mutation rate of the DNA region of interest. Equation (2) reveals that differences in effective size can explain differences in the level of genetic diversity.

Africans are expected to have higher genetic diversity simply because their population sizes were larger during much of the last million years (Harpending et al., 1996; Relethford and Harpending, 1994, 1995). Indeed, the patterns of genetic diversity found in humans are more consistent with differences in population sizes and growth rates than with differences in population ages from presumed bottlenecks (Harding et al., 1997; Perez-Lezaun et al., 1997). The danger of using diversity levels as an indicator of population age from a bottleneck is illustrated by the observation that mitochondrial DNA diversity *within Africa* is higher in food-producing populations than in hunter-gatherers (Watson et al., 1996). By equating diversity to age, this result would imply that agricultural peoples in Africa represent the ancestral populations, whereas the hunter-gatherers are the recent descendant populations. Such a conclusion is not credible, and the diversity levels within Africa are interpreted as reflecting effective size differences (Watson et al., 1996).

Note that equation (2) has no time component. The reason is that equation (2) describes the diversity levels at equilibrium. When the equilibrium is disturbed by bottlenecks or rapid population growth, time enters as a factor (Templeton, 1997a). Fortunately, different causes of departure from equilibrium can be discriminated. For example, a bottleneck and split should affect all genetic systems. However, nuclear DNA and mitochondrial DNA show discordant patterns in humans, a result inconsistent with the presumed population bottleneck and the sharing by all genetic systems of a common demographic history (Hey, 1997; Jorde et al., 1995). One can also discriminate by the patterns of diversity across genetic systems that differ in mutation rate (Templeton, 1997a). A bottleneck reduces genetic variation, and temporal dependence enters because mutation takes time to restore genetic diversity. Hence, the longest lasting discrepancies in relative genetic diversity levels are for low mutation rate systems. Therefore, under the bottleneck hypothesis, Africans should show the greatest excess in relative genetic diversity for low mutation rate systems. However, the excess genetic diversity in Africans is found with the high mutation rate systems (Armour et al., 1996; Comas et al., 1997; Francalacci et al., 1996; Jorde et al., 1997; Perez-Lezaun et al., 1997), whereas the classic, low mutation rate systems show comparable levels of genetic diversity (Bowcock et al., 1994; Jorde et al., 1995), and a low polymorphic section of Y-DNA shows greater levels of diversity in Europeans than in Africans (Mitchell, 1996). An alternative non-equilibrium pattern can be generated by rapid population growth which causes an increase—not a decrease—in levels of genetic diversity. The high mutation rate systems show the earliest and strongest response to increased population size, which is consistent with the observed pattern. Hence, the observed diversity patterns reflect human population growth rather than population bottlenecks.

The within "race" genetic diversity levels do not support the idea that Eurasians split off from Africans via a small founder population, but they do not necessarily falsify the notion that a Eurasian/African split occurred

without a bottleneck. Therefore, the within population genetic diversity data are inconclusive on the status of Eurasians and Africans as separate evolutionary lineages and thereby valid races.

Genetic Distances and Evolutionary "Trees"

An alternative method to F_{st} of measuring the extent of genetic differentiation among populations is to convert the genetic differences into a genetic distance. There are several genetic distance measures available, and sometimes the biological conclusions are strongly dependent upon the precise measure chosen (Perez-Lezaun et al., 1997). However, this problem will be ignored in this paper because the relative distances among the major human "races" appear robust to differing genetic distance measures (Cavalli-Sforza, 1997). Genetic distances in turn can be converted into an evolutionary tree of populations by various computer algorithms. Figure 4A shows such a population tree (Cavalli-Sforza et al., 1996). This and most other human genetic distance trees have the deepest divergence between Africans and non-Africans, and this split is commonly estimated to have occurred around 100,000 years ago (Cavalli-Sforza et al., 1996; Cavalli-Sforza, 1997; Nei and Takezaki, 1996). All this seems consistent with the recent candelabra model, but non-zero genetic distances can also arise and persist between interbreeding populations with recurrent gene flow (Wright, 1931, 1943, 1969). As shown by Slatkin (1991), recurrent gene flow results in an average divergence time of gene lineages between populations even when no population-level split occurred and the divergence levels are at equilibrium and thereby time invariant. Therefore, an apparent genetic time of divergence does not necessarily imply a time of population splitting—or any population split at all. Under a trellis model, genetic distances reflect the patterns and amounts of gene flow and *not* the age since some "separation" or "split."

Fortunately, these two interpretations of genetic distance can be distinguished. If human populations can truly be represented as branches on an evolutionary tree, then the resulting genetic distances should satisfy several constraints. For example, under the candelabra model, all non-African human populations "split" from the Africans at the same time, and therefore all genetic distances between African and non-African populations have the same expected value (Figure 4A). When genetic distances instead reflect the amount of gene flow, "treeness" constraints are no longer applicable. Because gene flow is commonly restricted by geographical distance (Wright, 1943), gene flow models are expected to yield a strong positive relationship between geographical distance and genetic distance. Figure 4B places the populations on a two-dimensional plot in a manner that attempts to reflect their genetic distances from one another, particularly nearest-neighbor distances, while otherwise attempting to minimize the total sum of branch lengths (formally, a neighbor-joining dendrogram). Figure 4B uses the same genetic distance data used to generate the tree in Figure 4A, but without imposing all the constraints of treeness (Cavalli-Sforza et al.,

A.

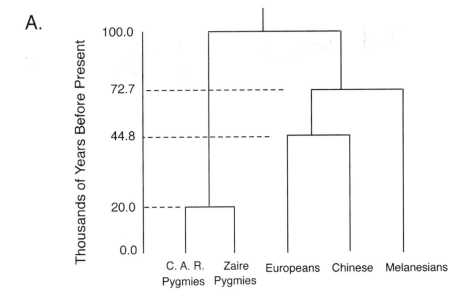

B.

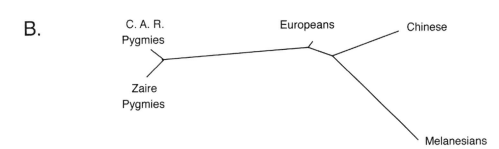

Figure 4. *Genetic distances and recent human evolution. Part A shows an evolutionary tree of human populations as estimated from the genetic distance data given in Bowcock et al. (1991). Human population evolution is depicted as a series of splits, and the numbers on the left indicate the estimated times of divergence in thousands of years. This figure is redrawn from Figure 2.4.4, Cavalli-Sforza et al. (1996:91). Part B shows the same genetic distance data drawn with the neighbor-joining method but without all the constraints of a tree. This figure is redrawn from Figure 2.4.5, Cavalli-Sforza et al. (1996:91).*

1996). Note that Europeans fall between Africans and Asians as predicted by their geographical location—in contrast to the candelabra model prediction of equal genetic distances of Europeans and Asians to Africans. The computer programs used to generate "trees" from genetic distance data will do so regardless of what evolutionary factors generated the distances. It is therefore the obligation of the users of such programs to ensure that the genetic distance data have the properties of treeness before representing their data as a tree. To present trees that do not have the properties of treeness is analytically indefensible, and worse, it is biologically misleading.

The failure of human genetic distances to fit treeness is ubiquitous whenever tested (Bowcock et al., 1991; Cavalli-Sforza et al., 1996; Nei and Roychoudhury, 1974, 1982). Nevertheless, these same authors persist in presenting the relationships of the major human "races" as an evolutionary tree. Worse, many recent papers do not even test for treeness. For example, Nei and Takezaki (1996) give several trees for both old and new genetic data sets, but not a single test of treeness is given or even mentioned. However, the older data sets given in Nei and Takezaki (1996) have long been known not to fit treeness (Nei and Roychoudhury, 1974, 1982). The

newer data sets in Nei and Takezaki (1996) were not tested for treeness in the original papers, so a test will be given here using a standard measure of treeness—the cophenetic correlation (Rohlf, 1993). Because the trees are themselves estimated from the genetic distance data, a large, positive cophenetic correlation is always expected and any correlation less than 0.8 is regarded as a "poor" fit (Rohlf, 1993). The cophenetic correlations for the new data sets given in Nei and Takezaki (1996) are 0.75 for the microsatellite data of Bowcock et al. (1994), 0.69 for the microsatellite data of Deka et al. (1995), 0.79 for the restriction fragment length data of Mountain and Cavalli-Sforza (1994), and 0.45 for the *Alu* insertion polymorphism data of Batzer et al. (1994). Not one of the data sets fits treeness.

In marked contrast, the genetic distance data fit well to a restricted gene flow model. In their analyses of the older data sets, Nei and Roychoudhury (1974,1982) not only rejected treeness, but showed that the deviations were those expected from genetic interchange among the "races." Similarly, Bowcock et al. (1991) not only rejected treeness for their data, but also showed that their data fit well to a model of "continuous admixture, in time, in space, or in both: a chain of populations somewhat similar to a stepping-stone model in which the ancestors of Europeans are geographically intermediate between the two extremes, Africans and Asians" (p. 841). The phrase "continuous admixture" is an oxymoron, as will be evident later, but in this case it is used as a synonym for recurrent gene flow (Cavalli-Sforza, personal communication). The "stepping-stone model" is a classic isolation by distance model, so Bowcock et al. (1991) show an excellent fit of their data to the recurrent gene flow model of isolation by distance. Santos et al. (1997) analyzed several human data sets with a variety of statistical procedures and found that the pattern is one of isolation by distance with high gene flow between geographically close populations. Finally, Cavalli-Sforza et al. assembled a comprehensive human data set and concluded that "the isolation-by-distance models hold for long distances as well as for short distances, and for large regions as well as for small and relatively isolated populations" (1996:124). Figure 5 is a redrawing of one of the figures from Cavalli-Sforza et al. (1996) that illustrates how well an isolation by distance model fits the human data.

Given that there is no tested human genetic distance data set consistent with treeness and that isolation by distance fits the human data well, proponents of the recent candelabra model have attempted to salvage the candelabra model by postulating a complex set of "admixtures between branches that had separated a long time before" (Cavalli-Sforza et al., 1996:19). The key phrase in this proposal is *between branches that had separated a long time before* (Terrell and Stewart, 1996). Admixture occurs when genetic interchange is reestablished between populations that had separated in the past and undergone genetic divergence (i.e., the gene flow patterns have been discontinuous). Proponents of the recent candelabra model then attempt to reconcile the genetic distance data with an admixture model that mimics some of the effects (and the good fit) of recurrent gene flow. By invoking admixture events as needed, human "races" can still be treated as separate evolutionary lineages, but now with the qualification

that the "races" were purer in the past—the paradigm of the "primitive isolate" (Terrell and Stewart, 1996). However, even advocates of the recent candelabra model acknowledge that these postulated admixture events are "extremely specific" and "unrealistic" (Bowcock et al., 1991:841).

For example, consider Melanesians and Africans. As shown in Figure 4B, these two human populations have nearly maximal genetic divergence within humanity as a whole with respect to molecular markers. Moreover, note that Europeans are closer to both Africans and to Melanesians than are Africans to Melanesians (Figure 4B). However, Melanesians and Africans share dark skin, hair texture, and cranial-facial morphology (Cavalli-Sforza et al., 1996; Nei and Roychoudhury, 1993)—the traits typically used to classify people into races. One obvious conclusion from this gross disparity between racially defining traits and the molecular genetic data is that classifications based on these "racial" traits have no evolutionary validity. However, in order to salvage the racial types emerging from the candelabra model, Nei and Roychoudhury (1993) propose two dispersal events out of Africa. The first group of people moved through the Middle East to Northeast Asia and then moved southward to occupy Southeast Asia. Later, a second group of humans migrated out of Africa to the Indian subcontinent and then to Southeast Asia, where admixture occurred with the earlier Asian group. Nei and Roychoudhury then propose that the resultant admixed population in Southeast Asia absorbed most of its gene pool from the older Asian group, but "retained the genes for dark skin, frizzled hair, etc. from Africans, because of natural selection in tropical conditions" (1993:937). This admixed group then moved out to the islands of the Pacific and Australia. The part of this admixed population that remained in Southeast Asia and India then experienced additional admixture events involving the older Asians and Europeans. This second round of admixture wiped out most of the "African traits" in India and Southeast Asia except for a few isolated subpopulations (Nei and Roychoudhury, 1993).

Nei and Roychoudhury argue that this complicated, ad hoc scheme is more plausible than the hypothesis of "independent evolution of African traits in this area" (1993: 938). However, no mention is even given to the trellis model interpretation in which these traits are not "African" traits at all, but rather tropical adaptive traits that are favored in human populations living in the appropriate environment—populations that are *not* evolutionarily independent because they were and are in genetic contact. Moreover, even this complicated scheme of multiple admixture and massive population movements still does not explain the genetic distance data. Admixed populations are expected to be intermediate in genetic distance between the original parental populations, but Melanesians are not intermediate between mainland Asian populations and Africans (Figure 4B). This example shows that although complex, multiple ad hoc admixture events are invoked to reconcile the recent candelabra model with the genetic distance data, they still fail to do so. In contrast, isolation by distance fits the human data well and all that it requires is that

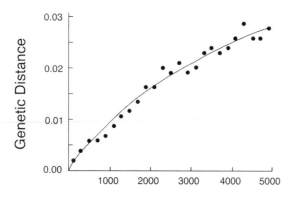

Figure 5. *Genetic distances and isolation by geographical distance. The global human genetic distances (the ordinate) are plotted against geographical distance in miles (the abscissa). The circles indicate the observed values, and the curved line is the theoretical expectation under an isolation-by-distance model. This figure is redrawn from Figure 2.9.2, Cavalli-Sforza et al. (1996:123).*

humans tend to mate primarily with others born nearby but often outside one's own natal group (Lasker and Crews, 1996; Santos et al., 1997).

The hypothesis of admixture can be tested directly. When admixture occurs between branches that have differentiated under past isolation, genetic clines are set up simultaneously for all differentiated loci. This results in a strong geographical concordance in the clines for all genetic systems, both neutral and selected. In contrast, isolation by distance may result in geographical concordance for systems under similar selective regimes (Endler, 1977; King and Lawson, 1997), but otherwise no concordance is expected. Hence, the lack of concordance of "African traits" with molecular genetic distances is not surprising under an isolation by distance model. The lack of concordance in the geographical distribution of different elements has been thoroughly and extensively documented by others and has been one of the primary traditional arguments against the biological validity of human races (Cavalli-Sforza et al., 1996; Futuyma, 1986). This lack of concordance across genetic systems falsifies the hypothesis of admixture of previously isolated branches and the idea that "races" were "pure" in the past.

The genetic distance data are therefore informative about the status of human "races" as evolutionary lineages. Genetic distance analyses strongly and uniformly indicate that human "races" cannot be represented as branches on an evolutionary tree as under the candelabra models, even by invoking ad hoc admixture events. Genetic distances, when properly analyzed, undermine the biological validity of human races as evolutionary lineages.

Haplotype Trees

The final type of genetic evidence to be considered is that arising from phylogenetic reconstructions of the genetic variation found in homologous regions of DNA that show little or no recombination. All the homologous copies of DNA in such a DNA region that are identical at every nucleotide (or in practice, identical at all scored nucleotide sites) constitute a single haplotype class. A mutation at any site in this DNA region will usually create a new haplotype that differs initially from its ancestral haplotype by that single mutational change. As time proceeds, some haplotypes can acquire multiple mutational changes from their ancestral type. All the different copies of a haplotype for each of the haplotypes in a species are subject to mutation, resulting in a diversity of haplotypes in the gene pool that vary in their mutational closeness to one another. If there is little or no recombination in the DNA region (as is the case for human mitochondrial DNA or for small segments of nuclear DNA), the divergence of haplotypes from one another reflects the order in which mutations occurred in evolutionary history. When mutational accumulation reflects evolutionary history, it is possible to estimate a network that shows how mutational changes transform one haplotype into another or from some common ancestral haplotype. Such a network represents an unrooted evolutionary tree of the haplotype

variation in that DNA region and is called a haplotype tree. In some circumstances, the ancestral haplotype is known or can be inferred, thereby providing a rooted haplotype tree. In practice, haplotype trees are sometimes difficult to infer from the mutational differences among a set of observed haplotypes because the same mutation may have occurred more than once, thereby destroying the relationship between mutational state and evolutionary history, and/or recombination may have scrambled up the DNA region so thoroughly that accumulated mutational differences reflect both evolutionary history and recombination in a confounded fashion. When they can be estimated, haplotype trees directly reflect only the evolutionary history of the genetic diversity being monitored in the DNA region under study. Haplotype trees are *not necessarily* evolutionary trees of species nor of subpopulations within species. For example, suppose a species is and always has been completely randomly mating as a single population and therefore has no subpopulation evolutionary history at all; yet that same randomly mating species will have haplotype trees for all homologous DNA regions that show little or no recombination.

The publication of mitochondrial haplotype trees (Cann et al., 1987; Vigilant et al., 1991) motivated much of the current debate over recent human evolution. These and subsequent papers (Stoneking, 1997) on mitochondrial haplotype trees make a threefold argument in favor of the recent candelabra model: (1) all mtDNA types in current human populations can be traced back to a single common ancestor (mitochondrial "Eve"), (2) the root of the mitochondrial tree is in Africa, and (3) the tree coalesces to its common ancestral type about 200,000 years ago. Although the original haplotype trees were estimated incorrectly because of an improper use of a computer program (Maddison, 1991; Templeton, 1992), this error is trivial in light of the fact that these three arguments are noninformative about the status of human populations as evolutionary lineages and therefore do not discriminate between the candelabra and trellis models (Templeton, 1994a). Point (1) is a universal for all models of human (and indeed, nonhuman) evolution because all homologous segments of DNA are expected to coalesce to a common ancestral molecule under any model of evolution in a finite population (Tavaré et al., 1997). Indeed, haplotype trees would not exist at all if this were not true. With respect to point (2), the trellis model is compatible with any root location occupied by humans at the time of coalescence, which includes Africa. Because the bulk of humanity lived in Africa hundreds of thousands of years ago (as previously noted), an African root is the most likely result under the trellis model. Argument (3) is based on the premise that mitochondrial DNA can spread only when populations expand geographically, so mitochondrial DNA either spread with *Homo erectus* (a million years ago or more) or with the presumed spread of anatomically modern humans about 100,000 years ago (Cann et al., 1987; Stoneking, 1997; Vigilant et al., 1991). This premise equates the mitochondrial haplotype tree to a population tree. Haplotype trees may or may not reflect population history (indeed, as pointed out above, there may be no population history at all), and this proposition needs to be tested rather than assumed. In particular, when dealing with populations that are exchanging genes (the premise of the trellis model), a haplotype can spread geographically at any time via gene flow. Hence, a coalescence time of 200,000 years ago is compatible with either model of human evolution (Templeton, 1994a).

A fourth argument, not present in the original "Eve" papers but related to mtDNA coalescence time, is that the human population size at the time of coalescence was too small to be compatible with the trellis model (Rogers, 1997). Under neutrality, the expected coalescence time of mtDNA is $2N_e$ generations, where N_e is the inbreeding effective size of females. Assuming a coalescence time of 200,000 years ago and a generation length of 20 years yields $N_e = 5,000$. More complicated coalescent models yield different estimates, but all are on the order of thousands for N_e (Rogers, 1997). N_e is not the census size of females. In general, effective sizes are much smaller than census size. For example, in conservation biology it is standard to assume that the effective size is only one-fifth the census size for large-bodied mammals. This fivefold correction factor from conservation biology assumes a stable or declining census size, but when population sizes are increasing, as seems to be the case for humans over the past hundred thousand years or so, inbreeding effective size can be orders of magnitude smaller than census size or other effective sizes, such as the variance effective size (Templeton, 1980). Hence, a fivefold correction for inbreeding effective size to census size is undoubtedly conservative for recent human evolution. Moreover, the census size should be doubled to include males. Thus, the estimate of $N_e = 5,000$ implies a census size of 50,000 humans or more. Also, coalescence time is not known to be exactly 200,000 years but rather has a broad confidence interval due to a lack of precise knowledge about the neutral mutation rate and evolutionary stochasticity (Tavaré et al., 1997; Templeton, 1993). Using the full range of ambiguity given in Templeton (1993), population sizes up to 200,000 cannot be excluded. Moreover, since 1993, the ambiguity on the mtDNA mutation rate has actually increased (Arnason et al., 1996; Howell et al., 1996; Parsons et al., 1997), taking the upper limits of the confidence range close to a population size of 500,000. All of these calculations depend upon the assumption of neutrality. Deleterious mutations will cause this procedure to underestimate effective size, and such mutations are known to exist (Hey, 1997; Nachman et al., 1996; Templeton, 1996). Therefore, all of the above calculations are *lower* bounds given this demonstrated violation of assumptions. More importantly, even a *single* advantageous mutation occurring *anywhere* within the mtDNA genome at *any time* during the past few hundreds of thousands of years of human evolution will make the effective size estimator quantitatively meaningless (Rogers, 1997). Given the broad confidence ranges associated with this estimation procedure and its extraordinary sensitivity to deviations from neutrality, it is patent that the population size argument does not discriminate among the alternatives.

Fortunately, there is much information in haplotype trees that can be used to test the hypothesis that human "races" are evolutionary sublineages whose past purity has been somewhat diminished by admixture. For example, in order to reconcile the candelabra model with the genetic distance data, it is necessary to regard Europeans as a heavily admixed population (Bowcock et al., 1991; Cavalli-Sforza et al., 1996). When admixture occurs, haplotypes that differ by multiple mutational events with no existing intermediate haplotypes should coexist in the admixed population's gene pool (Manderscheid and Rogers, 1996; Templeton et al., 1995). The detection of such highly divergent haplotypes requires large sample sizes of the presumed admixed population in order to have statistical power. When large sample surveys have been performed upon the presumed admixed European populations, no highly divergent haplotypes or evidence for admixture are observed for either mtDNA (Manderscheid and Rogers, 1996) or Y-DNA (Cooper et al., 1996). In contrast, isolation by distance (the trellis model) produces gene pools without strongly divergent haplotypes (i.e., most haplotypes differ by one or at most just a few mutational steps from some other haplotype found in the same population), as is observed.

The candelabra and trellis hypotheses are models of how genes spread across geographical space and through time, and hence a geographical analysis of haplotype trees provides a direct test of these two models. Statistical techniques exist that separate the influences of historical events (such as population range expansions) from recurrent events (such as gene flow with isolation by distance) when there is adequate sampling both in terms of numbers of individuals and of numbers and distribution of sampling sites (Templeton et al., 1995). This statistical approach first converts the haplotype tree into a nested statistical design. The lowest level of analysis is the haplotypes themselves, and the first level of nesting is created by starting at the tips of the haplotype network and moving one mutational step in, forming a union of any haplotypes that are reached by such a single mutational step or that converge upon a common node. This first set of "1-step clades" (Templeton et al., 1987) on the tips of the haplotype network is then pruned off and the process repeated until all haplotypes are included in 1-step clades. Now one has a tree of 1-step clades, and this tree can be nested into "2-step clades" using exactly the same nesting rules, but using 1-step clades instead of haplotypes as the base unit. These nesting rules are used at successively higher levels until the next level of nesting would place the entire original haplotype tree into a single clade (for more details, see Templeton and Sing, 1993).

The age of a higher order nesting clade has to be as old or older than the clades nested within it. Thus, even in the absence of a root for the haplotype tree, the nested design provides relative age information. By studying how a series of nested clades is distributed in space, it is therefore possible to make inferences about how haplotype lineages spread geographically through time. Moreover, the geographical range of a clade relative to that of the other clades it is nested with at the next higher level indicates how far spatially a haplotype lineage can spread during the time it takes to accumulate a single mutation. Hence, the nested design based on the haplotype tree automatically adds a temporal dimension to the spatial data gathered with the sample of current haplotypes. It is therefore possible to reconstruct the historical dynamics of the geographical spread of haplotype lineages, with the dynamical resolution being limited by the average amount of time it takes a lineage to accumulate a single mutation. Moreover, by making the analysis nested, no assumption of homogeneity is being made about how lineages spread geographically over time. That is, at one time or place, haplotype lineages may have spread through gene flow restricted by geographical distance; at another time or place, there may have been a rapid range expansion; and at yet another time or place, all genetic interchange between two geographical regions may have been severed. The nested analysis does not exclude any of these possibilities a priori, but rather regards all of them (or any mixture) as legitimate factors influencing the movement of haplotype lineages through time and space (Templeton et al., 1995). This statistical approach therefore treats historical and recurrent events as joint possibilities rather than as mutually exclusive alternatives.

These different factors, however, leave different signatures in the nested analyses. If gene flow restricted by isolation by distance dominated during the place and time when a certain subset of mutations occurred, then the older clades defined by these mutations should be more widespread and the younger but evolutionarily close clades should be in the same general area as the older clades. This expectation follows from the simple fact that under isolation by distance, genes spread only a little every generation, and the longer a gene lineage exists, the more generations it has to spread geographically and to accumulate additional mutations. If two geographical regions split from one another (i.e., severed genetic interchange), then the clades that mark those geographical regions and that time of isolation would accumulate many mutational differences but without movement into each other's space. Finally, if a subset of the original population (containing only a subset of the haplotype variation that existed at that time) suddenly expanded into and colonized a new geographical region, then the subset of haplotypes they carried and the lineages derived from them would have widespread geographical distributions for their frequency relative to the population as a whole. Thus, gene flow and different historical events leave distinct genetic-spatial signatures in a nested analysis and are thereby distinguishable. Moreover, the areas affected by these forces and events can be inferred, as can their time relative to the nested design of the haplotype tree.

The ability to discriminate the genetic signatures of range expansions from recurrent but restricted gene flow is critical to discriminating the candelabra from the trellis models and thereby inferring the evolutionary validity of race. The criteria used to identify range expansions in this nested approach have been empirically validated by analyzing data sets with strong prior evidence of range expansion and were found to be accurate and not prone to false positives (Templeton 1998a). Application of this statistical approach to human mtDNA haplotype trees yields the significant results summarized in Figure 6 (Templeton, 1993, 1997b, 1998a).

As shown in Figure 6, human mtDNA yields a pattern of isolation by distance between Africans and Eurasians throughout the *entire* time period marked by mtDNA coalescence (Templeton, 1993, 1997b), thereby significantly rejecting both the candelabra hypothesis of no gene flow between Africans and non-Africans and the admixture models used to reconcile the candelabra models with the genetic distance data. Recurrent gene flow in this analysis is relative to the time scale defined by the coalescence and mutation rates of mtDNA, so gene flow among Old World human populations could have been sporadic on a time scale of several tens of thousands of years.

Figure 6 also reveals that range expansions played a significant role in recent human evolution. Among the statistically significant range expansions is a relatively recent range expansion across Europe (Templeton, 1993, 1997b), an inference supported by other mtDNA data sets (Calafell et al., 1996; Comas et al., 1997; Francalacci et al., 1996). A recent study on mtDNA isolated from a Neandertal (Krings et al., 1997) is suggestive (but not conclusive as the sample size is one) that Neandertals were replaced in Europe. This inference is compatible with the statistically significant European expansion shown in Figure 6, but further data are obviously needed to determine if this recent European expansion event was also a replacement event. The other recent expansions (into northern Asia, the Pacific, and the Americas) appear to be range expansions into previously unoccupied areas.

Genetic interchange between Africans and Eurasians over long periods of human evolutionary history is also strongly suggested by a hemoglobin beta locus tree (Harding et al., 1997). The coalescence of an autosomal gene is expected to be about four times as old as that of mtDNA or Y-DNA, and this seems to be the case for the beta locus (Harding et al., 1997). Consequently, the patterns of widespread gene flow across Africa and Asia observed with the hemoglobin locus predate the hypothesized "replacement" event of the recent candelabra model (Harding et al., 1997). Obviously, if such a replacement had occurred, these earlier genetic signatures of gene flow should have been obliterated.

To reinforce these conclusions, the hemoglobin beta locus data of Harding et al. (1997) were subjected to a nested clade analysis of geographical associations (Templeton et al., 1995). First the estimated haplotype tree is converted into a series of nested branches (clades) (Templeton et al., 1987; Templeton and Sing, 1993). Figure 7 shows the hemoglobin haplotype network of Harding et al. (1997), along with the nested statistical design. Once the haplotype tree has been converted into a nested statistical design, the geographical data are quantified in two main fashions (Templeton et al., 1995): the clade distance, D_c, which measures the geographical range of a particular clade; and the nested

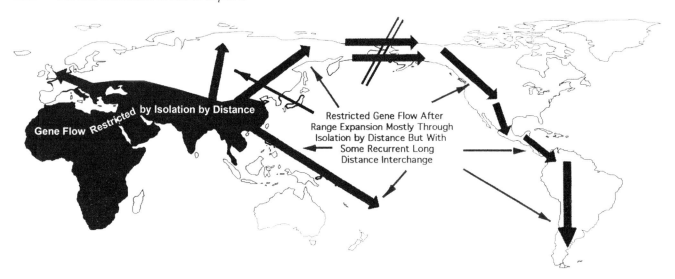

Figure 6. *Statistically significant inferences from geographical analyses of human mtDNA haplotype trees. As far back as is observable with mtDNA, there was gene flow restricted by isolation by distance in human populations living in Africa and southern Eurasia. More recent statistically significant range expansion events are indicated by wide arrows. There were expansions into Europe, northern Asia, the Pacific, and the Americas. Two arrows are indicated going into North America because this expansion either involved a colonization event with a large number of people, an extended colonization, or at least two separate colonization events. The lines drawn through these arrows indicate that after the colonization there was a significant reduction, perhaps cessation, of gene flow between Asia and North America. After the colonization of North America, there were further significant expansions into the remainder of the Americas. After these expansion events, there is statistically significant gene flow once again. Most of this postexpansion gene flow fits the expectations of isolation by distance, but some postexpansion gene flow occurred through long-distance interchanges.*

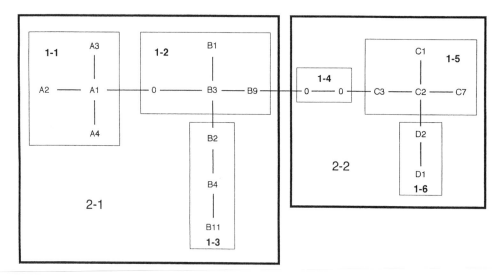

Figure 7. *The hemoglobin haplotype network of Harding et al. (1997), along with the nested statistical design. Haplotype designations are those given in Harding et al. (1997). Nested groupings above the haplotype level are designated by "C-N," where C is the nesting level of the clade and N is the number of a particular clade at a given nesting level. Boxes with thin lines nest together haplotypes into 1-step clades, and boxes with thick lines nest together 1-step clades with 2-step clades.*

clade distance, D_n, which measures how a particular clade is geographically distributed relative to its closest evolutionary sister clades (i.e., clades in the same next higher-level nesting category). Contrasts in these distance measures between older and younger clades are important in discriminating the potential causes of geographical structuring of the genetic variation (Templeton et al., 1995), as discussed above. In this case, temporal polarity is determined by an outgroup analysis that indicates that haplotype B3 in Figure 7 is the root (Harding et al., 1997) in addition to the polarity inherent in the nested design itself. The statistical significance

of the different distance measures and the old-young contrasts are determined by random permutation testing that simulates the null hypothesis of a random geographical distribution for all clades within a nesting category given the marginal clade frequencies and sample sizes per locality. Figure 8 presents the results of this nested clade analysis of geographical distributions.

The statistically significant patterns shown in Figure 8 need to be interpreted biologically. In order to make inferences explicit and consistent, a detailed inference key is provided as an appendix to Templeton et al. (1995) (hereafter referred to as the TRP key).

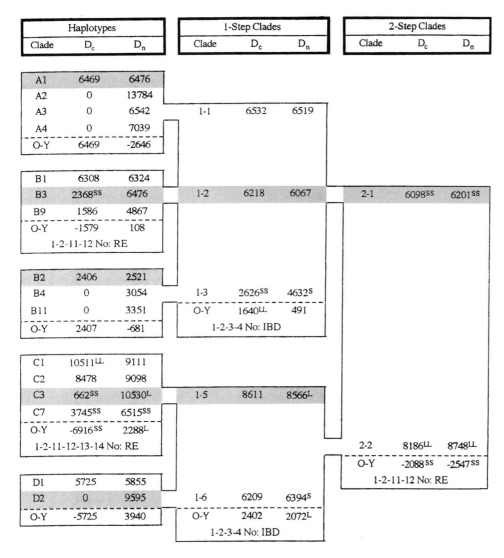

Haplotypes		
Clade	D_c	D_n
A1	6469	6476
A2	0	13784
A3	0	6542
A4	0	7039
O-Y	6469	-2646
B1	6308	6324
B3	2368^{SS}	6476
B9	1586	4867
O-Y	-1579	108
1-2-11-12 No: RE		
B2	2406	2521
B4	0	3054
B11	0	3351
O-Y	2407	-681
C1	10511^{LL}	9111
C2	8478	9098
C3	662^{SS}	10530^L
C7	3745^{SS}	6515^{SS}
O-Y	-6916^{SS}	2288^L
1-2-11-12-13-14 No: RE		
D1	5725	5855
D2	0	9595
O-Y	-5725	3940

1-Step Clades		
Clade	D_c	D_n
1-1	6532	6519
1-2	6218	6067
1-3	2626^{SS}	4632^S
O-Y	1640^{LL}	491
1-2-3-4 No: IBD		
1-5	8611	8566^L
1-6	6209	6394^S
O-Y	2402	2072^L
1-2-3-4 No: IBD		

2-Step Clades		
Clade	D_c	D_n
2-1	6098^{SS}	6201^{SS}
2-2	8186^{LL}	8748^{LL}
O-Y	-2088^{SS}	-2547^{SS}
1-2-11-12 No: RE		

Figure 8. *Results of the nested geographic analysis of the human beta chain hemoglobin haplotypes. The nested design is given in Figure 7, as are the haplotype and clade designations. Following the name or number of any given clade are the clade and nested clade distances. The oldest clade within a nested group is indicated by shading. The average difference between the oldest and younger clades within a nesting category (as determined by B3 being the root) for both distance measures is given in the row below a dashed line labeled "O-Y." A superscript S means that the distance measure is significantly small at the 5% level, and SS, at the 1% level. Similarly, a superscript L means that the distance measure is significantly large at the 5% level, and LL, at the 1% level. At the bottom of the boxes that indicate a nested set of clades in which one or more of the distance measures is significantly large or small is a line indicating the biological inference. The numbers refer to the sequence of questions in the TRP key that the pattern generated, followed by the answer to the final question in the TRP key. Following this answer is the biological inference generated by use of the TRP key, where RE is range expansion and IBD is recurrent gene flow restricted by isolation by distance.*

Templeton (1998a) gives an empirical validation of this key. This key provides for the objective and systematic identification of the distinct signatures associated with isolation by distance, fragmentation, and range expansion that were described qualitatively above. Moreover, the key also identifies the artifacts that can emerge from inadequate geographical sampling. Consequently, not all rejections of the null hypotheses can be interpreted biologically. Figure 8 shows the resulting inferences.

In comparing the mtDNA (Figure 6) and hemoglobin (Figure 8) inferences, it is important to keep two factors in mind. First, these two haplotype trees are detecting events on different time scales. In particular, the time depth of the hemoglobin network has a 95% confidence interval of 400,000 to 1,300,000 years ago (Harding et al., 1997). Once ultimate coalescence has occurred in a haplotype tree, there is no information about previous events or evolutionary forces. Therefore, the older events and forces detected in the hemoglobin analysis would be completely invisible to the mtDNA analysis. The oldest event detected in the hemoglobin analysis is an out-of-Africa range expansion found among 2-step clades as nested within the entire haplotype tree, and which therefore must have oc-

curred close to the time depth of the entire tree. This out-of-Africa expansion event is obviously too old to be the one postulated by the recent candelabra model. Because it spans the entire time depth of the hemoglobin haplotype tree, there is no information at all about the preexpansion population. Hence, this old out-of-Africa expansion could have been a colonization event of empty areas, a replacement event, or a hybridization event in which new migrants interbred with previous Eurasian inhabitants. There is simply no way of knowing. After this expansion, gene flow clearly occurred among Africans and Eurasians as constrained by isolation by distance as shown by the 1-step clades nested within both 2-step clades (Figure 8). The mutations defining these mid-level clades are expected to be ≥ 200,000 years old (Harding et al., 1997). Given that the mtDNA shows recurrent gene flow with isolation by distance certainly for times < 200,000 years ago (Figure 6), the two data sets jointly imply a long time span of recurrent genetic contact among the major Old World human populations.

An out-of-Asia expansion event is detected within clade 1-5 in the hemoglobin analysis (Figure 8). One of the critical mutations defining this expansion event (the mutation on the branch between C3 and C2) has an estimated age of 137,000 ± 81,500 years and a second critical mutation (the one defining C7) of 69,000 ± 48,000 years (Harding et al., 1997). If this out-of-Asia expansion is older than 100,000, then it would be impossible for a complete genetic replacement of the ancestral Asian population to have occurred by Africans 100,000 years ago. If this out-of-Asia expansion is younger than 100,000, then there was genetic interchange between Asians and Africans, and therefore no "split" between Africans and Eurasians 100,000 years ago. Another range expansion is found within clade 1-2 (Figure 8), and the geographical distribution of the haplotypes implies that this is an out-of-Africa expansion. Because clade 1-2 includes the very oldest haplotypes, this may simply be a reflection of the old out-of-Africa range expansion detected among the 2-step clades. However, the significant effect of the old haplotype B3 may in this case be due in part to the nonsignificant but widespread distribution of haplotype B1. The mutation defining B1 has an estimated age of about 152,000 years, but its confidence interval spans virtually the entire past 300,000 years (Harding et al., 1997). Hence, the clade 1-2 inference may represent a more recent out-of-Africa expansion occurring sometime in the last 300,000 years. Even if clade 1-2 represents a recent out-of-Africa expansion event, it certainly *is not* a replacement event. A true replacement event at about 100,000 years ago would have obliterated all evidence for older gene flow; yet the clade 1-2 out-of-Africa event is nested-*within* a pattern of significant gene flow with isolation by distance (clade 2-1). There is no obvious way to reconcile the hemoglobin data with a recent out-of-Africa replacement event.

The second factor to keep in mind when comparing the mtDNA with the hemoglobin analysis is the level of dynamic resolution. The nested clade analysis can only detect population events and recurrent forces that are marked by mutational changes (Templeton, 1998a). MtDNA is evolving much more rapidly than the hemoglobin locus, and the attendant haplotype trees are far more resolved for mtDNA than for hemoglobin. Consequently, the hemoglobin analysis is on both an older and a coarser time scale than the mtDNA. Therefore, the most recent events and forces detected in the mtDNA analysis would be invisible to the hemoglobin analysis. This explains why the hemoglobin analysis does not detect the more recent range expansions revealed by the mtDNA (Figure 6): there are simply no or too few mutations in the hemoglobin data to mark these recent expansion events. Hence, the hemoglobin and mtDNA analyses are complementary, not contradictory.

Finally, genetic interchange between Africans and Eurasians is additionally suggested by a nested clade analysis of a Y-DNA haplotype tree (Hammer et al., 1998). Interestingly, a range expansion out of Africa and into Eurasia is detected in this nested analysis. However, in light of the mtDNA and hemoglobin results, this expansion was not a replacement event, at least for the maternal demographic component. Following this out-of-Africa expansion, the nested analysis reveals a pattern of significant recurrent gene flow restricted by isolation by distance, including inter-

change between African and Eurasian populations. Moreover, there was a subsequent range expansion out of Asia and into Africa, as was also detected in the hemoglobin analysis. The Y-chromosome therefore shows more evidence of long-range population movements than the mtDNA. One possible explanation for this pattern is that males dispersed more than females during long-range population movements. However, both mtDNA and Y-DNA show recurrent gene flow with isolation by distance interconnecting African and Eurasian populations, indicating that both males and females have dispersed during short-range migrations. Regardless, there is clearly genetic interchange between Africans and Eurasians due to a mixture of gene flow mediated by isolation by distance and population movements. No genetic split between Africans and Eurasians is found in the Y-DNA, as was also true for the mtDNA and hemoglobin beta region.

Combined, the mtDNA, Y-DNA, and hemoglobin data sets reveal that human evolution from about a million years ago to the last tens of thousands of years has been dominated by two evolutionary forces: (1) population movements and associated range expansions (perhaps with some local replacements, but definitely with no global replacement within the last 100,000 years), and (2) gene flow restricted by isolation by distance. The only evidence for any split or fragmentation event in human evolutionary history within this time frame is the one detected with mtDNA (Figure 6) involving the colonization of the Americas (Templeton, 1998a). However, this colonization was due to either multiple colonization events or involved movements by large numbers of peoples (Templeton, 1998a), resulting in extensive sharing of genetic polymorphisms of New World with Old World human populations. Moreover, the genetic isolation between the Old and New Worlds was brief and no longer exists. Other than this temporary fragmentation event, the major human populations have been interconnected by gene flow (recurrent at least on a time scale of the order of tens of thousands of years) during the last one to two hundred thousand years. Gene flow may have been more sporadic earlier, but multiple genetic interchanges certainly occurred among Old World populations ≥ 200,000 years ago. Hence, the haplotype analyses of geographical associations strongly reject the existence of evolutionary sublineages of humans, reject the separation of Eurasians from Africans 100,000 years ago, and reject the idea of "pure races" in the past. Thus, human "races" have no biological validity under the evolutionary lineage definition of subspecies.

CONCLUSIONS

The genetic data are consistently and strongly informative about human races. Humans show only modest levels of differentiation among populations when compared to other large-bodied mammals, and this level of differentiation is well below the usual threshold used to identify subspecies (races) in nonhuman species. Hence, human races do not exist under the traditional

concept of a subspecies as being a geographically circumscribed population showing sharp genetic differentiation. A more modern definition of race is that of a
distinct evolutionary lineage within a species. The
genetic evidence strongly rejects the existence of distinct evolutionary lineages within humans. The widespread representation of human "races" as branches on
an intraspecific population tree is genetically indefensible and biologically misleading, even when the ancestral node is presented as being at 100,000 years ago.
Attempts to salvage the idea of human "races" as evolutionary lineages by invoking greater racial purity in the
past followed by admixture events are unsuccessful and
falsified by multilocus comparisons of geographical
concordance and by haplotype analyses. Instead, all of
the genetic evidence shows that there never was a split
or separation of the "races" or between Africans and
Eurasians. Recent human evolution has been characterized by both population range expansions (with perhaps some local replacements but no global replacement within the last 100,000 years) and recurrent
genetic interchange. The 100,000 years ago "divergence
time" between Eurasians and Africans that is commonly
found in the recent literature is really only an "effective

divergence time" *in sensu* Nei and Roychoudhury
(1974, 1982). Since no split occurred between Africans
and Eurasians, it is meaningless to assign a date to an
"event" that never happened. Instead, the effective
divergence time measures the amount of restricted
gene flow among the populations (Slatkin, 1991).

Because of the extensive evidence for genetic interchange through population movements and recurrent
gene flow going back at least hundreds of thousands of
years ago, there is only one evolutionary lineage of
humanity and there are no subspecies or races under
either the traditional or phylogenetic definitions.
Human evolution and population structure have been
and are characterized by many locally differentiated
populations coexisting at any given time, but with sufficient genetic contact to make all of humanity a single
lineage sharing a common, long-term evolutionary fate.

ACKNOWLEDGMENTS

I would like to thank Dr. Robert Sussman, Dr. Erik
Trinkaus, and three anonymous reviewers for their
excellent suggestions for improving an earlier draft of
this paper.

REFERENCES CITED

Aiello, L. C. 1997. *Review of* "Race and Human Evolution: A Fatal Attraction." Nature 386:350.

Amato, G., and J. Gatesy. 1994. PCR Assays of Variable Nucleotide Sites for Identification of Conservation Units. *In* Molecular Ecology and Evolution: Approaches and Applications. B. Schierwater, B. Streit, G. P. Wagner, and R. DeSalle, eds. Pp. 215–226. Basel: Birkhäuser Verlag.

Arctander, P., P. W. Kat, B. T. Simonsen, and H. R. Siegismund. 1996. Population Genetics of Kenyan Impalas—Consequences for Conservation. *In* Molecular Genetic Approaches in Conservation. T. B. Smith and R. K. Wayne, eds. Pp. 399–412. Oxford: Oxford University Press.

Armour, J. A. L., T. Anttinen, C. A. May, E. E. Vega, A. Sajantila, J. R. Kidd, K. K. Kidd, J. Bertranpetit, S. Paabo, and A. J. Jeffreys. 1996. Minisatellite Diversity Supports a Recent African Origin for Modern Humans. Nature Genetics 13: 154–160.

Arnason, U., A. Gullberg, A. Janke, and X. Xu. 1996. Pattern and Timing of Evolutionary Divergences among Hominoids Based on Analyses of Complete mtDNAs. Journal of Molecular Evolution 43:650–661.

Avise, J. C. 1994. Molecular Markers, Natural History and Evolution. New York: Chapman and Hall.

Barbujani, G., A. Magagni, E. Minch, and L. L. Cavalli-Sforza. 1997. An Apportionment of Human DNA Diversity. Proceedings of the National Academy of Sciences USA 94:4516–4519.

Barton, N. H., and S. Rouhani. 1993. Adaptation and the "Shifting Balance." Genetical Research 61:57–74.

Batzer, M. A., M. Stoneking, M. Alegria-Hartman, H. Bazan, D. H. Kass, T. H. Shaikh, G. E. Novick, P. A. Ioannou, W. D. Scheer, R. J. Herrera, and P. L. Deininger. 1994. African Origin of Human-Specific Polymorphic *Alu* Insertions. Proceedings of the National Academy of Sciences USA 91:12288–12292.

Bowcock, A. M., J. R. Kidd, J. L. Mountain, J. M. Hebert, L. Carotenuto, K. K. Kidd, and L. L. Cavalli-Sforza. 1991. Drift, Admixture, and Selection in Human Evolution: A Study with DNA Polymorphisms. Proceedings of the National Academy of Sciences USA 88:839–843.

Bowcock, A. M., A. Ruiz-Linares, J. Tomfohrde, E. Minch, J. R. Kidd, and L. L. Cavalli-Sforza. 1994. High Resolution of Human Evolutionary Trees with Polymorphic Microsatellites. Nature 368:455–457.

Boyce, W. M., P. W. Hedrick, N. E. Mugglicockett, S. Kalinowski, M. C. T. Penedo, and R. R. Ramey. 1997. Genetic Variation of Major

Histocompatibility Complex and Microsatellite Loci—A Comparison in Bighorn Sheep. Genetics 145:421–433.

Brownlow, C. A. 1996. Molecular Taxonomy and the Conservation of the Red Wolf and Other Endangered Carnivores. Conservation Biology 10:390–396.

Calafell, F., P. Underhill, A. Tolun, D. Angelicheva, and L. Kalaydjieva. 1996. From Asia to Europe: Mitochondrial DNA Sequence Variability in Bulgarians and Turks. Annals of Human Genetics 60:35–49.

Cann, R. L., M. Stoneking, and A. C. Wilson. 1987. Mitochondrial DNA and Human Evolution. Nature 325:31–36.

Cavalli-Sforza, L., P. Menozzi, and A. Piazza. 1996. The History and Geography of Human Genes. Princeton, NJ: Princeton University Press.

Cavalli-Sforza, L. L. 1997. Genes, Peoples, and Languages. Proceedings of the National Academy of Sciences USA 94:7719–7724.

Comas, D., F. Calafell, E. Mateu, A. Perez-Lezaun, E. Bosch, and J. Bertranpetit. 1997. Mitochondrial DNA Variation and the Origin of the Europeans. Human Genetics 99:443–449.

Cooper, G., W. Amos, D. Hoffman, and D. C. Rubinsztein. 1996. Network Analysis of Human Y Microsatellite Haplotypes. Human Molecular Genetics 5:1759–1766.

Crow, J. F., and M. Kimura. 1970. An Introduction to Population Genetic Theory. New York: Harper and Row.

Deka, R., L. Jin, M. D. Shriver, L. M. Yu, S. DeCroo, J. Hundrieser, C. H. Bunker, R. E. Ferrell, and R. Chakraborty. 1995. Population Genetics of Dinucleotide $(dC-dA)_n \cdot (dG-dT)_n$ Polymorphisms in World Populations. American Journal of Human Genetics 56:461–474.

DeSalle, R., A. Templeton, I. Mori, S. Pletscher, and J. S. Johnston. 1987. Temporal and Spatial Heterogeneity of mtDNA Polymorphisms in Natural Populations of *Drosophila mercatorum*. Genetics 116:215–223.

Ellsworth, D. L., R. L. Honeycutt, N. J. Silvy, J. W. Bickham, and W. D. Klimstra. 1994. Historical Biogeography and Contemporary Patterns of Mitochondrial DNA Variation in White-Tailed Deer from the Southeastern United States. Evolution 48:122–136.

Endler, J. A. 1977. Geographic Variation, Speciation, and Clines. Princeton, NJ: Princeton University Press.

Francalacci, P., J. Bertranpetit, F. Calafell, and P. A. Underhill. 1996. Sequence Diversity of the Control Region of Mitochondrial DNA in Tuscany and Its Implications for the Peopling of Europe. American Journal of Physical Anthropology 100:443–460.

Futuyma, D. J. 1986. Evolutionary Biology. Sunderland, MA: Sinauer Associates, Inc.

Georgiadis, N., L. Bischof, A. Templeton, J. Patton, W. Karesh, and D. Western. 1994. Structure and History of African Elephant Populations: I. Eastern and Southern Africa. Journal of Heredity 85:100–104.

Hammer, M. F., A. B. Spurdle, T. Karafet, M. R. Bonner, E. T. Wood, A. Novelletto, P. Malaspina, R. J. Mitchell, S. Horai, T. Jenkins, and S. L. Zegura. 1997. The Geographic Distribution of Human Y Chromosome Variation. Genetics 145:787–805.

Hammer, M. F., T. Karafet, A. Rasanayagam, E. T. Wood, T. K. Altheide, T. Jenkins, R. C. Griffiths, A. R. Templeton, and S. L. Zegura. 1998. Out of Africa and Back Again: Nested Cladistic Analysis of Human Y Chromosome Variation. Molecular Biology and Evolution 15(4):427–441.

Harding, R. M., S. M. Fullerton, R. C. Griffiths, J. Bond, M. J. Cox, J. A. Schneider, D. S. Moulin, and J. B. Clegg. 1997. Archaic African *and* Asian Lineages in the Genetic Ancestry of Modem Humans. American Journal of Human Genetics 60:772–789.

Harpending, H. C., J. H. Relethford, and S. T. Sherry. 1996. Methods and Models for Understanding Human Diversity. *In* Molecular Biology and Human Diversity. A. J. Boyce and C. G. N. Mascie-Taylor, eds. Pp. 283–299. Cambridge: Cambridge University Press.

Hey, J. 1997. Mitochondrial and Nuclear Genes Present Conflicting Portraits of Human Origins. Molecular Biology and Evolution 14:166–172.

Hollocher, H., and A. R. Templeton. 1994. The Molecular through Ecological Genetics of Abnormal Abdomen in *Drosophila mercatorum* VI. The Nonneutrality of the Y-chromosome rDNA Polymorphism. Genetics 136:1373–1384.

Hollocher, H., A. R. Templeton, R. DeSalle, and J. S. Johnston. 1992. The Molecular through Ecological Genetics of *Abnormal Abdomen*. IV. Components of Genetic-Variation in a Natural-Population of *Drosophila mercatorum*. Genetics 130:355–366.

Howell, N., I. Kubacka, and D. A. Mackey. 1996. How Rapidly Does the Human Mitochondrial Genome Evolve? American Journal of Human Genetics 59:501–509.

Hudson, R. R., D. D. Boos, and N. L. Kaplan. 1992. A Statistical Test for Detecting Geographical Subdivision. Molecular Biology and Evolution 9:138–151.

Jorde, L. B., M. J. Bamshad, W. S. Watkins, R. Zenger, A. E. Fraley, P. A. Krakowiak, K. D. Carpenter, H. Soodyall, T. Jenkins, and A. R. Rogers. 1995. Origins and Affinities of Modern Humans: A Comparison of Mitochondrial and Nuclear Genetic Data. American Journal of Human Genetics 57:523–538.

Jorde, L. B., A. R. Rogers, M. Bamshad, W. S. Watkins, P. Krakowiak, S. Sung, J. Kere, and H. C. Harpending. 1997. Microsatellite Diversity and the Demographic History of Modern Humans. Proceedings of the National Academy of Sciences USA 94:3100–3103.

King, R. B., and R. Lawson. 1995. Color-Pattern Variation in Lake Erie Water Snakes—The Role of Gene Flow. Evolution 49:885–896.

King, R. B., and R. Lawson. 1997. Microevolution in Island Water Snakes. BioScience 47:279–286.

Krings, M., A. Stone, R. W. Schmitz, H. Krainitzki, M. Stoneking, and S. Pääbo. 1997. Neandertal DNA sequences and the Origin of Modern Humans. Cell 90:19–30.

Lasker, G. W., and D. E. Crews. 1996. Behavioral Influences on the Evolution of Human Genetic Diversity. Molecular Phylogenetics and Evolution 5:232–240.

Lawson, R., and R. B. King. 1996. Gene Flow and Melanism in Lake Erie Garter Snake Populations. Biological Journal of the Linnean Society 59:1–19.

Legge, J. T., R. Roush, R. Desalle, A. P. Vogler, and B. May. 1996. Genetic Criteria for Establishing Evolutionarily Significant Units in Cryans Buckmoth. Conservation Biology 10:85–98.

Lehman, N., and R. K. Wayne. 1991. Analysis of Coyote Mitochondrial-DNA Genotype Frequencies: Estimation of the Effective Number of Alleles. Genetics 128:405–416.

Lynch, M., and T. J. Crease. 1990. The Analysis of Population Survey Data on DNA Sequence Variation. Molecular Biology and Evolution 7:377–394.

Maddison, D. R. 1991. African Origin of Human Mitochondrial DNA Reexamined. Systematic Zoology 40:355–363.

Manderscheid, E. J., and A. R. Rogers. 1996. Genetic Admixture in the Late Pleistocene. American Journal of Physical Anthropology 100:1–5.

Mayr, E. 1970. Populations, Species, and Evolution. Cambridge, MA: Belknap Press of Harvard University Press.

Mitchell, R. J. 1996. Y-Chromosome-Specific Restriction Fragment Length Polymorphisms (RFLPs)—Relevance to Human Evolution and Human Variation. American Journal of Human Biology 8:573–586.

Miththapala, S., J. Seidensticker, and S. J. O'Brien. 1996. Phylogeographic Subspecies Recognition in Leopards (*Panthera pardus*)—Molecular Genetic Variation. Conservation Biology 10:1115–1132.

Mountain, J. L., and L. L. Cavalli-Sforza. 1994. Inference of Human Evolution through Cladistic Analysis of Nuclear DNA Restriction Polymorphisms. Proceedings of the National Academy of Science USA 91:6515–6519.

Nachman, M. W., W. M. Brown, M. Stoneking, and C. F. Aquadro. 1996. Nonneutral Mitochondrial DNA Variation in Humans and Chimpanzees. Genetics 142:953–963.

Nei, M., and A. K. Roychoudhury. 1974. Genic Variation within and between the Three Major Races of Man: Caucasoids, Negroids, and Mongoloids. American Journal of Human Genetics 26:421–443.

Nei, M., and A. K. Roychoudhury. 1982. Genetic Relationship and Evolution of Human Races. Evolutionary Biology 14:1–59.

Nei, M., and A. K. Roychoudhury. 1993. Evolutionary Relationships of Human Populations on a Global Scale. Molecular Biology and Evolution 10:927–943.

Nei, M., and N. Takezaki. 1996. The Root of the Phylogenetic Tree of Human Populations. Molecular Biology and Evolution 13:170–177.

Parsons, T. J., D. S. Muniec, K. Sullivan, N. Woodyatt, R. Allistongreiner, M. R. Wilson, D. L. Berry, K. A. Holland, V. W. Weedn, P. Gill, and M. M. Holland. 1997. A High Observed Substitution Rate in the Human Mitochondrial DNA Control Region. Nature Genetics 15:363–368.

Pennock, D. S., and W. W. Dimmick. 1997. Critique of the Evolutionarily Significant Unit as a Definition for Distinct Population Segments under the U.S. Endangered Species Act. Conservation Biology 11:611–619.

Perez-Lezaun, A., F. Calafell, E. Mateu, D. Comas, R. Ruiz-Pacheco, and J. Bertranpetit. 1997. Microsatellite Variation and the Differentiation of Modern Humans. Human Genetics 99:1–7.

Relethford, J. H., and H. C. Harpending. 1994. Craniometric Variation, Genetic Theory, and Modern Human Origins. American Journal of Physical Anthropology 95:249–270.

Relethford, J. H., and H. C. Harpending. 1995. Ancient Differences in Population Size Can Mimic a Recent African Origin of Modern Humans. Current Anthropology 36:667–674.

Rogers, A. R. 1997. Population Structure and Modern Human Origins. *In* Progress in Population Genetics and Human Evolution. P. Donnelly and S. Tavaré, eds. Pp. 55–79. New York: Springer.

Rohlf, F. J. 1993. NTSYS-pc: Numerical Taxonomy and Multivariate Analysis System, Version 1.80. Setauket, NY: Exeter Software.

Santos, E. J. M., J. T. Epplen, and C. Epplen. 1997. Extensive Gene Flow in Human Populations as Revealed by Protein and Microsatellite DNA Markers. Human Heredity 47:165–172.

Shaffer, H. B., and M. L. McKnight. 1996. The Polytypic Species Revisited—Genetic Differentiation and Molecular Phylogenetics of the Tiger Salamander *Ambystoma tigrinum* (Amphibia, Caudata) Complex. Evolution 50:417–433.

Slatkin, M. 1991. Inbreeding Coefficients and Coalescence Times. Genetical Research 58:167–175.

Smith, H. M., D. Chiszar, and R. R. Montanucci. 1997. Subspecies and Classification. Herpetological Review 28:13–16.

Stoneking, M. 1997. Recent African Origin of Human Mitochondrial DNA: Review of the Evidence and Current Status of the Hypothesis. *In* Progress in Population Genetics and Human Evolution. P. Donnelly and S. Tavaré, eds. Pp. 1–13. New York: Springer.

Tavaré, S., D. Balding, R. C. Griffiths, and P. Donnelly. 1997. Inferring Coalescence Times from DNA Sequence Data. Genetics 145:505–518.

Templeton, A. R. 1980. The Theory of Speciation via the Founder Principle. Genetics 94:1011–1038.

Templeton, A. R. 1992. Human Origins and Analysis of Mitochondrial DNA Sequences. Science 255:737.

Templeton, A. R. 1993. The "Eve" Hypothesis: A Genetic Critique and Reanalysis. American Anthropologist 95:51–72.

Templeton, A. R. 1994a. "Eve": Hypothesis Compatibility versus Hypothesis Testing. American Anthropologist 96:141–147.

Templeton, A. R. 1994b. The Role of Molecular Genetics in Speciation Studies. In Molecular Ecology and Evolution: Approaches and Applications. B. Schierwater, B. Streit, G. P. Wagner, and R. DeSalle, eds. Pp. 455–477. Basel: Birkhäuser-Verlag.

Templeton, A. R. 1996. Contingency Tests of Neutrality Using Intra/Interspecific Gene Trees: The Rejection of Neutrality for the Evolution of the Mitochondrial Cytochrome Oxidase II Gene in the Hominoid Primates. Genetics 144:1263–1270.

Templeton, A. R. 1997a. Out of Africa? What Do Genes Tell Us? Current Opinion in Genetics and Development 7:841–847.

Templeton, A. R. 1997b. Testing the Out-of-Africa Replacement Hypothesis with Mitochondrial DNA Data. In Conceptual Issues in Modern Human Origins Research. G. A. Clark and C. M. Willermet, eds. Pp. 329–360. New York: Aldine de Gruyter.

Templeton, A. R. 1998a. Nested Clade Analyses of Phylogeographic Data: Testing Hypotheses about Gene Flow and Population History. Molecular Ecology 7:381–397.

Templeton, A. R. 1998. Species and Speciation: Geography, Population Structure, Ecology, and Gene Trees. In Endless Forms: Species and Speciation. D. J. Howard and S. H. Berlocher, eds. Pp. 32–43. Oxford: Oxford University Press.

Templeton, A. R., E. Boerwinkle, and C. F. Sing. 1987. A Cladistic Analysis of Phenotypic Associations with Haplotypes Inferred from Restriction Endonuclease Mapping. I. Basic Theory and an Analysis of Alcohol Dehydrogenase Activity in Drosophila. Genetics 117:343–351.

Templeton, A. R., and N. J. Georgiadis. 1996. A Landscape Approach to Conservation Genetics: Conserving Evolutionary Processes in the African Bovidae. In Conservation Genetics: Case Histories from Nature. J. C. Avise and J. L. Hamrick, eds. Pp. 398–430. New York: Chapman and Hall.

Templeton, A. R., H. Hollocher, and J. S. Johnston 1993. The Molecular through Ecological Genetics of Abnormal Abdomen in Drosophila mercatorum. V. Female Phenotypic Expression on Natural Genetic Backgrounds and in Natural Environments. Genetics 134:475–485.

Templeton, A. R., H. Hollocher, S. Lawler, and J. S. Johnston. 1989. Natural Selection and Ribosomal DNA in Drosophila. Genome 31:296–303.

Templeton, A. R., E. Routman, and C. Phillips. 1995. Separating Population Structure from Population History: A Cladistic Analysis of the Geographical Distribution of Mitochondrial DNA Haplotypes in the Tiger Salamander, Ambystoma tigrinum. Genetics 140:767–782.

Templeton, A. R., and C. F. Sing. 1993. A Cladistic Analysis of Phenotypic Associations with Haplotypes Inferred from Restriction Endonuclease Mapping. IV. Nested Analyses with Cladogram Uncertainty and Recombination. Genetics 134:659–669.

Terrell, J. E., and P. J. Stewart. 1996. The Paradox of Human Population Genetics at the End of the Twentieth Century. Reviews in Anthropology 25:13–33.

Vigilant, L., M. Stoneking, H. Harpending, K. Hawkes, and A. C. Wilson. 1991. African Populations and the Evolution of Human Mitochondrial DNA. Science 253:1503–1507.

Vogler, A. P. 1994. Extinction and the Formation of Phylogenetic Lineages: Diagnosing Units of Conservation Management in the Tiger Beetle Cicindela dorsalis. In PCR Assays of Variable Nucleotide Sites for Identification of Conservation Units. B. Schierwater, B. Streit, G. P. Wagner, and R. DeSalle, eds. Pp. 261–273. Basel: Birkhäuser Verlag.

Watson, E., K. Bauer, R. Aman, G. Weiss, A. van Haeseler, and S. Pääbo. 1996. mtDNA Sequence Diversity in Africa. American Journal of Human Genetics 59:437–444.

Wayne, R. K., N. Lehman, M. W. Allard, and R. L. Honeycutt. 1992. Mitochondrial DNA Variability of the Gray Wolf: Genetic Consequences of Population Decline and Habitat Fragmentation. Conservation Biology 6:559–569.

Wilson, E. O., and W. L. Brown. 1953. The Subspecies Concept and Its Taxonomic Applications. Systematic Zoology 2:97–111.

Wolpoff, M., and R. Caspari. 1997. Race and Human Evolution. New York: Simon and Schuster.

Wright, S. 1931. Evolution in Mendelian Populations. Genetics 16:97–159.

Wright, S. 1943. Isolation by Distance. Genetics 28:114–138.

Wright, S. 1969. Evolution and the Genetics of Populations. 3 vols. Volume 2. The Theory of Gene Frequencies. Chicago: University of Chicago Press.

75

On Stony Ground

Lithic Technology, Human Evolution, and the Emergence of Culture

R. Foley and M. M. Lahr

ABSTRACT

Culture is the central concept of anthropology. Its centrality comes from the fact that all branches of the discipline use it, that it is in a way a shorthand for what makes humans unique, and therefore defines anthropology as a separate discipline. In recent years the major contributions to an evolution-ary approach to culture have come either from primatologists mapping the range of behaviors, among chimpanzees in particular, that can be referred to as cultural or "protocultural"[1,2] or from evolutionary theorists who have developed models to account for the pattern and process of human cultural diversification and its impact on human adaptation.[3–5]

Theoretically and empirically, paleoanthropology has played a less prominent role, but remains central to the problem of the evolution of culture. The gap between a species that includes Shakespeare and Darwin among its members and one in which a particular type of hand-clasp plays a major social role has to be significant. However, that gap is an arbitrary one, filled by the extinction of hominin species other than *Homo sapiens*. Paleoanthropology has the potential to fill that gap, and thus provide more of a continuum between humans and other animals. Furthermore, it provides the context, and hence the selective environment, in which cultural capabilities evolved, and so may provide insights into the costs and benefits involved in evolving cultural adaptations.

In this paper we focus on the role that paleoanthropology can play in the development of the science of cultural evolution. In particular, we want to consider the way in which information from stone-tool technology can be used to map the pattern of cultural evolution and thus throw light on the nature of the apparent gap that lies between humans and chimpanzees. First, we discuss the various meanings of the culture concept and the role of paleoanthropology in its use. Second, we look at how stone-tool technology can be used to map cultural evolution and provide insights into the cultural capacities of different hominin species. Third, we consider the inferences that can be made from stone-tool technology for the timing of major events in cultural evolution.

EVOLUTION, CULTURE AND ANTHROPOLOGY

Culture in Anthropology

Culture is the jam in the sandwich of anthropology. It is all-pervasive. It is used to distinguish humans from apes ("everything that man does that the monkeys do not" (Lord Raglan)) and to characterize evolutionarily derived behaviors in both living apes and humans. It is often both the explanation of what it is that has made human evolution different and what it is that is necessary to explain. It is at once part of our biology and the thing that sets the limits on biological approaches and explanations. Just to add further confusion to the subject, it is also that which is universally shared by all humans and, at the same time, the word used to demarcate differences between human societies and groups. As if this were not enough for any hard-worked concept, it is both a trait itself and also a process. When treated as a trait, culture can be considered to be the trait or the means by which that trait is acquired, transmitted, changed, and used (that is, learned, taught, and socially passed on). It exists in the heads of humans and is manifested in the products of actions. To add one further dimension, culture is seen by some as the equivalent of the gene, and hence a particulate unit (the meme) that can be added together in endless permutations and combinations, while to others it is as a large and indivisible whole that it takes on its significance. In other words, culture is everything to anthropology, and it could be argued that in the process it has also become nothing.[3,5–10]

The pervasive nature of the culture concept means that evolutionary anthropology must also tackle the problems it throws up. This is not the place either to argue that the concept should be abandoned as of little or no analytical utility (one of us attempted this several years ago, to no noticeable effect[11]) nor to come up with a cutting-edge redefinition that will clear away a century of obfuscation (we leave that in the capable hands of the Editor of Evolutionary Anthropology). Rather, we wish to consider how those aspects of anthropology that deal with the deep past of the human lineage—paleoanthropology—might throw light on the evolution of culture and the role it may have played in human evolution.[12]

The problem in attempting this is that the sources of such evidence are limited, especially if little recourse is made either to analogical or phylogenetic inferences from chimpanzees and other primates or extrapolation back from ethnography and psychology. Paleoanthropology is limited to the archeological record for the evidence it throws either on hominin cognition, and hence culture, or else on the cultural manifestations of behavior. In practice, this means using the record of stone tools, the primary source of information about the behavior of prehuman hominins.

Culture and Paleoanthropology

There are two reasons why both evolution and paleoanthropology are central to any discussion of culture. The first is that the distinction between humans and other species is usually drawn in some way around the concept of culture—put simply, we have it and they do not. Chimpanzees chipping away at the margins of tool making or grappling with the rudiments of American sign language do not really change this state of affairs. Given the fact that humans must have evolved from an acultural organism to one that possesses such capacities means that the evolution of culture is a major challenge to evolutionary theory. The second, related, aspect is that the evolution of culture must therefore be a diachronic process. Comparisons between two living species, humans and chimpanzees, can only examine outcomes, not the actual process of transition. This must be inferred. The actual development of more and more culture-bearing hominins must have occurred among species that are now extinct, to whom our only access is through the fossil and archeological record.

To search for something in the fossil and archeological records requires knowing what one is looking for, so that a consideration of definitions of culture cannot be entirely avoided. Definitions of culture largely fall into two broad groups. Either they involve the actual end products of behaviors that are inherently human (technology, for example) or they focus on the processes that produce these outcomes—that is, the cognitive underpinnings. Most recent approaches have concentrated on the latter or, in other words, trying to get into the minds of extinct species and populations. This can only be done in terms of correlates. Most definitions of culture involve three core elements: those associated with learning, its depth and extent, or the ability to acquire new information independent of a tightly constrained genetic basis; those associated with social organization and complexity; and those associated with symbolic

Table 1. Cultural Capacity Is Cognitively Based, but Is Correlated with a Number of Manifestations in the Realms of Learning, Social Organization, Symbolic Expression, and Patterns of Tradition. These expressions may in turn be visible in the archeological and fossil record

Broad Correlative Components of Culture	Potential Paleobiological Manifestations
Learning capacity	Technology and technological variation Brain size?
Social organization and structure	Archeological density, structure and distribution Sexual dimorphism in fossil hominins Nonecologically functional elements of material culture
Traits associated with symbolic thought	Brain size? Anatomical basis for language Variation in material culture
Tradition maintenance and change	Regional variation and longevity of archeological components

thought, both its underlying cognitive basis and its communication. In addition to these core elements is the extent to which the behaviors derived from these capacities are either capable of change and variability (a characteristic of cultural systems) and have a means of being maintained as traditions (persistence through time). The possible paleobiological correlates of these are shown in Table 1.[12]

EVOLUTIONARY HISTORY IN THE STONES: WHAT CAN THEY TELL US?

We can now turn to stone technology. From over two million years, lithic artifacts provide a rich and durable source of information about the behavior of extinct hominins, and thus greatly expand on the anatomical fossil evidence. The question to ask is what sort of information can be derived from stone tools?

Archeologists have basically come up with two answers to this question. On one hand, patterns in technology have been used to reconstruct population histories, in a sense to construct phylogenies of species and populations (cultures, in other words). Stone tools were, in effect, treated as population markers. This may be considered the phylogenetic and historical approach. On the other hand, stone tools can be and have been interpreted as adaptive markers, often with little or no phylogenetic signal, because they are endlessly thrown up convergently by the demands of the environment and social organization, which thus reflect variability in behavioral response. This can be termed the adaptive function approach.

By and large, these two approaches have been seen as alternatives, and to be in conflict with one another. Furthermore, from a historical perspective, the adaptive function approach has generally supplanted and succeeded the phylogenetic and historical approach, and has become the consensus on which most Paleolithic archeology operates. However, it is worth considering briefly the strengths and weaknesses of each approach.

Phylogeny and History: Human Evolutionary History from Stone Tools

The idea that human evolutionary history might be reflected in stone-tool typology is one of the oldest in the discipline and, in one form or another, has been a persistent theme over the last one hundred and fifty years or more. When Frere recognized the stone tools discovered in the eighteenth century as the product of humans, and at the same time recognized that they were very "primitive," he was drawing the first of many such conclusions. Stone-tool typology could be seen to reflect the stages of human history, from the first simple flakes and cores through to the Solutrean points. During the first part of the twentieth century, this became formalized in the schemes of Breuil, Burkitt, and Bordes.[13]

The phylogenetic and historical approach generally encapsulated two basic components. The first was that if stone tools were similar, then they were made by the same sort of people, usually taken to mean people belonging to the same culture, with greater or lesser implications for ethnic groups, depending on the time scale involved. The second was that the level of sophistication or complexity of the tools reflected the cognitive or cultural status of the population concerned, usually more or less advanced within the framework of the time. When these two components are put together, one has a model for explaining prehistoric change in terms of the movements of peoples through their particular set of tools with a process of evolution toward greater cultural and, by implication, cognitive complexity.

The idea of stone tools as the markers of chronology gradually fell into disrepute, especially as it was recognized that globally it was hard to maintain the model of universal stages and that there was not necessarily any chronological consistency to the pattern of change. Nonetheless, stone tools were still seen as markers of peoples as they ebbed and flowed across the Paleolithic landscape. The high tide of the phylogenetic and historical approach occurred when it was possible to draw simple boundaries around typological and technological clusters and to associate them with cultural history and narrative. Thus, the cultures of the Upper Paleolithic, for example, were essentially analogous to ethnographic units, an analogy that was sometimes drawn all too explicitly.[14]

This "from technology to culture to people to history" approach has been subject to many criticisms, and is largely associated with work by archeologists in the first half of the twentieth century. The move to a greater emphasis on adaptation and, more recently, raw-material constraints, has greatly altered the way Paleolithic archeology has been done and how the past is interpreted.

Adaptation and Function: Information from Design

The alternative to the idea that stone tools reflect population and thus evolutionary history is that of adaptive function, and is the consensus view of archeologists today.[15,16] Variability in stone tools, rather than reflecting the social and cultural groupings of the populations who made them, reflects the demands of the environment and the responses of the populations to those demands within the constraints of raw-material availability.

The switch in emphasis was encapsulated in the Mousterian debate of the 1970s, when Binford argued that the variation in the frequencies of tool types in the rock shelters of the Dordogne and the Levant reflected different activities being carried out, rather than the movements of different people. The form of stone tools and their frequencies in assemblages have been seen increasingly as the result of environmental and ecological demands and opportunities. Concomitant with this view is the corollary that if the signal in the shapes of stone is function, it could not at the same time be phylogenetic and historical.

To this strongly ecological approach has been added an additional element, that of the constraints of stone as a raw material and the process of knapping itself. It is clear that in some parts of the world good lithic materials are abundant, and in others scarce. The strategies of stone-tool manufacture would therefore be expected to reflect this. The classic example of this view has been the increasingly popular interpretation of the Movius Line as a raw material boundary within the Old World.[17,18] The way in which stone tools are made—through a process of core and flake reduction—is also important. It has been argued that the differences among typological elements are the product of different degrees of reduction, and that, for example, a few more blows and one type is transformed into another. Tool-type frequency thus reflects use and the need to retouch more or less. From an evolutionary perspective, the adaptive function approach sees homoplasies (convergent evolution brought about through a combination of selection and constraints) as being rife, and therefore the phylogenetic signal of stone tools as being very low.

Back to Population History

In recent years, however, there has been a resurgence of interest in the interpretation of archeological materials in an evolutionary, in the sense of phylogenetic, perspective.[19] This can be seen in areas of direct interest to human evolution. One example is the association of the Aurignacian industries with the dispersals of modern humans into Europe and, conversely, the issue of whether there is a link between Neanderthal populations and the Mousterian in general and the Chatelperronean in particular.[20,21] A further example is the suggestion by Klein[22] that the dispersal of *Homo heidelbergensis* into Europe is associated with the Acheulean. We have also proposed that stone tools are markers of hominin geographical patterns,[23] both in the long-term persistence of the Movius line and in the

spread of Mode 3 or prepared core technologies in Africa and Europe as part of a dispersal of later archaic populations, as well as modern humans.[24]

The Evolution of Culture through Stone Tools: Which Approach?

Given these two contrasting approaches to the information potentially locked in the stone tools, we ask which one can give the most useful insights into the problem of the evolution of culture, and thus make use of the archeological record within the field of anthropology more generally. Perhaps the common-sense answer is the adaptive functional approach. This would certainly be the preferred option for most archeologists, as it represents the prevailing paradigm for the analysis of stone tool variation. More importantly, as culture is presumably an adaptation, then it is only natural to use an adaptive approach to identify it in the past. The extent to which hominins might have possessed a greater or lesser degree of cultural capacity might be expected to be reflected in the extent to which we can see a good fit between the environment and technology. Here the proxy for culture is thus taken to be those aspects of the various definitions that emphasize the behavioral manifestations of culture, variability, and a high rate of change.

If, on the other hand, culture is seen as a cognitive state reflecting the ability of the mind to generate new behaviors, then this can be something that might be expected to reside in the characteristics of the various species and not to exhibit a great deal of sensitivity in relation to the environment. This allows us to consider whether stone-tool technology covaries with phylogeny and taxonomic status or with the environment, and thus provides an empirical route into the problem.

In summary, therefore, we need to consider stone tools both in an environmental context and in the context of phylogeny. Both history ecology are important, as is the case in most evolutionary problems. Testing the various possibilities requires a dualistic approach.

STONE-TOOL TECHNOLOGY AND HUMAN EVOLUTION

Against this historical background, we propose that embedded in the Paleolithic record are the signals of both adaptation and phylogeny. The ideas we will develop here are one attempt at disentangling these signals. First we look for the presence or absence of a correlation between biological evolution, based on morphological affinities, and technological change, based on the distribution of technological modes. Second, we use this derived relationship to consider whether there is an association between cultural output and the species involved, and where technological change occurs in relation to biological change. Finally, we consider how these might relate to inferred cognition. Central to our argument is that while environment is shaping the technological demands, the nature of hominins' behavioral response is circumscribed by their cognitive abilities. Thus, the link between technology and phylogeny is crucial for determining the pattern of cultural evolution.

The Pattern of Hominin Evolution

To provide a framework, we can briefly outline the pattern of hominin evolution from the origins of the genus *Homo*. Figure 1 shows the distribution of proposed genus *Homo* taxa by time and geography. The earliest *Homo*, as well as the australopithecines, are excluded: Although there is clear evidence that they did make stone tools,[25–27] this primarily suggests either that Mode 1 technologies are plesiomorphies of *Homo*, being developed among one or more australopithecine lineages, or else an apomorphy at the base of *Homo*. The subsequent distribution of Mode 1 technologies shows the diversification and geographical radiation of the descendants of *Homo ergaster* or possibly earlier members of *Homo*. Among these geographically widespread members of *Homo* there appears to be considerable diversity, with a distinctive pattern to be found in Eastern Asia that has led some authorities to distinguish between an African lineage (*H. ergaster*) and an Asian one (*H. erectus*).[28,29]

Newer finds, such as those from Dmanisi,[30] Ceprano,[31,32] and Buia[33] support this perspective,

although others such as the material from Baka[34] have been employed to question such a distinction. The evolutionary changes that occur from a little more than 0.6 Myr have led to the view that there is a new taxon, *H. heidelbergensis*, which had a larger cranial vault and a generally more modern appearance, although retaining the extreme robusticity of the Lower Pleistocene *Homo* species.[35] This taxon is found in Africa and Europe, and to some it may also be present in East Asia. A further element of diversity can be added to this essentially Middle Pleistocene pattern with *H. antecessor*, known from Spain.[36] Finally, the terminal Middle Pleistocene and the earlier parts of the Upper Pleistocene show the evolution of two highly encephalized and derived forms of hominin, Neanderthals in Eurasia and modern humans in Africa.[37] The latter, *H. sapiens*, are present in Africa probably from 150,000 years ago, but occur, presumably through population expansions, in other parts of the world considerably later: 100,000 years ago in Western Asia, 60,000 years ago in Australia, and around 40,000 years ago in Mediterranean Europe and Eurasia.[38]

Technological Modes, Hominin Phylogeny, and the Scale of Environmental Variation

How do stone tools map on to a phylogeny of the genus *Homo*? This raises the question of how we "measure" technological diversity. There is no generally agreed means of doing this, as different approaches emphasize different traits, including means of flake production, typological forms and frequencies, metrical variation, core reduction sequences, and microwear patterns. The geographical and chronological scale of variation in each of these is very variable, and many show high levels of local, small-scale diversity rather than the large-scale one that we associate with hominin phylogeny biologically. We argue that in terms of mapping the general patterns of change and stability, what is needed is a scheme that operates on a global scale and reflects broad-scale change rather than local site variation. To make a biological comparison, we need a system that has high interpopulation variation relative to intrapopulation variation. Against this criterion, the most appropriate classification system is that of technological modes, the major forms of lithic production (see Box 1).

The principles have been developed elsewhere,[23,24,39] but in brief consist in recognizing general technological traits and treating them cladistically. These traits refer to the basic means by which the stone tools were made and the broad nature of the artifactual outputs. Using Clark's modes,[40] five basic technologies have been recognized: Mode 1 being chopping tool and flake industries; Mode 2 being the production of bifaces and bifacially worked handaxes; Mode 3 being prepared core technology; Mode 4 being lamellar or blade technology; and Mode 5 being microliths. Although there are continuities between them, they express more complex ways of making stone tools, leading toward greater control and a more effective use of raw material to produce particular end products. They are particularly suitable to be considered cladistically and so phylogenetically,

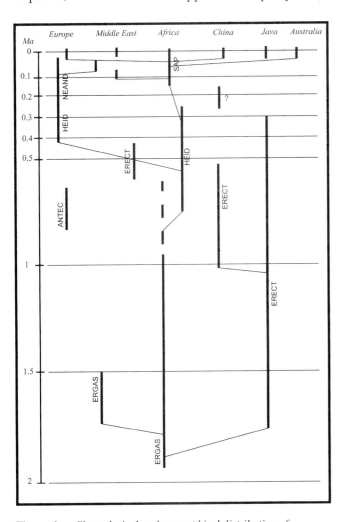

Figure 1. *Chronological and geographical distribution of recognized taxa of* Homo.

═══ BOX 1 ═══

Clark's Technological Modes

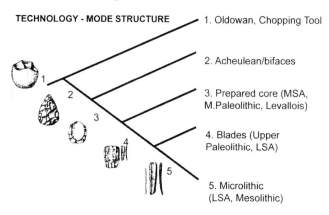

TECHNOLOGY - MODE STRUCTURE

1. Oldowan, Chopping Tool

2. Acheulean/bifaces

3. Prepared core (MSA, M.Paleolithic, Levallois)

4. Blades (Upper Paleolithic, LSA)

5. Microlithic (LSA, Mesolithic)

Clark, working in the context of a plethora of archeological cultures and terminological diversity, attempted to provide an overarching framework for summarizing variation in Paleolithic and Mesolithic lithics on a global scale. He suggested that across the range of lithic assemblages there could be seen some generalities that related to the way in which the stone tools were actually manufactured—hence, the term modes. Clark had in mind the technological modes of production for the Stone Age, upon which were superimposed the varieties brought about by cultural preference, economic need, and raw material availability. His modes provide a basic framework for grouping and separating stone-tool assemblages at a general rather than specific level. They are described here in outline form, with their broad geographical and temporal distribution.

Clark's modes were based essentially on the way in which the basic flake-core relationship occurred. Mode 1, comprising the Oldowan and Asian Pebble Tool and Chopping Tool Traditions, constituted the simplest mode of production, the striking of a flake off a core. The number of flakes could vary, but what held this system of production together was the simple platforms and lack of preparation involved. The flakes struck off tended to be relatively small compared to the size of the cores, and to lack, both on the cores and the flakes, significantly invasive retouch. This mode resulted in relatively little diversity of tool forms, relatively little by way of core reduction, and lack of any preparation of the striking platforms. Mode 1 occurs extensively throughout the Old World over

much of the Pleistocene and well into the Pliocene in sub-Saharan Africa. The African Mode 1 industries are primarily Pliocene and Lower Pleistocene, whereas in Eastern Asia they persist until the Upper Pleistocene. They also occur in the Middle Pleistocene in Europe.

Mode 2 saw the development of two elements, although of course it would have been possible for these to occur independently. The first of these was the ability to strike off relatively large flakes so that they would have some of the size properties of cores, but with a narrower cross-sectional area, and thus be suitable for a greater amount of invasive retouch. It was this that constituted the second development, for it became possible to retouch the resulting flakes in such a way that secondary flakes were removed across the whole surface of the flake and on both sides. The result was the bifacial tradition that is represented by the Acheulean and its variants. The Acheulean is known from Africa from dates close to 1.5 million years ago, although it often is difficult to draw a line between this and the developed Oldowan Mode 1 industries. The bulk of well-documented African Acheulean sites are less than 1 million years old, and usually belong to the Middle Pleistocene. In Europe, Western Asia, and the Indian subcontinent, the dated Acheulean sites fall mostly into the Middle Pleistocene, although there may be some evidence (at Ubeidiya) that it sporadically occurred earlier. There has been prolonged controversy over the presence of true Mode 2 industries in Eastern Asia. Although there is some evidence for bifacial stone tools in that region, there is nothing truly like the recurrent Acheulean of the west. It is this distinction that is represented by the Movius Line.

Mode 3 represents a major shift in the output of lithic production, although it shares with Mode 2 elements of the way tools are produced. The key difference is that the core is prepared prior to striking off a major flake as a means of having greater control over the shape and thickness of the flake. The actual means of preparation, however, is probably similar to that used in the production of handaxes. The outcome is a much more diverse set of finished tools, and hence a greater potential for variability and a greater emphasis on smaller items. Mode 3 constitutes the technologies of the European Middle Paleolithic and the African and Indian Middle Stone Age. Its presence in the Middle Pleistocene of Eastern Asia is disputed, but it may have had a more extensive eastern distribution in the Upper Pleistocene.

Mode 4 continues the trajectory of Mode 3 in the sense that it is concerned with producing pieces off a core with the shape

because they are built upon each other, and incorporate some of the elements of "descent" that are essential to an evolutionary approach. It is important to emphasize that one of the reasons that the technological modes are appropriate for evolutionary analysis is that they stress the most derived elements in an assemblage, for it is well-known that even after the development of more derived modes, more "primitive" ones, in the cladistic sense, persist.

Figure 2 shows the distribution of the technological modes represented in phylogenetic terms. It is perhaps striking that the overall shape of the two trees is remarkably similar: Both show deep African/Asian clades and relatively prolonged longevity of lineages. This con-

firms the continental rather than local scale of variation. These are, of course, two well-known and established facts, and it would perhaps be surprising if there was no concordance given that they are supposedly the records of the same populations. How, though, does this pattern relate to the expected scale of variation? The answer to this question is that the scale observed seems to reflect long-term phylogenetic patterns more than fine-grained adaptive ones. If environment was driving Lower Paleolithic variability, one would perhaps expect a far more fragmented distribution, with, for example, frequent oscillations between Mode 1 and Mode 2 industries as habitats changed and as the availability of raw material varied from region to region. This is not

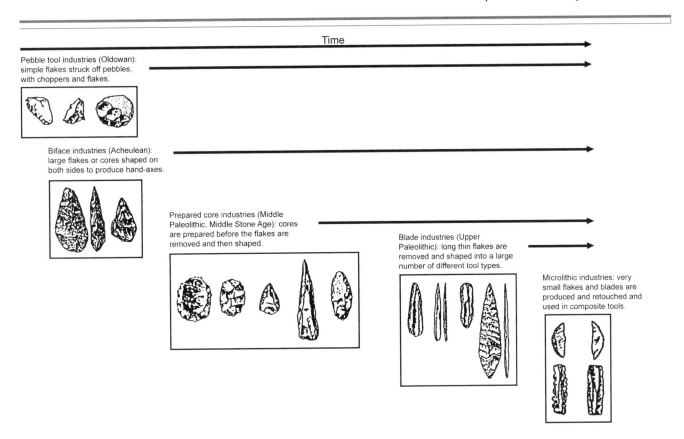

Time

Pebble tool industries (Oldowan): simple flakes struck off pebbles, with choppers and flakes.

Biface industries (Acheulean): large flakes or cores shaped on both sides to produce hand-axes.

Prepared core industries (Middle Paleolithic, Middle Stone Age): cores are prepared before the flakes are removed and then shaped.

Blade industries (Upper Paleolithic): long thin flakes are removed and shaped into a large number of different tool types.

Microlithic industries: very small flakes and blades are produced and retouched and used in composite tools.

of those pieces being determined by the way in which the core has been prepared. In this case, the preparation is designed to produce long flakes and results in cylindrical prismatic cores and fine, elongated blades with narrow cross-sections, which then are reworked extensively into diverse sets of subsidiary tool types. Although elongated flakes (that is, blades) are produced by the Mode 3 technologies, the Mode 4 system is different in that it is based on prismatic cores. Conventionally, Mode 4 industries are associated with the Eurasian and North African Upper Paleolithic and occur late (after 50,000 years) in the Upper Pleistocene. Blades are also known to occur in earlier deposits, for example in the Kapturin Beds in Kenya, and in the early Upper Pleistocene of Western Asia and Northern Africa, but these are seldom prismatic.

Mode 5 involves microlithic technologies: the production of very small flakes and blades that are retouched and worked into various shapes in some contexts or are used as composite unmodified tools in others. Microliths are widely known in the later parts of prehistory. They form the basis of the African Later Stone Age from approximately 30,000 years ago. However, there may have been earlier occurrences of this mode (for example, the Howieson's Poort in southern Africa around 80,000 years ago). Microliths are also known in Southern Asia from around 30,000 years ago, more widely across Europe and Asia in the latest parts of the Pleistocene, and in the early Holocene (the Mesolithic). Mode 5 industries are also known in the mid-Holocene in Australia.

what is seen. Instead, the best predictor of what an artifact is going to look like is what the earlier ones in the same region did—a measure of heritability, as it were, among (admittedly nonreproducing) artifacts. There is a fidelity of form that defies the scale of ecological variation and seems to suggest that the variation in stone tools as refuted in Clark's modes says more about the characteristics of their makers than the environments in which they were living.

There are, however, differences between the two. Where most interpretations of the fossil phylogeny suggest a divergence between European and African lineages dating back to the middle or early part of the Middle Pleistocene, the shared technology of the

Neanderthals and modern humans (Mode 3) suggests a later divergence or at least a period of contact and cultural diffusion around 300 Ka. Elsewhere we have proposed that Neanderthals and modern humans may have shared a more recent Middle Pleistocene ancestor than *H. heidelbergensis*, a population we named *H. helmei*.[24] It should be noted that our use of *H. helmei* differs from that made later by McBrearty and Brooks[48] to refer to the immediate African ancestor of modern humans only.

The preceding evidence suggests that there is a strong but not entirely straightforward relationship between phylogeny and technological modes. This may seem to indicate that in terms of the two approaches

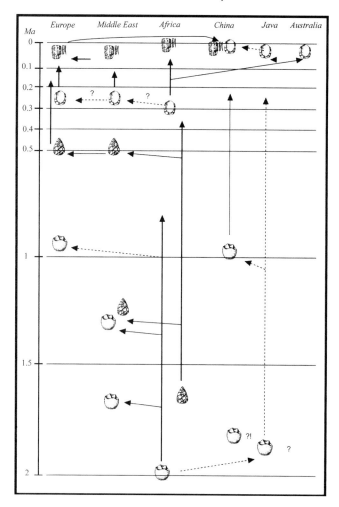

Figure 2. *Chronological and geographical distribution of lithic technologies in terms of modes.*

scale of variation. Typology, assemblage structure, and microwear analysis might well display diversity at either more general scales or more local ones. This in itself would not be surprising or necessarily a problem with this evolutionary history model. Microwear,[41] for example, might well be expected to map onto a very large scale of variability, as it is probably the case that different stone tools were used for the same purposes by different populations. In other words, there is only one way to skin a dead cat, but many tools that can be used to do it. At the other extreme, the detailed typological shape of the end-product artifacts may well be expected to display local variation, as these will be influenced both by the availability of raw materials and small-scale cultural tradition, the Paleolithic equivalent of the different ways of hand-clasping or nest-building found among chimpanzees. A prehistoric human example would be the differences in detailed bone harpoon shape found among the epi-Paleolithic populations of northern Europe, which shared the same basic stone-tool technology, and which Clark used to identify social territories.[42]

We argue that although the modes do not tell the whole story, they do tell an important one. This might perhaps be a pointer to the way in which we think about integrative approaches to human evolution. There are many sources of information about the evolutionary past, from fossils to archeology to genetics. While ultimately each must be the product of a single series of historical events, nonetheless each may have to some extent a private history. Genes may record events that are completely invisible archeologically—indeed, one would expect them to—while the stone tools might be highly sensitive to changes that are not seen in cranial morphology. Indeed, as the number of genetic systems studied increases, it is becoming clear that while they tell the same basic story, each one does have a private history: the Y chromosome compared to mtDNA, beta-globin compared to Alu insertions, and so on. Different elements of stone-tool technology may well also have their own private histories, and these histories may be regionally and chronologically specific. For this reason, technology may well not provide a single line of evidence and information, but separate ones relating to different evolutionary events—some to speciation, some to dispersals, some to behavioral grade shifts, some to cognition, some to ecology.

THE EVOLUTION OF CULTURE THROUGH HOMININ EVOLUTION

Technology and Evolution: Correlation and Causality

We can put this notion into practice by considering the relationship between the major changes in modes and the appearance of new taxa as shown in the fossil record.[23,24,39] In Figure 3 a phylogeny for *Homo* is shown, with the appearance and disappearance of the technological modes superimposed. It can be seen that the relationship is far from straightforward (Figure 4). It may be that this complexity is at least partly due to imprecise

discussed earlier, the phylogenetic and historical approach is the most consistent with these data. This may suggest that there is not a strongly adaptive element to technology. This is misleading in two ways. The first is that while the technology is adaptive—that is, carrying out particular functions that enhance survivorship—it is strongly mediated by the cognitive capacities of those hominins, who appear to have been limited at least in terms of their ability to innovate and vary their productions. This enhances the idea that the stone tools are providing insights into the evolution of the cognitive basis for culture. The second way in which we may be misled is if the approach through modes is insensitive to the scale of variation that is significant at an adaptive level. This has been one of the criticisms leveled at the approach and can be discussed in terms of "private histories."

Private Histories

There are many caveats to the broad interpretation of the archeological record presented, of which the most important one is that the modes clearly reflect only a small part of the variability in stone tools, and it could be argued that they are the only ones that reflect this

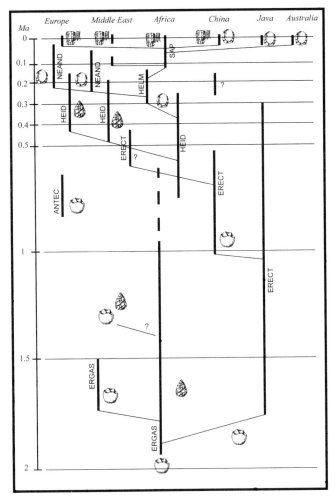

Figure 3. *Comparison of chronological and geographical distribution of lithic modes and* Homo *taxa.*

new technological mode, although there is some evidence to suggest that at this time there is an intensification of biface production. Finally, when we look at the later parts of human evolution, there is some tentative reason for suggesting that the emergence of Mode 3 technologies in Africa may be associated with a new morphology—what we have referred to elsewhere as *Homo helmei*. However, both *H. sapiens* and *H. neanderthalensis* make their appearance in the context of Mode 3 technologies, with Mode 4/5 only occurring tens of thousands of years after the first anatomical evidence for modernity.

To many, the complexities of the relationship between hominin lineages and technology might lead to the view that there is no relationship at all. Certainly there is no simple causal relationship between the development of new technologies and speciation. There is not even a consistent relationship, in the sense that technological change always precedes anatomical change or vice versa. There is, nonetheless, an important pattern that requires explanation. What is likely is that different elements are related to different events. Speciation or, more prosaically, the date of first appearances, is a demographic process, usually arising from the occurrence of small isolated populations. It is not inherent in this process that there should be a technological or behavioral or adaptive change. Rather, this process relates to genetic divergence, either through drift or selection. The major behavioral changes that might be associated with any new species could arise on either side of that geographical boundary. Major adaptive changes, in other words, are not necessarily related to speciation. What they may be associated with are dispersals. That is, where technology confers a major adaptive advantage it leads to a geographical range expansion, and this will be visible: Hence the often apparently rapid widespread distributions of novel technologies.[43] This may explain why the appearance of modern humans in Europe is associated with a new technology, the Aurignacian or Upper Paleolithic, but the anatomical features associated with these populations have been present in Africa for as much as 150,000 years.[44]

The Evolution of Culture: Inferences from Technology

What, though, can we learn about cultural evolution from modes? The most obvious point is that these

dating, but it may also reflect to some extent the fact that while both the stones and the fossils tell the same story they are sensitive to different parts of it. For example, we can see that the emergence of stone-tool technology predates the current evidence for the origins of *Homo*. In contrast, the earliest evidence for *Homo ergaster* does not relate to any significant change in technology, but rather technological change occurs considerably later, when Mode 2 appears, after 1.4 Myr. It is also the case that *Homo heidelbergensis*, which is known from about 600,000 years ago, is not associated with a

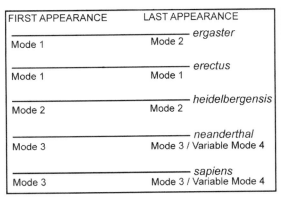

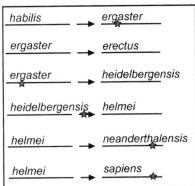

Figure 4. *Relationship between technological change and lineage change among hominins. The left diagram shows the major lineages of* Homo *and where Mode changes occur within them, while the right diagram shows how mode changes relate to "species" changes.*

technological systems of fossil hominins are deeply stable. Despite minor typological variation and raw-material constraints, there is little doubt that the Mode 2 industries, even subdivided into flake-based and nodule-based, are characteristic of particular periods and continents, and that they do not change much. It is perhaps a forgotten wonder of the archeological world that a French-trained archeologist who knows of nothing but the Dordogne could go to the Cape of Good Hope and recognize the artifacts and mode of production. What does this tell us about culture? Two things come to mind. The first is that across time there is clearly an increase in the complexity of the means by which tools are made, involving both more careful material selection, more forethought in the approach to production, and the potential for a greater diversity of outcomes. Unfashionable as it may be, this can be described as a progressive trend. However, the question to ask is where across this trend are significant changes occurring. This is not just "chronological" variation. The modes persist much longer in some places than others (for example in Eastern Asia with Mode 1), suggesting that the evolution of the underlying cognitive capacities of the hominins was not uniform across the world. If the modes reflect culture or cultural capacity, then culture is not evolving uniformly across the world's hominin population. At present there is insufficient data across Asia to understand the details of this and whether it is a case of isolation or local selection, but as a problem it emphasizes the need to situate the archeological record on the hominin phylogeny. It is no longer possible to refer to generalized evolution of cultural capacities within the genus *Homo*.

The second cultural aspect is the stability of the modes across the Pleistocene, which has been extensively discussed here and elsewhere. In one sense this stability mirrors a condition of culture—faithful replication of systems—but it does so on a scale that is manifestly very different from that of modern technologies. This argues either for a remarkable cultural template beyond the capacities of modern humans or for the absence of another cultural trait, the ability to innovate and make modifications. This latter possibility seems the more likely, with a sense that one part of the cultural program, imitation, was far more dominant in earlier hominins than it is in modern humans. As Byrne[45] has shown for gorillas, imitation is quite a complex cognitive process, so this does not mean that these creatures were not considerably more intelligent and culturally competent than living apes.

Finally, with regard to modes, we can ask whether the points at which they change are significant events in the evolution of culture or are what has been referred to earlier as private histories acting independently of the rest of the hominin evolutionary record. The mode change that has attracted the most attention recently is that of Mode 4, the blade technology associated with the Upper Paleolithic.[22,44,46] This has been strongly associated with the appearance of modern human behavior and the Out-of-Africa model of recent human evolution. However, as various authors have pointed out,[24,47,48] it is difficult to pinpoint a direct cognitive

change with this Mode. First, it is too regionally specific, essentially being confined to Eurasia. Second, it is too late, having occurred well after the first appearance of modern humans and after the diversification of the human population. If it was a cognitively and biologically based cultural shift, then it occurred only after the major populations of the world had separated, and therefore could not be a universal trait of humanity. Mode 4 and, we argue, Mode 5 as well, are important, not as markers of major cognitive evolution, but of the processes of demographic expansion into various environments, and probably reflect the processes described in Shennan's density model of cultural explosions.[49]

At the other end of the technological spectrum, the development of Mode 1 technologies has been seen as a significant cultural evolutionary event, distinguishing more advanced hominins from apes.[16] Although there is some experimental evidence that chimpanzees are capable of stone fracture techniques, these appear to be achieved with difficulty. *Homo habilis*, or whichever Pliocene hominin first made stone tools, was clearly able to replicate the process consistently. This does probably represent a significant change in the process of cultural evolution. Strout and coworkers have used PET scans of people carrying out stone knapping to explore the cognitive processes involved and shown that these do share similarities with cognitive responses to tasks of a cultural nature in the extent to which they coordinate motor control with other aspects of cognition, especially spatial processing.

Between these two extremes lie Modes 2 and 3. The development of Mode 2 at one level seems to show a major change: the ability to strike off large flakes and invasively retouch them in a controlled way, with a perception of the importance of final shape.[16,50] This shift occurs during the span of *Homo ergaster*. However, it is worth noting several points about the development of Mode 2. It does not appear with *H. ergaster* (1.8 Myr), but several hundred thousand years later; while the end product (the Acheulean) is distinctive, it does merge more gradually with the Developed Oldowan (Mode 1); and there is a considerable contrast between the earlier forms and the later modern derived Mode 2 that is associated with *H. heidelbergensis*, where there appears to be a much greater emphasis on symmetry and regular form, especially once access was gained to the flint sources of Europe. From the perspective of cultural evolution, Mode 2 does represent a major cognitive shift, but its full impact is a gradual process, not a sudden punctuated event followed by prolonged equilibrium. This seems to suggest that although the rate of change is glacial in comparison to modern cultural change, it does show a pattern of development that can be interpreted in terms of the refinement of a practice.

Mode 3 represents a different situation. It can be cogently argued that the basic technique of Mode 3, the preparation of the core prior to flaking, is inherent in the Mode 2 technologies, and a "Levallois component" has long been recognized as a part of many Acheulean assemblages. This has led some to suggest that the distinction between the two is insignificant.

However, although the actual technological aspects of change may be continuous, the outcomes are radically different. Rather than the repetitive and monomorphic production of handaxes, instead there is the diversity of flake forms. The shift represents a major change in the way stone cores (even if the cores are large flakes) are used and developed: They become the template from which diversity can be produced rather than the end product themselves. This can be seen in the increase in variation that occurs in the Middle Stone Age and Middle Paleolithic, both within and between assemblages.[51,52] With Mode 3 we see something that begins to approach the variation we would associate with modern cultural behavior, and its appearance may be related to other substantive changes in behavior.[53]

Cultural Status of Extinct Hominins

On the basis of the preceding discussion, we could argue that the technological modes do provide useful insights into the evolution of culture, but for this to be strengthened it needs to be more firmly rooted into other aspects of human evolution. We have shown (Figures 1–3) that there is considerable congruence in the broad distribution of modes and hominin populations, but this is far from simple, and that not all mode transitions show the same pattern in relation to biological evolution. This is summarized in Table 2.

From this two major points emerge. The first is that there is no simple relationship between modes and hominin species. For example, most technology-using hominins made Mode 1, itself an interesting insight

Table 2. Nature and Implications of Changes in Technological Modes

Transition	Nature of Change	Nature of Output	Change through Time	Cultural Inferences	Associated Hominins
Mode 0 ↓ Mode 1	Extension from stone-tool use to stone-tool modification, or extension of nonstone tool modification to stone	Relatively few different forms, with little formal shape Regional variation probably just raw-material related	Little, although the Developed Oldowan can be seen as a move toward Mode 2 and greater control, but the rate of change (100,000s of years) is very slow	Hominins probably not very dissimilar from apes, but control and foresight involved in consistent fracturing, choosing raw materials, and deploying tools shows a difference from the capabilities of living apes	*robustus? garhi? habilis rudolfensis ergaster erectus antecessor*
Mode 1 ↓ Mode 2	Ability to strike off large flake blanks from cobbles or to use large nodules in ways that allow invasive retouch on both sides	Relatively few forms, but these show signs of a preferred shape, and often exhibit symmetry Regional variation is probably largely determined by raw materials (flakes versus nodules)	Considerable change through time that may be related both to technical competence and the demand for particular preferred shapes (symmetry)	The emphasis in Mode 2 technology is on greater planning and goal-directed behavior associated with demand for particular shapes Some evidence for cultural variation on a large geographical scale (cleavers in Africa and India)	*ergaster heidelbergensis*
Mode 2 ↓ Mode 3	Transformation of the planning involved in Mode 2 toward the preparation of the core to allow greater control of flake production	Diverse, predetermined flakes, often very thin, with potential for modifying extensively into different tools (especially points) Regional variation may be increasingly associated with cultural patterns rather than raw materials	Some directional change from early generalized MSA to later, but most of the interassemblage variation is the development of local styles (MTS, Stillbay, Chatelperronean) Final Mode 3 in Europe undergoes major change	Clear evidence for cultural variants regionally Evidence for greater planning and awareness of indirect outputs	*helmei neanderthalensis sapiens*
Mode 3 ↓ Mode 4/5	Continuation of the strategy of emphasis on flake rather than core production, and predetermination of shape. But with emphasis on narrow flakes (blades), very thin flakes, and miniaturization (Mode 5, microliths)	Blade blanks for use as composite tools and for secondary shaping Major regional variation goes beyond raw material constraints, and probably reflects active strategies of use and cultural preference	Major change through time, although not in any unidirectional way toward greater technical competence or refinement	Evidence for ethnic marking by technology and other elements of material culture Localized cultural traditions and variants are endemic	*sapiens*

into the evolution of culture, suggesting a deep plesiomorphic conservatism for most of human evolution.
It is likely that the origins of each mode lie in one
lineage: Mode 1, an australopithecine?; Mode 2,
H. ergaster; Mode 3, *H. helmei;* Modes 4 and 5, *Homo
sapiens.* It is clear, however, that these lineages all diversified into a number of descendant populations that
persisted in making the same stone tools. If these are
species, then speciation was not the product of any technologically induced development. Indeed, in terms of
evolutionary process, it seems that technologies change
during the course of a lineage's existence.

The second point is that if the strongest evidence for
the evolution of enhanced cultural capacities and their
underlying cognition comes with freedom from the constraints of the environment (and, in the case of technology, this is presumably raw-material constraints), then
this occurs in a series of stages during the development
of later Mode 2, more fully in Mode 3, and certainly with
the elaboration of Modes 4 and 5. Certainly, it seems
that there is a strong contrast in behavior and apparent
cognitive flexibility between hominins prior to *H. heidelbergensis* and those after. It is perhaps significant that this
is also the period when brain-size evolution accelerated.

Who Has Culture, Whatever That Is?

We are aware that compared to the rich tapestry of culture in the other papers, our version is somewhat stony
and bare. There is no web of kinship or devious monkeys, no language, and no symbolic thought. In a way,
our intent has been to trace the most basic of patterns
in as broad a comparative context as possible, so that
we can see how cognitive states might map on to the
radiation of hominins as seen in the fossil record. This
has meant confining ourselves to a single source of
information, stone tools, and a large-scale approach,
technological modes. Given this limited approach, we
can see that the similarities between the fossil record
and the technological one suggest that the latter has a
strong phylogenetic signal, and that this can be interpreted as showing that the ability to generate technological solutions to adaptive problems was limited in
many species.

If we return to the larger questions relating to the
evolution of culture from the common ancestor with
chimpanzees to modern humans, we can consider
which among the many species of hominins can be said
to have possessed culture or, more accurately, how they
compared in their cultural capacities with either chimpanzees or modern humans. The cultural capacities of
those hominins making Mode 1 alone (early *Homo,*
early *H. ergaster,* and *H. erectus*) could be seen as very
close to that of chimpanzees in terms of their limited
control and formalization of functional output, although the ability to generate standardized stone tools
seems to represent some sort of shift (perhaps shared
with some australopithecines?). Those making Mode 2
(*H. ergaster* and *H. heidelbergensis*) show in the standardization of form and the remarkable stability of tradition
a considerable difference from the chimpanzee and the
earlier hominins. Furthermore, the fact that these

changes occur across the time of the lineages concerned suggests that this is not a case of behavioral
or cognitive stability. The development of Mode 3
(*H. helmei, H. neanderthalensis,* and *H. sapiens*) represents
an even greater shift, with both standardization of form
and diversification of end product. Comparison across
Modes 2 and 3 suggests that there is an earlier cognitive
shift related to the ability to imitate and to maintain
content and form (tradition?), and a later one associated with innovation. This latter change, when viewed
in the context of the evolution of modern humans and
the amazing accretion of diversity of material culture that occurs through the last 100,000 years, suggests
that the evolution of these cultural capabilities was not
a single event, but cumulative. Perhaps the most important conclusion is one that stresses the importance of
looking at evolution diachronically: The evolution of
culture is not a single step. Rather, the gap between humans and chimpanzees, between a few termites for
lunch and Beethoven, is filled with incremental steps.

While it has been possible to gain insights into the
cognitive states of extinct hominins via the relationship
between technological modes and morphological
affinities, it may be questioned how far we have demonstrated the absence or existence of culture. On one
hand, it may be argued that as all the hominins make
and use stone tools, they are culture-bearing; on the
other hand, some might say that as we have no access
to symbolic thought or language, there is no evidence
for culture. In other words, the final interpretation
depends on the definition of culture. The problem is
how to proceed out of the definitional problem.

One way is to recognize that culture is neither an
absolute, present-or-absent trait nor an indivisible
whole. It is made up of a series of potentialities, largely
resting in cognition, and depending on different mental thoughts. We can differentiate, for example, between imitation and copying as one element, which
forms the basis for social transmission, social learning,
and the maintenance of traditions, and innovation and
elaboration, which forms the basis for cultural diversification. Each of these, and many others, can be considered as a more finely graded scale. Whiten[54] has proposed that culture be tackled through the search for
contrasting features, which would include such things
as the existence or absence of traditions. Perhaps what
the paleoanthropological perspective adds to this is that
these contrasts are extremes on a continuous scale and,
furthermore, that they can vary independently. In this
sense, we return to the position that while culture as the
end product of evolution may be a qualitatively different "whole," its evolution is best treated in a more re-
ductionist and piecemeal manner.[11,12] In this way we can
track a series of different trajectories, each of which
contributes to the final outcome. Thus, although we
may never be able to speak in absolute terms about the
cultural status of extinct hominins, we may be able to
scale them relative to humans and chimpanzees, and
also gain insights into the process. For this to occur,
however, it is necessary for archeologists to work more
closely with the biological record that lies at the heart of
human evolutionary history.

REFERENCES

1. Whiten, A., Goodall, J., McGrew, W. C., Nishida, T., Reynolds, V., Sugiyama, Y., et al. 1999. Cultures in chimpanzees. Nature 399:682–685.

2. McGrew, W. C. 1992. Chimpanzee material culture. Cambridge: Cambridge University Press.

3. Cavalli-Sforza, L., Feldman, M. 1981. Cultural transmission and evolution. Princeton: Princeton University Press.

4. Boyd, R., Richerson, P. 1985. Culture and the evolutionary process. Chicago: University of Chicago Press.

5. Laland, K. N., Odling-Smee, J., Feldman, M. W. 2000. Niche construction, biological evolution, and cultural change. Behav Brain Sci 23:131–175.

6. Boesch, C., Boesch, H. 1983. Optimization of nut-cracking with natural hammers by wild chimpanzees. Behaviour 83:265–285.

7. Dawkins, R. 1976. The selfish gene. London: Oxford University Press.

8. Laland, K. N., Odling-Smee, J., Feldman, M. W. 2001. Cultural niche construction and human evolution. J Evol Biol 14:22–33.

9. Lumsden, C. J., Wilson, E. O. 1980. Translation of epigenetic rules of individual behaviour into ethnographic patterns. Proc Natl Acad Sci USA 77:4382–4386.

10. Tomasello, M. 2000. Culture and cognitive development. Curr Dir Psychol Sci 9:37–40.

11. Foley, R. A. 1991. How useful is the culture concept in early human studies. In: Foley, R. A., editor. The origins of human behaviour. London: Unwin Heinmann. p. 25–38.

12. Foley, R. A. n. d. The emergence of culture in the context of hominin evolutionary patterns. In: Levinson, S., Jaisson, P., editors. Evolution and culture. Boston: MIT Press. In press.

13. Bordes, F. 1961. Typologie du paleolithique ancien et modern. Bordeaux: Imprimeries Delmas.

14. Bordes, F. 1968. The old Stone Age. New York: McGraw-Hill.

15. Binford, L. R. 1973. Interassemblage variability—the Mousterian and the functional argument. In: Renfrew, A. C., editor. The exploration of culture change. Pittsburgh: University of Pittsburgh Press. p. 227–254.

16. Schick, K., Toth, N. 1993. Making silent stones speak. New York: Simon and Schuster.

17. Pope, G. G. 1988. Recent advances in Far Eastern paleoanthropology. Ann Rev Anthropol 17:43–77.

18. Schick, K. 1994. The Movius Line reconsidered: perspectives on the earlier Palaeolithic of Asia. In: Corruccini, R. S., Ciochon, R. L., editors. Integrative paths to the past: palaeoanthropological advances in honor of F. Clark Howell. Englewood Cliffs NJ: Prentice Hall. p. 569–596.

19. O'Brien, M. J., Lyman, R. L., Saab, Y., Saab, E., Darwent, J., Glover, D. S. 2002. Two issues in archaeological phylogenetics: taxon construction and outgroup selection. J Theor Biol 215:133–150.

20. Mellars, P. 1993. Archaeology and the population-dispersal hypothesis of modern human origins in Europe. In: Aitken, M. J., Stringer, C. B., Mellars, P. A., editors. The origins of modern humans and the impact of chronometric dating. Princeton: Princeton University Press. p. 196–216.

21. Clark, G. A., Lindly, J. M. 1989. The case of continuity: observations on the biocultural transition in Europe and Western Asia. In: Mellars, P., Stringer, C., editors. The human revolution. Edinburgh: Edinburgh University Press. p. 626–676.

22. Klein, R. G. 1995. Anatomy, behaviour and modern human origins. J World Prehist 9:167–198.

23. Foley, R. A. 1987. Hominid species and stone tools assemblages: how are they related? Antiquity 61:380–392.

24. Foley, R. A., Lahr, M. M. 1997. Mode 3 technologies and the evolution of modern humans. Cambridge Archaeol J 7:3–36.

25. Leakey, L. S. B. 1961. New finds at Olduvai Gorge. Nature 189:649–650.

26. Susman, R. L. 1994. Fossil evidence for early hominid tool use. Science 265:1570–1573.

27. Asfaw, B., White, T., Lovejoy, O., Latimer, B., Simpson, S., Suwa, G. 1999. *Australopithecus garhi*: a new species of early hominid from Ethiopia. Science 284:629–635.

28. Andrews, P. J. 1984. An alternative interpretation of the characters used to define *Homo erectus*. Courier Forschunginstitut Seckenberg 69:167–175.

29. Wood, B. 1984. The origins of *Homo erectus*. Courier Forschungsinstitut Senckenberg 69:99–111.

30. Lordkipanidze, D., Vekua, A. 2002. A new hominid mandible from Dmanisi (Georgia). J Hum Evol 42:A20–A.

31. Ascenzi, A., Mallegni, F., Manzi, G., Segre, A. G., Naldini, E. S. 2000. A re-appraisal of Ceprano calvaria affinities with *Homo erectus*, after the new reconstruction. J Hum Evol 39:443–450.

32. Manzi, G., Gracia, A., Arsuaga, J. L. 2000. Cranial discrete traits in the Middle Pleistocene humans from Sima de los Huesos (Sierra de Atapuerca, Spain): does hypostosis represent any increase in "ontogenetic stress" along the Neanderthal lineage? J Hum Evol 38:425–446.

33. Abbate, E., Albianelli, A., Azzaroli, A., Benvenuti, M., Tesfamariam, B., Bruni, P., Cipriani, N., Clarke, R. S., Ficcarelli, G., Macchiarelli, R., Napoleone, G., Papini, M., Rook, L., Sagri, M., Tecle, T. M., Torre, D., Villa, I. 1998. A one-million-year-old *Homo* cranium from the Danakil (Afar) Depression of Eritrea. Nature 393:458–460.

34. Asfaw, B., Gilbert, W. H., Beyene, Y., Hart, W. K., Renne, P. R., WoldeGabriel, G., Vrba, E. S., White, T. D. 2002. Remains of *Homo erectus* from Bouri, Middle Awash, Ethiopia. Nature 416:317–320.

35. Rightmire, G. P. 1998. Human evolution in the middle Pleistocene: the role of *Homo heidelbergensis*. Evol Anthropol 6:218–227.

36. deCastro, J. M. B., Arsuaga, J. L., Carbonell, E., Rosas, A., Martinez, I., Mosquera, M. 1997. A hominid from the lower Pleistocene of Atapuerca, Spain: possible ancestor to Neanderthals and modern humans. Science 276:1392–1395.

37. Stringer, C. B. 1995. The evolution and distribution of later Pleistocene human populations. In: Vrba, E. S., Denton, G. H., Partridge, T. C., Burckle, L. H., editors. Paleoclimate and evolution with emphasis on human origins. New Haven: Yale University Press. p. 524–531.

38. Lahr, M. M., Foley, R. A. 1994. Multiple dispersals and modern human origins. Evol Anthropol 3:48–60.

39. Lahr, M. M., Foley, R. A. 2001. Mode 3, *Homo helmei*, and the pattern of human evolution in the Middle Pleistocene. In: Barham, L., Robson Brown, K., editors. Human roots: Africa and Asia in the Middle Pleistocene. Bristol: Westbury Press.

40. Clark, J. G. D. 1968. World prehistory: a new outline, 2nd ed. Cambridge: Cambridge University Press.

41. Keeley, L., Toth, N. 1981. Microwear polishes on early stone tools from Kenya. Nature 293:464–465.

42. Clark, J. G. D. 1972. The archaeology of stone age settlement. Ulster J Archaeol 35:3–16.

43. Lahr, M. M., Foley, R. A. 1998. Towards a theory of modern human origins: geography, demography, and diversity in recent human evolution. Yearbook Phys Anthropol 41:137–176.

44. Klein, R. G. 1992. The archaeology of modern human origins. Evol Anthropol 1:5–14.

45. Byrne, R. W. 2002. Imitation of novel complex actions: what does the evidence from animals mean? Adv Stud Behav 31:77–105.

46. Klein, R. G. 2000. Archeology and the evolution of human behavior. Evol Anthropol 9:17–36.

47. Bar-Yosef, O., Kuhn, S. L. 1999. The big deal about blades: laminar technologies and human evolution. Am Anthropol 101:322–338.

48. McBrearty, S., Brooks, A. S. 2000. The revolution that wasn't: a new interpretation of the origin of modern human behavior. J Hum Evol 39:453–563.

49. Shennan, S. J. 2000. Population, culture history and the dynamics of culture change. Curr Anthropol 41:811–835.

50. Gamble, C., Marshall, G. 2001. A very remote period indeed. In: Milliken, S., Cook, J., editors. Papers on the Palaeolithic presented to Derek Roe. Oxford: Oxbow Books. p. 19–27.

51. Clark, J. D. 1992. African and Asian perspectives on the origins of modern humans. Philos Trans R Soc Series B 337:148–178.

52. McNabb, J. 1997. The Neanderthal legacy: an archaeological perspective from Western Europe—Mellars, P. J Archaeol Sci 24:575–576.

53. Stiner, M. C., Munro, N. D., Surovell, T. A., Tchernov, E., Bar-Yosef, O. 1999. Paleolithic population growth pulses evidenced by small animal exploitation. Science 283:190–194.

54. Whiten, A., Horner, V., Marshall-Pescini, S. 2003. Cultural panthropology. Evol Anthropol 2:92–105.

Glossary

Abduction   The movement of a limb or part of a limb away from the midline of the body.

Absolute dating   The determination of the age, in years, of a fossil site, usually on the basis of the amount of change in radioactive elements in rocks.

Acceleration   Faster rate of shape change or of developmental events.

Accretion   Growth through an increase in intercellular material.

Acculturation   Cultural change by borrowing from another individual or group.

Acetabulum   The hip socket.

Acheulean tradition   A stone tool technology containing large bifaces, often associated with *Homo erectus*.

Acme zone   A body of strata defined by the relatively high abundance of a designated taxon.

Adaptation   The process whereby an organism changes in order to survive in its given environment; or a specific new characteristic that enhances survival and/or reproductive success.

Adaptive radiation   A diverse array of related species with different morphological and ecological adaptations.

Adduction   The movement of a limb or part of a limb toward the midline of the body.

Admixture   Genetic interbreeding.

African hybridization and replacement model   A model for the spread of modern humans in which they originated in African and hybridized with other hominids as they spread throughout the rest of the world.

Air-fall volcanic ash   Ash from volcanic eruptions; forms tuff layers in the sedimentary sequence.

Albumin   The most prevalent blood protein.

Allele   Variant forms of a gene.

Allen's rule   A general physiological trend by which mammals in cold climates tend to have shorter and bulkier limbs, allowing less loss of body heat, whereas mammals in hot climates tend to have long, slender limbs, allowing greater loss of body heat. *See also* **Bergmann's rule.**

Allometry   The relationship between the shape of an organism or its parts to size; also, the study of such relationships.

Allopatric speciation   The emergence of a new species from similar populations that are separated geographically.

Alluvial   Geological sediments laid down by running water.

Altricial   Young born immature and helpless.

Alveolar prognathism   The forward projection of the portions of the jaws that bear teeth.

Alveolus (pl. **alveoli**)   The cavity in the bone for the root of the tooth.

Amino acid   The basic unit of which proteins are composed. Twenty different amino acids are found in biological compounds.

Amorphous   Formless.

Amplitude   The height or range of a repetitive movement or activity.

Anagenesis   Morphological change in a single species or lineage over time. Contrasts with **cladogenesis.**

Analogous   Describes the similarities in structure between species that do not share a common ancestor; due to convergent evolution.

Anatomically modern *Homo sapiens*   The extant modern form of *Homo* which characterizes all living populations that first appeared in the fossil record as early as 200,000 years ago.

Ancestral character   *See* **Primitive feature.**

Ankylosed   Fused.

Antemortem   Before death.

Anterior   Towards the front.

Anterior pillars   Thickened areas of bone on the face adjacent to the nasal region.

Anthropoid   A member of the suborder Anthropoidea that includes monkeys, apes, and humans.

Anthropometry   The measurement of the human body.

Antibody   Substance that reacts to other substances invading the body (antigens).

Antimere   The same tooth from the opposite side of the jaw.

Aperture   An opening.

Apex   The top or peak.

Aphelion   Farthest point in the earth's orbit around the sun.

Apical wear   Wear on the top of a tooth.

Apomorph   A new morphological feature that has appeared in an evolving lineage that may signify a point of divergence.

Arboreal   Habitually living in trees.

Archaeology   One of the four fields of anthropology; archaeologists attempt to reconstruct the past through the study of material remains.

Archaic *Homo sapiens*   A more primitive Pleistocene hominid than modern *Homo sapiens* now normally referred to as *Homo heidelbergensis*.

Archipelago   An area of water with a series of islands.

Aridification   The process of drying out thoroughly.

Articulation   A joint between two or more bones.

Artifact (or **artefact**)   Any movable object that has been altered or created by humans—tools, mobilary art, etc.

Ascending ramus   The vertical portion of the mandible.

Ash   Uncemented pyroclastic particles that are less than 2 mm in diameter.

Assemblage zone   A body of strata defined by the joint occurrence of a group of specified fossils.

Asterion   Where the lambdoid, parietomastoid, and occipitomastoid sutures meet on the skull.

Astragalus   *See* **Talus.**

Aterian tradition   A stone tool industry found primarily in North Africa.

Atlas   The first cervical vertebra which articulates with the skull.

Atlatl   A spear-thrower.

Auditory aperture (meatus)   External ear opening.

Aullan sea regression   A series of highly eroded sediments in northwest Tuscany (Italy) that indicates a cold, rainy climate associated with an abrupt, glacially induced drop in sea level. The Aullan sea regression coincides with the end of the Olduvai paleomagnetic episode, about 1.8 million years ago. Cold-adapted mammalian fossils are found in Aullan deposits.

Aurignacian tradition   An early Upper Paleolithic tool industry of the Old World, dating from about 33,000 to 18,000 B.P., characterized by bone tools and forms of art.

Australopithecine   General term for species in the genus *Australopithecus* or *Paranthropus.*

Autapomorph   A new morphological feature confined to one group in an evolving lineage.

Autocthonous   Indigenous; originating in the place where it is found.

Autosomal region   Part of any chromosomes other than the sex chromosomes.

B.P.   Before present.

Background radiation   The level of radiation in sediments surrounding an object being studied.

Basal   Near the base.

Basal metabolism   The energy requirements of an animal at rest.

Basalt   Fine-grained extrusive igneous rock of dark color, low in silica. Basalt can be dated radiometrically.

Basicranium   The underside of the cranium.

Basion   The anterior edge of the foramen magnum on the sagittal line.

Bauplan   A fundamental "body plan" or body structure for a group of organisms. From the German for "building plan" or "blueprint."

Bed   The smallest unit that can be depicted on geological maps; often applied to units that are made up of smaller, unmappable beds such as laminae or strata.

Benthic   Relating to the bottom of a body of water such as an ocean.

Bergmann's rule   A physiological trend whereby closely related mammals in colder climates are larger than their relatives in warmer climates. *See also* **Allen's rule.**

Beringia   Land bridge formed during the Cretaceous that lasted into the Tertiary; spanned the Bering Strait from Siberia to Alaska.

Biciliate cell   A cell with two ciliae.

Bicondylar angle   The angle that the shaft of a femur resting on its distal condyles makes with the vertical.

Biface   A stone tool with both sides worked.

Bilophodont   Having two transverse crests on a tooth.

Binomial nomenclature   The system of naming organisms using two names where the first is the genus designation and the second is the species designation.

Biochronology   Geohistorical analysis that divides time according to sequences of reconstructed paleobiological events.

Biogeography   The study of the geographic distribution of organisms.

Biological Species Concept (BSC)   A method of identifying species as a group of organisms that are not able to interbreed and produce fertile offspring with individuals of another species.

Biomass   The sum of the weights of the organisms in a particular area.

Biomechanics   The application of basic physics to biology; the study of forces and their effects in biological systems.

Biorbital breadth   Distance from outer orbit (eye socket) to outer orbit at widest point.

Biostratigraphy   A main branch of stratigraphy; sequential or temporal ordering of rocks based on the fossils they contain.

Biotope   Paleontological term for an environmentally governed set of fossils.

Bipedalism   Mode of locomotion using only the hindlimbs.

Bizygomatic breadth   Distance from cheekbone to cheekbone at widest point.

Blade technology   A method in which long, parallel-sided flakes are removed from a specially prepared core.

Bonobo   *Pan paniscus*, the pygmy chimpanzee.

Boss   Smooth, rounded, broad eminence.

Bottleneck   An isolating event in which the genotype of a small population eventually characterizes the entire population due to absence of gene flow.

Boundary-stratotype   A unique physical reference point that is a single stratigraphic plane in an easily correlatable section of beds.

Bovid   Related to the mammalian family containing cattle and antelopes.

Brachial index   Ratio of the radius length divided by the humerus length × 100.

Brachiation   A type of arboreal locomotion in which the animal moves below branches by grasping branches with alternating forelimbs.

Brachycephalic   Broad-headed, having a cephalic index above 80.

Breccia   Sedimentary rock composed of angular fragments of derived material embedded in fine cement.

Bregma   The point on the skull where the coronal and sagittal sutures join. The junction of the frontal bone with the two parietal bones.

Broca's area   An area on the left side of the frontal lobe in humans that is associated with language production.

Brow ridge   The large ridge above the orbits formed by an anterior projection of the frontal bone.

Buccal   The cheek side of a tooth or tooth row.

Bunodont   Teeth that possess low, rounded cusps.

Burin   An Upper Paleolithic chisel-like stone tool suitable for engraving bone, wood, horn, or soft stone.

Calcaneus   The heel bone.

Calcrete   Calcitic layers formed by the evaporation of soil water in the subsurface soil in arid and subarid regions.

Calibration   Standardization of a scale for measurement.

Calotte   Uppermost portion of the braincase.

Calvarium (pl. **calvaria**)   A skull without the bones of the face or mandible.

Canal   A tunnel-like, extended foramen.

Cancellous (spongy, trabecular) bone   The porous and lightweight portion of bone tissue found inside bones.

Candelabra model   A model of human evolution in which the hominid lineages in different regions remain separate from an early origin until the present with no interbreeding.

Canine diastema   The gap between the canine and first premolar or lateral incisor to accommodate the projecting canine from the opposing jaw; in the mandible, the diastema is between the canine and first premolar. On the maxilla, the diastema is between the lateral incisor and the canine.

Canine jugum   A ridge in the maxilla formed by an enlarged canine root.

Canine-premolar honing complex   A functional complex common among primates in which the lower anterior premolar has an anterior ridge that serves to sharpen the posterior edge of the upper canine.

Carabelli's cusp   An accessory cusp on the lingual surface of the crown of an upper molar tooth.

Carbon-14 dating   An absolute dating method based on the half-life of carbon-14. Based on measurements of the decay of the radioactive isotope ^{14}C to stable ^{14}N by emission of an electron charge from the nucleus, leaving a proton in place of a neutron. This method can be applied to organic remains up to a maximum age of about 50,000 years.

Carnivore   An animal that eats primarily the flesh of other animals; also often used to refer to the mammalian order Carnivora, which have tooth morphology adapted to this purpose.

Carpal   A wrist bone.

Catarrhine   A member of the group of higher primates consisting of Old World monkeys, apes, and humans (literally, "narrow-nosed").

Catchment scavenging   Natural resources managed by early *Homo* to minimize dependence on specific territories.

Caudal   Towards the tail end of the body.

Cenozoic   Youngest and briefest era in the geologic time scale, the last 65 myr from the end of the Cretaceous to the Present.

Cephalic index   A measure of cranial shape, length of skull divided by the width of the skull $\times$ 100.

Cercopithecine   A member of the subfamily of Old World monkeys with cheek pouches.

Cerebellum   A large dorsally projecting part of the brain concerned with movement.

Cerebrum   The area of the forebrain that consists of the outermost layer of brain cells; associated with memory, learning, and intelligence.

Chaîne opératoire   A sequence of actions involved in producing a stone tool.

Character   Morphological trait.

Character displacement   The tendency for enhanced character divergence in two closely related species occupying overlapping distributions, owing to the selective effects of competition.

Character redundance   Duplication in the description of anatomical features in phylogenetic analysis; counting the same structure more than once.

Châtelperronian tradition   Earliest Upper Paleolithic or final Middle Paleolithic industry of southwestern and central France and northeastern Spain; dated to 35–32 kya by radiocarbon.

Chignon   A protuberance of the occipital bone of the skull; characteristic of the Neandertals.

Chindadn biface   Very thin flaked blades or knives with a teardrop outline, associated with the Nenana complex.

Chopper   A stone chipped at one end to create a sharp edge; typical tool of the Oldowan and other pebble-chopper industries.

Chromosome   Visible structure in the nucleus during cell division; formed as a result of the condensation of the genetic material with proteins.

Chron   A small unit of geological time, especially in the Neogene of Europe.

Chronostratigraphy   A main branch of stratigraphy whereby strata are classified by age.

Cingulum   A band of enamel on the base of a tooth.

Circumduction   Movement of joint through 360 degrees.

Clade   A group composed of all the species descended from a single common ancestor; a monophyletic group.

Cladistics   Phylogenetic systematics; a method of phylogeny reconstruction and classification in which organisms are grouped on the basis of shared derived traits (synapomorphies).

Cladogenesis   The splitting of a lineage into two new species.

Cladogram   A branching tree diagram used to represent phyletic relationships among organisms.

Clast   A fragment of rock.

Clavicle   Bone connecting the sternum to the scapula.

Cleaver   A biface stone tool characterized by a broad, flat edge.

Clinal variation   The variation of a trait characterized by gradual transitions occurring over geographic distance, as opposed to a sharp disjuncture.

Clovis   An early North American stone tool tradition characterized by large, bifacially flaked lanceolate points manufactured by percussion flaking.

Coalescence date   The reconstructed time in which all the different alleles of a gene had a single common ancestor.

Coeval   Existing during the same time period.

Cognition   Mental awareness.

Colluvium   Sediments that accumulate at the base of a slope.

Colobine   A member of the subfamily of leaf-eating Old World monkeys with complex stomachs.

Colonization   Establishment of a colony or settlement in a new place.

Compact (cortical) bone   The outer tissue of bones.

Composite tools   Tools containing more than a single element.

Computed tomography (CT)   A radiographic technique that generates images with three dimensions.

Concurrent-range zone   The strata in which two designated taxa overlap.

Condensed section   A type of discontinuity where deposition was markedly slowed.

Condyle   The rounded part of a bone that articulates into a cavity of another bone.

Conglomerate   Consolidated pebble, gravel, or boulder beds that accumulate along waterways; often indicative of shallow water sedimentation and vigorous currents.

Conspecific   Belonging to the same species.

Continental drift   Theory that the Earth's surface is made up of constantly moving plates that split up and recombine through time.

Continuous trait   A trait that is expressed over a range of values and is measured rather than counted; length of a femur is a continuous trait. *See also* **Discrete trait.**

Convergent evolution   The independent evolution of similar morphological features from different ancestral conditions; for example, the wings of bats and birds or the tails of whales and fishes.

Coprolite   Fossilized fecal remains.

Core   A stone that serves as a source of stone flakes capable of being used either unaltered or modified for specific functions.

Coronal plane   A plane through the body that is parallel to the coronal suture of the skull and bisects the body into anterior and posterior halves.

Cortex   The outer part of an organ or structure.

Cranial capacity   The volume of the brain, usually determined by measuring the volume of the inside of the neurocranium.

Cranial frontal angulation   Slope of the forehead.

Cranial vault   Combination of bones that encase the brain.

Cranium (pl. **crania**)   The head.

Crest   A ridge or blade formed on a tooth or bone.

Cribriform plate   The upper part of the ethmoid bone that is exposed in the anterior cranial fossa and contains holes through which the olfactory nerves pass into the nasal region.

Crista galli   A crest of bone extending into the cranial cavity from the cribriform plate.

Cross-bedded   Sediments showing bedding planes set at an angle to one another.

Crural index   Ratio of the length of the tibia divided by the length of the femur $\times$ 100.

Crystal lattice   The interlocked three-dimensional array of atoms in a mineral.

Cuneiform   One of three small ankle bones.

Cusp   Pointed protuberance on the occlusal tooth surface.

Cyclostratigraphy   The analysis of the stratigraphic record using astronomical cycles; in particular, using earth-orbital cycles with periodicities from 0.1 and 1.0 myr that support an orbital-forcing time scale.

Cytogenetic data   Data derived from the study of chromosomes.

Datum event   The historical equivalent of a datum level.

Datum level   The limit of occurrence of a fossil in rock; emphasizes that the stratigraphic observations are different from inferred historical events that they only approximately record.

Death assemblage   A group of fossils found in the same place as a result of the processes leading to their burial, but not necessarily indicating that they were found together during their lifetimes.

Débitage   Unused or waste material resulting from the manufacture of a stone tool.

Deciduous dentition   The "milk teeth" or "baby teeth." The deciduous dentition is replaced by the permanent dentition.

Deme   A physically distinguishable group of organisms inhabiting the same general area and forming an interbreeding population within a species.

Dendrogram   A diagram which branches out from a single source.

Dental arcade   The tooth row.

Dental eruption sequence   The order in which the different teeth erupt in the mouth.

Dental formula   A notation of the number of incisors, canines, premolars, and molars in one side of the upper or lower dentition of a species; for example, the adult human dental formula is 2.1.2.3 in each quadrant.

Dental hypoplasias   Defects in the enamel of teeth, usually resulting from stress, such as poor nutrition or infection.

Denticulate   A tool with tooth-like projections along its working edge.

Derived feature   A specialized characteristic that departs from the condition found in the ancestors of a species or group of species. *See also* **Apomorph.**

Determinants of gait   The factors that influence the pattern of walking and running used by an animal.

Diagnostic   The features of a group or organisms that are characteristic or distinguish that group.

Diaphysis   The shaft of a long bone.

Diastema   Gap between adjacent teeth.

Diastems   A primary genetic type of rock record gap; due to the inherent transitions or pauses in a continuing depositional process.

Dietary hypothesis   A model first developed in the 1960s that posits two lineages of hominids during the Plio-Pleistocene with contrasting ecological adaptations—one group characterized by adaptations to a vegetarian diet and the other by an omnivorous diet.

Disconformities   A type of discontinuity where deposition was completely interrupted.

Discrete trait   A trait which can be counted and has a finite value. *See also* **Continuous trait.**

Distal   Away from the midline of the body.

Divergence   Where two or more descendant populations that differ from one another arose from a single ancestral population.

DNA   Genetic material that directs the synthesis of proteins.

DNA hybridization   A method for establishing the biological distance between species based on the ability of strands of DNA from each species to bond to another.

Dolichocephalic   Long-headed, having a cephalic index of less than 75.

Dome   A geologic feature in which all the strata dip away from a central point.

Dorsal   Toward the back side of the body; the opposite of ventral.

Dorsiflexion   Bending of a joint dorsally, such as raising the top of the foot towards the front of the leg.

East African Rift Valley   Long, narrow valley in Ethiopia, Kenya, and Tanzania caused by the separation of the Nubian, Somalian, and Arabian tectonic plates.

Eccentricity   The degree of ellipticity in the earth's orbit.

Ecological niche   The complex of features (such as diet, habitat, activity pattern) that characterize the role a species occupies in the ecosystem.

Ecology   The study of the relationship between an organism and all aspects of its environment; or all aspects of the environment of an organism that affect its way of life.

Ectocranial   On the outer surface of the neurocranium.

Egalitarian   Characterized by equality among members.

Electron   The negatively charged particle that circles the nucleus of an atom.

Electron spin resonance (ESR) dating   An absolute dating method usually applied to fossil teeth recovered from cave environments; the method measures the level of radioactive bombardment undergone by teeth by determining the number of electrons knocked off their shells that become trapped in crystals of apatite found in tooth enamel.

Eminence   A bony projection; not as prominent as a process.

Encephalization   Increase in brain size.

Endocast   An impression of the inside of the neurocranium which often preserves features of the surface of the brain.

Endocranial   On the inner surface of the neurocranium.

Endogamy   Marriage or mating within the same group.

Endogenous   Caused by factors within the organism.

Epiphyseal growth   The growth of bones characterized by the presence of epiphyseal cartilage alongside the zone of hypertrophic growth; seen at the ends of the long bones and at the superior and inferior borders of the vertebrae.

Epiphysis   The ossification at the end of a mammalian long bone.

Epoch   A unit of geologic time; a subdivision of a period.

Equid   A member of the family containing horses and zebras.

Equinox   One of the two days in the year (spring and fall) when the sun crosses the equator and day and night are of equal length everywhere.

Ethmoid   A small midline bone of the skull located between the orbits.

Ethnoarchaeology   The gathering of data on living populations to help reconstruct the past.

Eukaryote   An organism with cells containing a defined nucleus.

"Eve" hypothesis   The reconstructed common ancestor from which all of the mitochondrial genes in living humans descended.

Eversion   Turning (the foot) outward.

Evolution   Descent with modification.

Exogamy   Marriage or mating with a different group.

Exogenous   Caused by factors outside of an organism.

Extant   Living organisms, as opposed to extinct organisms.

Extension   A movement that straightens or increases the angle between the bones of a limb joint; the opposite of flexion.

Facet   A small articular surface on a bone that is smooth.

Facies   Rock types that change as the strata within a defined unit are traced laterally.

FAD   First Appearance Datum; the bottom of a fossil taxon's observed stratigraphic range.

Family   Principal category of the classification hierarchy below the order and above the genus.

Fauna   The Latin word for animal life.

Faunal analysis   The examination of animal remains from archaeological sites.

Faunal correlation   The determination of the relative ages of different geological strata by comparing the fossils within them and assigning similar ages to strata with similar fossils; a method of relative dating.

Fecundity   The ability to produce offspring.

Feldspar   A group of minerals containing aluminum silicates.

Femur (pl. **femora**)   The thigh bone.

Fibula (pl. **fibulae**)   The smaller of the two lower leg bones.

Findspot   The precise location of a fossil or artifact discovery, usually demarcated on a plan-view map.

Fission-track dating   An absolute dating method based on the number of tracks made across crystals in volcanic rock as uranium decays into lead.

Flake   A sharp fragment removed from a core.

Flexion   A movement indicating bending or a decreasing angle between the bones of a limb joint; the opposite of extension.

Flourine dating   A method of relative dating by measuring the amount of fluorine in a specimen.

Fluvial/riverine landscape   Landscape produced by the action of rivers and streams.

Folivore   An animal that feeds exclusively or primarily on leaves.

Folsom   The second fluted-point tradition in the Americas that follows the Clovis tradition.

Fontanelle   A cartilage-filled space between two skull bones usually early in development before the bones are fully grown.

Food web   The complex interaction between organisms based on their dietary habits.

Foraging strategy   The behavioral adaptations of a species related to its acquisition of food items.

Foramen (pl. **foramina**)   An opening or hole in a bone.

Foramen magnum   The large hole at the base of the skull through which the spinal cord passes from the vertebral column to the brain.

Formation   The basic unit of lithostratigraphy; any well-characterized set of beds with consistent mappable characteristics and clear stratigraphic boundaries.

Fossa   Any depression on a bone or tooth.

Fossil   The actual remains, or the indications, of past organisms.

Fossil bed   Layer or stratum, distinguishable from the layers above and below, that contains fossils.

Founder effect   Genetic drift caused by the formation of a new population by a small number of individuals.

Fovea   (1) A pit on a bone; or (2) the depression on the retina of anthropoid primates with an especially dense concentration of visual cells.

Frankfurt plane (or **Frankfurt horizontal**)   A predefined plane in which skulls may be oriented for comparative purposes. Arranged horizontally, it passes through the lower orbital margin and forms a tangent to the upper margin of the external auditory meatus (ear).

Frontal bone   Skull bone making up the forehead and upper portion of the eye sockets.

Frontal keel (or **torus**)   A vertical thickening of bone in the midline of the squama of the frontal bone.

Fructan   A polymer of fructose.

Frugivore   An animal that feeds primarily on fruit.

Functional anatomy   The study of anatomy in terms of movements and forces involved.

Gallery forest   A forest along a river or stream.

Gene   A section of DNA that determines a given biological feature or function in an organism.

Gene flow   A mechanism for evolutionary change resulting from the movement of genes from one population to another.

Gene pool   The genotypes of all the individuals in a population; their gametes.

Genetic drift   A mechanism for evolutionary change caused by the random fluctuations of gene frequencies from one generation to the next, or from any form of random sampling of a larger gene pool.

Genome   The sum total of genetic material, DNA, contained in a reproductive cell.

Genotype The genetic makeup of an organism.

Genus In the hierarchy of classification, the ranking that lies below the family group and above the species.

Geochronology Study of time in relationship to the history of the earth, especially by the absolute age and relative dating systems developed for this purpose.

Geochronometry The quantitative measurement of geologic time.

Geographic isolation Separation of different populations by geography.

Geology The study of the earth and earth materials, processes, and history.

Geometric morphometrics A series of approaches for multivariate statistical analysis of Cartesian coordinate data, usually limited to landmark point locations.

Gigantopithecus A genus of fossil ape found in Asia, dating between 0.2 and 8 million years B.P.

Glabella The midline prominence between the orbits.

Glaciation The formation and activities of glaciers.

Glacier A mass of ice on land that moves plastically.

Gluteals Large muscle group of the hips and buttocks essential for bipedal locomotion: Gluteus maximus is used for extension and rotation of the hip joint; gluteus medius is used for hip abduction and lateral balance; gluteus minimus is used for hip abduction and rotation as well as balance.

Gnathion The lowest point of the chin on the midline.

Gracile Relatively slender or delicately built.

Grade A level or stage of organization, or a group of organisms sharing a suite of features (either primitive or derived) that distinguishes them from more derived or more primitive animals but does not necessarily define a clade.

Gradistic classification A classification in which organisms are grouped by the grade or level of organization rather than according to ancestry or phylogeny.

Granivore An animal that eats primarily grains; also often used to describe an animal that eats seeds.

Gravel Unconsolidated natural accumulation of round rock pieces, mostly of particles larger than sand (diameter greater than 2 mm).

Gravettian An Upper Paleolithic industry of Europe.

Groups The combination of formations.

Growth allometry The relationship between size and shape during the growth (or ontogeny) of an organism.

Habitat The area where a species lives.

Haft Attaching an implement to a handle, i.e., a spear point or ax head.

Half-life Time period in which half the initial number of atoms of a radioactive element disintegrates into atoms of the element into which they change directly.

Hallux The big toe.

Hammerstone A stone tool that is used as a hammer in the production of other tools.

Hamstrings The large muscles on the back of the thigh that extend the hip and flex the knee.

Hamulus A small projection on a bone.

Hand ax A bifacially flaked stone tool shaped like a teardrop.

Haplotype A group of alleles of linked genes contributed by one parent.

Harpoon Barbed spear point artifact form found at many sites of the Late Paleolithic, in particular the Upper Paleolithic and Mesolithic of western Europe and the Later Stone Age of Africa.

Head Large, rounded, usually articular end of a bone.

Hearth The site of a man-made fire used for warmth or cooking.

Hegemony Influence or authority over others.

Hemoglobin An iron-containing pigment in red blood cells that functions to transport oxygen.

Herbivore An animal that consumes primarily plant material.

Heterochrony A change in the form of descendants relative to their ancestors that is brought about by an alteration in the timing of developmental events.

Heterodontism Tooth differentiation for different functions.

High-resolution mass spectrometry Determination, usually by electrical means, of molecular weights and relative abundances of isotopes within a compound.

Himalayan fore slope Essentially, the southern foothills of the Himalayan Mountains in current northeast Pakistan and north-central India. The fore slope has thick deposits of stream wash relating to the last burst of Himalayan uplift, 10–2 million years ago.

Holarctic Relating to the northern continents.

Holocene The most recent unit in the geologic time scale.

Holophyletic group A taxonomic group of organisms that has a single common ancestor and includes all descendants of that ancestor.

Home bases Campsites where members brought back food for sharing with other members of their group.

Homeobox gene A shared nucleotide segment involved in the formation of bodily segmentation during embryologic development.

Home range The area of land that is regularly used by a group of animals for a year or longer.

Hominid A member of the family Hominidae.

Hominidae The family of mammals comprising extant modern humans and extinct bipedal relatives.

Hominin *See* **footnote on page 31.**

Homininae A subfamily of the family Hominidae comprising all members of the genus *Homo*, both living and extinct.

Hominine A member of the subfamily Homininae.

Hominoid A member of the zoological superfamily Hominoidea; includes apes and humans.

Homo A genus of hominid characterized by a large brain with at least three recognized species: *Homo erectus, Homo habilis*, and *Homo sapiens*.

Homologous Having the same developmental and evolutionary origin. The bones in the hands of primates and the wings of bats are homologous bones.

Homoplasy Morphological similarity in two species that is not the result of common ancestry, including convergent evolution and parallel evolution.

Horizon A regionally mappable unit; a lithological level that can be recognized throughout a wide region by some distinctive fossil or mineral property.

Horst A block of the earth's crust that has been faulted upward relative to adjacent terrain.

Humerofemoral index   Ratio of the length of the humerus divided by the length of the femur × 100.

Humerus (pl. **humeri**)   The bone in the upper part of the arm or forelimb.

Hypermorphosis   Extension of a growth allometry that is common to both ancestor and descendant, to a larger size in the descendant by prolongation of the growth period (delayed offset of growth).

Hypodigm   The sample of all specimens attributed to a particular species.

Hypothesis   An initial explanation for observational data.

Igneous   In geology, rock formed under extreme heat, which then cools and hardens.

Ilium (pl. **ilia**)   One of three pelvis bones.

Imbricate   To overlap, as in tiles.

Imbrication zones   Areas where tectonic plates meet and overlap.

Immunology   The study of the interaction of antigens with specific antibodies.

Incision   Biting with the front teeth, the incisors.

Inert gaseous element (**noble gas**)   Nonreactive element in the gas state.

Inferior   Below.

Infradentale   A cranial landmark identified as the highest point on the gums between the lower central incisors.

Inion   The most posterior point on the occiput of the skull.

Insectivore   Animal that eats primarily insects.

Insertion   The attachment of a muscle or ligament farthest from the trunk or center of the body; the opposite of origin.

In situ   In place, such as archaeological remains or fossil found in sediments rather than on the surface.

Interglacial   The period of warm climate between two glaciations.

Intermembral index   A measure of the relative length of the forelimbs and hindlimbs of an animal; humerus plus radius length divided by femur plus tibia length × 100.

Interspecific allometry   The relationship between size and shape among different species; for example, a comparison between humans and chimpanzees.

Interstadial   The period of warm climate between two stadials of the same glacial.

Interstitial wear   The wear between adjacent teeth; also called *interdental wear*.

Inversion   Turning (the foot) inward.

Ischium (pl. **ischia**)   A pelvic bone.

Isotope stratigraphy   A branch of stratigraphy based on the relation between oxygen and carbon isotope ratios and astronomical cycles.

Isotope variation   Chemical elements that differ in mass or atomic number.

Isthmus   A narrow region of an organ or an area of land.

Javelin   A spear for throwing.

Karstic caves   Caves formed in limestone by the action of water; South African early hominids are found in karstic caves.

Keystone resources   Critical elements in a species' ecology that limit its population size and distribution.

Knapping   Stone tool production by percussion and pressure.

Knuckle-walking   A type of quadrupedal walking in which the upper body is supported on the dorsal surface of the middle phalanges of the hands, i.e., the knuckles. A form of locomotion used by chimpanzees and gorillas.

k-Selection   A reproductive pattern characterized by few offspring but extensive parental care.

Kya (or **kyr, Ka**)   Thousand years ago.

Labial   The side of the tooth nearer the lips.

Lacrimal bone   A small bone that forms a portion of the medial orbital wall in the skull.

Lacustrine landscape   Landscape characterized by lakes.

LAD   Last Appearance Datum; the top of a fossil taxon's observed stratigraphic range.

Lambda   The junction of the lambdoidal and sagittal sutures.

Lambdoidal suture   The horizontal or transverse suture at the back of the top of the cranium where the parietal and occipital bones join.

Laminar technology   Stone tool technology based on blade production and retouch.

Larynx   The voice box.

Lateral   Away from the midline of the body.

Laterite   Leeched tropical soils.

Lectotype   The designated type specimen of a species selected when the original author did not name one.

Lens   A thin discontinuous layer of sediments.

Levallois technique   Technique where three or four triangularly shaped flakes are detached from a specially prepared core.

Levant   The Middle East.

Lingual   The side of the teeth that face the tongue.

Lithic   Made of stone.

Lithostratigraphy   A main branch of stratigraphy whereby strata are classified using rocks.

Lithotope   The rocks of a particular sedimentary environment, without regard to coeval lateral relationships.

Living floor   An area of past activity in a hominid fossil site.

Locomotion   Movement from one place to another.

Loess   A fine-grained deposit of windblown material; glacial dust.

Lower Paleolithic   The Lower Old Stone Age. A general term used to refer collectively to the stone tool technologies of *Homo habilis* and *Homo erectus*.

Lumbar lordosis   The anterior curvature of the lumbar region of the vertebral column.

Luminescence   Emitting light.

Macroevolution   Large-scale evolutionary change such as the origin of species and higher taxa.

Magnetostratigraphy   A stratigraphic relationship based on the paleomagnetic record.

Malar   *See* **Zygomatic.**

Malleolus   Bony projection of the tibia or the fibula that articulates with the talus and forms the side of the ankle.

Mandible   The jawbone.

Mandibular symphysis   The joint between the right and left halves of the mandible. In human and other higher primates, this joint is fused.

Mantle   The zone surrounding the earth's core and comprising approximately 80 percent of its volume.

Manuport   Stones transported by humans.

Maritime   Related to the ocean.

Marrow   The blood-cell-producing tissue in the cavity within a long bone.

Masseter   A chewing muscle on the side of the mandible.

Mastication   Chewing.

Mastoid process   A prominence on the occipital bone behind the external auditory meatus on a human skull; in humans, more pronounced in males than females.

Maxilla (pl. **maxillae**)   The upper jaw.

Maxillary sinus   Air cavity within the maxillary bone.

Meatus   An opening in the skull.

Medial   Towards the midline of the body.

Megadonty   Large teeth relative to body size.

Member   In geology, the subdivision of a formation.

Menopause   The cessation of menstruation.

Mesial   Towards the front of the mouth.

Mesolithic   The Middle Stone Age of Europe and Southwestern Asia; began approximately 12 kya.

Messinian event   Refers to a time when the Mediterranean Sea was "drying up," around 6 mya.

Metacarpals   The bones at the base of the digits of the hand.

Metatarsals   The bones at the base of the digits of the foot.

Metopian   Related to the junction between the right and left frontal bones.

Microevolution   Small-scale evolutionary change such as that within populations and within species.

Microlith   Small blade an inch or less in length that was used alone or hafted; abundant in the Mesolithic.

Micromammal   Small mammal, such as a rodent or shrew.

Microwear analysis   The study of the patterns of damage on the edge of stone tools in order to find out what a particular tool was used for. Also can be applied to the dentition.

Middle Paleolithic   The Middle Old Stone Age; a term used to refer collectively to the Mousterian and Middle Stone Age industries.

Milankovitch cycles   Variations in the onset of ice ages and climate resulting from irregularities in the earth's rotation and orbit.

Miocene   The epoch and series that span the interval between 23.5 and 5.3 Ma in the later Cenozoic.

Mitochondrial DNA (mtDNA)   DNA that is found in the mitochondria of cells rather than the nucleus. Mitochondrial DNA is inherited only through females.

Modernity   Behavior or anatomy more characteristic of living humans rather than early hominids.

Molecular anthropology   Systematic study of primate taxa using comparative genetic methods.

Molecular clock   A technique for estimating the divergence times of two species based on biochemical differences between them.

Moment arm   The distance a force acts from the center of movement that helps determine its leverage.

Monogamy   A social system in which groups consist of a mated pair and their offspring.

Monophyletic group   A taxonomic group of organisms that has a single common ancestor.

Morphocline   A continuum of the morphological variations of a homologous character from primitive to derived states.

Morphogenesis   The formation and development of organs and tissues.

Morphology   The study of structure; the shape of anatomical structures.

Morphospecies   Species defined based on morphological differences.

Morphotype   A collection of character traits likely to be diagnostic of a species or a hypothetical ancestor.

Mosaic evolution   The concept that major evolutionary changes between taxa do not occur all together at the same time. For example, the sequential appearance of bipedalism and later brain enlargement in human evolution is mosaic evolution.

Mousterian tradition   A stone tool technology characterized by the careful preparation of a stone core from which finished flakes can be removed; usually associated with Neandertals.

Movius Line   An imaginary geographic boundary in Asia that divides western areas with hand axe industries from those to the east that apparently were lacking in these symmetrical forms.

Multiregional evolution model   A model of the evolution of *Homo sapiens* that posits changes from archaic to modern forms in many different regions of the Old World (although not necessarily at the same time); contrasts with **out of Africa model**. *See also* **Candelabra model**.

Mutagenesis   The forming of mutations.

Mutation   A change in the hereditary material in the genes of an organism.

Mya (or **myr, Ma**)   Million years ago.

Nasency   Birth.

Nasion   Where the two nasal bones and the frontal bone come together.

Nasoalveolar clivus   The region of the premaxilla between the bottom of the nasal aperture and the alveoli of the upper incisors.

Nasospinale   The inferior-most point on the nasal aperture at the midline.

Natural remnant magnetization   The magnetization in a rock after recent magnetic effects have been removed.

Natural selection   A nonrandom differential preservation of genotypes from one generation to the next which leads to changes in the genetic structure of a population; the basis for adaptation.

Navicular   A boat-shaped ankle bone at the base of the great toe.

Neandertal   A member of a regional population of archaic *Homo sapiens* characterized by very large brains, large brow ridges, large noses, and robust limbs. They lived in the circum-Mediterranean area between roughly 30,000 to 125,000 years B.P.

Nenana tradition   An early Paleo-Indian technology found in Alaska.

Neolithic period   The New Stone Age in Southwest Asia; began approximately 11 kya.

Neoteny   Heterochronic reduction in the developmental rate of change in shape, such that if the rate of growth in size and the ages at which growth begins and ends are the same in ancestor and descendant, the descendant will have an adult shape similar to that of a juvenile in the ancestor species (paedomorphic). The retention of juvenile characteristics into adulthood. The child-like rounded skull and large brain of adult humans are examples of neoteny.

Neurocranium   That part of a skull that houses the brain.

Neutron   An electrically neutral particle in the nucleus of an atom.

Niche   The role of an organism in the ecological system.

Nomenclature   The naming of organisms according to internationally accepted rules.

Nonmetric trait   A discrete characteristic described quantitatively rather than by measurements.

Normal polarity epoch   A geologic time period when magnetic north points north.

Nuchal plane   Area on rear of skull providing attachment for neck muscles.

Nuchal torus   Ridge where neck muscles attach to the back of the skull.

Nuclear magnetic resonance   The physical basis of a method of imaging (MRI) based on the differential reaction of body components to a strong magnetic field.

Nucleus   The center of an atom consisting of protons and neutrons.

Obelion   A posterior point on the sagittal suture between two parietal foramina.

Obliquity   Also known as tilt; the angle between the earth's rotational axis and the plane of the ecliptic.

Occipital   Rear bone of the skull.

Occipital bun   A posterior extension of the occipital bone above the nuchal plane.

Occipital plane   Rounded cranial area on rear of skull above nuchal plane.

Occipital torus   A horizontal ridge on the back of the skull in archaic *H. sapiens* and *H. erectus*.

Occlusal   Opposing tooth surfaces which meet during chewing.

Ochre   A red iron ore often used as pigment.

Oldowan tradition   A stone tool culture characterized by simple tools made by removing several flakes from a stone. The flakes removed could also be used as cutting tools. Generally considered the earliest stone tools.

Olduvai subchron   Brief period in the Plio-Pleistocene 1.98–1.79 mya, when the Tethys corridor was extremely unstable.

Olecranon fossa   The indentation on the posterior side of the distal humerus where the olecranon process of the ulna fits when the elbow is extended.

Olfactory   Pertaining to the sense of smell.

Omnivore   An animal whose diet consists of significant amounts of both plants and animals.

Ontogeny   The growth and development of an organism from conception to adulthood.

Opisthion   The midpoint of the posterior border of the foramen magnum.

Opisthocranion   The most posterior point on the occiput.

Opposition   The ability to bring the tip of the thumb in contact with the tips of the other fingers.

Orale   The midpoint between the central incisors.

Orbit   The bony eye socket.

Order   The taxonomic rank below class; humans are in the order Primates.

Origin   The attachment of a muscle or ligament closest to the center of the body.

Orthognathous   No forward projection of either upper or lower jaw.

Osteodontokeratic culture   Bone, tooth, and antler culture of australopithecines, hypothesized by Raymond Dart based on broken remains in South African cave sites.

Out of Africa model   A model of the evolution of *Homo sapiens* that posits a single, African origin for anatomically modern *Homo sapiens* and the replacement of other, archaic hominids in other regions of the Old World.

Oxygen isotope dating   A dating method based on changes in the ratio of oxygen isotopes during the Pleistocene, associated with climate fluctuations.

Oxygen isotope stage   A series of time periods during the Pleistocene characterized by differences in the ratios of oxygen isotopes.

Pachyostosis   Thickening of bone.

Paedomorphosis   The retention of ancestral juvenile shape in the adults of the descendant species.

Palate   The bony roof of the mouth.

Palearctic   The biogeographical region comprising Europe, the northwest coast of Africa, and Asia north of the Himalayas characterized by the distribution of animals.

Paleoanthropology   The multidisciplinary approach to the study of human biocultural evolution. Includes physical anthropology, archaeology, geology, paleontology, and ecology, as well as many other disciplines.

Paleocommunity   A community of organisms that lived in the past.

Paleodeme   A group of related fossil specimens that might represent some type of population.

Paleoecology   The study of the interaction between extinct organisms and their environments.

Paleo-Indian   First well-defined and widely recognized archaeological phase in the Americas, dated from the most ancient sites to 11 kya.

Paleolithic   The Old Stone Age, characterized by the manufacture of chipped stone tools.

Paleomagnetic column   A depiction of the epochs of normal and reversed polarity through geologic time.

Paleomagnetism   The study of the magnetism of rocks that were formed in earlier time periods. More broadly, the study of pole reversals in the earth's magnetic fields during geologic time.

Paleontology   The study of ancient life using fossils.

Paleopathology   The study of disease in prehistoric species.

Paleosol   A fossil soil.

Paleospecies   A group of similar fossils with a range of morphological variation that does not surpass that found in living groups of organisms.

Palimpsest   A collection of fossils or artifacts that are the result of multiple depositional events at different times.

Palmar   Referring to the palm side of the hand.

Palmigrade   Quadrupedal locomotion characterized by bearing weight on the palms rather than the digits or knuckles.

Palynology   The study of environmental conditions through the remains of fossilized pollen grains.

Panthera   Genus of primarily large cats; includes the modern species of lion, tiger, leopard, and jaguar.

Parallel evolution   Independent evolution of similar (and homologous) morphological features in separate lineages.

Paraphyletic classification   A classification in which a taxonomic group contains some of, but not all, the descendants of a common ancestor.

Parasagittal plane   Any plane parallel to the midsagittal plane that divides the body into right and left parts.

Paratype   The specimen other than the type specimen used to develop the description of a species.

Parietals   Right and left side bones at the top of the skull; joined by the sagittal suture.

Parsimony   The principle that the theory that accounts for all of the known facts with the fewest assumptions is preferred.

Partial-range zone   A variant of range zones; the strata between the FADs of two designated taxa or the interval between the LADs of two designated taxa.

Patella   Kneecap.

Pathogen   A disease-causing substance.

Patristic   The combination of both primitive and derived homologous similarities.

Pedal   Related to the foot.

Pelvis (pl. pelves)   The anatomical region enclosed by the hip bone, or the hip bones themselves consisting of a right and left ilium, ischium, and pubis.

Penecontemporaneous   Formed at almost the same time; also said of a structure or mineral that was formed immediately after deposition of a sediment but before its consolidation into rock.

Peninsula   Land surrounded on three sides by water.

Permafrost   Permanently frozen subsoil.

Peramorphosis   "Overdevelopment," or the development of traits in the descendant species beyond that seen in adult ancestors.

Percussion method   Manufacture of stone tools by striking the raw material against an anvil or using a hammerstone to remove flakes.

Periarctic   Near the North Pole.

Periglacial   Near a continental glacier.

Perigordian   An early Upper Paleolithic stone tool tradition that flourished in southwestern France and in Spain from about 33,000 to 18,000 B.P.

Perihelion   The nearest point in the earth's orbit to the sun.

Perikymata   Incremental bands of enamel exposed on the outer surface of a tooth; provide information on the time needed to form the tooth.

Perimortem   Near the time of death.

Periodicity   The time between repeated events.

Perennial   Present year-round.

Peroneal tubercle   Bony projection on the hallucal metatarsal bone for the insertion of the peroneus longus tendon.

Petrography   Branch of geology dealing with the description and systematic classification of rocks, especially igneous and metamorphic rocks, and especially by microscopic examination of thin sections.

Phalanx (pl. phalanges)   Manual (finger) and pedal (toe) bones.

Pharynx   Throat.

Phenocryst   One of the relatively large and ordinarily conspicuous crystals of an igneous rock.

Phenotype   The observable characteristics of an organism; in contrast to genotype.

Photosynthetic pathway   A biochemical process utilized by plants to obtain carbon using photosynthesis.

Phylum   The phylogenetic classification above class in size.

Phyletic classification   A classification in which taxonomic groups correspond to monophyletic groups.

Phyletic gradualism   A model of macroevolutionary change whereby evolutionary changes occur in small steps.

Phylogeny   The evolutionary or genealogical relationships among a group of organisms.

Physiology   The study of the function and activities of organisms.

Phytolith   Fossilized plant matter and wood.

Pisiform   A small bone on the medial side of the wrist.

Pithecanthropus   The early name given to *Homo erectus* fossils from Java.

Plagioclase   Class of common rock-forming minerals within the group of feldspars, including albite, oligoclase, andesine, labradorite, bytownite, and anorthite.

Plantar   Referring to the sole of the foot.

Plantarflexion   Flexion at the ankle joint causing the toes to point down.

Platycephalic   Broad-headed and flattened on top.

Platymeria   Anteroposterior flattening of the proximal portion of the femur shaft.

Platyrrhine   A member of the group of higher primates consisting of New World anthropoids, the "monkeys" of South and Central America (literally, "wide-nosed").

Pleiotropic   A trait produced by an allele with multiple effects on the biological makeup of an organism.

Pleistocene   The latest major geological epoch, also known as the "Ice Age" since this was a time of major glaciations; ca. 3,000,000–10,000 years B.P.

Plesiomorphic   Primitive traits shared by many groups.

Pliocene   Youngest epoch of the Cenozoic era, occupying the interval between 5.3 and 1.8 ma.

Plio-Pleistocene   Time period around 2 million years ago, spanning the end of the Pliocene period of the Tertiary era and the following Pleistocene period of the Quaternary.

Pluvial   A period of increased rainfall.

Pneumatization   Formation of the air spaces in skull bones, such as mastoid area, or nasal sinuses.

Polarity epoch   A period of geologic time of either normal or reversed magnetic polarity.

Polarity event   A short reversal of polarity that occurs within a polarity epoch.

Polarity of traits   A determination of the direction in which a series of features evolved.

Pollex   Thumb.

Polygenic trait   A characteristic governed by two or more genes.

Polygenism   The result of several sources of genetic influence.

Polygyny   Any type of social organization in which one male mates with more than one female.

Population   An interbreeding group of organisms; also referred to as a deme.

Population bottleneck   A constriction of the effective population relative to both earlier and later population sizes.

Postcrania Bones from any part of the body except the skull and face. The skeleton behind (below) the skull.

Postdisplacement Delayed onset of developmental change in shape. Assuming a common growth allometry between ancestor and descendant and similar ages of growth offset, postdisplacement will result in paedomorphic morphology in the descendant.

Posthumous Occurring after death.

Postmortem After death.

Posterior Towards the back.

Postorbital constriction The narrowness of the skull behind the eye orbits.

Potassium-argon dating An absolute dating method based on the half-life of radioactive potassium (which decays into argon gas); can be used to date volcanic rock older than 100,000 years.

Preadaptation The use of an existing structure, item of behavior, or physiological process for a different function than it originally evolved for.

Precession The shift of seasons with regard to the earth's orbit, due to the combined effect of a 26-kyr swing in the orientation of the earth's rotational axis with regard to the orbit and an independent, separate progression of the perihelion-aphelion nodes around the orbital path.

Precocial Young born advanced in development.

Predisplacement Early onset of developmental change in shape. Given common growth allometry between ancestor and descendant and similar ages of growth offset, predisplacement will result in peramorphic morphology in the descendant.

Prehallux Small sesamoid bone that sometimes occurs in the tarso-metatarsal joint of the hallux.

Prehensile Capable of grasping; for example, the prehensile tail of some platyrrhine monkeys.

Premaxilla The area of the maxilla below the nasal aperture and anterior to the canine roots.

Pressure flaking A technique where a bone, antler, or wooden tool is used to press flakes from a core.

Primates Order of mammals to which human beings, lemurs, lorises, tarsiers, monkeys, and apes belong.

Primitive feature A generalized characteristic found in a species and its ancestors. *See also* **Plesiomorphic.**

Principle of original horizontality States that strata are normally nearly horizontal when they are deposited.

Principle of original lateral continuity States that all parts of a stratum, however disrupted by later activity, once formed a single, connected layer.

Principle of superposition States that in an undisturbed sequence, younger strata overlie older strata.

Prismatic Formed by prisms.

Process General term for any bony projection.

Procumbent Inclined forward, protruding, as in the procumbent incisors of some primates.

Progenesis Early cessation (offset) of a growth allometry (common to both ancestor and descendant), resulting in paedomorphic descendants.

Prognathism Forward projection of the face; prominence of the snout.

Projectile A tool or weapon that is thrown or launched in some way.

Pronation Rotation of the forearm so that the palm faces dorsally or downward; the reverse movement from supination.

Prosthion The anterior-most point on the alveolar part of the premaxilla.

Protist A member of the kingdom of simple organisms.

Proton A positively charged particle in the nucleus of an atom.

Protozoa A group of single-celled organisms.

Provenance The place of origin.

Provisioning Bringing food to.

Proximal Closer to the midline of the body.

Pubis (pl. **pubes**) One of three pelvic bones.

Pumice A light-colored, cellular, glassy volcanic rock, often sufficiently buoyant to float on water.

Punctuated equilibrium A model of macroevolutionary change which argues that most evolutionary change takes place in brief, relatively large changes that occur sporadically during long periods of little evolutionary change (called *stasis*); contrast with **phyletic gradualism.**

Putative Accepted, presumed, recognized.

Pyriform aperture (or piriform aperture) The anterior nasal opening.

Quadriceps The four large muscles on the front of the thigh that insert in the patella and extend the knee.

Quadrupedalism Locomotion that involves both forelimbs and hindlimbs.

Quadrumanous Four-handed; as in quadrumanous climbing, in which many suspensory primates use their feet in the same manner as they use their hands.

Quantitative trait Traits that have both a genetic and environmental basis and vary continuously across a population; examples include intelligence and height.

Quaternary A unit of geologic time composed of the Pleistocene and recent epochs.

Race concept A now-discredited concept that modern humans can be easily divided into a series of distinct regional groups or races.

Radioactive isotope One of two or more variants of the same chemical element capable of changing spontaneously into another element by the emission of charged particles from its nucleus.

Radiocarbon dating *See* **Carbon-14 dating.**

Radiograph An X-ray.

Radiometric dating Calculation of an age in years for geological materials by measuring the presence of a short-life radioactive element (e.g., carbon-14) or a long-life radioactive element plus its decay product (e.g., potassium-40 and argon-40). The term applies to all methods of age determination based on nuclear decay of naturally occurring radioactive isotopes.

Radius (pl. **radii**) Lower arm bone on the thumb side.

Range zones Bodies of strata defined by the fossils of one or two specified taxa.

Regulatory gene A gene that controls the expression of other genes.

Relative dating A determination of whether a fossil or fossil site is younger or older than other fossils or sites, usually through study of the stratigraphic position or evolutionary relationships of the fauna; contrasts with **absolute dating.**

Reproductive strategy An organism's complex of behavioral and physiological features concerned with reproduction. *See also* **k-Selection, r-Selection.**

Reproductive success The contribution of an individual to the gene pool of the next generation.

Reticle A measuring device placed in the eyepiece of a microscope.

Retroflexion Bent backward.

Retromolar space or gap A space or gap between the last molar tooth and the ramus of the mandible.

Reversed polarity epoch A geological time period in which the magnetic field is opposite to that of the present time.

Rhinion The point at the anterior end of the suture between the two nasal bones.

Ridge Linear bony elevation, often roughened.

Rift system An elongated trough in the earth's crust that is bounded by faults.

Rift Valley (Great Rift Valley) A massive (1,200 miles long) geological feature in East Africa associated with mountain building, volcanoes, faulting, etc.

Robusticity Loosely used to refer to everything from brow-ridge size to degree of muscle scarring to overall bone size. Cranial robusticity refers to the degree of development of cranial vault superstructures and muscle attachment sites, while postcranial robusticity refers to the mechanical strength of skeletal elements relative to the overall size of the individual.

r-Selection A reproductive pattern characterized by large numbers of offspring and little parental care.

Sacroiliac joint The joint between the ilium and the sacrum.

Sagittal crest A bony ridge on the top of the neurocranium formed by the attachment of the temporalis muscles.

Sagittal keel A derived characteristic of *H. erectus*; a feature shaped like an upside-down V that runs along the midline of the skull.

Sagittal plane Imaginary line that transects the body along the midpoint into mirrored left and right sides.

Sahul The name given to the continent comprising Australia and New Guinea formed during low sea levels during a glaciation.

Savanna A type of vegetation zone characterized by grasslands with scattered trees.

Scapula Shoulder blade.

Sciatic notch A large notch on the posterior surface of the pelvis separating the ischium and the ilium.

Scientific method An orderly, logical process involving gathering data, formulating and testing hypotheses, and postulating theories.

Scramble competition A kind of interspecific competition, also known as exploitative competition. This does not mean that individuals will ever meet or compete directly but, rather, that they outcompete each other on the basis of how well they use the environment and exploit their niche. They do this by depleting as much of the available resources as possible so that no one else can use them.

Scraper A small stone tool with a sharp edge on one side.

Sectorial premolar The compressed, single-cusped first lower premolar that occludes with the upper canine. Seen in great apes, many extinct hominoids, and *Australopithecus afarensis*.

Sediment Rock debris produced by mechanical or chemical weathering processes.

Sella turcica The depression in the superior surface of the sphenoid bone that surrounds the pituitary gland.

Sensu lato In the broad sense.

Sensu stricto In the strict or narrow sense.

Sesamoid A bone formed within a tendon.

Sexual dichromatism The condition in which males and females of a species differ in color.

Sexual dimorphism Any condition in which males and females of a species differ in structural traits and/or nonreproductive anatomy, such as body size or canine tooth size.

Shovel-shaped incisors Incisor teeth that are scooped out on their lingual surfaces.

Side-scraper Flake with one or more edges with smooth, continuous retouching.

Single-species hypothesis The theory that there has never been more than one hominid lineage at any time because all hominids are characterized by culture and thus all occupy the same ecological niche.

Sinodonty Showing dental features characteristic of modern people from China.

Sinus A hollow space in a bone.

Sister group In cladistics, two lineages which are the most closely related due to divergence from a common ancestor.

Sivapithecus A genus of fossil ape found in Asia, between 8 and 17 million years B.P. On the basis of cranial and dental remains, the Asian form of *Sivapithecus* appears to be an ancestor of the modern-day orangutan.

Siwaliks Widespread Miocene-through-Present sediment deposits along the Himalayas.

Skull The bones of the head and jaw.

Soft percussion (soft hammer) A later Acheulean toolmaking technique that used wood, bone, or antler instead of rock to chip flakes from the core.

Solutrean An Upper Paleolithic cultural tradition that flourished only from 18,000 to 15,000 B.P.; it is limited to southwestern France and Spain and distinguished by its laurel-leaf blades.

Speciation The appearance of new species.

Species Associations of organisms that choose reproductive mates among themselves and do not, or cannot, mate successfully with organisms from other associations.

Speleothem A deposit formed in caves when mineral precipitates from drips or thin films of water; stalactites and stalagmites are common examples.

Sphenobasion The midline point on the junction between the sphenoid and occipital bones.

Squama The flattened or upper portion of the temporal bone.

Stable isotope One of two or more variants of the same chemical element (having the same number of protons in the nucleus, but differing in the number of neutrons) that is not spontaneously radioactive.

Stadial The cold period during a glaciation.

Stage Smallest chronostratigraphic unit capable of being correlated globally.

Stage stratotype A characterization of a stage that establishes its basic character and scope.

Stalactite An inverted cone-shaped formation of calcium carbonate on the roof of a cave.

Stalagmite A cone-shaped formation of calcium carbonate on the floor of a cave formed by water dripping from the roof.

Stasis Little or no evolutionary change occurring over a long period of time. *See also* **Punctuated equilibrium.**

Stratigraphy A branch of geology concerned with the sequence of stratified deposits and their correlation.

Stenosis A narrowing.

Stochastic Random.

Stratum (pl. strata) A geological layer.

Strepsirrhine A member of the taxonomic group made up of lemurs and lorises.

Structuralist perspective A view that morphological features are greatly influenced by the physical properties of biological tissues.

Subchron A division of chrons.

Subduction zone Long narrow belt where one tectonic plate descends beneath another.

Subnasal Below the nose.

Suid A member of the family containing pigs and warthogs.

Suite Regionally mappable unit; a composite unit like a group but organized laterally, rather than vertically, by the inclusion of coeval facies, in order to have a regional scope (e.g., the lake beds, river gravels, and peats of an interior montane valley).

Sulcus A depression; a groove on the surface of the brain.

Sunda Former subcontinent consisting of the Malaysian Peninsula, Sumatra, the Indonesian islands, and the currently submerged continental shelf.

Sundadonty Having dental features characteristic of the modern people of the Sunda Shelf, e.g., Indonesia, Malaysia.

Superciliary arch A bony arch over each eye, less prominent than a brow ridge.

Superior Above.

Supination The rotation of the forearm such that the palmar surface faces anteriorly or upward; the reverse movement from pronation.

Supramastoid crests Points of attachment on the temporal bones above the mastoid processes for the temporal muscles (major chewing muscles).

Supraorbital torus Bony ridge above the orbits (or eye sockets) on a skull; very pronounced in *H. erectus*, Neandertals, and some australopithecines.

Supratoral sulcus Depression above the supraorbital torus.

Suspensory behavior Locomotor and postural habits characterized by hanging or suspension of the body below or among branches rather than walking, running, or sitting on top of branches.

Suture A joint between two bones in which the bones interdigitate and can be separated by fibrous tissue. The joints between most of the bones of the skull are sutures.

Sylvian sulcus (sylvian fissure) The large groove on the lateral surface of the brain separating the temporal lobe from the frontal and parietal lobes.

Sympatry Overlap in the geographic range of two species.

Symphysis A bony junction between two bones, such as the joint between right and left sides of the lower jaw.

Symplesiomorphy A shared primitive morphological feature.

Synapomorphy A derived morphological feature shared between two or more groups in an evolving lineage that signifies their close and singular relationship.

Systematics The science of classifying organisms and the study of their genealogical relationships.

Szeletian An early Upper Paleolithic industry from central Europe.

Talus A large bone in the ankle which articulates with the tibia and fibula.

Talus deposit A geological deposit formed by debris on the slope of a hill.

Taphonomy The study of the processes that affect the remains of organisms from the death (or before) of the organism through its fossilization and collection.

Tarsal A bone of the ankle.

Taurodont Teeth having enlarged pulp cavities.

Taxon (pl. taxa) The general term for a group of organisms within the Linnaean classification, such as a species or a genus.

Taxonomy The science of describing, naming, and classifying organisms.

Tectonics The large-scale study of the movements and distortion of the earth's crust, including folding, faulting, and plate tectonics.

Tektite Pieces of glass formed when a large meteorite strikes the earth and melts the surrounding rock. Tektites are found in only a few regions on earth, called *tektite strewn fields.*

Temporal bone A paired bone on the sides of the skull that houses the organs of hearing and balance and the jaw articulation.

Temporalis A major chewing muscle which passes through the zygomatic arch.

Temporal line Area on the frontal bone of the skull where the temporalis, a major chewing muscle, attaches.

Temporomandibular joint (TMJ) The joint between the lower jaw and the skull.

Tephra Any ejected product of a volcanic eruption.

Terminus ante quem A date that is before or older than the object or layer in question, i.e., a maximum possible age.

Terminus post quem A date that is after or younger than the object or layer in question, i.e., a minimum possible age.

Terrestrial Living or moving on the ground.

Terrestrial quadrupedalism Four-limbed locomotion on the ground.

Tertiary First, and primary, period of the Cenozoic, including the Paleocene, Eocene, Oligocene, Miocene, and Pliocene epochs, in order of their age.

Tethys Corridor Zone along the former Tethys Ocean, which approximately occupied the current position of the mountain belt from the Alps to the Himalayas.

Tethys Sea Prehistoric sea during the early Tertiary that separated Eurasia from Arabia and Africa; what remains today is the Mediterranean Sea.

Theory An explanation for a natural phenomenon supported by a large body of evidence; must be testable and falsifiable.

Theropithecus A genus of Old World monkey, including the living gelada from Ethiopia, and several extinct relatives from the Pliocene and Pleistocene of Africa as well as of Europe and Asia.

Thermal emission spectrometer A device for measuring heat.

Thermoluminescence (TL) dating A method of dating archaeological material by the release of energy stored as electron displacements; the amount of energy released is proportional to the time elapsed since the formation of the material.

Thermoregulation Control of body temperature.

Thorax (thoracic) Pertaining to the chest region.

Tibia (pl. **tibiae**) Large long bone of the lower leg; the shin.

Time stratigraphic correlation The extension of chronostratigraphic boundaries accurately from region to region.

Time stratigraphic unit A body of rock strata formed during an interval of geologic time; represents all rocks formed during a specific span of the earth's history.

Torsion Twisting.

Torus A thickened bony ridge.

Total-range zone The strata between the FAD and the LAD of a designated taxon.

Trait A characteristic.

Transverse plane A horizontal plane that divides the body into upper and lower parts.

Trapezium A small wrist bone that lies at the base of the first metacarpal.

Travertine Spring-deposited limestone which can be very porous; crystalline layers are suitable for dating.

Trellis model A model of human evolution that hypothesizes interbreeding and gene flow among different lineages.

Trochanter A large prominence on a bone.

Trophic Related to diet and food.

Tuberosity A small prominence on a bone.

Tuff General term for all consolidated rocks formed by volcanic explosion or aerial expulsion from a volcanic vent; often laid down in water. A tuff can be radiometrically dated.

Type locality Site where the type specimen was found.

Type species The species for which a taxon was first named and described.

Type specimen A single designated individual of an organism which serves as the basis for the original name and description of the species.

Typology Grouping objects into distinct, ideal, often artificial categories, or types.

Ulna (pl. **ulnae**) Lower arm bone on the little finger side.

Uluzzian tradition An early Upper Paleolithic industry in Italy.

Unconformity An extreme form of discontinuity caused by erosion during exposure in which previously buried strata are eroded.

Upper Paleolithic The Upper Old Stone Age. A general term used to collectively refer to the stone tool technologies characterized by blades.

Uranium-series dating Age determinations based on decay of the short-lived isotopes of uranium and their daughter isotopes.

Valgus An angulation of the femur such that the knees are closer together than the hip joints; "knock-kneed."

Ventral Toward the belly side of an animal; the opposite of dorsal.

Vermiculate Worm-like.

Vertebrae (sing. **vertebra**) The bones of the spinal column.

Vertex The top of the skull.

Visual cortex The area of the brain associated with visual input and associations located on the posterior of the cerebrum.

Walther's law The fact that the sediments of coeval adjacent facies will also be deposited adjacent to one another in vertical succession.

Weathering The physical and chemical breakdown of rocks and minerals.

Wernicke's area A place on the left temporal lobe of the brain that is associated with comprehension of speech.

Woodland A vegetation type characterized by discontinuous stands of relatively short trees separated by grassland.

Wormian bones Small bones found in the sutures between cranial vault bones.

X chromosome The larger of the sex chromosomes. Females have two X chromosomes, males have one X chromosome and one Y chromosome.

X-linked regions Genes on the X chromosome.

Y chromosome The smaller of the sex chromosomes. Males have one Y chromosome and one X chromosome. Females have no Y chromosomes.

Zygomatic (or **Malar**) Bone of the face forming the cheekbone, the outer portion of the orbit (or eye socket) and its floor.

Zygomatic arch An arch formed by the zygomatic and temporal bones which encloses the temporalis muscle.

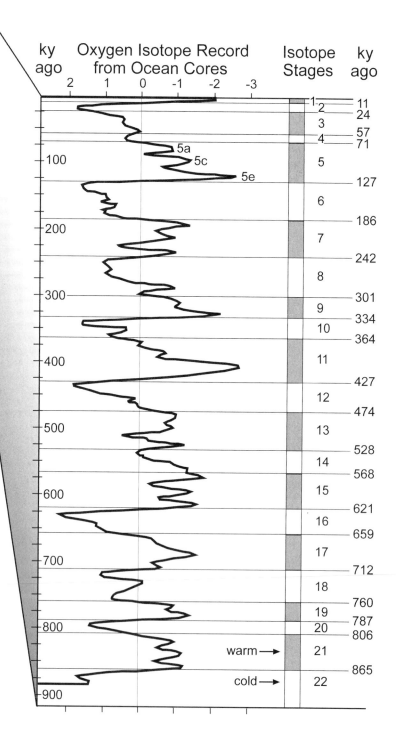

Time m yrs ago	Epochs	Paleomagnetic Chronology	
		Chrons	Events
1	PLEISTOCENE	BRUNHES (normal)	
			Jaramillo
		MATUYAMA (reversed)	
2			Olduvai
			Reunion
3	PLIOCENE	GAUSS (normal)	
			Kaena
			Mammoth
4		GILBERT (reversed)	
			Cochiti
			Nunivak
			Sidufjall
5			Thvera
24	Miocene	Hominoid Radiation	
34	Oligocene	Early Anthropoids	
55	Eocene	Prosimian Radiation	
65	Paleocene	Plesiadapiform Radiation	

HUMAN EVOLUTION TIME SCALE

Oxygen Isotope Record from Ocean Cores

ky ago

Isotope Stages	ky ago
1	11
2	24
3	57
4	71
5	127
6	186
7	242
8	301
9	334
10	364
11	427
12	474
13	528
14	568
15	621
16	659
17	712
18	760
19	787
20	806
21	865
22	

warm →

cold →

5a 5c 5e